MAP PAGES

06

108

110

KAZAKHSTAN

RUSSIA

FINLAND

EN

ESTONIA

LATVIA

EUROPE AND
COUNTRY INDEX
ENDPAPER

UKRAINE

NGARY

MOLDOVA

ROMANIA

TIA

BULG.

SERBIA

GREECE

104

TURKEY

GEORGIA

ARM. AZER.

(TURKMENISTAN

UZBEKISTAN

TAJIK.

KYRGYZSTAN

MONGOLIA

166

114

112

NORTH
KOREA

JAPAN

SOUTH
KOREA

128

SYRIA

130

IRAQ

122

AFGHAN.

IRAN

124

CHINA

116

137

JORDAN

KUWAIT

EGYPT

QATAR

SAUDI
ARABIA

U.A.E.

OMAN

PAKISTAN

NEPAL

126

BANGLA-
DESH

INDIA

BURMA

120

LAOS

TAIWAN

Tropic of Cancer

PACIFIC
OCEAN

156

CHAD

SUDAN

ERITREA

YEMEN

DJIBOUTI

SOUTH
SUDAN

ETHIOPIA

SOMALIA

CENTRAL
AFRICAN
REP.

142

UGANDA

KENYA

131

118

THAILAND

VIETNAM

CAMB.

PHILIPPINES

121

121

121

MALAYSIA

SRI
LANKA

CONGO
(DEM. REP. OF THE)

RWANDA

BURUNDI

TANZANIA

141

INDONESIA

Equator

INDIAN
OCEAN

146

PAPUA
NEW GUINEA

119

E. TIMOR

148

150

154

OLA

ZAMBIA

MALAWI

141

141

150

MOZAMBIQUE

ZIMBABWE

MADAGASCAR

141

Tropic of Capricorn

BIA

BOTSWANA

AUSTRALIA

SWAZILAND

SOUTH
AFRICA

LESOTHO

152

154

NEW
ZEALAND

SYMBOLS

The Royal Geographical Society

ESSENTIAL
WORLD
ATLAS

The Royal Geographical Society
ESSENTIAL
WORLD
ATLAS

PHILIP'S

Philip's would like to thank **Richard Chiles** and the staff at
NPA Satellite Mapping, Edenbridge, Kent, UK (www.npa.cgg.com)
for sourcing and processing the satellite imagery that appears in the atlas.

First published in Great Britain in 2013 by Philip's,
a division of Octopus Publishing Group Limited
(www.octopusbooks.co.uk)
Carmelite House, 50 Victoria Embankment, London EC4Y 0DZ
An Hachette UK Company (www.hachette.co.uk)

Second edition 2015

Copyright © 2015 Philip's

Reprinted 2016

Cartography by Philip's

ISBN 978–1–84907–392–9

A CIP catalogue record for this book is available from the British Library.

Printed in Hong Kong

Details of other Philip's titles and services can be found on our website at:
www.philips-maps.co.uk

Front cover image: Anton Balazh/Shutterstock

**Royal
Geographical
Society**
with IBG

Advancing geography
and geographical learning

PHILIP'S World Atlases are
published in association with
THE ROYAL GEOGRAPHICAL
SOCIETY (WITH THE INSTITUTE
OF BRITISH GEOGRAPHERS).

The Society was founded in
1830 and given a Royal Charter
in 1859 for 'the advancement of geographical science'.
It holds historical collections of national and international importance, many of which relate to the
Society's association with and support for scientific
exploration and research from the 19th century
onwards. It was pivotal in establishing geography as a
teaching and research discipline in British universities
close to the turn of the century, and has played a
key role in geographical and environmental education
ever since.

Today the Society is a leading world centre for
geographical learning – supporting education, teaching, research and expeditions, and promoting public
understanding of the subject. The Society welcomes
those interested in geography as members. For further
information, please visit the website at: **www.rgs.org**

Join us!

**Royal
Geographical
Society**
with IBG

Advancing geography
and geographical learning

Find out more
about your world.

**Visit our website www.rgs.org/joinus
to join the Society to discover:**

● **Why is the world changing and
what are the consequences?**

● **Enhance your understanding
of the world through Geography**

● **Be challenged and entertained
by great achievers**

Royal Geographical Society (with IBG) 1 Kensington Gore London SW7 2AR
☎ +44 (0) 20 7591 3000 🖷 +44 (0) 20 7591 3001

Image © NASA

USER GUIDE

The reference maps which form the main body of this atlas have been prepared in accordance with the highest standards of international cartography to provide an accurate and detailed representation of the Earth. The scales and projections used have been carefully chosen to give balanced coverage of the world, while emphasizing the most densely populated and economically significant regions. A hallmark of Philip's mapping is the use of hill shading and relief colouring to create a graphic impression of landforms: this makes the maps exceptionally easy to read. However, knowledge of the key features employed in the construction and presentation of the maps will enable the reader to derive the fullest benefit from the atlas.

MAP SEQUENCE

The atlas covers the Earth continent by continent: first Europe; then its land neighbour Asia (mapped north before south, in a clockwise sequence), then Africa, Australia and Oceania, North America and South America. This is the classic arrangement adopted by most cartographers since the 16th century. For each continent,

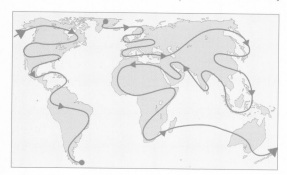

there are maps at a variety of scales. First, physical relief and political maps of the whole continent; then a series of larger-scale maps of the regions within the continent, each followed, where required, by still larger-scale maps of the most important or densely populated areas. The governing principle is that by turning the pages of the atlas, the reader moves steadily from north to south through each continent, with each map overlapping its neighbours.

MAP PRESENTATION

With very few exceptions (for example, for the Arctic and Antarctica), the maps are drawn with north at the top, regardless of whether they are presented upright or sideways on the page. In the borders will be found the map title; a locator diagram showing the area covered; continuation arrows showing the page numbers for maps of adjacent areas; the scale; the projection used; the degrees of latitude and longitude; and the letters and figures used in the index for locating place names and geographical features. Physical relief maps also have a height reference panel identifying the colours used for each layer of contouring.

MAP SYMBOLS

Each map contains a vast amount of detail which can only be conveyed clearly and accurately by the use of symbols. Points and circles of varying sizes locate and identify the relative importance of towns and cities; different styles of type are employed for administrative, geographical and regional place names to aid identification. A variety of pictorial symbols denote landforms such as glaciers, marshes and coral reefs, and man-made structures including roads, railways, airports and canals. International borders are shown by red lines. Where neighbouring countries are in dispute, for example in parts of the Middle East, the maps show the *de facto* boundary between nations, regardless of the legal or historical situation. The symbols are explained on the front endpaper of the atlas.

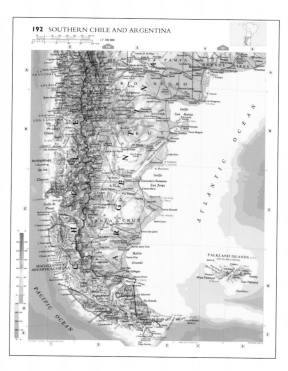

MAP SCALES

1:16 000 000
1 inch = 252 statute miles

The scale of each map is given in the numerical form known as the 'representative fraction'. The first figure is always one, signifying one unit of distance on the map; the second figure, usually in millions, is the number by which the map unit must be multiplied to give the equivalent distance on the Earth's surface. Calculations can easily be made in centimetres and kilometres, by dividing the Earth units figure by 100 000 (i.e. deleting the last five 0s). Thus 1:1 000 000 means 1 cm = 10 km. The calculation for inches and miles is more laborious, but 1 000 000 divided by 63 360 (the number of inches in a mile) shows that 1:1 000 000 means approximately 1 inch = 16 miles. The table below provides distance equivalents for scales down to 1:50 000 000.

LARGE SCALE		
1:1 000 000	1 cm = 10 km	1 inch = 16 miles
1:2 500 000	1 cm = 25 km	1 inch = 39.5 miles
1:5 000 000	1 cm = 50 km	1 inch = 79 miles
1:6 000 000	1 cm = 60 km	1 inch = 95 miles
1:8 000 000	1 cm = 80 km	1 inch = 126 miles
1:10 000 000	1 cm = 100 km	1 inch = 158 miles
1:15 000 000	1 cm = 150 km	1 inch = 237 miles
1:20 000 000	1 cm = 200 km	1 inch = 316 miles
1:50 000 000	1 cm = 500 km	1 inch = 790 miles
SMALL SCALE		

MEASURING DISTANCES

Although each map is accompanied by a scale bar, distances cannot always be measured with confidence because of the distortions involved in portraying the curved surface of the Earth on a flat page. As a general rule, the larger the map scale (that is, the lower the number of Earth units in the representative fraction), the more accurate and reliable will be the distance measured. On small-scale maps such as those of the world and of entire continents, measurement may only be accurate

along the 'standard parallels', or central axes, and should not be attempted without considering the map projection.

MAP PROJECTIONS

Unlike a globe, no flat map can give a true scale representation of the world in terms of area, shape and position of every region. Each of the numerous systems that have been devised for projecting the curved surface of the Earth on to a flat page involves the sacrifice of accuracy in one or more of these elements. The variations in shape and position of landmasses such as Alaska, Greenland and Australia, for example, can be quite dramatic when different projections are compared. For this atlas, the guiding principle has been to select projections that involve the least distortion of size and distance. The projection used for each map is noted in the border. Most fall into one of three categories – conic, azimuthal or cylindrical – whose basic concepts are shown above. Each involves plotting the forms of the Earth's surface on a grid of latitude and longitude lines, which may be shown as parallels, curves or radiating spokes.

LATITUDE AND LONGITUDE

Accurate positioning of individual points on the Earth's surface is made possible by reference to the geometrical system of latitude and longitude. Latitude *parallels* are drawn west–east around the Earth and numbered by degrees north and south of the equator, which is designated 0° of latitude. Longitude *meridians* are drawn north–south and numbered by degrees east and west of the *prime meridian*, 0° of longitude, which passes through Greenwich in England. By referring to these co-ordinates and their subdivisions of minutes (1/60th of a degree) and seconds (1/60th of a minute), any place on Earth can be located to within a few hundred metres. Latitude and longitude are indicated by blue lines on the maps; they are straight or curved according to the projection employed. Reference to these lines is the easiest way of determining the relative positions of places on different maps, and for plotting compass directions.

NAME FORMS

For ease of reference, both English and local name forms appear in the atlas. Oceans, seas and countries are shown in English throughout the atlas; country names may be abbreviated to their commonly accepted form (for example, Germany, not The Federal Republic of Germany). Conventional English forms are also used for place names on the smaller-scale maps of the continents. However, local name forms are used on all large-scale and regional maps, with the English form given in brackets only for important cities – the large-scale map of Russia and Northern Asia thus shows Moskva (Moscow). For countries which do not use a Roman script, place names have been transcribed according to the systems adopted by the British and US Geographic Names Authorities. For China, the Pin Yin system has been used, with some more widely known forms appearing in brackets, as with Beijing (Peking). Both English and local names appear in the index, the English form being cross-referenced to the local form.

CONTENTS

WORLD STATISTICS

COUNTRIES 8

CITIES 9

CLIMATE 10–11

PHYSICAL DIMENSIONS 12–13

IMAGES OF EARTH

LONDON, UNITED KINGDOM 16

AMSTERDAM, NETHERLANDS 17

ROME, ITALY 18

ATHENS, GREECE 19

ISLAMABAD AND RAWALPINDI, PAKISTAN 20

JAKARTA, INDONESIA 21

HONG KONG/SHENZHEN, CHINA 22

TOKYO, JAPAN 23

CAIRO, EGYPT 24

NAIROBI, KENYA 25

JOHANNESBURG, SOUTH AFRICA 26

CAPE TOWN, SOUTH AFRICA 27

SYDNEY, AUSTRALIA 28

AUCKLAND, NEW ZEALAND 29

VANCOUVER, CANADA 30

QUÉBEC, CANADA 31

NEW YORK CITY, USA 32

CHICAGO, USA 33

SALT LAKE CITY, USA 34

NEW ORLEANS, USA 35

MEXICO CITY, MEXICO 36

PANAMA CANAL, PANAMA 37

MARACAIBO, VENEZUELA 38

BRASILIA, BRAZIL 39

OCEAN SEAFLOORS

ARCTIC OCEAN SEAFLOOR 41

ATLANTIC OCEAN SEAFLOOR 42–43

PACIFIC OCEAN SEAFLOOR 44–45

INDIAN OCEAN SEAFLOOR 46

SOUTHERN OCEAN SEAFLOOR 47

WORLD MAPS

THE WORLD: PHYSICAL 50–51
1:84 000 000

THE WORLD: POLITICAL 52–53
1:84 000 000

ARCTIC OCEAN 54
1:31 100 000

ANTARCTICA 55
1:31 100 000

ATLANTIC OCEAN 56
1:45 000 000

GREENLAND 57
1:11 100 000

EUROPE

EUROPE: PHYSICAL 58
1:17 800 000

EUROPE: POLITICAL 59
1:17 800 000

SCANDINAVIA 60–61
1:5 300 000
Iceland 1:5 300 000
Færoe Islands 1:5 300 000

DENMARK AND SOUTHERN SWEDEN 62–63
1:2 200 000

IRELAND 64
1:1 800 000

SCOTLAND 65
1:1 800 000
Orkney Islands 1:1 800 000
Shetland Islands 1:1 800 000

ENGLAND AND WALES 66–67
1:1 800 000
Isles of Scilly 1:1 800 000

BRITISH ISLES 68
1:4 400 000

NETHERLANDS, BELGIUM
AND LUXEMBOURG 69
1:2 200 000

NORTHERN FRANCE 70–71
1:2 200 000

SOUTHERN FRANCE 72–73
1:2 200 000

CENTRAL EUROPE 74–75
1:4 400 000

GERMANY AND SWITZERLAND 76–77
1:2 200 000

AUSTRIA, CZECH REPUBLIC
AND SLOVAK REPUBLIC 78–79
1:2 200 000

HUNGARY, ROMANIA AND
THE LOWER DANUBE 80–81
1:2 200 000

POLAND AND THE SOUTHERN BALTIC 82–83
1:2 200 000

BALTIC STATES, BELARUS
AND UKRAINE 84–85
1:4 400 000

THE VOLGA BASIN AND
THE CAUCASUS 86–87
1:4 400 000

WESTERN SPAIN AND PORTUGAL 88–89
1:2 200 000

EASTERN SPAIN 90–91
1:2 200 000
Menorca 1:2 200 000

NORTHERN ITALY, SLOVENIA
AND CROATIA 92–93
1:2 200 000

SOUTHERN ITALY 94–95
1:2 200 000

THE BALKANS 96–97
1:2 200 000

SOUTHERN GREECE AND
WESTERN TURKEY 98–99
1:2 200 000

THE BALEARICS, THE CANARIES
AND MADEIRA 100
1:900 000 / 1:1 800 000

MALTA, CRETE, CORFU, RHODES
AND CYPRUS 101
1:900 000 / 1:1 200 000

ASIA

ASIA: PHYSICAL 102
1:44 400 000

ASIA: POLITICAL 103
1:44 400 000

TURKEY AND TRANSCAUCASIA 104–105
1:4 400 000

RUSSIA AND NORTHERN ASIA 106–107
1:17 800 000

KAZAKHSTAN AND CENTRAL ASIA 108–109
1:8 900 000

CHINA AND THE FAR EAST 110–111
1:13 300 000
Hong Kong, Macau and Shenzhen 1:890 000

JAPAN   112–113
1:4 400 000
Ryukyu Islands 1:4 400 000

NORTHERN CHINA AND KOREA   114–115
1:5 300 000

SOUTHERN CHINA AND TAIWAN   116–117
1:5 300 000
Hainan 1:5 300 000

INDONESIA AND THE PHILIPPINES   118–119
1:11 100 000
Java and Madura 1:6 700 000
Bali 1:1 800 000

MAINLAND SOUTH-EAST ASIA   120–121
1:5 300 000
Ko Phuket 1:900 000
Ko Samui 1:900 000
Pinang 1:900 000
Singapore 1:900 000

SOUTH ASIA   122–123
1:8 900 000

NORTHERN INDIA, PAKISTAN
    AND NEPAL   124–125
1:5 300 000
Jammu and Kashmir 1:5 300 000

SOUTHERN INDIA AND SRI LANKA   126–127
1:5 300 000
Lakshadweep Islands 1:5 300 000
Andaman and Nicobar Islands 1:5 300 000

THE MIDDLE EAST   128–129
1:6 200 000

THE NEAR EAST   130
1:2 200 000

ARABIA AND THE HORN OF AFRICA   131
1:13 300 000

AFRICA

AFRICA: PHYSICAL   132
1:37 300 000

AFRICA: POLITICAL   133
1:37 300 000

NORTHERN AFRICA   134–135
1:13 300 000
Azores 1:13 300 000
Cape Verde Islands 1:8 900 000

MOROCCO, ALGERIA AND TUNISIA   136
1:7 100 000

EGYPT   137
1:7 100 000

WEST AFRICA   138–139
1:7 100 000

CENTRAL AND SOUTHERN AFRICA   140–141
1:13 300 000
Seychelles 1:2 200 000
Réunion 1:2 200 000
Mauritius 1:2 200 000
Comoros 1:7 100 000
Madagascar 1:13 300 000

EAST AFRICA   142–143
1:7 100 000

SOUTHERN AFRICA   144–145
1:7 100 000

INDIAN OCEAN   146
1:45 000 000

AUSTRALIA AND OCEANIA

AUSTRALIA AND OCEANIA:
    PHYSICAL AND POLITICAL   147
1:44 400 000

WESTERN AUSTRALIA   148–149
1:7 100 000

EASTERN AUSTRALIA   150–151
1:7 100 000
Whitsunday Islands 1:2 200 000
Tasmania 1:7 100 000
Torres Strait 1:7 100 000

SOUTH-EASTERN AUSTRALIA   152–153
1:3 500 000

NEW ZEALAND – NORTH ISLAND   154
1:3 100 000
Fiji 1:5 300 000

NEW ZEALAND – SOUTH ISLAND   155
1:3 100 000
Tahiti and Moorea 1:900 000
Chatham Islands 1:3 100 000

PACIFIC OCEAN   156–157
1:48 000 000

NORTH AMERICA

NORTH AMERICA: PHYSICAL   158
1:31 100 000

NORTH AMERICA: POLITICAL   159
1:31 100 000

CANADA   160–161
1:13 300 000
Northern Canada 1:13 300 000

WESTERN CANADA   162–163
1:6 200 000

EASTERN CANADA   164–165
1:6 200 000

UNITED STATES   166–167
1:13 300 000
Hawai'i 1:13 300 000
Alaska 1:13 300 000

UNITED STATES – WEST   168–169
1:6 250 000

CENTRAL AND SOUTHERN
    CALIFORNIA AND
    WESTERN WASHINGTON   170–171
1:2 200 000

UNITED STATES – MIDWEST
    AND NORTH-EAST   172–173
1:6 250 000

NORTH-EASTERN UNITED STATES   174–175
1:2 200 000

UNITED STATES – SOUTH   176–177
1:6 250 000

SOUTH-EASTERN UNITED STATES   178–179
1:2 200 000

MEXICO   180–181
1:7 100 000

CENTRAL AMERICA AND
    THE WEST INDIES   182–183
1:7 100 000
Jamaica 1:2 700 000
Guadeloupe 1:1 800 000
Martinique 1:1 800 000
Puerto Rico 1:2 700 000
Virgin Islands 1:1 800 000
St Lucia 1:890 000
Barbados 1:890 000

SOUTH AMERICA

SOUTH AMERICA: PHYSICAL   184
1:31 100 000

SOUTH AMERICA: POLITICAL   185
1:31 100 000

SOUTH AMERICA – NORTH   186–187
1:14 200 000
Trinidad and Tobago 1:2 200 000

PERU AND THE CENTRAL ANDES   188
1:7 100 000

NORTH-EASTERN BRAZIL   189
1:7 100 000

CENTRAL SOUTH AMERICA   190–191
1:7 100 000

SOUTHERN CHILE AND ARGENTINA   192
1:7 100 000

INDEX TO WORLD
MAPS   193–288

WORLD STATISTICS: COUNTRIES

This alphabetical list includes the principal countries and territories of the world. If a territory is not completely independent, the country it is associated with is named. The area figures give the total area of land, inland water and ice. The population figures are 2014 estimates where available. The annual income is the Gross Domestic Product per capita (PPP) in US dollars. The figures are the latest available, usually 2014 estimates.

Country/Territory	Area km² Thousands	Area miles² Thousands	Population Thousands	Capital	Annual Income US $
Afghanistan	652	252	31,823	Kabul	2,000
Albania	28.7	11.1	3,020	Tirana	11,100
Algeria	2,382	920	38,814	Algiers	14,300
American Samoa (US)	0.20	0.08	55	Pago Pago	8,000
Andorra	0.47	0.18	85	Andorra La Vella	37,200
Angola	1,247	481	19,088	Luanda	8,200
Anguilla (UK)	0.10	0.04	16	The Valley	12,200
Antigua & Barbuda	0.44	0.17	91	St John's	22,600
Argentina	2,780	1,074	43,024	Buenos Aires	22,100
Armenia	29.8	11.5	3,061	Yerevan	7,400
Aruba (Netherlands)	0.19	0.07	111	Oranjestad	25,300
Australia	7,741	2,989	22,508	Canberra	46,600
Austria	83.9	32.4	8,223	Vienna	45,400
Azerbaijan	86.6	33.4	9,686	Baku	17,900
Azores (Portugal)	2.2	0.86	246	Ponta Delgada	15,197
Bahamas	13.9	5.4	322	Nassau	25,100
Bahrain	0.69	0.27	1,314	Manama	51,400
Bangladesh	144	55.6	166,281	Dhaka	3,400
Barbados	0.43	0.17	290	Bridgetown	16,200
Belarus	208	80.2	9,608	Minsk	18,200
Belgium	30.5	11.8	10,449	Brussels	41,700
Belize	23.0	8.9	341	Belmopan	8,100
Benin	113	43.5	10,161	Porto-Novo	1,900
Bermuda (UK)	0.05	0.02	70	Hamilton	86,000
Bhutan	47.0	18.1	734	Thimphu	7,700
Bolivia	1,099	424	10,631	La Paz/Sucre	6,200
Bosnia-Herzegovina	51.2	19.8	3,872	Sarajevo	9,800
Botswana	582	225	2,156	Gaborone	16,000
Brazil	8,514	3,287	202,657	Brasília	15,200
Brunei	5.8	2.2	423	Bandar Seri Begawan	77,700
Bulgaria	111	42.8	6,925	Sofia	17,100
Burkina Faso	274	106	18,365	Ouagadougou	1,700
Burma (Myanmar)	677	261	55,746	Rangoon/Naypyidaw	4,800
Burundi	27.8	10.7	10,396	Bujumbura	900
Cabo Verde	4.0	1.6	539	Praia	6,300
Cambodia	181	69.9	15,458	Phnom Penh	3,300
Cameroon	475	184	23,131	Yaoundé	3,000
Canada	9,971	3,850	34,835	Ottawa	44,500
Canary Is. (Spain)	7.2	2.8	1,682	Las Palmas/Santa Cruz	19,900
Cayman Is. (UK)	0.26	0.10	55	George Town	43,800
Central African Republic	623	241	5,278	Bangui	600
Chad	1,284	496	11,412	Ndjaména	2,600
Chile	757	292	17,364	Santiago	23,200
China	9,597	3,705	1,355,693	Beijing	12,900
Colombia	1,139	440	46,245	Bogotá	13,500
Comoros	2.2	0.86	767	Moroni	1,700
Congo	342	132	4,662	Brazzaville	6,600
Congo (Dem. Rep. of the)	2,345	905	77,434	Kinshasa	700
Cook Is. (NZ)	0.24	0.09	10	Avarua	9,100
Costa Rica	51.1	19.7	4,755	San José	14,900
Croatia	56.5	21.8	4,471	Zagreb	20,400
Cuba	111	42.8	11,047	Havana	10,200
Curaçao (Netherlands)	0.44	0.17	147	Willemstad	15,000
Cyprus	9.3	3.6	1,172	Nicosia	28,000
Czech Republic	78.9	30.5	10,627	Prague	28,400
Denmark	43.1	16.6	5,569	Copenhagen	44,300
Djibouti	23.2	9.0	810	Djibouti	3,000
Dominica	0.75	0.29	73	Roseau	10,700
Dominican Republic	48.5	18.7	10,350	Santo Domingo	12,800
East Timor	14.9	5.7	1,202	Dili	6,800
Ecuador	284	109	15,654	Quito	11,400
Egypt	1,001	387	86,895	Cairo	11,100
El Salvador	21.0	8.1	6,126	San Salvador	8,000
Equatorial Guinea	28.1	10.8	722	Malabo	32,600
Eritrea	118	45.4	6,381	Asmara	1,200
Estonia	45.1	17.4	1,258	Tallinn	26,600
Ethiopia	1,104	426	96,633	Addis Ababa	1,500
Falkland Is. (UK)	12.2	4.7	3	Stanley	55,400
Faroe Is. (Denmark)	1.4	0.54	50	Tórshavn	30,500
Fiji	18.3	7.1	903	Suva	8,200
Finland	338	131	5,269	Helsinki	40,500
France	552	213	66,259	Paris	40,400
French Guiana (France)	90.0	34.7	250	Cayenne	8,300
French Polynesia (France)	4.0	1.5	280	Papeete	26,100
Gabon	268	103	1,673	Libreville	21,600
Gambia, The	11.3	4.4	1,926	Banjul	1,700
Georgia	69.7	26.9	4,936	Tbilisi	7,700
Germany	357	138	80,997	Berlin	44,700
Ghana	239	92.1	25,758	Accra	4,200
Gibraltar (UK)	0.006	0.002	29	Gibraltar Town	43,000
Greece	132	50.9	10,776	Athens	25,800
Greenland (Denmark)	2,176	840	58	Nuuk	38,400
Grenada	0.34	0.13	110	St George's	11,800
Guadeloupe (France)	1.7	0.66	406	Basse-Terre	7,900
Guam (US)	0.55	0.21	161	Agana	28,700
Guatemala	109	42.0	14,647	Guatemala City	7,500
Guinea	246	94.9	11,474	Conakry	1,300
Guinea-Bissau	36.1	13.9	1,693	Bissau	1,400
Guyana	215	83.0	736	Georgetown	6,900
Haiti	27.8	10.7	9,997	Port-au-Prince	1,800
Honduras	112	43.3	8,599	Tegucigalpa	4,700
Hungary	93.0	35.9	9,919	Budapest	24,300
Iceland	103	39.8	317	Reykjavik	42,600
India	3,287	1,269	1,236,345	New Delhi	5,800
Indonesia	1,905	735	253,610	Jakarta	10,200
Iran	1,648	636	80,841	Tehran	16,500
Iraq	438	169	32,586	Baghdad	14,100
Ireland	70.3	27.1	4,833	Dublin	46,800
Israel	20.6	8.0	7,822	Jerusalem	33,400
Italy	301	116	61,680	Rome	34,500
Ivory Coast (Côte d'Ivoire)	322	125	22,849	Yamoussoukro	2,900
Jamaica	11.0	4.2	2,930	Kingston	8,700
Japan	378	146	127,103	Tokyo	37,800
Jordan	89.3	34.5	7,930	Amman	11,900
Kazakhstan	2,725	1,052	17,949	Astana	24,100
Kenya	580	224	45,010	Nairobi	3,100
Kiribati	0.73	0.28	104	Tarawa	1,600
Korea, North	121	46.5	24,852	Pyo˘ngyang	1,800
Korea, South	99.3	38.3	49,040	Seoul	35,400
Kosovo	10.9	4.2	1,859	Pristina	8,000
Kuwait	17.8	6.9	2,743	Kuwait City	71,000
Kyrgyzstan	200	77.2	5,604	Bishkek	3,400

Country/Territory	Area km² Thousands	Area miles² Thousands	Population Thousands	Capital	Annual Income US $
Laos	237	91.4	6,804	Vientiane	5,000
Latvia	64.6	24.9	2,165	Riga	23,900
Lebanon	10.4	4.0	5,883	Beirut	17,900
Lesotho	30.4	11.7	1,942	Maseru	2,900
Liberia	111	43.0	4,092	Monrovia	900
Libya	1,760	679	6,244	Tripoli	16,600
Liechtenstein	0.16	0.06	37	Vaduz	89,400
Lithuania	65.2	25.2	3,506	Vilnius	26,700
Luxembourg	2.6	1.0	521	Luxembourg	92,400
Macedonia (FYROM)	25.7	9.9	2,092	Skopje	13,200
Madagascar	587	227	23,202	Antananarivo	1,400
Madeira (Portugal)	0.78	0.30	268	Funchal	25,800
Malawi	118	45.7	17,377	Lilongwe	800
Malaysia	330	127	30,073	Kuala Lumpur/Putrajaya	24,500
Maldives	0.30	0.12	394	Malé	12,400
Mali	1,240	479	16,456	Bamako	1,600
Malta	0.32	0.12	413	Valletta	31,700
Marshall Is.	0.18	0.07	71	Majuro	3,200
Martinique (France)	1.1	0.43	386	Fort-de-France	14,400
Mauritania	1,026	396	3,517	Nouakchott	3,400
Mauritius	2.0	0.79	1,331	Port Louis	17,900
Mayotte (France)	0.37	0.14	213	Mamoudzou	4,900
Mexico	1,958	756	120,287	Mexico City	17,900
Micronesia, Fed. States of	0.70	0.27	106	Palikir	3,200
Moldova	33.9	13.1	3,583	Kishinev	4,800
Monaco	0.001	0.0004	31	Monaco	78,700
Mongolia	1,567	605	2,953	Ulan Bator	10,200
Montenegro	14.0	5.4	650	Podgorica	15,200
Montserrat (UK)	0.10	0.39	5	Brades	8,500
Morocco	447	172	32,987	Rabat	7,700
Mozambique	802	309	24,692	Maputo	1,100
Namibia	824	318	2,198	Windhoek	10,800
Nauru	0.02	0.008	9	Yaren	5,000
Nepal	147	56.8	30,987	Katmandu	2,400
Netherlands	41.5	16.0	16,877	Amsterdam/The Hague	47,400
New Caledonia (France)	18.6	7.2	268	Nouméa	38,800
New Zealand	271	104	4,402	Wellington	35,000
Nicaragua	130	50.2	5,849	Managua	4,800
Niger	1,267	489	17,466	Niamey	1,000
Nigeria	924	357	177,156	Abuja	6,100
Northern Mariana Is. (US)	0.46	0.18	51	Saipan	13,600
Norway	324	125	5,148	Oslo	65,900
Oman	310	119	3,220	Muscat	44,100
Pakistan	796	307	196,174	Islamabad	4,700
Palau	0.46	0.18	21	Melekeok	15,100
Panama	75.5	29.2	3,608	Panamá	20,300
Papua New Guinea	463	179	6,553	Port Moresby	2,400
Paraguay	407	157	6,704	Asunción	8,400
Peru	1,285	496	30,148	Lima	12,000
Philippines	300	116	107,668	Manila	7,000
Poland	323	125	38,346	Warsaw	24,400
Portugal	88.8	34.3	10,814	Lisbon	26,300
Puerto Rico (US)	8.9	3.4	3,621	San Juan	16,300
Qatar	11.0	4.2	2,123	Doha	144,400
Réunion (France)	2.5	0.97	841	St-Denis	6,200
Romania	238	92.0	21,730	Bucharest	19,400
Russia	17,075	6,593	142,470	Moscow	24,800
Rwanda	26.3	10.2	12,337	Kigali	1,700
St Kitts & Nevis	0.26	0.10	52	Basseterre	20,300
St Lucia	0.54	0.21	163	Castries	11,100
St Vincent & Grenadines	0.39	0.15	103	Kingstown	10,900
Samoa	2.8	1.1	197	Apia	5,200
San Marino	0.06	0.02	33	San Marino	55,000
São Tomé & Príncipe	0.96	0.37	190	São Tomé	3,100
Saudi Arabia	2,150	830	27,346	Riyadh	52,800
Senegal	197	76.0	13,636	Dakar	2,300
Serbia	77.5	29.9	7,210	Belgrade	12,500
Seychelles	0.46	0.18	92	Victoria	24,500
Sierra Leone	71.7	27.7	5,744	Freetown	2,100
Singapore	0.68	0.26	5,567	Singapore City	81,300
Slovak Republic	49.0	18.9	5,444	Bratislava	27,700
Slovenia	20.3	7.8	1,988	Ljubljana	29,400
Solomon Is.	28.9	11.2	610	Honiara	1,800
Somalia	638	246	10,428	Mogadishu	600
South Africa	1,221	471	48,376	Cape Town/Pretoria	12,700
Spain	498	192	47,738	Madrid	33,000
Sri Lanka	65.6	25.3	21,866	Colombo	10,400
Sudan	1,886	728	35,482	Khartoum	4,500
Sudan, South	620	239	11,563	Juba	2,000
Suriname	163	63.0	573	Paramaribo	16,700
Swaziland	17.4	6.7	1,420	Mbabane	7,800
Sweden	450	174	9,724	Stockholm	44,700
Switzerland	41.3	15.9	8,062	Berne	55,200
Syria	185	71.5	17,952	Damascus	5,100
Taiwan	36.0	13.9	23,360	Taipei	43,600
Tajikistan	143	55.3	8,052	Dushanbe	2,700
Tanzania	945	365	49,639	Dodoma	1,900
Thailand	513	198	67,741	Bangkok	14,400
Togo	56.8	21.9	7,351	Lomé	1,500
Tonga	0.65	0.25	106	Nuku'alofa	5,000
Trinidad & Tobago	5.1	2.0	1,224	Port of Spain	31,300
Tunisia	164	63.2	10,938	Tunis	11,400
Turkey	775	299	81,619	Ankara	19,600
Turkmenistan	488	188	5,172	Ashkhabad	14,200
Turks & Caicos Is. (UK)	0.43	0.17	49	Cockburn Town	29,100
Tuvalu	0.03	0.01	11	Fongafale	3,200
Uganda	241	93.1	35,919	Kampala	1,800
Ukraine	604	233	44,291	Kiev	8,200
United Arab Emirates	83.6	32.3	5,629	Abu Dhabi	65,000
United Kingdom	242	93.4	63,743	London	37,700
United States of America	9,629	3,718	318,892	Washington, DC	54,800
Uruguay	175	67.6	3,333	Montevideo	20,500
Uzbekistan	447	173	28,930	Tashkent	5,600
Vanuatu	12.2	4.7	267	Port-Vila	2,500
Vatican City	0.0004	0.0002	0.842	Vatican City	
Venezuela	912	352	28,868	Caracas	17,900
Vietnam	332	128	93,422	Hanoi	5,600
Virgin Is. (UK)	0.15	0.06	28	Road Town	42,300
Virgin Is. (US)	0.35	0.13	104	Charlotte Amalie	14,500
Yemen	528	204	26,053	Sana'	3,900
Zambia	753	291	14,639	Lusaka	4,100
Zimbabwe	391	151	13,772	Harare	2,000

WORLD STATISTICS: CITIES

This list shows the principal cities with more than 850,000 inhabitants. The figures are taken from the most recent census or estimate available, usually 2014, and as far as possible are the population of the metropolitan area or urban agglomeration. The list includes Metropolitan Statistical Areas from the United States Census Bureau. All the figures are in thousands. Local name forms have been used for the smaller cities (for example, Antwerpen).

AFGHANISTAN
Kabul 4,635
ALGERIA
Algiers 2,594
Oran 858
ANGOLA
Luanda 5,506
Huambo 1,269
ARGENTINA
Buenos Aires 15,180
Córdoba 1,511
Rosario 1,381
Mendoza 1,009
San Miguel de Tucumán 910
ARMENIA
Yerevan 1,044
AUSTRALIA
Sydney 4,505
Melbourne 4,203
Brisbane 2,202
Perth 1,861
Adelaide 1,256
AUSTRIA
Vienna 1,753
AZERBAIJAN
Baku 2,374
BANGLADESH
Dhaka 17,598
Chittagong 4,539
Khulna 1,022
BELARUS
Minsk 1,915
BELGIUM
Brussels 2,045
Antwerpen 994
BOLIVIA
Santa Cruz 2,107
La Paz 1,816
Cochabamba 1,240
BRAZIL
São Paulo 21,066
Rio de Janeiro 12,902
Belo Horizonte 5,716
Brasília 4,155
Fortaleza 3,880
Recife 3,739
Pôrto Alegre 3,603
Salvador 3,583
Curitiba 3,474
Campinas 3,047
Goiânia 2,285
Belém 2,182
Manaus 2,025
Vitória 1,636
Santos 1,539
São Luís 1,437
Maceió 1,266
Joinville 1,219
Florianópolis 1,180
Natal 1,167
João Pessoa 1,093
Teresina 959
BULGARIA
Sofia 1,226
BURKINA FASO
Ouagadougou 2,741
BURMA (MYANMAR)
Rangoon 4,802
Mandalay 1,167
Naypyidaw 1,030
CAMBODIA
Phnom Penh 1,731
CAMEROON
Yaoundé 3,066
Douala 2,943
CANADA
Toronto 5,993
Montréal 3,981
Vancouver 2,485
Calgary 1,337
Ottawa 1,326
Edmonton 1,272
CHAD
Ndjamena 1,260
CHILE
Santiago 6,507
Valparaíso 907
CHINA
Shanghai 23,741
Beijing 20,384
Chongqing 13,332
Guangzhou, Guangdong 12,458
Tianjin 11,210
Shenzhen 10,749
Wuhan 7,906
Chengdu 7,556
Dongguan, Guangdong 7,435
Nanjing, Jiangsu 7,369
Hong Kong 7,314
Foshan 7,036
Hangzhou 6,391
Shenyang 6,315
Xi'an, Shaanxi 6,044
Suzhou, Jiangsu 5,472
Harbin 5,457
Qingdao 4,566
Dalian 4,489
Xiamen 4,430
Zhengzhou 4,387
Jinan, Shandong 4,032
Shantou 3,949
Kunming 3,780
Changchun 3,762
Changsha 3,761
Zhongshan 3,691
Ürümqi 3,499
Taiyuan, Shanxi 3,482
Hefei 3,348
Fuzhou, Fujian 3,283
Shijiazhuang 3,264
Nanning 3,234
Wenzhou 3,208
Ningbo 3,132
Wuxi, Jiangsu 3,049
Guiyang 2,871
Tangshan 2,743
Lanzhou 2,723
Changzhou, Jiangsu 2,584
Nanchang 2,527
Zibo 2,430
Huizhou 2,312
Jinxi 2,268
Weifang 2,195
Yantai 2,114
Shaoxing 2,076
Luoyang 2,015
Huai'an 2,000
Nantong 1,978
Baotou 1,957
Xuzhou 1,918
Haikou 1,903
Hohhot 1,785
Yangzhou 1,765
Linyi 1,706
Taizhou, Zhejiang 1,648
Handan 1,634
Daqing 1,621
Liuzhou 1,619
Yinchuan 1,596
Jiangmen 1,572
Anshan 1,559
Zhuhai 1,542
Xiangyang 1,533
Datong 1,532
Jilin 1,520
Qiqihar 1,452
Putian 1,438
Yancheng 1,436
Quanzhou 1,395
Jining, Shandong 1,385
Chaozhou 1,333
Huainan 1,327
Xining 1,323
Cixi 1,303
Hengyang 1,301
Fushun 1,298
Tai'an 1,220
Taizhou, Jiangsu 1,184
Zhanjiang 1,149
Anyang 1,140
Qinhuangdao 1,109
Baoding 1,106
Lianyungang 1,099
Zhuzhou 1,083
Yiwu 1,080
Benxi 1,070
Mianyang 1,065
Rizhao 1,062
Zhenjiang 1,050
Suqian 1,050
Nanchong 1,050
Guilin 1,040
Jinzhou 1,035
Zaozhuang 1,028
Yingkou 1,026
Chifeng 1,018
Nanyang 1,011
Xiangtan 1,010
Puning 1,005
Baoji 1,001
Pingdingshan 995
Xinyang 991
Zhangjiakou 983
Huaibei 981
Ruian 973
Jiaxing 970
Jinhua 970
Dongying 967
Jingzhou 964
Yueyang 962
Jueyang 909
Fuyang 893
Jixi 890
Mudanjiang 851
COLOMBIA
Bogotá 9,765
Medellín 3,911
Cali 2,646
Barranquilla 1,991
Bucaramanga 1,215
Cartagena 1,092
Cúcuta 851
CONGO
Brazzaville 1,888
Pointe-Noire 969
CONGO (DEM. REP. OF THE)
Kinshasa 11,587
Lubumbashi 2,015
Mbuji-Mayi 2,007
Kananga 1,169
Kisangani 1,040
COSTA RICA
San José 1,170
CUBA
Havana 2,137
CZECH REPUBLIC
Prague 1,314
DENMARK
Copenhagen 1,268
DOMINICAN REPUBLIC
Santo Domingo 2,945
ECUADOR
Guayaquil 2,709
Quito 1,726
EGYPT
Cairo 18,772
Alexandria 4,778
EL SALVADOR
San Salvador 1,098
ETHIOPIA
Addis Ababa 3,238
FINLAND
Helsinki 1,180
FRANCE
Paris 10,843
Lyon 1,609
Marseilles 1,605
Lille 1,027
Nice 967
Toulouse 938
Bordeaux 891
GEORGIA
Tbilisi 1,147
GERMANY
Berlin 3,563
Hamburg 1,831
Munich 1,438
Cologne 1,037
GHANA
Kumasi 2,599
Accra 2,277
GREECE
Athens 3,052
GUATEMALA
Guatemala City 2,918
GUINEA
Conakry 1,936
HAITI
Port-au-Prince 2,440
HONDURAS
Tegucigalpa 1,123
San Pedro Sula 852
HUNGARY
Budapest 1,714
INDIA
Delhi 25,703
Mumbai 21,043
Kolkata 14,865
Bengaluru 10,087
Chennai 9,890
Hyderabad 8,944
Ahmedabad 7,343
Pune 5,728
Surat 5,650
Jaipur 3,461
Lucknow 3,222
Kanpur 3,021
Nagpur 2,675
Coimbatore 2,549
Calicut 2,476
Indore 2,441
Kochi 2,416
Thrissur 2,329
Malappuram 2,216
Patna 2,210
Kannur 2,153
Bhopal 2,102
Vadodara 1,975
Agra 1,966
Thiruvananthapuram 1,965
Vishakhapatnam 1,935
Nashik 1,779
Vijayawada 1,760
Ludhiana 1,716
Rajkot 1,599
Madurai 1,593
Meerut 1,550
Varanasi 1,541
Jamshedpur 1,451
Srinagar 1,429
Kollam 1,410
Raipur 1,374
Aurangabad 1,344
Jabalpur 1,337
Asansol 1,313
Allahabad 1,295
Jodhpur 1,284
Amritsar 1,265
Ranchi 1,262
Dhanbad 1,255
Tiruppur 1,230
Kota 1,163
Chandigarh 1,134
Bhilainagar-Durg 1,129
Bareilly 1,111
Tiruchchirapalli 1,106
Mysore 1,082
Guwahati 1,042
Aligarh 1,037
Moradabad 1,023
Hubli-Dharwad 1,020
Salem 1,003
Bhubaneswar 999
Solapur 986
Jalandhar 954
INDONESIA
Jakarta 10,323
Surabaya 2,853
Bandung 2,544
Medan 2,204
Semarang 1,630
Makassar 1,489
Palembang 1,455
Batam 1,391
Pekanbaru 1,121
Denpasar 1,107
Bogor 1,076
Bandar Lampung 965
Padang 903
Samarinda 865
Malang 856
IRAN
Tehran 8,432
Mashhad 3,014
Esfahan 1,880
Karaj 1,807
Shiraz 1,661
Tabriz 1,572
Ahvaz 1,216
Qom 1,204
Kermanshah 896
IRAQ
Baghdad 6,643
Mosul 1,694
Arbil 1,166
Basra 1,019
As Sulaymaniyah 1,004
IRELAND
Dublin 1,169
ISRAEL
Tel Aviv-Yafo 3,608
Haifa 1,097
ITALY
Rome 3,718
Milan 3,099
Naples 2,202
Turin 1,765
Palermo 853
IVORY COAST (CÔTE D'IVOIRE)
Abidjan 4,860
JAPAN
Tokyo–Yokohama 38,001
Osaka–Kobe 20,238
Nagoya 9,406
Fukuoka–Kitakyushu 5,510
Sapporo 2,571
Hiroshima 2,173
Sendai 2,091
Kyoto 1,470
JORDAN
Amman 1,155
KAZAKHSTAN
Almaty 1,523
KENYA
Nairobi 3,915
Mombasa 1,104
KOREA, NORTH
Pyongyang 2,863
KOREA, SOUTH
Seoul 9,774
Busan 3,216
Incheon 2,685
Daegu 2,244
Daejeon 1,564
Gwangju 1,536
Suwon 1,099
Yongin 1,048
Changwon 1,039
Seongnam 968
Goyang 942
Ulsan 904
KUWAIT
Kuwait City 2,779
KYRGYZSTAN
Bishkek 865
LEBANON
Beirut 2,226
LIBYA
Tripoli 1,126
MADAGASCAR
Antananarivo 2,610
MALAWI
Lilongwe 905
MALAYSIA
Kuala Lumpur 6,837
Johor Bahru 912
MALI
Bamako 2,515
MEXICO
Mexico City 20,999
Guadalajara 4,843
Monterrey 4,513
Puebla 2,984
Toluca 2,164
Tijuana 1,987
León 1,807
Ciudad Juárez 1,390
Torreón 1,332
Querétaro 1,267
San Luis Potosí 1,147
Mérida 1,068
Mexicali 1,034
Aguascalientes 1,031
Cuernavaca 993
Chihuahua 941
Saltillo 932
Tampico 920
Morelia 914
Acapulco 900
Veracruz 880
MONGOLIA
Ulan Bator 1,377
MOROCCO
Casablanca 3,515
Rabat 1,967
Fès 1,172
Marrakesh 1,134
Tangier 982
MOZAMBIQUE
Maputo 1,187
Matola 937
NEPAL
Katmandu 1,183
NETHERLANDS
Amsterdam 1,091
Rotterdam 993
NEW ZEALAND
Auckland 1,344
NICARAGUA
Managua 956
NIGER
Niamey 1,090
NIGERIA
Lagos 13,123
Kano 3,587
Ibadan 3,160
Abuja 2,440
Port Harcourt 2,343
Benin City 1,496
Onitsha 1,109
Kaduna 1,048
Aba 944
NORWAY
Oslo 986
PAKISTAN
Karachi 16,618
Lahore 8,741
Faisalabad 3,567
Rawalpindi 2,506
Gujranwala 2,122
Multan 1,921
Hyderabad 1,772
Peshawar 1,736
Islamabad 1,365
Quetta 1,109
Bahawalpur 913
PANAMA
Panamá 1,673
PARAGUAY
Asunción 2,356
PERU
Lima 9,897
Arequipa 850
PHILIPPINES
Manila 12,946
Davao 1,630
Cebu 951
Zamboanga 936
POLAND
Warsaw 1,722
PORTUGAL
Lisbon 2,884
Porto 1,299
PUERTO RICO
San Juan 2,463
ROMANIA
Bucharest 1,868
RUSSIA
Moscow 12,166
St Petersburg 4,993
Novosibirsk 1,497
Yekaterinburg 1,379
Nizhniy Novgorod 1,212
Samara 1,164
Kazan 1,162
Omsk 1,162
Chelyabinsk 1,157
Rostov 1,097
Ufa 1,070
Volgograd 1,022
Krasnoyarsk 1,008
Perm 982
Voronezh 911
RWANDA
Kigali 1,257
SAUDI ARABIA
Riyadh 6,370
Jedda 4,076
Mecca 1,771
Medina 1,280
Dammam 1,064
SENEGAL
Dakar 3,520
SERBIA
Belgrade 1,182
SIERRA LEONE
Freetown 1,007
SINGAPORE
Singapore City 5,619
SOMALIA
Mogadishu 2,138
SOUTH AFRICA
Johannesburg 9,399
Cape Town 3,660
Durban 2,901
Pretoria 2,059
Port Elizabeth 1,179
Vereeniging 1,155
SPAIN
Madrid 6,199
Barcelona 5,258
SUDAN
Khartoum 5,129
SWEDEN
Stockholm 1,486
SWITZERLAND
Zürich 1,246
SYRIA
Aleppo 3,562
Damascus 2,566
Homs 1,641
Hamah 1,237
TAIWAN
Taipei 2,666
T'aichung 1,225
Kaohsiung 1,523
TANZANIA
Dar es Salaam 5,116
THAILAND
Bangkok 9,270
Samut Prakan 1,814
TOGO
Lomé 956
TUNISIA
Tunis 1,993
TURKEY
Istanbul 14,164
Ankara 4,750
Izmir 3,040
Bursa 1,923
Adana 1,830
Gaziantep 1,528
Konya 1,194
Antalya 1,072
Diyarbakir 926
Kayseri 904
UGANDA
Kampala 1,936
UKRAINE
Kiev 2,942
Kharkov 1,441
Odessa 1,010
Dnepropetrovsk 957
Donetsk 934
UNITED ARAB EMIRATES
Dubai 2,415
Sharjah 1,279
Abu Dhabi 1,145
UNITED KINGDOM
London 10,313
Birmingham 2,515
Manchester 2,646
Glasgow 1,223
Liverpool 870
UNITED STATES OF AMERICA
New York 19,950
Los Angeles 13,131
Chicago 9,537
Dallas–Fort Worth 6,811
Houston 6,313
Philadelphia 6,035
Washington, DC 5,950
Miami 5,828
Atlanta 5,523
Boston 4,684
San Francisco 4,516
Phoenix–Mesa 4,399
Riverside–San Bernardino 4,381
Detroit 4,295
Seattle 3,610
Minneapolis–St Paul 3,459
San Diego 3,211
Tampa–St Petersburg 2,871
St Louis 2,801
Baltimore 2,771
Denver 2,697
Pittsburgh 2,361
Charlotte 2,335
Portland 2,314
San Antonio 2,278
Orlando 2,268
Sacramento 2,216
Cincinnati 2,137
Cleveland 2,065
Kansas City 2,054
Las Vegas 2,028
Columbus 1,967
Indianapolis 1,954
San Jose 1,920
Austin 1,883
Nashville 1,758
Virginia Beach–Norfolk 1,707
Providence 1,604
Milwaukee 1,570
Jacksonville 1,395
Memphis 1,342
Oklahoma 1,320
Louisville 1,262
Richmond 1,246
New Orleans 1,241
Hartford 1,215
Raleigh 1,215
Birmingham 1,140
Salt Lake City 1,140
Buffalo 1,134
Rochester 1,083
Grand Rapids 1,017
Tucson 997
Tulsa 961
Fresno 955
Worcester 927
Albuquerque 903
Omaha 895
Albany 878
New Haven 862
Honolulu 848
URUGUAY
Montevideo 1,707
UZBEKISTAN
Tashkent 2,251
VENEZUELA
Caracas 2,916
Maracaibo 2,196
Valencia 1,734
Maracay 1,166
Barquisimeto 1,039
VIETNAM
Ho Chi Minh City 7,298
Hanoi 3,629
Can Tho 1,175
Haiphong 1,075
Da Nang 952
YEMEN
Sana' 2,962
Aden 882
ZAMBIA
Lusaka 2,179
ZIMBABWE
Harare 1,501

WORLD STATISTICS: CLIMATE

Rainfall and temperature figures are provided for more than 70 cities. As climate is affected by altitude, the height of the weather station for each city is shown in metres beneath its name. For each location, the top row of figures shows the total rainfall or snow in millimetres, and the bottom row the average temperature in degrees Celsius; the total annual rainfall and average annual temperature are at the end of the rows. The map opposite shows the city locations.

CITY	JAN.	FEB.	MAR.	APR.	MAY	JUNE	JULY	AUG.	SEPT.	OCT.	NOV.	DEC.	YEAR
EUROPE													
Athens, Greece 107 m	62	37	37	23	23	14	6	7	15	51	56	71	402
	10	10	12	16	20	25	28	28	24	20	15	11	18
Berlin, Germany 55 m	42	33	41	37	54	69	56	58	45	37	44	55	571
	-1	0	4	9	14	17	19	18	15	9	5	1	9
Istanbul, Turkey 14 m	87	71	63	43	33	25	24	24	44	71	85	107	655
	5	6	7	11	16	20	23	23	20	16	12	8	14
Lisbon, Portugal 77 m	111	110	69	54	44	16	3	4	33	62	93	103	702
	11	12	14	16	17	20	22	23	21	18	14	12	17
London, UK 5 m	54	40	37	37	46	45	57	59	49	57	64	48	593
	4	5	7	9	12	16	18	17	15	11	8	5	11
Málaga, Spain 33 m	61	51	62	46	26	5	1	3	29	64	64	62	474
	12	13	16	17	19	29	25	26	23	20	16	13	18
Moscow, Russia 156 m	39	38	36	37	53	58	88	71	58	45	47	54	624
	-13	-10	-4	6	13	16	18	17	12	6	-1	-7	4
Odessa, Ukraine 64 m	57	62	30	21	34	34	42	37	37	13	35	71	473
	-3	-1	2	9	15	20	22	22	18	12	9	1	10
Paris, France 75 m	56	46	35	42	57	54	59	64	55	50	51	50	619
	3	4	8	11	15	18	20	19	17	12	7	4	12
Rome, Italy 17 m	71	62	57	51	46	37	15	21	63	99	129	93	744
	8	9	11	14	18	22	25	25	22	17	13	10	16
Shannon, Ireland 2 m	94	67	56	53	61	57	77	79	86	86	96	117	929
	5	5	7	9	12	14	16	16	14	11	8	6	10
Stockholm, Sweden 44 m	43	30	25	31	34	45	61	76	60	48	53	48	554
	-3	-3	-1	5	10	15	18	17	12	7	3	0	7
ASIA													
Bangkok, Thailand 2 m	8	20	36	58	198	160	160	175	305	206	66	5	1,397
	26	28	29	30	29	29	28	28	28	28	26	25	28
Beirut, Lebanon 34 m	191	158	94	53	18	3	3	3	5	51	132	185	892
	14	14	16	18	22	24	27	28	26	24	19	16	21
Colombo, Sri Lanka 7 m	89	69	147	231	371	224	135	109	160	348	315	147	2,365
	26	26	27	28	28	27	27	27	27	27	26	26	27
Harbin, China 160 m	6	5	10	23	43	94	112	104	46	33	8	5	488
	-18	-15	-5	6	13	19	22	21	14	4	-6	-16	3
Ho Chi Minh, Vietnam 9 m	15	3	13	43	221	330	315	269	335	269	114	56	1,984
	26	27	29	30	29	28	28	28	27	27	27	26	28
Hong Kong, China 33 m	33	46	74	137	292	394	381	361	257	114	43	31	2,162
	16	15	18	22	26	28	28	28	27	25	21	18	23
Jakarta, Indonesia 8 m	300	300	211	147	114	97	64	43	66	112	142	203	1,798
	26	26	27	27	27	27	27	27	27	27	27	26	27

CITY	JAN.	FEB.	MAR.	APR.	MAY	JUNE	JULY	AUG.	SEPT.	OCT.	NOV.	DEC.	YEAR
ASIA (continued)													
Kabul, Afghanistan 1,815 m	34	60	68	72	23	1	6	2	2	4	19	22	313
	-3	-1	6	13	18	22	25	24	20	14	7	3	12
Karachi, Pakistan 4 m	13	10	8	3	3	18	81	41	13	<3	3	5	196
	19	20	24	28	30	31	30	29	28	28	24	20	26
Kolkata, India 6 m	10	31	36	43	140	297	325	328	252	114	20	5	1,600
	20	22	27	30	30	30	29	29	29	28	23	19	26
Manama, Bahrain 5 m	8	18	13	8	3	0	0	0	0	0	18	18	81
	17	18	21	25	29	32	33	34	31	28	24	19	26
Mumbai, India 11 m	3	3	3	3	18	485	617	340	264	64	13	3	1,809
	24	24	26	28	30	29	27	27	27	28	27	26	27
New Delhi, India 218 m	23	18	13	8	13	74	180	172	117	10	3	10	640
	14	17	23	28	33	34	31	30	29	26	20	15	25
Omsk, Russia 85 m	15	8	8	13	31	51	51	51	28	25	18	20	318
	-22	-19	-12	-1	10	16	18	16	10	1	-11	-18	-1
Qazaly, Kazakhstan 63 m	10	10	13	13	15	5	5	8	8	10	13	15	125
	-12	-11	-3	6	18	23	25	23	16	8	-1	-7	7
Shanghai, China 7 m	48	58	84	94	94	180	147	142	130	71	51	36	1,135
	4	5	9	14	20	24	28	28	23	19	12	7	16
Singapore 10 m	252	173	193	188	173	173	170	196	178	208	254	257	2,413
	26	27	28	28	28	28	28	27	27	27	27	27	27
Tehran, Iran 1,220 m	46	38	46	36	13	3	3	3	3	8	20	31	246
	2	5	9	16	21	26	30	29	25	18	12	6	17
Tokyo, Japan 6 m	48	74	107	135	147	165	142	152	234	208	97	56	1,565
	3	4	7	13	17	21	25	26	23	17	11	6	14
Ulan Bator, Mongolia 1,325 m	3	3	3	5	10	28	76	51	23	5	5	3	208
	-26	-21	-13	-1	6	14	16	14	8	-1	-13	-22	-3
Verkhoyansk, Russia 100 m	5	5	3	5	8	23	28	25	13	8	8	5	134
	-50	-45	-32	-15	0	12	14	9	2	-15	-38	-48	-17
AFRICA													
Addis Ababa, Ethiopia 2,450 m	3	3	25	135	213	201	206	239	102	28	3	0	1,151
	19	20	20	20	19	18	18	19	21	22	21	20	20
Antananarivo, Madag. 1,372 m	300	279	178	53	18	8	8	10	18	61	135	287	1,356
	21	21	21	19	18	15	14	15	17	19	21	21	19
Cairo, Egypt 116 m	5	4	4	1	1	0	0	0	0	1	4	6	26
	13	15	18	21	25	28	28	28	26	24	20	15	22
Cape Town, S. Africa 17 m	15	8	18	48	79	84	89	66	43	31	18	10	508
	21	21	20	17	14	13	12	13	14	16	18	19	17
Jo'burg, S. Africa 1,665 m	114	109	89	38	25	8	8	8	23	56	107	125	709
	20	20	18	16	13	10	11	13	16	18	19	20	16

CITY	JAN.	FEB.	MAR.	APR.	MAY	JUNE	JULY	AUG.	SEPT.	OCT.	NOV.	DEC.	YEAR

AFRICA (continued)

CITY	JAN.	FEB.	MAR.	APR.	MAY	JUNE	JULY	AUG.	SEPT.	OCT.	NOV.	DEC.	YEAR
Khartoum, Sudan	3	3	3	3	3	8	53	71	18	5	3	0	158
390 m	24	25	28	31	33	34	32	31	32	32	28	25	29
Kinshasa, Congo (D.R.)	135	145	196	196	158	8	3	3	31	119	221	142	1,354
325 m	26	26	27	27	26	24	23	24	25	26	26	26	25
Lagos, Nigeria	28	46	102	150	269	460	279	64	140	206	69	25	1,836
3 m	27	28	29	28	28	26	26	25	26	26	28	28	27
Lusaka, Zambia	231	191	142	18	3	3	3	0	3	10	91	150	836
1,277 m	21	22	21	21	19	16	16	18	22	24	23	22	21
Monrovia, Liberia	31	56	97	216	516	973	996	373	744	772	236	130	5,138
23 m	26	26	27	27	26	25	24	25	25	25	26	26	26
Nairobi, Kenya	38	64	125	211	158	46	15	23	31	53	109	86	958
820 m	19	19	19	19	18	16	16	16	18	19	18	18	18
Timbuktu, Mali	1	0	0	1	4	16	54	74	29	4	0	0	183
301 m	22	24	28	32	34	35	32	30	32	31	28	23	29
Tunis, Tunisia	64	51	41	36	18	8	3	8	33	51	48	61	419
66 m	10	11	13	16	19	23	26	27	25	20	16	11	18
Walvis Bay, Namibia	3	5	8	3	3	3	3	3	3	3	3	3	23
7 m	19	19	19	18	17	16	15	14	14	15	17	18	18

AUSTRALIA, NEW ZEALAND AND ANTARCTICA

CITY	JAN.	FEB.	MAR.	APR.	MAY	JUNE	JULY	AUG.	SEPT.	OCT.	NOV.	DEC.	YEAR
Alice Springs, Aust.	43	33	28	10	15	13	8	8	8	18	31	38	252
579 m	29	28	25	20	15	12	12	14	18	23	26	28	21
Christchurch, NZ	56	43	48	48	66	66	69	48	46	43	48	56	638
10 m	16	16	14	12	9	6	6	7	9	12	14	16	11
Darwin, Australia	386	312	254	97	15	3	3	3	13	51	119	239	1,491
30 m	29	29	29	29	28	26	25	26	28	29	30	29	28
Mawson, Antarctica	11	30	20	10	44	180	4	40	3	20	0	0	362
14 m	0	−5	−10	−14	−15	−16	−18	−18	−19	−13	−5	−1	−11
Perth, Australia	8	10	20	43	130	180	170	149	86	56	20	13	881
60 m	23	23	22	19	16	14	13	13	15	16	19	22	18
Sydney, Australia	89	102	127	135	127	117	117	76	73	71	73	73	1,181
42 m	22	22	21	18	15	13	12	13	15	18	19	21	17

NORTH AMERICA

CITY	JAN.	FEB.	MAR.	APR.	MAY	JUNE	JULY	AUG.	SEPT.	OCT.	NOV.	DEC.	YEAR
Anchorage, USA	20	18	15	10	13	18	41	66	66	56	25	23	371
40 m	−11	−8	−5	2	7	12	14	13	9	2	−5	−11	2
Chicago, USA	51	51	66	71	86	89	84	81	79	66	61	51	836
251 m	−4	−3	2	9	14	20	23	22	19	12	5	−1	10
Churchill, Canada	15	13	18	23	32	44	46	58	51	43	39	21	402
13 m	−28	−26	−20	−10	−2	6	12	11	5	−2	−12	−22	−7
Edmonton, Canada	25	19	19	22	43	77	89	78	39	17	16	25	466
676 m	−15	−10	−5	4	11	15	17	16	11	6	−4	−10	3
Honolulu, USA	104	66	79	48	25	18	23	28	36	48	64	104	643
12 m	23	18	19	20	22	24	25	26	26	24	22	19	22
Houston, USA	89	76	84	91	119	117	99	99	104	94	89	109	1,171
12 m	12	13	17	21	24	27	28	29	26	22	16	12	21

NORTH AMERICA (continued)

CITY	JAN.	FEB.	MAR.	APR.	MAY	JUNE	JULY	AUG.	SEPT.	OCT.	NOV.	DEC.	YEAR
Kingston, Jamaica	23	15	23	31	102	89	38	91	99	180	74	36	800
34 m	25	25	25	26	26	28	28	28	27	27	26	26	26
Los Angeles, USA	79	76	71	25	10	3	3	3	5	15	31	66	381
95 m	13	14	14	16	17	19	21	22	21	18	16	14	17
Mexico City, Mexico	13	5	10	20	53	119	170	152	130	51	18	8	747
2,309 m	12	13	16	18	19	19	17	18	18	16	14	13	16
Miami, USA	71	53	64	81	173	178	155	160	203	234	71	51	1,516
8 m	20	20	22	23	25	27	28	28	27	25	22	21	24
Montréal, Canada	72	65	74	74	66	82	90	92	88	76	81	87	946
57 m	−10	−9	−3	−6	13	18	21	20	15	9	2	−7	6
New York City, USA	94	97	91	81	81	84	107	109	86	89	76	91	1,092
96 m	−1	−1	3	10	16	20	23	23	21	15	7	2	11
St Louis, USA	58	64	89	97	114	114	89	86	81	74	71	64	1,001
173 m	0	1	7	13	19	24	26	26	22	15	8	2	14
San José, Costa Rica	15	5	20	46	229	241	211	241	305	300	145	41	1,798
1,146 m	19	19	21	21	22	21	21	21	21	20	20	19	20
Vancouver, Canada	154	115	101	60	52	45	32	41	67	114	150	182	1,113
14 m	3	5	6	9	12	15	17	17	14	10	6	4	10
Washington, DC, USA	86	76	91	84	94	99	112	109	94	74	66	79	1,064
22 m	1	2	7	12	18	23	25	24	20	14	8	3	13

SOUTH AMERICA

CITY	JAN.	FEB.	MAR.	APR.	MAY	JUNE	JULY	AUG.	SEPT.	OCT.	NOV.	DEC.	YEAR
Antofagasta, Chile	0	0	0	3	3	3	5	3	3	3	3	0	13
94 m	21	21	20	18	16	15	14	14	15	16	18	19	17
Buenos Aires, Arg.	122	123	154	107	92	50	53	63	78	139	131	103	1,215
27 m	23	23	21	17	13	9	10	11	13	15	19	22	16
Lima, Peru	3	3	3	3	5	5	8	8	8	3	3	3	41
120 m	23	24	24	22	19	17	17	16	17	18	19	21	20
Manaus, Brazil	249	231	262	221	170	84	58	38	46	107	142	203	1,811
44 m	28	28	28	27	28	28	28	28	29	29	29	28	28
Paraná, Brazil	287	236	239	102	13	3	3	5	28	127	231	310	1,582
260 m	23	23	23	23	23	21	21	22	24	24	24	23	23
Rio de Janeiro, Brazil	125	122	130	107	79	53	41	43	66	79	104	137	1,082
61 m	26	26	25	24	22	21	21	21	21	22	23	25	23

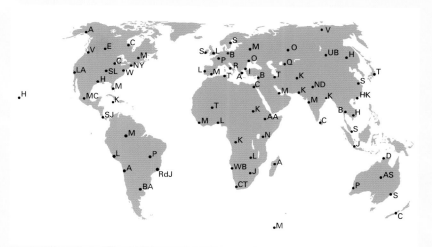

WORLD STATISTICS: PHYSICAL DIMENSIONS

Each topic list is divided into continents and within a continent the items are listed in order of size. The bottom part of many of the lists is selective in order to give examples from as many different countries as possible. The order of the continents is as in the atlas, Europe through to South America. The world top ten are shown in square brackets; in the case of mountains this has not been done because the world top 30 are all in Asia. The figures are rounded as appropriate.

WORLD, CONTINENTS, OCEANS

THE WORLD

	km²	miles²	%
The World	509,450,000	196,672,000	–
Land	149,450,000	57,688,000	29.3
Water	360,000,000	138,984,000	70.7
Asia	44,500,000	17,177,000	29.8
Africa	30,302,000	11,697,000	20.3
North America	24,241,000	9,357,000	16.2
South America	17,793,000	6,868,000	11.9
Antarctica	14,100,000	5,443,000	9.4
Europe	9,957,000	3,843,000	6.7
Australia and Oceania	8,557,000	3,303,000	5.7
Pacific Ocean	155,557,000	60,061,000	46.4
Atlantic Ocean	76,762,000	29,638,000	22.9
Indian Ocean	68,556,000	26,470,000	20.4
Southern Ocean	20,327,000	7,848,000	6.1
Arctic Ocean	14,056,000	5,427,000	4.2

SEAS

PACIFIC

	km²	miles²
South China Sea	2,974,600	1,148,500
Bering Sea	2,268,000	875,000
Sea of Okhotsk	1,528,000	590,000
East China and Yellow Sea	1,249,000	482,000
Sea of Japan	1,008,000	389,000
Gulf of California	162,000	62,500
Bass Strait	75,000	29,000

ATLANTIC

	km²	miles²
Caribbean Sea	2,766,000	1,068,000
Mediterranean Sea	2,516,000	971,000
Gulf of Mexico	1,543,000	596,000
Hudson Bay	1,232,000	476,000
North Sea	575,000	223,000
Black Sea	462,000	178,000
Baltic Sea	422,170	163,000
Gulf of St Lawrence	238,000	92,000

INDIAN

	km²	miles²
Red Sea	438,000	169,000
Persian Gulf	239,000	92,000

MOUNTAINS

EUROPE

		m	ft
Elbrus	Russia	5,642	18,510
Dykh Tau	Russia	5,203	17,070
Shkhara	Russia/Georgia	5,201	17,064
Koshtan Tau	Russia	5,152	16,903
Kazbek	Russia/Georgia	5,047	16,558
Pushkin	Russia/Georgia	5,033	16,512
Katyn Tau	Russia/Georgia	4,979	16,335
Shota Rustaveli	Russia/Georgia	4,860	15,945
Mont Blanc	France/Italy	4,808	15,774
Monte Rosa	Italy/Switzerland	4,634	15,203
Dom	Switzerland	4,545	14,911
Liskamm	Switzerland	4,527	14,852
Weisshorn	Switzerland	4,505	14,780
Tebulos	Russia/Georgia	4,492	14,737
Taschorn	Switzerland	4,490	14,730
Matterhorn/Cervino	Italy/Switzerland	4,478	14,691
Mont Maudit	France/Italy	4,465	14,649
Bazar Dyuzi	Russia/Azerbaijan	4,462	14,639
Grandes Jorasses	France/Italy	4,208	13,806
Jungfrau	Switzerland	4,158	13,642
Barre des Ecrins	France	4,102	13,458
Gran Paradiso	Italy	4,061	13,323
Piz Bernina	Italy/Switzerland	4,049	13,284
Eiger	Switzerland	3,970	13,025
Grossglockner	Austria	3,797	12,457
Mulhacén	Spain	3,478	11,411
Etna	Italy	3,323	10,902
Zugspitze	Germany	2,962	9,718
Olympus	Greece	2,917	9,570
Galdhøpiggen	Norway	2,469	8,100
Ben Nevis	UK	1,344	4,408

ASIA

		m	ft
Everest	China/Nepal	8,850	29,035
K2 (Godwin Austen)	China/Kashmir	8,611	28,251
Kanchenjunga	India/Nepal	8,598	28,208
Lhotse	China/Nepal	8,516	27,939
Makalu	China/Nepal	8,481	27,824
Cho Oyu	China/Nepal	8,201	26,906
Dhaulagiri	Nepal	8,167	26,795
Manaslu	Nepal	8,156	26,758
Nanga Parbat	Kashmir	8,126	26,660
Annapurna	Nepal	8,078	26,502
Gasherbrum	China/Kashmir	8,068	26,469
Broad Peak	China/Kashmir	8,051	26,414
Xixabangma Feng	China	8,012	26,286
Gayachung Kang	Nepal	7,897	25,909
Himalchuli	Nepal	7,893	25,896
Disteghil Sar	Kashmir	7,885	25,869
Nuptse	Nepal	7,879	25,849
Kangbachen	Nepal	7,858	25,781
Khunyang Chhish	Kashmir	7,852	25,761
Masherbrum	Kashmir	7,821	25,659
Nanda Devi	India	7,817	25,646
Rakaposhi	Kashmir	7,788	25,551
Batura	Kashmir	7,785	25,541
Namche Barwa	China	7,782	25,531
Kamet	India	7,756	25,447
Soltoro Kangri	Pakistan	7,742	25,400
Gurla Mandhata	China	7,728	25,354
Trivor	Pakistan	7,720	25,328
Kongur Shan	China	7,719	25,324
Jannu	Nepal	7,710	25,295
Tirich Mir	Pakistan	7,690	25,229
K'ula Shan	Bhutan/China	7,543	24,747
Pik Imeni Ismail Samani	Tajikistan	7,495	24,590
Demavend	Iran	5,604	18,386
Ararat	Turkey	5,165	16,945
Gunong Kinabalu	Malaysia (Borneo)	4,101	13,455
Yu Shan	Taiwan	3,952	12,966
Fuji-San	Japan	3,776	12,388

AFRICA

		m	ft
Kilimanjaro	Tanzania	5,895	19,340
Mt Kenya	Kenya	5,199	17,057
Ruwenzori (Margherita)	Uganda/Congo (D.R.)	5,109	16,762
Meru	Tanzania	4,565	14,977
Ras Dashen	Ethiopia	4,533	14,872
Karisimbi	Rwanda/Congo (D.R.)	4,507	14,787
Mt Elgon	Kenya/Uganda	4,321	14,176
Batu	Ethiopia	4,307	14,130
Guna	Ethiopia	4,231	13,882
Toubkal	Morocco	4,165	13,665
Irhil Mgoun	Morocco	4,071	13,356
Mt Cameroun	Cameroon	4,070	13,353
Amba Ferit	Ethiopia	3,875	13,042
Pico del Teide	Spain (Tenerife)	3,718	12,198
Thabana Ntlenyana	Lesotho	3,482	11,424
Emi Koussi	Chad	3,415	11,204
Mt aux Sources	Lesotho/South Africa	3,282	10,768
Piton des Neiges	Réunion	3,069	10,069

OCEANIA

		m	ft
Puncak Jaya	Indonesia	4,884	16,024
Puncak Trikora	Indonesia	4,730	15,518
Puncak Mandala	Indonesia	4,702	15,427
Mt Wilhelm	Papua New Guinea	4,508	14,790
Mauna Kea	USA (Hawai'i)	4,205	13,796
Mauna Loa	USA (Hawai'i)	4,169	13,678
Aoraki Mt Cook	New Zealand	3,753	12,313
Mt Popomanaseu	Solomon Islands	2,439	8,002
Mt Orohena	French Polynesia (Tahiti)	2,241	7,352
Mt Kosciuszko	Australia	2,228	7,310

NORTH AMERICA

		m	ft
Mt McKinley (Denali)	USA (Alaska)	6,168	20,237
Mt Logan	Canada	5,959	19,551
Pico de Orizaba	Mexico	5,610	18,405
Mt St Elias	USA/Canada	5,489	18,008
Popocatépetl	Mexico	5,452	17,887

NORTH AMERICA (continued)

		m	ft
Mt Foraker	USA (Alaska)	5,304	17,401
Iztaccíhuatl	Mexico	5,230	17,159
Mt Lucania	Canada	5,226	17,146
Mt Steele	Canada	5,073	16,644
Mt Bona	USA (Alaska)	5,005	16,420
Mt Blackburn	USA (Alaska)	4,996	16,391
Mt Sanford	USA (Alaska)	4,949	16,237
Mt Wood	Canada	4,840	15,880
Nevado de Toluca	Mexico	4,690	15,387
Mt Fairweather	USA (Alaska)	4,663	15,298
Mt Hunter	USA (Alaska)	4,442	14,573
Mt Whitney	USA	4,418	14,495
Mt Elbert	USA	4,399	14,432
Mt Harvard	USA	4,395	14,419
Mt Rainier	USA	4,392	14,409
Blanca Peak	USA	4,372	14,344
Longs Peak	USA	4,345	14,255
Tajumulco	Guatemala	4,220	13,845
Grand Teton	USA	4,197	13,770
Mt Waddington	Canada	4,019	13,186
Mt Robson	Canada	3,954	12,972
Chirripó Grande	Costa Rica	3,819	12,529
Pico Duarte	Dominican Rep.	3,175	10,417

SOUTH AMERICA

		m	ft
Aconcagua	Argentina	6,962	22,841
Ojos del Salado	Argentina/Chile	6,863	22,615
Monte Pissis	Argentina	6,793	22,287
Nevado Huascarán	Peru	6,768	22,205
Cerro Bonete	Argentina	6,759	22,175
Cerro Llullaillaco	Argentina/Chile	6,739	22,110
Cerro Mercedario	Argentina/Chile	6,720	22,047
Yerupaja	Peru	6,632	21,758
Nevado de Tres Cruces	Argentina/Chile	6,620	21,719
Tupungato	Argentina/Chile	6,570	21,555
Sajama	Bolivia	6,520	21,391
Coropuna	Peru	6,425	21,079
Illimani	Bolivia	6,402	21,004
Ausangate	Peru	6,384	20,945
Nevado de Cachi	Argentina	6,380	20,932
Cerro del Toro	Argentina	6,380	20,932
Siula Grande	Peru	6,356	20,853
Chimborazo	Ecuador	6,267	20,561
Incahuasi	Argentina/Chile	6,218	20,400
Alpamayo	Peru	5,947	19,511
Cerro Galan	Argentina	5,912	19,396
Cotapaxi	Ecuador	5,896	19,344
Pico Cristóbal Colón	Colombia	5,775	18,947
Pico Bolivar	Venezuela	4,981	16,342

ANTARCTICA

		m	ft
Vinson Massif		4,897	16,066
Mt Kirkpatrick		4,528	14,855
Mt Markham		4,349	14,268

OCEAN DEPTHS

ATLANTIC OCEAN

	m	ft	
Puerto Rico (Milwaukee) Deep	8,604	28,232	[7]
Cayman Trench	7,680	25,197	[10]
Gulf of Mexico	5,203	17,070	
Mediterranean Sea	5,121	16,801	
Black Sea	2,211	7,254	
North Sea	660	2,165	
Baltic Sea	463	1,519	
Hudson Bay	258	846	

INDIAN OCEAN

	m	ft
Java Trench	7,450	24,442
Red Sea	2,635	8,454
Persian Gulf	73	239

PACIFIC OCEAN

	m	ft	
Mariana Trench	11,022	36,161	[1]
Tonga Trench	10,882	35,702	[2]
Japan Trench	10,554	34,626	[3]
Kuril Trench	10,542	34,587	[4]
Mindanao Trench	10,497	34,439	[5]
Kermadec Trench	10,047	32,962	[6]

PACIFIC OCEAN (continued)

		m	ft	
Peru–Chile Trench		8,050	26,410	[8]
Aleutian Trench		7,822	25,662	[9]

ARCTIC OCEAN

		m	ft
Molloy Deep		5,608	18,399

SOUTHERN OCEAN

		m	ft
South Sandwich Trench		7,235	23,737

LAND LOWS

		m	ft
Caspian Sea	Europe	−28	−92
Dead Sea	Asia	−422	−1,384
Lake Assal	Africa	−156	−512
Lake Eyre North	Oceania	−16	−52
Death Valley	North America	−86	−282
Laguna del Carbón	South America	−105	−344

RIVERS

EUROPE

		km	miles
Volga	Caspian Sea	3,700	2,300
Danube	Black Sea	2,850	1,770
Ural	Caspian Sea	2,535	1,575
Dnieper	Black Sea	2,285	1,420
Kama	Volga	2,030	1,260
Don	Black Sea	1,990	1,240
Pechora	Arctic Ocean	1,790	1,110
Oka	Volga	1,480	920
Belaya	Kama	1,420	880
Dniester	Black Sea	1,400	870
Vyatka	Kama	1,370	850
Rhine	North Sea	1,320	820
Northern Dvina	Arctic Ocean	1,290	800
Desna	Dnieper	1,190	740
Elbe	North Sea	1,145	710
Vistula	Baltic Sea	1,090	675
Loire	Atlantic Ocean	1,020	635

ASIA

		km	miles	
Yangtse	Pacific Ocean	6,380	3,960	[3]
Yenisey–Angara	Arctic Ocean	5,550	3,445	[5]
Huang Ho	Pacific Ocean	5,464	3,395	[6]
Ob–Irtysh	Arctic Ocean	5,410	3,360	[7]
Mekong	Pacific Ocean	4,500	2,800	[9]
Amur	Pacific Ocean	4,442	2,760	
Lena	Arctic Ocean	4,402	2,735	
Irtysh	Ob	4,250	2,640	
Yenisey	Arctic Ocean	4,090	2,540	
Ob	Arctic Ocean	3,680	2,285	
Indus	Indian Ocean	3,100	1,925	
Brahmaputra	Indian Ocean	2,900	1,800	
Syrdarya	Aral Sea	2,860	1,775	
Salween	Indian Ocean	2,800	1,740	
Euphrates	Indian Ocean	2,700	1,675	
Vilyuy	Lena	2,650	1,645	
Kolyma	Arctic Ocean	2,600	1,615	
Amudarya	Aral Sea	2,540	1,578	
Ural	Caspian Sea	2,535	1,575	
Ganges	Indian Ocean	2,510	1,560	
Si Kiang	Pacific Ocean	2,100	1,305	
Irrawaddy	Indian Ocean	2,010	1,250	
Tarim–Yarkand	Lop Nur	2,000	1,240	
Tigris	Indian Ocean	1,900	1,180	

AFRICA

		km	miles	
Nile	Mediterranean	6,695	4,160	[1]
Congo	Atlantic Ocean	4,670	2,900	[8]
Niger	Atlantic Ocean	4,180	2,595	
Zambezi	Indian Ocean	3,540	2,200	
Oubangi/Uele	Congo (D.R.)	2,250	1,400	
Kasai	Congo (D.R.)	1,950	1,210	
Shaballe	Indian Ocean	1,930	1,200	
Orange	Atlantic Ocean	1,860	1,155	
Cubango	Okavango Delta	1,800	1,120	
Limpopo	Indian Ocean	1,770	1,100	
Senegal	Atlantic Ocean	1,640	1,020	
Volta	Atlantic Ocean	1,500	930	

AUSTRALIA

		km	miles
Murray–Darling	Southern Ocean	3,750	2,330
Darling	Murray	3,070	1,905
Murray	Southern Ocean	2,575	1,600
Murrumbidgee	Murray	1,690	1,050

NORTH AMERICA

		km	miles	
Mississippi–Missouri	Gulf of Mexico	5,971	3,710	[4]
Mackenzie	Arctic Ocean	4,240	2,630	
Missouri	Mississippi	4,088	2,540	

NORTH AMERICA (continued)

		km	miles
Mississippi	Gulf of Mexico	3,782	2,350
Yukon	Pacific Ocean	3,185	1,980
Rio Grande	Gulf of Mexico	3,030	1,880
Arkansas	Mississippi	2,340	1,450
Colorado	Pacific Ocean	2,330	1,445
Red	Mississippi	2,040	1,270
Columbia	Pacific Ocean	1,950	1,210
Saskatchewan	Lake Winnipeg	1,940	1,205
Snake	Columbia	1,670	1,040
Churchill	Hudson Bay	1,600	990
Ohio	Mississippi	1,580	980
Brazos	Gulf of Mexico	1,400	870
St Lawrence	Atlantic Ocean	1,170	730

SOUTH AMERICA

		km	miles	
Amazon	Atlantic Ocean	6,450	4,010	[2]
Paraná–Plate	Atlantic Ocean	4,500	2,800	[10]
Purus	Amazon	3,350	2,080	
Madeira	Amazon	3,200	1,990	
São Francisco	Atlantic Ocean	2,900	1,800	
Paraná	Plate	2,800	1,740	
Tocantins	Atlantic Ocean	2,750	1,710	
Orinoco	Atlantic Ocean	2,740	1,700	
Paraguay	Paraná	2,550	1,580	
Pilcomayo	Paraná	2,500	1,550	
Araguaia	Tocantins	2,250	1,400	
Juruá	Amazon	2,000	1,240	
Xingu	Amazon	1,980	1,230	
Ucayali	Amazon	1,900	1,180	
Uruguay	Plate	1,610	1,000	

LAKES

EUROPE

		km²	miles²
Lake Ladoga	Russia	17,700	6,800
Lake Onega	Russia	9,700	3,700
Saimaa system	Finland	8,000	3,100
Vänern	Sweden	5,500	2,100

ASIA

		km²	miles²	
Caspian Sea	Asia	371,000	143,000	[1]
Lake Baikal	Russia	30,500	11,780	[8]
Tonlé Sap	Cambodia	20,000	7,700	
Lake Balkhash	Kazakhstan	18,500	7,100	
Dongting Hu	China	12,000	4,600	
Aral Sea	Kazakhstan/ Uzbekistan	6,800	2,620	
Issyk Kul	Kyrgyzstan	6,200	2,400	
Koko Nur	China	5,700	2,200	
Poyang Hu	China	5,000	1,900	
Lake Khanka	China/Russia	4,400	1,700	
Lake Van	Turkey	3,500	1,400	

AFRICA

		km²	miles²	
Lake Victoria	East Africa	68,000	26,300	[3]
Lake Tanganyika	Central Africa	33,000	13,000	[6]
Lake Malawi/Nyasa	East Africa	29,600	11,430	[9]
Lake Chad	Central Africa	25,000	9,700	
Lake Bangweulu	Zambia	9,840	3,800	
Lake Turkana	Ethiopia/Kenya	8,500	3,290	
Lake Volta	Ghana	8,480	3,270	
Lake Kariba	Zambia/Zimbabwe	5,380	2,150	
Lake Albert	Uganda/Congo (D.R.)	5,300	2,050	
Lake Nasser	Egypt/Sudan	5,250	2,030	
Lake Mweru	Zambia/Congo (D.R.)	4,920	1,900	
Lake Kyoga	Uganda	4,430	1,710	
Lake Tana	Ethiopia	3,620	1,400	
Lake Cabora Bassa	Mozambique	2,750	1,070	
Lake Rukwa	Tanzania	2,600	1,000	
Lake Mai-Ndombe	Congo (D.R.)	2,300	890	

AUSTRALIA

		km²	miles²
Lake Eyre	Australia	8,900	3,400
Lake Torrens	Australia	5,800	2,200
Lake Gairdner	Australia	4,800	1,900

NORTH AMERICA

		km²	miles²	
Lake Superior	Canada/USA	82,350	31,800	[2]
Lake Huron	Canada/USA	59,600	23,010	[4]
Lake Michigan	USA	58,000	22,400	[5]
Great Bear Lake	Canada	31,800	12,280	[7]
Great Slave Lake	Canada	28,500	11,000	[10]
Lake Erie	Canada/USA	25,700	9,900	
Lake Winnipeg	Canada	24,400	9,400	
Lake Ontario	Canada/USA	19,500	7,500	
Lake Nicaragua	Nicaragua	8,200	3,200	
Lake Athabasca	Canada	8,100	3,100	
Smallwood Reservoir	Canada	6,530	2,520	
Reindeer Lake	Canada	6,400	2,500	
Nettilling Lake	Canada	5,500	2,100	

SOUTH AMERICA

		km²	miles²
Lake Titicaca	Bolivia/Peru	8,300	3,200
Lake Poopo	Bolivia	2,800	1,100

ISLANDS

EUROPE

		km²	miles²	
Great Britain	UK	229,880	88,700	[8]
Iceland	Atlantic Ocean	103,000	39,800	
Ireland	Ireland/UK	84,400	32,600	
Novaya Zemlya (N.)	Russia	48,200	18,600	
Spitsbergen	Norway	39,000	15,100	
Novaya Zemlya (S.)	Russia	33,200	12,800	
Sicily	Italy	25,500	9,800	
Sardinia	Italy	24,000	9,300	
Nordaustlandet	Norway	15,000	5,600	
Corsica	France	8,700	3,400	
Crete	Greece	8,350	3,200	
Sjælland	Denmark	6,850	2,600	

ASIA

		km²	miles²	
Borneo	South-east Asia	744,360	287,400	[3]
Sumatra	Indonesia	473,600	182,860	[6]
Honshu	Japan	230,500	88,980	[7]
Sulawesi (Celebes)	Indonesia	189,000	73,000	
Java	Indonesia	126,700	48,900	
Luzon	Philippines	104,700	40,400	
Mindanao	Philippines	101,500	39,200	
Hokkaido	Japan	78,400	30,300	
Sakhalin	Russia	74,060	28,600	
Sri Lanka	Indian Ocean	65,600	25,300	
Taiwan	Pacific Ocean	36,000	13,900	
Kyushu	Japan	35,700	13,800	
Hainan	China	34,000	13,100	
Timor	South-east Asia	33,600	13,000	
Shikoku	Japan	18,800	7,300	
Halmahera	Indonesia	18,000	6,900	
Ceram	Indonesia	17,150	6,600	
Sumbawa	Indonesia	15,450	6,000	
Flores	Indonesia	15,200	5,900	
Samar	Philippines	13,100	5,100	
Negros	Philippines	12,700	4,900	
Bangka	Indonesia	12,000	4,600	
Palawan	Philippines	12,000	4,600	
Panay	Philippines	11,500	4,400	
Sumba	Indonesia	11,100	4,300	
Mindoro	Philippines	9,750	3,800	

AFRICA

		km²	miles²	
Madagascar	Indian Ocean	587,040	226,660	[4]
Socotra	Indian Ocean	3,600	1,400	
Réunion	Indian Ocean	2,500	965	
Tenerife	Atlantic Ocean	2,350	900	
Mauritius	Indian Ocean	1,865	720	

OCEANIA

		km²	miles²	
New Guinea	Indonesia/Papua NG	821,030	317,000	[2]
New Zealand (S.)	Pacific Ocean	150,500	58,100	
New Zealand (N.)	Pacific Ocean	114,700	44,300	
Tasmania	Australia	67,800	26,200	
New Britain	Papua New Guinea	37,800	14,600	
New Caledonia	Pacific Ocean	19,100	7,400	
Viti Levu	Fiji	10,500	4,100	
Hawai'i	Pacific Ocean	10,450	4,000	
Bougainville	Papua New Guinea	9,600	3,700	
Guadalcanal	Solomon Islands	6,500	2,500	
Vanua Levu	Fiji	5,550	2,100	
New Ireland	Papua New Guinea	3,200	1,200	

NORTH AMERICA

		km²	miles²	
Greenland	Atlantic Ocean	2,175,600	839,800	[1]
Baffin Island	Canada	508,000	196,100	[5]
Victoria Island	Canada	212,200	81,900	[9]
Ellesmere Island	Canada	212,000	81,800	[10]
Cuba	Caribbean Sea	110,860	42,800	
Newfoundland	Canada	110,680	42,700	
Hispaniola	Dominican Rep./Haiti	76,200	29,400	
Banks Island	Canada	67,000	25,900	
Devon Island	Canada	54,500	21,000	
Melville Island	Canada	42,400	16,400	
Vancouver Island	Canada	32,150	12,400	
Somerset Island	Canada	24,300	9,400	
Jamaica	Caribbean Sea	11,400	4,400	
Puerto Rico	Atlantic Ocean	8,900	3,400	
Cape Breton Island	Canada	4,000	1,500	

SOUTH AMERICA

		km²	miles²	
Tierra del Fuego	Argentina/Chile	47,000	18,100	
Falkland Islands (East)	Atlantic Ocean	6,800	2,600	
South Georgia	Atlantic Ocean	4,200	1,600	
Galapagos (Isabela)	Pacific Ocean	2,250	870	

OF EARTH

Boston, on the curved bay in the north of the image, is the cultural, intellectual and commercial focus of New England. Now the tenth largest city in the United States, it was the scene of momentous events of the American Revolution. To the south and east of Boston, is the peninsula of Cape Cod, shaped like a spinnaker sail thrusting out into the Atlantic Ocean. The beaches of the peninsula, and the islands to the south, are a summer haven for thousands of tourists. Moving westwards around the coast leads to the bays and inlets (with the historic city of Providence at their apex) which are the defining feature of the state of Rhode Island. [Map page 173]
Source: RapidEye/NPA Satellite Mapping

The River Thames snakes from Chelsea Bridge in the west to Tower Bridge in the east in this image covering both the West End and the City of London. Despite having a population in excess of 10 million people, there are still many parks and open spaces around the city centre. St James's Park and Green Park, together with Buckingham Palace and its gardens, can be seen at centre left of the image, and, on the western edge, parts of Hyde Park and Regent's Park can also be seen. Just below the page title, at top centre, the newly developing area around Kings Cross and St Pancras railway stations can be seen. In addition, the low sun shows clearly the shadows of The Shard and the chimney of Tate Modern as well as the many high-rise buildings in the City. [Map page 67]
Source: GeoEye/NPA Satellite Mapping

As both the capital and the largest city in the Netherlands, with over 1 million inhabitants, Amsterdam is a major commercial and cultural centre. Its name is derived from its position at the mouth of the River Amstel, flowing in from the south. The urban area is split by the Nordzeekanaal, which connects the Ijsselmeer to the North Sea. There is also the important Rijnkanaal, which links it with the major inland waterways of Europe via the River Rhine. The ancient core of the settlement is to the south, where the concentric rings of the famous canal system can be seen. This network is evidence of city planning to accommodate and service a fast-rising population in the 17th century. [Map page 69]
Source: RapidEye/NPA Satellite Mapping

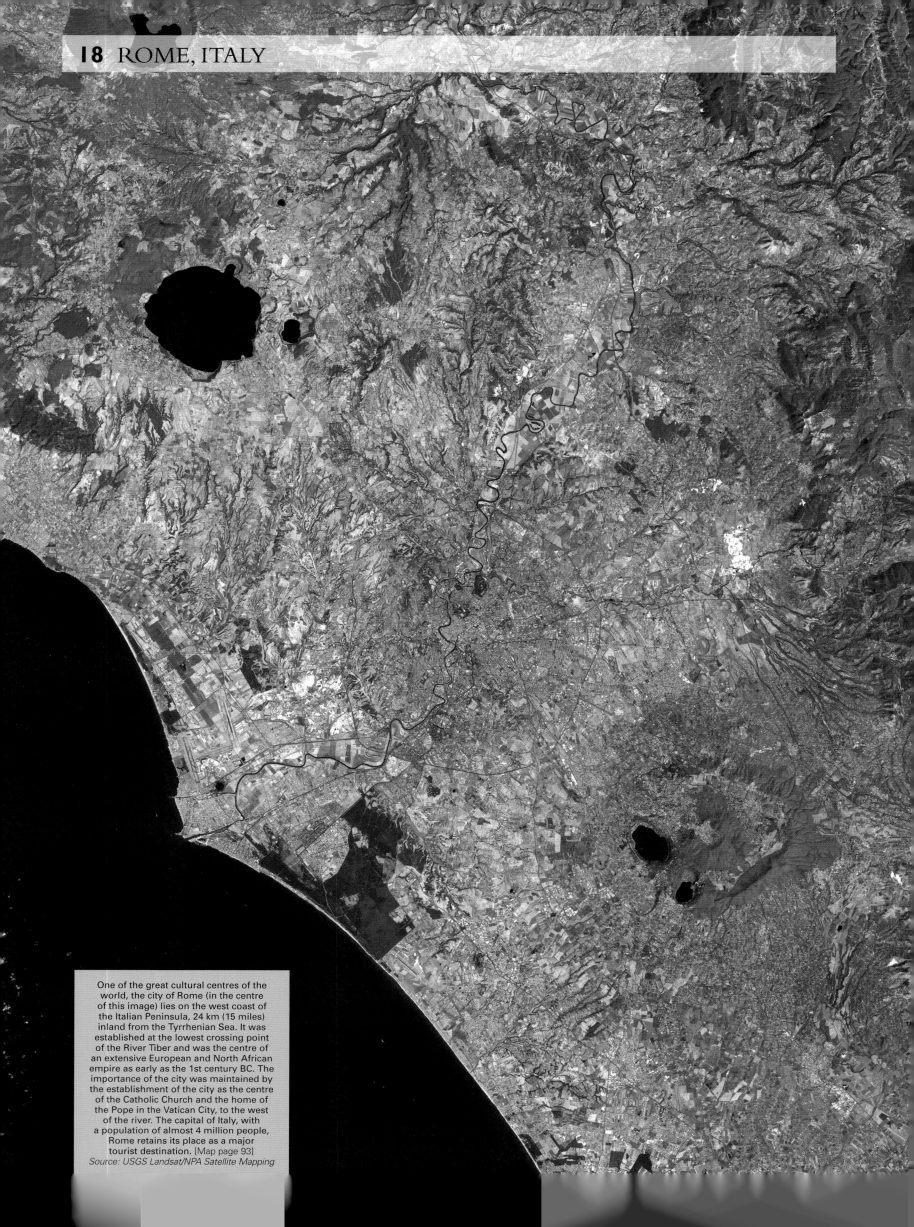

One of the great cultural centres of the world, the city of Rome (in the centre of this image) lies on the west coast of the Italian Peninsula, 24 km (15 miles) inland from the Tyrrhenian Sea. It was established at the lowest crossing point of the River Tiber and was the centre of an extensive European and North African empire as early as the 1st century BC. The importance of the city was maintained by the establishment of the city as the centre of the Catholic Church and the home of the Pope in the Vatican City, to the west of the river. The capital of Italy, with a population of almost 4 million people, Rome retains its place as a major tourist destination. [Map page 93]
Source: USGS Landsat/NPA Satellite Mapping

The metropolitan area of Athens, including its port of Piraeus, is home to nearly a third of the total population of Greece. The capital of the country, it was a powerful city state in the era of Ancient Greece, some 2,500 years ago. At the bottom left of the image is part of the Peloponnese Peninsula, connected to the mainland by the Isthmus of Corinth. To shorten the sailing time around the peninsula, the Corinth Canal was excavated at the end of the 19th century and can be seen here as a fine blue line. [Map page 98]
Source: USGS Landsat/NPA Satellite Mapping

This image shows part of the Pothohar Plateau in northern Pakistan, with the Margalla Hills to the north. The purple area to the south of the image is the city of Rawalpindi – the grid-like street pattern to the north of it is the country's capital, Islamabad. After independence in 1947, Islamabad gradually superseded Karachi, the old colonial capital. The capital was moved for a time to Rawalpindi whilst the new city was designed and established, after 1960. It is still being developed and the combined population of both settlements is now over 4 million inhabitants, with Islamabad acting as the administrative centre of the country. The city of Abbottabad is at the top right of the image. [Map page 124]
Source: USGS Landsat/NPA Satellite Mapping

On the north coast of Java, Jakarta is the capital city of Indonesia and, with a population of over 10 million, it is one of the world's largest urban agglomerations. Formerly known as Batavia, it was the centre of the trading empire of the Dutch East India Company. The city sprawls out from its colonial heart that has Javanese, Chinese and Arab quarters, through modern residential suburbs, to the shanty towns that form the fringes of the urban area. This image, taken in the wet season, shows the blurring of the line between land and sea in the north. Slumbering under the cloud cover in the centre bottom of the image, are the twin volcanic peaks of Gede-Pangrango. The surrounding national park provides a welcome contrast to the densely populated cities of Java. [Map page 118]
Source: USGS Landsat/NPA Satellite Mapping

This image covers one of the most dynamic areas in the world, Hong Kong, with Shenzhen to its north. Hong Kong became a major port and international financial centre during the period of British rule and retains a special status as a Special Administrative Region (SAR) with a high degree of economic autonomy, including the retention of the Hong Kong dollar. To its north Shenzhen was established by China as a Special Economic Zone (SEZ) in 1979, to attract foreign industry and investment. This has proved very successful and communications between the two have also improved, as can be seen by the sinuous Shenzhen Bay Bridge, at centre left in this image. [Map page 117]
Source: RapidEye/NPA Satellite Mapping

At the head of Tokyo Bay, the capital city forms the centre of one of the world's most densely populated areas. With its satellites of Kawasaki and Yokohama, the population of over 34 million people makes this metropolitan area the world's largest 'megacity'. Owing to the shortage of space for expansion, much development takes place on areas reclaimed from the sea, such as Haneda International Airport, visible at the mouth of the Tama River, towards the south-west of the image. The area is prone to earthquakes, and in 1923 the Great Kanto Earthquake devastated the city, killing 143,000 people. Consequently, modern buildings are reinforced to withstand seismic activity. [Map page 113]
Source: RapidEye/NPA Satellite Mapping

The largest city in Africa, with almost 19 million inhabitants, Cairo evolved in a strategic location on the eastern bank of the River Nile just below its delta, 165 km (100 miles) from the Mediterranean Sea. This image clearly shows the differences between the arid desert areas to the south-east and south-west, the fertile lands of the Nile flood plain, and the urban area itself. Air pollution from vehicle emissions and industry is a major concern in this rapidly expanding metropolitan area. To ease congestion, three metro lines have been built. The shadows of the Pyramids on the Giza Plateau can be seen at the bottom left of the image, showing the modern city's links with Ancient Egypt. [Map page 137]
Source: RapidEye/NPA Satellite Mapping

Nairobi sits at around one degree south of the equator, at an altitude of 1,700 m (5,580 ft), in the East African Highlands. It was founded as a construction camp on the Uganda railway in the 1890s, and rose to replace Mombasa as the capital of Kenya (then British East Africa) in 1907. Despite its proximity to the equator, the altitude and prevailing climate favour temperate zone crops, livestock and dairy farms. Nairobi National Park, lying south of the city, is a game reserve that attracts many visitors in search of the safari experience. The darker green area in the top left of the image is the southern end of the Aberdare National Park. The rougher landscape to the southwest of the city is part of the Ngong Hills that were home to many early colonial settlers. [Map page 142]
Source: USGS Landsat/NPA Satellite Mapping

26 JOHANNESBURG, SOUTH AFRICA

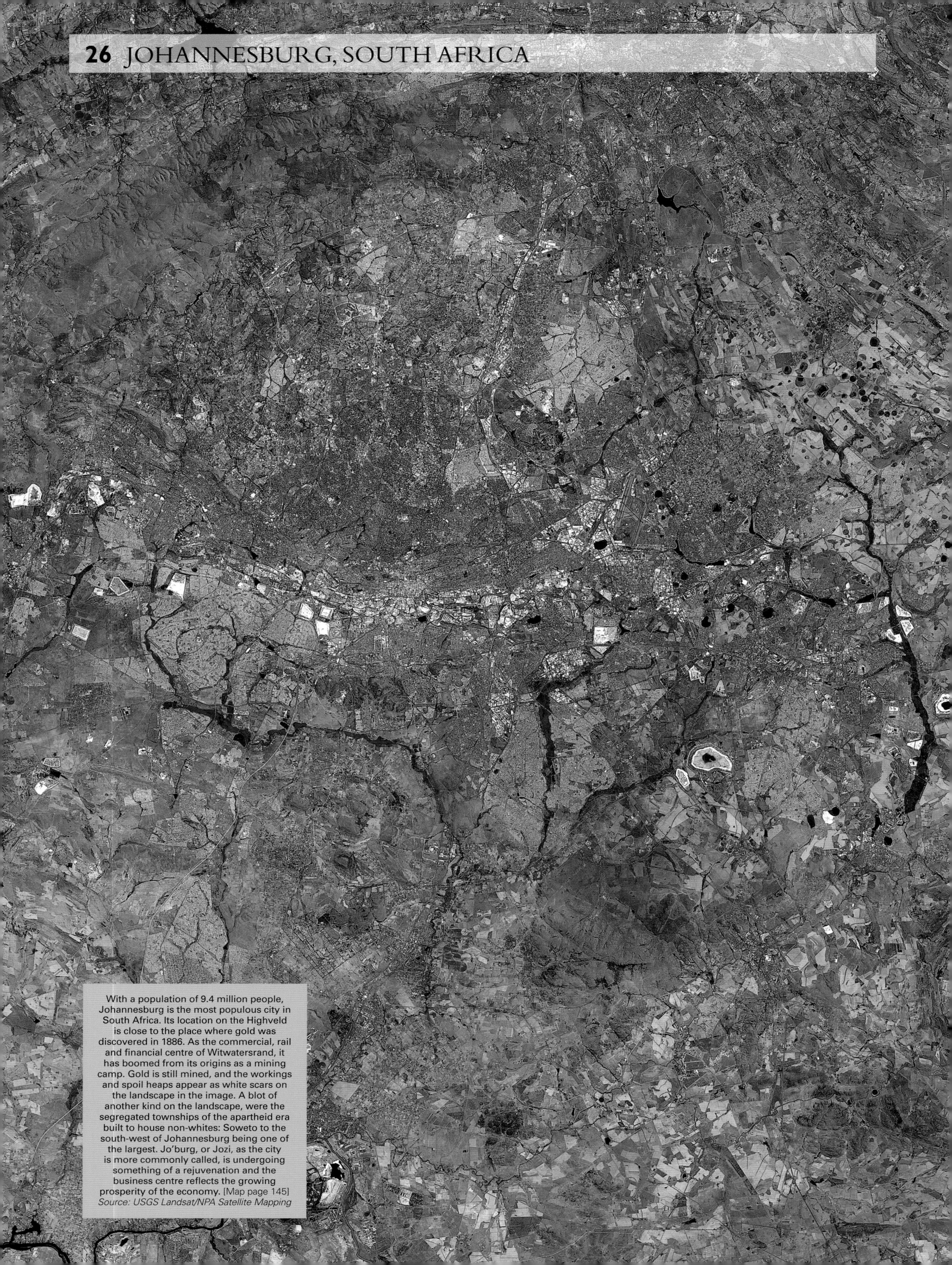

With a population of 9.4 million people, Johannesburg is the most populous city in South Africa. Its location on the Highveld is close to the place where gold was discovered in 1886. As the commercial, rail and financial centre of Witwatersrand, it has boomed from its origins as a mining camp. Gold is still mined, and the workings and spoil heaps appear as white scars on the landscape in the image. A blot of another kind on the landscape, were the segregated townships of the apartheid era built to house non-whites: Soweto to the south-west of Johannesburg being one of the largest. Jo'burg, or Jozi, as the city is more commonly called, is undergoing something of a rejuvenation and the business centre reflects the growing prosperity of the economy. [Map page 145]
Source: USGS Landsat/NPA Satellite Mapping

The city of Cape Town sits at the northern end of the Cape Peninsula beneath Table Mountain – the port facilities are clearly visible in this image. It developed from the first settlement in the 17th century, founded by the Dutch East India Company, because of its safe north-facing harbour, looking across Table Bay towards Robben Island. The urban area now spreads to the east of the peninsula down to False Bay. As well as being the second largest city in South Africa, after Johannesburg, Cape Town is also the seat of the National Parliament and is the country's legislative capital. To the west of the port can be seen the oval shape of the Cape Town Stadium. [Map page 144]
Source: RapidEye/NPA Satellite Mapping

28 SYDNEY, AUSTRALIA

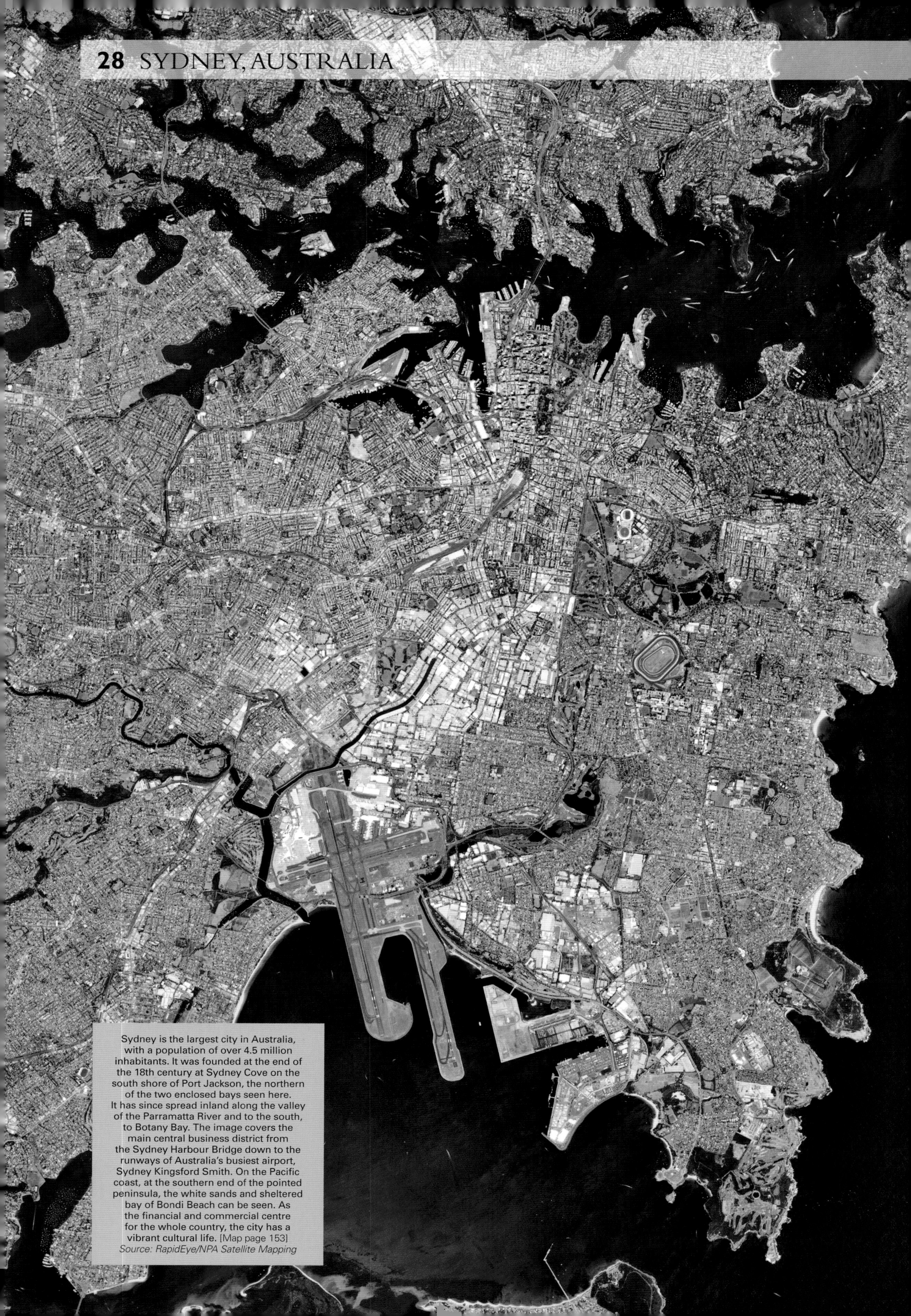

Sydney is the largest city in Australia, with a population of over 4.5 million inhabitants. It was founded at the end of the 18th century at Sydney Cove on the south shore of Port Jackson, the northern of the two enclosed bays seen here. It has since spread inland along the valley of the Parramatta River and to the south, to Botany Bay. The image covers the main central business district from the Sydney Harbour Bridge down to the runways of Australia's busiest airport, Sydney Kingsford Smith. On the Pacific coast, at the southern end of the pointed peninsula, the white sands and sheltered bay of Bondi Beach can be seen. As the financial and commercial centre for the whole country, the city has a vibrant cultural life. [Map page 153]
Source: RapidEye/NPA Satellite Mapping

Situated at the northern end of North Island, the city of Auckland was founded by the Maoris on the narrow isthmus at the top left of this image. It has since grown to become the largest settlement in the country. This is a landscape that has been shaped by volcanic forces – the dark circular shape to the east of the city is Rangitoto Island, the now-extinct remains of a volcano that erupted from the sea some 600 years ago. At the bottom of the image is the town of Hamilton. [Map page 154]
Source: USGS Landsat/NPA Satellite Mapping

On the north side of the Fraser River delta, the settlement grew up in the second half of the 19th century around its fine, natural harbour. It developed as the western railhead of the Canadian Pacific Railroad and is now the terminus of the Trans-Canada Highway, which crosses on the easternmost of the two road bridges visible here to the north. Vancouver is the largest cargo port in Canada. The larger metropolitan area of the city is home to over 2.5 million people. Downtown Vancouver is at the southern end of the peninsula which projects northwards and separates Vancouver Harbour from Burrard Inlet. The wooded area at the northern end is Stanley Park, which is connected to West and North Vancouver via the Lions Gate Bridge. [Map page 162]
Source: RapidEye/NPA Satellite Mapping

Québec was founded as a trading post
in 1608, at the narrowest point of the
St Lawrence River, just to the south-west
of the Île d'Orléans, and is one of the oldest
cities in North America. Strategically,
the city controlled the movement of
shipping between the Atlantic Ocean
and the Great Lakes, and consequently
developed fortifications on the cliffs of
Cape Diamond, 97 m (320 ft) above the
river. The port is 1,370 km (850 miles) from
the Atlantic, 2,404 km (1,495 miles) from
Duluth, and 2,252 km (1,400 miles) from
Chicago. It has a population of
over 750,000 people and is the capital
city of the French-speaking province
of the same name. [Map page 165]
Source: RapidEye/NPA Satellite Mapping

This image covers parts of New York City (to the east) and Jersey City (to the west). Flowing from the north, the Hudson River divides them, and the elongated island of Manhattan with Central Park at its heart is clearly visible. It is the centre of the most densely populated metropolitan area in the United States, with a population in excess of 20 million people. To the south-east is the end of Long Island, on which the suburbs of Brooklyn and Queens are situated. South-west of Manhattan are two small islands: the first is Ellis Island, where the early immigrants first disembarked, and beyond that is Liberty Island, where the famous Statue of Liberty is located. [Map page 175]
Source: RapidEye/NPA Satellite Mapping

Situated on the south-western shore of Lake Michigan, Chicago is the centre of the third largest metropolitan area in the United States, with a population of over 9.5 million people. The central area of the agglomeration, known by some as 'Chicagoland', can be seen on the lake shore. It developed as a major transport focus for the Midwest, with complex road and rail networks radiating out to its rich agricultural hinterland. It also developed as a large port, trading these commodities on a global scale. Chicago boasts the seventh busiest airport in the world, O'Hare International, which handles over 70 million passengers a year and which can be seen towards the north-west of the city. [Map page 172]
Source: USGS Landsat/NPA Satellite Mapping

Salt Lake City with a population of 1.1 million people, is the largest town and the state capital of Utah. It stretches between the south-western shore of the Great Salt Lake (top left), southwards towards the smaller Utah Lake. The settlement was founded in 1847 by Brigham Young and his Mormon followers as their headquarters. It subsequently played an important role as a trading centre during the California gold rush and has important transcontinental road and rail links. Tourism is an important industry and the 2002 Winter Olympic Games were held in the city and the nearby Wasatch Mountains, seen to the east. [Map page 168]
Source: USGS Landsat/NPA Satellite Mapping

Sometimes called 'The Crescent City', the settlement is situated between the south bank of Lake Pontchartrain (the largest in this view) and the Mississippi River. The latter can be seen meandering to the south of the city on its way to the delta, which lies to the south-east. In August 2005 the flood control system, which was constructed in the early 20th century, failed in the face of the category 5 Hurricane Katrina, which breached two dams and flooded and destroyed parts of the city, making many homeless. The wetlands to the south are themselves being eroded, since less silt is being deposited at the mouth to reinforce the delta. [Map page 177]
Source: USGS Landsat/NPA Satellite Mapping

With a population of over 22 million people for the continuous metropolitan area visible here, Mexico City is one of North America's most important commercial centres. It was originally founded by the Aztecs in 1325, on an island in Lake Texcoco, which has dried up over time. The city sits in a valley some 2,240 m (7,350 ft) above sea level. The relentless growth of the urban area has resulted in both air pollution and water-supply problems. To the south-east of the city can be seen three towering snow-covered volcanic peaks. The southernmost of these is Popocatépetl, an active volcano 5,452 m (17,887 ft) high, which has two glaciers near its summit. [Map page 181]
Source: USGS Landsat/NPA Satellite Mapping

The Panama Canal, originally dug
between 1904–14, crosses between
the Caribbean Sea, to the north of the
image, and the Pacific Ocean in the
south. Paradoxically, therefore, the Pacific
entrance is to the east of the Caribbean
entrance. Panama City, the capital of
Panama, is at the Pacific end of the canal.
The canal has until recently been able to
handle the world's largest cargo vessels,
carrying up to 5,000 containers, thus
cutting the ocean passage time between
Asia and the eastern USA. It is now being
upgraded so that by the end of 2016 it
will be able to handle the latest vessels –
these can carry a maximum load of
12,000 containers. [Map page 182]
Source: USGS Landsat/NPA Satellite Mapping

38 MARACAIBO, VENEZUELA

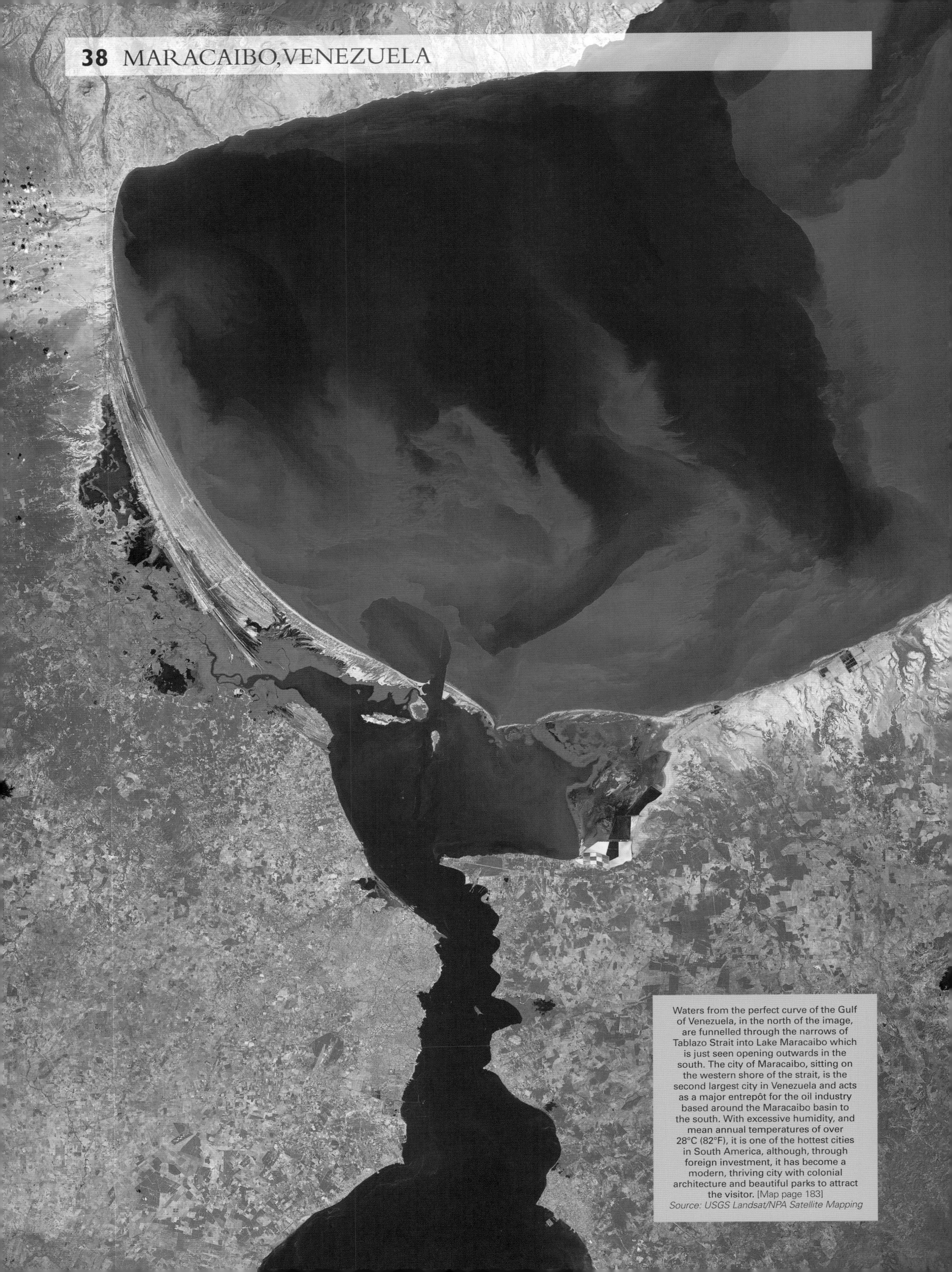

Waters from the perfect curve of the Gulf of Venezuela, in the north of the image, are funnelled through the narrows of Tablazo Strait into Lake Maracaibo which is just seen opening outwards in the south. The city of Maracaibo, sitting on the western shore of the strait, is the second largest city in Venezuela and acts as a major entrepôt for the oil industry based around the Maracaibo basin to the south. With excessive humidity, and mean annual temperatures of over 28°C (82°F), it is one of the hottest cities in South America, although, through foreign investment, it has become a modern, thriving city with colonial architecture and beautiful parks to attract the visitor. [Map page 183]

Source: USGS Landsat/NPA Satellite Mapping

Established in 1960 as the new capital of Brazil, Brasília, lies some 970 km (600 miles) north-west of Rio de Janeiro in the centre of the country. It took a scant five years for the city to be constructed from a blank canvas with Lucio Costa winning the competition to plan the design and layout. With its main buildings being designed by the architect Oscar Niemeyer, the modernist cityscape has had both admirers and critics, but it was declared a World Heritage Site by UNESCO in 1987. The main city centre lies to the west of the prominent Lake Paranoá to the right of centre in the image. The forest trees of the Brasília National Park can be seen almost encroaching into the suburbs to the north of the city. [Map page 189]
Source: USGS Landsat/NPA Satellite Mapping

OCEAN SEAFLOORS

– GREAT BARRIER REEF, AUSTRALIA –
First explored by Captain James Cook in
1770 and lying just off the east coast of
Queensland, the Great Barrier Reef is
composed of some 2,900 individual reefs
and over 900 islands, a few of which are
shown on this image. Designated a UNESCO
World Heritage Site and protected as
a Marine Park, this fragile environment
is home to over 1,500 species of fish and
400 species of coral, as well as turtles,
whales, and many species of birds.
[Map page 150]

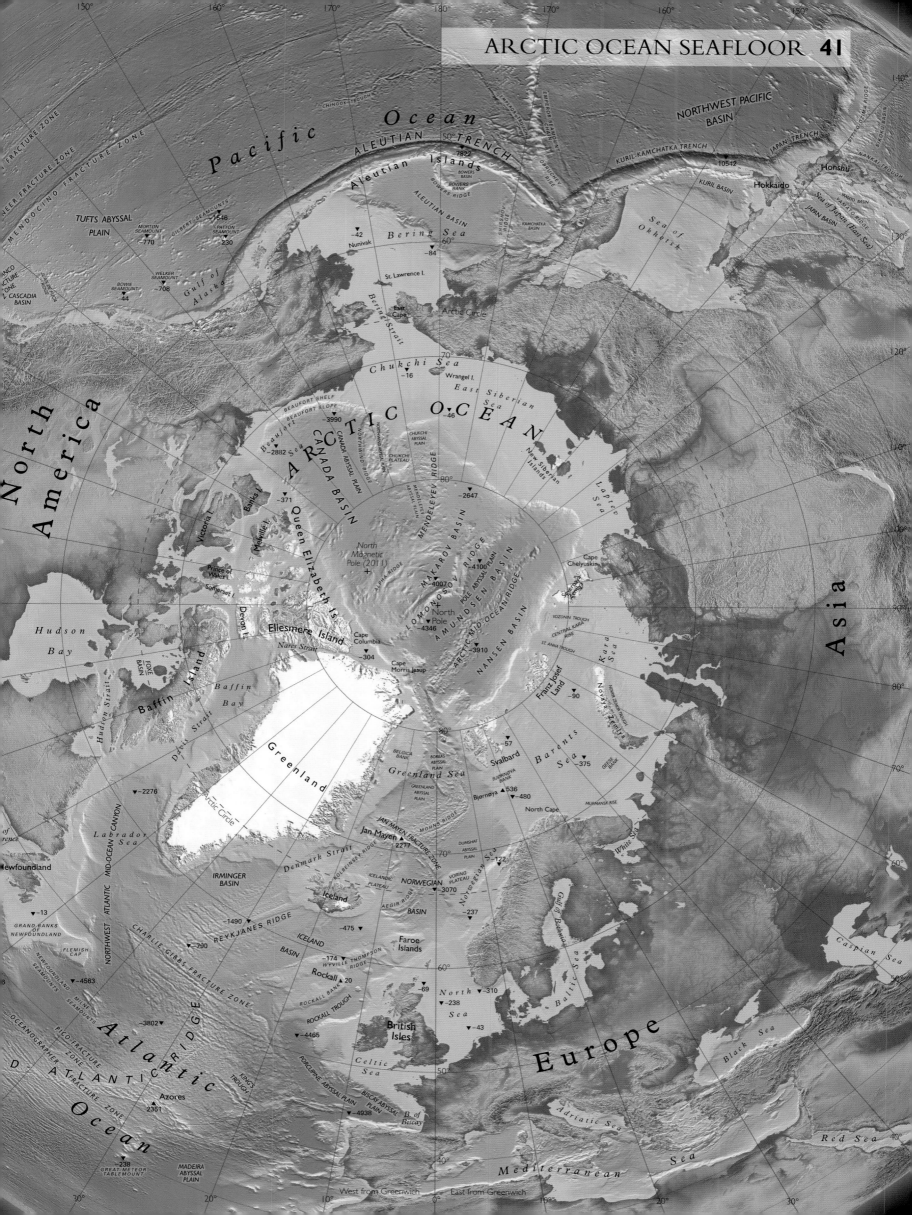

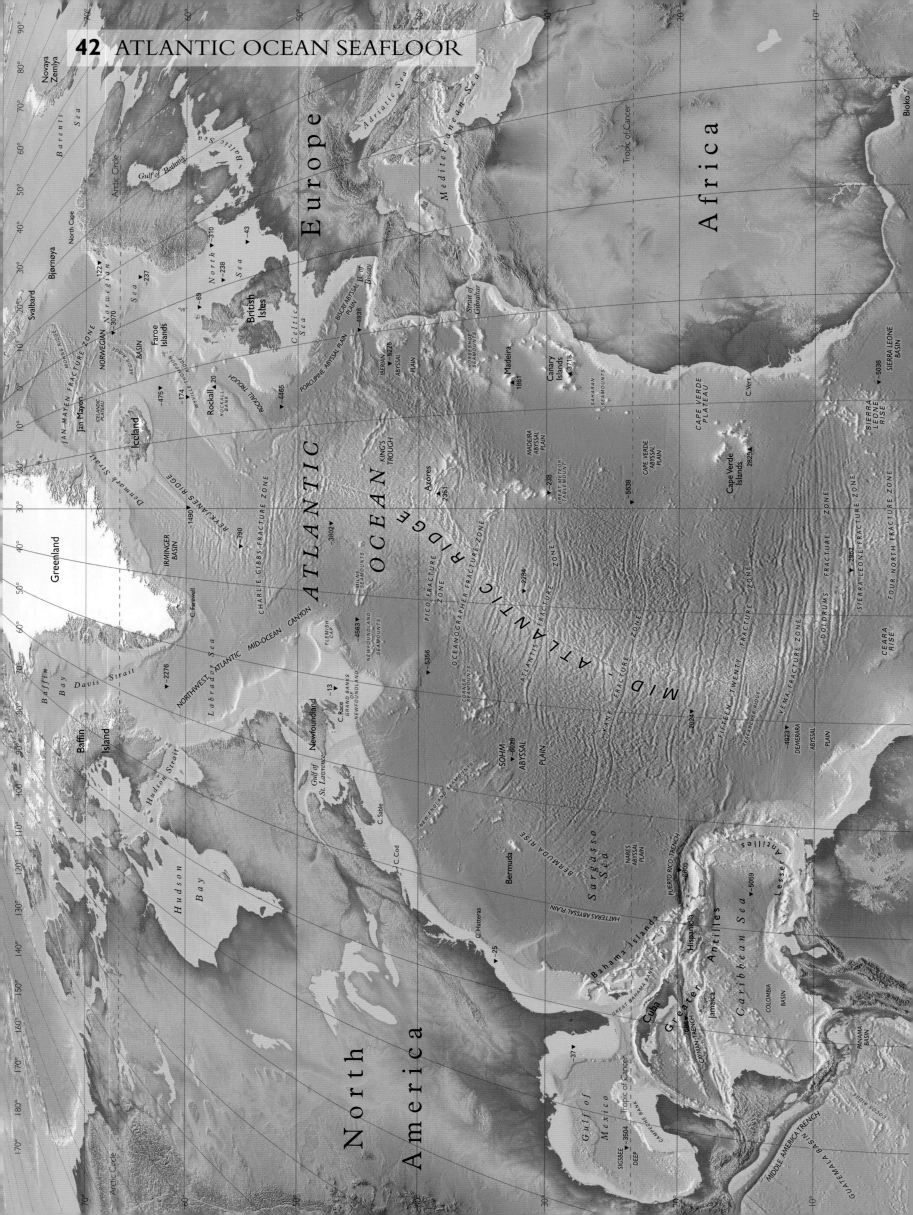

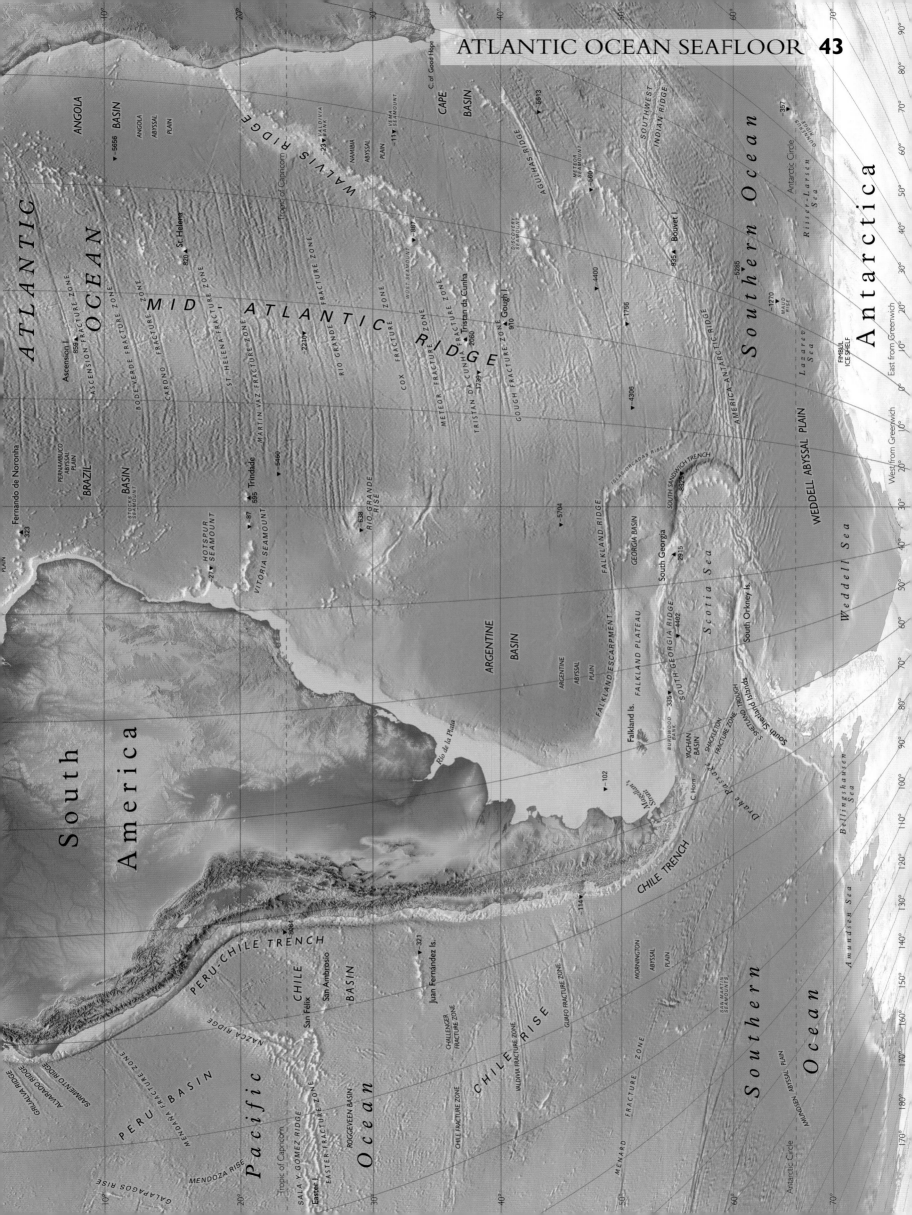

ATLANTIC

OCEAN

ANGOLA

ANGOLA BASIN

▶-5656

ANGOLA ABYSSAL PLAIN

NAMIBIA ABYSSAL PLAIN

▶-23

VALDIVIA BANK

C. of Good Hope

CAPE BASIN

▶-5613

SOUTHWEST

Southern Ocean

INDIAN RIDGE

Antarctica

▶-11 VEMA SEAMOUNT

MID-ATLANTIC FRACTURE ZONE

MID - *ATLANTIC*

WALVIS RIDGE

ASCENSION FRACTURE ZONE

Ascension I.

BODE-VERDE FRACTURE ZONE

CARDNO FRACTURE ZONE

ST. HELENA FRACTURE ZONE

820▶ St. Helena

Tropic of Capricorn

MARTIN VAZ FRACTURE ZONE

▶-2210

RIO GRANDE FRACTURE ZONE

COX FRACTURE ZONE

WEST SEAMOUNT

METEOR FRACTURE ZONE

METEOR SEAMOUNT

▶-560

RIDGE

GOUGH FRACTURE ZONE

Tristan da Cunha 2060▶

910▶ Gough I.

▶-4400

DISCOVERY SEAMOUNT

▶-1766

Bouvet I.
▶-895

▶-5285

Antarctic Circle

Riiser-Larsen Sea

Lazarev Sea

MAUD RISE

▶-1270

FIMBUL ICE SHELF

East from Greenwich

Fernando de Noronha
▶-323

PERNAMBUCO ABYSSAL PLAIN

BRAZIL

BASIN

STOCKS SEAMOUNT

▶-5460

Trindade 595▶

HOTSPUR SEAMOUNT
▶-27

▶-87 Vitoria Seamount

VITORIA SEAMOUNT

TRISTAN DA CUNHA FRACTURE ZONE

1739▶

GOUGH FRACTURE ZONE

▶-4306

ISLAS ORCADAS RISE

SOUTH SANDWICH TRENCH
▶-5826

West from Greenwich

WEDDELL ABYSSAL PLAIN

Weddell Sea

RIO GRANDE RISE

▶-838

▶-5704

FALKLAND RIDGE

GEORGIA BASIN

South Georgia
2915

Scotia Sea

South Orkney Is.

Rio de la Plata

South

America

ARGENTINE BASIN

ARGENTINE ABYSSAL PLAIN

FALKLAND ESCARPMENT

FALKLAND PLATEAU

SOUTH GEORGIA RIDGE
▶-4402

Falkland Is.

BURDWOOD BANK
▶-335

SHACKLETON FRACTURE ZONE

South Shetland Is.

South Sandwich Islands

Southern

Ocean

Bellingshausen Sea

▶-102

YAGHAN BASIN

C. Horn

Drake Passage

Strait of Magellan

Magallanes

CHILE TRENCH

Pacific

PERU-CHILE TRENCH

▶-114

MORNINGTON ABYSSAL PLAIN

SAN MARTIN SEAMOUNTS

Ocean

CHILE RISE

CHILE FRACTURE ZONE

GUAFO FRACTURE ZONE

VALDIVIA FRACTURE ZONE

▶-8064

Juan Fernandez Is.
▶-321

CHILE

San Ambrosio

San Felix

BASIN

CHALLENGER FRACTURE ZONE

CHILE FRACTURE ZONE

PERU BASIN

PERU

NAZCA RIDGE

SALA Y GOMEZ RIDGE

Easter I.

EASTER FRACTURE ZONE

MENDANA FRACTURE ZONE

ROGGEVEEN BASIN

MENDOZA RISE

GALAPAGOS RISE

SARMIENTO RIDGE

GRIJALVA RIDGE

ALVARADO RIDGE

MENARD FRACTURE ZONE

Amundsen Sea

AMUNDSEN ABYSSAL PLAIN

Antarctic Circle

Southern

Ocean

Arctic Circle

Asia

Bering Sea

St. Lawrence I.

ALEUTIAN BASIN

BOWERS RIDGE

BOWERS BASIN

Aleutian Islands

ALEUTIAN TRENCH

Kamchatka

OBRUCHEV RISE

Sea of Okhotsk

−1000

KURIL BASIN

OBRUCHEV

CHINOOK TROUGH

Hokkaido

−10542

KURIL-KAMCHATKA TRENCH

NORTHWEST PACIFIC BASIN

EMPEROR SEAMOUNT CHAIN

EMPEROR TROUGH

HESS RISE

NORTHWEST HAWAIIAN RIDGE

Sea of Japan (East Sea)

YAMATO RIDGE

KIMEI MON

Honshu

−8412

JAPAN TRENCH

SHATSKY RISE

−2450

HAWAIIAN RIDGE

Yellow Sea

Midway Is. 13

HAWAII

Tropic of Cancer

East China Sea

OKINAWA TROUGH

NANSEI SHOTO TRENCH

OKINAWA TROUGH

DAITO RIDGE

OKI-DAITO RIDGE

KYUSHU-PALAU RIDGE

MID-PACIFIC SEAMOUNTS

Taiwan

Taiwan Str.

MAPMAKERS SEAMOUNTS

MARSHALL SEAMOUNTS

Gulf of Tonkin

Hainan

Luzon

PHILIPPINE

WEST MARIANA BASIN

MARIANA RIDGE

MARIANA TROUGH

EAST MARIANA BASIN

Bay of Bengal

South China Sea

SOUTH CHINA BASIN

Philippine Sea

BASIN

Micronesia

CENTRAL PACIFIC BASIN

Maudin Sun

Andaman Is. ▲732

ANDAMAN BASIN

Philippine Islands

−10057

PHILIPPINE TRENCH

CHALLENGER DEEP −11022

MARIANA TRENCH

JAP TRENCH

CAROLINE SEAMOUNTS

Marshall Is.

PACIFIC

Andaman Sea

Palau Is.

EAURIPIK RISE

791

Pohnper

Ceylon

Nicobar Is. ▲642

−4267

Gulf of Thailand

Sulu Sea

SULU BASIN

Mindanao

WEST CAROLINE BASIN

EAST CAROLINE BASIN

MELANESIAN BASIN

Phoenix Is.

Dondra Head

−22

PALAWAN TROUGH

Celebes Sea

CELEBES BASIN

SOLOMON RISE

Str. of Malacca

SUNDA SHELF

ONTONG JAVA PLATEAU

MID-INDIAN

Celebes

NORTH BANDA BASIN

Banda Sea

Bismarck Sea

New Britain

CEYLON PLAIN

COCOS BASIN

MENTAWAI BASIN

Sumatra

Java Sea

SOUTH MAKASSAR BASIN

Flores Sea

SOUTH BANDA BASIN

New Guinea

−8940

Melanesia

OCEAN

−1550

MAKASSAR STRAIT

Sunda Is.

Solomon Sea

BASIN

AFANASY NIKITIN SEAMOUNT

Java

Arafura Sea

SOUTH SOLOMON TRENCH

−9165

Indian

SUNDA TRENCH (JAVA TRENCH)

SUNDA TROUGH

−7125

Timor

ARAFURA SHELF

Torres Str.

PAPUA PLATEAU

WEST FIJI BASIN

Samoa Is.

Christmas I. ▲361

−6204

ROO RISE

Timor Sea

PLATEAU

Espiritu Santo

Ocean

INVESTIGATOR RIDGE

Cocos Is.

NORTH AUSTRALIAN BASIN

Gulf of Carpentaria

Coral Sea

QUEENSLAND PLATEAU

New Caledonia

−570

Fiji Is.

OSBORN PLATEAU

GASCOGNE PLAIN

SAHUL SHELF

Great Barrier Reef

SOUTH FIJI BASIN

Tropic of Capricorn

WHARTON

EXMOUTH PLATEAU

North West C.

CUVIER BASIN

Australia

LORD HOWE RISE

Norfolk I. 319

BASIN

WALLABY PLATEAU

CUVIER PLATEAU

C. Inscription

NORFOLK RIDGE

NEW CALEDONIA CHAIN

HOWE TROUGH

TONGA TRENCH

−10822

BATAVIA KNOLL

PERTH BASIN

North I.

−10047

GULDEN DRAAK KNOLL

NATURALISTE PLATEAU

BROUWER SEAMOUNT

5746

BROKEN RIDGE

NATURALISTE FRACTURE ZONE

C. Leeuwin

Tasman Sea

New Zealand

KERMADEC TRENCH

Amsterdam I. 881

St. Paul Is. 284

EAST INDIAMAN RIDGE

−6602

DIAMANTINA FRACTURE ZONE

CHALLENGER PLATEAU

Chatham Is.

−2067

SOUTHEAST INDIAN RIDGE

SOUTH AUSTRALIAN BASIN

Bass Str.

Tasmania

TASMAN BASIN

South I.

CHATHAM RISE

BOUNTY TROUGH

DEL CAÑO RISE

Crozet Is.

AUSTRALIAN ANTARCTIC DISCORDANCE

TASMAN ABYSSAL PLAIN

EAST TASMAN PLATEAU

−60

Bounty Is.

BOUNTY PLATEAU

−1090

−4590

Kerguelen Is. 1850

CONRAD RISE

LENA SEAMOUNT

Heard I. 274

St. Paul

2745

KERGUELEN PLATEAU

SOUTH TASMAN RISE

Auckland Is.

Antipodes I.

CAMPBELL PLATEAU

Campbell I.

−272

Macquarie I.

BOLLONS SEAMOUNT

ELAN BANK

SOUTH INDIAN

−4650

−6240

ENDERBY ABYSSAL PLAIN

−6739

VALDIVIA ABYSSAL PLAIN

AMERY BASIN

AUSTRALIAN-ANTARCTIC BASIN

ABYSSAL PLAIN

Dumont d'Urville Sea

−6800

MACQUARIE RIDGE

Southern

−5325

C. Borley

PRINCESS ELIZABETH TROUGH

Davis Sea

Vincennes Bay

Paulding Bay

Porpoise Bay

Ocean

Balleny Is.

Scott I.

Antarctic Circle

Prydz Bay

North
America

South
America

*Atlantic
Ocean*

MID ATLANTIC RIDGE

OCEAN

EAST PACIFIC RISE

MIDDLE AMERICA TRENCH

Southern

Ocean

Gulf of
Alaska

PATTON
SEAMOUNT
−230
−1546

WELKER
SEAMOUNT
−708

−44
BOWIE
SEAMOUNT

−770
MORTON
SEAMOUNT

GILBERT SEAMOUNTS

TUFTS ABYSSAL
PLAIN

MENDOCINO FRACTURE ZONE

PIONEER FRACTURE ZONE

−6741

MURRAY FRACTURE ZONE

MOLOKAI FRACTURE ZONE

Hawaiian Is.

−4205 Hawaii
−975

RIDGE

CLARION FRACTURE ZONE

COOPER RIDGE

CLIPPERTON FRACTURE ZONE

Line Is.

Kiritimati

PENRHYN
BASIN

−5770

Marquesas Is.

MARQUESAS FRACTURE
ZONE

TUAMOTU FRACTURE ZONE

TIKI
BASIN

GARRETT
FRACTURE ZONE

Tuamotu Archipelago

Society Is.

Tahiti
2239

AUSTRAL FRACTURE ZONE

Austral Is.

2

Pitcairn I.
342

−1420

−5500

WEST PACIFIC BASIN

AGASSIZ FRACTURE ZONE

−5100

−2480

MENARD FRACTURE ZONE

−4100

ELTANIN FRACTURE ZONE SYSTEM

THARP FRACTURE ZONE

PACIFIC ANTARCTIC RIDGE FRACTURE ZONE

UDINTSEV FRACTURE ZONE

−3300

−2930

AMUNDSEN ABYSSAL PLAIN

−5100

AMUNDSEN RIDGES

Juan de Fuca
Ridge

CASCADIA
BASIN

BLANCO
FRACTURE
ZONE

Gulf of California

CEDROS TRENCH

−3790

Revillagigedo Is.

−5200

NORTH EAST
PACIFIC BASIN

MATHEMATICIANS
SEAMOUNTS

Clipperton I.
−4010

CLIPPERTON
SEAMOUNTS

GALAPAGOS FRACTURE
ZONE

GALLEGO
RISE

QUEBRADA
FRACTURE ZONE

BAUER
−4500
BASIN

MENDOZA RISE

YUPANQUI

BASIN

SALA Y GÓMEZ RIDGE
Easter I.
613   1247

EASTER FRACTURE ZONE

ROGGEVEEN BASIN

−4550

CHILE FRACTURE ZONE

VALDIVIA FRACTURE ZONE

GUAFO FRACTURE ZONE

−114

−102

MORNINGTON
ABYSSAL
PLAN
−5198

CHILE TRENCH

SAN MARTIN
SEAMOUNTS

BELLINGSHAUSEN ABYSSAL PLAIN

DE GERLACHE
SEAMOUNTS

Peter I Island

C. Byrd   Alexander I.

LARSEN
ICE SHELF

Labrador Sea

−790
NORTHWEST
ATLANTIC
MID-OCEAN
CANYON

CHARLIE GIBBS FRACTURE ZONE

Newfoundland

St. Lawrence
Gulf of
St. Lawrence

−13

FLEMISH
CAP

GRAND BANKS OF
NEWFOUNDLAND

C. Sable

NEWFOUNDLAND
SEAMOUNTS

ROCKALL
BANK

*British
Isles*

−4465

2351
Azor

Celtic S

−5356   PICO FRACTURE ZONE

−228

CORNER
SEAMOUNTS

OCEANOGRAPHER FRACTURE ZONE

NEW ENGLAND SEAMOUNTS

SOHM
ABYSSAL
PLAIN

ATLANTIS FRACTURE
ZONE

C. Hatteras
−25

Bermuda

BERMUDA RISE −6028

Gulf of −37
Mexico

SIGSBEE
DEEP −3504

CAMPECHE
BANK

HATTERAS ABYSSAL PLAIN

Bahama Islands

Cuba
Greater

GREAT BAHAMA BANK

7686 Antilles
CAYMAN TRENCH

Jamaica

Hispaniola

Caribbean Sea

COLOMBIA
BASIN

−5059

Tropic of Cancer

NARES
ABYSSAL
PLAIN

PUERTO RICO TRENCH −8605

Lesser
Antilles

KANE FRACTURE ZONE

−2024

FIFTEEN TWENT
FRACTURE ZONE
RESEARCHER RIDGE

−4923

DEMERARA
ABYSSAL
PLAIN

VEMA
FRACTURE
ZONE

TEHUANTEPEC
FRACTURE ZONE

−4210

SIQUEIROS
FRACTURE ZONE

GUATEMALA BASIN

COLÓN RIDGE

COCOS RIDGE

PANAMA
BASIN

Galapagos Is.
1696

CARNEGIE RIDGE

GRIJALVA RIDGE

ALVARADO RIDGE

GALAPAGOS RISE

SARMIENTO RIDGE

PERU BASIN

MENDAÑA FRACTURE ZONE

−6369

−6866

NAZCA RIDGE

PERU-CHILE TRENCH

−8064

Tropic of Capricorn

San Felix
San Ambrosio

CHILE
BASIN

Juan Fernández Is.
−321

CHALLENGER
FRACTURE ZONE

CHILE RISE

ARGENTINE

BASIN

−5704

ARGENTINE
ABYSSAL
PLAIN

Falkland Is.

FALKLAND PLATEAU

FALKLAND ESCARPMENT

FALKLAND RIDGE

−335
BURDWOOD
BANK

C. Horn

YAGHAN
BASIN

SOUTH GEORGIA RIDGE −4402

2915

South
Georgia

GEORGIA BASIN

−4306

−8525

SOUTH ORKNEY RISE

Drake Passage

S. SHETLAND TROUGH

South Shetland Islands

South Orkney Is.

Scotia Sea

AMERICA-ANTARCTIC RIDGE

SOUTH
SANDWICH TRENCH

WEDDELL ABYSSAL PLAIN

*Lazarev
Sea*

*Riiser-
Larsen
Sea*

Antarctic Circle

Equator

Arctic Circle

West from Greenwich   East from Greenwich

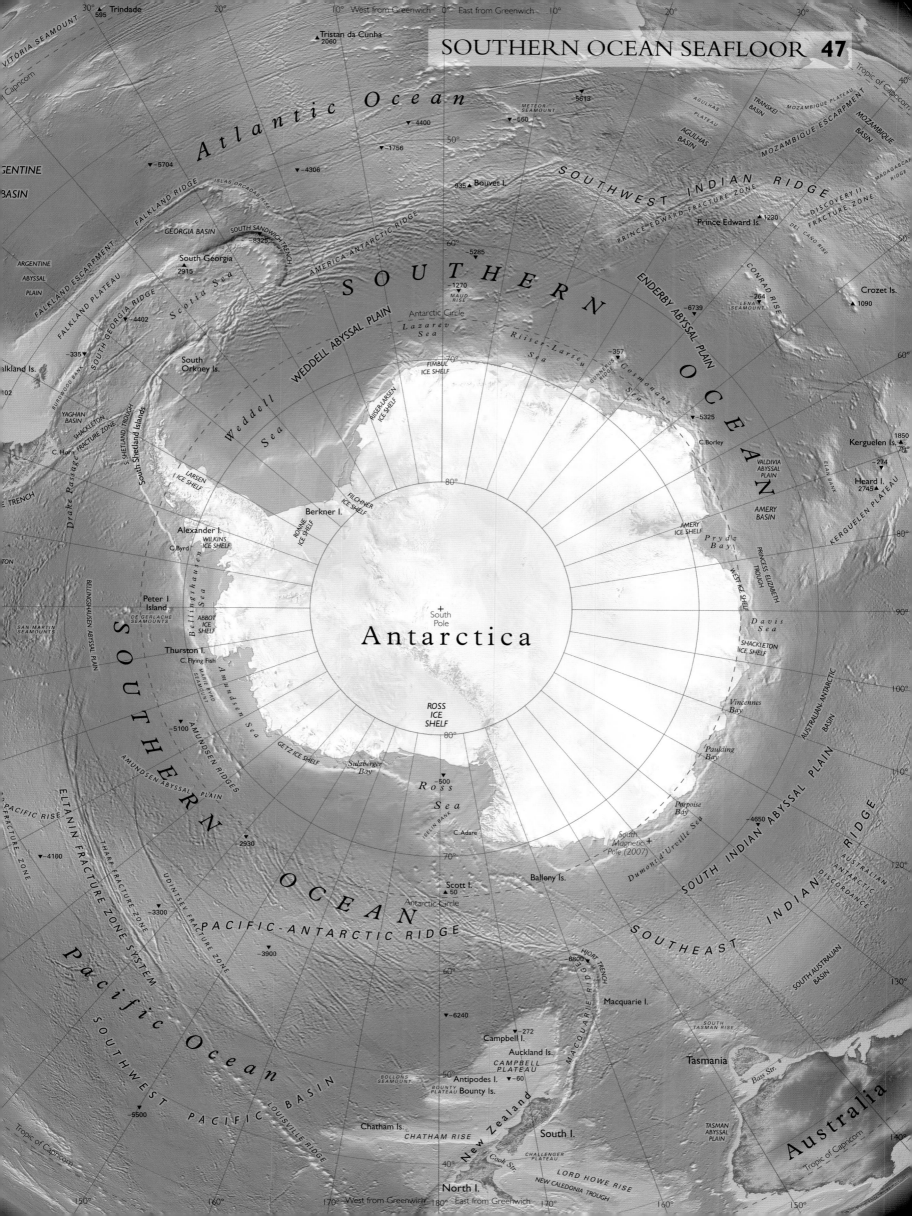

Atlantic Ocean

SOUTHERN OCEAN

Antarctica

South Pole

South Magnetic Pole (2007)

ROSS ICE SHELF

Weddell Sea

Ross Sea

Pacific Ocean

Australia

New Zealand

Tasmania

WORLD
MAPS

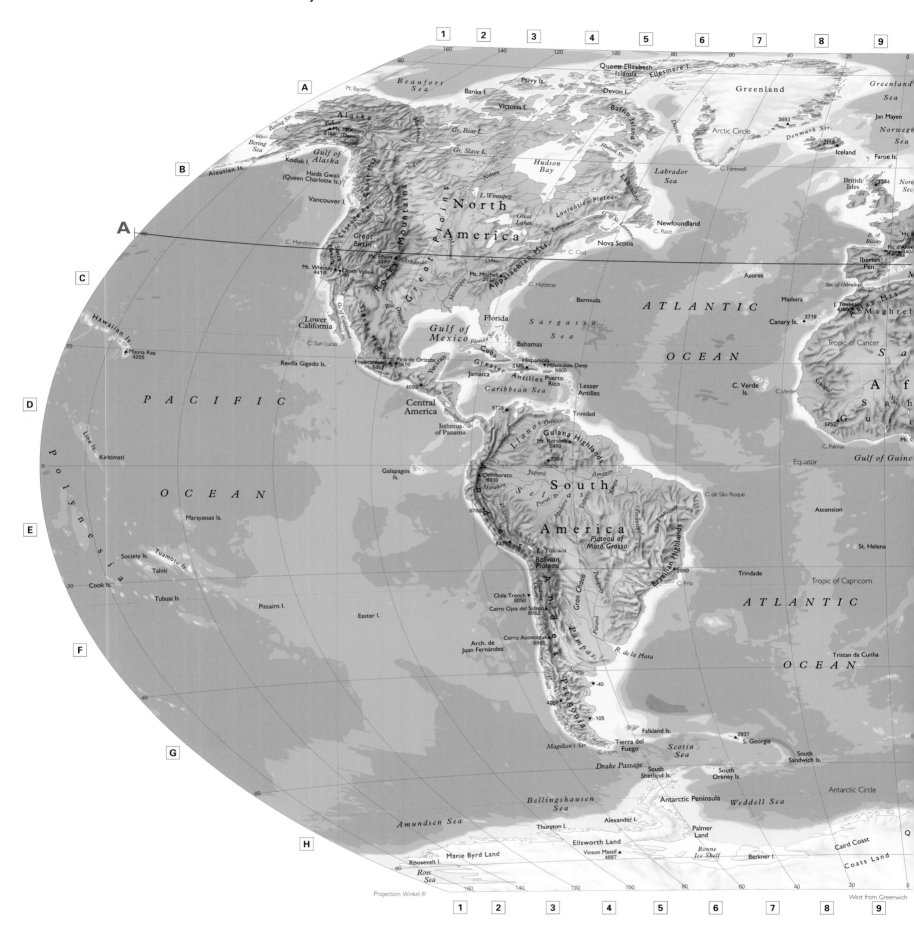

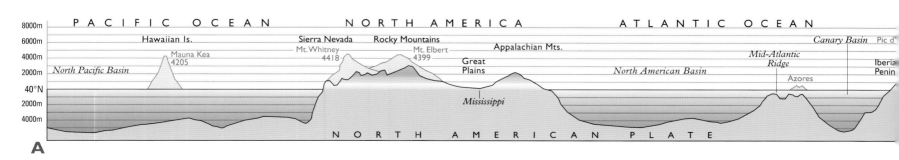

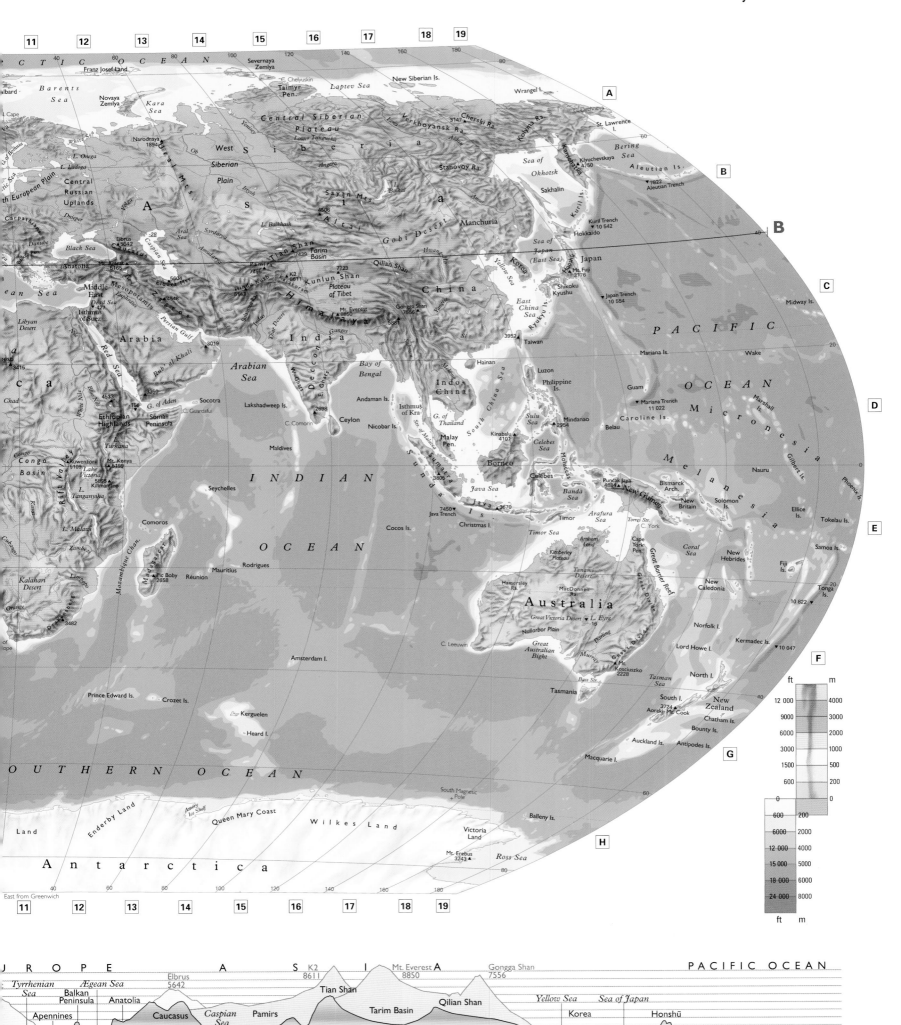

ARCTIC OCEAN
Franz Josef Land
Barents Sea
Novaya Zemlya
Kara Sea
Severnaya Zemlya
C. Chelyuskin
Taimyr Pen.
Laptev Sea
New Siberian Is.
Wrangel I.
Deznneva
St. Lawrence I.

A

L. Cape
Spitsbergen
Narodnaya 1894
West Siberian Plain
Central Siberian Plateau
Lower Tunguska
Lena
Verkhoyansk Ra.
3147 Cherski Ra.
Kolyma Ra.
Kamchatka
Klyuchevskaya 4750
Bering Sea
Aleutian Is.

7822 Aleutian Trench

B

L. Onega
L. Ladoga
Central Russian Uplands
Carpathians
Dnieper
Ural Mts.
Ob
Siberian Plain
Yenisey
Angara
Stanovoy Ra.
Amur
Sea of Okhotsk
Sakhalin
Kuril Is.
Kuril Trench 10 542
Hokkaido

B

Danube
Black Sea
Anatolia
Caspian Sea
Aral Sea
-28
Syrdarya
Amudarya
L. Balkhash
4506
Altai
Sayan Mts.
L. Baikal
Gobi Desert
Manchuria
Hwang-ho
Yellow Sea
Korea
Sea of Japan (East Sea)
Japan
Mt. Fuji 3776

Middle East
Mt. Ararat 5165
Mesopotamia
Elbrus 5642
Caucasus
5604
Elbruz 4546
Pamir
7495
Tian Shan 7439
Tarim Basin
K2 8611
Karakoram
Kunlun Shan
Qilian Shan
7723
Plateau of Tibet
China
East China Sea
Ryukyu Is.
Shikoku
Kyushu

C

Dead Sea -421
Red Sea
Isthmus of Suez
Arabia
Hindu Kush 7743
Thar Desert
Mt. Everest 8850
Himalaya
Gongga Shan 7556
Si
Taiwan 3952
PACIFIC
Midway Is.

Libyan Desert
3415
Persian Gulf
3019
India
Ganges
Deccan
Bay of Bengal
Hainan
Indo-China
Mariana Is.
Wake

Arabian Sea
Bab al Khali
Rub' al Khali
W. Ghats
E. Ghats
Andaman Is.
Isthmus of Kra
Luzon
Philippine Is.
Guam
Caroline Is.
Mariana Trench 11 022
OCEAN
Micronesia

D

Chad
3350
G. of Aden
Socotra
4533
Ethiopian Highlands
Somali Peninsula
C. Guardafui
Lakshadweep Is.
C. Comorin
Ceylon
Nicobar Is.
2898
G. of Thailand
South China Sea
Malay Pen.
Kinabalu 4101
Mindanao 2954
Sulu Sea
Celebes Sea
Belau
Marshall Is.

Nile
756
Turkana
Ruwenzori 5109
Mt. Kenya 5199
L. Victoria
Kilimanjaro 5895
INDIAN
Seychelles
Maldives
Cocos Is.
Sumatra
3805
Borneo
Celebes
Moluccas
Banda Sea
Puncak Jaya 4884
New Guinea
Bismarck Arch.
New Britain
Solomon Is.
Nauru
Gilbert Is.
Phoenix Is.

Conga Basin
Kasai
Rift Valley
L. Tanganyika
L. Malawi
Zambezi
Comoros
Madagascar
Pic Boby 2658
Réunion
Mauritius
Rodrigues
OCEAN
7450 Java Trench
Java
Java Sea
3670
Christmas I.
Timor
Arafura Sea
Torres Str.
C. York
Cape York Pen.
Coral Sea
New Hebrides
Ellice Is.
Tokelau Is.
Samoa Is.
Fiji Is.

E

Kalahari Desert
Limpopo
Orange
3482
Amsterdam I.
Cocos Is.
Timor Sea
Arnhem Land
Kimberley Plateau
Tanami Desert
Hamersley Ra.
MacDonnell Ra.
Great Barrier Reef
New Caledonia
Norfolk I.
Tonga Is.
10 822

Prince Edward Is.
Crozet Is.
Kerguelen
Heard I.
Australia
Great Victoria Desert
L. Eyre 16
Nullarbor Plain
Great Dividing Ra.
Murray
Darling
Mt. Kosciuszko 2228
Lord Howe I.
Kermadec Is.
10 047

F

SOUTHERN OCEAN
C. Leeuwin
Great Australian Bight
Bass Str.
Tasmania
Tasman Sea
North I.
South I.
Aoraki/Mt Cook 3724
New Zealand
Chatham Is.
Bounty Is.
Antipodes Is.
Auckland Is.
Macquarie I.

G

Enderby Land
Amery Ice Shelf
Queen Mary Coast
Wilkes Land
South Magnetic Pole
Balleny Is.
Victoria Land

H

Antarctica
Mt. Erebus 3743
Ross Sea

East from Greenwich

ft	m
12 000	4000
9000	3000
6000	2000
3000	1000
1500	500
600	200
0	0
600	200
6000	2000
12 000	4000
15 000	5000
18 000	6000
24 000	8000
ft	m

EUROPE ASIA PACIFIC OCEAN

Tyrrhenian Sea
Ægean Sea
Balkan Peninsula
Anatolia
Apennines
Elbrus 5642
Caucasus
Caspian Sea
Pamirs
K2 8611
Tian Shan
Tarim Basin
Mt. Everest 8850
Qilian Shan
Gongga Shan 7556
Yellow Sea
Sea of Japan
Korea
Honshū
40°N

EURASIAN PLATE
Japan Trench
Emperor Seamount Chain

B

Equatorial Scale 1:84 000 000

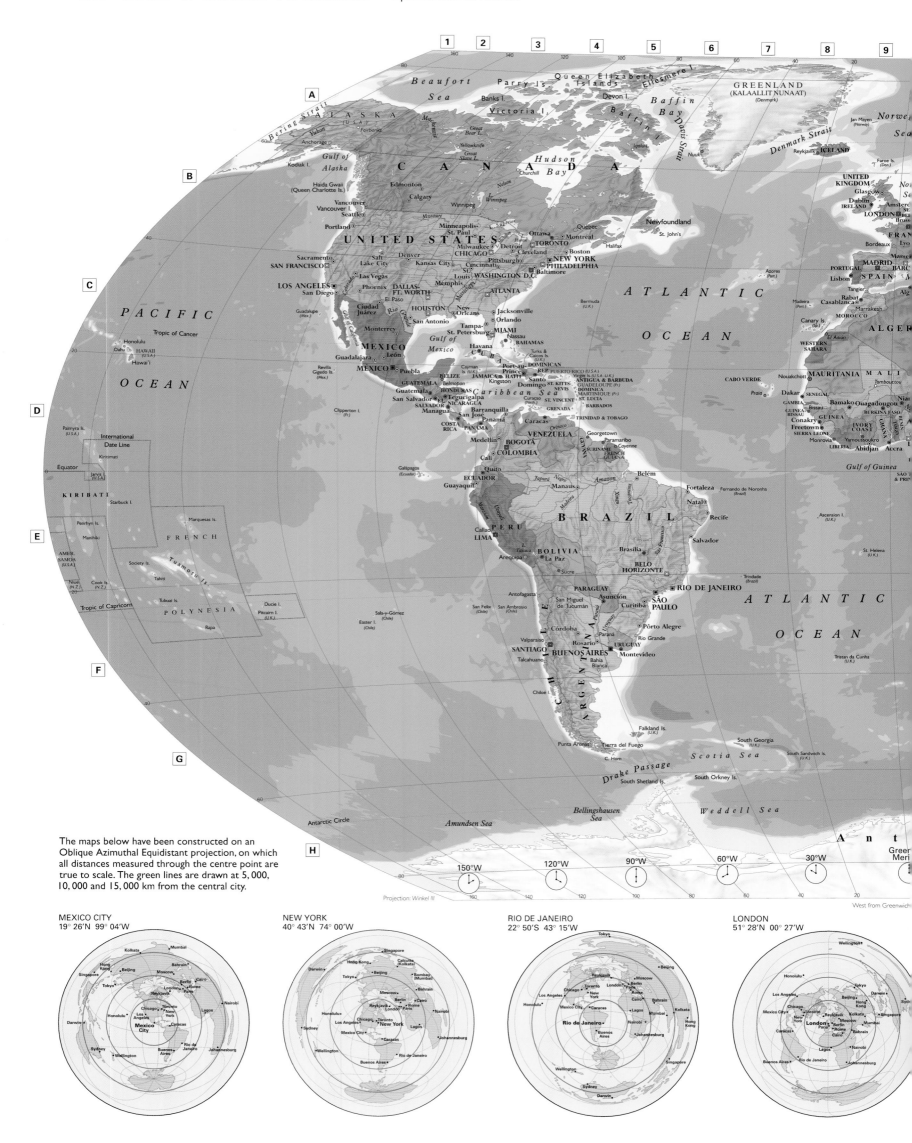

The maps below have been constructed on an Oblique Azimuthal Equidistant projection, on which all distances measured through the centre point are true to scale. The green lines are drawn at 5, 000, 10, 000 and 15, 000 km from the central city.

Projection: Winkel III

West from Greenwich

MEXICO CITY
19° 26'N 99° 04'W

NEW YORK
40° 43'N 74° 00'W

RIO DE JANEIRO
22° 50'S 43° 15'W

LONDON
51° 28'N 00° 27'W

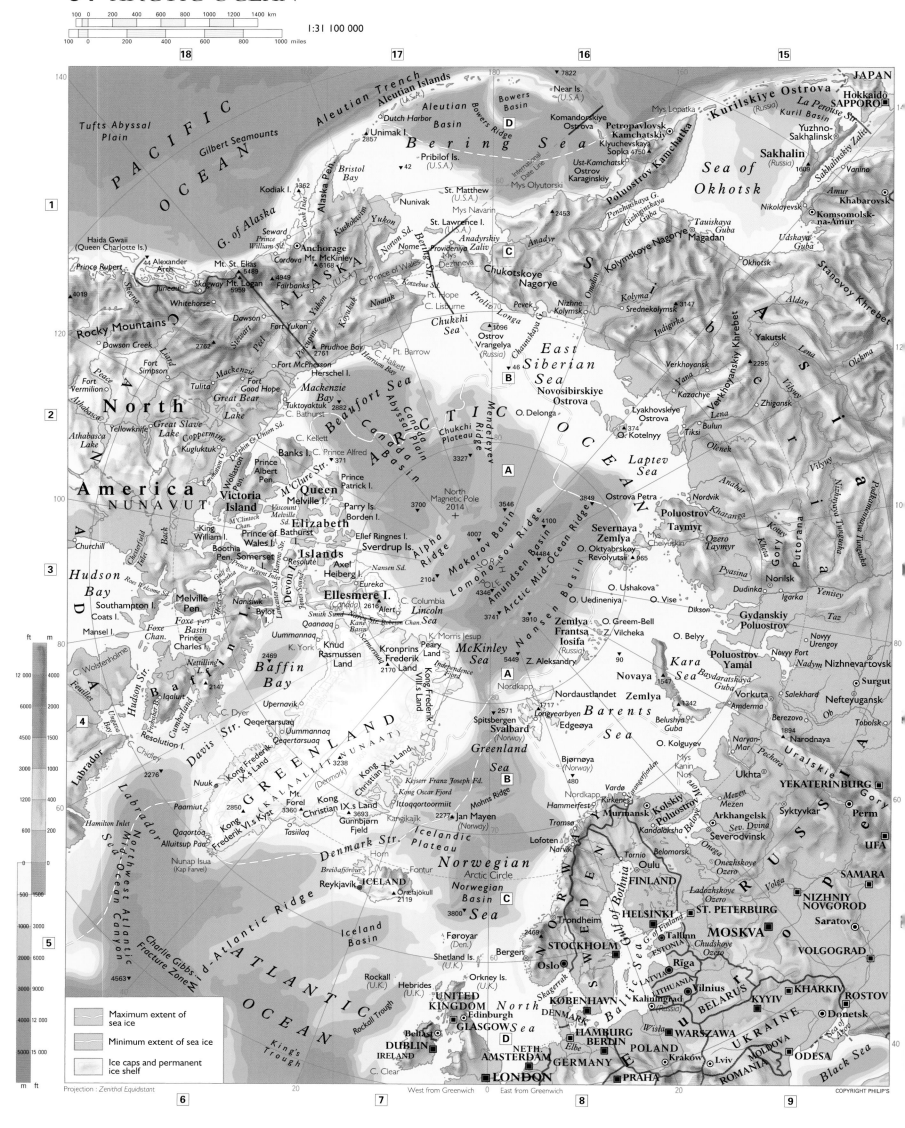

18   **17**   **16**   **15**

JAPAN

PACIFIC OCEAN

Tufts Abyssal Plain

Gilbert Seamounts

Aleutian Trench
Aleutian Islands (U.S.A.)

Bowers Basin

Komandorskiye Ostrova

Kurilskiye Ostrova (Russia)

Hokkaidō SAPPORO

La Pérouse Str.

Kuril Basin

Yuzhno-Sakhalinsk

Bering Sea

Dutch Harbor

Bowers Ridge

Near Is. (U.S.A.)

Petropavlovsk-Kamchatskiy

Klyuchevskaya Sopka 4750

Sakhalin (Russia) 1609

Sabghalinskiy Zaliv

Vanino

Unimak I. 2857

Pribilof Is. (U.S.A.)

Mys Olyutorski

Ust-Kamchatsk Ostrov Karaginskiy

Poluostrov Kamchatka

Sea of Okhotsk

Amur

Khabarovsk

Komsomolsk-na-Amur

Bristol Bay

Kodiak I. 1362

42

St. Matthew (U.S.A.)

Mys Navarin

Anadyr

Penzhinskaya G.

Gizhiginskaya Guba

Tauiskaya Guba

Magadan

Nikolayevsk

Udskaya Guba

G. of Alaska

Seward

Prince William Sd.

Anchorage

Cook Inlet

Mt. McKinley 6168

Nunivak

Nome

Norton Sd.

St. Lawrence I. (U.S.A.)

Provideniya Mys Dezhneva

Anadyrskiy Zaliv

2453

Chukotskoye Nagorye

Kolymskoye Nagorye

Tauiskaya Guba

Okhotsk

Stanovoy Khrebet

Haida Gwaii (Queen Charlotte Is.)

Alexander Arch.

Mt. St. Elias 5489

Cordova

Fairbanks

4949

Skagway Mt. Logan 5959

ALASKA (U.S.A.)

Yukon

C. Prince of Wales

Bering Str.

Prolio Longa

Pevek

Nizhne Kolymsk

Kolyma

Srednekolymsk 3147

Indigirka

Verkhoyansk

Yana

Aldan

Yakutsk

Lena

Olekma

Prince Rupert

44

Juneau

Whitehorse

4019

Rocky Mountains

Dawson Creek

Skeena

Liard

Dawson

Fort Yukon

Koyukuk

Pt. Hope

C. Lisburne

Pt. Barrow

Chukchi Sea

Ostrov Vrangelya (Russia) 1096

Chaunskaya G.

46

East Siberian Sea

Novosibirskiye Ostrova

Verkhoyanskiy Khrebet

2295

Kazachye

Zhigansk

Vilyuy

North America

Fort Simpson

Peace

Fort Vermilion

2762

Prudhoe Bay 2761

Fort McPherson

Herschel I.

Harrison Bay

C. Halkett

2882

C. Bathurst

Mackenzie

Tuktoyaktuk

Beaufort Sea

Canada Abyssal Plain

Canada Basin

Chukchi Plateau

Mendeleyev Ridge

3327

O. Delonga

374

Lyakhovskiye Ostrova

O. Kotelnyy

Tiksi

Bulun

Olenek

Laptev Sea

Anabar

Khatanga

NUNAVUT

Athabasca Lake

Yellowknife

Great Slave Lake

Coppermine

Kugluktuk

Great Bear Lake

Dolphin & Union Str.

Coronation G.

Banks I.

C. Prince Alfred 371

Prince Patrick I.

3700

North Magnetic Pole 2014 +

3546

4007

3849

Ostrova Petra

Nordvik

Poluostrov Taymyr

Gory Putorana

Norilsk

Vilyuy

Athabasca

Victoria Island

Wollaston Pen.

Prince Albert Pen.

Melville I.

Parry Is.

Borden I.

ARCTIC OCEAN

Alpha Ridge

Makarov Basin

Lomonosov Ridge

4100

NORTH POLE

4484

Amundsen Basin

Arctic Mid-Ocean Ridge

Severnaya Zemlya

Mys Chelyuskin

O. Oktyabrskoy Revolyutsii 965

Ozero Taymyr

Pyasina

Dudinka

Igarka

Yenisey

Taz

America

King William I.

M'Clintock Chan.

Prince of Wales I.

Queen Elizabeth Islands

Ellef Ringnes I.

Sverdrup I.

Axel Heiberg I.

Nansen Sd.

2104

Lomonosov Ridge

4346

Amundsen Basin

3741

3910

Nansen Basin

O. Ushakova

O. Vise

O. Uedineniya

Dikson

Gydanskiy Poluostrov

Novyy Urengoy

Hudson Bay

Churchill

Chesterfield Inlet

Boothia Pen.

Somerset I.

Gulf of Boothia

Prince Regent Inlet

Barrow Str.

Resolute

Devon I.

Ellesmere I. (Canada) 2616

Alert

Lincoln Sea

3741

McKinley Sea

5449

Zemlya Frantsa Iosifa (Russia)

Z. Aleksandry

90

Novaya

1547

Kara Sea

Baydaratskaya Guba

Poluostrov Yamal

Novyy Port

Nadym

Nizhnevartovsk

Surgut

Southampton I.

Coats I.

Mansel I.

Foxe Basin

Melville Pen.

Nanisivik

Bylot I.

Smith Sd.

Kane Basin

Qaanaaq

Str. Robeson Chan.

C. Columbia

Peary Land

K. Morris Jesup

Kong Frederik VIII's Land

Z. Vilcheka

O. Greem-Bell

O. Belyy

90

Z. Aleksandry

Zemlya

Novaya

1547

Zemlya

Salekhard

Vorkuta

Amderma

Berezovo

Ob

Nettilling L.

2147

Baffin Bay

2469

Knud Rasmussen Land

Kronprins Frederik Land 2170

Kong Frederik VIII's Land

Independence Fjord

McKinley Sea

A

Nordkapp

Nordaustlandet

Spitsbergen Svalbard (Norway)

Edgeøya

Barents Sea

Belushya Guba

1342

1894

Narodnaya

Pechora

Naryan-Mar

Neftеyugansk

Tobolsk

HUDSON BAY

Southampton I.

Iqaluit

Frobisher Bay

Resolution I.

Chidley

Davis Str.

Cumberland Sd.

C. Dyer

Upernavik

Qeqertarsuaq

Uummannaq

Kejser Franz Joseph Fd.

Kong Christian X's Land

Kong Oscar Fjord

Nordkapp

2571

1717

Longyearbyen

Greenland Sea

Bjørnøya (Norway)

480

Vardø

O. Kolguyev

Mys Kanin Nos

Ukhta

YEKATERINBURG

RUSSIA

Uralskie Gory

Labrador

Hamilton Inlet

2276

Nuuk

Paamiut

2850

Kong Frederik IX's Land

3238

Kong Christian IX's Land

Mt. Forel 3360

GREENLAND (KALAALLIT NUNAAT) (Denmark)

Kong Frederik VI's Kyst

Kangikajik

2277

Jan Mayen (Norway)

Mohns Ridge

Ittoqqortoormiit

Greenland Sea

Hammerfest

Kirkenes

Murmansk

Kolskiy Poluostrov

Varangerfjorden

Mezen

Mezen

Arkhangelsk

Sev. Dvina

Severodvinsk

Syktyvkar

Perm

UFA

Qaqortoq

Alluitsup Paa

Nunap Isua (Kap Farvel)

Tasiilaq

Gunnbjørn Fjeld 3693

3800

Icelandic Plateau

Norwegian Basin

Norwegian Sea

Lofoten

Tromsø

Narvik

Bodø

Nordkapp

Onega

Belomorsk

Onezhskoye Ozero

SAMARA

NIZHNIY NOVGOROD

Saratov

Labrador Sea

Northwest Atlantic Mid-Ocean Canyon

Charlie Gibbs Fracture Zone

Mid-Atlantic Ridge

Breiðafjörður

Horn

Reykjavik

ICELAND

Öræfajökull 2119

Fontur

Arctic Circle

2469

Trondheim

Gulf of Bothnia

FINLAND

HELSINKI

ST. PETERBURG

MOSKVA

Volga

Chudskoye Ozero

Ladozhskoye Ozero

VOLGOGRAD

Iceland Basin

Føroyar (Den.)

Shetland Is. (U.K.)

Bergen

NORWAY

Oslo

STOCKHOLM

SWEDEN

G. of Finland

Tallinn

ESTONIA

Rīga

LATVIA

KHARKIV

ROSTOV

ATLANTIC OCEAN

King's Trough

Rockall (U.K.)

Hebrides (U.K.)

Orkney Is. (U.K.)

Skagerrak

KØBENHAVN

DENMARK

Kaliningrad (Russia)

LITHUANIA

Vilnius

BELARUS

KYYIV

Donetsk

Rockall Trough

UNITED KINGDOM

Edinburgh

Belfast

GLASGOW

North Sea

HAMBURG

BERLIN

Baltic Sea

Sea of Azov

Black Sea

C. Clear

DUBLIN

IRELAND

LONDON

NETH.

AMSTERDAM

GERMANY

Elbe

POLAND

WARSZAWA

Kraków

Lviv

MOLDOVA

UKRAINE

ODESA

ROMANIA

PRAHA

Wisła

West from Greenwich 0 East from Greenwich

Projection: Zenithal Equidistant

COPYRIGHT PHILIP'S

Legend

	Maximum extent of sea ice
	Minimum extent of sea ice
	Ice caps and permanent ice shelf

ft   m

12 000   4000

6000   2000

4500   1500

3000   1000

1200   400

600   200

0   0

500   1500

1000   3000

2000   6000

3000   9000

4000   12 000

5000   15 000

m   ft

6   **7**   **8**   **9**

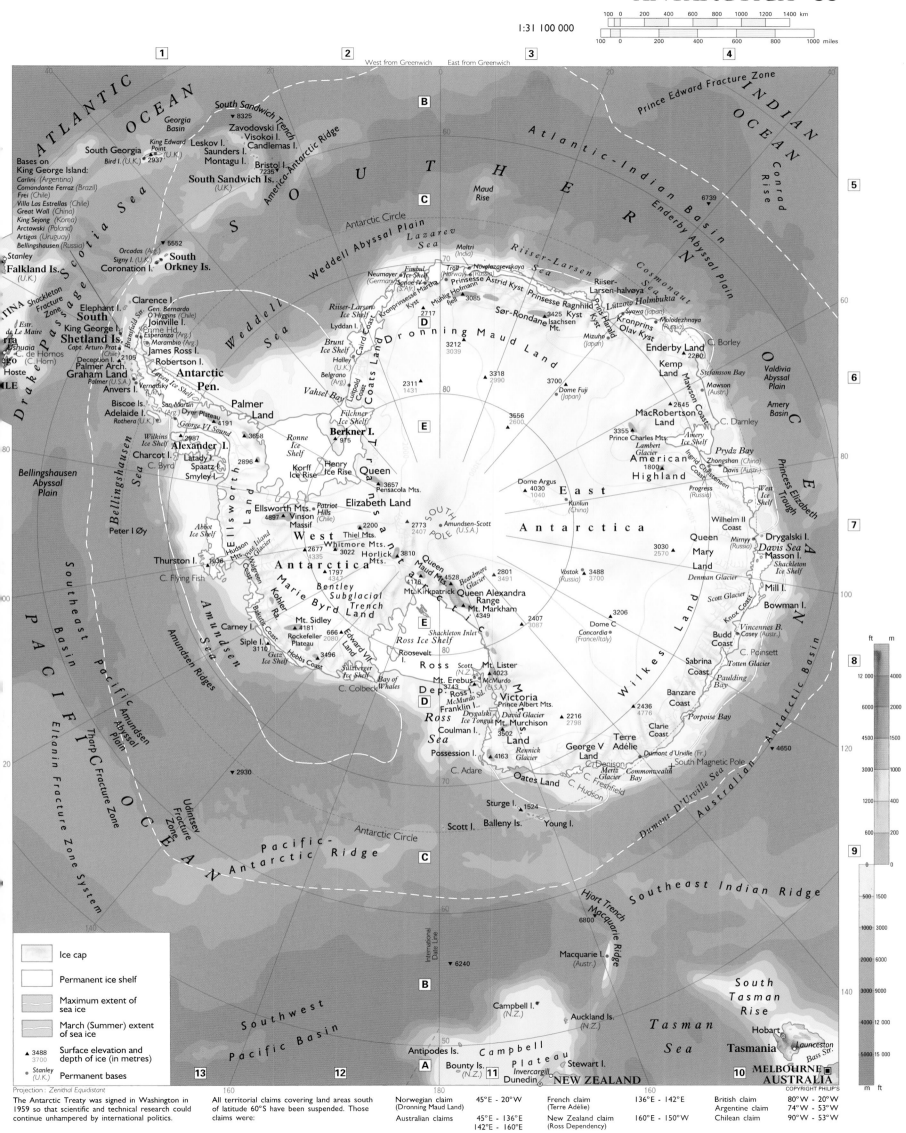

1:31 100 000

Projection : Zenithal Equidistant

The Antarctic Treaty was signed in Washington in 1959 so that scientific and technical research could continue unhampered by international politics.

All territorial claims covering land areas south of latitude 60°S have been suspended. Those claims were:

Norwegian claim (Dronning Maud Land)	45°E - 20°W	French claim (Terre Adélie)	136°E - 142°E
Australian claims	45°E - 136°E 142°E - 160°E	New Zealand claim (Ross Dependency)	160°E - 150°W
		British claim	80°W - 20°W
		Argentine claim	74°W - 53°W
		Chilean claim	90°W - 53°W

COPYRIGHT PHILIP'S

Map legend:

- Ice cap
- Permanent ice shelf
- Maximum extent of sea ice
- March (Summer) extent of sea ice
- ▲ 3488 / 3700 Surface elevation and depth of ice (in metres)
- • Stanley Permanent bases

Equatorial Scale 1:45 000 000

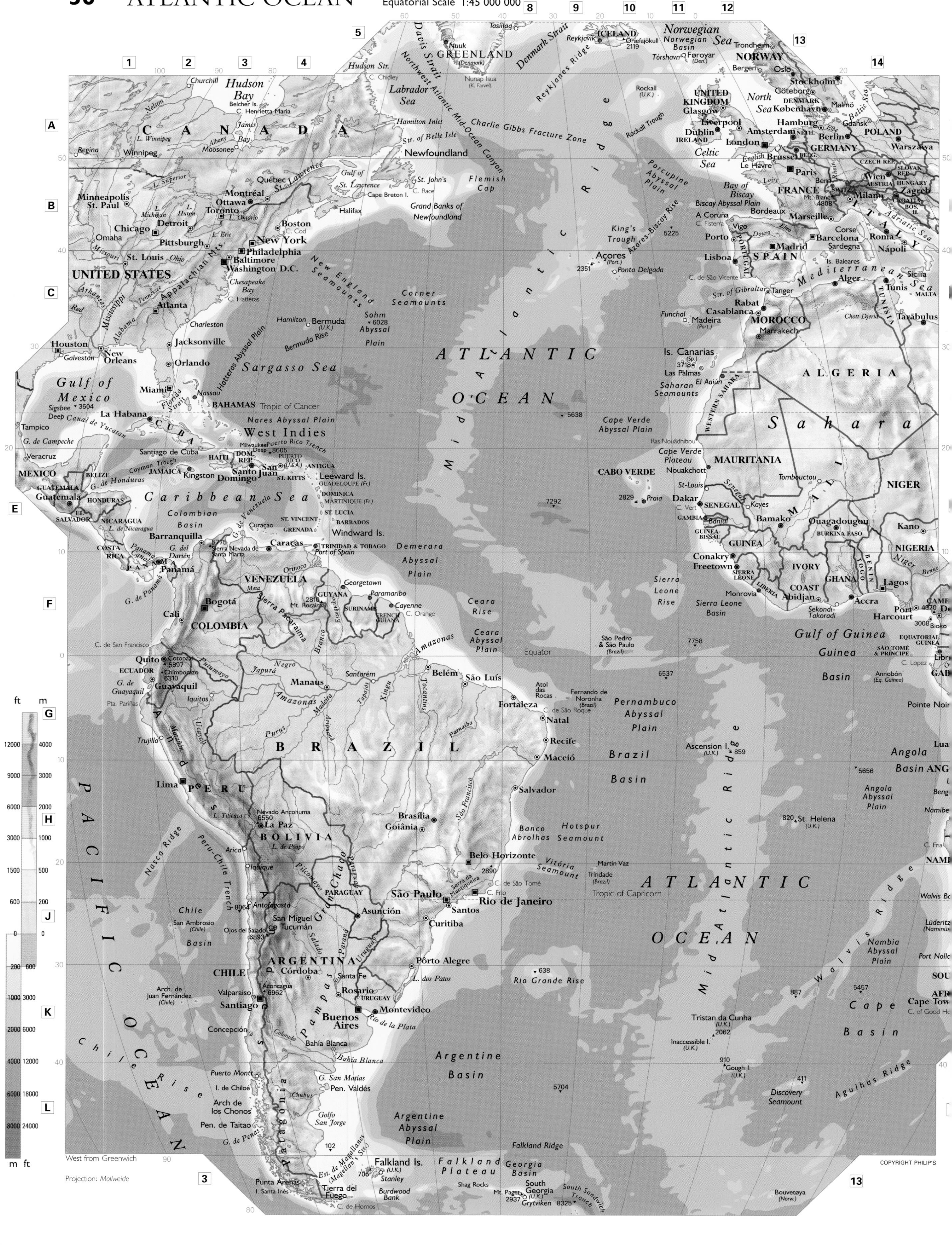
ATLANTIC OCEAN
ATLANTIC OCEAN
PACIFIC OCEAN
Hudson Bay
Labrador Sea
Davis Strait
GREENLAND
Denmark Strait
ICELAND
Norwegian Sea
Norwegian Basin
NORWAY
North Sea
UNITED KINGDOM
IRELAND
Celtic Sea
Bay of Biscay
FRANCE
SPAIN
PORTUGAL
ITALY
GERMANY
POLAND
Mediterranean Sea
MOROCCO
ALGERIA
WESTERN SAHARA
Sahara
MAURITANIA
MALI
NIGER
NIGERIA
SENEGAL
GUINEA
Gulf of Guinea
Guinea Basin
CANADA
UNITED STATES
Gulf of Mexico
MEXICO
CUBA
BAHAMAS
Tropic of Cancer
Caribbean Sea
West Indies
Sargasso Sea
COLOMBIA
VENEZUELA
GUYANA
SURINAME
ECUADOR
PERU
BRAZIL
BOLIVIA
PARAGUAY
CHILE
ARGENTINA
URUGUAY
Equator
Tropic of Capricorn
Mid-Atlantic Ridge
Reykjanes Ridge
Charlie Gibbs Fracture Zone
Northwest Atlantic Mid-Ocean Canyon
Newfoundland
Grand Banks of Newfoundland
Flemish Cap
New England Seamounts
Corner Seamounts
Sohm Abyssal Plain
Nares Abyssal Plain
Puerto Rico Trench
Cape Verde Abyssal Plain
CABO VERDE
Demerara Abyssal Plain
Ceara Rise
Ceara Abyssal Plain
Sierra Leone Rise
Sierra Leone Basin
Pernambuco Abyssal Plain
Brazil Basin
Angola Basin
Angola Abyssal Plain
Walvis Ridge
Cape Basin
Agulhas Ridge
Argentine Basin
Argentine Abyssal Plain
Rio Grande Rise
Falkland Plateau
Falkland Ridge
Georgia Basin
South Sandwich Trench
Falkland Is.
South Georgia
Tristan da Cunha
Gough I.
St. Helena
Ascension I.
Açores
Madeira
Is. Canarias
Bermuda
Chile Basin
Chile Rise
Peru-Chile Trench
Nasca Ridge
West from Greenwich
Projection: Mollweide
COPYRIGHT PHILIP'S

1:11 100 000

100   0   100   200   300   400   500 km
100   0   50   100   150   200   250   300   350 miles

54

A

B

C

D

E

F

ARCTIC OCEAN

3548

1626

Cape Columbia

QUTTINIRPAAQ NAT. PARK

2616 Lake Hazen

Meighen I.

Axel Heiberg I.

Ellef Ringnes I.

Nansen Sound

CANADA

Ellesmere Island

Eureka

3437

Alert

Lincoln Sea

Robeson Chan.

Nares Str.

Kennedy Chan.

Victoria Fjord

Nansen Land

J.P. Koch Fjord

Jørgen Brønlund Fjord

Peary Land

Kap Morris Jesup

Oodaaq

Frederick E. Hyde Fjord

1920

Station Nord

Nordostrundingen

Independence Fjord

Academy Gletscher

Heilprin Land

Dunmark Fjord

Kronprins Frederik Land

Mylius Erichsen Land

Kronprins Christian Land

Ingolf Fjord

Mallemukfjeld

Hans I.

Washington Land

Petermann Gletscher

Nyeboe Land

Wulff Land

Warming Land

Hall Land

Hagen Fjord

Smith Sound

Inglefield Land

Siorapaluk

Qaanaaq (Thule)

Kane Basin (Humboldt Gletscher)

Sermersuaq (Humboldt Gletscher)

Knud Rasmussen Land

2170

Hovgaard Ø

Nioghalvfjerdsfjorden

Norske Øer

Jøkel-bugten

Franske Øer

Île de France

Lambert Land

GREENLAND

2571

Grise Fiord

Jones Sd.

Coburg I.

Kap Atholl

Devon Island

Uummannaq (Dundas) (Thule Air Base)

Kap York

Qeqertarsuaq

Melville Bugt

Steenstrup Gletscher

Lauge Koch Kyst

Germania Land

Danmarkshavn

Store Koldewey

Dove Bugt

Hochstetter Forland

SEA

Baffin Bay

2469

Nuussuaq (Kraulshavn)

Upernavik

Kangersuatsiaq

Upernavik Kujalleq

QAASUITSUP

2935

Dronning Margrethe II Land

Shannon Ø

Clavering Ø

Daneborg

Wollaston Forland

Zackenberg

Ole Rømer Land

Waltershausen Gletscher

Andrée Land

Clyde River (Kangiqtugaapik)

Nunavik

Illorsuit

Maarmorilik

3238

2940

Petermann Bjerg

Geographical Society Ø

Ymer Ø

Kejserr Franz Joseph Fd.

Traill Ø

Mestersvig

Kong Oscar Fjord

Uunartoq Qeqertoq (Warming I.)

Jan Mayen (Norway)

Beerenberg 2277

Olonkinbyen

Mohns Ridge

Baffin I.

Qeqertarsuaq (Disko)

Qeqertarsuaq (Godhavn)

Aasiaat (Egedesminde)

Kangaatsiaq

Sullorsuaq

2602 Ikerasak

Saqqaq

Kangerluk

Disko Bugt

Illulissat (Jakobshavn)

Qasigiannguit (Christianshåb)

Ikamiut

Uummannaq

Renland

Milne Land

Jameson Land

Stauning Alper

Ittaqqimiut (Scoresbysund)

Scoresby Sund (Kangertittivaq)

Ittoqqortoormiit (Scoresbysund)

Uunarteq

Kangikajik (Kap Brewster)

Icelandic Plateau

C. Dyer

Nordre Strømfjord

Sisimiut (Holsteinsborg)

Kong Frederik IX.s Land

Kangerlussuaq (Søndre Strømfjord)

Itilleq

Kap Dalton

GREENLAND (KALAALLIT NUNAAT)

(Denmark)

SERMERSOOQ

Gunnbjørn Field

3693

Blosseville Kyst

Arctic Circle

Søndre Strømfjord

Kangaamiut

Maniitsoq (Sukkertoppen)

QEQQATA

Kangerdlugssuaq

Mt. Forel

3360

Kap Gustav Holm

Denmark Strait

ft   m

3000   1000

1200   400

600   200

Nuuk (Godthåb)

Kapisillit

Dronning Ingrid Land

Kong Christian IX.s Land

Helheim Gletscher

Kuummiut

Ikkatteq

Isortoq

Tasiilaq (Ammassalik)

Kulusuk

Ísafjörður

Blönduós

Breiðafjörður

Hrútafl.

Eyjafjörður

Akureyri

Húsavík

Neskaupstaður

ICELAND

Vatnajökull

Höfn

2119 Öræfajökull

200   600

500   1500

Kangerluarsoruseq (Færingehavn)

Qeqertarsuatsiaat (Fiskenæsset)

Paamiut (Frederikshåb)

Narsalik

2850

Gyldenløve Fjord

Kap Møsting

Kap Moltke

Kap Skjold

Faxaflói

Reykjavík

Vestmannaeyjar

Heimaey

Surtsey

1000   3000

2000   6000

Kangilinnguit (Grønnedal)

Arsuk

Ivittuut

Narsaq

Narsarsuaq

Qaqortoq (Julianehåb)

Alluitsup Paa (Sydprøven)

Timmiarmiut

Mogens Heinesen Fjord

Kong Frederik VI.s Kyst

Lindenow Fjord

ATLANTIC OCEAN

Reykjanes Ridge

3000   9000

4000   12000

Labrador Sea

Nanortalik

2045 Nunatsortoq

Nunap Isua (Kap Farvel)

Prins Christian Sund

KUJALLEQ

m   ft

Nordaustlandet

Kvitøya 270

Kong Karls Land

Nordkapp

Sjuøyane

Olgastredet

Barentsøya

Ny-Ålesund

Prins Karls Forland

1717

Newtontoppen

Longyearbyen

Edgeøya

Storfjorden

Svalbard (Spitsbergen) (Norway)

Barentsburg

Spitsbergen 1431

Sørkapp

McKinley Sea

Nansen Basin

1:17 800 000

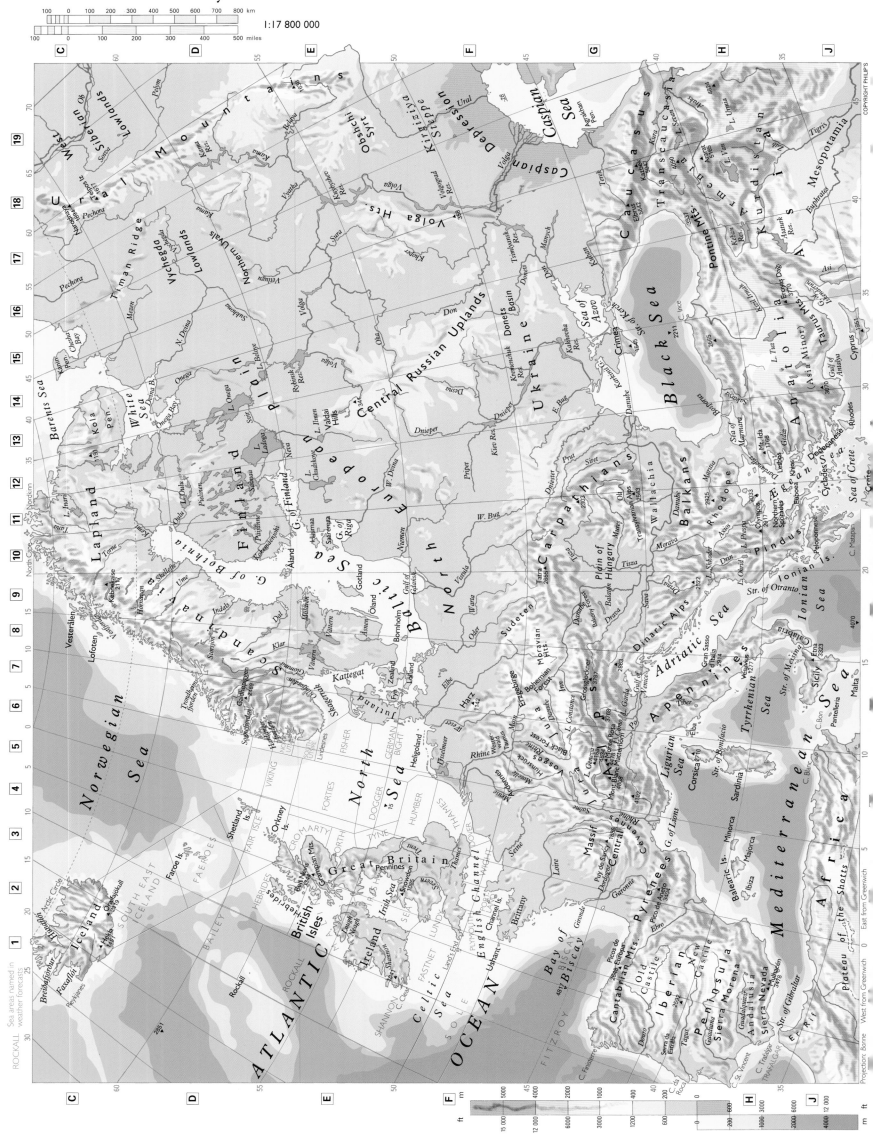

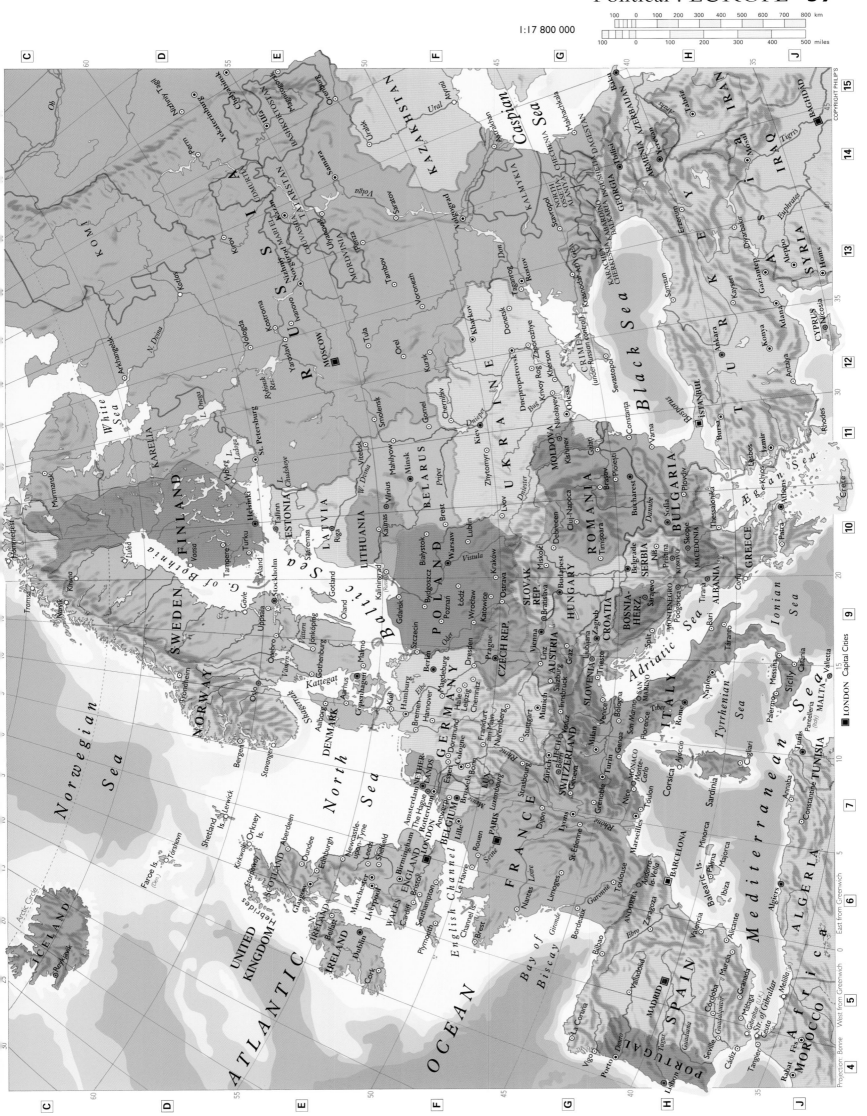

1:17 800 000

■ LONDON Capital Cities

COPYRIGHT PHILIP'S

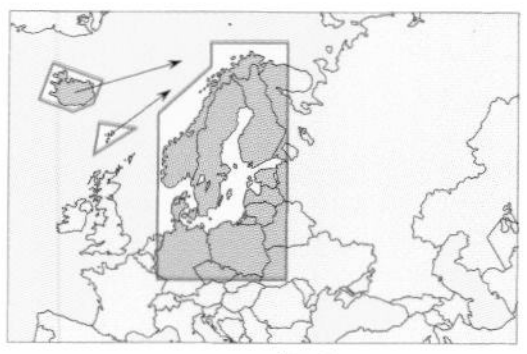

1:5 300 000

50 0 25 50 75 100 125 150 175 km
50 0 25 50 75 100 125 miles

BARENTS SEA

R U S S I A

KARELIA

F I N L A N D

Lappland

Norrland

NORGE

Jämtland

ATLANTIC OCEAN

Gulf of Bothnia

Murmansk
Kola
Kirkenes
Vadsø
Vardø
Hammerfest
Tromsø
Narvik
Bodø
Mo i Rana
Trondheim
Östersund
Umeå
Luleå
Skellefteå
Oulu
Rovaniemi
Tornio
Kemi
Kuopio
Vaasa
Kokkola
Tampere

ICELAND
on same scale

Reykjavik
Keflavik
Akureyri
Vatnajökull
Húnaflói
Faxaflói
Breiðafjörður

FÆROE ISLANDS
on same scale

Føroyar (Færoe Is.)
Tórshavn
Norðoyar
Streymoy
Eysturoy
Vágar
Sandoy
Suðuroy

West from Greenwich
Arctic Circle

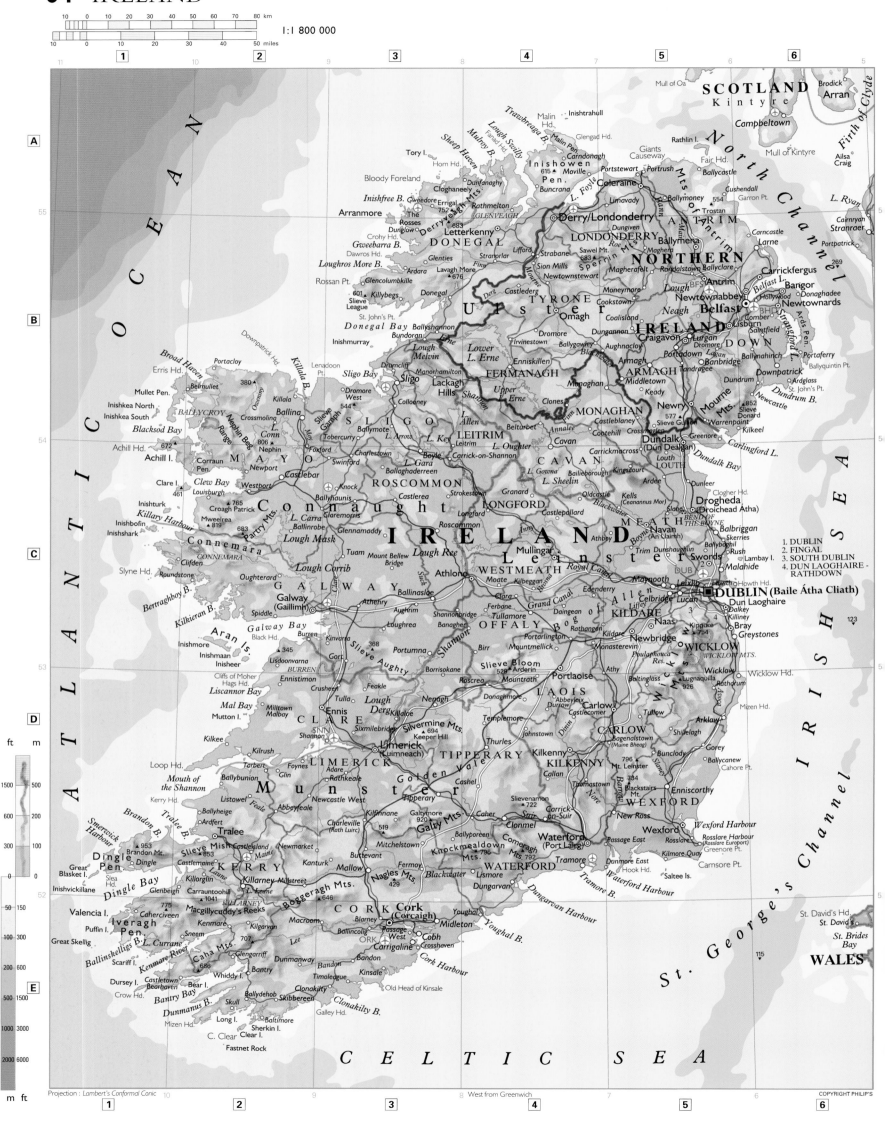

1 : 1 800 000

1. DUBLIN
2. FINGAL
3. SOUTH DUBLIN
4. DUN LAOGHAIRE - RATHDOWN

Projection : Lambert's Conformal Conic

West from Greenwich

COPYRIGHT PHILIP'S

1:1 800 000

10 0 10 20 30 40 50 60 70 80 km
10 0 10 20 30 40 50 miles

Key to Scottish unitary authorities on map
1 ABERDEEN CITY
2 DUNDEE CITY
3 WEST DUNBARTONSHIRE
4 EAST DUNBARTONSHIRE
5 GLASGOW CITY
6 INVERCLYDE
7 RENFREWSHIRE
8 EAST RENFREWSHIRE
9 NORTH LANARKSHIRE
10 FALKIRK
11 CLACKMANNANSHIRE
12 WEST LOTHIAN
13 CITY OF EDINBURGH
14 MIDLOTHIAN

ORKNEY IS. on same scale
ORKNEY
North Ronaldsay
Papa Westray
Westray
Eday
Sanday
Rousay
Stronsay
Shapinsay
Kirkwall
Stromness
Mainland
Brough Hd.
Hoy
Scapa Flow
St. Mary's
Burray
South Ronaldsay
Burwick
Dunnet Hd.
Stroma
Duncansby Head
John o' Groats
Thurso
Sinclair's Bay

SHETLAND IS. on same scale
Muckle Flugga
Unst
Haroldswick
Yell
Fetlar
Yell Sound
Ulsta
Out Skerries
Whalsay
St. Magnus Bay
Sullom Voe
Voe
Papa Stour
Walls
SHETLAND
Scalloway
Lerwick
Bressay
Foula
West Burra
Boddam
Sumburgh Hd.

SCOTLAND

ATLANTIC OCEAN

NORTH SEA

EILEAN SIAR (WESTERN ISLES)
OUTER HEBRIDES
Lewis
Stornoway
Butt of Lewis
Harris
North Uist
Benbecula
South Uist
Barra
Barra Hd.

Sea of the Hebrides
INNER HEBRIDES
Skye
Cuillin Hills
Rùm (Rhum)
Eigg
Muck
Coll
Tiree
Mull
Iona
Colonsay
Oronsay
Islay
Jura
Kintyre
Arran

C. Wrath
Cape Wrath
Durness
Reay Forest
SUTHERLAND
Caithness
Thurso
Wick
Dounreay
Pentland Firth
Ben Hope 927
Ben More Assynt 998
L. Shin
Lairg
Brora
Golspie
Helmsdale
Ord of Caithness

NORTH WEST HIGHLANDS
Ullapool
L. Maree
Gairloch
Kyle of Lochalsh
Fort Augustus
Loch Ness
Inverness
Dingwall
MORAY
Elgin
Buckie
Cullen
Banff
Macduff
Fraserburgh
Peterhead
Buchan Ness
Cruden Bay
Ellon
ABERDEENSHIRE
Aberdeen
Girdle Ness
Stonehaven

HIGHLAND
Glen More
Cairngorm Mts.
Ben Macdhui 1309
CAIRNGORMS
Aviemore
Grantown-on-Spey
Strath Spey
Tomintoul
Braemar
Ballater
Banchory

GRAMPIAN MOUNTAINS
Fort William
Ben Nevis 1344
Glen Coe
Rannoch Moor
ANGUS
Brechin
Montrose
Forfar
Arbroath
Carnoustie
PERTH AND KINROSS
Pitlochry
Blairgowrie
Perth
Dundee
Firth of Tay
St. Andrews
Fife Ness
FIFE
Glenrothes
Kirkcaldy
STIRLING
Stirling
Loch Lomond
LOCH LOMOND AND THE TROSSACHS
ARGYLL AND BUTE
Oban
Lochgilphead
Firth of Lorn
Bute
Rothesay
Campbeltown
Mull of Kintyre

Firth of Clyde
Greenock
Paisley
GLASGOW
Dumbarton
Clydebank
Hamilton
East Kilbride
Motherwell
Coatbridge
Airdrie
Cumbernauld
Falkirk
Grangemouth
Bo'ness
Dunfermline
EDINBURGH
Musselburgh
Haddington
Dunbar
North Berwick
EAST LOTHIAN
Livingston
Dalkeith
Bonnyrigg
Penicuik
WEST LOTHIAN
MIDLOTHIAN

NORTH AYRSHIRE
Ardrossan
Saltcoats
Irvine
Troon
Prestwick
Ayr
EAST AYRSHIRE
Kilmarnock
SOUTH AYRSHIRE
Maybole
Girvan
Ailsa Craig
Stranraer
Portpatrick
Wigtown
Whithorn
Mull of Galloway
Luce Bay
DUMFRIES & GALLOWAY
Dumfries
Annan
Gretna
Lockerbie
Langholm
Moffat
SOUTH LANARKSHIRE
Lanark
Biggar
Peebles
SCOTTISH BORDERS
Galashiels
Melrose
Kelso
Hawick
Jedburgh
Cheviot Hills
The Cheviot 816

NORTHUMBERLAND
Berwick-upon-Tweed
Alnwick
Amble
Morpeth
Newcastle-upon-Tyne
Gateshead
Blaydon
Stanley
Consett
ENGLAND
CUMBRIA
Carlisle
Penrith
Workington
Whitehaven
Keswick
DURHAM
Bishop Auckland
Crook
Barnard Castle
Solway Firth

NORTHERN IRELAND
Belfast
Bangor
Newtownards
Carrickfergus
Larne
North Channel

Projection: Lambert's Conformal Conic
West from Greenwich
COPYRIGHT PHILIP'S

ft m
3000 1000
1500 600
600 200
300 100
0 0
50 150
100 300
200 600
1000 3000
m ft

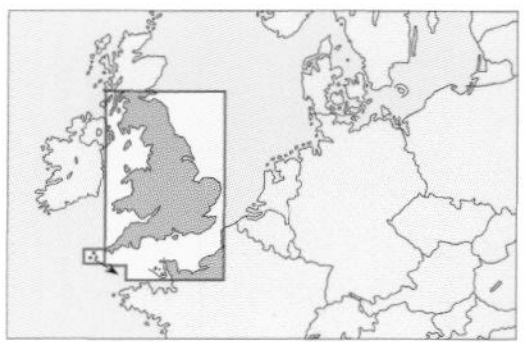

1:1 800 000

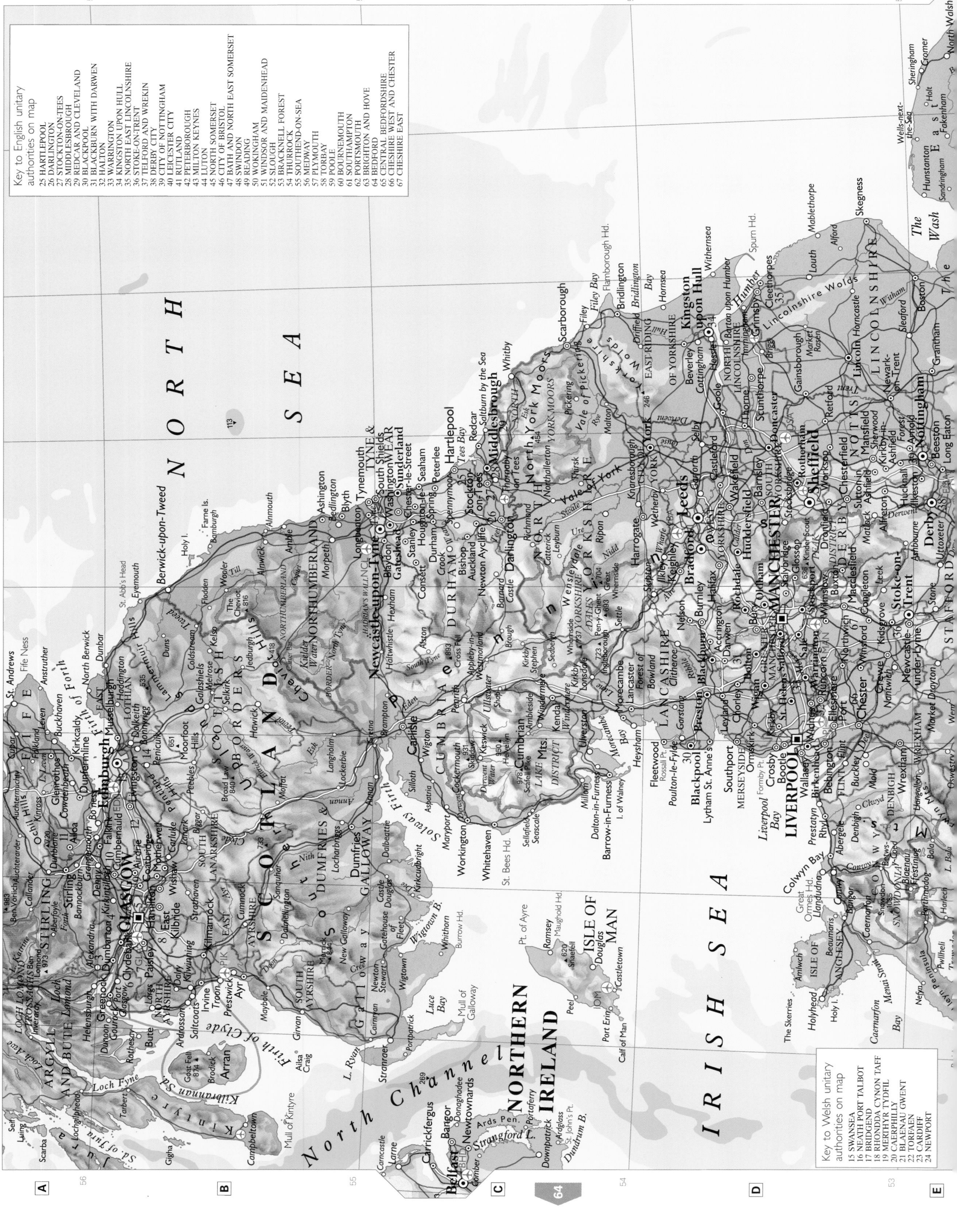

Key to English unitary authorities on map
25 HARTLEPOOL
26 DARLINGTON
27 STOCKTON-ON-TEES
28 MIDDLESBROUGH
29 REDCAR AND CLEVELAND
30 BLACKPOOL
31 BLACKBURN WITH DARWEN
32 HALTON
33 WARRINGTON
34 KINGSTON UPON HULL
35 NORTH EAST LINCOLNSHIRE
36 STOKE-ON-TRENT
37 TELFORD AND WREKIN
38 DERBY CITY
39 CITY OF NOTTINGHAM
40 LEICESTER CITY
41 RUTLAND
42 PETERBOROUGH
43 MILTON KEYNES
44 LUTON
45 NORTH SOMERSET
46 CITY OF BRISTOL
47 BATH AND NORTH EAST SOMERSET
48 SWINDON
49 READING
50 WOKINGHAM
51 WINDSOR AND MAIDENHEAD
52 SLOUGH
53 BRACKNELL FOREST
54 THURROCK
55 SOUTHEND-ON-SEA
56 MEDWAY
57 TORBAY
58 PLYMOUTH
59 POOLE
60 BOURNEMOUTH
61 SOUTHAMPTON
62 PORTSMOUTH
63 BRIGHTON AND HOVE
64 BEDFORD
65 CENTRAL BEDFORDSHIRE
66 CHESHIRE WEST AND CHESTER
67 CHESHIRE EAST

Key to Welsh unitary authorities on map
15 SWANSEA
16 NEATH PORT TALBOT
17 BRIDGEND
18 RHONDDA CYNON TAFF
19 MERTHYR TYDFIL
20 CAERPHILLY
21 BLAENAU GWENT
22 TORFAEN
23 CARDIFF
24 NEWPORT

NORTH SEA

IRISH SEA

North Channel

NORTHERN IRELAND

SCOTLAND

SCOTTISH BORDERS

SOUTHERN UPLANDS

DUMFRIES & GALLOWAY

ISLE OF MAN

ENGLAND

NORTHUMBERLAND

CUMBRIA

LAKE DISTRICT

DURHAM

NORTH YORKSHIRE

LANCASHIRE

WEST YORKSHIRE

SOUTH YORKSHIRE

LINCOLNSHIRE

LINCOLNSHIRE WOLDS

The Wash

WALES

ANGLESEY

Belfast
Glasgow
Edinburgh
Newcastle-upon-Tyne
Sunderland
Middlesbrough
Scarborough
Kingston upon Hull
Leeds
Bradford
Manchester
Liverpool
Sheffield
Chester
Stoke-on-Trent
Derby
Nottingham
Lincoln

Projection : Lambert's Conformal Conic

1:4 400 000

50   0   25   50   75   100   125   150   175 km

50   0   25   50   75   100 125 miles

Projection: Conical with two standard parallels

East from Greenwich
COPYRIGHT PHILIP'S

West from Greenwich

ATLANTIC OCEAN

Shetland Is.
(U.K.)

Yell
Unst
Fetlar
458
Foula
Mainland
Lerwick

Fair Isle

NORWAY
Bergen
Askøyna
Osøyro
Stord
Bømlo
Leir
Haugesund
Kopervik
Åkrahamn
Sandnes
Bryne
Stavanger
Boknai
Nærbø

Orkney Is.
Westray
Sanday
Stronsay
Mainland
Kirkwall
Hoy
South
Ronaldsay

Pentland Firth

C. Wrath
Thurso
Wick

Lewis
Stornoway
North Minch
Helmsdale

Outer Hebrides
Harris
789
Ullapool
Golspie
Lairg

North Uist
Benbecula
Skye
992
Portree
Inner Hebrides
Dingwall
Inverness
Nairn
Elgin
Buckie
Banff
Fraserburgh
Peterhead

South Uist
Mallaig
Rum
Eigg
1182
Glen Mor
L. Ness
Aviemore
CAIRNGORMS
Don
Huntly
Inverurie

Barra
Coll
SCOTLAND
Ben Nevis
1344
Fort William
1311
Ballater
Aberdeen
Stonehaven

Tiree
Tobermory
966
1214
Montrose

Mull
Iona
Oban
L. LOMOND
& TROSSACHS
Perth
Forfar
Arbroath
Dundee

Colonsay
L. Awe
L. Lomond
973
Stirling
St. Andrews

Jura
Islay
Greenock
Paisley
GLASGOW
Dumbarton
Cumbernauld
Hamilton
Edinburgh
Dunfermline
Kirkcaldy
Glenrothes

Campbeltown
Arran
East Kilbride
Irvine
Kilmarnock

Malin Hd.
Buncrana
Coleraine
Larne
Ayr
840
Jedburgh
Hawick
816
Cheviot Hills

Arranmore
Letterkenny
Derry/Londonderry
Ballymena
Antrim
Bangor
NORTHUMBERLAND

GLENVEAGH
Lifford
NORTHERN IRELAND
Lough Neagh
Belfast
Lisburn
Dumfries

Donegal
Omagh
Ulster
Craigavon
Armagh
Newry
Kirkcudbright
Annan
Carlisle
Hexham
893
Gateshead
Durham
Hartlepool

Bundoran
Lower L. Erne
Clones
Castleblaney
Mull of Galloway
Whitehaven
Cumbrian Mts.
978
Darlington
Middlesbrough
Stockton-on-Tees
Redcar

Ballina
Sligo
Leitrim
Cavan
Dundalk
Douglas
I. of Man
Barrow-in-Furness
Lancaster
YORKSHIRE DALES
N. YORK MOORS
Scarborough

Achill I.
Castlebar
L. Conn
852
Drogheda

Westport
Roscommon
Longford
Lough Ree
Mullingar
Boyne
Blackpool
Preston
Keighley
Leeds
York
Beverley
Kingston upon Hull

Lough Mask
Connemara
Lough Corrib
Athlone
Ballinasloe
Tullamore
DUBLIN
Burnley
Blackburn
Bradford
Huddersfield
Barnsley
Doncaster
Scunthorpe
Grimsby
Louth

Galway B.
Galway
Birr
Dun Laoghaire
Bray
Holyhead
Anglesey
Bangor
MANCHESTER
LIVERPOOL
Bolton
Oldham
636
Stockport
Rotherham
Sheffield
Lincoln
Skegness

Aran Is.
BURREN
Ennis
Lough Derg
Nenagh
Thurles
Kilkenny
Carlow
Arklow
Colwyn Bay
Wrexham
Chester
Warrington
Crewe
PEAK DISTRICT
Chesterfield
Mansfield
Nottingham
Boston
The Wash

Kilrush
Limerick
Tipperary
926
Snowdon
1085
Pwllheli
Stoke-on-Trent
Derby
Stafford
Grantham
King's Lynn
Cromer

Shannon
953
Listowel
Mallow
Clonmel
SNOWDONIA
Shrewsbury
Telford
Nuneaton
Leicester
Corby
Peterborough
Norwich
Great Yarmouth
Lowestoft

Dingle
Tralee
920
Waterford
Dungarvan
Cardigan Bay
Aberystwyth
Welshpool
Cambrian Mts.
BIRMINGHAM
Wolverhampton
Coventry
Rugby
Northampton
Ely
Bury St. Edmunds
Ipswich
THE BROADS

Carrantuohill
1041
Killarney
Blackwater
Youghal
Cork
WALES
886
Brecon
Hereford
Worcester
Redditch
Royal Leamington Spa
Bedford
Milton Keynes
Cambridge
Colchester
Felixstowe

Macgillycuddy's Reeks
Bandon
Cobh
Carmarthen
BRECON BEACONS
Merthyr Tydfil
Cheltenham
Gloucester
Stevenage
Luton
Harlow
Chelmsford

Valencia
Kinsale
Fishguard
Haverfordwest
Milford Haven
Pembroke
Llanelli
Neath
Rhondda
Cwmbran
Cardiff
Newport
Bristol
Bath
Swindon
Newbury
Reading
LONDON
Slough
Watford
Basildon
Southend-on-Sea
Margate

C. Clear
99
PEMBROKESHIRE COAST
Swansea
Port Talbot
Barry
Weston-super-Mare
EXMOOR
Bristol Channel
Chatham
Canterbury
Maidstone
Dover

CELTIC SEA
Bude
Barnstaple
Taunton
Yeovil
Salisbury
SOUTH DOWNS
Basingstoke
Winchester
Guildford
Reigate
Crawley
Ashford
Folkestone
Hastings

Newquay
Bideford
Exmouth
Bournemouth
Poole
Southampton
Fareham
Havant
Worthing
Brighton
Eastbourne

Truro
St. Austell
618
DARTMOOR
Torbay
Weymouth
Newport
Isle of Wight
Portsmouth
Str. of Dover

Land's End
Penzance
Falmouth
Plymouth
Exeter
NEW FOREST

Isles of Scilly
English Channel

IRELAND
IRISH SEA
UNITED KINGDOM
ENGLAND

NORTH SEA
238
16
36

Berwick-upon-Tweed
Galashiels
Southern Uplands
Alnwick
Newcastle-upon-Tyne
South Shields
Sunderland

NETHERLANDS
Haarler
Den Helde
Tex
Alkma
's-Gravenhage
(Den Haag)
Hoek van Holland
ROTTERDAM
Dordrecht
Zeeland
Vlissingen
Zeebrugge
Oostende
Brugge
Gent
Mechele
BELGIUM
BRUSSELS
(Bruxelles)
Antwerpen
Villeneuve d'Ascq
LILLE
Tourcoing
Roubaix

Calais
Gris-Nez
St-Omer
Boulogne-sur-Mer
Le Touquet-Paris-Plage
33
St-Béthune
Bruay-la-Buissière
Bruay-la-Buissière
Valenciennes
Cambrai

FRANCE
Alderney
C. de la Hague
Pte. de Barfleur
Cherbourg-Octeville
Valognes
Bayeux
Le Havre
Bolbec
Rouen
Trouville-sur-Mer
Lisieux
Elbeuf
Caen
Seine
Abbeville
Dieppe
Le Tréport
Fécamp
Pays de Caux
Amiens
Picardie
St. Quentin
Laon

Guernsey
St. Peter Port
Sark
Channel Is.
(U.K.)
St. Helier
Jersey
Cotentin

ft   m
3000   1000
1500   500
600   200
0   0
150
300
600
1500
3000
6000
m   ft

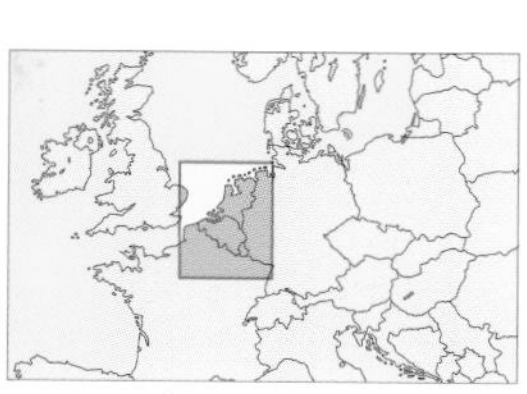

1:2 200 000

10 0 10 20 30 40 50 60 70 80 90 km
10 0 10 20 30 40 50 60 miles

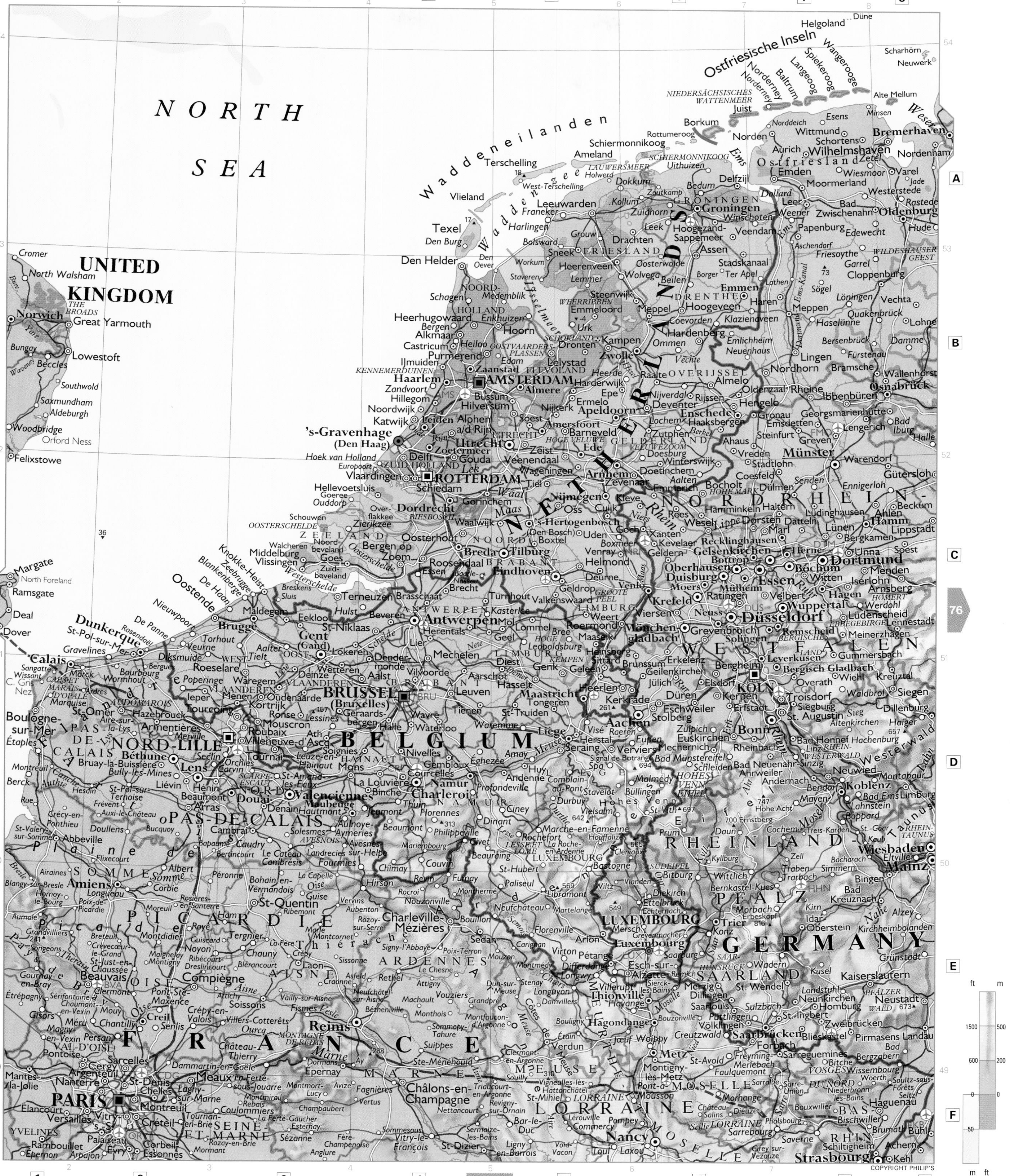

NORTH SEA

UNITED KINGDOM

Cromer
North Walsham
THE BROADS
Norwich
Bungay
Beccles
Lowestoft
Southwold
Saxmundham
Aldeburgh
Woodbridge
Orford Ness
Felixstowe
Margate
North Foreland
Ramsgate
Deal
Dover
Calais
C. Gris Nez

NETHERLANDS

Helgoland
Düne
Ostfriesische Inseln
Scharhörn
Neuwerk
Wangerooge
Spiekeroog
Langeoog
Baltrum
Norderney
Juist
Borkum
Rottumeroog
Schiermonnikoog
Ameland
Terschelling
Vlieland
Texel
Den Burg
Den Helder

Waddeneilanden
Waddenzee
NIEDERSÄCHSISCHES WATTENMEER

Bremerhaven
Nordenham
Wilhelmshaven
Emden
Oldenburg
Groningen
Leeuwarden
Franeker
Harlingen
Dokkum
Assen
Emmen
Hoogeveen
Meppel
Zwolle
Amsterdam
Haarlem
Hoorn
Alkmaar
Enkhuizen
Lelystad
Almere
's-Gravenhage (Den Haag)
Delft
Rotterdam
Dordrecht
Utrecht
Amersfoort
Apeldoorn
Deventer
Enschede
Arnhem
Nijmegen
Breda
Tilburg
Eindhoven
's-Hertogenbosch
Venlo
Roermond

FRIESLAND
DRENTHE
OVERIJSSEL
FLEVOLAND
GELDERLAND
NOORD-HOLLAND
ZUID-HOLLAND
ZEELAND
NOORD-BRABANT
LIMBURG

BELGIUM

Oostende
Brugge
Gent (Gand)
Antwerpen
Brussel (Bruxelles)
Mechelen
Leuven
Hasselt
Liège
Namur
Charleroi
Mons
Tournai
Maastricht
Aachen
Tongeren

VLAANDEREN
HAINAUT
BRABANT
NAMUR
LIÈGE
LUXEMBOURG

LUXEMBOURG

Luxembourg
Esch-sur-Alzette
Diekirch
Vianden
Ettelbrück

GERMANY

Dortmund
Essen
Düsseldorf
Köln
Bonn
Wuppertal
Bochum
Duisburg
Münster
Osnabrück
Wiesbaden
Mainz
Koblenz
Trier
Saarbrücken

NORDRHEIN-WESTFALEN
RHEINLAND-PFALZ
SAARLAND

FRANCE

Dunkerque
Lille
Valenciennes
Arras
Amiens
Reims
Charleville-Mézières
Sedan
Metz
Thionville
Nancy
Strasbourg
Paris
Beauvais
Compiègne
Soissons
Laon
St-Quentin
Boulogne-sur-Mer
Calais

PAS-DE-CALAIS
NORD
PICARDIE
SOMME
OISE
AISNE
ARDENNES
MARNE
LORRAINE
MOSELLE
VOSGES

——— High-speed rail routes

Underlined towns give their name to the administrative area in which they stand.

COPYRIGHT PHILIP'S

10 0 10 20 30 40 50 60 70 80 90 km
10 0 10 20 30 40 50 60 miles

1:2 200 000

DÉPARTEMENTS IN THE PARIS AREA
1 Ville de Paris   3 Val-de-Marne
2 Seine-St-Denis   4 Hauts-de-Seine

Projection : Lambert's Conformal Conic   West from Greenwich

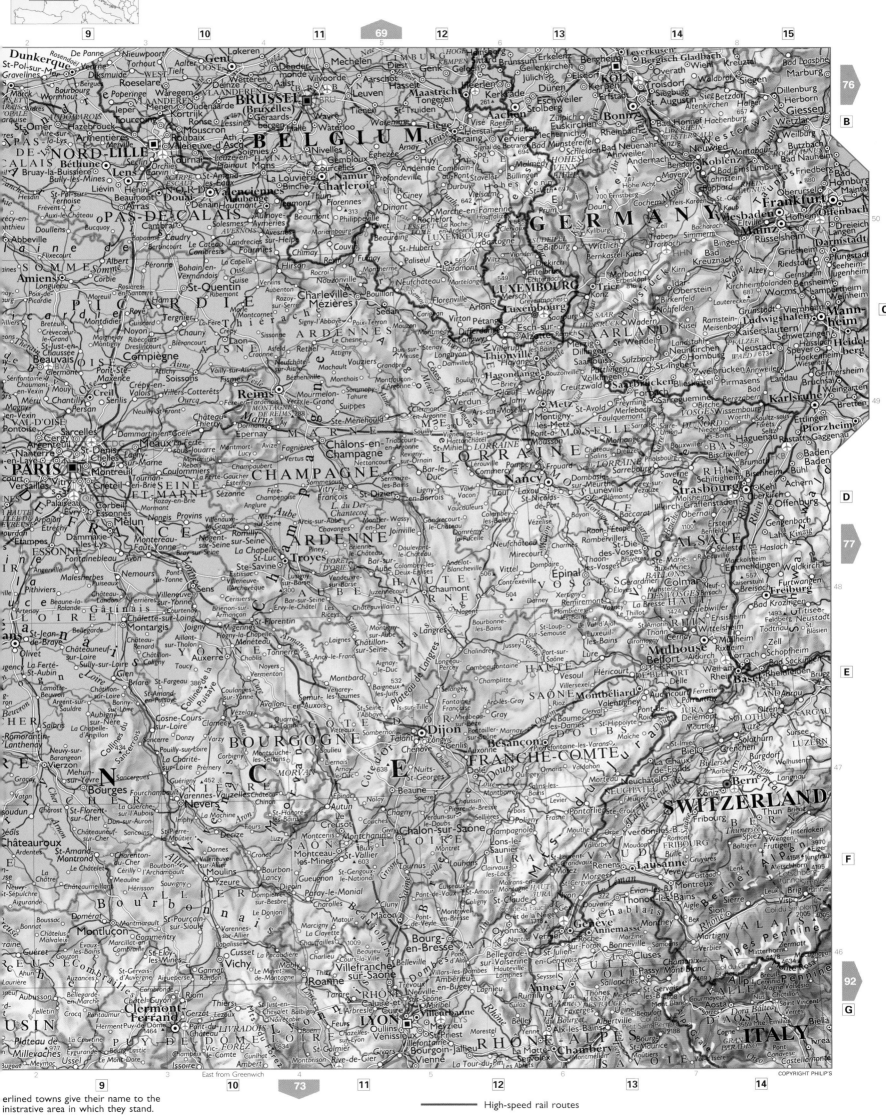

erlined towns give their name to the
inistrative area in which they stand.

High-speed rail routes

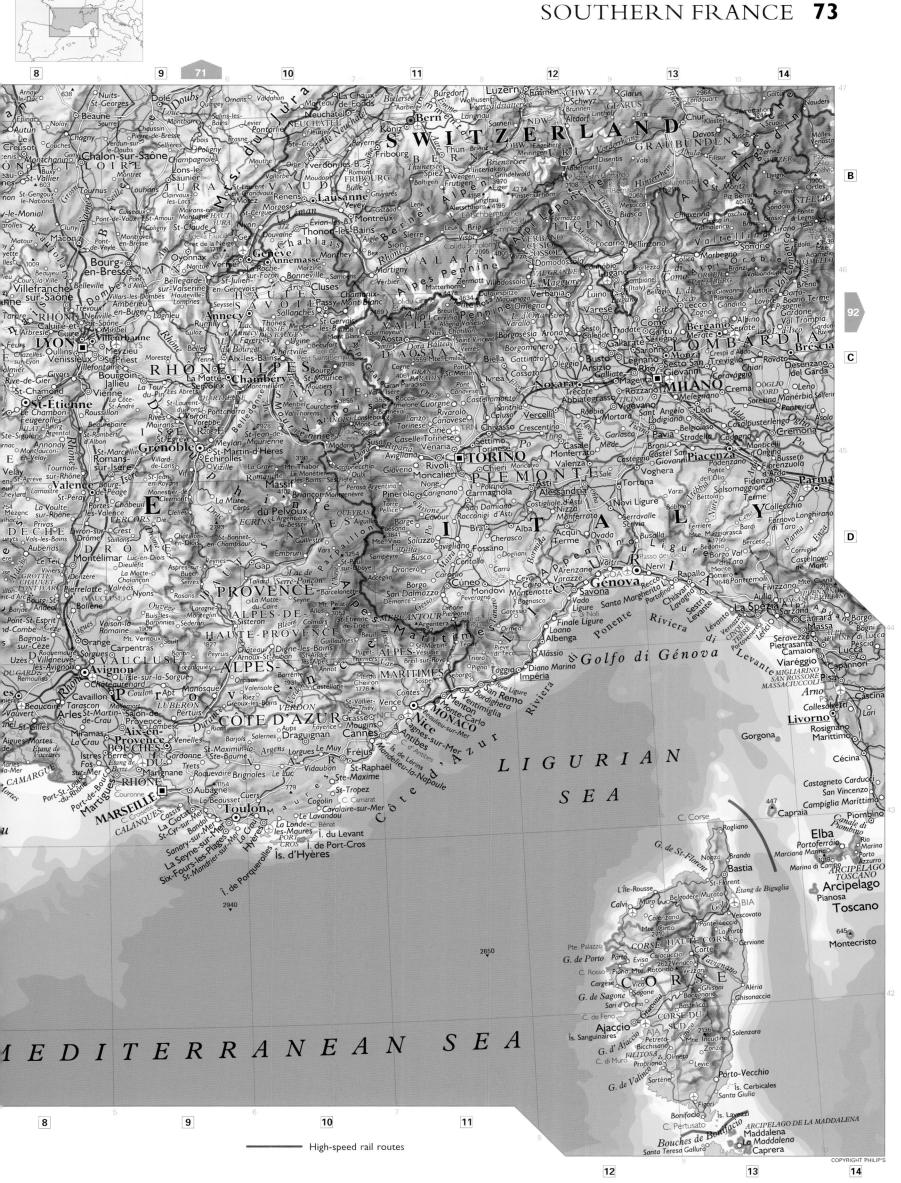

High-speed rail routes

1:4 400 000

Projection: Conical with two standard parallels

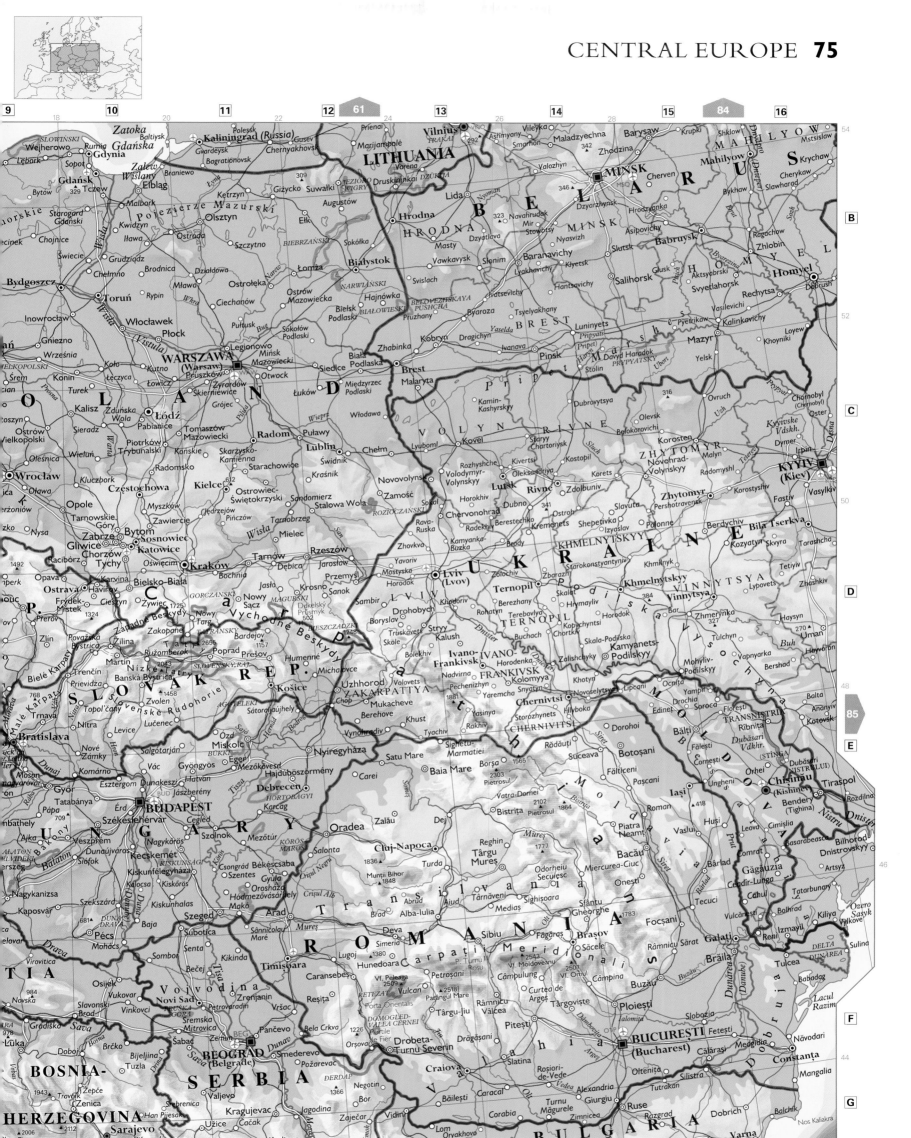

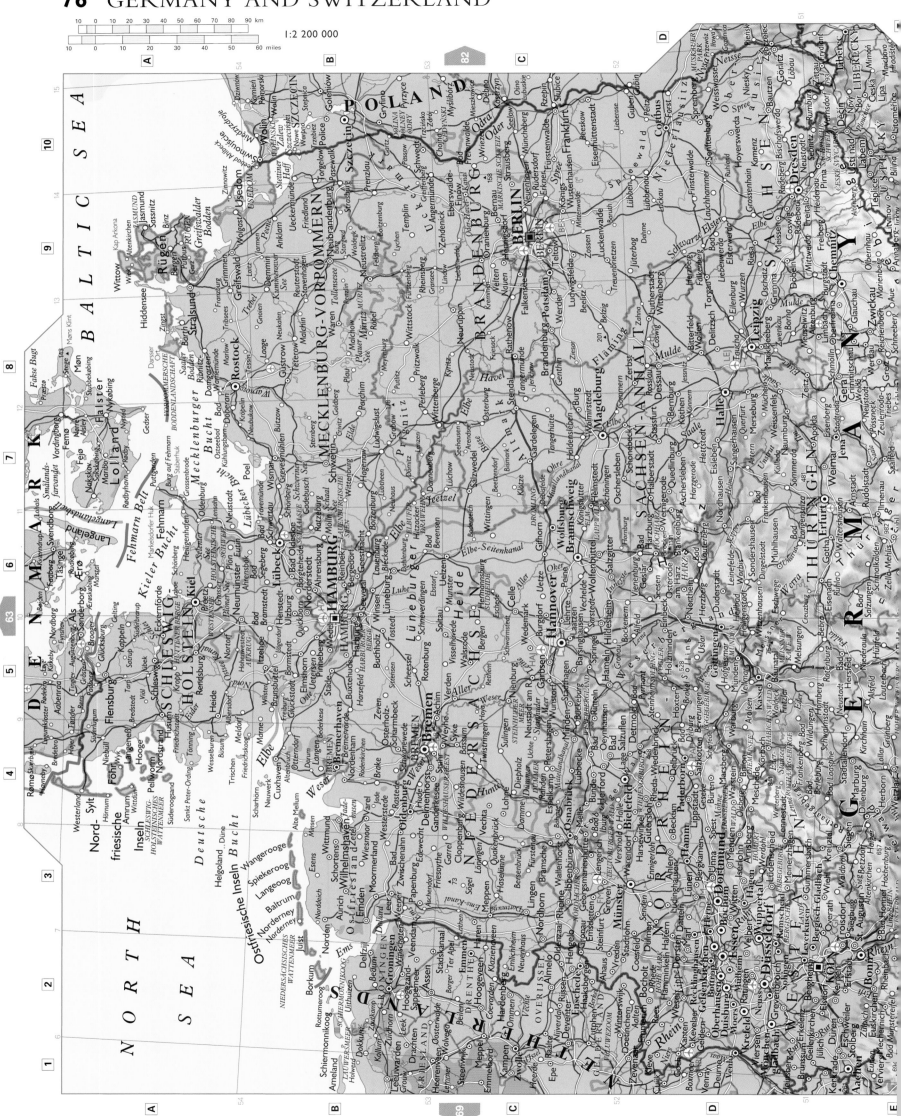

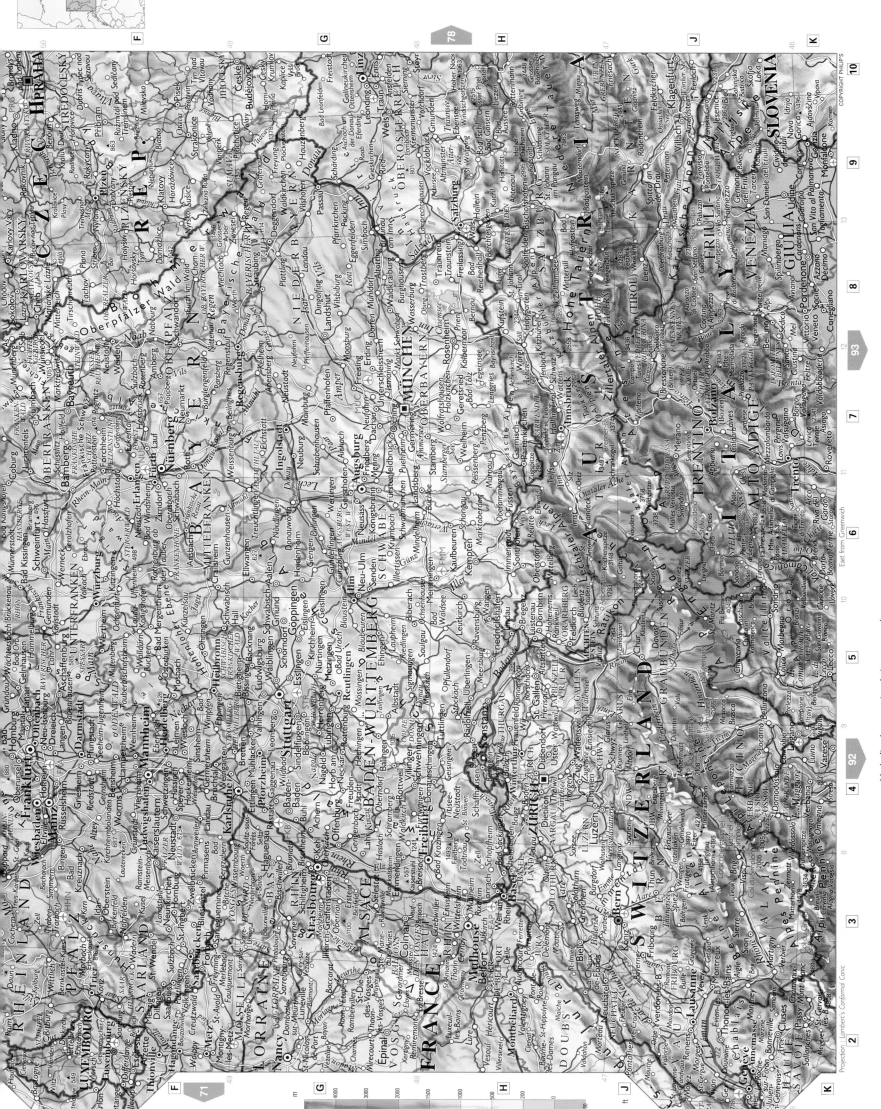

East from Greenwich

Projection: Lambert's Conformal Conic

—————— High-speed rail routes

Underlined towns give their name to the
administrative area in which they stand.

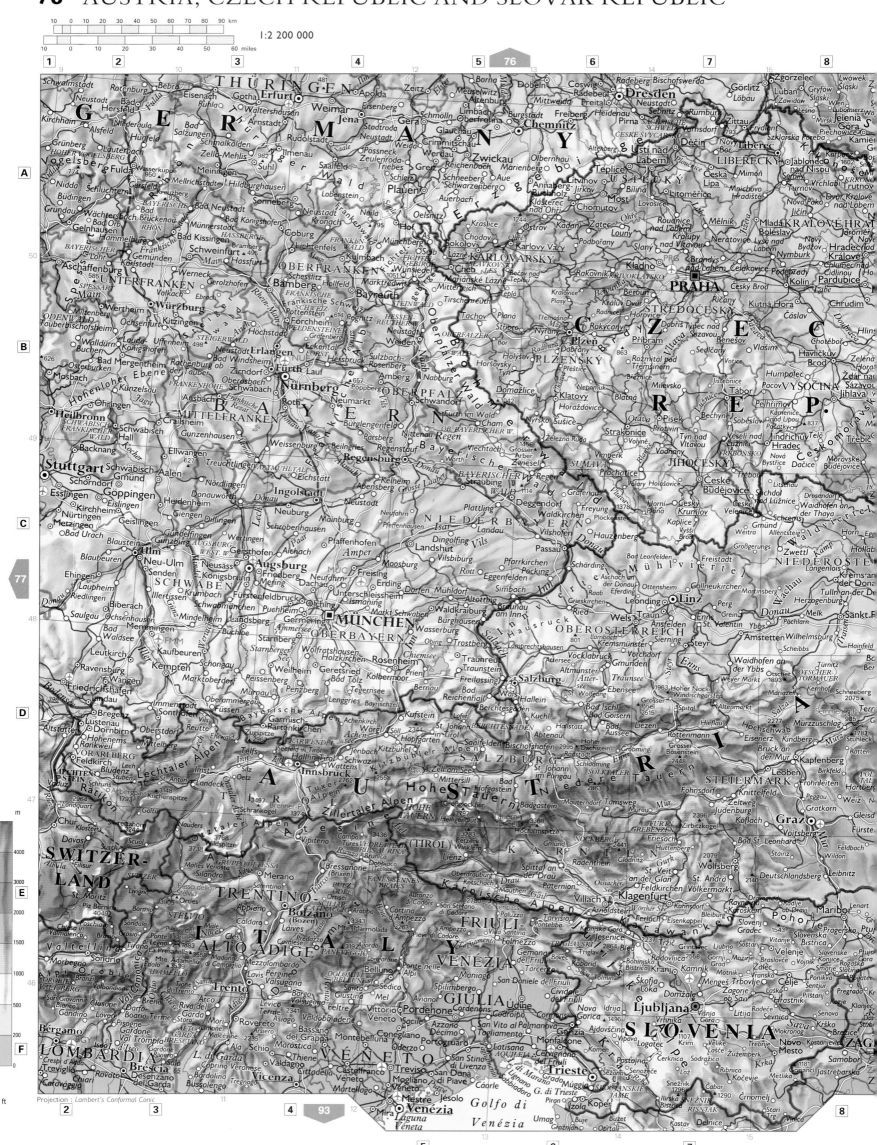

COPYRIGHT PHILIP'S

Underlined towns give their name to the
administrative area in which they stand.

Projection : Lambert's Conformal Conic

East from Greenwich

Administrative divisions in Croatia:
1 Brodsko-Posavska   5 Osječko-Baranjska   9 Vukovarsko-Srijemska
2 Koprivničko-Križevačka   6 Požeško-Slavonska
4 Medimurska   8 Virovitičko-Podravska

Underlined towns give their name to the
administrative area in which they stand.

COPYRIGHT PHILIP'S

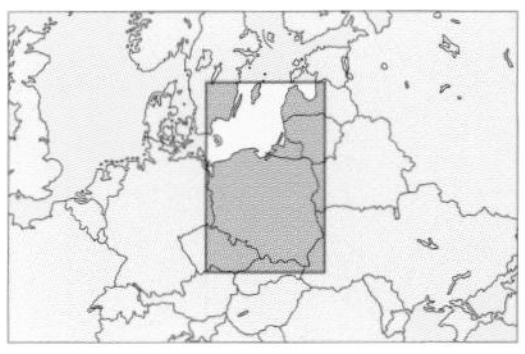

1:2 200 000

10 0 10 20 30 40 50 60 70 80 90 km
10 0 10 20 30 40 50 60 miles

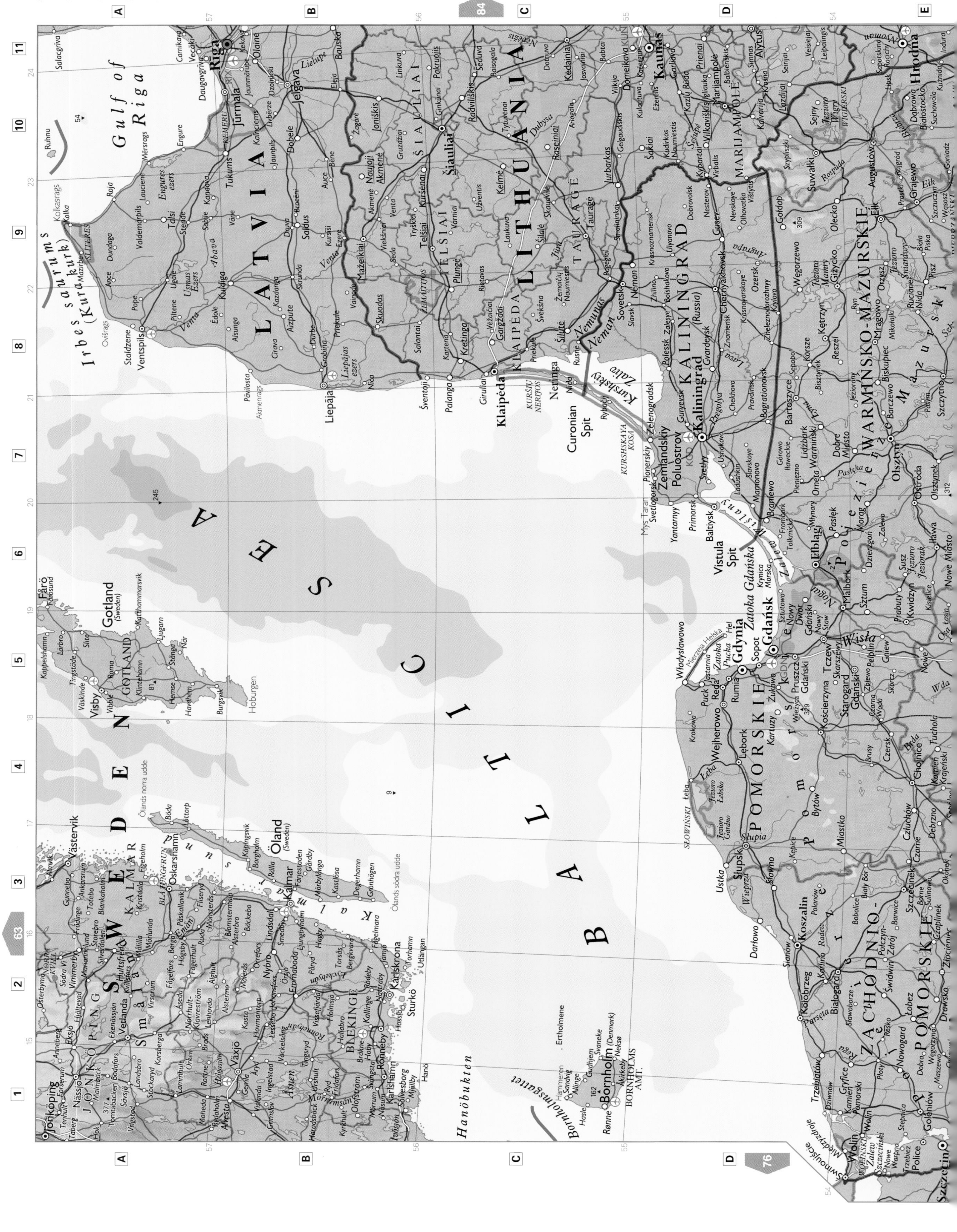

Gulf of Riga

BALTIC SEA

SWEDEN

LATVIA

LITHUANIA

KALININGRAD (Russia)

POLAND

Riga
Jūrmala
Jelgava
Šiauliai
Kaunas
MARIJAMPOLE
Klaipėda
Kaliningrad
Gdańsk
Gdynia
Sopot
Elbląg
Słupsk
Koszalin
Kołobrzeg

Gotland (Sweden)
Öland (Sweden)
Kalmar
Karlskrona
Visby
Bornholm (Denmark)

POMORSKIE
WARMIŃSKO-MAZURSKIE
ZACHODNIO-POMORSKIE

Curonian Spit
Vistula Spit
Zatoka Gdańska

Neman
Nemunas

Underlined towns give their name to the administrative area in which they stand.

East from Greenwich

Projection : Lambert's Conformal Conic

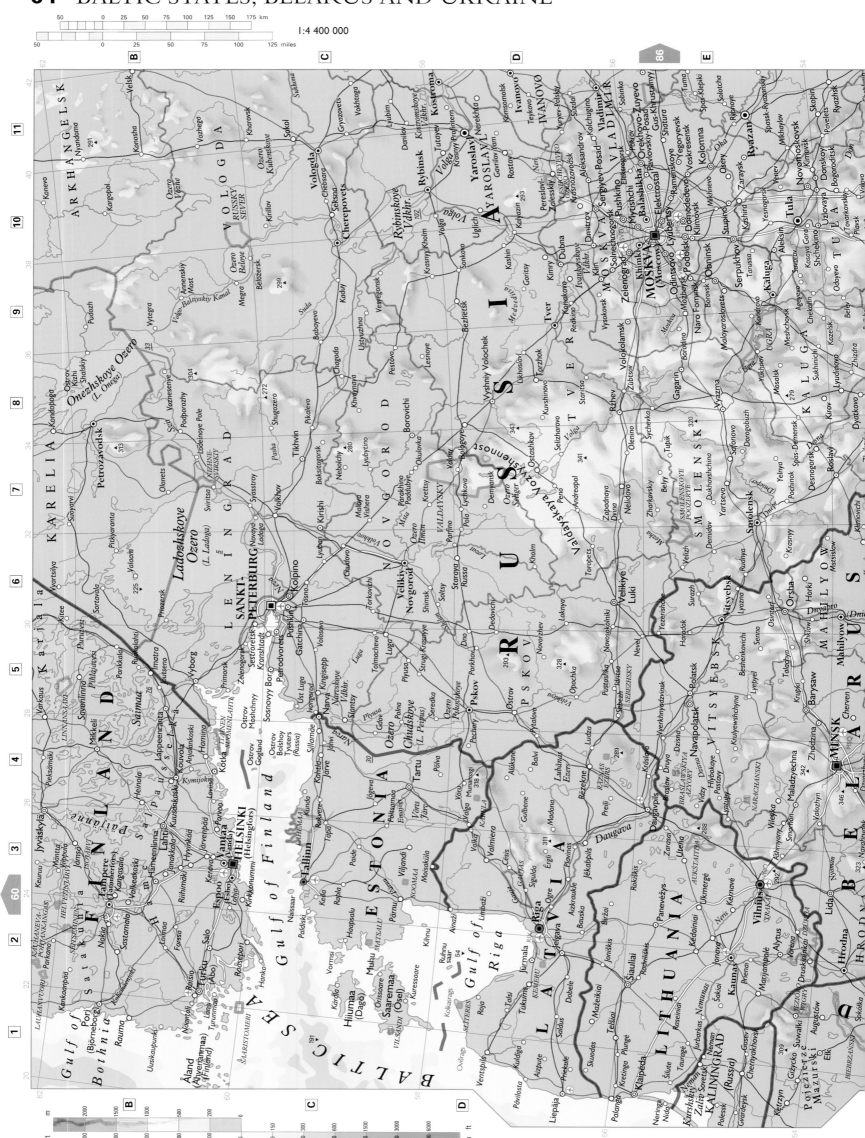

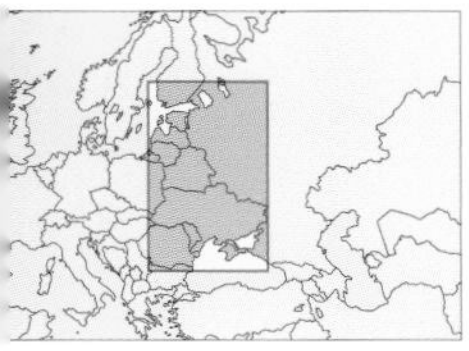

COPYRIGHT PHILIP'S

East from Greenwich

Projection: Conical with two standard parallels

Major labels

ORELL · VORONEZH · KURSK · BELGOROD · SUMY · POLTAVA · LUHANSK · DONETSK · KHARKIV (Kharkov) · DNIPROPETROVSK · ZAPORIZHZHYA · KHERSON · CRIMEA (under Russian control) · KRASNODAR

Sea of Azov · BLACK SEA · Taganrogskiy Zaliv · Kerchenskiy Proliv

CHERNIHIV · KYYIV (Kiev) · ZHYTOMYR · VOLYN · RIVNE · TERNOPIL · KHMELNYTSKYY · VINNYTSYA · CHERKASY · KIROVOHRAD · MYKOLAYIV · ODESA · ODESA

LVIV (Lvov) · IVANO-FRANKIVSK · ZAKARPATTYA · CHERNIVTSI · Podillya

MOLDOVA · TRANSNISTRIA · Chişinău (Kishinev) · Tiraspol · Bender (Tighina) · Gagauzia · TRANSNISTRIA

ROMANIA · BUCUREŞTI (Bucharest) · BULGARIA · HUNGARY · SLOVAK REP. · POLAND

HOMYEL · Homyel · BREST · Pinsk · Brest · Mazyr · Salihorsk

Rostov · Don · Lipetsk · Yelets · Starry Oskol · Kursk

Dnister · Dnipro · Desna · Don · Prut · Siret · Dunărea (Danube)

Map grid references

G · H · J · K · 6 · 7 · 8 · 9 · 10

86 · 87 · 75 · 81 · 104

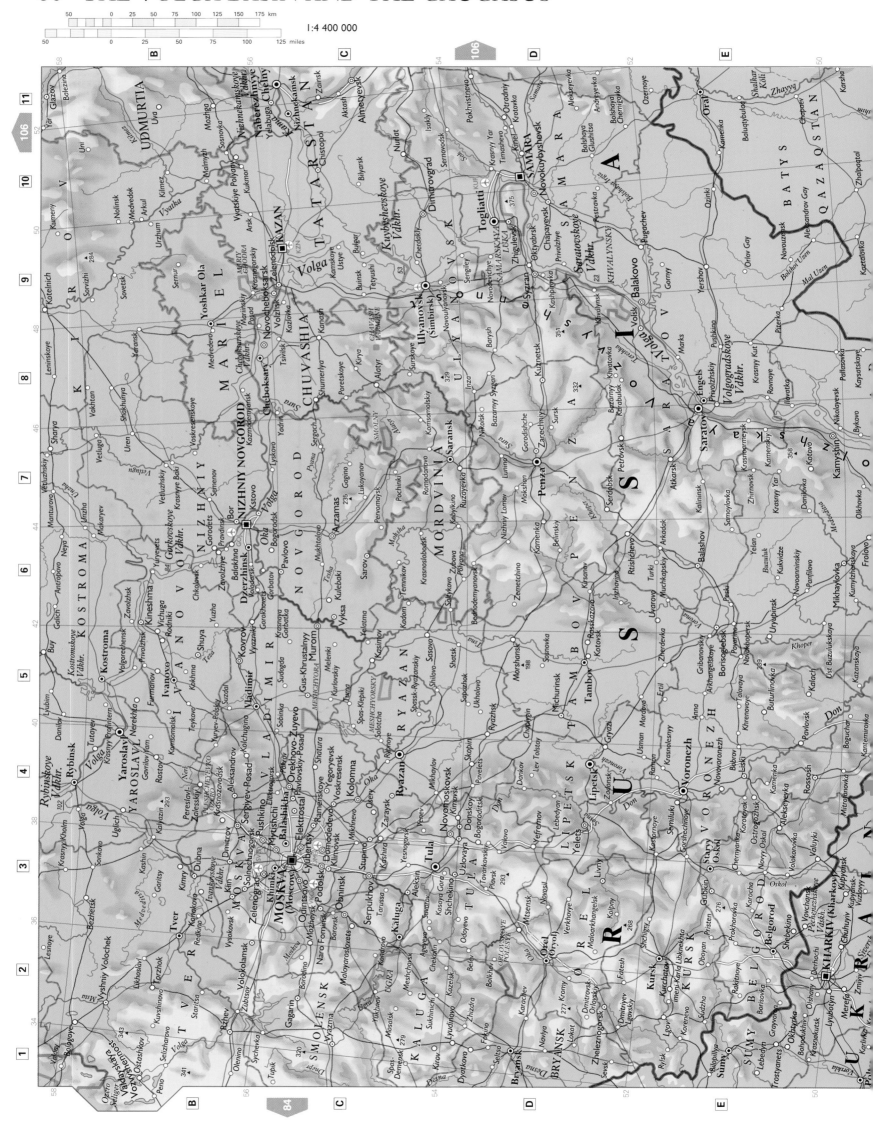

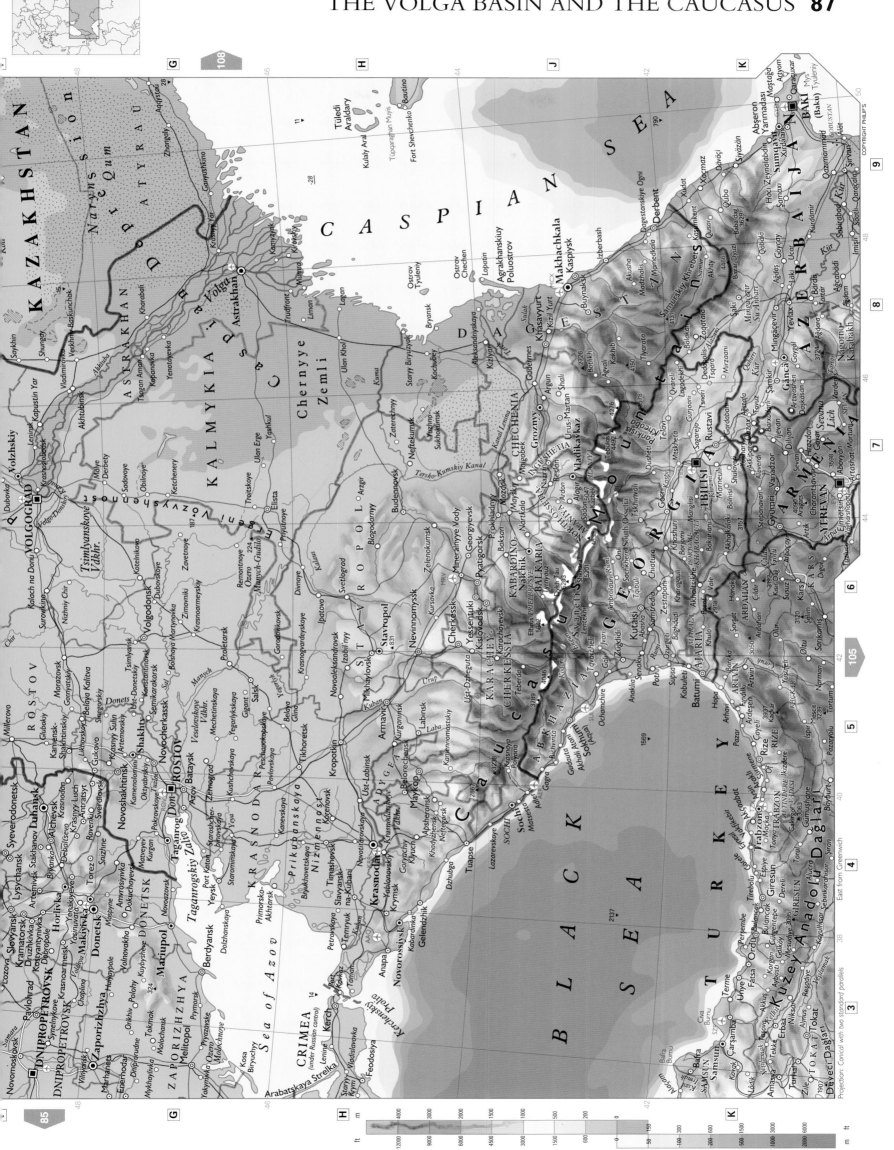

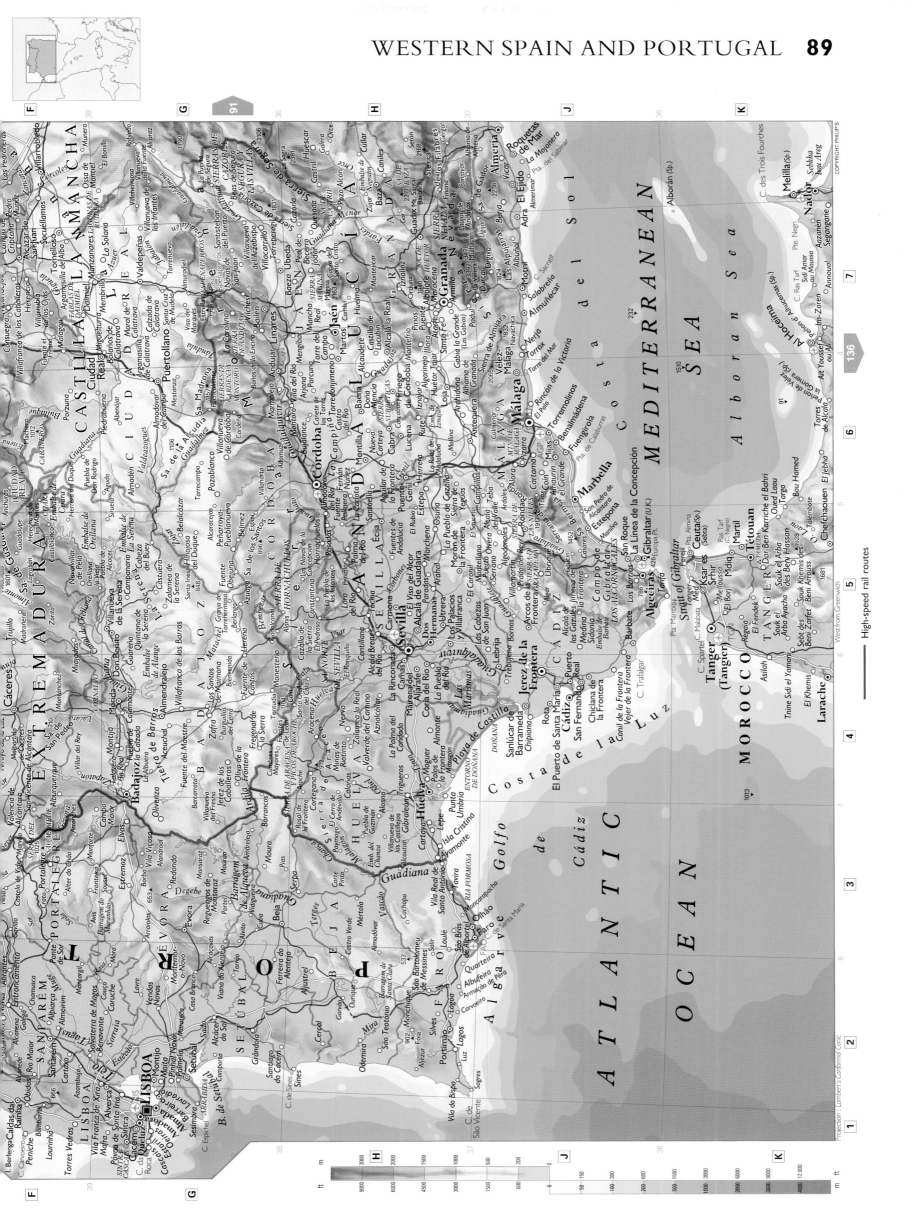

High-speed rail routes

Projection: Lambert's Conformal Conic

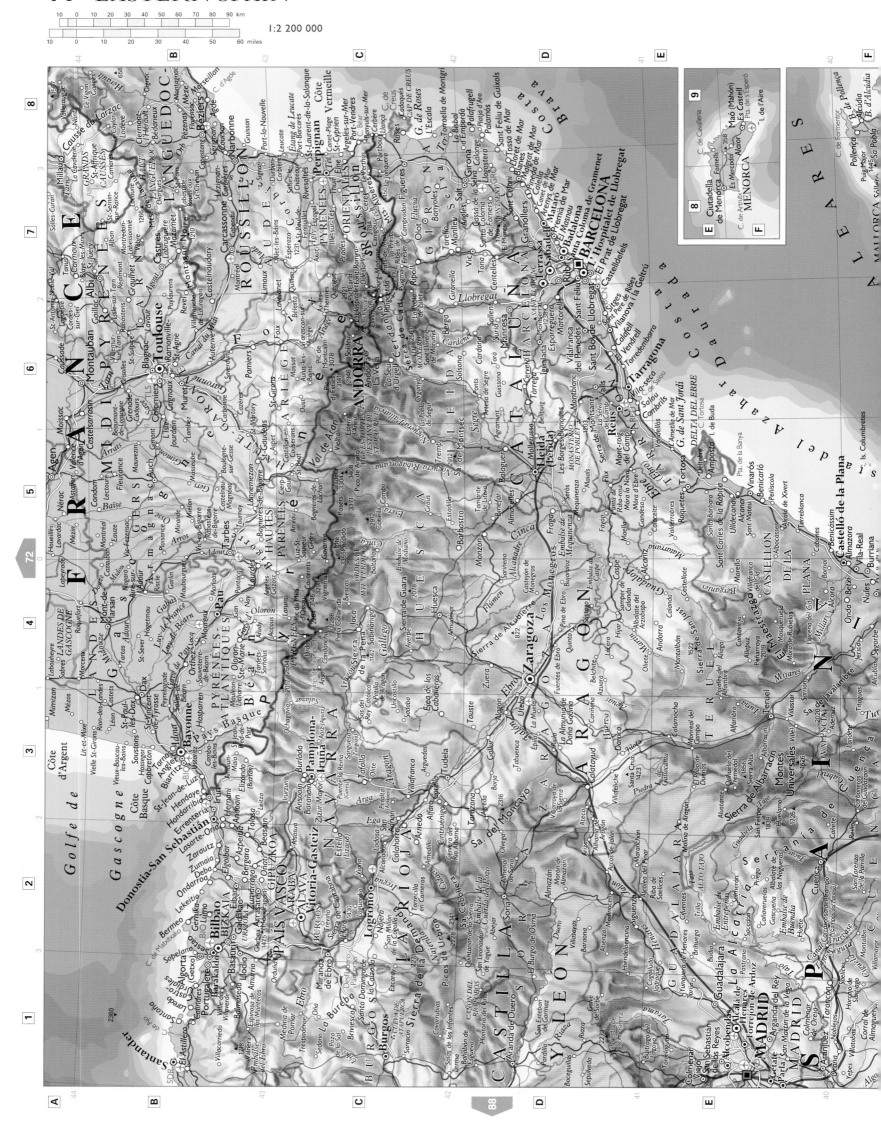

MEDITERRANEAN SEA

High-speed rail routes

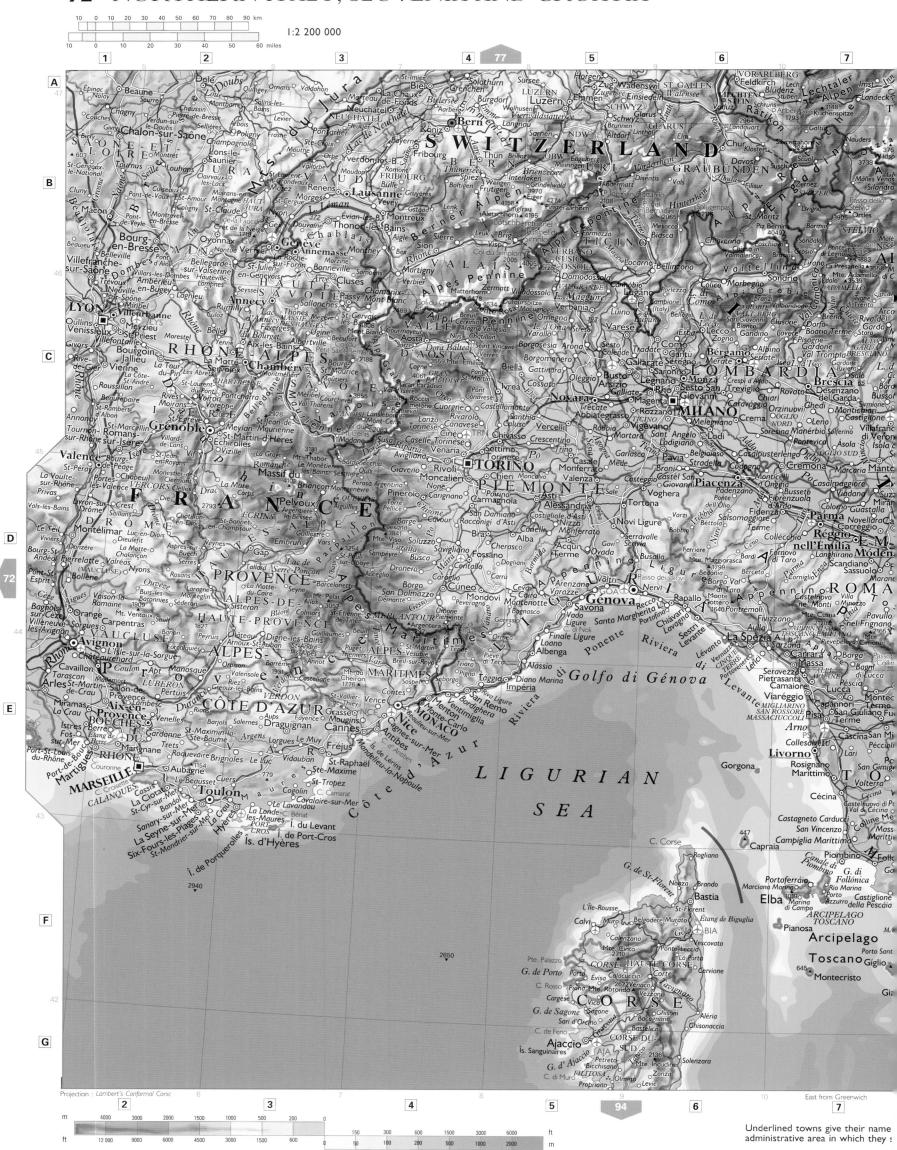

1:2 200 000

Underlined towns give their name
administrative area in which they s

Administrative divisions in Croatia:

...ko-Posavska	4 Medimurska	8 Virovitičko-Podravska
...vničko-Križevačka	6 Požeško-Slavonska	10 Zagreba čka
...sko-Zagorska	7 Varaždinska	

——— High-speed rail routes

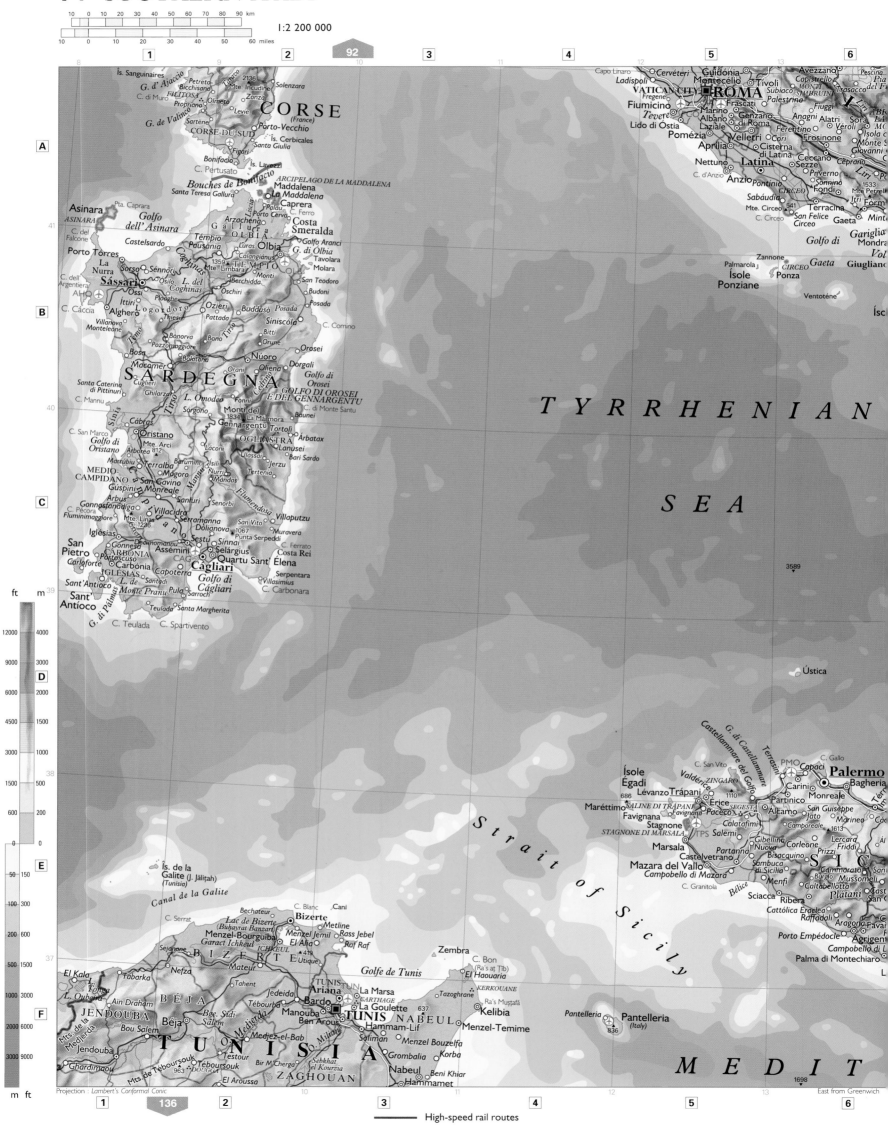

10 0 10 20 30 40 50 60 70 80 90 km

1:2 200 000

10 0 10 20 30 40 50 60 miles

High-speed rail routes

Projection : Lambert's Conformal Conic

East from Greenwich

COPYRIGHT PHILIP'S

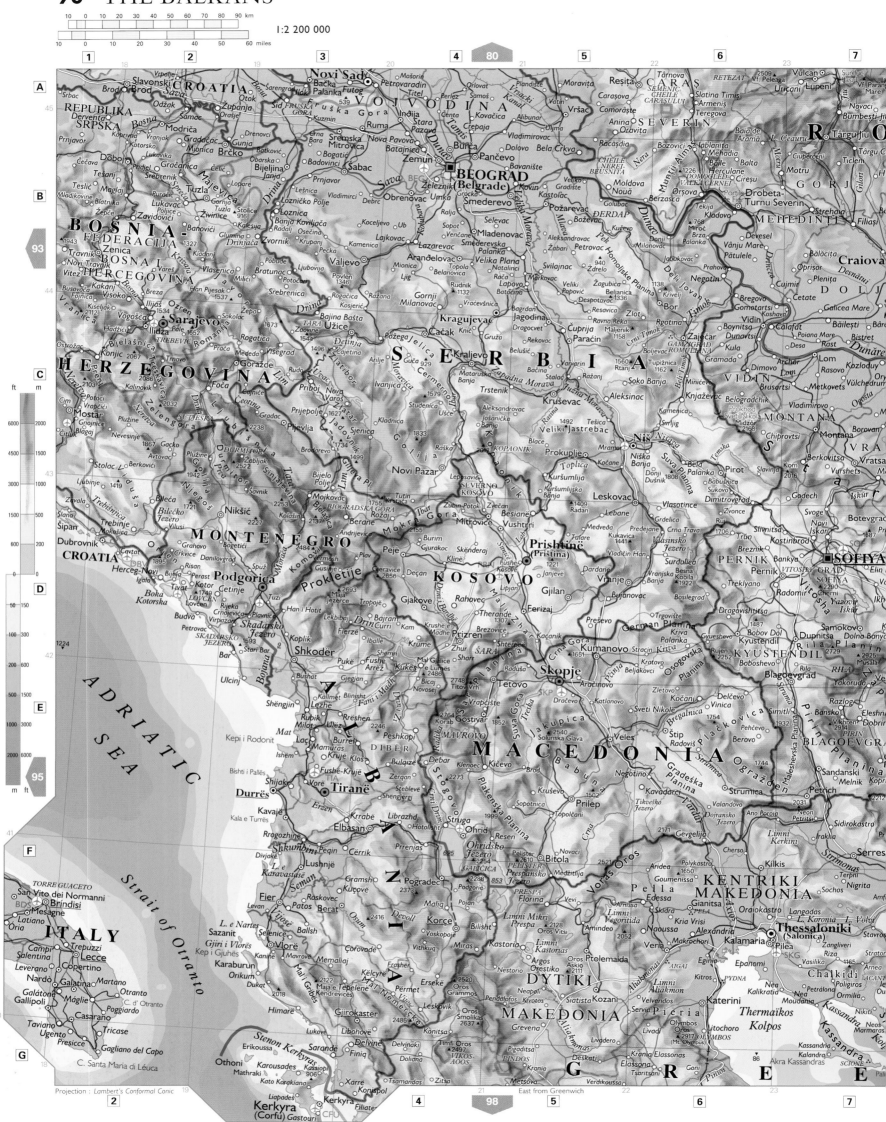

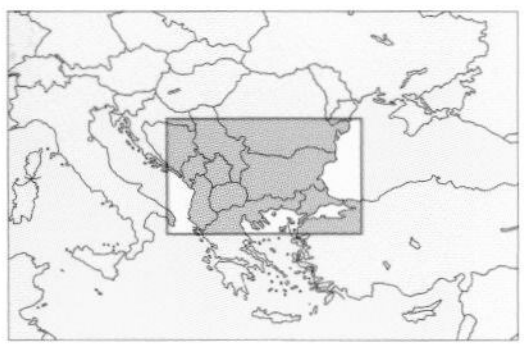

BLACK SEA

BULGARIA

TURKEY

ROMANIA

Marmara Denizi (Sea of Marmara)

Sea of Thrace

BUCUREŞTI (Bucharest)

ISTANBUL

BURSA

Varna

Constanţa

Burgas

Pleven

Plovdiv

Edirne

Sofia

Galaţi

Brăila

Buzău

Ploieşti

Piteşti

Târgovişte

Giurgiu

Ruse

Silistra

Dobrich

Shumen

Razgrad

Veliko Tŭrnovo

Gabrovo

Sliven

Stara Zagora

Yambol

Kazanlŭk

Pazardzhik

Asenovgrad

Dimitrovgrad

Khaskovo

Kŭrdzhali

Smolyan

Kavala

Xanthi

Komotini

Alexandroupoli

Thasos

Samothraki

Limnos

Bozcaada

Çanakkale

Gelibolu (Gallipoli)

Tekirdağ

Çorlu

Lüleburgaz

Kırklareli

Bandırma

İnegöl

Kocaeli (İzmit)

Gölcük

Gebze

Kartal

Üsküdar

Beyoğlu

ANATOLIKI MAKEDONIA KAI THRAKI

DELTA DUNĂREA

Underlined towns give their name to the administrative area in which they stand.

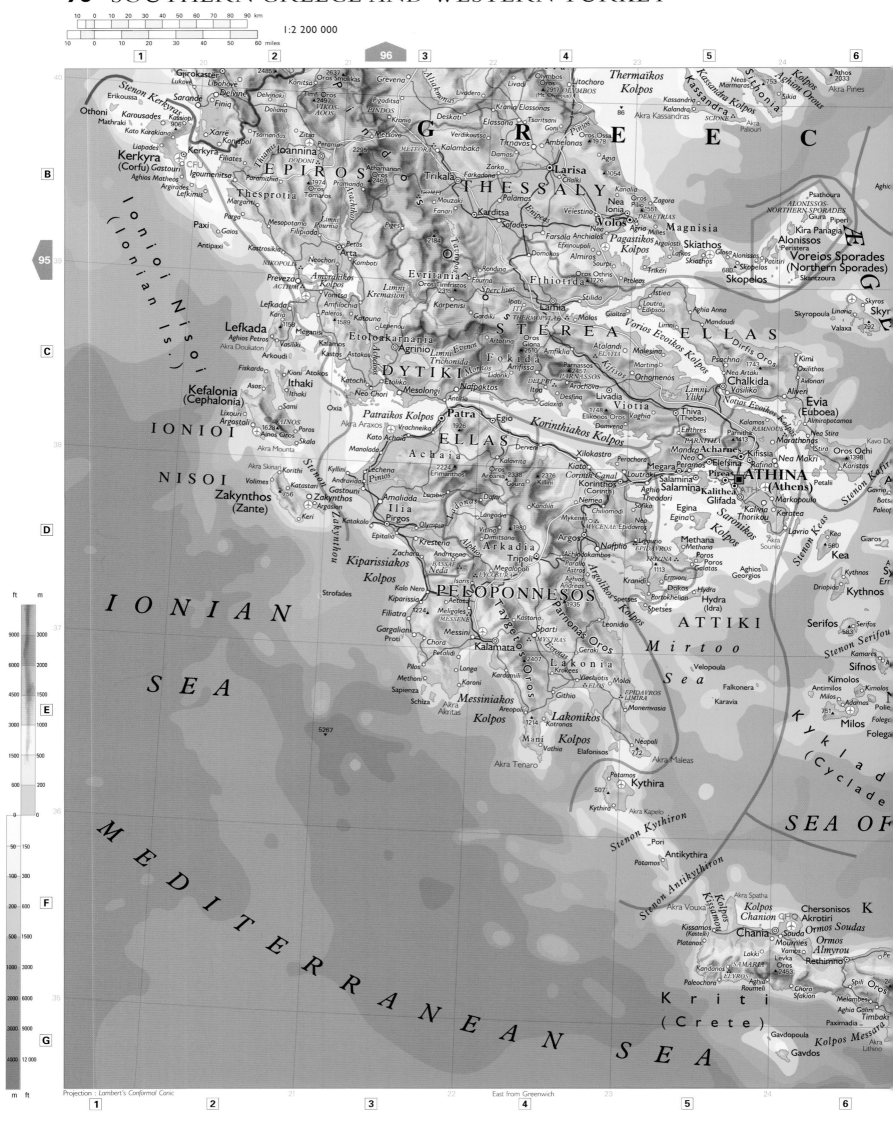

1:2 200 000

Projection : Lambert's Conformal Conic

East from Greenwich

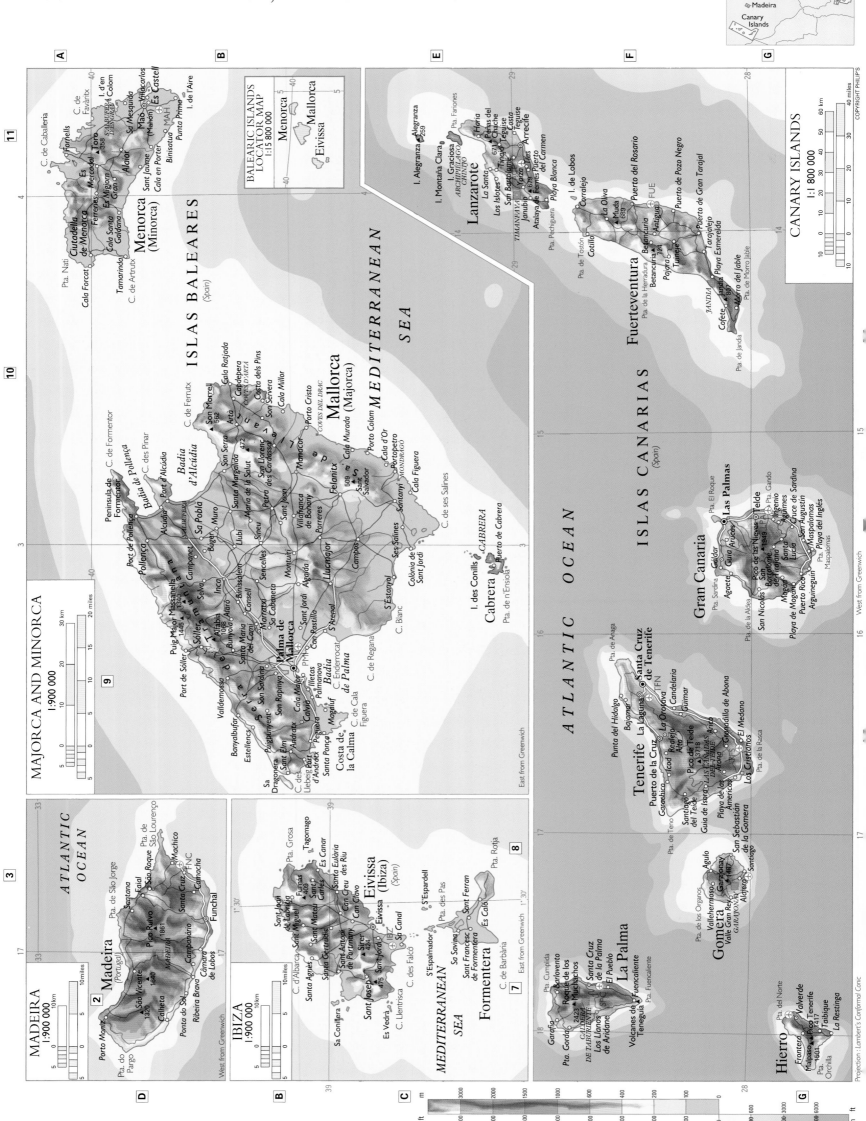

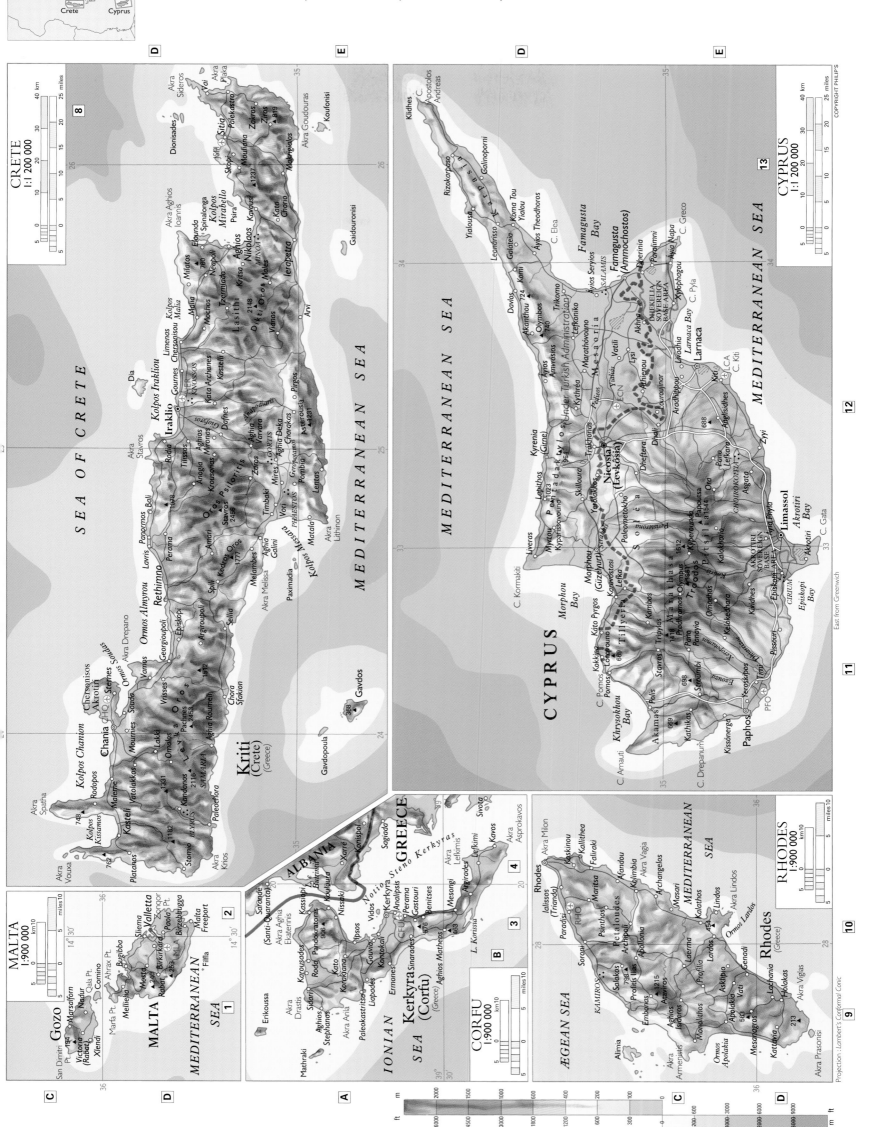

1:44 400 000

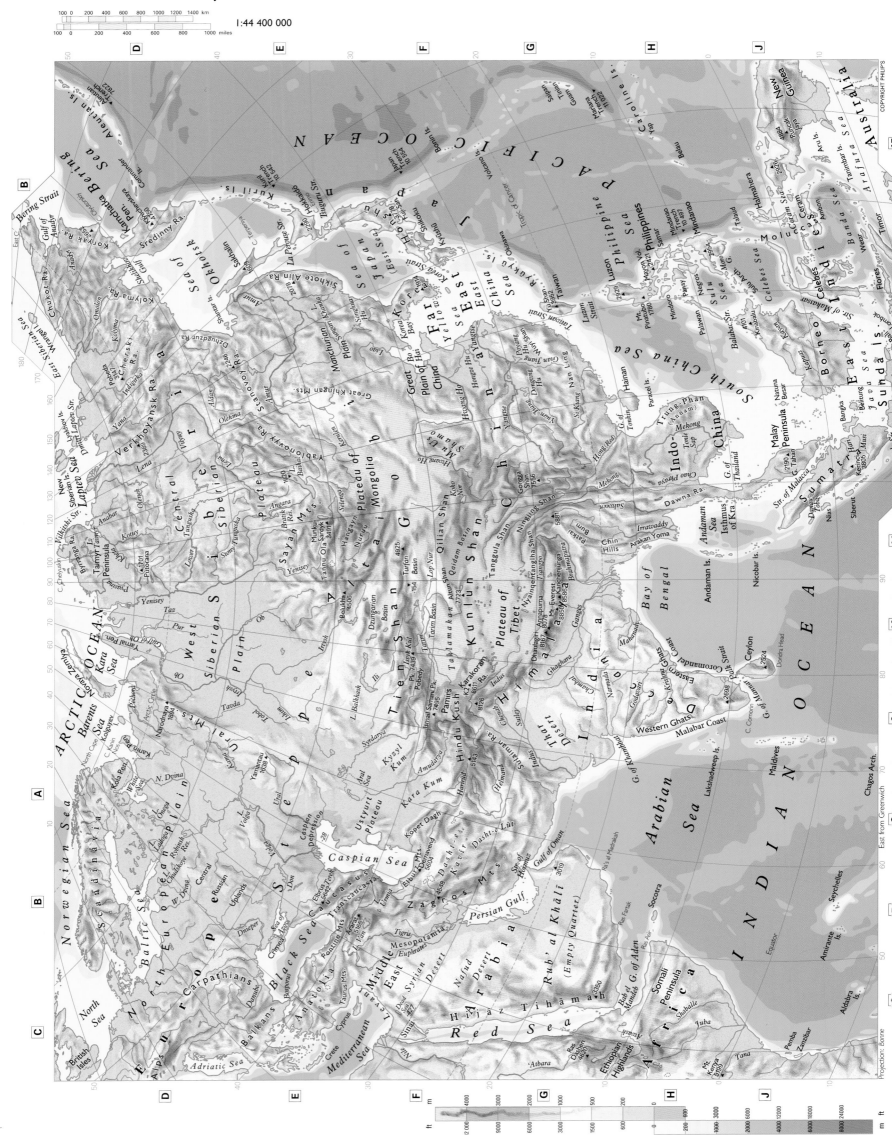

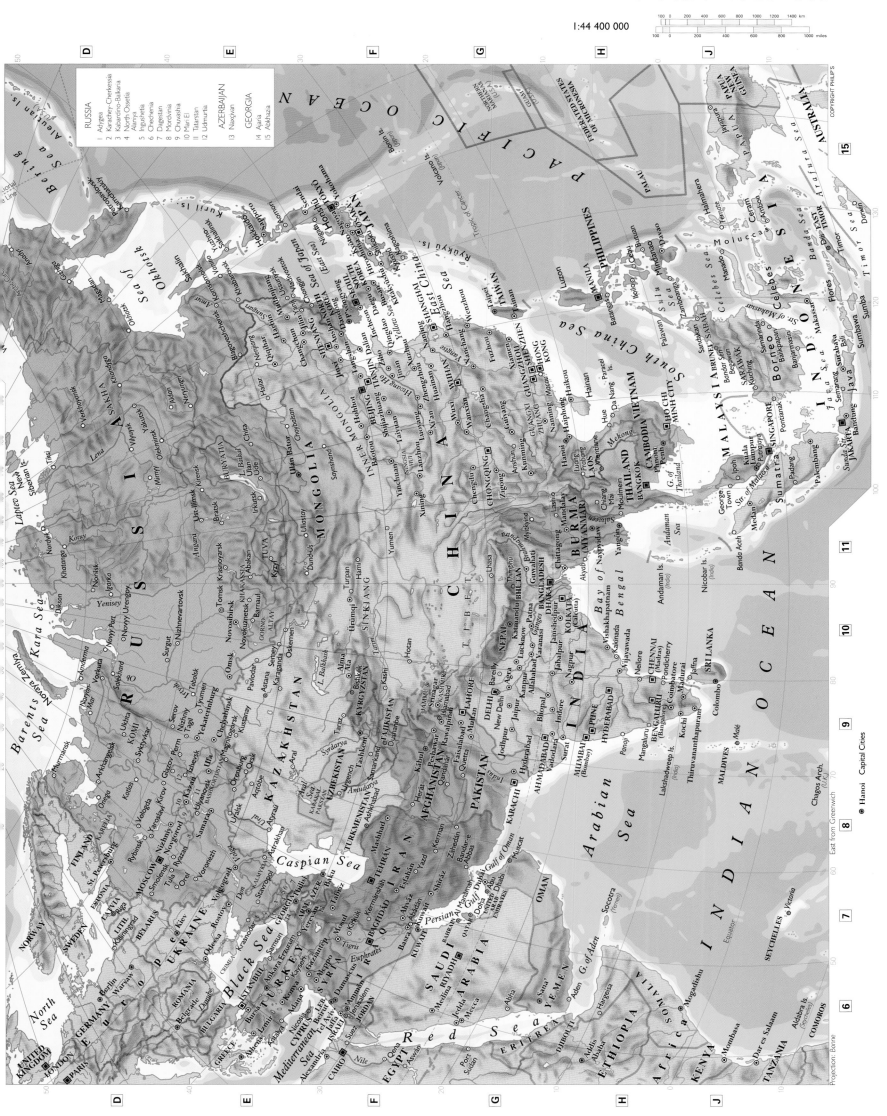

1:44 400 000

COPYRIGHT PHILIP'S

● Hanoi Capital Cities

East from Greenwich

Projection: Bonne

1: 4 400 000

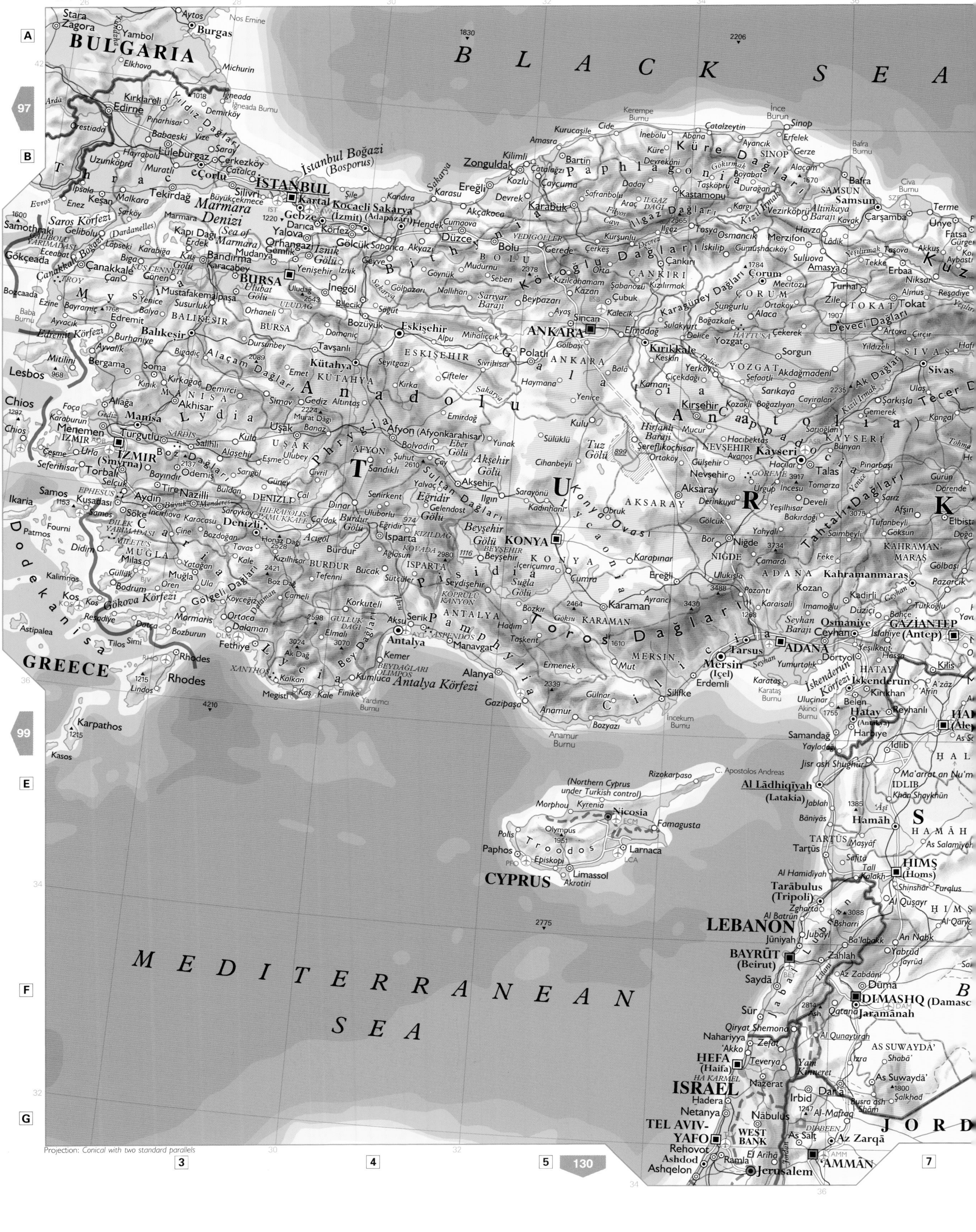

50 0 25 50 75 100 125 150 175 km
50 0 25 50 75 100 125 miles

BULGARIA

B L A C K   S E A

Stara Zagora
Yambol
Aytos
Burgas
Nos Emine
Elkhovo
Michurin
1830
2206

Kırklareli
Edirne
İğneada
İğneada Burnu
Demirköy
Pınarhisar
Babaeski
Saray
Vize
Kerempe Burnu
İnebolu
Abana
Çatalzeytin
Erfelek
Sinop
İnce Burun

Orestiada
Uzunköprü
Hayrabolu
Lüleburgaz
Çerkezköy
Çatalca
İstanbul Boğazı (Bosporus)
Şile
Kandıra
Kurucaşile
Amasra
Küre
Küre Dağları
Ayancık
Gerze
Bafra Burnu
Civa Burnu

Keşan
Malkara
Muratlı
Çorlu
İSTANBUL
Silivri
Büyükçekmece
Kartal
Gebze
Kocaeli (İzmit)
Sakarya (Adapazarı)
Hendek
Cumaova
Zonguldak
Kilimli
Kozlu
Ereğli
Akçakoca
Devrek
Çaycuma
Safranbolu
Karabük
Daday
Kastamonu
Boyabat
Durağan
SAMSUN
Samsun
Terme
Çarşamba
Ünye

Marmara Denizi (Sea of Marmara)

Gökçeada
Çanakkale
TROY
Biga
Gönen
Bandırma
BURSA
İnegöl
Bilecik
Eskişehir
ANKARA
Kırıkkale

MEDITERRANEAN SEA

CYPRUS
Nicosia
Famagusta
Kyrenia
Morphou
Larnaca
Limassol
Episkopi
Akrotiri
Troodos
Olympus
1951

Al Lādhiqīyah (Latakia)
Hamāh
HIMŞ (Homs)
Tarābulus (Tripoli)
LEBANON
BAYRŪT (Beirut)
DIMASHQ (Damas...)
ISRAEL
TEL AVIV-YAFO
WEST BANK
Jerusalem
AMMĀN
J O R D

İZMIR (Smyrna)
Manisa
Aydın
Denizli
KONYA
Antalya
ADANA
Mersin (İçel)
İskenderun
GAZİANTEP
KAHRAMANMARAŞ

GREECE
Rhodes
Kos
Karpathos

Projection: Conical with two standard parallels

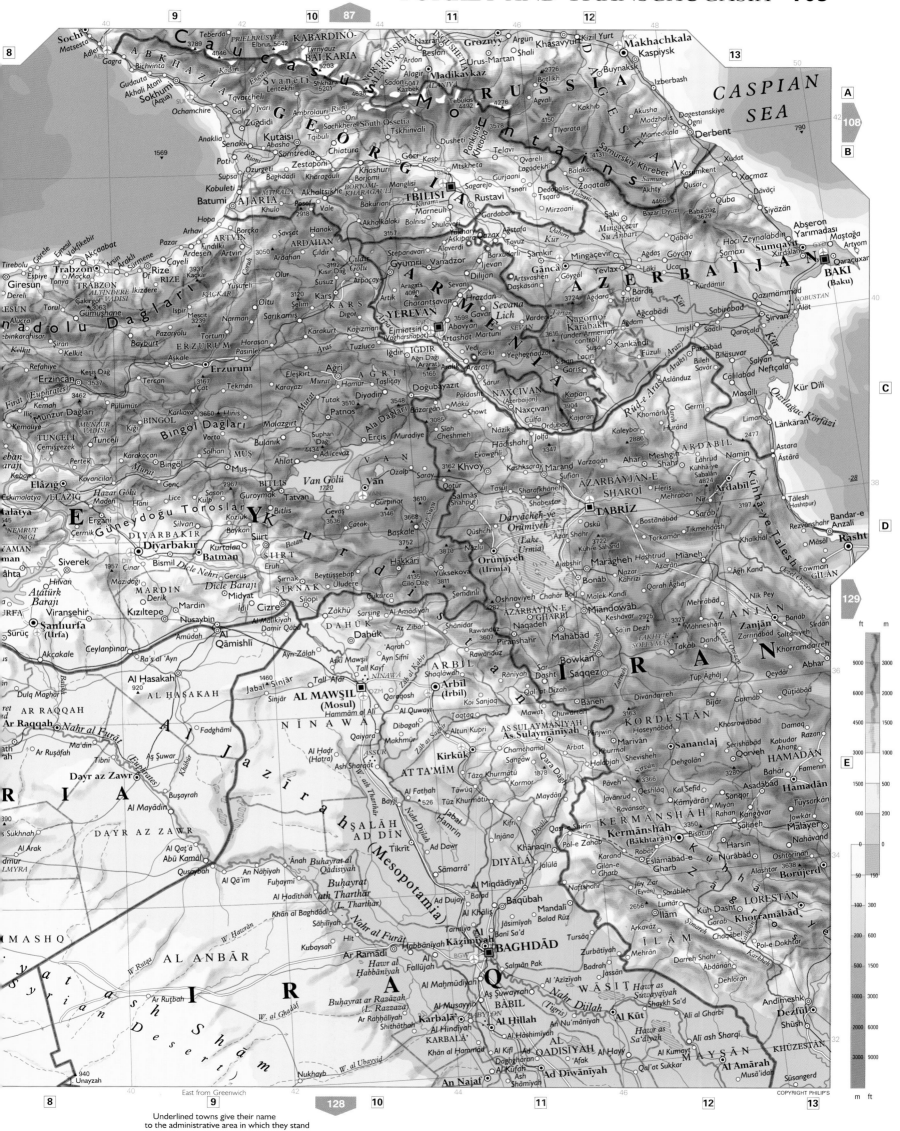

Underlined towns give their name
to the administrative area in which they stand

1:17 800 000

RUSSIA
1 Adygea
2 Karachey-Cherkessia
3 Kabardino-Balkaria
4 North Ossetia-Alaniya
5 Ingushetia
6 Chechenia
7 Dagestan
8 Mordvinia
9 Chuvashia
10 Mari El
11 Tatarstan
12 Udmurtia
13 Khakassia
AZERBAIJAN
14 Naxçivan
GEORGIA
15 Ajaria
16 Abkhazia

Projection: Conical Orthomorphic with two standard parallels

East from Greenwich

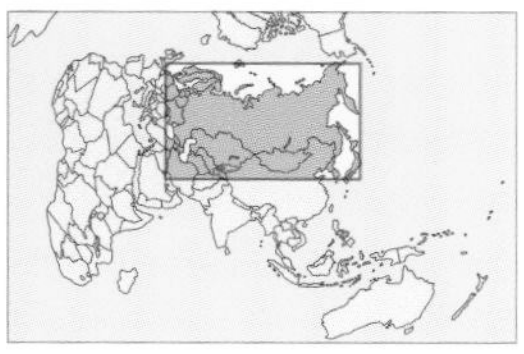

OCEAN

East Siberian Sea

Laptev Sea

Chukchi Sea

Bering Sea

Bering Str.

Sea of Okhotsk

Sea of Japan (East Sea)

Severnaya Zemlya

Ostrov Komsomolets
Ostrov Oktyabrskoy Revolyutsii
Ostrov Bolshevik
Ostrov Pioner
Ostrov Schmidta
Mys Arkticheskiy

Novosibirskiye Ostrova
Ostrova Delonga
Ostrova Bennetta
Ostrov Genrietty
Ostrov Zhannetty
Ostrov Faddeyevskiy
Ostrov Zhokhova
Novaya Sibir
Ostrov Kotelnyy
Ostrov Belkovskiy
Ostrov Malyy Lyakhovskiy
Ostrov Bolshoy Lyakhovskiy
Lyakhovskiye Ostrova
Ostrov Stolbovoy

Ostrova Medvezhi
Ostrov Ayon

Ostrov Vrangelya

Mys Dezhneva (East C.)
Proliv Longa
St. Lawrence I. (U.S.A.)
International Date Line

Poluostrov Taymyr
Gory Byrranga
Oz. Taymyr
Mys Chelyuskin
Nordvik
Novorybnoye

Kamchatka
Poluostrov Kamchatka
Petropavlovsk-Kamchatskiy

Sakhalin
Yuzhno-Sakhalinsk

Kurilskiye Ostrova

Hokkaidō
SAPPORO
Hakodate

Honshū

KYOTO
JAPAN
OSAKA
KŌBE

RUSSIA

Yakutsk
Lena
Verkhoyansk
Khrebet Cherskogo
Verkhoyanskiy Khrebet
Srednekolymsk
Kolyma
Zyryanka

Stanovoy Khrebet
Yablonovyy Khrebet
Khrebet Dzhugdzhur
Sikhote Alin

Vilyuysk
Nyurba
Suntar
Mirnyy
Olekminsk
Aldan
Neryungri
Tynda
Skovorodino

Bratsk
Irkutsk
Ulan Ude
Chita
Khabarovsk
Komsomolsk-na-Amur
Birobidzhan
Blagoveshchensk
Vladivostok
Nakhodka

Krasnoyarsk
Yeniseysk
Ust-Ilimsk

MONGOLIA
ULAANBAATAR
Darhan
Erdenet
Choybalsan
Hangayn Nuruu
Aerhtai Shan (Altay)
Gobi

CHINA
BEIJING
HOHHOT
BAOTOU
ZHANGJIAKOU
TANGSHAN
TIANJIN
SHENYANG
ANSHAN
FUSHUN
DALIAN
CHANGCHUN
JILIN
HARBIN
QIQIHAR
DAQING
JIAMUSI
JIXI
MUDANJIANG
CHIFENG
JINZHOU
Manchuria
Da Hinggan Ling

NORTH KOREA
PYONGYANG
NAMP'O
Hamhŭng
Wŏnsan
Ch'ŏngjin

SOUTH KOREA
SEOUL
INCHEON
DAEJEON
DAEGU
BUSAN
GWANGJU

Arctic Circle

50 0 100 200 300 400 km
50 0 50 100 150 200 250 miles

1:8 900 000

Projection : Modified Miller oblated stereographic

106

7 8 9 10 11 12 13

RUSSIA

Petukhovo · Bülaevo · Isil Kul · OMSK · Om · Tatarsk · Kalachinsk · NOVOSIBIRSK · Berdsk · Leninsk- · Belovo · Chernogorsk · Minusinsk
Mamlyutka · Petropavl · Kupino · Novosibirskoye Vdkhr. · Iskitim · Kuznetskiy · Kiselevsk · Shushenskoye · Toora-
SOLTÜSTIK · Kishkeneköl · Cherlak · Cherepanovo · Prokopyevsk · KEMEROVO · Abakan · KRASNOYARSK · Khem
QAZAQSTAN · Tayynsha · Karasuk · Kamen · Suzun · Novokuznetsk · Mezhdurechensk · Sayanogorsk · Khrebet Akademika
Taiynsha · Kökshetaü · Ozero · Novoaltaysk · Zarinsk · Temirtaü · HAKASSIA · Turan · Obrucheva
Rüzaevka · Makinsk · Chuny · Barnaul · Temirtaü · SHORSKY · Saiano- · Tuva
Esil · PAVLODAR · Slavgorod · Ob · Mayma · Shushensky · Shushenskoye · Kyzyl
Atbasar · Zhaltyr · Aqköl · Pavlodar · Aleysk · BOR · Uvs · TANNU OLA
Derzhavinsk · ASTANA · Nura · Ereymentaü · Aqsu · Volchikha · Pospelikha · Charysh · GORNO- · Nuur · Samagaltay · Erzin · Dzur
AQMOLA · Qorghalzhyn · Osakarovka · Ertis (Irtysh) · Rubtsovsk · Zmeinogorsk · ALTAY · ALTAI · Ölgiy · MONGOLIA
Arqalyk · Tengiz · Aqtaū · Sharbaqty · Shemonaikha · Gornyak · Ridder · Inya · Belukha · Hyargas · DZAVHAN
Köli · Temirtaū · Sorang · QARAGHANDY · Kürchatov · Semey · Glûbokoe · Belousovka · Zyryan · Tolbo · Har Us · Nuur
Qyzylzhar · Shakhtinsk · (Karaganda) · (Semipalatinsk) · Öskemen · Serebryansk · Qotanqaraghay · ALTAI · Dund-Us (Hövd)
Sätbaev · Zhayrang · Abay · Qorqaraly · Qaraghayly · Shan · Zaysan Köli · Habahe · Altay · HOVD · GOVI-ALTAY
Zhezqazghan · Qarazhal · Usaqshoghylyghy · QARAGHANDY · Qaynar · QAZAQSTAN · Kürshim · Burqin · Tögrog · Dörvi
Ulytau · Atasū · Barshatas · Ayaköz · Zaysan · Ulungur · Beitun · Fuyun · Qinghe · HOVD
Qyzylzhar · Qarazhal · Aqshataū · (Qoqek) · Tacheng · Emin · Toli · Karamay · Gurbantünggüt · Baytik Shan
Moyynty · Balqash · Ürzhar · Khrebet Tarbagatay · Alakol · Hoxtolgay · Shamo · Ertai
KAZAKHSTAN · Betpaqdala · Balqash · Saryshaghan · Gülshat · Qabanbay · Zaysan · Junggar Pendi · Fukang · Jimsar · Mori · Qijiaojing
Balqash Köli (L. Balkhash) · Saryesik-Atyraū Qumy · Üshtöbe · Alakol · Dostyq · Kuytun · Shihezi · Changji · ÜRÜMQI · Turpan · Shanshan
ONGTÜSTIK · Shyghanaq · Taldyqorghan · Molaly · Bole (Bortala) · Ušu · Manas · Miquan · Bogda Shan · Turpan Pendi
QAZAQSTAN · Bürylbaytal · Balpyk Bi · Ala Tau · Ebinur Hu · Borohoro Shan · Erbeng Shan · Toksun · Aydingkol Hu
ZHAMBYL · ALMATY · Saryözek · Zharkent · Huocheng · Yining (Gulja) · Hejing · Hoxud
Sozaq · Moyynqum · Qapshaghay · Köktal · Gongliu · Qapqal · Tiemenguan · Bosten Hu · Kuruktag
Zhangatas · Shelek · ALTYN-EMEL · Bögeni · Shonzhy · KALAJUN KU'ERDENING · Luntai · Korla · Hoxud · Lop Nur
Qarataū · Taraz (Zhambyl) · ALMATY (Alma Ata) · Talghar · Pik Khan Tengri · Halik Shan · Baicheng · Konqi He
Türkistan (Karataū) · Bishkek · Tokmak · Karakol · BAYANBULAK · Kuqa · Xayar · Tarim He
Shymkent (Chimkent) · Kara-Balta (Frunze) · ILE-ALA TAU · Cholpon-Ata · Tüp · Pik Pobedy (Jengish Chokusu) · Wensu · Aksu · Tarim Pendi
TOSHKENT (Tashkent) · KYRGYZSTAN · Ysyk-Köl · Kyzyl-Suu · YSYK-KÖL · Taklamakan
Angren · Naryn · At-Bashy · Wushi · Tumxuk · Alaer · XINJIANG UYGUR ZIZHIQU (SINKIANG)
Namangan · Andijon · Osh · Kochkor · Song Köl · Karateki Shan · Sugan · Bachu · Aksu · Ruoqiang
Chust · Marg'ilon · Sulaiman-Too · Gülcho · Alai Range · Artux · Kashi (Kashgar) · Shule · Shamo · Qiemo · Altun Shan
Qo'qon (Kokand) · Farg'ona · Torugarl Pass · Ulugqat · Wuqia · Yengisar · Markit · Hadilik · Waxxari · Zhen
Istaravshan · Batken · Kyzyl-Kyya · Sary-Tash · Kashi · Akto · Shache (Yarkand) · Muztagh-Ata · Moyu · Qira · Ayakkum Hu
Samarqand · TAJIKISTAN · Pik imeni Ismail Samani (Pik Kommunizma) · Karakul · Bulungkol · Zepu · Yecheng · Hotan · Kunlun Shan
Gharm · Khujand · GORNO-BADAKHSHON · Murghob · Taxkorgan · Pishan · Yutian · Minfeng · Karatax Shan
Dushanbe · Vahdat · Pamir · KUHISTON-BADAKHSHON · Tajik Zizhixian · Lop · Qiemo · Chagdo Kangri
SURXON-DARYO · KHATLON · Kulob · Khorugh · Feyzabad · Karakoram Range · Mazar · Xaidulla · Lazhuglung · XIZANG ZIZHIQU
Qürghonteppa · Ishkoshim · Rakaposhi · Aksai Chin · Sumdo · (TIBET)
Termiz · BADAKHSHON · Hindu Kush · Gilgit-Baltistan · Karakoram Pass · Sumxi · Duomula
Mazar-e Sharif · Kholm · Kondoz · Baghlan · Chilas · JAMMU & KASHMIR · Rutog
NISTAN · Chärikär · PAKISTAN · KHYBER PAKHTUNKHWA · SRINAGAR · INDIA
KĀBUL · Jalalabad · Mardan · Abbottabad · Leh

50 · 45 · 40 · 35

110 · 123

B · C · D · E · F

Underlined towns give their name to the administrative area in which they stand.

1:13 300 000

100   0   100   200   300   400   500   600 km
100   0   100   200   300   400 miles

Projection: Bonne

107

RUSSIA

Sakhalin

HEILONGJIANG

HOKKAIDO
SAPPORO

QIQIHAR
HARBIN
DAQING
JIAMUSI
JIXI
MUDANJIANG
CHANGCHUN
JILIN
FUSHUN
SHENYANG
Vladivostok

SEA OF JAPAN
(EAST SEA)

NORTH
KOREA
P'YONGYANG

SENDAI

SOUTH
KOREA
SEOUL
INCHEON
DAEJEON
DAEGU
ULSAN
BUSAN
GWANGJU

TŌKYŌ
KAWASAKI
YOKOHAMA
NAGOYA
KYŌTO
ŌSAKA
KŌBE
HAMAMATSU
HIROSHIMA
KITAKYUSHU
FUKUOKA

MONGOL ZIZHIQU
(INNER MONGOLIA)

CHIFENG
HOHHOT
DATONG
BEIJING
(Peking)
TIANJIN
TANGSHAN
BAODING
TAIYUAN
SHIJIAZHUANG

DALIAN

YELLOW
SEA

YANTAI
WEIFANG
JINAN
ZIBO
QINGDAO
LINYI

ZHENGZHOU
LUOYANG
XUZHOU
HUAI'AN
YANCHENG
NANJING
CHANGZHOU
WUXI
SUZHOU
SHANGHAI
HANGZHOU
NINGBO

WUHAN
NANCHANG
CHANGSHA
HENGYANG

TAIZHOU
WENZHOU

FUZHOU
T'AIPEI
T'AICHUNG
TAIWAN
KAOHSIUNG
T'AINAN

GUANGZHOU
(Canton)
FOSHAN
SHENZHEN
HONG KONG
(Xianggang)
Macau
ZHUHAI
ZHANJIANG
HAIKOU
HAINAN

EAST CHINA
SEA

PACIFIC
OCEAN

SOUTH CHINA
SEA

PHILIPPINES

119

HONG KONG, MACAU AND SHENZHEN

1:800 000

GUANGDONG

SHENZHEN
Futian
Nantou
Baolan

ZHONGSHAN

Tuen Mun

Kowloon
(Jiulong)
Victoria
HONG KONG
(Xianggang)
Hong Kong
Island
Aberdeen

Macau
(Aomen)
ZHUHAI

Lantau Island
(Tai Yue Shan)

Lingding Yang

Zhujiang Kou
(Mouth of the Pearl)

COPYRIGHT PHILIP'S

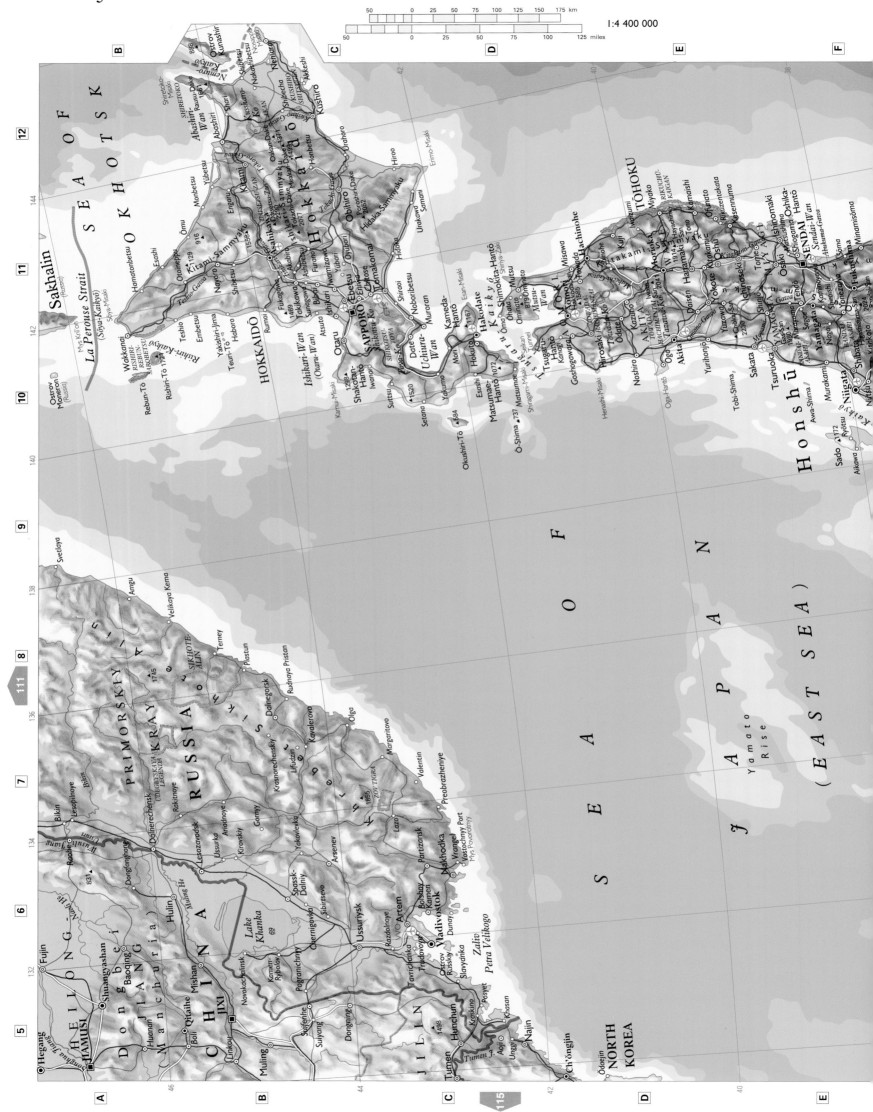

1:4 400 000

SEA OF OKHOTSK

Sakhalin
(Rossi)

La Perouse Strait
(Sōya-Kaikyō)

HOKKAIDŌ

SAPPORO

TŌHOKU

Honshū

SENDAI

AKITA

SEA OF JAPAN (EAST SEA)

Yamato Rise

RUSSIA

PRIMORSKIY KRAY

SIKHOTE ALIN

CHINA

Manchuria

HEILONGJIANG

Dongbei

Vladivostok

JILIN

NORTH KOREA

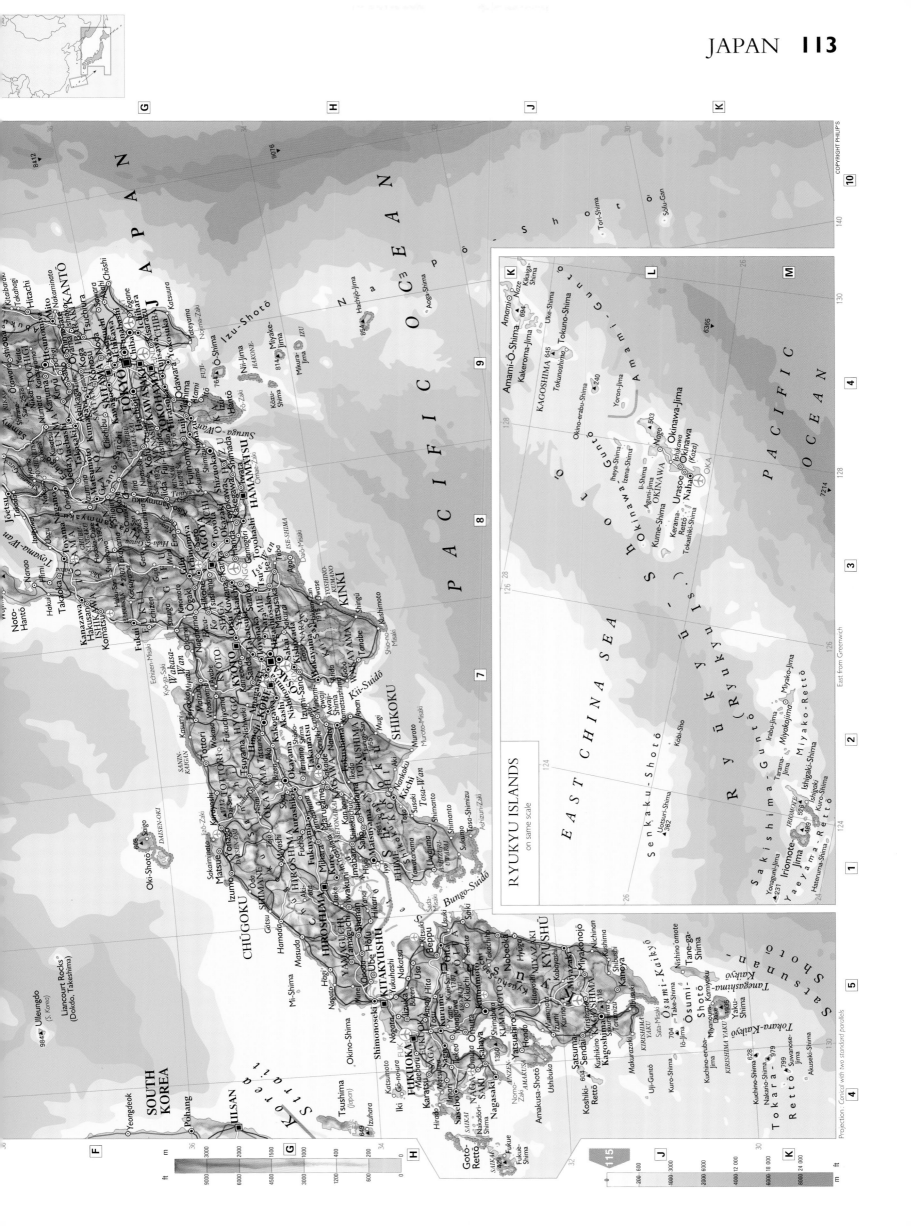

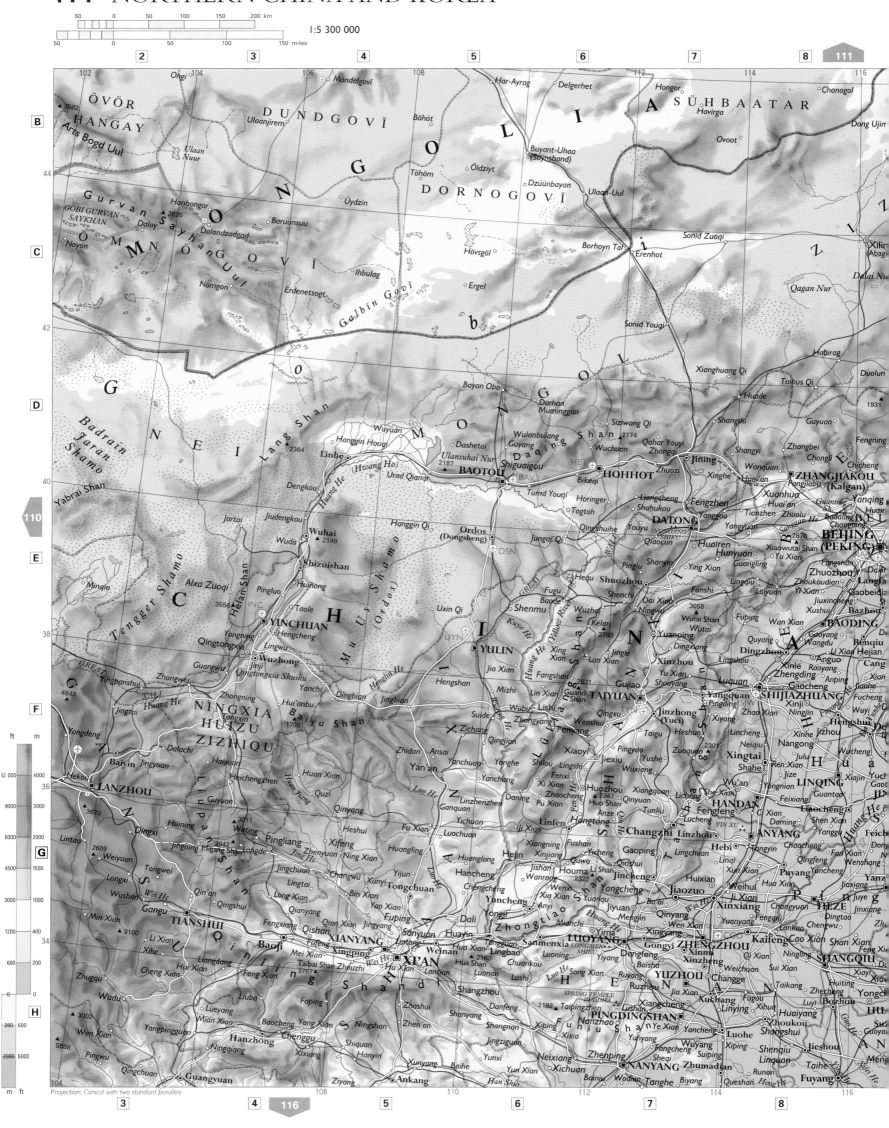

1:5 300 000

Projection: Conical with two standard parallels

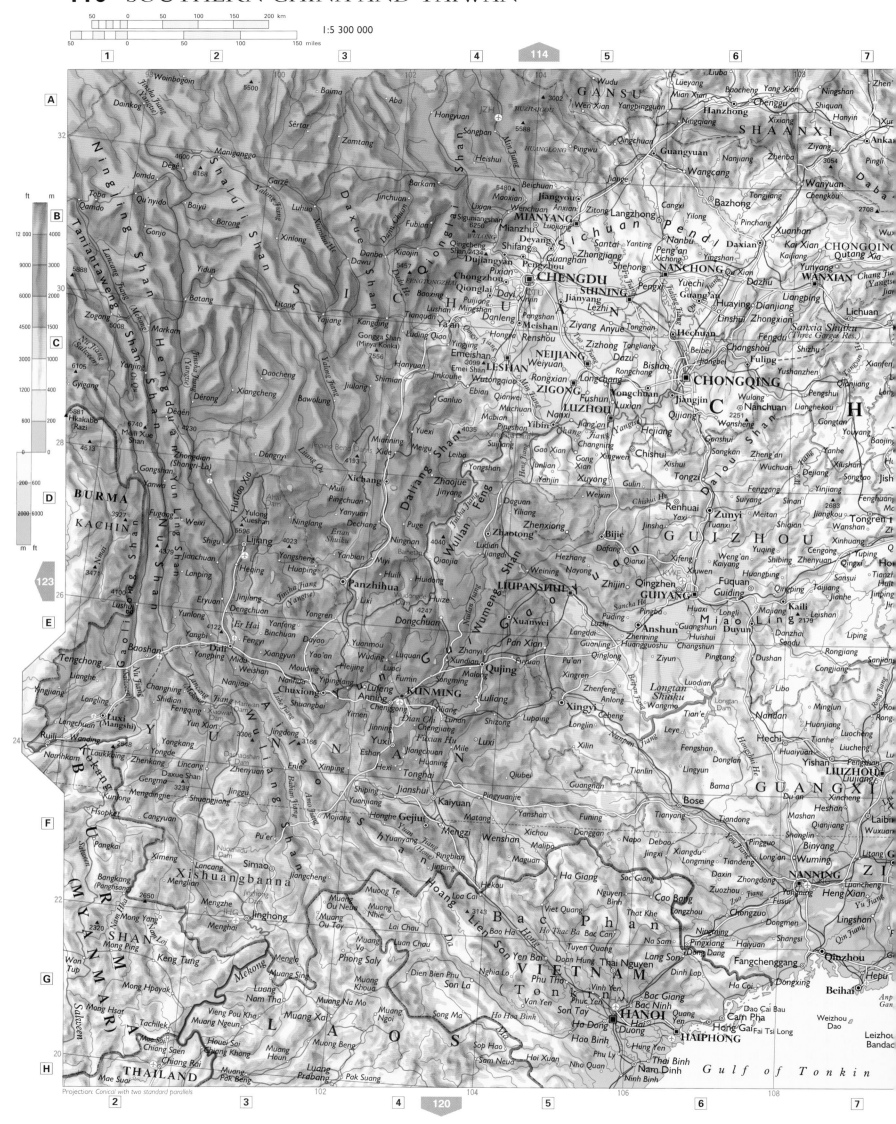

1:5 300 000

50   0   50   100   150   200 km
50   50   100   150 miles

Projection: Conical with two standard parallels

Gulf of Tonkin

JAVA AND MADURA
1:6 700 000

50 0 50 100 150 200 250 300 km
50 0 50 100 150 200 miles

BALI
1:1 600 000

10 0 10 20 30 km
10 0 10 20 miles

Seas and Oceans: CELEBES SEA, MOLUCCA SEA, BANDA SEA, ARAFURA SEA, HALMAHERA SEA, CERAM SEA, FLORES SEA, SAWU SEA, BALI SEA, PACIFIC OCEAN, INDIAN OCEAN

Major places (Philippines/Luzon area): Claveria, Bacarra, Laoag, Aparri, Babuyan Chan., C. Engaño, Batac, Bangued, 2360, Tuao, Tuguegarao, Vigan, Bontoc, Ilagan, Santiago, Palanan, Palanan Pt., Fernando, Pulog 2928, Bayombong, Casiguran, Baguio, Luzon, Dagupan, San Jose, C. San Ildefonso, Lingayen G., Tarlac, Cabanatuan, Baler, Angeles, Pinatubo 1759, San Fernando, Quezon City, MANILA, Cavite, Santa Cruz, Lamon Bay, Daet, Catanduanes, Batangas, Lipa, Calamba, Naga, Virac, Lucena, Marinduque, Tabaco, Legazpi, Mayon Volcano 2662, Sorsogon, Mindoro, Masbate, Samar, Romblon, Tablas, Panay, Roxas, Iloilo, Bacolod, Cebu, Mandaue, Negros, Dumaguete, Bohol, Tagbilaran, Surigao, Siargao, Butuan, Cagayan de Oro, Iligan, Ozamiz, Pagadian, Cotabato, Mindanao, DAVAO, Digos, General Santos, Zamboanga, Jolo, Basilan

Java/Madura area: JAKARTA, Tangerang, Serang, Merak, Bogor, Bekasi, Karawang, Indramayu, Cirebon, Tegal, Pekalongan, Semarang, BANDUNG, Sukabumi, Cianjur, Purwakarta, Subang, Kuningan, Brebes, Pemalang, Batang, Kendal, Demak, Kudus, Pati, Rembang, Tuban, Bojonegoro, Gresik, SURABAYA, Bangkalan, Sampang, Pamekasan, Sumenep, Madura, Garut, Tasikmalaya, Ciamis, Purwokerto, Wonosobo, Magelang, Salatiga, Purwodadi, Blora, Cepu, Ngawi, Mojokerto, Jombang, Sidoarjo, Selat Madura, Yogyakarta, Surakarta, Kediri, Malang, Probolinggo, Situbondo, Bondowoso, Jember, Banyuwangi, Bali, YOGYAKARTA, TIMUR, TENGAH, BARAT, Nusa Barung

Bali inset: Singaraja, Kubutambahan, Tejakula, Gerokgak, Lovina, Kintamani, Banyuwangi, Gilimanuk, Cekik, Melaya, Negara, Mendoyo, BALI, Bedugul, Gunung Batukau 2276, Gunung Agung 3142, Bangli, Klungkung (Semarapura), Gianyar, Tabanan, Denpasar, Sukawati, Ubud, Karangasem (Amlapura), Candi Dasa, Mataram, Lombok, Ampenan, Legian, Sanur, Kuta, Jimbaran, Uluwatu, Nusa Dua, Nusa Penida, Lembuak, Gerung

Sulawesi area: Manado, GORONTALO, Gorontalo, Toli-toli, Buol, Palu, Poso, Palopo, Kendari, Watampone, Bulukumba, Baubau, Buton, Muna, Kolaka, SELATAN, TENGGARA, TENGAH, Sulawesi (Celebes)

Maluku/Papua area: Ternate, Tidore, Halmahera, Morotai, Tobelo, Buru, Ambon, Seram (Ceram), MALUKU, Sorong, Manokwari, Biak, Jayapura, IRIAN JAYA BARAT, PAPUA, Pegunungan Maoke, Puncak Jaya 4702, Timika, Merauke, PAPUA NEW GUINEA

Lesser Sunda Islands: Flores, Ende, Maumere, Larantuka, Alor, Kupang, TIMOR, EAST TIMOR, Dili, Sumba, Waingapu, NUSA TENGGARA TIMUR, Kepulauan Tanimbar, Kepulauan Kai, Kepulauan Aru

Scale labels: 148, 140

COPYRIGHT PHILIP'S

1:5 300 000

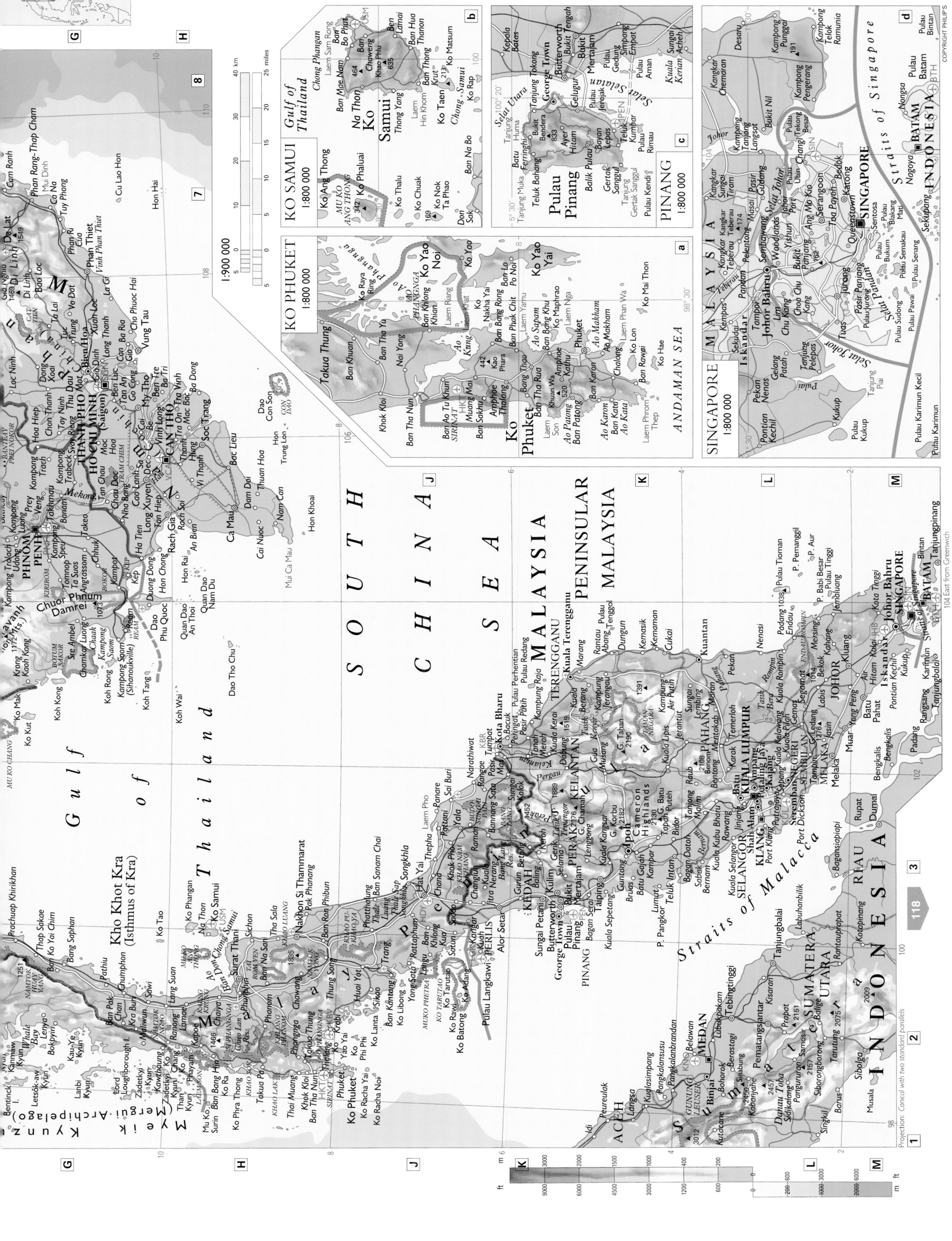

Inset maps

KO SAMUI
1:800 000

Gulf of Thailand

Ko Samui

KO PHUKET
1:800 000

ANDAMAN SEA

Ko
Phuket

PINANG
1:800 000

Pulau
Pinang

Selat Selatan

George Town
Butterworth

SINGAPORE
1:800 000

MALAYSIA

SINGAPORE

Johor Bahru

Straits of Singapore

INDONESIA

BATAM

Main map

SOUTH

CHINA

SEA

Gulf

of

Thailand

Kho Khot Kra
(Isthmus of Kra)

Mu Ko Chang

PHNOM
PENH

HO CHI MINH
(Saigon)

THANH PHO HO
CHI MINH

Chuor Phnum
Damrei

Mekong

CAN THO

PENINSULAR
MALAYSIA

MALAYSIA

TERENGGANU

KELANTAN

PERAK

PAHANG

KEDAH

PERLIS

PINANG

SELANGOR

KUALA LUMPUR

NEGERI
SEMBILAN

MELAKA

JOHOR

Kota Bharu

Ipoh

Klang

Seremban

Muar

Johor Bahru

SINGAPORE
BATAM

Straits of Malacca

SUMATERA
UTARA

RIAU

ACEH

MEDAN

INDONESIA

Mergui Archipelago

Kyunzu

Copyright Philip's

Projection: Conical with two standard parallels

104 East from Greenwich

1:8 900 000

Projection: Conical with two standard parallels

continuation southwards on same scale

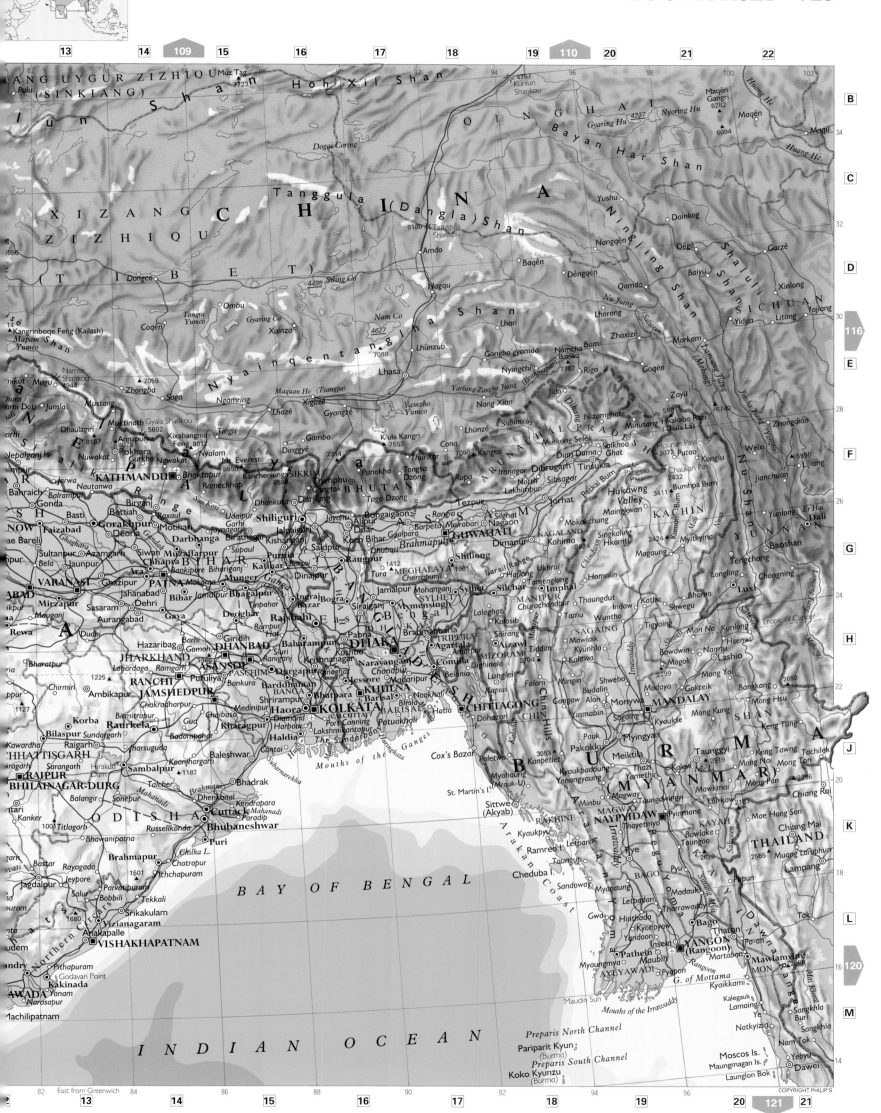

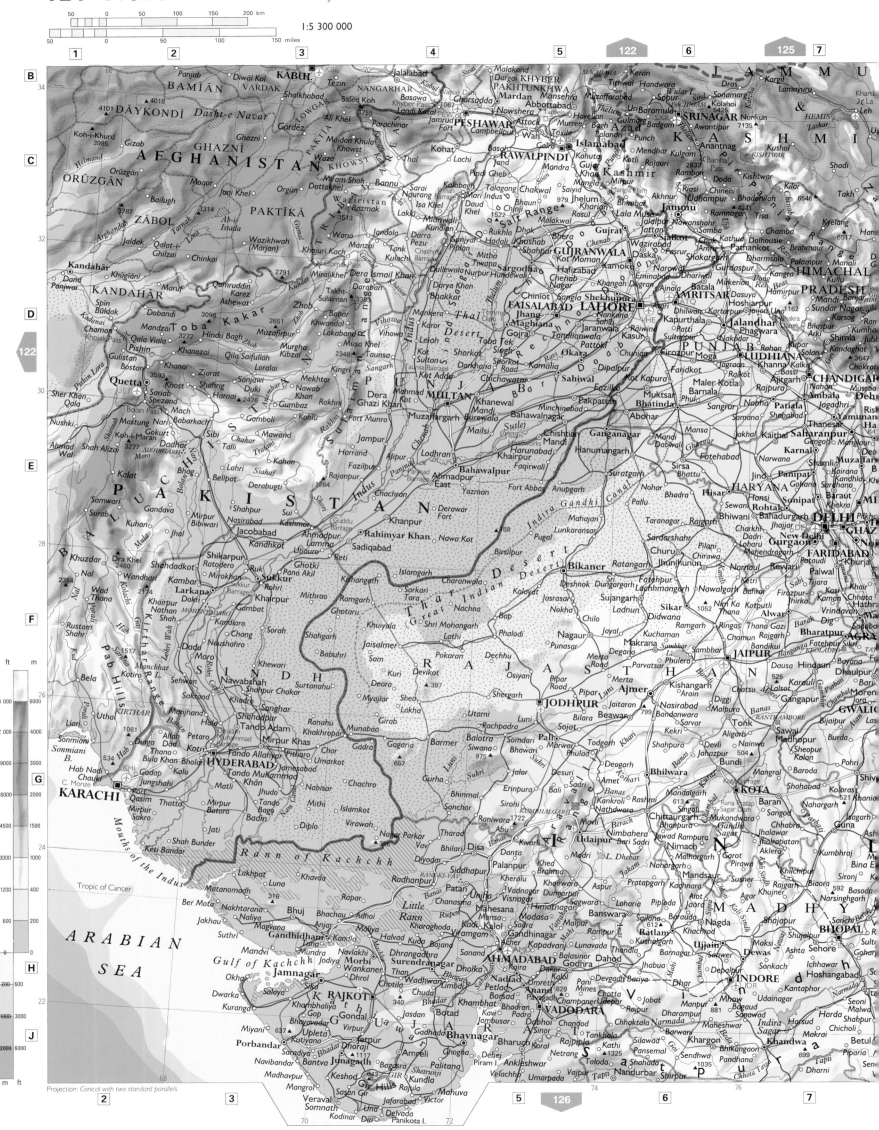

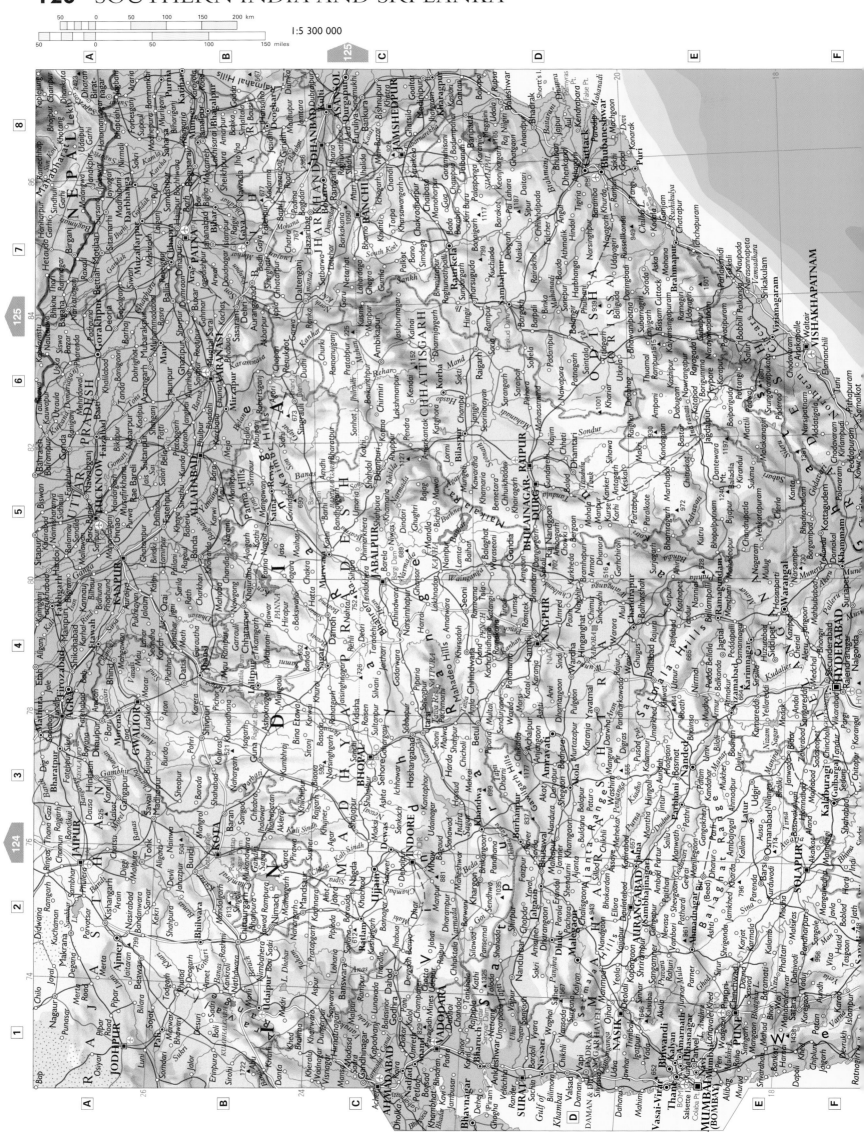

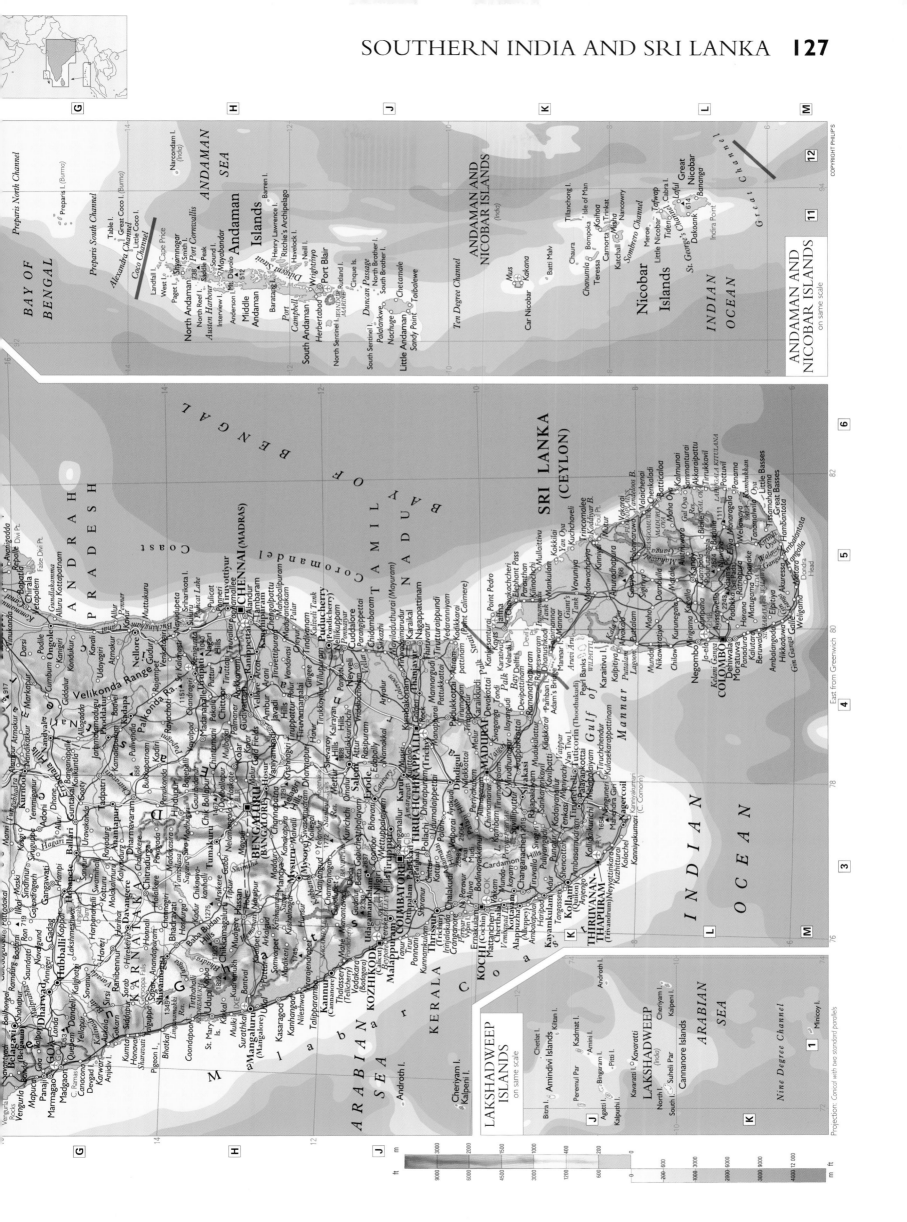

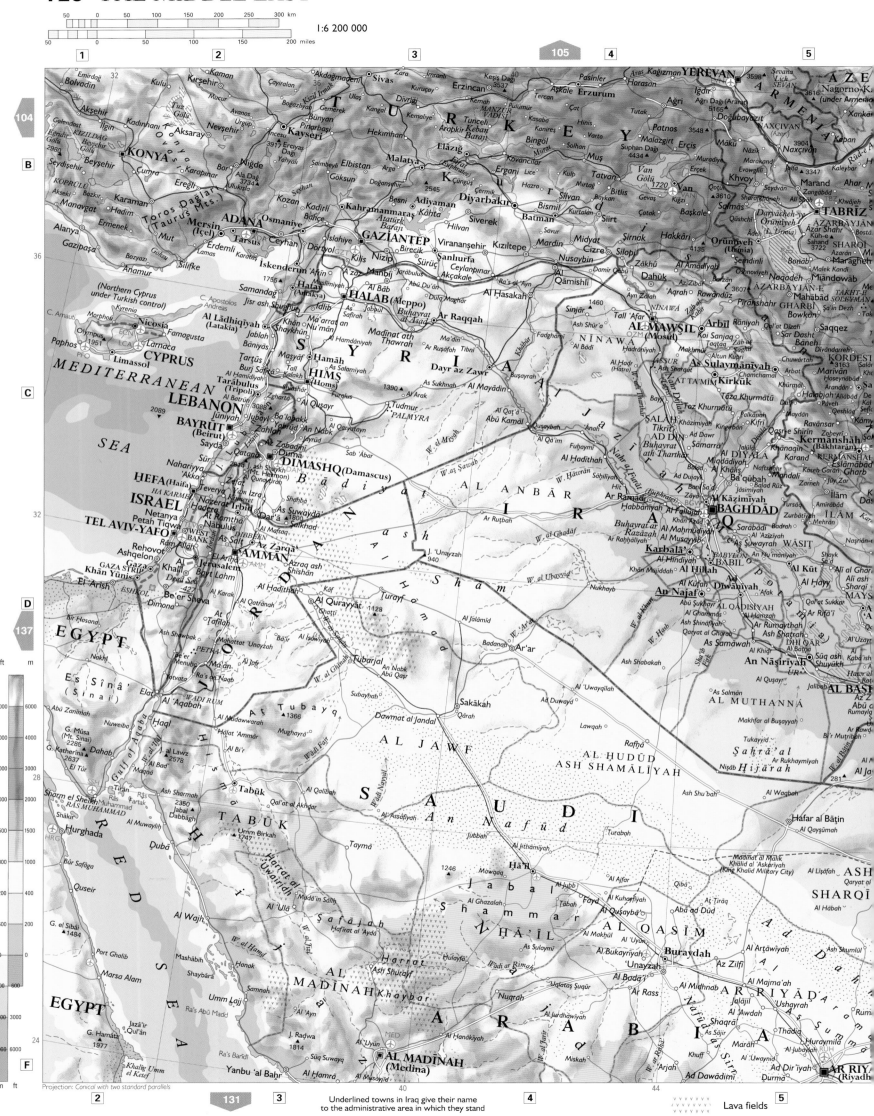

1:6 200 000

Underlined towns in Iraq give their name
to the administrative area in which they stand

v v v v v v
v v v v v v Lava fields
v v v v v v

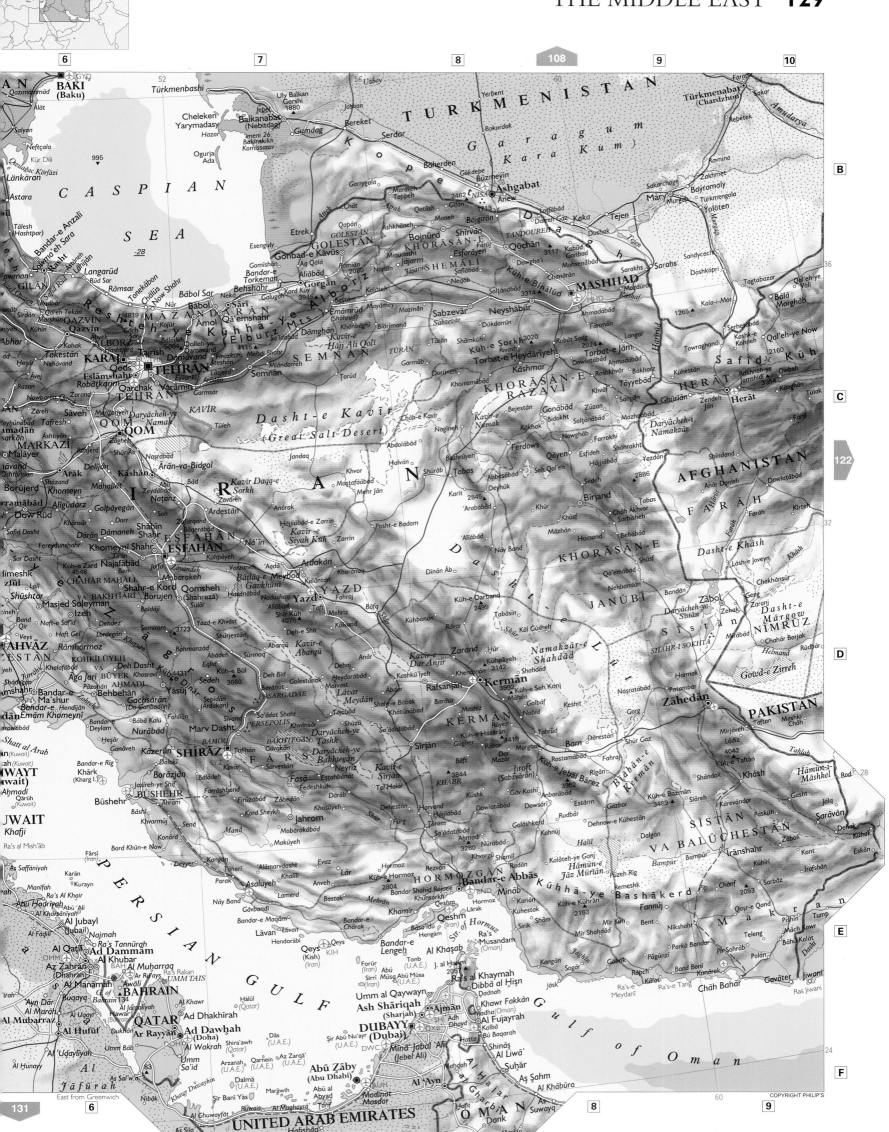

BAKI (Baku)

TURKMENISTAN
Türkmenbashi
Türkmenabat (Chardzhou)

CASPIAN SEA

GOLESTÄN
KHORÄSÄN-E SHEMÄLÏ
MASHHAD
HERÄT
AFGHANISTAN

TEHRÄN
QOM
SEMNÄN
Dasht-e Kavir (Great Salt Desert)
KHORÄSÄN-E RAZAVÏ

MARKAZÏ
I R A N
KHORÄSÄN-E JANÜBÏ

ESFAHÄN
YAZD
PAKISTAN
Zähedän

SHÏRÄZ
FÄRS
KERMÄN
Kermän
SISTÄN VA BALÜCHESTÄN

BÜSHEHR
HORMOZGÄN
Bandar-e Abbäs

PERSIAN GULF
BAHRAIN
QATAR
Ad Dawhah (Doha)
DUBAYY (Dubai)
ABÜ ZÄBY (Abu Dhabi)
UNITED ARAB EMIRATES
OMAN
Gulf of Oman

COPYRIGHT PHILIP'S

1:2 200 000

km / miles

Projection: Polyconic East from Greenwich COPYRIGHT PHILIP'S

1974 Cease Fire Lines

MEDITERRANEAN SEA

CYPRUS

Paphos Kividhes Zyyi
Episkopi PFO Limassol
Episkopi Bay Akrotiri Bay C. Gata

2775 2089

SYRIA

HIMS (Homs) Shinshār Furqlus
Al Hamīdīyah Tall Kalakh Halbā
Al Hirmil Al Qusayr HIMS
ASH SHAMĀLS Al Qaryatayn
Tarābulus (Tripoli) Zgharta Qurnat as Sawdā'
3088 Bsharrī Al Labwah 2464 Al Burayj
Al Batrūn Al Bārīq An Nabk Bi'r Ghadir
Jubayl Qartabā 2616 Yabrūd
Ibrāhīm Ba'labakk An Nabk
BAYRŪT (Beirut) BEY Biklayyā 2628 J. Sannin
Jūniyah Alayh Zahlah Shtūghāyā
Ash Shuwayfāt JABAL LUBNĀN Khān Abū Shāmat
Ad Dāmūr Az Zabadānī Dumayr
LEBANON Hawsh Mūssā Al Qutayfah DIMASHQ
1942 J. al Bārūk Dārayyā **DIMASHQ** (Damascus)
Saydā (Sidon) Qatana Jaramānah
Jazzīn 2814 (Mt. Hermon) Al Hājānah
An Nabatīyah at Tahta Q. Mas'ada Al Kiswah Burāq
AL JANŪB Marj 'Uyūn Az Zabadānī
Sūr (Tyre) Marj 'Uyūn Qilā As Sanamayn
Qiryat Shemona Qūnaytra As Sanamayn
1197 DARĀ
Nahariyya Zefat Ar Rafid Shahbā
Hagalil (Galilee) AS SUWAYDĀ
'Akko (Acre) Yam Kinneret (Sea of Galilee) As Salah 1900
Ma'alot-Tarshiha 1208 Fiq Shaykh Miskin Malah
Mifraz Hefa Karmi'el DARĀ
Qiryat Yam HAZAFON Saham al Jawlan
HEFA (Haifa) Teverya (Tiberias) 210
Qiryat Ata Nazerat (Nazareth) Darā As Suwayda
Har Ha Karmel 546 Afula Taiybe At Ramtha
HA KARMEL Yarmūk IRBID Salkhad
TEL MEGIDDO Bet She'an Irbid Umm al Qittayn
CAESAREA Jenin Tirat Zevi AJLŪN Bušrā ash Shām
Ummel Fahm J. Umm ad Daraj Al Mafraq
Hadera Shomron 2247 Jarash Umm al Qittayn
ISRAEL Tubās SAMARIA JARASH
Netanya Nāblus Al Mafraq AL MAFRAQ
HAMERKAZ SHILOH N. az Zarqā
Herzliyya Tulkarm AL BALQĀ
Ra'ananna Kefar Sava As Salt
Benē Beraq Petah Tiqwa Tila' al Ali **Az Zarqā**
TEL AVIV-YAFO Ramat Gan 289 Ar Ruşayfah
Bat Yam **WEST BANK** **AMMĀN** Azraq ash Shīshān
Holon Lod Wādī as Sīr Al Quwaysimah
Rishon le Ziyyon Ramla Na'ūr AZ ZARQĀ
Yavne Ram Allāh El Arīhā (Jericho) AMM
Rehovot Jerusalem (Yerushalayim) (Al Quds) Ma'daba
Ashdod Qiryat Mal'akhi Bet Shemesh Bayt Lahm (Bethlehem) AL 'ĀSIMAH
Qiryat Gat MA'DABA UMM AR RASAS
Ashqelon TEL LAKHISH Al Khalīl (Hebron) W. al Haydān
Beit Lāhīyā N. Shiqma Az Zāhiriya Dhibān
GAZA STRIP Jabalya Sederot 'En Gedi 422
Gaza Nuseirat Yehuda AL HADITHAH
Deir al Balah Rahat MASADA Al Hadithah
Khān Yūnis ESHKOL Arad W. al Mawjib
Rafah Be'er Sheva (Beersheba) W. Al Ghadaf
El Daheir Sedom AL KARAK W. Al Mawbag
Bor Mashash 333 Al Qatrānah
Dimona 'En Boqeq Al Karak
HADAROM Al Mazar W. Bā'ir

EGYPT

Bûr Sa'îd (Port Said) Bûr Fu'ad Râs Burûn
BÛR SA'ÎD Sabkhet el Bardawil
Qantara Suweis El 'Arîsh Khaliḡ el Tîna
Români Bîr el 'Abd W. el 'Arîsh
El Qantara Bîr Qatia Bîr Lahfân
Bîr ed Duweidar Bîr el Garârât Bîr Kaseiba
Wâḥid Bîr Madkûr **SHAMÂL SÎNÎ**
Ismâ'îlîya Bîr el Mâlḥi 121
Talâta Abu 'Aweigîla At Tafilah
ISMĀ'ILĪYA Qezi'ot Birein Dana
Khamsa 892 Muweilih
El Buheirat el Murrat el Kubra (Great Bitter L.) El Quşeima Sedé Boqér
G. Yi 'Allaq Bîr Ḥasana Mizpe Ramon Nijil
1094 Bîr Beiḍa 1305
Gineifa Bîr el Thamâda El 'Agrûd **Hanegev (Negev Desert)**
Mamarr Mitlâ W. el Bruk W. Qurāiya Rujm Tal'at al Jamâlah
W. el Sab 'a W. Mahashem 1736 Wādī Mûsā
El Suweis (Suez) Bûr Taufiq W. Giudi PETRA Ma'ān
Adabiya Ain Sudr N. Paran MA'ĀN
Uyûn Mûsa El Kuntilla N. Hiyyon
Khalîg es Suweis Nakhl Yotvata Al Jafr Qa'el Jafr
Ghubbet el Bûs Râs Sudr W. El Tamarâni En Avrona Bi'r al Mârî
Bîr Abu Sandûq 948 Râs Matarma W. Ruáq Al Aqabah Ra's an Naqb
1272 G. el Kabrît Gebel el Tîh El Thamad AL 'AQABAH 1435
EL SUWEIS El Wabeira 1165 Bîr el Biarât Mahattat ash Shidiyah
JANŪB SÎNÎ W. Abu Ga'da W. an Nukhei Elat 1592 1754 Batn al Ghûl
Bîr Abu Maţarma Bîr el Heisi Gulf of Aqaba WADI RUM
Abu Sandûq Râs Matarma Al 'Aqabah Rum **SAUDI ARABIA**
El Suweis Haql Al Mudawwarah At Tubaya

JORDAN

At Tafilah At Tafilah J. ash Shawmari
1072 Bā'ir

m / ft elevation scale:
9000 / 3000
6000 / 2000
4500 / 1500
3000 / 1200
1200 / 400
0 / 0
100 / 300
200 / 600
500 / 1500
1000 / 3000
2000 / 6000

1:13 300 000

100 0 100 200 300 400 500 600 km
100 0 100 200 300 400 miles

1 2 3 **128** 4 5 **129** 6 7

A
122
B
C
D

LEBANON
BAYRŪT (Beirut)
SYRIA
DIMASHQ (Damascus)
ISRAEL
TEL AVIV-YAFO
HAIFA
Ashqelon
AMMAN
Jerusalem
WEST BANK
GAZA
Būr Sa'īd
GAZA STRIP
Qanā es Suweis (Suez Canal)
Ismā'īlīya
El Suweis (Suez)
Jabal ad Durūz 1800
Ar Ramādī
Ar Ruṭbah
IRAQ
BAGHDAD
Al Kūt
Karbalā'
Al Ḥillah
An Najaf
Al 'Amārah
Dezfūl
Khorramābād
Arāk
Kāshān
Khomeynī Shahr
IRAN
Yazd
Birjand
Farāh
AFGHANISTAN

Ba'qūbah
Al Fallūjah
An Nāṣirīyah
AHVĀZ
Khorrāmshahr
Eṣfahān 4548
Shahr-e Kord
Zābol
Dāryācheh-ye Sīstān

Mōān
Al 'Aqabah
JORDAN
As Samāwah
Ar'ar
Sakākah
Al Jawf
Rafḥā
AL BAṢRAH (Basra)
Ābādān
Shatt al Arab
Būbiyān
Marv Dasht
PERSEPOLIS
SHĪRĀZ
Yāsūj 4431
Zāhedān
Es Sīnā'
G. Mûsa 2285
Sharm el Sheikh
Dubā
Tabūk
Al Muwayliḥ
Tamyā
Hā'il
Ḥafar al Bāṭin
AL KUWAYT
KUWAIT
Khārk
Būshehr
Deyyer
Kāzerūn
Neyrīz
Sīrjān
Bam 4042
Jīroft 4419
Kermān
Anār
Rafsanjān
Bandar-e Abbās
Īrānshahr
Gābrīk
4076

Hurghada 218
Būr Safāga
Qena
KARNAK
THEBES
El Uqsur (Luxor)
Isna
Idfū
Kôm Ombo
Marsa Alam
Quseir
Al Wajh
Yanbu al Baḥr
Jabal Shammar
Buraydah
'Unayzah
Ar Rass
Az Zilfī
SAUDI
Ad Dammām
Aẓ Ẓahrān (Dhahran)
Al Jubayl
Al Qaṭīf
Al Manāmah
BAHRAIN
QATAR
Ad Dawḥah (Doha)
Al Mubarraz
Al Hufūf
Ra's al-Khaymah
'Ajmān
Ash Shāriqah (Sharjah)
DUBAYY (Dubai)
Al Fujayrah
Ṣuḥār
As Suwayq
As Sīb
Maṭraḥ
Masqaṭ (Muscat)
Sūr
Ra's al Hadd
Ra's Musandam (Oman)
Str. of Hormuz
Gulf of Oman
Jāsk
Qeshm 2163
Khamīr
Qeys

Aswān
Sadd el Aali
Buheirat en Nasser (L. Nasser)
EGYPT
Es Sahrâ en Nûbîya
Bīr Shalatein
Ras Bānās
1977
Rābigh
AL MADĪNAH (Medina)
Tropic of Cancer
'Afīf
Ad Dawādimī
As Sulaymāniyah
Harad
Shaqrā'
AR RIYĀD (Riyadh)
UNITED ARAB EMIRATES
Abū Ẓaby (Abu Dhabi)
Al 'Ayn
Ibrī
Nizwā 3019
Izki
ARABIA
Ruwais
Al Hajar al Gharbī

Wadi Halfa
Halaib Triangle
Halaib
2216
King Abdullah Economic City
MAKKAH (Mecca)
JIDDAH (Jedda)
Ras Abu Shagara
Muhammad Qol 2259
ASIR
Al Ḥawīyah
Al Khurmah
Aṭ Ṭā'if 2565
Ar Rawḍah
Turabah
Al Līth
Qal'at Bīshah
As Sulayyil
Layla
Al 'Ubaylah
Rub' al Khālī
(Empty Quarter)
'Urūq ar Rumaylah
Khalūf
J. Maşīrah
Ḥaymā'
Ad Duqm
Ra's al Madrakah
Khalīj Maşīrah

Abu Hamed
Būr Sûdân
Suakin
Trinkitat
Sinkat
1596
Haiya
Karora
2780
Nakfa
Berber
Atbara
Ed Dāmer
Al Bāḥah 3039
Al Qunfudhah
Khamis Mushayṭ
Zahrān al Janub
Abha 3013
Najrān
Ash Sharawrah
Thamarīt
ZUFĀR
Salālah 1463
Mirbāṭ
Ra's Fartak
J. al Hallāniyat
OMAN
1132
Al Ghaydah

Wad Hamid
6th Cataract
SUDAN
5th Cataract
Omdurmân
EL KHARTÛM (Khartoum)
Kassalā
Asmera
Adarama
Akordat
Mitsiwa
Zula
Dahlak Kebir
Jīzān
Farasān
Sāmitah
Sa'dah
Khamir
Shibām
Say'ūn
Tarīm
Ḥaḍramawt
Al Luḥayyah
Kamarān
Hajjah 3760
ṢAN'Ā'
Mukalla
Ash Shiḥr
Sayḥūt

Manaqil
Wâd Medanî
El Gezira
Gedaref
Khashm el Girba
Badme
Adigrat
Aksum
Adwa
Mekele
ERITREA
Danakil Desert
Hanish
Al Ḥudaydah
Dhamār
Ibb
Ta'izz 3200
YEMEN
Niṣāb 2185
Al Mukallā

Ed Dueim
Sennar
Singa
Kôstî
Umm Ruwaba
Metema
Gonder
L. Tana
Bahir Dar
Debre Tabor
LALIBELA
Tekeze
Ras Dashen 4533
3018
Aseb
Al Mukha
Madinat ash Sha'b
Shaykh 'Uthmān
Shuqrā'
Aḥwar
Bāb el Mandeb
Tadjourah
DJIBOUTI
Djibouti
L. Assal
Saylac
Gulf of Aden
'Abd al Kūri (Yemen)
Hadīboh
Socotra (Yemen)
1503
Bereeda
Ras Asir
Boosaaso
Xaafuun
Ras Xaafuun

Jibalan Nubah
Ed Damazin
Roseires Res.
Dembidolo
Nekemte
Metu
Gore
ADDIS ABEBA
Debre Zeyit
Nazret
Debre Markos
Dese 4012
Dikhil
L. Abbé
Awash
3381
Dire Dawa
Harer
Jijiga
Somaliland
Berbera
Hargeisa
Burco (Burao)
Karin
Shimbiris 2416
Ceerigaabo
El Gal 2200
Qardho (Garda)
Bender Beyla
Garoowe

SOUTH SUDAN
Malakal
Juba
Bor
Pibor Post
Gambela
Jima 3686
Awasa
Yirga Alem
Gibe III
Batu 4307
Shashemene
Ginir
Goba
Dila
Kibre Mengist
Negele
Imi
Gode
Ogaden
Kebri Dehar
Ferfer
Las Anod (Laascaanood)
Eyl
Gaalkacyo (Galcaio)
Galmudug Puntland
Hobyo
Sina Dhago

ETHIOPIA
Ethiopian Highlands
3302
Arba Minch
L. Shamo
L. Abaya
Metu
Chew Bahir
Ilemi Triangle
Lokitaung 1794
375
L. Turkana
Mega
Moyale
El Wak
Dolo
Luuq (Lugh)
Baydhabo (Baidoa)
Buurhakaba (Bur Acaba)
Wanleweyne (Uanle Uen)
Beledweyne (Belet Uen)
Ceeldheere
Jawhar (Giohar)
Marka (Merca)
MUQDISHO (Mogadishu)
SOMALIA

INDIAN OCEAN

UGANDA
Gulu
Lira
Moroto
Soroti
Mt. Elgon 4321
Mbale
L. Kyoga
L. Albert
Masindi
Pakwach
Murchison Falls
Arua
KENYA
Kitale
South Horn
Lodwar
Marsabit
Wajir
Dif
Baardheere
Jamaame (Giamama)
Jilib (Gelib)
Equator
Kismaayo (Chisimaio)
2752
3187
Tali Post
Mongalla
Kapoeta
Torit
Yei
Kajo Kaji

Projection: Sanson-Flamsteed's Sinusoidal
1 2 **140** 3 East from Greenwich 4 5 6

ft m
12 000 4000
9000 3000
6000 2000
4500 1500
3000 1000
1200 400
600 200
0 0
200 600
1000 3000
2000 6000
4000 12 000
m ft

Lava fields

COPYRIGHT PHILIP'S

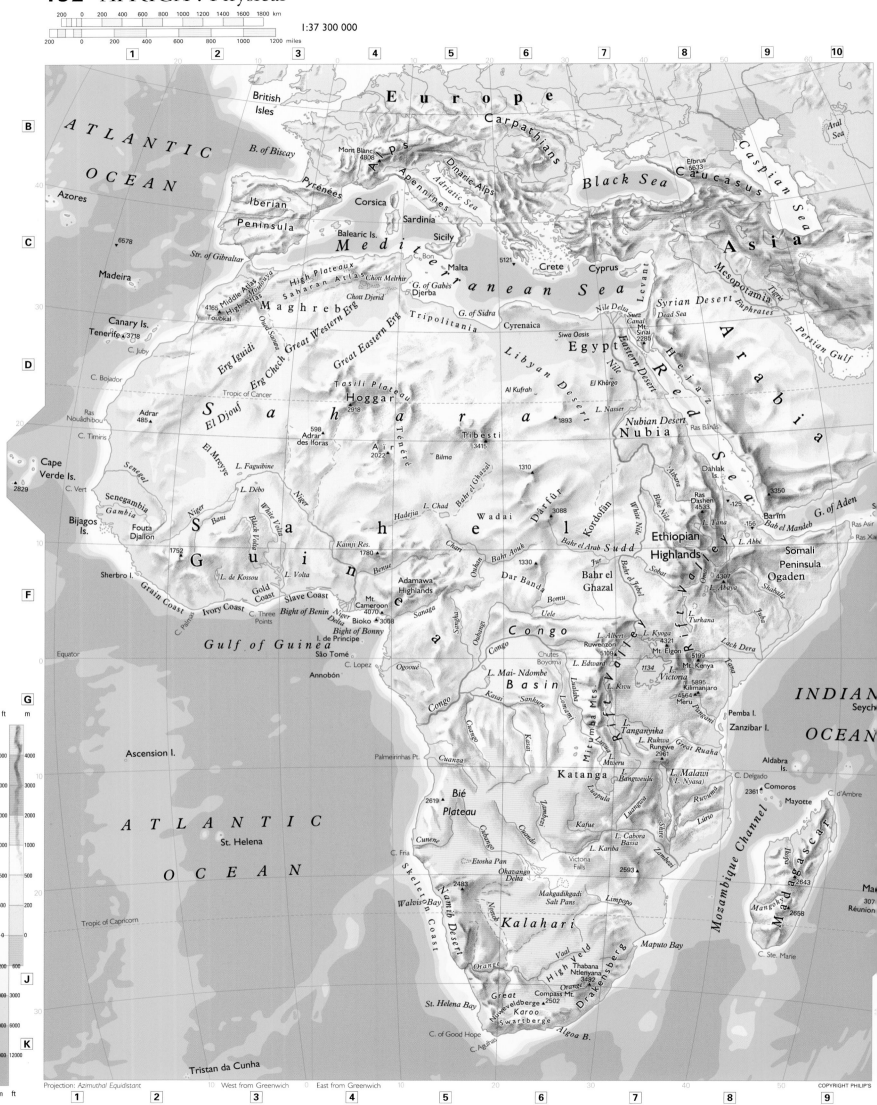

1:37 300 000

200 0 200 400 600 800 1000 1200 1400 1600 1800 km
200 0 200 400 600 800 1000 1200 miles

Projection: Azimuthal Equidistant

West from Greenwich   East from Greenwich

COPYRIGHT PHILIP'S

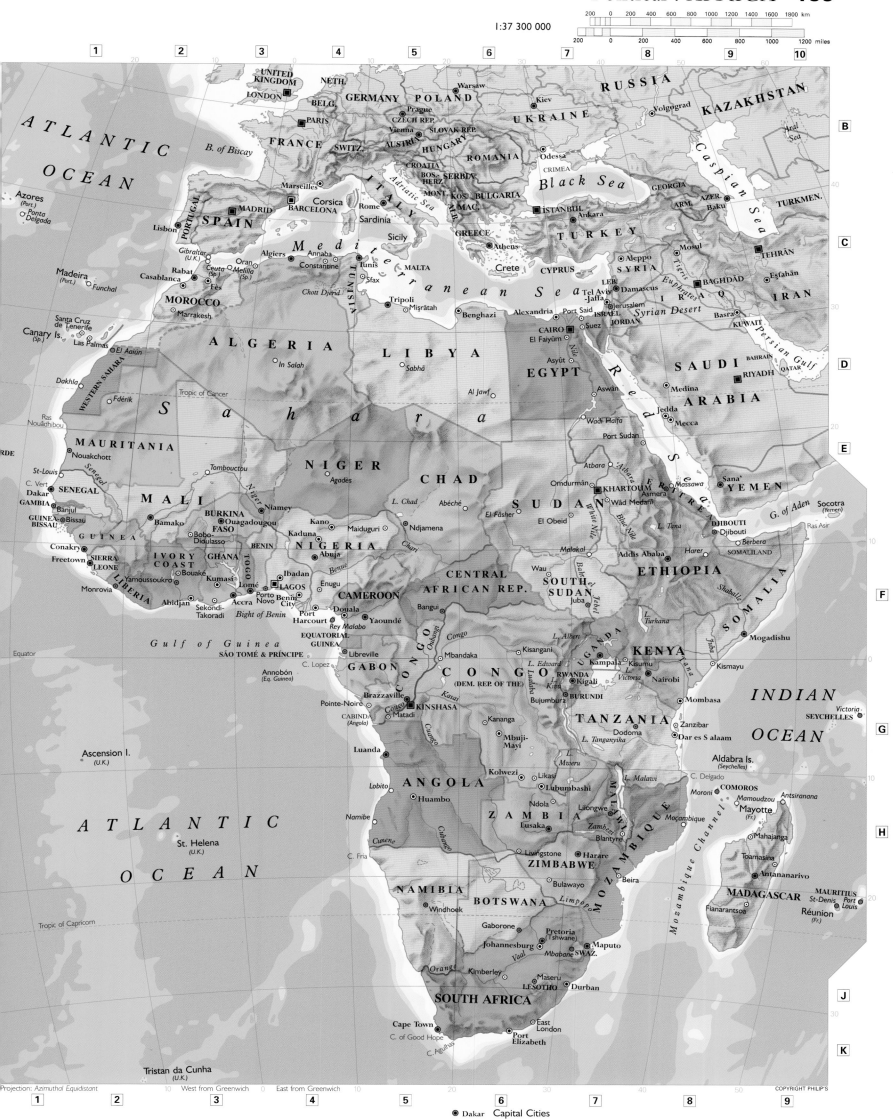

1:37 300 000

● Dakar   Capital Cities

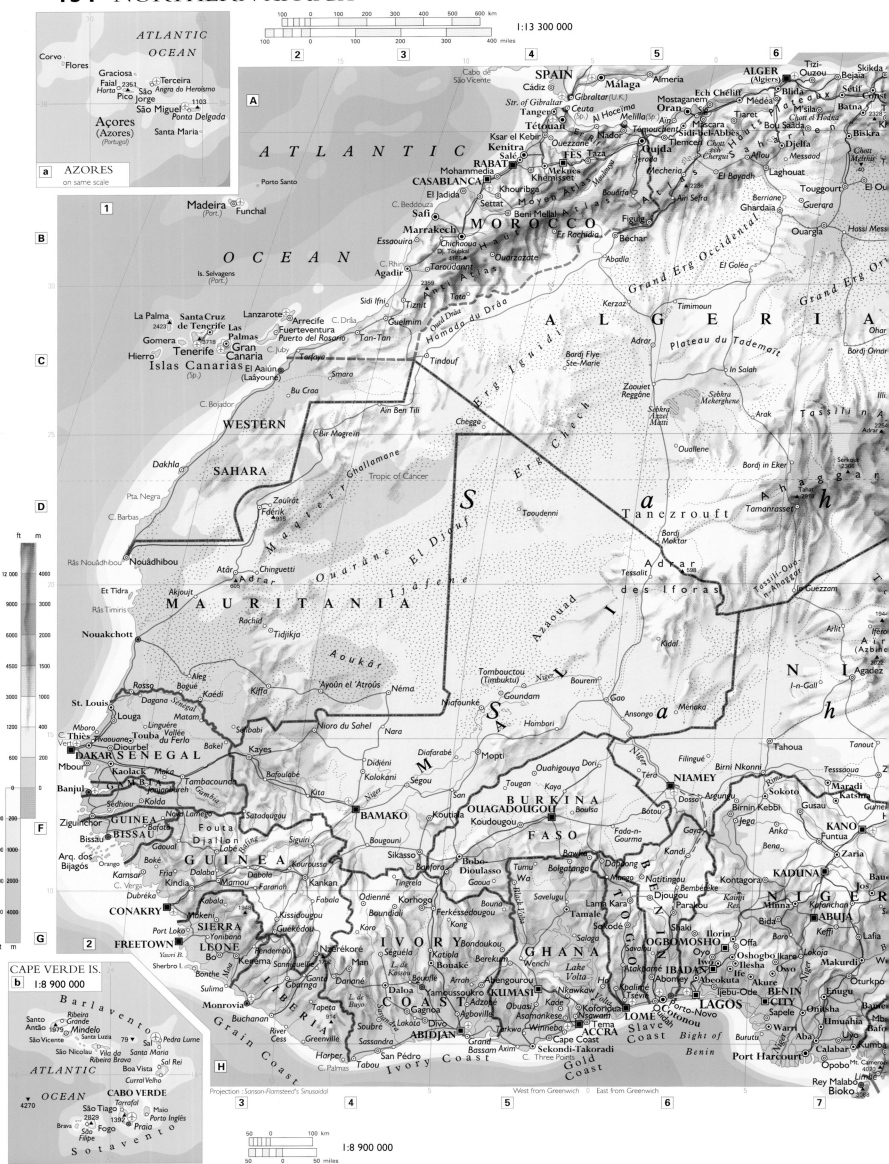

1:13 300 000

100 0 100 200 300 400 500 600 km
100 0 100 200 300 400 miles

a AZORES
on same scale

ATLANTIC OCEAN

Corvo
Flores
Graciosa
Faial ▲2351 Terceira
Horta São Angra do Heroísmo
Pico Jorge
São Miguel ▲1103
Ponta Delgada
Santa Maria
Açores
(Azores)
(Portugal)

1

Madeira
(Port.) Funchal
Porto Santo

Is. Selvagens
(Port.)

La Palma
Santa Cruz
Gomera de Tenerife Las
Palmas
Tenerife Gran
Hierro Canaria
El Aaiún
Islas Canarias (Laâyoune)
(Sp.)

SPAIN
Cádiz Málaga Almería
Str. of Gibraltar
Tanger Ceuta (Sp.) Al Hoceima Melilla (Sp.)
Tétouan Nador
Ksar el Kebir Oujda
Kenitra Salé FES Taza Tlemcen
RABAT Meknès
Mohammedia Khemisset
CASABLANCA Khouribga
El Jadida Settat Beni Mellal
Safi
Marrakech MOROCCO
Essaouira Chichaoua
Agadir Dj. Toubkal
4165▲
Taroudannt Ouarzazate
Sidi Ifni Tata
Tiznit Er Rachidia
Guelmim

ALGER
(Algiers)
Oran
Mostaganem
Mascara
Sidi-bel-Abbès
Tiaret
Saïda
Béchar

ALGERIA

WESTERN
SAHARA

Dakhla
Pta. Negra
C. Barbas

Nouâdhibou
Râs Nouâdhibou
Atâr Chinguetti
Et Tidra Adrar
Râs Timiris Akjoujt

MAURITANIA

Nouakchott

SENEGAL
St. Louis
Louga
DAKAR
Mbour Kaolack
Banjul GAMBIA
Ziguinchor GUINEA
BISSAU

GUINEA
CONAKRY

SIERRA
LEONE
FREETOWN

LIBERIA
Monrovia

MALI
BAMAKO

BURKINA
FASO
OUAGADOUGOU

Tombouctou
(Timbuktu)
Gao

NIAMEY
NIGER

IVORY
COAST
GHANA
ABIDJAN ACCRA

TOGO
BENIN
LOME
Porto-Novo
LAGOS

NIGERIA
ABUJA
KADUNA
KANO
IBADAN
BENIN CITY
Port Harcourt

Barlavento
Santo
Antão
São Vicente Mindelo
CABO VERDE
São Tiago
Praia
Sotavento

ATLANTIC
OCEAN

1:8 900 000

50 0 100 km
50 0 50 miles

Projection : Sanson-Flamsteed's Sinusoidal

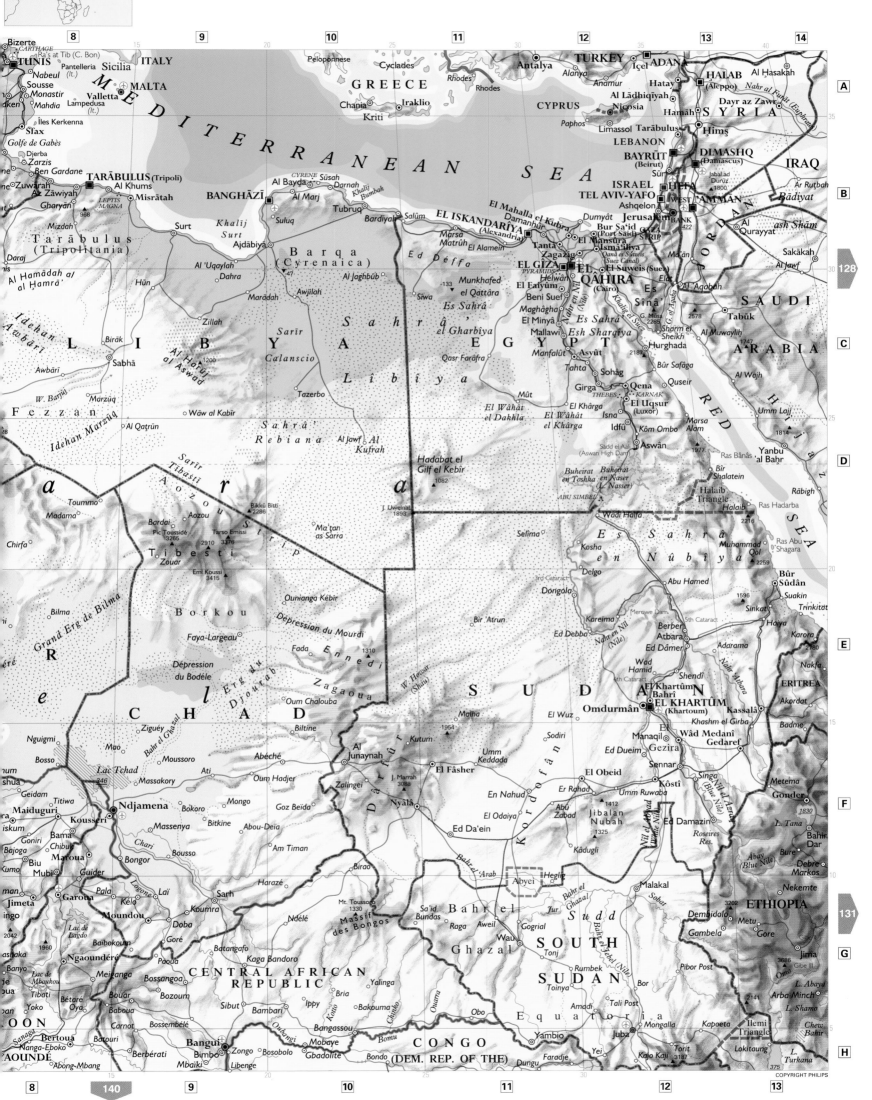

Lava fields

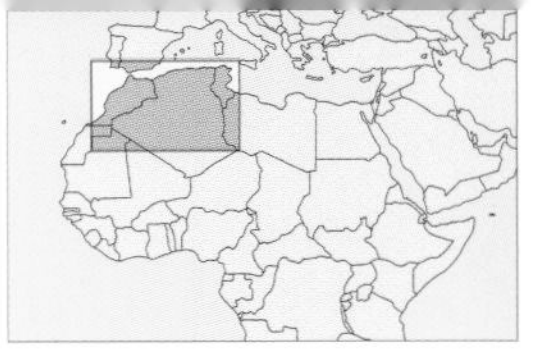

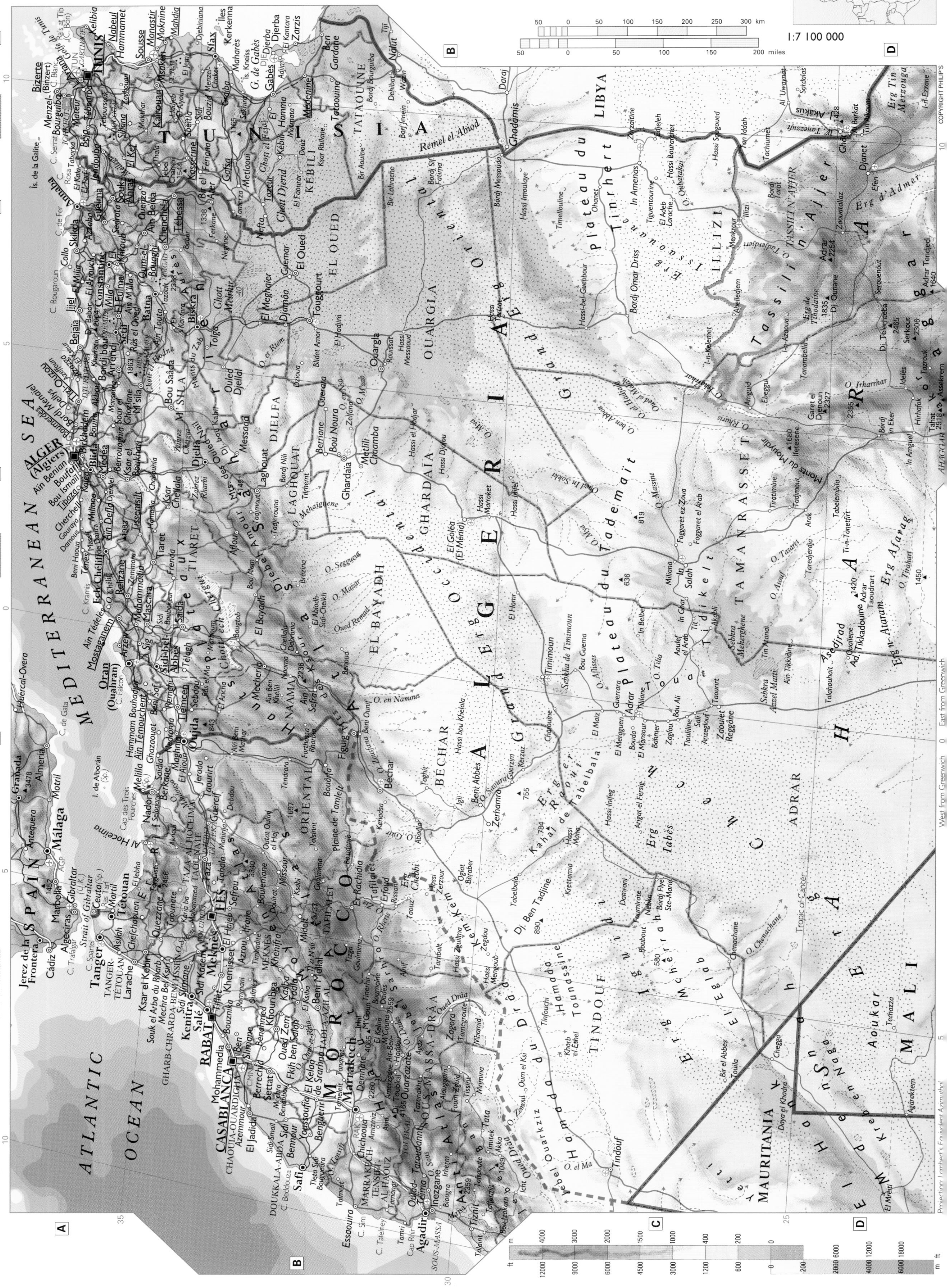

1:7 100 000

COPYRIGHT PHILIP'S

MEDITERRANEAN SEA

ATLANTIC OCEAN

SPAIN

MOROCCO

ALGERIA

TUNISIA

LIBYA

MALI

MAURITANIA

Tunis · Bizerte (Binzert) · Sousse · Monastir · Sfax · Nabeul · Hammamet · Kairouan · Gabès · Medenine · Tataouine · Kebili · Tozeur

Alger (Algiers) · Oran (Ouahran) · Constantine · Annaba · Béjaïa · Skikda · Sétif · Batna · Biskra · Ghardaïa · El Goléa (El Ménia) · Ouargla · Touggourt · El Oued · Laghouat · Djelfa · Béchar · Tindouf · Adrar · Timimoun · In Salah · Tamanrasset · Djanet

Rabat · Casablanca · Tanger (Tangier) · Fès · Meknès · Marrakech · Agadir · Oujda · Kenitra · Safi · Essaouira · Ouarzazate · Er-Rachidia · Figuig

Tropic of Cancer

West from Greenwich · East from Greenwich

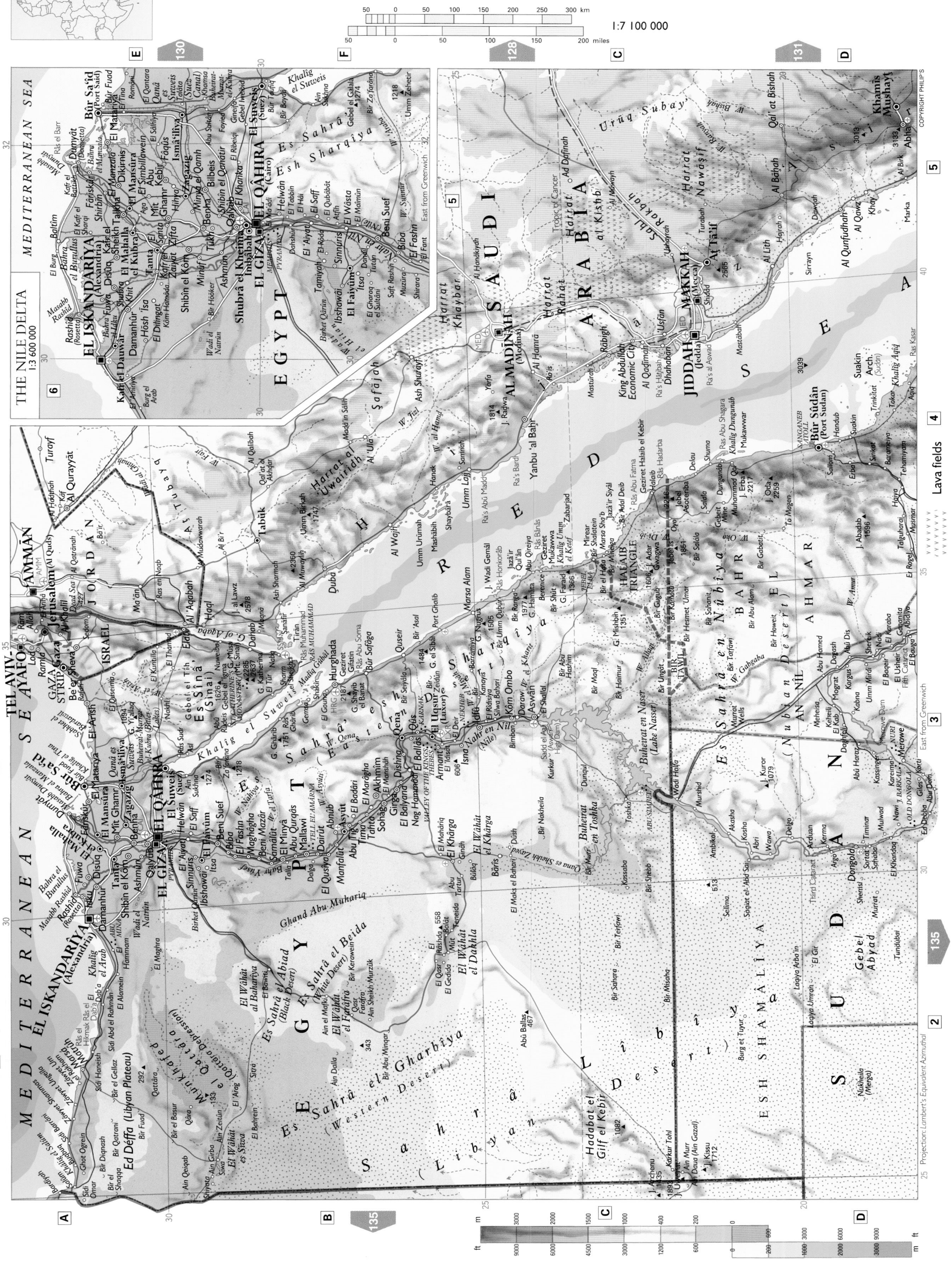

50 0 50 100 150 200 250 300 km

1:7 100 000

50 0 50 100 150 200 miles

THE NILE DELTA
1:3 600 000

COPYRIGHT PHILIP'S

Map labels

MEDITERRANEAN SEA

EGYPT

E G Y P T

S A U D I   A R A B I A

J O R D A N

ISRAEL

SINAI

Es Sahrâ el Gharbîya (Western Desert)

Libyan Desert

Sahrâ Lîbiyya

S U D A N

ESH SHAMÂLÎYA

RED SEA

BAHR EL AHMAR

Es Sahrâ en Nûbîya (Nubian Desert)

AN NÎL

Selected place names

Bûr Saʿîd (Port Said)
El Qâhira (Cairo)
EL GIZA
EL ISKANDARÎYA (Alexandria)
El Mansûra
El Suweis (Suez)
Damanhûr
Tanta
Benha
Zagazig
Bilbeis
Beni Suef
El Faiyûm
El Minya
Asyût
Sohâg
Qena
El Uqsur (Luxor)
Aswân
Hurghada
Quseir
Marsa Alam
Bûr Sûdân (Port Sudan)
Dongola
Merowe
OLD DONGOLA
Sîwa
El Wâhât el Baharîya
El Wâhât el Khârga
El Wâhât el Dâkhla
AL MADÎNAH (Medina)
MAKKAH (Mecca)
JIDDAH (Jedda)
Aṭ Ṭāʾif
AMMÂN
Jerusalem (Al Quds)
TEL AVIV-YAFO
GAZA STRIP
El ʿArîsh
Al ʿAqabah
Tabûk
Al Wajh
Yanbuʿ ʾal Baḥr

BÎR TAWÎL
HALAʿIB TRIANGLE

Buheirat en Nasser (Lake Nasser)

Tropic of Cancer

East from Greenwich

Projection: Lambert's Equivalent Azimuthal

Lava fields

m ft (elevation scale)

Projection : Lambert's Equivalent Azimuthal

Underlined towns give their name to the
administrative area in which they stand.

Administrative division in Ivory Coast:
1 Sassandra-Marahoué

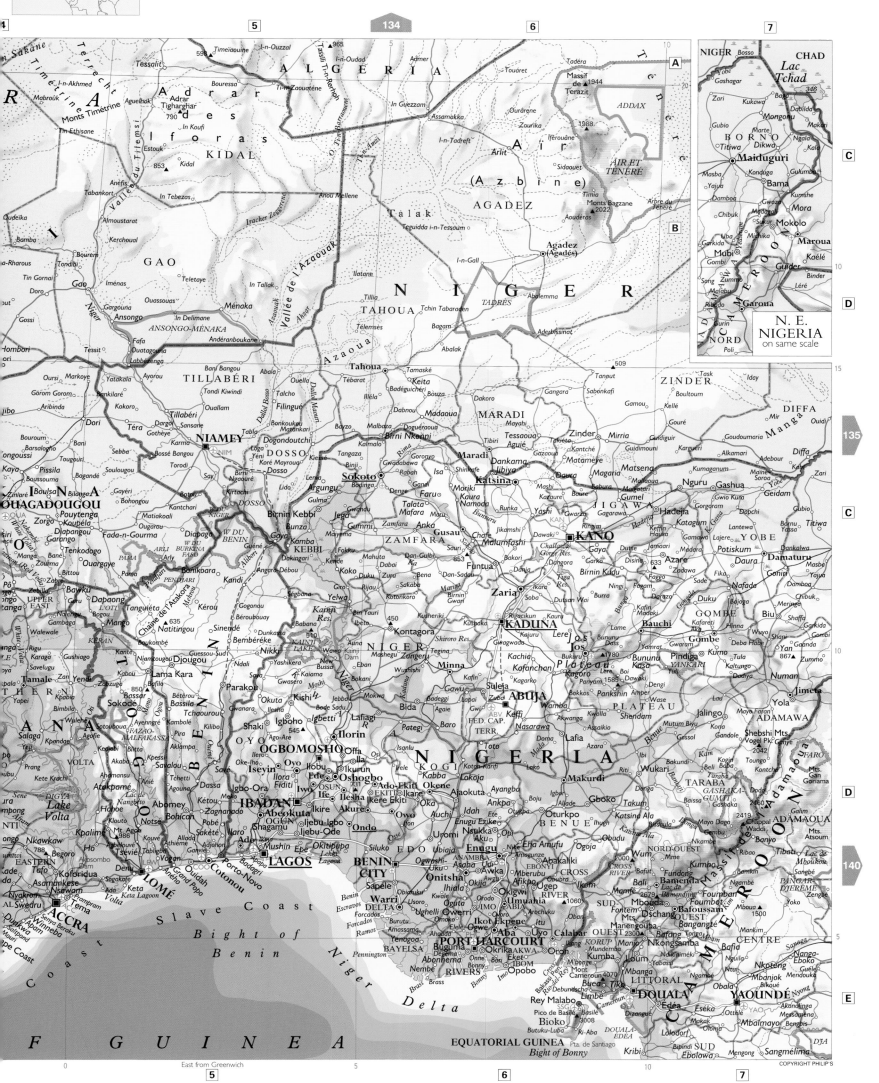

N. E.
NIGERIA
on same scale

East from Greenwich

COPYRIGHT PHILIP'S

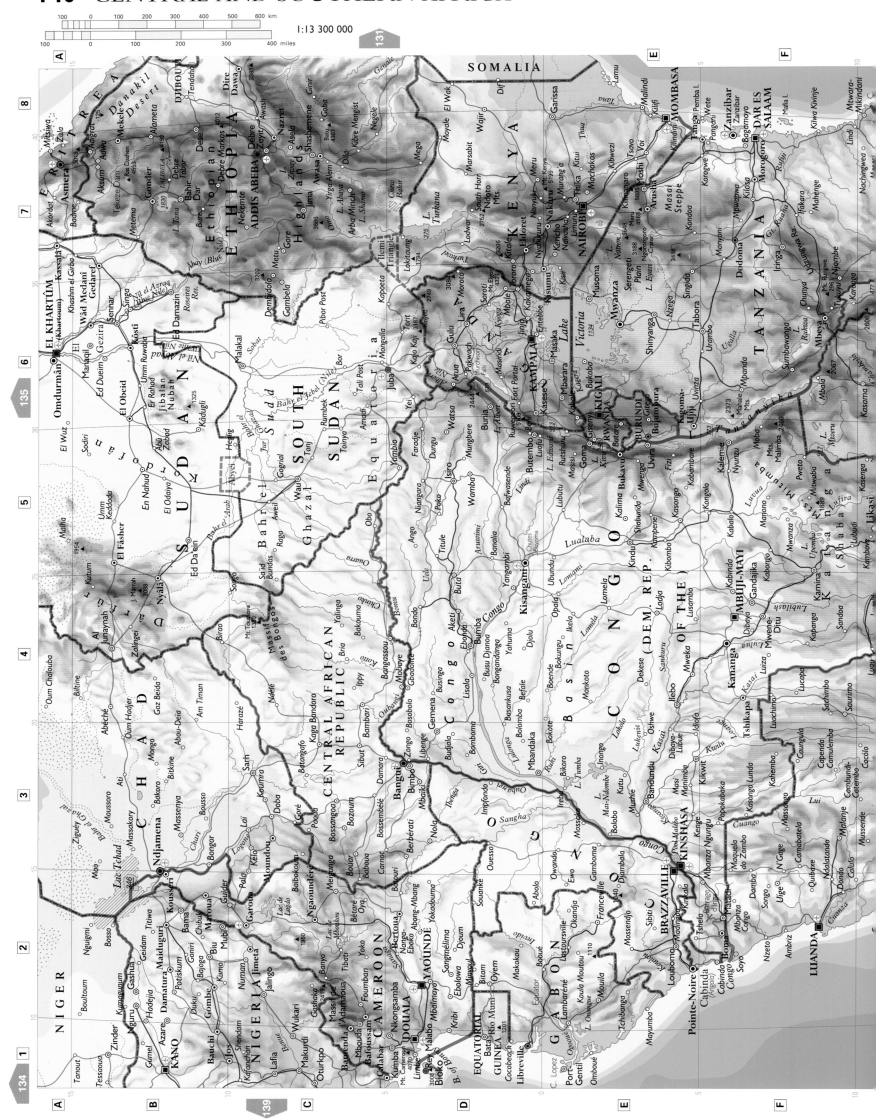

1:13 300 000

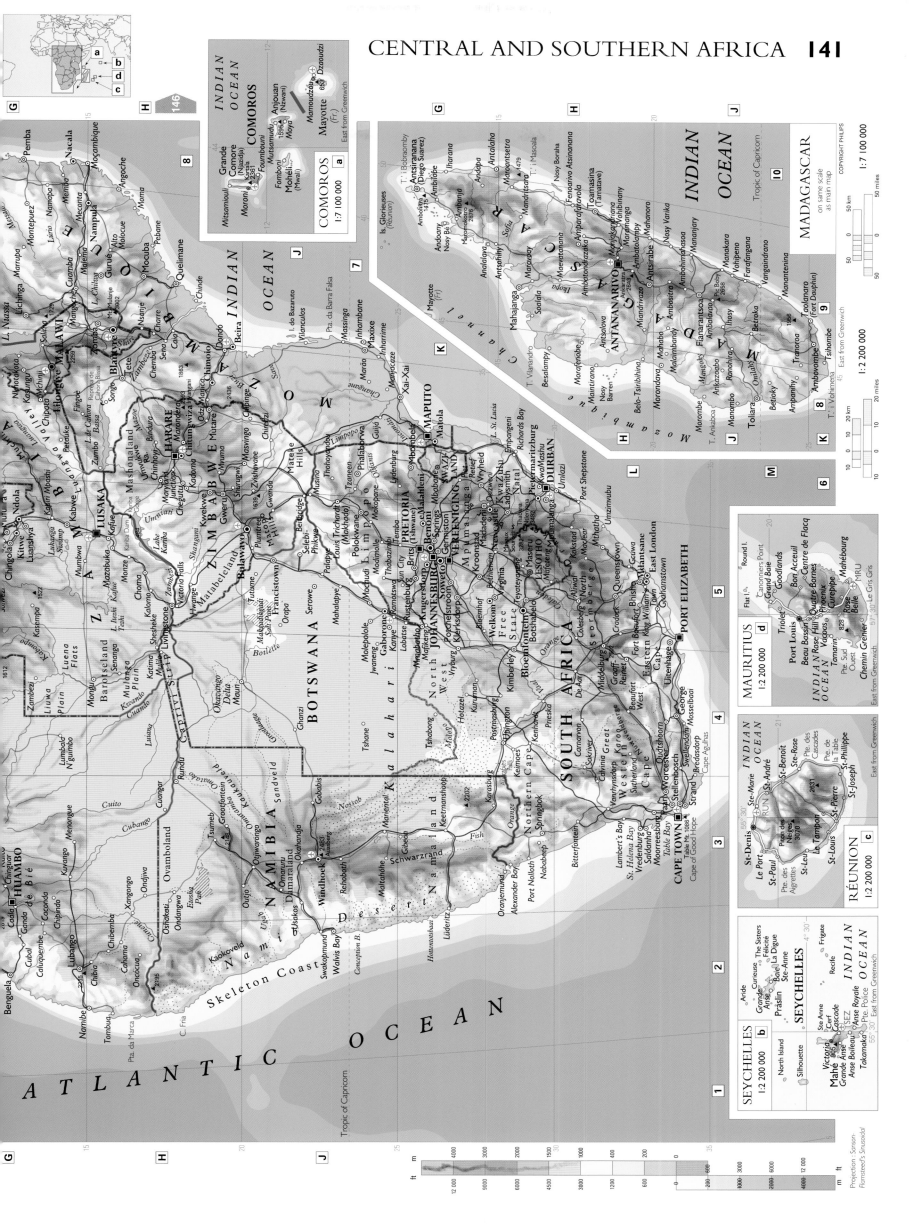

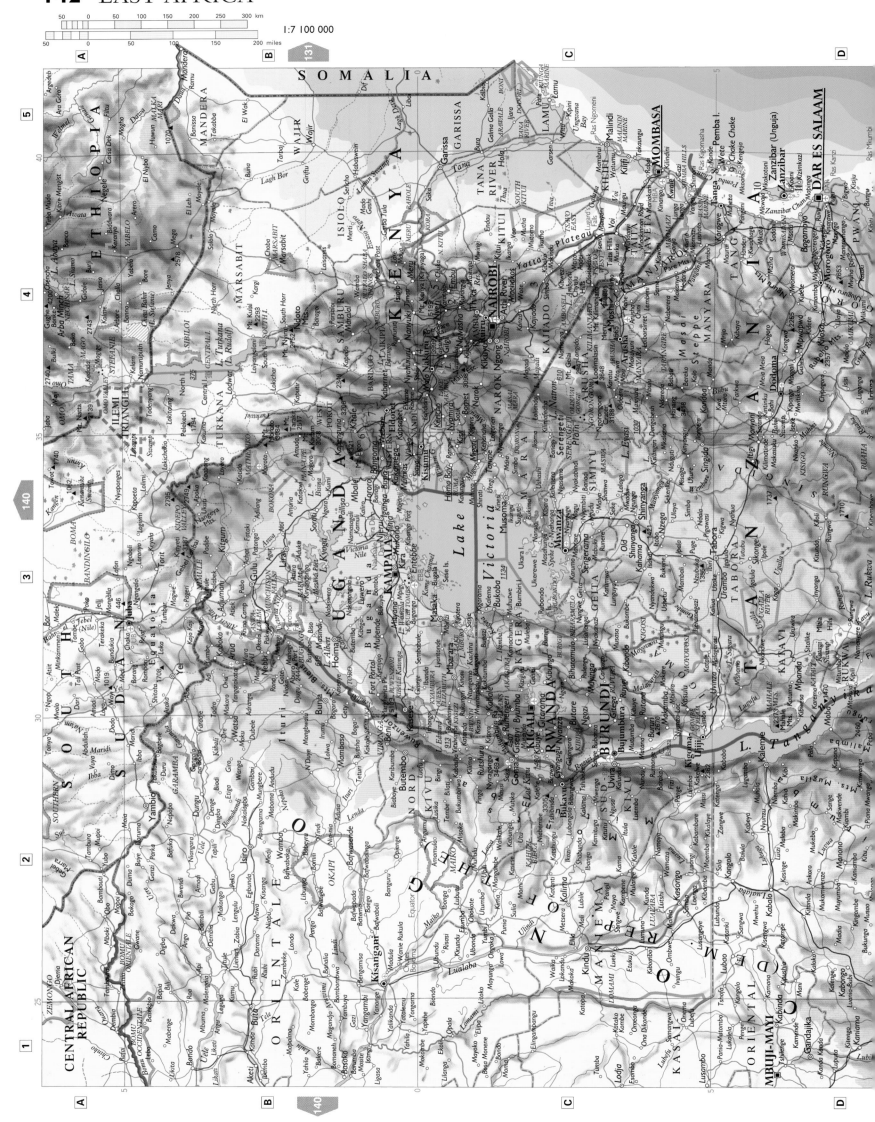

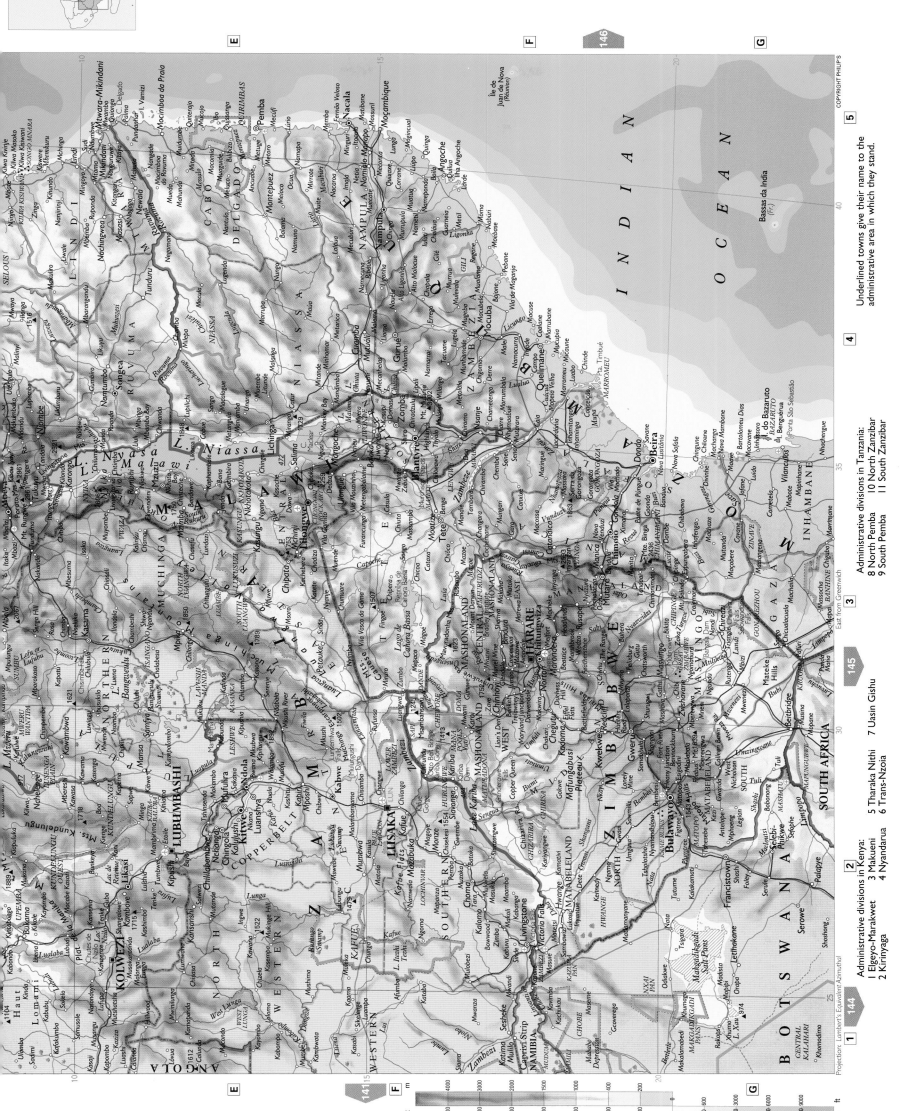

Administrative divisions in Kenya:
1 Elgeyo-Marakwet 3 Makueni   5 Tharaka Nithi 7 Uasin Gishu
2 Kirinyaga   4 Nyandarua   6 Trans-Nzoia

Administrative divisions in Tanzania:
8 North Pemba 10 North Zanzibar
9 South Pemba 11 South Zanzibar

Underlined towns give their name to the
administrative area in which they stand.

COPYRIGHT PHILIP'S

Projection: Lambert's Equivalent Azimuthal

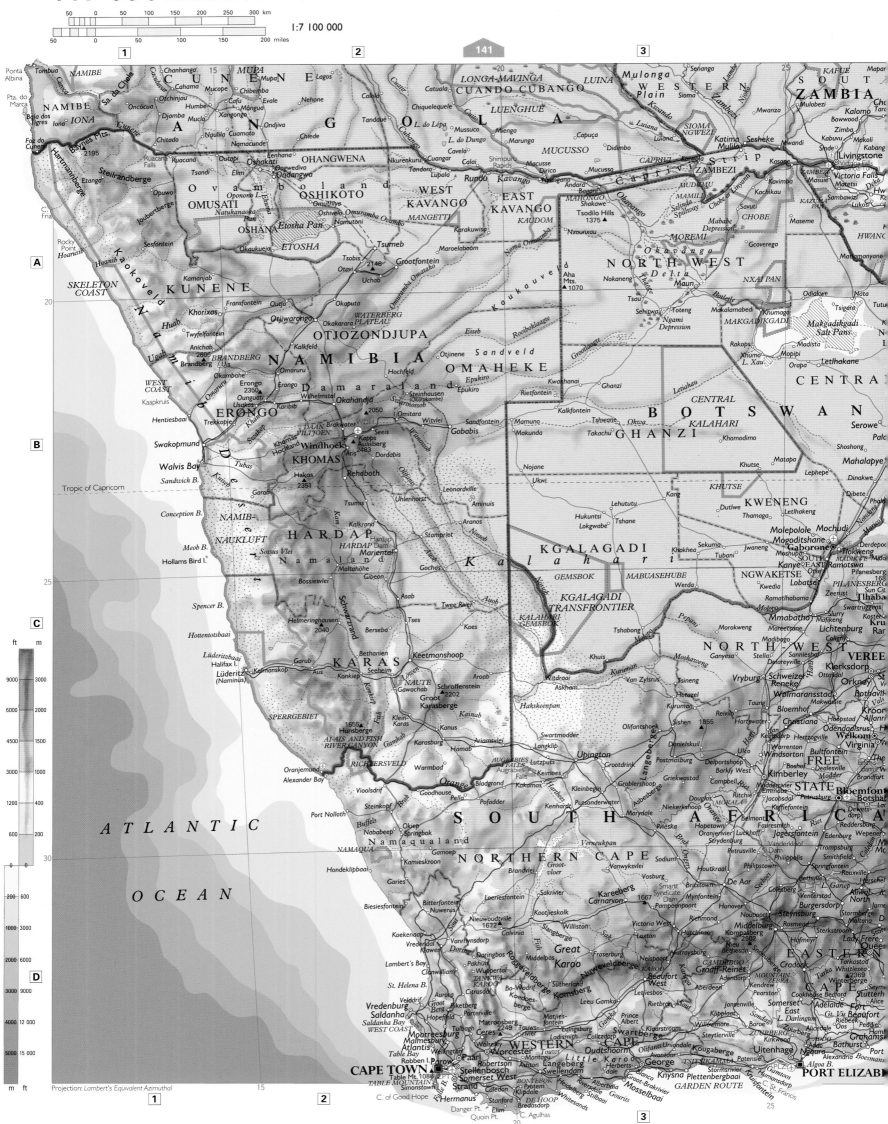

MOZAMBIQUE CHANNEL

Île de Júan de Nova (Fr.)

Bassas da India (Fr.)

Île Europa (Fr.)

Tropic of Capricorn

INDIAN

OCEAN

East from Greenwich

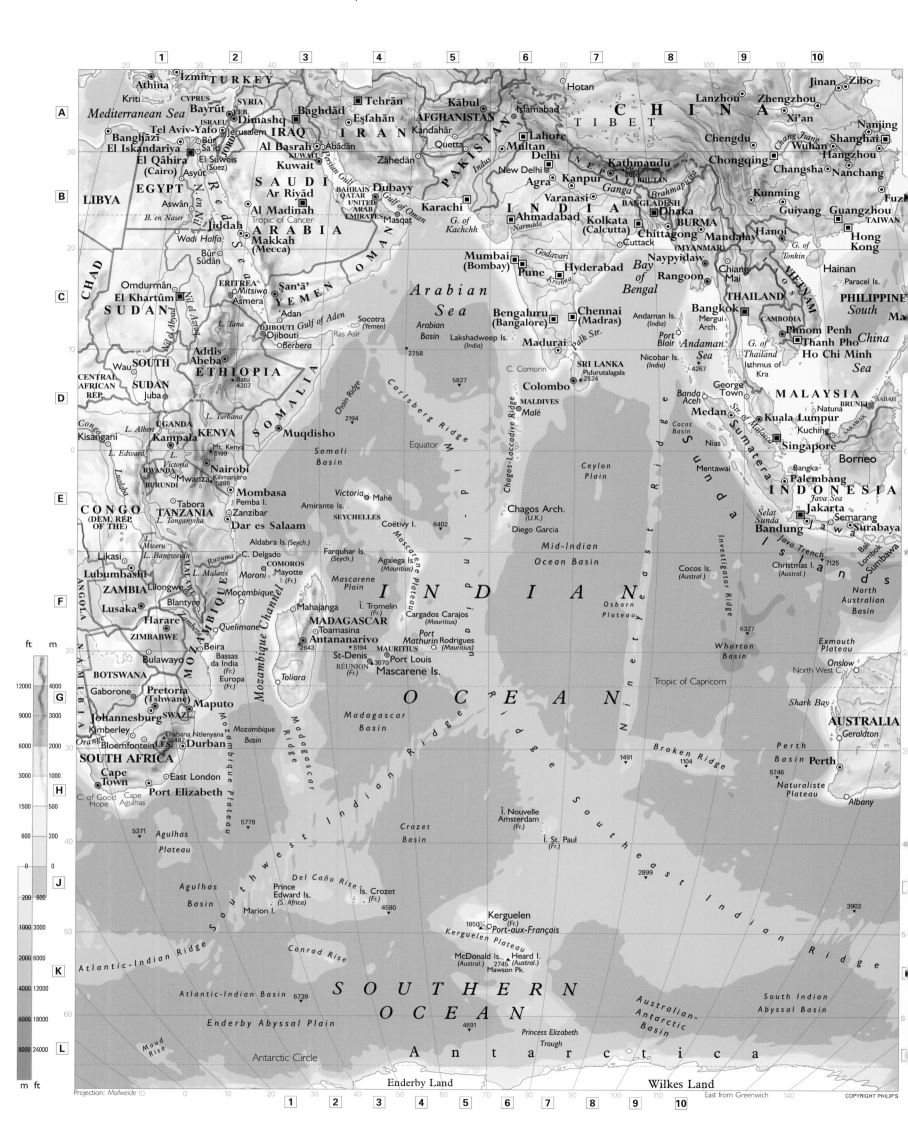

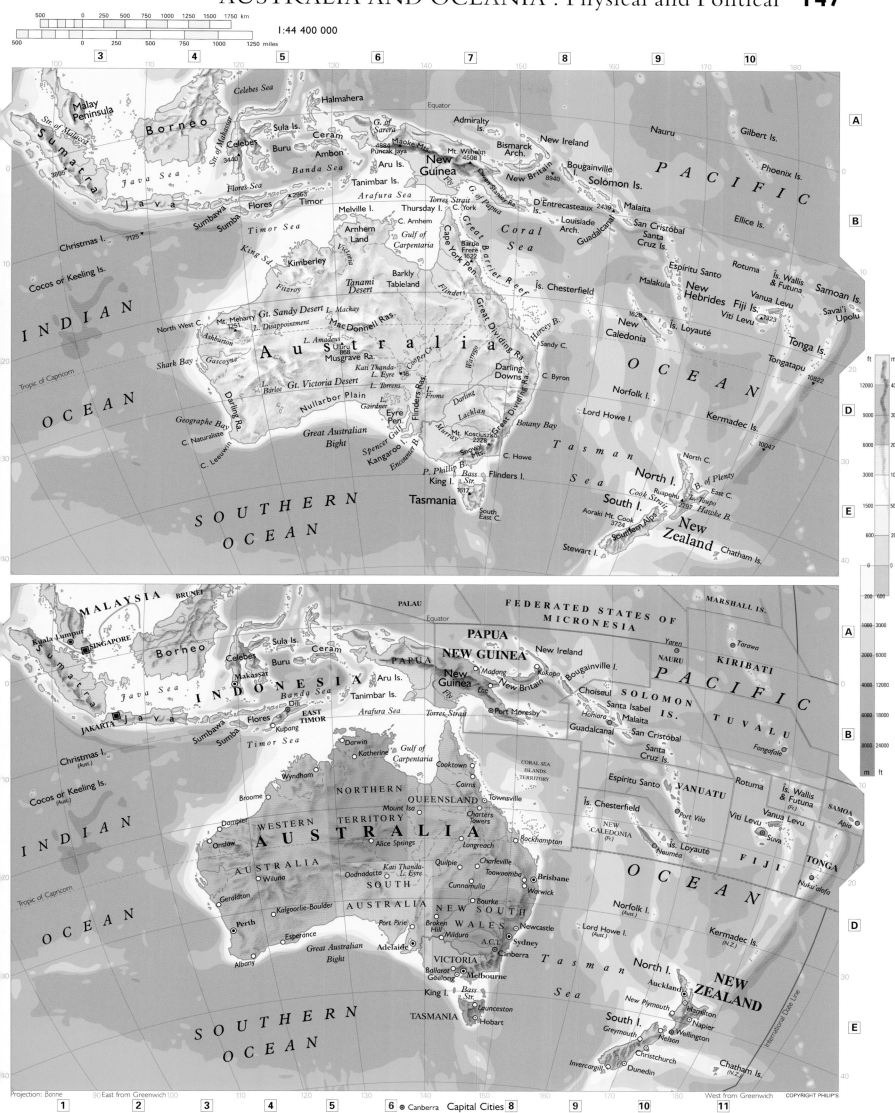

Scale 1:44 400 000

500 0 250 500 750 1000 1250 1500 1750 km
500 0 250 500 750 1000 1250 miles

Physical Map (top)

3   4   5   6   7   8   9   10

A   **B**   **D**   **E**

Malay Peninsula, Borneo, Celebes Sea, Str. of Makassar, Halmahera, Equator, Admiralty Is., New Ireland, Nauru, Gilbert Is., PACIFIC

Sumatra, Str. of Malacca, Celebes, Buru, Ceram, Ambon, Banda Sea, G. of Sarera, Maoke Mts. 4884, Puncak Jaya, Aru Is., New Guinea, Fly, Mt. Wilhelm 4508, Owen Stanley Ra., Bismarck Arch., New Britain 8940, Bougainville I., Solomon Is., Phoenix Is.

Java, Java Sea, Flores Sea, Sula Is., Flores, Timor 2963, Arafura Sea, Tanimbar Is., Melville I., Thursday I., C. York, C. Arnhem, Torres Strait, G. of Papua, Bartle Frere 1622, D'Entrecasteaux 2439, Malaita, Louisiade Arch., Guadalcanal, San Cristóbal, Santa Cruz Is., Coral Sea, Ellice Is.

Christmas I., 7125, Timor Sea, King Sd., Arnhem Land, Victoria, Gulf of Carpentaria, Cape York Pen., Great Barrier Reef, Îs. Chesterfield, Malakula, Espíritu Santo, New Hebrides, Rotuma, Îs. Wallis & Futuna, Samoan Is.

Cocos or Keeling Is., Kimberley, Fitzroy, Tanami Desert, Barkly Tableland, Flinders, Great Dividing Ra., Vanua Levu, Fiji Is., Viti Levu 1323, Savai'i, Upolu

INDIAN OCEAN, Gt. Sandy Desert, L. Mackay, Mt. Meharry 1251, L. Disappointment, MacDonnell Ras., L. Amadeus, Uluru 868, Musgrave Ra., Australia, Warrego, Hervey B., Sandy C., New Caledonia, 1628, Îs. Loyauté, OCEAN

North West C., Ashburton, Shark Bay, Gascoyne, Darling Ra., Geographe Bay, L. Barlee, Gt. Victoria Desert, Kati Thanda-L. Eyre 16, L. Torrens, Cooper Cr., Darling, Lachlan, Norfolk I., Tonga Is., 10822, Tongatapu

Tropic of Capricorn, Nullarbor Plain, Gairdner, Eyre Pen., Flinders Ras., L. Frome, Murray, Mt. Kosciuszko 2228, Snowy Mts., Botany Bay, C. Byron, Darling Downs, Lord Howe I., Tasman Sea

C. Naturaliste, C. Leeuwin, Great Australian Bight, Spencer Gulf, Kangaroo I., Encounter B., P. Phillip B., King I. 1617, Bass Str., Flinders I., C. Howe, Kermadec Is., 10047, North C., B. of Plenty, Ruapehu 2797, L. Taupo, East C., Hawke B.

SOUTHERN OCEAN, Tasmania, South East C., Stewart I., Aoraki Mt. Cook 3724, Southern Alps, North I., South I., New Zealand, Cook Strait, Chatham Is.

Political Map (bottom)

1   2   3   4   5   6   7   8   9   10   11

A   **B**   **D**   **E**

MALAYSIA, BRUNEI, PALAU, Equator, FEDERATED STATES OF MICRONESIA, MARSHALL IS.

Kuala Lumpur, SINGAPORE, Borneo, Celebes, Buru, Ceram, PAPUA, PAPUA NEW GUINEA, New Ireland, Yaren, Tarawa, NAURU, KIRIBATI, PACIFIC

Sumatra, INDONESIA, Sula Is., Aru Is., New Guinea, Madang, Kokopo, Bougainville I., Choiseul, SOLOMON IS., Santa Isabel

JAKARTA, Java, Java Sea, Makassar, Banda Sea, Dili, EAST TIMOR, Tanimbar Is., Fly, Lae, Port Moresby, Hohiara, Malaita, San Cristóbal, TUVALU

Christmas I. (Aust.), Sumbawa, Sumba, Flores, Kupang, Timor Sea, Arafura Sea, Torres Strait, Guadalcanal, Santa Cruz Is., Fongafale

Cocos or Keeling Is. (Aust.), Darwin, Katherine, Gulf of Carpentaria, Cooktown, Espíritu Santo, VANUATU, Rotuma, Îs. Wallis & Futuna (Fr.), SAMOA

INDIAN OCEAN, Broome, Wyndham, NORTHERN TERRITORY, Cairns, QUEENSLAND, Townsville, CORAL SEA ISLANDS TERRITORY, Îs. Chesterfield, Port Vila, Viti Levu, Vanua Levu, Apia

Dampier, WESTERN AUSTRALIA, Mount Isa, Charters Towers, NEW CALEDONIA (Fr.), Îs. Loyauté, Suva, FIJI, TONGA

Onslow, Alice Springs, Longreach, Rockhampton, Nouméa, Nuku'alofa

Tropic of Capricorn, Wiluna, Oodnadatta, Kati Thanda-L. Eyre, SOUTH, Quilpie, Charleville, Toowoomba, Brisbane, Norfolk I. (Aust.), OCEAN

Geraldton, Kalgoorlie-Boulder, AUSTRALIA, Cunnamulla, Warwick, Bourke, Lord Howe I. (Aust.), Kermadec Is. (N.Z.)

Perth, Port Pirie, Broken Hill, NEW SOUTH WALES, Mildura, Newcastle, Tasman Sea, North I.

Esperance, Adelaide, A.C.T., Sydney, Canberra, NEW ZEALAND, Auckland

Albany, Great Australian Bight, VICTORIA, Ballarat, Geelong, Melbourne, New Plymouth, Hamilton, Napier

King I., Bass Str., Launceston, South I., Greymouth, Nelson, Wellington

SOUTHERN OCEAN, TASMANIA, Hobart, Invercargill, Dunedin, Christchurch, Chatham Is. (N.Z.)

Projection: Bonne, 90 East from Greenwich 100, West from Greenwich, International Date Line

1:7 100 000

151

E   F   G

1   2   3   4   5

COPYRIGHT PHILIP'S

Projection: Bonne

East from Greenwich

Aboriginal lands

1. NGALIWURRU/ NUNGALI
2. WINIMIYN
3. WIMBARDN
4. LIIALALTUMA
5. RODNA
6. NTARLA
7. ROULPMALAULPMA
8. URUNA

SOUTH
AUSTRALIA

INDIAN
OCEAN

SOUTHERN

OCEAN

Great Victoria Desert

Great Australian Bight

Nullarbor Plain

Nullarbor Tableland

Hampton Tableland

SPINIFEX

CENTRAL DESERT

ANANGU PITJANTJATJARA

MARALINGA TJARUTJA

YALATA

Uluru (Ayers Rock) KATA TJUTA

Petermann Ranges

Musgrave Ranges

Mann Ranges

Everard Ranges

MUNGILLI

WARBURTON

NGAANYATJARRA

YAPURARRA

NGAANYATJARRA

TJIRRKARLI

Ernest Giles Ra.

WINDIDDA

Carnarvon Ra.

Robinson Ra.

Barr Smith Ra.

Waldburg Ra.

MT JAMES

KENNEDY RANGE

Gascoyne R.

SHARK BAY

FRANCOIS PERON

PERTH

Fremantle

Mandurah

Rockingham

Bunbury

Busselton

Geraldton

Kalbarri

Albany

Esperance

Norseman

Kalgoorlie
Boulder

Coolgardie

Kambalda

Leonora

Leinster

Laverton

Wiluna

Meekatharra

Mount Magnet

Cue

Sandstone

Menzies

GOONGARRIE

Southern Cross

Merredin

Northam

Midland

Armadale

Katanning

Nullarbor

Eucla

Madura

Cocklebiddy

Caiguna

Balladonia

Norseman

TRANS-AUSTRALIAN RWY

EYRE HWY

GREAT NORTHERN HWY

GREAT NORTHERN HWY

WESTERN HWY

COASTAL HWY

NORTHWEST COASTAL HWY

STIRLING RANGE

FRANKLAND

FITZGERALD RIVER

STOKES

CAPE ARID

CAPE LE GRAND

PEAK CHARLES

FRANK HANN

Archipelago of the Recherche

m   ft
3000   1000
1200   400
600   200
0   0

ft
6000   18 000
4000   12 000
2000   6000
1000   3000
400   1200
200   600
0   0

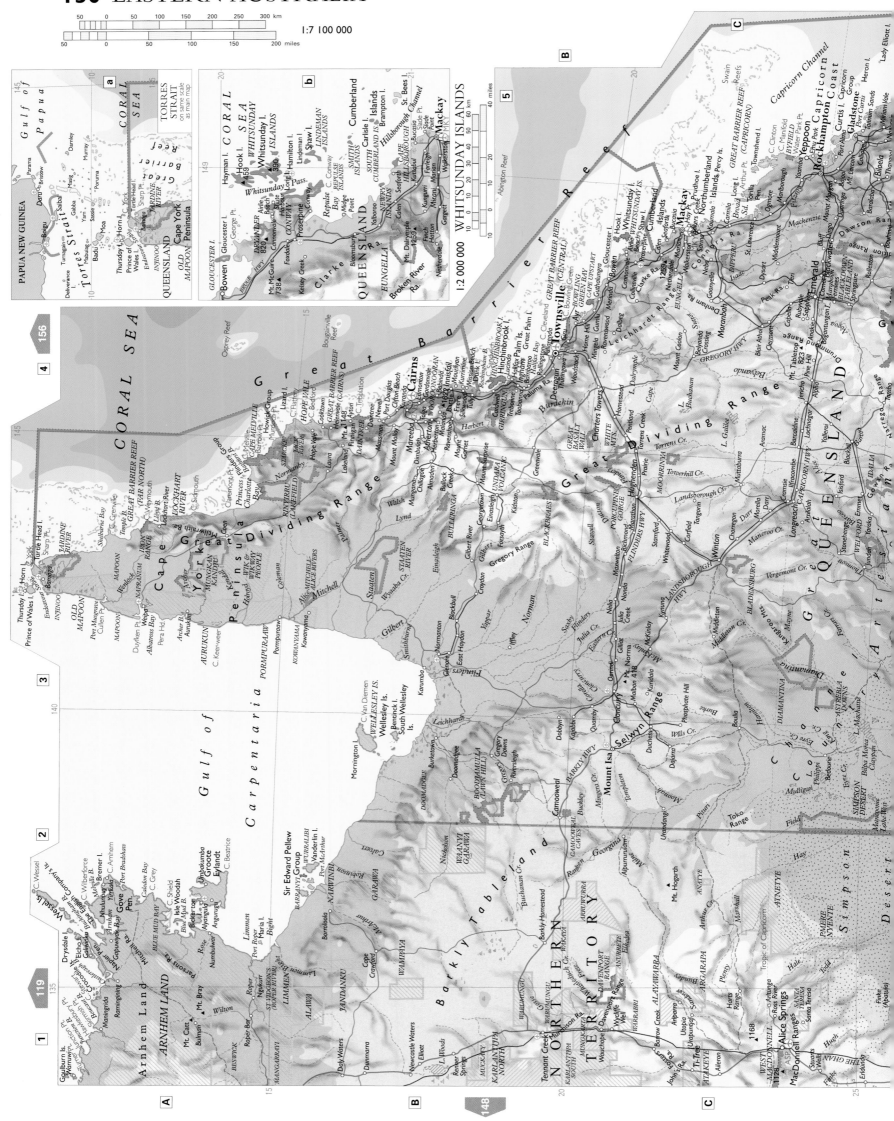

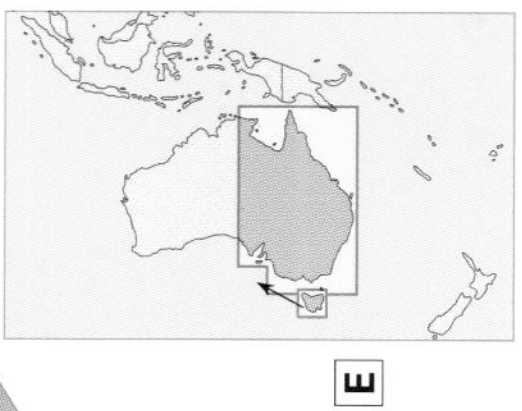

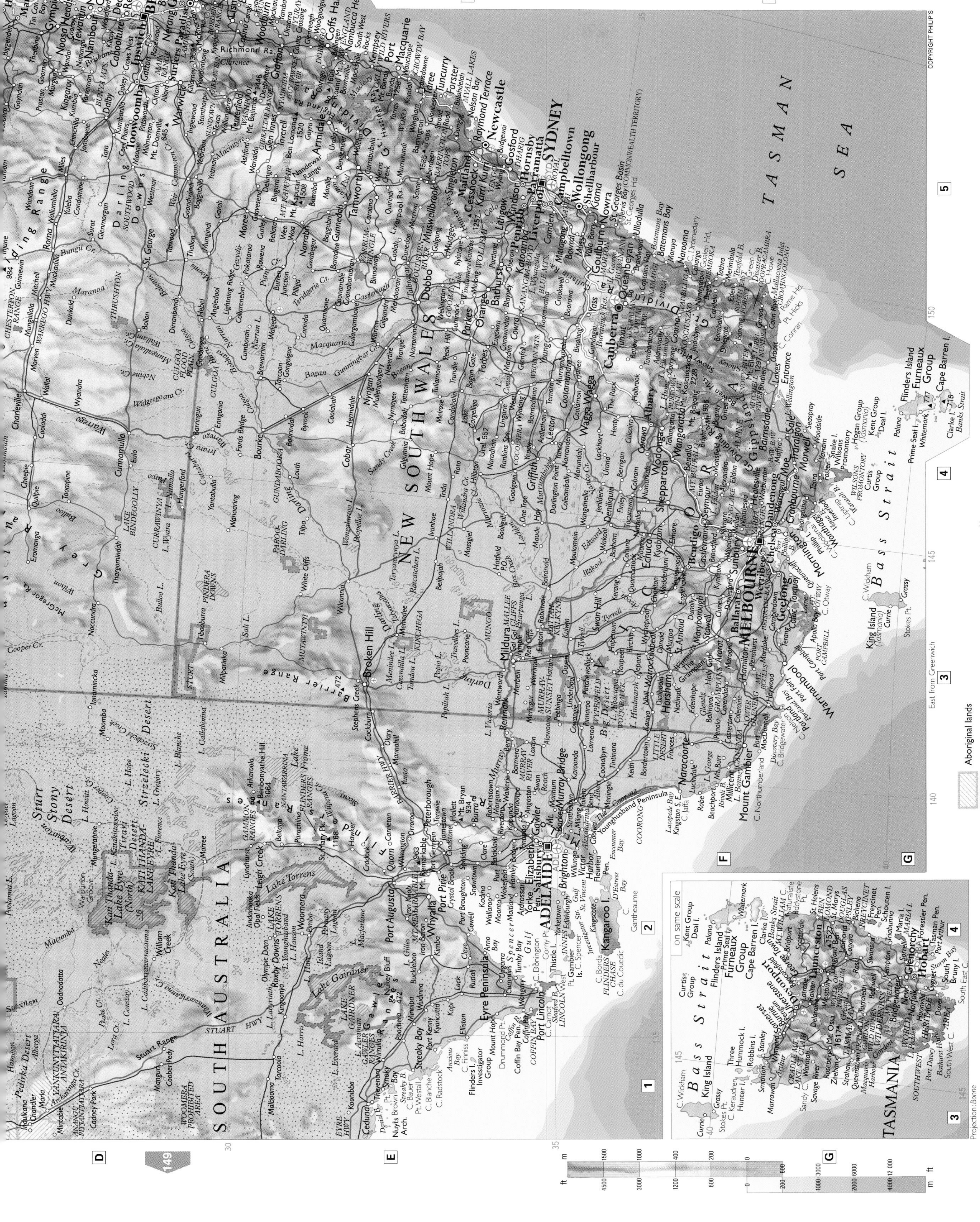

TASMAN SEA

NEW SOUTH WALES

SOUTH AUSTRALIA

QUEENSLAND

VICTORIA

TASMANIA

Bass Strait

Great Dividing Range

Darling Range

Grey Range

Barrier Range

Flinders Ranges

Gammon Ranges

Sturt Stony Desert

Strzelecki Desert

Tirari Desert

Simpson Desert

Sturt Desert

BRISBANE
SYDNEY
MELBOURNE
ADELAIDE
Canberra
Newcastle
Wollongong
Hobart

Sunshine Coast
Gold Coast
Coral Coast
Hervey Bay
Maryborough
Gympie
Noosa Heads
Nambour
Caloundra
Caboolture
Redcliffe
Ipswich
Toowoomba
Warwick
Tweed Heads
Surfers Paradise
Southport
Byron Bay
Ballina
Lismore
Grafton
Coffs Harbour
Port Macquarie
Taree
Forster
Raymond Terrace
Gosford
Hornsby
Parramatta
Liverpool
Campbelltown
Katoomba
Penrith
Windsor
Kurri Kurri
Cessnock
Maitland
Singleton
Muswellbrook
Scone
Tamworth
Armidale
Inverell
Moree
Narrabri
Gunnedah
Dubbo
Orange
Bathurst
Lithgow
Parkes
Forbes
Cowra
Young
Goulburn
Queanbeyan
Nowra
Kiama
Shellharbour
Bowral
Mittagong
Batemans Bay
Narooma
Cooma
Bega
Eden
Wagga Wagga
Albury
Wodonga
Griffith
Leeton
Narrandera
Deniliquin
Cobar
Bourke
Broken Hill
Wentworth
Mildura
Swan Hill
Echuca
Shepparton
Benalla
Wangaratta
Bendigo
Castlemaine
Maryborough
Ballarat
Geelong
Colac
Warrnambool
Portland
Mount Gambier
Naracoorte
Horsham
Stawell
Ararat
Hamilton
Sale
Bairnsdale
Traralgon
Morwell
Moe
Warragul
Dandenong
Frankston
Mornington
Werribee
Sunbury
Melton
Port Augusta
Port Pirie
Whyalla
Port Lincoln
Ceduna
Gawler
Elizabeth
Salisbury
Victor Harbor
Murray Bridge
Kangaroo I.
Eyre Peninsula
Yorke Peninsula
Spencer Gulf
Gulf St Vincent
Lake Eyre
Lake Torrens
Lake Gairdner
Lake Frome
Lake Blanche
Lake Callabonna
Cooper Cr.
Diamantina
Murray River
Darling River
Murrumbidgee River
Lachlan River

King Island
Flinders Island
Furneaux Group
Cape Barren I.
Launceston
Devonport
Burnie

Aboriginal lands

COPYRIGHT PHILIPS

East from Greenwich

Projection: Bonne

1:3 500 000

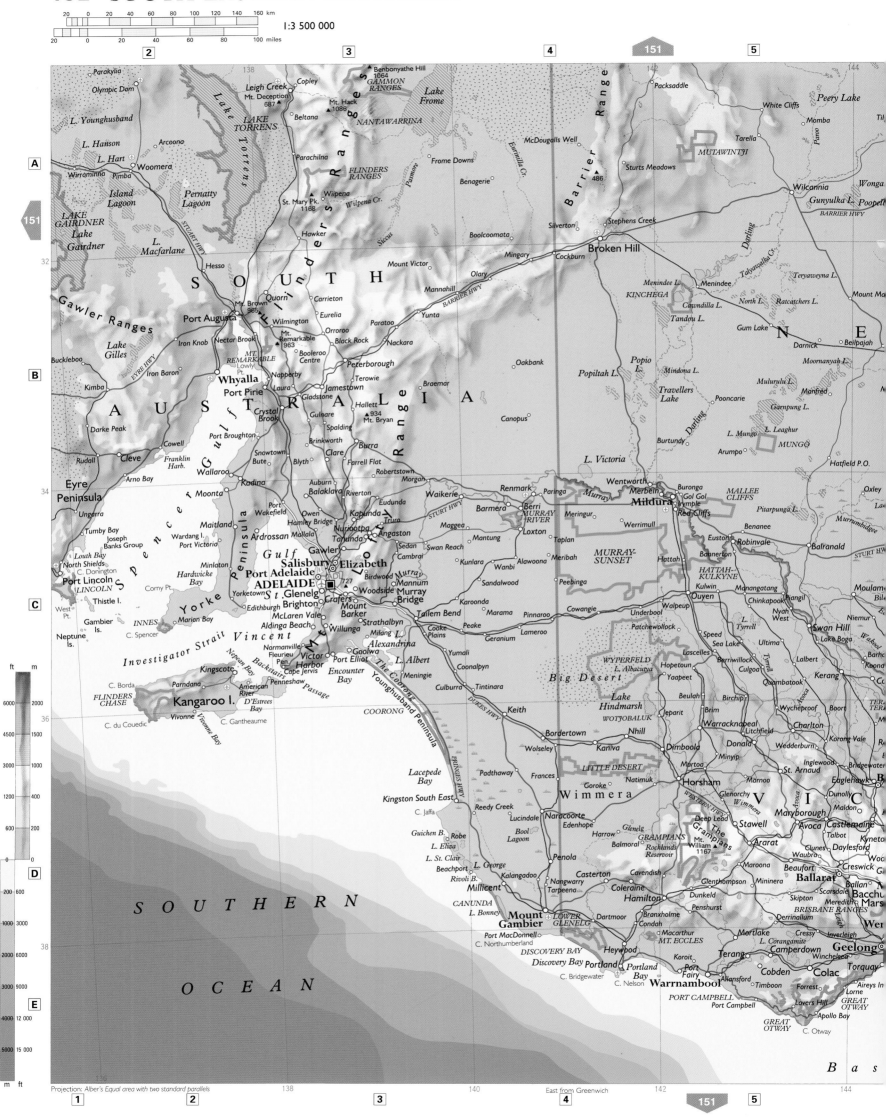

Projection: Alber's Equal area with two standard parallels

East from Greenwich

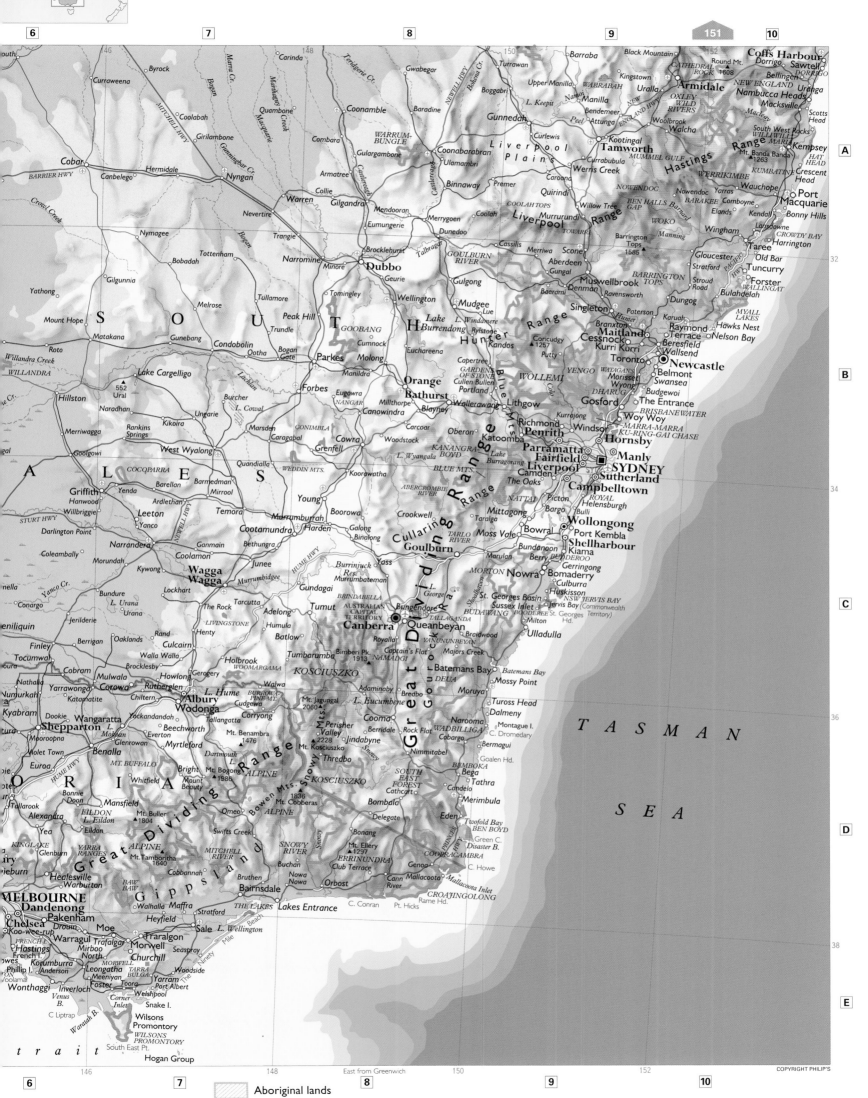

Aboriginal lands

10 0 20 40 60 80 100 120 140 km
10 0 20 40 60 80 100 miles

1:3 100 000

1 **2** **3** **4**

FIJI **a**

1:5 300 000

50 0 50 100 150 200 km
50 0 50 100 150 n

FIJI inset

PACIFIC OCEAN

Great Sea Reef Kia Udu Pt. Ringgold Is.
Yaqaga Labasa Natewa Bay Rabi
Vanua Levu 1031 Buca Qamea
Yadua Biua Savusavu Somosomo **Taveuni**
Yasawa Group Yasawa Nacula Nabouwalu Nasau Koro Vacata Kanacea Naitaba
Viwa Vomo Naviti BOUMA Mago Vanua Balavu
Waya Wakaya Makogai Vatu Vara Northern Lau Group
Malolo Lautoka Naval 1323 Lawaki Levuka **Ovalau** Cicia Tuvuca
Mamanuca Group Nadi KOROYANITU Korovou Yanuca Batiki Nairai Lakeba Passage Lakeba Tubou
Sigatoka Keiyasi Navua Nausori Gau Nayau Oneata
Viti Levu Korolevu **Suva** **FIJI** Moce
Vatulele Yanuca Beqa Moala Vanua Vatu Namuka-i-Lau Yagasa Cluster
Kadavu Passage Ono Totoya Kabara Fulaga Ogea Levu
Kadavu Tavuki Vunisea Matuku Ogea Driki
East from Greenwich West from Greenwich

North Island

C. Reinga Waitiki Landing North C.
C. Maria van Diemen Parengarenga Harbour
Houhora Heads Rangaunu B. C. Karikari
Awanui Mangonui Doubtless B. Cavalli Is.
Ahipara B. **Kaitaia** Kaeo Whangaroa Harb.
Herekino Kerikeri Paihia Russell B. of Islands C. Brett
Kohukohu Okaihau Opua Kawakawa Poor Knights Is.
Rawene Kaikohe Moerewa Whangaruru Harb.
NORTHLAND 744 Hikurangi
Hokianga Harbour 781 Kamo **Whangarei** Onerahi Whangarei Harb.
Omapere Waipoua Forest Kirikopuni Morsden Point Bream B. Hen & Chickens Is.
Donnelly's Crossing Wairoa Waiotira Bream Hd.
Aranga Waikiekie Waipu Maungaturoto Bream Tail Needles Pt.
Dargaville Paparoa Little Barrier I. 722 627 Port Fitzroy
Ruawai Te Kopuru Wellsford Matakana Tryphena Great Barrier I.
Warkworth Kawau I. 722 C. Barrier
Snells Beach C. Colville 892 Cuvier I. Port Charles
Helensville Whangaparaoa Pen. Coromandel Mercury Is.
AUCKLAND **Takapuna** Ostend Mercury B. Whitianga
Muriwai Beach **AUCKLAND** Waiheke I. Coromandel Pen.
Piha Howick Mount Wellington Tairua
Onehunga Otahuhu 846 Pauanui
Papatoetoe Manukau Harbour Papakura Firth of Thames Thames Whangamata
Manukau **Pukekohe** Waihi Mayor I.
Waiuku Tuakau Mercer Waihi Beach **BAY OF PLENTY**
Waikato Te Kauwhata L. Waikare Katikati Whakaari (White I.)
WAIKATO Huntly Te Aroha Tauranga Harb. C. Runaway Hicks Bay
Glen Afton Ngaruawahia Morrinsville Matakana I. **Tauranga** Te Araroa
Glen Massey Raglan **Hamilton** Waharoa Mount Maunganui East C.
Raglan Harbour Ohaupo **Cambridge** Matamata Te Puke **Bay of Plenty** Te Kaha 1067 1753
Aotea Harbour Te Awamutu Karapiro Paengaroa Matata Edgecumbe **Whakatane** Ohiwa Harbour Hikurangi
Kawhia Kihikihi Leamington Arapuni Tirau L. Rotorua Opotiki Ruatoria
Kawhia Harbour Otorohanga Putaruru Mamaku Kawerau Taneatua Raukumara Ra. Waipiro Bay
Albatross Pt. Waitomo Caves Tokoroa Ngongotaha **Rotorua** L. Tarawera L. Teko Tokomaru Bay
Te Kuiti Kinleith 1111 Mt. Tarawera **GISBORNE** Tolaga Bay
Tirua Pt. Mangakino Waiotapu UREWERA Matawai Puha
Herangi Ra. Aria Atiamuri Murupara Galatea Te Karaka Ormond
Mokau Ongarue 1185 Whakamaru Wairakei Ngatapa **Gisborne**
North Taranaki Bight Ohura Okahukura Mokai Taupo Rangitaiki 1392 L. Waikareiti Tuaheni Pt.
Pukearuhe Manunui Tokaanu 369 L. Taupo Waikaremoana Tuai Poverty B.
Waitara Taumarunui Turangi Rangitaiki 1383 Mohaka Frasertown
New Plymouth Tahora Owhango Mt. Tongariro 1968 Ahimanawa Ra. Nuhaka Waikokopu
Okato Inglewood Egmont Whangamomona Mt. Ngauruhoe 2291 Tarawera 403 Table C.
TARANAKI Huiroa TONGARIRO 1726 Putorino Mahia Pen.
Mt. Taranaki or Mt. Egmont 2518 Midhirst Ruapehu 2797 Kaweka Ra. Wairoa Portland I.
C. Egmont Stratford Ohakune Rangataua Portland I. Mahia Pen.
Rahotu Kaponga Eltham Raetihi Waiouru Bay View Hawke Bay
EGMONT Opunake Normanby 746 Pipiriki Taradale **Napier**
Manaia **Hawera** Ohakune Taihape Clive
South Taranaki Bight Pated Waverley Maxwell Mangaweka 1733 **Hastings** C. Kidnappers
Waitotara Hunterville Mangaweka Havelock North
Wanganui Apiti Opapa **HAWKE'S BAY**
Castlecliff Turakina Marton Norsewood Otane Waipawa
Bulls Halcombe Takapau Waipukurau Wanstead
MANAWATU-WANGANUI Feilding Ormondville **Dannevirke** C. Turnagain
Rangitikei Bunnythorpe Ashurst Woodville Porangahau
112 Rongotea Longburn Pahiatua Weber Herbertville
Palmerston North Foxton Shannon Eketahuna Alfredton Mauriceville
Manawatu Levin Woodville **PACIFIC**
Golden Bay C. Farewell Otaki Tinui **OCEAN**
Collingwood Farewell Spit Stephens I. Kapiti I. Castlepoint
Takaka Separation Pt. Rangitoto ke te tonga (D'Urville I.) **Paraparaumu** Mt. Mitre Mauriceville
Kahurangi Pt. Devil River Pk. 1780 French Pass **Porirua** Carterton **Masterton**
Riwaka Tasman Bay Pelorus Sd. **Lower Hutt** **Upper Hutt** Greytown
Motueka 1203 Forsyth I. **Wellington** Featherston Martinborough
KAHURANGI Karamea **NELSON** Queen Charlotte Sd. Johnsonville Petone L. Wairarapa **WELLINGTON**
Karamea 1780 Brightwater Havelock Pelorus Arapawa Eastbourne 665 Flat Pt.
Mokihinui Tadmor **Nelson** Stoke Pigeon Terawhiti Wainuiomata L. Onoke
Mt. Owen 1875 Wakefield Richmond Ra. **Blenheim** Ruamahanga Palliser B.
Glenhope Belgrove 1756 Tuamarina Pelorus C. Palliser
Lyell Richmond Ra. Renwick Port Nicholson Aorangi 981 Mts. C. Palliser
TASMAN NELSON LAKES 2120 Cloudy B. Eastbourne
Murchison Butler L. Rotoiti 1780 Seddon 3122
Glenhope Karamea Awatere Ward

TASMAN SEA

PACIFIC OCEAN

ft m (elevation scale) 9000 3000 / 6000 2000 / 3000 1000 / 1200 400 / 600 200 / 0 0 / 200 600 / 1000 3000 / 1500 4500 / 3000 9000 m ft

1:3 100 000

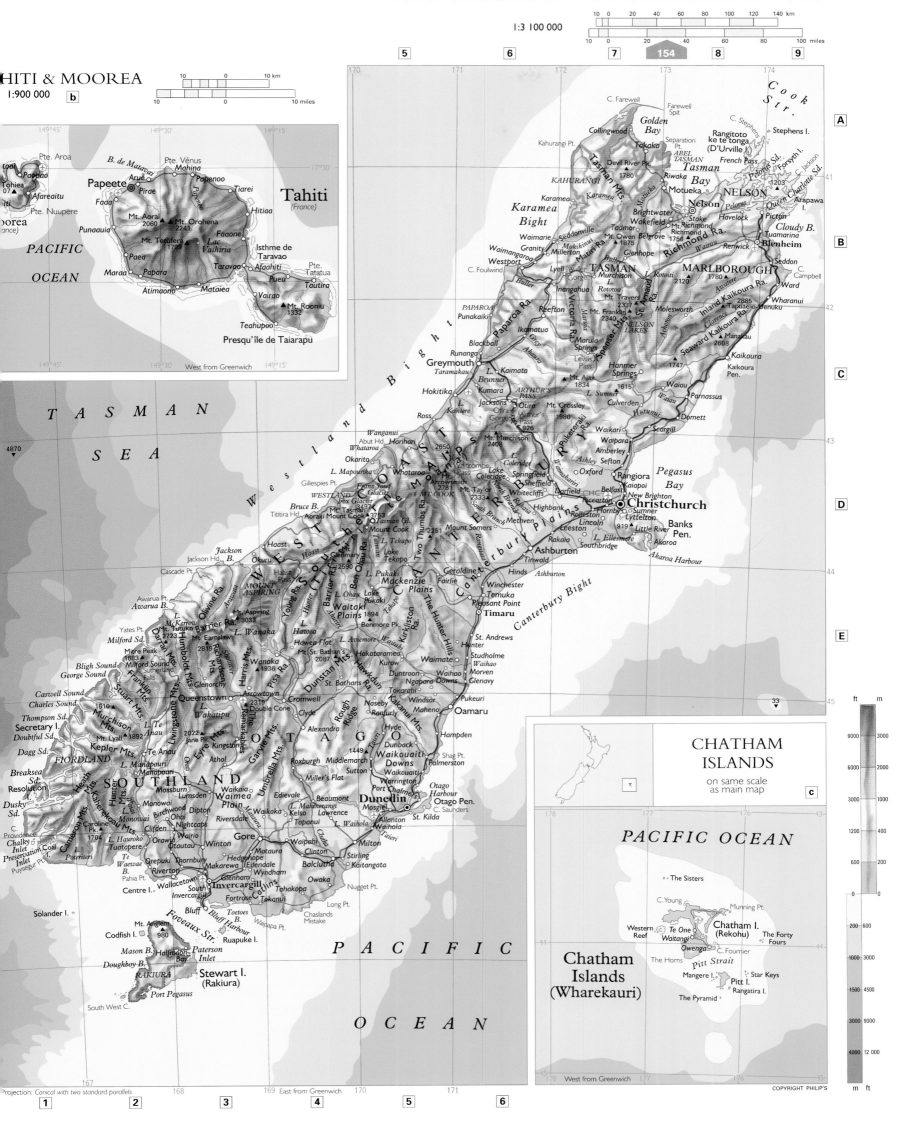

TAHITI & MOOREA
1:900 000

Tahiti
(France)

PACIFIC OCEAN

Presqu'île de Taiarapu

CHATHAM ISLANDS
on same scale as main map

PACIFIC OCEAN

Chatham Islands (Wharekauri)

COPYRIGHT PHILIP'S

Projection: Conical with two standard parallels

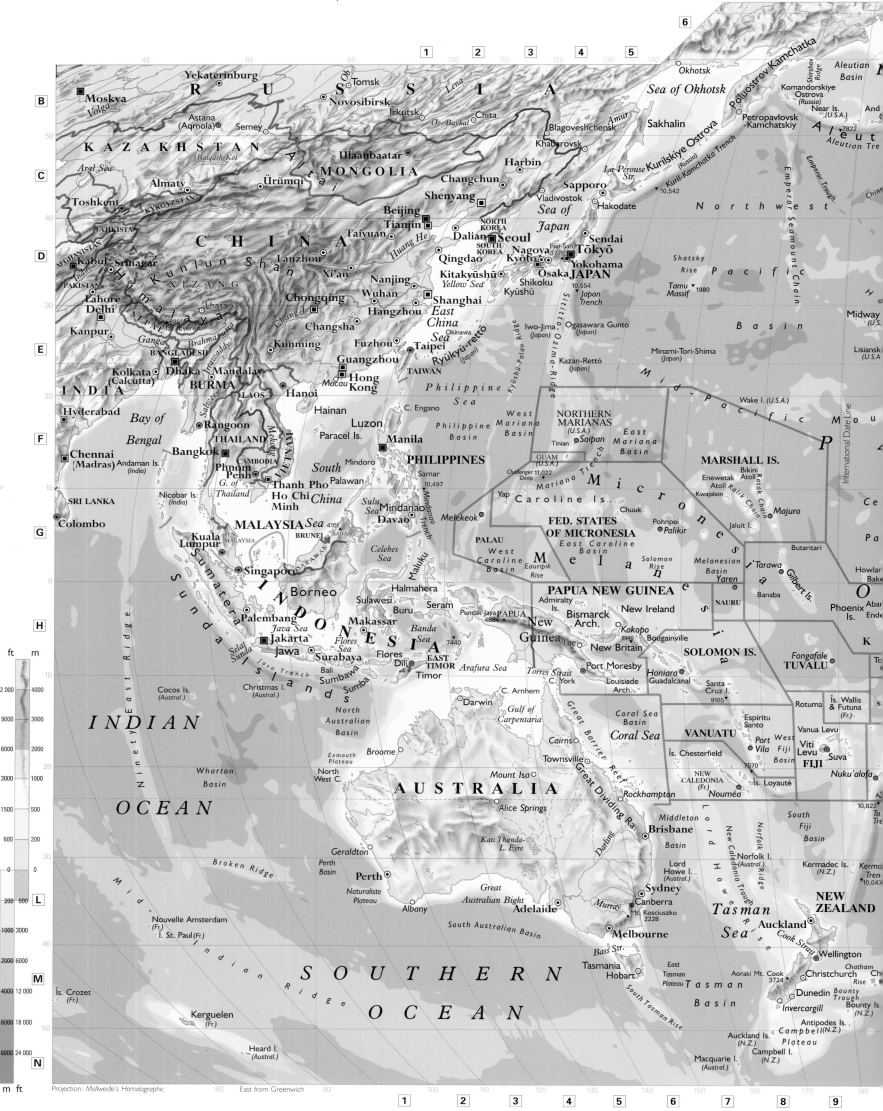

ft m

12 000 4000

9000 3000

6000 2000

3000 1000

1500 500

600 200

0 0

200 600

1000 3000

2000 6000

4000 12 000

6000 18 000

8000 24 000

m ft

Projection: Mollweide's Homalographic   East from Greenwich

12 13 14 15 16 17 18 19 20

Arctic Circle

ALASKA
(U.S.A.)
Anchorage
6959
Juneau

ol Bay
(U.S.A.)

Gulf of Alaska

Prince of Wales I.
(U.S.A.) Prince Rupert
Haida Gwaii
(Queen Charlotte Is.)
(Canada)
Tufts
Abyssal
Plain

CANADA

Edmonton

Calgary

L. Winnipeg

Winnipeg

Newfoundland

Vancouver
Vancouver I.
Victoria
Seattle
Portland
Boise
Snake

Regina

L. Superior

Minneapolis

Québec
Montréal
Ottawa
Toronto
Detroit
Chicago
Buffalo
Boston

St. Lawrence

St. John's

ortheast

Mendocino Fracture Zone C. Mendocino

Salt Lake
City
Denver
Kansas City
St. Louis
Pittsburgh

L. Michigan
L. Huron
L. Ontario
L. Erie

New York
Philadelphia
Baltimore
Washington D.C.

6741

Sacramento
San Francisco

Murray Fracture Zone

4418

UNITED STATES
Oklahoma City
Memphis

Cincinnati

Atlanta

C. Hatteras

ATLANTIC

Pacific

Los Angeles
San Diego

Phoenix
Dallas

Houston

Mississippi

Appalachian Mts.

Bermuda
(U.K.)

Guadalupe
(Mex.)

Molokai Fracture Zone

Ciudad
Juárez

San Antonio

New
Orleans

Monterrey

Tampa

Sargasso Sea

OCEAN

Basin

Tropic of Cancer

Ridge

Kauai
Honolulu
Oahu Maui
HAWAIIAN IS.
(U.S.A.)
Hilo Hawaii
4205

C. San Lucas

Gulf of Mexico
Miami

La Habana
Canal de Yucatán

BAHAMAS

West Indies

I.

Clarion Fracture Zone Is. Revilla Gigedo
(Mex.)

Guadalajara

Mexico
5610 Puebla

Mérida

JAMAICA

HAITI
8605
DOMINICAN REP.

Leeward
Is.

IFIC

Acapulco
6662

Î. Clipperton
(Fr.)

GUATEMALA
Guatemala
San Salvador
EL SALVADOR

Middle America Trench

Managua

BELIZE

HONDURAS
NICARAGUA

Caribbean Sea

Kingston

PUERTO
RICO
(U.S.A.)

BARBADOS
Windward Is.

Barranquilla
Maracaibo

Caracas

west Christmas Ridge

Imyra Is.
(U.S.A.)

Teraina
Tabuaeran
Kiritimati

Clipperton Fracture Zone

Guatemala
Basin

COSTA
RICA
Colón
PANAMA

San José
Panamá
Panama
Basin

I. del Coco
(Costa Rica)

Medellín

COSTA
Cocos Ridge

I. de Malpelo
(Colombia)

Cali
Bogotá

Orinoco

VENEZUELA

EAN

Jarvis I.
(U.S.A.)

Equator

Galápagos Fracture Zone

Galápagos
(Ecuador)

Carnegie Ridge

Quito
ECUADOR

COLOMBIA

A

Line Islands

Malden I.
Starbuck I.

Guayaquil

C. Pariñas

Iquitos

BRAZIL

ATI

Penrhyn
(Tongareva)

Manihiki
ukapuka
Manihiki
Suwarrow Is.

Vostok I.
Flint I.

Caroline I.
(Millennium I.)

Nuku Hiva

Îs. Marquises
Hiva Oa

Marquesas Fracture Zone

Yupanqui
Basin

Mendaña
Fracture Zone

6369

Trujillo

PERU

Galapagos Rise

Lima

Plateau

Îs. de la Société
Bora Bora
Huahine
Raiatea Tahiti
Papeete

Rangiroa

Îs. Tuamotu

Cusco
L. Titicaca

Nazca Ridge

Cook Is.
(N.Z.)
Aitutaki
Atiu
Rarotonga
Mangaia

Îs. Tubuai

FRENCH POLYNESIA

Îs. Gambier
Mururoa

Tuamotu

Arequipa

6866
Peru-

Arica

Nevado Ancohuma
6550

La Paz

BOLIVIA

Austral

Seamount Chain

Ridge

Tropic of Capricorn

Iquique
Chile

Antofagasta

PARAGUAY

Asunción

Oeno I.
Henderson I.
Pitcairn I. Ducie I.
(U.K.)

Rapa

Easter Fracture Zone

Sala-y-Gómez
(Chile)

I. de Pascua
(Chile)

Sala-y-Gómez Ridge

San Felix
(Chile)

San Ambrosio
(Chile)

8050

San Miguel
de Tucumán

Pôrto
Alegre

Roggeveen
Basin

Arch. de
Juan Fernández
(Chile)

Córdoba
Aconcagua
6962
Valparaíso
Santiago
Concepción

Rosario

URUGUAY

Buenos
Aires

Montevideo

Río de la Plata

Southwest

Pacific

Challenger Fracture Zone

Chile Rise

ARGENTINA

ATLANTIC

Basin

Menard Fracture Zone

OCEAN

6212

Patagonia

Pacific-Antarctic Ridge

East Pacific Rise

Southeast
Pacific Basin

Punta Arenas
Tierra del Fuego
C. de Hornos
Drake Passage

Est. de Magallanes

Falkland Is.
(U.K.)

South Georgia
(U.K.)

100 0 200 400 600 800 1000 1200 1400 km

1:31 100 000

100 0 200 400 600 800 1000 miles

Projection: Bonne

West from Greenwich

COPYRIGHT PHILIP'S

1:31 100 000

100 0 200 400 600 800 1000 1200 1400 km

100 0 200 400 600 800 1000 miles

C

B A B

RUSSIA

Asia

Bering
Sea

St. Lawrence
I.

Bering Strait

ARCTIC

OCEAN

International Date Line

Beaufort
Sea

70

80

Queen Elizabeth Is.

Ellesmere I.

GREENLAND

(Denmark)

Denmark Strait

ICELAND

Reykjavík

60

Baffin
Bay

Davis Strait

Nuuk

D

ALASKA
(USA)

Yukon

Anchorage

Fairbanks

Porcupine

Arctic Circle

Kodiak I.

Gulf of
Alaska

Whitehorse

Juneau

YUKON
TERRITORY

NORTHWEST

Mackenzie

Great Bear
L.

TERRITORIES

Yellowknife

Great
Slave L.

Liard

Back

Dubawnt

Victoria I.

NUNAVUT

Baffin Island

Iqaluit

Hudson Strait

Hudson

Bay

50

E

BRITISH

COLUMBIA

Skeena

Fraser

Peace

Athabasca

Athabasca

ALBERTA

Edmonton

Calgary

Saskatchewan

CANADA

Churchill

Nelson

MANITOBA

SASKATCHEWAN

L.
Winnipeg

D

NEWFOUNDLAND &

LABRADOR

Eastmain

QUÉBEC

St. Lawrence

St. John's

St-Pierre
et Miquelon
(Fr.)

PRINCE
EDWARD

Charlottetown

NOVA
SCOTIA

Halifax

NEW
BRUNSWICK

Fredericton

Québec

Montréal

40

F

Victoria

Vancouver

WASHINGTON

Olympia

Seattle

Portland

Salem

OREGON

Columbia

IDAHO

Boise

Snake

MONTANA

Helena

Missouri

WYOMING

ONTARIO

Winnipeg

Regina

NORTH
DAKOTA

Bismarck

SOUTH
DAKOTA

NEBRASKA

MINNESOTA

Minneapolis-
St. Paul

WISCONSIN

IOWA

Madison

L. Superior

L. Huron

L. Michigan

MICHIGAN

Milwaukee

Lansing

CHICAGO

ILLINOIS

INDIANA

Detroit

Toledo

OHIO

Cleveland

Columbus

L. Ontario

TORONTO

Buffalo

L. Erie

Pittsburgh

PA.

NEW YORK

Ottawa

VER.

N.H.

MAINE

Augusta

Concord

MASS.

Hartford

Boston

Providence

NEW YORK

PHILADELPHIA

N.J.

Baltimore

WASHINGTON D.C.

MD.

DEL.

30

G

Sacramento

SAN FRANCISCO

San Jose

CALIFORNIA

NEVADA

Carson
City

Salt Lake
City

UTAH

Denver

COLORADO

Lincoln

KANSAS

Topeka

Kansas City

MISSOURI

St.
Louis

Springfield

Indianapolis

Cincinnati

KENTUCKY

Nashville

TENNESSEE

Memphis

VIRGINIA

W.V.

Richmond

Raleigh

NORTH
CAROLINA

Charlotte

Columbia

SOUTH
CAROLINA

Charleston

Bermuda
(U.K.)

ATLANTIC

OCEAN

LOS ANGELES

Las Vegas

San Diego

Tijuana

Santa Fe

ARIZONA

Phoenix

Tucson

Mexicali

NEW MEXICO

Albuquerque

OKLAHOMA

Oklahoma
City

Little Rock

ARKANSAS

Birmingham

MISSISSIPPI

ALABAMA

Montgomery

GEORGIA

ATLANTA

Jacksonville

PACIFIC

OCEAN

Guadalupe
(Mex.)

El Paso

Ciudad Juárez

TEXAS

DALLAS-
FT. WORTH

Austin

HOUSTON

Baton
Rouge

Jackson

LOUISIANA

New
Orleans

Tallahassee

FLORIDA

Orlando

Tampa-
St. Petersburg

MIAMI

Nassau

Florida Str.

BAHAMAS

Turks & Caicos Is.
(U.K.)

20

Tropic of Cancer

Culiacán

Hermosillo

San Antonio

Rio Grande

Monterrey

Torreón

Gulf of Mexico

Havana

CUBA

Cayman Is.
(U.K.)

JAMAICA

Kingston

HAITI

Port-au-
Prince

DOMINICAN
REP.

Santo
Domingo

San Juan

PUERTO
RICO
(U.S.A.)

H

Revilla Gigedo Is.
(Mex.)

San Luis Potosí

León

Querétaro

Guadalajara

MÉXICO

Toluca

Puebla

Mérida

BELIZE

Belmopan

Caribbean Sea

Acapulco

GUATEMALA

Guatemala

San Salvador

EL SALVADOR

HONDURAS

Tegucigalpa

NICARAGUA

Managua

L. Nicaragua

Maracaibo

Barranquilla

VENEZUELA

10

J

COSTA

RICA

San José

PANAMA

Panamá

COLOMBIA

Medellín

South

America

80

Projection: Bonne

120

110

West from Greenwich

100

90

COPYRIGHT PHILIP'S

7 ■ MÉXICO Capital Cities 8 9 10 11 12

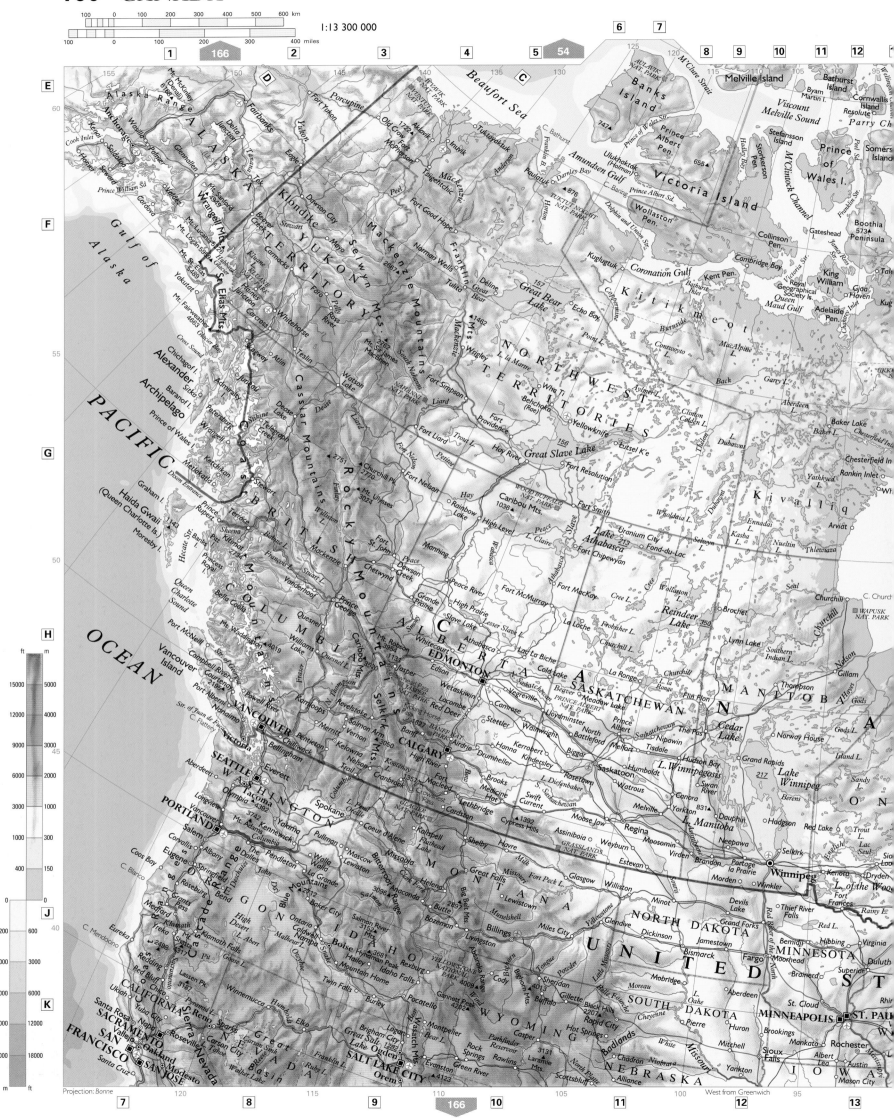

1:13 300 000

Projection: Bonne

West from Greenwich

NORTHERN CANADA
continuation northwards on same scale as main map

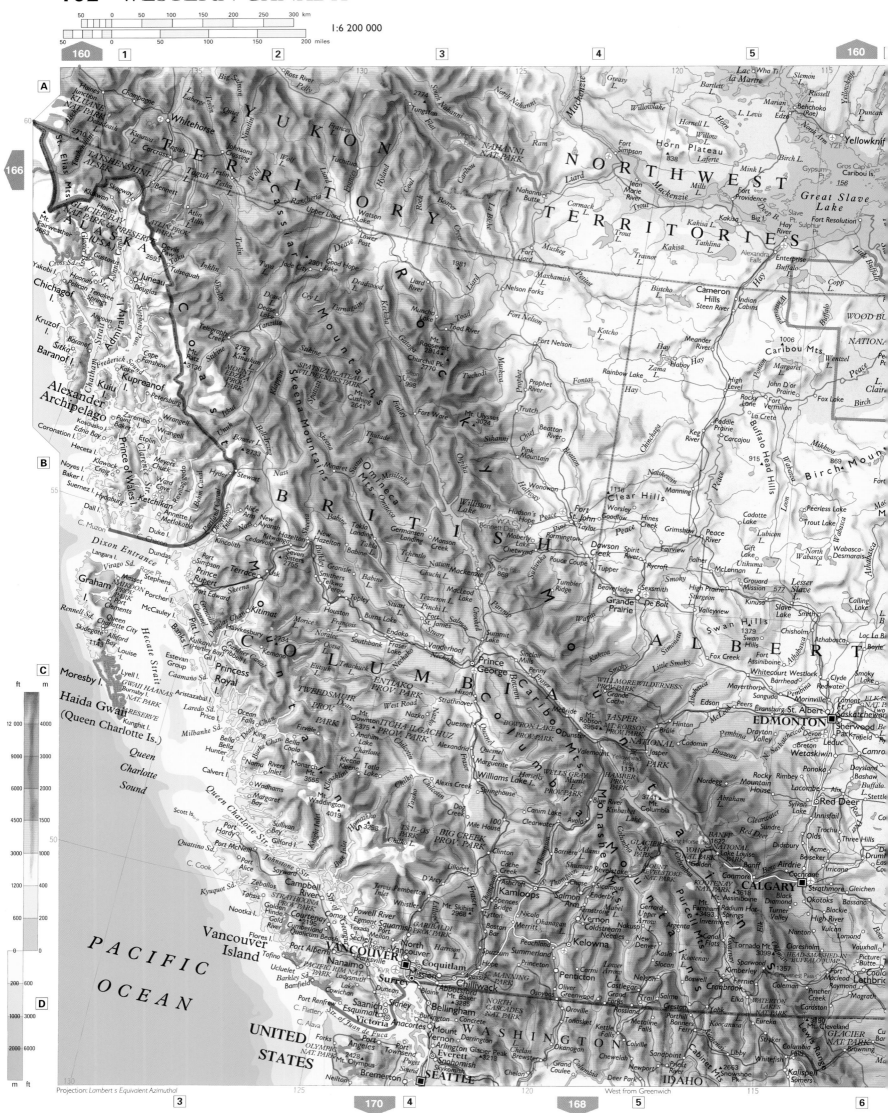

1:6 200 000

Projection: Lambert's Equivalent Azimuthal

A

B

C

50

C

45

D

L A B R A D O R

S E A

Nunatsiavut

Labrador

NEWFOUNDLAND &

Q U E B E C

LABRADOR

Newfoundland

Smallwood Reservoir

Happy Valley-Goose Bay

Churchill Falls

Twin Falls

Labrador City

Fermont

Sept-Îles

Port-Cartier

Île d'Anticosti

GULF OF

ST. LAWRENCE

Long Range Mts.

Corner Brook

Deer Lake

Grand Falls-Windsor

Gander

St. John's

Mt. Jacques-Cartier

Chic-Chocs

Gaspé

Pén. de la Gaspésie

Rimouski

Rivière-du-Loup

Edmundston

NEW

BRUNSWICK

PRINCE EDWARD

ISLAND

Charlottetown

Summerside

Moncton

Fredericton

Saint John

Bay of Fundy

NOVA SCOTIA

Truro

Halifax

Dartmouth

Cape Breton

Island

Sydney

Cabot Strait

ST-PIERRE-

ET-MIQUELON

(France)

Sable I.

(Nova Scotia)

A T L A N T I C

O C E A N

MAINE

Portland

Augusta

Bangor

U N I T E D

S T A T E S

BOSTON

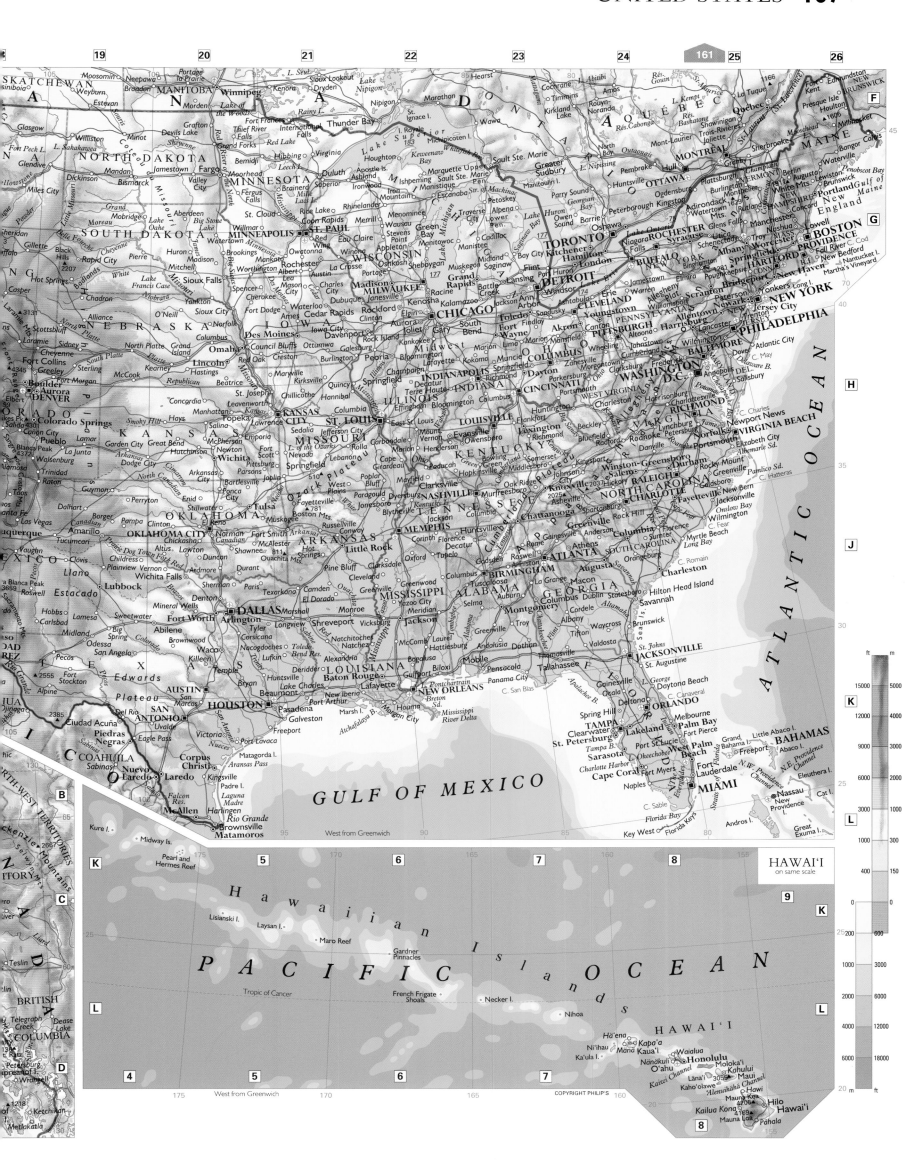

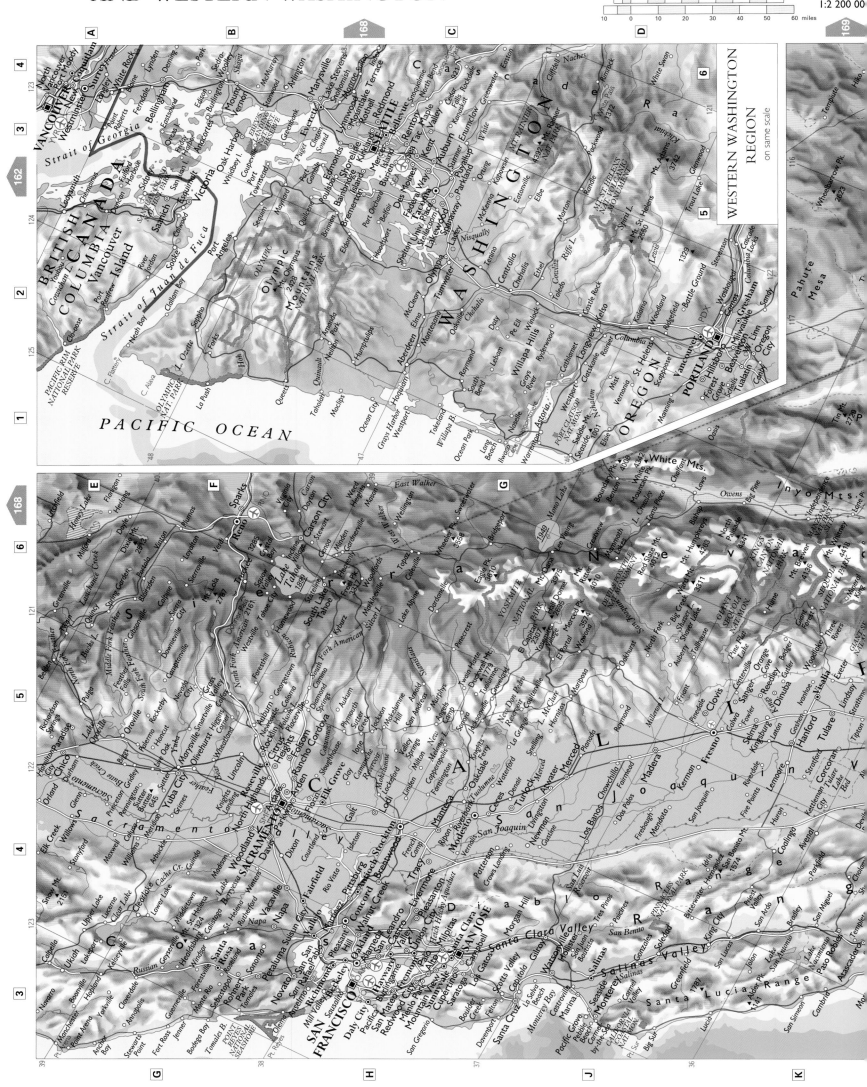

WESTERN WASHINGTON
REGION
on same scale

1:2 200 000

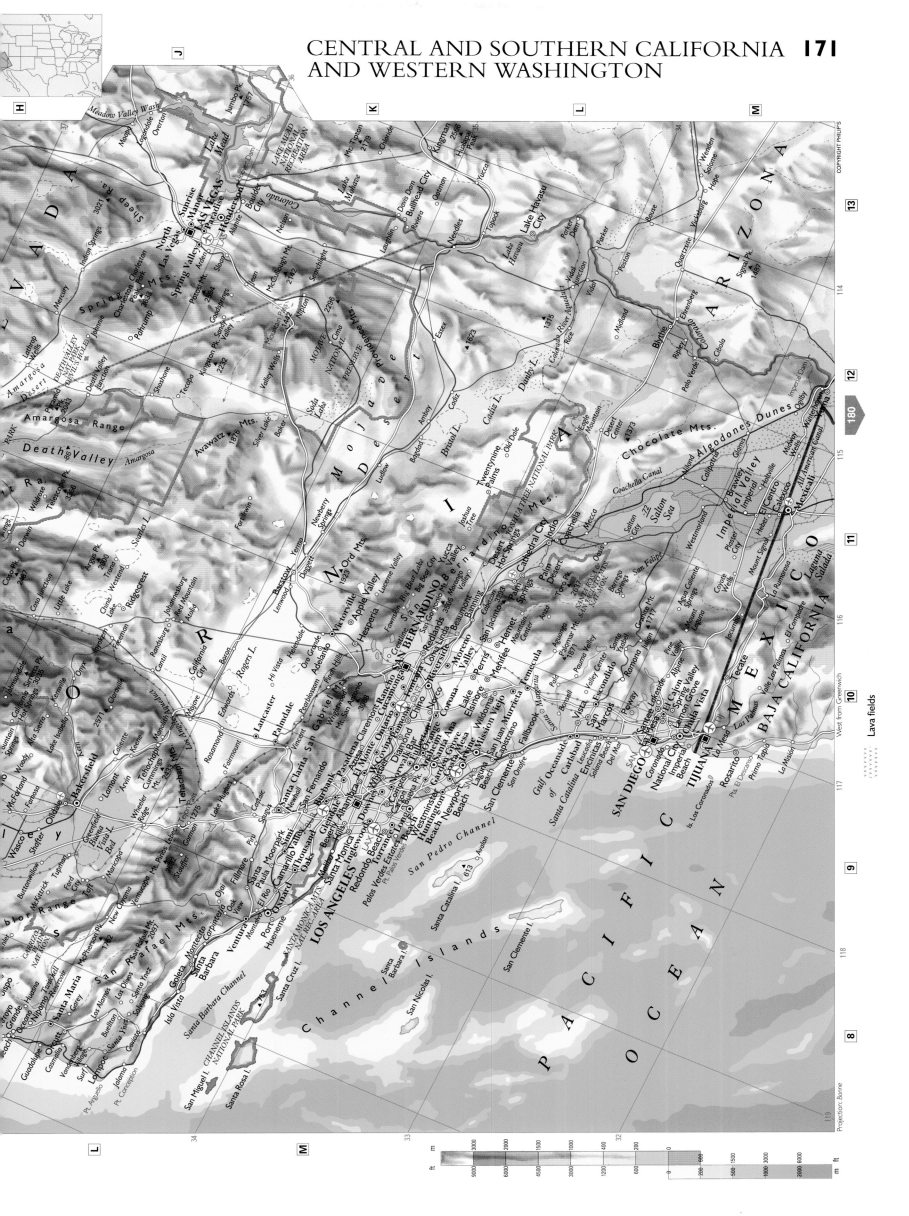

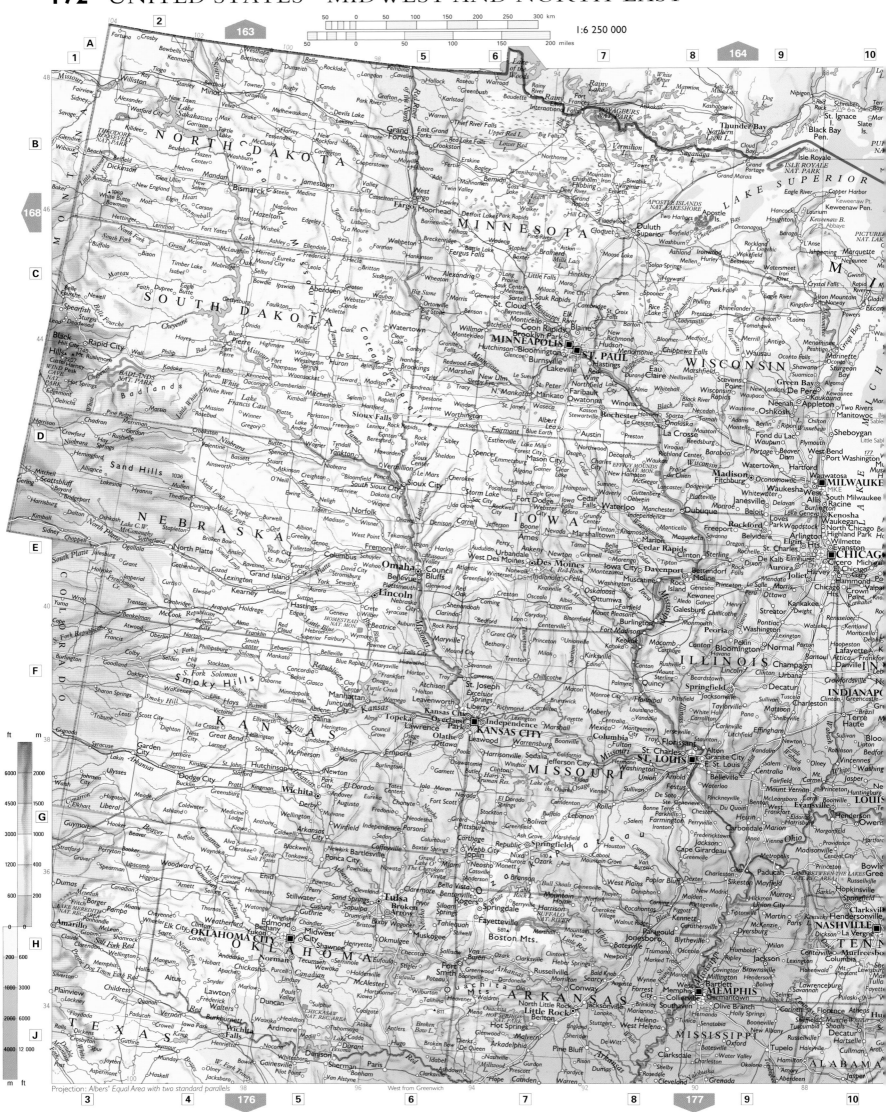

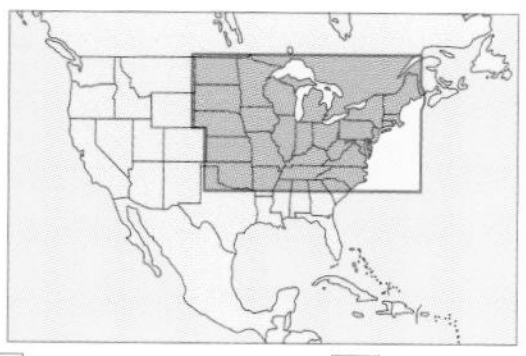

11
12
13
164
14
15
16
17
18
19
165
20
B
C
D
E
F
G
H
J
178
ONTARIO
QUEBEC
MAINE
NEW BRUNS.
VERMONT
NEW HAMPSHIRE
MA.
CT.
R.I.
NEW YORK
PENNSYLVANIA
NEW JERSEY
DELAWARE
MARYLAND
OHIO
WEST VIRGINIA
VIRGINIA
NORTH CAROLINA
SOUTH CAROLINA
GEORGIA
LAKE HURON
LAKE ERIE
LAKE ONTARIO
Georgian Bay
North Channel
Gulf of Maine
Cape Cod
Long Island Sound
Delaware Bay
Chesapeake Bay
Pamlico Sound
Albemarle Sd.
Onslow Bay
ATLANTIC OCEAN
Allegheny Plateau
Appalachian Plateau
Allegheny Mountains
Blue Ridge
Adirondack Mts.
White Mts.
Green Mts.
St. Lawrence
OTTAWA
MONTREAL
Québec
TORONTO
Hamilton
BUFFALO
ROCHESTER
Syracuse
Albany
DETROIT
Windsor
Toledo
CLEVELAND
Akron
Youngstown
PITTSBURGH
COLUMBUS
CINCINNATI
Dayton
PHILADELPHIA
NEW YORK
Newark
BOSTON
PROVIDENCE
HARTFORD
Springfield
Worcester
Portland
BALTIMORE
WASHINGTON D.C.
RICHMOND
VIRGINIA BEACH
Norfolk
RALEIGH
Durham
Greensboro
Winston-Salem
CHARLOTTE
Knoxville
Chattanooga
ATLANTA
Columbia
Wilmington
Lexington
Charleston
Scranton
Harrisburg
Allentown
Erie
Sault Ste. Marie
Greater Sudbury
North Bay
Kingston
Sherbrooke
Trois-Rivières
Bangor
Augusta
Concord
Manchester
Burlington
Montpelier
Binghamton
Utica
Trenton
Dover
Annapolis
C. Hatteras
C. Lookout
C. Fear
Nantucket I.
Martha's Vineyard
CAPE HATTERAS NAT. SEASHORE
CAPE COD NAT. SEASHORE
ASSATEAGUE ISLAND NAT. SEASHORE
SHENANDOAH NAT. PARK
GREAT SMOKY MTS. NAT. PARK
ALGONQUIN PROV. PARK
BAXTER STATE PARK
ACADIA NAT. PARK
ADIRONDACK PARK

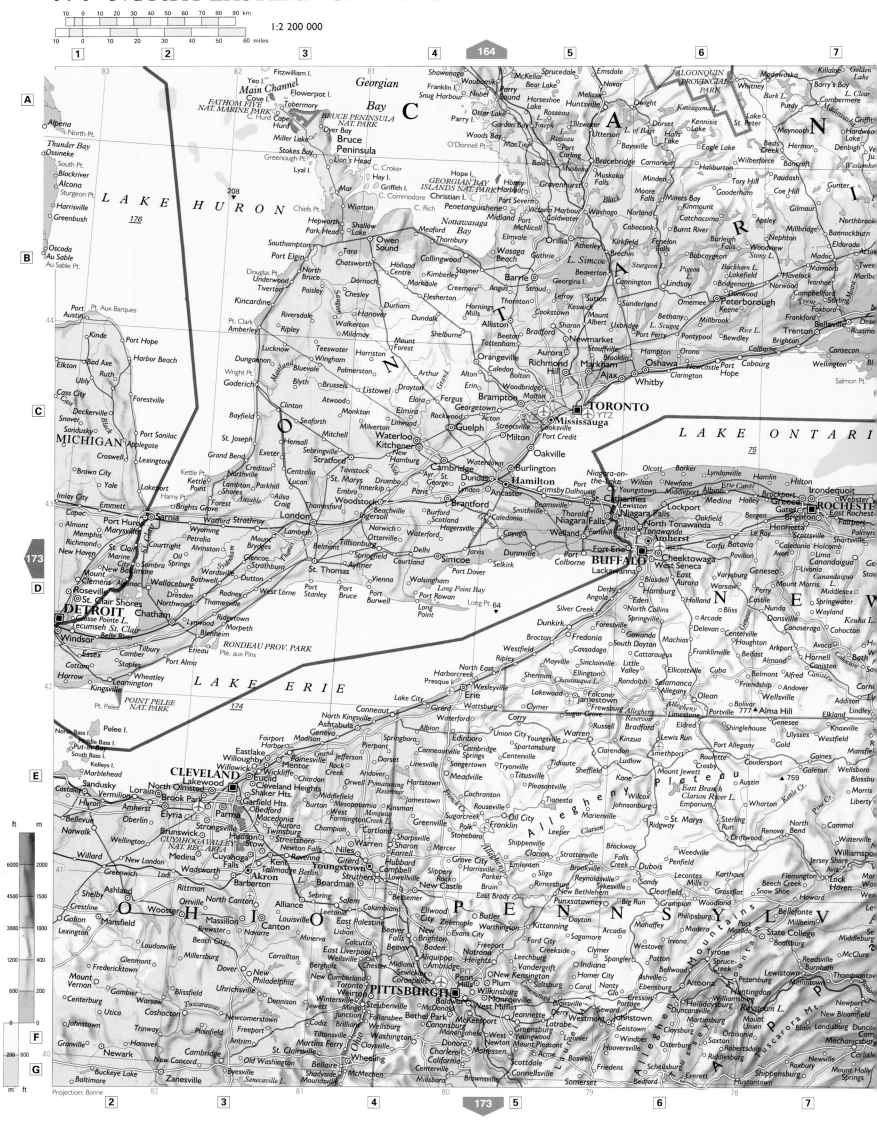

1:2 200 000

Projection: Bonne

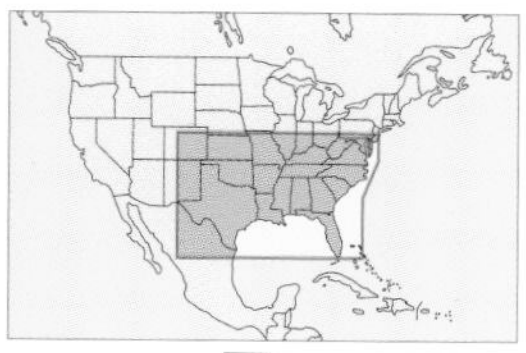

OHIO

INDIANA
INDIANAPOLIS

ILLINOIS

PENNSYLVANIA
PITTSBURGH
PHILADELPHIA

WEST VIRGINIA
Charleston

MARYLAND
BALTIMORE
WASHINGTON, D.C.

DELAWARE

VIRGINIA
RICHMOND
VIRGINIA BEACH

KENTUCKY
LOUISVILLE
Lexington
Frankfort

CINCINNATI

TENNESSEE
NASHVILLE
Knoxville
CHARLOTTE

NORTH CAROLINA
RALEIGH

SOUTH CAROLINA
Columbia
Charleston

MEMPHIS

MISSISSIPPI
Jackson

ALABAMA
BIRMINGHAM
Montgomery

GEORGIA
ATLANTA
Macon
Savannah
Columbus

NEW ORLEANS

FLORIDA
JACKSONVILLE
Tallahassee
ORLANDO
TAMPA
St. Petersburg
MIAMI
Fort Lauderdale
West Palm Beach
Cape Coral
Naples
Key West

ATLANTIC OCEAN

GULF OF MEXICO

BAHAMAS
Nassau
New Providence

Florida Keys
Str. of Florida

Mississippi River Delta

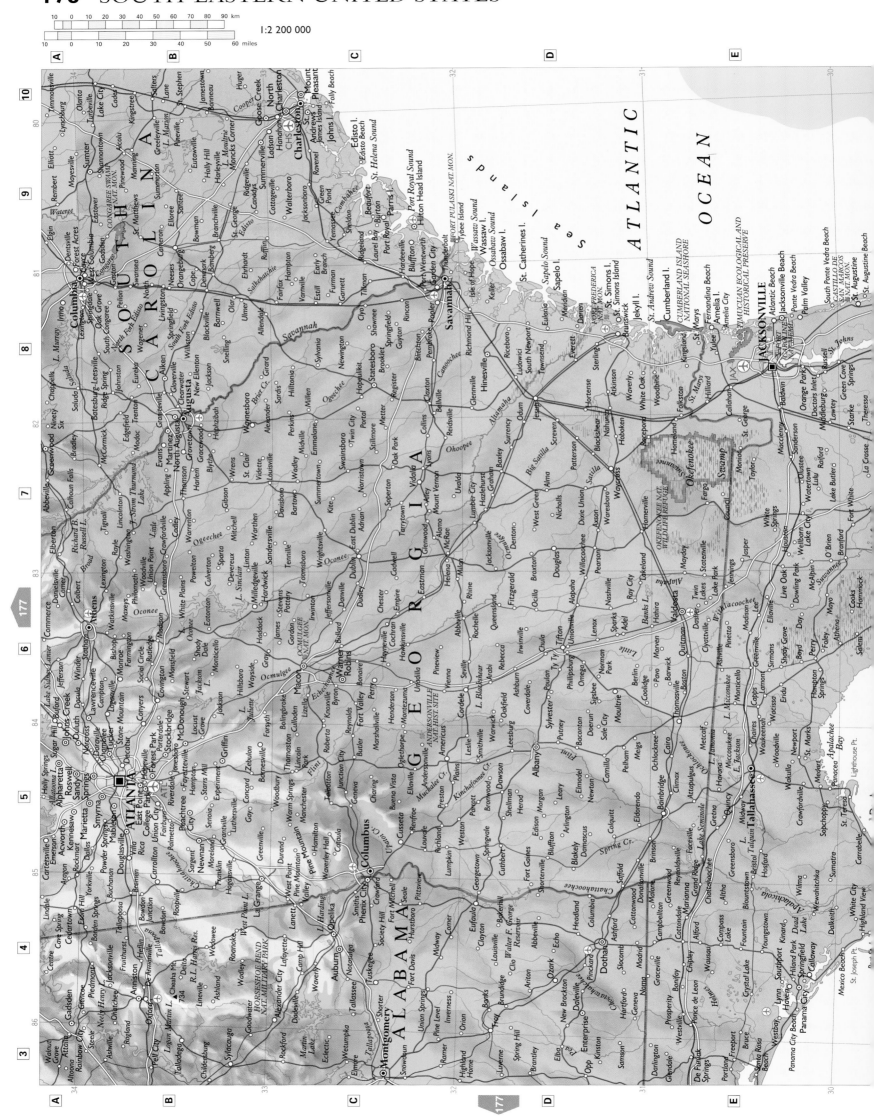

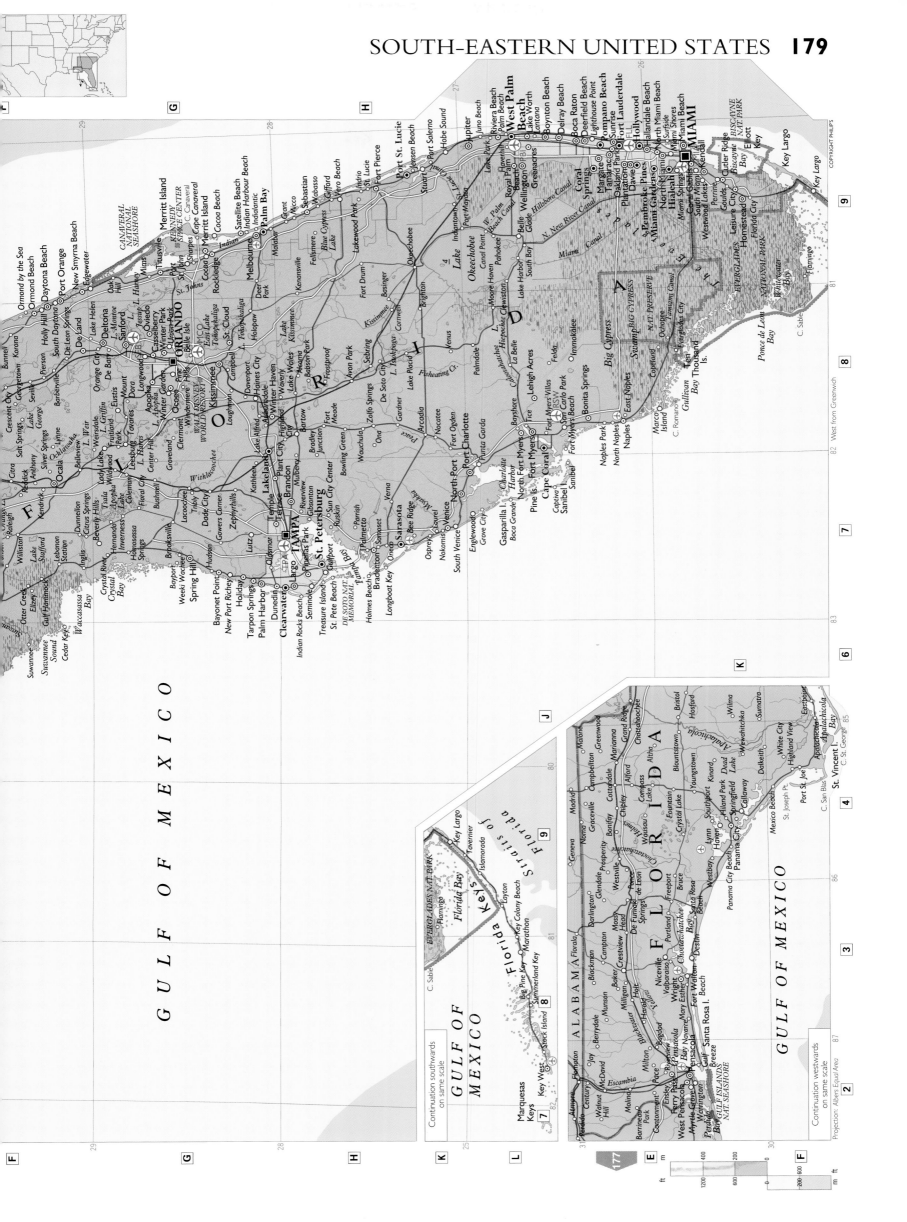

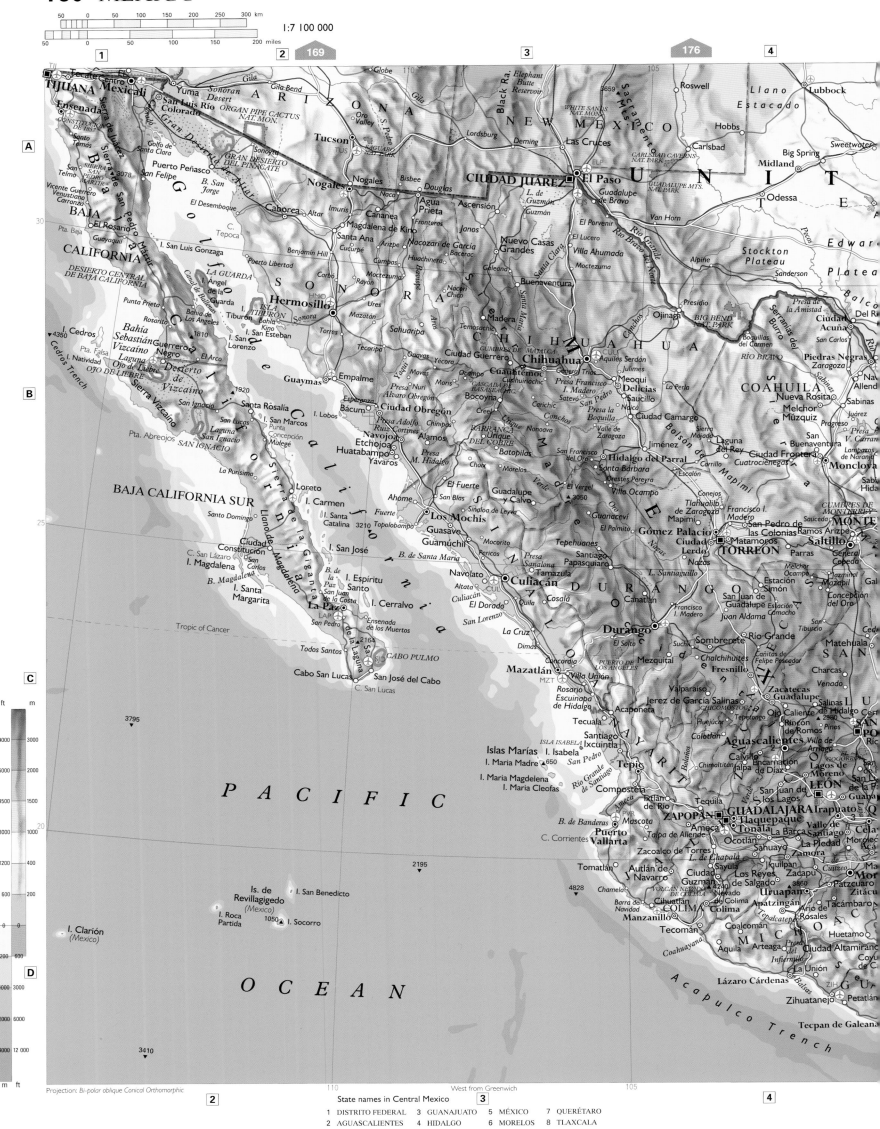

State names in Central Mexico

1 DISTRITO FEDERAL 3 GUANAJUATO 5 MÉXICO 7 QUERÉTARO
2 AGUASCALIENTES   4 HIDALGO   6 MORELOS 8 TLAXCALA

Projection: Bi-polar oblique Conical Orthomorphic

West from Greenwich

A

B

C

D

E

GULF OF MEXICO

G U L F   O F

M E X I C O

Sigsbee Deep

Tropic of Cancer

Banco Campeche

CUBA

ARKANSAS

MISSISSIPPI

ALABAMA

GEORGIA

FLORIDA

Fort Worth
DALLAS
AUSTIN
SAN ANTONIO
HOUSTON

New Orleans

Corpus Christi

McAllen
Reynosa
Matamoros

Golfo de Campeche

MÉRIDA
YUCATÁN
Campeche
CAMPECHE
QUINTANA ROO
Cancún
Cozumel

Costa Maya

Yucatan Basin

Chetumal

BELIZE
Belize City
Belmopan

TABASCO
Villahermosa
Coatzacoalcos

OAXACA
Oaxaca
Tuxtla Gutiérrez
CHIAPAS

GUATEMALA

HONDURAS

TEGUCIGALPA

JAMAICA
1:2 700 000

GUADELOUPE

MARTINIQUE

GUADELOUPE AND MARTINIQUE
1:1 800 000

PUERTO RICO d
1:2 700 000
10 0 10 20 30 40 50 km
10 0 10 20 30 miles

PUERTO RICO
(U.S.A.)

ATLANTIC OCEAN

Pta. Aguadilla
Pta. Borinquen
Isabela
Arecibo
Barceloneta
Manati
Vega Baja
Bayamón
SAN JUAN
SJU
Rio Grande
Fajardo
Pta. Puerca
Dewey
Culebra
Vieques
San Sebastián
Adjuntas
Utuado
Cordillera Central
Cerro 1338 de Punta
Caguas
Naguabo
Esperanza
Mayagüez
San German
Mts. de Uroyan
Yauco
Cayey
Coamo
Humacao
Yabucoa
Guanica
Ponce
Guayama
Pta. Aguila
I. Caja de Muertos

VIRGIN ISLANDS e
1:1 800 000
10 0 10 20 30 km
10 0 10 20 miles

Rufling Pt.
The Settlement
Anegada
East Pt.

Virgin Islands
(U.K.)

Great Camanoe
Jost Van Dyke I.
Guana I.
Virgin Gorda
Spanish Town
Virgin Is.
(U.S.A.)
Hans Lollik I.
Tortola
Beef I.
Road Town
Peter I.
Charlotte Amalie
Cruz Bay
St. John I.
St. Thomas I.
VIRGIN IS.

ST. LUCIA f
1:890 000
5 0 10 km
5 0 5 10 miles

Cap Point
Pte. Hardy
Gros Islet
Esperance Bay
Castries
Girard
Marquis
Anse la Raye
Millet
Dennery
Canaries
Soufrière
Mt. Gimie 950
750
Petit Piton
Trou Gras Pt.
Soufrière Bay
Micoud
796 Gros Piton
Vierge Pt.
Gros Piton Pt.
Choiseul
Laborie
Vieux Fort
UVF
C. Moule à Chique
ST. LUCIA

BARBADOS g
1:890 000
5 0 10 km
5 0 5 10 miles

ATLANTIC OCEAN
North Point
Crab Hill
Spring Hall
Fustic
Boscobelle
Portland
245 Belleplaine
Speightstown
Westmoreland
Bathsheba
BARBADOS
Alleynes Bay
840
Mt. Hillaby
Hillcrest
Holetown
Martin's Bay
Jackson
Massiah Street
Black Rock
Bridgefield
Ellerton
Ragged Pt.
Six Cross Roads
Bridgetown
Ivy
Edey
BGI
Oistins
St. Martins
The Crane
Carlisle Bay
Worthing
St. Philip
Chancery Lane
Oistins Bay
South Point

AS

A

ATLANTIC OCEAN

New Town
New Bight
Cat I.
Salvador I.
Conception I.
Rum Cay
Long I.
Clarence Town
Crooked I. Passage
Samana Cay
Albert Town
Snug Corner
Plana Cays
Acklins I.
Mira por vos Cay
Hogsty Reef
Little Inagua I.
Mayaguana Passage
Mayaguana I.
Tropic of Cancer
Crooked I.
Caicos Passage
Turks & Caicos Is. *(U.K.)*
PLS
Caicos Is.
Cockburn Town
Turks Island Passage
Turks Is.
INAGUA
Lake Rose
Great Inagua I.
Moa
Alejandro de Humboldt
Matthew Town
Mouchoir Bank
Silver Bank Passage
Silver Bank
Baracoa
Maisi
Pta. de Maisi
Navidad Bank
Guantánamo
Cap-Haïtien
Monte Cristi
LA ISABELA POP
Santiago de los Caballeros
San Francisco de Macoris
B
Windward Passage
Port-de-Paix
Fort Liberté
Puerto Plata
Milwaukee Deep 8605
Puerto Rico Trench
Jean Rabel
Cap-Foux
Cord. Central
La Vega
Nagua
Samana
Sánchez
St-Marc
Gonaïves
Hinche
Pico Duarte 3175
HAITISES
Sabana de la Mar
Jérémie
Dame Marie
Î. de la Gonâve
PORT-AU-PRINCE
DOMINICAN REP.
San Pedro de Macoris
Hato Mayor
C. Engaño
Higüey
Les Cayes
Massif de la Hotte
Petit Goave
Jacmel
Azua de Compostela
SDQ
La Romana
PUJ
Aguadilla
Arecibo
Bayamón
SAN JUAN
Carolina
St. Thomas
Virgin Gorda
Anegada
Virgin Is. *(U.K.)*
Sombrero *(U.K.)*
Pointe-à-Gravois
I. à Vache
Barahona
Pedernales
Santo Domingo
San Cristóbal
Isla Saona
Mona Passage
Isla Mona *(U.S.A.)*
Mayagüez
Ponce
Caguas
Fajardo
Culebra
Vieques
Guayama
Charlotte Amalie
Virgin Is. *(U.S.A.)*
Christiansted
St. Croix
Frederiksted
Road Town
St.-Martin *(Fr.)*
St. Maarten *(Neth.)*
St.-Barthélemy *(Fr.)*
Saba *(Neth.)*
Barbuda
ANTIGUA & BARBUDA
St. Eustatius *(Neth.)*
Mt. Liamuiga 1156
SKB
ST. KITTS & NEVIS
St. John's
Antigua
Redonda
ANU
Montserrat *(U.K.)*
914
Soufrière Hills
Guadeloupe Passage
Ste-Rose
Le Moule
La Désirade
GUADELOUPE *(Fr.)*
1467
Pointe-à-Pitre
PTP
Marie-Galante *(Fr.)*
Grand-Bourg
Basse-Terre
I. des Saintes
Portsmouth
1447
Dominica Passage
MORNE DIABLOTIN
DOMINICA
DOM
Roseau
TROIS PITONS
Martinique Passage
Mt. Pelée 1397
Ste-Marie
Le Robert
Fort-de-France
Rivière-Pilote
MARTINIQUE *(Fr.)*
FDF
St. Lucia Channel
Castries
950
ST. LUCIA
Soufrière
UVF
St. Vincent Passage
Soufrière 1234
St. Vincent
Speightstown
SVD
340
BGI
Kingstown
BARBADOS
Bequia
ST. VINCENT & THE GRENADINES
Bridgetown
Canouan
Carriacou
840
Tobago
St. George's
GRENADA
GND

C

Hispaniola

Antilles

Î. de la Gonâve
Gonâve
L. Enriquillo
San Juan
40
2680
SIERRA DE BAHORUCO
Bani
I. Beata
C. Beata
5500

Greater Antilles

Beata Ridge
4530

CARIBBEAN SEA
Muertas Trough

Venezuelan Basin

I. de Aves *(Venezuela)*

5420

Aves Ridge

Lesser Antilles

Leeward Islands

Windward Islands

Grenada Basin

The Grenadines

D

ABC Islands
Lesser Antilles

Aruba *(Neth.)*
Oranjestad
AUA
Curaçao *(Neth.)*
Willemstad
CUR
Bonaire *(Neth.)*
Pta. Gallinas
MACUIRA
ARC. LOS ROQUES
I. Orchila *(Ven.)*
I. Blanquilla *(Ven.)*
Is. Los Hermanos *(Ven.)*
Tobago
COLOMBIA
GUAJIRA
Puerto Bolívar
C. San Román
Pen. de Paraguaná
Is. Las Aves *(Ven.)*
Is. Los Roques *(Ven.)*
NUEVA ESPARTA
I. de Margarita *(Ven.)*
Is. Los Testigos *(Ven.)*
Scarborough
Ríohacha
Uribia
Pen. de la Guajira
Pta. Espada
Maicao
Golfo de Venezuela
Punta Cardón
Puerto Cumarebo
La Asunción
Porlamar
Port of Spain
Galera Pt.
Santa Marta
TAYRONA
Pta. Paraguaná
Coro
La Vela
PMV
Pen. de Paria
Güiria
Trinidad
Arima
Río Caribe
Caribe
POS
TRINIDAD & TOBAGO
MAR
SA. NEVADA DE STA. MARTA
San Rafael
MÉDANOS DE CORO
HENRI PITTIER
La Guaira
Maiquetía
CARACAS
Carúpano
Cumaná
Puerto La Cruz
Río Claro
San Fernando
Soledad
Sabanalarga
Fundación
Ciénaga
Santa Rita
Baragua
Mene de Mauroa
FALCÓN
Altagracia
Puerto Cabello
Los Teques
MIRANDA
SUCRE
2640
Guanta
Río Chico
Barcelona
Caripito
Serpent's Mouth
Calamar
Agustín Codazzi
Valledupar
La Concepción
MARACAIBO
Cabimas
Villa del Rosario
Ciudad Ojeda
LARA
YARACUY
San Felipe
CARABOBO
San Juan de los Morros
Ocumare del Tuy
Anaco
Maturín
MONAGAS
El Tigre
DELTA AMACURO
Plato
Calamar
El Banco
Machiques
Mene Grande
BARQUISIMETO
Yaritagua
VALENCIA
Aragua de Barcelona
Cantaura
Mompós
PERIJÁ
CIÉNAGAS DEL CATATUMBO
Trujillo
TRUJILLO
Valera
Betijoque
Guárico
Valle de la Pascua
Santa María de Ipire
Los Barrancos
Majagual
El Tigre
Magangué
ZULIA
EL GUACHE
Acarigua
Araure
PORTUGUESA
Guanare
Calabozo
GUÁRICO
ANZOÁTEGUI
Soledad
El Pao
Ciudad Guayana
Mariusa
Tucupita
Ciénaga
Barinas
Guanare
El Baúl
Ciudad Guayana
Sierra Imataca
El Banco
Simití
SANTANDER
Ocaña
CATATUMBO-BARI
NORTE DE SANTANDER
San Carlos del Zulia
CORD. DE MÉRIDA
PICO BOLÍVAR 4981
Mérida
Ciudad Bolivia
Libertad
BARINAS
San Fernando de Apure
El Tigre
Ciudad Bolívar
Upata
El Callao
Bolívar
Simití
TÁCHIRA
Cúcuta
Bruzual
Ciudad de Nutrias
Achaguas
Apure
Mapire
Guasipati
Tumeremo
Caucasia
Caicara
Embalse de Guri
San Cristóbal
San Antonio
San Carlos
Barinas
VENEZUELA

E

4000 3000 2000 1500 1000 400 200 0
2000 9000 4500 3000 1200 600 0
600 2000 4000 6000 8000
6000 12 000 18 000 24 000 ft
200 2000 4000 6000 8000 m

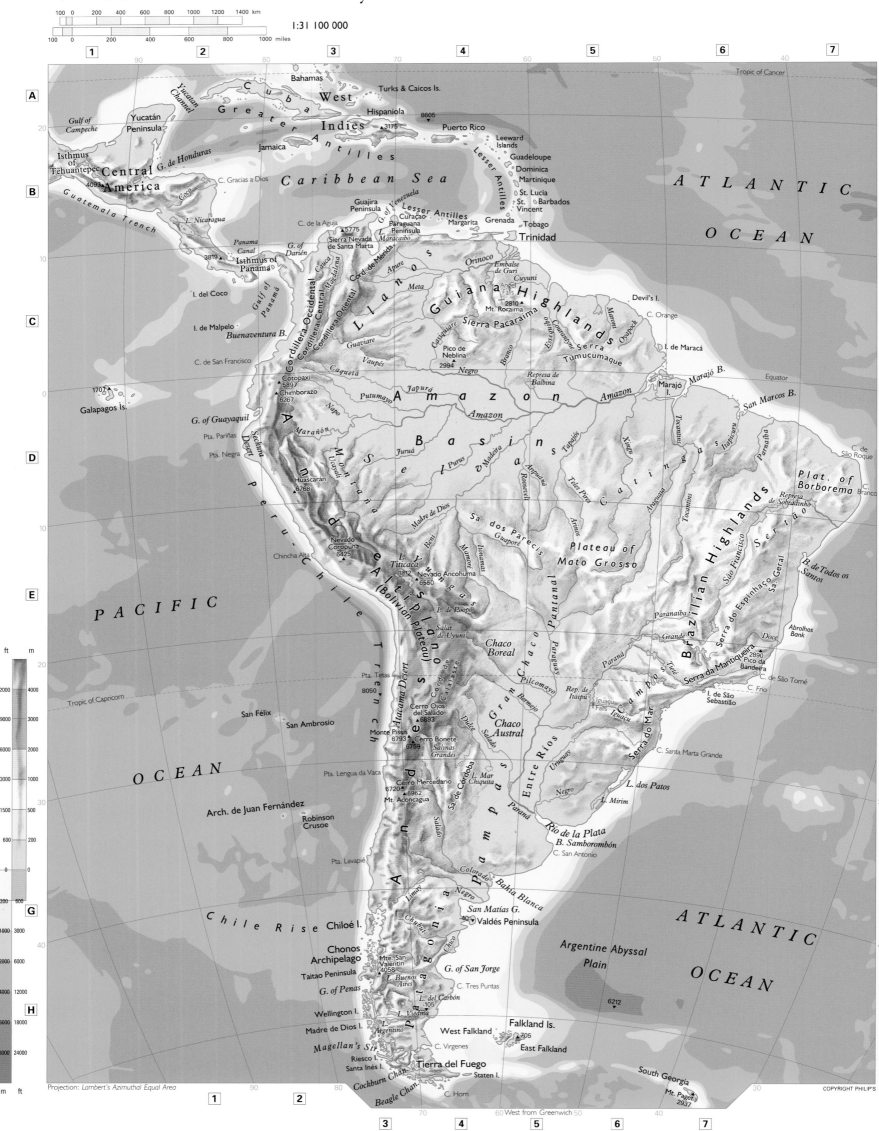

100 0   200 400 600 800 1000 1200 1400 km

1:31 100 000

100   200   400   600   800   1000 miles

ft   m

12000   4000

9000   3000

6000   2000

3000   1000

1500   500

600   200

0   0

200   600

1000   3000

2000   6000

4000   12000

6000   18000

8000   24000

m   ft

Projection: Lambert's Azimuthal Equal Area

COPYRIGHT PHILIP'S

A
Bahamas
West
Indies
Turks & Caicos Is.
Greater
Gulf of
Campeche
Yucatán
Peninsula
Antilles
Hispaniola
Puerto Rico
3175
8605
Leeward
Islands

B
Isthmus of
Tehuantepec
Central
America
G. de Honduras
Jamaica
Caribbean Sea
Lesser
Antilles
Guadeloupe
Dominica
Martinique
St. Lucia
Barbados
St.
Vincent
Grenada
Tobago
Trinidad
ATLANTIC

Guatemala Trench
C. Gracias a Dios
Coco
L. Nicaragua
Guajira
Peninsula
G. of Venezuela
Curaçao
Paraguana
Peninsula
Margarita
Lesser Antilles

OCEAN

C
Panama
Canal
G. of
Darién
3819
Isthmus of
Panamá
5775
Sierra Nevada
de Santa Marta
L.
Maracaibo
C. de la Aguja
Orinoco
Embalse
de Guri
Cuyuni
Angel
Falls
Devil's I.
C. Orange

I. del Coco
Gulf of
Panamá
Cauca
Cord. de Mérida
Apure
Meta
Llanos
Guiana
Highlands
Mt. Roraima
2810
Sierra Pacaraima
Caroni
Maroni
Oyapock
I. de Maracá

Cordillera Occidental
Cordillera Central
Cordillera Oriental
Magdalena
Casiquiare
Branco
Cotopaxi
5897
Pico de
Neblina
2994
Serra
Tumucumaque

D
I. de Malpelo
Buenaventura B.
Guaviare
Guainía
Negro
Represa de
Balbina
Amazon
Marajó
I.
Marajó B.
Equator
C. de
São Roque

C. de San Francisco
Caquetá
Vaupés
Putumayo
Napo
Amazon
Japurá
Amazon
Amazon
San Marcos B.
C. Branco

Chimborazo
6267
Marañón
Ucayali
Juruá
Purus
Madeira
Tapajós
Xingu
Tocantins
Iça
Araguaia
Parnaíba
Caatinga
Plat. of
Borborema

G. of Guayaquil
Pta. Pariñas
Pta. Negra
Andes
Montaña
Basin
Roosevelt
Telles Pires
Arinos
Tocantins
Brazilian
Highlands
Represa
de Sobradinho
Sertão

Galapagos Is.
1707
Sechura
Desert
Madre de Dios
Beni
Mamoré
Guaporé
Sa. dos Parecis
Plateau of
Mato Grosso
Araguaia
São Francisco
Serra do Espinhaço
B. de Todos os
Santos

E
Huascarán
6768
Nevado
Coropuna
6425
L.
Titicaca
3812
Nevado Ancohuma
6550
L. de Poopó
Pantanal
Grande
Serra Geral
Abrolhos
Bank

PACIFIC
Peru-Chile
Altiplano
(Bolivian Plateau)
Salar
de Uyuni
Chaco
Boreal
Paraguay
Paranaíba
Pico da
Bandeira
2890
Serra da Mantiqueira
C. de São Tomé

F
Tropic of Capricorn
Trench
Pta. Tetas
8050
Atacama Desert
Cerro Ojos
del Salado
6893
Gran
Chaco
Chaco
Austral
Pilcomayo
Bermejo
Rep. de
Itaipú
Iguaçu
Falls
Iguaçu
Paraná
Serra do Mar
C. Santa Marta Grande

San Félix
San Ambrosio
Monte Pissis
6793
Cerro Bonete
6759
Salinas
Grandes
Dulce
Salado
Paraná
Uruguay
Negro
L. Mirim
C. Frio
I. de São
Sebastião

OCEAN
Cerro Mercedario
6720
Mt. Aconcagua
6962
Sa. de Córdoba
L. Mar
Chiquita
Entre Ríos
L. dos Patos

G
Arch. de Juan Fernández
Robinson
Crusoe
Pta. Lengua da Vaca
Salado
Pampas
Colorado
Negro
Río de la Plata
B. Samborombón
C. San Antonio

Chile Rise
Chiloé I.
Bahía Blanca
Valdés Peninsula
San Matías G.
ATLANTIC

H
Chonos
Archipelago
Taitao Peninsula
G. of Penas
Mte. San
Valentín
4058
L. Buenos
Aires
Limay
Chubut
Chico
G. of San Jorge
C. Tres Puntas
Argentine Abyssal
Plain
6212
OCEAN

Wellington I.
Madre de Dios I.
Patagonia
L. Viedma
L.
Argentino
L. del Carbón
-105
West Falkland
Falkland Is.
705
East Falkland

Magellan's Str.
Riesco I.
Santa Inés I.
Tierra del Fuego
Staten I.
South Georgia
Mt. Paget
2937

Cockburn Chan.
Beagle Chan.
C. Horn
C. Virgenes

West from Greenwich

1:31 100 000

100 0   200   400   600   800   1000 1200 1400 km

100 0   200   400   600   800   1000 miles

1 **2** **3** **4** **5** **6** **7**

Tropic of Cancer

A

Havana BAHAMAS
CUBA
Cayman Is. Turks & Caicos Is.
(U.K.) (U.K.)
HAITI DOMINICAN
REP. San Juan Virgin Is. (U.S.A. - U.K.)
JAMAICA Port-au- Santo Anguilla (U.K.)
Kingston Prince Domingo PUERTO St. Martin (Fr. - Neth.)
RICO ANTIGUA &
(U.S.A.) ST. KITTS BARBUDA
& NEVIS Basse-Terre GUADELOUPE
DOMINICA (Fr.)
Fort-de-France MARTINIQUE
(Fr.)
Castries ST. LUCIA
ST. VINCENT BARBADOS
Kingstown Bridgetown
GRENADA St. George's

MEXICO
BELIZE
GUATEMALA
HONDURAS
Guatemala Tegucigalpa
San Salvador
EL SALVADOR **NICARAGUA**
Managua

Caribbean Sea

ATLANTIC

B

OCEAN

COSTA San José
RICA Panamá
I. del Coco **PANAMA**
(Costa Rica)
Barranquilla Maracaibo Caracas Port of
Cartagena Barquisimeto Valencia Spain **TRINIDAD &**
G. of Darién **TOBAGO**
Cúcuta San Cristóbal
I. de Malpelo Medellín Bucaramanga **VENEZUELA** Orinoco Ciudad Guayana
(Colombia)
Cali **BOGOTÁ** Georgetown
Galapagos Is. **COLOMBIA** **GUYANA** Paramaribo
(Ecuador) Boa Vista **SURINAME** Cayenne
Quito RORAIMA **FRENCH** C. Orange
ECUADOR **GUIANA**
Guayaquil AMAPÁ Macapá Equator
G. of Guayaquil *Japurá* *Amazon* Marajó Belém
Iquitos *Putumayo* I.
Napo Manaus Santarém São Luís
Marañón **AMAZONAS** *Amazon* Fortaleza
Chiclayo *Juruá* *Purus* *Madeira* **PARÁ** **MARANHÃO** Teresina
Trujillo *Acre* Pôrto Velho *Tapajós* *Xingu* Imperatriz CEARÁ RIO G. Natal
Chimbote **ACRE** Rio Branco *Tocantins* *Araguaia* PIAUÍ DO NORTE João
PERU Madre de Dios **RONDÔNIA** Palmas PERNAMBUCO PARAÍBA Pessoa
Callao Cusco **BRAZIL** TOCANTINS ALAGOAS Recife
LIMA L. **MATO GROSSO** SERGIPE Maceió
Titicaca La Paz Cuiabá GOIÁS Aracaju
Arequipa **BOLIVIA** DIS. FED. Brasília BAHÍA Salvador
Cochabamba Goiânia
Santa Cruz **MINAS GERAIS**
Sucre **MATO GROSSO** BELO
Iquique **DO SUL** Ribeirão HORIZONTE ESPÍRITO
Campo Prêto SANTO
Grande Juiz Vitória
Antofagasta **PARAGUAY** **PARANÁ** SÃO PAULO de Fora Campos
SÃO Campinas R. DE J.
Salta **ASUNCIÓN** PAULO RIO DE
San Miguel Curitiba Santos JANEIRO
de Tucumán Resistencia SANTA CATARINA
San Félix Corrientes URUGUAY Florianópolis
(Chile) RIO GRANDE
San Ambrosio Córdoba DO SUL Pôrto Alegre
(Chile) San Juan Santa Fé Paraná Pelotas
Viña del Mar Mendoza Rosario
Valparaíso **ARGENTINA** **URUGUAY**
Arch. de Juan Fernández **SANTIAGO** Montevideo
(Chile) Talca BUENOS AIRES Rio de la Plata
Robinson La Plata
Crusoe Concepción
Neuquen Bahía Mar del Plata
Valdivia Colorado Blanca
Puerto Montt Negro Viedma

C

D

Equator

E

Tropic of Capricorn

F

PACIFIC

OCEAN

20

10

0

10

20

30

G

Comodoro Rivadavia
Gulf of San Jorge

ATLANTIC

OCEAN

40

Gulf of Penas

H

West Falkland FALKLAND IS.
(U.K.)
Stanley
Magellan's Str. East Falkland
Punta Arenas
Tierra del Fuego South Georgia
C. Horn (U.K.)

■ LIMA Capital Cities

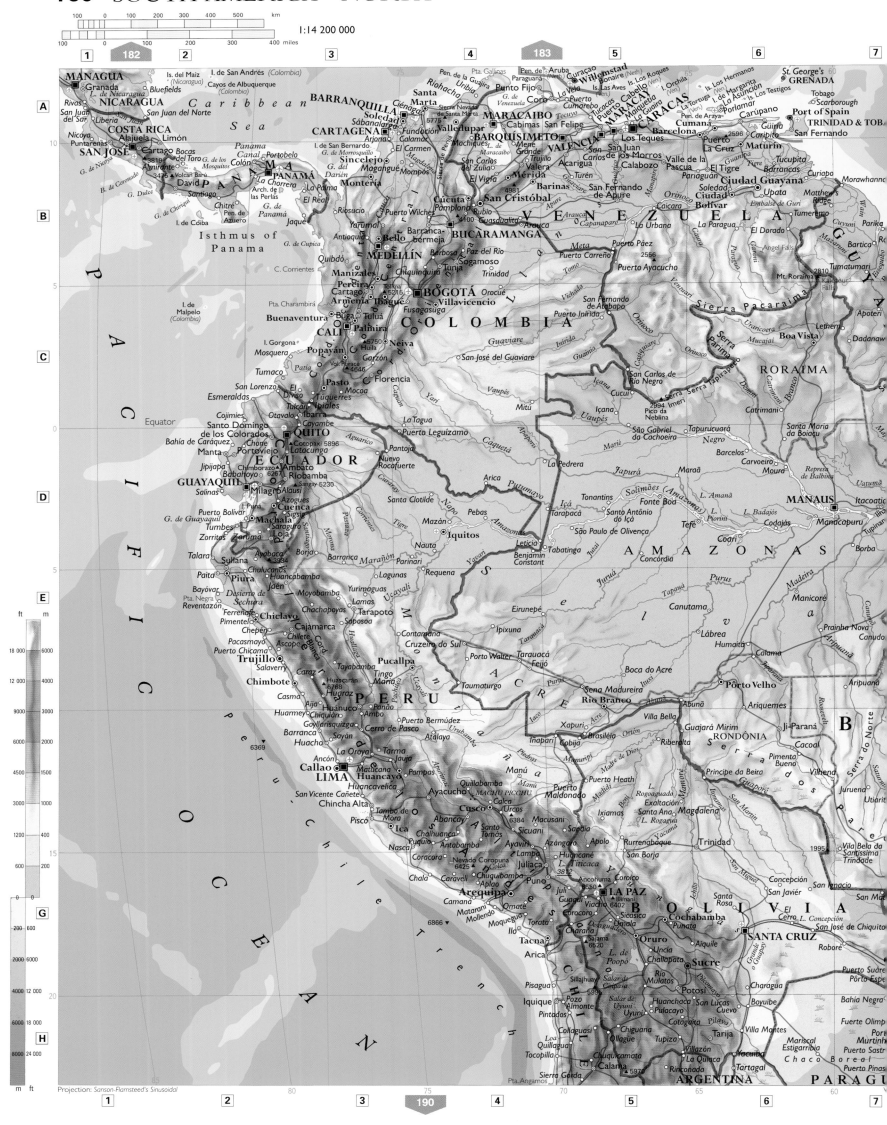

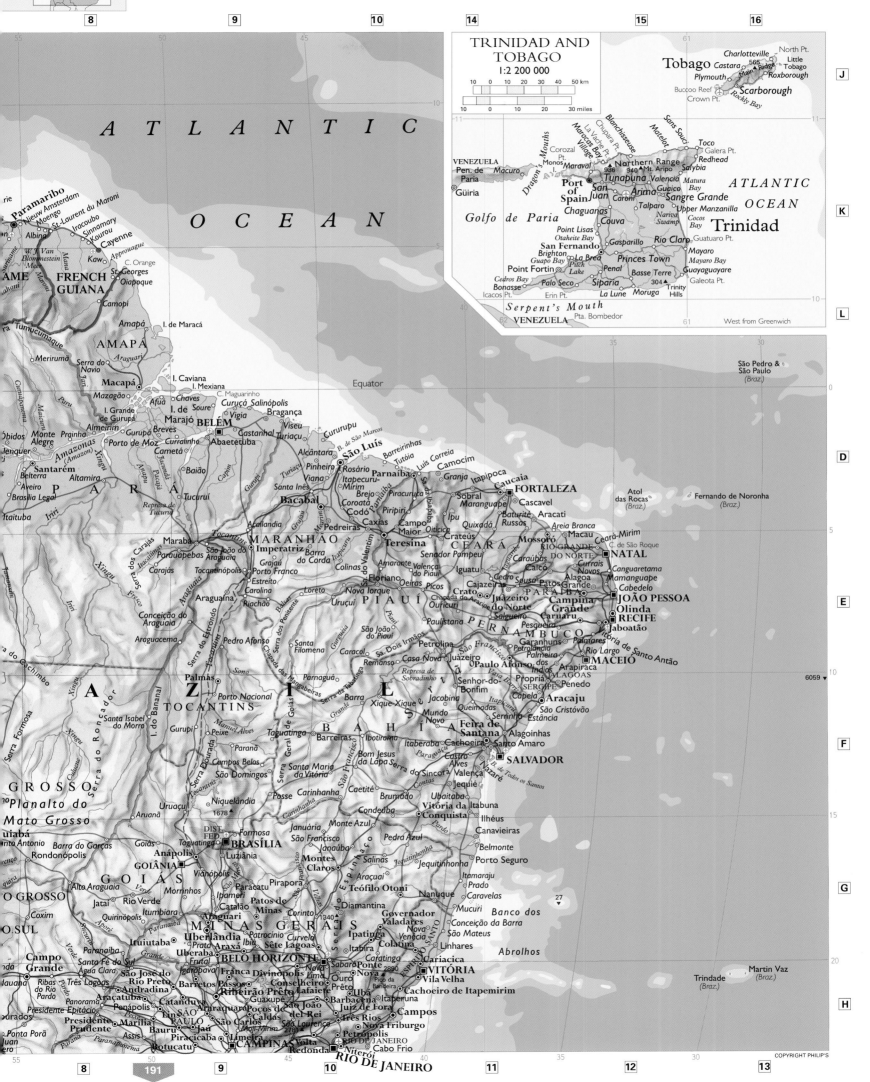

TRINIDAD AND TOBAGO
1:2 200 000

10 0 10 20 30 40 50 km
10 0 10 20 30 miles

J

Tobago
Charlotteville
Castara 565 North Pt.
Little Tobago
Plymouth Main Ridge Roxborough
Buccoo Reef Scarborough
Crown Pt. Rockly Bay

ATLANTIC OCEAN

VENEZUELA
Pen. de Paria
Macuro
Güiria

Corozal Pt.
Monos Maraval
La Vache Pt.
Chupara Pt.
Blanchisseuse
Matelot
Sans Souci
Toco Galera Pt.
Redhead
Salybia

Dragon's Mouths

Northern Range
936 940 ▲Mt. Aripo
Tunapuna Valencia
Port of Spain
San Juan Arima
Guaico
Matura Bay

ATLANTIC OCEAN

Golfo de Paria

Chaguanas
Caroni
Talparo
Sangre Grande
Upper Manzanilla
Nariva Swamp
Cocos Bay

Couva
Point Lisas
Otaheite Bay
San Fernando
Brighton
Guapo Bay La Brea
Point Fortin
Cedros Bay
Bonasse
Icacos Pt.
Palo Seco

Gasparillo
Rio Claro Guataro Pt.

Princes Town
Penal
Siparia
La Lune
Moruga
304 ▲
Trinity Hills

Trinidad

Mayaro
Mayaro Bay
Guayaguayare
Galeota Pt.

Pitch Lake
Basse Terre

K

Serpent's Mouth
VENEZUELA Pta. Bombedor

West from Greenwich

L

ATLANTIC

OCEAN

ame
Paramaribo
Nieuw Amsterdam
Moengo
St-Laurent du Maroni
Iracoubo
Sinnamary
Kourou
Cayenne
Albina
W.J. Van Blommestein Meer
Kaw
Approuague
St-Georges
Oiapoque
C. Orange
Camopi

FRENCH GUIANA

Tumucumaque

Amapá
I. de Maracá

Equator

São Pedro & São Paulo (Braz.)

D

Merirumã
Serra do Navio
AMAPÁ
Araguari
Macapá
Mazagão
I. Caviana
I. Mexiana
C. Maguarinho
Afuá Chaves
I. de Soure
Curuçá Salinópolis
Bragança

Óbidos
Monte Alegre
Prainha
Alenquer
Santarém
Belterra
Aveiro
Brasília Legal
Almeirim
Gurupá
I. Grande de Gurupá
Porto de Moz
Cametá
Breves
Marajó BELÉM
Castanhal
Abaetetuba
Curralinho

Vigia Viseu
Curururupu
B. de São Marcos
São Luís
Barreirinhas
Tutóia

Fernando de Noronha (Braz.)

Itaituba
Altamira
PARÁ
Baião
Capim
Tucuruí
Represa de Tucuruí

Alcântara
Rosário
Parnaíba
Luís Correia
Granja Itapipoca
Camocim

Caucaia
FORTALEZA

Atol das Rocas (Braz.)

Santa Inês
Bacabal
Pinheiro
Viana
Turiaçu

Piracuruca
Piripiri
Sobral
Maranguape
Cascavel
Aracati

5

Maraba
Serra dos Carajás
São João do Araguaia
Imperatriz
MARANHÃO
Brejo
Coroatá
Codó
Caxias
Campo Maior
Oiticica
Ipu
Quixadá
Crateús
Baturité
Russas
Mossoró
Areia Branca
Macau Ceará-Mirim

Parauapebas
Carajás
Tocantinópolis
Barra do Corda
Grajaú
Porto Franco
Teresina
Senador Pompeu
CEARÁ
Caraúbas RIO GRANDE
Calçó
NATAL

Araguaína
Estreito
Carolina
Colinas
Amarante
Valença do Piauí
Floriano
Oeiras
Picos
Iguatú
Cedro Sousa
Cajazeiras
Currais Novos
DO NORTE
Canguaretama
Mamanguape
Cabedelo

E

Conceição do Araguaia
Riachão
Loreto
Nova Iorque
Uruçuí
PIAUÍ
São João do Piauí
Juàzeiro
Chapada do Araripe
Crato Ouricuri
PARAÍBA
JOÃO PESSOA
Olinda
RECIFE
Jaboatão

Araguacema
Pedro Afonso
Santa Filomena
Dois Irmãos
Caracol
Remanso
Casa Nova
Juàzeiro
Petrolina
PERNAMBUCO
Salgueiro
Pesqueira
Caruaru
Vitória de Santo Antão
Palmares
Garanhuns
Petrolândia
Palmeira
Rio Largo
MACEIÓ

Palmas
BRAZIL
Porto Nacional
TOCANTINS
Parnaguá
Parnaíba
Xique-Xique
Mundo Novo
Senhor do Bonfim
Paulo Afonso
Indios dos
Represa de Sobradinho
Propriá
SERGIPE
Penedo
ALAGOAS
Arapiraca

6059

10

Santa Isabel do Morro
I. do Bananal
Gurupi
Peixe
Manuel Alves
Taguatinga
Barra
Jacobina
Queimadas
Serrinha
Estância
Capela
Aracaju
São Cristóvão

GROSSO
Planalto do Mato Grosso
Aruanã
1678
Niquelândia
Formosa
BAHIA
Barreiras
Ibotirama
Itaberaba
Cachoeira
Feira de Santana
Alagoinhas
Santo Amaro

F

uiabá
onto Antonio
Barra do Garças
Rondonópolis
Niquelândia
DIST FED
Formosa
Taguatinga
BRASÍLIA
Luziânia
São Domingos
Campos Belos
Paranã
Santa Maria da Vitória
Bom Jesus da Lapa
Posse
Carinhanha
Condeúba
Vitória da Conquista
Castro Alves
Valença
Jequié
SALVADOR
B. de Todos os Santos

GOIÁS
GOIÂNIA
Anápolis
Vianópolis
Januária
São Francisco
Monte Azul
Pedra Azul
Brumado
Ubaitaba
Ilhéus
Canavieiras

G

O GROSSO
OSUL
Coxim
Jataí
Rio Verde
Quirinópolis
Alto Araguaia
Mornhinos
Ipameri
Catalão
Paracatu
Patos de Minas
Diamantina
Salinas
Janaúba
Montes Claros
Araçuaí
Jequitinhonha
Itamaraju
Prado
Caravelas
Belmonte
Porto Seguro

Campo Grande
Santa Fé do Sul
Itumbiara
Araguari
MINAS GERAIS
Curvelo
Teófilo Otoni
Nanuque
Conceição da Barra
Banco dos Abrolhos
27

Ribas do Rio Pardo
Três Lagoas
Panorama
Uberlândia
Uberaba
Araxá
Sête Lagoas
Ipatinga
Governador Valadares
Mucuri
São Mateus
Nova Venécia

20

Presidente Epitácio
Aracatuba
Penápolis
Prata
Frutal
BELO HORIZONTE
Sabará
Itabira
Colatina
Linhares
Trindade (Braz.)
Martin Vaz (Braz.)

Presidente Prudente
Marília
Bauru
Jaú
SÃO PAULO
Franca
Divinópolis
Conselheiro Lafaiete
Ouro Prêto
Ponte Nova
2890
Pico da Bandeira
Cariacica
VITÓRIA
Vila Velha
Cachoeiro de Itapemirim

H

Ponta Porã
Paranaíba
Piracicaba
Limeira
CAMPINAS
Volta Redonda
RIO DE JANEIRO
Niterói
Cabo Frio
Nova Friburgo
Petrópolis
Três Rios
Juiz de Fora
Barbacena
São João del Rei
Campos
Itaperuna
Ubá

COPYRIGHT PHILIP'S

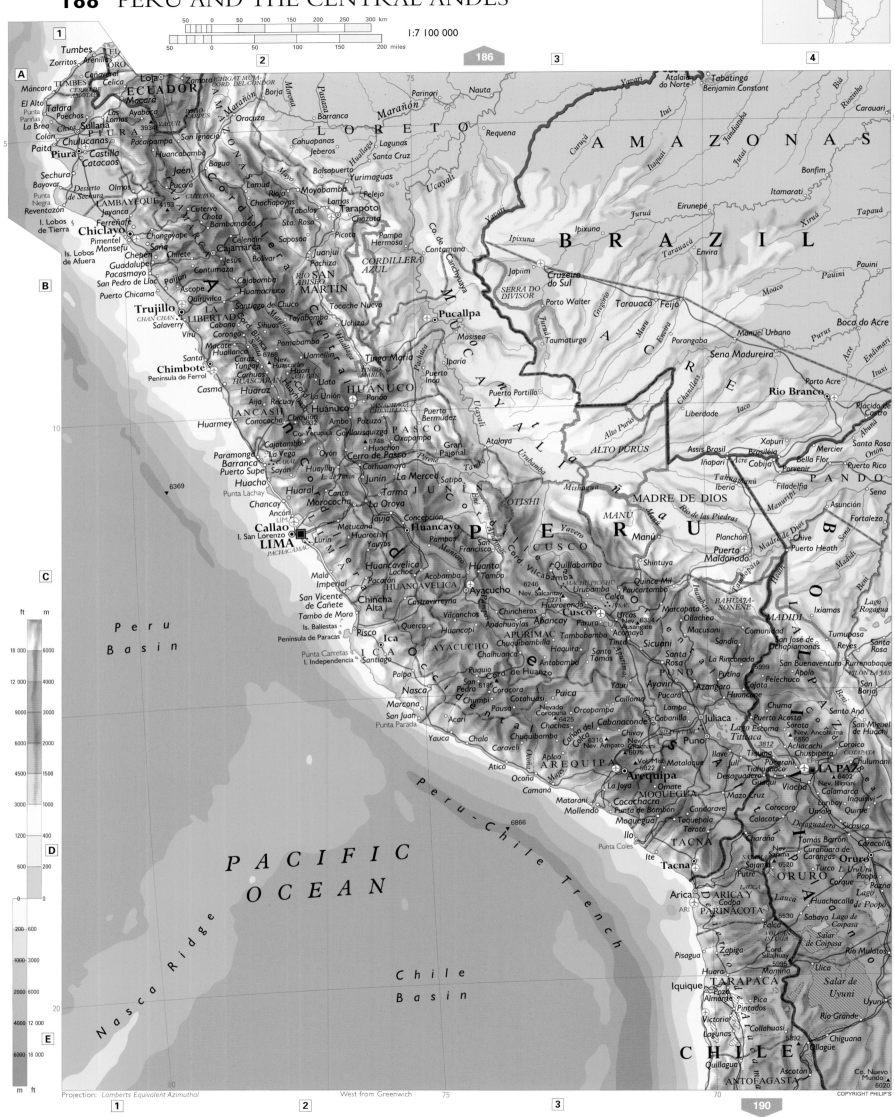

50 0 50 100 150 200 250 300 km
50 0 50 100 150 200 miles

1:7 100 000

Projection: Lamberts Equivalent Azimuthal

West from Greenwich

COPYRIGHT PHILIP'S

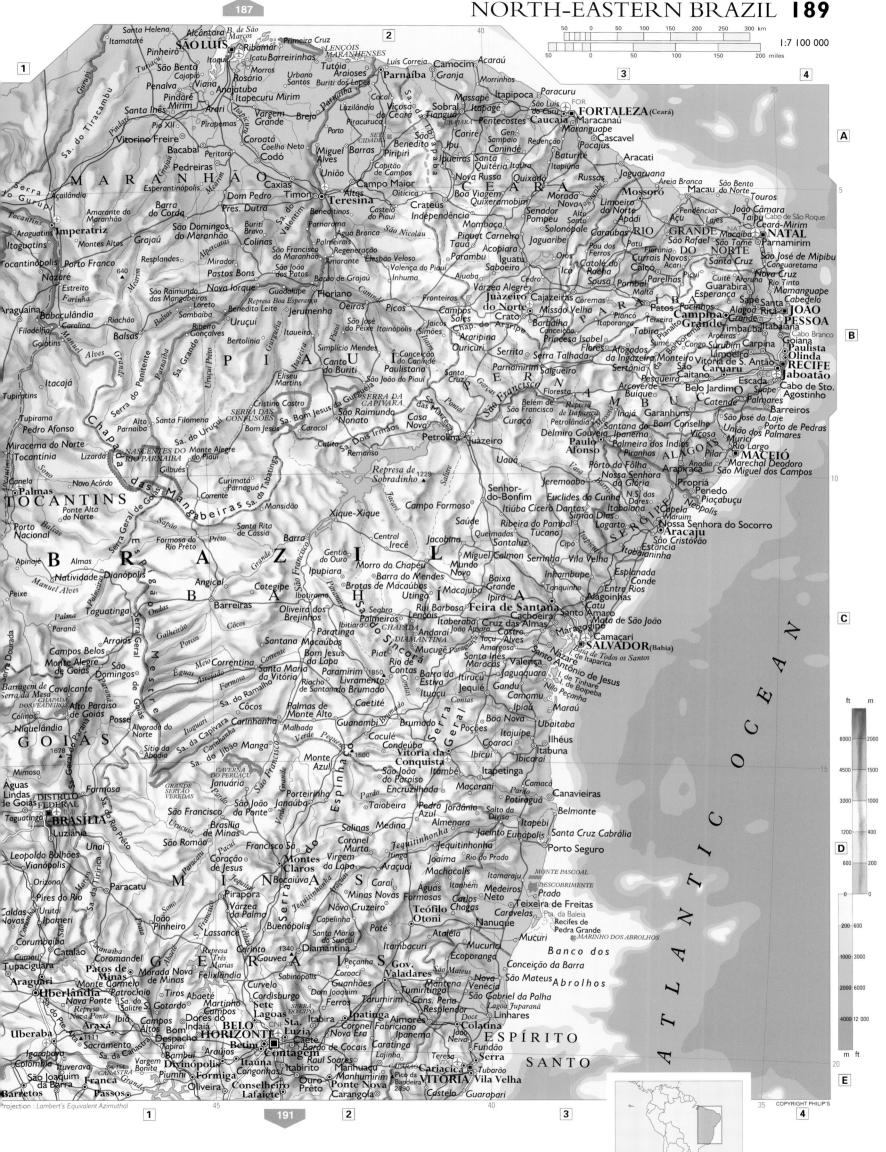

1:7 100 000

MARANHÃO

CEARÁ

RIO GRANDE DO NORTE

PARAÍBA

PERNAMBUCO

ALAGOAS

SERGIPE

PIAUÍ

TOCANTINS

BRAZIL

GOIÁS

BAHIA

MINAS GERAIS

ESPÍRITO SANTO

ATLANTIC OCEAN

SÃO LUIS

FORTALEZA (Ceará)

NATAL

JOÃO PESSOA

RECIFE

MACEIÓ

Aracaju

SALVADOR (Bahia)

Teresina

Imperatriz

BRASÍLIA

DISTRITO FEDERAL

BELO HORIZONTE

VITÓRIA

Uberlândia

Feira de Santana

Parnaíba

ft m

6000 2000

4500 1500

3000 1000

1200 400

600 200

0 0

200 600

1000 3000

2000 6000

4000 12 000

m ft

Projection : Lambert's Equivalent Azimuthal

COPYRIGHT PHILIP'S

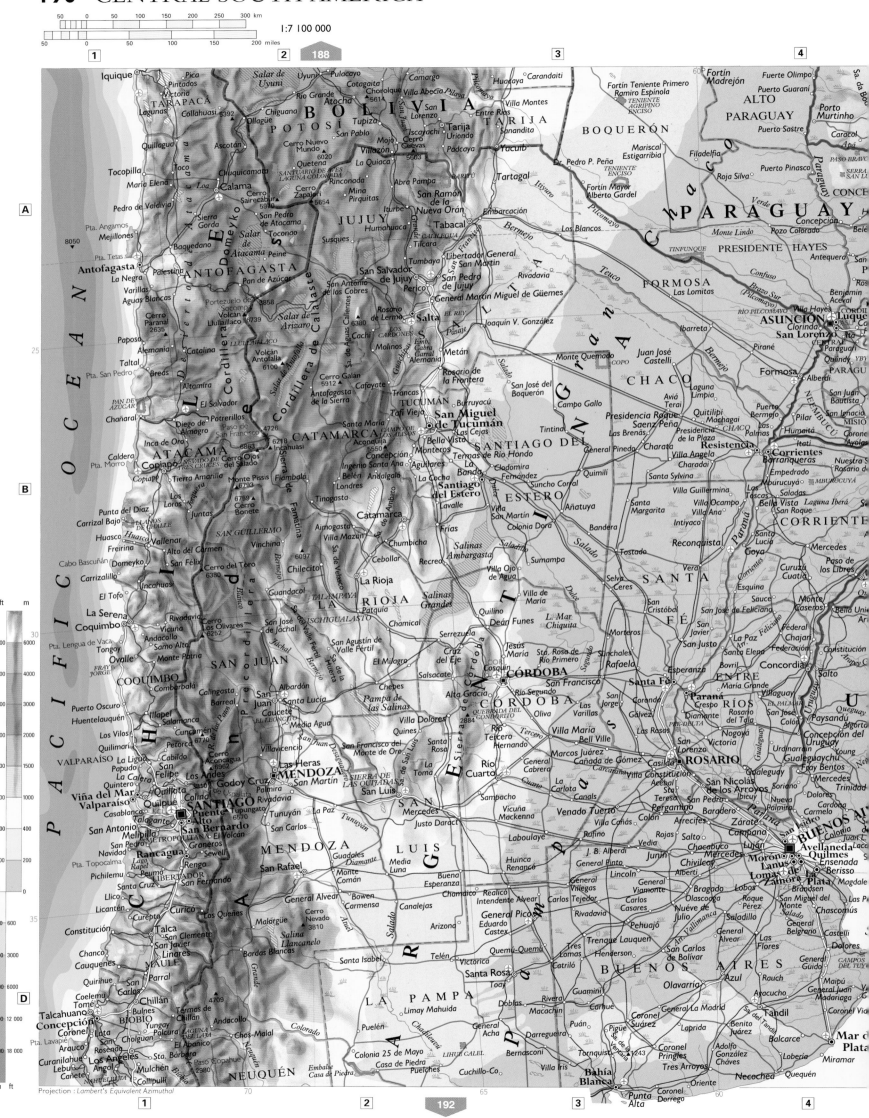

1:7 100 000

Projection : Lambert's Equivalent Azimuthal

COPYRIGHT PHILIP'S

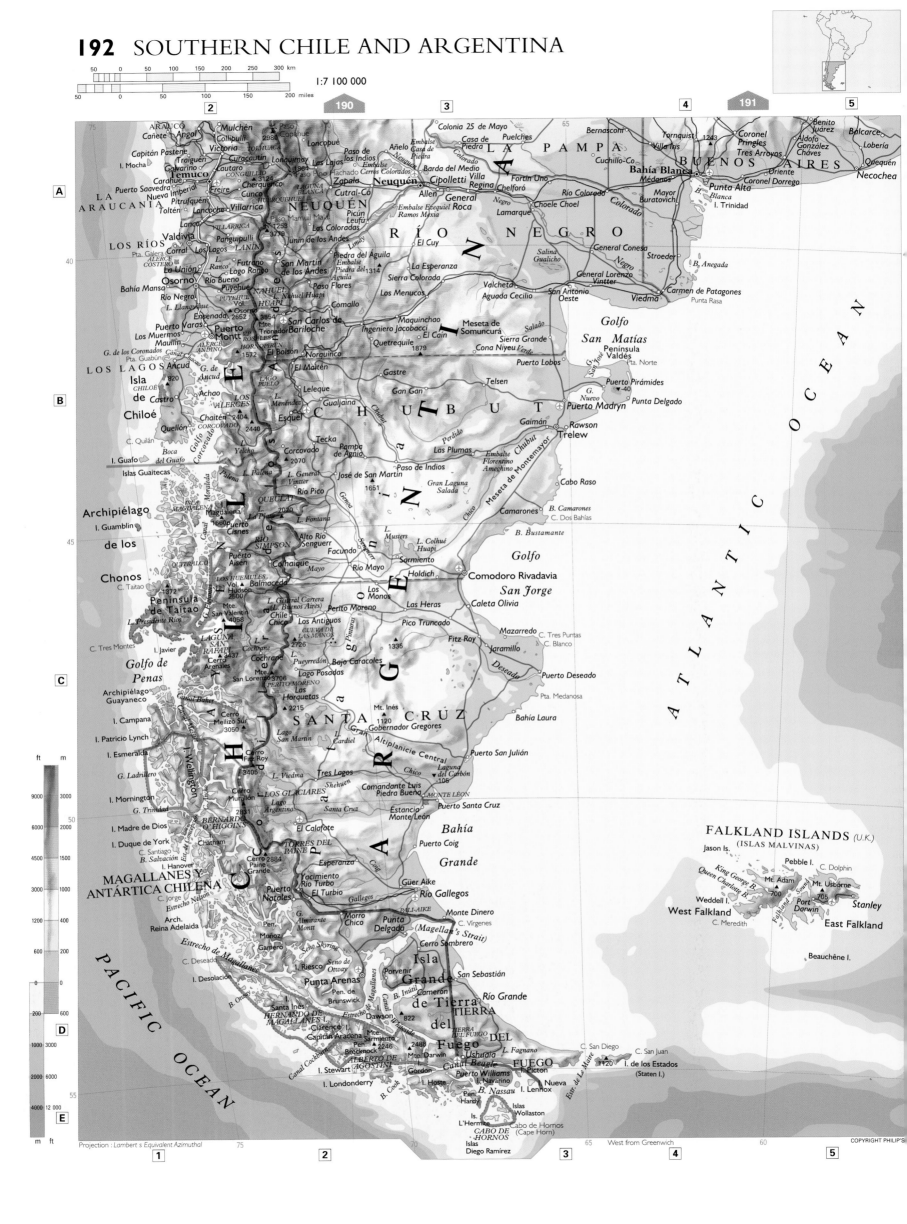

50 0   50 100 150 200 250 300 km

1:7 100 000

50   0   50   100   150
200 miles

2 **190** **3** **4** **191** **5**

A

Colonia 25 de Mayo

ARAUCO
Cañete
Angol
Mulchén
Collipulli
Victoria
Traiguen
Capitán Pastene
I. Mocha
Puerto Saavedra
Carahue
Nueva Imperial
Temuco
Cherquenco
Freire
Pitrufquen
Toltén
Lancoche
Villarrica
Loncopué
Las Lajas
Paso de los Indios
Zapala
Cutral-Co
Allen
Cipolletti
Neuquén
General Roca
Villa Regina
Choele Choel
Bahía Blanca
Médanos
Punta Alta
B. Blanca
I. Trinidad
Necochea

LA PAMPA
BUENOS AIRES
Benito Juárez
Coronel Pringles
Tres Arroyos
Aldofo Gonzáles Cháves
Balcarce
Lobería
Quequén

Bernasconi
Tornquist
Villa Iris
Coronel Dorrego
Oriente

NEUQUÉN
RÍO NEGRO
CHUBUT
SANTA CRUZ
LA ARGENTINA
PATAGONIA

Valdivia
LOS RÍOS
Osorno
LOS LAGOS
Ancud
Isla de Chiloé
Castro
Quellón

ATLANTIC OCEAN

PACIFIC OCEAN

FALKLAND ISLANDS (U.K.)
(ISLAS MALVINAS)
Jason Is.
King George B.
Queen Charlotte B.
Pebble I.
C. Dolphin
Mt. Adam 700
Mt. Usborne 705
Port Darwin
Stanley
West Falkland
East Falkland
Weddell I.
C. Meredith
Beauchêne I.

MAGALLANES Y ANTÁRTICA CHILENA

Punta Arenas
Isla Grande de Tierra del Fuego
TIERRA DEL FUEGO
Ushuaia
Río Grande
Puerto Williams
CABO DE HORNOS (Cape Horn)

Projection : Lambert's Equivalent Azimuthal

West from Greenwich

1 **2** **3** **4** **5**

INDEX TO WORLD MAPS

HOW TO USE THE INDEX

e index contains the names of all the principal places and features shown on the World Maps.
ch name is followed by an additional entry in italics giving the country or region within which it
ocated. The alphabetical order of names composed of two or more words is governed primarily
the first word, then by the second, and then by the country or region name that follows. This is
example of the rule:

Mir *Niger*	14°5N 11°59E	**139** C7
Mīr Kūh *Iran*	26°22N 58°55E	**129** E8
Mīr Shahdād *Iran*	26°15N 58°29E	**129** E8
Mira *Italy*	45°26N 12°8E	**93** C9

ysical features composed of a proper name (Erie) and a description (Lake) are positioned
habetically by the proper name. The description is positioned after the proper name and is
ually abbreviated:

Erie, L. *N. Amer.*	42°15N 81°0W	**174** D4

here a description forms part of a settlement or administrative name, however, it is always
itten in full and put in its true alphabetical position:

Mount Isa *Australia*	20°42S 139°26E	**150** C2

mes beginning with M' and Mc are indexed as if they were spelled Mac. Names beginning
are alphabetized under Saint, but Sankt, Sint, Sant', Santa and San are all spelt in full and are
habetized accordingly. If the same place name occurs two or more times in the index and all are in
same country, each is followed by the name of the administrative subdivision in which it is located.

e geographical co-ordinates which follow each name in the index give the latitude and longitude of
ch place. The first co-ordinate indicates latitude – the distance north or south of the Equator. The
ond co-ordinate indicates longitude – the distance east or west of the Greenwich Meridian. Both
itude and longitude are measured in degrees and minutes (there are 60 minutes in a degree).

e latitude is followed by N(orth) or S(outh) and the longitude by E(ast) or W(est).

e number in bold type which follows the geographical co-ordinates refers to the number of the
p page where that feature or place will be found. This is usually the largest scale at which the
ce or feature appears.

e letter and figure that are immediately after the page number give the grid square on the
p page, within which the feature is situated. The letter represents the latitude and the figure
longitude. A lower-case letter immediately after the page number refers to an inset map on
at page.

some cases the feature itself may fall within the specified square, while the name is outside.
is is usually the case only with features that are larger than a grid square.

vers are indexed to their mouths or confluences, and carry the symbol � after their names.
e following symbols are also used in the index: ■ country, ☑ overseas territory or dependency,
first-order administrative area, △ national park, ◠ other park (provincial park, nature
erve or game reserve), ☺ Australian Aboriginal land, ✈ (LHR) principal airport (and location
ntifier).

HOW TO PRONOUNCE PLACE NAMES

English-speaking people usually have no difficulty in reading and pronouncing correctly English
place names. However, foreign place name pronunciations may present many problems. Such
problems can be minimized by following some simple rules. However, these rules cannot be
applied to all situations, and there will be many exceptions.

1. In general, stress each syllable equally, unless your experience suggests otherwise.
2. Pronounce the letter 'a' as a broad 'a' as in 'arm'.
3. Pronounce the letter 'e' as a short 'e' as in 'elm'.
4. Pronounce the letter 'i' as a cross between a short 'i' and long 'e', as the two 'i's in 'California'.
5. Pronounce the letter 'o' as an intermediate 'o' as in 'soft'.
6. Pronounce the letter 'u' as an intermediate 'u' as in 'sure'.
7. Pronounce consonants hard, except in the Romance-language areas where 'g's are likely to
   be pronounced softly like 'j' in 'jam'; 'j' itself may be pronounced as 'y'; and 'x's may be
   pronounced as 'h'.
8. For names in mainland China, pronounce 'q' like the 'ch' in 'chin', 'x' like the 'sh' in 'she', 'zh'
   like the 'j' in 'jam', and 'z' as if it were spelled 'dz'. In general, pronounce 'a' as in 'father', 'e'
   as in 'but', 'i' as in 'keep', 'o' as in 'or', and 'u' as in 'rule'.

Moreover, English has no diacritical marks (accent and pronunciation signs), although some
languages do. The following is a brief and general guide to the pronunciation of those most
frequently used in the principal Western European languages.

		Pronunciation as in
French	é	day and shows that the 'e' is to be pronounced; e.g. Orléans.
	è	mare
	î	used over any vowel and does not affect pronunciation; shows contraction of the name, usually omission of 's' following a vowel.
	ç	's' before 'a', 'o' and 'u'.
	ë, ï, ü	over 'e', 'i' and 'u' when they are used with another vowel and shows that each is to be pronounced.
German	ä	fate
	ö	fur
	ü	no English equivalent; like French 'tu'.
Italian	à, é	over vowels and indicates stress.
Portuguese	ã, õ	vowels pronounced nasally.
	ç	boss
	á	shows stress.
	ô	shows that a vowel has an 'i' or 'u' sound combined with it.
Spanish	ñ	canyon
	ü	pronounced as 'w' and separately from adjoining vowels.
	á	usually indicates that this is a stressed vowel.

ABBREVIATIONS

C.T. – Australian Capital Territory
R. – Autonomous Region
ghan. – Afghanistan
r. – Africa
a. – Alabama
ta. – Alberta
ner. – America(n)
at. – Antilles
ch. – Archipelago
riz. – Arizona
k. – Arkansas
l. Oc. – Atlantic Ocean
– Baie, Bahía, Bay, Bucht, Bugt
C. – British Columbia
ngla. – Bangladesh
rr. – Barrage
os.-H. – Bosnia-Herzegovina
– Cabo, Cap, Cape, Coast
A.R. – Central African Republic
Prov. – Cape Province
lif. – California
it. – Catarata
nt. – Central
an. – Channel
olo. – Colorado
nn. – Connecticut
rd. – Cordillera
. – Creek
zech. – Czech Republic
C. – District of Columbia
el. – Delaware
em. – Democratic
ep. – Dependency
es. – Desert
ét. – Détroit
st. – District
. – Djebel
om. Rep. – Dominican Republic
– East

El Salv. – El Salvador
Eq. Guin. – Equatorial Guinea
Est. – Estrecho
Falk. Is. – Falkland Is.
Fd. – Fjord
Fla. – Florida
Fr. – French
G. – Golfe, Golfo, Gulf, Guba, Gebel
Ga. – Georgia
Gt. – Great, Greater
Guinea-Biss. – Guinea-Bissau
H.K. – Hong Kong
H.P. – Himachal Pradesh
Hants. – Hampshire
Harb. – Harbor, Harbour
Hd. – Head
Hts. – Heights
I.(s). – Île, Ilha, Insel, Isla, Island, Isle
Ill. – Illinois
Ind. – Indiana
Ind. Oc. – Indian Ocean
Ivory C. – Ivory Coast
J. – Jabal, Jebel
Jaz. – Jazīrah
Junc. – Junction
K. – Kap, Kapp
Kans. – Kansas
Kep. – Kepulauan
Ky. – Kentucky
L. – Lac, Lacul, Lago, Lagoa, Lake, Limni, Loch, Lough
La. – Louisiana
Ld. – Land
Liech. – Liechtenstein
Lux. – Luxembourg
Mad. P. – Madhya Pradesh
Madag. – Madagascar

Man. – Manitoba
Mass. – Massachusetts
Md. – Maryland
Me. – Maine
Medit. S. – Mediterranean Sea
Mich. – Michigan
Minn. – Minnesota
Miss. – Mississippi
Mo. – Missouri
Mont. – Montana
Mozam. – Mozambique
Mt.(s) – Mont, Montaña, Mountain
Mte. – Monte
Mti. – Monti
N. – Nord, Norte, North, Northern, Nouveau, Nahal, Nahr
N.B. – New Brunswick
N.C. – North Carolina
N. Cal. – New Caledonia
N. Dak. – North Dakota
N.H. – New Hampshire
N.I. – North Island
N.J. – New Jersey
N. Mex. – New Mexico
N.S. – Nova Scotia
N.S.W. – New South Wales
N.W.T. – North West Territory
N.Y. – New York
N.Z. – New Zealand
Nac. – Nacional
Nat. – National
Nebr. – Nebraska
Neths. – Netherlands
Nev. – Nevada
Nfld & L... – Newfoundland and Labrador
Nic. – Nicaragua
O. – Oued, Ouadi
Occ. – Occidentale

Okla. – Oklahoma
Ont. – Ontario
Or. – Orientale
Oreg. – Oregon
Os. – Ostrov
Oz. – Ozero
P. – Pass, Passo, Pasul, Pulau
P.E.I. – Prince Edward Island
Pa. – Pennsylvania
Pac. Oc. – Pacific Ocean
Papua N.G. – Papua New Guinea
Pass. – Passage
Peg. – Pegunungan
Pen. – Peninsula, Péninsule
Phil. – Philippines
Pk. – Peak
Plat. – Plateau
Prov. – Province, Provincial
Pt. – Point
Pta. – Ponta, Punta
Pte. – Pointe
Qué. – Québec
Queens. – Queensland
R. – Rio, River
R.I. – Rhode Island
Ra. – Range
Raj. – Rajasthan
Recr. – Recreational, Récréatif
Reg. – Region
Rep. – Republic
Res. – Reserve, Reservoir
Rhld-Pfz. – Rheinland-Pfalz
S. – South, Southern, Sur
Si. Arabia – Saudi Arabia
S.C. – South Carolina
S. Dak. – South Dakota
S.I. – South Island
S. Leone – Sierra Leone
Sa. – Serra, Sierra

Sask. – Saskatchewan
Scot. – Scotland
Sd. – Sound
Sev. – Severnaya
Sib. – Siberia
Sprs. – Springs
St. – Saint
Sta. – Santa
Ste. – Sainte
Sto. – Santo
Str. – Strait, Stretto
Switz. – Switzerland
Tas. – Tasmania
Tenn. – Tennessee
Terr. – Territory, Territoire
Tex. – Texas
Tg. – Tanjung
Trin. & Tob. – Trinidad & Tobago
U.A.E. – United Arab Emirates
U.K. – United Kingdom
U.S.A. – United States of America
Univ. – University, Université, Universidad
Ut. P. – Uttar Pradesh
Va. – Virginia
Vdkhr. – Vodokhranilishche
Vdskh. – Vodoskhovyshche
Vf. – Vírful
Vic. – Victoria
Vol. – Volcano
Vt. – Vermont
W. – Wadi, West
W. Va. – West Virginia
Wall. & F. Is. – Wallis and Futuna Is.
Wash. – Washington
Wis. – Wisconsin
Wlkp. – Wielkopolski
Wyo. – Wyoming
Yorks. – Yorkshire

A

A Baiuca Spain 43°19N 8°29W 88 B2
A Baña = San Vicenzo
  Spain 42°58N 8°46W 88 C2
A Cañiza Spain 42°13N 8°16W 88 C2
A Carballa Spain 43°13N 8°54W 88 B2
A Carreira Spain 43°21N 8°12W 88 B2
A Coruña Spain 43°20N 8°25W 88 B2
A Coruña □ Spain 43°10N 8°30W 88 B2
A Cruz do Incio Spain 42°39N 7°21W 88 C3
A Estrada Spain 42°43N 8°27W 88 C2
A Feira do Monte Spain 43°12N 7°34W 88 B3
A Fonsagrada Spain 43°8N 7°4W 88 B3
A Guarda Spain 41°56N 8°52W 88 D2
A Gudiña Spain 42°4N 7°8W 88 C3
A Pobre Spain 42°58N 7°3W 88 C3
A Ramallosa Spain 42°5N 8°30W 88 C2
A Rúa Spain 42°24N 7°6W 88 C3
A Serra de Outes Spain 42°52N 8°55W 88 C2
A Shau Vietnam 16°6N 107°22E 120 D6
Aabenraa Denmark 55°3N 9°25E 63 J3
Aabybro Denmark 57°10N 9°44E 63 G3
Aachen Germany 50°45N 6°6E 76 E2
Aalborg Denmark 57°2N 9°54E 63 G3
Aalborg Bugt Denmark 56°50N 10°35E 63 H4
Aalen Germany 48°51N 10°6E 77 G6
Aalestrup Denmark 56°42N 9°29E 63 H3
Aalst Belgium 50°56N 4°2E 69 D4
Aalten Neths. 51°56N 6°35E 69 C6
Aalter Belgium 51°5N 3°28E 69 C3
Äänekoski Finland 62°36N 25°44E 60 E21
Aarau Switz. 47°23N 8°4E 77 H4
Aarberg Switz. 47°2N 7°16E 77 H3
Aare → Switz. 47°33N 8°14E 77 H4
Aargau □ Switz. 47°26N 8°10E 77 H4
Aarhus Denmark 56°8N 10°11E 63 H4
Aars Denmark 56°48N 9°30E 63 H3
Aarschot Belgium 50°59N 4°49E 69 D4
Aasiaat Greenland 68°43N 52°56W 57 D5
Aba China 32°59N 101°42E 116 A3
Aba
  Dem. Rep. of the Congo 3°58N 30°17E 142 B3
Aba Nigeria 5°10N 7°19E 139 D6
Abaco I. Bahamas 26°25N 77°10W 182 A4
Abadab, J. Sudan 18°54N 35°56E 137 D4
Äbādān Iran 30°22N 48°20E 129 D6
Äbädeh Iran 31°8N 52°40E 129 D7
Abadin Spain 43°21N 7°29W 88 B3
Abadla Algeria 31°2N 2°45W 136 B3
Abaeté Brazil 19°9S 45°27W 189 D1
Abaeté → Brazil 18°2S 45°12W 189 D1
Abaetetuba Brazil 1°40S 48°50W 187 D9
Abagnar Qi = Xilinhot
  China 43°52N 116°2E 114 C9
Abah, Tanjung
  Indonesia 8°46S 115°38E 119 K18
Abai Paraguay 25°58S 55°54W 191 B4
Abakaliki Nigeria 6°22N 8°2E 139 D6
Abakan Russia 53°40N 91°10E 109 B12
Abala Niger 14°56N 3°22E 139 C5
Abalak Niger 15°22N 6°21E 139 B6
Abalemma Niger 16°12N 7°50E 139 B6
Abana Turkey 41°59N 34°1E 104 B6
Abancay Peru 13°35S 72°55W 188 C3
Abang, Gunung
  Indonesia 8°16S 115°25E 119 J18
Abano Terme Italy 45°22N 11°46E 93 C8
Abarán Spain 38°12N 1°23W 91 G3
Abariringa Kiribati 2°50S 171°40W 156 H10
Abarqū Iran 31°10N 53°20E 129 D7
Abasha Georgia 42°11N 42°13E 87 A6
Abashiri Japan 44°0N 144°15E 112 B12
Abashiri-Wan Japan 44°0N 144°30E 112 C12
Abaújszántó Hungary 48°16N 21°12E 80 B6
Abava → Latvia 57°6N 21°54E 82 A8
Äbay = Nîl el Azraq →
  Sudan 15°38N 32°31E 135 E12
Abay Kazakhstan 49°38N 72°53E 109 C8
Abaya, L. Ethiopia 6°30N 37°50E 131 F2
Abaza Russia 52°39N 90°6E 109 B12
Abbadia di Fiastra ○
  Italy 43°12N 13°24E 93 E10
Abbadia San Salvatore
  Italy 42°53N 11°41E 93 F8
'Abbāsābād Iran 33°34N 58°23E 129 C8
Abbay = Nîl el Azraq →
  Sudan 15°38N 32°31E 135 E12
Abbaye, Pt. U.S.A. 46°58N 88°8W 172 B9
Abbé, L. Ethiopia 11°8N 41°47E 131 E3
Abbeville France 50°6N 1°49E 71 B8
Abbeville Ala., U.S.A. 31°34N 85°15W 178 D4
Abbeville Ga., U.S.A. 31°59N 83°18W 178 D6
Abbeville La., U.S.A. 29°58N 92°8W 176 G8
Abbeville S.C., U.S.A. 34°11N 82°23W 178 A7
Abbeyfeale Ireland 52°23N 9°18W 64 D2
Abbeyleix Ireland 52°54N 7°22E 64 D4
Abbiategrasso Italy 45°24N 8°54E 92 C5
Abbot Ice Shelf
  Antarctica 73°0S 92°0W 55 D16
Abbotsford Canada 49°5N 122°20W 162 D4
Abbottabad Pakistan 34°10N 73°15E 124 B5
Abbou, O. ben →
  Algeria 28°32N 5°14E 136 C5
ABC Islands W. Indies 12°15N 69°0W 183 D6
Abd al Kūrī Yemen 12°5N 52°20E 131 D5
Äbdänän Iran 32°56N 47°28E 105 F12
Äbdar Iran 30°16N 55°19E 129 D7
'Abdolābād Iran 34°12N 56°30E 129 C8
Abdulino Russia 53°42N 53°40E 108 B4
Abdulpur Bangla. 24°15N 89°9E 125 G13
Abéché Chad 13°50N 20°35E 135 F10
Abejar Spain 41°48N 2°47W 90 D2
Abel Tasman △ N.Z. 40°59S 173°3E 155 M8
Abengourou Ivory C. 6°42N 3°27W 138 D4
Abenójar Spain 38°53N 4°21W 89 G6
Åbenrå = Aabenraa
  Denmark 55°3N 9°25E 63 J3
Abensberg Germany 48°48N 11°51E 77 G7
Abeokuta Nigeria 7°3N 3°19E 139 D5
Aberaeron U.K. 52°15N 4°15W 67 E3
Aberayron = Aberaeron
  U.K. 52°15N 4°15W 67 E3
Aberchirder U.K. 57°34N 2°37W 66 D6
Abercorn Australia 25°12S 151°5E 151 D5
Abercrombie River △
  Australia 34°5S 149°0E 153 C8
Aberdare U.K. 51°43N 3°27W 67 F4
Aberdare △ Kenya 0°22S 36°44E 142 C4

Aberdare Ra. Kenya 0°15S 36°50E 142 C4
Aberdaugleddau = Milford Haven
  U.K. 51°42N 5°7W 67 F2
Aberdeen Australia 32°9S 150°56E 153 B9
Aberdeen Canada 52°20N 106°8W 163 C7
Aberdeen China 22°14N 114°8E 111 a
Aberdeen S. Africa 32°28S 24°2E 144 D3
Aberdeen Idaho,
  U.S.A. 42°57N 112°50W 168 E7
Aberdeen Md., U.S.A. 39°31N 76°10W 173 F15
Aberdeen Miss.,
  U.S.A. 33°49N 88°33W 177 E10
Aberdeen S. Dak.,
  U.S.A. 45°28N 98°29W 172 C4
Aberdeen Wash.,
  U.S.A. 46°59N 123°50W 170 D3
Aberdeen City □ U.K. 57°10N 2°10W 65 D6
Aberdeen L. Canada 64°30N 99°0W 160 E12
Aberdeenshire □ U.K. 57°17N 2°36W 65 D6
Aberdovey = Aberdyfi
  U.K. 52°33N 4°3W 67 E3
Aberdyfi U.K. 52°33N 4°3W 67 E3
Aberfeldy U.K. 56°37N 3°51W 65 E5
Aberfoyle U.K. 56°11N 4°23W 65 E4
Abergavenny U.K. 51°49N 3°1W 67 F4
Abergele U.K. 53°17N 3°35W 66 D4
Abergwaun = Fishguard
  U.K. 52°0N 4°58W 67 E3
Aberhonddu = Brecon
  U.K. 51°57N 3°23W 67 F4
Abermaw = Barmouth
  U.K. 52°44N 4°4W 66 E3
Abernathy U.S.A. 33°50N 101°51W 176 E4
Aberpennar = Mountain Ash
  U.K. 51°40N 3°23W 67 F4
Abert, L. U.S.A. 42°38N 120°14W 168 E3
Abertawe = Swansea
  U.K. 51°37N 3°57W 67 F4
Aberteifi = Cardigan U.K. 52°5N 4°40W 67 E3
Aberystwyth U.K. 52°25N 4°5W 67 E3
Abhā Si. Arabia 18°0N 42°34E 137 D5
Abhayapuri India 26°24N 90°38E 125 F14
Abia □ Nigeria 5°30N 7°35E 139 D6
Abide Turkey 38°55N 29°20E 99 C11
Abidiya Sudan 18°18N 34°3E 137 D3
Abidjan Ivory C. 5°26N 3°58W 138 D4
Abidjan □ Ivory C. 5°20N 4°0W 138 D4
Abilene Kans., U.S.A. 38°55N 97°13W 172 F5
Abilene Tex., U.S.A. 32°28N 99°43W 176 E5
Abingdon U.S.A. 36°43N 81°59W 173 G13
Abingdon-on-Thames
  U.K. 51°40N 1°17W 67 F6
Abington Reef Australia 18°0S 149°35E 150 B4
Abiod, Remel el Tunisia 31°45N 9°35E 136 B5
Abisko △ Sweden 68°18N 18°44E 60 B18
Abitau → Canada 59°53N 109°3W 163 B7
Abitibi → Canada 51°3N 80°55W 164 B3
Abitibi, L. Canada 48°40N 79°40W 164 C4
Abkhaz Republic = Abkhazia □
  Georgia 43°12N 41°5E 87 J5
Abkhazia □ Georgia 43°12N 41°5E 87 J5
Abminga Australia 26°8S 134°51E 151 D1
Abnûb Egypt 27°18N 31°4E 137 B3
Åbo = Turku Finland 60°30N 22°19E 84 B2
Abohar India 30°10N 74°10E 124 D6
Aboisso Ivory C. 5°30N 3°5W 138 D4
Abomey Benin 7°10N 2°5E 139 D5
Abong-Mbang Cameroon 4°0N 13°8E 140 D2
Abonnema Nigeria 4°41N 6°49E 139 E6
Abony Hungary 47°12N 20°3E 80 C5
Aboso Ghana 5°23N 1°57W 138 D4
Abou-Deïa Chad 11°20N 19°20E 135 F9
Abovyan Armenia 40°16N 44°37E 87 K7
Aboyne U.K. 57°4N 2°47W 65 D6
Abra Pampa Argentina 22°43S 65°42W 190 A2
Abraham L. Canada 52°15N 116°35W 162 C5
Abrantes Portugal 39°24N 8°7W 89 F2
Abreojos, Pta. Mexico 26°50N 113°40W 180 B2
Abri Sudan 20°50N 30°27E 137 C3
Abrolhos, Banco dos
  Brazil 18°0S 38°0W 189 D3
Abrud Romania 46°19N 23°5E 80 D8
Abruzzo □ Italy 42°15N 14°0E 93 F10
Absaroka Range
  U.S.A. 44°45N 109°50W 168 D9
Abşeron Yarımadası
  Azerbaijan 40°28N 49°57E 87 K9
Abtenau Austria 47°33N 13°21E 78 D6
Abu India 24°41N 72°50E 124 G7
Abu al Abyad U.A.E. 24°11N 53°50E 129 E7
Abū al Khaşīb Iraq 30°25N 48°0E 128 D5
Abū 'Alī Si. Arabia 27°20N 49°27E 129 E6
Abū 'Alī → Lebanon 34°25N 35°50E 130 A4
Abu Ballas Egypt 24°26N 27°36E 137 C2
Abu Dhabi = Abū Ȥaby
  U.A.E. 24°28N 54°22E 129 E7
Abu Dis Sudan 19°12N 33°38E 137 D3
Abū Du'ān Syria 36°25N 38°15E 105 D8
Abu el Gaïn, W. →
  Egypt 29°35N 33°30E 130 F2
Abu Fatma, Ras Sudan 22°25N 36°25E 137 C4
Abu Ga'da, W. →
  Egypt 29°15N 32°53E 130 F1
Abū Ḩadrīyah
  Si. Arabia 27°20N 48°58E 129 E6
Abu Hamed Sudan 19°32N 33°13E 137 D3
Abu Haraz Sudan 19°8N 32°18E 137 D3
Abu Kamāl Syria 34°30N 41°0E 105 E9
Abū Kebīr Egypt 30°43N 31°40E 137 E2
Abū Madd, Ra's
  Si. Arabia 24°50N 37°7E 128 E3
Abu Mena = Abu Mina
  Egypt 30°51N 29°40E 137 E6
Abu Mina Egypt 30°51N 29°40E 137 E6
Abū Mūsā U.A.E. 25°52N 55°3E 129 E7
Abū Qaşr Si. Arabia 30°21N 38°34E 128 D3
Abū Qireiya Egypt 24°5N 35°28E 137 C4
Abū Qurqāş Egypt 28°1N 30°44E 137 C3
Abu Shagara, Ras Sudan 21°4N 37°19E 137 C4
Abu Simbel Egypt 22°18N 31°40E 137 C3
Abu Soma, Râs Egypt 26°50N 33°59E 137 C3
Abū Şukhayr Iraq 31°54N 44°30E 105 G11
Abū Sultān Egypt 30°24N 32°21E 137 E8
Abu Tig Egypt 27°4N 31°15E 137 C3
Abu Zabad Sudan 12°25N 29°10E 135 F11
Abū Ȥaby U.A.E. 24°28N 54°22E 129 E7
Abū Zeydābād Iran 33°54N 51°45E 129 C6
Abuja Nigeria 9°5N 7°32E 139 D6
Abukuma-Gawa →
  Japan 38°6N 140°52E 112 E10

Abukuma-Sammyaku
  Japan 37°30N 140°45E 112 F10
Abunã Brazil 9°40S 65°20W 186 E5
Abunã → Brazil 9°41S 65°20W 186 E5
Aburo
  Dem. Rep. of the Congo 2°4N 30°53E 142 B3
Abut Hd. N.Z. 43°7S 170°15E 155 D5
Åby Sweden 58°40N 16°10E 63 F10
Aby, Lagune Ivory C. 5°15N 3°14W 138 D4
Abyei ☑ Sudan 9°30N 28°30E 135 G11
Academy Gletscher
  Greenland 82°2N 34°0W 57 A7
Acadia U.S.A. 44°20N 68°13W 173 C19
Açailândia Brazil 4°57S 47°30W 189 A1
Acajutla El Salv. 13°36N 89°50W 182 D2
Acámbaro Mexico 20°2N 100°44W 180 C4
Acanthus Greece 40°27N 23°47E 96 F7
Acaponeta Mexico 22°30N 105°22W 180 C3
Acapulco Mexico 16°51N 99°55W 181 D5
Acapulco Trench
  Pac. Oc. 12°0N 88°0W 180 D4
Acarai, Serra Brazil 1°50N 57°50W 186 C7
Acarai Mts. = Acarai, Serra
  Brazil 1°50N 57°50W 186 C7
Acaraú Brazil 2°53S 40°7W 189 A2
Acari Brazil 6°31S 36°38W 189 B3
Acari Peru 15°25S 74°36W 188 C3
Acarigua Venezuela 9°33N 69°12W 186 B5
Acatlán Mexico 18°12N 98°3W 181 D5
Acayucan Mexico 17°57N 94°55W 181 D6
Accéglio Italy 44°28N 7°0E 92 D4
Accomac U.S.A. 37°43N 75°40W 173 G16
Accous France 43°0N 0°36W 72 E3
Accra Ghana 5°35N 0°6W 139 D4
Accrington U.K. 53°45N 2°22W 66 D5
Acebal Argentina 33°20S 60°50W 190 C3
Aceh □ Indonesia 4°15N 97°30E 118 D1
Acerra Italy 40°57N 14°22E 95 B7
Aceuchal Spain 38°39N 6°30W 89 G4
Achacachi Bolivia 16°3S 68°43W 188 D4
Achalia Greece 38°5N 21°45E 98 C3
Achalpur India 21°22N 77°32E 126 D3
Achao Chile 42°28S 73°30W 192 B2
Acharnes Greece 38°5S 23°44E 98 C5
Acheloos → Greece 38°19N 21°7E 98 C3
Acheng China 45°30N 126°58E 115 B14
Achenkirch Austria 47°32N 11°45E 78 D4
Achensee Austria 47°26N 11°45E 78 D4
Achentrias Greece 34°59N 25°13E 99 G7
Acher India 23°10N 72°32E 124 H5
Achern Germany 48°37N 8°4E 77 G4
Acheron → N.Z. 42°16S 173°4E 155 C8
Achill Hd. Ireland 53°58N 10°15W 64 C1
Achill I. Ireland 53°58N 10°1W 64 C1
Achim Germany 53°1N 9°3E 76 B5
Achinsk Russia 56°20N 90°20E 107 D10
Achladokambos Greece 37°31N 22°35E 98 D4
Acıgöl Turkey 37°50N 29°50E 99 D11
Acıpayam Turkey 37°26N 29°22E 99 D11
Acireale Italy 37°37N 15°10E 95 E8
Acklins I. Bahamas 22°30N 74°0W 183 B5
Acme Canada 51°33N 113°30W 162 C6
Acme U.S.A. 40°8N 79°26W 174 F5
Acobamba Peru 12°52S 74°35W 188 C3
Acomayo Peru 13°55S 71°38W 188 C3
Aconcagua, Cerro
  Argentina 32°39S 70°0W 190 C2
Aconquija, Mt. Argentina 27°0S 66°0W 190 B2
Acopiara Brazil 6°6S 39°27W 189 B3
Açores, Is. dos Atl. Oc. 38°0N 27°0W 134 a
Acornhoek S. Africa 24°37S 31°2E 145 B5
Acquapendente Italy 42°44N 11°52E 93 F8
Acquasanta Terme
  Italy 42°46N 13°24E 93 F10
Acquasparta Italy 42°41N 12°33E 93 F9
Acquaviva delle Fonti
  Italy 40°54N 16°50E 95 B9
Ácqui Terme Italy 44°41N 8°28E 92 D5
Acraman, L. Australia 32°2S 135°23E 151 E2
Acre = 'Akko Israel 32°55N 35°4E 130 C4
Acre □ Brazil 9°1S 71°0W 188 B3
Acre → Brazil 8°45S 67°22W 188 B4
Acri Italy 39°29N 16°23E 95 C9
Acs Hungary 47°42N 18°2E 80 C3
Actinolite Canada 44°32N 77°19W 174 B7
Actium Greece 38°57N 20°45E 98 C2
Acton Canada 43°38N 80°3W 174 C4
Açu Brazil 5°34S 36°54W 189 B3
Acworth U.S.A. 34°4N 84°41W 178 A5
Ad Dafinah Si. Arabia 23°18N 41°3E 128 D4
Ad Daghghāran Iraq 32°8N 44°55E 105 G11
Ad Dahnā Si. Arabia 24°30N 48°10E 131 C4
Ad Dammām Si. Arabia 26°20N 50°5E 129 E6
Ad Dāmūr Lebanon 33°43N 35°27E 130 B4
Ad Dawādimī Si. Arabia 24°35N 44°15E 128 E5
Ad Dawhah Qatar 25°15N 51°35E 129 E6
Ad Dawr Iraq 34°27N 43°47E 105 E10
Ad Dhakhīrah Qatar 25°44N 51°33E 129 E6
Ad Dir'īyah Si. Arabia 24°44N 46°35E 128 E5
Ad Dīwānīyah Iraq 32°0N 45°0E 105 F11
Ad Dujayl Iraq 33°51N 44°14E 105 F11
Ad Duwayd Si. Arabia 30°15N 42°17E 128 D4
Ada Ghana 5°44N 0°40E 139 D5
Ada Serbia 45°49N 20°9E 80 E5
Ada Minn., U.S.A. 47°18N 96°31W 172 B5
Ada Okla., U.S.A. 34°46N 96°41W 176 D6
Adabiya Egypt 29°53N 32°28E 130 F1
Adair, C. Canada 71°30N 71°34W 161 C17
Adaja → Spain 41°32N 4°52W 88 D6
Adak U.S.A. 51°45N 176°45W 166 E4
Adak I. U.S.A. 51°45N 176°45W 166 E4
Adam, Mt. Falk. Is. 51°34S 60°4W 192 D4
Adama = Nazret
  Ethiopia 8°32N 39°22E 131 F2
Adamaoua, Massif de l'
  Cameroon 7°20N 12°20E 139 D7
Adamawa □ Nigeria 9°20N 12°30E 139 D7
Adamawa Highlands =
  Adamaoua, Massif de l'
  Cameroon 7°20N 12°20E 139 D7
Adamello, Mte. Italy 46°10N 10°34E 92 B7
Adamello □ Italy 46°4N 10°28E 92 B7
Adaminaby Australia 36°0S 148°45E 153 D8
Adams Mass., U.S.A. 42°38N 73°7W 175 D11
Adams N.Y., U.S.A. 43°49N 76°1W 175 C8
Adams Wis., U.S.A. 43°57N 89°49W 172 D9
Adams, Mt. U.S.A. 46°12N 121°30W 170 D5
Adam's Bridge Sri Lanka 9°15N 79°40E 127 K4

Adams L. Canada 51°10N 119°40W 162 C5
Adam's Peak Sri Lanka 6°48N 80°30E 127 L5
Adamuz Spain 38°2N 4°32W 89 G6
'Adan Yemen 12°45N 45°0E 131 E4
Adana Turkey 37°0N 35°16E 104 D6
Adana □ Turkey 37°0N 35°0E 104 D6
Adanero Spain 40°56N 4°36W 88 E6
Adang, Ko Thailand 6°33N 99°18E 121 J2
Adapazarı = Sakarya
  Turkey 40°48N 30°25E 104 B4
Adarama Sudan 17°10N 34°52E 135 E12
Adare Ireland 52°34N 8°47W 64 D3
Adare, C. Antarctica 71°0S 171°0E 55 D11
Adaut Indonesia 8°8S 131°7E 119 F8
Adavale Australia 25°52S 144°32E 151 D3
Adda → Italy 45°8N 9°53E 92 C6
Addatigala India 17°31N 82°3E 126 F6
Addis Abeba = Addis Abeba
  Ethiopia 9°2N 38°42E 131 F2
Addis Abeba Ethiopia 9°2N 38°42E 131 F2
Addison U.S.A. 42°1N 77°14W 174 D7
Addo S. Africa 33°32S 25°45E 144 D4
Addo △ S. Africa 33°30S 25°45E 144 D4
Adebour Niger 13°17N 11°50E 139 C7
Ādeh Iran 37°42N 45°11E 128 B5
Adel U.S.A. 31°8N 83°25W 178 D6
Adel Bagrou Mauritania 15°29N 6°57W 138 B3
Adelaide Australia 34°52S 138°30E 152 C3
Adelaide S. Africa 32°42S 26°20E 144 D4
Adelaide I. Antarctica 67°15S 68°30W 55 C17
Adelaide Pen. Canada 68°15N 97°30W 160 D12
Adelaide River
  Australia 13°15S 131°7E 148 B5
Adelaide Village
  Bahamas 25°0N 77°31W 182 A4
Adelanto U.S.A. 34°35N 117°22W 171 L9
Adele I. Australia 15°32S 123°9E 148 C3
Adélie, Terre Antarctica 68°0S 140°0E 55 C10
Adélie Land = Adélie, Terre
  Antarctica 68°0S 140°0E 55 C10
Adelong Australia 35°16S 148°4E 153 C8
Adelsk Belarus 53°24N 23°47E 82 E10
Adelunga Toghi
  Uzbekistan 42°7N 70°58E 109 D8
Ademuz Spain 40°5N 1°13W 90 E3
Aden = 'Adan Yemen 12°45N 45°0E 131 E4
Aden, G. of Ind. Oc. 12°30N 47°30E 131 E4
Adendorp S. Africa 32°15S 24°30E 144 D3
Aderbissinat Niger 15°34N 7°54E 139 B6
Adh Dhayd U.A.E. 25°17N 55°53E 129 E7
Adhoi India 23°26N 70°32E 124 H4
Adi Indonesia 4°15S 133°30E 119 E8
Adieu, C. Australia 32°0S 132°10E 149 F5
Adieu Pt. Australia 15°14S 124°35E 148 C3
Adige → Italy 45°9N 12°20E 93 C9
Adigrat Ethiopia 14°20N 39°26E 131 E2
Adıgüzel Baraji Turkey 38°13N 29°14E 99 C11
Adilabad India 19°33N 78°20E 126 E4
Adilcevaz Turkey 38°47N 42°45E 105 C10
Adirondack △ U.S.A. 44°0N 74°20W 175 C10
Adirondack Mts. U.S.A. 44°0N 74°0W 175 C10
Adis Abeba = Addis Abeba
  Ethiopia 9°2N 38°42E 131 F2
Adıyaman Turkey 37°45N 38°16E 105 D8
Adıyaman □ Turkey 38°0N 38°10E 105 D8
Adjim Tunisia 33°47N 10°50E 136 B6
Adjohon Benin 6°41N 2°32E 139 D5
Adjud Romania 46°7N 27°10E 81 D12
Adjumani Uganda 3°20N 31°50E 142 B3
Adjuntas Puerto Rico 18°10N 66°43W 183 d
Adlavik Is. Canada 55°0N 58°40W 165 B8
Adler Russia 43°28N 39°52E 87 J4
Admer Algeria 20°21N 5°27E 139 A6
Admer, Erg d' Algeria 24°0N 9°5E 136 D6
Admiralty G. Australia 14°20S 125°55E 148 B4
Admiralty Gulf ○
  Australia 14°16S 125°52E 148 B4
Admiralty I. U.S.A. 57°30N 134°30W 162 B2
Admiralty Inlet Canada 72°30N 86°0W 161 C14
Admiralty Is. Papua N. G. 2°0S 147°0E 150 B7
Adnan Menderes, İzmir ✈ (ADB)
  Turkey 38°23N 27°9E 99 C9
Ado Nigeria 6°36N 2°56E 139 D5
Ado-Ekiti Nigeria 7°38N 5°12E 139 D6
Adolfo González Chaves
  Argentina 38°2S 60°5W 190 D3
Adolfo Ruiz Cortines, Presa
  Mexico 27°15N 109°6W 180 B3
Adonara Indonesia 8°15S 123°5E 119 F6
Adoni India 15°33N 77°18E 127 G3
Adony Hungary 47°6N 18°52E 80 C3
Adour → France 43°32N 1°32W 72 E2
Adra India 23°30N 86°42E 125 H12
Adra Spain 36°43N 3°3W 89 J7
Adrano Italy 37°40N 14°50E 95 E7
Adrar Mauritania 20°30N 7°30W 136 D2
Adrar Algeria 27°51N 0°19W 136 C3
Adrar □ Mauritania 20°0N 12°0W 136 D2
Adrar des Iforas Africa 19°40N 1°40E 133 E5
Ádria Italy 45°3N 12°3E 93 C9
Adrian Mich., U.S.A. 41°54N 84°2W 173 E11
Adrian Tex., U.S.A. 35°16N 102°40W 176 D3
Adriatic Sea Medit. S. 43°0N 16°0E 58 G9
Adua Indonesia 1°45S 129°50E 119 E7
Adur India 9°8N 76°43E 127 K3
Adwa Ethiopia 14°15N 38°52E 131 E2
Adygea □ Russia 45°0N 40°0E 87 A8
Adzhar Republic = Ajaria □
  Georgia 41°30N 42°0E 87 K6
Aegean Ivory C. 6°7N 3°49W 138 D4
Aegean = Aigai Greece 40°28N 22°19E 96 E6
Ægean Sea Medit. S. 38°30N 25°0E 98 C7
Aerht'ai Shan
  Mongolia 46°40N 92°45E 109 C12
Ærø Denmark 54°52N 10°25E 63 K4
Ærøskøbing Denmark 54°53N 10°24E 63 K4
Aetdia-Akarnania =
  Etoloakarnania
  Greece 38°45N 21°18E 98 C3
Aetos Greece 37°15N 21°50E 98 D3
Afaahiti Tahiti 17°45S 149°17W 155 b
'Afak Iraq 32°4N 45°15E 105 F11
Afandou Greece 36°18N 28°12E 101 C10
Afarag, Erg Algeria 23°50N 2°47E 136 D4
Afghanistan ■ Asia 33°0N 65°0E 122 C4
Afikpo Nigeria 5°53N 7°55E 139 D6
Aflisses, O. → Algeria 28°40N 0°50E 136 C4
Aflou Algeria 34°7N 2°3E 136 B4

Afogados da Ingàzeira
  Brazil 7°45S 37°39W 189 B3
Afognak I. U.S.A. 58°15N 152°30W 166 D9
Afram → Ghana 7°0N 0°52W 139 D4
Afrin Syria 36°32N 36°50E 104 C7
Afşin Turkey 38°14N 36°55E 104 C7
Afton N.Y., U.S.A. 42°14N 75°32W 175 D9
Afton Wyo., U.S.A. 42°44N 110°56W 168 E8
Afuá Brazil 0°15S 50°20W 187 D8
'Afula Israel 32°37N 35°17E 130 C4
Afyon Turkey 38°45N 30°33E 99 C12
Afyonkarahisar = Afyon
  Turkey 38°45N 30°33E 99 C12
Aga Egypt 30°55N 31°10E 137 E7
Ağa Jarı Iran 30°42N 49°50E 129 D6
Agadez Niger 16°58N 7°59E 139 B6
Agadez □ Niger 16°58N 7°59E 139 B6
Agadir Morocco 30°28N 9°55W 136 B2
Agaete Canary Is. 28°6N 15°43W 100 F4
Agaie Nigeria 9°1N 6°18E 139 D6
Agalega Is. Mauritius 11°0S 57°0E 146 F4
Ağapınar Turkey 39°48N 30°47E 99 C13
Agar India 23°40N 76°2E 124 H7
Agar → India 21°0N 82°57E 126 D6
Agartala India 23°50N 91°23E 125 H17
Ağaş Romania 46°28N 26°15E 81 D11
Agassiz Canada 49°14N 121°46W 162 D4
Agassiz Icecap Canada 80°15N 76°0W 161 A16
Agats Indonesia 5°33S 138°0E 119 F9
Agatti I. India 10°50N 72°12E 127 J7
Agawam U.S.A. 42°5N 72°37W 175 D12
Agboville Ivory C. 5°55N 4°15W 138 D4
Ağcabädi Azerbaijan 40°5N 47°27E 87 K8
Ağdam Azerbaijan 40°0N 46°58E 87 K8
Ağdara Azerbaijan 40°13N 46°49E 87 K8
Ağdaş Azerbaijan 40°44N 47°22E 87 K8
Agde France 43°19N 3°28E 72 E7
Agde, C. d' France 43°16N 3°28E 72 E7
Agdz Morocco 30°47N 6°30W 136 B2
Agen France 44°12N 0°38E 72 D4
Agerbæk Denmark 55°36N 8°48E 63 J2
Agersø Denmark 55°13N 11°12E 63 J5
Ageyevo Russia 54°10N 36°27E 84 E9
Aggteleki △ Hungary 48°27N 20°36E 80 B5
Aghia Anna Greece 38°52N 23°24E 98 C5
Aghia Deka Greece 35°3N 24°58E 101 D6
Aghia Ekaterinis, Akra
  Greece 39°50N 19°50E 101 A3
Aghia Galini Greece 35°6N 24°41E 101 D6
Aghia Marina Kasos,
  Greece 35°20N 26°53E 99 F8
Aghia Marina Leros,
  Greece 37°11N 26°48E 99 D8
Aghia Paraskevi Greece 39°14N 26°21E 99 B8
Aghia Roumeli Greece 35°14N 23°58E 98 F5
Aghia Varvara Greece 35°8N 25°1E 101 D7
Aghiasos Greece 39°5N 26°23E 99 B8
Aghio Theodori Greece 37°55N 23°9E 98 D5
Aghion Oros □ Greece 40°25N 24°6E 97 F8
Aghios Andreas Greece 37°21N 22°45E 98 D4
Aghios Efstratios Greece 39°34N 24°58E 98 B7
Aghios Georgios Greece 37°28N 23°57E 98 D5
Aghios Ioannis, Akra
  Greece 35°20N 25°40E 101 D7
Aghios Isidoros Greece 36°9N 27°51E 101 C9
Aghios Kirikos Greece 37°34N 26°17E 99 D8
Aghios Matheos Greece 39°30N 19°47E 101 B3
Aghios Mironas Greece 35°15N 25°1E 99 F7
Aghios Nikolaos Greece 35°11N 25°41E 101 D7
Aghios Petros Greece 38°40N 20°36E 98 C2
Aghios Stephanos
  Greece 39°46N 19°39E 101 A3
Aghiou Orous, Kolpos
  Greece 40°6N 24°0E 96 F7
Aghireşu Romania 46°53N 23°15E 81 D8
Agia Greece 39°43N 22°45E 98 B4
Aginskoye Russia 51°6N 114°32E 107 D12
Agjert Mauritania 16°23N 9°17W 138 B3
Ağlasun Turkey 37°39N 30°31E 99 D12
Agly → France 42°46N 3°3E 72 F7
Agnew Australia 28°1S 120°31E 149 E3
Agnibilékrou Ivory C. 7°10N 3°11W 138 D4
Agnita Romania 45°59N 24°40E 81 E9
Agnone Italy 41°48N 14°22E 93 G11
Ago-Are Nigeria 8°27N 3°28E 139 D5
Agofie Ghana 8°27N 0°15E 139 D5
Agogna → Italy 45°4N 8°54E 92 C5
Agoitz = Aoiz Spain 42°46N 1°22W 90 C3
Agón Sweden 61°34N 17°23E 62 C11
Agon-Coutainville France 49°2N 1°34W 70 C5
Agordo Italy 46°18N 12°2E 93 B9
Agori India 24°33N 82°57E 125 G10
Agoué Benin 7°39N 1°47E 139 D5
Agout → France 43°47N 1°41E 72 E5
Agra India 27°17N 77°58E 124 F7
Agrakhanskiuy Poluostrov
  Russia 43°42N 47°36E 87 J8
Agramunt Spain 41°48N 1°6E 90 D6
Ágreda Spain 41°51N 1°55W 90 D3
Ağrı Turkey 39°44N 43°3E 105 C10
Ağrı → Italy 40°13N 16°44E 95 B9
Ağrı Dağı Turkey 39°50N 44°15E 105 C11
Ağrı Karakose = Ağrı
  Turkey 39°44N 43°3E 105 C10
Agrigento Italy 37°19N 13°34E 94 E6
Agrinio Greece 38°37N 21°27E 98 C3
Agrópoli Italy 40°21N 14°59E 95 B7
Ağstafa Azerbaijan 41°7N 45°27E 87 K7
Água Branca Brazil 7°25S 37°38W 189 B3
Agua Caliente
  Mexico 26°28N 108°20W 180 B3
Agua Caliente Springs
  U.S.A. 32°56N 116°19W 171 N10
Água Clara Brazil 20°25S 52°45W 187 H8
Agua Fria △ U.S.A. 34°14N 112°0W 169 J8
Agua Hechicera
  Mexico 32°28N 116°15W 171 N10
Agua Prieta Mexico 31°18N 109°34W 180 A3
Aguada Cecilio
  Argentina 40°50S 65°4W 192 E3

Aguadilla Puerto Rico 18°26N 67°10W 183 d
Aguadulce Panama 8°15N 80°32W 182 E3
Aguanga U.S.A. 33°27N 116°51W 171 M10
Aguanish Canada 50°14N 62°2W 165 B7
Aguapey → Argentina 29°7S 56°36W 191 B4
Aguaray Guazú →
  Paraguay 24°47S 57°19W 191 B4
Aguarico → Ecuador 0°59S 75°11W 186 D3
Aguaro-Guariquito △
  Venezuela 8°20N 66°35W 186 B5
Aguas → Spain 41°20N 0°30W 90 D4
Aguas Blancas Chile 24°15S 69°55W 190 A2
Aguas Calientes, Sierra de
  Argentina 25°26S 66°40W 190 B2
Águas Formosas Brazil 17°5S 40°57W 189 D2
Águas Lindas de Goiás
  Brazil 15°46S 48°15W 187 G9
Aguascalientes
  Mexico 21°53N 102°18W 180 C4
Aguascalientes □
  Mexico 22°0N 102°20W 180 C4
Agudo Spain 38°59N 4°52W 89 G5
Águeda Portugal 40°34N 8°27W 88 E2
Águeda → Spain 41°2N 6°56W 88 D3
Aguelhok Mali 19°29N 0°52E 138 B5
Aguié Niger 13°31N 7°46E 139 C6
Aguila, Punta
  Puerto Rico 17°57N 67°13W 183 d
Aguilafuente Spain 41°13N 4°7W 88 D6
Aguilar de Campóo
  Spain 42°47N 4°15W 88 C6
Aguilar de la Frontera
  Spain 37°31N 4°40W 89 H6
Aguilares Argentina 27°26S 65°35W 190 B2
Águilas Spain 37°23N 1°35W 91 H3
Aguja, C. de la
  Colombia 11°18N 74°12W 186 A3
Agujereada, Pta.
  Puerto Rico 18°30N 67°8W 183 d
Agulhas, C. S. Africa 34°52S 20°0E 144 E3
Agulhas Ridge Atl. Oc. 42°0S 15°0E 58 L9
Agulo Canary Is. 28°11N 17°12W 100 F2
Agung, Gunung
  Indonesia 8°20S 115°28E 119 K18
Aguni-Jima Japan 26°35N 127°14E 113 L3
Agur Uganda 2°28N 32°55E 142 B3
Agusan → Phil. 9°0N 125°30E 117 C7
Ağva Turkey 41°8N 29°51E 97 d
Agvali Russia 42°36N 46°8E 87 J8
Aha Mts. Botswana 19°45S 21°0E 144 B3
Ahaggar Algeria 23°0N 6°30E 133 E6
Ahaggar △ Algeria 23°0N 4°50E 133 E5
Ahai Dam China 27°21N 100°30E 116 D3
Ahar Iran 38°35N 47°0E 128 B5
Ahaus Germany 52°4N 7°6E 76 C3
Ahelledjem Algeria 26°37N 6°58E 133 E6
Ahipara B. N.Z. 35°5S 173°5E 154 a
Ahiri India 19°30N 80°0E 126 E5
Ahlat Turkey 38°45N 42°29E 105 C10
Ahlen Germany 51°45N 7°53E 76 D3
Ahmad Wal Pakistan 29°18N 65°58E 124 E1
Ahmadabad India 23°0N 72°40E 124 H5
Ahmadābād Khorāsān,
  Iran 35°3N 60°50E 123 E9
Ahmadābād Khorāsān,
  Iran 35°49N 59°42E 123 F9
Ahmadī Iran 27°56N 56°42E 129 E8
Ahmadnagar India 19°7N 74°46E 126 E2
Ahmadpur India 18°40N 76°57E 126 E3
Ahmadpur East
  Pakistan 29°12N 71°10E 124 E4
Ahmadpur Lamma
  Pakistan 28°19N 70°3E 124 E4
Ahmedabad = Ahmadabad
  India 23°0N 72°40E 124 H5
Ahmednagar = Ahmadnagar
  India 19°7N 74°46E 126 E2
Ahmetbey Turkey 41°26N 27°34E 97 c
Ahmetler Turkey 38°28N 29°56E 99 C11
Ahmetli Turkey 38°32N 27°57E 99 C9
Ahoada Nigeria 5°8N 6°36E 139 D6
Ahome Mexico 25°55N 109°11W 180 B3
Ahoskie U.S.A. 36°17N 76°59W 177 C16
Ahr → Germany 50°35N 7°16E 76 E3
Ahram Iran 28°52N 51°16E 129 D6
Ahrax Pt. Malta 35°59N 14°22E 94 a
Ahrensburg Germany 53°40N 10°14E 76 B6
Ahuachapán El Salv. 13°54N 89°52W 182 D2
Ahun France 46°4N 2°5E 72 F5
Ahuriri → N.Z. 44°31S 170°12E 155 L3
Åhus Sweden 55°56N 14°18E 63 J6
Ahvāz Iran 31°20N 48°40E 129 D6
Ahvenanmaa = Åland
  Finland 60°15N 20°0E 63 E11
Ahwar Yemen 13°30N 46°40E 131 E4
Ahzar → Mali 15°30N 3°20E 133 E6
Ai → India 26°26N 90°4E 125 F14
Ai-Ais Namibia 27°54S 17°59E 144 D2
Ai-Ais and Fish River Canyon △
  Namibia 27°30S 17°30E 144 D2
Aichach Germany 48°27N 11°8E 77 G7
Aichi □ Japan 35°0N 137°15E 113 B9
Aigai Greece 40°28N 22°19E 96 E6
Aigle Switz. 46°18N 6°58E 78 E3
Aignay-le-Duc France 47°40N 4°43E 71 E11
Aigoual, Mt. France 44°8N 3°35E 72 D7
Aigre France 45°54N 0°1E 72 C4
Aigrettes, Pte. des
  Réunion 21°3S 55°13E 146 b
Aiguá Uruguay 34°13S 54°46W 191 C5
Aigueperse France 46°3N 3°13E 72 C6
Aigues → France 44°7N 4°43E 72 D8
Aigues-Mortes France 43°35N 4°12E 72 E8
Aigues-Mortes, G. d'
  France 43°31N 4°12E 72 E8
Aigües-Tortes i Estany de St.
  Maurici △ Spain 42°35N 0°58E 90 C6
Aiguilles France 44°47N 6°51E 73 D10
Aiguillon France 44°18N 0°21E 72 D4
Aigurande France 46°27N 1°49E 72 F5
Aihui = Heihe China 50°10N 127°30E 115 A13
Aija Peru 9°50S 77°45W 188 B2

kawa Japan 38°2N 138°15E 112 E9
ken U.S.A. 33°34N 81°43W 178 B8
lao Shan China 24°0N 101°20E 116 F3
leron Australia 22°39S 133°20E 150 C1
ley U.S.A. 32°11N 82°34W 178 C7
llant-sur-Tholon France 47°52N 3°20E 71 E10
llik Canada 55°11N 59°18W 165 A8
lsa Craig Canada 43°8N 81°33W 174 C3
lsa Craig U.K. 55°15N 5°6W 65 F3
m Russia 59°0N 133°55E 107 D14
mogasta Argentina 28°33S 66°50W 190 B2
morés Brazil 19°30S 41°4W 189 D2
n □ France 46°5N 5°20E 71 F12
n → France 45°45N 5°11E 73 C9
n Beïda Algeria 35°50N 7°29E 136 A5
n Ben Khellil Algeria 33°15N 0°49W 136 B3
n Ben Tili Mauritania 25°59N 9°27W 134 C4
n Beni Mathar Morocco 34°1N 2°0W 136 B3
n Benian Algeria 36°48N 2°55E 136 A4
n Dalla Egypt 27°20N 27°23E 137 B2
n Defla Algeria 36°16N 1°58E 136 A4
n Defla □ Algeria 36°10N 2°10E 136 A4
n el Mafki Egypt 27°30N 28°15E 137 B2
n Girba Egypt 29°20N 25°14E 137 B2
n M'lila Algeria 36°2N 6°35E 136 A5
n Murr Sudan 21°50N 25°9E 137 C2
n Qeiqab Egypt 29°42N 24°58E 137 B1
n Sefra Algeria 32°47N 0°37W 136 B3
n Sheikh Murzûk Egypt 26°47N 27°45E 137 B2
n Sudr Egypt 29°50N 33°6E 130 F2
n Sukhna Egypt 29°32N 32°20E 137 F8
n Tédelès Algeria 36°0N 0°21E 136 A4
n Témouchent Algeria 35°16N 1°8W 136 A3
n Témouchent □ Algeria 35°20N 1°5W 136 A3
n Tikkidine Algeria 25°33N 1°24E 136 A4
n Touta Algeria 35°26N 5°54E 136 A5
n Zeïtûn Egypt 29°10N 25°48E 137 B2
n Zorah Morocco 34°37N 3°32W 136 B3
naži Latvia 57°50N 24°24E 84 D3
nos Oros Greece 38°9N 20°40E 98 E2
nsworth U.S.A. 42°33N 99°52W 172 D4
quile Bolivia 18°10S 65°10W 186 G5
' Niger 18°30N 8°0E 139 B6
' et Ténéré □ Niger 18°12N 9°56E 139 B6
' Force I. Canada 67°58N 74°5W 161 D17
' Hitam Malaysia 1°55N 103°11E 121 M4
' raines France 49°58N 1°55E 70 B4
' drie Canada 51°18N 114°2W 162 C6
' drie U.K. 55°52N 3°57W 65 F5
' e → France 49°18N 4°49E 71 C11
' e → U.K. 53°43N 0°55W 66 D7
' e, I. de l' Spain 39°48N 4°16E 100 B11
' e-sur-la-Lys France 50°37N 2°22E 71 B9
' e-sur-l'Adour France 43°42N 0°15W 72 E3
' eys Inlet Australia 38°29S 144°5E 152 E6
' le Beach Australia 20°16S 148°43E 150 b
' vault France 46°50N 0°9W 70 F6
' ch → Germany 49°49N 10°58E 74 F6
' France 49°42N 3°40E 71 C10
' ne → France 49°26N 2°50E 71 C9
' ne → France 48°57N 1°30W 70 B4
Ben Haddou Morocco 31°3N 7°7W 136 B2
ana, Sierra de Spain 38°35N 0°24W 91 G4
kin U.S.A. 46°32N 93°42W 172 B7
utaki Cook Is. 18°52S 159°45W 157 J12
braž Brazil 6°38S 40°7W 189 B2
ad Romania 46°19N 23°44E 81 D8
-en-Provence France 43°32N 5°27E 73 E9
-la-Chapelle = Aachen
France 50°45N 6°6E 76 E2
-les-Bains France 45°41N 5°53E 73 C9
e-sur-Vienne France 45°47N 1°9E 72 C5
ina = Egina Greece 37°45N 23°26E 98 D5
awl India 23°40N 92°44E 123 H18
enay France 46°44N 1°38W 70 F5
kraukle Latvia 56°36N 25°11E 84 D3
pute Latvia 56°33N 21°40E 84 D1
uwakamatsu Japan 37°30N 139°56E 112 F9
bshïr Iran 37°28N 45°54E 105 D11
ccio France 41°55N 8°40E 73 G12
ccio, G. d' France 41°52N 8°40E 73 G12
i □ Uganda 2°52N 31°16E 142 B3
igarh India 24°52N 80°16E 125 G9
pan Mexico 18°22N 97°15W 181 D5
nta India 20°30N 75°48E 126 D2
nta Ra. India 20°30N 75°0E 126 D2
okuta Nigeria 7°28N 6°42E 139 D6
ri Rep. = Ajaria □
Georgia 41°30N 42°0E 87 K6
ria □ Georgia 41°30N 42°0E 87 K6
x Canada 43°50N 79°1W 174 C5
x, Mt. N.Z. 42°35S 172°0E 155 C5
ibïyä Libya 30°54N 20°4E 135 B10
ovščina Slovenia 45°54N 13°54E 93 C10
garh India 47°4N 76°41E 124 D7
a Hungary 47°4N 17°31E 80 C2
ün □ Jordan 32°18N 35°47E 130 C4
ün □ Jordan 32°18N 35°47E 130 C4
nän U.A.E. 25°25N 55°30E 129 E7
ner India 26°28N 74°37E 124 F6
ala India 31°50N 74°48E 124 D6
, C. de Spain 43°31N 3°35W 88 B7
Dağ Turkey 38°30N 29°32E 99 E11
Dağlar Turkey 39°32N 36°12E 104 C7
Dağları Turkey 36°30N 29°30E 99 E11
Dovurak Russia 51°11N 90°36E 109 D12
aba Togo 8°10N 1°2E 139 D5
abira Algeria 26°49N 1°31E 136 C4
abli Algeria 26°49N 1°31E 136 C4
ademika Obrucheva, Khrebet
Russia 51°50N 96°0E 109 D13
agera △ Rwanda 1°31S 30°33E 142 C3
amas Cyprus 35°3N 32°18E 101 D11
anthou Cyprus 35°20N 144°20E 101 D12
aroa N.Z. 43°49S 172°59E 155 D7
aroa Harbour N.Z. 43°50S 172°55E 155 D7
ashi Japan 34°45N 134°58E 113 G7
parpara Bihar, India 25°39N 83°58E 125 G10
parpara Ut. P., India 26°25N 82°32E 125 F10
bulak Russia 51°31N 55°37E 108 B5
aabat Turkey 41°1N 39°34E 105 B8
adağ Turkey 38°27N 37°43E 104 C7

Akçakale Turkey 36°41N 38°56E 105 D8
Akçakoca Turkey 41°5N 31°8E 104 B4
Akçaova Turkey 41°3N 29°57E 97 E13
Akçay Turkey 36°36N 29°45E 99 C8
Akçay → Turkey 37°50N 28°15E 99 D10
Akdağ Turkey 38°33N 26°30E 99 C8
Akdağmadeni Turkey 39°39N 35°53E 104 C6
Akdoğan = Lysi Cyprus 35°6N 33°41E 101 D12
Akelamo Indonesia 1°35N 129°40E 119 D7
Åkers styckebruk
Sweden 59°0N 17°5E 62 E11
Åkersberga Sweden 59°29N 18°18E 62 E12
Aketi Dem. Rep. of the Congo 2°38N 23°47E 140 D4
Akhali Atoni Georgia 43°7N 40°50E 87 J5
Akhalkalaki Georgia 41°27N 43°25E 87 K6
Akhaltsikhe Georgia 41°40N 43°0E 87 K6
Akhisar Turkey 38°56N 27°48E 99 C9
Akhmîm Egypt 26°31N 31°47E 137 B3
Akhnur India 32°52N 74°45E 125 C6
Akhtopol Bulgaria 42°6N 27°56E 97 D11
Akhtuba → Russia 47°41N 46°55E 87 F8
Akhtubinsk Russia 48°13N 46°7E 87 F8
Akhty Russia 41°30N 47°45E 87 K8
Akhtyrka = Okhtyrka
Ukraine 50°25N 35°0E 85 G8
Aki Japan 33°30N 133°54E 113 H6
Akimiski I. Canada 52°50N 81°30W 164 B3
Åkirkeby Denmark 55°4N 14°55E 63 J8
Akita Japan 39°45N 140°7E 112 E10
Akita □ Japan 39°40N 140°30E 112 E10
Akjoujt Mauritania 19°45N 14°15W 138 D2
Akka Mali 15°24N 4°11W 138 B4
Akka Morocco 29°22N 8°9W 136 C2
Akkaraipattu Sri Lanka 7°13N 81°51E 127 L5
Akkaya Tepesi Turkey 37°25N 29°38E 99 D11
Akkeshi Japan 43°2N 144°51E 112 C12
'Akko Israel 32°55N 35°4E 130 C4
Akköy Turkey 37°29N 27°15E 99 D9
Akkuş Turkey 40°47N 37°0E 104 B7
Aklampa Benin 8°15N 2°10E 139 D5
Aklavik Canada 68°12N 135°0W 160 D4
Aklera India 24°26N 76°32E 124 G7
Akmenė Lithuania 56°15N 22°45E 82 B9
Akmenrags Latvia 56°50N 21°4E 82 B8
Akmonte = Almonte
Spain 37°13N 6°38W 89 H4
Aknoul Morocco 34°39N 3°39W 136 B3
Akō Japan 34°45N 134°24E 113 G7
Akola Nigeria 10°19N 10°48E 139 C7
Akola Maharashtra, India 20°42N 77°2E 126 D3
Akola Maharashtra, India 19°32N 73°42E 126 E2
Akor Mali 14°59N 6°58W 138 C3
Akordat Eritrea 15°30N 37°40E 131 D2
Akosombo Dam Ghana 6°20N 0°5E 139 D5
Akpatok I. Canada 60°25N 68°8W 161 E18
Akrahamn Norway 59°15N 5°10E 61 G11
Akranes Iceland 64°19N 22°5W 60 D2
Akreïjit Mauritania 18°19N 9°11W 138 B3
Akritas, Akra Greece 36°43N 21°54E 98 E3
Akron Colo., U.S.A. 40°10N 103°13W 168 F12
Akron Ohio, U.S.A. 41°5N 81°31W 174 E3
Akrotiri Cyprus 34°36N 32°57E 101 E11
Akrotiri, Akra Greece 40°26N 25°27E 97 F9
Akrotiri Bay Cyprus 34°35N 33°10E 101 E12
Aksai Chin China 35°15N 79°55E 125 B8
Aksaray Turkey 38°25N 34°2E 104 C6
Aksaray □ Turkey 38°20N 33°45E 104 C5
Aksay = Aqsay
Kazakhstan 51°11N 53°0E 108 B4
Akşehir Turkey 38°18N 31°30E 104 C5
Akşehir Gölü Turkey 38°30N 31°25E 104 C4
Akstafa = Ağstafa
Azerbaijan 41°7N 45°27E 87 K7
Aksu China 41°5N 80°10E 109 D10
Aksu Turkey 36°57N 30°50E 104 D5
Aksu → Turkey 36°52N 30°57E 104 D4
Aksu He → China 40°26N 80°59E 109 D10
Aksum Ethiopia 14°5N 38°40E 131 E2
Aktash Russia 55°2N 52°3E 86 C11
Akto China 37°59N 75°6E 109 E9
Aktsyabrski Belarus 52°38N 28°53E 75 B15
Aktyubinsk = Aqtöbe
Kazakhstan 50°17N 57°10E 108 B5
Aku Nigeria 6°40N 7°18E 139 D6
Akure Nigeria 7°15N 5°5E 139 D6
Akuressa Sri Lanka 6°5N 80°29E 127 L5
Akurenri Iceland 65°40N 18°6W 60 D4
Akuseki-Shima Japan 29°27N 129°37E 113 K4
Akusha Russia 42°18N 47°30E 87 J8
Akwa-Ibom □ Nigeria 4°50N 7°30E 139 E6
Akwanga Nigeria 8°55N 8°23E 139 D6
Akyab = Sittwe
Burma 20°18N 92°45E 123 J18
Akyazı Turkey 40°40N 30°38E 104 B4
Al 'Adan = 'Adan
Yemen 12°45N 45°0E 131 E4
Al Aḥsā = Hasa
Si. Arabia 25°50N 49°0E 128 E6
Al Ajfar Si. Arabia 27°26N 43°0E 128 E4
Al Amādīyah Iraq 37°5N 43°30E 105 D10
Al 'Amārah Iraq 31°55N 47°15E 105 G12
Al Anbar □ Iraq 33°25N 42°0E 128 C4
Al 'Aqabah Jordan 29°31N 35°0E 130 F4
Al 'Aqabah □ Jordan 29°40N 35°5E 130 F4
Al Arak Syria 34°38N 38°35E 128 C3
Al 'Aramah Si. Arabia 25°30N 46°0E 128 E5
Al Arṭāwīyah
Si. Arabia 26°31N 45°20E 128 E5
Al 'Āşimah □ Jordan 31°40N 36°30E 130 D5
Al 'Assāfīyah Si. Arabia 28°17N 38°59E 128 E3
Al 'Ayn Si. Arabia 25°4N 38°6E 128 E3
Al 'Ayn U.A.E. 24°15N 55°45E 129 E7
Al 'Azīzīyah Iraq 32°54N 45°4E 105 F11
Al Bad' Si. Arabia 28°28N 35°1E 128 D2
Al Bad'ī' Si. Arabia 22°0N 46°35E 128 D4
Al Bādī Iraq 35°56N 41°32E 128 C4
Al Bahrah Kuwait 29°40N 47°52E 128 D5
Al Bahral Mayyit = Dead Sea
Asia 31°30N 35°30E 130 D4

Al Balqā' □ Jordan 32°5N 35°45E 130 C4
Al Bārūk, J. Lebanon 33°39N 35°40E 130 B4
Al Baṣrah Iraq 30°30N 47°50E 128 D5
Al Batḥā Iraq 31°6N 45°53E 128 D5
Al Batrūn Lebanon 34°15N 35°40E 130 A4
Al Baydā Libya 32°50N 21°44E 135 B10
Al Biqā Lebanon 34°10N 36°10E 130 A5
Al Bi'r Si. Arabia 28°51N 36°16E 128 D3
Al Bukayrīyah Si. Arabia 26°9N 43°40E 128 E4
Al Burayj Syria 34°15N 36°46E 130 A5
Al Faḍilī Si. Arabia 26°58N 49°10E 128 E6
Al Fallūjah Iraq 33°20N 43°55E 105 F10
Al Fatḥah Iraq 35°3N 43°33E 105 E10
Al Fāw Iraq 30°0N 48°30E 129 D6
Al Fujayrah U.A.E. 25°7N 56°18E 129 E8
Al Ghadaf, W. → Jordan 31°26N 36°43E 130 D5
Al Ghammās Iraq 31°45N 44°37E 128 D5
Al Ghazālah Si. Arabia 26°48N 41°19E 128 E4
Al Ghuwayfāt U.A.E. 24°5N 51°38E 129 E6
Al Ḥadīthah Iraq 34°0N 41°13E 105 E10
Al Ḥadīthah Si. Arabia 31°28N 37°8E 128 D3
Al Ḥaḍr Iraq 35°35N 42°44E 105 E10
Al Ḥājānah Syria 33°20N 36°33E 130 B5
Al Hajar al Gharbī
Oman 24°10N 56°15E 129 E8
Al Ḥāmad Si. Arabia 31°30N 39°30E 128 D3
Al Ḥamdānīyah Syria 35°25N 36°50E 128 C3
Al Ḥamīdīyah Syria 34°42N 35°57E 130 A4
Al Ḥammār Iraq 30°57N 46°51E 128 D5
Al Ḥamrā' Si. Arabia 24°2N 38°55E 128 E3
Al Ḥamzah Iraq 31°30N 44°58E 128 D5
Al Ḥanākīyah
Si. Arabia 24°51N 40°31E 128 E4
Al Harūj al Aswad Libya 27°0N 17°10E 135 C9
Al Ḥasakah Si. Arabia 36°35N 40°45E 105 D9
Al Ḥasakah □ Syria 36°45N 40°50E 105 D9
Al Hāshimīyah Iraq 32°22N 44°39E 105 G11
Al Ḥayy Iraq 32°5N 46°5E 105 F12
Al Ḥillah Iraq 32°30N 44°25E 105 F11
Al Hindīyah Iraq 32°30N 44°10E 105 F11
Al Hirmil Lebanon 34°26N 36°24E 130 A5
Al Hoceïma Morocco 35°8N 3°58W 136 A3
Al Ḥudaydah Yemen 14°50N 43°0E 131 E3
Al Ḥudūd ash Shamālīyah □
Si. Arabia 29°10N 42°30E 128 D4
Al Ḥufūf Si. Arabia 25°25N 49°45E 129 E6
Al Ḥumaydah
Si. Arabia 29°14N 34°56E 128 D2
Al Ḥunayy Si. Arabia 25°58N 48°45E 129 E6
Al 'Īsāwīyah Si. Arabia 30°43N 37°59E 128 D3
Al Jāfūrah Si. Arabia 25°0N 50°15E 129 E7
Al Jaghbūb Libya 29°42N 24°38E 135 C10
Al Jahrah Kuwait 29°25N 47°40E 128 D5
Al Jalāmīd Si. Arabia 31°20N 40°6E 128 D3
Al Jamalīyah Qatar 25°37N 51°5E 129 E6
Al Janūb □ Lebanon 33°0N 35°18E 130 B4
Al Jawf Libya 24°10N 23°24E 135 D10
Al Jawf □ Si. Arabia 29°55N 39°40E 128 D3
Al Jazair = Algeria ■
Africa 28°30N 2°0E 136 C4
Al Jazirah Iraq 33°30N 44°0E 105 D10
Al Jithāmīyah Si. Arabia 27°41N 41°43E 128 E4
Al Jubayl Si. Arabia 27°0N 49°50E 129 E6
Al Jubaylah Si. Arabia 24°55N 46°25E 128 E5
Al Jubb Si. Arabia 27°11N 42°17E 128 E4
Al Junaynah Sudan 13°27N 22°45E 135 F10
Al Kabā'ish Iraq 30°58N 47°0E 128 D5
Al Karak Jordan 31°11N 35°42E 130 D4
Al Karak □ Jordan 31°11N 35°42E 130 D4
Al Kāẓimīyah Iraq 33°22N 44°18E 105 F11
Al Khābūrah Oman 23°57N 57°5E 129 F8
Al Khafji Si. Arabia 28°24N 48°29E 129 E6
Al Khalīl West Bank 31°32N 35°6E 130 D4
Al Khāliṣ Iraq 33°49N 44°32E 105 F11
Al Kharsānīyah
Si. Arabia 27°13N 49°18E 129 E6
Al Khaṣab Oman 26°14N 56°15E 129 E8
Al Khawr Qatar 25°41N 51°30E 129 E6
Al Khiḍr Iraq 31°12N 45°33E 128 D5
Al Khiyām Lebanon 33°20N 35°36E 130 B4
Al Khubar Si. Arabia 26°17N 50°12E 129 E6
Al Khums Libya 32°40N 14°17E 135 B8
Al Khurmah Si. Arabia 21°54N 42°3E 131 C3
Al Kiflt Iraq 32°13N 44°22E 105 G11
Al Kiswah Syria 33°23N 36°14E 130 B5
Al Kūfah Iraq 32°2N 44°45E 105 F11
Al Kufrah Libya 24°17N 23°15E 135 D10
Al Kuhayfiyah Si. Arabia 27°12N 43°3E 128 E4
Al Kumayt Iraq 32°2N 46°52E 105 G12
Al Kūt Iraq 32°30N 46°0E 105 F11
Al Kuwayt Kuwait 29°30N 48°0E 128 D5
Al Labwah Lebanon 34°11N 36°20E 130 A5
Al Lādhiqīyah Si. Arabia 35°30N 35°45E 104 C6
Al Lādhiqīyah □ Syria 35°28N 35°48E 130 A4
Al Līth Si. Arabia 20°9N 40°15E 131 C3
Al Liwā' Oman 24°31N 56°36E 129 E8
Al Luḥayyah Yemen 15°45N 42°40E 131 D3
Al Madīnah Iraq 30°57N 47°16E 128 D5
Al Madīnah Si. Arabia 24°35N 39°52E 128 E3
Al Mafraq Jordan 32°17N 36°14E 130 C5
Al Maghreb = Morocco ■
N. Afr. 32°0N 5°50W 134 B4
Al Maḥmūdīyah Iraq 33°3N 44°21E 105 F11
Al Majma'ah Si. Arabia 25°57N 45°22E 128 E5
Al Makhruq, W. → Jordan 31°28N 37°0E 130 D6
Al Makhūl Si. Arabia 35°26N 42°0E 105 E11
Al Mālikīyah Syria 37°10N 42°0E 105 D10
Al Manāmah Bahrain 26°10N 50°30E 129 E6
Al Maqwa' Kuwait 29°10N 47°59E 128 D5
Al Marj Libya 32°25N 20°30E 135 B10
Al Maṭlā Kuwait 29°24N 47°40E 128 D5
Al Mayādin Iraq 35°1N 40°27E 105 D9
Al Mazār Jordan 31°4N 35°41E 130 D4
Al Midhnab Si. Arabia 25°50N 44°18E 128 E5
Al Minā' Lebanon 34°24N 35°49E 130 A4
Al Miqdādīyah Iraq 34°0N 45°0E 105 F11
Al Mubarraz Si. Arabia 25°30N 49°40E 129 E6
Al Mudawwarah Jordan 29°19N 36°0E 128 D2
Al Mughayrā' U.A.E. 24°5N 53°32E 129 E7
Al Muharraq Bahrain 26°15N 50°40E 129 E6
Al Mukallā Yemen 14°33N 49°2E 131 E4
Al Mukhā Yemen 13°18N 43°15E 131 E3
Al Musayjīd Si. Arabia 24°5N 39°5E 128 E3
Al Musayyib Iraq 32°49N 44°20E 105 F11
Al Muthanná □ Iraq 30°30N 45°15E 128 D5

Al Muwayh Si. Arabia 22°41N 41°37E 137 C5
Al Muwaylih Si. Arabia 27°40N 35°30E 128 E2
Al Owuho = Otukpa
Nigeria 7°9N 7°41E 139 D6
Al Qādisīyah □ Iraq 30°0N 45°0E 128 D5
Al Qa'im Iraq 34°21N 41°7E 105 E9
Al Qalībah Si. Arabia 28°24N 37°42E 128 D3
Al Qāmishlī Syria 37°2N 41°14E 105 D9
Al Qaryatayn Syria 34°12N 37°13E 130 A6
Al Qaşīm □ Si. Arabia 26°0N 43°0E 128 E4
Al Qaţ'ā Syria 34°40N 40°48E 105 E9
Al Qaţīf Si. Arabia 26°35N 50°0E 129 E6
Al Qaţrānah Jordan 31°12N 36°56E 130 D5
Al Qaţrūn Libya 24°56N 15°3E 135 D9
Al Qawz Si. Arabia 18°58N 41°26E 137 D5
Al Qayşūmah Si. Arabia 28°20N 46°7E 128 D5
Al Quds = Jerusalem
Israel/West Bank 31°47N 35°10E 130 D4
Al Qunayţirah Syria 33°5N 35°45E 130 B4
Al Qunfudhah Si. Arabia 19°3N 41°4E 137 D5
Al Qurayyāt Si. Arabia 31°20N 37°20E 128 D3
Al Qurnah Iraq 31°1N 47°25E 128 D5
Al Quşayr Iraq 30°39N 45°50E 128 D5
Al Quşayr Syria 34°31N 36°34E 130 A5
Al Qutayfah Syria 33°44N 36°36E 130 B5
Al Quwayr Iraq 36°2N 43°29E 105 D10
Al Quwaysimah Jordan 31°55N 35°57E 130 D4
Al 'Ubaylah Si. Arabia 21°59N 50°57E 131 C5
Al 'Udayliyah Si. Arabia 25°8N 49°18E 129 E6
Al 'Ulā Si. Arabia 26°35N 38°0E 128 E3
Al 'Uqayr Si. Arabia 25°40N 50°15E 129 E6
Al 'Uwaynid
Si. Arabia 24°50N 46°0E 128 E5
Al 'Uwayqilah
Si. Arabia 30°30N 42°10E 128 D4
Al 'Uyūn Ḥijāz,
Si. Arabia 24°33N 39°35E 128 E3
Al 'Uyūn Najd,
Si. Arabia 26°30N 43°50E 128 E4
Al Wajh Si. Arabia 26°10N 36°30E 128 E3
Al Wakrah Qatar 25°10N 51°40E 129 E6
Al Waqbah Si. Arabia 28°48N 45°33E 128 D5
Al Yaman = Yemen ■
Asia 15°0N 44°0E 131 E3
Ala Italy 45°45N 11°0E 92 C8
Ala Archa △ Kyrgyzstan 42°32N 74°28E 108 D8
Ala Dağ Turkey 37°44N 35°9E 128 B2
Ala Dağları Turkey 39°15N 43°33E 105 C10
Ala Tau Asia 45°30N 80°40E 109 C10
Ala Tau Shankou = Dzungarian
Gate Asia 45°10N 82°0E 109 C10
Alabama □ U.S.A. 33°0N 87°0W 177 E11
Alabama → U.S.A. 31°8N 87°57W 177 E11
Alabaster U.S.A. 33°15N 86°49W 177 E11
Alaca Turkey 40°10N 34°51E 104 B6
Alacaatlı Turkey 39°15N 28°3E 99 C9
Alaçam Turkey 41°36N 35°36E 104 B6
Alaçam Dağları Turkey 39°18N 28°49E 99 B10
Alacant = Alicante
Spain 38°23N 0°30W 91 G4
Alaçatı Turkey 38°15N 26°22E 99 C8
Alachua U.S.A. 29°47N 82°30W 178 F7
Alaejos Spain 41°18N 5°13W 88 D5
Alaer China 40°30N 81°16E 109 D10
Alagir Russia 43°3N 44°14E 87 J7
Alagna Valsésia Italy 45°51N 7°56E 92 C4
Alagoa Grande Brazil 7°3S 35°35W 189 B3
Alagoas □ Brazil 9°0S 36°0W 189 D3
Alagoinhas Brazil 12°7S 38°20W 189 C3
Alagón Spain 41°46N 1°12W 90 D3
Alagón → Spain 39°44N 6°53W 88 F4
Alaheaiatnu = Altaelva →
Norway 69°54N 23°17E 60 B20
Alai Range Asia 39°45N 72°0E 108 D8
Alaior Spain 39°57N 4°8E 100 B11
Alajero Canary Is. 28°3N 17°13W 100 F2
Alajuela Costa Rica 10°2N 84°8W 182 D3
Alaknanda → India 30°8N 78°36E 125 D8
Alaköl Kazakhstan 46°0N 81°5E 109 C10
Alakurtti Russia 66°58N 30°25E 60 C24
Alamarvdasht Iran 27°37N 52°59E 129 E7
Alameda Calif., U.S.A. 37°46N 122°15W 170 H4
Alameda N. Mex.,
U.S.A. 35°11N 106°37W 169 J10
Alamo Ga., U.S.A. 32°9N 82°47W 178 E7
Alamo Nev., U.S.A. 37°22N 115°10W 171 H11
Alamogordo U.S.A. 32°54N 105°57W 169 K11
Alamos Mexico 27°1N 108°56W 180 B3
Alamosa U.S.A. 37°28N 105°52W 169 H11
Åland Finland 60°15N 20°0E 61 F19
Alandroal Portugal 38°41N 7°24W 89 G3
Ålands hav Europe 60°0N 19°30E 61 G18
Ålandsbro Sweden 62°40N 17°51E 62 B11
Alange, Embalse d' Spain 38°45N 6°18W 89 G4
Alanis Spain 38°3N 5°43W 89 G5
Alaniya = North Ossetia-
Alaniya □ Russia 43°0N 44°30E 87 J7
Alaniya □ Russia 42°55N 44°30E 87 J7
Alanya Turkey 36°38N 32°0E 104 D5
Alapaha → U.S.A. 30°30N 83°12W 178 F6
Alappuzha India 9°30N 76°28E 127 K3
Alar del Rey Spain 42°38N 4°20E 88 C6
Alaraz Spain 40°45N 5°17W 88 E5
Alarcón, Embalse de
Spain 39°36N 2°10W 91 F3
Alaró Spain 39°42N 2°47E 100 B9
Alaşehir Turkey 38°23N 28°30E 99 C10
Alashtar Iran 33°51N 48°15E 105 F13
Alaska □ U.S.A. 64°0N 154°0W 166 D9
Alaska, G. of Pac. Oc. 58°0N 145°0W 160 F3
Alaska Peninsula
U.S.A. 56°0N 159°0W 166 D8
Alaska Range U.S.A. 62°50N 151°0W 160 E1
Alássio Italy 44°1N 8°10E 92 E5
Alatau Shan = Ala Tau
Asia 45°30N 80°40E 109 C10
Alatri Italy 41°43N 13°21E 94 D6
Alatyr Russia 54°55N 46°35E 86 C8
Alatyr → Russia 54°52N 46°35E 86 C8
Alausi Ecuador 2°0S 78°50W 186 D3
Álava □ Spain 42°48N 2°28W 90 C2
Alava, C. U.S.A. 48°10N 124°44W 170 B2
Alaverdi Armenia 41°15N 44°37E 87 K7

Alavo = Alavus Finland 62°35N 23°36E 60 E20
Alavus Finland 62°35N 23°36E 60 E20
Alawa ◊ Australia 15°42S 134°39E 150 B1
Alawoona Australia 34°45S 140°30E 152 C4
Alayawarra ◊
Australia 22°0S 134°30E 150 C1
'Alayh Lebanon 33°46N 35°33E 130 B4
Alayköy = Yerolakkos
Cyprus 35°11N 33°15E 101 D12
Alazani → Azerbaijan 41°5N 46°40E 87 K8
Alba Italy 44°42N 8°2E 92 D5
Alba □ Romania 46°10N 23°30E 81 D8
Alba Adriática Italy 42°50N 13°56E 93 F10
Alba de Tormes Spain 40°50N 5°30W 88 E5
Alba-Iulia Romania 46°8N 23°39E 81 D8
Albac Romania 46°28N 22°58E 80 D7
Albacete Spain 39°0N 1°50W 91 F3
Albacete □ Spain 38°50N 2°0W 91 G3
Albacutya, L. Australia 35°45S 141°58E 152 C4
Ålbæk Denmark 57°36N 10°25E 63 G4
Ålbæk Bugt Denmark 57°35N 10°40E 63 G4
Albaida Spain 38°51N 0°31W 91 G4
Albalate de las Nogueras
Spain 40°22N 2°18W 90 E2
Albalate del Arzobispo
Spain 41°6N 0°31W 90 D4
Alban France 43°53N 2°28E 72 E6
Albanel, L. Canada 50°55N 73°12W 164 B5
Albania ■ Europe 41°0N 20°0E 96 E4
Albano Laziale Italy 41°44N 12°39E 93 G9
Albany Australia 35°1S 117°58E 149 G2
Albany Ga., U.S.A. 31°35N 84°10W 178 E5
Albany N.Y., U.S.A. 42°39N 73°45W 175 D11
Albany Oreg., U.S.A. 44°38N 123°6W 168 D2
Albany Tex., U.S.A. 32°44N 99°18W 176 E5
Albany → Canada 52°17N 81°31W 164 B3
Albarca, C. d' Spain 39°4N 1°22E 100 B7
Albardón Argentina 31°20S 68°30W 190 C2
Albarracín Spain 40°25N 1°26W 90 E3
Albarracín, Sierra de
Spain 40°30N 1°30W 90 E3
Albatera Spain 38°11N 0°52W 91 G4
Albâtre, Côte d' France 49°55N 0°50E 70 C7
Albatross B. Australia 12°45S 141°30E 150 A3
Albatross Pt. N.Z. 38°7S 174°44E 154 E3
Albegna → Italy 42°30N 11°11E 92 F8
Albemarle U.S.A. 35°21N 80°12W 177 D14
Albemarle Sd. U.S.A. 36°5N 76°0W 177 C16
Albenga Italy 44°3N 8°13E 92 D5
Alberche → Spain 39°58N 4°46W 88 F6
Alberdi Paraguay 26°14S 58°20W 190 B4
Alberga → Australia 27°6S 135°33E 151 D2
Albersdorf Germany 54°8N 9°17E 76 A5
Albert France 50°0N 2°38E 71 C9
Albert, L. Africa 1°30N 31°0E 142 B3
Albert, L. Australia 35°30S 139°10E 152 C3
Albert Edward Ra.
Australia 18°17S 127°57E 148 C4
Albert Lea U.S.A. 43°39N 93°22W 172 D7
Albert Nile → Uganda 3°36N 32°2E 142 B3
Albert Town Bahamas 22°37N 74°33W 183 B5
Alberta □ Canada 54°40N 115°0W 162 C6
Alberti Argentina 35°1S 60°16W 190 D3
Albertinia S. Africa 34°11S 21°34E 144 D3
Albertirsa Hungary 47°14N 19°37E 80 C4
Alberto de Agostini △
Chile 54°38S 71°37W 192 D2
Alberton Canada 46°50N 64°0W 165 C7
Albertville France 45°40N 6°22E 73 C10
Albertville U.S.A. 34°16N 86°13W 177 D11
Albi France 43°56N 2°9E 72 E6
Albia U.S.A. 41°2N 92°48W 172 E7
Albina Suriname 5°37N 54°15W 187 B8
Albina, Ponta Angola 15°52S 11°44E 144 A1
Albino Italy 45°46N 9°47E 92 C6
Albion Mich., U.S.A. 42°15N 84°45W 173 D11
Albion Nebr., U.S.A. 41°42N 98°0W 172 E4
Albion Pa., U.S.A. 41°53N 80°22W 174 E4
Albocàsser Spain 40°21N 0°1E 90 E5
Albolote Spain 37°14N 3°39W 89 H7
Alborán Medit. S. 35°57N 3°0W 89 K7
Alboran Sea Medit. S. 36°0N 3°0W 89 K7
Ålborg = Aalborg Denmark 57°2N 9°54E 63 G3
Ålborg Bugt = Aalborg Bugt
Denmark 56°50N 10°35E 63 H4
Alborz □ Iran 35°57N 50°58E 129 B6
Alborz, Reshteh-ye Kūhhā-ye
Iran 36°0N 52°0E 129 C7
Albox Spain 37°23N 2°8W 91 H2
Albstadt Germany 48°13N 9°1E 77 G5
Albufeira Portugal 37°5N 8°15W 89 H2
Albula → Switz. 46°38N 9°28E 77 J5
Albuñol Spain 36°48N 3°11W 89 J7
Albuquerque U.S.A. 35°5N 106°39W 169 J10
Albuquerque, Cayos de
Caribbean 12°10N 81°50W 182 D3
Alburg U.S.A. 44°59N 73°18W 175 B11
Alburno, Mte. Italy 40°33N 15°17E 95 B8
Alburquerque Spain 39°15N 6°59W 89 F4
Albury Australia 35°3S 146°56E 153 D7
Alby Sweden 62°30N 15°28E 62 B9
Alcácer do Sal Portugal 38°22N 8°33W 89 G2
Alcáçovas Portugal 38°23N 8°9W 89 G2
Alcalá de Guadaira
Spain 37°20N 5°50W 89 H5
Alcalá de Henares Spain 40°28N 3°22W 88 E7
Alcalá de los Gazules
Spain 36°29N 5°43W 89 J5
Alcalá de Xivert Spain 40°19N 0°13E 90 E5
Alcalá del Júcar Spain 39°12N 1°25W 91 F3
Alcalá del Río Spain 37°30N 5°58W 89 H5
Alcalá del Valle Spain 36°54N 5°10W 89 J5
Alcalá la Real Spain 37°27N 3°57W 89 H7
Álcamo Italy 37°59N 12°55E 94 F5
Alcanadre → Spain 41°43N 0°12W 90 D4
Alcanar Spain 40°33N 0°28E 90 E5
Alcanede Portugal 39°25N 8°49W 89 F2
Alcanena Portugal 39°27N 8°40W 89 F2
Alcañices Spain 41°41N 6°21W 88 D4
Alcañiz Spain 41°2N 0°8W 90 D4
Alcântara Brazil 2°20S 44°30W 189 B2
Alcántara Spain 39°41N 6°57W 88 F4
Alcántara, Embalse de
Spain 39°44N 6°50W 88 F4
Alcantarilla Spain 37°59N 1°12W 91 H3
Alcaracejos Spain 38°24N 4°58W 89 G6
Alcaraz Spain 38°40N 2°29W 91 G2

Alcaraz, Sierra de Spain 38°40N 2°20W 91 G2
Alcaudete Spain 37°35N 4°5W 89 H6
Alcázar de San Juan
Spain 39°24N 3°12W 88 F7
Alchevsk Ukraine 48°30N 38°45E 85 H10
Alcira = Alzira Spain 39°9N 0°30W 91 F4
Alcobaça Portugal 39°32N 8°58W 89 F2
Alcobendas Spain 40°32N 3°38W 88 E7
Alcolea del Pinar Spain 41°2N 2°28W 90 D2
Alcoma U.S.A. 27°54N 81°29W 179 M5
Alcorcón Spain 40°20N 3°48W 88 E7
Alcoutim Portugal 37°25N 7°28W 89 H3
Alcova U.S.A. 42°34N 106°43W 168 E10
Alcoy Spain 38°43N 0°30W 91 G4
Alcubierre, Sierra de
Spain 41°45N 0°22W 90 D4
Alcublas Spain 39°48N 0°43W 90 F4
Alcúdia Spain 39°51N 3°7E 100 B10
Alcúdia, B. d' Spain 39°47N 3°15E 100 B10
Alcúdia, Sierra de la
Spain 38°34N 4°30W 89 G6
Aldabra Is. Seychelles 9°22S 46°28E 133 G8
Aldama Mexico 22°55N 98°4W 181 C5
Aldan Russia 58°40N 125°30E 107 D13
Aldan → Russia 63°28N 129°35E 107 C13
Aldea, Pta. de la
Canary Is. 28°0N 15°50W 100 G4
Aldeburgh U.K. 52°10N 1°37E 67 E9
Alder Pk. U.S.A. 35°53N 121°22W 170 K5
Alderney U.K. 49°42N 2°11W 67 H5
Aldershot U.K. 51°15N 0°44W 67 F7
Aldinga Beach
Australia 35°17S 138°27E 152 C3
Åled Sweden 56°44N 12°57E 63 H6
Aledo U.S.A. 41°12N 90°45W 172 E8
Aleg Mauritania 17°3N 13°55W 138 D2
Alegranza Canary Is. 29°23N 13°32W 100 E6
Alegranza, I. Canary Is. 29°23N 13°32W 100 E6
Alegre Brazil 20°50S 41°30W 191 B4
Alegrete Brazil 29°40S 56°0W 191 B4
Aleksandriya = Oleksandriya
Kirovohrad, Ukraine 48°42N 33°3E 85 H7
Aleksandriya = Oleksandriya
Rivne, Ukraine 50°37N 26°19E 75 C14
Aleksandriyskaya
Russia 43°58N 47°14E 87 J8
Aleksandrov Russia 56°23N 38°44E 84 D10
Aleksandrov Gay Russia 50°9N 48°34E 86 E9
Aleksandrovac Serbia 43°28N 21°3E 96 C5
Aleksandrovac Serbia 44°28N 21°13E 96 B5
Aleksandrovka = Oleksandrivka
Ukraine 48°55N 32°20E 85 H7
Aleksandrovo Bulgaria 43°14N 24°51E 97 C8
Aleksandrovsk-Sakhalinskiy
Russia 50°50N 142°20E 111 A17
Aleksandrów Kujawski
Poland 52°53N 18°43E 83 F5
Aleksandrów Łódzki
Poland 51°49N 19°17E 83 G6
Aleksandry, Zemlya
Russia 80°25N 48°0E 106 A5
Alekseyevka Samara,
Russia 52°35N 51°17E 86 D9
Alekseyevka Voronezh,
Russia 50°43N 38°40E 85 G10
Aleksin Russia 54°31N 37°9E 84 E9
Aleksinac Serbia 43°31N 21°42E 96 C5
Além Paraíba Brazil 21°52S 42°41W 191 B7
Alemania Argentina 25°40S 65°30W 190 B2
Alemania Chile 25°10S 69°55W 190 B2
Alençon France 48°27N 0°4E 70 D7
Alenquer Brazil 1°56S 54°46W 187 D8
'Alenuihähä Channel
U.S.A. 20°30N 156°0W 167 L8
Alépé Ivory C. 5°29N 3°40W 138 D4
Aleppo = Ḥalab Syria 36°10N 37°15E 104 D7
Alerce Andino △ Chile 41°33S 72°29W 192 B2
Alerce Costero △ Chile 40°10S 73°30W 192 B2
Aléria France 42°5N 9°26E 73 F13
Alert Canada 83°2N 60°0W 161 A20
Aleru India 17°39N 79°3E 126 F4
Alès France 44°9N 4°5E 73 D8
Aleşd Romania 47°3N 22°22E 80 C7
Alessándria Italy 44°54N 8°37E 92 D5
Alet-les-Bains France 42°59N 2°14E 72 F6
Aletschhorn Switz. 46°28N 8°0E 77 J4
Aleutian Basin Pac. Oc. 57°0N 177°0E 156 B9
Aleutian Is. Pac. Oc. 52°0N 175°0W 166 D7
Aleutian Range U.S.A. 60°0N 154°0W 166 D9
Aleutian Trench
Pac. Oc. 48°0N 180°0E 54 D17
Alexander Ga., U.S.A. 33°1N 81°53W 178 D8
Alexander N. Dak.,
U.S.A. 47°51N 103°39W 172 B2
Alexander, Mt.
Australia 28°58S 120°16E 149 E3
Alexander Arch. U.S.A. 56°0N 136°0W 160 F6
Alexander Bay S. Africa 28°40S 16°30E 144 D2
Alexander City U.S.A. 32°56N 85°58W 177 E11
Alexander I. Antarctica 69°0S 70°0W 55 C17
Alexandra Australia 37°8S 145°40E 153 D6
Alexandra N.Z. 45°14S 169°25E 155 F4
Alexandra Channel
Burma 14°7N 93°13E 127 L21
Alexandra Falls
Canada 60°29N 116°18W 162 A5
Alexandria = El Iskandarîya
Egypt 31°13N 29°58E 137 B2
Alexandria B.C.,
Canada 52°35N 122°27W 162 C4
Alexandria Ont.,
Canada 45°19N 74°38W 175 A10
Alexandria Romania 43°57N 25°24E 81 G10
Alexandria S. Africa 33°38S 26°28E 144 D4
Alexandria U.K. 55°59N 4°35W 65 F4
Alexandria La., U.S.A. 31°18N 92°27W 176 F8
Alexandria Minn.,
U.S.A. 45°53N 95°22W 172 C6
Alexandria S. Dak.,
U.S.A. 43°39N 97°47W 172 D5
Alexandria Va., U.S.A. 38°49N 77°5W 174 F8
Alexandria Bay U.S.A. 44°20N 75°55W 175 B9
Alexandrina, L.
Australia 35°25S 139°10E 152 C3
Alexandroupoli Greece 40°50N 25°54E 97 D8
Alexis → Canada 52°33N 56°8W 165 B8
Alexis Creek Canada 52°10N 123°20W 162 C4
Aley → Russia 52°40N 83°0E 108 D9
Alfabia Spain 39°44N 2°44E 100 B9

Alfambra Spain 40°33N 1°5W **90** E3
Alfândega da Fé Portugal 41°20N 6°59W **88** D4
Alfaro Spain 42°10N 1°50W **90** C3
Alfatar Bulgaria 43°59N 27°13E **97** C11
Alfeld Germany 51°59N 9°50E **76** D5
Alfenas Brazil 21°20S 46°10W **191** A6
Alföld Hungary 46°30N 20°0E **80** D5
Alfonsine Italy 44°30N 12°3E **93** D9
Alford Aberds., U.K. 57°14N 2°41W **65** D6
Alford Lincs., U.K. 53°15N 0°10E **66** D8
Alford U.S.A. 30°42N 85°24W **178** E4
Alfred Maine, U.S.A. 43°29N 70°43W **175** C14
Alfred N.Y., U.S.A. 42°16N 77°48W **174** D7
Alfreton U.K. 53°6N 1°24W **66** D6
Alfta Sweden 61°21N 16°4E **62** C10
Algaida Spain 39°33N 2°53E **100** B9
Algar Spain 36°40N 5°39W **89** J5
Ålgård Norway 58°46N 5°53E **61** G11
Algarinejo Spain 37°19N 4°9W **89** H6
Algarve Portugal 36°58N 8°20W **89** J2
Algeciras Spain 36°9N 5°28W **89** J5
Algemesí Spain 39°11N 0°27W **91** F4
Alger Algeria 36°42N 3°8E **136** A4
Alger ☐ Algeria 36°45N 3°10E **91** J8
Alger ✈ (ALG) Algeria 36°39N 3°13E **91** J8
Algeria ■ Africa 28°30N 2°0E **136** C4
Algha Kazakhstan 49°53N 57°20E **108** C5
Alghero Italy 40°33N 8°19E **94** B1
Älghult Sweden 57°0N 15°35E **63** G9
Algiers = Alger Algeria 36°42N 3°8E **136** A4
Algoa B. S. Africa 33°50S 25°45E **144** D4
Algodonales Spain 36°54N 5°24W **89** J5
Algodones Dunes U.S.A. 32°50N 115°5W **171** N11
Algodor → Spain 39°55N 3°53W **88** F7
Algoma U.S.A. 44°36N 87°26W **172** C10
Algona U.S.A. 43°4N 94°14W **172** D6
Algonac U.S.A. 42°37N 82°32W **174** D2
Algonquin ○ Canada 45°50N 78°30W **164** C4
Algorta Spain 43°21N 2°59W **90** B2
Algorta Uruguay 32°25S 57°24W **190** C4
Alhama de Almería Spain 36°57N 2°34W **89** J8
Alhama de Aragón Spain 41°18N 1°54W **90** D3
Alhama de Granada Spain 37°0N 3°59W **89** H7
Alhama de Murcia Spain 37°51N 1°25W **91** H3
Alhambra U.S.A. 34°5N 118°7W **171** L8
Alhaurín el Grande Spain 36°39N 4°41W **89** J6
Alhucemas = Al Hoceïma Morocco 35°8N 3°58W **136** A3
'Alī al Gharbī Iraq 32°30N 46°45E **105** F12
'Alī ash Sharqī Iraq 32°7N 46°44E **105** F12
Āli Bayramlı = Şirvan Azerbaijan 39°59N 48°52E **87** L9
'Alī Khēl Afghan. 33°57N 69°43E **124** C3
Alī Shāh Iran 38°9N 45°50E **128** B5
Ália Italy 37°47N 13°43E **94** E6
'Alīābād Golestān, Iran 36°40N 54°33E **129** B7
'Alīābād Khorāsān, Iran 32°30N 57°30E **129** C8
'Alīābād Kordestān, Iran 35°4N 46°58E **128** C5
'Alīābād Yazd, Iran 31°41N 53°49E **129** D7
Aliade Nigeria 7°18N 8°29E **139** D6
Aliaga Spain 40°40N 0°42W **90** E4
Aliağa Turkey 38°47N 26°59E **99** C8
Aliákmonas → Greece 40°30N 22°36E **96** F6
Alibag India 18°38N 72°56E **126** E1
Alibori → Benin 11°56N 3°17E **139** C5
Alibunar Serbia 45°5N 20°57E **80** C5
Alicante Spain 38°23N 0°30W **91** G4
Alicante ☐ Spain 38°30N 0°37W **91** G4
Alicante ✈ (ALC) Spain 38°14N 0°36W **91** G4
Alice S. Africa 32°48S 26°55E **144** D4
Alice U.S.A. 27°45N 98°5W **176** H5
Alice → Queens., Australia 24°2S 144°50E **150** C3
Alice → Queens., Australia 15°35S 142°20E **150** B3
Alice, Punta Italy 39°24N 17°9E **95** C10
Alice Arm Canada 55°29N 129°31W **162** B3
Alicedale S. Africa 33°15S 26°4E **144** D4
Aliceville U.S.A. 33°8N 88°9W **177** E10
Alicudi Italy 38°33N 14°20E **95** D7
Aliganj India 27°30N 79°10E **125** F8
Aligarh Raj., India 25°55N 76°15E **124** G7
Aligarh Ut. P., India 27°55N 78°10E **124** F8
Alīgūdarz Iran 33°25N 49°45E **129** C6
Alijó Portugal 41°16N 7°27W **88** D3
Alimia Greece 36°16N 27°43E **101** C9
Alingsås Sweden 57°56N 12°31E **63** G6
Alipur Pakistan 29°25N 70°55E **124** E4
Alipur Duar India 26°30N 89°35E **123** F16
Aliquippa U.S.A. 40°37N 80°15W **174** E4
Alishan Taiwan 23°31N 120°48E **117** F13
Aliste → Spain 41°34N 5°58W **88** D5
Aliveri Greece 38°24N 24°2E **98** C6
Aliwal North S. Africa 30°45S 26°45E **144** D4
Alix Canada 52°24N 113°11W **162** D6
Aljezur Portugal 37°18N 8°49W **89** H2
Aljustrel Portugal 37°55N 8°10W **89** H2
Alkamari Niger 13°27N 11°10E **139** C7
Alkhanay △ Russia 51°0N 113°30E **107** D12
Alkmaar Neths. 52°37N 4°45E **69** B4
All American Canal U.S.A. 32°45N 115°15W **171** N11
Allada Benin 6°41N 2°9E **139** D5
Allagadda India 15°8N 78°30E **127** G4
Allagash → U.S.A. 47°5N 69°3W **173** B19
Allah Dad Pakistan 25°38N 67°34E **124** G2
Allahabad India 25°25N 81°58E **125** G9
Allan Canada 51°53N 106°4W **163** C7
Allanche France 45°14N 2°57E **72** C6
Allanridge S. Africa 27°45S 26°40E **144** C4
Allansford Australia 38°25S 142°39E **152** E5
Allanton N.Z. 45°55S 170°15E **155** F5
Allaqi, Wadi → Egypt 23°7N 32°47E **137** C3
Allariz Spain 42°11N 7°50W **88** C3
Allassac France 45°15N 1°29E **72** C5
Allatoona L. U.S.A. 34°10N 84°44W **178** A5
Alleberg Sweden 58°8N 13°36E **63** F7
Allegany U.S.A. 42°6N 78°30W **174** D6
Allegheny → U.S.A. 40°27N 80°1W **174** E5
Allegheny Mts. U.S.A. 38°15N 80°10W **173** F13
Allegheny Plateau U.S.A. 41°30N 78°30W **173** E14

Allegheny Res. U.S.A. 41°50N 79°0W **174** E6
Allègre France 45°12N 3°41E **72** C7
Allègre, Pte. Guadeloupe 16°22N 61°46W **182** b
Allen Argentina 38°58S 67°50W **192** A3
Allen, Bog of Ireland 53°15N 7°0W **64** C5
Allen, L. Ireland 54°8N 8°4W **64** B3
Allendale U.S.A. 33°1N 81°18W **178** E5
Allende Mexico 28°20N 100°51W **180** B4
Allentown U.S.A. 40°37N 75°29W **175** F9
Allentsteig Austria 48°41N 15°20E **78** C8
Alleppey = Alappuzha India 9°30N 76°28E **127** K3
Allepuz Spain 40°29N 0°44W **90** E4
Aller → Germany 52°56N 9°12E **76** C5
Alleynes B. Barbados 13°13N 59°39W **183** g
Alliance Nebr., U.S.A. 42°6N 102°52W **172** D2
Alliance Ohio, U.S.A. 40°55N 81°6W **174** F3
Allier ☐ France 46°25N 2°40E **71** F10
Allier → France 46°57N 3°4E **71** F10
Alliford Bay Canada 53°12N 131°58W **162** C2
Alligator Pond Jamaica 17°52N 77°34W **182** a
Allinagaram India 10°2N 77°30E **127** J3
Allinge Denmark 55°17N 14°50E **63** J8
Alliston Canada 44°9N 79°52W **174** B5
Alloa U.K. 56°7N 3°47W **65** E5
Allones France 48°20N 1°40E **70** D8
Allora Australia 28°2S 152°0E **151** D5
Allos France 44°15N 6°38E **73** D10
Alluitsup Paa Greenland 60°30N 45°35W **57** E6
Allur India 14°40N 80°4E **127** G5
Alluru Kottapatnam India 15°24N 80°7E **127** G5
Alma Canada 48°35N 71°40W **165** C5
Alma Ga., U.S.A. 31°33N 82°28W **178** D7
Alma Kans., U.S.A. 39°1N 96°17W **172** F5
Alma Mich., U.S.A. 43°23N 84°39W **173** D11
Alma Nebr., U.S.A. 40°6N 99°22W **172** E4
Alma Wis., U.S.A. 44°20N 91°55W **172** C8
Alma Ata = Almaty Kazakhstan 43°15N 76°57E **109** D9
Alma Hill U.S.A. 42°2N 78°0W **174** D7
Almacelles Spain 41°43N 0°27E **90** D5
Almada Portugal 38°41N 9°8W **89** G1
Almaden Australia 17°22S 144°40E **150** B3
Almadén Spain 38°49N 4°52W **89** G6
Almalyk = Olmaliq Uzbekistan 40°50N 69°35E **109** D7
Almanor, L. U.S.A. 40°14N 121°9W **168** F3
Almansa Spain 38°51N 1°5W **91** G3
Almanza Spain 42°39N 5°3W **88** C5
Almanzor, Pico Spain 40°15N 5°18W **88** E5
Almanzora → Spain 37°14N 1°46W **91** H3
Almas Brazil 11°33S 47°9W **189** C11
Almaş, Munţii Romania 44°49N 22°12E **80** F7
Almaty Kazakhstan 43°15N 76°57E **109** D9
Almaty ☐ Kazakhstan 44°30N 78°0E **109** D9
Almazán Spain 41°30N 2°30W **90** D2
Almazora Spain 39°57N 0°3W **90** F4
Almeirim Brazil 1°30S 52°34W **187** D8
Almeirim Portugal 39°12N 8°37W **89** F2
Almelo Neths. 52°22N 6°42E **69** B6
Almenar de Soria Spain 41°43N 2°12W **90** D2
Almenara Spain 16°11S 40°42W **189** D12
Almenara Spain 39°46N 0°14W **90** F4
Almenara, Sierra de Spain 37°34N 1°32W **91** H3
Almendra, Embalse de Spain 41°10N 6°5W **88** D4
Almendralejo Spain 38°41N 6°26W **89** G4
Almere Neths. 52°20N 5°15E **69** B5
Almería Spain 36°52N 2°27W **89** J8
Almería ☐ Spain 37°20N 2°20W **91** H2
Almería, G. de Spain 36°41N 2°28W **91** J2
Almetyevsk Russia 54°53N 52°20E **86** C11
Älmhult Sweden 56°33N 14°8E **63** H8
Almirante Panama 9°10N 82°30W **182** E3
Almirante Montt, G. Chile 51°52S 72°50W **192** D2
Almiropotamos Greece 38°16N 24°11E **98** C6
Almiros Greece 39°11N 22°45E **98** B4
Almodôvar Portugal 37°31N 8°2W **89** H2
Almodóvar del Campo Spain 38°43N 4°10W **89** G6
Almodóvar del Río Spain 37°48N 5°1W **89** H5
Almond U.S.A. 42°19N 77°44W **174** D7
Almont U.S.A. 42°55N 83°3W **174** D1
Almonte Canada 45°14N 76°12W **175** A8
Almonte Spain 37°13N 6°38W **89** H4
Almora India 29°38N 79°40E **125** E8
Almoradí Spain 38°7N 0°46W **91** G4
Almorox Spain 40°14N 4°24W **88** E6
Almoustarat Mali 17°35N 0°8E **139** B5
Älmsta Sweden 59°58N 18°50E **62** E12
Almudévar Spain 42°3N 0°35W **90** C4
Almuñécar Spain 36°43N 3°41W **89** J7
Almunge Sweden 59°53N 18°3E **62** E12
Almuradiel Spain 38°32N 3°28W **89** G7
Almus Turkey 40°22N 36°54E **104** B7
Almvik Sweden 57°49N 16°30E **63** G10
Almyrou, Ormos Greece 35°23N 24°20E **101** D6
Alness U.K. 57°41N 4°16W **65** D4
Alnif Morocco 31°10N 5°8W **136** B4
Alnmouth U.K. 55°24N 1°37W **66** B6
Alnwick U.K. 55°24N 1°42W **66** B6
Aloi Uganda 2°16N 33°10E **142** B3
Alon Burma 22°12N 95°5E **123** H19
Alonissos Greece 39°15N 23°55E **98** B5
Alonissos-Northern Sporades △ Greece 39°15N 24°30E **98** B6
Alor Indonesia 8°15S 124°30E **119** F6
Alor Setar Malaysia 6°7N 100°22E **121** J3
Alosno Spain 36°49N 4°46W **89** J6 *(Alosno Spain)*
Alot India 23°56N 75°40E **124** H6
Alougoum Morocco 30°17N 6°56W **136** B2
Aloysius, Mt. Australia 26°0S 128°38E **149** E4
Alpaugh U.S.A. 35°53N 119°29W **170** K7
Alpe Apuane Italy 44°N 10°15E **92** D7
Alpedrinha Portugal 40°6N 7°27W **88** E3
Alpena U.S.A. 45°4N 83°27W **174** C4
Alpercatas → Brazil 9°25S 44°19W **189** D11
Alpes-de-Haute-Provence ☐ France 44°8N 6°0E **73** D10
Alpes-Maritimes ☐ France 43°55N 7°10E **73** E11
Alpha Australia 23°39S 146°37E **150** C4
Alpha Ridge Arctic 84°0N 118°0W **54** A2
Alpharetta U.S.A. 34°5N 84°18W **178** A5
Alphen aan den Rijn Neths. 52°7N 4°40E **69** B4

Alphios → Greece 37°40N 21°33E **98** D3
Alpiarça Portugal 39°15N 8°35W **89** F2
Alpine Ariz., U.S.A. 33°51N 109°9W **169** K9
Alpine Calif., U.S.A. 32°50N 116°46W **171** N10
Alpine Tex., U.S.A. 30°22N 103°40W **176** F3
Alpine ☐ Australia 36°56S 148°10E **153** D7
Alps Europe 46°30N 9°30E **74** E5
Alpu Turkey 39°46N 30°58E **104** C4
Alpurrurulam Australia 20°59S 137°50E **150** C2
Alqueta, Barragem do Portugal 38°20N 7°25W **89** G3
Alro Denmark 55°52N 10°5E **63** J4
Als Denmark 54°59N 9°55E **63** K3
Alsace ☐ France 48°15N 7°25E **71** D14
Alsask Canada 51°21N 109°59W **163** C7
Alsasua Spain 42°54N 2°10W **90** C2
Alsek → U.S.A. 59°10N 138°12W **162** B1
Alsfeld Germany 50°44N 9°16E **76** E5
Alsta Norway 65°58N 12°40E **60** D15
Alsterbro Sweden 56°57N 15°55E **63** H9
Alstermo Sweden 56°58N 15°38E **63** H9
Alston U.K. 54°49N 2°25W **66** C5
Alta Norway 69°57N 23°10E **60** B20
Alta, Sierra Spain 40°31N 1°30W **90** E3
Alta Gracia Argentina 31°40S 64°30W **190** C3
Alta Murgia △ Italy 40°55N 16°30E **95** B9
Alta Sierra U.S.A. 35°42N 118°33W **171** K8
Altaelva → Norway 69°54N 23°17E **60** B20
Altafjorden Norway 70°5N 23°5E **60** A20
Altai = Aerhtai Shan Mongolia 46°40N 92°45E **109** C12
Altai = Gorno-Altay ☐ Russia 51°0N 86°0E **109** B11
Altai → Russia 50°30N 85°0E **109** B11
Altamaha → U.S.A. 31°20N 81°20W **178** D8
Altamira Brazil 3°12S 52°10W **187** D8
Altamira Chile 25°47S 69°51W **190** B2
Altamira, Cuevas de Spain 43°20N 4°5W **88** B6
Altamont U.S.A. 42°42N 74°2W **175** D10
Altamura Italy 40°49N 16°33E **95** B9
Altanbulag Mongolia 50°16N 106°30E **110** A5
Altar Mexico 30°43N 111°44W **180** A2
Altar, Gran Desierto de Mexico 31°50N 114°10W **180** B2
Altata Mexico 24°40N 107°55W **180** C3
Altavista U.S.A. 37°6N 79°17W **173** G14
Altay China 47°48N 88°10E **109** C11
Altay Mongolia 46°22N 96°15E **110** B8
Altdorf Switz. 46°52N 8°36E **77** J4
Alte Mellum Germany 53°43N 8°10E **76** B4
Altea Spain 38°38N 0°2W **91** G4
Altenberg Germany 50°45N 13°45E **76** E9
Altenbruch Germany 53°49N 8°46E **76** B4
Altenburg Germany 50°59N 12°25E **76** E8
Altenkirchen Mecklenburg-Vorpommern, Germany 54°38N 13°22E **76** A9
Altenkirchen Rhld-Pfz., Germany 50°41N 7°39E **76** E3
Altenmarkt Austria 47°43N 14°39E **78** D7
Alter do Chão Portugal 39°12N 7°40W **89** F3
Altha U.S.A. 30°34N 85°8W **178** E4
Altınkaya Barajı Turkey 41°18N 35°30E **104** B6
Altınoluk Turkey 39°34N 26°45E **99** B8
Altınova Turkey 39°12N 26°47E **99** B8
Altıntaş Turkey 39°4N 30°7E **99** B12
Altınyaka Turkey 36°33N 30°20E **99** E12
Altınyayla Turkey 37°0N 29°33E **99** D11
Altiplano Bolivia 17°0S 68°0W **188** D4
Altkirch France 47°37N 7°15E **71** E14
Altmark Germany 52°45N 11°30E **76** C7
Altmühl → Germany 48°54N 11°52E **77** G7
Altmühltal △ Germany 48°55N 11°15E **77** G7
Altmunster Austria 47°54N 13°45E **78** D6
Alto Adige = Trentino-Alto Adige ☐ Italy 46°30N 11°0E **92** B8
Alto Araguaia Brazil 17°15S 53°20W **187** G8
Alto Cuchumatanes = Cuchumatanes, Sierra de los Guatemala 15°35N 91°25W **182** C1
Alto del Carmen Chile 28°46S 70°30W **190** B1
Alto Douro Portugal 41°6N 7°47W **88** D3
Alto Garda Bresciano △ Italy 45°42N 10°38E **92** C7
Alto Ligonha Mozam. 15°30S 38°11E **143** F4
Alto Molocue Mozam. 15°50S 37°35E **143** F4
Alto Paraguay ☐ Paraguay 21°0S 58°30W **190** A4
Alto Paraíso de Goiás Brazil 14°7S 47°31W **189** D9
Alto Paraná ☐ Paraguay 25°30S 54°50W **191** B5
Alto Parnaíba Brazil 9°6S 45°57W **189** D9
Alto Purús → Peru 9°12S 70°28W **188** B3
Alto Río Senguerr Argentina 45°2S 70°50W **192** C2
Alto Santo Brazil 5°31S 38°15W **189** D12
Alto Tajo △ Spain 40°44N 2°30W **90** E2
Alton Canada 43°54N 80°5W **174** C4
Alton U.K. 51°9N 0°59W **67** F7
Alton Ill., U.S.A. 38°53N 90°11W **172** F8
Alton N.H., U.S.A. 43°27N 71°13W **175** C13
Altona Canada 49°6N 97°33W **163** D9
Altoona Ala., U.S.A. 34°2N 86°20W **178** A4
Altoona Pa., U.S.A. 40°31N 78°24W **174** F6
Altos Brazil 5°3S 42°28W **189** D10
Altötting Germany 48°12N 12°39E **77** G8
Altsasu = Alsasua Spain 42°54N 2°10W **90** C2
Altstätten Switz. 47°22N 9°33E **77** H5
Altun Kupri Iraq 35°45N 44°9E **105** E11
Altun Shan China 38°30N 88°0E **110** D6
Alturas U.S.A. 41°29N 120°32W **168** F3
Altus U.S.A. 34°38N 99°20W **176** D5
Altyn-Emel △ Kazakhstan 44°20N 78°47E **109** B8
Alucra Turkey 40°22N 38°47E **105** B8
Alūksne Latvia 57°24N 27°3E **64** B4
Alunda Sweden 60°4N 18°5E **62** D12
Alūnite U.S.A. 35°59N 114°55W **171** K12
Alupka Ukraine 44°23N 34°2E **85** K8
Alur India 15°24N 77°15E **127** G3
Alushta Ukraine 44°40N 34°25E **85** K8
Alusi Indonesia 7°35S 131°40E **119** F8
Alutgama Sri Lanka 6°26N 79°59E **127** L4
Alutnuwara Sri Lanka 7°19N 80°55E **127** L5
Aluva India 10°8N 76°24E **127** J3

Alva U.S.A. 36°48N 98°40W **176** C5
Alvaiázere Portugal 39°49N 8°23W **88** D2
Älvängen Sweden 57°58N 12°8E **63** G6
Alvarado Mexico 18°46N 95°46W **181** D5
Alvarado U.S.A. 32°24N 97°13W **176** E6
Alvaro Obregón, Presa Mexico 27°52N 109°52W **180** B3
Älvdalen Sweden 61°13N 14°4E **62** C8
Alvear Argentina 29°5S 56°30W **190** B4
Alverca Portugal 38°56N 9°1W **89** G1
Alvesta Sweden 56°54N 14°35E **63** H8
Alvinston Canada 42°49N 81°52W **174** D3
Alvito Portugal 38°15N 7°58W **89** G3
Älvkarleby Sweden 60°34N 17°26E **62** D11
Alvord Desert U.S.A. 42°30N 118°25W **168** E4
Älvros Sweden 62°3N 14°38E **62** B8
Älvsbyn Sweden 65°40N 21°0E **60** D19
Alwar India 27°38N 76°34E **124** F7
Alwaye = Aluva India 10°8N 76°24E **127** J3
Alxa Zuoqi China 38°50N 105°40E **114** E3
Alyangula Australia 13°55S 136°30E **150** A2
Alyata = Älät Azerbaijan 39°58N 49°25E **87** L9
Alyth U.K. 56°38N 3°13W **65** E5
Alytus Lithuania 54°24N 24°3E **64** E3
Alzada U.S.A. 45°2N 104°25W **168** D11
Alzamay Russia 55°33N 98°39E **107** D10
Alzey Germany 49°45N 8°7E **77** F4
Alzira Spain 39°9N 0°30W **91** F4
Am Timan Chad 11°0N 20°10E **137** F10
Amādalen Sweden 61°20N 14°44E **62** C8
Amadeus, L. Australia 24°54S 131°0E **149** D5
Amadi Dem. Rep. of the Congo 3°40N 26°40E **142** B5
Amadi South Sudan 5°29N 30°25E **135** G12
Amadjuak L. Canada 65°0N 71°8W **161** E17
Amadora Portugal 38°45N 9°13W **89** G1
Amagansett U.S.A. 40°59N 72°9W **175** E12
Amagasaki Japan 34°42N 135°23E **113** G7
Amager Denmark 55°36N 12°35E **63** J6
Amagi Japan 33°25N 130°39E **113** H5
Amagunze Nigeria 6°20N 7°40E **139** D6
Amahai Indonesia 3°20S 128°55E **119** E7
Amaiun-Maia Spain 43°12N 1°29W **90** B3
Amakusa = Hondo Japan 32°32N 130°12E **113** H5
Amakusa-Shotō Japan 32°15N 130°10E **113** H5
Åmål Sweden 59°3N 12°42E **62** E6
Amalapuram India 16°35N 81°55E **127** F5
Amalfi Italy 40°38N 14°36E **95** B7
Amaliada Greece 37°47N 21°22E **98** D3
Amalner India 21°5N 75°5E **126** D2
Amamapare Indonesia 4°53S 136°38E **119** E9
Amambaí Brazil 23°22S 55°4W **191** A4
Amambaí → Brazil 23°22S 53°56W **191** A5
Amambay ☐ Paraguay 23°0S 56°0W **191** A4
Amambay, Cordillera de S. Amer. 23°0S 55°45W **191** A4
Amami Japan 28°22N 129°27E **113** K4
Amami-Guntō Japan 27°16N 129°21E **113** L4
Amami-Ō-Shima Japan 28°16N 129°21E **113** K4
Amal, Pulau Malaysia 5°16N 100°24E **121** c
Amaná, L. Brazil 2°35S 64°40W **186** D6
Amanat → India 24°7N 84°4E **125** G11
Amanda Park U.S.A. 47°28N 123°55W **170** C3
Amankeldi Kazakhstan 50°10N 65°10E **108** B7
Amantea Italy 39°8N 16°4E **95** C9
Amapá Brazil 2°5N 50°50W **187** C8
Amapá ☐ Brazil 1°40N 52°0W **187** C8
Amarante Brazil 6°14S 42°50W **189** D10
Amarante Portugal 41°16N 8°5W **88** D2
Amarante do Maranhão Brazil 5°36S 46°45W **189** B1
Amaranth Canada 50°36N 98°43W **163** C9
Amaravati → India 11°0N 78°15E **127** J4
Amareleja Portugal 38°12N 7°13W **89** G3
Amargosa Brazil 13°2S 39°36W **189** C3
Amargosa → U.S.A. 36°14N 116°51W **171** J10
Amargosa Desert U.S.A. 36°40N 116°30W **171** J10
Amargosa Range U.S.A. 36°20N 116°45W **171** J10
Amari Greece 35°13N 24°40E **101** D6
Amarillo U.S.A. 35°13N 101°50W **176** D4
Amarkantak India 22°40N 81°45E **125** H9
'Amārna, Tell el Egypt 27°38N 30°52E **137** B3
Amarnath India 19°12N 73°22E **126** E1
Amaro, Mte. Italy 42°5N 14°5E **93** F11
Amarpur India 25°5N 87°0E **125** G12
Amarwara India 22°18N 79°10E **125** H8
Amasra Turkey 41°45N 32°23E **104** B5
Amassama Nigeria 5°1N 6°2E **139** D6
Amasya Turkey 40°40N 35°50E **104** B6
Amasya ☐ Turkey 40°40N 35°50E **104** B6
Amata Australia 26°9S 131°9E **149** E5
Amatikulu S. Africa 29°3S 31°33E **145** C5
Amatitlán Guatemala 14°29N 90°38W **182** D1
Amatrice Italy 42°38N 13°17E **93** F10
Amay Belgium 50°33N 5°19E **69** D5
Amazon = Amazonas → S. Amer. 0°5S 50°0W **187** D8
Amazonas ☐ Brazil 5°0S 65°0W **186** E6
Amazonas ☐ Peru 5°0S 78°0W **188** B2
Amazonas → S. Amer. 0°5S 50°0W **187** D8
Ambad India 19°38N 75°50E **126** E2
Ambah India 26°43N 78°13E **124** F8
Ambahakily Madag. 21°36S 43°41E **145** C7
Ambahita Madag. 24°1S 45°16E **145** C8
Ambala India 30°23N 76°56E **124** D7
Ambalangoda Sri Lanka 6°15N 80°5E **127** L5
Ambalantota Sri Lanka 6°7N 81°1E **127** L5
Ambalapulai India 9°N 76°E **127** K3
Ambalavao Madag. 21°50S 46°56E **145** C8
Ambanja Madag. 13°40S 48°27E **145** A8
Ambarchik Russia 69°40N 162°20E **107** C17
Ambarli Turkey 40°58N 28°40E **99** B13
Ambasamudram India 8°43N 77°25E **127** K3
Ambato Ecuador 1°5S 78°42W **186** D3
Ambato, Sierra de Argentina 28°25S 66°10W **190** B3
Ambatolampy Madag. 19°20S 47°35E **145** B8
Ambatondrazaka Madag. 17°55S 48°28E **145** B8
Ambelonas Greece 39°45N 22°23E **98** B4
Amberg Germany 49°26N 11°52E **77** F7
Ambergris Cay Belize 18°0N 87°55W **181** D7
Ambérieu-en-Bugey France 45°57N 5°20E **73** C9
Ambert France 45°33N 3°44E **72** C7
Ambikapur India 23°15N 83°15E **125** H10

Amberley N.Z. 43°9S 172°44E **155** D7
Ambert France 45°33N 3°44E **72** C7
Ambidédi Mali 14°35N 11°47W **138** C2
Ambikapur India 23°15N 83°15E **125** H10
Ambikol Sudan 21°20N 30°50E **137** C3
Amble U.K. 55°20N 1°36W **66** B6
Ambleside U.K. 54°26N 2°58W **66** C5
Ambo Peru 10°5S 76°10W **188** B2
Ambohitra Madag. 12°30S 49°10E **141** G9
Amboise France 47°24N 1°2E **70** E8
Ambon Indonesia 3°43S 128°12E **119** E7
Ambositra Madag. 20°31S 47°25E **141** J9
Ambovombe Madag. 25°11S 46°5E **141** K9
Amboy Cay S. China Sea 7°50N 112°50E **118** C4
Amboy U.S.A. 34°33N 115°45W **171** L11
Ambridge U.S.A. 40°36N 80°14W **174** F4
Ambriz Angola 7°48S 13°8E **143** D2
Ambrolauri Georgia 42°31N 43°9E **105** A7
Ambur India 12°48N 78°43E **127** H4
Amchitka I. U.S.A. 51°32N 179°0E **166** E3
Amderma Russia 69°45N 61°30E **106** C7
Amdhi India 23°51N 81°27E **125** H9
Amdo China 32°20N 91°40E **110** E7
Ameca Mexico 20°33N 104°2W **180** C4
Ameca → Mexico 20°41N 105°18W **180** C3
Amecameca de Juárez Mexico 19°8N 98°46W **181** D5
Amed Indonesia 8°19S 115°39E **119** J18
Ameland Neths. 53°27N 5°45E **69** A5
Amélia Italy 42°33N 12°25E **93** F9
Amelia City U.S.A. 30°35N 81°28W **178** E8
Amelia I. U.S.A. 30°40N 81°25W **178** E8
Amendolara Italy 39°57N 16°35E **95** C9
Amenia U.S.A. 41°51N 73°33W **175** E11
America-Antarctica Ridge S. Ocean 59°0S 16°0W **55** B2
American Falls U.S.A. 42°47N 112°51W **168** E7
American Falls Res. U.S.A. 42°47N 112°52W **168** E7
American Fork U.S.A. 40°23N 111°48W **168** F8
American Highland Antarctica 73°0S 75°0E **55** D6
American River Australia 35°47S 137°46E **152** C2
American Samoa ☑ Pac. Oc. 14°20S 170°0W **157** J11
Americana Brazil 22°45S 47°20W **191** A6
Amerigo Vespucci, Firenze ✈ (FLR) Italy 43°49N 11°13E **93** E8
Amersfoort Neths. 52°9N 5°23E **69** B5
Amersfoort S. Africa 26°59S 29°53E **145** C4
Amery Basin S. Ocean 68°15S 74°30E **55** C6
Amery Ice Shelf Antarctica 69°30S 72°0E **55** C6
Amerzgane Morocco 31°4N 7°14W **136** B2
Ames = Bertamirans Spain 42°54N 8°38W **88** C2
Ames U.S.A. 42°2N 93°37W **172** D7
Amesbury U.K. 51°10N 1°46W **67** F6
Amesbury U.S.A. 42°51N 70°56W **175** D14
Amet India 25°18N 73°56E **124** G5
Amfiklia Greece 38°38N 22°35E **98** C4
Amfilochia Greece 38°52N 21°9E **98** C3
Amfipoli Greece 40°48N 23°52E **96** F7
Amfissa Greece 38°32N 22°22E **98** C4
Amga Russia 60°50N 132°0E **107** C14
Amga → Russia 62°38N 134°32E **107** C14
Amgaon India 21°22N 80°22E **125** H8
Amgu Russia 45°45N 137°15E **112** B8
Amguid Algeria 26°26N 5°22E **136** C7
Amgun → Russia 52°56N 139°38E **107** D14
Amherst Canada 45°48N 64°8W **165** C7
Amherst Mass., U.S.A. 42°23N 72°31W **175** D12
Amherst N.Y., U.S.A. 42°59N 78°48W **174** D6
Amherst Ohio, U.S.A. 41°24N 82°14W **174** E2
Amherst I. Canada 44°8N 76°43W **175** B8
Amherstburg Canada 42°6N 83°6W **174** D2
Amiata, Mte. Italy 42°53N 11°37E **93** F8
Amidon U.S.A. 46°29N 103°19W **172** B2
Amiens France 49°54N 2°16E **71** C9
Amindivi Is. India 11°23N 72°23E **127** J1
Amini I. India 11°7N 72°23E **127** J1
Aminuis Namibia 23°43S 19°21E **144** B2
Amīrābād Iran 33°20N 46°16E **128** C5
Amirante Is. Seychelles 6°0S 53°0E **132** J7
Amisk L. Canada 54°35N 102°15W **163** B8
Amistad, Presa de la Mexico 29°26N 101°3W **180** B4
Amite U.S.A. 30°44N 90°30W **177** F9
Amizmiz Morocco 31°12N 8°15W **136** B3
Amla India 21°56N 78°7E **124** J8
Amlapura = Karangasem Indonesia 8°27S 115°37E **119** J18
Amlia I. U.S.A. 52°4N 173°30W **166** E5
Amlwch U.K. 53°24N 4°20W **66** D3
'Ammān Jordan 31°57N 35°52E **130** D4
'Ammān ✈ (AMM) Jordan 31°45N 36°2E **130** D5
Ammanford U.K. 51°48N 3°59W **67** F4
Ammassalik = Tasiilaq Greenland 65°40N 37°20W **57** D7
Ammerån → Sweden 63°9N 16°13E **62** A10
Ammersee Germany 48°0N 11°7E **77** G7
Ammochostos = Famagusta Cyprus 35°8N 33°55E **101** D12
Ammon U.S.A. 43°28N 111°58W **168** E8
Amnat Charoen Thailand 15°51N 104°38E **120** E5
Amnura Bangla. 24°37N 88°25E **125** G13
Amo Jiang → China 22°53N 102°20E **116** E4
Amol Iran 36°23N 52°20E **128** B7
Amorgós Greece 36°50N 25°57E **99** E7
Amory U.S.A. 33°59N 88°29W **177** E10
Amos Canada 48°35N 78°5W **164** C4
Åmot Norway 59°57N 9°54E **63** D2
Åmotfors Sweden 59°47N 12°22E **62** E6
Amoy = Xiamen China 24°25N 118°4E **117** F12
Ampang Malaysia 3°8N 101°45E **121** L3
Ampanihy Madag. 24°40S 44°45E **141** J8

Ampato, Nevado Peru 15°40S 71°56W **188**
Ampenan Indonesia 8°34S 116°4E **119**
Amper Nigeria 9°25N 9°40E **139**
Amper → Germany 48°29N 11°55E **77**
Ampezzo Italy 46°25N 12°48E **9**
Amphitrite Group S. China Sea 16°50N 112°20E **11**
Amphoe Kathu Thailand 7°55N 98°21E **1**
Amphoe Thalang Thailand 8°1N 98°20E **1**
Amposta Spain 40°43N 0°34E **9**
Amqui Canada 48°28N 67°27W **16**
Amrabad India 16°23N 78°50E **12**
Amravati India 20°55N 77°45E **12**
Amreli India 21°35N 71°17E **12**
Amritsar India 31°35N 74°57E **12**
Amroha India 28°53N 78°30E **12**
Amrum Germany 54°38N 8°21E **7**
Amsterdam Neths. 52°23N 4°54E **6**
Amsterdam U.S.A. 42°56N 74°11W **175**
Amsterdam ✈ (AMS) Neths. 52°18N 4°45E **6**
Amsterdam I. = Nouvelle Amsterdam, Î. Ind. Oc. 38°30S 77°30E **1**
Amstetten Austria 48°7N 14°51E **7**
'Amūdah Syria 37°6N 40°55E **10**
Amudarya → Turkmenistan 37°53N 65°15E **10**
Amudarya → Uzbekistan 43°58N 59°34E **10**
Amukta Pass U.S.A. 52°0N 171°0W **16**
Amund Ringnes I. Canada 78°20N 96°25W **161**
Amundsen Abyssal Plain S. Ocean 65°0S 125°0W **55**
Amundsen Basin Arctic 87°30N 80°0E
Amundsen Gulf Canada 70°0N 124°0W **16**
Amundsen Ridges S. Ocean 69°15S 123°0W **55**
Amundsen-Scott Antarctica 90°0S 166°0E
Amundsen Sea Antarctica 72°0S 115°0W **55**
Amungen Sweden 61°10N 15°40E **6**
Amuntai Indonesia 2°28S 115°25E **11**
Amur → Russia 52°56N 141°10E **107**
Amur, W. → Sudan 18°56N 33°34E **13**
Amurang Indonesia 1°5N 124°40E **11**
Amurrio Spain 43°3N 3°0W **9**
Amursk Russia 50°14N 136°54E **107**
Amusco Spain 42°10N 4°28W **8**
Amvrakikos Kolpos Greece 39°0N 20°55E **9**
Amvrosiyivka Ukraine 47°43N 38°30E **85**
Amyderya = Amudarya → Uzbekistan 43°58N 59°34E **10**
An Bang, Dao = Amboyna Cay S. China Sea 7°50N 112°50E **11**
An Bien Vietnam 9°45N 105°0E **12**
An Hoa Vietnam 15°40N 108°5E **12**
An Khe Vietnam 13°57N 108°51E **12**
An Nabatīyah at Tahta Lebanon 33°23N 35°27E **13**
An Nabk Syria 34°2N 36°44E **13**
An Nafūd Si. Arabia 28°15N 41°0E **12**
An Nāhiyah Iraq 34°26N 41°33E **10**
An Najaf Iraq 32°3N 44°15E **10**
An Nāşirīyah Iraq 31°0N 46°15E **12**
An Nhon = Binh Dinh Vietnam 13°55N 109°7E **12**
An Nīl ☐ Sudan 19°30N 33°0E **13**
An Nu'ayrīyah Si. Arabia 27°30N 48°30E **12**
An Nu'mānīyah Iraq 32°32N 45°25E **105**
An Ros = Rush Ireland 53°31N 6°6W **6**
An Thoi, Quan Dao Vietnam 9°58N 104°0E **12**
Anabar → Russia 73°8N 113°36E **107**
Anaconda U.S.A. 46°8N 112°57W **11**
Anacortes U.S.A. 48°30N 122°37W **17**
Anadarko U.S.A. 35°4N 98°15W **17**
Anadia Brazil 9°42S 36°18W **18**
Anadia Portugal 40°26N 8°27W **8**
Anadolu Turkey 39°0N 30°0E **10**
Anadyr Russia 64°35N 177°20E **107**
Anadyr → Russia 64°55N 176°5E **10**
Anadyrskiy Zaliv Russia 64°0N 180°0E **10**
Anafi Greece 36°22N 25°48E **9**
Anaga, Pta. de Canary Is. 28°34N 16°9W **10**
Anagni Italy 41°44N 13°9E **9**
'Ānah Iraq 34°25N 42°0E **10**
Anaheim U.S.A. 33°50N 117°55W **17**
Anahim Lake Canada 52°28N 125°18W **16**
Anai Mudi India 10°12N 77°4E **12**
Anaimalai Hills India 10°20N 76°40E **12**
Anajatuba Brazil 3°16S 44°37W **18**
Anakapalle India 17°42N 83°6E **12**
Anakie Australia 23°32S 147°45E **15**
Anaklia Georgia 42°22N 41°35E **8**
Analalava Madag. 14°35S 48°0E **14**
Analipsis Greece 39°36N 19°55E **10**
Anambar → Pakistan 30°15N 68°50E **12**
Anambas, Kepulauan Indonesia 3°20N 106°30E **11**
Anambas Is. = Anambas, Kepulauan Indonesia 3°20N 106°30E **11**
Anambra ☐ Nigeria 6°20N 7°40E **13**
Anamosa U.S.A. 42°7N 91°17W **17**
Anamur Turkey 36°8N 32°58E **10**
Anamur Burnu Turkey 36°4N 32°57E **10**
Anan Japan 33°54N 134°40E **11**
Anand India 22°32N 72°59E **12**
Anandapur India 21°16N 86°13E **12**
Ananes Greece 36°33N 24°9E **9**
Anangu Pitjantjatjara ◎ Australia 27°0S 132°0E **1**
Anantapur India 14°39N 77°42E **1**
Anantnag India 33°45N 75°10E **12**
Ananyiv Ukraine 47°44N 29°58E **8**
Anapa Russia 44°55N 37°25E **8**
Anápolis Brazil 16°15S 48°50W **18**
Anapu → Brazil 1°53S 50°53W **18**
Anār Iran 30°55N 55°13E **12**
Anārak Iran 33°25N 53°40E **12**
Anarfjällen Sweden 63°6N 13°10E **6**
Anas → India 23°26N 74°0E **12**
Anatolia = Anadolu Turkey 39°0N 30°0E **104**

NDEX TO WORLD MAPS
Archipiélago Los Roques 197

toliki Makedonia kai
araki □ Greece 41°10N 24°30E 97 E8
tuya Argentina 28°20S 62°50W 190 B3
tye ✪ Australia 22°29S 137°3E 150 C2
unethad L.
nada 60°55N 104°25W 163 A8
yŏn N. Korea 39°1N 127°35E 115 E14
ares, Sierra dos
ain 42°51N 6°52W 88 C4
ares ⌂ Spain 42°50N 6°40W 88 C4
ash □ Peru 9°30S 77°45W 188 B2
aster Canada 43°13N 79°59W 174 C5
enis France 47°21N 1°10W 70 E5
ho, Canal Chile 50°0S 74°20W 192 D2
hor Bay U.S.A. 38°48N 123°34W 170 G3
horage U.S.A. 61°13N 149°54W 160 E2
huras Spain 39°29N 4°50W 89 F6
huthengu India 8°40N 76°46E 127 K3
China 39°20N 116°40E 114 E9
ohuma, Nevado
livia 16°0S 68°50W 188 D4
ón Peru 11°50S 77°10W 188 C2
na Italy 43°38N 13°30E 93 E10
ud Chile 42°0S 73°50W 192 B2
ud, G. de Chile 42°0S 73°0W 192 B2
y-le-Franc France 47°46N 4°10E 71 E11
a China 46°24N 125°19E 111 B14
acollo Argentina 37°10S 70°42W 190 D1
acollo Chile 30°14S 71°6W 190 C1
ahuaylas Peru 13°40S 73°25W 188 C3
algalá Argentina 27°40S 66°30W 190 B2
alsnes Norway 62°35N 7°43E 60 E12
alucía □ Spain 37°35N 5°0W 89 H6
alusia = Andalucía □
ain 37°35N 5°0W 89 H6
alusia U.S.A. 31°18N 86°29W 177 F11
aman & Nicobar Is. □
dia 10°0N 93°0E 127 K11
aman Is. Ind. Oc. 12°30N 92°45E 127 H11
aman Sea Ind. Oc. 13°0N 96°0E 118 B1
amooka Australia 30°27S 137°9E 151 E2
apa Madag. 14°39S 49°39E 141 G9
ara Namibia 18°2S 21°9E 144 A3
araí Brazil 12°48S 41°20W 189 C2
elot-Blancheville
ance 48°15N 5°18E 71 D12
enes Norway 69°19N 16°18E 60 B17
enne Belgium 50°28N 5°5E 69 D5
éranboukane Mali 15°26N 3°2E 139 B5
ermatt Switz. 46°38N 8°35E 77 J4
ernach Germany 50°26N 7°24E 76 E3
ernos-les-Bains
ance 44°44N 1°6W 72 D2
erslöv Sweden 55°26N 13°19E 63 J7
erson Australia 38°31S 145°26E 153 E6
erson Alaska,
S.A. 64°25N 149°15W 166 C10
erson Calif.,
S.A. 40°27N 122°18W 168 F2
erson Ind., U.S.A. 40°10N 85°41W 173 E11
erson Mo., U.S.A. 36°39N 94°27W 172 G6
erson S.C., U.S.A. 34°31N 82°39W 177 D13
erson → Canada 69°42N 129°0W 160 D6
erson I. India 12°46N 92°43E 127 H11
ersonville U.S.A. 32°12N 84°9W 178 C5
ersonville ⌂ U.S.A. 32°12N 84°1W 178 C5
erstorp Sweden 57°19N 13°39E 63 G7
es U.S.A. 42°12N 74°47W 175 D10
es, Cord. de los
Amer. 20°0S 68°0W 188 E4
fjorden Norway 69°10N 16°20E 60 B17
hra, L. India 18°54N 73°32E 126 E1
hra Pradesh □ India 18°0N 79°0E 126 F4
ijon Uzbekistan 41°10N 72°15E 109 D8
ijon □ Uzbekistan 40°45N 72°20E 109 D8
ikithira = Antikythira
eece 35°52N 23°15E 98 F5
imeshk Iran 32°27N 48°21E 105 F13
imilos = Antimilos
eece 36°47N 24°12E 98 E6
iparos = Antiparos
eece 37°0N 25°3E 99 D7
ipaxoi = Antipaxi
eece 39°9N 20°13E 98 B2
ipsara = Antipsara
eece 38°30N 25°29E 99 C7
izhan = Andijon
bekistan 41°10N 72°15E 109 D8
khvoy Afghan. 36°52N 65°8E 109 E7
oain Spain 43°13N 2°1W 90 B2
oany Madag. 13°25S 48°16E 141 G9
ol India 17°51N 78°4E 126 F4
ola India 16°57N 76°50E 126 F3
ong S. Korea 36°40N 128°43E 115 F15
orra Spain 40°59N 0°28W 90 E4
orra ■ Europe 42°30N 1°30E 72 F5
orra La Vella Andorra 42°31N 1°32E 72 F5
over U.K. 51°12N 1°29W 67 F6
over Kans., U.S.A. 37°43N 97°7W 172 G5
over Maine,
S.A. 44°38N 70°45W 175 B14
over Mass., U.S.A. 42°40N 71°8W 175 D13
over N.J., U.S.A. 40°59N 74°45W 175 F10
over N.Y., U.S.A. 42°10N 77°48W 174 D7
over Ohio, U.S.A. 41°36N 80°34W 174 E4
øya Norway 69°10N 15°50E 60 B16
radina Brazil 20°54S 51°23W 187 H8
ratx Spain 39°39N 2°25E 100 B9
ravida Greece 37°54N 21°16E 98 D3
reanof Is. U.S.A. 51°30N 176°0W 166 E4
reapol Russia 56°40N 32°17E 84 D7
rée Land Greenland 73°40N 26°0W 57 C8
rews S.C., U.S.A. 33°27N 79°34W 177 E15
rews Tex., U.S.A. 32°19N 102°33W 176 E3
reyevka Russia 52°19N 51°55E 86 D10
ria Italy 41°13N 16°17E 95 A9
rijevica Montenegro 42°45N 19°48E 96 D3
ritsena Greece 37°29N 21°52E 98 D3
ros Greece 37°50N 24°57E 98 D6
ros I. Bahamas 24°30N 78°0W 182 B4
ros Town Bahamas 24°43N 77°47W 182 B4
roth I. India 10°50N 73°41E 127 J1
rychów Poland 49°51N 19°18E 83 J6
selv Norway 69°4N 18°34E 60 B18
újar Spain 38°3N 4°5W 89 G6
ulo Angola 11°25S 16°45E 140 G3
by Sweden 57°48N 14°49E 63 G8
fis Mali 18°2N 0°36E 139 B5
gada Br. Virgin Is. 18°45N 64°20W 183 e
gada, B. Argentina 40°20S 62°20W 192 B4
gada Passage
. Indies 18°15N 63°45W 183 C7
Anécho Togo 6°12N 1°34E 139 D5
Añelo Argentina 38°20S 68°45W 192 A3
Anenni-Noi Moldova 46°53N 29°15E 81 D14
Aneto, Pico de Spain 42°37N 0°40E 90 C5
Ănew Turkmenistan 37°52N 58°31E 108 E5
Anfu China 27°21N 114°40E 117 D10
Ang Mo Kio Singapore 1°23N 103°50E 121 d
Ang Thong Thailand 14°35N 100°31E 120 E3
Ang Thong, Ko Thailand 9°37N 99°41E 121 b
Ang Thong, Mu Ko △
Thailand 9°40N 99°43E 121 b
Angamos, Punta Chile 23°1S 70°32W 190 A1
Angara → Russia 58°5N 94°20E 107 D10
Angara-Débou Benin 11°19N 3°3E 139 C5
Angarsk Russia 52°30N 104°0E 110 A9
Angas Hills Australia 23°0S 127°50E 148 D4
Angaston Australia 34°30S 139°8E 152 C3
Ånge Sweden 62°31N 15°35E 62 B9
Ángel, Salto = Angel Falls
Venezuela 5°57N 62°30W 186 B6
Ángel de la Guarda, I.
Mexico 29°20N 113°25W 180 B2
Angel Falls Venezuela 5°57N 62°30W 186 B6
Angeles Phil. 15°9N 120°33E 119 A6
Ängelholm Sweden 56°15N 12°50E 63 H6
Angels Camp U.S.A. 38°4N 120°32W 170 G6
Ängelsberg Sweden 59°58N 16°0E 62 E10
Ångermanälven →
Sweden 63°0N 17°20E 62 A11
Ångermanland Sweden 63°36N 17°45E 60 E17
Angermünde Germany 53°0N 14°0E 76 B9
Angers Canada 45°31N 75°29W 175 A9
Angers France 47°30N 0°35W 70 E6
Angerville France 48°19N 2°0E 71 D9
Ångesån → Sweden 66°16N 22°47E 60 C20
Angical Brazil 12°0S 44°42W 189 C2
Angikuni L. Canada 62°12N 99°59W 163 A9
Angkor Cambodia 13°22N 103°50E 120 F4
Angledool Australia 29°5S 147°55E 151 D4
Anglem, Mt. N.Z. 46°45S 167°53E 155 G2
Anglès Spain 41°57N 2°38E 90 D7
Anglesey U.K. 53°17N 4°20W 66 D3
Anglesey, Isle of □ U.K. 53°16N 4°18W 66 D3
Anglet France 43°29N 1°31W 72 E2
Angleton U.S.A. 29°10N 95°26W 176 G7
Anglin → France 46°42N 0°52E 72 B4
Anglisidhes Cyprus 34°51N 33°27E 101 E12
Anglure France 48°35N 3°50E 71 D10
Angmagssalik = Tasiilaq
Greenland 65°40N 37°20W 57 D7
Ango
Dem. Rep. of the Congo 4°10N 26°5E 142 B2
Angoche Mozam. 16°8S 39°55E 143 F4
Angoche, I. Mozam. 16°20S 39°50E 143 F4
Angol Chile 37°56S 72°45W 190 D1
Angola Ind., U.S.A. 41°38N 85°0W 173 E11
Angola N.Y., U.S.A. 42°38N 79°2W 174 D5
Angola ■ Africa 12°0S 18°0E 141 G3
Angola Abyssal Plain
Atl. Oc. 15°0S 2°0E 56 H12
Angola Basin Atl. Oc. 15°0S 3°0E 56 H12
Angoulême France 45°39N 0°10E 72 C4
Angoumois France 45°50N 0°25E 72 C4
Angra do Heroismo
Azores 38°39N 27°13W 134 a
Angra dos Reis Brazil 23°0S 44°10W 191 A7
Angrapa → Russia 54°37N 21°54E 82 D8
Angren Uzbekistan 41°1N 70°12E 109 D8
Angtassom Cambodia 11°1N 104°41E 121 G5
Angu
Dem. Rep. of the Congo 3°23N 24°30E 142 B1
Anguang China 45°15N 123°45E 115 B12
Anguilla ☑ W. Indies 18°14N 63°5W 183 C7
Angul India 20°51N 85°6E 126 D7
Anguo China 38°28N 115°15E 114 E8
Angurugu Australia 14°0S 136°25E 150 A2
Angus Canada 44°19N 79°53W 174 B5
Angus □ U.K. 56°46N 2°56W 65 E6
Angwa → Zimbabwe 16°0S 30°23E 145 A5
Anhanduí → Brazil 21°46S 52°9W 191 A5
Anholt Denmark 56°42N 11°33E 63 H5
Anhua China 28°23N 111°12E 117 C8
Anhui □ China 32°0N 117°0E 117 B11
Anhwei = Anhui □
China 32°0N 117°0E 117 B11
Anichab Namibia 21°0S 14°46E 144 B1
Anidros Greece 36°38N 25°43E 99 E7
Anié Togo 7°42N 1°8E 139 D5
Animas → U.S.A. 36°43N 108°13W 169 H9
Anin Burma 15°36N 97°50E 120 E1
Anina Romania 45°6N 21°51E 80 E6
Aninoasa Romania 44°47N 24°10E 81 F9
Anjalankoski Finland 60°45N 26°51E 84 B4
Anjangaon India 21°10N 77°20E 126 D3
Anjar = Hawsh Müssá
Lebanon 33°45N 35°55E 130 B4
Anjar India 23°6N 70°10E 124 H4
Anjengo = Anchuthengu
India 8°40N 76°46E 127 K3
Anji China 30°46N 119°40E 117 B12
Anjidiv I. India 14°40N 74°10E 127 G2
Anjou France 47°20N 0°15W 70 E6
Anjouan Comoros Is. 12°15S 44°20E 141 a
Anju N. Korea 39°36N 125°40E 115 E13
Anka Nigeria 12°13N 5°58E 139 C6
Ankaboa, Tanjona
Madag. 21°58S 43°20E 141 J8
Ankang China 32°40N 109°1E 114 H5
Ankara Turkey 39°57N 32°54E 104 C5
Ankara □ Turkey 39°55N 32°50E 104 C5
Ankaratra Madag. 19°25S 47°12E 141 H9
Ankarsrum Sweden 57°41N 16°20E 63 G10
Ankazoabo Madag. 22°18S 44°31E 141 J8
Ankeny U.S.A. 41°44N 93°36W 172 E7
Anklam Germany 53°51N 13°41E 76 B9
Ankleshwar India 21°38N 73°3E 126 D1
Ankola India 14°40N 74°18E 127 G2
Ankoro
Dem. Rep. of the Congo 6°45S 26°55E 142 D2
Ankpa Nigeria 7°22N 7°38E 139 D6
Anlong China 25°2N 105°27E 116 E5
Anlong Veng Cambodia 14°14N 104°5E 120 E5
Anlu China 31°15N 113°45E 117 B9
Anmyeondo S. Korea 36°25N 126°25E 115 F14
Ann Sweden 63°19N 12°33E 62 A6
Ann, C. U.S.A. 42°38N 70°35W 175 D14
Ann Arbor U.S.A. 42°17N 83°45W 173 D12
Anna Russia 51°28N 40°23E 86 E5
Anna U.S.A. 37°28N 89°15W 172 G9
Annaba Algeria 36°50N 7°46E 136 A5
Annaba □ Algeria 36°12N 7°45E 136 A5
Annaberg-Buchholz
Germany 50°34N 13°0E 76 E9
Annalee → Ireland 54°2N 7°24W 64 B4
Annam = Trung Phan
Vietnam 17°0N 109°0E 120 D6
Annamitique, Chaîne
Asia 17°0N 106°0E 120 D6
Annan U.K. 54°59N 3°16W 65 G5
Annan → U.K. 54°58N 3°16W 65 G5
Annapolis U.S.A. 38°59N 76°30W 173 F15
Annapolis Royal
Canada 44°44N 65°32W 165 D6
Annapurna Nepal 28°34N 83°50E 125 E10
Annean, L. Australia 26°54S 118°14E 149 E2
Anneberg Sweden 57°44N 14°49E 63 G8
Annecy France 45°55N 6°8E 73 C10
Annecy, Lac d' France 45°52N 6°10E 73 C10
Annemasse France 46°12N 6°16E 71 F13
Annenskiy Most Russia 60°45N 37°10E 84 B9
Annette I. U.S.A. 55°9N 131°28W 162 B2
Annigeri India 15°26N 75°26E 127 G2
Anning China 24°55N 102°26E 116 E4
Anniston U.S.A. 33°39N 85°50W 178 B4
Annobón Atl. Oc. 1°25S 5°36E 133 G4
Annonay France 45°15N 4°40E 73 C8
Annot France 43°58N 6°38E 73 E10
Annotto B. Jamaica 18°17N 76°45W 182 a
Ånnsjön Sweden 63°19N 12°34E 62 A6
Annville U.S.A. 40°20N 76°31W 175 F8
Annweiler Germany 49°12N 7°57E 77 F3
Ano Poroia Greece 41°17N 23°2E 96 E7
Ano Siros Greece 37°29N 24°56E 98 D6
Anogia Greece 35°16N 24°52E 101 D6
Anou Mellene Mali 17°29N 0°33E 139 B5
Anoumaba Ivory C. 6°23N 4°38W 138 D4
Anping Hebei, China 38°15N 115°30E 114 E8
Anping Liaoning, China 41°5N 123°30E 115 D12
Anpu Gang China 21°25N 109°50E 116 G7
Anqing China 30°30N 117°3E 117 B11
Anqiu China 36°25N 119°10E 115 F10
Anren China 26°43N 113°18E 117 D9
Ansager Denmark 55°43N 8°45E 63 J2
Ansai China 36°50N 109°20E 114 F5
Ansan S. Korea 37°21N 126°52E 115 F14
Ansbach Germany 49°28N 10°34E 77 F6
Anse Boileau Seychelles 4°43S 55°29E 141 b
Anse la Raye St. Lucia 13°55N 61°3W 183 f
Anse Royale Seychelles 4°44S 55°31E 141 b
Ansfelden Austria 48°12N 14°17E 78 C7
Anshan China 41°5N 122°58E 115 D12
Anshun China 26°18N 105°57E 116 D5
Ansião Portugal 39°56N 8°27W 88 F2
Ansley U.S.A. 41°18N 99°23W 172 E4
Ansó Spain 42°51N 0°48W 90 C4
Ansoáin Spain 42°50N 1°38W 90 C3
Anson U.S.A. 32°45N 99°54W 176 E5
Anson B. Australia 13°20S 130°6E 148 B5
Ansongo Mali 15°25N 0°35E 139 B5
Ansongo-Ménaka ⌂
Mali 15°3N 1°37E 139 B5
Ansonia U.S.A. 41°21N 73°5W 175 E11
Anstruther U.K. 56°14N 2°41W 65 E6
Ansudu Indonesia 2°11S 139°22E 119 E9
Antabamba Peru 14°40S 73°0W 188 C3
Antagarh India 20°6N 81°9E 126 D5
Antakya = Hatay
Turkey 36°14N 36°10E 104 D7
Antalaha Madag. 14°57S 50°20E 141 G10
Antalya Turkey 36°52N 30°45E 104 D4
Antalya □ Turkey 36°50N 30°45E 104 D4
Antalya ✕ (AYT)
Turkey 36°54N 30°47E 104 D4
Antalya Körfezi Turkey 36°15N 31°30E 104 D4
Antananarivo Madag. 18°55S 47°31E 141 H9
Antarctic Pen. Antarctica 67°0S 60°0W 55 C18
Antarctica 90°0S 0°0 55 E3
Antelope Zimbabwe 21°2S 28°31E 143 G2
Antep = Gaziantep
Turkey 37°6N 37°23E 104 D7
Antequera Paraguay 24°8S 57°7W 190 A4
Antequera Spain 37°5N 4°33W 89 H6
Antero, Mt. U.S.A. 38°41N 106°15W 168 G10
Anthony Fla., U.S.A. 29°18N 82°7W 179 F7
Anthony Kans., U.S.A. 37°9N 98°2W 172 G4
Anthony N. Mex.,
U.S.A. 32°0N 106°36W 169 K10
Anti Atlas Morocco 30°0N 8°30W 136 C2
Anti-Lebanon = Sharqi, Al Jabal
ash Lebanon 33°40N 36°10E 130 B5
Antibes France 43°34N 7°6E 73 E11
Antibes, C. d' France 43°31N 7°7E 73 E11
Anticosti, Î. d' Canada 49°30N 63°0W 165 C7
Antifer, C. d' France 49°41N 0°10E 70 C7
Antigo U.S.A. 45°9N 89°9W 172 C9
Antigonish Canada 45°38N 61°58W 165 C7
Antigua Canary Is. 28°24N 14°1W 100 F5
Antigua Guatemala 14°34N 90°41W 182 D1
Antigua W. Indies 17°0N 61°50W 183 C7
Antigua & Barbuda ■
W. Indies 17°20N 61°48W 183 C7
Antikythira Greece 35°52N 23°15E 98 F5
Antilla Cuba 20°40N 75°50W 182 B4
Antilles = West Indies
Cent. Amer. 15°0N 65°0W 183 D7
Antimilos Greece 36°47N 24°12E 98 E6
Antioch U.S.A. 38°1N 121°48W 170 G5
Antioche, Pertuis d'
France 46°6N 1°20W 72 B2
Antioquia Colombia 6°40N 75°55W 186 B3
Antiparos Greece 37°0N 25°3E 99 D7
Antipaxi Greece 39°9N 20°13E 98 B2
Antipodes Is. Pac. Oc. 49°45S 178°40E 156 M9
Antipsara Greece 38°30N 25°29E 99 C7
Antirio Greece 38°20N 21°46E 98 C3
Antlers U.S.A. 34°14N 95°37W 176 D7
Antofagasta Chile 23°50S 70°30W 190 A1
Antofagasta □ Chile 24°0S 69°0W 190 A2
Antofagasta de la Sierra
Argentina 26°5S 67°20W 190 B2
Antofalla Argentina 25°30S 68°5W 190 B2
Antofalla, Salar de
Argentina 25°40S 67°45W 190 B2
Anton U.S.A. 33°49N 102°10W 176 E3
Antonina Brazil 25°26S 48°42W 191 B6
Antrain France 48°28N 1°30W 70 D5
Antratsyt Ukraine 48°7N 39°5E 85 H10
Antrim U.K. 54°43N 6°14W 64 B5
Antrim U.S.A. 40°7N 81°21W 174 F3
Antrim □ U.K. 54°56N 6°25W 64 B5
Antrim, Mts. of U.K. 55°3N 6°14W 64 A5
Antrim Plateau
Australia 18°8S 128°20E 148 C4
Antrodoco Italy 42°25N 13°5E 93 F10
Antropovo Russia 58°24N 43°6E 86 A6
Antsalova Madag. 18°40S 44°37E 141 H8
Antsirabe Madag. 19°55S 47°2E 141 H9
Antsiranana Madag. 12°25S 49°20E 141 G9
Antsohihy Madag. 14°50S 47°59E 141 G9
Antu China 42°30N 128°20E 115 C15
Antwerp = Antwerpen
Belgium 51°13N 4°25E 69 C4
Antwerp U.S.A. 44°12N 75°37W 175 B9
Antwerpen Belgium 51°13N 4°25E 69 C4
Antwerpen □ Belgium 51°15N 4°40E 69 C4
Anupgarh India 29°10N 73°10E 124 E5
Anuppur India 23°6N 81°41E 125 H9
Anuradhapura Sri Lanka 8°22N 80°28E 127 K5
Anurrete ✪ Australia 20°50S 135°38E 150 C2
Anveh Iran 27°23N 54°11E 129 E7
Anvers = Antwerpen
Belgium 51°13N 4°25E 69 C4
Anvers I. Antarctica 64°30S 63°40W 55 C17
Anwen China 29°4N 120°26E 117 C13
Anxi Fujian, China 25°2N 118°12E 117 E12
Anxi Gansu, China 40°30N 95°43E 110 C8
Anxian China 31°40N 104°25E 116 B5
Anxiang China 29°27N 112°11E 117 C9
Anxious B. Australia 33°24S 134°45E 151 E1
Anyama Ivory C. 5°30N 4°3W 138 D4
Anyang China 36°5N 114°21E 114 F8
Anyang S. Korea 37°23N 126°55E 115 F14
Anyer Indonesia 6°4S 105°53E 119 G11
Anyi Jiangxi, China 28°49N 115°25E 117 C10
Anyi Shanxi, China 35°2N 111°2E 114 G6
Anyuan China 25°9N 115°21E 117 E10
Anyue China 30°9N 105°50E 116 B5
Anza U.S.A. 33°35N 116°39W 171 M10
Anze China 36°10N 112°12E 114 F7
Anzeglouf Algeria 26°50N 0°1E 136 C4
Anzhero-Sudzhensk
Russia 56°10N 86°0E 106 D9
Ánzio Italy 41°27N 12°37E 94 A5
Ao Makham Thailand 7°50N 98°24E 121 a
Ao Phangnga △ Thailand 8°10N 98°32E 121 a
Aoga-Shima Japan 32°28N 139°46E 113 H9
Aohan Qi China 43°18N 119°43E 115 C10
Aoiz Spain 42°46N 1°22W 90 C3
Aoji N. Korea 42°31N 130°23E 115 C16
Aomen = Macau
China 22°12N 113°33E 117 F9
Aomori Japan 40°45N 140°45E 112 D10
Aomori □ Japan 40°45N 140°40E 112 D10
tAonach, An = Nenagh
Ireland 52°52N 8°11W 64 D3
Aonla India 28°16N 79°11E 125 E8
Aorai, Mt. Tahiti 17°34S 149°30W 155 b
Aoraki Mount Cook
N.Z. 43°36S 170°9E 155 D5
Aoral, Phnum
Cambodia 12°0N 104°15E 121 G5
Aorangi Ra. N.Z. 41°28S 175°22E 154 H4
Aosta Italy 45°45N 7°20E 92 C4
Aotea Harbour N.Z. 38°0S 174°50E 154 E3
Aotearoa = New Zealand ■
Oceania 40°0S 176°0E 154 G5
Aoudéras Niger 17°45N 8°20E 139 B6
Aoukâr Mauritania 17°40N 10°0W 138 B3
Aoulef el Arab Algeria 26°55N 1°2E 136 C4
Aozou, Couloir d' Chad 22°0N 19°0E 135 D9
Apá → S. Amer. 22°6S 58°2W 190 A4
Apache U.S.A. 34°54N 98°22W 176 D5
Apache Junction
U.S.A. 33°25N 111°33W 169 K8
Apalachee B. U.S.A. 30°0N 84°0W 178 E5
Apalachicola U.S.A. 29°43N 84°59W 178 F5
Apalachicola →
U.S.A. 29°43N 84°58W 178 F5
Apalachicola B. U.S.A. 29°40N 85°0W 178 F3
Apam Ghana 5°19N 0°42W 139 D4
Apapa Nigeria 6°26N 3°21E 139 D5
Apaporis → Colombia 1°23S 69°25W 186 D5
Aparados da Serra △
Brazil 29°10S 50°8W 191 B5
Aparri Phil. 18°22N 121°38E 119 A6
Apateu Romania 46°36N 21°47E 80 D6
Apatin Serbia 45°40N 19°0E 80 E4
Apatity Russia 67°34N 33°22E 60 C25
Apatula = Finke
Australia 25°34S 134°35E 150 D1
Apatzingán Mexico 19°5N 102°21W 180 D4
Apeldoorn Neths. 52°13N 5°57E 69 B5
Apen Germany 53°13N 7°48E 76 B3
Apennines = Appennini
Italy 44°30N 10°0E 92 D7
Aphrodisias Turkey 37°42N 28°46E 99 D10
Api Nepal 30°0N 80°57E 110 F5
Apia Samoa 13°50S 171°50W 147 C11
Apiacás, Serra dos Brazil 9°50S 57°0W 186 E7
Apies → S. Africa 25°15S 28°8E 145 C4
Apinajé Brazil 11°31S 48°18W 189 C1
Apiti N.Z. 39°58S 175°54E 154 F4
Apizaco Mexico 19°25N 98°8W 181 D5
Aplao Peru 16°0S 72°40W 188 D3
Apo, Mt. Phil. 6°53N 125°14E 119 C7
Apodi Brazil 5°39S 37°48W 189 B3
Apolakia Greece 36°5N 27°48E 101 C9
Apolakia, Ormos Greece 36°5N 27°45E 101 C9
Apolda Germany 51°2N 11°32E 76 D7
Apollo Bay Australia 38°45S 143°40E 152 E5
Apollonia = Sūsah
Libya 32°52N 21°59E 135 B10
Apollonia Greece 36°15N 27°58E 101 C9
Apolo Bolivia 14°30S 68°30W 188 C4
Apolonia Greece 36°58N 24°43E 98 E6
Apopa El Salv. 13°48N 89°10W 182 D2
Apopka U.S.A. 28°40N 81°31W 179 G8
Apopka, L. U.S.A. 28°37N 81°37W 179 G8
Aporé → Brazil 19°27S 50°57W 187 G8
Apostle Is. U.S.A. 47°0N 90°40W 172 B8
Apostle Islands ⌂
U.S.A. 46°55N 91°0W 172 B8
Apóstoles Argentina 28°0S 56°0W 191 B4
Apostolos Andreas, C.
Cyprus 35°42N 34°35E 101 D13
Apostolovo Ukraine 47°39N 33°39E 85 J7
Apoteri Guyana 4°2N 58°32W 186 C7
Appalachian Mts.
U.S.A. 38°0N 80°0W 173 G14
Äppelbo Sweden 60°29N 14°1E 62 D8
Appenino Lucano-Val d'Agri-
Lagonegrese ⌂ Italy 40°5N 16°10E 95 B9
Appennino Tosco-Emiliano ⌂
Italy 44°10N 10°25E 92 D7
Appennini Italy 44°30N 10°0E 92 D7
Appennino Ligure Italy 44°30N 9°0E 92 D6
Appenzell-Ausser Rhoden □
Switz. 47°23N 9°23E 77 H5
Appenzell-Inner Rhoden □
Switz. 47°20N 9°25E 77 H5
Appiano Italy 46°28N 11°15E 93 B8
Apple Hill Canada 45°13N 74°46W 175 A10
Apple Valley U.S.A. 34°32N 117°14W 171 L9
Appleby-in-Westmorland
U.K. 54°35N 2°29W 66 C5
Appledore U.K. 51°3N 4°13W 67 F3
Appleton U.S.A. 44°16N 88°25W 172 C9
Appling U.S.A. 33°33N 82°19W 178 B7
Approuague →
Fr. Guiana 4°30N 51°57W 187 C8
Apricena Italy 41°47N 15°27E 93 G12
Aprilia Italy 41°36N 12°39E 94 A5
Apsheronsk Russia 44°28N 39°42E 87 H4
Apsley Canada 44°45N 78°6W 174 B6
Apt France 43°53N 5°24E 73 E9
Apuane, Alpi Italy 44°7N 10°14E 92 D7
Apucarana Brazil 23°55S 51°33W 191 A5
Apulia = Púglia □ Italy 41°15N 16°15E 95 A9
Apure → Venezuela 7°37N 66°25W 186 B5
Apurímac □ Peru 14°0S 73°0W 188 C3
Apurímac → Peru 12°17S 73°56W 188 C3
Apuseni, Munţii
Romania 46°30N 22°45E 80 D7
Āq Qālā Iran 37°10N 54°30E 129 B7
Aqaba = Al 'Aqabah
Jordan 29°31N 35°0E 130 F4
Aqaba, G. of Red Sea 29°0N 34°40E 128 D2
'Aqabah, Khalīj al = Aqaba, G. of
Red Sea 29°0N 34°40E 128 D2
Aqadyr Kazakhstan 48°17N 74°50E 109 C8
Āqchah Afghan. 36°56N 66°11E 109 E7
'Aqdā Iran 32°26N 53°37E 129 C7
Aqiq Sudan 18°14N 38°12E 137 D4
Aqīq, Khalīg Sudan 18°20N 38°10E 137 D4
Aqköl Kazakhstan 51°59N 70°56E 109 B8
Aqmola □ Kazakhstan 51°30N 70°0E 109 B8
'Aqrah Iraq 36°46N 43°45E 105 D10
Aqsay Kazakhstan 51°11N 53°0E 108 B4
Aqshataū Kazakhstan 47°59N 74°3E 109 C8
Aqsū Ongtüstik Qazaqstan,
Kazakhstan 42°25N 69°50E 109 D7
Aqsū Pavlodar,
Kazakhstan 52°2N 76°55E 109 B9
Aqsūgek Kazakhstan 44°37N 74°30E 109 D8
Aqtaū Mangghystaū,
Kazakhstan 43°39N 51°12E 108 D4
Aqtaū Qaraghandy,
Kazakhstan 50°14N 73°3E 109 B8
Aqtöbe Kazakhstan 50°17N 57°10E 108 B5
Aqtoghay Kazakhstan 46°57N 79°40E 109 C9
Aqua = Sokhumi Georgia 43°0N 41°0E 87 J5
Aquidauana Brazil 20°30S 55°50W 187 H7
Aquila Mexico 18°36N 103°30W 180 D4
Aquileia Italy 45°46N 13°22E 93 C10
Aquiles Serdán
Mexico 28°36N 105°53W 180 B3
Aquin Haiti 18°16N 73°24W 183 C5
Aquitaine □ France 44°25N 0°30W 72 D3
Ar Horqin Qi China 43°45N 120°0E 115 C11
Ar Rafid Syria 32°57N 35°52E 130 C4
Ar Rahhāliyah Iraq 32°44N 43°23E 105 F10
Ar Ramādī Iraq 33°25N 43°20E 105 F10
Ar Ramthā Jordan 32°34N 36°0E 130 C5
Ar Raqqah Syria 35°59N 39°8E 105 E8
Ar Raqqah □ Syria 36°20N 39°10E 105 D8
Ar Rashidiya = Er Rachidia
Morocco 31°58N 4°20W 136 B3
Ar Rass Si. Arabia 25°50N 43°40E 128 E4
Ar Rawḍah Si. Arabia 21°16N 42°50E 131 C3
Ar Rayyan Qatar 25°17N 51°25E 129 E6
Ar Rifā'ī Iraq 31°50N 46°10E 128 D5
Ar Riyāḍ Si. Arabia 24°41N 46°42E 128 E5
Ar Ru'ays Qatar 26°8N 51°12E 129 E6
Ar Rukhaymīyah Iraq 29°22N 45°38E 128 D5
Ar Rumaythah Iraq 31°31N 45°12E 128 D5
Ar Ruşāfah Syria 35°45N 38°49E 105 E8
Ar Rutbah Iraq 33°0N 40°15E 105 F9
Ara India 25°35N 84°32E 125 G11
Arab U.S.A. 34°19N 86°30W 177 D11
'Arab, Bahr el →
South Sudan 9°0N 29°30E 135 G11
Arab, Khalîg el Egypt 30°55N 29°0E 137 E6
Arab, Shatt al → Asia 29°57N 48°34E 129 D6
'Araba, W. → Egypt 28°19N 33°31E 137 F8
'Arabābād Iran 33°2N 57°41E 129 C8
Araban Turkey 37°28N 37°44E 104 D7
Arabatskaya Strelka
Ukraine 45°40N 35°0E 85 K8
Araba/Álava □ Spain 42°48N 2°28W 90 C2
Arabba Italy 46°30N 11°52E 93 B8
Arabi U.S.A. 31°50N 83°44W 178 D6
Arabia Asia 25°0N 45°0E 102 F6
Arabian Basin Ind. Oc. 11°30N 65°0E 146 C5
Arabian Desert = Sharqîya, Es
Sahrâ esh Egypt 27°30N 32°30E 137 B3
Arabian Gulf = Persian Gulf
Asia 27°0N 50°0E 129 E6
Arabian Sea Ind. Oc. 16°0N 65°0E 102 G8
Araç Turkey 41°15N 33°21E 104 B5
Aracaju Brazil 10°55S 37°4W 189 C3
Aracati Brazil 4°30S 37°44W 189 A3
Araçatuba Brazil 21°10S 50°30W 191 A5
Aracena Spain 37°53N 6°38W 89 H4
Aracena, Sierra de Spain 37°50N 6°50W 89 H4
Arachova Greece 38°28N 22°35E 98 C4
Arachthos → Greece 39°20N 21°4E 98 B3
Aračinovo Macedonia 42°1N 21°34E 96 D5
Araçuaí Brazil 16°52S 42°4W 189 D2
Araçuaí → Brazil 16°46S 42°2W 189 D2
'Arad Israel 31°15N 35°12E 130 D4
Arad Romania 46°10N 21°20E 80 D6
Arad □ Romania 46°20N 22°0E 80 D6
Arādān Iran 35°21N 52°30E 129 C7
Aradhippou Cyprus 34°57N 33°36E 101 E12
Arafura Sea E. Indies 9°0S 135°0E 147 B6
Aragats Armenia 40°30N 44°15E 87 K7
Aragon U.S.A. 34°2N 85°3W 178 A4
Aragón □ Spain 41°25N 0°40W 90 D4
Aragón → Spain 42°13N 1°44W 90 C3
Aragona Italy 37°24N 13°27E 94 E6
Araguacema Brazil 8°50S 49°20W 187 E9
Araguaia → Brazil 5°21S 48°41W 189 B1
Araguaína Brazil 7°12S 48°12W 189 B1
Araguari Brazil 18°38S 48°11W 189 D1
Araguari → Brazil 1°15N 49°55W 187 C9
Araguatins Brazil 5°38S 48°7W 189 B1
Arahal Spain 37°15N 5°33W 89 H5
Arain India 26°27N 75°2E 124 F6
Araioses Brazil 2°53S 41°55W 189 A2
Arak Algeria 25°20N 3°45E 136 C4
Arāk Iran 34°0N 49°40E 129 C6
Arakan = Rakhine □
Burma 19°0N 94°15E 123 K18
Arakan Coast Burma 19°0N 94°0E 123 K19
Arakan Yoma Burma 20°0N 94°40E 123 K19
Arakkonam India 13°7N 79°43E 127 H4
Araklı Turkey 41°6N 40°2E 105 B9
Araks = Aras, Rūd-e →
Asia 40°5N 48°29E 105 B13
Araks → Iran 39°10N 47°10E 108 E3
Aral Kazakhstan 46°41N 61°45E 108 C6
Aral Mangy Qaraqumy
Kazakhstan 46°50N 63°10E 108 C6
Aral Sea Asia 45°0N 58°20E 108 C5
Aral Tengizi = Aral Sea
Asia 45°0N 58°20E 108 C5
Aralık Turkey 39°52N 44°31E 105 C11
Aralkum Asia 44°30N 60°35E 108 D6
Aralsk = Aral
Kazakhstan 46°41N 61°45E 108 C6
Aralskoye More = Aral Sea
Asia 45°0N 58°20E 108 C5
Aralsor, Ozero = Aralsor Köli
Kazakhstan 49°5N 48°12E 87 F9
Aralsor Köli Kazakhstan 49°5N 48°12E 87 F9
Aramac Australia 22°58S 145°14E 150 C4
Aran → India 19°55N 78°12E 126 E4
Aran, Val de Spain 42°50N 0°55E 90 C5
Aran I. = Arranmore
Ireland 55°0N 8°30W 64 A3
Aran Is. Ireland 53°6N 9°38W 64 C2
Aranda de Duero Spain 41°39N 3°42W 88 D7
Arandān Iran 35°23N 46°55E 128 C5
Aranđelovac Serbia 44°18N 20°34E 96 B4
Aranga N.Z. 35°44S 173°40E 154 B2
Arani India 12°43N 79°19E 127 H4
Aranjuez Spain 40°1N 3°40W 88 E7
Aranos Namibia 24°9S 19°7E 144 B2
Aransas Pass U.S.A. 27°55N 97°9W 176 H6
Aranyaprathet
Thailand 13°41N 102°30E 120 F4
Araouane Mali 18°55N 3°30W 138 B4
Arapahoe U.S.A. 40°18N 99°54W 172 E4
Arapawa I. N.Z. 41°11S 174°17E 155 B9
Arapey Grande →
Uruguay 30°55S 57°49W 190 C4
Arapgir Turkey 39°5N 38°30E 105 C8
Arapiraca Brazil 9°45S 36°39W 189 B3
Arapis, Akra Greece 40°27N 24°0E 97 F8
Arapongas Brazil 23°29S 51°28W 191 A5
Arapuni N.Z. 38°4S 175°39E 154 E4
Ar'ar Si. Arabia 30°59N 41°2E 128 D4
Araranguá Brazil 29°0S 49°30W 191 B6
Araraquara Brazil 21°50S 48°0W 187 H9
Ararás, Serra das Brazil 25°0S 53°10W 191 B5
Ararat Armenia 39°48N 44°50E 105 C11
Ararat Australia 37°16S 142°58E 152 D5
Ararat, Mt. = Ağrı Dağı
Turkey 39°50N 44°15E 105 C11
Arari Brazil 3°28S 44°47W 189 A2
Araria India 26°9N 87°33E 125 F12
Araripe, Chapada do
Brazil 7°20S 40°0W 189 B3
Araripina Brazil 7°33S 40°34W 189 B2
Araruama, L. de Brazil 22°53S 42°12W 191 A7
Araruna Brazil 6°52S 35°44W 189 B3
Aras, Rūd-e → Asia 40°5N 48°29E 105 B13
Aratâne Mauritania 18°24N 8°32W 138 B3
Arauca Colombia 7°0N 70°40W 186 B4
Arauca → Venezuela 7°24N 66°35W 186 B5
Arauco Chile 37°16S 73°25W 190 D1
Araújos Brazil 19°56S 45°14W 189 D1
Aravalli Range India 25°0N 73°30E 124 G5
Arawale ⌂ Kenya 1°24S 40°9E 142 C5
Arawhata → N.Z. 44°0S 168°40E 155 E3
Araxá Brazil 19°35S 46°55W 189 D1
Araxos, Akra Greece 38°13N 21°20E 98 C3
Araya, Pen. de
Venezuela 10°40N 64°0W 186 A6
Arba Minch Ethiopia 6°0N 37°30E 131 F2
Arbat Iraq 35°25N 45°35E 105 E11
Árbatax Italy 39°56N 9°42E 94 C2
Arbīl Iraq 36°15N 44°5E 105 D11
Arbīl □ Iraq 36°20N 44°20E 105 D11
Arboga Sweden 59°24N 15°52E 62 E9
Arbois France 46°55N 5°46E 71 F12
Arborea Italy 39°46N 8°35E 94 C1
Arborfield Canada 53°6N 103°39W 163 C8
Arborg Canada 50°54N 97°13W 163 C9
Arbre du Ténéré Niger 17°50N 10°4E 139 B7
Arbroath U.K. 56°34N 2°35W 65 E6
Arbuckle U.S.A. 39°1N 122°3W 170 F4
Arbus Italy 39°30N 8°33E 94 C1
Arc → France 45°34N 6°12E 73 C10
Arc-lès-Gray France 47°28N 5°34E 71 E12
Arcachon France 44°40N 1°10W 72 D2
Arcachon, Bassin d'
France 44°42N 1°10W 72 D2
Arcade U.S.A. 42°32N 78°25W 174 D6
Arcadia = Arkadia
Greece 37°30N 22°20E 98 D4
Arcadia Fla., U.S.A. 27°13N 81°52W 179 H8
Arcadia La., U.S.A. 32°33N 92°55W 176 E8
Arcadia Pa., U.S.A. 40°47N 78°51W 174 F6
Arcata U.S.A. 40°52N 124°5W 168 F1
Arcévia Italy 43°30N 12°56E 93 E9
Archanes Greece 35°16N 25°11E 101 D7
Archangel = Arkhangelsk
Russia 64°38N 40°36E 106 C5
Archangelos Greece 36°13N 28°7E 101 C10
Archar Bulgaria 43°50N 22°54E 96 C6
Archbald U.S.A. 41°30N 75°32W 175 E9
Archena Spain 38°9N 1°16W 91 G3
Archer U.S.A. 29°32N 82°32W 179 F7
Archer → Australia 13°28S 141°41E 150 A3
Archer B. Australia 13°20S 141°30E 150 A3
Archer Bend = Mungkan
Kandju △ Australia 13°35S 142°52E 150 A3
Archers Post Kenya 0°35N 37°35E 142 B4
Arches △ U.S.A. 38°45N 109°25W 168 G9
Archidona Spain 37°6N 4°22W 89 H6
Archipel-de-Mingan △
Canada 50°13N 63°10W 165 B7
Archipiélago Chinijo △
Canary Is. 29°20N 13°30W 100 E6
Archipiélago Los Roques △
Venezuela 11°50N 66°44W 183 D6

Arci, Mte. *Italy* 39°47N 8°45E 94 C1
Arcidosso *Italy* 42°52N 11°33E 93 F8
Arcila = Asilah *Morocco* 35°29N 6°0W 136 A2
Arcipelago de la Maddalena △ *Italy* 41°14N 9°24E 94 A2
Arcipelago Toscano △ *Italy* 42°45N 10°15E 92 F7
Arcis-sur-Aube *France* 48°32N 4°10E 71 D11
Arckaringa Cr. → *Australia* 28°10S 135°22E 151 D2
Arco *Italy* 45°55N 10°53E 92 C7
Arco *U.S.A.* 43°38N 113°18W 168 E7
Arcoona *Australia* 31°2S 137°1E 152 A2
Arcos de Jalón *Spain* 41°12N 2°16W 90 D2
Arcos de la Frontera *Spain* 36°45N 5°49W 89 J5
Arcos de Valdevez *Portugal* 41°55N 8°22W 88 D2
Arcot *India* 12°53N 79°20E 127 H4
Arcoverde *Brazil* 8°25S 37°4W 189 B3
Arcozelo *Portugal* 40°32N 7°47W 88 E3
Arctic Bay *Canada* 73°1N 85°7W 161 C14
Arctic Mid-Ocean Ridge *Arctic* 87°0N 90°0E 54 A
Arctic Ocean *Arctic* 78°0N 160°0W 54 B18
Arctic Red River = Tsiigehtchic *Canada* 67°15N 134°0W 160 D5
Arctowski *Antarctica* 62°30S 58°0W 55 C18
Arda → *Bulgaria* 41°40N 26°30E 97 E10
Arda → *Italy* 45°2N 10°2E 92 C7
Ardabīl *Iran* 38°15N 48°18E 105 C13
Ardabīl □ *Iran* 38°15N 48°20E 129 B6
Ardahan *Turkey* 41°7N 42°41E 105 B10
Ardahan □ *Turkey* 41°10N 42°50E 105 B10
Ardakān = Sepīdān *Iran* 30°20N 52°5E 129 D7
Ardakān *Iran* 32°19N 53°59E 129 C7
Ardala *Sweden* 58°22N 13°19E 63 F7
Ardales *Spain* 36°53N 4°51W 89 J6
Ardara *Ireland* 54°46N 8°25W 64 B3
Ardas → *Greece* 41°40N 26°30E 97 E10
Ardèche □ *France* 44°42N 4°16E 73 D8
Ardèche → *France* 44°16N 4°39E 73 D8
Ardee *Ireland* 53°52N 6°33W 64 C5
Arden *Canada* 44°43N 76°56W 174 B8
Arden *Denmark* 56°46N 9°52E 63 H3
Arden *Calif., U.S.A.* 38°36N 121°33W 170 G5
Arden *Nev., U.S.A.* 36°1N 115°14W 171 J11
Ardenne *Belgium* 49°50N 5°5E 69 E5
Ardennes = Ardenne *Belgium* 49°50N 5°5E 69 E5
Ardennes □ *France* 49°35N 4°40E 71 C11
Ardentes *France* 46°45N 1°50E 71 F8
Arderin *Ireland* 53°2N 7°39W 64 C4
Ardeşen *Turkey* 41°12N 41°2E 105 B9
Ardestān *Iran* 33°20N 52°25E 129 C7
Ardfert *Ireland* 52°20N 9°47W 64 D2
Ardglass *U.K.* 54°16N 5°36W 64 B6
Ardhéa = Aridea *Greece* 40°58N 22°3E 96 F6
Ardila → *Portugal* 38°12N 7°28W 89 G3
Ardino *Bulgaria* 41°34N 25°9E 97 E9
Ardivachar Pt. *U.K.* 57°23N 7°26W 65 D1
Ardlethan *Australia* 34°22S 146°53E 153 C7
Ardmore *Okla., U.S.A.* 34°10N 97°8W 176 D6
Ardmore *Pa., U.S.A.* 40°2N 75°17W 175 F9
Ardnamurchan, Pt. of *U.K.* 56°43N 6°14W 65 E2
Ardnave Pt. *U.K.* 55°53N 6°20W 65 F2
Ardon *Russia* 43°10N 44°18E 87 J7
Ardore *Italy* 38°11N 16°10E 95 D9
Ardres *France* 50°50N 1°59E 71 B8
Ardrossan *Australia* 34°26S 137°53E 152 C2
Ardrossan *U.K.* 55°39N 4°49W 65 F4
Ards Pen. *U.K.* 54°33N 5°34W 64 B6
Arduan *Sudan* 19°54N 30°20E 137 D3
Arð *Romania* 47°37N 22°52E 80 C7
Åre *Sweden* 63°22N 13°15E 62 A7
Arecibo *Puerto Rico* 18°29N 66°43W 183 d
Areia Branca *Brazil* 5°0S 37°0W 189 A3
Arena, Pt. *U.S.A.* 38°57N 123°44W 170 G3
Arenal *Honduras* 15°21N 86°50W 182 C2
Arenales, Cerro *Chile* 47°5S 73°40W 192 C2
Arenas = Las Arenas *Spain* 43°17N 4°50W 88 B6
Arenas de San Pedro *Spain* 40°12N 5°5W 88 E5
Arendal *Norway* 58°28N 8°46E 61 G13
Arendsee *Germany* 52°52N 11°27E 76 C7
Arenys de Mar *Spain* 41°35N 2°33E 90 D7
Arenzano *Italy* 44°24N 8°41E 92 D5
Areopoli *Greece* 36°40N 22°22E 98 E4
Arequipa *Peru* 16°20S 71°30W 188 D3
Arequipa □ *Peru* 16°0S 72°50W 188 D3
Arès *France* 44°47N 1°8W 72 D2
Arévalo *Spain* 41°3N 4°43W 88 D6
Arezzo *Italy* 43°25N 11°53E 93 E8
Arga *Turkey* 38°21N 37°59E 128 B3
Arga → *Spain* 42°18N 1°47W 90 C3
Argalasti *Greece* 39°13N 23°13E 98 B5
Argamasilla de Alba 39°8N 3°5W 89 F7
Argamasilla de Calatrava *Spain* 38°44N 4°4W 89 G6
Arganda del Rey *Spain* 40°19N 3°26W 88 E7
Arganil *Portugal* 40°13N 8°3W 88 E2
Argarapa → *Australia* 22°20S 134°58E 150 C1
Argelès-Gazost *France* 43°0N 0°6W 72 E3
Argelès-sur-Mer *France* 42°34N 3°1E 72 F7
Argens → *France* 43°24N 6°44E 73 E10
Argent, Côte d' *France* 44°15N 1°30W 72 D2
Argent-sur-Sauldre *France* 47°33N 2°25E 71 E9
Argenta *Canada* 50°11N 116°56W 162 C5
Argenta *Italy* 44°37N 11°50E 92 D8
Argentan *France* 48°45N 0°1W 70 D6
Argentário, Mte. *Italy* 42°24N 11°9E 93 F8
Argentat *France* 45°6N 1°56E 72 D5
Argentera *Italy* 44°12N 7°5E 92 D4
Argenteuil *France* 48°57N 2°14E 71 C9
Argentia *Canada* 47°18N 53°58W 165 C9
Argentiera, C. dell' *Italy* 40°44N 8°8E 94 B1
Argentina ■ *S. Amer.* 35°0S 66°0W 185 G4
Argentine Abyssal Plain *Atl. Oc.* 45°0S 45°0W 56 L6
Argentine Basin *Atl. Oc.* 45°0S 45°0W 56 L7
Argentino, L. *Argentina* 50°10S 73°0W 192 D2
Argenton-les-Vallées *France* 46°59N 0°27W 70 F6
Argenton-sur-Creuse *France* 46°36N 1°30E 71 F8
Argeș □ *Romania* 45°0N 24°45E 81 F9
Argeș → *Romania* 44°5N 26°38E 81 F11
Arghandab → *Afghan.* 31°30N 64°15E 124 D1

Argirades *Greece* 39°27N 19°58E 101 B3
Argiroupoli *Greece* 35°17N 24°20E 101 D6
Argo *Sudan* 19°28N 30°30E 137 D3
Argolikos Kolpos *Greece* 37°20N 22°52E 98 D4
Argonne *France* 49°10N 5°0E 71 C12
Argos *Greece* 37°40N 22°43E 98 D4
Argos Orestiko *Greece* 40°27N 21°18E 96 F5
Argostoli *Greece* 38°11N 20°29E 98 C2
Arguedas *Spain* 42°11N 1°36W 90 C3
Arguello, Pt. *U.S.A.* 34°35N 120°39W 171 L6
Arguineguín *Canary Is.* 27°46N 15°41W 100 G4
Argun *Russia* 43°18N 45°52E 87 J7
Argun → *Russia* 53°20N 121°28E 111 A13
Argungu *Nigeria* 12°40N 4°31E 139 C5
Argus Pk. *U.S.A.* 35°52N 117°26W 171 K9
Argyle, L. *Australia* 16°20S 128°40E 148 C4
Argyll & Bute □ *U.K.* 56°13N 5°28W 65 E3
Arhavi *Turkey* 41°21N 41°18E 105 B9
Århus = Aarhus *Denmark* 56°8N 10°11E 63 H4
Aria *N.Z.* 38°33S 175°0E 154 E4
Ariadnoye *Russia* 45°8N 134°25E 112 B7
Ariamsvlei *Namibia* 28°9S 19°51E 144 C2
Ariana, L' *Tunisia* 36°50N 9°52E 136 A6
Ariana, L' □ *Tunisia* 36°50N 9°52E 136 A6
Ariano Irpino *Italy* 41°9N 15°5E 95 A8
Aribinda *Burkina Faso* 14°17N 0°52W 139 C4
Arica *Chile* 18°32S 70°20W 188 D3
Arica *Colombia* 2°0S 71°50W 186 D4
Arica o Parinacota □ *Chile* 17°40S 69°50W 188 D4
Arico *Canary Is.* 28°9N 16°29W 100 F3
Arid, C. *Australia* 34°1S 123°10E 149 F3
Arida *Japan* 34°5N 135°8E 113 G7
Aride *Seychelles* 4°13S 55°40E 141 b
Aridea *Greece* 40°58N 22°3E 96 F6
Ariège □ *France* 42°56N 1°30E 72 F5
Ariège → *France* 43°30N 1°25E 72 E5
Aries → *Romania* 46°24N 23°20E 81 D8
Arigat el Fersig *Algeria* 27°35N 2°7W 136 C3
Arihā *Israel* 31°51N 35°27E 137 A4
Arila, Akra *Greece* 39°43N 19°39E 101 A3
Arilje *Serbia* 43°44N 20°7E 96 C4
Arima *Trin. & Tob.* 10°38N 61°17W 187 K15
Arinos → *Brazil* 10°25S 58°20W 186 F7
Ario de Rosales *Mexico* 19°12N 101°43W 180 D4
Ariogala *Lithuania* 55°16N 23°28E 62 C10
Aripo, Mt. *Trin. & Tob.* 10°45N 61°15W 187 K15
Aripuanã *Brazil* 9°25S 60°30W 186 E6
Aripuanã → *Brazil* 5°7S 60°25W 186 E6
Ariquemes *Brazil* 9°55S 63°6W 186 E6
Arisaig *U.K.* 56°55N 5°51W 65 E3
Arish, W. el → *Egypt* 31°9N 33°49E 137 E8
Aristazabal I. *Canada* 52°40N 129°10W 162 C3
Ariton *U.S.A.* 31°36N 85°43W 178 D4
Ariyalur *India* 11°8N 79°8E 127 J4
Ariza *Spain* 41°19N 2°3W 90 D2
Arizaro, Salar de *Argentina* 24°40S 67°50W 190 A2
Arizona *Argentina* 35°45S 65°25W 190 D2
Arizona □ *U.S.A.* 34°0N 112°0W 169 J8
Arizpe *Mexico* 30°20N 110°10W 180 A2
'Arjah *Si. Arabia* 24°43N 44°17E 128 E5
Arjäng *Sweden* 59°24N 12°8E 62 E6
Arjeplog *Sweden* 66°3N 17°54E 60 C17
Arjepluovve = Arjeplog *Sweden* 66°3N 17°54E 60 C17
Arjona *Colombia* 10°14N 75°22W 186 A3
Arjona *Spain* 37°56N 4°4W 89 H6
Arjuna *Indonesia* 7°49S 112°34E 119 G15
Arka *Russia* 60°15N 142°0E 107 C15
Arkadak *Russia* 51°58N 43°30E 86 E6
Arkadelphia *U.S.A.* 34°7N 93°4W 176 D8
Arkadia *Greece* 37°30N 22°20E 98 D4
Arkaig, L. *U.K.* 56°59N 5°10W 65 E3
Arkalgud *India* 12°46N 76°3E 127 H3
Arkalyk = Arqalyk *Kazakhstan* 50°13N 66°50E 109 B7
Arkansas □ *U.S.A.* 35°0N 92°30W 176 D8
Arkansas → *U.S.A.* 33°47N 91°4W 176 E9
Arkansas City *U.S.A.* 37°4N 97°2W 177 D6
Arkaroola *Australia* 30°20S 139°22E 151 E2
Arkavaz *Iran* 33°22N 46°35E 105 F12
Arkhangelsk *Russia* 64°38N 40°36E 106 C5
Arkhangelskoye *Russia* 51°32N 40°58E 86 E5
Arki *Greece* 37°22N 26°44E 99 D8
Arki *India* 31°9N 76°58E 124 D7
Arklow *Ireland* 52°48N 6°10W 64 D5
Arkona, Kap *Germany* 54°42N 13°26E 76 A9
Arköșund *Sweden* 58°29N 16°56E 63 F10
Arkport *U.S.A.* 42°24N 77°42W 174 D7
Arkticheskiy, Mys *Russia* 81°10N 95°0E 107 A10
Arkul *Russia* 57°17N 50°3E 86 B10
Arkville *U.S.A.* 42°9N 74°37W 175 D10
Ärla *Sweden* 59°17N 16°40E 62 E10
Arlanda, Stockholm ✈ (ARN) *Sweden* 59°41N 17°56E 62 E11
Arlanza → *Spain* 42°6N 4°9W 88 C6
Arlanzón → *Spain* 42°3N 4°17W 88 C6
Arlberg Pass *Austria* 47°9N 10°12E 78 B3
Arlbergtunnel *Austria* 47°9N 10°12E 78 B3
Arles *France* 43°41N 4°40E 73 E8
Arli *Burkina Faso* 11°35N 1°28E 139 C5
Arli △ *Burkina Faso* 11°35N 1°28E 145 C4
Arlington *S. Africa* 28°1S 27°53E 145 C4
Arlington *Ga., U.S.A.* 31°26N 84°44W 178 D5
Arlington *N.Y., U.S.A.* 41°42N 73°54W 175 E11
Arlington *Oreg., U.S.A.* 45°43N 120°12W 168 D3
Arlington *S. Dak., U.S.A.* 44°22N 97°8W 172 C5
Arlington *Tex., U.S.A.* 32°44N 97°6W 176 E6
Arlington *Va., U.S.A.* 38°53N 77°7W 173 F15
Arlington *Vt., U.S.A.* 43°5N 73°9W 175 C11
Arlington *Wash., U.S.A.* 48°12N 122°8W 170 B4
Arlington Heights *U.S.A.* 42°5N 87°59W 172 D10
Arlit *Niger* 19°28N 10°38E 134 E7
Arlon *Belgium* 49°42N 5°49E 69 E5
Arlparra *Australia* 22°11S 134°30E 150 C1
Arltunga *Australia* 23°26S 134°41E 150 C1
Armação de Pêra *Portugal* 37°6N 8°22W 89 H2
Armadale *Australia* 32°9S 116°0E 149 F2
Armagh *U.K.* 54°21N 6°39W 64 B5
Armagh □ *U.K.* 54°18N 6°37W 64 B5
Armagnac *France* 43°44N 0°10E 72 E4
Armançon → *France* 47°59N 3°30E 71 E10
Armando Bermudez △ *Dom. Rep.* 19°3N 71°0W 183 C5

Armant *Egypt* 25°37N 32°32E 137 B3
Armatree *Australia* 31°26S 148°28E 153 A8
Armavir *Armenia* 40°5N 44°0E 87 K7
Armavir *Russia* 45°2N 41°7E 87 H5
Armenia *Colombia* 4°35N 75°45W 186 C3
Armenia ■ *Asia* 40°20N 45°0E 87 K7
Armeniș *Romania* 45°13N 22°17E 80 E7
Armenistís, Akra *Greece* 36°8N 27°42E 101 C9
Armentières *France* 50°40N 2°50E 71 B9
Armidale *Australia* 30°30S 151°40E 153 A9
Armilla *Spain* 37°9N 3°37W 89 H7
Armori *India* 20°28N 79°59E 126 D4
Armorique △ *France* 48°22N 3°50W 70 D3
Armour *U.S.A.* 43°19N 98°21W 172 D4
Armstrong *B.C., Canada* 50°25N 119°10W 162 C5
Armstrong *Ont., Canada* 50°18N 89°4W 164 B2
Armur *India* 18°48N 78°16E 126 E4
Arnarfjörður *Iceland* 65°48N 23°40W 60 D2
Arnaud → *Canada* 59°59N 69°46W 161 F18
Arnauti, C. *Cyprus* 35°6N 32°17E 101 D11
Arnay-le-Duc *France* 47°10N 4°27E 71 E11
Arnedillo *Spain* 42°13N 2°14W 90 C2
Arnedo *Spain* 42°12N 2°5W 90 C2
Arnett *U.S.A.* 36°8N 99°46W 176 C5
Arnhem *Neths.* 51°58N 5°55E 69 C5
Arnhem, C. *Australia* 12°20S 137°30E 150 A2
Arnhem B. *Australia* 12°20S 136°10E 150 A2
Arnhem Land *Australia* 13°10S 134°30E 150 A1
Arnhem Land ○ *Australia* 12°50S 134°30E 150 A1
Arnissa *Greece* 40°47N 21°49E 96 F5
Arno → *Italy* 43°41N 10°17E 92 E7
Arno Bay *Australia* 33°54S 136°34E 152 B2
Arnold *U.K.* 53°1N 1°7W 66 D6
Arnold *Calif., U.S.A.* 38°15N 120°21W 170 G6
Arnold *Mo., U.S.A.* 38°26N 90°23W 172 F8
Arnoldstein *Austria* 46°33N 13°43E 78 E6
Arnon → *France* 47°13N 2°1E 71 E9
Arnot *Canada* 55°56N 96°41W 163 B9
Arnøya *Norway* 70°9N 20°40E 60 A19
Arnprior *Canada* 45°26N 76°21W 175 A8
Arnsberg *Germany* 51°24N 8°5E 76 D4
Arnsberger Wald ○ *Germany* 51°25N 8°20E 76 D4
Arnstadt *Germany* 50°50N 10°56E 76 E6
Aroab *Namibia* 26°41S 19°39E 144 C2
Aroania Oros *Greece* 37°56N 22°12E 98 D4
Aroche *Spain* 37°56N 6°57W 89 H4
Arochuku *Nigeria* 5°21N 7°54E 139 D6
Aroeiras *Brazil* 7°31S 35°41W 189 B3
Arolsen *Germany* 51°23N 9°2E 76 D5
Aron *India* 25°57N 77°56E 124 G6
Aron → *France* 46°50N 3°28E 71 F10
Arona *Canary Is.* 28°6N 16°40W 100 F3
Arona *Italy* 45°46N 8°34E 92 C5
Aros → *Mexico* 29°9N 107°57W 180 B3
Arousa, Ría de → *Spain* 42°28N 8°57W 88 C2
Arpa → *Asia* 39°28N 44°56E 105 C11
Arpaçay *Turkey* 40°50N 43°19E 105 B10
Arpajon *France* 48°36N 2°15E 71 D9
Arpajon-sur-Cère *France* 44°54N 2°28E 72 D6
Arpașu de Jos *Romania* 45°47N 24°37E 81 E9
Arqalyk *Kazakhstan* 50°13N 66°50E 109 B7
Arrah = Ara *India* 25°35N 84°32E 125 G11
Arraias *Brazil* 12°56S 46°57W 189 C1
Arraiolos *Portugal* 38°44N 7°59W 89 G3
Arran *U.K.* 55°34N 5°12W 65 F3
Arranmore *Ireland* 55°0N 8°30W 64 A3
Arras *France* 50°17N 2°46E 71 B9
Arrasate *Spain* 43°4N 2°30W 90 B2
Arrats → *France* 44°6N 0°52E 72 D4
Arreau *France* 42°54N 0°22E 72 F4
Arrecife *Canary Is.* 28°57N 13°37W 100 F6
Arrecifes *Argentina* 34°6S 60°9W 190 C3
Arrée, Mts. d' *France* 48°26N 3°55W 70 D3
Arreso *Denmark* 55°58N 12°6E 63 J6
Arriaga *Mexico* 16°14N 93°54W 181 D6
Arribes del Duero ○ *Spain* 41°11N 6°39W 88 D4
Arrilalah *Australia* 23°43S 143°54E 150 C3
Arrino *Australia* 29°30S 115°40E 149 E2
Arriondas *Spain* 43°23N 5°11W 88 B5
Arrojado → *Brazil* 13°24S 44°20W 189 C2
Arromanches-les-Bains *France* 49°20N 0°38W 70 C6
Arronches *Portugal* 39°8N 7°16W 89 F3
Arros → *France* 43°40N 0°2W 72 E3
Arrow, L. *Ireland* 54°3N 8°19W 64 B3
Arrowsmith, Mt. *N.Z.* 43°20S 170°57E 155 D5
Arrowtown *N.Z.* 44°57S 168°50E 155 E3
Arroyo de la Luz *Spain* 39°30N 6°38W 89 F4
Arroyo Grande *U.S.A.* 35°7N 120°35W 171 K6
Ars *Iran* 37°9N 47°46E 128 B5
Ars-sur-Moselle *France* 49°5N 6°4E 71 C13
Arsenault L. *Canada* 55°6N 108°32W 163 B7
Arsenev *Russia* 44°10N 133°15E 112 B6
Arsiero *Italy* 45°48N 11°13E 93 C8
Arsikere *India* 13°15N 76°15E 127 H3
Arsin *Turkey* 41°8N 39°55E 105 B8
Arsk *Russia* 56°10N 49°50E 86 B9
Årsunda *Sweden* 60°31N 16°45E 62 D10
Arta *Greece* 39°8N 21°2E 98 B3
Artà, Coves d' *Spain* 39°40N 3°24E 90 B10
Artashat *Armenia* 39°53N 44°38E 105 B11
Arteaga *Mexico* 18°28N 102°25W 180 D4
Arteixo = A Baiuca *Spain* 43°19N 8°29W 88 B2
Artem = Artyom *Azerbaijan* 40°28N 50°20E 87 K10
Artem *Russia* 43°22N 132°13E 112 C6
Artemivsk *Ukraine* 48°35N 38°0E 83 H10
Artemovsk *Russia* 54°45N 93°35E 107 D10
Artemovskiy *Russia* 57°45N 40°16E 87 G5
Artenay *France* 48°5N 1°50E 71 D8
Artern *Germany* 51°22N 11°18E 76 D7
Artesa de Segre *Spain* 41°54N 1°3E 90 D6
Artesia = Mosomane *Botswana* 24°2S 26°19E 144 B4
Artesia *U.S.A.* 32°51N 104°24W 169 K11
Arthington *Liberia* 6°35N 10°45W 138 D2
Arthur *Canada* 43°50N 80°32W 174 C4
Arthur → *Australia* 41°2S 144°40E 151 G3
Arthur Cr. → *Australia* 22°30S 136°25E 150 C2
Arthur Pt. *Australia* 22°7S 150°3E 150 C5

Arthur River *Australia* 33°20S 117°2E 149 F2
Arthur's Pass *N.Z.* 42°54S 171°35E 155 C6
Arthur's Pass △ *N.Z.* 42°53S 171°42E 155 C6
Arthur's Town *Bahamas* 24°38N 75°42W 183 F4
Artigas *Antarctica* 62°30S 58°0W 55 C18
Artigas *Uruguay* 30°20S 56°30W 190 C4
Artik *Armenia* 40°38N 43°58E 87 K6
Artillery L. *Canada* 63°9N 107°52W 163 A7
Artois *France* 50°20N 2°30E 71 B9
Artotina *Greece* 38°42N 22°2E 98 C4
Artova *Turkey* 40°5N 36°28E 104 B7
Artrutx, C. de *Spain* 39°55N 3°49E 100 B10
Arts Bogd Uul *Mongolia* 44°40N 102°20E 114 B2
Artsvashen *Armenia* 40°38N 45°30E 105 B11
Artsyz *Ukraine* 46°4N 29°26E 81 D14
Artux *China* 39°40N 76°10E 109 E9
Artvin *Turkey* 41°14N 41°44E 105 B9
Artvin □ *Turkey* 41°10N 41°50E 105 B9
Artyk *Russia* 64°12N 145°6E 107 C15
Artyom *Azerbaijan* 40°28N 50°20E 87 K10
Aru, Kepulauan *Indonesia* 6°0S 134°30E 119 F8
Aru Is. = Aru, Kepulauan *Indonesia* 6°0S 134°30E 119 F8
Arua *Uganda* 3°1N 30°58E 142 B3
Aruanã *Brazil* 14°54S 51°10W 187 F8
Aruba ☑ *W. Indies* 12°30N 70°0W 183 D6
Arucas *Canary Is.* 28°7N 15°32W 100 F4
Arudy *France* 43°7N 0°28W 72 E3
Arué *Tahiti* 17°31S 149°30W 155 b
Arumpo *Australia* 33°48S 142°55E 152 B5
Arun → *Nepal* 26°55N 87°10E 125 F12
Arun → *U.K.* 50°49N 0°33W 67 G7
Arunachal Pradesh □ *India* 28°0N 95°0E 123 F19
Aruppukottai *India* 9°31N 78°8E 127 K4
Arusha *Tanzania* 3°20S 36°40E 142 C4
Arusha □ *Tanzania* 3°20S 36°30E 142 C4
Arusha △ *Tanzania* 3°16S 36°47E 142 C4
Arusha Chini *Tanzania* 3°32S 37°20E 142 C4
Aruvi → *Sri Lanka* 8°48N 79°53E 127 K4
Aruwimi → *Dem. Rep. of the Congo* 1°13N 23°36E 142 B1
Arvada *Colo., U.S.A.* 39°48N 105°5W 168 G11
Arvada *Wyo., U.S.A.* 44°39N 106°8W 168 D10
Arvagh *Ireland* 53°55N 7°35W 64 C4
Arvayheer *Mongolia* 46°15N 102°48E 110 B9
Arve → *France* 46°11N 6°8E 71 F13
Arvi *Greece* 34°59N 25°28E 101 E7
Arvi *India* 20°59N 78°16E 126 D4
Arviat *Canada* 61°6N 93°59W 163 A10
Arvidsjaur *Sweden* 65°35N 19°10E 60 D18
Arvika *Sweden* 59°40N 12°36E 62 E7
Arvin *U.S.A.* 35°12N 118°50W 171 K8
Arwal *India* 25°15N 84°41E 125 G11
Arxan *China* 47°11N 119°57E 111 B12
Åryd *Sweden* 56°49N 14°59E 63 H8
Arys *Kazakhstan* 42°26N 68°48E 109 D7
Arzachena *Italy* 41°5N 9°23E 94 A2
Arzamas *Russia* 55°27N 43°55E 86 C6
Arzanah *U.A.E.* 24°47N 52°34E 129 E7
Arzew *Algeria* 35°50N 0°23W 136 A3
Arzgir *Russia* 45°18N 44°23E 87 H7
Arzignano *Italy* 45°31N 11°20E 93 C8
Arzúa *Spain* 42°56N 8°9W 88 C2
Aš *Czech Rep.* 50°13N 12°12E 78 A5
Ås *Sweden* 63°15N 14°34E 62 A8
Aşağı = Assur *Iraq* 35°27N 43°15E 105 C10
Asahi *Japan* 35°43N 140°47E 113 G10
Asahi-Gawa → *Japan* 34°36N 133°58E 113 G6
Asahigawa = Asahikawa *Japan* 43°46N 142°22E 112 C11
Asahikawa *Japan* 43°46N 142°22E 112 C11
Asaluyeh *Iran* 27°29N 52°37E 129 E7
Asamankese *Ghana* 5°50N 0°40W 138 D4
Asan → *India* 26°37N 78°24E 125 F8
Asansol *India* 23°40N 87°1E 125 H12
Asärna *Sweden* 62°39N 14°22E 62 B8
Åsbesberg *S. Africa* 29°0S 23°0E 144 C3
Asbestos *Canada* 45°47N 71°58W 165 C5
Asbury Park *U.S.A.* 40°13N 74°1W 175 F10
Ascea *Italy* 40°8N 15°12E 95 B8
Ascensión *Mexico* 31°6N 107°59W 180 A3
Ascensión, B. de la *Mexico* 19°40N 87°30W 181 D7
Ascension I. *Atl. Oc.* 7°57S 14°23W 133 G2
Aschach an der Donau *Austria* 48°22N 14°2E 78 D7
Aschaffenburg *Germany* 49°58N 9°6E 78 D4
Aschendorf *Germany* 53°3N 7°19E 76 B3
Aschersleben *Germany* 51°45N 11°29E 76 D7
Asciano *Italy* 43°14N 11°33E 93 E8
Ascó *Spain* 41°11N 0°34E 90 D6
Áscoli Piceno *Italy* 42°51N 13°34E 93 F10
Áscoli Satriano *Italy* 41°11N 15°32E 95 A8
Ascope *Peru* 7°46S 79°8W 188 B2
Ascotán *Chile* 21°45S 68°17W 190 A2
Aseb *Eritrea* 13°0N 42°40E 131 E4

Åseda *Sweden* 57°10N 15°20E 63 G9
Asedjrad *Algeria* 24°51N 1°29E 136 D4
Asela *Ethiopia* 8°0N 39°0E 131 F2
Åsen *Sweden* 61°17N 13°50E 62 C7
Asenovgrad *Bulgaria* 42°1N 24°51E 97 D8
Asfeld *France* 49°27N 4°5E 71 C11
Asfûn el Matâ'na *Egypt* 25°26N 32°30E 137 B3
Asgata *Cyprus* 34°46N 33°15E 101 E12
Aşgabat = Ashgabat *Turkmenistan* 37°58N 58°24E 129 B8
Asha *Russia* 55°0N 57°16E 108 D5
Ashbourne *U.K.* 53°2N 1°43W 66 D6
Ashburn *U.S.A.* 31°43N 83°39W 178 D6
Ashburton *N.Z.* 43°53S 171°48E 155 D6
Ashburton → *Australia* 21°40S 114°56E 148 D1
Ashburton, North Branch → *N.Z.* 43°54S 171°44E 155 D6
Ashburton, South Branch → *N.Z.* 43°45S 171°44E 155 D6
Ashcroft *Canada* 50°40N 121°20W 162 C4
Ashdod *Israel* 31°49N 34°35E 130 D3
Asheboro *U.S.A.* 35°43N 79°49W 177 D15
Asherton *U.S.A.* 28°27N 99°46W 176 G5
Asheville *U.S.A.* 35°36N 82°33W 177 D13
Ashewat *Pakistan* 31°22N 68°32E 124 D3
Asheweig → *Canada* 54°17N 87°12W 164 B2
Ashford *Australia* 29°15S 151°3E 153 A9
Ashford *U.K.* 51°8N 0°53E 67 F8
Ashgabat *Turkmenistan* 37°58N 58°24E 129 B8
Ashibetsu *Japan* 43°31N 142°11E 112 C11
Ashikaga *Japan* 36°28N 139°29E 113 F9
Ashington *U.K.* 55°11N 1°33W 66 B6
Ashizuri-Uwakai △ *Japan* 32°56N 132°32E 113 H6
Ashizuri-Zaki *Japan* 32°44N 133°0E 113 H6
Ashkarkot *Afghan.* 33°3N 67°58E 124 C2
Ashkhabad = Ashgabat *Turkmenistan* 37°58N 58°24E 129 B8
Ashland *Ala., U.S.A.* 33°16N 85°50W 178 C4
Ashland *Kans., U.S.A.* 37°11N 99°46W 172 G4
Ashland *Maine, U.S.A.* 46°38N 68°24W 173 B19
Ashland *Mont., U.S.A.* 45°36N 106°16W 168 D10
Ashland *Ohio, U.S.A.* 40°52N 82°19W 174 F2
Ashland *Oreg., U.S.A.* 42°12N 122°43W 168 E2
Ashland *Pa., U.S.A.* 40°45N 76°22W 175 F15
Ashland *Wis., U.S.A.* 46°35N 90°53W 172 B8
Ashley *N. Dak., U.S.A.* 46°2N 99°22W 172 B4
Ashley *Pa., U.S.A.* 41°12N 75°55W 175 E9
Ashley → *N.Z.* 43°17S 172°44E 155 D5
Ashmore and Cartier Is. *Ind. Oc.* 12°15S 123°0E 148 B3
Ashmore Reef *Australia* 12°14S 123°5E 148 B3
Ashmûn *Egypt* 30°18N 30°55E 137 B4
Ashmyany *Belarus* 54°26N 25°52E 75 A13
Ashokan Reservoir *U.S.A.* 41°56N 74°13W 175 E10
Ashqelon *Israel* 31°42N 34°35E 130 D3
Ashta *India* 23°1N 76°43E 124 H7
Ashtabula *U.S.A.* 41°52N 80°47W 174 E4
Ashti *Maharashtra, India* 21°12N 78°11E 126 D4
Ashti *Maharashtra, India* 18°50N 75°15E 126 E2
Ashtiyan *Iran* 34°31N 50°0E 129 C6
Ashton *S. Africa* 33°50S 20°5E 144 E3
Ashton *U.S.A.* 44°4N 111°27W 168 D8
Ashuanipi, L. *Canada* 52°45N 66°15W 165 B6
Ashur = Assur *Iraq* 35°27N 43°15E 105 C10
Ashville *U.S.A.* 40°34N 78°33W 174 F6
Asia 45°0N 75°0E 102 E9
Asia, Kepulauan *Indonesia* 1°0N 131°13E 119 D8
Asiago *Italy* 45°52N 11°30E 93 C8
Asifabad *India* 19°20N 79°24E 126 E4
Asilah *Morocco* 35°29N 6°0W 136 A2
Asinara *Italy* 41°4N 8°16E 94 A1
Asinara, G. dell' *Italy* 41°0N 8°30E 94 A1
Asino *Russia* 57°0N 86°0E 106 D9
Asipovichy *Belarus* 53°19N 28°33E 75 B15
'Asīr *Si. Arabia* 18°40N 42°30E 131 D5
Asir, Ras *Somalia* 11°55N 51°10E 131 E6
Aşkale *Turkey* 39°56N 40°41E 105 C9
Askersund *Sweden* 58°53N 14°55E 63 F8
Askham *S. Africa* 26°59S 20°47E 144 D3
Åskim *Norway* 59°35N 11°10E 61 G14
Askio, Oros *Greece* 40°25N 21°35E 96 F5
Askja *Iceland* 65°3N 16°48W 60 D6
Askøy *Norway* 60°29N 5°10E 60 F11
Asl *Egypt* 29°33N 32°44E 137 C4
Aslan Burnu *Turkey* 38°28N 26°35E 99 E8
Asmara = Asmera *Eritrea* 15°19N 38°55E 131 D2
Asmera *Eritrea* 15°19N 38°55E 131 D2
Asnæs *Denmark* 55°40N 11°0E 63 J4
Åsnen *Sweden* 56°37N 14°45E 63 H8

Asni *Morocco* 31°17N 7°58W 13
Aso Kujū △ *Japan* 32°53N 131°6E 11
Ásola *Italy* 45°13N 10°24E 9
Asos *Greece* 38°22N 20°33E 9
Asoteriba, Jebel *Sudan* 21°51N 36°30E 13
Asouf, O. → *Algeria* 25°40N 2°8E 13
Aspatria *U.K.* 54°47N 3°19W 6
Aspe *Spain* 38°20N 0°40W 9
Aspen *U.S.A.* 39°11N 106°49W 168
Aspermont *U.S.A.* 33°8N 100°14W 17
Aspet *France* 43°1N 0°48E 7
Aspiring, Mt. *N.Z.* 44°23S 168°46E 15
Aspres-sur-Buëch *France* 44°32N 5°44E 7
Asprókavos, Akra *Greece* 39°21N 20°6E 10
Aspromonte △ *Italy* 38°10N 15°55E 9
Aspur *India* 23°58N 74°7E 12
Asquith *Canada* 52°8N 107°13W 16
Assab = Aseb *Eritrea* 13°0N 42°40E 13
Assâba □ *Mauritania* 16°40N 11°40W 13
Assâba, Massif de l' *Mauritania* 16°10N 11°45W 13
Assagny △ *Ivory C.* 5°10N 4°48W 13
Assaikio *Nigeria* 8°34N 8°55E 13
Assal, L. *Djibouti* 11°40N 42°26E 13
Assam □ *India* 26°0N 93°0E 123
Assamakka *Niger* 19°21N 5°38E 13
Assateague Island △ *U.S.A.* 38°15N 75°10W 173
Assaye *India* 20°15N 75°53E 12
Asse *Belgium* 50°24N 4°10E 6
Assekrem *Algeria* 23°16N 5°49E 13
Assémini *Italy* 39°17N 9°0E 9
Assen *Neths.* 53°0N 6°35E 6
Assens *Denmark* 55°16N 9°55E 6
Assini *Ivory C.* 5°9N 3°17W 13
Assiniboia *Canada* 49°40N 105°59W 16
Assiniboine → *Canada* 49°53N 97°8W 16
Assiniboine, Mt. *Canada* 50°52N 115°39W 16
Assis *Brazil* 22°40S 50°20W 19
Assis Brasil *Brazil* 10°55S 69°32W 18
Assisi *Italy* 43°4N 12°37E 9
Assur *Iraq* 35°27N 43°15E 105
Assynt, L. *U.K.* 58°10N 5°3W 6
Astaffort *France* 44°4N 0°40E 7
Astakida *Greece* 35°53N 26°50E 9
Astakos *Greece* 38°32N 21°5E 9
Astana *Kazakhstan* 51°10N 71°30E 10
Ästäneh *Iran* 37°17N 49°59E 12
Astara *Azerbaijan* 38°30N 48°50E 10
Ästärä *Iran* 38°20N 48°52E 105
Astarabad = Gorgān *Iran* 36°55N 54°30E 12
Asterousia *Greece* 34°59N 25°3E 10
Asti *Italy* 44°54N 8°12E 9
Astipalea *Greece* 36°32N 26°22E 9
Astorga *Spain* 42°29N 6°8W 8
Astoria *U.S.A.* 46°11N 123°50W 16
Åstorp *Sweden* 56°6N 12°55E 6
Astrakhan *Russia* 46°25N 48°5E 8
Astrakhan □ *Russia* 47°45N 46°20E 8
Astrebla Downs *Australia* 24°12S 140°34E 15
Astudillo *Spain* 42°12N 4°22W 8
Asturias □ *Spain* 43°15N 6°0W 8
Asturias ✈ (OVD) *Spain* 43°33N 6°3W 8
Asunción *Bolivia* 11°45S 67°50W 18
Asunción *Paraguay* 25°10S 57°30W 19
Asunción Nochixtlán *Mexico* 17°28N 97°14W 18
Åsunden *Sweden* 58°0N 15°51E 6
Aswa → *Uganda* 3°43N 31°55E 14
Aswa-Lolim △ *Uganda* 2°43N 31°35E 14
Aswad, Ra's al *Si. Arabia* 21°16N 39°37E 13
Aswân *Egypt* 24°4N 32°57E 13
Aswân High Dam = Sadd el Aali *Egypt* 23°54N 32°54E 13
Asyût *Egypt* 27°11N 31°4E 13
Asyûti, Wadi → *Egypt* 27°11N 31°16E 13
Aszód *Hungary* 47°39N 19°28E 8
At-Bashy *Kyrgyzstan* 41°10N 75°48E 10
Aţ Ţafilah *Jordan* 30°45N 35°30E 13
Aţ Ţafilah □ *Jordan* 30°45N 35°30E 13
Aṭ Ṭā'if *Si. Arabia* 21°5N 40°27E 13
Aṭ Ta'mīm □ *Iraq* 35°30N 44°33E 12
Aṭ Ţīraq *Si. Arabia* 27°19N 44°33E 12
Aṭ Tubayq *Si. Arabia* 29°30N 37°0E 12
Aṭ Ţunayb *Jordan* 31°48N 35°57E 13
Atabey *Turkey* 37°57N 30°39E 99
Atacama *Chile* 27°30S 70°0W 19
Atacama, Desierto de *Chile* 24°0S 69°20W 19
Atacama, Salar de *Chile* 23°30S 68°20W 19
Atakeye ◎ *Australia* 22°30S 133°45E 14
Atakor *Algeria* 23°27N 5°31E 13
Atakpamé *Togo* 7°31N 1°13E 13
Atalandi *Greece* 38°39N 22°58E 9
Atalaya *Peru* 10°45S 73°50W 18
Atalaya de Femes *Canary Is.* 28°56N 13°47W 10
Ataléia *Brazil* 18°3S 41°6W 18
Atami *Japan* 35°5N 139°4E 11
Atamyrat *Turkmenistan* 37°50N 65°12E 10
Atapuerca, Cueva de *Spain* 42°22N 3°32W 8
Atapupu *Indonesia* 9°0S 124°51E 11
Atâr *Mauritania* 20°30N 13°5W 13
Atarfe *Spain* 37°13N 3°40W 8
Atari *Pakistan* 31°34N 74°38E 12
Atascadero *U.S.A.* 35°29N 120°40W 17
Atasu *Kazakhstan* 48°30N 71°0E 10
Atatürk, İstanbul ✈ (IST) *Turkey* 40°59N 28°49E 99
Atatürk Baraji *Turkey* 37°28N 38°30E 10
Atauro *E. Timor* 8°10S 125°30E 11
Ataviros *Greece* 36°12N 27°50E 9
Atbara *Sudan* 17°42N 33°59E 13
'Atbara, Nahr → *Sudan* 17°40N 33°56E 13
Atbasar *Kazakhstan* 51°48N 68°20E 10
Atbashi = At-Bashy *Kyrgzstan* 41°10N 75°48E 10
Atça *Turkey* 37°53N 28°10E 9
Atchafalaya B. *U.S.A.* 29°25N 91°25W 17
Atchison *U.S.A.* 39°34N 95°7W 17
Atebubu *Ghana* 7°47N 1°0W 13
Ateca *Spain* 41°20N 1°49W 9

→ *Italy* 42°11N 13°51E **93** F10
shān *Iran* 35°35N 52°37E **129** C7
sine, Alpi *Italy* 46°55N 11°30E **93** B8
ssa *Italy* 42°4N 14°27E **93** F11
h *Egypt* 29°25N 31°15E **137** F7
Belgium 50°38N 3°47E **69** D3
abasca *Canada* 54°45N 113°20W **162** C6
abasca → *Canada* 58°40N 110°50W **163** B6
abasca, L. *Canada* 59°15N 109°15W **163** B7
abasca Sand Dunes
Canada 59°4N 108°43W **163** B7
agarh *India* 20°32N 85°37E **126** D7
amanon Oros *Greece* 39°30N 21°26E **98** B3
boy *Ireland* 53°36N 6°56W **64** C5
ena *U.S.A.* 29°59N 83°30W **178** G4
enry *Ireland* 53°18N 8°44W **64** C3
ens = Athina *Greece* 37°58N 23°43E **98** D5
ens Ala., *U.S.A.* 34°48N 86°58W **177** D11
ens Ga., *U.S.A.* 33°57N 83°23W **177** D12
ens Ohio, *U.S.A.* 39°20N 82°6W **173** F12
ens N.Y., *U.S.A.* 41°57N 76°31W **176** D8
ens Tenn., *U.S.A.* 35°27N 84°36W **177** D12
ens Tex., *U.S.A.* 32°12N 95°51W **176** E7
erley *Canada* 44°37N 79°20W **174** B5
erton *Australia* 17°15S 145°30E **150** B4
i River *Kenya* 1°28S 36°58E **142** C4
ièmé *Benin* 6°37N 1°40E **139** D5
ienou *Cyprus* 35°3N 33°32E **101** D12
ína *Greece* 37°58N 23°43E **98** D5
ssa *Greece* 37°56N 23°56E **98** D5
inai = Athina *Greece* 37°58N 23°43E **98** D5
lone *Ireland* 53°25N 7°56W **64** C4
malik *India* 20°43N 84°22E **126** F2
ol *N.Z.* 45°30S 168°35E **155** F3
ol *U.S.A.* 42°36N 72°14W **175** D12
oll, Forest of *U.K.* 56°51N 3°50W **65** E5
oll, Kap *Greenland* 76°25N 69°30W **58** C7
olville *Canada* 47°59N 66°43W **165** C6
os *Greece* 40°9N 24°22E **97** F8
y *Ireland* 53°0N 7°0W **64** C5
k *Uganda* 3°12N 32°2E **142** B3
Chad 13°13N 18°20E **135** F9
o *Peru* 16°14S 73°40W **188** D3
rnza *Spain* 41°12N 2°52W **90** D2
L. *Canada* 55°15N 96°0W **163** B9
kaki ⌀ *Canada* 51°30N 95°31W **163** C9
kameg → *Canada* 52°30N 82°46W **164** B3
okan *Canada* 48°45N 91°37W **164** C1
konak L. *Canada* 52°40N 64°32W **165** B7
naono *Tahiti* 17°46S 149°28W **155** b
ampattinam *India* 10°28N 79°20E **127** J4
a *Russia* 60°50N 151°48E **107** C16
Cook Is. 20°0S 158°10W **157** J12
a I. *U.S.A.* 52°7N 174°30W **166** E5
arsk *Russia* 51°55N 45°2E **86** E7
inson Ga., *U.S.A.* 31°13N 81°47W **178** D6
inson Nebr., *U.S.A.* 42°32N 98°59W **172** D4
anta Ga., *U.S.A.* 33°45N 84°23W **178** B5
anta Tex., *U.S.A.* 33°7N 94°10W **176** E7
anta Hartsfield-Jackson Int. ✈
U.S.A. 33°38N 84°26W **178** B5
antic *U.S.A.* 41°24N 95°1W **172** E6
antic Beach *U.S.A.* 30°20N 81°24W **178** D6
antic City *U.S.A.* 39°21N 74°27W **173** F16
antic-Indian Basin
Antarctica 60°0S 30°0E **55** B4
tic Ocean 0°0 20°0W **55** C8
antis *S. Africa* 33°34S 18°29E **144** D2
as Mts. = Haut Atlas
Morocco 32°30N 5°0W **136** B3
n *Canada* 59°31N 133°41W **162** B2
n, L. *Canada* 59°10N 133°45W **162** B2
o → *Canada* 59°10N 134°30W **162** B2
akur *Andhra Pradesh,*
dia 14°37N 79°40E **127** G4
akur *Andhra Pradesh,*
dia 15°53N 78°35E **127** G4
aku *Telangana,*
dia 18°45N 78°39E **126** E4
rone *U.S.A.* 31°2N 87°29W **179** D2
ka *U.S.A.* 34°23N 96°8W **176** D6
kos *Greece* 38°28N 20°49E **98** C2
asuk *U.S.A.* 35°19N 117°37W **171** K9
nai *U.S.A.* 70°28N 157°24W **166** A4
k = Atrek →
urkmenistan 37°35N 53°58E **129** B8
n *Sweden* 57°7N 12°57E **63** G6
→ *Sweden* 56°53N 12°30E **63** H6
ek → *Turkmenistan* 37°35N 53°58E **129** B8
Italy 39°35N 13°58E **93** F10
ki *Greece* 39°56N 25°13E **99** B7
um, Mt. *Cameroon* 6°41N 12°57E **139** D7
uta *Japan* 33°24N 141°26E **112** C10
eba *U.S.A.* 34°1N 86°6W **178** A3
apeu *Laos* 14°48N 106°50E **120** E6
apulgus *U.S.A.* 30°45N 84°29W **178** F5
awapiskat *Canada* 52°56N 82°24W **164** B3
anada 52°57N 82°18W **164** B3
awapiskat L.
anada 52°18N 87°54W **164** B2
ersee *Austria* 47°35N 13°32E **78** D6
ca = Attiki *Greece* 37°10N 23°40E **98** D5
ca *U.S.A.* 40°18N 87°15W **172** E10
ca Ohio, *U.S.A.* 41°4N 82°53W **174** E2
chy *France* 49°25N 3°3E **71** C11
kamagen *L. Canada* 51°30N 66°30W **165** B6
ki □ *Greece* 37°10N 23°40E **98** D5
eboro *U.S.A.* 33°52N 77°17W **175** C8
pu = Attapeu
Laos 14°48N 106°50E **120** E6
I. *U.S.A.* 52°55N 172°55E **166** E2
nga *Australia* 30°55S 150°50E **153** A9
ur *India* 11°35N 78°30E **127** J4
ra *Uganda* 2°7N 32°20E **142** B3
idaberg *Sweden* 58°12N 16°0E **63** F10
ater *U.S.A.* 37°21N 120°37W **170** H6
ood *Canada* 43°40N 81°1W **174** C3
rau *Kazakhstan* 47°5N 52°0E **108** C4
ala *U.S.A.* 44°15N 73°2W **173** B17
Sable → *U.S.A.* 44°25N 83°20W **173** C12
Sable Forks
U.S.A. 44°27N 73°41W **175** B11

Au Sable Pt. *U.S.A.* 44°20N 83°20W **174** B1
Auas *Honduras* 15°29N 84°20W **182** C3
Auasberg *Namibia* 22°37S 17°13E **144** B2
Aubagne *France* 43°17N 5°37E **73** E9
Aube → *France* 48°15N 4°10E **71** D11
Aube □ *France* 48°34N 3°43E **71** D10
Auberry *U.S.A.* 37°7N 119°29W **170** H7
Aubin *France* 44°33N 2°15E **72** D6
Aubrac, Mts. d' *France* 44°40N 3°2E **72** D7
Auburn *Australia* 34°1S 138°42E **152** C3
Auburn Ala., *U.S.A.* 32°36N 85°29W **178** C4
Auburn Calif., *U.S.A.* 38°54N 121°4W **170** G5
Auburn Ind., *U.S.A.* 41°22N 85°4W **173** E11
Auburn Maine, *U.S.A.* 44°6N 70°14W **173** C18
Auburn N.Y., *U.S.A.* 42°56N 76°34W **175** C8
Auburn Nebr., *U.S.A.* 40°23N 95°51W **172** E6
Auburn Pa., *U.S.A.* 40°36N 76°6W **173** E8
Auburn Wash., *U.S.A.* 47°18N 122°14W **170** C4
Auburn Ra. *Australia* 25°15S 150°30E **151** D5
Auburndale *U.S.A.* 28°4N 81°48W **179** G8
Aubusson *France* 45°57N 2°11E **72** D6
Auce *Latvia* 56°28N 22°53E **82** B9
Auch *France* 43°39N 0°36E **72** E4
Auchi *Nigeria* 7°6N 6°13E **139** D6
Auchterarder *U.K.* 56°18N 3°41W **65** E5
Auchtermuchty *U.K.* 56°18N 3°13W **65** E5
Auckland *N.Z.* 36°52S 174°46E **154** C3
Auckland □ *N.Z.* 36°50S 175°0E **154** C3
Auckland Is. *Pac. Oc.* 50°40S 166°5E **156** N8
Aude □ *France* 43°8N 2°28E **72** E6
Aude → *France* 43°13N 3°14E **72** E7
Auden *Canada* 50°14N 87°53W **164** B2
Auderville *France* 49°43N 1°57W **70** C5
Audierne *France* 48°1N 4°34W **70** D2
Audincourt *France* 47°30N 6°50E **71** E13
Audomarois □ *France* 50°50N 2°30E **71** B9
Audubon *U.S.A.* 41°43N 94°56W **172** E6
Aue *Germany* 50°35N 12°41E **76** E8
Auerbach *Germany* 50°30N 12°24E **76** E8
Augathella *Australia* 25°48S 146°35E **151** D4
Aughnacloy *U.K.* 54°25N 6°59W **64** B5
Aughrim *Ireland* 53°18N 8°19W **64** C3
Augrabies Falls
S. Africa 28°35S 20°20E **144** C3
Augrabies Falls △
S. Africa 28°40S 20°22E **144** C3
Augsburg *Germany* 48°25N 10°52E **77** G6
Augsburg-Westliche Wälder ⌀
Germany 48°20N 10°40E **77** G6
Augusta *Australia* 34°19S 115°9E **149** F2
Augusta *Italy* 37°13N 15°13E **95** E8
Augusta Ark., *U.S.A.* 35°17N 91°22W **176** D9
Augusta Ga., *U.S.A.* 33°28N 81°58W **178** B8
Augusta Kans., *U.S.A.* 37°41N 96°59W **172** G5
Augusta Maine,
U.S.A. 44°19N 69°47W **173** C19
Augusta Mont., *U.S.A.* 47°30N 112°24W **168** C7
Augustenborg *Denmark* 54°57N 9°53E **63** J3
Augustów *Poland* 53°51N 23°0E **82** E9
Augustus, Mt.
Australia 24°20S 116°50E **149** D2
Augustus I. *Australia* 15°20S 124°30E **148** C3
Aujuittuq = Grise Fiord
Canada 76°25N 82°57W **161** B15
Aukrug ⌀ *Canada* 54°5N 9°45E **76** A5
Aukštaitija △ *Lithuania* 55°15N 26°0E **61** J22
Aul *India* 20°41N 86°39E **126** D8
Aulavik △ *Canada* 73°42N 119°55W **160** C8
Auld, L. *Australia* 22°25S 123°50E **148** D3
Aülieköl *Kazakhstan* 52°32N 62°45E **108** B6
Aulifeltet *Norway* 60°30N 11°21E **62** D5
Aulla *Italy* 44°12N 9°58E **92** D6
Aulnay *France* 46°2N 0°22E **72** B3
Aulne → *France* 48°17N 4°16W **70** D2
Aulnoye-Aymeries
France 50°12N 3°50E **71** B10
Ault *France* 50°5N 1°29E **70** A4
Ault *U.S.A.* 40°35N 104°44W **168** F11
Aulus-les-Bains *France* 42°49N 1°19E **72** F5
Aumale *France* 49°46N 1°46E **71** C8
Aumont-Aubrac *France* 44°43N 3°17E **72** D7
Auna *Nigeria* 10°9N 4°42E **139** C5
Aundah *India* 19°32N 77°22E **126** E3
Aundh *India* 17°33N 74°23E **126** F2
Auning *Denmark* 56°26N 10°22E **63** H4
Aunis *France* 46°5N 0°50W **72** B3
Auponhia *Indonesia* 1°58S 125°27E **119** E7
Aups *France* 43°37N 6°15E **73** E10
Aur, Pulau *Malaysia* 2°35N 104°10E **121** L5
Auraiya *India* 26°28N 79°33E **125** F8
Aurangabad *Bihar,*
India 24°45N 84°18E **125** G11
Aurangabad *Maharashtra,*
India 19°50N 75°23E **126** E2
Auray *France* 47°40N 2°59W **70** E4
Aurès *Algeria* 35°8N 6°30E **136** A5
Aurich *Germany* 53°28N 7°28E **76** B3
Auronzo di Cadore *Italy* 46°33N 12°26E **93** B9
Aurora *Canada* 44°0N 79°28W **174** C5
Aurora *S. Africa* 32°40S 18°29E **144** D2
Aurora Colo., *U.S.A.* 39°43N 104°49W **168** G11
Aurora Ill., *U.S.A.* 41°45N 88°19W **172** E9
Aurora Mo., *U.S.A.* 36°58N 93°43W **172** G7
Aurora N.Y., *U.S.A.* 42°45N 76°42W **175** C8
Aurora Nebr., *U.S.A.* 40°52N 98°0W **172** E5
Aurora Ohio, *U.S.A.* 41°21N 81°20W **174** E3
Aurukun *Australia* 13°20S 141°45E **150** A3
Aurukun ⌀ *Australia* 13°36S 141°48E **150** A3
Aus *Namibia* 26°35S 16°12E **144** C2
Ausable → *Canada* 43°19N 81°46W **174** C3
Auschwitz = Oświęcim
Poland 50°2N 19°11E **83** H6
Auski Roadhouse
Australia 22°22S 118°41E **148** D2
Austen Harbour *India* 12°55N 92°45E **127** H11
Austerlitz = Slavkov u Brna
Czech Rep. 49°10N 16°52E **79** B9
Austin Minn., *U.S.A.* 43°40N 92°58W **172** D7
Austin Nev., *U.S.A.* 39°30N 117°4W **168** G5
Austin Pa., *U.S.A.* 41°38N 78°6W **174** E6
Austin Tex., *U.S.A.* 30°17N 97°45W **176** E6
Austin, L. *Australia* 27°40S 118°0E **149** E2
Austin I. *Canada* 61°10N 94°0W **163** A10
Austra *Norway* 65°8N 11°55E **62** D6
Austral Is. = Tubuaï, Is.
French Polynesia 25°0S 150°0W **157** K13

Austral Seamount Chain
Pac. Oc. 24°0S 150°0W **157** K13
Australia ■ *Oceania* 23°0S 135°0E **147** D6
Australian-Antarctic Basin
S. Ocean 60°0S 120°0E **55** C9
Australian Capital Territory □
Australia 35°30S 149°0E **153** C8
Australind *Australia* 33°17S 115°42E **149** F2
Austria ■ *Europe* 47°0N 14°0E **78** E7
Austvågøya *Norway* 68°20N 14°40E **60** B16
Auterive *France* 43°21N 1°29E **72** E5
Authie → *France* 50°22N 1°38E **71** B8
Authon-du-Perche
France 48°12N 0°54E **70** D7
Autlán de Navarro
Mexico 19°46N 104°22W **180** D4
Autun *France* 46°58N 4°17E **71** F11
Auvergne □ *France* 45°20N 3°15E **72** C7
Auvergne, Mts. d' *France* 45°20N 2°55E **72** C6
Auvézère → *France* 45°12N 0°50E **72** C4
Auxerre *France* 47°48N 3°32E **71** E10
Auxi-le-Château *France* 50°15N 2°8E **71** B9
Auxonne *France* 47°10N 5°20E **71** E12
Auyuittuq △ *Canada* 67°30N 66°0W **161** D18
Auzances *France* 46°2N 2°30E **71** F9
Auzangate, Nevado
Peru 13°47S 71°13W **188** C3
Av-Dovurak *Russia* 51°17N 91°35E **107** D10
Ava *U.S.A.* 36°57N 92°40W **172** G7
Avachinskaya Sopka
Russia 53°15N 158°50E **107** D16
Avallon *France* 47°30N 3°53E **71** E10
Avalon *U.S.A.* 33°21N 118°20W **171** M8
Avalon Pen. *Canada* 47°30N 53°20W **165** D9
Avanigadda *India* 16°0N 80°56E **127** G5
Avanos *Turkey* 38°43N 34°51E **104** C6
Avantas *Greece* 40°57N 25°56E **97** F9
Avaré *Brazil* 23°4S 48°58W **191** A6
Avawatz Mts. *U.S.A.* 35°40N 116°30W **171** K10
Avdan Dağı *Turkey* 40°23N 29°46E **97** F13
Aveiro *Brazil* 3°10S 55°5W **187** D7
Aveiro *Portugal* 40°37N 8°38W **88** E2
Aveiro □ *Portugal* 40°40N 8°35W **88** E2
Āvej *Iran* 35°40N 49°15E **129** C6
Avellaneda *Argentina* 34°40S 58°22W **190** C4
Avellino *Italy* 40°54N 14°47E **95** B7
Avenal *U.S.A.* 36°0N 120°8W **170** K6
Aversa *Italy* 40°58N 14°12E **95** B7
Avery *U.S.A.* 47°15N 115°49W **168** C6
Aves, I. de *W. Indies* 15°45N 63°55W **183** C7
Aves, Is. las *Venezuela* 12°0N 67°30W **183** D6
Avesnes-sur-Helpe
France 50°8N 3°55E **71** B10
Avesnois □ *France* 50°10N 3°45E **71** B10
Avesta *Sweden* 60°9N 16°10E **62** D10
Aveyron □ *France* 44°22N 2°45E **72** D6
Aveyron → *France* 44°5N 1°16E **72** D5
Avezzano *Italy* 42°2N 13°25E **93** F10
Avgó *Greece* 35°33N 25°37E **99** F7
Aviá Terai *Argentina* 26°45S 60°50W **190** B3
Aviano *Italy* 46°4N 12°36E **93** B9
Aviemore *U.K.* 57°12N 3°50W **65** D5
Aviemore, L. *N.Z.* 44°37S 170°18E **155** E5
Avigliana *Italy* 45°5N 7°23E **92** C4
Avigliano *Italy* 40°44N 15°43E **95** B8
Avignon *France* 43°57N 4°50E **73** E8
Ávila *Spain* 40°39N 4°43W **88** E6
Ávila □ *Spain* 40°30N 5°0W **88** E6
Ávila, Sierra de *Spain* 40°40N 5°15W **88** E5
Avila Beach *U.S.A.* 35°11N 120°44W **171** K6
Avilés *Spain* 43°35N 5°57W **88** A5
Aviño *Spain* 43°36N 8°8W **88** B2
Avintes *Portugal* 41°7N 8°33W **88** D2
Avis *Portugal* 39°4N 7°53W **89** F3
Avis *U.S.A.* 41°11N 77°19W **174** E7
Avissawella *Sri Lanka* 6°56N 80°11E **127** L5
Aviz = Avis *Portugal* 39°4N 7°53W **89** F3
Avize *France* 48°59N 4°1E **71** D11
Avlonari *Greece* 38°31N 24°5E **98** C6
Avlum *Denmark* 56°16N 8°47E **63** H2
Avoca *Australia* 37°5S 143°26E **152** D5
Avoca *U.S.A.* 42°25N 77°25W **174** D7
Avoca → *Australia* 35°40S 143°43E **152** C5
Avoca → *Ireland* 52°48N 6°10W **64** D5
Avola *Canada* 51°45N 119°19W **162** C5
Avola *Italy* 36°56N 15°7E **95** F8
Avon *U.S.A.* 42°55N 77°45W **174** D7
Avon → *Australia* 31°40S 116°7E **149** F2
Avon → *Bristol, U.K.* 51°29N 2°41W **67** F5
Avon → *Dorset, U.K.* 50°44N 1°46W **67** G6
Avon → *Warks., U.K.* 52°0N 2°8W **67** E5
Avon Park *U.S.A.* 27°36N 81°31W **179** H8
Avondale *Zimbabwe* 17°43S 30°58E **143** F3
Avonlea *Canada* 50°0N 105°0W **163** D8
Avonmore *Canada* 45°10N 74°58W **175** A10
Avonmouth *U.K.* 51°30N 2°42W **67** F5
Avramov *Bulgaria* 42°45N 26°38E **97** D10
Avranches *France* 48°40N 1°20W **70** D5
Avre → *France* 48°47N 1°22E **70** D8
Avrig *Romania* 45°43N 24°21E **81** E9
Avrillé *France* 47°28N 7°28E **76** B6
Avtovac *Bos.-H.* 43°9N 18°35E **96** C3
Awa-Shima *Japan* 38°27N 139°14E **112** E9
A'waj → *Syria* 33°23N 36°20E **130** B5
Awaji-Shima *Japan* 34°30N 134°50E **113** G7
'Awālī *Bahrain* 26°0N 50°30E **129** E6
Awantipur *India* 33°55N 75°3E **125** C6
Awanui *N.Z.* 35°4S 173°17E **154** B3
Awarja B. *N.Z.* 44°28S 168°4E **155** E3
Awarua Ra. *N.Z.* 44°15S 168°5E **155** E3
Awasa *Ethiopia* 7°2N 38°28E **131** F2
Awash *Ethiopia* 9°1N 40°10E **131** F4
Awaso *Ghana* 6°15N 2°22W **138** D4
Awat *China* 40°36N 80°22E **109** E12
Awatere → *N.Z.* 41°37S 174°10E **155** D5
Awbārī *Libya* 26°46N 12°57E **135** C8
Awbārī, Idehan *Libya* 27°10N 11°30E **135** C8
Awe, L. *U.K.* 56°17N 5°16W **65** E3
Awgu *Nigeria* 6°4N 7°24E **139** D6
Awjilah *Libya* 29°8N 21°7E **135** C10
Awkaman *Morocco* 31°52N 6°7W **136** B4
Awka *Nigeria* 6°12N 7°5E **139** D6
Ax-les-Thermes *France* 42°44N 1°50E **72** F5
Axat *France* 42°48N 2°13E **72** F6
Axe → *U.K.* 50°42N 3°4W **67** G5
Axel Heiberg I. *Canada* 80°0N 90°0W **161** B14
Axim *Ghana* 4°51N 2°15W **138** E4
Axintele *Romania* 44°37N 26°47E **81** F11
Axios → *Greece* 40°57N 22°35E **96** F6
Axminster *U.K.* 50°46N 3°0W **67** G4

Axson *U.S.A.* 31°17N 82°44W **178** D7
Axvall *Sweden* 58°23N 13°34E **63** F7
Ay *France* 49°3N 4°1E **71** C11
Ayabaca *Peru* 4°40S 79°53W **188** A2
Ayabe *Japan* 35°20N 135°20E **113** G7
Ayacucho *Argentina* 37°5S 58°20W **190** D4
Ayacucho *Peru* 13°0S 74°0W **188** C3
Ayacucho □ *Peru* 14°0S 74°0W **188** C3
Ayakkum Hu *China* 37°30N 89°20E **109** E11
Ayaköz *Kazakhstan* 47°30N 80°10E **109** C10
Ayaköz → *Kazakhstan* 46°40N 79°14E **109** C9
Ayakudi *India* 10°28N 77°56E **127** J3
Ayamé *Ivory C.* 5°35N 3°9W **138** D4
Ayamonte *Spain* 37°12N 7°24W **89** D3
Ayan *Russia* 56°30N 138°16E **107** D14
Ayanck *Turkey* 41°57N 34°35E **104** B6
Ayangba *Nigeria* 7°31N 7°8E **139** D6
Ayas *Turkey* 40°10N 32°50E **104** B5
Ayas *Afghan.* 36°15N 68°5E **109** E7
Ayaviri *Peru* 14°50S 70°35W **188** C3
Aybak *Afghan.* 36°15N 68°5E **109** E7
Aybasti *Turkey* 40°41N 37°23E **104** B7
Aydarko'l Ko'li
Uzbekistan 40°50N 67°10E **109** C10
Aydın *Turkey* 37°51N 27°51E **104** D2
Aydın □ *Turkey* 37°50N 28°0E **99** D9
Aydın Dağları *Turkey* 38°0N 28°0E **99** D10
Aydıngkol Hu *China* 42°40N 89°15E **109** D11
Ayenngré *Togo* 8°40N 1°1E **139** D5
Ayer Hitam *Malaysia* 5°24N 100°16E **121** c
Ayerbe *Spain* 42°17N 0°41W **90** C4
Ayer's Cliff *Canada* 45°10N 72°3W **175** A12
Ayers Rock = Uluru
Australia 25°23S 131°5E **149** E5
Ayeyarwady = Ayeyawadi →
Burma 15°50N 95°6E **123** M19
Ayeyawadi → *Burma* 15°50N 95°6E **123** M19
Áyia Napa *Cyprus* 34°59N 34°0E **101** E13
Áyia Phyla *Cyprus* 34°43N 33°1E **101** E12
Áyios Amvrósios
Cyprus 35°20N 33°35E **101** D12
Áyios Seryios *Cyprus* 35°12N 33°53E **101** D12
Áyios Theodhoros
Cyprus 35°22N 34°1E **101** D13
Áyios Yeóryios = Aghios Georgios
Greece 37°28N 23°57E **98** D5
Aykhal *Russia* 66°0N 111°30E **107** C12
Aykırıkçı *Turkey* 39°8N 30°9E **99** E12
Aylesbury *U.K.* 51°49N 0°49W **67** F7
Aylmer *Canada* 42°46N 80°59W **174** D4
Aylmer, L. *Canada* 64°5N 108°30W **160** E10
Ayn Dār *Si. Arabia* 25°55N 49°10E **129** E7
Ayn Sifni *Iraq* 36°41N 43°20E **105** D10
Ayn Zālah *Iraq* 36°45N 42°35E **105** D10
Ayna *Spain* 38°34N 2°3W **91** G2
Ayolas *Paraguay* 27°10S 56°59W **190** B4
Ayon, Ostrov *Russia* 69°50N 169°0E **107** C17
Ayora *Spain* 39°3N 1°3W **91** G3
Ayorou *Niger* 14°50N 0°52E **139** C5
'Ayoûn el 'Atroûs
Mauritania 16°38N 9°37W **138** B3
Ayr *Australia* 19°35S 147°25E **150** B4
Ayr *Canada* 43°17N 80°27W **174** C4
Ayr *U.K.* 55°28N 4°38W **65** F4
Ayr → *U.K.* 55°28N 4°38W **65** F4
Ayrancı *Turkey* 37°21N 33°41E **104** D5
Ayrancılar *Turkey* 38°15N 27°18E **99** C9
Ayre, Pt. of I. of Man 54°25N 4°21W **66** C3
Ayribaba *Turkmenistan* 37°50N 66°34E **109** E7
Aysén □ *Chile* 46°30S 73°0W **192** C2
Ayteke Bi *Kazakhstan* 45°48N 62°6E **108** C6
Ayton *Australia* 15°56S 145°22E **150** B4
Aytos *Bulgaria* 42°42N 27°16E **97** D11
Aytoska Planina
Bulgaria 42°45N 27°30E **97** D11
Ayu, Kepulauan
Indonesia 0°35N 131°5E **119** D8
Ayutla *Guatemala* 14°40N 92°10W **182** D1
Ayutla de los Libres
Mexico 16°54N 99°13W **181** D5
Ayutthaya = Phra Nakhon Si
Ayutthaya *Thailand* 14°25N 100°30E **120** E3
Ayvacık *Turkey* 39°36N 26°24E **104** C2
Ayvalık *Turkey* 39°20N 26°46E **99** B8
Az Zabadānī *Syria* 33°43N 36°5E **130** B5
Az Ẓāhirīyah
West Bank 31°25N 34°58E **130** D3
Az Zahrān *Si. Arabia* 26°10N 50°7E **129** E6
Az Zarqā *Jordan* 32°5N 36°4E **130** C5
Az Zarqā' *U.A.E.* 24°53N 53°4E **129** E7
Az Zarqā □ *Jordan* 32°5N 36°12E **130** C5
Az Zāwiyah *Libya* 32°52N 12°56E **135** B8
Az Zibār *Iraq* 36°52N 44°4E **105** D11
Az Zilfi *Si. Arabia* 26°12N 44°52E **128** E5
Az Zubayr *Iraq* 30°26N 47°40E **128** D5
Azad Kashmir □
Pakistan 33°50N 73°50E **125** C5
Azahar, Costa del *Spain* 40°0N 0°10E **90** F5
Azambuja *Portugal* 39°4N 8°51W **89** F2
Azamgarh *India* 26°5N 83°13E **125** E10
Azangaro *Peru* 14°55S 70°13W **188** C3
Azaouad *Mali* 19°0N 3°0W **138** B4
Azaouak, → *Mali* 15°50N 4°0E **139** B5
Azaouak, Vallée de l'
Mali 15°50N 3°20E **139** B5
Āzār Shahr *Iran* 37°45N 45°59E **105** D11
Azara *Nigeria* 8°22N 9°12E **139** D6
Azarān *Iran* 37°25N 47°16E **105** D12
Azärbayjan = Azerbaijan ■
Asia 40°20N 48°0E **87** K9
Āzärbāyjān-e Gharbī □
Iran 37°0N 44°30E **128** B5
Āzärbāyjān-e Sharqī □
Iran 37°20N 47°0E **128** B5
Azay-le-Rideau *France* 47°16N 0°30E **70** E7
Azazga *Algeria* 36°36N 37°4E **136** A7
A'zāz *Syria* 36°36N 37°4E **130** A3
Azbine = Aïr *Niger* 18°30N 8°0E **139** A6
Azeffoun *Algeria* 36°51N 4°26E **136** A6
Azemmour *Morocco* 33°20N 9°20W **136** B4
Azerbaijan ■ *Asia* 40°20N 48°0E **87** K9
Azkoien = Peralta *Spain* 42°20N 1°48W **90** C3
Azilal *Morocco* 31°57N 6°13W **136** B4
Azilda *Canada* 46°33N 81°9W **174** A3
Azimganj *India* 24°14S 88°15E **125** G12
Azizçıye *France* 36°17N 11°49E **136** A5
Azores = Açores, Is. dos
Atl. Oc. 38°0N 27°0W **134** a
Azores-Biscay Rise
Atl. Oc. 42°0N 20°0W **56** B9
Azov *Russia* 47°3N 39°25E **87** G4
Azov, Sea of *Europe* 46°0N 36°30E **87** J6
Azov, Sea of = Azov, Sea of
Europe 46°0N 36°30E **87** J6
Azovskoye More = Azov, Sea of
Europe 46°0N 36°30E **87** J6
Azpeitia *Spain* 43°12N 2°19W **90** B2
Azraq ash Shīshān
Jordan 31°50N 36°49E **130** D5
Azrou *Morocco* 33°28N 5°19W **136** B3
Aztec *U.S.A.* 36°49N 107°59W **169** H10
Azua de Compostela
Dom. Rep. 18°25N 70°44W **183** C5
Azuaga *Spain* 38°16N 5°39W **89** G5
Azuara *Spain* 41°15N 0°53W **90** D4
Azuer → *Spain* 39°8N 3°36W **89** F7
Azuero, Pen. de *Panama* 7°30N 80°30W **182** E3
Azuga *Romania* 45°27N 25°33E **81** E10
Azul *Argentina* 36°42S 59°43W **190** D4
Azumino *Japan* 36°20N 137°50E **113** F8
Azur, Côte d' *France* 43°25N 7°10E **73** E11
Azusa *U.S.A.* 34°8N 117°52W **171** L9
Azzaba *Algeria* 36°48N 7°6E **136** A6
Azzano Décimo *Italy* 45°52N 12°56E **93** C9
Azzel Matti, Sebkra
Algeria 26°10N 0°43E **136** C4

B

Ba Be △ *Vietnam* 22°25N 105°37E **120** A5
Ba Don *Vietnam* 17°45N 106°26E **120** D6
Ba Dong *Vietnam* 9°40N 106°33E **121** H6
Ba Ngoi *Vietnam* 11°54N 109°10E **121** G7
Ba Ria *Vietnam* 10°30N 107°10E **121** G6
Ba Tri *Vietnam* 10°2N 106°36E **121** G6
Ba Vì △ *Vietnam* 21°1N 105°22E **120** B5
Ba Xian = Bazhou
China 39°8N 116°22E **114** E9
Baa *Indonesia* 10°50S 123°0E **148** B3
Baalbek = Ba'labakk
Lebanon 34°0N 36°10E **130** B5
Baamonde *Spain* 43°7N 7°44W **88** B3
Baardheere *Somalia* 2°20N 42°27E **131** G3
Baarle-Nassau *Belgium* 51°27N 4°56E **69** C4
Bab al Mandeb *Red Sea* 12°35N 43°25E **131** E3
Bābā, Koh-i- *Afghan.* 34°30N 67°0E **109** F7
Baba Budan Hills *India* 13°30N 75°44E **127** H2
Baba Burnu *Turkey* 39°29N 26°2E **99** B8
Baba dag *Azerbaijan* 41°0N 48°19E **87** K9
Bābā Kalū *Iran* 30°7N 50°49E **129** D6
Babaçulândia *Brazil* 7°13S 47°46W **189** D1
Babadag *Romania* 44°53N 28°44E **81** F13
Babadağ *Turkey* 37°49N 28°53E **99** D10
Babaeski *Turkey* 41°26N 27°6E **97** E11
Babahoyo *Ecuador* 1°40S 79°30W **186** D3
Babai = Sarju → *India* 27°21N 81°23E **125** F9
Babai = Nepal 28°10N 82°2E **125** E10
Babana *Nigeria* 10°31N 3°46E **139** C5
Babar *Indonesia* 8°0S 129°30E **119** F7
Babar *Pakistan* 31°7N 69°32E **124** D3
Babarkach *Pakistan* 29°45N 68°0E **124** E3
Babayevo *Russia* 59°24N 35°55E **84** C8
Babb *U.S.A.* 48°51N 113°27W **168** B7
Babenhausen *Germany* 49°57N 8°57E **77** F4
Băbeni *Romania* 44°59N 24°11E **81** F9
Baberu *India* 25°33N 80°43E **125** G9
Babi Besar, Pulau
Malaysia 2°25N 103°59E **121** L4
Babia Gora *Europe* 49°38N 19°38E **83** J6
Babian Jiang → *China* 22°55N 101°47E **116** F3
Bābil □ *Iraq* 32°30N 44°30E **128** C5
Babimost *Poland* 52°10N 15°49E **81** F2
Babinda *Australia* 17°20S 145°56E **150** B4
Babine *Canada* 55°22N 126°37E **162** B3
Babine → *Canada* 55°45N 127°44W **162** B3
Babine L. *Canada* 54°48N 126°0W **162** C3
Babiogórski △ *Poland* 49°38N 19°38E **83** J6
Babo *Indonesia* 2°30S 133°30E **119** E8
Babócsa *Hungary* 46°2N 17°21E **80** D2
Bābol *Iran* 36°40N 52°50E **129** B7
Bābol Sar *Iran* 36°45N 52°45E **129** B7
Babor, Dj. *Algeria* 36°31N 5°25E **136** A5
Baborów *Poland* 50°7N 18°1E **83** H5
Baboua *C.A.R.* 5°49N 14°58E **140** C2
Babruysk *Belarus* 53°10N 29°15E **75** D15
Babson Park *U.S.A.* 27°49N 81°32W **179** H8
Babuhri *India* 26°49N 69°43E **124** F3
Babuna *Macedonia* 41°30N 21°40E **96** D5
Babura *Nigeria* 12°51N 8°59E **139** C6
Babusar Pass *Pakistan* 35°12N 73°59E **125** B5
Babušnica *Serbia* 43°7N 22°27E **96** C8
Babuyan Chan. *Phil.* 18°40N 121°30E **119** A6
Babylon *Iraq* 32°34N 44°22E **128** C5
Bač *Serbia* 45°29N 19°17E **80** E4
Bắc = *Moldova* 45°9N 28°4E **81** F14
Bac Can *Vietnam* 22°8N 105°49E **116** F5
Bac Giang *Vietnam* 21°16N 106°11E **116** G6
Bac Lieu *Vietnam* 9°17N 105°43E **121** H5
Bac Ninh *Vietnam* 21°13N 106°4E **116** G6
Bac Phan *Vietnam* 22°0N 105°0E **116** G5
Bacabal *Brazil* 4°15S 44°45W **189** A2
Bacalar *Mexico* 18°43N 87°27W **181** D7
Bacan, Kepulauan
Indonesia 0°35S 127°30E **119** E7
Baccarat *France* 48°28N 6°42E **71** D13
Bacchus Marsh
Australia 37°43S 144°27E **152** D6
Bacerac *Mexico* 30°18N 108°50W **180** A3
Băcești *Romania* 46°50N 27°11E **81** D12
Bach Long Vi, Dao
Vietnam 20°10N 107°40E **120** B6
Bach Ma △ *Vietnam* 16°11N 107°49E **120** D6
Bacharach *Germany* 50°3N 7°46E **77** E3
Bachhwara *India* 25°35N 85°54E **125** G11
Bachu *China* 39°48N 78°12E **124** B6
Bačina *Serbia* 43°42N 21°23E **96** C9
Back → *Canada* 65°10N 104°0W **161** D9
Bačka Palanka *Serbia* 45°17N 19°27E **80** E4
Bačka Topola *Serbia* 45°49N 19°39E **80** E4
Bäckefors *Sweden* 58°48N 12°9E **63** F6
Bäckhammar *Sweden* 59°10N 14°11E **62** F7
Bački Petrovac *Serbia* 45°29N 19°32E **80** E4
Backnang *Germany* 48°56N 9°26E **77** G5
Backstairs Passage
Australia 35°40S 138°5E **152** D2
Bacolod *Phil.* 10°40N 122°57E **119** B6

Baconton *U.S.A.* 31°23N 84°10W **178** D5
Bacqueville-en-Caux
France 49°47N 1°0E **70** C8
Bács-Kiskun □ *Hungary* 46°43N 19°30E **80** D4
Bácsalmás *Hungary* 46°8N 19°17E **80** D4
Bacuk *Malaysia* 6°4N 102°25E **121** J4
Bácum *Mexico* 27°33N 110°5W **180** B2
Bād *Iran* 33°41N 52°1E **129** C7
Bad → *U.S.A.* 44°21N 100°22W **172** C3
Bad Aussee *Austria* 47°43N 13°45E **78** D6
Bad Axe *U.S.A.* 43°48N 83°0W **174** C2
Bad Bergzabern *Germany* 49°6N 7°59E **77** F3
Bad Berleburg *Germany* 51°2N 8°26E **76** D4
Bad Bevensen *Germany* 53°5N 10°35E **76** B6
Bad Bramstedt *Germany* 53°55N 9°53E **76** B5
Bad Brückenau *Germany* 50°18N 9°47E **77** E5
Bad Doberan *Germany* 54°6N 11°55E **76** A7
Bad Driburg *Germany* 51°43N 9°1E **76** D5
Bad Ems *Germany* 50°20N 7°43E **77** E3
Bad Frankenhausen
Germany 51°21N 11°5E **76** D7
Bad Freienwalde
Germany 52°46N 14°1E **76** C10
Bad Goisern *Austria* 47°38N 13°38E **78** D6
Bad Harzburg *Germany* 51°52N 10°34E **76** D6
Bad Hersfeld *Germany* 50°52N 9°42E **76** E5
Bad Hofgastein *Austria* 47°17N 13°6E **78** D6
Bad Homburg *Germany* 50°13N 8°37E **77** E4
Bad Honnef *Germany* 50°38N 7°13E **76** E3
Bad Iburg *Germany* 52°10N 8°3E **76** C4
Bad Ischl *Austria* 47°44N 13°38E **78** D6
Bad Kissingen *Germany* 50°11N 10°4E **77** E6
Bad Königshofen
Germany 50°18N 10°29E **77** E6
Bad Kreuznach *Germany* 49°50N 7°51E **77** F3
Bad Krozingen *Germany* 47°54N 7°42E **77** H3
Bad Laasphe *Germany* 50°56N 8°25E **76** E4
Bad Langensalza
Germany 51°5N 10°38E **76** D6
Bad Lauterberg *Germany* 51°38N 10°28E **76** D6
Bad Leonfelden *Austria* 48°31N 14°18E **78** C7
Bad Liebenwerda
Germany 51°31N 13°24E **76** D9
Bad Mergentheim
Germany 49°29N 9°42E **77** F5
Bad Münstereifel
Germany 50°33N 6°46E **76** E2
Bad Nauheim *Germany* 50°22N 8°44E **77** E4
Bad Neuenahr-Ahrweiler
Germany 50°32N 7°5E **76** E3
Bad Neustadt *Germany* 50°18N 10°13E **77** E6
Bad Oeynhausen
Germany 52°12N 8°46E **76** C4
Bad Oldesloe *Germany* 53°48N 10°22E **76** B6
Bad Orb *Germany* 50°13N 9°20E **77** E5
Bad Pyrmont *Germany* 51°59N 9°16E **76** D5
Bad Reichenhall
Germany 47°43N 12°54E **77** H8
Bad Säckingen *Germany* 47°33N 7°56E **77** H3
Bad Salzuflen *Germany* 52°6N 8°45E **76** C4
Bad Salzungen *Germany* 50°48N 10°14E **76** E6
Bad Sankt Leonhard
Austria 46°58N 14°47E **78** E7
Bad Schwartau *Germany* 53°55N 10°41E **76** B6
Bad Segeberg *Germany* 53°56N 10°18E **76** B6
Bad Tölz *Germany* 47°45N 11°34E **77** H7
Bad Urach *Germany* 48°29N 9°23E **77** G5
Bad Vöslau *Austria* 47°58N 16°12E **79** D9
Bad Waldsee *Germany* 47°55N 9°45E **77** H5
Bad Wildungen *Germany* 51°6N 9°7E **76** D5
Bad Wimpfen *Germany* 49°13N 9°11E **77** F5
Bad Windsheim
Germany 49°36N 10°25E **77** F6
Bad Zwischenahn
Germany 53°12N 8°1E **76** B4
Bada Barabil *India* 22°7N 85°24E **125** H11
Badagara = Vadakara
India 11°35N 75°40E **127** J2
Badagri *Nigeria* 6°25N 2°55E **139** D5
Badain Jaran Shamo
China 40°23N 102°0E **110** C9
Badajós, L. *Brazil* 3°15S 62°50W **186** D6
Badajoz *Spain* 38°50N 6°59W **89** G4
Badajoz □ *Spain* 38°40N 6°30W **89** G5
Badakhshān □ *Afghan.* 36°30N 71°0E **109** E8
Badaling *China* 40°20N 116°0E **114** D9
Badalona *Spain* 41°26N 2°15E **90** D7
Badalzai *Afghan.* 29°50N 65°35E **124** E1
Badami *India* 15°55N 75°41E **127** G2
Badampahar *India* 22°10N 86°10E **125** H11
Badanah *Si. Arabia* 30°58N 41°30E **128** D4
Badarinath *India* 30°45N 79°29E **125** D8
Badas, Kepulauan
Indonesia 0°45N 107°5E **118** D3
Baddo → *Pakistan* 28°0N 64°20E **122** F4
Bade *Indonesia* 7°10S 139°35E **119** F9
Badeggi *Nigeria* 9°3N 6°9E **139** D6
Badéguichéri *Niger* 13°42N 5°32E **139** C6
Baden *Austria* 48°1N 16°13E **79** C9
Baden *Switz.* 47°28N 8°18E **72** a
Baden *U.S.A.* 40°38N 80°14W **174** F4
Baden-Baden *Germany* 48°44N 8°13E **77** G4
Baden-Württemberg □
Germany 48°20N 8°40E **77** G4
Badgam *India* 34°1N 74°45E **125** B6
Badgastein *Austria* 47°7N 13°9E **78** D6
Badger *Canada* 49°0N 56°4W **165** C8
Badger *U.S.A.* 36°38N 119°1W **170** J7
Bādghīs □ *Afghan.* 35°0N 63°0E **108** F2
Badgingarra
Australia 30°23S 115°22E **149** F2
Badia Polésine *Italy* 45°6N 11°30E **92** C8
Badin *Pakistan* 24°38N 68°54E **124** G3
Badiar △ *Guinea* 13°10N 13°20E **138** C2
Badin *U.S.A.* 35°24N 80°7W **179** B6
Badlands *U.S.A.* 43°38N 102°56W **172** D2
Badme *Africa* 14°43N 37°48E **131** E2
Badnera *India* 20°48N 77°44E **126** D3
Badogo *Mali* 11°2N 8°13W **138** C3
Badoumbé *Mali* 13°42N 10°59E **138** C2
Badrah *Iraq* 33°6N 45°58E **105** F11
Badrain Jaran Shamo
China 40°40N 103°0E **114** D2
Badrinath *India* 30°44N 79°29E **125** D8
Badulla *Sri Lanka* 7°1N 81°7E **127** L5
Badung, Bukit
Indonesia 8°49S 115°10E **119** K18
Badung, Selat
Indonesia 8°40S 115°22E **119** K18

Badvel India 14°45N 79°3E **127** G4
Baena Spain 37°37N 4°20W **89** H6
Baengnyeongdo
  S. Korea 37°57N 124°40E **115** F13
Baerami Australia 32°27S 150°27E **153** B9
Baetov Kyrgyzstan 41°13N 74°54E **109** D8
Baeza Spain 37°57N 3°25W **89** H7
Bafang Cameroon 5°9N 10°11E **139** D7
Bafatá Guinea-Biss. 12°8N 14°40W **138** C2
Baffin B. N. Amer. 72°0N 64°0W **158** B13
Baffin I. Canada 68°0N 75°0W **161** D17
Bafia Cameroon 4°40N 11°10E **139** E7
Bafilo Togo 9°22N 1°22E **139** D5
Bafing → Mali 13°49N 10°50W **138** C2
Bafing △ Mali 12°38N 10°28W **138** C2
Bafliyūn Syria 36°37N 36°59E **128** B3
Bafoulabé Mali 13°50N 10°55W **138** C2
Bafoussam Cameroon 5°28N 10°25E **139** D7
Bāfq Iran 31°40N 55°25E **129** D7
Bafra Turkey 41°34N 35°54E **104** B6
Bafra Burnu Turkey 41°45N 36°2E **104** B7
Bāft Iran 29°15N 56°38E **129** D8
Bafut Cameroon 6°6N 10°2E **139** D7
Bafwasende
  Dem. Rep. of the Congo 1°3N 27°5E **142** B2
Bagaha India 27°6N 84°5E **126** A7
Bagalkot India 16°10N 75°40E **127** F2
Bagam Niger 15°43N 6°35E **139** B6
Bagamoyo Tanzania 6°28S 38°55E **142** D4
Bagan Datoh Malaysia 3°59N 100°47E **121** L3
Bagan Serai Malaysia 5°1N 100°32E **121** K3
Baganga Phil. 7°34N 126°33E **119** C7
Bagani Namibia 18°7S 21°41E **144** A3
Bagansiapiapi Indonesia 2°12N 100°50E **118** D2
Bagasra India 21°30N 71°0E **124** J4
Bagaud India 22°19N 75°53E **124** H6
Bagdad Calif., U.S.A. 34°35N 115°53W **171** L11
Bagdad Fla., U.S.A. 30°36N 87°2W **179** E2
Bagdarin Russia 54°26N 113°36E **107** D12
Bagé Brazil 31°20S 54°15W **191** C5
Bagenalstown Ireland 52°42N 6°58W **64** D5
Bagepalli India 13°47N 77°47E **127** H3
Bageshwar India 29°51N 79°46E **125** E8
Bagevadi India 16°35N 75°58E **126** F2
Baggs U.S.A. 41°2N 107°39W **168** F10
Bagh Pakistan 33°59N 73°45E **125** C5
Baghain → India 25°32N 81°1E **125** G9
Baghdād Iraq 33°20N 44°23E **105** F11
Baghdadi Georgia 42°5N 42°49E **105** A10
Bagheria Italy 38°5N 13°30E **94** D6
Baghlān Afghan. 32°12N 68°46E **109** E7
Baghlān □ Afghan. 36°0N 68°30E **109** E7
Bagley U.S.A. 47°32N 95°24W **172** B6
Baglung Nepal 28°16N 83°36E **125** E10
Bagnara Cálabra Italy 38°17N 15°48E **95** D8
Bagnasco Italy 44°18N 8°2E **92** D5
Bagnères-de-Bigorre France 43°5N 0°9E **72** E4
Bagnères-de-Luchon
  France 42°47N 0°38E **72** F4
Bagni di Lucca Italy 44°1N 10°35E **92** D7
Bagno di Romagna Italy 43°50N 11°57E **93** E8
Bagnoles-de-l'Orne
  France 48°32N 0°25W **70** D6
Bagnols-sur-Cèze France 44°10N 4°36E **73** D8
Bagnorégio Italy 42°37N 12°5E **93** F9
Bago Burma 17°20N 96°29E **123** L20
Bagodar India 24°5N 85°52E **125** G11
Bagrationovsk Russia 54°23N 20°39E **82** D7
Bagrdan Serbia 44°5N 21°11E **96** B5
Bagua Peru 5°35S 78°22W **188** B2
Baguio Phil. 16°26N 120°34E **119** A6
Bagyurdu Turkey 38°25N 27°41E **99** C9
Bagzane, Monts Niger 17°43N 8°45E **139** B6
Bahabón de Esgueva
  Spain 41°52N 3°43W **88** D7
Bahadurganj India 26°16N 87°49E **125** F12
Bahadurgarh India 28°40N 76°57E **124** E7
Bahama, Canal Viejo de
  W. Indies 22°10N 77°30W **182** B4
Bahamas ■ N. Amer. 24°0N 75°0W **183** B5
Bahār Iran 34°54N 48°26E **105** E13
Baharampur India 24°2N 88°27E **125** G13
Baharîya, El Wâhât al
  Egypt 28°0N 28°50E **137** F6
Baharu Pandan = Pandan
  Malaysia 1°32N 103°46E **121** d
Bahawalnagar Pakistan 30°0N 73°15E **124** E5
Bahawalpur Pakistan 29°24N 71°40E **124** E4
Bahçe Turkey 37°13N 36°34E **104** D7
Bahçecik Turkey 40°41N 29°44E **97** F13
Bäherden Turkmenistan 38°25N 57°26E **129** B8
Baheri India 28°45N 79°34E **125** E8
Bahgul → India 27°45N 79°36E **125** E8
Bahi Tanzania 5°58S 35°21E **142** D4
Bahi Swamp Tanzania 6°10S 35°0E **142** D4
Bahía = Salvador Brazil 13°0S 38°30W **189** D3
Bahía □ Brazil 12°0S 42°0W **189** C2
Bahía, Is. de la
  Honduras 16°45N 86°15W **182** C2
Bahía Blanca Argentina 38°35S 62°13W **190** D3
Bahía de Caráquez
  Ecuador 0°40S 80°27W **186** D2
Bahía de Los Angeles
  Mexico 28°56N 113°34W **180** B2
Bahía Honda Cuba 22°54N 83°10W **182** B3
Bahía Kino Mexico 28°47N 111°58W **180** B2
Bahía Laura Argentina 48°10S 66°30W **192** C3
Bahía Mansa Chile 40°33S 73°46W **192** D2
Bahía Negra Paraguay 20°5S 58°5W **186** H7
Bahir Dar Ethiopia 11°37N 37°10E **131** E2
Bahmanzād Iran 31°15N 51°47E **129** D6
Bahmer Algeria 27°19N 0°32E **138** C6
Bahr el Ahmar □ Sudan 20°0N 35°0E **137** D4
Bahraich India 27°38N 81°37E **125** F9
Bahrain ■ Asia 26°0N 50°35E **129** E6
Bahror India 27°51N 76°20E **124** F6
Bāhū Kalāt Iran 25°43N 61°25E **129** E9
Bai Mali 13°35N 3°28W **138** C4
Bai Bung, Mui = Ca Mau, Mui
  Vietnam 8°38N 104°44E **121** H5
Bai Thuong Vietnam 19°54N 105°23E **120** C5
Baia de Aramă Romania 45°0N 22°50E **80** E7
Baia Mare Romania 47°40N 23°35E **81** C8
Baia-Sprie Romania 47°41N 23°43E **81** C8
Baião Brazil 2°40S 49°40W **187** D9
Baïbokoum Chad 7°46N 15°43E **135** G9
Baicheng Jilin, China 45°38N 122°42E **115** B12
Baicheng Xinjiang Uygur,
  China 41°46N 81°52E **109** D10
Băicoi Romania 45°3N 25°52E **81** E10
Baidoa = Baydhabo
  Somalia 3°8N 43°30E **131** G3

Baie-Comeau Canada 49°12N 68°10W **165** C6
Baie-St-Paul Canada 47°28N 70°32W **165** C5
Baie Ste-Anne Seychelles 4°18S 55°45E **141** b
Baie-Trinité Canada 49°25N 67°20W **165** C6
Baie Verte Canada 49°55N 56°12W **165** C8
Baignes-Ste-Radegonde
  France 45°23N 0°25W **72** C3
Baigneux-les-Juifs
  France 47°31N 4°39E **71** E11
Baihar India 22°6N 80°33E **125** H9
Baihe Hubei, China 32°50N 110°5E **117** A8
Baihe Jilin, China 42°27N 128°9E **115** C15
Ba'ījī Iraq 35°0N 43°30E **105** F10
Baijnath India 29°55N 79°37E **125** E8
Baikal, L. = Baykal, Oz.
  Russia 53°0N 108°0E **107** D11
Baikonur = Bayqonyr
  Kazakhstan 45°40N 63°20E **108** C6
Baikunthpur India 23°15N 82°33E **125** H10
Bailadila, Mt. India 18°43N 81°15E **126** E5
Baile Átha Cliath = Dublin
  Ireland 53°21N 6°15W **64** C5
Baile Átha Fhirdhia = Ardee
  Ireland 53°52N 6°33W **64** C5
Baile Átha Í = Athy Ireland 53°0N 7°0W **64** C5
Baile Átha Luain = Athlone
  Ireland 53°25N 7°56W **64** C4
Baile Átha Troim = Trim
  Ireland 53°33N 6°48W **64** C5
Baile Brigín = Balbriggan
  Ireland 53°37N 6°11W **64** C5
Bāile Govora Romania 45°5N 24°11E **81** E9
Bāile Herculane Romania 44°53N 22°26E **80** F7
Baile Olănești Romania 45°12N 24°14E **81** E9
Baile Sear = Baleshare
  U.K. 57°31N 7°22W **65** D1
Bāile Tușnad Romania 46°9N 25°51E **81** D10
Bailén Spain 38°8N 3°48W **89** G7
Bāilești Romania 44°1N 23°20E **81** F8
Bailhongal India 15°55N 74°53E **127** G2
Bailieborough Ireland 53°56N 6°59W **64** C5
Baima China 33°0N 100°26E **116** A3
Bain-de-Bretagne France 47°50N 1°40W **70** E5
Bainbridge Ga., U.S.A. 30°55N 84°35W **178** E5
Bainbridge N.Y.,
  U.S.A. 42°18N 75°29W **175** D9
Bainbridge Island
  U.S.A. 47°38N 122°32W **170** C4
Baine China 42°0N 128°0E **111** C14
Baing Indonesia 10°14S 120°34E **119** G6
Bainiu China 32°50N 112°15E **117** A9
Baiona Spain 42°6N 8°52W **88** C2
Bā'ir Jordan 30°45N 36°55E **130** D5
Baird Mts. U.S.A. 67°0N 160°0W **166** B8
Bairiki = Tarawa
  Kiribati 1°30N 173°0E **156** G9
Bairin Youqi China 43°30N 118°35E **115** C10
Bairin Zuoqi China 43°58N 119°15E **115** C10
Bairnsdale Australia 37°48S 147°36E **153** D7
Baisha China 34°20N 112°32E **114** G7
Baisha Li China 19°12N 109°20E **117** a
Baishan = Hunjiang
  China 41°54N 126°26E **115** C14
Baishan China 42°43N 127°14E **115** C14
Baissa Nigeria 7°14N 10°38E **139** D7
Baitadi Nepal 29°35N 80°25E **125** E9
Baitarani → India 20°45N 86°48E **126** D8
Baixa Grande Brazil 11°57S 40°11W **189** C2
Baixa Limia-Sierra do Xurés △
  Spain 41°50N 8°0W **88** C3
Baiyin China 36°45N 104°14E **114** F3
Baiyü China 31°16N 98°50E **116** B2
Baiyu Shan China 37°15N 107°30E **114** F4
Baj Baj India 22°30N 88°5E **125** H13
Baja Hungary 46°12N 18°59E **80** D3
Baja, Pta. Mexico 29°58N 115°49W **180** B1
Baja California
  Mexico 31°10N 115°12W **180** A1
Baja California □
  Mexico 30°0N 115°0W **180** B2
Baja California Sur □
  Mexico 25°50N 111°50W **180** B2
Bajag India 22°40N 81°21E **125** H9
Bajamar Canary Is. 28°33N 16°20W **100** F3
Bajana India 23°7N 71°49E **124** H4
Bajatrejo Indonesia 8°29S 114°19E **119** J17
Bajawa Indonesia 8°47S 120°59E **119** F6
Bajera Indonesia 8°31S 115°2E **119** J18
Bājgīrān Iran 37°36N 58°24E **129** B8
Bajimba, Mt. Australia 29°17S 152°6E **151** D5
Bajina Bašta Serbia 43°58N 19°35E **96** C3
Bajmok Serbia 45°57N 19°24E **80** E4
Bajo Boquete Panama 8°46N 82°27W **182** E3
Bajo Caracoles
  Argentina 47°27S 70°56W **192** C2
Bajo Nuevo Caribbean 15°40N 78°50W **183** D4
Bajoga Nigeria 10°57N 11°20E **139** C7
Bajool Australia 23°40S 150°35E **150** C5
Bak Hungary 46°43N 16°51E **80** D1
Bakar Croatia 45°18N 14°32E **93** C11
Bakassi Pen. Cameroon 4°42N 8°20E **139** E6
Bakel Senegal 14°56N 12°20W **138** C2
Bakel Calif., U.S.A. 35°16N 116°4W **171** K10
Baker Fla., U.S.A. 30°48N 86°41W **179** E3
Baker Mont., U.S.A. 46°22N 104°17W **168** C11
Baker, Canal Chile 47°45S 74°44W **192** C2
Baker, L. Canada 64°0N 96°0W **160** E12
Baker, Mt. U.S.A. 48°50N 121°49W **168** A3
Baker City U.S.A. 44°47N 117°50W **168** D5
Baker I. Pac. Oc. 0°10N 176°35W **156** G10
Baker I. U.S.A. 55°20N 133°40W **162** B2
Baker Lake Canada 64°20N 96°3W **160** E12
Bakerhill U.S.A. 31°47N 85°18W **178** D4
Bakers Creek Australia 21°13S 149°7E **150** C4
Bakers Dozen Is.
  Canada 56°45N 78°45W **164** A4
Bakersfield Calif.,
  U.S.A. 35°23N 119°1W **171** K8
Bakersfield Vt., U.S.A. 44°45N 72°48W **175** B12
Bakharden = Bäherden
  Turkmenistan 38°25N 57°26E **129** B8
Bakhchysaray Ukraine 44°40N 33°45E **85** K7
Bakhmach Ukraine 51°10N 32°45E **85** G7
Bākhtarān = Kermānshāh
  Iran 34°23N 47°0E **105** E12
Bākhtarān = Kermānshāh □
  Iran 34°0N 46°30E **128** C5
Bakhtegān, Daryācheh-ye
  Iran 29°40N 53°50E **129** D7

Bakhtegān △ Iran 29°51N 53°40E **129** D7
Bakır Azerbaijan 40°29N 49°56E **87** K9
Bakır → Turkey 38°55N 27°0E **99** C9
Bakırdağı Turkey 38°13N 35°46E **104** C6
Bakkafjörður Iceland 66°2N 14°48W **60** C6
Bakkagerði Iceland 65°31N 13°49W **60** D7
Baklan Turkey 38°0N 29°36E **99** C11
Bako Ivory C. 9°8N 7°40W **138** D3
Bakony Hungary 47°10N 17°30E **80** C2
Bakony Forest = Bakony
  Hungary 47°10N 17°30E **80** C2
Bakori Nigeria 11°34N 7°25E **139** C6
Bakouma C.A.R. 5°40N 22°56E **140** C4
Baksan Russia 43°42N 43°32E **87** J6
Bakswaho India 24°15N 79°18E **125** G8
Baku = Bakı Azerbaijan 40°29N 49°56E **87** K9
Bakundi Nigeria 8°2N 10°45E **139** D7
Bakuriani Georgia 41°44N 43°31E **105** B10
Baky = Bakı Azerbaijan 40°29N 49°56E **87** K9
Bala Senegal 14°1N 13°8W **138** C2
Balâ Turkey 39°32N 33°7E **104** C5
Bala U.K. 52°54N 3°36W **66** E4
Bala, L. U.K. 52°53N 3°37W **66** E4
Bālā Morghāb Afghan. 35°35N 63°20E **108** E6
Balabac I. Phil. 8°0N 117°0E **118** C5
Balabac Str. E. Indies 7°53N 117°5E **118** C5
Balabagh Afghan. 34°25N 70°12E **124** B4
Ba'labakk Lebanon 34°0N 36°10E **130** B5
Balabalangan, Kepulauan
  Indonesia 2°20S 117°30E **118** E5
Bălăcița Romania 44°23N 23°8E **81** F8
Balad Iraq 34°0N 44°9E **105** F11
Balad Rūz Iraq 33°42N 45°5E **105** F11
Bālādeh Fārs, Iran 29°17N 51°56E **129** D6
Bālādeh Māzandaran,
  Iran 36°12N 51°48E **129** B6
Balaghat India 21°49N 80°12E **125** J9
Balaghat Ra. India 18°50N 76°30E **126** E3
Balaguer Spain 41°50N 0°50E **90** D6
Balakän Azerbaijan 41°43N 46°24E **87** K8
Balakhna Russia 56°25N 43°32E **86** B6
Balaklava Australia 34°7S 138°22E **152** C3
Balaklava Ukraine 44°30N 33°30E **85** K7
Balakliya Ukraine 49°28N 36°55E **85** H9
Balakovo Russia 52°4N 47°55E **86** D8
Balamau India 27°10N 80°21E **125** F9
Bālan Romania 46°39N 25°49E **81** D10
Balancán Mexico 17°48N 91°32W **181** D6
Balangir India 20°43N 83°35E **126** D6
Balapur India 20°40N 76°45E **126** D3
Balashikha Russia 55°48N 37°58E **84** E9
Balashov Russia 51°30N 43°10E **86** E6
Balasinor India 22°57N 73°23E **124** H5
Balasore = Baleshwar
  India 21°35N 87°3E **126** D8
Balassagyarmat Hungary 48°4N 19°15E **80** B4
Balāt Egypt 25°36N 29°19E **137** B2
Balaton Hungary 46°50N 17°40E **80** D2
Balaton-Felvidéki △
  Hungary 46°52N 17°30E **80** D2
Balatonboglár Hungary 46°46N 17°40E **80** D2
Balatonfüred Hungary 46°58N 17°54E **80** D2
Balatonszentgyörgy
  Hungary 46°41N 17°19E **80** D2
Balazote Spain 38°54N 2°9W **91** G2
Balbieriškis Lithuania 54°32N 23°52E **82** D10
Balbigny France 45°49N 4°11E **73** C8
Balbina, Represa de
  Brazil 2°0S 59°30W **186** D7
Balboa Panama 8°57N 79°34W **182** E4
Balbriggan Ireland 53°37N 6°11W **64** C5
Balcarce Argentina 38°0S 58°10W **190** D4
Balcarres Canada 50°50N 103°35W **163** C8
Balchik Bulgaria 43°28N 28°11E **97** C12
Bălcești Romania 44°37N 23°57E **81** F8
Balclutha N.Z. 46°15S 169°45E **155** G4
Balcones Escarpment
  U.S.A. 29°30N 99°15W **176** G5
Balçova Turkey 38°22N 27°4E **99** C9
Bald I. Australia 34°57S 118°27E **149** F2
Bald Knob U.S.A. 35°19N 91°34W **176** D9
Baldock L. Canada 56°33N 97°57W **163** B9
Baldoyle Ireland 53°24N 6°10W **64** C5
Baldwin Fla., U.S.A. 30°18N 81°59W **178** E4
Baldwin Mich., U.S.A. 43°54N 85°51W **173** D11
Baldwin Pa., U.S.A. 40°21N 79°58W **174** F5
Baldwinsville U.S.A. 43°10N 76°20W **175** C8
Baldy Peak U.S.A. 33°54N 109°34W **169** K9
Bale Croatia 45°4N 13°46E **93** C10
Baleares, Is. Spain 39°30N 3°0E **90** B10
Balearic Is. = Baleares, Is.
  Spain 39°30N 3°0E **90** B10
Baleia, Pta. da Brazil 17°40S 39°7W **189** D3
Baleine → Canada 58°15N 67°40W **165** A6
Baleine, Petite R. de la →
  Canada 56°0N 76°45W **164** A4
Băleni Romania 45°48N 27°51E **81** E12
Baler Phil. 15°46N 121°34E **119** A6
Baleshare U.K. 57°31N 7°22W **65** D1
Baleshwar India 21°35N 87°3E **126** D8
Baley Russia 51°36N 116°37E **107** D12
Balezino Russia 58°2N 53°6E **86** B11
Balfate Honduras 15°48N 86°25W **182** C2
Balgo Australia 20°9S 127°58E **148** D4
Balharshah India 19°10N 79°45E **126** E4
Bali Cameroon 5°54N 10°0E **139** D7
Bali Greece 35°25N 24°47E **101** D6
Bali India 25°11N 73°17E **124** G5
Bali Indonesia 8°20S 115°0E **118** F5
Bali □ Indonesia 8°20S 115°0E **118** F5
Bali, Selat Indonesia 8°18S 114°25E **119** J17
Bali Barat △ Indonesia 8°12S 114°35E **119** J17
Bali Sea Indonesia 8°0S 115°0E **118** F5
Balia S. Leone 9°22N 11°1W **138** D2
Baliapal India 21°40N 87°17E **125** J12
Baligród Poland 49°20N 22°17E **83** J9
Baliguda India 20°12N 83°55E **126** D6
Balik Pulau Malaysia 5°21N 100°14E **121** c
Balıkeşir Turkey 39°39N 27°53E **99** B9
Balıkeşir □ Turkey 39°45N 28°0E **99** B9
Balıklıçeşme Turkey 40°10N 27°35E **97** F11
Balikpapan Indonesia 1°10S 116°55E **118** E5
Balimbing Phil. 5°5N 119°58E **119** C5
Baling Malaysia 5°41N 100°55E **121** K3
Bälinge Sweden 59°57N 17°33E **62** E11
Balingen Germany 48°16N 8°51E **77** G4
Balingian Malaysia 2°50N 112°0E **118** D4
Balintang Channel Phil. 19°50N 121°50E **119** ?
Balkan □ Turkmenistan 40°0N 54°30E **108** D5
Balkan Mts. = Stara Planina
  Bulgaria 43°15N 23°0E **96** C7

Balkanabat
  Turkmenistan 39°30N 54°22E **129** B7
Balkh Afghan. 36°44N 66°47E **109** E7
Balkh □ Afghan. 36°50N 67°0E **109** E7
Balkhash = Balqash
  Kazakhstan 46°50N 74°50E **106** E8
Balkhash, Ozero = Balqash Köli
  Kazakhstan 46°0N 74°50E **109** C8
Balkonda India 18°52N 78°21E **126** E4
Balla Bangladesh 24°10N 91°35E **125** G17
Ballachulish U.K. 56°41N 5°8W **65** E3
Balladonia Australia 32°27S 123°51E **149** F3
Ballaghaderreen Ireland 53°55N 8°34W **64** C3
Ballan Australia 37°33S 144°13E **152** D6
Ballarat Australia 37°33S 143°50E **152** D6
Ballard, L. Australia 29°20S 120°40E **149** E3
Ballater U.K. 57°3N 3°3W **65** D5
Ballé Mali 15°18N 8°33W **138** B3
Ballena, Canal de
  Mexico 29°10N 113°29W **180** B2
Balleny Is. Antarctica 66°30S 163°0E **55** C11
Balleroy France 49°11N 0°50W **70** C6
Ballerup Denmark 55°43N 12°21E **63** J6
Ballestas, Is. Peru 13°44S 76°25W **188** C2
Balli Turkey 40°50N 27°3E **97** F11
Ballia India 25°46N 84°12E **125** G11
Ballina Australia 28°50S 153°31E **151** D5
Ballina Ireland 54°7N 9°9W **64** B2
Ballinasloe Ireland 53°20N 8°13W **64** C3
Ballincollig Ireland 51°53N 8°33W **64** E3
Ballinger U.S.A. 31°45N 99°57W **176** F5
Ballinrobe Ireland 53°38N 9°13W **64** C2
Ballinskelligs B. Ireland 51°48N 10°13W **64** E1
Ballon France 48°10N 0°14E **70** D7
Ballons des Vosges △
  France 48°0N 7°0E **71** E14
Ballsh Albania 40°36N 19°44E **96** F3
Ballston Spa U.S.A. 43°0N 73°51W **175** D11
Ballyboghil Ireland 53°32N 6°16W **64** C5
Ballybunion Ireland 52°31N 9°40W **64** D2
Ballycanew Ireland 52°37N 6°19W **64** D5
Ballycastle U.K. 55°12N 6°15W **64** A5
Ballyclare U.K. 54°46N 6°0W **64** B5
Ballycroy △ Ireland 54°5N 9°50W **64** B2
Ballydehob Ireland 51°34N 9°28W **64** E2
Ballygawley U.K. 54°27N 7°2W **64** B4
Ballyhaunis Ireland 53°46N 8°46W **64** C3
Ballyheige Ireland 52°23N 9°49W **64** D2
Ballymena U.K. 54°52N 6°17W **64** B5
Ballymoney U.K. 55°5N 6°31W **64** A5
Ballymote Ireland 54°5N 8°31W **64** B3
Ballynahinch U.K. 54°24N 5°54W **64** B6
Ballyporeen Ireland 52°16N 8°6W **64** D3
Ballyquintin Pt. U.K. 54°20N 5°30W **64** B6
Ballyshannon Ireland 54°30N 8°11W **64** B3
Balmaceda Chile 46°0S 71°50W **192** C2
Balmaseda Spain 43°11N 3°12W **90** B1
Balmazújváros Hungary 47°37N 21°21E **80** C5
Balmertown Canada 51°4N 93°41W **163** C10
Balmoral Australia 37°15S 141°48E **152** D4
Balmorhea U.S.A. 30°59N 103°45W **176** F3
Balneário Camboriú
  Brazil 26°59S 48°38W **191** B6
Balochistan = Baluchistan □
  Pakistan 27°30N 65°0E **122** F4
Balod India 20°44N 81°13E **126** D5
Balonne → Australia 28°47S 147°56E **151** D4
Balotra India 25°50N 72°14E **124** G5
Balpyq Bi Kazakhstan 44°52N 78°12E **109** D9
Balqash Kazakhstan 46°50N 74°50E **106** E8
Balqash Köli Kazakhstan 46°0N 74°50E **109** C8
Balrampur India 27°30N 82°20E **125** F10
Balranald Australia 34°38S 143°33E **152** C5
Bals Romania 44°22N 24°5E **81** F9
Balsapuerto Peru 5°48S 76°33W **188** B2
Balsas → Maranhão,
  Brazil 7°15S 44°35W **189** B1
Balsas Mexico 18°0N 99°46W **181** D5
Balsas → Tocantins,
  Brazil 9°58S 47°52W **189** B1
Balsas → Mexico 17°55N 102°10W **180** D4
Bålsta Sweden 59°35N 17°30E **62** E11
Balta Ukraine 47°56N 29°45E **81** D15
Balta Ialomiței Romania 44°20N 27°55E **81** F12
Baltakol Kazakhstan 43°7N 67°46E **109** D7
Baltanás Spain 41°56N 4°15W **88** D6
Bălți Moldova 47°48N 27°58E **81** C14
Baltic Sea Europe 57°0N 19°0E **61** H18
Baltîm Egypt 31°35N 31°10E **137** E7
Baltimore Ireland 51°29N 9°22W **64** E2
Baltimore Md., U.S.A. 39°17N 76°36W **173** F15
Baltimore Ohio, U.S.A. 39°51N 82°36W **174** G2
Baltimore-Washington Int. ✈
  (BWI) U.S.A. 39°10N 76°40W **173** F15
Baltinglass Ireland 52°56N 6°43W **64** D5
Baltit Pakistan 36°15N 74°40E **125** A6
Baltiysk Russia 54°41N 19°58E **82** D6
Baltrum Germany 53°43N 7°24E **76** B3
Baluchistan □ Pakistan 27°30N 65°0E **122** F4
Baluqtybulaq Kazakhstan 50°51N 51°8E **86** E10
Balurghat India 25°15N 88°44E **125** G13
Balvi Latvia 57°8N 27°15E **84** D4
Balya Turkey 39°44N 27°35E **99** B9
Bam Iran 29°7N 58°14E **129** D8
Bama China 24°8N 107°12E **116** E5
Bama Nigeria 11°33N 13°41E **139** C7
Bamaga Australia 10°50S 142°25E **150** A3
Bamaji L. Canada 51°9N 91°25W **164** B1
Bamako Mali 12°34N 7°55W **138** C3
Bamba Mali 17°5N 1°24W **138** B5
Bambamarca Peru 6°36S 78°32W **188** B2
Bambaroo Australia 18°50S 146°10E **150** B4
Bambari C.A.R. 5°40N 20°35E **140** C4
Bambaroo Mali 13°26N 4°33W **138** C4
Bamberg Germany 49°54N 10°54E **77** F6
Bamberg U.S.A. 33°18N 81°2W **178** D6
Bambey Senegal 14°42N 16°28W **138** C2
Bambili
  Dem. Rep. of the Congo 3°40N 26°0E **142** B2
Bamboi Ghana 8°13N 2°1W **138** D4
Bambui Brazil 20°1S 45°58W **189** E1
Bamburgh U.K. 55°37N 1°43W **66** B6
Bamenda Cameroon 5°57N 10°11E **139** D7
Bamendjing, L. de
  Cameroon 5°45N 10°30E **139** D7
Bamfield Canada 48°45N 125°10W **162** D3
Bāmiān Afghan. 34°49N 67°49E **109** E7

Bāmiān □ Afghan. 35°0N 67°0E **122** B5
Bamiancheng China 43°15N 124°2E **115** C13
Bamkin Cameroon 6°3N 11°27E **139** D7
Bamou △ Iran 29°45N 52°35E **129** D7
Bampūr Iran 27°15N 60°21E **129** E9
Bampūr → Iran 27°24N 59°0E **129** E8
Ban Ao Tu Khun Thailand 8°9N 98°20E **121** a
Ban Ban Laos 19°31N 103°30E **120** C4
Ban Bang Hin Thailand 9°32N 98°35E **121** H2
Ban Bang Khu Thailand 7°57N 98°23E **121** a
Ban Bang Rong Thailand 8°3N 98°25E **121** a
Ban Bo Phut Thailand 9°33N 100°2E **121** b
Ban Chaweng Thailand 9°32N 100°3E **121** b
Ban Chiang Thailand 17°30N 103°10E **120** D4
Ban Chiang Klang
  Thailand 19°25N 100°55E **120** C3
Ban Choho Thailand 15°2N 102°9E **120** E4
Ban Dan Lan Hoi
  Thailand 17°0N 99°35E **120** D2
Ban Don = Surat Thani
  Thailand 9°6N 99°20E **121** H2
Ban Don Vietnam 12°53N 107°48E **120** F6
Ban Don, Ao → Thailand 9°20N 99°25E **121** H2
Ban Dong Thailand 19°30N 100°59E **120** C3
Ban Hong Thailand 18°18N 98°50E **120** C2
Ban Hua Thanon
  Thailand 9°26N 100°1E **121** b
Ban Kantang Thailand 7°25N 99°31E **121** J2
Ban Karon Thailand 7°51N 98°18E **121** a
Ban Kata Thailand 7°50N 98°18E **121** a
Ban Keun Laos 18°22N 102°35E **120** C4
Ban Khai Thailand 12°46N 101°18E **120** F3
Ban Khlong Kua
  Thailand 6°57N 100°8E **121** J3
Ban Khlong Khian
  Thailand 8°10N 98°26E **121** a
Ban Khuan Thailand 8°20N 98°25E **121** a
Ban Ko Yai Chim
  Thailand 11°17N 99°26E **121** G2
Ban Laem Thailand 13°13N 99°59E **120** F2
Ban Lamai Thailand 9°28N 100°3E **121** b
Ban Lao Ngam Laos 15°28N 106°10E **120** E6
Ban Le Kathe Thailand 15°49N 98°53E **120** E2
Ban Lo Po Noi Thailand 8°1N 98°34E **121** a
Ban Mae Chedi
  Thailand 19°11N 99°31E **120** C2
Ban Mae Nam Thailand 9°34N 100°0E **121** b
Ban Mae Sariang
  Thailand 18°10N 97°56E **120** C1
Ban Mê Thuôt = Buon Ma Thuot
  Vietnam 12°40N 108°3E **120** F7
Ban Mi Thailand 15°3N 100°32E **120** E3
Ban Muang Mo Laos 19°9N 99°41E **121** b
Ban Na Bo Thailand 9°19N 99°41E **121** b
Ban Na San Thailand 8°53N 99°52E **121** H2
Ban Na Tong Laos 20°56N 101°47E **120** B3
Ban Nam Bac Laos 20°38N 102°20E **120** B4
Ban Nammi Thailand 17°7N 100°9E **120** D5
Ban Nong Bok Laos 17°5N 104°48E **120** D5
Ban Nong Pling
  Thailand 15°40N 100°10E **120** E3
Ban Pak Chan Thailand 10°32N 98°51E **121** G2
Ban Patong Thailand 7°54N 98°18E **121** a
Ban Phai Thailand 16°4N 102°44E **120** D4
Ban Phak Chit Thailand 8°0N 98°24E **121** a
Ban Pong Thailand 13°50N 99°55E **120** F2
Ban Rawai Thailand 7°47N 98°20E **121** a
Ban Ron Phibun Thailand 8°9N 99°51E **121** H2
Ban Sakhu Thailand 8°4N 98°14E **121** a
Ban Sanam Chai
  Thailand 7°33N 100°25E **121** J3
Ban Tak Thailand 17°2N 99°4E **120** D2
Ban Tha Nun Thailand 8°12N 98°17E **121** a
Ban Tha Rua Thailand 7°59N 98°22E **121** a
Ban Tha Yu Thailand 8°17N 98°22E **121** a
Ban Thong Krut Thailand 9°25N 99°57E **121** b
Ban Xien Kok Laos 20°54N 100°39E **120** B3
Ban Yen Nhan Vietnam 20°57N 106°2E **120** B6
Banaba Kiribati 0°45S 169°50E **156** H8
Banagher Ireland 53°11N 7°59W **64** C3
Banalia
  Dem. Rep. of the Congo 1°32N 25°5E **142** B2
Banam Cambodia 11°20N 105°17E **120** G5
Banamba Mali 13°29N 7°22W **138** C3
Banana Is. S. Leone 8°7N 13°15W **138** D2
Banana, I. do Brazil 11°30N 50°30W **187** F8
Bananga India 6°57N 93°54E **127** L11
Banas → Gujarat, India 23°45N 71°25E **124** H4
Banas → Mad. P., India 24°15N 81°30E **125** G9
Bânâs, Ras Egypt 23°57N 35°59E **137** C4
Banaz Turkey 38°44N 29°46E **99** C11
Banaz → Turkey 38°42N 29°7E **99** C11
Banbridge U.K. 54°21N 6°16W **64** B5
Banbury U.K. 52°4N 1°20W **67** E6
Banchory U.K. 57°3N 2°29W **65** D6
Bancroft Canada 45°3N 77°51W **174** B7
Band Bonī Iran 25°30N 59°33E **129** E8
Band Qīr Iran 31°39N 48°53E **129** D6
Banda Mad. P., India 24°3N 78°57E **125** G8
Banda Ut. P., India 25°30N 80°26E **125** G9
Banda Maharashtra,
  India 15°49N 73°52E **127** G2
Banda, Kepulauan
  Indonesia 4°37S 129°50E **119** E7
Banda Aceh Indonesia 5°35N 95°20E **118** C1
Banda Banda, Mt.
  Australia 31°10S 152°28E **153** A10
Banda Elat Indonesia 5°40S 133°5E **119** F8
Banda Is. = Banda, Kepulauan
  Indonesia 4°37S 129°50E **119** E7
Banda Sea Indonesia 6°0S 130°0E **119** F7
Bandai-Asahi △ Japan 37°38N 140°5E **112** F10
Bandai-San Japan 37°36N 140°4E **112** F10
Bandama → Ivory C. 6°32N 5°30W **138** D3
Bandama Blanc →
  Ivory C. 7°1N 7°29W **138** D3
Bandama Rouge →
  Ivory C. 6°54S 5°31W **138** D3
Bandān Iran 31°23N 60°44E **129** D9
Bandanaira Indonesia 4°32S 129°54E **119** E7
Bandanwara India 26°9N 74°38E **124** F6
Bandar = Machilipatnam
  India 16°12N 81°8E **127** F5
Bandar-e Abbās Iran 27°15N 56°15E **129** E8

Bandar-e Anzalī Iran 37°30N 49°30E **105**
Bandar-e Bushehr = Büshehr
  Iran 28°55N 50°55E **12**
Bandar-e Chārak Iran 26°45N 54°20E **1**
Bandar-e Deylam Iran 30°5N 50°10E **12**
Bandar-e Emām Khomeynī
  Iran 30°30N 49°5E **12**
Bandar-e Lengeh Iran 26°35N 54°58E **1**
Bandar-e Maqām Iran 26°56N 53°29E **1**
Bandar-e Ma'shur Iran 30°35N 49°10E **12**
Bandar-e Rīg Iran 29°29N 50°38E **12**
Bandar-e Torkeman
  Iran 37°0N 54°10E **12**
Bandar Labuan
  Malaysia 5°20N 115°14E **11**
Bandar Lampung
  Indonesia 5°20S 105°10E **1**
Bandar Maharani = Muar
  Malaysia 2°3N 102°34E **1**
Bandar Penggaram = Batu Pahat
  Malaysia 1°50N 102°56E **1**
Bandar Seri Begawan
  Brunei 4°52N 115°0E **11**
Bandar Shahid Rajaee
  Iran 27°7N 56°4E **12**
Bandar Sri Aman
  Malaysia 1°15N 111°32E **11**
Bande Spain 42°3N 7°58W **8**
Bandeira, Pico da
  Brazil 20°26S 41°47W **18**
Bandera Argentina 28°55S 62°20W **19**
Banderas, B. de
  Mexico 20°40N 105°25W **1**
Bandhavgarh India 23°40N 81°2E **12**
Bandhavgarh △ India 23°45N 81°10E **12**
Bandi → India 26°12N 75°47E **12**
Bandia → India 19°2N 80°28E **12**
Bandiagara Mali 14°12N 3°29W **13**
Bandikui India 27°3N 76°34E **12**
Bandipur △ India 11°45N 76°30E **12**
Bandırma Turkey 40°20N 28°0E **9**
Bandjarmasin = Banjarmasin
  Indonesia 3°20S 114°35E **11**
Bandol France 43°8S 5°46E **7**
Bandon Ireland 51°44N 8°44W **6**
Bandon → Ireland 51°43N 8°37W **6**
Bandula Mozam. 19°0S 33°7E **14**
Bandundu
  Dem. Rep. of the Congo 3°15S 17°22E **14**
Bandung Indonesia 6°54S 107°36E **11**
Bané Burkina Faso 11°42N 0°15W **13**
Bâneasa Romania 45°56N 27°55E **8**
Bāneh Iran 35°59N 45°53E **10**
Banes Cuba 21°0N 75°42W **18**
Banff Canada 51°10N 115°34W **16**
Banff U.K. 57°40N 2°33W **6**
Banff △ Canada 51°30N 116°15W **16**
Banfora Burkina Faso 10°40N 4°40W **13**
Bang Fai → Laos 16°57N 104°45E **12**
Bang Hieng → Laos 16°10N 105°10E **12**
Bang Krathum
  Thailand 16°34N 100°18E **12**
Bang Lang △ Thailand 5°58N 101°19E **12**
Bang Lang Res. Thailand 6°6N 101°17E **12**
Bang Mun Nak
  Thailand 16°2N 100°23E **12**
Bang Pa In Thailand 14°14N 100°35E **12**
Bang Rakam Thailand 16°45N 100°7E **12**
Bang Saphan Thailand 11°14N 99°28E **12**
Bang Thao Thailand 7°59N 98°18E **1**
Bangaduni I. India 21°34N 88°52E **12**
Bangala Dam Zimbabwe 21°7S 31°25E **14**
Bangalore = Bengaluru
  India 12°59N 77°40E **12**
Banganapalle India 15°19N 78°14E **12**
Banganga → India 26°6N 79°25E **12**
Bangangté Cameroon 5°8N 10°32E **13**
Bangaon India 23°0N 88°47E **12**
Bangassou C.A.R. 4°55N 23°7E **14**
Banggai Indonesia 1°34S 123°30E **11**
Banggai, Kepulauan
  Indonesia 1°40S 123°30E **11**
Banggai Arch. = Banggai,
  Kepulauan Indonesia 1°40S 123°30E **11**
Banggi, Pulau Malaysia 7°17N 117°12E **11**
Banghāzī Libya 32°11N 20°3E **13**
Bangka Sulawesi,
  Indonesia 1°50N 125°5E **11**
Bangka Sumatera,
  Indonesia 2°0S 105°50E **11**
Bangka, Selat Indonesia 2°30S 105°30E **11**
Bangka-Belitung □
  Indonesia 2°30S 107°0E **11**
Bangkalan Indonesia 7°2S 112°46E **11**
Bangkinang Indonesia 0°18N 101°5E **11**
Bangko Indonesia 2°5S 102°9E **11**
Bangkok Thailand 13°45N 100°35E **12**
Bangkok, Bight of
  Thailand 13°0N 100°30E **12**
Bangla = Paschimbanga □
  India 23°0N 88°0E **12**
Bangladesh ■ Asia 24°0N 90°0E **12**
Bangli Indonesia 8°27S 115°21E **11**
Bangong Co China 33°45N 78°43E **12**
Bangor Down, U.K. 54°40N 5°40W **6**
Bangor Gwynedd, U.K. 53°14N 4°8W **6**
Bangor Maine, U.S.A. 44°48N 68°46W **17**
Bangor Pa., U.S.A. 40°52N 75°13W **1**
Bangued Phil. 17°40N 120°37E **11**
Banguru
  Dem. Rep. of the Congo 0°30N 27°10E **14**
Bangweulu, L. Zambia 11°0S 30°0E **14**
Bangweulu Swamp
  Zambia 11°20S 30°15E **14**
Banhine △ Mozam. 22°49S 32°55E **14**
Banhine Blanc →
  Ivory C.
Bani Dom. Rep. 18°16N 70°22W **18**
Bani → Mali 14°30N 4°12W **13**
Bani, Jebel Morocco 29°16N 8°0W **13**
Bani Bangou Niger 15°3N 2°42E **13**
Bani Sa'd Iraq 33°34N 44°32E **10**
Bania Cent. Afr. Rep.
Banihal Pass India 33°30N 75°12E **12**
Banikoara Benin 11°18N 2°26E **13**
Banissa Kenya 3°55N 40°19E **14**

niyâs Syria 35°10N 36°0E 104 E6
nja Luka Bos.-H. 44°49N 17°11E 80 F2
njar India 31°38N 77°21E 124 D7
njar → India 22°36N 80°22E 125 H9
njarmasin Indonesia 3°20S 114°35E 118 E4
njul Gambia 13°28N 16°40W 138 C1
nkas Mali 14°4N 3°31W 138 C4
nkeryd Sweden 57°53N 14°6E 63 G8
nket Zimbabwe 17°27S 30°19E 143 F3
nkilare Niger 14°35N 0°44E 139 C5
nkipore India 25°35N 85°10E 123 G14
nkot India 17°58N 73°2E 126 F1
nks U.S.A. 31°49N 85°51W 178 D4
nks I. = Moa
Australia 10°11S 142°16E 150 a
nks I. B.C., Canada 53°20N 130°0W 162 C3
nks I. N.W.T.,
Canada 73°15N 121°30W 160 C7
nks Pen. N.Z. 43°45S 173°15E 155 D8
nks Str. Australia 40°40S 148°10E 151 G4
nkura India 23°11N 87°18E 125 H12
nkya Bulgaria 42°43N 23°8E 96 D7
nmankhi India 25°53N 87°11E 125 G12
nmu → Armagh, U.K. 54°30N 6°31W 64 B5
nn → L'derry., U.K. 55°8N 6°41W 64 A5
nnalec France 47°57N 3°42W 70 E3
nnang Sata Thailand 6°16N 101°16E 121 J3
nnerton U.S.A. 34°42S 142°47E 152 C5
nning U.S.A. 33°56N 116°53W 171 M10
nnockburn Canada 44°39N 77°33W 174 B7
nnockburn 56°5N 3°55W 65 E5
nnockburn
Zimbabwe 20°17S 29°48E 143 G2
nnu Pakistan 33°0N 70°18E 122 C7
no India 22°40N 84°55E 125 H11
nolas = Banyoles Spain 42°16N 2°44E 90 C7
non France 44°2N 5°38E 73 D9
nos de la Encina Spain 38°10N 3°46W 89 G7
nos de Molgas Spain 42°15N 7°40W 88 C3
novce nad Bebravou
Slovak Rep. 48°44N 18°16E 79 C11
novići Bos.-H. 44°25N 18°32E 80 F3
nsagar Dam India 24°11N 81°17E 126 B5
nsgaon India 26°33N 83°21E 125 F10
nská Bystrica
Slovak Rep. 48°46N 19°14E 79 C12
nská Štiavnica
Slovak Rep. 48°25N 18°55E 79 C11
nsko Bulgaria 41°52N 23°28E 96 E7
nskobystrický □
Slovak Rep. 48°20N 19°0E 79 C12
nswara India 23°32N 74°24E 124 H6
ntaeng Indonesia 5°32S 119°56E 119 F5
ntaji → Nigeria 8°6N 10°15E 139 D7
nteay Prei Nokor
Cambodia 11°56N 105°40E 121 G5
ntina Indonesia 6°30S 106°0E 119 G11
ntry Ireland 51°41N 9°27W 64 E2
ntry B. Ireland 51°37N 9°44W 64 E2
ntval India 21°29N 70°12E 124 J4
ntval India 12°55N 75°0E 127 H2
nya Bulgaria 42°33N 24°50E 97 D8
nya, Pta. de la Spain 40°33N 0°36E 90 E5
nyak, Kepulauan
Indonesia 2°10N 97°10E 118 D1
nyalburlar Spain 39°42N 2°31E 100 B9
nyeres de Mariola
Spain 38°44N 0°38W 91 G4
nyoke Cameroon 6°52N 11°45E 139 D7
nyoles Spain 42°16N 2°44E 90 C7
nyuls-sur-Mer France 42°28N 3°8E 72 F7
nyuwangi Indonesia 8°13S 114°21E 119 J17
nzare Coast Antarctica 68°0S 125°0E 55 C9
o Ha Vietnam 22°11N 104°2E 116 F5
o Lac Vietnam 22°57N 105°40E 120 A5
o Loc Vietnam 11°32N 107°48E 121 G6
o'an China 22°34N 113°52E 111 a
ocheng China 33°12N 106°56E 116 A6
ode China 39°1N 111°5E 114 E6
oding China 39°38N 117°20E 115 E9
oding China 38°50N 115°28E 114 E8
oji China 34°20N 107°5E 114 G4
ojing China 28°45N 109°41E 116 C7
okang China 31°54N 111°12E 117 B8
okang Shanghai,
China 31°24N 121°28E 117 B13
oshan Yunnan, China 25°10N 99°5E 116 D2
otou China 30°32N 110°2E 114 D6
oué Mali 12°36N 9°45W 138 C3
oxing China 30°24N 102°50E 116 B4
oying China 33°17N 119°20E 115 H10
oyou = Ledong China 18°41N 109°5E 117 a
p India 27°23N 72°18E 124 F5
patla India 15°55N 80°32E 127 M6
paume France 50°7N 2°50E 71 B9
qerâbâd Iran 33°2N 51°58E 129 C6
qūbah Iraq 33°45N 44°50E 105 F11
quedano Chile 23°20S 69°52W 190 A2
r Montenegro 42°8N 19°6E 96 D3
r Ukraine 49°4N 27°40E 75 D14
r Bigha India 25°21N 85°4E 125 G11
r Harbor U.S.A. 44°23N 68°13W 173 C19
ra India 27°23N 77°18E 124 F7
ra Romania 47°2N 27°3E 81 C12
ra Banki India 26°55N 81°12E 125 F9
rabai Indonesia 2°32S 115°34E 118 E5
raboo U.S.A. 43°28N 89°45W 172 D9
racoa Cuba 20°20N 74°30W 183 B5
radä → India 25°33N 86°34E 125 G12
radero Argentina 33°52S 59°30W 190 C4
radine Australia 30°56S 149°4E 153 A3
radol Romania 46°47N 28°0E 172 B9
răganul Romania 44°49N 27°31E 81 F12
rail Kenya 0°47N 36°16E 142 B4
rah → India 27°42N 77°5E 124 F6
rahona Dom. Rep. 18°13N 71°7E 183 C5
rail Range India 25°15N 93°20E 123 G18
rajas, Madrid ✈ (MAD)
Spain 40°28N 3°34W 88 E7
rakaldo Spain 43°18N 2°59W 90 B2
rakerd → India 24°7N 86°14E 125 G15
rakpur India 22°47N 88°21E 125 H13
ralba Australia 24°13S 149°50E 150 C4
ralla Spain 42°53N 7°15W 88 C3

Baralzon L. Canada 60°0N 98°3W 163 B10
Baramati India 18°11N 74°33E 126 E2
Baramba India 20°25N 85°23E 126 D7
Barameiya Sudan 18°32N 36°38E 137 D4
Baramula India 34°15N 74°20E 125 B6
Baran India 25°9N 76°40E 124 G7
Baran → Pakistan 25°13N 68°17E 124 G3
Barañain Spain 42°48N 1°40W 90 C3
Baranavichy Belarus 53°10N 26°0E 75 B14
Barani Burkina Faso 13°9N 3°51W 138 C4
Baranof I. U.S.A. 57°5N 134°50W 162 B2
Baranof I. U.S.A. 57°0N 135°0W 160 F4
Baranów Sandomierski
Poland 50°29N 21°30E 83 H8
Baranya □ Hungary 46°0N 18°15E 80 E3
Barão de Cocais Brazil 19°56S 43°28W 189 D2
Barão de Grajaú Brazil 6°45S 43°1W 189 D2
Baraolt Romania 46°5N 25°34E 81 D10
Baraona Spain 41°17N 2°39W 90 D2
Barapasi Indonesia 2°15S 137°5E 119 E9
Barasat India 22°46N 88°31E 125 H13
Barat Daya, Kepulauan
Indonesia 7°30S 128°0E 119 F7
Baratang I. India 12°13N 92°45E 127 H11
Barataria B. U.S.A. 29°20N 89°55W 177 G10
Barauda India 23°33N 75°15E 124 H6
Baraut India 29°13N 77°7E 124 E7
Barbacena Brazil 21°15S 43°56W 191 A7
Barbados ■ W. Indies 13°10N 59°30W 183 b
Barbalha Brazil 7°19S 39°17W 189 B3
Barban Croatia 45°5N 14°2E 93 C11
Barbària, C. de Spain 38°39N 1°24E 100 C7
Barbaros Turkey 40°54N 27°27E 97 F11
Barbas, C. W. Sahara 22°20N 16°42W 134 D2
Barbastro Spain 42°2N 0°5E 90 C5
Barbate Spain 36°13N 5°56W 89 J5
Barbeau Pk. Canada 81°54N 75°1W 161 A16
Barberino di Mugello
Italy 44°0N 11°15E 93 E8
Barberton S. Africa 25°42S 31°2E 145 C5
Barberton U.S.A. 41°1N 81°39W 174 E3
Barberville U.S.A. 29°11N 81°26W 179 F8
Barbezieux-St-Hilaire
France 45°28N 0°9W 72 C3
Barbosa Colombia 5°57N 73°37W 186 B4
Barbourville U.S.A. 36°52N 83°53W 173 G12
Barbuda W. Indies 17°30N 61°40W 183 C7
Bârca Romania 43°59N 23°36E 81 G8
Barcaldine Australia 23°43S 145°6E 150 C4
Barcarrota Spain 38°31N 6°51W 89 G4
Barcellona Pozzo di Gotto
Italy 38°9N 15°13E 95 D8
Barcelona Spain 41°22N 2°10E 90 D7
Barcelona Venezuela 10°10N 64°40W 186 A6
Barcelona, El Prat ✈ (BCN)
Spain 41°18N 2°5E 90 D7
Barceloneta Puerto Rico 18°27N 66°32W 183 d
Barcelonnette France 44°23N 6°40E 73 D10
Barcelos Brazil 1°0S 63°0W 186 D6
Barcin Poland 52°52N 17°55E 83 F4
Barclayville Liberia 4°48N 8°10W 138 E3
Barcoo → Australia 25°30S 142°50E 150 D3
Barcs Hungary 45°58N 17°28E 80 E2
Barczewo Poland 53°50N 20°42E 82 E7
Bärdä Azerbaijan 40°25N 47°10E 87 K8
Barda del Medio
Argentina 38°45S 68°11W 192 A3
Bardaï Chad 21°25N 17°0E 135 D9
Bardas Blancas
Argentina 35°49S 69°45W 190 D2
Barddhaman India 23°14N 87°39E 125 H12
Bardejov Slovak Rep. 49°18N 21°15E 79 B14
Bardera = Baardheere
Somalia 2°20N 42°27E 131 G3
Bardi Italy 44°38N 9°44E 92 D6
Bardīyah Libya 31°45N 25°5E 135 B10
Bardoli India 21°12N 73°5E 126 D1
Bardolino Italy 45°33N 10°43E 92 C7
Bardonécchia Italy 45°5N 6°42E 92 C4
Bardsey I. U.K. 52°45N 4°47W 66 E3
Bardstown U.S.A. 37°49N 85°28W 173 G11
Bareilly India 28°22N 79°27E 125 E8
Barela India 23°6N 80°3E 125 H9
Barellan Australia 34°16S 146°24E 153 C7
Barentin France 49°33N 0°58E 70 C7
Barenton France 48°38N 0°50W 70 D6
Barentsøya Svalbard 78°25N 21°20E 57 B13
Barfleur France 49°40N 1°17W 70 C5
Barfleur, Pte. de France 49°42N 1°16W 70 C5
Barga China 44°4N 10°2E 92 D7
Bargara Australia 24°50S 152°25E 150 C5
Bargarh India 21°20N 83°37E 126 D6
Bargas Spain 39°56N 4°3W 88 F6
Barge Italy 44°43N 7°20E 92 D4
Bargi Dam India 22°59N 80°0E 126 C5
Barguzin Russia 53°37N 109°37E 107 D11
Barh India 25°29N 85°46E 125 G11
Barhaj India 26°18N 83°44E 125 F10
Barham Australia 35°36S 144°8E 152 C6
Barharwa India 24°52N 87°47E 125 G12
Barhi India 26°30N 77°39E 124 F7
Bari Italy 41°8N 16°51E 95 A9
Bari Doab Pakistan 30°20N 73°0E 124 D5
Bari Sadri India 24°28N 74°30E 124 G6
Bari Sardo Italy 39°50N 9°38E 94 C2
Bariadi Tanzania 2°48S 34°0E 142 C3
Baria Bangla. 22°45N 90°20E 123 H17
Barim Yemen 12°39N 43°25E 132 E8
Barinas Venezuela 8°36N 70°15W 186 B4
Baring, C. Canada 70°0N 117°30W 160 D8
Baringo □ Kenya 0°47N 36°16E 142 B4
Baringo, L. Kenya 0°47N 36°16E 142 B4
Baripada India 21°57N 86°45E 126 D8
Bâris Egypt 24°42N 30°31E 137 C12
Barisal Bangla. 22°45N 90°20E 123 H17
Barisan, Pegunungan
Indonesia 3°30S 102°15E 118 E2
Barito → Indonesia 4°0S 114°50E 118 E4
Baritú △ Argentina 22°43S 64°40W 190 A3
Barjols France 43°34N 6°2E 73 E10
Barjūj, Wadi → Libya 25°26N 12°12E 135 C8
Bark L. Canada 45°27N 77°51W 174 A7

Barkakana India 23°37N 85°29E 125 H11
Barkal, J. Sudan 18°32N 31°50E 137 D3
Barkam China 31°51N 102°28E 116 B4
Barker U.S.A. 43°20N 78°33W 174 C6
Barkley, L. U.S.A. 37°1N 88°14W 177 C10
Barkley Sound
Canada 48°50N 125°10W 162 D3
Barkly East S. Africa 30°58S 27°33E 144 D4
Barkly Homestead
Australia 19°52S 135°50E 150 B2
Barkly Tableland
Australia 17°50S 136°40E 150 B2
Barkly West S. Africa 28°5S 24°31E 144 C3
Barkol Kazak Zizhixian
China 43°37N 93°2E 110 C7
Barla Daği Turkey 37°10N 72°45E 125 A5
Bârlad Romania 46°15N 27°38E 81 D12
Bârlad → Romania 45°38N 27°32E 81 E12
Barlee, L. Australia 29°15S 119°30E 149 E2
Barlee, Mt. Australia 24°38S 128°13E 149 D4
Barletta Italy 41°19N 16°17E 95 A9
Barlinek Poland 53°0N 15°15E 83 F2
Barlovento Canary Is. 28°48N 17°48W 100 F2
Barlovento C. Verde Is. 17°0N 25°0W 134 b
Barlow L. Canada 62°0N 103°0W 163 A8
Barmedman Australia 34°9S 147°21E 153 C7
Barmer India 25°45N 71°20E 124 G4
Barmera Australia 34°15S 140°28E 152 C4
Barmouth U.K. 52°44N 4°4W 66 E3
Barmstedt Germany 53°47N 9°46E 76 B5
Barnagar India 23°7N 75°19E 124 H6
Barnala India 30°23N 75°33E 124 D6
Barnard Castle U.K. 54°33N 1°55W 66 C6
Barnaul Russia 53°20N 83°40E 108 D10
Barnes Australia 36°2S 144°49E 152 D6
Barnesville Ga., U.S.A. 33°3N 84°9W 178 D5
Barnesville Minn.,
U.S.A. 46°43N 96°28W 172 B5
Barnet □ U.K. 51°38N 0°9W 67 F7
Barnetwold Neths. 52°7N 5°36E 69 B5
Barneville-Cartevert
France 49°23N 1°46W 70 C5
Barnhart U.S.A. 31°8N 101°10W 176 F4
Barnsley U.K. 53°34N 1°27W 66 D6
Barnstable U.S.A. 41°42N 70°18W 173 E18
Barnstaple U.K. 51°5N 4°4W 67 F3
Barnstaple Bay = Bideford Bay
U.K. 51°5N 4°20W 67 F3
Barnwell U.S.A. 33°15N 81°23W 178 D7
Baro Nigeria 8°35N 6°18E 139 D6
Baroda = Vadodara
India 22°20N 73°10E 124 H5
Baroda India 25°29N 76°35E 124 G7
Baroe S. Africa 33°13S 24°33E 144 D3
Baron Ra. Australia 23°30S 127°45E 148 D4
Barong China 31°39N 99°0E 116 B3
Barotseland Zambia 15°0S 24°0E 141 H4
Barouéli Mali 13°4N 6°50W 138 C3
Barpali India 21°11N 83°35E 126 D6
Barpeta India 26°20N 91°10E 123 F17
Barqa Libya 27°0N 23°0E 135 C10
Barques, Pt. Aux U.S.A. 44°4N 82°58W 174 B2
Barquísimeto Venezuela 10°4N 69°19W 186 A5
Barr, Ras el Egypt 31°32N 31°50E 137 E7
Barr Smith Range
Australia 27°4S 120°20E 149 E3
Barra Brazil 11°5S 43°10W 189 C2
Barra Gambia 13°28N 16°32W 138 C1
Barra U.K. 57°0N 7°29W 65 E1
Barra, Pta. Mozam. 23°48S 35°32E 145 B6
Barra, Sd. of U.K. 57°4N 7°25W 65 D1
Barra da Estiva Brazil 13°38S 41°19W 189 C2
Barra de Navidad
Mexico 19°12N 104°41W 180 D4
Barra do Corda Brazil 5°30S 45°10W 189 B1
Barra do Garças Brazil 15°54S 52°16W 187 G8
Barra do Mendes Brazil 11°43S 42°4W 189 C2
Barra do Piraí Brazil 22°30S 43°50W 191 A7
Barra Falsa, Pta. da
Mozam. 22°58S 35°37E 145 B6
Barra Hd. U.K. 56°47N 7°40W 65 E1
Barra Mansa Brazil 22°35S 44°12W 191 A7
Barraba Australia 30°21S 150°35E 153 A9
Barrackpur = Barakpur
India 22°47N 88°21E 125 H13
Barrafranca Italy 37°22N 14°12E 95 E7
Barrãmîya Egypt 24°59N 34°57E 137 C13
Barranca Lima, Peru 10°45S 77°50W 186 D2
Barranca Loreto, Peru 4°50S 76°50W 186 D3
Barranca del Cobre △
Mexico 27°18N 107°40W 180 B3
Barrancabermeja
Colombia 7°0N 73°50W 186 B4
Barrancas Venezuela 8°55N 62°5W 186 B6
Barrancos Portugal 38°10N 6°58W 89 G4
Barranqueras Argentina 27°30S 59°0W 190 B4
Barranquilla Colombia 11°0N 74°50W 186 A4
Barras Brazil 4°15S 42°18W 189 A2
Barraute Canada 48°26N 77°38W 164 C4
Barre Mass., U.S.A. 42°25N 72°6W 173 D16
Barre Vt., U.S.A. 44°12N 72°30W 175 B12
Barreal Argentina 31°33S 69°28W 190 C2
Barreiras Brazil 12°8S 45°0W 189 C2
Barreirinhas Brazil 2°30S 42°50W 189 A2
Barreiro Portugal 38°39N 9°5W 89 G1
Barreiros Brazil 8°49S 35°12W 189 B3
Barrème France 43°57N 6°23E 73 E10
Barren, Nosy Madag. 18°25S 43°40E 141 H8
Barretos Brazil 20°30S 48°35W 189 E1
Barrie Canada 44°24N 79°40W 174 D5
Barrier, C. N.Z. 36°25S 175°32E 154 F4
Barrier Ra. Australia 31°0S 141°30E 152 A4
Barrier Ra. Otago, N.Z. 44°35S 169°32E 155 E4
Barrier Ra. W. Coast,
N.Z. 44°30S 168°30E 155 E3
Barrière Canada 51°12N 120°7W 162 C4
Barrineau Park U.S.A. 30°42N 87°26W 179 E12
Barrington L. Canada 56°55N 100°15W 163 B8
Barrington Tops
Australia 32°6S 151°28E 153 B9
Barrington Tops △
Australia 32°4S 151°25E 153 B9
Barringun Australia 29°1S 145°41E 151 D4
Barron U.S.A. 45°24N 91°51W 172 C8
Barrow U.S.A. 71°18N 156°47W 166 A8

Barrow → Ireland 52°25N 6°58W 64 D5
Barrow, Pt. U.S.A. 71°23N 156°29W 166 A8
Barrow Creek
Australia 21°30S 133°55E 150 C1
Barrow I. Australia 20°45S 115°20E 148 D2
Barrow-in-Furness U.K. 54°7N 3°14W 66 C4
Barrow Pt. Australia 14°20S 144°40E 150 A3
Barrow Pt. U.S.A. 71°20N 156°30W 166 A8
Barrow Ra. Australia 26°0S 127°40E 149 E4
Barrow Str. Canada 74°20N 95°0W 161 C13
Barruecopardo Spain 41°4N 6°40W 88 D4
Barruelo de Santullán
Spain 42°54N 4°17W 88 C6
Barry U.K. 51°24N 3°16W 67 F4
Barry's Bay Canada 45°29N 77°41W 174 A7
Barsalogho Burkina Faso 13°25N 1°3W 139 C4
Barsat Pakistan 36°10N 72°45E 125 A5
Barsham Syria 35°21N 40°33E 105 E9
Barshatas Kazakhstan 48°10N 78°39E 109 C9
Barsi India 18°10N 75°50E 126 E2
Barsinghausen Germany 52°18N 9°28E 76 C5
Barso India 25°48N 87°57E 123 G15
Barstow U.S.A. 34°54N 117°1W 171 L9
Barth Germany 54°22N 12°42E 76 A8
Bartica Guyana 6°25N 58°40W 186 B7
Bartin Turkey 41°38N 32°21E 104 B5
Bartle Frere Australia 17°27S 145°50E 150 B4
Bartlesville U.S.A. 36°45N 95°59W 176 C7
Bartlett Calif., U.S.A. 36°29N 118°2W 170 J8
Bartlett Tenn., U.S.A. 35°12N 89°52W 177 D10
Bartlett, L. Canada 63°5N 118°20W 162 A5
Bartolomeu Dias
Mozam. 21°10S 35°8E 143 G4
Barton U.S.A. 44°45N 72°11W 175 B12
Barton-upon-Humber
U.K. 53°41N 0°25W 66 D7
Bartoszyce Poland 54°15N 20°55E 82 D7
Bartow Fla., U.S.A. 27°54N 81°50W 179 H8
Bartow Ga., U.S.A. 32°53N 82°29W 178 D7
Barú, Volcan Panama 8°55N 82°35E 182 E3
Barumba
Dem. Rep. of the Congo 1°3N 23°37E 142 B1
Barúmini Italy 39°42N 8°59E 94 C1
Barung, Nusa
Indonesia 8°30S 113°30E 119 H15
Baruth Germany 52°4N 13°30E 76 C9
Baruun Urt Mongolia 46°46N 113°15E 111 B11
Baruunsuu Mongolia 43°43N 105°35E 114 C3
Barvinkove Ukraine 48°57N 37°0E 85 H9
Barwani India 22°2N 74°57E 126 D2
Barwice Poland 53°44N 16°21E 82 E3
Barwick Poland 53°54N 83°54E 178 E5
Barxudarlı Azerbaijan 41°0N 45°14E 105 B11
Barycz → Poland 51°42N 16°15E 83 G3
Barysaw Belarus 54°17N 28°28E 75 A15
Barysh Russia 53°39N 47°8E 88 D8
Barzán Iraq 36°55N 44°3E 128 B5
Bârzava Romania 46°7N 21°59E 80 D6
Bas-Rhin □ France 48°40N 7°30E 71 D14
Bas-Sassandra □ Ivory C. 5°30N 7°0W 138 D3
Bašaïd Serbia 45°38N 20°25E 80 E5
Bāsa'idū Iran 26°35N 55°20E 129 E7
Basal Pakistan 33°33N 72°13E 124 C5
Basankusu
Dem. Rep. of the Congo 1°5N 19°50E 140 D3
Basarabeasca Moldova 46°21N 28°58E 81 D13
Basarabi Romania 44°10N 28°26E 81 F13
Basarabia = Bessarabia
Moldova 47°0N 28°10E 75 E15
Basauri Spain 43°13N 2°53W 90 B2
Basavakalyan India 17°52N 76°57E 126 F3
Basawa Afghan. 34°15N 70°50E 124 B4
Bascuñán, C. Chile 28°52S 71°35W 190 B1
Basel Switz. 47°35N 7°35E 77 H3
Basel-Landschaft □
Switz. 47°26N 7°45E 77 H3
Basento → Italy 40°20N 16°49E 95 B9
Bashäkerd, Kühhä-ye
Iran 26°42N 58°35E 129 E8
Bashaw Canada 52°35N 112°58W 162 C6
Bāshī Iran 28°41N 51°4E 129 D6
Bashkand = Artsvashen
Armenia 40°38N 45°30E 105 B11
Bashkir Republic =
Bashkortostan □
Russia 54°0N 57°0E 108 D5
Bashkiriya △ Russia 52°58N 56°30E 108 D5
Bashkortostan □ Russia 54°0N 57°0E 108 D5
Bashtanivka Ukraine 45°46N 29°29E 81 E14
Basilan □ Phil. 6°35N 122°0E 119 C6
Basilan Str. Phil. 6°50N 122°0E 119 C6
Basildon U.K. 51°34N 0°28E 67 F8
Basile Eq. Guin. 3°42N 8°48E 139 E6
Basile, Pico de Eq. Guin. 3°36N 8°49E 139 E6
Basilicata □ Italy 40°30N 16°30E 95 B9
Basim = Washim India 20°3N 77°0E 126 D3
Basin U.S.A. 44°23N 108°2W 174 D9
Basingstoke U.K. 51°15N 1°5W 67 F6
Baška Croatia 44°58N 14°45E 93 D11
Başkale Turkey 38°2N 43°59E 105 C10
Baskatong, Rés.
Canada 46°46N 75°50W 164 C4
Basle = Basel Switz. 47°35N 7°35E 77 H3
Basle Euroairport ✈ (EAP)
France 47°36N 7°33E 71 E14
Başmakçı Turkey 37°54N 30°1E 99 D13
Basmat India 19°15N 77°12E 126 D3
Basoda India 23°52N 77°54E 124 H7
Basoko
Dem. Rep. of the Congo 1°16N 23°40E 142 B1
Basque, Côte France 43°30N 2°0W 72 E2
Basque Provinces = País Vasco □
Spain 42°50N 2°45W 90 C2
Basra = Al Başrah Iraq 30°30N 47°50E 128 D5
Bass Str. Australia 39°15S 146°30E 151 F4
Bassae Greece 37°26N 21°53E 98 D3
Bassano Canada 50°48N 112°20W 162 C6
Bassano del Grappa
Italy 45°46N 11°44E 93 C8
Bassar Togo 9°19N 0°57E 139 D5
Bassas da India Ind. Oc. 22°0S 39°0E 143 G4
Basse-Normandie □
France 48°45N 0°10W 70 D6
Basse-Pointe Martinique 14°52N 61°8W 182 c
Basse Santa-Su
Gambia 13°13N 14°15W 138 C2
Basse-Terre Guadeloupe 16°0N 61°44W 182 b
Basse Terre Trin. & Tob. 10°7N 61°19W 187 K15
Bassein = Pathein
Burma 16°45N 94°30E 123 L19

Basses, Pte. des
Guadeloupe 15°52N 61°17W 182 b
Basseterre
St. Kitts & Nevis 17°17N 62°43W 183 C7
Bassett U.S.A. 42°35N 99°32W 172 D4
Bassi India 30°44N 76°21E 124 D7
Bassigny France 48°0N 5°30E 71 E12
Bassikounou Mauritania 15°55N 6°1W 138 B3
Bassila Benin 9°1N 1°46E 139 D5
Bassum Germany 52°50N 8°40E 76 C4
Båstad Sweden 56°25N 12°51E 63 H6
Bastak Iran 27°15N 54°25E 129 E7
Bastām Iran 36°29N 55°4E 129 B7
Bastar India 19°15N 81°40E 126 E5
Bastelica France 42°1N 9°3E 73 F13
Basti India 26°52N 82°55E 125 F10
Bastia France 42°40N 9°30E 73 F13
Bastogne Belgium 50°1N 5°43E 69 D5
Bastrop La., U.S.A. 32°47N 91°55W 176 E9
Bastrop Tex., U.S.A. 30°7N 97°19W 176 F6
Basuo = Dongfang
China 18°50N 108°33E 117 a
Bat Yam Israel 32°2N 34°44E 138 C3
Bata Eq. Guin. 1°57N 9°50E 140 D1
Bata Romania 46°1N 22°4E 80 D7
Bataan □ Phil. 14°40N 120°25E 119 B6
Batabanó Cuba 22°41N 82°18W 182 B3
Batabanó, G. de Cuba 22°30N 82°30W 182 B3
Batac Phil. 18°3N 120°34E 119 A6
Batagai Russia 67°38N 134°38E 107 C14
Batajnica Serbia 44°54N 20°17E 96 B4
Batak Bulgaria 41°57N 24°12E 97 E8
Batala India 31°48N 75°12E 124 D6
Batalha Portugal 39°40N 8°50W 88 F2
Batam Indonesia 1°10N 104°2E 121 d
Batama
Dem. Rep. of the Congo 0°58N 26°33E 142 B2
Batamay Russia 63°30N 129°15E 107 C13
Batang China 30°1N 99°0E 116 B2
Batang Indonesia 6°55S 109°45E 119 G13
Batangafo C.A.R. 7°25N 18°20E 140 C3
Batangas Phil. 13°35N 121°10E 119 B6
Batatais Brazil 20°54S 47°37W 191 A6
Batavia U.S.A. 43°0N 78°11W 174 C6
Bataysk Russia 47°3N 39°45E 85 J10
Batchelor Australia 13°4S 131°1E 148 B5
Batdambang Cambodia 13°7N 103°12E 120 F4
Batemans B. Australia 35°40S 150°12E 153 C9
Batemans Bay
Australia 35°44S 150°11E 153 C9
Batesburg-Leesville
U.S.A. 33°54N 81°33W 178 D6
Batesville Ark., U.S.A. 35°46N 91°39W 176 D8
Batesville Miss.,
U.S.A. 34°19N 89°57W 177 D10
Batesville Tex., U.S.A. 28°58N 99°37W 176 G5
Bath Canada 44°11N 76°47W 175 B8
Bath U.K. 51°23N 2°22W 67 F5
Bath Maine, U.S.A. 43°55N 69°49W 173 D19
Bath N.Y., U.S.A. 42°20N 77°19W 174 D7
Bath & North East Somerset □
U.K. 51°21N 2°27W 67 F5
Batheay Cambodia 11°59N 104°57E 121 G5
Bathsheba Barbados 13°13N 59°32W 183 g
Bathurst Australia 33°25S 149°31E 153 B8
Bathurst Canada 47°37N 65°43W 165 C6
Bathurst S. Africa 33°30S 26°50E 144 D4
Bathurst, C. Canada 70°34N 128°0W 160 C6
Bathurst B. Australia 14°16S 144°25E 150 A3
Bathurst Harb.
Australia 43°15S 146°10E 151 G4
Bathurst I. Australia 11°30S 130°10E 148 B5
Bathurst I. Canada 76°0N 100°30W 161 B11
Bathurst Inlet Canada 66°50N 108°1W 160 D10
Batie Burkina Faso 9°53N 2°53W 138 D4
Batiki Fiji 17°48S 179°10E 154 a
Batken Kyrgyzstan 39°50N 71°0E 109 E8
Batken □ Kyrgyzstan 39°50N 71°0E 109 E8
Batlow U.S.A. 35°31S 148°9E 153 C8
Batman Turkey 37°55N 41°5E 105 C9
Batn al Ghūl Jordan 29°36N 35°56E 130 F4
Batna Algeria 35°34N 6°15E 134 A7
Batna □ Algeria 35°30N 5°55E 134 A6
Batočina Serbia 44°7N 21°5E 96 B5
Batoka Zambia 16°45S 27°15E 143 F2
Baton Rouge U.S.A. 30°27N 91°11W 176 F9
Batong, Ko Thailand 6°32N 99°12E 121 J2
Bátonyterenye Hungary 47°59N 19°50E 80 C4
Batopilas Mexico 27°1N 107°44W 180 B3
Batouri Cameroon 4°30N 14°25E 140 D2
Båtsfjord Norway 70°38N 29°39E 60 A23
Batsi Greece 37°52N 24°47E 98 D6
Battambang = Batdambang
Cambodia 13°7N 103°12E 121 F4
Batticaloa Sri Lanka 7°43N 81°45E 127 L5
Battipáglia Italy 40°37N 14°58E 95 B7
Battle → Canada 52°43N 108°15W 162 C7
Battle Creek U.S.A. 42°19N 85°11W 173 D11
Battle Ground U.S.A. 45°47N 122°32W 170 E4
Battle Harbour Canada 52°16N 55°35W 165 B8
Battle Lake U.S.A. 46°17N 95°43W 172 B6
Battle Mountain
U.S.A. 40°38N 116°56W 168 F5
Battlefields Zimbabwe 18°37S 29°47E 143 F2
Battlefields Canada 52°45N 108°15W 163 C7
Battonya Hungary 46°16N 21°3E 80 E6
Batu Ethiopia 6°55N 39°45E 131 F2
Batu Malaysia 3°15N 101°40E 121 L3
Batu, Kepulauan
Indonesia 0°30S 98°25E 118 E1
Batu Ferringhi Malaysia 5°28N 100°15E 121 K3
Batu Gajah Malaysia 4°28N 101°3E 121 K3
Batu Is. = Batu, Kepulauan
Indonesia 0°30S 98°25E 118 E1
Batu Pahat Malaysia 1°50N 102°56E 121 M4
Batu Puteh, Gunung
Malaysia 4°15N 101°31E 121 K3
Batuata Indonesia 6°12S 122°42E 119 F6
Batugondang, Tanjung
Indonesia 8°6S 114°29E 119 J17
Batukaru, Gunung
Indonesia 8°20S 115°5E 119 J18
Batumi Georgia 41°30N 41°30E 87 J5
Batur, Gunung
Indonesia 8°20S 115°23E 119 J18
Baturaja Indonesia 4°11S 104°15E 118 E2
Baturité Brazil 4°7S 38°45W 189 A3

Baturiti Indonesia 8°19S 115°11E 119 J18
Batys Qazaqstan □
Kazakhstan 50°0N 50°0E 108 C3
Bau Malaysia 1°25N 110°9E 118 D4
Baubau Indonesia 5°25S 122°38E 119 F6
Baucau E. Timor 8°27S 126°27E 119 F7
Bauchi Nigeria 10°22N 9°48E 139 C6
Bauchi □ Nigeria 10°30N 10°0E 139 C7
Baud France 47°52N 3°1W 70 E3
Bauda India 20°50N 84°25E 126 D7
Baudette U.S.A. 48°43N 94°36W 172 A7
Bauer, C. Australia 32°44S 134°4E 151 E1
Bauhinia Australia 24°35S 149°18E 150 C4
Baukau = Baucau
E. Timor 8°27S 126°27E 119 F7
Baunatal Germany 51°14N 9°24E 76 D5
Baunei Italy 40°2N 9°40E 94 B2
Baure Nigeria 12°52N 9°50E 139 C6
Bauru Brazil 22°10S 49°0W 191 A6
Bausi India 24°48N 87°1E 125 G12
Bauska Latvia 56°24N 24°15E 82 B11
Bautino Kazakhstan 44°35N 50°14E 87 H10
Bautzen Germany 51°10N 14°26E 76 D10
Bauya S. Leone 8°12N 12°38W 138 D2
Bāvānāt Iran 30°28N 53°27E 129 D7
Bavanište Serbia 44°49N 20°55E 80 F5
Bavaria = Bayern □
Germany 48°50N 12°0E 77 G7
Båven Sweden 59°0N 16°56E 62 E10
Bavispe → Mexico 29°15N 109°11W 180 B3
Baw Burma 23°5N 97°20E 123 H20
Bawdwin Burma 23°5N 97°20E 123 H20
Bawean Indonesia 5°46S 112°35E 118 F4
Bawku Ghana 11°3N 0°19W 139 C4
Bawlake Burma 19°11N 97°21E 123 K20
Bawolung China 28°50N 101°16E 116 C3
Baxley U.S.A. 31°47N 82°21W 178 D7
Baxter U.S.A. 46°21N 94°17W 172 B6
Baxter Springs U.S.A. 37°2N 94°44W 172 G6
Bay City Mich., U.S.A. 43°36N 83°54W 173 D12
Bay City Tex., U.S.A. 28°59N 95°58W 176 G7
Bay Is. = Bahía, Is. de la
Honduras 16°45N 86°15W 182 C2
Bay Minette U.S.A. 30°53N 87°46W 177 F11
Bay of Plenty □ N.Z. 38°0S 177°0E 154 C5
Bay Roberts Canada 47°36N 53°16W 165 C9
Bay St. Louis U.S.A. 30°19N 89°20W 177 F10
Bay Springs U.S.A. 31°59N 89°17W 177 F10
Bay View N.Z. 39°25S 176°50E 154 F5
Baya
Dem. Rep. of the Congo 11°53S 27°25E 143 E2
Bayamo Cuba 20°20N 76°40W 182 B4
Bayamón Puerto Rico 18°24N 66°9W 183 d
Bayan Har Shan China 34°0N 98°0E 110 E8
Bayan Hot = Alxa Zuoqi
China 38°50N 105°40E 114 E3
Bayan Lepas Malaysia 5°17N 100°16E 121 c
Bayan Obo China 41°52N 109°59E 114 D5
Bayan-Ovoo = Erdenetsogt
Mongolia 42°55N 106°5E 114 C4
Bayana India 26°55N 77°18E 124 F7
Bayanaul Kazakhstan 50°45N 75°45E 108 D9
Bayanbulak △ China 42°30N 84°0E 109 D10
Bayanhongor Mongolia 46°8N 102°43E 110 B9
Bayard N. Mex., U.S.A. 32°46N 108°8W 169 K9
Bayard Nebr., U.S.A. 41°45N 103°20W 172 E2
Baybay Turkey 40°15N 40°20E 105 B9
Bayburt Turkey 40°15N 40°20E 105 B9
Baydaratskaya Guba
Russia 69°0N 67°30E 108 C7
Baydhabo Somalia 3°8N 43°30E 131 G3
Bayelsa □ Nigeria 4°30N 6°0E 139 E6
Bayerische Alpen
Germany 47°35N 11°30E 77 H7
Bayerische Rhön △
Germany 50°10N 10°5E 77 E6
Bayerischer Spessart △
Germany 49°58N 10°15E 77 F6
Bayerischer Wald
Germany 48°58N 12°50E 77 G8
Bayern □ Germany 48°50N 12°0E 77 G7
Bayeux France 49°17N 0°42W 70 C6
Bayfield Canada 43°34N 81°42W 174 C3
Bayfield U.S.A. 46°49N 90°49W 172 B8
Bayındır Turkey 38°13N 27°39E 99 D9
Baykal, Oz. Russia 53°0N 108°0E 107 D11
Baykan Turkey 38°7N 41°44E 105 C9
Baymak Russia 52°36N 58°19E 108 D5
Baynes Mts. Namibia 17°15S 13°0E 144 A1
Bayombong Phil. 16°30N 121°10E 119 A6
Bayon France 48°30N 6°20E 71 D13
Bayona = Baiona Spain 42°6N 8°52W 88 C2
Bayonet Point U.S.A. 28°19N 82°42W 179 G8
Bayonne France 43°30N 1°28W 72 E2
Bayonne U.S.A. 40°40N 74°6W 175 F10
Bayovar Peru 5°50S 81°0W 188 B1
Bayport U.S.A. 28°32N 82°39W 179 G8
Bayqongyr Kazakhstan 45°40N 63°20E 108 C6
Bayram-Ali = Bayramaly
Turkmenistan 37°37N 62°10E 109 F7
Bayramaly
Turkmenistan 37°37N 62°10E 109 F7
Bayramiç Turkey 39°48N 26°36E 99 B8
Bayreuth Germany 49°56N 11°35E 77 F7
Bayrischzell Germany 47°41N 12°0E 77 H8
Bayrūt Lebanon 33°53N 35°31E 130 B4
Bays, L. of Canada 45°15N 79°4W 174 A6
Bayshore U.S.A. 26°43N 81°59W 179 J8
Baysville Canada 45°9N 79°7W 174 A6
Baytik Shan China 45°45N 90°37E 110 B6
Baytown U.S.A. 29°43N 94°59W 176 G7
Bayuquan China 40°16N 122°28E 115 D12
Bayyo China 31°52N 106°46E 116 B6
Baza Spain 37°30N 2°47W 89 H8
Bazarak Afghanistan 35°17N 69°40E 124 B3
Bazardüzü = Bazar Dyuzi
Russia 41°13N 47°50E 87 K8
Bāzārgān Iran 39°22N 44°26E 128 B5
Bazarny Karabulak
Russia 52°20N 46°29E 86 D8
Bazarnyy Syzgan Russia 53°45N 46°40E 86 D8
Bazaruto △ Mozam. 21°40S 35°28E 145 B6
Bazaruto, I. do. Mozam. 21°42S 35°26E 145 B6
Bazas France 44°27N 0°13W 72 D3
Bazhong China 31°52N 106°46E 116 B6

Bazhou China 39°8N 116°22E 114 E9
Bazmān, Kūh-e Iran 28°4N 60°1E 129 D9
Baztan = Elizondo Spain 43°12N 1°30W 90 B3
Bé, Nosy Madag. 13°25S 48°15E 141 G9
Beach U.S.A. 46°58N 104°0W 172 B2
Beach City U.S.A. 40°39N 81°35W 174 F3
Beachport Australia 37°29S 140°0E 152 D4
Beachville Canada 43°5N 80°49W 174 C4
Beachy Hd. U.K. 50°44N 0°15E 67 G8
Beacon Australia 30°26S 117°52E 149 F2
Beacon U.S.A. 41°30N 73°58W 175 E11
Beaconsfield Australia 41°11S 146°48E 151 G4
Beagle, Canal S. Amer. 55°0S 68°30W 192 E3
Beagle Bay Australia 16°58S 122°40E 148 C3
Beagle Bay ○ Australia 16°53S 122°40E 148 C3
Beagle G. Australia 12°15S 130°25E 148 B5
Béal an Átha = Ballina
  Ireland 54°7N 9°9W 64 B2
Béal Átha na Sluaighe =
  Ballinasloe Ireland 53°20N 8°13W 64 C3
Beals Cr. → U.S.A. 32°10N 100°51W 176 E4
Beamsville Canada 43°12N 79°28W 174 C5
Bear → Calif., U.S.A. 38°56N 121°36W 170 G5
Bear → Utah, U.S.A. 41°30N 112°8W 166 G17
Béar, C. France 42°31N 3°8E 72 F7
Bear I. = Bjørnøya Arctic 74°30N 19°0E 54 B8
Bear I. Ireland 51°38N 9°50W 64 E2
Bear L. Canada 55°8N 96°0W 163 B9
Bear L. U.S.A. 41°59N 111°21W 168 F8
Bear Lake Canada 45°27N 79°35W 174 A5
Beardmore Canada 49°36N 87°57W 164 C2
Beardmore Glacier
  Antarctica 84°30S 170°0E 55 E11
Beardstown U.S.A. 40°1N 90°26W 172 E8
Bearma → India 24°20N 79°51E 125 G8
Bearpaw Mts. U.S.A. 48°10N 109°30W 168 B9
Bearskin Lake Canada 53°58N 91°2W 164 B1
Beas → India 31°10N 74°59E 124 D6
Beas de Segura Spain 38°15N 2°53W 89 G8
Beasain Spain 43°3N 2°11W 90 B2
Beata, C. Dom. Rep. 17°40N 71°30W 183 C5
Beata, I. Dom. Rep. 17°34N 71°31W 183 C5
Beatrice U.S.A. 40°16N 96°45W 172 E5
Beatrice Zimbabwe 18°15S 30°55E 143 F3
Beatrice, C. Australia 14°20S 136°55E 150 A2
Beatton → Canada 56°15N 120°45W 162 B4
Beatton River Canada 57°26N 121°20W 162 B4
Beatty U.S.A. 36°54N 116°46W 170 J10
Beau Bassin Mauritius 20°13S 57°27E 141 d
Beaucaire France 43°48N 4°39E 73 E8
Beauce, Plaine de la
  France 48°10N 1°45E 71 D8
Beauceville Canada 46°13N 70°46W 165 C5
Beauchêne, I. Falk. Is. 52°55S 59°15W 192 D5
Beaudesert Australia 27°59S 153°0E 151 D5
Beaufort Australia 37°25S 143°25E 152 D5
Beaufort France 45°44N 6°34E 73 C10
Beaufort Malaysia 5°30N 115°40E 118 C5
Beaufort N.C., U.S.A. 34°43N 76°40W 177 D16
Beaufort S.C., U.S.A. 32°26N 80°40W 178 C9
Beaufort Sea Arctic 72°0N 140°0W 158 B5
Beaufort West S. Africa 32°18S 22°36E 144 E3
Beaugency France 47°47N 1°38E 71 E8
Beauharnois Canada 45°20N 73°52W 175 A11
Beaujeu France 46°10N 4°35E 71 F11
Beaujolais France 46°0N 4°22E 71 F11
Beaulieu → Canada 62°3N 113°11W 162 A6
Beaulieu-sur-Dordogne
  France 44°58N 1°50E 72 D5
Beaulieu-sur-Mer
  France 43°42N 7°20E 73 E11
Beauly U.K. 57°30N 4°28W 65 D4
Beauly → U.K. 57°29N 4°27W 65 D4
Beaumaris U.K. 53°16N 4°6W 66 D3
Beaumont Belgium 50°15N 4°14E 69 D4
Beaumont N.Z. 45°50S 169°33E 155 F4
Beaumont Calif.,
  U.S.A. 33°57N 116°59W 171 M9
Beaumont Tex., U.S.A. 30°5N 94°6W 176 F7
Beaumont-de-Lomagne
  France 43°53N 1°0E 72 E5
Beaumont-du-Périgord
  France 44°45N 0°46E 72 D4
Beaumont-le-Roger
  France 49°4N 0°47E 70 C7
Beaumont-sur-Sarthe
  France 48°13N 0°8E 70 D7
Beaune France 47°2N 4°50E 71 E11
Beaune-la-Rolande France 48°4N 2°25E 71 D9
Beaupré Canada 47°3N 70°54W 165 C5
Beaupréau France 47°12N 1°0W 70 E6
Beauraing Belgium 50°7N 4°57E 69 D4
Beaurepaire France 45°20N 5°3E 73 C9
Beausejour Canada 50°5N 96°35W 163 C9
Beauvais France 49°25N 2°8E 71 C9
Beauval Canada 55°9N 107°37W 163 B7
Beauvoir-sur-Mer France 46°55N 2°2W 70 F4
Beauvoir-sur-Niort
  France 46°12N 0°30W 72 B3
Beaver Okla., U.S.A. 36°49N 100°31W 176 C4
Beaver Pa., U.S.A. 40°42N 80°19W 174 F4
Beaver Utah, U.S.A. 38°17N 112°38W 168 G7
Beaver → B.C.,
  Canada 59°52N 124°20W 162 B4
Beaver → Ont., Canada 55°55N 87°48W 164 A2
Beaver → Sask.,
  Canada 55°26N 107°45W 163 B7
Beaver City U.S.A. 40°8N 99°50W 172 E5
Beaver Creek Canada 63°0N 141°0W 160 E3
Beaver Dam U.S.A. 43°28N 88°50W 172 D9
Beaver Falls U.S.A. 40°46N 80°20W 174 F4
Beaver Hill L. Canada 54°5N 94°50W 163 C10
Beaver I. U.S.A. 45°40N 85°33W 173 C11
Beavercreek U.S.A. 39°43N 84°11W 173 F11
Beaverhill L. Canada 53°27N 112°32W 162 C6
Beaverlodge Canada 55°11N 119°29W 162 B5
Beaverstone →
  Canada 54°59N 89°25W 164 B2
Beaverton Canada 44°26N 79°9W 174 B5
Beaverton U.S.A. 45°29N 122°48W 174 B5
Beawar India 26°3N 74°18E 124 F5
Bebedouro Brazil 21°0S 48°25W 191 A6
Bebera, Tanjung
  Indonesia 8°44S 115°51E 119 K18
Bebington U.K. 53°22N 3°0W 66 D4
Bebra Germany 50°58N 9°48E 76 E5
Becán Mexico 18°34N 89°31W 181 D7
Bécancour Canada 46°20N 72°26W 173 B17
Beccles U.K. 52°27N 1°35E 67 E9

Bečej Serbia 45°36N 20°3E 80 E5
Beceni Romania 45°23N 26°48E 81 E11
Becerreá Spain 42°51N 7°10W 88 C3
Béchar Algeria 31°38N 2°18W 136 B4
Béchar □ Algeria 30°15N 3°5E 136 B4
Becharre = Bsharri
  Lebanon 34°15N 36°0E 130 A3
Bechyně Czech Rep. 49°17N 14°29E 76 D7
Beckley U.S.A. 37°47N 81°11W 173 G13
Beckum Germany 51°45N 8°3E 76 D4
Beclean Romania 47°11N 24°11E 81 C9
Bečov nad Teplou
  Czech Rep. 50°5N 12°49E 78 A5
Bečva → Czech Rep. 49°31N 17°20E 79 B10
Bédar Spain 37°11N 1°59W 91 H3
Bédarieux France 43°37N 3°10E 72 E7
Beddouza, C. Morocco 32°33N 9°9W 136 B4
Bederkesa Germany 53°37N 8°50E 76 B4
Bedford Canada 45°7N 72°59W 175 A12
Bedford S. Africa 32°40S 26°10E 144 D4
Bedford U.K. 52°8N 0°28W 67 E7
Bedford Ind., U.S.A. 38°52N 86°29W 172 F10
Bedford Iowa, U.S.A. 40°40N 94°44W 172 E6
Bedford Ohio, U.S.A. 41°23N 81°32W 174 E3
Bedford Pa., U.S.A. 40°1N 78°30W 174 F6
Bedford Va., U.S.A. 37°20N 79°31W 173 G14
Bedford □ U.K. 52°4N 0°28W 67 E7
Bedford, C. Australia 15°14S 145°21E 150 B4
Bedków Poland 51°36N 19°44E 83 D6
Bednja → Croatia 46°20N 16°52E 93 B13
Bednodemyanovsk
  Russia 53°55N 43°15E 86 D6
Bedok Singapore 1°19N 103°56E 121 d
Bedónia Italy 44°30N 9°38E 92 D6
Bedourie Australia 24°30S 139°30E 150 C2
Bedti → India 14°50N 74°44E 127 G2
Bedugul Indonesia 8°17S 115°10E 119 J18
Bedum Neths. 53°18N 6°36E 69 A6
Będzin Poland 50°19N 19°7E 83 H6
Bee Ridge U.S.A. 27°17N 82°29W 179 H7
Beebe Plain Canada 45°1N 72°9W 175 A12
Beech Creek U.S.A. 41°5N 77°36W 174 E7
Beechworth Australia 36°22S 146°43E 153 D7
Beechy Canada 50°53N 107°24W 163 C7
Beef I. Br. Virgin Is. 18°26N 64°30W 183 e
Beelitz Germany 52°14N 12°58E 76 C8
Beenleigh Australia 27°43S 153°10E 151 D5
Beerenberg Norway 71°0N 8°20W 57 C10
Beersheba = Be'er Sheva
  Israel 31°15N 34°48E 130 D3
Beeskow Germany 52°10N 14°15E 76 C10
Beesteraal S. Africa 25°23S 27°38E 145 C4
Beeston U.K. 52°56N 1°14W 66 E6
Beeton Canada 44°5N 79°47W 174 B5
Beetzendorf Germany 52°42N 11°6E 76 C7
Beeville U.S.A. 28°24N 97°45W 176 G6
Befale
  Dem. Rep. of the Congo 0°25N 20°45E 140 D4
Bega Australia 36°41S 149°51E 153 D8
Bega, Canalul Romania 45°37N 20°46E 80 E5
Bégard France 48°38N 3°18W 70 D3
Beğendik Turkey 40°55N 26°34E 97 F10
Begoro Ghana 6°23N 0°23W 139 D4
Begusarai India 25°24N 86°9E 125 G12
Behābād Iran 32°24N 59°47E 129 C8
Behbehān Iran 30°30N 50°15E 129 D6
Behchoko Canada 62°50N 116°3W 162 A5
Behm Canal U.S.A. 55°10N 131°0W 162 B2
Behshahr Iran 36°45N 53°35E 129 B7
Bei Jiang → China 23°2N 112°58E 117 F9
Bei Shan China 41°30N 96°0E 110 C8
Bei'an China 48°10N 126°20E 111 B14
Beibei China 29°47N 106°22E 116 C6
Beida, Es Sahrā al
  Egypt 27°50N 28°45E 137 B2
Beihai China 21°28N 109°6E 116 G7
Beijing China 39°53N 116°21E 114 E9
Beijing Capital Int. ✈ (PEK)
  China 40°5N 116°35E 114 D9
Beijing Shi □ China 39°55N 116°20E 114 E9
Beilen Neths. 52°52N 6°27E 69 B6
Beiliu China 22°41N 110°21E 117 F8
Beilngries Germany 49°2N 11°28E 77 F7
Beilpajah Australia 32°54S 143°52E 152 B5
Beinn na Faoghla = Benbecula
  U.K. 57°26N 7°21W 65 D1
Beipan Jiang → China 24°55N 106°5E 116 E6
Beipiao China 41°52N 120°32E 115 D11
Beira Mozam. 19°50S 34°52E 143 F3
Beirut = Bayrūt
  Lebanon 33°53N 35°31E 130 B4
Beiseker Canada 51°23N 113°32W 162 C6
Beit Lāḥiyā Gaza Strip 31°33N 34°30E 130 D3
Beit Lahm = Bayt Lahm
  West Bank 31°43N 35°12E 130 D4
Beitaolaizhao China 44°58N 125°58E 115 B13
Beitbridge Zimbabwe 22°12S 30°0E 143 G3
Beitun China 47°22N 87°4E 109 D11
Beiuș Romania 46°40N 22°21E 80 D7
Beizhen = Binzhou
  China 37°20N 118°2E 115 F10
Beizhen China 41°38N 121°54E 115 D11
Beizhengzhen China 44°31N 123°30E 115 B12
Beja Portugal 38°2N 7°53W 89 G3
Beja Tunisia 36°43N 9°12E 136 A1
Beja □ Portugal 37°55N 7°55W 89 H3
Beja → Portugal 38°17N 7°43W 89 G3
Bejaïa Algeria 36°42N 5°2E 136 A6
Bejaïa □ Algeria 36°40N 4°55E 136 A6
Béjar Spain 40°23N 5°46W 88 E5
Bejestān Iran 34°30N 58°5E 129 C8
Bekaa Valley = Al Biqā'
  Lebanon 34°10N 36°10E 130 A5
Bekasi Indonesia 6°14S 106°59E 119 G12
Bekçiler Turkey 36°56N 29°44E 99 E11
Bekdash Turkmenistan 41°34N 52°32E 108 D4
Békés Hungary 46°47N 21°9E 80 D6
Békés □ Hungary 46°45N 21°30E 80 D6
Békéscsaba Hungary 46°40N 21°5E 80 D6
Bekilli Turkey 38°17N 29°22E 99 C11
Bekok Malaysia 2°20N 103°7E 121 L4
Bekwai Ghana 6°30N 1°34W 139 D4
Bela India 25°50N 82°0E 125 G10
Bela Pakistan 26°12N 66°20E 124 F2
Bela Bela S. Africa 24°51S 28°19E 145 B4
Bela Crkva Serbia 44°55N 21°27E 80 F6

Bela Palanka Serbia 43°13N 22°17E 96 C5
Bela Vista Brazil 22°12S 56°20W 190 A4
Bela Vista Mozam. 26°10S 32°44E 145 C5
Bélâbre France 46°34N 1°8E 72 B5
Belagavi India 15°55N 74°35E 127 G2
Belalcázar Spain 38°35N 5°10W 89 G5
Belan → India 24°2N 81°45E 125 G9
Belanovica Serbia 44°15N 20°23E 96 B4
Belarus ■ Europe 53°30N 27°0E 75 B14
Belau = Palau ■ Palau 7°30N 134°30E 156 G5
Belawan Indonesia 3°33N 98°32E 118 D1
Belaya → Russia 54°40N 56°0E 108 B5
Belaya Glina Russia 46°5N 40°48E 87 G5
Belaya Kalitva Russia 48°13N 40°50E 87 F5
Belaya Tserkov = Bila Tserkva
  Ukraine 49°45N 30°10E 75 D16
Belaya Zemlya, Ostrova
  Russia 81°36N 62°18E 106 A7
Belcești Romania 47°19N 27°7E 81 C12
Belchatów Poland 51°21N 19°22E 83 G6
Belcher Is. Canada 56°15N 78°45W 164 A3
Belchite Spain 41°18N 0°43W 90 D4
Belden U.S.A. 40°2N 121°17W 170 D5
Belebey Russia 54°7N 54°7E 108 B4
Beledweyne Somalia 4°30N 45°5E 131 G4
Belém Brazil 1°20S 48°30W 187 D9
Belém de São Francisco
  Brazil 8°46S 38°58W 189 B3
Belén Argentina 27°40S 67°5W 190 B2
Belén Paraguay 23°30S 57°6W 190 A4
Belen Turkey 36°31N 36°10E 104 D7
Belen U.S.A. 34°40N 106°46W 169 J10
Belene Bulgaria 43°39N 25°10E 97 C9
Belesar France 42°55N 1°56E 72 F5
Belet Uen = Beledweyne
  Somalia 4°30N 45°5E 131 G4
Belev Russia 53°50N 36°5E 84 F9
Belevi Turkey 38°0N 27°28E 99 C9
Belfair U.S.A. 47°27N 122°50W 170 C4
Belfast S. Africa 25°42S 30°2E 145 C5
Belfast N.Z. 43°27S 172°39E 155 D7
Belfast U.K. 54°37N 5°56W 64 B6
Belfast Maine, U.S.A. 44°26N 69°1W 173 C19
Belfast N.Y., U.S.A. 42°21N 78°7W 174 D6
Belfast □ U.K. 54°40N 5°50W 64 B6
Belfield U.S.A. 46°53N 103°12W 172 B2
Belfort France 47°38N 6°50E 71 E13
Belfort, Territoire de □
  France 47°40N 6°55E 71 E13
Belfry U.S.A. 45°9N 109°1W 168 D9
Belgaum = Belagavi
  India 15°55N 74°35E 127 G2
Belgioioso Italy 45°10N 9°19E 92 C6
Belgium ■ Europe 50°30N 5°0E 69 D4
Belgodère France 42°35N 9°1E 73 F13
Belgorod Russia 50°35N 36°35E 85 G9
Belgorod □ Russia 50°45N 36°45E 85 G9
Belgorod-Dnestrovskiy =
  Bilhorod-Dnistrovskyy
  Ukraine 46°11N 30°23E 85 J6
Belgrade = Beograd
  Serbia 44°50N 20°37E 96 B4
Belgrade U.S.A. 45°47N 111°11W 168 D8
Belgrano Antarctica 77°52S 34°37W 55 D1
Belgrove N.Z. 41°27S 172°59E 155 B7
Belhaven U.S.A. 35°33N 76°37W 177 D16
Béli Guinea-Biss. 11°51N 13°56W 138 C2
Beli Nigeria 7°52N 10°55E 139 D7
Beli Drim → Europe 42°6N 20°25E 96 C4
Beli Manastir Croatia 45°45N 18°36E 80 E3
Beli Timok → Serbia 43°53N 22°14E 96 C6
Bélice → Italy 37°35N 12°55E 94 E5
Belimbing Indonesia 8°24S 115°2E 119 J18
Belinskiy Russia 53°0N 43°26E 86 D6
Belinyu Indonesia 1°35S 105°50E 118 E3
Beliton Is. = Belitung
  Indonesia 3°10S 107°50E 118 E3
Belitung Indonesia 3°10S 107°50E 118 E3
Beliu Romania 46°30N 22°0E 80 D6
Belize ■ Cent. Amer. 17°0N 88°30W 181 D7
Belize Barrier Reef Belize 17°9N 88°3W 181 D7
Belize City Belize 17°25N 88°10W 181 D7
Beljakovci Macedonia 42°6N 21°59E 96 D5
Beljanica Serbia 44°8N 21°43E 96 B5
Belkovskiy, Ostrov
  Russia 75°32N 135°44E 107 B14
Bell U.S.A. 29°45N 82°52W 179 F7
Bell → Canada 49°48N 77°38W 164 C4
Bell I. Canada 50°46N 55°35W 165 B8
Bell-Irving → Canada 56°12N 129°5W 162 B3
Bell Peninsula Canada 63°50N 82°0W 161 E15
Bell Ville Argentina 32°40S 62°40W 190 C3
Bella Italy 40°45N 15°32E 95 B8
Bella Bella Canada 52°10N 128°10W 162 C3
Bella Coola Canada 52°25N 126°40W 162 C3
Bella Flor Bolivia 11°9S 67°54W 188 C4
Bella Unión Uruguay 30°15S 57°40W 190 C4
Bella Vista Corrientes,
  Argentina 28°33S 59°0W 190 B4
Bella Vista Tucuman,
  Argentina 27°10S 65°25W 190 B2
Bellac France 46°7N 1°3E 72 B5
Bellágio Italy 45°59N 9°15E 92 C6
Bellaire U.S.A. 40°1N 80°45W 174 F4
Bellária Italy 44°9N 12°28E 93 D9
Bellata Australia 29°53S 149°46E 151 D4
Belle Fourche U.S.A. 44°40N 103°51W 172 C2
Belle Fourche →
  U.S.A. 44°26N 102°18W 172 C2
Belle Glade U.S.A. 26°41N 80°40W 179 J9
Belle-Île France 47°20N 3°10W 70 E3
Belle Isle Canada 51°57N 55°25W 165 B8
Belle Isle, Str. of
  Canada 51°30N 56°30W 165 B8
Belle Plaine U.S.A. 41°54N 92°17W 172 E7
Belle River Canada 42°18N 82°43W 174 D2
Belle Yella Liberia 7°24N 10°0W 138 D3
Belledonne France 45°20N 6°10E 73 C10
Bellefontaine U.S.A. 40°22N 83°46W 173 E12
Bellefonte U.S.A. 40°55N 77°47W 174 F7
Bellegarde France 47°59N 2°26E 71 E9
Bellegarde-en-Marche
  France 45°59N 2°18E 72 C6
Bellegarde-sur-Valserine
  France 46°4N 5°50E 71 F12
Bellême France 48°22N 0°34E 70 D7
Belleoram Canada 47°31N 55°25W 165 C8
Belleplaine Barbados 13°15N 59°34W 183 g

Belleview U.S.A. 29°4N 82°3W 179 F7
Belleville Canada 44°10N 77°23W 174 B7
Belleville France 46°7N 4°45E 71 F11
Belleville Ill., U.S.A. 38°31N 89°59W 172 F9
Belleville Kans., U.S.A. 39°50N 97°38W 172 F5
Belleville N.J., U.S.A. 40°47N 74°9W 175 F10
Belleville N.Y., U.S.A. 43°46N 76°10W 175 C8
Belleville-sur-Vie France 46°46N 1°25W 70 F5
Bellevue Idaho, U.S.A. 43°28N 114°16W 168 E6
Bellevue Nebr., U.S.A. 41°9N 95°54W 172 E6
Bellevue Ohio, U.S.A. 41°17N 82°51W 174 E2
Bellevue Wash.,
  U.S.A. 47°37N 122°12W 170 C4
Belley France 45°46N 5°41E 73 C9
Bellin = Kangirsuk
  Canada 60°0N 70°0W 161 F18
Bellinge Denmark 55°20N 10°20E 63 J4
Bellingen Australia 30°25S 152°50E 153 A10
Bellingham U.S.A. 48°46N 122°29W 170 B4
Bellingshausen Abyssal Plain
  S. Ocean 65°0S 90°0W 55 C16
Bellingshausen Sea
  Antarctica 66°0S 80°0W 55 C17
Bellinzona Switz. 46°11N 9°1E 77 J5
Bello Colombia 6°20N 75°33W 186 B3
Bellows Falls U.S.A. 43°8N 72°27W 175 C12
Belluno Italy 46°9N 12°13E 93 B9
Bellville U.S.A. 40°36N 78°20W 174 F6
Bélmez Spain 38°17N 5°17W 89 G5
Belmont Australia 33°4S 151°42E 153 B9
Belmont Canada 42°53N 81°5W 174 D3
Belmont S. Africa 29°28S 24°22E 144 C3
Belmont U.S.A. 42°14N 78°2W 174 D6
Belmonte Brazil 16°0S 39°0W 189 D3
Belmonte Portugal 40°21N 7°20W 88 E3
Belmonte Spain 39°34N 2°43W 91 F2
Belmopan Belize 17°18N 88°30W 181 D7
Belmullet Ireland 54°14N 9°58W 64 B2
Belo Horizonte Brazil 19°55S 43°56W 189 D2
Belo Jardim Brazil 8°20S 36°26W 189 B3
Belo-Tsiribihina Madag. 19°40S 44°30E 141 H8
Belogorsk = Bilohirsk
  Ukraine 45°3N 34°35E 85 K8
Belogorsk Russia 51°0N 128°20E 107 D13
Belogradchik Bulgaria 43°53N 22°42E 96 C6
Belogradets Bulgaria 43°22N 27°18E 97 C11
Beloit Kans., U.S.A. 39°28N 98°6W 172 F4
Beloit Wis., U.S.A. 42°31N 89°2W 172 D9
Belokorovichi Ukraine 51°7N 28°2E 75 C15
Belomorsk Russia 64°35N 34°54E 106 C4
Belonia India 23°15N 91°30E 123 H17
Belopolye = Bilopillya
  Ukraine 51°14N 34°20E 85 G8
Belorechensk Russia 44°46N 39°52E 87 H4
Beloretsk Russia 53°58N 58°24E 108 B5
Belorussia = Belarus ■
  Europe 53°30N 27°0E 75 B14
Beloslav Bulgaria 43°11N 27°42E 97 C11
Beloūsovka Kazakhstan 50°8N 82°31E 109 B10
Belovezhskaya Pushcha =
  Białowieża △ Poland 52°43N 23°50E 83 F10
Belovo Bulgaria 42°13N 24°11E 97 D8
Belovo Russia 54°30N 86°0E 109 D11
Beloyarskiy Russia 63°42N 66°40E 106 C7
Beloye, Ozero Russia 60°10N 37°35E 84 B9
Beloye More Russia 66°30N 38°0E 58 B13
Belozem Bulgaria 42°12N 25°2E 97 D9
Belozersk Russia 60°1N 37°45E 84 B9
Belpasso Italy 37°35N 14°58E 95 E7
Belpre U.S.A. 39°17N 81°34W 173 F13
Belrain India 28°23N 80°55E 125 E9
Belt U.S.A. 47°23N 110°55W 168 C8
Beltana Australia 30°48S 138°25E 152 A3
Belterra Brazil 2°45S 55°0W 187 D8
Beltinci Slovenia 46°37N 16°20E 93 B13
Belton U.S.A. 31°3N 97°28W 176 F6
Beltsy = Bălți Moldova 47°48N 27°58E 81 C12
Belturbet Ireland 54°6N 7°26W 64 B4
Belukha Russia 49°50N 86°50E 109 C11
Beluran Malaysia 5°48N 117°35E 118 C5
Belušia Slovak Rep. 49°5N 18°17E 79 B11
Belushya Guba Russia 71°32N 52°19E 106 B6
Belušić Serbia 43°47N 21°10E 96 C5
Belvédère Maríttimo
  Italy 39°37N 15°52E 95 C8
Belvès France 44°46N 1°0E 72 D5
Belvidere Ill., U.S.A. 42°15N 88°50W 172 D9
Belvidere N.J., U.S.A. 40°50N 75°5W 175 F9
Belvís de la Jara Spain 39°45N 4°57W 88 F6
Belyando → Australia 21°38S 146°50E 150 C4
Belyando Crossing
  Australia 21°32S 146°51E 150 C4
Belyuen Australia 12°34S 130°42E 148 B5
Belyy Russia 55°49N 33°3E 84 E7
Belyy, Ostrov Russia 73°30N 71°0E 106 B8
Belyy Yar Russia 58°26N 84°39E 106 D9
Belyye Vody = Aqsū
  Kazakhstan 42°25N 69°50E 108 D7
Belz Ukraine 50°23N 24°1E 83 H11
Bełżec Poland 50°23N 23°26E 83 H10
Bełżyce Poland 51°11N 22°17E 83 G9
Belzoni U.S.A. 33°11N 90°29W 177 E10
Bembéréke Benin 10°11N 2°43E 139 C5
Bembesi Zimbabwe 20°0S 28°58E 143 G2
Bembesi → Zimbabwe 18°57S 27°47E 143 F2
Bembézar → Spain 37°45N 5°13W 89 H5
Bembibre Spain 42°41N 6°20W 88 C4
Bemboka Australia 36°35S 149°41E 153 D8
Bemetara India 21°42N 81°32E 125 J9
Bemidji U.S.A. 47°28N 94°53W 172 B6
Ben Iran 32°32N 50°45E 129 C6
Ben Boyd △ Australia 37°0S 149°55E 153 D8
Ben Cruachan U.K. 56°26N 5°8W 65 E3
Ben Dearg U.K. 57°47N 4°56W 65 D4
Ben En △ Vietnam 19°37N 105°30E 120 C5
Ben Gardane Tunisia 33°11N 11°11E 136 B8
Ben Halls Gap △
  Australia 31°37S 151°1E 153 A9
Ben Hope U.K. 58°25N 4°36W 65 C4
Ben Lawers U.K. 56°32N 4°14W 65 E4
Ben Lomond N.S.W.,
  Australia 30°1S 151°43E 153 A9
Ben Lomond Tas.,
  Australia 41°38S 147°42E 151 G4
Ben Lomond △
  Australia 41°38S 147°42E 151 G4
Ben Lomond △ U.K. 56°11N 4°38W 65 E4

Ben Luc Vietnam 10°39N 106°29E 121 G6
Ben Macdhui U.K. 57°4N 3°40W 65 D5
Ben Mhor U.K. 57°15N 7°18W 65 D1
Ben More Argyll & Bute,
  U.K. 56°26N 6°1W 65 E2
Ben More Stirling, U.K. 56°23N 4°32W 65 E4
Ben More Assynt U.K. 58°8N 4°52W 65 C4
Ben Nevis U.K. 56°48N 5°1W 65 E3
Ben Ohau Ra. N.Z. 44°15S 170°4E 155 E5
Ben Quang Vietnam 17°3N 106°55E 120 D6
Ben Slimane Morocco 33°38N 7°7W 136 B2
Ben Tadjine, Djebel
  Algeria 29°0N 3°30W 136 C3
Ben Tre Vietnam 10°14N 106°23E 121 G6
Ben Vorlich U.K. 56°21N 4°14W 65 E4
Ben Wyvis U.K. 57°40N 4°35W 65 D4
Bena Nigeria 11°20N 5°50E 139 C6
Benaco = Garda, L. di
  Italy 45°40N 10°41E 92 C7
Benagerie Australia 31°25S 140°22E 152 B3
Benahmed Morocco 33°4N 7°9W 136 B2
Benalla Australia 36°30S 146°0E 153 D7
Benalmádena Spain 36°36N 4°34W 89 J6
Benambra, Mt.
  Australia 36°31S 147°34E 153 D7
Benamejí Spain 37°16N 4°33W 89 H6
Benares = Varanasi
  India 25°22N 83°0E 125 G10
Benavente Portugal 38°59N 8°49W 89 G2
Benavente Spain 42°2N 5°43W 88 C5
Benavides Spain 42°30N 5°54W 88 C5
Benavides de Órbigo
  Spain 42°30N 5°54W 88 C5
Benbecula U.K. 57°26N 7°21W 65 D1
Benbonyathe Hill
  Australia 30°25S 139°11E 152 A3
Bend U.S.A. 44°4N 121°19W 168 D3
Bendemeer Australia 30°53S 151°8E 153 A9
Bender Beyla Somalia 9°30N 50°48E 131 F5
Bendery = Tighina
  Moldova 46°50N 29°30E 81 D14
Bendigo Australia 36°40S 144°15E 152 D6
Bendorf Germany 50°25N 7°35E 76 E3
Bene Beraq Israel 32°6N 34°51E 130 C3
Benenitra Madag. 23°27S 45°5E 141 J8
Benešov Czech Rep. 49°46N 14°41E 78 B7
Bénestroff France 48°54N 6°45E 71 D13
Benevento Italy 41°8N 14°45E 95 A7
Benfeld France 48°22N 7°34E 71 D14
Beng Mealea Cambodia 13°28N 104°14E 120 F5
Bengal, Bay of Ind. Oc. 15°0N 90°0E 123 M17
Bengbis Cameroon 3°27N 12°36E 139 E7
Bengbu China 32°58N 117°20E 117 A11
Benghazi = Banghāzī
  Libya 32°11N 20°3E 135 B10
Bengkalis Indonesia 1°30N 102°10E 121 M4
Bengkulu Indonesia 3°50S 102°12E 118 E2
Bengkulu □ Indonesia 3°48S 102°16E 118 E2
Bengough Canada 49°25N 105°10W 163 D7
Bengtsfors Sweden 59°2N 12°14E 63 E6
Benguela Angola 12°37S 13°25E 141 G2
Benguérir Morocco 32°16N 7°56W 136 B2
Benguérua, I. Mozam. 21°58S 35°28E 145 B6
Benha Egypt 30°26N 31°8E 137 E7
Beni
  Dem. Rep. of the Congo 0°30N 29°27E 142 B2
Beni → Bolivia 10°23S 65°24W 186 F5
Beni Abbès Algeria 30°5N 2°5W 136 B3
Beni Hammad Algeria 35°49N 4°47E 136 A4
Beni Haoua Algeria 36°30N 1°30E 136 A5
Beni Mazâr Egypt 28°32N 30°44E 137 C7
Beni Mellal Morocco 32°21N 6°21W 136 B2
Beni Ounif Algeria 32°0N 1°10W 136 B3
Beni Suef Egypt 29°5N 31°6E 137 C7
Beniah L. Canada 63°23N 112°17W 162 A6
Benicarló Spain 40°23N 0°23E 90 E5
Benicássim Spain 40°3N 0°9E 90 E5
Benidorm Spain 38°33N 0°9W 91 G4
Benin ■ Africa 10°0N 2°0E 139 D5
Benin, Bight of W. Afr. 5°0N 3°0E 139 E5
Benin City Nigeria 6°20N 5°31E 139 D6
Benissa Spain 38°43N 0°3E 91 G5
Benito Juárez Argentina 37°40S 59°43W 190 D4
Benitses Greece 39°32N 19°55E 101 A3
Benjamin Aceval
  Paraguay 24°58S 57°34W 190 A4
Benjamin Constant
  Brazil 4°40S 70°15W 186 D4
Benjamin Hill Mexico 30°9N 111°7W 180 A2
Benkelman U.S.A. 40°3N 101°32W 172 E4
Benkovac Croatia 44°2N 15°37E 93 D12
Benmore, L. N.Z. 44°25S 170°8E 155 F3
Benmore Pk. N.Z. 44°28S 170°13E 155 F3
Bennett Canada 59°51N 135°0W 162 B2
Bennett, L. Australia 22°50S 131°2E 148 D5
Bennetta, Ostrov
  Russia 76°21N 148°56E 107 B15
Bennettsville U.S.A. 34°37N 79°41W 177 D15
Bennichchâb
  Mauritania 19°32N 15°12W 138 B1
Bennington N.H.,
  U.S.A. 43°0N 71°55W 175 D11
Bennington Vt.,
  U.S.A. 42°53N 73°12W 175 D11
Bénodet France 47°53N 4°7W 70 E2
Bénoni S. Africa 26°11S 28°18E 145 C4
Benque Viejo del Carmen
  Belize 17°5N 89°8W 181 D7
Bensheim Germany 49°40N 8°38E 77 F4
Benson Ariz., U.S.A. 31°58N 110°18W 169 L8
Benson Minn., U.S.A. 45°19N 95°36W 172 C6
Bent Iran 26°20N 59°31E 129 E8
Benteng Indonesia 6°10S 120°30E 119 F6
Bentinck I. Australia 17°3S 139°35E 150 B2
Bentley Subglacial Trench
  Antarctica 80°0S 115°0W 55 F16
Bento Gonçalves Brazil 29°10S 51°31W 191 B5
Benton Ark., U.S.A. 34°34N 92°35W 176 D8
Benton Calif., U.S.A. 37°48N 118°32W 170 H8
Benton Ill., U.S.A. 38°0N 88°55W 172 G9
Benton Pa., U.S.A. 41°12N 76°23W 174 E8
Benton Harbor U.S.A. 42°6N 86°27W 172 D10
Bentong Malaysia 3°31N 101°55E 121 L3

Bentonville U.S.A. 36°22N 94°13W 176 C7
Benue □ Nigeria 7°20N 8°45E 139 D7
Benue → Nigeria 7°48N 6°46E 139 D6
Benxi China 41°20N 123°48E 115 D12
Beo Indonesia 4°25N 126°50E 119 D7
Beograd Serbia 44°50N 20°37E 96 B4
Beograd ✈ (BEG) Serbia 43°49N 20°17E 96 C4
Beolgyo S. Korea 34°51N 127°21E 115 G14
Beoumi Ivory C. 7°45N 5°23W 138 D3
Beppu Japan 33°15N 131°30E 112 G5
Beqa Fiji 18°23S 178°8E 153 a
Beqaa Valley = Al Biqā'
  Lebanon 34°10N 36°10E 130 A5
Ber Mota India 23°27N 68°34E 124 H3
Bera, Tasik Malaysia 3°5N 102°38E 121 L4
Berach → India 25°15N 75°2E 124 G6
Berane Montenegro 42°51N 19°52E 96 C3
Berastagi Indonesia 3°1N 98°31E 118 D1
Berat Albania 40°43N 19°59E 96 E2
Berau = Tanjungredeb
  Indonesia 2°9N 117°29E 119 D5
Berau, Teluk Indonesia 2°30S 132°30E 119 E8
Beraun Sudan 18°0N 34°0E 135 E12
Berber Sudan 18°0N 34°0E 135 E12
Berbera Somalia 10°30N 45°2E 131 E4
Berbérati C.A.R. 4°15N 15°40E 142 D3
Berbice → Guyana 6°20N 57°32W 186 B7
Berceto Italy 44°31N 9°59E 92 D7
Berchidda Italy 40°47N 9°10E 94 B2
Berchtesgaden Germany 47°38N 13°0E 77 J7
Berchtesgaden △
  Germany 47°34N 12°55E 77 J7
Berck France 50°25N 1°36E 71 B8
Berdichev = Berdychiv
  Ukraine 49°57N 28°30E 75 D15
Berdsk Russia 54°47N 83°2E 109 D9
Berdyansk Ukraine 46°45N 36°50E 85 J9
Berdychiv Ukraine 49°57N 28°30E 75 D15
Berea U.S.A. 37°34N 84°17W 173 G11
Berebere Indonesia 2°25N 128°45E 119 D7
Bereeda Somalia 11°45N 51°0E 131 E6
Berehomet Ukraine 48°10N 25°19E 81 B8
Berehove Ukraine 48°15N 22°35E 81 B8
Bereket Turkmenistan 39°16N 55°32E 129 B7
Berekum Ghana 7°29N 2°34W 138 D4
Berenice Egypt 24°2N 35°25E 135 D12
Berens → Canada 52°18N 97°18W 163 C9
Berens I. Canada 52°18N 97°18W 163 C9
Berens River Canada 52°25N 97°0W 163 C9
Beresford Australia 32°50S 151°43E 153 B9
Beresford U.S.A. 43°5N 96°47W 172 D5
Berestechko Ukraine 50°22N 25°5E 81 A8
Berettyó → Hungary 46°59N 21°7E 80 E6
Berettyóújfalu Hungary 47°13N 21°33E 80 D6
Bereza = Byaroza
  Belarus 52°31N 24°51E 75 B13
Berezhany Ukraine 49°26N 24°58E 81 B8
Berezina = Byarezina →
  Belarus 52°33N 30°14E 75 B16
Berezivka Ukraine 47°14N 30°55E 85 J6
Berezna Ukraine 51°35N 31°46E 85 G6
Bereznik Russia 62°51N 42°40E 108 A3
Berezniki Russia 59°24N 56°46E 108 B5
Berezovo Russia 64°0N 65°0E 108 A7
Berezyne Ukraine 46°14N 29°12E 81 D15
Berga Spain 42°6N 1°48E 90 C6
Berga Sweden 57°14N 16°3E 63 F7
Bergama Turkey 39°8N 27°11E 99 C9
Bérgamo Italy 45°41N 9°43E 92 C6
Bergantiños Spain 43°13N 8°50W 88 B2
Bergara Spain 43°9N 2°28W 90 B2
Bergby Sweden 60°57N 17°2E 63 E7
Berge Norway 59°34N 8°10E 63 F5
Bergedorf Germany 53°28N 10°12E 76 B6
Bergen Mecklenburg-Vorpommern,
  Germany 54°25N 13°25E 76 A9
Bergen Niedersachsen,
  Germany 52°49N 9°58E 76 C5
Bergen Neths. 52°40N 4°43E 69 B4
Bergen Norway 60°20N 5°20E 63 E4
Bergen U.S.A. 43°5N 77°57W 174 C7
Bergen op Zoom Neths. 51°28N 4°18E 69 C4
Bergerac France 44°51N 0°30E 72 D4
Bergheim Germany 50°57N 6°38E 76 E2
Bergholz U.S.A. 40°31N 80°53W 174 F4
Bergisch Gladbach
  Germany 50°59N 7°8E 76 E3
Bergisches Land
  Germany 51°0N 7°30E 76 E3
Bergkamen Germany 51°37N 7°38E 76 D3
Bergkvara Sweden 56°23N 16°5E 63 H7
Bergshamra Sweden 59°38N 18°37E 62 F4
Bergsjö Sweden 61°59N 17°3E 62 E7
Bergstrasse-Odenwald △
  Germany 49°45N 5°55E 77 F4
Bergues France 50°58N 2°24E 71 B9
Bergviken Sweden 61°15N 16°40E 62 E7
Bergville S. Africa 28°52S 29°18E 145 D4
Berhala, Selat Indonesia 1°0S 104°15E 118 E2
Berhampore = Baharampur
  India 24°2N 88°27E 125 G13
Berhampur = Brahmapur
  India 19°15N 84°54E 126 E8
Berheci → Romania 45°58N 27°28E 81 C12
Bering Glacier
  U.S.A. 60°20N 143°30W 160 E5
Bering Sea Pac. Oc. 58°0N 171°0W 158 C1
Bering Strait Pac. Oc. 65°30N 169°0W 160 C3
Beringovskiy Russia 63°3N 179°19E 107 C18
Berisso Argentina 34°56S 57°50W 190 C4
Berja Spain 36°50N 2°56W 89 J8
Berkane Morocco 34°52N 2°20W 136 B4
Berkeley U.S.A. 37°52N 122°16W 170 H4
Berkner I. Antarctica 79°30S 50°0W 55 D18
Berkovitsa Bulgaria 43°16N 23°8E 96 C7
Berkshire U.S.A. 42°19N 76°11W 175 D8
Berkshire Downs U.K. 51°33N 1°29W 67 F6
Berlanga Spain 38°17N 5°50W 89 G5
Berlenga, I. Portugal 39°25N 9°30W 88 F1
Berlin Germany 52°31N 13°23E 76 C9
Berlin Ga., U.S.A. 31°4N 83°37W 178 D6
Berlin Md., U.S.A. 38°20N 75°13W 173 F18
Berlin N.H., U.S.A. 44°28N 71°11W 175 B13
Berlin N.Y., U.S.A. 42°42N 73°23W 175 D11
Berlin Wis., U.S.A. 43°58N 88°57W 172 D9
Berlin, L. U.S.A. 39°3N 81°0W 174 F5
Berlin Tegel ✈ (TXL)
  Germany 52°33N 13°14E 76 C9

magui *Australia* 36°25S 150°4E **153 D9**
meja, Sierra *Spain* 36°30N 5°11W **89 J5**
mejo ➤ *Formosa,*
Argentina 26°51S 58°23W **190 B4**
mejo ➤ *San Juan,*
Argentina 32°30S 67°30W **190 C2**
mejo, Paso = Uspallata, P. de
Argentina 32°37S 69°22W **190 C2**
men, L. *Canada* 53°35N 68°55W **165 B6**
meo *Spain* 43°25N 2°47W **90 B2**
millo de Sayago *Spain* 41°22N 6°8W **88 D4**
muda ☒ *Atl. Oc.* 32°18N 64°45W **159 F13**
n ☐ *Switz.* 46°57N 7°28E **77 J3**
n ☐ *Switz.* 46°45N 7°40E **77 J3**
nalda *Italy* 40°24N 16°41E **95 B9**
nalillo *U.S.A.* 35°18N 106°33W **169 J10**
nardo de Irigoyen
Argentina 26°15S 53°40W **191 B5**
nardo O'Higgins ➤
Chile 48°50S 75°36W **192 C1**
nardsville *U.S.A.* 40°43N 74°34W **175 F10**
nasconi *Argentina* 37°55S 63°44W **190 D3**
nau *Bayern, Germany* 47°47N 12°22E **77 H8**
nau *Brandenburg,*
Germany 52°40N 13°35E **76 C9**
nay *France* 49°5N 0°35E **70 C7**
nburg *Germany* 51°47N 11°44E **76 D7**
ndorf *Austria* 47°59N 16°1E **78 D9**
ne = Bern *Switz.* 46°57N 7°28E **77 J3**
ne = Bern ☐ *Switz.* 46°45N 7°40E **77 J3**
ner Alpen *Switz.* 46°25N 7°30E **77 J3**
neray *U.K.* 57°43N 7°11W **65 D1**
nier I. *Australia* 24°50S 113°12E **149 D1**
nina, Piz *Switz.* 46°20N 9°54E **77 J5**
nkastel-Kues *Germany* 49°55N 7°3E **77 F3**
nobouay *Benin* 10°34N 2°46E **139 C5**
noun *Czech Rep.* 49°57N 14°5E **78 B7**
nounka ➤ *Czech Rep.* 50°0N 14°22E **78 B7**
novo *Macedonia* 41°38N 22°51E **96 E6**
ne, Étang de *France* 43°27N 5°5E **73 E9**
ne-l'Étang *France* 43°27N 5°10E **73 E9**
rechid *Morocco* 33°18N 7°36W **136 B2**
ri *Australia* 34°14S 140°35E **152 C4**
ridale *Australia* 36°22S 148°48E **153 C8**
rigan *Australia* 35°38S 145°49E **153 C6**
riwillock *Australia* 35°38S 142°59E **152 C5**
rouaghia *Algeria* 36°10N 2°53E **136 A4**
ry *Australia* 34°46S 150°43E **153 C9**
ry *France* 46°50N 2°0E **71 F8**
ry Is. *Bahamas* 25°40N 77°50W **182 A4**
rydale *U.S.A.* 30°53N 87°29W **179 E2**
ryessa, L. *U.S.A.* 38°31N 122°6W **170 C4**
ryville *U.S.A.* 36°22N 93°34W **176 C8**
seba *Namibia* 26°0S 17°46E **144 C2**
senbrück *Germany* 52°34N 7°56E **76 C3**
shad *Ukraine* 48°22N 29°31E **81 B14**
tamirans *Spain* 42°54N 8°38W **88 C2**
thoud *U.S.A.* 48°19N 101°44W **172 A3**
tincourt *France* 50°5N 2°58E **71 B9**
tolinia *Brazil* 7°38S 43°57W **189 B2**
toua *Cameroon* 4°30N 13°45E **140 A3**
traghboy B. *Ireland* 53°22N 9°54W **64 C2**
uniy *Uzbekistan* 41°41N 60°45E **108 D6**
uwala *Sri Lanka* 8°0N 80°0E **127 L4**
wick *U.S.A.* 41°3N 76°14W **175 E8**
wick-upon-Tweed
U.K. 55°46N 2°0W **66 B6**
wyn Mts. *U.K.* 52°54N 3°26W **66 E4**
yslav *Ukraine* 46°50N 33°30E **85 J7**
zasca *Romania* 44°39N 21°58E **80 F6**
zence *Hungary* 46°12N 17°11E **80 D2**
al *Pakistan* 35°4N 73°56E **125 B5**
alampy *Madag.* 16°43S 44°29E **141 B8**
ançon *France* 47°15N 6°2E **71 E13**
ar *Indonesia* 2°40S 116°0E **118 E5**
henkovichi *Belarus* 55°2N 29°29E **84 E5**
iani *Kosovo* 42°54N 21°10E **96 D5**
ka *Serbia* 45°8N 20°6E **80 E5**
lan *Russia* 43°15N 44°28E **87 J7**
na Kobila *Serbia* 42°31N 22°10E **96 D6**
nard L. *Canada* 52°35N 106°0W **163 B7**
nil *Turkey* 37°41N 37°52E **104 D7**
or, N. ➤ *Egypt* 31°28N 34°22E **130 D3**
sarabiya *Moldova* 28°20N 28°10E **75 E15**
sarabka = Basarabeasca
Moldova 46°21N 28°58E **81 D13**
sèges *France* 44°18N 4°8E **73 D8**
semer *Ala., U.S.A.* 33°24N 86°58W **177 E11**
semer *Pa., U.S.A.* 40°59N 80°30W **174 F4**
ssin *France* 46°18N 1°0W **70 C6**
ssines-sur-Gartempe
France 46°6N 1°22E **72 B5**
wick *Australia* 14°34S 132°53E **148 B5**
wick ☐ *Australia* 14°31S 132°51E **148 B5**
She'an *Israel* 32°30N 35°30E **130 C4**
Shemesh *Israel* 31°44N 35°0E **130 D4**
hulie *S. Africa* 30°30S 25°59E **144 D4**
hune *France* 50°30N 3°28E **71 B9**
hune *France* 49°53N 1°4E **70 D8**
hungra *Australia* 34°45S 147°51E **153 C7**
im *Brazil* 19°58S 44°0W **189 D2**
idu *Madag.* 20°0N 48°0E **141 J8**
ong *Malaysia* 1°24N 111°31E **118 D4**
ong *Thailand* 5°45N 101°5E **121 K3**
roka *Madag.* 23°16S 46°0E **141 J9**

Betsiamites *Canada* 48°56N 68°40W **165 B6**
Betsiamites ➤ *Canada* 48°56N 68°38W **165 B6**
Bettendorf *U.S.A.* 41°32N 90°30W **172 E8**
Bettiah *India* 26°48N 84°33E **125 F11**
Bettna *Sweden* 58°55N 16°38E **63 F10**
Béttola *Italy* 44°47N 9°36E **92 D6**
Betul *India* 21°58N 77°59E **126 D3**
Betws-y-Coed *U.K.* 53°5N 3°48W **66 D4**
Betxi *Spain* 39°56N 0°12W **90 F4**
Betzdorf *Germany* 50°46N 7°52E **76 E3**
Beuil *France* 44°6N 6°59E **73 D10**
Beulah *Australia* 35°58S 142°29E **152 C5**
Beulah *Mich., U.S.A.* 44°38N 86°6W **172 C10**
Beulah *N. Dak., U.S.A.* 47°16N 101°47W **172 B3**
Beuvron ➤ *France* 47°29N 1°15E **70 E8**
Beverley *Australia* 32°9S 116°56E **149 F2**
Beverley *U.K.* 53°51N 0°26W **67 E7**
Beverly *U.S.A.* 42°33N 70°53W **175 D14**
Beverly Hills *Calif.,*
U.S.A. 34°5N 118°24W **171 L8**
Beverly Hills *Fla.,*
U.S.A. 28°55N 82°28W **179 G7**
Beverungen *Germany* 51°39N 9°22E **76 D5**
Bewas ➤ *India* 23°59N 79°21E **125 H8**
Bewdley *Canada* 44°5N 78°19W **174 B6**
Bexhill *U.K.* 50°51N 0°29E **67 H8**
Bey Dağları *Turkey* 36°38N 30°29E **99 E12**
Beyānlū *Iran* 36°0N 47°51E **126 A5**
Beyazköy *Turkey* 41°21N 27°42E **97 E11**
Beyçayırı *Turkey* 40°15N 26°55E **97 F10**
Beydağ *Turkey* 38°5N 28°13E **99 D10**
Beyşağ *Turkey* 37°14N 28°53E **99 D10**
Beyin *Ghana* 5°1N 2°41W **138 D4**
Beykoz *Turkey* 41°7N 29°7E **97 E13**
Beyla *Guinea* 8°30N 8°38W **138 D3**
Beynat *France* 45°8N 1°44E **72 C5**
Beyneu *Kazakhstan* 45°18N 55°9E **108 D5**
Beyoba *Turkey* 38°48N 27°47E **99 C9**
Beyoğlu *Turkey* 41°1N 28°58E **97 E12**
Beypazarı *Turkey* 40°10N 31°56E **104 B4**
Beypore ➤ *India* 11°10N 75°47E **127 J2**
Beysehir *Turkey* 37°41N 31°43E **104 D4**
Beysehir Gölü *Turkey* 37°41N 31°33E **104 D4**
Beytüşşebap *Turkey* 37°35N 43°10E **105 D10**
Bezdan *Serbia* 45°50N 18°57E **80 E3**
Bezhetsk *Russia* 57°47N 36°39E **84 D9**
Béziers *France* 43°20N 3°12E **72 E7**
Bezwada = Vijayawada
India 16°31N 80°39E **126 F5**
Bhabua *India* 25°3N 83°37E **125 G10**
Bhachau *India* 23°20N 70°16E **124 H4**
Bhadar ➤ *Gujarat,*
India 22°17N 72°20E **124 H5**
Bhadar ➤ *Gujarat,*
India 21°27N 69°47E **124 J3**
Bhadarwah *India* 32°58N 75°46E **125 C6**
Bhadgaon = Bhaktapur
Nepal 27°38N 85°24E **125 F11**
Bhadohi *India* 25°25N 82°34E **125 G10**
Bhadra *India* 29°8N 75°14E **124 E6**
Bhadra ➤ *India* 14°0N 75°20E **127 H2**
Bhadrachalam *India* 17°40N 80°52E **126 F5**
Bhadrak *India* 21°10N 86°30E **126 D8**
Bhadravati *India* 13°49N 75°40E **127 H2**
Bhag *Pakistan* 29°2N 67°49E **124 E2**
Bhagalpur *India* 25°10N 87°0E **125 G12**
Bhagirathi ➤ *Paschimbanga,*
India 23°25N 88°23E **125 H13**
Bhagirathi ➤ *Uttarakhand,*
India 30°8N 78°35E **125 D8**
Bhainsa *India* 19°10N 77°58E **126 E3**
Bhakkar *Pakistan* 31°40N 71°5E **124 D4**
Bhakra Dam *India* 31°30N 76°45E **124 D7**
Bhaktapur *Nepal* 27°38N 85°24E **125 F11**
Bhalki *India* 18°2N 77°13E **126 E3**
Bhamo *Burma* 24°15N 97°15E **123 G20**
Bhamragarh *India* 19°30N 80°40E **126 E5**
Bhandara *India* 21°5N 79°42E **126 D4**
Bhanpura *India* 24°31N 75°44E **124 G6**
Bhanrer Ra. *India* 23°40N 79°45E **125 H8**
Bhaptiahi *India* 26°19N 86°44E **125 F12**
Bharat = India ■ *Asia* 20°0N 78°0E **122 K11**
Bharatpur *Chhattisgarh,*
India 23°44N 81°46E **125 H9**
Bharatpur *Raj., India* 27°15N 77°30E **124 F7**
Bharatpur *Nepal* 27°34N 84°10E **125 F10**
Bharno *India* 23°14N 84°53E **125 H11**
Bharuch *India* 21°47N 73°0E **126 D1**
Bharraig = Barra *U.K.* 57°0N 7°29W **65 E1**
Bharraig, Caolas = Barra, Sd. of
U.K. 56°55N 7°32W **65 E1**
Bharatsaigh = Vatersay
U.K. 56°55N 7°32W **65 E1**
Bhatghar L. *India* 18°10N 73°48E **126 E1**
Bhatinda *India* 30°15N 74°57E **124 D6**
Bhatkal *India* 13°58N 74°35E **127 H2**
Bhatpara *India* 22°50N 88°25E **125 H13**
Bhattu *India* 29°36N 75°19E **124 E6**
Bhaun *Pakistan* 32°55N 72°40E **124 C5**
Bhaunagar = Bhavnagar
India 21°45N 72°10E **126 D1**
Bhavani *India* 11°27N 77°43E **127 J3**
Bhavani ➤ *India* 11°27N 77°43E **127 J3**
Bhawanipatna *India* 19°55N 83°10E **126 E5**
Bhayavadar *India* 21°51N 70°15E **124 J4**
Bhearnaraigh = Berneray
U.K. 57°43N 7°11W **65 D1**
Bhera *Pakistan* 32°29N 72°57E **124 C5**
Bhera = Nepal 32°29N 72°57E **124 C5**
Bhikangaon *India* 21°52N 75°57E **124 J6**
Bhilai = Bhilainagar-Durg
India 21°13N 81°26E **126 D5**
Bhilainagar-Durg *India* 21°13N 81°26E **126 D5**
Bhilsa = Vidisha *India* 23°28N 77°53E **124 H7**
Bhima ➤ *India* 16°25N 77°17E **126 F3**
Bhimavaram *India* 16°30N 81°30E **126 F5**
Bhimbar *Pakistan* 32°59N 74°3E **125 C6**
Bhind *India* 26°30N 78°46E **125 F8**
Bhinmal *India* 25°0N 72°15E **124 G5**
Bhisho *S. Africa* 32°50S 27°23E **144 D4**
Bhiwandi *India* 19°20N 73°0E **126 E1**
Bhiwani *India* 28°50N 76°9E **124 E7**
Bhogava ➤ *India* 22°26N 72°20E **124 H5**
Bhojpur *Nepal* 27°10N 87°3E **125 F12**
Bhokardan *India* 20°16N 75°46E **126 D2**

Bhola *Bangla.* 22°45N 90°35E **123 H17**
Bholari *Pakistan* 25°19N 68°13E **124 G3**
Bhongir *India* 17°30N 78°56E **126 F4**
Bhopal *India* 23°20N 77°30E **124 H7**
Bhopalpatnam *India* 18°52N 80°23E **126 E5**
Bhor *India* 18°12N 73°53E **126 E1**
Bhuban *India* 20°53N 85°50E **126 D7**
Bhubaneshwar *India* 20°15N 85°50E **126 D7**
Bhuj *India* 23°15N 69°49E **124 H3**
Bhumiphol Res.
Thailand 17°20N 98°40E **120 D2**
Bhusawal *India* 21°3N 75°46E **126 D2**
Bhutan ■ *Asia* 27°25N 90°30E **123 F17**
Biafra, B. of = Bonny, Bight of
Africa 3°30N 9°20E **139 E6**
Biak *Indonesia* 1°10S 136°6E **119 E9**
Biała *Poland* 50°24N 17°40E **83 H4**
Biała ➤ *Poland* 50°3N 20°55E **83 H7**
Biała Piska *Poland* 53°37N 22°5E **82 E9**
Biała Podlaska *Poland* 52°4N 23°6E **83 F10**
Biała Rawska *Poland* 51°48N 20°29E **83 G7**
Białobrzegi *Poland* 51°39N 20°57E **83 G7**
Białogard *Poland* 54°2N 15°58E **82 D2**
Białowieski △ *Poland* 52°43N 23°50E **83 F10**
Białowieża *Poland* 52°41N 23°49E **83 F10**
Biały Bór *Poland* 53°53N 16°51E **82 E3**
Białystok *Poland* 53°10N 23°10E **83 E10**
Biancavilla *Italy* 37°38N 14°52E **95 E7**
Bianco *Italy* 38°5N 16°9E **95 D9**
Biankouma *Ivory C.* 7°50N 7°40W **138 D3**
Biaora *India* 36°6N 55°53E **124 H7**
Biaro *Indonesia* 2°5N 125°26E **119 D7**
Biarjmand *Iran* 36°6N 55°53E **129 B7**
Biarritz *France* 43°29N 1°33W **72 E2**
Biasca *Switz.* 46°22N 8°58E **77 J4**
Biba *Egypt* 28°55N 31°0E **137 F7**
Bibai *Japan* 43°19N 141°52E **112 C10**
Bibbiena *Italy* 43°42N 11°49E **93 E8**
Bibby L. *Canada* 61°55N 93°0W **163 A10**
Bibei ➤ *Spain* 42°24N 7°13W **88 C3**
Biberach *Germany* 48°5N 9°47E **77 G5**
Bibiani *Ghana* 6°30N 2°8W **138 D4**
Bibile *Sri Lanka* 7°10N 81°25E **127 L5**
Bibungwa
Dem. Rep. of the Congo 2°40S 28°15E **142 C2**
Bicaj *Albania* 41°59N 20°25E **96 D3**
Bicaz *Romania* 46°53N 26°5E **81 D11**
Bicazu Ardelean
Romania 46°51N 25°56E **81 D10**
Biccari *Italy* 41°23N 15°12E **95 A8**
Bicester *U.K.* 51°54N 1°9W **67 F6**
Bicheno *Australia* 41°52S 148°18E **151 E4**
Bichia *India* 22°27N 80°42E **124 H4**
Bichvinta *Georgia* 43°9N 40°21E **87 J5**
Bickerton I. *Australia* 13°45S 136°10E **150 A2**
Bicske *Hungary* 47°29N 18°38E **80 C3**
Bid = Bir *India* 19°4N 75°46E **126 E2**
Bida *Nigeria* 9°3N 5°58E **139 D6**
Bidar *India* 17°55N 77°35E **126 F3**
Biddeford *U.S.A.* 43°30N 70°28W **173 D18**
Bideford *U.K.* 51°1N 4°13W **67 F3**
Bideford Bay *U.K.* 51°5N 4°20W **67 F3**
Bidhuna *India* 26°49N 79°31E **125 F8**
Bidokht *Iran* 34°20N 58°46E **129 C8**
Bidor *Malaysia* 4°6N 101°15E **121 K3**
Bidyadanga *Australia* 18°45S 121°43E **148 C3**
Bie, Planalto de *Angola* 12°0S 16°0E **141 G3**
Bieber *U.S.A.* 41°7N 121°8W **168 F3**
Biebrza ➤ *Poland* 53°13N 22°25E **83 E9**
Biebrzański △ *Poland* 53°36N 22°42E **83 E9**
Biecz *Poland* 49°44N 21°15E **83 J8**
Biel *Switz.* 47°8N 7°14E **77 H3**
Bielawa *Poland* 50°43N 16°37E **83 H3**
Bielefeld *Germany* 52°1N 8°33E **76 C4**
Bielersee *Switz.* 47°6N 7°5E **77 H3**
Biella *Italy* 45°34N 8°3E **92 C5**
Bielsk Podlaski *Poland* 52°47N 23°12E **83 F10**
Bielsko-Biała *Poland* 49°50N 19°2E **83 J6**
Bien Hoa *Vietnam* 10°57N 106°49E **121 G6**
Bienne = Biel *Switz.* 47°8N 7°14E **77 H3**
Bienvenida *Spain* 38°18N 6°12W **89 G4**
Bienville, L. *Canada* 55°5N 72°40W **164 A5**
Bierné *France* 47°48N 0°33W **70 E5**
Bierun *Poland* 50°6N 19°6E **83 H6**
Bierutów *Poland* 51°7N 17°32E **83 G4**
Biesbosch △ *Neths.* 51°45N 4°48E **69 C4**
Biescas *Spain* 42°37N 0°20W **90 C4**
Biese ➤ *Germany* 52°53N 11°46E **76 C7**
Biesiesfontein *S. Africa* 30°57S 17°58E **144 D2**
Bietigheim-Bissingen
Germany 48°58N 9°8E **77 G5**
Bieżuń *Poland* 52°58N 19°58E **82 E6**
Biferno ➤ *Italy* 41°59N 15°2E **93 G12**
Big ➤ *Canada* 54°50N 58°55W **165 B8**
Big B. = Awarua B.
N.Z. 44°28S 168°4E **155 E3**
Big B. *Canada* 55°43N 60°35W **165 B8**
Big Bear City *U.S.A.* 34°16N 116°51W **171 L10**
Big Bear Lake *U.S.A.* 34°15N 116°56W **171 L10**
Big Belt Mts. *U.S.A.* 46°30N 111°25W **168 C8**
Big Bend *Swaziland* 26°50S 31°58E **145 D5**
Big Bend △ *U.S.A.* 29°20N 103°5W **176 G3**
Big Black ➤ *U.S.A.* 32°3N 91°4W **177 F9**
Big Blue ➤ *U.S.A.* 39°35N 96°34W **172 F6**
Big Buddha
Hong Kong, China 22°15N 113°54E **111 a**
Big Creek *U.S.A.* 37°11N 119°14W **170 H7**
Big Creek ☐ *Canada* 51°18N 123°10W **162 C4**
Big Cypress ➤ *U.S.A.* 26°0N 81°10W **179 H7**
Big Cypress Swamp
U.S.A. 26°12N 81°10W **179 J8**
Big Desert *Australia* 35°45S 141°10E **151 F3**
Big Falls *U.S.A.* 48°12N 93°48W **172 A7**
Big Fork ➤ *U.S.A.* 48°31N 93°43W **172 A7**
Big Horn Mts. = Bighorn Mts.
U.S.A. 44°25N 107°0W **168 D10**
Big I. *Canada* 61°7N 116°45W **162 A5**
Big Lake *U.S.A.* 31°12N 101°28W **176 F4**
Big Moose *U.S.A.* 43°49N 74°58W **175 C10**
Big Muddy Cr. ➤
U.S.A. 48°8N 104°36W **168 B11**
Big Pine *U.S.A.* 37°10N 118°17W **170 H8**
Big Pine Key *U.S.A.* 24°40N 81°21W **179 J7**
Big Piney *U.S.A.* 42°32N 110°7W **168 E8**
Big Quill L. *Canada* 51°55N 104°50W **163 C8**
Big Rapids *U.S.A.* 43°42N 85°29W **173 D11**
Big Rideau L. *Canada* 44°40N 76°15W **174 B8**
Big River *Canada* 53°50N 107°0W **163 C7**
Big Run *U.S.A.* 40°57N 78°55W **174 F6**

Big Sable Pt. *U.S.A.* 44°3N 86°1W **172 C10**
Big Salmon ➤
Canada 61°52N 134°55W **162 A2**
Big Sand L. *Canada* 57°45N 99°45W **163 B9**
Big Sandy *U.S.A.* 48°11N 110°7W **168 B8**
Big Sandy ➤ *U.S.A.* 38°25N 82°36W **173 F12**
Big Sandy Cr. = Sandy Cr. ➤
U.S.A. 41°51N 109°47W **168 F9**
Big Sandy Cr. ➤
U.S.A. 38°7N 102°29W **168 G12**
Big Satilla Cr. ➤ *U.S.A.* 31°27N 82°23W **178 D7**
Big Sioux ➤ *U.S.A.* 42°29N 96°27W **172 D5**
Big South Fork △
U.S.A. 36°27N 84°47W **177 C12**
Big Spring *U.S.A.* 32°15N 101°28W **176 E4**
Big Stone City *U.S.A.* 45°18N 96°28W **172 C5**
Big Stone Gap *U.S.A.* 36°52N 82°47W **173 G12**
Big Stone L. *U.S.A.* 45°18N 96°27W **172 C5**
Big Sur *U.S.A.* 36°15N 121°48W **170 J5**
Big Timber *U.S.A.* 45°50N 109°57W **168 D9**
Big Trout L. *Canada* 53°40N 90°0W **164 B2**
Big Trout Lake *Canada* 53°45N 90°0W **164 B2**
Biğa *Turkey* 40°13N 27°14E **97 F11**
Biga ➤ *Turkey* 40°20N 27°14E **97 F11**
Bigadiç *Turkey* 39°22N 28°7E **99 B10**
Biganos *France* 44°39N 0°59W **72 D3**
Biggar *Canada* 52°4N 108°0W **163 C7**
Biggar *U.K.* 55°38N 3°32W **65 F5**
Bigge I. *Australia* 14°35S 125°10E **148 B4**
Biggenden *Australia* 25°31S 152°4E **151 D5**
Biggleswade *U.K.* 52°5N 0°14W **67 E7**
Biggs *U.S.A.* 39°25N 121°43W **170 F5**
Bighorn *U.S.A.* 46°10N 107°27W **168 C10**
Bighorn ➤ *U.S.A.* 46°10N 107°28W **168 C10**
Bighorn Canyon △
U.S.A. 45°10N 108°0W **168 D10**
Bighorn L. *U.S.A.* 44°55N 108°15W **168 D9**
Bighorn Mts. *U.S.A.* 44°25N 107°0W **168 D10**
Bignona *Senegal* 12°52N 16°14W **138 C1**
Bigorre *France* 43°10N 0°5E **72 E4**
Bigstone L. *Canada* 53°42N 95°44W **163 C9**
Bigugila, Étang de
France 42°36N 9°29E **73 F13**
Biha *Tanzania* 7°10S 39°10E **142 D4**
Bihać *Bos.-H.* 44°49N 15°57E **93 D12**
Bihar *India* 25°5N 85°40E **125 G11**
Bihar ☐ *India* 25°0N 86°0E **125 G12**
Biharamulo *Tanzania* 2°25S 31°25E **142 C3**
Biharamulo *Tanzania* 2°24S 31°26E **142 C3**
Bihariganj *India* 25°44N 86°59E **125 G12**
Biharkeresztes *Hungary* 47°8N 21°44E **80 C6**
Bihor *Romania* 47°0N 22°10E **80 D7**
Bihor, Munții *Romania* 46°29N 22°47E **80 D7**
Bijagós, Arquipélago dos
Guinea-Biss. 11°15N 16°10W **138 C1**
Bijaipur *India* 26°2N 77°20E **124 F7**
Bijapur = Vijayapura
India 16°50N 75°55E **126 F2**
Bijapur *India* 18°50N 80°50E **126 E5**
Bijar *Iran* 35°52N 47°35E **126 C2**
Bijawar *India* 24°38N 79°30E **125 G8**
Bijeljina *Bos.-H.* 44°46N 19°14E **80 F4**
Bijelo Polje *Montenegro* 43°1N 19°45E **96 C3**
Bijie *China* 27°20N 105°16E **116 D5**
Bijnor *India* 29°27N 78°11E **124 E8**
Bikaner *India* 28°2N 73°18E **124 E5**
Bikapur *India* 26°30N 82°7E **125 F10**
Bikeqi *China* 40°43N 111°20E **114 D6**
Bikfayyā *Lebanon* 33°55N 35°41E **130 B4**
Bikin *Russia* 46°50N 134°20E **112 A7**
Bikin ➤ *Russia* 46°51N 134°2E **112 A7**
Bikini Atoll *Marshall Is.* 12°0N 167°30E **156 F8**
Bikita *Zimbabwe* 20°6S 31°41E **145 B5**
Bikkū Bīttī *Libya* 22°0N 19°12E **135 D9**
Bikoué *Cameroon* 3°55N 11°50E **139 E7**
Bila Tserkva *Ukraine* 49°45N 30°10E **75 D16**
Bilanga *Burkina Faso* 12°40N 0°1W **138 C4**
Bilara *India* 26°14N 73°53E **124 F5**
Bilaspur *Chhattisgarh,*
India 22°2N 82°15E **125 H10**
Bilaspur *Punjab, India* 31°19N 76°50E **124 D7**
Bīlāsuvar *Azerbaijan* 39°27N 48°32E **105 C13**
Bilauk Taungdan
Thailand 13°0N 99°0E **120 F2**
Bilauri *Nepal* 28°41N 80°21E **125 E9**
Bilbao *Spain* 43°16N 2°56W **90 B2**
Bilbao ✈ (BIO) *Spain* 43°18N 2°57W **90 B2**
Bilbeis *Egypt* 30°25N 31°34E **137 E7**
Bilbo = Bilbao *Spain* 43°16N 2°56W **90 B2**
Bilce-Zolote *Ukraine* 48°47N 25°53E **81 B10**
Bilciureşti *Romania* 44°44N 25°48E **81 F10**
Bildudalur *Iceland* 65°41N 23°36W **60 D2**
Bílé Karpaty *Europe* 49°5N 18°0E **79 B11**
Bileća *Bos.-H.* 42°53N 18°27E **96 D2**
Bilecik *Turkey* 40°5N 30°5E **104 B4**
Bilecik ☐ *Turkey* 40°10N 29°50E **104 B4**
Bilecko Jezero *Bos.-H.* 42°48N 18°8E **96 D2**
Bileh Savār *Iran* 39°21N 48°21E **105 C13**
Bilgoraj *Poland* 50°33N 22°42E **83 H9**
Bilgram *India* 27°11N 80°2E **125 F9**
Bilhaur *India* 26°51N 80°5E **125 F9**
Bilhorod-Dnistrovskyy
Ukraine 46°11N 30°23E **85 J6**
Bilibino *Russia* 68°3N 166°20E **107 C17**
Biliran *Phil.* 11°36N 124°33E **119 F6**
Biliza *Mozam.* 12°30S 40°20E **143 E5**
Bilibiza *Mozam.* 12°30S 40°20E **143 E5**
Bilimora *India* 20°45N 72°57E **126 D1**
Bilisht *Albania* 40°37N 21°2E **96 F5**
Billabong ➤
Australia 35°5S 144°2E **152 C6**
Billdal *Sweden* 57°22N 11°57E **63 G5**
Billiluna *Australia* 19°37S 127°41E **148 C4**
Billings *U.S.A.* 45°47N 108°30W **168 D9**
Billiton Is. = Belitung
Indonesia 3°10S 107°50E **118 E3**
Billsta *Sweden* 63°20N 18°28E **62 A12**
Billund *Denmark* 55°44N 9°6E **63 J3**
Bilma *Niger* 18°50N 13°30E **135 E8**
Bilma, Grand Erg de
Niger 18°30N 14°0E **135 E8**
Bilo Gora *Croatia* 45°53N 17°15E **80 E2**
Biloela *Australia* 24°24S 150°31E **150 C5**
Bilohirsk *Ukraine* 45°3N 34°35E **85 K8**
Biloli *India* 18°46N 77°44E **126 E3**
Bilopillya *Ukraine* 51°14N 34°20E **85 G8**
Bilovodsk *Ukraine* 49°13N 39°36E **85 H10**
Biloxi *U.S.A.* 30°24N 88°53W **177 F10**
Bilpa Morea Claypan
Australia 25°0S 140°0E **150 D3**

Biltine *Chad* 14°40N 20°50E **135 F10**
Bilyarsk *Russia* 54°58N 50°22E **86 C10**
Bima *Indonesia* 8°22S 118°49E **119 F5**
Bimban *Egypt* 8°54N 0°58E **135 B14**
Bimbe *C.A.R.* 5°40N 22°50E **140 A3**
Bimbila *Ghana* 8°54N 0°5E **139 D5**
Bimbo *C.A.R.* 4°15N 18°33E **140 D3**
Bimini Is. *Bahamas* 25°42N 79°25W **182 A4**
Bin Xian *Heilongjiang,*
China 45°42N 127°32E **115 B14**
Bin Xian *Shaanxi, China* 35°2N 108°4E **114 G5**
Bin Yauri *Nigeria* 10°46N 4°45E **139 C5**
Bina-Etawah *India* 24°13N 78°14E **124 G8**
Binalong *Australia* 34°40S 148°39E **153 C8**
Bīnālūd, Kūh-e *Iran* 36°30N 58°30E **129 B8**
Binatang = Bintangau
Malaysia 2°10N 111°40E **118 D4**
Binche *Belgium* 50°26N 4°10E **69 D4**
Binchuan *China* 25°42N 100°38E **116 E3**
Binder *Chad* 9°56N 14°27E **139 D7**
Bindki *India* 26°2N 80°36E **125 F9**
Bindslev *Denmark* 57°33N 10°11E **63 F9**
Bindura *Zimbabwe* 17°18S 31°18E **143 F3**
Binéfar *Spain* 41°51N 0°18E **90 D5**
Bingara *Australia* 29°52S 150°36E **153 D5**
Bingaram I. *India* 10°56N 72°17E **127 J1**
Bingen *Germany* 49°57N 7°55E **77 F3**
Bingerville *Ivory C.* 5°18N 3°49W **138 D4**
Bingham *U.S.A.* 45°3N 69°53W **173 C19**
Binghamton *U.S.A.* 42°6N 75°55W **175 D9**
Bingöl *Turkey* 38°53N 40°29E **105 C9**
Bingöl ☐ *Turkey* 38°55N 40°30E **105 C9**
Bingöl Dağları *Turkey* 39°16N 41°9E **105 C9**
Bingsjö *Sweden* 61°1N 15°39E **62 C9**
Binh Dinh *Vietnam* 13°55N 109°7E **120 F7**
Binh Son *Vietnam* 15°20N 108°40E **120 E7**
Binhai *China* 34°2N 119°49E **115 G10**
Binic *France* 48°46N 2°50W **70 D4**
Binisatua *Spain* 39°50N 4°11E **100 B11**
Binissalem *Spain* 39°41N 2°50E **100 B9**
Binjai *Indonesia* 3°20N 98°30E **118 D1**
Binji *Nigeria* 13°10N 4°55E **139 C5**
Binka *India* 21°2N 83°48E **125 J5**
Binnaway *Australia* 31°28S 149°24E **153 A8**
Binongko *Indonesia* 5°57S 124°2E **119 F6**
Binscarth *Canada* 50°37N 101°17W **163 C8**
Bintan *Indonesia* 1°0N 104°0E **118 D2**
Bintangau *Malaysia* 2°10N 111°40E **118 D4**
Bintulu *Malaysia* 3°10N 113°0E **118 D4**
Bintuni *Indonesia* 2°7S 133°32E **119 E8**
Binyang *China* 23°12N 108°47E **116 F7**
Binz *Germany* 54°24N 13°35E **76 A9**
Binzert = Bizerte *Tunisia* 37°15N 9°50E **136 A5**
Binzhou *China* 37°20N 118°2E **115 F10**
Biobio ☐ *Chile* 37°35S 72°0W **190 D1**
Biobio ➤ *Chile* 36°49S 73°10W **190 D1**
Biograd na Moru
Croatia 43°56N 15°29E **93 E12**
Biogradska Gora △
Montenegro 42°55N 19°40E **96 D3**
Bioko *Eq. Guin.* 3°30N 8°40E **139 E6**
Biokovo *Croatia* 43°23N 17°0E **93 E14**
Biougra *Morocco* 30°15N 9°14W **136 B2**
Bipindi *Cameroon* 3°6N 10°30E **139 E7**
Bir *India* 19°4N 75°46E **126 E2**
Bīr Abu Hashim *Egypt* 23°42N 34°5E **137 C7**
Bir Abu Minqar *Egypt* 26°33N 27°33E **137 B2**
Bīr Abū Muḩammad
Egypt 29°44N 34°14E **130 F3**
Bi'r al Butayyihat
Jordan 29°45N 35°20E **130 F4**
Bi'r al Mārī *Jordan* 30°4N 35°33E **130 E4**
Bi'r al Qattār *Jordan* 30°5N 35°20E **130 F4**
Bir Aouine *Tunisia* 32°25N 9°18E **136 B5**
Bīr 'Asal *Egypt* 25°55N 34°20E **137 C7**
Bir Atrun *Sudan* 18°15N 26°40E **137 D3**
Bîr Beida *Egypt* 30°25N 34°29E **130 E3**
Bîr Diqnash *Egypt* 31°3N 25°23E **137 B2**
Bir el Abbes *Algeria* 26°7N 6°9W **136 C2**
Bîr el 'Abd *Egypt* 31°2N 33°0E **130 D2**
Bir el Ater *Algeria* 34°46N 8°3E **136 B6**
Bîr el Basur *Egypt* 29°51N 25°49E **137 C2**
Bîr el Biarât *Egypt* 29°30N 34°43E **130 F3**
Bîr el Duweidar *Egypt* 30°56N 32°32E **130 E1**
Bir el Gellaz *Egypt* 30°50N 28°30E **137 B2**
Bîr el Heisi *Egypt* 29°22N 34°36E **130 F3**
Bîr el Jafir *Egypt* 30°50N 32°41E **130 E1**
Bir el Lahrache *Algeria* 32°1N 8°12E **136 B6**
Bîr el Mâlhi *Egypt* 30°38N 32°31E **130 E1**
Bir el Shaqqa *Egypt* 30°54N 25°1W **137 B2**
Bîr el Thamâda *Egypt* 30°12N 33°27E **130 E2**
Bîr Fuad *Egypt* 30°35N 26°28E **137 B2**
Bir Gebeil Ḥişn *Egypt* 30°2N 33°18E **130 E2**
Bir Haimur *Egypt* 22°45N 33°40E **137 C7**
Bīr Ḩasana *Egypt* 30°29N 33°46E **130 E2**
Bîr Hōoker *Egypt* 30°23N 30°19E **137 E5**
Bir Kanayis *Egypt* 24°59N 33°15E **137 C7**
Bir Kaseiba *Egypt* 31°0N 33°17E **130 E2**
Bir Kerawein *Egypt* 27°30N 28°50E **137 C4**
Bir Lahfân *Egypt* 30°48N 33°51E **130 E2**
Bir Lahrache *Algeria* 32°1N 8°12E **136 B6**
Bîr Madkûr *Egypt* 30°44N 32°33E **130 E1**
Bir Mineiga *Sudan* 22°7N 33°40E **137 C7**
Bir Misaha *Egypt* 22°13N 27°59E **137 C3**
Bir Mogreïn *Mauritania* 25°10N 11°25W **134 C3**
Bîr Murr *Egypt* 23°28N 30°10E **137 C5**
Bi'r Muṭribah *Kuwait* 29°54N 47°17E **128 D5**
Bîr Nakheila *Egypt* 24°1N 30°50E **137 C5**
Bîr Qatia *Egypt* 30°58N 32°45E **130 E1**
Bir Qatrani *Egypt* 30°55N 26°10E **137 B2**
Bîr Ranga *Egypt* 24°25N 35°15E **137 C7**
Bîr Sahara *Egypt* 22°54N 28°40E **137 C3**
Bir Seiyâla *Egypt* 26°10N 33°50E **137 C7**
Bir Shalatein *Egypt* 23°5N 35°25E **137 C7**
Bir Shebb *Egypt* 22°25N 29°40E **137 C5**
Bîr Shût *Egypt* 23°50N 35°15E **137 C7**
Bir Terfawi *Egypt* 22°57N 28°55E **137 C3**
Bir Umm Qubûr *Egypt* 24°35N 34°2E **137 C7**
Bîr Ungât *Egypt* 22°8N 33°48E **137 C7**
Bîr Za'farâna *Egypt* 29°10N 32°40E **137 B7**
Bîr Zeidûn *Egypt* 25°45N 33°40E **137 C7**
Birāk *Libya* 27°32N 14°11E **135 C8**
Biramféro *Guinea* 11°40N 9°10W **138 C3**
Biratnagar *Nepal* 26°27N 87°17E **125 F12**
Birawa
Dem. Rep. of the Congo 2°20S 28°48E **142 C2**
Birch ➤ *Canada* 58°28N 112°17W **162 B6**

Birch Hills *Canada* 52°59N 105°25W **163 C7**
Birch I. *Canada* 52°26N 99°54W **163 C9**
Birch L. *N.W.T., Canada* 62°4N 116°33W **162 A5**
Birch L. *Ont., Canada* 51°23N 92°18W **164 B1**
Birch Mts. *Canada* 57°30N 113°10W **162 B6**
Birch River *Canada* 52°24N 101°6W **163 C8**
Birchip *Australia* 35°56S 142°55E **152 C5**
Birchiş *Romania* 45°58N 22°9E **80 E7**
Birchwood *N.Z.* 46°55S 167°53E **155 F2**
Bird *Canada* 56°30N 94°13W **163 B10**
Bird I. = Aves, I. de
W. Indies 15°45S 63°55W **183 C7**
Bird I. *S. Georgia* 54°0S 38°3W **55 B1**
Birds Creek *Canada* 45°6N 77°52W **174 A7**
Birdsville *Australia* 25°51S 139°20E **150 D2**
Birdum Cr. ➤ *Australia* 15°14S 133°0E **148 C5**
Birdwood *Australia* 34°51S 138°58E **152 C3**
Birecik *Turkey* 37°3N 38°0E **105 C6**
Birein *Israel* 30°50N 34°28E **130 E3**
Bireuen *Indonesia* 5°14N 96°39E **118 C1**
Birganj *Nepal* 27°1N 84°52E **125 F11**
Birifo *Gambia* 13°30N 14°0W **138 C2**
Birigüi *Brazil* 21°18S 50°16W **191 A5**
Bīrjand *Iran* 32°53N 59°13E **129 C8**
Birka *Sweden* 59°20N 17°32E **62 E11**
Birkenfeld *Germany* 49°38N 7°9E **77 F3**
Birkenhead *U.K.* 53°23N 3°2W **66 D4**
Birkerød *Denmark* 55°50N 12°25E **63 J6**
Birket Qârûn *Egypt* 29°30N 30°40E **137 F7**
Birkfeld *Austria* 47°21N 15°45E **78 D8**
Birkhadem *Algeria* 36°43N 3°3E **136 A4**
Bîrlad = Bârlad
Romania 46°15N 27°38E **81 D12**
Birmingham *U.K.* 52°29N 1°52W **67 E6**
Birmingham *U.S.A.* 33°31N 86°48W **177 E11**
Birmingham Int. ✈ (BHX)
U.K. 52°26N 1°45W **67 E6**
Birmitrapur *India* 22°24N 84°46E **126 C6**
Birni Ngaouré *Niger* 13°5N 2°51E **139 C5**
Birni Nkonni *Niger* 13°55N 5°15E **139 C6**
Birni Gwari *Nigeria* 11°0N 6°45E **139 C6**
Birnin Kebbi *Nigeria* 12°32N 4°12E **139 C5**
Birnin Kudu *Nigeria* 11°30N 9°29E **139 C6**
Birobidzhan *Russia* 48°50N 132°50E **111 B15**
Birr *Ireland* 53°6N 7°54W **64 C4**
Birrie ➤ *Australia* 29°43S 146°37E **151 D4**
Birsilpur *India* 28°11N 72°15E **124 E5**
Birsk *Russia* 55°25N 55°30E **106 D6**
Birtle *Canada* 50°30N 101°5W **163 C8**
Birur *India* 13°30N 75°55E **127 J2**
Biryuchiy *Ukraine* 46°10N 35°0E **85 J8**
Biržai *Lithuania* 56°11N 24°45E **84 D3**
Birzebbugga *Malta* 35°50N 14°32E **101 D2**
Bisa *Indonesia* 1°15S 127°28E **119 E7**
Bisáccia *Italy* 41°0N 15°22E **94 E6**
Bisacquino *Italy* 37°42N 13°15E **94 E6**
Bisalpur *India* 28°14N 79°48E **125 E8**
Bisbee *U.S.A.* 31°27N 109°55W **169 L9**
Biscarrosse *France* 44°22N 1°20W **72 D2**
Biscarrosse et de Parentis, Étang
de *France* 44°21N 1°10W **72 D2**
Biscay, B. of *Atl. Oc.* 45°0N 2°0W **58 F5**
Biscay Abyssal Plain
Atl. Oc. 45°0N 8°0W **56 B1**
Biscayne *U.S.A.* 25°40N 80°12W **179 K9**
Biscayne B. *U.S.A.* 25°40N 80°12W **179 K9**
Biscéglie *Italy* 41°14N 16°30E **95 A8**
Bischheim *France* 48°37N 7°46E **71 D14**
Bischofshofen *Austria* 47°26N 13°14E **78 D7**
Bischofswerda *Germany* 51°7N 14°10E **76 D10**
Bischwiller *France* 48°41N 7°50E **71 D14**
Biscoe Is. *Antarctica* 66°0S 67°0W **55 C17**
Biscotasing *Canada* 47°18N 82°9W **164 C3**
Bisert ➤ *Russia* 56°52N 59°16E **93 F13**
Bishah, W. ➤
Si. Arabia 21°24N 43°26E **137 C5**
Bishan *China* 29°33N 106°12E **116 C6**
Bishkek *Kyrgyzstan* 42°54N 74°46E **109 D8**
Bishnupur *India* 23°8N 87°20E **125 H12**
Bisho = Bhisho *S. Africa* 32°50S 27°23E **144 D4**
Bishoftu = Debre Zeyit
Ethiopia 8°50N 39°0E **131 F2**
Bishop *Calif., U.S.A.* 37°22N 118°24W **170 H8**
Bishop *Ga., U.S.A.* 33°49N 83°26W **178 B3**
Bishop *Tex., U.S.A.* 27°35N 97°48W **176 H6**
Bishop Auckland *U.K.* 54°39N 1°40W **66 C6**
Bishop's Falls *Canada* 49°2N 55°30W **165 C8**
Bishop's Stortford *U.K.* 51°52N 0°10E **67 F8**
Bisignano *Italy* 39°31N 16°17E **95 C9**
Bisina, L. *Uganda* 1°38N 33°56E **142 B3**
Biskra *Algeria* 34°50N 5°44E **136 B6**
Biskupiec *Poland* 53°53N 20°58E **82 E7**
Bismarck *U.S.A.* 46°48N 100°47W **172 B3**
Bismarck Arch.
Papua N. G. 2°30S 150°0E **147 B7**
Bismark *Germany* 52°40N 11°33E **76 C7**
Bismil *Turkey* 37°51N 40°40E **105 C9**
Biso *Uganda* 1°44N 31°26E **142 B3**
Bison *U.S.A.* 45°31N 102°28W **172 C2**
Bispgården *Sweden* 63°2N 16°40E **62 A10**
Bissagos = Bijagós, Arquipélago
dos *Guinea-Biss.* 11°15N 16°10W **138 C1**
Bissam Cuttack *India* 19°31N 83°31E **126 E6**
Bissau *Guinea-Biss.* 11°45N 15°45W **138 C1**
Bissaula *Nigeria* 7°0N 10°2E **139 D7**
Bissikrima *Guinea* 10°50N 10°58W **138 C2**
Bissorã *Guinea-Biss.* 12°16N 15°13W **138 C1**
Bistcho L. *Canada* 59°45N 118°50W **162 B5**
Bistret *Romania* 43°54N 23°23E **81 G8**
Bistrica = Ilirska-Bistrica
Slovenia 45°34N 14°14E **93 C11**
Bistrița *Romania* 47°9N 24°35E **81 C9**
Bistrița ➤ *Romania* 46°30N 26°57E **81 D11**
Bistrița Năsăud ☐
Romania 47°15N 24°30E **81 C9**
Bistriței, Munții
Romania 47°15N 25°0E **81 C10**
Biswan *India* 27°29N 81°2E **125 F9**
Bisztynek *Poland* 54°8N 20°53E **82 D7**
Bitam *Gabon* 2°5N 11°25W **140 D2**
Bitburg *Germany* 49°58N 6°32E **77 F2**
Bitche *France* 49°2N 7°25E **71 C14**
Bithynia *Turkey* 40°40N 31°0E **104 B4**
Bitkine *Chad* 11°59N 18°13E **135 F9**
Bitlis *Turkey* 38°20N 42°3E **105 C10**
Bitlis ☐ *Turkey* 38°20N 42°5E **105 C10**
Bitola *Macedonia* 41°1N 21°20E **96 E5**
Bitola = Bitola *Macedonia* 41°1N 21°20E **96 E5**
Bitonto *Italy* 41°6N 16°41E **95 A9**

Bitra I. India 11°33N 72°9E 127 J1
Bitter Creek U.S.A. 41°33N 108°33W 168 F9
Bitter L. = Buheirat-Murrat-el-
  Kubra Egypt 30°18N 32°26E 137 E8
Bitterfeld-Wolfen
  Germany 51°37N 12°20E 76 D8
Bitterfontein S. Africa 31°1S 18°32E 144 D2
Bitterroot → U.S.A. 46°52N 114°7W 168 C6
Bitterroot Range
  U.S.A. 46°0N 114°20W 168 C6
Bitterwater U.S.A. 36°23N 121°0W 170 J6
Bitti Italy 40°29N 9°23E 94 B2
Bittou Burkina Faso 11°17N 0°18W 139 C4
Biu Nigeria 10°40N 12°3E 139 C7
Bivolari Romania 47°31N 27°27E 81 C12
Bivolu, Vf. Romania 47°16N 25°58E 81 C10
Biwa-Ko Japan 35°15N 136°10E 113 G8
Biwabik U.S.A. 47°32N 92°21W 172 B7
Bixad Romania 47°56N 23°28E 81 C8
Bixby U.S.A. 35°57N 95°53W 176 D7
Biya → Russia 52°25N 85°0E 109 B11
Biyang China 32°38N 113°21E 117 A9
Biysk Russia 52°40N 85°0E 109 B11
Bizana S. Africa 30°50S 29°52E 145 D4
Bizen Japan 34°43N 134°8E 113 G7
Bizerte Tunisia 37°15N 9°50E 136 A5
Bizerte = Tunisia 37°5N 9°35E 136 A5
Bizkaia □ Spain 43°15N 2°45W 90 B2
Bjargtangar Iceland 65°30N 24°30W 60 D1
Bjärnum Sweden 56°17N 13°43E 63 H7
Bjästa Sweden 63°12N 18°29E 62 A12
Bjelasica Montenegro 42°50N 19°40E 96 D3
Bjelašnica Bos.-H. 43°43N 18°9E 80 G3
Bjelovar Croatia 45°56N 16°49E 93 C13
Bjerringbro Denmark 56°23N 9°39E 63 H3
Björbo Sweden 60°27N 14°44E 62 D8
Björklinge Sweden 60°2N 17°33E 62 D11
Björkö Sweden 59°52N 19°2E 62 E13
Björneborg = Pori
  Finland 61°29N 21°48E 84 B1
Björneborg Sweden 59°14N 14°16E 62 E8
Bjørnevatn Norway 69°40N 30°0E 60 B24
Bjørnøya Arctic 74°30N 19°0E 54 B8
Bjursås Sweden 60°44N 15°25E 62 D9
Bjuv Sweden 56°5N 12°55E 63 H6
Bla Mali 12°56N 5°47W 138 C3
Blå Jungfrun △ Sweden 57°16N 16°47E 63 G10
Blace Serbia 43°18N 21°17E 96 C5
Blachownia Poland 50°49N 18°56E 83 H5
Black = Da →
  Vietnam 21°15N 105°20E 116 G5
Black → Canada 44°42N 79°19W 174 B5
Black → Ariz., U.S.A. 33°44N 110°13W 169 K8
Black → Ark., U.S.A. 35°38N 91°20W 176 D9
Black → La., U.S.A. 31°16N 91°50W 176 F9
Black → Mich., U.S.A. 43°59N 82°27W 174 D2
Black → N.Y., U.S.A. 43°59N 76°4W 175 C8
Black → Wis., U.S.A. 43°57N 91°22W 172 D8
Black Bay Pen. Canada 48°38N 88°21W 164 C2
Black Birch L. Canada 56°53N 107°45W 163 B7
Black Canyon of the Gunnison △
  U.S.A. 38°40N 107°35W 168 G10
Black Diamond
  Canada 50°45N 114°14W 162 C6
Black Duck → Canada 56°51N 89°2W 164 A2
Black Forest = Schwarzwald
  Germany 48°30N 8°20E 77 G4
Black Forest U.S.A. 39°0N 104°43W 168 G11
Black Hd. Ireland 53°9N 9°16W 64 C2
Black Hills U.S.A. 44°0N 103°45W 172 D2
Black I. Canada 51°12N 96°30W 163 C9
Black L. Canada 59°12N 105°15W 163 B7
Black L. Mich., U.S.A. 45°28N 84°16W 173 C11
Black L. N.Y., U.S.A. 44°31N 75°36W 175 B9
Black Lake Canada 59°11N 105°20W 163 B7
Black Mesa U.S.A. 36°58N 102°58W 176 C3
Black Mountain
  Australia 30°18S 151°39E 153 A9
Black Mt. = Mynydd Du
  U.K. 51°52N 3°50W 67 F4
Black Mts. U.K. 51°55N 3°7W 67 F4
Black Range U.S.A. 33°15N 107°50W 169 K10
Black River Jamaica 18°0N 77°50W 182 a
Black River U.S.A. 44°0N 75°47W 175 C9
Black River Falls
  U.S.A. 44°18N 90°51W 172 C8
Black Rock Australia 32°50S 138°44E 152 B3
Black Rock Barbados 13°7N 59°37W 183 g
Black Rock Desert
  U.S.A. 41°10N 118°50W 168 F4
Black Sea Eurasia 43°30N 35°0E 58 G12
Black Tickle Canada 53°28N 55°45W 165 B8
Black Volta → Africa 8°41N 1°33W 138 D4
Black Warrior →
  U.S.A. 32°32N 87°51W 177 E11
Blackall Australia 24°25S 145°45E 150 C4
Blackball N.Z. 42°22S 171°26E 155 C6
Blackbraes △
  Australia 19°10S 144°10E 150 B3
Blackbull Australia 17°55S 141°45E 150 B3
Blackburn U.K. 53°45N 2°29W 66 D5
Blackburn, Mt.
  U.S.A. 61°44N 143°26W 166 C11
Blackburn with Darwen □
  U.K. 53°45N 2°29W 66 D5
Blackdown Tableland △
  Australia 23°52S 149°8E 150 C4
Blackfoot U.S.A. 43°11N 112°21W 168 E7
Blackfoot → U.S.A. 46°52N 113°53W 168 C7
Blackfoot Res. U.S.A. 42°55N 111°39W 168 E8
Blackman U.S.A. 30°56N 86°38W 179 E3
Blackpool U.S.A. 53°49N 3°3W 66 D4
Blackpool □ U.K. 53°49N 3°3W 66 D4
Blackriver U.S.A. 44°83N 83°17W 174 B1
Blacks Harbour Canada 45°3N 66°49W 165 C6
Blacksburg U.S.A. 37°14N 80°25W 173 G12
Blackshear U.S.A. 31°18N 82°14W 177 F13
Blackshear, L. U.S.A. 31°51N 83°56W 178 D6
Blacksod B. Ireland 54°6N 10°0W 64 B1
Blackstairs Mt. Ireland 52°33N 6°48W 64 D5
Blackstone U.S.A. 37°4N 78°0W 173 G14
Blackstone Ra.
  Australia 26°0S 128°30E 149 E4
Blackville Canada 46°44N 65°50W 165 C6
Blackville U.S.A. 33°22N 81°16W 178 D8
Blackwater = West Road →
  Canada 53°18N 122°53W 162 C4
Blackwater Australia 23°35S 148°53E 150 C4
Blackwater → Meath,
  Ireland 53°39N 6°41W 64 C4
Blackwater → Waterford,
  Ireland 52°4N 7°52W 64 D4

Blackwater → U.K. 54°31N 6°35W 64 B5
Blackwater → U.K. 30°36N 87°2W 179 E2
Blackwell U.S.A. 36°48N 97°17W 176 C6
Blackwells Corner
  U.S.A. 35°37N 119°47W 171 K7
Blackwood U.K. 51°39N 3°12W 67 F4
Bladenburg △
  Australia 22°30S 142°59E 150 C3
Blaenau Ffestiniog U.K. 53°0N 3°56W 66 E4
Blaenau Gwent □ U.K. 51°48N 3°12W 67 F4
Blåfjella-Skjækerfjella △
  Norway 64°15N 13°8E 60 D15
Blagaj Bos.-H. 43°16N 17°55E 96 C1
Blagnac France 43°37N 1°23E 72 E5
Blagnac, Toulouse ✈ (TLS)
  France 43°37N 1°22E 72 E5
Blagodarnyy Russia 45°7N 43°37E 87 H6
Blagoevgrad Bulgaria 42°2N 23°5E 96 D7
Blagoevgrad □ Bulgaria 42°2N 23°5E 96 D7
Blagoveshchensk
  Russia 50°20N 127°30E 111 A14
Blahkiuh Indonesia 8°31S 115°12E 119 J18
Blain France 47°29N 1°45W 70 E5
Blain U.S.A. 40°20N 77°31W 174 F7
Blaine Minn., U.S.A. 45°10N 93°13W 172 C7
Blaine Wash., U.S.A. 48°59N 122°45W 170 B4
Blaine Lake Canada 52°51N 106°52W 163 C7
Blair U.S.A. 41°33N 96°8W 172 E5
Blair Athol Australia 22°42S 147°31E 150 C4
Blair Atholl U.K. 56°46N 3°50W 65 E5
Blairgowrie U.K. 56°35N 3°21W 65 E5
Blairsden U.S.A. 39°47N 120°37W 170 F6
Blairsville U.S.A. 40°26N 79°16W 174 F5
Blaj Romania 46°10N 23°57E 81 D8
Blakang Mati, Pulau
  Singapore 1°15N 103°50E 121 d
Blake Pt. U.S.A. 48°11N 88°25W 172 A9
Blakely U.S.A. 31°23N 84°56W 178 D5
Blakely Pa., U.S.A. 41°28N 75°37W 175 E9
Blambangan, Semenanjung
  Indonesia 8°42S 114°29E 119 K17
Blâmont France 48°35N 6°50E 71 D13
Blanc, C. Spain 39°21N 2°51E 100 B9
Blanc, C. Tunisia 37°15N 9°56E 136 A5
Blanc, Mont Europe 45°48N 6°50E 73 C10
Blanca, B. Argentina 39°10S 61°30W 192 A4
Blanca, Cord. Peru 9°10S 77°35W 186 E3
Blanca, Costa Spain 38°25N 0°10W 91 G4
Blanca Peak U.S.A. 37°35N 105°29W 169 H11
Blanche, C. Australia 33°1S 134°9E 151 E1
Blanche, L. S. Austral.,
  Australia 29°15S 139°40E 151 D2
Blanche, L. W. Austral.,
  Australia 22°25S 123°17E 148 D3
Blanchisseuse
  Trin. & Tob. 10°48N 61°18W 187 K15
Blanco S. Africa 33°55S 22°23E 144 D3
Blanco U.S.A. 30°6N 98°25W 176 F5
Blanco → Argentina 30°20S 68°42W 190 C2
Blanco, C. Costa Rica 9°34N 85°8W 182 E2
Blanco, C. U.S.A. 42°51N 124°34W 168 E1
Blanda → Iceland 65°37N 20°9W 60 D3
Blandford Forum U.K. 50°51N 2°9W 67 G5
Blanding U.S.A. 37°37N 109°29W 169 H9
Blanes Spain 41°40N 2°48E 90 D7
Blangy-sur-Bresle France 49°55N 1°37E 71 C8
Blanice → Czech Rep. 49°10N 14°5E 78 B7
Blankaholm Sweden 57°36N 16°31E 63 G10
Blankenberge Belgium 51°20N 3°9E 69 C3
Blankenburg Germany 51°47N 10°57E 76 D6
Blanquefort France 44°53N 0°38W 72 D3
Blanquilla, I. Venezuela 11°51N 64°37W 187 D7
Blanquillo Uruguay 32°53S 55°37W 191 C4
Blansko Czech Rep. 49°22N 16°40E 79 B9
Blantyre Malawi 15°45S 35°0E 143 F4
Blarney Ireland 51°56N 8°33W 64 E3
Blasdell U.S.A. 42°48N 78°50W 174 D6
Blaszki Poland 51°38N 18°30E 83 G5
Blatná Czech Rep. 49°25N 13°52E 78 B6
Blato Croatia 42°56N 16°48E 93 F13
Blaubeuren Germany 48°24N 9°46E 77 G5
Blaustein Germany 48°25N 9°58E 77 G5
Blåvands Huk Denmark 55°33N 8°4E 63 J2
Blaydon U.K. 54°58N 1°42W 66 C6
Blaye France 45°8N 0°40W 72 C3
Blaye-les-Mines France 44°1N 2°8E 72 D6
Blayney Australia 33°32S 149°14E 153 B8
Blaze, Pt. Australia 12°56S 130°11E 148 B5
Blażowa Poland 49°53N 22°7E 83 J9
Bleckede Germany 53°17N 10°43E 76 B6
Bled Slovenia 46°27N 14°7E 93 B11
Bleiburg Austria 46°35N 14°49E 78 E7
Blejești Romania 44°19N 25°27E 81 F10
Blekinge □ Sweden 56°20N 15°20E 63 H9
Blenheim Canada 42°20N 82°0W 174 D3
Blenheim N.Z. 41°38S 173°57E 155 D5
Bléone → France 44°5N 6°0E 73 D10
Blérancourt France 49°31N 3°9E 71 C10
Bletchley U.K. 51°59N 0°44W 67 F7
Bleus, Monts
  Dem. Rep. of the Congo 1°30N 30°30E 142 B3
Blida Algeria 36°30N 2°49E 136 A4
Blida □ Algeria 36°35N 3°0E 136 A4
Blidet Amor Algeria 32°59N 5°58E 136 B5
Blidö Sweden 59°37N 18°53E 62 E12
Blidsberg Sweden 57°56N 13°30E 63 G7
Blieskastel Germany 49°14N 7°12E 77 F3
Bligh Sound N.Z. 44°47S 167°32E 155 E2
Bligh Water Fiji 17°0S 178°0E 154 a
Blind River Canada 46°10N 82°58W 164 C3
Blinisht Albania 41°52N 19°59E 96 E3
Bliss Idaho, U.S.A. 42°56N 114°57W 168 E6
Bliss N.Y., U.S.A. 42°34N 78°15W 174 D6
Blissfield U.S.A. 41°50N 83°51W 173 E12
Blitar Indonesia 8°5S 112°11E 119 H15
Blitta Togo 8°23N 1°6E 139 D5
Block I. U.S.A. 41°11N 71°35W 175 E13
Block Island Sd.
  U.S.A. 41°15N 71°40W 175 E13
Bloemfontein S. Africa 29°6S 26°7E 144 C4
Bloemhof S. Africa 27°38S 25°32E 144 C4
Blois France 47°35N 1°20E 70 E4
Blomskog Sweden 59°16N 12°2E 62 E6
Blomstermåla Sweden 56°59N 16°21E 63 H10
Blönduós Iceland 65°40N 20°12W 60 D3
Blongas Indonesia 8°53S 116°2E 119 K19
Blonie Poland 52°12N 20°37E 83 F7
Bloodvein → Canada 51°47N 96°43W 163 C9
Bloody Foreland Ireland 55°10N 8°17W 64 A3

Bloomer U.S.A. 45°6N 91°29W 172 C8
Bloomfield Canada 43°59N 77°14W 174 C7
Bloomfield Iowa, U.S.A. 40°45N 92°25W 172 E7
Bloomfield N. Mex.,
  U.S.A. 36°43N 107°59W 169 H10
Bloomfield Nebr.,
  U.S.A. 42°36N 97°39W 172 D5
Bloomington Ill., U.S.A. 40°28N 89°0W 172 E9
Bloomington Ind.,
  U.S.A. 39°10N 86°32W 172 F10
Bloomington Minn.,
  U.S.A. 44°50N 93°17W 172 C7
Bloomsburg U.S.A. 41°0N 76°27W 175 E8
Bloomsbury Australia 20°48S 148°38E 150 b
Blora Indonesia 6°57S 111°25E 119 G14
Blossburg U.S.A. 41°41N 77°4W 174 E7
Blosseville Kyst
  Greenland 68°50N 26°30W 57 D8
Blouberg S. Africa 23°8S 28°59E 145 A4
Blountstown U.S.A. 30°27N 85°3W 178 E4
Blue → Canada 47°10N 9°50E 78 D2
Blue Cypress L. U.S.A. 27°44N 80°45W 179 H9
Blue Earth U.S.A. 43°38N 94°6W 172 D6
Blue Hole △ Belize 17°9N 88°40W 182 C2
Blue Lagoon △ Zambia 15°28S 27°26E 143 F2
Blue Mesa Res.
  U.S.A. 38°28N 107°20W 168 G10
Blue Mountain Lake
  U.S.A. 43°51N 74°27W 175 C10
Blue Mountain Pk.
  Jamaica 18°3N 76°36W 182 a
Blue Mt. U.S.A. 40°30N 76°39W 175 F8
Blue Mts. Australia 33°40S 150°15E 153 B9
Blue Mts. Jamaica 18°3N 76°36W 182 a
Blue Mts. Maine,
  U.S.A. 44°50N 70°35W 175 B14
Blue Mts. Oreg., U.S.A. 45°0N 118°20W 168 D4
Blue Mts. △ U.S.A. 34°2S 150°15E 153 C9
Blue Mud B. Australia 13°30S 136°0E 150 A2
Blue Mud Bay ⊙
  Australia 13°25S 136°2E 150 A2
Blue Nile = Nil el Azraq →
  Sudan 15°38N 32°31E 135 E12
Blue Rapids U.S.A. 39°41N 96°39W 172 F5
Blue Ridge U.S.A. 36°40N 80°50W 173 G13
Blue River Canada 52°6N 119°18W 162 C5
Bluefield U.S.A. 37°15N 81°17W 173 G13
Bluefields Nic. 12°20N 83°50W 182 D3
Bluevale Canada 43°51N 81°15W 174 C3
Bluff Australia 23°35S 149°4E 150 C4
Bluff N.Z. 46°37S 168°20E 155 G3
Bluff U.S.A. 37°17N 109°33W 169 H9
Bluff Harbour → U.S.A. 36°36S 168°21E 155 G3
Bluff Knoll Australia 34°24S 118°15E 149 F2
Bluff Pt. Australia 27°50S 114°5E 149 E1
Bluffton Ga., U.S.A. 31°31N 84°52W 178 D5
Bluffton Ind., U.S.A. 40°44N 85°11W 173 E11
Bluffton S.C., U.S.A. 32°14N 80°52W 178 E5
Blumenau Brazil 27°0S 49°0W 191 B6
Blunt U.S.A. 44°31N 99°59W 172 C4
Bly U.S.A. 42°24N 121°3W 168 E3
Blyde River Canyon △
  S. Africa 24°37S 31°2E 145 B5
Blyth Australia 33°49S 138°28E 152 B3
Blyth Canada 43°44N 81°26W 174 C3
Blyth U.K. 55°8N 1°31W 66 B6
Blythe Calif., U.S.A. 33°37N 114°36W 171 M12
Blythe → U.S.A. 33°17N 82°12W 178 D7
Blytheville U.S.A. 35°56N 89°55W 177 D10
Bo S. Leone 7°55N 11°50W 138 D2
Bo Duc Vietnam 11°58N 106°50E 121 G6
Bo Hai China 39°0N 119°0E 115 E10
Bo Hai Haixia Asia 38°25N 121°10E 115 E11
Bo Xian = Bozhou
  China 33°55N 115°41E 114 H8
Boa Esperança, Represa
  Brazil 6°5S 43°50W 189 D2
Boa Nova Brazil 14°22S 40°10W 189 C2
Boa Viagem Brazil 5°7S 39°44W 189 D3
Boa Vista Brazil 2°48N 60°30W 186 C6
Boa Vista C. Verde Is. 16°0N 22°49W 134 b
Boaco Nic. 12°29N 85°35W 182 D2
Bo'ai China 35°10N 113°3E 114 G7
Boal Spain 43°25N 6°49W 88 B4
Boalsburg U.S.A. 40°47N 77°49W 174 F7
Boane Mozam. 26°6S 32°19E 145 C5
Boao China 19°8N 110°34E 117 a
Boardman U.S.A. 41°2N 80°40W 174 E4
Boath India 19°20N 78°20E 126 E4
Bobadah Australia 32°19S 146°41E 153 B7
Bobai China 22°17N 109°59E 116 F7
Bobbili India 18°35N 83°30E 126 E6
Bóbbio Italy 44°46N 9°23E 92 D6
Bobcaygeon Canada 44°33N 78°33W 174 B6
Böblingen Germany 48°40N 9°1E 77 G5
Bobo-Dioulasso
  Burkina Faso 11°8N 4°13W 138 C4
Bobolice Poland 53°58N 16°37E 82 E3
Bobonong Botswana 21°58S 28°20E 145 B4
Boboshevo Bulgaria 42°9N 23°0E 96 D7
Bobov Dol Bulgaria 42°20N 23°0E 96 D6
Bóbr → Poland 52°4N 15°4E 83 F2
Bobraomby, Tanjon' i
  Madag. 12°40S 49°10E 141 G9
Bobrov Russia 51°5N 40°2E 86 E5
Bobrovytsya Ukraine 50°44N 31°12E 86 G6
Bobruysk = Babruysk
  Belarus 53°10N 29°15E 75 B15
Bobrynets Ukraine 48°4N 32°5E 85 H7
Boby, Pic Madag. 22°12S 46°55E 141 J9
Boca del Río Mexico 19°5N 96°4W 181 D5
Boca do Acre Brazil 8°50S 67°27W 188 D5
Boca Grande U.S.A. 26°45N 82°16W 179 J7
Boca Raton Ivory C. 26°45N 82°16W 179 J7
Bocaiúva Brazil 17°7S 43°49W 189 D2
Bocas del Dragón = Dragon's
  Mouths Trin. & Tob. 11°0N 61°50W 187 K15
Bocas del Toro Panama 9°15N 82°20W 182 E3
Boceguillas Spain 41°20N 3°39W 88 D7
Bochalema Ukraine 47°40N 29°34E 81 C14
Bochnia Poland 49°58N 20°27E 83 J7
Bocholt Germany 51°50N 6°36E 76 D2
Bochum = Senwabarana
  S. Africa 23°17S 29°7E 145 B4
Bochum Germany 51°28N 7°13E 76 D3
Bockenem Germany 52°1N 10°8E 76 C6
Bočki Poland 52°39N 23°3E 83 F10
Bocognano France 42°5N 9°4E 73 F13
Bocoyna Mexico 27°52N 107°35W 180 B3

Bocşa Romania 45°21N 21°47E 80 E6
Boda Dalarna, Sweden 61°1N 15°13E 62 C9
Böda Kalmar, Sweden 57°15N 17°3E 63 G11
Boda Västernorrland,
  Sweden 62°52N 16°39E 62 B10
Bodafors Sweden 57°48N 14°23E 63 G8
Bodaybo Russia 57°50N 114°0E 107 D12
Boddam Australia 32°50S 116°30E 149 F2
Boddington Australia 32°50S 116°30E 149 F2
Bode Sadu Nigeria 9°0N 4°47E 139 D5
Bodega Bay U.S.A. 38°20N 123°3W 170 G3
Boden Sweden 65°50N 21°42E 60 D19
Bodensee Europe 47°35N 9°25E 77 H5
Bodenteich Germany 52°50N 10°42E 76 C6
Bodh Gaya India 24°41N 84°59E 125 G11
Bodhan India 18°40N 77°44E 126 E3
Bodinayakkanur India 10°2N 77°10E 127 J3
Bodinga Nigeria 12°58N 5°10E 139 C6
Bodmin U.K. 50°28N 4°43W 67 G3
Bodmin Moor U.K. 50°33N 4°36W 67 G3
Bodø Norway 67°17N 14°24E 60 C16
Bodrog → Hungary 48°11N 21°22E 80 B6
Bodrum Turkey 37°3N 27°30E 99 D9
Bódva → Hungary 48°19N 20°45E 80 B5
Boën France 45°44N 4°1E 73 C8
Boende
  Dem. Rep. of the Congo 0°24S 21°12E 140 E4
Boeotia = Viotia Greece 38°20N 23°0E 97 E10
Boerne U.S.A. 29°47N 98°44W 176 G5
Boesmans → S. Africa 33°42S 26°39E 144 D4
Boffa Guinea 10°16N 14°3W 138 C2
Bogalusa U.S.A. 30°47N 89°52W 177 F10
Bogan → Australia 30°20S 146°55E 153 A7
Bogan Gate Australia 33°7S 147°49E 153 B7
Bogandé Burkina Faso 12°2N 0°9W 139 C4
Bogantungan
  Australia 23°41S 147°17E 150 C4
Bogata U.S.A. 33°28N 95°13W 176 E7
Bogatić Serbia 44°51N 19°30E 96 B4
Boğazkale Turkey 40°2N 34°37E 104 B6
Boğazlıyan Turkey 39°11N 35°14E 104 C6
Bogda Shan China 43°35N 89°40E 109 D11
Bogen Sweden 60°4N 12°33E 62 C6
Bogense Denmark 55°34N 10°5E 63 J4
Bogetići Montenegro 42°41N 18°58E 96 D2
Boggabilla Australia 28°36S 150°24E 153 D5
Boggabri Australia 30°45S 150°5E 153 A9
Boggeragh Mts. Ireland 52°2N 8°55W 64 D3
Boglan = Solhan Turkey 38°57N 41°3E 105 C9
Bognes Norway 68°13N 16°5E 60 B17
Bognor Regis U.K. 50°47N 0°40W 67 G7
Bogo Phil. 11°3N 124°0E 119 B6
Bogodukhov = Bohodukhiv
  Ukraine 50°9N 35°33E 85 G8
Bogong, Mt. Australia 36°47S 147°17E 153 D7
Bogor Indonesia 6°36S 106°48E 118 F3
Bogoroditsk Russia 53°47N 38°8E 84 F10
Bogorodsk Russia 56°6N 43°30E 84 C13
Bogoso Ghana 5°38N 2°3W 138 D4
Bogotá Colombia 4°34N 74°0W 186 C4
Bogotol Russia 56°15N 89°50E 106 D9
Bogou Togo 10°40N 0°12E 139 C5
Bogra Bangla. 24°51N 89°22E 123 G16
Boguchanskoye Vdkhr.
  Russia 58°40N 97°30E 107 D10
Boguchany Russia 58°40N 97°30E 107 D10
Boguchar Russia 49°55N 40°32E 86 F5
Bogué Mauritania 16°45N 14°10W 138 B2
Boguszów-Gorce Poland 50°45N 16°12E 83 H3
Bohain-en-Vermandois
  France 49°59N 3°28E 71 C10
Bohdan Ukraine 48°0N 24°22E 81 B9
Bohemian Forest = Böhmerwald
  Germany 49°8N 13°14E 77 F9
Bohena Cr. →
  Australia 30°17S 149°42E 153 A8
Bohinjska Bistrica
  Slovenia 46°17N 14°1E 93 B11
Böhmerwald Germany 49°8N 13°14E 77 F9
Bohodukhiv Ukraine 50°9N 35°33E 85 G8
Bohol □ Phil. 9°50N 124°10E 119 C6
Bohol Sea Phil. 9°0N 124°0E 119 C6
Bohongou Burkina Faso 12°30N 0°40E 139 C5
Böhönye Hungary 46°25N 17°28E 80 D2
Bohorodchany Ukraine 48°50N 24°32E 81 B9
Bohorok Indonesia 3°30N 98°12E 121 L2
Bohotleh Somalia 8°20N 46°25E 133 F4
Bohu China 41°58N 86°37E 109 D11
Bohuslän Sweden 58°25N 12°0E 63 F6
Bohuslav Ukraine 49°30N 30°56E 85 H6
Boi Nigeria 9°35N 9°27E 139 D6
Boi, Pta. do Brazil 23°55S 45°15W 191 A6
Boiaçu Brazil 0°27S 61°46W 186 D6
Boigu Australia 9°16S 142°13E 150 a
Boileau, C. Australia 17°40S 122°7E 148 C3
Boipariguda India 18°46N 82°26E 126 E6
Boipeba, I. de Brazil 13°39S 38°55W 189 C3
Boiro Spain 42°39N 8°54W 88 C2
Boise U.S.A. 43°37N 116°13W 168 E5
Boise City U.S.A. 36°44N 102°31W 176 C3
Boissevain Canada 49°15N 100°5W 163 D8
Bóite → Italy 46°5N 12°5E 92 B4
Boitzenburg Germany 53°16N 13°36E 76 B9
Boizenburg Germany 53°23N 10°43E 76 B6
Bojador, C. W. Sahara 26°0N 14°30W 134 C3
Bojana → Albania 41°52N 19°22E 96 E3
Bojano Italy 41°29N 14°29E 95 A7
Bojanowo Poland 51°43N 16°42E 83 G3
BojnHe Denmark 54°56N 10°7E 63 J4
Bojnúrd Iran 37°30N 57°20E 129 B8
Bojonegoro Indonesia 7°11S 111°54E 119 G14
Boju Nigeria 7°22N 7°55E 139 D6
Boka Serbia 45°22N 20°52E 80 E5
Boka Kotorska
  Montenegro 42°23N 18°32E 96 D2
Bokala Ivory C. 8°31N 4°33W 138 D4
Bokani Nigeria 9°28N 5°10E 139 D6
Bokaro India 23°46N 85°55E 125 H11
Boké Guinea 10°56N 14°17W 138 C2
Bokhara → Australia 29°55S 146°42E 151 D4
Bokkos Nigeria 9°17N 9°1E 139 D6
Boknafjorden Norway 59°14N 5°40E 63 E11
Bokor △ Cambodia 10°50N 104°1E 121 G5
Bokoro Chad 12°25N 17°14E 135 F9
Bokpyin Burma 11°18N 98°42E 121 G2
Boksitogorsk Russia 59°32N 33°56E 84 C7
Bokungu
  Dem. Rep. of the Congo 0°35S 22°50E 140 E4
Bol Croatia 43°18N 16°38E 93 E13

Bolama Guinea-Biss. 11°30N 15°30W 138 C1
Bolan → Pakistan 28°38N 67°42E 124 E2
Bolan Pass Pakistan 29°50N 67°20E 122 E5
Bolaños → Mexico 21°12N 104°5W 180 C4
Bolaños de Calatrava
  Spain 38°54N 3°40W 89 C7
Bolayir Turkey 40°31N 26°45E 97 F10
Bolbec France 49°30N 0°30E 70 C7
Boldājī Iran 31°56N 51°3E 129 D6
Boldeşti-Scăeni Romania 45°3N 26°2E 81 E11
Bole China 44°55N 81°37E 109 C10
Bole Ghana 9°3N 2°23E 138 D4
Bolekhiv Ukraine 49°0N 23°57E 75 D12
Boleslawiec Poland 51°17N 15°37E 83 G2
Bolgatanga Ghana 10°44N 0°53W 139 C4
Bolgrad = Bolhrad
  Ukraine 45°40N 28°32E 81 E13
Bolhrad Ukraine 45°40N 28°32E 81 E13
Bolinao Phil. 16°23N 119°54E 119 A5
Bolintin-Vale Romania 44°27N 25°46E 81 F10
Bolívar Peru 7°18S 77°48W 188 B2
Bolívar Mo., U.S.A. 37°37N 93°25W 172 G7
Bolívar N.Y., U.S.A. 42°4N 78°10W 174 D6
Bolívar Tenn., U.S.A. 35°12N 89°0W 177 D10
Bolívar, Pico Venezuela 8°32N 71°2W 183 E5
Bolivia ■ S. Amer. 17°6S 64°0W 186 G6
Bolivian Plateau = Altiplano
  Bolivia 17°0S 68°0W 188 D4
Boljevac Serbia 43°51N 21°58E 96 C5
Bolkhov Russia 53°25N 36°0E 84 F9
Bolków Poland 50°55N 16°6E 83 H3
Bollebygd Sweden 57°40N 12°35E 63 G6
Bollène France 44°18N 4°45E 73 D8
Bollnäs Sweden 61°21N 16°24E 62 C10
Bollon Australia 28°2S 147°29E 151 D4
Bollstabruk Sweden 62°59N 17°40E 62 B11
Bolmen Sweden 56°55N 13°40E 63 H7
Bolnisi Georgia 41°26N 44°32E 87 K7
Bolobo
  Dem. Rep. of the Congo 2°6S 16°20E 140 E3
Bologna Italy 44°29N 11°20E 93 D8
Bologna ✈ (BLQ) Italy 44°34N 11°16E 93 D8
Bologoye Russia 57°55N 34°5E 84 D8
Bolomba
  Dem. Rep. of the Congo 0°35N 19°0E 140 D3
Bolonchén Mexico 20°1N 89°45W 181 D7
Bolotana Italy 40°20N 8°52E 94 B1
Boloven, Cao Nguyen
  Laos 15°10N 106°30E 120 E6
Bolpur India 23°40N 87°45E 125 H12
Bolsena Italy 42°39N 11°59E 92 F8
Bolsena, L. di Italy 42°36N 11°56E 92 F8
Bolshakovo Russia 54°53N 21°40E 82 D8
Bolshaya Chernigovka
  Russia 52°6N 50°52E 86 D10
Bolshaya Glushitsa
  Russia 52°28N 50°30E 86 D10
Bolshaya Martynovka
  Russia 47°19N 41°37E 87 G5
Bolshaya Vradiyevka
  Russia 47°50N 30°34E 85 J6
Bolshevik, Ostrov
  Russia 78°30N 102°0E 107 B11
Bolshoy Anyuy →
  Russia 68°30N 160°49E 107 C17
Bolshoy Begichev, Ostrov
  Russia 74°20N 112°30E 107 B12
Bolshoy Kamen Russia 43°7N 132°19E 112 C6
Bolshoy Kavkaz = Caucasus
  Mountains Eurasia 42°50N 44°0E 87 J7
Bolshoy Lyakhovskiy, Ostrov
  Russia 73°35N 142°0E 107 B15
Bolshoy Tyuters, Ostrov
  Russia 59°51N 27°13E 84 C4
Bolsward Neths. 53°3N 5°32E 69 A5
Bolt Head U.K. 50°12N 3°48W 67 G4
Boltaña Spain 42°28N 0°4E 90 C5
Boltigen Switz. 46°38N 7°24E 77 J3
Bolton Canada 43°54N 79°45W 174 C5
Bolton U.K. 53°35N 2°26W 66 D5
Bolton Landing
  U.S.A. 43°32N 73°35W 175 C11
Bolu Turkey 40°45N 31°35E 104 B4
Bolu □ Turkey 40°40N 31°30E 104 B4
Bolungavík Iceland 66°9N 23°15W 60 C2
Boluo China 23°13N 114°21E 117 F10
Bolvadin Turkey 38°45N 31°4E 104 C5
Bolzano Italy 46°31N 11°22E 93 B8
Bom Despacho Brazil 19°43S 45°15W 189 D1
Bom Jesus Brazil 9°0S 44°0W 189 D2
Bom Jesus da Gurguéia, Serra
  Brazil 9°0S 43°0W 189 D2
Bom Jesus da Lapa
  Brazil 13°15S 43°25W 189 C2
Boma
  Dem. Rep. of the Congo 5°50S 13°4E 140 F2
Bomaderry Australia 34°52S 150°37E 153 C9
Bombala Australia 36°56S 149°15E 153 D8
Bombarral Portugal 39°15N 9°9W 89 F1
Bombay = Mumbai
  India 18°56N 72°50E 126 F6
Bombay U.S.A. 44°56N 74°34W 175 B10
Bombedor, Pta.
  Venezuela 9°53N 61°37W 187 L15
Bomboma
  Dem. Rep. of the Congo 2°25N 18°55E 140 D3
Bombombwa
  Dem. Rep. of the Congo 1°40N 25°40E 142 B2
Bomi Liberia 7°1N 10°38W 138 D2
Bomili
  Dem. Rep. of the Congo 1°45N 27°5E 142 B2
Bomokandi →
  Dem. Rep. of the Congo 3°39N 26°8E 142 B2
Bomongo
  Dem. Rep. of the Congo 1°27N 18°21E 140 D3
Bomu → C.A.R. 4°40N 22°30E 140 D4

Bonaire W. Indies 12°10N 68°15W 183
Bonampak Mexico 16°44N 91°5W 181
Bonang Australia 37°11S 148°41E 153
Bonanza Nic. 13°54N 84°35W 182
Bonaparte Arch.
  Australia 14°0S 124°30E 148
Boñar Spain 42°52N 5°19W 88
Bonar Bridge U.K. 57°54N 4°20W 65
Bonasse Trin. & Tob. 10°5N 61°54W 187
Bonaventure Canada 48°5N 65°32W 165
Bonavista Canada 48°40N 53°5W 165
Bonavista, C. Canada 48°42N 53°5W 165
Bonavista B. Canada 48°45N 53°25W 165
Bondeno Italy 44°53N 11°25E 92
Bondo
  Dem. Rep. of the Congo 3°55N 23°53E 142
Bondokodi Indonesia 9°35S 119°0E 119
Bondoukou Ivory C. 8°2N 2°47W 138
Bondowoso Indonesia 7°55S 113°49E 119
Bone, Teluk Indonesia 4°10S 120°50E 119
Bonerate Indonesia 7°25S 121°5E 119
Bonerate, Kepulauan
  Indonesia 6°30S 121°10E 119
Bo'ness U.K. 56°1N 3°37W 65
Bonete, Cerro
  Argentina 27°55S 68°40W 190
Bong Son = Hoai Nhon
  Vietnam 14°28N 109°1E 120
Bongaigaon India 26°28N 90°34E 118
Bongandanga
  Dem. Rep. of the Congo 1°24N 21°3E 140
Bongor Chad 10°35N 15°20E 135
Bongos, Massif des
  C.A.R. 8°40N 22°25E 140
Bongouanou Ivory C. 6°42N 4°15W 138
Bonham U.S.A. 33°35N 96°11W 176
Boni Mali 15°3N 2°10W 138
Boni □ Kenya 1°35S 41°18E 142
Bonifacio France 41°24N 9°10E 73
Bonifacio, Bouches de
  Medit. S. 41°12N 9°15E 94
Bonifay U.S.A. 30°47N 85°41W 178
Bonin Is. = Ogasawara Gunto
  Pac. Oc. 27°0N 142°0E 156
Bonita Springs U.S.A. 26°21N 81°47W 179
Bonkoukou Niger 14°0N 3°15E 139
Bonn Germany 50°46N 7°6E 76
Bonnat France 46°20N 1°54E 71
Bonne Terre U.S.A. 37°55N 90°33W 172
Bonneau U.S.A. 33°16N 79°58W 178
Bonners Ferry U.S.A. 48°42N 116°19W 168
Bonnétable France 48°11N 0°25E 70
Bonneval France 48°11N 1°24E 70
Bonneval-sur-Arc France 45°22N 7°3E 73
Bonneville France 46°4N 6°24E 73
Bonney, L. Australia 37°50S 140°20E 152
Bonnie Doon Australia 37°2S 145°53E 153
Bonnie Rock Australia 30°29S 118°22E 149
Bonny Nigeria 4°25N 7°13E 139
Bonny → Nigeria 4°20N 7°10E 139
Bonny, Bight of Africa 3°30N 9°20E 139
Bonnyrigg U.K. 55°53N 3°6W 65
Bonnyville Canada 54°20N 110°45W 163
Bono Italy 40°25N 9°2E 94
Bonoi Indonesia 1°45S 137°41E 119
Bonorva Italy 40°25N 8°46E 94
Bonsall U.S.A. 33°16N 117°14W 171
Bontang Indonesia 0°10N 117°30E 118
Bonthe S. Leone 7°30N 12°33W 138
Bontoc Phil. 17°7N 120°58E 119
Bonyeri Ghana 5°1N 2°46W 138
Bonyhád Hungary 46°18N 18°32E 80
Bonython Ra.
  Australia 23°40S 128°45E 148
Booderee △ Australia 35°12S 150°42E 153
Boodjamulla △
  Australia 18°15S 138°6E 150
Bookabie Australia 31°50S 132°41E 149
Booker U.S.A. 36°27N 100°32W 176
Bool Lagoon Australia 37°7S 140°40E 152
Boola Guinea 8°22N 8°41W 138
Boolcoomata Australia 31°55S 140°33E 152
Boolindal Australia 30°22S 146°11E 153
Boorowa Australia 34°28S 148°44E 153
Boort Australia 36°7S 143°46E 153
Boosaaso Somalia 11°12N 49°18E 131
Boothia, Gulf of Canada 71°0N 90°0W 166
Boothia Pen. Canada 71°0N 94°0W 166
Bootle U.K. 53°28N 3°1W 66
Booué Gabon 0°5S 11°55E 140
Bopolu Liberia 7°4N 10°29W 138
Boppard Germany 50°13N 7°35E 76
Boquilla, Presa de la
  Mexico 27°31N 105°30W 180
Boquillas del Carmen
  Mexico 29°12N 102°58W 180
Bor Czech Rep. 49°41N 12°45E 78
Bor Russia 56°28N 43°59E 86
Bor Serbia 44°5N 22°7E 96
Bor South Sudan 6°10N 31°40E 135
Bor Sweden 57°9N 14°10E 63
Bor Turkey 37°35N 34°32E 104
Bor Mashash Israel 31°7N 34°50E 108
Bora Bora
  French Polynesia 16°30S 151°45W 157
Borah Peak U.S.A. 44°8N 113°47W 168
Boraha, Nosy Madag. 16°50S 49°55E 141
Borankul Kazakhstan 44°0N 54°0E 87
Borås Sweden 57°43N 12°56E 63
Borăzjăn Iran 29°22N 51°10E 129
Borba Brazil 4°12S 59°34W 186
Borba Portugal 38°50N 7°26W 89

rborema, Planalto da Brazil 7°0S 37°0W 189 B3
rča Serbia 44°52N 20°28E 96 B4
rcea Romania 44°20N 27°45E 81 F12
rçka Turkey 41°25N 41°41E 105 B9
rd Khūn-e Now Iran 28°3N 51°28E 129 D6
rda, C. Australia 35°45S 136°34E 152 C2
rdeaux France 44°50N 0°36W 72 D3
rdeaux ✈ (BOD) France 44°50N 0°35W 72 D3
rden Australia 34°3S 118°12E 149 F2
rden-Carleton Canada 46°18N 63°47W 165 C7
rden I. Canada 78°30N 111°30W 161 B9
rden Pen. Canada 73°0N 83°0W 161 C15
rden Springs U.S.A. 33°56N 85°28W 178 B4
rder Ranges △ Australia 28°24S 152°56E 151 D5
rders = Scottish Borders □ U.K. 55°35N 2°50W 65 F6
rdertown Australia 36°19S 140°45E 152 D4
rðeyri Iceland 65°12N 21°6W 60 D3
rdighera Italy 43°46N 7°39E 92 E4
rdj bou Arreridj Algeria 36°4N 4°45E 136 A4
rdj Bourguiba Tunisia 32°12N 10°2E 136 B6
rdj Flye Ste-Marie Algeria 27°19N 2°32W 136 C3
rdj in Eker Algeria 24°9N 5°3E 136 D5
rdj Menaïel Algeria 36°46N 3°43E 136 A4
rdj Messouda Algeria 30°12N 9°25E 136 B5
rdj Mokhtar Algeria 21°20N 0°56E 134 D6
rdj Nili Algeria 33°28N 3°2E 136 B4
rdj Omar Driss Algeria 28°10N 6°40E 136 C5
rdj Sif Fatima Algeria 31°6N 8°41E 136 B5
rdj Tarat Algeria 25°55N 9°3E 136 C5
rehamwood U.K. 51°40N 0°15W 67 F7
rek Wielkopolski Poland 51°54N 17°11E 83 G4
rensberg Sweden 58°34N 15°17E 63 F9
rgå = Porvoo Finland 60°24N 25°40E 84 B3
rgampad India 17°39N 80°52E 126 F5
rgarnes Iceland 64°32N 21°55W 60 D3
rgefjellet Norway 65°20N 13°45E 60 D15
rger Neths. 52°54N 6°44E 69 B6
rger U.S.A. 35°39N 101°24W 176 D4
rgholm Sweden 56°52N 16°39E 63 H10
rgia Italy 38°49N 16°30E 95 D9
rgo San Dalmazzo Italy 44°20N 7°30E 92 D4
rgo San Lorenzo Italy 43°57N 11°23E 93 E8
rgo Val di Taro Italy 44°29N 9°46E 92 D6
rgo Valsugana Italy 46°3N 11°27E 93 B8
rgomanero Italy 45°42N 8°28E 92 C5
rgorose Italy 42°11N 13°13E 93 F10
rgosésia Italy 45°43N 8°16E 92 C5
rhoyn Tal Mongolia 43°50N 111°58E 114 C6
ri Nigeria 4°42N 7°21E 139 E6
rigumma India 19°3N 82°33E 126 E6
rikhane Laos 18°33N 103°43E 120 C4
risoglebsk Russia 51°27N 42°5E 86 E6
risov = Barysaw Belarus 54°17N 28°28E 75 A15
risovka Russia 50°36N 36°1E 85 G9
rj Jeneïn Tunisia 31°45N 10°9E 136 B6
rja Peru 4°20S 77°40W 186 D3
rja Spain 41°48N 1°34W 90 D3
rjas Blancas = Les Borges Blanques Spain 41°31N 0°52E 90 D5
rjomi Georgia 41°48N 43°28E 87 K6
rkop Denmark 55°39N 9°39E 63 J3
rkou Chad 18°15N 18°50E 135 E9
rkum Germany 53°34N 6°40E 76 B2
rlänge Sweden 60°29N 15°26E 62 D9
rley, C. Antarctica 66°15S 52°30E 55 C5
rlu Turkey 38°44N 28°27E 99 C10
rmida → Italy 44°23N 8°13E 92 D5
rmio Italy 46°28N 10°22E 92 B7
rna Germany 51°7N 12°29E 76 D8
rne Sulinowo Poland 53°32N 16°36E 82 E3
rneo E. Indies 1°0N 115°0E 118 D5
rnholm Denmark 55°10N 15°0E 63 J8
rnholmsgattet Europe 55°15N 14°20E 63 J8
rno □ Nigeria 11°30N 13°0E 139 C7
rnos Spain 36°48N 5°42W 89 J5
rnova Turkey 38°27N 27°14E 99 C9
rnu Yassa Nigeria 12°14N 12°25E 139 C7
robudur △ Indonesia 7°36S 110°12E 119 G14
rodino Russia 55°31N 35°40E 84 E8
rodino Ukraine 46°18N 29°15E 81 D14
rogontsy Russia 62°42N 131°8E 107 C14
rohoro Shan China 44°6N 83°10E 109 D10
romo Burkina Faso 11°45N 2°58W 138 C4
ron U.S.A. 35°0N 117°39W 171 L9
rongan Phil. 11°37N 125°26E 119 B7
rotou Ivory C. 8°46N 7°30W 138 D3
rovan Bulgaria 43°27N 23°45E 96 C7
rovichi Russia 58°25N 33°55E 84 C7
rovsk Russia 55°12N 36°24E 84 E9
rovskoy Kazakhstan 53°48N 64°9E 108 B6
rrby Sweden 55°27N 14°10E 63 J8
rrego Springs U.S.A. 33°15N 116°23W 171 M10
rriol Spain 40°4N 0°4W 90 E4
rrisokane Ireland 53°0N 8°7W 64 D3
rroloola Australia 16°4S 136°17E 150 B2
rşa Cluj, Romania 46°56N 23°40E 81 D8
rşa Maramureş, Romania 47°41N 24°50E 81 C9
rsad India 22°25N 72°54E 124 H5
rsec Romania 46°57N 25°34E 81 D10
rshchiv Ukraine 48°48N 26°3E 81 B11
rsod-Abaúj-Zemplén □ Hungary 48°20N 21°0E 80 B6
rt-les-Orgues France 45°24N 2°29E 72 C6
rtala = Bole China 44°55N 81°37E 109 C10
rth U.K. 52°29N 4°2W 67 E3
rtnan Sweden 62°45N 13°50E 62 B7
rūjerd Iran 33°55N 48°50E 105 F13
ryeong S. Korea 36°21N 126°36E 115 F14
rynya Ukraine 49°4N 23°0E 83 J10
ryslav Ukraine 49°18N 23°28E 83 J10
ryspil Ukraine 50°21N 30°59E 85 G6
rzhomi = Borjomi Georgia 41°48N 43°28E 87 K6
rzna Ukraine 51°18N 32°26E 85 G7
rzya Russia 50°24N 116°31E 111 A12
sa Italy 40°18N 8°30E 94 B1
sanska Dubica = Dubica Bos.-H. 45°10N 16°50E 93 C13
Bosanska Gradiška = Gradiška Bos.-H. 45°10N 17°15E 80 E2
Bosanska Kostajnica = Kostajnica Bos.-H. 45°11N 16°33E 93 C13
Bosanska Krupa Bos.-H. 44°53N 16°10E 93 D13
Bosanski Brod = Brod Bos.-H. 45°10N 18°0E 80 E2
Bosanski Novi = Novi Grad Bos.-H. 45°2N 16°22E 93 C13
Bosanski Petrovac Bos.-H. 44°35N 16°21E 93 D13
Bosanski Šamac = Šamac Bos.-H. 45°3N 18°29E 80 E3
Bosansko Grahovo Bos.-H. 44°12N 16°26E 93 D13
Boscastle U.K. 50°41N 4°42W 67 G3
Boscobelle Barbados 13°17N 59°35W 183 g
Bose China 23°53N 106°35E 116 F6
Boseong S. Korea 34°46N 127°5E 115 G14
Boshan China 36°28N 117°49E 115 F9
Boshof S. Africa 28°31S 25°13E 144 C4
Boshrūyeh Iran 33°50N 57°30E 129 C8
Bosilegrad Serbia 42°30N 22°27E 96 D6
Boskovice Czech Rep. 49°29N 16°40E 79 B9
Bosna → Bos.-H. 45°4N 18°29E 80 E3
Bosna i Hercegovina = Bosnia-Herzegovina ■ Europe 44°0N 18°0E 80 G2
Bosnia-Herzegovina ■ Europe 44°0N 18°0E 80 G2
Bosnik Indonesia 1°5S 136°10E 119 E9
Bosobolo Dem. Rep. of the Congo 4°15N 19°50E 140 D3
Bosporus = İstanbul Boğazı Turkey 41°5N 29°3E 97 E13
Bosque Farms U.S.A. 35°51N 106°42W 169 J10
Bosra = Buşra ash Shām Syria 32°30N 36°25E 130 C5
Bossangoa C.A.R. 6°35N 17°30E 140 C3
Bossé Bangou Niger 13°20N 1°18E 139 C5
Bossier City U.S.A. 32°31N 93°44W 176 E8
Bossiesvlei Namibia 25°1S 16°44E 144 C2
Bosso Niger 13°43N 13°19E 139 C7
Bosso, Dallol → Niger 12°25N 2°50E 139 C5
Bostan Pakistan 30°26N 67°2E 124 D2
Bostānābād Iran 37°50N 46°50E 105 D12
Bosten Hu China 41°55N 87°40E 109 D11
Boston U.K. 52°59N 0°2W 66 E7
Boston Ga., U.S.A. 30°47N 83°47W 178 E6
Boston Mass., U.S.A. 42°22N 71°3W 175 D13
Boston Bar Canada 49°52N 121°30W 162 D4
Boston Mts. U.S.A. 35°42N 93°15W 176 D8
Bostwick U.S.A. 29°46N 81°38W 178 F8
Bosumtwi, L. Ghana 6°30N 1°25W 139 D4
Bosut → Croatia 45°20N 18°45E 80 E3
Boswell Canada 49°28N 116°45W 162 D5
Boswell U.S.A. 40°10N 79°2W 174 F5
Botad India 22°15N 71°40E 124 H4
Botan → Turkey 37°57N 42°2E 105 D10
Botany B. Australia 33°58S 151°11E 147 E8
Botene Laos 17°35N 101°12E 120 D3
Botev Bulgaria 42°44N 24°52E 97 D8
Botevgrad Bulgaria 42°55N 23°47E 96 D7
Bothaville S. Africa 27°23S 26°34E 144 C4
Bothnia, G. of Europe 62°0N 20°0E 60 F19
Bothwell Australia 42°20S 147°1E 151 G4
Bothwell Canada 42°38N 81°52W 174 D3
Boticas Portugal 41°41N 7°40W 88 D3
Botletle → Botswana 20°10S 23°15E 144 B3
Botlikh Russia 42°39N 46°11E 87 J8
Botna → Moldova 46°45N 29°34E 81 D14
Botoroaga Romania 44°8N 25°32E 81 F10
Botoşani Romania 47°42N 26°41E 81 C11
Botoşani □ Romania 47°50N 26°50E 81 C11
Botou Burkina Faso 12°42N 1°59E 139 C5
Botou China 38°4N 116°34E 114 E9
Botricello Italy 38°56N 16°51E 95 D9
Botro Ivory C. 7°51N 5°19W 138 D3
Botshabelo S. Africa 29°14S 26°44E 144 C4
Botswana ■ Africa 22°0S 24°0E 144 B3
Bottineau U.S.A. 48°50N 100°27W 172 A3
Bottnaryd Sweden 57°47N 13°50E 63 G7
Bottrop Germany 51°31N 6°58E 76 D2
Botucatu Brazil 22°55S 48°30W 191 A6
Botum Sakor △ Cambodia 11°5N 103°15E 121 G4
Botwood Canada 49°6N 55°23W 165 C8
Bou Alam Algeria 33°50N 1°26E 136 B4
Bou Ali Algeria 27°11N 0°4W 136 C3
Bou Djébéha Mali 18°25N 2°45W 138 B4
Bou Guema Algeria 28°49N 0°19E 136 C4
Bou Ismaïl Algeria 36°38N 2°42E 136 A4
Bou Izakarn Morocco 29°12N 9°46W 136 C2
Boû Naga Mauritania 18°49N 13°20W 138 B2
Bou Noura Algeria 32°29N 3°43E 136 B4
Boû Rjeïmât Mauritania 19°4N 15°3W 138 B1
Bou Saâda Algeria 35°11N 4°9E 136 A4
Bou Salem Tunisia 36°45N 9°2E 136 A5
Bouaflé Ivory C. 7°1N 5°47W 138 D3
Bouaké Ivory C. 7°40N 5°2W 138 D3
Bouar C.A.R. 6°0N 15°40E 140 C3
Bouârfa Morocco 32°32N 1°58W 136 B3
Boubout Algeria 27°26N 4°30W 136 C3
Boucaut B. Australia 12°0S 134°25E 150 A1
Bouches-du-Rhône □ France 43°37N 5°2E 73 E9
Boucle de Baoulé △ Mali 13°53N 9°0W 138 C3
Boucles de la Seine Normande ⌓ France 49°32N 0°35E 70 C7
Bouctouche Canada 46°30N 64°45W 165 C7
Bouda Algeria 27°50N 0°27W 136 C3
Boudenib Morocco 31°59N 3°31W 136 B3
Boufarik Algeria 36°34N 2°58E 136 A4
Bougainville, C. Australia 13°57S 126°4E 148 B4
Bougainville I. Papua N. G. 6°0S 155°0E 147 B8
Bougainville Reef Australia 15°30S 147°5E 150 B4
Bougaroun, C. Algeria 37°6N 6°30E 136 A5
Bougie = Bejaïa Algeria 36°42N 5°2E 136 A5
Bougouni Mali 11°30N 7°20W 138 C3
Bougtob Algeria 34°2N 0°5E 136 B4
Bouillon Belgium 49°44N 5°3E 69 E5
Bouïra Algeria 36°20N 3°59E 136 A4
Bouïra □ Algeria 36°15N 3°55E 136 A4
Boukombé Benin 10°13N 1°9E 139 C5
Boulal Mali 15°8N 8°21W 138 B3
Boulazac France 45°10N 0°47E 72 C4
Boulder Colo., U.S.A. 40°1N 105°17W 168 F11
Boulder Mont., U.S.A. 46°14N 112°7W 168 C7
Boulder City U.S.A. 35°58N 114°49W 171 K12
Boulder Creek U.S.A. 37°7N 122°7W 170 H4
Boulder Dam = Hoover Dam U.S.A. 36°1N 114°44W 171 K12
Bouli Mauritania 15°17N 12°18W 138 B2
Boulia Australia 22°52S 139°51E 150 C2
Bouligny France 49°17N 5°45E 71 C12
Boulogne → France 47°12N 1°47W 70 E5
Boulogne-sur-Gesse France 43°18N 0°38E 72 E4
Boulogne-sur-Mer France 50°42N 1°36E 71 B8
Bouloire France 47°59N 0°45E 70 E7
Boulouli Mali 15°30N 9°25W 138 B3
Boulsa Burkina Faso 12°39N 0°34W 139 C4
Boultoum Niger 14°45N 10°25E 139 C7
Bouma △ Fiji 16°50S 179°52W 154 a
Boumalne Dadès Morocco 31°25N 6°0W 136 B2
Boûmdeïd Mauritania 17°25N 11°50W 138 B2
Boumerdès Algeria 36°46N 3°28E 136 A4
Boumerdès □ Algeria 36°45N 3°40E 136 A4
Boun Neua Laos 21°38N 101°54E 120 B3
Boun Tai Laos 21°23N 101°58E 120 B3
Bouna Ivory C. 9°10N 3°0W 138 D4
Boundary Peak U.S.A. 37°51N 118°21W 170 H8
Boundiali Ivory C. 9°30N 6°20W 138 D3
Bountiful U.S.A. 40°53N 111°52W 168 F8
Bounty Is. Pac. Oc. 48°0S 178°30E 156 M9
Bounty Trough Pac. Oc. 46°0S 178°0E 156 M9
Boura Mali 12°25N 4°33W 138 C4
Bourbon-Lancy France 46°37N 3°45E 71 F10
Bourbon-l'Archambault France 46°36N 3°4E 71 F10
Bourbonnais France 46°28N 3°0E 71 F10
Bourbonne-les-Bains France 47°54N 5°45E 71 E12
Bourbourg France 50°56N 2°12E 71 B9
Bourdel L. Canada 56°43N 74°10W 164 A5
Bourem Mali 17°0N 0°24W 139 B4
Bourg France 45°3N 0°34W 72 C3
Bourg-Argental France 45°18N 4°32E 73 C8
Bourg-de-Péage France 45°2N 5°3E 73 C9
Bourg-en-Bresse France 46°13N 5°12E 71 F12
Bourg-Lastic France 45°39N 2°35E 72 C6
Bourg-Madame France 42°26N 1°55E 72 F5
Bourg-St-Andéol France 44°23N 4°39E 73 D8
Bourg-St-Maurice France 45°35N 6°46E 73 C10
Bourganeuf France 45°57N 1°45E 72 C5
Bourgas = Burgas Bulgaria 42°33N 27°29E 97 D11
Bourges France 47°9N 2°25E 71 E9
Bourget Canada 45°26N 75°9W 175 A9
Bourget, Lac du France 45°44N 5°52E 73 C9
Bourgneuf, B. de France 47°3N 2°10W 70 E4
Bourgneuf-en-Retz France 47°2N 1°58W 70 E5
Bourgogne □ France 47°0N 4°50E 71 F11
Bourgoin-Jallieu France 45°36N 5°17E 73 C9
Bourgueil France 47°17N 0°10E 70 E7
Bourke Australia 30°8S 145°55E 151 E4
Bourne U.K. 52°47N 0°22W 66 E7
Bournemouth U.K. 50°43N 1°52W 67 G6
Bournemouth □ U.K. 50°43N 1°52W 67 G6
Bouroum Burkina Faso 13°37N 0°39W 139 C4
Bouse U.S.A. 33°56N 114°0W 171 M13
Boussac France 46°22N 2°13E 71 F9
Boussé Burkina Faso 12°39N 1°53W 139 C4
Bousso Chad 10°34N 16°52E 135 F9
Boussouma Burkina Faso 12°52N 1°13W 139 C4
Boutilimit Mauritania 17°45N 14°40W 138 B2
Boutonne → France 45°54N 0°50W 72 C3
Bouvet I. = Bouvetøya Antarctica 54°26S 3°24E 56 M12
Bouvetøya Antarctica 54°26S 3°24E 56 M12
Bouxwiller France 48°49N 7°27E 71 D14
Bouza Niger 14°29N 6°2E 139 C6
Bouznika Morocco 33°46N 7°6W 136 B2
Bouzonville France 49°17N 6°32E 71 C13
Bova Marina Italy 37°56N 15°55E 95 E8
Bovalino Italy 38°10N 16°10E 95 D9
Bovanenkovo Russia 70°22N 68°40E 106 B7
Bovec Slovenia 46°20N 13°33E 93 B10
Bovill U.S.A. 46°51N 116°24W 168 C5
Bovino Italy 41°15N 15°20E 95 A8
Bovril Argentina 31°21S 59°26W 190 C4
Bow → Canada 49°57N 111°41W 162 C6
Bow Island Canada 49°50N 111°23W 168 B8
Bowbells U.S.A. 48°48N 102°15W 172 A2
Bowdle U.S.A. 45°27N 99°39W 172 C4
Bowdon U.S.A. 33°32N 85°15W 178 B4
Bowdon Junction U.S.A. 33°40N 85°9W 178 B4
Bowelling Australia 33°25S 116°30E 149 F2
Bowen Argentina 35°0S 67°31W 190 D2
Bowen Australia 20°0S 148°16E 150 J6
Bowen Mts. Australia 37°0S 147°50E 153 D7
Bowers Basin Pac. Oc. 53°45N 176°0E 54 D16
Bowers Ridge Pac. Oc. 54°0N 180°0E 54 D17
Bowie Ariz., U.S.A. 32°19N 109°29W 169 K9
Bowie Tex., U.S.A. 33°34N 97°51W 176 E6
Bowkān Iran 36°31N 46°12E 105 D12
Bowland, Forest of U.K. 54°0N 2°30W 66 D5
Bowling Green Fla., U.S.A. 27°38N 81°50W 179 H8
Bowling Green Ky., U.S.A. 36°59N 86°27W 172 G10
Bowling Green Ohio, U.S.A. 41°23N 83°39W 173 E12
Bowling Green, C. Australia 19°19S 147°25E 150 B4
Bowling Green Bay △ Australia 19°26S 146°57E 150 B4
Bowman N. Dak., U.S.A. 46°11N 103°24W 172 B2
Bowman S.C., U.S.A. 33°21N 80°41W 178 B9
Bowman I. Antarctica 65°0S 104°0E 55 C8
Bowmanville = Clarington Canada 43°55N 78°41W 174 C6
Bowmore U.K. 55°45N 6°17W 65 F2
Bowral Australia 34°26S 150°27E 153 C9
Bowraville Australia 30°37S 152°52E 151 E5
Bowron → Canada 54°3N 121°50W 162 C4
Bowron Lake ⌓ Canada 53°10N 121°5W 162 C4
Bowser L. Canada 56°30N 129°30W 162 B3
Bowsman Canada 52°14N 101°12W 163 C8
Bowwood Zambia 17°5S 26°20E 143 F2
Box Cr. → Australia 34°10S 143°50E 151 E3
Boxholm Sweden 58°12N 15°3E 63 F9
Boxmeer Neths. 51°38N 5°56E 69 C5
Boxtel Neths. 51°36N 5°20E 69 C5
Boyabat Turkey 41°28N 34°47E 104 B6
Boyalıca Turkey 40°29N 29°33E 97 F13
Boyang China 29°0N 116°38E 117 C11
Boyany Ukraine 48°17N 26°8E 81 B11
Boyce U.S.A. 31°23N 92°40W 176 F8
Boyd U.S.A. 30°11N 83°37W 178 E6
Boyd L. Canada 52°46N 76°42W 164 B4
Boyle Canada 54°35N 112°49W 162 C6
Boyle Ireland 53°59N 8°18W 64 C3
Boyne → Ireland 53°43N 6°15W 64 C5
Boyne, Bend of the Ireland 53°41N 6°27W 64 C5
Boyne City U.S.A. 45°13N 85°1W 173 C11
Boynitsa Bulgaria 43°58N 22°32E 96 C6
Boynton Beach U.S.A. 26°32N 80°4W 179 J9
Boyoma, Chutes Dem. Rep. of the Congo 0°35N 25°23E 142 B2
Boysen Res. U.S.A. 43°25N 108°11W 168 E9
Boyuibe Bolivia 20°25S 63°17W 186 G6
Boyup Brook Australia 33°50S 116°23E 149 F2
Boz Burun Turkey 40°32N 28°46E 97 F12
Boz Dağ Turkey 37°18N 29°11E 99 D11
Boz Dağları Turkey 38°20N 28°0E 99 C10
Bozburun Turkey 36°43N 28°4E 99 E10
Bozcaada Turkey 39°49N 26°3E 104 C2
Bozdoğan Turkey 37°40N 28°17E 99 D10
Bozeman U.S.A. 45°41N 111°2W 168 D8
Bozen = Bolzano Italy 46°31N 11°22E 93 B8
Boževac Serbia 44°32N 21°24E 96 B5
Bozhou China 33°55N 115°41E 114 H8
Bozkır Turkey 37°11N 32°14E 104 D5
Bozkurt Turkey 37°50N 29°37E 99 D11
Bozouls France 44°28N 2°43E 72 D6
Bozoum C.A.R. 6°25N 16°35E 140 C3
Bozova Antalya, Turkey 37°13N 30°18E 99 D12
Bozova Sanliurfa, Turkey 37°21N 38°32E 105 D8
Bozovici Romania 44°56N 22°0E 80 F7
Bozüyük Turkey 39°54N 30°3E 99 B12
Bozyazı Turkey 36°6N 33°0E 128 B2
Bra Italy 44°42N 7°51E 92 D4
Braås Sweden 57°4N 15°3E 63 G9
Brabant □ Belgium 50°46N 4°30E 69 D4
Brabant L. Canada 55°58N 103°43W 163 B8
Brabrand Denmark 56°9N 10°7E 63 H4
Brač Croatia 43°20N 16°40E 93 E13
Bracadale, L. U.K. 57°20N 6°30W 65 D2
Bracciano Italy 42°6N 12°10E 93 F9
Bracciano, L. di Italy 42°7N 12°14E 93 F9
Bracebridge Canada 45°2N 79°19W 174 A5
Bracieux France 47°30N 1°30E 70 E8
Bräcke Sweden 62°45N 15°26E 62 B9
Brackettville U.S.A. 29°19N 100°25W 176 G4
Bračk Kanal Croatia 43°24N 16°40E 93 E13
Bracknell U.K. 51°25N 0°43W 67 F7
Bracknell Forest □ U.K. 51°25N 0°44W 67 F7
Brad Romania 46°10N 22°50E 80 D7
Brádano → Italy 40°23N 16°51E 95 B9
Bradenton U.S.A. 27°30N 82°34W 179 H7
Bradford Canada 44°7N 79°34W 174 B5
Bradford U.K. 53°47N 1°45W 66 D6
Bradford Pa., U.S.A. 41°58N 78°38W 174 E6
Bradford Vt., U.S.A. 43°59N 72°9W 175 C12
Bradley Ark., U.S.A. 33°6N 93°39W 176 E8
Bradley Calif., U.S.A. 35°52N 120°48W 170 K6
Bradley Institute Zimbabwe 17°7S 31°25E 143 F3
Bradley Junction U.S.A. 27°48N 81°59W 179 H8
Brady U.S.A. 31°9N 99°20W 176 F5
Brædstrup Denmark 55°58N 9°37E 63 J3
Braemar Australia 33°12S 139°35E 152 B3
Braeside Canada 45°28N 76°24W 175 A8
Braga Portugal 41°35N 8°25W 88 D2
Braga □ Portugal 41°30N 8°30W 88 D2
Bragadiru Romania 43°46N 25°31E 81 G10
Bragado Argentina 35°2S 60°27W 190 D3
Bragança Brazil 1°0S 47°2W 187 D9
Bragança Portugal 41°48N 6°50W 88 D4
Bragança □ Portugal 41°30N 6°45W 88 D4
Bragança Paulista Brazil 22°55S 46°32W 191 A6
Brahestad = Raahe Finland 64°40N 24°28E 60 D21
Brahmanbaria Bangla. 23°58N 91°15E 123 H17
Brahmani → India 20°39N 86°46E 126 D8
Brahmapur India 19°15N 84°54E 126 E7
Brahmaputra → Asia 23°40N 90°35E 125 H13
Braich-y-pwll U.K. 52°47N 4°46W 66 E3
Braidwood Australia 35°27S 149°49E 153 C8
Brăila Romania 45°19N 27°59E 81 E12
Brăila □ Romania 45°5N 27°30E 81 E12
Brainerd U.S.A. 46°22N 94°12W 172 B6
Braintree U.K. 51°53N 0°34E 67 F8
Braintree U.S.A. 42°13N 71°0W 175 D14
Brak → S. Africa 29°35S 22°55E 144 C3
Brake Germany 53°20N 8°28E 76 B4
Brakel Germany 51°42N 9°11E 76 D5
Brakna □ Mauritania 17°0N 13°20W 138 B2
Bräkne-Hoby Sweden 56°14N 15°6E 63 H9
Brakwater Namibia 22°28S 17°3E 144 B2
Brålanda Sweden 58°34N 12°21E 63 F6
Bramberg Germany 50°6N 10°40E 77 E6
Bramdrupdam Denmark 55°31N 9°28E 63 J3
Bramhapuri India 20°36N 79°52E 126 D4
Bramming Denmark 55°28N 8°42E 63 J2
Brämön Sweden 62°14N 17°40E 62 B11
Brampton Canada 43°45N 79°45W 174 C5
Brampton U.K. 54°57N 2°44W 66 C5
Brampton I. Australia 20°49S 149°16E 150 b
Bramsche Germany 52°24N 7°59E 76 C3
Branchville U.S.A. 33°15N 80°49W 178 B9
Branco → Brazil 1°20S 61°50W 186 D6
Branco, C. Brazil 7°9S 34°47W 189 B4
Brandberg Namibia 21°10S 14°33E 144 B1
Brandberg ⌓ Namibia 21°10S 14°30E 144 B1
Brande Denmark 55°57N 9°8E 63 J3
Brandenburg = Neubrandenburg Germany 53°33N 13°15E 76 B9
Brandenburg Germany 52°25N 12°33E 76 C8
Brandenburg □ Germany 52°50N 13°0E 76 C9
Brandfort S. Africa 28°40S 26°30E 144 C4
Brando France 42°47N 9°27E 73 F13
Brandon Canada 49°50N 99°57W 163 D9
Brandon Fla., U.S.A. 27°56N 82°17W 179 H7
Brandon Vt., U.S.A. 43°48N 73°6W 175 C11
Brandon B. Ireland 52°17N 10°8W 64 D1
Brandon Mt. Ireland 52°15N 10°15W 64 D1
Brandsen Argentina 35°10S 58°15W 190 D4
Brandvlei S. Africa 30°25S 20°30E 144 D3
Brandýs nad Labem Czech Rep. 50°10N 14°40E 78 A7
Branford Conn., U.S.A. 41°17N 72°49W 175 E12
Branford Fla., U.S.A. 29°58N 82°56W 178 F7
Braniewo Poland 54°25N 19°50E 82 D6
Bransfield Str. Antarctica 63°0S 59°0W 55 C18
Brańsk Poland 52°45N 22°50E 83 F9
Branson U.S.A. 36°39N 93°13W 172 G7
Brantford Canada 43°10N 80°15W 174 C4
Brantley U.S.A. 31°35N 86°16W 178 D3
Brantôme France 45°22N 0°39E 72 C4
Branxholme Australia 37°52S 141°49E 152 D4
Branxton Australia 32°38S 151°21E 153 B9
Branzi Italy 46°1N 9°46E 92 B6
Bras d'Or L. Canada 45°50N 60°50W 165 C7
Brasher Falls U.S.A. 44°49N 74°47W 175 B10
Brasil = Brazil ■ S. Amer. 12°0S 50°0W 187 F9
Brasil, Planalto Brazil 18°0S 46°30W 184 E6
Brasiléia Brazil 11°0S 68°45W 188 C4
Brasília Distrito Federal, Brazil 15°47S 47°55W 189 D1
Brasília Minas Gerais, Brazil 16°12S 44°26W 189 D2
Brasília Legal Brazil 3°49S 55°36W 187 D7
Braslaw Belarus 55°38N 27°0E 84 E4
Braslawskiya Azyory △ Belarus 55°36N 27°3E 84 E4
Braslovče Slovenia 46°21N 15°3E 93 B12
Braşov Romania 45°38N 25°35E 81 E10
Braşov □ Romania 45°45N 25°15E 81 E10
Brass Nigeria 4°35N 6°14E 139 E6
Brass → Nigeria 4°15N 6°13E 139 E6
Brassac-les-Mines France 45°24N 3°20E 72 C7
Brasschaat Belgium 51°19N 4°27E 69 C4
Brassey, Banjaran Malaysia 5°0N 117°15E 118 D5
Brassey Ra. Australia 25°8S 122°15E 149 E3
Brasstown Bald U.S.A. 34°53N 83°49W 177 D13
Brastad Sweden 58°23N 11°30E 63 F5
Brastavăţu Romania 43°55N 24°24E 81 G9
Bratan = Morozov Bulgaria 42°30N 25°10E 97 D9
Brateş Romania 45°50N 26°4E 81 E11
Bratislava Slovak Rep. 48°10N 17°7E 79 C10
Bratislava M.R. Štefánik ✈ (BTS) Slovak Rep. 48°11N 17°9E 79 C10
Bratislavský □ Slovak Rep. 48°15N 17°20E 79 C10
Bratsigovo Bulgaria 42°1N 24°22E 97 D8
Bratsk Russia 56°10N 101°30E 107 D11
Bratskoye Vdkhr. Russia 56°0N 101°40E 107 D11
Brattleboro U.S.A. 42°51N 72°34W 175 D12
Bratunac Bos.-H. 44°13N 19°21E 80 F4
Braunau am Inn Austria 48°15N 13°3E 78 C6
Braunschweig Germany 52°15N 10°31E 76 C6
Braunton U.K. 51°7N 4°10W 67 F3
Brava C. Verde Is. 15°0N 24°40W 134 b
Brava, Costa Spain 41°30N 3°0E 90 D8
Bravicea Moldova 47°22N 28°27E 81 C13
Bråviken Sweden 58°38N 16°32E 63 F10
Bravo del Norte, Rio = Grande, Rio → N. Amer. 25°58N 97°9W 176 J6
Brawley U.S.A. 32°59N 115°31W 171 N11
Bray Ireland 53°13N 6°7W 64 C5
Bray, Mt. Australia 14°0S 134°30E 150 A1
Bray, Pays de France 49°46N 1°26E 71 C8
Bray-sur-Seine France 48°25N 3°14E 71 D10
Brazeau → Canada 52°55N 115°14W 162 C5
Brazil U.S.A. 39°32N 87°8W 172 F10
Brazil ■ S. Amer. 12°0S 50°0W 187 F9
Brazil Basin Atl. Oc. 15°0S 25°0W 56 H9
Brazilian Highlands = Brasil, Planalto Brazil 18°0S 46°30W 184 E6
Brazo Sur → S. Amer. 25°21S 57°42W 190 B4
Brazos → U.S.A. 28°53N 95°23W 176 G7
Brazzaville Congo 4°9S 15°12E 140 E3
Brčko Bos.-H. 44°54N 18°46E 80 F3
Brda → Poland 53°8N 18°8E 83 E5
Brdy Czech Rep. 49°43N 13°55E 78 B6
Bré = Bray Ireland 53°13N 6°7W 64 C5
Breaden, L. Australia 25°51S 125°28E 149 E4
Breaksea Sd. N.Z. 45°35S 166°35E 155 F1
Bream B. N.Z. 35°56S 174°28E 154 B3
Bream Hd. N.Z. 35°51S 174°36E 154 B3
Bream Tail N.Z. 36°3S 174°36E 154 C3
Breas Chile 25°29S 70°24W 190 B1
Breaza Romania 45°11N 25°40E 81 E10
Brebes Indonesia 6°52S 109°3E 119 G13
Brechin Canada 44°32N 79°10W 174 B5
Brechin U.K. 56°44N 2°39W 65 E6
Brecht Belgium 51°21N 4°38E 69 C4
Breckenridge Colo., U.S.A. 39°29N 106°3W 168 G10
Breckenridge Minn., U.S.A. 46°16N 96°35W 172 B5
Breckenridge Tex., U.S.A. 32°45N 98°54W 176 E5
Breckland U.K. 52°30N 0°40E 67 E8
Brecknock, Pen. Chile 54°35S 71°30W 192 D2
Břeclav Czech Rep. 48°46N 16°53E 79 C9
Brecon U.K. 51°57N 3°23W 67 F4
Brecon Beacons U.K. 51°53N 3°26W 67 F4
Brecon Beacons △ U.K. 51°50N 3°30W 67 F4
Breda Neths. 51°35N 4°45E 69 C4
Bredaryd Sweden 57°10N 13°45E 63 G7
Bredasdorp S. Africa 34°33S 20°2E 144 D3
Bredbo Australia 35°58S 149°10E 153 C8
Bredebro Denmark 55°4N 8°50E 63 J2
Bredstedt Germany 54°37N 8°55E 76 A4
Bredy Russia 52°26N 60°21E 108 B6
Bree Belgium 51°8N 5°35E 69 C5
Bregalnica → Macedonia 41°43N 22°9E 96 E6
Bregenz Austria 47°30N 9°45E 78 D2
Bregovo Bulgaria 44°9N 22°39E 96 B6
Bréhal France 48°53N 1°30W 70 D5
Bréhat, Î. de France 48°51N 3°0W 70 D4
Breiðafjörður Iceland 65°15N 23°15W 60 D2
Breil-sur-Roya France 43°56N 7°31E 73 E11
Breisach Germany 48°1N 7°36E 77 G3
Brejo Brazil 3°41S 42°47W 189 A2
Bremen Germany 53°4N 8°47E 76 B4
Bremen U.S.A. 33°43N 85°9W 178 B4
Bremen □ Germany 53°4N 8°50E 76 B4
Bremer Bay Australia 34°21S 119°20E 149 F2
Bremer I. Australia 12°5S 136°45E 150 A2
Bremerhaven Germany 53°33N 8°36E 76 B4
Bremerton U.S.A. 47°34N 122°37W 170 C4
Bremervörde Germany 53°29N 9°8E 76 B5
Brenes Spain 37°32N 5°54W 89 H5
Brenham U.S.A. 30°10N 96°24W 176 F6
Brenne France 46°44N 1°14E 72 B5
Brenne ⌓ France 46°40N 1°15E 72 B5
Brennerpass Austria 47°2N 11°30E 78 D4
Breno Italy 45°57N 10°18E 92 C7
Brent U.S.A. 32°56N 87°10W 177 E11
Brenta → Italy 45°11N 12°18E 93 C9
Brentwood U.K. 51°37N 0°19E 67 F8
Brentwood Calif., U.S.A. 37°56N 121°42W 170 H5
Brentwood N.Y., U.S.A. 40°47N 73°15W 175 F11
Bréscia Italy 45°33N 10°15E 92 C7
Breskens Neths. 51°23N 3°33E 69 C3
Breslau = Wrocław Poland 51°5N 17°5E 83 G4
Bresle → France 50°4N 1°22E 70 B8
Bressanone Italy 46°43N 11°39E 93 B8
Bressay U.K. 60°9N 1°6W 65 A7
Bresse France 46°50N 5°10E 71 F12
Bressuire France 46°51N 0°30W 70 F6
Brest Belarus 52°10N 23°40E 75 B12
Brest France 48°24N 4°31W 70 D2
Brest □ Belarus 52°30N 26°10E 75 B13
Brest-Litovsk = Brest Belarus 52°10N 23°40E 75 B12
Bretagne □ France 48°10N 3°0W 70 D3
Bretçu Romania 46°7N 26°18E 81 D11
Bretenoux France 44°54N 1°51E 72 D5
Breteuil Eure, France 48°50N 0°57E 70 D7
Breteuil Oise, France 49°38N 2°18E 71 C9
Breton Canada 53°7N 114°28W 162 C6
Breton, Pertuis France 46°17N 1°25W 72 B2
Breton Sd. U.S.A. 29°35N 89°15W 177 G10
Brett, C. N.Z. 35°10S 174°20E 154 B3
Bretten Germany 49°2N 8°42E 77 F4
Breuil-Cervínia Italy 45°56N 7°38E 92 C4
Brevard U.S.A. 35°14N 82°44W 177 D13
Breves Brazil 1°40S 50°29W 187 D8
Brewarrina Australia 30°0S 146°51E 151 E4
Brewer U.S.A. 44°48N 68°46W 173 C19
Brewer, Mt. U.S.A. 36°44N 118°28W 170 J8
Brewerville Liberia 6°26N 10°47W 138 D2
Brewster N.Y., U.S.A. 41°24N 73°36W 175 E11
Brewster Ohio, U.S.A. 40°43N 81°36W 174 F3
Brewster Wash., U.S.A. 48°6N 119°47W 168 B4
Brewster, Kap = Kangikajik Greenland 70°7N 22°0W 57 C8
Brewton U.S.A. 31°7N 87°4W 177 F11
Breyten S. Africa 26°16S 30°0E 145 C5
Breza Bos.-H. 44°2N 18°16E 80 F3
Brežice Slovenia 45°54N 15°35E 93 C12
Brézina Algeria 33°4N 1°14E 136 B4
Březnice Czech Rep. 49°32N 13°57E 78 B6
Breznik Bulgaria 42°44N 22°55E 96 D6
Brezno Slovak Rep. 48°50N 19°40E 79 C12
Brezoi Romania 45°21N 24°15E 81 E9
Brezovicë Kosovo 42°15N 21°3E 96 D5
Brezovo Bulgaria 42°21N 25°5E 97 D9
Bria C.A.R. 6°30N 21°58E 140 C4
Briançon France 44°54N 6°39E 73 D10
Briare France 47°38N 2°45E 71 E9
Briático Italy 38°43N 16°2E 95 D9
Bribie I. Australia 27°0S 153°10E 151 D5
Bribri Costa Rica 9°38N 82°50W 182 E3
Briceni Moldova 48°22N 27°6E 81 B12
Bricquebec France 49°28N 1°38W 70 C5
Bridgefield Barbados 13°9N 59°36W 183 g
Bridgehampton U.S.A. 40°56N 72°19W 175 F12
Bridgend U.K. 51°30N 3°34W 67 F4
Bridgend □ U.K. 51°36N 3°36W 67 F4
Bridgenorth Canada 44°23N 78°23W 174 B6
Bridgeport Calif., U.S.A. 38°15N 119°14W 170 G7
Bridgeport Conn., U.S.A. 41°11N 73°12W 175 E11
Bridgeport N.Y., U.S.A. 43°9N 75°58W 175 C9
Bridgeport Nebr., U.S.A. 41°40N 103°6W 172 E2
Bridgeport Tex., U.S.A. 33°13N 97°45W 176 E6
Bridger U.S.A. 45°18N 108°55W 168 D9
Bridgeton U.S.A. 39°26N 75°14W 173 F16
Bridgetown Australia 33°58S 116°7E 149 F2
Bridgetown Barbados 13°6N 59°37W 183 g
Bridgetown Canada 44°55N 65°18W 165 D6
Bridgewater Tas., Australia 42°44S 147°14E 151 G4
Bridgewater Vic., Australia 36°36S 143°59E 152 D5
Bridgewater Canada 44°25N 64°31W 165 D7
Bridgewater Mass., U.S.A. 41°59N 70°58W 175 E14
Bridgewater N.Y., U.S.A. 42°53N 75°15W 175 D9
Bridgewater, C. Australia 38°23S 141°23E 152 E4
Bridgnorth U.K. 52°32N 2°25W 67 E5
Bridgton U.S.A. 44°3N 70°42W 175 B14
Bridgwater U.K. 51°8N 2°59W 67 F5
Bridgwater B. U.K. 51°15N 3°15W 67 F4
Bridlington U.K. 54°5N 0°12W 66 C7
Bridlington B. U.K. 54°4N 0°10W 66 C7
Bridport Australia 40°59S 147°23E 151 G4
Bridport U.K. 50°44N 2°45W 67 G5
Briec France 48°6N 4°0W 70 D2
Brienne-le-Château France 48°24N 4°30E 71 D11
Brienon-sur-Armançon France 47°59N 3°38E 71 E10
Brienz Switz. 46°46N 8°2E 77 J4
Brienzersee Switz. 46°44N 7°53E 77 J3
Brier Cr. → U.S.A. 32°44N 81°26W 178 C8
Brière ⌓ France 47°22N 2°13W 70 E4
Brig Switz. 46°18N 7°59E 77 J3
Brigg U.K. 53°34N 0°28W 66 D7
Brigham City U.S.A. 41°31N 112°1W 168 F7
Bright Australia 36°42S 146°56E 153 D7
Brighton Australia 35°5S 138°30E 152 C3
Brighton Canada 44°2N 77°44W 174 B7
Brighton Trin. & Tob. 10°15N 61°39W 187 K15
Brighton U.K. 50°49N 0°7W 67 G7
Brighton Fla., U.S.A. 27°14N 81°6W 179 H8
Brighton N.Y., U.S.A. 43°8N 77°34W 174 C7
Brightside Canada 45°7N 76°29W 175 A8
Brightwater N.Z. 41°22S 173°9E 155 B8
Brignogan-Plage France 48°40N 4°20W 70 D2
Brignoles France 43°25N 6°5E 73 E10
Brihuega Spain 40°45N 2°52W 90 E2
Brikama Gambia 13°15N 16°45W 138 C1
Brilliant U.S.A. 40°15N 80°39W 174 F4
Brilon Germany 51°23N 8°35E 76 D4

Brim Australia 36°3S 142°27E **152** D5
Brindabella △ Australia 35°14S 148°5E **153** C8
Brindisi Italy 40°39N 17°55E **95** B10
Brinje Croatia 44°59N 15°9E **93** D12
Brinkley U.S.A. 34°53N 91°12W **176** D9
Brinkworth Australia 33°42S 138°26E **152** B3
Brinnon U.S.A. 47°41N 122°54W **170** C4
Brinson U.S.A. 30°59N 84°44W **178** E5
Brion, Î. Canada 47°46N 61°26W **165** C7
Brionne France 49°11N 0°43E **70** C7
Brionski Croatia 44°55N 13°45E **93** D10
Brioude France 45°18N 3°24E **72** C7
Briouze France 48°42N 0°23W **70** D6
Brisay Canada 54°26N 70°31W **165** B5
Brisbane Australia 27°25S 153°2E **151** D5
Brisbane → Australia 27°24S 153°9E **151** D5
Brisbane ✈ (BNE)
  Australia 27°35S 153°7E **151** D5
Brisbane Ranges △
  Australia 37°47S 144°16E **152** D6
Brisbane Water △
  Australia 33°26S 151°13E **153** B9
Brisighella Italy 44°13N 11°46E **93** D8
Bristol Italy 51°26N 2°35W **67** F5
Bristol Conn., U.S.A. 41°40N 72°57W **175** E12
Bristol Fla., U.S.A. 30°26N 84°59W **178** E5
Bristol Pa., U.S.A. 40°6N 74°51W **175** F10
Bristol R.I., U.S.A. 41°40N 71°16W **175** E13
Bristol Tenn., U.S.A. 36°36N 82°11W **177** C13
Bristol Vt., U.S.A. 44°8N 73°4W **175** B11
Bristol, City of □ U.K. 51°27N 2°36W **67** F5
Bristol B. U.S.A. 58°0N 160°0W **166** D8
Bristol Channel U.K. 51°18N 4°30W **67** F3
Bristol I. Antarctica 58°45S 28°0W **55** B1
Bristol L. U.S.A. 34°28N 115°41W **171** L11
Bristow U.S.A. 35°50N 96°23W **176** D6
Britain = Great Britain
  Europe 54°0N 2°15W **58** E5
British Columbia □
  Canada 55°0N 125°15W **162** C3
British Indian Ocean Terr. =
  Chagos Arch. ☑ Ind. Oc. 6°0S 72°0E **146** E6
British Isles Europe 54°0N 4°0W **68** D5
British Mts. N. Amer. 68°50N 140°0W **166** B12
British Virgin Is. ☑
  W. Indies 18°30N 64°30W **183** e
Brits S. Africa 25°37S 27°48E **145** C4
Britstown S. Africa 30°37S 23°30E **144** D3
Britt Canada 45°46N 80°34W **164** C3
Brittany = Bretagne □
  France 48°10N 3°0W **70** D3
Britton U.S.A. 45°48N 97°45W **172** C5
Brive-la-Gaillarde France 45°10N 1°32E **72** C5
Briviesca Spain 42°32N 3°19W **88** C7
Brixen = Bressanone
  Italy 46°43N 11°39E **93** B8
Brixham U.K. 50°23N 3°31W **67** G4
Brnaze Croatia 43°41N 16°40E **93** E13
Brnenský = Jihomoravský □
  Czech Rep. 49°5N 16°30E **79** B9
Brno Czech Rep. 49°10N 16°35E **79** B9
Broach = Bharuch India 21°47N 73°0E **126** D1
Broad → Ga., U.S.A. 33°59N 82°39W **178** B7
Broad → S.C., U.S.A. 34°1N 81°4W **177** D14
Broad Arrow Australia 30°23S 121°15E **149** F3
Broad B. U.K. 58°14N 6°18W **65** C2
Broad Haven Ireland 54°20N 9°55W **64** B2
Broad Law U.K. 55°30N 3°21W **65** F5
Broad Pk. = Faichan Kangri
  India 35°48N 76°34E **125** B7
Broad Sd. Australia 22°0S 149°45E **150** C4
Broadalbin U.S.A. 43°4N 74°12W **175** C10
Broadback → Canada 51°21N 78°52W **164** B4
Broadford Australia 37°14S 145°4E **153** D6

Bronwood U.S.A. 31°50N 84°22W **178** D5
Brook Park U.S.A. 41°23N 81°48W **174** E4
Brookhaven U.S.A. 31°35N 90°26W **177** F9
Brookings Oreg., U.S.A. 42°3N 124°17W **168** E1
Brookings S. Dak.,
  U.S.A. 44°19N 96°48W **172** C5
Brooklet U.S.A. 32°23N 81°40W **178** D8
Brooklin Canada 43°55N 78°55W **174** C6
Brooklyn Park U.S.A. 45°6N 93°23W **172** C7
Brooks Canada 50°35N 111°55W **162** C6
Brooks Range U.S.A. 68°0N 152°0W **166** B9
Brooksville U.S.A. 28°33N 82°23W **179** G2
Brookton Australia 32°22S 117°0E **149** F2
Brookville U.S.A. 41°10N 79°5W **174** E5
Broom, L. U.K. 57°55N 5°15W **65** D3
Broome Australia 18°0S 122°15E **148** C3
Broons France 48°20N 2°16W **70** D4
Brora U.K. 58°0N 3°52W **65** C5
Brora → U.K. 58°0N 3°51W **65** C5
Brørup Denmark 55°29N 9°1E **63** J2
Brösarp Sweden 55°43N 14°6E **63** J8
Brosna → Ireland 53°14N 7°58W **64** C4
Broșteni Mehedinți,
  Romania 44°45N 22°59E **80** F7
Broșteni Suceava,
  Romania 47°14N 25°43E **81** C10
Brotas de Macaúbas
  Brazil 12°0S 42°38W **189** D2
Brothers U.S.A. 43°49N 120°36W **168** E3
Brou France 48°13N 1°11E **70** D8
Brouage France 45°52N 1°4W **72** C2
Brough U.K. 54°32N 2°18W **66** C5
Brough Hd. U.K. 59°8N 3°20W **65** B5
Broughton Island = Qikiqtarjuaq
  Canada 67°33N 63°0W **161** D19
Broumov Czech Rep. 50°35N 16°20E **79** A9
Brovary Ukraine 50°34N 30°48E **85** G6
Brovst Denmark 57°6N 9°31E **63** G3
Brown, L. Australia 31°5S 118°15E **149** F2
Brown, Mt. Australia 32°30S 138°0E **152** B3
Brown, Pt. Australia 32°33S 133°50E **151** E1
Brown City U.S.A. 43°13N 82°59W **174** C2
Brownfield U.S.A. 33°11N 102°17W **176** E3
Browning U.S.A. 48°34N 113°1W **168** B7
Brownsville Oreg.,
  U.S.A. 44°24N 122°59W **168** D2
Brownsville Pa., U.S.A. 40°1N 79°53W **174** F5
Brownsville Tenn.,
  U.S.A. 35°36N 89°16W **177** D10
Brownsville Tex.,
  U.S.A. 25°54N 97°30W **176** J6
Brownville U.S.A. 44°0N 75°59W **175** C9
Brownwood U.S.A. 31°43N 98°59W **176** F5
Browse I. Australia 14°7S 123°33E **148** B3
Broxton U.S.A. 31°38N 82°53W **178** D7
Bruas Malaysia 4°30N 100°47E **121** K3
Bruay-la-Buissière France 50°29N 2°33E **71** B9
Bruce U.S.A. 30°28N 85°58W **178** E4
Bruce, Mt. Australia 22°37S 118°8E **148** D2
Bruce Pen. Canada 45°0N 81°30W **174** B3
Bruce Peninsula △
  Canada 45°14N 81°36W **174** A3
Bruce Rock Australia 31°52S 118°8E **149** F2
Bruche → France 48°34N 7°43E **71** D14
Bruchsal Germany 49°7N 8°35E **77** F4
Bruck an der Leitha
  Austria 48°1N 16°47E **79** C9
Bruck an der Mur
  Austria 47°24N 15°16E **78** D8
Brue → U.K. 51°13N 2°59W **67** F5
Bruges = Brugge Belgium 51°13N 3°13E **69** C3
Brugg Switz. 47°29N 8°11E **77** H4
Brugge Belgium 51°13N 3°13E **69** C3
Bruin U.S.A. 41°3N 79°43W **174** E5
Brûk, W. el → Egypt 30°35N 30°58E **130** E2
Bruksvallarna Sweden 62°38N 12°27E **62** B6
Brûlé Canada 53°15N 117°58W **162** C5
Brûlé, L. Canada 53°35N 64°4W **165** B7
Brûlon France 47°58N 0°15W **70** E6
Brumado Brazil 14°14S 41°40W **189** D3
Brumado → Brazil 14°13S 41°40W **189** D2
Brumath France 48°43N 7°40E **71** D14
Brumunddal Norway 60°53N 10°56E **63** F14
Brundidge U.S.A. 31°43N 85°49W **178** E4
Bruneau U.S.A. 42°53N 115°48W **168** E6
Bruneau → U.S.A. 42°56N 115°57W **168** E6
Bruneck = Brunico Italy 46°48N 11°56E **93** B8
Brunei = Bandar Seri Begawan
  Brunei 4°52N 115°0E **118** D5
Brunei ■ Asia 4°50N 115°0E **118** D5
Brunflo Sweden 63°5N 14°50E **62** A8
Brunico Italy 46°48N 11°56E **93** B8
Brunn Switz. 46°59N 8°37E **77** J4
Brunner, N.Z. 42°37S 171°27E **155** C6
Brunnsberg Sweden 61°17N 13°56E **62** C8
Brunsbüttel Germany 53°53N 9°6E **76** B5
Brunssum Neths. 50°57N 5°59E **69** D5
Brunswick = Braunschweig
  Germany 52°15N 10°31E **76** C6
Brunswick Ga., U.S.A. 31°10N 81°30W **178** D8
Brunswick Maine,
  U.S.A. 43°55N 69°58W **173** D19
Brunswick Md.,
  U.S.A. 39°19N 77°38W **173** F15
Brunswick Mo., U.S.A. 39°26N 93°8W **172** F7
Brunswick Ohio, U.S.A. 41°14N 81°51W **174** E3
Brunswick, Pen. de
  Chile 53°30S 71°30W **192** G2
Brunswick B. Australia 15°15S 124°50E **148** C3
Brunswick Junction
  Australia 33°15S 115°50E **149** F2
Brunt Ice Shelf Antarctica 75°30S 25°0W **55** D2
Bruntál Czech Rep. 49°59N 17°27E **79** B10
Brus Laguna Honduras 15°47N 84°35W **182** C3
Brusartsi Bulgaria 43°40N 23°5E **96** C7
Brush U.S.A. 40°15N 103°37W **168** F12
Brushton U.S.A. 44°50N 74°31W **175** B10
Brusio Switz. 46°14N 10°8E **77** J6
Brusque Brazil 27°5S 49°0W **191** B6
Brussel Belgium 50°51N 4°21E **69** D4
Brussel ✈ (BRU) Belgium 50°54N 4°29E **69** D5
Brussels = Brussel
  Belgium 50°51N 4°21E **69** D4
Brussels Canada 43°44N 81°15W **174** C3
Brusy Poland 53°53N 17°43E **82** E4
Bruthen Australia 37°42S 147°50E **153** D7
Bruxelles = Brussel
  Belgium 50°51N 4°21E **69** D4
Bruyères France 48°10N 6°40E **71** D13

Bruz France 48°1N 1°46W **70** D5
Brwinów Poland 52°9N 20°40E **83** F7
Bryagovo Bulgaria 41°58N 25°8E **97** E9
Bryan Ohio, U.S.A. 41°28N 84°33W **173** E11
Bryan Tex., U.S.A. 30°40N 96°22W **176** F6
Bryanka Ukraine 48°32N 38°45E **85** H10
Bryansk Bryansk, Russia 53°13N 34°25E **85** F8
Bryansk Dagestan, Russia 44°20N 47°10E **87** H8
Bryansk □ Russia 53°10N 33°10E **85** F7
Bryce Canyon △
  U.S.A. 37°30N 112°10W **169** H7
Bryne Norway 58°44N 5°38E **61** G11
Bryson City U.S.A. 35°26N 83°27W **177** D13
Bryukhovetskaya
  Russia 45°48N 39°0E **85** K10
Brza Palanka Serbia 44°28N 22°27E **96** B6
Brzeg Poland 50°52N 17°30E **83** H4
Brzeg Dolny Poland 51°16N 16°41E **83** H3
Brześć Kujawski Poland 52°36N 18°55E **83** F5
Brzeziny Poland 51°49N 19°42E **83** G6
Brzozów Poland 49°41N 22°3E **83** J9
Bsharri Lebanon 34°15N 36°0E **130** A5
Bū Baqarah U.A.E. 25°35N 56°25E **129** E8
Bu Craa W. Sahara 26°45N 12°50W **134** C3
Bū Ḩasā U.A.E. 23°30N 53°20E **129** F7
Bua Fiji 16°48S 178°37E **154** a
Bua Sweden 57°14N 12°7E **63** G6
Bua → Malawi 12°45S 34°16E **143** E3
Bua Yai Thailand 15°33N 102°26E **120** E4
Buan S. Korea 35°44N 126°44E **115** G14
Buapinang Indonesia 4°40S 121°30E **119** E6
Buba Guinea-Biss. 11°40N 14°59W **138** C2
Bubanza Burundi 3°6S 29°23E **142** C2
Bubaque Guinea-Biss. 11°16N 15°51W **138** C1
Bubi → Zimbabwe 22°0S 31°7E **145** B5
Bubye Fiji 16°38S 179°52E **154** a
Buca Turkey 38°22N 27°11E **99** C9
Bucak Turkey 37°28N 30°36E **99** D12
Bucaramanga Colombia 7°0N 73°0W **186** B4
Bucasia Australia 21°2S 149°10E **150** b
Buccaneer Arch.
  Australia 16°7S 123°20E **148** C3
Buccheri Italy 40°38N 15°22E **95** B8
Buccoo Reef
  Trin. & Tob. 11°10N 60°51W **187** J16
Bucecea Romania 47°47N 26°28E **81** C11
Bucegi △ Romania 45°25N 25°25E **81** E10
Buchach Ukraine 49°5N 25°25E **81** D10
Buchan U.K. 57°32N 2°21W **65** D6
Buchan Ness U.K. 57°29N 1°46W **65** D7
Buchanan Canada 51°40N 102°45W **163** C8
Buchanan Liberia 5°57N 10°2W **138** D2
Buchanan, L.
  Queens.,
  Australia 21°35S 145°52E **150** C4
Buchanan, L. W. Austral.,
  Australia 25°33S 123°2E **149** E3
Buchanan, L. U.S.A. 30°45N 98°25W **176** F5
Buchanan Cr. →
  Australia 19°13S 136°33E **150** B2
Buchans Canada 48°50N 56°52W **165** C8
Bucharest = București
  Romania 44°27N 26°10E **81** F11
Buchen Germany 49°32N 9°20E **77** F5
Bucheon S. Korea 37°28N 126°45E **115** F14
Buchholz Germany 53°19N 9°52E **76** B5
Buchloe Germany 48°1N 10°44E **77** G6
Buchon, Pt. U.S.A. 35°15N 120°54W **170** K6
Buciumi Romania 47°4N 23°1E **80** C8
Buck Hill Falls U.S.A. 41°11N 75°16W **175** E9
Bückeburg Germany 52°16N 9°7E **76** C5
Buckeye Lake U.S.A. 39°55N 82°29W **174** G2
Buckhannon U.S.A. 39°0N 80°8W **173** F13
Buckhaven U.K. 56°11N 3°3W **65** E5
Buckhorn L. Canada 44°29N 78°23W **174** B6
Buckie U.K. 57°41N 2°58W **65** D6
Buckingham Canada 45°37N 75°24W **164** C4
Buckingham U.K. 51°59N 0°57W **67** F7
Buckingham B.
  Australia 12°10S 135°40E **150** A2
Buckingham Canal India 14°0N 80°5E **127** H5
Buckinghamshire □ U.K. 51°53N 0°55W **67** F7
Buckland U.S.A. 65°59N 161°8W **166** C9
Buckleboo Australia 32°54S 136°12E **152** B2
Buckley U.S.A. 47°10N 122°2W **170** C4
Buckley → Australia 20°10S 138°49E **150** C2
Bucks L. U.S.A. 39°54N 121°12W **170** F5
Bucquoy France 50°9N 2°43E **71** B9
București Romania 44°27N 26°10E **81** F11
București Otopeni ✈ (OTP)
  Romania 44°34N 26°5E **81** E11
Bucyrus U.S.A. 40°48N 82°59W **173** E12
Budacu, Vf. Romania 47°7N 25°4E **81** C10
Budalin Burma 22°20N 95°10E **123** H19
Budaörs Hungary 47°27N 18°57E **80** C2
Budapest Hungary 47°29N 19°3E **80** C4
Budapest □ Hungary 47°29N 19°5E **80** C4
Budapest Ferihegy ✈ (BUD)
  Hungary 47°26N 19°14E **80** C4
Budaun India 28°5N 79°10E **125** E8
Budawang △ Australia 35°10S 150°12E **153** C9
Budd Coast Antarctica 68°0S 112°0E **55** C8
Budderoo △ Australia 34°40S 150°41E **153** C9
Buddusò Italy 40°35N 9°15E **94** B2
Bude U.K. 50°49N 4°34W **67** G3
Budennovsk Russia 44°50N 44°10E **87** H7
Budești Romania 44°13N 26°30E **81** F11
Budge Budge = Baj Baj
  India 22°30N 88°5E **125** H13
Budgewoi Australia 33°13S 151°34E **153** B9
Budia Spain 40°38N 2°46W **90** E2
Büdingen Germany 50°16N 9°7E **77** E5
Budjala
  Dem. Rep. of the Congo 2°50N 19°40E **140** D3
Budo-Sungai Padi △
  Thailand 6°19N 101°42E **121** J3
Budoni Italy 40°40N 9°45E **94** B2
Búðir Iceland 64°49N 23°23W **61** D2
Budva Montenegro 42°17N 18°50E **96** C6
Budzyń Poland 52°54N 16°59E **83** F3
Buea Cameroon 4°10N 9°9E **138** E6
Buellton U.S.A. 34°37N 120°12W **171** L6
Buena Esperanza
  Argentina 34°45S 65°15W **190** C2

Buena Park U.S.A. 33°52N 117°59W **171** M9
Buena Vista Colo.,
  U.S.A. 38°51N 106°8W **168** G10
Buena Vista Ga.,
  U.S.A. 32°19N 84°31W **178** C5
Buena Vista Va.,
  U.S.A. 37°44N 79°21W **173** G14
Buena Vista Lake Bed
  U.S.A. 35°12N 119°18W **171** K7
Buenaventura Colombia 3°53N 77°4W **186** C3
Buenaventura Mexico 29°51N 107°29W **180** B3
Buendia, Embalse de
  Spain 40°25N 2°43W **90** E2
Buenópolis Brazil 17°54S 44°11W **189** D2
Buenos Aires Argentina 34°36S 58°22W **190** C4
Buenos Aires Costa Rica 9°10N 83°20W **182** E3
Buenos Aires □
  Argentina 36°30S 60°0W **190** D4
Buenos Aires, L. = General
  Carrera, L. S. Amer. 46°35S 72°0W **192** C2
Buffalo Mo., U.S.A. 37°39N 93°6W **172** G7
Buffalo N.Y., U.S.A. 42°53N 78°53W **174** D6
Buffalo Okla., U.S.A. 36°50N 99°38W **176** C5
Buffalo S. Dak., U.S.A. 45°35N 103°33W **172** C2
Buffalo Wyo., U.S.A. 44°21N 106°42W **168** D10
Buffalo → Canada 60°5N 115°5W **162** A5
Buffalo → S. Africa 28°43S 30°37E **145** C5
Buffalo △ U.S.A. 36°14N 92°36W **176** C8
Buffalo Head Hills
  Canada 57°25N 115°55W **162** B5
Buffalo L. Alta.,
  Canada 52°27N 112°54W **162** C6
Buffalo L. N.W.T.,
  Canada 60°12N 115°25W **162** A5
Buffalo Narrows
  Canada 55°51N 108°29W **163** B7
Buffalo Springs △ Kenya 0°32N 37°35E **142** B4
Buffels → S. Africa 29°36S 17°3E **144** C2
Buford U.S.A. 34°7N 83°59W **178** B5
Bug → Poland 52°31N 21°5E **83** F8
Bug = Buh → Ukraine 46°59N 31°58E **85** J6
Buga Colombia 4°0N 76°15W **186** C3
Bugala I. Uganda 0°0 31°30E **142** C3
Buganda Uganda 0°0S 31°30E **142** C3
Buganga Uganda 0°3S 32°0E **142** C3
Bugeat France 45°36N 1°55E **72** C5
Bugel, Tanjung
  Indonesia 6°26S 111°3E **119** G14
Búger Spain 39°45N 2°59E **100** B9
Bugibba Malta 35°57N 14°25E **101** D1
Bugojno Bos.-H. 44°2N 17°25E **96** B7
Bugsuk I. Phil. 8°12N 117°18E **118** C5
Bugulma Russia 54°33N 52°48E **88** D9
Buguma Nigeria 4°42N 6°55E **138** E6
Bugungu → Uganda 2°17N 31°50E **142** B3
Buguruslan Russia 53°39N 52°26E **108** D8
Buh → Ukraine 46°59N 31°58E **85** J6
Buharkent Turkey 37°58N 28°44E **99** D10
Buheirat-Murrat-el-Kubra
  Egypt 30°18N 32°26E **137** E2
Buhera Zimbabwe 19°18S 31°29E **145** A5
Bühl Germany 48°40N 8°8E **77** G4
Buhuși Romania 46°41N 26°45E **81** D11
Bui → Ghana 8°21N 2°21E **138** D4
Buila-Vanturariţa △
  Romania 45°15N 24°0E **81** E8
Builth Wells U.K. 52°9N 3°25W **67** E4
Buinsk Russia 55°0N 48°18E **86** C9
Buïque Brazil 8°37S 37°9W **189** D3
Buir Nur Mongolia 47°50N 117°42E **111** B12
Buis-les-Baronnies
  France 44°17N 5°16E **73** D9
Buitrago del Lozoya
  Spain 40°58N 3°38W **88** E7
Bujalance Spain 37°54N 4°23W **89** H6
Bujanovac Serbia 42°28N 21°44E **96** D5
Bujaraloz Spain 41°29N 0°10W **90** D4
Buje Croatia 45°24N 13°39E **93** C10
Buji China 22°37N 114°5E **111** a
Bujumbura Burundi 3°16S 29°18E **142** C2
Bük Hungary 47°22N 16°45E **80** C1
Buk Poland 52°21N 16°30E **83** F3
Bukachacha Russia 52°55N 116°50E **107** D12
Bukama
  Dem. Rep. of the Congo 9°10S 25°50E **143** D2
Bukavu
  Dem. Rep. of the Congo 2°20S 28°52E **142** C2
Bukene Tanzania 4°15S 32°48E **142** C3
Bukhara = Buxoro
  Uzbekistan 39°48N 64°25E **108** E6
Bukhoro = Buxoro
  Uzbekistan 39°48N 64°25E **108** E6
Bukhtarma Res. = Zaysan Köli
  Kazakhstan 48°0N 83°0E **109** C10
Bukima Tanzania 1°50S 33°25E **142** C3
Bukit Bendera Malaysia 5°25N 100°15E **121** c
Bukit Mertajam
  Malaysia 5°22N 100°28E **121** c
Bukit Nil Malaysia 1°22N 104°12E **121** d
Bukit Tengah Malaysia 5°21N 100°28E **121** c
Bukittinggi Indonesia 0°20S 100°20E **118** E2
Bükk △ Hungary 48°0N 20°30E **80** B5
Bukkapatnam India 14°14N 77°46E **127** G3
Bükki △ Hungary 48°3N 20°30E **80** B5
Bukoba Tanzania 1°20S 31°49E **142** C3
Bukum, Pulau Singapore 1°14N 103°46E **121** d
Bukuru Nigeria 9°42N 8°48E **138** D6
Bukuya Uganda 0°40N 31°52E **142** B3
Bül, Kuh-e Iran 34°3N 52°5E **128** C7
Bula Guinea-Biss. 12°7N 15°43W **138** C1
Bula Indonesia 3°6S 130°30E **119** E8
Bülach Switz. 47°31N 8°32E **77** H4
Bulahdelah Australia 32°23S 152°13E **153** B10
Bulan Phil. 12°40N 123°52E **119** B6
Bulancak Turkey 40°59N 38°54E **99** D2
Bulanık Turkey 39°4N 42°14E **105** C10
Bûlâq Egypt 25°10N 30°38E **137** C12
Bulawayo Zimbabwe 20°7S 28°32E **143** G2
Buldan Turkey 38°2N 28°58E **99** C10
Buldana India 20°6N 76°18E **126** D3
Buldir I. U.S.A. 52°21N 175°56E **166** E3
Bulgan Mongolia 48°45N 103°34E **110** B9
Bulgar Russia 54°57N 49°4E **86** C9
Bulgaria ■ Europe 42°35N 25°30E **97** D9
Bulgheria, Monte Italy 40°4N 15°26E **95** B8
Bulgurca Turkey 37°45N 30°0E **99** D11
Buli, Teluk Indonesia 0°48N 128°25E **119** D7

Bulkley → Canada 55°15N 127°40W **162** B3
Bull Shoals L. U.S.A. 36°22N 92°35W **176** C8
Bullaque → Spain 38°59N 4°17W **89** G6
Bullard U.S.A. 32°8N 95°19W **176** E6
Bullas Spain 38°2N 1°40W **91** G3
Bulle Switz. 46°37N 7°3E **77** J3
Buller → N.Z. 41°44S 171°36E **155** D6
Buller, Mt. Australia 37°10S 146°28E **153** D7
Buller Gorge N.Z. 41°40S 172°10E **155** B7
Bullering a Australia 17°39S 143°56E **150** B3
Bullhead City U.S.A. 35°8N 114°32W **171** L12
Bulli Australia 34°15S 150°57E **153** C9
Büllingen Belgium 50°25N 6°16E **69** D6
Bullock Creek
  Australia 17°43S 144°31E **150** B3
Bulloo → Australia 28°43S 142°30E **151** D3
Bulloo L. Australia 28°43S 142°25E **151** D3
Bulls N.Z. 40°10S 175°24E **154** D6
Bully-les-Mines France 50°27N 2°44E **71** B9
Bulman Australia 13°39S 134°20E **150** A1
Bulnes Chile 36°42S 72°19W **190** D1
Bulqizë Albania 41°30N 20°21E **96** E4
Bulsar = Valsad India 20°40N 72°58E **126** D1
Bultfontein S. Africa 28°18S 26°10E **144** C4
Bulukumba Indonesia 5°33S 120°11E **119** F6
Bulun Russia 70°37N 127°30E **107** B13
Bulungkol China 38°36N 74°58E **109** E8
Bumba
  Dem. Rep. of the Congo 2°13N 22°30E **140** D4
Bumbah, Khalīj Libya 32°20N 23°15E **135** B10
Bumbești-Jiu Romania 45°10N 23°24E **81** E8
Bumbiri I. Tanzania 1°40S 31°55E **142** C3
Bumbuna S. Leone 9°2N 11°49W **138** D2
Bumhpa Bum Burma 26°51N 97°14E **123** F20
Bumi → Zimbabwe 17°0S 28°20E **143** F2
Buna Kenya 2°58N 39°30E **142** B4
Bunaken Indonesia 1°37N 124°46E **119** D6
Bunazi Tanzania 1°3S 31°23E **142** C3
Bunbury Australia 33°20S 115°35E **149** F2
Bunclody Ireland 52°39N 6°40W **64** D5
Buncrana Ireland 55°8N 7°27W **64** A4
Bundaberg Australia 24°54S 152°22E **151** C5
Bundanoon Australia 34°40S 150°16E **153** C9
Bünde Germany 52°11N 8°35E **76** C4
Bundey → Australia 21°46S 135°37E **150** C2
Bundi India 25°30N 75°35E **124** G6
Bundjalung △
  Australia 29°16S 153°21E **155** D5
Bundoran Ireland 54°28N 8°18W **64** B3
Bundure Australia 35°10S 146°1E **153** C7
Bung Kan Thailand 18°23N 103°37E **120** C4
Bunga → Nigeria 11°23N 9°56E **139** C6
Bungay U.K. 52°29N 1°28E **67** E9
Bungendore Australia 35°14S 149°30E **153** C8
Bungil Cr. → Australia 27°5S 149°5E **151** D4
Bungle Bungle = Purnululu △
  Australia 17°20S 128°20E **148** C4
Bungo-Suidō Japan 33°0N 132°15E **113** H6
Bungoma Kenya 0°34N 34°34E **142** B3
Bungotakada Japan 33°35N 131°25E **113** H5
Bungu Tanzania 7°35S 39°0E **142** D4
Bunia
  Dem. Rep. of the Congo 1°35N 30°20E **142** B3
Bunji Pakistan 35°45N 74°40E **125** B6
Bunkie U.S.A. 30°57N 92°11W **176** F8
Bunnell U.S.A. 29°28N 81°16W **179** F8
Bunnythorpe N.Z. 40°16S 175°39E **154** G4
Buñol Spain 39°25N 0°47W **91** F4
Bunsuru → Nigeria 13°21N 6°23E **139** C5
Buntok Indonesia 1°40S 114°58E **118** E4
Bunya Mts. △
  Australia 26°51S 151°34E **151** D5
Bünyan Turkey 38°51N 35°51E **104** C6
Bunyola Spain 39°41N 2°42E **100** B9
Bunyu Indonesia 3°35N 117°50E **118** D5
Bunza Nigeria 12°8N 4°0E **138** C5
Buol Indonesia 1°15N 121°32E **119** D6
Buon Brieng Vietnam 13°9N 108°12E **120** F7
Buon Ho Vietnam 12°40N 108°3E **120** F7
Buon Ma Thuot
  Vietnam 12°40N 108°3E **120** F7
Buong Long Cambodia 13°44N 106°59E **120** F6
Buorkhaya, Mys
  Russia 71°50N 132°40E **107** B14
Buqayq Si. Arabia 26°0N 49°45E **129** E6
Buqbuq Egypt 31°29N 25°29E **137** A2
Bur Acaba = Buurhakaba
  Somalia 3°12N 44°20E **131** G3
Bûr Safâga Egypt 26°43N 33°57E **128** E2
Bûr Sa'îd Egypt 31°16N 32°18E **137** A12
Bûr Sûdân Sudan 19°32N 37°9E **137** D4
Bûr Taufiq Egypt 29°54N 32°32E **137** F8
Bura Kenya 1°4S 39°58E **142** C4
Burakin Australia 30°31S 117°10E **149** F2
Burang China 30°15N 81°10E **110** E5
Burao = Burco Somalia 9°32N 45°32E **132** F4
Buraq Syria 33°11N 36°29E **130** B5
Burathum Nepal 28°4N 84°50E **125** E11
Buraydah Si. Arabia 26°20N 43°59E **128** E4
Burbank U.S.A. 34°12N 118°14W **171** L8
Burcher Australia 33°30S 147°16E **153** B7
Burco Somalia 9°32N 45°32E **132** F4
Burda India 25°50N 77°35E **124** G7
Burdekin → Australia 19°38S 147°25E **150** B4
Burdur Turkey 37°45N 30°0E **99** D12
Burdur □ Turkey 37°45N 30°0E **99** D12
Burdur Gölü Turkey 37°50N 30°0E **99** D12
Burdwan = Barddhaman
  India 23°14N 87°39E **125** H12
Bure Ethiopia 10°40N 37°4E **132** E2
Bure → U.K. 52°38N 1°43E **67** E9
Burela Spain 43°39N 7°24W **88** B3
Bureya → Russia 49°27N 129°30E **107** E13
Burford Canada 43°7N 80°27W **174** D4
Burg Germany 52°16N 11°51E **76** C7
Burg auf Fehmarn
  Germany 54°18N 11°10E **76** A7

Burgdorf Switz. 47°3N 7°37E **77** H3
Burgenland □ Austria 47°20N 16°20E **79** D9
Burgeo Canada 47°37N 57°38W **165** C8
Burgersdorp S. Africa 31°0S 26°20E **144** D4
Burgess, Mt. Australia 30°50S 121°5E **149** E3
Burghausen Germany 48°9N 12°49E **77** G8
Burghead U.K. 57°43N 3°30W **65** D5
Bürgio Italy 37°36N 13°17E **94** F5
Burglengenfeld Germany 49°12N 12°2E **77** F8
Burgohondo Spain 40°24N 4°47W **88** E6
Burgos Spain 42°21N 3°41W **88** C7
Burgos □ Spain 42°21N 3°42W **88** C7
Burgstädt Germany 50°54N 12°49E **76** E8
Burgsvik Sweden 57°3N 18°19E **63** H15
Burguillos del Cerro
  Spain 38°23N 6°35W **89** G4
Burgundy = Bourgogne □
  France 47°0N 4°50E **73** E6
Burhaniye Turkey 39°30N 26°58E **99** B8
Burhanpur India 21°18N 76°14E **126** D3
Burhi Gandak →
  India 25°20N 86°37E **125** G12
Burhner → India 22°43N 80°31E **125** H8
Burias, Pta. Costa Rica 8°3N 82°51W **182** E3
Burien U.S.A. 47°28N 122°20W **170** C4
Burigi, L. Tanzania 2°2S 31°22E **142** C3
Burigi □ Tanzania 2°20S 31°6E **142** C3
Burin Kosovo 42°45N 20°24E **96** C3
Burin Canada 47°1N 55°14W **165** C8
Buriram Thailand 15°0N 103°0E **120** E4
Buriti Bravo Brazil 5°50S 43°50W **189** C3
Buriti dos Lopes Brazil 3°10S 41°52W **189** C4
Burkburnett U.S.A. 34°6N 98°34W **176** D5
Burke → Australia 23°12S 139°33E **150** C2
Burke Chan. Canada 52°10N 127°30W **162** C3
Burketown Australia 17°45S 139°33E **150** B2
Burkina Faso ■ Africa 12°0N 1°0W **138** C4
Burk's Falls Canada 45°37N 79°24W **164** C5
Burladingen Germany 48°17N 9°7E **77** G5
Burleigh Falls Canada 44°33N 78°12W **174** B6
Burley U.S.A. 42°32N 113°48W **168** E7
Burlingame U.S.A. 37°35N 122°21W **170** H4
Burlington Canada 43°18N 79°45W **174** D5
Burlington Colo.,
  U.S.A. 39°18N 102°16W **168** G3
Burlington Iowa,
  U.S.A. 40°49N 91°14W **172** E8
Burlington Kans.,
  U.S.A. 38°12N 95°45W **172** F6
Burlington N.C., U.S.A. 36°6N 79°26W **177** C15
Burlington N.J., U.S.A. 40°4N 74°51W **175** F10
Burlington Vt., U.S.A. 44°29N 73°12W **175** B11
Burlington Wash.,
  U.S.A. 48°28N 122°20W **170** B4
Burlington Wis.,
  U.S.A. 42°41N 88°17W **172** D9
Burlyu-Tobe Kazakhstan 46°30N 79°10E **108** E8
Burma ■ Asia 21°0N 96°30E **123** J20
Burnaby I. Canada 52°25N 131°19W **162** C2
Burnet U.S.A. 30°45N 98°14W **176** F5
Burney U.S.A. 40°53N 121°40W **168** F3
Burnham U.S.A. 40°38N 77°34W **174** F7
Burnham-on-Sea U.K. 51°14N 3°0W **67** F4
Burnie Australia 41°4S 145°56E **153** G4
Burnley U.K. 53°47N 2°14W **66** D5
Burns U.S.A. 43°35N 119°3W **168** E4
Burns Junction
  U.S.A. 42°47N 117°51W **168** E5
Burnside → Canada 66°51N 108°4W **166** C10
Burnside, L. Australia 25°22S 123°0E **149** E3
Burnsville U.S.A. 44°46N 93°17W **172** C7
Burnt River Canada 44°41N 78°42W **174** B6
Burntwood → Canada 56°8N 96°34W **163** B9
Burntwood L. Canada 55°22N 100°26W **163** B8
Burqan Kuwait 29°0N 47°57E **128** D5
Burqin China 47°43N 87°0E **110** B6
Burra Australia 33°40S 138°55E **152** B3
Burra Nigeria 11°0N 8°56E **139** C6
Burragorang, L.
  Australia 33°52S 150°37E **153** C9
Burray U.K. 58°51N 2°54W **65** C6
Burrel Albania 41°36N 20°1E **96** E4
Burren △ Ireland 53°9N 9°5W **64** C2
Burren Junction
  Australia 30°7S 148°59E **153** A8
Burrendong, L.
  Australia 32°45S 149°10E **153** B8
Burriana Spain 39°50N 0°4W **91** E4
Burrinjuck, L. Australia 35°0S 148°36E **153** C8
Burro, Serranías del
  Mexico 29°0N 102°0W **180** B4
Burrow Hd. U.K. 54°41N 4°24W **66** C4
Burrowa-Pine Mountain △
  Australia 36°6S 147°45E **153** C8
Burruyacú Argentina 26°30S 64°40W **190** B3
Burry Port U.K. 51°41N 4°15W **67** F3
Bursa Turkey 40°15N 29°5E **99** B11
Bursa □ Turkey 40°10N 29°5E **99** B11
Burseryd Sweden 57°12N 13°17E **63** H7
Burstall Canada 50°39N 109°54W **163** C7
Burton Ohio, U.S.A. 41°28N 81°8W **174** E3
Burton, S.C., U.S.A. 32°26N 80°43W **177** E14
Burton, L. Canada 54°45N 78°20W **164** B4
Burton upon Trent U.K. 52°48N 1°38W **66** E6
Burtundy Australia 33°45S 142°15E **152** B3
Buru Indonesia 3°30S 126°30E **119** E7
Burullus, Bahra el Egypt 31°25N 31°0E **137** A12
Burûn, Râs Egypt 31°14N 33°7E **130** D2
Burundi ■ Africa 3°15S 30°0E **142** C3
Bururi Burundi 3°57S 29°37E **142** C2
Burutu Nigeria 5°20N 5°29E **138** D6
Burwell U.S.A. 41°47N 99°8W **172** E4
Burwick U.K. 58°45N 2°58W **65** C6
Bury U.K. 53°35N 2°17W **66** D5
Bury St. Edmunds U.K. 52°15N 0°43E **67** E8
Buryatia □ Russia 53°0N 110°0E **107** D11
Bürylbaytal Kazakhstan 44°56N 74°0E **108** E8
Buryn Ukraine 51°13N 33°50E **85** G5
Burzenin Poland 51°28N 18°47E **83** G5
Busalla Italy 44°34N 8°57E **93** D6
Busan S. Korea 35°5N 129°0E **115** G15
Busango Swamp
  Zambia 14°15S 25°45E **143** E2
Busayrah Syria 35°9N 40°26E **105** C9
Busca Italy 44°31N 7°29E **93** D6

hat Albania 41°58N 19°34E 96 E3
ehr Iran 28°55N 50°55E 129 D6
ehr □ Iran 28°20N 51°45E 129 D6
henyi Uganda 0°35S 30°10E 142 C3
hire = Būshehr
an 28°55N 50°55E 129 D6
nnell U.S.A. 28°40N 82°7W 179 G7
ntyna Ukraine 48°3N 23°28E 81 B8
e Ghana 10°29N 2°22W 138 C4
nga
m. Rep. of the Congo 3°16N 20°59E 140 D4
ngen Germany 47°42N 8°41E 77 H4
ko-Zdrój Poland 50°28N 20°42E 83 H7
ovača Bos.-H. 44°6N 17°53E 80 F2
a ash Shām Syria 32°30N 36°25E 130 C5
elton Australia 33°42S 115°15E 149 F2
eto Italy 44°59N 10°2E 92 D7
ière-Badil France 45°39N 0°36E 72 C4
sol, Proliv Russia 46°30N 151°0E 107 E16
solengo Italy 45°28N 10°51E 92 C7
sum Neths. 52°16N 5°10E 69 B5
amante, B.
gentina 45°5S 66°18W 192 C3
eni Romania 45°24N 25°32E 81 E10
o, C. Spain 43°34N 6°28W 88 B4
o Arsízio Italy 45°37N 8°51E 92 C5
a Djanoa
m. Rep. of the Congo 1°43N 21°23E 140 D4
uanga I. Phil. 12°10N 120°0E 119 B6
um Germany 54°7N 8°51E 76 A4
ungbiu Indonesia 8°16S 114°58E 119 J17
m. Rep. of the Congo 2°50N 24°53E 142 B1
are Rwanda 2°31S 29°52E 142 C2
aritari Kiribati 3°30N 174°0E 156 G9
e Australia 33°51S 138°0E 152 B3
e U.K. 55°48N 5°2W 65 F3
e Inlet Canada 50°40N 124°53W 162 C4
emba Uganda 1°9N 31°37E 142 B3
mbo
m. Rep. of the Congo 0°9N 29°18E 142 B2
eni Romania 46°19N 22°7E 80 D7
era Italy 37°11N 14°11E 95 E7
ere Kenya 0°13N 34°30E 142 B3
aa-Buthe Lesotho 28°47S 28°14E 145 C4
aba Uganda 1°50N 31°20E 142 B3
er Ga., U.S.A. 32°33N 84°14W 178 C5
er Mo., U.S.A. 38°16N 94°20W 172 F6
er Pa., U.S.A. 40°52N 79°54W 174 F5
on Indonesia 5°0S 122°45E 119 E6
e Mont., U.S.A. 46°0N 112°32W 168 C7
e Nebr., U.S.A. 42°58N 98°51W 172 D4
e Creek → U.S.A. 39°12N 121°56W 170 F5
erworth = Gcuwa
Africa 32°20S 28°11E 145 D4
erworth Malaysia 5°24N 100°23E 121 c
evant Ireland 52°14N 8°40W 64 D3
field, Mt. Australia 24°45S 128°9E 149 D4
on B. Canada 58°45N 94°23W 163 B10
onwillow U.S.A. 35°24N 119°28W 171 K7
y Hd. Australia 33°54S 121°39E 149 F3
uan Phil. 8°57N 125°33E 119 C7
uku-Luba Eq. Guin. 3°29N 8°33E 139 E6
ung = Buton
donesia 5°0S 122°45E 119 E6
urlinovka Russia 50°50N 40°35E 86 E5
wal Nepal 27°33N 83°31E 125 F10
bach Germany 50°25N 8°40E 77 E4
row Germany 53°50N 11°58E 76 B7
rhakaba Somalia 3°12N 44°20E 131 G3
a Duar India 27°45N 89°35E 125 F13
ar India 25°34N 83°58E 125 G10
oro Uzbekistan 39°48N 64°25E 108 E6
tehude Germany 53°28N 9°39E 76 B5
ton U.K. 53°16N 1°54W 66 D6
y France 46°44N 4°40E 71 F11
Russia 58°28N 41°28E 86 A5
ant-Uhaa
ongolia 44°55N 110°11E 114 B6
naksk Russia 42°48N 47°7E 87 J8
o Ivory C. 6°21N 7°5W 138 D3
o, L. de Ivory C. 6°16N 7°10W 138 D3
ük Menderes →
rkey 37°28N 27°11E 99 D9
ükçekmece Turkey 41°2N 28°35E 97 E12
ükkariştiran
rkey 41°18N 27°33E 97 E11
ükkemikli Burnu
rkey 40°18N 26°14E 97 F10
ükkonuk = Komi
yprus 35°24N 34°0E 101 D13
ükorhan Turkey 39°46N 28°56E 99 B10
ükyoncalı Turkey 41°20N 27°55E 97 E11
un Shan China 40°4N 122°43E 115 D12
ançais France 46°54N 1°25E 70 F8
iu Romania 45°10N 26°50E 81 E11
iu □ Romania 45°20N 26°30E 81 E11
iu → Romania 45°26N 27°44E 81 E11
iu, Pasul Romania 45°35N 26°12E 81 E11
en Japan 33°35N 131°5E 113 H5
et Croatia 45°24N 13°58E 93 C10
e → Mozam. 19°50S 34°43E 143 F3
aş Romania 45°38N 21°36E 80 E6
meyin Turkmenistan 38°3N 58°12E 129 B8
luk Russia 52°48N 52°12E 108 B4
luk → Russia 50°15N 42°7E 86 E6
ards Bay U.S.A. 41°45N 70°37W 175 E14
na Mkubwa Zambia 13°8S 28°38E 143 E2
ndi △ Uganda 1°2S 29°42E 142 C2
a Ruse, Bulgaria 43°28N 25°44E 97 C9
a Varna, Bulgaria 42°53N 27°55E 97 D11
a Slatina Bulgaria 43°26N 23°58E 96 C7
n Martin I.
anada 75°15N 104°15W 161 B11
ezina → Belarus 52°33N 30°14E 75 B16
oza Belarus 52°31N 24°51E 75 B13
os = Jubayl Lebanon 34°5N 35°39E 130 A4
nawa Poland 51°1N 22°36E 83 G9
zyna Poland 51°7N 18°12E 83 G5
goszcz Poland 53°10N 18°0E 83 E5
orussia = Belarus ■
urope 53°30N 27°0E 75 B14
s U.S.A. 39°43N 104°14W 168 G11
ville U.S.A. 39°58N 81°32W 174 G3
eld △ Australia 22°52S 150°45E 150 C5
haw Belarus 53°31N 30°14E 75 B16
hov = Bykhaw
elarus 53°31N 30°14E 75 B16
ovo Russia 49°50N 45°25E 86 F7
s U.S.A. 33°8N 110°7W 169 K8
t Canada 58°25N 94°8W 163 B10
Bylot I. Canada 73°13N 78°34W 161 C16
Byram U.S.A. 32°11N 90°15W 177 E9
Byrd, C. Antarctica 69°38S 76°7W 55 C17
Byrock Australia 30°40S 146°27E 153 A7
Byron U.S.A. 32°39N 83°46W 178 C6
Byron, C. Australia 28°43S 153°38E 151 D5
Byron Bay Australia 28°43S 153°37E 151 D5
Byrranga, Gory Russia 75°0N 100°0E 107 B11
Byrranga Mts. = Byrranga, Gory
Russia 75°0N 100°0E 107 B11
Byrum Denmark 57°16N 11°0E 63 G5
Byske Sweden 64°57N 21°11E 60 D19
Byskeälven → Sweden 64°57N 21°13E 60 D19
Bystrytsya Ukraine 48°27N 24°14E 81 B9
Bystrzyca → Dolnośląskie,
Poland 51°12N 16°55E 83 G3
Bystrzyca → Lubelskie,
Poland 51°21N 22°46E 83 G9
Bystrzyca Kłodzka
Poland 50°19N 16°39E 83 H3
Bytča Slovak Rep. 49°13N 18°34E 79 B11
Bytkiv Ukraine 48°38N 24°28E 81 B9
Bytom Poland 50°25N 18°54E 83 H5
Bytom Odrzański Poland 51°44N 15°48E 83 G2
Bytów Poland 54°10N 17°30E 82 D4
Byumba Rwanda 1°35S 30°4E 142 C3
Bzenec Czech Rep. 48°58N 17°18E 79 C10
Bzura → Poland 52°25N 20°15E 83 F7

C

C.W. McConaughy, L.
U.S.A. 41°14N 101°40W 172 E3
Ca → Vietnam 18°45N 105°45E 120 C5
Ca Mau Vietnam 9°7N 105°8E 121 H5
Ca Mau, Mui Vietnam 8°38N 104°44E 121 H5
Ca Na Vietnam 11°20N 108°54E 121 G7
Caacupé Paraguay 25°23S 57°5W 190 B4
Caaguazú △ Paraguay 26°5S 55°31W 191 B4
Caála Angola 12°46S 15°30E 141 G3
Caamaño Sd. Canada 52°55N 129°25W 162 C3
Caazapá Paraguay 26°8S 56°19W 190 B4
Caazapá □ Paraguay 26°10S 56°0W 191 B4
Cabana Peru 8°25S 78°5W 188 B2
Cabana de Bergantiños =
Carballo Spain 43°13N 8°54W 88 B2
Cabanaconde Peru 15°38S 71°58W 188 D3
Cabañaquinta Spain 43°10N 5°38W 88 B5
Cabanatuan Phil. 15°30N 120°58E 119 A6
Cabañeros ⌂ Spain 39°18N 4°35W 89 F6
Cabanes Spain 40°9N 0°2E 90 E5
Cabanilla Peru 15°36S 70°28W 188 D3
Cabano Canada 47°40N 68°56W 165 C6
Čabar Croatia 45°36N 14°39E 93 C11
Cabazon U.S.A. 33°55N 116°47W 171 M10
Cabedelo Brazil 7°0S 34°50W 189 B4
Cabeza del Buey Spain 38°44N 5°13W 89 G5
Cabezón de la Sal Spain 43°18N 4°14W 88 B6
Cabhán, An = Cavan
Ireland 54°0N 7°22W 64 B4
Cabildo Chile 32°30S 71°5W 190 C1
Cabimas Venezuela 10°23N 71°25W 186 A4
Cabinda Angola 5°33S 12°11E 140 F2
Cabinda □ Angola 5°0S 12°30E 140 F2
Cabinet Mts. U.S.A. 48°10N 115°50W 168 B6
Cabo Blanco Argentina 47°15S 65°47W 192 C3
Cabo de Gata-Níjar ⌂
Spain 36°51N 2°6W 91 J2
Cabo de Hornos △
Chile 55°42S 67°20W 192 E3
Cabo de Santo Agostinho
Brazil 8°20S 34°55W 189 B4
Cabo Frio Brazil 22°51S 42°3W 191 A7
Cabo Pantoja Peru 1°0S 75°10W 186 D3
Cabo Pulmo △
Mexico 23°20N 109°28W 180 C3
Cabo Raso Argentina 44°20S 65°15W 192 B3
Cabo San Lucas
Mexico 22°53N 109°54W 180 C3
Cabo Verde ■ Atl. Oc. 16°0N 24°0W 134 b
Cabonga, Réservoir
Canada 47°20N 76°40W 164 C4
Cabool U.S.A. 37°7N 92°6W 172 G7
Caboolture Australia 27°5S 152°58E 151 D5
Cabora Bassa Dam = Cahora
Bassa, Lago de
Mozam. 15°20S 32°50E 143 F3
Caborca Mexico 30°37N 112°6W 180 A2
Cabot, Mt. U.S.A. 44°30N 71°25W 175 B13
Cabot Hd. Canada 45°14N 81°17W 174 A3
Cabot Str. Canada 47°15N 59°40W 165 C8
Cabourg France 49°17N 0°7W 70 C6
Cabra Spain 37°30N 4°28W 89 H6
Cabra del Santo Cristo
Spain 37°42N 3°16W 89 H7
Cabra I. India 7°18N 93°50E 127 L11
Cábras Italy 39°56N 8°32E 94 C1
Cabrera Spain 39°8N 2°57E 100 B9
Cabrera, Sierra de la
Spain 42°12N 6°40W 88 C4
Cabrera △ Spain 39°13N 2°53E 91 F7
Cabri Canada 50°35N 108°25W 163 C7
Cabriel → Spain 39°14N 1°3W 91 F3
Cacabelos Spain 42°36N 6°44W 88 C4
Caçador Brazil 26°47S 51°0W 191 B5
Čačak Serbia 43°54N 20°20E 96 C4
Caçapava do Sul Brazil 30°30S 53°30W 191 C5
Cáccamo Italy 37°56N 13°40E 94 E6
Cacém Portugal 38°46N 9°18W 89 G1
Cáceres Brazil 16°5S 57°40W 186 G7
Cáceres Spain 39°26N 6°23W 89 F4
Cáceres □ Spain 39°45N 6°0W 88 F5
Cache Bay Canada 46°22N 80°0W 164 C4
Cache Cr. → U.S.A. 38°42N 121°42W 170 G5
Cache Creek Canada 50°48N 121°19W 162 C4
Cacheu Guinea-Biss. 12°14N 16°8W 138 C1
Cachi Argentina 25°5S 66°10W 190 B2
Cachimbo, Serra do
Brazil 9°30S 55°30W 187 E7
Cachinal de la Sierra
Chile 24°58S 69°32W 190 A2
Cachoeira Brazil 12°30S 39°0W 189 C3
Cachoeira do Sul Brazil 30°3S 52°53W 191 C5
Cachoeiro de Itapemirim
Brazil 20°51S 41°7W 191 A7
Cachopo Portugal 37°20N 7°49W 89 H3
Cacine Guinea-Biss. 11°8N 14°57W 138 C1
Cacoal Brazil 11°32S 61°18W 186 F6
Cacólo Angola 10°9S 19°21E 140 G3
Caconda Angola 13°48S 15°8E 141 G3
Caculé Brazil 14°30S 42°13W 189 C2
Cadaqués Spain 42°17N 3°17E 90 C8
Čadca Slovak Rep. 49°26N 18°45E 79 B11
Caddo U.S.A. 34°7N 96°16W 176 D6
Cader Idris U.K. 52°42N 3°53W 67 E4
Cadereyta de Jiménez
Mexico 25°36N 100°0W 180 B5
Cades U.S.A. 33°47N 79°47W 178 B10
Cadí, Serra del Spain 42°17N 1°42E 90 C6
Cadí-Moixeró ⌂ Spain 42°17N 1°44W 90 C3
Cadibarrawirracanna, L.
Australia 28°52S 135°27E 151 D2
Cadillac France 44°38N 0°20W 72 D3
Cadillac U.S.A. 44°15N 85°24W 173 C11
Cadiz Phil. 10°57N 123°15E 119 B6
Cádiz Spain 36°30N 6°20W 89 J4
Cadiz Calif., U.S.A. 34°30N 115°28W 171 L11
Cadiz Ohio, U.S.A. 40°22N 81°0W 174 F4
Cádiz □ Spain 36°36N 5°45W 89 J5
Cádiz, G. de Spain 36°40N 7°0W 89 J3
Cadiz L. U.S.A. 34°18N 115°24W 171 L11
Cadley U.S.A. 33°32N 82°40W 178 B7
Cadney Park Australia 27°55S 134°3E 151 D1
Cadomin Canada 53°2N 117°20W 162 C5
Cadotte Lake Canada 56°26N 116°23W 162 B5
Cadours France 43°44N 1°2E 72 E5
Cadoux Australia 30°46S 117°7E 149 F2
Cadwell U.S.A. 32°20N 83°3W 178 C6
Caen France 49°10N 0°22W 70 C6
Caerdydd = Cardiff U.K. 51°29N 3°10W 67 F4
Caerfyrddin = Carmarthen
U.K. 51°52N 4°19W 67 F3
Caergybi = Holyhead
U.K. 53°18N 4°38W 66 D3
Caernarfon U.K. 53°8N 4°16W 66 D3
Caernarfon B. U.K. 53°4N 4°40W 66 D3
Caernarvon = Caernarfon
U.K. 53°8N 4°16W 66 D3
Caerphilly U.K. 51°35N 3°13W 67 F4
Caerphilly □ U.K. 51°37N 3°12W 67 F4
Caesarea Israel 32°30N 34°53E 130 C3
Caeté Brazil 19°55S 43°40W 189 D2
Caetité Brazil 13°50S 42°32W 189 C2
Cafayate Argentina 26°2S 66°0W 190 B2
Cafu Angola 16°30S 15°8E 144 A2
Cagayan de Oro Phil. 8°30N 124°40E 119 C6
Cagli Italy 43°33N 12°39E 93 E9
Cágliari Italy 39°13N 9°7E 94 C2
Cágliari, G. di Italy 39°8N 9°11E 94 C2
Cagnano Varano Italy 41°49N 15°47E 93 G12
Cagnes-sur-Mer France 43°40N 7°9E 73 E11
Caguán → Colombia 0°8S 74°18W 186 D4
Caguas Puerto Rico 18°14N 66°2W 183 d
Caha Mts. Ireland 51°45N 9°40W 64 E2
Cahama Angola 16°17S 14°19E 144 A1
Caherciveen Ireland 51°56N 10°14W 64 E1
Cahir Ireland 52°22N 7°56W 64 D4
Cahora Bassa, Lago de
Mozam. 15°20S 32°50E 143 F3
Cahore Pt. Ireland 52°33N 6°12W 64 D5
Cahors France 44°27N 1°27E 72 D5
Cahuapanas Peru 5°15S 77°0W 188 B2
Cahul Moldova 45°50N 28°15E 81 E13
Cai Bau, Dao Vietnam 21°10N 107°27E 116 G6
Cai Be Vietnam 10°20N 106°2E 121 G6
Cai Nuoc Vietnam 8°56N 105°1E 121 H5
Caia Mozam. 17°51S 35°24E 143 F4
Caianda Angola 11°2S 23°31E 143 E1
Caibarién Cuba 22°30N 79°30W 182 B4
Caicara Venezuela 7°38N 66°10W 186 B5
Caicó Brazil 6°20S 37°0W 189 B3
Caicos Is.
Turks & Caicos 21°40N 71°40W 183 B5
Caicos Passage
W. Indies 22°45N 72°45W 183 B5
Caidian China 30°35N 114°2E 117 B10
Caiguna Australia 32°16S 125°29E 149 F4
Cailloma Peru 15°9S 71°45W 188 D3
Căinari Moldova 46°41N 29°3E 81 D14
Caird Coast Antarctica 75°0S 25°0W 55 D1
Cairn Gorm U.K. 57°7N 3°39W 65 D5
Cairngorm Mts. U.K. 57°6N 3°42W 65 D5
Cairngorms △ U.K. 57°10N 3°50W 65 D5
Cairnryan U.K. 54°59N 5°1W 65 G3
Cairns Australia 16°57S 145°45E 150 B4
Cairns L. Canada 51°42N 94°30W 163 C10
Cairo = El Qâhira Egypt 30°2N 31°13E 137 E7
Cairo Ga., U.S.A. 30°52N 84°13W 178 E5
Cairo Ill., U.S.A. 37°0N 89°11W 172 G9
Cairo N.Y., U.S.A. 42°18N 74°0W 175 D10
Cairo Montenotte Italy 44°23N 8°16E 92 D5
Caiseal = Cashel Ireland 52°30N 7°53W 64 D4
Caisleán an Bharraigh = Castlebar
Ireland 53°52N 9°18W 64 C2
Caithness U.K. 58°25N 3°35W 65 C5
Caithness, Ord of U.K. 58°8N 3°36W 65 C5
Caja de Muertos, I.
Puerto Rico 17°54N 66°32W 183 d
Cajabamba Peru 7°38S 78°4W 188 B2
Cajamarca Peru 7°5S 78°28W 188 B2
Cajamarca □ Peru 6°15S 78°50W 188 B2
Cajapió Brazil 2°58S 44°48W 189 A2
Cajarc France 44°29N 1°50E 72 D5
Cajatambo Peru 10°30S 77°2W 188 C2
Cajazeiras Brazil 6°52S 38°30W 189 B3
Ćajetina Serbia 43°47N 19°42E 96 C3
Çakirgol Turkey 40°33N 39°40E 105 B8
Çakırlar Turkey 36°52N 30°33E 99 E12
Čakovec Croatia 46°23N 16°26E 93 B13
Çal Turkey 38°4N 29°23E 99 C11
Cala Spain 37°59N 6°21W 89 H4
Cala → Spain 37°38N 6°5W 89 H4
Cala Cadolar, Punta de = Rotja,
Pta. Spain 38°38N 1°35E 91 G6
Cala d'Or Spain 39°23N 3°14E 100 B10
Cala en Porter Spain 39°52N 4°8E 100 B11
Cala Figuera Spain 39°20N 3°10E 100 B10
Cala Figuera, C. de Spain 39°27N 2°31E 100 B9
Cala Forcat Spain 40°0N 3°47E 100 B10
Cala Major Spain 39°33N 2°37E 100 B9
Cala Mezquida = Sa Mesquida
Spain 39°55N 4°16E 100 B11
Cala Millor Spain 39°35N 3°22E 100 B10
Cala Murada Spain 39°27N 3°17E 100 B10
Cala Ratjada Spain 39°43N 3°27E 100 B10
Cala Santa Galdana
Spain 39°56N 3°58E 100 B10
Calabar Nigeria 4°57N 8°20E 139 E6
Calabogie Canada 45°18N 76°43W 175 A8
Calabozo Venezuela 9°0N 67°28W 186 B5
Calábria □ Italy 39°0N 16°30E 95 C9
Calábria △ Italy 39°6N 16°35E 95 C9
Calaburras, Pta. de Spain 36°30N 4°38W 89 J6
Calaceite Spain 41°1N 0°11E 90 D5
Calacoto Bolivia 17°16S 68°38W 188 D4
Calacuccia France 42°21N 9°1E 73 F13
Calafat Romania 43°58N 22°59E 80 G7
Calafell Spain 41°11N 1°34E 90 D6
Calahorra Spain 42°18N 1°59W 90 C3
Calais France 50°57N 1°56E 71 B8
Calais U.S.A. 45°11N 67°17W 173 C20
Calakmul ⌂ Mexico 18°14N 89°48W 181 D7
Calalaste, Cord. de
Argentina 25°0S 67°0W 190 B2
Calama Brazil 8°0S 62°50W 186 E6
Calama Chile 22°30S 68°55W 190 A2
Calamar Colombia 10°15N 74°55W 186 A4
Calamarca Bolivia 16°55S 68°9W 188 D4
Calamian Group Phil. 11°50N 119°55E 119 B5
Calamocha Spain 40°50N 1°17W 90 E3
Calamonte Spain 38°53N 6°23W 89 G4
Călan Romania 45°44N 22°59E 80 E7
Calañas Spain 37°40N 6°53W 89 H4
Calanda Spain 40°56N 0°15W 90 E4
Calang Indonesia 4°37N 95°37E 118 D1
Calangiánus Italy 40°56N 9°11E 94 B2
Calanques △ France 43°14N 5°30E 73 E9
Calanscio, Sarîr Libya 27°30N 22°30E 135 C10
Calapan Phil. 13°25N 121°7E 119 B6
Călăraşi Moldova 47°16N 28°19E 81 C13
Călăraşi Romania 44°12N 27°20E 81 F12
Călăraşi □ Romania 44°10N 27°0E 81 F12
Calasparra Spain 38°14N 1°41W 91 G3
Calatafimi Italy 37°55N 12°52E 94 E5
Calatayud Spain 41°20N 1°40W 90 D3
Călăţele Romania 46°46N 23°1E 80 D8
Calato = Kalathos Greece 36°9N 28°8E 99 E10
Calauag Phil. 13°55N 122°15E 119 B6
Calavà, C. Italy 38°11N 14°55E 95 D7
Calavite, C. Phil. 13°26N 120°20E 119 B6
Calbayog Phil. 12°4N 124°38E 119 B6
Calca Peru 13°22S 72°0W 188 C3
Calcasieu L. U.S.A. 29°55N 93°18W 176 G8
Calcium U.S.A. 44°1N 75°50W 175 B9
Calcutta = Kolkata
India 22°34N 88°21E 125 H13
Calcutta U.S.A. 40°40N 80°34W 174 F4
Caldaro Italy 46°25N 11°14E 93 B8
Caldas da Rainha Portugal 39°24N 9°8W 89 F1
Caldas de Reis Spain 42°36N 8°39W 88 C2
Caldas Novas Brazil 17°45S 48°38W 189 D1
Calder → U.K. 53°44N 1°22W 66 D6
Caldera Chile 27°5S 70°55W 190 B1
Caldera de Taburiente △
Canary Is. 28°43N 17°52W 100 F2
Caldwell Idaho, U.S.A. 43°40N 116°41W 168 E5
Caldwell Kans., U.S.A. 37°2N 97°37W 172 G5
Caldwell Tex., U.S.A. 30°32N 96°42W 176 F6
Caledon Canada 43°51N 79°51W 174 C5
Caledon S. Africa 34°14S 19°26E 144 D2
Caledon → S. Africa 30°31S 26°5E 144 D4
Caledon B. Australia 12°45S 137°0E 150 A2
Caledonia Canada 43°7N 79°58W 174 C5
Caledonia U.S.A. 42°58N 77°51W 174 D7
Calella Spain 41°37N 2°40E 90 D7
Calemba Angola 16°0S 15°44E 144 A2
Calen Australia 20°56S 148°48E 150 b
Calenzana France 42°31N 8°51E 73 F12
Caleta Olivia Argentina 46°25S 67°25W 192 C3
Caletones Chile 34°6S 70°27W 190 C1
Calexico U.S.A. 32°40N 115°30W 171 N11
Calf of Man I. of Man 54°3N 4°48W 66 C3
Calgary Canada 51°0N 114°10W 162 C6
Calheta Madeira 32°44N 17°11W 100 D2
Calhoun U.S.A. 34°30N 84°57W 177 D12
Calhoun Falls U.S.A. 34°6N 82°36W 178 A7
Cali Colombia 3°25N 76°35W 186 C3
Calicut = Kozhikode
India 11°15N 75°43E 127 J2
Cálida, Costa Spain 37°30N 1°30W 91 H3
Caliente U.S.A. 37°37N 114°31W 169 H6
California Mo., U.S.A. 38°38N 92°34W 172 F7
California Pa., U.S.A. 40°4N 79°54W 174 F5
California □ U.S.A. 37°30N 119°30W 170 H7
California, Baja, T.N. = Baja
California □ Mexico 30°0N 115°0W 180 B2
California, Baja, T.S. = Baja
California Sur □
Mexico 25°50N 111°50W 180 B2
California, G. de Mexico 27°0N 111°0W 180 B2
California City U.S.A. 35°10N 117°55W 171 K9
California Hot Springs
U.S.A. 35°51N 118°41W 171 K8
Călilabad Azerbaijan 39°12N 48°29E 105 C13
Calilegua △ Argentina 25°36S 64°50W 190 B3
Călimăneşti Romania 45°14N 24°20E 81 E9
Călimani, Munţii
Romania 47°12N 25°0E 81 C10
Călimani △ Romania 47°7N 25°10E 81 C10
Calingasta Argentina 31°15S 69°30W 190 C2
Calipatria U.S.A. 33°8N 115°31W 171 M11
Calistoga U.S.A. 38°35N 122°35W 170 G4
Calitri Italy 40°54N 15°26E 95 B8
Calitzdorp S. Africa 33°33S 21°42E 144 D3
Callabonna, L.
Australia 29°40S 140°5E 151 D3
Callac France 48°25N 3°27W 70 D3
Callahan U.S.A. 30°34N 81°50W 178 E8
Callan Ireland 52°32N 7°24W 64 D4
Callander U.K. 56°15N 4°13W 65 E4
Callao Peru 12°3S 77°8W 188 C2
Callaway U.S.A. 30°8N 85°36W 178 E4
Callicoon U.S.A. 41°46N 75°3W 175 E9
Calling Lake Canada 55°15N 113°12W 162 B6
Calliope Australia 24°0S 151°16E 150 C5
Callosa de Segura Spain 38°7N 0°53W 91 G4
Callosa d'En Sarrià Spain 38°40N 0°8W 91 G4
Calma, Costa de la Spain 39°28N 2°26E 100 B9
Calne U.K. 51°26N 2°0W 67 F6
Calola Angola 16°25S 17°48E 144 A2
Calonge Spain 41°52N 3°5E 90 D8
Caloosahatchee →
U.S.A. 26°31N 82°1W 179 J7
Calore → Italy 41°11N 14°28E 95 A7
Caloundra Australia 26°45S 153°10E 151 D5
Calpe Spain 38°39N 0°3E 91 G5
Calpella U.S.A. 39°14N 123°12W 170 F3
Calpine U.S.A. 39°40N 120°27W 170 F6
Calstock Canada 49°47N 84°9W 164 C3
Caltabellotta Italy 37°34N 13°13E 94 E6
Caltagirone Italy 37°14N 14°31E 95 E7
Caltanissetta Italy 37°29N 14°4E 95 E7
Çaltılıbük Turkey 39°57N 28°36E 97 G12
Caluire-et-Cuire France 45°48N 4°52E 71 G11
Calulo Angola 10°1S 14°56E 140 G2
Caluso Italy 45°18N 7°53E 92 C4
Calvados □ France 49°5N 0°15W 70 C6
Calvert → Australia 16°17S 137°44E 150 B2
Calvert I. Canada 51°30N 128°0W 162 C3
Calvert Ra. Australia 24°0S 122°30E 148 D3
Calvi France 42°34N 8°45E 73 F12
Calvià Spain 39°34N 2°31E 100 B9
Calvillo Mexico 21°51N 102°43W 180 C4
Calvinia S. Africa 31°28S 19°45E 144 D2
Calvo, Mte. Italy 41°44N 15°46E 93 G12
Calwa U.S.A. 36°42N 119°46W 170 J7
Calzada Almuradiel = Almuradiel
Spain 38°32N 3°28W 89 G7
Calzada de Calatrava
Spain 38°42N 3°46W 89 G7
Cam → U.K. 52°21N 0°16E 67 E8
Cam Lam = Ba Ngoi
Vietnam 11°54N 109°10E 121 G7
Cam Pha Vietnam 21°7N 107°18E 116 G6
Cam Ranh Vietnam 11°54N 109°12E 121 G7
Cam Xuyen Vietnam 18°15N 106°0E 120 C6
Camabatela Angola 8°20S 15°26E 140 F3
Camacã Brazil 15°24S 39°30W 189 D3
Camaçari Brazil 12°41S 38°18W 189 C3
Camacha Madeira 32°41N 16°49W 100 D3
Camacupa Angola 11°58S 17°22E 141 G3
Camagüey Cuba 21°20N 77°55W 182 B4
Camaiore Italy 43°56N 10°18E 92 E7
Camamu Brazil 13°57S 39°7W 189 C3
Camaná Peru 16°30S 72°50W 188 D3
Camanche Res. U.S.A. 38°14N 121°1W 170 G6
Camaquã Brazil 30°51S 51°49W 191 C5
Camaquã → Brazil 31°17S 51°47W 191 C5
Câmara de Lobos
Madeira 32°39N 16°59W 100 D3
Camarat, C. France 43°12N 6°41E 73 E10
Çamardı Turkey 37°49N 34°58E 104 D6
Camarès France 43°49N 2°53E 72 E6
Camaret-sur-Mer France 48°16N 4°37W 70 D2
Camargo Mexico 26°19N 98°50W 181 B5
Camargue France 43°34N 4°34E 73 E8
Camargue ⌂ France 43°30N 4°40E 73 E8
Camarillo U.S.A. 34°13N 119°2W 171 L7
Camariñas Spain 43°8N 9°12W 88 B1
Camarón, C. Honduras 16°0N 85°5W 182 C2
Camarones Argentina 44°50S 65°40W 192 B3
Camarones, B.
Argentina 44°45S 65°35W 192 B3
Camas Spain 37°24N 6°2W 89 H4
Camas U.S.A. 45°35N 122°24W 170 E4
Camas Valley U.S.A. 43°2N 123°40W 168 E2
Camballin Australia 17°59S 124°12E 148 C3
Cambará Brazil 23°2S 50°5W 191 A5
Cambay = Khambhat
India 22°23N 72°33E 124 H5
Cambay, G. of = Khambhat, G. of
India 20°45N 72°30E 122 J8
Cambil Spain 37°40N 3°33W 89 H7
Cambo-les-Bains France 43°22N 1°23W 72 E2
Cambodia ■ Asia 12°15N 105°0E 120 F5
Camborne U.K. 50°12N 5°19W 67 G2
Cambrai Australia 34°40S 139°16E 152 C3
Cambrai France 50°11N 3°14E 71 B10
Cambre Spain 43°17N 8°20W 88 B2
Cambria U.S.A. 35°34N 121°5W 170 K5
Cambrian Mts. U.K. 52°3N 3°57W 67 E4
Cambridge Canada 43°23N 80°15W 174 C4
Cambridge Jamaica 18°18N 77°54W 182 a
Cambridge N.Z. 37°54S 175°29E 154 D4
Cambridge U.K. 52°12N 0°8E 67 E8
Cambridge Mass.,
U.S.A. 42°23N 71°7W 175 D13
Cambridge Minn.,
U.S.A. 45°34N 93°13W 172 C7
Cambridge N.Y., U.S.A. 43°2N 73°22W 175 C11
Cambridge Nebr.,
U.S.A. 40°17N 100°10W 172 E3
Cambridge Ohio, U.S.A. 40°2N 81°35W 174 F3
Cambridge Bay
Canada 69°10N 105°0W 160 D11
Cambridge G.
Australia 14°55S 128°15E 148 B4
Cambridge Springs
U.S.A. 41°48N 80°4W 174 E4
Cambridgeshire □ U.K. 52°25N 0°7W 67 E7
Cambrils Spain 41°8N 1°3E 90 D6
Cambuci Brazil 21°35S 41°55W 191 A7
Cambundi-Catembo
Angola 10°10S 17°35E 140 G3
Camdeboo △ S. Africa 32°28S 24°25E 144 D3
Camden Australia 34°1S 150°43E 153 C9
Camden Ala., U.S.A. 31°59N 87°17W 177 F11
Camden Ark., U.S.A. 33°35N 92°50W 176 E8
Camden Maine, U.S.A. 44°13N 69°4W 173 C19
Camden N.J., U.S.A. 39°55N 75°7W 175 G9
Camden N.Y., U.S.A. 43°20N 75°45W 175 C9
Camden S.C., U.S.A. 34°16N 80°36W 177 D14
Camden Sd. Australia 15°27S 124°25E 148 C3
Camdenton U.S.A. 38°1N 92°45W 172 F7
Camelford U.K. 50°37N 4°52W 67 G3
Çameli Turkey 37°5N 29°24E 99 D11
Camenca Moldova 48°3N 28°42E 81 B13
Camerino Italy 43°8N 13°4E 93 E10
Camerón Chile 53°38S 69°39W 192 D3
Cameron Ariz., U.S.A. 35°53N 111°25W 169 J8
Cameron La., U.S.A. 29°48N 93°20W 176 G8
Cameron Mo., U.S.A. 39°44N 94°14W 172 F6
Cameron S.C., U.S.A. 33°34N 80°43W 178 B9
Cameron Tex., U.S.A. 30°51N 96°59W 176 F6
Cameron Highlands
Malaysia 4°27N 101°22E 121 K3
Cameron Hills Canada 59°48N 118°0W 162 B5
Cameron Mts. N.Z. 46°1S 167°0E 155 G2
Cameroon ■ Africa 6°0N 12°30E 135 G7
Camerota Italy 40°2N 15°22E 95 B8
Cameroun → Cameroon 4°0N 9°35E 139 E6
Cameroun, Mt. Cameroon 4°13N 9°10E 139 E6
Cametá Brazil 2°12S 49°30W 187 D9
Çamiçi Gölü Turkey 37°29N 27°28E 99 D9
Camilla U.S.A. 31°14N 84°12W 178 D5
Caminha Portugal 41°50N 8°50W 88 D2
Camino U.S.A. 38°44N 120°41W 170 G6
Camlıbel = Myrtou
Cyprus 35°18N 33°4E 101 D12
Cammal U.S.A. 41°24N 77°28W 174 E7
Cammarata Italy 37°38N 13°38E 94 E6
Camocim Brazil 2°55S 40°50W 189 A2
Camonica, Val Italy 46°0N 10°20E 92 B7
Camooweal Australia 19°56S 138°7E 150 B2
Camooweal Caves △
Australia 20°1S 138°11E 150 C2
Camopi Fr. Guiana 3°12N 52°17W 187 C8
Camorta India 8°8N 93°30E 127 K11
Camp Hill Ala., U.S.A. 32°48N 85°39W 178 C4
Camp Hill Pa., U.S.A. 40°14N 76°55W 174 F8
Camp Nelson U.S.A. 36°8N 118°39W 171 J8
Camp Pendleton
U.S.A. 33°13N 117°24W 171 M9
Camp Verde U.S.A. 34°34N 111°51W 169 J8
Camp Wood U.S.A. 29°40N 100°1W 176 G4
Campagna Italy 40°40N 15°6E 95 B8
Campana Argentina 34°10S 58°55W 190 C4
Campana, I. Chile 48°20S 75°20W 192 C1
Campanário Madeira 32°39N 17°2W 100 D2
Campanario Spain 38°52N 5°36W 89 G5
Campanet Spain 39°46N 2°58E 100 B9
Campánia □ Italy 41°0N 14°30E 95 B7
Campas del Tuyú △
Argentina 36°17S 56°50W 190 D4
Campbell S. Africa 28°48S 23°44E 144 C3
Campbell Calif., U.S.A. 37°17N 121°57W 170 H5
Campbell Fla., U.S.A. 28°16N 81°27W 179 G8
Campbell Ohio, U.S.A. 41°5N 80°37W 174 E4
Campbell, C. N.Z. 41°47S 174°18E 155 B9
Campbell I. Pac. Oc. 52°30S 169°0E 156 N8
Campbell L. Canada 63°14N 106°55W 163 A7
Campbell Plateau
S. Ocean 50°0S 170°0E 55 A11
Campbell River Canada 50°5N 125°20W 162 C3
Campbellford Canada 44°18N 77°48W 174 B7
Campbellpur Pakistan 33°46N 72°26E 124 C5
Campbellsville U.S.A. 37°21N 85°20W 173 G11
Campbellton Canada 47°57N 66°43W 165 C6
Campbellton U.S.A. 30°57N 85°24W 178 E4
Campbelltown
Australia 34°4S 150°49E 153 C9
Campbeltown U.K. 55°26N 5°36W 65 F3
Campeche Mexico 19°51N 90°32W 181 D6
Campeche □ Mexico 19°0N 90°30W 181 D6
Campeche, Banco
Mexico 22°30N 88°0W 181 C7
Campeche, Golfo de
Mexico 19°30N 93°0W 181 D6
Câmpeni Romania 46°22N 23°3E 80 D8
Camperdown Australia 38°14S 143°9E 152 E5
Camperville Canada 51°59N 100°9W 163 C8
Campi Salentina Italy 40°24N 18°1E 95 B11
Câmpia Turzii Romania 46°34N 23°53E 81 D8
Campidano Italy 39°30N 8°47E 94 C1
Campíglia Maríttima
Italy 43°4N 10°37E 92 E7
Campillo de Altobuey
Spain 39°36N 1°49W 91 F3
Campillos Spain 37°4N 4°51W 89 H6
Câmpina Romania 45°10N 25°45E 81 E10
Campina Grande Brazil 7°20S 35°47W 189 B3
Campinas Brazil 22°50S 47°0W 191 A6
Campione Italy 45°58N 8°58E 73 C12
Campli Italy 42°43N 13°41E 93 F10
Campo Spain 42°25N 0°24E 90 C5
Campo de Criptana Spain 39°24N 3°7W 89 F7
Campo de Gibraltar
Spain 36°15N 5°25W 89 J5
Campo de los Alisos △
Argentina 27°15S 66°0W 190 B2
Campo Formoso Brazil 10°30S 40°20W 189 C2
Campo Grande Brazil 20°25S 54°40W 187 H8
Campo Maior Brazil 4°50S 42°12W 189 A2
Campo Maior Portugal 39°2N 7°7W 89 F3
Campo Mourão Brazil 24°3S 52°22W 191 A5
Campo Túres Italy 46°53N 11°55E 93 B8
Campobasso Italy 41°34N 14°39E 95 A7
Campobello di Licata
Italy 37°15N 13°55E 94 E6
Campobello di Mazara
Italy 37°38N 12°45E 94 E5
Campofelice di Roccella
Italy 37°59N 13°53E 94 E6
Campomarino Italy 41°57N 15°2E 93 G12
Camporeale Italy 37°54N 13°6E 94 E6
Camporrobles Spain 39°39N 1°24W 90 F3
Campos Brazil 21°50S 41°20W 191 A7
Campos Spain 39°26N 3°1E 100 B10
Campos Altos Brazil 19°47S 46°10W 189 D1
Campos Belos Brazil 13°10S 47°3W 189 C1
Campos del Paraíso = Carrascosa
del Campo Spain 40°2N 2°45W 90 E2
Campos Novos Brazil 27°21S 51°50W 191 B5
Campos Sales Brazil 7°4S 40°23W 189 B2
Camprodon Spain 42°19N 2°23E 90 C7
Campton Fla., U.S.A. 30°53N 86°31W 179 E3
Campton Ga., U.S.A. 33°52N 83°43W 178 B6
Camptonville U.S.A. 39°27N 121°3W 170 F5
Camptown U.S.A. 41°44N 76°14W 175 E8
Câmpulung Romania 45°17N 25°3E 81 E10
Câmpulung Moldovenesc
Romania 47°32N 25°30E 81 C10
Câmpuri Romania 46°0N 26°50E 81 D11
Campville U.S.A. 29°40N 82°7W 178 F7
Camrose Canada 53°0N 112°50W 162 C6
Camsell Portage
Canada 59°37N 109°15W 163 B7
Çamyuva Turkey 36°30N 30°30E 99 E12
Çan Turkey 40°2N 27°3E 97 F11
Can Clavo Spain 38°57N 1°27E 100 C7
Can Creu Spain 38°58N 1°28E 100 C7
Can Gio Vietnam 10°25N 106°58E 121 G6
Can Pastilla Spain 39°32N 2°42E 100 B9
Can Tho Vietnam 10°2N 105°46E 121 G5
Canaan U.S.A. 42°2N 73°20W 175 D11
Canacona India 15°1N 74°4E 127 G2
Canada ■ N. Amer. 60°0N 100°0W 160 G11
Canada Abyssal Plain
Arctic 80°0N 140°0W 54 B18
Canada Basin Arctic 75°0N 145°0W 54 B18
Cañada de Gómez
Argentina 32°40S 61°30W 190 C3
Canadian U.S.A. 35°55N 100°23W 176 D4
Canadian → U.S.A. 35°28N 95°3W 176 D7
Canadian Shield Canada 53°0N 75°0W 158 D12
Canadys U.S.A. 33°3N 80°37W 178 B9
Canajoharie U.S.A. 42°54N 74°35W 175 D10
Çanakkale Turkey 40°8N 26°24E 97 F10
Çanakkale □ Turkey 40°10N 26°25E 97 F10
Çanakkale Boğazı
Turkey 40°17N 26°32E 97 F10
Canal Flats Canada 50°10N 115°48W 162 C5
Canal Point U.S.A. 26°52N 80°38W 179 J9
Canalejas Argentina 35°15S 66°34W 190 D2

Canals _Argentina_ 33°35S 62°53W **190** C3
Canals _Spain_ 38°58N 0°35W **91** G4
Canandaigua _U.S.A._ 42°54N 77°17W **174** D7
Canandaigua L. _U.S.A._ 42°47N 77°19W **174** D7
Cananea _Mexico_ 31°0N 110°18W **180** A2
Canarias, Is. _Atl. Oc._ 28°30N 16°0W **100** F4
Canaries _St. Lucia_ 13°55N 61°4W **183** f
Canarreos, Arch. de los
Cuba 21°35S 81°40W **182** B3
Canary Is. = Canarias, Is.
Atl. Oc. 28°30N 16°0W **100** F4
Canaseraga _U.S.A._ 42°27N 77°45W **174** D7
Canastra, Serra da
Brazil 20°0S 46°20W **189** E1
Canatlán _Mexico_ 24°31N 104°47W **180** C4
Canaveral, C. _U.S.A._ 28°27N 80°32W **179** G9
Canaveral _U.S.A._ 28°28N 80°34W **179** G9
Cañaveruelas _Spain_ 40°24N 2°38W **90** E2
Canavieiras _Brazil_ 15°39S 39°0W **189** D3
Canbelego _Australia_ 31°32S 146°18E **153** A7
Canberra _Australia_ 35°15S 149°8E **153** C8
Canby _Calif., U.S.A._ 41°27N 120°52W **168** F3
Canby _Minn., U.S.A._ 44°43N 96°16W **172** C5
Canby _Oreg., U.S.A._ 45°16N 122°42W **170** E4
Cancale _France_ 48°40N 1°50W **70** D5
Canche → _France_ 50°31N 1°39E **71** B8
Canchungo _Guinea-Biss._ 12°26N 16°5W **138** C1
Canchyuaya, Cordillera de
Peru 7°30S 74°0W **188** B3
Cancún _Mexico_ 21°8N 86°44W **181** C7
Candanchú _Spain_ 42°47N 0°32W **90** C4
Candarave _Peru_ 17°15S 70°13W **188** D3
Çandarlı _Turkey_ 38°56N 26°56E **99** C8
Çandarlı Körfezi _Turkey_ 38°52N 26°55E **99** C8
Candás _Spain_ 43°35N 5°45W **88** B5
Candé _France_ 47°34N 1°2W **70** E5
Candela _Italy_ 41°8N 15°31E **95** A8
Candelaria _Argentina_ 27°29S 55°44W **191** B4
Candelaria _Canary Is._ 28°22N 16°22W **100** F3
Candelario ○ _Spain_ 40°20N 5°46W **88** E5
Candeleda _Spain_ 40°10N 5°14W **88** E5
Candelo _Australia_ 36°47S 149°43E **153** D8
Candi Dasa _Indonesia_ 8°30S 115°34E **119** J18
Candia = Iraklio _Greece_ 35°20N 25°12E **101** D7
Candia, Sea of = Crete, Sea of
Greece 36°0N 25°0E **99** E7
Candle L. _Canada_ 53°50N 105°18W **163** C7
Candlemas I. _Antarctica_ 57°3S 26°40W **55** B1
Cando _U.S.A._ 48°32N 99°12W **172** A4
Canea = Chania _Greece_ 35°30N 24°4E **101** D6
Canela _Brazil_ 10°15S 48°25W **189** C1
Canelli _Italy_ 44°43N 8°17E **92** D5
Canelones _Uruguay_ 34°32S 56°17W **191** C4
Canet de Mar _Spain_ 41°35N 2°35E **90** D7
Canet-Plage _France_ 42°41N 3°2E **72** F7
Cañete _Chile_ 37°50S 73°30W **190** D1
Cañete _Spain_ 40°3N 1°54W **90** E3
Cañete de las Torres
Spain 37°53N 4°19W **89** H6
Cangas _Spain_ 42°16N 8°47W **88** C2
Cangas de Onis _Spain_ 43°21N 5°8W **88** B5
Cangas del Narcea _Spain_ 43°10N 6°32W **88** B4
Cangnan _China_ 27°30N 120°23E **117** D13
Cangshan _China_ 34°50N 118°2E **115** G10
Canguaretama _Brazil_ 6°20S 35°5W **189** B3
Canguçu _Brazil_ 31°22S 52°43W **191** C5
Canguçu, Serra do
Brazil 31°20S 52°40W **191** C5
Cangxi _China_ 31°47N 105°59E **116** B5
Cangyuan _China_ 23°12N 99°14E **116** F2
Cangzhou _China_ 38°19N 116°52E **114** E9
Caniapiscau →
Canada 56°40N 69°30W **165** A6
Caniapiscau, L. _Canada_ 54°10N 69°55W **165** B6
Canicatti _Italy_ 37°21N 13°51E **94** E6
Canicattini Bagni _Italy_ 37°2N 15°4E **95** E8
Canigou _France_ 42°31N 2°27E **72** F6
Caniles _Spain_ 37°26N 2°43W **89** H8
Canim Lake _Canada_ 51°47N 120°54W **162** C4
Canindé _Brazil_ 4°22S 39°19W **189** A3
Canindé → _Brazil_ 6°15S 42°52W **189** B2
Canindeyu □ _Paraguay_ 24°10S 55°0W **191** A5
Canino _Italy_ 42°28N 11°45E **93** F8
Canisteo _U.S.A._ 42°16N 77°36W **174** D7
Canisteo → _U.S.A._ 42°7N 77°8W **174** D7
Cañitas de Felipe Pescador
Mexico 23°36N 102°43W **180** C4
Cañizal _Spain_ 41°12N 5°22W **88** D5
Canjáyar _Spain_ 37°1N 2°44W **89** H8
Çankırı _Turkey_ 40°40N 33°37E **104** B5
Çankırı □ _Turkey_ 40°40N 33°30E **104** B5
Cankuzo _Burundi_ 3°10S 30°31E **142** C3
Canmore _Canada_ 51°7N 115°18W **162** C5
Cann River _Australia_ 37°35S 149°7E **153** D8
Canna _U.K._ 57°3N 6°33W **65** D2
Cannanore = Kannur
India 11°53N 75°27E **127** J2
Cannanore Is. _India_ 10°30N 72°30E **127** J1
Cannes _France_ 43°32N 7°1E **73** E11
Canning Town = Port Canning
India 22°23N 88°40E **125** H13
Cannington _Canada_ 44°20N 79°2W **174** B5
Cannóbio _Italy_ 46°4N 8°42E **92** B5
Cannock _U.K._ 52°41N 2°1W **67** E5
Cannonball →
_U.S.A._ 46°26N 100°35W **172** B3
Cannondale Mt.
Australia 25°13S 148°57E **150** D4
Cannonsville Res.
_U.S.A._ 42°4N 75°22W **175** D9
Cannonvale _Australia_ 20°17S 148°43E **150** b
Canoas _Brazil_ 29°56S 51°11W **191** B5
Canoe L. _Canada_ 55°10N 108°15W **167** B7
Cañon City _U.S.A._ 38°27N 105°14W **168** G11
Cañon de Rio Blanco △
Mexico 18°43N 97°15W **181** D5
Cañon del Río Lobos ○
Spain 41°46N 3°28W **88** D7
Canonniers Pt. _Mauritius_ 20°2S 57°32E **141** d
Canoochee → _U.S.A._ 31°59N 81°19W **178** D4
Canopus _Australia_ 33°29S 140°42E **154** D2
Canora _Canada_ 51°40N 102°30W **167** C8
Canosa di Púglia _Italy_ 41°13N 16°4E **95** A9
Canowindra _Australia_ 33°35S 148°38E **153** B8
Canso _Canada_ 45°20N 61°0W **165** C7
Canso, Str. of _Canada_ 45°37N 61°22W **165** C7
Canta _Peru_ 11°29S 76°37W **188** C2
Cantabria □ _Spain_ 43°10N 4°0W **88** B7
Cantabria, Sierra de
Spain 42°40N 2°30W **90** C2
Cantabrian Mts. = Cantábrica,
Cordillera _Spain_ 43°0N 5°10W **88** C5

Cantábrica, Cordillera
Spain 43°0N 5°10W **88** C5
Cantal □ _France_ 45°5N 2°45E **72** C6
Cantal, Plomb du _France_ 45°3N 2°45E **72** C6
Cantanhede _Portugal_ 40°20N 8°36W **88** E2
Cantavieja _Spain_ 40°31N 0°25W **90** E4
Čantavir _Serbia_ 45°55N 19°46E **80** E4
Cantemir _Moldova_ 46°17N 28°14E **81** D13
Canterbury _Australia_ 25°23S 141°53E **150** D3
Canterbury _U.K._ 51°16N 1°6E **67** F9
Canterbury □ _N.Z._ 43°45S 171°19E **155** D6
Canterbury Bight _N.Z._ 44°16S 171°55E **155** E6
Canterbury Plains
_N.Z._ 43°55S 171°22E **155** D6
Cantil _U.S.A._ 35°18N 117°58W **171** K9
Cantillana _Spain_ 37°36N 5°50W **89** H5
Canto do Buriti _Brazil_ 8°7S 42°58W **189** B2
Canton = Guangzhou
China 23°6N 113°13E **117** F9
Canton _Ga., U.S.A._ 34°14N 84°29W **177** D12
Canton _Ill., U.S.A._ 40°33N 90°2W **172** E8
Canton _Miss., U.S.A._ 32°37N 90°2W **177** E9
Canton _Mo., U.S.A._ 40°8N 91°32W **172** E8
Canton _N.Y., U.S.A._ 44°36N 75°10W **175** B9
Canton _Ohio, U.S.A._ 40°48N 81°23W **174** F3
Canton _Pa., U.S.A._ 41°39N 76°51W **174** E8
Canton _S. Dak., U.S.A._ 43°18N 96°35W **172** D5
Canton L. _U.S.A._ 36°6N 98°35W **176** D5
Cantonment _U.S.A._ 30°37N 87°20W **179** E2
Cantù _Italy_ 45°44N 9°8E **92** C6
Canudos _Brazil_ 7°13S 58°5W **186** D7
Canumã → _Australia_ 37°42S 140°16E **152** D4
Canunda △ _Australia_ 37°42S 140°16E **152** D4
Canutama _Brazil_ 6°30S 64°20W **186** E6
Canutillo _U.S.A._ 31°55N 106°36W **176** F1
Canvey Island _U.K._ 51°31N 0°37E **67** F8
Canyon _U.S.A._ 34°59N 101°55W **176** D4
Canyon De Chelly ○
_U.S.A._ 36°10N 109°20W **169** H9
Canyonlands △ _U.S.A._ 38°15N 110°0W **169** G9
Canyons of the Ancients ○
_U.S.A._ 37°30N 108°55W **169** H9
Canyonville _U.S.A._ 42°56N 123°17W **168** E2
Cao Bang _Vietnam_ 22°40N 106°15E **116** F6
Cao He → _China_ 40°10N 124°32E **115** D13
Cao Lanh _Vietnam_ 10°27N 105°38E **121** G5
Cao Xian _China_ 34°50N 115°35E **114** G8
Caofeidian _China_ 38°56N 118°23E **115** E10
Cáorle _Italy_ 45°36N 12°53E **93** C9
Cap-aux-Meules
Canada 47°23N 61°52W **165** C7
Cap-Chat _Canada_ 49°6N 66°40W **165** C6
Cap-de-la-Madeleine
Canada 46°22N 72°31W **164** C5
Cap-Haïtien _Haiti_ 19°40N 72°20W **183** C5
Cap Pt. _St. Lucia_ 14°7N 60°57W **183** f
Capac _U.S.A._ 43°1N 82°56W **174** C2
Capáccio _Italy_ 40°25N 15°5E **95** B8
Capaci _Italy_ 38°10N 13°14E **94** D6
Capanaparo → _Venezuela_ 7°1N 67°7W **186** B5
Capánnori _Italy_ 43°50N 10°34E **92** E7
Caparaó → _Brazil_ 20°25S 41°46W **189** E2
Capbreton _France_ 43°39N 1°26W **72** E2
Capdenac _France_ 44°34N 2°5E **72** D6
Capdepera _Spain_ 39°42N 3°26E **90** F8
Cape → _Australia_ 20°59S 146°51E **150** C4
Cape Arid △ _Australia_ 33°56S 123°13E **149** F3
Cape Barren I.
Australia 40°25S 148°15E **151** G4
Cape Basin _Atl. Oc._ 34°0S 7°0W **56** K12
Cape Breton Highlands △
Canada 46°50N 60°40W **165** C7
Cape Breton I. _Canada_ 46°0N 60°30W **165** C7
Cape Canaveral _U.S.A._ 28°24N 80°36W **179** G9
Cape Charles _U.S.A._ 37°16N 76°1W **173** G15
Cape Coast _Ghana_ 5°5N 1°15W **139** D4
Cape Cod △ _U.S.A._ 41°56N 70°6W **173** E18
Cape Coral _U.S.A._ 26°33N 81°57W **179** J8
Cape Crawford
Australia 16°41S 135°43E **150** B2
Cape Dorset = Kinngait
Canada 64°14N 76°32W **161** E16
Cape Fear → _U.S.A._ 33°53N 78°1W **177** E15
Cape Girardeau _U.S.A._ 37°19N 89°32W **172** G9
Cape Hatteras ○
_U.S.A._ 35°30N 75°28W **177** D17
Cape Hillsborough △
Australia 20°54S 149°2E **150** b
Cape Jervis _Australia_ 35°40S 138°5E **152** C3
Cape Lambert
Australia 20°36S 117°11E **148** D2
Cape Le Grand △
Australia 33°54S 122°26E **149** F3
Cape Lookout ○
_U.S.A._ 35°45N 76°25W **177** D16
Cape May _U.S.A._ 38°56N 74°56W **173** F16
Cape May Point
_U.S.A._ 38°56N 74°58W **173** F16
Cape Melville △
Australia 14°26S 144°28E **150** A3
Cape Mount → _Liberia_ 6°44N 11°24W **138** D2
Cape Range △ _Australia_ 22°3S 114°0E **148** D1
Cape St. George
Canada 48°28N 59°14W **165** C8
Cape Tormentine
Canada 46°8N 63°47W **165** C7
Cape Town _S. Africa_ 33°55S 18°22E **144** D2
Cape Upstart △
Australia 19°45S 147°48E **150** B4
Cape Verde Abyssal Plain
Atl. Oc. 23°0N 26°0W **56** D9
Cape Verde Is. = Cabo Verde ■
Atl. Oc. 16°0N 24°0W **134** b
Cape Verde Plateau
Atl. Oc. 18°0N 20°0W **56** E10
Cape Vincent _U.S.A._ 44°8N 76°20W **175** B8
Cape York Peninsula
Australia 12°0S 142°30E **150** A3
Capela _Brazil_ 10°30S 37°0W **189** C3
Capelinha _Brazil_ 17°42S 42°31W **189** D2
Capella _Australia_ 23°2S 148°1E **150** C4
Capendu _France_ 43°11N 2°31E **72** E6
Capertree _Australia_ 33°8S 149°58E **153** B8
Capesterre-Belle-Eau
Guadeloupe 16°4N 61°36W **182** b
Capesterre-de-Marie-Galante
Guadeloupe 15°53N 61°14W **182** b
Capim → _Brazil_ 1°40S 47°47W **187** D9
Capistrello _Italy_ 41°57N 13°23E **93** G10
Capitan _U.S.A._ 33°35N 105°35W **169** K11

Capitán Aracena, I.
Chile 54°10S 71°20W **192** D2
Capitán Arturo Prat
Antarctica 63°0S 61°0W **55** C17
Capitán Pastene _Chile_ 38°13S 73°1W **192** A2
Capitão de Campos
Brazil 4°40S 41°55W **189** A2
Capitol Reef △ _U.S.A._ 38°15N 111°10W **169** G8
Capitola _U.S.A._ 36°59N 121°57W **170** J5
Capivara, Serra da
Brazil 14°35S 45°0W **189** C2
Capizzi _Italy_ 37°51N 14°29E **95** E7
Capoche → _Mozam._ 15°35S 33°0E **143** F3
Capodichino, Nápoli ✈ (NAP)
Italy 40°53N 14°16E **95** B7
Capodistria = Koper
Slovenia 45°31N 13°44E **93** C10
Ca포terra _Italy_ 39°11N 8°58E **94** C1
Cappadocia _Turkey_ 39°0N 35°0E **104** C6
Capraia _Italy_ 43°2N 9°50E **92** E6
Caprara, Pta. _Italy_ 41°7N 8°19E **94** A1
Caprarola _Italy_ 42°19N 12°14E **93** F9
Caprera _Italy_ 41°12N 9°28E **94** A2
Capri _Italy_ 40°33N 14°14E **95** B7
Capricorn Coast
Australia 23°16S 150°49E **150** C5
Capricorn Group
Australia 23°30S 151°55E **150** C5
Capricorn Ra.
Australia 23°20S 116°50E **148** D2
Caprino Veronese _Italy_ 45°36N 10°47E **92** C7
Caprivi □ _Namibia_ 17°55S 22°37E **144** A3
Caprivi Strip _Namibia_ 18°0S 23°0E **144** A3
Caps et Marais d'Opale ○
France 50°40N 2°0E **71** B9
Captains Flat _Australia_ 35°35S 149°27E **153** C8
Captieux _France_ 44°18N 0°16W **72** D3
Captiva _U.S.A._ 26°31N 82°11W **179** J7
Capulin Volcano ○
_U.S.A._ 36°47N 103°58W **176** C3
Caquetá → _Colombia_ 1°15S 69°15W **186** D5
Car Nicobar _India_ 9°10N 92°47E **127** K11
Caracal _Romania_ 44°8N 24°22E **81** F9
Caracas _Venezuela_ 10°30N 66°55W **186** A5
Caracol _Belize_ 16°45N 89°6W **182** C2
Caracol _Mato Grosso do Sul,
Brazil_ 22°18S 57°1W **190** A4
Caracol _Piauí, Brazil_ 9°15S 43°22W **189** B2
Caracollo _Bolivia_ 17°39S 67°10W **188** D4
Caragabal _Australia_ 33°49S 147°45E **153** B7
Caráglio _Italy_ 44°25N 7°26E **92** D4
Carahue _Chile_ 38°43S 73°12W **192** A2
Caraí _Brazil_ 17°12S 41°42W **189** D2
Carajas _Brazil_ 6°5S 50°23W **187** E8
Carajás, Serra dos _Brazil_ 6°0S 51°30W **187** E8
Caral _Peru_ 10°53S 77°31W **188** C2
Carangola _Brazil_ 20°44S 42°5W **189** E2
Caransebeş _Romania_ 45°28N 22°18E **80** E7
Carantec _France_ 48°40N 3°55W **70** D3
Caraquet _Canada_ 47°48N 64°57W **165** C6
Caraş Severin □
Romania 45°10N 22°10E **80** E7
Caraşova _Romania_ 45°11N 21°51E **80** E6
Caratasca, L. de
Honduras 15°20N 83°40W **182** C3
Caratinga _Brazil_ 19°50S 42°10W **189** D2
Caraúbas _Brazil_ 5°43S 37°33W **189** B3
Caravaca de la Cruz _Spain_ 38°8N 1°52W **91** G3
Caravela _Guinea-Biss._ 11°30N 16°30W **138** C1
Caravelas _Brazil_ 17°45S 39°15W **189** D3
Caraveli _Peru_ 15°45S 73°25W **188** D3
Caravelle, Presqu'île de la
Martinique 14°46N 60°48W **182** c
Caraz _Peru_ 9°3S 77°47W **188** B2
Carazinho _Brazil_ 28°16S 52°46W **191** B5
Carballia _Moldova_ 45°52N 28°27E **81** E13
Carballino = O Carballiño
Spain 42°26N 8°5W **88** C2
Carballo _Spain_ 43°13N 8°41W **88** B2
Carberry _Canada_ 49°50N 99°25W **167** D9
Carbó _Mexico_ 29°42N 110°58W **180** B2
Carbón, L. del
Argentina 49°35S 68°21W **192** C3
Carbonara, C. _Italy_ 39°6N 9°31E **94** C2
Carbondale _Colo.,
U.S.A._ 39°24N 107°13W **168** G10
Carbondale _Ill., U.S.A._ 37°44N 89°13W **172** G9
Carbondale _Pa., U.S.A._ 41°35N 75°30W **175** E9
Carbonear _Canada_ 47°42N 53°13W **165** C9
Carboneras _Spain_ 36°59N 1°53W **91** J3
Carboneras de Guadazaón
Spain 39°54N 1°50W **90** F3
Carbónia _Italy_ 39°10N 8°30E **94** C1
Carbonne _France_ 43°18N 1°11E **72** E5
Carcabuey _Spain_ 37°27N 4°17W **89** H6
Carcagente = Carcaixent
Spain 39°8N 0°28W **91** F4
Carcaixent _Spain_ 39°8N 0°28W **91** F4
Carcajou _Canada_ 57°47N 117°6W **162** B5
Carcar _Phil._ 10°8N 123°38E **125** F6
Carcarana → _Argentina_ 32°27S 60°48W **190** D3
Carcasse, C. _Haiti_ 18°30N 74°28W **183** C5
Carcassonne _France_ 43°13N 2°20E **72** E6
Carcar _Australia_ 35°3S 149°8E **153** B8
Carcross _Canada_ 60°13N 134°45W **162** A2
Çardak _Çanakkale,
Turkey_ 40°22N 26°43E **97** F10
Cardak _Spain_ 38°16N 4°20W **89** G6
Çardak _Denizli, Turkey_ 37°49N 29°39E **99** D11
Cardamon Hills _India_ 9°30N 77°15E **127** K3
Cardamom Hills = Kravanh,
Chuor Phnum
Cambodia 12°0N 103°32E **121** G4
Cárdenas _Cuba_ 23°0N 81°30W **182** B3
Cárdenas _San Luis Potosí,
Mexico_ 22°0N 99°38W **181** C5
Cárdenas _Tabasco,
Mexico_ 17°59N 93°22W **181** D6
Cardener → _Spain_ 41°41N 1°51E **90** D6
Cardenete _Spain_ 39°46N 1°41W **90** F3
Cardiel, L. _Argentina_ 48°55S 71°0W **192** C2
Cardiff _U.K._ 51°29N 3°10W **67** F4
Cardiff □ _U.K._ 51°31N 3°12W **67** F4
Cardiff-by-the-Sea
_U.S.A._ 33°1N 117°17W **171** M9
Cardigan _U.K._ 52°5N 4°40W **67** E3
Cardigan B. □ _U.K._ 52°30N 4°30W **67** E3

Cardinal _Canada_ 44°47N 75°23W **175** B9
Cardona _Spain_ 41°56N 1°40E **90** D6
Cardona _Uruguay_ 33°53S 57°18W **190** C4
Cardoso, Ilha do _Brazil_ 25°8S 47°58W **191** B5
Cardston _Canada_ 49°15N 113°20W **162** D6
Cardwell _Australia_ 18°14S 146°2E **150** B4
Careen L. _Canada_ 57°0N 108°11W **167** B7
Carei _Romania_ 47°40N 22°29E **80** C7
Carentan _France_ 49°19N 1°15W **70** C5
Carey _U.S.A._ 43°19N 113°57W **168** E7
Carey, L. _Australia_ 29°0S 122°15E **149** E3
Carey L. _Canada_ 62°12N 102°55W **163** A8
Careysburg _Liberia_ 6°34N 10°30W **138** D2
Cargados Carajos _Ind. Oc._ 17°0S 59°0E **146** F4
Cargèse _France_ 42°7N 8°35E **73** F12
Carhaix-Plouguer
France 48°18N 3°36W **70** D3
Carhuamayo _Peru_ 10°51S 76°4W **188** C2
Carhuás _Peru_ 9°15S 77°39W **188** B2
Caria _Turkey_ 37°20N 28°10E **99** D10
Cariacica _Brazil_ 20°16S 40°25W **189** E2
Cariati _Italy_ 39°30N 16°57E **95** C9
Caribbean Sea _W. Indies_ 15°0N 75°0W **183** D5
Cariboo Mts. _Canada_ 53°0N 121°0W **162** C4
Caribou _U.S.A._ 46°52N 68°1W **173** B19
Caribou → _Man.,
Canada_ 59°20N 94°44W **163** B10
Caribou → _N.W.T.,
Canada_ 61°27N 125°45W **162** A3
Caribou Group
Australia 23°30S 151°55E **150** C5
Caribou Is. _Canada_ 61°55N 113°15W **162** A6
Caribou L. _Man._,
Canada 59°21N 96°10W **163** B9
Caribou Mts. _Canada_ 59°12N 115°40W **162** B5
Caribou River ○
Canada 59°35N 96°35W **163** B9
Caribrod = Dimitrovgrad
Serbia 43°2N 22°48E **98** C6
Carichic _Mexico_ 27°56N 107°3W **180** B3
Carignan _France_ 49°38N 5°10E **71** C12
Carignano _Italy_ 44°55N 7°40E **92** D4
Cariñena _Spain_ 41°20N 1°13W **90** D3
Carinhanha _Brazil_ 14°15S 44°46W **189** C2
Carinhanha → _Brazil_ 14°20S 43°47W **189** C2
Carini _Italy_ 38°8N 13°11E **94** D6
Cariño _Spain_ 43°45N 7°52W **88** B3
Carinola _Italy_ 41°11N 13°58E **94** A5
Carinthia = Kärnten □
Austria 46°52N 13°30E **78** E6
Caripito _Venezuela_ 10°8N 63°6W **186** A6
Cariré _Brazil_ 3°57S 40°27W **189** A2
Carlet _Spain_ 39°14N 0°31W **91** F4
Carleton, Mt. _Canada_ 47°23N 66°53W **165** C6
Carleton Place _Canada_ 45°8N 76°9W **175** A8
Carletonville _S. Africa_ 26°23S 27°22E **144** C4
Carlin _U.S.A._ 40°43N 116°7W **168** F5
Carlingford L. _U.K._ 54°3N 6°9W **64** B5
Carlini Base _Antarctica_ 62°30S 58°0W **55** C18
Carlinville _U.S.A._ 39°17N 89°53W **172** F9
Carlisle _U.K._ 54°54N 2°56W **66** C5
Carlisle _U.S.A._ 40°12N 77°12W **174** F7
Carlisle B. _Barbados_ 13°5N 59°37W **183** g
Carlisle I. _Australia_ 20°49S 149°18E **150** b
Carlit, Pic _France_ 42°35N 1°55E **72** F5
Carloforte _Italy_ 39°8N 8°18E **94** C1
Carlos Casares
Argentina 35°32S 61°20W **190** D3
Carlos Chagas _Brazil_ 17°43S 40°45W **189** D2
Carlos Tejedor
Argentina 35°25S 62°25W **190** D3
Carlow _Ireland_ 52°50N 6°56W **64** D5
Carlow □ _Ireland_ 52°43N 6°50W **64** D5
Carlsbad _Calif., U.S.A._ 33°10N 117°21W **171** M9
Carlsbad _N. Mex.,
U.S.A._ 32°25N 104°14W **169** K11
Carlsbad Caverns △
_U.S.A._ 32°10N 104°35W **169** K11
Carlsberg Ridge _Ind. Oc._ 1°0N 66°0E **146** D5
Carluke _U.K._ 55°45N 3°50W **65** F5
Carlyle _Canada_ 49°40N 102°20W **167** D8
Carmacks _Canada_ 62°5N 136°16W **160** E4
Carmagnola _Italy_ 44°51N 7°43E **92** D4
Carman _Canada_ 49°30N 98°0W **163** D9
Carmarthen _U.K._ 51°52N 4°19W **67** F3
Carmarthen B. _U.K._ 51°40N 4°30W **67** F3
Carmarthenshire □ _U.K._ 51°55N 4°13W **67** F3
Carmaux _France_ 44°3N 2°10E **72** D6
Carmel, Mt. = Ha Karmel, Har
Israel 32°44N 35°3E **130** C4
Carmel-by-the-Sea
_U.S.A._ 36°33N 121°55W **170** J5
Carmel Valley _U.S.A._ 36°29N 121°43W **170** J5
Carmelo _Uruguay_ 34°0S 58°20W **190** C4
Carmen _Bolivia_ 11°0S 67°0W **188** C4
Carmen _Paraguay_ 27°13S 56°12W **191** B4
Carmen, L. _Mexico_ 25°57N 111°12W **180** B2
Carmen de Patagones
Argentina 40°50S 63°0W **192** B4
Cármenes _Spain_ 42°58N 5°34W **88** C5
Carmensa _Argentina_ 35°15S 67°40W **190** D2
Carmi _Canada_ 49°36N 119°8W **162** D5
Carmi _U.S.A._ 38°5N 88°10W **172** F9
Carmila _Australia_ 21°55S 149°24E **150** C4
Carmona _Costa Rica_ 10°0N 85°15W **182** E2
Carmona _Spain_ 37°28N 5°42W **89** H5
Carn Ban _U.K._ 57°7N 4°15W **65** D4
Carn Eige _U.K._ 57°17N 5°8W **65** D3
Carnac _France_ 47°35N 3°5W **70** E3
Carnamah _Australia_ 29°41S 115°53E **149** E2
Carnarvon _Canada_ 45°3N 78°41W **174** A6
Carnarvon _Queens.,
Australia_ 24°54S 113°42E **149** D1
Carnarvon _W. Austral.,
Australia_ 25°20S 120°45E **149** E3
Carnarvon _S. Africa_ 30°56S 22°8E **144** D3
Carnarvon △ _Queens.,
Australia_ 24°54S 148°2E **150** D4
Carnarvon Ra. _Queens.,
Australia_ 25°15S 148°30E **150** D4
Carnarvon Ra. _W. Austral.,
Australia_ 25°20S 120°45E **149** E3
Carnatic _India_ 9°40N 77°50E **127** K3
Carnation _U.S.A._ 47°39N 121°55W **170** C5
Carncastle _U.K._ 54°54N 5°53W **64** B6
Carndonagh _Ireland_ 55°16N 7°15W **64** A4
Carnduff _Canada_ 49°10N 101°50W **167** D8
Carnegie _U.S.A._ 40°24N 80°5W **174** F4
Carnegie, L. _Australia_ 26°5S 122°30E **149** E3
Carnegie Ridge _Pac. Oc._ 1°0S 87°0W **157** H19

Carnic Alps = Karnische Alpen
Europe 46°36N 13°0E **78** E6
Carniche Alpi = Karnische Alpen
Europe 46°36N 13°0E **78** E6
Carnot _C.A.R._ 4°59N 15°56E **140** D3
Carnot, C. _Australia_ 34°57S 135°38E **151** E2
Carnot B. _Australia_ 17°20S 122°15E **148** C3
Caroustie _U.K._ 56°30N 2°42W **65** E6
Caro _U.S.A._ 43°29N 83°24W **173** D12
Caroga Lake _U.S.A._ 43°8N 74°28W **175** C10
Carol City _U.S.A._ 25°56N 80°14W **177** J14
Carolina _Brazil_ 7°10S 47°30W **189** B1
Carolina _Puerto Rico_ 18°23N 65°58W **183** d
Carolina _S. Africa_ 26°5S 30°6E **145** C5
Caroline I. _Kiribati_ 9°58S 150°13W **157** H12
Caroline Is. _Micronesia_ 8°0N 150°0E **156** G6
Caroline Pk. _N.Z._ 45°57S 167°15E **155** F2
Caroni _Trin. & Tob._ 10°34N 61°23W **187** K15
Caroni → _Venezuela_ 8°21N 62°43W **186** B6
Caronie = Nébrodi, Monti
Italy 37°54N 14°35E **95** E7
Caroona _Australia_ 31°24S 150°26E **153** A9
Carpathians _Europe_ 49°30N 21°0E **75** D11
Carpații Meridionali
Romania 45°30N 25°0E **81** E9
Carpentaria, G. of
Australia 14°0S 139°0E **150** A2
Carpentras _France_ 44°3N 5°2E **73** D9
Carpi _Italy_ 44°47N 10°53E **92** D7
Carpina _Brazil_ 7°51S 35°15W **189** B3
Cărpineni _Moldova_ 46°46N 28°22E **81** D13
Carpinteria _U.S.A._ 34°24N 119°31W **171** L7
Carpio _Spain_ 41°13N 5°7W **88** D5
Carr Boyd Ra.
Australia 16°15S 128°35E **148** C4
Carra, L. _Ireland_ 53°41N 9°14W **64** C2
Carrabelle _U.S.A._ 29°51N 84°40W **178** F5
Carraig Mhachaire Rois =
Carrickmacross
Ireland 53°59N 6°43W **64** C5
Carraig na Siúire = Carrick-on-
Suir _Ireland_ 52°21N 7°24W **64** D4
Carral _Spain_ 43°14N 8°21W **88** B2
Carranya ○ _Australia_ 19°13S 127°46E **148** C4
Carrara _Italy_ 44°5N 10°6E **92** D7
Carrascosa del Campo
Spain 40°2N 2°45W **90** E2
Carrauntoohill _Ireland_ 52°0N 9°45W **64** D2
Carretas, Punta _Peru_ 14°12S 76°17W **188** C2
Carrick-on-Shannon
Ireland 53°57N 8°7W **64** C3
Carrick-on-Suir _Ireland_ 52°21N 7°24W **64** D4
Carrickfergus _U.K._ 54°43N 5°49W **64** B6
Carrickmacross _Ireland_ 53°59N 6°43W **64** C5
Carrieton _Australia_ 32°25S 138°31E **152** B3
Carrigaline _Ireland_ 51°48N 8°23W **64** E3
Carrillo _Mexico_ 26°54N 103°55W **180** B4
Carrington _U.S.A._ 47°27N 99°8W **172** B4
Carrión de los Condes
Spain 42°20N 4°37W **88** C6
Carrión → _Spain_ 41°53N 4°32W **88** D6
Carrizal Bajo _Chile_ 28°5S 71°20W **190** B1
Carrizalillo _Chile_ 29°5S 71°30W **190** B1
Carrizo Cr. →
_U.S.A._ 36°55N 103°55W **169** H12
Carrizo Plain ○
_U.S.A._ 35°11N 119°47W **170** K7
Carrizo Springs _U.S.A._ 28°31N 99°52W **176** G5
Carrizozo _U.S.A._ 33°38N 105°53W **169** K11
Carroll _U.S.A._ 42°4N 94°52W **172** D6
Carrollton _Ga., U.S.A._ 33°35N 85°5W **178** D4
Carrollton _Ill., U.S.A._ 39°18N 90°24W **172** F8
Carrollton _Ky., U.S.A._ 38°41N 85°11W **173** F11
Carrollton _Mo., U.S.A._ 39°22N 93°30W **172** F7
Carrollton _Ohio, U.S.A._ 40°34N 81°5W **174** F3
Carron → _U.K._ 57°53N 4°22W **65** D4
Carron, L. _U.K._ 57°22N 5°35W **65** D3
Carrot → _Canada_ 53°50N 101°17W **163** C8
Carrot River _Canada_ 53°17N 103°35W **167** C8
Carrouges _France_ 48°34N 0°10W **70** D6
Carruthers _Canada_ 52°52N 109°16W **167** C7
Çarşamba _Turkey_ 41°11N 36°44E **104** B7
Carsóli _Italy_ 42°6N 13°5E **93** F10
Carson _Calif., U.S.A._ 33°49N 118°16W **171** M8
Carson _N. Dak., U.S.A._ 46°25N 101°34W **172** B3
Carson → _U.S.A._ 39°45N 118°40W **168** G4
Carson City _U.S.A._ 39°10N 119°46W **170** F7
Carson Sink _U.S.A._ 39°50N 118°25W **168** G4
Cartagena _Colombia_ 10°25N 75°33W **186** A3
Cartagena _Spain_ 37°38N 0°59W **91** H4
Cartago _Colombia_ 4°45N 75°55W **186** C3
Cartago _Costa Rica_ 9°50N 83°55W **182** E3
Cártama _Spain_ 36°43N 4°39W **89** J6
Cartaxo _Portugal_ 39°10N 8°47W **89** F2
Cartaya _Spain_ 37°16N 7°9W **89** H3
Carter Bar _U.K._ 55°21N 2°29W **66** B5
Cartersville _N.Z._ 41°2S 175°31E **154** H4
Carterton _N.Z._ 41°2S 175°31E **154** H4
Carthage _Tunisia_ 36°52N 10°20E **95** F8
Carthage _Ill., U.S.A._ 40°25N 91°8W **172** E8
Carthage _Mo., U.S.A._ 37°11N 94°19W **172** G6
Carthage _N.Y., U.S.A._ 43°59N 75°37W **175** C9
Carthage _Tex., U.S.A._ 32°9N 94°20W **176** E7
Cartier I. _Australia_ 12°31S 123°29E **148** B3
Cartwright _Canada_ 53°41N 56°58W **165** B8
Caruaru _Brazil_ 8°15S 35°55W **189** B3
Carúpano _Venezuela_ 10°39N 63°15W **186** A6
Caruthersville _U.S.A._ 36°11N 89°39W **177** C10
Carvin _France_ 50°30N 2°57E **71** B9
Carvoeiro _Brazil_ 1°30S 61°59W **186** D6
Carvoeiro, C. _Portugal_ 39°21N 9°24W **89** F1
Casa Branca _Portugal_ 38°29N 8°12W **89** G2
Casa Grande _U.S.A._ 32°53N 111°45W **169** K8
Casa Nova _Brazil_ 9°25S 41°5W **189** B2
Casablanca _Chile_ 33°20S 71°25W **190** C1
Casablanca _Morocco_ 33°36N 7°36W **136** B4
Casacalenda _Italy_ 41°44N 14°51E **93** G11
Casale Monferrato _Italy_ 45°8N 8°27E **92** C5

Casalmaggiore _Italy_ 44°59N 10°26E **92** C7
Casalpusterlengo _Italy_ 45°11N 9°39E **92** C6
Casamance _Senegal_ 13°0N 15°30W **138** C1
Casamance → _Senegal_ 12°33N 16°46W **138** C1
Casarano _Italy_ 40°0N 18°10E **95** B11
Casares _Spain_ 36°27N 5°16W **89** J5
Casas Ibáñez _Spain_ 39°17N 1°30W **91** F3
Casasimarro _Spain_ 39°22N 2°3W **91** F3
Casatejada _Spain_ 39°54N 5°40W **88** F5
Casavieja _Spain_ 40°17N 4°46W **88** E6
Cascada de Basaseachic △
Mexico 28°9N 108°15W **180** B3
Cascade _Seychelles_ 4°39S 55°29E **145** b
Cascade _Idaho, U.S.A._ 44°31N 116°2W **168** D6
Cascade _Mont., U.S.A._ 47°16N 111°42W **168** C8
Cascade Locks _U.S.A._ 45°40N 121°54W **170** E5
Cascade Pt. _N.Z._ 44°1S 168°20E **155** D1
Cascade Ra. _U.S.A._ 47°0N 121°30W **168** C3
Cascade Res. _U.S.A._ 44°32N 116°3W **168** D6
Cascades, Pte. des
Réunion 21°9S 55°51E **141** c
Cascais _Portugal_ 38°41N 9°25W **89** G1
Cascavel _Ceará, Brazil_ 4°7S 38°14W **189** A3
Cascavel _Paraná, Brazil_ 24°57S 53°28W **191** A5
Cáscina _Italy_ 43°41N 10°33E **92** E7
Casco B. _U.S.A._ 43°45N 70°0W **173** D18
Caselle Torinese _Italy_ 45°10N 7°39E **92** C4
Caserta _Italy_ 41°4N 14°20E **95** A7
Caseyr, Raas = Asir, Ras
Somalia 11°55N 51°10E **133** E5
Cashel _Ireland_ 52°30N 7°53W **64** D4
Casigua _Venezuela_ 11°2N 71°1W **186** B4
Casiguran _Phil._ 16°22N 122°7E **125** A6
Casilda _Argentina_ 33°10S 61°10W **190** C3
Casimcea _Romania_ 44°45N 28°23E **81** F11
Casino _Australia_ 28°52S 153°3E **153** A9
Casiquiare → _Venezuela_ 2°1N 67°7W **186** C5
Casitas _Peru_ 3°54S 80°39W **188** B1
Časlav _Czech Rep._ 49°54N 15°22E **76** D8
Casma _Peru_ 9°30S 78°20W **188** B2
Casmalia _U.S.A._ 34°50N 120°32W **171** L6
Casnewydd = Newport
_U.K._ 51°35N 3°0W **67** F4
Cásola Valsénio _Italy_ 44°12N 11°40E **92** D8
Cásoli _Italy_ 42°7N 14°18E **93** F11
Caspe _Spain_ 41°14N 0°1W **90** D4
Casper _U.S.A._ 42°51N 106°19W **168** E10
Caspian Depression
Eurasia 47°0N 48°0E **87** E8
Caspian Sea _Eurasia_ 43°0N 50°0E **102** F8
Cass City _U.S.A._ 43°36N 83°10W **173** D12
Cass Lake _U.S.A._ 47°23N 94°37W **172** B7
Cassà de la Selva _Spain_ 41°53N 2°52E **90** D7
Cassadaga _U.S.A._ 42°20N 79°19W **174** D4
Cássano allo Iónio _Italy_ 39°47N 16°20E **95** C9
Casselberry _U.S.A._ 28°41N 81°20W **179** G9
Casselman _Canada_ 45°19N 75°5W **175** A9
Casselton _U.S.A._ 46°54N 97°13W **172** B5
Cassiar Mts. _Canada_ 59°30N 130°30W **162** B2
Cassilis _Australia_ 32°3S 149°58E **153** B8
Cassino _Italy_ 41°30N 13°49E **93** G10
Cassis _France_ 43°14N 5°32E **73** E9
Cassville _U.S.A._ 36°41N 93°52W **172** G7
Castagneto Carducci
Italy 43°9N 10°36E **92** E7
Castaic _U.S.A._ 34°30N 118°38W **171** L8
Castalia _U.S.A._ 41°24N 82°49W **174** E2
Castanhal _Brazil_ 1°18S 47°55W **187** D9
Castasegna _Trin. & Tob._ 11°17N 60°42W **183** D7
Castéggio _Italy_ 45°0N 9°8E **92** C6
Castejón de Monegros
Spain 41°37N 0°15W **90** D4
Castèl del Monte _Italy_ 41°5N 16°16E **95** A9
Castèl di Sangro _Italy_ 41°47N 14°6E **93** G11
Castèl San Giovanni _Italy_ 45°4N 9°26E **92** C6
Castèl San Pietro Terme
Italy 44°24N 11°35E **92** D8
Castelbuono _Italy_ 37°56N 14°5E **95** E7
Castelfidardo _Italy_ 43°28N 13°33E **93** E10
Castelfiorentino _Italy_ 43°36N 10°58E **92** E7
Castelfranco Véneto
Italy 45°40N 11°55E **93** C8
Casteljaloux _France_ 44°19N 0°6E **72** D4
Castell-Nedd = Neath
_U.K._ 51°39N 3°48W **67** F4
Castellabate _Italy_ 40°17N 14°57E **95** B7
Castellammare, G. di
Italy 38°8N 12°54E **94** D5
Castellammare del Golfo
Italy 38°1N 12°53E **94** D5
Castellammare di Stábia
Italy 40°42N 14°29E **95** B7
Castellane _France_ 43°50N 6°31E **73** E10
Castellaneta _Italy_ 40°38N 16°57E **95** B9
Castelli _Argentina_ 36°7S 57°47W **190** D4
Castelló de la Plana _Spain_ 39°58N 0°3W **90** E5
Castellón de la Plana □
Spain 40°15N 0°5W **90** E4
Castellote _Spain_ 40°48N 0°15W **90** E4
Castelmáuro _Italy_ 41°50N 14°43E **93** G11
Castelnau-de-Médoc
France 45°2N 0°48W **72** C3
Castelnau-Magnoac
France 43°17N 0°31E **72** E4
Castelnaudary _France_ 43°20N 1°58E **72** E5
Castelnovo ne' Monti
Italy 44°26N 10°24E **92** D7
Castelnuovo di Val di Cécina
Italy 43°12N 10°55E **92** E7
Castelo _Brazil_ 20°33S 41°14W **189** E2
Castelo Branco _Portugal_ 39°50N 7°31W **89** F3
Castelo Branco □
Portugal 39°52N 7°45W **89** F3
Castelo de Paiva _Portugal_ 41°2N 8°16W **88** D2
Castelo de Vide _Portugal_ 39°25N 7°27W **89** F3
Castelo do Piauí _Brazil_ 5°20S 41°33W **189** B2
Castelsardo _Italy_ 40°55N 8°43E **94** A1
Castelsarrasin _France_ 44°2N 1°7E **72** D5
Castéltermini _Italy_ 37°32N 13°38E **94** E6
Casterton _Australia_ 37°30S 141°30E **152** D4
Castets _France_ 43°53N 1°9W **72** E2
Castiglion Fiorentino
Italy 43°20N 11°55E **92** E8
Castiglione del Lago _Italy_ 43°7N 12°3E **93** E9
Castiglione della Pescáia
Italy 42°46N 10°53E **92** F7
Castiglione delle Stiviere
Italy 45°23N 10°30E **92** C7

lblanco Spain 39°17N 5°5W 89 F5
le U.S.A. 42°38N 78°3W 174 D6
illa Peru 5°12S 80°38W 188 B1
illa, Playa de Spain 37°0N 6°33W 89 J4
atin 39°30N 3°30W 89 F7
la y Leon □ Spain 42°0N 5°0W 88 D6
illo de Locubín Spain 37°32N 3°56W 89 H7
S.A. 29°54N 81°19W 178 F4
illon-en-Couserans
France 42°56N 1°1E 72 F5
ilonès France 44°39N 0°37E 72 D4
les Uruguay 34°12S 53°52W 191 C5
e Dale U.S.A. 39°13N 111°1W 168 G8
le Douglas U.K. 54°56N 3°56W 65 G5
le Rock Colo.,
S.A. 39°22N 104°51W 168 G11
le Rock Wash.,
S.A. 46°17N 122°54W 170 D4
ebar Ireland 53°52N 9°18W 64 C2
ebay U.K. 56°57N 7°31W 65 E1
eblayney Ireland 54°7N 6°44W 64 B5
ecliff N.Z. 39°57S 175°5E 154 F4
ecomer Ireland 52°48N 7°14W 64 D4
ederg U.K. 54°42N 7°36W 64 B4
eford U.K. 53°43N 1°21W 66 D6
egar Canada 49°20N 117°40W 162 D5
eisland Ireland 52°14N 9°42W 64 D2
emaine Australia 37°2S 144°12E 152 D6
epoint N.Z. 40°54S 176°15E 154 G5
epollard Ireland 53°41N 7°19W 64 C4
erea Ireland 53°46N 8°29W 64 C3
ereagh →
ustralia 30°12S 147°32E 153 A7
ereagh B.
ustralia 12°10S 135°10E 150 A2
eton U.S.A. 43°37N 73°11W 175 C11
eton-on-Hudson
letown I. of Man 54°5N 4°38W 66 C3
letown Bearhaven
land 51°39N 9°55W 64 E2
or Canada 52°15N 111°50W 162 C6
or → Canada 53°24N 78°58W 164 B4
orland U.S.A. 43°53N 75°31W 175 C9
res France 43°37N 2°13E 72 E6
ricum Neths. 52°33N 4°40E 69 B4
ries St. Lucia 14°2N 60°58W 183 f
ro Brazil 37°48N 2°46W 89 H8
ril Spain 24°45S 50°0W 191 A6
ro Chile 42°30S 73°50W 192 B2
ro Alves Brazil 12°46S 39°33W 189 C3
ro del Rio Spain 37°41N 4°29W 89 H6
ro-Urdiales Spain 43°23N 3°11W 88 B7
ro Valley U.S.A. 37°41N 122°5W 170 H4
ro Verde Portugal 37°41N 8°4W 89 H2
rojeriz Spain 42°17N 4°9W 88 C6
ropol Spain 43°32N 7°0W 88 B4
roreale Italy 38°6N 15°12E 95 D8
rovillari Italy 39°50N 16°13E 95 C9
roville U.S.A. 36°46N 121°45W 170 J5
rovirreyna Peru 13°20S 75°18W 188 C2
uera Spain 38°43N 5°37W 89 G5
vell Sound N.Z. 40°59S 167°8E 155 E2
Turkey 39°40N 41°3E 105 C9
Ba, Dao Vietnam 20°50N 107°0E 120 B6
Ba △ Vietnam 20°47N 107°3E 120 B6
. Bahamas 24°30N 75°30W 183 B4
. Canada 51°40N 91°50W 164 B1
Lake Canada 51°40N 91°50W 164 B1
Tien △ Vietnam 11°25N 107°17E 121 G6
Slovak Rep. 47°58N 18°38E 79 D11
camas Honduras 14°54N 85°56W 182 D2
caos Peru 5°20S 80°45W 188 B1
guases Brazil 21°23S 42°39W 191 A7
k Turkey 41°30N 31°59E 104 B4
lağa Turkey 41°30N 31°59E 104 B4
lâo Brazil 18°10S 47°57W 189 D1
lca Turkey 41°8N 28°27E 97 E12
lina Canada 48°31N 53°4W 165 C9
lina Chile 25°13S 69°43W 190 B2
lina U.S.A. 32°30N 110°43W 169 K8
onia = Cataluña □
Spain 41°40N 1°15E 90 B6
luña □ Spain 41°40N 1°15E 90 B6
Izeytin Turkey 41°57N 34°12E 104 B6
marca France 28°30S 65°50W 190 B2
marca □ Argentina 27°30S 65°50W 190 B2
nduanes □ Phil. 13°50N 124°20E 119 B6
nia Italy 37°30N 15°6E 95 E8
nia, G. di Italy 37°24N 15°9E 95 E8
nzaro Italy 38°54N 16°35E 95 D9
rman Phil. 12°28N 124°35E 119 B6
tumbo-Bari △
lombia 9°3N 73°12W 183 C3
ula U.S.A. 32°39N 84°52W 178 C5
acoma Canada 44°44N 78°19W 174 B6
el Phil. 7°47N 126°24E 119 C7
nde Mozam. 26°0S 32°33E 145 C5
rham U.K. 8°40S 35°43W 189 D4
rham U.K. 51°15N 0°4W 67 F7
air na Mart = Westport
cart Australia 33°48N 9°31W 64 C2
cart Australia 36°52S 149°24E 153 D8
er S. Africa 32°18S 27°10E 144 D4
edral City
ustralia 30°24S 152°15E 153 A10
lamet U.S.A. 46°12N 123°23W 170 D3
n Guinea-Biss. 11°17N 15°15W 138 C1
ttsburg U.S.A. 9°31S 43°1W 189 D2
na Dağı Turkey 38°25N 29°50E 99 C11
che, C. Mexico 21°35N 87°5W 181 C7
ia do Rocha Brazil 6°21S 37°45W 189 C4
ia, Mte. Italy 36°21N 12°42E 93 E9
imani Brazil 0°27N 61°41W 186 C6
imani → Brazil 2°0S 67°57W 186 D5
kill U.S.A. 42°14N 73°52W 175 D11
kill Mts. U.S.A. 42°10N 74°25W 175 D10
Mt. Australia 13°49S 134°23E 150 A1
araugus U.S.A. 42°20N 78°52W 174 D6
rrick U.K. 54°23N 1°37W 66 C6
Italy 43°58N 12°44E 93 E9

Cattólica Eraclea Italy 37°26N 13°24E 94 E6
Catu Brazil 12°21S 38°23W 189 C3
Catuala Angola 16°25S 19°2E 144 A2
Catuane Mozam. 26°48S 32°18E 145 C5
Catur Mozam. 13°45S 35°30E 143 E4
Caubvick, Mt. = Iberville, Mt. d'
Canada 58°50N 63°50W 161 F19
Cauca → Colombia 8°54N 74°28W 186 B4
Caucaia Brazil 3°40S 38°35W 189 A3
Caucasus Mountains
Eurasia 42°50N 44°0E 87 J7
Caucete Argentina 31°38S 68°20W 190 C2
Caudete Spain 38°42N 1°2W 91 G3
Caudry France 50°7N 3°22E 71 B10
Cauese Mts. Mozam. 15°14S 30°33E 143 F3
Caulnes France 48°18N 2°10W 70 D4
Caulónia Italy 38°23N 16°24E 95 D9
Caungula Angola 8°26S 18°38E 140 F3
Caura → Venezuela 7°38N 64°53W 186 B6
Căuşani Moldova 46°38N 29°25E 81 D14
Causapscal Canada 48°19N 67°12W 165 C6
Causse-Méjean France 44°18N 3°42E 72 D7
Causses du Quercy △
France 44°35N 1°35E 72 D5
Cauterets France 42°52N 0°8E 72 F3
Cauvery → India 11°9N 78°52E 127 J4
Caux, Pays de France 49°38N 0°35E 70 C7
Cava de' Tirreni Italy 40°42N 14°42E 95 B7
Cávado → Portugal 41°32N 8°48W 88 D2
Cavagrande del Cassibile △
Italy 36°58N 15°6E 95 F8
Cavaillon France 43°50N 5°2E 73 E9
Cavalaire-sur-Mer
France 43°10N 6°33E 73 E10
Cavalcante Brazil 13°48S 47°30W 189 C1
Cavalese Italy 46°17N 11°27E 93 B8
Cavalier U.S.A. 48°48N 97°37W 172 A5
Cavalla = Cavally →
Africa 4°22N 7°32W 138 E3
Cavalla △ Liberia 5°8N 7°20W 138 D3
Cavalli Is. N.Z. 35°0S 173°58E 154 B2
Cavally → Africa 4°22N 7°32W 138 E3
Cavan Ireland 54°0N 7°22W 64 B4
Cavan □ Ireland 54°1N 7°16W 64 C4
Cavárzere Italy 45°8N 12°5E 93 C9
Çavdarhisar Turkey 39°12N 29°37E 99 B11
Çavdır Turkey 37°10N 29°42E 99 D11
Cave U.S.A. 33°50N 111°57W 169 K8
Cave Spring U.S.A. 34°6N 85°20W 178 A4
Cavenagh Ra.
Australia 26°12S 127°55E 149 E4
Cavendish Australia 37°31S 142°2E 152 D5
Caverna do Peruaçu △
Brazil 15°0S 44°35W 189 D2
Caviana, I. Brazil 0°10N 50°10W 187 C8
Cavite Phil. 14°29N 120°54E 119 B6
Cavnic Romania 47°40N 23°52E 81 C8
Cavour Italy 44°47N 7°22E 92 D4
Cavtat Croatia 42°35N 18°13E 96 D2
Cawndilla L. Australia 32°30S 142°15E 152 E5
Cawnpore = Kanpur
India 26°28N 80°20E 125 F9
Caxias Brazil 4°55S 43°20W 189 A2
Caxias do Sul Brazil 29°10S 51°10W 191 B5
Çay Turkey 38°35N 31°1E 104 C4
Cay Sal Bank Bahamas 23°45N 80°0W 182 B4
Cayambe Ecuador 0°3N 78°8W 186 C3
Cayce U.S.A. 33°58N 81°4W 178 B8
Çaycuma Turkey 41°25N 32°4E 104 B5
Çayeli Turkey 41°5N 40°45E 105 B9
Cayenne Fr. Guiana 5°5N 52°18W 187 B8
Cayey Puerto Rico 18°7N 66°10W 183 d
Caygören Baraji Turkey 39°15N 28°12E 99 B10
Cayiralan Turkey 39°17N 35°38E 104 C6
Çayırova = Áyios Theodhoros
Cyprus 35°22N 34°1E 101 D13
Caylus France 44°15N 1°47E 72 D5
Cayman Brac
Cayman Is. 19°43N 79°49W 182 C4
Cayman Is. ☑
W. Indies 19°40N 80°30W 182 C3
Cayman Trench
Caribbean 17°0N 83°0W 158 H11
Cayres France 44°55N 3°48E 72 D7
Cayuga Canada 42°59N 79°50W 174 D5
Cayuga U.S.A. 42°54N 76°44W 175 D8
Cayuga Heights U.S.A. 42°27N 76°29W 175 D8
Cayuga L. U.S.A. 42°41N 76°41W 175 D8
Cazalla de la Sierra Spain 37°56N 5°45W 89 H5
Căzănești Romania 44°36N 27°3E 81 F12
Cazaubon France 43°56N 0°3W 72 E3
Cazaux et Sanguinet, Étang de
France 44°29N 1°10W 72 D2
Cazenovia U.S.A. 42°56N 75°51W 175 D9
Cazères France 43°13N 1°5E 72 E5
Cazin Bos.-H. 44°57N 15°57E 93 D12
Čazma Croatia 45°45N 16°39E 93 C13
Cazombo Angola 11°54S 22°56E 141 G4
Cazorla Spain 38°5N 3°2W 89 H7
Cazorla, Sierra de Spain 38°5N 2°55W 89 H8
Cea → Spain 42°0N 5°36W 88 C5
Ceadîr-Lunga Moldova 46°3N 28°51E 81 D13
Ceahlău □ Romania 46°58N 25°55E 81 D10
Ceamurlia de Jos
Romania 44°43N 28°47E 81 F13
Ceanannus Mor = Kells
Ireland 53°44N 6°53W 64 C5
Ceará = Fortaleza Brazil 3°45S 38°35W 189 A4
Ceará □ Brazil 5°0S 40°0W 189 B3
Ceara Abyssal Plain
Atl. Oc. 0°0 30°0W 56 F7
Ceará-Mirim Brazil 5°38S 35°25W 189 B3
Ceara Rise Atl. Oc. 3°30N 43°30W 56 F7
Ceatharlach = Carlow
Ireland 52°50N 6°56W 64 D5
Ceauru, L. Romania 44°58N 23°11E 81 F8
Cébaco, I. de Panama 7°33N 81°9W 182 E3
Cebollar Argentina 29°10S 66°35W 190 B2
Cebollera, Sierra Spain 42°0N 2°30W 90 C2
Cebreros Spain 40°27N 4°28W 88 E6
Cebu Phil. 10°18N 123°54E 119 B6
Čečava Bos.-H. 44°42N 17°44E 80 F2
Ceccano Italy 41°34N 13°20E 94 A6
Cece Hungary 46°46N 18°39E 80 D3
Cechi Ivory C. 6°15N 4°25W 138 D4
Cecil Plains Australia 27°30S 151°11E 151 D5
Cécina Italy 43°18N 10°33E 92 E7
Cécina → Italy 43°19N 10°31E 92 E7

Cécina → Italy 43°18N 10°29E 92 E7
Ceclavín Spain 39°50N 6°45W 88 F4
Cedar → U.S.A. 41°17N 91°21W 172 E8
Cedar City U.S.A. 37°41N 113°4W 169 H7
Cedar Creek Res. U.S.A. 32°11N 96°4W 176 E6
Cedar Falls Iowa,
U.S.A. 42°32N 92°27W 172 D7
Cedar Falls Wash.,
U.S.A. 47°25N 121°45W 170 C5
Cedar Key U.S.A. 29°8N 83°2W 179 F6
Cedar L. Canada 53°10N 100°0W 163 C9
Cedar Park U.S.A. 30°30N 97°49W 176 E6
Cedar Rapids U.S.A. 41°59N 91°40W 172 E8
Cedartown U.S.A. 34°1N 85°15W 178 A4
Cedarvale Canada 55°1N 128°22W 162 B3
Cedarville S. Africa 30°23S 29°3E 145 D4
Cedeira Spain 43°39N 8°2W 88 B2
Cedral Mexico 23°50N 100°45W 180 C4
Cedrino → Italy 40°11N 9°24E 94 B2
Cedro Brazil 6°34S 39°3W 189 B3
Cedros, I. Mexico 28°12N 115°15W 180 B1
Cedros B. Trin. & Tob. 10°16N 61°54W 187 K15
Ceduna Australia 32°7S 133°46E 151 E1
Cedynia Poland 52°53N 14°12E 83 F1
Cée Spain 42°57N 9°10W 88 C1
Ceel Gaal Somalia 10°58N 50°20E 131 E5
Ceel Waaq Kenya 2°49N 40°56E 140 D8
Ceeldheere Somalia 3°50N 47°8E 131 G4
Ceerigaabo Somalia 10°35N 47°20E 131 E4
Cefalù Italy 38°2N 14°1E 95 D7
Cega → Spain 41°33N 4°46W 88 D6
Cegléd Hungary 47°11N 19°47E 80 D4
Céglie Messápica Italy 40°39N 17°31E 95 B10
Cehegín Spain 38°6N 1°48W 91 G3
Ceheng China 24°58N 105°48E 116 E5
Cehu-Silvaniei Romania 47°24N 23°9E 81 C8
Ceica Romania 46°53N 22°10E 80 D7
Ceira → Portugal 40°13N 8°16W 88 E2
Çekerek Turkey 40°4N 35°29E 104 B6
Cekik Indonesia 8°12S 114°27E 119 J17
Čelákovice Czech Rep. 50°10N 14°46E 78 A7
Celano Italy 42°5N 13°33E 93 F10
Celanova Spain 42°9N 7°58W 88 C3
Celaque △ Honduras 14°30N 88°43W 182 D2
Celaya Mexico 20°31N 100°37W 180 C4
Celbridge Ireland 53°20N 6°32W 64 C5
Celebes = Sulawesi
Indonesia 2°0S 120°0E 119 E6
Celebes Sea Indonesia 3°0N 123°0E 119 D6
Celendín Peru 6°52S 78°10W 188 B2
Čelić Bos.-H. 44°43N 18°49E 80 F3
Celina U.S.A. 40°33N 84°35W 173 E11
Celinac Bos.-H. 44°44N 17°22E 80 F2
Celje Slovenia 46°16N 15°18E 93 B12
Celldömölk Hungary 47°16N 17°10E 80 C2
Celle Germany 52°37N 10°4E 76 C6
Celorico da Beira
Portugal 40°38N 7°24W 88 E3
Celtic Sea Atl. Oc. 50°9N 9°34W 68 F2
Çeltikçi Turkey 37°32N 30°29E 99 D12
Çemişgezek Turkey 39°3N 38°56E 105 C8
Cenderawasih, Teluk
Indonesia 3°0S 135°20E 119 E9
Cengong China 27°13N 108°44E 116 D7
Ceno → Italy 44°43N 10°5E 92 D7
Centallo Italy 44°30N 7°35E 92 D4
Centelles Spain 41°50N 2°14E 90 D7
Centennial U.S.A. 39°34N 104°52W 168 G11
Center N. Dak., U.S.A. 47°7N 101°18W 172 B3
Center Tex., U.S.A. 31°48N 94°11W 176 F7
Center Hill U.S.A. 28°38N 82°3W 179 G7
Centerburg U.S.A. 40°18N 82°42W 174 F2
Centerville Calif.,
U.S.A. 36°44N 119°30W 170 J7
Centerville Iowa, U.S.A. 40°44N 92°52W 172 E7
Centerville Pa., U.S.A. 39°6N 79°59W 174 F5
Centerville Tenn.,
U.S.A. 35°47N 87°28W 177 D11
Centerville Tex., U.S.A. 31°16N 95°59W 176 F7
Cento Italy 44°43N 11°17E 93 D8
Central = Tsentralnyy □
Russia 52°0N 40°0E 106 D7
Central □ Brazil 11°8S 42°8W 189 D2
Central □ Botswana 22°0S 26°30E 144 B4
Central □ Ghana 5°30N 1°0W 139 D4
Central □ Malawi 13°30S 33°30E 143 E3
Central □ Zambia 14°25S 28°50E 143 E2
Central, Cordillera
Colombia 5°0N 75°0W 186 C4
Central, Cordillera
Costa Rica 10°10N 84°5W 182 D3
Central, Cordillera
Dom. Rep. 19°15N 71°0W 183 C5
Central, Cordillera Peru 7°0S 77°30W 188 B2
Central, Cordillera
Puerto Rico 18°8N 66°35W 183 d
Central African Rep. ■
Africa 7°0N 20°0E 135 G9
Central America
America 12°0N 85°0W 158 H11
Central Australia ♢
Australia 20°30S 128°30E 148 D4
Central Bedfordshire □
U.K. 52°5N 0°20W 67 E7
Central Butte Canada 50°48N 106°31W 163 C7
Central City Colo.,
U.S.A. 39°48N 105°31W 168 G11
Central City Ky.,
U.S.A. 37°18N 87°7W 172 G10
Central City Nebr., U.S.A. 41°7N 98°0W 172 E4
Central Desert ♢
Australia 19°56S 130°46E 148 C5
Central I. Kenya 3°30N 36°0E 142 B4
Central Island △ Kenya 2°33N 36°1E 142 B4
Central Japan Int. ✈ (NGO)
Japan 34°53N 136°45E 113 G8
Central Kalahari ♢
Botswana 22°36S 23°58E 144 B3
Central Makran Range
Pakistan 26°30N 64°15E 122 F4
Central Pacific Basin
Pac. Oc. 8°0N 175°0W 156 G10
Central Patricia Canada 51°30N 90°9W 164 B1
Central Point U.S.A. 42°23N 122°55W 168 E2
Central Russian Uplands
Europe 54°0N 36°0E 58 E13
Central Siberian Plateau
Russia 65°0N 105°0E 102 B12
Central Square U.S.A. 43°17N 76°9W 175 C8
Centralia Canada 43°17N 81°28W 174 D3
Centralia Ill., U.S.A. 38°32N 89°8W 172 F9

Centralia Mo., U.S.A. 39°13N 92°8W 172 F7
Centralia Wash.,
U.S.A. 46°43N 122°58W 170 D4
Centre □ Cameroon 4°45N 12°0E 139 D7
Centre de Flacq
Mauritius 20°12S 57°43E 141 d
Centreville N.Y., U.S.A. 42°28N 78°14W 174 D6
Centreville Pa., U.S.A. 41°44N 79°45W 174 E5
Century U.S.A. 30°58N 87°16W 179 E2
Cenxi China 22°57N 110°57E 117 F8
Ceotina → Bos.-H. 43°36N 18°50E 96 C2
Cephalonia = Kefalonia
Greece 38°15N 20°30E 98 C2
Cepin Croatia 45°32N 18°34E 80 E3
Ceprano Italy 41°33N 13°31E 94 A6
Ceptura Romania 45°1N 26°21E 81 E11
Cepu Indonesia 7°9S 111°35E 119 G14
Ceram = Seram
Indonesia 3°10S 129°0E 119 E7
Ceram Sea = Seram Sea
Indonesia 2°30S 128°30E 119 E7
Cerbère France 42°26N 3°10E 72 F7
Cerbicales, Îs. France 41°33N 9°22E 73 G13
Cercal Portugal 37°48N 8°40W 89 H2
Cerdanya Spain 42°22N 1°50E 90 D6
Cère → France 44°55N 1°49E 72 D5
Cerea Italy 45°12N 11°13E 93 C8
Ceres Argentina 29°55S 61°55W 190 B3
Ceres S. Africa 33°21S 19°18E 144 D2
Ceres U.S.A. 37°35N 120°57W 170 H6
Cerignola Italy 41°17N 15°53E 95 A8
Cerigo = Kythira Greece 36°8N 23°0E 98 E5
Cerilly France 46°37N 2°50E 71 F9
Cerisiers France 48°8N 3°30E 71 D10
Cerizay France 46°50N 0°40W 70 F6
Çerkeş Turkey 40°49N 32°52E 104 B5
Çerkezköy Turkey 41°17N 28°0E 97 E12
Cerknica Slovenia 45°48N 14°21E 93 C11
Cerkovica Bulgaria 43°41N 24°50E 97 C8
Cermei Romania 46°35N 21°17E 80 D6
Çermik Turkey 38°8N 39°26E 105 C8
Cerna Romania 45°4N 28°17E 81 E13
Cerna → Romania 44°38N 23°58E 81 F8
Cernavodă Romania 44°22N 28°3E 81 F13
Cernay France 47°44N 7°10E 71 E14
Cernik Croatia 45°17N 17°22E 80 E2
Cerralvo, I. Mexico 24°15N 109°55W 180 C3
Cêrrik Albania 41°2N 19°58E 98 B4
Cerritos Mexico 22°25N 100°16W 180 C4
Cerro Chato Uruguay 33°6S 55°8W 191 C4
Cerro Cofre de Perote △
Mexico 19°29N 97°8W 181 D5
Cerro Corá □ Paraguay 22°35S 56°2W 191 A4
Cerro de Pasco Peru 10°45S 76°10W 188 C2
Cerro el Copey △
Venezuela 10°59N 63°53W 183 D7
Cerro Hoya △ Panama 7°17N 80°45W 182 E3
Cerro Saroche △
Venezuela 10°9N 69°38W 183 D6
Cerro Sombrero Chile 52°45S 69°15W 192 D3
Cerros Colorados, Embalse
Argentina 38°30S 68°50W 192 A3
Certaldo Italy 43°33N 11°2E 92 E8
Cervaro → Italy 41°30N 15°52E 95 A8
Cervati, Monte Italy 40°17N 15°29E 95 B8
Cerventes Australia 30°31S 115°3E 149 F2
Cervera Spain 41°40N 1°16E 90 D6
Cervera de Pisuerga
Spain 42°51N 4°30W 88 C6
Cervera del Río Alhama
Spain 42°2N 1°58W 90 C3
Cervéteri Italy 42°0N 12°6E 93 F9
Cérvia Italy 44°14N 12°20E 93 D9
Cervignano del Friuli
Italy 45°49N 13°20E 93 C10
Cervione France 42°20N 9°29E 73 F13
Cervo Spain 43°40N 7°24W 88 B3
Cesaro Italy 37°50N 14°38E 95 E7
Cesena Italy 44°8N 12°15E 93 D9
Cesenático Italy 44°12N 12°24E 93 D9
Cēsis Latvia 57°18N 25°15E 84 D3
Česká Lipa Czech Rep. 50°45N 14°30E 78 A7
Česká Rep. = Czech Rep. ■
Europe 50°0N 15°0E 78 B8
Česká Třebová
Czech Rep. 49°54N 16°27E 79 B9
České Budějovice
Czech Rep. 48°55N 14°25E 78 C7
České Švýcarsko △
Czech Rep. 50°54N 14°20E 78 A7
České Velenice
Czech Rep. 48°45N 14°57E 78 C7
Českobudějovický = Jihočeský □
Czech Rep. 49°0N 14°40E 78 C8
Českomoravská Vrchovina
Czech Rep. 49°30N 15°40E 78 B8
Český Brod Czech Rep. 50°4N 14°52E 78 A7
Český Krumlov
Czech Rep. 48°43N 14°21E 78 C7
Český Těšín Czech Rep. 49°45N 18°39E 79 B11
Çeşme Turkey 38°20N 26°23E 99 C8
Çeşme → Croatia 45°35N 16°19E 93 C13
Çesma → Croatia 45°35N 16°19E 93 C13
Çeşme Yarımadası
Turkey 38°20N 26°30E 99 C8
Cessnock Australia 32°50S 151°21E 153 B9
Cesson-Sévigné France 48°8N 1°36W 70 D5
Cestas France 44°44N 0°41W 72 D3
Cestos → Liberia 5°40N 9°10W 138 D3
Cestos Sehnkwehn △
Liberia 5°40N 9°10W 138 D3
Cetate Romania 44°7N 23°2E 80 F8
Cetin Grad Croatia 45°9N 15°45E 93 C12
Cetina → Croatia 43°26N 16°42E 93 E13
Cetinje Montenegro 42°23N 18°59E 96 D2
Cetraro Italy 39°31N 15°55E 95 C9
Ceuta N. Afr. 35°52N 5°18W 134 A4
Ceva Italy 44°23N 8°2E 92 D5
Cévennes France 44°10N 3°50E 72 D7
Cévennes → France 44°15N 3°42E 72 D7
Ceyhan Turkey 37°4N 35°47E 104 D6
Ceyhan → Turkey 36°38N 35°40E 104 D6
Ceylanpınar Turkey 36°50N 40°2E 105 D9
Ceylon = Sri Lanka ■
Asia 7°30N 80°50E 127 L5

Ceylon Plain Ind. Oc. 4°0S 82°0E 146 E7
Cèze → France 44°6N 4°43E 73 D8
Cha-am Thailand 12°48N 99°58E 120 F2
Chabanais France 45°52N 0°48E 72 C4
Chabeuil France 44°54N 5°3E 73 D9
Chablais France 46°20N 6°36E 71 F13
Chablis France 47°47N 3°48E 71 E10
Chabounia Algeria 35°30N 2°38E 136 A4
Chacabuco Argentina 34°40S 60°27W 190 C3
Chacao, Canal Chile 41°47S 73°42W 192 B2
Chachani, Nevado
Peru 16°11S 71°31W 188 D3
Chachapoyas Peru 6°15S 77°50W 188 B2
Chachasp Peru 6°20S 73°0W 188 B2
Chachoengsao Thailand 13°42N 101°5E 120 F3
Chachran Pakistan 28°55N 70°30E 124 E4
Chachro Pakistan 25°5N 70°15E 124 G4
Chaco □ Argentina 26°30S 61°0W 190 B3
Chaco □ Paraguay 26°0S 60°0W 190 B4
Chaco → U.S.A. 36°46N 108°39W 169 H9
Chaco Boreal S. Amer. 22°0S 60°0W 186 H6
Chaco Culture △
U.S.A. 36°3N 107°58W 169 H10
Chacon, C. U.S.A. 54°42N 132°0W 162 C2
Chad ■ Africa 15°0N 17°15E 135 F8
Chad, L. = Tchad, L.
Chad 13°30N 14°30E 135 F8
Chadileuvú →
Argentina 37°46S 66°0W 190 D2
Chadiza Zambia 14°45S 32°27E 143 E3
Chadron U.S.A. 42°50N 103°0W 172 D2
Chadyr-Lunga = Ceadîr-Lunga
Moldova 46°3N 28°51E 81 D13
Chae Hom Thailand 18°43N 99°35E 120 C2
Chae Son △ Thailand 18°42N 99°20E 120 C2
Chaem → Thailand 18°11N 98°38E 120 C2
Chaeryŏng N. Korea 38°24N 125°36E 115 E13
Chafe Nigeria 11°56N 6°55E 139 C6
Chagai Hills = Chāh Gay Hills
Afghan. 29°30N 64°0E 122 E3
Chagda Russia 58°45N 130°38E 107 D14
Chagdo Kangri China 34°15N 84°10E 109 F10
Chaghcharān Afghan. 34°31N 65°15E 122 B5
Chagny France 46°57N 4°45E 71 F11
Chagoda Russia 59°10N 35°15E 84 B6
Chagos Arch. ☑ Ind. Oc. 6°0S 72°0E 146 E6
Chagos-Laccadive Ridge
Ind. Oc. 3°0N 73°0E 146 D6
Chagres △ Panama 9°33N 79°37W 182 E4
Chaguanas
Trin. & Tob. 10°30N 61°26W 187 K15
Chāh Bahar Iran 25°20N 60°40E 129 E9
Chāh Gay Hills Afghan. 29°30N 64°0E 122 E3
Chāh-e Kavīr Iran 34°29N 56°52E 129 C8
Chahar Borj Iran 37°6N 45°59E 105 D11
Chāhār Mahāll va Bakhtiārī □
Iran 32°0N 49°0E 129 C6
Chai Badan Thailand 15°12N 101°8E 120 E3
Chaibasa India 22°42N 85°49E 125 H11
Chaillé-les-Marais France 46°25N 1°2W 72 B2
Chain Ridge Ind. Oc. 6°0N 54°0E 146 D4
Chainat Thailand 15°11N 100°8E 120 E2
Chainpur Nepal 27°17N 87°19E 125 F12
Chaires U.S.A. 30°28N 84°13W 179 F6
Chaitén Chile 42°55S 72°43W 192 B2
Chaiya Thailand 9°23N 99°14E 121 H2
Chaiyaphum Thailand 15°48N 102°2E 120 E4
Chaj Doab Pakistan 32°15N 73°0E 124 C5
Chajari Argentina 30°42S 58°0W 190 C4
Chak Amru Pakistan 32°22N 75°11E 124 C6
Chakar → Pakistan 29°29N 68°2E 124 E3
Chakari Zimbabwe 18°5S 29°51E 145 B4
Chake Chake Tanzania 5°15S 39°45E 142 D4
Chakhānsūr Afghan. 31°10N 62°0E 122 D3
Chakonipau, L. Canada 56°18N 68°30W 165 A6
Chakradharpur India 22°45N 85°40E 125 H11
Chakrata India 30°42N 77°51E 124 D7
Chakwal Pakistan 32°56N 72°53E 124 C5
Chala Peru 15°48S 74°20W 188 D3
Chalais France 45°16N 0°3E 72 C4
Chalakudi India 10°18N 76°20E 127 J3
Chalchihuites Mexico 23°29N 103°53W 180 C4
Chalcis = Chalkida
Greece 38°27N 23°42E 98 C5
Chaleur B. Canada 47°55N 65°30W 165 C6
Chalfant U.S.A. 37°32N 118°21W 170 H8
Chalhuanca Peru 14°15S 73°15W 188 C3
Chalindrey France 47°43N 5°26E 71 E12
Chalisgaon India 20°30N 75°10E 124 J9
Chalk River Canada 46°1N 77°27W 164 C4
Chalkar, Ozero = Shalkar Köli
Kazakhstan 50°35N 51°47E 86 E15
Chalki Dodekanisa, Greece 36°17N 27°35E 99 E12
Chalki Thessaly, Greece 39°36N 22°30E 98 B4
Chalkida Greece 38°27N 23°42E 98 C5
Chalkidiki Greece 40°25N 23°20E 98 A5
Chalky Inlet N.Z. 46°3S 166°31E 155 G1
Challakere India 14°19N 76°33E 127 J3
Challans France 46°50N 1°52W 70 F5
Challapata Bolivia 18°53S 66°50W 186 G5
Challenger Deep
Pac. Oc. 11°30N 142°0E 156 F6
Challenger Fracture Zone
Pac. Oc. 35°0S 105°0W 157 L17
Challis U.S.A. 44°30N 114°14W 168 D6
Chalmette U.S.A. 29°56N 89°57W 177 G10
Chaloem Rattanakosin △
Thailand 14°40N 99°17E 120 E2
Chalon-sur-Saône
France 46°48N 4°50E 71 F11
Chalong Thailand 7°50N 98°22E 121 a
Chalonnes-sur-Loire
France 47°20N 0°45W 70 E6
Châlons-en-Champagne
France 48°58N 4°20E 71 D11
Chālūs Iran 36°38N 51°26E 129 B6
Cham Germany 49°12N 12°40E 77 D8
Cham, Cu Lao Vietnam 15°57N 108°30E 120 E7
Chama U.S.A. 36°54N 106°35W 169 H10
Chamaicó Argentina 35°3S 64°58W 190 D3
Chaman Pakistan 30°58N 66°25E 122 D5

Chamba India 32°35N 76°10E 124 C7
Chamba Tanzania 11°37S 37°0E 143 E4
Chambal → India 26°29N 79°15E 125 F8
Chamberlain U.S.A. 43°49N 99°20W 172 D4
Chamberlain →
Australia 15°30S 127°54E 148 C4
Chamberlain L.
U.S.A. 46°14N 69°19W 173 B19
Chambers U.S.A. 35°11N 109°26W 169 J9
Chambersburg U.S.A. 39°56N 77°40W 173 F15
Chambéry France 45°34N 5°55E 73 C9
Chambeshi → Zambia 11°53S 29°48E 140 G6
Chambi, Jebel Tunisia 35°11N 8°35E 136 A5
Chamblee U.S.A. 33°53N 84°18W 178 B5
Chambly Canada 45°27N 73°17W 175 A11
Chambord Canada 48°25N 72°6W 165 C5
Chamboulive France 45°26N 1°42E 72 C5
Chamchamal Iraq 35°32N 44°50E 105 C11
Chamela Mexico 19°32N 105°5W 180 D3
Chamical Argentina 30°22S 66°27W 190 C2
Chamili Greece 35°50N 26°15E 99 F8
Chamkar Luong
Cambodia 11°0N 103°45E 121 G4
Chamoli India 30°24N 79°21E 125 D8
Chamonix-Mont Blanc
France 45°55N 6°51E 73 C10
Chamouchuane =
Ashuapmushuan →
Canada 48°37N 72°20W 164 C5
Champa India 22°2N 82°43E 125 H10
Champagne Canada 60°49N 136°30W 162 A1
Champagne France 48°40N 4°20E 71 D11
Champagnole France 46°45N 5°55E 71 F12
Champaign U.S.A. 40°7N 88°15W 172 E9
Champaner India 22°29N 73°32E 124 H5
Champassak Laos 14°53N 105°52E 120 E5
Champawat India 29°20N 80°6E 125 E9
Champdeniers-St-Denis
France 46°29N 0°25W 72 B3
Champeix France 45°37N 3°8E 72 C7
Champion U.S.A. 41°19N 80°51W 174 E4
Champlain U.S.A. 44°59N 73°27W 175 B11
Champlain, L. U.S.A. 44°40N 73°20W 175 B11
Champlitte France 47°37N 5°31E 71 E12
Champotón Mexico 19°21N 90°43W 181 D6
Champua India 22°5N 85°40E 125 H11
Chamrajnagar India 11°52N 76°52E 127 J3
Chamusca Portugal 39°21N 8°29W 89 F2
Chan Chan Peru 8°7S 79°9W 188 B2
Chana Thailand 6°55N 100°44E 121 J3
Chañaral Chile 26°23S 70°40W 190 B1
Chanārān Iran 36°39N 59°6E 129 B8
Chanasma India 23°44N 72°5E 124 H5
Chancay Peru 11°32S 77°25W 188 C2
Chancery Lane Barbados 13°3N 59°30W 183 g
Chanco Chile 35°44S 72°32W 190 D1
Chand India 21°57N 79°7E 125 J8
Chandan Chauki India 28°33N 80°47E 125 E9
Chandannagar India 22°52N 88°24E 125 H13
Chandausi India 28°27N 78°49E 125 E8
Chandeleur Is. U.S.A. 29°55N 88°57W 177 G10
Chandeleur Sd. U.S.A. 29°55N 89°0W 177 G10
Chandigarh India 30°43N 76°47E 124 D7
Chandil India 22°58N 86°3E 125 H12
Chandler Australia 27°0S 133°19E 151 D1
Chandler Canada 48°18N 64°46W 165 C7
Chandler Ariz., U.S.A. 33°18N 111°50W 169 K8
Chandler Okla., U.S.A. 35°42N 96°53W 176 D6
Chandless → Brazil 9°35S 69°51W 188 B4
Chandod India 21°59N 73°28E 124 J5
Chandpur Bangla. 23°8N 90°45E 125 H17
Chandra → India 35°3N 26°9E 99 F8
Chandragiri India 13°35N 79°19E 127 H4
Chandrapur India 19°57N 79°25E 124 K8
Chandrupatla India 18°43N 84°24E 125 E6
Chânf Iran 26°38N 60°29E 129 E9
Chang Pakistan 26°59N 68°30E 124 F3
Chang, Ko Thailand 12°0N 102°23E 121 G4
Chang, Ko Thailand 9°50N 98°27E 121 H2
Ch'ang Chiang = Chang Jiang →
China 31°48N 121°10E 117 B13
Chang Jiang →
China 31°48N 121°10E 117 B13
Chang-won S. Korea 35°16N 128°37E 115 G15
Changan China 22°48N 113°48E 111 a
Changanacheri India 9°25N 76°31E 127 K3
Changanassery = Changanacheri
India 9°25N 76°31E 127 K3
Changane → Mozam. 24°30S 33°30E 145 B5
Changbai China 41°25N 128°5E 115 D15
Changbai Shan China 42°20N 129°0E 115 C15
Changchiak'ou = Zhangjiakou
China 40°48N 114°55E 114 D8
Ch'angchou = Changzhou
China 31°47N 119°58E 117 B12
Changchun China 43°57N 125°17E 115 C13
Changchunling China 45°18N 125°27E 115 B13
Changde China 29°4N 111°35E 117 C8
Changdo-ri N. Korea 38°30N 127°40E 115 E14
Changfeng China 32°28N 117°10E 117 A11
Changge China 34°13N 113°46E 116 G7
Changhai = Shanghai
China 31°15N 121°26E 117 B13
Changhua China 30°12N 119°12E 117 B12
Changhua Taiwan 24°2N 120°30E 117 E13
Changhüngni
N. Korea 40°24N 128°19E 115 D14
Changi Singapore 1°23N 103°59E 121 d
Changi, Singapore ✈ (SIN)
Singapore 1°23N 103°59E 121 d
Changji China 44°1N 87°19E 109 D11
Changjin China 40°23N 127°15E 115 D14
Changjiang Shuiku
China 22°29N 113°27E 111 a
Changjin N. Korea 40°23N 127°15E 115 D14
Changjin-ho N. Korea 40°30N 127°15E 115 D14
Changli China 39°40N 119°19E 115 E10
Changlun Malaysia 6°25N 100°26E 121 J3
Changning Hunan,
China 26°28N 112°22E 117 D9
Changning Sichuan,
China 28°40N 104°56E 116 D5
Changning Yunnan,
China 24°45N 99°30E 116 E2
Changping China 40°14N 116°12E 114 D9
Changsha China 28°12N 113°0E 117 C9

210 Changshan
INDEX TO WORLD MAP

Changshan China 28°55N 118°27E 117 C12
Changshan Qundao China 39°11N 122°32E 115 E12
Changshou China 29°50N 107°4E 116 C6
Changshu China 31°38N 120°43E 117 B13
Changshun China 26°3N 106°25E 116 D6
Changtai China 24°35N 117°42E 117 E11
Changting China 25°50N 116°22E 117 E11
Changtu China 42°46N 124°6E 115 C13
Changuinola Panama 9°26N 82°31W 182 E3
Changwu Guangxi Zhuangzu, China 23°25N 111°17E 117 F8
Changwu Shaanxi, China 35°10N 107°45E 114 G4
Changxing China 31°0N 119°55E 117 B12
Changyang China 30°30N 111°10E 117 B8
Changyi China 36°40N 119°30E 115 F10
Changyŏn N. Korea 38°15N 125°6E 115 E13
Changyuan China 35°15N 114°42E 114 G8
Changzhi China 36°10N 113°6E 114 F7
Changzhou China 31°47N 119°58E 117 B12
Chanhanga Angola 16°0S 14°8E 144 A1
Chania Greece 35°30N 24°4E 101 D6
Chanion, Kolpos Greece 35°33N 23°55E 101 D5
Chanlar = Goygöl Azerbaijan 40°37N 46°12E 87 K8
Channagiri India 14°2N 75°56E 127 G2
Channapatna India 12°40N 77°15E 127 H3
Channel Is. U.K. 49°19N 2°24W 67 H5
Channel Is. U.S.A. 33°40N 119°15W 171 M7
Channel Islands △ U.S.A. 34°0N 119°24W 171 L7
Channel-Port aux Basques Canada 47°30N 59°9W 165 C8
Channel Tunnel Europe 51°0N 1°30E 67 F9
Channing U.S.A. 35°41N 102°20W 176 D3
Chantada Spain 42°36N 7°46W 88 C3
Chanthaburi Thailand 12°38N 102°12E 120 F4
Chantilly France 49°12N 2°29E 71 C9
Chantonnay France 46°40N 1°3W 70 F5
Chantrey Inlet Canada 67°48N 96°20W 160 D12
Chanumla India 8°19N 93°5E 127 K11
Chanute U.S.A. 37°41N 95°27W 172 G6
Chany, Ozero Russia 54°49N 77°29E 109 B9
Chanza → Spain 37°32N 7°30W 89 H3
Chao Hu China 31°30N 117°30E 117 B11
Chao Phraya → Thailand 13°40N 100°31E 120 F3
Chao Phraya Lowlands Thailand 15°30N 100°0E 120 E3
Chaocheng China 36°4N 115°37E 114 F8
Chaohu China 31°38N 117°50E 117 B11
Chaouia-Ouardigha □ Morocco 33°0N 7°30W 136 B2
Chaoyang Guangdong, China 23°17N 116°30E 117 F11
Chaoyang Liaoning, China 41°35N 120°22E 115 D11
Chaozhou China 23°42N 116°32E 117 F11
Chapada Diamantina △ Brazil 12°52S 41°30W 189 C2
Chapada dos Veadeiros △ Brazil 14°0S 47°30W 189 C1
Chapaev Kazakhstan 50°25N 51°10E 86 E10
Chapais Canada 49°47N 74°51W 164 C5
Chapala Mozam. 15°50S 37°35E 143 F4
Chapala, L. de Mexico 20°15N 103°0W 180 C4
Chapayevsk Russia 53°0N 49°40E 86 D9
Chapecó Brazil 27°14S 52°41W 191 B5
Chapel Hill U.S.A. 35°55N 79°4W 177 D15
Chapleau Canada 47°50N 83°24W 164 C3
Chaplin Canada 50°28N 106°40W 163 C7
Chaplin L. Canada 50°22N 106°36W 163 C7
Chaplino Ukraine 48°8N 36°15E 85 H9
Chaplygin Russia 53°15N 40°0E 84 F11
Chappell U.S.A. 41°6N 102°28W 172 E2
Chappells U.S.A. 34°11N 81°52W 178 A8
Chapra = Chhapra India 25°48N 84°44E 125 G11
Chaqābel Iran 33°16N 47°30E 105 F12
Chara Russia 56°54N 118°20E 107 D12
Charadai Argentina 27°35S 59°55W 190 B4
Charagua Bolivia 19°45S 63°10W 186 G6
Charakas Greece 35°1N 25°7E 101 D7
Charambirá, Punta Colombia 4°16N 77°32W 186 C3
Charaña Bolivia 17°30S 69°25W 188 D4
Charantsavan Armenia 40°35N 44°41E 87 K7
Charanwala India 27°51N 72°10E 124 F5
Charata Argentina 27°13S 61°14W 190 B3
Charcas Mexico 23°8N 101°7W 180 C4
Charcot I. Antarctica 70°0S 70°0W 55 C17
Chard U.K. 50°52N 2°58W 67 G5
Chardon U.S.A. 41°35N 81°12W 174 E3
Chardzhou = Türkmenabat Turkmenistan 39°6N 63°34E 129 B9
Charente □ France 45°50N 0°16E 72 C4
Charente → France 45°57N 1°5W 72 C2
Charente-Maritime □ France 45°45N 0°45W 72 C3
Charenton-du-Cher France 46°44N 2°39E 71 F9
Chari → Chad 12°58N 14°31E 135 F8
Chārīkār Afghan. 35°0N 69°10E 109 E7
Charing U.S.A. 32°28N 84°22W 178 C5
Chariton U.S.A. 41°1N 93°19W 172 E7
Chariton → U.S.A. 39°19N 92°58W 172 F7
Chärjew = Türkmenabat Turkmenistan 39°6N 63°34E 129 B9
Charkhari India 25°24N 79°45E 125 G8
Charkhi Dadri India 28°37N 76°17E 124 E7
Charleroi Belgium 50°24N 4°27E 69 D4
Charleroi U.S.A. 40°9N 79°57W 174 F5
Charles, C. U.S.A. 37°7N 75°58W 173 G16
Charles, Peak Australia 32°52S 121°11E 149 F3
Charles City U.S.A. 43°4N 92°41W 172 D7
Charles de Gaulle, Paris ✗ (CDG) France 49°0N 2°32E 71 D9
Charles I. Canada 62°39N 74°15W 161 E17
Charles L. Canada 59°50N 110°33W 163 B6
Charles Sound N.Z. 45°2S 167°4E 155 F2
Charles Town U.S.A. 39°17N 77°52W 173 F15
Charlesbourg Canada 46°51N 71°16W 173 B18
Charleston Ill., U.S.A. 39°30N 88°10W 172 F9
Charleston Miss., U.S.A. 34°1N 90°4W 177 D9
Charleston Mo., U.S.A. 36°55N 89°21W 172 G9
Charleston S.C., U.S.A. 32°46N 79°56W 178 C10
Charleston W. Va., U.S.A. 38°21N 81°38W 173 F13
Charleston L. Canada 44°32N 76°0W 175 B9
Charleston Peak U.S.A. 36°16N 115°42W 171 J11
Charlestown Ireland 53°58N 8°48W 64 C3
Charlestown S. Africa 27°26S 29°53E 145 C4
Charlestown Ind., U.S.A. 38°27N 85°40W 173 F11
Charlestown N.H., U.S.A. 43°14N 72°25W 175 C12
Charlestown of Aberlour U.K. 57°28N 3°14W 65 D5
Charleville Australia 26°24S 146°15E 151 D4
Charleville Ireland 52°21N 8°40W 64 D3
Charleville-Mézières France 49°44N 4°40E 71 C11
Charlevoix U.S.A. 45°19N 85°16W 173 C11
Charlie Gibbs Fracture Zone Atl. Oc. 52°45N 35°30W 56 A8
Charlieu France 46°10N 4°10E 71 F11
Charlotte Mich., U.S.A. 42°34N 84°50W 173 D11
Charlotte N.C., U.S.A. 35°13N 80°50W 177 D14
Charlotte Vt., U.S.A. 44°19N 73°16W 175 B11
Charlotte Amalie U.S. Virgin Is. 18°21N 64°56W 183 e
Charlotte-Douglas Int. ✗ (CLT) U.S.A. 35°12N 80°56W 177 D14
Charlotte Harbor U.S.A. 26°57N 82°4W 179 J7
Charlotte L. Canada 52°12N 125°19W 162 C3
Charlottenberg Sweden 59°54N 12°17E 62 E6
Charlottesville U.S.A. 38°2N 78°30W 173 F14
Charlottetown Nfld. & L., Canada 52°46N 56°7W 165 B8
Charlottetown P.E.I., Canada 46°14N 63°8W 165 C7
Charlotteville Trin. & Tob. 11°20N 60°33W 187 J16
Charlton Australia 36°16S 143°24E 152 D5
Charlton I. Canada 52°0N 79°20W 164 B4
Charmes France 48°22N 6°17E 71 D13
Charny Canada 46°43N 71°15W 165 C5
Charnyany Belarus 51°59N 24°12E 83 G11
Charolles France 46°27N 4°16E 71 F11
Chârost France 47°0N 2°7E 71 F9
Charouine Algeria 29°0N 0°15W 136 C3
Charre Mozam. 17°13S 35°10E 143 F4
Charroux France 46°9N 0°25E 72 B4
Charsadda Pakistan 34°7N 71°45E 124 B4
Charters Towers Australia 20°5S 146°13E 150 C4
Chartres France 48°29N 1°30E 70 D8
Chartreuse ⌂ France 45°22N 5°42E 73 C9
Charysh → Russia 52°22N 83°45E 109 B10
Chascomús Argentina 35°30S 58°0W 190 D4
Chase Canada 50°50N 119°41W 162 C5
Chasefu Zambia 11°55S 33°8E 143 E3
Chashma Barrage Pakistan 32°27N 71°20E 124 C4
Chaslands Mistake N.Z. 46°38S 169°22E 155 G4
Chasseneuil-sur-Bonnieure France 45°52N 0°29E 72 C4
Chāt Iran 37°59N 55°16E 129 B7
Chatal Balkan = Udvoy Balkan Bulgaria 42°50N 26°50E 97 D10
Château-Arnoux-St-Auban France 44°6N 6°0E 73 D10
Château-Chinon France 47°4N 3°56E 71 E10
Château-d'Olonne France 46°30N 1°44W 72 B2
Château-du-Loir France 47°40N 0°25E 70 E7
Château-Gontier France 47°50N 0°48W 70 E6
Château-la-Vallière France 47°30N 0°20E 70 E7
Château-Landon France 48°8N 2°40E 71 D9
Château-Renard France 47°56N 2°55E 71 E9
Château-Renault France 47°36N 0°56E 70 E7
Château-Salins France 48°50N 6°30E 71 D13
Château-Thierry France 49°3N 3°20E 71 C10
Châteaubourg France 48°7N 1°25W 70 D5
Châteaubriant France 47°43N 1°23W 70 E5
Châteaudun France 48°3N 1°20E 70 D8
Chateaugay U.S.A. 44°56N 74°5W 175 B10
Châteaugiron France 48°3N 1°30W 70 D5
Châteauguay, L. Canada 56°26N 70°3W 165 A5
Châteaulin France 48°11N 4°8W 70 D2
Châteaumeillant France 46°35N 2°12E 71 F9
Châteauneuf-du-Faou France 48°11N 3°50W 70 D3
Châteauneuf-sur-Charente France 45°36N 0°3W 72 C3
Châteauneuf-sur-Cher France 46°52N 2°18E 71 F9
Châteauneuf-sur-Loire France 47°52N 2°13E 71 E9
Châteaurenard France 43°53N 4°51E 73 E8
Châteauroux France 46°50N 1°40E 71 F8
Châteauvillain France 48°2N 4°55E 71 D11
Châteaux, Pte. des Guadeloupe 16°15N 61°10W 182 b
Châtel-Guyon France 45°55N 3°4E 72 C7
Châtelaillon-Plage France 46°5N 1°5W 72 B2
Châtellerault France 46°50N 0°30E 70 F7
Châtelus-Malvaleix France 46°18N 2°1E 71 F9
Chatham = Miramichi Canada 47°2N 65°28W 165 C6
Chatham Canada 42°24N 82°11W 174 D2
Chatham U.K. 51°22N 0°32E 67 F8
Chatham U.S.A. 42°21N 73°36W 175 D11
Chatham, I. Chile 50°40S 74°25W 192 D2
Chatham Is. Pac. Oc. 44°0S 176°40W 155 c
Chatham Rise Pac. Oc. 43°30S 180°0E 156 M10
Châtillon Italy 45°45N 7°37E 92 C4
Châtillon-Coligny France 47°50N 2°51E 71 E9
Châtillon-en-Diois France 44°41N 5°29E 73 D9
Châtillon-sur-Indre France 46°59N 1°10E 70 F8
Châtillon-sur-Loire France 47°35N 2°44E 71 E9
Châtillon-sur-Seine France 47°50N 4°33E 71 E11
Chatmohar Bangla. 24°15N 89°15E 125 G13
Chatra India 24°12N 84°56E 125 G11
Chatrapur India 19°22N 85°2E 126 E7
Chats, L. des Canada 45°30N 76°20W 175 A8
Chatsu India 26°36N 75°57E 124 F6
Chatsworth Canada 44°27N 80°54W 174 B4
Chatsworth Zimbabwe 19°38S 31°13E 143 F3
Chāttāgām = Chittagong Bangla. 22°19N 91°48E 123 H17
Chattahoochee U.S.A. 30°42N 84°51W 178 E5
Chattahoochee → U.S.A. 30°54N 84°57W 178 E5
Chattanooga U.S.A. 35°3N 85°19W 177 D12
Chatteris U.K. 52°28N 0°2E 67 E8
Chatturat Thailand 15°40N 101°51E 120 E3
Chau Doc Vietnam 10°42N 105°7E 121 G5
Chaudes-Aigues France 44°51N 3°1E 72 D7
Chauffailles France 46°13N 4°20E 71 F11
Chaukan Pass Burma 27°8N 97°10E 123 F20
Chaumont France 48°7N 5°8E 71 D12
Chaumont U.S.A. 44°4N 76°8W 175 B8
Chaumont-en-Vexin France 49°16N 1°53E 71 C8
Chaumont-sur-Loire France 47°29N 1°11E 70 E8
Chaunay France 46°13N 0°9E 72 B4
Chaunskaya G. Russia 69°0N 169°0E 107 C17
Chauny France 49°37N 3°12E 71 C10
Chaura India 8°27N 93°2E 127 K11
Chausey, Îs. France 48°52N 1°49W 70 D5
Chaussin France 46°59N 5°22E 71 F12
Chautara Nepal 27°46N 85°42E 125 F11
Chautauqua L. U.S.A. 42°10N 79°24W 174 D5
Chauvigny France 46°34N 0°39E 70 F7
Chauvin Canada 52°45N 110°10W 163 C6
Chavakachcheri Sri Lanka 9°39N 80°9E 127 K5
Chavanges France 48°30N 4°35E 71 D11
Chavash Varmane △ Russia 54°50N 47°10E 86 C8
Chaves Brazil 0°15S 49°55W 187 D9
Chaves Portugal 41°45N 7°32W 88 D3
Chavín de Huantar Peru 9°35S 77°10W 188 B2
Chawang Thailand 8°25N 99°30E 121 H2
Chazelles-sur-Lyon France 45°39N 4°22E 73 C8
Chazuta Peru 6°30S 76°0W 188 B2
Chazy U.S.A. 44°53N 73°26W 175 B11
Cheaha Mt. U.S.A. 33°29N 85°49W 178 B4
Cheb Czech Rep. 50°9N 12°28E 78 A5
Chebbi, Erg Africa 31°12N 3°58W 136 B3
Cheboksarskoye Vdkhr. Russia 56°13N 46°58E 86 B8
Cheboksary Russia 56°8N 47°12E 86 B8
Cheboygan U.S.A. 45°39N 84°29W 173 C11
Chebsara Russia 59°10N 38°59E 84 C10
Chech, Erg Africa 25°0N 2°15W 136 D3
Chechelnyk Ukraine 48°13N 29°22E 81 B14
Chechen, Ostrov Russia 43°59N 47°40E 87 H8
Chechenia □ Russia 43°30N 45°29E 87 J7
Checheno-Ingush Republic = Chechenia □ Russia 43°30N 45°29E 87 J7
Chechnya = Chechenia □ Russia 43°30N 45°29E 87 J7
Chęciny Poland 50°46N 20°28E 83 H7
Checotah U.S.A. 35°28N 95°31W 176 D7
Chedabucto B. Canada 45°25N 61°8W 165 C7
Cheduba I. Burma 18°45N 93°40E 123 K18
Cheektowaga U.S.A. 42°54N 78°45W 174 D6
Cheepie Australia 26°33S 145°0E 151 D4
Chef-Boutonne France 46°7N 0°4W 72 B3
Chefchaouen Morocco 35°9N 5°15W 136 A2
Chegdomyn Russia 51°7N 133°1E 107 D14
Chegga Mauritania 25°27N 5°40W 134 C4
Chegutu Zimbabwe 18°10S 30°14E 143 F3
Chehalis U.S.A. 46°40N 122°58W 170 D4
Chehalis → U.S.A. 46°57N 123°50W 170 D3
Cheile Bicazului-Hăşmaş △ Romania 46°55N 25°50E 81 D10
Cheile Nerei-Beusnita △ Romania 44°56N 21°52E 80 F6
Cheiron, Mt. du France 43°49N 6°58E 73 E10
Cheju = Jeju S. Korea 33°31N 126°32E 115 H14
Cheju-do = Jeju-do S. Korea 33°29N 126°34E 115 H14
Cheju Str. = Jeju Haehyop S. Korea 33°50N 126°30E 115 H14
Chek Lap Kok China 22°18N 113°56E 111 a
Chek Lap Kok ✗ (HKG) China 22°19N 113°57E 111 a
Chekalin Russia 54°10N 36°10E 84 E9
Chekhovo Russia 54°33N 20°43E 82 D7
Chekiang = Zhejiang □ China 29°0N 120°0E 117 C13
Chela, Sa. da Angola 16°20S 13°20E 144 A1
Chelan U.S.A. 47°51N 120°1W 168 C3
Chelan, L. U.S.A. 48°11N 120°30W 168 B3
Cheleken = Hazar Turkmenistan 39°34N 53°16E 108 E4
Cheleken Yarymadasy Turkmenistan 39°30N 53°15E 129 B7
Chelforó Argentina 39°0S 66°33W 192 A3
Chéliff, O. → Algeria 36°0N 0°8E 136 A4
Chelkar = Shalqar Kazakhstan 47°48N 59°39E 108 C5
Chellala Dahrania Algeria 33°2N 0°1E 136 B4
Chelles France 48°53N 2°35E 71 D9
Chełm Poland 51°8N 23°30E 83 G10
Chełmno Poland 53°20N 18°30E 83 E5
Chelmsford U.K. 51°44N 0°29E 67 F8
Chełmża Poland 53°10N 18°39E 83 E5
Chelsea Australia 38°5S 145°8E 153 E6
Chelsea U.S.A. 43°59N 72°27W 175 C12
Cheltenham U.K. 51°54N 2°4W 67 F5
Chelva Spain 39°45N 1°0W 90 F4
Chelyabinsk Russia 55°10N 61°24E 108 A6
Chelyuskin, C. = Chelyuskin, Mys Russia 77°30N 103°0E 107 B11
Chelyuskin, Mys Russia 77°30N 103°0E 107 B11
Chemainus Canada 48°55N 123°42W 170 B3
Chemba Mozam. 17°9S 34°53E 141 H6
Chembar = Belinskiy Russia 53°0N 43°25E 86 D6
Chemillé France 47°14N 0°45W 70 E6
Chemin Grenier Mauritius 20°29S 57°28E 141 d
Chemnitz Germany 50°51N 12°54E 76 E8
Chemult U.S.A. 43°14N 121°47W 168 E3
Chen, Gora Russia 65°16N 141°50E 107 C15
Chenab → Pakistan 30°23N 71°2E 124 D4
Chenab Nagar Pakistan 31°45N 72°55E 124 D5
Chenachane Algeria 26°0N 4°15W 136 C3
Chenachane, O. → Algeria 25°20N 3°20W 136 C3
Chenango Forks U.S.A. 42°15N 75°51W 175 D9
Chenchiang = Zhenjiang China 32°11N 119°26E 117 A12
Cheney U.S.A. 47°30N 117°35W 168 C5
Cheng Xian China 33°43N 105°42E 114 H3
Chengalpattu India 12°42N 79°58E 127 H4
Chengbu China 26°18N 110°16E 117 D8
Chengcheng China 35°8N 109°56E 114 G5
Chengchou = Zhengzhou China 34°45N 113°34E 114 G7
Chengde China 40°59N 117°58E 115 D9
Chengdong Hu China 32°15N 116°20E 117 A11
Chengdu China 30°38N 104°2E 116 B5
Chengdu Shuangliu Int. ✗ (CTU) China 30°35N 103°57E 116 B4
Chenggong China 24°52N 102°56E 116 E4
Chenggu China 33°10N 107°21E 116 A6
Chenghai China 23°30N 116°42E 117 F11
Chengjiang China 24°39N 103°0E 116 E4
Chengkou China 31°54N 108°31E 116 B7
Chengmai China 19°50N 109°58E 117 a
Chengshan Jiao China 37°25N 122°44E 115 F12
Ch'engtu = Chengdu China 30°38N 104°2E 116 B5
Chengwu China 34°58N 115°50E 114 G8
Chengxi Hu China 32°15N 116°10E 117 A11
Chengyang China 36°18N 120°21E 115 F11
Chenjiagang China 34°23N 119°47E 115 G10
Chenkaladi Sri Lanka 7°47N 81°35E 127 L5
Chennai India 13°8N 80°19E 127 H5
Chenôve France 47°16N 5°1E 71 E12
Chenxi China 28°2N 110°12E 117 C8
Chenzhou China 25°47N 113°1E 117 E9
Cheò, Eilean a' = Skye U.K. 57°15N 6°10W 65 D2
Cheo Reo Vietnam 13°20N 108°25E 120 F7
Cheom Ksan Cambodia 14°13N 104°56E 120 E5
Cheonan S. Korea 36°48N 127°9E 115 F14
Cheongdo S. Korea 35°38N 128°42E 115 G15
Cheongju S. Korea 36°39N 127°27E 115 F14
Cheorwon S. Korea 38°15N 127°10E 115 E14
Chepelare Bulgaria 41°44N 24°40E 97 E8
Chepelarska → Bulgaria 42°9N 24°54E 97 D8
Chepén Peru 7°15S 79°23W 188 B2
Chepes Argentina 31°20S 66°35W 190 C2
Chepo Panama 9°10N 79°6W 182 E4
Chepstow U.K. 51°38N 2°41W 67 F5
Chequamegon B. U.S.A. 46°39N 90°51W 172 B8
Cher □ France 47°10N 2°30E 71 E9
Cher → France 47°21N 0°29E 70 E7
Chéradi Italy 40°27N 17°10E 95 B10
Cherasco Italy 44°39N 7°51E 92 D4
Cheraw U.S.A. 34°42N 79°53W 177 D15
Cherbourg-Octeville France 49°39N 1°40W 70 C5
Cherchell Algeria 36°35N 2°12E 136 A4
Cherdakly Russia 54°25N 48°50E 86 C9
Cherdyn Russia 60°24N 56°29E 106 C6
Cheremkhovo Russia 53°8N 103°1E 110 A9
Cherepanovo Russia 54°15N 83°30E 109 B10
Cherepovets Russia 59°5N 37°55E 84 C9
Chergui, Chott ech Algeria 34°21N 0°25E 136 B4
Chergui, Zahrez Algeria 35°11N 3°31E 136 A4
Cherial India 17°55N 78°59E 126 F4
Cherikov = Cherykaw Belarus 53°32N 31°20E 75 B16
Cheriyam I. India 10°9N 73°40E 127 J1
Cherkasy Ukraine 49°27N 32°4E 85 H7
Cherkasy □ Ukraine 48°55N 30°50E 85 H6
Cherkessk Russia 44°15N 42°5E 87 H6
Cherla India 18°5N 80°49E 126 E5
Cherlak Russia 54°15N 74°55E 109 B8
Chernaya Russia 70°30N 89°10E 107 B9
Chernelytsya Ukraine 48°49N 25°26E 81 B10
Cherni Bulgaria 42°35N 23°18E 96 D7
Chernigov = Chernihiv Ukraine 51°28N 31°20E 85 G6
Chernigovka Russia 44°19N 132°34E 112 B6
Chernihiv Ukraine 51°28N 31°20E 85 G6
Chernihiv □ Ukraine 51°10N 32°5E 85 G7
Chernivtsi Chernivtsi, Ukraine 48°15N 25°52E 81 B10
Chernivtsi Vinnyts'ka, Ukraine 48°32N 28°9E 81 B13
Chernivtsi □ Ukraine 48°5N 25°30E 81 B10
Chernobyl = Chornobyl Ukraine 51°20N 30°15E 75 C16
Chernogorsk Russia 53°49N 91°18E 109 B12
Chernomorskoye = Chornomorske Ukraine 45°31N 32°40E 85 K7
Chernovtsy = Chernivtsi Ukraine 48°15N 25°52E 81 B10
Chernyakhovsk Russia 54°36N 21°48E 82 D8
Chernyanka Russia 50°56N 37°49E 85 G9
Chernysheyskiy Russia 63°0N 112°30E 107 C12
Chernyye Zemli Russia 46°10N 46°0E 87 H8
Cherokee Iowa, U.S.A. 42°45N 95°33W 172 D6
Cherokee Okla., U.S.A. 36°45N 98°21W 176 C5
Cherokee Village U.S.A. 36°18N 91°31W 176 C9
Cherokees, Grand Lake O' The U.S.A. 36°28N 94°55W 176 C7
Cherquenco Chile 38°35S 72°0W 192 A2
Cherrapunji India 25°17N 91°47E 123 G17
Cherry Valley U.S.A. 42°48N 74°45W 175 D10
Cherskiy Russia 68°45N 161°18E 107 C17
Cherskogo Khrebet Russia 65°0N 143°0E 107 C15
Cherso Greece 41°5N 22°47E 96 E6
Chersonesus Ukraine 44°37N 33°30E 85 K7
Chersonisos Greece 35°18N 25°22E 101 D7
Chersonisos Akrotiri Greece 35°30N 24°10E 101 D6
Cherthala India 9°42N 76°20E 127 K3
Chertkovo Russia 49°25N 40°19E 85 H11
Cherven Belarus 53°45N 28°28E 75 B15
Cherven-Bryag Bulgaria 43°17N 24°7E 97 C8
Chervonoarmiyske Ukraine 45°47N 28°44E 81 E13
Chervonohrad Ukraine 50°25N 24°10E 75 C13
Cherwell → U.K. 51°44N 1°14W 67 F6
Cherykaw Belarus 53°32N 31°20E 75 B16
Chesapeake U.S.A. 36°49N 76°16W 173 G15
Chesapeake B. U.S.A. 38°0N 76°10W 173 F14
Cheshire East □ U.K. 53°15N 2°15W 66 D5
Cheshire West and Chester □ U.K. 53°15N 2°40W 66 D5
Cheshskaya Guba Russia 67°20N 47°0E 106 C5
Cheshunt U.K. 51°43N 0°1W 67 F7
Chesil Beach U.K. 50°37N 2°33W 67 G5
Chesley Canada 44°17N 81°5W 174 B3
Cheste Spain 39°30N 0°41W 91 F4
Chester U.K. 53°12N 2°53W 66 D5
Chester Calif., U.S.A. 40°19N 121°14W 168 F3
Chester Ga., U.S.A. 32°24N 83°9W 178 C6
Chester Ill., U.S.A. 37°55N 89°49W 172 G9
Chester Mont., U.S.A. 48°31N 110°58W 168 B8
Chester Pa., U.S.A. 39°51N 75°22W 173 F16
Chester S.C., U.S.A. 34°43N 81°12W 177 D14
Chester Vt., U.S.A. 43°16N 72°36W 175 C12
Chester W. Va., U.S.A. 40°37N 80°34W 174 F4
Chester-le-Street U.K. 54°51N 1°34W 66 C6
Chesterfield U.K. 53°15N 1°25W 66 D6
Chesterfield, Îs. N. Cal. 19°52S 158°15E 147 C8
Chesterfield Inlet Canada 63°30N 90°45W 160 E13
Chesterton Ra. Australia 25°30S 147°27E 151 D4
Chesterton Range △ Australia 26°16S 147°22E 151 D4
Chestertown U.S.A. 43°40N 73°48W 175 C11
Chesterville Canada 45°6N 75°14W 175 A9
Chesuncook L. U.S.A. 46°0N 69°21W 173 C19
Chetamale India 10°43N 92°33E 127 J11
Chéticamp Canada 46°37N 60°59W 165 C7
Chetlat I. India 11°42N 72°42E 127 J1
Chetrosu Moldova 48°5N 27°54E 81 B12
Chetumal Mexico 18°30N 88°20W 181 D7
Chetumal, B. de Cent. Amer. 18°40N 88°10W 181 D7
Chetwynd Canada 55°45N 121°36W 162 B4
Cheung Chau China 22°13N 114°1E 111 a
Chevanceaux France 45°18N 0°14W 72 C3
Cheviot, The U.K. 55°29N 2°9W 66 B5
Cheviot Hills U.K. 55°20N 2°30W 66 B5
Cheviot Ra. Australia 25°20S 143°45E 150 D3
Chew Bahir Ethiopia 4°40N 36°50E 131 G2
Chewelah U.S.A. 48°17N 117°43W 168 B5
Chewore ⌂ Zimbabwe 16°0S 29°52E 143 F2
Cheyenne Okla., U.S.A. 35°37N 99°40W 176 D5
Cheyenne Wyo., U.S.A. 41°8N 104°49W 168 F11
Cheyenne → U.S.A. 44°41N 101°18W 172 C3
Cheyenne Wells U.S.A. 38°49N 102°21W 168 G12
Cheyne B. Australia 34°35S 118°50E 149 F2
Cheyur India 12°21N 80°0E 127 H5
Chhabra India 24°40N 76°54E 124 G7
Chhaktala India 22°6N 74°11E 124 H6
Chhapra India 25°48N 84°44E 125 G11
Chhata India 27°42N 77°30E 124 F7
Chhatarpur Jharkhand, India 24°23N 84°11E 125 G11
Chhatarpur Mad. P., India 24°55N 79°35E 125 G8
Chhati India 20°47N 81°40E 126 D5
Chhattisgarh □ India 22°0N 82°0E 125 J10
Chhep Cambodia 13°45N 105°24E 120 F5
Chhindwara Mad. P., India 23°3N 79°29E 125 H8
Chhindwara Mad. P., India 22°2N 78°59E 125 H8
Chhinhdipada India 21°6N 84°52E 126 D7
Chhlong Cambodia 12°15N 105°58E 121 F5
Chhota Tawa → India 22°14N 76°36E 124 H7
Chhoti Kali Sindh → India 24°2N 75°31E 124 G6
Chhuikhadan India 21°32N 80°59E 125 J9
Chhuk Cambodia 10°46N 104°28E 121 G5
Chi → Thailand 15°11N 104°43E 120 E5
Chi Thanh Vietnam 13°17N 109°16E 120 F7
Chiai Taiwan 23°29N 120°25E 117 F13
Chiali Taiwan 23°9N 120°10E 117 F13
Chianciano Terme Italy 43°2N 11°49E 93 E8
Chiang Dao Thailand 19°22N 98°58E 120 C2
Chiang Dao, Doi Thailand 19°23N 98°54E 120 C2
Chiang Kham Thailand 19°32N 100°18E 120 C3
Chiang Khan Thailand 17°52N 101°36E 120 D3
Chiang Khong Thailand 20°17N 100°24E 116 G3
Chiang Mai Thailand 18°47N 98°59E 120 C2
Chiang Rai Thailand 19°52N 99°50E 116 H2
Chiang Saen Thailand 20°16N 100°5E 116 G3
Chianti Italy 43°32N 11°25E 93 E8
Chiapa de Corzo Mexico 16°42N 93°0W 181 D6
Chiapas □ Mexico 16°30N 92°30W 181 D6
Chiapas, Sa. Madre de Mexico 15°40N 93°0W 181 D6
Chiaramonte Gulfi Italy 37°2N 14°42E 95 E7
Chiaravalle Italy 43°36N 13°19E 93 E10
Chiaravalle Centrale Italy 38°41N 16°25E 95 D9
Chiari Italy 45°32N 9°56E 92 C6
Chiatura Georgia 42°15N 43°17E 87 J6
Chiautla de Tapia Mexico 18°18N 98°36W 181 D5
Chiávari Italy 44°19N 9°19E 92 D6
Chiavenna Italy 46°19N 9°24E 92 B6
Chiba Japan 35°30N 140°7E 113 G10
Chiba □ Japan 35°30N 140°20E 113 G10
Chibabava Mozam. 20°17S 33°35E 145 B5
Chibemba Cunene, Angola 15°48S 14°8E 141 H2
Chibemba Huila, Angola 16°20S 15°20E 144 A2
Chibi Zimbabwe 20°18S 30°25E 145 B5
Chibia Angola 15°10S 13°42E 141 H2
Chibougamau Canada 49°56N 74°24W 164 C5
Chibougamau, L. Canada 49°50N 74°20W 164 C5
Chibuk Nigeria 10°52N 12°50E 139 C7
Chibuto Mozam. 24°40S 33°33E 145 B5
Chic-Chocs, Mts. Canada 48°55N 66°0W 165 C6
Chicacole = Srikakulam India 18°14N 83°58E 126 E6
Chicago U.S.A. 41°52N 87°38W 172 E10
Chicago Heights U.S.A. 41°30N 87°38W 172 E10
Chichagof I. U.S.A. 57°30N 135°30W 160 F4
Chichaoua Morocco 31°32N 8°44W 136 B2
Chichawatni Pakistan 30°32N 72°42E 124 D5
Chichén-Itzá Mexico 20°37N 88°35W 181 C7
Chicheng China 40°55N 115°55E 114 D8
Chichester U.K. 50°50N 0°47W 67 G7
Chichester Ra. Australia 22°12S 119°15E 148 D2
Chichibu Japan 35°59N 139°10E 113 F9
Chichibu-Tama-Kai △ Japan 35°52N 138°42E 113 G9
Ch'ich'ihaerh = Qiqihar China 47°26N 124°0E 11
Chicholi India 22°1N 77°40E 1
Chickasaw ⌂ U.S.A. 34°26N 97°0W 1
Chickasha U.S.A. 35°3N 97°58W 1
Chiclana de la Frontera Spain 36°26N 6°9W
Chiclayo Peru 6°42S 79°50W 1
Chico U.S.A. 39°44N 121°50W 1
Chico → Chubut, Argentina 44°0S 67°0W 1
Chico → Santa Cruz, Argentina 50°0S 68°30W 1
Chicoa Mozam. 15°36S 32°20E 1
Chicomo Mozam. 24°31S 34°6E 1
Chicomostoc Mexico 22°28N 102°46W 1
Chicontepec Mexico 20°58N 98°10W 1
Chicopee U.S.A. 42°9N 72°37W 17
Chicoutimi Canada 48°28N 71°5W 1
Chicualacuala Mozam. 22°6S 31°42E 1
Chidambaram India 11°20N 79°45E 1
Chidenguele Mozam. 24°55S 34°11E 1
Chidley, C. Canada 60°23N 64°26W 16
Chiducuane Mozam. 24°35S 34°25E 1
Chiede Angola 17°15S 16°22E 1
Chiefland U.S.A. 29°29N 82°52W 1
Chiefs Pt. Canada 44°41N 81°18W 1
Chiem Hoa Vietnam 22°12N 105°17E 1
Chiemsee Germany 47°53N 12°28E
Chiengi Zambia 8°45S 29°10E 1
Chiengmai = Chiang Mai Thailand 18°47N 98°59E 1
Chienti → Italy 43°18N 13°45E 9
Chieri Italy 45°1N 7°49E
Chiers → France 49°39N 4°59E 7
Chiesa in Valmalenco Italy 46°16N 9°51E
Chiese → Italy 45°8N 10°25E
Chieti Italy 42°21N 14°10E
Chifeng China 42°18N 118°58E 11
Chigirin Ukraine 49°4N 32°38E
Chignecto B. Canada 45°30N 64°40W 1
Chiguana Bolivia 21°0S 67°58W 1
Chigwell U.K. 51°37N 0°6E
Chihli, G. of = Bo Hai China 39°0N 119°0E 11
Chihuahua Mexico 28°38N 106°5W 1
Chihuahua □ Mexico 28°30N 106°0W 1
Chiili = Shīeli Kazakhstan 44°20N 66°15E 1
Chik Bollapur India 13°25N 77°45E 1
Chikalda India 21°24N 77°19E 1
Chikhli Ahmadabad, India 20°45N 73°4E 1
Chikhli Maharashtra, India 20°20N 76°18E 1
Chikkamagaluru India 13°15N 75°45E 1
Chiknayakanhalli India 13°26N 76°37E 1
Chikodi India 16°26N 74°38E 1
Chikwawa Malawi 16°2S 34°50E 1
Chilanga Zambia 15°33S 28°16E 1
Chilapa Mexico 17°36N 99°10W 1
Chilas Pakistan 35°25N 74°5E 1
Chilaw Sri Lanka 7°30N 79°50E 1
Chilcotin → Canada 51°44N 122°23W 1
Childers Australia 25°15S 152°17E 1
Childersburg U.S.A. 33°16N 86°21W 1
Childress U.S.A. 34°25N 100°13W 1
Chile ■ S. Amer. 35°0S 72°0W 1
Chile Chico Chile 46°33S 71°44W 1
Chile Rise Pac. Oc. 38°0S 92°0W 15
Chilecito Argentina 29°10S 67°30W 1
Chilete Peru 7°10S 78°50W 1
Chilia, Braţul → Romania 45°14N 29°42E 8
Chilik = Shelek Kazakhstan 43°33N 78°17E 1
Chililabombwe Zambia 12°18S 27°43E 1
Chilim Pakistan 35°5N 75°5E 1
Chilin = Jilin China 43°44N 126°30E 11
Chiliomodi Greece 37°48N 22°51E
Chilka L. India 19°40N 85°25E 1
Chilko → Canada 52°0N 123°40W 1
Chilko L. Canada 51°20N 124°10W 1
Chillagoe Australia 17°7S 144°33E 1
Chillán Chile 36°40S 72°10W 1
Chillicothe Ill., U.S.A. 40°55N 89°29W 1
Chillicothe Mo., U.S.A. 39°48N 93°33W 1
Chillicothe Ohio, U.S.A. 39°20N 82°59W 17
Chilliwack Canada 49°10N 121°54W 1
Chilo India 27°25N 73°32E 1
Chiloane, I. Mozam. 20°40S 34°55E 1
Chiloé, I. de Chile 42°30S 73°50W 1
Chiloé △ Chile 42°11S 73°59W 1
Chilpancingo Mexico 17°33N 99°30W 1
Chiltern Australia 36°10S 146°36E 1
Chiltern Hills U.K. 51°40N 0°53W
Chilton U.S.A. 44°2N 88°10W 1
Chilubi Zambia 11°5S 29°58E 1
Chilubula Zambia 10°14S 30°51E 1
Chilumba Malawi 10°28S 34°12E 1
Chilung Taiwan 25°3N 121°45E 11
Chilwa, L. Malawi 15°15S 35°40E 1
Chimaltitán Mexico 21°35N 103°50W 1
Chimán Panama 8°45N 78°40W 1
Chimanimani Zimbabwe 19°48S 32°52E 1
Chimanimani △ Zimbabwe 19°48S 33°0E 1
Chimay Belgium 50°3N 4°20E
Chimayo U.S.A. 36°0N 105°56W 16
Chimba Zambia 9°54S 31°28E 1
Chimborazo Ecuador 1°29S 78°55W 1
Chimbote Peru 9°0S 78°35W 1
Chimboy Uzbekistan 42°57N 59°47E 1
Chimkent = Shymkent Kazakhstan 42°18N 69°36E 1
Chimoio Mozam. 19°4S 33°30E 1
Chimpembe Zambia 9°31S 29°33E 1
Chimur India 20°30N 79°23E 1
Chin □ Burma 22°0N 93°0E 12
Chin Hills Burma 22°30N 93°30E 12
Chin Ling Shan = Qinling Shandi China 33°50N 108°10E 11
China Mexico 25°42N 99°14W 1
China ■ Asia 30°0N 110°0E 11
China, Great Plain of Asia 35°0N 115°0E 10
China Lake U.S.A. 35°44N 117°37W 1
Chinan = Jinan China 36°38N 117°1E 1
Chinandega Nic. 12°35N 87°12W 1

...ati Peak *U.S.A.* 29°57N 104°29W **176** G2
...cha Alta *Peru* 13°25S 76°47W **188** C2
...chaga → *Canada* 58°53N 118°20W **162** B5
...cheros *Peru* 13°30S 73°44W **188** C3
...chilla *Australia* 26°45S 150°38E **151** D5
...chilla de Monte Aragón
    ... 38°53N 1°40W **91** G3
...choli *India* 17°28N 77°26E **126** E3
...chorro, Banco
...exico 18°35N 87°22W **181** D7
...chou = Jinzhou
...ina 41°5N 121°3E **115** D11
...coteague *U.S.A.* 37°56N 75°23W **173** G16
 de Mozam. 18°35S 36°34E **143** F4
...dwin → *Burma* 21°26N 95°15E **123** J19
...ga *Mozam.* 33°2N 75°15E **125** C6
...gole *Malawi* 13°4S 34°17E **143** E3
...gtao = Qingdao
...ina 36°5N 120°20E **115** F11
...guetti *Mauritania* 20°25N 12°24W **134** D3
...gune *Mozam.* 20°33S 34°58E **145** B5
...hanguanine
...ina 25°21S 32°30E **145** C5
...hoyi *Zimbabwe* 17°20S 30°8E **143** F3
...iot *Pakistan* 31°45N 73°0E **124** D5
...ipas *Mexico* 27°23N 108°32W **180** B3
...ji *Pakistan* 32°42N 72°22E **124** C5
...ju = Jinju
...Korea 35°12N 128°2E **115** G15
...kapook *Australia* 35°11S 142°57E **152** C5
...ko → *C.A.R.* 4°50N 23°53E **140** D4
 de *U.S.A.* 36°9N 109°33W **169** H9
...men *Taiwan* 24°26N 118°19E **117** E12
...men Tao *Taiwan* 24°26N 118°22E **117** E12
...namanur *India* 9°50N 77°24E **127** K3
...nampo = Namp'o
...Korea 38°52N 125°10E **115** E13
...o *Japan* 35°59N 138°9E **113** G9
...o Valley *U.S.A.* 34°45N 112°27W **169** J17
...on *France* 47°10N 0°15E **70** E7
...ook *U.S.A.* 48°35N 109°14W **168** B9
...ook Trough
...t. Oc. 44°0N 175°0W **156** C10
...sali *Zambia* 10°30S 32°2E **143** E3
...sura = Chunchura
...lia 22°53N 88°27E **125** H13
...tamani *India* 13°26N 78°3E **127** H4
...ggia *Italy* 45°13N 12°17E **93** C9
...ata *Zambia* 13°38S 32°28E **143** E3
...erceni *Moldova* 47°31N 28°50E **81** C13
...indo *Angola* 13°49S 15°48E **141** G3
...inge → *U.S.A.* 20°13S 32°28E **143** G3
...inge ○ *Zimbabwe* 20°14S 33°0E **143** G3
...iona *Spain* 36°44N 6°26W **89** J4
...ley *U.S.A.* 30°47N 85°32W **178** E4
...lun *India* 17°31N 73°34E **126** F1
...man *Canada* 46°6N 65°53W **165** C6
...oka *Malawi* 13°57S 34°28E **143** E3
...penham *U.K.* 51°27N 2°6W **67** F5
...pewa → *U.S.A.* 44°25N 92°5W **172** C7
...pewa Falls *U.S.A.* 44°56N 91°24W **172** C8
...ping Norton *U.K.* 51°56N 1°32W **67** F6
...rovtsi *Bulgaria* 43°24N 22°52E **96** C6
...utneticook Lakes
...Amer. 45°35N 67°35W **173** C20
...uián *Peru* 10°10S 77°0W **188** C2
...uibul △ *Belize* 16°49N 88°52W **182** C2
...uimula *Guatemala* 14°51N 89°37W **182** D2
...uinquira *Colombia* 5°38N 73°36W **186** B4
 → *Russia* 48°30N 43°0E **87** F6
...ala *India* 15°50N 80°26E **127** G5
...amba *Mozam.* 16°55S 34°39E **143** F3
...awa *India* 28°14N 75°42E **124** E6
...hiq *Uzbekistan* 41°29N 69°35E **109** D7
...cahua △ *U.S.A.* 32°0N 109°20W **169** K9
...cahua Peak
...S.A. 31°51N 109°18W **169** K9
...kofi *U.S.A.* 55°50N 155°40W **166** D8
...qui, G. de *Panama* 8°0N 82°10W **182** E3
...qui, L. de *Panama* 9°10N 82°0W **182** E3
...tira Falls
...mbia 21°10S 32°12E **143** G3
...miri *India* 23°15N 82°20E **125** H10
...nogi *Russia* 44°7N 26°32E **81** F11
...pan *Bulgaria* 42°10N 25°19E **97** D9
...ripó Grande, Cerro
...sta Rica 9°29N 83°29W **182** E3
...undu *Zimbabwe* 16°3S 28°50E **145** A4
...amba *Zambia* 14°55S 28°20E **143** E2
...apani *Nepal* 28°37N 81°16E **125** E9
...asibi *Canada* 53°50N 79°0W **164** B4
...han *Taiwan* 22°44N 120°31E **117** F13
...holm *Canada* 54°55N 114°10W **162** C6
...holm *U.S.A.* 47°29N 92°53W **172** B7
...htian Mandi
...kistan 29°50N 72°55E **124** E5
...hui *China* 28°30N 105°42E **116** C5
...imaio = Kismaayo
...malia 0°22S 42°32E **131** H3
...Falls *Zambia* 28°49N 105°50E **116** C5
...ânău *Moldova* 47°2N 28°50E **81** C13
...ânău ✈ (KIV)
...oldova 47°3N 28°46E **81** C13
...ineu Criș *Romania* 46°32N 21°37E **80** D6
...one → *Italy* 44°49N 7°22E **92** D5
...os Mts. *U.S.A.* 29°5N 103°15W **176** A2
...a *Russia* 52°0N 113°35E **111** A11
...pa *Italy* 17°10N 72°9E **143** D3
...pa *Malawi* 9°41S 33°19E **143** D3
...se *Japan* 42°49N 141°39E **112** C10
...adurga *India* 14°14N 76°24E **127** G3
...rakot *India* 19°10N 81°44E **126** E5
...nal *Pakistan* 35°50N 71°15E **122** B7
...ravati → *India* 14°45N 78°15E **127** G4
...pa *India* 7°59N 80°27E **132** L1
...tagong *Bangla.* 22°19N 91°48E **123** H17
...tagong □ *Bangla.* 24°5N 91°0E **123** G17
...taurgarh *India* 24°53N 74°38E **124** G6
...toor *India* 13°15N 79°5E **127** H4
...tor *India* 10°40N 76°45E **127** J3
...ngwiza *Zimbabwe* 18°0S 31°6E **143** F3
...i *Italy* 43°1N 11°57E **93** E8

Chiva *Spain* 39°27N 0°41W **91** F4
Chivasso *Italy* 45°11N 7°53E **92** C4
Chivay *Peru* 15°40S 71°35W **188** D3
Chive *Bolivia* 12°23S 68°35W **188** C4
Chivhu *Zimbabwe* 19°2S 30°52E **143** F3
Chivilcoy *Argentina* 34°55S 60°0W **190** C4
Chiwanda *Tanzania* 11°23S 34°55E **143** E3
Chixi *China* 22°0N 112°58E **117** G9
Chizarira = *Zimbabwe* 17°44S 27°52E **143** F2
Chizarira Ra. *Zimbabwe* 17°36S 27°45E **143** F2
Chizela *Zambia* 13°8S 25°0E **143** E2
Chkalov = Orenburg
 Russia 51°45N 55°6E **108** B5
Chkolovsk *Russia* 56°50N 43°10E **86** B6
Chloride *U.S.A.* 35°25N 114°12W **171** K12
Chlumec nad Cidlinou
 Czech Rep. 50°9N 15°29E **78** A8
Chmielnik *Poland* 50°37N 20°43E **83** H7
Cho-do *N. Korea* 38°30N 124°40E **115** E13
Cho Phuoc Hai
 Vietnam 10°26N 107°18E **121** G6
Choa Chu Kang
 Singapore 1°22N 103°41E **121** d
Chobe △ *Botswana* 18°37S 24°23E **144** A4
Chociánow *Poland* 51°27N 15°55E **83** G2
Chociwel *Poland* 53°29N 15°21E **82** E2
Chocolate Mts.
 U.S.A. 33°15N 115°15W **171** M11
Choctawhatchee →
 U.S.A. 30°25N 86°8W **178** E3
Choctawhatchee B.
 U.S.A. 30°20N 86°20W **179** E3
Chodavaram *Andhra Pradesh,*
 India 17°50N 82°57E **126** F6
Chodavaram *Andhra Pradesh,*
 India 17°27N 81°46E **126** F5
Chodecz *Poland* 52°24N 19°2E **83** F6
Chodov *Czech Rep.* 50°15N 12°45E **78** A5
Chodziez *Poland* 52°58N 16°58E **83** F3
Choele Choel *Argentina* 39°11S 65°40W **192** A3
Chogha Zanbil *Iran* 32°1N 48°32E **128** D6
Choiseul *St. Lucia* 13°47N 61°3W **183** f
Choiseul *Solomon Is.* 7°0S 156°40E **147** B8
Choix *Mexico* 26°43N 108°17W **180** B3
Chojna *Poland* 52°58N 14°25E **83** F1
Chojnice *Poland* 53°42N 17°32E **82** E4
Chojnów *Poland* 51°18N 15°58E **83** G2
Chok Chai *Thailand* 14°44N 102°10E **120** E4
Chōkai-San *Japan* 39°6N 140°3E **112** E10
Choke Canyon Res.
 U.S.A. 28°30N 98°20W **176** G5
Chokurdakh *Russia* 70°38N 147°55E **107** B15
Chokwé *Mozam.* 24°32S 32°59E **145** B5
Cholame *U.S.A.* 35°44N 120°18W **170** K6
Cholet *France* 47°4N 0°52W **70** E6
Cholguan *Chile* 37°10S 72°3W **190** D1
Choloma *Honduras* 15°37N 87°57W **182** C2
Cholpon-Ata *Kyrgyzstan* 42°40N 77°6E **109** D9
Choluteca *Honduras* 13°20N 87°14W **182** D2
Choluteca → *Honduras* 13°0N 87°20W **182** D2
Chom Bung *Thailand* 13°37N 99°36E **120** F2
Chom Thong *Thailand* 18°25N 98°41E **120** C2
Choma *Zambia* 16°48S 26°59E **143** F2
Chomolungma = Everest, Mt.
 Nepal 28°5N 86°58E **125** E12
Chomun *India* 27°15N 75°40E **124** F6
Chomutov *Czech Rep.* 50°28N 13°23E **78** A6
Chon Buri *Thailand* 13°21N 101°1E **120** F3
Chon Thanh *Vietnam* 11°24N 106°36E **121** G6
Chone *Ecuador* 0°40S 80°0W **186** D3
Chong Kai *Cambodia* 13°57N 103°35E **120** F4
Chong Mek *Thailand* 15°10N 105°27E **120** E5
Chong Phangan *Thailand* 9°39N 100°0E **121** b
Chong Samui *Thailand* 9°30N 100°0E **121** b
Chongde *China* 30°38N 120°52E **117** B13
Ch'ŏngjin *N. Korea* 41°47N 129°50E **115** D15
Chŏngju *N. Korea* 39°40N 125°5E **115** E13
Chongli *China* 40°58N 115°15E **114** D8
Chongming *China* 31°38N 121°30E **117** B13
Chongming Dao
 China 31°40N 121°30E **117** B13
Chongoni Rock Art
 Malawi 14°17S 34°16E **143** E3
Chongoyape *Peru* 6°35S 79°25W **188** B2
Chŏngp'yŏng
 N. Korea 39°47N 127°23E **115** E14
Chongqing *Chongqing,*
 China 29°35N 106°25E **116** C6
Chongqing *Sichuan,*
 China 30°38N 103°40E **116** B4
Chongqing Jiangbei Int. ✈ (CKG)
 China 29°35N 106°25E **116** C6
Chongqing Shi □ *China* 30°0N 108°0E **116** C6
Chongren *China* 27°46N 116°3E **117** D11
Chongwe *Zambia* 15°21S 28°42E **143** F2
Chongyi *China* 25°45N 114°29E **117** E10
Chongzuo *China* 22°23N 107°20E **116** E6
Chonogol *Mongolia* 45°54N 115°22E **114** B8
Chonos, Arch. de los
 Chile 45°0S 75°0W **192** C2
Chop *Ukraine* 48°26N 22°12E **80** B7
Chopda *India* 21°20N 75°15E **126** D2
Chopim → *Brazil* 25°35S 53°5W **191** B5
Chor *Pakistan* 25°31N 69°46E **124** G3
Chora *Greece* 37°3N 21°42E **98** D3
Chora Sfakion *Greece* 35°15N 24°9E **101** D6
Chorbat La *India* 34°42N 76°37E **125** B7
Chorley *U.K.* 53°39N 2°38W **66** D5
Chorna *Ukraine* 47°36N 29°20E **81** C14
Chornobyl *Ukraine* 51°20N 30°15E **75** C16
Chornomorske *Ukraine* 45°31N 32°40E **85** K7
Chorolque, Cerro
 Bolivia 20°59S 66°5W **190** A2
Choroszcz *Poland* 53°10N 22°59E **83** E9
Chorregon *Australia* 22°40S 143°32E **150** C3
Chorro el Indio △
 Venezuela 7°43N 72°9W **183** E5
Chortkiv *Ukraine* 49°2N 25°46E **75** D13
Chorzele *Poland* 53°15N 20°55E **83** E7
Chorzów *Poland* 50°18N 18°57E **83** H5
Chos-Malal *Argentina* 37°20S 70°15W **190** D1
Ch'osan *N. Korea* 40°50N 125°47E **115** D13
Choszczno *Poland* 53°7N 15°25E **82** E2
Chota *Peru* 6°33S 78°39W **188** B2
Choteau *U.S.A.* 47°49N 112°11W **168** C7
Chotěboř *Czech Rep.* 49°43N 15°40E **78** B8
Chotila *India* 22°23N 71°15E **124** H7
Chotta Udepur *India* 22°19N 74°1E **124** H6
Chowchilla *U.S.A.* 37°7N 120°16W **170** H6
Choybalsan *Mongolia* 48°4N 114°30E **111** B11

Choyr *Mongolia* 46°24N 108°30E **111** B10
Chrisoupoli *Greece* 40°58N 24°42E **97** F8
Chrissi = Gaidouronisi
 Greece 34°53N 25°41E **101** E7
Christchurch *N.Z.* 43°33S 172°47E **155** D7
Christchurch *U.K.* 50°44N 1°47W **67** G6
Christian I. *Canada* 44°50N 80°12W **174** B7
Christian Sd. *U.S.A.* 55°56N 134°40W **167** D13
Christiana *Greece* 36°14N 25°13E **96** D7
Christiana *S. Africa* 27°52S 25°8E **144** C4
Christiansfeld *Denmark* 55°21N 9°29E **63** J3
Christianshåb = Qasigiannguit
 Greenland 68°50N 51°18W **57** D5
Christiansted
 U.S. Virgin Is. 17°45N 64°42W **183** C7
Christie B. *Canada* 62°32N 111°10W **163** A6
Christmas Cr. →
 Australia 18°29S 125°23E **148** C4
Christmas I. = Kiritimati
 Kiribati 1°58N 157°27W **157** G12
Christmas I. *Ind. Oc.* 10°30S 105°40E **146** N9
Christopher, L.
 Australia 24°49S 127°42E **149** D4
Chrudim *Czech Rep.* 49°58N 15°43E **78** B8
Chrzanów *Poland* 50°10N 19°21E **83** H6
Chtimba *Malawi* 10°35S 34°13E **143** E3
Chū = Shū *Kazakhstan* 43°36N 73°42E **109** D8
Chū = Shū →
 Kazakhstan 45°0N 67°44E **109** D7
Chu → *Vietnam* 19°53N 105°45E **120** C5
Chu Lai *Vietnam* 15°28N 108°45E **120** E7
Chu Mom Ray △
 Vietnam 14°29N 107°38E **120** E6
Chu Se *Vietnam* 13°40N 108°8E **120** F7
Chuadanga *Bangla.* 23°38N 88°51E **125** H13
Chuak, Ko *Thailand* 9°28N 99°41E **121** b
Ch'uanchou = Quanzhou
 China 24°55N 118°34E **117** E12
Chuankou *China* 32°0N 110°59E **114** G6
Chubbuck *U.S.A.* 42°55N 112°28W **168** E7
Chūbu □ *Japan* 36°45N 137°30E **113** F8
Chūbu-Sangaku △
 Japan 36°30N 137°40E **113** F8
Chubut □ *Argentina* 43°30S 69°0W **192** B3
Chubut → *Argentina* 43°20S 65°5W **192** B3
Chuçand = Khŭjand
 Tajikistan 40°17N 69°37E **109** D7
Chuchi L. *Canada* 55°12N 124°30W **162** B4
Chuda *India* 22°29N 71°41E **124** H4
Chudovo *Russia* 59°10N 31°41E **84** C6
Chudskoye, Ozero
 Russia 58°13N 27°30E **84** C4
Chugach Mts. *U.S.A.* 60°45N 147°0W **166** C10
Chūgoku □ *Japan* 35°0N 133°0E **113** G6
Chūgoku-Sanchi *Japan* 35°0N 133°0E **113** G6
Chuguyev = Chuhuyiv
 Ukraine 49°55N 36°45E **85** H9
Chugwater *U.S.A.* 41°46N 104°50W **168** F11
Chuhuyiv *Ukraine* 49°55N 36°45E **85** H9
Chuka *Kenya* 0°20S 37°39E **142** C4
Chukchi Plateau *Arctic* 78°0N 165°0W **54** B17
Chukchi Sea *Russia* 68°0N 175°0W **107** C19
Chukotskiy, Mys
 Russia 64°14N 173°8W **166** C1
Chukotskiy Poluostrov
 Russia 66°0N 174°0W **166** B5
Chukotskoye Nagorye
 Russia 68°0N 175°0E **107** C18
Chula *U.S.A.* 31°33N 83°32W **178** D6
Chula Vista *U.S.A.* 32°38N 117°5W **171** N9
Chulband → *India* 20°40N 79°54E **126** B6
Chulucanas *Peru* 5°8S 80°10W **188** B1
Chulumani *Bolivia* 16°24S 67°31W **188** D4
Chulym → *Russia* 57°43N 83°51E **106** D9
Chum Phae *Thailand* 16°40N 102°6E **120** D4
Chum Saeng *Thailand* 15°55N 100°15E **120** E3
Chuma *Bolivia* 15°24S 68°56W **188** D4
Chumar *India* 32°40N 78°35E **125** C8
Chumbicha *Argentina* 29°0S 66°10W **190** B2
Chumerna *Bulgaria* 42°45N 25°55E **97** D9
Chumikan *Russia* 54°40N 135°10E **107** D14
Chumphon *Thailand* 10°35N 99°14E **121** G2
Chumpi *Peru* 15°4S 73°46W **188** D3
Chumuare *Mozam.* 14°31S 31°50E **143** E3
Chuna → *Russia* 57°47N 94°37E **107** D10
Chun'an *China* 29°35N 119°3E **117** C12
Chuncheon *S. Korea* 37°58N 127°44E **115** F14
Chunchura *India* 22°53N 88°27E **125** H13
Chunga *Zambia* 15°0S 26°2E **143** F2
Chunggang-ŭp
 N. Korea 41°48N 126°48E **115** D14
Chunghwa *N. Korea* 38°52N 125°47E **115** E13
Chungju *S. Korea* 36°58N 127°58E **115** F14
Chungking = Chongqing
 China 29°35N 106°25E **116** C6
Chungli *Taiwan* 24°57N 121°13E **117** E13
Chungt'iaoshan = Zhongtiao
 Shan *China* 35°0N 111°10E **114** G6
Chungyang Shanmo
 Taiwan 23°10N 121°0E **117** F13
Chunian *Pakistan* 30°57N 74°0E **124** D6
Chunya *Tanzania* 8°30S 33°27E **143** D3
Chunyang *China* 43°38N 129°23E **115** C15
Chupara Pt.
 Trin. & Tob. 10°49N 61°22W **187** K15
Chuquibamba *Peru* 15°47S 72°44W **188** D3
Chuquibambilla *Peru* 14°7S 72°41W **188** D3
Chuquicamata *Chile* 22°15S 69°0W **190** A2
Chur *Switz.* 46°52N 9°32E **77** J5
Churachandpur *India* 24°20N 93°40E **123** H18
Church Stretton *U.K.* 52°32N 2°48W **67** E5
Churchill *Canada* 58°47N 94°11W **163** B10
Churchill → *Man.,*
 Canada 58°47N 94°12W **163** B10
Churchill → *Nfld. & L.,*
 Canada 53°19N 60°10W **165** B7
Churchill, C. *Canada* 58°46N 93°12W **163** B10
Churchill Falls *Canada* 53°36N 64°19W **165** B7
Churchill L. *Canada* 55°55N 108°20W **162** B7
Churchill Pk. *Canada* 58°10N 125°10W **162** B3
Churki *India* 23°50N 83°12E **125** H10
Churu *India* 28°20N 74°50E **124** E6
Churún Merú = Angel Falls
 Venezuela 5°57N 62°30W **186** B6
Chushal *India* 33°40N 78°40E **125** C8
Chuska Mts. *U.S.A.* 36°15N 108°50W **169** H9
Chusovoy *Russia* 58°22N 57°50E **106** D6
Chuspipata *Bolivia* 16°18S 67°48W **188** D4
Chust *Uzbekistan* 40°0N 71°13E **109** D7

Chute-aux-Outardes
 Canada 49°7N 68°24W **165** C6
Chuuk = Truk
 Micronesia 7°25N 151°46E **156** G7
Chuvash Republic = Chuvashia □
 Russia 55°30N 47°0E **86** C8
Chuvashia □ *Russia* 55°30N 47°0E **86** C8
Chuwārtah *Iraq* 35°43N 45°34E **105** E11
Chuxiong *China* 25°2N 101°28E **116** E3
Chūy □ *Kyrgyzstan* 42°55N 75°15E **109** D9
Chuy *Uruguay* 33°41S 53°27W **191** C5
Chūy □ *Kyrgyzstan* 42°55N 75°16E **109** D9
Chuzhou *China* 32°19N 118°20E **117** A12
Chynadiyeve *Ukraine* 48°29N 22°50E **80** B7
Chyulu Hills *Kenya* 2°35S 37°50E **142** C4
Ci Xian *China* 36°20N 114°25E **114** F8
Ciacova *Romania* 45°35N 21°10E **80** E6
Ciamis *Indonesia* 7°20S 108°21E **119** G13
Cianjur *Indonesia* 6°49S 107°8E **119** G12
Cianorte *Brazil* 23°37S 52°37W **191** A5
Cibola *U.S.A.* 33°17N 114°42W **171** M12
Cicero *U.S.A.* 41°51N 87°44W **172** E10
Cicero Dantas *Brazil* 10°36S 38°23W **189** C3
Cicia *Fiji* 17°45S 179°18W **154** a
Cícero *Turkey* 36°30N 34°0E **104** D5
Cicia *Turkey* 41°53N 33°1E **104** B5
Ciéagas del Cataumbo △
 Venezuela 9°25N 71°54W **183** E5
Ciechanów *Poland* 52°52N 20°38E **83** F7
Ciechanowiec *Poland* 52°40N 22°31E **83** F9
Ciechocinek *Poland* 52°53N 18°45E **83** F5
Ciego de Ávila *Cuba* 21°50N 78°50W **182** B4
Ciénaga *Colombia* 11°1N 74°15W **186** A4
Cienfuegos *Cuba* 22°10N 80°30W **182** B3
Cierp-Gaud *France* 42°55N 0°40E **72** F4
Cieszanów *Poland* 50°14N 23°8E **83** H10
Cieszyn *Poland* 49°45N 18°35E **83** J5
Cieza *Spain* 38°17N 1°23W **91** G3
Çifteler *Turkey* 39°22N 31°2E **104** C4
Cifuentes *Spain* 40°47N 2°37W **90** E2
Cihanbeyli *Turkey* 38°40N 32°55E **104** C5
Cihuatlán *Mexico* 19°14N 104°35W **180** D4
Cijara, Embalse de *Spain* 39°18N 4°52W **89** F6
Cijara △ *Spain* 39°18N 4°35W **89** F6
Cijulang *Indonesia* 7°42S 108°27E **119** G13
Cilacap *Indonesia* 7°43S 109°0E **119** G13
Çıldır *Turkey* 41°7N 43°5E **105** B10
Çıldır Gölü *Turkey* 41°5N 43°15E **105** B10
Cilento e Vallo di Diano △
 Italy 40°15N 15°20E **95** B8
Cili *China* 29°30N 111°8E **117** C8
Cilibia *Romania* 45°4N 27°4E **81** E12
Cilicia *Turkey* 36°30N 35°0E **104** D5
Cill Airne = Killarney
 Ireland 52°4N 9°30W **64** D2
Cill Chainnigh = Kilkenny
 Ireland 52°39N 7°15W **64** D4
Cill Dara = Kildare *Ireland* 53°9N 6°55W **64** C5
Cill Droichid = Celbridge
 Ireland 53°20N 6°32W **64** C5
Cill Mhantáin = Wicklow
 Ireland 52°59N 6°3W **64** D5
Cilo Dağı *Turkey* 36°35N 5°45E **71** F12
Cima *U.S.A.* 35°14N 115°30W **171** K11
Cimarron *Kans.,*
 U.S.A. 37°48N 100°21W **172** G3
Cimarron *N. Mex.,*
 U.S.A. 36°31N 104°55W **169** H11
Cimarron → *U.S.A.* 36°10N 96°16W **176** C6
Cimişlia *Moldova* 46°34N 28°44E **81** C13
Cimone, Mte. *Italy* 44°12N 10°42E **92** D7
Çinar *Turkey* 37°46N 40°19E **105** D9
Çınarcık *Turkey* 40°38N 29°5E **97** F13
Cinca → *Spain* 41°26N 0°21E **90** D5
Cincar *Bos.-H.* 43°55N 17°5E **80** G2
Cincinnati *U.S.A.* 39°9N 84°27W **173** F11
Cincinnatus *U.S.A.* 42°33N 75°54W **173** D9
Çine *Turkey* 37°37N 28°2E **99** D10
Ciney *Belgium* 50°18N 5°5E **69** D5
Cíngoli *Italy* 43°23N 13°10E **93** E10
Cinigiano *Italy* 42°53N 11°23E **93** F8
Cinque I. *India* 11°16N 92°42E **127** J11
Cinque Terre △ *Italy* 44°10N 9°45E **92** D6
Cinto, Mte. *France* 42°24N 8°54E **73** F12
Cintruénigo *Spain* 42°5N 1°49W **90** C3
Ciocile *Romania* 44°49N 27°1E **81** F12
Ciolănești din Deal
 Romania 44°19N 25°5E **81** F10
Ciorani *Romania* 44°45N 26°25E **81** F11
Čiovo *Croatia* 43°30N 16°17E **93** E13
Cipó *Brazil* 11°6S 38°3W **189** C3
Cipolletti *Argentina* 38°56S 67°59W **192** A3
Circeo, Mte. *Italy* 41°14N 13°3E **94** A6
Circir *Turkey* 40°3N 36°47E **104** C7
Circle *Alaska, U.S.A.* 65°50N 144°4W **166** B11
Circle *Mont., U.S.A.* 47°25N 105°35W **168** C11
Circleville *U.S.A.* 39°36N 82°57W **173** F12
Cirebon *Indonesia* 6°45S 108°32E **118** F3
Cirencester *U.K.* 51°43N 1°57W **67** F6
Cireşu *Romania* 44°47N 22°31E **80** F7
Cirey-sur-Vezouze
 France 48°35N 6°57E **71** D13
Ciriè *Italy* 45°14N 7°36E **92** C4
Cirium *Cyprus* 34°40N 32°53E **101** E11
Cirò *Italy* 39°23N 17°3E **95** C10
Cirò Marina *Italy* 39°22N 17°8E **95** C10
Ciron → *France* 44°36N 0°18W **72** D3
Cisco *U.S.A.* 32°23N 98°59W **176** E5
Cislău *Romania* 45°14N 26°20E **81** E11
Cisna *Poland* 49°12N 22°20E **83** J9
Cisnădie *Romania* 45°42N 24°9E **81** E9
Cisterna di Latina *Italy* 41°35N 12°49E **94** A5
Cisternino *Italy* 40°44N 17°25E **95** B10
Citeli-Ckaro = Dedoplis Tsqaro
 Georgia 41°33N 46°0E **87** K8
Citlaltépetl = Orizaba, Pico de
 Mexico 18°58N 97°15W **181** D5
Citra *U.S.A.* 29°25N 82°7W **179** F7
Citrus Heights *U.S.A.* 38°42N 121°17W **170** G5
Citrus Springs *U.S.A.* 29°2N 82°27W **178** F7
Città del Vaticano = Vatican
 City *Europe* 41°54N 12°27E **93** G9
Città della Pieve *Italy* 42°57N 12°1E **93** F9
Città di Castello *Italy* 43°27N 12°14E **93** E9
Città Sant' Angelo *Italy* 42°32N 14°5E **93** F11
Cittadella *Italy* 45°39N 11°47E **93** C8

Cittaducale *Italy* 42°23N 12°57E **93** F9
Cittanova *Italy* 38°21N 16°5E **95** D9
Ciuc, Munții *Romania* 46°26N 26°5E **81** D11
Ciucaş, Vf. *Romania* 45°31N 25°56E **81** E10
Ciucea *Romania* 46°57N 22°49E **80** D7
Ciulnița *Romania* 44°26N 27°22E **81** F12
Ciumeghiu *Romania* 46°44N 21°35E **80** D6
Ciuperceni *Romania* 44°54N 23°4E **80** F8
Civa Burnu *Turkey* 41°21N 36°38E **104** B7
Cividale del Friuli *Italy* 46°6N 13°26E **93** B10
Civita Castellana *Italy* 42°18N 12°24E **93** F9
Civitanova Marche
 Italy 43°18N 13°44E **93** E10
Civitavécchia *Italy* 42°6N 11°48E **93** F8
Civray *France* 46°10N 0°17E **72** B4
Çivril *Turkey* 38°20N 29°43E **99** C11
Cixerri → *Italy* 39°17N 8°59E **94** C1
Cixi *China* 30°17N 121°9E **117** B13
Cizre *Turkey* 37°19N 42°10E **105** D10
Clackmannanshire □
 U.K. 56°10N 3°43W **65** E5
Clacton-on-Sea *U.K.* 51°47N 1°11E **67** F9
Clain → *France* 46°47N 0°33E **70** F7
Claire, L. *Canada* 58°35N 112°5W **162** B6
Clairton *U.S.A.* 40°18N 79°53W **174** F5
Clairvaux-les-Lacs
 France 46°35N 5°45E **71** F12
Claise → *France* 46°56N 0°42E **70** F7
Clallam Bay *U.S.A.* 48°15N 124°16W **170** B2
Clamecy *France* 47°28N 3°30E **71** E10
Clanton *U.S.A.* 32°51N 86°38W **177** E11
Clanwilliam *S. Africa* 32°11S 18°52E **144** D2
Clara *Ireland* 53°21N 7°37W **64** C4
Clare *Australia* 33°50S 138°37E **152** B3
Clare *U.S.A.* 43°49N 84°46W **173** D11
Clare □ *Ireland* 52°45N 9°0W **64** D3
Clare → *Ireland* 53°20N 9°2W **64** C2
Clare I. *Ireland* 53°49N 10°0W **64** C1
Claremont *Calif., U.S.A.* 34°6N 117°43W **171** L9
Claremont *N.H.,*
 U.S.A. 43°23N 72°20W **175** C12
Claremont Pt. *Australia* 14°1S 143°41E **150** A3
Claremore *U.S.A.* 36°19N 95°36W **176** C7
Claremorris *Ireland* 53°45N 9°0W **64** C3
Clarence → *Australia* 29°25S 153°22E **151** D5
Clarence → *N.Z.* 42°10S 173°56E **155** D5
Clarence I. *Antarctica* 61°10S 54°0W **55** C18
Clarence Str. *Australia* 12°0S 131°0E **148** B5
Clarence Town
 Bahamas 23°6N 74°59W **183** B5
Clarendon *Pa., U.S.A.* 41°47N 79°6W **174** E5
Clarendon *Tex.,*
 U.S.A. 34°56N 100°53W **176** D4
Clarenville *Canada* 48°10N 54°1W **165** C9
Claresholm *Canada* 50°0N 113°33W **162** D6
Clarie Coast *Antarctica* 68°0S 135°0E **55** C9
Clarinda *U.S.A.* 40°44N 95°2W **172** E6
Clarington *Canada* 43°55N 78°41W **174** C6
Clarion *Iowa, U.S.A.* 42°44N 93°44W **172** D7
Clarion *Pa., U.S.A.* 41°13N 79°23W **174** E5
Clarion → *U.S.A.* 41°7N 79°41W **174** E5
Clarion Fracture Zone
 Pac. Oc. 20°0N 120°0W **158** F17
Clark *U.S.A.* 44°53N 97°44W **172** C5
Clark, Pt. *Canada* 44°4N 81°45W **174** B3
Clark Fork *U.S.A.* 48°9N 116°11W **168** B5
Clark Fork → *U.S.A.* 48°9N 116°15W **168** B5
Clarkdale *U.S.A.* 34°46N 112°3W **169** J7
Clarke City *Canada* 50°12N 66°38W **165** B6
Clarke I. *Australia* 40°32S 148°10E **151** G4
Clarke Ra. *Australia* 20°40S 148°30E **150** b
Clark's Harbour
 Canada 43°25N 65°38W **165** D6
Clarks Hill L. = J. Strom
 Thurmond L. *U.S.A.* 33°40N 82°12W **178** C6
Clarks Summit *U.S.A.* 41°30N 75°42W **175** D9
Clarksburg *U.S.A.* 39°17N 80°30W **173** F13
Clarksdale *U.S.A.* 34°12N 90°35W **177** D9
Clarkston *U.S.A.* 46°25N 117°3W **168** C5
Clarksville *Ark., U.S.A.* 35°28N 93°28W **176** D8
Clarksville *Tenn.,*
 U.S.A. 36°32N 87°21W **177** C11
Clarksville *Tex., U.S.A.* 33°37N 95°3W **176** E7
Clatskanie *U.S.A.* 46°6N 123°12W **170** D3
Claude *U.S.A.* 35°7N 101°22W **176** D4
Claveria *Phil.* 18°37N 121°4E **119** A6
Clay *U.S.A.* 38°17N 121°10W **170** G5
Clay Center *U.S.A.* 39°23N 97°8W **172** F5
Claypool *U.S.A.* 33°25N 110°51W **169** K8
Claysburg *U.S.A.* 40°17N 78°27W **174** F6
Claysville *U.S.A.* 40°7N 80°25W **174** F4
Clayton *Canada* 45°11N 76°19W **175** A8
Clayton *Ala., U.S.A.* 31°53N 85°27W **177** F12
Clayton *N. Mex.,*
 U.S.A. 36°27N 103°11W **169** H12
Clayton *N.Y., U.S.A.* 44°14N 76°5W **175** B8
Clear, C. *Ireland* 51°25N 9°32W **64** E2
Clear, L. *Canada* 45°26N 77°12W **174** A7
Clear Hills *Canada* 56°40N 119°30W **162** B5
Clear I. *Ireland* 51°26N 9°30W **64** E2
Clear L. *U.S.A.* 39°2N 122°47W **170** F4
Clear Lake *Iowa, U.S.A.* 43°8N 93°23W **172** D7
Clear Lake *S. Dak.,*
 U.S.A. 44°45N 96°41W **172** C5
Clear Lake Res. *U.S.A.* 41°56N 121°5W **168** F3
Clearfield *Pa., U.S.A.* 41°2N 78°27W **174** E6
Clearfield *Utah, U.S.A.* 41°7N 112°2W **168** F7
Clearlake *U.S.A.* 38°57N 122°38W **170** G4
Clearwater *U.S.A.* 27°59N 82°48W **179** H7
Clearwater → *Alta.,*
 Canada 52°22N 114°57W **162** C6
Clearwater → *Alta.,*
 Canada 56°44N 111°23W **163** B6
Clearwater L. *Canada* 53°34N 99°49W **163** C9
Clearwater Lake ○
 Canada 54°0N 101°0W **163** C8
Clearwater Mts. *U.S.A.* 46°5N 115°20W **168** C6
Clearwater River △
 Canada 56°55N 109°10W **163** B7
Cleburne *U.S.A.* 32°21N 97°23W **176** E6
Clee Hills *U.K.* 52°26N 2°35W **67** E5
Cleethorpes *U.K.* 53°33N 0°3W **66** D7
Cleeve Cloud *U.K.* 51°56N 2°0W **67** F6
Clelles *France* 44°50N 5°38E **73** D9
Clemson *U.S.A.* 34°41N 82°50W **177** D13
Clerke Reef *Australia* 17°22S 119°20E **148** C2
Clermont *Australia* 22°49S 147°39E **150** C4
Clermont *France* 49°23N 2°24E **71** C9
Clermont *U.S.A.* 28°33N 81°46W **179** G8
Clermont-en-Argonne
 France 49°5N 5°4E **71** C12
Clermont-Ferrand *France* 45°46N 3°4E **72** C7
Clermont-l'Hérault
 France 43°38N 3°26E **72** E7
Clerval *France* 47°25N 6°30E **71** E13
Clervaux *Lux.* 50°4N 6°2E **69** D6
Cles *Italy* 46°22N 11°2E **92** B8
Cleve *Australia* 33°43S 136°30E **152** B2
Clevedon *U.K.* 51°26N 2°52W **67** F5
Cleveland *Miss., U.S.A.* 33°45N 90°43W **177** E9
Cleveland *Ohio, U.S.A.* 41°29N 81°41W **174** E3
Cleveland *Okla., U.S.A.* 36°19N 96°28W **176** C6
Cleveland *Tenn.,*
 U.S.A. 35°10N 84°53W **177** D12
Cleveland *Tex., U.S.A.* 30°21N 95°5W **176** F7
Cleveland, C. *Australia* 19°11S 147°1E **150** B4
Cleveland Heights
 U.S.A. 41°31N 81°33W **174** E3
Clevelândia *Brazil* 26°24S 52°23W **191** B5
Clew B. *Ireland* 53°50N 9°49W **64** C2
Clewiston *U.S.A.* 26°45N 80°56W **179** J9
Clifden *Ireland* 53°29N 10°1W **64** C1
Clifden *N.Z.* 46°1S 167°42E **155** G2
Cliffdell *U.S.A.* 46°56N 121°5W **170** D5
Cliffy Hd. *Australia* 35°1S 116°29E **149** G2
Clifton *Australia* 27°59S 151°53E **151** D5
Clifton *Ariz., U.S.A.* 33°3N 109°18W **169** K9
Clifton *Colo., U.S.A.* 39°7N 108°25W **168** G9
Clifton *Tex., U.S.A.* 31°47N 97°35W **176** F6
Clifton Beach *Australia* 16°46S 145°39E **150** B4
Climax *Canada* 49°10N 108°20W **162** D7
Clinch → *U.S.A.* 35°53N 84°29W **177** D12
Clingmans Dome
 U.S.A. 35°34N 83°30W **177** D13
Clint *U.S.A.* 31°35N 106°14W **176** F1
Clinton *B.C., Canada* 51°6N 121°35W **162** C4
Clinton *Ont., Canada* 43°37N 81°32W **174** C3
Clinton *N.Z.* 46°12S 169°23E **155** G4
Clinton *Ark., U.S.A.* 35°36N 92°28W **176** D8
Clinton *Conn., U.S.A.* 41°17N 72°32W **175** E12
Clinton *Ill., U.S.A.* 40°9N 88°57W **172** E9
Clinton *Ind., U.S.A.* 39°40N 87°24W **172** F10
Clinton *Iowa, U.S.A.* 41°51N 90°12W **172** E8
Clinton *Mass., U.S.A.* 42°25N 71°41W **175** D13
Clinton *Miss., U.S.A.* 32°20N 90°20W **177** E9
Clinton *Mo., U.S.A.* 38°22N 93°46W **172** F7
Clinton *N.C., U.S.A.* 35°0N 78°22W **177** D15
Clinton *Okla., U.S.A.* 35°31N 98°58W **176** D5
Clinton *S.C., U.S.A.* 34°29N 81°53W **177** D14
Clinton *Tenn., U.S.A.* 36°6N 84°8W **177** C12
Clinton *Wash., U.S.A.* 47°59N 122°21W **170** C4
Clinton, C. *Australia* 22°30S 150°45E **150** C5
Clinton Colden L.
 Canada 63°58N 107°27W **160** E10
Clio *U.S.A.* 43°11N 83°44W **174** D4
Clipperton, Î.
 Pac. Oc. 10°18N 109°13W **157** F17
Clipperton Fracture Zone
 Pac. Oc. 19°0N 122°0W **157** G16
Clisham *U.K.* 57°58N 6°49W **65** D2
Clisson *France* 47°5N 1°16W **70** E5
Clitheroe *U.K.* 53°53N 2°22W **66** D5
Clive *N.Z.* 39°36S 176°58E **154** F5
Clo-oose *Canada* 48°39N 124°49W **170** D2
Cloates, Pt. *Australia* 22°43S 113°40E **148** D1
Clocolan *S. Africa* 28°55S 27°34E **145** C4
Clodomira *Argentina* 27°35S 64°14W **190** B3
Cloghaneely *Ireland* 55°8N 8°4W **64** A3
Clogher Hd. *Ireland* 53°48N 6°14W **64** C5
Clonakilty *Ireland* 51°37N 8°53W **64** E3
Clonakilty B. *Ireland* 51°35N 8°51W **64** E3
Cloncurry *Australia* 20°40S 140°28E **150** C3
Cloncurry → *Australia* 18°37S 140°40E **150** B3
Clondalkin *Ireland* 53°19N 6°25W **64** C5
Clones *Ireland* 54°11N 7°15W **64** B4
Clonmel *Ireland* 52°21N 7°42W **64** D4
Cloppenburg *Germany* 52°51N 8°1E **76** C4
Cloquet *U.S.A.* 46°43N 92°28W **172** B7
Clorinda *Argentina* 25°16S 57°45W **190** B4
Cloud Peak *U.S.A.* 44°23N 107°11W **168** D10
Cloudcroft *U.S.A.* 32°58N 105°45W **169** K11
Cloudy B. *N.Z.* 41°25S 174°10E **155** D5
Cloverdale *U.S.A.* 38°48N 123°1W **170** G4

Clovis Calif., U.S.A. 36°49N 119°42W 170 J7
Clovis N. Mex., U.S.A. 34°24N 103°12W 169 J12
Cloyes-sur-le-Loir France 48°0N 1°14E 70 E8
Cloyne Ireland 44°49N 77°11W 174 B7
Cluain Meala = Clonmel
Ireland 52°21N 7°42W 64 D4
Club Terrace Australia 37°35S 148°58E 153 D8
Cluj □ Romania 46°45N 23°30E 81 D8
Cluj-Napoca Romania 46°47N 23°38E 81 D8
Clunes Australia 37°20S 143°45E 152 D5
Cluny France 46°26N 4°38E 71 F11
Cluses France 46°5N 6°35E 71 F13
Clusone Italy 45°53N 9°57E 92 C6
Clutha → N.Z. 46°20S 169°49E 155 G4
Clwyd → U.K. 53°19N 3°31W 66 D4
Clyattville U.S.A. 30°42N 83°19W 178 E6
Clyde Canada 54°9N 113°39W 162 C6
Clyde N.Z. 45°12S 169°20E 155 F3
Clyde → U.S.A. 43°5N 76°52W 174 C8
Clyde → U.K. 55°55N 4°30W 65 F4
Clyde, Firth of U.K. 55°22N 5°1W 65 F3
Clyde River Canada 70°30N 68°30W 161 C18
Clydebank U.K. 55°54N 4°23W 65 F4
Clymer N.Y., U.S.A. 42°1N 79°37W 174 D5
Clymer Pa., U.S.A. 40°40N 79°1W 174 D5
Clyo U.S.A. 32°29N 81°16W 178 C8
Ćmielów Poland 50°53N 21°31E 83 H8
Côa → Portugal 41°5N 7°6W 88 D3
Coachella U.S.A. 33°41N 116°10W 171 M10
Coachella Canal
U.S.A. 32°43N 114°57W 171 N12
Coahoma U.S.A. 32°18N 101°18W 176 E4
Coahuayana →
Mexico 18°41N 103°45W 180 D4
Coahuila □ Mexico 27°20N 102°0W 180 B4
Coal → Canada 59°39N 126°57W 162 B3
Coal I. N.Z. 46°8S 166°40E 155 G1
Coalane Mozam. 17°48S 37°2E 143 F4
Coalcomán Mexico 18°47N 103°9W 180 D4
Coaldale Canada 49°45N 112°35W 162 D6
Coalgate U.S.A. 34°32N 96°13W 176 D6
Coalinga U.S.A. 36°9N 120°21W 170 J6
Coalisland U.K. 54°33N 6°42W 64 B5
Coalville U.K. 52°44N 1°23W 66 E6
Coalville U.S.A. 40°55N 111°24W 168 F8
Coamo Puerto Rico 18°5N 66°22W 183 d
Coaraci Brazil 14°38S 39°32W 189 C3
Coari Brazil 4°8S 63°7W 186 D6
Coast Mts. Canada 55°0N 129°20W 162 C3
Coast Ranges U.S.A. 39°0N 123°0W 170 G4
Coatbridge U.K. 55°52N 4°6W 65 F4
Coatepec Mexico 19°27N 96°58W 181 D5
Coatepeque Guatemala 14°46N 91°55W 182 D1
Coatesville U.S.A. 39°59N 75°50W 173 F16
Coaticook Canada 45°10N 71°46W 175 A13
Coats I. Canada 62°30N 83°0W 161 E15
Coats Land Antarctica 77°0S 25°0W 55 D1
Coatzacoalcos Mexico 18°7N 94°25W 181 D6
Cobá Mexico 20°31N 87°45W 181 C7
Cobadin Romania 44°5N 28°13E 81 F13
Cobalt Canada 47°25N 79°42W 164 C4
Cobán Guatemala 15°30N 90°21W 182 C1
Çobanlar Turkey 38°41N 30°47E 99 C12
Cobar Australia 31°27S 145°48E 153 A6
Cobargo Australia 36°20S 149°55E 153 D8
Cobbannah Australia 37°37S 147°13E 153 D7
Cobberas, Mt.
Australia 36°53S 148°12E 153 D8
Cobden Australia 38°20S 143°3E 152 E5
Cobden Canada 45°38N 76°53W 174 B7
Cobh Ireland 51°51N 8°17W 64 E3
Cóbh, An = Cobh Ireland 51°51N 8°17W 64 E3
Cobija Bolivia 11°0S 68°50W 188 C4
Cobleskill U.S.A. 42°41N 74°29W 175 D10
Coboconk Canada 44°39N 78°48W 174 B6
Cobourg Canada 43°58N 78°10W 174 C6
Cobourg Pen.
Australia 11°20S 132°15E 148 B5
Cobram Australia 35°54S 145°40E 153 C6
Cóbué Mozam. 12°0S 34°58E 143 E3
Coburg Germany 50°15N 10°58E 77 E6
Coburg I. Canada 75°57N 79°26W 161 B16
Coca → Ecuador 0°3S 76°58W 186 D3
Cocachacra Peru 17°5S 71°45W 188 D3
Cocal Brazil 3°28S 41°34W 189 A2
Cocanada = Kakinada
India 16°57N 82°11E 126 F6
Cocentaina Spain 38°45N 0°27W 91 G4
Cochabamba Bolivia 17°26S 66°10W 188 D5
Cochem Germany 50°9N 7°9E 77 E3
Cochemane Mozam. 17°0S 32°54E 143 F3
Cochin = Kochi India 9°58N 76°20E 127 K3
Cochin China = Nam Phan
Vietnam 10°30N 106°0E 121 G6
Cochran U.S.A. 32°23N 83°21W 178 D6
Cochrane Alta.,
Canada 51°11N 114°30W 162 C6
Cochrane Ont., Canada 49°0N 81°0W 164 C3
Cochrane Chile 47°15S 72°33W 192 C2
Cochrane → Canada 59°0N 103°40W 163 B8
Cochrane, L. Chile 47°10S 72°0W 192 C2
Cochranton U.S.A. 41°31N 80°3W 174 E4
Cockburn Australia 32°5S 141°0E 152 B4
Cockburn, Canal Chile 54°30S 72°0W 192 D2
Cockburn I. Canada 45°55N 83°22W 164 C3
Cockburn Ra. Australia 15°46S 128°0E 148 C4
Cockermouth U.K. 54°40N 3°22W 66 C4
Cocklebiddy Australia 32°0S 126°3E 149 F4
Cockpit Country, The
Jamaica 18°15N 77°45W 182 a
Coco → Cent. Amer. 15°0N 83°8W 182 D3
Coco, I. del Pac. Oc. 5°25N 87°55W 157 G19
Coco Channel Asia 14°5N 93°10E 127 H11
Cocoa U.S.A. 28°21N 80°44W 179 G9
Cocoa Beach U.S.A. 28°19N 80°37W 179 G9
Cocobeach Gabon 0°59N 9°34E 140 D1
Cocoparra △ Australia 34°5S 146°12E 153 C7
Cocora Romania 44°45N 27°3E 81 F12
Côcos Brazil 14°10S 44°33W 189 C2
Côcos → Brazil 12°44S 44°44W 189 C2
Cocos B. Trin. & Tob. 10°24N 61°2W 187 K15
Cocos Basin Ind. Oc. 1°0N 94°0E 146 D8
Cocos I. = Coco, I. del
Pac. Oc. 5°25N 87°55W 157 G19
Cocos Is. Ind. Oc. 12°10S 96°55E 146 F8
Cocos Ridge Pac. Oc. 4°0N 88°0W 157 G19
Cod, C. U.S.A. 42°5N 70°10W 173 D18
Codajás Brazil 3°55S 62°0W 186 D6
Codfish I. N.Z. 46°45S 167°38E 155 G2
Codigoro Italy 44°49N 12°8E 93 D9
Codlea Romania 45°42N 25°27E 81 E10
Codó Brazil 4°30S 43°55W 189 A2

Codogno Italy 45°9N 9°42E 92 C6
Codpa Chile 18°50S 69°44W 188 D4
Codróipo Italy 45°58N 13°0E 93 C10
Codru, Munții Romania 46°30N 22°15E 80 D7
Cody U.S.A. 44°32N 109°3W 168 D9
Coe Hill Canada 44°52N 77°50W 174 B7
Coelemu Chile 36°30S 72°48W 190 D1
Coelho Neto Brazil 4°15S 43°0W 189 A2
Coen Australia 13°52S 143°12E 150 D11
Coesfeld Germany 51°56N 7°10E 76 D3
Coetivy I. Seychelles 7°8S 56°16E 146 E4
Coeur d'Alene U.S.A. 47°41N 116°46W 168 C5
Coeur d'Alene L.
U.S.A. 47°32N 116°49W 168 C5
Coevorden Neths. 52°40N 6°44E 69 B6
Cofete Canary Is. 28°6N 14°23W 100 F5
Coffeyville U.S.A. 37°2N 95°37W 172 G6
Coffin B. Australia 34°38S 135°28E 151 E2
Coffin Bay Australia 34°37S 135°29E 151 E2
Coffin Bay △ Australia 34°34S 135°19E 151 E2
Coffin Bay Peninsula
Australia 34°32S 135°15E 151 E2
Coffs Harbour
Australia 30°16S 153°5E 153 A10
Cofrentes Spain 39°13N 1°5W 91 F3
Cogalnic = Kohylnyk →
Ukraine 45°49N 29°40E 81 E14
Cogealac Romania 44°36N 28°36E 81 F13
Coghinas → Italy 40°55N 8°48E 94 B1
Coghinas, L. del Italy 40°46N 9°3E 94 B2
Cognac France 45°41N 0°20W 72 C3
Cogne Italy 45°37N 7°21E 92 C4
Cogolin France 43°15N 6°32E 73 E10
Cogolludo Spain 40°59N 3°10W 90 E1
Cohocton U.S.A. 42°30N 77°30W 174 D7
Cohocton → U.S.A. 42°9N 77°6W 174 D7
Cohoes U.S.A. 42°46N 73°42W 175 D11
Cohuna Australia 35°45S 144°15E 152 C6
Coiba, I. de Panama 7°30N 81°40W 182 E3
Coig → Argentina 51°0S 69°10W 192 D3
Coigeach, Rubha U.K. 58°6N 5°26W 65 D7
Coihaique Chile 45°30S 71°45W 192 C2
Coimbatore India 11°2N 76°59E 127 J3
Coimbra Brazil 19°55S 57°48W 186 G7
Coimbra Portugal 40°15N 8°27W 88 E2
Coimbra □ Portugal 40°12N 8°25W 88 E2
Coín Spain 36°40N 4°48W 89 J6
Coipasa, L. de Bolivia 19°12S 68°7W 188 D4
Coipasa, Salar de
Bolivia 19°26S 68°9W 188 D4
Cojata Peru 15°2S 69°25W 188 D4
Cojimies Ecuador 0°20N 80°0W 186 C3
Cojocna Romania 46°45N 23°50E 81 D8
Cojutepeque El Salv. 13°41N 88°54W 182 D2
Čoka Serbia 45°57N 20°12E 80 E5
Cokeville U.S.A. 42°5N 110°57W 168 E8
Colaba Pt. India 18°53N 72°48E 126 E7
Colac Australia 38°21S 143°35E 152 E5
Colachel = Kolachel
India 8°10N 77°15E 127 K3
Colán Peru 5°0S 81°0W 188 B1
Colatina Brazil 19°32S 40°37W 189 D2
Colbeck, C. Antarctica 77°6S 157°48W 55 D13
Colbert U.S.A. 34°2N 83°13W 178 A6
Colborne Canada 44°0N 77°53W 174 C7
Colby U.S.A. 39°24N 101°3W 172 F3
Colca → Peru 15°55S 72°43W 186 G4
Colca, Cañón del Peru 15°41N 88°54W 182 E8
Colchester U.K. 51°54N 0°55E 67 F8
Colchester U.S.A. 41°35N 72°20W 175 E12
Cold L. Canada 54°33N 110°5W 163 C7
Cold Lake Canada 54°27N 110°10W 163 C6
Coldstream Canada 50°13N 119°11W 162 C5
Coldstream U.K. 55°39N 2°15W 65 F6
Coldwater Canada 44°42N 79°40W 174 B5
Coldwater Kans.,
U.S.A. 37°16N 99°20W 172 G4
Coldwater Mich.,
U.S.A. 41°57N 85°0W 173 E11
Coleambally Australia 34°49S 145°52E 153 C6
Colebrook U.S.A. 44°54N 71°30W 175 B13
Coleman Canada 49°40N 114°30W 162 D6
Coleman Fla., U.S.A. 28°48N 82°4W 179 G7
Coleman Tex., U.S.A. 31°50N 99°26W 176 F5
Coleman → Australia 15°6S 141°38E 150 D3
Colenso S. Africa 28°44S 29°50E 145 D4
Coleraine Australia 37°36S 141°40E 152 D4
Coleraine U.K. 55°8N 6°41W 64 A5
Coleridge, L. N.Z. 43°17S 171°30E 155 D6
Coleroon → India 11°25N 79°50E 127 J4
Colesberg S. Africa 30°45S 25°5E 144 D4
Coleville U.S.A. 38°34N 119°30W 170 G7
Colfax Calif., U.S.A. 39°6N 120°57W 170 F6
Colfax La., U.S.A. 31°31N 92°42W 176 F8
Colfax Wash., U.S.A. 46°53N 117°22W 168 C5
Colhué Huapi, L.
Argentina 45°30S 69°0W 192 C3
Colibași = Mioveni
Romania 44°56N 24°54E 81 F9
Colibași Moldova 45°43N 28°11E 81 E13
Cólico Italy 46°8N 9°22E 92 B6
Coligny France 46°23N 5°21E 71 F12
Coligny S. Africa 26°17S 26°15E 145 C4
Colima Mexico 19°14N 103°43W 180 D4
Colima □ Mexico 19°10N 104°0W 180 D4
Colima, Nevado de
Mexico 19°33N 103°38W 180 D4
Colina Chile 33°13S 70°45W 190 C1
Colina do Norte
Guinea-Biss. 12°28N 15°0W 138 C2
Colinas Brazil 7°14S 44°15W 189 B2
Colinas Maranhão, Brazil 6°0S 44°10W 189 B2
Colindres Spain 43°24N 3°27W 88 B7
Coll U.K. 56°39N 6°34W 65 E2
Collahuasi Chile 21°5S 68°45W 188 E5
Collarada, Peña Spain 42°43N 0°29W 90 C4
Collarenebri Australia 29°33S 148°34E 151 D5
Colle di Val d'Elsa Italy 43°25N 11°7E 92 E8
Collécchio Italy 44°45N 10°13E 92 D7
Colleen Bawn Zimbabwe 21°0S 29°12E 143 G2
College U.S.A. 64°52N 147°49W 166 C10
College Park U.S.A. 33°39N 84°27W 178 B5
College Station U.S.A. 30°37N 96°21W 176 F6
Collesalvetti Italy 43°34N 10°27E 92 E7
Colli Euganei △ Italy 45°18N 11°43E 93 C8
Collie N.S.W., Australia 31°41S 148°18E 153 A8
Collie W. Austral.,
Australia 33°22S 116°8E 149 F2
Collier B. Australia 16°10S 124°15E 148 C3
Collier Ra. Australia 24°45S 119°10E 149 D2
Collier Range △
Australia 24°33S 119°7E 149 D2

Collierville U.S.A. 35°3N 89°40W 177 D10
Collina, Passo di Italy 44°2N 10°56E 92 D7
Collingwood Canada 44°29N 80°13W 174 B4
Collingwood N.Z. 40°41S 172°40E 155 D4
Collins Canada 50°17N 89°27W 164 B2
Collins U.S.A. 32°11N 82°7W 178 C7
Collins Bay Canada 44°14N 76°36W 175 B8
Collinson Pen.
Canada 69°58N 101°24W 160 D11
Collinsville Australia 20°30S 147°56E 150 C4
Collipulli Chile 37°55S 72°30W 190 D1
Collo Algeria 36°58N 6°37E 136 A5
Collooney Ireland 54°11N 8°29W 64 B3
Colmar France 48°5N 7°20E 71 D14
Colmars France 44°11N 6°39E 73 D10
Colmenar Spain 36°54N 4°20W 89 J6
Colmenar de Oreja Spain 40°6N 3°25W 88 E7
Colmenar Viejo Spain 40°39N 3°47W 88 E7
Colo → Australia 33°25S 150°52E 153 B9
Cologne = Köln Germany 50°56N 6°57E 76 E2
Colom, I. d'en Spain 39°58N 4°16E 100 B11
Coloma U.S.A. 38°48N 120°53W 170 G6
Colomb-Béchar = Béchar
Algeria 31°38N 2°18W 136 B3
Colombey-les-Belles
France 48°32N 5°54E 71 D12
Colombey-les-Deux-Églises
France 48°13N 4°50E 71 D11
Colômbia Brazil 20°10S 48°40W 189 E1
Colombia ■ S. Amer. 3°45N 73°0W 186 C4
Colombian Basin
Caribbean 14°0N 76°0W 182 D4
Colombo Sri Lanka 6°56N 79°58E 127 L4
Colomiers France 43°36N 1°21E 72 E5
Colón B. Aires, Argentina 33°53S 61°7W 190 C3
Colón Entre Ríos,
Argentina 32°12S 58°10W 190 C4
Colón Cuba 22°42N 80°54W 182 B3
Colón Panama 9°20N 79°54W 182 E4
Colón, Arch. de Ecuador 0°0 91°0W 184 D1
Colonia 25 de Mayo
Argentina 37°48S 67°41W 192 A3
Colònia de Sant Jordi
Spain 39°19N 2°59E 100 B9
Colonia del Sacramento
Uruguay 34°25S 57°50W 190 C4
Colonia Dora Argentina 28°34S 62°59W 190 B3
Colonial Beach U.S.A. 38°15N 76°58W 173 F15
Colonie U.S.A. 42°43N 73°50W 175 D11
Colonna, C. Italy 39°2N 17°12E 95 C10
Colonsay Canada 51°59N 105°52W 163 C7
Colonsay U.K. 56°5N 6°12W 65 E2
Colorado □ U.S.A. 39°30N 105°30W 168 G11
Colorado → Argentina 39°50S 62°8W 192 A4
Colorado → N. Amer. 31°45N 114°40W 169 L6
Colorado → U.S.A. 28°36N 95°59W 176 G7
Colorado City U.S.A. 32°24N 100°52W 176 E4
Colorado Plateau
U.S.A. 37°0N 111°0W 169 H8
Colorado River Aqueduct
U.S.A. 33°50N 117°23W 171 L12
Colorado Springs
U.S.A. 38°50N 104°49W 168 G11
Colorno Italy 44°56N 10°22E 92 D7
Colotlán Mexico 22°6N 103°16W 180 C4
Colquitt U.S.A. 31°10N 84°44W 178 D5
Colstrip U.S.A. 45°53N 106°38W 168 D10
Colton U.S.A. 44°33N 74°56W 175 B10
Columbia Ala., U.S.A. 31°18N 85°7W 178 D4
Columbia Ky., U.S.A. 37°6N 85°18W 173 G11
Columbia La., U.S.A. 32°6N 92°5W 176 E8
Columbia Miss.,
U.S.A. 31°15N 89°50W 177 F10
Columbia Mo., U.S.A. 38°57N 92°20W 172 F7
Columbia Pa., U.S.A. 40°2N 76°30W 175 F8
Columbia S.C., U.S.A. 34°0N 81°2W 178 A8
Columbia Tenn., U.S.A. 35°37N 87°2W 177 D11
Columbia → N. Amer. 46°15N 124°5W 170 D2
Columbia, C. Canada 83°6N 69°57W 161 A18
Columbia, District of □
U.S.A. 38°55N 77°0W 173 F15
Columbia, Mt. Canada 52°8N 117°20W 162 C5
Columbia Basin U.S.A. 46°45N 119°5W 168 C4
Columbia Falls U.S.A. 48°23N 114°11W 168 B6
Columbia Mts. Canada 52°0N 119°0W 162 C5
Columbia Plateau
U.S.A. 44°0N 117°30W 168 E5
Columbiana U.S.A. 40°53N 80°42W 174 F4
Columbretes, Is. Spain 39°50N 0°0E 90 F5
Columbus Ga., U.S.A. 32°28N 84°59W 178 C5
Columbus Ind., U.S.A. 39°13N 85°55W 173 F11
Columbus Kans.,
U.S.A. 37°10N 94°50W 172 G6
Columbus Miss.,
U.S.A. 33°30N 88°25W 177 E10
Columbus Mont.,
U.S.A. 45°38N 109°15W 168 D9
Columbus N. Mex.,
U.S.A. 31°50N 107°38W 169 L10
Columbus Nebr., U.S.A. 41°26N 97°22W 172 E5
Columbus Ohio, U.S.A. 39°58N 83°0W 173 F12
Columbus Tex., U.S.A. 29°42N 96°33W 176 G6
Colunga Spain 43°29N 5°16W 88 B5
Colusa U.S.A. 39°13N 122°1W 170 F4
Colville U.S.A. 48°33N 117°54W 168 B5
Colville → U.S.A. 70°25N 150°30W 166 A9
Colville, C. N.Z. 36°29S 175°21E 154 C4
Colville Channel N.Z. 36°25S 175°27E 154 C4
Colwood Canada 48°26N 123°29W 170 B3
Colwyn Bay U.K. 53°18N 3°44W 66 D4
Comácchio Italy 44°42N 12°11E 93 D9
Comalcalco Mexico 18°16N 93°13W 181 D6
Comallo Argentina 41°0S 70°5W 192 B2
Comana Romania 44°10N 26°10E 81 F10
Comanche U.S.A. 31°54N 98°36W 176 F5
Comandante Ferraz
Antarctica 62°30S 58°0W 55 C18
Comandante Luis Piedrabuena
Argentina 49°59S 68°54W 192 C3
Comănești Romania 46°25N 26°26E 81 D11
Comarnic Romania 45°15N 25°38E 81 E10
Comayagua Honduras 14°25N 87°37W 182 D2
Combahee → U.S.A. 32°31N 80°31W 178 D8
Combarbalá Chile 31°11S 71°2W 190 C1
Combeaufontaine
France 47°38N 5°54E 71 E12
Comber Canada 42°14N 82°33W 174 D2
Comber U.K. 54°33N 5°45W 64 B6
Combermere Canada 45°22N 77°37W 174 A7

Comblain-au-Pont
Belgium 50°29N 5°35E 69 D5
Combourg France 48°25N 1°46W 70 D5
Comboyne Australia 31°34S 152°27E 153 A10
Combrailles France 46°8N 2°8E 71 F9
Combronde France 45°58N 3°5E 72 C7
Comer Ala., U.S.A. 32°2N 85°23W 178 C4
Comer Ga., U.S.A. 34°4N 83°8W 178 A6
Comeragh Mts. Ireland 52°18N 7°34W 64 D4
Comet Australia 23°36S 148°38E 150 C4
Comilla Bangla. 23°28N 91°10E 123 H17
Comino Malta 36°1N 14°20E 101 C1
Comino, C. Italy 40°32N 9°49E 94 B2
Cómiso Italy 36°56N 14°36E 95 F7
Comitán de Domínguez
Mexico 16°15N 92°8W 181 D6
Commentry France 46°20N 2°46E 71 F9
Commerce Ga., U.S.A. 34°12N 83°28W 178 A6
Commerce Tex., U.S.A. 33°15N 95°54W 176 E7
Commercy France 48°46N 5°34E 71 D12
Committee B. Canada 68°30N 86°30W 161 D14
Commodore, C. Canada 44°47N 80°54W 174 B4
Commonwealth B.
Antarctica 67°0S 144°0E 55 C10
Commoron Cr. →
Australia 28°22S 150°8E 151 D5
Communism Pk. = imeni Ismail
Samani, Pik Tajikistan 39°0N 72°2E 109 E8
Como Italy 45°47N 9°5E 92 C6
Como, L. di Italy 46°0N 9°11E 92 B6
Comodoro Rivadavia
Argentina 45°50S 67°40W 192 C3
Comoé □ Ivory C. 6°48N 3°30W 138 D4
Comoé → Ivory C. 5°12N 3°44W 138 D4
Comoé △ Ivory C. 9°0N 3°35W 138 D4
Comorâște Romania 45°10N 21°35E 80 E6
Comorin, C. = Kannyakumari
India 8°3N 77°40E 127 K3
Comoros ■ Ind. Oc. 12°10S 44°15E 141 a
Comox Canada 49°42N 124°55W 162 D4
Compass Lake U.S.A. 30°36N 85°24W 178 E4
Compiègne France 49°24N 2°50E 71 C9
Comporta Portugal 38°22N 8°46W 89 G2
Compostela Mexico 21°14N 104°55W 180 C4
Comprida, I. Brazil 24°50S 47°42W 191 A6
Compton Canada 45°14N 71°49W 175 A13
Compton U.S.A. 33°53N 118°13W 171 M8
Comrat Moldova 46°18N 28°40E 81 D13
Comrie U.K. 56°22N 3°59W 65 E5
Comstock U.S.A. 29°41N 101°10W 176 G4
Con Cuong Vietnam 19°2N 104°54E 120 C5
Con Dao △ Vietnam 8°42N 106°35E 121 H6
Con Son, Dao Vietnam 8°41N 106°37E 121 H6
Cona Niyeu Argentina 41°58S 67°0W 192 B3
Conakry Guinea 9°29N 13°49W 138 D2
Conara Australia 41°50S 147°26E 153 G4
Conargo Australia 35°16S 145°10E 153 C6
Concarneau France 47°52N 3°56W 70 E3
Conceição Brazil 7°33S 38°31W 189 B3
Conceição Mozam. 18°47S 36°7E 143 F4
Conceição da Barra
Brazil 18°35S 39°45W 189 D3
Conceição do Araguaia
Brazil 8°0S 49°2W 187 E9
Conceição do Canindé
Brazil 7°54S 41°34W 189 B2
Concepción Bolivia 16°15S 62°8W 186 G6
Concepción Chile 36°50S 73°0W 190 D1
Concepción Peru 11°54S 75°19W 188 D2
Concepción Paraguay 23°22S 57°26W 190 A4
Concepción, Est. de
Chile 50°30S 74°55W 192 D2
Concepción, L. Bolivia 17°20S 61°20W 186 G6
Concepción, Pta.
Mexico 26°53N 111°50W 180 B2
Concepción del Oro
Mexico 24°38N 101°25W 180 C4
Concepción del Uruguay
Argentina 32°35S 58°20W 190 C4
Conception, Pt.
U.S.A. 34°27N 120°28W 171 L6
Conception B. Canada 47°45N 53°0W 165 C9
Conception B. Namibia 23°55S 14°22E 144 B1
Conception I. Bahamas 23°52N 75°9W 183 B4
Concession Zimbabwe 17°27S 30°56E 143 F3
Conchas Dam U.S.A. 35°22N 104°11W 169 J11
Conches-en-Ouche
France 48°58N 0°56E 70 D7
Concho U.S.A. 34°28N 109°36W 169 J9
Concho → U.S.A. 31°34N 99°43W 176 F5
Conchos → Chihuahua,
Mexico 29°35N 104°25W 180 B4
Conchos → Tamaulipas,
Mexico 24°55N 97°38W 181 B5
Concord Calif., U.S.A. 37°59N 122°2W 170 H4
Concord Ga., U.S.A. 33°5N 84°27W 178 B5
Concord N.C., U.S.A. 35°25N 80°35W 177 D14
Concord N.H., U.S.A. 43°12N 71°32W 175 C13
Concordia Antarctica 75°6S 123°23E 55 D9
Concórdia Argentina 31°20S 58°2W 190 C4
Concórdia Amazonas,
Brazil 4°36S 66°36W 186 D5
Concórdia Sta. Catarina,
Brazil 27°14S 52°1W 191 B5
Concordia Mexico 23°17N 106°4W 180 C3
Concrete U.S.A. 48°32N 121°45W 168 B3
Condah Australia 37°57S 141°44E 152 D4
Condamine Australia 26°56S 150°9E 151 D5
Condat France 45°21N 2°46E 72 C6
Condé Brazil 11°49S 37°37W 189 C3
Conde U.S.A. 45°9N 98°6W 172 C4
Condé-sur-Noireau
France 48°51N 0°33W 70 D6
Condeúba Brazil 14°52S 42°0W 189 D3
Condobolin Australia 33°4S 147°6E 153 B8
Condom France 43°57N 0°22E 72 E4
Condon U.S.A. 45°14N 120°11W 168 D3
Conegliano Italy 45°53N 12°18E 93 C9
Conejera, I. = Conills, I. des
Spain 39°11N 2°58E 100 B9
Conejos Mexico 26°14N 103°53W 180 B4
Conemaugh → U.S.A. 40°28N 79°19W 174 F5
Conero △ Italy 43°32N 13°35E 93 C10
Confolens France 46°2N 0°40E 72 B4
Confuso → Paraguay 25°9S 57°34W 190 B4
Congaree △ U.S.A. 33°47N 80°47W 178 B8
Congleton U.K. 53°10N 2°13W 66 D5
Congo (Brazzaville) = Congo ■
Africa
Congo (Kinshasa) = Congo, Dem.
Rep. of the ■ Africa
Congo ■ Africa 1°0S 16°0E 140 E3
Congo → Africa 6°4S 12°24E 140 F2
Congo, Dem. Rep. of the ■
Africa 3°0S 23°0E 140 E4
Congo Basin Africa 0°10S 24°30E 140 E4
Congonhas Brazil 20°30S 43°52W 189 E2
Congress U.S.A. 34°9N 112°51W 169 J7
Conguillío △ Chile 38°40S 71°42W 192 A2
Conil de la Frontera
Spain 36°17N 6°10W 89 J4
Conills, I. des Spain 39°11N 2°58E 100 B9
Conimbla △ Australia 33°45S 148°28E 153 B8
Coniston Canada 46°29N 80°51W 164 C3
Conjeeveram = Kanchipuram
India 12°52N 79°45E 127 H4
Conklin Canada 55°38N 111°5W 163 B6
Conklin U.S.A. 42°2N 75°49W 175 D9
Connacht □ Ireland 53°43N 9°12W 64 C2
Conneaut U.S.A. 41°57N 80°34W 174 E4
Conneautville U.S.A. 41°45N 80°22W 174 E4
Connecticut □ U.S.A. 41°30N 72°45W 175 E12
Connecticut →
U.S.A. 41°16N 72°20W 175 E12
Connell U.S.A. 46°40N 118°52W 168 C4
Connellsville U.S.A. 40°1N 79°35W 174 F5
Connemara △ Ireland 53°29N 9°45W 64 C2
Connemara □ Ireland 53°32N 9°52W 64 C2
Connerré France 48°3N 0°30E 70 D7
Connersville U.S.A. 39°39N 85°8W 173 F11
Connors Ra. Australia 21°40S 149°10E 150 C4
Conoble Australia 32°55S 144°33E 153 B6
Conococha Peru 10°7S 77°18W 188 C2
Conques France 44°36N 2°23E 72 D6
Conquest Canada 51°32N 107°14W 163 C7
Conrad U.S.A. 48°10N 111°57W 168 B8
Conrad Rise S. Ocean 53°0S 41°0E 55 B5
Conran, C. Australia 37°49S 148°44E 153 D8
Conroe U.S.A. 30°19N 95°27W 176 F7
Consecon Canada 44°0N 77°31W 174 C7
Conselheiro Lafaiete
Brazil 20°40S 43°48W 189 E2
Conselheiro Pena
Brazil 19°10S 41°30W 189 D2
Consell Spain 39°40N 2°48E 100 B9
Conselve Italy 45°14N 11°52E 93 C8
Consett U.K. 54°51N 1°50W 66 C6
Consort Canada 52°1N 110°46W 163 C6
Constance = Konstanz
Germany 47°40N 9°10E 77 H5
Constance, L. = Bodensee
Europe 47°35N 9°25E 77 H5
Constanța Romania 44°14N 28°38E 81 F13
Constanța □ Romania 44°15N 28°15E 81 F13
Constantina Spain 37°51N 5°40W 89 H5
Constantine Algeria 36°25N 6°42E 136 A5
Constantine □ Algeria 36°30N 6°40E 136 A5
Constitución Chile 35°20S 72°30W 190 D1
Constitución Uruguay 31°0S 57°50W 190 C4
Constitución de 1857 △
Mexico 32°4N 115°55W 180 A1
Consuegra Spain 39°28N 3°36W 89 F7
Consul Canada 49°20N 109°30W 163 D7
Contact U.S.A. 41°46N 114°45W 168 F6
Contagem Brazil 19°55S 44°6W 189 E2
Contai India 21°54N 87°46E 125 J12
Contamana Peru 7°19S 74°55W 188 B3
Contas → Brazil 14°17S 39°1W 189 D3
Contes France 43°49N 7°19E 73 E11
Contoocook U.S.A. 43°13N 71°45W 175 C13
Contra Costa Mozam. 25°9S 33°30E 145 C5
Contres France 47°24N 1°26E 70 E8
Contrexéville France 48°10N 5°53E 71 D12
Contumazá Peru 7°23S 78°57W 188 B2
Contwoyto L. Canada 65°42N 110°50W 160 D8
Conversano Italy 40°58N 17°8E 95 B10
Conway = Conwy U.K. 53°17N 3°50W 66 D4
Conway = Conwy →
U.K. 53°17N 3°50W 66 D4
Conway Australia 20°24S 148°41E 150 b
Conway Ark., U.S.A. 35°5N 92°26W 176 D8
Conway N.H., U.S.A. 43°59N 71°7W 175 C13
Conway S.C., U.S.A. 33°51N 79°3W 178 B9
Conway, C. Australia 20°34S 148°46E 150 b
Conway, L. Australia 28°17S 135°35E 151 D2
Conwy U.K. 53°17N 3°50W 66 D4
Conwy □ U.K. 53°10N 3°44W 66 D4
Conwy → U.K. 53°17N 3°50W 66 D4
Cooch Behar = Koch Bihar
India 26°22N 89°29E 123 F16
Cooinda Australia 13°15S 130°5E 148 B5
Cook Australia 30°37S 130°25E 149 F5
Cook, B. Chile 55°10S 70°0W 192 E2
Cook, Mt. = Aoraki Mount Cook
N.Z. 43°36S 170°9E 155 D5
Cook Inlet U.S.A. 60°0N 152°0W 166 D9
Cook Is. ⬚ Pac. Oc. 17°0S 160°0W 157 J12
Cook Strait N.Z. 41°15S 174°29E 154 D4
Cooke Plains Australia 35°23S 139°34E 152 C3
Cookeville U.S.A. 36°10N 85°30W 177 C12
Cookhouse S. Africa 32°44S 25°47E 144 D4
Cooks Hammock
U.S.A. 29°56N 83°17W 178 F6
Cooks Harbour Canada 51°36N 55°52W 165 B8
Cookshire Canada 45°25N 71°38W 175 A13
Cookstown Canada 44°11N 79°42W 174 B5
Cookstown U.K. 54°38N 6°45W 64 B5
Cooksville U.S.A. 40°24N 88°43W 172 E9
Coolabah Australia 31°1S 146°43E 153 B8
Cooladdi Australia 26°37S 145°23E 151 D4
Coolah Australia 31°48S 149°41E 153 A8
Coolah Tops △
Australia 31°52S 150°9E 153 A9
Coolamon Australia 34°46S 147°8E 153 C7
Coolgardie Australia 30°55S 121°8E 149 F3
Coolibah Australia 15°33S 130°56E 148 C5
Coolidge Ariz., U.S.A. 32°59N 111°31W 169 K8
Coolidge Ga., U.S.A. 31°1N 83°52W 178 E6
Coolidge Dam U.S.A. 33°10N 110°32W 169 K8

Cooma Australia 36°12S 149°8E 153 D8
Coon Rapids U.S.A. 45°9N 93°19W 172 C7
Coonabarabran
Australia 31°14S 149°18E 153 A8
Coonalpyn Australia 35°43S 139°52E 152 C3
Coonamble Australia 30°56S 148°27E 153 A8
Coonana Australia 31°0S 123°0E 149 F3
Coondapoor India 13°42N 74°40E 127 E2
Cooninie, L. Australia 26°4S 139°59E 151 D3
Coonoor India 11°21N 76°45E 127 J3
Cooper U.S.A. 33°23N 95°42W 176 E7
Cooper Cr. →
Australia 32°50N 79°56W 178 B8
Cooper Cr. →
Australia 28°29S 137°46E 151 D3
Cooper Ridge Pac. Oc. 10°0N 150°30W 157 F12
Cooperstown N. Dak.,
U.S.A. 47°27N 98°8W 172 B4
Cooperstown N.Y.,
U.S.A. 42°42N 74°56W 175 D10
Coopracambra △
Australia 37°15S 149°2E 153 D8
Coorabie Australia 31°54S 132°18E 149 F5
Coorong, The
Australia 35°50S 139°20E 152 C3
Coorong △ Australia 36°0S 139°29E 152 C3
Coorow Australia 29°53S 116°2E 149 E2
Cooroy Australia 26°22S 152°54E 151 D5
Coos Bay U.S.A. 43°22N 124°13W 168 E1
Coosa → U.S.A. 32°30N 86°16W 177 E11
Cootamundra Australia 34°36S 148°1E 153 C8
Cootehill Ireland 54°4N 7°5W 64 B4
Copahue Paso Argentina 37°49S 71°8W 190 D2
Copainalá Mexico 17°4N 93°18W 181 D6
Copake U.S.A. 42°7N 73°31W 175 D11
Copalnic Mănăştur
Romania 47°30N 23°41E 81 C8
Copán Honduras 14°50N 89°9W 182 D2
Copceac Moldova 45°51N 28°42E 81 E13
Cope Colo., U.S.A. 39°40N 102°51W 168 G12
Cope, C. Spain 37°26N 1°28W 91 H3
Copeland U.S.A. 25°57N 81°22W 179 H7
Copenhagen = København
Denmark 55°40N 12°26E 63 F7
Copenhagen U.S.A. 43°54N 75°41W 175 C9
Copertino Italy 40°16N 18°3E 95 B11
Copiapó Chile 27°30S 70°20W 190 B1
Copiapó → Chile 27°19S 70°56W 190 B1
Copley Australia 30°36S 138°26E 152 B2
Copo △ Argentina 25°53S 61°41W 190 B3
Copp L. Canada 60°14N 114°40W 162 A6
Copparo Italy 44°54N 11°49E 92 D8
Coppename → Suriname 5°48N 55°55W 187 B7
Copper Canyon = Barranca del
Cobre △ Mexico 27°18N 107°40W 180 B3
Copper Center
U.S.A. 61°58N 145°18W 166 C11
Copper Harbor U.S.A. 47°28N 87°53W 172 B9
Copper Queen
Zimbabwe 17°29S 29°18E 143 F2
Copperas Cove U.S.A. 31°8N 97°54W 176 F6
Copperbelt □ Zambia 13°15S 27°30E 143 E2
Coppermine = Kugluktuk
Canada 67°50N 115°5W 160 D8
Coppermine →
Canada 67°49N 116°4W 160 D8
Copperopolis U.S.A. 37°58N 120°38W 170 H6
Copșa Mică Romania 46°7N 24°15E 81 D9
Coquet → U.K. 55°20N 1°32W 66 B6
Coquille U.S.A. 43°11N 124°11W 168 E1
Coquimbo Chile 30°0S 71°20W 190 C1
Coquimbo □ Chile 31°0S 71°0W 190 C1
Coquitlam Canada 49°17N 122°45W 170 A4
Corabia Romania 43°48N 24°30E 81 G9
Coração de Jesus
Brazil 16°43S 44°22W 189 D2
Coracora Peru 15°5S 73°45W 188 D3
Coraki Australia 28°59S 153°17E 153 A9
Coral U.S.A. 40°29N 79°10W 174 F5
Coral Bay Australia 23°5S 113°46E 148 D1
Coral Gables U.S.A. 25°43N 80°16W 179 H7
Coral Harbour Canada 64°8N 83°10W 161 E15
Coral Sea Pac. Oc. 15°0S 150°0E 154 C6
Coral Sea Basin Pac. Oc. 14°0S 152°0E 150 b
Coral Sea Islands Terr. □
Australia 20°0S 155°0E 154 C8
Coral Springs U.S.A. 26°16N 80°16W 179 H7
Corangamite, L.
Australia 38°0S 143°30E 152 E5
Corantijn = Courantyne →
S. Amer. 5°50N 57°8W 187 B7
Coraopolis U.S.A. 40°31N 80°10W 174 F4
Corato Italy 41°9N 16°25E 95 A9
Corbeil-Essonnes France 48°36N 2°26E 70 D9
Corbett △ India 29°20N 79°0E 125 E8
Corbie France 49°54N 2°30E 70 B9
Corbières France 42°55N 2°35E 72 F6
Corbigny France 47°16N 3°40E 71 E10
Corbin U.S.A. 36°57N 84°6W 173 G11
Corbones → Spain 37°36N 5°39W 89 H5
Corbu Romania 44°25N 28°39E 81 F13
Corby U.K. 52°30N 0°41W 67 E7
Corcaigh = Cork Ireland 51°54N 8°29W 64 E3
Corcoran U.S.A. 36°6N 119°33W 170 J7
Corcovado △ Chile 43°25S 72°45W 192 C2
Corcovado, G. del Chile 43°30S 73°30W 192 C2
Corcubión Spain 42°56N 9°12W 88 C1
Cordele U.S.A. 31°58N 83°47W 178 D6
Cordell U.S.A. 35°17N 98°59W 176 D5
Cordenons Italy 45°59N 12°42E 93 C9
Cordes-sur-Ciel France 44°5N 1°57E 72 D5
Cordillera Azul △ Peru 7°30S 76°0W 186 E3
Cordisburgo Brazil 19°5S 44°21W 189 E2
Córdoba Argentina 31°20S 64°10W 190 C3
Córdoba Mexico 18°53N 96°56W 181 D5
Córdoba Spain 37°50N 4°50W 89 H6
Córdoba □ Argentina 31°22S 64°15W 190 C3
Córdoba □ Spain 38°5N 5°0W 89 H6
Córdoba, Sierra de
Argentina 31°10S 64°25W 190 C3
Cordova U.S.A. 60°33N 145°45W 166 C11
Corella Spain 42°7N 1°48W 90 C3
Corella → Australia 19°34S 140°47E 150 C3
Coremas Brazil 7°1S 37°20W 189 B3
Corentyne = Courantyne →
S. Amer. 5°50N 57°8W 187 B7
Corfield Australia 21°40S 143°21E 150 C3
Corfu = Kerkyra Greece 39°38N 19°50E 105 E3
Corfu U.S.A. 42°57N 78°24W 174 D6

orfu ✗ (CFU) Greece 39°35N 19°54E 98 B1
Steno Greece 39°34N 20°0E 101 A4
orgo □ O Corgo Spain 42°56N 7°25W 88 C3
oria Italy 41°39N 12°55E 94 A5
oria Spain 39°58N 6°33W 88 F4
oria del Río Spain 37°16N 6°3W 89 H4
oricudgy Australia 32°51S 150°24E 153 B9
oringa Is. Australia 16°58S 149°58E 150 B4
orinth = Korinthos Greece
orinth Miss., U.S.A. 34°56N 88°31W 177 D10
orinth N.Y., U.S.A. 43°15N 73°49W 175 C11
orinth, G. of = Korinthiakos Kolpos Greece 38°16N 22°30E 98 C4
orinth Canal Greece 37°58N 23°0E 98 D4
orinto Brazil 18°20S 44°30W 189 D2
orinto Nic. 12°30N 87°10W 182 D2
ork Ireland 51°54N 8°29W 64 E3
ork □ Ireland 51°57N 8°40W 64 E3
ork Harbour Ireland 51°47N 8°16W 64 E3
orlay France 48°20N 3°5W 70 D3
orleone Italy 37°49N 13°18E 94 E6
orleto Perticara Italy 40°23N 16°8E 95 C8
orlu Turkey 41°11N 27°49E 97 E11
ormack L. Canada 60°56N 121°37W 162 A4
ormòns Italy 54°58N 13°28E 93 C10
ormorant Canada 54°14N 100°35W 163 C8
ormorant L. Canada 54°15N 100°50W 163 C8
orn Is. = Maíz, Is. del Nic. 12°15N 83°4W 182 D3
ornalvo □ Spain 39°1N 6°13W 89 F4
ornélio Procópio Brazil 23°7S 50°40W 191 A5
orner Brook Canada 48°57N 57°58W 161 C8
orner Inlet Australia 38°45S 146°20E 153 E7
orner Seamounts Atl. Oc. 35°0N 52°0W 56 C6
orneşti Moldova 47°21N 28°1E 81 C13
orníglio Italy 44°29N 10°5E 92 D7
orning Ark., U.S.A. 36°25N 90°35W 177 C9
orning Calif., U.S.A. 39°56N 122°11W 168 G2
orning Iowa, U.S.A. 40°59N 94°44W 172 E6
orning N.Y., U.S.A. 42°9N 77°3W 174 D7
orno Grande Italy 42°28N 13°34E 93 F10
ornwall Canada 45°2N 74°44W 175 A10
ornwall U.S.A. 40°17N 76°25W 175 F8
ornwall □ U.K. 50°26N 4°40W 67 G3
ornwall I. Canada 77°37N 94°38W 161 B13
ornwallis I. Canada 75°8N 95°0W 161 B13
orny Pt. Australia 34°55S 137°0E 152 C2
oro Venezuela 11°25N 69°41W 186 A5
oroaci Brazil 18°35S 42°57W 189 D3
oroatá Brazil 4°8S 44°0W 189 A2
orocoro Bolivia 17°15S 68°28W 188 D4
oroico Bolivia 16°0S 67°50W 188 D4
oromandel Brazil 18°28S 47°13W 189 D1
oromandel N.Z. 36°45S 175°31E 154 C4
oromandel Coast India 12°30N 81°0E 127 H5
oromandel Pen. N.Z. 37°0S 175°45E 154 C4
oromandel Ra. N.Z. 37°0S 175°40E 154 C4
orona Calif., U.S.A. 33°53N 117°34W 171 M9
orona N. Mex., U.S.A. 34°15N 105°36W 169 J11
oronado U.S.A. 32°41N 117°10W 171 N9
oronado, B. de Costa Rica 9°0N 83°40W 182 E3
oronados, G. de los Chile 41°40S 74°0W 192 B2
oronados, Is. Los Mexico 32°26N 117°19W 171 N9
oronation Canada 52°5N 111°27W 162 C6
oronation Gulf Canada 68°25N 110°0W 160 D10
oronation I. Antarctica 60°45S 46°0W 55 C18
oronation Is. Australia 14°57S 124°55E 148 B3
oronda Argentina 31°58S 60°56W 190 C4
oronel Chile 37°0S 73°10W 190 D1
oronel Bogado Paraguay 27°11S 56°18W 190 B4
oronel Dorrego Argentina 38°40S 61°10W 190 D3
oronel Fabriciano Brazil 19°31S 42°38W 189 D2
oronel Murta Brazil 16°37S 42°11W 189 D2
oronel Oviedo Paraguay 25°24S 56°30W 190 B4
oronel Pringles Argentina 38°0S 61°30W 190 D3
oronel Suárez Argentina 37°30S 61°52W 190 D3
oronel Vidal Argentina 37°28S 57°45W 190 D4
orongo Peru 8°30S 77°53W 188 B2
oropuna, Nevado Peru 15°30S 72°41W 188 D3
orovodě Albania 40°31N 20°14E 96 F4
orowa Australia 35°58S 146°21E 153 C7
orozal □ Belize 18°23N 88°23W 181 D7
orozal Pt. Trin. & Tob. 10°45N 61°37W 187 K15
orps U.S.A. 44°50N 5°56E 73 D9
orpus Argentina 27°10S 55°30W 191 B4
orpus Christi U.S.A. 27°47N 97°24W 176 H6
orpus Christi, L. U.S.A. 28°2N 97°52W 176 G6
orque Bolivia 18°20S 67°41W 188 D4
orral Chile 39°52S 73°26W 192 A2
orral de Almaguer Spain 39°45N 3°10W 88 F7
orraun Pen. Ireland 53°54N 9°54W 64 C2
orréggio Italy 44°46N 10°47E 92 D7
orrente Brazil 10°27S 45°10W 189 C2
orrente → Brazil 13°8S 43°28W 189 C2
orrentes, C. das Mozam. 24°6S 35°34E 145 B6
orrentina Brazil 13°20S 44°39W 189 C2
orrèze □ France 45°20N 1°45E 72 C5
orrèze → France 45°10N 1°28E 72 C5
orrib, L. Ireland 53°27N 9°16W 64 C2
orridónia Italy 43°15N 13°30E 93 E10
orrientes Argentina 27°30S 58°45W 190 B4
orrientes □ Argentina 28°0S 57°0W 190 B4
orrientes → Argentina 30°42S 59°38W 190 C4
orrientes → Peru 3°43S 74°35W 188 A3
orrientes, C. Colombia 5°30N 77°34W 186 B3

Corrientes, C. Cuba 21°43N 84°30W 182 B3
Corrientes, C. Mexico 20°25N 105°42W 180 C3
Corrigan U.S.A. 31°0N 94°52W 176 F7
Corrigin Australia 32°20S 117°53E 149 F2
Corriverton Guyana 5°55N 57°20W 186 B7
Corry U.S.A. 41°55N 79°39W 174 E5
Corryong Australia 36°12S 147°53E 153 D7
Corse □ France 42°0N 9°0E 73 G13
Corse, C. France 43°1N 9°25E 73 F13
Corse □ France 42°14N 9°10E 73 F13
Corse-du-Sud □ France 41°45N 9°0E 73 G13
Corsica = Corse □ France 42°0N 9°0E 73 G13
Corsicana U.S.A. 32°6N 96°28W 176 E6
Corte France 42°19N 9°11E 73 F13
Corte Pinto Portugal 37°42N 7°29W 89 H3
Cortegana Spain 37°52N 6°49W 89 H4
Cortés, Mar de = California, G. de Mexico 27°0N 111°0W 180 B2
Cortez U.S.A. 37°21N 108°35W 169 H9
Cortina d'Ampezzo Italy 46°32N 12°8E 93 B9
Cortland N.Y., U.S.A. 42°36N 76°11W 175 D8
Cortland Ohio, U.S.A. 41°20N 80°44W 174 E4
Cortona Italy 43°16N 12°0E 93 E8
Corubal → Guinea-Biss. 11°57N 15°5W 138 C2
Coruche Portugal 38°57N 8°30W 89 G2
Çoruh → Turkey 41°38N 41°38E 87 K5
Çorum Turkey 40°30N 34°57E 104 B6
Çorum □ Turkey 40°40N 35°0E 104 B6
Corumbá Brazil 19°0S 57°30W 186 G7
Corumbá → Brazil 18°19S 48°55W 189 D1
Corumbaíba Brazil 18°9S 48°34W 189 D1
Corund Romania 46°30N 25°13E 81 D10
Corunna = A Coruña Spain 43°20N 8°25W 88 B2
Corvallis U.S.A. 44°34N 123°16W 168 D2
Corvette, L. de la Canada 53°25N 74°3W 164 B5
Corvo Azores 39°43N 31°8W 134 a
Corydon U.S.A. 40°46N 93°19W 172 E7
Cosalá Mexico 24°23N 106°41W 180 C3
Cosamaloapan de Carpio Mexico 18°22N 95°48W 181 D5
Cosenza Italy 39°18N 16°15E 95 C9
Coşereni Romania 44°38N 26°35E 81 F11
Coshocton U.S.A. 40°16N 81°51W 174 F3
Cosmo Newberry Australia 28°0S 122°54E 149 E3
Cosmo Newberry ◇ Australia 27°59S 122°53E 149 E3
Cosmonaut Sea S. Ocean 66°30S 40°0E 55 C5
Cosne-Cours-sur-Loire France 47°24N 2°54E 71 E9
Coso Junction U.S.A. 36°3N 117°57W 171 J9
Coso Pk. U.S.A. 36°13N 117°44W 171 J9
Cospeito = A Feira do Monte Spain 43°21N 7°34W 88 B3
Cosquín Argentina 31°15S 64°30W 190 C3
Cossato Italy 45°34N 8°10E 92 C5
Cossé-le-Vivien France 47°57N 0°54W 70 E6
Cosson → France 47°30N 1°15E 70 E8
Costa dels Pins Spain 39°36N 3°26E 100 B11
Costa Mesa U.S.A. 33°38N 117°55W 171 M9
Costa Rica ■ Cent. Amer. 10°0N 84°0W 182 E3
Costa Teguise Canary Is. 29°0N 13°31W 100 F6
Costeşti Romania 44°40N 24°53E 81 F9
Costigliole d'Asti Italy 44°47N 8°11E 92 D5
Cosumnes → U.S.A. 38°16N 121°26W 170 G5
Coswig Sachsen, Germany 51°7N 13°34E 76 D9
Coswig Sachsen-Anhalt, Germany 51°53N 12°27E 76 D8
Cotabato Phil. 7°14N 124°15E 119 C6
Cotacaes → Bolivia 16°0S 67°1W 188 D4
Cotagaita Bolivia 20°45S 65°40W 190 A2
Cotahuasi Peru 15°12S 72°50W 188 D3
Côte-d'Ivoire = Ivory Coast ■ Africa 7°30N 5°0W 138 D4
Côte d'Or □ France 47°30N 4°50E 71 E11
Coteau des Prairies U.S.A. 45°20N 97°50W 172 C5
Coteau du Missouri U.S.A. 47°0N 100°0W 172 B4
Cotegipe Brazil 12°2S 44°15W 189 C2
Cotentin France 49°15N 1°30W 70 C5
Côtes-d'Armor □ France 48°25N 2°40W 70 D4
Côtes de Meuse France 49°15N 5°22E 71 C12
Côtes-du-Nord = Côtes-d'Armor □ France 48°25N 2°40W 70 D4
Cotiella Spain 42°31N 0°19E 90 C5
Cotiujeni Moldova 47°51N 28°33E 81 C13
Cotonou Benin 6°20N 2°25E 139 D5
Cotopaxi Ecuador 0°40S 78°30W 186 D3
Cotronei Italy 39°9N 16°47E 95 C9
Cotswold Hills U.K. 51°42N 2°10W 67 F5
Cottage Grove U.S.A. 43°48N 123°3W 168 E2
Cottageville U.S.A. 32°56N 80°29W 178 C9
Cottam Canada 42°8N 82°45W 174 D2
Cottbus Germany 51°45N 14°20E 76 D10
Cottingham U.K. 53°48N 0°25W 66 D7
Cottondale U.S.A. 30°48N 85°23W 178 E4
Cottonwood Ala., U.S.A. 31°3N 85°18W 178 D4
Cottonwood Ariz., U.S.A. 34°45N 112°1W 169 J7
Cotulla U.S.A. 28°26N 99°14W 176 G5
Coubre, Pte. de la France 45°42N 1°15W 72 C3
Couches France 46°53N 4°30E 71 F11
Couço Portugal 38°59N 8°17W 89 G2
Couedic, C. du Australia 36°5S 136°40E 152 D2
Couesnon → France 48°38N 1°32W 70 D5
Couhé France 46°18N 0°11E 72 B4
Coulanges-sur-Yonne France 47°31N 3°33E 71 E10
Coulee City U.S.A. 47°37N 119°17W 168 C4
Coulman I. Antarctica 73°35S 170°0E 55 D11
Coulommiers France 48°50N 3°3E 71 D10
Coulon → France 43°51N 5°0E 73 E9
Coulonge → Canada 45°52N 76°46W 164 C4
Coulonges-sur-l'Autize France 46°29N 0°36W 72 B3
Coulounieix-Chamiers France 45°11N 0°42E 72 C4
Coultervílle U.S.A. 37°43N 120°12W 170 H6
Council Alaska, U.S.A. 64°53N 163°41W 166 C7
Council Ga., U.S.A. 30°37N 82°31W 178 E7

Council Idaho, U.S.A. 44°44N 116°26W 168 D5
Council Bluffs U.S.A. 41°16N 95°52W 172 E6
Council Grove U.S.A. 38°40N 96°29W 172 F5
Coupeville U.S.A. 48°13N 122°41W 170 B4
Courantyne → S. Amer. 5°50N 57°8W 186 B7
Courcelles Belgium 50°28N 4°22E 69 D4
Courchevel France 45°25N 6°36E 73 C10
Courçon France 46°15N 0°50W 72 B3
Courmayeur Italy 45°47N 6°58E 92 C3
Couronne, C. France 43°19N 5°3E 73 E9
Cours-la-Ville France 46°7N 4°19E 71 F11
Coursan France 43°14N 3°4E 72 E7
Courseulles-sur-Mer France 49°20N 0°29W 70 C6
Courtenay Canada 49°45N 125°0W 162 D4
Courtenay France 48°3N 3°1E 71 D10
Courtland Canada 42°51N 80°38W 174 D4
Courtland U.S.A. 38°20N 121°34W 170 G5
Courtrai = Kortrijk Belgium 50°50N 3°17E 69 D3
Courtright Canada 42°49N 82°28W 174 D2
Coushatta U.S.A. 32°1N 93°21W 176 E8
Coutances France 49°3N 1°28W 70 C5
Coutras France 45°3N 0°8W 72 C3
Coutts Crossing Australia 29°49S 152°55E 151 D5
Couva Trin. & Tob. 10°25N 61°27W 187 K15
Couvin Belgium 50°3N 4°29E 69 D4
Covarrubias Spain 42°4N 3°31W 88 D7
Covasna Romania 45°50N 26°10E 81 E11
Covasna □ Romania 45°50N 26°0E 81 E10
Cove L. Canada 45°1N 78°14W 174 A3
Coventry U.K. 52°25N 1°28W 67 E6
Coverdale U.S.A. 31°38N 83°58W 178 D6
Covilhã Portugal 40°17N 7°31W 88 E3
Covington Ga., U.S.A. 33°36N 83°51W 178 C6
Covington Ky., U.S.A. 39°5N 84°30W 173 F11
Covington Tenn., U.S.A. 35°34N 89°39W 177 D10
Covington Va., U.S.A. 37°47N 79°59W 173 G14
Cowal, L. Australia 33°40S 147°25E 153 B8
Cowan, L. Australia 31°45S 121°45E 149 F3
Cowan, L. Canada 54°0N 107°15W 163 C7
Cowangie Australia 35°12S 141°26E 152 C4
Cowansville Canada 45°14N 72°46W 175 A12
Coward Springs Australia 29°24S 136°49E 151 D2
Cowcowing Lakes Australia 30°55S 117°20E 149 F2
Cowdenbeath U.K. 56°7N 3°21W 65 E5
Cowell Australia 33°39S 136°56E 152 B2
Cowes U.K. 50°45N 1°18W 67 G6
Cowichan L. Canada 48°53N 124°17W 170 B2
Cowlitz → U.S.A. 46°6N 122°55W 170 D4
Cowra Australia 33°49S 148°42E 153 B8
Cox Spain 38°8N 0°53W 91 G4
Coxilha Grande Brazil 28°18S 51°30W 191 B5
Coxim Brazil 18°30S 54°55W 189 D6
Cox's Bazar Bangla. 21°26N 91°59E 123 J17
Coyah Guinea 9°42N 13°22W 138 D2
Coyote Wells U.S.A. 32°44N 115°58W 171 N11
Coyuca de Benitez Mexico 17°2N 100°4W 181 D4
Coyuca de Catalán Mexico 18°20N 100°39W 181 D4
Cozad U.S.A. 40°52N 99°59W 172 E4
Cozes France 45°34N 0°49W 72 C3
Cozia △ Romania 45°25N 24°16E 81 E9
Cozumel Mexico 20°31N 86°55W 181 C7
Cozumel, Isla Mexico 20°30N 86°40W 181 C7
Crab Hill Barbados 13°19N 59°38W 183 g
Cracow = Kraków Poland 50°4N 19°57E 83 H6
Cracow Australia 25°17S 150°17E 151 D5
Craddock Channel N.Z. 36°0S 175°13E 154 C4
Cradle Mt.-Lake St. Clair △ Australia 41°49S 147°56E 151 G4
Cradock S. Africa 32°8S 25°36E 144 D4
Crafers Australia 35°0S 138°42E 152 C3
Craig U.S.A. 40°31N 107°33W 168 F10
Craigavon U.K. 54°27N 6°23W 64 B5
Craigieburn Australia 37°35S 144°56E 153 D6
Craigmore Zimbabwe 20°28S 32°50E 143 G3
Craik Canada 51°3N 105°49E 163 C7
Crailsheim Germany 49°8N 10°5E 77 F6
Craiova Romania 44°21N 23°48E 81 F8
Cramsie Australia 23°20S 144°15E 150 C3
Cranberry L. U.S.A. 44°11N 74°50W 175 B10
Cranberry Portage Canada 54°35N 101°23W 163 C8
Cranbrook Australia 34°18S 117°33E 149 F2
Cranbrook Canada 49°30N 115°46W 162 D5
Crandon U.S.A. 45°34N 88°54W 172 C9
Crane Oreg., U.S.A. 43°25N 118°35W 168 E4
Crane Tex., U.S.A. 31°24N 102°21W 176 F3
Crane, The Barbados 13°6N 59°27W 183 g
Cranganore India 10°13N 76°13E 127 J3
Cranston U.S.A. 41°47N 71°26W 175 E13
Craon France 47°50N 0°58W 70 E6
Craonne France 49°27N 3°46E 71 C10
Craponne-sur-Arzon France 45°19N 3°51E 72 C7
Crasna Romania 46°32N 27°51E 81 D12
Crasna → Romania 47°44N 22°35E 80 C7
Crasnei, Munţii Romania 47°0N 23°20E 81 C8
Crater L. △ U.S.A. 42°55N 122°6W 168 E2
Crater L. △ U.S.A. 42°55N 122°10W 168 E2
Craters of the Moon △ U.S.A. 43°25N 113°30W 168 E7
Crateús Brazil 5°10S 40°39W 189 B2
Crati → Italy 39°43N 16°31E 95 C9
Crato Brazil 7°10S 39°25W 189 B3
Crato Portugal 39°16N 7°39W 89 F3
Craven, L. Canada 54°20N 76°56W 164 B4
Crawford Ala., U.S.A. 32°27N 85°11W 178 C4
Crawford Nebr., U.S.A. 42°41N 103°25W 172 D2
Crawfordsville U.S.A. 40°2N 86°54W 172 E8
Crawfordville Fla., U.S.A. 30°11N 84°23W 178 E6
Crawfordville Ga., U.S.A. 33°33N 82°54W 178 B7
Crawley U.K. 51°7N 0°11W 67 F7
Crazy Mts. U.S.A. 46°12N 110°20W 168 C8
Crean L. Canada 54°5N 106°9W 163 C7
Crécy-en-Ponthieu France 50°15N 1°53E 71 B8
Crediton Canada 43°17N 81°33W 174 C3

Crediton U.K. 50°47N 3°40W 67 G4
Cree → Canada 58°57N 105°47W 163 B7
Cree → U.K. 54°55N 4°25W 65 G4
Cree L. Canada 57°30N 106°30W 163 B7
Creede U.S.A. 37°51N 106°56W 169 H10
Creekside U.S.A. 40°40N 79°11W 174 F5
Creel Mexico 27°45N 107°38W 180 B3
Creemore Canada 44°19N 80°6W 174 B4
Creighton Canada 54°45N 101°54W 163 C8
Creighton U.S.A. 42°28N 97°54W 172 D5
Creil France 49°15N 2°29E 71 C9
Crema Italy 45°22N 9°41E 92 C6
Cremona Italy 45°7N 10°2E 92 C7
Crepaja Serbia 45°1N 20°38E 80 E5
Crépy France 49°35N 3°32E 71 C10
Crépy-en-Valois France 49°14N 2°54E 71 C9
Cres Croatia 44°58N 14°25E 93 D11
Crescent City Calif., U.S.A. 41°45N 124°12W 168 F1
Crescent City Fla., U.S.A. 29°26N 81°31W 179 F8
Crescent Group S. China Sea 16°30N 111°40E 118 A4
Crescent Hd. Australia 31°11S 152°59E 153 A10
Crescent L. U.S.A. 29°28N 81°30W 179 F8
Crescentino Italy 45°11N 8°6E 92 C5
Crespi d'Adda Italy 45°35N 9°32E 92 C6
Crespo Argentina 32°2S 60°19W 190 C3
Cresson U.S.A. 40°28N 78°36W 174 F6
Cressy Australia 38°2S 143°40E 152 E5
Crest France 44°44N 5°2E 73 D9
Crestline Calif., U.S.A. 34°14N 117°18W 171 L9
Crestline Ohio, U.S.A. 40°47N 82°44W 174 F2
Creston Canada 49°10N 116°31W 162 D5
Creston Calif., U.S.A. 35°32N 120°33W 170 K6
Creston Iowa, U.S.A. 41°4N 94°22W 172 E6
Crestview Calif., U.S.A. 37°46N 118°58W 170 H8
Crestview Fla., U.S.A. 30°46N 86°34W 179 F3
Creswick Australia 37°25S 143°58E 152 D5
Crêt de la Neige France 46°16N 5°58E 71 F12
Crete = Kríti Greece 35°15N 25°0E 101 D7
Crete U.S.A. 40°38N 96°58W 172 E5
Crete, Sea of Greece 36°0N 25°0E 99 F7
Créteil France 48°47N 2°27E 71 D9
Creus, C. de Spain 42°20N 3°19E 90 C8
Creuse □ France 46°10N 2°0E 71 F9
Creuse → France 47°0N 0°34E 72 B4
Creutzwald France 49°12N 6°42E 71 C13
Creuzburg Germany 51°3N 10°14E 76 D6
Crèvecoeur-le-Grand France 49°37N 2°5E 71 C9
Crevillent Spain 38°12N 0°48W 91 G4
Crewe U.K. 53°6N 2°26W 66 D5
Crewkerne U.K. 50°53N 2°48W 67 G5
Crianlarich U.K. 56°24N 4°37W 65 E4
Criciúma Brazil 28°40S 49°23W 191 B6
Cricova Moldova 47°8N 28°52E 81 C13
Crieff U.K. 56°22N 3°50W 65 E5
Crikvenica Croatia 45°11N 14°40E 93 C11
Crimea □ Ukraine 45°30N 33°10E 85 K8
Crimean Pen. = Krymskyy Pivostriv Ukraine 45°0N 34°0E 85 K8
Crimmitschau Germany 50°48N 12°24E 76 E8
Cristino Castro Brazil 8°49S 44°13W 189 B2
Cristuru Secuiesc Romania 46°17N 25°2E 81 D10
Crişul Alb → Romania 46°42N 21°17E 80 D6
Crişul Negru → Romania 46°42N 21°16E 80 D6
Crişul Repede → Romania 46°55N 20°59E 80 D5
Criuleni Moldova 47°13N 29°10E 81 C14
Crivitz Germany 53°34N 11°39E 76 B7
Crna Gora = Montenegro ■ Europe 42°40N 19°20E 96 D3
Crna Gora Macedonia 42°10N 21°30E 96 D5
Crna Reka → Macedonia 41°33N 21°59E 96 E5
Crna Trava Serbia 42°49N 22°19E 96 D6
Crni Drim → Macedonia 41°17N 20°40E 96 E4
Crni Timok → Serbia 43°53N 22°15E 96 C6
Crnoljeva Planina = Zhar, Mali Kosovo 42°20N 21°0E 96 D5
Črnomelj Slovenia 45°33N 15°10E 93 C12
Croagh Patrick Ireland 53°46N 9°40W 64 C2
Croajingolong △ Australia 37°45S 149°26E 153 D8
Croatia ■ Europe 45°20N 16°0E 93 C13
Crocker, Banjaran Malaysia 5°40N 116°30E 118 C5
Crockett U.S.A. 31°19N 95°27W 176 F7
Crocodile = Umgwenya → Mozam. 25°14S 32°18E 145 C5
Crocodile → S. Africa 24°12S 26°53E 144 B4
Crocodile Is. Australia 12°3S 134°58E 150 A1
Crocq France 45°52N 2°21E 72 C6
Crohy Hd. Ireland 54°55N 8°26W 64 B3
Croisette, C. France 43°14N 5°22E 73 E9
Croisic, Pte. du France 47°19N 2°31W 70 E4
Croix, L. La Canada 48°20N 92°15W 164 C1
Croker, C. Canada 44°58N 80°59W 174 B4
Croker, C. Australia 10°58S 132°35E 148 B5
Croker I. Australia 11°12S 132°32E 148 B5
Croker Islands Seas ◇ Australia 11°20S 132°30E 148 B5
Cromarty U.K. 57°40N 4°2W 65 D4
Cromer U.K. 52°56N 1°17E 66 E9
Cromwell N.Z. 45°3S 169°14E 155 F4
Cromwell U.S.A. 41°36N 72°39W 175 E12
Cronat France 46°43N 3°40E 71 F10
Crook U.K. 54°43N 1°45W 66 C6
Crooked → Canada 54°50N 122°54W 162 C4
Crooked → U.S.A. 44°32N 121°16W 168 D3
Crooked I. Bahamas 22°50N 74°10W 183 B5
Crooked Island Passage Bahamas 22°55N 74°35W 183 B5
Crookston Minn., U.S.A. 47°47N 96°37W 172 B5
Crookston Nebr., U.S.A. 42°56N 100°45W 172 D3
Crookwell Australia 34°28S 149°24E 153 B8
Cropane-Micone → Italy 38°31N 16°18E 95 D9
Crosby N. Dak., U.S.A. 48°55N 103°18W 172 A2
Crosby Pa., U.S.A. 41°45N 78°23W 174 E6
Crosbyton U.S.A. 33°40N 101°14W 176 E4
Cuiabá Brazil 15°30S 56°0W 187 G7

Crosia Italy 39°35N 16°45E 95 C9
Cross → Nigeria 4°42N 8°21E 139 E6
Cross City U.S.A. 29°38N 83°7W 179 F6
Cross Fell U.K. 54°43N 2°28W 66 C5
Cross L. Canada 54°37N 97°47W 163 C9
Cross Lake Canada 54°37N 97°47W 163 C9
Cross River □ Nigeria 6°0N 8°0E 139 D6
Cross River △ Nigeria 5°50N 9°50E 139 D6
Cross Sound U.S.A. 58°0N 135°0W 160 F4
Crossett U.S.A. 33°8N 91°58W 176 E8
Crosshaven Ireland 51°47N 8°17W 64 E3
Crossley, Mt. N.Z. 42°50S 172°5E 155 C7
Crossmaglen U.K. 54°5N 6°36W 64 B5
Crossmolina Ireland 54°6N 9°20W 64 B2
Crossville U.S.A. 35°57N 85°2W 177 D12
Croswell U.S.A. 43°16N 82°37W 174 C2
Croton-on-Hudson U.S.A. 41°12N 73°55W 175 E11
Crotone Italy 39°5N 17°8E 95 C10
Crow → Canada 59°41N 124°20W 162 B4
Crow Agency U.S.A. 45°36N 107°28W 168 D10
Crow Hd. Ireland 51°35N 10°9W 64 E1
Crowdy Bay △ Australia 31°45S 152°45E 153 A10
Crowl Cr. → Australia 32°0S 145°30E 153 B6
Crowley U.S.A. 30°13N 92°22W 176 F8
Crowley, L. U.S.A. 37°35N 118°42W 170 H8
Crown Point Ind. U.S.A. 41°25N 87°22W 172 E10
Crown Point N.Y., U.S.A. 43°57N 73°26W 175 C11
Crownpoint U.S.A. 35°41N 108°9W 169 J9
Crows Landing U.S.A. 37°23N 121°6W 170 H5
Crows Nest Australia 27°16S 152°4E 151 D5
Crowsnest Pass Canada 49°40N 114°40W 162 D6
Croydon Australia 18°13S 142°14E 150 B3
Croydon □ U.K. 51°22N 0°5W 67 F7
Crozet, Îs. Ind. Oc. 46°27S 52°0E 146 J4
Crozet Basin Ind. Oc. 39°0S 60°0E 146 H5
Crozon France 48°15N 4°30W 70 D2
Cruce de Sardina Canary Is. 27°52N 15°22W 100 G4
Crusheen Ireland 52°57N 8°53W 64 D3
Cruz, C. Cuba 19°50N 77°50W 182 C4
Cruz Alta Brazil 28°40S 53°40W 191 B5
Cruz das Almas Brazil 12°0S 39°6W 189 C3
Cruz Bay U.S. Virgin Is. 18°20N 64°48W 183 e
Cruz del Eje Argentina 30°45S 64°50W 190 C3
Cruzeiro Brazil 22°33S 45°0W 191 A7
Cruzeiro do Oeste Brazil 23°46S 53°4W 191 A5
Cruzeiro do Sul Brazil 7°35S 72°35W 186 E3
Cry L. Canada 58°45N 129°0W 162 B3
Crystal B. U.S.A. 28°50N 82°35W 179 G7
Crystal Bay U.S.A. 39°15N 120°0W 170 F7
Crystal Brook Australia 33°21S 138°12E 152 B3
Crystal City U.S.A. 28°41N 99°50W 176 G5
Crystal Falls U.S.A. 46°5N 88°20W 172 B9
Crystal Lake U.S.A. 30°26N 85°42W 178 E4
Crystal River U.S.A. 28°54N 82°35W 179 G7
Crystal Springs U.S.A. 31°59N 90°21W 177 F9
Csenger Hungary 47°50N 22°41E 80 C7
Csongrád Hungary 46°43N 20°12E 80 D5
Csongrád □ Hungary 46°32N 20°15E 80 D5
Csorna Hungary 47°38N 17°18E 80 C2
Csurgo Hungary 46°16N 17°9E 80 D2
Cu Lao Hon Vietnam 10°54N 108°18E 121 G7
Cua Rao Vietnam 19°16N 104°27E 120 C5
Cuácua → Mozam. 17°54S 37°0E 143 F4
Cuamato Angola 17°2S 15°7E 144 A2
Cuamba Mozam. 14°45S 36°22E 143 E4
Cuando → Angola 17°30S 23°15E 141 H4
Cuando Cubango □ Angola 16°25S 20°0E 144 A3
Cuangar Angola 17°36S 18°39E 144 A2
Cuango = Kwango → Dem. Rep. of the Congo 3°14S 17°22E 140 E3
Cuanza → Angola 9°21S 13°9E 140 F2
Cuarto → Argentina 33°25S 63°2W 190 C3
Cuatrociénegas Mexico 26°59N 102°5W 180 B4
Cuauhtémoc Mexico 28°25N 106°52W 180 B3
Cuba Portugal 38°10N 7°54W 89 G3
Cuba N. Mex., U.S.A. 36°1N 107°4W 169 H10
Cuba N.Y., U.S.A. 42°13N 78°17W 174 D6
Cuba ■ W. Indies 22°0N 79°0W 182 B4
Cubango → Africa 18°50S 22°25E 144 B3
Çubuk Turkey 40°14N 33°3E 104 B5
Cuc Phuong △ Vietnam 20°17N 105°38E 120 B5
Cuchillo-Co Argentina 38°20S 64°37W 192 A4
Cuchumatanes, Sierra de los Guatemala 15°35N 91°25W 182 C1
Cucui Brazil 1°12N 66°50W 186 C5
Cucurpe Mexico 30°20N 110°43W 180 A2
Cúcuta Colombia 7°54N 72°31W 186 B4
Cudalbi Romania 45°46N 27°41E 81 E12
Cuddalore India 11°46N 79°45E 127 J4
Cuddapah = Kadapa India 14°30N 78°47E 127 J4
Cudgewa Australia 36°10S 147°42E 153 D7
Cudillero Spain 43°33N 6°9W 88 B4
Cue Australia 27°25S 117°54E 149 E2
Cuéllar Spain 41°23N 4°21W 88 D6
Cuenca Ecuador 2°50S 79°9W 186 D3
Cuenca Spain 40°5N 2°10W 90 E2
Cuenca □ Spain 40°0N 2°0W 90 E2
Cuenca, Serranía de Spain 39°55N 1°50W 90 E3
Cuerda del Pozo, Embalse de la Spain 41°51N 2°44W 90 D2
Cuernavaca Mexico 18°55N 99°15W 181 D5
Cuero U.S.A. 29°6N 97°17W 176 G6
Cuers France 43°14N 6°5E 73 E10
Cueva de la Quebrada del Toro △ Venezuela 10°6N 69°3W 186 A4
Cuevas del Almanzora Spain 37°18N 1°58W 91 H3
Cuevo Bolivia 20°15S 63°30W 188 E5
Cugir Romania 45°48N 23°25E 81 E8
Cugnaux France 43°32N 1°20E 72 E5
Cuhai-Bakony → Hungary 47°35N 17°54E 80 C2
Cuiabá Brazil 15°30S 56°0W 187 G7

Cuiabá → Brazil 17°5S 56°36W 187 G7
Cuihangcun China 22°27N 113°32E 111 a
Cuijk Neths. 51°44N 5°50E 69 C5
Cuilco Guatemala 15°24N 91°58W 182 C1
Cuillin Hills U.K. 57°13N 6°15W 65 D2
Cuillin Sd. U.K. 57°4N 6°20W 65 D2
Cuilo = Kwilu → Dem. Rep. of the Congo 3°22S 17°22E 140 E3
Cuiseaux France 46°30N 5°22E 71 F12
Cuité Brazil 6°29S 36°9W 189 B3
Cuito → Angola 18°1S 20°48E 144 A3
Cuitzeo, L. de Mexico 19°55N 101°5W 180 D4
Cujmir Romania 44°13N 22°57E 80 F7
Çukai Malaysia 4°13N 103°25E 121 K4
Çukurca Turkey 37°14N 43°36E 105 D10
Çukurova = Cilicia Turkey 36°30N 34°0E 104 D5
Culbertson U.S.A. 48°9N 104°31W 168 B12
Culburra N.S.W., Australia 34°56S 150°46E 153 C9
Culburra S. Austral., Australia 35°50S 139°58E 152 C3
Culcairn Australia 35°41S 147°3E 153 C7
Culebra Puerto Rico 18°19N 65°18W 183 d
Culebra, Sierra de la Spain 41°55N 6°20W 88 D4
Culfa Azerbaijan 38°57N 45°38E 105 C11
Culgoa → Australia 29°56S 146°20E 151 D4
Culgoa Flood Plain △ Australia 28°58S 147°5E 151 D4
Culiacán Mexico 24°50N 107°23W 180 C3
Culiacán → Mexico 24°30N 107°42W 180 C3
Culik Indonesia 8°21S 115°37E 119 J18
Culion Phil. 11°54N 119°58E 119 B6
Cúllar Spain 37°35N 2°34W 91 H2
Cullarin Ra. Australia 34°30S 149°30E 153 B8
Cullen U.K. 57°42N 2°49W 65 D6
Cullen Bullen Australia 33°18S 150°1E 153 B9
Cullen Pt. Australia 11°57S 141°54E 150 A3
Cullera Spain 39°9N 0°17W 91 F4
Cullman U.S.A. 34°11N 86°51W 177 D11
Culloden U.S.A. 32°52N 84°6W 178 C5
Cullompton U.K. 50°51N 3°24W 67 G4
Culoz France 45°47N 5°46E 73 C9
Culpeper U.S.A. 38°30N 78°0W 173 F14
Culuene → Brazil 12°56S 52°51W 187 F8
Culver, Pt. Australia 32°54S 124°43E 149 F3
Culverden N.Z. 42°47S 172°49E 155 C7
Culverton U.S.A. 33°19N 82°54W 178 B7
Cumaná Venezuela 10°30N 64°5W 186 A6
Cumaovası Turkey 38°15N 27°9E 99 C9
Cumari Brazil 18°16S 48°11W 189 D1
Cumberland B.C., Canada 49°40N 125°0W 162 D4
Cumberland Ont., Canada 45°29N 75°24W 175 A9
Cumberland U.S.A. 39°39N 78°46W 173 F14
Cumberland → U.S.A. 37°9N 88°25W 172 G9
Cumberland, L. U.S.A. 36°52N 85°9W 173 G11
Cumberland Gap △ U.S.A. 36°36N 83°40W 173 G12
Cumberland I. U.S.A. 30°50N 81°25W 178 E8
Cumberland Is. Australia 20°35S 149°10E 150 b
Cumberland Island △ U.S.A. 30°12N 81°24W 178 E8
Cumberland L. Canada 54°3N 102°18W 163 C8
Cumberland Pen. Canada 67°0N 64°0W 161 D19
Cumberland Plateau U.S.A. 36°0N 85°0W 177 D12
Cumberland Sd. Canada 65°30N 66°0W 161 D18
Cumbernauld U.K. 55°57N 3°58W 65 F5
Cumborah Australia 29°40S 147°45E 151 D4
Cumbres de Majalca △ Mexico 28°48N 106°30W 180 B3
Cumbres de Monterrey △ Mexico 25°26N 100°25W 180 B4
Cumbres Mayores Spain 38°4N 6°39W 89 G4
Cumbria □ U.K. 54°42N 2°52W 66 C5
Cumbrian Mts. U.K. 54°30N 3°0W 66 C5
Cumbum India 15°40N 79°10E 127 G4
Cuminá → Brazil 1°30S 56°0W 187 D7
Cummings Mt. U.S.A. 35°2N 118°34W 171 K8
Cummins Australia 34°16S 135°43E 152 B2
Cumnock Australia 32°59S 148°46E 153 B8
Cumnock U.K. 55°28N 4°17W 65 F4
Cumpas Mexico 30°2N 109°48W 180 B3
Cumplida, Pta. Canary Is. 28°50N 17°48W 100 F3
Çumra Turkey 37°34N 32°54E 104 D5
Cuncumén Chile 31°53S 70°38W 190 C1
Cundeelee Australia 30°43S 123°25E 149 F3
Cunderdin Australia 31°37S 117°12E 149 F2
Cunene → Angola 17°20S 11°50E 144 A1
Cúneo Italy 44°23N 7°32E 92 D4
Cung Son Vietnam 13°2N 108°58E 120 F7
Çüngüş Turkey 38°13N 39°17E 105 C8
Cunillera, I. = Sa Conillera Spain 38°59N 1°13E 100 C7
Cunhat France 45°38N 3°32E 72 C7
Cunnamulla Australia 28°2S 145°38E 151 D4
Cuorgné Italy 45°23N 7°39E 92 C4
Cupar Canada 50°57N 104°10W 163 C8
Cupar U.K. 56°19N 3°1W 65 E5
Cupcini Moldova 48°6N 27°3E 81 B12
Cupertino U.S.A. 37°19N 122°2W 170 H4
Cupica, G. de Colombia 6°25N 77°30W 186 B3
Ćuprija Serbia 43°57N 21°26E 96 C5
Curaçá Brazil 8°5S 39°54W 189 B3
Curaçao W. Indies 12°10N 69°0W 187 D6
Curacautín Chile 38°26S 71°53W 192 A2
Curahuara de Carangas Bolivia 17°55S 68°26W 188 D4
Curanilahue Chile 37°29S 73°28W 190 D1
Curaray → Peru 2°20S 74°5W 186 D4
Cure → France 47°40N 3°41E 71 E10
Curepipe Mauritius 20°19N 57°31E 141 d
Curepto Chile 35°8S 72°1W 190 D1
Curia Portugal 40°22N 8°22W 88 E2
Curiapo Venezuela 8°33N 61°0W 187 B6
Curicó Chile 34°55S 71°20W 190 C1
Curieuse Seychelles 4°15S 55°44E 141 b
Curimatá Brazil 10°25S 44°17W 189 C2
Curinga Italy 38°49N 16°19E 95 D9
Curitiba Brazil 25°20S 49°10W 191 B6
Curitibanos Brazil 27°18S 50°36W 191 B5
Curlewis Australia 31°7S 150°16E 153 A9
Curonian Lagoon = Kurshskiy Zaliv Russia 55°9N 21°6E 82 C4

Curonian Spit *Europe* 55°20N 20°55E **82** C7
Currabubula *Australia* 31°16S 150°44E **153** A9
Currais Novos *Brazil* 6°13S 36°30W **189** B3
Curral Velho *C. Verde Is.* 16°8N 22°48W **134** b
Curralinho *Brazil* 1°45S 49°46W **187** D9
Currane, L. *Ireland* 51°49N 10°4W **64** E1
Currant *U.S.A.* 38°44N 115°28W **168** G6
Curraweena *Australia* 30°47S 145°54E **153** A6
Currawinya △
  Australia 28°55S 144°27E **151** D3
Current → *U.S.A.* 36°15N 90°55W **176** C9
Currie *Australia* 39°56S 143°53E **151** F3
Currie *U.S.A.* 40°16N 114°45W **168** F6
Curtea de Argeş
  Romania 45°12N 24°42E **81** E9
Curtici *Romania* 46°21N 21°18E **80** D6
Curtin Springs
  Australia 25°20S 131°45E **149** E5
Curtis *U.S.A.* 40°38N 100°31W **172** E3
Curtis Group *Australia* 39°30S 146°37E **151** F4
Curtis I. *Australia* 23°35S 151°10E **150** C5
Curuápanema → *Brazil* 2°25S 55°2W **187** D7
Curuçá *Brazil* 0°43S 47°50W **187** D9
Curuçá → *Brazil* 4°27S 71°23W **188** A3
Curuguaty *Paraguay* 24°31S 55°42W **191** A4
Çürüksu Çayi = Büyük
  Menderes → *Turkey* 37°28N 27°11E **99** D9
Curup *Indonesia* 4°26S 102°13E **118** E2
Cururupu *Brazil* 1°50S 44°50W **187** D10
Curuzú Cuatiá
  Argentina 29°50S 58°5W **190** B4
Curvelo *Brazil* 18°45S 44°27W **189** D2
Cusco *Peru* 13°32S 72°0W **188** C3
Cusco □ *Peru* 13°31S 71°59W **188** C3
Cushendall *U.K.* 55°5N 6°4W **64** A5
Cushing *U.S.A.* 35°59N 96°46W **176** D6
Cushing, Mt. *Canada* 57°35N 126°57W **162** B3
Cusihuiriáchic
  Mexico 28°14N 106°50W **180** B3
Cusna, Mte. *Italy* 44°17N 10°23E **92** D7
Cusset *France* 46°8N 3°28E **71** F10
Cusseta *U.S.A.* 32°18N 84°47W **178** C5
Custer *U.S.A.* 43°46N 103°36W **172** D2
Cut Bank *U.S.A.* 48°38N 112°20W **168** B7
Cutchogue *U.S.A.* 41°1N 72°30W **175** E12
Cutervo *Peru* 6°25S 78°55W **188** B2
Cuthbert *U.S.A.* 31°46N 84°48W **178** D5
Cutler *U.S.A.* 36°31N 119°17W **170** J7
Cutler Ridge *U.S.A.* 25°35N 80°20W **179** K9
Cutral-Có *Argentina* 38°58S 69°15W **192** A3
Cutro *Italy* 39°2N 16°59E **95** C9
Cuttaburra →
  Australia 29°43S 144°22E **151** D3
Cuttack *India* 20°25N 85°57E **126** D7
Cuvier, C. *Australia* 23°14S 113°22E **149** D1
Cuvier I. *N.Z.* 36°27S 175°50E **154** C4
Cuxhaven *Germany* 53°51N 8°41E **76** B4
Cuyahoga Falls *U.S.A.* 41°8N 81°29W **174** E3
Cuyahoga Valley △
  U.S.A. 41°24N 81°33W **174** E3
Cuyo *Phil.* 10°51N 121°2E **119** B6
Cuyuni → *Guyana* 6°23N 58°41W **186** B7
Cuzco = Cusco *Peru* 13°32S 72°0W **188** C3
Cuzco *Bolivia* 20°0S 66°50W **186** H5
Čvrsnica *Bos.-H.* 43°36N 17°35E **80** G2
Cwmbran *U.K.* 51°39N 3°2W **67** F4
Cyangugu *Rwanda* 2°29S 28°54E **142** C2
Cybinka *Poland* 52°12N 14°46E **83** F1
Cyclades = Kyklades
  Greece 37°0N 24°30E **98** E6
Cygnet *Australia* 43°8S 147°1E **151** G4
Cynthiana *U.S.A.* 38°23N 84°18W **173** F11
Cypress Hills *Canada* 49°40N 109°30W **163** D7
Cypress Hills △
  Canada 49°40N 109°30W **163** D7
Cyprus ■ *Asia* 35°0N 33°0E **101** E12
Cyrenaica = Barqa
  Libya 27°0N 23°0E **135** C10
Cyrene *Libya* 32°53N 21°52E **135** B10
Czaplinek *Poland* 53°34N 16°14E **82** E3
Czar *Canada* 52°27N 110°50W **163** C6
Czarna → *Łódzkie,*
  Poland 51°18N 19°55E **83** G6
Czarna → *Świętokrzyskie,*
  Poland 50°28N 21°21E **83** H8
Czarna Białostocka
  Poland 53°18N 23°17E **83** E10
Czarna Woda *Poland* 53°51N 18°6E **82** E5
Czarne *Poland* 53°42N 16°58E **82** E3
Czarnków *Poland* 52°55N 16°38E **83** F3
Czech Rep. ■ *Europe* 50°0N 15°0E **78** B8
Czechowice-Dziedzice
  Poland 49°54N 18°59E **83** J5
Czempiń *Poland* 52°9N 16°43E **83** F3
Czeremcha *Poland* 52°31N 23°21E **83** F10
Czersk *Poland* 53°46N 17°58E **82** E4
Czerwieńsk *Poland* 52°1N 15°23E **83** F2
Czerwionka-Leszczyny
  Poland 50°7N 18°37E **83** H5
Częstochowa *Poland* 50°49N 19°7E **83** H6
Człopa *Poland* 53°6N 16°6E **83** E3
Człuchów *Poland* 53°41N 17°22E **82** E4
Czyżew-Osada *Poland* 52°48N 22°19E **83** F9

D

Da → *Vietnam* 21°15N 105°20E **116** G5
Da Hinggan Ling *China* 48°0N 121°0E **111** B13
Da Lat *Vietnam* 11°56N 108°25E **121** G7
Da Nang *Vietnam* 16°4N 108°13E **120** D7
Da Qaidam *China* 37°50N 95°15E **110** D8
Da Yunhe → *Hopei,*
  China 39°10N 117°10E **115** E9
Da Yunhe → *Jiangsu,*
  China 34°25N 120°5E **115** H10
Da'an *China* 45°30N 124°7E **115** B13
Daan Viljoen → *Namibia* 22°2S 16°45E **144** B2
Dab'a, Ras el *Egypt* 31°3N 28°31E **137** A1
Daba Shan *China* 32°0N 109°0E **116** B7
Dabai *Nigeria* 11°25N 5°15E **139** C6
Dabakala *Ivory C.* 8°15N 4°20W **138** D4
Dabas *Hungary* 47°11N 19°19E **80** C4
Dabbagh, Jabal
  Si. Arabia 27°52N 35°45E **128** E2
Dabhoi *India* 22°10N 73°20E **124** H5
Dąbie *Poland* 52°5N 18°50E **83** F5
Dabie Shan *China* 31°20N 115°20E **117** B10
Dabilda *Cameroon* 12°45N 14°35E **139** D7
Dabnou *Niger* 14°10N 5°22E **139** C6

Dabola *Guinea* 10°50N 11°5W **138** C2
Dabou *Ivory C.* 5°20N 4°23W **138** D4
Daboya *Ghana* 9°30N 1°20W **139** D4
Dąbrowa Białostocka
  Poland 53°40N 23°21E **82** E10
Dąbrowa Górnicza
  Poland 50°15N 19°10E **83** H6
Dąbrowa Tarnowska
  Poland 50°10N 20°59E **83** H7
Dabu *China* 24°22N 116°41E **117** E11
Dabugam *India* 19°27N 82°26E **126** E6
Dabung *Malaysia* 5°23N 102°1E **121** K4
Dacca = Dhaka
  Bangla. 23°43N 90°26E **125** H14
Dachang *China* 32°13N 118°45E **117** A12
Dachaoshan Dam
  China 24°1N 100°22E **116** E3
Dachau *Germany* 48°15N 11°26E **77** G7
Dachigam △ *India* 34°10N 75°0E **124** B6
Dachstein, Hoher
  Austria 47°28N 13°35E **78** D6
Dačice *Czech Rep.* 49°5N 15°26E **78** D8
Dacre *Canada* 45°22N 76°57W **174** A8
Dacula *U.S.A.* 33°59N 83°54W **178** B6
Dadanawa *Guyana* 2°50N 59°30W **186** C7
Daday *Turkey* 41°28N 33°27E **104** B5
Dade City *U.S.A.* 28°22N 82°11W **179** G7
Dadès, Oued →
  Morocco 30°58N 6°44W **136** B2
Dadeville *U.S.A.* 32°50N 85°46W **178** C4
Dadhar *Pakistan* 29°28N 67°39E **124** E2
Dadiya *Nigeria* 9°35N 11°24E **139** D7
Dadra & Nagar Haveli □
  India 20°5N 73°0E **126** D1
Dadri = Charkhi Dadri
  India 28°37N 76°17E **124** E7
Dadu *Pakistan* 26°45N 67°45E **124** F2
Dadu He → *China* 29°31N 103°46E **116** C4
Daegu *S. Korea* 35°50N 128°37E **115** G15
Daejeon *S. Korea* 36°20N 127°28E **115** F14
Daejeong *S. Korea* 33°8N 126°17E **115** H14
Daet *Phil.* 14°2N 122°55E **119** B6
Dafang *China* 27°9N 105°39E **116** D5
Dafeng *China* 33°3N 120°45E **115** H11
Dafnes *Greece* 35°13N 25°3E **101** D7
Dafni *Greece* 37°48N 22°1E **98** D4
Dağ *Turkey* 37°12N 30°31E **99** D12
Dagana *Senegal* 16°30N 15°35W **138** B1
Dagash *Sudan* 19°19N 33°25E **137** D3
Dagestan □ *Russia* 42°30N 47°0E **87** J8
Dagestanskiye Ogni
  Russia 42°6N 48°12E **87** J9
Dagg Sd. *N.Z.* 45°23S 166°45E **155** F1
Daggett *U.S.A.* 34°52N 116°52W **171** L10
Daghestan Republic =
  Dagestan □ *Russia* 42°30N 47°0E **87** J8
Daghfeli *Sudan* 19°18N 32°40E **137** D3
Dağlıq Qarabağ =
  Nagorno-Karabakh □
  Azerbaijan 39°55N 46°45E **105** C12
Dagö = Hiiumaa *Estonia* 58°50N 22°45E **84** C2
Dagu *China* 38°59N 117°40E **115** E9
Daguan *China* 27°43N 103°56E **116** D4
Dagupan *Phil.* 16°3N 120°20E **119** A6
Daguragu *Australia* 17°33S 130°30E **148** C5
Daguragu ☉ *Australia* 17°24S 130°48E **148** C5
Dahab *Egypt* 28°31N 34°31E **128** D2
Dahanu *India* 19°58N 72°44E **126** E1
Dahivadi *India* 17°43N 74°33E **126** F2
Dahlak Kebir *Eritrea* 15°50N 40°10E **131** D3
Dahlenburg *Germany* 53°11N 10°44E **76** B6
Dahlonega *U.S.A.* 34°32N 83°59W **177** D13
Dahod *India* 22°50N 74°15E **124** H6
Dahong Shan *China* 31°25N 113°0E **117** B9
Dahongliutan *China* 35°45N 79°20E **125** B8
Dahra *Libya* 29°30N 17°50E **135** C9
Dahra *Senegal* 15°22N 15°30W **138** B1
Dahra, Massif de *Algeria* 36°7N 1°21E **136** A4
Dahūk *Iraq* 36°50N 43°1E **105** D10
Dahūk □ *Iraq* 36°50N 42°50E **105** D10
Dai Hao *Vietnam* 18°1N 106°25E **120** D6
Dai-Sen *Japan* 35°22N 133°32E **113** G6
Dai Xian *China* 39°4N 112°58E **114** E7
Daicheng *China* 38°42N 116°38E **114** E9
Daikondi = Dāykondī □
  Afghan. 34°0N 66°0E **122** C5
Dailekh *Nepal* 28°50N 81°44E **125** E9
Daimiel *Spain* 39°5N 3°35W **89** F7
Daingean *Ireland* 53°18N 7°17W **64** C4
Daingean, An = Dingle
  Ireland 52°9N 10°17W **64** D1
Dainkog *China* 32°30N 97°58E **116** A1
Daintree *Australia* 16°20S 145°20E **150** B4
Daintree △ *Australia* 16°8S 145°2E **150** B4
Daiō-Misaki *Japan* 34°15N 136°45E **113** G8
Dairût *Egypt* 27°34N 30°43E **137** B3
Daisen *Japan* 39°27N 140°29E **112** E10
Daisen-Oki □ *Japan* 35°23N 133°34E **113** G6
Daisetsu-Zan *Japan* 43°30N 142°57E **112** C11
Daisetsu-Zan △
  Japan 43°38N 142°55E **112** C11
Daitari *India* 21°10N 85°46E **126** D7
Daiyun Shan *China* 25°50N 118°15E **117** E12
Dajarra *Australia* 21°42S 139°30E **150** C2
Dajiawa *China* 37°3N 119°0E **115** F10
Dajin Chuan → *China* 31°16N 101°59E **116** B3
Dak Dam *Cambodia* 12°20N 107°21E **120** F6
Dak Nhe *Vietnam* 15°28N 107°48E **120** E6
Dak Pek *Vietnam* 15°4N 107°44E **120** E6
Dak Song *Vietnam* 12°19N 107°35E **120** F6
Dak Sui *Vietnam* 14°55N 107°43E **120** E6
Dakar *Senegal* 14°34N 17°29W **138** C1
Dakar □ *Senegal* 14°45N 17°20W **138** C1
Dakhla *W. Sahara* 23°50N 15°53W **134** D2
Dakhla, El Wâhât el
  Egypt 25°30N 28°50E **137** B2
Dakingari *Nigeria* 11°37N 4°1E **139** C5
Dakoank *India* 7°2N 93°43E **127** L11
Dakor *India* 22°45N 73°11E **124** H5
Dakoro *Niger* 14°31N 6°46E **139** C6
Dakota City *U.S.A.* 42°25N 96°25W **172** D5
Đakovica = Gjakovë
  Kosovo 42°22N 20°26E **96** D4
Đakovo *Croatia* 45°19N 18°24E **80** E3
Dala-Järna *Sweden* 60°33N 14°26E **62** D8
Dalaba *Guinea* 10°47N 12°12W **138** C2

Dalachi *China* 36°48N 105°0E **114** F3
Dalai Nur *China* 43°20N 116°45E **114** C9
Dālakī *Iran* 29°26N 51°17E **129** D6
Dalälven → *Sweden* 60°12N 16°43E **62** D10
Dalaman *Turkey* 36°48N 28°47E **99** E10
Dalaman → *Turkey* 36°41N 28°43E **99** E10
Dalandzadgad
  Mongolia 43°27N 104°30E **114** C3
Dalap-Uliga-Darrit = Majuro
  Marshall Is. 7°9N 171°12E **156** G9
Dalarna *Sweden* 61°0N 14°0E **62** D8
Dalarna □ *Sweden* 61°0N 14°15E **62** D8
Dalay *Mongolia* 43°28N 103°30E **114** C2
Dālbandīn *Pakistan* 29°0N 64°23E **122** E4
Dalbeattie *U.K.* 54°56N 3°50W **65** G5
Dalbeg *Australia* 20°16S 147°18E **150** C4
Dalby *Australia* 27°10S 151°17E **151** D5
Dalby *Sweden* 55°40N 13°22E **63** J6
Dalby Söderskog △
  Sweden 55°41N 13°21E **63** J7
Dale City *U.S.A.* 38°38N 77°19W **173** F15
Dale Hollow L. *U.S.A.* 36°32N 85°27W **177** C12
Daleville *U.S.A.* 31°19N 85°43W **178** D4
Dalga *Egypt* 27°39N 30°41E **137** B3
Dalgān *Iran* 27°31N 59°19E **129** E8
Dalhart *U.S.A.* 36°4N 102°31W **176** C3
Dalhousie *Canada* 48°5N 66°26W **165** C6
Dalhousie *India* 32°38N 75°58E **124** C6
Dali *Shaanxi, China* 34°48N 109°58E **114** G5
Dali *Yunnan, China* 25°40N 100°10E **116** E3
Dalian *China* 38°50N 121°40E **115** E11
Daliang Shan *China* 28°0N 102°45E **116** D4
Daling He → *China* 40°55N 121°40E **115** D11
Dāliyat el Karmel *Israel* 32°43N 35°2E **130** C4
Dalj *Croatia* 45°29N 18°59E **80** E3
Dalkeith *U.K.* 55°54N 3°4W **65** F5
Dalkeith *U.K.* 30°0N 85°9W **178** E4
Dalkey *Ireland* 53°16N 6°6W **64** C5
Dallas *Ga., U.S.A.* 33°55N 84°51W **178** B3
Dallas *Oreg., U.S.A.* 44°55N 123°19W **168** D2
Dallas *Tex., U.S.A.* 32°47N 96°48W **176** E6
Dallas-Fort Worth Int. ✈ (DFW)
  U.S.A. 32°54N 97°2W **176** E6
Dalles, The *U.S.A.* 45°36N 121°10W **168** D3
Dalmacija *Croatia* 43°20N 17°0E **80** C7
Dalmacija *Croatia* 43°20N 17°0E **93** E13
Dalmas, L. *Canada* 53°30N 71°50W **165** B5
Dalmatia = Dalmacija
  Croatia 43°20N 17°0E **93** E13
Dalmellington *U.K.* 55°19N 4°23W **65** F4
Dalnegorsk *Russia* 44°32N 135°33E **112** B7
Dalnerechensk *Russia* 45°50N 133°40E **112** B6
Dalnevostochnyy □
  Russia 67°0N 140°0E **107** C14
Daloa *Ivory C.* 7°0N 6°30W **138** D3
Dalou Shan *China* 28°15N 107°0E **116** C6
Dalry *U.K.* 55°42N 4°43W **65** F4
Dalrymple, L. *Australia* 20°40S 147°0E **150** C4
Dalrymple, Mt. *Australia* 21°1S 148°39E **150** C4
Dals Långed *Sweden* 58°56N 12°18E **63** F6
Dalsjöfors *Sweden* 57°46N 13°5E **63** G7
Dalskog *Sweden* 58°50N 12°15E **63** F6
Daltenganj *India* 24°0N 84°4E **125** H11
Dalton *Ga., U.S.A.* 34°46N 84°58W **177** D12
Dalton *Mass., U.S.A.* 42°28N 73°11W **175** D11
Dalton *Nebr., U.S.A.* 41°25N 102°58W **172** E2
Dalton, Kap *Greenland* 69°26N 24°3W **57** B8
Dalton-in-Furness *U.K.* 54°10N 3°11W **66** C4
Dalvík *Iceland* 65°58N 18°32W **60** D4
Dálvvadis = Jokkmokk
  Sweden 66°35N 19°50E **60** C18
Dalwallinu *Australia* 30°17S 116°40E **149** F2
Daly → *Australia* 13°35S 130°19E **148** B5
Daly City *U.S.A.* 37°42N 122°27W **170** H4
Daly L. *Canada* 56°32N 105°39W **163** B7
Daly River *Australia* 13°46S 130°42E **148** B5
Daly River-Port Keats ☉
  Australia 14°13S 129°36E **148** B4
Daly Waters *Australia* 16°15S 133°24E **150** B1
Dalyan *Turkey* 36°50N 28°39E **99** E10
Dam Doi *Vietnam* 8°50N 105°12E **121** H5
Dam Ha *Vietnam* 21°21N 107°36E **120** B6
Damachova *Belarus* 51°45N 23°36E **83** G10
Daman *India* 20°25N 72°57E **126** D1
Daman & Diu □ *India* 20°25N 72°57E **126** D1
Damanhûr *Egypt* 31°0N 30°30E **137** A3
Damanganga → *India* 20°25N 72°56E **126** D1
Damant L. *Canada* 61°45N 105°5W **163** A7
Damaq *Iran* 35°25N 48°49E **105** E13
Damar *Indonesia* 7°7S 128°40E **119** F7
Damara *C.A.R.* 4°58N 18°42E **140** D3
Damaraland *Namibia* 20°0S 15°0E **144** B2
Damascus = Dimashq
  Syria 33°30N 36°18E **130** B5
Damascus *U.S.A.* 31°18N 84°43W **178** D5
Damasi *Greece* 39°43N 22°11E **98** B4
Damaturu *Nigeria* 11°45N 11°55E **139** C7
Damāvand *Iran* 35°47N 52°0E **129** C7
Damāvand, Qolleh-ye
  Iran 35°56N 52°10E **129** C7
Damba *Angola* 6°44S 15°20E **140** F3
Damboa *Nigeria* 11°51N 12°50E **139** C7
Dâmbovița □ *Romania* 45°0N 25°30E **81** F10
Dâmbovița → *Romania* 44°12N 26°26E **81** F11
Dâmbovnic →
  Romania 44°28N 25°18E **81** F10
Dambulla *Sri Lanka* 7°51N 80°39E **127** L5
Dame Marie *Haiti* 18°34N 74°26W **183** C5
Dāmghān *Iran* 36°10N 54°17E **129** B7
Dămieneşti *Romania* 46°44N 26°59E **81** D11
Damietta = Dumyât
  Egypt 31°24N 31°48E **137** A3
Damīr Qābū *Syria* 36°58N 41°51E **128** B4
Dammam = Ad Dammām
  Si. Arabia 26°20N 50°5E **131** B7
Dammartin-en-Goële
  France 49°3N 2°41E **71** C9
Damme *Germany* 52°32N 8°11E **76** C4
Damodar → *India* 23°17N 87°35E **125** H12
Damoh *India* 23°50N 79°28E **125** H8
Damous *Algeria* 36°31N 1°42E **136** A4
Dampier *Australia* 20°41S 116°42E **148** D2
Dampier, Selat *Indonesia* 0°40S 131°0E **119** E8
Dampier Arch.
  Australia 20°38S 116°32E **148** D2

Damrani *Algeria* 27°45N 2°56W **136** C3
Damrei, Chuor Phnm
  Cambodia 11°30N 103°0E **121** G4
Damyang *S. Korea* 35°19N 126°59E **115** G14
Dan-Gulbi *Nigeria* 11°40N 6°15E **139** C6
Dan-Sadau *Nigeria* 11°17N 6°29E **139** C6
Dana *Indonesia* 11°0S 121°15E **119** F6
Dana *Jordan* 30°41N 35°37E **130** E4
Dana *Nepal* 28°32N 83°37E **125** E10
Dana, L. *Canada* 50°53N 77°20W **164** B4
Dana, Mt. *U.S.A.* 37°54N 119°12W **170** H7
Danakil Desert *Ethiopia* 12°45N 41°0E **131** E3
Danané *Ivory C.* 7°16N 8°9W **138** D3
Danba *China* 30°34N 101°48E **116** B3
Danbury *U.S.A.* 41°24N 73°28W **175** E11
Danby L. *U.S.A.* 34°13N 115°5W **171** L11
Dand *Afghan.* 31°28N 65°32E **124** D1
Dande → *Zimbabwe* 15°56S 30°16E **143** F3
Dandeldhura *Nepal* 29°20N 80°35E **125** E9
Dandeli *India* 15°5N 74°30E **126** M9
Dandenong *Australia* 38°0S 145°15E **153** E6
Dandī *Iran* 36°32N 47°37E **105** D12
Dandil *Egypt* 29°10N 31°2E **137** F7
Dandong *China* 40°10N 124°20E **115** D13
Daneborg *Greenland* 74°18N 20°14W **57** C8
Danfeng *China* 33°45N 110°25E **114** H6
Dangan Liedao *China* 22°3N 114°18E **117** F10
Dangé-St-Romain *France* 46°56N 0°36E **72** B4
Dângeni *Romania* 47°51N 26°58E **81** C11
Danger Is. = Pukapuka
  Cook Is. 10°53S 165°49W **157** J11
Danger Pt. *S. Africa* 34°40S 19°17E **144** D2
Dangla Shan = Tanggula Shan
  China 32°40N 92°10E **110** E7
Dangora *Nigeria* 11°30N 8°7E **139** C6
Dangouadougou
  Burkina Faso 10°9N 4°56W **138** D4
Dangrek, Mts. = Dangrek,
  Phnom *Thailand* 14°20N 104°0E **120** E5
Dangrek, Phnom
  Thailand 14°20N 104°0E **120** E5
Dangriga *Belize* 17°0N 88°13W **181** D7
Dangshan *China* 34°27N 116°22E **114** G9
Dangtu *China* 31°32N 118°25E **117** B12
Dangyang *China* 30°52N 111°44E **117** B8
Daniel *U.S.A.* 42°52N 110°4W **168** E8
Daniel's Harbour
  Canada 50°13N 57°35W **165** B8
Danielskuil *S. Africa* 28°11S 23°33E **144** C3
Danielson *U.S.A.* 41°48N 71°53W **175** E13
Danielsville *U.S.A.* 34°8N 83°13W **178** A6
Danilov *Russia* 58°16N 40°13E **84** C11
Danilovgrad *Montenegro* 42°38N 19°4E **96** D3
Danilovka *Russia* 50°25N 44°12E **86** E7
Daning *China* 36°28N 110°45E **114** F6
Danja *Nigeria* 11°21N 7°30E **139** C6
Danjiangkou *China* 32°31N 111°30E **117** A8
Danjiangkou Shuiku
  China 32°37N 111°30E **117** A8
Dank *Oman* 23°33N 56°16E **129** F8
Dankalwa *Nigeria* 11°52N 12°12E **139** C7
Dankama *Nigeria* 13°20N 7°44E **139** C6
Dankhar Gompa *India* 32°10N 78°10E **124** C8
Dankov *Russia* 53°20N 39°5E **84** F10
Danleng *China* 30°1N 103°31E **116** B4
Danli *Honduras* 14°4N 86°35W **182** D2
Danmark = Denmark ■
  Europe 55°45N 10°0E **63** J3
Danmark Fjord
  Greenland 81°30N 22°0W **57** A8
Danmarkshavn
  Greenland 76°45N 18°50W **57** B9
Dannemora *U.S.A.* 44°43N 73°44W **175** B11
Dannenberg *Germany* 53°6N 11°5E **76** B7
Dannevirke *N.Z.* 40°12S 176°8E **154** G5
Dannhauser *S. Africa* 28°0S 30°3E **145** C5
Dansville *U.S.A.* 42°34N 77°42W **174** D7
Danta *India* 24°11N 72°46E **124** G5
Dantan *India* 21°57N 87°20E **125** J12
Dante = Xaafuun
  Somalia 10°25N 51°16E **131** E5
Dantewara *India* 18°54N 81°21E **126** E5
Danube = Dunărea →
  Europe 45°20N 29°40E **81** F15
Danvers *U.S.A.* 42°34N 70°56W **175** D14
Danville *Ga., U.S.A.* 32°37N 83°15W **178** C6
Danville *Ill., U.S.A.* 40°8N 87°37W **172** E10
Danville *Ky., U.S.A.* 37°39N 84°46W **173** G11
Danville *Pa., U.S.A.* 40°58N 76°37W **175** F8
Danville *Va., U.S.A.* 36°36N 79°23W **177** C15
Danville *Vt., U.S.A.* 44°25N 72°9W **175** B12
Danyang *China* 32°0N 119°31E **117** B12
Danzhai *China* 26°11N 107°48E **116** D6
Danzhou *China* 19°31N 109°33E **117** a
Danzig = Gdańsk *Poland* 54°22N 18°40E **82** D5
Dão → *Portugal* 40°20N 8°11W **88** E2
Dao Xian *China* 25°36N 111°31E **117** E8
Daocheng *China* 29°20N 100°10E **116** D3
Daoud = Aïn Beïda
  Algeria 35°50N 7°29E **136** A6
Daoukro *Ivory C.* 7°10N 3°58W **138** D4
Dapaong *Togo* 10°55N 0°16E **139** C5
Dapchi *Nigeria* 12°32N 11°31E **139** C7
Dapoli *India* 17°46N 73°11E **126** F1
Daqing *China* 46°35N 125°0E **115** B11
Daqing Shan *China* 40°40N 111°0E **114** D6
Daqq-e Sorkh, Kavīr
  Iran 33°45N 52°50E **129** C7
Daqu Shan *China* 30°25N 122°20E **117** B14
Dar Banda *Africa* 8°0N 23°0E **132** F6
Dar el Beida = Casablanca
  Morocco 33°36N 7°36W **136** B4
Dar es Salaam *Tanzania* 6°50S 39°12E **142** D4
Dar Mazār *Iran* 29°14N 57°20E **129** D8
Dar'ā *Syria* 32°36N 36°7E **130** C5
Dar'ā □ *Syria* 32°55N 36°10E **130** C5
Dārāb *Iran* 28°50N 54°30E **129** D7
Daraban *Pakistan* 31°44N 70°20E **124** D4
Darabani *Romania* 48°10N 26°39E **81** B11
Daraj *Libya* 30°10N 10°28E **135** B8
Dārān *Iran* 32°59N 50°24E **129** C6
Daravica = Gjeravicë
  Kosovo 42°32N 20°8E **96** D4
Daraw *Egypt* 24°22N 32°51E **137** C3
Darazo *Nigeria* 11°1N 10°24E **139** C7
Darband *Pakistan* 34°20N 72°50E **124** B5
Darband, Kūh-e *Iran* 31°34N 57°8E **129** D8
Darbhanga *India* 26°15N 85°55E **125** F11
D'Arcy *Canada* 50°33N 122°29W **162** C4

Darda *Croatia* 45°40N 18°41E **80** E3
Dardanë *Kosovo* 42°35N 21°35E **96** D5
Dardanelle *Ark., U.S.A.* 35°13N 93°9W **176** D8
Dardanelle *Calif.,*
  U.S.A. 38°20N 119°50W **170** G7
Dardanelles = Çanakkale Boğazı
  Turkey 40°17N 26°32E **97** F10
Darende *Turkey* 38°31N 37°30E **104** C7
Dārestān *Iran* 29°9N 58°42E **129** D8
Darfield *N.Z.* 43°29S 172°7E **155** D7
Darfo-Boario Terme
  Italy 45°53N 10°11E **92** C7
Dârfûr *Sudan* 13°40N 24°0E **135** F10
Dargai *Pakistan* 34°25N 71°55E **124** B4
Dargaville *N.Z.* 35°57S 173°52E **154** B2
Darhan *Mongolia* 49°37N 106°21E **110** B10
Darhan Muminggan
  China 41°40N 110°28E **114** D6
Darica *Turkey* 40°45N 29°23E **104** B3
Darien *U.S.A.* 31°23N 81°26W **178** D8
Darién, G. del *Caribbean* 9°0N 77°0W **186** B3
Darién, P. de *Panama* 7°36N 77°57W **182** E4
Dariganga = Ovoot
  Mongolia 45°21N 113°45E **114** B7
Daringbadi *India* 19°54N 84°8E **126** E7
Darjeeling = Darjiling
  India 27°3N 88°18E **125** F13
Darjiling *India* 27°3N 88°18E **125** F13
Darkan *Australia* 33°20S 116°43E **149** F2
Darke Peak *Australia* 33°27S 136°12E **152** B2
Darkhana *Pakistan* 30°39N 72°11E **124** D5
Darkhazīneh *Iran* 31°54N 48°39E **129** D6
Darkot Pass *Pakistan* 36°45N 73°26E **125** A5
Darling → *Australia* 34°4S 141°54E **152** C4
Darling Downs
  Australia 27°30S 150°30E **151** D5
Darling Ra. *Australia* 32°30S 116°20E **149** F2
Darlington *U.K.* 54°32N 1°33W **66** C6
Darlington *Fla., U.S.A.* 30°57N 86°3W **178** D3
Darlington *S.C.,*
  U.S.A. 34°18N 79°52W **177** D15
Darlington *Wis., U.S.A.* 42°41N 90°7W **172** D8
Darlington, L. *S. Africa* 33°10S 25°9E **144** D4
Darlington Point
  Australia 34°37S 146°1E **153** E7
Darłowo *Poland* 54°25N 16°25E **82** D3
Dărmănești *Bacău,*
  Romania 46°21N 26°33E **81** D11
Dărmănești *Suceava,*
  Romania 47°44N 26°9E **81** C11
Darmstadt *Germany* 49°51N 8°39E **77** F4
Darnah *Libya* 32°45N 22°45E **135** B10
Darnall *S. Africa* 29°23S 31°18E **145** D5
Darney *France* 48°5N 6°2E **71** D13
Darnick *Australia* 32°48S 143°38E **152** B5
Darnley, B. *Australia* 9°35S 143°46E **150** a
Darnley, C. *Antarctica* 68°0S 69°0E **5** C6
Darou-Mousti *Senegal* 15°3N 16°3W **138** B1
Darr → *Australia* 23°39S 143°50E **150** C3
Darra Pezu *Pakistan* 32°19N 70°44E **124** C4
Darran Mts. *N.Z.* 44°37S 167°59E **155** D1
Darrah Shahr *Iran* 33°7N 47°22E **105** F12
Darrequeira *Argentina* 37°42S 63°10W **190** D3
Darrington *U.S.A.* 48°15N 121°36W **168** B3
Darsi *India* 15°46N 79°44E **127** M8
Darsser Ort *Germany* 54°28N 12°32E **76** A8
Dart → *U.K.* 50°24N 3°39W **67** G4
Dartford *U.K.* 51°26N 0°13E **67** F8
Dartmoor *Australia* 37°56S 141°19E **152** C4
Dartmoor *U.K.* 42°35N 57°3W **67** G4
Dartmoor △ *U.K.* 50°37N 3°59W **67** G4
Dartmouth *Australia* 23°31S 144°44E **150** C3
Dartmouth *Canada* 44°40N 63°30W **165** D7
Dartmouth *U.K.* 50°21N 3°36W **67** G4
Dartmouth, L. *Queens.,*
  Australia 26°4S 145°18E **151** D4
Dartmouth, L. *Vic.,*
  Australia 36°34S 147°32E **153** D7
Dartuch, C. = Artrutx, C. de
  Spain 39°55N 3°49E **91** B10
Daruvar *Croatia* 45°35N 17°14E **80** E2
Darvel, Teluk = Lahad Datu,
  Telok *Malaysia* 4°50N 118°20E **119** D5
Darvi *Mongolia* 46°27N 94°7E **109** C12
Darwen *U.K.* 53°42N 2°29W **66** D5
Darwendale *Zimbabwe* 17°41S 30°33E **145** A5
Darwin *Australia* 12°25S 130°51E **148** B5
Darwin *U.S.A.* 36°15N 117°35W **171** J9
Darwin, Mt. *Chile* 54°47S 69°5W **192** D3
Darya Khan *Pakistan* 31°48N 71°6E **124** D4
Daryapur *India* 20°55N 77°20E **126** D3
Daryoi Amu = Amudarya →
  Uzbekistan 43°58N 59°34E **108** E6
Dās *U.A.E.* 25°20N 53°30E **129** E7
Dashen, Ras *Ethiopia* 13°8N 38°26E **133** E12
Dasher, Ras *Ethiopia* 30°45N 83°19W **178** E6
Dashetai *China* 41°0N 109°5E **114** D5
Dashiqiao *China* 40°21N 122°30E **115** D12
Dashkesan = Daşkäsän
  Azerbaijan 40°31N 46°15E **87** K7
Daska *Pakistan* 32°20N 74°20E **124** C6
Dasoguz = Dashowuz
  Turkmenistan 41°49N 59°58E **108** E6
Dassa *Benin* 7°46N 2°14E **139** D5
Dasuya *India* 31°49N 75°40E **124** D6
Datça *Turkey* 36°46N 27°40E **99** E9
Date *Japan* 42°28N 140°5E **112** C10
Datia *India* 25°39N 78°27E **125** G8
Datian *China* 25°40N 117°50E **117** E12
Datong *Anhui, China* 30°48N 117°44E **117** B11
Datong *Shanxi, China* 40°6N 113°18E **114** D7
Dattakhel *Pakistan* 32°54N 69°46E **124** C3
Dattapur = Dhamangaon
  India 20°48N 78°8E **126** D3
Datu, Tanjung *Indonesia* 2°5N 109°39E **118** D3
Datu Piang *Phil.* 7°2N 124°30E **119** C6
Datuk, Tanjong = Datu, Tanjung
  Indonesia 2°5N 109°39E **118** D3
Daugava → *Latvia* 57°4N 24°3E **84** C4
Daugavpils *Latvia* 55°53N 26°32E **84** D4

Daulpur *India* 26°45N 77°59E **124** F7
Daun *Germany* 50°11N 6°49E **76** E2
Daund *India* 18°26N 74°40E **124** K6
Daung Kyun *Burma* 12°13N 98°4E **121** G1
Dauphin *Canada* 51°9N 100°5W **163** C8
Dauphin L. *Canada* 40°22N 76°56W **175** F8
Dauphiné *France* 45°15N 5°25E **73** E12
Daura *Borno, Nigeria* 11°31N 11°24E **139** C7
Daura *Katsina, Nigeria* 13°2N 8°21E **139** C7
Daurada, Costa *Spain* 41°12N 1°15E **91** B9
Dausa *India* 26°52N 76°20E **124** F7
Dāvāçi *Azerbaijan* 41°15N 48°57E **87** K9
Davangere *India* 14°25N 75°55E **126** M9
Davao *Phil.* 7°0N 125°40E **119** D7
Davao, G. *Phil.* 6°30N 125°48E **119** D7
Dāvar Panāh = Sarāvān
  Iran 27°25N 62°15E **129** E9
Davenport *Calif.,*
  U.S.A. 37°1N 122°12W **170** H4
Davenport *Fla., U.S.A.* 28°10N 81°36W **179** G7
Davenport *Iowa, U.S.A.* 41°32N 90°35W **172** E8
Davenport *Wash.,*
  U.S.A. 47°39N 118°9W **168** C4
Davenport Ra.
  Australia 20°28S 134°0E **150** C1
Davenport Range △
  Australia 20°36S 134°22E **150** C1
Daventry *U.K.* 52°16N 1°10W **67** E6
David *Panama* 8°30N 82°30W **182** E3
David City *U.S.A.* 41°15N 97°8W **172** E5
David Glacier
  Antarctica 75°20S 162°0E **5** D11
David Gorodok = Davyd Haradok
  Belarus 52°4N 27°8E **84** F4
Davidson *Canada* 51°16N 105°59W **163** C7
Davidson Mts.
  U.S.A. 68°41N 142°22W **166** B5
Davie *U.S.A.* 26°3N 80°14W **179** H9
Davis *Antarctica* 68°34S 77°55E **5** C6
Davis *U.S.A.* 38°33N 121°44W **170** G5
Davis Dam *U.S.A.* 35°12N 114°34W **171** K12
Davis Mts. *U.S.A.* 30°50N 103°55W **176** F3
Davis Sea *Antarctica* 66°0S 92°0E **5** C7
Davis Str. *N. Amer.* 65°0N 58°0W **161** C14
Davisboro *U.S.A.* 32°59N 82°36W **178** C6
Davlos *Cyprus* 35°25N 33°54E **101** D12
Davo → *Ivory C.* 5°0N 6°10W **138** E3
Davos *Switz.* 46°48N 9°49E **78** E5
Davutlar *Turkey* 37°43N 27°17E **99** D9
Davy L. *Canada* 58°53N 108°18W **163** B7
Davyd Haradok *Belarus* 52°4N 27°8E **84** F4
Dawaki *Bauchi, Nigeria* 9°25N 9°33E **139** D7
Dawaki *Kano, Nigeria* 12°5N 8°23E **139** C7
Dawei *Burma* 14°2N 98°12E **120** E1
Dawes Ra. *Australia* 24°40S 150°40E **150** C5
Dawlish *U.K.* 50°35N 3°28W **67** G4
Dawmat al Jandal
  Si. Arabia 29°55N 39°40E **128** D3
Dawna Ra. *Burma* 16°30N 98°30E **120** D2
Dawros Hd. *Ireland* 54°50N 8°33W **64** B3
Dawson *U.S.A.* 31°46N 84°27W **178** D5
Dawson, I. *Chile* 53°50S 70°50W **192** D2
Dawson B. *Canada* 52°53N 100°49W **163** C8
Dawson City *Canada* 64°10N 139°30W **166** D4
Dawson Creek
  Canada 55°45N 120°15W **162** B4
Dawson Inlet *Canada* 61°50N 93°25W **163** A10
Dawson Ra. *Australia* 24°30S 149°48E **150** C4
Dawu *Hubei, China* 31°34N 114°7E **117** B9
Dawu *Sichuan, China* 30°55N 101°0E **116** B3
Dax *France* 43°44N 1°3W **73** E3
Daxian *China* 31°15N 107°23E **116** B6
Daxin *China* 22°50N 107°11E **116** F6
Daxindian *China* 37°30N 120°50E **115** F11
Daxing *China* 39°47N 116°26E **114** E9
Daxinggou *China* 43°25N 129°40E **115** C15
Daxue Shan *Sichuan,*
  China 30°30N 101°30E **116** B3
Daxue Shan *Yunnan,*
  China 23°42N 99°48E **116** E3
Day *U.S.A.* 30°12N 83°17W **178** F6
Dayao *China* 25°45N 101°20E **116** E3
Daye *China* 30°6N 114°58E **117** B9
Dayet en Naharat *Mali* 17°39N 3°10W **138** B4
Dayi *China* 30°41N 103°29E **116** B4
Daylesford *Australia* 37°21S 144°9E **153** D6
Dayong = Zhangjiajie
  China 29°11N 110°30E **117** C8
Daysland *Canada* 52°50N 112°20W **162** C6
Dayton *Nev., U.S.A.* 39°14N 119°36W **170** F7
Dayton *Ohio, U.S.A.* 39°45N 84°12W **173** F11
Dayton *Tenn., U.S.A.* 35°30N 85°1W **177** D12
Dayton *Wash., U.S.A.* 46°19N 117°59W **168** C5
Dayton *Wyo., U.S.A.* 44°53N 107°16W **168** D10
Daytona Beach *U.S.A.* 29°13N 81°1W **179** G7
Dayville *U.S.A.* 44°28N 119°32W **168** D4
Dazhu *China* 30°41N 107°15E **116** B6
Dazkırı *Turkey* 37°55N 29°52E **99** D11
Dazu *China* 29°40N 105°42E **116** C5
De Aar *S. Africa* 30°39S 24°0E **144** C3
De Armanville *U.S.A.* 33°35N 85°45W **178** B4
De Bary *U.S.A.* 28°54N 81°18W **179** G7
De Funiak Springs
  U.S.A. 30°43N 86°7W **178** D2
De Grey → *Australia* 20°12S 119°13E **148** D2
De Haan *Belgium* 51°16N 3°2E **75** C3
De Hoop △ *S. Africa* 34°30S 20°45E **144** D3
De Kalb Junction
  U.S.A. 44°30N 75°20W **175** A10
De Land *U.S.A.* 29°2N 81°18W **179** G7
De Leon *U.S.A.* 32°7N 98°32W **176** E5
De Long Mts. *U.S.A.* 68°10N 163°30W **166** B3
De Panne *Belgium* 51°6N 2°34E **75** C2
De Pere *U.S.A.* 44°27N 88°4W **172** C9
De Queen *U.S.A.* 34°2N 94°21W **176** D7
De Ruyters *U.S.A.* 42°45N 75°53W **175** D9
De Smet *U.S.A.* 44°23N 97°33W **172** C5
De Soto *U.S.A.* 38°8N 90°34W **172** F8
De Soto City *U.S.A.* 27°27N 81°24W **179** H7
De Tour Village *U.S.A.* 46°0N 83°56W **173** B12
De Witt *U.S.A.* 34°18N 91°20W **176** D9
Dead Sea *Asia* 31°30N 35°30E **130** E4

dman B. U.S.A. 29°30N 83°30W 179 F6
dwood U.S.A. 44°23N 103°44W 172 C2
dwood L. Canada 59°10N 128°30W 162 B3
l U.K. 51°13N 1°25E 67 F9
l I. Australia 39°30S 147°20E 151 F4
lesville S. Africa 28°41S 25°44E 144 C4
an China 29°21N 115°46E 117 C10
n → Canada 52°49N 126°58W 162 C3
n. Forest of U.K. 51°45N 2°33W 67 F5
n Chan. Canada 52°30N 127°15W 162 C3
se → Canada 59°56N 129°57W 162 B2
se L. Canada 58°40N 130°5W 162 B2
se Lake Canada 58°25N 130°35W 162 B2
th Valley U.S.A. 36°15N 116°50W 171 J10
th Valley △ U.S.A. 36°30N 117°6W 171 J9
th Valley Junction U.S.A. 36°20N 116°25W 171 J10
tnu = Tana → Norway 70°30N 28°14E 60 A23
uville France 49°23N 0°2E 70 C7
a Spain 43°18N 2°21W 90 B2
a Habe Nigeria 10°14N 11°20E 139 C7
agram India 23°41N 88°18E 125 H13
altsevo Ukraine 48°22N 38°26E 85 H10
ao China 23°21N 106°46E 116 F6
ar Macedonia 41°31N 20°30E 96 E4
dou Morocco 33°59N 3°W 136 B3
den Canada 53°30N 106°50W 163 C7
ica Poland 50°2N 21°25E 83 G8
lin Poland 51°34N 21°50E 83 G8
no Poland 52°44N 14°41E 83 F1
o, L. Mali 15°14N 4°15W 138 B4
olt Canada 55°12N 118°1W 162 B5
orah East, L. Australia 30°45S 119°30E 149 F2
orah West, L. Australia 30°45S 119°5E 149 F2
re Serbia 44°38N 19°53E 96 B3
re Markos Ethiopia 10°20N 37°40E 131 E2
re Tabor Ethiopia 11°50N 38°26E 131 E2
re Zeyit Ethiopia 8°50N 39°0E 131 F2
recen Hungary 47°33N 21°42E 80 C6
rzno Poland 53°31N 17°14E 82 E4
undscha Cameroon 4°7N 8°58E 139 E6
an Kosovo 42°30N 20°18E 96 D4
atur Ala., U.S.A. 34°36N 86°59W 177 D11
atur Ga., U.S.A. 33°46N 84°16W 178 B5
atur Ill., U.S.A. 39°51N 88°57W 172 F9
atur Ind., U.S.A. 40°50N 84°56W 173 E11
atur Tex., U.S.A. 33°14N 97°35W 176 E6
azeville France 44°34N 2°15E 72 D6
eption, Mt. Australia 30°42S 138°16E 152 A3
eption Bay Australia 27°10S 153°5E 151 D5
eption I. Antarctica 63°0S 60°15W 55 C17
eption L. Canada 56°33N 104°13W 163 B8
hhu India 26°46N 72°2E 124 F5
immannu Italy 39°19N 8°58E 94 C1
in Czech Rep. 50°47N 14°12E 78 A7
ize France 46°50N 3°28E 71 F10
kerville U.S.A. 43°32N 82°44W 174 C2
ollatura Italy 39°3N 16°21E 95 C9
orah U.S.A. 43°18N 91°48W 172 D8
a Romania 46°56N 24°50E 81 D9
éagach = Alexandroupoli Greece 40°50N 25°54E 97 F9
opolis Tsqaro Georgia 41°30N 46°0E 87 K8
ougou Burkina Faso 12°30N 3°25W 138 C4
ovichi Russia 58°22N 56°26E 84 D5
za Malawi 14°20S 34°20E 143 E3
→ Aberds., U.K. 57°9N 2°5W 65 D6
→ Dumf. & Gall., U.K. 54°51N 4°3W 65 G4
→ Wales, U.K. 53°22N 3°17W 66 D4
p B. Canada 61°15N 116°35W 162 A5
p Bay = Shenzhen Wan China 22°27N 113°55E 111 a
p Lead Australia 37°0S 142°43E 152 D5
pwater Australia 29°25S 151°51E 151 D5
r → Canada 58°23N 94°13W 163 B10
r L. Canada 52°40N 94°20W 163 C10
r Lake Nfld. & L., Canada 49°11N 57°27W 165 C8
r Lake Ont., Canada 52°36N 94°20W 163 C10
r Lodge U.S.A. 46°24N 112°44W 168 C7
r Park Fla., U.S.A. 28°6N 80°54W 179 G9
r Park Wash., U.S.A. 47°57N 117°28W 168 C5
r River U.S.A. 47°20N 93°48W 172 B7
ragun Australia 19°16S 146°33E 150 B4
rfield Beach U.S.A. 26°19N 80°6W 179 J9
fiance U.S.A. 41°17N 84°22W 173 E11
gana India 26°50N 74°20E 124 F6
gê China 31°44N 94°13E 110 E7
gebe → Portugal 38°13N 7°29W 89 G3
geberga Sweden 55°51N 14°5E 63 J8
gelis Canada 47°30N 68°35W 165 C6
gema Nigeria 4°50N 6°48E 139 E6
gerhamn Sweden 56°20N 16°24E 63 H10
gerfors Sweden 59°15N 14°27E 62 E8
gendorf Germany 48°50N 12°57E 77 G8
o → Pakistan 31°3N 73°21E 124 D5
geime Turkey 40°42N 29°47E 97 F13
girmenlik = Kythréa Cyprus 35°15N 33°29E 101 D12
Bid Iran 28°30N 55°35E 129 D7
ngolan Iran 35°17N 47°25E 105 E12
niwala Sri Lanka 6°50N 79°51E 127 L4
iloran Iran 35°14N 47°16E 105 F12
now-e Kūhestān Iran
ra Dun India 30°20N 78°4E 124 D8
nua India 26°50N 84°15E 125 G11
hua China 26°50N 118°14E 117 E12
nui China 44°32N 125°40E 115 B13
r al Balah Gaza Strip 31°25N 34°21E 130 D3
Romania 47°10N 23°52E 81 C8

Deje Sweden 59°35N 13°29E 62 E7
Dejiang China 28°18N 108°7E 116 C7
Deka → Zimbabwe 18°4S 26°42E 144 A4
DeKalb U.S.A. 41°56N 88°46W 172 E9
Dekese Dem. Rep. of the Congo 3°24S 21°24E 140 E4
Del Caño Rise Ind. Oc. 45°15S 44°15E 146 J3
Del Mar U.S.A. 32°58N 117°16W 171 N9
Del Norte U.S.A. 37°41N 106°21W 169 H10
Del Rio U.S.A. 29°22N 100°54W 176 G4
Delambre I. Australia 20°26S 117°5E 148 D2
Delano U.S.A. 35°46N 119°15W 171 K7
Delano Peak U.S.A. 38°22N 112°22W 168 G7
Delaronde L. Canada 54°31N 107°3W 163 C7
Delavan U.S.A. 42°38N 88°39W 172 D9
Delaware U.S.A. 40°18N 83°4W 173 E12
Delaware □ U.S.A. 39°0N 75°20W 173 F16
Delaware B. U.S.A. 39°0N 75°10W 173 F16
Delaware → U.S.A. 39°15N 75°20W 173 F16
Delaware Water Gap △ U.S.A. 41°0N 74°55W 175 E10
Delay → Canada 56°56N 71°28W 165 A5
Delbrück Germany 51°46N 8°34E 76 D4
Delčevo Macedonia 41°58N 22°46E 96 E6
Delegate Australia 37°4S 148°56E 153 D8
Delémont Switz. 47°22N 7°20E 77 H3
Delevan U.S.A. 42°29N 78°29W 174 D6
Delft Neths. 52°1N 4°22E 69 B4
Delft I. Sri Lanka 9°30N 79°40E 127 K4
Delfzijl Neths. 53°20N 6°55E 69 A6
Delgada, Punta Chile 52°28S 69°32W 192 D3
Delgado, C. Mozam. 10°45S 40°40E 143 E5
Delgerhet Mongolia 45°50N 110°30E 114 B6
Delgo Sudan 20°6N 30°40E 137 C3
Delhi Canada 42°51N 80°30W 174 D4
Delhi India 28°39N 77°13E 124 E7
Delhi La., U.S.A. 32°28N 91°30W 176 E9
Delhi N.Y., U.S.A. 42°17N 74°55W 175 D10
Deli Jovan Serbia 44°13N 22°9E 96 B6
Delia Canada 51°38N 112°23W 162 C6
Delice Turkey 39°54N 34°2E 104 C6
Delice → Turkey 40°45N 34°15E 104 B6
Delicias Mexico 28°13N 105°28W 180 B3
Deligrad Serbia 43°37N 21°27E 96 C5
Déline Canada 65°11N 123°25W 160 D7
Delingha China 37°23N 97°23E 110 D8
Delisle Canada 51°55N 107°8W 163 C7
Delitzsch Germany 51°31N 12°20E 76 D8
Deliverance I. Australia 9°31S 141°34E 150 a
Dell City U.S.A. 31°56N 105°12W 176 F2
Dell Rapids U.S.A. 43°50N 96°43W 172 D5
Delle France 47°30N 7°2E 71 E14
Dellys Algeria 36°57N 3°57E 136 A4
Delmar U.S.A. 42°37N 73°47W 175 D11
Delmenhorst Germany 53°3N 8°37E 76 B4
Delmiro Gouveia Brazil 9°24S 38°6W 189 B3
Delnice Croatia 45°23N 14°50E 93 C11
Delonga, Ostrova Russia 76°40N 149°20E 107 B15
Deloraine Australia 41°30S 146°40E 151 G4
Deloraine Canada 49°15N 100°29W 163 D8
Delos = Dilos Greece 37°23N 25°15E 99 D7
Delphi U.S.A. 40°36N 86°41W 172 E10
Delphi Greece 38°28N 22°30E 98 C4
Delphos U.S.A. 40°51N 84°21W 173 E11
Delportshoop S. Africa 28°22S 24°20E 144 C3
Delray Beach U.S.A. 26°28N 80°4W 179 J10
Delsbo Sweden 61°48N 16°32E 62 C10
Delta U.S.A. 39°21N 112°35W 168 G7
Delta Colo., U.S.A. 38°44N 108°4W 168 G9
Delta Utah, U.S.A. 39°21N 112°35W 168 G7
Delta □ Nigeria 5°30N 6°0E 139 D6
Delta del Ebre Spain 40°43N 0°43E 90 E5
Delta del Po → Italy 44°57N 12°15E 93 C9
Delta du Saloum △ Senegal 13°42N 16°43W 138 C1
Delta Dunărea △ Romania 45°15N 29°25E 81 E14
Deltebre Spain 40°43N 0°43E 90 E5
Deltona U.S.A. 28°54N 81°16W 179 G9
Delungra Australia 29°39S 150°51E 151 D5
Delvada India 20°46N 71°2E 124 J4
Delvinaki Greece 39°57N 20°32E 98 B2
Delvinë Albania 39°59N 20°6E 96 G4
Delyatyn Ukraine 48°32N 24°38E 81 B9
Demak Indonesia 6°53S 110°38E 119 G14
Demanda, Sierra de la Spain 42°15N 3°0W 90 C2
Demavend = Damāvand, Qolleh-ye Iran 35°56N 52°10E 129 C7
Dembia C.A.R. 5°10N 24°25E 142 a
Dembia Dem. Rep. of the Congo 3°33N 25°48E 142 B2
Dembidolo Ethiopia 8°34N 34°50E 131 F1
Demchok India 32°42N 79°29E 125 C8
Demer → Belgium 50°57N 4°42E 69 D4
Demini → Brazil 0°46S 62°56W 186 D6
Demirci Turkey 39°2N 28°38E 99 B10
Demirköprü Baraji Turkey 38°42N 28°25E 99 C10
Demirköy Turkey 41°49N 27°45E 97 E11
Demmin Germany 53°54N 13°2E 76 B9
Demnate Morocco 31°44N 6°59W 136 B2
Demonte Italy 44°19N 7°17E 92 D4
Demopolis U.S.A. 32°31N 87°50W 179 E11
Dempo Indonesia 4°2S 103°15E 118 E2
Demyansk Russia 57°30N 32°27E 84 D7
Den Bosch = 's-Hertogenbosch Neths. 51°42N 5°17E 69 C5
Den Burg Neths. 53°3N 4°47E 69 A4
Den Chai Thailand 17°59N 100°4E 120 D3
Den Haag = 's-Gravenhage Neths. 52°7N 4°17E 69 B4
Den Helder Neths. 52°57N 4°45E 69 B4
Den Oever Neths. 52°56N 5°2E 69 B5
Denain France 50°20N 3°22E 71 B10
Denair U.S.A. 37°32N 120°48W 170 H6
Denali = McKinley, Mt. U.S.A. 63°4N 151°0W 160 D10
Denau = Denov Uzbekistan 38°16N 67°54E 109 E7
Denbigh Canada 45°8N 77°15W 174 A7
Denbigh U.K. 53°12N 3°25W 66 D4

Denbighshire □ U.K. 53°8N 3°22W 66 D4
Dendang Indonesia 3°7S 107°56E 118 E3
Dendermonde Belgium 51°2N 4°5E 69 C4
Dengchuan China 25°59N 100°3E 116 E3
Denge Nigeria 12°52N 5°21E 139 C6
Dengfeng China 34°25N 113°2E 114 G7
Dengi Nigeria 9°25N 9°55E 139 D6
Dengkou China 40°18N 106°55E 114 D4
Denguélé □ Ivory C. 9°45N 7°30W 138 G3
Dengzhou China 32°34N 112°4E 117 A9
Denham Australia 25°56S 113°31E 149 E1
Denham, Mt. Jamaica 18°13N 77°32W 182 a
Denham Ra. Australia 21°55S 147°46E 150 C4
Denham Sd. Australia 25°45S 113°15E 149 E1
Denholm Canada 52°39N 108°1W 163 C7
Denia Spain 38°49N 0°8E 91 G5
Denial B. Australia 32°14S 133°32E 151 E1
Deniliquin Australia 35°30S 144°58E 153 C6
Denimoo = Fort Resolution Canada 61°10N 113°40W 162 A6
Denison Iowa, U.S.A. 42°1N 95°21W 172 D6
Denison Tex., U.S.A. 33°45N 96°33W 176 E6
Denison, C. Antarctica 67°0S 142°40E 55 C10
Denison Plains Australia 18°35S 128°0E 148 C4
Denisovka Kazakhstan 52°27N 61°39E 108 D6
Deniyaya Sri Lanka 6°21N 80°33E 127 L5
Denizli Turkey 37°42N 29°2E 99 D11
Denizli □ Turkey 37°45N 29°5E 99 D11
Denman Canada 32°24S 150°42E 153 B9
Denman Glacier Antarctica 66°45S 100°0E 55 C8
Denmark Australia 34°59S 117°25E 149 F2
Denmark ■ Europe 55°45N 10°0E 63 J3
Denmark Str. Atl. Oc. 66°0N 30°0W 57 D8
Dennery St. Lucia 13°55N 60°54W 183 f
Dennison U.S.A. 40°24N 81°19W 174 F3
Denny U.K. 56°1N 3°55W 65 E5
Denov Uzbekistan 38°16N 67°54E 109 E7
Denpasar Indonesia 8°39S 115°13E 118 F5
Denpasar ✈ (DPS) Indonesia 8°44S 115°10E 119 K18
Denton U.S.A. 34°36N 82°42W 178 D7 (hidden)
Denton Mont., U.S.A. 47°19N 109°57W 168 C9
Denton Tex., U.S.A. 33°13N 97°8W 176 E6
D'Entrecasteaux, Pt. Australia 34°50S 115°57E 149 F2
D'Entrecasteaux △ Australia 34°20S 115°33E 149 F2
D'Entrecasteaux Is. Papua N. G. 9°0S 151°0E 147 B8
Dentsville U.S.A. 34°4N 80°58W 178 A9
Denu Ghana 6°4N 1°8E 139 D5
Denver Colo., U.S.A. 39°42N 104°59W 168 G11
Denver U.S.A. 40°14N 76°8W 175 F8
Denver City U.S.A. 32°58N 102°50W 176 E3
Denver Int. ✈ (DEN) U.S.A. 39°52N 104°40W 168 G11
Deoband India 29°42N 77°43E 124 E7
Deobhog India 19°53N 82°44E 126 E6
Deodrug India 16°26N 76°55E 127 F3
Deogarh Odisha, India 21°31N 84°45E 126 D7
Deogarh Raj., India 25°32N 73°54E 124 G5
Deoghar India 24°30N 86°42E 125 G12
Deolali India 19°58N 73°50E 126 E1
Deoli = Devli India 25°50N 75°20E 124 G6
Déols France 46°50N 1°43E 71 F8
Deora India 26°22N 70°55E 124 F4
Deori India 23°24N 79°1E 125 H8
Deoria India 26°31N 83°48E 125 F10
Deosai Mts. Pakistan 35°40N 75°0E 125 B6
Deosri India 26°46N 90°29E 125 F14
Depalpur India 22°51N 75°33E 124 H6
Deposit U.S.A. 42°4N 75°25W 175 D9
Depuch I. Australia 20°37S 117°44E 148 D2
Deputatskiy Russia 69°18N 139°54E 107 C14
Déqên China 28°34N 98°51E 116 D2
Deqing China 23°8N 111°42E 117 F8
Der-Chantecoq, L. du France 48°35N 4°40E 71 D11
Dera Ghazi Khan Pakistan 30°5N 70°43E 124 D4
Dera Ismail Khan Pakistan 31°50N 70°50E 124 D4
Derabugti Pakistan 29°2N 69°9E 124 E3
Derawar Fort Pakistan 28°46N 71°20E 124 E4
Derbent Russia 42°5N 48°15E 87 J9
Derbent Turkey 38°11N 28°33E 99 C10
Derby Australia 17°18S 123°38E 148 C3
Derby U.K. 52°56N 1°28W 66 E6
Derby Conn., U.S.A. 41°19N 73°5W 175 E11
Derby Kans., U.S.A. 37°33N 97°16W 172 G5
Derby N.Y., U.S.A. 42°41N 78°58W 174 D6
Derby City □ U.K. 52°56N 1°28W 66 E6
Derby Line U.S.A. 45°0N 72°6W 175 B12
Derbyshire □ U.K. 53°11N 1°38W 66 D6
Derdap △ Serbia 44°40N 22°23E 96 B6
Derdepoort S. Africa 24°38S 26°24E 144 B4
Derecske Hungary 47°20N 21°33E 80 C6
Dereham U.K. 52°41N 0°57E 67 E8
Dereköy Turkey 41°28N 27°21E 97 E11
Dereli Turkey 40°45N 38°26E 105 B8
Dergachi = Derhachi Ukraine 50°9N 36°11E 85 G9
Derhachi Ukraine 50°9N 36°11E 85 G9
Deridder U.S.A. 30°51N 93°17W 176 F8
Derik Turkey 37°21N 40°18E 105 D9
Derinkuyu Turkey 38°22N 34°45E 104 C6
Dermantsi Bulgaria 43°8N 24°17E 97 C8
Dermott U.S.A. 33°32N 91°26W 176 E9
Dêrong China 28°44N 99°9E 116 C2
Derrinallum Australia 37°57S 143°15E 152 D5
Derry = Londonderry U.K. 55°0N 7°20W 64 B4
Derry = Londonderry □ U.K. 55°0N 7°20W 64 B4
Derry N.H., U.S.A. 42°53N 71°19W 175 D13
Derry Pa., U.S.A. 40°20N 79°18W 174 F5
Derryveagh Mts. Ireland 54°56N 8°11W 64 B3
Derval France 47°40N 1°41W 70 E5
Derveni Greece 38°8N 22°25E 98 C4
Derventa Bos.-H. 44°59N 17°55E 80 F7
Derwent → Cumb., U.K. 54°39N 3°33W 66 C4
Derwent → Derby, U.K. 52°57N 1°28W 66 E6
Derwent → N. Yorks., U.K. 53°45N 0°58W 66 D7
Derwent Water U.K. 54°35N 3°9W 66 C4

Des Moines Iowa, U.S.A. 41°35N 93°37W 172 E7
Des Moines N. Mex., U.S.A. 36°46N 103°50W 169 H12
Des Moines Wash., U.S.A. 47°24N 122°19W 170 C4
Des Moines → U.S.A. 40°23N 91°25W 172 E8
Desa Romania 43°52N 23°2E 80 G8
Desaguadero Peru 16°34S 69°3W 188 D4
Desaguadero → Argentina 34°30S 66°46W 190 C2
Desaguadero → Bolivia 16°35S 69°5W 188 D4
Desantne Ukraine 45°34N 29°32E 81 E14
Desaru Malaysia 1°31N 104°17E 121 d
Descanso, Pta. Mexico 32°21N 117°3W 171 N9
Descartes France 46°59N 0°42E 72 B4
Deschaillons-sur-St-Laurent Canada 46°32N 72°7W 165 C5
Deschambault L. Canada 54°50N 103°30W 163 C8
Deschutes → U.S.A. 45°38N 120°55W 168 D3
Dese Ethiopia 11°5N 39°40E 131 E2
Deseado → Argentina 47°45S 65°54W 192 F3
Deseado, C. Chile 52°45S 74°42W 192 D2
Desenzano del Garda Italy 45°28N 10°32E 92 C7
Deseronto Canada 44°12N 77°3W 174 B7
Desert Center U.S.A. 33°43N 115°24W 171 M11
Desert Hot Springs U.S.A. 33°58N 116°30W 171 M10
Desfina Greece 38°25N 22°31E 98 C4
Deshnok India 27°48N 73°21E 124 F5
Desierto Central de Baja California △ Mexico 29°40N 114°50W 180 B2
Deskati Greece 39°55N 21°49E 96 G5
Desna → Ukraine 50°33N 30°32E 75 C16
Desnăţui → Romania 43°53N 23°35E 81 G8
Desnogorsk Russia 54°9N 33°17E 84 E7
Desolación, I. Chile 53°0S 74°0W 192 D2
Despeñaperros, Paso Spain 38°24N 3°30W 89 G7
Despeñaperros △ Spain 38°23N 3°32W 89 G7
Despotiko Greece 36°57N 24°58E 98 E6
Despotovac Serbia 44°6N 21°30E 96 B5
Dessau Germany 51°51N 12°14E 76 D8
Dessau = Dese Ethiopia 11°5N 39°40E 131 E2
Destin U.S.A. 30°24N 86°30W 179 E3
D'Estrees B. Australia 35°55S 137°45E 152 C2
Det Udom Thailand 14°54N 105°5E 120 E5
Dete Zimbabwe 18°38S 26°50E 144 A4
Detinja → Serbia 43°51N 20°5E 96 C4
Detmold Germany 51°56N 8°52E 76 D4
Detour, Pt. U.S.A. 45°40N 86°40W 172 C10
Detroit U.S.A. 42°19N 83°12W 174 D1
Detroit Lakes U.S.A. 46°49N 95°51W 172 B6
Detva Slovak Rep. 48°34N 19°25E 79 C12
Deua △ Australia 35°32S 149°46E 153 C8
Deurne Neths. 51°27N 5°49E 69 C5
Deutsch-Luxemburgischer □ Germany 48°60N 6°12E 77 F2
Deutsche Bucht Germany 54°15N 8°0E 76 A4
Deutschland = Germany ■ Europe 51°0N 10°0E 76 E6
Deutschlandsberg Austria 46°49N 15°14E 78 E8
Deux-Sèvres □ France 46°35N 0°20W 70 F6
Deva Romania 45°53N 22°55E 80 E7
Devakottai India 9°55N 78°45E 127 K4
Devaprayag India 30°13N 78°35E 125 D8
Devarkonda India 16°42N 78°56E 126 F4
Dévaványa Hungary 47°2N 20°59E 80 C5
Deveci Dağları Turkey 39°55N 28°34E 97 G12
Devecikonağı Turkey 39°55N 28°34E 97 G12
Devecser Hungary 47°6N 17°26E 80 C2
Develi Turkey 38°35N 35°28E 104 C6
Deventer Neths. 52°15N 6°10E 69 B6
Devereux △ U.K. 33°13N 83°5W 178 B6
Deveron → U.K. 57°41N 2°32W 65 D6
Devesel Romania 44°28N 22°41E 80 F7
Devgad, I. India 14°48N 74°5E 127 H5
Devgadh Bariya India 22°40N 73°55E 124 H5
Devgarh India 18°26N 73°23E 127 F1
Devi → India 19°59N 86°24E 126 B8
Devikot India 26°42N 71°12E 124 F4
Devil River Pk. N.Z. 40°56S 172°37E 155 A7
Devils Den U.S.A. 35°46N 119°58W 170 K7
Devils Hole = Death Valley △ U.S.A. 36°30N 117°6W 171 J9
Devils Lake U.S.A. 48°7N 98°52W 172 A4
Devils Paw Canada 58°47N 134°0W 162 B2
Devils Postpile △ U.S.A. 37°37N 119°5W 170 H7
Devil's Pt. Sri Lanka 9°26N 80°6E 127 K5
Devils Tower U.S.A. 44°35N 104°42W 168 D11
Devils Tower △ U.S.A. 44°48N 104°55W 168 D11
Devin Bulgaria 41°44N 24°24E 97 E8
Devine U.S.A. 29°8N 98°54W 176 G5
Devizes U.K. 51°22N 1°58W 67 F6
Devli India 25°50N 75°20E 124 G6
Devnya Bulgaria 43°13N 27°33E 97 C11
Devoll → Albania 40°57N 19°36E 96 G4
Devon Canada 53°24N 113°44W 162 C6
Devon □ U.K. 50°50N 3°40W 67 G4
Devon I. Canada 75°10N 85°0W 161 B15
Devonport Australia 41°10S 146°22E 151 G4
Devonport N.Z. 36°49S 174°49E 154 B5
Devrek Turkey 41°13N 31°57E 104 B5
Devrekâni Turkey 41°33N 33°25E 104 B5
Devrukh India 17°3N 73°37E 126 F1
Dewas India 22°59N 76°3E 124 H7
Dewetsdorp S. Africa 29°33S 26°39E 144 C4
Dewey Puerto Rico 18°18N 65°18W 183 d
Dexing China 28°46N 117°30E 117 C11
Dexter Maine, U.S.A. 45°1N 69°18W 173 C19
Dexter Mo., U.S.A. 36°48N 89°57W 172 G9
Dexter N. Mex., U.S.A. 33°12N 104°22W 169 K11
Dey-Dey, L. Australia 29°12S 131°4E 149 E5
Deyang China 31°3N 104°27E 116 B5
Deyhūk Iran 33°15N 57°30E 129 C8
Deyyer Iran 27°55N 51°55E 129 E6
Dez → Iran 31°39N 48°52E 128 D5
Dezadeash L. Canada 60°28N 136°58W 162 A1
Dezfūl Iran 32°20N 48°30E 128 C5

Dezhneva, Mys Russia 66°5N 169°40W 107 C19
Dezhou China 37°26N 116°18E 114 F9
Dhadhar → India 24°56N 85°24E 125 G11
Dhahaban Si. Arabia 21°58N 39°3E 137 C4
Dhahiriya = Az Zāhiriyah West Bank 31°25N 34°58E 130 D3
Dhahran = Az Zahrān Si. Arabia 26°10N 50°7E 129 E6
Dhak Pakistan 32°25N 72°33E 124 C5
Dhaka Bangla. 23°43N 90°26E 125 H14
Dhaka □ Bangla. 24°25N 90°25E 125 G14
Dhali Cyprus 35°1N 33°25E 101 D12
Dhamangaon India 20°46N 78°15E 126 D8
Dhamār Yemen 14°30N 44°20E 131 E3
Dhampur India 29°19N 78°33E 124 E8
Dhamtari India 20°42N 81°35E 126 D6
Dhanbad India 23°50N 86°30E 125 H12
Dhangarhi Nepal 28°55N 80°40E 125 E9
Dhankuta Nepal 26°55N 87°40E 125 F12
Dhanora India 20°20N 80°22E 126 D5
Dhanpuri India 23°13N 81°30E 125 H9
Dhar India 22°35N 75°26E 124 H6
Dharampur India 22°13N 75°18E 124 H6
Dharamsala = Dharmsala India 32°16N 76°23E 124 C7
Dharan Nepal 26°49N 87°17E 125 F12
Dharangaon India 21°1N 75°10E 124 J6
Dharapuram India 10°45N 77°34E 127 J3
Dhariwal India 31°57N 75°19E 124 D6
Dharla → Bangla. 25°46N 89°42E 125 G13
Dharmapuri India 12°10N 78°10E 127 H4
Dharmavaram India 14°29N 77°44E 127 H3
Dharmjaygarh India 22°28N 83°13E 125 H10
Dharmsala India 32°16N 76°23E 124 C7
Dharni India 21°33N 76°53E 124 J7
Dharug △ Australia 33°20S 151°2E 153 B9
Dharur India 18°3N 76°8E 126 E3
Dharwad India 15°30N 75°4E 127 G2
Dhasan → India 25°48N 79°24E 125 G8
Dhaulagiri Nepal 28°39N 83°28E 125 E10
Dhebar, L. India 24°10N 74°0E 124 G6
Dheftera Cyprus 35°5N 33°16E 101 D12
Dhenkanal India 20°45N 85°35E 126 D7
Dherinia Cyprus 35°3N 33°57E 101 D12
Dheskáti = Deskati Greece 39°55N 21°49E 96 G5
Dhī Qār □ Iraq 31°0N 46°15E 128 D5
Dhiarrizos → Cyprus 34°41N 32°34E 101 E11
Dhībān Jordan 31°30N 35°46E 130 D4
Dhilwan India 31°31N 75°21E 124 D6
Dhimarkhera India 23°28N 80°22E 125 H9
Dholka India 22°44N 72°29E 124 H5
Dhomokós = Domokos Greece 39°10N 22°18E 98 B4
Dhond = Daund India 18°26N 74°40E 126 E2
Dhone India 15°25N 77°53E 127 E3
Dhoraji India 21°45N 70°37E 124 J4
Dhorpatan Nepal 28°29N 83°4E 125 E10
Dhragonisi = Tragonisi Greece 37°27N 25°29E 99 D7
Dhrangadhra India 22°59N 71°31E 124 H4
Dhrol India 22°33N 70°25E 124 H4
Dhuburi India 26°2N 89°59E 123 F16
Dhule India 20°58N 74°50E 126 D2
Di-b, → Sudan 22°38N 36°58E 137 C4
Di Linh Vietnam 11°35N 108°4E 121 G7
Di Linh, Cao Nguyen Vietnam 11°30N 108°0E 121 G7
Dia Greece 35°28N 25°14E 101 D7
Diablo Range U.S.A. 37°20N 121°25W 170 J5
Diabakania Guinea 10°38N 10°58W 138 G2
Diafarabé Mali 14°9N 4°57W 138 C4
Diala Mali 14°10N 9°58W 138 C3
Dialakoro Mali 12°18N 7°54W 138 C3
Dialakoto Senegal 13°21N 13°19W 138 C2
Diallassagou Mali 13°47N 3°41W 138 C4
Diamante Argentina 32°5S 60°40W 190 C3
Diamante → Argentina 34°30S 66°46W 190 C2
Diamantina Brazil 18°17S 43°40W 189 D2
Diamantina □ Australia 26°45S 139°10E 151 D2
Diamantina → Australia 23°33S 141°23E 150 C3
Diamantino Brazil 14°30S 56°30W 187 D6
Diamond Bar U.S.A. 34°1N 117°49W 171 L9
Diamond Harbour India 22°11N 88°14E 125 H13
Diamond Is. Australia 17°25S 151°5E 150 B5
Diamond Mts. U.S.A. 39°40N 115°50W 168 G6
Diamond Springs U.S.A. 38°42N 120°49W 170 G6
Dian Chi China 24°50N 102°43E 116 E4
Dianalund Denmark 55°32N 11°30E 63 J5
Dianbai China 21°33N 111°0E 117 G8
Diancheng China 21°30N 111°0E 117 G8
Dianjiang China 30°24N 107°20E 116 B6
Diano Marina Italy 43°55N 8°3E 92 E5
Dianópolis Brazil 11°38S 46°50W 189 D2
Dianra Ivory C. 8°45N 6°14W 138 G3
Diapaga Burkina Faso 12°5N 1°46E 139 C5
Diapangou Burkina Faso 12°5N 0°10E 138 C5
Diariguila Guinea 10°35N 10°2W 138 C2
Diavolo, Mt. India 12°40N 92°56E 127 H11
Diba = Dibbā al Ḩisn U.A.E. 25°45N 56°16E 129 E8
Dibagah Iraq 35°53N 43°48E 105 E10
Dibai India 28°13N 78°15E 124 E8
Dibaya Dem. Rep. of the Congo 6°30S 22°57E 140 F4
Dibaya-Lubue Dem. Rep. of the Congo 4°12S 19°54E 140 E3
Dibbeen △ Jordan 32°23N 35°42E 130 C4
Dibbā al Ḩisn U.A.E. 25°45N 56°16E 129 E8
Dibben △ Jordan 32°23N 35°42E 130 C4
Dibër □ Albania 41°40N 20°20E 96 G4
D'Iberville, Lac Canada 55°55N 73°15W 164 A5
Dibete Botswana 23°45S 26°32E 144 C4
Dibrugarh India 27°29N 94°55E 123 F19
Dickens U.S.A. 33°37N 100°50W 176 E4
Dickinson U.S.A. 46°53N 102°47W 172 B2
Dickson = Dikson Russia 73°40N 80°5E 106 B9
Dickson U.S.A. 36°5N 87°23W 177 C11
Dickson City U.S.A. 41°28N 75°37W 175 E9
Dicle Baraji Turkey 38°20N 40°11E 105 C10
Dicle Nehri → Turkey 37°43N 41°0E 105 D10

Dicomano Italy 43°53N 11°31E 93 E8
Didiéni Mali 13°53N 8°6W 138 C3
Didim Turkey 37°22N 27°16E 99 D9
Didimoticho Greece 41°22N 26°29E 97 E10
Didsbury Canada 51°35N 114°10W 162 C6
Didwana India 27°23N 74°36E 124 F6
Die France 44°47N 5°22E 73 D9
Diébougou Burkina Faso 11°0N 3°15W 138 C4
Diecke Guinea 7°27N 8°54W 138 D3
Diefenbaker, L. Canada 51°0N 106°55W 163 C7
Diego de Almagro Chile 26°22S 70°3W 190 B1
Diego Garcia Ind. Oc. 7°50S 72°50E 146 E6
Diego Ramírez, Islas Chile 56°30S 68°44W 192 E3
Diekirch Lux. 49°52N 6°10E 69 E6
Diéma Mali 14°32N 9°12W 138 C3
Diembéring Senegal 12°29N 16°47W 138 C1
Diemelsee = Germany 51°22N 8°40E 76 D4
Dien Ban Vietnam 15°53N 108°16E 120 D7
Dien Bien Phu Vietnam 21°20N 103°0E 116 G4
Dien Chau, Vinh Vietnam 19°0N 105°55W 120 C5
Dien Khanh Vietnam 12°15N 109°6E 121 F7
Diepholz Germany 52°37N 8°22E 76 C4
Dieppe France 49°54N 1°4E 70 C8
Dierks U.S.A. 34°7N 94°1W 176 D7
Diest Belgium 50°58N 5°4E 69 D5
Dietikon Switz. 47°24N 8°24E 73 C9
Dieulefit France 44°32N 5°4E 73 D9
Dieuze France 48°49N 6°43E 71 D13
Dif Somalia 0°59N 40°58E 131 G3
Diffa □ Niger 13°18N 12°36E 139 C7
Diffa □ Niger 14°0N 12°30E 139 C7
Differdange Lux. 49°31N 5°54E 69 E5
Dig India 27°28N 77°20E 124 F7
Digba Dem. Rep. of the Congo 4°25N 25°48E 142 B2
Digby Canada 44°38N 65°50W 165 D6
Digges Is. Canada 62°40N 77°50W 161 E16
Diggi India 26°22N 75°26E 124 F6
Dighinala Bangla. 23°15N 92°5E 123 H18
Dighton U.S.A. 38°29N 100°28W 172 F4
Diglur India 18°34N 77°33E 126 E3
Digna Mali 14°48N 8°10W 138 C3
Digne-les-Bains France 44°5N 6°12E 73 D10
Digoin France 46°29N 4°1E 71 F11
Digor Turkey 40°22N 43°25E 105 B10
Digos Phil. 6°45N 125°20E 119 C7
Digranes Iceland 66°4N 14°44W 60 C6
Digras India 20°6N 77°45E 126 D3
Digul → Indonesia 7°7S 138°42E 119 F9
Digya △ Ghana 7°15N 0°5E 139 D5
Dihang = Brahmaputra → Asia 23°40N 90°35E 125 H13
Dijlah, Nahr → Asia 31°0N 47°25E 128 D5
Dijon France 47°20N 5°3E 71 E12
Dikhil Djibouti 11°8N 42°20E 131 E3
Dikili Turkey 39°4N 26°53E 99 B8
Dikirnis Egypt 31°6N 31°35E 137 E7
Dikodougou Ivory C. 9°4N 5°45W 138 D3
Diksmuide Belgium 51°2N 2°52E 69 C2
Dikson Russia 73°40N 80°5E 106 B9
Dikti Oros Greece 35°8N 25°30E 101 D7
Dikwa Nigeria 12°4N 13°30E 139 C7
Dila Ethiopia 6°21N 38°22E 131 F2
Dilek Yarimadisi △ Turkey 37°40N 27°10E 99 D9
Dili E. Timor 8°39S 125°34E 119 F7
Diligent Strait India 12°11N 92°57E 127 H11
Dilijan Armenia 40°46N 44°57E 87 K7
Dilj Croatia 45°29N 18°1E 80 E3
Dillenburg Germany 50°43N 8°17E 76 E4
Dilley U.S.A. 28°40N 99°10W 176 G5
Dilli = Delhi India 29°7N 77°13E 124 E7
Dilli Mali 15°1N 7°10W 138 C3
Dillingen Bayern, Germany 48°36N 10°30E 77 F6
Dillingen Saarland, Germany 49°22N 6°43E 77 F2
Dillingham U.S.A. 59°3N 158°28W 166 D8
Dillon Canada 55°56N 108°35W 163 B7
Dillon Mont., U.S.A. 45°13N 112°38W 168 D7
Dillon S.C., U.S.A. 34°25N 79°22W 177 D15
Dillon → Canada 55°56N 108°56W 163 B7
Dillsburg U.S.A. 40°7N 77°2W 174 F7
Dilolo Dem. Rep. of the Congo 10°28S 22°18E 140 G4
Dilos Greece 37°23N 25°15E 99 D7
Dilove Ukraine 47°56N 24°11E 81 C9
Dimapur India 25°54N 93°45E 110 F7
Dimas Mexico 23°43N 106°47W 180 C3
Dimashq Syria 33°30N 36°18E 130 B5
Dimashq □ Syria 33°30N 36°30E 130 B5
Dimbaza S. Africa 32°50S 27°14E 145 D4
Dimbokro Ivory C. 6°45N 4°46W 138 D4
Dimboola Australia 36°28S 142°7E 152 D5
Dîmbovița = Dâmbovița → Romania 44°12N 26°26E 81 F11
Dimbulah Australia 17°8S 145°4E 150 B4
Dimitrovgrad Bulgaria 42°5N 25°35E 97 D9
Dimitrovgrad Russia 54°14N 49°39E 86 D9
Dimitrovgrad Serbia 43°2N 22°48E 96 C6
Dimitrovo = Pernik Bulgaria 42°35N 23°2E 96 C7
Dimitsana Greece 37°36N 22°3E 98 D4
Dimmitt U.S.A. 34°33N 102°19W 176 D3
Dimona Israel 31°2N 35°1E 130 D4
Dimovo Bulgaria 43°43N 22°50E 96 C7
Dinagat I. Phil. 10°10N 125°40E 119 B7
Dinajpur Bangla. 25°33N 88°43E 123 G16
Dinan France 48°28N 2°2W 70 D4
Dinān Āb Iran 32°4N 56°49E 129 C8
Dinant Belgium 50°16N 4°55E 69 D4
Dinapur India 25°38N 85°5E 125 G11
Dīnār, Kūh-e Iran 30°42N 51°46E 129 D6
Dinara Planina Croatia 44°0N 16°30E 93 C13
Dinard France 48°38N 2°6W 70 D4
Dinaric Alps = Dinara Planina Croatia 44°0N 16°30E 93 C13
Dinbych = Denbigh U.K. 53°12N 3°25W 66 D4
Dinbych-y-Pysgod = Tenby U.K. 51°40N 4°42W 67 F3
Dindanko Mali 12°38N 8°31W 138 C3
Dindi → India 16°24N 78°15E 126 F4
Dindigul India 10°25N 78°0E 127 J3
Dindori India 22°57N 81°5E 125 H9
Ding Xian = Dingzhou China 38°30N 114°59E 114 E8
Dinga Pakistan 25°26N 67°10E 124 G2

Ding'an China 19°42N 110°19E 117 a
Dingbian China 37°35N 107°32E 114 F4
Dingelstädt Germany 51°18N 10°19E 76 D6
Dingle Ireland 52°9N 10°17W 64 D1
Dingle Sweden 58°32N 11°35E 63 F5
Dingle B. Ireland 52°3N 10°20W 64 D1
Dingle Pen. Ireland 52°12N 10°5W 64 D1
Dingmans Ferry U.S.A. 41°13N 74°55W 175 E10
Dingnan China 24°45N 115°0E 117 E10
Dingo Australia 23°38S 149°19E 150 C4
Dingolfing Germany 48°37N 12°30E 77 G8
Dingtao China 35°5N 115°35E 114 G8
Dinguiraye Guinea 11°18N 10°49W 138 C2
Dingwall U.K. 57°36N 4°26W 65 D4
Dingxi China 35°30N 104°33E 114 G3
Dingxiang China 38°30N 112°58E 114 E7
Dingyuan China 32°32N 117°41E 117 A11
Dingzhou China 38°30N 114°59E 114 E8
Dinh, Mui Vietnam 11°22N 109°1E 121 G7
Dinh Lap Vietnam 21°33N 107°6E 116 G6
Dinin → Ireland 52°43N 7°18W 64 D4
Dinira △ Venezuela 9°57N 70°6W 183 E6
Dinokwe Botswana 23°29S 26°37E 144 B4
Dinorwic Canada 49°41N 92°30W 163 D10
Dinosaur △ Canada 50°47N 111°30W 162 C6
Dinosaur △ U.S.A. 40°30N 108°45W 168 F9
Dinuba U.S.A. 36°32N 119°23W 170 J7
Diö Sweden 56°37N 14°15E 63 H8
Dioila Mali 12°23N 6°50W 138 C3
Dioka Mali 14°57N 10°4W 138 C2
Diongoï Mali 14°38N 8°34W 138 C3
Dionisades Greece 35°20N 26°10E 101 D8
Diósgyőr Hungary 48°7N 20°43E 80 B5
Diosig Romania 47°18N 22°2E 80 C7
Diougani Mali 14°19N 2°44W 138 C4
Diouloulou Senegal 13°5N 16°38W 138 C1
Dioura Mali 14°59N 5°12W 138 C3
Diourbel Senegal 14°39N 16°12W 138 C1
Diourbel □ Senegal 14°45N 16°15W 138 C1
Dipalpur Pakistan 30°40N 73°39E 124 D5
Dipkarpaz = Rizokarpaso Cyprus 35°36N 34°23E 101 D13
Diplo Pakistan 24°35N 69°35E 124 G3
Dipolog Phil. 8°36N 123°20E 119 C6
Dipperu △ Australia 21°56S 148°42E 150 C4
Dipton N.Z. 45°54S 168°22E 155 F3
Dir Pakistan 35°8N 71°59E 122 B7
Diré Mali 16°20N 3°25W 138 B4
Dire Dawa Ethiopia 9°35N 41°45E 131 F3
Dirfis Oros Greece 38°40N 23°54E 98 C5
Diriamba Nic. 11°51N 86°19W 182 D2
Dirk Hartog I. Australia 25°50S 113°5E 149 E1
Dirranbandi Australia 28°33S 148°17E 151 D4
Disa India 24°18N 72°10E 124 G5
Disappointment, C. U.S.A. 46°18N 124°5W 170 D2
Disappointment, L. Australia 23°20S 122°40E 148 D3
Disaster B. Australia 37°15S 149°58E 153 D8
Discovery B. Australia 38°10S 140°40E 152 E4
Discovery B. China 22°18N 114°1E 111 a
Discovery Bay △ Australia 38°9S 141°16E 152 E4
Discovery Seamount Atl. Oc. 42°0S 0°10E 56 L12
Disentis Muster Switz. 46°42N 8°50E 77 J4
Dishna Egypt 26°9N 32°32E 137 B3
Disina Nigeria 11°35N 9°50E 139 C6
Disko = Qeqertarsuaq Greenland 69°45N 53°30W 57 D5
Disko Bugt Greenland 69°10N 52°0W 57 D5
Disna = Dzisna → Belarus 55°34N 28°12E 84 E5
Disneyland Hong Kong China 22°19N 114°2E 111 a
Diss U.K. 52°23N 1°7E 67 E9
Disteghil Sar Pakistan 36°20N 75°12E 125 A6
District of Columbia □ U.S.A. 38°55N 77°0W 173 F15
Distrito Federal □ Brazil 15°45S 47°45W 189 D1
Distrito Federal □ Mexico 19°15N 99°10W 181 D5
Disûq Egypt 31°8N 30°35E 137 E7
Diu India 20°45N 70°58E 124 J4
Divândarreh Iran 35°55N 47°2E 105 E12
Dives → France 49°18N 0°7W 70 C6
Dives-sur-Mer France 49°18N 0°8W 70 C6
Divi Pt. India 15°59N 81°9E 127 G5
Divichi = Dāvāçi Azerbaijan 41°15N 48°57E 87 K9
Divide U.S.A. 45°45N 112°45W 168 D7
Dividing Ra. Australia 27°45S 116°0E 149 E2
Divinópolis Brazil 20°10S 44°54W 189 E2
Divjake Albania 41°0N 19°32E 96 F3
Divnoye Russia 45°55N 43°21E 87 H6
Divo Ivory C. 5°48N 5°15W 138 D3
Divriği Turkey 39°23N 38°7E 105 C8
Diwāl Kol Afghan. 34°23N 67°52E 124 B2
Dixie Mt. U.S.A. 39°55N 120°16W 170 F6
Dixie Union U.S.A. 31°20N 82°28W 178 D7
Dixon Calif., U.S.A. 38°27N 121°49W 170 G5
Dixon Ill., U.S.A. 41°50N 89°29W 172 E9
Dixon Entrance U.S.A. 54°30N 132°0W 160 G5
Dixville Canada 45°4N 71°46W 175 A13
Diyadin Turkey 39°33N 43°40E 105 C10
Diyālā □ Iraq 33°45N 44°50E 128 C5
Diyālā → Iraq 33°13N 44°30E 108 F11
Diyarbakır Turkey 37°55N 40°18E 105 D9
Diyarbakır □ Turkey 37°50N 40°30E 105 D9
Diyodar India 24°8N 71°50E 124 G4
Dizangué Cameroon 3°46N 9°59E 139 E6
Djakarta = Jakarta Indonesia 6°9S 106°49E 118 b
Djamâa Algeria 33°32N 5°59E 136 B5
Djamba Angola 16°45S 13°58E 144 A1
Djambala Congo 2°32S 14°30E 140 E2
Djanet Algeria 24°35N 9°32E 136 D5
Djawa = Jawa Indonesia 7°0S 110°0E 118 F4
Djebel Tazzeka △ Morocco 34°6N 4°11W 136 B3
Djebiniana Tunisia 35°1N 11°0E 136 A6
Djelfa Algeria 34°40N 3°15E 136 B5
Djelfa □ Algeria 34°20N 3°40E 136 B4
Djema C.A.R. 6°3N 25°15E 142 A2
Djémila Algeria 36°19N 5°15E 136 A5
Djendel Algeria 36°15N 2°25E 136 A4
Djenné Mali 14°0N 4°30W 138 C4
Djenoun, Garet el Algeria 25°4N 5°31E 136 D5
Djerba Tunisia 33°48N 10°54E 136 B6
Djerba, Î. de Tunisia 33°48N 10°48E 135 B8

Djerid, Chott Tunisia 33°42N 8°30E 136 B5
Djibo Burkina Faso 14°9N 1°35W 139 C4
Djibouti Djibouti 11°30N 43°5E 131 E3
Djibouti ■ Africa 12°0N 43°0E 131 E3
Djolu Dem. Rep. of the Congo 0°35N 22°5E 140 D4
Djoudj △ Senegal 16°24N 16°14W 138 B1
Djougou Benin 9°40N 1°45E 139 D5
Djoum Cameroon 2°41N 12°35E 140 D2
Djourab, Erg du Chad 16°40N 18°50E 135 E9
Djugu Dem. Rep. of the Congo 1°55N 30°35E 142 B3
Djukbinj △ Australia 12°11S 131°12E 148 B5
Djúpivogur Iceland 64°39N 14°17W 60 D6
Djursland Denmark 56°27N 10°45E 63 H4
Dmitriya Lapteva, Proliv Russia 73°0N 140°0E 107 B15
Dmitriyev Lgovskiy Russia 52°10N 35°0E 85 F8
Dmitrov Russia 56°25N 37°32E 84 D9
Dmitrovsk-Orlovskiy Russia 52°29N 35°10E 85 F8
Dnepr = Dnipro → Ukraine 46°30N 32°18E 85 J7
Dneprodzerzhinsk = Dniprodzerzhynsk Ukraine 48°32N 34°37E 85 H8
Dneprodzerzhinskoye Vdkhr. = Dniprodzerzhynske Vdskh. Ukraine 48°49N 34°8E 85 H8
Dnepropetrovsk = Dnipropetrovsk Ukraine 48°30N 35°0E 85 H8
Dneprorudnoye = Dniprorudne Ukraine 47°21N 34°58E 85 J8
Dnestr = Dnister → Europe 46°18N 30°17E 75 E16
Dnieper = Dnipro → Europe 46°30N 32°18E 85 J7
Dniester = Dnister → Europe 46°18N 30°17E 75 E16
Dnipro → Ukraine 46°30N 32°18E 85 J7
Dniprodzerzhynsk Ukraine 48°32N 34°37E 85 H8
Dniprodzerzhynske Vdskh. Ukraine 48°49N 34°8E 85 H8
Dnipropetrovsk Ukraine 48°30N 35°0E 85 H8
Dnipropetrovsk □ Ukraine 48°15N 34°50E 85 H8
Dniprorudne Ukraine 47°21N 34°58E 85 J8
Dnister → Europe 46°18N 30°17E 75 E16
Dnistrovskyy Lyman Ukraine 46°15N 30°17E 85 J6
Dno Russia 57°50N 29°58E 84 D5
Dnyapro = Dnipro → Ukraine 46°30N 32°18E 85 J7
Do Gonbadān = Gachsārān Iran 30°15N 50°45E 129 D6
Doaktown Canada 46°33N 66°8W 165 C6
Doan Hung Vietnam 21°30N 105°10E 116 G5
Doba Chad 8°40N 16°50E 135 G9
Dobandi Pakistan 31°13N 66°50E 124 D2
Dobbiaco Italy 46°44N 12°14E 93 B9
Dobbyn Australia 19°44S 140°2E 150 B3
Dobczyce Poland 49°52N 20°5E 83 J7
Dobele Latvia 56°37N 23°16E 82 B10
Döbeln Germany 51°6N 13°7E 76 D9
Doberai, Jazirah Indonesia 1°25S 133°0E 119 E8
Dobiegniew Poland 52°59N 15°45E 83 F2
Doblas Argentina 37°5S 64°0W 190 D3
Dobo Indonesia 5°45S 134°15E 119 F8
Doboj Bos.-H. 44°46N 18°4E 80 F3
Dobra Wielkopolskie, Poland 51°55N 18°37E 83 G5
Dobra Zachodnio-Pomorskie, Poland 53°34N 15°20E 82 E2
Dobra Dâmbovita, Romania 44°52N 25°40E 81 F10
Dobra Hunedoara, Romania 45°54N 22°36E 80 E7
Dobre Miasto Poland 53°58N 20°26E 82 E7
Dobreşti Romania 46°51N 22°18E 80 D7
Dobrich Bulgaria 43°37N 27°49E 97 C11
Dobrich □ Bulgaria 43°37N 27°49E 97 C11
Dobrinishte Bulgaria 41°49N 23°34E 96 E7
Dobříš Czech Rep. 49°46N 14°10E 78 B7
Dobrodzień Poland 50°45N 18°25E 83 H5
Dobromyl Ukraine 49°34N 22°46E 83 J9
Dobropole Ukraine 48°25N 37°2E 85 H9
Dobrovolsk Russia 54°46N 22°31E 82 D9
Dobruja Europe 44°30N 28°15E 81 F13
Dobrush Belarus 52°25N 31°22E 75 E16
Dobrzany Poland 53°22N 15°25E 82 E2
Dobrzyń nad Wisłą Poland 52°39N 19°22E 83 F6
Doc, Mui Vietnam 17°58N 106°30E 120 D6
Doce → Brazil 19°37S 39°49W 189 D3
Docker River = Kaltukatjara Australia 24°52S 129°5E 149 D4
Docksta Sweden 63°3N 18°18E 62 A12
Doctor Arroyo Mexico 23°40N 100°11W 180 C4
Doctor Pedro P. Peña Paraguay 22°27S 62°21W 190 A3
Doctors Inlet U.S.A. 30°6N 81°47W 178 E6
Doda India 33°10N 75°34E 125 C6
Doda, L. Canada 49°25N 75°13W 164 C4
Doda Betta India 11°24N 76°44E 127 J3
Dodballapur India 13°18N 77°22E 127 H3
Dodecanese = Dodekanisa Greece 36°35N 27°0E 99 E8
Dodekanisa Greece 36°35N 27°0E 99 E8
Dodge City U.S.A. 37°45N 100°1W 172 G3
Dodge L. Canada 59°50N 105°36W 163 B7
Dodgeville U.S.A. 42°58N 90°8W 172 D8
Dodo Cameroon 7°30N 12°3E 139 D7
Dodoma Tanzania 6°8S 35°45E 142 D4
Dodoma □ Tanzania 6°0S 36°0E 142 D4
Dodoni Greece 39°40N 20°46E 98 B2
Dodori △ Kenya 1°55S 41°7E 142 C5
Dodsland Canada 51°50N 108°45W 163 C7
Dodurga Turkey 40°49N 29°57E 99 B13
Doerun U.S.A. 31°19N 83°55W 178 D6
Doesburg Neths. 52°1N 6°9E 70 B6
Doetinchem Neths. 51°59N 6°18E 69 C6
Dog Creek Canada 51°35N 122°14W 162 C4

Dog I. U.S.A. 29°48N 84°36W 178 F5
Dog L., Man., Canada 51°2N 98°31W 163 C9
Dog L., Ont., Canada 48°48N 89°30W 164 C2
Doğanşehir Turkey 38°5N 37°53E 104 C7
Dogliani Italy 44°32N 7°56E 92 D4
Dogondoutchi Niger 13°38N 4°2E 139 C5
Dogons, Land of the = Bandiagara, Falaise de Mali 14°14N 3°29W 138 D4
Dogran Pakistan 31°48N 73°35E 124 D5
Doğubayazıt Turkey 39°31N 44°5E 105 C11
Doguéraoua Niger 14°0N 5°31E 139 C6
Doha = Ad Dawḥah Qatar 25°15N 51°35E 129 E6
Doha Int. ✈ (DOH) Qatar 25°16N 51°34E 129 E6
Dohazari Bangla. 22°10N 92°5E 123 H18
Dohrighat India 26°16N 83°31E 125 F10
Doi Indonesia 2°14N 127°49E 119 D7
Doi Inthanon Thailand 18°35N 98°29E 120 C2
Doi Inthanon △ Thailand 18°33N 98°34E 120 C2
Doi Khuntan △ Thailand 18°33N 99°14E 120 C2
Doi Luang Thailand 18°30N 101°0E 120 D3
Doi Luang △ Thailand 19°39N 99°35E 120 C2
Doi Phukha △ Thailand 19°8N 101°9E 120 C3
Doi Saket Thailand 18°52N 99°9E 120 C2
Doi Suthep Pui △ Thailand 18°49N 98°53E 120 C2
Doi Toa Thailand 17°55N 98°30E 120 D2
Dois Irmãos, Sa. Brazil 9°0S 42°30W 189 B2
Dojransko Jezero Macedonia 41°13N 22°44E 96 E6
Dokdo = Liancourt Rocks Asia 37°15N 131°52E 113 F5
Dokkum Neths. 53°20N 5°59E 69 A5
Dokos Greece 37°20N 23°20E 98 D5
Dokri Pakistan 27°25N 68°7E 124 F3
Dokuchayevsk Ukraine 47°44N 37°40E 85 J9
Dol-de-Bretagne France 48°34N 1°47W 70 D5
Dolak, Pulau Indonesia 8°0S 138°30E 119 F9
Dolbeau-Mistassini Canada 48°53N 72°14W 165 C5
Dole France 47°7N 5°31E 71 E12
Dolenji Logatec = Logatec Slovenia 45°56N 14°15E 93 C11
Dolgellau U.K. 52°45N 3°53W 66 E4
Dolgelley = Dolgellau U.K. 52°45N 3°53W 66 E4
Dolhasca Romania 47°26N 26°36E 81 C11
Doliana Greece 39°54N 20°32E 98 B2
Dolianova Italy 39°22N 9°10E 94 C2
Dolinsk Russia 47°21N 142°48E 107 E15
Dolinskaya = Dolynska Ukraine 48°6N 32°46E 85 H7
Dolj □ Romania 44°10N 23°30E 81 F8
Dollard Neths. 53°20N 7°10E 69 A7
Dolna Banya Bulgaria 42°26N 23°44E 96 D7
Dolni Chiflik Bulgaria 42°59N 27°43E 97 D11
Dolni Dŭbnik Bulgaria 43°24N 24°26E 97 C8
Dolnośląskie □ Poland 51°0N 16°30E 83 G3
Dolný Kubín Slovak Rep. 49°12N 19°18E 79 B12
Dolo Ethiopia 4°11N 42°3E 131 G3
Dolo Italy 45°25N 12°5E 93 C9
Dolomites = Dolomiti Italy 46°23N 11°51E 93 B8
Dolomiti Italy 46°23N 11°51E 93 B8
Dolomiti Bellunesi △ Italy 46°10N 12°5E 93 B9
Dolores Argentina 36°20S 57°40W 190 D4
Dolores Uruguay 33°34S 58°15W 190 C4
Dolores U.S.A. 37°28N 108°30W 169 H9
Dolores → U.S.A. 38°49N 109°17W 168 G9
Dolovo Serbia 44°55N 20°52E 80 F5
Dolphin, C. Falk. Is. 51°10S 59°0W 192 D5
Dolphin and Union Str. Canada 69°5N 114°45W 160 D9
Dolsk Poland 51°59N 17°3E 83 G4
Dolyna Ukraine 48°58N 24°1E 81 B9
Dolynska Ukraine 48°6N 32°46E 85 H7
Dolzhanskaya Russia 46°37N 37°48E 85 J9
Dom Joaquim Brazil 18°57S 43°16W 189 D2
Dom Pedrito Brazil 31°0S 54°40W 191 C5
Dom Pedro Brazil 4°59S 44°27W 189 A2
Doma Nigeria 8°25N 8°18E 139 D6
Doma □ Zimbabwe 16°28S 30°12E 143 F3
Domanic Turkey 39°48N 29°36E 99 B11
Domariaganj → India 26°17N 83°44E 125 F10
Domasi Malawi 15°15S 35°22E 143 F4
Domažlice Czech Rep. 49°28N 12°58E 78 B5
Dombarovskiy Russia 50°46N 59°32E 106 D6
Dombås Norway 62°4N 9°8E 60 E13
Dombasle-sur-Meurthe France 48°38N 6°21E 71 D13
Dombes France 45°58N 5°0E 73 C9
Dombóvár Hungary 46°21N 18°9E 80 D3
Dombrád Hungary 48°13N 21°54E 80 B6
Dome Argus Antarctica 80°50S 76°30E 55 E6
Dome C. Antarctica 75°12S 123°37E 55 D9
Dome Rock Mts. U.S.A. 33°30N 114°20W 171 M12
Domel I. = Letsôk-aw Kyun Burma 11°30N 98°25E 121 G2
Domérat France 46°21N 2°32E 71 F9
Domett N.Z. 42°53S 173°12E 155 D5
Domeyko Chile 29°0S 71°0W 190 B1
Domeyko, Cordillera Chile 24°30S 69°0W 190 A2
Domfront France 48°37N 0°40W 70 D6
Dominador Chile 24°21S 69°20W 190 A2
Dominica ■ W. Indies 15°20N 61°20W 183 C7
Dominica Passage W. Indies 15°10N 61°20W 183 C7
Dominican Rep. ■ W. Indies 19°0N 70°30W 183 C5
Dömitz Germany 53°8N 11°15E 76 B7
Domme France 44°48N 1°12E 72 D5
Domnești Romania 45°12N 24°50E 81 F9
Domodedovo Int., Moscow ✈ (DME) Russia 55°24N 37°54E 84 C9
Domodóssola Italy 46°7N 8°17E 92 B5
Domogled-Valea Cernei △ Romania 44°52N 22°27E 80 F7
Domokos Greece 39°10N 22°18E 98 B4
Dompaire France 48°14N 6°14E 71 D13
Dompierre-sur-Besbre France 46°31N 3°41E 71 F10
Dompim Ghana 5°10N 2°5W 138 D4

Domrémy-la-Pucelle France 48°26N 5°40E 71 D12
Domvena Greece 38°15N 22°59E 98 C4
Domville, Mt. Australia 28°1S 151°15E 151 D5
Dômzale Slovenia 46°9N 14°35E 93 B11
Don → India 16°20N 76°15E 127 F3
Don → Russia 47°4N 39°18E 85 J10
Don → Aberds., U.K. 57°11N 2°5W 65 D6
Don → S. Yorks., U.K. 53°41N 0°52W 66 D7
Don, C. Australia 11°18S 131°46E 148 B5
Don Benito Spain 38°53N 5°51W 89 G5
Don Figuerroa Mts. Jamaica 18°5N 77°36W 182 a
Don Sak Thailand 9°18N 99°41E 121 b
Dona Ana = Nhamaabué Mozam. 17°25S 35°5E 143 F4
Doña Mencía Spain 37°33N 4°21W 89 H6
Donaghadee U.K. 54°39N 5°33W 64 B6
Donaghmore Ireland 52°52N 7°36W 64 D4
Donald Australia 36°23S 143°0E 152 D5
Donaldsonville U.S.A. 30°6N 90°59W 176 F9
Donalsonville U.S.A. 31°3N 84°53W 178 D5
Doñana △ Spain 36°59N 6°23W 89 J4
Donau = Dunărea → Europe 45°20N 29°40E 81 E14
Donau → Austria 48°10N 17°0E 79 C10
Donau Auen △ Austria 48°10N 16°49E 79 C9
Donaueschingen Germany 47°56N 8°29E 77 H4
Donauwörth Germany 48°43N 10°47E 77 G6
Doncaster U.K. 53°32N 1°6W 66 D6
Dondo Angola 9°45S 14°25E 140 F2
Dondo Mozam. 19°33S 34°46E 143 F3
Dondo, Teluk Indonesia 0°50N 120°30E 119 D6
Dondra Head Sri Lanka 5°55N 80°40E 127 M5
Donduşeni Moldova 48°14N 27°36E 81 B12
Donegal Ireland 54°39N 8°5W 64 B3
Donegal □ Ireland 54°53N 8°0W 64 B4
Donegal B. Ireland 54°31N 8°49W 64 B3
Donets → Russia 47°33N 40°55E 87 G5
Donets Basin Ukraine 49°0N 38°0E 58 F13
Donetsk Ukraine 48°0N 37°45E 85 J9
Donetsk □ Ukraine 48°0N 37°50E 85 J9
Dong Ba Thin Vietnam 12°8N 109°13E 121 F7
Dong Dang Vietnam 21°54N 106°42E 116 G6
Dong Giam Vietnam 19°25N 105°31E 120 C5
Dong Ha Vietnam 16°55N 107°8E 120 D6
Dong Hene Laos 16°40N 105°18E 120 D5
Dong Hoi Vietnam 17°29N 106°36E 120 D6
Dong Jiang → China 23°6N 114°0E 117 F10
Dong Khe Vietnam 22°26N 106°27E 116 A6
Dong Phayayen Thailand 14°20N 101°22E 120 E3
Dong Ujimqin Qi China 45°32N 116°55E 114 B9
Dong Van Vietnam 23°16N 105°22E 116 A5
Dong Xoai Vietnam 11°32N 106°55E 121 G6
Donga Nigeria 7°45N 10°2E 139 D7
Donga → Nigeria 8°20N 9°58E 139 D7
Dong'an China 26°23N 111°12E 117 D8
Dongara Australia 29°14S 114°57E 149 E1
Dongargarh India 21°10N 80°40E 126 D5
Dongbei China 45°0N 125°0E 115 C13
Dongchuan China 26°8N 103°1E 116 D4
Dongfang China 18°50N 108°33E 117 a
Dongfeng China 42°40N 125°34E 115 C13
Dongfanghong China 46°16N 133°34E 115 B16
Donggala Indonesia 0°30S 119°40E 119 E5
Donggan China 23°22N 105°9E 116 F5
Donggang China 39°52N 124°10E 115 E13
Dongguan China 22°58N 113°44E 117 F9
Dongguang China 37°50N 116°30E 114 F9
Donghae S. Korea 37°29N 129°7E 115 F15
Donghai Dao China 21°0N 110°15E 117 G8
Dongjingcheng China 44°5N 129°10E 115 B15
Dongkou China 27°6N 110°35E 117 D8
Dongliao He → China 42°58N 123°32E 115 C12
Dongliu China 30°13N 116°55E 117 B11
Dongmen China 22°20N 107°48E 116 F5
Dongning China 44°2N 131°5E 115 B16
Dongnyi China 28°30N 100°15E 116 D3
Dongola Sudan 19°9N 30°22E 137 D3
Dongping China 35°55N 116°20E 114 G9
Dongsha Dao S. China Sea 20°45N 116°43E 111 G12
Dongshan China 23°43N 117°30E 117 F11
Dongsheng = Ordos China 39°50N 110°0E 114 E6
Dongtai China 32°51N 120°21E 117 A13
Dongting Hu China 29°18N 112°45E 117 D9
Dongtou China 27°51N 121°10E 117 D13
Dongxiang China 28°11N 116°34E 117 C11
Dongxing China 21°34N 108°0E 116 F7
Dongyang China 29°13N 120°15E 117 C13
Dongying China 37°37N 118°37E 115 F10
Dongyinggang China 38°5N 118°27E 115 F10
Dongzhi China 30°9N 117°0E 117 B11
Donington, C. Australia 34°45S 136°0E 152 C2
Doniphan U.S.A. 36°37N 90°50W 172 G8
Donja Stubica Croatia 45°59N 15°59E 93 C12
Donji Dušnik Serbia 43°12N 22°5E 96 C8
Donji Miholjac Croatia 45°45N 18°10E 80 E3
Donji Milanovac Serbia 44°28N 22°6E 96 B6
Donji Vakuf Bos.-H. 44°8N 17°24E 80 F2
Donna Norway 66°6N 12°30E 60 C15
Donna U.S.A. 26°9N 98°4W 176 H5
Donnacona Canada 46°41N 71°41W 165 C5
Donnelly's Crossing N.Z. 35°42S 173°38E 154 B2
Donner Pass U.S.A. 39°19N 120°20W 170 F6
Donnybrook Australia 33°34S 115°48E 149 F2
Donnybrook S. Africa 29°59S 29°48E 145 D4
Donostia = Donostia-San Sebastián Spain 43°17N 1°58W 90 B3
Donostia-San Sebastián Spain 43°17N 1°58W 90 B3
Donousa Greece 37°8N 25°48E 99 D7
Donwood Canada 44°19N 78°16W 174 B6
Donzère France 44°26N 4°43E 73 D8
Donzy France 47°20N 3°6E 71 E10
Dookie Australia 36°20S 145°41E 153 D6
Doomadgee Australia 17°56S 138°49E 150 B2
Doomadgee □ Australia 17°56S 138°49E 150 B2
Doon → U.K. 55°27N 4°39W 65 F4
Doon Doon Australia 16°18S 128°14E 148 C4
Dora, L. Australia 22°0S 123°0E 148 D3

Dover-Foxcroft U.S.A. 45°11N 69°13W 173 C7
Dover Plains U.S.A. 41°43N 73°35W 175 E11
Dovey = Dyfi → U.K. 52°32N 4°3W 67 E4
Dovhe Ukraine 48°22N 23°17E 81 B8
Dovrefjell Norway 62°15N 9°33E 60 E13
Dovrefjell-Sunndalsfjella △ Norway 62°23N 9°11E 60 E13
Dow Rūd Iran 33°28N 49°4E 129 C7
Dowa Malawi 13°38S 33°58E 143 E3
Dowagiac U.S.A. 41°59N 86°6W 172 F11
Dowerin Australia 31°12S 117°2E 149 F2
Dowgha'i Iran 36°54N 58°32E 129 B8
Dowlatabad Kermān, Iran 28°20N 56°40E 129 D8
Dowlatabad Khorāsān, Iran 28°20N 56°40E 129 D8
Dowling Park U.S.A. 30°15N 83°15W 178 F6
Down □ U.K. 54°23N 6°2W 64 B6
Downey Calif., U.S.A. 33°56N 118°9W 171 M8
Downey Idaho, U.S.A. 42°26N 112°7W 168 E7
Downham Market U.K. 52°37N 0°23E 67 E8
Downieville U.S.A. 39°34N 120°50W 170 F6
Downpatrick U.K. 54°20N 5°43W 64 B6
Downpatrick Hd. Ireland 54°20N 9°21W 64 B2
Downsville U.S.A. 42°5N 75°0W 175 D10
Downton, Mt. Canada 52°42N 124°52W 162 C4
Dowsāri Iran 28°25N 57°59E 129 D8
Doxato Greece 41°9N 24°16E 97 B8
Doyle U.S.A. 40°2N 120°6W 170 E6
Doylestown U.S.A. 40°21N 75°10W 175 E9
Dozois, Rés. Canada 47°30N 77°5W 164 C4
Dra Khel Pakistan 27°58N 66°45E 124 F2
Drâa, C. Morocco 28°47N 11°0W 136 C3
Drâa, Oued → Morocco 28°40N 11°10W 136 C3
Drac → France 45°13N 5°42E 73 D9
Drac, Coves del Spain 39°31N 3°19E 100 B10
Dračevo Macedonia 41°56N 21°31E 96 B2
Drachten Neths. 53°7N 6°5E 69 A6
Drăgănești Ukraine 47°43N 28°15E 81 C10
Dragalina Romania 44°30N 27°15E 81 F12
Drăgănești-Olt Romania 44°9N 24°32E 81 F9
Draganeşti-Vlasça Romania 44°5N 25°33E 81 F10
Dragaš = Sharr Kosovo 42°5N 20°41E 96 C3
Drăgășani Romania 44°39N 24°17E 81 F9
Dragichyn Belarus 52°15N 25°8E 75 B8
Dragocvet Serbia 43°58N 21°15E 96 C5
Dragon's Mouths Trin. & Tob. 11°0N 61°50W 187 K15
Dragovishtitsa Bulgaria 42°22N 22°39E 96 C6
Draguignan France 43°32N 6°27E 73 E10
Drahovo Ukraine 48°14N 23°33E 81 B8
Drain U.S.A. 43°40N 123°19W 168 E2
Drake U.S.A. 47°55N 100°23W 172 B4
Drake Passage S. Ocean 58°0S 68°0W 55 B17
Drakensberg S. Africa 31°0S 28°0E 145 E4
Drama Greece 41°9N 24°10E 97 B8
Drammen Norway 59°42N 10°12E 61 G14
Drangajökull Iceland 66°9N 22°15W 60 A2
Dras India 34°25N 75°48E 125 B6
Drastis, Akra Greece 39°48N 19°40E 98 B1
Drau = Drava → Croatia 45°33N 18°55E 80 E3
Drava → Croatia 45°33N 18°55E 80 E3
Dravograd Slovenia 46°36N 15°5E 93 B12
Drawa → Poland 52°52N 15°59E 82 E3
Drawieński △ Poland 53°6N 15°58E 82 E3
Drawno Poland 53°13N 15°46E 82 E3
Drawsko Pomorskie Poland 53°35N 15°50E 82 E3
Drayton Canada 43°46N 80°40W 174 C4
Drayton Valley Canada 53°12N 114°58W 162 C5
Dreieich Germany 50°1N 8°41E 77
Drenthe □ Neths. 52°52N 6°40E 69 B6
Drepano, Akra Greece 35°28N 24°14E 101
Drepanum, C. Cyprus 34°54N 32°19E 101 E11
Dresden Canada 42°35N 82°11W 174 D2
Dresden Germany 51°3N 13°44E 76 D9
Dresden U.S.A. 42°41N 76°57W 174
Dreux France 48°44N 1°23E 70 D7
Drezdenko Poland 52°50N 15°49E 83 F2
Driffield U.K. 54°0N 0°26W 66
Driftwood U.S.A. 41°20N 78°8W 174
Driggs U.S.A. 43°44N 111°6W 168
Drin → Albania 41°39N 20°28E 96
Drin i Zi → Albania 41°37N 20°28E 96
Drina → Bos.-H. 44°53N 19°21E 80 F4
Drincea → Romania 44°20N 22°55E 80
Drinjača → Bos.-H. 44°15N 19°8E 80
Driopida Greece 37°22N 24°35E 99
Drissa = Vyerkhnyadzvinsk Belarus 55°45N 27°58E 84
Drniš Croatia 43°51N 16°10E 93
Drøbak Norway 59°39N 10°39E 61
Drobeta-Turnu Severin Romania 44°39N 22°41E 80
Drobin Poland 52°42N 19°58E 83
Drochia Moldova 48°2N 27°48E 81
Drogheda Ireland 53°43N 6°22W 64
Drogichin = Dragichyn Belarus 52°15N 25°8E 75
Drogobych = Drohobych Ukraine 49°20N 23°30E 81
Drohiczyn Poland 52°24N 22°39E 83
Drohobych Ukraine 49°20N 23°30E 81
Droichead Átha = Drogheda Ireland 53°43N 6°22W 64
Droichead na Bandan = Bandon Ireland 51°44N 8°44W 64
Droichead Nua = Newbridge Ireland 53°11N 6°48W 64
Droitwich U.K. 52°16N 2°8W 67
Drôme □ France 44°38N 5°15E 73
Drôme → France 44°46N 4°46E 73
Dromedary, C. Australia 36°17S 150°10E 153
Drömling Germany 52°29N 11°3E 76
Dromore Down, U.K. 52°29N 6°9W 64
Dromore Tyrone, U.K. 54°31N 7°28W 64
Dromore West Ireland 54°15N 8°52W 64
Dronero Italy 44°28N 7°22E 92
Dronfield U.K. 53°19N 1°27W 66
Dronne → France 45°2N 0°9W 72
Dronning Ingrid Land Greenland 64°20N 50°55W 57
Dronning Maud Land Antarctica 72°30S 12°0E 55

nninglund Denmark 57°10N 10°19'E **63** G4
nten Neths. 52°32N 5°43E **69** B5
pt → France 44°35N 0°6W **72** D3
sendorf Austria 48°52N 15°37E **78** C8
ué France 48°3N 1°6E **70** D8
uin Austria 38°10S 145°53E **153** E6
ak Yul = Bhutan ■
　sia 27°25N 90°30E **123** F17
mbo Canada 43°16N 80°35W **174** C4
mcliff Ireland 54°20N 8°29W **64** B3
mheller Canada 51°25N 112°40W **162** C6
mmond I. U.S.A. 46°1N 83°39W **173** B12
mmond Pt.
　ustralia 30°9S 135°16E **151** E2
mmond Ra.
　ustralia 23°45S 147°10E **150** C4
mmondville
　ustralia 45°55N 72°25W **164** C5
mright U.S.A. 35°59N 96°36W **176** D6
skininkai Lithuania 54°33N 23°58E **84** E2
at → Russia 53°8N 30°55 **75** B16
aya Belarus 55°45N 27°28E **84** E4
zhba Bulgaria 43°15N 28°1E **97** C12
zhina Russia 68°14N 145°18E **107** C15
zhkivka Ukraine 48°38N 37°32E **85** H9
ar Bos.-H. 44°21N 16°23E **93** D13
enik Croatia 43°2N 16°3E **93** E13
weca → Poland 53°0N 18°42E **83** E5
amaica 18°19N 77°24W **182** a
Tortugas U.S.A. 24°38N 82°55W **177** J13
ander △ Australia 20°13S 148°34E **150** b
anovo Bulgaria 42°30N 25°28E **97** D9
den Canada 49°47N 92°50W **163** D10
galski I. Antarctica 66°0S 92°0E **55** C7
galski Ice Tongue
　Antarctica 75°24S 163°30E **55** D11
sdale → Australia 13°59S 126°51E **148** B4
sdale I. Australia 11°45S 136°0E **150** A2
sdale River △
　ustralia 14°56S 127°2E **148** B4
ewica Poland 51°27N 20°29E **83** G7
ewiczka → Poland 51°36N 20°36E **83** G7
hang Cameroon 5°32N 10°3E **139** D7
Gué → Canada 57°21N 70°45W **164** A5
He → China 32°48N 110°40E **117** A8
Quoin U.S.A. 38°1N 89°14W **172** F9
an China 23°59N 108°3E **116** F7
anesburg U.S.A. 42°45N 74°11W **175** D10
aringa Australia 24°32S 149°42E **150** C4
arte, Pico Dom. Rep. 19°2N 70°59W **183** D5
ai → U.A.E. 25°18N 55°20E **129** E7
ãsari Moldova 47°15N 29°10E **81** C14
ãsari Vdkhr.
　Moldova 47°30N 29°0E **81** C13
awnt → Canada 64°33N 100°6W **163** A8
awnt L. Canada 63°8N 101°28W **163** A8
ary U.A.E. 25°18N 55°20E **129** E7
bo Australia 32°11S 148°35E **153** E8
e → Liberia 5°16N 7°29W **138** D3
ele
em. Rep. of the Congo 2°56N 29°35E **140** D5
bendorf Switz. 47°24N 8°37E **77** H4
ica Bos.-H. 45°10N 16°50E **93** C13
ica Croatia 45°11N 16°48E **93** C13
olin Ireland 53°21N 6°15W **64** C5
olin Ga., U.S.A. 32°32N 82°54W **178** C7
olin Tex., U.S.A. 32°5N 98°21W **176** E5
olin ✈ (DUB) Ireland 53°26N 6°15W **64** C5
ona Russia 56°44N 37°10E **84** D9
onica nad Váhom
　ovak Rep. 48°58N 18°11E **79** C11
bno Ukraine 50°25N 25°45E **75** C13
bois Idaho, U.S.A. 44°10N 112°14W **168** D7
Bois Pa., U.S.A. 41°7N 78°46W **174** E6
bysa → Lithuania 55°5N 23°26E **82** C10
c Tho Vietnam 18°32N 105°35E **120** C5
chang China 29°18N 116°12E **117** C11
chesne U.S.A. 40°10N 110°24W **168** F8
chess Australia 21°20S 139°50E **150** C2
cie I. Pac. Oc. 24°40S 124°48W **157** K15
ck → A. 36°2N 87°52W **177** C11
ck Cr. → Australia 23°21S ... **150** C4
ck Lake Canada 52°50N 106°16W **163** C7
ck Mountain △
　anada 51°45N 101°0W **163** C8
ckwall, Mt. U.S.A. 37°58N 120°7W **170** H6
erstadt Germany 51°31N 10°15E **76** D6
dhi India 24°15N 83°10E **125** G10
dinka Russia 69°30N 86°13E **107** C9
dley U.K. 52°31N 2°5W **67** E5
dley U.S.A. 42°32N 83°5W **178** C6
dna → India 19°17N 76°54E **126** E3
dna India 28°30N 80°41E **125** E9
ékoué Ivory C. 6°40N 7°10E **138** D3
eñas Spain 41°54N 4°33W **88** D2
ero = Douro → Europe 41°8N 8°40W **88** D2
ftown U.K. 57°27N 3°8W **66** D5
gi Otok Croatia 44°0N 15°3E **93** D11
go Selo Croatia 45°53N 17°18E **93** C14
isburg Germany 51°26N 6°45E **76** D2
iwelskloof = Modjadjiskloof
　. Africa 23°42S 30°10E **145** B5
jiangxin China 30°21N 103°38E **116** B4
kat Albania 40°16N 19°32E **96** F3
kdamin Iran 35°59N 57°43E **129** C8
kelský Průsmyk
　ovak Rep. 49°25N 21°42E **79** B14
khãn Iran 37°50N 57°40E **127** B8
khovshchina Russia 55°15N 32°27E **84** E7
kla Poland 49°30N 21°35E **83** J8
ku Bauchi, Nigeria 10°43N 10°43E **139** C7
ku Sokoto, Nigeria 11°11N 4°55E **139** C5

Dukuza = Stanger
　S. Africa 29°27S 31°14E **145** C5
Dulan China 36°0N 97°11E **110** D8
Dulce U.S.A. 36°56N 107°0W **169** H10
Dulce → Argentina 30°32S 62°33W **190** C3
Dulce, G. Costa Rica 8°40N 83°20E **182** E3
Dulf Iraq 35°7N 45°51E **128** C5
Dŭlgopol Bulgaria 43°3N 27°22E **97** C11
Duliu China 39°2N 116°55E **114** E9
Dulles Int. ✈ (IAD)
　U.S.A. 38°57N 77°27W **173** F15
Dullewala Pakistan 31°50N 71°25E **124** D4
Dullstroom S. Africa 25°27S 30°7E **145** C5
Dülmen Germany 51°49N 7°17E **76** D3
Dulovo Bulgaria 43°48N 27°9E **97** C11
Dulq Maghãr Syria 36°22N 38°39E **105** D8
Duluth Ga., U.S.A. 34°0N 84°9W **178** A5
Duluth Minn., U.S.A. 46°47N 92°6W **172** B7
Dum Dum India 22°39N 88°26E **125** H13
Dum Duma India 27°40N 95°40E **123** F19
Dūmã Syria 33°34N 36°24E **130** B5
Dumaguete Phil. 9°17N 123°15E **119** C6
Dumai Indonesia 1°35N 101°28E **118** D2
Dumaran Phil. 10°33N 119°50E **119** B5
Dumas Ark., U.S.A. 33°53N 91°29W **176** E9
Dumas Tex., U.S.A. 35°52N 101°58W **176** D4
Dumayr Syria 33°39N 36°42E **130** B5
Dumbarton U.K. 55°57N 4°33W **65** F4
Dúmbier Slovak Rep. 48°58N 19°58E **79** C12
Dumbleyung Australia 33°17S 117°42E **149** F2
Dumbrǎveni Romania 46°14N 24°34E **81** D9
Dumfries U.K. 55°4N 3°37W **65** F5
Dumfries & Galloway □
　U.K. 55°9N 3°58W **65** F5
Dumitreşti Romania 45°33N 26°55E **81** E11
Dumka India 24°12N 87°15E **125** G12
Dumlupınar Turkey 38°53N 30°0E **99** C12
Dümmer Germany 52°31N 8°20E **76** C4
Dümmer → Germany 52°31N 8°21E **76** C4
Dumoine → Canada 46°13N 77°51W **164** C4
Dumoine, L. Canada 46°55N 77°55W **164** C4
Dumont d'Urville
　Antarctica 66°40S 140°0E **55** C10
Dumont d'Urville Sea
　S. Ocean 63°30S 138°0E **55** C9
Dumyât Egypt 31°24N 31°48E **137** D2
Dumyât, Masabb Egypt 31°28N 31°51E **137** D2
Dún Dealgan = Dundalk
　Ireland 54°1N 6°24W **64** B5
Dún Garbhán = Dungarvan
　Ireland 52°5N 7°37W **64** D4
Dun Laoghaire Ireland 53°17N 6°8W **64** C5
Dun Laoghaire-Rathdown □
　Ireland 53°14N 6°11W **64** C5
Dun-le-Palestel France 46°18N 1°39E **71** F8
Dun-sur-Auron France 46°53N 2°33E **71** F9
Dun-sur-Meuse France 49°23N 5°11E **71** C12
Duna = Dunărea →
　Europe 45°20N 29°40E **81** E14
Duna-Drava △ Hungary 46°15N 18°50E **80** D3
Duna-völgyi-főcsatorna
　Hungary 46°40N 19°14E **80** D4
Dunafalva Hungary 46°10N 18°57E **80** D3
Dunaföldvár Hungary 46°50N 18°57E **80** D3
Dunagiri India 30°31N 79°52E **125** D8
Dunaj = Dunărea →
　Europe 45°20N 29°40E **81** E14
Dunajec → Poland 50°15N 20°44E **83** H7
Dunajská Streda
　Slovak Rep. 48°0N 17°37E **79** C10
Dunakeszi Hungary 47°37N 19°8E **80** D4
Dunapataj Hungary 46°39N 19°4E **80** D4
Dunărea → Europe 45°20N 29°40E **81** E14
Dunaszekcső Hungary 46°6N 18°45E **80** D3
Dunaújváros Hungary 46°58N 18°57E **80** D3
Dunav = Dunărea →
　Europe 45°20N 29°40E **81** E14
Dunavaţu de Jos
　Romania 44°59N 29°13E **81** F14
Dunavtsi Bulgaria 43°57N 22°53E **96** C6
Dunay Russia 42°52N 132°22E **112** C6
Dunayivtsi Ukraine 48°54N 26°50E **81** B11
Dunback N.Z. 45°23S 170°36E **155** F5
Dunbar U.K. 56°0N 2°31W **65** E6
Dunblane U.K. 56°11N 3°58W **65** E5
Duncan Canada 48°45N 123°40W **170** B3
Duncan Ariz., U.S.A. 32°43N 109°6W **169** K9
Duncan Okla., U.S.A. 34°30N 97°57W **176** D6
Duncan, L. Canada 53°29N 77°58W **164** B4
Duncan, L. Canada 62°51N 113°58W **162** A6
Duncan Passage India 11°0N 92°0E **127** L4
Duncan Town
　Bahamas 22°15N 75°45W **182** B4
Duncannon U.S.A. 40°23N 77°2W **174** F7
Duncansby Head U.K. 58°38N 3°1W **66** C5
Dund-Us Mongolia 48°1N 91°38E **109** C12
Dundaga Latvia 57°30N 22°21E **82** A9
Dundalk Canada 44°10N 80°24W **174** B4
Dundalk Ireland 54°1N 6°24W **64** B5
Dundalk U.S.A. 39°15N 76°31W **173** F15
Dundalk Bay Ireland 53°55N 6°15W **64** C5
Dundas = Uummannaq
　Greenland 77°33N 68°52W **57** B4
Dundas Canada 43°17N 79°59W **174** C5
Dundas, L. Australia 32°35S 121°50E **149** F3
Dundas I. Canada 54°30N 130°50W **162** C2
Dundas Str. Australia 11°15S 131°35E **148** B5
Dundee S. Africa 28°11S 30°15E **145** C5
Dundee U.K. 56°28N 2°59W **66** E6
Dundee U.S.A. 42°32N 76°59W **174** D8
Dundee City □ U.K. 56°30N 2°58W **66** E6
Dundgovĭ □ Mongolia 45°10N 106°0E **114** B4
Dundrum U.K. 54°16N 5°52W **64** B6
Dundrum B. U.K. 54°13N 5°47W **64** B6
Dunedin U.S.A. 28°1N 82°46W **179** G7
Dunedin N.Z. 45°50S 170°33E **155** F5
Dunedoo Australia 32°0S 149°25E **153** A8
Dunfanaghy Ireland 55°11N 7°58W **64** A4
Dunfermline U.K. 56°5N 3°27W **65** E5
Dungannon Canada 43°51N 81°36W **174** C3
Dungannon U.K. 54°31N 6°46W **64** B5
Dungarpur India 23°52N 73°45E **124** H5
Dungarvan Ireland 52°5N 7°37W **64** D4
Dungarvan Harbour
　Ireland 52°4N 7°35W **64** D4
Dungeness U.K. 50°54N 0°59E **67** G8
Dunglow Ireland 54°57N 8°21W **64** B3
Dungo, L. do Angola 17°15S 19°0E **144** A2
Dungog Australia 32°22S 151°46E **153** E9
Dungu
　Dem. Rep. of the Congo 3°40N 28°32E **142** B2

Dungun Malaysia 4°45N 103°25E **121** K4
Dungunâb Sudan 21°10N 37°9E **137** C4
Dungunâb, Khalig
　Sudan 21°5N 37°12E **137** C4
Dunhua China 43°20N 128°14E **115** C15
Dunhuang China 40°8N 94°36E **110** C7
Dunk I. Australia 17°59S 146°29E **150** B4
Dunkassa Benin 10°21N 3°10E **139** C5
Dunkeld Queens.,
　Australia 33°25S 149°29E **151** E4
Dunkeld Vic., Australia 37°40S 142°22E **152** D5
Dunkeld U.K. 56°34N 3°35W **65** E5
Dunkerque France 51°2N 2°20E **71** A9
Dunkery Beacon U.K. 51°9N 3°36W **67** F4
Dunkirk = Dunkerque
　France 51°2N 2°20E **71** A9
Dunkirk U.S.A. 42°29N 79°20W **174** D5
Dunkwa Central, Ghana 6°0N 1°47W **138** D4
Dunkwa Central, Ghana 5°30N 1°0W **139** D4
Dunleary = Dún Laoghaire
　Ireland 53°17N 6°8W **64** C5
Dunleer Ireland 53°50N 6°24W **64** C5
Dunmanus B. Ireland 51°31N 9°50W **64** E2
Dunmanway Ireland 51°43N 9°6W **64** E2
Dunmarra Australia 16°42S 133°25E **150** B1
Dunmore U.S.A. 41°25N 75°38W **175** E9
Dunmore East Ireland 52°9N 7°0W **64** D5
Dunmore Town
　Bahamas 25°30N 76°39W **182** A4
Dunn U.S.A. 35°19N 78°37W **177** D15
Dunnellon U.S.A. 29°3N 82°28W **179** F7
Dunnet Hd. U.K. 58°40N 3°21W **66** C5
Dunning U.S.A. 41°50N 100°6W **172** E3
Dunnville Australia 42°54N 79°36W **174** D5
Dunolly Australia 36°51S 143°44E **152** D5
Dunoon U.K. 55°57N 4°56W **65** F4
Dunqul Egypt 23°26N 31°37E **137** C3
Duns U.K. 55°47N 2°20W **65** F6
Dunseith U.S.A. 48°50N 100°3W **172** A3
Dunshaughlin Ireland 53°31N 6°33W **64** C5
Dunsmuir U.S.A. 41°13N 122°16W **168** F2
Dunstable U.K. 51°53N 0°32W **67** F7
Dunstan Mts. N.Z. 44°53S 169°35E **155** E4
Dunster Canada 53°8N 119°50W **162** C5
Duntroon N.Z. 44°51S 170°40E **155** E5
Dunvegan U.K. 57°27N 6°35W **66** D2
Dunvegan L. Canada 60°8N 107°10W **163** A7
Dunwich Australia 27°12N 116°28E **114** C9
Duolun China 34°8N 82°29E **109** F10
Duong Dong Vietnam 10°13N 103°58E **121** G4
Dupree U.S.A. 45°4N 101°35W **172** C3
Dupuyer U.S.A. 48°13N 112°30W **168** B7
Duque de Caxias Brazil 22°46S 43°18W **191** A7
Duque de York, I.
　Chile 50°37S 75°25W **192** D1
Durack → Australia 15°33S 127°52E **148** C4
Durack Ra. Australia 16°50S 127°40E **148** C4
Durack River
　Australia 15°32S 127°39E **148** C4
Durağan Turkey 41°25N 35°3E **104** B6
Durak Turkey 39°42N 28°17E **99** B10
Durakovac = Gjurakoc
　Kosovo 42°43N 20°29E **96** D4
Durance → France 43°55N 4°45E **73** E8
Durand Ga., U.S.A. 32°55N 84°46W **178** C5
Durand Wis., U.S.A. 44°38N 91°58W **172** C8
Durango Mexico 24°3N 104°39W **180** C4
Durango U.S.A. 37°16N 107°53W **169** H10
Durango □ Mexico 24°50N 105°20W **180** C4
Durankulak Bulgaria 43°41N 28°32E **97** C12
Durant Miss., U.S.A. 33°4N 89°51W **177** E10
Durant Okla., U.S.A. 33°59N 96°25W **176** E6
Duratón → Spain 41°37N 4°7W **88** D6
Durazno Uruguay 33°25S 56°31W **190** C4
Durazzo = Durrës
　Albania 41°19N 19°28E **96** E3
Durban France 42°59N 2°49E **72** E6
Durban S. Africa 29°49S 31°1E **145** C5
Durban ✈ (DUR)
　S. Africa 29°37S 31°7E **145** C5
Durbuy Belgium 50°21N 5°28E **69** D5
Dúrcal Spain 36°59N 3°34W **89** J7
Đurđevac Croatia 46°2N 17°3E **80** D2
Düren Germany 50°48N 6°29E **76** E2
Durg = Bhilainagar-Durg
　India 21°13N 81°26E **126** D5
Durgapur India 23°30N 87°20E **125** H12
Durham Canada 44°10N 80°49W **174** B4
Durham U.K. 54°47N 1°34W **66** C6
Durham Calif., U.S.A. 39°39N 121°48W **170** F5
Durham N.C., U.S.A. 35°59N 78°54W **177** D15
Durham N.H., U.S.A. 43°8N 70°56W **175** C14
Durham □ U.K. 54°42N 1°45W **66** C6
Durlas = Thurles Ireland 52°41N 7°49W **64** D4
Durleşti Moldova 47°2N 28°46E **81** C15
Durmã Si. Arabia 24°37N 46°8E **128** E5
Durmitor Montenegro 43°10N 19°0E **96** C2
Durmitor △ Montenegro 43°15N 19°5E **96** C2
Durness U.K. 58°34N 4°45W **66** C4
Durrës Albania 41°19N 19°28E **96** E3
Durrow Ireland 52°51N 7°24W **64** D4
Dursey I. Ireland 51°36N 10°12W **64** E1
Dursley U.K. 51°40N 2°21W **67** F5
Dursunbey Turkey 39°35N 28°37E **99** B10
Durtal France 47°40N 0°18W **70** E6
Duru
　Dem. Rep. of the Congo 4°14N 28°50E **142** B2
Duru Gölü Turkey 41°20N 27°35E **97** E12
Durusu Turkey 41°21N 28°41E **97** E12
Durûz, Jabal ad Jordan 32°35N 36°40E **130** C5
D'Urville, Tanjung
　Indonesia 1°28S 137°54E **119** E9
D'Urville I. N.Z. 40°50S 173°55E **155** A8
Duryea U.S.A. 41°20N 75°45W **175** E9
Dûsh Egypt 24°35N 30°41E **137** C3
Dushak Turkmenistan 37°13N 60°1E **129** B9
Dushan China 25°48N 107°30E **116** E6
Dushanbe Tajikistan 38°33N 68°48E **108** F7
Dusheti Georgia 42°10N 44°42E **87** J7
Dushore U.S.A. 41°31N 76°24W **175** E8
Dusky Sd. N.Z. 45°47S 166°30E **155** F1
Dussejour, C. Australia 14°45S 128°13E **148** B4
Düsseldorf Germany 51°14N 6°47E **76** D2
Düsseldorf Rhein-Ruhr ✈ (DUS)
　Germany 51°17N 6°46E **76** D2
Dusti Tajikistan 37°30N 68°40E **129** B12
Dutch Harbor U.S.A. 53°53N 166°32W **166** E6
Dutlwe Botswana 23°58S 23°46E **144** C3
Dutsan Wai Nigeria 10°50N 8°10E **139** C6
Dutse Nigeria 11°46N 9°20E **139** C6
Dutton Canada 42°39N 81°30W **174** D3

Dutton → Australia 20°44S 143°10E **150** C3
Dutywa S. Africa 32°8S 28°18E **145** D4
Duved Sweden 63°23N 12°55E **62** A6
Düvertepe Turkey 39°14N 28°27E **99** B10
Duwayhin, Khawr
　U.A.E. 24°20N 51°25E **129** E6
Duyfken Pt. Australia 12°33S 141°38E **150** A3
Duyun China 26°18N 107°29E **116** C6
Düzağaç Turkey 38°45N 30°6E **99** C12
Duzce = Akhna Cyprus 35°3N 33°47E **101** D12
Düzce Turkey 40°50N 31°10E **104** B4
Düzce □ Turkey 40°50N 31°10E **104** B4
Düziçi Turkey 37°15N 36°28E **104** D7
Dve Mogili Bulgaria 43°35N 25°55E **97** C9
Dvina, Severnaya →
　Russia 64°32N 40°30E **58** C14
Dvinsk = Daugavpils
　Latvia 55°53N 26°32E **84** E4
Dvor Croatia 45°4N 16°22E **93** C13
Dvůr Králové nad Labem
　Czech Rep. 50°27N 15°50E **78** A8
Dwarka India 22°18N 69°8E **124** H3
Dwellingup Australia 32°43S 116°4E **149** F2
Dwight Canada 45°20N 79°1W **174** A5
Dwight U.S.A. 41°5N 88°26W **172** E9
Dyakove Ukraine 48°1N 23°0E **80** B7
Dyatkovo Russia 53°40N 34°27E **84** F8
Dyatlovo = Dzyatlava
　Belarus 53°28N 25°28E **75** B13
Dyce U.K. 57°13N 2°12W **65** D6
Dyer, C. Canada 66°37N 61°16W **161** D19
Dyer Bay Canada 45°10N 81°20W **174** A3
Dyer Plateau
　Antarctica 70°45S 65°30W **55** D17
Dyersburg U.S.A. 36°3N 89°23W **177** C10
Dyersville U.S.A. 42°29N 91°8W **172** D8
Dyfi → U.K. 52°32N 4°3W **67** E3
Dyje → Czech Rep. 48°37N 16°56E **79** C9
Dykh Tau Russia 43°3N 43°8E **87** J6
Dymer Ukraine 50°47N 30°18E **75** C16
Dynów Poland 49°50N 22°11E **83** J9
Dysart Australia 22°32S 148°23E **150** C4
Dytiki Ellas ◇ Greece 38°20N 21°30E **98** C3
Dyviziya Ukraine 45°55N 29°59E **81** E14
Dzamin Üüd = Zamyn-Üüd
　Mongolia 43°50N 111°58E **114** C7
Dzaoudzi Mayotte 12°47S 45°16E **141** a
Dzavhan Gol →
　Mongolia 48°54N 93°23E **110** B7
Dzerzhinsk Russia 56°14N 43°30E **86** B6
Dzhalal-Abad = Jalal-Abad
　Kyrgyzstan 40°56N 73°0E **109** D8
Dzhalinda Russia 53°26N 124°0E **107** D13
Dzhambeyty = Zhympity
　Kazakhstan 50°16N 52°35E **108** B4
Dzhambul = Taraz
　Kazakhstan 42°54N 71°22E **109** D8
Dzhankoy Ukraine 45°40N 34°20E **85** K8
Dzhanybek = Zhänibek
　Kazakhstan 49°25N 46°50E **86** F3
Dzharylhach, Ostriv
　Ukraine 46°2N 32°55E **85** J7
Dzhezkazgan = Zhezqazghan
　Kazakhstan 47°44N 67°40E **109** C7
Dzhizak = Jizzax
　Uzbekistan 40°6N 67°50E **109** D7
Dzhugba Russia 44°19N 38°48E **87** H4
Dzhugdzur, Khrebet
　Russia 57°30N 138°0E **107** D14
Dzhulynka Ukraine 48°26N 29°45E **81** B14
Dzhumgoltau, Khrebet
　Kyrgyzstan 42°15N 74°30E **109** D8
Dzhungarskiye Vorota =
　Dzungarian Gate
　Asia 45°10N 82°0E **109** C10
Dzhuryn Ukraine 48°41N 28°18E **81** B13
Dzhvari = Jvari Georgia 42°42N 42°4E **87** J6
Działdowo Poland 53°15N 20°15E **83** E7
Działoszyce Poland 50°22N 20°20E **83** H7
Działoszyn Poland 51°6N 18°50E **83** G5
Dzibilchaltún Mexico 21°10N 89°35W **181** C7
Dzierżoniów Poland 50°45N 16°39E **83** H3
Dzilam de Bravo
　Mexico 21°24N 88°53W **181** C7
Dzioua Algeria 33°14N 5°14E **136** B5
Dzisna Belarus 55°34N 28°12E **84** E5
Dzisna → Belarus 55°34N 28°12E **84** E5
Dziwnów Poland 54°2N 14°45E **82** D1
Dzükija △ Lithuania 54°10N 24°30E **61** J21
Dzungarian Basin = Junggar
　Pendi China 44°30N 86°0E **109** D11
Dzungarian Gate Asia 45°10N 82°0E **109** C10
Dzur Mongolia 49°39N 95°46E **109** C13
Dzüünbayan Mongolia 44°29N 110°2E **114** B6
Dzüünharaa
　Mongolia 48°52N 106°28E **110** B10
Dzüünmod Mongolia 47°45N 106°58E **110** B10
Dzyarzhynsk Belarus 53°40N 27°1E **75** B14
Dzyatlava Belarus 53°28N 25°28E **75** B13

Dutton U.S.A. 33°52N 80°41W **178** B9
Dutywa S. Africa 29°44N 84°53W **178** F5
Eagles Mere U.S.A. 41°25N 76°33W **175** E8
Ealing □ U.K. 51°31N 0°20W **67** F7
Ear Falls Canada 50°38N 93°13W **163** C10
Earlimart U.S.A. 35°53N 119°16W **171** K7
Earlville U.S.A. 42°45N 75°32W **175** D9
Early Branch U.S.A. 32°45N 80°55W **178** C9
Earn → U.K. 56°21N 3°18W **65** E5
Earn, L., U.K. 56°23N 4°13W **65** E4
Earnslaw, Mt. N.Z. 44°32S 168°27E **155** E3
Earth U.S.A. 34°14N 102°24W **176** D3
Easley U.S.A. 34°50N 82°36W **177** D13
East Anglia □ U.K. 52°50N 1°0E **66** E9
East Angus Canada 45°30N 71°40W **165** C5
East Antarctica Antarctica 80°0S 90°0E **55** D7
East Aurora U.S.A. 42°46N 78°37W **174** D6
East Ayrshire □ U.K. 55°26N 4°11W **65** F4
East Bengal Bangla. 24°0N 90°0E **123** G17
East Brady U.S.A. 40°59N 79°37W **174** F5
East Branch Clarion River L.
　U.S.A. 41°35N 78°35W **174** E6
East C. = Dezhneva, Mys
　Russia 66°5N 169°40W **107** C19
East C. N.Z. 37°42S 178°35E **154** C7
East Caroline Basin
　Pac. Oc. 4°0N 146°45E **156** G6
East Chicago U.S.A. 41°38N 87°27W **172** E9
East China Sea Asia 30°0N 126°0E **111** F14
East Coulee Canada 51°23N 112°27W **162** C6
East Dereham = Dereham
　U.K. 52°41N 0°57E **67** E8
East Dublin U.S.A. 32°32N 82°52W **178** C7
East Dunbartonshire □
　U.K. 55°57N 4°13W **65** F4
East Falkland Falk. Is. 51°30S 58°30W **192** D5
East Grand Forks
　U.S.A. 47°56N 97°1W **172** B5
East Greenwich
　U.S.A. 41°40N 71°27W **175** E13
East Grinstead U.K. 51°7N 0°0 **67** F8
East Hartford U.S.A. 41°46N 72°39W **175** E12
East Haydon Australia 18°0S 141°30E **150** B3
East Helena U.S.A. 46°35N 111°56W **168** C8
East Indies Asia 0°0 120°0E **102** J14
East Kavango □
　Namibia 18°0S 20°15E **144** A3
East Kilbride U.K. 55°47N 4°11W **65** F4
East Lamma Channel
　China 22°14N 114°9E **111** a
East Lansing U.S.A. 42°44N 84°29W **173** D11
East Liverpool U.S.A. 40°37N 80°35W **174** F4
East London S. Africa 33°0S 27°55E **145** D4
East Lothian □ U.K. 55°58N 2°44W **65** F6
East Main = Eastmain
　Canada 52°10N 78°30W **164** B4
East Mariana Basin
　Pac. Oc. 12°0N 153°0E **156** F7
East Naples U.S.A. 26°8N 81°46W **179** J8
East Northport U.S.A. 40°53N 73°19W **175** F11
East Orange U.S.A. 40°46N 74°12W **175** F10
East Pacific Rise
　Pac. Oc. 15°0S 110°0W **157** J17
East Palatka U.S.A. 29°39N 81°36W **178** F8
East Palestine U.S.A. 40°50N 80°32W **174** F4
East Pine Canada 55°48N 120°12W **162** B4
East Point U.S.A. 33°41N 84°25W **178** B5
East Providence
　U.S.A. 41°49N 71°23W **175** E13
East Pt. Br. Virgin Is. 18°40N 64°18W **183** e
East Pt. Canada 46°27N 61°58W **165** C7
East Renfrewshire □
　U.K. 55°46N 4°21W **65** F4
East Retford = Retford
　U.K. 53°19N 0°56W **66** D7
East Riding of Yorkshire □
　U.K. 53°55N 0°30W **66** D7
East Rochester U.S.A. 43°7N 77°29W **174** D7
East St. Louis U.S.A. 38°37N 90°9W **172** F8
East Schelde = Oosterschelde →
　Neths. 51°33N 4°0E **69** C4
East Sea = Japan, Sea of
　Asia 40°0N 135°0E **112** E7
East Siberian Sea
　Russia 73°0N 160°0E **107** B17
East Stroudsburg U.S.A. 41°1N 75°11W **175** E9
East Sussex □ U.K. 50°56N 0°19E **67** G8
East Tasman Plateau
　Pac. Oc. 43°30S 152°0E **156** M7
East Tawas U.S.A. 44°17N 83°29W **173** C12
East Timor ■ Asia 8°50S 126°0E **119** F7
East Toorale Australia 30°27S 145°28E **151** E4
East Walker →
　U.S.A. 38°52N 119°10W **170** F7
East Windsor U.S.A. 41°17N 74°34W **175** F10
Eastbourne N.Z. 41°19S 174°55E **154** H3
Eastbourne U.K. 50°46N 0°18E **67** G8
Eastend Canada 49°32N 108°50W **163** D7
Easter Fracture Zone
　Pac. Oc. 25°0S 110°0W **157** K16
Easter I. = Pascua, I. de
　Chile 27°7S 109°23W **157** K17
Eastern □ Ghana 6°30N 0°30W **139** D4
Eastern □ S. Leone 8°15N 11°0W **138** D2
Eastern Cape □ S. Africa 32°0S 26°0E **144** C4
Eastern Cr. →
　Australia 20°40S 141°35E **150** C3
Eastern Desert = Sharqîya, Es
　Sahrâ esh Egypt 27°30N 32°30E **137** B3
Eastern Ghats India 14°0N 78°50E **127** B3
Eastern Group = Lau Group
　Fiji 17°0S 178°30W **154** a
Eastern Group
　Australia 33°30S 124°30E **149** F3
Eastern Guruma ◇
　Australia 22°0S 117°30E **148** D2
Eastern Transvaal =
　Mpumalanga □
　S. Africa 26°0S 30°0E **145** C5
Easterville Canada 53°8N 99°49W **163** C9
Easthampton U.S.A. 42°16N 72°40W **175** D12
Eastlake U.S.A. 41°40N 81°26W **174** E4
Eastleigh U.K. 50°58N 1°21W **67** G6
Eastmain Canada 52°10N 78°30W **164** B4
Eastmain → Canada 52°27N 78°26W **164** B4
Eastman Canada 45°18N 72°19W **175** A12
Eastman U.S.A. 32°12N 83°11W **178** C6
Easton Md., U.S.A. 38°47N 76°5W **173** F15
Easton Pa., U.S.A. 40°41N 75°13W **175** F9
Easton Wash., U.S.A. 47°14N 121°11W **170** C5

Eastover U.S.A. 33°52N 80°41W **178** B9
Eastport U.S.A. 44°54N 66°59W **165** D12
Eastsound U.S.A. 48°42N 122°55W **170** B4
Eaton U.S.A. 40°32N 104°42W **168** F11
Eatonia Canada 51°13N 109°25W **163** C7
Eatonton U.S.A. 33°20N 83°23W **178** B6
Eatontown U.S.A. 40°19N 74°4W **175** F10
Eatonville U.S.A. 46°52N 122°16W **170** D4
Eau Claire U.S.A. 44°49N 91°30W **172** C8
Eau Claire, L. à l'
　Canada 56°10N 74°25W **164** A5
Eauripik Rise Pac. Oc. 2°0N 142°0E **156** G6
Eauze France 43°53N 0°7E **72** E4
Eban Nigeria 9°40N 4°50E **139** D5
Ebano Mexico 22°13N 98°24W **181** C5
Ebbegebirge △ Germany 51°10N 7°55E **76** D3
Ebbw Vale U.K. 51°46N 3°12W **67** F4
Ebeltoft Denmark 56°12N 10°41E **63** H4
Ebeltoft Vig Denmark 56°10N 10°35E **63** H4
Ebensburg U.S.A. 40°29N 78°44W **174** F6
Ebensee Austria 47°48N 13°46E **78** D6
Eber Gölü Turkey 38°38N 31°11E **104** C4
Eberbach Germany 49°28N 8°59E **77** F4
Eberswalde-Finow
　Germany 52°50N 13°49E **76** C9
Ebetsu Japan 43°7N 141°34E **112** C10
Ebey's Landing △
　U.S.A. 48°12N 122°41W **170** B4
Ebian China 29°11N 103°13E **116** C4
Ebingen = Albstadt
　Germany 48°13N 9°1E **77** G5
Ebinur Hu China 44°55N 82°55E **109** D10
Ěboli Italy 40°39N 15°2E **95** B8
Ebolowa Cameroon 2°55N 11°10E **139** E7
Ebonda
　Dem. Rep. of the Congo 2°12N 22°21E **140** D4
Ebonyi □ Nigeria 6°20N 8°0E **139** D6
Ebrach Germany 49°51N 10°29E **77** F6
Ebre = Ebro → Spain 40°43N 0°54E **90** D5
Ébrié, Lagune Ivory C. 5°12N 4°26W **138** D4
Ebro → Spain 40°43N 0°54E **90** D5
Ebro, Embalse del Spain 43°0N 3°58W **88** C7
Ebstorf Germany 53°2N 10°24E **76** B6
Ecatepec de Morelos
　Mexico 19°36N 99°3W **181** D5
Ecbatana = Hamadān
　Iran 34°52N 48°32E **105** E13
Eceabat Turkey 40°11N 26°21E **97** F10
Ech Chéliff Algeria 36°10N 1°20E **136** A4
Ech Chéliff □ Algeria 36°15N 1°30E **136** A4
Echechonnee →
　U.S.A. 32°39N 83°36W **178** C6
Echigo-Sammyaku
　Japan 36°50N 139°50E **113** F9
Echinos Greece 41°16N 25°1E **97** E9
Échirolles France 45°8N 5°44E **73** C9
Echizen Japan 35°50N 136°10E **113** G8
Echizen-Misaki Japan 35°59N 135°57E **113** G7
Echmiadzin = Ejmiatsin
　Armenia 40°12N 44°19E **87** K7
Echo U.S.A. 31°29N 85°28W **178** D4
Echo Bay N.W.T.,
　Canada 66°5N 117°55W **160** D8
Echo Bay Ont., Canada 46°29N 84°4W **164** C3
Echoing → Canada 55°51N 92°5W **163** C10
Echterdingen, Stuttgart ✈ (STR)
　Germany 48°42N 9°11E **77** G5
Echternach Lux. 49°49N 6°25E **69** E6
Echuca Australia 36°10S 144°45E **153** D6
Écija Spain 37°30N 5°10W **89** H5
Eckental Germany 54°28N 9°50E **76** A5
Eckernförde Germany 54°28N 9°50E **76** A5
Eclectic U.S.A. 32°38N 86°2W **178** C3
Eclipse I. Australia 35°5S 117°58E **149** G2
Eclipse Is. Australia 13°54S 126°19E **148** B4
Eclipse Sd. Canada 72°38N 79°0W **161** C16
Écommoy France 47°50N 0°17E **70** E7
Ecoporanga Brazil 18°23S 40°50W **189** D2
Écouché France 48°42N 0°7W **70** D6
Écrins → France 44°50N 6°18E **73** D10
Ecuador ■ S. Amer. 2°0S 78°0W **186** D3
Écueillé France 47°5N 1°21E **70** E8
Ed Sweden 58°55N 11°55E **63** F5
Ed Da'ein Sudan 11°26N 26°9E **140** B5
Ed Damazin Sudan 11°46N 34°21E **135** F12
Ed Dâmer Sudan 17°27N 34°0E **135** E12
Ed Dar el Beida = Casablanca
　Morocco 33°36N 7°36W **136** B2
Ed Debba Sudan 18°0N 30°51E **137** D3
Ed Déffa Egypt 30°40N 26°30E **137** A2
Ed Dueim Sudan 14°0N 32°10E **135** F12
Edam Canada 53°11N 108°46W **163** C7
Edam Neths. 52°31N 5°3E **69** B5
Edane Sweden 59°38N 12°49E **62** E6
Edapally India 11°19N 78°3E **127** J4
Edavanna India 11°36N 76°14E **127** J3
Eday U.K. 59°11N 2°47W **66** B6
Edco Nigeria 5°54N 5°30E **139** D5
Edd Eritrea 14°0N 41°38E **135** F13
Ede Neths. 52°4N 5°40E **69** B5
Ede Nigeria 7°45N 4°29E **139** D5
Édéa Cameroon 3°51N 10°9E **139** E7
Edebäck Sweden 60°4N 13°32E **62** D7
Edehon L. Canada 60°25N 97°15W **163** A9
Eden N.C., U.S.A. 36°29N 79°53W **177** C15
Eden N.Y., U.S.A. 42°39N 78°55W **174** D6
Eden U.S.A. 31°13N 99°51W **176** F5
Eden → U.K. 54°57N 3°1W **66** C4
Edenburg S. Africa 29°43S 25°58E **144** C4
Edendale N.Z. 46°19S 168°48E **155** G3
Edendale S. Africa 29°39S 30°18E **145** C5
Edenderry Ireland 53°21N 7°4W **64** C4
Edenhope Australia 37°4S 141°19E **152** D4
Edenton U.S.A. 36°4N 76°39W **177** C16
Edenville S. Africa 27°37S 27°34E **145** C4
Eder → Germany 51°12N 9°28E **76** D5
Eder-Stausee Germany 51°10N 8°57E **76** D4
Edessa Greece 40°48N 22°5E **98** A4
Edewecht Germany 53°8N 7°58E **76** B4
Edfu = Idfû Egypt 24°55N 32°49E **137** C3
Edgar U.S.A. 40°22N 97°58W **172** E5
Edgartown U.S.A. 41°23N 70°31W **175** E14
Edge Hill U.K. 52°8N 1°26W **67** E6
Edgefield U.S.A. 33°47N 81°56W **178** B8
Edgeley U.S.A. 46°22N 98°43W **172** B4
Edgemont U.S.A. 43°18N 103°50W **172** D2
Edgeøya Svalbard 77°45N 22°30E **54** B9

Edgewater U.S.A. 28°59N 80°54W 179 G9
Édhessa = Edessa Greece 40°48N 22°5E 96 F6
Edievale N.Z. 45°49S 169°22E 155 F4
Edina Liberia 6°0N 10°10W 138 D2
Edina U.S.A. 40°10N 92°11W 172 E7
Edinboro U.S.A. 41°52N 80°8W 174 E4
Edinburg U.S.A. 26°18N 98°10W 176 H5
Edinburgh U.K. 55°57N 3°13W 65 F5
Edinburgh ✕ (EDI) U.K. 55°54N 3°22W 65 F5
Edinburgh, City of □ U.K. 55°57N 3°17W 65 F5
Edineţ Moldova 48°9N 27°18E 81 B12
Edirne Turkey 41°40N 26°34E 97 E10
Edirne □ Turkey 41°12N 26°30E 97 E10
Edison Ga., U.S.A. 31°34N 84°44W 178 D5
Edison Wash., U.S.A. 48°33N 122°27W 170 B4
Edisto → U.S.A. 32°29N 80°21W 178 C9
Edisto Beach U.S.A. 32°29N 80°20W 178 C9
Edisto I. U.S.A. 32°35N 80°20W 178 C9
Edithburgh Australia 35°5S 137°43E 152 C2
Edjeleh Algeria 28°38N 9°50E 136 C5
Edmeston U.S.A. 42°42N 75°15W 175 D9
Edmond U.S.A. 35°39N 97°29W 176 D6
Edmonds U.S.A. 47°48N 122°22W 170 C4
Edmonton Australia 17°2S 145°46E 150 B4
Edmonton Canada 53°30N 113°30W 162 C6
Edmund L. Canada 54°45N 93°17W 164 B1
Edmundston Canada 47°23N 68°20W 165 C6
Edna U.S.A. 28°59N 96°39W 176 G6
Edo □ Nigeria 6°30N 6°0E 139 D6
Edolo Italy 46°10N 10°21E 92 B7
Edremit Turkey 39°34N 27°0E 99 B9
Edremit Körfezi Turkey 39°30N 26°45E 99 B8
Edsbro Sweden 59°54N 18°29E 62 E12
Edsbruk Sweden 58°1N 16°29E 63 F10
Edsbyn Sweden 61°23N 15°49E 62 C9
Edson Canada 53°35N 116°28W 162 C5
Eduardo Castex Argentina 35°50S 64°18W 190 D3
Eduardo Frei Montalva = Frei Antarctica 62°30S 58°0W 55 C18
Edward → Australia 35°5S 143°30E 152 C5
Edward, L. Africa 0°25S 29°40E 142 C2
Edward VII Land Antarctica 80°0S 150°0W 55 E13
Edwards Calif., U.S.A. 34°50N 117°40W 171 L9
Edwards N.Y., U.S.A. 44°20N 75°15W 175 B9
Edwards Plateau U.S.A. 30°45N 101°20W 176 F4
Edwardsville U.S.A. 41°15N 75°56W 175 E9
Edzná Mexico 19°39N 90°19W 181 D6
Edzo = Behchoko Canada 62°50N 116°3W 162 A5
Eeklo Belgium 51°11N 3°33E 69 C3
Eenhana Namibia 17°30S 16°23E 144 A2
Eesti = Estonia ■ Europe 58°30N 25°30E 84 C3
Eferding Austria 48°18N 14°1E 78 C7
Effigy Mounds △ U.S.A. 43°5N 91°11W 172 D8
Effingham U.S.A. 39°7N 88°33W 172 F9
Eforie Romania 44°1N 28°37E 81 F13
Efxinoupoli Greece 39°12N 22°42E 98 B4
Ega → Spain 42°19N 1°55W 90 C3
Égadi, Ísole Italy 37°55N 12°16E 94 E5
Egan Range U.S.A. 39°35N 114°55W 168 G6
Eganville Canada 45°32N 77°5W 174 A7
Egedesminde = Aasiaat Greenland 68°43N 52°56W 57 D5
Eger = Cheb Czech Rep. 50°9N 12°28E 78 A5
Eger Hungary 47°53N 20°27E 80 C5
Eger → Hungary 47°38N 20°50E 80 C5
Egersund Norway 58°26N 6°1E 61 G12
Egg L. Canada 55°5N 105°30W 163 B7
Eggegebirge Südlicher Teutoburger Wald △ Germany 51°40N 8°59E 76 D4
Eggenburg Austria 48°38N 15°50E 78 C8
Eggenfelden Germany 48°23N 12°46E 77 G8
Éghezée Belgium 50°35N 4°55E 69 D4
Egilsstaðir Iceland 65°16N 14°25W 60 D6
Egina Greece 37°45N 23°26E 98 D5
Eginio Greece 40°28N 22°28E 96 F6
Egio Greece 38°15N 22°5E 98 C4
Égletons France 45°24N 2°3E 72 C6
Eglinton I. Canada 75°48N 118°30W 161 B8
Egmont Canada 49°45N 123°56W 162 D4
Egmont, C. N.Z. 39°16S 173°45E 154 F2
Egmont, Mt. = Taranaki, Mt. N.Z. 39°17S 174°5E 154 F3
Egmont △ N.Z. 39°17S 174°4E 154 F3
Egra India 21°54N 87°32E 125 J12
Eğridir Turkey 37°52N 30°51E 104 D4
Eğridir Gölü Turkey 37°53N 30°50E 104 D4
Egtved Denmark 55°38N 9°18E 63 J3
Éguas → Brazil 13°26S 44°14W 189 C2
Éguzon-Chantôme France 46°27N 1°33E 71 F8
Egvekinot Russia 66°19N 179°50W 107 C19
Egyek Hungary 47°39N 20°52E 80 C5
Egypt ■ Africa 28°0N 31°0E 137 F7
Eha Amufu Nigeria 6°30N 7°46E 139 D6
Ehime □ Japan 33°30N 132°40E 113 H6
Ehingen Germany 48°16N 9°43E 77 G5
Ehrenberg U.S.A. 33°36N 114°31W 171 M12
Ehrhardt U.S.A. 33°6N 81°1W 178 B8
Ehrwald Austria 47°24N 10°56E 78 D3
Eibar Spain 43°11N 2°28W 90 B2
Eichstätt Germany 48°54N 11°11E 77 G7
Eider → Germany 54°19N 8°57E 76 A4
Eidsvold Australia 25°25S 151°12E 151 D5
Eidsvoll Norway 60°19N 11°14E 61 F14
Eielson U.S.A. 64°40N 147°4W 166 C10
Eifel Germany 50°15N 6°50E 77 E2
Eiffel Flats Zimbabwe 18°20S 30°0E 143 F3
Eiger Switz. 46°34N 8°1E 92 B5
Eigg U.K. 56°54N 6°10W 65 E2
Eighty Mile Beach Australia 19°30S 120°40E 148 C3
Eil, L. U.K. 56°51N 5°16W 65 E3
Eilat = Elat Israel 29°30N 34°56E 130 F3
Eildon Australia 37°14S 145°55E 153 D6
Eildon, L. Australia 37°10S 146°0E 153 D7
Eilean Siar □ U.K. 57°30N 7°10W 65 D1
Eilenburg Germany 51°27N 12°36E 76 D8
Einasleigh Australia 18°32S 144°5E 150 B3
Einasleigh → Australia 17°30S 142°17E 150 B3
Einbeck Germany 51°49N 9°53E 76 D5
Eindhoven Neths. 51°26N 5°28E 69 C5
Einsiedeln Switz. 47°7N 8°46E 77 H4
Eire = Ireland ■ Europe 53°50N 7°52W 64 C4
Eiríksjökull Iceland 64°46N 20°24W 60 D3
Eiriosgaigh = Eriskay U.K. 57°4N 7°18W 65 D1
Eirunepé Brazil 6°35S 69°53W 188 B4
Eiseb → Namibia 20°33S 20°59E 144 B2
Eisenach Germany 50°58N 10°19E 76 E6
Eisenberg Germany 50°58N 11°54E 76 E7
Eisenerz Austria 47°32N 14°54E 78 D7
Eisenhüttenstadt Germany 52°9N 14°38E 76 C10
Eisenkappel Austria 46°29N 14°36E 78 E7
Eisenstadt Austria 47°51N 16°31E 79 D9
Eisleben Germany 51°32N 11°32E 76 D7
Eislingen Germany 48°41N 9°42E 77 G5
Eivissa Spain 38°54N 1°26E 100 C7
Eixe, Serra do Spain 42°24N 6°54W 88 C4
Ejea de los Caballeros Spain 42°7N 1°9W 90 C3
Ejmiatsin Armenia 40°12N 44°19E 87 K7
Ejura Ghana 7°23N 1°15W 139 D4
Ejutla Mexico 16°34N 96°44W 181 D5
Ekalaka U.S.A. 45°53N 104°33W 168 D11
Ekaterinburg = Yekaterinburg Russia 56°50N 60°30E 106 D7
Ekenäs = Raasepori Finland 60°0N 23°26E 84 B2
Ekenässjön Sweden 57°28N 15°1E 63 G9
Ekerö Sweden 59°16N 17°45E 62 E11
Eket Nigeria 4°38N 7°56E 139 E6
Eketahuna N.Z. 40°38S 175°43E 154 G4
Ekibastuz Kazakhstan 51°50N 75°10E 109 B9
Ekiti □ Nigeria 7°25N 5°20E 139 D6
Ekoli Dem. Rep. of the Congo 0°23S 24°13E 142 C1
Ekoln Sweden 59°45N 17°37E 62 E11
Ekshärad Sweden 60°10N 13°30E 62 D7
Eksjö Sweden 57°40N 14°58E 63 G8
Ekuma → Namibia 18°40S 16°2E 144 A2
Ekwan → Canada 53°12N 82°15W 164 B3
Ekwan Pt. Canada 53°16N 82°7W 164 B3
El Aaiún W. Sahara 27°9N 13°12W 134 C3
El Abanico Chile 37°20S 71°31W 190 D1
El Abiodh-Sidi-Cheikh Algeria 32°53N 0°31E 136 B4
El Adeb Larache Algeria 27°22N 8°52E 136 C5
El 'Agrûd Egypt 30°14N 34°24E 130 E3
El Aïoun Morocco 34°33N 2°30W 136 B3
El 'Aiyat Egypt 29°36N 31°15E 137 F7
El Alamein Egypt 30°48N 28°58E 137 E6
El Alto Peru 4°15S 81°14W 188 A1
El 'Aqaba, W. → Egypt 30°7N 33°54E 130 E2
El 'Arag Egypt 28°40N 26°20E 137 B2
El Aricha Algeria 34°13N 1°10W 136 B3
El Arīḥā West Bank 31°52N 35°27E 130 D4
El 'Arish Egypt 31°8N 33°50E 130 D2
El 'Arish, W. → Egypt 31°8N 33°47E 130 D2
El Arrouch Algeria 36°37N 6°53E 136 A5
El Asnam = Ech Chéliff Algeria 36°10N 1°20E 136 A4
El Astillero Spain 43°24N 3°49W 88 B7
El Badâri Egypt 27°4N 31°25E 137 B3
El Bahrein Egypt 28°30N 26°25E 137 B2
El Ballâs Egypt 26°2N 32°43E 137 B3
El Balyana Egypt 26°10N 32°3E 137 B3
El Baqeir Sudan 18°40N 33°40E 137 D3
El Barco de Ávila Spain 40°21N 5°31W 88 E5
El Barco de Valdeorras = O Barco Spain 42°23N 6°58W 88 C4
El Bauga Sudan 18°18N 33°52E 137 D3
El Bawiti Egypt 28°25N 28°45E 137 F6
El Bayadh Algeria 33°40N 1°1E 136 B4
El Bayadh □ Algeria 32°30N 1°10E 136 B4
El Bierzo Spain 42°45N 6°30W 88 C4
El Bluff Nic. 11°59N 83°40W 182 D3
El Bolsón Argentina 41°55S 71°30W 192 B2
El Bonillo Spain 38°57N 2°35W 91 G2
El Burgo de Osma Spain 41°35N 3°4W 90 D1
El Caín Argentina 41°38S 68°19W 192 B3
El Cajon U.S.A. 32°48N 116°58W 171 N10
El Calafate Argentina 50°19S 72°15W 192 D2
El Campello Spain 38°26N 0°24W 91 G4
El Campo U.S.A. 29°12N 96°16W 176 G6
El Capitan U.S.A. 37°44N 119°38W 170 H7
El Carbón Honduras 15°25N 85°32W 182 C2
El Carmen Colombia 9°43N 75°8W 186 B3
El Centro U.S.A. 32°48N 115°34W 171 N11
El Cerro Bolivia 17°30S 61°40W 186 G6
El Cerro de Andévalo Spain 37°45N 6°57W 89 H4
El Chaltén Argentina 49°19S 72°56W 192 C2
El Compadre Mexico 32°20N 116°14W 171 N10
El Corcovado Argentina 43°25S 71°35W 192 B2
El Coronil Spain 37°5N 5°38W 89 H5
El Cotillo Canary Is. 28°41N 14°1W 100 F5
El Cuy Argentina 39°55S 68°25W 192 A3
El Cuyo Mexico 21°31N 87°41W 181 C7
El Dab'a Egypt 31°0N 28°27E 137 E6
El Daheir Egypt 31°13N 34°10E 130 D3
El Deir Egypt 25°25N 32°20E 137 B3
El Descanso Mexico 32°12N 116°58W 171 N10
El Desemboque Mexico 30°33N 113°1W 180 A2
El Dilingat Egypt 30°50N 30°31E 137 E7
El Diviso Colombia 1°22N 78°14W 186 C3
El Djouf Mauritania 21°25N 6°40W 134 D4
El Dorado Mexico 24°17N 107°21W 180 C3
El Dorado Ark., U.S.A. 33°12N 92°40W 176 E8
El Dorado Kans., U.S.A. 37°49N 96°52W 172 G5
El Dorado Venezuela 6°55N 61°37W 186 B6
El Dorado Springs U.S.A. 37°52N 94°1W 172 G6
El Eglab Algeria 26°20N 4°30W 136 C3
El Ejido Spain 36°47N 2°49W 89 J8
El Escorial Spain 40°35N 4°7W 88 E6
El Espinar Spain 41°43N 4°15W 88 D6
El Eulma Algeria 36°9N 5°42E 136 A5
El Faiyûm Egypt 29°19N 30°50E 137 F7
El Faouar Tunisia 33°22N 8°45E 136 B5
El Fâsher Sudan 13°33N 25°26E 135 F11
El Fashn Egypt 28°50N 30°54E 137 F7
El Ferrol = Ferrol Spain 43°29N 8°15W 88 B2
El Fuerte Mexico 26°25N 108°39W 180 B3
El Gedida Egypt 25°40N 28°30E 137 B2
El Geneina = Al Junaynah Sudan 13°27N 22°45E 135 F10
El Gezira □ Sudan 15°0N 33°0E 135 F12
El Gir Sudan 19°50N 28°18E 137 D2
El Giza Egypt 30°0N 31°12E 137 F7
El Gogorrón △ Mexico 21°49N 100°57W 180 C4
El Goléa Algeria 30°30N 2°50E 136 B4
El Gouna Egypt 27°5N 33°47E 137 B3
El Guácharo △ Venezuela 10°8N 63°21W 183 D7
El Guache △ Venezuela 9°45N 69°30W 183 E6
El Hadjira Algeria 32°36N 5°30E 136 B5
El Hâi Egypt 29°39N 31°18E 137 F7
El Hajeb Morocco 33°43N 5°13W 136 B2
El Hamma Tunisia 33°54N 9°48E 136 B5
El Hammam Egypt 30°52N 29°25E 137 E6
El Homr Algeria 29°43N 1°45E 136 C4
El 'Idisât Egypt 25°30N 32°35E 137 B3
El Iskandarîya Egypt 31°13N 29°58E 137 H6
El Istiwa'iya Sudan 5°0N 28°0E 135 G11
El Jadida Morocco 33°11N 8°17W 136 B2
El Jardal Honduras 14°54N 88°50W 182 D2
El Jebha Morocco 35°11N 4°43W 136 A3
El Jem Tunisia 35°19N 10°41E 136 A6
El Kab Sudan 19°27N 32°46E 137 D3
El Kafr el Sharqi Egypt 31°16N 31°10E 137 E7
El Kala Algeria 36°53N 8°26E 136 A5
El Kantara Algeria 35°14N 5°45E 136 A5
El Kantara Tunisia 33°45N 10°58E 136 B6
El Karaba Sudan 18°32N 33°41E 137 D3
El Kef Tunisia 36°12N 8°47E 136 A5
El Kef □ Tunisia 36°0N 9°0E 136 A5
El Kelaâ de Srahna Morocco 32°4N 7°27W 136 B2
El Kelaâ M'Gouna Morocco 31°14N 6°7W 136 B2
El Khandaq Sudan 18°30N 30°30E 137 D3
El Khanka Egypt 30°13N 31°21E 137 E7
El Khârga Egypt 25°30N 30°33E 137 B3
El Khartûm Sudan 15°31N 32°35E 135 E12
El Khartûm Bahrî Sudan 15°40N 32°31E 135 E12
El Khroub Algeria 36°10N 6°55E 136 A5
El Kseur Algeria 36°46N 4°49E 136 A4
El Ksiba Morocco 32°45N 6°1W 136 B2
El Kuntilla Egypt 30°1N 34°45E 130 E3
El Leoncito △ Argentina 31°58S 69°10W 190 C2
El Lucero Mexico 30°37N 106°31W 180 A3
El Maestrazgo Spain 40°30N 0°25W 90 E4
El Maghra Egypt 30°15N 28°55E 137 E6
El Mahalla el Kubra Egypt 31°0N 31°0E 137 E7
El Mahâriq Egypt 25°35N 30°35E 137 B3
El Maîmûn Egypt 29°14N 31°12E 137 F7
El Maitén Argentina 42°3S 71°10W 192 B2
El Maiz Algeria 28°19N 0°9W 136 C3
El Maks el Bahari Egypt 24°30N 30°40E 137 C3
El Malpais △ U.S.A. 34°53N 108°0W 169 J10
El Manshâh Egypt 26°26N 31°50E 137 B3
El Mansour Algeria 27°47N 0°14W 136 C3
El Mansûra Egypt 31°0N 31°19E 137 E7
El Manzala Egypt 31°10N 31°50E 137 E7
El Marâgha Egypt 26°35N 31°10E 137 B3
El Masnou Spain 41°28N 2°20E 90 D7
El Matarîya Egypt 31°15N 32°0E 137 E8
El Medano Canary Is. 28°3N 16°32W 100 F3
El Meghaier Algeria 33°55N 5°58E 136 B5
El Ménia = El Goléa Algeria 30°30N 2°50E 136 B4
El Meraguen Algeria 28°0N 0°7W 136 C3
El Milagro Argentina 30°59S 65°59W 190 C2
El Milia Algeria 36°51N 6°13E 136 A5
El Minyâ Egypt 28°7N 30°33E 137 F7
El Monte U.S.A. 34°4N 118°1W 171 L8
El Montseny Spain 41°55N 2°25E 90 D7
El Mreyye Mauritania 18°0N 6°0W 138 B3
El Obeid Sudan 13°8N 30°10E 135 F12
El Odaiya Sudan 12°8N 28°12E 135 F11
El Oro Mexico 19°51N 100°7W 181 D4
El Oued Algeria 33°20N 6°58E 136 B5
El Oued □ Algeria 33°10N 7°15E 136 B5
El Palmar △ Argentina 32°10S 58°31W 190 C4
El Paso U.S.A. 31°45N 106°29W 176 F1
El Paso de Robles = Paso Robles U.S.A. 35°38N 120°41W 170 K6
El Pedernoso Spain 39°29N 2°45W 91 F2
El Pedroso Spain 37°51N 5°45W 89 H5
El Pinacate y Gran Desierto del Altar = Gran Desierto del Pinacate △ Mexico 31°51N 113°32W 180 A2
El Pobo de Dueñas Spain 40°46N 1°39W 90 E3
El Portal U.S.A. 37°41N 119°47W 170 H7
El Porvenir Mexico 31°15N 105°51W 180 A3
El Prat Barcelona ✕ (BCN) Spain 41°18N 2°5E 90 D7
El Prat de Llobregat Spain 41°19N 2°5E 90 D7
El Progreso Honduras 15°26N 87°51W 182 C2
El Pueblo Canary Is. 28°36N 17°47W 100 F2
El Puente del Arzobispo Spain 39°48N 5°10W 88 F5
El Puerto de Santa María Spain 36°36N 6°13W 89 J4
El Qâhira Egypt 30°2N 31°13E 137 E7
El Qantara Egypt 30°51N 32°20E 130 E1
El Qasr Egypt 25°44N 28°42E 137 B2
El Qubâbât Egypt 29°28N 31°16E 137 F7
El Quseima Egypt 30°40N 34°15E 130 E3
El Qusîya Egypt 27°29N 30°44E 137 B3
El Râshda Egypt 25°36N 28°57E 137 B2
El Real de Santa María Panama 8°0N 77°40W 186 B3
El Reno U.S.A. 35°32N 97°57W 167 H20
El Rey △ Argentina 24°40S 64°34W 190 A3
El Rîdisiya Egypt 24°56N 32°51E 137 C3
El Rio U.S.A. 34°14N 119°10W 171 L7
El Ronquillo Spain 37°44N 6°10W 89 H4
El Roque, Pta. Canary Is. 28°10N 15°25W 100 F4
El Rosario Mexico 30°1N 115°45W 180 A1
El Rubio Spain 37°22N 5°0W 89 H5
El Saff Egypt 29°34N 31°16E 137 F7
El Salto Mexico 23°47N 105°22W 180 C3
El Salvador ■ Cent. Amer. 13°50N 89°0W 182 D2
El Sauce Nic. 13°0N 86°40W 182 D2
El Saucejo Spain 37°4N 5°6W 89 H5
El Shallal Egypt 24°0N 32°53E 137 C3
El Simbillawein Egypt 30°48N 31°13E 137 E7
El Suweis Egypt 29°58N 32°31E 137 F8
El Tabbîn Egypt 29°47N 31°18E 137 F7
El Tamarâni, W. → Egypt 30°7N 34°43E 130 E3
El Tarf Algeria 36°46N 8°19E 136 A5
El Tarf □ Algeria 36°45N 8°10E 136 A5
El Thamad Egypt 29°40N 34°28E 130 F3
El Tigre Venezuela 8°44N 64°15W 186 B6
El Tîh, Gebel Egypt 29°40N 33°50E 130 F2
El Tîna Egypt 31°3N 32°22E 137 E8
El Tofo Chile 29°22S 71°18W 190 B1
El Tránsito Chile 28°52S 70°17W 190 B1
El Tûr Egypt 28°14N 33°36E 128 D2
El Turbio Argentina 51°45S 72°5W 192 D2
El Uqsur Egypt 25°41N 32°38E 137 B3
El Valle △ Spain 37°56N 1°6W 91 H3
El Vendrell Spain 41°10N 1°30E 90 D6
El Vergel Mexico 26°28N 106°22W 180 B3
El Vigía Venezuela 8°38N 71°39W 186 B4
El Viso del Alcor Spain 37°23N 5°43W 89 H5
El Wabeira Egypt 29°34N 33°6E 130 F2
El Wuz Sudan 15°5N 30°7E 135 E12
Elafonisos Greece 36°29N 22°56E 98 E4
Elamanchili India 17°33N 82°50E 126 F6
Élancourt France 48°47N 1°58E 71 D8
Elands Australia 31°37S 152°20E 153 A10
Elasa Greece 35°18N 26°21E 99 F8
Elassona Greece 39°53N 22°12E 98 B4
Elat Israel 29°30N 34°56E 130 F3
Elatia Greece 38°37N 22°46E 98 C4
Elâzığ Turkey 38°37N 39°14E 105 C8
Elâzığ □ Turkey 38°40N 39°15E 105 C8
Elba Italy 42°46N 10°17E 92 F7
Elba U.S.A. 31°25N 86°4W 178 D3
Elbasan Albania 41°9N 20°9E 96 E4
Elbe U.S.A. 46°45N 122°10W 170 D4
Elbe → Europe 53°50N 9°0E 76 B4
Elbe-Seitenkanal Germany 52°45N 10°32E 76 C6
Elbert, Mt. U.S.A. 39°7N 106°27W 168 G10
Elberton U.S.A. 34°7N 82°52W 178 A7
Elbeuf France 49°17N 1°2E 70 C8
Elbing = Elbląg Poland 54°10N 19°25E 82 D6
Elbistan Turkey 38°13N 37°15E 104 C7
Elbląg Poland 54°10N 19°25E 82 D6
Elbow Canada 51°7N 106°35W 163 C7
Elbrus Russia 43°21N 42°30E 87 J6
Elbufer-Drawehn △ Germany 53°8N 10°58E 76 B6
Elburz Mts. = Alborz, Reshteh-ye Kūhhā-ye Iran 36°0N 52°0E 129 C7
Elche Spain 38°15N 0°42W 91 G4
Elche de la Sierra Spain 38°27N 2°3W 91 G2
Elcho I. Australia 11°55S 135°45E 150 A2
Elda Spain 38°29N 0°47W 91 G4
Eldama Ravine Kenya 0°3N 35°43E 142 B4
Elde → Germany 53°7N 11°15E 76 B7
Eldon Mo., U.S.A. 38°21N 92°35W 172 F7
Eldon Wash., U.S.A. 47°33N 123°3W 170 C3
Eldora U.S.A. 42°22N 93°5W 172 D7
Eldorado Argentina 26°28S 54°43W 191 B5
Eldorado Canada 44°35N 77°31W 174 B7
Eldorado Ill., U.S.A. 37°49N 88°26W 172 G9
Eldorado Tex., U.S.A. 30°52N 100°36W 176 F4
Eldorendo U.S.A. 31°3N 84°39W 178 D5
Eldoret Kenya 0°30N 35°17E 142 B4
Eldred U.S.A. 41°58N 78°23W 174 E6
Elea, C. Cyprus 35°19N 34°4E 101 D13
Eleanora, Pk. Australia 32°57S 121°9E 149 F3
Elefantes → Africa 24°10S 32°40E 145 B5
Elefantes, G. Chile 46°28S 73°49W 192 C2
Elefsina Greece 38°4N 23°26E 98 C5
Eleftherios Venizelos ✕ (ATH) Greece 37°56N 23°56E 98 D5
Elektrogorsk Russia 55°56N 38°50E 84 E10
Elektrostal Russia 55°41N 38°32E 84 E10
Elele Nigeria 5°5N 6°50E 139 D6
Elemi Triangle = Ilemi Triangle Africa 5°0N 35°20E 142 B4
Elena Bulgaria 42°55N 25°53E 97 D9
Elephant Butte Res. U.S.A. 33°9N 107°11W 169 K10
Elephant I. Antarctica 61°0S 55°0W 55 C18
Elephant Pass Sri Lanka 9°35N 80°25E 127 K5
Elesbão Veloso Brazil 6°13S 42°8W 189 B2
Eleshnitsa Bulgaria 41°52N 23°36E 96 E7
Eleşkirt Turkey 39°50N 42°50E 105 C10
Eleuthera I. Bahamas 25°0N 76°20W 182 B4
Eleutheroupoli Greece 40°52N 24°20E 97 F8
Elgeyo-Marakwet □ Kenya 0°50N 35°35E 142 B4
Elgin Canada 44°36N 76°13W 175 B8
Elgin U.K. 57°39N 3°19W 65 D5
Elgin Ill., U.S.A. 42°2N 88°17W 172 D9
Elgin N. Dak., U.S.A. 46°24N 101°51W 172 B3
Elgin Oreg., U.S.A. 45°34N 117°55W 168 D5
Elgin S.C., U.S.A. 34°10N 80°48W 178 A9
Elgin Tex., U.S.A. 30°21N 97°22W 176 F6
Elgoibar Spain 43°13N 2°24W 90 B2
Elgon, Mt. Africa 1°10N 34°30E 142 B3
Eliase Indonesia 8°21S 130°48E 119 F8
Elikonos Oros Greece 38°18N 22°45E 98 C4
Elim Namibia 17°48S 15°31E 144 A2
Elim S. Africa 34°35S 19°45E 144 D2
Elin Pelin Bulgaria 42°40N 23°36E 96 D7
Elis = Ilia Greece 37°45N 21°35E 98 D3
Eliseu Martins Brazil 8°13S 43°42W 189 B2
Elista Russia 46°16N 44°14E 87 G7
Eliza, L. Australia 37°15S 139°50E 152 D3
Elizabeth Australia 34°42S 138°41E 152 C3
Elizabeth U.S.A. 40°39N 74°12W 175 F10
Elizabeth City U.S.A. 36°18N 76°14W 177 C16
Elizabethton U.S.A. 36°21N 82°13W 177 C13
Elizabethtown Ky., U.S.A. 37°42N 85°52W 173 G11
Elizabethtown N.Y., U.S.A. 44°13N 73°36W 175 B11
Elizabethtown Pa., U.S.A. 40°9N 76°36W 175 F8
Elizondo Spain 43°12N 1°30W 90 B3
Ełk Poland 53°50N 22°21E 82 E9
Elk → Canada 49°11N 115°14W 162 C5
Ełk → Poland 53°41N 22°28E 82 E9
Elk → U.S.A. 34°46N 87°16W 177 D11
Elk City U.S.A. 35°25N 99°25W 176 D5
Elk Creek U.S.A. 39°36N 122°32W 170 F4
Elk Grove U.S.A. 38°25N 121°22W 170 G5
Elk Island △ Canada 53°35N 112°59W 162 C6
Elk Lake Canada 47°40N 80°25W 164 C3
Elk Point Canada 53°54N 110°55W 163 C6
Elk River Idaho, U.S.A. 46°47N 116°11W 168 C5
Elk River Minn., U.S.A. 45°18N 93°35W 172 C7
Elkedra → Australia 21°8S 136°22E 150 C2
Elkhart Ind., U.S.A. 41°41N 85°58W 173 E11
Elkhart Kans., U.S.A. 37°0N 101°54W 172 G3
Elkhorn Canada 49°59N 101°14W 163 D8
Elkhorn → U.S.A. 41°8N 96°19W 172 E5
Elkhovo Bulgaria 42°10N 26°35E 97 D10
Elkin U.S.A. 36°15N 80°51W 177 C14
Elkins U.S.A. 38°55N 79°51W 173 F14
Elkland U.S.A. 41°59N 77°19W 174 E7
Elko Canada 49°20N 115°10W 162 D5
Elko U.S.A. 40°50N 115°46W 168 F6
Elkton U.S.A. 43°49N 83°11W 174 C1
Ellas = Greece ■ Europe 40°0N 23°0E 98 B3
Ellaville Fla., U.S.A. 30°23N 83°10W 178 E6
Ellaville Ga., U.S.A. 32°14N 84°19W 178 C5
Ellef Ringnes I. Canada 78°30N 102°2W 161 B11
Ellen, Mt. U.S.A. 44°9N 72°56W 175 B12
Ellenburg U.S.A. 44°54N 73°48W 175 B11
Ellendale U.S.A. 46°0N 98°32W 172 B4
Ellensburg U.S.A. 46°59N 120°34W 168 C3
Ellenville U.S.A. 41°43N 74°24W 175 E10
Ellerton Barbados 13°7N 59°33W 183 g
Ellery, Mt. Australia 37°28S 148°47E 153 D8
Ellesmere, L. N.Z. 43°47S 172°28E 155 D7
Ellesmere I. Canada 79°30N 80°0W 161 B16
Ellesmere Port U.K. 53°17N 2°54W 66 D5
Ellice Is. = Tuvalu ■ Pac. Oc. 8°0S 178°0E 147 B10
Ellicottville U.S.A. 42°17N 78°40W 174 D6
Ellington U.S.A. 42°13N 79°6W 174 D5
Elliot Australia 17°33S 133°32E 150 B1
Elliot S. Africa 31°22S 27°48E 145 D4
Elliot Lake Canada 46°25N 82°35W 164 C3
Elliotdale = Xhora S. Africa 31°55S 28°38E 145 D4
Elliott U.S.A. 34°6N 80°10W 178 A9
Elliott Key U.S.A. 25°27N 80°12W 179 K9
Ellis U.S.A. 38°56N 99°34W 172 F4
Elliston Australia 33°39S 134°53E 151 E1
Ellisville U.S.A. 31°36N 89°12W 177 F10
Ellon U.K. 57°22N 2°4W 65 D6
Ellora India 20°1N 75°10E 126 D2
Ellore = Eluru India 16°48N 81°8E 126 F5
Elloree U.S.A. 33°32N 80°34W 178 B9
Ellsworth Kans., U.S.A. 38°44N 98°14W 172 F4
Ellsworth Maine, U.S.A. 44°33N 68°25W 173 C19
Ellsworth Land Antarctica 76°0S 89°0W 55 D16
Ellsworth Mts. Antarctica 78°30S 85°0W 55 D16
Ellwangen Germany 48°57N 10°8E 77 G6
Ellwood City U.S.A. 40°52N 80°17W 174 F4
Ellzey U.S.A. 29°19N 82°48W 179 F7
Elm Switz. 46°54N 9°10E 77 J5
Elm-Lappwald △ Germany 52°15N 10°50E 76 C6
Elma Canada 49°52N 95°55W 163 D9
Elma U.S.A. 47°0N 123°25W 170 D3
Elmadağ Turkey 39°55N 33°14E 104 C5
Elmalı Turkey 36°44N 29°56E 99 E11
Elmhurst U.S.A. 41°53N 87°56W 172 E10
Elmina Ghana 5°5N 1°21W 139 D4
Elmira Canada 43°36N 80°33W 174 C4
Elmira U.S.A. 42°6N 76°48W 174 D8
Elmira Heights U.S.A. 42°8N 76°50W 174 D8
Elmodel U.S.A. 31°21N 84°29W 178 D5
Elmore Australia 36°30S 144°37E 152 D6
Elmore U.S.A. 32°32N 86°19W 178 C3
Elmshorn Germany 53°43N 9°40E 76 B5
Elmvale Canada 44°35N 79°52W 174 B5
Elne France 42°36N 2°58E 72 F6
Elora Canada 43°41N 80°26W 174 C4
Elos Greece 36°46N 22°43E 98 E4
Elounda Greece 35°16N 25°42E 101 D7
Eloy U.S.A. 32°45N 111°33W 169 K8
Éloyes France 48°6N 6°36E 71 D13
Elphin Canada 44°55N 76°37W 175 B8
Elpitiya Sri Lanka 6°17N 80°10E 127 L5
Elrose Canada 51°12N 108°0W 163 C7
Elsby △ Australia 14°55S 133°10E 148 B5
Elsdorf Germany 50°55N 6°34E 76 E2
Elsie U.S.A. 45°52N 123°36W 170 E3
Elsinore = Helsingør Denmark 56°2N 12°35E 63 H6
Elster → Germany 51°25N 11°57E 76 D7
Elsterwerda Germany 51°27N 13°31E 76 D9
Eltanin Fracture Zone System S. Ocean 54°0S 130°0W 55 B14
Eltham N.Z. 39°26S 174°19E 154 F3
Elton Russia 49°5N 46°52E 87 F8
Elton, Ozero Russia 49°5N 46°42E 87 F8
Eltville Germany 50°2N 8°7E 77 E4
Eluru India 16°48N 81°8E 126 F5
Elvas Portugal 38°50N 7°10W 89 G3
Elven France 47°44N 2°36W 70 E4
Elverum Norway 60°53N 11°34E 60 F14
Elvire → Australia 17°51S 128°11E 148 C4
Elvire, Mt. Australia 29°22S 119°36E 149 E2
Elvo → Italy 45°23N 8°21E 92 C5
Elwell, L. = Tiber Res. U.S.A. 48°19N 111°6W 168 B8
Elwood Ind., U.S.A. 40°17N 85°50W 173 E11
Elwood Nebr., U.S.A. 40°36N 99°52W 172 E4
Elx = Elche Spain 38°15N 0°42W 91 G4
Ely U.K. 52°24N 0°16E 67 E8
Ely Minn., U.S.A. 47°55N 91°51W 172 B8
Ely Nev., U.S.A. 39°15N 114°54W 168 G6
Elyria U.S.A. 41°22N 82°7W 174 E2
Elyros Greece 35°15N 23°45E 98 F5
Elz → Germany 48°18N 7°44E 77 G3
Emajõgi → Estonia 58°25N 27°20E 84 C4
eMakhazeni S. Africa 25°42S 30°2E 145 C5
eMalahleni S. Africa 25°51S 29°14E 145 C4
Emāmrūd Iran 36°30N 55°0E 129 B7
Emån → Sweden 57°8N 16°30E 63 G10
eMbalenhle S. Africa 26°32S 29°4E 145 C4
Embarcación Argentina 23°10S 64°0W 190 A3
Embetsu Japan 44°44N 141°47E 112 B10
Embi Kazakhstan 48°50N 58°8E 108 C5
Embi → Kazakhstan 46°55N 53°28E 108 C4
Embonas Greece 36°13N 27°51E 101 C9
Embro Canada 43°9N 80°54W 174 C4
Embrun France 44°34N 6°30E 73 D10
Embu Kenya 0°32S 37°38E 142 C4
Emden Germany 53°21N 7°12E 76 B3
Emecik Turkey 36°46N 27°49E 99 E9
Emei Shan China 29°32N 103°46E 116 C4
Emeishan China 29°31N 103°23E 116 C4
Emerald Australia 23°32S 148°10E 150 C4
Emerald I. Canada 76°48N 114°10W 161 B9
Émeraude, Côte d' France 48°45N 2°40W 70 D4
Emerson Canada 49°0N 97°10W 163 D9
Emerson U.S.A. 34°8N 84°45W 178 A5
Emet Turkey 39°20N 29°15E 99 B11
Emgwenya S. Africa 25°40S 30°18E 145 C5
Emi Koussi Chad 19°45N 18°55E 135 E9
Emilia-Romagna □ Italy 44°45N 11°0E 92 D8
Emilius, Mte. Italy 45°45N 7°20E 92 C4
Emin China 46°34N 83°36E 109 C10
Eminabad Pakistan 32°2N 74°8E 124 C6
Emine, Nos Bulgaria 42°40N 27°56E 97 D11
Emirdağ Turkey 39°2N 31°8E 104 C4
Emissi, Tarso Chad 21°27N 18°36E 135 D9
eMkhondo = Piet Retief S. Africa 27°1S 30°50E 14
Emlenton U.S.A. 41°11N 79°43W 17
Emlichheim Germany 52°37N 6°51E 7
Emmaboda Sweden 56°37N 15°32E 6
Emmalane U.S.A. 32°46N 82°0W 17
Emmaus S. Africa 29°2S 25°15E 14
Emmaus U.S.A. 40°32N 75°30W 17
Emme → Switz. 47°14N 7°32E 7
Emmeloord Neths. 52°44N 5°46E 6
Emmen Neths. 52°48N 6°57E 6
Emmen Switz. 47°5N 8°18E 7
Emmendingen Germany 48°6N 7°51E 7
Emmental Switz. 46°55N 7°40E 7
Emmerich Germany 51°50N 6°14E 7
Emmet Australia 24°45S 144°30E 15
Emmetsburg U.S.A. 43°7N 94°41W 17
Emmett Idaho, U.S.A. 43°52N 116°30W 16
Emmett Mich., U.S.A. 42°59N 82°46W 17
Emmiganuru = Yemmiganur India 15°44N 77°29E 12
Emmonak U.S.A. 62°47N 164°31W 16
Emo Canada 48°38N 93°50W 163
Emőd Hungary 47°57N 20°47E 8
Emona Bulgaria 42°43N 27°53E 97
Empalme Mexico 27°58N 110°51W 18
Empangeni S. Africa 28°50S 31°52E 14
Empedrado Argentina 28°0S 58°46W 19
Emperor Seamount Chain Pac. Oc. 40°0N 170°0E 15
Emperor Trough Pac. Oc. 43°0N 175°30E 15
Empire U.S.A. 32°21N 83°18W 17
Empoli Italy 43°43N 10°57E 9
Emporia Kans., U.S.A. 38°25N 96°11W 17
Emporia Va., U.S.A. 36°42N 77°32W 173
Emporium U.S.A. 41°31N 78°14W 17
Empress Canada 50°57N 110°0W 16
Empty Quarter = Rub' al Khālī Si. Arabia 19°0N 48°0E 13
Ems → Germany 53°20N 7°12E 7
Emsdale Canada 45°32N 79°19W 17
Emsdetten Germany 52°10N 7°32E 7
Emu China 43°40N 128°6E 115
Emu Park Australia 23°13S 150°50E 15
eMuziwezinto S. Africa 30°15S 30°45E 14
'En 'Avrona Israel 29°43N 35°0E 13
'En Boqeq Israel 31°12N 35°21E 12
'En Gedi Israel 31°28N 35°25E 12
En Nahud Sudan 12°45N 28°25E 13
Ena Japan 35°25N 137°25E 11
Enånger Sweden 61°30N 17°9E 62
Enard B. U.K. 58°5N 5°20W 6
Enare träsk = Inarijärvi Finland 69°0N 28°0E 60
Enarotali Indonesia 3°55S 136°21E 11
Encampment U.S.A. 41°12N 106°47W 168
Encantadas, Serra Brazil 30°40S 53°0W 19
Encarnación Paraguay 27°15S 55°50W 19
Encarnación de Díaz Mexico 21°31N 102°14W 18
Enchi Ghana 5°53N 2°48W 13
Encinitas U.S.A. 33°3N 117°17W 17
Encino U.S.A. 34°39N 105°28W 169
Encounter B. Australia 35°45S 138°45E 15
Encruzilhada Brazil 15°31S 40°54W 18
Encs Hungary 48°20N 21°8E 8
Endako Canada 54°6N 125°2W 16
Endau Kenya 1°18S 38°31E 14
Endau Rompin △ Malaysia 2°27N 103°45E 12
Ende Indonesia 8°45S 121°40E 11
Endeavour Str. Australia 10°45S 142°0E 15
Endelave Denmark 55°46N 10°18E 6
Enderbury Kiribati 3°8S 171°5W 156
Enderby Canada 50°35N 119°10W 162
Enderby Abyssal Plain S. Ocean 60°0S 40°0E 5
Enderby I. Australia 20°35S 116°30E 14
Enderby Land Antarctica 66°0S 53°0E 5
Enderlin U.S.A. 46°38N 97°36W 17
Enderrocat, C. Spain 39°28N 2°43E 10
Endicott U.S.A. 42°6N 76°4W 17
Endicott Mts. U.S.A. 68°0N 152°0W 16
Endimari → Brazil 8°46S 66°7W 18
Endwell U.S.A. 42°6N 76°2W 17
Endyalgout I. Australia 11°40S 132°35E 14
Ené → Peru 11°10S 74°18W 18
Eneabba Australia 29°49S 115°16E 14
Enerhodar Ukraine 47°30N 34°28E 8
Enewetak Atoll Marshall Is. 11°30N 162°15E 15
Enez Turkey 40°45N 26°5E 97
Enfer, Pte. d' Martinique 14°22N 60°54W 1
Enfield Canada 44°56N 63°32W 16
Enfield Conn., U.S.A. 41°58N 72°36W 17
Enfield N.C., U.S.A. 36°11N 77°41W 17
Enfield N.H., U.S.A. 43°39N 72°9W 17
Engadin Switz. 46°45N 10°10E 7
Engaño, C. Dom. Rep. 18°30N 68°20W 18
Engaño, C. Phil. 18°35N 122°23E 11
Engaru Japan 44°3N 143°31E 112
Engcobo = Ngcobo S. Africa 31°37S 28°0E 14
Engelberg Switz. 46°48N 8°26E 7
Engels Russia 51°28N 46°6E 8
Engelsberg = Ängelsberg Sweden 59°58N 16°0E 62
Engemann L. Canada 58°0N 106°55W 16
Enggano Indonesia 5°20S 102°40E 11
England U.S.A. 34°33N 91°58W 17
England □ U.K. 53°0N 2°0W 6
Englee Canada 50°45N 56°5W 16
Englehart Canada 47°49N 79°52W 16
Englewood U.S.A. 26°58N 82°21W 17
English → Canada 49°12N 91°5W 16
English Bazar = Ingraj Bazar India 24°58N 88°10E 12
English Channel Europe 50°0N 2°0W 6
English Company's Is., The Australia 11°50S 136°32E 15
English River Canada 49°14N 91°0W 16
Engures ezers Latvia 57°16N 23°8E 82
Enguri → Georgia 42°27N 41°38E 8
Enid U.S.A. 36°24N 97°53W 17
Enipeas → Greece 39°22N 22°17E 9
Eniwa Japan 43°0N 141°30E 112
Enkhuizen Neths. 52°42N 5°17E 6
Enköping Sweden 59°37N 17°4E 6
Enle China 24°0N 101°9E 11

a Italy 37°34N 14°16E **95** E7
adai I. Canada 60°58N 101°20W **163** A8
gonia Australia 29°21S 145°50E **151** D4
gierloh Germany 51°50N 8°2E **76** D4
is Ireland 52°51N 8°59W **64** D3
is Mont., U.S.A. 45°21N 111°44W **168** D8
is Tex., U.S.A. 32°20N 96°38W **176** E6
iscorthy Ireland 52°30N 6°34W **64** D5
iskillen U.K. 54°21N 7°39W **64** B4
istimon Ireland 52°57N 9°11W **64** D3
Austria 48°12N 14°28E **78** C7
Austria 48°14N 14°32E **78** C7
Finland 62°47N 30°10E **60** E24
sburg Falls U.S.A. 44°55N 72°48W **175** B12
iquillo, L. Dom. Rep. 18°20N 71°40W **183** C5
chede Neths. 52°13N 6°53E **69** B6
enada Argentina 34°55S 57°55W **190** C4
enada Chile 41°12S 72°33W **192** B2
enada Mexico 31°52N 116°37W **180** A1
enada de los Muertos
Mexico 23°59N 109°51W **180** C2
hi China 30°18N 109°29E **116** B7
iola, Pta. de n' Spain 39°7N 2°55E **100** B9
isheim France 47°50N 7°12E **71** E14
ley U.S.A. 30°31N 87°16W **177** F2
ebbe Uganda 0°4N 32°28E **142** B3
erprise Canada 60°47N 115°45W **162** A5
erprise Ala., U.S.A. 31°19N 85°51W **178** D4
erprise Oreg.,
U.S.A. 45°25N 117°17W **168** D5
iako ○ Canada 53°15N 125°26W **162** C3
orno de Doñana ○
pain 37°0N 6°26W **89** A4
rance, The
ustralia 33°21S 151°30E **153** B9
raygues-sur-Truyère
rance 44°38N 2°35E **72** D6
re Rios Bolivia 21°30S 64°25W **190** A3
re Rios Brazil 11°56S 38°59W **189** C3
re Rios □ Argentina 30°30S 58°30W **190** C4
repeñas, Embalse de
pain 40°34N 2°42W **90** B2
roncamento Portugal 39°28N 8°28W **89** F2
gu Nigeria 6°30N 7°30E **139** D6
gu □ Nigeria 6°30N 7°45E **139** D6
gu Ezike Nigeria 7°0N 7°29E **139** D6
mclaw U.S.A. 47°12N 121°59W **170** C5
alira, Port d' Europe 42°33N 1°43E **90** C6
ermeu France 49°53N 1°15E **70** D8
iken Sweden 60°49N 15°46E **62** D9
ira Brazil 7°18S 70°13W **188** D5
ira → Brazil 7°19S 70°15W **188** D5
a → Italy 46°56N 18°15E **80** D3
a → Italy 44°54N 10°31E **92** D7
haili = Youghal
reland 51°56N 7°52W **64** E4
e, Ís. Italy 38°30N 14°57E **95** D7
nomi Greece 40°25N 22°50E **96** F6
Neths. 52°21N 5°59E **69** B5
Nigeria 6°36N 3°58E **139** D5
rnay France 49°3N 3°56E **71** C10
rnon France 48°35N 1°40E **71** D8
esus Turkey 37°55N 27°22E **99** D9
raim U.S.A. 39°22N 111°35W **168** G8
rata Pa., U.S.A. 40°11N 76°11W **175** F8
rata Wash., U.S.A. 47°19N 119°33W **168** C4
taurus = Epidavros
reece 37°40N 23°7E **98** D5
avros Greece 40°39N 23°7E **98** D5
avros Limira Greece 36°46N 23°0E **98** E5
a Spain 41°36N 1°17W **92** D2
nac France 46°59N 4°31E **71** F11
nal France 48°10N 6°27E **71** D13
ros □ Greece 39°30N 20°30E **98** B2
skopi Cyprus 34°40N 32°54E **101** E11
skopi Greece 35°20N 24°4E **101** D6
skopi Bay Cyprus 34°35N 32°50E **101** E11
talio Greece 37°35N 22°50E **98** D4
alock, L. Australia 36°52S 144°34E **152** D6
an = Appiano Italy 46°28N 11°15E **92** B8
ingen Germany 49°8N 8°53E **77** F4
om U.K. 51°19N 0°16W **67** F7
kiro Namibia 21°40S 19°9E **144** B2
ataria = El Istiwa'iya
udan 5°0N 28°0E **135** G11
atorial Guinea ■ Africa 2°0N 8°0E **140** D1
ai China 25°48N 100°11E **116** E3
achidia Morocco 31°58N 4°20W **136** B3
ahad Sudan 12°45N 30°32E **137** E12
if Morocco 35°1N 4°1W **136** B4
ogel Sudan 18°10N 35°25E **137** D4
clea Italy 45°35N 12°40E **93** C9
ndol India 20°56N 75°20E **126** D2
wadi Myit = Ayeyawady →
urma 15°50N 95°6E **123** M19
wadi Myitwanya = Irrawaddy,
louths of the
urma 15°30N 95°0E **123** M19
wan △ Thailand 14°25N 98°58E **120** E2
a Italy 45°48N 9°15E **92** C6
a Sudan 19°5N 36°51E **137** D4
a, J. Sudan 20°48N 36°47E **137** C4
sa Turkey 40°42N 36°36E **104** B7
eng Shan China 42°50N 84°59E **109** D10
eskopf Germany 49°44N 7°2E **77** F3
esk Turkey 38°39N 43°36E **105** C10
wyaş Dağı Turkey 38°30N 35°30E **104** C6
ao Jiang → China 42°37N 128°0E **115** C14
ek Turkey 40°23N 27°47E **97** F11
emli Turkey 36°27N 29°16E **99** E11
ene = Ulaan-Uul
Mongolia 46°4N 100°49E **110** B9
net Mongolia 49°2N 104°5E **110** B9
ing Germany 48°18N 11°54E **77** G7
bus, Mt. Antarctica 77°35S 167°0E **55** D11
chim Brazil 27°35S 52°15W **191** B5
gli Zonguldak, Turkey 41°15N 31°24E **104** B4
nhot China 43°48N 112°2E **114** C7
sa → Spain 41°26N 4°45W **88** D6
sos Greece 39°11N 25°57E **99** B7
lek Turkey 41°15N 34°42E **104** B5
nisdam S. Africa 28°30S 26°50E **144** C4
ad Morocco 31°30N 4°15W **136** B3

Erfstadt Germany 50°50N 6°50E **76** E2
Erft → Germany 51°11N 6°44E **76** D2
Erfurt Germany 50°58N 11°2E **76** E7
Ergani Turkey 38°17N 39°49E **105** C8
Ergel Mongolia 43°8N 109°5E **114** C5
Ergene → Turkey 41°1N 26°22E **97** E10
Ergeni Vozvyshennost
Russia 47°0N 44°0E **87** G7
Ergli Latvia 56°54N 25°38E **84** D3
Ergun He = Argun →
Russia 53°20N 121°28E **111** A13
Ergun Youqi China 50°15N 120°11E **111** A13
Erhlin Taiwan 23°54N 120°22E **117** F13
Eria → Spain 42°3N 5°44W **88** C5
Érice Italy 38°2N 12°35E **94** D5
Eridu Iraq 30°18N 83°45W **178** E6
Erie U.S.A. 42°8N 80°5W **174** D4
Erie, L. N. Amer. 42°15N 81°0W **174** D4
Erie Canal U.S.A. 43°5N 78°43W **174** D3
Erieau Canada 42°16N 81°57W **174** D3
Erigavo = Ceerigaabo
Somalia 10°35N 47°20E **131** E4
Erikoussa Greece 39°53N 19°34E **101** A3
Eriksdale Canada 50°52N 98°7E **163** C9
Erimanthos Greece 37°57N 21°50E **98** D3
Erimo-Misaki Japan 41°50N 143°15E **112** D11
Erin Japan 43°45N 80°7W **174** C4
Erin Pt. Trin. & Tob. 10°3N 61°39W **187** K15
Erinpura India 25°9N 73°3E **124** G5
Eriskay U.K. 57°4N 7°18W **65** D1
Erithres Greece 38°13N 23°20E **98** C5
Eritrea ■ Africa 14°0N 38°30E **131** D2
Erjas → Portugal 39°40N 7°1W **88** F3
Erkech-Tam Pass Asia 39°46N 74°2E **109** E8
Erkelenz Germany 51°4N 6°19E **76** D2
Erkner Germany 52°25N 13°44E **76** C9
Erlangen Germany 49°36N 11°0E **77** F6
Erldunda Australia 25°14S 133°12E **150** D1
Ermelo Neths. 52°18N 5°35E **69** B5
Ermelo S. Africa 26°31S 29°59E **145** C4
Ermenek Turkey 36°38N 33°0E **104** D5
Ermioni Greece 37°23N 23°15E **98** D5
Ermones Greece 39°37N 19°46E **101** A3
Ermoupoli Greece 37°28N 24°57E **98** D6
Ernakulam India 9°59N 76°22E **127** K3
Erne → Ireland 54°30N 8°16W **64** B3
Erne, Lower L. U.K. 54°28N 7°47W **64** B4
Erne, Upper L. U.K. 54°14N 7°32W **64** B4
Ernée France 48°18N 0°56W **70** D6
Ernest Giles Ra.
Australia 27°0S 123°45E **149** E3
Ernstberg Germany 50°13N 6°47E **77** E2
Erode India 11°24N 77°45E **127** J3
Eromanga Australia 26°40S 143°11E **151** D3
Erongo Namibia 21°39S 15°58E **144** B2
Erongo □ Namibia 22°0S 15°0E **144** B2
Erquy France 48°38N 2°29W **70** D4
Erramala Hills India 15°30N 78°15E **127** G4
Errenteria Spain 43°19N 1°54W **90** B3
Errigal Ireland 55°2N 8°6W **64** A3
Errinundra △
Australia 37°20S 148°47E **153** D8
Erris Hd. Ireland 54°17N 10°0W **64** B1
Erseke Albania 40°22N 20°40E **96** F4
Erskine U.S.A. 47°40N 96°0W **172** B6
Ertai China 46°3N 90°5E **109** C12
Ertan Shuiku China 27°5N 101°52E **116** D3
Erthlemne Denmark 55°19N 15°11E **63** J9
Ertil Russia 51°55N 40°50E **86** E5
Ertis = Irtysh → Russia 61°4N 68°52E **106** C7
Ertis Kazakhstan 53°20N 75°20E **109** C7
Ertis → Kazakhstan 52°20N 84°16E **109** C10
Eruh Turkey 37°46N 42°13E **105** D10
Ervy-le-Châtel France 48°2N 3°55E **71** D10
Erwin U.S.A. 36°9N 82°25W **177** C13
Eryuan China 26°7N 99°57E **116** D2
Erzgebirge Germany 50°27N 12°55E **76** E8
Erzin Russia 50°15N 95°10E **109** B13
Erzincan Turkey 39°46N 39°30E **105** C8
Erzincan □ Turkey 39°30N 39°30E **105** C8
Erzurum Turkey 39°57N 41°15E **105** C9
Erzurum □ Turkey 39°55N 41°15E **105** C9
Es Caló Spain 38°40N 1°30E **100** C8
Es Canar Spain 39°2N 1°36E **100** B8
Es Mercadal Spain 39°59N 4°5E **100** B11
Es Migjorn Gran Spain 39°57N 4°3E **100** B11
Es Sînâ' Egypt 29°0N 34°0E **130** F2
Es Vedrà Spain 38°52N 1°12E **100** C7
Esambo
Dem. Rep. of the Congo 3°48S 23°30E **142** C1
Esan-Misaki Japan 41°40N 141°10E **112** D10
Esashi Hokkaidō, Japan 44°56N 142°35E **112** B11
Esashi Hokkaidō, Japan 41°52N 140°7E **112** D10
Esbjerg Denmark 55°29N 8°29E **63** J2
Esbo = Espoo Finland 60°12N 24°40E **64** B3
Escada Brazil 8°22S 35°8W **189** B3
Escalante U.S.A. 37°47N 111°36W **169** H8
Escalante → U.S.A. 37°24N 110°57W **169** H8
Escalón Mexico 26°45N 104°20W **180** B4
Escambia → U.S.A. 30°32N 87°11W **179** F2
Escanaba U.S.A. 45°45N 87°4W **172** C10
Escárcega Mexico 18°37N 90°43W **181** D6
Esch-sur-Alzette Lux. 49°32N 6°0E **69** E6
Eschede Germany 52°44N 10°14E **76** C6
Eschwege Germany 51°11N 10°2E **76** D6
Eschweiler Germany 50°49N 6°15E **76** E2
Escoma Bolivia 15°40S 69°8W **188** D4
Escondido → Nicaragua 5°35N 5°10E **139** D6
Escondido U.S.A. 33°7N 117°5W **171** M9
Escuinapa de Hidalgo
Mexico 22°50N 105°50W **180** C3
Escuintla Guatemala 14°20N 90°48E **182** D1
Eséka Cameroon 3°41N 10°44E **139** E7
Esenguly Turkmenistan 37°37N 53°59E **108** F6
Esentepe = Áyios Amvrósios
Cyprus 35°20N 33°20E **101** D12
Esenyurt Turkey 41°3N 28°48E **97** E12
Esera → Spain 42°6N 0°15E **90** C5
Esfahān Iran 32°50N 51°43E **129** C6
Esfahān □ Iran 32°50N 51°50E **129** C6
Esfarāyen Iran 37°4N 57°30E **129** B8
Esfideh Iran 33°39N 59°46E **129** C8
Esgueva → Spain 41°40N 4°43W **88** D6
Esh Sham = Dimashq
Syria 33°30N 36°18E **130** B5
Esh Shamâlîya □ Sudan 19°0N 29°0E **137** D2
Esha Ness U.K. 60°29N 1°38W **65** A7
Eshan China 24°11N 102°2E **116** E4

Esher U.K. 51°21N 0°20W **67** F7
Eshkāshem = Ishkahim
Tajikistan 36°44N 71°37E **109** E8
Eshkol △ Israel 31°20N 34°30E **130** D3
Eshowe S. Africa 28°50S 31°30E **145** C5
Esigodini Zimbabwe 20°18S 28°56E **145** B4
Esil = Ishim → Russia 57°45N 71°10E **106** D8
Esil Kazakhstan 51°55N 66°25E **108** D7
Esino → Italy 43°39N 13°22E **93** E10
Esk → Dumf. & Gall., U.K. 54°58N 3°2W **65** D5
Esk → N. Yorks., U.K. 54°30N 0°37W **66** C7
Eskån Iran 26°48N 63°9E **129** E9
Esker Siding Canada 53°53N 66°25W **165** B6
Eskifjörður Iceland 65°3N 13°55W **60** D7
Eskilstuna Sweden 59°22N 16°32E **62** E10
Eskimalatya Turkey 38°24N 38°22E **105** C8
Eskimo Point = Arviat
Canada 61°6N 93°59W **163** A10
Eskişehir Turkey 39°50N 30°30E **99** B12
Eskişehir □ Turkey 39°40N 31°0E **99** B12
Esla → Spain 41°29N 6°3W **88** D4
Eslāmābād-e Gharb
Iran 34°10N 46°30E **105** E12
Eslāmshahr Iran 35°40N 51°10E **129** C6
Eslöv Sweden 55°50N 13°20E **63** J7
Eşme Turkey 38°23N 28°58E **99** C10
Esmeralda, I. Chile 48°55S 75°25W **192** C1
Esmeraldas Ecuador 1°0N 79°40W **186** C3
Esna = Isna Egypt 25°17N 32°30E **137** B3
Esnagi L. Canada 48°36N 84°33W **164** C3
Esom Hill U.S.A. 33°57N 85°23W **178** B4
Espalion France 44°32N 2°47E **72** D6
España = Spain ■ Europe 39°0N 4°0W **98** F5
Espanola Canada 46°15N 81°46W **164** C3
Espanola U.S.A. 35°59N 106°5W **169** J10
Esparraguera Spain 41°33N 1°52E **90** D6
Esparza Costa Rica 9°59N 84°40W **182** E3
Espelkamp Germany 52°24N 8°36E **76** C4
Esperança Brazil 7°1S 35°51W **189** B3
Esperance Australia 33°45S 121°55E **149** F3
Esperance B. Australia 33°48S 121°55E **149** F4
Esperance Harbour
St. Lucia 14°4N 60°55W **183** f
Esperantinópolis Brazil 4°53S 44°53W **189** A2
Esperanza Antarctica 65°0S 55°0W **55** C18
Esperanza Santa Cruz,
Argentina 51°1S 70°49W **192** D2
Esperanza Santa Fe,
Argentina 31°29S 61°3W **190** C3
Esperanza Puerto Rico 18°6N 65°28W **183** d
Espéraza France 42°56N 2°14E **72** F6
Espichel, C. Portugal 38°22N 9°16W **89** G1
Espiel Spain 38°11N 5°1W **89** G5
Espigão, Serra do
Brazil 26°35S 50°30W **191** B5
Espinar Peru 14°51S 71°24W **188** C3
Espinazo, Sierra del = Espinhaço,
Serra do Brazil 17°30S 43°30W **189** D2
Espinhaço, Serra do
Brazil 17°30S 43°30W **189** D2
Espinho Portugal 41°1N 8°38W **88** D2
Espinilho, Serra do
Brazil 28°30S 55°0W **191** B5
Espinosa de los Monteros
Spain 43°5N 3°34W **88** B7
Espírito Santo Brazil 20°0S 40°45W **189** E2
Espírito Santo do Pinhal
Brazil 22°10S 46°46W **191** A6
Espiritu Santo Vanuatu 15°15S 166°50E **147** C9
Espíritu Santo, B. del
Mexico 19°20N 87°35W **181** D7
Espiritu Santo, I.
Mexico 24°30N 110°22W **180** C2
Espita Mexico 21°1N 88°19W **181** C7
Espiye Turkey 40°56N 38°43E **105** B8
Esplanada Brazil 11°47S 37°57W **189** C3
Espoo Finland 60°12N 24°40E **64** B3
Espuña, Sierra de Spain 37°51N 1°35W **91** H3
Espungabera Mozam. 20°29S 32°45E **145** B5
Esquel Argentina 42°55S 71°20W **192** B2
Esquimalt Canada 48°26N 123°25W **170** B3
Esquina Argentina 30°0S 59°30W **190** C4
Essaouira Morocco 31°32N 9°42W **136** B2
Essen Belgium 51°28N 4°28E **69** B4
Essen Germany 51°28N 7°2E **76** D3
Essendon, Mt. Australia 25°0S 120°29E **149** E3
Essequibo → Guyana 6°50N 58°30W **186** B7
Essex Canada 42°10N 82°49W **174** D1
Essex Calif., U.S.A. 34°44N 115°15W **171** L11
Essex □ U.K. 51°54N 0°27E **67** F8
Essex Junction U.S.A. 44°29N 73°7W **175** B11
Esslingen Germany 48°44N 9°18E **77** G5
Essonne □ France 48°30N 2°20E **71** D9
Estaca de Bares, C. de
Spain 43°46N 7°42W **88** B3
Estación Camacho
Mexico 24°25N 102°18W **180** C4
Estación Simón
Mexico 24°42N 102°35W **180** C4
Estadilla Spain 42°4N 0°16E **90** C5
Estados, I. de Los
Argentina 54°40S 64°30W **192** G4
Estagel France 42°47N 2°40E **72** F6
Eştahbānāt Iran 29°8N 54°4E **129** D7
Estância Brazil 11°16S 37°26W **189** C3
Estancia U.S.A. 34°46N 106°4W **169** J10
Estancia Monte León
Argentina 50°14S 68°55W **192** D3
Estarreja Portugal 40°45S 8°35W **88** E2
Estats, Pic d' Spain 42°40N 1°24E **90** C6
Estcourt S. Africa 29°0S 29°53E **145** C4
Este Italy 45°14N 11°39E **92** C8
Este △ Dom. Rep. 18°14N 68°42W **183** C6
Estel' Nic. 13°9N 86°22W **182** D2
Estella = Lizarra Spain 42°40N 2°2W **90** C2
Estellencs Spain 39°39N 2°29E **100** B9
Estena → Spain 39°3N 4°44W **89** H6
Estepa Spain 37°17N 4°52W **89** H6
Estepona Spain 36°24N 5°7W **89** J5
Esterhazy Canada 50°37N 102°5W **163** C8
Esternay France 48°44N 3°33E **71** D10
Esterri d'Aneu Spain 42°38N 1°5E **90** C6
Estevan Canada 49°10N 102°59W **163** D8
Estevan Group Canada 53°3N 129°38W **162** C3
Estherville U.S.A. 43°24N 94°50W **172** D6
Estill U.S.A. 32°45N 81°15W **178** E6
Estissac France 48°16N 3°48E **71** D10
Eston Canada 51°8N 108°40W **163** C7

Estonia ■ Europe 58°30N 25°30E **84** C3
Estoril Portugal 38°42N 9°23W **89** G1
Estouk Mali 18°14N 1°2E **139** B5
Estreito Brazil 6°32S 47°25W **187** E9
Estreito Maranhão, Brazil 6°34S 47°27W **189** B1
Estrela Spain 38°25N 3°35W **89** G7
Estrela, Serra da Portugal 40°10N 7°45W **88** E3
Estremoz Portugal 38°51N 7°39W **89** G3
Estrondo, Serra do Brazil 7°20S 48°0W **189** D1
Esztergom Hungary 47°47N 18°44E **81** E11
Et Tidra Mauritania 19°45N 16°20W **138** B1
Etah India 27°35N 78°40E **125** F8
Étain France 49°13N 5°38E **71** C12
Étampes France 48°26N 2°10E **71** D9
Etanga Namibia 17°55S 13°0E **144** A1
Étaples France 50°30N 1°39E **71** B8
Etawah India 26°48N 79°6E **125** F8
Etawney L. Canada 57°50N 96°50W **163** B9
Ete Nigeria 7°2N 7°28E **139** D6
eThekwini = Durban
S. Africa 29°49S 31°1E **145** C5
Ethel U.S.A. 46°32N 122°46W **170** D4
Ethelbert Canada 51°32N 100°25W **163** C8
Ethiopia ■ Africa 8°0N 40°0E **131** F3
Ethiopian Highlands
Ethiopia 10°0N 37°0E **131** F2
Etili Turkey 39°59N 26°54E **97** G10
Etive, L. U.K. 56°29N 5°10W **65** E3
Etna, I. Italy 37°50N 14°55E **95** E7
Etoile
Dem. Rep. of the Congo 11°33S 27°30E **143** E2
Etoliko Greece 38°26N 21°21E **98** C3
Etolin Strait U.S.A. 60°20N 165°15W **166** C3
Etoloakarnania Greece 38°45N 21°18E **98** C3
Etosha △ Namibia 19°0S 16°0E **144** A2
Etosha Pan Namibia 18°40S 16°30E **144** A2
Etowah U.S.A. 35°20N 84°32W **177** D12
Étréchy France 48°30N 2°12E **71** D9
Etrek Turkmenistan 37°36N 54°46E **129** B7
Étrépagny France 49°18N 1°36E **71** C8
Étretat France 49°42N 0°12E **70** C7
Etropole Bulgaria 42°50N 24°0E **97** D8
Ettelbruck Lux. 49°51N 6°5E **69** E6
Ettlingen Germany 48°58N 8°25E **77** G4
Ettrick Water → U.K. 55°31N 2°55W **65** F6
Etuku
Dem. Rep. of the Congo 3°42S 25°45E **142** C2
Etulia Moldova 45°32N 28°27E **81** E13
Etzná-Tixmucuy = Edzná
Mexico 19°39N 90°19W **181** D6
Eu France 50°3N 1°26E **70** B8
Euboea = Evia Greece 38°30N 24°0E **98** C6
Eucharena Australia 32°57S 149°6E **153** B8
Eucla Australia 31°41S 128°52E **149** F4
Euclid U.S.A. 41°34N 81°32W **174** E3
Euclides da Cunha
Brazil 10°31S 39°1W **189** C3
Eucumbene, L.
Australia 36°2S 148°40E **153** D8
Eudora U.S.A. 33°7N 91°16W **176** D9
Eudunda Australia 34°12S 139°7E **152** C3
Eufaula Ala., U.S.A. 31°54N 85°9W **178** D4
Eufaula Okla., U.S.A. 35°17N 95°35W **176** D7
Eufaula L. U.S.A. 35°18N 95°21W **176** D7
Eugene U.S.A. 44°5N 123°4W **168** D2
Eugowra Australia 33°22S 148°24E **153** B8
Eulo Australia 28°10S 145°3E **151** D4
Eulonia U.S.A. 31°32N 81°26W **178** D8
Eumungerie Australia 31°56S 148°32E **153** A8
Eungella △ Australia 20°57S 148°40E **150** b
Eunice La., U.S.A. 30°30N 92°25W **176** F8
Eunice N. Mex.,
U.S.A. 32°26N 103°10W **169** K12
Eupen Belgium 50°37N 6°3E **69** D6
Euphrates = Furāt, Nahr al →
Asia 31°0N 47°25E **128** D5
Eure □ France 49°10N 1°0E **70** C8
Eure → France 49°18N 1°12E **70** C8
Eure-et-Loir □ France 48°22N 1°30E **70** D8
Eureka Canada 80°0N 85°56W **161** B14
Eureka Calif., U.S.A. 40°47N 124°9W **168** F1
Eureka Kans., U.S.A. 37°49N 96°17W **172** G5
Eureka Mont., U.S.A. 48°53N 115°3W **168** A6
Eureka Nev., U.S.A. 39°31N 115°58W **168** G6
Eureka S. Dak., U.S.A. 45°46N 99°38W **172** C4
Eureka Utah, U.S.A. 39°58N 112°7W **168** G7
Eureka, Mt. Australia 26°35S 121°35E **149** E3
Eureka Sd. Canada 79°0N 85°0W **161** B15
Eurelia Australia 32°3S 138°55E **152** B3
Eurinilla Cr. →
Australia 30°53S 140°11E **152** A4
Euroa Australia 36°44S 145°35E **153** D6
Europa, Île Ind. Oc. 22°20S 40°22E **145** B7
Europa, Picos de Spain 43°10N 4°49W **88** B6
Europa, Pt. Gib. 36°3N 5°21W **89** J5
Europe 50°0N 20°0E **58** E10
Europoort Neths. 51°57N 4°10E **69** C4
Euskadi = País Vasco □
Spain 42°50N 2°45W **90** C2
Euskirchen Germany 50°39N 6°45E **76** E2
Eustis U.S.A. 28°51N 81°41W **179** G8
Euston Australia 34°30S 142°46E **152** C5
Eutaw U.S.A. 32°50N 87°53W **178** D3
Eutin Germany 54°7N 10°38E **76** A6
Eutsuk L. Canada 53°20N 126°45W **162** C3
Evale Angola 16°33S 15°44E **144** A2
Evans U.S.A. 40°23N 104°41W **168** F11
Evans, L. Canada 50°50N 77°0W **164** B4
Evans City U.S.A. 40°46N 80°4W **174** F4
Evans Head Australia 29°7S 153°27E **151** D5
Evansburg Canada 53°36N 114°59W **162** C5
Evanston Ill., U.S.A. 42°3N 87°40W **172** D10
Evanston Wyo.,
U.S.A. 41°16N 110°58W **168** F8
Evansville U.S.A. 37°58N 87°35W **172** G9
Évaux-les-Bains France 46°12N 2°29E **71** F9
Evaz Iran 27°46N 53°59E **129** E7
Evciler Afyon, Turkey 38°4N 29°54E **99** C11
Evciler Çanakkale, Turkey 39°47N 26°44E **97** G9
Eveleth U.S.A. 47°28N 92°32W **172** B7
Evensk Russia 62°12N 159°30E **107** C16
Everard, L. Australia 31°30S 135°0E **151** E2
Everard Ranges
Australia 27°5S 132°28E **149** E5
Everest, Mt. Nepal 28°5N 86°58E **125** E12
Everett Pa., U.S.A. 40°1N 78°23W **174** F5
Everett Wash., U.S.A. 47°59N 122°12W **170** C4
Everglades, The U.S.A. 25°50N 81°0W **179** K9

Everglades △ U.S.A. 25°30N 81°0W **179** K9
Everglades City U.S.A. 25°52N 81°23W **179** K8
Evergreen Ala., U.S.A. 31°26N 86°57W **177** F11
Evergreen Mont.,
U.S.A. 48°14N 114°17W **168** B6
Everöd Sweden 55°53N 14°5E **63** J8
Everton Australia 36°25S 146°33E **153** D7
Evertsberg Sweden 61°8N 13°58E **62** D7
Evesham U.K. 52°6N 1°56W **67** E6
Evia Greece 38°30N 24°0E **98** C6
Évian-les-Bains France 46°24N 6°35E **71** F13
Evinos → Greece 38°27N 21°40E **98** C3
Évisa France 42°15N 8°48E **73** F12
Évora Portugal 38°33N 7°57W **89** G3
Évora □ Portugal 38°33N 7°50W **89** G3
Evowghlí Iran 38°43N 45°13E **105** C11
Évreux France 49°3N 1°8E **70** C8
Évron France 48°10N 0°24W **70** D6
Évros → Greece 41°40N 26°34E **97** F10
Évry France 48°38N 2°27E **71** D9
Évvoia = Evia Greece 38°30N 24°0E **98** C6
Ewe, L. U.K. 57°49N 5°38W **65** D3
Ewing U.S.A. 42°16N 98°21W **172** D4
Ewo Congo 0°48S 14°45E **140** E2
Exaltación Bolivia 13°10S 65°20W **188** C5
Excelsior Springs
U.S.A. 39°20N 94°13W **172** F6
Excideuil France 45°20N 1°4E **72** C5
Exe → U.K. 50°41N 3°29W **67** G4
Exeter Canada 43°21N 81°29W **174** C3
Exeter U.K. 50°43N 3°31W **67** G4
Exeter Calif., U.S.A. 36°18N 119°9W **170** J7
Exeter N.H., U.S.A. 42°59N 70°57W **175** D14
Exmoor U.K. 51°12N 3°45W **67** F4
Exmoor △ U.K. 51°8N 3°42W **67** F4
Exmouth Australia 21°54S 114°10E **148** D1
Exmouth U.K. 50°37N 3°25W **67** G4
Exmouth G. Australia 22°15S 114°15E **148** D1
Exmouth Plateau
Ind. Oc. 19°0S 114°0E **152** D2
Expedition △ Australia 25°41S 149°7E **151** D4
Expedition Ra.
Australia 24°30S 149°12E **150** C4
Experiment = Highland Mills
U.S.A. 33°17N 84°17W **178** B5
Extremadura □ Spain 39°30N 6°5W **89** F4
Exuma Sound
Bahamas 24°30N 76°20W **182** B4
Eyasi, L. Tanzania 3°30S 35°0E **142** C4
Eye Pen. U.K. 58°13N 6°10W **65** C2
Eyemouth U.K. 55°52N 2°5W **65** F6
Eygues = Aigues →
France 44°7N 4°43E **73** D8
Eygurande France 45°40N 2°26E **71** G9
Eyjafjallajökull Iceland 63°38N 19°36W **60** E4
Eyjafjörður Iceland 66°15N 18°30W **60** C4
Eyl Somalia 8°0N 49°50E **131** F4
Eymet France 44°40N 0°25E **72** D4
Eymoutiers France 45°40N 1°45E **72** C5
Eynesil Turkey 41°4N 39°9E **105** B8
Eyre → France 44°39N 1°1W **72** D2
Eyre, L. = Kati Thanda-Lake Eyre
Australia 29°30S 137°26E **147** D6
Eyre Mts. N.Z. 45°25S 168°25E **155** F3
Eyre Pen. Australia 33°30S 136°17E **152** C1
Eysturoy Færoe Is. 62°13N 6°54W **60** F9
Eyvān = Jūy Zar Iran 33°50N 46°18E **105** F12
Eyvānkī Iran 35°24N 51°56E **129** C6
Ezcaray Spain 42°19N 3°0W **90** C1
Ežerélis Lithuania 54°53N 23°37E **82** D10
Ezhou China 30°23N 114°50E **117** B10
Ezine Turkey 39°48N 26°20E **99** B8
Ezouza → Cyprus 34°44N 32°27E **101** E11

F

F.Y.R.O.M. = Macedonia ■
Europe 41°53N 21°40E **96** E5
Faaa Tahiti 17°34S 149°35W **155** b
Faaborg Denmark 55°6N 10°15E **63** J4
Faaone Tahiti 17°40S 149°21W **155** b
Fabala Guinea 9°44N 9°5W **138** D3
Fabens U.S.A. 31°30N 106°10W **176** F1
Fåberg Norway 61°15N 10°22E **63** E5
Fabero Spain 42°46N 6°37W **88** C4
Fabius U.S.A. 42°50N 75°59W **175** D9
Fabriano Italy 43°20N 12°54E **93** E9
Făcăeni Romania 44°32N 27°53E **81** F12
Faceville U.S.A. 30°45N 84°38W **178** E5
Fachi Niger 18°6N 11°34E **139** B8
Facundo Argentina 45°10S 69°58W **192** C3
Fada Chad 17°13N 21°34E **135** E10
Fada-n-Gourma
Burkina Faso 12°10N 0°30E **139** C5
Fadd Hungary 46°28N 18°49E **80** D3
Faddeyevskiy, Ostrov
Russia 76°0N 144°0E **107** B15
Fadghāmī Syria 35°53N 40°52E **105** D9
Faenza Italy 44°17N 11°53E **93** D8
Færingehavn =
Kangerluarsoruseq
Greenland 63°45N 51°27W **57** c5
Færoe Is. = Føroyar ☐
Atl. Oc. 62°0N 7°0W **60** F9
Fafa Mali 15°22N 0°48E **139** B5
Fafe Portugal 41°27N 8°11W **88** D2
Fagam Nigeria 11°1N 10°1E **139** C7
Făgăraş Romania 45°48N 24°58E **81** E9
Făgăraş, Munţii
Romania 45°40N 24°40E **81** E8
Fagersta Sweden 60°1N 15°46E **62** D9
Făget Romania 45°52N 22°10E **81** E7
Făget, Munţii Romania 47°40N 23°10E **81** C8
Fagnano, L. Argentina 54°30S 68°0W **192** G3
Fagnières France 48°58N 4°20E **71** D11
Faguibine, L. Mali 16°45N 4°0W **138** B4
Fahlīān Iran 30°11N 51°28E **129** D6
Fahraj Kermān, Iran 29°0N 59°0E **129** D8
Fahraj Yazd, Iran 31°46N 54°36E **129** D7
Fai Tsi Long Vietnam 21°0N 107°30E **122** B5
Faial Madeira 32°47N 16°53E **134** D3
Faial Azores 38°34N 28°42W **134** a
Faichan Kangri India 35°8N 76°54E **125** B7
Fair Haven N.Y.,
U.S.A. 43°18N 76°42W **175** C8

Fair Haven Vt., U.S.A. 43°36N 73°16W **175** C11
Fair Hd. U.K. 55°14N 6°9W **64** A5
Fair Isle U.K. 59°32N 1°38W **68** B6
Fair Oaks U.S.A. 38°39N 121°16W **170** G5
Fairbanks Alaska,
U.S.A. 64°51N 147°43W **160** E2
Fairbanks Fla., U.S.A. 29°44N 82°16W **178** F7
Fairburn U.S.A. 33°34N 84°35W **178** B5
Fairbury U.S.A. 40°8N 97°11W **172** E5
Fairfax S.C., U.S.A. 32°59N 81°15W **178** E6
Fairfax Tex., U.S.A. 44°40N 73°1W **175** B11
Fairfield Australia 33°53S 150°57E **153** B9
Fairfield Calif., U.S.A. 38°15N 122°3W **170** G4
Fairfield Conn., U.S.A. 41°9N 73°16W **175** E11
Fairfield Idaho, U.S.A. 43°21N 114°44W **168** E6
Fairfield Ill., U.S.A. 38°23N 88°22W **172** F9
Fairfield Iowa, U.S.A. 40°56N 91°57W **172** E8
Fairfield Tex., U.S.A. 31°44N 96°10W **176** F6
Fairford Canada 51°37N 98°38W **163** C9
Fairhope U.S.A. 30°31N 87°54W **177** F11
Fairlie N.Z. 44°5S 170°49E **155** E5
Fairmead U.S.A. 37°5N 120°10W **170** H6
Fairmont Minn., U.S.A. 43°39N 94°28W **172** D6
Fairmont W. Va.,
U.S.A. 39°29N 80°9W **173** F13
Fairmount Calif.,
U.S.A. 34°45N 118°26W **171** L8
Fairmount N.Y., U.S.A. 43°5N 76°12W **175** C8
Fairplay U.S.A. 39°15N 106°2W **168** G10
Fairport U.S.A. 43°6N 77°27W **174** C7
Fairport Harbor U.S.A. 41°45N 81°17W **174** E3
Fairview Canada 56°5N 118°25W **162** B5
Fairview Mont.,
U.S.A. 47°51N 104°3W **168** C11
Fairview Okla., U.S.A. 36°16N 98°29W **176** C5
Fairweather, Mt.
U.S.A. 58°55N 137°32W **162** A4
Faisalabad Pakistan 31°30N 73°5E **124** D5
Faith U.S.A. 45°2N 102°2W **172** C2
Faizabad India 26°45N 82°10E **125** F10
Faizabad India 21°41N 75°49E **126** D2
Fajardo Puerto Rico 18°20N 65°39W **183** d
Fajr, W. → Si. Arabia 29°10N 38°10E **128** D3
Fakenham U.K. 52°51N 0°51E **66** E8
Fåker Sweden 63°0N 14°34E **62** A8
Fakfak Indonesia 2°55S 132°18E **119** E8
Fakiya Bulgaria 42°10N 27°6E **97** D11
Fakobli Ivory C. 7°23N 7°23W **138** D3
Fakse Denmark 55°15N 12°8E **63** J6
Fakse Bugt Denmark 55°11N 12°15E **63** J6
Fakse Ladeplads Denmark 55°11N 12°9E **63** J6
Faku China 42°32N 123°21E **115** C12
Falaba S. Leone 9°54N 11°32W **138** D2
Falaise France 48°54N 0°12W **70** D6
Falakro Oros Greece 41°15N 23°58E **96** E7
Falam Burma 23°0N 93°45E **123** H18
Fălciu Romania 46°17N 28°7E **81** D13
Falcó, C. des Spain 38°50N 1°23E **100** C7
Falcon, C. Algeria 35°50N 0°50W **136** A3
Falcón, Presa Mexico 26°35N 99°10W **181** B5
Falcon Lake Canada 49°42N 95°15W **163** D9
Falcon Res. U.S.A. 26°34N 99°10W **176** H5
Falconara Maríttima
Italy 43°37N 13°24E **93** E10
Falcone, C. del Italy 40°58N 8°12E **94** B1
Falconer U.S.A. 42°7N 79°12W **174** D5
Faléa Mali 12°16N 11°17W **138** C2
Falémé → Senegal 14°46N 12°14W **138** C2
Falerum Sweden 58°9N 16°13E **63** F10
Faleshty = Fălești
Moldova 47°32N 27°44E **81** C12
Fălești Moldova 47°32N 27°44E **81** C12
Falfurrias U.S.A. 27°14N 98°9W **176** H5
Falher Canada 55°44N 117°15W **162** B5
Faliraki Greece 36°22N 28°12E **101** C10
Falkenberg Germany 51°35N 13°14E **76** D9
Falkenberg Sweden 56°54N 12°30E **63** H6
Falkensee Germany 52°34N 13°4E **76** C9
Falkirk U.K. 56°0N 3°47W **65** F5
Falkirk □ U.K. 55°58N 3°49W **65** F5
Falkland U.K. 56°16N 3°12W **65** E5
Falkland, East, I.
Falk. Is. 51°40S 58°30W **192** G5
Falkland, West, I.
Falk. Is. 51°40S 60°0W **192** G5
Falkland Is. ☑ Atl. Oc. 51°30S 59°0W **192** D5
Falkland Plateau Atl. Oc. 51°0S 50°0W **56** M7
Falkland Ridge Atl. Oc. 49°20S 40°0W **56** L8
Falkland Sd. Falk. Is. 52°0S 60°0W **192** D5
Fabriano Italy 43°20N 12°54E **93** E9
Falkonera Greece 36°50N 23°52E **98** E5
Falköping Sweden 58°12N 13°33E **63** F7
Fall River U.S.A. 41°43N 71°10W **175** E13
Fallbrook U.S.A. 33°23N 117°15W **171** M9
Fallon U.S.A. 39°28N 118°47W **168** G4
Falls City U.S.A. 40°3N 95°36W **172** E6
Falls Creek U.S.A. 41°9N 78°48W **174** E6
Falmouth Jamaica 18°30N 77°40W **182** a
Falmouth U.K. 50°9N 5°5W **67** G2
Falmouth U.S.A. 41°33N 70°37W **175** E14
False B. S. Africa 34°15S 18°40E **144** E2
False Divi Pt. India 15°43N 80°50E **127** G5
False Pt. India 20°18N 86°48E **126** D8
Falso, C. Honduras 15°12N 83°21W **182** C3
Falster Denmark 54°45N 11°55E **63** K5
Fălticeni Romania 47°21N 26°20E **81** C11
Falun Sweden 60°37N 15°37E **62** D9
Famagusta Cyprus 35°8N 33°55E **101** D12
Famagusta Bay Cyprus 35°15N 34°0E **101** D13
Famatina, Sierra de
Argentina 27°30S 68°0W **190** B2
Famenin Iran 35°5N 48°58E **105** D13
Family L. Canada 51°54N 95°27W **163** C9
Famoso U.S.A. 35°37N 119°12W **171** K7
Fan Xian China 35°55N 115°38E **114** G8
Fanad Hd. Ireland 55°17N 7°38W **64** A4
Fanárion Greece 39°24N 21°47E **98** B3
Fánes-Sénnes-Braies △
Italy 46°38N 12°5E **92** B8
Fang Thailand 19°55N 99°13E **120** C2
Fang Xian China 32°3N 110°40E **117** A8
Fangchang China 31°5N 118°4E **117** B12
Fangcheng China 33°18N 112°59E **114** H7
Fangchenggang China 21°50N 108°21E **117** E7
Fangliao Taiwan 22°22N 120°38E **117** F13
Fangshan Beijing, China 39°41N 116°0E **114** E8
Fangshan Shanxi, China 38°3N 111°25E **114** E6
Fangzi China 36°33N 119°10E **115** F10
Fani i Madh → Albania 41°56N 20°16E **96** G4
Fanjiatun China 43°40N 125°15E **115** C13
Fanling China 22°30N 114°8E **111** a

Fannich, L. U.K. 57°38N 4°59W **65** D4
Fannūj Iran 26°35N 59°38E **129** E8
Fanø Denmark 55°25N 8°25E **63** J2
Fano Italy 43°50N 13°1E **93** E10
Fanshi China 39°12N 113°20E **114** E7
Fao = Al Fāw Iraq 30°0N 48°30E **129** D6
Faqirwāl Pakistan 29°27N 73°0E **124** E5
Fâqûs Egypt 30°44N 31°47E **137** E7
Far East = Dalnevostochnyy □
　Russia 67°0N 140°0E **107** C14
Far East Asia 40°0N 130°0E **102** E14
Fara in Sabina Italy 42°12N 12°43E **93** F9
Faradje
　Dem. Rep. of the Congo 3°50N 29°45E **142** B2
Farafangana Madag. 22°49S 47°50E **141** J9
Farafenni Gambia 13°34N 15°36W **138** C1
Farâfra, El Wâhât el
　Egypt 27°15N 28°20E **137** B2
Farāh Afghan. 32°20N 62°7E **122** C3
Farāh □ Afghan. 32°25N 62°10E **122** C3
Faraid, Gebel Egypt 23°33N 35°19E **137** C4
Farako Ivory C. 10°45N 6°50W **138** D4
Faramana Burkina Faso 11°56N 4°45W **138** C4
Faranah Guinea 10°3N 10°45W **138** C2
Farap Turkmenistan 39°9N 63°36E **108** E6
Farasān, Jazā'ir
　Si. Arabia 16°45N 41°55E **131** D3
Farasan Is. = Farasān, Jazā'ir
　Si. Arabia 16°45N 41°55E **131** D3
Fardes → Spain 37°35N 3°0W **89** H7
Fareham U.K. 50°51N 1°11W **67** G6
Farewell, C. = Nunap Isua
　Greenland 59°48N 43°55W **57** F6
Farewell, C. N.Z. 40°29S 172°43E **155** A7
Farewell Spit N.Z. 40°35S 173°0E **155** A8
Färgelanda Sweden 58°34N 12°0E **63** F5
Fargo Ga., U.S.A. 30°41N 82°34W **178** F7
Fargo N. Dak., U.S.A. 46°53N 96°48W **172** B5
Farg'ona Uzbekistan 40°23N 71°19E **109** D8
Farg'ona □ Uzbekistan 40°30N 71°15E **109** D8
Farg'ona vodiysi Asia 40°46N 71°30E **109** D8
Fār'iah, W. al →
　West Bank 32°12N 35°27E **130** C4
Faribault U.S.A. 44°18N 93°16W **172** C7
Faridabad India 28°26N 77°19E **124** E6
Faridkot India 30°44N 74°45E **124** D6
Faridpur Bangla. 23°15N 89°55E **125** H13
Faridpur India 28°13N 79°33E **125** E8
Färila Sweden 61°48N 15°50E **62** C9
Farim Guinea-Biss. 12°27N 15°9W **138** C1
Farīmān Iran 35°40N 59°49E **129** C8
Farinha → Brazil 6°51S 47°30W **189** B1
Fariones, Pta.
　Canary Is. 29°13N 13°28W **100** E6
Fâriskûr Egypt 31°20N 31°43E **137** C7
Färjestaden Sweden 56°39N 16°27E **63** H10
Farkadóna Greece 39°36N 22°4E **98** B4
Farleigh Australia 21°4S 149°8E **150** b
Farmakonisi Greece 37°17N 27°5E **99** D9
Farmerville U.S.A. 32°47N 92°24W **176** E8
Farmingdale U.S.A. 40°12N 74°10W **175** F10
Farmington Canada 55°54N 120°30W **162** B4
Farmington Calif.,
　U.S.A. 37°55N 120°59W **170** H6
Farmington Ga., U.S.A. 33°47N 83°26W **178** B6
Farmington Maine,
　U.S.A. 44°40N 70°9W **173** C18
Farmington Mo.,
　U.S.A. 37°47N 90°25W **172** G8
Farmington N.H.,
　U.S.A. 43°24N 71°4W **175** C13
Farmington N. Mex.,
　U.S.A. 36°44N 108°12W **169** H9
Farmington Utah,
　U.S.A. 40°59N 111°53W **168** F8
Farmington →
　U.S.A. 41°51N 72°38W **175** E12
Farmville U.S.A. 37°18N 78°24W **173** G14
Färnäs Sweden 61°0N 14°39E **62** D8
Farne Is. U.K. 55°38N 1°37W **66** B6
Färnebofjärden △
　Sweden 60°10N 16°48E **62** D10
Farnham Canada 45°17N 72°59W **175** A12
Farnham, Mt. Canada 50°29N 116°30W **162** C5
Faro Brazil 2°10S 56°39W **187** D7
Faro Canada 62°11N 133°22W **160** E5
Faro Portugal 37°2N 7°55W **89** H3
Fårö Sweden 57°55N 19°5E **63** G13
Faro □ Portugal 37°12N 8°10W **89** H2
Faro ✠ (FAO) Portugal 37°2N 7°57W **89** H3
Fårösund Sweden 57°52N 19°2E **63** G13
Farquhar, C. Australia 23°50S 113°36E **149** D1
Farquhar Is. Seychelles 11°0S 52°0E **146** F4
Farrars Cr. →
　Australia 25°35S 140°43E **150** D3
Farrāshband Iran 28°57N 52°5E **129** D7
Farrell U.S.A. 41°13N 80°30W **174** E4
Farrell Flat Australia 33°48S 138°48E **152** B3
Farrokhī Iran 33°50N 59°31E **129** C8
Farruch, C. = Ferrutx, C. de
　Spain 39°47N 3°21E **100** B10
Farrukhabad India 27°24N 79°34E **124** A4
Fārs □ Iran 29°30N 55°0E **129** D7
Fársala Greece 39°17N 22°23E **98** B4
Fârsî Iran 27°58N 50°11E **129** E6
Farsø Denmark 56°46N 9°19E **63** H3
Farson U.S.A. 42°7N 109°26W **168** E9
Farsund Norway 58°5N 6°55E **61** G12
Fartak, Râs Si. Arabia 28°5N 34°34E **128** D2
Fartak, Ra's Yemen 15°38N 52°15E **131** D5
Fârțânești Romania 45°49N 27°59E **81** E12
Fartura, Serra da
　Brazil 26°21S 52°52W **191** B5
Faru Nigeria 12°12N 6°12E **139** C6
Fārûj Iran 37°14N 58°14E **129** B8
Fårup Denmark 56°33N 9°51E **63** H3
Farvel, Kap = Nunap Isua
　Greenland 59°48N 43°55W **57** F6
Farwell U.S.A. 34°23N 103°2W **176** D3
Fâryâb □ Afghan. 36°0N 65°0E **128** B4
Fasā Iran 29°0N 53°39E **129** D7
Fasano Italy 40°50N 17°22E **95** B10
Fassa Mali 13°26N 8°15W **138** C3
Fassalé Mauritania 15°33N 5°31W **138** B3
Fastiv Ukraine 50°7N 29°57E **75** C15
Fastnet Rock Ireland 51°22N 9°37W **64** E2
Fastov = Fastiv Ukraine 50°7N 29°57E **75** C15
Fatagartuting, Tanjung
　Indonesia 2°46S 131°57E **119** E8
Fatehabad Haryana,
　India 29°31N 75°27E **124** E6
Fatehabad Ut. P., India 27°1N 78°19E **124** F8

Fatehgarh India 27°25N 79°35E **125** F8
Fatehpur Bihar, India 24°38N 85°14E **125** G11
Fatehpur Raj., India 28°0N 74°40E **124** F6
Fatehpur Ut. P., India 25°56N 81°13E **125** G9
Fatehpur Ut. P., India 27°10N 81°13E **125** F9
Fatehpur Sikri India 27°6N 77°40E **124** F6
Fatesh Russia 52°8N 35°57E **85** F8
Fathom Five △ Canada 45°17N 81°40W **174** A3
Fatick Senegal 14°19N 16°27W **138** C1
Fatick □ Senegal 14°15N 16°30W **138** C1
Fatima Canada 47°24N 61°53W **165** C7
Fátima Portugal 39°37N 8°39W **89** F2
Fatoya Guinea 11°37N 9°10W **138** C3
Fatsa Turkey 41°2N 37°31E **104** B7
Faucille, Col de la France 46°22N 6°2E **71** F13
Faulkton U.S.A. 45°2N 99°8W **172** C4
Faulquemont France 49°3N 6°36E **71** C13
Faure I. Australia 25°52S 113°50E **149** E1
Fauresmith S. Africa 29°44S 25°17E **144** C4
Fauske Norway 67°17N 15°25E **60** C16
Favara Italy 37°19N 13°39E **94** E6
Favāritx, C. de Spain 40°0N 4°15E **100** B11
Faverges France 45°45N 6°17E **73** C10
Favignana Italy 37°56N 12°20E **94** E5
Favignana, I. Italy 37°56N 12°19E **94** E5
Fawcett, Pt. Australia 11°46S 130°2E **148** B5
Fawn → Canada 55°20N 87°35W **164** A2
Fawnskin U.S.A. 34°16N 116°56W **171** L10
Faxaflói Iceland 64°29N 23°0W **60** D2
Faxälven → Sweden 63°13N 17°13E **62** A10
Faya-Largeau Chad 17°58N 19°6E **135** E9
Fayd Si. Arabia 27°1N 42°52E **128** E4
Fayence France 43°38N 6°42E **73** E10
Fayette Ala., U.S.A. 33°41N 87°50W **177** E11
Fayette Mo., U.S.A. 39°9N 92°41W **172** F7
Fayette N.Y., U.S.A. 42°48N 76°48W **175** D8
Fayetteville Ark., U.S.A. 36°4N 94°10W **176** C7
Fayetteville Ga., U.S.A. 33°27N 84°27W **178** B5
Fayetteville N.C.,
　U.S.A. 35°3N 78°53W **177** D15
Fayetteville N.Y., U.S.A. 43°1N 76°0W **175** C9
Fayetteville Tenn.,
　U.S.A. 35°9N 86°34W **177** D11
Fayied Egypt 30°18N 32°16E **137** E8
Faylakah Kuwait 29°27N 48°20E **129** D6
Fayón Spain 41°15N 0°20E **90** D5
Fazao-Malfakassa △
　Togo 8°45N 0°50E **139** D5
Fazilka India 30°27N 74°2E **124** D6
Fazilpur Pakistan 29°18N 70°29E **124** E4
Fdérik Mauritania 22°40N 12°45W **134** D3
Feakle Ireland 52°56N 8°40W **64** D3
Feale → Ireland 52°27N 9°37W **64** D2
Fear, C. U.S.A. 33°50N 77°58W **177** E16
Feather → U.S.A. 38°47N 121°36W **170** G5
Feather Falls U.S.A. 39°36N 121°16W **170** F5
Featherston N.Z. 41°6S 175°20E **154** H4
Featherstone Zimbabwe 18°42S 30°55E **143** F3
Fécamp France 49°45N 0°22E **70** C7
Fedala = Mohammedia
　Morocco 33°44N 7°21W **136** B2
Federación Argentina 31°0S 57°55W **190** C4
Féderal Argentina 30°57S 58°48W **190** C4
Federal Capital Terr. □
　Nigeria 9°0N 7°10E **139** D6
Federal Way U.S.A. 47°18N 122°19W **170** C4
Fedeshküh Iran 28°49N 53°50E **129** D7
Fedorovka Kazakhstan 53°37N 62°42E **108** B6
Fehérgyarmat Hungary 47°58N 22°30E **80** C7
Fehmarn Germany 54°27N 11°7E **76** A7
Fehmarn Bælt Europe 54°35N 11°20E **63** K5
Fehmarn Belt = Fehmarn Bælt
　Europe 54°35N 11°20E **63** K5
Fei Xian China 35°18N 117°59E **115** G9
Feicheng China 36°14N 116°45E **114** F9
Feidong China 32°0N 117°35E **117** B11
Feijó Brazil 8°9S 70°21W **188** B3
Feilding N.Z. 40°13S 175°35E **154** G4
Feira de Santana
　Brazil 12°15S 38°57W **189** C3
Feixi China 31°43N 117°9E **117** B11
Feixiang China 36°30N 114°45E **114** F8
Fejaj, Chott el Tunisia 33°52N 9°14E **136** B5
Fejér □ Hungary 47°9N 18°30E **80** C3
Fejø Denmark 54°55N 11°30E **63** K5
Feke Turkey 37°48N 35°56E **104** D6
Fekete → Hungary 45°47N 18°15E **80** E3
Felanitx Spain 39°28N 3°9E **100** B10
Felda → Australia 26°34N 81°26W **179** J8
Feldbach Austria 46°57N 15°52E **78** E8
Feldberg Baden-W.,
　Germany 47°52N 8°0E **77** H3
Feldberg Mecklenburg-Vorpommern,
　Germany 53°20N 13°26E **76** B9
Feldkirch Austria 47°15N 9°37E **78** D2
Feldkirchen Austria 46°44N 14°6E **78** E7
Félicité Seychelles 4°19S 55°52E **141** b
Felipe Carrillo Puerto
　Mexico 19°38N 88°3W **181** D7
Felixburg Zimbabwe 19°29S 30°51E **145** A5
Felixlândia Brazil 18°47S 44°55W **191** A2
Felixstowe U.K. 51°58N 1°23E **67** F9
Felletin France 45°53N 2°11E **72** C6
Fellingsbro Sweden 59°26N 15°37E **62** E9
Fellsmere U.S.A. 27°46N 80°36W **179** H9
Felton U.S.A. 37°3N 122°4W **170** H4
Feltre Italy 46°1N 11°54E **93** B8
Femer Bælt = Fehmarn Bælt
　Europe 54°35N 11°20E **63** K5
Femø Denmark 54°58N 11°33E **63** K5
Femunden Norway 62°10N 11°53E **60** E14
Femundsmarka △
　Norway 62°18N 12°6E **60** E15
Fen He → China 35°36N 110°42E **114** G6
Fene Spain 43°27N 8°9W **88** B2
Fenelon Falls Canada 44°32N 78°45W **174** B6
Fener Burnu Turkey 36°58N 27°18E **99** E9
Feng Xian Jiangsu,
　China 34°43N 116°35E **114** G9
Feng Xian Shaanxi,
　China 33°54N 106°40E **114** H4
Fengari Greece 40°25N 25°32E **97** F9
Fengcheng Jiangxi,
　China 28°12N 115°48E **117** C10
Fengcheng Liaoning,
　China 40°28N 124°5E **115** D13
Fengdu China 29°55N 107°38E **116** C6
Fengfeng China 36°28N 114°8E **114** F8
Fenggang China 27°57N 107°47E **116** D6
Fenghua China 29°40N 121°25E **117** C13
Fenghuang China 27°57N 109°29E **116** D7

Fengjie China 31°3N 109°31E **116** B7
Fengkai China 23°24N 111°30E **117** F8
Fengkang Taiwan 22°12N 120°41E **117** F13
Fengle China 31°29N 112°29E **117** B9
Fenglin Taiwan 23°45N 121°26E **117** F13
Fengning China 41°10N 116°33E **114** D9
Fengqing China 24°38N 99°55E **116** E2
Fengqiu China 35°2N 114°25E **114** G8
Fengrun China 39°48N 118°8E **115** E10
Fengshan Guangxi Zhuangzu,
　China 24°39N 109°15E **116** E7
Fengshan Guangxi Zhuangzu,
　China 24°31N 107°3E **116** E6
Fengshan Taiwan 22°38N 120°21E **117** F13
Fengshun China 23°46N 116°10E **117** F11
Fengtai China 32°50N 116°40E **117** A11
Fengxiang China 34°29N 107°25E **114** G4
Fengxin China 28°41N 115°18E **117** C10
Fengyang China 32°51N 117°29E **117** A11
Fengyi China 25°37N 100°20E **116** E3
Fengyüan Taiwan 24°15N 120°35E **117** E13
Feno, C. de France 41°58N 8°33E **73** G12
Fenoarivo Atsinanana
　Madag. 17°22S 49°25E **141** H9
Fens, The U.K. 52°38N 0°2E **66** E7
Fensmark Denmark 55°17N 11°48E **63** J5
Fenton U.S.A. 42°48N 83°42W **173** D12
Fenxi China 36°40N 111°31E **114** F6
Fenyang China 37°18N 111°48E **114** F6
Fenyi China 27°45N 114°47E **117** D10
Feodosiya Ukraine 45°2N 35°16E **85** K8
Fer, C. de Algeria 37°3N 7°10E **136** A5
Ferbane Ireland 53°16N 7°50W **64** C4
Ferdows Iran 33°58N 58°2E **129** C8
Fère-Champenoise
　France 48°45N 3°59E **71** D10
Fère-en-Tardenois
　France 49°10N 3°30E **71** C10
Ferentino Italy 41°42N 13°15E **93** G10
Feres Greece 40°53N 26°10E **97** F10
Ferfer Somalia 5°4N 45°9E **131** F4
Fergana = Farg'ona
　Uzbekistan 40°23N 71°19E **109** D8
Fergana Range Asia 40°50N 73°0E **109** D8
Fergus Canada 43°43N 80°24W **174** C4
Fergus Falls U.S.A. 46°17N 96°4W **172** B5
Fériana Tunisia 34°59N 8°33E **136** B5
Feričanci Croatia 45°32N 18°0E **80** E2
Ferihegy, Budapest ✠ (BUD)
　Hungary 47°26N 19°14E **80** C4
Ferizaj Kosovo 42°23N 21°10E **96** D5
Ferkane Algeria 34°37N 7°26E **136** B5
Ferkéssédougou Ivory C. 9°35N 5°6W **138** D3
Ferlach Austria 46°32N 14°18E **78** E7
Ferland Canada 50°19N 88°27W **164** B2
Ferlo, Vallée du
　Senegal 15°15N 14°15W **138** B2
Ferlo-Nord △ Senegal 15°43N 14°0W **138** B2
Ferlo-Sud △ Senegal 15°43N 14°0W **138** B2
Fermanagh □ U.K. 54°21N 7°40W **64** B4
Fermo Italy 43°9N 13°43E **93** E10
Fermont Canada 52°47N 67°5W **165** B6
Fermoselle Spain 41°19N 6°27W **88** D4
Fermoy Ireland 52°9N 8°16W **64** D3
Fernán Núñez Spain 37°40N 4°44W **89** H6
Fernández Argentina 27°55S 63°50W **190** B3
Fernandina Beach
　U.S.A. 30°40N 81°27W **178** E8
Fernando de Noronha
　Brazil 4°0S 33°10W **187** D12
Fernando Póo = Bioko
　Eq. Guin. 3°30N 8°40E **139** E6
Ferndale Canada 44°58N 81°17W **174** B3
Ferndale U.S.A. 48°51N 122°36W **170** B4
Fernie Canada 49°30N 115°5W **162** D5
Fernlees Australia 23°51S 148°7E **150** C4
Fernley U.S.A. 39°36N 119°15W **168** G4
Fernwood U.S.A. 43°16N 73°38W **175** C11
Feroke India 11°9N 75°46E **127** J2
Ferozepore = Firozpur
　India 30°55N 74°40E **124** D6
Ferrandina Italy 40°29N 16°27E **95** B9
Ferrara Italy 44°50N 11°35E **93** D8
Ferrato, C. Italy 39°18N 9°38E **94** C2
Ferreira do Alentejo
　Portugal 38°4N 8°6W **89** G2
Ferreñafe Peru 6°42S 79°50W **188** B2
Ferreries Spain 39°59N 4°1E **100** B11
Ferret, C. France 44°38N 1°15W **72** D2
Ferrette France 47°30N 7°20E **71** E14
Ferriday U.S.A. 31°38N 91°33W **176** F9
Ferrières France 48°5N 2°48E **71** D9
Ferrières Italy 44°40N 9°30E **92** D6
Ferro, Capo Italy 41°9N 9°31E **94** A2
Ferrol Spain 43°29N 8°15W **88** B2
Ferrol, Pen. de Peru 9°10S 78°35W **188** B2
Ferron U.S.A. 39°5N 111°8W **168** G8
Ferros Brazil 19°14S 43°2W **191** A2
Ferrutx, C. de Spain 39°47N 3°21E **100** B10
Ferry Pass U.S.A. 30°31N 87°13W **179** E2
Ferryland Canada 47°2N 52°53W **165** C9
Fertile U.S.A. 47°32N 96°17W **172** B5
Fertő-Hanság △
　Hungary 47°25N 16°50E **80** C1
Fertőszentmiklós
　Hungary 47°35N 16°53E **80** C1
Fès Morocco 34°0N 5°0W **136** B3
Fès □ Morocco 34°1N 5°0W **136** B3
Fessenden U.S.A. 47°39N 99°38W **172** B4
Festus U.S.A. 38°13N 90°24W **172** F8
Fetě Bowé Senegal 14°56N 13°30W **138** C2
Fethiye Turkey 36°36N 29°6E **99** E11
Fethiye Körfezi Turkey 36°40N 28°50E **99** E11
Fetlar U.K. 60°36N 0°52W **65** A8
Fetsund Norway 59°54N 11°10E **63** D6
Fetești Romania 44°22N 27°51E **81** F12
Feuilles → Canada 58°47N 70°4W **161** F17
Feurs France 45°45N 4°13E **73** C8
Feyzābād Afghan. 37°7N 70°33E **109** E8
Fez = Fès Morocco 34°0N 5°0W **136** B3
Fezzan Libya 27°0N 13°0E **135** C8
Fiambalá Argentina 27°45S 67°37W **190** B2
Fianarantsoa Madag. 21°26S 47°5E **141** J9
Fichtelgebirge Germany 50°9N 11°55E **77** E7
Fichtelgebirge = Germany 50°8N 12°0E **77** E8
Ficksburg S. Africa 28°51S 27°53E **145** D4
Fidenza Italy 44°52N 10°3E **92** D7
Fiditi Nigeria 7°45N 3°53E **139** D5
Field → Australia 23°48N 138°0E **150** C2
Field I. Australia 12°5S 132°23E **148** B5
Fieni Romania 45°8N 25°25E **81** E10

Fier Albania 40°43N 19°33E **96** F3
Fierzë Albania 42°15N 20°1E **96** D4
Fife □ U.K. 56°16N 3°1W **65** E5
Fife Ness U.K. 56°17N 2°35W **65** E6
Fifth Cataract Sudan 18°22N 33°50E **137** D3
Figari France 41°29N 9°7E **73** G13
Figeac France 44°37N 2°2E **72** D6
Figeholm Sweden 57°22N 16°33E **63** G10
Figline Valdarno Italy 43°37N 11°28E **93** E8
Figtree Zimbabwe 20°22S 28°20E **143** G2
Figueira Castelo Rodrigo
　Portugal 40°57N 6°58W **88** E4
Figueira da Foz Portugal 40°7N 8°54W **88** E2
Figueiró dos Vinhos
　Portugal 39°55N 8°16W **88** F2
Figueres Spain 42°18N 2°58E **90** C7
Figuig Morocco 32°5N 1°11W **136** B3
Fiji ■ Pac. Oc. 17°20S 179°0E **154** a
Fika Nigeria 11°15N 11°13E **139** C7
Filabres, Sierra de los
　Spain 37°13N 2°20W **89** H8
Filabus Zimbabwe 20°34S 29°20E **145** B4
Filadélfia Brazil 7°21S 47°30W **189** B1
Filadelfia Italy 38°47N 16°17E **95** D9
Filadélfia Paraguay 22°21S 60°2W **190** A3
Fil'akovo Slovak Rep. 48°17N 19°50E **79** C12
Filchner Ice Shelf
　Antarctica 79°0S 40°0W **55** D1
Filey U.K. 54°12N 0°18W **66** C7
Filey B. U.K. 54°12N 0°15W **66** C7
Filfla Malta 35°47N 14°24E **101** D1
Filiași Romania 44°32N 23°31E **81** F8
Filiates Greece 39°38N 20°16E **98** B2
Filiatra Greece 37°9N 21°35E **98** D3
Filicudi Italy 38°35N 14°33E **95** D7
Filingué Niger 14°21N 3°22E **139** C5
Filiouri = Lissos →
　Greece 41°15N 25°40E **97** E9
Filipiada Greece 39°12N 20°53E **98** B2
Filipstad Sweden 59°43N 14°9E **62** E8
Filisur Switz. 46°41N 9°40E **77** J5
Filitosa France 41°45N 8°52E **73** G12
Fillmore Calif., U.S.A. 34°24N 118°55W **171** L8
Fillmore Utah, U.S.A. 38°58N 112°20W **168** G7
Filotio Greece 37°3N 25°30E **99** D7
Filottrano Italy 43°26N 13°21E **93** E10
Filyos Çayı → Turkey 41°35N 32°10E **104** B5
Fimbul Ice Shelf S. Ocean 69°30S 1°0W **55** C2
Fina △ Mali 13°15N 8°46W **138** C3
Finale Emília Italy 44°50N 11°18E **93** D8
Finale Ligure Italy 44°10N 8°20E **92** D5
Fiñana Spain 37°10N 2°50W **89** H8
Finch Canada 45°11N 75°7W **175** A9
Finch Hatton Australia 20°25S 148°39E **150** b
Findhorn → U.K. 57°38N 3°38W **65** D5
Findlay U.S.A. 41°2N 83°39W **173** E12
Fine U.S.A. 44°14N 75°8W **175** B9
Fingal □ Ireland 53°29N 6°14W **64** C5
Finger L. Canada 53°33N 93°30W **164** B1
Finger Lakes U.S.A. 42°40N 76°30W **175** D8
Fingoè Mozam. 15°55S 31°50E **143** F3
Finike Turkey 36°21N 30°10E **99** E12
Finike Körfezi Turkey 36°17N 30°16E **99** E12
Finiq Albania 39°54N 20°3E **96** G4
Finistère □ France 48°20N 4°0W **70** D3
Finisterre = Fisterra
　Spain 42°54N 9°16W **88** C1
Finisterre, C. = Fisterra, C.
　Spain 42°50N 9°19W **88** C1
Finke Australia 25°34S 134°35E **150** D1
Finke Gorge △
　Australia 24°8S 132°49E **148** D5
Finland ■ Europe 63°0N 27°0E **60** E22
Finland, G. of Europe 60°0N 26°0E **63** B22
Finlay → Canada 57°0N 125°10W **162** B3
Finley Australia 35°38S 145°35E **153** C6
Finley U.S.A. 47°31N 97°50W **172** B5
Finn → Ireland 54°51N 7°28W **64** B4
Finnerödja Sweden 58°57N 14°24E **63** F8
Finnigan, Mt.
　Australia 15°49S 145°17E **150** B4
Finniss, C. Australia 33°8S 134°51E **151** E1
Finnmark Norway 69°37N 23°57E **60** B20
Finnsnes Norway 69°14N 18°0E **60** B18
Finspång Sweden 58°43N 15°47E **63** F9
Finsteraarhorn Switz. 46°31N 8°10E **77** J4
Finsterwalde Germany 51°37N 13°42E **76** D9
Fiora → Italy 42°20N 11°34E **93** F8
Fiordland △ N.Z. 45°46S 167°0E **155** F2
Fiorenzuola d'Arda Italy 44°56N 9°55E **92** D6
Fiq Syria 32°46N 35°41E **130** C4
Firat = Furāt, Nahr al →
　Asia 31°0N 47°25E **128** D5
Fire Island △ U.S.A. 40°38N 73°8W **175** F11
Firebag → Canada 57°45N 111°21W **163** B6
Firebaugh U.S.A. 36°52N 120°27W **170** J6
Firedrake L. Canada 61°25N 104°30W **163** A8
Firenze Italy 43°46N 11°15E **93** E8
Firenze Amerigo Vespucci ✠
　(FLR) Italy 43°49N 11°13E **93** E8
Firenze Pisa ✠ (PSA)
　Italy 43°40N 10°22E **92** E7
Firenzuola Italy 44°7N 11°23E **93** D8
Firk, Sha'ib → Iraq 30°59N 44°34E **128** D5
Firmi France 44°33N 2°19E **72** D6
Firminy France 45°23N 4°18E **73** C8
Firozabad India 27°10N 78°25E **125** F8
Firozpur India 30°55N 74°40E **124** D6
Firozpur-Jhirka India 27°48N 76°57E **124** F7
Fīrūzābād Iran 28°52N 52°35E **129** D7
Fīrūzkūh Iran 35°50N 52°50E **129** C7
Firvale Canada 52°27N 126°13W **162** C3
Fish → Namibia 28°7S 17°10E **144** D2
Fish → S. Africa 31°30S 20°16E **144** D3
Fish River Canyon
　Namibia 27°40S 17°35E **144** C2
Fisheating Cr. →
　U.S.A. 26°57N 81°7W **179** H8
Fisher B. Canada 51°35N 97°13W **163** C9
Fishers I. U.S.A. 41°15N 72°0W **175** E13
Fishguard U.K. 52°0N 4°58W **67** E3
Fishing L. Canada 52°10N 95°24W **163** C9
Fishkill U.S.A. 41°32N 73°54W **175** E11
Fiskardo Greece 38°28N 20°37E **98** C2
Fiskenæsset = Qeqertarsuatsiaat
　Greenland 63°5N 50°45W **57** E5
Fismes France 49°20N 3°40E **71** C10
Fisterra Spain 42°50N 9°19W **88** C1
Fisterra, C. Spain 42°50N 9°19W **88** C1
Fitéri Romania 45°8N 25°29E **81** E10

Flores Azores 39°26N 31°13W 1...
Flores Brazil 7°51S 37°59W 18...
Flores Guatemala 16°59N 89°50W 18...
Flores Indonesia 8°35S 121°0E 11...
Flores I. Canada 49°20N 126°10W 16...
Floresta Brazil 8°40S 37°26W 18...
Florești Moldova 47°53N 28°17E 81...
Floresville U.S.A. 29°8N 98°10W 17...
Floriano Brazil 6°50S 43°0W 18...
Florianópolis Brazil 27°30S 48°30W 19...
Florida Cuba 21°32N 78°14W 18...
Florida Uruguay 34°7S 56°10W 19...
Florida □ Uruguay 34°0S 56°0W 19...
Florida □ U.S.A. 28°0N 82°0W 17...
Florida, Straits of U.S.A. 25°0N 80°0W 18...
Florida B. U.S.A. 25°0N 80°45W 18...
Florida City U.S.A. 25°27N 80°29W 17...
Florida Keys U.S.A. 24°40N 81°0W 17...
Floridia Italy 37°5N 15°9E 9...
Florina Greece 40°48N 21°26E 9...
Florissant U.S.A. 38°47N 90°19W 17...
Florø Norway 61°35N 5°1E 6...
Flower Station Canada 45°10N 76°22W 17...
Flowerpot I. Canada 45°18N 81°38W 17...
Floydada U.S.A. 33°59N 101°20W 17...
Fluk Indonesia 1°42S 127°44E 11...
Flúmen → Spain 41°43N 0°9W 9...
Flumendosa → Italy 39°26N 9°37E 9...
Fluminimaggiore Italy 39°26N 8°30E 9...
Flushing = Vlissingen
　Neths. 51°26N 3°34E 6...
Fluvià → Spain 42°12N 3°7E 9...
Fly → Papua N.G. 8°25S 143°0E 14...
Flying Fish, C.
　Antarctica 72°6S 102°29W 5...
Foam Lake Canada 51°40N 103°32W 16...
Foča Bos.-H. 43°31N 18°47E 9...
Foça Turkey 38°39N 26°46E 9...
Fochabers U.K. 57°37N 3°6W 6...
Focșani Romania 45°41N 27°15E 8...
Fodécontéa Guinea 9°35N 12°30W 13...
Fogang China 23°52N 113°30E 11...
Foggáret el Arab Algeria 27°13N 2°49E 13...
Foggáret ez Zoua Algeria 27°20N 2°53E 13...
Fóggia Italy 41°27N 15°34E 9...
Foglia → Italy 43°55N 12°54E 9...
Fogo Canada 49°43N 54°17W 16...
Fogo C. Verde Is. 15°5N 24°20W 1...
Fogo I. Canada 49°40N 54°5W 16...
Fohnsdorf Austria 47°12N 14°40E 7...
Föhr Germany 54°43N 8°30E 7...
Fóia Portugal 37°19N 8°37W 8...
Foix France 42°58N 1°38E 7...
Fojnica Bos.-H. 43°59N 17°51E 8...
Fokida Greece 38°30N 22°15E 9...
Fokino Russia 53°30N 34°22E 8...
Fokku Nigeria 11°36N 4°32E 13...
Folda Nord-Trøndelag,
　Norway 64°32N 10°30E 6...
Folda Nordland, Norway 67°38N 14°50E 6...
Földeák Hungary 46°19N 20°30E 8...
Folégandros Greece 36°40N 24°55E 9...
Foley Botswana 21°34S 27°21E 14...
Foley U.S.A. 30°24N 87°41W 17...
Foley I. Canada 68°30N 75°10W 16...
Foleyet Canada 48°15N 82°25W 16...
Folgefonna Norway 60°3N 6°23E 6...
Foligno Italy 42°57N 12°42E 9...
Folkestone U.K. 51°5N 1°12E 6...
Folkston U.S.A. 30°50N 82°0W 17...
Follansbee U.S.A. 40°19N 80°35W 17...
Follónica Italy 42°55N 10°45E 9...
Follónica, G. di Italy 42°54N 10°43E 9...
Folsom U.S.A. 38°40N 121°9W 17...
Folsom L. U.S.A. 38°42N 121°9W 17...
Foltești Romania 45°45N 28°3E 8...
Fomboni Comoros Is. 12°18S 43°46E 1...
Fombuena Spain 59°19N 107°12W 16...
Fond-du-Lac Canada 59°17N 106°0W 16...
Fond du Lac U.S.A. 43°47N 88°27W 17...
Fond-du-Lac → Canada 59°17N 106°0W 16...
Fonda U.S.A. 42°57N 74°22W 17...
Fondi Italy 41°21N 13°25E 9...
Fonfría Spain 41°37N 6°9W 8...
Fongafale Tuvalu 8°31S 179°13E 14...
Fonni Italy 40°7N 9°15E 9...
Fonsagrada = A Fonsagrada
　Spain 43°8N 7°4W 8...
Fonseca, G. de
　Cent. Amer. 13°10N 87°40W 18...
Font-Romeu-Odeillo-Via
　France 42°31N 2°3E 7...
Fontaine-Française
　France 47°32N 5°21E 7...
Fontainebleau France 48°24N 2°40E 7...
Fontana U.S.A. 34°6N 117°26W 17...
Fontana, L. Argentina 44°55S 71°30W 19...
Fontas → Canada 58°14N 121°48W 16...
Fonte Boa Brazil 2°33S 66°0W 13...
Fontem Cameroon 5°32N 9°52E 13...
Fontenay-le-Comte
　France 46°28N 0°48W 7...
Fontenelle Res. U.S.A. 42°1N 110°3W 16...
Fontur Iceland 66°23N 14°32W 6...
Fonyód Hungary 46°44N 17°33E 8...
Foochow = Fuzhou
　China 26°5N 119°16E 117...
Foping China 33°41N 108°0E 11...
Foraker, Mt. U.S.A. 62°58N 151°24W 16...
Forbach France 49°10N 6°52E 7...
Forbes Australia 33°22S 148°5E 15...
Forbesganj India 26°17N 87°18E 12...
Forcados Nigeria 5°26N 5°26E 13...
Forcados → Nigeria 5°25N 5°19E 13...
Forcalquier France 43°58N 5°47E 7...
Forchheim Germany 49°43N 11°2E 7...
Ford City Calif., U.S.A. 35°9N 119°27W 17...
Ford City Pa., U.S.A. 40°46N 79°32W 17...
Førde Norway 61°27N 5°53E 6...
Ford's Bridge Australia 29°41S 145°29E 15...
Fordyce U.S.A. 33°49N 92°25W 17...
Forécariah Guinea 9°28N 13°10W 13...
Forel, Mt. Greenland 66°52N 36°55W 5...
Foremost Canada 49°26N 111°34W 16...
Forest Canada 43°6N 82°0W 17...
Forest U.S.A. 32°22N 89°29W 17...
Forest Acres U.S.A. 34°1N 80°58W 17...
Forest City Iowa, U.S.A. 43°16N 93°39W 17...
Forest City N.C.,
　U.S.A. 35°20N 81°52W 17...
Forest City Pa., U.S.A. 41°39N 75°28W 17...

st Grove U.S.A. 45°31N 123°7W 170 E3
t Park U.S.A. 33°7N 84°22W 178 B5
stburg Canada 52°35N 112°1W 162 C6
ste Casentinesi-Monte
 alterona-Campigna △
 aly 43°50N 11°48E 93 E8
sthill U.S.A. 39°1N 120°49W 170 F6
tier Park Australia 43°0S 148°0E 151 G4
stville Canada 48°48N 69°2W 165 C6
stville Calif.,
 U.S.A. 38°28N 122°54W 170 G4
stville N.Y., U.S.A. 42°28N 79°10W 174 D5
t d'Orient □ France 45°16N 4°25E 71 D11
ez, Mts. du France 45°40N 3°50E 72 C7
ar U.K. 56°39N 2°53W 65 E6
llon △ Canada 48°46N 64°12W 165 C7
ks U.S.A. 47°57N 124°23W 170 C2
i Italy 44°13N 12°3E 93 D9
i-Cesena □ Italy 44°10N 12°20E 93 D9
man U.S.A. 46°N 97°38W 172 B5
mazza Italy 46°22N 8°26E 92 B5
mby Pt. U.K. 53°33N 3°6W 66 D4
mentera Spain 38°43N 1°27E 100 C7
mentor, C. de Spain 39°58N 3°13E 100 B10
mentor, Pen. de
 xain 39°56N 3°11E 100 B10
ner Yugoslav Republic of
 Macedonia = Macedonia ■
 urope 41°53N 21°40E 96 E5
nia Italy 41°15N 13°23E 94 A6
niga Brazil 20°27S 45°25W 189 E1
nigine Italy 44°37N 10°51E 92 D7
nosa = Taiwan ■
 sia 23°30N 121°0E 117 F13
nosa Argentina 26°15S 58°10W 190 B4
nosa Brazil 15°32S 47°20W 189 D1
nosa □ Argentina 25°0S 60°0W 190 B4
nosa, Serra Brazil 12°0S 55°0W 187 F8
enya 2°45S 40°20E 142 C5
nosa do Rio Prêto
 ortugal 11°2S 45°3W 189 C1
nos de Algodres
 ortugal 40°38N 7°32W 88 E3
novo di Taro Italy 44°42N 10°6E 92 D7
ollhogna △ Norway 62°39N 10°41E 60 E14
oyar ☑ Atl. Oc. 62°0N 7°0W 60 F9
res U.K. 57°37N 3°37W 65 D5
rest Vic., Australia 38°33S 143°47E 152 E5
rest W. Austral.,
 ustralia 30°51S 128°6E 149 F4
rest, Mt. Australia 24°48S 127°45E 149 D4
rest City U.S.A. 35°1N 90°47W 177 D9
s Sweden 60°14N 16°20E 62 D10
sayth Australia 18°33S 143°34E 150 B3
serum Sweden 57°42N 14°30E 63 G8
shaga Sweden 59°33N 13°29E 62 E7
slöv Sweden 56°21N 12°48E 63 H6
ssa Finland 63°16N 17°41E 62 B11
ssa Finland 60°49N 23°38E 84 B2
st Germany 48°8N 14°37E 76 D10
ster Australia 32°12S 152°31E 153 E10
rvik Sweden 58°35N 14°26E 63 F9
syth Ga., U.S.A. 33°2N 83°56W 178 B6
syth Mont.,
 .A. 46°16N 106°41W 168 C10
yth I. N.Z. 40°58S 174°5E 155 A9
t Abbas Pakistan 29°12N 72°52E 124 E5
t Albany Canada 52°15N 81°35W 164 B3
anada 54°20N 114°45W 162 C6
t Augustus U.S.A. 57°9N 4°42W 65 D4
t Beaufort S. Africa 32°46S 26°40E 144 D4
t Benton U.S.A. 47°49N 110°40W 168 G2
t Bragg U.S.A. 39°26N 123°48W 168 G2
t Bridger U.S.A. 41°19N 110°23W 168 F8
t Caroline △ U.S.A. 30°30N 87°11W 178 E18
t Chipewyan
 anada 58°42N 111°8W 163 B6
t Clatsop = Lewis and Clark △
 .S.A. 46°8N 123°53W 170 D3
t Collins U.S.A. 40°35N 105°5W 168 F11
t-Coulonge Canada 45°50N 76°45W 164 C4
t Covington
 .A. 44°59N 74°29W 175 B10
t Dauphin = Taolanaro
 Madag. 25°2S 47°0E 141 K9
t Davis Ala., U.S.A. 32°25N 85°43W 178 C4
t Davis Tex., U.S.A. 30°35N 103°54W 176 F3
t-de-France
 artinique 14°36N 61°5W 182 c
t Defiance U.S.A. 35°45N 109°5W 169 J9
t Dodge U.S.A. 42°30N 94°11W 172 D6
t Drum U.S.A. 27°32N 80°48W 179 M9
t Edward U.S.A. 43°16N 73°35W 175 C11
t Erie Canada 42°54N 78°56W 174 D6
t Fairfield U.S.A. 46°46N 67°50W 173 B20
t Frances Canada 48°36N 93°24W 163 D10
t Franklin = Déline
 anada 65°11N 123°25W 160 D7
t Frederica △
 .S.A. 31°13N 81°23W 178 D8
t Gaines U.S.A. 31°36N 85°3W 178 D4
t Garland U.S.A. 37°26N 105°26W 169 H11
t George = Chisasibi
 anada 53°50N 79°0W 164 B4
t Good Hope
 anada 66°14N 128°40W 160 D6
t Hancock U.S.A. 31°18N 105°51W 176 F2
t Hope = Eabametoong
 anada 51°30N 88°0W 164 B2
t Irwin U.S.A. 35°16N 116°41W 171 K10
t Kent U.S.A. 45°41N 68°36W 173 B19
t Klamath U.S.A. 42°42N 122°0W 168 D3
t Laramie U.S.A. 42°13N 104°31W 168 F2
t Lauderdale U.S.A. 26°7N 80°8W 179 J9
t Liard Canada 60°14N 123°30W 162 A4
t Liberté Haiti 19°42N 71°51E 183 C5
t Lupton U.S.A. 40°5N 104°49W 168 F2
t MacKay Canada 57°12N 111°41W 162 B6
t Macleod Canada 49°45N 113°30W 162 D6
t McMurray
 anada 56°44N 111°7W 162 B6
t McPherson
 anada 67°30N 134°55W 160 D5
t Madison U.S.A. 40°38N 91°27W 172 E8
t Matanzas △
 .A. 29°43N 81°14W 178 E8
t Meade U.S.A. 27°45N 81°48W 179 H8
t Mitchell U.S.A. 32°20N 85°1W 178 C4

Fort Morgan U.S.A. 40°15N 103°48W 168 F12
Fort Myers U.S.A. 26°39N 81°52W 179 J8
Fort Myers Beach
 U.S.A. 26°26N 81°52W 179 J8
Fort Myers Villas
 U.S.A. 26°33N 81°52W 179 J8
Fort Nelson Canada 58°50N 122°44W 162 B4
Fort Nelson → Canada 59°32N 124°0W 162 B4
Fort Norman = Tulita
 Canada 64°57N 125°30W 160 E6
Fort Ogden U.S.A. 27°5N 81°57W 179 H8
Fort Payne U.S.A. 34°26N 85°43W 177 D12
Fort Peck U.S.A. 48°1N 106°27W 168 B10
Fort Peck Dam U.S.A. 48°0N 106°26W 168 C10
Fort Peck L. U.S.A. 48°0N 106°26W 168 C10
Fort Pierce U.S.A. 27°27N 80°20W 179 M9
Fort Pierre U.S.A. 44°21N 100°22W 172 C3
Fort Plain U.S.A. 42°56N 74°37W 175 D10
Fort Portal Uganda 0°40N 30°20E 142 B3
Fort Providence
 Canada 61°3N 117°40W 162 A5
Fort Pulaski △ U.S.A. 32°2N 80°56W 178 C9
Fort Qu'Appelle
 Canada 50°45N 103°50W 163 C8
Fort Resolution
 Canada 61°10N 113°40W 162 A6
Fort Rixon Zimbabwe 20°2S 29°17E 143 G2
Fort Ross U.S.A. 38°32N 123°13W 170 G3
Fort Rupert = Waskaganish
 Canada 51°30N 78°40W 164 B4
Fort St. James Canada 54°30N 124°10W 162 C4
Fort St. John Canada 56°15N 120°50W 162 B4
Fort Saskatchewan
 Canada 53°40N 113°15W 162 C6
Fort Scott U.S.A. 37°50N 94°42W 172 G6
Fort Severn Canada 56°0N 87°40W 164 A2
Fort Shevchenko
 Kazakhstan 44°35N 50°23E 87 H10
Fort Simpson Canada 61°45N 121°15W 162 A4
Fort Smith Canada 60°0N 111°51W 162 B6
Fort Smith U.S.A. 35°23N 94°25W 176 D7
Fort Stockton U.S.A. 30°53N 102°53W 176 F3
Fort Sumner U.S.A. 34°28N 104°15W 169 J11
Fort Thompson U.S.A. 44°3N 99°26W 172 C4
Fort Union △ U.S.A. 35°54N 105°1W 169 J11
Fort Valley U.S.A. 32°33N 83°53W 178 C6
Fort Vermilion Canada 58°24N 116°0W 162 B5
Fort Walton Beach
 U.S.A. 30°25N 86°36W 179 E3
Fort Ware Canada 57°26N 125°41W 162 B3
Fort Wayne U.S.A. 41°4N 85°9W 173 E11
Fort White U.S.A. 29°55N 82°43W 178 F7
Fort William U.K. 56°49N 5°7W 65 E3
Fort Worth U.S.A. 32°43N 97°19W 176 E6
Fort Yates U.S.A. 46°5N 100°38W 172 B4
Fort Yukon U.S.A. 66°34N 145°16W 160 D2
Fortaleza Bolivia 12°6S 66°49W 188 C4
Fortaleza Brazil 3°45S 38°35W 189 A3
Forteau Canada 51°28N 56°58W 165 B8
Fortescue → Australia 21°0S 116°4E 148 D2
Fortescue River Roadhouse
 Australia 21°17S 116°8E 148 D2
Forth → U.K. 56°9N 3°50W 65 E5
Forth, Firth of U.K. 56°5N 2°55W 65 E6
Forthassa Rharbia
 Algeria 32°52N 1°18W 136 B3
Fortín Uno Argentina 38°50S 65°18W 192 A3
Fortore → Italy 41°55N 15°17E 93 G12
Fortrose N.Z. 46°38S 168°45E 155 G3
Fortrose U.K. 57°35N 4°9W 65 D4
Fortuna Spain 38°11N 1°7W 91 G3
Fortuna Calif., U.S.A. 40°36N 124°9W 168 F1
Fortuna N. Dak.,
 U.S.A. 48°55N 103°47W 172 A2
Fortune Canada 47°4N 55°50W 165 C8
Fortune B. Canada 47°30N 55°22W 165 C8
Forūr Iran 26°17N 54°32E 129 E7
Fos-sur-Mer France 43°26N 4°56E 73 E8
Fosen Norway 63°50N 10°20E 60 E14
Foshan China 23°3N 113°9E 117 F9
Fosnavåg Norway 62°22N 5°38E 60 E11
Foso Ghana 5°43N 1°15W 139 D4
Fossano Italy 44°33N 7°43E 92 D4
Fossil U.S.A. 45°0N 120°9W 168 D3
Fossil Butte △ U.S.A. 41°50N 110°27W 168 F8
Fossombrone Italy 43°41N 12°48E 93 E9
Foster Australia 38°40S 146°15E 153 F7
Foster → Canada 55°47N 105°49W 163 B7
Fosters Ra. Australia 21°35S 133°48E 150 C1
Fostoria U.S.A. 41°10N 83°25W 173 E12
Fouesnant France 47°53N 4°1W 70 E2
Fougères France 48°21N 1°14W 70 D5
Foul Pt. Sri Lanka 8°35N 81°18E 127 K5
Foula U.K. 60°10N 2°5W 65 A6
Foulalaba Mali 10°40N 7°20W 138 C3
Foulness I. U.K. 51°36N 0°55E 67 F8
Foulwind, C. N.Z. 41°45S 171°28E 155 B6
Foum Zguid Morocco 30°2N 6°59W 136 B2
Foumban Cameroon 5°45N 10°50E 139 D7
Foumbot Cameroon 5°31N 10°28E 139 D7
Foumbouni Comoros Is. 11°51S 43°29E 141 a
Fourmirate Algeria 27°30N 13°0E 136 C3
Foundiougne Senegal 14°5N 16°32W 138 C1
Fountain Colo.,
 U.S.A. 38°41N 104°42W 168 G11
Fountain Fla., U.S.A. 30°29N 85°25W 178 F4
Fountain Hills U.S.A. 33°37N 111°43W 169 K8
Fountain Springs
 U.S.A. 35°54N 118°51W 171 K8
Four Mountains, Is. of
 U.S.A. 53°0N 170°0W 166 E5
Fourchambault France 47°2N 3°3E 71 E10
Fouriesburg S. Africa 28°38S 28°14E 145 C4
Fourmies France 50°1N 4°2E 71 B11
Fourna Greece 39°3N 21°52E 98 B3
Fourni Greece 37°36N 26°32E 99 D8
Fours France 46°50N 3°42E 71 F10
Fourth Cataract Sudan 18°47N 32°3E 135 E12
Fouta Djalon Guinea 11°20N 12°10W 138 C2
Foux, Cap-à- Haiti 19°43N 73°27W 183 C5
Foveaux Str. N.Z. 46°42S 168°10E 155 G2
Fowey U.K. 50°20N 4°39W 67 G3
Fowler Calif., U.S.A. 36°38N 119°41W 170 J7
Fowler Colo., U.S.A. 38°8N 104°2W 168 G11
Fowler, Pt. Australia 32°2S 132°32E 149 F5
Fowlers B. Australia 31°59S 132°34E 149 F5
Fowman Iran 37°13N 49°19E 105 D13
Fox → Canada 56°3N 93°18W 163 B10
Fox Creek Canada 54°24N 116°48W 162 C5
Fox Is. U.S.A. 53°0N 168°0W 166 E6
Fox Lake Canada 58°14N 114°31W 162 B6

Fox Valley Canada 50°30N 109°25W 163 C7
Foxboro Canada 44°14N 77°26W 174 B7
Foxboro U.S.A. 42°4N 71°16W 175 D13
Foxdale Australia 20°22S 148°35E 150 b
Foxe Basin Canada 66°0N 77°0W 161 D16
Foxe Chan. Canada 65°0N 80°0W 161 E16
Foxe Pen. Canada 65°0N 76°0W 161 E16
Foxen Sweden 59°25N 11°55E 62 E5
Foxford Ireland 53°59N 9°7W 64 C2
Foxton N.Z. 40°29S 175°18E 154 C4
Foyle, Lough U.K. 55°7N 7°4W 64 A4
Foynes Ireland 52°37N 9°7W 64 D2
Foz Spain 43°33N 7°20W 88 A3
Foz do Cunene Angola 17°15S 11°48E 144 A1
Foz do Gregório Brazil 6°47S 70°44W 188 B3
Foz do Iguaçu Brazil 25°30S 54°30W 191 B5
Fraga Spain 41°32N 0°21E 90 D5
Fraile Muerto Uruguay 32°31S 54°32W 191 C5
Framingham U.S.A. 42°18N 71°24W 175 D13
Frampol Poland 50°41N 22°40E 83 H9
Franca Brazil 20°33S 47°30W 189 E1
Francavilla al Mare
 Italy 42°25N 14°17E 93 F11
Francavilla Fontana
 Italy 40°32N 17°35E 95 B10
France ■ Europe 47°0N 3°0E 59 F6
Frances Australia 36°41S 140°55E 152 D4
Frances → Canada 60°16N 129°10W 162 A3
Frances L. Canada 61°23N 129°30W 162 A3
Franceville Gabon 1°40S 13°32E 140 E2
Franche-Comté □
 France 46°50N 5°55E 71 F12
Francis Case, L. U.S.A. 43°4N 98°34W 172 D4
Francisco Beltrão Brazil 26°5S 53°4W 191 B5
Francisco Ignacio Madero
 Coahuila, Mexico 25°48N 103°18W 180 B4
Francisco Ignacio Madero
 Durango, Mexico 24°26N 104°18W 180 C4
Francisco Ignacio Madero, Presa
 Mexico 28°10N 105°37W 180 B3
Francisco Sá Brazil 16°28S 43°30W 189 D2
Francistown Botswana 21°7S 27°33E 145 B4
Francofonte Italy 37°14N 14°53E 95 E7
François Canada 47°35N 56°45W 165 C8
François L. Canada 54°0N 125°30W 162 C3
Francois Peron △
 Australia 25°42S 113°33E 149 E1
Francs Pk. U.S.A. 43°58N 109°20W 168 E9
Franeker Neths. 53°12N 5°33E 69 A5
Frank Hann △
 Australia 32°52S 120°19E 149 F3
Frankenberg Germany 51°3N 8°48E 76 D4
Frankenhöhe △
 Germany 49°20N 10°25E 77 F6
Frankenwald Germany 50°20N 11°30E 77 E7
Frankenwald △
 Germany 50°15N 11°30E 77 E7
Frankford Canada 44°12N 77°36W 174 B7
Frankfort S. Africa 27°17S 28°30E 145 C4
Frankfort Ind., U.S.A. 40°17N 86°31W 172 E10
Frankfort Kans., U.S.A. 39°42N 96°25W 172 F5
Frankfort Ky., U.S.A. 38°12N 84°52W 173 F11
Frankfort N.Y., U.S.A. 43°2N 75°4W 175 C9
Frankfurt Brandenburg,
 Germany 52°20N 14°32E 76 C10
Frankfurt Hessen, Germany 50°7N 8°41E 77 E4
Frankfurt ✈ (FRA)
 Germany 50°1N 8°34E 77 E4
Fränkische Alb Germany 49°10N 11°23E 77 F7
Fränkische Rezat →
 Germany 49°11N 11°1E 77 F7
Fränkische Saale →
 Germany 50°3N 9°42E 77 E5
Fränkische Schweiz
 Germany 49°50N 11°16E 77 F7
Fränkische Schweiz-Veldensteiner
 Forst △ Germany 49°45N 11°22E 77 F7
Frankland → Australia 35°0S 116°48E 149 G2
Franklin Ga., U.S.A. 33°17N 85°6W 178 B4
Franklin Ky., U.S.A. 36°43N 86°35W 172 G10
Franklin La., U.S.A. 29°48N 91°30W 177 D13
Franklin Mass., U.S.A. 42°5N 71°24W 175 D13
Franklin N.H., U.S.A. 43°27N 71°39W 175 C13
Franklin Nebr., U.S.A. 40°6N 98°57W 172 E4
Franklin Pa., U.S.A. 41°24N 79°50W 174 E5
Franklin Va., U.S.A. 36°41N 76°56W 173 G15
Franklin W. Va.,
 U.S.A. 38°39N 79°20W 173 F14
Franklin B. Canada 69°45N 126°0W 160 D6
Franklin D. Roosevelt L.
 U.S.A. 48°18N 118°9W 168 B4
Franklin-Gordon Wild Rivers △
 Australia 42°19S 145°51E 151 G4
Franklin Harb.
 Australia 33°43S 136°55E 152 B2
Franklin I. Antarctica 76°10S 168°30E 55 D11
Franklin I. Canada 45°24N 80°20W 174 A4
Franklin Mts. Canada 40°25N 115°22W 168 F6
Franklin Mts. N.Z. 45°0N 125°0W 160 D6
Franklin Str. Canada 72°0N 96°0W 160 C12
Franklinton U.S.A. 30°51N 90°9W 177 F9
Franklinville U.S.A. 42°20N 78°27W 174 D6
Franklyn Mt. N.Z. 42°4S 172°42E 155 C7
Frankston Australia 38°8S 145°8E 153 E6
Frånö Sweden 62°51N 17°48E 62 B11
Fransfontein Namibia 20°12S 15°1E 144 B2
Fränsta Sweden 62°30N 16°11E 62 B10
Frantsa Iosifa, Zemlya
 Arctic 82°0N 55°0E 106 A6
Franz Canada 48°25N 84°30W 164 C3
Franz Josef Land = Frantsa Iosifa,
 Zemlya Arctic 82°0N 55°0E 106 A6
Franz Josef Strauss ✈ (MUC)
 Germany 48°21N 11°47E 77 G7
Franzburg Germany 54°11N 12°51E 76 A8
Frascati Italy 41°48N 12°41E 93 G9
Fraser → B.C., Canada 49°7N 123°11W 170 A3
Fraser → Nfld. & L.,
 Canada 56°39N 62°10W 165 A7
Fraser, Mt. Australia 25°35S 118°20W 149 E2
Fraser I. Australia 25°15S 153°10E 151 E5
Fraser Lake Canada 54°0N 124°50W 162 C4
Fraserburg S. Africa 31°55S 21°30E 144 E3
Fraserburgh U.K. 57°42N 2°1W 65 D6
Fraserdale Canada 49°55N 81°37W 164 C3
Frasertown N.Z. 38°58S 177°34E 154 E6
Frashër Albania 40°23N 20°26E 98 D9
Frasne France 46°50N 6°10E 71 F13

Frătești Romania 43°58N 25°58E 81 G10
Frauenfeld Switz. 47°34N 8°54E 77 H4
Fray Bentos Uruguay 33°10S 58°15W 190 C4
Fray Jorge △ Chile 30°42S 71°40W 190 C1
Frazier Downs ○
 Australia 18°48S 121°42E 148 C3
Frechilla Spain 42°8N 4°50W 88 C6
Fredericia Denmark 55°34N 9°45E 63 J3
Frederick Md., U.S.A. 39°25N 77°25W 173 F15
Frederick Okla., U.S.A. 34°23N 99°1W 176 D5
Frederick S. Dak.,
 U.S.A. 45°50N 98°31W 172 C4
Frederick E. Hyde Fjord
 Greenland 83°25N 29°0W 57 A4
Fredericksburg Pa.,
 U.S.A. 40°27N 76°26W 175 F8
Fredericksburg Tex.,
 U.S.A. 30°16N 98°52W 176 F5
Fredericksburg Va.,
 U.S.A. 38°18N 77°28W 173 F15
Fredericktown Mo.,
 U.S.A. 37°34N 90°18W 172 G8
Fredericktown Ohio,
 U.S.A. 40°29N 82°33W 174 F2
Frederico Westphalen
 Brazil 27°22S 53°24W 191 B5
Fredericton Canada 45°57N 66°40W 165 C6
Fredericton Junction
 Canada 45°41N 66°40W 165 C6
Frederikshåb = Paamiut
 Greenland 62°0N 49°43W 57 E6
Frederikshamn = Hamina
 Finland 60°34N 27°12E 84 B4
Frederikshavn Denmark 57°28N 10°31E 63 G4
Frederikssund Denmark 55°50N 12°3E 63 J6
Frederiksted
 U.S. Virgin Is. 17°43N 64°53W 183 C7
Frederiksværk Denmark 55°58N 12°4E 63 J6
Fredonia Ariz., U.S.A. 36°57N 112°32W 169 H7
Fredonia Kans., U.S.A. 37°32N 95°49W 172 G6
Fredonia N.Y., U.S.A. 42°26N 79°20W 174 D5
Fredriksberg Sweden 60°8N 14°23E 62 D8
Fredrikstad Norway 59°13N 10°57E 63 G14
Free State □ S. Africa 28°30S 27°0E 144 C4
Freehold U.S.A. 40°16N 74°17W 175 F10
Freeland U.S.A. 41°1N 75°54W 175 E9
Freels, C., Nfld. & L.,
 Canada 49°15N 53°30W 165 C9
Freels, C., Nfld. & L.,
 Canada 46°37N 53°32W 165 C9
Freeman Calif., U.S.A. 35°35N 117°53W 171 K9
Freeman S. Dak.,
 U.S.A. 43°21N 97°26W 172 D5
Freeport Bahamas 26°30N 78°47W 182 A4
Freeport Fla., U.S.A. 30°30N 86°8W 178 E3
Freeport Ill., U.S.A. 42°17N 89°36W 172 D9
Freeport N.Y., U.S.A. 40°39N 73°35W 175 F11
Freeport Ohio, U.S.A. 40°12N 81°15W 174 F3
Freeport Pa., U.S.A. 40°41N 79°41W 174 F5
Freeport Tex., U.S.A. 28°57N 95°21W 176 G7
Freetown S. Leone 8°30N 13°17W 138 D2
Freeville U.S.A. 42°30N 76°20W 175 D8
Frégate, L. de la
 Canada 53°15N 74°45W 164 B5
Fregenal de la Sierra
 Spain 38°10N 6°39W 89 G4
Fregene Italy 41°51N 12°12E 93 G9
Fregon Australia 26°45S 132°1E 149 E5
Fréhel, C. France 48°40N 2°20W 70 D4
Frei Antarctica 62°30S 58°0W 55 C18
Freiberg Germany 50°55N 13°20E 76 E9
Freiburg = Fribourg
 Switz. 46°49N 7°9E 77 J3
Freiburg Baden-W.,
 Germany 47°59N 7°51E 77 H3
Freiburg Niedersachsen,
 Germany 53°49N 9°16E 76 B5
Freilassing Germany 47°50N 12°58E 77 H8
Freire Chile 38°54S 72°38W 192 A2
Freirina Chile 28°30S 71°10W 190 B1
Freising Germany 48°24N 11°45E 77 G7
Freistadt Austria 48°30N 14°30E 78 C7
Freital Germany 51°1N 13°39E 76 D9
Fréjus France 43°25N 6°44E 73 E10
Fremantle Australia 32°7S 115°47E 149 F2
Fremont Calif., U.S.A. 37°32N 121°57W 170 H4
Fremont Mich., U.S.A. 43°28N 85°57W 173 D11
Fremont Nebr., U.S.A. 41°26N 96°30W 172 E5
Fremont Ohio, U.S.A. 41°21N 83°7W 173 E12
Fremont → U.S.A. 38°24N 110°42W 169 G8
Fremont L. U.S.A. 42°57N 109°48W 168 E9
French Camp U.S.A. 37°53N 121°16W 170 H5
French Cays = Plana Cays
 Bahamas 22°38N 73°30W 183 B5
French Creek → U.S.A. 41°24N 79°50W 174 E5
French Frigate Shoals
 U.S.A. 23°45N 166°10W 167 L6
French Guiana ☑
 S. Amer. 4°0N 53°0W 187 C8
French I. Australia 38°20S 145°22E 153 F6
French Island △
 Australia 38°20S 145°22E 153 F6
French Pass N.Z. 40°55S 173°55E 155 A8
French Polynesia ☑
 Pac. Oc. 20°0S 145°0W 157 J13
French Riviera = Azur, Côte d'
 France 43°25N 7°10E 73 E11
Frenchman Cr. →
 N. Amer. 48°31N 107°10W 168 B10
Frenchman Cr. →
 U.S.A. 40°14N 100°50W 172 E3
Frenda Algeria 35°2N 1°1E 136 A4
Frenštát pod Radhoštěm
 Czech Rep. 49°33N 18°13E 79 B11
Freona Ivory C. 5°3N 5°31W 138 D3
Fresco → Brazil 7°15S 51°30W 187 E8
Freshfield, C.
 Antarctica 68°25S 151°10E 55 C10
Fresnay-sur-Sarthe France 48°17N 0°1E 70 D7
Fresnillo Mexico 23°10N 102°53W 180 C4
Fresno U.S.A. 36°44N 119°47W 170 J7
Fresno Alhándiga Spain 40°42N 5°37W 88 E5
Fresno Res. U.S.A. 48°36N 109°57W 168 B9
Freudenstadt Germany 48°27N 8°24E 77 G4
Frévent France 50°15N 2°17E 70 B9
Frew → Australia 20°0S 135°38E 150 C2
Frewsburg U.S.A. 42°3N 79°10W 174 D5
Freycinet △ Australia 42°11S 148°19E 151 G4
Freycinet Pen.
 Australia 42°10S 148°25E 151 G4
Freyming-Merlebach
 France 49°8N 6°48E 71 C13

Freyung Germany 48°48N 13°31E 77 G9
Fria Guinea 10°27N 13°38W 138 C2
Fria, C. Namibia 18°0S 12°0E 144 A1
Frias Argentina 28°40S 65°5W 190 B2
Fribourg Switz. 46°49N 7°9E 77 J3
Fribourg □ Switz. 46°40N 7°0E 77 J3
Fridafors Sweden 56°25N 14°39E 63 H8
Friday Harbor U.S.A. 48°32N 123°1W 170 B3
Friedberg Bayern,
 Germany 48°21N 10°59E 77 G6
Friedberg Hessen, Germany 50°19N 8°45E 77 E4
Friedens U.S.A. 40°3N 78°59W 174 F6
Friedland Germany 53°40N 13°33E 76 B9
Friedrichshafen Germany 47°39N 9°30E 77 H5
Friedrichskoog Germany 54°1N 8°53E 76 A4
Friedrichstadt Germany 54°23N 9°6E 76 A5
Friendship U.S.A. 42°12N 78°8W 174 D6
Friesach Austria 46°57N 14°24E 78 E7
Friesack Germany 52°44N 12°34E 76 C8
Friesland □ Neths. 53°5N 5°50E 69 A5
Friesoythe Germany 53°1N 7°51E 76 B3
Frigate Seychelles 4°35S 55°56E 141 b
Friggesund Sweden 61°54N 16°33E 62 C10
Frillesås Sweden 57°20N 12°12E 63 G6
Frinnaryd Sweden 57°55N 14°50E 63 G8
Frio → U.S.A. 28°26N 98°11W 176 G5
Frio, C. Brazil 22°50S 41°50W 184 F6
Friol Spain 43°2N 7°47W 88 B3
Friona U.S.A. 34°38N 102°43W 176 D3
Frisco U.S.A. 33°8N 96°49W 176 E6
Fristad Sweden 57°50N 13°0E 63 G6
Fritch U.S.A. 35°38N 101°36W 176 D4
Fritsla Sweden 57°33N 12°47E 63 G6
Fritzlar Germany 51°7N 9°16E 76 D5
Friuli-Venézia Giulia □
 Italy 46°0N 13°0E 93 B9
Friza, Proliv Russia 45°30N 149°0E 107 E15
Frobisher B. Canada 62°30N 66°0W 161 E18
Frobisher Bay = Iqaluit
 Canada 63°44N 68°31W 161 E18
Frobisher L. Canada 56°20N 108°15W 163 B7
Frohavet Norway 64°0N 9°30E 60 E13
Frohnleiten Austria 47°16N 15°19E 78 D8
Frolovo Russia 49°45S 43°40E 86 F6
Frombork Poland 54°21N 19°41E 82 D6
Frome → U.K. 51°14N 2°19W 67 F5
Frome, L. Australia 30°45S 139°45E 152 A3
Frome Downs
 Australia 31°13S 139°45E 152 A3
Frómista Spain 42°16N 4°25W 88 C6
Front Range U.S.A. 40°25N 105°45W 168 F11
Front Royal U.S.A. 38°55N 78°12W 173 F14
Fronteira Portugal 39°3N 7°39W 89 F3
Fronteiras Brazil 7°5S 40°37W 189 B2
Frontenac Canada 45°55N 76°15W 175 B8
Frontenac Canary Is. 27°47N 17°59W 100 G2
Frontera Mexico 18°42N 92°38W 181 D6
Fronteras Mexico 30°56N 109°31W 180 A3
Frontignan France 43°27N 3°45E 72 E7
Frosinone Italy 41°38N 13°19E 94 A6
Frostburg U.S.A. 39°39N 78°56W 173 F14
Frostisen Norway 68°14N 17°10E 60 B17
Frostproof U.S.A. 27°45N 81°31W 179 H8
Frouard France 48°47N 6°8E 71 D13
Frövi Sweden 59°28N 15°24E 62 E9
Frøya Norway 63°43N 8°40E 60 E13
Fruita U.S.A. 39°9N 108°44W 168 G9
Fruithurst U.S.A. 33°44N 85°26W 178 B4
Fruitland Park U.S.A. 28°51N 81°54W 179 G8
Frumoasa Romania 46°28N 25°48E 81 D10
Frunze = Bishkek
 Kyrgyzstan 42°54N 74°46E 108 D8
Frunzivka Ukraine 47°20N 29°43E 81 C14
Fruška Gora Serbia 45°7N 19°30E 80 E4
Fruška Gora △ Serbia 45°8N 19°40E 96 A3
Frutal Brazil 20°0S 49°0W 187 H9
Frutigen Switz. 46°35N 7°38E 77 J3
Frýdek-Místek
 Czech Rep. 49°40N 18°20E 79 B11
Frýdlant Czech Rep. 50°56N 15°9E 78 A8
Fryeburg U.S.A. 44°1N 70°59W 175 B14
Fryvaldov = Jeseník
 Czech Rep. 50°0N 17°8E 79 A9
Fthiotida Greece 38°50N 22°25E 98 C4
Fu Jiang → China 30°0N 106°16E 116 C6
Fu Xian = Wafangdian
 China 39°38N 121°58E 115 E11
Fu Xian China 36°0N 109°20E 116 E10
Fu'an China 27°11N 119°36E 117 D12
Fubian China 31°17N 102°22E 116 B4
Fucécchio Italy 43°44N 10°48E 92 E7
Fucheng China 37°50N 116°10E 114 F9
Fuchou = Fuzhou
 China 26°5N 119°16E 117 D12
Fuchū Japan 34°34N 133°14E 113 G6
Fuchuan China 24°50N 111°5E 117 E8
Fuchun Jiang → China 30°5N 120°5E 117 B13
Fúcino, Piana del Italy 42°1N 13°31E 93 F10
Fuding China 27°20N 120°12E 117 D13
Fuencaliente Canary Is. 28°28N 17°50W 100 F2
Fuencaliente Spain 38°25N 4°18W 89 G6
Fuencaliente, Pta.
 Canary Is. 28°27N 17°51W 100 F2
Fuengirola Spain 36°32N 4°41W 89 J6
Fuenlabrada Spain 40°17N 3°48W 88 E7
Fuensalida Spain 40°3N 4°12W 88 E6
Fuente-Álamo Spain 38°44N 1°24W 91 G3
Fuente-Álamo de Murcia
 Spain 37°42N 1°6W 91 H3
Fuente de Cantos Spain 38°15N 6°18W 89 G4
Fuente del Maestre Spain 38°15N 6°18W 89 G4
Fuente el Fresno Spain 39°14N 3°46W 89 F7
Fuentes de Ebro Spain 41°31N 0°38W 90 D4
Fuentes de León Spain 38°5N 6°32W 89 G4
Fuentes de Oñoro Spain 40°33N 6°52W 88 E4
Fuentesaúco Spain 41°15N 5°30W 88 D5
Fuerte → Mexico 25°54N 109°22W 180 B3
Fuerte Olimpo Paraguay 21°0S 57°51W 190 A4
Fuerteventura
 Canary Is. 28°30N 14°0W 100 F6
Fuerteventura ✈ (FUE)
 Canary Is. 28°24N 13°52W 100 F6

Fuhai China 47°2N 87°25E 109 C11
Fubaymi Iraq 34°16N 42°10E 105 E10
Fuhlsbüttel, Hamburg ✈ (HAM)
 Germany 53°35N 9°59E 76 B6
Fuidhaigh = Wiay U.K. 57°24N 7°13W 65 D1
Fuji-Hakone-Izu △
 Japan 35°15N 138°45E 113 G9
Fuji-San Japan 35°22N 138°44E 113 G9
Fuji-Yoshida Japan 35°30N 138°46E 113 G9
Fujian □ China 26°0N 118°0E 117 E12
Fujin China 47°16N 132°1E 111 B15
Fujinomiya Japan 35°10N 138°40E 113 G9
Fujisawa Japan 35°22N 139°29E 113 G9
Fujiyama, Mt. = Fuji-San
 Japan 35°22N 138°44E 113 G9
Fukagawa Japan 43°43N 142°2E 112 C11
Fukien = Fujian □ China 26°0N 118°0E 117 E12
Fukuchiyama Japan 35°19N 135°9E 113 G7
Fukue Japan 32°41N 128°51E 113 H4
Fukue-Shima Japan 32°40N 128°45E 113 H4
Fukui Japan 36°5N 136°10E 113 F8
Fukui □ Japan 36°0N 136°12E 113 G8
Fukuoka Japan 33°39N 130°21E 113 H5
Fukuoka □ Japan 33°30N 131°0E 113 H5
Fukushima Japan 37°44N 140°28E 112 F10
Fukushima □ Japan 37°30N 140°15E 112 F10
Fukuyama Japan 34°35N 133°20E 113 G6
Fulacunda Guinea-Biss. 11°33N 15°1W 138 C1
Fulaga Fiji 19°8S 178°33W 154 a
Fulan → Sweden 61°18N 13°4E 62 C7
Fulda Germany 50°32N 9°40E 76 E5
Fulda → Germany 51°25N 9°39E 76 D5
Fulford Harbour
 Canada 48°47N 123°27W 170 B3
Fuliang China 29°23N 117°14E 117 C11
Fuling China 29°39N 107°1E 116 C6
Fullerton Calif.,
 U.S.A. 33°53N 117°56W 171 M9
Fullerton Nebr., U.S.A. 41°22N 97°58W 172 E5
Fulongquan China 44°20N 124°42E 115 B13
Fulton Mo., U.S.A. 38°52N 91°57W 172 F8
Fulton N.Y., U.S.A. 43°19N 76°25W 175 C8
Fulufjället Sweden 61°32N 12°41E 62 C6
Fumay France 49°58N 4°40E 71 C11
Fumel France 44°30N 0°58E 72 D4
Fumin China 25°10N 102°20E 116 E4
Funabashi Japan 35°45N 140°0E 113 G10
Funäsdalen Sweden 62°33N 12°32E 62 B6
Funchal Madeira 32°38N 16°54W 100 D3
Funchal ✈ (FNC)
 Madeira 32°42N 16°45W 100 D3
Fundación Colombia 10°31N 74°11W 186 A4
Fundão Brazil 19°55S 40°24W 189 D2
Fundão Portugal 40°8N 7°30W 88 E3
Fundong Cameroon 6°15N 10°16E 139 D7
Fundu Moldovei
 Romania 47°32N 25°24E 81 C10
Fundulea Romania 44°28N 26°31E 81 F11
Fundy, B. of Canada 45°0N 66°0W 165 D6
Fundy △ Canada 45°35N 65°10W 165 C6
Funhalouro Mozam. 23°3S 34°25E 145 B5
Funing Hebei, China 39°53N 119°12E 115 E10
Funing Jiangsu, China 33°45N 119°50E 115 H10
Funing Yunnan, China 23°35N 105°45E 116 F5
Funiu Shan China 33°30N 112°20E 114 H7
Funsi Ghana 10°21N 1°54W 138 C4
Funtua Nigeria 11°30N 7°18E 139 C6
Fuping Hebei, China 38°48N 114°12E 114 E8
Fuping Shaanxi, China 34°42N 109°10E 114 G5
Fuqing China 25°41N 119°21E 117 E12
Fuquan China 26°41N 107°27E 116 D6
Furano Japan 43°21N 142°23E 112 C11
Furāt, Nahr al → Asia 31°0N 47°25E 128 D5
Fürg Iran 28°18N 55°13E 129 D7
Furman U.S.A. 32°41N 81°11W 178 D4
Furmanov Russia 57°10N 41°8E 86 B6
Furnás Spain 39°3N 1°32E 100 B8
Furnas, Represa de
 Brazil 20°50S 45°30W 191 A6
Furneaux Group
 Australia 40°10S 147°50E 151 G4
Furqlus Syria 34°36N 37°8E 130 A3
Fürstenberg Germany 53°11N 13°9E 76 B9
Fürstenfeld Austria 47°3N 16°3E 78 D9
Fürstenfeldbruck
 Germany 48°10N 11°15E 77 G7
Fürstenwalde Germany 52°22N 14°3E 76 C10
Fürth Germany 49°28N 10°59E 77 F6
Fürth im Wald Germany 49°18N 12°51E 77 F8
Furtwangen Germany 48°3N 8°12E 77 G4
Furudal Sweden 61°10N 15°11E 62 C9
Furukawa = Ōsaki
 Japan 38°34N 140°58E 112 E10
Furulund Sweden 55°46N 13°6E 63 J7
Furuvik Sweden 61°38N 17°20E 62 D11
Fury and Hecla Str.
 Canada 69°56N 84°0W 161 D15
Fusagasugá Colombia 4°21N 74°22W 186 C4
Fuscaldo Italy 39°25N 16°2E 95 C9
Fushan Shandong,
 China 37°30N 121°15E 115 F11
Fushë Arrëz Albania 42°4N 20°2E 96 G4
Fushë Kosovë Kosovo 42°40N 21°5E 96 G5
Fushë Kruje Albania 41°29N 19°43E 96 E3
Fushun Liaoning,
 China 41°50N 123°56E 115 D12
Fushun Sichuan, China 29°13N 104°52E 116 C5
Füssen Germany 47°34N 10°42E 77 H6
Fustic Barbados 13°16N 59°38W 183 g
Fusui China 22°40N 107°56E 116 F6
Futian China 22°32N 114°4E 111 a
Futrono Chile 40°8S 72°24W 192 A2
Fuxian Hu China 24°30N 102°52E 116 E4
Fuxin China 42°5N 121°48E 115 C11
Fuyang Anhui, China 33°0N 115°48E 114 H8
Fuyang Zhejiang, China 30°5N 119°57E 117 B13
Fuyang He → China 38°12N 117°0E 114 E9
Fuying Dao China 26°34N 120°9E 117 D13
Fuyu Heilongjiang,
 China 47°49N 124°27E 111 B13
Fuyu Jilin, China 45°12N 124°43E 115 B13

Fuyuan China 25°40N 104°16E 116 E5
Fuyuan China 47°0N 89°28E 109 C11
Füzesgyarmat Hungary 47°6N 21°14E 80 C6
Fuzhou = Linchuan
China 27°57N 116°15E 117 D11
Fuzhou China 26°5N 119°16E 117 D12
Füzuli Azerbaijan 39°36N 47°8E 105 C12
Fyn Denmark 55°20N 10°30E 63 J4
Fyne, L. U.K. 55°59N 5°23W 65 F3
Fynshav Denmark 54°59N 9°59E 63 K3

G

Ga Ghana 9°47N 2°30W 138 D4
Gaalkacyo Somalia 6°30N 47°30E 131 F4
Gaanda Nigeria 10°10N 12°27E 139 C7
Gabas → France 43°46N 0°42W 72 E3
Gabba Australia 9°45S 142°38E 150 a
Gabela Angola 11°0S 14°24E 140 G2
Gabès Tunisia 33°53N 10°2E 136 B6
Gabès □ Tunisia 33°35N 9°30E 136 B5
Gabès, G. de Tunisia 34°0N 10°30E 136 B6
Gabgaba, W. → Egypt 22°10N 33°5E 137 C3
Gabia la Grande Spain 37°8N 3°40W 89 H7
Gąbin Poland 52°23N 19°41E 83 F6
Gabon ■ Africa 0°10S 10°0E 140 E2
Gaborone Botswana 24°45S 25°57E 144 B4
Gabriels U.S.A. 44°26N 74°12W 175 B10
Gābrīk Iran 25°44N 58°28E 129 E8
Gabrovo Bulgaria 42°52N 25°19E 97 D9
Gacé France 48°49N 0°20E 70 D7
Gāch Sār Iran 36°7N 51°19E 129 B6
Gachsārān Iran 30°15N 50°45E 129 D6
Gacko Bos.-H. 43°10N 18°33E 96 C2
Gad Hinglaj India 16°14N 74°21E 127 F2
Gadag India 15°30N 75°45E 127 G2
Gadap Pakistan 25°5N 67°28E 124 G2
Gadarwara India 22°50N 78°50E 125 H8
Gadebusch Germany 53°42N 11°7E 76 B7
Gadhada India 22°0N 71°35E 124 J4
Gádor, Sierra de Spain 36°57N 2°45W 89 J8
Gadra Pakistan 25°40N 70°38E 124 G4
Gadsden Ala., U.S.A. 34°1N 86°1W 178 A3
Gadsden S.C., U.S.A. 33°51N 80°46W 178 B9
Gadwal India 16°10N 77°50E 127 F3
Gadyach = Hadyach
Ukraine 50°21N 34°0E 85 G8
Găeşti Romania 44°48N 25°19E 81 F10
Gaeta Italy 41°12N 13°35E 94 A6
Gaeta, G. di Italy 41°6N 13°30E 94 A6
Gaffney U.S.A. 35°5N 81°39W 177 D14
Gafsa Tunisia 34°24N 8°43E 136 B5
Gafsa □ Tunisia 34°30N 8°48E 136 B5
Gagarawa Nigeria 12°25N 9°32E 139 C6
Gagaria India 25°43N 70°46E 124 G4
Gagarin Russia 55°38N 35°0E 84 E8
Găgăuzia □ Moldova 46°10N 28°40E 81 D13
Gaggenau Germany 48°48N 8°18E 77 G4
Gagino Russia 55°15N 45°1E 86 C7
Gagliano del Capo Italy 39°50N 18°22E 95 C11
Gagnef Sweden 60°36N 15°5E 62 D9
Gagnoa Ivory C. 6°56N 6°16W 138 D3
Gagnon Canada 51°50N 68°5W 165 B6
Gagnon, L. Canada 62°3N 110°27W 163 A6
Gagra Georgia 43°20N 40°10E 87 J5
Gahini Rwanda 1°50S 30°30E 142 C3
Gahmar India 25°27N 83°49E 125 G10
Gahnpa = Ganta Liberia 7°15N 8°59W 138 D3
Gai Xian = Gaizhou
China 40°22N 122°20E 115 D12
Gaidouronisi Greece 34°53N 25°41E 101 E7
Gail U.S.A. 32°46N 101°27W 176 E4
Gail → Austria 46°36N 13°53E 78 E6
Gaillac France 43°54N 1°54E 72 E5
Gaillimh = Galway
Ireland 53°17N 9°3W 64 C2
Gaillon France 49°10N 1°20E 70 C8
Gaimán Argentina 43°10S 65°25W 192 B3
Gaines U.S.A. 41°46N 77°35W 174 E7
Gainesville Fla., U.S.A. 29°40N 82°20W 179 F7
Gainesville Ga.,
U.S.A. 34°18N 83°50W 177 D13
Gainesville Mo., U.S.A. 36°36N 92°26W 172 G7
Gainesville Tex., U.S.A. 33°38N 97°8W 176 E6
Gainsborough U.K. 53°24N 0°46W 66 D7
Gairdner, L. Australia 31°30S 136°0E 152 A2
Gairloch U.K. 57°43N 5°41W 65 D3
Gairloch, L. U.K. 57°43N 5°45W 65 D3
Gaizhou China 40°22N 122°20E 115 D12
Gaj Croatia 45°28N 17°3E 80 E2
Gaj → Pakistan 26°26N 67°21E 124 F2
Gajendragarh India 15°44N 75°59E 127 G2
Gakuch Pakistan 36°7N 73°45E 125 A5
Gal Oya △ Sri Lanka 7°0N 81°20E 127 L5
Gal Oya Res. Sri Lanka 7°5N 81°30E 127 L5
Galâla, Gebel el Egypt 29°21N 32°22E 137 F8
Galán, Cerro Argentina 25°55S 66°52W 190 B2
Galana → Kenya 3°9S 40°8E 142 C5
Galanta Slovak Rep. 48°11N 17°45E 79 C10
Galapagar Spain 40°36N 3°58W 88 E7
Galápagos = Colón, Arch. de
Ecuador 0°0 91°0W 184 D1
Galapagos Fracture Zone
Pac. Oc. 3°0N 110°0W 157 G17
Galapagos Rise Pac. Oc. 15°0S 95°0W 157 J18
Galashiels U.K. 55°37N 2°49W 65 F6
Galatas Greece 37°30N 23°26E 98 D5
Galatea N.Z. 38°24S 176°45E 154 E5
Galateia Cyprus 35°25N 34°4E 101 D13
Galaţi Romania 45°27N 28°2E 81 E13
Galaţi □ Romania 45°45N 27°30E 81 E12
Galatia Turkey 39°30N 33°0E 104 C5
Galatina Italy 40°10N 18°10E 95 B11
Galátone Italy 40°9N 18°4E 95 B11
Galax U.S.A. 36°40N 80°56W 173 G13
Galaxidi Greece 38°22N 22°23E 98 C4
Galbīn Govĭ Mongolia 43°0N 107°0E 114 C4
Galcaio = Gaalkacyo
Somalia 6°30N 47°30E 131 F4
Galdhøpiggen Norway 61°38N 8°18E 60 F13
Galeana Chihuahua,
Mexico 30°7N 107°38W 180 A3
Galeana Nuevo León,
Mexico 24°50N 100°4W 180 A4
Galela Indonesia 1°50N 127°49E 119 D7
Galeota Pt. Trin. & Tob. 10°8N 60°59W 187 K16
Galera Spain 37°45N 2°33W 91 H2
Galera, Pta. Chile 39°59S 73°43W 192 A2
Galera Pt. Trin. & Tob. 10°49N 60°54W 183 D7
Galesburg U.S.A. 40°57N 90°22W 172 E8
Galestan △ Iran 37°30N 56°0E 129 B8
Galeton U.S.A. 41°44N 77°39W 174 E7
Galheirão → Brazil 12°23S 45°5W 189 C1
Gali Georgia 42°37N 41°46E 87 J5
Galicea Mare Romania 44°4N 23°19E 81 F8
Galich Russia 58°22N 42°24E 86 A6
Galiche Bulgaria 43°34N 23°53E 96 C7
Galicia □ Spain 42°43N 7°45W 88 C3
Galičica △ Macedonia 41°2N 20°55E 96 E4
Galilee = Hagalil Israel 32°53N 35°18E 130 C4
Galilee, L. Australia 22°20S 145°50E 150 C4
Galilee, Sea of = Yam Kinneret
Israel 32°45N 35°35E 130 C4
Galim Cameroon 7°6N 12°25E 139 D7
Galina Pt. Jamaica 18°24N 76°58W 182 a
Galinoporni Cyprus 35°31N 34°18E 101 D13
Galion U.S.A. 40°44N 82°47W 174 F2
Galite, Îs. de la Tunisia 37°30N 8°59E 136 A5
Galiuro Mts. U.S.A. 32°30N 110°20W 169 K8
Galiwinku Australia 12°2S 135°34E 150 A2
Gallan Hd. U.K. 58°15N 7°2W 65 C1
Gallarate Italy 45°40N 8°48E 92 C5
Gallatin U.S.A. 36°24N 86°27W 177 C11
Galle Sri Lanka 6°5N 80°10E 127 L5
Gállego → Spain 41°39N 0°51W 90 D4
Gallegos → Argentina 51°35S 69°0W 192 D3
Galley Hd. Ireland 51°32N 8°55W 64 E3
Galliate Italy 45°29N 8°42E 92 C5
Gallinas, Pta. Colombia 12°28N 71°40W 186 A4
Gallipoli = Gelibolu
Turkey 40°28N 26°43E 97 F10
Gallipoli Italy 40°3N 17°58E 95 B10
Gallipolis U.S.A. 38°49N 82°12W 173 F12
Gällivare Sweden 67°9N 20°40E 60 C19
Gallneukirchen Austria 48°21N 14°25E 78 C7
Gällö Sweden 62°55N 15°13E 62 B9
Gallo, C. Italy 38°13N 13°19E 94 D6
Gallocanta, L. de Spain 40°58N 1°30W 90 E3
Galloo I. U.S.A. 43°55N 76°25W 175 C8
Galloway U.K. 55°1N 4°29W 65 F4
Galloway, Mull of U.K. 54°39N 4°52W 65 G4
Gallup U.S.A. 35°32N 108°45W 169 J9
Gallur Spain 41°52N 1°19W 90 D3
Gallura Italy 41°5N 9°20E 94 A2
Galmudug Somalia 6°30N 48°0E 131 F4
Galong Australia 34°37S 148°34E 153 C8
Galoya Sri Lanka 8°10N 80°55E 127 K5
Galt U.S.A. 38°15N 121°18W 170 G5
Galten Denmark 56°9N 9°54E 63 H3
Galtür Austria 46°58N 10°11E 78 E3
Galty Mts. Ireland 52°22N 8°10W 64 D3
Galtymore Ireland 52°21N 8°11W 64 D3
Galugāh Iran 36°43N 53°48E 129 B7
Galva U.S.A. 41°10N 90°3W 172 E8
Galvarino Chile 38°24S 72°47W 192 A2
Galve de Sorbe Spain 41°13N 3°10W 90 D1
Galveston U.S.A. 29°18N 94°48W 176 G7
Galveston B. U.S.A. 29°36N 94°50W 176 G7
Gálvez Argentina 32°0S 61°14W 190 C3
Galway Ireland 53°17N 9°3W 64 C2
Galway □ Ireland 53°22N 9°1W 64 C2
Galway B. Ireland 53°13N 9°10W 64 C2
Gam → Vietnam 21°55N 105°12E 120 B5
Gamagōri Japan 34°50N 137°14E 113 G8
Gamawa Nigeria 12°10N 10°31E 139 C7
Gambaga Ghana 10°30N 0°28W 139 C4
Gambat Pakistan 27°17N 68°26E 124 F3
Gambhir → India 26°58N 77°27E 124 F6
Gambia ■ W. Afr. 13°25N 16°0W 138 C1
Gambia → W. Afr. 13°28N 16°34W 138 C1
Gambier U.S.A. 40°22N 82°23W 174 F2
Gambier, C. Australia 11°56S 130°57E 148 B5
Gambier, Îs.
French Polynesia 23°8S 134°58W 157 K14
Gambier Is. Australia 35°3S 136°30E 152 C2
Gambo Canada 48°47N 54°13W 165 C9
Gamboli Pakistan 29°53N 68°24E 124 E3
Gamboma Congo 1°55S 15°52E 140 E3
Gamka → S. Africa 33°18S 21°39E 144 D3
Gamkab → Namibia 28°4S 17°54E 144 C2
Gamla Uppsala Sweden 59°54N 17°40E 62 E11
Gamlakarleby = Kokkola
Finland 63°50N 23°8E 60 E20
Gamleby Sweden 57°54N 16°24E 63 G10
Gammon → Canada 51°24N 95°44W 163 C9
Gammon Ranges △
Australia 30°38S 139°8E 151 E2
Gamou Niger 14°20N 9°55E 139 C6
Gampaha Sri Lanka 7°5N 79°59E 127 L4
Gampola Sri Lanka 7°10N 80°34E 127 L5
Gamtoos → S. Africa 33°58S 25°1E 144 D4
Gamzigrad-Romuliana
Serbia 43°53N 22°11E 96 C6
Gan France 43°12N 0°27W 72 E3
Gan Gan Argentina 42°30S 68°10W 192 B3
Gan Goriama, Mts.
Cameroon 7°44N 12°45E 139 D7
Gan Jiang → China 29°15N 116°0E 117 C11
Ganado U.S.A. 35°43N 109°33W 169 J9
Gananita Sudan 18°22N 33°50E 137 D3
Gananoque Canada 44°20N 76°10W 175 B8
Ganāveh Iran 29°35N 50°35E 129 D6
Gäncä Azerbaijan 40°45N 46°20E 87 K8
Gancheng China 18°51N 108°37E 117 a
Gand = Gent Belgium 51°2N 3°42E 69 C3
Ganda Angola 13°3S 14°35E 141 G2
Gandajika
Dem. Rep. of the Congo 6°46S 23°58E 140 F4
Gandak → India 25°39N 85°13E 125 G11
Gandava Pakistan 28°32N 67°32E 124 E2
Gander Canada 48°58N 54°35W 165 C9
Gander L. Canada 48°58N 54°35W 165 C9
Ganderkesee Germany 53°2N 8°32E 76 B4
Ganderowe Falls
Zimbabwe 17°20S 29°10E 143 F2
Gandesa Spain 41°3N 0°26E 90 D5
Gandhi Sagar India 24°40N 75°40E 124 G6
Gandhinagar India 23°15N 72°45E 124 H5
Gandi Nigeria 12°55N 5°49E 139 C6
Gandia Spain 38°58N 0°9W 91 G4
Gandino Italy 45°49N 9°54E 92 C6
Gando, Pta. Canary Is. 27°55N 15°22W 100 G4
Gandole Nigeria 8°28N 11°35E 139 D7
Gandu Brazil 13°45S 39°30W 189 C3
Gâneb Mauritania 18°29N 10°8W 138 B2
Ganedidalem = Gani
Indonesia 0°48S 128°14E 119 E7
Ganga → India 23°20N 90°30E 125 H14
Ganga Sagar India 21°38N 88°5E 125 J13
Gangafani Mali 14°20N 2°20W 138 C4
Gangakher India 18°57N 76°45E 126 E3
Gangan → India 28°38N 78°58E 125 E8
Ganganagar India 29°56N 73°56E 124 E5
Gangapur Maharashtra,
India 19°41N 75°1E 126 E2
Gangapur Raj., India 26°32N 76°49E 124 F7
Gangara Niger 14°35N 8°29E 139 C6
Gangaw Burma 22°5N 94°5E 123 H19
Gangawati India 15°30N 76°36E 127 G3
Gangdisê Shan China 31°20N 81°0E 125 D9
Ganges = Ganga →
India 23°20N 90°30E 125 H14
Ganges Canada 48°51N 123°31W 162 D4
Ganges France 43°56N 3°42E 72 E7
Ganges, Mouths of the
India 21°30N 90°0E 125 J14
Ganggyeong S. Korea 36°10N 127°0E 115 F14
Gånghester Sweden 57°42N 13°1E 63 G7
Gangi Italy 37°48N 14°12E 95 E7
Gângiova Romania 43°54N 23°50E 81 G8
Gangneung S. Korea 37°45N 128°54E 115 F15
Gangoh India 29°46N 77°18E 124 E7
Gangotri India 30°50N 79°10E 125 D8
Gangotri △ India 30°50N 79°10E 125 D8
Gangseong S. Korea 38°24N 128°30E 115 E15
Gangtok India 27°20N 88°37E 123 F16
Gangu China 34°40N 105°15E 114 G3
Gangyao China 44°12N 126°37E 115 B14
Gani Indonesia 0°48S 128°14E 119 E7
Ganj India 27°45N 78°57E 125 F8
Ganjam India 19°23N 85°4E 126 E7
Ganluo China 28°58N 102°59E 116 C4
Ganmain Australia 34°47S 147°1E 153 C7
Gannat France 46°7N 3°11E 71 F10
Gannett Peak U.S.A. 43°11N 109°39W 168 E9
Ganquan China 36°20N 109°20E 114 F5
Gänserdorf Austria 48°20N 16°43E 79 C9
Ganshui China 28°40N 106°40E 116 C6
Gansu □ China 36°0N 104°0E 114 G3
Ganta Liberia 7°15N 8°59W 138 D3
Gantheaume, C.
Australia 36°4S 137°32E 152 D2
Gantheaume B.
Australia 27°40S 114°10E 149 E1
Gantsevichi = Hantsavichy
Belarus 52°49N 26°30E 75 B14
Ganvie Benin 6°28N 2°25E 139 D5
Ganye Nigeria 8°25N 12°4E 139 D7
Ganyem = Genyem
Indonesia 2°46S 140°12E 119 E10
Ganyu China 34°50N 119°8E 115 G10
Ganyushkino
Kazakhstan 46°35N 49°20E 87 G9
Ganzhou China 25°51N 114°56E 117 E10
Gao Mali 16°15N 0°5W 139 B4
Gao Xian China 28°21N 104°32E 116 C5
Gao'an China 28°26N 115°17E 117 C10
Gaobeidian China 39°19N 115°51E 114 E8
Gaocheng China 38°2N 114°49E 114 E8
Gaochun China 31°20N 118°49E 117 B12
Gaohebu China 30°43N 116°49E 117 B11
Gaokeng China 27°40N 113°58E 117 D9
Gaolan Dao China 21°55N 113°10E 117 G9
Gaoligong Shan China 24°45N 98°45E 116 E2
Gaomi China 36°20N 119°42E 115 F10
Gaoping China 35°45N 112°55E 114 G7
Gaotang China 36°50N 116°15E 114 F9
Gaoua Burkina Faso 10°20N 3°8W 138 C4
Gaoual Guinea 11°45N 13°25W 138 C2
Gaoyang China 38°40N 115°45E 114 E8
Gaoyao China 23°3N 112°27E 117 F9
Gaoyou China 32°47N 119°26E 117 A12
Gaoyou Hu China 32°45N 119°20E 117 A12
Gaoyuan China 37°8N 117°58E 115 F9
Gaozhou China 21°58N 110°50E 117 G8
Gap France 44°33N 6°5E 73 D10
Gapat → India 24°30N 82°28E 125 G10
Gapuwiyak Australia 12°25S 135°43E 150 A2
Gar China 32°10N 79°58E 110 E4
Gara, L. Ireland 53°57N 8°26W 64 C3
Garāb Iran 33°27N 47°16E 105 F12
Garabogazköl Aylagy
Turkmenistan 41°0N 53°30E 108 D4
Garachico Canary Is. 28°22N 16°46W 100 F3
Garachiné Panama 8°0N 78°12W 182 E4
Garafía Canary Is. 28°48N 17°57W 100 F2
Garagum Turkmenistan 39°30N 60°0E 129 B8
Garah Australia 29°5S 149°38E 151 D4
Garajonay Canary Is. 28°7N 17°14W 100 F2
Garajonay △ Canary Is. 28°7N 17°14W 100 F2
Garamba △
Dem. Rep. of the Congo 4°10N 29°40E 142 B2
Garango Burkina Faso 11°48N 0°34W 139 C4
Garanhuns Brazil 8°50S 36°30W 189 B3
Garautha India 25°34N 79°18E 125 G8
Garawa ✪ Australia 16°43S 136°51E 150 B2
Garawe Liberia 4°35N 8°0W 138 E3
Garba Tula Kenya 0°30N 38°32E 142 B4
Garberville U.S.A. 40°6N 123°48W 168 F2
Garbiyang India 30°8N 80°54E 125 D9
Garbsen Germany 52°26N 9°31E 76 C5
Garças → Brazil 8°43S 39°41W 189 B3
Gard □ France 44°2N 4°10E 73 D8
Gard → France 43°51N 4°37E 73 E8
Garda, L. di Italy 45°40N 10°41E 92 C7
Gardabani Georgia 41°27N 45°5E 87 K7
Gardanne France 43°27N 5°27E 73 E9
Gårdby Sweden 56°36N 16°38E 63 H10
Garde L. Canada 62°50N 106°13W 163 A7
Gardelegen Germany 52°32N 11°24E 76 C7
Garden City Ga., U.S.A. 32°6N 81°9W 178 C8
Garden City Kans.,
U.S.A. 37°58N 100°53W 172 G3
Garden City Tex.,
U.S.A. 31°52N 101°29W 176 F4
Garden Grove U.S.A. 33°47N 117°55W 171 M9
Gardens of Stone △
Australia 33°14S 150°11E 153 B9
Gardēz Afghan. 33°37N 69°9E 124 C3
Gardiki Greece 38°50N 21°55E 98 C3
Gardiner Maine,
U.S.A. 44°14N 69°47W 173 C19
Gardiner Mont., U.S.A. 45°2N 110°22W 168 D8
Gardiners I. U.S.A. 41°6N 72°6W 175 E12
Gardner Fla., U.S.A. 27°21N 81°48W 179 H8
Gardner Mass., U.S.A. 42°34N 71°59W 175 D13
Gardner Canal Canada 53°27N 128°8W 162 C3
Gardner Pinnacles
U.S.A. 25°0N 167°55W 167 L6
Gardnerville U.S.A. 38°56N 119°45W 170 G7
Gardno, Jezioro Poland 54°40N 17°7E 82 D4
Gardo = Qardho Somalia 9°30N 49°6E 131 F4
Gardone Riviera Italy 45°37N 10°34E 92 C7
Gardone Val Trómpia
Italy 45°41N 10°11E 92 C7
Gárdony Hungary 47°12N 18°39E 80 C3
Gares = Puente la Reina
Spain 42°40N 1°49W 90 C3
Garešnica Croatia 45°36N 16°56E 93 C13
Garéssio Italy 44°12N 8°2E 92 D5
Garey U.S.A. 34°53N 120°19W 171 L6
Garfield U.S.A. 47°1N 117°9W 168 C5
Garforth U.K. 53°47N 1°24W 66 D6
Gargaliani Greece 37°4N 21°38E 98 D3
Gargan, Mt. France 45°37N 1°39E 72 C5
Gargano △ Italy 41°43N 15°52E 93 G12
Gargantua, C. Canada 47°36N 85°2W 173 B11
Gargett Australia 21°9S 148°46E 150 b
Gargouna Mali 15°56N 0°13E 139 B5
Gargždai Lithuania 55°43N 21°24E 82 C8
Garhchiroli India 20°10N 80°0E 126 D5
Garibaldi ⌂ Canada 49°50N 122°40W 162 D4
Gariep, L. S. Africa 30°40S 25°40E 144 D4
Garies S. Africa 30°32S 17°59E 144 D2
Garig Gunak Barlu △
Australia 11°26S 131°58E 148 B5
Garigliano → Italy 41°13N 13°45E 94 A6
Garissa Kenya 0°25S 39°40E 142 C4
Garissa □ Kenya 0°20S 40°10E 142 C5
Garkida Nigeria 10°27N 12°36E 139 C7
Garko Nigeria 11°45N 8°35E 139 C6
Garland Tex., U.S.A. 32°54N 96°38W 176 E6
Garland Utah, U.S.A. 41°45N 112°10W 168 F7
Garlasco Italy 45°12N 8°55E 92 C5
Garliava Lithuania 54°49N 23°52E 82 D10
Garlin France 43°33N 0°16W 72 E3
Garmāb Semnān, Iran 35°25N 56°45E 129 C8
Garmāb Zanjān, Iran 35°50N 48°11E 105 E13
Garmisch-Partenkirchen
Germany 47°30N 11°6E 77 H7
Garmsār Iran 35°20N 52°25E 129 C7
Garner U.S.A. 43°6N 93°36W 172 D7
Garnett U.S.A. 38°17N 95°14W 172 F6
Garnpung L. Australia 33°25S 143°10E 152 B5
Garo Hills India 25°30N 90°30E 125 G14
Garoe = Garoowe
Somalia 8°25N 48°33E 131 F4
Garonne → France 45°2N 0°36W 72 C3
Garonne, Canal Latéral à la
France 44°15N 0°18E 72 D4
Garoowe Somalia 8°25N 48°33E 131 F4
Garot India 24°19N 75°41E 124 G6
Garou, L. Mali 16°2N 2°45W 138 B4
Garoua Cameroon 9°19N 13°21E 139 D7
Garpenberg Sweden 60°19N 16°12E 62 D10
Garphyttan Sweden 59°18N 14°56E 62 E8
Garrauli India 25°5N 79°22E 125 G8
Garrel Germany 52°57N 8°1E 76 C4
Garrison Mont.,
U.S.A. 46°31N 112°49W 168 C7
Garrison N. Dak.,
U.S.A. 47°40N 101°25W 172 B3
Garrison Res. = Sakakawea, L.
U.S.A. 47°30N 101°25W 172 B3
Garron Pt. U.K. 55°3N 5°59W 64 A6
Garrovillas de Alconétar
Spain 39°40N 6°33W 89 F4
Garrucha Spain 37°11N 1°49W 91 H3
Garry → U.K. 56°44N 3°47W 65 E5
Garry, L. Canada 65°58N 100°18W 160 D11
Garrygala Turkmenistan 38°31N 56°29E 129 B8
Garsen Kenya 2°20S 40°5E 142 C5
Gärsnäs Sweden 55°32N 14°10E 63 J8
Garson L. Canada 56°19N 110°2W 163 B6
Garstang U.K. 53°55N 2°46W 66 D5
Gartempe → France 46°47N 0°49E 72 B4
Gartz Germany 53°13N 14°22E 76 B10
Garu Ghana 10°55N 0°11W 139 C4
Garu India 23°40N 84°14E 125 H11
Garub Namibia 26°37S 16°0E 144 C2
Garut Indonesia 7°14S 107°53E 119 G12
Garvão Portugal 37°42N 8°21W 89 H2
Garvie Mts. N.Z. 45°30S 168°50E 155 F3
Garwa = Garoua
Cameroon 9°19N 13°21E 139 D7
Garwa India 24°11N 83°47E 125 G10
Garwolin Poland 51°55N 21°38E 83 G8
Gary U.S.A. 41°36N 87°20W 172 E10
Garz Germany 54°19N 13°21E 76 A9
Garzê China 31°38N 100°1E 116 B3
Garzón Colombia 2°10N 75°40W 186 C3
Gas-San Japan 38°32N 140°1E 112 E10
Gasan Kuli = Esenguly
Turkmenistan 37°37N 53°59E 108 E4
Gascogne France 43°45N 0°20E 72 E4
Gascogne, G. de Europe 44°0N 2°0W 72 E2
Gascony = Gascogne
France 43°45N 0°20E 72 E4
Gascoyne → Australia 24°52S 113°37E 149 D1
Gascoyne Junction
Australia 25°2S 115°17E 149 E2
Gascueña Spain 40°18N 2°31W 90 E2
Gashagar Nigeria 13°22N 12°47E 139 C7
Gashaka Nigeria 7°20N 11°29E 139 D7
Gashaka-Gumti △
Nigeria 7°23N 11°34E 139 D7
Gasherbrum Pakistan 35°40N 76°40E 125 B7
Gashua Nigeria 12°54N 11°0E 139 C7
Gaspar Str. = Gelasa, Selat
Indonesia 2°50S 107°0E 118 E3
Gasparilla I. U.S.A. 26°46N 82°16W 179 J7
Gasparillo Trin. & Tob. 10°18N 61°26W 187 K15
Gaspé Canada 48°52N 64°30W 165 C7
Gaspé, C. de Canada 48°48N 64°7W 165 C7
Gaspé Pen. = Gaspésie, Pén. de la
Canada 48°45N 65°40W 165 C6
Gaspésie, Pén. de la
Canada 48°45N 65°40W 165 C6
Gaspésie ⌂ Canada 48°55N 66°10W 165 C6
Gassan Burkina Faso 12°49N 3°12W 138 C4
Gassol Nigeria 8°34N 10°25E 139 D7
Gasteiz = Vitoria-Gasteiz
Spain 42°50N 2°41W 90 C2
Gaston U.S.A. 33°49N 81°5W 178 B8
Gastonia U.S.A. 35°16N 81°11W 177 D14
Gastouni Greece 37°51N 21°15E 98 D3
Gastouri Greece 39°34N 19°54E 98 B1
Gastre Argentina 42°20S 69°15W 192 B3
Gästrikland Sweden 60°45N 16°40E 62 D10
Gata, C. Cyprus 34°34N 33°2E 101 E12
Gata, C. de Spain 36°41N 2°13W 91 J2
Gata, Sierra de Spain 40°20N 6°45W 88 E4
Gataga → Canada 58°35N 126°59W 162 B3
Gătaia Romania 45°26N 21°30E 80 E6
Gatchina Russia 59°35N 30°9E 84 C6
Gatehouse of Fleet U.K. 54°53N 4°12W 65 G4
Gates U.S.A. 43°9N 77°42W 174 C7
Gateshead U.K. 54°57N 1°35W 66 C6
Gateshead I. Canada 70°36N 100°26W 160 C11
Gatesville U.S.A. 31°26N 97°45W 176 F6
Gateway ⌂ U.S.A. 40°38N 73°51W 175 F11
Gaths Zimbabwe 20°2S 30°32E 143 G3
Gâtinais France 48°5N 2°40E 71 D9
Gâtine, Hauteurs de
France 46°35N 0°45W 72 B3
Gatineau Canada 45°29N 75°39W 175 A9
Gatineau → Canada 45°27N 75°42W 164 C4
Gatineau △ Canada 45°40N 76°0W 164 C4
Gattinara Italy 45°37N 8°22E 92 C5
Gatton Australia 27°32S 152°17E 151 D5
Gatún, L. Panama 9°7N 79°56W 182 E4
Gatwick, London ✕ (LGW)
U.K. 51°10N 0°11W 67 F7
Gatyana S. Africa 32°16S 28°31E 145 D4
Gau Fiji 18°2S 179°18E 154 a
Gaucín Spain 36°31N 5°19W 89 J5
Gauer L. Canada 57°0N 97°50W 163 B9
Gauhati = Guwahati
India 26°10N 91°45E 123 F17
Gauja → Latvia 57°10N 24°16E 84 D3
Gaujas △ Latvia 57°10N 24°50E 61 H21
Gaula → Norway 63°21N 10°14E 60 E14
Gaurdak = Gowurdak
Turkmenistan 37°50N 66°4E 109 E7
Gauri Phanta India 28°41N 80°36E 125 E9
Gauribidanur India 13°37N 77°32E 127 H3
Gaustatoppen Norway 59°48N 8°40E 61 G13
Gauteng □ S. Africa 26°0S 28°0E 145 C4
Gāv Koshī Iran 28°38N 57°12E 129 D8
Gāvakān Iran 29°37N 53°10E 129 D7
Gavar Armenia 40°21N 45°7E 87 K7
Gavarnie France 42°44N 0°1W 72 F3
Gavāter Iran 25°10N 61°31E 129 E9
Gāvbandī Iran 27°12N 53°4E 129 E7
Gavdopoula Greece 34°56N 24°0E 101 E6
Gavdos Greece 34°50N 24°5E 101 E6
Gavi Italy 44°41N 8°49E 92 D5
Gavião Portugal 39°28N 7°56W 89 F3
Gaviota U.S.A. 34°29N 120°13W 171 L6
Gāvkhūnī, Bāṭlāq-e Iran 32°6N 52°52E 129 C7
Gävle Sweden 60°40N 17°9E 62 D11
Gävleborg □ Sweden 61°30N 16°15E 62 C10
Gävlebukten Sweden 60°40N 17°20E 62 D11
Gavorrano Italy 42°55N 10°54E 92 F7
Gavray France 48°55N 1°20W 70 D5
Gavrilov Yam Russia 57°18N 39°49E 84 D10
Gavrio Greece 37°54N 24°44E 98 D6
Gawachab Namibia 27°4S 17°55E 144 C2
Gawilgarh Hills India 21°15N 76°45E 126 D3
Gawler Australia 34°30S 138°42E 152 C3
Gawler Ranges
Australia 32°30S 135°45E 152 B2
Gawu Nigeria 9°14N 6°52E 139 D6
Gaxun Nur China 42°22N 100°30E 110 C9
Gay Russia 51°27N 58°27E 108 B5
Gay U.S.A. 33°6N 84°35W 178 B5
Gaya India 24°47N 85°4E 125 G11
Gaya Niger 11°52N 3°28E 139 C5
Gaya Nigeria 11°57N 9°0E 139 C6
Gayéri Burkina Faso 12°39N 0°29E 139 C5
Gaylord U.S.A. 45°2N 84°41W 173 C11
Gayndah Australia 25°35S 151°32E 151 D5
Gaysin = Haysyn
Ukraine 48°57N 29°25E 81 B14
Gayvoron = Hayvoron
Ukraine 48°22N 29°52E 81 B14
Gaza Gaza Strip 31°30N 34°28E 130 D3
Gaza □ Moz. 23°10S 32°45E 145 B5
Gaza Strip ■ Asia 31°29N 34°25E 130 D3
Gazanjyk = Bereket
Turkmenistan 39°16N 55°32E 129 B7
Gazaoua Niger 13°32N 7°55E 139 C6
Gāzbor Iran 28°5N 58°51E 129 D8
Gazi Dem. Rep. of the Congo 1°3N 24°30E 142 B1
Gaziantep Turkey 37°6N 37°23E 104 D7
Gaziantep □ Turkey 37°0N 37°0E 104 D7
Gazimağusa = Famagusta
Cyprus 35°8N 33°55E 101 D12
Gazipaşa Turkey 36°16N 32°18E 104 D5
Gazli Uzbekistan 40°8N 63°27E 108 D6
Gazojak Turkmenistan 41°11N 61°24E 108 D6
Gbadolite
Dem. Rep. of the Congo 4°17N 21°1E 140 D4
Gbarnga Liberia 7°19N 9°13W 138 D3
Gboko Nigeria 7°17N 9°4E 139 D6
Gcoverega Botswana 19°8S 24°18E 144 A3
Gcuwa S. Africa 32°20S 28°11E 145 D4
Gdańsk Poland 54°22N 18°40E 82 D5
Gdańsk ✕ (GDN) Poland 54°22N 18°30E 82 D5
Gdańsk B. = Gdańska, Zatoka
Poland 54°30N 19°20E 82 D6
Gdańska, Zatoka Poland 54°30N 19°20E 82 D6
Gdov Russia 58°48N 27°55E 84 C4
Gdynia Poland 54°35N 18°33E 82 D5
Geba → Guinea-Biss. 11°46N 15°36W 138 C1
Gebe Indonesia 0°5N 129°25E 119 D7
Gebeciler Turkey 38°46N 30°46E 99 C12
Gebeit Mine Sudan 21°3N 36°29E 137 C4
Gebel Abyad Sudan 19°0N 28°0E 137 D2
Gebel Iweibid Egypt 30°8N 32°13E 137 E8
Gebze Turkey 40°47N 29°25E 97 F13
Geçitkale = Lefkoniko
Cyprus 35°18N 33°44E 101 D12
Gedaref Sudan 14°2N 35°28E 135 F13
Gede, Tanjung
Indonesia 6°46S 105°12E 119 G11
Gediz Turkey 39°1N 29°24E 99 B11
Gediz → Turkey 38°35N 26°48E 99 C8
Gèdre France 42°47N 0°2E 72 F4
Gedser Denmark 54°35N 11°55E 63 K5
Gedung, Pulau Malaysia 5°17N 100°23E 121 c
Geegully Cr. →
Australia 18°32S 123°41E 148 C3
Geel Belgium 51°10N 4°59E 69 C4
Geelong Australia 38°10S 144°22E 152 E6
Geelvink B. = Cenderawasih,
Teluk Indonesia 3°0S 135°20E 119 E9
Geelvink Chan.
Australia 28°30S 114°0E 149 E1
Geesthacht Germany 53°26N 10°22E 76 B6
Geidam Nigeria 12°57N 11°57E 139 C7
Geikie → Canada 57°45N 103°52W 163 B8
Geikie Gorge △
Australia 18°3S 125°41E 148 C4
Geilenkirchen Germany 50°57N 6°8E 76 E2
Geisingen Germany 47°54N 8°38E 77 H4
Geislingen Germany 48°37N 9°50E 77 G5
Geistown U.S.A. 40°18N 78°52W 174 F6
Geita Tanzania 2°48S 32°12E 142 C3
Geita □ Tanzania 2°50S 32°10E 14
Gejiu China 23°20N 103°10E 1
Gel, Meydān-e Iran 29°4N 54°50E 12
Gela Italy 37°4N 14°15E
Gela, G. di Italy 37°0N 14°20E
Gelahun Liberia 7°55N 10°28W 13
Gelang Patah Malaysia 1°27N 103°35E
Gelasa, Selat Indonesia 2°50S 107°0E 1
Gelderland □ Neths. 52°5N 6°10E
Geldern Germany 51°31N 6°20E
Geldrop Neths. 51°25N 5°32E
Geleen Neths. 50°57N 5°49E
Gelehun S. Leone 8°20N 11°40W 13
Gelembe Turkey 39°10N 27°50E
Gelendost Turkey 38°7N 31°1E 1
Gelendzhik Russia 44°33N 38°10E 8
Gelib = Jilib Somalia 0°29N 42°46E 1
Gelibolu Turkey 40°28N 26°43E 9
Gelibolu Yarımadası
Turkey 40°20N 26°30E 9
Gelidonya Burnu
Turkey 36°12N 30°24E 1
Gelnhausen Germany 50°11N 9°11E
Gelnica Slovak Rep. 48°51N 20°55E 7
Gelsenkirchen Germany 51°32N 7°6E
Gelting Germany 54°45N 9°53E
Gelugur Malaysia 5°22N 100°18E
Gemas Malaysia 2°37N 102°36E 1
Gembloux Belgium 50°34N 4°43E
Gembu Nigeria 6°42N 11°10E 1
Gemena
Dem. Rep. of the Congo 3°13N 19°48E 1
Gemerek Turkey 39°15N 36°10E 1
Gemikonağı = Karavostasi
Cyprus 35°8N 32°50E 10
Gemla Sweden 56°52N 14°39E
Gemlik Turkey 40°26N 29°9E
Gemlik Körfezi Turkey 40°25N 28°55E 9
Gemona del Friuli Italy 46°16N 13°9E 9
Gemsa Egypt 27°39N 33°35E 1
Gemsbok △ Botswana 25°5S 21°1E 1
Gemünden Germany 50°3N 9°42E
Genadi Greece 36°2N 27°56E 1
Genale → Ethiopia 6°2N 39°1E 1
Genç Turkey 38°44N 40°34E 1
Gençay France 46°23N 0°23E
General Acha
Argentina 37°20S 64°38W 1
General Alvear B. Aires,
Argentina 36°0S 60°0W 1
General Alvear Mendoza,
Argentina 35°0S 67°40W 1
General Artigas
Paraguay 26°52S 56°16W 1
General Belgrano
Argentina 36°35S 58°47W 1
General Bernardo O'Higgins
Antarctica 63°0S 58°3W 5
General Cabrera
Argentina 32°53S 63°52W 1
General Carrera, L.
S. Amer. 46°35S 72°0W 1
General Cepeda
Mexico 25°21N 101°22W 1
General Conesa
Argentina 40°6S 64°25W 1
General Guido
Argentina 36°40S 57°50W 1
General Juan Madariaga
Argentina 37°0S 57°0W 1
General La Madrid
Argentina 37°17S 61°20W 1
General Lorenzo Vintter
Argentina 40°45S 64°26W 1
General MacArthur
Phil. 11°18N 125°28E 1
General Martin Miguel de Güemes
Argentina 24°50S 65°0W 1
General Pico Argentina 35°45S 63°50W 1
General Pinedo
Argentina 27°15S 61°20W 1
General Pinto
Argentina 34°45S 61°50W 1
General Roca Argentina 39°2S 67°35W 1
General Sampaio Brazil 4°2S 39°29W 1
General Santos Phil. 6°5N 125°14E 1
General Toshevo
Bulgaria 43°42N 28°6E 9
General Treviño
Mexico 26°14N 99°29W 1
General Trías Mexico 28°21N 106°22W 1
General Viamonte
Argentina 35°1S 61°3W 1
General Villegas
Argentina 35°5S 63°0W 1
General Vintter, L.
Argentina 43°55S 71°40W 1
Genesee Idaho, U.S.A. 46°33N 116°56W 1
Genesee Pa., U.S.A. 41°59N 77°54W 1
Genesee → U.S.A. 43°16N 77°36W 1
Geneseo Ill., U.S.A. 41°27N 90°9W 1
Geneseo N.Y., U.S.A. 42°48N 77°49W 1
Geneva = Genève Switz. 46°12N 6°9E 7
Geneva Ala., U.S.A. 31°2N 85°52W 1
Geneva Ga., U.S.A. 32°35N 84°33W 1
Geneva N.Y., U.S.A. 42°52N 76°59W 1
Geneva Nebr., U.S.A. 40°32N 97°36W 1
Geneva Ohio, U.S.A. 41°48N 80°57W 1
Geneva, L. = Léman, L.
Europe 46°26N 6°30E 71
Genève Switz. 46°12N 6°9E 7
Gengenbach Germany 48°24N 8°1E 7
Gengma China 23°32N 99°20E 11
Genhe China 50°47N 121°31E 111
Genichesk = Henichesk
Ukraine 46°12N 34°50E 8
Genil → Spain 37°42N 5°19W 8
Genisea Greece 41°1N 24°57E 9
Genk Belgium 50°58N 5°32E 6
Genlis France 47°11N 5°12E 71
Gennargentu, Mti. del
Italy 40°1N 9°19E 9
Gennes France 47°20N 0°17W 7
Genoa = Gênova Italy 44°25N 8°57E 9
Genoa Australia 37°29S 149°35E 15
Genoa N.Y., U.S.A. 42°40N 76°32W 17
Genoa Nebr., U.S.A. 41°27N 97°44W 17
Genoa Nev., U.S.A. 39°2N 119°50W 17
Genoa → Argentina 44°55S 70°5W 19
Génova Italy 44°25N 8°57E 9
Génova ✕ (GOA) Italy 44°25N 8°56E 9
Génova, G. di Italy 44°0N 9°0E 9

riyetty, Ostrov
 ussia 77°6N 156°30E 107 B16
t Belgium 51°2N 3°42E 69 C3
teng Jawa Barat,
 donesia 7°22S 106°24E 119 G12
teng Jawa Timur,
 donesia 8°22S 114°9E 119 J17
thin Germany 52°25N 12°9E 76 C8
tio do Ouro Brazil 11°25S 42°30W 189 C2
yem Indonesia
zano di Lucánia Italy 40°51N 16°2E 95 B9
zano di Roma Italy 41°42N 12°41E 93 G9
chang S. Korea 34°55N 127°55E 115 G14
agiu Romania 45°55N 23°12E 81 E8
graphe B. Australia 33°30S 115°15E 149 F2
graphe Chan.
 ustralia 24°30S 113°0E 149 D1
graphical Society Ø
 reenland 72°57N 23°15W 57 C8
ie S. Korea 34°51N 128°35E 115 G15
kchay = Göyçay
 zerbaijan 40°42N 47°43E 87 K8
rga, Zemlya Russia 80°30N 49°0E 106 A5
rga S. Africa 33°58S 22°29E 144 D3
rge → Canada 58°49N 66°10W 165 A6
rge, L. N.S.W.,
 ustralia 35°10S 149°25E 153 C8
rge, L. S. Austral.,
 ustralia 37°25S 140°0E 152 D4
rge, L. W. Austral.,
 ustralia 22°45S 123°40E 148 D3
rge, L. Uganda 0°5N 30°10E 142 B3
rge, L. Fla., U.S.A. 29°17N 81°36W 177 G5
rge, L. N.Y.,
 .S.A. 43°37N 73°33W 175 C11
rge Bush Intercontinental,
 ouston ✕ (IAH)
 .S.A. 29°59N 95°20W 176 G7
rge Gill Ra.
 ustralia 24°22S 131°45E 148 D5
rge Pt. Australia 20°6S 148°36E 150 b
rge River = Kangiqsualujjuaq
 anada 58°30N 65°59W 161 F18
rge Sound N.Z. 44°52S 167°25E 155 E2
rge Town Australia 41°6S 146°49E 151 G4
rge Town Bahamas 23°33N 75°47W 182 B4
rge Town
 ayman Is. 19°20N 81°24W 182 C3
rge Town Malaysia 5°25N 100°20E 121 c
rge V Land
 ntarctica 69°0S 148°0E 55 C10
rge VI Sound
 ntarctica 71°0S 68°0W 55 D17
rge West U.S.A. 28°20N 98°7W 176 G5
rgetown = Janjanbureh
 ambia 13°30N 14°47W 138 C2
rgetown Australia 18°17S 143°33E 150 B3
rgetown Ont.,
 anada 43°40N 79°56W 174 C5
rgetown P.E.I.,
 anada 46°13N 62°24W 165 C7
rgetown Guyana 6°50N 58°12W 186 B7
rgetown Calif.,
 .S.A. 38°54N 120°50W 170 G6
rgetown Colo.,
 .S.A. 39°42N 105°42W 168 G11
rgetown Fla.,
 .S.A. 29°23N 81°38W 179 F8
rgetown Ga., U.S.A. 31°53N 85°6W 178 D4
rgetown Ky.,
 .S.A. 38°13N 84°33W 173 F11
rgetown N.Y.,
 .S.A. 42°46N 75°44W 175 D9
rgetown Ohio,
 .S.A. 38°52N 83°54W 173 F12
rgetown S.C.,
 .S.A. 33°23N 79°17W 177 E15
rgetown Tex.,
 .S.A. 30°38N 97°41W 176 F4
rgia □ U.S.A. 32°50N 83°15W 178 C6
rgia □ Asia 42°0N 43°0E 87 J6
rgia, Str. of
 Amer. 49°25N 124°0W 170 A3
rgia Basin S. Ocean 50°45S 35°30W 55 B1
rgia B. Canada 45°15N 81°0W 174 A4
rgian Bay Islands ✕
 anada 44°53N 79°52W 174 B5
rgievka
 azakhstan 49°19N 84°34E 109 C10
rgina → Australia 23°30S 139°47E 150 C2
rgina I. Canada 44°22N 79°17W 174 B5
rgioupoli Greece 35°20N 24°15E 101 D6
rgiyevsk Russia 44°12N 43°28E 87 H6
rgsmarienhütte
 Germany 52°13N 8°3E 76 C4
a Germany 50°53N 12°4E 76 E8
aardsbergen Belgium 50°45N 3°53E 69 D3
aki Greece 37°0N 22°42E 98 D4
al, Serra Bahia, Brazil 14°0S 41°0W 189 D2
al, Serra Goiás,
 razil 11°15S 46°30W 189 C1
al, Serra Sta. Catarina,
 razil 26°25S 50°0W 191 B6
de Goiás, Serra
 razil 12°0S 46°0W 189 C1
do Paraná, Serra
 razil 15°0S 47°30W 189 D1
aldine N.Z. 44°5S 171°15E 155 E6
aldton U.S.A. 47°36N 110°16W 168 C8
aldton Australia 28°48S 114°32E 149 E1
aldton Canada 49°44N 87°10W 164 C2
anium Australia 35°23S 140°11E 152 C4
üş Turkey 37°34N 41°23E 105 D9
s, Sierra do Portugal 41°48N 8°0W 88 B3
eshk Azerbaijan 31°47N 64°35E 122 D4
etsried Germany 47°51N 11°28E 77 H7
gal Spain 57°2N 3°31W 91 H2
k Malaysia 5°50N 101°15E 121 K3
ach U.S.A. 41°50N 103°40W 172 E3
achovský štít
 ovak Rep. 49°11N 20°7E 79 B13
man Bight = Deutsche Bucht
 ermany 54°15N 8°0E 76 A4
man Planina
 acedonia 42°20N 22°0E 96 B6
mania Land
 reenland 77°5N 19°30W 57 B9

Germansen Landing
 Canada 55°43N 124°40W 162 B4
Germantown U.S.A. 35°5N 89°49W 177 D10
Germany ■ Europe 51°0N 10°0E 76 E6
Germencik Turkey 37°52N 27°37E 99 D9
Germering Germany 48°8N 11°22E 77 G7
Germersheim Germany 49°12N 8°22E 77 F4
Germī Iran 39°1N 48°3E 105 C13
Germiston S. Africa 26°13S 28°10E 145 C4
Gernika-Lumo Spain 43°19N 2°40W 90 B2
Gernsheim Germany 49°45N 8°30E 77 F4
Gero Japan 35°48N 137°14E 113 G8
Gerogery Australia 35°50S 147°1E 153 C7
Gerokgak Indonesia 8°11S 114°27E 119 J17
Gerolzhofen Germany 49°54N 10°21E 77 F6
Gerona = Girona Spain 41°58N 2°46E 90 D7
Geropotamos → Greece 35°3N 24°50E 101 D6
Gerrard Canada 50°30N 117°17W 162 C5
Gerringong Australia 34°46S 150°47E 153 C9
Gersoppa Falls India 14°12N 74°46E 127 G2
Gersthofen Germany 48°25N 10°53E 77 G6
Gertak Sanggul
 Malaysia 5°17N 100°12E 121 c
Gertak Sanggul, Tanjung
 Malaysia 5°16N 100°11E 121 c
Gerung Indonesia 8°43S 116°7E 119 K19
Gerzat France 45°48N 3°8E 72 C7
Gerze Turkey 41°48N 35°12E 104 B6
Geseke Germany 51°38N 8°31E 76 D4
Geser Indonesia 3°50S 130°54E 119 E8
Gesso → Italy 44°24N 7°33E 92 D4
Getafe Spain 40°18N 3°43W 88 E7
Getinge Sweden 56°49N 12°44E 63 H6
Gettysburg Pa., U.S.A. 39°50N 77°14W 173 F15
Gettysburg S. Dak.,
 U.S.A. 45°1N 99°57W 172 C4
Getxo = Algorta Spain 43°21N 2°59W 90 B2
Getz Ice Shelf Antarctica 75°0S 130°0W 55 D14
Gevas Turkey 38°15N 43°6E 105 C10
Gévora → Spain 38°53N 6°57W 89 G4
Gevrai India 19°16N 75°45E 126 E2
Gex France 46°21N 6°3E 71 F13
Geyikli Turkey 39°48N 26°12E 99 B8
Geyser U.S.A. 47°16N 110°30W 168 C8
Geyserville U.S.A. 38°42N 122°54W 170 G4
Geyve Turkey 40°30N 30°18E 104 B4
Gezhouba Dam China 30°40N 111°20E 117 B8
Ghadaf, W. al → Iraq 32°56N 43°30E 105 F10
Ghadāmis Libya 30°11N 9°29E 135 B8
Ghaggar → India 29°30N 74°53E 124 E6
Ghaghara → India 25°45N 84°40E 125 G11
Ghaghat → Bangla. 25°19N 89°38E 125 G13
Ghagra India 23°17N 84°33E 125 H11
Ghallamane Mauritania 23°15N 10°0W 134 D4
Ghana ■ W. Afr. 8°0N 1°0W 139 D4
Ghanpokhara Nepal 28°17N 84°14E 125 E10
Ghansor India 22°39N 80°1E 125 H9
Ghanzi Botswana 21°50S 21°34E 144 B3
Ghanzi □ Botswana 22°30S 22°30E 144 B3
Gharb-Chrarda-Beni Hssen □
 Morocco 35°35N 6°0W 136 A2
Gharbīya, Es Sahrâ el
 Egypt 27°40N 26°30E 137 B2
Ghardaïa Algeria 32°20N 3°37E 136 B4
Ghardaïa □ Algeria 31°5N 3°10E 136 B4
Ghârib, G. Egypt 28°6N 32°54E 137 B8
Gharm Tajikistan 39°0N 70°20E 106 F8
Gharyān Libya 32°10N 13°0E 135 B8
Ghāt Libya 24°59N 10°11E 135 D8
Ghatal India 22°40N 87°46E 125 H12
Ghatampur India 26°8N 80°13E 125 F9
Ghatgaon India 21°24N 85°53E 126 D7
Ghatprabha → India 16°15N 75°20E 127 F2
Ghats, Eastern India 14°0N 78°50E 127 H4
Ghats, Western India 14°0N 75°0E 127 H2
Ghatsila India 22°36N 86°29E 125 H12
Ghaṭṭī Si. Arabia 31°16N 37°31E 114 D3
Ghawdex = Gozo Malta 36°3N 14°15E 101 C1
Ghazal, Bahr el → Chad 13°0N 15°47E 135 F9
Ghazal, Bahr el →
 South Sudan 9°31N 30°25E 135 G12
Ghazaouet Algeria 35°8N 1°50W 136 A4
Ghaziabad India 28°42N 77°26E 124 E7
Ghazipur India 25°38N 83°35E 125 G10
Ghaznī Afghan. 33°30N 68°28E 124 C3
Ghaznī □ Afghan. 32°10N 68°20E 124 C3
Ghedi Italy 45°24N 10°16E 92 C7
Ghelari Romania 45°38N 22°45E 80 E7
Ghent = Gent Belgium 51°2N 3°42E 69 C3
Gheorghe Gheorghiu-Dej = Oneşti
 Romania 46°17N 26°47E 81 D11
Gheorgheni Romania 46°43N 25°41E 81 D10
Gherla Romania 47°2N 23°57E 81 C8
Ghidigeni Romania 46°3N 27°30E 81 D12
Ghilarza Italy 40°7N 8°50E 94 B1
Ghimeş-Făget Romania 46°35N 26°2E 81 D11
Ghinah, Wādī al →
 Si. Arabia 30°27N 38°14E 128 D3
Ghisonaccia France 42°1N 9°26E 73 F13
Ghisoni France 42°8N 9°23E 73 F13
Ghizar → Pakistan 36°15N 73°43E 125 A5
Ghod → India 18°30N 74°35E 126 D2
Ghogha India 21°40N 72°20E 126 D1
Ghot Ogrein Egypt 31°10N 25°20E 137 A2
Ghotaru India 27°20N 70°1E 124 F4
Ghotki Pakistan 28°5N 69°21E 124 E3
Ghowr □ Afghan. 34°0N 64°20E 122 C4
Ghughus India 22°39N 80°41E 126 A4
Ghulam Mohammad Barrage
 Pakistan 25°30N 68°20E 124 G3
Ghūrīān Afghan. 34°17N 61°25E 122 C3
Gia Dinh Vietnam 10°49N 106°42E 121 G6
Gia Lai = Plei Ku
 Vietnam 13°57N 108°0E 120 F7
Gia Nghia Vietnam 11°58N 107°42E 121 G6
Gia Ngoc Vietnam 14°50N 108°58E 120 E7
Gia Vuc Vietnam 14°42N 108°34E 120 E7
Giali Greece 36°41N 27°11E 99 E9
Gialtra Greece 38°51N 22°59E 98 C4
Giamama = Jamaame
 Somalia 0°4N 42°44E 131 G3
Gianitsa Greece 40°46N 22°24E 98 A4
Giannutri Italy 42°15N 11°6E 92 F8
Giant Forest U.S.A. 36°36N 118°43W 170 J8

Giant Mts. = Krkonoše
 Czech Rep. 50°50N 15°35E 78 A8
Giant Sequoia △
 U.S.A. 36°10N 118°35W 170 K8
Giants Causeway U.K. 55°16N 6°29W 64 A5
Giant's Tank Sri Lanka 8°51N 80°2E 127 K5
Gianyar Indonesia 8°35S 115°20E 119 K18
Giàrabub = Al Jaghbūb
 Libya 29°42N 24°38E 135 C10
Giaros Greece 37°32N 24°40E 98 D6
Giarre Italy 37°43N 15°11E 95 B8
Giaveno Italy 45°2N 7°21E 92 C4
Gibara Cuba 21°9N 76°11W 182 B4
Gibbon U.S.A. 40°45N 98°51W 172 E4
Gibe II Ethiopia 8°0N 37°30E 131 F2
Gibe III Ethiopia 7°0N 37°30E 131 F2
Gibellina Nuova Italy 37°47N 12°58E 94 E5
Gibeon Namibia 25°9S 17°43E 144 C2
Gibraleón Spain 37°23N 6°58W 89 H4
Gibraltar ☑ Europe 36°7N 5°22W 89 J5
Gibraltar, Str. of Medit. S. 35°55N 5°40W 89 K5
Gibraltar Range △
 Australia 29°31S 152°19E 151 D5
Gibson U.S.A. 33°14N 82°36W 178 D7
Gibson Desert Australia 24°0S 126°0E 148 D4
Gibsons Canada 49°24N 123°32W 162 D4
Gibsonton U.S.A. 27°51N 82°23W 179 H7
Gibsonville U.S.A. 39°46N 120°54W 170 F6
Giddalur India 15°20N 78°57E 127 G4
Giddings U.S.A. 30°11N 96°56W 176 F6
Giebnegáisi = Kebnekaise
 Sweden 67°53N 18°33E 60 C18
Gien France 47°40N 2°36E 71 E9
Giengen Germany 48°37N 10°14E 77 G6
Giessen Germany 50°34N 8°41E 76 E4
Gīfān Iran 37°54N 57°28E 129 B8
Gifatin, Geziret Egypt 27°10N 33°50E 137 B3
Gifford U.S.A. 27°40N 80°25W 179 H9
Gifhorn Germany 52°30N 10°33E 76 C6
Gift Lake Canada 55°53N 115°49W 162 B5
Gifu Japan 35°30N 136°45E 113 G8
Gifu □ Japan 35°40N 137°0E 113 G8
Gigant Russia 46°28N 41°20E 87 G5
Giganta, Sa. de la
 Mexico 26°0N 111°39W 180 B2
Gigen Bulgaria 43°40N 24°28E 97 C8
Gigha U.K. 55°42N 5°44W 65 F3
Gíglio Italy 42°20N 10°52E 92 F7
Gignac France 43°39N 3°32E 72 E7
Gigüela → Spain 39°8N 3°44W 88 E7
Gijón = Xixón Spain 43°32N 5°42W 88 B5
Gikongoro Rwanda 2°28S 29°34E 142 C2
Gil I. Canada 53°12N 129°15W 162 C3
Gila → U.S.A. 32°43N 114°33W 169 K6
Gila Bend U.S.A. 32°57N 112°43W 169 K7
Gila Bend Mts. U.S.A. 33°10N 113°0W 169 K7
Gila Cliff Dwellings △
 U.S.A. 33°12N 108°16W 169 K9
Gīlān □ Iran 37°0N 50°0E 129 B6
Gīlān-e Gharb Iran 34°8N 45°55E 105 E11
Gilău Romania 46°45N 23°23E 81 D8
Gilbert → Australia 16°35S 141°15E 150 B3
Gilbert Is. Kiribati 1°0N 172°0E 147 A10
Gilbert River Australia 18°9S 142°52E 150 B3
Gilbert Seamounts
 Pac. Oc. 52°50N 150°10W 54 D18
Gilbués Brazil 9°50S 45°21W 189 B1
Gilead U.S.A. 44°24N 70°59W 175 B14
Gilf el Kebîr, Hadabat el
 Egypt 23°50N 25°50E 137 C2
Gilford I. Canada 50°40N 126°30W 162 C3
Gilgandra Australia 31°43S 148°39E 153 A8
Gilgil Kenya 0°30S 36°20E 142 C4
Gilgit India 35°50N 74°15E 125 B6
Gilgit → Pakistan 35°44N 74°37E 125 B6
Gilgit-Baltistan □
 Pakistan 36°30N 73°0E 125 A5
Gilgunnia Australia 32°26S 146°2E 153 B7
Gili □ Mozam. 16°39S 38°27E 143 F4
Gilimanuk Indonesia 8°10S 114°26E 119 J17
Giljeva Planina Europe 43°9N 20°0E 96 C3
Gillam Canada 56°20N 94°40W 163 B10
Gilleleje Denmark 56°8N 12°19E 63 H6
Gillen, L. Australia 26°11S 124°38E 149 E3
Gilles, L. Australia 32°50S 136°45E 152 B2
Gillespies Pt. N.Z. 43°24S 169°49E 155 D4
Gillette U.S.A. 44°18N 105°30W 168 D11
Gilliat Australia 20°40S 141°28E 150 C3
Gillingham U.K. 51°23N 0°33E 67 D8
Gilmer U.S.A. 32°44N 94°57W 176 E7
Gilmore, L. Australia 32°29S 121°37E 149 F3
Gilmour Canada 44°48N 77°37W 174 B7
Gilort → Romania 44°38N 23°32E 81 E8
Gilroy U.S.A. 37°1N 121°34W 170 H5
Gimcheon S. Korea 36°11N 128°4E 115 F15
Gimhae S. Korea 35°14N 128°53E 115 G15
Gimhwa S. Korea 38°17N 127°28E 115 E14
Gimie, Mt. St. Lucia 13°54N 61°0W 183 f
Gimje S. Korea 35°48N 126°45E 115 G14
Gimli Canada 50°40N 97°0W 163 C9
Gimo Sweden 60°11N 18°12E 62 D12
Gimone → France 44°0N 1°6E 72 E5
Gimont France 43°38N 0°52E 72 E5
Gin → Sri Lanka 6°5N 80°7E 127 L5
Gin Gin Australia 25°0S 151°58E 151 D5
Gināh Egypt 25°21N 30°30E 137 C7
Gineifa Egypt 30°12N 32°25E 137 E8
Gingee India 12°15N 79°25E 127 H4
Gingin Australia 31°22S 115°54E 149 F2
Gingindlovu S. Africa 29°2S 31°30E 145 C5
Ginir Ethiopia 7°6N 40°40E 131 F3
Ginosa Italy 40°35N 16°45E 95 B9
Ginzo de Limia = Xinzo de Limia
 Spain 42°3N 7°47W 88 C3
Giófyros → Greece 35°20N 25°6E 101 D7
Gióia, G. di Italy 38°30N 15°45E 95 D8
Gióia del Colle Italy 40°48N 16°55E 95 B9
Gióia Táuro Italy 38°25N 15°54E 95 D8
Gioiosa Iónica Italy 38°20N 16°19E 95 D9
Gioiosa Marea Italy 38°10N 14°54E 95 D7
Giona, Oros Greece 38°38N 22°14E 98 C4
Giovi, Passo dei Italy 44°33N 8°57E 92 D5
Giovinazzo Italy 41°11N 16°40E 95 A9
Gippsland Australia 37°52S 147°0E 153 D7
Gipuzkoa □ Spain 43°12N 2°15W 90 B2
Gir Hills India 21°0N 71°0E 124 J4
Girab India 26°2N 70°38E 124 F3
Girâfi, W. → Egypt 29°58N 34°39E 130 F3
Giraltovce Slovak Rep. 49°7N 21°32E 79 B14

Girard St. Lucia 13°59N 60°57W 183 D7
Girard Ga., U.S.A. 33°3N 81°43W 178 D8
Girard Kans., U.S.A. 37°31N 94°51W 172 G6
Girard Ohio, U.S.A. 41°9N 80°42W 174 E4
Girard Pa., U.S.A. 42°0N 80°19W 174 E4
Girdle Ness U.K. 57°9N 2°3W 65 D6
Giresun Turkey 40°55N 38°30E 105 B8
Girga Egypt 26°17N 31°55E 137 B3
Giri → India 30°28N 77°41E 124 D7
Giridih India 24°10N 86°21E 125 G12
Girifalco Italy 38°49N 16°25E 95 D9
Giriftu Kenya 1°59N 39°46E 142 B4
Girilambone Australia 31°16S 146°57E 153 A7
Girne = Kyrenia
 Cyprus 35°20N 33°20E 101 D12
Giro Nigeria 11°7N 4°42E 139 C5
Giromagny France 47°45N 6°50E 71 E13
Girona Spain 41°58N 2°46E 90 D7
Girona □ Spain 42°11N 2°30E 90 D7
Gironde □ France 44°45N 0°30W 72 D3
Gironde → France 45°32N 1°7W 72 C2
Gironella Spain 42°2N 1°53E 90 C6
Girvan U.K. 55°14N 4°51W 65 F4
Gisborne Australia 37°29S 144°36E 152 D6
Gisborne N.Z. 38°39S 178°5E 154 E7
Gisborne □ N.Z. 38°30S 178°0E 154 E7
Gisenyi Rwanda 1°41S 29°15E 142 C2
Gislaved Sweden 57°19N 13°32E 63 G7
Gisors France 49°15N 1°47E 71 C8
Gitarama Rwanda 2°4S 29°45E 142 C2
Gitega Burundi 3°26S 29°56E 142 C2
Githio Greece 36°46N 22°34E 98 E4
Giuba = Juba →
 Somalia 1°30N 42°35E 131 G3
Giugliano in Campania
 Italy 40°56N 14°12E 95 B7
Giulianova Italy 42°45N 13°57E 93 F10
Giura Greece 39°23N 24°10E 98 B6
Giurgeni Romania 44°45N 27°48E 81 F12
Giurgiu Romania 43°52N 25°57E 81 G10
Giurgiu □ Romania 44°20N 26°0E 81 F10
Give Denmark 55°51N 9°13E 63 J3
Givet France 50°8N 4°49E 71 B11
Givors France 45°35N 4°45E 73 C8
Givry France 46°41N 4°46E 71 F11
Giyani S. Africa 23°19S 30°43E 145 B5
Giza = El Giza Egypt 30°0N 31°12E 137 F7
Giza Pyramids Egypt 29°58N 31°9E 137 F7
Gizab Afghan. 33°22N 66°17E 124 C5
Gizhiga Russia 62°3N 160°30E 107 C17
Gizhiginskaya Guba
 Russia 61°0N 158°0E 107 C16
Giżycko Poland 54°2N 21°48E 82 D8
Gizzeria Italy 38°59N 16°12E 95 D9
Gjakovë Kosovo 42°22N 20°26E 96 D4
Gjalicë e Lumës, Mal.
 Albania 42°2N 20°25E 96 D4
Gjegjan Albania 41°58N 20°3E 96 D4
Gjeračicë Kosovo 42°32N 20°8E 96 D4
Gjilan Kosovo 42°28N 21°29E 96 D5
Gjirokastër Albania 40°7N 20°10E 96 F4
Gjoa Haven Canada 68°38N 95°53W 160 D12
Gjøvik Norway 60°47N 10°43E 60 F14
Gjuhës, Kep i Albania 40°28N 19°15E 96 F3
Gjurakoc Kosovo 42°34N 20°29E 96 D4
Glace Bay Canada 46°11N 59°58W 165 C8
Glacier △ U.S.A. 48°42N 113°48W 168 B7
Glacier △ Canada 58°40N 136°0W 160 F4
Glacier Bay △ U.S.A. 58°45N 136°30W 162 B1
Glacier Peak U.S.A. 48°7N 121°7W 168 B3
Gladewater U.S.A. 32°33N 94°56W 176 E7
Gladstone Queens.,
 Australia 23°52S 151°16E 150 C5
Gladstone S. Austral.,
 Australia 33°15S 138°22E 152 B2
Gladstone Canada 50°13N 98°57W 163 C9
Gladstone U.S.A. 45°51N 87°1W 172 C10
Gladwin U.S.A. 43°59N 84°29W 173 D11
Glafsfjorden Sweden 59°30N 12°37E 62 E6
Glagah Indonesia 8°13S 114°18E 119 J17
Głagów Malopolski
 Poland 50°10N 21°56E 83 H8
Glâma = Glomma →
 Norway 59°12N 10°57E 61 G14
Gláma Iceland 65°48N 23°0W 60 D2
Glamis U.S.A. 32°55N 115°5W 171 N11
Glamoč Bos.-H. 44°3N 16°51E 93 F7
Glamorgan, Vale of □
 U.K. 51°28N 3°25W 67 F4
Glasco Kans., U.S.A. 39°22N 97°50W 172 F5
Glasco N.Y., U.S.A. 42°3N 73°57W 175 D11
Glasgow U.K. 55°51N 4°15W 65 F4
Glasgow Ky., U.S.A. 37°0N 85°55W 173 G11
Glasgow Mont.,
 U.S.A. 48°12N 106°38W 168 B10
Glasgow City □ U.K. 55°51N 4°12W 65 F4
Glasgow Int. ✕ (GLA)
 U.K. 55°51N 4°21W 65 F4
Glaslyn Canada 53°22N 108°21W 163 C7
Glastonbury U.K. 51°9N 2°43W 67 F5
Glastonbury U.S.A. 41°43N 72°37W 175 E12
Glauchau Germany 50°49N 12°33E 76 E8
Glava Sweden 59°33N 12°35E 62 E6
Glavice Croatia 43°33N 16°41E 93 E13
Glazov Russia 58°9N 52°40E 86 A11
Gleichen Canada 50°52N 113°3W 162 C6
Gleisdorf Austria 47°6N 15°44E 78 D8
Gleiwitz = Gliwice
 Poland 50°22N 18°41E 83 H5
Glen U.S.A. 44°7N 71°11W 175 B13
Glen Affric U.K. 57°17N 5°1W 65 D3
Glen Afton N.Z. 37°37S 175°4E 154 D4
Glen Canyon U.S.A. 37°15N 111°0W 169 H8
Glen Canyon △ U.S.A. 37°15N 111°0W 169 H8
Glen Canyon Dam
 U.S.A. 36°57N 111°29W 169 H8
Glen Coe U.K. 56°40N 5°0W 65 E3
Glen Cove U.S.A. 40°52N 73°38W 175 E13
Glen Garry U.K. 57°3N 5°7W 65 D3
Glen Innes Australia 29°44S 151°44E 151 D5
Glen Lyon U.S.A. 41°10N 76°5W 175 E8
Glen Massey N.Z. 37°38S 175°2E 154 D4

Glen Mor U.K. 57°9N 4°37W 65 D4
Glen Moriston U.K. 57°11N 4°52W 65 D4
Glen Robertson
 Canada 45°22N 74°30W 175 A10
Glen Spean U.K. 56°53N 4°40E 65 E4
Glen Ullin U.S.A. 46°49N 101°50W 172 B3
Glénan, Îs. de France 47°43N 4°0W 70 E3
Glenavy N.Z. 44°54S 171°7E 155 E6
Glenbeigh Ireland 52°3N 9°58W 64 D2
Glenburn Australia 37°27S 145°26E 153 D6
Glencoe Canada 42°45N 81°43W 174 D3
Glencoe S. Africa 28°11S 30°11E 145 C5
Glencoe Ala., U.S.A. 33°57N 85°56W 178 D4
Glencoe Minn., U.S.A. 44°46N 94°9W 172 C6
Glencolumbkille Ireland 54°43N 8°42W 64 B3
Glendale Ariz., U.S.A. 33°32N 112°11W 169 K7
Glendale Calif., U.S.A. 34°9N 118°15W 171 L8
Glendale Fla., U.S.A. 30°52N 86°7W 178 E3
Glendale Zimbabwe 17°22S 31°5E 143 F3
Glendive U.S.A. 47°7N 104°43W 168 C2
Glendo U.S.A. 42°30N 105°2W 168 E11
Glenelg Australia 34°58S 138°31E 152 C3
Glenelg → Australia 38°4S 140°59E 152 D4
Glenfield U.S.A. 43°43N 75°24W 175 C9
Glengad Hd. Ireland 55°20N 7°10W 64 A4
Glengarriff Ireland 51°45N 9°34W 64 E2
Glenham N.Z. 46°26S 168°52E 155 F2
Glenhope N.Z. 41°40S 172°39E 155 D5
Glenmary, Mt. N.Z. 43°45S 169°59E 155 D4
Glenmont U.S.A. 40°31N 82°6W 174 F2
Glenmorgan Australia 27°14S 149°42E 151 D4
Glenn U.S.A. 39°31N 122°1W 170 F4
Glennallen U.S.A. 62°7N 145°33W 160 D5
Glennamaddy Ireland 53°37N 8°33W 64 C3
Glenns Ferry U.S.A. 42°57N 115°18W 168 E6
Glenville U.S.A. 31°56N 81°56W 178 D8
Glenora Canada 44°2N 77°3W 174 B7
Glenorchy Tas.,
 Australia 42°49S 147°18E 151 G4
Glenorchy Vic.,
 Australia 36°55S 142°41E 152 C5
Glenorchy N.Z. 44°51S 168°24E 155 E3
Glenore Australia 17°50S 141°12E 150 B3
Glenreagh Australia 30°2S 153°1E 151 E5
Glenrock U.S.A. 42°52N 105°52W 168 E11
Glenrothes U.K. 56°12N 3°10W 65 E5
Glenrowan
 Australia 36°29S 146°13E 153 D7
Glens Falls U.S.A. 43°19N 73°39W 175 C11
Glenside U.S.A. 40°6N 75°9W 175 F9
Glenthompson
 Australia 37°38S 142°35E 152 D5
Glenties Ireland 54°48N 8°17W 64 B3
Glenveagh △ Ireland 55°3N 8°1W 64 A3
Glenville U.S.A. 38°56N 80°50W 173 F13
Glenwood Ark., U.S.A. 34°20N 93°33W 176 D8
Glenwood Ala., U.S.A. 31°40N 86°11W 178 E4
Glenwood Iowa, U.S.A. 41°3N 95°45W 172 E6
Glenwood Minn.,
 U.S.A. 45°39N 95°23W 172 C6
Glenwood Wash.,
 U.S.A. 46°1N 121°17W 170 D5
Glenwood Springs
 U.S.A. 39°33N 107°19W 168 G10
Glettinganes Iceland 65°30N 13°37W 60 D7
Glifada Greece 37°52N 23°45E 98 D5
Glímákra Sweden 56°19N 14°7E 63 H8
Glin Ireland 52°34N 9°17W 64 D2
Glina Croatia 45°20N 16°6E 93 C13
Glinojeck Poland 52°49N 20°21E 83 F7
Gliwice Poland 50°22N 18°41E 83 H5
Globe U.S.A. 33°24N 110°47W 169 K8
Glodeanu Siliştea
 Romania 44°50N 26°48E 81 F11
Glodeni Moldova 47°45N 27°31E 81 C12
Glödnitz Austria 46°53N 14°7E 78 E7
Gloggnitz Austria 47°41N 15°56E 78 D8
Głogów Poland 51°37N 16°5E 83 G3
Głogówek Poland 50°21N 17°53E 83 H4
Glomma → Norway 59°12N 10°57E 61 G14
Glorieuses, Îs. Ind. Oc. 11°30S 47°20E 141 G9
Glosa Greece 39°10N 23°45E 98 B5
Glossop U.K. 53°27N 1°56W 66 D6
Gloucester Australia 32°0S 151°59E 153 B9
Gloucester Canada 45°18N 75°35W 175 A9
Gloucester U.K. 51°53N 2°15W 67 F5
Gloucester U.S.A. 42°37N 70°40W 175 D14
Gloucester I. Australia 20°0S 148°30E 150 b
Gloucester Island △
 Australia 20°2S 148°30E 150 b
Gloucester Point
 U.S.A. 37°15N 76°30W 173 G15
Gloucestershire □ U.K. 51°46N 2°15W 67 F5
Gloversville U.S.A. 43°3N 74°21W 175 C10
Glovertown Canada 48°40N 54°3W 165 C9
Gloverville = Warrenville
 U.S.A. 33°33N 81°48W 178 D8
Glowno Poland 51°59N 19°42E 83 G6
Glubczyce Poland 50°13N 17°38E 83 H4
Glubokiy Russia 48°35N 40°25E 87 F11
Głubokoe Kazakhstan 50°9N 82°18E 109 B10
Glubokoye = Hlybokaye
 Belarus 55°10N 27°45E 84 E4
Gluchołazy Poland 50°19N 17°24E 83 H4
Glücksburg Germany 54°50N 9°33E 76 A5
Glückstadt Germany 53°48N 9°29E 76 B5
Glukhov = Hlukhiv
 Ukraine 51°42N 33°45E 85 F7
Glusk Belarus 52°53N 28°41E 85 B15
Głuszyca Poland 50°41N 16°22E 83 H3
Glyfada = Glifada Greece 37°52N 23°45E 98 D5
Glyn Ebwy = Ebbw Vale
 U.K. 51°46N 3°12W 67 F4
Glyngøre Denmark 56°46N 8°52E 63 H2
Gmünd Kärnten, Austria 46°54N 13°31E 78 E6
Gmünd Niederösterreich,
 Austria 48°45N 15°0E 78 C8
Gmunden Austria 47°55N 13°48E 78 D6
Gnarp Sweden 62°3N 17°16E 62 D11
Gnesta Sweden 59°3N 17°18E 62 E11
Gniew Poland 53°50N 18°50E 83 E5
Gniewkowo Poland 52°54N 18°25E 83 F5
Gniezno Poland 52°30N 17°35E 83 F4
Gnjilane = Gjilan Kosovo 42°28N 21°29E 96 D5
Gnoien Germany 53°58N 12°41E 76 B8
Gnosjö Sweden 57°22N 13°43E 63 H7
Gnowangerup
 Australia 33°58S 117°59E 149 F2
Go Cong Vietnam 10°22N 106°40E 121 G6
Gō-no-ura Japan 33°44N 129°40E 113 H4
Goa India 15°33N 73°59E 127 G2
Goa □ India 15°33N 73°59E 127 G2
Goalen Hd. Australia 36°33S 150°4E 153 D9

Goalpara India 26°10N 90°40E 123 F17
Goaltor India 22°43N 87°10E 125 H12
Goalundo Ghat
 Bangla. 23°50N 89°47E 125 H13
Goaso Ghana 6°48N 2°30W 138 D4
Goat Fell U.K. 55°38N 5°11W 65 F3
Goba Ethiopia 7°1N 39°59E 131 F2
Goba Mozam. 26°15S 32°13E 145 D5
Gobabis Namibia 22°30S 19°0E 144 B2
Göbel Turkey 40°9N 28°9E 99 B9
Gobernador Gregores
 Argentina 48°46S 70°15W 192 C2
Gobi Asia 44°0N 110°0E 114 C6
Gobi Gurvan Saykhan △
 Mongolia 43°42N 101°24E 114 C2
Gobichettipalayam
 India 11°31N 77°21E 127 J3
Gobō Japan 33°53N 135°10E 113 H7
Göçbeyli Turkey 39°13N 27°25E 99 B9
Goch Germany 51°41N 6°9E 76 D2
Gochas Namibia 24°59S 18°55E 144 B2
Godalming U.K. 51°11N 0°36W 67 F7
Godavari → India 16°25N 82°18E 126 F6
Godavari Pt. India 17°0N 82°20E 126 F6
Godbout Canada 49°20N 67°38W 165 C6
Godda India 24°50N 87°13E 125 G12
Goderich Bulgaria 43°1N 23°4E 96 C7
Goderich Canada 43°45N 81°41W 174 C3
Goderville France 49°38N 0°22E 70 C7
Godfrey Ra. Australia 24°0S 117°0E 149 D2
Godhavn = Qeqertarsuaq
 Greenland 69°15N 53°38W 57 D5
Godhra India 22°49N 73°40E 124 H5
Gödöllő Hungary 47°38N 19°25E 80 C4
Godoy Cruz Argentina 32°56S 68°52W 190 C2
Gods → Canada 56°22N 92°51W 164 A1
Gods L. Canada 54°40N 94°15W 164 B1
Gods River Canada 54°50N 94°5W 163 C10
Godthåb = Nuuk
 Greenland 64°10N 51°35W 57 E5
Goeie Hoop, Kaap die = Good
 Hope, C. of S. Africa 34°24S 18°30E 144 E2
Goéland, L. au Canada 49°50N 76°48W 164 C4
Goélands, L. aux
 Canada 55°27N 64°17W 165 A7
Goeree Neths. 51°50N 4°0E 69 C3
Goes Neths. 51°30N 3°55E 69 C3
Goffstown U.S.A. 43°1N 71°36W 175 C13
Gogama Canada 47°35N 81°43W 164 C3
Gogebic, L. U.S.A. 46°30N 89°35W 172 B8
Gogolin Poland 50°30N 18°0E 83 H5
Gogonou Benin 10°50N 2°50E 139 C5
Gogra = Ghaghara →
 India 25°45N 84°40E 125 G11
Gogriâl South Sudan 8°30N 28°8E 135 G11
Gogui Mali 15°32N 9°25W 138 B3
Goh-Djiboua □ Ivory C. 6°2N 5°33W 138 D3
Gohana India 29°8N 76°42E 124 E7
Goharganj India 23°1N 77°41E 124 H7
Goi → India 22°4N 74°46E 124 H6
Goiana Brazil 7°33S 34°59W 189 E4
Goiânia Brazil 16°43S 49°20W 187 B3
Goiás Brazil 15°55S 50°10W 187 B3
Goiás □ Brazil 12°10S 48°0W 187 B3
Goio-Erê Brazil 24°12S 53°1W 191 A5
Góis Portugal 40°10N 8°6W 88 E2
Gojō Japan 34°21N 135°42E 113 G7
Gojra Pakistan 31°10N 72°40E 124 D5
Gokarn India 14°33N 74°17E 127 G2
Gökçeada Turkey 40°10N 25°55E 97 F9
Gökçedağ Turkey 39°58N 27°41E 99 B9
Gökçeören Turkey 38°37N 28°35E 99 C10
Gökırmak → Turkey 41°25N 35°58E 104 B6
Gökova Turkey 37°4N 28°0E 99 E9
Gökova Körfezi Turkey 36°55N 27°50E 99 E9
Göksu → Turkey 36°30N 34°4E 104 D6
Göksun Turkey 38°2N 36°30E 104 C7
Gokteik Burma 22°26N 97°0E 123 H20
Goktepe Turkey 37°25N 32°34E 104 D5
Gokurt Pakistan 29°40N 67°26E 124 E2
Gokwe Zimbabwe 18°7S 28°58E 145 A4
Gol Gol Australia 34°12S 142°14E 152 B5
Gola India 28°3N 80°32E 125 F9
Golakganj India 26°8N 89°52E 125 F13
Golan Heights = Hagolan
 Syria 33°0N 35°45E 130 C4
Golancz Poland 52°57N 17°18E 83 F4
Gölbaşı Adıyaman,
 Turkey 37°39N 37°25E 104 D8
Gölbaşı Ankara, Turkey 39°47N 32°49E 104 C5
Golconda U.S.A. 40°58N 117°30W 168 F5
Gölcük Kocaeli, Turkey 40°42N 29°48E 97 F13
Gölcük Niğde, Turkey 38°14N 34°44E 104 C6
Gold U.S.A. 41°52N 77°50W 175 E7
Gold Beach U.S.A. 42°25N 124°25W 168 E1
Gold Coast W. Afr. 4°0N 1°40W 139 E4
Gold Hill U.S.A. 42°26N 123°3W 168 E2
Gold River Canada 49°46N 126°3W 162 D3
Goldap Poland 54°19N 22°18E 82 D9
Goldberg Germany 53°35N 12°4E 76 B8
Golden Canada 51°20N 116°59W 162 C5
Golden B. N.Z. 40°40S 172°50E 154 J4
Golden Gate U.S.A. 37°48N 122°29W 169 H2
Golden Gate Highlands △
 S. Africa 28°40S 28°40E 145 C4
Golden Hinde Canada 49°40N 125°44W 162 D3
Golden Lake Canada 45°34N 77°21W 174 A7
Golden Spike △
 U.S.A. 41°37N 112°33W 168 F7
Goldendale U.S.A. 45°49N 120°50W 168 D3
Goldfield U.S.A. 37°42N 117°14W 171 H9
Goldsand L. Canada 57°2N 101°8W 163 B8
Goldsboro U.S.A. 35°23N 77°59W 177 D16
Goldsmith U.S.A. 31°59N 102°37W 176 E3
Goldthwaite U.S.A. 31°27N 98°34W 176 F5
Golega Portugal 39°24N 8°29W 88 F2
Goleniów Poland 53°35N 14°50E 82 E1
Golestān □ Iran 37°20N 55°25E 129 B8
Golestānak Iran 30°36N 54°14E 129 D7
Goleta U.S.A. 34°27N 119°50W 171 L7

Golfito Costa Rica 8°41N 83°5W 182 E3
Golfo Aranci Italy 40°59N 9°38E 94 B2
Golfo de Santa Clara Mexico 31°42N 114°30W 180 A2
Golfo di Orosei e del Gennargentu △ Italy 40°5N 9°15E 94 B2
Gölgeli Dağları Turkey 37°10N 28°55E 99 D10
Gölhisar Turkey 37°8N 29°31E 99 D11
Goliad U.S.A. 28°40N 97°23W 176 G6
Golija Montenegro 43°5N 18°45E 96 C2
Golija Serbia 43°22N 20°15E 96 C4
Golina Poland 52°15N 18°4E 83 F5
Gölköy Turkey 40°41N 37°37E 104 B7
Göllersdorf Austria 48°29N 16°7E 78 C9
Gölmarmara Turkey 38°42N 27°55E 99 C9
Golmud China 36°25N 94°53E 110 D7
Golo → France 42°31N 9°32E 73 F13
Gölova Turkey 36°48N 30°5E 99 E12
Golpāyegān Iran 33°27N 50°18E 129 C6
Gölpazarı Turkey 40°16N 30°18E 104 B4
Golra Pakistan 33°37N 72°56E 124 C5
Golspie U.K. 57°58N 3°59W 65 D5
Golub-Dobrzyń Poland 53°7N 19°2E 83 E6
Golubac Serbia 44°38N 21°38E 96 B5
Golyam Perelik Bulgaria 41°36N 24°33E 97 E8
Golyama Kamchiya → Bulgaria 43°10N 27°55E 97 C11
Goma Dem. Rep. of the Congo 1°37S 29°10E 142 C2
Gomal Pass Pakistan 31°56N 69°20E 124 D3
Gomati → India 25°32N 83°11E 125 G10
Gombari Dem. Rep. of the Congo 2°45N 29°3E 142 B2
Gombe Nigeria 10°19N 11°2E 139 C7
Gömbe Turkey 36°33N 29°38E 99 E11
Gombe □ Nigeria 10°0N 11°10E 139 C7
Gombe → Tanzania 4°38S 31°40E 142 C3
Gombe Stream △ Tanzania 4°42S 29°37E 142 C2
Gombi Nigeria 10°12N 12°30E 139 C7
Gomel = Homyel Belarus 52°28N 31°0E 75 B16
Gomera Canary Is. 28°7N 17°14W 100 F2
Gómez Palacio Mexico 25°34N 103°30W 180 B4
Gomfi Greece 39°26N 21°36E 98 B3
Gomīshān Iran 37°4N 54°6E 129 B7
Gommern Germany 52°4N 11°50E 76 C7
Gomogomo Indonesia 6°39S 134°43E 119 F8
Gomoh India 23°52N 86°10E 125 H12
Gomotartsi Bulgaria 44°6N 22°57E 96 B6
Gompa = Ganta Liberia 7°15N 8°59W 138 D3
Gonābād Iran 34°15N 58°45E 129 C8
Gonaïves Haiti 19°20N 72°42W 183 C5
Gonarezhou △ Zimbabwe 21°32S 31°55E 143 G3
Gonâve, G. de la Haiti 19°29N 72°42W 183 C5
Gonâve, Île de la Haiti 18°51N 73°3W 183 C5
Gonbad-e Kāvūs Iran 37°20N 55°25E 129 B7
Gönc Hungary 48°28N 21°14E 80 B6
Gonda India 27°9N 81°58E 125 F9
Gondal India 21°58N 70°52E 124 J4
Gonder Ethiopia 12°39N 37°30E 131 E2
Gondia India 21°23N 80°10E 126 D5
Gondola Mozam. 19°10S 33°37E 143 F3
Gondomar Portugal 41°10N 8°35W 88 D2
Gondrecourt-le-Château France 48°31N 5°30E 71 D12
Gönen Balıkesir, Turkey 40°6N 27°39E 97 F11
Gönen Isparta, Turkey 37°57N 30°31E 99 D12
Gönen → Turkey 40°6N 27°39E 97 F11
Gong Xian China 28°23N 104°47E 116 C5
Gong'an China 30°7N 112°12E 117 B9
Gongbei China 22°12N 113°32E 111 a
Gongchangling China 41°7N 123°27E 115 D12
Gongcheng China 24°50N 110°49E 117 E8
Gongga Shan China 29°40N 101°55E 116 C3
Gonggar China 29°23N 91°7E 110 F7
Gongguan China 21°48N 109°36E 116 G7
Gonghe China 36°18N 100°32E 110 D9
Gongju S. Korea 36°27N 127°7E 115 F14
Gongliu China 43°28N 82°8E 109 D10
Gongming China 22°47N 113°53E 111 a
Gongola → Nigeria 9°30N 12°4E 139 D7
Gongolgon Australia 30°21S 146°54E 151 E4
Gongshan China 27°43N 98°29E 116 D2
Gongtan China 28°55N 108°20E 116 C7
Gongyi China 34°45N 112°58E 114 G7
Gongzhuling China 43°30N 124°40E 115 C13
Goni Greece 39°52N 22°29E 98 B4
Goniadz Poland 53°30N 22°44E 82 E9
Goniri Nigeria 11°30N 12°15E 139 C7
Gonjo China 30°52N 98°17E 116 B2
Gonnesa Italy 39°16N 8°28E 94 C1
Gonnosfanadiga Italy 39°29N 8°39E 94 C1
Gonzales Calif., U.S.A. 36°30N 121°26W 170 J5
Gonzales Tex., U.S.A. 29°30N 97°27W 176 G6
González Mexico 22°48N 98°25W 181 C5
Goobang △ Australia 33°0S 148°32E 153 B8
Good Hope, C. of S. Africa 34°24S 18°30E 144 D2
Good Hope Lake Canada 59°16N 129°18W 162 B3
Gooderham Canada 44°54N 78°21W 174 B6
Goodhouse S. Africa 28°57S 18°13E 144 C2
Gooding U.S.A. 42°56N 114°43W 168 E6
Goodland U.S.A. 39°21N 101°43W 172 F3
Goodlands Mauritius 20°2S 57°39E 141 d
Goodlow Canada 56°20N 120°8W 162 B4
Goodooga Australia 29°3S 147°28E 151 D4
Goodsprings U.S.A. 35°49N 115°27W 171 K11
Goodwater U.S.A. 33°4N 86°3W 178 B3
Goole U.K. 53°42N 0°53W 66 D7
Goolgowi Australia 33°58S 145°41E 153 B6
Goolwa Australia 35°30S 138°47E 152 C3
Goomalling Australia 31°15S 116°49E 149 F2
Goomeri Australia 26°12S 152°6E 151 D5
Goonda Mozam. 19°48S 33°57E 143 F3
Goondiwindi Australia 28°30S 150°21E 151 D5
Goongarrie, L. Australia 30°3S 121°9E 149 F3
Goongarrie △ Australia 30°7S 121°30E 149 F3
Goonyella Australia 21°47S 147°58E 150 C4
Goose → Canada 53°20N 60°35W 165 B7
Goose Creek U.S.A. 32°59N 80°2W 178 C9
Goose L. U.S.A. 41°56N 120°26W 168 F3
Gooty India 15°7N 77°41E 127 G3
Gop India 22°5N 69°50E 124 H3
Gopalganj India 26°28N 84°30E 125 F11
Göppingen Germany 48°42N 9°39E 77 G5
Gor Spain 37°23N 2°58W 89 H8
Góra Dolnośląskie, Poland 51°40N 16°31E 83 G3
Góra Mazowieckie, Poland 52°39N 20°6E 83 F7
Góra Kalwaria Poland 51°59N 21°14E 83 G8
Gorakhpur India 26°47N 83°23E 125 F10
Goražde Bos.-H. 43°38N 18°58E 80 G3
Gorbatov Russia 56°12N 43°2E 86 B6
Gorbea Spain 43°1N 2°50W 90 B2
Gorczański △ Poland 49°30N 20°10E 83 J7
Gorda, Pta. Canary Is. 28°45N 18°0W 100 F2
Gorda, Pta. Nic. 14°20N 83°10W 182 D3
Gordan B. Australia 11°35S 130°10E 148 B5
Gördes Turkey 38°54N 28°17E 99 C10
Gordon Ga., U.S.A. 32°54N 83°20W 178 C6
Gordon Nebr., U.S.A. 42°48N 102°12W 172 D2
Gordon → Australia 42°27S 145°30E 151 G4
Gordon, I. Chile 54°55S 69°30W 192 D3
Gordon Bay Canada 45°12N 79°47W 174 A5
Gordon L. Alta., Canada 56°30N 110°25W 163 B6
Gordon L. N.W.T., Canada 63°5N 113°11W 162 A6
Gordonvale Australia 17°5S 145°50E 150 B4
Goré Chad 7°59N 16°31E 135 G9
Gore Ethiopia 8°12N 35°32E 131 F2
Gore N.Z. 46°5S 168°58E 155 G3
Gore Bay Canada 45°57N 82°28W 164 C3
Gorée, Île de Senegal 14°40N 17°23W 138 C1
Görele Turkey 41°2N 39°0E 105 B8
Göreme Turkey 38°35N 34°52E 104 C6
Gorey Ireland 52°41N 6°18W 64 D5
Gorg Iran 29°29N 59°43E 129 D8
Gorgān Iran 36°55N 54°30E 129 B7
Gorgol □ Mauritania 15°45N 13°0W 138 B2
Gorgona Italy 43°26N 9°54E 92 E6
Gorgona, I. Colombia 3°0N 78°10W 186 C3
Gorgoram Nigeria 12°40N 10°45E 139 C7
Gorham U.S.A. 44°23N 71°10W 175 B13
Gori Georgia 42°0N 44°7E 87 J7
Goribidnur = Gauribidanur India 13°37N 77°32E 127 H3
Goriganga → India 29°45N 80°23E 125 E9
Gorinchem Neths. 51°50N 4°59E 69 C4
Goris Armenia 39°31N 46°22E 105 C12
Goritsy Russia 57°4N 36°43E 84 D9
Gorízia Italy 45°56N 13°37E 93 C10
Gorj □ Romania 45°5N 23°25E 81 E8
Gorki = Horki Belarus 54°17N 30°59E 84 E6
Gorkiy = Nizhniy Novgorod Russia 56°20N 44°0E 86 B7
Gorkovskoye Vdkhr. Russia 57°2N 43°4E 86 B6
Gorleston-on-Sea U.K. 52°35N 1°44E 67 E9
Gorlice Poland 49°35N 21°11E 83 J8
Görlitz Germany 51°9N 14°58E 76 D10
Gorlovka = Horlivka Ukraine 48°19N 38°5E 85 H10
Gorman U.S.A. 34°47N 118°51W 171 L8
Gorna Dzhumayo = Blagoevgrad Bulgaria 42°2N 23°5E 96 D7
Gorna Oryakhovitsa Bulgaria 43°7N 25°40E 97 C9
Gornja Radgona Slovenia 46°40N 16°2E 93 B13
Gornja Tuzla Bos.-H. 44°35N 18°46E 80 F3
Gornji Grad Slovenia 46°20N 14°52E 93 B11
Gornji Milanovac Serbia 44°3N 20°29E 96 B4
Gornji Vakuf Bos.-H. 43°57N 17°34E 80 G2
Gorno Ablanovo Bulgaria 43°37N 25°43E 97 C9
Gorno-Altay □ Russia 51°0N 86°0E 109 B11
Gorno-Altaysk Russia 51°50N 86°5E 109 B11
Gorno-Badakhshan = Kŭhiston-Badakhshon □ Tajikistan 38°30N 73°0E 109 E8
Gornozavodsk Russia 46°33N 141°50E 107 E15
Gornyak Russia 50°59N 81°27E 109 B10
Gornyatskiy Russia 48°18N 40°56E 87 F5
Gornyy Primorsk, Russia 44°57N 133°59E 112 B6
Gornyy Saratov, Russia 51°50N 48°30E 86 E9
Gorodenka = Horodenka Ukraine 48°41N 25°29E 81 B10
Gorodets Russia 56°38N 43°28E 86 B6
Gorodishche = Horodyshche Ukraine 49°17N 31°27E 85 H6
Gorodishche Russia 53°13N 45°40E 86 D7
Gorodnya = Horodnya Ukraine 51°55N 31°33E 85 G6
Gorodok = Haradok Belarus 55°30N 30°3E 84 E6
Gorodok = Horodok Ukraine 49°46N 23°32E 75 D12
Gorodovikovsk Russia 46°8N 41°58E 87 G5
Goroke Australia 36°43S 141°29E 152 D4
Gorokhov = Horokhiv Ukraine 50°30N 24°45E 75 C13
Gorokhovets Russia 56°13N 42°39E 86 B6
Gorom Gorom Burkina Faso 14°26N 0°14W 139 C4
Goromonzi Zimbabwe 17°52S 31°22E 143 F3
Gorong, Kepulauan Indonesia 3°59S 131°25E 119 E8
Gorongose → Mozam. 20°30S 34°40E 145 B5
Gorongoza Mozam. 18°44S 34°2E 143 F3
Gorongoza, Sa. da Mozam. 18°27S 34°2E 143 F3
Gorongoza △ Mozam. 18°50S 34°29E 145 A5
Gorontalo Indonesia 0°35N 123°5E 119 D6
Gorontalo □ Indonesia 0°50N 122°20E 119 D6
Goronyo Nigeria 13°29N 5°39E 139 C6
Górowo Iławeckie Poland 54°17N 20°30E 82 D7
Gorron France 48°25N 0°50W 70 D6
Gorshechnoye Russia 51°31N 38°2E 85 G10
Gort Ireland 53°3N 8°49W 64 C3
Gortis Greece 35°4N 24°58E 101 D6
Gorumahisani India 22°20N 86°24E 126 C8
Góry Bystrzyckie Poland 50°16N 16°33E 83 H3
Goryachiy Klyuch Russia 44°38N 39°8E 87 H4
Goryeong S. Korea 35°44N 128°15E 115 G15
Gorzkowice Poland 51°13N 19°36E 83 G6
Górzno Poland 53°12N 19°38E 83 E6
Gorzów Śląski Poland 51°3N 18°22E 83 G5
Gorzów Wielkopolski Poland 52°43N 15°15E 83 F2
Gosford Australia 33°23S 151°18E 153 B9
Goshen Calif., U.S.A. 36°21N 119°25W 170 J7
Goshen Ind., U.S.A. 41°35N 85°50W 173 E11
Goshen N.Y., U.S.A. 41°24N 74°20W 175 E10
Goshogawara Japan 40°48N 140°27E 112 D10
Goslar Germany 51°54N 10°25E 76 D6
Gospič Croatia 44°35N 15°23E 93 D12
Gosport U.K. 50°48N 1°9W 67 G6
Gossas Senegal 14°28N 16°0W 138 C1
Gosse → Australia 19°32S 134°37E 150 B1
Gossi Mali 15°48N 1°20W 139 B4
Gostivar Macedonia 41°48N 20°57E 96 E4
Gostyń Poland 51°50N 17°3E 83 G4
Gostynin Poland 52°26N 19°29E 83 F6
Göta älv → Sweden 57°42N 11°54E 63 G5
Göta kanal Sweden 58°30N 15°58E 63 F10
Götaland Sweden 57°30N 14°30E 63 G8
Göteborg Sweden 57°43N 11°59E 63 G5
Götene Sweden 58°32N 13°30E 63 F7
Gotești Moldova 46°9N 28°10E 81 D13
Gotha Germany 50°56N 10°42E 76 E6
Gothenburg = Göteborg Sweden 57°43N 11°59E 63 G5
Gothenburg U.S.A. 40°56N 100°10W 172 E3
Gothèye Niger 13°52N 1°34E 139 C5
Gotland Sweden 57°30N 18°33E 63 G12
Gotland □ Sweden 57°15N 18°30E 63 G12
Gotō = Fukue Japan 32°41N 128°51E 113 H4
Gotō-Rettō Japan 32°55N 129°5E 113 H4
Gotse Delchev Bulgaria 41°36N 23°46E 96 E7
Gotska Sandön Sweden 58°24N 19°15E 63 F13
Göttero, Monte Italy 44°22N 9°42E 92 D6
Göttingen Germany 51°31N 9°55E 76 D5
Gottskär Sweden 57°25N 12°2E 63 G6
Gottwald = Zmiyev Ukraine 49°39N 36°27E 85 H9
Gottwaldov = Zlín Czech Rep. 49°14N 17°40E 79 B10
Goubangzi China 41°20N 121°52E 115 D11
Gouda Neths. 52°1N 4°42E 69 B4
Goudiri Senegal 14°15N 12°45W 138 C2
Goudoumaria Niger 13°40N 11°10E 139 C7
Goudouras, Akra Greece 34°59N 26°6E 101 E8
Gouéké Guinea 8°2N 8°43W 138 D3
Gough I. Atl. Oc. 40°10S 9°45W 56 L11
Gouin, Rés. Canada 48°35N 74°40W 164 C5
Gouitafla Ivory C. 7°30N 5°53W 138 D3
Goulburn Australia 34°44S 149°44E 153 C8
Goulburn Is. Australia 11°40S 133°20E 150 A1
Goulburn River △ Australia 32°19S 150°10E 153 B9
Goulds U.S.A. 25°33N 80°23W 179 K9
Goulia Ivory C. 10°1N 7°11W 138 C3
Goulimma Morocco 31°41N 4°57W 136 B3
Goumbou Mali 15°2N 7°25W 138 B3
Goumenissa Greece 40°56N 22°37E 96 F6
Goundam Mali 16°27N 3°40W 138 B4
Goura Greece 37°56N 22°20E 98 D4
Gouraya Algeria 36°31N 1°56E 136 A4
Gourbassi Mali 13°24N 11°38W 138 C2
Gourdon France 44°44N 1°23E 72 D5
Gouré Niger 14°0N 10°10E 139 C7
Gourin France 48°8N 3°37W 70 D3
Gourits → S. Africa 34°21S 21°52E 144 D3
Gourma-Rharous Mali 16°55N 1°50W 139 B4
Gournay-en-Bray France 49°29N 1°44E 71 C8
Gournes Greece 35°19N 25°16E 101 D7
Gourock U.K. 55°57N 4°49W 65 F4
Gourock Ra. Australia 36°0S 149°25E 153 D8
Goursi Burkina Faso 12°42N 2°37W 138 C4
Gouvea Brazil 18°27S 43°44W 189 D2
Gouverneur U.S.A. 44°20N 75°28W 175 B9
Gouvia Greece 39°39N 19°50E 101 A3
Gouzon France 46°12N 2°14E 71 F9
Gove Peninsula Australia 12°17S 136°49E 150 A2
Governador Valadares Brazil 18°15S 41°57W 189 D2
Governor's Harbour Bahamas 25°10N 76°14W 182 A4
Govĭaltay □ Mongolia 45°30N 96°0E 109 C13
Govindgarh India 24°23N 81°18E 125 G9
Gowan Ra. Australia 25°0S 145°0E 150 D4
Gowanda U.S.A. 42°28N 78°56W 174 D6
Gower U.K. 51°35N 4°10W 67 F3
Gowers Corner U.S.A. 28°20N 82°30W 179 G7
Gowna, L. Ireland 53°51N 7°34W 64 C4
Gowurdak Turkmenistan 37°50N 66°4E 109 E7
Goya Argentina 29°10S 59°10W 190 B4
Goyang S. Korea 37°39N 126°50E 115 F14
Göyçay Azerbaijan 40°42N 47°43E 87 K8
Goyder Lagoon Australia 27°3S 138°58E 151 D2
Goygöl Azerbaijan 40°37N 46°12E 87 K8
Goyllarisquizga Peru 10°31S 76°24W 188 C2
Göynük Antalya, Turkey 36°41N 30°33E 99 E12
Göynük Bolu, Turkey 40°24N 30°48E 104 B4
Goz Beïda Chad 12°10N 21°20E 135 F10
Gozdnica Poland 51°28N 15°4E 83 G2
Gozo Malta 36°3N 14°15E 101 C1
Graaff-Reinet S. Africa 32°13S 24°32E 144 D3
Grabo Ivory C. 4°57N 7°30W 138 D3
Grabow Germany 53°17N 11°34E 76 B7
Grabów nad Prosną Poland 51°31N 18°7E 83 G5
Gračac Croatia 44°18N 15°57E 93 D12
Gračanica Bos.-H. 44°43N 18°18E 80 F3
Graçay France 47°10N 1°50E 71 E8
Graceville U.S.A. 30°58N 85°31W 178 E4
Gracewood U.S.A. 33°22N 82°2W 178 B7
Gracias a Dios, C. Honduras 15°0N 83°10W 182 D3
Graciosa Azores 39°4N 28°0W 134 a
Graciosa, I. Canary Is. 29°15N 13°32W 100 E6
Grad Sofiya □ Bulgaria 42°35N 23°20E 96 D7
Gradac Montenegro 43°23N 19°9E 96 C3
Gradačac Bos.-H. 44°52N 18°26E 80 F3
Gradeška Planina Macedonia 41°30N 22°15E 96 E6
Gradets Bulgaria 42°46N 26°30E 97 D10
Gradišče Slovenia 46°37N 15°50E 93 B12
Gradiška Bos.-H. 45°10N 17°15E 80 E2
Grădiştea de Munte Romania 45°37N 23°13E 81 E8
Grado Italy 45°40N 13°23E 93 C10
Grado Spain 43°23N 6°4W 88 B4
Grady U.S.A. 34°49N 103°19W 169 J12
Graeca, Lacul Romania 44°5N 26°10E 81 F11
Grafenau Germany 48°51N 13°22E 77 G9
Gräfenberg Germany 49°39N 11°14E 77 F7
Grafham Water U.K. 52°19N 0°18W 67 E7
Grafton Australia 29°38S 152°58E 151 D5
Grafton N. Dak., U.S.A. 48°25N 97°25W 172 A5
Grafton W. Va., U.S.A. 39°21N 80°2W 173 F13
Graham Canada 49°20N 90°30W 164 C1
Graham Ga., U.S.A. 31°50N 82°30W 178 D7
Graham Tex., U.S.A. 33°6N 98°35W 176 E5
Graham, Mt. U.S.A. 32°42N 109°52W 169 K9
Graham Bell, Ostrov = Greem-Bell, Ostrov Russia 81°0N 62°0E 106 A7
Graham I. B.C., Canada 53°40N 132°30W 162 C2
Graham I. Nunavut, Canada 77°25N 90°30W 161 B13
Graham Land Antarctica 65°0S 64°0W 55 C17
Grahamstown S. Africa 33°19S 26°31E 144 D4
Grahamsville U.S.A. 41°51N 74°33W 175 E10
Grahovo Montenegro 42°40N 18°40E 96 D2
Graïba Tunisia 34°30N 10°13E 136 B6
Graie, Alpi Europe 45°30N 7°10E 73 C11
Grain Coast W. Afr. 4°20N 10°0W 138 E3
Grajagan Indonesia 8°35S 114°13E 119 K17
Grajaú Brazil 5°50S 46°4W 189 B1
Grajaú → Brazil 3°41S 44°48W 189 A2
Grajewo Poland 53°39N 22°30E 82 E9
Gramada Bulgaria 43°49N 22°39E 96 C6
Gramat France 44°48N 1°43E 72 D5
Grammichele Italy 37°13N 14°38E 95 E7
Grámmos, Óros Greece 40°18N 20°47E 96 F4
Grampian U.S.A. 40°58N 78°37W 174 F6
Grampian Highlands = Grampian Mts. U.K. 56°50N 4°0W 65 E5
Grampian Mts. U.K. 56°50N 4°0W 65 E5
Grampians, The Australia 37°15S 142°20E 152 D5
Grampians △ Australia 37°15S 142°28E 152 D5
Gramsh Albania 40°52N 20°12E 96 F4
Gran Altiplanicie Central Argentina 49°0S 69°30W 192 C3
Gran Canaria Canary Is. 27°55N 15°35W 100 G4
Gran Chaco S. Amer. 25°0S 61°0W 190 B3
Gran Desierto del Pinacate ⌂ Mexico 31°51N 113°32W 180 A2
Gran Laguna Salada Argentina 44°24S 67°23W 192 B3
Gran Pajonal Peru 10°45S 74°30W 188 C3
Gran Paradiso Italy 45°33N 7°17E 92 C4
Gran Sasso d'Itália Italy 42°27N 13°42E 93 F10
Gran Sasso e Monti Della Laga △ Italy 42°32N 13°22E 93 F10
Gran Tarajal Canary Is. 28°13N 14°1W 100 F5
Granada Nic. 11°58N 86°0W 182 D2
Granada Spain 37°10N 3°35W 89 H7
Granada U.S.A. 38°4N 102°19W 168 G12
Granada □ Spain 37°18N 3°0W 89 H7
Granadilla de Abona Canary Is. 28°7N 16°33W 100 F3
Granard Ireland 53°47N 7°30W 64 C4
Granbury U.S.A. 32°27N 97°47W 176 E6
Granby Canada 45°25N 72°45W 175 A12
Granby U.S.A. 40°5N 105°56W 168 F11
Grand → Canada 42°51N 79°34W 174 D5
Grand → Mo., U.S.A. 39°23N 93°7W 172 F7
Grand → S. Dak., U.S.A. 45°40N 100°45W 172 C3
Grand-Anse = Portsmouth Dominica 15°34N 61°27W 183 C7
Grand Bahama I. Bahamas 26°40N 78°30W 182 A4
Grand Baie Mauritius 20°0S 57°35E 141 d
Grand Bank Canada 47°6N 55°48W 165 C8
Grand Banks Atl. Oc. 45°0N 52°0W 56 B6
Grand Bassam Ivory C. 5°10N 3°49W 138 D4
Grand Bend Canada 43°18N 81°45W 174 C3
Grand Béréby Ivory C. 4°38N 6°55W 138 E3
Grand-Bourg Guadeloupe 15°53N 61°19W 182 b
Grand Canal = Da Yunhe → China 34°25N 120°5E 115 H10
Grand Canyon U.S.A. 36°3N 112°9W 169 H7
Grand Canyon △ U.S.A. 36°15N 112°30W 169 H7
Grand Canyon-Parashant ⌂ U.S.A. 36°30N 113°45W 169 H7
Grand Cayman Cayman Is. 19°20N 81°20W 182 C3
Grand Cess Liberia 4°40N 8°12W 138 E3
Grand Coulee U.S.A. 47°57N 119°0W 168 C4
Grand Coulee Dam U.S.A. 47°57N 118°59W 168 C4
Grand Falls Canada 47°3N 67°44W 165 C6
Grand Falls-Windsor Canada 48°56N 55°40W 165 C8
Grand Forks Canada 49°0N 118°30W 162 D5
Grand Forks U.S.A. 47°55N 97°3W 172 B5
Grand Gorge U.S.A. 42°21N 74°29W 175 D10
Grand Haven U.S.A. 43°4N 86°13W 172 D10
Grand I. Mich., U.S.A. 46°31N 86°40W 172 B10
Grand I. N.Y., U.S.A. 43°0N 78°58W 174 D6
Grand Island U.S.A. 40°55N 98°21W 172 E4
Grand Isle La., U.S.A. 29°14N 90°0W 177 G9
Grand Isle Vt., U.S.A. 44°43N 73°18W 175 B11
Grand Junction U.S.A. 39°4N 108°33W 168 G9
Grand L. N.B., Canada 45°57N 66°7W 165 C6
Grand L. Nfld. & L., Canada 49°0N 57°30W 165 C8
Grand L. Nfld. & L., Canada 53°40N 60°30W 165 B7
Grand L. U.S.A. 29°55N 92°47W 176 G8
Grand Lahou Ivory C. 5°10N 5°5W 138 D3
Grand Lake U.S.A. 40°15N 105°49W 168 F11
Grand-Lieu, L. de France 47°6N 1°40W 70 E5
Grand Manan I. Canada 44°45N 66°52W 165 D6
Grand Marais Mich., U.S.A. 46°40N 85°59W 173 B11
Grand Marais Minn., U.S.A. 47°45N 90°25W 164 C1
Grand-Mère Canada 46°36N 72°40W 164 C5
Grand Popo Benin 6°15N 1°57E 139 D5
Grand Portage U.S.A. 47°58N 89°41W 172 B9
Grand Prairie U.S.A. 32°44N 96°59W 176 E6
Grand Rapids Canada 53°12N 99°19W 163 C9
Grand Rapids Mich., U.S.A. 42°58N 85°40W 173 D11
Grand Rapids Minn., U.S.A. 47°14N 93°31W 172 B7
Grand Ridge U.S.A. 30°43N 85°1W 178 E4
Grand St-Bernard, Col du Europe 45°50N 7°10E 77 K3
Grand Staircase-Escalante ⌂ U.S.A. 37°25N 111°33W 169 H8
Grand Teton U.S.A. 43°54N 110°50W 168 E8
Grand Teton △ U.S.A. 43°50N 110°50W 168 E8
Grand Union Canal U.K. 52°7N 0°53W 67 E7
Grandas Spain 43°13N 6°53W 88 B4
Grande → Jujuy, Argentina 24°20S 65°2W 190 A2
Grande → Mendoza, Argentina 36°52S 69°45W 190 D2
Grande → Bolivia 15°51S 64°39W 186 G6
Grande → Bahia, Brazil 11°30S 44°30W 189 C2
Grande → Minas Gerais, Brazil 20°6S 51°4W 187 H8
Grande, B. Argentina 50°30S 68°20W 192 D3
Grande, Rio → N. Amer. 25°58N 97°9W 176 J6
Grande, Serra Piauí, Brazil 8°0S 45°10W 189 B1
Grande, Serra Tocantins, Brazil 11°15S 46°30W 189 C1
Grande Anse Seychelles 4°18S 55°45E 141 b
Grande Baleine → Canada 55°16N 77°47W 164 A4
Grande Cache Canada 53°53N 119°8W 162 C5
Grande Casse, Pte. de la France 45°24N 6°49E 73 C10
Grande Comore Comoros Is. 11°35S 43°20E 141 a
Grande-Entrée Canada 47°30N 61°40W 165 C7
Grande Prairie Canada 55°10N 118°50W 162 B5
Grande-Rivière Canada 48°26N 64°30W 165 C7
Grande Sertão Veredas △ Brazil 15°10S 45°40W 189 D1
Grande-Terre Guadeloupe 16°20N 61°25W 182 b
Grande-Vallée Canada 49°14N 65°8W 165 C6
Grande Vigie, Pte. de la Guadeloupe 16°32N 61°27W 182 b
Grandfalls U.S.A. 31°20N 102°51W 176 F3
Grândola Portugal 38°12N 8°35W 89 G2
Grandpré France 49°20N 4°50E 71 C11
Grands Causses ⌂ France 44°5N 2°58E 72 D6
Grands-Jardins ⌂ Canada 47°41N 70°51W 165 C5
Grandview Canada 51°10N 100°42W 163 C8
Grandview U.S.A. 46°15N 119°54W 168 C4
Grandvilliers France 49°40N 1°57E 71 C8
Graneros Chile 34°5S 70°45W 190 C1
Grangemouth U.K. 56°1N 3°42W 65 E5
Granger U.S.A. 41°35N 109°58W 168 F9
Grängesberg Sweden 60°6N 15°1E 62 D9
Grangeville U.S.A. 45°56N 116°7W 168 D5
Granisle Canada 54°53N 126°13W 162 C3
Granit Rose, Côte France 48°50N 4°10W 70 D2
Granite City U.S.A. 38°42N 90°8W 172 F8
Granite Falls U.S.A. 44°49N 95°33W 172 C6
Granite L. Canada 48°8N 57°5W 165 C8
Granite Mt. U.S.A. 33°5N 116°28W 171 M10
Granite Pk. U.S.A. 45°10N 109°48W 168 D9
Graniteville S.C., U.S.A. 33°34N 81°49W 178 B8
Graniteville Vt., U.S.A. 44°8N 72°29W 175 B12
Granitola, C. Italy 37°34N 12°39E 94 E5
Granity N.Z. 41°39S 171°51E 155 B6
Granja Brazil 3°7S 40°50W 189 A2
Granja de Moreruela Spain 41°48N 5°44W 88 D5
Granja de Torrehermosa Spain 38°19N 5°35W 89 G5
Gränna Sweden 58°1N 14°28E 63 F8
Granollers Spain 41°39N 2°18E 90 D7
Gransee Germany 53°1N 13°8E 76 B9
Grant Fla., U.S.A. 27°56N 80°32W 179 H9
Grant Nebr., U.S.A. 40°50N 101°43W 172 E3
Grant, Mt. U.S.A. 38°34N 118°48W 168 G4
Grant City U.S.A. 40°29N 94°25W 172 E6
Grant I. Australia 11°10S 132°52E 148 B5
Grant Range U.S.A. 38°30N 115°25W 168 G6
Grantham U.K. 52°55N 0°38W 66 E7
Grantown-on-Spey U.K. 57°20N 3°36W 65 D5
Grants U.S.A. 35°9N 107°52W 169 J10
Grants Pass U.S.A. 42°26N 123°19W 168 E2
Grantsville U.S.A. 40°36N 112°28W 168 F7
Grantville U.S.A. 33°14N 84°50W 178 B5
Granville France 48°50N 1°35W 70 D5
Granville N. Dak., U.S.A. 48°16N 100°47W 172 A3
Granville N.Y., U.S.A. 43°24N 73°16W 175 C11
Granville Ohio, U.S.A. 40°4N 82°31W 174 F2
Granville L. Canada 56°18N 100°30W 163 B8
Graskop S. Africa 24°56S 30°49E 145 B5
Gräsö Sweden 60°28N 18°35E 62 D12
Grass → Canada 56°3N 96°33W 163 B9
Grass Range U.S.A. 47°2N 108°48W 168 C9
Grass River ⌂ Canada 54°40N 100°50W 163 C8
Grass Valley Calif., U.S.A. 39°13N 121°4W 170 F6
Grass Valley Oreg., U.S.A. 45°22N 120°47W 168 D3
Grassano Italy 40°38N 16°17E 95 B9
Grasse France 43°38N 6°56E 73 E10
Grassflat U.S.A. 41°0N 78°6W 174 E6
Grasslands △ Canada 49°11N 107°38W 163 D7
Grassy Australia 40°3S 144°5E 151 G3
Gråsten Denmark 54°55N 9°35E 63 K3
Grästorp Sweden 58°20N 12°40E 63 F6
Gratkorn Austria 47°8N 15°21E 78 D8
Graubünden □ Switz. 46°45N 9°30E 77 J5
Graulhet France 43°45N 1°59E 72 E5
Graus Spain 42°11N 0°20E 90 C5
Grave, Pte. de France 45°34N 1°4W 72 C2
Gravelbourg Canada 49°50N 106°35W 163 D7
Gravelines France 51°1N 2°10E 71 A9
's-Gravenhage Neths. 52°7N 4°17E 69 B4
Gravenhurst Canada 44°52N 79°20W 174 B5
Gravesend Australia 29°35S 150°20E 151 D5
Gravesend U.K. 51°26N 0°22E 67 F8
Gravina in Púglia Italy 40°49N 16°25E 95 B9
Gravois, Pointe-à- Haiti 18°2N 73°56W 183 C5
Gravona → France 41°58N 8°45E 73 G12
Gray France 47°22N 5°35E 71 E12
Gray U.S.A. 33°1N 83°32W 178 B6
Grayling U.S.A. 44°40N 84°43W 173 C11
Grays U.K. 51°28N 0°21E 67 F8
Grays Harbor U.S.A. 46°59N 124°1W 170 D2
Grays L. U.S.A. 43°4N 111°26W 168 E8
Grays River U.S.A. 46°21N 123°37W 170 D3
Grayvoron Russia 50°29N 35°39E 85 G8
Graz Austria 47°4N 15°27E 78 D8
Grdelica Serbia 42°55N 22°3E 96 D6
Greasy L. Canada 62°55N 122°12W 162 A4
Great Abaco I. = Abaco I. Bahamas 26°25N 77°10W 182 A4
Great Artesian Basin Australia 23°0S 144°0E 150 C3
Great Australian Bight Australia 33°30S 130°0E 149 F5
Great Bahama Bank Bahamas 23°15N 78°0W 18
Great Barrier I. N.Z. 36°11S 175°25E 15
Great Barrier Reef Australia 18°0S 146°50E 15
Great Barrier Reef ⌂ Australia 20°0S 150°0E 15
Great Barrington U.S.A. 42°12N 73°22W 175
Great Basalt Wall △ Australia 19°52S 145°43E 15
Great Basin U.S.A. 40°0N 117°0W 16
Great Basin △ U.S.A. 38°56N 114°15W 16
Great Basses Sri Lanka 6°11N 81°29E 12
Great Bear → Canada 65°0N 126°0W 16
Great Bear L. Canada 65°30N 120°0W 16
Great Belt = Store Bælt Denmark 55°20N 11°0E 6
Great Bend Kans., U.S.A. 38°22N 98°46W 17
Great Bend Pa., U.S.A. 41°58N 75°45W 17
Great Blasket I. Ireland 52°6N 10°32W 6
Great Britain Europe 54°0N 2°15W 5
Great Camanoe Br. Virgin Is. 18°30N 64°35W 1
Great Channel Asia 6°0N 94°0E 12
Great Coco I. = Koko Kyunzu Burma 14°7N 93°22E 12
Great Codroy Canada 47°51N 59°16W 16
Great Divide, The = Great Dividing Ra. Australia 23°0S 146°0E 15
Great Divide Basin U.S.A. 42°0N 108°0W 16
Great Dividing Ra. Australia 23°0S 146°0E 15
Great Driffield = Driffield U.K. 54°0N 0°26W 6
Great Exuma I. Bahamas 23°30N 75°50W 18
Great Falls U.S.A. 47°30N 111°17W 16
Great Fish = Groot-Vis → S. Africa 33°28S 27°5E 14
Great Guana Cay Bahamas 24°0N 76°20W 18
Great Himalayan △ India 31°30N 77°30E 12
Great Inagua I. Bahamas 21°0N 73°20W 18
Great Indian Desert = Thar Desert India 28°0N 72°0E 12
Great Karoo S. Africa 31°55S 21°0E 14
Great Khingan Mts. = Da Hinggan Ling China 48°0N 121°0E 11
Great Lake Australia 41°50S 146°40E 15
Great Lakes N. Amer. 46°0N 84°0W 15
Great Limpopo Transfrontier △ Africa 23°0S 31°45E 14
Great Malvern U.K. 52°7N 2°18W 6
Great Miami → U.S.A. 39°7N 84°49W 17
Great Nicobar India 7°0N 93°50E 12
Great Ormes Head U.K. 53°20N 3°52W 6
Great Otway △ Australia 38°50S 143°50E 15
Great Ouse → U.K. 52°48N 0°21E 6
Great Palm I. Australia 18°45S 146°40E 15
Great Pedro Bluff Jamaica 17°51N 77°44W 1
Great Pee Dee → U.S.A. 33°21N 79°10W 17
Great Plains N. Amer. 47°0N 105°0W 15
Great Ruaha → Tanzania 7°56S 37°52E 14
Great Sacandaga L. U.S.A. 43°6N 74°16W 175
Great Saint Bernard Pass = Grand St-Bernard, Col du Europe 45°50N 7°10E 7
Great Salt Desert = Kavīr, Dasht-e Iran 34°30N 55°0E 12
Great Salt L. U.S.A. 41°15N 112°40W 16
Great Salt Lake Desert U.S.A. 40°50N 113°30W 16
Great Salt Plains L. U.S.A. 36°45N 98°8W 1
Great Sand Dunes ⌂ U.S.A. 37°48N 105°45W 169
Great Sandy △ Australia 26°13S 153°2E 15
Great Sandy Desert Australia 21°0S 124°0E 14
Great Sangi = Sangihe, Pulau Indonesia 3°35N 125°30E 11
Great Scarcies → S. Leone 9°0N 13°0W 13
Great Sea Reef Fiji 16°15S 179°0E 1
Great Sitkin I. U.S.A. 52°3N 176°6W 16
Great Skellig Ireland 51°47N 10°33W 6
Great Slave L. Canada 61°23N 115°38W 16
Great Smoky Mts. △ U.S.A. 35°40N 83°40W 17
Great Stour = Stour → U.K. 51°18N 1°22E 6
Great Victoria Desert Australia 29°30S 126°30E 14
Great Wall Antarctica 62°30S 58°0W 55
Great Wall China 38°30N 109°30E 11
Great Whernside U.K. 54°10N 1°58W 6
Great Yarmouth U.K. 52°37N 1°44E 6
Great Zab = Zāb al Kabīr → Iraq 36°1N 43°24E 105
Great Zimbabwe Zimbabwe 20°16S 30°54E 14
Greater Antilles W. Indies 17°40N 74°0W 18
Greater London □ U.K. 51°31N 0°6W 6
Greater Manchester □ U.K. 53°30N 2°15W 6
Greater Sudbury Canada 46°30N 81°0W 16
Greater Sunda Is. Indonesia 7°0S 112°0E 11
Grebbestad Sweden 58°42N 11°15E 6
Grebenka = Hrebenka Ukraine 50°9N 32°22E 8
Greco, C. Cyprus 34°57N 34°5E 10
Greco, Mte. Italy 41°48N 13°58E 93
Gredos, Sierra de Spain 40°20N 5°0W 8
Greece U.S.A. 43°13N 77°41W 17
Greece ■ Europe 40°0N 23°0E 9
Greeley Colo., U.S.A. 40°25N 104°42W 168
Greeley Nebr., U.S.A. 41°33N 98°32W 17
Greeleyville U.S.A. 33°40N 79°59W 178
Greely Fd. Canada 80°30N 85°0W 161

n-Bell, Ostrov
  ssia 81°0N 62°0E 106 A7
n → Ky., U.S.A. 37°54N 87°30W 172 G10
n → Utah, U.S.A. 38°11N 109°53W 168 G9
n B. U.S.A. 45°0N 87°30W 172 C10
n Bay U.S.A. 44°31N 88°0W 172 C9
n C. Australia 37°13S 150°1E 153 D9
n Cove Springs
  S.A. 29°59N 81°42W 178 F8
n I. = Lütao
  iwan 22°40N 121°30E 117 F13
n Lake Canada 54°17N 107°47W 163 C7
n Mts. U.S.A. 43°45N 72°45W 175 C12
n Pond U.S.A. 32°44N 80°37W 178 C9
n River Utah,
  S.A. 38°59N 110°10W 168 G8
n River Wyo.,
  S.A. 41°32N 109°28W 168 F9
n Valley U.S.A. 31°52N 110°56W 169 L8
nacres U.S.A. 26°38N 80°7W 179 J9
nbank U.S.A. 48°6N 122°34W 170 B4
nbush Mich.,
  S.A. 44°35N 83°19W 174 B1
nbush Minn.,
  S.A. 48°42N 96°11W 172 A6
ncastle U.S.A. 39°38N 86°52W 172 F10
ne U.S.A. 42°20N 75°46W 175 D9
neville U.S.A. 36°10N 82°50W 177 C13
nfield Calif.,
  S.A. 36°19N 121°15W 170 J5
nfield Calif., U.S.A. 35°15N 119°0W 171 K8
nfield Ind., U.S.A. 39°47N 85°46W 173 F11
nfield Iowa, U.S.A. 41°18N 94°28W 172 E6
nfield Mass.,
  S.A. 42°35N 72°36W 175 D12
nfield Mo., U.S.A. 37°25N 93°51W 172 G7
nfield Park
  nada 45°29N 73°28W 175 A11
nland ☐ N. Amer. 60°N 45°0W 57 D6
nland Sea Arctic 73°0N 10°0W 57 B10
nock U.K. 55°57N 4°46W 65 F4
nore Ireland 54°1N 6°9W 64 B5
nore Pt. Ireland 52°14N 6°19W 64 D5
nough Australia 28°58S 114°43E 149 E1
nough →
  stralia 28°51S 114°38E 149 E1
nough Pt. Canada 44°58N 81°26W 174 B3
nport U.S.A. 41°6N 72°22W 175 E12
nsboro Fla., U.S.A. 30°34N 84°45W 178 E5
nsboro Ga., U.S.A. 33°35N 83°11W 178 B6
nsboro N.C.,
  S.A. 36°4N 79°48W 177 C15
nsboro Vt.,
  S.A. 44°36N 72°18W 175 B12
nsburg Ind.,
  S.A. 39°20N 85°29W 173 F11
nsburg Kans.,
  S.A. 37°36N 99°18W 172 G4
nsburg Pa., U.S.A. 40°18N 79°33W 174 F5
nstone = Geraldton
  nada 49°44N 87°10W 164 C2
nstone Pt. U.S.A. 57°55N 5°37W 65 D3
nvale Australia 18°55S 145°7E 150 B4
nville Liberia 5°1N 9°6W 138 D3
nville Ala., U.S.A. 31°50N 86°38W 177 F11
nville Calif., U.S.A. 40°8N 120°57W 170 E6
nville Fla., U.S.A. 30°28N 83°38W 178 F6
nville Ga., U.S.A. 33°2N 84°43W 178 B5
nville Maine,
  S.A. 45°28N 69°35W 173 C19
nville Mich.,
  S.A. 43°11N 85°15W 173 D11
nville Miss., U.S.A. 33°24N 91°4W 177 E9
nville Mo., U.S.A. 37°8N 90°27W 172 G8
nville N.C.,
  S.A. 35°37N 77°23W 177 D16
nville N.H.,
  S.A. 42°46N 71°49W 175 D13
nville N.Y., U.S.A. 42°25N 74°1W 175 D10
nville Ohio, U.S.A. 40°6N 84°38W 173 E11
nville S.C., U.S.A. 34°51N 82°24W 177 D13
nville Tex., U.S.A. 33°8N 96°7W 176 E6
nwater Lake ○
  nada 52°30N 103°30W 163 C8
nwich Conn.,
  S.A. 41°2N 73°38W 175 E11
nwich N.Y.,
  S.A. 43°5N 73°30W 175 C11
nwich Ohio, U.S.A. 41°2N 82°31W 174 E2
nwich ☐ U.K. 51°29N 0°1E 67 F8
nwood Canada 49°10N 118°40W 162 D5
nwood Ark.,
  S.A. 35°13N 94°16W 176 D7
nwood Fla., U.S.A. 30°52N 85°3W 178 E4
nwood Ind., U.S.A. 39°37N 86°7W 172 F10
nwood Miss.,
  S.A. 33°31N 90°11W 177 E9
nwood S.C.,
  S.A. 34°12N 82°10W 178 A7
nwood, Mt.
  stralia 13°48S 130°4E 148 B5
be Ivory C. 6°48N 6°43W 138 D3
ório → Brazil 6°50S 70°46W 188 E3
ório U.S.A. 43°14N 99°26W 172 D4
os Australia 17°53S 139°17E 150 B2

Grenadines, The
  St. Vincent 12°40N 61°20W 183 D12
Grenchen Switz. 47°12N 7°24E 77 H3
Grenen Denmark 57°44N 10°40E 63 G4
Grenfell Australia 33°52S 148°8E 153 E8
Grenfell Canada 50°30N 102°56W 163 C8
Grenoble France 45°12N 5°42E 73 D9
Grenville, C. Australia 12°0S 143°13E 150 A3
Grenville Chan.
  Canada 53°40N 129°46W 162 C3
Gréoux-les-Bains France 43°45N 5°52E 73 E9
Gresham U.S.A. 45°30N 122°25W 170 E4
Gresik Indonesia 7°13S 112°38E 119 G15
Gretna U.K. 55°0N 3°3W 65 F5
Gretna Fla., U.S.A. 30°37N 84°40W 178 E5
Gretna La., U.S.A. 29°54N 90°3W 177 G9
Greve Strand Denmark 55°34N 12°18E 63 J6
Greven Germany 52°6N 7°37E 76 C3
Grevená Greece 40°4N 21°25E 96 F5
Grevenbroich Germany 51°5N 6°35E 76 D2
Grevenmacher Lux. 49°41N 6°26E 69 E6
Grevesmühlen Germany 53°52N 11°12E 76 B7
Grey → Canada 47°34N 57°6W 165 C8
Grey → N.Z. 42°27S 171°12E 155 C6
Grey, C. Australia 13°0S 136°35E 150 A2
Grey Is. Canada 50°50N 55°35W 161 G20
Grey Ra. Australia 27°0S 143°30E 151 D3
Greybull U.S.A. 44°30N 108°3W 168 D9
Greymouth N.Z. 42°29S 171°13E 155 C6
Greystones Ireland 53°9N 6°5W 64 C5
Greytown S. Africa 29°1S 30°36E 145 C5
Greytown N.Z. 41°5S 175°29E 154 H4
Gribanovskiy Russia 51°28N 41°50E 86 E5
Gribbell I. Canada 53°23N 129°0W 162 C3
Gribës, Mal i Albania 40°17N 19°45E 96 F3
Gridley U.S.A. 39°22N 121°42W 170 F5
Griekwastad S. Africa 28°49S 23°15E 144 C3
Griesheim Germany 49°51N 8°33E 77 F4
Grieskirchen Austria 48°16N 13°48E 78 C6
Griffin U.S.A. 33°15N 84°16W 178 B5
Griffin, L. U.S.A. 28°52N 81°51W 179 G8
Griffith Australia 34°18S 146°2E 153 C7
Griffith Canada 45°15N 77°10W 174 A7
Griffith I. Canada 44°50N 80°55W 174 B4
Grignols France 44°23N 0°2W 72 D3
Grigoriopol Moldova 47°9N 29°18E 81 C14
Grimes U.S.A. 39°4N 121°54W 170 F5
Grimma Germany 51°14N 12°43E 76 D8
Grimmen Germany 54°7N 13°3E 76 A9
Grimsay U.K. 57°29N 7°14W 65 D1
Grimsby Canada 43°12N 79°34W 174 C5
Grimsby U.K. 53°34N 0°5W 66 D7
Grimsey Iceland 66°33N 17°58W 60 C5
Grimshaw Canada 56°10N 117°40W 162 B5
Grimslöv Sweden 56°44N 14°34E 63 H8
Grimstad Norway 58°20N 8°35E 61 G13
Grindelwald Switz. 46°38N 8°2E 77 J4
Grindsted Denmark 55°46N 8°55E 63 J2
Grindu Romania 44°44N 26°50E 81 F11
Grinnell Pen. Canada 76°40N 95°0W 161 B13
Grintavec Slovenia 46°22N 14°32E 93 B11
Griomasaigh = Grimsay
  U.K. 57°29N 7°14W 65 D1
Gris-Nez, C. France 50°52N 1°35E 71 B8
Grise Fiord Canada 76°25N 82°57W 161 B15
Grisolles France 43°49N 1°19E 72 E5
Grisons = Graubünden ☐
  Switz. 46°45N 9°30E 77 J5
Grisslehamn Sweden 60°5N 18°49E 62 D12
Groais I. Canada 50°55N 55°35W 165 B8
Grobiņa Latvia 56°33N 21°10E 62 B8
Groblersdal S. Africa 25°15S 29°25E 145 C4
Grobming Austria 47°27N 13°54E 78 D6
Grocka Serbia 44°40N 20°42E 96 B4
Gródek Poland 53°6N 23°40E 83 E10
Grodków Poland 50°43N 17°21E 83 H4
Grodno = Hrodna
  Belarus 53°42N 23°52E 82 E10
Grodzisk Mazowiecki
  Poland 52°7N 20°37E 83 F7
Grodzisk Wielkopolski
  Poland 52°15N 16°22E 83 F3
Grodzyanka = Hrodzyanka
  Belarus 53°31N 28°42E 75 B15
Groesbeck U.S.A. 31°31N 96°32W 176 F6
Groix France 47°38N 3°29W 70 E3
Groix, Î. de France 47°38N 3°28W 70 E3
Grójec Poland 51°50N 20°58E 83 G7
Gronau Niedersachsen,
  Germany 52°5N 9°47E 76 C5
Gronau Nordrhein-Westfalen,
  Germany 52°12N 7°2E 76 C3
Grong Norway 64°25N 12°8E 60 D15
Grönhögen Sweden 56°16N 16°24E 63 H10
Groningen Neths. 53°15N 6°35E 69 A6
Groningen ☐ Neths. 53°16N 6°40E 69 A6
Grønlands ☐ Greenland 75°0N 35°0W 57 C7
Grønnedal = Kangilinnguit
  Greenland 61°20N 47°57W 57 E6
Groom U.S.A. 35°12N 101°6W 176 D4
Groot → S. Africa 33°45S 24°36E 144 D3
Groot-Berg → S. Africa 32°47S 18°8E 144 D2
Groot-Brakrivier
  S. Africa 34°2S 22°18E 144 D3
Groot Karasberge
  Namibia 27°20S 18°40E 144 C2
Groot-Kei → S. Africa 32°41S 28°22E 145 D4
Groot-Vis → S. Africa 33°28S 27°5E 144 D4
Grootdrink S. Africa 28°33S 21°42E 144 C3
Groote Eylandt
  Australia 14°0S 136°40E 150 A2
Groote Peel ○ Neths. 51°22N 5°49E 69 C5
Grootfontein Namibia 19°31S 18°6E 144 A2
Grootlaagte → S. Africa 20°55S 21°27E 144 B3
Grootvloer → S. Africa 30°0S 20°40E 144 D3
Gros C. Canada 61°59N 113°32W 162 A6
Gros Islet St. Lucia 14°5N 60°58W 183 f
Gros Morne ○ Canada 49°40N 57°50W 165 C8
Gros Piton St. Lucia 13°49N 61°5W 183 f
Gros Piton Pt. St. Lucia 13°49N 61°5W 183 f
Grósio Italy 46°18N 10°16E 92 B7
Grosne → France 46°42N 4°56E 71 F11
Grossa, Pta. Spain 39°6N 1°36E 100 B8
Grosse Point U.S.A. 42°23N 82°54W 174 C2
Grossenbrode Germany 54°21N 11°4E 76 A6
Grossenhain Germany 51°17N 13°32E 76 D9
Grosser Arber Germany 49°6N 13°8E 77 F9

Grosser Plöner See
  Germany 54°10N 10°22E 76 A6
Grosseto Italy 42°46N 11°8E 93 F8
Grossgerungs Austria 48°34N 14°57E 78 C7
Grossglockner Austria 47°5N 12°40E 78 E5
Groswater B. Canada 54°20N 57°40W 165 B8
Groton Conn., U.S.A. 41°21N 72°5W 175 E12
Groton N.Y., U.S.A. 42°36N 76°22W 175 D8
Groton S. Dak., U.S.A. 45°27N 98°6W 172 C4
Grottáglie Italy 40°32N 17°26E 95 B10
Grottaminarda Italy 41°4N 15°2E 95 A8
Grottammare Italy 42°59N 13°52E 93 F10
Grotte Chauvet-Pont d'Arc
  France 44°23N 4°25E 73 D8
Grouard Mission
  Canada 55°33N 116°9W 162 B5
Grouin, Pte. du France 48°43N 1°51W 70 D5
Groulx, Mts. Canada 51°27N 68°41W 165 B6
Groundhog → Canada 48°45N 82°58W 164 C3
Grouw Neths. 53°5N 5°51E 69 A5
Grove City Fla., U.S.A. 26°55N 82°20W 179 H7
Grove City Pa., U.S.A. 41°10N 80°5W 174 E4
Grove Hill U.S.A. 31°42N 87°47W 177 F11
Groveland Calif.,
  U.S.A. 37°50N 120°14W 170 H6
Groveland Fla., U.S.A. 28°34N 81°51W 179 G8
Grover Beach U.S.A. 35°7N 120°37W 171 K6
Groves U.S.A. 29°57N 93°54W 176 G8
Groveton U.S.A. 44°36N 71°31W 175 B13
Grovetown U.S.A. 33°27N 82°12W 178 B7
Groźnjan Croatia 45°22N 13°43E 93 C10
Groznyy Russia 43°20N 45°45E 87 J7
Grubišno Polje Croatia 45°44N 17°12E 80 E2
Grudovo Bulgaria 42°21N 27°10E 97 D11
Grudusk Poland 53°30N 20°38E 83 E7
Grudziądz Poland 53°30N 18°47E 82 E5
Gruinard B. U.K. 57°56N 5°35W 65 D3
Gruissan France 43°8N 3°7E 72 E7
Grumo Áppula Italy 41°1N 16°42E 95 A9
Grums Sweden 59°22N 13°5E 62 E7
Grünberg Germany 50°35N 8°58E 76 E4
Gründau Germany 50°10N 9°9E 77 E5
Grundy Center U.S.A. 42°22N 92°47W 172 D7
Gruppo di Tessa ○ Italy 46°47N 11°0E 92 B8
Gruvberget Sweden 61°6N 16°10E 62 C10
Gruver U.S.A. 36°16N 101°24W 176 C4
Gruyères Switz. 46°35N 7°4E 77 J3
Gruža Serbia 43°54N 20°46E 96 C4
Gryazi Russia 52°30N 39°58E 85 F10
Gryazovets Russia 58°50N 40°10E 84 C11
Grybów Poland 49°36N 20°55E 83 J7
Grycksbo Sweden 60°40N 15°29E 62 D9
Gryfice Poland 53°55N 15°13E 82 E2
Gryfino Poland 53°9N 14°28E 83 E1
Gryfów Śląski Poland 51°2N 15°24E 83 G2
Gryt Sweden 58°12N 16°48E 63 F10
Grythyttan Sweden 59°41N 14°32E 62 E8
Grytviken S. Georgia 54°19S 36°33W 56 M8
Gstaad Switz. 46°28N 7°18E 77 J3
Gua India 22°18N 85°20E 125 H11
Gua Musang Malaysia 4°53S 101°58E 121 K3
Guabún, Pta. Chile 41°48S 74°2W 192 B2
Guacanayabo, G. de
  Cuba 20°40N 77°20W 182 B4
Guachipas →
  Argentina 25°40S 65°30W 190 B2
Guadajoz → Spain 37°50N 4°51W 89 H6
Guadalajara Mexico 20°40N 103°20W 180 C4
Guadalajara Spain 40°37N 3°12W 90 E1
Guadalajara ☐ Spain 40°47N 2°30W 90 E2
Guadalaviar = Turia →
  Spain 39°27N 0°19W 91 F4
Guadalcanal
  Solomon Is. 9°32S 160°12E 147 B9
Guadalcanal Spain 38°5N 5°52W 89 G5
Guadalén → Spain 38°5N 3°32W 89 G7
Guadales Argentina 34°30S 67°55W 190 C2
Guadalete → Spain 36°35N 6°13W 89 J4
Guadalimar → Spain 38°5N 3°28W 89 G7
Guadalmena → Spain 38°19N 2°56W 89 G8
Guadalmez → Spain 38°46N 5°4W 89 G5
Guadalquivir → Spain 36°47N 6°22W 89 J4
Guadalupe = Guadeloupe ☑
  W. Indies 16°15N 61°40W 182 b
Guadalupe Brazil 6°44S 43°47W 189 D2
Guadalupe Mexico 22°45N 102°31W 180 C4
Guadalupe Spain 39°27N 5°17W 89 F5
Guadalupe U.S.A. 34°58N 120°34W 171 L6
Guadalupe → U.S.A. 28°27N 96°47W 176 G6
Guadalupe, Sierra de
  Spain 39°28N 5°30W 89 F5
Guadalupe de Bravo
  Mexico 31°23N 106°7W 180 A3
Guadalupe I. Pac. Oc. 29°0N 118°50W 158 G8
Guadalupe Mts. △
  U.S.A. 31°40N 104°30W 176 F2
Guadalupe Peak
  U.S.A. 31°50N 104°52W 176 F2
Guadalupe y Calvo
  Mexico 26°6N 106°58W 180 B3
Guadarrama, Sierra de
  Spain 41°0N 4°0W 88 E7
Guadeloupe ☑ W. Indies 16°15N 61°40W 182 b
Guadeloupe △
  Guadeloupe 16°10N 61°40W 182 b
Guadeloupe Passage
  W. Indies 16°50N 62°15W 183 C7
Guadiamar → Spain 7°15S 79°29W 188 B2
Guadiana → Portugal 37°14N 7°22W 89 H3
Guadiana Menor →
  Spain 37°56N 3°15W 89 H7
Guadiaro → Spain 36°17N 5°17W 89 J5
Guadiato → Spain 37°52N 5°5W 89 H5
Guadiela → Spain 40°22N 2°49W 90 E2
Guadix Spain 37°18N 3°11W 89 H7
Guafo, Boca del Chile 43°35S 74°0W 192 B2
Guafo, I. Chile 43°35S 74°50W 192 B2
Guahán = Guam ☑
  Pac. Oc. 13°27N 144°45E 156 F6
Guaico Trin. & Tob. 10°35N 61°9W 187 K15
Guainía → Colombia 2°1N 67°7W 186 C5
Guaíra Brazil 24°5S 54°10W 191 A5
Guáira → Paraguay 25°45S 56°30W 191 B4
Guaíre = Gorey Ireland 52°41N 6°18W 64 D5
Guajará-Mirim Brazil 10°50S 65°20W 186 F5
Guajira, Pen. de la
  Colombia 12°0N 72°0W 186 A4
Gualán Guatemala 15°8N 89°22W 182 C2

Gualdo Tadino Italy 43°14N 12°47E 93 E9
Gualeguay Argentina 33°10S 59°14W 190 C4
Gualeguaychú
  Argentina 33°3S 59°31W 190 C4
Gualeguay →
  Argentina 33°19S 59°39W 190 C4
Gualicho, Salina
  Argentina 40°25S 65°20W 192 B3
Guam ☑ Pac. Oc. 13°27N 144°45E 156 F6
Guamblin, I. Chile 44°50S 75°0W 192 B2
Guamini Argentina 37°1S 62°28W 190 D3
Guamúchil Mexico 25°28N 108°6W 180 B3
Guana I. Br. Virgin Is. 18°30N 64°30W 183 e
Guanabacoa Cuba 23°8N 82°18W 182 B3
Guanacaste, Cordillera de
  Costa Rica 10°40N 85°4W 182 D2
Guanacaste △
  Costa Rica 10°57N 85°30W 182 D2
Guanacevi Mexico 25°56N 105°57W 180 B3
Guanahani = San Salvador I.
  Bahamas 24°0N 74°30W 183 B5
Guanaja Honduras 16°30N 85°55W 182 C2
Guanajay Cuba 22°56N 82°42W 182 B3
Guanajuato Mexico 21°1N 101°15W 180 C4
Guanajuato ☐ Mexico 21°0N 101°0W 180 C4
Guanambi Brazil 14°13S 42°47W 189 C2
Guanare Venezuela 9°3N 69°45W 186 B4
Guandacol Argentina 29°30S 68°40W 190 B2
Guandi Shan China 37°53N 111°29E 114 F6
Guane Cuba 22°10N 84°7W 182 B3
Guang'an China 30°28N 106°35E 116 B6
Guangchang China 26°50N 116°21E 117 D11
Guangde China 30°54N 119°25E 117 B12
Guangdong ☐ China 23°0N 113°0E 117 F9
Guangfeng China 28°20N 118°15E 117 C12
Guanghan China 30°58N 104°17E 116 B5
Guangling China 39°47N 114°22E 116 C10
Guangnan China 24°5N 105°4E 116 E5
Guangning China 23°40N 112°22E 117 F9
Guangrao China 37°5N 118°25E 115 F10
Guangshui China 31°37N 114°0E 117 B10
Guangshun China 26°9N 106°21E 116 D6
Guangwu China 37°48N 105°57E 114 F3
Guangxi Zhuangzu Zizhiqu ☐
  China 24°0N 109°0E 116 F7
Guangyuan China 32°26N 105°51E 114 H3
Guangze China 27°30N 117°12E 117 D11
Guangzhou China 23°6N 113°13E 117 F9
Guangzhou Baiyun Int. ✕ (CAN)
  China 23°23N 113°18E 117 F9
Guanhães Brazil 18°47S 42°57W 189 D2
Guanica Puerto Rico 17°58N 66°55W 183 d
Guanipa → Venezuela 9°56N 62°26W 186 B6
Guanling China 26°56N 105°35E 116 E5
Guannan China 34°8N 119°21E 115 G10
Guantánamo Cuba 20°10N 75°14W 183 B4
Guantánamo B. Cuba 19°59N 75°10W 183 C4
Guantao China 36°42N 115°25E 114 F8
Guanting Shuiku
  China 40°14N 115°35E 114 D8
Guanyang China 25°30N 111°9E 117 E8
Guanyun China 34°20N 119°18E 115 G10
Guapay = Grande →
  Bolivia 15°51S 64°39W 186 G6
Guápiles Costa Rica 10°10N 83°46W 182 D3
Guapo B. Trin. & Tob. 10°12N 61°41W 187 K15
Guaporé Brazil 28°51S 51°54W 191 B5
Guaporé → Brazil 11°55S 65°4W 186 F5
Guaqui Bolivia 16°41S 68°54W 186 G4
Guara, Sierra de Spain 42°19N 0°15W 90 C4
Guarabira Brazil 6°51S 35°29W 189 D3
Guaramacal △
  Venezuela 9°13N 70°12W 183 E5
Guarapari Brazil 20°40S 40°30W 189 E2
Guarapuava Brazil 25°20S 51°30W 191 B5
Guaratinguetá Brazil 22°49S 45°9W 191 A6
Guaratuba Brazil 25°53S 48°38W 191 B6
Guarda Portugal 40°32N 7°20W 88 E3
Guarda ☐ Portugal 40°40N 7°20W 88 E3
Guardafui, C. = Asir, Ras
  Somalia 11°55N 51°10E 131 E5
Guardamar del Segura
  Spain 38°5N 0°39W 91 G4
Guardavalle Italy 38°30N 16°30E 95 D9
Guárdia Sanframondi
  Italy 41°15N 14°36E 95 A7
Guardiagrele Italy 42°11N 14°13E 93 F11
Guardo Spain 42°47N 4°50W 88 C6
Guareña Spain 38°51N 6°6W 89 G4
Guareña → Spain 41°29N 5°23W 88 D5
Guárico ☐ Venezuela 8°40N 66°35W 186 B5
Guarujá Brazil 24°2S 46°25W 191 A6
Guarulhos Brazil 23°29S 46°33W 191 A6
Guasave Mexico 25°34N 108°27W 180 B3
Guasdualito Venezuela 7°15N 70°44W 186 B4
Guastalla Italy 44°55N 10°39E 92 D7
Guatemala Guatemala 14°40N 90°22W 182 D1
Guatemala ■
  Cent. Amer. 15°40N 90°30W 182 C1
Guatemala Basin
  Pac. Oc. 11°0N 95°0W 157 F18
Guatemala Trench
  Pac. Oc. 14°0N 95°0W 158 H10
Guatopo △ Venezuela 10°5N 66°30W 183 D6
Guatuaro Pt.
  Trin. & Tob. 10°19N 60°59W 187 K16
Guaviare → Colombia 4°3N 67°44W 186 C5
Guaxupé Brazil 21°10S 47°5W 191 A6
Guayaguayare
  Trin. & Tob. 10°8N 61°2W 187 K15
Guayama Puerto Rico 17°59N 66°7W 183 d
Guayaneco, Arch.
  Chile 47°45S 75°10W 192 C1
Guayaquil Ecuador 2°15S 79°52W 186 D3
Guayaquil Mexico 27°59N 110°54W 180 B2
Guayaquil, G. de Ecuador 3°10S 81°0W 186 D2
Guaymas Mexico 27°56N 110°54W 180 B2
Guba
  Dem. Rep. of the Congo 10°38S 26°27E 143 E2
Gûbâl, Madîq Egypt 27°30N 33°42E 137 L3
Gubbi India 13°19N 76°56E 127 H3
Gúbbio Italy 43°21N 12°35E 93 E9
Guben Germany 51°57N 14°43E 76 D10
Gubin Poland 51°57N 14°43E 83 G1
Gubio Nigeria 12°30N 12°39E 139 C7
Gubkin Russia 51°17N 37°32E 85 G9
Gubkinskiy Russia 64°28N 76°36E 106 C8
Gúča Serbia 43°46N 20°15E 96 C4
Gudalur India 11°30N 76°29E 127 J3
Gudauta Georgia 43°7N 40°32E 87 J5

Gudbrandsdalen
  Norway 61°33N 10°10E 60 F14
Guddu Barrage
  Pakistan 28°30N 69°50E 124 E3
Gudenå → Denmark 56°29N 10°13E 63 H4
Gudermes Russia 43°24N 46°5E 87 J8
Gudhjem Denmark 55°12N 14°58E 63 J8
Gudivada India 16°30N 81°3E 127 F5
Gudiyattam India 12°57N 78°55E 127 H4
Gudur India 14°12N 79°55E 127 M4
Guebwiller France 47°55N 7°12E 71 E14
Guecho = Algorta Spain 43°21N 2°59W 90 B2
Guékédou Guinea 8°40N 10°5W 138 D2
Guele Mendouka
  Cameroon 4°23N 12°55E 139 E7
Guelma Algeria 36°25N 7°29E 136 A5
Guelma ☐ Algeria 36°25N 7°25E 136 A5
Guelmim Morocco 28°56N 10°0W 134 C3
Guelph Canada 43°35N 80°20W 174 C4
Guemar Algeria 33°30N 6°49E 136 B5
Guémené-Penfao France 47°38N 1°50W 70 E5
Guémené-sur-Scorff
  France 48°4N 3°13W 70 D3
Guéné Benin 11°44N 3°16E 139 C5
Guer France 47°54N 2°8W 70 E4
Güer Aike Argentina 51°39S 69°35W 192 D3
Guérande France 47°20N 2°26W 70 E4
Guercif Morocco 34°14N 3°21E 136 B4
Guéret France 46°11N 1°51E 71 F8
Guérigny France 47°6N 3°10E 71 E10
Guerneville U.S.A. 38°30N 123°0W 170 G4
Guernica = Gernika-Lumo
  Spain 43°19N 2°40W 90 B2
Guernsey U.K. 49°26N 2°35W 67 H5
Guernsey U.S.A. 42°16N 104°45W 168 E11
Guerrara Oasis, Algeria 32°51N 4°22E 136 B4
Guerrara Saoura, Algeria 28°5N 0°8W 136 C3
Guerrero ☐ Mexico 17°40N 100°0W 181 D5
Guerzim Algeria 29°39N 1°40W 136 C4
Guessou-Sud Benin 10°30N 2°38E 139 C5
Gueugnon France 46°36N 4°4E 71 F11
Guéyo Ivory C. 5°25N 6°5W 138 D3
Gûgher Iran 29°28N 56°27E 129 D8
Guglionesi Italy 41°55N 14°55E 93 F11
Gui Jiang → China 23°30N 111°15E 117 F8
Guia Canary Is. 28°8N 15°38W 100 F4
Guia de Isora
  Canary Is. 28°12N 16°46W 100 F3
Guia Lopes da Laguna
  Brazil 21°26S 56°7W 191 A4
Guiana Highlands
  S. Amer. 5°10N 60°40W 184 C4
Guibéroua Ivory C. 6°14N 6°10W 138 D3
Guichen B. Australia 37°10S 139°45E 152 D3
Guichi China 30°39N 117°27E 117 B11
Guider Cameroon 9°55N 13°57E 139 D7
Guidiguir Niger 13°40N 9°50E 139 C6
Guidimaka ☐
  Mauritania 15°20N 12°30E 138 B2
Guiding China 26°34N 107°11E 116 D6
Guidong China 26°7N 113°57E 117 D9
Guiglo Ivory C. 6°45N 7°30W 138 D3
Guijá Mozam. 24°27S 33°0E 145 C5
Guijuelo Spain 40°33N 5°40W 88 E5
Guildford U.K. 51°14N 0°34W 67 F7
Guildford U.S.A. 41°17N 72°41W 175 E12
Guilford U.S.A. 45°10N 69°23W 173 C19
Guilin China 25°18N 110°15E 117 E8
Guillaume-Delisle, L.
  Canada 56°15N 76°17W 164 A4
Guillaumes France 44°5N 6°52E 73 D10
Guillestre France 44°39N 6°40E 73 D10
Guilvinec France 47°48N 4°17W 70 E2
Güímar Canary Is. 28°18N 16°24W 100 F3
Guimarães Portugal 41°28N 8°24W 88 D2
Guimaras ☐ Phil. 10°35N 122°37E 119 B6
Guinda U.S.A. 38°50N 122°12W 170 G4
Guinea ■ W. Afr. 10°20N 11°30W 138 C2
Guinea, Gulf of Atl. Oc. 3°0N 2°30E 139 E5
Guinea Basin Atl. Oc. 0°0 0°0 56 G11
Guinea-Bissau ■ Africa 12°0N 15°0W 138 C1
Güines Cuba 22°50N 82°0W 182 B3
Guingamp France 48°34N 3°10W 70 D3
Guinguinéo Senegal 14°0N 15°57W 138 C1
Guipavas France 48°26N 4°29W 70 D2
Guiping China 23°21N 110°2E 117 F8
Guir Mali 18°52N 2°52W 138 B4
Guir, O. → Algeria 31°29N 2°17W 136 B3
Guiratinga Brazil 16°25S 53°40W 187 G8
Güiria Venezuela 10°32N 62°18W 186 A6
Guiscard France 49°40N 3°1E 71 C10
Guise France 49°52N 3°35E 71 C10
Guiuan Phil. 11°5N 125°55E 119 B7
Guixi China 28°16N 117°15E 117 C11
Guiyang Guizhou,
  China 26°32N 106°40E 116 D6
Guiyang Hunan, China 25°36N 112°42E 117 E9
Guizhou ☐ China 27°0N 107°0E 116 D6
Guiar ☐ India 23°20N 71°0E 124 H4
Gujar Khan Pakistan 33°16N 73°19E 124 C5
Gujarat ☐ India 23°20N 71°0E 124 H4
Gujiang China 27°11N 114°47E 117 D10
Gujiao China 37°54N 112°8E 114 F7
Gujō Japan 35°45N 136°57E 113 G8
Gujranwala Pakistan 32°10N 74°12E 124 C6
Gujrat Pakistan 32°40N 74°2E 124 C6
Gukovo Russia 48°1N 39°58E 87 F5
Gulargambone
  Australia 31°20S 148°30E 153 A8
Gulbarga = Kalaburagi
  India 17°20N 76°50E 126 F3
Gulbene Latvia 57°8N 26°52E 84 D4
Gülchö Kyrgyzstan 40°48N 73°18E 107 F8
Guledagudda India 16°3N 75°48E 127 G2
Gulf, The = Persian Gulf
  Asia 27°0N 50°0E 129 E6
Gulf Breeze U.S.A. 30°21N 87°10W 177 F11
Gulf Hammock U.S.A. 29°15N 82°43W 179 F7
Gulf Islands △ U.S.A. 30°10N 87°10W 177 F11
Gulfport Fla., U.S.A. 27°45N 82°42W 179 H7
Gulfport Miss., U.S.A. 30°22N 89°6W 177 F10
Gulgong Australia 32°20S 149°49E 153 B8
Gulian China 52°56N 122°21E 111 A13
Gulin China 28°1N 105°50E 116 C5

Gulistan Pakistan 30°30N 66°35E 124 D2
Guliston Uzbekistan 40°29N 68°46E 109 E7
Gulja = Yining China 43°58N 81°10E 109 D10
Gull Lake Canada 50°10N 108°29W 163 C7
Gullbrandstorp Sweden 56°42N 12°43E 63 H6
Gullspång Sweden 58°59N 14°6E 63 F8
Gullivan B. U.S.A. 25°45N 81°40W 179 H8
Gullträsk Sweden 66°44N 20°21E 60 C12
Güllük Turkey 37°14N 27°35E 99 E9
Güllük Dağı △ Turkey 36°42N 30°27E 99 E12
Güllük Körfezi Turkey 37°12N 27°30E 99 E9
Gulma Nigeria 12°40N 4°23E 139 C5
Gulmarg India 34°3N 74°25E 125 B6
Gülnar Turkey 36°19N 33°24E 104 D5
Gülpınar Turkey 39°32N 26°7E 99 B8
Gülşehir Turkey 38°44N 34°37E 104 C6
Gülshat Kazakhstan 46°38N 74°21E 109 E8
Gulu Uganda 2°48N 32°17E 142 B3
Gülübovo Bulgaria 42°8N 25°55E 97 D9
Gulwe Tanzania 6°30S 36°25E 142 D4
Gulyaipole = Hulyaipole
  Ukraine 47°45N 36°21E 85 J9
Gum Lake Australia 32°42S 143°9E 152 B5
Gumal → Pakistan 31°40N 71°50E 124 C4
Gumbaz Pakistan 30°2N 69°0E 124 D3
Gumdag Turkmenistan 39°9N 54°36E 108 E4
Gumel Nigeria 12°39N 9°22E 139 C6
Gumi S. Korea 36°10N 128°11E 115 F15
Gumiel de Izán Spain 41°46N 3°41W 88 D7
Gumla India 23°3N 84°40E 125 H11
Gumlu Australia 19°53S 147°41E 150 B4
Gummersbach Germany 51°1N 7°34E 76 D3
Gummi Nigeria 12°4N 5°9E 139 C6
Gümüldür Turkey 38°6N 27°0E 99 C9
Gümüşçay Turkey 40°16N 27°17E 97 F11
Gümüşhaciköy Turkey 40°50N 35°18E 104 B6
Gümüşhane Turkey 40°30N 39°30E 105 B10
Gümüşsu Turkey 38°14N 30°1E 99 C12
Gumzai Indonesia 5°28S 134°42E 119 F8
Guna India 24°40N 77°19E 124 G7
Gunbalanya Australia 12°20S 133°4E 148 B5
Gundabooka △
  Australia 30°30S 145°0E 151 E4
Gundagai Australia 35°3S 148°6E 153 C8
Gundarehi India 20°57N 81°17E 126 D5
Gundelfingen Germany 48°34N 10°22E 77 G6
Gundlakamma →
  India 15°30N 80°15E 127 G5
Gundlupet India 11°48N 76°41E 127 J3
Güney Burdur, Turkey 37°29N 29°34E 99 D11
Güney Denizli, Turkey 38°9N 29°4E 99 C11
Güneydoğu Toroslar
  Turkey 38°20N 40°30E 105 C9
Gungal Australia 32°17S 150°32E 153 B9
Gunisao → Canada 53°56N 97°53W 163 C9
Gunisao L. Canada 53°33N 96°15W 163 C9
Gunjur Gambia 13°12N 16°44W 138 C1
Gunjyal Pakistan 32°20N 71°55E 124 C4
Gunlüce Turkey 36°50N 28°0E 99 E10
Gunma ☐ Japan 36°30N 138°20E 113 F9
Gunnarskog Sweden 59°49N 12°34E 62 E6
Gunnbjørn Fjeld
  Greenland 68°55N 29°47W 57 C8
Gunnebo Sweden 57°44N 16°32E 63 G10
Gunnedah Australia 30°59S 150°15E 153 A9
Gunnewin Australia 25°59S 148°33E 151 D4
Gunningbar Cr. →
  Australia 31°14S 147°6E 153 A7
Gunnison Colo.,
  U.S.A. 38°33N 106°56W 168 G10
Gunnison Utah, U.S.A. 39°9N 111°49W 168 G8
Gunnison → U.S.A. 39°4N 108°35W 168 G9
Gunsan S. Korea 35°59N 126°45E 115 G14
Guntakal India 15°11N 77°27E 127 G3
Gunter Canada 44°52N 77°32W 174 B7
Guntersville U.S.A. 34°21N 86°18W 177 D11
Guntong Malaysia 4°36N 101°3E 121 K3
Guntur India 16°23N 80°30E 127 F5
Gunung Ciremay △
  Indonesia 6°53S 108°24E 119 G13
Gunungapi Indonesia 6°45S 126°30E 119 F7
Gunungsitoli Indonesia 1°15N 97°30E 118 D1
Gunupur India 19°5N 83°50E 126 E6
Günz → Germany 48°27N 10°16E 77 G6
Günzburg Germany 48°27N 10°16E 77 G6
Günzhong China 33°32N 116°12E 114 H9
Gunza Angola 10°50S 13°50E 140 G2
Gunzenhausen Germany 49°7N 10°44E 77 F6
Guo He → China 32°59N 117°10E 117 A11
Guoyang China 33°32N 116°12E 114 H9
Gupis Pakistan 36°15N 73°20E 125 A5
Gura Humorului
  Romania 47°35N 25°53E 81 C10
Gura-Teghii Romania 45°30N 26°28E 81 E11
Gurahonț Romania 46°16N 22°21E 80 D7
Gurban Obo China 43°20N 112°18E 114 C7
Gurbantünggüt Shamo
  China 45°8N 87°0E 109 C11
Gurdaspur India 32°5N 75°31E 124 C6
Gurdon U.S.A. 33°55N 93°9W 176 E8
Güre Balıkesir, Turkey 39°36N 26°54E 99 B8
Güre Uşak, Turkey 38°39N 29°10E 99 C11
Gurgaon India 28°27N 77°1E 124 E7
Gurgueia → Brazil 6°50S 43°24W 189 D2
Gurha India 25°12N 71°39E 124 G4
Guri, Embalse de
  Venezuela 7°50N 62°52W 186 B6
Gurin Nigeria 9°5N 12°54E 139 D7
Gurjaani Georgia 41°43N 45°52E 87 K7
Gurk → Austria 46°35N 14°31E 78 E7
Gurkha Nepal 28°5N 84°40E 125 E11
Gurla Mandhata = Naimona'nyi
  Feng 30°26N 81°18E 125 D9
Gurley Australia 29°45S 149°48E 153 A9
Gurnet Point U.S.A. 42°1N 70°34W 175 D14
Guro Mozam. 17°26S 32°30E 143 F3
Güroymak Turkey 38°35N 41°55E 105 C10
Gürpınar İstanbul,
  Turkey 40°59N 28°13E 97 F12
Gürpınar Van, Turkey 38°18N 43°25E 105 C10
Gurué Mozam. 15°25S 36°58E 143 F4
Gurun Malaysia 5°49N 100°27E 121 K3
Gürün Turkey 38°43N 37°15E 104 C7
Gurupá Brazil 1°25S 51°35W 187 D8
Gurupá, I. Grande de
  Brazil 1°25S 51°45W 187 D8
Gurupi Brazil 11°43S 49°4W 187 F9
Gurupi → Brazil 1°13S 46°6W 187 D9
Gurupi, Serra do Brazil 5°0S 47°50W 189 B1

Guruwe *Zimbabwe* 16°40S 30°42E **145** A5
Gurvan Sayhan Uul
Mongolia 43°50N 104°0E **114** C3
Guryev = Atyraū
Kazakhstan 47°5N 52°0E **108** C4
Guryevsk *Russia* 54°47N 20°38E **82** D7
Gus-Khrustalnyy *Russia* 55°42N 40°44E **86** C5
Gusau *Nigeria* 12°12N 6°40E **139** C6
Gusev *Russia* 54°35N 22°10E **82** D9
Gushan *China* 39°50N 123°35E **115** E12
Gushgy = Serhetabat
Turkmenistan 35°20N 62°18E **129** C9
Gushi *China* 32°11N 115°41E **117** A10
Gushiago *Ghana* 9°55N 0°15W **139** D4
Gusinje *Montenegro* 42°35N 19°50E **96** D3
Gusinoozersk *Russia* 51°16N 106°27E **107** D11
Gúspini *Italy* 39°32N 8°37E **94** C1
Güssing *Austria* 47°3N 16°20E **79** D9
Gustav Holm, Kap
Greenland 66°36N 34°15W **57** D7
Gustavus *U.S.A.* 58°25N 135°44W **162** B1
Gustine *U.S.A.* 37°16N 121°0W **170** H6
Güstrow *Germany* 53°47N 12°10E **76** B8
Gusum *Sweden* 58°16N 16°30E **63** F10
Guta = Kolárovo
Slovak Rep. 47°54N 18°0E **79** D10
Gütersloh *Germany* 51°54N 8°24E **76** D4
Gutha *Australia* 28°58S 115°55E **149** E2
Guthalungra *Australia* 19°52S 147°50E **150** B4
Guthrie *Canada* 44°28N 79°32W **174** B5
Guthrie *Okla., U.S.A.* 35°53N 97°25W **176** D6
Guthrie *Tex., U.S.A.* 33°37N 100°19W **176** E4
Gutian *China* 26°32N 118°43E **117** D12
Gutu *Zimbabwe* 19°41S 31°9E **145** A5
Guwahati *India* 26°10N 91°45E **123** F17
Guy Fawkes River △
Australia 30°0S 152°20E **151** D5
Guyana ■ *S. Amer.* 5°0N 59°0W **186** C7
Guyane française = French
Guiana ☒ *S. Amer.* 4°0N 53°0W **187** C8
Guyang *China* 41°0N 110°5E **114** D6
Guyenne *France* 44°30N 0°40E **72** D4
Guymon *U.S.A.* 36°41N 101°29W **176** C4
Guyra *Australia* 30°15S 151°40E **151** E5
Guyton *U.S.A.* 32°20N 81°24W **178** E5
Guyuan *Hebei, China* 41°37N 115°40E **114** D8
Guyuan *Ningxia Huizu,*
China 36°0N 106°20E **114** F4
Güzelbahçe *Turkey* 38°21N 26°54E **99** C8
Güzelyurt = Morphou
Cyprus 35°12N 32°59E **101** D11
Guzhang *China* 28°42N 109°58E **116** C7
Guzhen *China* 33°22N 117°18E **115** H9
Guzmán, L. de *Mexico* 31°20N 107°30W **180** A3
G'uzor *Uzbekistan* 38°36N 66°15E **109** E7
Gvardeysk *Russia* 54°39N 21°5E **82** D8
Gvardeyskoye *Ukraine* 45°7N 34°1E **85** K8
Gwa *Burma* 17°36N 94°34E **123** L19
Gwaai *Zimbabwe* 19°15S 27°45E **143** F2
Gwaai → *Zimbabwe* 17°59S 26°52E **143** F2
Gwabegar *Australia* 30°37S 148°59E **153** A8
Gwadabawa *Nigeria* 13°28N 5°15E **139** C6
Gwādar *Pakistan* 25°10N 62°18E **122** G3
Gwagwada *Nigeria* 10°15N 7°15E **139** C6
Gwaii Haanas △
Canada 52°21N 131°26W **162** C2
Gwalior *India* 26°12N 78°10E **124** F8
Gwanara *Nigeria* 8°55N 3°9E **139** D5
Gwanda *Zimbabwe* 20°55S 29°0E **143** G2
Gwandu *Nigeria* 12°30N 4°41E **139** C5
Gwane
Dem. Rep. of the Congo 4°45N 25°48E **142** B2
Gwangju *S. Korea* 35°9N 126°54E **115** G14
Gwangyang *S. Korea* 34°56N 127°41E **115** G14
Gwanju = Gwangju
S. Korea 35°9N 126°54E **115** G14
Gwaram *Nigeria* 10°15N 10°25E **139** C7
Gwarzo *Nigeria* 12°20N 8°55E **139** C6
Gwasero *Nigeria* 9°29N 3°30E **139** D5
Gwda → *Poland* 53°3N 16°44E **83** E3
Gweebarra B. *Ireland* 54°51N 8°23W **64** B3
Gweedore *Ireland* 55°3N 8°14W **64** A3
Gweru *Zimbabwe* 19°28S 29°45E **143** F2
Gwi *Nigeria* 9°0N 7°10E **139** D6
Gwinn *U.S.A.* 46°19N 87°27W **172** B10
Gwio Kura *Nigeria* 12°30N 11°2E **139** C7
Gwoza *Nigeria* 11°5N 13°40E **139** C7
Gwydir → *Australia* 29°27S 149°48E **151** E4
Gwynedd □ *U.K.* 52°52N 4°10W **66** E3
Gyandzha = Gäncä
Azerbaijan 40°45N 46°20E **87** K8
Gyangzê *China* 29°5N 89°47E **110** F6
Gyaring Hu *China* 34°50N 97°40E **110** E8
Gydanskiy Poluostrov
Russia 70°0N 78°0E **106** C3
Gyeonggi-man
S. Korea 37°0N 125°30E **115** F13
Gyeongju *S. Korea* 35°51N 129°14E **115** G15
Gyldenløve Fjord
Greenland 64°15N 40°30W **57** E6
Gympie *Australia* 26°11S 152°38E **151** D5
Gyomaendrőd *Hungary* 46°56N 20°50E **80** D5
Gyöngyös *Hungary* 47°48N 19°56E **80** C4
Győr *Hungary* 47°41N 17°40E **80** C2
Győr-Moson-Sopron □
Hungary 47°40N 17°20E **80** C2
Gypsum Pt. *Canada* 61°53N 114°35W **162** A6
Gypsumville *Canada* 51°45N 98°40W **163** C9
Gyueshevo *Bulgaria* 42°14N 22°28E **96** D6
Gyula *Hungary* 46°38N 21°17E **80** D6
Gyumri *Armenia* 40°47N 43°50E **87** K6
Gyzylarbat = Serdar
Turkmenistan 39°4N 56°23E **129** B8
Gyzyletrek = Etrek
Turkmenistan 37°36N 54°46E **129** B7
Gyzylgaya *Turkmenistan* 40°40N 55°30E **108** D5
Gzhatsk = Gagarin
Russia 55°38N 35°0E **84** E8

H

H. Neely Henry L.
U.S.A. 33°55N 86°2W **178** B3
Ha 'Arava → *Israel* 30°50N 35°20E **130** E4
Ha Coi *Vietnam* 21°26N 107°46E **116** G6
Ha Dong *Vietnam* 20°58N 105°46E **116** G5
Ha Giang *Vietnam* 22°50N 104°59E **116** F5
Ha Karmel, Har *Israel* 32°44N 35°3E **130** C4
Ha Karmel △ *Israel* 32°45N 35°5E **130** C4

Ha Long = Hong Gai
Vietnam 20°57N 107°5E **116** G6
Ha Long, Vinh *Vietnam* 20°56N 107°3E **120** B6
Ha Tien *Vietnam* 10°23N 104°29E **121** G5
Ha Tinh *Vietnam* 18°20N 105°54E **120** C5
Ha Trung *Vietnam* 19°58N 105°50E **120** C5
Haakon VII Topp = Beerenberg
Norway 71°0N 8°20W **57** C10
Haaksbergen *Neths.* 52°9N 6°45E **69** B6
Haapsalu *Estonia* 58°56N 23°30E **84** C2
Haarby *Denmark* 55°13N 10°7E **63** J4
Haarlem *Neths.* 52°23N 4°39E **68** B5
Haast *N.Z.* 43°51S 169°1E **155** D4
Haast → *N.Z.* 43°50S 169°2E **155** D4
Haast Pass *N.Z.* 44°6S 169°21E **155** E4
Haasts Bluff *Australia* 23°22S 132°0E **148** D5
Haasts Bluff ◌
Australia 23°39S 130°34E **148** D5
Hab → *Pakistan* 24°53N 66°41E **124** G3
Hab Nadi Chauki
Pakistan 25°0N 66°50E **124** G2
Habahe *China* 48°3N 86°23E **109** C11
Habaswein *Kenya* 1°2N 39°30E **142** B4
Habay *Canada* 58°50N 118°44W **162** B5
Ḥabbāniyah *Iraq* 33°17N 43°29E **105** F10
Ḥabbāniyah, Hawr al
Iraq 33°17N 43°29E **105** F10
Habibas, Îles *Algeria* 35°44N 1°8W **91** K3
Habichtswald △ *Germany* 51°15N 9°15E **76** D5
Habirag *China* 42°17N 115°42E **114** C8
Habo *Sweden* 57°55N 14°6E **63** G8
Haboro *Japan* 44°22N 141°42E **112** B10
Ḥabshān *U.A.E.* 23°50N 53°37E **129** F7
Hachenburg *Germany* 50°40N 7°49E **76** E3
Hachijō-Jima *Japan* 33°5N 139°45E **113** H9
Hachiman = Gujō
Japan 35°45N 136°57E **113** G8
Hachinohe *Japan* 40°30N 141°29E **112** D10
Hachiōji *Japan* 35°40N 139°20E **113** G9
Hacı Zeynalabdin
Azerbaijan 40°37N 49°33E **87** K9
Hacıbektaş *Turkey* 38°56N 34°33E **104** C6
Hacılar *Turkey* 38°38N 35°26E **104** C6
Hack, Mt. *Australia* 30°45S 138°55E **152** A3
Hackås *Sweden* 62°56N 14°30E **62** B8
Hackensack *U.S.A.* 40°52N 74°4W **175** F10
Hackettstown *U.S.A.* 40°51N 74°50W **175** F10
Håckrenmagasinet
Sweden 63°15N 13°30E **62** C7
Hadali *Pakistan* 32°16N 72°11E **124** C5
Hadarba, Ras *Sudan* 22°4N 36°51E **137** C4
Hadarom □ *Israel* 31°0N 35°0E **130** E4
Ḥadd, Ra's al *Oman* 22°35N 59°50E **131** C6
Haddington *U.K.* 55°57N 2°47W **65** F6
Haddock *U.S.A.* 33°2N 83°26W **178** D6
Hadejia *Nigeria* 12°30N 10°5E **139** C7
Hadejia → *Nigeria* 12°50N 10°51E **139** C7
Hadera *Israel* 32°28N 34°55E **130** C3
Hadera, N. → *Israel* 32°28N 34°52E **130** C3
Haderslev *Denmark* 55°15N 9°30E **63** J3
Hadgaon *India* 19°30N 77°40E **126** E3
Hadhramaut = Ḥaḍramawt □
Yemen 15°30N 49°30E **131** D4
Hadiboh *Yemen* 12°39N 54°2E **131** E5
Hadilik *China* 37°56N 86°6E **109** E11
Hadım *Turkey* 36°58N 32°26E **104** D5
Hādīshahr *Iran* 38°51N 45°40E **105** C11
Hadjadj, O. el → *Algeria* 28°18N 5°20E **136** C5
Hadjeb el Aïoun *Tunisia* 35°21N 9°32E **136** A5
Hadley B. *Canada* 72°31N 108°12W **160** C10
Ḥaḍramawt □ *Yemen* 15°30N 49°30E **131** D4
Ḥadrānīyah *Iraq* 35°38N 43°14E **128** C4
Hadrian's Wall *U.K.* 55°0N 2°30W **66** B5
Hadsten *Denmark* 56°19N 10°3E **63** H4
Hadsund *Denmark* 56°44N 10°8E **63** H4
Hadyach *Ukraine* 50°21N 34°0E **85** F8
Hae, Ko *Thailand* 7°44N 98°22E **121** a
Haeju *N. Korea* 38°3N 125°45E **115** E13
Hā'ena *U.S.A.* 22°14N 159°34W **167** L8
Haenam *S. Korea* 34°34N 126°35E **115** H14
Haenertsburg *S. Africa* 24°0S 29°50E **145** B4
Haerhpin = Harbin
China 45°48N 126°40E **115** B14
Hafar al Bāṭin
Si. Arabia 28°32N 45°52E **128** D5
Hafik *Turkey* 39°51N 37°23E **104** C7
Ḥafirat al 'Aydā
Si. Arabia 26°26N 39°12E **128** E3
Hafit *Oman* 23°59N 55°49E **129** F7
Hafizabad *Pakistan* 32°5N 73°40E **124** C5
Haflong *India* 25°10N 93°5E **123** G18
Haft Gel *Iran* 31°30N 49°32E **129** D6
Hagalil *Israel* 32°53N 35°18E **130** C4
Hagari → *India* 15°40N 77°0E **127** G3
Hagby *Sweden* 56°34N 16°11E **63** H10
Hagemeister I. *U.S.A.* 58°39N 160°54W **166** D7
Hagen *Germany* 51°21N 7°27E **76** D3
Hagenow *Germany* 53°26N 11°12E **76** B7
Hagerman *U.S.A.* 33°7N 104°20W **169** K11
Hagerman Fossil Beds ◌
U.S.A. 42°48N 114°57W **168** E6
Hagerstown *U.S.A.* 39°39N 77°43W **173** F15
Hagersville *Canada* 42°58N 80°3W **174** D4
Hagetmau *France* 43°39N 0°37W **72** E3
Hagfors *Sweden* 60°3N 13°45E **63** F7
Hagi *Japan* 34°30N 131°22E **113** G5
Hagolan *Syria* 33°0N 35°45E **130** C4
Hagondange *France* 49°16N 6°11E **71** C13
Hags Hd. *Ireland* 52°57N 9°28W **64** D2
Hague, C. de la *France* 49°44N 1°56W **70** C5
Hague, The = 's-Gravenhage
Neths. 52°7N 4°17E **69** B4
Haguenau *France* 48°49N 7°47E **71** D14
Hahira *U.S.A.* 30°59N 83°22W **178** F6
Hai Duong *Vietnam* 20°56N 106°19E **116** G6
Hai'an *Guangdong, China* 20°18N 110°11E **117** a
Hai'an *Jiangsu, China* 32°37N 120°17E **117** A13
Haicheng *China* 40°50N 122°45E **115** D12
Haida Gwaii *Canada* 53°20N 132°10W **162** C2
Haidar Khel *Afghan.* 33°58N 68°38E **124** C3
Haidarâbâd = Hyderabad
India 17°22N 78°29E **126** F4
Haidargarh *India* 26°37N 81°22E **125** F9
Haifa = Ḥefa *Israel* 32°46N 35°0E **130** C4
Haifeng *China* 22°58N 115°10E **117** F10
Haiger *Germany* 50°44N 8°12E **76** E4
Haikou *China* 20°1N 110°16E **117** a
Hā'il *Si. Arabia* 27°28N 41°45E **128** E4
Hā'il □ *Si. Arabia* 26°40N 41°45E **128** E4
Hailar *China* 49°10N 119°38E **111** B12
Hailey *U.S.A.* 43°31N 114°19W **168** E6

Haileybury *Canada* 47°30N 79°38W **164** C4
Hailin *China* 44°37N 129°30E **115** B15
Hailing Dao *China* 21°35N 111°47E **117** G8
Hailun *China* 47°28N 126°50E **111** B14
Hailuoto *Finland* 65°3N 24°45E **60** D21
Haimen *Guangdong,*
China 23°15N 116°38E **117** F11
Haimen *Jiangsu,*
China 31°52N 121°10E **117** B13
Hainan □ *China* 19°0N 109°30E **117** a
Hainan Dao *China* 19°0N 109°30E **117** a
Hainan Str. = Qiongzhou Haixia
China 20°10N 110°15E **117** a
Hainaut □ *Belgium* 50°30N 4°0E **69** D4
Hainburg *Austria* 48°9N 16°56E **79** C9
Haines *Alaska, U.S.A.* 59°14N 135°26W **162** B1
Haines *Oreg., U.S.A.* 44°55N 117°56W **168** D5
Haines City *U.S.A.* 28°7N 81°38W **179** G8
Haines Junction
Canada 60°45N 137°30W **162** A1
Hainfeld *Austria* 48°3N 15°48E **78** C8
Haining *China* 30°28N 120°40E **117** B13
Haiphong *Vietnam* 20°47N 106°41E **116** G6
Haitan Dao *China* 25°30N 119°45E **117** E12
Haiti ■ *W. Indies* 19°0N 72°30W **183** C5
Haiya *Sudan* 18°20N 36°21E **137** D4
Haiyan *Qinghai, China* 36°53N 100°59E **110** D9
Haiyan *Zhejiang,*
China 30°28N 120°57E **117** B13
Haiyang *China* 36°47N 121°9E **115** F11
Haizhou *China* 34°37N 119°7E **115** G10
Haizhou Wan *China* 34°50N 119°20E **115** G10
Hajdú-Bihar □ *Hungary* 47°30N 21°30E **80** C6
Hajdúböszörmény
Hungary 47°40N 21°30E **80** C6
Hajdúdorog *Hungary* 47°48N 21°30E **80** C6
Hajdúhadház *Hungary* 47°40N 21°40E **80** C6
Hajdúnánás *Hungary* 47°50N 21°26E **80** C6
Hajdúsámson *Hungary* 47°37N 21°42E **80** C6
Hajdúszoboszló *Hungary* 47°27N 21°22E **80** C6
Haji Ibrahim *Iraq* 36°40N 44°30E **105** D11
Hajipur *India* 25°45N 85°13E **125** G11
Ḥājj Ali Qolī, Kavīr-e
Iran 35°55N 54°50E **129** C7
Ḥajjah *Yemen* 15°42N 43°36E **131** D3
Ḥājjīābād *Hormozgān,*
Iran 28°19N 55°55E **129** D7
Ḥājjīābād □ *Iran* 35°0N 49°0E **129** C6
Ḥājjīābād Khorāsān, Iran 33°37N 60°0E **129** C9
Ḥājjīābād-e Zarrīn *Iran* 33°9N 54°51E **129** C7
Hajnówka *Poland* 52°47N 23°35E **83** E10
Hakansson, Mts.
Dem. Rep. of the Congo 8°40S 25°45E **143** D2
Hakataramea *N.Z.* 44°43S 170°30E **155** E5
Hakkâri *Turkey* 37°34N 43°44E **105** D10
Hakkâri □ *Turkey* 37°30N 44°0E **105** D10
Hakkôda San *Japan* 40°50N 141°0E **112** D10
Hakodate *Japan* 41°45N 140°44E **112** C10
Hakos *Namibia* 23°13S 16°21E **144** B2
Haku-San *Japan* 36°9N 136°46E **113** F8
Haku-San □ *Japan* 36°15N 136°45E **113** F8
Hakui *Japan* 36°53N 136°47E **113** F8
Hakusan *Japan* 36°31N 136°34E **113** F8
Hala *Pakistan* 25°43N 68°20E **122** G6
Ḥalab *Syria* 36°10N 37°15E **104** D7
Ḥalab □ *Syria* 36°10N 37°10E **104** D7
Ḥalabjah *Iraq* 35°10N 45°58E **105** E11
Halabjah *Sudan* 22°12N 36°30E **137** C4
Halaib Triangle *Africa* 22°30N 35°20E **137** C4
Ḥalat 'Ammār *Si. Arabia* 29°10N 36°4E **128** D3
Halbā *Lebanon* 34°34N 36°6E **130** A5
Halberstadt *Germany* 51°54N 11°3E **76** D7
Halcombe *N.Z.* 40°8S 175°30E **154** G4
Halcon, Mt. *Phil.* 13°16N 121°0E **119** B6
Halde Fjäll = Haltiatunturi
Finland 69°17N 21°18E **60** B19
Halden *Norway* 59°9N 11°23E **61** G14
Haldensleben *Germany* 52°17N 11°41E **76** C7
Haldia *Bangla.* 21°1N 88°3E **125** H13
Haldwani *India* 29°31N 79°30E **125** E8
Hale → *Australia* 24°56S 135°53E **150** C2
Halesowen *U.K.* 52°27N 2°3W **67** E5
Halesworth *U.K.* 52°20N 1°32E **67** E9
Haleyville *U.S.A.* 34°14N 87°37W **177** D11
Half Assini *Ghana* 5°1N 2°50W **138** D4
Half Dome *U.S.A.* 37°44N 119°32E **170** H7
Halfeti *Turkey* 37°8N 37°52E **104** D7
Halfmoon Bay *N.Z.* 46°50S 168°5E **155** G3
Halfway → *Canada* 56°12N 121°32W **162** B4
Halia *India* 24°50N 82°19E **125** G10
Haliburton *Canada* 45°3N 78°30W **174** A6
Halifax *Australia* 18°32S 146°22E **150** B4
Halifax *Canada* 44°38N 63°35W **165** D7
Halifax *U.K.* 53°43N 1°52W **66** D6
Halifax *U.S.A.* 40°25N 76°55W **174** F8
Halifax B. *Australia* 18°50S 147°0E **150** B4
Halifax I. *Namibia* 26°38S 15°4E **144** C2
Halkida = Chalkida
Greece 38°27N 23°42E **98** C5
Halkidiki = Chalkidiki
Greece 40°25N 23°20E **96** F7
Hall Beach *Canada* 68°46N 81°12W **161** D15
Hall in Tirol *Austria* 47°17N 11°30E **78** D4
Hall Pen. *Canada* 63°30N 66°0W **161** E18
Hall Pt. *Australia* 15°40S 124°23E **148** C3
Halland *Sweden* 57°8N 12°47E **61** H15
Halland □ *Sweden* 56°50N 12°50E **63** H6
Hallands Väderö *Sweden* 56°27N 12°34E **63** H5
Hällanyiat, Jazâ'ir al
Oman 17°30N 56°0E **129** F8
Hallasan *S. Korea* 33°22N 126°31E **115** H14
Hällbybrunn *Sweden* 59°24N 16°25E **62** E10
Halle *Belgium* 50°44N 4°13E **69** D4
Halle *Nordrhein-Westfalen,*
Germany 52°3N 8°22E **76** C4

Halle *Sachsen-Anhalt,*
Germany 51°30N 11°56E **76** D7
Hällefors *Sweden* 59°47N 14°31E **62** E8
Hälleforsnäs *Sweden* 59°10N 16°30E **62** E10
Hallein *Austria* 47°40N 13°5E **78** D6
Hällekis *Sweden* 58°38N 13°27E **63** F7
Hallsberg *Sweden* 59°5N 15°7E **62** E9
Hallett *Australia* 33°25S 138°55E **152** B3
Hallettsville *U.S.A.* 29°27N 96°57W **176** G6
Halley *Antarctica* 75°35S 26°39W **55** D1
Hallia → *India* 16°55N 79°20E **126** F4
Hallim *S. Korea* 33°24N 126°15E **115** H14
Hallingdalselva →
Norway 60°23N 9°35E **60** F13
Hallock *U.S.A.* 48°47N 96°57W **172** A5
Halls Creek *Australia* 18°16S 127°38E **148** C4
Halls Gap *Australia* 37°8S 142°34E **151** F3
Halls Lake *Canada* 45°7N 78°45W **174** A6
Hallstahammar *Sweden* 59°38N 16°15E **62** E10
Hallstatt *Austria* 47°33N 13°38E **78** D6
Hallstavik *Sweden* 60°5N 18°37E **62** D12
Hallstead *U.S.A.* 41°58N 75°45W **175** E9
Halmahera *Indonesia* 0°40N 128°0E **119** D7
Halmahera Sea *Indonesia* 2°0N 130°0E **119** D7
Halmeu *Romania* 47°57N 23°2E **80** C8
Halmstad *Sweden* 56°41N 12°52E **63** H6
Halong Bay = Ha Long, Vinh
Vietnam 20°56N 107°3E **120** B6
Halq el Oued = La Goulette
Tunisia 36°53N 10°18E **94** F3
Hals *Denmark* 57°0N 10°18E **63** H4
Hälsingborg = Helsingborg
Sweden 56°3N 12°42E **63** H6
Hälsingland *Sweden* 61°40N 16°5E **62** C10
Halstead *U.K.* 51°57N 0°40E **67** F8
Haltern *Germany* 51°45N 7°11E **76** D3
Haltiatunturi *Finland* 69°17N 21°18E **60** B19
Halton □ *U.K.* 53°22N 2°45W **66** D5
Haltwhistle *U.K.* 54°58N 2°26W **66** C5
Ḥālūl *Qatar* 25°40N 52°40E **129** E7
Halvad *India* 23°1N 71°11E **124** H4
Halvān *Iran* 33°57N 56°15E **129** C8
Ham *France* 49°45N 3°4E **71** C10
Hamab *Namibia* 28°7S 19°16E **144** C2
Hamada *Japan* 34°56N 132°4E **113** G6
Hamadān *Iran* 34°52N 48°32E **105** E13
Hamadān □ *Iran* 35°0N 49°0E **129** C6
Hamadia *Algeria* 35°28N 1°57E **136** A4
Hamāh *Syria* 35°5N 36°40E **104** E7
Hamāh □ *Syria* 35°10N 37°0E **104** E7
Hamale *Ghana* 10°56N 2°45W **138** C4
Hamamatsu *Japan* 34°45N 137°45E **113** G8
Hamar *Norway* 60°48N 11°7E **60** F14
Hamāṭah, Gebel *Egypt* 24°17N 35°0E **128** E2
Hamatonbetsu *Japan* 45°10N 142°20E **112** B11
Hambantota *Sri Lanka* 6°10N 81°10E **127** L5
Hamber △ *Canada* 52°20N 118°0W **162** C5
Hamburg *Germany* 53°33N 9°59E **76** B5
Hamburg *Ark., U.S.A.* 33°14N 91°48W **176** E9
Hamburg *N.Y., U.S.A.* 42°43N 78°50W **174** D6
Hamburg *Pa., U.S.A.* 40°33N 75°59W **175** F9
Hamburg □ *Germany* 53°30N 10°0E **76** B5
Hamburg Fuhlsbüttel ✈ *(HAM)*
Germany 53°38N 9°59E **76** B5
Ḥamḍ, W. al →
Si. Arabia 24°55N 36°20E **128** E3
Hamden *U.S.A.* 41°23N 72°54W **175** E12
Hämeenlinna *Finland* 61°0N 24°28E **63** E21
Hamelin Pool *Australia* 26°22S 114°20E **149** E1
Hameln *Germany* 52°6N 9°21E **76** C5
Hamerkaz □ *Israel* 32°15N 34°55E **130** C3
Hamersley Ra.
Australia 22°0S 117°45E **148** D2
Hamhŭng *N. Korea* 39°54N 127°30E **115** E14
Hami *China* 42°55N 93°25E **110** B4
Hamilton *Australia* 37°45S 142°2E **151** F3
Hamilton *Bermuda* 32°17N 64°47W **183** b
Hamilton *Canada* 43°15N 79°50W **174** D5
Hamilton *N.Z.* 37°47S 175°19E **154** C4
Hamilton *U.K.* 55°46N 4°2W **65** F4
Hamilton *Ala., U.S.A.* 34°9N 87°59W **177** D11
Hamilton *Mont.,*
U.S.A. 46°15N 114°10W **168** C6
Hamilton *N.Y., U.S.A.* 42°50N 75°33W **175** D9
Hamilton *Ohio, U.S.A.* 39°24N 84°34W **173** F11
Hamilton *Tex., U.S.A.* 31°42N 98°7W **176** F5
Hamilton → *Queens.,*
Australia 23°30S 139°47E **150** C2
Hamilton → *S. Austral.,*
Australia 26°40S 135°19E **152** D2
Hamilton City *U.S.A.* 39°45N 122°1W **170** F4
Hamilton I. *Australia* 20°21S 148°56E **150** b
Hamilton Inlet *Canada* 54°0N 57°30W **165** B8
Hamilton Mt. *U.S.A.* 43°25N 74°22W **175** C10
Hamina *Finland* 60°34N 27°12E **84** B4
Hamirpur *H.P., India* 31°41N 76°31E **124** D7
Hamirpur *U.P., India* 25°57N 80°9E **125** G9
Hamitabat *Turkey* 41°30N 27°17E **97** E11
Hamlet *U.S.A.* 34°53N 79°42W **177** D15
Hamley Bridge
Australia 34°17S 138°35E **152** B2
Hamlin = Hameln
Germany 52°6N 9°21E **76** C5
Hamlin *N.Y., U.S.A.* 43°17N 77°55W **174** C7
Hamlin *Tex., U.S.A.* 32°53N 100°8W **176** E4
Hamm *Germany* 51°40N 7°50E **76** D3
Hammām Bouhadjar
Algeria 35°23N 0°58W **136** A3
Ḥammām, Hawr al *Iraq* 30°50N 47°10E **128** D5
Hammamet *Tunisia* 36°24N 10°38E **95** A1
Hammamet, G. de *Tunisia* 36°10N 10°48E **95** A1
Hammarstrand *Sweden* 63°7N 16°20E **62** A10
Hammeren *Denmark* 55°18N 14°47E **63** J8
Hammerfest *Norway* 70°39N 23°41E **60** A20
Hammerum *Denmark* 56°9N 9°3E **63** H3
Hammln *Indonesia* 7°30S 110°20E **119** G14
Hammond *Ind.,*
U.S.A. 41°38N 87°30W **172** E10
Hammond *La.,*
U.S.A. 30°30N 90°28W **177** F9
Hammond *N.Y., U.S.A.* 44°27N 75°42W **175** B9
Hammondsport *U.S.A.* 42°25N 77°13W **174** D7
Hampden *N.Z.* 45°18N 170°50E **155** F3
Hampi *India* 15°18N 76°28E **127** G3
Hampshire □ *U.K.* 51°7N 1°23W **67** F6

Hampshire Downs *U.K.* 51°15N 1°10W **67** F6
Hampton *N.B., Canada* 45°32N 65°51W **165** C6
Hampton *Ark., U.S.A.* 33°32N 92°28W **176** E8
Hampton *Ga., U.S.A.* 33°23N 84°17W **178** D5
Hampton *Iowa, U.S.A.* 42°45N 93°13W **172** D7
Hampton *N.H., U.S.A.* 42°57N 70°50W **175** D14
Hampton *S.C., U.S.A.* 32°52N 81°7W **178** C8
Hampton *Va., U.S.A.* 37°2N 76°21W **173** G15
Hampton Bays *U.S.A.* 40°53N 72°30W **175** F12
Hampton Springs
U.S.A. 30°5N 83°40W **178** E6
Hampton Tableland
Australia 32°0S 127°0E **149** F4
Hamra *Sweden* 61°39N 14°59E **62** C8
Ḥamrīn, Jabal *Iraq* 34°30N 44°30E **105** E11
Hamur *Turkey* 39°37N 43°3E **105** C10
Hamyang *S. Korea* 35°32N 127°42E **115** G14
Han = Hangang →
S. Korea 37°50N 126°30E **115** F14
Han i Hotit *Albania* 42°19N 19°27E **96** D3
Han Jiang → *China* 23°25N 116°40E **117** F11
Han Shui → *China* 30°34N 114°17E **117** B10
Hanahan *U.S.A.* 32°55N 80°0W **178** D10
Hanak *Si. Arabia* 25°32N 37°0E **128** E3
Hanak *Turkey* 41°14N 42°50E **105** B10
Hanamaki *Japan* 39°23N 141°7E **112** E10
Hanang *Tanzania* 4°30S 35°25E **142** C4
Hanau *Germany* 50°7N 8°56E **77** E4
Hançalar *Turkey* 38°8N 29°24E **99** C11
Hancheng *China* 35°31N 110°25E **114** G6
Hanchuan *China* 30°40N 113°50E **117** B9
Hancock *Mich., U.S.A.* 47°8N 88°35W **172** B9
Hancock *N.Y., U.S.A.* 41°57N 75°17W **175** E9
Hancock *Vt., U.S.A.* 43°55N 72°50W **175** C12
Handa *Japan* 34°53N 136°55E **113** G8
Handan *China* 36°35N 114°28E **114** F8
Handeni *Tanzania* 5°25S 38°2E **142** D4
Handlová *Slovak Rep.* 48°45N 18°35E **79** C11
Handub *Sudan* 19°15N 37°16E **137** D4
Handwara *India* 34°21N 74°20E **125** B6
Hanegev *Israel* 30°50N 35°0E **130** E4
Hanford *U.S.A.* 36°20N 119°39W **170** J7
Hanford Reach ◌
U.S.A. 46°40N 119°30W **168** C4
Hang Chat *Thailand* 18°20N 99°21E **120** C2
Hangang → *S. Korea* 37°50N 126°30E **115** F14
Hangayn Nuruu
Mongolia 47°30N 99°0E **110** B8
Hangchou = Hangzhou
China 30°18N 120°11E **117** B13
Hanger *Sweden* 57°5N 13°58E **63** G7
Hanggin Houqi *China* 40°58N 107°4E **114** D4
Hanggin Qi *China* 39°52N 108°50E **114** E5
Hangu *China* 39°18N 117°53E **115** E9
Hangzhou *China* 30°18N 120°11E **117** B13
Hangzhou Wan
China 30°15N 120°45E **117** B13
Hangzhou Xiaoshan Int. ✈ *(HGH)*
China 30°14N 120°26E **117** B13
Hanh *Mongolia* 51°32N 100°35E **110** A9
Hanhöhiy Uul
Mongolia 49°30N 94°30E **109** B10
Hanhongor *Mongolia* 43°55N 104°28E **114** C3
Hani *Turkey* 38°24N 40°23E **105** C9
Hania = Chania *Greece* 35°30N 24°4E **101** D6
Hanidh *Si. Arabia* 26°35N 48°38E **128** E6
Hanish *Yemen* 13°45N 42°46E **131** E3
Haniska *Slovak Rep.* 48°37N 21°15E **79** C14
Hanjiang *China* 25°26N 119°9E **117** E12
Hankinson *U.S.A.* 46°4N 96°54W **172** B5
Hankö *Finland* 59°50N 22°57E **84** C2
Hankou *China* 30°35N 114°30E **117** B10
Hanksville *U.S.A.* 38°22N 110°43W **168** G8
Hanle *India* 32°42N 79°4E **125** C8
Hanmer Springs *N.Z.* 42°32S 172°50E **155** D5
Hann → *Australia* 17°26S 126°17E **148** C4
Hann, Mt. *Australia* 15°45S 126°0E **148** C4
Hanna *Canada* 51°40N 111°54W **162** C6
Hannah *U.S.A.* 48°58N 98°42W **172** A4
Hannah B. *Canada* 51°40N 80°0W **164** B3
Hannibal *Mo., U.S.A.* 39°42N 91°22W **172** F8
Hannibal *N.Y., U.S.A.* 43°19N 76°35W **175** C8
Hannik *Sudan* 18°12N 32°20E **137** D3
Hannover *Germany* 52°22N 9°46E **76** C5
Hanö *Sweden* 56°0N 14°50E **63** H8
Hanöbukten *Sweden* 55°35N 14°30E **63** J8
Hanoi *Vietnam* 21°5N 105°55E **116** G5
Hanover = Hannover
Germany 52°22N 9°46E **76** C5
Hanover *Canada* 44°9N 81°2W **174** B3
Hanover *S. Africa* 31°4S 24°29E **144** E7
Hanover *N.H., U.S.A.* 43°42N 72°17W **175** C12
Hanover *Ohio, U.S.A.* 40°4N 82°16W **174** F2
Hanover *Pa., U.S.A.* 39°48N 76°59W **173** F15
Hanover *I., Chile* 51°0S 74°50W **192** G2
Hans Lollik I.
U.S. Virgin Is. 18°24N 64°53W **183** e
Hansdiha *India* 24°36N 87°5E **125** G12
Hansi *Haryana, India* 29°10N 75°57E **124** E6
Hanson, L. *Australia* 31°0S 136°15E **152** B2
Hansholm *Denmark* 57°7N 8°39E **63** G2
Hanting *China* 36°46N 119°12E **115** F10
Hantsavichy *Belarus* 52°49N 26°30E **83** E14
Hanumangarh *India* 29°35N 74°19E **124** E6
Hanyin *China* 32°54N 108°28E **116** A7
Hanyuan *China* 29°21N 102°39E **116** C4
Hanzhong *China* 33°10N 107°1E **116** A6
Haora *India* 22°37N 88°20E **125** H12
Haoxue *China* 30°3N 112°16E **117** B9
Haparanda *Sweden* 65°52N 24°8E **60** D21
Haparanda Skärgård △
Sweden 65°35N 23°44E **60** D20
Hapeville *U.S.A.* 33°33N 84°24W **178** E8
Happy *U.S.A.* 34°45N 101°52W **176** D4
Happy Camp *U.S.A.* 41°48N 123°23W **168** F2
Happy Valley-Goose Bay
Canada 53°15N 60°20W **165** B7
Hapsu *N. Korea* 41°13N 128°51E **115** D15
Hapur *India* 28°45N 77°45E **124** E7
Haql *Si. Arabia* 29°10N 34°58E **128** D2
Haquira *Peru* 14°14S 72°21W **187** G4
Har *Indonesia* 5°16S 133°14E **119** F8
Har-Ayrag *Mongolia* 45°47N 109°16E **114** B5
Har Hu *China* 38°20N 97°38E **110** D8

Har Us Nuur *Mongolia* 48°0N 92°0E **110** B7
Har Yehuda *Israel* 31°35N 34°57E **130** D3
Ḥarad *Si. Arabia* 24°22N 49°0E **131** C5
Haradok *Belarus* 55°30N 30°0E **84** D5
Härädsbäck *Sweden* 56°32N 14°26E **63** H8
Haramosh *Pakistan* 35°50N 74°54E **124** C6
Haranomachi = Minamisōma
Japan 37°38N 140°58E **112** F10
Harar = Harer *Ethiopia* 9°20N 42°8E **131** F4
Harare *Zimbabwe* 17°43S 31°2E **145** A5
Harazé *Chad* 9°57N 20°48E **137** G9
Harbel *Liberia* 6°16N 10°20W **138** D2
Harbhanga *India* 20°38N 84°36E **125** J11
Harbin *China* 45°48N 126°40E **115** B14
Harbiye *Turkey* 36°10N 36°8E **105** D7
Harboøre *Denmark* 56°38N 8°10E **63** H2
Harbor Beach *U.S.A.* 43°51N 82°39W **172** D12
Harbourcreek *U.S.A.* 42°9N 79°57W **174** D4
Harbour Breton
Canada 47°29N 55°50W **165** D9
Harbour Deep *Canada* 50°25N 56°32W **165** B8
Harburg *Germany* 53°27N 9°58E **76** B5
Harburger Berge ◌
Germany 53°26N 9°51E **76** B5
Harda *India* 22°27N 77°5E **124** H7
Hardangerfjorden *Norway* 60°5N 6°0E **63** B1
Hardangervidda *Norway* 60°7N 7°20E **63** B2
Hardap □ *Namibia* 24°0S 17°0E **144** B2
Hardap ◌ *Namibia* 24°9S 17°41E **144** B2
Hardap Dam *Namibia* 24°32S 17°50E **144** B2
Hardeeville *U.S.A.* 32°17N 81°5W **178** E8
Hardenberg *Neths.* 52°34N 6°37E **69** B6
Harderwijk *Neths.* 52°21N 5°38E **69** B5
Hardey → *Australia* 22°45S 116°8E **148** D2
Hardin *U.S.A.* 45°44N 107°37W **168** D10
Harding *S. Africa* 30°35S 29°55E **145** E4
Harding, L. *U.S.A.* 32°40N 85°5W **177** E12
Harding Ra. *Australia* 16°17S 124°55E **148** C3
Hardisty *Canada* 52°40N 111°18W **162** C6
Hardoi *India* 27°26N 80°6E **125** F9
Hardwar = Haridwar
India 29°58N 78°9E **124** E8
Hardwick *Ga., U.S.A.* 33°4N 83°14W **178** D6
Hardwick *Vt., U.S.A.* 44°30N 72°22W **175** B12
Hardwicke B.
Australia 34°55S 137°20E **152** B2
Hardwood Lake
Canada 45°12N 77°26W **174** A7
Hardy, Pen. *Chile* 55°30S 68°20W **192** H3
Hardy, Pte. *St. Lucia* 14°6N 60°56W **183** D7
Hare B. *Canada* 51°15N 55°45W **165** B8
Hareid *Norway* 62°22N 6°1E **63** B1
Harer *Ethiopia* 9°20N 42°8E **131** F4
Harfleur *France* 49°30N 0°10E **70** C7
Hargeisa *Somalia* 9°30N 44°2E **131** F4
Harghita, Munţii
Romania 46°25N 25°35E **80** E8
Hargshamn *Sweden* 60°12N 18°30E **62** D12
Hari → *Indonesia* 1°16S 104°5E **118** E2
Haría *Canary Is.* 29°8N 13°32E **91** E6
Haridwar *India* 29°58N 78°9E **124** E8
Harihari *N.Z.* 43°9S 170°32E **155** E3
Hariharpur Garhi
Nepal 27°19N 85°29E **125** E11
Harim, Jabal al *Oman* 25°58N 56°14E **129** E8
Haringhata → *Bangla.* 22°0N 89°58E **125** J12
Haripad *India* 9°14N 76°28E **127** J3
Harīr, W. al → *Syria* 32°44N 35°59E **130** C4
Harirūd → *Asia* 37°24N 60°38E **128** B9
Härjedalen *Sweden* 37°30N 13°20E **62** C7
Harlan *Iowa, U.S.A.* 41°39N 95°19W **172** E6
Harlan *Ky., U.S.A.* 36°51N 83°19W **173** G12
Hârlău *Romania* 47°28N 26°51E **81** C12
Harlech *U.K.* 52°52N 4°6W **66** E3
Harlem *U.S.A.* 33°25N 82°19W **178** D6
Harlem *Mont., U.S.A.* 48°32N 108°47W **168** B9
Harlev *Denmark* 55°21N 12°44E **63** J7
Harleyville *U.S.A.* 33°13N 80°27W **178** D8
Harlingen *Neths.* 53°11N 5°25E **69** A5
Harlingen *U.S.A.* 26°12N 97°42W **176** H6
Harlow *U.K.* 51°46N 0°8E **67** F8
Harlowton *U.S.A.* 46°26N 109°50W **168** C9
Harney Basin *U.S.A.* 43°30N 119°0W **168** E4
Harney L. *U.S.A.* 43°14N 119°8W **168** E4
Harney Peak *U.S.A.* 43°52N 103°32W **172** D2
Härnön *Sweden* 62°36N 18°0E **62** B11
Härnösand *Sweden* 62°38N 17°55E **62** B11
Haro *Spain* 42°35N 2°55W **73** A4
Haroldswick *U.K.* 60°48N 0°50W **65** A8
Harp L. *Canada* 55°5N 61°50W **165** A7
Harpanahalli *India* 14°47N 75°56E **127** G3
Harper *Liberia* 4°25N 7°43W **138** E4
Harper, Mt. *U.S.A.* 64°14N 143°51W **166** C6
Harplinge *Sweden* 56°45N 12°45E **63** H6
Harrai *India* 22°37N 79°13E **124** H8
Harrand *Pakistan* 29°28N 70°3E **124** E4
Harricana → *Canada* 50°56N 79°32W **164** B4
Harriman *U.S.A.* 35°56N 84°33W **177** C12
Harrington Harbour
Canada 50°31N 59°30W **165** B8
Harris *U.K.* 57°50N 6°55W **65** D2
Harris, L. *Australia* 31°10S 135°10E **152** B2
Harris, Sd. of *U.K.* 57°44N 7°6W **65** D1
Harris Mts. *N.Z.* 44°49S 168°49E **155** E2
Harris Pt. *Canada* 43°6N 82°9W **174** C2
Harrisburg *Ill., U.S.A.* 37°44N 88°32W **172** G10
Harrisburg *Nebr.,*
U.S.A. 41°33N 103°44W **172** E2
Harrisburg *Pa., U.S.A.* 40°16N 76°53W **174** F7
Harrismith *S. Africa* 28°15S 29°8E **145** D4
Harrison *Ark., U.S.A.* 36°14N 93°7W **176** C8
Harrison *Maine, U.S.A.* 44°7N 70°39W **175** B14
Harrison, C. *Canada* 54°55N 57°55W **165** B8
Harrison, C. *Canada* 54°55N 57°55W **165** B8
Harrison Bay *U.S.A.* 70°40N 151°0W **166** A4
Harrison L. *Canada* 49°33N 121°50W **162** D4
Harrisonburg *U.S.A.* 38°27N 78°52W **173** F14
Harrisonville *U.S.A.* 38°39N 94°21W **172** F6
Harriston *Canada* 43°57N 80°53W **174** C4

isville Mich., S.A. 44°39'N 83°17'W 174 B1
isville N.Y., U.S.A. 44°9'N 75°19'W 175 B9
isville Pa., U.S.A. 41°8'N 80°0'W 174 E5
odsburg U.K. 54°0'N 1°33W 66 C6
ow Australia 37°9S 141°35E 152 D4
ow Canada 42°2N 82°30W 174 D2
ow □ U.K. 51°55N 0°21W 67 F7
owsmith Canada 44°24N 76°40W 175 B8
y S. Truman Res. S.A. 38°16N 93°24W 172 F7
efeld Germany 53°27N 9°30E 76 B5
inwinkel Germany 51°56N 8°14E 76 D4
n Iran 34°18N 47°33E 105 E12
nova Romania 44°40N 27°59E 81 F12
rtad Norway 68°48N 16°30E 60 B17
ud U.S.A. 43°42N 86°22W 172 D10
L. Australia 31°10S 136°25E 152 A2
bees → S. Africa 28°45S 20°32E 144 C3
berg Austria 47°17N 15°58E 78 D8
ford Ala., U.S.A. 31°6N 85°42W 178 D4
ford Conn., U.S.A. 41°46N 72°41W 175 E12
ford Ky., U.S.A. 37°27N 86°55W 172 G5
ford S. Dak., U.S.A. 43°38N 96°55W 172 D5
ford Vt., U.S.A. 43°40N 72°20W 175 C13
ford Wis., U.S.A. 43°19N 88°22W 172 D9
ford City U.S.A. 40°27N 85°22W 173 E11
iland Canada 46°20N 67°32W 165 C6
iland Pt. U.K. 51°1N 4°32W 67 F3
iepool U.K. 54°42N 1°13W 66 C6
iepool □ U.K. 54°42N 1°17W 66 C6
iey Bay Canada 53°25N 129°15W 162 C3
imannberge Namibia 17°0S 13°0E 144 A1
iney Canada 49°30N 100°35W 163 D8
op Moldova 46°39N 28°40E 81 C15
→ S. Africa 28°24S 24°17E 144 C3
s Range Australia 23°6S 134°55E 150 C5
selle L. 34°27N 86°56W 177 D11
TL.) 33°38N 84°26W 178 B5
shorne U.S.A. 34°51N 95°34W 176 D7
stown U.S.A. 41°33N 80°23W 174 E4
sville U.S.A. 34°23N 80°4W 177 D14
swater S. Africa 34°21N 82°56W 177 D13
nabad Pakistan 29°35N 73°8E 124 E5
r India 12°3N 78°29E 127 H4
and Iran 28°25N 55°43E 129 D7
ey Australia 33°5S 115°54E 149 F2
ey Ill., U.S.A. 41°36N 87°50W 172 E10
ey N. Dak., U.S.A. 47°47N 99°56W 172 B5
vich U.K. 51°56N 1°17E 67 F9
ana □ India 29°0N 76°10E 124 E7
n → Belarus 52°7N 27°17E 75 B14
Germany 51°38N 10°44E 76 D6
□ Germany 51°40N 10°18E 76 D6
gerode Germany 51°38N 11°8E 76 D7
Si. Arabia 25°50N 49°0E 129 E6
, W. al → Jordan 31°4N 35°29E 130 D4
nabad Iran 32°9N 52°44E 129 C7
nkeyf Turkey 37°42N 41°24E 105 D9
nparti India 18°4N 79°32E 126 E4
W. → Iraq 31°45N 44°17E 128 D5
lo → India 21°44N 82°44E 125 J10
lünne Germany 52°40N 7°29E 76 C3
imoto Japan 34°19N 135°37E 113 G7
tjerd Iran 37°58N 48°58E 105 D13
tpur = Tālesh 37°58N 48°58E 105 D13
trud Iran 37°28N 47°4E 105 D12
ell U.S.A. 33°10N 99°44W 176 E5
lgaria 41°56N 25°30E 97 F8
köy Turkey 41°38N 26°52E 97 E10
ach Germany 48°16N 8°5E 77 G4
emere U.K. 55°11N 14°44E 63 J8
emere U.K. 51°5N 0°43W 67 F7
n Denmark 55°18N 11°57E 63 J5
arren France 43°24N 1°18W 72 E2
a Turkey 36°48N 36°29E 104 D7
an India 13°0N 76°5E 127 H3
berge → Germany 50°8N 10°44E 76 E6
ela Sweden 62°7N 16°42E 62 B10
elt Belgium 50°56N 5°21E 69 D5
furt Germany 50°20N 10°30E 77 E6
i bel Guebbour 28°30N 6°41E 136 C5
i bou Khelala Algeria 30°17N 0°18W 136 B3
i Bourachet Algeria 27°26N 9°19E 136 C5
i Djafou Algeria 30°55N 3°35E 136 B4
i el Hadjar Algeria 32°38N 4°45E 136 B4
i Imoulaye Algeria 29°54N 9°10E 136 C5
i Inifeg Algeria 28°15N 1°30W 136 C4
i Inifel Algeria 29°50N 3°41E 136 C4
i Mana Algeria 28°48N 2°37W 136 C3
i Marroket Algeria 30°10N 3°30E 136 B4
i Mengoub Algeria 29°56N 6°26E 136 C5
i Messaoud Algeria 31°51N 6°1E 136 B5
i Sougoued Algeria 26°50N 9°28E 136 C5
i Tartrat Algeria 30°5N 6°28E 136 B5
i Zerzour Morocco 30°51N 3°56W 136 B3
i Zguilma Morocco 30°19N 6°10W 136 B3
eleholm Sweden 56°10N 13°46E 63 H7
ild Sweden 56°7N 15°28E 63 H9
sloch Germany 49°22N 8°16E 77 F4
holmen Sweden 58°38N 145°12E 153 E6
ings Australia 39°39S 176°52E 154 F5
ings N.Z. 50°51N 0°35E 67 G8
ings Fla., U.S.A. 29°43N 81°31W 178 F8
ings Minn., U.S.A. 44°44N 92°51W 172 C7
ings Nebr., U.S.A. 40°35N 98°23W 172 E4
ings Ra.
  ustralia 31°15S 152°14E 153 A10
veda Sweden 63°6N 14°51E 62 A7
Ukraine 48°19N 22°38E 80 B7
Head □ Australia 31°3S 153°1E 153 A10
Lot Vietnam 21°15N 104°7E 120 B5
Yai Thailand 7°1N 100°27E 121 J3
anbulag = Ergel
  ongolia 43°8N 109°5E 114 C6
ay □ Australia 34°30S 116°8E 149 F2
ay □ Australia 36°25N 36°15E 104 C7
chet L. Canada 58°36N 102°22W 163 B8
ruma-Shima
  an 24°3N 123°47E 113 M1

Hatfield Australia 33°54S 143°49E 152 B5
Hatgal Mongolia 50°26N 100°9E 110 A9
Hathras India 27°36N 78°6E 124 F8
Hatia Bangla. 22°30N 91°5E 123 H17
Hatia Nepal 27°43N 75°3E 126 F2
Hātībah, Ra's Si. Arabia 21°55N 38°57E 137 C4
Hatid India 17°47N 75°3E 126 F2
Hato Mayor Dom. Rep. 18°46N 69°15W 183 C6
Hatra = Al Ḩaḑr Iraq 35°35N 42°44E 105 E10
Hatta India 24°7N 79°36E 125 G8
Hatta U.A.E. 24°45N 56°4E 129 E8
Hattah Australia 34°48S 142°17E 152 C5
Hattah Kulkyne △
  Australia 34°16S 142°33E 152 C5
Hatteras, C. U.S.A. 35°14N 75°32W 177 D17
Hatteras Abyssal Plain
  Atl. Oc. 28°0N 72°0W 56 D4
Hattiesburg U.S.A. 31°20N 89°17W 177 F10
Hattingen Germany 51°24N 7°11E 76 D4
Hattusa Turkey 40°0N 34°37E 104 B6
Hatvan Hungary 47°40N 19°45E 80 C4
Hau → Vietnam 9°30N 106°13E 121 H6
Haugesund Norway 59°23N 5°13E 61 G11
Hauhungaroa Ra.
  N.Z. 38°42S 175°40E 154 E4
Haukipudas Finland 65°12N 25°20E 60 D21
Haultain → Canada 55°51N 106°46W 163 B7
Hauraki G. N.Z. 36°35S 175°5E 154 C4
Hauroko L. N.Z. 45°59S 167°21E 155 F2
Hausruck Austria 48°6N 13°30E 78 C6
Haut Atlas Morocco 32°30N 5°0W 136 B3
Haut-Jura △ France 46°23N 2°23E 71 F9
Haut-Languedoc △
  France 43°30N 2°43E 72 E6
Haut-Niger △ Guinea 10°20N 10°20W 138 C2
Haut-Rhin □ France 48°0N 7°15E 71 E14
Haut-Languedoc □
  France 43°30N 2°43E 72 E6
Haute-Corse □ France 42°30N 9°30E 73 F13
Haute-Garonne □ France 43°28N 1°30E 72 E5
Haute-Loire □ France 45°5N 3°50E 72 C7
Haute-Marne □ France 48°10N 5°20E 71 D12
Haute-Normandie □
  France 49°20N 1°0E 70 C7
Haute-Saône □ France 47°45N 6°10E 71 E13
Haute-Savoie □ France 46°0N 6°20E 73 C10
Haute-Vienne □ France 45°50N 1°10E 72 C5
Hautes-Alpes □ France 44°42N 6°20E 73 D10
Hautes-Fagnes = Hohes Venn
  Belgium 50°30N 6°5E 69 D6
Hautes-Pyrénées □ France 43°0N 0°10E 72 F4
Hauteville-Lompnès
  France 45°58N 5°36E 73 C9
Hautmont France 50°15N 3°55E 71 B10
Hauts-de-Seine □ France 48°52N 2°15E 71 D9
Hauts Plateaux □ Algeria 35°0N 1°0E 136 B4
Hauzenberg Germany 48°40N 13°37E 77 G9
Havana = La Habana
  Cuba 23°8N 82°22W 182 B3
Havana Fla., U.S.A. 30°37N 84°25W 178 E5
Havana Ill., U.S.A. 40°18N 90°4W 172 E8
Havant U.K. 50°51N 0°58W 67 G7
Havârna Romania 48°4N 26°43E 81 B11
Havasu = Kiẕa Turkey 38°18N 43°25E 128 B4
Havasu, L. U.S.A. 34°18N 114°28W 171 L12
Havdhem Sweden 57°10N 18°20E 63 G12
Havel → Germany 52°50N 12°3E 76 B7
Havelian Pakistan 34°2N 73°10E 124 B5
Havelock Canada 44°26N 77°53W 174 B7
Havelock N.Z. 41°17S 173°48E 155 B8
Havelock U.S.A. 34°53N 76°54W 177 D16
Havelock I. Canada 11°58N 93°0E 127 F2
Havelock North N.Z. 39°40S 176°53E 154 F5
Haverfordwest U.K. 51°48N 4°58W 67 F3
Haverhill U.K. 52°5N 0°28E 67 E8
Haverhill Fla., U.S.A. 26°42N 80°7W 179 J3
Haverhill Mass., U.S.A. 42°47N 71°5W 175 D13
Haveri India 14°53N 75°24E 127 G2
Havern Sweden 62°18N 15°7E 62 B9
Haverstraw U.S.A. 41°12N 73°58W 175 E11
Håverud Sweden 58°50N 12°2E 63 F6
Havirga Mongolia 45°41N 113°5E 114 B7
Havířov Czech Rep. 49°46N 18°20E 79 B11
Havlíčkův Brod
  Czech Rep. 49°36N 15°33E 78 B8
Havneby Denmark 55°5N 8°34E 63 J2
Havran Turkey 39°33N 27°6E 99 B9
Havre U.S.A. 48°33N 109°41W 168 B9
Havre-Aubert Canada 47°12N 61°56W 165 C7
Havre-St.-Pierre
  Canada 50°18N 63°33W 165 B7
Havsa Turkey 41°31N 26°48E 97 E10
Havza Turkey 41°0N 34°0W 104 B6
Haw → U.S.A. 35°36N 79°3W 177 D15
Hawai'i U.S.A. 19°30N 155°30W 167 M8
Hawai'i □ U.S.A. 19°30N 156°30W 167 M8
Hawaiian Is. Pac. Oc. 19°30N 156°0W 157 E12
Hawaiian Ridge
  Pac. Oc. 24°0N 165°0W 157 E11
Hawarden U.S.A. 43°0N 96°29W 172 D5
Hawea, L. N.Z. 44°28S 169°19E 155 E4
Hawea Flat N.Z. 44°40S 169°19E 155 E4
Hawera N.Z. 39°35S 174°19E 154 E4
Hawi U.S.A. 20°14N 155°50W 167 L8
Hawick U.K. 55°26N 2°47W 65 F6
Hawk Junction Canada 48°5N 84°38W 164 C3
Hawkdun Ra. N.Z. 44°53S 170°5E 155 E5
Hawke, B. N.Z. 39°25S 177°20E 154 E6
Hawker Australia 31°59S 138°22E 152 A3
Hawke's Bay Canada 50°36N 57°10W 165 B8
Hawke's Bay □ N.Z. 39°45S 176°35E 154 E5
Hawkesbury Canada 45°37N 74°37W 165 D5
Hawkesbury I. Canada 53°37N 129°3W 162 C3
Hawkesbury Pt.
  Australia 11°55S 134°5E 150 A1
Hawkinsville U.S.A. 32°17N 83°28W 178 C6
Hawks Nest Australia 32°41S 152°11E 153 B10
Hawley Minn., U.S.A. 46°53N 96°19W 172 B5
Hawley Pa., U.S.A. 41°28N 75°11W 175 E10
Ḩawrān, W. → Iraq 33°58N 42°34E 105 F10
Hawsh Mūssá Lebanon 33°45N 35°55E 130 B4
Hawthorne Fla., U.S.A. 29°36N 82°5W 179 F7
Hawthorne Nev.,
  U.S.A. 38°32N 118°38W 168 G4
Hay Australia 34°30S 144°51E 153 C6
Hay → Australia 24°50S 138°0E 150 C2
Hay → Canada 60°50N 116°26W 162 A5
Hay, C. Australia 14°5S 129°29E 148 B4
Hay L. Canada 58°50N 118°50W 162 B5
Hay-on-Wye U.K. 52°5N 3°8W 67 E4
Hay Point Australia 21°18S 149°17E 150 C4
Hay River Canada 60°51N 115°44W 162 A5
Hay Springs U.S.A. 42°41N 102°41W 172 D2
Hayachine-San Japan 39°34N 141°29E 112 E10

Hayange France 49°20N 6°2E 71 C13
Hayastan = Armenia ■
  Asia 40°20N 45°0E 87 K7
Haydān, W. al →
  Jordan 31°29N 35°34E 130 D4
Haydarlı Turkey 38°16N 30°23E 99 C12
Hayden U.S.A. 40°30N 107°16W 168 F10
Hayes U.S.A. 44°23N 101°1W 172 C3
Hayes → Canada 57°3N 92°12W 163 B10
Hayes, Mt. U.S.A. 63°37N 146°43W 166 C5
Hayle U.K. 50°11N 5°26W 67 G2
Hayling I. U.K. 50°48N 0°59W 67 G7
Hayman I. Australia 20°4S 148°53E 150 b
Haymana Turkey 39°26N 32°31E 104 C5
Hayneville U.S.A. 32°23N 83°37W 178 C6
Hayrabolu Turkey 41°12N 27°5E 97 E11
Hays Canada 50°6N 111°48W 162 C6
Hays U.S.A. 38°53N 99°20W 172 F4
Haysyn Ukraine 48°57N 29°25E 81 B14
Hayvoron Ukraine 48°22N 29°52E 81 B13
Hayward Calif., U.S.A. 37°40N 122°4W 170 H4
Hayward Wis., U.S.A. 46°1N 91°29W 172 B8
Haywards Heath U.K. 51°0N 0°5W 67 G7
Hazafon □ Israel 32°40N 35°20E 130 C4
Hazar Turkmenistan 39°34N 53°16E 108 E4
Hazārān, Kūh-e Iran 29°35N 57°20E 129 D8
Hazard U.S.A. 37°15N 83°12W 173 G12
Hazaribag India 23°58N 85°26E 125 H11
Hazaribag Road India 24°12N 85°57E 125 G11
Hazebrouck France 50°42N 2°31E 71 B9
Hazelton Canada 55°20N 127°42W 162 B3
Hazelton U.S.A. 46°29N 100°17W 172 B3
Hazen U.S.A. 47°18N 101°38W 172 B3
Hazen, L. Canada 81°47N 71°1W 57 A3
Hazlehurst Ga., U.S.A. 31°52N 82°36W 178 D7
Hazlehurst Miss.,
  U.S.A. 31°52N 90°24W 177 F9
Hazlet U.S.A. 40°25N 74°12W 175 F10
Hazleton U.S.A. 40°57N 75°59W 175 F9
Hazlett, L. Australia 21°30S 128°48E 148 C4
Hazro Turkey 38°15N 40°47E 128 B4
He Xian = Hezhou
  China 24°27N 111°30E 117 E8
He Xian China 31°45N 118°20E 117 B12
Head of Bight Australia 31°30S 131°25E 149 F5
Headland U.S.A. 31°21N 85°21W 178 D4
Headlands Zimbabwe 18°15S 32°2E 143 F3
Healdsburg U.S.A. 38°37N 122°52W 170 G4
Healdton U.S.A. 34°14N 97°29W 176 D6
Healesville Australia 37°35S 145°30E 153 D6
Healy U.S.A. 63°52N 148°58W 166 C10
Heany Junction
  Zimbabwe 20°6S 28°54E 145 A4
Heard I. Ind. Oc. 53°6S 72°36E 146 K6
Hearne U.S.A. 30°53N 96°36W 176 F6
Hearst Canada 49°40N 83°41W 164 C3
Heart → U.S.A. 46°46N 100°50W 172 B3
Heart's Content
  Canada 47°54N 53°27W 165 C9
Heath → Bolivia 12°31S 68°38W 188 C4
Heath, Pte. Canada 49°8N 61°40W 165 C7
Heath Mts. N.Z. 45°39S 167°9E 155 F2
Heathcote Australia 36°55S 144°45E 153 D6
Heathrow, London ✈ (LHR)
  U.K. 51°28N 0°27W 67 F7
Heavener U.S.A. 34°53N 94°36W 176 D7
Hebbronville U.S.A. 27°18N 98°41W 176 H5
Hebei □ China 39°0N 116°0E 114 E9
Hebel Australia 28°58S 147°47E 151 D4
Heber U.S.A. 32°44N 115°32W 171 N11
Heber Springs U.S.A. 35°30N 92°2W 176 D8
Hebgen L. U.S.A. 44°52N 111°20W 168 D8
Hebi China 35°57N 114°7E 114 G8
Hebrides U.K. 57°30N 7°0W 65 D2
Hebrides, Sea of the U.K. 57°5N 7°0W 65 D2
Hebron = Al Khalīl
  West Bank 31°32N 35°6E 130 D4
Hebron Canada 58°5N 62°30W 161 F19
Hebron N. Dak., U.S.A. 46°54N 102°3W 172 B2
Hebron Nebr., U.S.A. 40°10N 97°35W 172 E5
Heby Sweden 59°56N 16°53E 62 E10
Hecate Str. Canada 53°10N 130°30W 162 C2
Heceta I. U.S.A. 55°46N 133°40W 162 B2
Hechi China 24°40N 108°2E 116 E7
Hechingen Germany 48°21N 8°57E 77 G4
Hechuan China 30°2N 106°12E 116 B6
Hecla U.S.A. 45°53N 98°9W 172 C4
Hecla I. Canada 51°10N 96°43W 163 C9
Hedal Norway 60°37N 9°41E 62 D3
Hédé France 48°18N 1°49W 70 D5
Hede Sweden 62°23N 13°30E 62 B7
Hedemora Sweden 60°18N 15°58E 62 D9
Hedensted Sweden 55°46N 9°42E 63 J3
Hedesunda Sweden 60°24N 17°12E 62 D10
Hedgehope N.Z. 46°12S 168°34E 155 G3
Heerde Neths. 52°24N 6°2E 69 B6
Heerenveen Neths. 52°57N 5°55E 69 B5
Heerhugowaard Neths. 52°40N 4°51E 69 B4
Heerlen Neths. 50°55N 5°58E 69 D5
Ḩefa Israel 32°46N 35°0E 130 C4
Ḩefa □ Israel 32°40N 35°0E 130 C4
Hefei China 31°52N 117°18E 117 B11
Hefeng China 29°55N 109°52E 116 C7
Heflin U.S.A. 33°39N 85°35W 178 B4
Hegang China 47°20N 130°19E 111 B15
Heglig Sudan 10°0N 29°24E 135 G1
Hei Ling Chau China 22°15N 114°2E 111 a
Heichengzhen China 36°24N 106°3E 114 F4
Heide Germany 54°11N 9°6E 76 A5
Heidelberg Germany 49°24N 8°42E 77 F4
Heidelberg S. Africa 26°30S 28°21E 145 C4
Heidenau Germany 50°59N 13°55E 76 D9
Heidenheim Germany 48°41N 10°9E 77 G6
Heihe China 50°10N 127°30E 111 A14
Heijing China 25°22N 101°44E 116 E3
Heilbad Heiligenstadt
  Germany 51°22N 10°8E 76 D6
Heilbron S. Africa 27°16S 27°59E 145 D4
Heilbronn Germany 49°9N 9°13E 77 F5
Heiligenblut Austria 47°2N 12°51E 78 D5
Heiligenhafen Germany 54°22N 10°59E 76 A6
Heilongjiang □ China 48°0N 126°0E 111 B14
Heilongjiang → =
  Amur → Russia 52°56N 141°10E 111 A17
Heiloo Neths. 52°36N 4°42E 69 B4
Heilprin Land Greenland 82°15N 33°0W 57 A7
Heilunkiang = Heilongjiang □
  China 48°0N 126°0E 111 B14
Heimaey Iceland 63°26N 20°17W 60 b3
Heinola Finland 61°13N 26°2E 84 B4

Heinsberg Germany 51°3N 6°5E 76 D2
Heinze Chaung Burma 14°42N 97°52E 120 E1
Heinze Kyun Burma 14°25N 97°45E 120 E1
Heishan China 41°40N 122°5E 115 D12
Heishui Liaoning, China 42°8N 119°30E 115 C10
Heishui Sichuan, China 32°4N 103°2E 116 A4
Hejaz = Ḩijāz Si. Arabia 24°0N 40°0E 128 E3
Hejian China 38°25N 116°5E 114 E9
Hejiang China 28°43N 105°46E 116 C5
Hejin China 35°35N 110°42E 114 G6
Hejing China 42°18N 86°22E 109 D11
Hekimhan Turkey 38°50N 37°55E 104 C7
Hekla Iceland 63°56N 19°35W 60 E4
Hekou Gansu, China 36°10N 103°26E 114 F2
Hekou Guangdong,
  China 23°13N 112°45E 117 F9
Hekou Yunnan, China 22°30N 103°59E 116 F4
Helan Shan China 38°30N 105°55E 114 E3
Helchosa de los Montes
  Spain 39°22N 4°53W 89 F6
Helen Atoll Palau 2°40N 132°0E 119 D8
Helena Ga., U.S.A. 32°5N 82°55W 178 C7
Helena Mont., U.S.A. 46°36N 112°2W 168 C7
Helena -West Helena
  U.S.A. 34°44N 117°19W 171 L9
Helendale U.S.A. 34°44N 117°19W 171 L9
Helensburgh Australia 34°11S 151°1E 153 C9
Helensburgh U.K. 56°1N 4°43W 65 E4
Helensville N.Z. 36°41S 174°29E 154 C4
Helenvale Australia 15°43S 145°14E 150 B4
Helgeland Norway 66°7N 13°29E 60 C15
Helgasjön Sweden 56°55N 14°50E 63 H8
Helgoland Germany 54°10N 7°53E 76 A3
Helgoland B. = Deutsche Bucht
  Germany 54°15N 8°0E 76 A4
Heligoland = Helgoland
  Germany 54°10N 7°53E 76 A3
Heligoland B. = Deutsche Bucht
  Germany 54°15N 8°0E 76 A4
Heliopolis = Masr el Gedida
  Egypt 30°5N 31°21E 137 E7
Hell Hole Gorge △
  Australia 25°26S 144°12E 150 D3
Hella Iceland 63°50N 20°24W 60 E3
Hellertown U.S.A. 40°35N 75°21W 175 F9
Hellespont = Çanakkale Boğazı
  Turkey 40°17N 26°32E 97 F10
Hellevoetsluis Neths. 51°50N 4°8E 69 C4
Hellin Spain 38°31N 1°40W 91 G3
Hells Canyon △
  U.S.A. 45°30N 117°45W 168 D5
Hell's Gate △ Kenya 0°54S 36°19E 142 C4
Helmand □ Afghan. 31°20N 64°0E 124 D4
Helmand → Afghan. 31°12N 61°34E 122 D2
Helme → Germany 51°20N 11°12E 76 D7
Helmeringhausen
  Namibia 25°54S 16°57E 144 C2
Helmond Neths. 51°29N 5°41E 69 C5
Helmsdale U.K. 58°7N 3°39W 65 C5
Helmsdale → U.K. 58°8N 3°43W 65 C5
Helmstedt Germany 52°12N 11°0E 76 B6
Helong China 42°40N 129°0E 115 C15
Helper U.S.A. 39°41N 110°51W 168 G8
Helsingborg Sweden 56°3N 12°42E 63 H6
Helsingør Denmark 56°2N 12°12E 63 H6
Helsinki Finland 60°10N 24°55E 84 B3
Helska, Mierzeja Poland 54°45N 18°40E 82 D5
Helston U.K. 50°6N 5°17W 67 G2
Helvellyn U.K. 54°32N 3°1W 66 C4
Helvetinjärvi △ Finland 62°5N 23°47E 60 E20
Helwân Egypt 29°50N 31°20E 137 F7
Hemavati → India 12°30N 76°20E 127 H3
Hemel Hempstead U.K. 51°44N 0°28W 67 F7
Hemet U.S.A. 33°45N 116°58W 171 M10
Hemingford U.S.A. 42°19N 103°4W 172 D2
Hemis △ India 34°10N 77°15E 124 B7
Hemmingford Canada 45°3N 73°35W 175 A11
Hempstead N.Y.,
  U.S.A. 40°42N 73°37W 175 F11
Hempstead Tex., U.S.A. 30°6N 96°5W 176 F6
Hemse Sweden 57°15N 18°22E 63 G12
Hemsö Sweden 62°42N 18°5E 62 B12
Hen and Chickens Is.
  N.Z. 35°58S 174°45E 154 B3
Henán □ China 34°0N 114°0E 114 H8
Henan □ China 34°0N 114°0E 114 H8
Henares → Spain 40°24N 3°30W 88 E7
Henashi-Misaki Japan 40°37N 139°51E 112 D9
Hendaye France 43°23N 1°47W 72 E2
Hendek Turkey 40°48N 30°44E 104 B4
Henderson Argentina 36°18S 61°43W 190 D3
Henderson Argentina 36°18S 61°43W 190 D3
Henderson Ky.,
  U.S.A. 37°50N 87°35W 172 G10
Henderson N.C.,
  U.S.A. 36°20N 78°25W 177 C15
Henderson N.Y.,
  U.S.A. 43°50N 76°10W 175 C8
Henderson Nev.,
  U.S.A. 36°2N 114°58W 171 J12
Henderson Tenn.,
  U.S.A. 35°26N 88°38W 177 D10
Henderson Tex., U.S.A. 32°9N 94°48W 176 E7
Henderson I. Pac. Oc. 24°22S 128°19W 157 K15
Hendersonville N.C.,
  U.S.A. 35°19N 82°28W 177 D13
Hendersonville Tenn.,
  U.S.A. 36°18N 86°37W 177 D13
Hendijān Iran 30°14N 49°43E 129 D6
Hendorābī Iran 26°40N 53°37E 129 E7
Heng Jiang → China 28°40N 104°25E 116 C5
Heng Xian China 22°40N 109°17E 116 F7
Hengcheng China 38°18N 106°28E 114 E4
Hengdaohezi China 44°52N 129°0E 115 B15
Hengduan Shan China 25°10N 99°10E 116 E2
Hengelo Neths. 52°16N 6°48E 69 B6
Henggang China 22°33N 114°12E 111 a
Hengshan Hunan,
  China 27°16N 112°45E 117 D9
Hengshan Shaanxi,
  China 37°58N 109°5E 114 F5
Hengshui China 37°41N 115°40E 114 F8
Hengyang China 26°52N 112°22E 117 D9

Henichesk Ukraine 46°12N 34°50E 85 J8
Hénin-Beaumont France 50°25N 2°58E 71 B9
Henley-on-Thames U.K. 51°32N 0°54W 67 F7
Henlopen, C. U.S.A. 38°48N 75°6W 173 F16
Hennan Sweden 62°2N 15°54E 62 B9
Hennebont France 47°49N 3°19W 70 E3
Hennenman S. Africa 27°59S 27°1E 144 C4
Hennessey U.S.A. 36°6N 97°54W 176 C6
Hennigsdorf Germany 52°38N 13°12E 76 B9
Henri Pittier △
  Venezuela 10°26N 67°37W 183 D6
Henrietta N.Y., U.S.A. 43°4N 77°37W 174 C7
Henrietta Tex., U.S.A. 33°49N 98°12W 176 E5
Henrietta, Ostrov = Genriyetty,
  Ostrov Russia 77°6N 156°30E 107 B16
Henrietta Maria, C.
  Canada 55°9N 82°20W 164 A3
Henry U.S.A. 41°7N 89°22W 172 E9
Henry Ice Rise
  Antarctica 80°35S 62°0W 55 E17
Henry Lawrence I. India 12°9N 93°5E 127 H11
Henryetta U.S.A. 35°27N 95°59W 176 D7
Henryville Canada 45°8N 73°11W 175 A11
Hensall Canada 43°26N 81°30W 174 C3
Henstedt-Ulzburg
  Germany 53°47N 10°0E 76 B6
Hentiesbaai Namibia 22°8S 14°18E 144 B1
Hentiyn Nuruu
  Mongolia 48°30N 108°30E 111 B10
Henty Australia 35°30S 147°3E 153 C7
Henzada = Hinthada
  Burma 17°38N 95°26E 123 L19
Hephaestia Greece 39°55N 25°14E 99 B7
Hephzibah U.S.A. 33°19N 82°6W 178 C7
Heping China 24°29N 115°0E 117 E10
Heppner U.S.A. 45°21N 119°33W 168 D4
Hepu China 21°40N 109°12E 116 F7
Hepworth Canada 44°37N 81°9W 174 B3
Heqing China 26°37N 100°11E 116 D3
Hequ China 39°20N 111°15E 114 E6
Héraðsflói Iceland 65°42N 14°12W 60 D6
Héraðsvötn → Iceland 65°45N 19°25W 60 D4
Heraklion = Iraklio
  Greece 35°20N 25°12E 101 D7
Herald Cays Australia 16°58S 149°9E 150 B4
Herangi N.Z. 38°33S 174°48E 154 D4
Herät Afghan. 34°20N 62°7E 108 F6
Herät □ Afghan. 35°0N 62°0E 122 B3
Hérault □ France 43°34N 3°15E 72 E7
Hérault → France 43°17N 3°26E 72 E7
Herbault France 47°36N 1°8E 70 E8
Herbert Canada 50°30N 107°10W 163 C7
Herbert → Australia 18°31S 146°17E 150 B4
Herbertabad India 11°43N 92°37E 127 J11
Herberton Australia 17°20S 145°25E 150 B4
Herbertsdale S. Africa 34°1S 21°46E 144 D3
Herbertville N.Z. 40°30S 176°33E 154 E5
Herbignac France 47°27N 2°18W 70 E4
Herborn Germany 50°41N 8°18E 76 E4
Herby Poland 50°45N 18°50E 83 H5
Herceg-Novi Montenegro 42°30N 18°33E 96 D2
Herchmer Canada 57°22N 94°10W 163 B10
Herðubreið Iceland 65°11N 16°21W 60 D5
Hereford U.K. 52°4N 2°43W 67 E5
Hereford U.S.A. 34°49N 102°24W 176 D3
Herefordshire □ U.K. 52°8N 2°40W 67 E5
Herekino N.Z. 35°18S 173°11E 154 B2
Herencia Spain 39°21N 3°22W 89 F7
Herentals Belgium 51°12N 4°51E 69 C4
Herford Germany 52°7N 8°39E 76 C4
Héricourt France 47°32N 6°45E 71 E13
Herington U.S.A. 38°40N 96°57W 172 F5
Heris Iran 38°46N 47°6E 105 C12
Herisau Switz. 47°22N 9°17E 77 H5
Herkimer U.S.A. 43°2N 74°59W 175 D10
Herlen → Asia 48°48N 117°0E 111 B12
Herlong U.S.A. 40°8N 120°8W 170 E6
Herm U.K. 49°30N 2°28W 67 H5
Hermann U.S.A. 38°42N 91°27W 172 F8
Hermannsburg
  Australia 23°57S 132°45E 148 D5
Hermanus S. Africa 34°27S 19°12E 144 D2
Herment France 45°45N 2°24E 72 C6
Hermidale Australia 31°30S 146°42E 153 B7
Hermiston U.S.A. 45°51N 119°17W 168 D4
Hermon U.S.A. 44°28N 75°14W 175 B9
Hermon, Mt. = Shaykh, J. ash
  Lebanon 33°25N 35°50E 130 B4
Hermosillo Mexico 29°10N 111°0W 180 B2
Hernád → Hungary 47°56N 21°8E 80 C6
Hernandarias
  Paraguay 25°20S 54°40W 191 B5
Hernandez U.S.A. 36°24N 120°46W 170 J6
Hernando Argentina 32°28S 63°40W 190 C3
Hernando Fla., U.S.A. 28°54N 82°23W 179 G7
Hernando Miss., U.S.A. 34°50N 90°0W 177 D10
Hernani Spain 43°16N 1°58W 90 B3
Herndon U.S.A. 40°43N 76°51W 174 F8
Herne Germany 51°32N 7°14E 76 D3
Herne Bay U.K. 51°21N 1°8E 67 F9
Herning Denmark 56°8N 8°58E 63 H2
Herod U.S.A. 31°42N 84°26W 178 D5
Heroica Caborca = Caborca
  Mexico 30°37N 112°6W 180 A2
Heroica Nogales = Nogales
  Mexico 31°19N 110°56W 180 A2
Heron Bay Canada 48°40N 86°25W 164 C2
Heron I. Australia 23°27S 151°55E 150 C5
Herradura, Pta. de la
  Canary Is. 28°26N 14°8W 100 G3
Herreid U.S.A. 45°50N 100°4W 172 C3
Herrenberg Germany 48°35N 8°52E 77 G4
Herrera Spain 37°30N 7°25W 89 F2
Herrera de Alcántara
  Spain 39°39N 7°25W 89 F2
Herrera de Pisuerga
  Spain 42°35N 4°20W 88 C6
Herrera del Duque Spain 39°10N 5°3W 89 F5
Herrestad Sweden 58°18N 12°2E 63 F6
Herrin U.S.A. 37°48N 89°2W 172 G9
Herriot Canada 56°22N 101°16W 163 B9
Herrljunga Sweden 58°5N 13°1E 63 F7
Hersbruck Germany 49°30N 11°25E 77 F7
Herschel I. Canada 69°35N 139°5W 166 B11
Hershey U.S.A. 40°17N 76°39W 175 F8
Herso = Cherso Greece 41°5N 22°47E 96 C5

Herstal Belgium 50°40N 5°38E 69 D5
Hertford U.K. 51°48N 0°4W 67 F7
Hertford □ U.K. 51°51N 0°5W 67 F7
's-Hertogenbosch Neths. 51°42N 5°17E 69 C5
Hertsa Ukraine 48°9N 26°15E 81 B11
Hertzogville S. Africa 28°9S 25°30E 144 C4
Hervás Spain 40°16N 5°52W 88 E5
Hervey B. Australia 25°0S 152°52E 150 C5
Herzberg Brandenburg,
  Germany 51°41N 13°14E 76 D9
Herzberg Niedersachsen,
  Germany 51°38N 10°20E 76 D6
Herzliyya Israel 32°10N 34°50E 130 C3
Ḩeşār Färs, Iran 29°52N 50°16E 129 D6
Ḩeşār Markazī, Iran 35°50N 49°12E 129 C6
Hesdin France 50°21N 2°2E 71 B9
Heshan Guangdong,
  China 22°34N 113°4E 117 F9
Heshan Guangxi Zhuangzu,
  China 23°50N 108°53E 116 E7
Heshui China 35°48N 108°0E 114 G5
Heshun China 37°22N 113°32E 114 F7
Hesperia U.S.A. 34°25N 117°18W 171 L9
Hesse = Hessen □
  Germany 50°30N 9°0E 76 E4
Hessen □ Germany 50°30N 9°0E 76 E4
Hessenreuther und Manteler
  Wald △ Germany 49°45N 12°1E 77 F8
Hessle U.K. 53°44N 0°24W 66 D7
Hesso Australia 32°8S 137°27E 152 B2
Hestra Sweden 57°26N 13°35E 63 G7
Hetauda Nepal 27°25N 85°2E 125 F11
Hetch Hetchy Aqueduct
  U.S.A. 37°29N 122°19W 170 H5
Hetta Enontekiö
  Finland 68°23N 23°37E 60 B20
Hettinger U.S.A. 46°0N 102°42W 172 B2
Hettstedt Germany 51°39N 11°31E 76 D7
Heuksando S. Korea 34°40N 125°30E 115 G13
Heunghae S. Korea 36°12N 129°21E 115 F15
Heuvelton U.S.A. 44°37N 75°25W 175 B9
Heves Hungary 47°36N 20°17E 80 C5
Heves □ Hungary 47°50N 20°0E 80 C5
Hewitt U.S.A. 31°28N 97°12W 176 F6
Hexham U.K. 54°58N 2°4W 66 C5
Hexi Yunnan, China 24°9N 102°38E 116 E4
Hexi Zhejiang, China 27°58N 119°38E 117 D12
Hexigten Qi China 43°18N 117°30E 115 C9
Heydarābād Iran 30°33N 55°38E 129 D7
Heyfield Australia 37°59S 146°47E 153 D7
Heysham U.K. 54°3N 2°53W 66 C5
Heyuan China 23°39N 114°0E 117 F10
Heywood Australia 38°8S 141°37E 152 D4
Heze China 35°14N 115°20E 114 G8
Hezhang China 27°8N 104°41E 116 D5
Hezhou China 24°27N 111°30E 117 E8
Hi Vista U.S.A. 34°45N 117°46W 171 L9
Hialeah U.S.A. 25°51N 80°16W 179 K9
Hiawatha U.S.A. 39°51N 95°32W 172 F6
Hibbing U.S.A. 47°25N 92°56W 172 B7
Hibernia Reef Australia 12°0S 123°23E 148 B3
Hickman U.S.A. 36°34N 89°11W 172 G9
Hickory U.S.A. 35°44N 81°21W 177 D14
Hicks, Pt. Australia 37°49S 149°17E 153 D8
Hicks L. Canada 61°25N 100°0W 163 A9
Hico U.S.A. 31°59N 98°2W 176 E5
Hicpochee, L. U.S.A. 26°48N 81°19W 179 J8
Hida Romania 47°10N 23°19E 81 C8
Hida-Gawa → Japan 35°26N 137°3E 113 G8
Hida-Sammyaku Japan 36°30N 137°40E 113 F8
Hidaka Japan 42°30N 142°10E 112 C11
Hidaka-Sammyaku
  Japan 42°35N 142°45E 112 C11
Hidalgo Mexico 20°30N 99°0W 181 C5
Hidalgo del Parral
  Mexico 26°56N 105°40W 180 B3
Hiddensee Germany 54°30N 13°6E 76 A9
Hieflau Austria 47°36N 14°46E 78 D7
Hienghène New Caledonia 41°5N 3°0W 90 D2
Hierapolis-Pamukkale
  Turkey 37°55S 29°7E 99 D11
Hierro Canary Is. 27°44N 18°0W 100 G1
Higashihijima-San
  Japan 37°40N 140°10E 112 F10
Higashiōsaka Japan 34°39N 135°37E 113 G7
Higgins U.S.A. 36°7N 100°2W 176 C4
Higgins Corner U.S.A. 39°2N 121°5W 170 F5
High Bridge U.S.A. 40°40N 74°54W 175 F10
High Island Res. China 22°24N 114°21E 111 a
High Level Canada 58°31N 117°8W 162 B5
High Point U.S.A. 35°57N 80°0W 177 D15
High Prairie Canada 55°30N 116°30W 162 B5
High River Canada 50°30N 113°50W 162 C6
High Springs U.S.A. 29°50N 82°36W 179 F7
High Tatra = Tatry
  Slovak Rep. 49°20N 20°0E 79 B13
High Veld Africa 27°0S 27°0E 132 J6
High Wycombe U.K. 51°37N 0°45W 67 F7
Highbank N.Z. 43°37S 171°45E 155 D6
Highland □ U.K. 57°17N 4°21W 65 D4
Highland City U.S.A. 27°58N 81°53W 179 H8
Highland Home U.S.A. 31°57N 86°19W 178 D4
Highland Mills U.S.A. 41°21N 74°7W 175 E10
Highland Park U.S.A. 42°11N 87°48W 172 D10
Highland View U.S.A. 29°50N 85°4W 178 F5
Highmore U.S.A. 44°31N 99°27W 172 C4
Highrock L. Canada 55°45N 100°30W 163 B8
Hihya Egypt 30°40N 31°36E 137 D7
Hiiumaa Estonia 58°50N 22°45E 84 C2
Ḩijāz Si. Arabia 24°0N 40°0E 128 E3
Hijo = Tagum Phil. 7°33N 125°53E 119 C7
Hikari Japan 33°58N 131°58E 113 H5
Hikkaduwa Sri Lanka 6°10N 80°7E 127 L4
Hikmak, Ras el Egypt 31°15N 27°15W 137 A12
Hikone Japan 35°15N 136°10E 113 G8
Hikurangi Gisborne,
  N.Z. 37°55S 178°4E 154 E7
Hikurangi Northland,
  N.Z. 35°36S 174°17E 154 B3
Hiland Park U.S.A. 30°12N 85°33W 178 F4
Hildburghausen
  Germany 50°25N 10°42E 76 E6
Hildesheim Germany 52°9N 9°56E 76 C5

Hill → Australia 30°23S 115°3E **149** F2
Hill City Idaho, U.S.A. 43°18N 115°3W **168** E6
Hill City Kans., U.S.A. 39°22N 99°51W **172** F4
Hill City Minn., U.S.A. 46°59N 93°36W **172** B7
Hill City S. Dak.,
　U.S.A. 43°56N 103°35W **172** D2
Hill Island L. Canada 60°30N 109°50W **163** A7
Hillaby, Mt. Barbados 13°12N 59°35W **183** g4
Hillared Sweden 57°37N 13°10E **63** G7
Hillcrest Barbados 13°13N 59°31W **183** g4
Hillegom Neths. 52°18N 4°35E **69** B4
Hillerød Denmark 55°56N 12°19E **63** J6
Hillerstorp Sweden 57°20N 13°52E **63** G7
Hilliard U.S.A. 30°41N 81°55W **178** E8
Hillsboro Ga., U.S.A. 33°11N 83°38W **178** B6
Hillsboro Kans., U.S.A. 38°21N 97°12W **172** F5
Hillsboro N. Dak., U.S.A. 47°26N 97°3W **172** B5
Hillsboro Ohio, U.S.A. 39°12N 83°37W **173** F12
Hillsboro Oreg., U.S.A. 45°31N 122°59W **170** E4
Hillsboro Tex., U.S.A. 32°1N 97°8W **176** E6
Hillsboro Canal U.S.A. 26°30N 80°15W **179** J9
Hillsborough Grenada 12°28N 61°28W **183** D7
Hillsborough U.S.A. 43°7N 71°54W **175** C13
Hillsborough Channel
　Australia 20°56S 149°15E **150** J
Hillsdale Mich., U.S.A. 41°56N 84°38W **173** E11
Hillsdale N.Y., U.S.A. 42°11N 73°32W **175** D11
Hillsport Canada 49°27N 85°34W **164** C2
Hillston Australia 33°30S 145°31E **153** B6
Hilltonia U.S.A. 32°53N 81°40W **178** C8
Hilo U.S.A. 19°44N 155°5W **167** M8
Hilton U.S.A. 43°17N 77°48W **174** C7
Hilton Head Island
　U.S.A. 32°13N 80°45W **178** C9
Hilvan Turkey 37°34M 38°58E **105** D8
Hilversum Neths. 52°14N 5°10E **69** B5
Himachal Pradesh □
　India 31°30N 77°0E **124** D7
Himalaya Asia 29°0N 84°0E **125** E11
Himalchuli Nepal 28°27N 84°38E **125** E11
Himarë Albania 40°8N 19°43E **96** F3
Himatnagar India 23°37N 72°57E **124** H5
Himeji Japan 34°50N 134°40E **113** G7
Himi Japan 36°50N 136°55E **113** F8
Himmerland Denmark 56°45N 9°30E **63** H3
Ḥimş Syria 34°40N 36°45E **130** A5
Ḥimş □ Syria 34°30N 37°0E **130** A6
Hin Khom, Laem Thailand 9°25N 99°56E **121** b
Hinche Haiti 19°9N 72°1W **183** C5
Hinchinbrook I.
　Australia 18°20S 146°15E **150** B4
Hinchinbrook Island △
　Australia 18°14S 146°6E **150** B4
Hinckley U.K. 52°33N 1°22W **67** E6
Hinckley U.S.A. 46°1N 92°56W **172** B7
Hindaun India 26°44N 77°5E **124** F7
Hindmarsh, L. Australia 36°5S 141°55E **152** D4
Hindol India 20°40N 85°10E **126** D7
Hinds N.Z. 43°59S 171°36E **155** D6
Hindsholm Denmark 55°30N 10°40E **63** J4
Hindu Bagh Pakistan 30°56N 67°50E **124** D2
Hindu Kush Asia 36°0N 71°0E **109** E8
Hindupur India 13°49N 77°32E **127** H3
Hines Creek Canada 56°20N 118°40W **162** B5
Hinesville U.S.A. 31°51N 81°36W **178** D8
Hinganghat India 20°30N 78°52E **126** D4
Hingham U.S.A. 48°33N 110°25W **168** B8
Hingir India 21°57N 83°41E **125** J10
Hingoli India 19°41N 77°15E **126** E3
Hinis Turkey 39°22N 41°43E **105** C9
Hinna = Imi Ethiopia 6°28N 42°10E **131** F3
Hinna Nigeria 10°25N 11°35E **139** C7
Hinnerup Denmark 56°16N 10°4E **63** H4
Hinnøya Norway 68°35N 15°50E **60** B16
Hinojosa del Duque Spain 38°30N 5°9W **89** G5
Hinsdale U.S.A. 42°47N 72°29W **175** D12
Hinterrhein → Switz. 46°40N 9°25E **77** J5
Hinthada Burma 17°38N 95°26E **123** L19
Hinton Canada 53°26N 117°34W **162** C5
Hinton U.S.A. 37°40N 80°54W **173** G13
Hios = Chios Greece 38°27N 26°9E **99** C8
Hirado Japan 33°22N 129°33E **113** H4
Hirakud Dam India 21°32N 83°45E **126** D6
Hiran → India 23°6N 79°21E **125** H8
Hirapur India 24°22N 79°13E **125** G8
Hirara = Miyakojima
　Japan 24°48N 125°17E **113** M2
Hiratsuka Japan 35°19N 139°21E **113** G9
Hirekerur India 14°28N 75°23E **127** G2
Hirfanlı Baraji Turkey 39°18N 33°31E **104** C5
Hirhafok Algeria 23°49N 5°45E **136** D6
Hiroo Japan 42°17N 143°19E **112** C11
Hirosaki Japan 40°34N 140°28E **112** D10
Hiroshima Japan 34°24N 132°30E **113** G6
Hiroshima □ Japan 34°50N 133°0E **113** G6
Hirson France 49°55N 4°4E **71** C11
Hirtshals Denmark 57°36N 9°57E **63** G3
Hisar India 29°12N 75°45E **124** E6
Hisarcık Turkey 39°15N 29°14E **99** B11
Hisaria Bulgaria 42°30N 24°44E **97** D8
Hisb, Sha'ib → Ḥasab, W. →
　Iraq 31°45N 44°17E **128** D5
Ḥismā Si. Arabia 28°30N 36°0E **128** D3
Hispaniola W. Indies 19°0N 71°0W **183** C5
Hīt Iraq 33°38N 42°49E **105** F10
Hita Japan 33°20N 130°58E **113** H5
Hitachi Japan 36°36N 140°39E **113** F10
Hitan, W. el Egypt 29°19N 30°10E **137** F7
Hitchin U.K. 51°58N 0°16W **67** F7
Hitiaa Tahiti 17°36S 149°18W **155** b
Hitoyoshi Japan 32°13N 130°45E **113** H5
Hitra Norway 63°30N 8°45E **60** E13
Hitzacker Germany 53°9N 11°2E **76** B7
Hiva Oa
　French Polynesia 9°45S 139°0W **157** H14
Hixon Canada 53°25N 122°35W **162** C4
Hiyyon, N. → Israel 30°25N 35°10E **130** E4
Hjalmar L. Canada 61°33N 109°25W **163** A7
Hjälmaren Sweden 59°18N 15°40E **62** E9
Hjältevad Sweden 57°38N 15°20E **63** G8
Hjo Sweden 58°22N 14°17E **63** F8
Hjørring Denmark 57°29N 9°59E **63** G3
Hjort Trench S. Ocean 58°0S 157°30E **55** B10
Hjortkvarn Sweden 58°54N 15°26E **63** F9
Hkakabo Razi Burma 28°25N 97°23E **114** b
Hkamti Burma 26°0N 95°39E **123** G19
Hlinsko Czech Rep. 49°45N 15°54E **78** D8
Hlobane S. Africa 27°42S 31°0E **145** C5
Hlohovec Slovak Rep. 48°26N 17°49E **79** C10
Hlučín Czech Rep. 49°54N 18°11E **79** B11
Hluhluwe S. Africa 28°1S 32°15E **145** C5
Hluhluwe ← S. Africa 22°10S 32°5E **145** B5

Hlukhiv Ukraine 51°40N 33°58E **85** G7
Hlyboka Ukraine 48°5N 25°56E **81** B10
Hlybokaye Belarus 55°10N 27°45E **84** E4
Hnúšťa Slovak Rep. 48°35N 19°58E **79** C12
Ho Ghana 6°37N 0°27E **139** D5
Ho Chi Minh City = Thanh Pho
　Ho Chi Minh
　Vietnam 10°58N 106°40E **121** G6
Ho Hoa Binh Vietnam 20°50N 105°0E **116** B5
Ho Thac Ba Vietnam 21°42N 105°1E **120** A5
Ho Thuong Vietnam 20°50N 105°48E **120** C5
Hoa Binh Vietnam 20°50N 105°20E **116** B5
Hoa Hiep Vietnam 11°34N 105°51E **121** G5
Hoai Nhon Vietnam 14°28N 109°1E **120** E7
Hoang Lien △ Vietnam 22°18N 103°32E **120** B5
Hoang Lien Son Vietnam 22°0N 104°0E **116** F4
Hoang Sa, Dao = Paracel Is.
　S. China Sea 15°50N 112°0E **118** A4
Hoanib → Namibia 19°27S 12°46E **144** A2
Hoare B. Canada 65°17N 62°30W **161** D19
Hoarusib → Namibia 19°3S 12°36E **144** A2
Hobart Australia 42°50S 147°21E **151** G4
Hobart U.S.A. 35°1N 99°6W **176** D5
Hobbs U.S.A. 32°42N 103°8W **169** K12
Hobbs Coast Antarctica 74°50S 131°0W **55** D14
Hobe Sound U.S.A. 27°4N 80°8W **179** H9
Hoboken Ga., U.S.A. 31°11N 82°8W **178** D7
Hoboken N.J., U.S.A. 40°44N 74°3W **175** F10
Hobro Denmark 56°39N 9°46E **63** H3
Hoburgen Sweden 56°55N 18°7E **63** H12
Hocalar Turkey 38°36N 30°0E **99** C11
Hochfeld Namibia 21°28S 17°58E **144** B2
Hochharz △ Germany 51°48N 10°38E **76** D6
Hochschwab Austria 47°35N 15°0E **78** D8
Hochstadt Germany 49°42N 10°47E **77** F6
Hochtaunus △ Germany 50°20N 8°30E **77** E4
Hockenheim Germany 49°19N 8°32E **77** F4
Hodaka-Dake Japan 36°17N 137°39E **113** F8
Hodeida = Al Ḩudaydah
　Yemen 14°50N 43°0E **131** E3
Hodgeville Canada 50°7N 106°58W **163** C7
Hodgson Canada 51°13N 97°36W **163** C9
Hodh El Gharbi □
　Mauritania 16°30N 10°0W **138** B3
Hódmezővásárhely
　Hungary 46°28N 20°22E **80** D5
Hodna, Chott el Algeria 35°26N 4°43E **136** A4
Hodonín Czech Rep. 48°50N 17°0E **79** C10
Hœdic, Î. de France 47°20N 2°53W **70** E4
Hoek van Holland Neths. 52°0N 4°7E **69** C4
Hoengseong S. Korea 37°29N 127°59E **115** F14
Hoeryong N. Korea 42°30N 129°45E **115** C15
Hoeyang N. Korea 38°43N 127°36E **115** E14
Hof Germany 50°19N 11°55E **77** E7
Hofgeismar Germany 51°29N 9°23E **76** D5
Hofheim Germany 50°8N 10°31E **77** E6
Hofmeyr S. Africa 31°39S 25°50E **144** D4
Höfn Iceland 64°15N 15°13W **60** D6
Hofors Sweden 60°31N 16°15E **62** D10
Hofsjökull Iceland 64°49N 18°48W **60** D4
Höfu Japan 34°3N 131°34E **113** G5
Hogan Group Australia 39°13S 147°1E **151** F4
Höganäs Sweden 56°12N 12°33E **63** H6
Hogansville U.S.A. 33°10N 84°55W **178** B5
Hogarth, Mt. Australia 21°48S 136°58E **150** C2
Hoge Kempen △ Belgium 51°6N 5°35E **69** C5
Hoge Veluwe ⌂ Neths. 52°5N 5°46E **69** B5
Hogenakal Falls India 12°6N 77°50E **127** H3
Hoggar = Ahaggar
　Algeria 23°0N 6°30E **136** D6
Högsäter Sweden 58°38N 12°5E **63** F6
Högsby Sweden 57°10N 16°1E **63** G10
Högsjö Sweden 59°4N 15°44E **62** E9
Hogsty Reef Bahamas 21°41N 73°48W **183** B5
Hoh → U.S.A. 47°45N 124°29W **170** C2
Hoh Xil Shan China 36°30N 89°0E **110** D6
Hohd ech Chargui □
　Mauritania 19°0N 7°15W **138** B3
Hohe Acht Germany 50°22N 7°0E **77** E3
Hohe Tauern Austria 47°11N 12°40E **78** D5
Hohe Tauern △ Austria 47°5N 12°20E **78** D5
Hohenau Austria 48°36N 16°55E **79** C9
Hohenems Austria 47°22N 9°42E **78** D2
Hohenloher Ebene
　Germany 49°14N 9°36E **77** F5
Hohenwald U.S.A. 35°33N 87°33W **177** D11
Hohenwestedt Germany 54°5N 9°40E **76** A5
Hoher Rhön = Rhön
　Germany 50°24N 9°58E **76** E5
Hoher Vogelsberg △
　Germany 51°45N 9°35E **76** D5
Hohes Venn Belgium 50°30N 6°5E **69** D6
Hohes Venn-Eifel ⌂
　Europe 50°30N 6°5E **69** D6
Hohhot China 40°52N 111°40E **114** D6
Hohoe Ghana 7°8N 0°32E **139** D5
Hoi An Vietnam 15°30N 108°19E **120** E7
Hoi Xuan Vietnam 20°25N 105°9E **116** G5
Hoisington U.S.A. 38°31N 98°47W **172** F4
Hojambaz Turkmenistan 38°7N 65°0E **108** E6
Hojer Denmark 54°58N 8°42E **63** K2
Hōjō Japan 33°58N 132°46E **113** H6
Hok Sweden 57°31N 14°16E **63** G8
Hökensås Sweden 58°0N 14°5E **63** F7
Hökerum Sweden 57°51N 13°16E **63** G7
Hokianga Harbour
　N.Z. 35°31S 173°22E **154** B2
Hokitika N.Z. 42°42S 171°0E **155** D6
Hokkaidō □ Japan 43°30N 143°0E **112** C11
Hokuto Japan 41°49N 140°39E **112** D10
Hola Kenya 1°29S 40°2E **142** B4
Hola Prystan Ukraine 46°29N 32°32E **85** J7
Holakas Greece 35°57N 27°53E **109** D11
Holalkere India 14°2N 76°11E **127** G3
Holašovice Czech Rep. 48°57N 14°15E **78** D7
Holbæk Denmark 55°43N 11°43E **63** J5
Holborn Australia 35°42S 147°18E **153** C7
Holbrook Australia 35°42S 147°18E **153** C7
Holbrook U.S.A. 34°54N 110°10W **169** J8
Holcomb U.S.A. 42°54N 77°25W **174** D7
Holden U.S.A. 39°6N 112°16W **168** G7
Holdenville U.S.A. 35°5N 96°24W **176** D6
Holdich Argentina 45°57S 68°13W **192** F3
Holdrege U.S.A. 40°26N 99°23W **172** E4
Hole-Narsipur India 12°48N 76°16E **127** H3
Holešov Czech Rep. 49°20N 17°35E **79** B10
Holetown Barbados 13°11N 59°38W **183** g4
Holguín Cuba 20°50N 76°20W **182** B4
Holič Slovak Rep. 48°49N 17°7E **79** C10
Holice Czech Rep. 50°5N 16°7E **78** D8
Holiday U.S.A. 28°11N 82°44W **179** G7
Höljes Sweden 60°50N 12°35E **62** D6

Hollabrunn Austria 48°34N 16°5E **78** C9
Hollams Bird I. Namibia 24°40S 14°30E **144** B1
Holland = Netherlands ■
　Europe 52°0N 5°30E **69** C5
Holland Mich., U.S.A. 42°47N 86°7W **172** D10
Holland N.Y., U.S.A. 42°38N 78°32W **174** D6
Holland Centre Canada 44°23N 80°47W **174** B4
Holland Patent U.S.A. 43°14N 75°15W **175** C9
Hollandale U.S.A. 33°10N 90°51W **177** E9
Hollandia = Jayapura
　Indonesia 2°28S 140°38E **119** E10
Holley U.S.A. 43°14N 78°2W **174** C6
Hollfeld Germany 49°56N 11°18E **77** F7
Hollidaysburg U.S.A. 40°26N 78°24W **174** F6
Hollis U.S.A. 34°41N 99°55W **176** D5
Hollister Calif., U.S.A. 36°51N 121°24W **170** J5
Hollister Idaho, U.S.A. 42°21N 114°35W **168** E6
Holly U.S.A. 38°3N 102°7W **172** G2
Holly Hill Fla., U.S.A. 29°16N 81°3W **179** F8
Holly Hill S.C., U.S.A. 33°19N 80°25W **178** C8
Holly Springs Ark.,
　U.S.A. 34°10N 84°30W **178** A5
Holly Springs Miss.,
　U.S.A. 34°46N 89°27W **177** D10
Hollywood Ireland 53°6N 6°35W **64** B6
Hollywood U.S.A. 26°0N 80°8W **179** J9
Holman = Ulukhaktok
　Canada 70°44N 117°44W **160** C8
Hólmavík Iceland 65°42N 21°40W **60** D3
Holmen U.S.A. 43°58N 91°15W **172** D8
Holmes Beach U.S.A. 27°31N 82°43W **179** H7
Holmes Cr. → U.S.A. 30°30N 85°50W **178** F4
Holmes Reefs Australia 16°27S 148°0E **150** B4
Holmsjö Sweden 56°25N 15°32E **63** H9
Holmsjön Västernorrland,
　Sweden 62°41N 16°33E **62** B10
Holmsjön Västernorrland,
　Sweden 62°26N 15°20E **62** B9
Holmsland Klit Denmark 56°0N 8°5E **63** J2
Holmsund Sweden 63°41N 20°20E **60** E19
Holod Romania 46°49N 22°8E **80** D9
Holon Israel 32°0N 34°46E **130** C3
Holopaw U.S.A. 28°8N 81°5W **179** G8
Holovne Ukraine 51°20N 24°5E **83** G11
Holozubyntsi Ukraine 48°50N 26°55E **81** B11
Holroyd → Australia 14°10S 141°36E **150** A3
Holstebro Denmark 56°22N 8°37E **63** H2
Holsteinische Schweiz ⌂
　Germany 54°8N 10°30E **76** A6
Holsteinsborg = Sisimiut
　Greenland 66°40N 53°30W **57** D5
Holsworthy U.K. 50°48N 4°22W **67** G3
Holt U.S.A. 30°43N 86°45W **179** E3
Holton Canada 54°31N 57°12W **165** B8
Holton U.S.A. 39°28N 95°44W **172** F7
Holtville U.S.A. 32°49N 115°23W **171** N11
Holwerd Neths. 53°22N 5°54E **69** A5
Holy Cross U.S.A. 62°12N 159°46W **166** C8
Holy I. Anglesey, U.K. 53°17N 4°37W **66** D3
Holy I. Northumberland,
　U.K. 55°40N 1°47W **66** B6
Holyhead U.K. 53°18N 4°38W **66** D3
Holyoke Colo., U.S.A. 40°35N 102°18W **168** F12
Holyoke Mass., U.S.A. 42°12N 72°37W **175** D12
Holyrood Canada 47°27N 53°8W **165** C9
Holzkirchen Germany 47°52N 11°42E **77** H7
Holzminden Germany 51°50N 9°28E **76** D5
Homa Bay Kenya 0°36S 34°30E **142** C3
Homalin Burma 24°55N 95°0E **123** G19
Homand Iran 32°28N 59°37E **129** C8
Homathko → Canada 51°0N 124°56W **162** C4
Homberg Germany 51°2N 9°23E **76** D5
Hombori Mali 15°20N 1°38W **138** B5
Hombori Tondo Mali 15°16N 1°40W **139** A4
Homburg Germany 49°19N 7°18E **77** F3
Home B. Canada 68°40N 67°10W **161** D18
Home Hill Australia 19°43S 147°25E **150** B4
Homedale U.S.A. 43°37N 116°56W **168** E5
Homeland U.S.A. 30°51N 82°1W **178** F7
Homer Alaska, U.S.A. 59°39N 151°33W **166** D9
Homer La., U.S.A. 32°48N 93°4W **176** E8
Homer N.Y., U.S.A. 42°38N 76°10W **175** D8
Homer City U.S.A. 40°32N 79°10W **174** F5
Homestead Australia 20°20S 145°40E **150** C4
Homestead U.S.A. 25°28N 80°29W **179** K9
Homestead ⌂ U.S.A. 40°17N 96°50W **172** E5
Homoine Mozam. 23°55S 35°8E **145** B6
Homolje Planina
　Serbia 44°10N 21°45E **96** B5
Homorod Romania 46°5N 25°15E **81** D10
Homosassa Springs
　U.S.A. 28°48N 82°35W **179** G7
Homs = Ḩimş Syria 34°40N 36°45E **130** A5
Homyel Belarus 52°28N 31°0E **85** B16
Homyel □ Belarus 52°30N 30°10E **85** F6
Hon Chong Vietnam 10°25N 104°30E **121** G5
Hon Hai Vietnam 10°0N 109°0E **121** H7
Hon Me Vietnam 19°23N 105°56E **120** C5
Honan = Henan □
　China 34°0N 114°0E **114** H8
Honavar India 14°17N 74°27E **127** G2
Honaz Turkey 37°46N 29°18E **99** D11
Honbetsu Japan 43°7N 143°37E **112** C11
Honcut U.S.A. 39°20N 121°32W **170** F5
Hondarribia Spain 43°22N 1°47W **90** B3
Hondeklipbaai S. Africa 30°19S 17°17E **144** D2
Hondo Japan 32°27N 130°12E **113** H5
Hondo U.S.A. 29°21N 99°9W **176** G5
Hondo, Río → Belize 18°25N 88°21W **181** D7
Honduras ■
　Cent. Amer. 14°40N 86°30W **182** D2
Honduras, G. de
　Caribbean 16°50N 87°0W **182** C2
Honey Harbour
　Canada 44°52N 79°49W **174** B5
Honey L. U.S.A. 40°15N 120°19W **170** E6
Honfleur France 49°25N 0°13E **70** C7
Høng Denmark 55°31N 11°18E **63** J5
Hong → Asia 20°16N 106°34E **120** B5
Hong He → China 32°25N 115°35E **117** A10
Hong Hu China 29°50N 113°30E **117** C9
Hong Kong □ China 22°11N 114°14E **111** a
Hong Kong I. China 22°16N 114°12E **111** a
Hong Kong Int. ✈ (HKG)
　China 22°19N 113°57E **111** a
Hong'an China 31°20N 114°40E **117** B10

Hongcheon S. Korea 37°44N 127°53E **115** F14
Honghai Wan China 22°40N 115°0E **117** F10
Honghe China 23°22N 102°25E **116** F4
Honghu China 29°50N 113°30E **117** C9
Hongjiang China 27°7N 109°59E **116** D7
Hongliu He → China 38°0N 109°50E **114** F5
Hongor Mongolia 45°45N 112°50E **114** B7
Hongseong S. Korea 36°37N 126°38E **115** F14
Hongshan China 36°38N 117°58E **115** F9
Hongshui He →
　China 23°48N 109°30E **116** F7
Hongtong China 36°16N 111°40E **114** F6
Honguedo, Détroit d'
　Canada 49°15N 64°0W **165** C7
Hongwon N. Korea 40°0N 127°56E **115** E14
Hongya China 29°57N 103°22E **116** C4
Hongyuan China 32°51N 102°40E **116** A4
Honge Hu China 33°15N 118°35E **115** H10
Honiara Solomon Is. 9°27S 159°57E **147** B8
Honiton U.K. 50°47N 3°11W **67** G4
Honjō = Yurihonjō
　Japan 39°23N 140°3E **112** E10
Honkorâb, Ras Egypt 24°35N 35°10E **137** C4
Honnali India 14°15N 75°40E **127** G2
Honningsvåg Norway 70°59N 25°59E **60** A21
Hönö Sweden 57°41N 11°39E **63** G5
Honolulu U.S.A. 21°19N 157°52W **167** L8
Honshū Japan 36°0N 138°0E **113** F9
Hontoria del Pinar Spain 41°50N 3°10W **90** D1
Hood, Mt. U.S.A. 45°23N 121°42W **168** D3
Hood, Pt. Australia 34°23S 119°34E **149** F2
Hood River U.S.A. 45°43N 121°31W **168** D3
Hoodsport U.S.A. 47°24N 123°9W **170** C3
Hooge Germany 54°34N 8°33E **76** A4
Hoogeveen Neths. 52°44N 6°28E **69** B6
Hoogezand-Sappemeer
　Neths. 53°9N 6°45E **69** A6
Hooghly = Hugli →
　India 21°56N 88°4E **125** J13
Hooghly-Chinsura = Chunchura
　India 22°53N 88°27E **125** H13
Hook Hd. Ireland 52°7N 6°56W **64** D5
Hook I. Australia 20°4S 149°0E **150** b
Hook of Holland = Hoek van
　Holland Neths. 52°0N 4°7E **69** C4
Hooker U.S.A. 36°52N 101°13W **176** C4
Hooker Creek = Lajamanu
　Australia 18°23S 130°38E **148** C5
Hooker Creek ⌂
　Australia 18°6S 130°23E **148** C5
Hoonah U.S.A. 58°7N 135°27W **162** B1
Hooper Bay U.S.A. 61°32N 166°6W **166** D6
Hoopeston U.S.A. 40°28N 87°40W **172** E10
Hoopstad S. Africa 27°50S 25°55E **144** C4
Höör Sweden 55°56N 13°33E **63** J7
Hoorn Neths. 52°38N 5°4E **69** B5
Hoover U.S.A. 33°24N 86°49W **177** E11
Hoover Dam U.S.A. 36°1N 114°44W **171** K12
Hooversville U.S.A. 40°9N 78°55W **174** F6
Hop Bottom U.S.A. 41°42N 75°46W **175** E9
Hopa Turkey 41°28N 41°30E **105** B9
Hope Canada 49°25N 121°25W **162** D4
Hope Ariz., U.S.A. 33°43N 113°42W **171** M13
Hope Ark., U.S.A. 33°40N 93°36W **176** E8
Hope, L. S. Austral.,
　Australia 28°24S 139°18E **151** D2
Hope, L. W. Austral.,
　Australia 32°35S 120°15E **149** F3
Hope, Pt. U.S.A. 68°21N 166°47W **158** C3
Hope I. Canada 44°55N 80°11W **174** B4
Hope Town Bahamas 26°35N 76°57W **182** A4
Hope Vale Australia 15°16S 145°20E **150** B4
Hope Vale ⌂ Australia 15°8S 145°15E **150** B4
Hopedale Canada 55°28N 60°13W **165** A7
Hopedale U.S.A. 42°8N 71°33W **175** D13
Hopefield S. Africa 33°3S 18°22E **144** D2
Hopei = Hebei □ China 39°0N 116°0E **114** H8
Hopelchén Mexico 19°46N 89°51W **181** D7
Hopetoun Vic.,
　Australia 35°42S 142°22E **152** C5
Hopetown S. Africa 29°34S 24°3E **144** C3
Hopewell U.S.A. 37°18N 77°17W **173** G15
Hopgarten Austria 47°27N 12°10E **78** D5
Hopkins, L. Australia 24°15S 128°35E **149** D4
Hopkinsville U.S.A. 36°52N 87°29W **172** G10
Hopland U.S.A. 38°58N 123°7W **170** G3
Hoquiam U.S.A. 46°59N 123°53W **170** C2
Hora Hoverla Ukraine 48°7N 24°41E **81** B9
Horana Sri Lanka 6°43N 80°4E **127** L5
Horasan Turkey 40°3N 42°11E **105** C10
Horaždovice Czech Rep. 49°19N 13°42E **78** B6
Horb Germany 48°26N 8°42E **77** G4
Hørby Denmark 57°5N 13°40E **63** F7
Horcajo de Santiago Spain 39°50N 3°1W **90** F1
Hordern Hills Australia 20°15S 130°0E **148** D5
Horezu Romania 45°6N 24°0E **81** E8
Horgen Switz. 47°15N 8°35E **77** H4
Horgos Serbia 46°10N 20°0E **80** D4
Horgoš Serbia 46°10N 20°0E **80** D4
Horinchove Ukraine 48°16N 23°26E **81** B8
Horinger China 40°28N 111°48E **114** D6
Horizontina Brazil 27°37S 54°19W **191** B5
Horki Belarus 54°17N 30°59E **84** E6
Horlick Mts. Antarctica 84°0S 102°0W **55** E15
Hormak Iran 29°58N 60°51E **129** D9
Hormoz Iran 27°35N 55°0E **129** E7
Hormoz, Jaz.-ye Iran 27°8N 56°28E **129** E8
Hormozgan □ Iran 27°30N 56°0E **129** E8
Hormuz, Kūh-e Iran 27°27N 55°10E **129** E7
Hormuz, Str. of The Gulf 26°30N 56°30E **129** E8
Horn Austria 48°39N 15°40E **78** C8
Horn Sweden 57°54N 15°51E **63** G9
Horn → Canada 61°30N 118°1W **162** A5
Horn, Cape = Hornos, C. de
　Chile 55°50S 67°30W **192** E3
Horn Head Ireland 55°14N 8°0W **64** A3
Horn I. Australia 10°37S 142°17E **150** A3
Horn Plateau Canada 62°15N 119°15W **162** A5
Hornachuelos Spain 37°50N 5°14W **89** H5
Hornavan Sweden 66°15N 17°30E **60** D17
Hornbæk Denmark 56°5N 12°26E **63** H6
Hornbeck U.S.A. 31°20N 93°24W **176** F8
Hornbrook U.S.A. 41°55N 122°33W **168** F2
Hornburg Germany 52°2N 10°37E **76** C6
Hornby N.Z. 43°33S 172°33E **155** D7
Horncastle U.K. 53°13N 0°7W **66** D7
Horndal Sweden 60°18N 16°23E **62** D10
Hornell U.S.A. 42°20N 77°40W **174** D7
Hornell L. Canada 62°20N 119°25W **162** A5
Hornepayne Canada 49°14N 84°48W **164** C3

Howar, Wadi → Sudan 17°30N 27°8E **13**
Howard Australia 25°16S 152°32E **1**
Howard Pa., U.S.A. 41°1N 77°40W **1**
Howard S. Dak., U.S.A. 44°1N 97°32W **1**
Howe U.S.A. 43°48N 113°0W **1**
Howe, C. Australia 37°30S 150°0E **1**
Howe, West Cape
　Australia 35°8S 117°36E **1**
Howe I. Canada 44°16N 76°17W **1**
Howell U.S.A. 42°36N 83°56W **1**
Howick Canada 45°11N 73°51W **1**
Howick N.Z. 36°54S 174°56E **1**
Howick S. Africa 29°28S 30°14E **1**
Howick Group
　Australia 14°20S 145°30E **1**
Howitt, L. Australia 27°40S 138°40E **1**
Howland I. Pac. Oc. 0°48S 176°38W **1**
Howlong Australia 35°59S 146°38E **1**
Howrah = Haora
　India 22°34N 88°18E **12**
Howth Ireland 53°23N 6°7W
Howth Hd. Ireland 53°22N 6°4W
Höxter Germany 51°46N 9°22E
Hoxtolgay China 46°35N 85°59E **10**
Hoxud China 42°15N 86°51E **10**
Hoy U.K. 58°50N 3°15W
Hoya Germany 52°49N 9°8E
Høyanger Norway 61°13N 6°4E
Hoyerswerda Germany 51°26N 14°14E **7**
Hoyos Spain 40°9N 6°45W
Hpa-an = Pa-an
　Burma 16°51N 97°40E **12**
Hpunan Pass Asia 27°30N 96°55E **12**
Hpyu = Pyu Burma 18°30N 96°28E **12**
Hradec Králové
　Czech Rep. 50°15N 15°50E
Hrádek Czech Rep. 48°46N 16°16E
Hranice Czech Rep. 49°34N 17°45E **7**
Hrazdan Armenia 40°30N 44°46E
Hrebenka Ukraine 50°9N 32°22E
Hrisoupoli = Chrisoupoli
　Greece 40°58N 24°42E
Hrodna Belarus 53°42N 23°52E **8**
Hrodna □ Belarus 53°20N 24°45E
Hrodzyanka Belarus 53°31N 28°42E **7**
Hron → Slovak Rep. 47°49N 18°45E **7**
Hrubieszów Poland 50°49N 23°51E **8**
Hrubý Jeseník Czech Rep. 50°5N 17°10E **7**
Hrvatska = Croatia ■
　Europe 45°20N 16°0E **9**
Hrymayliv Ukraine 49°20N 26°5E **8**
Hrynyava Ukraine 47°59N 24°53E
Hsenwi Burma 23°22N 97°55E **12**
Hsiamen = Xiamen
　China 24°25N 118°4E **11**
Hsian = Xi'an China 34°15N 109°0E **1**
Hsinchu Taiwan 24°48N 120°58E **11**
Hsinhailien = Lianyungang
　China 34°40N 119°11E **11**
Hsinkai = Bhamo
　Burma 24°15N 97°15E **12**
Hsinying Taiwan 23°21N 120°17E **11**
Hsopket Burma 23°11N 98°26E **12**
Hsüchou = Xuzhou
　China 34°18N 117°10E **11**
Htawei = Dawei Burma 14°2N 98°12E **1**
Hu Xian China 34°8N 108°42E **1**
Hua Hin Thailand 12°34N 99°58E **1**
Hua Muang Laos 20°13N 103°52E **1**
Hua Shan China 34°28N 110°4E **1**
Hua Xian Henan, China 35°30N 114°30E **1**
Hua Xian Shaanxi,
　China 34°30N 109°48E **1**
Huab → Namibia 20°52S 13°25E **1**
Huacaya Bolivia 20°45S 63°40W **1**
Huachacalla Bolivia 18°45S 68°17W **1**
Huacheng China 24°4N 115°37E **1**
Huachinera Mexico 30°9N 108°55W **1**
Huacho Peru 11°10S 77°35W **1**
Huade China 41°55N 113°59E **1**
Huadian China 43°0N 126°40E **1**
Huadu China 23°22N 113°12E **1**
Huahine,
　French Polynesia 16°46S 150°58W **15**
Huai Hat ⌂ Thailand 16°20N 104°17E **1**
Huai He → China 33°0N 118°30E **11**
Huai Kha Khaeng ⌂
　Thailand 15°20N 99°55E **1**
Huai Nam Dang △
　Thailand 19°30N 98°30E **1**
Huai Yot Thailand 7°45N 99°37E **1**
Huai'an Jiangsu,
　China 33°30N 119°10E **11**
Huaibei China 33°10N 116°48E **11**
Huaibin China 32°32N 115°27E **11**
Huaide = Gongzhuling
　China 43°30N 124°40E **11**
Huaidezhen China 43°48N 124°50E **11**
Huaihua China 27°32N 109°57E **1**
Huaiji China 23°55N 112°18E **11**
Huainan China 32°38N 116°58E **11**
Huairen China 39°48N 113°20E **11**
Huairou China 40°20N 116°35E **11**
Huaiyang China 33°40N 114°52E **11**
Huaiyin China 33°30N 119°2E **11**
Huaiyuan Anhui,
　China 32°55N 117°10E **11**
Huaiyuan Guangxi Zhuangzu,
　China 24°31N 108°22E **1**
Huajuápan de León
　Mexico 17°48N 97°46W **18**
Hualapai Peak U.S.A. 35°5N 113°54W **17**
Hualian Taiwan 23°59N 121°36E **11**
Huallaga → Peru 5°15S 75°30W **1**
Huamachuco Peru 7°50S 78°5W **1**
Huambo Angola 12°42S 15°54E **14**
Huan Jiang → China 34°28N 109°0E **1**
Huan Xian China 36°33N 107°7E **1**
Huancabamba Peru 5°10S 79°15W **1**
Huancane Peru 15°10S 69°44W **1**
Huancapi Peru 13°40S 74°0W **1**
Huancavelica Peru 12°50S 75°5W **1**
Huancayo Peru 12°5S 75°12W **1**
Huanchaca Bolivia 20°15S 66°40W **1**
Huang Hai = Yellow Sea
　China 35°0N 123°0E **11**
Huang He → China 37°55N 118°50E **11**

ng Xian *China* 37°38N 120°30E 115 F11
ngchuan *China* 32°15N 115°10E 117 A10
ngdao *China* 36°0N 120°7E 115 G11
nggang *China* 30°29N 114°52E 117 B10
ngguoshu *China* 26°0N 105°40E 116 E5
nghuagang *China* 38°22N 117°54E 115 E9
nghua *China* 38°22N 117°20E 115 E9
ngling *China* 35°34N 109°15E 114 G5
nglong *China* 35°30N 109°59E 114 G5
nglong *China* 32°44N 103°50E 116 A4
nglongtan *China* 32°40N 110°33E 117 A9
ngmei *China* 30°5N 115°56E 117 B10
ngpi *China* 30°50N 114°22E 117 B10
ngping *China* 26°52N 107°54E 116 D6
ngshan *Anhui,*
ina 30°8N 118°9E 117 B12
ngshan *Anhui,*
ina 29°42N 118°25E 117 C12
ngshi *China* 30°10N 115°3E 117 B10
ngsongdian *China* 43°45N 127°25E 115 C14
ngyan *China* 28°38N 121°19E 117 C13
ngyangxi *China* 26°33N 111°39E 117 D8
ning *China* 24°17N 102°56E 116 E4
njiang *China* 24°50N 108°18E 116 E7
nren *China* 41°23N 125°20E 115 D13
nta *Peru* 12°55S 74°20W 188 C3
ntai *China* 36°58N 117°56E 115 F9
nuco *Peru* 9°55S 76°15W 188 B2
nuco *Peru* 9°55S 76°14W 188 B2
nzo, Cordillera de
ping *China* 26°46N 101°25E 116 D3
ra *Chile* 19°59S 69°47W 188 D4
ral *Peru* 11°32S 77°13W 188 C2
raz *Peru* 9°30S 77°32W 188 B2
ri *Peru* 9°14S 77°14W 188 B2
rmey *Peru* 10°5S 78°5W 188 C2
rochiri *Peru* 12°9S 76°15W 188 C2
rocondo *Peru* 13°26S 72°14W 188 C3
rong *China* 29°29N 112°30E 117 C9
scarán, Nevado *Peru* 9°7S 77°37W 188 B2
sco *Chile* 28°30S 71°15W 190 B1
sco ~ *Chile* 28°27S 71°13W 190 B1
sna *U.S.A.* 35°6N 120°24W 171 K6
tabampo *Mexico* 26°30N 109°3W 180 B3
uchinango *Mexico* 20°12N 98°3W 181 C5
utla de Jiménez
exico 18°8N 96°51W 181 D5
xi *China* 26°25N 106°40E 116 D6
yhuash, Cordillera
ru 10°35S 76°45W 188 B2
ying *China* 34°35N 110°5E 114 G6
ying *China* 30°8N 106°44E 116 B6
yllay *Peru* 11°3S 76°21W 188 C2
yuan *China* 28°37N 109°29E 116 C7
zhou *China* 21°33N 110°33E 117 G8
balli *China* 15°22N 75°15E 127 G2
bard *Ohio, U.S.A.* 41°9N 80°34W 174 E4
bard *Tex., U.S.A.* 31°51N 96°48W 176 F6
bard Glacier
nada 60°18N 139°22W 163 B6
ei ~ *China* 31°0N 112°0E 117 B9
e *Germany* 53°7N 8°26E 76 B4
iksvall *Sweden* 61°43N 17°10E 62 C11
son *Fla., U.S.A.* 50°6N 92°9W 164 B1
son *Fla., U.S.A.* 28°22N 82°42W 179 G7
son *Mass., U.S.A.* 42°23N 71°34W 175 D13
son *N.Y., U.S.A.* 42°15N 73°46W 175 D11
son *Wis., U.S.A.* 44°58N 92°45W 172 C7
son *Wyo., U.S.A.* 42°54N 108°35W 168 E9
son, C. *Antarctica* 68°21S 153°45E 55 C10
son, Vol. *Chile* 46°4S 72°55W 192 C2
son Bay *Nunavut,*
nada 60°0N 86°0W 161 F14
son Bay *Sask.,*
nada 52°51N 102°23W 163 C8
son Falls *U.S.A.* 35°12N 83°35W 175 C15
son Mts. *Antarctica* 74°32S 99°20W 55 D16
son Str. *Canada* 62°0N 70°0W 161 E18
son's Hope *Canada* 56°0N 121°54W 162 B4
Vietnam 16°30N 107°35E 120 D6
bra ~ *Spain* 41°2N 6°48W 88 D4
din *Romania* 46°52N 23°2E 80 D8
huetenango
atemala 15°20N 91°28W 182 C1
júcar *Spain* 22°21N 103°13W 180 C4
lamo *Spain* 40°17N 1°48W 90 E3
lgoat *France* 48°22N 3°46W 70 D3
lma *Spain* 37°39N 3°28W 89 H7
lva *Spain* 37°18N 6°57W 89 H4
lva *Spain* 37°39N 5°33W 89 H5
lva ~ *Spain* 37°27N 6°0W 89 H5
ntelauquén *Chile* 31°38S 71°33W 190 C1
rcal-Overa *Spain* 37°23N 1°57W 91 H3
ruehue △ *Chile* 39°6S 71°42W 192 A2
rgentina 31°10S 67°30W 190 C2
rtas, C. de la *Spain* 38°21N 0°24W 91 G4
rva ~ *Spain* 37°27N 6°0W 89 H5
sca □ *Spain* 42°20N 0°1E 90 C5
scar *Spain* 37°44N 2°35W 91 H2
tamo *Mexico* 18°35N 100°53W 180 D4
te *Spain* 40°10N 2°43W 90 E2
h ~ *Australia* 25°1S 134°1E 150 D1
henden *Australia* 20°50S 142°20E 152 C3
hesville *U.S.A.* 41°14N 76°44W 175 E8
li ~ *India* 21°56N 88°4E 125 H12
o *Colo., U.S.A.* 39°8N 103°28W 168 G12
o *Okla., U.S.A.* 34°1N 95°31W 176 D7
oton *U.S.A.* 37°11N 101°21W 172 G3
Xian = Huixian
China 35°27N 113°12E 114 G7
Xian *China* 33°50N 106°4E 114 H4
'an *China* 25°11N 118°43E 117 D12
anbu *China* 37°28N 106°38E 114 F4
arau Ra. *N.Z.* 38°45S 176°55E 154 E6
chang *China* 34°21N 109°42E 114 G5
chapan *Mexico* 20°23N 99°39W 181 C5
chon *N. Guangdong,*
chon *China* 40°10N 126°15E 115 D14
dong *Guangdong,*
China 22°58N 114°43E 117 F10

Huidong *Sichuan,*
China 26°34N 102°35E 116 D4
Huifa He ~ *China* 43°0N 127°50E 115 C14
Huila, Nevado del
Colombia 3°0N 76°0W 186 C3
Huilai *China* 23°0N 116°18E 117 F11
Huili *China* 26°35N 102°17E 116 D4
Huimin *China* 37°27N 117°28E 115 F9
Huinan *China* 42°40N 126°2E 115 C14
Huinca Renancó
Argentina 34°51S 64°22W 190 C3
Huining *China* 35°38N 105°0E 114 G3
Huinong *China* 39°5N 106°35E 114 E4
Huiroa *N.Z.* 39°15S 174°30E 154 F3
Huishui *China* 26°7N 106°38E 116 D6
Huisne ~ *France* 47°59N 0°11E 70 E7
Huiting *China* 34°5N 116°5E 114 G9
Huixian *China* 26°51N 109°45E 116 D7
Huixian *China* 35°27N 113°12E 114 G7
Huixtla *Mexico* 15°9N 92°28W 181 D6
Huize *China* 26°24N 103°15E 116 D4
Huizhou *China* 23°0N 114°23E 117 F10
Hukawng Valley
Burma 26°30N 96°30E 123 F20
Hukeri *India* 16°14N 74°36E 127 F2
Hukou *China* 29°45N 116°21E 117 C11
Hukuntsi *Botswana* 23°58S 21°45E 144 B3
Ḩulayfā' *Si. Arabia* 25°58N 40°45E 128 E4
Hulin *China* 45°48N 132°59E 111 B15
Hulin He ~ *China* 45°0N 122°10E 115 B12
Hull = Kingston upon Hull
U.K. 53°45N 0°21W 66 D7
Hull *Canada* 45°26N 75°43W 175 A9
Hull ~ *U.K.* 53°44N 0°20W 66 D7
Hulst *Neths.* 51°17N 4°2E 69 C4
Hultsfred *Sweden* 57°30N 15°52E 63 G9
Huludao *China* 40°45N 120°55E 115 D11
Hulun Nur *China* 49°0N 117°30E 111 B12
Hulunbuir = Hailar
China 49°10N 119°38E 111 B12
Hulyaypole *Ukraine* 47°45N 36°21E 85 J9
Huma, Tanjung
Malaysia 5°29N 100°16E 121 c
Humahuaca *Argentina* 23°10S 65°25W 190 A2
Humaitá *Brazil* 7°35S 63°1W 186 E6
Humaitá *Paraguay* 27°2S 58°31W 190 B4
Humansdorp *S. Africa* 34°2S 24°46E 144 D3
Humbe *Angola* 16°40S 14°55E 144 A1
Humber ~ *U.K.* 53°42N 0°27W 66 D7
Humboldt *Canada* 52°15N 105°9W 163 C7
Humboldt *Iowa, U.S.A.* 42°44N 94°13W 172 D6
Humboldt *Tenn.,*
U.S.A. 35°50N 88°55W 177 D10
Humboldt ~ *U.S.A.* 39°59N 118°36W 168 G4
Humboldt Gletscher =
Sermersuaq *Greenland* 79°30N 62°0W 57 B4
Humboldt Mts. *N.Z.* 44°30S 168°15E 155 E3
Hume, L. *Australia* 36°0S 147°5E 153 D7
Humen *China* 22°50N 113°40E 111 a
Humenné *Slovak Rep.* 48°55N 21°50E 79 C14
Hummelsta *Sweden* 59°34N 16°58E 62 E10
Humphreys, Mt.
U.S.A. 37°17N 118°40W 170 H8
Humphreys Peak
U.S.A. 35°21N 111°41W 169 J8
Humpolec *Czech Rep.* 49°31N 15°20E 78 B8
Humptulips *U.S.A.* 47°14N 123°57W 168 C2
Humula *Australia* 35°30S 147°46E 153 C7
Hūn *Libya* 29°2N 16°0E 135 C9
Hun Jiang ~ *China* 40°50N 125°38E 115 D13
Húnaflói *Iceland* 65°50N 20°50W 60 D3
Hunan □ *China* 27°30N 112°0E 117 D9
Hunchun *China* 42°52N 130°28E 115 C16
Hundested *Denmark* 55°58N 11°52E 63 J5
Hundewali *Pakistan* 31°55N 72°38E 124 D5
Hundred Mile House
Canada 51°38N 121°18W 162 C4
Hunedoara *Romania* 45°40N 22°50E 80 E7
Hunedoara □ *Romania* 45°50N 22°54E 80 E7
Hünfeld *Germany* 50°39N 9°46E 76 E5
Hung Yen *Vietnam* 20°39N 106°4E 116 G6
Hungary ■ *Europe* 47°20N 19°20E 79 D12
Hungary, Plain of *Europe* 47°0N 20°0E 58 F10
Hungerford *Australia* 28°58S 144°24E 151 D3
Hüngnam *N. Korea* 39°49N 127°45E 115 E14
Hungt'ou Hsü = Lan Yü
Taiwan 22°4N 121°25E 117 F13
Hungt'ou Hsü = Lan Yü
Vietnam 16°30N 107°35E 120 D6
Huni Valley *Ghana* 5°33N 1°56W 138 D4
Hunjiang *China* 41°54N 126°26E 115 D14
Hunneberg *Sweden* 58°18N 12°30E 63 F6
Hunnebostrand *Sweden* 58°27N 11°18E 63 F5
Hunsberge *Namibia* 27°45S 17°12E 144 C2
Hunsrück *Germany* 49°56N 7°27E 77 F3
Hunstanton *U.K.* 52°56N 0°29E 66 E8
Hunsur *India* 12°16N 76°16E 127 H3
Hunte ~ *Germany* 53°14N 8°28E 76 B4
Hunter *N.Z.* 44°36S 171°2E 155 E6
Hunter *U.S.A.* 42°13N 74°13W 175 D10
Hunter ~ *Australia* 32°52S 151°46E 153 B9
Hunter I. *Canada* 51°55N 128°0W 162 C3
Hunter Hills, The *N.Z.* 44°21S 169°27E 155 E4
Hunter Ra. *Australia* 32°45S 150°15E 153 B9
Hunters Road *Zimbabwe* 19°9S 29°49E 143 F2
Huntingburg *U.S.A.* 38°18N 86°57W 172 F10
Huntingdon *U.K.* 52°20N 0°11W 67 E7
Huntington *Ind.,*
U.S.A. 40°53N 85°30W 173 E11
Huntington *N.Y.,*
U.S.A. 40°52N 73°26W 175 F11
Huntington *Oreg.,*
U.S.A. 44°21N 117°16W 168 D5
Huntington *Utah,*
U.S.A. 39°20N 110°58W 168 G8
Huntington *W. Va.,*
U.S.A. 38°25N 82°27W 173 F12
Huntington Beach
U.S.A. 33°40N 118°5W 171 M9
Huntly *N.Z.* 37°34S 175°11E 154 D4
Huntly *U.K.* 57°27N 2°47W 65 D6
Huntsville *Canadá* 45°20N 79°14W 174 A5
Huntsville *Ala., U.S.A.* 34°44N 86°35W 177 D11
Huntsville *Tex., U.S.A.* 30°43N 95°33W 176 F7
Hunyani ~ *Zimbabwe* 15°57S 30°39E 143 F3
Hunyuan *China* 39°42N 113°42E 114 E7
Hunza ~ *India* 35°54N 74°20E 125 B6

Huo Shan *China* 36°26N 111°52E 114 F6
Huo Xian = Huozhou
China 36°36N 111°42E 114 F6
Huocheng *China* 44°0N 80°48E 109 D10
Huolin Gol *China* 45°32N 119°38E 115 B10
Huoln Gol *China* 45°32N 119°38E 115 B10
Huong Khe *Vietnam* 18°13N 105°41E 120 C5
Huonville *Australia* 43°0S 147°5E 151 G4
Huoqiu *China* 32°20N 116°12E 117 A11
Huoshan *China* 31°25N 116°20E 117 B11
Huoshao Dao = Lütao
Taiwan 22°40N 121°30E 117 F13
Huozhou *China* 36°36N 111°42E 114 F6
Hupeh = Hubei □ *China* 31°0N 112°0E 117 B9
Ḩūr *Iran* 30°50N 57°7E 129 D8
Hurānd *Iran* 38°51N 47°22E 105 C12
Ḩuraymilā *Si. Arabia* 25°8N 46°8E 128 E5
Hurbanovo *Slovak Rep.* 47°51N 18°11E 79 D11
Hurd, C. *Canada* 45°13N 81°44W 174 A3
Hure Qi *China* 42°45N 121°45E 115 C11
Hurezani *Romania* 44°49N 23°40E 81 F8
Hurghada *Egypt* 27°15N 33°50E 137 B3
Hurley *N. Mex., U.S.A.* 32°42N 108°8W 169 K9
Hurley *Wis., U.S.A.* 46°27N 90°11W 172 B8
Huron *Calif., U.S.A.* 36°12N 120°6W 170 J6
Huron *Ohio, U.S.A.* 41°24N 82°33W 174 E2
Huron *S. Dak., U.S.A.* 44°22N 98°13W 172 C4
Huron, L. *U.S.A.* 44°30N 82°40W 174 B3
Huron East *Canada* 43°37N 81°18W 174 C3
Hurricane *U.S.A.* 37°11N 113°17W 169 H7
Hurtsboro *U.S.A.* 32°15N 85°25W 177 E12
Hurungwe ~ *Zimbabwe* 16°7S 29°5E 143 F2
Hurunui ~ *N.Z.* 42°54S 173°18E 155 C6
Hurup *Denmark* 56°46N 8°25E 63 H2
Húsavík *Iceland* 66°3N 17°21W 60 C5
Huşi *Romania* 46°41N 28°7E 81 D13
Huskisson *Australia* 35°2S 150°41E 153 C9
Huskvarna *Sweden* 57°47N 14°15E 63 G8
Hustadvika *Norway* 63°0N 7°0E 60 E12
Hustontown *U.S.A.* 40°3N 78°2W 174 F6
Hustopeče *Czech Rep.* 48°57N 16°43E 79 C9
Husum *Germany* 54°28N 9°4E 76 A5
Husum *Sweden* 63°21N 19°12E 62 A13
Hutchinson *Kans.,*
U.S.A. 38°5N 97°56W 172 F5
Hutchinson *Minn.,*
U.S.A. 44°54N 94°22W 172 C6
Hutiao Xia *China* 27°13N 100°9E 116 D3
Hutte Sauvage, L. de la
Canada 56°15N 64°45W 165 A7
Hüttenberg *Austria* 46°56N 14°33E 78 E7
Hüttener Berge △
Germany 54°24N 9°40E 76 A5
Hutton, Mt. *Australia* 25°51S 148°20E 151 D4
Huwaki *Indonesia* 7°55S 126°30E 119 F7
Huy *Belgium* 50°31N 5°15E 69 D5
Huzhou *China* 30°51N 120°8E 117 B13
Huzurabad *India* 18°12N 79°25E 126 E4
Huzurnagar *India* 16°54N 79°53E 126 F4
Hvalpsund *Denmark* 56°42N 9°11E 63 H3
Hvammstangi *Iceland* 65°24N 20°57W 60 D3
Hvar *Croatia* 43°11N 16°28E 93 E13
Hvarski Kanal *Croatia* 43°15N 16°35E 93 E13
Hvítá ~ *Iceland* 64°30N 21°58W 60 D3
Hvizdets *Ukraine* 48°35N 25°17E 81 B10
Hwacheon-Cheosuji
S. Korea 38°5N 127°50E 115 E14
Hwang Ho = Huang He ~
China 37°55N 118°50E 115 F10
Hwange *Zimbabwe* 18°18S 26°30E 144 B4
Hwange △ *Zimbabwe* 19°0S 26°30E 144 A4
Hwlffordd = Haverfordwest
U.K. 51°48N 4°58W 67 F3
Hyannis *Mass., U.S.A.* 41°39N 70°17W 173 E18
Hyannis *Nebr., U.S.A.* 42°0N 101°46W 172 E3
Hyargas Nuur *Mongolia* 49°0N 93°0E 109 C12
Hybo *Sweden* 61°49N 16°15E 62 C10
Hydaburg *U.S.A.* 55°15N 132°50W 162 B2
Hyde *U.K.* 53°26N 2°4W 66 D5
Hyde Park *U.S.A.* 41°47N 73°56W 175 E11
Hyden *Australia* 32°24S 118°53E 149 F2
Hyder *U.S.A.* 55°55N 130°5W 162 B2
Hyderabad *India* 17°22N 78°29E 126 F4
Hyderabad *Pakistan* 25°23N 68°24E 124 G3
Hydra *Greece* 37°20N 23°28E 98 D5
Hyères *France* 43°8N 6°9E 73 E10
Hyères, Îs. d' *France* 43°0N 6°20E 73 F10
Hyesan *N. Korea* 41°20N 128°10E 115 D15
Hyland ~ *Canada* 59°52N 128°12W 162 B3
Hyltebruk *Sweden* 56°59N 13°15E 63 H7
Hyndman Peak *U.S.A.* 43°45N 114°8W 168 E6
Hyōgo □ *Japan* 35°15N 134°50E 113 G7
Hyrum *U.S.A.* 41°38N 111°51W 168 F8
Hythe *U.K.* 51°4N 1°5E 67 F9
Hyūga *Japan* 32°25N 131°35E 113 H5
Hyvinge = Hyvinkää
Finland 60°38N 24°50E 84 B3
Hyvinkää *Finland* 60°38N 24°50E 84 B3

I

I-n-Akhmed *Mali* 19°49N 0°56W 139 B4
I-n-Azaoua *Algeria* 25°42N 6°54E 136 C5
I-n-Ezzane *Algeria* 23°29N 11°15E 136 D6
I-n-Gall *Niger* 16°51N 7°1E 139 B6
I-n-Kelemet *Algeria* 26°57N 5°47E 136 C5
I-n-Oudad *Algeria* 20°17N 4°38E 139 A5
I-n-Ouzzal *Algeria* 20°41N 2°33E 139 A5
I-n-Tadreft *Niger* 19°5N 6°38E 139 B6
Iabès, Erg *Algeria* 27°30N 2°2W 136 C3
Iablanița *Romania* 45°8N 22°19E 80 F7
Iaco ~ *Brazil* 9°3S 68°34W 188 B4
Iacobeni *Romania* 47°25N 25°20E 81 C10
Iaçu *Brazil* 12°45S 40°13W 189 C2
Ialissos *Greece* 36°24N 28°10E 101 C10
Ialomița □ *Romania* 44°30N 27°30E 81 F12
Ialomița ~ *Romania* 44°42N 27°51E 81 F13
Ialoveni *Moldova* 46°54N 28°47E 81 D13
Ialpug ~ *Moldova* 45°41N 28°35E 81 F15
Iamonia, L. *U.S.A.* 30°38N 84°14W 178 E15
Ianca *Romania* 45°6N 27°29E 81 E12
Iara *Brazil* 34°31N 23°35E 81 D8
Iargara *Moldova* 46°24N 28°23E 81 D13
Iași *Romania* 47°10N 27°40E 81 C12
Iași □ *Romania* 47°20N 27°0E 81 C12
Iasmos *Greece* 41°8N 25°11E 97 E9
Iba *Phil.* 15°22N 120°0E 119 A6
Ibadan *Nigeria* 7°22N 3°58E 139 D5
Ibagué *Colombia* 4°20N 75°20W 186 C3
Iballë *Albania* 42°12N 20°2E 96 D4

Ibănești *Botoșani,*
Romania 48°4N 26°22E 81 B11
Ibănești *Mureș, Romania* 46°45N 24°57E 81 D9
Ibar ~ *Serbia* 43°43N 20°45E 96 C4
Ibaraki □ *Japan* 36°10N 140°10E 113 F10
Ibarra *Ecuador* 0°21N 78°7W 186 C3
Ibba ~ *Sudan* 4°49N 29°2E 135 H11
Ibbenbüren *Germany* 52°16N 7°43E 76 C3
Ibembo
Dem. Rep. of the Congo 2°35N 23°35E 142 B1
Ibenga ~ *Congo* 2°19N 18°9E 140 D3
Ibera, L. *Argentina* 28°30S 57°9W 190 B4
Iberia *Peru* 11°21S 69°35W 188 C4
Iberian Peninsula *Europe* 40°0N 5°0W 58 H5
Iberville *Canada* 45°19N 73°17W 175 A11
Iberville, Mt. d'
Canada 58°50N 63°50W 161 F19
Ibeto *Nigeria* 10°29N 5°8E 139 D6
Ibi *Nigeria* 8°15N 9°44E 139 D6
Ibi *Spain* 38°38N 0°34W 91 G4
Ibiá *Brazil* 19°30S 46°30W 189 C3
Ibiapaba, Sa. da *Brazil* 4°0S 41°30W 189 A2
Ibicaraí *Brazil* 14°51S 39°36W 189 C3
Ibicuí *Brazil* 14°51S 39°59W 189 C3
Ibicuí ~ *Brazil* 29°25S 56°47W 191 B4
Ibicuy *Argentina* 33°55S 59°10W 190 C4
Ibitiara *Brazil* 12°39S 42°13W 189 C2
Ibiza = Eivissa *Spain* 38°54N 1°26E 91 G6
Iblei, Monti *Italy* 37°15N 14°45E 95 E7
Ibo *Mozam.* 12°22S 40°40E 143 E5
Ibonma *Indonesia* 3°29S 133°31E 119 E8
Ibotirama *Brazil* 12°13S 43°12W 189 C2
Ibrāhīm ~ *Lebanon* 34°4N 35°38E 130 A4
'Ibrī *Oman* 23°14N 56°30E 131 C6
Ibrktepe *Turkey* 41°0N 26°30E 97 E10
Ibshawāi *Egypt* 29°21N 30°40E 137 F7
Ibu *Indonesia* 1°35N 127°33E 119 D7
Ibusuki *Japan* 31°12N 130°40E 113 J5
Ica *Peru* 14°0S 75°48W 188 C2
Ica □ *Peru* 14°0S 75°30W 188 C2
Iça ~ *Brazil* 2°55S 67°58W 186 D5
Içana *Brazil* 0°21N 67°19W 186 C5
Içana ~ *Brazil* 0°26N 67°19W 186 C5
Icatu *Brazil* 2°46S 44°0W 189 A2
İçel = Mersin *Turkey* 36°51N 34°36E 104 D6
Iceland ■ *Europe* 64°45N 19°0W 60 D4
Iceland Basin *Atl. Oc.* 61°0N 19°0W 54 C7
Icelandic Plateau *Arctic* 64°0N 10°0W 54 C7
İçeriçumra *Turkey* 37°34N 32°59E 104 D5
Ichalkaranji *India* 16°40N 74°33E 126 F2
Ich'ang = Yichang
China 30°40N 111°20E 117 B8
Ichchapuram *India* 19°10N 84°40E 126 E7
Ichhawar *India* 23°1N 77°1E 124 H7
Ichigat Muja-Cordillera del
Condor ~ *Peru* 2°0S 77°30W 188 A2
Ichihara *Japan* 35°28N 140°5E 113 G10
Ichikawa *Japan* 35°44N 139°55E 113 G9
Ichilo ~ *Bolivia* 15°57S 64°50W 186 G6
Ichinohe *Japan* 40°13N 141°17E 112 D10
Ichinomiya *Japan* 35°18N 136°48E 113 G8
Ichinoseki *Japan* 38°55N 141°8E 112 E10
Ichkeul △ *Tunisia* 37°9N 9°37E 136 A5
Ichnya *Ukraine* 50°52N 32°24E 85 G7
Icht *Morocco* 29°6N 8°54W 134 C4
Icó *Brazil* 6°24S 38°51W 189 B3
Icod *Canary Is.* 28°22N 16°43W 100 F3
İçoguz *Turkmenistan* 40°11N 58°24E 108 D5
Icy C. *U.S.A.* 70°20N 161°52W 159 B7
Ida Grove *U.S.A.* 42°21N 95°28W 172 D6
Idabel *U.S.A.* 33°54N 94°50W 176 E7
Idah *Nigeria* 7°5N 6°40E 139 D6
Idaho □ *U.S.A.* 45°0N 115°0W 168 D6
Idaho City *U.S.A.* 43°50N 115°50W 168 E6
Idaho Falls *U.S.A.* 43°30N 112°2W 168 E7
Idalia △ *Australia* 24°49S 144°36E 150 C3
Idanha-a-Nova *Portugal* 39°50N 7°15W 88 F3
Idar-Oberstein *Germany* 49°43N 7°16E 77 F3
Idelès *Algeria* 23°50N 5°53E 136 D6
Idensalmi = Iisalmi
Finland 63°32N 27°10E 60 E22
Idfû *Egypt* 24°55N 32°49E 137 C3
Idi *Indonesia* 5°2N 97°37E 118 C1
Idi, Oros = Psiloritis, Oros
Greece 35°15N 24°45E 101 D6
İdil *Turkey* 37°20N 41°53E 105 D9
Idiofa
Dem. Rep. of the Congo 4°55S 19°42E 140 E3
Idkerberget *Sweden* 60°22N 15°15E 62 D9
Idku *Egypt* 31°18N 30°17E 137 E7
Idku, Bahra el *Egypt* 31°18N 30°18E 137 E7
Idlib *Syria* 35°55N 36°36E 104 E7
Idlib □ *Syria* 35°45N 36°45E 104 E7
Idra = Hydra *Greece* 37°20N 23°28E 98 D5
Idre *Sweden* 61°52N 12°42E 62 C6
Idria *U.S.A.* 36°25N 120°41W 170 J6
Idrija *Slovenia* 46°0N 14°5E 93 C11
Idritsa *Russia* 56°17N 28°53E 84 D5
Idutywa = Dutywa
S. Africa 32°8S 28°18E 145 D4
Ieper *Belgium* 50°51N 2°53E 69 D2
Ierapetra *Greece* 35°1N 25°44E 101 E7
Ierissos *Greece* 40°22N 23°52E 96 F7
Ierissos Kolpos *Greece* 40°27N 23°57E 96 F7
Iernut *Romania* 46°27N 24°15E 81 D9
Iesi *Italy* 43°31N 13°14E 93 E10
Ifac, Penyal d' *Spain* 38°38N 0°5E 91 G5
Ifakara *Tanzania* 8°8S 36°41E 140 F7
'Ifāl, W. al ~ *Si. Arabia* 28°7N 35°3E 128 D2
Ife *Nigeria* 7°30N 4°31E 139 D5
Iferouâne *Niger* 19°5N 8°24E 137 D1
Ifetesene *Algeria* 25°30N 4°33E 136 D6
Iffley *Australia* 18°53S 141°12E 150 B3
Ifôghas, Adrar des *Africa* 20°0N 2°0E 136 E6
Ifould, L. *Australia* 30°52S 132°6E 149 F5
Ifrane *Morocco* 33°33N 5°7W 136 B2
Igalo *Montenegro* 42°33N 18°30E 96 D2
Iganga *Uganda* 0°37N 33°28E 142 B3
Igarapava *Brazil* 20°3S 47°47W 189 C1
Igarka *Russia* 67°30N 86°33E 106 C9
Igatimi *Paraguay* 24°5S 55°40W 190 A4
Igbetti *Nigeria* 8°44N 4°8E 139 D5
Igbo-Ora *Nigeria* 7°29N 3°15E 139 D5
Igbor *Nigeria* 7°27N 8°43E 139 D6
Iğdır *Turkey* 39°55N 44°2E 105 D11
Iggesund *Sweden* 61°39N 17°10E 62 C11

Ighil Izane = Relizane
Algeria 35°44N 0°31E 136 A4
Iglésias *Italy* 39°19N 8°32E 94 C1
Igli *Algeria* 30°25N 2°19W 136 B3
Igloolik = Iglulik
Canada 69°20N 81°49W 161 D12
Iglulik *Canada* 69°20N 81°49W 161 D12
Igluligaarjuk = Chesterfield Inlet
Canada 63°30N 90°45W 160 E13
Ignace *Canada* 49°30N 91°40W 164 C1
Iğneada *Turkey* 41°52N 27°59E 97 E11
İğneada Burnu *Turkey* 41°53N 28°2E 97 E12
Igoumenitsa *Greece* 39°32N 20°18E 98 B2
Igrim *Russia* 63°12N 64°30E 106 C7
Iguaçu ~ *Brazil* 25°36S 54°36W 191 B5
Iguaçu, Cat. del *Brazil* 25°41S 54°26W 191 B5
Iguaçu △ *Brazil* 25°30S 54°0W 191 B5
Iguaçu Falls = Iguaçu, Cat. del
Brazil 25°41S 54°26W 191 B5
Iguala *Mexico* 18°21N 99°32W 181 D5
Igualada *Spain* 41°37N 1°37E 90 D6
Iguassu = Iguaçu ~
Brazil 25°36S 54°36W 191 B5
Iguatu *Brazil* 6°20S 39°18W 189 B3
Iguazú △ *Argentina* 25°42S 54°22W 191 B5
Iguidi, Erg *Africa* 27°0N 6°0W 134 C4
Iharana *Madag.* 13°25S 50°0E 141 G10
Iheya-Shima *Japan* 27°4N 127°58E 113 L3
Ihiala *Nigeria* 5°51N 6°55E 139 D6
Ihosy *Madag.* 22°24S 46°8E 141 J9
Ihugh *Nigeria* 7°2N 9°0E 139 D6
Ii *Finland* 65°19N 25°22E 60 D21
Ii-Shima *Japan* 26°43N 127°47E 113 L3
Iida *Japan* 35°35N 137°50E 113 G8
Iijoki ~ *Finland* 65°20N 25°20E 60 D21
Iisalmi *Finland* 63°32N 27°10E 60 E22
Iiyama *Japan* 36°51N 138°22E 113 F9
Iizuka *Japan* 33°38N 130°42E 113 H5
Ijâfene *Mauritania* 20°40N 8°0W 134 D4
Ijebu-Igbo *Nigeria* 6°56N 4°1E 139 D5
Ijebu-Ode *Nigeria* 6°47N 3°58E 139 D5
IJevan *Armenia* 40°52N 45°8E 87 K7
IJmuiden *Neths.* 52°28N 4°35E 69 B4
Ijo älv = Iijoki ~
Finland 65°20N 25°20E 60 D21
IJssel ~ *Neths.* 52°35N 5°50E 69 B5
IJsselmeer *Neths.* 52°45N 5°20E 69 B5
Ijuí *Brazil* 28°23S 53°55W 191 B5
Ijuí ~ *Brazil* 27°58S 55°20W 191 B4
Ikamatua *N.Z.* 42°16S 171°41E 155 C6
Ikang *Nigeria* 4°49N 8°30E 139 E6
Ikanga *Kenya* 1°42S 38°4E 142 C4
Ikara *Nigeria* 11°12N 8°15E 139 C6
Ikare *Nigeria* 7°32N 5°40E 139 D6
Ikaria *Greece* 37°35N 26°10E 99 D8
Ikast *Denmark* 56°8N 9°10E 63 H3
Ikeda *Japan* 34°1N 133°48E 113 G6
Ikeja *Nigeria* 6°36N 3°20E 139 D5
Ikela *Dem. Rep. of the Congo* 1°6S 23°6E 140 E4
Ikere *Nigeria* 7°25N 5°19E 139 D6
Ikhtiman *Bulgaria* 42°27N 23°48E 96 C7
Iki *Japan* 33°45N 129°42E 113 H4
Ikimba L. *Tanzania* 1°30S 31°20E 142 C3
Ikire *Nigeria* 7°25N 4°17E 139 D5
Ikizdere *Turkey* 40°46N 40°32E 105 B9
Ikom *Nigeria* 6°0N 8°42E 139 D6
Ikopa ~ *Madag.* 16°45S 46°40E 141 H9
Ikorongo △ *Tanzania* 1°50S 34°53E 142 C3
Ikot Ekpene *Nigeria* 5°12N 7°40E 139 D6
Ikparjuk = Arctic Bay
Canada 73°1N 85°7W 161 C14
Iksan *S. Korea* 35°59N 127°0E 115 G14
Ikungu *Tanzania* 1°33S 33°42E 142 C3
Ikuntji = Haasts Bluff
Australia 23°22S 132°0E 148 D5
Ikurun *Nigeria* 7°54N 4°40E 139 D5
Ila *Nigeria* 8°0N 4°39E 139 D5
Ilagan *Phil.* 17°7N 121°53E 119 A6
Ïlâm *Iran* 33°36N 46°36E 128 C5
Ilam *Nepal* 26°58N 87°58E 125 F12
Ïlâm □ *Iran* 33°0N 47°0E 128 C5
Ilan *Taiwan* 24°45N 121°44E 117 E13
Ilanskiy *Russia* 56°14N 96°3E 111 D10
Ilaro *Nigeria* 6°53N 3°3E 139 D5
Ilatane *Niger* 16°36N 4°45E 139 B5
Ilave *Peru* 16°5S 69°40W 188 D4
Ilawa *Poland* 53°36N 19°34E 85 F5
Ilayangudi *India* 9°34N 78°37E 127 K4
Ilbenge *Russia* 57°6N 115°3E 111 D12
Île-à-la-Crosse *Canada* 55°27N 107°53W 163 B7
Île-à-la-Crosse, Lac
Canada 55°40N 107°45W 163 B7
Île-de-France *France* 49°0N 2°20E 70 B5
Ileanda *Romania* 47°20N 23°48E 81 C8
Ilebo
Dem. Rep. of the Congo 4°17S 20°55E 140 E4
Ilek *Russia* 51°32N 53°21E 108 B4
Ilemi Triangle *Africa* 5°0N 35°0E 142 B4
Ilero *Nigeria* 8°0N 3°20E 139 D5
Ilesha *Kwara, Nigeria* 8°57N 3°28E 139 D5
Ilesha *Oyo, Nigeria* 7°37N 4°40E 139 D5
Ilford *Canada* 56°4N 95°35W 163 B9
Ilfov □ *Romania* 44°36N 26°7E 81 F11
Ilfracombe *Australia* 23°30S 144°30E 150 C3
Ilfracombe *U.K.* 51°12N 4°8W 67 F3
Ilgaz *Turkey* 40°55N 33°35E 104 B5
Ilgaz Dağları *Turkey* 41°0N 33°50E 104 B5
Ilgın *Turkey* 38°18N 31°55E 104 C4
Ilha Grande, Represa
Brazil 23°10S 53°5W 191 A5
Ilha Grande △ *Brazil* 23°20S 45°10W 189 C3
Ilhavo *Portugal* 40°33N 8°43W 88 E2
Ili = Ile ~ *Kazakhstan* 45°53N 77°10E 109 C9
Ilia *Greece* 37°45N 21°35E 98 D3
Ilia *Romania* 45°57N 22°40E 80 E7
Iliamna L. *U.S.A.* 59°30N 155°0W 166 D8
Ilias, Profitis *Greece* 36°17N 27°56E 101 E9
Iliç *Turkey* 39°27N 38°37E 105 C8
Ilica *Turkey* 39°34N 28°43E 99 C9
Iligan *Phil.* 8°12N 124°13E 119 C6
Ilion *U.S.A.* 43°1N 75°2W 175 C9
Ilirska-Bistrica *Slovenia* 45°34N 14°14E 93 C11
Ilkal *India* 15°57N 76°8E 127 G3
Ilkeston *U.K.* 52°58N 1°19W 66 E6
Ilkley *U.K.* 53°56N 1°48W 66 D6
Illampu = Ancohuma, Nevado
Bolivia 16°0S 68°50W 188 D4
Illana B. *Phil.* 7°35N 123°45E 119 C6

Illapel *Chile* 32°0S 71°10W 190 C1
Ille-et-Vilaine □ *France* 48°10N 1°30W 70 D5
Ille-sur-Têt *France* 42°40N 2°38E 72 F6
Illéla *Niger* 14°32N 5°20E 139 C6
Iller ~ *Germany* 48°23N 9°58E 77 G5
Illertissen *Germany* 48°12N 10°7E 77 G6
Illes Balears = Baleares, Is.
Spain 39°30N 3°0E 100 B10
Illescas *Spain* 40°8N 3°51W 88 E7
Illetas *Spain* 39°32N 2°35E 100 B9
Illichivsk *Ukraine* 46°20N 30°35E 85 J6
Illiers-Combray *France* 48°18N 1°15E 70 D8
Illimani, Nevado
Bolivia 16°30S 67°50W 188 D4
Illinois □ *U.S.A.* 40°15N 89°30W 172 E8
Illinois ~ *U.S.A.* 38°58N 90°28W 172 F8
Illizi *Algeria* 26°31N 8°32E 136 C5
Illizi *Algeria* 26°50N 8°10E 136 C5
Illkirch-Graffenstaden
France 48°34N 7°42E 71 D7
Íllora *Spain* 37°17N 3°53W 89 H7
Ilm ~ *Germany* 51°6N 11°40E 76 D7
Ilma, L. *Australia* 29°13S 127°46E 149 E4
Ilmajoki *Finland* 62°44N 22°34E 60 E20
Ilmen, Ozero *Russia* 58°15N 31°10E 84 C6
Ilmenau *Germany* 50°41N 10°54E 76 E6
Ilnytsya *Ukraine* 48°21N 23°5E 80 B8
Ilo *Peru* 17°40S 71°20W 188 D3
Ilobu *Nigeria* 7°45N 4°25E 139 D5
Iloilo *Phil.* 10°45N 122°33E 119 B6
Ilomantsi *Finland* 62°38N 30°57E 60 E24
Ilora *Nigeria* 7°45N 3°50E 139 D5
Ilorin *Nigeria* 8°30N 4°35E 139 D5
Ilovatka *Russia* 50°30N 45°50E 86 E7
Ilovlya *Russia* 49°15N 44°2E 87 F7
Ilovlya ~ *Russia* 49°14N 44°0E 87 F7
Iłowa *Poland* 51°30N 15°10E 83 G2
Ilulissat *Greenland* 69°12N 51°10W 57 D5
Ilva Mică *Romania* 47°17N 24°40E 81 C9
Ilwaco *U.S.A.* 46°19N 124°3W 170 D2
Ilyichevsk = Illichivsk
Ukraine 46°20N 30°35E 85 J6
Iłża *Poland* 51°10N 21°15E 83 G8
Iłżanka ~ *Poland* 51°14N 21°48E 83 G8
Imabari *Japan* 34°4N 133°0E 113 G6
İmamoğlu *Turkey* 37°15N 35°38E 104 D6
Imandra, Ozero *Russia* 67°30N 33°0E 60 C25
Imari *Japan* 33°15N 129°52E 113 H4
Imatra *Finland* 61°12N 28°48E 84 B5
Imênas *Mali* 16°20N 0°40E 139 B5
imeni 26 Bakinskikh
Komissarov = Neftçala
Azerbaijan 39°19N 49°12E 105 C13
imeni 26 Bakinskikh Komissarov
Turkmenistan 39°22N 54°10E 129 B7
imeni Ismail Samani, Pik
Tajikistan 39°0N 72°2E 109 E8
imeni Karl Libknekhta
Russia 51°40N 35°35E 85 G8
Imeri, Serra *Brazil* 0°50N 65°25W 186 C5
Imfolozi △ *S. Africa* 28°18S 31°50E 145 C5
Imi *Ethiopia* 6°28N 42°10E 131 F3
Imişli *Azerbaijan* 39°55N 48°4E 105 C13
Imitek *Morocco* 29°43N 8°10W 136 C2
Imlay *U.S.A.* 40°40N 118°9W 168 F4
Imlay City *U.S.A.* 43°2N 83°5W 174 D1
Immenstadt *Germany* 47°33N 10°13E 77 H6
Immingham *U.K.* 53°37N 0°13W 66 D7
Immokalee *U.S.A.* 26°25N 81°25W 179 J8
Imo □ *Nigeria* 5°40N 7°0E 139 D6
Imo ~ *Nigeria* 4°36N 7°35E 139 E6
Ímola *Italy* 44°20N 11°42E 93 D8
Imotski *Croatia* 43°27N 17°12E 93 E14
Imperatriz *Amazonas,*
Brazil 5°18S 67°11W 188 B4
Imperatriz *Maranhão,*
Brazil 5°30S 47°29W 189 B1
Impéria *Italy* 43°53N 8°3E 92 E5
Imperial *Canada* 51°21N 105°28W 163 C7
Imperial *Calif.,*
U.S.A. 32°51N 115°34W 171 N11
Imperial *Nebr., U.S.A.* 40°31N 101°39W 172 E3
Imperial Beach *U.S.A.* 32°35N 117°6W 171 N9
Imperial Dam *U.S.A.* 32°55N 114°25W 171 N12
Imperial Res. *U.S.A.* 32°53N 114°28W 171 N12
Imperial Valley
U.S.A. 33°0N 115°30W 171 N11
Imperieuse Reef
Australia 17°36S 118°50E 148 C2
Impfondo *Congo* 1°40N 18°0E 140 D3
Imphal *India* 24°48N 93°56E 123 G18
Imphy *France* 46°55N 3°16E 71 F10
İmranlı *Turkey* 39°54N 38°9E 105 C8
Imroz = Gökçeada
Turkey 40°10N 25°50E 99 E9
Imst *Austria* 47°15N 10°44E 78 E3
Imuris *Mexico* 30°47N 110°52W 180 A2
Imuruan B. *Phil.* 10°40N 119°10E 119 B5
In Aleï *Mali* 17°42N 2°30W 138 B4
In Amenas *Algeria* 28°5N 9°35E 136 C6
In Amguel *Algeria* 28°25N 5°33E 136 D6
In Belbel *Algeria* 27°55N 1°12E 136 C5
In Delimane *Mali* 15°52N 1°31E 138 B5
In Guezzam *Algeria* 19°37N 5°52E 137 D1
In Koufi *Mali* 22°1N 1°28E 138 B5
In Salah *Algeria* 27°10N 2°32E 136 C5
In Tallak *Mali* 16°19N 3°15E 138 B5
In Tebezas *Mali* 17°47N 1°3E 138 B5
Ina *Japan* 35°50N 137°55E 113 G8
Inaccessible I. *Atl. Oc.* 37°17S 12°40W 54 K2
Inagua △ *Bahamas* 21°5N 73°24W 183 B5
Inajá *Brazil* 8°54S 37°49W 189 B3
Inambari ~ *Peru* 12°41S 69°44W 188 C4
Inangahua *N.Z.* 41°52S 171°59E 155 C5
Iñapari *Peru* 11°0S 69°40W 188 C4
Inari *Finland* 68°54N 27°1E 60 C22
Inarijärvi *Finland* 69°0N 28°0E 60 C23
Inawashiro-Ko *Japan* 37°29N 140°6E 112 F10
tInbhear Mór, An = Arklow
Ireland 52°48N 6°10E 67 D5
Inca *Spain* 39°43N 2°54E 100 B10
Inca de Oro *Chile* 26°45S 69°54W 190 B2
Incahuasi *Argentina* 27°2S 68°10W 190 B2
Incahuasi *Chile* 29°12S 71°5W 190 B1
İnce Burun *Turkey* 42°7N 34°56E 104 A6
İncekum Burnu *Turkey* 36°13N 33°58E 104 D5
Incesu *Turkey* 38°38N 35°11E 104 C6
Incheon *S. Korea* 37°27N 126°40E 115 F14
Inchiri □ *Mauritania* 20°0N 15°0W 138 B2

Incio = A Cruz do Incio
  Spain 42°39N 7°21W **88** C3
Încirliova Turkey 37°50N 27°41E **99** D9
Incline Village U.S.A. 39°10N 119°58W **170** F7
Incomáti → Mozam. 25°46S 32°43E **145** C5
Incudine, Mte. France 41°50N 9°12E **73** G13
Indal Sweden 62°35N 17°5E **62** B11
Indalsälven → Sweden 62°36N 17°30E **62** B11
Indaw Burma 24°15N 96°5E **123** G20
Independence Calif.,
  U.S.A. 36°48N 118°12W **170** J8
Independence Iowa,
  U.S.A. 42°28N 91°54W **172** D8
Independence Kans.,
  U.S.A. 37°14N 95°42W **172** G6
Independence Ky.,
  U.S.A. 38°57N 84°33W **173** F11
Independence Mo.,
  U.S.A. 39°6N 94°25W **172** F6
Independence Fjord
  Greenland 82°10N 29°0W **57** A8
Independence Mts.
  U.S.A. 41°20N 116°0W **168** F5
Independência Brazil 5°23S 40°19W **189** B2
Independencia, I. Peru 14°16S 76°12W **188** C2
Independența Romania 45°25N 27°42E **81** E12
Înderbor Kazakhstan 48°33N 51°47E **108** C4
Index U.S.A. 47°50N 121°33W **170** C5
Indi India 17°10N 75°58E **126** F2
India ■ Asia 20°0N 78°0E **122** K11
Indialantic U.S.A. 28°6N 80°34W **177** G5
Indian → U.S.A. 27°59N 80°34W **179** G9
Indian Cabins Canada 59°52N 117°40W **162** B5
Indian Harbour
  Canada 54°27N 57°13W **165** B8
Indian Harbour Beach
  U.S.A. 28°10N 80°35W **179** G9
Indian Head Canada 50°30N 103°41W **163** C8
Indian L. U.S.A. 43°46N 74°16W **175** C10
Indian Lake U.S.A. 43°47N 74°16W **175** C10
Indian Ocean 5°0S 75°0E **146** E6
Indian Rocks Beach
  U.S.A. 27°52N 82°51W **179** H7
Indian Springs
  U.S.A. 36°35N 115°40W **171** J11
Indiana U.S.A. 40°37N 79°9W **174** F5
Indiana □ U.S.A. 40°0N 86°0W **173** F11
Indianapolis U.S.A. 39°46N 86°9W **172** F10
Indianola Iowa, U.S.A. 41°22N 93°34W **172** E7
Indianola Miss., U.S.A. 33°27N 90°39W **177** D9
Indiantown U.S.A. 27°1N 80°28W **179** H9
Indigirka → Russia 70°48N 148°54E **107** B15
Indija Serbia 45°6N 20°7E **80** E5
Indio U.S.A. 33°43N 116°13W **171** M10
Indira Gandhi Canal
  India 28°0N 72°0E **124** F5
Indira Pt. India 6°44N 93°49E **127** L11
Indira Sagar India 22°15N 76°40E **124** H7
Indo-China Asia 15°0N 102°0E **102** G12
Indonesia ■ Asia 5°0S 115°0E **118** F5
Indore India 22°42N 75°53E **124** H6
Indramayu Indonesia 6°20S 108°19E **119** G13
Indravati → India 19°20N 80°20E **126** E5
Indre □ France 46°50N 1°39E **71** F8
Indre → France 47°16N 0°11E **70** E7
Indre-et-Loire □ France 47°12N 0°40E **70** E7
Indrio U.S.A. 27°31N 80°21W **179** H9
Indulkana Australia 26°58S 133°5E **151** D1
Indura Belarus 53°26N 23°53E **82** E10
Indus → Pakistan 24°20N 67°47E **124** G2
Indus, Mouths of the
  Pakistan 24°0N 68°0E **124** H3
İnebolu Turkey 41°55N 33°40E **104** B5
İnecik Turkey 40°56N 27°16E **97** F11
İnegöl Turkey 40°5N 29°31E **97** F13
Inés, Mt. Argentina 48°30S 69°40W **192** C3
Ineu Romania 46°26N 21°51E **80** D6
Inezgane Morocco 30°25N 9°29W **136** B2
Infantes = Villanueva de los
  Infantes Spain 38°43N 3°1W **89** G7
Infiernillo, Presa del
  Mexico 18°35N 101°50W **180** D4
Infiesto Spain 43°21N 5°21W **88** B5
Inga, Barrage d'
  Dem. Rep. of the Congo 5°39S 13°39E **140** F2
Ingaro Sweden 59°12N 18°45E **62** E12
Ingelstad Sweden 56°45N 14°56E **63** H8
Ingeniero Jacobacci
  Argentina 41°20S 69°36W **192** B3
Ingenio Canary Is. 27°55N 15°26W **100** G4
Ingenio Santa Ana
  Argentina 27°25S 65°40W **190** B2
Ingersoll Canada 43°4N 80°55W **174** C4
Ingham Australia 18°43S 146°10E **150** B4
Ingleborough U.K. 54°10N 2°22W **66** C5
Inglefield Land Greenland 78°30N 70°0W **57** B4
Inglewood Queens.,
  Australia 28°25S 151°2E **151** D5
Inglewood Vic.,
  Australia 36°29S 143°53E **152** C5
Inglewood N.Z. 39°9S 174°14E **154** F3
Inglewood U.S.A. 33°58N 118°21W **171** M8
Inglis U.S.A. 29°2N 82°40W **179** F7
Ingolf Fjord Greenland 80°35N 17°30W **57** A9
Ingólfshöfði Iceland 63°48N 16°39W **60** E5
Ingolstadt Germany 48°46N 11°26E **77** G7
Ingomar Canada 46°35N 107°23W **168** C10
Ingonish Canada 46°42N 60°18W **165** C7
Ingore Guinea-Biss. 12°24N 15°48W **134** C2
Ingraj Bazar India 24°58N 88°10E **125** G13
Ingrid Christensen Coast
  Antarctica 69°30S 76°0E **55** C6
Ingul = Inhul → Ukraine 46°50N 32°0E **85** J7
Ingulec = Inhulec
  Ukraine 47°42N 33°14E **85** J7
Ingulets = Inhulets →
  Ukraine 46°46N 32°47E **85** J7
Inguri = Enguri →
  Georgia 42°27N 41°38E **87** J5
Ingushetia □ Russia 43°20N 44°50E **87** J7
Ingwavuma S. Africa 27°9S 31°59E **145** D5
Inhaca Mozam. 26°1S 32°57E **145** C5
Inhaca Pen. Mozam. 26°15S 32°54E **145** C5
Inhafenga Mozam. 20°36S 33°53E **145** B5
Inhambane Mozam. 23°54S 35°30E **145** C6
Inhambane □ Mozam. 22°30S 34°20E **145** C5
Inhambupe Brazil 11°47S 38°21W **189** D3
Inhaminga Mozam. 18°26S 35°0E **145** B6
Inharrime Mozam. 24°30S 35°0E **145** C6
Inharrime → Mozam. 24°30S 35°0E **145** C6
Inhisar Turkey 40°3N 30°23E **99** A12
Inhul → Ukraine 46°50N 32°0E **85** J7

Inhulec Ukraine 47°42N 33°14E **85** J7
Inhulets → Ukraine 46°46N 32°47E **85** J7
Inhuma Brazil 6°40S 41°42W **189** B2
Iniesta Spain 39°27N 1°45W **91** F3
Ining = Yining China 43°58N 81°10E **109** D10
Inírida → Colombia 3°55N 67°52W **186** C5
Inis = Ennis Ireland 52°51N 8°59W **64** D3
Inishbofin Ireland 53°37N 10°13W **64** C1
Inisheer Ireland 53°3N 9°32W **64** C2
Inishfree B. Ireland 55°4N 8°23W **64** A3
Inishkea North Ireland 54°9N 10°11W **64** B1
Inishkea South Ireland 54°7N 10°12W **64** B1
Inishmaan Ireland 53°5N 9°35W **64** C2
Inishmore Ireland 53°8N 9°45W **64** C2
Inishmurray Ireland 54°26N 8°39W **64** B3
Inishowen Pen. Ireland 55°14N 7°15W **64** A4
Inishshark Ireland 53°37N 10°16W **64** C1
Inishturk Ireland 53°42N 10°7W **64** C1
Inishvickillane Ireland 52°3N 10°37W **64** D1
Injana Iraq 34°29N 44°38E **105** E11
Injinoo ◇ Australia 10°56S 142°15E **150** A3
Injune Australia 25°53S 148°32E **151** D4
Inklin → N. Amer. 58°50N 133°10W **162** B2
Inland Kaikoura Ra.
  N.Z. 41°59S 173°41E **155** B8
Inland Sea = Setonaikai
  Japan 34°20N 133°30E **113** G6
Inle L. Burma 20°30N 96°58E **123** J20
Inlet U.S.A. 43°45N 74°48W **175** C10
Inn → Austria 48°35N 13°28E **78** C6
Innamincka Australia 27°44S 140°46E **151** D3
Inner Hebrides U.K. 57°0N 6°30W **65** E2
Inner Mongolia = Nei Mongol
  Zizhiqu □ China 42°0N 112°0E **114** D7
Inner Sound U.K. 57°30N 5°55W **65** D3
Innerkip Canada 43°13N 80°42W **174** C4
Innes ◇ Australia 35°52S 136°53E **152** C2
Innetalling I. Canada 56°0N 79°0W **164** A4
Innisfail Australia 17°33S 146°5E **150** B4
Innisfail Canada 52°2N 113°57W **162** C6
In'noshima Japan 34°19N 133°10E **113** G6
Innop U.K. 57°2N 4°30W **65** D4
Innsbruck Austria 47°16N 11°23E **78** D4
Inny → Ireland 53°32N 7°51W **64** C4
Inongo
  Dem. Rep. of the Congo 1°55S 18°30E **140** E3
İnönü Turkey 39°48N 30°9E **99** B12
Inoucdjouac = Inukjuak
  Canada 58°25N 78°15W **161** F16
Inousses Greece 38°33N 26°14E **99** C8
Inowrocław Poland 52°50N 18°12E **83** F5
Inquisivi Bolivia 16°50S 67°10W **188** D4
Inscription, C.
  Australia 25°29S 112°59E **149** E1
Insein Burma 16°50N 96°5E **123** L20
Insjön Sweden 60°41N 15°5E **62** D9
Ínsko Poland 53°25N 15°32E **82** E2
İnsurăței Romania 44°50N 27°40E **81** F12
Inta Russia 66°5N 60°8E **106** C6
Intendente Alvear
  Argentina 35°12S 63°32W **190** D3
İntepe Turkey 40°1N 26°20E **99** A8
Interlachen U.S.A. 29°37N 81°53W **179** F8
Interlaken Switz. 46°41N 7°50E **77** J3
Interlaken U.S.A. 42°37N 76°44W **175** D8
International Falls
  U.S.A. 48°36N 93°25W **172** A7
Interview I. India 12°55N 92°43E **127** H11
Intiyaco Argentina 28°43S 60°5W **190** B3
Întorsura Buzăului
  Romania 45°41N 26°2E **81** E11
Inukjuak Canada 58°25N 78°15W **161** F16
Inútil, B. Chile 53°30S 70°15W **192** D2
Inuvik Canada 68°16N 133°40W **160** D5
Inveraray U.K. 56°14N 5°5W **65** E3
Inverbervie U.K. 56°51N 2°17W **65** E6
Invercargill N.Z. 46°24S 168°24E **155** G2
Inverclyde □ U.K. 55°55N 4°49W **65** F4
Invergordon U.K. 57°41N 4°10W **65** D4
Inverleigh Australia 38°6S 144°3E **152** E6
Inverloch Australia 38°38S 145°45E **151** F4
Inverloch Canada 50°30N 116°2W **162** C5
Inverness Canada 46°15N 61°19W **165** C7
Inverness U.K. 57°29N 4°13W **65** D4
Inverness Ala., U.S.A. 32°1N 85°45W **178** C4
Inverness Fla., U.S.A. 28°50N 82°20W **179** G7
Inverurie U.K. 57°17N 2°23W **65** D6
Investigator Group
  Australia 34°45S 134°20E **151** E1
Investigator Ridge
  Ind. Oc. 11°30S 98°10E **146** F8
Investigator Str.
  Australia 35°30S 137°0E **152** C2
Inya Russia 50°28N 86°37E **109** B11
Inyanga Zimbabwe 18°12S 32°40E **143** F3
Inyangani Zimbabwe 18°5S 32°50E **143** F3
Inyantue Zimbabwe 18°33S 26°39E **144** B4
Inyo Mts. U.S.A. 36°40N 118°0W **170** J9
Inyokern U.S.A. 35°39N 117°49W **171** K9
Inyonga Tanzania 6°45S 32°5E **142** D3
Inza Russia 53°55N 46°25E **86** D8
Inzhavino Russia 52°22N 42°30E **86** D6
Iñ-Jima Japan 30°48N 130°18E **113** J5
Ioannina Greece 39°42N 20°47E **98** B2
Iola U.S.A. 37°55N 95°24W **172** G6
Ion Corvin Romania 44°7N 27°50E **81** F12
Iona U.K. 56°20N 6°25W **65** E2
Ione U.S.A. 38°21N 120°56W **170** G6
Ionia U.S.A. 42°59N 85°4W **173** D11
Ionian Is. = Ionioi Nisoi
  Greece 38°40N 20°0E **98** C2
Ionian Sea Medit. S. 37°30N 17°30E **58** H9
Ionioi Nisoi Greece 38°40N 20°0E **98** C2
Ionioi Nisoi □ Greece 38°40N 20°0E **98** C2
Ios, Ostrov Russia 56°24N 143°22E **107** D15
Ios Greece 36°41N 25°20E **99** E7
Iowa □ U.S.A. 42°18N 93°30W **172** D7
Iowa → U.S.A. 41°10N 91°1W **172** E8
Iowa City U.S.A. 41°40N 91°32W **172** E8
Iowa Falls U.S.A. 42°31N 93°16W **172** D7
Iowa Park U.S.A. 33°57N 98°40W **176** E5
Ipala Tanzania 4°30S 32°52E **142** C3
Ipameri Brazil 17°44S 48°9W **189** E1
Ipanema Brazil 19°47S 41°44W **189** E2
Iparía Peru 9°17S 74°29W **188** B2
Ipati Greece 38°52N 22°14E **98** C4
Ipatinga Brazil 19°32S 42°30W **189** E2
Ipatovo Russia 45°45N 42°50E **87** H6
Ipel' → Europe 47°48N 18°53E **79** D11
Ipiales Colombia 0°50N 77°37W **186** C3
Ipiaú Brazil 14°8S 39°44W **189** D3

Ipin = Yibin China 28°45N 104°32E **116** C5
Ipirá Brazil 12°10S 39°44W **189** D3
Ipixuna Brazil 7°0S 71°40W **188** B3
Ipixuna → Brazil 7°11S 71°51W **188** B3
Ipoh Malaysia 4°35N 101°5E **121** K3
Ippy C.A.R. 6°5N 21°7E **140** C4
İpsala Turkey 40°55N 26°23E **97** F10
Ipsario, Oros Greece 40°40N 24°40E **97** F8
Ipswich Australia 27°35S 152°40E **151** D5
Ipswich U.K. 52°4N 1°10E **67** E9
Ipswich Mass., U.S.A. 42°41N 70°50W **175** D14
Ipswich S. Dak., U.S.A. 45°27N 99°2W **172** C4
Ipu Brazil 4°23S 40°44W **189** A2
Ipueiras Brazil 4°33S 40°43W **189** A2
Ipupiara Brazil 11°49S 42°37W **189** C2
Iqaluit Canada 63°44N 68°31W **161** E18
Iqaluktuutiaq = Cambridge Bay
  Canada 69°10N 105°0W **160** D10
Iquique Chile 20°19S 70°5W **188** E3
Iquitos Peru 3°45S 73°10W **186** D4
Irabu-Jima Japan 24°50N 125°10E **113** M2
Iracoubo Fr. Guiana 5°30N 53°10W **187** B8
Irafshān Iran 26°42N 61°56E **129** E9
Iraklia Cyclades, Greece 36°50N 25°28E **99** E7
Iraklia Serres, Greece 41°10N 23°16E **96** C7
Iraklio Greece 35°20N 25°12E **101** D7
Iráklion = Iraklio
  Greece 35°20N 25°12E **101** D7
Irakliou, Kolpos Greece 35°23N 25°8E **101** D7
Irala Paraguay 25°55S 54°35W **191** B5
Iran ■ Asia 33°0N 53°0E **129** C7
Iran, Pegunungan
  Malaysia 2°20N 114°50E **118** D4
Iran Ra. = Iran, Pegunungan
  Malaysia 2°20N 114°50E **118** D4
Iranamadu Tank
  Sri Lanka 9°23N 80°29E **127** K5
Īrānshahr Iran 27°15N 60°40E **129** E9
Irapuato Mexico 20°41N 101°28W **180** C4
Iraq ■ Asia 33°0N 44°0E **105** F10
Irati Brazil 25°25S 50°38W **191** B5
Irazú, Volcan Costa Rica 9°59N 83°51W **182** D3
Irbes saurums Latvia 57°45N 22°5E **82** A9
Irbid Jordan 32°35N 35°48E **130** C4
Irbid □ Jordan 32°30N 35°50E **130** C5
Irbil = Arbil Iraq 36°15N 44°5E **105** D11
Irebu
  Dem. Rep. of the Congo 0°40S 17°46E **140** E3
Irecê Brazil 11°18S 41°52W **189** C2
Iregua → Spain 42°27N 2°24E **90** C7
Ireland ■ Europe 53°50N 7°52W **64** C4
Irele Nigeria 7°40N 5°40E **139** D6
Irgiz = Yrghyz
  Kazakhstan 48°37N 61°16E **108** C7
Irgiz = Yrghyz →
  Kazakhstan 48°6N 62°30E **108** C6
Irgiz, Bolshaya →
  Russia 52°10N 49°10E **86** D9
Irharrar, O. → Algeria 28°3N 6°15E **136** C5
Irherm Morocco 30°7N 8°18W **136** B2
Irhil M'Goun Morocco 31°30N 6°28W **136** B2
Iri = Iksan S. Korea 35°59N 127°0E **115** G14
Irian Jaya = Papua □
  Indonesia 4°0S 137°0E **119** E9
Irian Jaya Barat □
  Indonesia 2°5S 132°50E **119** E8
Irié Guinea 8°15N 9°10W **138** D3
Iriklinskoye Vdkhr.
  Russia 52°0N 59°0E **108** B5
Iringa Tanzania 7°48S 35°43E **142** D4
Iringa □ Tanzania 7°48S 35°43E **142** D4
Irinjalakuda India 10°21N 76°14E **127** J3
Iriomote ◇ Japan 24°26S 123°52E **113** M1
Iriomote-Jima Japan 24°19N 123°48E **113** M1
Iriona Honduras 15°57N 85°11W **182** C2
Iriri → Brazil 3°52S 52°37W **187** D8
Irish Sea Europe 53°38N 4°48W **66** D3
Irkeshtam Pass = Erkech-Tam
  Pass Asia 39°46N 74°2E **109** E8
Irkutsk Russia 52°18N 104°20E **110** D11
Irlanganj Turkey 37°53N 29°9E **99** D11
Irma Canada 52°55N 111°14W **163** C6
Irō-Zaki Japan 34°36N 138°51E **113** G9
Iroise, Mer d' France 48°15N 4°45W **70** D2
Iron Baron Australia 32°58S 137°11E **152** B2
Iron Gate = Portile de Fier
  Europe 44°44N 22°30E **80** F7
Iron Knob Australia 32°46S 137°8E **152** B2
Iron Mountain U.S.A. 45°49N 88°4W **172** C9
Iron Range △
  Australia 12°34S 143°18E **150** A3
Iron River U.S.A. 46°6N 88°39W **172** B9
Irondequoit U.S.A. 43°13N 77°35W **174** C7
Ironton Mo., U.S.A. 37°36N 90°38W **172** G8
Ironton Ohio, U.S.A. 38°32N 82°41W **173** F13
Ironwood U.S.A. 46°27N 90°9W **172** B8
Ironwood Forest ◇
  U.S.A. 32°30N 111°28W **169** K8
Iroquois Canada 44°51N 75°19W **175** B9
Iroquois Falls Canada 48°46N 80°41W **164** C3
Irpin Ukraine 50°30N 30°15E **75** C16
Irrara Cr. → Australia 29°35S 145°31E **151** D4
Irrawaddy □ Burma 17°0N 95°0E **123** L19
Irrawaddy → Burma 15°50N 95°6E **123** M19
Irrawaddy, Mouths of the
  Burma 15°30N 95°0E **123** M19
Irricana Canada 51°19N 113°37W **162** C6
Irrunytju Australia 26°3S 128°56E **149** E4
Irshava Ukraine 48°19N 23°9E **80** B8
Irsina Italy 40°45N 16°14E **95** B9
Irtysh → Russia 61°4N 68°52E **106** C7
Irumu
  Dem. Rep. of the Congo 1°32N 29°53E **142** B2
Irún Spain 43°20N 1°52W **90** B3
Irunea = Pamplona-Iruña
  Spain 42°48N 1°38W **90** C3
Irurzun Spain 42°55N 1°50W **90** C3
Irvine Canada 49°57N 110°16W **163** D6
Irvine U.K. 55°37N 4°41W **65** F4
Irvine Calif., U.S.A. 33°41N 117°46W **179** B5
Irvine Ky., U.S.A. 37°42N 83°58W **173** G12
Irving U.S.A. 32°48N 96°56W **176** E6
Irvona U.S.A. 40°46N 78°33W **174** F6
Irwin → Australia 29°15S 114°54E **149** E1
Irwin U.S.A. 40°19N 79°42W **174** F5
Irymple Australia 34°14S 142°8E **152** C5
Is, Jebel Sudan 22°8N 35°9E **137** D4
Is-sur-Tille France 47°30N 5°8E **71** E12
Isa Nigeria 13°14N 6°24E **139** C6

Isa Khel Pakistan 32°41N 71°17E **124** C4
Isaac → Australia 22°55S 149°20E **150** C4
Isabel U.S.A. 45°24N 101°26W **172** C3
Isabel, I. Mexico 21°51N 105°55W **180** C3
Isabela Phil. 6°40N 121°59E **119** C6
Isabela Puerto Rico 18°30N 67°2W **183** d
Isabela, Cord. Nic. 13°30N 85°25W **182** D2
Isabella Ra. Australia 21°0S 121°4E **148** D3
Isaccea Romania 45°16N 28°28E **81** E13
Isachsen, C. Canada 79°20N 105°28W **161** B10
Isachsen Mt. Antarctica 72°8S 26°5E **55** D4
İşafjarðardjúp Iceland 66°10N 23°0W **60** C2
İşafjörður Iceland 66°5N 23°9W **60** C2
Isagarh India 24°48N 77°51E **124** G7
Isahaya Japan 32°52N 130°2E **113** H5
Isaka Tanzania 3°56S 32°59E **142** C3
İşalnița Romania 44°24N 23°44E **81** F8
Isan → India 26°51N 80°7E **125** F9
Isana = Içana → Brazil 0°26N 67°19W **186** C5
Isangano □ Zambia 11°8S 30°35E **143** E3
Isanlu Makutu Nigeria 8°20N 5°50E **139** D6
Isar → Germany 48°48N 12°57E **77** G8
Isarco → Italy 46°27N 11°18E **93** B8
Ísaris Greece 37°22N 22°0E **98** D3
İscar Spain 41°22N 4°32W **88** D6
Iscehisar Turkey 38°51N 30°45E **99** C12
Ischia Italy 40°44N 13°57E **94** B6
Ischigualasto △
  Argentina 30°0S 68°0W **190** B2
Isdell → Australia 16°27S 124°51E **148** C3
Ise Japan 34°25N 136°45E **113** G8
Ise-Shima △ Japan 34°25N 136°48E **113** G8
Ise-Wan Japan 34°43N 136°43E **113** G8
Isefjord Denmark 55°53N 11°50E **63** J5
Isel → Austria 46°50N 12°47E **78** E5
Iseo Italy 45°39N 10°3E **92** C7
Iseo, L. d' Italy 45°43N 10°4E **92** C7
Iseramagazi Tanzania 4°37S 32°10E **142** C3
Isère □ France 44°59N 4°51E **73** D8
Isère → France 51°22N 7°41E **76** D3
Isérnia Italy 41°36N 14°14E **95** A7
Iseyin Nigeria 8°0N 3°36E **139** D5
Isfahan = Eşfahān Iran 32°39N 51°43E **129** C6
Ishëm Albania 41°33N 19°34E **98** A1
Ishigaki Japan 24°26N 124°10E **113** M2
Ishigaki-Shima Japan 24°20N 124°10E **113** M2
Ishikari → Japan 43°20N 141°15E **112** C10
Ishikari-Gawa →
  Japan 43°15N 141°23E **112** C10
Ishikari-Sammyaku
  Japan 43°30N 143°0E **112** C11
Ishikari-Wan Japan 43°25N 141°1E **112** C10
Ishikawa □ Japan 36°30N 136°30E **113** F8
Ishim → Russia 56°10N 69°30E **106** D7
Ishim Russia 56°10N 69°30E **106** D7
Ishimbay Russia 53°28N 56°2E **108** B5
Ishinomaki Japan 38°32N 141°20E **112** E10
Ishioka Japan 36°11N 140°16E **113** F10
Ishkashim Tajikistan 36°44N 71°37E **109** E8
Ishkoman Pakistan 36°30N 73°50E **125** A5
Ishpeming U.S.A. 46°29N 87°40W **172** B10
Isigny-sur-Mer France 49°19N 1°6W **70** C5
Isıklar Daği Turkey 40°45N 27°15E **97** F11
Işıklı Turkey 38°19N 29°51E **99** C11
Isil Kul Russia 54°55N 71°16E **109** B8
İsili Italy 39°44N 9°6E **94** C2
iSimangaliso △
  S. Africa 27°50S 32°32E **145** C5
Isiolo Kenya 0°24N 37°33E **142** B4
Isiolo □ Kenya 1°0N 37°30E **142** B4
Isiro
  Dem. Rep. of the Congo 2°53N 27°40E **142** B2
Isisford Australia 24°15S 144°21E **150** C3
İskele = Trikomo
  Cyprus 35°17N 33°52E **101** D12
İskenderun Turkey 36°32N 36°10E **104** D7
İskenderun Körfezi
  Turkey 36°40N 35°50E **104** D6
İskilip Turkey 40°45N 34°29E **104** B6
Iskitim Russia 54°38N 83°18E **109** D10
Iskür → Bulgaria 43°45N 24°25E **98** C8
Iskür, Yazovir Bulgaria 42°23N 23°30E **96** D7
Iskut → Canada 56°45N 131°49W **162** B2
Isla → U.K. 56°32N 3°20W **65** E5
Isla Coiba △ Panama 7°33N 81°36W **182** E3
Isla Cristina Spain 37°13N 7°17W **89** H3
Isla de Salamanca △
  Colombia 10°59N 74°40W **183** D5
Isla Gorge △ Australia 25°10S 149°57E **150** C4
Isla Guamblin △ Chile 44°50S 75°4W **192** B1
Isla Isabel △ Mexico 21°54N 105°58W **180** C3
Isla Magdalena △
  Chile 44°25S 73°13W **192** B2
Isla Tiburón y San Esteban △
  Mexico 29°0N 112°27W **180** B2
Isla Vista U.S.A. 34°25N 119°53W **171** L7
İslahiye Turkey 37°0N 36°35E **104** D7
Islam Headworks
  Pakistan 29°49N 72°33E **124** E5
Islamabad Pakistan 33°40N 73°10E **124** C5
Islamgarh Pakistan 27°51N 70°48E **124** F4
Islamkot Pakistan 24°42N 70°13E **124** G4
Islamorada U.S.A. 24°55N 80°37W **179** L9
Islampur Bihar, India 25°9N 85°12E **125** G11
Islampur Maharashtra,
  India 17°2N 74°20E **126** F2
Islampur Paschimbanga,
  India 26°16N 88°12E **125** F13
Island = Iceland ■
  Europe 64°45N 19°0W **60** D4
Island L. Canada 53°47N 94°25W **163** C10
Island Lagoon
  Australia 31°30S 136°40E **152** A2
Island Pond U.S.A. 44°49N 71°53W **175** B13
Islands, B. of Canada 49°11N 58°15W **165** C8
Islands, B. of N.Z. 35°15S 174°6E **154** B5
Islas Atlánticas de Galicia △
  Spain 42°23N 8°55W **88** C2
Islay U.K. 55°46N 6°10W **65** F2
Isle → France 44°55N 0°15W **72** D3
Isle aux Morts Canada 47°35N 59°0W **165** C8
Isle of Hope U.S.A. 31°58N 81°5W **178** E8
Isle of Wight □ U.K. 50°41N 1°17W **67** G6
Isle Royale △ U.S.A. 48°0N 88°55W **172** A9
Isleton U.S.A. 38°10N 121°37W **170** G5
Ismail = Izmayil
  Ukraine 45°22N 28°46E **81** F13
Ismâ'ilîya Egypt 30°37N 32°18E **137** B6
Ismaning Germany 48°14N 11°40E **77** G7
Isna Egypt 25°17N 32°30E **137** D4

Isojärvi △ Finland 61°40N 25°0E **60** F21
Ísola del Liri Italy 41°41N 13°34E **93** G10
Ísola della Scala Italy 45°16N 11°0E **92** C7
Ísola di Capo Rizzuto
  Italy 38°58N 17°6E **95** D10
Isparta Turkey 37°47N 30°30E **99** D12
Isperih Bulgaria 43°43N 26°50E **97** C12
İspica Italy 36°47N 14°55E **95** F7
İspir Turkey 40°28N 40°59E **105** B9
Israel ■ Asia 32°0N 34°50E **130** D3
Ivalojoki → Finland 68°40N 27°40E **62** C9
Ivanava Belarus 52°7N 25°29E **75** C15
Ivănești Romania 46°39N 27°27E **81** D12
Ivangorod Russia 59°27N 28°13E **62** C15
İsțálós-ko Hungary 48°4N 20°26E **80** B5
İstanbul Turkey 41°0N 28°58E **97** F12
İstanbul □ Turkey 41°0N 29°0E **97** E12
İstanbul ✈ (IST) Turkey 40°59N 28°49E **97** F12
İstanbul Boğazı Turkey 41°10N 29°10E **97** E13
Istaravshan Tajikistan 39°55N 69°1E **109** E7
Istiea Greece 38°57N 23°9E **98** C5
Isto, Mt. U.S.A. 69°12N 143°48W **166** B11
Istok = Burim Kosovo 42°45N 20°24E **96** D4
Istokpoga, L. U.S.A. 27°23N 81°17W **179** H8
Istra Croatia 45°10N 14°0E **93** C10
Istres France 43°31N 4°59E **73** E8
Istria = Istra Croatia 45°10N 14°0E **93** C10
Itá Paraguay 25°29S 57°21W **190** B4
Itabaiana Paraíba, Brazil 7°18S 35°19W **189** B3
Itabaiana Sergipe,
  Brazil 10°41S 37°37W **189** C3
Itabaianinha Brazil 11°16S 37°47W **189** C3
Itaberaba Brazil 12°32S 40°18W **189** D2
Itabira Brazil 19°37S 43°13W **189** D2
Itabirito Brazil 20°15S 43°48W **189** E2
Itabuna Brazil 14°48S 39°16W **189** D3
Itacajá Brazil 8°19S 47°46W **189** B1
Itacaunas → Brazil 5°21S 49°8W **187** E9
Itacoatiara Brazil 3°8S 58°25W **186** D7
Itaguaí Brazil 22°15S 43°46W **189** E2
Itaguari → Brazil 14°11S 44°40W **189** C2
Itaguatins Brazil 5°47S 47°29W **189** B1
Itaim → Brazil 7°2S 42°9W **189** B2
Itainópolis Brazil 7°35S 41°31W **189** B2
Itaipú, Represa de
  Brazil 25°30S 54°30W **191** B5
Itaituba Brazil 4°10S 55°50W **187** D7
Itajaí Brazil 27°50S 48°39W **191** B6
Itajubá Brazil 22°24S 45°30W **191** A6
Itajuípe Brazil 14°41S 39°22W **189** D3
Itala △ S. Africa 27°30S 31°7E **145** D5
Itala □ Italy 42°0N 13°0E **59** G8
Italy ■ Europe 42°0N 13°0E **59** G8
Itamaraju Brazil 17°5S 39°8W **189** E3
Itamarati Brazil 6°24S 68°15W **186** B4
Itamataré Brazil 2°16S 46°24W **189** A1
Itambacuri Brazil 18°1S 41°42W **189** E2
Itambé Brazil 15°15S 40°37W **189** E2
Itanhém Brazil 17°9S 40°20W **189** E2
Itapagé Brazil 3°40S 39°30W **189** A2
Itaparica, I. de Brazil 12°54S 38°42W **189** D3
Itaparica, Represa de
  Brazil 11°3S 42°47W **189** C2
Itapebi Brazil 15°56S 39°32W **189** D3
Itapecuru Mirim Brazil 3°24S 44°20W **189** A2
Itaperuna Brazil 21°10S 41°54W **189** E2
Itapetinga Brazil 15°15S 40°15W **189** D2
Itapetininga Brazil 23°36S 48°7W **191** A6
Itapeva Brazil 23°59S 48°59W **191** A6
Itapicuru → Bahia,
  Brazil 11°47S 37°32W **189** C3
Itapicuru → Maranhão,
  Brazil 2°52S 44°12W **189** A2
Itapipoca Brazil 3°30S 39°35W **189** A3
Itapiúna Brazil 4°33S 38°57W **189** A3
Itapuá □ Paraguay 26°40S 55°40W **191** B4
Itaquí Maranhão, Brazil 2°34S 44°22W **189** A2
Itaquí Rio Grande do S.,
  Brazil 29°8S 56°30W **190** B4
Itararé Brazil 24°6S 49°23W **191** A6
Itarsi India 22°36N 77°51E **124** H7
Itati Argentina 27°16S 58°15W **190** B4
Itatiaia △ Brazil 22°30S 44°35W **191** A7
Itatira Brazil 4°30S 39°37W **189** A3
Itaueira Brazil 7°36S 43°2W **189** B2
Itaueira → Brazil 6°41S 42°54W **189** B2
Itaúna Brazil 20°4S 44°34W **189** E2
Itbayat Phil. 20°45N 121°50E **113** H11
Itchen → U.K. 50°55N 1°22W **67** G6
Itcha Ilgachuz △
  Canada 52°42N 124°58W **162** C3
Ite Peru 17°55S 70°57W **188** D3
Itezhi Tezhi, L. Zambia 15°30S 25°30E **143** F2
Ithaca = Ithaki Greece 38°25N 20°40E **98** C2
Ithaca U.S.A. 42°27N 76°30W **175** D8
Ithaki Greece 38°25N 20°40E **98** C2
Iti △ Greece 38°47N 22°16E **98** C4
Itinga Brazil 16°36S 41°47W **189** E2
Itiquira → Brazil 17°18S 56°44W **187** G7
Itiruçu Brazil 13°31S 40°9W **189** D2
Itiúba Brazil 10°43S 39°51W **189** D3
Ityuro → Argentina 22°50S 63°50W **190** A3
Itō Japan 34°58N 139°5E **113** G9
Iton → France 49°9N 1°12E **70** C8
Itoigawa Japan 37°5N 137°51E **113** F8
Itonamas → Bolivia 12°28S 64°24E **186** F6
Itri Italy 41°17N 13°32E **94** A6
Itsa Egypt 29°15N 30°47E **137** C7
Ittoqqortoormiit
  Greenland 70°20N 23°0W **57** C6
Itu Brazil 23°17S 47°15W **191** A6
Itu Aba I. S. China Sea 10°23N 114°21E **118** B4
Itu → Nigeria 5°10N 7°58E **138** D2
Ituaçu Brazil 13°50S 41°18W **189** D2
Ituiutaba Brazil 19°0S 49°25W **189** E1
Itumbiara Brazil 18°20S 49°10W **189** E1
Ituna Canada 51°10N 103°24W **163** C8
Itunge Port Tanzania 9°40S 33°55E **143** D3
Iturbe Argentina 23°0S 65°25W **190** A2
Iturup, Ostrov Russia 45°0N 148°0E **107** E15
Itxassou France 43°20N 1°24W **72** E3
Iuka U.S.A. 34°49N 88°11W **177** D11

Ituri
  Dem. Rep. of the Congo 2°30N 29°30E **14**
Ituri →
  Dem. Rep. of the Congo 1°40N 27°1E **14**
Iturama Brazil 19°44S 50°13W **18**
Iturbide Mexico 24°43N 99°53W **18**
Ituverava Brazil 20°20S 47°47W **18**
Ituxi → Brazil 7°18S 64°51W **18**
Itzehoe Germany 53°55N 9°31E **7**
Ivaí → Brazil 23°18S 53°42W **19**
Ivalo Finland 68°38N 27°35E **6**
Ivalojoki → Finland 68°40N 27°40E **6**
Ivanava Belarus 52°7N 25°29E **7**
Ivanhoe N.S.W.,
  Australia 32°56S 144°20E **15**
Ivanhoe Vic., Australia 37°45S 145°3E **15**
Ivanhoe Calif., U.S.A. 36°23N 119°13W **17**
Ivanhoe Minn., U.S.A. 44°28N 96°15W **17**
Ivanhorod Ukraine 48°48N 29°50E **8**
Ivanić Grad Croatia 45°41N 16°25E **9**
Ivanjica Serbia 43°35N 20°12E **9**
Ivanjska Bos.-H. 44°55N 17°4E **9**
Ivankoyskoye Vdkhr.
  Russia 56°37N 36°32E **8**
Ivano-Frankivsk
  Ukraine 48°40N 24°40E **8**
Ivano-Frankivsk □
  Ukraine 48°45N 24°30E **8**
Ivanovo = Ivanava
  Belarus 52°7N 25°29E **7**
Ivanovo Bulgaria 43°43N 25°58E **9**
Ivanovo Russia 57°5N 41°0E **8**
Ivanovo □ Russia 57°10N 41°0E **8**
Ivanščica Croatia 46°12N 16°13E **9**
Ivatsevichy Belarus 52°43N 25°21E **7**
Ivaylovgrad Bulgaria 41°32N 26°8E **9**
Iveragh Pen. Ireland 51°52N 10°15W **6**
Ivinheima → Brazil 23°14S 53°42W **19**
Ivinhema Brazil 22°10S 53°37W **19**
Iviittuut Greenland 61°14N 48°12W **5**
Ivohibe Madag. 22°31S 46°57E **14**
Ivory Coast W. Afr. 4°20N 5°0W **13**
Ivory Coast ■ Africa 7°30N 5°0W **13**
Ivösjön Sweden 56°8N 14°25E **6**
Ivrea Italy 45°28N 7°52E **9**
İvrindi Turkey 39°34N 27°30E **9**
Ivujivik Canada 62°24N 77°55W **16**
Ivvavik △ Canada 69°10N 139°30W **16**
Ivybridge U.K. 50°23N 3°56W **6**
Iwaizumi Japan 39°50N 141°45E **11**
Iwaki Japan 37°3N 140°55E **11**
Iwakuni Japan 34°15N 132°8E **11**
Iwamizawa Japan 43°12N 141°46E **11**
Iwanai Japan 42°58N 140°30E **11**
Iwata Japan 34°42N 137°51E **11**
Iwate □ Japan 39°30N 141°30E **11**
Iwate-San Japan 39°51N 141°0E **11**
Iwo Nigeria 7°39N 4°9E **13**
Iwŏn N. Korea 40°19N 128°39E **11**
Iwonicz-Zdrój Poland 49°37N 21°47E **8**
Ixiamas Bolivia 13°50S 68°5W **18**
Ixopo S. Africa 30°11S 30°5E **14**
Ixtepec Mexico 16°34N 95°6W **18**
Ixtlán del Río Mexico 21°2N 104°22W **18**
Iyo Japan 33°45N 132°45E **11**
Izabal, L. de Guatemala 15°30N 89°10W **18**
Izamal Mexico 20°56N 89°1W **18**
Izberbash Russia 42°35N 47°52E **8**
Izbica Poland 50°53N 23°10E **8**
Izbica Kujawska Poland 52°25N 18°40E **8**
Izbiceni Romania 43°45N 24°40E **8**
Izena-Shima Japan 26°56N 127°56E **11**
Izgrev Bulgaria 43°36N 26°58E **9**
Izhevsk Russia 56°51N 53°14E **8**
Izmayil Ukraine 45°22N 28°46E **8**
İzmir Turkey 38°25N 27°8E **9**
İzmir Adnan Menderes ✈ (ADB)
  Turkey 38°23N 27°6E **9**
İzmir Körfezi Turkey 38°30N 26°50E **9**
İzmit = Kocaeli Turkey 40°45N 29°50E **9**
İznájar Spain 37°15N 4°19W **8**
İznalloz Spain 37°24N 3°30W **8**
İznik Turkey 40°27N 29°30E **9**
İznik Gölü Turkey 40°27N 29°30E **9**
Izobil'nyy Russia 45°25N 41°44E **8**
Izola Slovenia 45°32N 13°39E **9**
Izra Syria 32°51N 36°15E **13**
Iztochni Rodopi Bulgaria 41°45N 25°30E **9**
Izu-Hantō Japan 34°45N 139°0E **11**
Izu-Shotō Japan 34°30N 140°0E **11**
Izúcar de Matamoros
  Mexico 18°36N 98°28W **18**
Izumi Japan 32°5N 130°22E **11**
Izumi-Sano Japan 34°23N 135°18E **11**
Izumo Japan 35°20N 132°46E **11**
Izyaslav Ukraine 50°5N 26°50E **7**
Izyum Ukraine 49°12N 37°19E **8**

J

J.F.K. Int. ✈ (JFK)
  U.S.A. 40°38N 73°47W **17**
J.P. Koch Fjord Greenland 82°45N 44°0W **5**
J. Strom Thurmond L.
  U.S.A. 33°40N 82°12W **17**
Ja-ela Sri Lanka 7°5N 79°53E **12**
Jabalón → Spain 38°53N 4°5W **8**
Jabalpur India 23°9N 79°58E **12**
Jabālya Gaza Strip 31°32N 34°27E **13**
Jabbūl Syria 36°4N 37°30E **13**
Jabiru Australia 12°40S 132°53E **15**
Jablah Syria 35°20N 36°0E **13**
Jablanac Croatia 44°42N 14°56E **9**
Jablanica Bos.-H. 43°40N 17°45E **9**
Jablonec nad Nisou
  Czech Rep. 50°43N 15°10E **8**
Jablonowo Pomorskie
  Poland 53°23N 19°10E **8**
Jablunkov Czech Rep. 49°35N 18°46E **8**
Jaboatão Brazil 8°7S 35°1W **18**
Jaboatão = Jakarta
  Indonesia 6°9S 106°52E **11**
Jaboticabal Brazil 21°15S 48°17W **19**
Jabukovac Serbia 44°22N 22°21E **8**
Jaca Spain 42°35N 0°33W **9**
Jacaré → Brazil 10°3S 42°23W **18**
Jacaré → Brazil 10°3S 42°23W **18**

reí Brazil 23°20S 46°0W 191 A6
arêzinho Brazil 23°5S 49°58W 191 A6
nto Brazil 16°10S 40°17W 189 D2
River △ Australia 14°58S 144°19E 150 A3
man U.S.A. 45°37N 70°15W 173 C18
sboro U.S.A. 33°13N 98°10W 176 E5
son Barbados 13°7N 59°36W 183 d
son Ala., U.S.A. 31°31N 87°53W 177 F11
son Calif., U.S.A. 38°21N 120°46W 170 G6
son Ga., U.S.A. 33°20N 83°57W 178 B6
son Ky., U.S.A. 37°33N 83°23W 173 G4
son Mich., U.S.A. 42°15N 84°24W 173 D11
son Minn., U.S.A. 43°37N 95°1W 172 D6
son Miss., U.S.A. 32°18N 90°12W 177 E9
son Mo., U.S.A. 38°25N 89°40W 172 G9
son N.H., U.S.A. 44°10N 71°11W 175 B13
son Ohio, U.S.A. 39°3N 82°39W 173 F12
son S.C., U.S.A. 33°20N 81°47W 178 D6
son Tenn., U.S.A. 35°37N 88°49W 177 D10
son Wyo., U.S.A. 43°29N 110°46W 168 E8
son, C., N.Z. 40°59S 174°20E 155 A9
son B. N.Z. 43°58S 168°42E 155 D3
son Hd. N.Z. 43°58S 168°37E 155 D3
son L. Fla., U.S.A. 30°30N 84°17W 178 E5
son L. Wyo., ...S.A. 43°52N 110°36W 168 E8
sons N.Z. 42°46S 171°32E 155 C6
son's Arm Canada 49°52N 56°47W 165 C8
sonville Ark., ...S.A. 35°49N 85°46W 178 B4
sonville Calif., ...S.A. 34°52N 92°7W 176 D8
sonville Fla., ...S.A. 37°52N 120°24W 170 H6
sonville Ga., ...S.A. 30°20N 81°39W 178 E8
sonville Ill., U.S.A. 39°44N 90°14W 172 F8
sonville N.C., ...S.A. 34°45N 77°26W 177 D16
sonville Tex., ...S.A. 31°58N 95°17W 176 F7
sonville Beach ...S.A. 30°17N 81°24W 178 E8
sonville Int. ✈ (JAX) ...S.A. 30°30N 81°41W 178 E8
nel Haiti 18°14N 72°32W 183 C5
b Lake U.S.A. 36°43N 112°13W 169 H7
babad Pakistan 28°20N 68°29E 124 E3
bina Brazil 11°11S 40°30W 189 C2
ques-Cartier, Dét. de Canada 50°0N 63°30W 165 C7
ques-Cartier, Mt. Canada 48°57N 66°0W 165 C6
ques-Cartier ○ Canada 47°15N 71°33W 165 C5
queville Ivory C. 5°12N 4°25W 138 D4
ai → Brazil 30°2S 51°15W 191 C5
mba U.S.A. 32°37N 116°11W 171 N10
ndá → Brazil 1°57S 50°26W 187 D8
herla India 16°46N 78°9E 126 F4
 Germany 53°20N 8°4E 76 B4
, Côte de France 46°40N 2°0W 70 F4
 City Canada 51°29N 129°37W 162 B3
 Dragon Snow Mt. = Yulong
ueshan China 27°6N 100°10E 116 D3
 Mt. = Yü Shan Taiwan 23°25N 120°52E 117 F13
busen Germany 53°29N 8°12E 76 B4
ovnik Serbia 43°20N 19°45E 96 C3
aque Spain 40°55N 2°55W 90 E2
 Peru 5°25S 78°40W 188 B2
 Spain 37°44N 3°43W 89 H7
 Spain 37°50N 3°30W 89 H7
rabad India 20°52N 71°22E 124 J4
 is = Tel Aviv-Yafo Israel 32°4N 34°48E 130 C3
, C. Australia 36°58S 139°40E 152 D3
na Sri Lanka 9°45N 80°2E 127 K5
ey U.S.A. 42°49N 72°2W 175 D12
dhri India 30°10N 77°20E 124 D7
dishpur India 25°30N 84°21E 125 G11
t Nepal 28°19N 84°53E 125 E11
dalpur India 19°30N 82°0E 126 E6
laqi China 50°25N 124°7E 111 A13
rsfontein S. Africa 29°44S 25°27E 144 C4
ñn → Iran 27°17N 53°13E 128 E4
odina Serbia 44°5N 21°15E 96 B5
st → Germany 50°50N 75°25E 124 D6
 Germany 49°14N 9°10E 77 F5
ial India 18°50N 79°0E 126 E4
aquara Brazil 13°32S 39°58W 189 C3
ariaíva Brazil 24°10S 49°50W 191 A6
aribe Brazil 5°53S 38°37W 189 A3
aribe → Brazil 4°25S 37°45W 189 A3
aruana Brazil 4°50S 37°47W 189 A3
ey Grande Cuba 22°35N 81°7W 182 B3
nabad India 25°13N 84°59E 125 G11
anabad India 25°37N 75°17E 124 G6
zwari Pakistan 28°30N 53°31E 128 D7
rom Iran 28°30N 53°31E 128 D7
ós Brazil 7°21S 41°8W 189 B2
arh India 17°17N 73°13E 126 F1
o India 31°21N 76°9E 124 D7
olo Indonesia 1°5N 127°30E 119 D7
olo, Selat Indonesia 0°5N 129°5E 119 D7
almer India 26°15N 81°32E 125 F9
inghnagar India 23°38N 78°34E 125 H8
aran India 12°26N 73°56E 124 F5
hari India 25°38N 83°3E 125 H8
rkot Nepal 28°42N 82°14E 125 E10
 Bos.-H. 44°19N 17°17E 80 F2
um → India 23°54N 74°13E 124 H6
am → India 23°5S 45°59W 191 A6
arta Sukarno-Hatta Int. ✈
 (CGK) Indonesia 6°7S 106°40E 119 G12
hal India 29°40N 80°52E 124 D7
ihau India 23°11N 68°43E 124 H3
 India 28°42N 82°14E 125 E10
 Bos.-H. 44°19N 17°17E 80 F2
upica Macedonia 41°43N 21°22E 96 E5
jil Si. Arabia 27°37N 103°12W 169 K12
jil Si. Arabia 25°40N 45°27E 128 E5
 Abad Kyrgyzstan 40°56N 73°0E 109 D8

Jalal-Abad □
 Kyrgyzstan 41°30N 72°30E 109 D8
Jalālābād Afghan. 34°30N 70°29E 124 B4
Jalalabad India 27°41N 79°42E 125 F8
Jalalpur Jattan Pakistan 32°38N 74°11E 124 C6
Jalama U.S.A. 34°29N 120°29W 171 L6
Jalandhar India 31°20N 75°40E 124 D6
Jalapa Guatemala 14°39N 89°59W 182 D2
Jalapa Enríquez = Xalapa
 Mexico 19°32N 96°55W 181 D5
Jalasjärvi Finland 62°29N 22°47E 60 E20
Jalaun India 26°8N 79°25E 125 F8
Jaldhaka → Bangla. 26°16N 89°16E 125 F13
Jalesar India 27°29N 78°19E 124 F8
Jaleswar Nepal 26°38N 85°48E 125 F11
Jalgaon India 21°0N 75°42E 126 D2
Jalibah Iraq 30°35N 46°32E 128 D5
Jalingo Nigeria 8°55N 11°25E 139 D7
Jalisco □ Mexico 20°20N 103°40W 180 D4
Jalkot Pakistan 35°14N 73°24E 125 B5
Jalna India 19°48N 75°38E 126 E2
Jalón → Spain 41°47N 1°4W 90 D3
Jalor India 25°21N 72°37E 124 G5
Jalpa Mexico 21°38N 102°58W 180 C4
Jalpaiguri India 26°32N 88°46E 123 F16
Jalpan Mexico 21°14N 99°29W 181 C5
Jaluit I. Marshall Is. 6°0N 169°30E 156 G8
Jalūlā Iraq 34°16N 45°10E 105 E11
Jamaame Somalia 0°4N 42°44E 131 G3
Jamaari Nigeria 11°44N 9°53E 139 C6
Jamaica ■ W. Indies 18°10N 77°30W 182 a
Jamalpur Bangla. 24°52N 89°56E 125 G16
Jamalpur India 25°18N 86°28E 125 G12
Jamalpurganj India 23°2N 87°59E 125 H13
Jamanxim → Brazil 4°43S 56°18W 187 D7
Jambewangi Indonesia 8°17S 114°7E 119 K18
Jambi Indonesia 1°38S 103°30E 118 E2
Jambi □ Indonesia 1°30S 102°30E 118 E2
Jambongan, Pulau
 Malaysia 6°45N 117°20E 118 C5
Jambusar India 22°3N 72°51E 124 H5
James → U.S.A. 32°58N 83°29W 178 C6
James → S. Dak.,
 U.S.A. 42°52N 97°18W 172 D5
James → Va., U.S.A. 36°56N 76°27W 173 G15
James B. Canada 54°0N 80°0W 164 B3
James I. Gambia 13°19N 16°21W 138 C1
James Island U.S.A. 32°45N 79°55W 178 C10
James → N. Dak.,
 U.S.A. 46°54N 98°42W 172 B4
Jamestown N.Y., U.S.A. 42°6N 79°14W 174 D5
Jamestown Pa., U.S.A. 41°29N 80°27W 174 E4
Jamestown S.C.,
 U.S.A. 33°17N 79°42W 178 B10
Jamīlābād Iran 34°24N 48°28E 129 C6
Jamira → India 21°35N 88°28E 125 H13
Jämjö Sweden 56°12N 15°49E 63 H9
Jamkhandi India 16°30N 75°15E 126 F2
Jamkhed India 18°43N 75°19E 126 E2
Jammalamadugu India 14°51N 78°25E 127 G4
Jammerbugten Denmark 57°15N 9°20E 63 G3
Jammu India 32°43N 74°54E 124 C6
Jammu & Kashmir □
 India 34°25N 77°0E 125 B7
Jamnagar India 22°30N 70°6E 124 H4
Jamner India 20°45N 75°52E 126 D3
Jamni → India 25°13N 78°35E 125 G8
Jampur Pakistan 29°39N 70°40E 124 E5
Jamrud Pakistan 33°59N 71°24E 124 C4
Jämsä Finland 61°53N 25°10E 64 B3
Jamshedpur India 22°44N 86°12E 125 H12
Jamtara India 23°59N 86°49E 125 H12
Jämtland □ Sweden 63°31N 14°0E 60 E16
Jämtland ○ Sweden 63°0N 14°40E 62 B7
Jan L. Canada 54°56N 102°55W 163 C8
Jan Mayen Arctic 71°0N 9°0W 54 B7
Janakkala Finland 60°54N 24°36E 64 B3
Janakpur Nepal 26°42N 85°55E 125 E11
Janaúba Brazil 15°48S 43°19W 189 D2
Jand Pakistan 33°30N 72°6E 124 C5
Jandaq Iran 34°3N 54°22E 129 C7
Jandia Canary Is. 28°6N 14°21W 100 F5
Jandia, Pta. de
 Canary Is. 28°3N 14°31W 100 F5
Jandola Pakistan 32°20N 70°9E 124 C4
Jandowae Australia 26°45S 151°7E 153 D5
Jándula → Spain 38°3N 4°6W 89 G6
Jane Pk. N.Z. 45°15S 168°20E 155 F3
Janesville U.S.A. 42°41N 89°1W 172 D9
Janga Ghana 10°5N 1°0W 139 C4
Jangamo Mozam. 24°6S 35°21E 145 B6
Janghai India 25°33N 82°19E 125 G9
Jangheung S. Korea 34°41N 126°52E 115 G14
Jangipur India 24°28N 88°4E 125 G12
Janikowo Poland 52°45N 18°7E 83 F5
Janja Bos.-H. 44°40N 19°4E 96 B4
Janjanbureh Gambia 13°30N 14°47W 138 C2
Janjgir India 22°1N 82°34E 125 J10
Janjina Croatia 42°58N 17°25E 80 G2
Janos Mexico 30°54N 108°10W 180 A3
Jánoshalma Hungary 46°18N 19°21E 80 D4
Jánosháza Hungary 47°8N 17°12E 80 C2
Jánossomorja Hungary 47°47N 17°11E 80 C2
Janów Lubelski Poland 50°48N 22°23E 83 H9
Janów Podlaski Poland 52°11N 23°11E 83 F10
Janowiec Wielkopolski
 Poland 52°45N 17°30E 83 F4
Januária Brazil 15°25S 44°25W 189 D2
Janūb Sīnī □ Egypt 29°30N 33°50E 130 F2
Janville France 48°10N 1°50E 71 D8
Janzé France 47°55N 1°28W 70 E5
Jaora India 23°40N 75°10E 124 H6
Japan ■ Asia 36°0N 136°0E 113 G8
Japan, Sea of Asia 40°0N 135°0E 112 E7
Japan Trench Pac. Oc. 32°0N 142°0E 156 D6

Japen = Yapen Indonesia 1°50S 136°0E 119 E9
Japiim Brazil 7°37S 72°54W 188 B3
Japla India 24°33N 84°1E 125 G11
Japurá → Brazil 3°8S 65°46W 186 D5
Jaquarão Brazil 32°34S 53°23W 191 C5
Jaqué Panama 7°27N 78°8W 182 E4
Jarábulus Syria 36°49N 38°1E 105 D8
Jaraguá do Sul Brazil 26°29S 49°4W 191 B6
Jaraicejo Spain 39°40N 5°49W 89 F5
Jaraíz de la Vera Spain 40°4N 5°45W 88 E5
Jarama → Spain 40°24N 3°32W 88 E7
Jaramānah Syria 33°29N 36°21E 104 F7
Jarandilla de la Vera Spain 40°8N 5°39W 88 E5
Jaranwala Pakistan 31°15N 73°26E 124 D5
Jarash Jordan 32°17N 35°54E 130 C4
Jarash □ Jordan 32°17N 35°54E 130 C4
Järbo Sweden 60°43N 16°36E 64 A10
Jardim Brazil 21°28S 56°2W 190 A4
Jardín → Spain 38°50N 2°10W 91 G2
Jardín América
 Argentina 27°3S 55°14W 191 B4
Jardine River △
 Australia 11°9S 142°21E 150 A3
Jardines de la Reina, Arch. de los
 Cuba 20°50N 78°50W 182 B4
Jargalang China 43°5N 122°55E 115 C12
Jari → Brazil 1°9S 51°54W 187 D8
Jarīr, W. al → Si. Arabia 25°38N 42°30E 128 E4
Järlåsa Sweden 59°53N 17°12E 62 E11
Jarmen Germany 53°54N 13°20E 76 B9
Järna Sweden 59°6N 17°34E 62 E11
Jarnac France 45°40N 0°11W 72 C3
Jarny France 49°9N 5°53E 71 C12
Jarocin Poland 51°59N 17°29E 83 G4
Jaroměř Czech Rep. 50°22N 15°52E 78 A8
Jarosław Poland 50°2N 22°42E 83 H9
Järpås Sweden 58°23N 12°57E 63 F6
Järpen Sweden 63°21N 13°26E 62 A7
Jarrahdale Australia 32°24S 116°5E 149 F2
Jarrahi → Iran 30°49N 48°48E 129 D6
Jartai China 39°45N 105°48E 114 E3
Jarud Qi China 44°28N 120°50E 115 B11
Järvenpää Finland 60°29N 25°5E 64 B3
Jarvis Canada 42°53N 80°6W 174 D4
Jarvis I. Pac. Oc. 0°15S 160°5W 157 H11
Jarvornik Czech Rep. 50°23N 17°2E 79 A10
Järvsö Sweden 61°43N 16°10E 62 C10
Jarwa India 27°38N 82°30E 125 F9
Jaša Tomić Serbia 45°26N 20°50E 80 E5
Jasdan India 22°2N 71°12E 124 H4
Jashpurnagar India 22°54N 84°9E 125 H11
Jasidih India 24°31N 86°39E 125 G12
Jasień Poland 51°46N 15°0E 83 G2
Jāsimīyah Iraq 33°45N 44°41E 105 F11
Jasin Malaysia 2°20N 102°26E 121 L4
Jāsk Iran 25°38N 57°45E 129 E8
Jasliq Uzbekistan 43°58N 57°10E 108 D5
Jasło Poland 49°45N 21°30E 83 J8
Jasmund Germany 54°32N 13°38E 76 A9
Jasmund △ Germany 54°31N 13°38E 76 A9
Jaso India 24°30N 80°29E 125 G9
Jason Is. Falk. Is. 51°0S 61°0W 192 G4
Jastarnia Poland 54°42N 18°40E 83 A5
Jastrebarsko Croatia 45°41N 15°39E 93 C12
Jastrowie Poland 53°26N 16°49E 82 E3
Jastrzębie Zdrój Poland 49°57N 18°35E 83 J5
Jász-Nagykun-Szolnok □
 Hungary 47°15N 20°30E 80 C5
Jászapáti Hungary 47°32N 20°10E 80 C5
Jászárokszállás Hungary 47°39N 19°58E 80 C4
Jászberény Hungary 47°30N 19°55E 80 C4
Jászkisér Hungary 47°27N 20°20E 80 C5
Jászladány Hungary 47°23N 20°18E 80 C5
Jataí Brazil 17°58S 51°48W 187 G8
Jath India 17°3N 75°13E 126 F2
Jati Pakistan 24°20N 68°19E 124 G3
Jatibarang Indonesia 6°28S 108°18E 119 G13
Jatiluwih Indonesia 8°23S 115°8E 119 J18
Jatinegara Indonesia 6°13S 106°52E 119 G12
Játiva = Xàtiva Spain 38°59N 0°32W 91 G4
Jättendal Sweden 61°58N 17°12E 62 C11
Jaú Brazil 22°10S 48°30W 191 A6
Jauja Peru 11°45S 75°15W 188 C2
Jaunpur India 25°46N 82°44E 125 G10
Java = Jawa Indonesia 7°0S 110°0E 118 F3
Java Sea Indonesia 4°35S 107°15E 118 E3
Java Trench Ind. Oc. 9°0S 105°0E 118 F3
Javadi Hills India 12°40N 78°40E 127 H4
Javalambre, Sa. de Spain 40°10N 1°0W 90 E5
Javänrud Iran 34°47N 46°31E 105 E12
Jávea Spain 38°48N 0°10E 91 G5
Javier, I. Chile 47°55S 74°25W 192 C2
Javla India 17°18N 75°9E 126 F2
Jawa Indonesia 7°0S 110°0E 118 F3
Jawa Barat □ Indonesia 7°0S 107°0E 119 G12
Jawa Tengah □
 Indonesia 7°0S 110°0E 119 G14
Jawa Timur □ Indonesia 8°0S 113°0E 119 G15
Jawad India 24°36N 74°51E 124 G6
Jawhar Somalia 2°48N 45°30E 131 G4
Jawor Poland 51°4N 16°11E 83 G3
Jaworzno Poland 50°13N 19°11E 83 H6
Jaworzyna Śląska
 Poland 50°55N 16°28E 83 H3
Jay Peak U.S.A. 44°55N 72°32W 175 B12
Jaya, Puncak Indonesia 3°57S 137°17E 119 E9
Jayanca Peru 6°24S 79°50W 188 B2
Jayanti India 26°45S 89°40E 125 F13
Jayapura Indonesia 2°28S 140°38E 119 E10
Jayawijaya, Pegunungan
 Indonesia 5°0S 139°0E 119 F9
Jaynagar India 26°43N 86°9E 125 F12
Jaypur = Jeypore India 18°50N 82°38E 126 E6
Jayrūd Syria 33°49N 36°44E 104 F7
Jaza'ir India 31°30N 100°34W 176 E4
Jāz Mūrīān, Hāmūn-e
 Iran 27°20N 58°55E 129 E8
Jazīreh-ye Shīf Iran 29°4N 50°54E 129 D6

Jazminal Mexico 24°52N 101°24W 180 C4
Jazzīn Lebanon 33°31N 35°35E 130 B4
Jean U.S.A. 35°47N 115°20W 171 K11
Jean Marie River
 Canada 61°32N 120°38W 162 A4
Jean-Rabel Haiti 19°50N 73°5W 183 C5
Jeanerette U.S.A. 29°55N 91°40W 176 D9
Jeanette, Ostrov = Zhannetty,
 Ostrov Russia 76°43N 158°0E 107 B16
Jeannette U.S.A. 40°20N 79°36W 174 F5
Jebäl Bärez, Küh-e Iran 28°30N 58°20E 129 D8
Jebba Nigeria 9°9N 4°48E 139 D5
Jebel, Bahr el →
 South Sudan 9°30N 30°25E 135 G12
Jebel Ali = Minā' Jabal 'Alī
 U.A.E. 25°2N 55°8E 129 E7
Jebel Elba △ Egypt 22°11N 36°22E 137 C4
Jeberos Peru 5°15S 76°10W 188 B2
Jecheon S. Korea 37°8N 128°12E 115 F15
Jedburgh U.K. 55°29N 2°33W 65 F6
Jedda = Jiddah
 Si. Arabia 21°29N 39°10E 131 C2
Jedlicze Poland 49°43N 21°40E 83 J8
Jędrzejów Poland 50°35N 20°15E 83 H7
Jedwabne Poland 53°17N 22°18E 83 E9
Jeetzel → Germany 53°9N 11°3E 76 B7
Jefferson Iowa, U.S.A. 42°1N 94°23W 172 D6
Jefferson Ohio, U.S.A. 41°44N 80°46W 174 E4
Jefferson Tex., U.S.A. 32°46N 94°21W 176 E7
Jefferson, Mt. Nev.,
 U.S.A. 38°47N 116°56W 168 G5
Jefferson, Mt. Oreg.,
 U.S.A. 44°41N 121°48W 168 D3
Jefferson City Mo.,
 U.S.A. 38°34N 92°10W 172 F7
Jefferson City Tenn.,
 U.S.A. 36°7N 83°30W 177 C13
Jeffersontown U.S.A. 38°12N 85°35W 173 F11
Jeffersonville Ga.,
 U.S.A. 32°41N 83°20W 178 C6
Jeffersonville Ind.,
 U.S.A. 38°17N 85°44W 173 F11
Jeffrey City U.S.A. 42°30N 107°49W 168 E10
Jega Nigeria 12°15N 4°23E 139 C5
Jeju S. Korea 33°31N 126°32E 115 H14
Jeju-do S. Korea 33°29N 126°34E 115 H14
Jeju Haehyop
 S. Korea 33°50N 126°30E 115 H14
Jēkabpils Latvia 56°29N 25°57E 84 D3
Jekyll I. U.S.A. 31°4N 81°25W 178 D8
Jelcz-Laskowice Poland 51°2N 17°19E 83 G4
Jelenia Góra Poland 50°50N 15°45E 83 H2
Jelgava Latvia 56°41N 23°49E 82 B10
Jelica Serbia 43°50N 20°17E 96 C4
Jelšava Slovak Rep. 48°37N 20°15E 79 C13
Jemaja Indonesia 3°5N 105°45E 118 D3
Jemaluang Malaysia 2°16N 103°52E 121 L4
Jember Indonesia 8°11S 113°41E 119 H15
Jena Germany 50°54N 11°35E 76 E7
Jena U.S.A. 31°41N 92°8W 176 F8
Jenbach Austria 47°24N 11°47E 78 D4
Jendouba Tunisia 36°29N 8°47E 136 A1
Jengish Chokusu = Pobedy, Pik
 Asia 42°0N 79°58E 109 D9
Jenīn West Bank 32°28N 35°18E 130 C4
Jenkins U.S.A. 37°10N 82°38W 173 G12
Jenner U.S.A. 38°27N 123°7W 170 G3
Jennings Fla., U.S.A. 30°36N 83°6W 178 E6
Jennings La., U.S.A. 30°13N 92°40W 176 F8
Jensen Beach U.S.A. 27°15N 80°14W 179 H9
Jeong-eup S. Korea 35°35N 126°50E 115 G14
Jeongseon S. Korea 37°23N 128°45E 115 F15
Jeonju S. Korea 35°50N 127°4E 115 G14
Jepara Indonesia 7°40S 109°14E 119 G14
Jeparit Australia 36°8S 142°1E 152 D5
Jequié Brazil 13°51S 40°5W 189 D2
Jequitaí → Brazil 17°4S 44°50W 189 D2
Jequitinhonha Brazil 16°30S 41°0W 189 D2
Jequitinhonha →
 Brazil 15°51S 38°53W 189 D3
Jerada Morocco 34°17N 2°10W 136 B3
Jerantut Malaysia 3°56N 102°22E 121 L4
Jerejak, Pulau Malaysia 5°19N 100°19E 121 c
Jérémie Haiti 18°40N 74°10W 183 C5
Jeremoabo Brazil 10°4S 38°21W 189 C3
Jerez, Pta. Mexico 22°58N 97°40W 181 C5
Jerez de García Salinas
 Mexico 22°39N 103°0W 180 C4
Jerez de la Frontera
 Spain 36°41N 6°7W 89 J4
Jerez de los Caballeros
 Spain 38°20N 6°45W 89 G4
Jericho = El Arīḥā
 West Bank 31°52N 35°27E 130 D4
Jericho Australia 23°38S 146°6E 150 C4
Jerichow Germany 52°30N 12°1E 76 C8
Jerid, Chott el = Djerid, Chott
 Tunisia 33°42N 8°30E 136 B5
Jerilderie Australia 35°20S 145°41E 153 C4
Jermyn U.S.A. 41°32N 75°33W 175 E9
Jerome U.S.A. 42°44N 114°31W 168 E6
Jerramungup Australia 33°55S 118°55E 149 F2
Jersey U.K. 49°11N 2°7W 67 H5
Jersey City U.S.A. 40°42N 74°4W 175 F10
Jersey Shore U.S.A. 41°12N 77°15W 174 E7
Jerseyville U.S.A. 39°7N 90°20W 172 F8
Jerumenha Brazil 7°5S 43°30W 189 B2
Jerusalem
 Israel/West Bank 31°47N 35°10E 130 D4
Jervis B. Australia 35°8S 150°46E 153 C5
Jervis Bay △ Australia 35°9S 150°44E 153 C5
Jervis Inlet Canada 50°0N 123°57W 162 C4
Jerzu Italy 39°47N 9°31E 94 C2
Jesenice Slovenia 46°28N 14°3E 93 B11
Jeseník Czech Rep. 50°14N 17°8E 79 A10
Jesenké Slovak Rep. 48°20N 20°10E 79 C13
Jesi = Iesi Italy 43°31N 13°14E 93 E10
Jēsólo Italy 45°32N 12°38E 93 C9
Jessnitz Germany 51°40N 12°18E 76 D8
Jessore Bangla. 23°10N 89°10E 125 H16
Jesup U.S.A. 31°36N 81°53W 178 D8
Jesup, L. U.S.A. 28°43N 81°14W 179 G8
Jesús Peru 7°15S 78°20W 188 B2
Jesús Carranza Mexico 17°26N 95°2W 181 D5
Jesús María Argentina 30°59S 64°5W 190 C3
Jesús María Mexico 21°57N 102°20W 180 C4
Jetmore U.S.A. 38°4N 99°54W 176 A4
Jetpur India 21°45N 70°10E 124 J4
Jevnaker Norway 60°15N 10°26E 63 F14
Jewett U.S.A. 31°22N 96°9W 176 F6
Jewett City U.S.A. 41°36N 71°59W 175 E13

Jeyḩūnābād Iran 34°58N 48°59E 129 C6
Jeypore India 18°50N 82°38E 126 E6
Jeziorak, Jezioro Poland 53°40N 19°35E 82 E6
Jeziorany Poland 53°58N 20°46E 82 E7
Jeziorka → Poland 52°8N 21°9E 83 F8
Jha Jha India 24°46N 86°22E 125 G12
Jhabua India 22°46N 74°36E 124 H6
Jhajjar India 28°37N 76°42E 124 E7
Jhal Pakistan 28°17N 67°27E 124 E2
Jhal Jhao Pakistan 26°20N 65°35E 124 F2
Jhalawar India 24°40N 76°10E 124 G7
Jhalida India 23°22N 85°58E 125 H11
Jhalrapatan India 24°33N 76°10E 124 G7
Jhang Maghiana
 Pakistan 31°15N 72°22E 124 D5
Jhang Sadr = Jhang Maghiana
 Pakistan 31°15N 72°22E 124 D5
Jhansi India 25°30N 78°36E 125 G8
Jhargram India 22°27N 86°59E 125 H12
Jharia India 23°45N 86°26E 125 H12
Jharkhand □ India 24°0N 85°50E 125 H11
Jharsuguda India 21°56N 84°5E 126 D7
Jhelum Pakistan 33°0N 73°45E 124 C5
Jhelum → Pakistan 31°20N 72°10E 124 D5
Jhilmilli India 23°24N 82°51E 125 H10
Jhudo Pakistan 24°58N 69°18E 124 G3
Jhunjhunun India 28°10N 75°30E 124 E6
Ji-Paraná Brazil 10°52S 62°57W 186 F6
Ji Xian China 36°7N 110°40E 114 F6
Jia Xian Henan, China 33°59N 113°12E 114 H7
Jia Xian Shaanxi, China 38°12N 110°28E 114 E6
Jiahe China 25°38N 112°30E 117 E9
Jiaji = Qionghai China 19°15N 110°26E 117 a
Jialing Jiang → China 29°30N 106°20E 114 E6
Jiamusi China 46°40N 130°26E 111 B15
Ji'an Jiangxi, China 27°6N 114°59E 117 D10
Ji'an Jilin, China 41°5N 126°10E 115 D14
Jianchang China 40°55N 120°35E 115 D11
Jianchuan China 26°38N 99°55E 116 D2
Jiang'an China 29°30N 105°30E 114 C5
Jiangbei China 29°40N 106°34E 114 C6
Jiangcheng China 22°36N 101°52E 116 F3
Jiangchuan China 24°8N 102°39E 116 E4
Jiangdi China 26°57N 103°38E 114 D4
Jiangdu China 32°27N 119°36E 117 A12
Jiange China 32°4N 105°32E 114 A5
Jianghua China 25°0N 111°47E 117 E8
Jiangjin China 29°14N 106°14E 114 C6
Jiangkou China 27°40N 108°58E 117 C7
Jiangle China 26°42N 117°23E 117 D11
Jiangling China 30°25N 112°12E 117 B9
Jiangmen China 22°32N 113°0E 117 F9
Jiangshan China 28°40N 118°37E 117 C12
Jiangsu □ China 33°0N 120°0E 115 H11
Jiangxi □ China 27°30N 116°0E 117 D11
Jiangyin China 31°54N 120°17E 117 B13
Jiangyong China 25°20N 111°22E 117 E8
Jiangyou China 31°44N 104°43E 116 B5
Jiangyuan China 42°2N 126°34E 115 C14
Jianhe China 26°37N 108°31E 117 D7
Jianli China 29°46N 112°55E 117 C9
Jianning China 26°50N 116°50E 117 D11
Jian'ou China 27°3N 118°17E 117 D12
Jianping China 41°53N 119°42E 115 D10
Jianshi China 30°37N 109°38E 116 B7
Jianshui China 23°36N 102°43E 116 F4
Jianyang Fujian, China 27°20N 118°5E 117 D12
Jianyang Sichuan,
 China 30°24N 104°33E 116 B5
Jiao Xian = Jiaozhou
 China 36°18N 120°1E 115 F11
Jiaohe Hebei, China 38°2N 116°20E 114 E9
Jiaohe Jilin, China 43°40N 127°22E 115 C14
Jiaoling China 24°41N 116°12E 117 D11
Jiaonan China 35°52N 119°58E 115 G10
Jiaozhou China 36°18N 120°1E 115 F11
Jiaozhou Wan China 36°5N 120°10E 115 F11
Jiaozuo China 35°16N 113°12E 114 G7
Jiawang China 34°28N 117°26E 115 G9
Jiaxiang China 35°25N 116°20E 114 G9
Jiaxing China 30°49N 120°45E 117 B13
Jiayu China 29°49N 113°53E 117 C9
Jiayuguan China 39°49N 98°18E 110 D8
Jibão, Serra do Brazil 14°48S 45°0W 189 D2
Jibiya Nigeria 13°5N 7°12E 139 C6
Jibou Romania 47°15N 23°17E 81 E6
Jibuti = Djibouti ■ Africa 12°0N 43°0E 131 E3
Jicarón, I. Panama 7°10N 81°50W 182 E3
Jičín Czech Rep. 50°25N 15°58E 78 A8
Jiddah Si. Arabia 21°29N 39°10E 131 C2
Jido India 29°2N 94°58E 125 E19
Jieshou China 33°18N 115°22E 114 H8
Jiexiu China 37°2N 111°55E 114 F6
Jieyang China 23°35N 116°21E 117 F11
Jigalong Australia 23°21S 120°47E 148 D3
Jigalong ○ Australia 23°21S 120°46E 148 D3
Jigawa □ Nigeria 12°0N 9°0E 139 C6
Jigni India 25°45N 79°25E 125 G8
Jihlava Czech Rep. 49°28N 15°35E 78 B8
Jihlava → Czech Rep. 48°55N 16°36E 77 G9
Jihočeský □ Czech Rep. 49°8N 14°35E 78 B7
Jihomoravský □
 Czech Rep. 49°5N 16°30E 78 B9
Jijel Algeria 36°52N 5°50E 136 A6
Jijel □ Algeria 36°45N 5°50E 136 A6
Jijiga Ethiopia 9°20N 42°50E 131 F3
Jikamshi Nigeria 12°12N 7°45E 139 C6
Jilib Somalia 0°29N 42°46E 131 G3
Jilin China 43°44N 126°30E 115 C14
Jilin □ China 44°0N 127°0E 115 C14
Jiloca → Spain 41°21N 1°39W 90 D3
Jílové Czech Rep. 50°14N 17°8E 78 C7
Jim Thorpe U.S.A. 40°52N 75°44W 175 F9
Jima Ethiopia 7°40N 36°47E 131 F2
Jimbaran, Teluk
 Indonesia 8°46S 115°9E 119 K18
Jimbolia Romania 45°47N 20°57E 80 E5
Jimena de la Frontera
 Spain 36°27N 5°24W 89 J5
Jiménez Mexico 27°8N 104°54W 180 B4
Jimeta Nigeria 9°17N 12°28E 139 D7
Jimo China 36°23N 120°30E 115 F11
Jimsar China 43°56N 89°4E 110 B6
Jin Xian = Jinzhou
 China 38°2N 121°12E 115 E11
Jinan China 36°38N 117°1E 114 F9
Jinchang China 38°30N 102°10E 110 D8
Jincheng China 35°29N 112°50E 114 G7

Jinchuan China 31°30N 102°3E 116 B4
Jind India 29°19N 76°22E 124 E7
Jindabyne Australia 36°25S 148°35E 153 D8
Jinding China 22°22N 113°33E 111 a
Jindo S. Korea 34°28N 126°15E 115 G14
Jindřichův Hradec
 Czech Rep. 49°10N 15°2E 78 B8
Jing He → China 34°27N 109°4E 114 G5
Jing Shan China 31°20N 111°35E 117 B8
Jing Xian China 30°38N 118°25E 117 B12
Jing'an China 28°50N 115°17E 117 C10
Jingbian China 37°20N 108°30E 114 F5
Jingchuan China 35°20N 107°20E 114 G4
Jingde China 30°15N 118°27E 117 B12
Jingdezhen China 29°20N 117°11E 117 C11
Jingdong China 24°23N 100°47E 116 E3
Jinggangshan China 26°58N 114°15E 117 D10
Jinggu China 23°35N 100°41E 116 F3
Jinghai Guangdong,
 China 22°59N 116°31E 117 F11
Jinghai Tianjin, China 38°55N 116°55E 114 E9
Jinghong China 22°0N 100°45E 116 G3
Jinghong Dam China 22°10N 100°46E 116 G3
Jingjiang China 32°2N 120°16E 117 A13
Jingle China 38°20N 111°55E 114 E6
Jingning China 35°30N 105°43E 114 G3
Jingpo Hu China 43°55N 128°55E 115 C15
Jingshan China 31°1N 113°7E 117 B9
Jingtai China 37°10N 104°6E 114 F3
Jingtang China 39°10N 119°5E 115 E10
Jingxi China 23°8N 106°27E 116 F6
Jingyang China 34°30N 108°50E 114 G5
Jingyu China 42°25N 126°45E 115 C14
Jingyuan China 36°30N 104°40E 114 F3
Jingzhou Hubei, China 30°21N 112°11E 117 B9
Jingzhou Hunan, China 26°33N 109°40E 117 D7
Jingziguan China 33°15N 111°0E 114 H6
Jinhua China 29°8N 119°38E 117 C12
Jining Nei Monggol Zizhiqu,
 China 41°5N 113°0E 114 D7
Jining Shandong, China 35°22N 116°34E 114 G9
Jinja Uganda 0°25N 33°12E 142 B3
Jinjang Malaysia 3°13N 101°39E 121 L3
Jinji China 37°58N 106°8E 114 F4
Jinjiang Fujian, China 24°43N 118°33E 117 E12
Jinjiang Yunnan, China 26°14N 100°34E 116 D3
Jinju S. Korea 35°12N 128°2E 115 G15
Jinkou China 30°20N 114°8E 117 B10
Jinkouhe China 29°18N 103°4E 116 C4
Jinmu Jiao China 18°9N 109°34E 117 a
Jinnah Barrage
 Pakistan 32°58N 71°33E 124 C4
Jinning China 24°38N 102°38E 116 E4
Jinotega Nic. 13°6N 85°59W 182 D2
Jinotepe Nic. 11°50N 86°10W 182 E2
Jinping Guizhou, China 26°40N 109°10E 117 D7
Jinping Yunnan, China 22°45N 103°3E 116 F4
Jinping Bend Dams
 China 28°1N 101°39E 116 C3
Jinsha China 27°29N 106°12E 117 D6
Jinsha Jiang → China 28°50N 104°36E 116 C5
Jinshi China 29°40N 111°50E 117 C8
Jintan China 31°42N 119°36E 117 B12
Jintur India 19°37N 76°42E 126 E3
Jinxi Jiangxi, China 27°56N 116°45E 117 D11
Jinxi Liaoning, China 40°52N 120°50E 115 D11
Jinxian China 28°26N 116°17E 117 C11
Jinxiang China 35°5N 116°22E 114 G9
Jinzhai China 31°39N 115°43E 117 B10
Jinzhong China 37°42N 112°46E 114 F7
Jinzhou Liaoning,
 China 38°55N 121°42E 115 E11
Jinzhou Liaoning, China 41°5N 121°3E 115 D11
Jiparaná → Brazil 8°3S 62°52W 186 E6
Jipijapa Ecuador 1°0S 80°40W 186 D2
Jiquilpan Mexico 19°59N 102°43W 180 D4
Jirisan S. Korea 35°20N 127°44E 115 G14
Jiroft Iran 28°45N 57°50E 129 D8
Jishan China 35°34N 110°58E 114 G6
Jishou China 28°21N 109°43E 117 C7
Jishui China 27°12N 115°8E 117 D10
Jisr ash Shughūr Syria 35°49N 36°18E 104 C7
Jitarning Australia 32°48S 117°57E 149 F2
Jitra Malaysia 6°16N 100°25E 121 J3
Jiu → Romania 43°47N 23°48E 81 G8
Jiudengkou China 39°56N 106°40E 114 E4
Jiujiang Jiangxi,
 China 22°50N 113°0E 117 F9
Jiujiang Jiangxi, China 29°42N 115°58E 117 C10
Jiuling Shan China 28°40N 114°40E 117 C10
Jiulong = Kowloon
 China 22°19N 114°11E 117 F10
Jiulong China 28°57N 101°31E 116 C3
Jiuquan China 39°50N 98°20E 110 D8
Jiutai China 44°10N 125°50E 115 B13
Jiuxincheng China 39°17N 115°59E 114 E8
Jiuzhaigou China 33°38N 103°58E 116 A4
Jiwani Pakistan 25°1N 61°44E 122 G2
Jixi Anhui, China 30°5N 118°34E 117 B12
Jixi Heilongjiang, China 45°20N 130°50E 115 B16
Jiyang China 37°0N 117°12E 114 F9
Jiyuan China 35°7N 112°57E 114 G7
Jīzān Si. Arabia 17°0N 42°20E 131 D3
Jize China 36°54N 114°56E 114 F8
Jizera → Czech Rep. 50°10N 14°43E 78 A7
Jizl, Wādī al →
 Si. Arabia 25°39N 38°25E 128 E3
Jīzō-Zaki Japan 35°34N 133°20E 113 G6
Jizzax Uzbekistan 40°6N 67°50E 108 D7
Jizzax □ Uzbekistan 40°20N 67°50E 108 D7
Joaçaba Brazil 27°5S 51°31W 191 B5
Joaima Brazil 16°39S 41°2W 189 D3
Joal Fadiout Senegal 14°28N 16°56W 138 C1
João Amaro Brazil 12°46S 40°22W 189 D3
João Câmara Brazil 5°33S 35°25W 189 B4
João Neiva Brazil 19°45S 40°24W 189 E3
João Pessoa Brazil 7°10S 34°52W 189 B4
João Pinheiro Brazil 17°45S 46°10W 189 D1
Joaquín V. González
 Argentina 25°10S 64°0W 190 B3
Jobat India 22°25N 74°34E 124 H6
Jobourg, Nez de France 49°41N 1°57W 70 C4
Jódar Spain 37°50N 3°21W 89 H7
Jodhpur India 26°23N 73°8E 124 F5
Jodiya India 22°42N 70°18E 124 H4
Joensuu Finland 62°37N 29°49E 60 E23
Jōetsu Japan 37°12N 138°10E 113 F9

Jœuf France 49°12N 6°0E 71 C12
Jofane Mozam. 21°15S 34°18E 145 B5
Jog Falls = Gersoppa Falls
India 14°12N 74°46E 127 G2
Jogbani India 26°25N 87°15E 125 F12
Jõgeva Estonia 58°45N 26°24E 84 C4
Jogjakarta = Yogyakarta
Indonesia 7°49S 110°22E 118 F4
Johannesburg S. Africa 26°11S 28°2E 145 D4
Johannesburg U.S.A. 35°22N 117°38W 171 K9
Johansfors Sweden 56°42N 15°32E 63 H9
Johilla → India 23°37N 81°14E 125 H9
John Crow Mts. Jamaica 18°5N 76°25W 182 a
John Day U.S.A. 44°25N 118°57W 168 D4
John Day → U.S.A. 45°44N 120°39W 168 D3
John Day Fossil Beds ○
U.S.A. 44°33N 119°38W 168 D4
John D'or Prairie
Canada 58°30N 115°8W 162 B5
John F. Kennedy Space Center
U.S.A. 28°40N 80°42W 179 G9
John H. Kerr Res.
U.S.A. 36°36N 78°18W 177 C15
John o' Groats U.K. 58°38N 3°4W 65 C5
Johnnie U.S.A. 36°25N 116°5W 171 J10
Johns Creek U.S.A. 34°2N 84°12W 178 A5
Johns I. U.S.A. 32°47N 80°7W 178 C9
John's Ra. Australia 21°55S 133°23E 150 C1
Johnson U.S.A. 44°38N 72°41W 175 B12
Johnson City Kans.,
U.S.A. 37°34N 101°45W 172 G3
Johnson City N.Y.,
U.S.A. 42°7N 75°58W 175 D9
Johnson City Tenn.,
U.S.A. 36°19N 82°21W 177 C13
Johnson City Tex.,
U.S.A. 30°17N 98°25W 176 F5
Johnsonburg U.S.A. 41°29N 78°41W 174 E6
Johnsondale U.S.A. 35°58N 118°32W 171 K8
Johnsons Crossing
Canada 60°29N 133°18W 162 A2
Johnsonville N.Z. 41°13S 174°48E 154 H3
Johnston U.S.A. 33°50N 81°48W 178 B8
Johnston, L. Australia 32°25S 120°30E 149 F3
Johnston Atoll
Pac. Oc. 17°10N 169°8W 157 F11
Johnston Falls = Mambilima Falls
Zambia 10°31S 28°45E 143 E2
Johnstone Str. Canada 50°28N 126°0W 162 C3
Johnstown Ireland 52°45N 7°33W 64 D4
Johnstown N.Y.,
U.S.A. 43°0N 74°22W 175 C10
Johnstown Ohio, U.S.A. 40°9N 82°41W 174 F2
Johnstown Pa., U.S.A. 40°20N 78°55W 174 F6
Johor □ Malaysia 2°5N 103°20E 121 M4
Johor, Selat Asia 1°28N 103°47E 121 d
Johor Bahru Malaysia 1°28N 103°46E 121 d
Johor Port Malaysia 1°26N 103°53E 121 d
Jõhvi Estonia 59°22N 27°27E 84 C4
Joigny France 47°58N 3°20E 71 E10
Joinville Brazil 26°15S 48°55W 191 B6
Joinville France 48°27N 5°10E 71 D12
Joinville I. Antarctica 65°0S 55°30W 55 C18
Jojutla Mexico 18°37N 99°11W 181 D5
Jøkelbugten Greenland 78°25N 20°20W 57 B9
Jokkmokk Sweden 66°35N 19°50E 60 C18
Jökulsá á Bru →
Iceland 65°40N 14°16W 60 D6
Jökulsá á Fjöllum →
Iceland 66°10N 16°30W 60 C5
Jökulsárgljúfur △
Iceland 65°56N 16°31W 60 D5

Josselin France 47°57N 2°33W 70 E4
Jost Van Dyke I.
Br. Virgin Is. 18°29N 64°47W 183 e
Jostedalsbreen Norway 61°40N 6°59E 60 F12
Jotunheimen Norway 61°35N 8°25E 60 F13
Joubertberge Namibia 18°30S 14°0E 144 A1
Joué-lès-Tours France 47°21N 0°40E 70 E7
Jourdanton U.S.A. 28°55N 98°33W 176 G5
Joutseno Finland 61°7N 28°31E 84 B5
Jovellanos Cuba 22°40N 81°10W 182 B3
Jowkār Iran 34°25N 48°40E 105 E13
Jowzjān □ Afghan. 36°10N 66°0E 109 E7
Joyeuse France 44°29N 4°16E 73 D8
Józefów Lubelskie, Poland 50°28N 23°2E 83 H10
Józefów Mazowieckie,
Poland 52°10N 21°11E 83 F8
Ju Xian China 35°35N 118°20E 115 G10
Juan Aldama Mexico 24°19N 103°21W 180 C4
Juan Bautista Alberdi
Argentina 34°26S 61°48W 190 C3
Juan de Fuca, Str. of.
N. Amer. 48°15N 124°0W 170 B3
Juan de Nova Ind. Oc. 17°3S 43°45E 145 A7
Juan Fernández, Arch. de
Pac. Oc. 33°50S 80°0W 184 G2
Juan José Castelli
Argentina 25°27S 60°57W 190 B3
Juan L. Lacaze
Uruguay 34°26S 57°25W 190 C4
Juanjui Peru 7°10S 76°45W 188 B2
Juankoski Finland 63°3N 28°19E 60 E23
Juárez Mexico 27°37N 100°44W 180 B4
Juárez, Sa. de Mexico 32°0N 115°50W 180 A1
Juàzeiro Brazil 9°30S 40°30W 189 D3
Juàzeiro do Norte Brazil 7°10S 39°18W 189 D3
Juazohn Liberia 5°22N 8°50W 138 D3
Juba South Sudan 4°51N 31°35E 135 H12
Juba → Somalia 1°30N 42°35E 131 G3
Jubail = Al Jubayl
Si. Arabia 27°0N 49°50E 129 E6
Jubany = Carlini Base
Antarctica 62°30S 58°0W 55 C18
Jubayl Lebanon 34°5N 35°39E 130 A4
Jubbah Si. Arabia 28°2N 40°56E 128 D4
Jubbal India 31°5N 77°40E 124 D7
Jubbulpore = Jabalpur
India 23°9N 79°58E 124 H8
Jübek Germany 54°33N 9°22E 76 A5
Jubilee L. Australia 29°0S 126°50E 149 E4
Juby, C. Morocco 28°0N 12°59W 134 C3
Júcar = Xúquer → Spain 39°5N 0°10W 91 F4
Júcaro Cuba 21°37N 78°51W 182 B4
Juchitán de Zaragoza
Mexico 16°26N 95°1W 181 D5
Judea = Har Yehuda
Israel 31°35N 34°57E 130 D3
Judenburg Austria 47°12N 14°38E 78 D7
Judith → U.S.A. 47°44N 109°39W 168 C9
Judith, Pt. U.S.A. 41°22N 71°29W 175 E13
Judith Gap U.S.A. 46°41N 109°45W 168 C9
Juelsminde Denmark 55°43N 10°1E 63 J4
Juigalpa Nic. 12°6N 85°26W 182 D2
Juillac France 45°20N 1°19E 72 C5
Juiz de Fora Brazil 21°43S 43°19W 191 A7
Jujuy □ Argentina 23°20S 65°40W 190 A3
Julesburg U.S.A. 40°59N 102°16W 168 F12
Juli Peru 16°10S 69°25W 188 G5
Julia Cr. → Australia 20°0S 141°11E 150 C3
Julia Creek Australia 20°39S 141°44E 150 C3
Juliaca Peru 15°25S 70°10W 188 G3
Julian U.S.A. 33°4N 116°38W 171 M10
Julian, L. Canada 54°25N 77°57W 164 B4
Julian Alps = Julijske Alpe
Slovenia 46°15N 14°1E 93 B11
Julianatop Suriname 3°40N 56°30W 187 C7
Julianehåb = Qaqortoq
Greenland 60°43N 46°0W 57 E6
Jülich Germany 50°55N 6°22E 76 E2
Juliette, L. U.S.A. 33°2N 83°50W 178 B6
Julijske Alpe Slovenia 46°15N 14°1E 93 B11
Julimes Mexico 28°25N 105°27W 180 B3
Jullundur = Jalandhar
India 31°20N 75°40E 124 D6
Julu China 37°15N 115°2E 114 F8
Jumbo Zimbabwe 17°30S 30°58E 143 F3
Jumbo Pk. U.S.A. 36°12N 114°11W 171 J12
Jumentos Cays Bahamas 23°0N 75°40W 182 B4
Jumilla Spain 38°28N 1°19W 91 G3
Jumla Nepal 29°15N 82°13E 125 E10
Jumna = Yamuna →
India 25°30N 81°53E 125 G9
Jumunjin S. Korea 37°55N 128°54E 115 F15
Junagadh India 21°30N 70°30E 124 J4
Junan China 35°12N 118°53E 115 G10
Junction Tex., U.S.A. 30°29N 99°46W 176 F5
Junction Utah, U.S.A. 38°14N 112°13W 169 G7
Junction B. Australia 11°52S 133°55E 150 A1
Junction City Ga.,
U.S.A. 32°36N 84°28W 178 C5
Junction City Kans.,
U.S.A. 39°2N 96°50W 172 F5
Junction City Oreg.,
U.S.A. 44°13N 123°12W 168 D2
Junction Pt. Australia 11°45S 133°50E 150 A1
Jundah Australia 24°46S 143°2E 150 C3
Jundiaí Brazil 24°30S 47°0W 191 A6
Juneau U.S.A. 58°18N 134°25W 162 B2
Junee Australia 34°53S 147°35E 153 C7
Jungar Qi China 39°49N 110°57E 114 E6
Jungfrau Switz. 46°32N 7°58E 77 J3
Junggar Pendi China 44°30N 86°0E 109 D11
Jungshahi Pakistan 24°52N 67°44E 124 G2
Juniata → U.S.A. 40°24N 77°1W 174 F7
Junín Argentina 34°33S 60°57W 190 C3
Junín Peru 11°12S 76°0W 188 C2
Junín, L. de Peru 11°2S 76°0W 188 C2
Junín de los Andes
Argentina 39°45S 71°0W 192 A2
Jūniyah Lebanon 33°59N 35°38E 130 B4
Junkerdal △ Norway 66°50N 15°50E 60 C16
Junlian China 28°8N 104°29E 116 C5
Junnar India 19°12N 73°58E 126 E1
Juno Beach U.S.A. 26°52N 80°3W 179 J9
Juntas Chile 28°24S 69°58W 190 B2
Juntura U.S.A. 43°45N 118°5W 168 E4
Juparaná, L. Brazil 19°16S 40°8W 189 D2
Jupiter U.S.A. 26°57N 80°6W 179 J9
Jur → South Sudan 8°45N 29°15E 135 G11
Jura = Jura, Mts. du
Europe 46°40N 6°5E 71 F13

Jura = Schwäbische Alb
Germany 48°20N 9°30E 77 G5
Jura U.K. 56°0N 5°50W 65 F3
Jura □ France 46°47N 5°45E 71 F12
Jura □ Switz. 47°20N 7°0E 77 H3
Jura, Mts. du Europe 46°40N 6°5E 71 F13
Jura, Sd. of U.K. 55°57N 5°45W 65 F3
Jurassic Coast U.K. 50°42N 2°50W 67 G5
Jurbarkas Lithuania 55°4N 22°46E 82 C9
Jurien Bay Australia 30°18S 115°2E 149 F2
Jurilovca Romania 44°46N 28°52E 81 F13
Jūrmala Latvia 56°58N 23°34E 82 B10
Jurong China 31°57N 119°9E 117 B12
Jurong Singapore 1°19N 103°42E 121 d
Juruá → Brazil 2°37S 65°44W 186 D5
Juruena Brazil 13°0S 58°10W 186 F7
Juruena → Brazil 7°20S 58°3W 186 E7
Juruti Brazil 2°9S 56°4W 187 D7
Jussey France 47°50N 5°55E 71 E12
Justo Daract Argentina 33°52S 65°12W 190 C2
Jutaí Brazil 5°11S 68°54W 188 B4
Jutaí → Brazil 2°43S 66°57W 186 D5
Jüterbog Germany 51°59N 13°5E 76 D9
Juticalpa Honduras 14°40N 86°12W 182 D2
Jutland = Jylland
Denmark 56°25N 9°30E 63 H3
Juuka Finland 63°13N 29°17E 60 E23
Juventud, I. de la Cuba 21°40N 82°40W 182 B3
Juvigny-sous-Andaine
France 48°32N 0°30W 70 D6
Jüy Zar Iran 33°50N 46°18E 105 F12
Juye China 35°22N 116°5E 114 G9
Juzennecourt France 48°10N 4°58E 71 D11
Jvari Georgia 42°42N 42°4E 87 J6
Jwaneng Botswana 24°45S 24°50E 141 J4
Jyderup Denmark 55°40N 11°25E 63 J5
Jylland Denmark 56°25N 9°30E 63 H3
Jyväskylä Finland 62°14N 25°50E 84 A3

K

K2 Pakistan 35°58N 76°32E 125 B7
Ka → Nigeria 11°40N 4°10E 139 C5
Kaakha = Kaka
Turkmenistan 37°21N 59°36E 129 B8
Kaap Plateau S. Africa 28°30S 24°0E 144 D3
Kaapkruis Namibia 21°55S 13°57E 144 B1
Kaapstad = Cape Town
S. Africa 33°55S 18°22E 144 D2
Kaba Guinea 10°9N 11°40W 138 C2
Kabaena Indonesia 5°15S 122°0E 119 F6
Kabala S. Leone 9°38N 11°37W 138 D2
Kabale Uganda 1°15S 30°0E 142 C3
Kabalo
Dem. Rep. of the Congo 6°0S 27°0E 142 D2
Kabambare
Dem. Rep. of the Congo 4°41S 27°39E 142 C2
Kabango
Dem. Rep. of the Congo 8°35S 28°30E 143 D2
Kabanjahe Indonesia 3°6N 98°30E 118 D1
Kabankalan Phil. 9°59N 122°49E 119 C6
Kabara Fiji 18°59S 178°56W 154 a
Kabardinka Russia 44°40N 37°57E 85 K10
Kabardino-Balkaria □
Russia 43°30N 43°30E 87 J6
Kabarega Falls = Murchison Falls
Uganda 2°15N 31°30E 142 B3
Kabarnet Kenya 0°30N 35°45E 142 B4
Kabasalan Phil. 7°47N 122°44E 119 C6
Kabat Indonesia 8°16S 114°19E 119 J17
Kabba Nigeria 7°50N 6°3E 139 D6
Kabbani → India 12°13N 76°54E 127 H3
Kabin Buri Thailand 13°57N 101°43E 120 F3
Kabinakagami L.
Canada 48°54N 84°25W 164 C3
Kabinda
Dem. Rep. of the Congo 6°19S 24°20E 140 F4
Kabna Sudan 19°6N 32°40E 137 D3
Kabompo Zambia 13°36S 24°14E 143 E1
Kabompo → Zambia 14°11S 23°11E 141 G4
Kabondo
Dem. Rep. of the Congo 8°58S 25°40E 143 D2
Kabongo
Dem. Rep. of the Congo 7°22S 25°33E 142 D2
Kabot Guinea 10°48N 14°57W 138 C2
Kabou Togo 9°28N 0°55E 139 D5
Kabrit, G. el Egypt 29°42N 33°16E 130 F2
Kabrousse Senegal 12°25N 16°45W 138 C1
Kabūd Gonbad Iran 37°5N 59°45E 129 B8
Kabudar Ahang Iran 35°11N 48°43E 105 E13
Kabul Afghan. 34°28N 69°11E 124 B3
Kābul □ Afghan. 34°30N 69°0E 109 F7
Kābul → Pakistan 33°55N 72°14E 124 C5
Kabunga
Dem. Rep. of the Congo 1°38S 28°3E 142 C2
Kaburuang Indonesia 3°50N 126°30E 119 D7
Kabwe Zambia 14°30S 28°29E 143 E2
Kaçanik Kosovo 42°13N 21°12E 96 D5
Kachchh, Gulf of India 22°50N 69°15E 124 H3
Kachchh, Rann of India 24°0N 70°0E 124 H4
Kachchhidhana India 21°44N 78°46E 125 J8
Kachebera Zambia 13°50S 32°50E 143 E3
Kachia Nigeria 9°50N 7°55E 139 D6
Kachikau Botswana 18°8S 24°26E 144 A3
Kachin □ Burma 26°0N 97°30E 110 D1
Kachira, L. Uganda 0°40S 31°7E 142 C3
Kachnara India 23°50N 75°6E 124 H6
Kachot Cambodia 11°30N 103°3E 121 G4
Kaçkar Turkey 40°45N 41°10E 105 B9
Kadaiyanallur India 9°3N 77°22E 127 K3
Kadam, Mt. Uganda 1°45N 34°45E 142 B3
Kadan Kyun Burma 12°30N 98°20E 120 F2
Kadanai → Afghan. 31°22N 65°45E 124 D1
Kadapa India 14°30N 78°47E 127 G4
Kadarkút Hungary 46°13N 17°39E 80 D2
Kadavu Fiji 19°0S 178°15E 154 a
Kadavu Passage Fiji 18°45S 178°0E 154 a
Kade Ghana 6°7N 0°56W 139 D4
Kadhimain = Al Kāẓimīyah
Iraq 33°22N 44°18E 105 F11
Kadi India 23°18N 72°23E 124 H5
Kadiana Mali 10°45N 6°30W 138 C3
Kadina Australia 33°55S 137°43E 152 B2
Kadınhanı Turkey 38°14N 32°13E 104 C5
Kadiolo Mali 10°35N 7°41W 138 C3

Kadipur India 26°10N 82°23E 125 F10
Kadirabad India 19°51N 75°54E 126 E2
Kadiri India 14°12N 78°13E 127 G4
Kadirli Turkey 37°23N 36°5E 104 D7
Kadiyevka = Stakhanov
Ukraine 48°35N 38°40E 85 H10
Kadmat I. India 11°14N 72°47E 127 J1
Kadoka U.S.A. 43°50N 101°31W 172 D3
Kadom Russia 54°37N 42°30E 86 D6
Kadoma Zimbabwe 18°20S 29°52E 143 F2
Kádugli Sudan 11°0N 29°45E 135 F11
Kaduna Nigeria 10°30N 7°21E 139 C6
Kaduna → Nigeria 8°45N 5°48E 139 D6
Kadur India 13°34N 76°1E 127 H3
Kaduy Russia 59°12N 37°9E 84 C9
Kaédi Mauritania 16°9N 13°28W 138 B2
Kaélé Cameroon 10°7N 14°27E 137 F7
Kaeng Khoi Thailand 14°35N 101°0E 120 E3
Kaeng Krachan △
Thailand 12°57N 99°23E 120 F2
Kaeng Krung △
Thailand 9°30N 98°50E 121 H2
Kaeng Tana △
Thailand 15°25N 105°32E 120 E5
Kaeo N.Z. 35°6S 173°49E 154 B4
Kaesŏng N. Korea 37°58N 126°35E 115 F14
Kāf Si. Arabia 31°25N 37°29E 128 D3
Kafan = Kapan
Armenia 39°18N 46°27E 105 C12
Kafanchan Nigeria 9°40N 8°20E 139 D6
Kafareti Nigeria 10°25N 11°12E 139 C7
Kaffrine Senegal 14°8N 15°36W 138 C1
Kafin Nigeria 9°30N 7°4E 139 D6
Kafin Madaki Nigeria 10°41N 9°46E 139 C6
Kafinda Zambia 12°32S 30°20E 143 E3
Kafireos, Stenon Greece 37°55N 24°35E 98 D6
Kafr el Battikh Egypt 31°25N 31°44E 137 E7
Kafr el Dauwâr Egypt 31°8N 30°8E 137 E7
Kafr el Sheikh Egypt 31°15N 30°50E 137 E7
Kafr el Zaiyât Egypt 30°49N 30°48E 137 E7
Kafue Zambia 15°46S 28°9E 143 F2
Kafue → Zambia 15°30S 29°0E 141 H5
Kafue △ Zambia 15°12S 25°35E 143 E1
Kafue Flats Zambia 15°40S 27°25E 143 E2
Kafulwe Zambia 9°0S 29°1E 143 D2
Kaga Japan 34°14N 70°10E 124 B4
Kaga Bandoro C.A.R. 7°0N 19°10E 140 C3
Kagawa □ Japan 34°15N 134°0E 113 G7
Kagera □ Tanzania 2°0S 31°30E 142 C3
Kagera → Tanzania 0°57S 31°47E 142 C3
Kağizman Turkey 40°5N 43°10E 105 B10
Kagoro Nigeria 9°36N 8°23E 139 D6
Kagoshima Japan 31°35N 130°33E 113 J5
Kagoshima □ Japan 31°30N 130°30E 113 J5
Kagul = Cahul Moldova 45°50N 28°15E 81 E13
Kahak Iran 36°6N 49°46E 129 B6
Kahama Tanzania 4°8S 32°30E 142 C3
Kahan Pakistan 29°18N 68°54E 124 E3
Kahang Malaysia 2°12N 103°32E 121 L4
Kahayan → Indonesia 3°40S 114°0E 118 E4
Kahe Tanzania 3°30S 37°25E 142 C4
Kahemba
Dem. Rep. of the Congo 7°18S 18°55E 140 F3
Kaherekoau Mts. N.Z. 45°45S 167°15E 155 F2
Kahil, Djebel bou Algeria 34°26N 4°0E 136 B4
Kahnūj Iran 27°55N 57°40E 129 E8
Kahoka U.S.A. 40°25N 91°44W 172 E8
Kaho'olawe U.S.A. 20°33N 156°37W 167 L8
Kahramanmaraş
Turkey 37°37N 36°53E 104 D7
Kahramanmaraş □
Turkey 37°35N 36°50E 104 D7
Kâhta Turkey 37°46N 38°36E 105 D8
Kahuku U.S.A. 21°41N 157°57W 167 L8
Kahului U.S.A. 20°54N 156°28W 167 L8
Kahurangi △ N.Z. 41°10S 172°32E 155 D3
Kahurangi Pt. N.Z. 40°50S 172°10E 155 D3
Kahuta Pakistan 33°35N 73°24E 124 C5
Kahuzi-Biega △
Dem. Rep. of the Congo 1°50S 27°55E 142 C2
Kai, Kepulauan
Indonesia 5°55S 132°45E 119 F8
Kai Besar Indonesia 5°35S 133°0E 119 F8
Kai Is. = Kai, Kepulauan
Indonesia 5°55S 132°45E 119 F8
Kai Kecil Indonesia 5°45S 132°40E 119 F8
Kai Xian China 31°11N 108°21E 116 B7
Kaiama Nigeria 9°36N 4°1E 139 D5
Kaiapoi N.Z. 43°24S 172°40E 155 E4
Kaidu He → China 41°46N 86°31E 110 C6
Kaieteur Falls Guyana 5°1N 59°10W 186 B7
Kaifeng China 34°48N 114°21E 114 G8
Kaihua China 29°12N 118°20E 117 C12
Kaijiang China 31°7N 107°55E 116 B6
Kaikohe N.Z. 35°25S 173°49E 154 B4
Kaikoura N.Z. 42°25S 173°43E 155 E4
Kaikoura Pen. N.Z. 42°25S 173°43E 155 E4
Kailahun S. Leone 8°18N 10°39W 138 D2
Kailas = Kangrinboqê Feng
China 31°0N 81°25E 125 D9
Kaili China 26°33N 107°59E 116 D6
Kailu China 43°38N 121°18E 115 C11
Kailua Kona U.S.A. 19°39N 155°59W 167 M8
Kaimaganj India 27°33N 79°24E 125 F8
Kaimana Indonesia 3°39S 133°45E 119 E8
Kaimanawa Mts. N.Z. 39°15S 175°56E 154 F4
Kaimata N.Z. 42°34S 171°28E 155 E3
Kaimganj India 27°33N 79°24E 125 F8
Kaimur Hills India 24°30N 82°0E 125 G10
Kainab → Namibia 28°32S 19°34E 144 C2
Kainji Dam Nigeria 9°55N 4°35E 139 C5
Kainji Lake △ Nigeria 10°1N 4°40E 139 C5
Kainuu Finland 64°30N 29°7E 60 D23
Kaipara Harbour N.Z. 36°25S 174°14E 154 B4
Kaiping China 22°23N 112°42E 117 F9
Kaipokok B. Canada 54°54N 59°47W 165 B8
Kaira India 22°75N 72°57E 124 H5
Kairana India 29°24N 77°15E 124 E7
Kairouan Tunisia 35°45N 10°5E 136 A1
Kairouan □ Tunisia 35°30N 9°45E 136 A1
Kaiserslautern Germany 49°26N 7°45E 77 D3
Kaiserstuhl Germany 48°4N 7°40E 77 G3
Kaitaia N.Z. 35°8S 173°17E 154 B4
Kaitangata N.Z. 46°17S 169°51E 155 G2
Kaithal India 29°48N 76°26E 124 E7
Kaitu → Pakistan 33°10N 70°30E 124 C4
Kaiwi Channel U.S.A. 21°15N 157°30W 167 L8

Kaiyang China 27°4N 106°59E 116 D6
Kaiyuan Liaoning,
China 42°28N 124°1E 115 C13
Kaiyuan Yunnan,
China 23°40N 103°12E 116 F4
Kaiyuh Mts. U.S.A. 64°30N 158°0W 166 C8
Kajaani Finland 64°17N 27°46E 60 D22
Kajabbi Australia 20°0S 140°1E 150 C3
Kajana = Kajaani
Finland 64°17N 27°46E 60 D22
Kajang Malaysia 2°59N 101°48E 121 L3
Kajaran Armenia 39°10N 46°7E 105 C12
Kajiado Kenya 1°53S 36°48E 142 C4
Kajiado □ Kenya 2°0S 36°30E 142 C4
Kajo Kaji South Sudan 3°58N 31°40E 135 H12
Kajuru Nigeria 10°15N 7°34E 139 C6
Kaka Turkmenistan 37°21N 59°36E 129 B8
Kakabeka Falls
Canada 48°24N 89°37W 164 C2
Kakadu △ Australia 12°0S 132°3E 148 B5
Kakamas S. Africa 28°45S 20°33E 144 C3
Kakamega Kenya 0°20N 34°46E 142 B3
Kakana India 9°7N 92°48E 127 K11
Kakanj Bos.-H. 44°4N 18°4E 80 F3
Kakanui Mts. N.Z. 45°10S 170°30E 155 F5
Kakata Liberia 6°35N 10°20W 138 D2
Kakdwip India 21°53N 88°11E 125 J13
Kake Japan 34°36N 132°19E 113 G6
Kake U.S.A. 56°59N 133°57W 162 B2
Kakegawa Japan 34°45N 138°1E 113 G9
Kakeroma-Jima Japan 28°8N 129°14E 113 K4
Kākhak Iran 34°9N 58°38E 129 C8
Kakhib Russia 42°28N 46°34E 87 J8
Kakhovka Ukraine 46°45N 33°30E 85 J7
Kakhovske Vdskh.
Ukraine 47°5N 34°0E 85 J7
Kakinada India 16°57N 82°11E 126 F6
Kakisa → Canada 60°56N 117°25W 162 A5
Kakisa L. Canada 60°56N 117°43W 162 A5
Kakogawa Japan 34°46N 134°51E 113 G7
Kakum △ Ghana 5°24N 1°20W 139 D4
Kakuma Kenya 3°43N 34°52E 142 B3
Kakwa → Canada 54°37N 118°28W 162 C5
Kāl Gūsheh Iran 30°59N 58°12E 129 D8
Kal Sefid Iran 34°52N 47°23E 105 E12
Kala Nigeria 12°2N 14°40E 139 C7
Kala Oya → Sri Lanka 8°20N 79°45E 127 K4
Kalaallit Nunaat = Greenland ☑
N. Amer. 66°0N 45°0W 57 D6
Kalabagh Pakistan 33°0N 71°28E 124 C4
Kalabahi Indonesia 8°13S 124°31E 119 F6
Kalabana Mali 14°10N 8°35W 138 C3
Kalaburagi India 17°20N 76°50E 126 F3
Kalach Russia 50°22N 41°0E 86 E5
Kalach na Donu Russia 48°43N 43°32E 87 F6
Kalachinsk Russia 55°3N 74°33E 109 A8
Kaladan → Burma 20°20N 93°5E 123 J18
Kaladar Canada 44°37N 77°5W 174 B7
Kalahari Africa 24°0S 21°30E 144 B3
Kalahari Gemsbok △
S. Africa 25°30S 20°30E 144 C3
Kalaikhum Tajikistan 38°28N 70°6E 109 F8
Kalajoki Finland 64°12N 24°10E 60 D21
Kalajun-Ku'erdening ○
China 43°10N 81°50E 109 D10
Kalakamati Botswana 20°40S 27°25E 145 B4
Kalakan Russia 55°15N 116°45E 107 D12
K'alak'unlun Shank'ou =
Karakoram Pass
Asia 35°33N 77°50E 125 B7
Kalam Pakistan 35°34N 72°30E 124 B5
Kalama
Dem. Rep. of the Congo 2°52S 28°35E 142 C2
Kalama U.S.A. 46°1N 122°51W 170 E4
Kalamaria Greece 40°33N 22°55E 96 F6
Kalamata Greece 37°3N 22°10E 98 D4
Kalamazoo U.S.A. 42°17N 85°35W 173 D11
Kalamazoo → U.S.A. 42°40N 86°10W 172 D10
Kalamb India 18°3N 74°48E 126 E1
Kalambaka Greece 39°42N 21°39E 98 E3
Kalambo Falls Tanzania 8°37S 31°35E 143 D3
Kalannuri India 19°0N 77°16E 126 F4
Kalaotoa Indonesia 7°20S 121°50E 119 F6
Kalárne Sweden 62°59N 16°5E 62 E10
Kalasin Thailand 16°26N 103°30E 120 D4
Kalāt Iran 25°29N 59°22E 129 E9
Kalāt Pakistan 29°8N 66°31E 124 E2
Kalāteh Iran 36°33N 55°41E 129 B7
Kalāteh-ye Ganj Iran 27°31N 57°55E 129 E8
Kalathos Greece 36°9N 28°8E 101 D9
Kalaus → Russia 45°40N 44°7E 87 H7
Kalávrita Greece 38°3N 22°8E 98 C4
Kalb, Ras Yemen 14°2N 48°41E 131 E4
Kalba U.A.E. 25°5N 56°22E 129 E8
Kalbarri Australia 27°40S 114°10E 149 E1
Kalbarri △ Australia 27°45S 114°30E 149 E1
Kalce Slovenia 45°54N 14°13E 74 F8
Kale Antalya, Turkey 36°27N 29°55E 99 E4
Kale Denizli, Turkey 37°27N 28°49E 99 D3
Kalecik Turkey 40°4N 33°26E 104 B5
Kalegauk Kyun Burma 15°33N 97°35E 120 E1
Kalehe
Dem. Rep. of the Congo 2°6S 28°50E 142 C2
Kalema Tanzania 1°12S 31°55E 142 C3
Kalemie
Dem. Rep. of the Congo 5°55S 29°9E 142 D2
Kalety Poland 50°35N 18°52E 83 E5
Kalewa Burma 23°10N 94°15E 123 H19
Kaleybar Iran 38°47N 47°2E 105 B12
Kalgan = Zhangjiakou
China 40°48N 114°55E 114 B8
Kalghatgi India 15°11N 74°58E 127 G2
Kalgoorlie-Boulder
Australia 30°40S 121°22E 149 F3
Kali → India 27°6N 79°52E 125 F8
Kali Sindh → India 26°20N 76°17E 124 G6
Kaliakra, Nos Bulgaria 43°21N 28°30E 97 C12
Kalianda Indonesia 5°50S 105°45E 118 F3
Kalibo Phil. 11°43N 122°22E 119 B6
Kalima
Dem. Rep. of the Congo 2°33S 26°32E 142 C2
Kalimantan Indonesia 0°0 114°0E 118 E4
Kalimantan Barat □
Indonesia 0°0 110°30E 118 E4

Kalimantan Selatan □
Indonesia 2°30S 115°30E 118
Kalimantan Tengah □
Indonesia 2°0S 113°30E 118
Kalimantan Timur □
Indonesia 1°30N 116°30E 118
Kálimnos Greece 37°0N 27°0E 99
Kalimpong India 27°4N 88°35E 125
Kalinadi → India 14°50N 74°7E 127
Kalinikinsk Russia 51°29N 44°28E 108
Kaliningrad Russia 54°42N 20°32E 82
Kaliningrad ✈ (KGD)
Russia 54°45N 20°33E 82
Kalininsk Russia 51°30N 44°40E 86
Kalinkavichy Belarus 52°12N 29°20E 75
Kalinkovichi = Kalinkavichy
Belarus 52°12N 29°20E 75
Kalinovik Bos.-H. 43°31N 18°25E 96
Kalipetrovo Bulgaria 44°3N 27°14E 97
Kaliráchi Greece 40°40N 24°35E 97
Kaliro Uganda 0°56N 33°30E 142
Kalispell U.S.A. 48°12N 114°19W 168
Kalisz Poland 51°45N 18°8E 83
Kalisz Pomorski Poland 53°17N 15°55E 83
Kalithea Greece 37°56N 23°43E 98
Kaliua Tanzania 5°5S 31°48E 142
Kaliveli Tank India 12°5N 79°50E 127
Kalivia Thorikou Greece 37°50N 23°55E 98
Kalix Sweden 65°53N 23°12E 60
Kalixälven → Sweden 65°50N 23°11E 60
Kalka India 30°46N 76°57E 124
Kalkan Turkey 36°15N 29°23E 99
Kalkarindji Australia 17°30S 130°47E 148
Kalkaska U.S.A. 44°44N 85°11W 173
Kalkfeld Namibia 20°57S 16°14E 144
Kalkfontein Botswana 22°4S 20°57E 144
Kalkım Turkey 39°42N 27°13E 99
Kalkrand Namibia 24°1S 17°35E 144
Kallakurichi India 11°44N 79°1E 127
Kallam India 18°36N 76°2E 126
Kållandsö Sweden 58°40N 13°5E 63
Kallavesi Finland 62°58N 27°30E 60
Källby Sweden 58°30N 13°8E 63
Kållered Sweden 57°32N 12°4E 63
Kallidaikurichi India 8°38N 77°31E 127
Kallimasia Greece 38°18N 26°6E 99
Kallinge Sweden 56°15N 15°18E 63
Kallmet Albania 41°51N 19°41E 96
Kallsjön Sweden 63°38N 13°0E 60
Kalmalo Nigeria 13°40N 5°20E 139
Kalmar Sweden 56°40N 16°20E 63
Kalmar □ Sweden 57°25N 16°0E 63
Kalmar sund Sweden 56°40N 16°25E 63
Kalmunai Sri Lanka 7°25N 81°49E 127
Kalmykia □ Russia 46°5N 46°1E 87
Kalna India 23°13N 88°25E 125
Kalnai India 22°46N 83°30E 125
Kalo Nero Greece 37°30N 21°38E 98
Kalocsa Hungary 46°32N 19°0E 80
Kalofer Bulgaria 42°37N 24°59E 97
Kalokhorio Cyprus 34°51N 33°2E 101
Kaloko
Dem. Rep. of the Congo 6°47S 25°48E 142
Kalol Gujarat, India 22°37N 73°31E 124
Kalol Gujarat, India 23°15N 72°33E 124
Kalolimnos Greece 37°4N 27°5E 99
Kalomo Zambia 17°0S 26°30E 143
Kaloni Greece 39°14N 26°12E 99
Kaloni, Kolpos Greece 39°10N 26°10E 99
Kalpeni I. India 10°5N 73°38E 127
Kalpi India 26°8N 79°47E 125
Kalputhi I. India 10°49N 72°10E 127
Kalrayan Hills India 11°45N 78°40E 127
Kalsubai India 19°35N 73°45E 126
Kaltag U.S.A. 64°20N 158°43W 166
Kaltern = Caldaro Italy 46°25N 11°14E 93
Kaltukatjara Australia 24°52S 129°5E 149
Kaltungo Nigeria 9°48N 11°19E 139
Kalu Pakistan 25°5N 67°39E 124
Kaluga Russia 54°35N 36°10E 84
Kaluga □ Russia 54°35N 35°0E 84
Kalulushi Zambia 12°50S 28°3E 143
Kalumburu Australia 13°55S 126°35E 148
Kalumburu ○
Australia 14°17S 126°38E 148
Kalundborg Denmark 55°41N 11°5E 63
Kalush Ukraine 49°3N 24°23E 75
Kaluszyn Poland 52°13N 21°52E 83
Kalutara Sri Lanka 6°35N 80°0E 127
Kalvarija Lithuania 54°25N 23°14E 82
Kalwakurti India 16°41N 78°33E 126
Kalyan = Basavakalyan
India 17°52N 76°57E 126
Kalyan Maharashtra,
India 20°30N 74°3E 126
Kalyan Maharashtra,
India 19°15N 73°9E 126
Kalyandurg India 14°33N 77°6E 127
Kalyansingapuram
India 19°30N 83°19E 126
Kalyazin Russia 57°15N 37°58E 84
Kam Albania 42°17N 20°18E 96
Kam → Nigeria 8°15N 11°0E 139
Kama
Dem. Rep. of the Congo 3°30S 27°5E 142
Kama Japan 33°33N 130°49E 113
Kama → Russia 55°45N 52°0E 86
Kamachumu Tanzania 1°37S 31°37E 142
Kamaishi Japan 39°16N 141°53E 112
Kamalapuram India 14°35N 78°39E 127
Kamalia Pakistan 30°44N 72°42E 124
Kaman India 27°39N 77°16E 124
Kamanjab Namibia 19°35S 14°51E 144
Kamapanda Zambia 12°5S 24°0E 143
Kamaran Yemen 15°21N 42°35E 131
Kamativi Zimbabwe 18°19N 78°21E 145
Kamba Nigeria 11°50N 3°45E 139
Kambalda West
Australia 31°10S 121°37E 149
Kambam India 9°45N 77°16E 127
Kambangan, Nusa
Indonesia 7°40S 108°10E 119
Kambar India 27°37N 68°1E 124
Kambarka Russia 56°15N 54°11E 86
Kambia S. Leone 9°3N 12°53W 138
Kamboké Zambia 8°47S 30°48E 143
Kambos Cyprus 35°2N 32°44E 101

ambove
Dem. Rep. of the Congo 10°51S 26°33E 143 E2
amchatka, Poluostrov
Russia 57°0N 160°0E 107 D17
amchatka Pen. = Kamchatka,
Poluostrov Russia 57°0N 160°0E 107 D17
amchiya → Bulgaria 43°4N 27°44E 97 C11
ame Ruins Zimbabwe 20°7S 28°25E 143 G2
ameda-Hantō Japan 41°50N 141°0E 112 D10
amen Russia 53°50N 81°30E 109 B10
amen-Rybolov Russia 44°46N 132°2E 112 B5
amenica Serbia 43°27N 22°27E 96 C6
amenica Serbia 44°25N 19°45E 96 B3
amenice nad Lipou
Czech Rep. 49°18N 15°2E 78 B8
amenjak, Rt Croatia 44°47N 13°55E 93 D10
amenka = Kamyanka
Ukraine 49°3N 32°6E 85 H7
amenka Kazakhstan 51°7N 50°19E 86 E10
amenka Penza, Russia 53°10N 44°5E 86 D6
amenka Voronezh,
Russia 50°47N 39°20E 85 G10
amenka Bugskaya =
Kamyanka-Buzka
Ukraine 50°8N 24°16E 75 C13
amenka Dneprovskaya =
Kamyanka-Dniprovska
Ukraine 47°29N 34°28E 85 J8
amennomosstskiy
Russia 44°18N 40°13E 87 H5
ameno Bulgaria 42°34N 27°18E 97 D11
amenolomini Russia 47°40N 40°14E 87 G5
amensk-Shakhtinskiy
Russia 48°23N 40°20E 87 F5
amensk Uralskiy
Russia 56°25N 62°2E 106 D7
amenskiy Russia 50°48N 45°25E 86 E7
amenskoye Russia 62°45N 165°30E 107 C17
amenyak Bulgaria 43°24N 26°57E 97 C10
amenz Germany 51°15N 14°5E 76 D10
ameoka Japan 35°0N 135°35E 113 G7
amet India 30°55N 79°35E 125 D8
amiah U.S.A. 46°14N 116°2W 168 C5
amień Krajeński
Poland 53°32N 17°32E 82 E4
amień Pomorski
Poland 53°57N 14°43E 82 E1
amienna → Poland 51°6N 21°47E 83 G8
amienna Góra Poland 50°47N 16°2E 83 H3
amieńsk Poland 51°12N 19°29E 83 G6
amieskuak L. S. Africa 30°9S 17°56E 144 D2
amilukuak L.
Canada 62°22N 101°40W 163 A8
amin-Kashyrskyy
Ukraine 51°39N 24°56E 75 C13
amina
Dem. Rep. of the Congo 8°45S 25°0E 143 D2
aminak L. Canada 62°10N 95°0W 163 A10
aminoyama Japan 38°9N 140°17E 112 E10
amiros Greece 36°20N 27°56E 101 C9
amituga
Dem. Rep. of the Congo 3°2S 28°10E 142 C2
amla → India 25°35N 86°36E 125 G12
amloops Canada 50°40N 120°20W 162 C4
amnik Slovenia 46°14N 14°37E 93 B11
amo Japan 37°39N 139°3E 112 F9
amo N.Z. 35°42S 174°20E 154 B5
amoke Pakistan 32°4N 74°4E 124 C6
amp → Austria 48°23N 15°42E 78 C8
ampala Uganda 0°20N 32°32E 142 B3
ampar Malaysia 4°18N 101°9E 121 K3
ampar → Indonesia 0°30N 103°8E 118 D2
ampen Neths. 52°33N 5°53E 69 B5
ampene
Dem. Rep. of the Congo 3°36S 26°40E 140 E5
amphaeng Phet
Thailand 16°28N 99°30E 120 D2
ampinoski △ Poland 52°21N 20°40E 83 F7
ampolombo, I.
Zambia 11°37S 29°42E 143 E2
ampong Cham
Cambodia 12°0N 105°30E 121 G5
ampong Chhnang
Cambodia 12°20N 104°35E 121 F5
ampong Pengerang
Malaysia 1°22N 104°7E 121 d
ampong Punggai
Malaysia 1°27N 104°18E 121 d
ampong Saom
Cambodia 10°38N 103°30E 121 G4
ampong Saom, Chaak
Cambodia 10°50N 103°32E 121 G4
ampong Tanjong Langsat
Malaysia 1°28N 104°12E 121 d
ampong Telok Ramunia
Malaysia 1°22N 104°15E 121 d
ampung Air Putih
Malaysia 4°15N 103°10E 121 K4
ampung Jerangau
Malaysia 4°50N 103°10E 121 K4
ampung Raja
Malaysia 5°45N 102°35E 121 K4
ampungbaru = Tolitoli
Indonesia 1°5N 120°50E 119 D6
amrau, Teluk
Indonesia 3°30S 133°36E 119 E8
amsack Canada 51°34N 101°54W 163 C8
amsar Guinea 10°40N 14°36W 138 C2
amskoye Ustye Russia 55°10N 49°20E 86 C9
amthi India 21°9N 79°19E 126 D4
amuchawie L. Canada 56°18N 101°59W 163 B8
amui-Misaki Japan 43°20N 140°21E 112 C10
amyanets-Podilskyy
Ukraine 48°45N 26°40E 81 B11
amyanka Ukraine 49°3N 32°6E 85 H7
amyanka-Buzka
Ukraine 50°8N 24°16E 75 C13
amyanka-Dniprovska
Ukraine 47°29N 34°28E 85 J8
amyanets Belarus 52°32N 23°49E 83 F10
amyanyuki Belarus 52°57N 23°49E 83 F11
amyārān Iran 34°47N 46°56E 105 E12
amyshin Russia 50°10N 45°24E 86 E7
amysheve Russia 46°4N 48°10E 87 G9
anaaupscow →
Canada 54°2N 76°30W 164 B4
anab U.S.A. 37°3N 112°32W 169 H7

Kanab Cr. → U.S.A. 36°24N 112°38W 169 H7
Kanacea Lau Group, Fiji 17°15S 179°6W 154 a
Kanacea Taveuni, Fiji 16°59S 179°56E 154 a
Kanagi Japan 40°54N 140°27E 112 D10
Kanairiktok → Canada 55°2N 60°18W 165 A7
Kanakapura India 12°33N 77°28E 127 H3
Kanalia Greece 39°30N 22°53E 98 B4
Kananga
Dem. Rep. of the Congo 5°55S 22°18E 140 F4
Kanangra-Boyd △
Australia 33°57S 150°15E 153 B9
Kanash Russia 55°30N 47°32E 86 C8
Kanaskat U.S.A. 47°19N 121°54W 170 C5
Kanastraíon, Ákra = Paliouri,
Akra Greece 39°57N 23°45E 96 G7
Kanawha → U.S.A. 38°50N 82°9W 173 F12
Kanazawa Japan 36°30N 136°38E 113 F8
Kanchanaburi Thailand 14°2N 99°31E 120 E2
Kanchenjunga Nepal 27°50N 88°10E 125 F12
Kanchenjunga △ India 27°42N 88°8E 125 F13
Kanchipuram India 12°52N 79°45E 127 H4
Kańczuga Poland 49°59N 22°25E 83 J9
Kandaghat India 30°59N 77°7E 124 D7
Kandahār Afghan. 31°32N 65°43E 122 D4
Kandahar India 18°52N 77°12E 126 E3
Kandahār □ Afghan. 31°0N 65°0E 122 D4
Kandalaksha Russia 67°9N 32°30E 60 C25
Kandangan Indonesia 2°50S 115°20E 118 E5
Kandanos Greece 35°19N 23°44E 101 D5
Kandava Latvia 57°2N 22°46E 82 A9
Kandavu = Kadavu Fiji 19°0S 178°15E 154 a
Kandavu Passage = Kadavu
Passage Fiji 18°45S 178°0E 154 a
Kandé = Kanté Togo 9°57N 1°3E 139 D5
Kandhkot Pakistan 28°16N 69°8E 124 E3
Kandhla India 29°18N 77°19E 124 E7
Kandi Benin 11°7N 2°55E 139 C5
Kandi India 23°58N 88°5E 125 H13
Kandiaro Pakistan 27°4N 68°13E 124 F3
Kandila Greece 37°46N 22°2E 98 D4
Kandra Turkey 41°4N 30°9E 104 B4
Kandla India 23°0N 70°10E 124 H4
Kandos Australia 32°45S 149°58E 153 B8
Kandy Sri Lanka 7°18N 80°43E 127 L5
Kane U.S.A. 41°40N 78°49W 174 E6
Kane Basin Greenland 79°1N 70°0W 57 B4
Kane Senegal 15°30N 13°18W 138 B2
Kanevskaya Russia 46°3N 38°57E 87 G4
Kanfanar Croatia 45°7N 13°50E 93 C10
Kang Botswana 23°41S 22°50E 144 B3
Kangaamiut Greenland 65°50N 53°20W 57 D5
Kangaatsiaq Greenland 68°18N 53°28W 57 D5
Kangaba Mali 11°56N 8°25W 138 C3
Kangal Turkey 39°14N 37°23E 104 C7
Kangān Fārs, Iran 27°50N 52°3E 129 E7
Kangān Hormozgān,
Iran 25°48N 57°28E 129 E8
Kangar Malaysia 6°27N 100°12E 121 J3
Kangaré Mali 11°36N 8°4W 138 C3
Kangaroo I. Australia 35°45S 137°0E 152 C2
Kangaroo Mts.
Australia 23°29S 141°51E 150 C3
Kangasala Finland 61°28N 24°4E 84 B3
Kangāvar Iran 34°40N 48°0E 105 E12
Kangdong China 30°2N 101°57E 116 B3
Kangdong N. Korea 39°9N 126°5E 115 E14
Kangean, Kepulauan
Indonesia 6°55S 115°23E 118 F5
Kangean Is. = Kangean,
Kepulauan Indonesia 6°55S 115°23E 118 F5
Kangerdlugssuak
Greenland 68°10N 32°20W 57 D7
Kangerluarsoruseq
Greenland 63°45N 51°27W 57 E5
Kangerluarsoruset =
Kangerluarsoruseq
Greenland 63°45N 51°27W 57 E5
Kangerlussuaq
Greenland 66°59N 50°40W 57 D5
Kangertittivaq = Scoresby Sund
Greenland 70°29N 21°46W 57 C8
Kanggye N. Korea 41°0N 126°35E 115 D14
Kangiqliniq = Rankin Inlet
Canada 62°30N 93°0W 160 E13
Kangiqsualujjuaq
Canada 58°30N 65°59W 161 F18
Kangiqsujuaq Canada 61°30N 72°0W 161 E17
Kangiqtugaapik = Clyde River
Canada 70°30N 68°30W 161 C18
Kangirsuk Canada 60°0N 70°0W 161 F18
Kangkar Chemaran
Malaysia 1°34N 104°12E 121 d
Kangkar Sungai Tiram
Malaysia 1°35N 103°55E 121 d
Kangkar Teberau
Malaysia 1°32N 103°51E 121 d
Kangping China 42°43N 123°18E 115 C12
Kangrinboqê Feng
China 31°0N 81°25E 125 D9
Kangto China 27°50N 92°35E 125 F18
Kanha △ India 22°15N 80°40E 125 H9
Kanhan → India 21°4N 79°34E 126 D4
Kanhangad India 12°21N 74°58E 127 H2
Kani Ivory C. 8°29N 6°36W 138 D3
Kaniama
Dem. Rep. of the Congo 7°30S 24°12E 142 D1
Kaniapiskau = Caniapiscau →
Canada 54°40N 69°30W 165 A6
Kaniapiskau, L. = Caniapiscau, L.
Canada 54°10N 69°55W 165 B6
Kaniere, L. N.Z. 42°50S 171°10E 155 C6
Kanigiri India 15°24N 79°31E 127 G4
Kanin, Poluostrov Russia 68°0N 45°0E 58 B14
Kanin Nos, Mys Russia 68°39N 43°32E 106 C5
Kanin Pen. = Kanin, Poluostrov
Russia 68°0N 45°0E 58 B14
Kaniva Australia 36°22S 141°18E 152 C4
Kanjiza Serbia 46°3N 20°4E 80 D5
Kanjut Sar Pakistan 36°7N 75°25E 125 A6
Kankaanpää Finland 61°44N 22°50E 84 B2
Kankakee U.S.A. 41°7N 87°52W 172 E12
Kankakee → U.S.A. 41°23N 88°15W 172 E19
Kankan Guinea 10°23N 9°15W 138 C3
Kanker India 20°10N 81°40E 125 D5

Kankesanturai Sri Lanka 9°49N 80°2E 127 K5
Kankossa Mauritania 15°54N 11°31W 138 B2
Kankroli India 25°4N 73°53E 124 G5
Kanmaw Kyun Burma 11°40N 98°28E 121 G2
Kannapolis U.S.A. 35°30N 80°37W 177 D14
Kannauj India 27°3N 79°56E 125 F8
Kanniyakumari India 8°5N 77°34E 127 K3
Kannod India 22°45N 76°40E 124 H7
Kannur India 11°53N 75°27E 127 J2
Kano Nigeria 12°2N 8°30E 139 C6
Kan'onji Japan 34°7N 133°39E 113 G6
Kanoroba Ivory C. 9°7N 6°8W 138 D3
Kanowit Malaysia 2°14N 112°20E 118 D4
Kanoya Japan 31°25N 130°50E 113 J5
Kanpetlet Burma 21°10N 93°59E 123 J18
Kanpur India 26°28N 80°20E 125 F8
Kansas □ U.S.A. 38°30N 99°0W 172 F4
Kansas → U.S.A. 39°7N 94°38W 172 F6
Kansas City Kans.,
U.S.A. 39°7N 94°38W 172 F6
Kansas City Mo., U.S.A. 39°6N 94°35W 172 F6
Kansenia
Dem. Rep. of the Congo 10°20S 26°0E 143 E2
Kansk Russia 56°20N 95°37E 107 D10
Kansu = Gansu □ China 36°0N 104°0E 114 G3
Kantaphor India 22°35N 76°34E 124 H7
Kantchari Burkina Faso 12°37N 1°37E 139 C5
Kantché Niger 13°31N 8°30E 139 C6
Kanté Togo 9°57N 1°3E 139 D5
Kantemirovka Russia 49°43N 39°55E 85 H10
Kantharalak Thailand 14°39N 104°39E 120 E5
Kanthi = Contai India 21°54N 87°46E 125 J12
Kantli → India 28°20N 75°30E 124 E6
Kantō □ Japan 36°15N 139°30E 113 F9
Kantō-Sanchi Japan 35°59N 138°50E 113 G9
Kanturk Ireland 52°11N 8°54W 64 D3
Kanuma Japan 36°34N 139°42E 113 F9
Kanus Namibia 27°50S 18°39E 144 C2
Kanye Botswana 24°55S 25°28E 144 B4
Kanzenze
Dem. Rep. of the Congo 10°30S 25°12E 143 E2
Kanzi, Ras Tanzania 7°1S 39°33E 142 D4
Kao Phara Thailand 8°0N 98°30E 121 a
Kaohsiung Taiwan 22°35N 120°16E 117 F13
Kaokoveld Namibia 19°15S 14°30E 144 A1
Kaolack Senegal 14°5N 16°8W 138 C1
Kaolack □ Senegal 14°10N 15°15W 138 C1
Kaoshan China 44°38N 124°50E 115 B13
Kapa'a U.S.A. 22°5N 159°19W 167 L8
Kapadvanj India 23°5N 73°0E 124 H5
Kapan Armenia 39°18N 46°27E 105 C12
Kapanga
Dem. Rep. of the Congo 8°30S 22°40E 140 F4
Kapchagai = Qapshaghay
Kazakhstan 43°51N 77°14E 109 D9
Kapchagaiskoye Vdkhr. =
Qapshaghay Bögeni
Kazakhstan 43°45N 77°50E 109 D9
Kapedo Kenya 1°10N 36°6E 142 B4
Kapela = Velika Kapela
Croatia 45°10N 15°5E 93 C12
Kapellskär Sweden 59°44N 19°2E 62 E13
Kapelo, Akra Greece 36°9N 23°3E 98 E5
Kapema
Dem. Rep. of the Congo 10°45S 28°22E 143 E2
Kapenguria Kenya 1°14N 35°7E 142 B4
Kapfenberg Austria 47°26N 15°18E 78 D8
Kapı Daği Turkey 40°28N 27°50E 97 F11
Kapiri Mposhi Zambia 13°59S 28°43E 143 E2
Kāpīsā □ Afghan. 35°0N 69°20E 122 B6
Kapiskau → Canada 52°47N 81°55W 164 B3
Kapit Malaysia 2°0N 112°55E 118 D4
Kapiti I. N.Z. 40°50S 174°56E 154 G3
Kaplan U.S.A. 30°0N 92°17W 176 F8
Kaplica = Davlos
Cyprus 35°25N 33°54E 101 D12
Kaplice Czech Rep. 48°42N 14°30E 78 C7
Kapoe Thailand 9°34N 98°32E 121 H2
Kapoeta South Sudan 4°50N 33°35E 135 H12
Kápolnásnyék Hungary 47°16N 18°41E 80 C3
Kaponga N.Z. 39°29S 174°9E 154 F3
Kapos → Hungary 46°44N 18°30E 80 D3
Kaposvár Hungary 46°25N 17°47E 80 D2
Kapowsin U.S.A. 46°59N 122°13W 170 D4
Kappeln Germany 54°40N 9°55E 76 A5
Kappelshamn Sweden 57°52N 18°47E 63 G12
Kapps Namibia 22°32S 17°18E 144 B2
Kaprije Croatia 43°42N 15°43E 93 E12
Kapsabet Kenya 0°12N 35°5E 142 B4
Kapsan N. Korea 41°4N 128°19E 115 D15
Kapsukas = Marijampolė
Lithuania 54°33N 23°19E 82 D10
Kaptai L. Bangla. 22°40N 92°20E 123 H18
Kapuas → Indonesia 0°25S 109°20E 118 E3
Kapuas Hulu, Pegunungan
Malaysia 1°30N 113°30E 118 D4
Kapuas Hulu Ra. = Kapuas Hulu,
Pegunungan
Malaysia 1°30N 113°30E 118 D4
Kapulo
Dem. Rep. of the Congo 8°18S 29°15E 143 D2
Kapunda Australia 34°20S 138°56E 152 C3
Kapuni N.Z. 39°29S 174°8E 154 F3
Kapurthala India 31°23N 75°25E 124 D6
Kapuskasing Canada 49°25N 82°30W 164 C3
Kapuskasing →
Canada 49°49N 82°0W 164 C3
Kaputar, Mt. Australia 30°15S 150°10E 151 E5
Kaputir Kenya 2°5N 35°28E 142 B4
Kapuvár Hungary 47°36N 17°1E 80 C2
Kara, W. → Si. Arabia 20°45N 41°42E 137 C5
Kara Ada Turkey 36°58N 27°28E 99 E9
Kara-Balta Kyrgyzstan 42°50N 73°49E 109 D8
Kara Bogaz Gol, Zaliv =
Garabogazköl Aylagy
Turkmenistan 41°0N 53°30E 108 D4
Kara Burun Turkey 38°32N 27°58E 99 C8
Kara Kala = Garrygala
Turkmenistan 38°31N 56°29E 129 B8
Kara Kalpak Republic =
Qoraqalpog'iston □
Uzbekistan 43°0N 58°0E 108 D6
Kara-Köl Kyrgyzstan 41°40N 72°43E 109 D8
Kara Kum = Garagum
Turkmenistan 39°30N 60°0E 129 B8
Kara Sea Russia 75°0N 70°0E 106 B8
Karaadilli Turkey 38°18N 30°37E 99 C5

Karabiğa Turkey 40°23N 27°17E 97 F11
Karabük Turkey 41°12N 32°37E 104 B5
Karabük □ Turkey 41°10N 32°30E 104 B5
Karaburun Albania 40°25N 19°20E 96 F3
Karaburun Turkey 38°41N 26°28E 99 C8
Karabutak = Qarabutaq
Kazakhstan 50°0N 60°14E 108 C6
Karacabey Turkey 40°12N 28°21E 97 F12
Karacakılavuz Turkey 41°8N 27°21E 97 F11
Karacaköy Turkey 41°24N 28°22E 97 E12
Karacasu Turkey 37°43N 28°35E 99 D11
Karachala = Qaraçala
Azerbaijan 39°45N 48°53E 87 L9
Karachayevsk Russia 43°50N 41°55E 87 J5
Karachey-Cherkessia □
Russia 43°40N 41°30E 87 J5
Karachi Pakistan 24°50N 67°0E 129 E8
Karad India 17°15N 74°10E 126 F2
Karadirek Turkey 38°34N 30°11E 99 C5
Karaga Ghana 9°58N 0°28W 139 D4
Karaganda = Qaraghandy
Kazakhstan 49°50N 73°10E 108 C8
Karagayly = Qaraghayly
Kazakhstan 49°26N 76°0E 108 E8
Karaginskiy, Ostrov
Russia 58°45N 164°0E 107 D17
Karagola Road India 25°29N 87°23E 125 G12
Karagüney Dağları
Turkey 40°30N 34°40E 104 B6
Karahallı Turkey 38°21N 29°33E 99 C11
Karaikal India 10°59N 79°50E 127 J4
Karaikkudi India 10°5N 78°45E 127 J4
Karaisalı Turkey 37°16N 35°2E 104 D6
Karaj Iran 35°48N 51°0E 129 B6
Karajarri ◌ Australia 19°0S 122°30E 148 C3
Karak Malaysia 3°25N 102°2E 121 L4
Karakalpakstan =
Qoraqalpog'iston □
Uzbekistan 43°0N 58°0E 108 D5
Karakaya Barajı
Turkey 38°31N 38°23E 105 C8
Karakelong Indonesia 4°35N 126°50E 119 D7
Karakitang Indonesia 3°14N 125°28E 119 D7
Karakoçan Turkey 38°57N 40°2E 105 C9
Karakol Kyrgyzstan 42°30N 78°20E 109 D9
Karakoram Pass Asia 35°33N 77°50E 125 B7
Karakoram Ra. Pakistan 35°30N 77°0E 125 B7
Karakul = Qorako'l
Uzbekistan 39°32N 63°50E 108 E6
Karakul Tajikistan 39°2N 73°33E 109 E8
Karakul, Ozero
Tajikistan 39°5N 73°25E 109 E8
Karakurt Turkey 40°10N 42°37E 105 B10
Karakuwisa Namibia 18°56S 19°40E 144 A2
Karalon Russia 57°5N 115°50E 107 D12
Karama Jordan 31°57N 35°35E 130 D4
Karaman Balıkesir, Turkey 39°39N 28°0E 99 B9
Karaman Konya, Turkey 37°14N 33°13E 104 D5
Karamanlı Turkey 37°23N 29°47E 99 D11
Karamay China 45°30N 84°58E 109 C10
Karambu Indonesia 3°53S 116°6E 118 E5
Karamea N.Z. 41°14S 172°6E 155 B7
Karamea → N.Z. 41°13S 172°26E 155 B7
Karamea Bight N.Z. 41°22S 171°40E 155 B6
Karamnasa → India 25°31N 83°52E 125 G10
Karamürsel Turkey 40°41N 29°36E 97 F13
Karand Iran 34°16N 46°15E 105 E12
Karanganyar Indonesia 7°38S 109°37E 119 G13
Karangasem = Amlapura
Indonesia 8°27S 115°37E 119 J18
Karanja Maharashtra,
India 21°11N 78°24E 126 D4
Karanja Maharashtra,
India 20°29N 77°31E 126 D3
Karanjia India 21°47N 85°58E 125 J11
Karankasso
Burkina Faso 10°50N 3°53W 138 C4
Karaova Turkey 37°5N 27°40E 99 D9
Karapınar Turkey 37°43N 33°6E 104 D5
Karapiro N.Z. 37°53S 175°32E 154 G5
Karas □ Namibia 25°0S 18°0E 144 C2
Karasburg Namibia 28°0S 18°44E 144 C2
Karasino Russia 66°50N 86°50E 106 C9
Karasjok Norway 69°27N 25°30E 60 B21
Karasu Turkey 41°4N 30°46E 104 B4
Karasu → Turkey 36°18N 37°0E 104 C7
Karasuk Russia 53°44N 78°2E 108 D8
Karasuyama Japan 36°39N 140°9E 113 F10
Karatas Adana, Turkey 36°36N 35°21E 104 D6
Karataş Manisa, Turkey 38°35N 28°16E 99 C10
Karataş Burnu Turkey 36°31N 35°24E 104 D6
Karatau, Khrebet = Qarataū
Kazakhstan 43°30N 69°30E 108 E7
Karatax Shan China 35°57N 81°0E 109 E10
Karateki Shan China 40°30N 77°50E 109 D9
Karativu Sri Lanka 8°22N 79°47E 127 K4
Karatoprak = Turgutreis
Turkey 37°2N 27°15E 99 D9
Karatsu Japan 33°26N 129°58E 113 H5
Karaul Russia 70°6N 83°15E 106 B9
Karauli India 26°30N 77°4E 124 F7
Karavastasë, L. e Albania 40°55N 19°30E 96 F3
Karavia Greece 36°49N 23°37E 98 E5
Karavostasi Cyprus 35°8N 32°50E 101 D11
Karawang Indonesia 6°30S 107°15E 119 G12
Karawanken Europe 46°30N 14°40E 78 B7
Karayazı Turkey 39°41N 42°9E 105 C10
Karazhal = Qarazhal
Kazakhstan 48°2N 70°49E 108 C4
Karbalā' Iraq 32°36N 44°3E 105 F11
Karbalā' □ Iraq 32°36N 44°3E 105 F10
Kårböle Sweden 61°59N 15°22E 62 C9
Karcag Hungary 47°19N 20°57E 80 C5
Karcha → Pakistan 34°45N 76°10E 125 B7
Karchana India 25°17N 81°56E 125 G9
Karczew Poland 52°5N 21°15E 83 F8
Kardam Bulgaria 43°45N 28°6E 97 C12
Kardamaina Greece 36°47N 27°8E 99 E10
Kardamili Greece 36°53N 22°2E 98 E4
Kardeljovo = Ploče
Croatia 43°4N 17°26E 93 E14
Karditsa Greece 39°23N 21°54E 98 B3
Kärdla Estonia 59°0N 22°4E 84 C2
Kardzhali = Kŭrdzhali
Bulgaria 41°38N 25°21E 97 E10
Kareeberge S. Africa 30°59S 21°50E 144 E3
Kareha → India 25°44N 86°21E 125 G12

Kareima Sudan 18°30N 31°49E 137 D3
Karelia □ Russia 65°30N 32°30E 106 C4
Karelian Republic = Karelia □
Russia 65°30N 32°30E 106 C4
Karera India 25°32N 78°9E 124 G8
Kärevändar Iran 27°53N 60°44E 129 E9
Kargasok Russia 59°3N 80°53E 106 D9
Kargat Russia 55°10N 80°15E 106 D9
Kargı Turkey 41°11N 34°30E 104 B6
Kargil India 34°32N 76°12E 125 B7
Kargopol Russia 61°30N 38°58E 84 B10
Karguéri Niger 13°27N 10°30E 139 C7
Karia ba Mohammed
Morocco 34°22N 5°12W 136 B2
Kariān Iran 26°57N 57°14E 129 E8
Kariba Zimbabwe 16°28S 28°50E 143 F2
Kariba, L. Zimbabwe 16°40S 28°25E 143 F2
Kariba Dam Zimbabwe 16°30S 28°35E 143 F2
Kariba Gorge Zambia 16°30S 28°50E 143 F2
Karibib Namibia 22°0S 15°56E 144 B2
Karies Greece 40°14N 24°19E 97 F8
Karijini △ Australia 23°15S 118°33E 148 D2
Karikari, C. N.Z. 34°46S 173°24E 154 A2
Karimata, Kepulauan
Indonesia 1°25S 109°0E 118 E3
Karimata, Selat
Indonesia 2°0S 108°40E 118 E3
Karimata Is. = Karimata,
Kepulauan Indonesia 1°25S 109°0E 118 E3
Karimnagar India 18°26N 79°10E 126 E4
Karimun, Pulau Indonesia 1°3N 103°22E 121 d
Karimun Kecil, Pulau
Indonesia 1°8N 103°22E 121 d
Karimunjawa, Kepulauan
Indonesia 5°50S 110°30E 118 F4
Karin Somalia 10°50N 45°52E 131 E4
Karistos Greece 38°1N 24°29E 98 C6
Karīt Iran 33°29N 56°55E 128 C8
Kariya Japan 34°58N 137°1E 113 G8
Kariyangwe Zimbabwe 18°0S 27°38E 145 A4
Karjala Finland 62°0N 30°25E 84 A5
Karjat India 18°33N 75°0E 126 E2
Karkal India 13°15N 74°56E 127 H2
Karkaralinsk = Qarqaraly
Kazakhstan 49°26N 75°30E 109 C9
Karkheh → Iran 31°2N 47°29E 128 D5
Karki Azerbaijan 39°47N 44°57E 105 C11
Karkinitska Zatoka
Ukraine 45°56N 33°0E 85 K7
Karkinitskiy Zaliv = Karkinitska
Zatoka Ukraine 45°56N 33°0E 85 K7
Karkuk = Kirkūk
Iraq 35°30N 44°21E 105 E11
Karkur Tohl Egypt 22°5N 25°5E 137 C2
Karl Liebknecht = imeni Karl
Libknekhta Russia 51°40N 35°35E 85 G8
Karla, L. = Volvi, L.
Greece 40°40N 23°34E 96 F7
Karlantijpa North ◌
Australia 19°27S 133°33E 148 C5
Karlantijpa South ◌
Australia 20°31S 133°9E 148 D5
Karleby = Kokkola
Finland 63°50N 23°8E 60 E20
Karlholmsbruk Sweden 60°31N 17°37E 62 D11
Karlino Poland 54°3N 15°53E 82 D2
Karlova Turkey 39°17N 41°0E 105 C9
Karlovac Croatia 45°31N 15°36E 93 D12
Karlovarský □
Czech Rep. 50°10N 12°50E 78 A5
Karlovasi Greece 37°45N 26°42E 99 D8
Karlovka = Karlivka
Ukraine 49°29N 35°8E 85 H8
Karlovo Bulgaria 42°38N 24°47E 97 D8
Karlovy Vary Czech Rep. 50°13N 12°51E 78 A5
Karlsbad = Karlovy Vary
Czech Rep. 50°13N 12°51E 78 A5
Karlsborg Sweden 58°33N 14°33E 63 F8
Karlshamn Sweden 56°10N 14°51E 63 H8
Karlskoga Sweden 59°28N 14°33E 63 F7
Karlskrona Sweden 56°10N 15°35E 63 H9
Karlsruhe Germany 49°0N 8°23E 77 F4
Karlstad Sweden 59°23N 13°30E 63 F7
Karlstad U.S.A. 48°35N 96°31W 172 A5
Karlstadt Germany 49°57N 9°46E 77 F5
Karma Niger 13°38N 1°52E 139 C5
Karmala India 18°26N 75°22E 126 E2
Karmi'el Israel 32°55N 35°18E 130 C4
Karnak Egypt 25°43N 32°39E 137 B3
Karnal India 29°42N 77°2E 124 E7
Karnali = Ghaghara →
India 25°45N 84°40E 125 G11
Karnali → Nepal 28°45N 81°16E 125 E9
Karnaphuli Res. = Kaptai L.
Bangla. 22°40N 92°20E 123 H18
Karnataka □ India 13°15N 77°0E 127 H3
Karnes City U.S.A. 28°53N 97°54W 176 G6
Karnische Alpen Europe 46°36N 13°0E 78 E6
Karnobat Bulgaria 42°39N 26°59E 97 D10
Kärnten □ Austria 46°52N 13°30E 78 E6
Karo Mali 12°16N 3°18W 138 C4
Karoi Zimbabwe 16°48S 29°45E 143 F2
Karon, Ao Thailand 7°51N 98°17E 121 a
Karonga Malawi 9°57S 33°55E 143 D3
Karoo △ S. Africa 32°18S 22°27E 144 E3
Karoonda Australia 35°1S 139°59E 152 C2
Karor Pakistan 31°15N 70°59E 124 D4
Karora Sudan 17°44N 38°15E 137 D4
Karounga Mali 16°5N 3°30W 138 B4
Karousades Greece 39°47N 19°45E 98 B1
Karpasia Cyprus 35°32N 34°15E 101 D13
Karpathos Greece 35°37N 27°10E 99 F10
Karpathou, Stenon
Greece 36°0N 27°30E 99 F10
Karpatsky △ Ukraine 48°30N 24°0E 81 B9
Karpenisi Greece 38°55N 21°40E 98 C3
Karpuzlu Turkey 37°33N 27°43E 99 D9
Karpuzlu Burnu = Apostolos
Andreas, C. Cyprus 35°42N 34°35E 101 D13
Karratha Australia 20°44S 116°52E 148 D2
Kars Turkey 40°40N 43°5E 105 B10
Kars □ Turkey 40°40N 43°0E 105 B10
Karsakpay Kazakhstan 47°55N 66°40E 108 C7
Karsha Kazakhstan 49°45N 51°35E 86 F10

Karshi = Qarshi
Uzbekistan 38°53N 65°48E 109 E7
Karsiyang India 26°56N 88°18E 125 F13
Karsog India 31°23N 77°12E 124 D7
Karst = Kras Slovenia 45°35N 14°0E 93 C10
Kartal Turkey 40°53N 29°11E 97 F13
Kartala Comoros Is. 11°45S 43°21E 141 a
Kartaly Russia 53°3N 60°40E 108 D6
Kartapur India 31°27N 75°32E 124 D6
Karthaus U.S.A. 41°8N 78°9W 174 E6
Kartuzy Poland 54°22N 18°10E 82 D5
Karuah Australia 32°37S 151°56E 153 B9
Karufa Indonesia 3°50S 133°20E 119 E8
Karula △ Estonia 57°43N 26°30E 84 D4
Karuma △ Uganda 2°5N 32°15E 142 B3
Karumba Australia 17°31S 140°50E 150 B3
Karumo Tanzania 2°25S 32°50E 142 C3
Karumwa Tanzania 3°12S 32°38E 142 C3
Kārūn → Iran 30°26N 48°10E 129 D6
Karungu Kenya 0°50S 34°10E 142 C3
Karup Denmark 56°19N 9°10E 63 H3
Karur India 10°59N 78°2E 127 J4
Karviná Czech Rep. 49°53N 18°31E 79 B11
Karwan → India 27°26N 78°4E 124 F8
Karwar India 14°55N 74°13E 127 H2
Karwendel △ Austria 47°25N 11°30E 78 D4
Karwi India 25°12N 80°57E 125 G9
Karymskoye Russia 51°36N 114°21E 107 D12
Kaş Turkey 36°11N 29°37E 99 E11
Kasaba Turkey 36°18N 29°44E 99 E11
Kasache Malawi 13°25S 34°20E 143 E3
Kasai →
Dem. Rep. of the Congo 3°30S 16°10E 140 E3
Kasai-Oriental □
Dem. Rep. of the Congo 5°0S 24°30E 142 D1
Kasaji
Dem. Rep. of the Congo 10°25S 23°27E 143 E1
Kasama Zambia 10°16S 31°9E 143 E3
Kasan-dong N. Korea 41°18N 126°55E 115 D14
Kasane Namibia 17°34S 24°50E 144 A3
Kasanga Tanzania 8°30S 31°10E 143 D3
Kasanka △ Zambia 11°34S 30°15E 143 E3
Kasar, Ras Sudan 18°2N 38°35E 137 D4
Kasaragod India 12°30N 74°58E 127 H2
Kasba L. Canada 60°20N 102°10W 163 A8
Kasba Tadla Morocco 32°36N 6°17W 136 B2
Käseh Garän Iran 34°5N 46°2E 128 C5
Kasempa Zambia 13°30S 25°44E 142 E1
Kasenga
Dem. Rep. of the Congo 10°20S 28°45E 143 E2
Kasese Uganda 0°13N 30°3E 142 B3
Kasganj India 27°48N 78°42E 125 F8
Kashabowie Canada 48°40N 90°26W 164 C1
Kashaf Iran 35°58N 61°7E 129 C9
Kāshān Iran 34°5N 51°30E 129 C6
Kashechewan Canada 52°18N 81°37W 164 B3
Kashgar = Kashi China 39°30N 76°2E 109 E9
Kashi China 39°30N 76°2E 109 E9
Kashimbo
Dem. Rep. of the Congo 11°12S 26°19E 143 E2
Kashin Russia 57°20N 37°36E 84 D9
Kashipur Odisha, India 19°16N 83°3E 126 E6
Kashipur Uttarakhand,
India 29°15N 79°0E 125 E8
Kashira Russia 54°45N 38°10E 84 E10
Kashiwazaki Japan 37°22N 138°33E 113 F9
Kashk-e Kohneh
Afghan. 34°55N 62°30E 122 B3
Kashksaray Iran 38°37N 45°34E 105 C11
Kashkū'īyeh Iran 30°31N 55°40E 129 D7
Kāshmar Iran 35°16N 58°26E 129 C8
Kashmir Asia 34°0N 76°0E 125 C7
Kashmor Pakistan 28°28N 69°32E 124 E3
Kashpirovka Russia 53°0N 48°30E 86 D9
Kashun Noerh = Gaxun Nur
China 42°22N 100°30E 110 C9
Kasiari India 22°8N 87°14E 125 H12
Kasimov Russia 54°55N 41°20E 86 D6
Kasinge
Dem. Rep. of the Congo 6°15S 26°58E 142 D2
Kasiruta Indonesia 0°25S 127°12E 119 E7
Kaskaskia → U.S.A. 37°58N 89°57W 172 G9
Kaskattama → Canada 57°3N 90°4W 163 B10
Kaskinen Finland 62°22N 21°15E 63 E16
Kaskö = Kaskinen
Finland 62°22N 21°15E 60 E16
Kaslo Canada 49°55N 116°55W 162 D5
Kasmere L. Canada 59°34N 101°10W 163 B8
Kasongo
Dem. Rep. of the Congo 4°30S 26°33E 142 C2
Kasongo Lunda
Dem. Rep. of the Congo 6°35S 16°49E 140 F3
Kasos Greece 35°20N 26°55E 99 F8
Kasou, Stenon Greece 35°30N 26°30E 99 F8
Kaspi Georgia 41°59N 44°26E 87 K7
Kaspichan Bulgaria 43°18N 27°11E 97 C11
Kaspiysk Russia 42°52N 47°40E 87 J8
Kaspiyskiy Russia 45°22N 47°23E 87 H8
Kassaba Egypt 22°40N 29°55E 137 C2
Kassalâ Sudan 15°30N 36°0E 135 E13
Kassandra Greece 40°0N 23°30E 96 F7
Kassandra Kolpos Greece 40°5N 23°30E 96 F7
Kassandras, Akra
Greece 39°57N 23°30E 96 G7
Kassándria Greece 40°2N 23°30E 96 F7
Kassel Germany 51°18N 9°26E 76 D5
Kasserine Tunisia 35°15N 8°50E 136 A5
Kassinger Sudan 18°46N 31°51E 137 D3
Kassiopi Greece 39°48N 19°53E 101 A3
Kasson U.S.A. 44°2N 92°45W 172 C7
Kastamonu Turkey 41°25N 33°43E 104 B5
Kastamonu □ Turkey 41°30N 33°40E 104 B5
Kastav Croatia 45°22N 14°20E 93 C11
Kasteli = Kissamos
Greece 35°29N 23°38E 101 D5
Kastelli Greece 35°12N 25°20E 101 D7
Kastellorizo = Megisti
Greece 36°8N 29°34E 99 E11
Kastelo, Akra Greece 35°30N 27°15E 99 F9
Kasterlee Belgium 51°15N 4°59E 69 C4
Kastlösa Sweden 56°26N 16°25E 63 H10
Kastoria Greece 40°30N 21°19E 96 F5
Kastorias, L. Greece 40°30N 21°20E 96 F5
Kastorio Greece 37°10N 22°17E 98 D5
Kastornoye Russia 51°55N 38°2E 85 G10
Kastos Greece 38°35N 20°55E 98 C2
Kastrom Mefa'a = Umm al Rasas
Jordan 31°30N 35°55E 130 D4
Kastrosikia Greece 39°6N 20°36E 98 B2

Kastrup, København ✈ (CPH)
  Denmark 55°37N 12°39E 63 J6
Kastsyukovichy Belarus 53°20N 32°4E 85 F7
Kasubi Tombs Uganda 0°2'0N 32°30E 142 B3
Kasulu Tanzania 4°37S 30°5E 142 C3
Kasumi Japan 35°38N 134°38E 113 G7
Kasumkent Russia 41°47N 48°15E 87 K9
Kasungu Malawi 13°0S 33°29E 143 E3
Kasungu △ Malawi 12°53S 33°9E 143 E3
Kasur Pakistan 31°5N 74°25E 124 D6
Kata, Ao Thailand 7°48N 98°18E 121 J2
Kata Archanes Greece 35°15N 25°10E 101 D7
Kata Tjuta Australia 25°20S 130°50E 149 E5
Kataba Zambia 16°5S 25°10E 143 E2
Katagum Nigeria 12°18N 10°21E 139 C7
Katahdin, Mt. U.S.A. 45°54N 68°56W 173 C19
Kataka = Cuttack
  India 20°25N 85°57E 126 D7
Katako Kombe
  Dem. Rep. of the Congo 3°25S 24°20E 142 C1
Katakolo Greece 37°38N 21°19E 98 D3
Katale Tanzania 4°52S 31°7E 142 C3
Katamatite Australia 36°6S 145°41E 153 D6
Katanda,
  Dem. Rep. of the Congo 7°52S 24°13E 142 D1
Katanda Nord-Kivu,
  Dem. Rep. of the Congo 0°55S 29°21E 142 C2
Katanga □
  Dem. Rep. of the Congo 8°0S 25°0E 142 D2
Katangi India 21°56N 79°50E 126 D4
Katanning Australia 33°40S 117°33E 149 F2
Katastari Greece 37°50N 20°45E 98 D2
Katavi □ Tanzania 6°0S 31°0E 142 D2
Katavi L. Tanzania 6°51S 31°3E 142 D3
Katavi Swamp Tanzania 6°50S 31°10E 142 D3
Katchall India 7°57N 93°22E 127 L11
Katerini Greece 40°18N 22°37E 96 F6
Katghora India 22°30N 82°33E 125 H10
Katha Burma 24°10N 96°30E 123 G20
Katherîna, Gebel Egypt 28°30N 33°57E 128 D2
Katherine Australia 14°27S 132°20E 148 B5
Katherine Gorge = Nitmiluk △
  Australia 14°6S 132°15E 148 B5
Kathi India 21°47N 74°3E 124 J6
Kathiawar India 22°20N 71°0E 124 H4
Kathikas Cyprus 34°55N 32°25E 101 E11
Kathleen U.S.A. 28°7N 82°2W 179 G7
Kathmandu Nepal 27°45N 85°20E 125 F11
Kathua India 32°23N 75°34E 124 C6
Kati Mali 12°41N 8°4W 138 C3
Kati Thanda-Lake Eyre
  Australia 29°30S 137°26E 147 D6
Kati Thanda-Lake Eyre (North)
  Australia 28°30S 137°20E 151 D2
Kati Thanda-Lake Eyre (South)
  Australia 29°18S 137°25E 151 D2
Katihar India 25°34N 87°36E 125 G12
Katikati N.Z. 37°32S 175°57E 154 C4
Katima Mulilo Namibia 17°28S 24°13E 144 A3
Katimbira Malawi 12°40S 34°0E 143 E3
Katingan = Mendawai →
  Indonesia 3°30S 113°0E 118 E4
Katiola Ivory C. 8°10N 5°10W 138 D3
Katiti ○ Australia 25°1S 131°11E 149 E5
Katlabukh, Ozero
  Ukraine 45°30N 29°20E 87 K5
Katlanovo Macedonia 41°52N 21°40E 96 E5
Katmandu = Kathmandu
  Nepal 27°45N 85°20E 125 F11
Katni India 23°51N 80°24E 125 H9
Kato Achaia Greece 38°8N 21°33E 98 C3
Kato Chorio Greece 35°3N 25°47E 101 D7
Kato Korakiana Greece 39°42N 19°45E 101 A3
Kato Pyrgos Cyprus 35°11N 32°41E 101 D11
Katochi Greece 38°26N 21°15E 98 C3
Katol India 21°17N 78°38E 126 D4
Katompe
  Dem. Rep. of the Congo 6°2S 26°23E 142 D2
Katong Singapore 1°18N 103°53E 121 d
Katonga → Uganda 0°34N 31°50E 142 B3
Katoomba Australia 33°41S 150°19E 153 B9
Katouna Greece 38°47N 21°7E 98 C3
Katowice Poland 50°17N 19°5E 83 H6
Katrancı Dağı Turkey 37°27N 30°25E 99 D12
Katrine, L. U.K. 56°15N 4°30W 65 E4
Katrineholm Sweden 59°0N 16°12E 62 E11
Katsina Nigeria 13°0N 7°32E 139 C6
Katsina □ Nigeria 12°30N 7°30E 139 C6
Katsina Ala Nigeria 7°10N 9°30E 139 D6
Katsina Ala → Nigeria 7°10N 9°20E 139 D6
Katsumoto Japan 33°51N 129°42E 113 H4
Katsuura Japan 35°10N 140°20E 113 G10
Katsuyama Japan 36°3N 136°30E 113 F8
Kattaqo'rg'on
  Uzbekistan 39°55N 66°15E 109 E7
Kattavia Greece 35°57N 27°46E 101 D9
Kattegat Denmark 56°40N 11°20E 63 H5
Katthammarsvik
  Sweden 57°26N 18°51E 63 G12
Katumba
  Dem. Rep. of the Congo 7°40S 25°17E 142 D2
Katun → Russia 52°25N 85°1E 109 B11
Katwa India 23°30N 88°5E 125 H13
Katwijk Neths. 52°12N 4°24E 69 B4
Kąty Wrocławskie
  Poland 51°2N 16°45E 83 G3
Kau-Ye Kyun Burma 11°1N 98°32E 121 G2
Kaua'i U.S.A. 22°3N 159°30W 167 L8
Kaub Germany 50°5N 7°46E 77 E3
Kaudom ○ Namibia 18°45S 20°51E 144 A3
Kaufbeuren Germany 47°53N 10°37E 77 E6
Kaufman U.S.A. 32°36N 96°19W 176 E6
Kauhajoki Finland 62°25N 22°10E 60 E20
Kauhaneva-Pohjankangas △
  Finland 62°13N 22°20E 60 E20
Kaukauna U.S.A. 44°17N 88°17W 172 C8
Kaukauveld Namibia 20°0S 20°15E 144 B3
Ka'ula U.S.A. 21°40N 160°33W 167 L7
Kaunas Lithuania 54°54N 23°54E 82 D13
Kaunas ✈ (KUN)
  Lithuania 54°57N 24°3E 82 D11
Kaunia Bangla. 25°46N 89°26E 125 G13
Kaunos Turkey 36°49N 28°40E 99 E11
Kaura Namoda Nigeria 12°37N 6°33E 139 C6
Kauru Nigeria 10°33N 8°12E 139 C6
Kautokeino Norway 69°0N 23°4E 60 B20
Kauwapur India 12°53N 82°18E 125 F10
Kavacha Russia 60°16N 169°51E 107 C17
Kavadarci Macedonia 41°26N 22°3E 96 E5
Kavajë Albania 41°11N 19°33E 96 E3
Kavak Turkey 41°4N 36°3E 104 B7
Kavak Dağı Turkey 37°10N 28°12E 99 D10

Kavaklı Turkey 41°39N 27°10E 97 E11
Kavaklıdere Turkey 37°27N 28°21E 99 D10
Kavala Greece 40°57N 24°28E 97 F8
Kavala Kolpos Greece 40°50N 24°25E 97 F8
Kavalerovo Russia 44°15N 135°4E 112 B7
Kavali India 14°55N 80°1E 127 G5
Kavango = Cubango →
  Africa 18°50S 22°25E 144 A3
Kavār Iran 29°11N 52°44E 129 D7
Kavaratti India 10°34N 72°37E 127 J1
Kavaratti I. India 10°33N 72°38E 127 J1
Kavarna Bulgaria 43°26N 28°22E 97 C12
Kaveri = Cauvery →
  India 11°9N 78°52E 127 J4
Kavi India 22°12N 72°38E 124 H5
Kavimba Botswana 18°2S 24°38E 144 A3
Kavīr, Dasht-e Iran 34°30N 55°0E 129 C7
Kavīr △ Iran 34°40N 52°0E 129 C7
Kävlinge Sweden 55°47N 13°9E 63 J7
Kavos Greece 39°23N 20°3E 101 B4
Kavousi Greece 35°7N 25°51E 99 F7
Kaw Fr. Guiana 4°30N 52°15W 187 C8
Kawagama L. Canada 45°18N 78°45W 174 A6
Kawagoe Japan 35°55N 139°29E 113 G9
Kawaguchi Japan 35°52N 139°45E 113 G9
Kawah Ijen □ Indonesia 8°3S 114°14E 119 H15
Kawakawa N.Z. 35°23S 174°6E 154 B3
Kawambwa Zambia 9°48S 29°3E 143 D2
Kawanoe = Shikokuchūō
  Japan 34°1N 133°34E 113 G6
Kawardha India 22°0N 81°17E 125 J9
Kawasaki Japan 35°31N 139°43E 113 G9
Kawasi Indonesia 1°38S 127°28E 119 E7
Kawau I. N.Z. 36°25S 174°52E 154 C3
Kawawachikamach
  Canada 54°48N 66°50W 165 B6
Kaweka Ra. N.Z. 39°17S 176°19E 154 F5
Kawerau N.Z. 38°7S 176°42E 154 E5
Kawhia N.Z. 38°4S 174°49E 154 E3
Kawhia Harbour N.Z. 38°5S 174°51E 154 E3
Kawio, Kepulauan
  Indonesia 4°30N 125°30E 119 D7
Kawthaung Burma 10°5N 98°36E 121 H2
Kawthoolei = Kayin □
  Burma 18°0N 97°30E 123 L20
Kawthule = Kayin □
  Burma 18°0N 97°30E 123 L20
Kaxgar He → China 39°45N 78°24E 109 E9
Kaxholmen Sweden 57°51N 14°19E 63 G8
Kaya Burkina Faso 13°4N 1°10W 139 C4
Kayah □ Burma 19°15N 97°15E 123 K20
Kayak I. U.S.A. 59°56N 144°23W 166 D11
Kayalıköy Baraji Turkey 41°50N 27°5E 97 E11
Kayamkulam India 9°10N 76°33E 127 K3
Kayan → Indonesia 2°55N 117°35E 118 D5
Kaycee U.S.A. 43°43N 106°38W 168 E10
Kayeli Indonesia 3°20S 127°10E 119 E7
Kayenta U.S.A. 36°44N 110°15W 169 H8
Kayes Mali 14°25N 11°30W 138 C2
Kayes □ Mali 14°0N 11°0W 138 C2
Kayı Turkey 39°12N 30°46E 99 B12
Kayima S. Leone 8°54N 11°15W 138 D2
Kayin □ Burma 18°0N 97°30E 123 L20
Kaymakçı Turkey 38°10N 28°8E 99 C10
Kayoa Indonesia 0°1N 127°28E 119 D7
Kayombo Zambia 13°3S 23°51E 143 E1
Kaysatskoye Russia 49°47N 46°49E 86 F8
Kayseri Turkey 38°45N 35°30E 104 C6
Kayseri □ Turkey 38°40N 36°0E 104 C7
Kaysville U.S.A. 41°2N 111°56W 168 F8
Kayts Sri Lanka 9°42N 79°51E 127 K4
Kaz Dağı Turkey 39°42N 26°50E 99 B8
Kazachye Russia 70°52N 135°58E 107 B14
Kazakhstan ■ Asia 50°0N 70°0E 109 C8
Kazaly = Qazaly
  Kazakhstan 45°45N 62°6E 108 C6
Kazan Russia 55°50N 49°10E 86 C9
Kazan Turkey 40°14N 32°41E 104 B5
Kazan → Canada 64°2N 95°29W 163 A9
Kazan-Rettō Pac. Oc. 25°0N 141°0E 156 E6
Kazanlŭk Bulgaria 42°38N 25°20E 97 D9
Kazanskaya Russia 49°50N 41°10E 86 F5
Kazatin = Kozyatyn
  Ukraine 49°45N 28°50E 75 D15
Kazaure Nigeria 12°42N 8°28E 139 C6
Kazbek Russia 42°42N 44°30E 87 J7
Kāzerūn Iran 29°38N 51°40E 129 D6
Kazi Magomed = Qazımämmäd
  Azerbaijan 40°3N 49°0E 87 K9
Kazimierz Dolny Poland 51°19N 21°57E 83 G8
Kazimierza Wielka
  Poland 50°15N 20°30E 83 H7
Kazincbarcika Hungary 48°17N 20°36E 80 B5
Kazipet India 17°58N 79°30E 126 F4
Kazlų Rūda Lithuania 54°45N 23°30E 82 D10
Kaztalovka Kazakhstan 49°47N 48°43E 86 F9
Kazuma Pan △
  Zimbabwe 18°20S 25°48E 143 F2
Kazuno Japan 40°10N 140°45E 112 D10
Kazym → Russia 63°54N 65°50E 106 C7
Kcynia Poland 53°0N 17°30E 83 F4
Ké-Macina Mali 13°58N 5°22W 138 C3
Kea Greece 37°35N 24°22E 98 D6
Keady U.K. 54°15N 6°42W 64 B5
Kearney U.S.A. 40°42N 99°5W 172 E4
Kearney ○ Australia 20°10S 128°4E 148 D4
Kearny U.S.A. 33°3N 110°55W 169 K8
Kearsarge, Mt. U.S.A. 43°22N 71°50W 175 C13
Keban Turkey 38°50N 38°50E 105 C8
Keban Baraji Turkey 38°41N 38°33E 105 C8
Kebbi □ Nigeria 11°35N 4°0E 139 C5
Kébémèr Senegal 15°23N 16°34W 138 C1
Kebili Tunisia 33°30N 8°50E 138 B6
Kebnekaise Sweden 67°53N 18°33E 60 D18
Kebri Dehar Ethiopia 6°45N 44°17E 131 F3
Kebumen Indonesia 7°42S 109°40E 119 G13
Kecel Hungary 46°31N 19°16E 80 D4
Kechika → Canada 59°41N 127°12W 162 B3
Keçiborlu Turkey 37°57N 30°18E 99 D12
Kecskemét Hungary 46°57N 19°42E 80 D4
Kedah □ Malaysia 6°0N 100°40E 121 K3
Kėdainiai Lithuania 55°15N 24°2E 82 C11
Kedarnath India 30°44N 79°4E 125 D8
Kedgwick Canada 47°40N 67°20W 165 C6
Kedia India 7°51S 112°1E 119 H17
Kedjebi Ghana 8°12N 0°25E 139 D5
Kédougou Senegal 12°35N 12°10W 138 C2
Kedros Oros Greece 35°11N 24°37E 101 D6
Kędzierzyn-Koźle Poland 50°20N 18°12E 83 H5
Keeler U.S.A. 36°29N 117°52W 170 J9

Keeley L. Canada 54°54N 108°8W 163 C7
Keeling Is. = Cocos Is.
  Ind. Oc. 12°10S 96°55E 146 F8
Keelung = Chilung
  Taiwan 25°3N 121°45E 117 E13
Keene Canada 44°15N 78°10W 174 B6
Keene Calif., U.S.A. 35°13N 118°33W 171 K8
Keene N.H., U.S.A. 42°56N 72°17W 175 D12
Keene N.Y., U.S.A. 44°16N 73°46W 175 B11
Keep River △ Australia 15°49S 129°8E 148 C4
Keeper Hill Ireland 52°45N 8°16W 64 D3
Keepit, L. Australia 30°50S 150°30E 153 A9
Keerweer, C. Australia 14°0S 141°32E 150 A3
Keeseville U.S.A. 44°29N 73°30W 175 B11
Keetmanshoop Namibia 26°35S 18°8E 144 C2
Keewatin Canada 49°46N 94°34W 163 D10
Keewatin → Canada 56°29N 100°46W 163 B8
Kefalonia Greece 38°15N 20°30E 98 C2
Kefalos Greece 36°45N 26°59E 99 E8
Kefamenanu Indonesia 9°28S 124°29E 119 F6
Kefar Sava Israel 32°11N 34°54E 130 C3
Keffi Nigeria 8°55N 7°43E 139 D6
Keffin Hausa Nigeria 12°13N 9°59E 139 C6
Keflavík Iceland 64°2N 22°35W 60 D2
Keg River Canada 57°54N 117°55W 162 B5
Kegalla Sri Lanka 7°15N 80°21E 127 L5
Kegaska Canada 50°9N 61°18W 165 B7
Kehancha Kenya 1°11S 34°37E 142 C3
Keheili Sudan 19°25N 32°50E 131 D3
Kehl Germany 48°34N 7°50E 77 G3
Keighley U.K. 53°52N 1°54W 66 D6
Keila Estonia 59°18N 24°25E 84 C3
Keimoes S. Africa 28°41S 20°59E 144 C3
Keita Niger 14°46N 5°56E 139 C6
Keitele Finland 63°10N 26°20E 60 E22
Keith Australia 36°6S 140°0E 152 D4
Keith U.K. 57°32N 2°57W 65 D6
Keiyasi Fiji 17°53S 177°46E 154 a
Keizer U.S.A. 44°57N 123°1W 168 D2
Kejimkujik △ Canada 44°25N 65°25W 165 D14
Kejser Franz Joseph Fd.
  Greenland 73°30N 24°30W 57 C8
Kekri India 26°0N 75°10E 124 G6
Kelan China 38°43N 111°31E 114 E6
Kelang = Klang
  Malaysia 3°2N 101°26E 121 L3
Kelantan □ Malaysia 5°10N 102°0E 121 K3
Kelantan → Malaysia 6°13N 102°14E 121 J4
Kēlcyrë Albania 40°20N 20°12E 96 F4
Kelekçi Turkey 37°15N 29°20E 99 D11
Keles Turkey 39°54N 29°14E 97 G13
Keleti-főcsatorna
  Hungary 47°45N 21°20E 80 C6
Kelheim Germany 48°54N 11°52E 77 G7
Kelibia Tunisia 36°50N 11°3E 138 A6
Kelkit Turkey 40°7N 39°16E 105 B8
Kelkit → Turkey 40°45N 36°32E 104 B7
Kellé Niger 14°16N 10°7E 139 C7
Keller U.S.A. 31°50N 81°15W 178 D8
Kellerberrin Australia 31°36S 117°38E 149 F2
Kellett, C. Canada 72°0N 126°0W 54 B1
Kelleys I. U.S.A. 41°36N 82°42W 174 E2
Kellogg U.S.A. 47°32N 116°7W 168 C5
Kells Ireland 53°44N 6°53W 64 C5
Kelmė Lithuania 55°38N 22°56E 82 C9
Kelmentsi Ukraine 48°28N 26°50E 81 H3
Kélo Chad 9°10N 15°45E 135 G9
Kelokedhara Cyprus 34°48N 32°39E 101 E11
Kelowna Canada 49°50N 119°25W 162 D5
Kelsey Creek Australia 20°26S 148°31E 150 b
Kelseyville U.S.A. 38°59N 122°50W 170 G4
Kelso N.Z. 45°54S 169°15E 155 F4
Kelso U.K. 55°36N 2°26W 65 F6
Kelso U.S.A. 46°9N 122°54W 170 D4
Keluang = Kluang
  Malaysia 2°3N 103°18E 121 L4
Kelud Indonesia 7°56N 112°18E 119 H15
Kelvington Canada 52°10N 103°30W 163 C8
Kem Russia 65°0N 34°38E 106 C4
Kem-Kem Morocco 30°40N 4°30W 136 B3
Kema Indonesia 1°22N 125°8E 119 D7
Kemah Turkey 39°32N 39°5E 105 C8
Kemaliye Erzincan,
  Turkey 39°16N 38°28E 105 C8
Kemaliye Manisa,
  Turkey 38°27N 28°25E 99 C10
Kemalpaşa Turkey 38°25N 27°27E 99 C9
Kemaman Malaysia 4°12N 103°18E 121 K4
Kemano Canada 53°35N 128°0W 162 C3
Kemasik Malaysia 4°25N 103°27E 121 K4
Kemer Antalya, Turkey 36°36N 30°34E 99 E12
Kemer Burdur, Turkey 37°21N 30°4E 99 D12
Kemer Muğla, Turkey 36°40N 29°22E 99 E11
Kemer Baraji Turkey 37°30N 28°37E 99 D10
Kemerovo Russia 55°20N 86°5E 108 D9
Kemerovo □ Russia 55°0N 86°0E 109 D11
Kemi Finland 65°44N 24°34E 60 D21
Kemi älv = Kemijoki →
  Finland 65°47N 24°32E 60 D21
Kemi träsk = Kemijärvi
  Finland 66°43N 27°22E 60 C22
Kemijärvi Finland 66°43N 27°22E 60 C22
Kemijoki → Finland 65°47N 24°32E 60 D21
Kemmerer U.S.A. 41°48N 110°32W 168 F8
Kemmuna = Comino
  Malta 36°1N 14°20E 101 C1
Kemp, L. U.S.A. 33°46N 99°9W 176 E5
Kemp Land Antarctica 69°0S 55°0E 55 C5
Kempas Malaysia 1°33N 103°42E 121 d
Kempsey Australia 31°1S 152°50E 153 A10
Kempt, L. Canada 47°25N 74°22W 164 C5
Kempten Germany 47°45N 10°17E 77 H6
Kemptville Canada 45°0N 75°38W 175 B9
Ken → India 25°13N 80°27E 125 G9
Kenadsa Algeria 31°48N 2°26W 136 B3
Kenai U.S.A. 60°33N 151°16W 166 D9
Kenai Mts. U.S.A. 60°0N 150°0W 166 D9
Kenamuke Swamp
  South Sudan 5°55N 33°48E 142 A3
Kenaston Canada 51°30N 106°17W 163 C7
Kendai India 22°45N 82°37E 125 H9
Kendal Indonesia 6°56N 110°14E 119 G14
Kendal U.K. 54°20N 2°44W 66 C5
Kendall Australia 31°35S 152°44E 153 A10
Kendall → Australia 14°4S 141°35E 150 A3
Kendallville U.S.A. 41°27N 85°16W 172 E11
Kendari Indonesia 3°50S 122°30E 119 E6

Kendawangan
  Indonesia 2°32S 110°17E 118 E4
Kende Nigeria 11°30N 4°12E 139 C5
Kendi, Pulau Malaysia 5°13N 100°11E 121 c
Kendrapara India 20°35N 86°30E 126 D8
Kendrew S. Africa 32°32S 24°30E 144 D3
Kendrick U.S.A. 29°15N 82°10W 179 F7
Kene Thao Laos 17°44N 101°10E 120 D3
Kenedy U.S.A. 28°49N 97°51W 176 G6
Kenema S. Leone 7°50N 11°14W 138 D2
Keng Kok Laos 16°26N 105°12E 120 D5
Keng Tawng Burma 20°45N 98°18E 123 J21
Keng Tung Burma 21°18N 99°39E 120 B2
Kengeja Tanzania 5°26S 39°45E 142 D4
Kenhardt S. Africa 29°19S 21°12E 144 C3
Kenitra Morocco 34°15N 6°40W 136 B2
Kenli China 37°30N 118°20E 115 F10
Kenmare Ireland 51°53N 9°36W 64 E2
Kenmare U.S.A. 48°41N 102°5W 172 A2
Kenmare River →
  Ireland 51°48N 9°51W 64 E2
Kennebago Lake
  U.S.A. 45°4N 70°40W 175 A14
Kennebec U.S.A. 43°54N 99°52W 172 D4
Kennebec → U.S.A. 43°45N 69°46W 173 D19
Kennebunk U.S.A. 43°23N 70°33W 175 C14
Kennedy Zimbabwe 18°52S 27°10E 144 A4
Kennedy Channel Arctic 80°50N 66°0W 57 A4
Kennedy Ra. Australia 24°45S 115°10E 149 D2
Kennedy Range △
  Australia 24°34S 115°2E 149 D2
Kennedy Space Center
  U.S.A. 28°40N 80°42W 179 G9
Kennemerduinen △
  Neths. 52°27N 4°33E 69 B4
Kenner U.S.A. 29°59N 90°14W 177 G9
Kennesaw U.S.A. 34°1N 84°37W 178 A5
Kennet → U.K. 51°27N 0°57W 67 F7
Kenneth Ra. Australia 23°50S 117°8E 149 D2
Kennett U.S.A. 36°14N 90°3W 172 G8
Kennewick U.S.A. 46°12N 119°7W 168 C4
Kennisis Lake Canada 45°13N 78°36W 174 A6
Kenogami → Canada 51°6N 84°28W 164 B3
Kenora Canada 49°47N 94°29W 163 D10
Kenosha U.S.A. 42°35N 87°49W 172 D12
Kenozersky △ Russia 62°5N 38°10E 106 C1
Kensington Canada 46°28N 63°34W 165 C7
Kent Ohio, U.S.A. 41°9N 81°22W 174 E3
Kent Tex., U.S.A. 31°4N 104°13W 176 F2
Kent Wash., U.S.A. 47°22N 122°14W 170 C4
Kent □ U.K. 51°12N 0°40E 67 F8
Kent Group Australia 39°30S 147°20E 151 F4
Kent Pen. Canada 68°30N 107°0W 160 D10
Kentau Kazakhstan 43°32N 68°36E 109 D7
Kentland U.S.A. 40°46N 87°27W 172 E10
Kenton U.S.A. 40°39N 83°37W 173 E12
Kentucky □ U.S.A. 37°0N 84°0W 173 G11
Kentucky → U.S.A. 38°41N 85°11W 173 F11
Kentucky L. U.S.A. 37°1N 88°16W 172 G9
Kentville Canada 45°6N 64°29W 165 C7
Kentwood U.S.A. 30°56N 90°31W 177 F9
Kenya ■ Africa 1°0N 38°0E 142 B4
Kenya, Mt. Kenya 0°10S 37°18E 142 C4
Kenyir, Tasik Malaysia 5°1N 102°54E 121 K4
Keo Neua, Deo
  Vietnam 18°23N 105°10E 120 C5
Keokuk U.S.A. 40°24N 91°24W 172 E8
Keoladeo △ India 27°0N 77°20E 124 F7
Keonjhargarh India 21°28N 85°35E 125 J11
Kep Cambodia 10°29N 104°12E 120 C3
Kep Vietnam 21°24N 106°16E 120 B6
Kep □ Cambodia 10°30N 104°12E 120 L5
Kepala Batas Malaysia 5°31N 100°26E 121 c
Kepez Turkey 40°5N 26°24E 97 F10
Kepi Indonesia 6°32S 139°19E 119 F9
Kepice Poland 54°16N 16°51E 82 D3
Kepler Mts. N.Z. 45°25S 167°20E 155 F2
Kepno Poland 51°18N 17°58E 83 G4
Kepsut Turkey 39°40N 28°9E 99 B10
Kerala □ India 11°0N 76°15E 127 J3
Kerama-Rettō Japan 26°5N 127°15E 113 L3
Keramoti Greece 40°52N 24°42E 97 F8
Keran Pakistan 34°35N 73°59E 125 B5
Keran △ Togo 10°9N 0°41E 139 C5
Kerang Australia 35°40S 143°55E 152 C5
Keratea Greece 37°48N 23°58E 98 D5
Keraudren, C.
  Australia 19°58S 119°45E 148 C2
Kerava Finland 60°25N 25°5E 84 B3
Kerch Ukraine 45°20N 36°20E 85 K9
Kerchoual Mali 17°12N 0°20E 139 B5
Kerempe Burnu Turkey 42°2N 33°20E 104 A5
Keren Eritrea 15°45N 38°28E 131 D4
Kerewan Gambia 13°29N 16°10W 138 C1
Kerguelen Ind. Oc. 49°15S 69°10E 146 J5
Kerguelen Plateau
  S. Ocean 55°0S 75°0E 146 K6
Keri Greece 37°40N 20°49E 98 D2
Kerian, Kuala Malaysia 5°10N 100°25E 121 c
Kericho Kenya 0°22S 35°15E 142 C4
Kerikeri N.Z. 35°12S 173°59E 154 B2
Kerinci Indonesia 1°40S 101°15E 118 E2
Keriya He → China 36°1N 84°1E...
Kerki = Atamyrat
  Turkmenistan 37°50N 65°12E 109 F7
Kerkini, L. Greece 41°12N 23°10E 96 E7
Kerkouane Tunisia 36°58N 11°2E 94 F4
Kerkrade Neths. 50°53N 6°4E 69 D6
Kerkyra ✈ (CFU) Greece 39°37N 19°54E 98 B1
Kerkyras, Notio Steno
  Greece 39°34N 20°0E 101 A4
Kerma Sudan 19°33N 30°32E 137 E3
Kermadec Is. Pac. Oc. 30°0S 178°15W 147 E11
Kermadec Trench
  Pac. Oc. 30°30S 176°0W 156 L10
Kermān Iran 30°15N 57°1E 129 D8
Kermān □ Iran 30°0N 57°0E 129 D8
Kermān, Bīābān-e Iran 28°45N 59°45E 129 D9
Kermānshāh Iran 34°23N 47°0E 105 C12
Kermānshāh □ Iran 34°0N 46°30E 128 C5
Kermen Bulgaria 42°30N 26°16E 97 D10
Kermit U.S.A. 31°52N 103°6W 176 F3
Kern → U.S.A. 35°16N 119°18W 171 K7

Khān al Baghdādī
  Iraq 33°51N 42°32E 105 G10
Khān al Ḩammād
  Iraq 32°19N 44°16E 105 F10
Khān Āzād Iraq 33°7N 44°22E 128 C5
Khān Mujiddah Iraq 32°21N 43°48E 128 C5
Khān Shaykhūn Syria 35°26N 36°38E 104 E7
Khān Tengri, Pik Asia 42°12N 80°10E 109 E9
Khanai Pakistan 30°30N 67°8E 124 D2
Khānaqīn Iraq 34°23N 45°25E 105 F11
Khānbāghī Iran 36°10N 55°25E 129 B7
Khandwa India 21°49N 76°22E 126 D2
Khandyga Russia 62°42N 135°35E 107 C14
Khanewal Pakistan 30°20N 71°55E 124 D5
Khangah Dogran
  Pakistan 31°50N 73°37E 124 D5
Khangchendzonga =
  Kanchenjunga △
  India 27°42N 88°8E 125 F13
Khanh Duong
  Vietnam 12°44N 108°44E 120 F7
Khaniá = Chania Greece 35°30N 24°4E 101 D6
Khaniadhana India 25°1N 78°8E 124 G8
Khanka, L. Asia 45°0N 132°24E 112 B6
Khankendy = Xankändi
  Azerbaijan 39°52N 46°49E 105 C12
Khanna India 30°42N 76°16E 124 D7
Khanozai Pakistan 30°37N 67°19E 124 D2
Khanpur Pakistan 28°42N 70°35E 124 E5
Khanty-Mansiysk Russia 61°0N 69°0E 106 C7
Khao Khitchakut □
  Thailand 12°50N 102°10E 120 F4
Khao Laem △ Thailand 14°50N 98°31E 120 E2
Khao Laem Res.
  Thailand 14°50N 98°30E 120 E2
Khao Lak △ Malaysia 8°38N 98°18E 121 H2
Khao Luang △ Thailand 8°34N 99°42E 121 H2
Khao Nam Khang △
  Thailand 6°32N 100°35E 121 J3
Khao Phlu Thailand 9°29N 99°59E 121 b
Khao Pu -Khao Ya △
  Thailand 7°26N 99°57E 121 J2
Khao Sam Roi Yot △
  Thailand 12°13N 99°57E 121 F2
Khao Sok △ Thailand 8°55N 98°38E 121 H2
Khao Yai △ Thailand 14°21N 101°29E 120 E3
Khaoen Si Nakarin △
  Thailand 14°47N 99°0E 120 E2
Khapalu Pakistan 35°10N 76°20E 125 B7
Khapcheranga
  Russia 49°42N 112°24E 107 E12
Khaptao △ Nepal 29°20N 81°10E 125 E9
Kharabali Russia 47°25N 47°15E 87 J8
Kharagauli Georgia 42°1N 43°12E 87 J6
Kharaghoda India 23°11N 71°46E 124 H4
Kharagpur India 22°20N 87°25E 125 H12
Kharānaq Iran 32°20N 54°45E 129 C7
Kharda India 18°40N 75°34E 126 E2
Khardung La India 34°20N 77°43E 125 B7
Kharg = Khārk, Jazīreh-ye
  Iran 29°15N 50°28E 129 D6
Khârga, El Wâhât el
  Egypt 25°10N 30°35E 137 C3
Khargon India 21°45N 75°40E 124 J6
Khari → India 25°54N 74°31E 124 G6
Kharian Pakistan 32°49N 73°52E 124 C5
Khariar India 20°17N 82°46E 126 D6
Kharit, Wadi el →
  Egypt 24°26N 33°3E 137 C4
Khārk, Jazīreh-ye Iran 29°15N 50°28E 129 D6
Kharkiv Ukraine 49°58N 36°20E 85 G9
Kharkiv □ Ukraine 48°20N 36°20E 85 H9
Kharkov = Kharkiv
  Ukraine 49°58N 36°20E 85 G9
Kharmanli Bulgaria 41°55N 25°55E 97 E9
Kharovsk Russia 59°56N 40°13E 84 C11
Kharsawangarh India 22°48N 85°50E 125 H11
Kharta Turkey 40°55N 29°7E 104 B3
Khartoum = El Khartûm
  Sudan 15°31N 32°35E 135 E12
Khartum Canada 45°15N 77°5W 174 A7
Khasan Russia 42°25N 130°40E 112 C5
Khasavyurt Russia 43°16N 46°40E 87 J8
Khāsh Iran 28°15N 61°15E 129 D9
Khashm el Girba
  Sudan 14°59N 35°58E 131 E3
Khashuri Georgia 42°0N 43°15E 87 J6
Khaskovo □ Bulgaria 41°56N 25°30E 97 E9
Khaskovo Bulgaria 41°56N 25°30E 97 E9
Khat, Laem Thailand 8°6N 98°26E 121 a
Khatanga Russia 72°0N 102°20E 107 B11
Khatanga → Russia 72°55N 106°0E 107 B11
Khatauli India 29°17N 77°43E 124 E7
Khatlon □ Tajikistan 37°45N 69°30E 109 F7
Khatra India 23°0N 86°51E 125 H12
Khātūnābād Iran 30°1N 55°25E 129 D7
Khatyrka Russia 62°3N 175°15E 107 C18
Khavda India 23°51N 69°43E 124 H3
Khawr Fakkān U.A.E. 25°21N 56°22E 129 E8
Khay' Si. Arabia 18°45N 41°24E 137 D5
Khaybar, Ḩarrat
  Si. Arabia 25°0N 37°0E 137 D4
Khāzimiyah Iraq 34°46N 43°37E 128 C4
Khe Bo Vietnam 19°8N 104°41E 120 C5
Khe Long Vietnam 21°29N 104°46E 120 B5
Khe Sanh Vietnam 16°37N 106°45E 120 D6
Khed Maharashtra, India 17°43N 73°27E 126 F1
Khed Maharashtra, India 18°51N 73°56E 126 E1
Khed Brahma India 24°7N 73°5E 124 G5
Khekra India 28°52N 77°20E 124 E7
Khemarak Phouminville = Krong
  Kaoh Kong
  Cambodia 11°37N 102°59E 121 G4
Khemis Miliana Algeria 36°11N 2°14E 136 A6
Khemisset Morocco 33°50N 6°1W 136 B4
Khemmarat Thailand 16°10N 105°15E 120 D5
Khenāmān Iran 30°27N 56°29E 129 D8
Khenchela Algeria 35°28N 7°11E 136 A7
Khenchela □ Algeria 35°0N 7°0E 136 B7
Khenifra Morocco 32°58N 5°46W 136 B4
Kherrata Algeria 36°27N 5°31E 136 A7
Khersān → Iran 31°33N 50°22E 129 D6
Kherson Ukraine 46°35N 32°35E 85 J7
Kherson □ Ukraine 46°30N 32°30E 85 J7
Kheta → Russia 71°54N 102°6E 107 B11
Khewari Pakistan 26°36N 68°52E 124 F3
Khilchipur India 24°2N 76°34E 124 G7
Khilok Russia 51°30N 110°45E 107 D12
Khimki Russia 55°50N 37°20E 84 E9
Khios = Chios Greece 38°27N 26°9E 99 C8
Khirsadoh India 22°11N 78°47E 125 H8

uma = Hiiumaa 58°50N 22°45E **84** C2
stonia
va = Xiva 41°30N 60°18E **108** D6
zbekistan
wa = Xiva 41°30N 60°18E **108** D6
ebarovo Bulgaria 43°37N 26°15E **97** C10
ong Khlung
Dem. Rep. of the Congo 8°40S 24°48E **143** D1
hailand 16°12N 99°43E **120** D2
ong Lan △ Thailand 16°12N 99°13E **120** D2
ong Phanom △
hailand 8°45N 98°38E **121** H2
melnik Ukraine 33°30N 27°58E **75** D14
melnytskyy Ukraine 49°23N 27°0E **75** D14
melnytskyy □ 49°50N 26°40E **75** D14
ner Rep. = Cambodia ■
sia 12°15N 105°0E **120** F5
ai, Hon Vietnam 8°26N 104°50E **121** H5
. Arabia 26°17N 50°12E **129** E6
doriv Ukraine 49°24N 24°19E **75** D13
dzent = Khŭjand
ajikistan 40°17N 69°37E **109** D7
jak Pass Afghan. 30°51N 66°34E **124** D2
jayli = Xo'jayli
zbekistan 42°29N 59°31E **108** D5
k Kloi Thailand 8°17N 98°19E **121** a
k Pho Thailand 6°43N 101°6E **121** J3
k Samrong
ailand 15°3N 100°43E **120** E3
lm Afghan. 36°45N 67°40E **129** B9
lm Russia 57°10N 31°15E **84** D6
lmsk Russia 47°40N 142°5E **107** E15
märlu Iran 39°6N 47°3E **105** C12
mas □ Namibia 23°30S 17°0E **144** B2
mas Hochland
amibia 22°40S 16°0E **144** B2
mbole Senegal 14°43N 16°42W **138** C1
meyn Iran 33°40N 50°7E **129** C6
meynī Shahr Iran 32°41N 51°31E **129** C6
modino Botswana 22°46S 23°52E **144** B3
n Kaen Thailand 16°30N 102°47E **120** D4
ng → Cambodia 13°32N 105°58E **120** F5
ng Sedone Laos 15°34N 105°49E **120** E5
nuu Russia 66°30N 143°12E **107** C15
per → Russia 49°30N 42°20E **86** B6
rāsān-e Janūb □
an 32°0N 59°0E **129** C8
rāsān-e Razavī □
an 35°0N 59°0E **129** C8
rāsān-e Shemālī □
an 37°0N 57°0E **129** B8
rat = Nakhon Ratchasima
ailand 14°59N 102°12E **120** E4
rat, Cao Nguyen
ailand 15°30N 102°50E **120** E4
razm = Xorazm □
zbekistan 43°0N 60°0E **108** D6
rel Ethel Algeria 36°N 6°17W **136** C2
rixas Namibia 20°16S 14°59E **144** B1
rol Ukraine 49°48N 33°15E **85** H7
rramābād Khorāsān,
an 35°6N 57°57E **129** C8
rramābād Lorestān,
an 33°30N 48°25E **129** C6
rramdarreh Iran 36°11N 49°11E **105** D13
rramshahr Iran 30°29N 48°15E **129** D6
rugh Tajikistan 37°30N 71°36E **109** E8
sravī □ Iran 30°48N 51°28E **129** D6
srowābād Khuzestān,
an 30°10N 48°25E **129** D6
srowābād Kordestān,
an 35°31N 47°38E **105** E12
st Pakistan 30°13N 67°35E **124** D2
süyeh Iran 28°32N 54°26E **129** D7
tang Nepal 27°1N 86°51E **125** F12
tyn Ukraine 48°31N 26°27E **81** D11
uriba Morocco 32°58N 6°57E **136** B2
wst □ Afghan. 33°22N 69°58E **124** C3
wst □ Afghan. 33°20N 70°0E **122** C6
yniki Russia 51°54N 29°55E **75** C15
am, Ko Thailand 12°42N 100°47E **120** F3
ami → Georgia 41°25N 45°0E **87** K7
enovoye Russia 51°4N 40°16E **86** E5
omtaū Kazakhstan 50°17N 58°27E **108** B5
ysokhou B. Cyprus 35°6N 32°25E **101** D11
tan Wa Thailand 7°53N 98°17E **121** a
dzhand = Khŭjand
ajikistan 40°17N 69°37E **109** D7
aff Si. Arabia 24°55N 44°53E **128** E5
agiāni Afghan. 31°34N 62°32E **124** D2
ais Botswana 26°40S 21°49E **144** C3
aiyala India 27°9N 70°25E **124** F4
ajand Tajikistan 40°17N 69°37E **124** H7
ajner India 23°47N 76°36E **124** H7
akhan Thailand 14°42N 104°12E **120** E5
alna Bangla. 22°45N 89°34E **123** H16
alna □ Bangla. 22°25N 89°35E **123** H16
alo Georgia 41°33N 42°19E **87** K6
amago Botswana 20°26S 24°32E **144** B3
anjerab △ Pakistan 36°40N 75°30E **125** A6
anjerab Pass = Kinjirap Daban
sia
insorkh Iran 27°9N 56°7E **129** E8
anti India 23°5N 85°17E **125** H11
ir Iran 34°33N 50°0E **129** C6
āf Iran 34°33N 60°0E **129** C9
vājeh Iran 38°9N 46°35E **128** B5
alynsk Russia 50°17N 46°50E **86** D9
vānsār Iran 34°23N 46°55E **128** C5
atovka Russia 52°24N 46°32E **86** D8
orgū Iran 33°45N 55°0E **129** C7
orgū Iran 27°34N 56°6E **129** E8
ormūj Iran 28°40N 51°30E **105** C11
oynaya Russia 58°50N 34°28E **84** C4
ae Noi → Thailand 14°1N 99°32E **120** E2

Khyber Pakhtunkhwa □
Pakistan 34°0N 72°0E **124** B5
Khyber Pass Afghan. 34°10N 71°8E **124** B4
Khyriv Ukraine 49°32N 22°50E **83** J9
Kia Fiji 16°15S 179°8E **154** a
Kiabukwa
Dem. Rep. of the Congo 8°40S 24°48E **143** D1
Kiadho → India 19°37N 77°40E **126** E3
Kiama Australia 34°40S 150°50E **153** C9
Kiamba Phil. 6°2N 124°46E **119** C6
Kiambi
Dem. Rep. of the Congo 7°15S 28°0E **142** D2
Kiambu Kenya 1°10S 36°50E **142** C4
Kiang West △ Gambia 13°25N 15°50W **138** C1
Kiangsi = Jiangxi □
China 27°30N 116°0E **117** D11
Kiangsu = Jiangsu □
China 33°0N 120°0E **115** H11
Kiato Greece 38°1N 22°45E **98** C4
Kibæk Denmark 56°2N 8°51E **63** H2
Kibale △ Uganda 0°16N 30°18E **142** B3
Kibanga Port Uganda 0°10N 32°58E **142** B3
Kibara, Mts.
Dem. Rep. of the Congo 8°25S 27°10E **142** D2
Kibira △ Burundi 3°6S 30°24E **142** C2
Kiboga Uganda 0°58N 31°45E **142** B3
Kibombo
Dem. Rep. of the Congo 3°57S 25°53E **142** C2
Kibondo Tanzania 3°35S 30°45E **142** C2
Kibre Mengist Ethiopia 5°54N 38°59E **131** F2
Kibumbu Burundi 3°32S 29°45E **142** C2
Kibungo Rwanda 2°10S 30°32E **142** C3
Kibuye Burundi 3°39S 29°59E **142** C2
Kibuye Rwanda 2°3S 29°21E **142** C2
Kibwesa Tanzania 6°30S 29°58E **142** D2
Kibwezi Kenya 2°27S 37°57E **142** C4
Kicasalih Turkey 41°23N 26°48E **97** E10
Kičevo Macedonia 41°34N 20°59E **96** E4
Kichha → India 28°41N 79°18E **125** E8
Kicking Horse Pass
Canada 51°28N 116°16W **162** C5
Kidal Mali 18°26N 1°22E **139** B5
Kidal □ Mali 19°55N 1°5E **139** B5
Kidderminster U.K. 52°24N 2°15W **67** E5
Kidepo Valley △ Uganda 3°52N 33°50E **142** B3
Kidete Tanzania 6°25S 37°17E **142** D4
Kidira Senegal 14°28N 12°13W **138** C2
Kidnappers, C. N.Z. 39°38S 177°5E **154** F6
Kidsgrove U.K. 53°5N 2°14W **66** D5
Kidston Australia 18°52S 144°8E **150** B3
Kidugallo Tanzania 6°49S 38°15E **142** D4
Kiel Germany 54°19N 10°8E **76** A6
Kiel Canal = Nord-Ostsee-Kanal
Germany 54°12N 9°32E **76** A5
Kielce Poland 50°52N 20°42E **83** H7
Kielder Water U.K. 55°11N 2°31W **66** B5
Kieler Bucht Germany 54°35N 10°25E **76** A6
Kiembara Burkina Faso 13°15N 2°44W **138** C4
Kienge
Dem. Rep. of the Congo 10°30S 27°30E **143** E2
Kiessé Niger 13°29N 4°1E **139** D5
Kiev = Kyyiv Ukraine 50°30N 30°28E **75** C16
Kifaya Guinea 12°10N 13°4W **138** C2
Kiffa Mauritania 16°37N 11°24W **138** B2
Kifisos → Greece 38°35N 23°20E **98** C5
Kifissia Greece 38°4N 23°49E **98** C5
Kifri Iraq 34°45N 45°0E **105** E11
Kigali Rwanda 1°59S 30°4E **142** C3
Kigarama Tanzania 1°1S 31°50E **142** C3
Kigezi △ Uganda 0°34S 29°55E **142** C2
Kiği Turkey 39°18N 40°21E **105** C9
Kigoma □ Tanzania 5°0S 30°0E **142** D2
Kigoma-Ujiji Tanzania 4°55S 29°36E **142** C2
Kigomasha, Ras
Tanzania 4°58S 38°58E **142** C4
Kigosi ○ Tanzania 4°10S 31°45E **142** C3
Kığzı Turkey 38°18N 43°25E **128** B4
Kihikihi N.Z. 38°2S 175°22E **154** E4
Kihnu Estonia 58°9N 24°1E **84** C3
Kii-Sanchi Japan 34°20N 136°0E **113** G8
Kii-Suidō Japan 33°40N 134°45E **113** H7
Kiira Dam Uganda 0°25N 33°0E **142** B3
Kikaiga-Shima Japan 28°19N 129°59E **113** K4
Kikiak = Rigolet
Canada 54°10N 58°23W **165** B8
Kikinda Serbia 45°50N 20°30E **80** B5
Kikládhes = Kyklades
Greece 37°0N 24°30E **98** F6
Kikoira Australia 33°39S 146°40E **153** B7
Kikuchi Japan 32°59N 130°47E **113** H5
Kikuyu Kenya 1°15S 36°40E **142** C4
Kikwit
Dem. Rep. of the Congo 5°0S 18°45E **140** F3
Kil Sweden 59°30N 13°20E **62** E7
Kilafors Sweden 61°14N 16°36E **62** C10
Kilakkarai India 9°12N 78°47E **127** K4
Kilar India 33°6N 76°25E **124** C7
Kilbeggan Ireland 53°22N 7°30W **64** C4
Kilbrannan Sd. U.K. 55°37N 5°26W **65** F3
Kilbuck Mts. U.S.A. 60°36N 159°53W **166** C8
Kilchu N. Korea 40°57N 129°25E **115** D15
Kilcoy Australia 26°59S 152°30E **151** D5
Kildare Ireland 53°9N 6°55W **64** C5
Kildare □ Ireland 53°10N 6°50W **64** C5
Kildinstroy Russia 68°48N 33°6E **80** B25
Kilfinnane Ireland 52°21N 8°28W **64** D3
Kilgarvan Ireland 51°54N 9°27W **64** E2
Kilgore U.S.A. 32°23N 94°53W **176** E7
Kilgoris Kenya 1°0S 34°53E **142** C3
Kilibo Benin 8°32N 2°38E **139** D5
Kilifi Kenya 3°40S 39°48E **142** C4
Kilimanjaro Tanzania 3°7S 37°20E **142** C4
Kilimanjaro □ Tanzania 4°0S 38°0E **142** C4
Kilimli Turkey 41°28N 31°50E **104** B4
Kilindini Kenya 4°4S 39°40E **142** C4
Kilinochchi Sri Lanka 9°24N 80°25E **127** K5
Kilis Turkey 36°42N 37°6E **104** D7
Kilis □ Turkey 36°50N 37°10E **104** D7
Kiliya Ukraine 45°28N 29°16E **81** E14
Kilkee Ireland 52°41N 9°39W **64** D2
Kilkeel U.K. 54°7N 5°55W **64** B5
Kilkenny Ireland 52°39N 7°15W **64** D4
Kilkenny □ Ireland 52°35N 7°15W **64** D4
Kilkieran B. Ireland 53°20N 9°41W **64** C2
Kilkis Greece 40°58N 22°57E **96** F5
Kilkis □ Greece 41°5N 22°50E **96** E5
Killadysert Ireland 52°41N 9°6W **64** D2
Killala Ireland 54°13N 9°13W **64** B2
Killala B. Ireland 54°16N 9°8W **64** B2
Killaloe Canada 45°33N 77°25W **174** A7
Killaloe Ireland 52°48N 8°28W **64** D3

Killarney Australia 28°20S 152°18E **151** D5
Killarney Canada 49°10N 99°40W **163** D9
Killarney Ireland 52°4N 9°30W **64** D2
Killarney ○ Canada 46°2N 81°35W **164** C3
Killarney □ Ireland 52°0N 9°33W **64** D2
Killary Harbour Ireland 53°38N 9°52W **64** C2
Killdeer U.S.A. 47°22N 102°45W **172** B2
Killeberg Sweden 56°29N 14°5E **63** H8
Killeen U.S.A. 31°7N 97°44W **176** F6
Killin U.K. 56°28N 4°19W **65** E4
Killiney Ireland 53°15N 6°7W **64** C5
Killington Pk. U.S.A. 43°36N 72°49W **175** C12
Killini = Kyllini Greece 37°55N 21°8E **98** D3
Killini Greece 37°54N 22°25E **98** D4
Killiniq I. Canada 60°24N 64°37W **161** E19
Killorglin Ireland 52°6N 9°47W **64** D2
Killybegs Ireland 54°38N 8°26W **64** B3
Kilmarnock U.K. 55°37N 4°29W **65** F4
Kilmez Russia 56°58N 50°59E **86** B10
Kilmez → Russia 56°58N 50°28E **86** B10
Kilmore Australia 37°25S 144°53E **153** D6
Kilmore Quay Ireland 52°10N 6°36W **64** D5
Kilondo Tanzania 9°45S 34°20E **143** D3
Kilosa Tanzania 6°48S 37°0E **142** D4
Kilrush Ireland 52°38N 9°29W **64** D2
Kiltan I. India 11°29N 73°0E **127** J1
Kilwa Kisiwani Tanzania 8°58S 39°32E **143** D4
Kilwa Kivinje Tanzania 8°45S 39°25E **143** D4
Kilwa Masoko Tanzania 8°55S 39°30E **143** D4
Kilwinning U.K. 55°39N 4°43W **65** F4
Kim U.S.A. 37°15N 103°21W **169** H12
Kim → Cameroon 5°28N 11°7E **139** D7
Kimaam Indonesia 7°58S 138°53E **119** F9
Kimamba Tanzania 6°45S 37°10E **142** D4
Kimba Australia 33°8S 136°23E **152** B2
Kimball Nebr., U.S.A. 41°14N 103°40W **172** E2
Kimball S. Dak., U.S.A. 43°45N 98°57W **172** D4
Kimberley Australia 16°20S 127°0E **148** C4
Kimberley B.C.,
Canada 49°40N 115°59W **162** C5
Kimberley Ont., Canada 44°23N 80°32W **174** B4
Kimberley S. Africa 28°43S 24°46E **144** C3
Kimberly U.S.A. 42°32N 114°22W **168** E6
Kimch'aek N. Korea 40°40N 129°10E **115** D15
Kimhae = Gimhae
S. Korea 35°14N 128°53E **115** G15
Kimi Greece 38°38N 24°6E **98** C6
Kimmirut Canada 62°50N 69°50W **161** E18
Kimolos Greece 36°48N 24°37E **98** E6
Kimovsk Russia 54°0N 38°29E **84** E4
Kimparana Mali 12°48N 5°0W **138** C4
Kimpese
Dem. Rep. of the Congo 5°33S 14°26E **140** F2
Kimry Russia 56°55N 37°15E **84** D6
Kimstad Sweden 58°35N 15°58E **63** F9
Kinabalu, Gunung
Malaysia 6°3N 116°14E **118** C5
Kinango Kenya 4°8S 39°19E **142** C4
Kinard U.S.A. 30°16N 85°15W **178** A3
Kinaros Greece 36°59N 26°15E **99** E8
Kinaskan L. Canada 57°38N 130°8W **162** B2
Kinbasket L. Canada 52°0N 118°10W **162** C5
Kincardine Canada 44°10N 81°40W **174** B3
Kinchafoonee Cr. →
U.S.A. 31°38N 84°10W **178** D1
Kincolith Canada 55°0N 129°57W **162** B3
Kinda
Dem. Rep. of the Congo 9°18S 25°4E **143** D2
Kindberg Austria 47°30N 15°27E **78** D8
Kinde U.S.A. 43°56N 83°0W **174** C2
Kinder Scout U.K. 53°24N 1°52W **66** D6
Kindersley Canada 51°30N 109°10W **163** C7
Kindia Guinea 10°0N 12°52W **138** D2
Kindu
Dem. Rep. of the Congo 2°55S 25°50E **142** C2
Kinel Russia 53°15N 50°40E **86** D10
Kineshma Russia 57°30N 42°5E **86** B6
Kinesi Tanzania 1°25S 33°50E **142** C3
King, L. Australia 33°10S 119°35E **149** F2
King, Mt. Australia 25°10S 147°30E **150** D4
King Abdullah Economic City
Si. Arabia 22°24N 39°5E **137** C4
King Christian I.
Canada 77°48N 101°40W **161** B11
King City U.S.A. 36°13N 121°8W **170** J5
King Cr. → Australia 24°35S 139°30E **150** C2
King Edward →
Australia 14°14S 126°35E **148** B4
King Edward Point
S. Georgia 54°17S 36°30W **55** B1
King Frederick VI Land = Kong
Frederik VI.s Kyst
Greenland 63°0N 43°0W **57** E6
King George B.
Falk. Is. 51°30S 60°30W **192** G4
King George I. Antarctica 60°0S 60°0W **55** C18
King George Is.
Canada 57°20N 80°30W **161** F15
King George Sd.
Australia 35°5S 118°0E **149** G2
King I. = Kadan Kyun
Burma 12°30N 98°20E **120** F2
King I. Australia 39°50S 144°0E **153** D3
King I. Canada 52°10N 127°40W **162** C3
King Khalid Int. ✈ (RUH)
Si. Arabia 24°57N 46°42E **128** E5
King Khalid Military City =
Madinat al Malik Khalid al
Askariyah Si. Arabia 27°54N 45°31E **128** E5
King Leopold Ranges
Australia 17°30S 125°45E **148** C4
King of Prussia U.S.A. 40°5N 75°23W **175** F9
King Sd. Australia 16°50S 123°20E **148** C3
King Sejong Antarctica 62°30S 58°0W **55** C18
King Shaka Int. ✈ (DUR)
S. Africa 29°37S 31°7E **145** C5
King William I.
Canada 69°10N 97°25W **160** D12
King William's Town
S. Africa 32°51S 27°22W **144** D4
Kingaok = Bathurst Inlet
Canada 66°50N 108°1W **160** D10
Kingaroy Australia 26°32S 151°51E **151** D5
Kingfisher U.S.A. 35°52N 97°56W **176** D6
Kingirbān Iraq 34°40N 44°54E **128** C5
Kingisepp = Kuressaare
Estonia 58°15N 22°30E **84** C2
Kingisepp Russia 59°25N 28°40E **84** C5
Kinglake △ Australia 37°30S 145°22E **153** D6
Kingman Ariz., U.S.A. 35°12N 114°4W **171** K12
Kingman Kans., U.S.A. 37°39N 98°7W **172** G4

Kingoonya Australia 30°55S 135°19E **151** E2
Kingri Pakistan 30°27N 69°49E **124** D3
Kings → U.S.A. 36°3N 119°50W **170** J7
Kings Canyon
Australia 24°15S 131°34E **148** D5
Kings Canyon □
U.S.A. 36°50N 118°40W **170** J8
King's Lynn U.K. 52°45N 0°24E **66** E8
Kings Park U.S.A. 40°53N 73°16W **175** F11
Kings Peak U.S.A. 40°46N 110°23W **168** F8
King's Trough Atl. Oc. 43°48N 22°0W **54** D9
Kingsbridge U.K. 50°17N 3°47W **67** G4
Kingsburg U.S.A. 36°31N 119°33W **170** J7
Kingscote Australia 35°40S 137°38E **152** C2
Kingscourt Ireland 53°54N 6°48W **64** C5
Kingsford U.S.A. 45°48N 88°4W **172** C9
Kingsland U.S.A. 30°48N 81°41W **178** E4
Kingsport U.S.A. 36°33N 82°33W **178** B2
Kingston Canada 44°14N 76°30W **175** B8
Kingston Jamaica 17°55N 76°50W **182** a
Kingston N.Z. 45°20S 168°43E **155** F3
Kingston N.H., U.S.A. 42°56N 71°3W **175** D13
Kingston N.Y., U.S.A. 41°56N 73°59W **175** E11
Kingston Pa., U.S.A. 41°16N 75°54W **175** E9
Kingston R.I., U.S.A. 41°29N 71°30W **175** E13
Kingston Pk. U.S.A. 35°44N 115°55W **171** K11
Kingston South East
Australia 36°51S 139°55E **152** D3
Kingston upon Hull
U.K. 53°45N 0°21W **66** D7
Kingston upon Hull □
U.K. 53°45N 0°21W **66** D7
Kingston-upon-Thames □
U.K. 51°24N 0°17W **67** F7
Kingstown Australia 30°29S 151°6E **153** A9
Kingstown St. Vincent 13°10N 61°10W **183** D7
Kingstree U.S.A. 33°40N 79°50W **178** B10
Kingsville Canada 42°2N 82°45W **174** D2
Kingsville U.S.A. 27°31N 97°52W **176** H6
Kingussie U.K. 57°6N 4°2W **65** D4
Kingwood U.S.A. 30°2N 95°16W **176** E7
Kınık Antalya, Turkey 36°20N 29°20E **99** E11
Kınık İzmir, Turkey 39°6N 27°24E **99** B9
Kinkala Congo 4°18S 14°49E **140** E2
Kinki □ Japan 33°45N 136°0E **113** H8
Kinleith N.Z. 38°20S 175°56E **154** E4
Kinlochleven U.K. 56°43N 5°0W **65** E4
Kinmount Canada 44°48N 78°45W **174** B6
Kinna Sweden 57°32N 12°42E **63** G6
Kinnairds Hd. U.K. 57°43N 2°1W **65** D6
Kinnared Sweden 57°2N 13°7E **63** G7
Kinnarodden = Nordkinn
Norway 71°8N 27°40E **60** A22
Kinnarp Sweden 58°5N 13°32E **63** F7
Kinngait Canada 64°14N 76°32W **161** E16
Kinniyai Sri Lanka 8°29N 81°11E **127** K5
Kino Nuevo Mexico 28°52N 112°33W **180** B2
Kinoje → Canada 52°8N 81°25W **164** B3
Kinomoto Japan 35°30N 136°13E **113** G8
Kinoni Uganda 0°41S 30°28E **142** C3
Kinoosao Canada 57°5N 102°1W **163** B8
Kinross U.K. 56°13N 3°25W **65** E5
Kinsale Ireland 51°42N 8°31W **64** E3
Kinsale, Old Hd. of
Ireland 51°37N 8°33W **64** E3
Kinsha = Chang Jiang →
China 31°48N 121°10E **117** B13
Kinshasa
Dem. Rep. of the Congo 4°20S 15°15E **140** E3
Kinsley U.S.A. 37°55N 99°25W **172** G4
Kinsman U.S.A. 41°26N 80°35W **174** E4
Kinston Ala., U.S.A. 31°13N 86°10W **178** D3
Kinston N.C., U.S.A. 35°16N 77°35W **177** D16
Kintampo Ghana 8°5N 1°41W **138** D4
Kintore U.K. 57°14N 2°20W **65** D6
Kintore Ra. Australia 23°15S 128°47E **148** D4
Kintyre U.K. 55°30N 5°35W **65** F3
Kintyre, Mull of U.K. 55°17N 5°47W **65** F3
Kinushseo → Canada 55°15N 83°45W **164** A3
Kinuso Canada 55°20N 115°25W **162** B5
Kinyangiri Tanzania 4°25S 34°37E **142** C3
Kinyeti South Sudan 3°57N 32°54E **142** B3
Kinzig → Germany 48°36N 7°49E **77** G3
Kinzua U.S.A. 41°52N 78°58W **174** E6
Kioni Greece 38°27N 20°41E **98** C2
Kiosk Canada 46°6N 78°53W **164** C4
Kiowa Kans., U.S.A. 37°1N 98°29W **172** G4
Kiowa Okla., U.S.A. 34°43N 95°54W **176** D7
Kipahigan L. Canada 55°20N 101°55W **163** B8
Kipanga Tanzania 6°15S 35°20E **142** D4
Kiparissia Greece 37°15N 21°40E **98** D3
Kiparissiakos Kolpos
Greece 37°25N 21°25E **98** D3
Kipawa, L. Canada 46°50N 79°0W **164** C4
Kipembawe Tanzania 7°38S 33°27E **142** D3
Kipengere Ra. Tanzania 9°12S 34°15E **143** D3
Kipili Tanzania 7°28S 30°32E **142** D3
Kipini Kenya 2°30S 40°32E **142** C5
Kipling Canada 50°6N 102°38W **163** C8
Kippure Ireland 53°11N 6°21W **64** C5
Kipushi
Dem. Rep. of the Congo 11°48S 27°12E **143** E2
Kira Panagia Greece 39°17N 24°4E **98** B6
Kirandul India 18°33N 81°10E **126** D5
Kirane Mali 15°20N 10°0W **138** D2
Kiraz Turkey 38°14N 28°13E **99** D10
Kırazlı Turkey 26°26N 26°41E **97** F10
Kirchain Germany 50°47N 8°56E **76** E4
Kirchheim Germany 48°9N 9°27E **77** G5
Kirchheimbolanden
Germany 49°40N 8°0E **77** F3
Kirchschlag Austria 47°30N 16°19E **79** D9
Kireç Turkey 39°30N 28°12E **99** D10
Kirensk Russia 57°50N 107°55E **107** D11
Kirghiz Range Asia 42°40N 73°40E **109** D8
Kirghizia = Kyrgyzstan ■
Asia 42°0N 75°0E **109** D9
Kirgiziya Steppe Eurasia 50°0N 55°0E **87** E11
Kiri Dem. Rep. of the Congo 1°29S 19°0E **140** E3
Kiribati ■ Pac. Oc. 3°0S 180°0E **157** H10
Kırıkhan Turkey 36°31N 36°22E **104** D7
Kırıkkale Turkey 39°51N 33°32E **104** C5
Kirikopuni N.Z. 35°50S 174°1E **154** C5
Kirillov Russia 59°49N 38°24E **84** C6
Kirin = Jilin China 43°44N 126°30E **115** C14

Kirindi Oya → Sri Lanka 6°15N 81°20E **127** L5
Kirinyaga = Kenya, Mt.
Kenya 0°10S 37°18E **142** C4
Kirinyaga □ Kenya 0°35S 37°15E **142** C4
Kirirom △ Cambodia 11°18N 104°5E **121** G5
Kirishi Russia 59°28N 32°0E **84** C7
Kirishima Japan 31°44N 130°46E **113** J5
Kirishima Yaku △
Japan 31°24N 130°50E **113** J5
Kiritimati Kiribati 1°58N 157°27W **157** G12
Kirka Turkey 39°17N 30°33E **99** B12
Kirkby U.K. 53°30N 2°54W **66** D5
Kirkby-in-Ashfield U.K. 53°6N 1°14W **66** D6
Kirkby Lonsdale U.K. 54°12N 2°36W **66** C5
Kirkby Stephen U.K. 54°29N 2°21W **66** C5
Kirkcaldy U.K. 56°7N 3°9W **65** E5
Kirkcudbright U.K. 54°50N 4°2W **65** G4
Kirkenes Norway 69°40N 30°5E **60** B24
Kirkfield Canada 44°34N 78°59W **174** B6
Kirkintilloch U.K. 55°56N 4°8W **65** F4
Kirkjubæjarklaustur
Iceland 63°47N 18°4W **60** E4
Kirkkonummi Finland 60°8N 24°26E **84** B3
Kirkland U.S.A. 47°40N 122°12W **170** C4
Kirkland Lake Canada 48°9N 80°2W **164** C3
Kırklareli Turkey 41°44N 27°15E **97** E11
Kırklareli □ Turkey 41°45N 27°15E **97** E11
Kirkliston Ra. N.Z. 44°25S 170°34E **155** E5
Kirkpatrick, Mt.
Antarctica 84°20S 166°25E **55** E11
Kirksville U.S.A. 40°12N 92°35W **172** E7
Kirkūk Iraq 35°30N 44°21E **105** E11
Kirkwall U.K. 58°59N 2°58W **65** B6
Kirkwood S. Africa 33°22S 25°15E **144** D4
Kirlampudi India 17°12N 82°12E **126** F6
Kirn Germany 49°47N 7°26E **77** F3
Kirov Kaluga, Russia 54°3N 34°20E **84** E8
Kirov Kirov, Russia 58°35N 49°40E **106** D5
Kirovabad = Gäncä
Azerbaijan 40°45N 46°20E **87** K8
Kirovograd = Kirovohrad
Ukraine 48°35N 32°20E **85** H7
Kirovohrad Ukraine 48°35N 32°20E **85** H7
Kirovohrad □ Ukraine 48°30N 31°30E **85** H6
Kirovskiy = Balpyq Bī
Kazakhstan 44°52N 78°12E **109** D9
Kirovskiy Astrakhan,
Russia 45°51N 48°11E **87** H9
Kirovskiy Kamchatka,
Russia 54°27N 155°42E **107** D16
Kirovskiy Primorsk,
Russia 45°7N 133°30E **112** B6
Kirriemuir U.K. 56°41N 3°1W **65** E5
Kirsanov Russia 52°35N 42°40E **86** D6
Kırşehir Turkey 39°14N 34°5E **104** C6
Kirtachi Niger 12°52N 2°30E **139** C5
Kirthar △ Pakistan 25°45N 67°30E **124** F2
Kirthar Range Pakistan 27°0N 67°0E **124** F2
Kirtland U.S.A. 36°44N 108°21W **169** H9
Kiruna Sweden 67°52N 20°15E **60** C19
Kirundu
Dem. Rep. of the Congo 0°50S 25°35E **142** C2
Kirya Russia 55°5N 46°45E **86** C8
Kiryū Japan 36°24N 139°20E **113** F9
Kisa Sweden 58°0N 15°39E **63** G9
Kisaga Tanzania 4°30S 34°23E **142** C3
Kisalföld Hungary 47°30N 17°0E **80** C2
Kisanga
Dem. Rep. of the Congo 2°30S 26°35E **142** C2
Kisangani
Dem. Rep. of the Congo 0°35N 25°15E **142** B2
Kisar Indonesia 8°5S 127°10E **119** F7
Kisarawe Tanzania 6°53S 39°0E **142** D4
Kisarazu Japan 35°23N 139°55E **113** G9
Kisbér Hungary 47°30N 18°2E **80** D3
Kiselevsk Russia 54°5N 86°39E **108** B11
Kish = Qeys Iran 26°32N 53°58E **129** E7
Kishanganga →
Pakistan 34°18N 73°28E **125** B5
Kishanganj India 26°3N 88°14E **125** F13
Kishangarh Raj., India 26°34N 74°52E **124** F6
Kishangarh Raj., India 27°50N 70°30E **124** F4
Kishi Nigeria 9°1N 3°52E **139** D5
Kishinev = Chișinău
Moldova 47°2N 28°50E **81** C13
Kishiwada Japan 34°28N 135°22E **113** G7
Kishkeneköl
Kazakhstan 53°38N 72°20E **109** D8
Kishtwar India 33°20N 75°48E **124** C6
Kisielice Poland 53°35N 19°16E **82** E6
Kisigo → Tanzania 6°23S 34°17E **142** D3
Kisii Kenya 0°40S 34°45E **142** C3
Kisiju Tanzania 7°23S 39°19E **142** D4
Kisir Turkey 41°0N 43°5E **105** B10
Kisizi Uganda 1°0S 29°58E **142** C2
Kiska I. U.S.A. 51°59N 177°30E **166** E3
Kiskatinaw → Canada 56°8N 120°10W **162** B4
Kiskomárom = Zalakomár
Hungary 46°33N 17°10E **80** D2
Kiskőrei-víztároló
Hungary 47°31N 20°36E **80** C5
Kiskőrös Hungary 46°37N 19°20E **80** D4
Kiskundorozsma
Hungary 46°16N 20°5E **80** D5
Kiskunfélegyháza
Hungary 46°42N 19°53E **80** D4
Kiskunhalas Hungary 46°28N 19°37E **80** D4
Kiskunmajsa Hungary 46°30N 19°48E **80** D4
Kiskunsági △ Hungary 46°53N 19°17E **80** D4
Kislovodsk Russia 43°50N 42°45E **87** J6
Kismaayo Somalia 0°22S 42°32E **131** H3
Kiso-Gawa → Japan 35°20N 136°45E **113** G8
Kiso-Sammyaku
Japan 35°45N 137°45E **113** G8
Kisofukushima Japan 35°52N 137°43E **113** G8
Kisoro Uganda 1°17S 29°48E **142** C2
Kissamos Greece 35°30N 23°38E **101** D5
Kissamos, Kolpos
Greece 35°30N 23°38E **101** D5
Kissidougou Guinea 9°5N 10°5W **138** D2
Kissimmee U.S.A. 28°18N 81°24W **178** G5
Kissimmee → U.S.A. 27°58N 80°55W **178** H5
Kississing L. Canada 55°10N 101°20W **163** B8
Kissónerga Cyprus 34°49N 32°24E **101** E11
Kissu, J. Sudan 21°35N 25°5E **137** D12
Kistanje Croatia 43°58N 15°58E **78** G13
Kisújszállás Hungary 47°12N 20°50E **80** C5
Kisumu Kenya 0°3S 34°45E **142** C3
Kisvárda Hungary 48°14N 22°4E **80** B7
Kiswani Tanzania 4°5S 37°57E **142** C4
Kiswere Tanzania 9°27S 39°30E **143** D4

Kit Carson U.S.A. 38°46N 102°48W **168** G12
Kitaibaraki Japan 36°50N 140°45E **113** F10
Kitakami Japan 39°20N 141°10E **112** E10
Kitakami-Gawa →
Japan 38°25N 141°19E **112** E10
Kitakami-Sammyaku
Japan 39°30N 141°30E **112** E10
Kitakata Japan 37°39N 139°52E **112** F9
Kitakyūshū Japan 33°50N 130°50E **113** H5
Kitale Kenya 1°0N 35°0E **142** B4
Kitami Japan 43°48N 143°54E **112** C11
Kitami-Sammyaku
Japan 44°22N 142°43E **112** B11
Kitangiri, L. Tanzania 4°5S 34°20E **142** C3
Kitaya Tanzania 10°38S 40°8E **143** E5
Kitchener Canada 43°27N 80°29W **174** C4
Kitee Finland 62°15N 30°9E **84** A8
Kitega = Gitega Burundi 3°26S 29°56E **142** C2
Kitengo
Dem. Rep. of the Congo 7°26S 24°8E **142** D1
Kitgum Uganda 3°17N 32°52E **142** B3
Kithira = Kythira Greece 36°9N 23°0E **98** E5
Kithnos = Kythnos
Greece 37°26N 24°27E **98** D6
Kiti Cyprus 34°50N 33°34E **101** E12
Kiti, C. Cyprus 34°48N 33°36E **101** E12
Kitikmeot Canada 67°0N 110°0W **160** D9
Kitimat Canada 54°3N 128°38W **162** C3
Kitinen → Finland 67°14N 27°27E **60** C22
Kitros Greece 40°22N 22°34E **96** F5
Kitsman Ukraine 48°26N 25°46E **81** D10
Kitsuki Japan 33°25N 131°37E **113** H5
Kittakittaooloo, L.
Australia 28°3S 138°14E **151** D2
Kittanning U.S.A. 40°49N 79°31W **174** E5
Kittatinny Mt. U.S.A. 41°19N 74°39W **175** F10
Kittery U.S.A. 43°5N 70°45W **175** C14
Kittilä Finland 67°40N 24°51E **60** C21
Kitui Kenya 1°17S 38°0E **142** C4
Kitui □ Kenya 1°30S 38°25E **142** C4
Kitwanga Canada 55°6N 128°4W **162** B3
Kitwe Zambia 12°54S 28°13E **143** E2
Kitzbühel Austria 47°27N 12°24E **78** D5
Kitzbüheler Alpen
Austria 47°20N 12°20E **78** D5
Kitzingen Germany 49°44N 10°9E **77** F6
Kiunga Marine △ Kenya 2°1S 41°14E **142** C5
Kivalliq Canada 62°0N 97°30W **160** E12
Kivarli India 24°33N 72°46E **124** G5
Kivertsi Ukraine 50°50N 25°28E **75** C13
Kividhes Cyprus 34°46N 32°51E **101** E11
Kivik Sweden 55°41N 14°13E **63** J8
Kivotos Greece 40°13N 21°26E **96** F5
Kivu, L.
Dem. Rep. of the Congo 1°48S 29°0E **142** C2
Kiwirrkurra Australia 22°49S 127°45E **148** D4
Kiwirrkurra ○
Australia 22°49S 127°45E **148** D4
Kiyev = Kyyiv Ukraine 50°30N 30°28E **75** C16
Kiyevskoye Vdkhr. = Kyyivske
Vdskh. Ukraine 51°0N 30°25E **75** C16
Kıyıköy Turkey 41°38N 28°5E **97** E12
Kizhi, Ostrov Russia 62°4N 35°13E **84** B8
Kiziba-Baluba ○
Dem. Rep. of the Congo 11°50S 28°0E **143** E2
Kiziguru Rwanda 1°46S 30°23E **142** C3
Kızıl Adalar Turkey 40°49N 29°10E **99** A11
Kızıl Irmak → Turkey 41°44N 35°58E **104** B6
Kizil Jilga China 35°26N 78°50E **125** B8
Kizil Yurt Russia 43°13N 46°54E **87** J8
Kızılcabölük Turkey 37°37N 29°1E **99** D11
Kızılcahamam Turkey 40°30N 32°30E **104** B5
Kizilhisar Turkey 35°5N 31°20E **128** B1
Kızılhisar Turkey 37°25N 29°17E **104** D3
Kızılırmak Turkey 40°21N 33°59E **104** B5
Kızılkaya Turkey 37°9N 30°39E **99** E12
Kızılören Turkey 38°15N 30°10E **99** D12
Kızıltepe Turkey 37°12N 40°35E **105** D9
Kizimkazi Tanzania 6°28S 39°30E **142** D4
Kizlyar Russia 43°51N 46°40E **87** J8
Kizyl-Arvat = Serdar
Turkmenistan 39°4N 56°23E **129** B8
Kjellerup Denmark 56°17N 9°25E **63** H3
Kjölur Iceland 64°50N 19°25W **60** D4
Kladanj Bos.-H. 44°14N 18°42E **80** F3
Kladnica Serbia 43°23N 20°2E **80** G4
Kladno Czech Rep. 50°10N 14°7E **78** A7
Kladovo Serbia 44°36N 22°33E **96** B6
Klaeng Thailand 12°47N 101°39E **120** F3
Klagenfurt Austria 46°38N 14°20E **78** E7
Klaipėda Lithuania 55°43N 21°10E **84** D2
Klaipėda □ Lithuania 55°43N 21°17E **82** C8
Klaksvík Føroe Is. 62°14N 6°35W **60** E9
Klamath → U.S.A. 41°33N 124°5W **168** F1
Klamath Falls U.S.A. 42°13N 121°46W **168** E3
Klamath Mts. U.S.A. 41°20N 123°0W **168** F2
Klamono Indonesia 1°8S 131°30E **119** E8
Klang Malaysia 3°2N 101°26E **121** L3
Klanjec Croatia 46°3N 15°45E **78** C12
Klappan → Canada 58°0N 129°43W **162** B3
Klarälven → Sweden 59°23N 13°32E **62** E7
Klässbol Sweden 59°33N 12°50E **62** E6
Klatovy Czech Rep. 49°23N 13°18E **78** B6
Klawer S. Africa 31°44S 18°36E **144** D2
Klazienaveen Neths. 52°44N 7°0E **76** B8
Klé Mali 12°0N 6°28W **138** C3
Klecko Poland 52°38N 17°27E **83** F4
Kleczew Poland 52°22N 18°9E **83** F5
Kleena Kleene Canada 52°0N 124°59W **162** C4
Klein-Karas Namibia 27°33S 18°7E **144** C2
Kleinbegin S. Africa 28°55S 21°40E **144** C3
Klekovača Bos.-H. 44°25N 16°32E **93** D13
Klembivka Ukraine 48°23N 28°25E **81** B13
Klenovec Slovak Rep. 48°36N 19°54E **83** C11
Klerksdorp S. Africa 26°53S 26°38E **145** B4
Kletnya Russia 53°23N 33°12E **84** E8
Kletsk = Klyetsk Belarus 53°5N 26°45E **84** E4
Kletskiy Russia 49°16N 43°11E **87** F7
Kleve Germany 51°47N 6°11E **76** D2
Klickitat U.S.A. 45°49N 121°9W **170** D5
Klickitat → U.S.A. 45°42N 121°17W **170** E5
Klidhes Cyprus 35°42N 34°36E **101** D13
Klimovichi Belarus 53°36N 32°0E **84** E7
Klin Russia 56°20N 36°45E **84** D6
Klinaklini → Canada 51°21N 125°40W **162** C3
Klintě Kosovo 42°37N 20°35E **96** C3
Klintehamn Sweden 57°24N 18°12E **63** G12

Klintsy Russia 52°50N 32°10E 85 F7
Klip → S. Africa 27°3S 29°3E 145 C4
Klipdale S. Africa 34°19S 19°57E 144 D2
Klippan Sweden 56°8N 13°10E 83 H7
Klipplaat S. Africa 33°1S 24°22E 144 D3
Klishkivtsi Ukraine 48°26N 26°16E 81 B11
Klisura Bulgaria 42°40N 24°28E 97 D8
Kljajićevo Serbia 45°45N 19°17E 80 E4
Ključ Bos.-H. 44°32N 16°48E 93 D13
Klobuck Poland 50°55N 18°55E 83 H5
Klockestrand Sweden 62°53N 17°55E 62 B11
Klodawa Poland 52°15N 18°55E 83 F5
Klodzko Poland 50°28N 16°38E 83 H3
Klondike Canada 64°0N 139°26W 160 E4
Klong Wang Chao △
  Thailand 16°20N 99°9E 120 D2
Klos Albania 41°28N 20°10E 96 E4
Klosterneuburg Austria 48°18N 16°19E 79 C9
Klosters Switz. 46°52N 9°52E 77 J5
Klötze Germany 52°37N 11°10E 76 C7
Klouto Togo 6°57N 0°44E 139 D5
Klövsjö Sweden 62°32N 14°11E 62 B8
Kluane △ Canada 60°45N 139°30W 162 A1
Kluane L. Canada 61°15N 138°40W 160 E4
Kluang Malaysia 2°3N 103°18E 121 L4
Kluczbork Poland 50°58N 18°12E 83 H5
Klukwan U.S.A. 59°24N 135°54W 162 B1
Klungkung Indonesia 8°32S 115°24E 119 K18
Klyetsk Belarus 53°5N 26°45E 75 B14
Klyuchevskaya, Sopka
  Russia 55°50N 160°30E 107 D17
Klyuchi Russia 56°18N 160°51E 107 D17
Knäred Sweden 56°31N 13°19E 63 H7
Knaresborough U.K. 54°1N 1°28W 66 C6
Knee L. Man., Canada 55°3N 94°45W 164 A1
Knee L. Sask., Canada 55°51N 107°0W 163 B7
Kneiss, Îs. Tunisia 34°22N 10°18E 136 B6
Knezha Bulgaria 43°30N 24°5E 97 C8
Knight Inlet Canada 50°45N 125°40W 162 C3
Knighton U.K. 52°21N 3°3W 67 E4
Knights Ferry U.S.A. 37°50N 120°40W 170 H6
Knights Landing
  U.S.A. 38°48N 121°43W 170 G5
Knin Croatia 44°3N 16°17E 93 D13
Knislinge Sweden 56°12N 14°5E 63 H8
Knittelfeld Austria 47°13N 14°51E 78 D7
Knivsta Sweden 59°43N 17°48E 62 E11
Knjaževac Serbia 43°35N 22°18E 96 C6
Knob, C. Australia 34°32S 119°16E 149 F2
Knock Ireland 53°48N 8°55W 64 C3
Knockmealdown Mts.
  Ireland 52°14N 7°56W 64 D4
Knokke-Heist Belgium 51°21N 3°17E 69 C3
Knossos Greece 35°16N 25°10E 101 D7
Knowlton Canada 53°20N 72°31W 175 A12
Knox U.S.A. 41°18N 86°37W 172 E10
Knox Coast Antarctica 66°30S 108°0E 55 C8
Knoxville Ga., U.S.A. 32°47N 83°59W 178 C6
Knoxville Iowa, U.S.A. 41°19N 93°6W 172 E7
Knoxville Pa., U.S.A. 41°57N 77°27W 174 E7
Knoxville Tenn.,
  U.S.A. 35°58N 83°55W 177 D13
Knud Rasmussen Land
  Greenland 78°0N 60°0W 57 B4
Knysna S. Africa 34°2S 23°2E 144 D3
Knyszyn Poland 53°20N 22°56E 82 E9
Ko Kha Thailand 18°11N 99°24E 120 C2
Ko Tarutao △ Thailand 6°31N 99°26E 121 J2
Ko Yao Thailand 8°7N 98°35E 121 a
Koani Tanzania 6°8S 39°17E 142 D4
Koartac = Quaqtaq
  Canada 60°55N 69°40W 161 E18
Koba Indonesia 6°37S 134°37E 119 F8
Kobarid Slovenia 46°15N 13°30E 93 B10
Kobayashi Japan 31°56N 130°59E 113 J5
Kōbe Japan 34°41N 135°13E 113 G7
Kobelyaky Ukraine 49°11N 34°9E 85 H8
København Denmark 55°40N 12°26E 63 J6
København ✈ (CPH)
  Denmark 55°37N 12°39E 63 J6
Kobenni Mauritania 15°58N 9°24W 138 B3
Kōbi-Sho E. China Sea 25°56N 123°41E 113 M1
Koblenz Germany 50°21N 7°36E 77 E3
Kobryn Belarus 52°15N 24°22E 75 B3
Kobuk → U.S.A. 66°54N 160°39W 166 B7
Kobuleti Georgia 41°55N 41°45E 87 K5
Kobyletska Polyana
  Ukraine 48°3N 24°4E 81 B9
Kobylin Poland 51°43N 17°12E 83 G4
Kobylka Poland 52°21N 21°12E 83 F8
Kobylkino Russia 54°8N 43°56E 86 C6
Koca → Turkey 40°8N 27°57E 97 F11
Kocabas Turkey 37°49N 29°20E 99 D11
Kocaeli Turkey 40°45N 29°50E 97 F13
Kocaeli □ Turkey 40°45N 29°55E 97 F13
Kočane Serbia 43°12N 21°52E 96 C5
Kočani Macedonia 41°55N 22°25E 96 E6
Koçarlı Turkey 37°45N 27°43E 99 D9
Koceljevo Serbia 44°28N 19°50E 96 B3
Kočevje Slovenia 45°39N 14°50E 93 C11
Koch Bihar India 26°22N 89°29E 123 F16
Kochas India 25°15N 83°56E 125 G10
Kocher → Germany 49°13N 9°12E 77 F5
Kochi India 9°58N 76°20E 127 K3
Kōchi Japan 33°30N 133°35E 113 H6
Kōchi □ Japan 33°40N 133°30E 113 H6
Kochiu = Gejiu China 23°20N 103°10E 110 D4
Kochkor Kyrgyzstan 42°13N 75°46E 109 D9
Kochubey Russia 44°23N 46°32E 87 H8
Kock Poland 51°38N 22°27E 83 G9
Kodala India 19°38N 84°57E 126 E7
Kodarma India 24°28N 85°36E 125 G11
Koddiyar B. Sri Lanka 8°33N 81°15E 127 K5
Kode Sweden 57°53N 11°53E 63 G5
Kodiak U.S.A. 57°47N 152°24W 166 D9
Kodiak I. U.S.A. 57°30N 152°45W 166 D9
Kodikkarai = Point Calimere
  India 10°17N 79°49E 127 J4
Kodinar India 20°46N 70°46E 124 J4
Kodinsk Russia 58°40N 99°10E 107 D10
Kodlipet India 12°48N 75°53E 127 H2
Kodori → Georgia 42°47N 41°10E 87 J5
Kodungallur = Cranganore
  India 10°13N 76°13E 127 J3
Kodyma Ukraine 48°25N 29°35E 81 A13
Koedoesberge S. Africa 32°40S 20°11E 144 D3
Koes Namibia 26°0S 19°15E 144 C2
Kofarnihon Tajikistan 38°33N 69°1E 109 E7
Kofçaz Turkey 41°58N 27°12E 97 E11
Koffiefontein S. Africa 29°30S 25°0E 144 C4
Kofiau Indonesia 1°11S 129°50E 119 E7
Köflach Austria 47°4N 15°5E 78 D8

Koforidua Ghana 6°3N 0°17W 139 D4
Kōfu Japan 35°40N 138°30E 113 G9
Koga Japan 36°11N 139°43E 113 F9
Kogaluc → Canada 56°12N 61°44W 165 A7
Køge Denmark 55°27N 12°11E 63 J6
Køge Bugt Denmark 55°34N 12°24E 63 J6
Kogi □ Nigeria 7°45N 6°45E 139 D6
Kogin Baba Nigeria 7°55N 11°35E 139 D7
Kogon Uzbekistan 39°43N 64°33E 108 E6
Koh-i-Khurd Afghan. 33°30N 65°59E 124 C1
Koh-i-Maran Pakistan 29°18N 66°50E 124 E2
Koh Ker Cambodia 13°47N 104°32E 120 F5
Koh Wai Thailand 11°54N 102°25E 121 H4
Kohat Pakistan 33°40N 71°29E 124 C4
Kohima India 25°35N 94°10E 123 G19
Kohkīlūyeh va Būyer Aḥmadī □
  Iran 31°30N 50°30E 129 D6
Kohler Ra. Antarctica 77°0S 110°0W 55 D15
Kohlu Pakistan 29°54N 69°15E 124 E3
Kohtla-Järve Estonia 59°20N 27°20E 84 C4
Kohukohu N.Z. 35°22S 173°38E 154 B2
Kohylnyk → Ukraine 45°49N 29°40E 81 E14
Koi Sanjaq Iraq 36°5N 44°38E 105 D11
Koidu S. Leone 8°38N 10°59W 138 D2
Koihoa India 8°12N 93°29E 127 K11
Koilkuntla India 15°14N 78°19E 127 G4
Koillismaa Finland 65°44N 28°36E 60 D23
Koin N. Korea 40°28N 126°18E 115 D14
Koinare Bulgaria 43°21N 24°8E 97 C8
Koindu S. Leone 8°26N 10°19W 138 D2
Kojetín Czech Rep. 49°21N 17°20E 79 B10
Kojō N. Korea 38°58N 127°58E 115 E14
Kojonup Australia 33°48S 117°10E 149 F2
Kojūr Iran 36°23N 51°43E 129 B6
Kokand = Qo'qon
  Uzbekistan 40°31N 70°56E 109 D8
Kokang Burma 23°45N 98°30E 116 F2
Kokas Indonesia 2°42S 132°26E 119 E8
Kokava Slovak Rep. 48°35N 19°50E 79 C12
Kokcha → Afghan. 37°9N 69°24E 109 E7
Kokchetav = Kökshetaū
  Kazakhstan 53°20N 69°25E 109 B7
Kokemäenjoki →
  Finland 61°32N 21°44E 84 B1
Kokhma Russia 56°57N 41°8E 86 B5
Koki Senegal 15°30N 15°59W 138 B1
Kokkilai Sri Lanka 9°0N 80°57E 127 K5
Kokkola Finland 63°50N 23°8E 60 E20
Koko Nigeria 11°28N 4°29E 139 C5
Koko Kyunzu Burma 14°7N 93°22E 127 G11
Koko Nur = Qinghai Hu
  China 36°40N 100°10E 110 D9
Kokologo Burkina Faso 12°11N 1°53W 138 C4
Kokolopozo Ivory C. 5°8N 6°5W 138 D3
Kokomo U.S.A. 40°29N 86°8W 172 E10
Kokopo Papua N. G. 4°22S 152°19E 156 H7
Kokoro Niger 14°12N 0°55E 139 C5
Koksan N. Korea 38°46N 126°40E 115 E14
Kökshetaū Kazakhstan 53°20N 69°25E 109 B7
Koksoak → Canada 58°30N 68°10W 161 F18
Kokstad S. Africa 30°32S 29°29E 145 D4
Kōktal Kazakhstan 44°8N 79°48E 109 D9
Kokubu = Kirishima
  Japan 31°44N 130°46E 113 J5
Kokyar China 37°23N 77°10E 109 E9
Kola Indonesia 5°35S 134°30E 119 F8
Kola Russia 68°45N 33°8E 60 B25
Kola Pen. = Kolskiy Poluostrov
  Russia 67°30N 38°0E 58 B13
Kolachel India 8°10N 77°15E 127 K3
Kolachi → Pakistan 27°8N 67°2E 124 F2
Kolahoi India 34°12N 75°22E 125 B6
Kolahun Liberia 8°15N 10°4W 138 D2
Kolaka Indonesia 4°3S 121°46E 119 E6
Kolar India 13°12N 78°15E 127 H4
Kolar Gold Fields India 12°58N 78°16E 127 H4
Kolaras India 25°14N 77°36E 124 G6
Kolari Finland 67°20N 23°48E 60 C20
Kolárovo Slovak Rep. 47°54N 18°0E 79 D10
Kolasib India 24°15N 92°45E 123 G18
Kolašin Montenegro 42°50N 19°31E 96 D3
Kolayat India 27°50N 72°50E 124 F5
Kolbäck Sweden 59°34N 16°15E 62 E10
Kolbäcksån → Sweden 59°3N 16°9E 62 E10
Kolbermoor Germany 47°51N 12°4E 77 H8
Kolbuszowa Poland 50°15N 21°46E 83 H8
Kolchugino Russia 56°17N 39°22E 84 D10
Kolda Senegal 12°55N 14°57W 138 C2
Kolding Denmark 55°30N 9°29E 63 J3
Koléa Algeria 36°38N 2°46E 136 A4
Kolepom = Dolak, Pulau
  Indonesia 8°0S 138°30E 119 F9
Kolguyev, Ostrov
  Russia 69°20N 48°30E 106 C5
Kolhapur India 16°43N 74°15E 127 F2
Kolia Ivory C. 9°46N 6°28W 138 D3
Kolimbia Greece 36°15N 28°10E 101 C10
Kolín Czech Rep. 50°2N 15°9E 78 A8
Kolind Denmark 56°21N 10°34E 63 H4
Kolkas rags Latvia 57°46N 22°37E 82 H9
Kolkata India 22°34N 88°21E 125 H13
Kollam India 8°50N 76°38E 127 K3
Kölleda Germany 51°11N 11°15E 76 D7
Kollegal India 12°9N 77°9E 127 H3
Kolleru L. India 16°40N 81°10E 126 F5
Kollum Neths. 53°17N 6°10E 69 A6
Kolmanskop Namibia 26°45S 15°14E 144 C2
Köln Germany 50°56N 6°57E 76 E2
Kolno Poland 53°25N 21°56E 82 E8
Kolo Poland 52°14N 18°40E 83 F5
Kolobrzeg Poland 54°10N 15°35E 82 D2
Kolochava Ukraine 48°26N 23°41E 81 B8
Kolokani Mali 13°35N 7°45W 138 C3
Koloko Burkina Faso 11°5N 5°19W 138 C3
Kolomna Russia 55°8N 38°45E 84 E10
Kolomyya Ukraine 48°31N 25°2E 81 B10
Kolondiéba Mali 11°5N 6°54W 138 C3
Kolonodale Indonesia 2°0S 121°19E 119 E6
Kolonowskie Poland 50°38N 18°22E 83 H5
Kolpashevo Russia 58°20N 83°5E 106 D9
Kolpino Russia 59°44N 30°39E 84 C6
Kolskiy Poluostrov
  Russia 67°30N 38°0E 58 B13
Kolskiy Zaliv Russia 69°23N 34°0E 60 B26
Kolsva Sweden 59°36N 15°53E 62 E10
Kolubara → Serbia 44°35N 20°15E 96 B4
Koluszki Poland 51°45N 19°46E 83 G6
Kolwezi
  Dem. Rep. of the Congo 10°40S 25°25E 143 E2
Kolyma → Russia 69°30N 161°0E 107 C17

Kolymskoye Nagorye
  Russia 63°0N 157°0E 107 C16
Kôm Hamâda Egypt 30°46N 30°41E 137 E7
Kôm Ombo Egypt 24°25N 32°52E 137 C3
Koma Tou Yialou
  Cyprus 35°25N 34°8E 101 D13
Komadugu Gana →
  Nigeria 13°5N 12°24E 139 C7
Komandorskiye Is. =
  Komandorskiye Ostrova
  Russia 55°0N 167°0E 107 D17
Komandorskiye Ostrova
  Russia 55°0N 167°0E 107 D17
Komárno Slovak Rep. 47°49N 18°5E 79 D11
Komárom Hungary 47°43N 18°7E 80 D3
Komárom-Esztergom □
  Hungary 47°35N 18°20E 80 C3
Komatipoort S. Africa 25°25S 31°55E 145 C5
Komatsu Japan 36°25N 136°30E 113 F8
Komatsushima Japan 34°0N 134°35E 113 H7
Kombissiri Burkina Faso 12°4N 1°20W 139 C4
Komboti Greece 39°6N 21°5E 98 B3
Kome Channel Uganda 0°1S 32°35E 142 C3
Komen Slovenia 45°49N 13°45E 93 C10
Komenda Ghana 5°4N 1°28W 139 D4
Komi Cyprus 35°24N 34°0E 101 D13
Komi □ Russia 64°0N 55°0E 106 C6
Komiža Croatia 43°3N 16°11E 93 E13
Komló Hungary 46°15N 18°16E 80 D3
Kommamur Canal India 16°0N 80°25E 127 G5
Kommunarsk = Alchevsk
  Ukraine 48°30N 38°45E 85 H10
Kommunizma, Pik = imeni Ismail
  Samani, Pik Tajikistan 39°0N 72°2E 109 E8
Komodo Indonesia 8°37S 119°20E 119 F5
Komoran, Pulau
  Indonesia 8°18S 138°45E 119 F9
Komoro Japan 36°19N 138°26E 113 F9
Komotini Greece 41°9N 25°26E 97 E9
Komovi Montenegro 42°41N 19°39E 96 D3
Kompasberg S. Africa 31°45S 24°32E 144 D3
Kompong Chhnang = Kampong
  Chhnang Cambodia 12°20N 104°35E 121 F5
Kompong Chikreng
  Cambodia 13°5N 104°18E 120 F5
Kompong Kleang
  Cambodia 13°6N 104°8E 120 F5
Kompong Luong
  Cambodia 11°49N 104°48E 121 G5
Kompong Pranak
  Cambodia 13°35N 104°55E 120 F5
Kompong Som = Kampong Saom
  Cambodia 10°38N 103°30E 121 G4
Kompong Som, Chhung =
  Kampong Saom, Chaak
  Cambodia 10°50N 103°32E 121 G4
Kompong Speu
  Cambodia 11°26N 104°32E 121 G5
Kompong Sralau
  Cambodia 14°5N 105°46E 120 E5
Kompong Thom
  Cambodia 12°35N 104°51E 120 F5
Kompong Trabeck
  Cambodia 13°6N 105°14E 120 F5
Kompong Trach
  Cambodia 11°25N 105°48E 121 G5
Kompong Tralach
  Cambodia 11°54N 104°47E 121 G5
Komrat = Comrat
  Moldova 46°18N 28°40E 81 D13
Komsberg S. Africa 32°40S 20°45E 144 D3
Komsomolets = Qarabalyq
  Kazakhstan 53°45N 62°0E 108 B6
Komsomolets, Ostrov
  Russia 80°30N 95°0E 107 A10
Komsomolsk Russia 57°2N 40°20E 84 D11
Komsomolsk Ukraine 49°1N 33°38E 85 H7
Komsomolsk-na-Amur
  Russia 50°30N 137°0E 111 A16
Komsomolskiy Russia 54°27N 45°33E 86 C7
Komsomolskoe
  Kazakhstan 50°17N 52°40E 87 B9
Kōmür Burnu Turkey 38°39N 26°12E 99 C8
Kon Ka Kinh △
  Vietnam 14°19N 107°23E 120 E6
Kon Tum Vietnam 14°24N 108°0E 120 E7
Kon Tum, Plateau du
  Vietnam 14°30N 108°30E 120 E7
Kona Mali 14°57N 3°53W 138 C4
Kona Nigeria 8°57N 11°21E 139 D7
Konakovo Russia 56°40N 36°51E 84 D9
Konar □ Afghan. 34°30N 71°3E 122 B7
Konarak India 19°54N 86°7E 126 E8
Konārī Iran 28°13N 51°36E 129 D6
Konch India 26°0N 79°10E 125 G8
Konda → Russia 60°40N 69°48E 106 C7
Kondagaon India 19°35N 81°35E 126 E5
Konde Tanzania 4°57S 39°45E 142 C4
Kondiás Greece 39°49N 25°10E 99 B7
Kondinin Australia 32°34S 118°8E 149 F2
Kondoa Tanzania 4°55S 35°50E 142 C4
Kondopoga Russia 62°12N 34°17E 84 A8
Kondoz Afghan. 36°50N 68°50E 127 A6
Kondoz → Afghan. 37°0N 68°16E 109 E7
Kondratyevo Russia 57°22N 98°15E 107 D10
Kondrovo Russia 54°48N 35°56E 84 E9
Kondukur India 15°12N 79°57E 127 G4
Konduz □ Afghan. 36°50N 68°50E 127 A6
Köneürgench
  Turkmenistan 42°19N 59°10E 108 D5
Kong Ivory C. 8°54N 4°36W 138 D4
Kong, Koh Cambodia 11°20N 103°0E 121 G4
Kong Christian IX.s Land
  Greenland 68°0N 36°0W 57 D7
Kong Christian X.s Land
  Greenland 74°0N 29°0W 57 C8
Kong Frederik IX.s Land
  Greenland 67°0N 52°0W 57 D5
Kong Frederik VI.s Kyst
  Greenland 63°0N 43°0W 57 E6
Kong Frederik VIII.s Land
  Greenland 78°30N 26°0W 57 B8
Kong Karls Land Svalbard 79°0N 28°0E 57 B13
Kong Oscar Fjord
  Greenland 72°20N 24°0W 57 C8
Kongeå → Denmark 55°23N 8°39E 63 J2

Kongernes Nordsjælland △
  Denmark 56°5N 12°15E 63 H6
Kongerslev Denmark 56°54N 10°6E 63 H4
Konglu Burma 27°13N 97°57E 123 F20
Kongo Liberia 7°20N 11°6W 138 D2
Kongola Namibia 17°45S 23°20E 144 A3
Kongolo Kasai-Or.,
  Dem. Rep. of the Congo 5°26S 24°49E 142 D1
Kongolo Katanga,
  Dem. Rep. of the Congo 5°22S 27°0E 142 D2
Kongossambougou △
  Mali 14°0N 9°30W 138 C3
Kongoussi Burkina Faso 13°19N 1°32W 139 C4
Kongsberg Norway 59°39N 9°39E 61 G13
Kongsvinger Norway 60°12N 12°2E 61 F15
Kongur Shan China 38°34N 75°18E 109 E9
Kongwa Tanzania 6°11S 36°26E 142 D4
Koni
  Dem. Rep. of the Congo 10°40S 27°11E 143 E2
Koniakari Mali 14°30N 10°50W 138 C2
Koniecpol Poland 50°46N 19°40E 83 H6
Königs Wusterhausen
  Germany 52°19N 13°38E 76 C9
Königsbrunn Germany 48°16N 10°54E 77 G6
Königslutter Germany 52°15N 10°49E 76 C6
Konin Poland 52°12N 18°15E 83 F5
Konispol Albania 39°42N 20°10E 96 G4
Kónitsa Greece 40°5N 20°48E 98 A2
Köniz Switz. 46°56N 7°25E 77 J3
Konjic Bos.-H. 43°42N 17°58E 80 G2
Konkiep Namibia 26°49S 17°15E 144 C2
Konkouré → Guinea 9°50N 13°42E 138 D2
Könnern Germany 51°41N 11°47E 76 D7
Konnur India 16°14N 74°49E 127 F2
Kono S. Leone 8°30N 11°5W 138 D2
Konongo Ghana 6°40N 1°15W 139 D4
Konosha Russia 61°0N 40°5E 84 B11
Kōnosu Japan 36°3N 139°31E 113 F9
Konotop Ukraine 51°12N 33°7E 85 G7
Konqi He → China 40°45N 90°10E 109 D11
Konsankoro Guinea 9°2N 9°9W 138 D3
Końskie Poland 51°15N 20°23E 83 G7
Konstancin-Jeziorna
  Poland 52°5N 21°7E 83 F8
Konstantinovka =
  Kostyantynivka
  Ukraine 48°32N 37°39E 85 H9
Konstantinovsk Russia 47°33N 41°10E 87 G5
Konstantynów Łódzki
  Poland 51°45N 19°20E 83 G6
Konstanz Germany 47°40N 9°10E 77 H5
Kont Iran 26°55N 61°50E 129 E9
Konta India 17°48N 81°23E 126 F5
Kontagora Nigeria 10°23N 5°27E 139 C6
Kontcha Cameroon 7°59N 12°15E 139 D7
Kontiolahti Finland 62°46N 29°50E 60 E23
Kontokali Greece 39°38N 19°51E 101 A3
Konya Turkey 37°52N 32°35E 104 D5
Konya □ Turkey 37°46N 32°20E 104 D5
Konz Germany 49°42N 6°34E 77 F2
Konza Kenya 1°45S 37°7E 142 C4
Koo-wee-rup Australia 38°13S 145°28E 153 E6
Koocanusa, L. Canada 49°20N 115°15W 168 B6
Kookynie Australia 29°17S 121°22E 149 E3
Koolyanobbing
  Australia 30°48S 119°36E 149 F2
Koondrook Australia 35°33S 144°8E 152 C6
Koonibba Australia 31°54S 133°25E 151 E1
Koorawatha Australia 34°2S 148°33E 153 C8
Koorda Australia 30°48S 117°35E 149 F2
Kooskia U.S.A. 46°9N 115°59W 168 C6
Kootenay → Canada 49°19N 117°39W 162 D5
Kootenay L. Canada 51°0N 116°0W 162 C5
Kootenay L. Canada 49°45N 116°50W 162 D5
Kootingal Australia 31°3S 151°4E 153 E9
Kootjieskolk S. Africa 31°15S 20°21E 144 D3
Kopanovka Russia 47°28N 46°50E 87 G8
Kopaonik Serbia 43°10N 20°50E 96 C4
Kopargaon India 19°51N 74°28E 126 E2
Kópavogur Iceland 64°6N 21°55W 60 D3
Koper Slovenia 45°31N 13°44E 93 C10
Kopervik Norway 59°17N 5°17E 61 G11
Kopet Dagh Asia 38°0N 58°0E 129 B8
Kopeysk Russia 55°7N 61°37E 108 A7
Kopi Australia 33°24S 135°40E 151 E2
Köping Sweden 59°31N 16°3E 62 E10
Köpingsvik Sweden 56°53N 16°43E 63 H10
Kopiste Croatia 42°48N 16°42E 93 F13
Koplik Albania 42°15N 19°25E 96 D3
Köpmanholmen
  Sweden 63°10N 18°35E 62 A12
Koppa India 13°32N 75°21E 127 H2
Koppal India 15°23N 76°5E 127 G3
Kopparberg Sweden 59°52N 15°0E 62 E10
Koppeh Dāgh = Kopet Dagh
  Asia 38°0N 58°0E 129 B8
Koppies S. Africa 27°20N 27°30E 145 D4
Koppom Sweden 59°43N 12°10E 62 E8
Koprivlen Bulgaria 41°31N 23°53E 96 E7
Koprivnica Croatia 46°12N 16°45E 80 D2
Kopřivnice Czech Rep. 49°38N 18°9E 79 B11
Koprivshtitsa Bulgaria 42°40N 24°19E 97 D8
Köprübaşı Turkey 38°43N 28°23E 99 C10
Köprülü □ Turkey 37°0N 31°0E 104 D4
Kopychyntsi Ukraine 49°7N 25°58E 81 B9
Kora △ Kenya 0°35S 38°35E 142 C4
Korab Macedonia 41°44N 20°40E 96 E4
Koral India 21°50N 73°12E 124 J5
Korangal India 17°6N 77°42E 126 F3
Koraput India 18°50N 82°40E 126 E6
Korarou, L. Mali 15°55N 3°10W 138 C4
Korba India 22°20N 82°45E 125 H13
Korba Tunisia 36°34N 10°57E 95 F1
Korbu, Gunong
  Malaysia 4°41N 101°18E 121 K3
Korçë Albania 40°37N 20°50E 96 E4
Korčula Croatia 42°56N 16°57E 93 F13
Korčulanski Kanal
  Croatia 43°3N 16°40E 93 F13
Kord Kūy Iran 36°48N 54°7E 129 B7
Kord Sheykh Iran 28°31N 52°53E 129 D7
Kordestān = Kurdistan
  Asia 37°30N 43°30E 105 D10
Kordestān □ Iran 36°0N 47°0E 129 C5
Kordié Burkina Faso 12°0N 3°30W 138 C4
Kordofân Sudan 13°0N 29°0E 137 F2
Koré Mayroua Niger 13°18N 3°55E 139 C5
Korea, North ■ Asia 40°0N 127°0E 115 E14
Korea, South ■ Asia 36°0N 128°0E 115 G15

Korea Bay Korea 39°0N 124°0E 115 E13
Korea Strait Asia 34°0N 129°30E 115 H15
Koregaon India 17°40N 74°10E 126 F2
Korenevo Russia 51°27N 34°55E 85 G8
Korenovsk Russia 45°30N 39°22E 87 H4
Korets Ukraine 50°40N 27°5E 75 C14
Kőszeg Hungary 47°23N 16°33E 80 A1
Körfantów Poland 50°29N 17°36E 83 H4
Körfez Turkey 40°47N 29°44E 97 F13
Korff Ice Rise Antarctica 79°0S 69°30W 55 D17
Korgalzhyn = Qorghalzhyn
  Kazakhstan 50°25N 69°11E 109 B7
Korgan Turkey 40°44N 37°13E 104 B7
Korgus Sudan 19°16N 33°29E 137 D3
Korhogo Ivory C. 9°29N 5°28W 138 D3
Koribundu S. Leone 7°41N 11°46W 138 D2
Korienzé Mali 15°22N 3°30E 138 B4
Korinthiakos Kolpos
  Greece 38°16N 22°30E 98 C4
Korinthos Greece 37°56N 22°55E 98 C4
Koriouné Mali 18°3N 1°16W 138 B4
Korissia, L. Greece 39°27N 19°53E 101 A3
Kōriyama Japan 37°24N 140°23E 112 F10
Korkino Russia 54°54N 61°23E 108 B6
Korkuteli Turkey 37°4N 30°13E 99 D12
Korla China 41°45N 86°4E 109 C11
Kormakiti, C. Cyprus 35°23N 32°56E 101 D11
Körmend Hungary 47°5N 16°35E 80 C1
Kornat Croatia 43°50N 15°20E 93 E12
Kornešty = Corneşti
  Moldova 47°21N 28°1E 81 C13
Korneuburg Austria 48°20N 16°20E 79 C9
Kórnik Poland 52°15N 17°6E 83 F4
Koro Fiji 17°19S 179°23E 154 a
Koro Ivory C. 8°32N 7°30W 138 D3
Koro Mali 14°1N 2°58W 138 C4
Koro Sea Fiji 17°30S 179°45W 154 a
Korocha Russia 50°55N 37°30E 85 G9
Köroğlu Dağları Turkey 40°30N 31°30E 104 B5
Korogwe Tanzania 5°5S 38°25E 142 D4
Koroit Australia 38°18S 142°24E 152 F5
Korolevu Fiji 18°12S 177°46E 154 a
Koronadal Phil. 6°12N 124°51E 119 C6
Korong Vale Australia 36°22S 143°45E 152 D5
Koroni Greece 36°48N 21°57E 98 D3
Koronia, L. Greece 40°47N 23°37E 98 A4
Koronowo Poland 53°19N 17°55E 83 E4
Körös → Hungary 46°43N 20°12E 80 D5
Körös Maros △ Hungary 47°8N 20°42E 80 C5
Köröstarcsa Hungary 46°53N 21°3E 80 C5
Korosten Ukraine 50°54N 28°36E 75 C15
Korostyshev Ukraine 50°19N 29°4E 75 C15
Korotoyak Russia 51°1N 39°2E 85 G10
Korovou Fiji 17°47S 178°32E 154 a
Koroyanitu △ Fiji 17°40S 177°35E 154 a
Korsakov Russia 46°36N 142°42E 107 E15
Korsberga Sweden 57°19N 15°7E 63 G9
Korshiv Ukraine 48°39N 25°1E 81 B10
Korshunovo Russia 58°37N 110°10E 107 D12
Korsør Denmark 55°20N 11°9E 63 J5
Korsun Shevchenkovskiy
  Ukraine 49°26N 31°16E 85 H6
Korsze Poland 54°11N 21°9E 82 D8
Korti Sudan 18°6N 31°33E 137 D3
Kortrijk Belgium 50°50N 3°17E 69 D3
Korucu Turkey 39°28N 27°22E 99 B9
Korumburra Australia 38°26S 145°50E 153 E6
Koryakskoye Nagorye
  Russia 61°0N 171°0E 107 C18
Koryong S. Korea 35°44N 128°15E 115 G15
Kos Greece 36°50N 27°15E 99 E9
Kosan N. Korea 38°52N 127°25E 115 E14
Kosaya Gora Russia 54°10N 37°30E 84 E9
Kościan Poland 52°5N 16°40E 83 F3
Kościerzyna Poland 54°8N 17°59E 83 D4
Kosciusko U.S.A. 33°4N 89°35W 177 E10
Kosciuszko, Mt.
  Australia 36°27S 148°16E 153 E8
Kosciuszko △ Australia 36°0S 148°35E 153 F8
Kosha Sudan 20°50N 30°30E 137 C3
Kōshiki-Rettō Japan 31°45N 129°49E 113 J4
Koshim → Kazakhstan 49°20N 50°0E 87 E9
Kosi India 27°48N 77°29E 124 F6
Kosi → India 26°0N 78°45E 124 F6
Košice Slovak Rep. 48°42N 21°15E 79 C14
Kosický □ Slovak Rep. 48°45N 21°0E 79 C14
Kosiv Ukraine 48°19N 25°4E 81 B10
Kosjerić Serbia 44°0N 19°55E 96 B3
Kŏsŏng N. Korea 38°40N 128°22E 115 E15
Koskhinou Greece 36°6N 28°8E 101 C10
Koslan Russia 63°34N 49°14E 106 C8
Kosŏng N. Korea 38°40N 128°22E 115 E15
Kosovo ■ Europe 42°30N 21°0E 96 D4
Kosovo Polje = Fushë Kosovë
  Kosovo 42°40N 21°7E 96 D4
Kosovska Kamenica = Dardanë
  Kosovo 42°35N 21°19E 96 D4
Kosovska Mitrovica = Mitrovicë
  Kosovo 42°54N 20°52E 96 D4
Kossou, L. de Ivory C. 6°59N 5°31W 138 D3
Kostajnica Bos.-H. 45°11N 16°33E 93 B13
Kostanjevica Slovenia 45°51N 15°27E 93 C12
Kostenets Bulgaria 42°15N 23°52E 96 E7
Koster S. Africa 25°52S 26°54E 144 C4
Kôsti Sudan 13°8N 32°43E 137 E3
Kostinbrod Bulgaria 42°49N 23°13E 96 D7
Kostroma Russia 57°50N 40°58E 84 C11
Kostromskoye Vdkhr.
  Russia 57°52N 40°49E 84 C11

Kostrzyn Wielkopolskie,
  Poland 52°24N 17°14E 83 F4
Kostyantynivka Ukraine 48°32N 37°39E 85 H9
Kostyukovichi = Kastsyukovichy
  Belarus 53°20N 32°4E 85 E7
Koszalin Poland 54°11N 16°8E 82 D3
Kőszeg Hungary 47°23N 16°33E 80 A1
Kot Addu Pakistan 30°30N 71°0E 124 D4
Kot Kapura India 30°35N 74°50E 124 D6
Kot Moman Pakistan 32°13N 73°0E 124 C5
Kot Sultan Pakistan 30°46N 70°56E 124 D4
Kota India 25°14N 75°49E 124 G6
Kota Barrage India 25°6N 75°51E 124 G6
Kota Belud Malaysia 6°21N 116°26E 118 C5
Kota Bharu Malaysia 6°7N 102°14E 121 J4
Kota I. = Loaita I.
  S. China Sea 10°41N 114°25E 116 B4
Kota Kinabalu Malaysia 6°0N 116°4E 118 C5
Kota Tinggi Malaysia 1°44N 103°53E 121 M4
Kotaagung Indonesia 5°38S 104°29E 118 F2
Kotabaru Indonesia 3°20S 116°20E 118 E5
Kotabumi Indonesia 4°49S 104°54E 118 E2
Kotamobagu Indonesia 0°57N 124°31E 119 D6
Kotapad India 19°9N 82°21E 126 E6
Kotapinang Indonesia 1°53N 100°5E 118 D2
Kotcho L. Canada 59°7N 121°12W 162 B4
Kotdwara India 29°45N 78°32E 124 E8
Kotel Bulgaria 42°52N 26°26E 97 C10
Kotelnich Russia 58°22N 48°24E 86 B9
Kotelnikovo Russia 47°38N 43°8E 87 G7
Kotelnyy, Ostrov
  Russia 75°10N 139°0E 107 B14
Kothapet India 19°21N 79°28E 126 E4
Kothari → India 25°20N 75°4E 124 G6
Köthen Germany 51°45N 11°59E 76 D7
Kothi Chhattisgarh, India 23°21N 82°3E 125 H10
Kothi Mad. P., India 24°45N 80°40E 125 G9
Kotiro India 26°17N 67°13E 124 F2
Kotka Finland 60°28N 26°58E 63 E22
Kotlas Russia 61°17N 46°43E 106 C8
Kotlenska Planina
  Bulgaria 42°56N 26°30E 97 C10
Kotli Pakistan 33°30N 73°55E 124 C5
Kotlik U.S.A. 63°2N 163°33W 166 C6
Kotma India 23°12N 81°58E 125 H9
Koton-Karifi Nigeria 8°0N 6°48E 139 D6
Kotonkoro Nigeria 11°3N 5°58E 139 C6
Kotor Montenegro 42°25N 18°47E 96 D3
Kotor Varoš Bos.-H. 44°38N 17°22E 93 B14
Kotoriba Croatia 46°20N 16°48E 93 B13
Kotovo Russia 50°22N 44°45E 86 E7
Kotovsk Russia 52°36N 41°32E 86 D5
Kotovsk Ukraine 47°45N 29°35E 81 D13
Kotputli India 27°43N 76°12E 124 F6
Kotri → India 19°15N 80°35E 126 E4
Kotronas Greece 36°38N 22°29E 98 E4
Kötschach-Mauthen
  Austria 46°41N 13°1E 73 E7
Kottagudem India 17°30N 80°40E 126 F5
Kottayam India 9°35N 76°33E 127 K3
Kotto → C.A.R. 4°14N 22°2E 140 D4
Kottur India 10°34N 76°56E 127 J3
Kotturu India 14°45N 76°10E 127 G3
Kotuy → Russia 71°54N 102°6E 107 B11
Kotyuzhany Russia 48°48N 27°42E 81 B14
Kotzebue U.S.A. 66°53N 162°39W 166 B6
Kotzebue Sound
  U.S.A. 66°20N 163°0W 166 B6
Kouchibouguac △
  Canada 46°50N 65°0W 173 C14
Koudougou
  Burkina Faso 12°10N 2°20W 138 C4
Koufonisi Iraklio, Greece 34°56N 26°8E 101 E8
Koufonisi Notio Aigaio,
  Greece 36°57N 25°35E 99 E7
Kougaberge S. Africa 33°48S 23°50E 144 D3
Kouibli Ivory C. 7°15N 7°14W 138 D3
Kouilou → Congo 4°10S 12°5E 142 E2
Koukdjuak → Canada 66°43N 73°0W 161 C17
Koula Greece 41°23N 24°44E 97 E8
Koula Moutou Gabon 1°15S 12°25E 142 E2
Koulen = Kulen
  Cambodia 13°50N 104°40E 120 F5
Koulikoro Mali 12°40N 7°50W 138 C3
Koulikoro □ Mali 13°0N 7°45W 138 C3
Kouloura Greece 39°45N 19°54E 101 A3
Koumala Australia 21°38S 149°15E 150 C4
Koumankou Mali 11°58N 6°5W 138 C3
Koumbia Burkina Faso 11°10N 3°50W 138 C4
Koumbia Guinea 11°48N 13°29W 138 C2
Koumboum Guinea 10°25N 13°0W 138 D2
Koumpenntoum
  Senegal 13°59N 14°34W 138 C2
Koumra Chad 8°50N 17°35E 137 G9
Kouna-Fao Ivory C. 7°30N 3°15W 138 D4
Koundara Guinea 12°29N 13°18W 138 C2
Koungheul Senegal 14°0N 14°50W 138 C2
Koupéla Burkina Faso 12°11N 0°21W 139 C5
Kouremalé Mali 11°58N 8°42W 138 C3
Kouris → Cyprus 34°38N 32°54E 101 E11
Kourou Fr. Guiana 5°9N 52°39W 197 B8
Kouroudjeli Mauritania 12°35N 10°59W 138 C2
Kourouninkoto Mali 12°35N 10°59W 138 C2
Kouroussa Guinea 10°45N 9°45W 138 C3
Koussanar Senegal 13°52N 14°11W 138 C2
Koussané Mali 14°10N 11°22W 138 C2
Kousseri Cameroon 12°0N 14°55E 138 B8
Koutiala Mali 12°25N 5°23W 138 C4
Kouvé Togo 6°25N 1°25E 139 D5
Kouvola Finland 60°52N 26°43E 63 E22
Kovačica Serbia 45°5N 20°38E 96 B5
Kovdor Russia 67°34N 30°24E 60 C25
Kovel Ukraine 51°11N 24°38E 81 A9
Kovilpatti India 9°10N 77°50E 127 K3
Kovrov Russia 56°25N 41°25E 84 C12
Kovur Andhra Pradesh,
  India 14°30N 80°1E 127 G4
Kowal Poland 52°32N 19°7E 83 F6
Kowalewo Pomorskie
  Poland 53°10N 18°52E 83 E5
Kowanyama Australia 15°29S 141°44E 150 B3

...wanyama ☉
Australia 15°20S 141°47E **150** B3
...wloon China 22°19N 114°11E **117** F10
...wön N. Korea 39°26N 127°14E **115** E14
...wampattur = Coimbatore
India 11°2N 76°59E **127** J3
...vceğiz Turkey 36°57N 28°40E **99** E10
...vceğiz Gölü Turkey 36°56N 28°42E **99** E10
...vyukuk ✈ U.S.A. 64°55N 157°32W **166** C8
...vunyeri Turkey 40°50N 26°26E **97** F10
...ta = Okinawa
Japan 26°19N 127°46E **113** L3
...tak Turkey 39°15N 27°6E **99** B9
...taklı Turkey 39°13N 34°49E **104** C6
...tan Turkey 37°26N 35°50E **104** D6
...tani Greece 40°19N 21°47E **96** F5
...tara Bos.-H. 45°0N 17°0E **93** D14
...tara △ Bos.-H. 45°0N 17°0E **80** F2
...belts Ukraine 50°55N 31°7E **85** G6
...telsk Russia 54°2N 35°48E **84** E6
...thikode India 11°15N 75°43E **127** J2
...tieglowy Poland 50°37N 19°8E **83** H6
...tienice Poland 51°35N 21°34E **83** G8
...tje Slovenia 46°5N 15°35E **93** B12
...tloduy Bulgaria 43°45N 23°42E **96** C7
...tlovets Bulgaria 43°30N 25°0E **97** C9
...tlovka Russia 55°52N 48°14E **86** C9
...tlu Turkey 41°26N 31°45E **104** B4
...tluk Turkey 38°11N 41°31E **105** C9
...min Turkey 51°48N 17°27E **83** G4
...modemyansk Russia 56°20N 46°36E **86** B8
...tu-Shima Japan 34°13N 139°10E **113** G9
...tuchów Poland 51°45N 15°31E **83** G2
...yatyn Ukraine 49°45N 28°50E **75** D15
...tyrevsk Russia 56°3N 159°51E **107** D16
...abia Ghana 9°10N 0°20W **139** D4
...gero Norway 58°52N 9°25E **61** G13
...gujevac Serbia 44°2N 20°56E **96** B4
...andae Ghana 8°30N 0°2W **139** D4
...ssi Togo 6°57N 0°44E **139** D5
..., Isthmus of = Kra, Kho Khot
Thailand 10°15N 99°30E **121** G2
..., Kho Khot Thailand 10°15N 99°30E **121** G2
...Buri Thailand 10°22N 98°46E **121** G2
...ai = S. Africa 30°40S 26°45E **144** D4
...bi Thailand 8°4N 98°55E **121** H2
...cheh = Kratie
Cambodia 12°32N 106°10E **120** F6
...gan Indonesia 6°43S 111°38E **119** G14
...ksaan Indonesia 7°43S 113°23E **119** G16
...lanh Cambodia 13°35N 103°25E **120** F4
...liky Czech Rep. 50°6N 16°45E **79** A9
...ljevo Serbia 43°44N 20°41E **96** C4
...lovéhradecký □
Czech Rep. 50°25N 15°50E **78** A8
...lovský Chlmec
Slovak Rep. 48°27N 22°0E **79** C14
...lupy nad Vltavou
Czech Rep. 50°13N 14°20E **78** A7
...matorsk Ukraine 48°50N 37°30E **85** H9
...mfors Sweden 62°55N 17°48E **62** E11
...mis, C. Algeria 36°26N 0°45E **136** A4
...nia Greece 39°53N 21°18E **96** G5
...nia Elassonas Greece 39°57N 22°2E **98** B4
...nidi Greece 37°20N 23°10E **98** D5
...nj Slovenia 46°16N 14°22E **93** B11
...njska Gora Slovenia 46°29N 13°48E **93** B10
...nksskop S. Africa 28°0S 30°47E **145** C5
...pina Croatia 45°50N 15°50E **93** C12
...pina = Croatia 45°50N 15°50E **93** C12
...pkowice Poland 52°29N 17°56E **83** H4
...s Slovenia 45°35N 14°0E **93** C10
...sieo Res. Thailand 14°49N 99°30E **120** E2
...skino Russia 52°44N 130°48E **112** C15
...slava Latvia 55°54N 27°10E **84** B5
...slice Czech Rep. 50°19N 12°31E **78** A5
...ussaya Gorbatka
Russia 55°52N 41°45E **86** C5
...snaya Polyana
Russia 43°40N 40°13E **87** J5
...sne Ukraine 46°7N 29°15E **81** D14
...sni Okny Ukraine 47°32N 29°27E **81** C14
...śnik Poland 50°37N 22°15E **83** H9
...snoarmeysk Ukraine 48°13N 37°11E **85** H9
...snoarmeysk = Tayynsha
Kazakhstan 53°50N 69°45E **108** B7
...snoarmeysk Russia 51°0N 45°42E **86** E7
...snoarmeyskiy Russia 47°0N 42°12E **87** G6
...snobrod Poland 50°33N 23°12E **83** H10
...snodar Russia 45°5N 39°0E **87** H4
...snodar □ Russia 45°0N 38°0E **87** H4
...snodarskoye Vdkhr.
Russia 45°1N 39°23E **87** H4
...snodon Ukraine 48°17N 39°44E **85** H10
...snogorskiy Russia 56°10N 48°28E **86** B9
...snograd = Krasnohrad
Ukraine 49°27N 35°27E **85** H8
...snogvardeysk
Ukraine 45°32N 34°16E **85** K8
...snogvardeyskoye
Russia 45°52N 41°33E **87** H5
...snohrad Ukraine 49°27N 35°27E **85** H8
...snokamensk
Russia 50°3N 118°0E **107** D12
...snoinsk Russia 50°10N 34°50E **85** G8
...snolesnyy Russia 51°53N 39°35E **85** G10
...snoperekopsk Ukraine 46°0N 33°54E **85** J7
...snosel Russia 54°25N 43°45E **86** C6
...snoselkup Russia 65°20N 82°10E **106** C9
...snoslobodsk Mordvinia,
Russia 54°25N 43°45E **86** C6
...snoslobodsk Volgograd,
Russia 48°42N 44°33E **87** F7
...snoturinsk Russia 59°46N 60°12E **106** D7
...snoyarsk Russia 56°8N 93°0E **106** D10
...snoyarskoye Vdkhr.
Russia 54°31N 21°56E **82** D8
...snoye = Krasnyy
Russia 54°25N 31°30E **84** E6

Krasnoyarsk Ukraine 47°59N 25°38E **81** C10
Krasnozavodsk Russia 56°27N 38°25E **84** D10
Krasnoznamensk
Russia 54°57N 22°30E **82** D9
Krasnystaw Poland 50°57N 23°5E **83** H10
Krasnyy Russia 54°25N 31°30E **84** E6
Krasnyy Kholm Russia 58°10N 37°10E **84** C9
Krasnyy Kut Russia 50°50N 47°0E **86** E8
Krasnyy Liman Ukraine 48°58N 37°50E **85** H9
Krasnyy Luch Ukraine 48°13N 39°0E **85** H10
Krasnyy Profintern
Russia 57°45N 40°27E **84** D11
Krasnyy Sulin Russia 47°52N 40°8E **87** G5
Krasnyy Yar Astrakhan,
Russia 46°43N 48°23E **87** G9
Krasnyy Yar Samara,
Russia 53°30N 50°22E **86** D10
Krasnyy Yar Volgograd,
Russia 50°42N 44°45E **86** E7
Krasnyy Baki Russia 57°8N 45°10E **86** B7
Krasnyyoskolske Vdskh.
Ukraine 49°27N 37°40E **85** H9
Kraszna → Hungary 48°4N 22°20E **80** B7
Kratie Cambodia 12°32N 106°10E **120** F6
Kratovo Macedonia 42°6N 22°10E **96** D6
Krau Indonesia 3°19S 140°5E **119** E10
Kraulshavn = Nuussuaq
Greenland 74°8N 57°3W **57** C5
Kravanh, Chuor Phnum
Cambodia 12°0N 103°32E **121** G4
Krefeld Germany 51°20N 6°33E **76** D2
Kremaston, L. Greece 38°52N 21°30E **98** C3
Kremen Croatia 44°28N 15°53E **93** D12
Kremenchuk Ukraine 49°5N 33°25E **85** H7
Kremenchuksk Vdskh.
Ukraine 49°20N 32°30E **85** H7
Kremenets Ukraine 50°8N 25°43E **75** C13
Kremennaya Ukraine 49°1N 38°10E **85** H10
Kremges = Svitlovodsk
Ukraine 49°2N 33°13E **85** H7
Kremmen Germany 52°45N 13°1E **76** C9
Kremming U.S.A. 40°4N 106°24W **168** F10
Kremnica Slovak Rep. 48°45N 18°50E **79** C11
Krems an der Donau
Austria 48°25N 15°36E **78** C8
Kremsmünster Austria 48°3N 14°8E **78** C7
Krestena Greece 37°35N 21°37E **98** D3
Kretinga Lithuania 55°53N 21°15E **82** C8
Krettsy Russia 58°15N 32°30E **84** C7
Kreuzberg Germany 50°22N 9°58E **77** E5
Kreuztal Germany 50°57N 8°0E **76** E4
Kria Vrisi Greece 40°41N 22°18E **96** F6
Krichem Bulgaria 42°8N 24°28E **97** D8
Krichev = Krychaw
Belarus 53°40N 31°41E **75** B16
Kril'on, Mys Russia 45°53N 142°5E **112** B11
Krim Slovenia 45°53N 14°30E **93** C11
Krios, Akra Greece 35°13N 23°34E **101** D5
Krishna → India 15°57N 80°59E **127** G5
Krishnagiri India 12°32N 78°16E **127** H4
Krishnanagar India 23°24N 88°33E **125** H13
Krishnaraja Sagar
India 12°20N 76°30E **127** H3
Kristdala Sweden 57°24N 16°13E **63** G10
Kristiansand Norway 58°8N 8°1E **61** G13
Kristianstad Sweden 56°2N 14°9E **63** H8
Kristiansund Norway 63°7N 7°45E **60** E12
Kristiinankaupunki
Finland 62°16N 21°21E **60** E19
Kristinehamn Sweden 59°18N 14°7E **62** E8
Kristinestad =
Kristiinankaupunki
Finland 62°16N 21°21E **60** E19
Kriti Greece 35°15N 25°0E **101** D7
Kritsa Greece 35°10N 25°41E **101** D7
Kriva → Macedonia 42°5N 21°47E **96** D5
Kriva Palanka
Macedonia 42°11N 22°19E **96** D6
Krivaja → Bos.-H. 44°27N 18°9E **80** F3
Krivelj Serbia 44°10N 22°5E **96** B6
Křivoklátsko △
Czech Rep. 50°1N 13°51E **78** A6
Krivoy Rog = Kryvyy Rih
Ukraine 47°51N 33°20E **85** J7
Križevci Croatia 46°3N 16°32E **93** B13
Krk Croatia 45°8N 14°40E **93** C11
Krka → Slovenia 45°50N 15°30E **93** C12
Krka △ Croatia 43°53N 15°56E **93** E12
Krnov Czech Rep. 50°5N 17°40E **79** A10
Krobia Poland 51°47N 16°59E **83** G3
Krokees Greece 36°53N 22°32E **98** E4
Krokek Sweden 58°40N 16°24E **63** F10
Krokodil = Umgwenya →
Mozam. 25°14S 32°18E **145** C5
Krokom Sweden 63°20N 14°30E **62** E6
Krokowa Poland 54°47N 18°9E **82** D5
Krolevets Ukraine 51°35N 33°20E **85** G5
Kroměříž Czech Rep. 49°18N 17°21E **79** B10
Krompachy Slovak Rep. 48°54N 20°52E **79** C13
Kromy Russia 52°48N 35°48E **85** F8
Kronach Germany 50°14N 11°19E **77** E7
Krong Kaoh Kong
Cambodia 11°37N 102°59E **121** G4
Kronoberg □ Sweden 56°45N 14°30E **63** H8
Kronprins Christian Land
Greenland 80°30N 22°0W **57** A8
Kronprins Frederik Land
Greenland 81°0N 45°0W **57** A6
Kronprins Olav Kyst
Antarctica 69°0S 42°0E **55** C5
Kronprinsesse Märtha Kyst
Antarctica 73°30S 10°0W **55** D2
Kronshtadt Russia 59°57N 29°51E **84** C5
Kroonstad S. Africa 27°43S 27°19E **144** D4
Kröpelin Germany 54°4N 11°47E **76** A7
Kropotkin Russia 45°28N 40°28E **87** H5
Kropp Germany 54°24N 9°31E **76** A5
Krosna Lithuania 54°32N 23°33E **82** D10
Krośniewice Poland 52°15N 19°11E **83** F6
Krosno Poland 49°42N 21°46E **83** J8
Krosno Odrzańskie Poland 52°3N 15°7E **83** F2
Krotoszyn Poland 51°42N 17°23E **83** G3
Krousonas Greece 35°13N 24°59E **101** D6
Krrabë Albania 41°13N 20°0E **96** E3
Krško Slovenia 45°57N 15°30E **93** C12
Krstača Serbia 42°57N 20°8E **96** C4
Kruger △ S. Africa 24°0S 31°40E **145** B4

Krugersdorp S. Africa 26°5S 27°46E **145** C4
Kruisfontein S. Africa 33°59S 24°43E **144** D3
Krujë Albania 41°32N 19°46E **96** E3
Krulevshchina =
Krulyewshchyna
Belarus 55°5N 27°45E **84** E4
Krulyewshchyna Belarus 55°5N 27°45E **84** E4
Krumbach Germany 48°13N 10°22E **77** G6
Krumë Albania 42°14N 20°28E **96** D4
Krumovgrad Bulgaria 41°29N 25°38E **97** E9
Krung Thep = Bangkok
Thailand 13°45N 100°35E **120** F3
Krupanj Serbia 44°25N 19°22E **96** B3
Krupina Slovak Rep. 48°22N 19°5E **79** C12
Krupki Belarus 54°19N 29°8E **75** A15
Kruševac Serbia 43°35N 21°28E **96** C5
Kruševo Macedonia 41°23N 21°19E **96** E4
Krushë e Madhe Kosovo 42°19N 20°39E **96** D4
Krushelnyksya Ukraine 49°7N 23°29E **83** J10
Kruszwica Poland 52°40N 18°20E **83** F5
Kruzenshterna, Proliv
Russia 48°0N 154°0E **107** E16
Krychaw Belarus 53°40N 31°41E **75** B16
Krymsk Russia 44°50N 38°0E **85** K10
Krymskiy Poluostrov =
Krymskyy Pivostriv
Ukraine 45°0N 34°0E **85** K8
Krymskyy Pivostriv
Ukraine 45°0N 34°0E **85** K8
Krynica Poland 49°25N 20°57E **83** J7
Krynica Morska Poland 54°23N 19°28E **82** D6
Krynki Poland 53°17N 23°43E **83** H10
Krynychne Ukraine 45°32N 28°40E **81** E13
Kryvyy Rih Ukraine 47°51N 33°20E **85** J7
Kryzhopil Ukraine 48°23N 28°53E **81** B13
Krzepice Poland 50°58N 18°50E **83** H5
Krzeszów Poland 50°24N 22°21E **83** H9
Krzna → Poland 52°8N 23°32E **83** F10
Krzywiń Poland 51°58N 16°50E **83** G3
Krzyż Wielkopolski
Poland 52°52N 16°0E **83** F2
Ksabi Morocco 32°51N 4°13W **136** B5
Ksar Chellala Algeria 35°13N 2°19E **136** A4
Ksar el Boukhari Algeria 35°51N 2°52E **136** A4
Ksar el Kebir Morocco 35°0N 6°0W **136** B2
Ksar es Souk = Er Rachidia
Morocco 31°58N 4°20W **136** B3
Ksar es Srhir Morocco 35°51N 5°34W **89** E3
Ksar Rhilane Tunisia 33°0N 9°39E **136** B5
Ksiaz Wielkopolski
Poland 52°4N 17°14E **83** F4
Ksour, Mts. des Algeria 32°45N 0°30W **136** B3
Kstovo Russia 56°12N 44°13E **86** B7
Ku-Ring-Gai Chase △
Australia 33°39S 151°14E **153** A10
Kuah Malaysia 6°19N 99°51E **121** J2
Kuala Belait Malaysia 4°35N 114°11E **118** D4
Kuala Berang Malaysia 5°5N 103°1E **121** K4
Kuala Dungun = Dungun
Malaysia 4°45N 103°25E **121** K4
Kuala Kangsar
Malaysia 4°46N 100°56E **121** K3
Kuala Kelawang
Malaysia 2°56N 102°5E **121** L4
Kuala Kerai Malaysia 5°30N 102°12E **121** K4
Kuala Kubu Bharu
Malaysia 3°34N 101°39E **121** L3
Kuala Lipis Malaysia 4°10N 102°3E **121** K4
Kuala Lumpur Malaysia 3°9N 101°41E **121** L3
Kuala Lumpur Int. ✈ (KUL)
Malaysia 2°44N 101°42E **121** L3
Kuala Nerang Malaysia 6°16N 100°37E **121** J3
Kuala Pilah Malaysia 2°45N 102°15E **121** L4
Kuala Rompin
Malaysia 2°49N 103°29E **121** L4
Kuala Selangor
Malaysia 3°20N 101°15E **121** L3
Kuala Sepetang
Malaysia 4°49N 100°28E **121** K3
Kuala Terengganu
Malaysia 5°20N 103°8E **121** K4
Kualajelai Indonesia 2°58S 110°46E **118** E4
Kualakapuas Indonesia 2°55S 114°20E **118** E4
Kualakurun Indonesia 1°10S 113°50E **118** E4
Kualapembuang
Indonesia 3°14S 112°38E **118** E4
Kualasimpang Indonesia 4°17N 98°3E **118** D1
Kuancheng China 40°37N 118°30E **115** D10
Kuandang Indonesia 0°56N 123°1E **119** D6
Kuandian China 40°45N 124°45E **115** D13
Kuangchou = Guangzhou
China 23°6N 113°13E **117** F9
Kuanshan Taiwan 23°3N 121°9E **117** F13
Kuantan Malaysia 3°49N 103°20E **121** L4
Kuba = Quba Azerbaijan 41°21N 48°32E **87** K9
Kuban → Russia 45°20N 37°30E **85** K9
Kuban Depression =
Prikubanskaya Nizmennost
Russia 45°39N 38°33E **87** H4
Kubaysah Iraq 33°35N 42°37E **105** G10
Kubenskoye, Ozero
Russia 59°40N 39°25E **84** C10
Kubokawa = Shimanto
Japan 33°12N 133°8E **113** H6
Kubrat Bulgaria 43°49N 26°31E **97** C10
Kubu Indonesia 8°16S 115°35E **119** J18
Kubutambahan
Indonesia 8°9S 115°10E **119** J18
Kucar, Tanjung
Indonesia 8°39S 114°34E **119** K18
Kučevo Serbia 44°30N 21°40E **96** B5
Kuchaman India 27°13N 74°47E **124** F6
Kuchchaveli Sri Lanka 8°49N 81°6E **127** K5
Kuchinda India 21°44N 84°21E **125** J11
Kuchino-eruba-Jima
Japan 30°28N 130°12E **113** J5
Kuchino-Shima Japan 29°57N 129°55E **113** K4
Kuchinotsu Japan 32°36N 130°11E **113** H5
Kuchl Austria 47°37N 13°9E **78** D6
Kuchurhan → Ukraine 46°39N 29°57E **81** D14
Kucing = Kuching
Malaysia 1°33N 110°25E **118** D4
Kuçovë Albania 40°47N 19°57E **96** F3
Küçükköy Turkey 39°33N 26°24E **99** B8
Küçükkuyu Turkey 39°36N 26°26E **99** B8
Küçükmenderes →
Turkey 37°57N 27°16E **99** D9
Kud → Pakistan 26°5N 66°20E **124** F2

Kuda India 23°10N 71°15E **124** H3
Kudal India 16°2N 73°41E **127** F1
Kudalier → India 18°35N 79°48E **126** E4
Kudat Malaysia 6°55N 116°55E **118** C5
Kudirkos Naumiestis
Lithuania 54°46N 22°53E **82** D9
Kudremukh India 13°15N 75°20E **127** H2
Kudus Indonesia 6°48S 110°51E **119** G14
Kudymkar Russia 59°1N 54°39E **106** D6
Kueiyang = Guiyang
China 26°32N 106°40E **116** D6
Kufra Oasis = Al Kufrah
Libya 24°17N 23°15E **135** D10
Kufstein Austria 47°35N 12°11E **78** D5
Kugaaruk = Pelly Bay
Canada 68°38N 89°50W **161** D14
Kugluktuk Canada 67°50N 115°5W **160** D8
Kugong I. Canada 56°18N 79°50W **164** A4
Kūh Dasht Iran 33°32N 47°36E **107** G6
Kūhak Iran 27°12N 63°10E **129** E9
Kühbonän Iran 31°23N 56°19E **129** D8
Kühestak Iran 26°47N 57°2E **129** E8
Kuhin Iran 36°22N 49°40E **129** B6
Kühiri Iran 26°55N 61°2E **129** E9
Kūhak Iran 28°19N 67°14E **124** F2
Kühbonän Iran 31°23N 56°19E **129** D8
Kühpäyeh Eşfahan, Iran 32°44N 52°20E **129** C7
Kühpäyeh Kermān, Iran 30°35N 57°15E **129** D8
Kührän, Küh-e Iran 26°46N 58°12E **129** E8
Kuhmo Finland 64°7N 29°31E **60** D23
Kühn Chae △ Thailand 19°8N 99°24E **120** C2
Kuhnsdorf Austria 46°37N 14°38E **78** E7
Kuiburi △ Thailand 12°10N 99°37E **121** F2
Kuichong China 22°38N 114°25E **111** a
Kuiseb → Namibia 22°59S 14°31E **144** B1
Kuito Angola 12°22S 16°55E **141** G3
Kuiu I. U.S.A. 57°45N 134°10W **162** B2
Kujalleq □ Greenland 61°0N 44°0W **57** E6
Kujang N. Korea 39°57N 126°1E **115** E14
Kujawsko-Pomorskie □
Poland 53°20N 18°30E **82** E5
Kuji Japan 40°11N 141°46E **112** D10
Kujū-San Japan 33°5N 131°15E **113** H5
Kukava Ukraine 48°37N 27°43E **81** B12
Kukawa Nigeria 12°58N 13°27E **139** C7
Kukës Albania 42°5N 20°27E **96** D4
Kukmor Russia 56°11N 50°54E **86** B10
Kukup Malaysia 1°20N 103°27E **121** d
Kukup, Pulau Malaysia 1°18N 103°25E **121** d
Kukvidze Russia 50°40N 43°0E **86** E6
Kula Bulgaria 43°52N 22°36E **96** C6
Kula Serbia 45°37N 19°32E **80** E4
Kula Turkey 38°32N 28°40E **99** C10
Kulachi Pakistan 31°56N 70°27E **124** D4
Kulai Malaysia 1°44N 103°35E **121** M4
Kulaly Aral Kazakhstan 45°0N 50°5E **87** H10
Kulasekarappattinam
India 8°20N 78°5E **127** K4
Kulautuva Lithuania 54°56N 23°36E **82** D10
Kuldiga Latvia 56°58N 21°59E **82** B8
Kulebaki Russia 55°22N 42°25E **86** C6
Kulen Cambodia 13°50N 104°40E **120** F5
Kulen Vakuf Bos.-H. 44°35N 16°2E **93** D13
Kulgam India 33°36N 75°2E **125** C6
Kulgera Australia 25°50S 133°18E **150** D1
Kulim Malaysia 5°22N 100°34E **121** K3
Kulin Australia 32°40S 118°2E **149** F2
Kulittalai India 10°55N 78°22E **127** J4
Kulkayu = Hartley Bay
Canada 53°25N 129°15W **162** C3
Kullen Sweden 56°18N 12°26E **63** H6
Kulm U.S.A. 31°58N 77°6E **124** D7
Kulmbach Germany 50°6N 11°26E **77** E7
Kulob Tajikistan 37°55N 69°50E **109** F7
Kulp Turkey 38°29N 41°2E **105** C9
Kulpawn → Ghana 10°20N 1°5W **139** D4
Kulsary = Qulsary
Kazakhstan 46°59N 54°1E **108** C2
Kulti India 23°43N 86°50E **125** H12
Kulu Turkey 39°5N 33°4E **104** C5
Kulu India 31°58N 77°6E **124** D7
Kulunda Russia 52°35N 78°57E **109** D9
Kulundinskoye, Ozero
Russia 53°0N 79°36E **109** B9
Kulungar Afghan. 34°0N 69°2E **124** C3
Külvand Iran 31°21N 54°35E **129** D7
Kulwin Australia 35°2S 142°42E **152** C5
Kulyab = Külob
Tajikistan 37°55N 69°50E **109** F7
Kuma → Russia 44°55N 47°0E **87** H8
Kumafşari Turkey 37°19N 29°32E **99** D11
Kumaganum Nigeria 13°8N 10°38E **139** C7
Kumagaya Japan 36°9N 139°22E **113** F9
Kumai Indonesia 2°44S 111°43E **118** E4
Kumamba, Kepulauan
Indonesia 1°36S 138°45E **119** E9
Kumamoto Japan 32°45N 130°45E **113** H5
Kumamoto □ Japan 32°55N 130°55E **113** H5
Kumanovo Macedonia 42°9N 21°42E **96** D5
Kumara N.Z. 42°37S 171°12E **155** C6
Kumara → Afghan. 34°30N 70°28E **109** F8
Kumarina Roadhouse
Australia 24°41S 119°32E **149** D2
Kumasi Ghana 6°41N 1°38W **138** D4
Kumba Cameroon 4°36N 9°24E **139** E6
Kumbakonam India 10°58N 79°25E **127** J4
Kumbarilla Australia 27°15S 150°55E **151** D5
Kumbhalgarh △ India 25°10N 73°35E **124** G5
Kumbhraj India 24°22N 77°3E **124** G7
Kumbia Australia 26°41S 151°39E **151** D5
Kumbo Cameroon 6°15N 10°36E **139** D7
Kumbukkan Oya →
Sri Lanka 6°35N 81°40E **127** L5
Kumch'on N. Korea 38°10N 126°29E **115** E14
Kume-Shima Japan 26°20N 126°47E **113** L3
Kumeny Russia 58°10N 49°47E **86** A9
Kumharsain India 31°19N 77°27E **124** D7
Kumi Uganda 1°30N 33°58E **142** B3
Kumkale Turkey 39°59N 26°11E **97** G10
Kumla Sweden 59°8N 15°10E **62** E9
Kumluca Turkey 36°22N 30°20E **99** E12
Kumo Nigeria 10°1N 11°12E **139** C7

Kummerower See
Germany 53°49N 12°51E **76** B8
Kumo Nigeria 10°1N 11°12E **139** C7
Kumo älv = Kokemäenjoki →
Finland 61°32N 21°44E **84** B1
Kumon Bum Burma 26°30N 97°15E **123** F20
Kumta India 14°29N 74°25E **127** G2
Kumtag Shamo China 39°40N 92°0E **110** D7
Kumul = Hami China 42°55N 93°25E **110** D7
Kumylzhenskaya Russia 49°51N 42°38E **86** F6
Kuna U.S.A. 43°30N 116°25W **168** E5
Kunágota Hungary 46°26N 21°3E **80** D6
Kunashir, Ostrov
Russia 44°0N 146°0E **107** E15
Kunchha Nepal 28°8N 84°20E **125** E11
Kunda Estonia 59°30N 26°34E **84** C4
Kunda India 25°43N 81°31E **125** G9
Kundar → Pakistan 31°56N 69°19E **124** D3
Kundelungu △
Dem. Rep. of the Congo 9°30S 27°50E **143** E2
Kundelungu Ouest △
Dem. Rep. of the Congo 9°55S 27°17E **143** D2
Kundian Pakistan 32°27N 71°28E **124** C4
Kundla India 21°21N 71°25E **124** J4
Kunene → Namibia 20°0S 14°0E **144** A1
Kung, Ao Thailand 8°5N 98°24E **121** a
Kunga → Bangla. 21°46N 89°30E **125** J13
Kunghit I. Canada 52°6N 131°3W **162** C2
Kungrad = Qŭnghirot
Uzbekistan 43°2N 58°50E **108** D5
Kungsängen Sweden 59°29N 17°45E **62** E11
Kungsbacka Sweden 57°30N 12°5E **63** G6
Kungsgården Sweden 60°37N 16°35E **62** D10
Kungshamn Sweden 58°22N 11°15E **63** F5
Kungsör Sweden 59°25N 16°5E **62** E10
Kungur Russia 57°25N 56°57E **106** D6
Kungurri Australia 21°4S 148°45E **150** b
Kunhar → Pakistan 34°20N 73°30E **124** J4
Kunhegyes Hungary 47°22N 20°36E **80** C5
Kuningan Indonesia 6°59S 108°29E **119** G13
Kunlara Australia 34°54S 139°55E **152** C3
Kunlong Burma 23°20N 98°50E **116** G2
Kunlun Antarctica 80°25S 77°7E **55** E6
Kunlun Shan Asia 36°0N 86°30E **109** E11
Kunlun Shankou China 35°38N 94°4E **110** D7
Kunmadaras Hungary 47°28N 20°45E **80** D7
Kunming Changshui Int. ✈
(KMG) China 24°59N 102°45E **116** E4
Kunming China 25°1N 102°41E **116** E4
Kunmunya
Australia 15°26S 124°42E **148** C3
Kunnamkulam India 10°38N 76°7E **127** J3
Kunów Poland 50°57N 21°17E **83** H8
Kunshan China 31°22N 120°58E **117** B13
Kunszentmárton
Hungary 46°50N 20°20E **80** D5
Kunszentmiklós Hungary 47°2N 19°8E **80** C4
Kuntaur Senegal 13°40N 14°48W **138** C2
Kununurra Australia 15°40S 128°50E **148** C4
Kunwari → India 26°26N 79°11E **125** F8
Kunya-Urgench = Köneürgench
Turkmenistan 42°19N 59°10E **108** D5
Künzelsau Germany 49°17N 9°42E **77** F5
Kuopio Finland 62°53N 27°35E **60** E22
Kupa → Croatia 45°28N 16°24E **93** C13
Kupang Indonesia 10°19S 123°39E **119** F6
Kupino Russia 54°21N 77°16E **108** D8
Kupreanof I. U.S.A. 56°50N 133°30W **162** B2
Kupres Bos.-H. 43°56N 17°18E **80** G2
Kupyansk Ukraine 49°52N 37°35E **85** H9
Kupyansk-Uzlovoi
Ukraine 49°40N 37°43E **85** H9
Kuqa China 41°35N 82°30E **109** D10
Kür → Azerbaijan 39°29N 49°15E **105** C13
Kür Dili Azerbaijan 39°3N 49°13E **105** C13
Kura = Kür →
Azerbaijan 39°29N 49°15E **105** C13
Kuranda Australia 16°48S 145°35E **150** B4
Kuranga India 22°4N 69°10E **124** H3
Kurashiki Japan 34°40N 133°50E **113** G6
Kurayn Si. Arabia 27°38N 49°50E **129** E6
Kurayoshi Japan 35°26N 133°50E **113** G6
Kürchatov Kazakhstan 50°45N 78°32E **109** D9
Kurchatov Russia 51°40N 35°38E **85** G8
Kürdämir Azerbaijan 40°25N 48°3E **87** K9
Kurdistan Asia 37°20N 43°30E **105** C10
Kurduvadi India 18°8N 75°29E **126** E2
Kürdzhali Bulgaria 41°38N 25°21E **97** E9
Kürdzhali □ Bulgaria 41°38N 25°21E **97** E9
Kure Japan 34°14N 132°32E **113** G6
Küre Turkey 41°50N 33°20E **104** B5
Küre Dağları Turkey 41°50N 33°50E **104** B5
Kure I. U.S.A. 28°25N 178°25W **167** K4
Kuressaare Estonia 58°15N 22°30E **84** C2
Kurgan Russia 55°26N 65°18E **108** D7
Kurgan-Tyube = Qŭrghonteppa
Tajikistan 37°50N 68°47E **109** F7
Kurganinsk Russia 44°54N 40°34E **87** H5
Kurgannaya = Kurganinsk
Russia 44°54N 40°34E **87** H5
Kuri India 26°37N 70°43E **124** F4
Kurikka Finland 62°36N 22°24E **62** B8
Kuril Basin Pac. Oc. 47°0N 150°0E **54** E15
Kuril Is. = Kurilskiye Ostrova
Pac. Oc. 45°0N 150°0E **107** E16
Kuril-Kamchatka Trench
Pac. Oc. 44°0N 153°0E **54** C17
Kurilsk Russia 45°14N 147°53E **107** E15
Kurilskiye Ostrova
Pac. Oc. 45°0N 150°0E **107** E16
Kurino Japan 31°57N 130°43E **113** J5
Kurinskaya Kosa = Kür Dili
Azerbaijan 39°3N 49°13E **105** C13
Kurkheda India 20°37N 80°12E **126** D5
Kurkur Egypt 23°50N 32°0E **135** C12
Kurla India 19°4N 72°52E **126** D1
Kurlkuta △
Australia 24°45S 127°45E **149** D4
Kurmuk Sudan 10°33N 34°21E **135** F12
Kurnool India 15°45N 78°0E **127** G3
Kuro-Shima Kagoshima,
Japan 30°50N 129°57E **113** J4
Kuro-Shima Okinawa,
Japan 24°14N 124°1E **113** M2
Kurow N.Z. 44°44S 170°29E **155** E5
Kurów Poland 51°23N 22°12E **83** G9
Kurrajong Australia 33°33S 150°42E **153** B9
Kurram → Pakistan 32°36N 71°20E **124** C4
Kurri Kurri Australia 32°50S 151°28E **153** B9
Kurrimine Australia 17°47S 146°6E **150** B4
Kursavka Russia 44°29N 42°32E **87** H5
Kurseong = Karsiyang
India 26°56N 88°18E **125** F13
Kürshim Kazakhstan 48°34N 83°39E **109** C10
Kürshskaya Kosa △
Russia 55°7N 20°45E **82** C7
Kurshskiy Zaliv Russia 55°9N 21°6E **82** C7
Kuršiu Nerijos □
Lithuania 55°30N 21°6E **82** C8
Kursk Russia 51°42N 36°11E **85** G9
Kursk □ Russia 51°50N 36°10E **85** G9
Kuršumlija Serbia 43°9N 21°19E **96** C5
Kuršumlijska Banja
Serbia 43°3N 21°11E **96** C5
Kurşunlu Bursa, Turkey 40°3N 29°40E **97** F13
Kurşunlu Çankırı,
Turkey 40°51N 33°15E **104** B5
Kurtalan Turkey 37°56N 41°44E **105** D9
Kurtbey Turkey 41°9N 26°35E **97** E10
Kurucaşile Turkey 41°49N 32°42E **104** B5
Kuruçay Turkey 39°39N 38°29E **128** E3
Kurukshetra = Thanesar
India 30°1N 76°52E **124** D7
Kuruktag China 41°0N 89°0E **109** D11
Kuruman S. Africa 27°28S 23°28E **144** D3
Kuruman → S. Africa 26°56S 20°39E **144** C3
Kurume Japan 33°15N 130°30E **113** H5
Kurunegala Sri Lanka 7°30N 80°23E **127** L5
Kurya Russia 61°42N 57°9E **61** C16
Kus Gölü Turkey 40°10N 27°55E **97** F11
Kuşadası Turkey 37°52N 27°15E **104** D2
Kuşadası Körfezi Turkey 37°56N 27°0E **99** D8
Kusamba Indonesia 8°34S 115°27E **119** K18
Kusatsu Japan 36°37N 138°36E **113** F9
Kusawa L. Canada 60°20N 136°13W **162** A1
Kusel Germany 49°32N 7°24E **77** F3
Kushaka Nigeria 10°32N 6°58E **139** C6
Kushalnagar India 12°14N 75°57E **127** J2
Kushchevskaya Russia 46°33N 39°35E **87** G4
Kusheriki Nigeria 10°28N 6°28E **139** C6
Kushima Japan 31°29N 131°14E **113** J5
Kushimoto Japan 33°28N 135°47E **113** H7
Kushiro-Gawa →
Japan 42°59N 144°23E **112** C12
Kushiro Shitsugen △
Japan 43°9N 144°26E **112** C12
Kushk Iran 33°31N 58°45E **108** G5
Kushka = Serhetabat
Turkmenistan 35°20N 62°18E **129** C9
Kushmurun = Qusmuryn
Kazakhstan 52°27N 64°36E **108** B6
Kushnytsya Ukraine 48°27N 23°15E **81** B8
Kushol India 33°40N 76°36E **125** C7
Kushtia Bangla. 23°55N 89°5E **123** H16
Kuskokwim → U.S.A. 60°5N 162°25W **166** C7
Kuskokwim B.
U.S.A. 59°45N 162°25W **166** C7
Kuskokwim Mts.
U.S.A. 62°30N 156°0W **166** C8
Kusmi India 23°17N 83°55E **125** H10
Kusöng N. Korea 39°59N 125°25E **115** E13
Kussharo-Ko Japan 43°38N 144°21E **112** C12
Kustanay = Qostanay
Kazakhstan 53°10N 63°35E **108** B6
Kut, Ko Thailand 11°40N 102°35E **121** G4
Kuta Indonesia 8°43S 115°11E **119** K18
Kütahya Turkey 39°30N 30°2E **99** C12
Kütahya □ Turkey 39°15N 29°46E **99** C11
Kutaisi Georgia 42°19N 42°40E **87** J6
Kutaraja = Banda Aceh
Indonesia 5°35N 95°20E **118** C1
Kutch, Gulf of = Kachchh, Gulf of
India 22°50N 69°15E **124** H3
Kutch, Rann of = Kachchh, Rann
of India 24°0N 70°0E **124** H4
Kutina Croatia 45°29N 16°48E **93** C13
Kutiyana India 21°36N 70°2E **124** J3
Kutkashen = Qäbälä
Azerbaijan 40°59N 47°52E **87** K8
Kutná Hora Czech Rep. 49°57N 15°16E **78** B8
Kutno Poland 52°15N 19°23E **83** F6
Kutse Botswana 21°7S 22°16E **144** C3
Kutu
Dem. Rep. of the Congo 2°40S 18°11E **140** E3
Kutum Sudan 14°10N 24°40E **135** F10
Küty Slovak Rep. 48°40N 17°3E **79** C10
Kúty Ukraine 48°16N 25°11E **81** B10
Kuujjuaq Canada 58°6N 68°15W **161** D13
Kuujjuarapik Canada 55°20N 77°35W **164** A4
Kuusamo Finland 65°57N 29°8E **60** D23
Kuusankoski Finland 60°55N 26°38E **84** B4
Kuvshinovo Russia 57°2N 34°11E **84** C8
Kuwait = Al Kuwayt
Kuwait 29°30N 48°0E **128** D5
Kuwait ■ Asia 29°30N 47°30E **128** D5
Kuwana Japan 35°5N 136°43E **113** G8
Kuwana → India 26°25N 83°15E **125** F10
Kuybyshev = Samara
Russia 53°8N 50°6E **86** D10
Kuybyshev Russia 55°27N 78°19E **106** D8
Kuybyshevo Ukraine 47°35N 36°40E **85** J9
Kuybyshevskoye Vdkhr.
Russia 55°2N 49°30E **86** C10

Kuye He → China 38°23N 110°46E **114** E6
Küyeh Iran 38°45N 47°57E **128** B5
Kuyto, Ozero Russia 65°6N 31°0E **60** D24
Kuytun China 44°25N 85°0E **110** B6
Kuyucak Turkey 37°55N 28°27E **99** D10
Kuyumba Russia 60°58N 96°59E **107** C10
Kuzey Anadolu Dağları
Turkey 41°30N 35°0E **104** B6
Kuzhithurai India 8°18N 77°11E **127** K3
Kuzmin Serbia 45°2N 19°5E **80** E4
Kuznetsk Russia 53°12N 46°40E **86** D8
Kuzomen Russia 66°22N 36°50E **84** A5
Kvænangen Norway 70°5N 21°15E **60** A19
Kværndrup Denmark 55°10N 10°31E **63** J4
Kvaløya Norway 69°40N 18°30E **60** B18
Kvänum Sweden 58°18N 13°11E **63** F7

Kvareli = Qvareli *Georgia* 41°57N 45°47E **87** K7
Kvarner *Croatia* 44°50N 14°10E **93** D11
Kvarnerič *Croatia* 44°43N 14°37E **93** D11
Kvicksund *Sweden* 59°27N 16°19E **62** E10
Kvillsfors *Sweden* 57°24N 15°29E **63** G9
Kvismare kanal *Sweden* 59°11N 15°35E **62** E9
Kvissleby *Sweden* 62°18N 17°22E **62** B11
Kvitøya *Svalbard* 80°8N 32°35E **57** A14
Kwabhaca *S. Africa* 30°51S 29°0E **145** D4
Kwai = Khwae Noi → *Thailand* 14°1N 99°32E **120** E2
Kwajalein *Marshall Is.* 9°5N 167°20E **156** G8
Kwakhanai *Botswana* 21°39S 21°16E **144** B3
Kwakoegron *Suriname* 5°12N 55°25W **187** B7
Kwale *Kenya* 4°15S 39°31E **142** C4
Kwale *Nigeria* 5°46N 6°26E **139** D6
KwaMashu *S. Africa* 29°45S 30°58E **145** C5
Kwando → *Africa* 18°27S 23°32E **144** A3
Kwangchow = Guangzhou *China* 23°6N 113°13E **117** F9
Kwangdaeri *N. Korea* 40°34N 127°33E **115** D14
Kwango → *Dem. Rep. of the Congo* 3°14S 17°22E **140** E3
Kwangsi-Chuang = Guangxi Zhuangzu Zizhiqu □ *China* 24°0N 109°0E **116** F7
Kwangtung = Guangdong □ *China* 23°0N 113°0E **117** F9
Kwara □ *Nigeria* 8°45N 4°30E **139** D6
Kwataboahegan → *Canada* 51°9N 80°50W **164** B3
Kwatisore *Indonesia* 3°18S 134°50E **119** E8
KwaZulu Natal □ *S. Africa* 29°0S 30°0E **145** C5
Kweichow = Guizhou □ *China* 27°0N 107°0E **116** D6
Kwekwe *Zimbabwe* 18°58S 29°48E **143** F2
Kweneng □ *Botswana* 24°0S 25°0E **144** B3
Kwidzyn *Poland* 53°44N 18°55E **82** E5
Kwilu → *Dem. Rep. of the Congo* 3°22S 17°22E **140** E3
Kwinana *Australia* 32°15S 115°47E **149** F2
Kwisa → *Poland* 51°34N 15°24E **83** G2
Kwoka *Indonesia* 0°31S 132°27E **119** E8
Kwolla *Nigeria* 9°0N 9°15E **139** D6
Kwun Tong *China* 22°19N 114°13E **111** a
Kyabra Cr. → *Australia* 25°36S 142°55E **151** D3
Kyabram *Australia* 36°19S 145°4E **153** D6
Kyaikto *Burma* 17°20N 97°3E **120** D1
Kyaing Tong = Keng Tung *Burma* 21°18N 99°39E **120** B2
Kyakhta *Russia* 50°30N 106°25E **107** D11
Kyambura ⌓ *Uganda* 0°7S 30°9E **142** C3
Kyancutta *Australia* 33°8S 135°33E **151** E2
Kyaukpadaung *Burma* 20°52N 95°8E **123** J19
Kyaukpyu *Burma* 19°28N 93°30E **123** K18
Kyaukse *Burma* 21°36N 96°10E **123** J20
Kybartai *Lithuania* 54°39N 22°45E **82** D9
Kyburz *U.S.A.* 38°47N 120°18W **170** G6
Kyelang *India* 32°35N 77°2E **124** C7
Kyenjojo *Uganda* 0°40N 30°37E **142** B3
Kyjov *Czech Rep.* 49°1N 17°7E **79** B10
Kyklades *Greece* 37°0N 24°30E **98** E6
Kyle *Canada* 50°50N 108°2W **163** C7
Kyle *U.S.A.* 29°59N 97°53W **176** F6
Kyle Dam = Mutirikwe Dam *Zimbabwe* 20°15S 31°0E **143** G3
Kyle of Lochalsh *U.K.* 57°17N 5°44W **65** D3
Kyll → *Germany* 49°48N 6°41E **77** F2
Kyllburg *Germany* 50°2N 6°34E **77** E2
Kyllini *Greece* 37°55N 21°8E **98** D3
Kymijoki → *Finland* 60°30N 26°55E **84** B4
Kymmene älv = Kymijoki → *Finland* 60°30N 26°55E **84** B4
Kyneton *Australia* 37°10S 144°29E **152** D6
Kynuna *Australia* 21°37S 141°55E **150** C3
Kyō-ga-Saki *Japan* 35°45N 135°15E **113** G7
Kyoga, L. *Uganda* 1°35N 33°0E **142** B3
Kyogle *Australia* 28°40S 153°0E **151** D5
Kyŏngju = Gyeongju *S. Korea* 35°51N 129°14E **115** G15
Kyŏngsŏng *N. Korea* 41°35N 129°36E **115** D15
Kyonpyaw *Burma* 17°12N 95°10E **123** L19
Kyōto *Japan* 35°0N 135°45E **113** G7
Kyōto □ *Japan* 35°15N 135°45E **113** G7
Kyparissovouno *Cyprus* 35°19N 33°10E **101** D12
Kyperounda *Cyprus* 34°56N 32°58E **101** E11
Kypros = Cyprus ■ *Asia* 35°0N 33°0E **101** E12
Kyrenia *Cyprus* 35°20N 33°20E **101** D12
Kyrgyzstan ■ *Asia* 42°0N 75°0E **109** D9
Kyritz *Germany* 52°56N 12°24E **76** C8
Kyrkhult *Sweden* 56°22N 14°34E **63** H8
Kyrnasivka *Ukraine* 48°35N 28°58E **81** B13
Kyrnychky *Ukraine* 45°42N 29°4E **81** E14
Kyro älv = Kyrönjoki → *Finland* 63°14N 21°45E **60** E19
Kyrönjoki → *Finland* 63°14N 21°45E **60** E19
Kystatyam *Russia* 67°20N 123°10E **107** C13
Kysucké Nové Mesto *Slovak Rep.* 49°18N 18°47E **79** B11
Kytay, Ozero *Ukraine* 45°40N 29°13E **81** E14
Kythira *Greece* 36°8N 23°0E **98** E5
Kythnos *Greece* 37°26N 24°27E **98** D6
Kythréa *Cyprus* 35°15N 33°29E **101** D12
Kyunhla *Burma* 23°25N 95°15E **123** H19
Kyuquot Sound *Canada* 50°2N 127°22W **162** D3
Kyurdamir = Kürdämir *Azerbaijan* 40°25N 48°3E **87** K9
Kyūshū *Japan* 33°0N 131°0E **113** H5
Kyūshū □ *Japan* 33°0N 131°0E **113** H5
Kyūshū-Palau Ridge *Pac. Oc.* 20°0N 136°0E **156** E5
Kyūshū-Sanchi *Japan* 32°35N 131°17E **113** H5
Kyustendil *Bulgaria* 42°16N 22°41E **96** D6
Kyustendil □ *Bulgaria* 42°25N 22°41E **96** D6
Kyusyur *Russia* 70°19N 127°30E **107** B13
Kywong *Australia* 34°58S 146°44E **153** C7
Kyyiv *Ukraine* 50°30N 30°28E **75** C16
Kyyiv □ *Ukraine* 50°5N 30°45E **85** G6
Kyyivske Vdskh. *Ukraine* 51°0N 30°25E **75** C16
Kyzyl *Russia* 51°50N 94°30E **109** B12
Kyzyl-Adyr *Kyrgyzstan* 42°39N 71°35E **109** D8
Kyzyl Kum *Uzbekistan* 42°30N 65°0E **109** D7
Kyzyl-Kyya *Kyrgyzstan* 40°16N 72°8E **109** D8
Kyzyl Orda = Qyzylorda *Kazakhstan* 44°48N 65°28E **108** D7
Kyzyl-Suu *Kyrgyzstan* 42°20N 78°0E **109** D9

L

La Albuera *Spain* 38°45N 6°49W **89** G4
La Alcarria *Spain* 40°31N 2°45W **90** E2
La Almarcha *Spain* 39°41N 2°24W **90** F2
La Almunia de Doña Godina *Spain* 41°29N 1°23W **90** D3
La Amistad △ *Cent. Amer.* 9°28N 83°18W **182** E3
La Asunción *Venezuela* 11°2N 63°51W **186** A6
La Baie *Canada* 48°19N 70°53W **165** C5
La Banda *Argentina* 27°45S 64°10W **190** B3
La Bañeza *Spain* 42°17N 5°54W **88** C5
La Barca *Mexico* 20°17N 102°34W **180** C4
La Barge *U.S.A.* 42°16N 110°12W **168** E8
La Barra *Nic.* 12°54N 83°33W **182** D3
La Bastide-Puylaurent *France* 44°35N 3°55E **72** D7
La Baule *France* 47°17N 2°24W **70** E4
La Belle *U.S.A.* 26°46N 81°26W **179** J8
La Biche → *Canada* 59°57N 123°50W **162** B4
La Biche, L. *Canada* 54°50N 112°3W **162** C6
La Bisbal d'Empordà *Spain* 41°58N 3°2E **90** D8
La Brea *Peru* 4°40S 81°7W **188** A1
La Brea *Trin. & Tob.* 10°15N 61°37W **187** K15
La Brède *France* 44°41N 0°32W **72** D3
La Bresse *France* 48°2N 6°53E **71** D13
La Bureba *Spain* 42°36N 3°24W **88** C7
La Calera *Chile* 32°50S 71°10W **190** C1
La Campana △ *Chile* 32°58S 71°14W **190** C1
La Campiña *Spain* 37°45N 4°45W **89** H6
La Canal = Sa Canal *Spain* 38°51N 1°23E **100** C7
La Cañiza = A Cañiza *Spain* 42°13N 8°16W **88** C2
La Canourgue *France* 44°26N 3°13E **72** D7
La Capelle *France* 49°59N 3°50E **71** C10
La Carlota *Argentina* 33°30S 63°20W **190** C3
La Carlota *Spain* 37°40N 4°56W **89** H6
La Carolina *Spain* 38°17N 3°38W **89** G7
La Cavalerie *France* 44°1N 3°10E **72** D7
La Ceiba *Honduras* 15°40N 86°50W **182** C2
La Chaise-Dieu *France* 45°18N 3°42E **72** C7
La Chapelle d'Angillon *France* 47°21N 2°25E **71** E9
La Chapelle-St-Luc *France* 48°20N 4°3E **71** D11
La Chapelle-sur-Erdre *France* 47°18N 1°34W **70** E5
La Charité-sur-Loire *France* 47°10N 3°1E **71** E10
La Chartre-sur-le-Loir *France* 47°44N 0°34E **70** E7
La Châtaigneraie *France* 46°39N 0°44W **72** B3
La Châtre *France* 46°35N 2°0E **71** F9
La Chaux-de-Fonds *Switz.* 47°7N 6°50E **77** H2
La Chorrera *Panama* 8°53N 79°47W **182** E4
La Ciotat *France* 43°10N 5°37E **73** E9
La Clayette *France* 46°17N 4°19E **71** F11
La Cocha *Argentina* 27°50S 65°40W **190** B2
La Concepción *Panama* 8°31N 82°37W **182** E3
La Concordia *Mexico* 16°5N 92°38W **181** D6
La Coruña = A Coruña *Spain* 43°20N 8°25W **88** B2
La Côte-St-André *France* 45°24N 5°15E **73** C9
La Courtine *France* 45°41N 2°15E **72** C6
La Crau *Bouches-du-Rhône, France* 43°32N 4°40E **73** E8
La Crau *Var, France* 43°9N 6°4E **73** E10
La Crescent *U.S.A.* 43°50N 91°18W **172** D8
La Crete *Canada* 58°11N 116°24W **162** B5
La Crosse *Fla., U.S.A.* 29°51N 82°24W **178** F7
La Crosse *Kans., U.S.A.* 38°32N 99°18W **172** F4
La Crosse *Wis., U.S.A.* 43°48N 91°15W **172** D8
La Cruz *Costa Rica* 11°4N 85°39W **182** D2
La Cruz *Mexico* 23°55N 106°54W **180** C3
La Désirade *Guadeloupe* 16°18N 61°3W **182** b
La Digue *Seychelles* 4°20S 55°51E **141** b
La Esperanza *Argentina* 40°26S 68°32W **192** B3
La Esperanza *Cuba* 22°46N 83°44W **182** B3
La Esperanza *Honduras* 14°15N 88°10W **182** D2
La Estrada = A Estrada *Spain* 42°43N 8°27W **88** C2
La Faouët *France* 48°2N 3°30W **70** D3
La Fayette *U.S.A.* 34°42N 85°17W **177** D12
La Fé *Cuba* 22°2N 84°15W **182** B3
La Fère *France* 49°39N 3°21E **71** C10
La Ferté-Bernard *France* 48°10N 0°40E **70** D7
La Ferté-Gaucher *France* 48°47N 3°19E **71** D10
La Ferté-Macé *France* 48°35N 0°22W **70** D6
La Ferté-St-Aubin *France* 47°42N 1°57E **71** E8
La Ferté-sous-Jouarre *France* 48°56N 3°8E **71** D10
La Ferté-Vidame *France* 48°37N 0°53E **70** D7
La Flèche *France* 47°42N 0°4W **70** E6
La Follette *U.S.A.* 36°23N 84°7W **177** C12
La Fregeneda *Spain* 40°58N 6°54W **88** E4
La Fuente de San Esteban *Spain* 40°49N 6°15W **88** E4
La Gacilly *France* 47°45N 2°8W **70** E4
La Gi *Vietnam* 10°40N 107°45E **121** G6
La Gineta *Spain* 39°8N 2°1W **91** F2
La Goulette *Tunisia* 36°53N 10°18E **94** F3
La Grand'Combe *France* 44°13N 4°2E **73** D8
La Grande *U.S.A.* 45°20N 118°5W **168** D4
La Grande → *Canada* 53°50N 79°0W **164** B5
La Grande 3, Rés. *Canada* 53°40N 75°10W **164** B4
La Grande 4, Rés. *Canada* 54°0N 73°15W **164** B5
La Grande-Motte *France* 43°23N 4°5E **73** E8
La Grange *Calif., U.S.A.* 37°42N 120°27W **170** H6
La Grange *Ga., U.S.A.* 33°2N 85°2W **178** B4
La Grange *Ky., U.S.A.* 38°24N 85°22W **173** F11
La Grange *Tex., U.S.A.* 29°54N 96°52W **176** G6
La Grave *France* 45°3N 6°18E **73** C10
La Guaira *Venezuela* 10°36N 66°56W **186** A5
La Guarda △ *Mexico* 29°20N 113°27W **180** B2
La Guardia = A Guarda *Spain* 41°56N 8°52W **88** D2
La Gudiña = A Gudiña *Spain* 42°4N 7°8W **88** C3
La Guerche-de-Bretagne *France* 47°57N 1°16W **70** E5
La Guerche-sur-l'Aubois *France* 46°58N 2°56E **71** F9
La Habana *Cuba* 23°8N 82°22W **182** B3
La Haute Vallée de Chevreuse ⌓ *France* 48°35N 1°58E **71** D8
La Haye-du-Puits *France* 49°17N 1°33W **70** C5
La Horra *Spain* 41°44N 3°53W **88** D7
La Independencia *Mexico* 16°15N 92°1W **181** D6
La Isabela *Dom. Rep.* 19°58N 71°2W **183** C5
La Jonquera *Spain* 42°25N 2°53E **90** C7
La Joya *Peru* 16°43S 71°52W **188** D3
La Junta *U.S.A.* 37°59N 103°33W **168** H12
La Laguna = San Cristóbal de La Laguna *Canary Is.* 28°28N 16°18W **100** F3
La Libertad = Puerto Libertad *Mexico* 29°55N 112°43W **180** B2
La Libertad *Guatemala* 16°47N 90°7W **182** C1
La Libertad □ *Peru* 8°0S 78°30W **188** B2
La Ligua *Chile* 32°30S 71°16W **190** C1
La Línea de la Concepción *Spain* 36°15N 5°23W **89** J5
La Loche *Canada* 56°29N 109°26W **163** B7
La Londe-les-Maures *France* 43°8N 6°14E **73** E10
La Lora *Spain* 42°45N 4°0W **88** C7
La Loupe *France* 48°29N 1°0E **70** D8
La Louvière *Belgium* 50°27N 4°10E **69** D4
La Lune *Trin. & Tob.* 10°3N 61°22W **187** K15
La Machine *France* 46°54N 3°27E **71** F10
La Maddalena *Italy* 41°13N 9°24E **94** A2
La Malbaie *Canada* 47°40N 70°10W **165** C5
La Malinche △ *Mexico* 19°15N 98°3W **181** D5
La Mancha *Spain* 39°10N 2°54W **91** F2
La Mariña *Spain* 43°30N 7°40W **88** B3
La Martre, L. *Canada* 63°15N 117°55W **162** A5
La Merced *Peru* 11°3S 75°19W **188** C2
La Mercy ✈ (DUR) *S. Africa* 29°37S 31°7E **145** C5
La Mesa *Mexico* 32°30N 116°57W **171** N10
La Mesa *U.S.A.* 32°46N 117°1W **171** N9
La Mesilla *U.S.A.* 32°16N 106°48W **169** K10
La Mothe-Achard *France* 46°37N 1°40W **70** F5
La Motte-Chalançon *France* 44°30N 5°21E **73** D9
La Motte-du-Caire *France* 44°20N 6°3E **73** D10
La Motte-Servolex *France* 45°35N 5°53E **73** C9
La Moure *U.S.A.* 46°21N 98°18W **172** B4
La Muela *Spain* 41°36N 1°7W **90** D3
La Mure *France* 44°55N 5°48E **73** D9
La Negra *Chile* 23°46S 70°18W **190** A1
La Oliva *Canary Is.* 28°36N 13°57W **100** F6
La Oraya *Peru* 11°32S 75°54W **188** C2
La Orotava *Canary Is.* 28°22N 16°31W **100** F3
La Oroya *Peru* 11°32S 75°54W **188** C2
La Pacaudière *France* 46°11N 3°52E **71** F10
La Palma *Canary Is.* 28°40N 17°50W **100** F2
La Palma *Panama* 8°15N 78°0W **182** E4
La Palma del Condado *Spain* 37°21N 6°38W **89** H4
La Palmyre *France* 45°43N 1°9W **72** C2
La Paloma *Chile* 30°35S 71°0W **190** C1
La Pampa □ *Argentina* 36°50S 66°0W **190** D2
La Paragua *Venezuela* 6°50N 63°20W **186** B6
La Paz *Entre Ríos, Argentina* 30°50S 59°45W **190** C4
La Paz *San Luis, Argentina* 33°30S 67°20W **190** C2
La Paz *Bolivia* 16°20S 68°10W **188** D4
La Paz *Honduras* 14°20N 87°47W **182** D2
La Paz *Mexico* 24°10N 110°18W **180** C2
La Paz □ *Bolivia* 15°30S 68°0W **188** D4
La Paz Centro *Nic.* 12°20N 86°41W **182** D2
La Pedrera *Colombia* 1°18S 69°43W **186** D5
La Pérade *Canada* 46°35N 72°12W **165** C5
La Perla *Mexico* 28°18N 104°32W **180** B4
La Perouse Str. *Asia* 45°40N 142°0E **112** B11
La Pesca *Mexico* 23°46N 97°47W **181** C5
La Piedad *Mexico* 20°21N 102°0W **180** C4
La Pine *U.S.A.* 43°40N 121°30W **168** E3
La Plata *Argentina* 35°0S 57°55W **190** C4
La Plata, L. *Argentina* 44°55S 71°50W **192** B2
La Pobla de Lillet *Spain* 42°16N 1°59E **90** C6
La Pobla de Segur *Spain* 42°15N 0°58E **90** C5
La Pocatière *Canada* 47°22N 70°2W **165** C5
La Pola de Gordón *Spain* 42°51N 5°41W **88** C5
La Porta *France* 42°25N 9°21E **73** F13
La Porte *U.S.A.* 29°40N 95°1W **176** G7
La Presanella *Italy* 46°13N 10°40E **92** B7
La Puebla = Sa Pobla *Spain* 39°46N 3°1E **90** F8
La Puebla de Cazalla *Spain* 37°10N 5°20W **89** H5
La Puebla de los Infantes *Spain* 37°47N 5°24W **89** H5
La Puebla de Montalbán *Spain* 39°52N 4°22W **88** F6
La Puebla del Río *Spain* 37°16N 6°3W **89** H4
La Puerta de Segura *Spain* 38°22N 2°45W **89** G8
La Purísima *Mexico* 26°10N 112°4W **180** B2
La Push *U.S.A.* 47°55N 124°38W **170** C2
La Quiaca *Argentina* 22°5S 65°35W **190** A2
La Réole *France* 44°35N 0°1W **72** D3
La Restinga *Canary Is.* 27°38N 17°59W **100** G2
La Rinconada *Peru* 14°38S 69°27W **188** C4
La Rioja *Argentina* 29°20S 67°0W **190** B2
La Rioja □ *Argentina* 29°30S 67°0W **190** B2
La Rioja □ *Spain* 42°20N 2°20W **90** C2
La Robla *Spain* 42°50N 5°41W **88** C5
La Roche-Bernard *France* 47°31N 2°19W **70** E4
La Roche-Canillac *France* 45°12N 1°57E **72** C5
La Roche-en-Ardenne *Belgium* 50°11N 5°35E **69** D5
La Roche-sur-Foron *France* 46°4N 6°19E **71** F13
La Roche-sur-Yon *France* 46°40N 1°25W **70** F5
La Rochefoucauld *France* 45°44N 0°24E **72** C4
La Rochelle *France* 46°10N 1°9W **72** B2
La Roda *Spain* 39°13N 2°15W **91** F2
La Roda de Andalucía *Spain* 37°12N 4°46W **89** H6
La Romaine *Canada* 50°13N 60°40W **165** B7
La Romana *Dom. Rep.* 18°27N 68°57W **183** C6
La Ronge *Canada* 55°5N 105°20W **163** B7
La Rumorosa *Mexico* 32°34N 116°6W **171** N10
La Sabina = Sa Savina *Spain* 38°44N 1°25E **100** C7
La Sagra *Spain* 37°57N 2°35W **91** H2
La Salle *U.S.A.* 41°20N 89°6W **172** E9
La Sanabria *Spain* 42°0N 6°30W **88** C4
La Santa *Canary Is.* 29°5N 13°40W **100** E6
La Sarre *Canada* 48°45N 79°15W **164** C4
La Scie *Canada* 49°57N 55°36W **165** C8
La Selva *Spain* 42°0N 2°45E **90** C7
La Selva Beach *U.S.A.* 36°56N 121°51W **170** J5
La Selva del Camp *Spain* 41°13N 1°8E **90** D6
La Serena *Chile* 29°55S 71°10W **190** B1
La Serena *Spain* 38°45N 5°40W **89** G5
La Seu d'Urgell *Spain* 42°22N 1°23E **90** C6
La Seyne-sur-Mer *France* 43°7N 5°52E **73** E9
La Sila *Italy* 39°15N 16°35E **95** C9
La Solana *Spain* 38°59N 3°14W **89** G7
La Soufrière *St. Vincent* 13°20N 61°11W **183** D7
La Souterraine *France* 46°15N 1°30E **71** F8
La Spézia *Italy* 44°7N 9°50E **92** D6
La Suze-sur-Sarthe *France* 47°53N 0°2E **70** E7
La Tagua *Colombia* 0°3N 74°40W **186** C4
La Teste-de-Buch *France* 44°37N 1°8W **72** D2
La Tortuga, I. *Venezuela* 11°0N 65°22W **183** D6
La Tour-du-Pin *France* 45°33N 5°27E **73** C9
La Tranche-sur-Mer *France* 46°20N 1°27W **70** F5
La Tremblade *France* 45°46N 1°8W **72** C2
La Trinité *Martinique* 14°45N 60°58W **182** c
La Tuque *Canada* 47°30N 72°50W **164** C5
La Unión *Chile* 40°10S 73°0W **192** B2
La Unión *El Salv.* 13°20N 87°50W **182** D2
La Unión *Mexico* 17°58N 101°49W **180** D4
La Unión *Peru* 9°43S 76°45W **188** B2
La Unión *Spain* 37°38N 0°53W **91** H4
La Urbana *Venezuela* 7°8N 66°56W **186** B5
La Vache Pt. *Trin. & Tob.* 10°47N 61°28W **187** K15
La Vall d'Uixó *Spain* 39°49N 0°15W **90** F4
La Vecilla *Spain* 42°51N 5°27W **88** C5
La Vega *Dom. Rep.* 19°20N 70°30W **183** C5
La Vega *Peru* 10°41S 77°44W **188** C2
La Vela de Coro *Venezuela* 11°27N 69°34W **186** A5
La Veleta *Spain* 37°1N 3°22W **89** H7
La Venta *Mexico* 18°5N 94°3W **181** D6
La Vergne *U.S.A.* 36°1N 86°35W **177** C11
La Villa Joiosa = Villajoyosa *Spain* 38°30N 0°12W **91** G4
La Voulte-sur-Rhône *France* 44°48N 4°46E **73** D8
Laa an der Thaya *Austria* 48°43N 16°23E **79** C9
Laaber, Grosse → *Germany* 48°55N 12°30E **77** G8
Laage *Germany* 53°55N 12°21E **76** B8
Laascaanood = Las Anod *Somalia* 8°26N 47°19E **131** F4
Laatzen *Germany* 52°19N 9°48E **76** C5
Laba → *Russia* 45°11N 39°42E **87** H4
Labasa *Fiji* 16°30S 179°27E **154** a
Labastide-Murat *France* 44°39N 1°33E **72** D5
Labastide-Rouairoux *France* 43°28N 2°39E **72** E6
Labbézenga *Mali* 15°2N 0°48E **139** B5
Labdah = Leptis Magna *Libya* 32°40N 14°12E **135** B8
Labe = Elbe → *Europe* 53°50N 9°0E **76** B4
Labé *Guinea* 11°24N 12°16W **138** C2
Laberge, L. *Canada* 61°11N 135°12W **162** A1
Labin *Croatia* 45°5N 14°8E **93** C11
Labinsk *Russia* 44°40N 40°48E **87** H5
Labis *Malaysia* 2°22N 103°2E **121** L4
Łabiszyn *Poland* 52°57N 17°54E **83** F4
Laboe *Germany* 54°24N 10°13E **76** A6
Laborec → *Slovak Rep.* 48°37N 21°58E **79** C14
Laborie *St. Lucia* 13°45N 61°2W **183** f
Labouheyre *France* 44°13N 0°55W **72** D3
Laboulaye *Argentina* 34°10S 63°30W **190** C3
Labrador *Canada* 53°20N 61°0W **165** B7
Labrador City *Canada* 52°57N 66°55W **165** B6
Labrador Sea *Atl. Oc.* 57°0N 54°0W **161** F21
Lábrea *Brazil* 7°15S 64°51W **186** E6
Labruguière *France* 43°31N 2°16E **72** E6
Labuan □ *Malaysia* 5°20N 115°12E **118** C4
Labuha *Indonesia* 0°30S 127°30E **119** E7
Labuhan *Indonesia* 6°22S 105°50E **119** G11
Labuhanbajo *Indonesia* 8°28S 119°54E **119** F6
Labuhanbilik *Indonesia* 2°31N 100°10E **121** L3
Labuk, Telok *Malaysia* 6°10N 117°50E **118** C5
Labyrinth, L. *Australia* 30°40S 135°11E **151** E2
Labytnangi *Russia* 66°39N 66°21E **106** C7
Laç *Albania* 41°38N 19°43E **96** E3
Lac-Bouchette *Canada* 48°16N 72°11W **165** C5
Lac-Édouard *Canada* 47°40N 72°16W **165** C5
Lac La Biche *Canada* 54°45N 111°58W **162** C6
Lac la Martre = Wha Ti *Canada* 63°8N 117°16W **160** E8
Lac La Ronge ⌓ *Canada* 55°9N 104°41W **163** B7
Lac-Mégantic *Canada* 45°35N 70°53W **165** C5
Lac Thien *Vietnam* 12°25N 108°11E **120** F7
Lacanau *France* 44°58N 1°5W **72** D2
Lacanau, L. de *France* 44°58N 1°7W **72** D2
Lacantún → *Mexico* 16°36N 90°39W **181** D6
Lácara → *Spain* 38°55N 6°25W **89** G4
Lacaune *France* 43°43N 2°40E **72** E6
Lacaune, Mts. de *France* 43°43N 2°50E **72** E6
Laccadive Is. = Lakshadweep Is. *India* 10°0N 72°30E **127** J1
Lacepede B. *Australia* 36°40S 139°40E **152** D3
Lacepede Is. *Australia* 16°55S 122°0E **148** C3
Lacerdónia *Mozam.* 18°3S 35°35E **143** F4
Lacey *U.S.A.* 47°7N 122°49W **170** C4
Lachania *Greece* 35°58N 27°54E **101** D9
Lachay, Pta. *Peru* 11°17S 77°44W **188** C2
Lachhmangarh *India* 27°50N 75°4E **124** F6
Lachi *Pakistan* 33°25N 71°20E **124** C4
Lachine *Canada* 45°26N 73°42W **164** C5
Lachlan → *Australia* 34°22S 143°55E **152** C5
Lachoc *Peru* 12°50S 75°6W **188** C2
Lachute *Canada* 45°39N 74°21W **164** C5
Laçın *Azerbaijan* 39°38N 46°33E **105** C12
Lackagh Hills *Ireland* 54°16N 8°10W **64** B3
Lackawanna *U.S.A.* 42°50N 78°50W **174** D6
Lackawaxen *U.S.A.* 41°29N 74°59W **175** E10
Lacolle *Canada* 45°5N 73°22W **175** A11
Lacombe *Canada* 52°30N 113°44W **162** C6
Lacona *U.S.A.* 43°39N 76°10W **175** C8
Láconi *Italy* 39°54N 9°4E **94** C2
Laconia = Lakonia *Greece* 36°55N 22°30E **98** E4
Laconia *U.S.A.* 43°32N 71°28W **175** C13
Lacoochee *U.S.A.* 28°28N 82°11W **179** G7
Lacq *France* 43°25N 0°35W **72** E3
Lacs □ *Ivory C.* 7°1N 4°46W **138** D4
Ladakh Ra. *India* 34°0N 78°0E **125** C8
Lądek-Zdrój *Poland* 50°21N 16°53E **83** H3
Lâdik *Turkey* 40°57N 35°58E **104** B6
Ladismith *S. Africa* 33°28S 21°15E **144** D3
Ladíspoli *Italy* 41°56N 12°5E **93** G9
Lādīz *Iran* 28°55N 61°15E **129** D9
Ladnun *India* 27°38N 74°25E **124** F6
Ladoga, L. = Ladozhskoye Ozero *Russia* 61°15N 30°30E **84** B6
Ladonas → *Greece* 37°40N 21°50E **98** D3
Ladozhskoye Ozero *Russia* 61°15N 30°30E **84** B6
Ladrillero, G. *Chile* 49°20S 75°35W **192** C1
Ladson *U.S.A.* 32°59N 80°6W **178** C9
Ladushkin *Russia* 54°34N 20°10E **82** D7
Lady Elliott I. *Australia* 24°7S 152°42E **150** C5
Lady Frere *S. Africa* 31°42S 27°14E **144** D4
Lady Grey *S. Africa* 30°43S 27°13E **144** D4
Lady Lake *U.S.A.* 28°55N 81°55W **179** G8
Ladybrand *S. Africa* 29°9S 27°29E **144** C4
Ladysmith *Canada* 49°0N 123°49W **170** B3
Ladysmith *S. Africa* 28°32S 29°46E **145** C4
Ladysmith *U.S.A.* 45°28N 91°12W **172** C8
Ladyznyn *Ukraine* 48°40N 29°15E **81** B14
Lae *Papua N. G.* 6°40S 147°2E **147** B7
Laem Chabang *Thailand* 13°5N 100°53E **120** F3
Laem Ngop *Thailand* 12°10N 102°26E **121** F4
Laem Son △ *Thailand* 9°29N 98°24E **121** H2
Laerma *Greece* 36°9N 27°57E **101** C9
Læsø *Denmark* 57°15N 11°5E **63** G5
Læsø Rende *Denmark* 57°20N 10°45E **63** G4
Lafayette *Ala., U.S.A.* 32°54N 85°24W **178** C4
Lafayette *Ind., U.S.A.* 40°25N 86°54W **172** E10
Lafayette *La., U.S.A.* 30°14N 92°1W **176** F8
Lafayette *Tenn., U.S.A.* 36°31N 86°2W **177** C11
Laferte → *Canada* 61°53N 117°44W **162** A5
Lafia *Nigeria* 8°30N 8°34E **139** D6
Lafiagi *Nigeria* 8°52N 5°20E **139** D6
Lafkos *Greece* 39°9N 23°14E **98** B5
Lafleche *Canada* 49°45N 106°40W **163** D7
Laful *India* 7°10N 93°52E **127** L11
Lagan *Sweden* 56°56N 13°58E **63** H7
Lagan → *Sweden* 56°30N 12°58E **63** H6
Lagan → *U.K.* 54°36N 5°55W **64** B6
Lagarfljót → *Iceland* 65°40N 14°18W **60** D6
Lagarto *Brazil* 10°54S 37°41W **189** C3
Lagdo, L. de *Cameroon* 8°40N 14°0E **135** G8
Lage *Germany* 51°59N 8°48E **76** D4
Lågen → *Oppland, Norway* 61°8N 10°25E **60** F14
Lågen → *Vestfold, Norway* 59°3N 10°3E **61** G14
Lägerdorf *Germany* 53°53N 9°34E **76** B5
Lages *Brazil* 27°48S 50°20W **191** B5
Laghouat *Algeria* 33°50N 2°59E **136** B4
Laghouat □ *Algeria* 33°35N 2°40E **136** B4
Lagnieu *France* 45°55N 5°20E **73** C9
Lagny-sur-Marne *France* 48°52N 2°44E **71** D9
Lago *Italy* 39°10N 16°9E **95** C9
Lago de Sanabria y Entorno ⌓ *Spain* 42°9N 6°45W **88** C4
Lago Posadas *Argentina* 47°30S 71°40W **192** C2
Lago Puelo △ *Argentina* 42°30S 71°55W **192** B2
Lago Ranco *Chile* 40°19S 72°30W **192** B2
Lagoa *Portugal* 37°8N 8°27W **89** H2
Lagoa do Peixe △ *Brazil* 31°12S 50°55W **191** C5
Lagoa Vermelha *Brazil* 28°13S 51°32W **191** B5
Lagoaça *Portugal* 41°11N 6°44W **88** D4
Lagodekhi *Georgia* 41°50N 46°22E **87** K8
Lagónegro *Italy* 40°8N 15°45E **95** B8
Lagonoy G. *Phil.* 13°35N 123°50E **119** B6
Lagos *Greece* 41°1N 25°6E **97** E9
Lagos *Nigeria* 6°25N 3°27E **139** D5
Lagos *Portugal* 37°5N 8°41W **89** H2
Lagos □ *Nigeria* 6°28N 3°25E **139** D5
Lagos de Moreno *Mexico* 21°21N 101°55W **180** C4
Lagrange = Bidyadanga *Australia* 18°45S 121°43E **148** C3
Lagrange B. *Australia* 18°38S 121°42E **148** C3
Laguardia *Spain* 42°33N 2°35W **90** C2
Laguépie *France* 44°8N 1°57E **72** D5
Laguna *Brazil* 28°30S 48°50W **191** B6
Laguna *U.S.A.* 35°2N 107°25W **169** J10
Laguna, Sa. de la *Mexico* 23°35N 109°55W **180** C3
Laguna Beach *U.S.A.* 33°33N 117°47W **171** M9
Laguna Blanca △ *Argentina* 39°0S 70°5W **192** A2
Laguna de Duero *Spain* 41°35N 4°43W **88** D6
Laguna de la Restinga △ *Venezuela* 10°58N 64°0W **183** D6
Laguna de Lachuá △ *Guatemala* 15°55N 90°40W **182** C1
Laguna del Laja △ *Chile* 37°27S 71°20W **190** D1
Laguna del Tigre △ *Guatemala* 17°32N 90°56W **182** C1
Laguna Limpia *Argentina* 26°32S 59°45W **190** B4
Laguna San Rafael △ *Chile* 46°54S 73°31W **192** C2
Lagunas *Chile* 21°0S 69°45W **190** A2
Lagunas *Peru* 5°10S 75°35W **188** B2
Lagunas de Chacahua △ *Mexico* 16°0N 97°43W **181** D5
Lagunas de Montebello △ *Mexico* 16°4N 91°42W **181** D6
Lagunas de Ruidera ⌓ *Spain* 38°57N 2°52W **91** G2
Lagunes □ *Ivory C.* 5°47N 4°12W **138** D4
Lahad Datu *Malaysia* 5°0N 118°20E **119** D5
Lahad Datu, Telok *Malaysia* 4°50N 118°20E **119** D5
Lahan Sai *Thailand* 14°25N 102°52E **120** E4
Lahanam *Laos* 16°16N 105°16E **120** D5
Lahar *India* 26°12N 78°57E **125** F8
Laharpur *India* 27°43N 80°56E **125** F9
Lahat *Indonesia* 3°45S 103°30E **118** E2
Lahewa *Indonesia* 1°22N 97°12E **118** D1
Lāhījān *Iran* 37°10N 50°6E **129** B6
Lahn → *Germany* 50°19N 7°37E **77** E3
Lahnstein *Germany* 50°19N 7°37E **77** E3
Laholm *Sweden* 56°30N 13°2E **63** H7
Laholmsbukten *Sweden* 56°30N 12°45E **63** H6
Lahore *Pakistan* 31°32N 74°22E **124** D6
Lahr *Germany* 48°20N 7°53E **77** G3
Lahri *Pakistan* 29°11N 68°13E **124** E3
Lāhrūd *Iran* 38°30N 47°52E **105** C12
Lahti *Finland* 60°58N 25°40E **84** B3
Lahtis = Lahti *Finland* 60°58N 25°40E **84** B3
Lahugala Kitulana △ *Sri Lanka* 6°50N 81°40E **127** L5
Laï *Chad* 9°25N 16°18E **135** G9
Lai Chau *Vietnam* 22°5N 103°3E **116** F4
Lai'an *China* 32°28N 118°30E **117**
Laibin *China* 23°42N 109°14E **116**
Laifeng *China* 29°27N 109°20E **116**
L'Aigle *France* 48°46N 0°38E **70**
Laignes *France* 47°50N 4°20E **71**
L'Aiguillon-sur-Mer *France* 46°20N 1°18W **72**
Laikipia □ *Kenya* 0°10N 36°40E **142**
Laila = Layla *Si. Arabia* 22°10N 46°40E **131**
Laingsburg *S. Africa* 33°9S 20°52E **144**
Lainioälven → *Sweden* 67°35N 22°40E **60**
Lairg *U.K.* 58°2N 4°24W **65**
Laisamis *Kenya* 1°36N 37°48E **142**
Laissac *France* 44°23N 2°50E **72**
Láives *Italy* 46°26N 11°20E **93**
Laiwu *China* 36°15N 117°40E **115**
Laixi *China* 36°50N 120°31E **115**
Laiyang *China* 36°59N 120°45E **115**
Laiyuan *China* 39°20N 114°40E **114**
Laizhou *China* 37°8N 119°57E **115**
Laizhou Wan *China* 37°30N 119°30E **115**
Lajamanu *Australia* 18°23S 130°38E **148**
Lajere *Nigeria* 12°10N 11°25E **139**
Lajes *Brazil* 5°41S 36°14W **189**
Lajinha *Brazil* 20°9S 41°37W **189**
Lajkovac *Serbia* 44°27N 20°14E **96**
Lajosmizse *Hungary* 47°3N 19°32E **80**
Lak Sao *Laos* 18°11N 104°59E **120**
Lakaband *Pakistan* 31°2N 69°15E **124**
Lakamané *Mali* 14°35N 9°44W **138**
Lake *U.S.A.* 44°33N 110°24W **168**
Lake Alfred *U.S.A.* 28°6N 81°44W **179**
Lake Alpine *U.S.A.* 38°29N 120°0W **170**
Lake Andes *U.S.A.* 43°9N 98°32W **172**
Lake Arthur *U.S.A.* 30°5N 92°41W **176**
Lake Bindegolly △ *Australia* 28°0S 144°12E **151**
Lake Boga *Australia* 35°26S 143°38E **152**
Lake Butler *U.S.A.* 30°1N 82°21W **178**
Lake Cargelligo *Australia* 33°15S 146°22E **153**
Lake Charles *U.S.A.* 30°14N 93°13W **176**
Lake City *Colo., U.S.A.* 38°2N 107°19W **168**
Lake City *Fla., U.S.A.* 30°11N 82°38W **178**
Lake City *Mich., U.S.A.* 44°20N 85°13W **173**
Lake City *Minn., U.S.A.* 44°27N 92°16W **172**
Lake City *Pa., U.S.A.* 42°1N 80°21W **174**
Lake City *S.C., U.S.A.* 33°52N 79°45W **178**
Lake Coleridge *N.Z.* 43°17S 171°30E **155**
Lake Cowichan *Canada* 48°49N 124°3W **162**
Lake District △ *U.K.* 54°30N 3°21W **66**
Lake Eildon △ *Australia* 37°10S 145°56E **153**
Lake Elsinore *U.S.A.* 33°38N 117°20W **171**
Lake Eyre △ *Australia* 28°40S 137°31E **151**
Lake Gairdner △ *Australia* 31°41S 135°51E **151**
Lake George *U.S.A.* 43°26N 73°43W **175**
Lake Grace *Australia* 33°7S 118°28E **149**
Lake Gregory ☼ *Australia* 20°12S 127°27E **148**
Lake Harbor *U.S.A.* 26°42N 80°48W **179**
Lake Harbour = Kimmirut *Canada* 62°50N 69°50W **161**
Lake Havasu City *U.S.A.* 34°27N 114°22W **171**
Lake Helen *U.S.A.* 28°59N 81°14W **179**
Lake Hughes *U.S.A.* 34°41N 118°26W **171**
Lake Isabella *U.S.A.* 35°38N 118°28W **171**
Lake Jackson *U.S.A.* 29°3N 95°27W **176**
Lake King *Australia* 33°5S 119°45E **149**
Lake Lenore *Canada* 52°24N 104°59W **163**
Lake Louise *Canada* 51°30N 116°10W **162**
Lake Mackay ☼ *Australia* 21°48S 129°46E **148**
Lake Mburo △ *Uganda* 0°33S 30°56E **142**
Lake Mead ⌓ *U.S.A.* 36°30N 114°22W **171**
Lake Meredith ⌓ *U.S.A.* 35°50N 101°50W **176**
Lake Mills *U.S.A.* 43°25N 93°32W **172**
Lake Nakura △ *Kenya* 0°21S 36°8E **142**
Lake Park *Fla., U.S.A.* 26°48N 80°3W **179**
Lake Park *Ga., U.S.A.* 30°41N 83°11W **178**
Lake Placid *Fla., U.S.A.* 27°18N 81°22W **179**
Lake Placid *N.Y., U.S.A.* 44°17N 73°59W **175**
Lake Pleasant *U.S.A.* 43°28N 74°25W **175**
Lake Providence *U.S.A.* 32°48N 91°10W **176**
Lake Pukaki *N.Z.* 44°11S 170°8E **155**
Lake Roosevelt ⌓ *U.S.A.* 48°5N 118°14W **168**
Lake St. Peter *Canada* 45°18N 78°2W **174**
Lake Stevens *U.S.A.* 48°1N 122°4W **170**
Lake Superior ⌓ *Canada* 47°45N 84°45W **164**
Lake Tekapo *N.Z.* 44°0S 170°30E **155**
Lake Torrens △ *Australia* 30°55S 137°40E **151**
Lake Village *U.S.A.* 33°20N 91°17W **176**
Lake Wales *U.S.A.* 27°54N 81°35W **179**
Lake Worth *U.S.A.* 26°37N 80°3W **179**
Lakeba *Fiji* 18°13S 178°47W **15**
Lakeba Passage *Fiji* 18°0S 178°45W **15**
Lakefield = Rinyirru △ *Australia* 15°24S 144°26E **150**
Lakefield *Canada* 44°25N 78°16W **174**
Lakehurst *U.S.A.* 40°1N 74°19W **175**
Lakeland *Australia* 15°49S 144°57E **150**
Lakeland *Fla., U.S.A.* 28°3N 81°57W **179**
Lakeland *Ga., U.S.A.* 31°2N 83°4W **178**
Lakemba = Lakeba *Fiji* 18°13S 178°47W **15**
Lakeport *Calif., U.S.A.* 39°3N 122°55W **170**
Lakeport *Mich., U.S.A.* 43°7N 82°30W **174**
Lakes Entrance *Australia* 37°50S 148°0E **153**
Lakeside *Calif., U.S.A.* 32°52N 116°55W **171**
Lakeside *Nebr., U.S.A.* 42°3N 102°26W **172**
Lakeview *U.S.A.* 42°11N 120°21W **168**
Lakeville *U.S.A.* 44°39N 93°14W **172**
Lakewood *Colo., U.S.A.* 39°42N 105°4W **168**
Lakewood *N.J., U.S.A.* 40°6N 74°13W **175**
Lakewood *N.Y., U.S.A.* 42°6N 79°19W **174**
Lakewood *Ohio, U.S.A.* 41°28N 81°47W **174**
Lakewood *Wash., U.S.A.* 47°11N 122°32W **170**

- cewood Park U.S.A. 27°53N 80°24W 179 H9
- cha India 26°9N 70°54E 124 F4
- chimpur India 27°57N 80°46E 125 F9
- chisarai India 25°11N 86°5E 125 G12
- chnadon India 22°36N 79°36E 125 H8
- cin U.S.A. 38°57N 101°15W 172 G3
- chonpheng Laos 15°54N 105°34E 120 E5
- india 26°50N 81°0E 125 F9
- ci Azerbaijan 40°34N 47°22E 87 K8
- itusaki → Canada 54°21N 82°25W 164 B3
- cki Greece 35°24N 23°57E 101 D5
- cki Pakistan 32°51N 70°55E 124 C4
- conia Greece 36°55N 22°30E 98 E4
- onikos Kolpos
  - reece 36°40N 22°40E 98 E4
- cor Indonesia 8°15S 128°17E 119 F7
- cota Ivory C. 5°50N 5°30W 138 D3
- cota U.S.A. 48°2N 98°21W 174 A4
- csar India 29°46N 78°3E 124 E8
- csefjorden Norway 70°45N 26°50E 60 A22
- cselv Norway 70°26N 25°0E 60 A21
- csettipet India 18°52N 79°13E 126 E4
- cshadweep ☐ India 10°0N 72°30E 127 J1
- cshadweep Is. India 10°0N 72°30E 127 J1
- cshmanpur India 22°58N 83°3E 125 H10
- cshmeshwar India 15°9N 75°28E 127 G2
- cshmikantapur
  - india 22°5N 88°20E 125 H13
- caghat India 24°30N 92°40E 123 G18
- cago Tanzania 3°28S 33°58E 142 C3
- capanzi Zimbabwe 19°20S 30°15E 143 F3
- capaşa Turkey 41°49N 26°44E 97 E10
- cbenque France 44°19N 1°34E 72 D5
- cbert Australia 35°38S 143°20E 152 C5
- clbufera Spain 39°20N 0°27W 91 F4
- clcora Spain 40°5N 0°14W 90 E4
- clfas del Pi Spain 38°35N 0°5W 91 G4
- cganj India 25°52N 85°13E 125 G11
- cgola India 24°25N 88°15E 125 G13
- cbela Ethiopia 12°3N 39°0E 131 E2
- n Iran 32°21N 49°6E 126 C6
- n China 45°12N 127°0E 115 B14
- n Spain 42°40N 8°5W 88 C2
- cn He → China 45°32N 125°40E 115 B13
- cnde France 44°50N 0°44E 72 D4
- cndi Kotal Pakistan 34°7N 71°6E 124 B4
- ctpur India 24°42N 78°28E 125 G8
- ctpur Nepal 27°40N 85°20E 125 F11
- cxua India 29°5N 79°31E 125 E8
- csot India 26°34N 76°20E 124 F7
- c Nam Nan △
  - Thailand 17°55N 100°28E 120 D3
- cn Pao Res. Thailand 16°50N 103°15E 120 D4
- cna Kara Togo 9°30N 1°15E 139 D5
- cae Thailand 9°51N 99°5E 121 H2
- cnaing Burma 15°25N 97°53E 120 E1
- cnar Colo., U.S.A. 38°5N 102°37W 168 G12
- car Mo., U.S.A. 37°30N 94°16W 172 G6
- carque Argentina 39°24S 65°40W 192 A3
- cas Peru 6°28S 76°31W 188 B2
- castre France 44°59N 4°35E 73 D8
- cayuru India 34°25N 76°56E 125 B6
- cbach Austria 48°6N 13°51E 78 C6
- caballe Austria 48°29N 2°31W 70 D4
- cabaréné Gabon 0°41S 10°12E 140 E2
- cbasa = Labasa Fiji 16°30S 179°27E 154 a
- cbay I. Ireland 53°29N 6°1W 64 C5
- cbayeque ☐ Peru 6°45S 80°0W 188 B2
- cbert's Bay S. Africa 28°38S 18°17E 144 D2
- cbesc France 43°39N 5°16E 73 E9
- cbeth Canada 42°54N 81°18W 174 D3
- cbia Greece 37°52N 21°53E 98 D3
- cbro → Italy 45°8N 9°32E 92 C6
- cbe Nigeria 10°30N 9°20E 139 C6
- ce Deer U.S.A. 45°37N 106°40W 168 D10
- cnego Portugal 41°5N 7°52W 88 D3
- cnèque Canada 47°45N 64°38W 165 C7
- cneroo Australia 35°19S 140°33E 152 C4
- cnesa U.S.A. 32°44N 101°58W 176 E4
- cmetlla de Mar Spain 40°53N 0°48E 90 E5
- cnezia Terme Italy 38°55N 16°16E 95 D9
- cnia France 38°55N 22°26E 98 C4
- cnington △
  - Australia 28°13S 153°12E 151 D5
- cma I. China 22°12N 114°7E 111 a
- cnmermühle Hills U.K. 55°50N 2°40W 65 F6
- cmhult Sweden 57°10N 14°33E 63 G8
- cnoille → U.S.A. 44°38N 73°13W 175 B11
- cnon B. Phil. 14°30N 122°20E 119 B6
- cnont Canada 53°46N 112°50W 162 C6
- cnont Calif., U.S.A. 35°15N 118°55W 171 K8
- cnont Fla., U.S.A. 30°23N 83°49W 178 F6
- cnont Wyo., U.S.A. 42°13N 107°29W 168 E10
- cnotte-Beuvron France 47°36N 2°2E 70 E5
- cpa Peru 15°22S 70°22W 188 D3
- cpang Thailand 18°16N 99°32E 120 C2
- cpasas U.S.A. 31°4N 98°11W 176 F5
- cpazos de Naranjo
  - Mexico 27°1N 100°31W 180 B4
- cpertheim Germany 49°35N 8°27E 77 F9
- cpeter U.K. 52°7N 4°4W 67 E3
- cphun Thailand 18°40N 99°2E 120 C2
- cnu Kenya 2°16S 40°55E 142 C5
- cnud Peru 6°10S 77°57W 188 B2
- cny U.S.A. 35°29N 105°53W 169 J11
- cn Xian China 38°15N 111°35E 114 E6
- cni Yü Taiwan 22°4N 121°25E 117 F13
- cna'i U.S.A. 20°50N 156°55W 167 L8
- cak La China 32°42N 79°32E 125 B8
- cak'o Shank'ou = Lanak La
- cnark Canada 45°1N 76°22W 175 A8
- cnbi Kyun Burma 10°50N 98°20E 121 G2
- ccang China 23°26N 99°58E 116 F2
- cang Jiang →
  - China 21°40N 101°10E 116 G3
- ccashire ☐ U.K. 53°50N 2°48W 66 D5
- ccaster Canada 54°1N 74°30W 175 A10
- ccaster Calif., U.S.A. 34°42N 118°8W 171 L8
- ccaster N.H.,
  - U.S.A. 44°29N 71°34W 175 B13
- ccaster Ohio, U.S.A. 39°43N 82°36W 173 F12

- Lancaster Pa., U.S.A. 40°2N 76°19W 175 F8
- Lancaster S.C., U.S.A. 34°43N 80°46W 177 D14
- Lancaster Wis., U.S.A. 42°51N 90°43W 172 D8
- Lancelin Australia 31°0S 115°18E 149 F2
- Lanchow = Lanzhou
  - China 36°1N 103°52E 114 F7
- Lanchyn Ukraine 48°33N 24°45E 81 B9
- Lanciano Italy 42°14N 14°23E 93 F11
- Lanco Chile 39°24S 72°46W 192 A2
- Lancones Peru 4°30S 80°30W 188 A1
- Lancun China 36°25N 120°10E 115 F11
- Lańcut Poland 50°10N 22°13E 83 H9
- Land Between the Lakes
  - U.S.A. 36°25N 88°0W 177 C11
- Landau Bayern, Germany 48°40N 12°41E 77 G8
- Landau Rhld-Pfz., Germany 49°12N 8°6E 77 F4
- Landeck Austria 47°9N 10°34E 78 E4
- Lander → Australia 22°0S 132°0E 148 D5
- Lander U.S.A. 42°50N 108°44W 168 E9
- Landerneau France 48°28N 4°17W 70 D2
- Landeryd Sweden 57°7N 13°15E 63 G7
- Landes ☐ France 44°0N 1°0W 72 D2
- Landes de Gascogne △
  - France 44°23N 0°50W 72 D3
- Landete Spain 39°56N 1°25W 91 C4
- Landfall I. India 13°40N 93°2E 127 H11
- Landi Kotal Pakistan 34°7N 71°6E 124 B4
- Landivisiau France 48°31N 4°6W 70 D2
- Landmannalaugar
  - Iceland 63°59N 19°4W 60 E4
- Landquart Switz. 46°58N 9°32E 78 E5
- Landrecies France 50°7N 3°40E 71 B10
- Land's End U.K. 50°4N 5°44W 67 G2
- Landsberg Germany 48°2N 10°53E 77 G6
- Landsborough Cr. →
  - Australia 22°28S 144°35E 150 C3
- Landsbro Sweden 57°24N 14°56E 63 G8
- Landshut Germany 48°34N 12°8E 77 G8
- Landskrona Sweden 55°53N 12°50E 63 J6
- Landstuhl Germany 49°24N 7°33E 77 F3
- Landvetter Sweden 57°41N 12°17E 63 G6
- Lane U.S.A. 33°32N 79°53W 178 B10
- Lanesboro U.S.A. 41°57N 75°34W 175 E9
- Lanester France 47°46N 3°22W 70 E3
- Lanett U.S.A. 32°52N 85°12W 178 C4
- Lang Shan China 41°0N 106°30E 114 D4
- Lang Son Vietnam 21°52N 106°42E 116 G6
- Lang Suan Thailand 9°57N 99°4E 121 H2
- Långå Denmark 56°23N 9°54E 63 H3
- La'nga Co China 30°45N 81°15E 125 D9
- Langadás Greece 40°46N 23°36E 96 F7
- Langadia Greece 37°43N 22°1E 98 D4
- Långan → Sweden 63°19N 14°44E 62 A8
- Langar Iran 35°23N 60°25E 129 C9
- Langara I. Canada 54°14N 133°1W 162 C2
- Langärud Iran 37°11N 50°8E 129 B6
- Långås Sweden 56°58N 12°26E 63 H6
- Langdai China 26°6N 105°21E 116 D5
- Langdon U.S.A. 48°45N 98°22W 172 A4
- Länge Jan = Ölands södra udde
  - Sweden 56°12N 16°24E 63 H10
- Langeac France 45°7N 3°29E 72 C7
- Langeais France 47°20N 0°24E 70 E7
- Langeb Baraka →
  - Sudan 17°28N 36°50E 137 D4
- Langeberg S. Africa 33°55S 21°0E 144 D3
- Langeberge S. Africa 28°15S 22°33E 144 D3
- Langeland Denmark 54°56N 10°48E 63 K4
- Langelands Bælt
  - Denmark 54°50N 10°55E 63 K4
- Langen Hessen, Germany 49°59N 8°40E 77 F4
- Langen Niedersachsen,
  - Germany 53°36N 8°36E 76 B4
- Langenburg Canada 50°51N 101°43W 163 C8
- Langeneß Germany 54°38N 8°36E 76 A4
- Langenlois Austria 48°29N 15°40E 78 C8
- Langeoog Germany 53°45N 7°32E 76 B3
- Langesköv Denmark 55°22N 10°35E 63 J4
- Langfang China 39°30N 116°41E 114 E9
- Länghem Sweden 57°36N 13°14E 63 G7
- Langhirano Italy 44°37N 10°16E 92 D7
- Langholm U.K. 55°9N 3°0W 65 F5
- Langjökull Iceland 64°39N 20°12W 60 D3
- Langkawi, Pulau
  - Malaysia 6°25N 99°45E 121 J2
- Langklip S. Africa 28°12S 20°20E 144 D3
- Langkon Malaysia 6°30N 116°40E 118 C5
- Langley Canada 49°7N 122°39W 170 A4
- Langnau Switz. 46°56N 7°47E 78 E4
- Langogne France 44°43N 3°50E 72 D7
- Langon France 44°33N 0°16W 72 D3
- Langøya Norway 68°45N 14°50E 60 B16
- Langreo Spain 43°18N 5°40W 88 B5
- Langres France 47°52N 5°20E 71 E12
- Langres, Plateau de
  - France 47°45N 5°3E 71 E12
- Langsa Indonesia 4°30N 97°57E 118 D1
- Långsele Sweden 63°12N 17°4E 62 A11
- Långshyttan Sweden 60°27N 16°2E 62 F10
- Langtang △ Nepal 28°10N 85°30E 125 E11
- Langtou China 40°1N 124°19E 115 D13
- Langtry U.S.A. 29°49N 101°34W 176 G4
- Langu Thailand 6°53N 99°47E 121 J2
- Langue de Barbarie △
  - Senegal 14°54N 16°30W 138 C1
- Languedoc France 43°25N 3°0E 72 E6
- Languedoc-Roussillon ☐
  - France 43°58N 3°55E 72 E7
- Langwang China 22°38N 113°27E 111 a
- Langxi China 31°10N 119°12E 117 B12
- Langzhong China 31°38N 105°58E 116 B5
- Lanigan Canada 51°51N 105°2W 163 C7
- Lanín △ Argentina 40°0S 71°55W 192 A2
- Lanjigarh India 19°43N 83°23E 126 E6
- Lankao China 34°48N 114°50E 114 G8
- Länkäran Azerbaijan 38°48N 48°52E 105 C13
- Lannemezan France 43°8N 0°23E 72 E4
- Lannilis France 48°35N 4°33W 70 D2
- Lannion France 48°46N 3°29W 70 D3
- L'Annonciation
  - Canada 46°25N 74°55W 164 C5
- Lanouaille France 45°24N 1°9E 72 C5
- Lanping China 26°28N 99°12E 116 D2
- Lansang △ Thailand 16°45N 99°0E 120 D2
- Lansdowne Australia 31°48S 152°30E 153 A10
- Lansdowne Canada 44°24N 76°1W 175 B8
- Lansdowne India 29°50N 78°41E 125 E8

- Lansdowne House = Neskantaga
  - Canada 52°14N 87°53W 164 B2
- L'Anse U.S.A. 46°45N 88°27W 172 B9
- L'Anse au Loup
  - Canada 51°32N 56°50W 165 B10
- L'Anse aux Meadows
  - Canada 51°36N 55°32W 165 B8
- Lansford U.S.A. 40°50N 75°53W 175 F9
- Lanshan China 25°24N 112°10E 117 E9
- Lanshantou China 35°5N 119°20E 115 G10
- Länsi-Turunmaa
  - Finland 60°18N 22°18E 84 B2
- Lansing U.S.A. 42°44N 84°33W 173 D11
- Lanslebourg-Mont-Cenis
  - France 45°17N 6°52E 73 C10
- Lanta, Ko Thailand 7°35N 99°3E 121 J2
- Lantana U.S.A. 26°35N 80°3W 179 J9
- Lantau I. China 22°15N 113°56E 111 a
- Lantewa Nigeria 12°16N 11°44E 139 C7
- Lantian China 34°11N 109°20E 114 G5
- Lanus Argentina 34°42S 58°23W 190 C4
- Lanusei Italy 39°52N 9°34E 94 C2
- Lanxi China 29°13N 119°28E 117 C12
- Lanzarote Canary Is. 29°0N 13°40W 100 F6
- Lanzarote ✈ (ACE)
  - Canary Is. 28°57N 13°40W 100 E6
- Lanzhou China 36°1N 103°52E 114 F7
- Lanzo Torinese Italy 45°16N 7°28E 92 C4
- Lao → Italy 39°47N 15°48E 95 C8
- Lao Cai Vietnam 22°30N 103°57E 116 F4
- Laoag Phil. 18°7N 120°34E 119 A6
- Laoang Phil. 12°32N 125°8E 119 B7
- Laoha He → China 43°25N 120°35E 115 C11
- Laohekou China 32°22N 111°38E 117 A8
- Laois ☐ Ireland 52°57N 7°27W 64 D4
- Laon France 49°33N 3°35E 71 C10
- Laona U.S.A. 45°34N 88°40W 172 C9
- Laos ■ Asia 17°45N 105°0E 120 D5
- Lapa Brazil 25°46S 49°44W 191 B6
- Lapai Nigeria 9°5N 6°32E 139 D6
- Lapalisse France 46°15N 3°38E 71 F10
- Lapeer U.S.A. 43°3N 83°19W 173 D12
- Lapeyrade France 44°4N 0°30E 72 D3
- Lapithos Cyprus 35°21N 33°11E 101 D12
- Lapland = Lappland
  - Europe 68°7N 24°0E 60 B21
- LaPorte Ind., U.S.A. 41°36N 86°43W 172 E10
- Laporte Pa., U.S.A. 41°25N 76°30W 175 E8
- Lapovo Serbia 44°10N 21°2E 96 B5
- Lappeenranta Finland 61°3N 28°12E 84 B5
- Lappland Europe 68°7N 24°0E 60 B21
- Lappo = Lapua Finland 62°58N 23°0E 60 E20
- Laprida Argentina 37°34S 60°45W 190 D3
- Lâpseki Turkey 40°20N 26°41E 97 F10
- Lapta = Lapithos
  - Cyprus 35°21N 33°11E 101 D12
- Laptev Sea Russia 76°0N 125°0E 107 B13
- Lapua Finland 62°58N 23°0E 60 E20
- L'Áquila Italy 42°22N 13°22E 93 F10
- Lār Iran 27°40N 54°14E 129 E7
- Lara Australia 38°2S 144°26E 152 E6
- Larabanga Ghana 9°16N 1°56W 138 D4
- Larache Morocco 35°10N 6°5W 136 A2
- Laragne-Montéglin
  - France 44°18N 5°49E 73 D9
- Lārak Iran 26°51N 56°21E 129 E8
- Laramie U.S.A. 41°19N 105°35W 168 F11
- Laramie Mts., U.S.A. 42°0N 105°30W 168 F11
- Laranda = Karaman
  - Turkey 37°14N 33°13E 104 D5
- Laranjeiras do Sul
  - Brazil 25°23S 52°23W 191 B5
- Larantuka Indonesia 8°21S 122°55E 119 F6
- Larat Indonesia 7°0S 132°0E 119 F8
- L'Arbresle France 45°50N 4°36E 73 C8
- Lärbro Sweden 57°47N 18°50E 63 G12
- Larde Mozam. 16°28S 39°43E 143 F4
- Larder Lake Canada 48°5N 79°40W 164 C4
- Lardos Greece 36°6N 28°3E 97 C10
- Lardos, Akra = Líndos, Akra
  - Greece 36°4N 28°10E 101 C10
- Lardos, Ormos Greece 36°4N 28°2E 101 C10
- Laredo Spain 43°26N 3°28W 88 B7
- Laredo U.S.A. 27°30N 99°30W 176 H5
- Laredo Sd. Canada 52°30N 128°53W 162 C3
- Largo U.S.A. 27°54N 82°47W 179 H7
- Largo, Key U.S.A. 25°15N 80°15W 179 J9
- Largs U.K. 55°47N 4°52W 65 F4
- Lari Italy 43°34N 10°35E 92 E7
- Lariang Indonesia 1°26S 119°17E 119 E5
- Larimore U.S.A. 47°54N 97°38W 172 B5
- Larino Italy 41°48N 14°54E 93 G11
- Lario, Il = Como, L. di
  - Italy 46°0N 9°17E 92 B6
- Larisa Greece 39°36N 22°27E 98 B4
- Larkana Pakistan 27°32N 68°18E 124 F3
- Larnaca Cyprus 34°55N 33°38E 101 E12
- Larnaca Bay Cyprus 34°53N 33°45E 101 E12
- Larne U.K. 54°51N 5°51W 64 B6
- Larned U.S.A. 38°11N 99°6W 172 F4
- Laroquebrou France 44°58N 2°12E 72 D6
- Larose U.S.A. 29°34N 90°23W 177 G9
- Larrimah Australia 15°35S 133°12E 148 C5
- Larsen Ice Shelf
  - Antarctica 67°0S 62°0W 55 C17
- Larvik Norway 59°4N 10°2E 63 E14
- Larzac, Causse du France 43°58N 3°20E 72 E7
- Las Alpujarras Spain 36°55N 3°20W 91 E7
- Las Animas U.S.A. 38°4N 103°13W 169 G12
- Las Anod Somalia 8°26N 47°19E 131 F4
- Las Arenas Spain 43°17N 4°50W 88 B6
- Las Batuecas △ Spain 40°30N 6°5W 88 E4
- Las Brenãs Argentina 27°5S 61°7W 190 B3
- Las Cañadas de San Juan
  - Spain 36°57N 5°58W 89 J5
- Las Cañadas del Teide
  - Canary Is. 28°15N 16°37W 100 F3
- Las Cejas Argentina 26°53S 64°44W 190 B3
- Las Chimeneas Mexico 31°8N 116°5W 171 N10
- Las Coloradas
  - Argentina 39°34S 70°36W 192 A2

- Las Cruces U.S.A. 32°19N 106°47W 169 K10
- Las Flores Argentina 36°10S 59°7W 190 D4
- Las Gabias = Gabia la Grande
  - Spain 37°8N 3°40W 89 H7
- Las Heras Mendoza,
  - Argentina 32°51S 68°49W 190 C2
- Las Heras Santa Cruz,
  - Argentina 46°33S 68°57W 192 C3
- Las Horquetas
  - Argentina 48°14S 71°11W 192 C2
- Las Lajas Argentina 38°30S 70°25W 192 A2
- Las Lomas Peru 4°40S 80°10W 188 A1
- Las Lomitas Argentina 24°43S 60°35W 190 A3
- Las Manos, Cueva de
  - Argentina 47°9S 70°40W 192 C2
- Las Marismas Spain 37°5N 6°20W 89 H4
- Las Médulas Spain 42°28N 6°46W 88 C4
- Las Minas Spain 38°20N 1°41W 91 G3
- Las Navas de la Concepción
  - Spain 37°56N 5°30W 89 H5
- Las Navas del Marqués
  - Spain 40°36N 4°20W 88 E6
- Las Palmas Argentina 27°8S 58°45W 190 B4
- Las Palmas →
  - Mexico 32°31N 116°58W 171 N10
- Las Palmas Canary Is. 28°7N 15°25W 100 G4
- Las Palmas ✈ (LPA)
  - Canary Is. 27°55N 15°25W 100 G4
- Las Palmas de Gran Canaria
  - Canary Is. 28°7N 15°26W 100 F4
- Las Pedroñeras Spain 39°26N 2°40W 91 F2
- Las Piedras Uruguay 34°44S 56°14W 191 C4
- Las Pipinas Argentina 35°30S 57°19W 190 D4
- Las Plumas Argentina 43°40S 67°15W 192 B3
- Las Rosas Argentina 32°30S 61°35W 190 C3
- Las Rozas Spain 40°29N 3°52W 88 E7
- Las Tablas Panama 7°49N 80°14W 182 E3
- Las Toscas Argentina 28°21S 59°18W 190 B4
- Las Tunas Cuba 20°58N 76°59W 182 B4
- Las Varillas Argentina 31°50S 62°50W 190 C3
- Las Vegas N. Mex.,
  - U.S.A. 35°36N 105°13W 169 J11
- Las Vegas Nev., U.S.A. 36°10N 115°8W 171 J11
- Las Vegas McCarran Int. ✈ (LAS)
  - U.S.A. 36°5N 115°9W 171 J11
- Lasarte-Oria Spain 43°16N 2°1W 90 B2
- Lascano Uruguay 33°35S 54°12W 191 C5
- Lascelles Australia 35°34S 142°34E 152 C5
- Lash-e Joveyn Afghan. 31°45N 61°30E 128 D2
- Lashburn Canada 53°10N 109°40W 163 C7
- Lashio Burma 22°56N 97°45E 123 H20
- Lashkar India 26°10N 78°10E 124 F8
- Lasin Poland 53°30N 19°2E 82 E6
- Lasithi Greece 35°11N 25°31E 101 D7
- Lask Poland 51°34N 19°8E 83 G6
- Laskarzew Poland 51°48N 21°36E 83 G8
- Laško Slovenia 46°10N 15°16E 92 B12
- Lassance Brazil 17°54S 44°34W 189 D2
- Lassay-les-Châteaux
  - France 48°27N 0°30W 70 D6
- Lassen Pk. U.S.A. 40°29N 121°30W 168 F3
- Lassen Volcanic △
  - U.S.A. 40°30N 121°20W 168 F3
- Last Mountain L.
  - Canada 51°5N 105°14W 163 C7
- Lastchance Cr. →
  - U.S.A. 40°2N 121°15W 170 E5
- Lastoursville Gabon 0°55S 12°38E 140 E2
- Lastovo Croatia 42°46N 16°55E 93 F13
- Lastovski Kanal Croatia 42°50N 17°0E 93 F14
- Lat Yao Thailand 15°45N 99°48E 120 E2
- Latacunga Ecuador 0°50S 78°35W 186 D3
- Latady I. Antarctica 70°45S 74°35W 55 D17
- Latakia = Al Lādhiqīyah
  - Syria 35°30N 35°45E 104 E6
- Latchford Canada 47°20N 79°50W 164 C4
- Latehar India 23°45N 84°30E 125 H11
- Laterza Italy 40°37N 16°48E 95 B9
- Latham Australia 29°44S 116°20E 149 E2
- Lathen Germany 52°52N 7°19E 76 C3
- Lathi India 27°43N 71°23E 124 F4
- Lathrop Wells U.S.A. 36°39N 116°24W 171 J10
- Latiano Italy 40°33N 17°43E 95 B10
- Latina Italy 41°28N 12°52E 94 A5
- Latisana Italy 45°47N 13°0E 93 C10
- Latium = Lazio ☐ Italy 42°10N 12°30E 93 F9
- Laton U.S.A. 36°26N 119°41W 170 J7
- Latorytsya →
  - Slovak Rep. 48°28N 21°50E 81 B11
- Latouche Treville, C.
  - Australia 18°27S 121°49E 148 C3
- Latrobe Australia 41°14S 146°30E 151 G4
- Latrobe U.S.A. 40°19N 79°23W 174 F5
- Latrónico Italy 40°5N 16°1E 95 B9
- Latur India 18°25N 76°40E 126 E3
- Latvia ■ Europe 56°50N 24°0E 84 D2
- Lau Nigeria 9°11N 11°19E 139 D7
- Lau Group Fiji 17°0S 178°30W 154 a
- Lauca → Bolivia 19°9S 68°10W 188 D4
- Lauchhammer Germany 51°29N 13°47E 76 D9
- Lauda-Königshofen
  - Germany 49°33N 9°42E 77 F5
- Laudio = Llodio Spain 43°9N 2°58W 90 B2
- Lauenburg Germany 53°22N 10°33E 76 B6
- Lauenburgische Seen △
  - Germany 53°38N 10°45E 76 B6
- Laughlin U.S.A. 35°10N 114°34W 171 K12
- Lauhanvuori △ Finland 62°8N 22°4E 60 E20
- Laujar de Andarax Spain 37°0N 2°54W 91 H2
- Laukaa Finland 62°24N 25°56E 60 E21
- Launceston Australia 41°24S 147°8E 151 G4
- Launceston U.K. 50°38N 4°22W 67 G3
- Laune → Ireland 52°7N 9°47W 64 D2
- Launglon Bok Burma 13°50N 97°54E 121 F2
- Laupheim Germany 48°14N 9°52E 77 G5
- Laura Queens.,
  - Australia 15°32S 144°32E 150 B3
- Laura S. Austral.,
  - Australia 33°10S 138°18E 152 B3
- Laureana di Borrello
  - Italy 38°30N 16°5E 95 D9
- Laurel Fla., U.S.A. 27°8N 82°27W 179 H7
- Laurel Miss., U.S.A. 31°41N 89°8W 177 F10
- Laurel Mont., U.S.A. 45°40N 108°46W 168 D9
- Laurel Bay U.S.A. 32°26N 80°48W 178 E6
- Laurel Hill U.S.A. 40°14N 79°6W 174 F5
- Laurencekirk U.K. 56°50N 2°28W 65 E6
- Laurens U.S.A. 34°30N 82°1W 177 D13

- Laurentian Plateau
  - Canada 52°0N 70°0W 165 B6
- Lauria Italy 40°2N 15°50E 95 B8
- Laurie L. Canada 56°35N 101°57W 163 B8
- Laurinburg U.S.A. 34°47N 79°28W 177 D15
- Laurium U.S.A. 47°14N 88°27W 172 B9
- Lausanne Switz. 46°32N 6°38E 77 J2
- Laut Indonesia 4°45N 108°0E 118 D3
- Laut, Pulau Indonesia 3°40S 116°10E 118 E5
- Laut Kecil, Kepulauan
  - Indonesia 4°45S 115°40E 118 E5
- Lautaro Chile 38°31S 72°27W 192 A2
- Lauterbach Germany 50°37N 9°24E 76 E5
- Lauterecken Germany 49°38N 7°35E 77 F3
- Lautoka Fiji 17°37S 177°27E 154 a
- Lauwersmeer △ Neths. 53°22N 6°11E 69 A6
- Lauzès France 44°34N 1°35E 72 D5
- Lava → Russia 54°34N 21°14E 82 D8
- Lava Beds △ U.S.A. 41°40N 121°30W 168 F3
- Lavagh More Ireland 54°46N 8°6W 64 B3
- Lavagna Italy 44°18N 9°22E 92 D6
- Laval France 48°4N 0°48W 70 D6
- Laval-des-Rapides
  - Canada 45°33N 73°42W 164 C5
- Lavalle Argentina 28°15S 65°15W 190 B2
- Lāvān Iran 26°48N 53°22E 129 E7
- Lavant Canada 45°3N 76°42W 175 A8
- Lāvar Meydān Iran 30°20N 54°30E 129 D7
- Lavara Greece 41°19N 26°22E 97 E10
- Lavardac France 44°12N 0°20E 72 D4
- Lavaur France 43°40N 1°49E 72 E5
- Lavelanet France 42°57N 1°51E 72 F5
- Lavello Italy 41°3N 15°48E 95 A8
- Lavers Hill Australia 38°40S 143°25E 152 E5
- Laverton Australia 28°44S 122°29E 149 E3
- Lavezzi, Ís. France 41°22N 9°16E 73 G13
- Lavis Italy 46°8N 11°7E 92 B8
- Lavos Portugal 40°6N 8°49W 88 E2
- Lavradio Portugal 38°40N 9°2W 89 G1
- Lavras Brazil 21°20S 45°0W 191 A7
- Lavre Portugal 38°46N 8°22W 89 G2
- Lavrio Greece 37°40N 24°4E 98 D6
- Lavris Greece 35°25N 24°40E 101 D6
- Lavumisa Swaziland 27°20S 31°55E 145 D5
- Lavushi Manda △
  - Zambia 12°46S 31°0E 143 E3
- Lawak I. = Nanshan I.
  - S. China Sea 10°45N 115°49E 118 B5
- Lawas Malaysia 4°55N 115°25E 118 D5
- Lawele Indonesia 5°13S 122°57E 119 F6
- Lawn Hill = Boodjamulla △
  - Australia 18°15S 138°6E 150 B2
- Lawqah Si. Arabia 29°49N 42°45E 128 D4
- Lawra Ghana 10°39N 2°51W 138 C4
- Lawrence N.Z. 45°55S 169°41E 155 F4
- Lawrence Ind., U.S.A. 39°50N 86°2W 172 F10
- Lawrence Kans., U.S.A. 38°58N 95°14W 172 F6
- Lawrence Mass.,
  - U.S.A. 42°43N 71°10W 175 D13
- Lawrenceburg Ind.,
  - U.S.A. 39°6N 84°52W 173 F11
- Lawrenceburg Tenn.,
  - U.S.A. 35°14N 87°20W 177 D11
- Lawrenceville Ga.,
  - U.S.A. 33°57N 83°59W 178 B6
- Lawrenceville Pa.,
  - U.S.A. 41°59N 77°8W 174 E7
- Laws U.S.A. 37°24N 118°20W 170 H8
- Lawtey U.S.A. 30°3N 82°5W 178 F7
- Lawton U.S.A. 34°37N 98°25W 176 D5
- Lawu Indonesia 7°40S 111°13E 119 G14
- Lawz, J. al Si. Arabia 28°39N 35°18E 137 B4
- Laxá Sweden 58°59N 14°37E 63 F8
- Laxford, L. U.K. 58°24N 5°6W 65 C3
- Laxiwa Dam China 36°4N 101°1E 110 D9
- Laxou France 48°41N 6°8E 71 D13
- Lay → France 46°18N 1°17W 72 B3
- Layla Si. Arabia 22°10N 46°40E 131 C4
- Laylán Iraq 35°18N 44°31E 128 C5
- Layon → France 47°20N 0°45W 70 E6
- Laysan I. U.S.A. 25°30N 171°50W 167 K5
- Layton Fla., U.S.A. 24°50N 80°47W 179 L9
- Layton Utah, U.S.A. 41°4N 111°58W 168 E8
- Laytonville U.S.A. 39°41N 123°29W 168 G2
- Lazarev Russia 52°13N 141°30E 107 D15
- Lazarev Sea S. Ocean 62°0S 15°0E 55 D2
- Lazarevac Serbia 44°23N 20°17E 96 B4
- Lazarevskoye Russia 43°55N 39°21E 87 J4
- Lázaro Cárdenas
  - Mexico 17°55N 102°11W 180 D4
- Lazdijai Lithuania 54°14N 23°31E 82 D10
- Lazhuglung China 34°52N 81°24E 109 F13
- Lazio ☐ Italy 42°10N 12°30E 93 F9
- Lazo Moldova 47°30N 28°25E 81 C13
- Lazo Russia 43°25N 133°55E 112 C6
- Le Beausset France 43°12N 5°48E 73 E9
- Le Bic Canada 48°20N 68°41W 165 C6
- Le Blanc France 46°37N 1°3E 72 B4
- Le Bleymard France 44°30N 3°42E 72 D7
- Le Bourgneuf-la-Fôret
  - France 48°10N 0°59W 70 D6
- Le Bugue France 44°55N 0°56E 72 D4
- Le Cateau Cambrésis
  - France 50°10N 3°38E 71 B10
- Le Caylar France 43°51N 3°19E 72 E7
- Le Chambon-Feugerolles
  - France 45°24N 4°19E 73 C8
- Le Châtelet France 46°38N 2°16E 71 F9
- Le Chesne France 49°30N 4°45E 71 C11
- Le Cheylard France 44°55N 4°25E 73 D8
- Le Conquet France 48°21N 4°46W 70 D2
- Le Creusot France 46°48N 4°24E 71 F11
- Le Croisic France 47°18N 2°30W 70 E4
- Le Donjon France 46°22N 3°48E 71 F10
- Le Dorat France 46°14N 1°5E 72 B5
- Le François Martinique 14°38N 60°57W 182 c
- Le Gosier Guadeloupe 16°14N 61°29W 182 b
- Le Grand-Lucé France 47°52N 0°28E 70 E7
- Le Grand-Pressigny
  - France 46°55N 0°48E 70 F7
- Le Grand-Quevilly France 49°24N 1°2E 70 C8
- Le Gris Gris Mauritius 20°31S 57°32E 141 d
- Le Havre France 49°30N 0°5E 70 C7
- Le Lamentin Martinique 14°35N 61°2W 182 c
- Le Lavandou France 43°8N 6°22E 73 E10
- Le Lion-d'Angers France 47°37N 0°43W 70 E6
- Le Louroux-Béconnais
  - France 47°30N 0°55W 70 E6
- Le Luc France 43°23N 6°21E 73 E10
- Le Lude France 47°39N 0°9E 70 E7

- Le Maire, Estr. de
  - Argentina 54°50S 65°0W 192 D4
- Le Mans France 48°0N 0°10E 70 E7
- Le Marin Martinique 14°27N 60°55W 182 c
- Le Mars U.S.A. 42°47N 96°10W 172 D5
- Le Mayet-de-Montagne
  - France 46°4N 3°40E 71 F10
- Le Mêle-sur-Sarthe
  - France 48°31N 0°22E 70 D7
- Le Monastier-sur-Gazeille
  - France 44°57N 3°59E 72 D7
- Le Monêtier-les-Bains France 44°58N 6°30E 73 D10
- Le Mont-Dore France 45°35N 2°49E 72 C6
- Le Mont-St-Michel
  - France 48°40N 1°30W 70 D5
- Le Moule Guadeloupe 16°20N 61°22W 182 b
- Le Moyne, L. Canada 56°45N 68°47W 165 A6
- Le Muy France 43°28N 6°34E 73 E10
- Le Palais France 47°20N 3°10W 70 E4
- Le Perthus France 42°28N 2°53E 72 F6
- Le Port Réunion 20°56S 55°18E 141 c
- Le Prêcheur Martinique 14°50N 61°12W 182 c
- Le Puy-en-Velay France 45°3N 3°52E 72 C7
- Le Raysville U.S.A. 41°50N 76°10W 175 E8
- Le Robert Martinique 14°40N 60°56W 182 c
- Le Roy U.S.A. 42°58N 77°59W 174 D7
- Le St-Esprit Martinique 14°34N 60°56W 182 c
- Le Sueur U.S.A. 44°28N 93°55W 172 C7
- Le Tampon Réunion 21°16S 55°32E 141 c
- Le Teil France 44°33N 4°40E 73 D8
- Le Teilleul France 48°16N 0°53W 70 D6
- Le Theil France 48°16N 0°42E 70 D7
- Le Thillot France 47°53N 6°46E 71 E13
- Le Thuy Vietnam 17°14N 106°49E 120 D6
- Le Touquet-Paris-Plage
  - France 50°30N 1°36E 71 B8
- Le Tréport France 50°3N 1°20E 70 B8
- Le Val-André France 48°35N 2°32W 70 D4
- Le Val-d'Ajol France 47°55N 6°30E 71 E13
- Le Verdon-sur-Mer
  - France 45°33N 1°4W 72 C2
- Le Vigan France 43°59N 3°36E 72 E7
- Lea → U.K. 51°31N 0°1E 67 F8
- Leach Cambodia 12°21N 103°46E 121 F4
- Lead U.S.A. 44°21N 103°46W 172 C2
- Leader Canada 50°50N 109°30W 163 C7
- Leadville U.S.A. 39°15N 106°18W 168 G10
- Leaf → U.S.A. 30°59N 88°44W 177 F10
- Leaf Rapids Canada 56°30N 99°59W 163 B8
- Leaghur, L. Australia 33°35S 143°3E 152 B5
- League City U.S.A. 29°31N 95°6W 176 C7
- Leamington Canada 42°3N 82°36W 174 D2
- Leamington N.Z. 37°55S 175°30E 154 D4
- Leamington U.S.A. 39°32N 112°17W 168 G7
- Leamington Spa = Royal
  - Leamington Spa U.K. 52°18N 1°31W 67 E6
- Le'an China 27°22N 115°48E 117 D10
- Leandro Norte Alem
  - Argentina 27°34S 55°15W 191 B4
- Leane, L. Ireland 52°2N 9°32W 64 D2
- Learmonth Australia 22°13S 114°10E 148 D1
- Leary U.S.A. 31°29N 84°31W 178 D5
- Leask Canada 53°5N 106°45W 163 C7
- Leatherhead U.K. 51°18N 0°20W 67 F7
- Leavdnja = Lakselv
  - Norway 70°2N 25°0E 60 A21
- Leavenworth Kans.,
  - U.S.A. 39°19N 94°55W 172 F6
- Leavenworth Wash.,
  - U.S.A. 47°36N 120°40W 168 C3
- Leawood U.S.A. 38°58N 94°37W 172 F6
- Łeba Poland 54°45N 17°32E 82 A4
- Łeba → Poland 54°46N 17°33E 82 A4
- Lebach Germany 49°25N 6°54E 77 F2
- Lebak Phil. 6°32N 124°5E 119 C6
- Lebane Serbia 42°56N 21°44E 96 D5
- Lebanon Fla., U.S.A. 29°10N 82°37W 179 F7
- Lebanon Ind., U.S.A. 40°3N 86°28W 172 E10
- Lebanon Kans., U.S.A. 39°49N 98°33W 172 F4
- Lebanon Ky., U.S.A. 37°34N 85°15W 173 G11
- Lebanon Mo., U.S.A. 37°41N 92°40W 172 G7
- Lebanon N.H., U.S.A. 43°39N 72°15W 175 C12
- Lebanon Oreg., U.S.A. 44°32N 122°55W 168 D2
- Lebanon Pa., U.S.A. 40°20N 76°26W 175 F8
- Lebanon Tenn., U.S.A. 36°12N 86°18W 177 C11
- Lebanon ■ Asia 34°0N 36°0E 130 B5
- Lebap Turkmenistan 40°0N 63°0E 108 D6
- Lebec U.S.A. 34°51N 118°52W 171 L8
- Lebedyan Russia 53°0N 39°10E 85 F10
- Lebel-sur-Quévillon
  - Canada 49°3N 76°59W 164 C4
- Lebomboberge S. Africa 24°30S 32°0E 145 D5
- Łebork Poland 54°33N 17°46E 82 A4
- Lebowakgomo S. Africa 24°12S 29°30E 145 D4
- Lebrija Spain 36°53N 6°5W 89 J4
- Łebsko, Jezioro Poland 54°40N 17°25E 82 A4
- Lebu Chile 37°40S 73°47W 190 D1
- Leça da Palmeira
  - Portugal 41°12N 8°42W 88 D2
- Lecce Italy 40°23N 18°11E 95 B11
- Lecco Italy 45°51N 9°23E 92 C6
- Lecco, L. di Italy 45°51N 9°25E 92 C6
- Lécera Spain 41°13N 0°43W 90 D4
- Lech Austria 47°13N 10°9E 78 E3
- Lech → Germany 48°43N 10°56E 77 G6
- Lechang China 25°10N 113°20E 117 E9
- Lechena Greece 37°57N 21°16E 98 D3
- Lechtaler Alpen Austria 47°15N 10°30E 78 E3
- Lecontes Mills U.S.A. 41°5N 78°17W 174 E6
- Lectoure France 43°56N 0°38E 72 E4
- Łęczna Poland 51°18N 22°53E 83 G9
- Łęczyca Poland 52°5N 19°15E 83 F6
- Ledang, Gunung
  - Malaysia 2°22N 102°37E 121 L4
- Ledesma Spain 41°6N 5°59W 88 D5
- Lednice Czech Rep. 48°48N 16°48E 79 G9
- Ledong China 18°41N 109°5E 117 a
- Leduc Canada 53°15N 113°30W 162 C6
- Lee Fla., U.S.A. 30°25N 83°18W 178 F6
- Lee Mass., U.S.A. 42°19N 73°15W 175 D11
- Lee → Ireland 51°53N 8°56W 64 E3
- Lee Vining U.S.A. 37°58N 119°7W 170 H7
- Leech L. U.S.A. 47°10N 94°24W 172 B6
- Leechburg U.S.A. 40°37N 79°36W 174 F5
- Leeds U.K. 53°48N 1°33W 66 D6
- Leeds U.S.A. 33°33N 86°33W 177 D11
- Leek Neths. 53°10N 6°24E 69 A6
- Leek U.K. 53°7N 2°1W 66 D5

Leeman Australia 29°57S 114°58E **149** E1
Leeper U.S.A. 41°22N 79°18W **174** E5
Leer Germany 53°13N 7°26E **76** B3
Leesburg Fla., U.S.A. 28°49N 81°53W **179** G8
Leesburg Ga., U.S.A. 31°44N 84°10W **178** D5
Leeston N.Z. 43°45S 172°19E **155** D7
Leesville U.S.A. 31°8N 93°16W **176** F8
Leeton Australia 34°33S 146°23E **153** C7
Leetonia U.S.A. 40°53N 80°45W **174** F4
Leeu Gamka S. Africa 32°47S 21°59E **144** D3
Leeuwarden Neths. 53°15N 5°48E **69** A5
Leeuwin, C. Australia 34°20S 115°9E **149** F2
Leeuwin Naturaliste △
  Australia 34°6S 115°3E **149** F2
Leeward Is. Atl. Oc. 16°30N 63°30W **183** C7
Lefka Cyprus 35°6N 32°51E **101** D11
Lefkada Greece 38°40N 20°43E **98** C2
Lefkimi Greece 39°25N 20°3E **101** B4
Lefkimis, Akra Greece 39°29N 20°4E **101** B4
Lefkoniko Cyprus 35°18N 33°44E **101** D12
Lefkosia = Nicosia
  Cyprus 35°10N 33°25E **101** D12
Lefroy Canada 44°16N 79°34W **174** B5
Lefroy, L. Australia 31°21S 121°40E **149** F3
Leg → Poland 50°42N 21°50E **83** H8
Leganés Spain 40°19N 3°45W **88** E7
Legazpi Phil. 13°10N 123°45E **119** E6
Lège-Cap-Ferret France 44°48N 1°9W **72** D2
Legendre I. Australia 20°22S 116°55E **148** D2
Leghorn = Livorno Italy 43°33N 10°19E **92** E7
Legian Indonesia 8°42S 115°10E **119** K18
Legionowo Poland 52°25N 20°50E **83** F7
Legnago Italy 45°11N 11°18E **93** C8
Legnano Italy 45°36N 8°54E **92** C5
Legnica Poland 51°12N 16°10E **83** G3
Legrad Croatia 46°17N 16°51E **93** B13
Leh India 34°9N 77°35E **125** B7
Lehigh Acres U.S.A. 26°36N 81°39W **179** J8
Lehighton U.S.A. 40°50N 75°43W **175** F9
Lehliu Romania 44°29N 26°50E **81** F11
Lehrte Germany 52°22N 9°58E **76** C5
Lehututu Botswana 23°54S 21°55E **144** B3
Lei Shui → China 26°55N 112°35E **117** D9
Leiah Pakistan 30°58N 70°58E **124** D4
Leibnitz Austria 46°47N 15°34E **78** E8
Leibo China 28°11N 103°34E **116** C4
Leicester U.K. 52°38N 1°8W **67** E6
Leicester City □ U.K. 52°38N 1°8W **67** E6
Leicestershire □ U.K. 52°41N 1°17W **67** E6
Leichhardt →
  Australia 17°35S 139°48E **150** B2
Leichhardt Ra.
  Australia 20°46S 147°40E **150** C4
Leiden Neths. 52°9N 4°30E **69** B4
Leie → Belgium 51°2N 3°45E **69** C3
Leifers = Láives Italy 46°26N 11°20E **93** B8
Leigh → Australia 38°18S 144°30E **152** E3
Leigh Creek Australia 30°38S 138°26E **152** A3
Leimen Germany 49°21N 8°41E **77** F4
Leimus Nic. 14°40N 84°3W **182** D3
Leine → Germany 52°43N 9°36E **76** C5
Leinefelde-Worbris
  Germany 51°23N 10°19E **76** D6
Leinster Australia 27°51S 120°36E **149** E3
Leinster □ Ireland 53°3N 7°8W **64** C4
Leinster, Mt. Ireland 52°37N 6°46W **64** D5
Leipalingis Lithuania 54°5N 23°51E **82** D10
Leipzig Germany 51°18N 12°22E **76** D8
Leiria Portugal 39°46N 8°53E **88** F2
Leiria □ Portugal 39°46N 8°53E **88** F2
Leirvik Norway 59°47N 5°28E **61** G11
Leishan China 26°15N 108°20E **116** D7
Leisler, Mt. Australia 23°23S 129°20E **148** D4
Leisure City U.S.A. 25°30N 80°26W **179** K9
Leith U.K. 55°59N 3°11W **65** F5
Leith Hill U.K. 51°11N 0°22W **67** F7
Leitha → Europe 47°50N 17°15E **79** D10
Leitir Ceanainn = Letterkenny
  Ireland 54°57N 7°45W **64** B4
Leitrim Ireland 54°0N 8°5W **64** B3
Leitrim □ Ireland 54°8N 8°0W **64** B4
Leitza Spain 43°5N 1°55W **90** B3
Leixlip Ireland 53°22N 6°30W **64** C5
Leiyang China 26°27N 112°45E **117** D9
Leizhou China 20°52N 110°8E **117** G8
Leizhou Bandao China 21°0N 110°0E **116** G7
Leizhou Wan China 20°50N 110°20E **117** G8
Lek → Neths. 51°54N 4°35E **69** C4
Leka Norway 65°5N 11°35E **60** D14
Lekani Greece 41°10N 24°35E **97** E8
Lekbibaj Albania 42°17N 19°56E **96** D3
Lekeitio Spain 43°20N 2°32W **90** B2
Lekki Lagoon Nigeria 6°30N 4°7E **139** D5
Léko Mali 13°37N 9°2W **138** C3
Lekoui Burkina Faso 12°37N 3°40W **138** C4
Leksand Sweden 60°44N 15°1E **62** D9
Leland Mich., U.S.A. 45°1N 85°45W **173** C11
Leland Miss., U.S.A. 33°24N 90°54W **177** E9
Lelång Sweden 59°10N 12°5E **62** E6
Leleque Argentina 42°28S 71°0W **192** B2
Leling China 37°44N 117°13E **115** F9
Lelystad Neths. 52°30N 5°25E **69** B5
Lem Denmark 56°1N 8°24E **63** H2
Lema Nigeria 12°58N 4°13E **139** C5
Léman, L. Europe 46°26N 6°30E **71** F13
Lembar Indonesia 8°45S 116°4E **119** K19
Lembongan, Nusa
  Indonesia 8°40S 115°27E **119** K18
Lembuak Indonesia 8°36S 116°11E **119** K19
Lemera
  Dem. Rep. of the Congo 3°0S 28°55E **142** C2
Lemesós = Limassol
  Cyprus 34°42N 33°1E **101** E12
Lemhi Ra. U.S.A. 44°30N 113°30E **168** D7
Lemmenjoki △ Finland 68°40N 25°30E **60** B21
Lemmer Neths. 52°51N 5°43E **69** B5
Lemmon U.S.A. 45°57N 102°10W **172** C2
Lemon Grove U.S.A. 32°44N 117°1W **166** N9
Lemoore U.S.A. 36°18N 119°46W **170** J7
Lempdes-sur-Allagnon
  France 45°22N 3°17E **72** C7
Lemvig Denmark 56°33N 8°20E **63** H2
Lena → Russia 72°52N 126°40E **107** B13
Lena Pillars = Lenskiy Stolby
  Russia 60°55N 126°0E **107** C13
Lenadoon Pt. Ireland 54°18N 9°3W **64** B2
Lenart Slovenia 46°36N 15°48E **93** B12
Lenartovce Slovak Rep. 48°18N 20°19E **79** C13
Lencloître France 46°50N 0°20E **70** F7
Lençóis Brazil 12°35S 41°24W **189** C2

Lençóis Maranhenses △
  Brazil 2°30S 43°0W **189** A2
Lendava Slovenia 46°35N 16°25E **93** B13
Lendinara Italy 45°5N 11°36E **93** C8
Lenger Kazakhstan 42°12N 69°54E **109** D7
Lengerich Germany 52°11N 7°52E **76** C3
Lenggong Malaysia 5°6N 100°58E **121** K3
Lenggries Germany 47°41N 11°35E **77** H7
Lengshuijiang China 27°46N 111°26E **117** D8
Lengshuitan China 26°27N 111°35E **117** D8
Lengua de Vaca, Pta.
  Chile 30°14S 71°38W **190** C1
Lengwe △ Malawi 16°14S 34°45E **143** F3
Lengyeltóti Hungary 46°40N 17°40E **80** D2
Lenhovda Sweden 57°0N 15°16E **63** G9
Lenina, Kanal → Russia 43°44N 45°17E **87** J7
Lenine Ukraine 45°17N 35°46E **85** K8
Leningrad □ Russia 59°40N 32°0E **84** C7
Leningorsk = Ridder
  Kazakhstan 50°20N 83°30E **109** B10
Leningorsk Russia 54°36N 52°30E **108** B4
Leninsk Russia 48°40N 45°15E **87** F7
Leninsk-Kuznetskiy
  Russia 54°44N 86°10E **109** B11
Leninskoye Russia 58°23N 47°3E **86** A8
Lenk Switz. 46°27N 7°28E **77** J3
Lenkoran = Länkäran
  Azerbaijan 38°48N 48°52E **105** C13
Lenmalu Indonesia 1°45S 130°15E **119** E8
Lennartsfors Sweden 59°20N 11°55E **62** E5
Lenne → Germany 51°25N 7°29E **76** D3
Lennestadt Germany 51°8N 8°2E **76** D4
Lennox U.S.A. 43°21N 96°53W **172** D5
Lennox, I. Chile 55°18S 66°50W **192** E3
Lennoxville Canada 45°22N 71°51W **175** A13
Leno Italy 45°22N 10°13E **92** C7
Lenoir U.S.A. 35°55N 81°32W **177** D14
Lenoir City U.S.A. 35°48N 84°16W **177** D12
Lenore L. Canada 52°30N 104°59W **163** C8
Lenox Ga., U.S.A. 31°16N 83°28W **178** D6
Lenox Mass., U.S.A. 42°22N 73°17W **175** D11
Lens France 50°26N 2°50E **71** B9
Lensahn Germany 54°13N 10°53E **76** A6
Lensk Russia 60°48N 114°55E **107** C12
Lenskiy Stolby Russia 60°55N 126°0E **107** C13
Lentas Greece 34°56N 24°56E **101** E6
Lenti Hungary 46°37N 16°33E **80** C1
Lentini Italy 37°17N 15°0E **95** E8
Lenwood U.S.A. 34°53N 117°7W **171** L9
Lenya Burma 11°33N 98°57E **121** G2
Lenzen Germany 53°5N 11°29E **76** B7
Léo Burkina Faso 11°3N 2°2W **138** C4
Leoben Austria 47°22N 15°5E **78** D8
Leodhais = Lewis U.K. 58°9N 6°40W **65** C2
Leola U.S.A. 45°43N 98°56W **172** C4
Leominster U.K. 52°14N 2°43W **67** E5
Leominster U.S.A. 42°32N 71°46W **175** D13
Léon Mexico 21°6N 101°41W **180** C4
León Nic. 12°27N 86°51W **182** D2
León Spain 42°38N 5°34W **88** C5
León □ Spain 42°40N 5°55W **88** C5
León, Montes de Spain 42°30N 6°18W **88** C4
Leonardo da Vinci, Roma × (FCO)
  Italy 41°48N 12°15E **94** A5
Leonardtown U.S.A. 38°17N 76°38W **173** F15
Leonardville Namibia 23°29S 18°49E **144** B2
Leonárisso Cyprus 35°28N 34°8E **101** D13
Leonberg Germany 48°48N 9°1E **77** G5
Leonding Austria 48°16N 14°15E **78** C7
Leonessa Italy 42°34N 12°58E **93** F9
Leonforte Italy 37°38N 14°23E **95** E7
Leongatha Australia 38°30S 145°58E **153** E6
Leonia U.S.A. 30°55N 86°1W **178** E3
Leonidio Greece 37°9N 22°52E **98** D4
Leonora Australia 28°49S 121°19E **149** E3
Leopoldina Brazil 21°28S 42°40W **191** A7
Leopoldo Bulhões
  Brazil 16°37S 48°46W **189** D1
Leopoldsburg Belgium 51°7N 5°13E **69** C5
Leoti U.S.A. 38°29N 101°21W **172** F3
Leova Moldova 46°28N 28°15E **81** D13
Leoville Canada 53°39N 107°33W **163** C7
Lepe Spain 37°15N 7°12W **89** H3
Lepel = Lyepyel Belarus 54°50N 28°40E **84** E5
Lepenou Greece 38°42N 21°17E **98** C3
Leping China 28°47N 117°7E **117** C11
Lépo, L. do Angola 17°0S 19°0E **144** A2
Lépontine, Alpi Italy 46°22N 8°27E **92** B5
Leposavić Kosovo 43°7N 20°48E **96** C5
Leppävirta Finland 62°29N 27°46E **60** E22
Lepsény Hungary 47°0N 18°15E **80** D3
Leptis Magna Libya 32°40N 14°12E **135** B8
Lequeitio = Lekeitio
  Spain 43°20N 2°32W **90** B2
Lercara Friddi Italy 37°45N 13°36E **94** E6
Léré Chad 9°39N 14°13E **139** D7
Léré Mali 15°45N 4°55W **138** B4
Lere Bauchi, Nigeria 9°43N 9°18E **139** D6
Lere Kaduna, Nigeria 10°23N 8°35E **139** C6
Leribe Lesotho 28°51S 28°3E **145** C4
Lérici Italy 44°4N 9°55E **92** D6
Lérida = Lleida Spain 41°37N 0°39E **90** D5
Lérins, Îs. de France 43°31N 7°3E **73** E11
Lerma Spain 42°0N 3°47W **88** C7
Léronville France 48°44N 5°30E **71** D12
Lerum Sweden 57°46N 12°16E **63** G6
Lerwick U.K. 60°9N 1°9W **65** A7
Les Romania 46°58N 21°50E **80** D6
Les Abrets France 45°32N 5°35E **73** C9
Les Andelys France 49°15N 1°25E **70** C4
Les Borges Blanques
  Spain 41°31N 0°52E **90** D5
Les Cayes Haiti 18°15N 73°46W **183** C5
Les Coteaux Canada 45°15N 74°13W **175** A10
Les Escoumins Canada 48°21N 69°24W **165** C6
Les Essarts France 46°47N 1°12W **70** F5
Les Herbiers France 46°52N 1°1W **70** F5
Les Minquiers, Plateau des
  Chan. Is. 48°58N 2°8W **70** D4
Les Pieux France 49°30N 1°48W **70** C5
Les Ponts-de-Cé France 47°25N 0°30W **70** E6
Les Riceys France 47°59N 4°22E **71** E11
Les Sables-d'Olonne
  France 46°30N 1°45W **70** F4
Les Vans France 44°25N 4°7E **73** D8
Lesbos Greece 39°10N 26°20E **98** B5
L'Escala Spain 42°7N 3°8E **90** C8

Leshan China 29°33N 103°41E **116** C4
Leshwe △
  Dem. Rep. of the Congo 12°45S 29°30E **143** E2
Lésina Italy 41°52N 15°21E **93** G12
Lésina, L. di Italy 41°53N 15°26E **93** G12
Lesjöfors Sweden 59°58N 14°11E **62** E8
Lesko Poland 49°30N 22°23E **83** J9
Leskov I. Antarctica 56°0S 28°0W **55** B1
Leskovac Serbia 43°0N 21°58E **96** C5
Leskovik Albania 40°10N 20°34E **96** F4
Leslie U.S.A. 31°57N 84°5W **178** D5
Leśna Poland 51°1N 15°15E **83** G2
Leśnica Poland 50°26N 18°11E **83** H5
Leśnica Serbia 44°39N 19°20E **96** B3
Lesnoye Russia 58°15N 35°18E **84** C8
Lesopilnoye Russia 46°44N 134°20E **112** A7
Lesotho ■ Africa 29°40S 28°0E **145** C4
Lesozavodsk Russia 45°30N 133°29E **112** B6
Lesparre-Médoc France 45°18N 0°57W **72** C3
L'Espluga de Francolí
  Spain 41°24N 1°7E **90** D6
Lesse → Belgium 50°15N 4°54E **69** D4
Lessebo Sweden 56°45N 15°16E **63** H9
Lesser Antilles W. Indies 15°0N 61°0W **183** D7
Lesser Slave L. Canada 55°30N 115°25W **162** B5
Lesser Sunda Is. Indonesia 8°0S 120°0E **119** F6
Lessines Belgium 50°42N 3°50E **69** D3
Lester B. Pearson Int., Toronto ×
  (YYZ) Canada 43°46N 79°35W **174** C5
Lestock Canada 51°19N 103°59W **163** C8
Lesuer △ Australia 30°11S 115°10E **149** F2
Lésvos = Lesbos Greece 39°10N 26°20E **98** B5
Leszno Poland 51°50N 16°30E **83** G3
Letaba S. Africa 23°59S 31°50E **145** B5
Letälven → Sweden 59°5N 14°20E **62** E8
Li Shan China 35°30N 111°56E **114** G6
Letchworth Garden City
  U.K. 51°59N 0°13W **67** F7
Letea, Ostrovul
  Romania 45°18N 29°20E **81** E14
Lethbridge Canada 49°45N 112°45W **162** D6
Lethem Guyana 3°20N 59°50W **186** C7
Leti, Kepulauan
  Indonesia 8°10S 128°0E **119** F7
Leti Is. = Leti, Kepulauan
  Indonesia 8°10S 128°0E **119** F7
Letiahau → Botswana 21°16S 24°0E **144** B3
Leticia Colombia 4°9S 70°0W **186** D5
Leting China 39°23N 118°55E **115** E10
Letjiesbos S. Africa 32°34S 22°16E **144** D3
Letlhakane Botswana 21°27S 25°30E **144** B4
Letlhakeng Botswana 24°0S 24°59E **144** B3
Letpadan Burma 17°45N 95°45E **123** L19
Letpan Burma 19°28N 94°10E **123** K19
Letsôk-aw Kyun
  Burma 11°30N 98°25E **121** G2
Letterkenny Ireland 54°57N 7°45W **64** B4
Leu Romania 44°10N 24°0E **81** F9
Leucadia U.S.A. 33°4N 117°18W **171** M9
Leucate France 42°56N 3°3E **72** F7
Leucate, Étang de France 42°50N 3°0E **72** F7
Leuchars U.K. 56°24N 2°53W **65** E6
Leuk Switz. 46°19N 7°37E **77** J3
Leuşeni Moldova 46°49N 28°12E **81** D13
Leuser, Gunung
  Indonesia 3°46N 97°12E **118** D1
Leutkirch Germany 47°49N 10°1E **77** H6
Leuven Belgium 50°52N 4°42E **69** D4
Leuze-en-Hainaut
  Belgium 50°36N 3°37E **69** D3
Lev Tolstoy Russia 53°13N 39°29E **84** F10
Levan Albania 40°40N 19°28E **96** F3
Levanger Norway 63°45N 11°19E **60** E14
Levant, Î. du France 43°3N 6°28E **73** E10
Lévanto Italy 44°10N 9°38E **92** D6
Lévanzo Italy 38°0N 12°20E **94** D5
Levelland U.S.A. 33°35N 102°23W **176** E3
Leven U.K. 56°12N 3°0W **65** E6
Leven, L. U.K. 56°12N 3°22W **65** E5
Leverano Italy 40°17N 18°0E **95** B10
Leverkusen Germany 51°1N 7°1E **76** D3
Levice Slovak Rep. 48°13N 18°35E **79** C11
Lévico Terme Italy 46°0N 11°18E **93** C8
Levie France 41°40N 9°7E **73** G13
Levin N.Z. 40°37S 175°18E **154** G4
Lévis Canada 46°48N 71°9W **165** C5
Levis, L. Canada 46°37N 117°58W **162** A5
Levithà Greece 37°0N 26°28E **98** D8
Levittown N.Y.,
  U.S.A. 40°44N 73°31W **175** F11
Levittown Pa., U.S.A. 40°9N 74°51W **175** F10
Levka Bulgaria 41°52N 26°15E **97** E10
Levka Oros Greece 35°18N 24°3E **101** D6
Levkás = Lefkada Greece 38°40N 20°43E **98** C2
Levoča Slovak Rep. 49°2N 20°35E **79** B13
Levroux France 46°59N 1°38E **70** F8
Levski Bulgaria 43°21N 25°10E **97** C9
Levskigrad = Karlovo
  Bulgaria 42°38N 24°47E **97** D8
Levuka Fiji 17°34S 179°0E **154** a
Lewes U.K. 50°52N 0°1E **67** G8
Lewes U.S.A. 38°46N 75°9W **173** F16
Lewin Brzeski Poland 50°45N 17°37E **83** H4
Lewis U.K. 58°9N 6°40W **65** C2
Lewis → U.S.A. 45°51N 122°48W **170** E4
Lewis, Butt of U.K. 58°31N 6°16W **65** C2
Lewis and Clark △
  U.S.A. 46°8N 123°53W **170** D3
Lewis Pass N.Z. 42°31S 172°11E **155** D7
Lewis Ra. Australia 20°3S 128°50E **148** D4
Lewis Range U.S.A. 48°5N 113°5W **168** B7
Lewis Run U.S.A. 41°52N 78°40W **174** E6
Lewisburg Pa., U.S.A. 40°58N 76°54W **174** F7
Lewisburg Tenn.,
  U.S.A. 35°27N 86°48W **177** D11
Lewisburg W. Va.,
  U.S.A. 37°48N 80°27W **173** G12
Lewisporte Canada 49°15N 55°3W **165** C8
Lewiston Idaho, U.S.A. 46°25N 117°1W **168** C5
Lewiston Maine, U.S.A. 44°6N 70°13W **175** C18
Lewiston N.Y., U.S.A. 43°11N 79°3W **174** C5
Lewistown Mont.,
  U.S.A. 47°4N 109°26W **169** C9
Lewistown Pa., U.S.A. 40°36N 77°34W **174** F7
Lewisville U.S.A. 33°2N 96°59W **176** E6
Lexington → U.S.A. 39°6N 84°30W **173** D11
Lexington Ga., U.S.A. 33°52N 83°7W **178** B6
Lexington Ill., U.S.A. 40°39N 88°47W **172** E9
Licata Italy 37°6N 13°56E **94** E6

Lexington Ky., U.S.A. 38°3N 84°30W **173** F11
Lexington Mich.,
  U.S.A. 43°16N 82°32W **174** C2
Lexington Mo., U.S.A. 39°11N 93°52W **172** F7
Lexington N.C.,
  U.S.A. 35°49N 80°15W **177** D14
Lexington Nebr., U.S.A. 40°47N 99°45W **172** E4
Lexington Ohio, U.S.A. 40°41N 82°35W **174** F2
Lexington S.C., U.S.A. 33°59N 81°11W **178** B8
Lexington Tenn.,
  U.S.A. 35°39N 88°24W **177** D10
Lexington Va., U.S.A. 37°47N 79°27W **173** G14
Lexington Park
  U.S.A. 38°16N 76°27W **173** F15
Leyburn U.K. 54°19N 1°48W **66** C6
Leye China 24°48N 106°29E **116** E6
Leyland U.K. 53°42N 2°43W **66** D5
Leyte □ Phil. 11°0N 125°0E **119** E7
Lezajsk Poland 50°16N 22°25E **83** H9
Lezay France 46°15N 0°1W **72** B3
Lezhë Albania 41°47N 19°39E **96** E3
Lezhi China 30°19N 104°58E **116** B5
Lézignan-Corbières
  France 43°13N 2°43E **72** E6
Lezoux France 45°49N 3°21E **72** C7
Lgov Russia 51°42N 35°16E **85** G8
Lhasa China 29°25N 90°58E **110** F7
Lhazê China 29°5N 87°38E **110** F6
L'Hermite, I. Chile 55°50S 68°0W **192** E3
Lhokkruet Indonesia 4°55N 95°24E **118** D1
Lhokseumawe Indonesia 5°10N 97°10E **118** C1
L'Hospitalet de Llobregat
  Spain 41°21N 2°6E **90** D7
Li Thailand 17°48N 98°57E **120** D2
Li Jiang → China 24°40N 110°40E **117** E8
Li Jiang △ China 24°38N 110°38E **117** E8
Li Shan China 35°30N 111°56E **114** G6
Li Shui → China 29°24N 112°1E **117** C9
Li Xian Gansu, China 34°10N 105°5E **114** G3
Li Xian Hebei, China 38°30N 115°35E **114** E8
Li Xian Hunan, China 29°36N 111°42E **117** C8
Liadi Greece 36°50N 26°11E **99** E8
Liancheng China 25°42N 116°40E **117** E11
Liancourt Rocks Asia 37°15N 131°52E **113** F5
Lianga Phil. 8°38N 126°6E **119** C7
Liangcheng Nei Monggol Zizhiqu,
  China 40°28N 112°25E **114** D7
Liangcheng Shandong,
  China 35°32N 119°37E **115** G10
Liangdang China 33°56N 106°18E **114** H4
Lianghe China 24°50N 98°20E **116** E2
Lianghekou China 29°11N 108°44E **116** C6
Liangping China 30°38N 107°47E **116** B6
Liangpran Indonesia 1°4N 114°23E **118** D4
Lianhua China 27°3N 113°54E **117** D9
Lianhua Shan China 23°40N 115°48E **117** F10
Lianjiang Fujian,
  China 26°12N 119°27E **117** D12
Lianjiang Guangdong,
  China 21°40N 110°20E **117** G8
Lianping China 24°26N 114°30E **117** E10
Lianshan China 24°38N 112°8E **117** E9
Lianshanguan China 40°53N 123°43E **115** D12
Lianshui China 33°42N 119°20E **115** H10
Lianyuan China 27°40N 111°38E **117** D8
Lianyungang China 34°40N 119°11E **115** G10
Lianzhou China 24°51N 112°22E **117** E9
Liao He → China 41°0N 121°50E **115** D11
Liaocheng China 36°28N 115°58E **114** F8
Liaodong Bandao
  China 40°0N 122°30E **115** E12
Liaodong Wan China 40°20N 121°10E **115** D11
Liaoning □ China 41°40N 122°30E **115** D12
Liaotung, G. of = Liaodong Wan
  China 40°20N 121°10E **115** D11
Liaoyang China 41°15N 122°58E **115** D12
Liaoyuan China 42°58N 125°2E **115** C13
Liaozhong China 41°23N 122°50E **115** D12
Liapades Greece 39°42N 19°40E **101** A3
Liard → Canada 61°51N 121°18W **162** A4
Liard River Canada 59°25N 126°5W **162** B3
Liari Pakistan 25°37N 66°30E **124** G2
Libanggaon Nepal 28°18N 82°38E **125** E10
Libau = Liepāja Latvia 56°30N 21°0E **82** B8
Libby U.S.A. 48°23N 115°33W **168** B5
Libenge
  Dem. Rep. of the Congo 3°40N 18°55E **140** D3
Liberal U.S.A. 37°3N 100°55W **172** G3
Liberdade Brazil 10°5S 70°20W **188** C3
Liberec Czech Rep. 50°47N 15°7E **78** A8
Liberecký □ Czech Rep. 50°45N 15°0E **78** A8
Liberia Costa Rica 10°40N 85°30W **182** D2
Liberia ■ W. Afr. 6°30N 9°30W **138** D3
Libertador □ Chile 34°15S 70°45W **190** C1
Liberty Mo., U.S.A. 39°15N 94°25W **172** F7
Liberty N.Y., U.S.A. 41°48N 74°45W **175** E10
Liberty Pa., U.S.A. 41°34N 77°6W **174** E7
Liberty Tex., U.S.A. 30°3N 94°48W **176** F7
Liberty-Newark Int. × (EWR)
  U.S.A. 40°42N 74°10W **175** F10
Libiąż Poland 50°7N 19°21E **83** H6
Libîya, Sahrâ' Africa 25°0N 25°0E **135** C10
Libo China 25°22N 107°53E **116** E6
Libobo, Tanjung
  Indonesia 0°54S 128°28E **119** E7
Libode S. Africa 31°33S 29°2E **145** D4
Libohovë Albania 40°3N 20°10E **96** F4
Libong, Ko Thailand 7°15N 99°23E **121** J2
Libourne France 44°55N 0°14W **72** D3
Libramont Belgium 49°55N 5°23E **69** E5
Librazhd Albania 41°12N 20°22E **96** E4
Libreville Gabon 0°25N 9°26E **140** D1
Libya ■ N. Afr. 27°0N 17°0E **135** C8
Libyan Desert = Libîya, Sahrâ'
  Africa 25°0N 25°0E **135** C10
Libyan Plateau = Ed Déffa
  Egypt 30°40N 26°30E **137** A2
Licantén Chile 35°55S 72°0W **190** D1
Licata Italy 37°6N 13°56E **94** E6
Lice Turkey 38°27N 40°55E **105** C9
Licheng China 36°28N 113°20E **114** F7
Lichfield U.K. 52°41N 1°49W **67** E6
Lichinga Mozam. 13°13S 35°11E **143** E4
Lichtenburg S. Africa 26°8S 26°8E **144** C4
Lichtenfels Germany 50°9N 11°4E **76** E7
Lichuan Hubei, China 30°18N 108°57E **116** B7
Lichuan Jiangxi,
  China 27°18N 116°55E **117** D11
Licking → U.S.A. 39°6N 84°30W **173** F11
Licosa, Punta Italy 40°15N 14°54E **95** B7

Licungo → Mozam. 17°40S 37°15E **143** F4
Lida Belarus 53°53N 25°15E **75** B13
Liden Sweden 62°42N 16°48E **62** E10
Lidhult Sweden 56°50N 13°27E **63** H7
Lidköping Sweden 58°31N 13°7E **63** F7
Lido Niger 12°54N 3°44E **139** C5
Lido di Roma = Óstia, Lido di
  Italy 41°43N 12°17E **93** G9
Lidoríki Greece 38°32N 22°12E **98** C4
Lidzbark Poland 53°15N 19°49E **83** E6
Lidzbark Warmiński
  Poland 54°7N 20°34E **82** D7
Liebenwalde Germany 52°52N 13°24E **76** C9
Lieberose Germany 51°59N 14°17E **76** D10
Liebig, Mt. Australia 23°18S 131°22E **148** D5
Liebling Romania 45°36N 21°20E **80** F6
Liechtenstein ■ Europe 47°8N 9°35E **77** H5
Liège Belgium 50°38N 5°35E **69** D5
Liège □ Belgium 50°32N 5°35E **69** D5
Liegnitz = Legnica
  Poland 51°12N 16°10E **83** G3
Lieksa Finland 63°18N 30°2E **60** E24
Lienart
  Dem. Rep. of the Congo 3°3N 25°31E **142** B2
Lienyünchiangshih =
  Lianyungang
  China 34°40N 119°11E **115** G10
Lienz Austria 46°50N 12°46E **78** E5
Liepāja Latvia 56°30N 21°0E **82** B8
Liepājas ezers Latvia 56°27N 21°3E **82** B8
Lier Belgium 51°7N 4°34E **69** C4
Liernais France 47°13N 4°16E **71** E11
Lieto Finland 60°38N 22°26E **63** E13
Lietuva = Lithuania ■
  Europe 55°30N 24°0E **84** C2
Liévin France 50°24N 2°47E **71** B9
Lièvre → Canada 45°31N 75°26W **164** C4
Liezen Austria 47°34N 14°15E **78** D7
Liffey → Ireland 53°21N 6°13W **64** C5
Lifford Ireland 54°51N 7°29W **64** B4
Liffré France 48°12N 1°30W **70** D5
Lifudzin Russia 44°21N 134°58E **112** B7
Lighthouse Point U.S.A. 26°15N 80°7W **179** J9
Lighthouse Pt. U.S.A. 29°54N 84°21W **178** F5
Lightning Ridge
  Australia 29°22S 148°0E **151** D4
Lignano Sabbiadoro
  Italy 45°42N 13°9E **93** C10
Ligny-en-Barrois France 48°36N 5°20E **71** D12
Ligonha → Mozam. 16°54S 39°9E **143** F4
Ligonier U.S.A. 40°15N 79°14W **174** F5
Ligourio Greece 37°37N 23°2E **98** D5
Ligueil France 47°2N 0°49E **70** F7
Liguria □ Italy 44°30N 8°50E **92** D5
Ligurian Sea Medit. S. 43°20N 9°0E **92** E5
Lihou Reefs and Cays
  Australia 17°25S 151°40E **150** B5
Lihue Calel △ Argentina 38°0S 65°10W **190** D2
L'Île-Bouchard France 47°7N 0°26E **70** F7
L'Île-Rousse France 42°38N 8°57E **73** F12
Lijiang China 27°42N 113°29E **117** D9
Likasi
  Dem. Rep. of the Congo 10°55S 26°48E **143** E2
Likenäs Sweden 60°37N 13°3E **62** D7
Likhoslavl Russia 57°12N 35°30E **84** D8
Likhovskoy Russia 48°10N 40°10E **87** F5
Likoma I. Malawi 12°3S 34°45E **143** E3
Likumburu Tanzania 9°43S 35°8E **143** D4
L'Île-Bouchard France 47°7N 0°26E **70** F7
Likoma I. Malawi 12°3S 34°45E **143** E3
Liku Indonesia 0°53N 128°28E **119** E7
Lille France 50°38N 3°3E **71** B10
Lille Bælt Denmark 55°20N 9°45E **63** J3
Lillehammer Norway 61°8N 10°30E **60** F14
Lillesand Norway 58°15N 8°23E **61** G13
Lillhärdal Sweden 61°51N 14°4E **62** C7
Lillian Pt. Australia 27°40S 126°6E **149** E4
Lillooet Canada 50°44N 121°57W **162** C4
Lillooet → Canada 49°15N 121°57W **162** D4
Lilongwe Malawi 14°0S 33°48E **143** E3
Liloy Phil. 8°4N 122°39E **119** C6
Lim → Europe 43°0N 19°40E **96** C4
Lim Chu Kang Singapore 1°26N 103°43E **121** d
Lima Indonesia 3°39S 127°58E **119** F7
Lima Peru 12°3S 77°2W **188** D2
Lima Mont., U.S.A. 44°38N 112°36W **168** D7
Lima N.Y., U.S.A. 42°54N 77°36W **174** D7
Lima Ohio, U.S.A. 40°44N 84°6W **173** E11
Lima □ Peru 12°0S 77°0W **188** D2
Lima → Portugal 41°41N 8°50W **88** D2
Liman Azerbaijan 38°53N 48°47E **105** C13
Liman Russia 45°45N 47°12E **87** H8
Limanowa Poland 49°42N 20°22E **83** J7
Limassol Cyprus 34°42N 33°1E **101** E12
Limavady U.K. 55°3N 6°56W **64** A5
Limay → Argentina 39°0S 68°0W **190** D3
Limay Mahuida
  Argentina 37°10S 66°45W **190** D2
Limbach-Oberfrohna
  Germany 50°52N 12°43E **76** E8
Limbang Malaysia 4°42N 115°6E **118** D5
Limbara, Mte. Italy 40°51N 9°10E **94** B2
Limbaži Latvia 57°31N 24°42E **84** D3
Limbdi India 22°34N 71°51E **124** H4
Limbe Cameroon 4°1N 9°10E **139** E6
Limburg Germany 50°22N 8°4E **77** E4
Limburg □ Belgium 51°2N 5°25E **69** C5
Limburg □ Neths. 51°20N 5°55E **69** C5
Limedsforsen Sweden 60°52N 13°26E **62** D7
Limeira Brazil 22°35S 47°28W **191** A6
Limenaria Greece 40°38N 24°32E **97** F8
Limenas Chersonisou
  Greece 35°18N 25°21E **101** D6
Limerick Ireland 52°40N 8°37W **64** D3
Limerick □ Ireland 52°30N 8°50W **64** D3
Limestone U.S.A. 42°2N 78°38W **174** D6
Limestone → Canada 56°31N 94°7W **163** B10
Limfjorden Denmark 56°55N 9°0E **63** H3
Limia = Lima →
  Portugal 41°41N 8°50W **88** D2
Limingen Norway 64°48N 13°35E **60** D15
Limmared Sweden 57°32N 13°20E **63** H7
Limmen ○ Australia 15°15S 135°30E **150** B2
Limmen Bight
  Australia 14°40S 135°35E **150** A2

Limmen Bight →
  Australia 15°7S 135°44E **150** B2
Limni Greece 38°43N 23°18E **98** C5
Limnos Greece 39°50N 25°5E **98** B5
Limoeiro Brazil 7°52S 35°27W **189** D4
Limoeiro do Norte Brazil 5°5S 38°0W **189** C4
Limoges Canada 45°20N 75°16W **175** A9
Limoges France 45°50N 1°15E **72** C4
Limón Costa Rica 10°0N 83°2W **182** E3
Limon U.S.A. 39°16N 103°41W **169** G12
Limone Italy 45°48N 10°47E **92** C7
Limone Piemonte Italy 44°12N 7°34E **92** D4
Limousin □ France 45°30N 1°30E **72** C5
Limousin, Plateaux du
  France 45°45N 1°15E **72** C4
Limoux France 43°4N 2°12E **72** E6
Limpopo → S. Africa 24°5S 33°30E **145** B5
Limpopo → Africa 25°5S 33°30E **145** B5
Limuru Kenya 1°2S 36°35E **142** C4
Lin'an China 30°15N 119°42E **117** B12
Linares Chile 35°50S 71°40W **190** D1
Linares Mexico 24°52N 99°34W **181** C5
Linares Spain 38°10N 3°40W **89** G7
Linaria Greece 38°52N 24°31E **98** C6
Linaro, Capo Italy 42°2N 11°50E **93** G8
Linas Mte. Italy 39°25N 8°38E **94** C1
Linate, Milano × (LIN)
  Italy 45°27N 9°16E **92** C6
Lincang China 23°58N 100°1E **116** F3
Lincheng China 37°25N 114°30E **114** F8
Linchuan China 27°57N 116°15E **117** D11
Lincoln = Beamsville
  Canada 43°12N 79°28W **174** C6
Lincoln Argentina 34°55S 61°30W **190** C4
Lincoln N.Z. 43°38S 172°30E **155** D8
Lincoln U.K. 53°14N 0°32W **67** D7
Lincoln Calif., U.S.A. 38°54N 121°17W **170** G5
Lincoln Ill., U.S.A. 40°9N 89°22W **172** E9
Lincoln Kans., U.S.A. 39°3N 98°9W **172** F4
Lincoln Maine, U.S.A. 45°22N 68°30W **173** B19
Lincoln N.H., U.S.A. 44°3N 71°40W **175** B13
Lincoln N. Mex.,
  U.S.A. 33°30N 105°23W **169** K11
Lincoln Nebr., U.S.A. 40°49N 96°41W **172** E5
Lincoln City U.S.A. 44°57N 124°1W **168** D1
Lincoln Hav = Lincoln Sea
  Arctic 84°0N 55°0W **54** A5
Lincoln Park U.S.A. 32°52N 84°20W **178** C5
Lincoln Sea Arctic 84°0N 55°0W **54** A5
Lincolnshire □ U.K. 53°14N 0°32W **67** D7
Lincolnshire Wolds U.K. 53°26N 0°13W **66** D7
Lincolnton Ga., U.S.A. 33°48N 82°29W **178** B6
Lincolnton N.C.,
  U.S.A. 35°29N 81°16W **177** D14
Lind U.S.A. 46°58N 118°37W **168** C4
Lindale U.S.A. 34°11N 85°11W **178** B4
Lindau Germany 47°33N 9°41E **77** H5
Lindeman I. Australia 20°27S 149°3E **150** C4
Linden Guyana 6°0N 58°10W **186** B7
Linden Ala., U.S.A. 32°18N 87°48W **177** E9
Linden Calif., U.S.A. 38°1N 121°5W **170** G5
Linden Tex., U.S.A. 33°1N 94°22W **176** E7
Lindenhurst U.S.A. 40°41N 73°23W **175** F11
Lindenow Fjord
  Greenland 60°30N 43°25W **54** C5
Lindesberg Sweden 59°36N 15°15E **63** E9
Lindesnes Norway 57°58N 7°3E **61** H11
Líndhos Greece 36°6N 28°4E **101** B4
Líndhos, Ákra Greece 36°4N 28°10E **101** B4
Lindi Tanzania 9°58S 39°38E **143** D4
Lindi □ Tanzania 9°40S 38°30E **143** D4
Lindi →
  Dem. Rep. of the Congo 0°33N 25°5E **142** B2
Lindley U.S.A. 42°1N 77°8W **174** D7
Lindö Sweden 58°37N 16°15E **63** F9
Lindome Sweden 57°34N 12°5E **63** G6
Líndos Greece 36°6N 28°4E **101** B4
Líndos, Ákra Greece 36°4N 28°10E **101** B4
Lindoso Portugal 41°52N 8°11W **88** D2
Lindow Germany 52°58N 12°59E **76** C8
Lindsay Canada 44°22N 78°43W **174** B6
Lindsay Calif., U.S.A. 36°12N 119°5W **170** J7
Lindsay Okla., U.S.A. 34°50N 97°38W **176** D6
Lindsborg U.S.A. 38°35N 97°40W **172** F5
Lindsdal Sweden 56°44N 16°18E **63** H10
Line Islands Pac. Oc. 7°0N 160°0W **157** G12
Linesville U.S.A. 41°39N 80°26W **174** E4
Lineville U.S.A. 33°19N 85°45W **177** E11
Linfen China 36°3N 111°30E **114** F6
Ling Xian Hunan,
  China 26°29N 113°48E **117** D9
Ling Xian Shandong,
  China 37°22N 116°30E **115** F9
Lingal India 16°17N 78°31E **125** E4
Linganamakki Res.
  India 14°6N 74°52E **125** G2
Lingao China 19°56N 109°42E **116** G7
Lingayen Phil. 16°1N 120°14E **119** A6
Lingayen G. Phil. 16°10N 120°15E **119** A6
Lingbao China 34°31N 110°51E **114** G6
Lingbi China 33°33N 117°33E **115** H9
Lingbo Sweden 61°3N 16°41E **62** D10
Lingchuan Guangxi Zhuangzu,
  China 25°26N 110°21E **117** E8
Lingchuan Shanxi,
  China 35°45N 113°12E **114** G7
Lingding Yang China 22°25N 113°44E **117** a
Lingen Germany 52°31N 7°19E **76** C3
Lingga Indonesia 0°12S 104°37E **118** E2
Lingga, Kepulauan
  Indonesia 0°10S 104°30E **118** E2
Lingga Arch. = Lingga,
  Kepulauan Indonesia 0°10S 104°30E **118** E2
Linghed Sweden 60°48N 15°55E **62** D9
Lingle U.S.A. 42°8N 104°21W **168** E12
Lingqiu China 39°28N 114°22E **114** E8
Lingshan China 22°25N 109°18E **116** E7
Lingshi China 36°48N 111°48E **114** F6
Lingshou China 38°20N 114°20E **114** E8
Lingshui China 18°27N 110°0E **116** H8
Lingtai China 35°0N 107°40E **114** G4
Lingyang China 25°21N 110°20E **117** E8
Lingui China 25°12N 110°2E **117** E8
Lingwu China 38°6N 106°20E **114** E4
Lingyuan China 41°10N 119°15E **115** D10
Lingyun China 24°20N 106°31E **116** E6
Linhai China 28°50N 121°8E **117** C13

...ares Brazil 19°25S 40°4W 189 D2
...e China 40°48N 107°20E 114 D4
...iang China 41°50N 127°0E 115 D14
...ou China 45°15N 130°18E 115 B16
...China 29°27N 111°30E 117 C8
...ansaari △ Finland 62°3N 28°40E 60 E23
...he, L. U.K. 56°36N 5°25W 65 E3
...China 35°45N 113°52E 114 G7
...jing China 36°50N 115°42E 114 F8
...ging China 36°25N 118°30E 115 F10
...quan China 33°5N 115°17E 117 A10
...Brazil 21°40S 49°44W 191 A6
...hu China 34°53N 118°38E 115 G10
...hui China 30°21N 106°57E 116 B6
...ead Jamaica 18°8N 77°2W 182 a
...ao China 35°26N 103°58E 114 G2
...n Switz. 47°7N 9°7E 77 H5
...hal Switz. 46°54N 9°0E 77 J5
...Ind., U.S.A. 39°2N 87°10W 172 F2
...n N. Dak., U.S.A. 46°16N 100°14W 172 B3
...wood Canada 34°35N 80°43W 174 C4
...ru China 25°19N 112°31E 117 E9
...i Hebei, China 39°42N 118°26E 115 E10
...i Liaoning, China 43°36N 118°2E 115 C10
...ia China 35°36N 103°10E 117 D9
...iang China 29°28N 113°23E 117 C9
...anti → Africa 17°50S 25°5E 144 A4
...i Shandong, China 37°13N 116°54E 114 F9
...i Shandong, China 35°5N 118°21E 115 G10
...ia China 33°48N 113°56E 114 H7
...Austria 48°18N 14°18E 78 C7
...Germany 50°34N 7°17E 76 E3
...henzhen China 36°30N 109°59E 114 F5
...hou China 36°15N 113°49E 114 F7
...China 36°50N 118°20E 115 F10
...,G. du France 43°10N 4°0E 72 E7
...i Italy 40°52N 15°11E 95 B8

s, G. of = Lion, G. du ance 43°10N 4°0E 72 E7
's Den Zimbabwe 17°15S 30°5E 143 F3
...'s Head Canada 54°8N 81°15W 174 B3
...o = Lyozna Belarus 55°0N 30°50E 84 E6
...Phil. 13°57N 121°10E 119 B6
...i Mozam. 15°50S 35°50E 143 F4
...ny Slovak Rep. 49°9N 20°58E 79 B13
...ri Italy 38°26N 14°58E 95 D7
...i, I., Italy 38°29N 14°56E 95 D7
...ly 38°30N 14°57E 95 C7
...ri Moldova 48°14N 26°48E 81 B11
...i Finland 62°31N 29°24E 60 E23
...tsk Russia 52°37N 39°35E 85 F10
...sk □ Russia 52°50N 38°50E 86 D4
...any Poland 53°2N 14°58E 83 E1
...ng China 26°15N 109°7E 116 D7
...i Greece 37°19N 26°50E 99 D8
...i Kosovo 42°31N 21°7E 96 D5
...any = Lipcani oldova 48°14N 26°48E 81 B11
...ech Rep. 49°32N 17°36E 79 B10
...o Poland 52°14N 19°15E 83 F6
...va Romania 46°8N 21°42E 80 D6
...vets Ukraine 49°12N 29°1E 75 D15
...e = Germany 51°39N 6°36E 76 D2
...stadt Germany 51°34N 8°22E 76 D4
...comb U.S.A. 36°14N 100°16W 176 C4
...k Poland 53°44N 23°24E 82 E10
...ko Poland 51°9N 21°40E 83 G8
...vský Hrádok ovak Rep. 49°2N 19°44E 79 B12
...ovský Milkuláš ovak Rep. 49°6N 19°35E 79 B12
...ap, C. Australia 38°50S 145°55E 153 E6
...China 24°30N 110°22E 117 E8
...Uganda 2°17N 32°57E 142 B3
...ly 41°25N 13°52E 94 A6
... = Lliria Spain 39°37N 0°35W 91 F4
...kovsk Kazakhstan 52°33N 62°37E 108 B6
...m. Rep. of the Congo 2°12N 21°38E 140 D4
...ba Portugal 38°42N 9°9W 89 G1
...ba □ Portugal 39°0N 9°12W 89 F1
...ba ✈ (LIS) Portugal 38°46N 9°8W 89 G1
... = Lisboa Portugal 38°46N 9°8W 89 G1
...n N. Dak., U.S.A. 47°6N 99°26W 176 B5
...n N.H., U.S.A. 44°13N 71°55W 175 B13
...n N.Y., U.S.A. 44°43N 75°19W 175 B9
...n Ohio, U.S.A. 40°46N 80°46W 174 F4
...n Falls U.S.A. 44°0N 70°4W 173 D18
...rne, C. U.S.A. 68°53N 166°13W 166 B6
...nnor B. Ireland 52°55N 9°24W 64 D2
...a → Italy 41°11N 9°9E 94 A2
...onvarna Ireland 53°2N 9°18W 64 C2
...e Jiang → China 24°15N 101°35E 116 E3
...China 37°31N 111°8E 114 F6
...i China 43°20N 124°18E 115 C13
...ti Jiangsu, China 31°38N 119°2E 117 B12
...ti Zhejiang, China 28°28N 119°54E 117 C12
...nski I. U.S.A. 26°2N 174°0W 167 K5
...thansk = Lysychansk

Litchfield Minn., U.S.A. 45°8N 94°32W 172 C6
Litchfield △ Australia 13°14S 131°1E 148 B5
Liteni Romania 47°32N 26°32E 81 C11
Lithgow Australia 33°25S 150°8E 153 B9
Lithino, Akra Greece 34°55N 24°44E 101 E6
Lithuania ■ Europe 55°30N 24°0E 84 E2
Litija Slovenia 46°3N 14°50E 93 B11
Lititz U.S.A. 40°9N 76°18W 175 F8
Litochoro Greece 40°8N 22°34E 96 F6
Litoměřice Czech Rep. 50°33N 14°10E 78 A7
Litomyšl Czech Rep. 49°52N 16°20E 79 B9
Litschau Austria 48°58N 15°4E 78 C8
Little Abaco Bahamas 26°50N 77°30W 182 A4
Little Andaman I. India 10°45N 92°30E 127 J11
Little Aral Sea = Northern Aral Sea Kazakhstan 46°0N 60°30E 108 C6
Little Barrier I. N.Z. 36°12S 175°8E 154 B5
Little Basses Sri Lanka 6°24N 81°43E 127 L5
Little Belt Mts. U.S.A. 46°40N 110°45W 168 C8
Little Bighorn Battlefield △ U.S.A. 45°34N 107°25W 168 D10
Little Blue → U.S.A. 39°42N 96°41W 172 F5
Little Buffalo → Canada 61°0N 113°46W 162 A6
Little Cayman Cayman Is. 19°41N 80°3W 182 C3
Little Churchill → Canada 57°30N 95°22W 163 B9
Little Coco I. Burma 14°0N 93°13E 127 H11
Little Colorado → U.S.A. 36°12N 111°48W 169 H8
Little Current Canada 45°55N 82°0W 164 C3
Little Current → Canada 50°57N 84°36W 164 B3
Little Desert △ Australia 37°25S 141°30E 152 D4
Little Diomede I. U.S.A. 65°45N 168°56W 166 B6
Little Falls Minn., U.S.A. 45°59N 94°22W 172 C6
Little Falls N.Y., U.S.A. 43°3N 74°51W 175 C10
Little Fork → U.S.A. 48°31N 93°35W 172 A7
Little Grand Rapids Canada 52°0N 95°29W 163 C9
Little Humboldt → U.S.A. 41°1N 117°43W 168 F5
Little Inagua I. Bahamas 21°40N 73°50W 183 B5
Little Karoo S. Africa 33°45S 21°0E 144 D3
Little Khingan Mts. = Xiao Hinggan Ling China 49°0N 127°0E 111 B14
Little Lake U.S.A. 35°56N 117°55W 171 K9
Little Laut Is. = Laut Kecil, Kepulauan Indonesia 4°45S 115°40E 118 E5
Little Mecatina = Petit-Mécatina → Canada 50°40N 59°30W 165 B8
Little Minch U.K. 57°35N 6°45W 65 D2
Little Missouri → U.S.A. 47°36N 102°25W 172 B2
Little Nicobar India 7°20N 93°40E 127 L11
Little Ouse → U.K. 52°22N 1°12E 67 E9
Little Rann India 23°25N 71°25E 124 H4
Little Red → U.S.A. 35°11N 91°27W 176 D9
Little River N.Z. 43°45S 172°49E 155 D7
Little Rock U.S.A. 34°45N 92°17W 176 D8
Little Ruaha → Tanzania 7°57S 37°53E 142 D4
Little Sable Pt. U.S.A. 43°38N 86°33W 172 D10
Little Sioux → U.S.A. 41°48N 96°4W 172 E5
Little Smoky → Canada 54°44N 117°11W 162 C5
Little Snake → U.S.A. 40°27N 108°26W 168 F9
Little Tobago Trin. & Tob. 11°18N 60°30W 187 J16
Little Valley U.S.A. 42°15N 78°48W 174 D6
Little Wabash → U.S.A. 37°55N 88°5W 172 G9
Little White → U.S.A. 43°40N 100°40W 172 D3
Little Zab = Zāb aş Şaghīr → Iraq 35°17N 43°29E 105 E10
Littlefield U.S.A. 33°55N 102°20W 176 E3
Littlehampton U.K. 50°49N 0°32W 67 G7
Littleton U.S.A. 44°18N 71°46W 175 B13
Littoral □ Cameroon 4°0N 10°0E 139 E7
Litvinov Czech Rep. 50°36N 13°37E 78 A6
Liu He → China 40°55N 121°35E 115 D11
Liu Jiang → China 23°55N 109°30E 116 F7
Liuba China 33°38N 106°55E 114 A6
Liucheng China 24°38N 109°14E 116 E7
Liugou China 40°57N 118°15E 115 D10
Liuhe China 42°17N 125°43E 115 C13
Liuheng Dao China 29°40N 122°5E 117 C14
Liujiang China 24°26N 109°11E 116 E7
Liukang Tenggaja = Sabalana, Kepulauan Indonesia 6°45S 118°50E 119 F5
Liuli Tanzania 11°3S 34°38E 143 E3
Liupan Shan China 35°39N 106°12E 114 G4
Liupanshui China 26°38N 104°48E 116 D5
Liuwa Plain Zambia 14°20S 22°30E 143 E1
Liuyang China 28°10N 113°37E 117 C9
Liuzhou China 24°22N 109°22E 116 E7
Liuzhuang China 33°12N 120°18E 115 H11
Livada Romania 47°52N 23°5E 80 C8
Livadero Greece 40°2N 21°57E 96 F5
Livadhia Cyprus 34°57N 33°38E 101 E12
Livadi Greece 40°0N 22°9E 98 A4
Livarot France 48°58N 0°9E 70 D7
Live Oak Calif., U.S.A. 39°17N 121°40W 170 F5
Live Oak Fla., U.S.A. 30°18N 82°59W 179 F7
Lively Canada 46°26N 81°9W 173 B13
Liveras Cyprus 35°23N 32°57E 101 D11
Livermore, Mt. U.S.A. 30°38N 104°11W 176 F2
Livermore Falls U.S.A. 44°29N 70°11W 173 C18
Liverpool Australia 33°54S 150°58E 153 B9
Liverpool Canada 44°5N 64°41W 165 D7
Liverpool U.K. 53°25N 3°0W 66 D4
Liverpool Bay U.K. 53°30N 3°20W 66 D4
Liverpool Plains Australia 31°15S 150°15E 153 A9
Liverpool Ra. Australia 31°50S 150°30E 153 A9
Livigno Italy 46°35N 10°10E 92 B7
Livingston Guatemala 15°50N 88°50W 182 C2
Livingston U.K. 55°54N 3°30W 65 F5

Livingston Ala., U.S.A. 32°35N 88°11W 177 E10
Livingston Calif., U.S.A. 37°23N 120°43W 170 H6
Livingston Mont., U.S.A. 45°40N 110°34W 168 D8
Livingston S.C., U.S.A. 33°38N 81°7W 178 D6
Livingston Tenn., U.S.A. 35°23N 85°19W 177 C12
Livingston Tex., U.S.A. 30°43N 94°56W 176 F7
Livingston, L., U.S.A. 30°50N 95°10W 176 F7
Livingston Manor U.S.A. 41°54N 74°50W 175 E10
Livingstone Zambia 17°46S 25°52E 143 F2
Livingstone △ Australia 35°22S 147°22E 153 C7
Livingstone Mts. N.Z. 45°15S 168°9E 155 F3
Livingstone Mts. Tanzania 9°40S 34°20E 143 D3
Livingstonia Malawi 10°38S 34°5E 143 E3
Livno Bos.-H. 43°50N 17°1E 80 G2
Livny Russia 52°30N 37°30E 85 F9
Livonia Mich., U.S.A. 42°23N 83°23W 173 D12
Livonia N.Y., U.S.A. 42°49N 77°40W 174 D7
Livorno Italy 43°33N 10°19E 92 E7
Livramento Brazil 30°55S 55°30W 191 C4
Livramento do Brumado Brazil 13°39S 41°50W 189 C2
Livron-sur-Drôme France 44°46N 4°51E 73 D8
Livyntsi Ukraine 48°25N 26°37E 81 B11
Liwale Tanzania 9°48S 37°58E 143 D4
Liwiec → Poland 52°36N 21°34E 83 F8
Liwonde Malawi 15°4S 35°13E 143 F4
Liwonde △ Malawi 14°48S 35°20E 143 E4
Lixi China 26°23N 101°59E 116 D3
Lixian China 31°23N 103°13E 116 B4
Lixin China 33°8N 116°13E 117 A11
Lixouri Greece 38°12N 20°26E 98 C2
Liyang China 31°26N 119°28E 117 B12
Lizard I. Australia 14°42S 145°30E 150 A4
Lizard Pt. U.K. 49°57N 5°13W 67 H2
Lizarra = Estella Spain 42°40N 2°2W 92 D2
Lizella U.S.A. 32°48N 83°49W 178 C6
Lizzano Italy 40°23N 17°27E 95 B10
Ljig Serbia 44°13N 20°18E 96 B4
Ljubija Bos.-H. 44°55N 16°35E 93 D13
Ljubinje Bos.-H. 42°58N 18°5E 96 D2
Ljubišnja Europe 43°18N 19°6E 96 C3
Ljubljana Slovenia 46°4N 14°33E 93 B11
Ljubljana ✈ (LJU) Slovenia 46°14N 14°33E 93 B11
Ljubno Slovenia 46°25N 14°46E 93 B11
Ljubovija Serbia 44°11N 19°22E 96 B3
Ljugarn Sweden 57°20N 18°43E 63 G12
Ljung Sweden 57°59N 13°3E 63 G7
Ljungan → Sweden 62°18N 17°23E 62 B11
Ljungaverk Sweden 62°30N 16°5E 62 B10
Ljungby Sweden 56°49N 13°55E 63 H7
Ljungbyholm Sweden 56°39N 16°5E 63 H10
Ljungdalen Sweden 62°51N 12°47E 62 B6
Ljungsbro Sweden 58°31N 15°30E 63 D9
Ljungskile Sweden 58°14N 11°55E 63 F5
Ljusdal Sweden 61°46N 16°3E 62 C10
Ljusfallshammar Sweden 58°48N 15°30E 63 F9
Ljusnan → Sweden 61°12N 17°8E 62 C11
Ljusne Sweden 61°13N 17°7E 62 C11
Ljusterö Sweden 59°31N 18°37E 62 E12
Ljustorp Sweden 62°38N 17°19E 62 B11
Ljutomer Slovenia 46°31N 16°11E 93 B13
Llagostera Spain 41°50N 2°54E 90 D7
Llamellín Peru 9°0S 76°54W 188 B2
Llançà Spain 42°22N 3°9E 90 C8
Llancanelo, Salina Argentina 35°40S 69°8W 190 D2
Llandeilo U.K. 51°53N 3°59W 67 F4
Llandovery U.K. 51°59N 3°48W 67 F4
Llandrindod Wells U.K. 52°14N 3°22W 67 E4
Llandudno U.K. 53°19N 3°50W 66 D4
Llanelli U.K. 51°41N 4°10W 67 F3
Llanes Spain 43°25N 4°50W 88 B6
Llanfair-ym-Muallt = Builth Wells U.K. 52°9N 3°25W 67 E4
Llangollen U.K. 52°58N 3°11W 66 E4
Llanidloes U.K. 52°27N 3°31W 67 E4
Llano U.S.A. 30°45N 98°41W 176 F5
Llano → U.S.A. 30°39N 98°26W 176 F5
Llano Estacado U.S.A. 33°30N 103°0W 176 D3
Llanos S. Amer. 5°0N 71°35W 188 C4
Llanos de Challe △ Chile 28°8S 71°1W 190 B1
Llanquihue, L. Chile 41°10S 72°50W 192 B1
Llanwrtyd Wells U.K. 52°7N 3°38W 67 E4
Llata Peru 9°25S 76°47W 188 B2
Llebeig, C. des Spain 39°33N 2°18E 90 B9
Lleida Spain 41°37N 0°39E 90 D5
Lleida □ Spain 42°6N 1°0E 90 C6
Llentrisca, C. Spain 38°52N 1°15E 90 C7
Llera de Canales Mexico 23°19N 99°1W 181 C5
Llerena Spain 38°17N 6°0W 89 G5
Llica Bolivia 19°52S 68°16W 188 D4
Llico Chile 34°46S 72°5W 190 C1
Lliria Spain 39°37N 0°35W 91 F4
Llivia Spain 42°28N 1°59E 72 F5
Llobregat → Spain 41°19N 2°5E 90 D7
Llodio Spain 43°9N 2°58W 90 B2
Lloyd B. Australia 12°45S 143°27E 150 A3
Lloyd L. Canada 57°22N 108°57W 163 B7
Lloydminster Canada 53°17N 110°0W 163 C7
Llubí Spain 39°42N 3°0E 90 B10
Llucena del Cid Spain 40°9N 0°17W 90 E4
Llucmajor Spain 39°29N 2°53E 90 B9
Llullaillaco, Volcán S. Amer. 24°43S 68°30W 190 A2
Llullaillaco △ Chile 24°50S 68°51W 190 A2
Lo → Vietnam 21°18N 105°25E 120 B5
Loa U.S.A. 38°24N 111°39W 168 G8
Loa → Chile 21°26S 70°41W 190 A1
Loaita I. S. China Sea 10°41N 114°25E 118 B4
Loange → Dem. Rep. of the Congo 4°17S 20°2E 140 D4
Loano Italy 44°8N 8°14E 92 D5
Lobamba Swaziland 26°28S 31°12E 145 D5
Lobatse Botswana 25°12S 25°40E 144 D4
Löbau Germany 51°5N 14°40E 76 D10
Lobenstein Germany 50°25N 11°39E 76 E7
Loberia Argentina 38°10S 58°40W 190 D4
Łobez Poland 53°38N 15°39E 82 E2

Lobito Angola 12°18S 13°35E 141 G2
Lobo → Ivory C. 6°2N 6°45W 138 D3
Lobos Argentina 35°10S 59°0W 190 D4
Lobos, I. Mexico 27°20N 110°36W 180 B2
Lobos, I. de Canary Is. 28°45N 13°50W 100 F6
Lobos de Afuera, Islas Peru 6°57S 80°42W 188 B1
Lobos de Tierra, I. Peru 6°27S 80°52W 188 B1
Łobżenica Poland 53°18N 17°15E 83 E4
Loc Binh Vietnam 21°46N 106°54E 120 B6
Loc Ninh Vietnam 11°50N 106°34E 121 G6
Locarno Switz. 46°10N 8°47E 77 J4
Loch Garman = Wexford Ireland 52°20N 6°28W 64 D5
Loch Lomond and the Trossachs △ U.K. 56°10N 4°40W 65 E4
Lochaber U.K. 56°59N 5°1W 65 E3
Locharbriggs U.K. 55°7N 3°35W 65 F5
Lochboisdale U.K. 57°9N 7°20W 65 D1
Loche, L. La Canada 56°30N 109°30W 163 B7
Loches France 47°7N 1°0E 70 E7
Lochgilphead U.K. 56°2N 5°26W 65 E3
Lochinvar △ Zambia 15°55S 27°15E 143 F2
Lochinver U.K. 58°9N 5°14W 65 C3
Lochloosa L. U.S.A. 29°30N 82°7W 179 F7
Lochmaddy U.K. 57°36N 7°10W 65 D1
Lochnagar Australia 23°33S 145°38E 150 C4
Lochnagar U.K. 56°57N 3°15W 65 E5
Lochów Poland 52°33N 21°42E 83 F8
Lochy, L. U.K. 57°0N 4°53W 65 E4
Lock Australia 33°34S 135°46E 151 G2
Lock Haven U.S.A. 41°8N 77°28W 174 E7
Lockeford U.S.A. 38°10N 121°9W 170 G5
Lockeport Canada 43°47N 65°4W 165 D6
Lockerbie U.K. 55°7N 3°21W 65 F5
Lockhart Australia 35°14S 146°40E 153 C7
Lockhart U.S.A. 29°53N 97°40W 176 G6
Lockhart, L. Australia 33°15S 119°3E 149 F2
Lockhart River Australia 12°58S 143°30E 150 A3
Lockhart River ○ Australia 12°47S 143°20E 150 A3
Lockney U.S.A. 34°7N 101°27W 176 D4
Lockport U.S.A. 43°10N 78°42W 174 C6
Locminé France 47°54N 2°51W 70 E4
Locri Italy 38°14N 16°16E 95 D9
Locronan France 48°7N 4°15W 70 D2
Locust Grove U.S.A. 33°21N 84°7W 178 B5
Lod Israel 31°57N 34°54E 130 D3
Lodeinoye Pole Russia 60°44N 33°33E 84 B7
Lodève France 43°44N 3°19E 72 E7
Lodge Bay Canada 52°14N 55°51W 165 B8
Lodge Grass U.S.A. 45°19N 107°22W 168 D10
Lodhran Pakistan 29°32N 71°30E 124 E4
Lodi Italy 45°19N 9°30E 92 C6
Lodi Calif., U.S.A. 38°8N 121°16W 170 G5
Lodi Ohio, U.S.A. 41°2N 82°1W 174 E3
Lodja Dem. Rep. of the Congo 3°30S 23°23E 142 C1
Lodosa Spain 42°25N 2°4W 90 C2
Lödöse Sweden 58°2N 12°9E 63 F6
Lodwar Kenya 3°7N 35°36E 142 B4
Łódź Poland 51°45N 19°27E 83 G6
Łódzkie □ Poland 51°30N 19°30E 83 G6
Loei Thailand 17°29N 101°35E 120 D3
Loengo Dem. Rep. of the Congo 4°48S 26°30E 142 C2
Loeriesfontein S. Africa 31°0S 19°26E 144 D2
Lofa □ Liberia 6°35N 11°8W 138 D2
Lofa Mano → Liberia 7°55N 10°25W 138 D2
Lofer Austria 47°35N 12°41E 78 D5
Lofoten Norway 68°30N 13°59E 60 B16
Lofsdalen Sweden 62°10N 13°20E 62 B7
Lofsen → Sweden 62°7N 13°57E 62 B7
Loftahammar Sweden 57°54N 16°41E 63 G10
Loga Niger 13°40N 3°15E 139 C5
Logan Iowa, U.S.A. 41°39N 95°47W 172 E6
Logan Ohio, U.S.A. 39°32N 82°25W 173 F12
Logan Utah, U.S.A. 41°44N 111°50W 168 F8
Logan W. Va., U.S.A. 37°51N 81°59W 173 G13
Logan, Mt. Canada 60°34N 140°23W 160 E3
Logan Martin L. U.S.A. 33°26N 86°20W 178 B3
Logandale U.S.A. 36°36N 114°29W 171 J12
Logansport Ind., U.S.A. 40°45N 86°22W 172 E10
Logansport La., U.S.A. 31°58N 94°0W 176 F8
Loganville U.S.A. 33°50N 83°54W 178 B6
Logatec Slovenia 45°56N 14°15E 93 C11
Logodoro Italy 40°35N 8°45E 94 B1
Logone → Chad 12°6N 15°2E 135 F9
Logroño Spain 42°28N 2°27W 90 C2
Logrosán Spain 39°20N 5°32W 89 F5
Løgstør Denmark 56°58N 9°14E 63 H3
Løgten Denmark 56°23N 10°23E 63 H4
Løgumkloster Denmark 55°4N 8°57E 63 J2
Lohals Denmark 55°8N 10°55E 63 J4
Lohardaga India 23°27N 84°45E 125 H11
Loharia India 23°45N 74°14E 124 H6
Loharu India 28°27N 75°49E 124 E6
Lohja Finland 60°12N 24°5E 63 E21
Löhne Germany 52°12N 8°40E 76 C4
Lohr Germany 49°59N 9°35E 76 E5
Lohri Wah → Pakistan 27°27N 67°37E 124 F2
Loikaw Burma 19°40N 97°17E 123 K20
Loimaa Finland 60°50N 23°5E 63 E20
Loir → France 47°33N 0°32W 70 E6
Loir-et-Cher □ France 47°40N 1°20E 70 E8
Loire □ France 45°40N 4°5E 73 C8
Loire → France 47°16N 2°10W 70 E4
Loire-Anjou-Touraine △ France 47°14N 0°5W 70 E6
Loire-Atlantique □ France 47°25N 1°40W 70 E5
Loiret □ France 47°58N 2°10E 70 E5
Loitz Germany 53°58N 13°8E 76 B9
Loja Ecuador 3°59S 79°16W 188 A2
Loja Spain 37°10N 4°10W 89 H6
Loji = Kawasi Indonesia 1°38S 127°28E 119 E7
Lojo = Lohja Finland 60°12N 24°5E 63 E21
Løjt Kirkeby Denmark 55°7N 9°26E 63 J3
Lojung China 24°27N 109°36E 116 E7
Lokandu Dem. Rep. of the Congo 2°30S 25°45E 142 C2
Lokeren Belgium 51°6N 3°59E 69 C3
Lokgwabe Botswana 24°10S 21°50E 144 C3
Lokhvytsya Ukraine 50°25N 33°18E 85 G7
Lokichar Kenya 2°23N 35°39E 142 B4
Lokichokio Kenya 4°19N 34°13E 142 B3
Lokitaung Kenya 4°12N 35°48E 142 B4

Løkken Denmark 57°22N 9°41E 63 G3
Loknya Russia 56°49N 30°4E 84 D6
Loko Nigeria 8°1N 7°53E 139 D6
Lokoja Nigeria 7°47N 6°45E 139 D6
Lokolo → Dem. Rep. of the Congo 1°43S 18°23E 140 E3
Lokot Russia 52°31N 34°36E 85 F8
Lola Guinea 7°52N 8°29W 138 D3
Lola, Mt. U.S.A. 39°26N 120°22W 170 F6
Lolgorien Kenya 1°14S 34°48E 142 C3
Loliondo Tanzania 2°2S 35°39E 142 C4
Lolland Denmark 54°45N 11°30E 63 K5
Lollar Germany 50°37N 8°43E 76 E4
Lolo U.S.A. 46°45N 114°5W 168 C6
Lolodorf Cameroon 3°16N 10°49E 139 E7
Lom → Bulgaria 43°48N 23°12E 96 C7
Lom Bulgaria 43°45N 23°15E 96 C7
Lom Kao Thailand 16°53N 101°14E 120 D3
Lom Sak Thailand 16°47N 101°15E 120 D3
Loma U.S.A. 47°57N 110°30W 168 C8
Loma Linda U.S.A. 34°3N 117°16W 171 L9
Loma Mansa S. Leone 9°13N 11°7W 138 D2
Lomas, Mts. S. Leone 9°0N 11°0W 138 D2
Lomaloma Fiji 17°17S 178°59W 154 a
Lomami → Dem. Rep. of the Congo 0°46N 24°16E 142 B1
Lomas de Zamora Argentina 34°45S 58°24W 190 C4
Lombadina Australia 16°31S 122°54E 148 C3
Lombárdia □ Italy 45°40N 9°30E 92 C6
Lombardy = Lombárdia □ Italy 45°40N 9°30E 92 C6
Lombez France 43°29N 0°55E 72 E4
Lomblen Indonesia 8°30S 123°32E 119 F6
Lombok Indonesia 8°45S 116°30E 118 F5
Lombok, Selat Indonesia 8°30S 115°50E 119 K18
Lomé Togo 6°9N 1°20E 139 D5
Lomela Dem. Rep. of the Congo 2°19S 23°15E 140 E4
Lomela → Dem. Rep. of the Congo 0°15S 20°40E 140 E4
Lomianki Poland 52°21N 20°54E 83 F7
Lomma Sweden 55°43N 13°6E 63 J7
Lommel Belgium 51°14N 5°19E 69 C5
Lomond Canada 50°24N 112°36W 162 C6
Lomond, L. U.K. 56°8N 4°38W 65 E4
Lomonosov Ridge Arctic 88°0N 140°0E 54 A
Lomphat Cambodia 13°30N 106°59E 120 F6
Lompobatang Indonesia 5°24S 119°56E 119 F5
Lompoc U.S.A. 34°38N 120°28W 171 L6
Lomża Poland 53°10N 22°2E 83 E9
Lon, Ko Thailand 7°47N 98°23E 121 a
Lonavale India 18°46N 73°29E 124 F6
Loncoche Chile 39°20S 72°50W 192 A2
Loncopué Argentina 38°4S 70°37W 192 A2
Londa India 15°30N 74°30E 122 G2
Londiani Kenya 0°10S 35°33E 142 C4
Londinières France 49°50N 1°25E 70 D8
London Canada 42°59N 81°15W 174 D3
London U.K. 51°30N 0°3W 67 F7
London Ky., U.S.A. 37°8N 84°5W 173 G11
London Ohio, U.S.A. 39°53N 83°27W 173 F12
London, Greater □ U.K. 51°36N 0°5W 67 F7
London Gateway U.K. 51°31N 0°29E 67 F8
London Gatwick ✈ (LGW) U.K. 51°10N 0°11W 67 F7
London Heathrow ✈ (LHR) U.K. 51°28N 0°27W 67 F7
London Stansted ✈ (STN) U.K. 51°54N 0°14E 67 F8
Londonderry U.K. 55°0N 7°20W 64 B4
Londonderry □ U.K. 55°0N 7°20W 64 B4
Londonderry, C. Australia 13°45S 126°55E 148 B4
Londonderry, I. Chile 55°0S 71°0W 192 L2
Londres Argentina 27°43S 67°7W 190 B2
Londrina Brazil 23°18S 51°10W 191 A5
Lone Pine U.S.A. 36°36N 118°4W 170 J8
Lonely Mine Zimbabwe 19°30S 28°49E 145 A4
Long B. U.S.A. 33°35N 78°45W 177 E11
Long Beach Calif., U.S.A. 33°46N 118°11W 171 M8
Long Beach N.Y., U.S.A. 40°35N 73°39W 175 F11
Long Beach Wash., U.S.A. 46°21N 124°3W 170 D2
Long Branch U.S.A. 40°18N 74°0W 175 F11
Long Creek U.S.A. 44°43N 119°6W 168 D4
Long Eaton U.K. 52°53N 1°15W 66 E6
Long I. Australia 20°22S 148°51E 150 b
Long I. Bahamas 23°20N 75°10W 183 B4
Long I. Canada 54°50N 79°20W 164 B4
Long I. Ireland 51°30N 9°34W 64 E2
Long I. U.S.A. 40°45N 73°30W 175 F11
Long Island Sd. U.S.A. 41°10N 73°0W 175 E12
Long L. Canada 49°30N 86°50W 164 C2
Long L. U.S.A. 44°0N 74°25W 175 C10
Long Lake U.S.A. 43°58N 74°25W 175 C10
Long Point B. Canada 42°40N 80°10W 174 D4
Long Prairie U.S.A. 45°59N 94°52W 172 C6
Long Prairie → U.S.A. 46°20N 94°36W 172 B6
Long Pt. Ont., Canada 42°35N 80°2W 174 D4
Long Pt. Ont., Canada 42°40N 80°10W 174 D4
Long Pt. N.Z. 46°34S 169°36E 155 G4
Long Range Mts. Canada 49°30N 57°30W 165 C8
Long Reef Australia 14°1S 125°48E 148 B4
Long Sault Canada 45°2N 74°53W 175 A10
Long Str. = Longa, Proliv Russia 70°0N 175°0E 107 C18
Long Thanh Vietnam 10°47N 106°57E 121 G6
Long Xian China 34°55N 106°55E 114 G4
Long Xuyen Vietnam 10°19N 105°28E 121 G5
Longa, Proliv Russia 70°0N 175°0E 107 C18
Long'an China 23°10N 107°40E 116 F6
Longarone Italy 46°16N 12°18E 93 B9
Longbenton U.K. 55°1N 1°31W 66 B6
Longboat Key U.S.A. 27°23N 82°39W 179 H7
Longburn N.Z. 40°23S 175°35E 154 D6
Longchang China 29°18N 105°15E 116 C5
Longchuan Guangdong, China 24°5N 115°17E 117 E10
Longchuan Yunnan, China 24°27N 97°58E 116 E1
Longde China 35°30N 106°20E 114 G4
Longeau-Percey France 47°47N 5°20E 71 E12
Longford Australia 41°32S 147°3E 153 G4
Longford Ireland 53°43N 7°49W 64 C4
Longford □ Ireland 53°42N 7°45W 64 C4

Longfort, An = Longford Ireland 53°43N 7°49W 64 C4
Longhai China 24°25N 117°46E 117 E11
Longhua Guangdong, China 22°39N 114°0E 111 a
Longhua Hebei, China 41°18N 117°45E 115 D9
Longido Tanzania 2°43S 36°42E 142 C4
Longiram Indonesia 0°5S 115°45E 118 E5
Longjing China 42°46N 129°25E 115 C15
Longkou Jiangxi, China 26°8N 115°10E 117 D10
Longkou Shandong, China 37°40N 120°18E 115 F11
Longlac Canada 49°45N 86°25W 164 C2
Longli China 26°25N 106°58E 116 D6
Longlin China 24°47N 105°20E 116 E5
Longling China 24°37N 98°39E 116 E2
Longmeadow U.S.A. 42°3N 72°34W 175 D12
Longmen China 23°40N 114°18E 117 F10
Longmen Shiku China 34°28N 112°28E 114 G7
Longming China 22°59N 107°7E 116 F6
Longmont U.S.A. 40°10N 105°6W 168 F11
Longnawan Indonesia 1°51N 114°55E 118 D4
Longobucco Italy 39°27N 16°37E 95 C9
Longquan China 28°7N 119°10E 117 C12
Longreach Australia 23°28S 144°14E 150 C3
Longshan China 29°29N 109°25E 116 C7
Longsheng China 25°48N 110°0E 117 E8
Longtan China 25°5N 107°0E 116 E6
Longtan Shuiku China 25°10N 106°50E 116 E6
Longué-Jumelles France 47°22N 0°8W 70 E6
Longueau France 49°52N 2°21E 71 C9
Longueuil Canada 45°31N 73°29W 175 A11
Longuyon France 49°27N 5°35E 71 C12
Longvic France 47°17N 5°4E 71 E12
Longview Wash., U.S.A. 46°8N 122°57W 170 D4
Longwood U.S.A. 28°42N 81°21W 179 G8
Longwy France 49°30N 5°46E 71 C12
Longxi China 34°53N 104°40E 114 G3
Longxue Dao China 22°41N 113°38E 111 a
Longyan China 25°10N 117°0E 117 E11
Longyearbyen Svalbard 78°13N 15°40E 54 B8
Longyou China 29°1N 119°8E 117 C12
Longzhou China 22°22N 106°50E 116 F6
Lonigo Italy 45°23N 11°23E 93 C8
Löningen Germany 52°44N 7°46E 76 C3
Lonja → Croatia 45°22N 16°40E 93 C13
Lonoke U.S.A. 34°47N 91°54W 176 D9
Lonquimay Chile 38°26S 71°14W 192 A2
Lons-le-Saunier France 46°40N 5°31E 71 F12
Lönsboda Sweden 56°24N 14°19E 63 H8
Looe U.K. 50°22N 4°28W 67 G3
Lookout, C. Canada 55°18N 83°56W 164 A3
Lookout, C. U.S.A. 34°35N 76°32W 177 D16
Loolmalasin Tanzania 3°0S 35°53E 142 C4
Loon → Alta., Canada 57°8N 115°3W 162 B5
Loon → Man., Canada 55°53N 101°59W 163 B8
Loon Lake Canada 54°2N 109°10W 163 C7
Loongana Australia 30°52S 127°5E 149 F4
Loop Hd. Ireland 52°34N 9°56W 64 D2
Lop Ireland 52°33N 9°56W 64 D2
Lop Nor = Lop Nur China 40°20N 90°10E 109 D12
Lop Nur China 40°20N 90°10E 109 D12
Lopare Bos.-H. 44°39N 18°46E 80 F3
Lopatin Russia 43°50N 47°35E 87 J8
Lopatina, Gora Russia 50°47N 143°10E 107 D15
Lopatka, Mys Russia 50°52N 156°40E 107 D16
Lopburi Thailand 14°48N 100°37E 120 E3
Lopez U.S.A. 41°27N 76°20W 175 E8
Lopez, C. Gabon 0°47S 8°40E 140 E1
Lopphavet Norway 70°27N 21°15E 60 A19
Lora → Afghan. 31°35N 66°32E 122 D4
Lora, Hämün-i- Pakistan 29°38N 64°58E 122 E4
Lora Cr. → Australia 28°10S 135°22E 151 D2
Lora del Rio Spain 37°39N 5°33W 89 H5
Lorain U.S.A. 41°28N 82°11W 174 E2
Loralai Pakistan 30°20N 68°41E 124 D3
Lorca Spain 37°41N 1°42W 91 H3
Lord Howe I. Pac. Oc. 31°33S 159°6E 147 E8
Lord Howe Rise Pac. Oc. 30°0S 162°30E 156 L8
Lord Loughborough I. Burma 10°25N 97°54E 121 G1
Lordsburg U.S.A. 32°21N 108°43W 169 K9
Lorestān □ Iran 33°30N 48°40E 129 C6
Loreto Brazil 7°5S 45°10W 189 B1
Loreto Italy 43°26N 13°36E 93 E10
Loreto Mexico 26°0N 111°21W 180 B2
Lorgues France 43°28N 6°22E 73 E10
Lorhosso = Loropéni Burkina Faso 10°17N 3°38W 138 C4
Lorient France 47°45N 3°23W 70 E3
Lőrinci Hungary 47°44N 19°41E 80 C4
Lormi India 22°17N 81°41E 125 H9
Lorn U.K. 56°26N 5°10W 65 E3
Lorn, Firth of U.K. 56°20N 5°40W 65 E3
Lorne Australia 38°33S 143°59E 152 E5
Loropéni Burkina Faso 10°17N 3°38W 138 C4
Lorovouno Cyprus 35°8N 32°36E 101 D11
Lörrach Germany 47°36N 7°40E 77 H3
Lorraine □ France 48°53N 6°0E 71 D13
Lorraine △ France 48°55N 5°50E 71 D12

Los Sweden 61°45N 15°10E 62 C9
Los, Îles de Guinea 9°30N 13°50W 138 D2
Los Alamos Calif., U.S.A. 34°44N 120°17W 171 L6
Los Alamos N. Mex., U.S.A. 35°53N 106°19W 169 J10
Los Alerces △ Argentina 42°55S 71°55W 192 B2
Los Altos U.S.A. 37°23N 122°7W 170 H4
Los Andes Chile 32°50S 70°40W 190 C1
Los Angeles Chile 37°28S 72°23W 190 D1
Los Angeles U.S.A. 34°4N 118°15W 171 M8
Los Angeles Aqueduct U.S.A. 35°22N 118°5W 171 K9
Los Angeles Int. ✈ (LAX) U.S.A. 33°57N 118°25W 171 M8
Los Antiguos Argentina 46°35S 71°0W 192 C2
Los Banos U.S.A. 37°4N 120°51W 170 H6
Los Barrios Spain 36°11N 5°30W 89 J5
Los Blancos Argentina 23°40S 62°30W 190 A3
Los Cabos Int. ✈ (SJD) Mexico 23°9N 109°43W 180 C3

Los Cardones △ Argentina 25°8S 65°55W 190 B2
Los Chiles Costa Rica 11°2N 84°43W 182 D3
Los Corrales de Buelna Spain 43°16N 4°4W 88 B6
Los Cristianos Canary Is. 28°3N 16°42W 100 F3
Los Gallardos Spain 37°10N 1°57W 91 H3
Los Gatos U.S.A. 37°14N 121°59W 170 H5
Los Glaciares △ Argentina 50°0S 73°55W 192 C2
Los Haïtises △ Dom. Rep. 19°4N 69°36W 183 C6
Los Hermanos, Is. Venezuela 11°45N 64°25W 183 D7
Los Huemules △ Chile 46°10S 73°23W 192 C2
Los Islotes Canary Is. 29°4N 13°44W 100 E6
Los Lagos Chile 39°51S 72°50W 192 A2
Los Llanos de Aridane Canary Is. 28°38N 17°54W 100 F2
Los Loros Chile 27°50S 70°6W 190 B1
Los Lunas U.S.A. 34°48N 106°44W 169 J10
Los Menucos Argentina 40°50S 68°10W 192 B3
Los Mochis Mexico 25°45N 108°57W 180 B3
Los Monegros Spain 41°29N 0°13W 90 D4
Los Monos Argentina 46°1S 69°36W 192 C3
Los Muermos Chile 41°24S 73°29W 192 B2
Los Nietos Spain 37°39N 0°47W 91 H4
Los Olivos U.S.A. 34°40N 120°7W 171 L6
Los Palacios Cuba 22°35N 83°15W 182 B3
Los Palacios y Villafranca Spain 37°10N 5°55W 89 H5
Los Queñes Chile 35°1S 70°48W 190 D1
Los Reyes de Salgado Mexico 19°35N 102°29W 180 D4
Los Roques, Is. Venezuela 11°50N 66°45W 183 D6
Los Santos de Maimona Spain 38°27N 6°22W 89 G4
Los Teques Venezuela 10°21N 67°2W 186 A5
Los Testigos, Is. Venezuela 11°23N 63°6W 186 A6
Los Vilos Chile 32°10S 71°30W 190 C1
Los Yébenes Spain 39°36N 3°55W 89 F7
Łosice Poland 52°13N 22°43E 83 F9
Lošinj Croatia 44°30N 14°30E 93 D11
Loskop Dam S. Africa 25°23S 29°20E 145 C4
Løsning Denmark 55°48N 9°42E 63 J3
Lossiemouth U.K. 57°42N 3°17W 65 D5
Lossnen Sweden 62°26N 12°45E 62 B6
Lostwithiel U.K. 50°24N 4°41W 67 G3
Lot □ France 44°39N 1°40E 72 D5
Lot → France 44°18N 0°20E 72 D4
Lot-et-Garonne □ France 44°22N 0°30E 72 D4
Lota Chile 37°5S 73°10W 190 D1
Lotagipi Swamp Kenya 4°36N 34°55E 142 B3
Lotfābād Iran 37°32N 59°20E 129 B8
Lothair S. Africa 26°22S 30°27E 145 C5
Lotorp Sweden 58°44N 15°50E 63 F9
Lötschbergtunnel Switz. 46°26N 7°43E 77 J3
Lotta → Europe 68°42N 31°6E 60 B24
Lottefors Sweden 61°25N 16°24E 62 C10
Löttorp Sweden 57°10N 17°0E 63 G11
Lotung Taiwan 24°41N 121°46E 117 E13
Loubomo Congo 4°9S 12°47E 140 E2
Loudéac France 48°11N 2°47W 70 D4
Loudi China 27°42N 111°59E 117 D8
Loudonville U.S.A. 40°38N 82°14W 174 F2
Loudun France 47°3N 0°5E 70 E7
Loue → France 47°1N 5°28E 71 E12
Louga Senegal 15°45N 16°5W 138 B1
Louga □ Senegal 15°20N 15°35W 138 B1
Loughborough U.K. 52°47N 1°11W 66 E6
Lougheed I. Canada 77°26N 105°6W 161 B10
Loughman U.S.A. 28°14N 81°34W 179 G8
Loughrea Ireland 53°12N 8°33W 64 C3
Loughros More B. Ireland 54°48N 8°32W 64 B3
Louhans France 46°38N 5°12E 71 F12
Louis Trichardt S. Africa 23°1S 29°43E 145 B4
Louis XIV, Pte. Canada 54°37N 79°45W 164 B4
Louisa U.S.A. 38°7N 82°36W 173 F12
Louisbourg Canada 45°55N 60°0W 165 C8
Louisburgh Ireland 53°46N 9°49W 64 C2
Louise I. Canada 52°55N 131°50W 162 C2
Louiseville Canada 46°20N 72°56W 164 C5
Louisiade Arch. Papua N. G. 11°10S 153°0E 147 C8
Louisiana U.S.A. 39°27N 91°3W 172 F8
Louisiana □ U.S.A. 30°50N 92°0W 176 F9
Louisville Ala., U.S.A. 31°47N 85°33W 178 D4
Louisville Ga., U.S.A. 33°0N 82°25W 178 B7
Louisville Ky., U.S.A. 38°15N 85°46W 173 F11
Louisville Miss., U.S.A. 33°7N 89°3W 177 E10
Louisville Ohio, U.S.A. 40°50N 81°16W 174 F3
Louisville Ridge Pac. Oc. 31°0S 172°30W 156 L10
Loulay France 46°3N 0°30W 72 B3
Loulé Portugal 37°9N 8°0W 89 H3
Loulouni Mali 10°54N 5°36W 138 C3
Loum Cameroon 4°42N 9°44E 139 E6
Louny Czech Rep. 50°20N 13°48E 78 A6
Loup City U.S.A. 41°17N 98°58W 172 E4
Loups Marins, Lacs des Canada 56°30N 73°45W 164 A5
Lourdes France 43°6N 0°3W 72 E3
Lourdes-de-Blanc-Sablon Canada 51°24N 57°12W 165 B8
Lourinhã Portugal 39°14N 9°17W 89 F1
Louroujina Cyprus 35°0N 33°28E 101 E12
Lousã Portugal 40°7N 8°14W 88 E2
Louta Burkina Faso 13°30N 3°10W 138 C4
Louth Australia 30°30S 145°8E 153 B6
Louth Ireland 53°58N 6°32W 64 C5
Louth U.K. 53°22N 0°1W 66 D7
Louth □ Ireland 53°56N 6°34W 64 C5
Loutra Edipsou Greece 38°54N 23°2E 98 C5
Loutraki Greece 37°58N 22°57E 98 D4
Loutropoli Thermis Greece 39°11N 26°29E 99 B8
Louvain = Leuven Belgium 50°52N 4°42E 69 D4
Louvale U.S.A. 32°10N 84°50W 178 C5
Louviers France 49°12N 1°10E 70 C8
Louwsburg S. Africa 27°37S 31°7E 145 C5
Lovat → Russia 58°14N 31°28E 84 C6
Lovćen Montenegro 42°23N 18°51E 96 D2
Lovćen △ Montenegro 42°20N 18°50E 96 D2
Lovech Bulgaria 43°8N 24°42E 97 C8
Lovech □ Bulgaria 43°0N 24°45E 97 D8
Loveland U.S.A. 40°24N 105°5W 168 F11
Lovell U.S.A. 44°50N 108°24W 168 D9
Lovelock U.S.A. 40°11N 118°28W 168 F4
Lövere Italy 45°49N 10°4E 92 C7
Lövestad Sweden 55°40N 13°54E 63 J7
Loviisa Finland 60°28N 26°12E 84 B4
Lovina Indonesia 8°9S 115°1E 119 J18
Loving U.S.A. 32°17N 104°6W 169 K11
Lovington U.S.A. 32°57N 103°21W 169 K12
Lovisa = Loviisa Finland 60°28N 26°12E 84 B4
Lovosice Czech Rep. 50°30N 14°2E 78 A7
Lovran Croatia 45°18N 14°15E 93 C11
Lovrin Romania 45°58N 20°48E 80 E5
Lövstabruk Sweden 60°25N 17°53E 62 D11
Lövstabukten Sweden 60°35N 17°45E 62 D11
Low, L. Canada 52°29N 76°17W 164 B4
Low Pt. Australia 32°25S 127°25E 149 F4
Low Tatra = Nízké Tatry Slovak Rep. 48°55N 19°30E 79 C12
Lowa Dem. Rep. of the Congo 1°25S 25°47E 142 C2
Lowa → Dem. Rep. of the Congo 1°24S 25°51E 142 C2
Lowell U.S.A. 42°38N 71°19W 175 D13
Lowellville U.S.A. 41°2N 80°32W 174 E4
Löwen → Namibia 26°51S 18°17E 144 C2
Lower Alkali L. U.S.A. 41°16N 120°2W 168 F3
Lower Arrow L. Canada 49°40N 118°5W 162 D5
Lower Austria = Niederösterreich □ Austria 48°25N 15°40E 78 C8
Lower California = Baja California Mexico 31°10N 115°12W 180 A1
Lower Glenelg △ Australia 38°4S 141°41E 152 E4
Lower Hutt N.Z. 41°10S 174°55E 154 H3
Lower Lake U.S.A. 38°55N 122°37W 170 G4
Lower Manitou L. Canada 49°15N 93°0W 163 D10
Lower Post Canada 59°58N 128°30W 162 B3
Lower Red L. U.S.A. 47°58N 95°0W 172 B6
Lower Saxony = Niedersachsen □ Germany 52°50N 9°0E 76 C4
Lower Tunguska = Tunguska, Nizhnyaya → Russia 65°48N 88°4E 107 C9
Lower Zambezi △ Zambia 15°25S 29°40E 143 F2
Lowestoft U.K. 52°29N 1°45E 67 E9
Lowgar □ Afghan. 34°0N 69°0E 122 B6
Łowicz Poland 52°6N 19°55E 83 F6
Lowly, Pt. Australia 33°0S 137°46E 152 B2
Lowther I. Canada 74°33N 97°30W 161 C12
Lowville U.S.A. 43°47N 75°29W 175 C9
Loxton Australia 34°28S 140°31E 152 C4
Loxton S. Africa 31°30S 22°22E 144 D3
Loyalton U.S.A. 39°41N 120°14W 170 F6
Loyalty Is. = Loyauté, Îs. N. Cal. 20°50S 166°30E 147 D9
Loyang = Luoyang China 34°40N 112°26E 114 G7
Loyauté, Îs. N. Cal. 20°50S 166°30E 147 D9
Loyev = Loyew Belarus 51°56N 30°46E 75 C16
Loyew Belarus 51°56N 30°46E 75 C16
Loyoro Uganda 3°22N 34°14E 142 B3
Lož Slovenia 45°43N 14°30E 93 C11
Lozère □ France 44°35N 3°30E 72 D7
Loznica Serbia 44°32N 19°12E 96 B3
Lozova Ukraine 49°0N 36°20E 85 H9
Ltalaltuma ☼ Australia 23°57S 132°25E 148 D5
Lü Shan China 29°30N 115°55E 117 C10
Lü Shan △ China 29°26N 115°52E 117 C10
Lu Wo China 22°33N 114°6E 111 a
Luachimo Angola 7°23S 20°48E 140 F4
Luajan → India 24°44N 85°1E 125 G11
Lualaba → Dem. Rep. of the Congo 0°26N 25°20E 142 B2
Luambe △ Zambia 12°30S 32°15E 143 E3
Luampa Zambia 15°4S 24°20E 143 F1
Lu'an China 31°45N 116°29E 117 B11
Luan Chau Vietnam 21°38N 103°24E 116 G4
Luan He → China 39°20N 119°5E 115 E10
Luan Xian China 39°40N 118°40E 115 E10
Luancheng Guangxi Zhuangzu, China 22°48N 108°55E 116 F7
Luancheng Hebei, China 37°53N 114°40E 114 F8
Luanco Spain 43°37N 5°48W 88 B5
Luanda Angola 8°50S 13°15E 140 F2
Luang, Doi Thailand 18°30N 101°15E 120 C3
Luang, Thale Thailand 7°30N 100°15E 121 J3
Luang Nam Tha Laos 20°58N 101°30E 116 G3
Luang Prabang Laos 19°52N 102°10E 116 H4
Luangwa Zambia 15°35S 30°16E 143 F3
Luangwa → Zambia 14°25S 30°25E 143 E3
Luangwa Valley Zambia 13°30S 31°30E 143 E3
Luangwe = Loange → Dem. Rep. of the Congo 4°17S 20°2E 140 E4
Luanne China 40°55N 117°40E 115 D9
Luanping China 40°53N 117°23E 115 D9
Luanshya Zambia 13°3S 28°28E 143 E2
Luapula □ Zambia 11°0S 29°0E 143 E2
Luapula → Africa 9°26S 28°33E 143 D2
Luarca Spain 43°32N 6°32W 88 B4
Luashi Dem. Rep. of the Congo 10°50S 23°36E 143 E1
Luau Angola 10°40S 22°10E 140 G4
Lubaczów Poland 50°10N 23°8E 83 H10
Lubań Poland 51°5N 15°15E 83 G2
Lubana, Ozero = Lubānas Ezers Latvia 56°45N 27°0E 84 D4
Lubānas Ezers Latvia 56°45N 27°0E 84 D4
Lubang Is. Phil. 13°50N 120°12E 119 B6
Lubango Angola 14°55S 13°30E 141 G2
Lubao Dem. Rep. of the Congo 5°17S 25°42E 142 D2
Lubartów Poland 51°28N 22°42E 83 G9
Lubawa Poland 53°30N 19°48E 82 E6
Lübbecke Germany 52°18N 8°37E 76 C4
Lübben Germany 51°56N 13°54E 76 D9
Lübbenau Germany 51°52N 13°57E 76 D9
Lubbock U.S.A. 33°35N 101°51W 176 E4
Lübeck Germany 53°52N 10°40E 76 B6
Lübecker Bucht Germany 54°3N 10°54E 76 A6
Lubefu Dem. Rep. of the Congo 4°47S 24°27E 142 C1
Lubefu → Dem. Rep. of the Congo 4°10S 23°0E 142 C1
Lubelskie □ Poland 51°20N 22°50E 83 G9
Lubero = Luofu Dem. Rep. of the Congo 0°10S 29°15E 142 C2
Luberon △ France 43°52N 5°25E 73 E9
Lubersac France 45°26N 1°23E 72 C5
Lubicon L. Canada 56°23N 115°56W 162 B5
Lubień Kujawski Poland 52°23N 19°9E 83 F6
Lubilash → Dem. Rep. of the Congo 6°2S 23°45E 140 F4
Lubin Poland 51°24N 16°11E 83 G3
Lublin Poland 51°12N 22°38E 83 G9
Lubliniec Poland 50°43N 18°45E 83 H5
Lubnān = Lebanon ■ Asia 34°0N 36°0E 130 B5
Lubnān, Jabal Lebanon 33°45N 35°40E 130 B4
Lubniewice Poland 52°31N 15°15E 83 F2
Lubny Ukraine 50°3N 32°58E 85 G7
Lubomierz Poland 51°1N 15°31E 83 G2
Luboń Poland 52°21N 16°51E 83 F3
Lubongola Dem. Rep. of the Congo 2°35S 27°50E 142 C2
L'ubotín Slovak Rep. 49°17N 20°53E 79 B13
Lubraniec Poland 52°33N 18°50E 83 F5
Lubsko Poland 51°45N 14°57E 83 G1
Lübtheen Germany 53°18N 11°5E 76 B7
Lubudi Dem. Rep. of the Congo 9°57S 25°58E 140 F5
Lubudi → Dem. Rep. of the Congo 9°0S 25°35E 143 D2
Lubuklinggau Indonesia 3°15S 102°55E 118 E2
Lubuksikaping Indonesia 0°10N 100°15E 118 D2
Lubumbashi Dem. Rep. of the Congo 11°40S 27°28E 143 E2
Lubunda Dem. Rep. of the Congo 5°12S 26°41E 142 D2
Lubungu Zambia 14°35S 26°24E 143 E2
Lubuskie □ Poland 52°10N 15°20E 83 F2
Lubutu Dem. Rep. of the Congo 0°45S 26°30E 142 C2
Luc-en-Diois France 44°36N 5°28E 73 D9
Lucan Canada 43°11N 81°24W 174 C3
Lucan Ireland 53°22N 6°28W 64 C5
Lucania, Mt. Canada 61°1N 140°27W 160 E3
Lucas Channel = Main Channel Canada 45°21N 81°45W 174 A3
Lucca Italy 43°50N 10°29E 92 E7
Lucé France 48°26N 1°27E 70 D8
Luce Bay U.K. 54°45N 4°48W 65 G4
Lucea Jamaica 18°27N 78°10W 182 a
Lucedale U.S.A. 30°56N 88°35W 177 F10
Lucena Phil. 13°56N 121°37E 119 B6
Lucena Spain 37°27N 4°31W 89 H6
Lučenec Slovak Rep. 48°18N 19°42E 79 C12
Lucera Italy 41°30N 15°20E 95 A8
Lucerne = Luzern Switz. 47°3N 8°18E 77 H4
Lucerne U.S.A. 39°6N 122°48W 170 F4
Lucerne Valley U.S.A. 34°27N 116°57W 171 L10
Luchena → Spain 37°44N 1°50W 91 H3
Lucheng China 36°20N 113°11E 114 F7
Lucheringo → Mozam. 11°43S 36°17E 143 E4
Lüchow Germany 52°58N 11°8E 76 C7
Luchuan China 22°21N 110°12E 117 F8
Lucia U.S.A. 36°2N 121°33W 170 J5
Lucinda Australia 18°32S 146°20E 150 B4
Lucindale Australia 36°58S 140°26E 152 D4
Luckau Germany 51°50N 13°42E 76 D9
Luckenwalde Germany 52°5N 13°10E 76 C9
Luckhoff S. Africa 29°44S 24°43E 144 C3
Lucknow Canada 43°57N 81°31W 174 C3
Lucknow India 26°50N 81°0E 125 F9
Luçon France 46°28N 1°10W 72 B2
Lüda = Dalian China 38°50N 121°40E 115 E11
Luda Kamchiya → Bulgaria 43°3N 27°29E 97 C11
Ludbreg Croatia 46°15N 16°38E 93 B13
Lüdenscheid Germany 51°13N 7°37E 76 D3
Lüderitz Namibia 26°41S 15°8E 144 C2
Lüderitzbaai Namibia 26°36S 15°8E 144 C2
Ludhiana India 30°57N 75°56E 124 D6
Ludian China 27°10N 103°33E 116 D4
Luding Qiao China 29°53N 102°12E 116 C4
Lüdinghausen Germany 51°46N 7°27E 76 D3
Ludington U.S.A. 43°57N 86°27W 172 D10
Ludlow U.K. 52°22N 2°42W 67 E5
Ludlow Calif., U.S.A. 34°43N 116°10W 171 L10
Ludlow Pa., U.S.A. 41°43N 78°56W 174 E6
Ludlow Vt., U.S.A. 43°24N 72°42W 175 C12
Ludowici U.S.A. 31°43N 81°45W 178 D8
Luduş Romania 46°29N 24°5E 81 D9
Ludvika Sweden 60°8N 15°14E 62 D9
Ludwigsburg Germany 48°53N 9°11E 77 G5
Ludwigsfelde Germany 52°17N 13°17E 76 C9
Ludwigshafen Germany 49°29N 8°26E 77 F4
Ludwigslust Germany 53°19N 11°30E 76 B7
Ludza Latvia 56°32N 27°43E 84 D4
Lue Australia 32°38S 149°50E 153 B8
Lueki Dem. Rep. of the Congo 3°20S 25°48E 142 C2
Luena Dem. Rep. of the Congo 9°28S 25°43E 143 D2
Luena Zambia 10°40S 30°25E 143 E3
Luena Flats Zambia 14°47S 23°17E 141 G4
Luenha = Ruenya → Africa 16°24S 33°48E 143 F3
Lüeyang China 33°22N 106°10E 116 A6
Lufeng Guangdong, China 22°57N 115°38E 117 F10
Lufeng Yunnan, China 25°0N 102°5E 116 E4
Lufira → Dem. Rep. of the Congo 9°30S 27°0E 143 D2
Lufkin U.S.A. 31°21N 94°44W 176 F7
Lufupa Dem. Rep. of the Congo 10°37S 24°56E 143 E1
Luga Russia 58°40N 29°55E 84 C5
Luga → Russia 59°40N 28°18E 84 C5
Lugano Switz. 46°1N 8°57E 77 J4
Lugano, L. di Switz. 46°0N 9°0E 92 C6
Lugansk = Luhansk Ukraine 48°38N 39°15E 85 H10
Lugard's Falls Kenya 3°6S 38°41E 142 C4
Lugela Mozam. 16°25S 36°43E 143 F4
Lugenda → Mozam. 11°25S 38°33E 143 E4
Lugh = Luuq Somalia 3°48N 42°34E 131 G3
Lugnaquilla Ireland 52°58N 6°28W 64 D5
Lugnvik Sweden 62°56N 17°55E 62 B11
Lugo Italy 44°25N 11°54E 93 D8
Lugo Spain 43°2N 7°35W 88 B3
Lugo □ Spain 43°0N 7°30W 88 C3
Lugoj Romania 45°42N 21°57E 80 E6
Lugovoy = Qulan Kazakhstan 42°55N 72°43E 106 E8
Luhansk Ukraine 48°38N 39°15E 85 H10
Luhansk □ Ukraine 49°10N 38°40E 85 H10
Luhe China 32°19N 118°50E 117 A12
Luhe → Germany 53°23N 10°13E 76 B6
Luhuo China 31°21N 100°48E 116 B3
Lui → Angola 8°21S 17°33E 140 F3
Luiana Angola 17°25S 22°59E 144 A3
Luiana → Angola 17°24S 23°3E 141 H4
Luichow Pen. = Leizhou Bandao China 21°0N 110°0E 116 G7
Luimneach = Limerick Ireland 52°40N 8°37W 64 D3
Luing U.K. 56°14N 5°39W 65 E3
Luino Italy 45°59N 8°44E 92 C5
Luís Correia Brazil 3°0S 41°35W 189 A2
Luitpold Coast Antarctica 78°30S 32°0W 55 D1
Luiza Dem. Rep. of the Congo 7°40S 22°30E 140 F4
Luizi Dem. Rep. of the Congo 6°0S 27°25E 142 D2
Luján Argentina 34°45S 59°5W 190 C4
Lujiang China 31°20N 117°15E 117 B11
Lukang Taiwan 24°1N 120°22E 117 E13
Lukanga Swamp Zambia 14°30S 27°40E 143 E2
Lukavac Bos.-H. 44°33N 18°32E 80 F3
Lukenie → Dem. Rep. of the Congo 3°0S 18°50E 140 E3
Lŭki Bulgaria 41°50N 24°43E 97 E8
Lukla Nepal 27°42N 86°43E 125 F12
Lukolela Dem. Rep. of the Congo 5°23S 24°32E 142 D1
Lukosi Zimbabwe 18°30S 26°30E 143 F2
Lukovë Albania 39°59N 19°54E 96 G3
Lukovit Bulgaria 43°13N 24°11E 97 C8
Łuków Poland 51°55N 22°23E 83 G9
Lukoyanov Russia 55°2N 44°29E 86 C7
Lukusuzi △ Zambia 12°43S 32°36E 143 E3
Lülang Shan China 38°0N 111°15E 114 F6
Luleå Sweden 65°35N 22°10E 60 D20
Luleälven → Sweden 65°35N 22°10E 60 D20
Lüleburgaz Turkey 41°23N 27°22E 97 E11
Luliang China 25°0N 103°40E 116 E4
Lulima Dem. Rep. of the Congo 4°12S 25°36E 142 C2
Luling U.S.A. 29°41N 97°39W 176 G6
Lulong China 39°53N 118°51E 115 E10
Lulonga → Dem. Rep. of the Congo 1°0N 18°10E 140 D3
Lulu U.S.A. 30°7N 82°29W 178 E7
Lulua → Dem. Rep. of the Congo 4°30S 20°30E 140 E4
Lumajang Indonesia 8°8S 113°13E 119 H15
Lumār Iran 33°33N 46°49E 105 F12
Lumbala N'guimbo Angola 14°18S 21°18E 141 G4
Lumber City U.S.A. 31°56N 82°41W 178 D7
Lumberton N.C., U.S.A. 34°37N 79°0W 177 D15
Lumberton Tex., U.S.A. 30°16N 94°12W 176 F7
Lumière, Côte de France 46°50N 2°10W 70 F4
Lumpkin U.S.A. 32°3N 84°48W 178 C5
Lumsden Canada 50°39N 104°52W 163 C8
Lumsden N.Z. 45°44S 168°27E 155 F3
Lumut Malaysia 4°13N 100°37E 121 K3
Lumut, Tanjung Indonesia 3°50S 105°58E 118 E3
Lumwana Zambia 11°50S 25°8E 143 E2
Luna India 23°43N 69°16E 124 H3
Lunan China 24°40N 103°18E 116 E4
Lunavada India 23°8N 73°37E 124 H5
Lunca Romania 47°22N 25°1E 81 C10
Lunca Corbului Romania 44°42N 24°45E 81 F9
Lund Sweden 55°44N 13°12E 63 J7
Lundazi Zambia 12°20S 33°7E 143 E3
Lunde Sweden 62°53N 17°51E 62 B11
Lunderskov Denmark 55°29N 9°19E 63 J3
Lundi → Zimbabwe 21°43S 32°34E 143 G3
Lundu Malaysia 1°40N 109°50E 118 D3
Lundy U.K. 51°10N 4°41W 67 F3
Lune → U.K. 54°0N 2°51W 66 C5
Lüneburg Germany 53°15N 10°24E 76 B6
Lüneburg Heath = Lüneburger Heide Germany 53°10N 10°12E 76 B6
Lüneburger Heide Germany 53°10N 10°12E 76 B6
Lunel France 43°39N 4°9E 73 E8
Lünen Germany 51°37N 7°32E 76 D3
Lunenburg Canada 44°22N 64°18W 165 D7
Lunéville France 48°36N 6°30E 71 D13
Lunga → Zambia 14°34S 26°25E 143 E2
Lunga Lunga Kenya 4°33S 39°7E 142 C4
Lungi S. Leone 8°40N 13°17W 138 D2
Lunglei India 22°55N 92°45E 123 H18
Luni India 26°0N 73°6E 124 G5
Luni → India 24°41N 71°14E 124 G4
Luninets = Luninyets Belarus 52°15N 26°50E 75 B14
Luning U.S.A. 38°30N 118°11W 168 G4
Lunino Russia 53°38N 45°18E 86 D7
Luninyets Belarus 52°15N 26°50E 75 B14
Lunkaransar India 28°29N 73°44E 124 E5
Lunsar S. Leone 8°41N 12°32W 138 D2
Lunsemfwa → Zambia 14°54S 30°12E 143 E3
Lunsemfwa Falls Zambia 14°30S 29°6E 143 E2
Luntai China 41°46N 84°14E 109 D10
Luo He → China 34°35N 110°20E 114 G6
Luocheng China 24°48N 108°53E 116 E7
Luochuan China 35°45N 109°26E 114 G5
Luoci China 25°19N 102°18E 116 E4
Luodian China 25°24N 106°43E 116 E6
Luoding China 22°45N 111°40E 117 F8
Luofu Dem. Rep. of the Congo 0°10S 29°15E 142 C2
Luohe China 33°32N 114°2E 114 H8
Luojiang China 31°18N 104°33E 116 B5
Luonan China 34°5N 110°10E 114 G6
Luoning China 34°35N 111°40E 114 G6
Luoshan China 32°13N 114°30E 117 A10
Luotian China 30°46N 115°22E 117 B10
Luoxiao Shan China 26°30N 114°1E 117 D10
Luoyang China 34°40N 112°26E 114 G7
Luoyuan China 26°28N 119°30E 117 D12
Luozigou China 43°42N 130°18E 115 C16
Lupeni Romania 45°21N 23°13E 81 E8
Lupilichi Mozam. 11°47S 35°13E 143 E4
Łupków Poland 49°15N 22°4E 83 J9
Lupoing China 24°53N 104°21E 116 E5
Luquan Hebei, China 38°4N 114°17E 114 E8
Luquan Yunnan, China 25°35N 102°25E 116 E4
Luque Paraguay 25°19S 57°25W 190 B4
Luquillo, Sierra de Puerto Rico 18°20N 65°47W 183 d
Lúras Italy 40°56N 9°10E 94 B2
Luray U.S.A. 38°40N 78°28W 173 F14
Lure France 47°40N 6°30E 71 E13
Lurgan U.K. 54°27N 6°20W 64 B5
Luribay Bolivia 17°6S 67°39W 188 D4
Lurín Peru 12°17S 76°52W 188 C2
Lúrio Mozam. 13°32S 40°30E 143 E5
Lusaka Zambia 15°28S 28°16E 143 F2
Lusaka □ Zambia 15°30S 29°0E 143 F2
Lusambo Dem. Rep. of the Congo 4°58S 23°28E 142 C1
Lusangaye Dem. Rep. of the Congo 4°54S 26°0E 142 C2
Luseland Canada 52°5N 109°24W 163 C7
Lusenga Plain △ Zambia 9°22S 29°14E 143 D2
Lushan Henan, China 33°45N 112°55E 114 H7
Lushan Sichuan, China 30°12N 102°52E 116 B4
Lushi China 34°3N 111°3E 114 G6
Lushnjë Albania 40°55N 19°41E 96 F3
Lushoto Tanzania 4°47S 38°20E 142 C4
Lushui China 25°58N 98°44E 116 E2
Lüshun China 38°45N 121°15E 115 E11
Lusignan France 46°26N 0°8E 72 B4
Lusigny-sur-Barse France 48°16N 4°15E 71 D11
Lusk U.S.A. 42°46N 104°27W 168 E11
Luso Portugal 40°23N 8°23W 88 E2
Lussac-les-Châteaux France 46°24N 0°43E 72 B4
Lustenau Austria 47°26N 9°39E 78 D2
Lūt, Dasht-e Iran 31°30N 58°0E 129 D8
Luta = Dalian China 38°50N 121°40E 115 E11
Lütao Taiwan 22°40N 121°30E 117 F13
Lutherstadt Wittenberg Germany 51°53N 12°39E 76 D8
Luthersville U.S.A. 33°13N 84°45W 178 B5
Luton U.K. 51°53N 0°24W 67 F7
Luton □ U.K. 51°53N 0°24W 67 F7
Łutsel K'e Canada 62°24N 110°44W 163 A6
Lutsk Ukraine 50°50N 25°15E 75 C13
Lutto = Lotta → Europe 68°42N 31°6E 60 B24
Lutz U.S.A. 28°9N 82°28W 179 G7
Lützow Holmbukta Antarctica 69°10S 37°30E 55 C4
Lutzputs S. Africa 28°3S 20°40E 144 C3
Luuq Somalia 3°48N 42°34E 131 G3
Luverne Ala., U.S.A. 31°43N 86°16W 178 D3
Luverne Minn., U.S.A. 43°39N 96°13W 172 D5
Luvua Dem. Rep. of the Congo 8°48S 25°17E 143 D2
Luvua → Dem. Rep. of the Congo 6°50S 27°30E 142 D2
Luvuvhu → S. Africa 22°25S 31°18E 145 B5
Luwegu → Tanzania 8°31S 37°23E 143 D4
Luwero Uganda 0°50N 32°28E 142 B3
Luwuk Indonesia 0°56S 122°47E 119 E6
Luxembourg Lux. 49°37N 6°9E 69 E6
Luxembourg □ Belgium 49°58N 5°30E 69 E5
Luxembourg ■ Europe 49°45N 6°0E 69 E5
Luxembourg ✈ (LUX) Lux. 49°37N 6°10E 69 E6
Luxeuil-les-Bains France 47°49N 6°24E 71 E13
Luxi Hunan, China 28°20N 110°7E 117 C8
Luxi Yunnan, China 24°40N 103°55E 116 E4
Luxi Yunnan, China 24°27N 98°36E 116 E2
Luxian China 29°9N 105°24E 116 C5
Luxor = El Uqsur Egypt 25°41N 32°38E 137 B3
Luy-de-Béarn → France 43°39N 0°48W 72 E3
Luy-de-France → France 43°39N 0°48W 72 E3
Luyi China 33°50N 115°35E 114 H8
Luykau = Loikaw Burma 19°40N 97°17E 123 K20
Luz-St-Sauveur France 42°53N 0°0 72 F4
Luzern Switz. 47°3N 8°18E 77 H4
Luzern □ Switz. 47°2N 7°55E 77 H3
Luzhai China 24°29N 109°42E 116 E7
Luzhany Ukraine 48°22N 25°47E 81 B10
Luzhi China 26°21N 105°16E 116 D5
Luzhou China 28°52N 105°20E 116 C5
Luziânia Brazil 16°20S 48°0W 189 D1
Luzilândia Brazil 3°28S 42°22W 189 A2
Lužnice → Czech Rep. 49°14N 14°23E 78 B7
Luzon Phil. 16°0N 121°0E 119 A6
Luzon Strait Asia 21°0N 120°40E 117 G13
Luzy France 46°47N 3°58E 71 F10
Luzzi Italy 39°27N 16°17E 95 C9
Lviv Ukraine 49°50N 24°0E 75 D13
Lviv □ Ukraine 49°30N 23°45E 75 D12
Lvov = Lviv Ukraine 49°50N 24°0E 75 D13
Lwówek Poland 52°28N 16°10E 83 F3
Lwówek Śląski Poland 51°7N 15°38E 83 G2
Lyakhavichy Belarus 53°2N 26°32E 75 B14
Lyakhovskiye, Ostrova Russia 73°40N 141°0E 107 B15
Lyaki = Läki Azerbaijan 40°34N 47°22E 87 K8
Lyal I. Canada 44°57N 81°24W 174 B3
Lyall Mt. N.Z. 45°16S 167°32E 155 F2
Lyaskovets Bulgaria 43°6N 25°44E 97 C9
Lyasnaya → Belarus 52°9N 23°31E 83 F10
Lybster U.K. 58°18N 3°15W 65 C5
Lycaonia Turkey 38°0N 33°0E 104 D5
Lychen Germany 53°12N 13°18E 76 B9
Lychkova Russia 57°55N 32°24E 84 D7
Lycia Turkey 36°30N 29°30E 99 E11
Lyckebyån → Sweden 56°12N 15°39E 63 H9
Lycksele Sweden 64°38N 18°40E 60 D18
Lycosura Greece 37°20N 22°3E 98 D4
Lydda = Lod Israel 31°57N 34°54E 130 D3
Lyddan I. Antarctica 74°0S 21°0W 55 D2
Lydenburg S. Africa 25°10S 30°29E 145 C5
Lydia Turkey 38°48N 28°19E 99 C10
Łydynia → Poland 52°43N 20°26E 83 F7
Lyell N.Z. 41°48S 172°4E 155 B7
Lyell I. Canada 52°40N 131°35W 162 C2
Lyepyel Belarus 54°50N 28°40E 84 E5
Lygnern Sweden 57°30N 12°15E 63 G6
Lykens U.S.A. 40°34N 76°42W 175 F8
Lyman Ukraine 45°41N 29°45E 81 E14
Lyman U.S.A. 41°20N 110°18W 168 F8
Lymanske Ukraine 46°40N 29°58E 81 D14
Lyme B. U.K. 50°42N 2°53W 67 G4
Lyme Regis U.K. 50°43N 2°57W 67 G5
Lymington U.K. 50°45N 1°32W 67 G6
Łyna → Poland 54°37N 21°14E 82 D8
Lynchburg S.C., U.S.A. 34°3N 80°4W 178 A9
Lynchburg Va., U.S.A. 37°25N 79°9W 173 G14
Lynd → Australia 16°28S 143°18E 150 B3
Lynd Ra. Australia 25°30S 149°20E 151 D4
Lynden Canada 43°14N 80°9W 174 C4
Lynden U.S.A. 48°57N 122°27W 170 B4
Lyndhurst Australia 30°15S 138°18E 151 E2
Lyndon → Australia 23°29S 114°6E 149 D1
Lyndonville N.Y., U.S.A. 43°20N 78°23W 174 C6
Lyndonville Vt., U.S.A. 44°31N 72°1W 175 B12
Lyngen Norway 69°45N 20°30E 60 B19
Lynher Reef Australia 15°27S 121°55E 1
Lynn U.S.A. 42°28N 70°57W 17
Lynn Canal U.S.A. 58°50N 135°15W 16
Lynn Haven U.S.A. 30°15N 85°39W 1
Lynn Lake Canada 56°51N 101°3W 1
Lynne U.S.A. 29°12N 81°55W 1
Lynnwood U.S.A. 47°49N 122°18W 1
Lynton U.K. 51°13N 3°50W
Lyntupy Belarus 55°4N 26°23E
Lynx L. Canada 62°25N 106°15W 1
Lyon France 45°46N 4°50E
Lyon St-Exupery ✈ (LYS) France 45°44N 5°2E
Lyonnais France 45°45N 4°15E
Lyons = Lyon France 45°46N 4°50E
Lyons Ga., U.S.A. 32°12N 82°19W 1
Lyons Kans., U.S.A. 38°21N 98°12W 1
Lyons N.Y., U.S.A. 43°5N 77°0W 1
Lyons → Australia 25°2S 115°9E 1
Lyons Falls U.S.A. 43°37N 75°22W 1
Lyozna Belarus 55°0N 30°50E
Lys = Leie → Belgium 51°2N 3°45E
Lysá nad Labem Czech Rep. 50°11N 14°51E
Lysekil Sweden 58°17N 11°26E
Lysi Cyprus 35°6N 33°41E 10
Lyskovo Russia 56°0N 45°3E
Lystrup Denmark 56°14N 10°14E
Lysvik Sweden 60°1N 13°9E
Lysychansk Ukraine 48°55N 38°30E 8
Lytham St. Anne's U.K. 53°45N 3°0W
Lyttelton N.Z. 43°35S 172°44E 1
Lytton Canada 50°13N 121°31W 1
Lyuban Russia 59°16N 31°18E
Lyubertsy Russia 55°40N 37°51E
Lyubim Russia 58°20N 40°39E 8
Lyubimets Bulgaria 41°50N 26°5E 9
Lyuboml Ukraine 51°11N 24°4E 8
Lyubotyn Ukraine 50°0N 36°0E
Lyubytino Russia 58°50N 33°16E
Lyudinovo Russia 53°52N 34°28E

M

M.R. Štefánik, Bratislava ✈ (BTS) Slovak Rep. 48°11N 17°9E 7
Ma → Vietnam 19°47N 105°56E 1
Ma, O. el → Algeria 27°45N 7°52W 1
Ma On Shan China 22°23N 114°12E
Ma'adaba Jordan 31°43N 35°47E 1
Ma'alot-Tarshiha Israel 33°1N 35°17E 1
Maamba Zambia 17°17S 26°28E 1
Ma'ān Jordan 30°12N 35°44E 1
Ma'ān □ Jordan 30°0N 36°0E 1
Maanselkä Finland 63°52N 28°32E 6
Ma'anshan China 31°44N 118°29E 1
Maarianhamina = Mariehamn Finland 60°5N 19°55E 6
Maarmorilik Greenland 71°3N 51°0W
Ma'arrat an Nu'mān Syria 35°43N 36°43E 1
Maas → Neths. 51°45N 4°32E
Maaseik Belgium 51°6N 5°45E
Maasin Phil. 10°8N 124°50E 1
Maastricht Neths. 50°50N 5°40E
Maave Mozam. 21°4S 34°47E 1
Mababe Depression Botswana 18°50S 24°15E 1
Mabalane Mozam. 23°37S 32°31E 1
Mabel L. Canada 50°35N 118°43W 1
Mabenge Dem. Rep. of the Congo 4°15N 24°12E 1
Maberly Canada 44°50N 76°32W 1
Mabesi, L. S. Leone 7°10N 11°42W 1
Mabian China 28°47N 103°37E 1
Mablethorpe U.K. 53°20N 0°15E
Mableton U.S.A. 33°49N 84°35W 1
Mably France 46°5N 4°4E 7
Maboma Dem. Rep. of the Congo 2°30N 28°10E 1
Mabonto S. Leone 8°53N 11°50W 1
Mabroûk Mali 19°29N 1°15W 1
Mabuasehube ⌓ Botswana 25°5S 21°10E 1
Mabuiag Australia 9°57S 142°11E
Mac Bac Vietnam 9°46N 106°7E 1
Macachín Argentina 37°10S 63°43W 1
Macaé Brazil 22°20S 41°43W 1
Macael Spain 37°20N 2°18W
Macaíba Brazil 5°51S 35°21W 1
Macajuba Brazil 12°9S 40°22W 1
McAlester U.S.A. 34°56N 95°46W 1
McAllen U.S.A. 26°12N 98°14W 1
McAlpin U.S.A. 30°8N 82°57W 1
MacAlpine L. Canada 66°32N 102°45W 16
Macamic Canada 48°45N 79°0W 1
Macao = Macau China 22°12N 113°33E 1
Macão Portugal 39°35N 7°59W
Macapá Brazil 0°5N 51°4W 1
Macarani Brazil 15°33S 40°24W 1
Macarao △ Venezuela 10°22N 67°7W 1
Macarthur Australia 38°5S 142°0E 1
McArthur → Australia 15°54S 136°40E 1
McArthur, Port Australia 16°4S 136°23E 1
Macate Peru 8°48S 78°7W 1
Macau Brazil 5°15S 36°40W 1
Macau China 22°12N 113°33E 1
Macaúbas Brazil 13°2S 42°42W 1
McBride Canada 53°20N 120°19W 1
McCall U.S.A. 44°55N 116°6W 1
McCamey U.S.A. 31°8N 102°14W 1
McCammon U.S.A. 42°39N 112°12W 1
McCarran Int., Las Vegas ✈ (LAS) U.S.A. 36°5N 115°9W 17
McCauley I. Canada 53°40N 130°15W 1
McCleary U.S.A. 47°3N 123°16W 1
Macclenny U.S.A. 30°17N 82°7W 1
Macclesfield U.K. 53°15N 2°8W 6
Macclesfield Bank S. China Sea 16°0N 114°30E 1
M'Clintock Chan. Canada 72°0N 102°0W 16
McClintock Ra. Australia 18°44S 127°38E 1
McCloud U.S.A. 41°15N 122°8W 1
McCluer I. Australia 11°5S 133°0E 1
McClure U.S.A. 40°42N 77°19W 1

ure, L. U.S.A. 37°35N 120°16W 170 H6
ure Str. Canada 75°0N 119°0W 161 C8
lusky U.S.A. 47°29N 100°27W 172 B3
omb U.S.A. 31°15N 90°27W 177 F9
ook U.S.A. 40°12N 100°38W 172 E3
ormick U.S.A. 33°55N 82°17W 178 B7
reary Canada 50°47N 99°29W 163 C9
ullough Mt.
S.A. 35°35N 115°13W 171 K11
usker → Canada 55°32N 108°39W 163 B7
avid U.S.A. 30°52N 87°19W 179 E2
ermitt U.S.A. 41°59N 117°43W 168 F5
onald U.S.A. 40°22N 80°14W 174 F4
onald, L. Australia 23°30S 129°0E 148 D4
onald Is. Ind. Oc. 53°0S 73°0E 146 K6
Donnell Ranges
stralia 23°40S 133°0E 148 D5
onough U.S.A. 33°27N 84°9W 178 B5
ougalls Well
stralia 31°8S 141°15E 152 A4
Dowell L. Canada 52°15N 92°45W 164 B1
duff U.K. 57°40N 2°31W 65 D6
eda Spain 42°16N 7°39W 88 C3
edonia U.S.A. 41°19N 81°31W 174 E3
edonia ■ Europe 41°53N 21°40E 96 E5
eió Brazil 9°40S 35°41W 189 B3
eira Portugal 39°41N 8°55W 88 F2
enta Guinea 8°35N 9°32W 138 D3
erata Italy 43°18N 13°27E 93 E10
arland U.S.A. 35°41N 119°14W 171 K7
arlane → Canada 59°12N 107°58W 163 B7
arlane, L. Australia 32°0S 136°40E 152 B2
ehee U.S.A. 33°38N 91°24W 176 E9
ill U.S.A. 39°23N 114°47W 168 G6
gillycuddy's Reeks
land 51°58N 9°45W 64 E2
raw U.S.A. 42°36N 76°8W 175 D8
regor U.S.A. 43°1N 91°11W 172 D8
regor Ra. Australia 27°0S 142°45E 151 D3
uire, Mt. Australia 20°18S 148°23E 150 b
n Pakistan 29°50N 67°20E 124 E2
n Kowr Iran 25°48N 61°28E 129 E9
acalis Brazil 17°5S 40°45W 189 D2
nado = Jiparaná →
azil 8°3S 62°52W 186 E6
nagai Argentina 26°56S 60°2W 190 B3
nakos Kenya 1°30S 37°15E 142 C4
nakos □ Kenya 1°15S 34°35E 142 C4
nala Ecuador 3°20S 79°57W 186 D3
nanga Mozam. 20°59S 35°0E 145 B6
nattie, L. Australia 24°50S 139°48E 150 C2
nault France 49°21N 4°29E 71 C11
nava Mozam. 25°54S 32°28E 145 C5
necoul France 47°0N 1°49W 70 F5
neke Zimbabwe 18°5S 31°51E 145 A5
neng China 31°12N 115°2E 117 B10
nerla India 16°29N 79°26E 126 F4
nero Spain 39°21N 4°20W 89 F6
ngaon India 20°5N 86°17E 126 D8
nhu → India 23°6N 70°46E 124 H4
niara △ Pakistan 34°40N 73°30E 124 B5
nias Maine,
S.A. 44°43N 67°28W 173 C20
nias N.Y., U.S.A. 42°25N 78°29W 174 D6
nichi → Canada 57°3N 92°6W 163 B10
nico Madeira 32°43N 16°44W 100 D3
nilipatnam India 16°12N 81°8E 127 F5
niques Venezuela 10°4N 72°34W 186 A4
nu Picchu Peru 13°8S 72°30W 188 C3
nynlleth U.K. 52°35N 3°50W 67 E4
a Mozam. 25°2S 33°8E 145 C5
ejowice Poland 51°36N 21°26E 83 G8
wraith Ra.
stralia 13°50S 143°20E 150 A3
n Romania 45°16N 28°8E 81 E13
na Mali 14°50N 5°0W 138 C4
nes L. Canada 52°13N 93°45W 163 C10
tosh U.S.A. 45°55N 101°21W 172 C3
tosh L. Canada 55°45N 105°0W 163 B8
ntosh Ra.
stralia 27°39S 125°32E 149 E4
ntyre →
stralia 28°37S 150°47E 151 D5
zo Galaico Spain 42°30N 7°30W 88 C3
ka Turkey 40°49N 39°36E 105 B8
kay Australia 21°8S 149°11E 150 K7
kay U.S.A. 43°55N 113°37W 168 E7
Kay → Canada 57°10N 111°38W 162 B6
kay, L. Australia 22°30S 129°0E 148 D4
ay Ra. Australia 23°0S 122°30E 148 D3
eesport U.S.A. 40°20N 79°51W 174 F5
ellar Canada 45°30N 79°55W 174 A5
enna U.S.A. 46°56N 122°33W 170 D4
kenzie = Linden
yana 6°0N 58°10W 186 B7
kenzie Canada 55°20N 123°5W 162 B4
enzie U.S.A. 36°8N 88°31W 177 C10
kenzie →
stralia 23°38S 149°46E 150 C4
kenzie → Canada 69°10N 134°20W 160 D5
enzie → U.S.A. 44°7N 123°6W 168 D2
kenzie Bay Canada 69°0N 137°30W 158 C6
kenzie King I.
nada 77°45N 111°0W 161 B9
kenzie Mts. Canada 64°0N 130°0W 158 C6
kenzie Plains N.Z. 44°10S 170°25E 155 E5
errow, L. N.Z. 44°25S 168°5E 155 E3
kinac, Straits of
S.A. 45°50N 84°40W 173 C11
kinaw City
S.A. 45°47N 84°44W 173 C11
inlay Australia 21°16S 141°18E 150 C3
inlay → Australia 20°50S 141°28E 150 C3
inley, Mt. U.S.A. 63°4N 151°0W 160 E1
inley Sea Arctic 82°0N 0°0 57 A11
inney U.S.A. 33°12N 96°37W 176 E6
kinnon Road Kenya 3°40S 39°1E 142 C4
ittrick U.S.A. 35°18N 119°37W 171 K7
klin Canada 52°20N 109°56W 163 C7
ksville Australia 30°40S 152°56E 153 A10
aren Vale
stralia 35°13S 138°31E 152 C3
aughlin U.S.A. 45°49N 100°49W 172 C3
ean Australia 29°26S 153°16E 151 D5
ean U.S.A. 35°14N 100°36W 176 D4
eansboro U.S.A. 38°6N 88°32W 172 F9
ear S. Africa 31°2S 28°23E 145 D4
ear, C. Malawi 13°58S 34°49E 143 E3
eay → Australia 30°56S 153°0E 153 A10
ennan Canada 55°42N 116°50W 162 B5
eod → Canada 54°9N 115°44W 162 C5
Leod, L. Australia 24°9S 113°47E 149 D1
MacLeod B. Canada 62°53N 110°0W 163 A7
MacLeod Lake Canada 54°58N 123°0W 162 C4
McLoughlin, Mt.
U.S.A. 42°27N 122°19W 168 E2
McMechen U.S.A. 39°57N 80°44W 174 G4
McMinnville Oreg.,
U.S.A. 45°13N 123°12W 168 D2
McMinnville Tenn.,
U.S.A. 35°41N 85°46W 177 D12
McMurdo Antarctica 77°51S 166°37E 55 D11
McMurdo Sd. Antarctica 77°0S 170°0E 55 D11
McMurray = Fort McMurray
Canada 56°44N 111°7W 162 B6
McMurray U.S.A. 48°19N 122°14W 170 B4
Maçobere Mozam. 21°13S 32°47E 143 G3
Macodoene Mozam. 23°32S 35°5E 145 B6
Macomb U.S.A. 40°27N 90°40W 172 E8
Macomer Italy 40°16N 8°47E 94 B1
Mâcon France 46°19N 4°50E 71 F11
Macon Ga., U.S.A. 32°51N 83°38W 178 C6
Macon Miss., U.S.A. 33°7N 88°34W 177 E10
Macon Mo., U.S.A. 39°44N 92°28W 172 F7
Macossa Mozam. 17°55S 33°56E 143 F3
Macoun L. Canada 56°32N 103°40W 163 B8
Macovane Mozam. 21°30S 35°2E 145 B6
McPherson U.S.A. 38°22N 97°40W 172 F5
McPherson Pk.
U.S.A. 34°53N 119°53W 171 L7
McPherson Ra.
Australia 28°15S 153°15E 151 D5
Macquarie → Australia 30°7S 147°24E 153 A7
Macquarie Harbour
Australia 42°15S 145°23E 151 G4
Macquarie I. Pac. Oc. 54°36S 158°55E 156 N7
Macquarie Ridge
S. Ocean 57°0S 159°0E 55 B10
McRae U.S.A. 32°4N 82°54W 178 C7
MacRobertson Land
Antarctica 71°0S 64°0E 55 D6
Macroom Ireland 51°54N 8°57W 64 E3
MacTier Canada 45°8N 79°47W 174 A5
Macubela Mozam. 16°53S 37°49E 143 F4
Macugnaga Italy 45°58N 7°58E 92 C4
Macuira △ Colombia 12°9N 71°21W 183 D5
Macumba →
Australia 27°52S 137°12E 151 D2
Macuro Venezuela 10°42N 61°55W 187 K15
Macusani Peru 14°4S 70°29W 188 C3
Macuse Mozam. 17°45S 37°10E 143 F4
Macuspana Mexico 17°46N 92°36W 181 D6
Macusse Angola 17°48S 20°23E 144 A3
Mada → Nigeria 7°59N 7°55E 139 D6
Ma'dabā □ Jordan 31°43N 35°47E 130 D4
Madadeni S. Africa 27°43S 30°3E 145 C5
Madagali Nigeria 10°56N 13°33E 139 C7
Madagascar ■ Africa 20°0S 47°0E 141 J9
Madā'in Sālih Si. Arabia 26°46N 37°57E 128 E3
Madakasira India 13°56N 77°16E 127 H3
Madama Niger 22°0N 13°40E 135 D8
Madame, I. Canada 45°30N 60°58W 165 C7
Madan Bulgaria 41°30N 24°57E 97 E8
Madanapalle India 13°33N 78°28E 127 H4
Madang Papua N. G. 5°12S 145°49E 147 B7
Madaoua Niger 14°5N 6°27E 139 C6
Madara Bulgaria 43°17N 27°8E 97 C11
Madara Nigeria 11°45N 10°35E 139 C7
Madaripur Bangla. 23°19N 90°15E 123 H17
Madauk Burma 17°56N 96°52E 123 L20
Madawaska Canada 45°30N 78°0W 174 A7
Madawaska →
Canada 45°27N 76°21W 174 A7
Madaya Burma 22°12N 96°10E 123 H20
Maddalena Italy 41°16N 9°23E 94 A2
Maddaloni Italy 41°2N 14°23E 95 A7
Maddur India 12°36N 77°4E 127 H3
Madeira Atl. Oc. 32°50N 17°0W 100 D3
Madeira → Brazil 3°22S 58°45W 186 D7
Madeleine, Îs. de la
Canada 47°30N 61°40W 165 C7
Maden Turkey 38°23N 39°40E 105 C8
Madera Mexico 29°12N 108°7W 180 B3
Madera Calif., U.S.A. 36°57N 120°3W 170 J6
Madera Pa., U.S.A. 40°49N 78°26W 174 F6
Madgaon India 15°12N 73°58E 127 G1
Madha India 18°0N 75°30E 126 F2
Madhavpur India 21°15N 69°58E 124 J3
Madhepura India 26°11N 86°23E 125 F12
Madhira India 16°55N 80°22E 126 F5
Madhubani India 26°21N 86°7E 125 F12
Madhugiri India 13°40N 77°12E 127 H3
Madhupur India 24°16N 86°39E 125 G12
Madhya Pradesh □
India 22°50N 78°0E 124 J8
Madidi → Bolivia 12°32S 66°52W 188 C4
Madikeri India 12°30N 75°45E 127 H2
Madikwe ⌂ S. Africa 27°38S 32°15E 145 C5
Madill U.S.A. 34°6N 96°46W 176 D6
Madimba
Dem. Rep. of the Congo 4°58S 15°5E 140 E3
Ma'din Syria 35°45N 39°36E 105 E8
Madina Mali 13°25N 8°50W 138 C3
Madinani Ivory C. 9°37N 6°57W 138 D3
Madinat al Malik Khālid al
Askarīyah Si. Arabia 27°54N 45°31E 128 E5
Madīnat ath Thawrah
Syria 35°50N 38°32E 105 E8
Madīnat Masdar
U.A.E. 24°26N 54°37E 129 E7
Madingou Congo 4°10S 13°33E 140 E2
Madison Calif., U.S.A. 38°41N 121°59W 170 G5
Madison Fla., U.S.A. 30°28N 83°25W 178 E6
Madison Ga., U.S.A. 33°36N 83°28W 178 B6
Madison Ind., U.S.A. 38°44N 85°23W 173 F11
Madison Nebr., U.S.A. 41°50N 97°27W 172 E5
Madison Ohio, U.S.A. 41°46N 81°3W 174 E3
Madison S. Dak., U.S.A. 44°0N 97°7W 172 C5
Madison Wis., U.S.A. 43°4N 89°24W 172 D9
Madison → U.S.A. 45°56N 111°31W 168 D8
Madison Heights
U.S.A. 37°25N 79°8W 173 G14
Madisonville Ky.,
U.S.A. 37°20N 87°30W 172 G10
Madisonville Tex.,
U.S.A. 30°57N 95°55W 176 F7
Madista Botswana 21°15S 25°6E 144 B4
Madiun Indonesia 7°38S 111°32E 118 F4
Mado Gashi Kenya 0°44N 39°10E 142 B4
Madoc Canada 44°30N 77°28W 174 B7
Madoi China 34°46N 98°18E 110 E8
Madon → France 48°36N 6°6E 71 D13
Madona Latvia 56°53N 26°5E 84 D4
Madonie Italy 37°50N 13°50E 94 E6
Madonna di Campiglio
Italy 46°14N 10°49E 92 B7
Madra Dağı Turkey 39°23N 27°12E 99 B9
Madrakah, Ra's al
Oman 19°0N 57°50E 131 D6
Madras = Chennai India 13°8N 80°19E 127 H5
Madras = Tamil Nadu □
India 11°0N 77°0E 127 J3
Madras U.S.A. 44°38N 121°8W 168 D3
Madre, L. U.S.A. 26°50N 97°30W 176 J6
Madre, Sierra Phil. 17°0N 122°0E 119 A6
Madre de Dios □ Peru 12°0S 70°15W 188 C3
Madre de Dios →
Bolivia 10°59S 66°8W 188 C4
Madre de Dios, I. Chile 50°20S 75°10W 192 D1
Madre del Sur, Sierra
Mexico 17°30N 100°0W 181 D5
Madre Occidental, Sierra
Mexico 27°0N 107°0W 180 B3
Madre Oriental, Sierra
Mexico 25°0N 100°0W 180 C5
Madri India 24°16N 73°32E 124 G5
Madrid Spain 40°24N 3°42W 88 E7
Madrid Ala., U.S.A. 31°2N 85°24W 178 D4
Madrid N.Y., U.S.A. 44°45N 75°8W 175 B9
Madrid □ Spain 40°30N 3°45W 88 E7
Madrid Barajas ✕ (MAD)
Spain 40°26N 3°34W 88 E7
Madridejos Spain 39°28N 3°33W 89 F7
Madrigal de las Altas Torres
Spain 41°5N 5°0W 88 D6
Madrona, Sierra Spain 38°27N 4°16W 89 G6
Madroñera Spain 39°26N 5°42W 89 F5
Madula
Dem. Rep. of the Congo 0°27N 25°22E 142 B2
Madura Australia 31°55S 127°0E 149 F4
Madura Indonesia 7°30S 114°0E 119 G15
Madura, Selat
Indonesia 7°30S 113°20E 119 G15
Madura Oya △ Sri Lanka 7°20N 81°10E 127 L5
Madurai India 9°55N 78°10E 127 K4
Madurantakam India 12°30N 79°50E 127 H4
Madzhalis Russia 42°9N 47°47E 87 J8
Mae Chan Thailand 20°9N 99°52E 120 B2
Mae Charim △
Thailand 18°17N 100°59E 120 C3
Mae Hong Son Thailand 19°16N 97°56E 120 C2
Mae Khlong →
Thailand 13°24N 100°0E 120 F3
Mae Moei △ Thailand 17°26N 98°7E 120 D2
Mae Phang △ Thailand 19°7N 99°13E 120 C2
Mae Phrik Thailand 17°27N 99°7E 120 D2
Mae Ping △ Thailand 17°37N 98°51E 120 D2
Mae Ramat Thailand 16°58N 98°31E 120 D2
Mae Rim Thailand 18°54N 98°57E 120 C2
Mae Sai Thailand 20°20N 99°55E 116 G2
Mae Sot Thailand 16°43N 98°34E 120 D2
Mae Suai Thailand 19°39N 99°33E 116 H2
Mae Tha Thailand 18°28N 99°8E 120 C2
Mae Tup Res. Thailand 17°52N 98°45E 120 D2
Mae Wa △ Thailand 17°23N 99°16E 120 D2
Mae Wong △ Thailand 15°54N 99°12E 120 E2
Mae Yom △ Thailand 18°43N 100°15E 120 C3
Maebaru Japan 33°33N 130°12E 113 H5
Maebashi Japan 36°24N 139°4E 113 F9
Maella Spain 41°8N 0°7E 90 D5
Maelpaeg L. Canada 48°20N 56°30W 165 C8
Maestra, Sierra Cuba 20°15N 77°0W 182 B4
Maevatanana Madag. 16°56S 46°49E 141 H9
Mafadi S. Africa 29°12S 29°21E 145 C4
Mafeking = Mafikeng
S. Africa 25°50S 25°38E 144 C4
Mafeking Canada 52°40N 101°10W 163 C8
Maféré Ivory C. 5°30N 3°2W 138 D4
Mafeteng Lesotho 29°51S 27°15E 144 C4
Maffra Australia 37°53S 146°58E 153 D7
Mafia I. Tanzania 7°45S 39°50E 142 D4
Mafikeng S. Africa 25°50S 25°38E 144 C4
Mafra Brazil 26°10S 49°55W 191 B6
Mafra Portugal 38°55N 9°20W 89 G1
Mafungabusi Plateau
Zimbabwe 18°30S 29°8E 143 F2
Magadan Russia 59°38N 150°50E 107 D16
Magadi India 12°58N 77°14E 127 H3
Magadi Kenya 1°54S 36°19E 142 C4
Magadi, L. Kenya 1°54S 36°19E 142 C4
Magaliesburg S. Africa 26°0S 27°32E 145 C4
Magallanes □ Chile 52°0S 72°0W 192 D2
Magallanes, Estrecho de
Chile 52°30S 75°0W 192 D2
Magaluf Spain 39°29N 2°32E 91 F7
Magangué Colombia 9°14N 74°45W 186 B4
Magaria Niger 13°4N 9°5E 139 C6
Magburaka S. Leone 8°47N 12°0W 138 D2
Magdagachi Russia 53°27N 125°48E 107 D13
Magdalen Is. = Madeleine, Îs. de
la Canada 47°30N 61°40W 165 C7
Magdalena Argentina 35°5S 57°30W 190 D4
Magdalena Bolivia 13°13S 63°57W 186 F6
Magdalena U.S.A. 34°7N 107°15W 169 J10
Magdalena → Colombia 11°6N 74°51W 186 A4
Magdalena, B. Mexico 24°35N 112°0W 180 C2
Magdalena, I. Chile 44°40S 73°0W 192 B2
Magdalena, I. Mexico 24°40N 112°15W 180 C2
Magdalena, Llano de
Mexico 25°0N 111°25W 180 C2
Magdalena de Kino
Mexico 30°38N 110°57W 180 A2
Magdeburg Germany 52°7N 11°38E 76 C7
Magdelaine Cays
Australia 16°33S 150°18E 150 B5
Magee U.S.A. 31°52N 89°44W 177 F10
Magelang Indonesia 7°29S 110°13E 118 F4
Magellan's Str. = Magallanes,
Estrecho de Chile 52°30S 75°0W 192 D2
Magenta Italy 45°28N 8°53E 92 C5
Magenta, L. Australia 33°30S 119°2E 149 F2
Magerøya Norway 71°3N 25°40E 60 A21
Maggea Australia 34°28S 140°2E 152 C4
Maggia → Switz. 46°18N 8°36E 77 J4
Maggiorasca, Mte. Italy 44°33N 9°29E 92 D6
Maggiore, L. Italy 45°57N 8°39E 92 B5
Maggotty Jamaica 18°9N 77°46W 182 a
Maghâgha Egypt 28°38N 30°50E 137 F7
Maghama Mauritania 15°32N 12°57W 138 B2
Maghera U.K. 54°51N 6°41W 64 B5
Magherafelt U.K. 54°45N 6°37W 64 B5
Maghnia Algeria 34°50N 1°43W 136 B3
Maghreb N. Afr. 32°0N 4°0W 132 C3
Magione Italy 43°8N 12°12E 93 E9
Magistralnyy Russia 56°16N 107°36E 107 D11
Maglaj Bos.-H. 44°33N 18°7E 80 F3
Magliano in Toscana
Italy 42°36N 11°17E 93 F8
Máglie Italy 40°7N 18°18E 95 B11
Magnac-Laval France 46°13N 1°11E 72 B5
Magnesia = Magnisia
Greece 39°15N 23°0E 98 B5
Magnetic Pole (North)
Arctic 85°9N 149°0W 54 A1
Magnetic Pole (South)
Antarctica 64°8S 138°8E 55 C9
Magnisia Greece 39°15N 23°0E 98 B5
Magnitogorsk Russia 53°27N 59°4E 108 B5
Magnolia Ark., U.S.A. 33°16N 93°14W 176 E8
Magnolia Miss., U.S.A. 31°9N 90°28W 177 F9
Magny-en-Vexin France 49°9N 1°47E 71 C8
Mago Fiji 17°26S 179°8W 154 a
Magog Canada 45°18N 72°9W 175 A12
Magoro Uganda 1°45N 34°12E 142 B3
Magoulades Greece 39°45N 19°42E 101 A3
Magoye Zambia 16°1S 27°30E 143 F2
Magpie, L. Canada 51°0N 64°41W 165 B7
Magrath Canada 49°25N 112°50W 162 D6
Magre → Spain 39°11N 0°25W 91 F4
Magta Lahjar
Mauritania 17°28N 13°17W 138 B2
Magu Tanzania 2°30S 33°30E 142 C3
Maguan China 23°0N 104°21E 116 F5
Maguarinho, C. Brazil 0°15S 48°30W 187 D9
Magude Mozam. 25°2S 32°40E 145 C5
Magurski △ Poland 49°30N 21°30E 83 J8
Mağusa = Famagusta
Cyprus 35°8N 33°55E 101 D12
Maguse L. Canada 61°37N 95°10W 163 A9
Maguse Pt. Canada 61°20N 93°50W 163 A10
Magvana India 23°13N 69°22E 124 H3
Magway Burma 20°10N 95°0E 123 J19
Magyarorszag = Hungary ■
Europe 47°20N 19°20E 79 D12
Maha Oya Sri Lanka 7°31N 81°22E 127 L5
Maha Sarakham
Thailand 16°12N 103°16E 120 D4
Mahābād Iran 36°50N 45°45E 105 D11
Mahabaleshwar India 17°58N 73°43E 126 F1
Mahabalipuram India 12°37N 80°11E 127 H5
Mahabharat Lekh
Nepal 28°30N 82°0E 125 E10
Mahabo Madag. 20°23S 44°40E 141 J8
Mahad India 18°6N 73°29E 126 E1
Mahadeo Hills India 22°20N 78°30E 125 H8
Mahadeopur India 18°48N 80°0E 126 E5
Mahaffey U.S.A. 40°53N 78°44W 174 F6
Mahagi
Dem. Rep. of the Congo 2°20N 31°0E 142 B3
Mahajan India 28°48N 73°56E 124 E5
Mahajanga Madag. 15°40S 46°25E 141 H9
Mahakam → Indonesia 0°35S 117°17E 118 E5
Mahalapye Botswana 23°1S 26°51E 144 B4
Mahale Mts. Tanzania 6°20S 30°0E 142 D3
Mahale Mts. △ Tanzania 6°10S 29°50E 142 D2
Maḩallāt Iran 33°55N 50°30E 129 C6
Māhān Iran 30°5N 57°18E 129 D8
Mahan → India 23°30N 82°50E 125 H10
Mahanadi → India 20°20N 86°25E 126 D8
Mahananda → India 25°12N 87°52E 125 G12
Mahanoro Madag. 19°54S 48°48E 141 H9
Mahanoy City U.S.A. 40°49N 76°9W 175 F8
Maharashtra □ India 20°30N 75°30E 126 D2
Maharès Tunisia 34°32N 10°29E 136 B6
Mahasamund India 21°6N 82°6E 126 D6
Mahasham, W. →
Egypt 30°15N 34°10E 130 E3
Mahattat ash Shīdīyah
Jordan 29°55N 35°55E 130 F4
Mahattat 'Unayzah
Jordan 30°30N 35°47E 130 E4
Mahaweli Ganga →
Sri Lanka 8°27N 81°13E 127 K5
Mahaxay Laos 17°22N 105°12E 120 D5
Mahbubabad India 17°42N 80°2E 126 F5
Mahbubnagar India 16°45N 77°59E 126 F3
Mahda U.A.E. 25°20N 56°15E 129 E8
Maḩḑah Oman 24°24N 55°59E 129 E7
Mahdia Tunisia 35°28N 11°0E 136 A6
Mahdia □ Tunisia 35°20N 10°35E 136 A6
Mahe Jammu & Kashmir,
India 33°10N 78°32E 125 C8
Mahé Pondicherry, India 11°42N 75°34E 127 J2
Mahé Seychelles 5°0S 55°30E 141 b
Mahé ✕ (SEZ) Seychelles 4°40S 55°31E 141 b
Mahébourg Mauritius 20°24S 57°42E 141 d
Mahendra Giri India 8°20N 77°30E 127 K3
Mahendragarh India 28°17N 76°14E 124 E7
Mahendranagar Nepal 28°55N 80°20E 125 E9
Mahenge Tanzania 8°45S 36°41E 143 D4
Maheno N.Z. 45°10S 170°50E 155 F5
Mahesana India 23°39N 72°26E 124 H5
Maheshwar India 22°11N 75°35E 124 H6
Mahgawan India 26°29N 78°37E 125 F8
Mahi → India 22°15N 72°55E 124 H5
Mahia Pen. N.Z. 39°9S 177°55E 154 F6
Mahikeng = Mafikeng
S. Africa 25°50S 25°38E 144 C4
Mahilyow Belarus 53°55N 30°18E 75 B16
Mahilyow □ Belarus 54°10N 30°50E 84 E6
Mahim India 19°39N 72°44E 126 E1
Mahina Tahiti 17°30S 149°27W 155 b
Mahirija Morocco 34°0N 3°16W 136 B3
Mahmud Kot Pakistan 30°16N 71°0E 124 D4
Mahmudia Romania 45°5N 29°5E 81 E14
Mahmudiye Turkey 39°48N 30°15E 99 B12
Mahmutbey Turkey 41°3N 28°49E 97 E12
Māhneshān Iran 36°44N 47°39E 105 D12
Mahnomen U.S.A. 47°19N 95°58W 172 B6
Maho Sri Lanka 7°49N 80°16E 127 L5
Mahoba India 25°15N 79°55E 125 G8
Mahón = Maó Spain 39°53N 4°16E 100 B11
Mahon, Menorca ✕ (MAH)
Spain 39°50N 4°16E 90 F9
Mahone Bay Canada 44°27N 64°23W 165 D7
Mahongo ⌂ Namibia 18°0S 23°15E 144 B3
Mahopac U.S.A. 41°22N 73°45W 175 E11
Mahuta Nigeria 11°32N 4°58E 139 C5
Mahuva India 21°5N 71°48E 124 J4
Mahya Dağı Turkey 41°47N 27°36E 97 E11
Mai-Ndombe, L.
Dem. Rep. of the Congo 2°0S 18°20E 140 E3
Mai Thon, Ko Thailand 7°40N 98°28E 121 a
Maia Portugal 41°14N 8°37W 88 D2
Maials Spain 41°22N 0°30E 90 D5
Maîche France 47°16N 6°48E 71 E13
Maicuru → Brazil 2°14S 54°17W 187 D8
Máida Italy 38°51N 16°22E 95 D9
Maidan Khula Afghan. 33°36N 69°50E 124 C3
Maidenhead U.K. 51°31N 0°42W 67 F7
Maidstone Canada 53°5N 109°20W 163 C7
Maidstone U.K. 51°16N 0°32E 67 F8
Maiduguri Nigeria 12°0N 13°20E 139 C7
Maiella △ Italy 42°5N 14°5E 93 F11
Măieruş Romania 45°53N 25°31E 81 E10
Maigatari Nigeria 12°46N 9°27E 139 C6
Maigh Nuad = Maynooth
Ireland 53°23N 6°34W 64 C5
Maignelay Montigny
France 49°32N 2°30E 71 C9
Maihar India 24°16N 80°45E 125 G9
Maikala Ra. India 22°0N 81°0E 126 D5
Maiko △
Dem. Rep. of the Congo 0°30S 27°50E 142 C2
Mailani India 28°17N 80°21E 125 E9
Maillezais France 46°22N 0°45W 72 B3
Mailsi Pakistan 29°48N 72°15E 124 E5
Main → Germany 50°0N 8°18E 77 F4
Main → U.K. 54°48N 6°18W 64 B5
Main Channel Canada 45°21N 81°45W 174 A3
Main Range △
Australia 28°11S 152°27E 151 D5
Main Ridge
Trin. & Tob. 11°16N 60°40W 187 J16
Mainburg Germany 48°38N 11°47E 77 G7
Maindargi India 17°28N 76°18E 126 F3
Maine France 48°20N 0°15W 70 D6
Maine □ U.S.A. 45°20N 69°0W 173 C19
Maine → Ireland 52°9N 9°45W 64 D2
Maine, G. of U.S.A. 43°0N 68°30W 167 G26
Maine-et-Loire □ France 47°31N 0°30W 70 E6
Maïne-Soroa Niger 13°13N 12°2E 139 C7
Maingkwan Burma 26°15N 96°37E 123 F20
Mainistir na Corann = Midleton
Ireland 51°55N 8°10W 64 E3
Mainit, L. Phil. 9°31N 125°30E 119 C7
Mainland Orkney, U.K. 58°59N 3°8W 65 C5
Mainland Shet., U.K. 60°15N 1°22W 65 A7
Mainpuri India 27°18N 79°4E 125 F8
Maintal Germany 50°7N 8°52E 77 E4
Maintenon France 48°35N 1°35E 71 D8
Maintirano Madag. 18°3S 44°1E 141 H8
Mainz Germany 50°1N 8°14E 77 E4
Maio C. Verde Is. 15°10N 23°10W 134 b
Maipú Argentina 36°52S 57°50W 190 D4
Maiquetía Venezuela 10°36N 66°57W 186 A5
Máira → Italy 44°49N 7°38E 92 D4
Mairabari India 26°30N 92°22E 123 F18
Mairena del Aljarafe
Spain 37°20N 6°4W 89 H4
Maisi Cuba 20°17N 74°9W 183 B5
Maisí, Pta. de Cuba 20°10N 74°10W 183 B5
Maitland N.S.W.,
Australia 32°33S 151°36E 153 B9
Maitland S. Austral.,
Australia 34°23S 137°40E 152 C2
Maitland → Canada 43°45N 81°43W 174 C3
Maitri Antarctica 70°0S 3°0W 55 D3
Maiyema Nigeria 12°5N 4°25E 139 C5
Maiyuan China 25°34N 117°28E 117 E11
Maiz, Is. del Nic. 12°15N 83°4W 182 D3
Maizuru Japan 35°25N 135°22E 113 G7
Majalengka Indonesia 6°50S 108°13E 119 G13
Majanji Uganda 0°16N 34°0E 142 B3
Majella = Maiella △ Italy 42°5N 14°5E 93 F11
Majene Indonesia 3°38S 118°57E 119 E5
Majete ⌂ Malawi 15°54S 34°34E 143 F3
Majevica Bos.-H. 44°45N 18°50E 80 F3
Majiang China 26°28N 107°32E 116 D6
Majorca = Mallorca
Spain 39°30N 3°0E 100 B10
Majors Creek Australia 35°33S 149°45E 153 C8
Majuro Marshall Is. 7°9N 171°12E 156 G9
Mak, Ko Thailand 11°49N 102°29E 121 G4
Maka Senegal 13°40N 14°10W 138 C2
Makaha Zimbabwe 17°20S 32°39E 145 A5
Makak Cameroon 3°36N 11°0E 139 E7
Makalamabedi
Botswana 20°19S 23°51E 144 B3
Makale Indonesia 3°6S 119°51E 119 E5
Makalu Nepal 27°55N 87°8E 125 F12
Makalu-Barun △
Nepal 27°45N 87°10E 125 F12
Makamba Burundi 4°8S 29°49E 142 C2
Makarewa Junction
N.Z. 46°20S 168°21E 155 G3
Makari Cameroon 12°35N 14°28E 139 C7
Makarikari = Makgadikgadi Salt
Pans Botswana 20°40S 25°45E 144 B4
Makarov Basin Arctic 87°0N 150°0W 54 A
Makarovo Russia 57°40N 107°45E 107 D11
Makarska Croatia 43°20N 17°2E 93 E14
Makaryev Russia 57°52N 43°50E 86 B6
Makassar Indonesia 5°10S 119°20E 119 F5
Makassar, Selat
Indonesia 1°0S 118°20E 119 E5
Makassar, Str. of = Makassar,
Selat Indonesia 1°0S 118°20E 119 E5
Makat = Maqat
Kazakhstan 47°39N 53°19E 108 C4
Makedonija = Macedonia ■
Europe 41°53N 21°40E 96 E5
Makeni S. Leone 8°55N 12°5W 138 D2
Makeyevka = Makiyivka
Ukraine 48°0N 38°0E 85 H9
Makgadikgadi △
Botswana 20°27S 24°47E 144 B3
Makgadikgadi Salt Pans
Botswana 20°40S 25°45E 144 B4
Makhachkala Russia 43°0N 47°30E 87 J8
Makhado = Louis Trichardt
S. Africa 23°1S 29°43E 145 B4
Makham, Ao Thailand 7°51N 98°25E 121 a
Makharadze = Ozurgeti
Georgia 41°55N 42°0E 87 K5
Makhfar al Buşayyah
Iraq 30°0N 46°10E 128 D5
Makhmūr Iraq 35°46N 43°35E 105 E10
Makhtal India 16°30N 77°31E 127 E3
Makian Indonesia 0°20N 127°20E 119 D7
Makindu Kenya 2°18S 37°50E 142 C4
Makīnsk Kazakhstan 52°37N 70°26E 109 B8
Makira = San Cristóbal
Solomon Is. 10°30S 161°0E 147 C9
Makiyivka Ukraine 48°0N 38°0E 85 H9
Makkah Si. Arabia 21°30N 39°54E 137 C4
Makkovik Canada 55°10N 59°10W 165 A8
Makó Hungary 46°14N 20°33E 80 D5
Mako Senegal 12°52N 12°20W 138 C2
Makogai Fiji 17°28S 179°0E 154 a
Makokou Gabon 0°40N 12°50E 140 D2
Makongo
Dem. Rep. of the Congo 3°25N 26°17E 142 B2
Makoro
Dem. Rep. of the Congo 3°10N 29°59E 142 B2
Maków Mazowiecki
Poland 52°52N 21°6E 83 F8
Maków Podhalański
Poland 49°43N 19°45E 83 J6
Makra Greece 36°15N 25°54E 99 E7
Makrai India 22°2N 77°0E 124 H7
Makran Coast Range
Pakistan 25°40N 64°0E 122 G4
Makrana India 27°2N 74°46E 124 F6
Makrany Belarus 51°48N 24°17E 83 G11
Makri Greece 40°52N 25°40E 97 F9
Makri India 19°46N 81°55E 126 E5
Makrigialos Greece 35°2N 25°59E 101 D7
Makthar Tunisia 35°48N 9°12E 136 A5
Mākū Iran 39°15N 44°31E 105 C11
Makueni □ Kenya 1°50S 37°40E 142 C4
Makunda Botswana 22°30S 20°7E 144 B3
Makung Taiwan 23°34N 119°34E 117 F12
Makurazaki Japan 31°15N 130°20E 113 J5
Makurdi Nigeria 7°43N 8°35E 139 D6
Makushin Volcano
U.S.A. 53°53N 166°55W 166 E6
Makūyeh Iran 28°7N 53°9E 129 D7
Makwassie S. Africa 27°17S 26°0E 144 C4
Makwiro Zimbabwe 17°58S 30°25E 145 A5
Mâl Mauritania 16°58N 13°23W 138 B2
Mal B. Ireland 52°50N 9°30W 64 D2
Mala = Mallow Ireland 52°8N 8°39W 64 D3
Mala Peru 12°40S 76°38W 188 C2
Mala ✿ Australia 21°39S 130°45E 148 D5
Mala, Pta. Panama 7°28N 80°2W 182 E3
Mala Belozërka Ukraine 47°12N 34°56E 85 J8
Malá Fatra △ Slovak Rep. 49°10N 19°0E 79 B12
Mala Kapela Croatia 44°45N 15°30E 93 D12
Mala Panew → Poland 50°43N 17°54E 83 H4
Mala Vyska Ukraine 48°39N 31°36E 85 H6
Malabar U.S.A. 28°0N 80°34W 179 H9
Malabar Coast India 11°0N 75°0E 127 J2
Malabu Nigeria 9°32N 12°48E 139 D7
Malacca, Straits of
Indonesia 3°0N 101°0E 121 L3
Malacky Slovak Rep. 48°27N 17°0E 79 C10
Malad City U.S.A. 42°12N 112°15W 168 E7
Maladeta Spain 42°39N 0°39E 90 C5
Maladzyechna Belarus 54°20N 26°50E 75 A14
Málaga Spain 36°43N 4°23W 89 J6
Málaga □ Spain 36°38N 4°58W 89 J6
Malagarasi Tanzania 5°5S 30°50E 142 D3
Malagarasi → Tanzania 5°12S 29°47E 142 D2
Malagasy Rep. = Madagascar ■
Africa 20°0S 47°0E 141 J9
Malagón Spain 39°11N 3°52W 89 F7
Malagón → Spain 37°35N 7°29W 89 H3
Malahide Ireland 53°26N 6°9W 64 C5
Malaimbandy Madag. 20°20S 45°36E 141 J9
Malaita Solomon Is. 9°0S 161°0E 147 B9
Malakal South Sudan 9°33N 31°40E 135 G12
Malakanagiri India 18°21N 81°54E 126 E5
Malakand Pakistan 34°40N 71°55E 124 B4
Malakula Vanuatu 16°15S 167°30E 147 C9
Malakwal Pakistan 32°34N 73°13E 124 C5
Malamala Indonesia 3°21S 120°55E 119 E6
Malanda Australia 17°22S 145°35E 150 B4
Malang Indonesia 7°59S 112°45E 118 F4
Malanga Mozam. 13°28S 36°7E 143 E4
Malangen Norway 69°24N 18°37E 60 B18
Malangwa Nepal 26°52N 85°34E 125 F11
Malanje Angola 9°36S 16°17E 140 F3
Malappuram India 11°7N 76°11E 127 J3
Mälaren Sweden 59°30N 17°10E 62 E11
Malargüe Argentina 35°32S 69°30W 190 D2
Malartic Canada 48°9N 78°9W 164 C4
Malaryta Belarus 51°50N 24°3E 83 G11
Malaspina Glacier
U.S.A. 59°50N 140°30W 166 D11
Malatya Turkey 38°25N 38°20E 105 C8
Malatya □ Turkey 38°15N 38°0E 104 C7
Malawi ■ Africa 11°55S 34°0E 143 E3
Malawi, L. Africa 12°30S 34°30E 143 E3
Malay Pen. Asia 7°25N 100°0E 121 J3
Malaya Belozërka = Mala
Belozërka Ukraine 47°12N 34°56E 85 J8
Malaya Vishera Russia 58°55N 32°25E 84 C7
Malaya Viska = Mala Vyska
Ukraine 48°39N 31°36E 85 H6
Malaybalay Phil. 8°5N 125°7E 119 C7
Malāyer Iran 34°19N 48°51E 105 E13
Malaysia ■ Asia 5°0N 110°0E 118 D4
Malazgirt Turkey 39°10N 42°33E 105 C10
Malbaza Niger 13°59N 5°38E 139 C6
Malbon Australia 21°5S 140°17E 150 C3
Malbooma Australia 30°41S 134°11E 151 E1
Malbork Poland 54°3N 19°1E 82 D6
Malcésine Italy 45°46N 10°48E 92 C7
Malchin Germany 53°44N 12°44E 76 B8
Malchow Germany 53°28N 12°25E 76 B8
Malcolm Australia 28°51S 121°25E 149 E3
Malcolm, Pt. Australia 33°48S 123°45E 149 F3
Malczyce Poland 51°14N 16°29E 83 G3
Maldah India 25°2N 88°9E 125 G13
Maldegem Belgium 51°14N 3°26E 69 C3
Malden Mass., U.S.A. 42°26N 71°3W 175 D13
Malden Mo., U.S.A. 36°34N 89°57W 172 G9
Malden I. Kiribati 4°3S 155°1W 157 H12
Maldives ■ Ind. Oc. 5°0N 73°0E 103 H9
Maldon Australia 37°0S 144°6E 152 D6
Maldon U.K. 51°44N 0°42E 67 F8
Maldonado Uruguay 34°59S 55°0W 191 C5
Maldonado, Pta.
Mexico 16°20N 98°33W 181 D5
Malè Italy 46°21N 10°55E 92 B7
Malé Maldives 4°10N 73°28E 146 D6
Malé Karpaty
Slovak Rep. 48°30N 17°20E 79 C10
Maleas, Akra Greece 36°28N 23°7E 98 E5
Malebo, Pool Africa 4°17S 15°20E 140 E3
Malegaon India 20°30N 74°38E 126 D2
Malei Mozam. 17°12S 36°58E 143 F4
Malek Kandī Iran 37°9N 46°6E 105 D12
Malela
Dem. Rep. of the Congo 4°22S 26°8E 142 C2
Malema Mozam. 14°57S 37°20E 143 E4
Maleme Greece 35°31N 23°49E 101 D5
Maler Kotla India 30°32N 75°58E 124 D6
Målerås Sweden 56°54N 15°34E 63 H9
Males Greece 35°6N 25°35E 101 D7
Malesherbes France 48°15N 2°24E 71 D9

Maleshevska Planina
Europe 41°38N 23°7E 96 E7
Malesina Greece 38°37N 23°14E 98 C5
Malestroit France 47°49N 2°25W 70 E4
Malfa Italy 38°35N 14°50E 95 D7
Malgobek Russia 43°30N 44°34E 87 J7
Malgomaj Sweden 64°40N 16°30E 60 D17
Malgrat de Mar Spain 41°39N 2°46E 90 D7
Malha Sudan 15°8N 25°10E 135 E11
Malhada Brazil 14°21S 43°47W 189 C2
Malhargarh India 24°17N 74°59E 124 G6
Malheur → U.S.A. 44°4N 116°59W 168 D5
Malheur L. U.S.A. 43°20N 118°48W 168 E4
Mali Guinea 12°10N 12°20W 138 C2
Mali ■ Africa 17°0N 3°0W 138 B4
Mali → Burma 25°42N 97°30E 123 G20
Mali Kanal Serbia 45°36N 19°24E 80 E4
Mali Kyun Burma 13°0N 98°20E 120 F2
Malia Greece 35°17N 25°32E 101 D7
Malia, Kolpos Greece 35°19N 25°27E 101 D7
Malibu U.S.A. 34°2N 118°41W 171 L8
Maliku = Minicoy I.
India 8°17N 73°2E 127 K1
Maliku Indonesia 0°39S 123°16E 119 E6
Malili Indonesia 2°42S 121°6E 119 E6
Mälilla Sweden 57°23N 15°48E 63 G9
Malimba, Mts.
Dem. Rep. of the Congo 7°30S 29°30E 142 D2
Malin Hd. Ireland 55°23N 7°23W 64 A4
Malin Pen. Ireland 55°20N 7°17W 64 A4
Malindi Kenya 3°12S 40°5E 142 C5
Malindi Marine △ Kenya 3°15S 40°7E 142 C5
Malines = Mechelen
Belgium 51°2N 4°29E 69 C4
Malino Indonesia 1°0N 121°0E 119 D6
Malinyi Tanzania 8°56S 36°0E 143 D4
Malipo China 23°7N 104°42E 116 F5
Malita Phil. 6°19N 125°39E 119 C7
Maliwun Burma 10°17N 98°40E 121 G2
Maliya India 23°5N 70°46E 124 H4
Maljenik Serbia 43°54N 21°43E 96 C5
Malka Mari △ Kenya 4°11N 40°46E 142 B5
Malkapur India 20°53N 76°12E 126 D3
Malkara Turkey 40°53N 26°53E 97 F10
Malkhangiri = Malakanagiri
India 18°21N 81°54E 126 E5
Malkinia Górna Poland 52°42N 22°5E 83 F9
Malko Tŭrnovo
Bulgaria 41°59N 27°31E 97 E11
Mallacoota Australia 37°40S 149°40E 153 D8
Mallacoota Inlet
Australia 37°34S 149°40E 153 D8
Mallaig U.K. 57°0N 5°50W 65 D3
Mallala Australia 34°26S 138°30E 152 C2
Mallaoua Niger 13°2N 9°36E 139 C6
Mallawan India 27°4N 80°12E 125 F9
Mallawi Egypt 27°44N 30°44E 137 B3
Mallee Cliffs △
Australia 34°16S 142°32E 152 C5
Mallemort France 43°43N 5°11E 73 E9
Málles Venosta Italy 46°41N 10°32E 92 B7
Mallicolo = Malakula
Vanuatu 16°15S 167°30E 147 C9
Mallorca Spain 39°30N 3°0E 100 B10
Mallorytown Canada 44°29N 75°53W 175 B9
Mallow Ireland 52°8N 8°39W 64 D3
Malmbäck Sweden 57°34N 14°28E 63 G8
Malmberget Sweden 67°11N 20°40E 60 C19
Malmédy Belgium 50°25N 6°2E 69 D6
Malmesbury S. Africa 33°28S 18°41E 144 D2
Malmivaara = Malmberget
Sweden 67°11N 20°40E 60 C19
Malmköping Sweden 59°8N 16°44E 62 E10
Malmö Sweden 55°36N 12°59E 63 J7
Malmslätt Sweden 58°27N 15°33E 63 F9
Malmyzh Russia 56°31N 50°41E 86 B10
Malnas Romania 46°2N 25°49E 81 D10
Malo Konare Bulgaria 42°12N 24°24E 97 D8
Maloarkhangelsk
Russia 52°28N 36°30E 85 F9
Malolo Fiji 17°45S 177°11E 154 a
Malolos Phil. 14°50N 120°49E 119 B6
Malolotja △ Swaziland 26°4S 31°6E 145 C5
Malombe L. Malawi 14°40S 35°15E 143 E4
Malomice Poland 51°34N 15°29E 83 G2
Malomir Bulgaria 42°16N 26°32E 97 D10
Malone Fla., U.S.A. 30°57N 85°10W 178 F4
Malone N.Y., U.S.A. 44°51N 74°18W 175 B10
Malong China 25°24N 103°34E 116 E4
Malopolskie □ Poland 49°50N 20°0E 83 J7
Malorad Bulgaria 43°28N 23°41E 96 C7
Maloti Mts. = Drakensberg
S. Africa 31°0S 28°0E 145 D4
Maløy Norway 61°57N 5°6E 60 F11
Maloyaroslovets Russia 55°2N 36°20E 84 E9
Malpartida de Cáceres
Spain 39°26N 6°30W 89 F4
Malpaso Canary Is. 27°43N 18°3W 100 G1
Malpaso, Presa =
Netzahualcóyotl, Presa
Mexico 17°8N 93°35W 181 D6
Malpelo, I. de Colombia 4°3N 81°35W 186 C2
Malpica de Bergantiños
Spain 43°19N 8°50W 88 B2
Malprabha → India 16°20N 76°5E 127 F3
Malpur India 23°21N 73°27E 124 H5
Malpura India 26°17N 75°23E 124 F6
Mals = Málles Venosta
Italy 46°41N 10°32E 92 B7
Malsiras India 17°52N 74°55E 126 F2
Malta Idaho, U.S.A. 42°18N 113°22W 168 F7
Malta Mont., U.S.A. 48°21N 107°52W 168 B10
Malta ■ Europe 35°55N 14°26E 101 D2
Malta Freeport Malta 35°49N 14°32E 101 D2
Maltahöhe Namibia 24°55S 17°0E 144 B2
Maltepe Turkey 40°52N 29°8E 97 F13
Malton Canada 43°42N 79°38W 174 C5
Malton U.K. 54°8N 0°49W 66 C7
Maluku Indonesia 1°0S 127°0E 119 E7
Maluku □ Indonesia 3°0S 128°0E 119 E7
Maluku Sea = Molucca Sea
Indonesia 0°0 125°0E 119 E6
Malumfashi Nigeria 11°48N 7°39E 139 C6
Malung Sweden 60°42N 13°44E 62 D7
Malungsfors Sweden 60°44N 13°33E 62 D7
Malur India 13°0N 77°55E 127 H3
Maluwe Ghana 8°40N 2°17W 138 D4
Malvalli India 12°28N 77°8E 127 H3
Malvan India 16°2N 73°30E 127 F1
Malvern U.S.A. 34°22N 92°49W 176 D8

Malvern Hills U.K. 52°0N 2°19W 67 E5
Malvinas, Is. = Falkland Is. ☒
Atl. Oc. 51°30S 59°0W 192 D5
Malý Dunaj →
Slovak Rep. 47°45N 18°9E 79 D11
Malya Tanzania 3°5S 33°38E 142 C3
Malye Derbety Russia 47°57N 44°42E 87 G7
Malyn Ukraine 50°46N 29°3E 75 C15
Malyy Lyakhovskiy, Ostrov
Russia 74°7N 140°36E 107 B15
Malyy Taymyr, Ostrov
Russia 78°6N 107°15E 107 B11
Mama Russia 58°18N 112°54E 107 D12
Mamaku N.Z. 38°5S 176°8E 154 E5
Mamanguape Brazil 6°50S 35°4W 189 B3
Mamanuca Group Fiji 17°35S 177°5E 154 a
Mamarr Mitlā Egypt 30°2N 32°54E 130 E1
Mamasa Indonesia 2°55S 119°20E 119 E5
Mambasa
Dem. Rep. of the Congo 1°22N 29°3E 142 B2
Mamberamo →
Indonesia 2°0S 137°50E 119 E9
Mambilima Falls
Zambia 10°31S 28°45E 143 E2
Mambirima
Dem. Rep. of the Congo 11°25S 27°33E 143 E2
Mambo Tanzania 4°52S 38°22E 142 C4
Mambrui Kenya 3°5S 40°5E 142 C5
Mamburao Phil. 13°13N 120°39E 119 B6
Mamedkala Russia 42°10N 48°7E 87 J9
Mameigwess L. Canada 52°35N 87°50W 164 B2
Mamers France 48°21N 0°22E 70 D7
Mamfe Cameroon 5°50N 9°15E 139 D6
Mamili △ Namibia 18°2S 24°1E 144 A3
Mamiña Chile 20°5S 69°14W 188 E4
Mamlyutka Kazakhstan 54°56N 68°32E 109 H7
Mammoth U.S.A. 32°43N 110°39W 169 K8
Mammoth Cave △
U.S.A. 37°8N 86°13W 172 G10
Mammoth Lakes
U.S.A. 37°39N 118°59W 170 H8
Mamonovo Russia 54°28N 19°55E 82 D6
Mamoré → Bolivia 10°23S 65°53W 186 F5
Mamou Guinea 10°15N 12°0W 138 C2
Mamoudzou Mayotte 12°48S 45°14E 141 a
Mampong Ghana 7°6N 1°26W 139 D4
Mamry, Jezioro Poland 54°5N 21°50E 82 D8
Mamuil Malal, Paso
S. Amer. 39°35S 71°28W 192 A2
Mamuju Indonesia 2°41S 118°50E 119 E5
Mamuno Botswana 22°16S 20°1E 144 B3
Mamuras Albania 41°34N 19°41E 96 E3
Man Ivory C. 7°30N 7°40W 138 D3
Man → India 17°31N 75°32E 126 F2
Man, I. of India 8°28N 93°36E 127 K11
Man, I. of U.K. 54°15N 4°30W 66 C3
Man-Bazar India 23°4N 86°39E 125 H12
Man Na Burma 23°27N 97°19E 123 H20
Mänä U.S.A. 22°2N 159°47W 167 L8
Mana → Fr. Guiana 5°45N 53°55W 187 B8
Mana Pools △
Zimbabwe 15°56S 29°25E 143 F2
Manaar, G. of = Mannar, G. of
Asia 8°30N 79°0E 127 K4
Manacapuru Brazil 3°16S 60°37W 186 D6
Manacor Spain 39°34N 3°13E 100 B10
Manado Indonesia 1°29N 124°51E 119 D6
Managua Nic. 12°6N 86°20W 182 D2
Managua, L. de Nic. 12°20N 86°30W 182 D2
Manaia N.Z. 39°33S 174°8E 154 F5
Manakara Madag. 22°8S 48°1E 141 J9
Manakau N.Z. 42°15S 173°42E 155 C8
Manali India 32°16N 77°10E 124 C7
Manama = Al Manāmah
Bahrain 26°10N 50°30E 129 E6
Manangatang Australia 35°5S 142°54E 152 C5
Mananjary Madag. 21°13S 48°20E 141 J9
Manankoro Mali 10°28N 7°25W 138 C3
Manantali, L. de Mali 13°12N 10°28W 138 C2
Manantavadi India 11°49N 76°1E 127 J3
Manantenina Madag. 24°17S 47°19E 141 J9
Manaos = Manaus Brazil 3°0S 60°0W 186 D7
Manapire → Venezuela 7°26N 66°7W 186 B5
Manapouri N.Z. 45°34S 167°39E 155 F2
Manapouri, L. N.Z. 45°32S 167°32E 155 F2
Manapparai India 10°36N 78°25E 127 J4
Manar → India 18°50N 77°20E 126 E3
Manār, Jabal Yemen 14°2N 44°17E 131 E3
Manas China 44°17N 86°10E 109 D11
Manas → China 46°12N 90°40E 123 F17
Manas He → China 45°38N 85°12E 110 B6
Manas Hu China 45°45N 85°55E 109 C11
Manaslu Nepal 28°33N 84°33E 125 E11
Manasquan U.S.A. 40°8N 74°3W 175 F10
Manassa U.S.A. 37°11N 105°56W 169 H11
Manati Puerto Rico 18°26N 66°29W 183 d
Manaus Brazil 3°0S 60°0W 186 D7
Manavgat Turkey 36°47N 31°26E 104 D4
Manawan L. Canada 55°24N 103°14W 163 B8
Manawatu → N.Z. 40°28S 175°12E 154 G4
Manawatu-Wanganui □
N.Z. 39°50S 175°30E 154 F4
Manbij Syria 36°31N 37°57E 104 D7
Mancha Real Spain 37°48N 3°39W 89 H7
Manche □ France 49°10N 1°20W 70 C5
Manchegorsk Russia 67°54N 32°58E 106 C4
Manchester U.K. 53°29N 2°12W 66 D5
Manchester Calif.,
U.S.A. 38°58N 123°41W 170 G3
Manchester Conn.,
U.S.A. 41°47N 72°31W 175 E12
Manchester Ga., U.S.A. 32°51N 84°37W 178 C5
Manchester Iowa,
U.S.A. 42°29N 91°27W 172 D8
Manchester Ky.,
U.S.A. 37°9N 83°46W 173 G12
Manchester N.H.,
U.S.A. 42°59N 71°28W 175 D13
Manchester N.Y.,
U.S.A. 42°56N 77°16W 174 D7
Manchester Pa., U.S.A. 40°4N 76°43W 175 F8
Manchester Tenn.,
U.S.A. 35°29N 86°5W 177 D11
Manchester Vt., U.S.A. 43°10N 73°5W 175 C11
Manchester Int. ✈ (MAN)
U.K. 53°21N 2°17W 66 D5
Manchester L. Canada 52°28N 107°29W 163 A7
Manchhar L. Pakistan 26°25N 67°39E 124 F2
Manchuria = Dongbei
China 45°0N 125°0E 115 D13
Manchurian Plain
China 47°0N 124°0E 102 D14

Manciano Italy 42°35N 11°31E 93 F8
Máncora Peru 4°9S 81°1W 188 A1
Mand → India 21°42N 83°15E 125 J10
Mand → Iran 28°20N 52°30E 129 D7
Manda Ludewe, Tanzania 10°30S 34°40E 143 E3
Manda Mbeya, Tanzania 7°58S 32°29E 142 D3
Manda Mbeya, Tanzania 8°30S 32°49E 143 D3
Mandaguari Brazil 23°32S 51°42W 191 A5
Mandah = Töhöm
Mongolia 44°27N 108°2E 114 B5
Mandal Norway 58°2N 7°25E 61 G12
Mandala, Puncak
Indonesia 4°44S 140°20E 119 E10
Mandalay Burma 22°0N 96°4E 123 J20
Mandale = Mandalay
Burma 22°0N 96°4E 123 J20
Mandalgarh India 25°12N 75°6E 124 G6
Mandalgovĭ Mongolia 45°45N 106°10E 114 B4
Mandalī Iraq 33°43N 45°28E 105 F11
Mandan U.S.A. 46°50N 100°54W 172 B3
Mandar, Teluk
Indonesia 3°35S 119°21E 119 E5
Mándas Italy 39°40N 9°8E 94 C2
Mandaue Phil. 10°20N 123°56E 119 B6
Mandelieu-la-Napoule
France 43°34N 6°57E 73 E10
Mandera Kenya 3°55N 41°53E 142 B5
Mandera □ Kenya 3°20N 40°40E 142 B5
Mandeville Jamaica 18°2N 77°31W 182 a
Mandi India 31°39N 76°58E 124 D7
Mandi Burewala
Pakistan 30°9N 72°41E 124 D5
Mandi Dabwali India 29°58N 74°42E 124 E6
Mandiana Guinea 10°37N 8°39W 138 C3
Mandimba Mozam. 14°20S 35°40E 143 E4
Mandioli Indonesia 0°40S 127°20E 119 E7
Mandla India 22°39N 80°30E 125 H9
Mando Denmark 55°18N 8°33E 63 J2
Mandorah Australia 12°32S 130°42E 148 B5
Mandoudi Greece 38°48N 23°29E 98 C5
Mandra Greece 38°4N 23°30E 98 C5
Mandra Pakistan 33°23N 73°12E 124 C5
Mandraki Greece 36°36N 27°11E 99 E9
Mandritsara Madag. 15°50S 48°49E 141 H9
Mandsaur India 24°3N 75°8E 124 G6
Mandurah Australia 32°36S 115°48E 149 F2
Mandúria Italy 40°24N 17°38E 95 B10
Mandvi India 22°51N 69°22E 124 H3
Mandya India 12°30N 77°0E 127 H3
Mandzai Pakistan 30°55N 67°6E 124 D2
Mané Burkina Faso 12°59N 1°21W 139 C4
Maneh Iran 37°39N 57°7E 129 B8
Manengouba, Mts.
Cameroon 5°0N 9°50E 139 E6
Maner → India 18°30N 79°40E 126 E4
Manérbio Italy 45°21N 10°8E 92 C7
Maneroo Cr. →
Australia 23°21S 143°53E 150 C3
Manfalût Egypt 27°20N 30°52E 137 B3
Manfred Australia 33°19S 143°45E 152 B5
Manfredónia Italy 41°38N 15°55E 93 G12
Manfredónia, G. di Italy 41°35S 16°5E 93 G13
Manga Brazil 14°46S 43°56W 189 C2
Manga Burkina Faso 11°40N 1°4W 139 C4
Manga Niger 15°0N 14°0E 139 C7
Mangabeiras, Chapada das
Brazil 10°0S 46°30W 189 C1
Mangaia Cook Is. 21°55S 157°55W 157 K12
Mangakino N.Z. 38°22S 175°47E 154 E4
Mangalagiri India 16°26N 80°36E 127 F5
Mangalia Romania 43°50N 28°35E 81 G13
Mangalore = Mangaluru
India 12°55N 74°47E 127 H2
Mangaluru India 12°55N 74°47E 127 H2
Mangalvedha India 17°31N 75°28E 126 F2
Mangan India 27°31N 88°32E 125 F13
Mangaon India 18°15N 73°20E 126 E1
Mangarrayi ⊙
Australia 15°5S 133°10E 150 B1
Mangawan India 24°41N 81°33E 125 G9
Mangaweka N.Z. 39°48S 175°47E 154 F4
Mangaweka, Mt. N.Z. 39°49S 176°5E 154 F5
Mangetti △ Namibia 18°43S 19°8E 144 A2
Manggar Indonesia 2°50S 108°10E 118 E3
Manggawitu Indonesia 4°8S 133°32E 119 E8
Mangghystaŭ
Kazakhstan 43°40N 51°13E 108 D4
Mangghystaŭ □
Kazakhstan 44°0N 52°30E 108 D4
Mangghystaŭ Tübegi
Kazakhstan 44°30N 52°30E 108 D4
Manggis Indonesia 8°29S 115°31E 119 J18
Mangkalihat, Tanjung
Indonesia 1°2N 118°59E 119 D5
Mangkururrpa ⊙
Australia 20°35S 129°43E 148 D4
Mangla Pakistan 33°7N 73°39E 124 C5
Mangla Dam Pakistan 33°9N 73°44E 125 C5
Manglaur India 29°44N 77°49E 124 E7
Manglisi Georgia 41°41N 44°22E 87 K7
Mangnai Zhen China 38°24N 90°14E 109 E12
Mango Togo 10°20N 0°30E 139 C5
Mangoche Malawi 14°25S 35°16E 143 E4
Mangoky → Madag. 21°29S 43°41E 141 J8
Mangole Indonesia 1°50S 125°55E 119 E6
Mangombe
Dem. Rep. of the Congo 1°20S 26°48E 142 C2
Mangonui N.Z. 35°1S 173°32E 154 B2
Mangrol Mad. P., India 21°7N 70°7E 124 J4
Mangrol Raj., India 25°20N 76°31E 124 G6
Mangrul Pir India 20°19N 77°21E 126 D3
Mangshi = Luxi China 24°27N 98°36E 116 E2
Mangualde Portugal 40°38N 7°48W 88 E3
Mangueira, L. da Brazil 33°0S 52°50W 191 C5
Mangum U.S.A. 34°53N 99°30W 176 D5
Mangyshlak, Poluostrov =
Mangghystaŭ Tübegi
Kazakhstan 44°30N 52°30E 108 D4
Manhattan U.S.A. 39°11N 96°35W 172 F7
Manhiça Mozam. 25°23S 32°49E 145 C5
Manhuaçu Brazil 20°15S 42°2W 191 A7
Manhumirim Brazil 20°22S 41°57W 189 E2
Mania → Madag. 19°42S 45°22E 141 H9
Manica Mozam. 18°58S 32°59E 145 A5
Manica □ Mozam. 19°0S 33°45E 145 A5
Manicoré Brazil 5°48S 61°16W 186 E6
Manicouagan →
Canada 49°30N 68°30W 165 C6

Manicouagan, Rés.
Canada 51°5N 68°40W 165 C6
Maniema □
Dem. Rep. of the Congo 3°0S 26°0E 142 C2
Manifah Si. Arabia 27°44N 49°0E 129 E6
Manifold, C. Australia 22°41S 150°50E 150 C5
Maniganggo China 31°56N 99°10E 116 B2
Manigotagan Canada 51°6N 96°18W 163 C9
Manigotagan →
Canada 51°7N 96°20W 163 C9
Manihari India 25°21N 87°38E 125 G12
Manihiki Cook Is. 10°24S 161°1W 157 J11
Manihiki Plateau
Pac. Oc. 11°0S 164°0W 157 J11
Maniitsoq Greenland 65°26N 52°55W 57 D5
Manika, Plateau de la
Dem. Rep. of the Congo 10°0S 25°5E 143 E2
Manikpur India 25°4N 81°7E 125 G9
Manila Phil. 14°35N 120°58E 119 B6
Manila U.S.A. 40°59N 109°43W 168 F9
Manila B. Phil. 14°40N 120°35E 119 B6
Manildra Australia 33°11S 148°41E 153 B8
Manilla Australia 30°45S 150°43E 153 E9
Manilva Spain 36°23N 5°15W 89 J5
Manimpé Mali 14°11N 5°28W 138 C3
Maningrida Australia 12°3S 134°13E 150 A1
Maninian Ivory C. 10°3N 7°52W 138 C3
Manipa, Selat Indonesia 3°20S 127°25E 119 E7
Manipur □ India 25°0N 94°0E 123 G19
Manipur → Burma 23°45N 94°20E 123 H19
Manisa Turkey 38°38N 27°30E 99 C9
Manisa □ Turkey 38°40N 28°0E 99 C10
Manistee U.S.A. 44°15N 86°19W 172 C10
Manistee → U.S.A. 44°15N 86°21W 172 C10
Manistique U.S.A. 45°57N 86°15W 172 C10
Manitoba □ Canada 53°30N 97°0W 163 B9
Manitoba, L. Canada 51°0N 98°45W 163 C9
Manitou Canada 49°15N 98°32W 163 D9
Manitou, L. Canada 50°55N 65°17W 165 B6
Manitou I. U.S.A. 45°8N 86°0W 172 C10
Manitou L. Canada 52°43N 109°43W 163 C7
Manitou Springs
U.S.A. 38°52N 104°55W 168 G11
Manitoulin I. Canada 45°40N 82°30W 164 C3
Manitouwadge Canada 49°8N 85°48W 164 C2
Manitowoc U.S.A. 44°5N 87°40W 172 C10
Maniyachi India 8°51N 77°55E 127 K3
Manizales Colombia 5°5N 75°32W 186 B3
Manja Madag. 21°26S 44°20E 141 J8
Manjacaze Mozam. 24°45S 34°0E 145 B5
Manjakandriana
Madag. 18°55S 47°47E 141 H9
Manjhand Pakistan 25°50N 68°10E 124 G3
Manjimup Australia 34°15S 116°6E 149 F2
Manjlegaon India 19°9N 76°14E 126 E3
Manjo Cameroon 4°50N 9°49E 139 E6
Manjra → India 18°49N 77°52E 126 E3
Mankato Kans., U.S.A. 39°47N 98°13W 172 F4
Mankato Minn., U.S.A. 44°10N 94°0W 172 C6
Mankayane Swaziland 26°40S 31°4E 145 C5
Mankera Pakistan 31°23N 71°26E 124 D4
Mankim Cameroon 5°6N 12°3E 139 D7
Mankono Ivory C. 8°1N 6°10W 138 D3
Mankota Canada 49°25N 107°5W 163 D7
Mankulam Sri Lanka 9°8N 80°26E 127 K5
Manlay = Üydzin
Mongolia 44°9N 107°0E 114 B4
Manlleu Spain 42°2N 2°17E 90 C7
Manly Australia 33°47S 151°17E 153 B9
Manmad India 20°18N 74°28E 126 D2
Mann Ranges Australia 26°6S 130°5E 149 E5
Manna Indonesia 4°25S 102°55E 118 E2
Mannahill Australia 32°25S 140°0E 152 B4
Mannar Sri Lanka 9°1N 79°54E 127 K4
Mannar, G. of Asia 8°30N 79°0E 127 K4
Mannar I. Sri Lanka 9°5N 79°45E 127 K4
Mannargudi India 10°45N 79°51E 127 J4
Mannheim Germany 49°29N 8°29E 77 F4
Manning Canada 56°53N 117°39W 162 B5
Manning Oreg., U.S.A. 45°45N 123°13W 170 E3
Manning S.C., U.S.A. 33°42N 80°13W 178 B9
Manning □
Australia 31°52S 152°43E 153 A10
Mannu → Italy 39°16N 9°0E 94 C2
Mannu, C. Italy 40°3N 8°21E 94 B1
Mannum Australia 34°50S 139°20E 152 C3
Mano S. Leone 8°3N 12°2W 138 D2
Mano → Liberia 6°56N 11°30W 138 D2
Manokwari Indonesia 0°54S 134°0E 119 E8
Manola Greece 38°4N 21°21E 98 C3
Manolo Madag. 22°57S 43°28E 141 J8
Manono
Dem. Rep. of the Congo 7°15S 27°25E 142 D2
Manoppello Italy 42°15N 14°3E 93 F11
Manorhamilton Ireland 54°18N 8°11W 64 B3
Manosque France 43°49N 5°47E 73 E9
Manotick Canada 45°13N 75°41W 175 A9
Manouane → Canada 49°30N 71°10W 165 C5
Manouane, L. Canada 50°45N 70°45W 165 B5
Manp'o N. Korea 41°6N 126°24E 115 D14
Manpojin = Manp'o
N. Korea 41°6N 126°24E 115 D14
Manpur Chhattisgarh,
India 23°17N 83°35E 125 H10
Manpur Mad. P., India 22°26N 75°37E 124 H6
Manresa Spain 41°48N 1°50E 90 D6
Mansa Gujarat, India 23°27N 72°45E 124 H5
Mansa Punjab, India 30°0N 75°27E 124 E6
Mansa Zambia 11°13S 28°55E 143 E2
Mansa Konko Gambia 13°28N 15°33E 138 C1
Månsåsen Sweden 63°5N 14°18E 62 A8
Mansehra Pakistan 34°20N 73°15E 124 B5
Mansel I. Canada 62°0N 79°50W 161 E15
Mansfield Australia 37°4S 146°6E 153 C7
Mansfield U.K. 53°9N 1°11W 66 D6
Mansfield La., U.S.A. 32°2N 93°43W 176 E7
Mansfield Mass.,
U.S.A. 42°2N 71°13W 175 D13
Mansfield Ohio, U.S.A. 40°45N 82°31W 174 F2
Mansfield Pa., U.S.A. 41°48N 77°5W 174 E7
Mansfield Tex., U.S.A. 32°35N 97°9W 176 E6
Mansfield, Mt. U.S.A. 44°33N 72°49W 175 B12
Mansidão Brazil 10°43S 44°3W 189 C2
Mansilla de las Mulas
Spain 42°30N 5°25W 88 C5
Mansle France 45°52N 0°12E 72 C4
Manso → Brazil 13°50S 43°24W 189 C2
Mansôa Guinea-Biss. 12°0N 15°20W 138 C1

Manson Creek
Canada 55°37N 124°32W 162 B4
Mansoura Algeria 36°1N 4°31E 136 A4
Manta Ecuador 1°0S 80°40W 186 D2
Mantalingajan, Mt.
Phil. 8°55N 117°45E 118 C5
Mantare Tanzania 2°42S 33°13E 142 C3
Mantaro → Peru 12°16S 73°57W 188 D3
Manteca U.S.A. 37°48N 121°13W 170 H5
Mantena Brazil 18°47S 40°59W 189 E2
Manteo U.S.A. 35°55N 75°40W 177 D17
Mantha India 19°40N 76°23E 126 E3
Manthani India 18°40N 79°35E 126 E4
Manti U.S.A. 39°16N 111°38W 168 G8
Mantiqueira, Serra da
Brazil 22°0S 44°0W 191 A7
Manton U.S.A. 44°25N 85°24W 173 C11
Mantorp Sweden 58°21N 15°20E 63 F9
Mántova Italy 45°9N 10°48E 92 C7
Mänttä Vilppula Finland 62°3N 24°40E 84 A3
Mantua = Mántova Italy 45°9N 10°48E 92 C7
Mantung Australia 34°35S 140°3E 152 C4
Manturovo Russia 58°23N 44°45E 86 A7
Manú Peru 12°10S 70°51W 188 C3
Manú → Peru 12°16S 70°55W 188 C3
Manuel Alves →
Brazil 11°19S 48°28W 189 C1
Manuel Alves Grande →
Brazil 7°27S 47°35W 189 B1
Manuel Urbano Brazil 8°53S 69°18W 188 B4
Manui Indonesia 3°35S 123°5E 119 E6
Manukau N.Z. 37°0S 174°52E 154 D3
Manukau Harbour
N.Z. 37°3S 174°45E 154 D3
Manunui N.Z. 38°54S 175°21E 154 F4
Manuoha N.Z. 38°39S 177°7E 154 E6
Manuripi → Bolivia 11°6S 67°36W 188 C4
Manvi India 15°57N 76°59E 127 G3
Manwan Dam China 24°44N 100°20E 116 E3
Manwath India 19°19N 76°32E 126 E3
Many U.S.A. 31°34N 93°29W 176 F8
Manyallaluk ⊙
Australia 14°16S 132°49E 148 B5
Manyani Kenya 3°5S 38°30E 142 C4
Manyara □ Tanzania 4°30S 37°10E 142 C4
Manyara, L. Tanzania 3°40S 35°50E 142 C4
Manyas Turkey 40°2N 27°59E 97 F11
Manyava Ukraine 48°39N 24°21E 81 B9
Manych → Russia 47°13N 40°0E 87 G6
Manych-Gudilo, Ozero
Russia 46°24N 42°38E 87 G6
Manyonga → Tanzania 4°10S 34°15E 142 C3
Manyoni Tanzania 5°45S 34°55E 142 D3
Manzai Pakistan 32°12N 70°15E 124 C4
Manzala, Bahra el
Egypt 31°10N 31°56E 137 E7
Manzanar △ U.S.A. 36°44N 118°9W 170 J7
Manzanares Spain 39°2N 3°22W 89 F7
Manzaneda Spain 42°12N 7°15W 88 C3
Manzanillo Cuba 20°20N 77°31W 182 B4
Manzanillo Mexico 19°3N 104°20W 180 D4
Manzanillo, Pta.
Panama 9°30N 79°40W 182 E4
Manzano Mts.
U.S.A. 34°40N 106°20W 169 J10
Manzariyeh Iran 34°53N 50°50E 129 C6
Manzhouli China 49°35N 117°25E 111 B12
Manzini Swaziland 26°30S 31°25E 145 C5
Manzouli = Manzhouli
China 49°35N 117°25E 111 B12
Manzur Vadisi △
Turkey 39°10N 39°30E 128 B3
Mao Chad 14°4N 15°19E 135 F9
Maó Spain 39°53N 4°16E 100 B11
Maoke, Pegunungan
Indonesia 3°40S 137°30E 119 E9
Maolin China 43°58N 123°30E 115 C12
Maoming China 21°50N 110°54E 117 G8
Maopi T'ou China 21°56N 120°43E 117 G13
Maouri, Dallol → Niger 12°5N 3°30E 139 C5
Maoxian China 31°41N 103°49E 116 B4
Maoxing China 45°28N 124°40E 115 B13
Mapam Yumco China 30°45N 81°28E 125 D9
Mapastepec Mexico 15°26N 92°54W 181 D6
Maphrao, Ko Thailand 7°56N 98°26E 121 a
Mapia, Kepulauan
Indonesia 0°50N 134°20E 119 D8
Mapimí Mexico 25°49N 103°51W 180 B4
Mapimí, Bolsón de
Mexico 27°0N 104°15W 180 B4
Maping China 31°34N 113°32E 117 B9
Mapinga Tanzania 6°40S 39°12E 142 D4
Mapinhane Mozam. 22°20S 35°0E 145 C6
Maple Creek Canada 49°55N 109°29W 163 D7
Maple Valley U.S.A. 47°22N 122°3W 170 C4
Mapleton U.S.A. 44°2N 123°52W 168 D2
Mapourika, L. N.Z. 43°16S 170°9E 155 D3
Mapuca India 15°36N 73°47E 127 H1
Mapuera → Brazil 1°5S 57°2W 187 D7
Mapulanguene Mozam. 24°29S 32°6E 145 B5
Mapungubwe △
S. Africa 22°12S 29°22E 145 B4
Maputo Mozam. 25°58S 32°32E 145 C5
Maputo □ Mozam. 26°0S 32°25E 145 C5
Maputo, B. de Mozam. 25°50S 32°45E 145 C5
Maputo △ Mozam. 26°30S 32°40E 145 C5
Maqanshy Kazakhstan 46°47N 82°15E 109 C10
Maqat Kazakhstan 47°39N 53°19E 108 E4
Maqên Gangri China 34°24N 100°0E 110 E9
Maqiaohe China 44°40N 130°30E 115 B16
Maqnā Si. Arabia 28°25N 34°50E 128 D2
Maqteïr Mauritania 23°30N 12°50W 138 A2
Maqu China 33°52N 102°12E 110 E9
Maquan He = Brahmaputra →
Asia 23°40N 90°35E 125 H13
Maquela do Zombo
Angola 6°0S 15°15E 140 F3
Maquinchao Argentina 41°15S 68°50W 192 E3
Maquoketa U.S.A. 42°4N 90°40W 172 D8
Mar, Serra do Brazil 25°30S 49°0W 191 B6
Mar Chiquita, L.
Argentina 30°40S 62°50W 190 C3
Mar del Plata Argentina 38°0S 57°30W 190 D4
Mar Menor Spain 37°40N 0°45W 89 H4
Mara Tanzania 1°30S 34°32E 142 C3
Mara □ Tanzania 1°45S 34°20E 142 C3

Maraã Brazil 1°52S 65°25W 186 D5
Maraa Tahiti 17°46S 149°34W 155 d
Marabá Brazil 5°20S 49°5W 187 E9
Maraboon, L. Australia 23°41S 148°0E 150 C4
Maracá, I. de Brazil 2°10N 50°30W 187 C8
Maracaibo Venezuela 10°40N 71°37W 186 A4
Maracaibo, L. de
Venezuela 9°40N 71°30W 186 B4
Maracaju Brazil 21°38S 55°9W 191 A4
Maracanaú Brazil 3°52S 38°38W 189 D4
Maracás Brazil 13°26S 40°18W 189 D3
Maracas Bay Village
Trin. & Tob. 10°46N 61°28W 183 D7
Maracay Venezuela 10°15N 67°28W 186 A5
Maracena Spain 37°12N 3°38W 89 H7
Marādah Libya 29°15N 19°15E 135 C9
Maradi Niger 13°29N 7°20E 139 C6
Marāgheh Iran 37°30N 46°12E 105 B12
Maragogipe Brazil 12°46S 38°55W 189 D3
Marāh Si. Arabia 25°0N 45°35E 128 E5
Marahoué △ Ivory C. 8°0N 7°8W 138 D3
Marais du Cotentin et du Bessin △
France 49°10N 1°30W 70 C5
Marais Poitevin, Val de Sèvre et
Vendée △ France 46°18N 0°35W 72 B3
Marajo, I. de Brazil 1°0S 49°30W 187 D9
Marākand Iran 38°51N 45°16E 105 B12
Marakele △ S. Africa 24°30S 25°30E 145 B4
Maralal Kenya 1°0N 36°38E 142 B4
Maralinga Australia 30°13S 131°32E 149 F5
Maralinga Tjarutja ⊙
Australia 29°30S 131°0E 149 F5
Marama Australia 35°10S 140°10E 152 C4
Maramaeregëlisi
Turkey 40°57N 27°57E 97 F11
Marambio Antarctica 64°0S 56°0W 5 C18
Maramureş □ Romania 47°45N 24°0E 81 C8
Marana U.S.A. 32°27N 111°13W 169 K8
Maranboy ⊙ Australia 14°40S 132°39E 148 B5
Maranchón Spain 41°6N 2°15W 89 D7
Marand Iran 38°30N 45°45E 105 B12
Maranello Italy 44°32N 10°52E 92 D7
Marang Malaysia 5°12N 103°13E 121 K4
Maranguape Brazil 3°55S 38°50W 189 D4
Maranhão = São Luís
Brazil 2°39S 44°15W 189 B2
Maranhão □ Brazil 5°0S 46°0W 189 B2
Marano, L. di Italy 45°44N 13°13E 92 C5
Maranoa → Australia 27°50S 148°37E 153 D9
Marañón → Peru 4°30S 73°35W 186 D3
Marão Mozam. 24°18S 34°2E 145 B5
Marari Brazil 5°43S 67°47W 186 E5
Maraş = Kahramanmaraş
Turkey 37°37N 36°53E 104 D7
Mărăşeşti Romania 45°52N 27°14E 81 D11
Maratea Italy 39°59N 15°43E 95 C8
Marateca Portugal 38°34N 8°40W 89 C2
Marathasa Cyprus 34°59N 32°51E 101 E11
Marathokambos Greece 37°43N 26°42E 99 D8
Marathon Canada 48°44N 86°23W 164 C2
Marathon Fla., U.S.A. 24°43N 81°5W 178 H9
Marathon N.Y., U.S.A. 42°27N 76°2W 175 D8
Marathon Tex., U.S.A. 30°12N 103°15W 176 F3
Marathonas Greece 38°11N 23°58E 98 C5
Marathóvounos
Cyprus 35°13N 33°37E 101 D12
Maratua Indonesia 2°10N 118°35E 119 D5
Maraú Brazil 14°6S 39°0W 189 D3
Maraval Trin. & Tob. 10°42N 61°31W 183 D7
Maravatío Mexico 19°54N 100°27W 180 C4
Marāwih U.A.E. 24°18N 53°18E 129 E7
Marazliyivka Ukraine 46°8N 30°3E 81 B10
Marbella Spain 36°30N 4°57W 89 J6
Marble Bar Australia 21°9S 119°44E 149 D2
Marblehead Mass.,
U.S.A. 42°29N 70°51W 175 D14
Marburg Germany 50°47N 8°46E 77 E4
Marca, Pta. do Angola 16°31S 11°43E 140 H2
Marcal → Hungary 47°41N 17°2E 81 E1
Marcali Hungary 46°35N 17°25E 81 E2
Marcapata Peru 13°31S 70°52W 188 D3
Marcaria Italy 45°7N 10°32E 92 C7
Mărculeşti Moldova 47°54N 28°12E 81 B10
March U.K. 52°33N 0°5E 67 E8
Marche France 46°5N 1°20E 72 B5
Marche □ Italy 43°30N 13°0E 92 E9
Marche-en-Famenne
Belgium 50°14N 5°19E 69 D5
Marchena Spain 37°18N 5°23W 89 H5
Marches = Marche □
Italy 43°30N 13°0E 92 E9
Marchesale △ Italy 38°32N 16°13E 95 D9
Marciana Marina Italy 42°48N 10°12E 92 F7
Marcianise Italy 41°2N 14°17E 95 A7
Marcigny France 46°17N 4°2E 72 B6
Marcillat-en-Combraille
France 46°12N 2°38E 72 B5
Marck France 50°57N 1°57E 70 A4
Marckolsheim France 48°10N 7°30E 70 D8
Marco Island U.S.A. 25°58N 81°44W 178 H8
Marcona Peru 15°10S 75°0W 188 D2
Marcos Juárez Argentina 32°42S 62°5W 190 C3

rennes *France* 45°49N 1°7W **72** C2
éttimo *Italy* 37°58N 12°4E **94** E5
reuil *France* 45°26N 0°29E **72** G4
fa *U.S.A.* 30°19N 104°1W **176** F2
fa Pt. *Malta* 35°59N 14°19E **101** D1
ganets = Marhanets
kraine 47°40N 34°40E **85** J8
gao = Madgaon
dia 15°12N 73°58E **127** G1
garet → *Australia* 18°9S 125°41E **148** C4
garet Bay *Canada* 51°20N 127°35W **162** C3
garet L. *Canada* 58°56N 115°25W **162** B5
garet River
Australia 33°57S 115°4E **149** F2
garita, I. de
Venezuela 11°0N 64°0W **186** A6
gariti *Greece* 39°22N 20°26E **98** B2
garitovo *Russia* 43°25N 134°5E **112** C7
gate *S. Africa* 30°50S 30°20E **145** D5
gate *U.K.* 51°23N 1°23E **67** F9
geride, Mts. de la
France 44°43N 3°38E **72** D7
gherita di Savóia
Italy 41°22N 16°9E **95** A9
gherita Pk. *Uganda* 0°22N 29°51E **142** B3
ghita *Romania* 47°22N 22°22E **80** C7
g'ilon *Uzbekistan* 40°27N 71°42E **109** D8
gow, Dasht-e
ghan. 30°40N 62°30E **122** D3
guerite *Canada* 52°30N 122°25W **162** C4
hanets *Ukraine* 47°40N 34°40E **85** J8
houm *Algeria* 34°27N 0°11W **136** B3
El □ *Russia* 56°30N 48°0E **86** B8
i *Indus Pakistan* 35°7N 71°34E **124** C4
i Republic = Mari El □
ussia 56°30N 48°0E **86** B8
ia, Sa. de *Spain* 37°39N 2°14W **91** H2
ia de la Salut *Spain* 39°40N 3°5E **100** B10
ia Elena *Chile* 22°18S 69°40W **190** A2
ia Grande
rgentina 31°45S 59°55W **190** C4
ia I. N. Terr.,
ustralia 14°52S 135°45E **150** A2
ia I. Tas., *Australia* 42°38S 148°5E **151** G4
ia Island △
ustralia 42°38S 148°5E **151** G4
Z. 34°29S 172°40E **154** A1
iager *Denmark* 56°40N 9°59E **63** H3
iager Fjord *Denmark* 56°42N 10°19E **63** H4
iakani *Russia* 3°50S 39°27E **142** C4
iala △ *Australia* 25°57S 145°2E **151** D4
ian *Australia* 21°9S 148°57E **150** b
ian L. *Canada* 63°0N 116°15W **162** A5
ianna Trench *Pac. Oc.* 13°0N 145°0E **156** F6
ianna *Ark., U.S.A.* 34°46N 90°46W **177** D9
iannelund *Sweden* 57°37N 15°35E **63** G9
iánské Lázně
ech Rep. 49°58N 12°41E **78** B5
ias → *U.S.A.* 47°56N 110°30W **168** C8
ias, Is. *Mexico* 21°25N 106°28W **180** C3
iato, Punta *Panama* 7°12N 80°52W **182** E3
iazell *Austria* 47°47N 15°19E **78** D8
ibo *Denmark* 54°48N 11°30E **63** K5
ibor *Slovenia* 46°36N 15°40E **93** B12
ico → *Africa* 23°35S 26°57E **144** B4
icopa *Ariz., U.S.A.* 33°4N 112°3W **169** K7
icopa *Calif., U.S.A.* 35°4N 119°24W **171** K7
ié → *Brazil* 0°27S 66°26W **186** D5
ie Byrd Land
ntarctica 79°30S 125°0W **55** D14
ie-Galante
adeloupe 15°56N 61°16W **182** b
iecourt = Kangiqsujuaq
nada 61°30N 72°0W **161** E17
iefred *Sweden* 59°15N 17°12E **62** E11
iehamn *Finland* 60°5N 19°55E **61** F18
ieholm *Sweden* 55°53N 13°10E **63** J7
iembourg *Belgium* 50°6N 4°31E **69** D4
ienbad = Mariánské Lázně
ech Rep. 49°58N 12°41E **78** B5
ienberg *Germany* 50°39N 13°9E **76** E9
iental *Namibia* 24°36S 18°0E **144** B2
ienville *U.S.A.* 41°28N 79°8W **174** E5
iestad *Sweden* 58°43N 13°50E **63** F7
ía, La., U.S.A. 33°57N 84°33W **178** B4
ietta *Ohio, U.S.A.* 39°25N 81°27W **173** F13
ieville *Canada* 45°26N 73°10W **175** A11
iga → *Nigeria* 9°40N 5°55E **139** C6
ignane *France* 43°25N 5°13E **73** E9
iinsk *Russia* 56°10N 87°20E **106** D9
iinskiy Posad *Russia* 56°10N 47°45E **86** B8
ijampolė *Lithuania* 54°33N 23°19E **82** D10
ijampolė >
huania 54°34N 23°21E **82** D10
ília *Brazil* 22°13S 50°0W **191** A5
in *Spain* 42°23N 8°42W **88** C2
ina *U.S.A.* 36°41N 121°48W **170** J5
induque *Phil.* 13°25N 122°0E **119** B6
ine City *U.S.A.* 42°43N 82°30W **174** D2
ineland *U.S.A.* 29°40N 81°13W **178** F4
ineo *Italy* 37°57N 13°25E **94** E6
inette *U.S.A.* 45°6N 87°38W **172** C10
ingá *Brazil* 23°26S 52°2W **191** A5
inha Grande
azil 39°45N 8°56W **88** F2
inho dos Abrolhos △
azil 17°50S 39°0W **189** D3
ino *Italy* 41°46N 12°39E **93** G9
ino di Campo *Italy* 42°46N 10°11E **92** F7
ion *Ala., U.S.A.* 32°38N 87°19W **177** E11
ion *Ark., U.S.A.* 35°13N 90°12W **177** H8
ion *Ill., U.S.A.* 37°44N 88°56W **172** G10
ion *Ind., U.S.A.* 40°32N 85°40W **173** E11
ion *Iowa, U.S.A.* 42°2N 91°36W **172** E8
ion *Kans., U.S.A.* 38°21N 97°1W **172** F5
ion *Ohio, U.S.A.* 40°35N 83°8W **173** E13
ion *S.C., U.S.A.* 34°11N 79°24W **177** D15
ion Bay *Canada* 50°25N 126°59W **162** C3
ion I. *Ind. Oc.* 47°0S 38°0E **146** J2
iscal Estigarribia
raguay 22°3S 60°40W **190** A3
itime Alps = Maritimes, Alpes
rope 44°10N 7°10E **73** D11
itimes, Alpes *Europe* 44°10N 7°10E **73** D11

Maritsa = Evros →
Greece 41°40N 26°34E **97** F10
Maritsa *Greece* 36°22N 28°8E **101** C10
Mariupol *Ukraine* 47°5N 37°31E **85** J9
Mariusa △ *Venezuela* 9°24N 61°27E **183** E7
Marivãn *Iran* 35°30N 46°25E **105** C12
Mariy Chodra △ *Russia* 56°10N 48°30E **86** B9
Marj *Si. Arabia* 18°14N 41°19E **137** D5
Marka *Somalia* 1°48N 44°50E **131** G3
Markam *China* 29°42N 98°38E **116** C2
Markapur *India* 15°44N 79°19E **127** G4
Markaryd *Sweden* 56°28N 13°35E **63** H7
Markazi □ *Iran* 34°0N 49°30E **129** C6
Markdale *Canada* 44°19N 80°39W **174** B4
Marked Tree *U.S.A.* 35°32N 90°25W **177** D9
Markelsdorfer Huk
Germany 54°33N 11°4E **76** A7
Market Drayton *U.K.* 52°54N 2°29W **66** E5
Market Harborough
U.K. 52°29N 0°55W **67** E7
Market Rasen *U.K.* 53°24N 0°20W **66** D7
Markham *Canada* 43°52N 79°16W **174** C5
Markham, Mt.
Antarctica 83°0S 164°0E **55** E11
Marki *Poland* 52°19N 21°6E **83** F8
Märkische Schweiz △
Germany 52°34N 14°2E **76** C10
Markit *China* 38°54N 77°40E **109** E9
Markleeberg *Germany* 51°16N 12°23E **76** D8
Markleeville *U.S.A.* 38°42N 119°47W **170** G7
Markopoulo *Greece* 37°53N 23°57E **98** D5
Markovac *Serbia* 44°14N 21°7E **96** B5
Markovo *Russia* 64°40N 170°24E **107** C17
Markoye *Burkina Faso* 14°39N 0°2E **139** C5
Marks *Russia* 51°45N 46°50E **86** E8
Marksville *U.S.A.* 31°8N 92°4W **176** F8
Markt Schwaben
Germany 48°11N 11°52E **77** G7
Marktoberdorf *Germany* 47°45N 10°37E **77** H6
Marktredwitz *Germany* 50°1N 12°6E **77** E8
Marl *Germany* 51°39N 7°4E **76** D3
Marla *Australia* 27°19S 133°33E **151** D1
Marlbank *Canada* 44°26N 77°6W **174** B7
Marlboro *U.S.A.* 41°36N 73°59W **175** E11
Marlborough *Australia* 22°46S 149°52E **150** C4
Marlborough *U.K.* 51°25N 1°43W **67** F6
Marlborough *U.S.A.* 42°21N 71°33W **175** D13
Marlborough □ *N.Z.* 41°40S 173°50E **155** B8
Marlborough Downs
U.K. 51°27N 1°53W **67** F6
Marle *France* 49°43N 3°47E **71** C10
Marlin *U.S.A.* 31°18N 96°54W **176** F6
Marlow *Germany* 54°9N 12°33E **76** A8
Marlow *U.K.* 51°34N 0°46W **67** F7
Marlow *U.S.A.* 34°39N 97°58W **176** D6
Marmagao *India* 15°25N 73°56E **127** G1
Marmande *France* 44°30N 0°10E **72** D4
Marmara *Turkey* 40°35N 27°34E **99** C3
Mármora, La *Italy* 39°59N 9°20E **94** C2
Marnay *France* 47°16N 5°48E **71** E12
Marne *Germany* 53°56N 9°2E **76** A5
Marne □ *France* 48°47N 2°29E **71** D9
Marne → *France* 48°48N 2°24E **71** D11
Marneuli *Georgia* 41°30N 44°48E **87** K7
Marnoo *Australia* 36°40S 142°52E **152** D5
Maro Reef *U.S.A.* 25°25N 170°35W **167** N23
Maroantsetra *Madag.* 15°26S 49°44E **141** H9
Maroelaboom *Namibia* 19°15S 18°53E **144** A2
Marondera *Zimbabwe* 18°5S 31°42E **143** F3
Maroni → *Fr. Guiana* 5°30N 54°0W **187** B8
Maronia *Greece* 40°53N 25°30E **97** F9
Maronne → *France* 45°5N 1°56E **72** C5
Maroochydore
Australia 26°29S 153°5E **151** D5
Maroona *Australia* 37°27S 142°54E **152** D5
Maros → *Hungary* 46°15N 20°13E **80** D5
Maróstica *Italy* 45°45N 11°39E **93** C8
Maroua *Cameroon* 10°40N 14°20E **139** C7
Marovoay *Madag.* 16°6S 46°39E **141** H9
Marqakõl *Kazakhstan* 48°45N 85°50E **109** C11
Marquard *S. Africa* 28°40S 27°28E **144** C4
Marquesas Fracture Zone
Pac. Oc. 9°0S 125°0W **157** H15
Marquesas Is. = Marquises, Îs.
French Polynesia 9°30S 140°0W **157** H14
Marquesas Keys
U.S.A. 24°35N 82°10W **179** L7
Marquette *U.S.A.* 46°33N 87°24W **172** B10
Marquis *St. Lucia* 14°2N 60°54W **183** f
Marquise *France* 50°50N 1°40E **71** B8
Marquises, Îs.
French Polynesia 9°30S 140°0W **157** H14
Marra, Djebel *Sudan* 13°10N 24°22E **135** F10
Marra Cr. → *Australia* 30°5S 147°15E **153** A7
Marra-Marra △
Australia 33°30S 151°4E **153** B9
Marracuene *Mozam.* 25°45S 32°35E **145** C5
Marradi *Italy* 44°4N 11°37E **93** D8
Marrakech *Morocco* 31°9N 8°0W **136** B2
Marratxí *Spain* 39°39N 2°48E **90** F7
Marrawah *Australia* 40°55S 144°42E **151** G3
Marrecas, Serra das
Brazil 9°0S 41°0W **189** B2
Marree *Australia* 29°39S 138°1E **151** D2
Marrero *U.S.A.* 29°53N 90°6W **177** G9
Marromeu *Mozam.* 18°15S 36°25E **145** A6
Marromeu △ *Mozam.* 19°0S 36°0E **145** A6
Marouqí, Punta *Spain* 35°57W **89** K5
Marrowie Cr. →
Australia 33°23S 145°40E **153** B6
Marrubane *Mozam.* 18°0S 37°0E **143** F4
Marrúbiu *Italy* 39°46N 8°33E **94** C1
Marrupa *Mozam.* 13°8S 37°30E **143** E4
Mars Hill *U.S.A.* 46°31N 67°52W **173** B20
Marsá 'Alam *Egypt* 25°5N 34°54E **137** E3
Marsá Matrûh *Egypt* 31°19N 27°9E **137** A2
Marsa Sha'b *Sudan* 22°35N 35°47E **137** C4

Marsabit *Kenya* 2°18N 38°0E **142** B4
Marsabit □ *Kenya* 3°0N 37°30E **142** B4
Marsabit △ *Kenya* 2°23N 37°56E **142** B4
Marsala *Italy* 37°48N 12°26E **94** E5
Marsalforn *Malta* 36°4N 14°16E **101** C1
Mârşani *Romania* 44°1N 24°1E **81** F9
Marsberg *Germany* 51°28N 8°52E **76** D4
Marsden *Australia* 42°54N 12°20E **93** F9
Marsden *Australia* 33°47S 147°32E **153** B7
Marsden Point *N.Z.* 35°50S 174°31E **154** B3
Marseillan *France* 43°23N 3°31E **72** E7
Marseille *France* 43°18N 5°23E **73** E9
Marseille-Marignane ✈ (MRS)
France 43°26N 5°14E **73** E9
Marseilles = Marseille
France 43°18N 5°23E **73** E9
Marsh I. *U.S.A.* 29°34N 91°53W **176** G9
Marshall *Liberia* 6°8N 10°22E **138** D2
Marshall *Ark., U.S.A.* 35°55N 92°38W **176** D8
Marshall *Mich.,
U.S.A.* 42°16N 84°58W **173** D11
Marshall *Minn., U.S.A.* 44°27N 95°47W **172** C6
Marshall *Mo., U.S.A.* 39°7N 93°12W **172** F7
Marshall *Tex., U.S.A.* 32°33N 94°23W **176** E7
Marshall → *Australia* 22°59S 136°59E **150** C2
Marshall Is. ■ *Pac. Oc.* 9°0N 171°0E **156** G9
Marshalltown *U.S.A.* 42°3N 92°55W **172** D7
Marshallville *U.S.A.* 32°27N 83°56W **178** C6
Marshbrook *Zimbabwe* 18°33S 31°9E **145** A5
Marshfield *Mo., U.S.A.* 37°15N 92°54W **172** G7
Marshfield *Vt., U.S.A.* 44°20N 72°20W **175** B12
Marshfield *Wis., U.S.A.* 44°40N 90°10W **172** C8
Marshūn *Iran* 36°19N 49°23E **129** B6
Mársico Nuovo *Italy* 40°25N 15°44E **95** B8
Märsta *Sweden* 59°37N 17°52E **62** E11
Marstal *Denmark* 54°51N 10°30E **63** K4
Marstrand *Sweden* 57°53N 11°35E **63** G5
Mart *U.S.A.* 31°33N 96°50W **176** F6
Marta → *Italy* 42°14N 11°42E **93** F8
Martaban *Burma* 16°30N 97°35E **123** L20
Martaban, G. of = Mottama, G. of
Burma 16°5N 96°30E **123** L20
Martano *Italy* 40°12N 18°18E **95** B11
Martapura *Kalimantan Selatan,
Indonesia* 3°22S 114°47E **118** E4
Martapura *Sumatera Selatan,
Indonesia* 4°19S 104°22E **118** E2
Marte R. Gómez, Presa
Mexico 26°10N 99°0W **181** B5
Martel *France* 44°57N 1°37E **72** D5
Martelange *Belgium* 49°49N 5°43E **69** E5
Martellago *Italy* 45°33N 12°9E **93** C9
Martés, Sierra *Spain* 39°20N 1°0W **91** F4
Martfű *Hungary* 47°1N 20°17E **80** C5
Marthaguy Cr. →
Australia 30°16S 147°35E **153** A7
Marthapal *India* 18°41N 81°37E **126** E5
Martha's Vineyard
U.S.A. 41°25N 70°38W **175** E14
Martigné-Ferchaud
France 47°50N 1°20W **70** E5
Martigny *Switz.* 46°6N 7°3E **77** J3
Martigues *France* 43°24N 5°4E **73** E9
Martil *Morocco* 35°36N 5°15W **136** A2
Martin *Slovak Rep.* 49°6N 18°58E **79** B11
Martin *S. Dak., U.S.A.* 43°11N 101°44W **172** D3
Martin *Tenn., U.S.A.* 36°21N 88°51W **177** C10
Martin → *Spain* 41°18N 0°19W **90** D4
Martin L. *U.S.A.* 32°41N 85°55W **178** C4
Martin Vaz *Atl. Oc.* 20°30S 28°51W **56** J9
Martina Franca *Italy* 40°42N 17°20E **95** B10
Martinborough *N.Z.* 41°14S 175°29E **154** H4
Martinez *Calif., U.S.A.* 38°1N 122°8W **170** G4
Martinez *Ga., U.S.A.* 33°31N 82°5W **178** B7
Martinho Campos
Brazil 19°20S 45°13W **189** D1
Martinique ☑ *W. Indies* 14°40N 61°0W **182** c
Martinique Passage
W. Indies 15°15N 61°0W **183** C7
Martino *Greece* 38°35N 23°12E **98** C5
Martinópolis *Brazil* 22°11S 51°12W **191** A5
Martins Bay *Barbados* 13°12N 59°29W **183** g
Martins Ferry *U.S.A.* 40°6N 80°44W **174** F4
Martinsberg *Austria* 48°22N 15°9E **78** C8
Martinsburg *Pa.,
U.S.A.* 40°19N 78°20W **174** F6
Martinsburg *W. Va.,
U.S.A.* 39°27N 77°58W **173** F15
Martinsicuro *Italy* 42°54N 13°54E **93** F10
Martinsville *Ind.,
U.S.A.* 39°26N 86°25W **172** F10
Martinsville *Va.,
U.S.A.* 36°41N 79°52W **173** G14
Marton *N.Z.* 40°4S 175°23E **154** G4
Martorell *Spain* 41°28N 1°56E **90** D6
Martos *Spain* 37°44N 3°58W **89** H7
Martu ☑ *Australia* 22°30S 122°30E **148** D3
Martuni *Armenia* 40°8N 45°20E **87** K7
Maru *Nigeria* 12°22N 6°22E **139** C6
Marudi *Malaysia* 4°11N 114°19E **118** D4
Maruf *Afghan.* 31°30N 67°6E **124** D5
Marugame *Japan* 34°15N 133°40E **113** G6
Maruia → *N.Z.* 41°47S 172°13E **155** B7
Maruim *Brazil* 10°45S 37°5W **189** C3
Marulan *Australia* 34°43S 150°3E **153** C9
Marunga *Angola* 17°28S 20°2E **144** A3
Marungu, Mts.
Dem. Rep. of the Congo 7°30S 30°0E **142** D3
Maruwa ☑ *Australia* 29°50S 127°30E **148** D4
Marv Dasht *Iran* 29°50N 52°40E **131** D7
Marvão *Portugal* 39°24N 7°20W **89** F3
Marvast *Iran* 30°30N 54°15E **129** D7
Marvel Loch *Australia* 31°28S 119°29E **149** F2
Marwar *India* 25°15N 73°0E **124** G5
Mary *Turkmenistan* 37°40N 61°50E **129** B9
Mary Esther *U.S.A.* 30°25N 86°40W **179** F13
Maryborough = Portlaoise
Ireland 53°2N 7°18W **64** C4
Maryborough *Queens.,
Australia* 25°31S 152°37E **151** D5
Maryborough *Vic.,
Australia* 37°0S 143°44E **152** D5
Maryfield *Canada* 49°50N 101°35W **163** D8
Maryland □ *U.S.A.* 39°0N 76°30W **173** F15
Maryland Junction
Zimbabwe 17°45S 30°31E **143** F3
Maryport *U.K.* 54°44N 3°28W **66** C4
Mary's Harbour
Canada 52°18N 55°51W **165** B8
Marystown *Canada* 47°10N 55°10W **165** C8

Marysville *Calif., U.S.A.* 39°9N 121°35W **170** F5
Marysville *Kans.,
U.S.A.* 39°51N 96°39W **172** F5
Marysville *Mich.,
U.S.A.* 42°54N 82°29W **174** D2
Marysville *Ohio,
U.S.A.* 40°14N 83°22W **173** E12
Marysville *Tenn.,
U.S.A.* 48°3N 122°11W **170** B4
Maryville *Mo., U.S.A.* 40°21N 94°52W **172** E6
Maryville *Tenn.,
U.S.A.* 35°46N 83°58W **177** D13
Masada *Israel* 31°18N 35°21E **130** D4
Masahunga *Tanzania* 2°6S 33°18E **142** C3
Masai *Malaysia* 1°29N 103°55E **121** d
Masai Mara △ *Kenya* 1°25S 35°5E **142** C4
Masai Steppe *Tanzania* 4°30S 36°30E **142** C4
Masaka *Uganda* 0°21S 31°45E **142** C3
Masalembo, Kepulauan
Indonesia 5°35S 114°30E **118** F4
Masalima, Kepulauan
Indonesia 5°4S 117°5E **118** F5
Masalli *Azerbaijan* 39°3N 48°40E **105** C13
Masamba *Indonesia* 2°30S 120°15E **119** E6
Masan *S. Korea* 35°11N 128°32E **115** G15
Masandam, Ra's *Oman* 26°30N 56°30E **129** E8
Masasi *Tanzania* 10°45S 38°52E **143** E4
Masaya *Nic.* 12°0N 86°7W **182** D2
Masbate *Phil.* 12°21N 123°36E **119** B6
Máscali *Italy* 37°45N 15°12E **95** E8
Mascara *Algeria* 35°26N 0°6E **136** A4
Mascarene Is. *Ind. Oc.* 22°0S 55°0E **132** J9
Mascota *Mexico* 20°32N 104°49W **180** C4
Masdar City = Madīnat Masdar
U.A.E. 24°26N 54°37E **129** E7
Masela *Indonesia* 8°9S 129°51E **119** F7
Maseru *Lesotho* 29°18S 27°30E **144** C4
Mashābih *Si. Arabia* 25°35N 36°30E **128** E3
Mashan *China* 23°40N 108°11E **116** F7
Mashang *China* 36°48N 117°57E **115** F9
Mashatu △ *Botswana* 22°45S 29°5E **145** B4
Mashegu *Nigeria* 10°0N 5°35E **139** D6
Masherbrum *Pakistan* 35°38N 76°18E **125** B7
Mashhad *Iran* 36°20N 59°35E **129** B8
Mashi *Nigeria* 13°0N 7°54E **139** C6
Mashīz *Iran* 29°56N 56°37E **129** D8
Mashki Chāh *Pakistan* 29°5N 62°30E **129** E3
Mashonaland *Zimbabwe* 16°30S 31°0E **143** F3
Mashonaland Central □
Zimbabwe 17°30S 31°0E **145** A5
Mashonaland East □
Zimbabwe 18°0S 32°0E **145** A5
Mashonaland West □
Zimbabwe 17°30S 29°30E **145** A4
Mashrakh *India* 26°7N 84°48E **125** F11
Masi Manimba
Dem. Rep. of the Congo 4°40S 17°54E **140** E3
Masig *Australia* 9°45S 143°24E **150** a
Masindi *Uganda* 1°40N 31°43E **142** B3
Masindi Port *Uganda* 1°43N 32°2E **142** B3
Masinga Res. *Kenya* 0°58S 37°38E **142** C4
Maşīrah, Jazīrat *Oman* 21°0N 58°50E **131** C6
Maşīrah, Khalīj *Oman* 20°10N 58°10E **131** C6
Masisea *Peru* 8°35S 74°22W **188** B3
Masisi
Dem. Rep. of the Congo 1°23S 28°49E **142** C2
Masjed Soleyman *Iran* 31°55N 49°18E **129** D6
Mask, L. *Ireland* 53°36N 9°22W **64** C2
Maski *India* 15°56N 76°46E **127** G3
Maskin *Oman* 23°44N 56°52E **129** F8
Maslen Nos *Bulgaria* 42°18N 27°48E **97** D11
Maslinica *Croatia* 43°24N 16°13E **93** E13
Masnou = El Masnou
Spain 41°28N 2°20E **90** D7
Masoala, Tanjon' i
Madag. 15°59S 50°13E **141** H10
Masohi = Amahai
Indonesia 3°20S 128°55E **119** E7
Mason *Nev., U.S.A.* 38°56N 119°8W **170** G7
Mason *Tex., U.S.A.* 30°45N 99°14W **176** F5
Mason B. *N.Z.* 46°55S 167°45E **155** G2
Mason City *U.S.A.* 43°9N 93°12W **172** D7
Maspalomas *Canary Is.* 27°46N 15°35W **100** G4
Maspalomas, Pta.
Canary Is. 27°43N 15°36W **100** G4
Masqat *Oman* 23°37N 58°36E **131** C6
Mas'ed Gedida *Egypt* 30°5N 31°21E **137** E7
Massa *Italy* 44°1N 10°9E **92** D7
Massa, O. → *Morocco* 30°2N 9°40W **136** B2
Massa e Carrara □ *Italy* 44°10N 10°10E **92** D7
Massa Maríttima *Italy* 43°3N 10°52E **92** E7
Massachusetts □
U.S.A. 42°30N 72°0W **175** D13
Massachusetts B.
U.S.A. 42°25N 70°50W **175** D14
Massafra *Italy* 40°35N 17°7E **95** B10
Massakory *Chad* 13°0N 15°49E **135** F8
Massamba *Mozam.* 15°58S 33°31E **143** F3
Massanella *Spain* 39°48N 2°51E **90** B9
Massangena *Mozam.* 21°34S 33°0E **145** B5
Massango *Angola* 8°2S 16°21E **140** F3
Massapê *Brazil* 3°31S 40°19W **189** A2
Massat *France* 42°53N 1°21E **72** F5
Massawa = Mitsiwa
Eritrea 15°35N 39°25E **131** D2
Massena *U.S.A.* 44°56N 74°54W **175** B10
Massenya *Chad* 11°21N 16°9E **135** F9
Masset *Canada* 54°2N 132°10W **162** C2
Masseube *France* 43°25N 0°34E **72** E4
Massiac *France* 45°15N 3°11E **72** C7
Massiah Street *Barbados* 13°9N 59°29W **183** g
Massif Central *France* 44°55N 3°0E **72** D7
Massif des Bauges △
France 45°40N 6°10E **71** G13
Massigui *Mali* 11°48N 6°50W **138** C4
Massillon *U.S.A.* 40°48N 81°32W **174** F3
Massine, O. → *Algeria* 36°13N 2°12E **136** A4
Massinga *Mozam.* 23°15S 35°22E **145** C6
Massingir *Mozam.* 23°51S 32°4E **145** C5
Masson I. *Antarctica* 66°10S 93°20E **55** C7
Masson-Angers
Canada 45°32N 75°25W **175** A9
Masson I. *Antarctica* 66°10S 93°20E **55** C7
Mastanli = Momchilgrad
Bulgaria 41°33N 25°23E **97** E9
Masterton *N.Z.* 40°56S 175°39E **154** G4

Mastic *U.S.A.* 40°47N 72°54W **175** F12
Mastuj *Pakistan* 36°20N 72°36E **125** A5
Mastung *Pakistan* 29°50N 66°56E **122** E5
Mastūrah *Si. Arabia* 23°7N 38°52E **137** C4
Masty *Belarus* 53°27N 24°38E **75** B13
Masuda *Japan* 34°40N 131°51E **113** G5
Masuku = Franceville
Gabon 1°40S 13°32E **140** E2
Masurian Lakes = Mazurski,
Pojezierze *Poland* 53°50N 21°0E **82** E7
Masvingo *Zimbabwe* 20°8S 30°49E **143** G3
Masvingo □ *Zimbabwe* 21°0S 31°30E **143** G3
Maswa □ *Tanzania* 2°58S 34°19E **142** C3
Maşyāf *Syria* 35°4N 36°20E **104** E7
Mat → *Albania* 41°40N 19°35E **96** E3
Mata-au = Clutha →
N.Z. 46°20S 169°49E **155** G4
Mata de São João
Brazil 12°31S 38°17W **189** C3
Matabeleland *Zimbabwe* 18°0S 27°0E **141** H5
Matabeleland North □
Zimbabwe 19°0S 28°0E **143** F2
Matabeleland South □
Zimbabwe 21°0S 29°0E **143** G2
Matachel → *Spain* 38°50N 6°17W **89** G4
Matachewan *Canada* 47°56N 80°39W **164** C3
Matadi
Dem. Rep. of the Congo 5°52S 13°31E **140** F2
Matagalpa *Nic.* 13°0N 85°58W **182** D2
Matagami *Canada* 49°45N 77°34W **164** C4
Matagami, L. *Canada* 49°50N 77°40W **164** C4
Matagorda B. *U.S.A.* 28°40N 96°12W **176** G6
Matagorda I. *U.S.A.* 28°15N 96°30W **176** G6
Mataiea *Tahiti* 17°46S 149°25W **155** b
Matak *Indonesia* 3°18N 106°16E **118** D3
Matakana *Australia* 32°59S 145°54E **153** B6
Matakana *N.Z.* 36°21S 174°43E **154** C3
Matala *Greece* 34°59N 24°45E **101** E6
Matalaque *Peru* 16°26S 70°49W **188** D3
Matale *Sri Lanka* 7°30N 80°37E **127** L5
Matam *Senegal* 15°34N 13°17W **138** B2
Matam □ *Senegal* 15°30N 13°19W **138** B2
Matamata *N.Z.* 37°48S 175°47E **154** D4
Matameye *Niger* 13°26N 8°28E **139** C6
Matamoros *Coahuila,
Mexico* 25°32N 103°15W **180** B4
Matamoros *Tamaulipas,
Mexico* 25°53N 97°30W **181** B5
Ma'tan as Sarra *Libya* 21°45N 22°0E **135** D10
Matane *Canada* 48°50N 67°33W **165** C6
Matang *China* 23°30N 104°7E **116** F5
Matankari *Niger* 13°46N 4°1E **139** C5
Matanomadh *India* 23°33N 68°57E **124** H3
Matanzas *Cuba* 23°0N 81°40W **182** B3
Matapa *Botswana* 23°11S 24°39E **144** B3
Matapan, C. = Tenaro, Akra
Greece 36°22N 22°27E **98** E4
Matapédia *Canada* 48°0N 66°59W **165** C6
Matapo △ *Zimbabwe* 20°30S 29°40E **143** G2
Mataporquera *Spain* 42°52N 4°10W **88** C6
Matara *Sri Lanka* 5°58N 80°30E **127** M5
Mataram *Indonesia* 8°35S 116°7E **118** F5
Matarani *Peru* 17°0S 72°10W **188** D3
Mataranka *Australia* 14°55S 133°4E **148** B5
Matarma, Râs *Egypt* 30°27N 32°44E **138** E1
Mataró *Spain* 41°32N 2°29E **90** D7
Matarraña → *Spain* 41°14N 0°22E **90** D5
Mataruška Banja *Serbia* 43°40N 20°40E **96** C4
Matata *N.Z.* 37°54S 176°48E **154** D5
Matatiele *S. Africa* 30°20S 28°49E **145** D4
Mataula Dam *India* 25°26S 72°58E **126** B4
Mataura → *N.Z.* 46°11S 168°51E **155** G3
Mataura *N.Z.* 46°34S 168°44E **155** G3
Matavai, B. de *Tahiti* 17°30S 149°23W **155** b
Matehuala *Mexico* 23°39N 100°39W **180** C4
Mateke Hills *Zimbabwe* 21°48S 31°0E **143** G3
Matelot *Trin. & Tob.* 10°50N 61°7W **183** K15
Matera *Italy* 40°40N 16°36E **95** B9
Matese, Monti del *Italy* 41°27N 14°22E **95** A7
Matese △ *Italy* 41°24N 14°23E **95** A7
Mátészalka *Hungary* 47°58N 22°20E **80** C7
Mateur *Tunisia* 37°0N 9°40E **136** A1
Matfors *Sweden* 62°21N 17°2E **62** B11
Matha *France* 45°52N 0°20W **72** C3
Matheniko △ *Uganda* 2°49N 34°27E **142** B3
Mathis *U.S.A.* 28°6N 97°50W **176** G6
Mathoura *Australia* 35°50S 144°55E **153** C6
Mathráki *Greece* 39°48N 19°31E **101** A3
Mathura *India* 27°30N 77°40E **124** F7
Mati *Phil.* 6°55N 126°15E **119** C7
Matiakoali *Burkina Faso* 12°28N 1°2E **139** C5
Matiali *India* 26°56N 88°49E **125** F13
Matías Romero *Mexico* 16°53N 95°2W **181** D5
Matibane *Mozam.* 14°49S 40°45E **143** E5
Matiri *N.Z.* 41°38S 172°20E **155** B7
Matjiesfontein *S. Africa* 33°14S 20°35E **144** E3
Matla → *India* 21°40N 88°40E **125** J13
Matlamanyane
Botswana 19°33S 25°57E **144** B4
Matli *Pakistan* 25°2N 68°39E **124** G3
Matlock *U.K.* 53°9N 1°33W **66** D6
Matmata *Tunisia* 33°37N 9°59E **136** B1
Mato Grosso □ *Brazil* 14°0S 55°0W **187** F8
Mato Grosso, Planalto do
Brazil 15°0S 55°0W **187** G8
Mato Grosso do Sul □
Brazil 18°0S 55°0W **187** G8
Matobo = Matapo △
Zimbabwe 20°30S 29°40E **143** G2
Matochkin Shar, Proliv
Russia 73°23N 55°12E **106** B6
Matola *Mozam.* 25°57S 32°27E **145** C5
Matopo Hills *Zimbabwe* 20°36S 28°20E **143** G2
Matopos *Zimbabwe* 20°20S 28°29E **143** G2
Matosinhos *Portugal* 41°11N 8°42W **88** D2
Matour *France* 46°19N 4°29E **71** F11
Matroosberg *S. Africa* 33°23S 19°40E **144** E2
Matruh *Oman* 23°37N 58°30E **131** C6
Matsalu △ *Estonia* 58°45N 23°36E **84** C2
Matsena *Nigeria* 13°5N 10°5E **139** C7
Matsesta *Russia* 43°34N 39°51E **87** K4
Matsu Tao *Taiwan* 26°8N 119°56E **117** D12
Matsue *Japan* 35°25N 133°10E **113** G6
Matsumae *Japan* 41°26N 140°7E **112** D10
Matsumae-Hantō
Japan 41°30N 140°15E **112** D10
Matsumoto *Japan* 36°15N 138°0E **113** F9
Matsusaka *Japan* 34°34N 136°32E **113** G8

Matsushima *Japan* 38°20N 141°10E **112** E10
Matsuura *Japan* 33°20N 129°49E **113** H4
Matsuyama *Japan* 33°45N 132°45E **113** H6
Mattagami → *Canada* 50°43N 81°29W **164** B3
Mattancheri *India* 9°50N 76°15E **127** K3
Mattawa *Canada* 46°20N 78°45W **164** C4
Matterhorn *Switz.* 45°58N 7°39E **77** K3
Mattersburg *Austria* 47°44N 16°24E **79** D9
Matthew Town
Bahamas 20°57N 73°40W **183** B5
Matthews Ridge
Guyana 7°37N 60°10W **186** B6
Mattice *Canada* 49°40N 83°20W **164** C3
Mattili *India* 18°33N 82°17E **126** E5
Mattituck *U.S.A.* 40°59N 72°32W **175** F12
Mattō = Hakusan
Japan 36°31N 136°34E **113** F8
Mattoon *U.S.A.* 39°29N 88°23W **172** F9
Matuba *Mozam.* 24°28S 32°49E **145** B5
Matucana *Peru* 11°55S 76°25W **188** C2
Matugama *Sri Lanka* 6°31N 80°7E **127** L5
Matuku *Fiji* 19°10S 179°44E **154** a
Matûn = Khowst
Afghan. 33°22N 69°58E **124** C3
Matura B. *Trin. & Tob.* 10°39N 61°1W **187** K15
Maturín *Venezuela* 9°45N 63°11W **186** B6
Matusadona △
Zimbabwe 16°58S 28°42E **143** F2
Matveyev Kurgan
Russia 47°35N 38°57E **85** J10
Matxitxako, C. *Spain* 43°28N 2°47W **90** B2
Mau *Mad. P., India* 26°17N 78°41E **125** F8
Mau *Ut. P., India* 25°56N 83°33E **125** G10
Mau *Ut. P., India* 25°17N 81°23E **125** G9
Mau Escarpment *Kenya* 0°40S 36°0E **142** C4
Mau Ranipur *India* 25°16N 79°8E **125** G8
Maua *Kenya* 0°14N 37°56E **142** B4
Maua *Mozam.* 13°53S 37°10E **143** E4
Maubeuge *France* 50°17N 3°57E **71** B10
Maubin *Burma* 16°44N 95°39E **123** L19
Maubourguet *France* 43°29N 0°1E **72** E4
Maud, Pt. *Australia* 23°6S 113°45E **148** D1
Maud Rise *S. Ocean* 66°0S 3°0E **55** C3
Maude *Australia* 34°29S 144°18E **152** C6
Maudin Sun *Burma* 16°0N 94°30E **123** M19
Maués *Brazil* 3°20S 57°45W **186** D7
Mauganj *India* 24°50N 81°55E **125** G9
Maughold Hd. *I. of Man* 54°18N 4°18E **64** C3
Maugúio *France* 43°37N 4°1E **72** E7
Maui *U.S.A.* 20°48N 156°20W **167** L8
Maulamyaing = Mawlamyine
Burma 16°30N 97°40E **123** L20
Maule □ *Chile* 36°5S 72°30W **190** D1
Mauléon-Licharre
France 43°14N 0°54W **72** E3
Maullín *Chile* 41°38S 73°37W **192** E2
Maumee → *U.S.A.* 41°34N 83°39W **173** E12
Maumee *U.S.A.* 41°42N 83°28W **173** E12
Maumere *Indonesia* 8°38S 122°13E **119** F6
Maumusson, Pertuis de
France 45°48N 1°14W **72** C2
Maun *Botswana* 20°0S 23°26E **144** B3
Mauna Kea *U.S.A.* 19°50N 155°28W **167** M8
Mauna Loa *U.S.A.* 19°30N 155°35W **167** M8
Maunath Bhanjan = Mau
India 25°56N 83°33E **125** G10
Maungaturoto *N.Z.* 36°6S 174°23E **154** C3
Maungmagan Kyunzu
Burma 14°0N 97°48E **120** E1
Maungu *Kenya* 3°33S 38°45E **142** C4
Maupin *U.S.A.* 45°11N 121°5W **168** D3
Maure-de-Bretagne
France 47°59N 1°58W **70** E5
Maurepas, L. *U.S.A.* 30°15N 90°30W **177** F9
Maures *France* 43°15N 6°15E **73** E10
Mauriac *France* 45°13N 2°19E **72** C6
Maurice, L. *Australia* 29°30S 131°0E **149** E5
Mauricievile △ *Canada* 46°45N 73°0W **164** C5
Mauritania ■ *Africa* 20°50N 10°0W **134** E3
Mauritius ■ *Ind. Oc.* 20°0S 57°0E **141** d
Mauron *France* 48°9N 2°18W **72** D2
Maurs *France* 44°43N 2°12E **72** D6
Mauston *U.S.A.* 43°48N 90°5W **172** D8
Mauterndorf *Austria* 47°9N 13°40E **78** D6
Mauthen *Austria* 46°39N 12°59E **78** E6
Mauvezin *France* 43°44N 0°53E **72** E4
Mauzé-sur-le-Mignon
France 46°12N 0°41W **72** B3
Mavli *India* 24°45N 73°55E **124** G5
Mavrové *Albania* 40°26N 19°32E **96** K5
Mavrovo △ *Macedonia* 41°36N 20°45E **96** K4
Mavuradonha Mts.
Zimbabwe 16°30S 31°30E **143** F3
Mawa
Dem. Rep. of the Congo 2°45N 26°40E **142** B2
Mawai *India* 22°30N 81°4E **125** H9
Mawana *India* 29°6N 77°58E **124** E7
Mawand *Pakistan* 29°33N 68°38E **124** E3
Mawat *Iraq* 35°54N 45°24E **105** E11
Mawjib, W. al →
Jordan 31°28N 35°36E **130** D4
Mawkmai *Burma* 20°14N 97°37E **123** J20
Mawlaik *Burma* 23°40N 94°26E **123** H19
Mawlamyine *Burma* 16°30N 97°40E **123** L20
Mawqaq *Si. Arabia* 27°25N 41°8E **128** E4
Mawson *Antarctica* 67°30S 62°53E **55** C6
Mawson Coast *Antarctica* 68°30S 63°0E **55** C6
Mawson Pk. *Heard I.* 53°6S 73°31E **146** K6
Max *U.S.A.* 47°49N 101°18W **172** B3
Maxcanú *Mexico* 20°35N 89°59W **181** C7
Maxesibeni *S. Africa* 30°49S 29°23E **145** D4
Maxeys *U.S.A.* 33°45N 83°11W **178** B6
Maxhamish L. *Canada* 59°50N 123°17W **162** B4
Maxixe *Mozam.* 23°54S 35°17E **145** C6
Maxville *Canada* 45°17N 74°51W **175** A10
Maxwell *N.Z.* 39°51S 174°49E **154** G4
Maxwell *U.S.A.* 39°17N 122°11W **170** F4
Maxwelton *Australia* 20°43S 142°41E **150** C3
May Pen *Jamaica* 17°58N 77°15W **182** a
Maya → *Russia* 60°28N 134°28E **107** D14
Maya, Costa *Mexico* 18°44N 87°42W **181** D7
Maya Mts. *Belize* 16°30N 89°0W **181** D7
Mayabandar *India* 12°56N 92°56E **127** H11
Mayaguana I.
Bahamas 22°30N 72°44W **183** B5
Mayaguana Passage
Bahamas 22°32N 73°15W **183** B5

Mayagüez *Puerto Rico* 18°12N 67°9W **183** d
Mayahi *Niger* 13°58N 7°40E **139** C6
Mayaky *Ukraine* 47°26N 29°33E **81** C14
Mayals = Maials *Spain* 41°22N 0°30E **90** D5
Mayámey *Iran* 36°24N 55°42E **129** B7
Mayang *China* 27°53N 109°49E **116** D7
Mayanup *Australia* 33°57S 116°27E **149** F2
Mayapán *Mexico* 20°29N 89°11W **181** C7
Mayarí *Cuba* 20°40N 75°41W **183** B4
Mayaro *Trin. & Tob.* 10°17N 61°1W **187** K15
Mayaro B.
  Trin. & Tob. 10°14N 60°59W **187** K16
Mayavaram = Mayiladuthurai
  India 11°3N 79°42E **127** J4
Maybell *U.S.A.* 40°31N 108°5W **168** F9
Maybole *U.K.* 55°21N 4°42W **65** F4
Maydän *Iraq* 34°55N 45°37E **105** E11
Maydan *Ukraine* 48°36N 23°29E **81** B8
Mayen *Germany* 50°19N 7°13E **77** E3
Mayenne *France* 48°20N 0°38W **70** D6
Mayenne □ *France* 48°10N 0°40W **70** D6
Mayenne → *France* 47°30N 0°32W **70** D6
Mayer *U.S.A.* 34°24N 112°14W **169** J7
Mayerthorpe *Canada* 53°57N 115°8W **162** C5
Mayesville *U.S.A.* 34°0N 80°12W **178** A9
Mayfield *Ky., U.S.A.* 36°44N 88°38W **172** G3
Mayfield *N.Y., U.S.A.* 43°6N 74°16W **175** C10
Mayhill *U.S.A.* 32°53N 105°29W **169** K11
Mayiladuthurai *India* 11°3N 79°42E **127** J4
Maykop *Russia* 44°35N 40°10E **87** K5
Mayma *Russia* 52°3N 85°55E **109** B11
Maymyo = Pyin-U-Lwin
  Burma 22°2N 96°28E **120** A1
Maynard *Mass.,*
  U.S.A. 42°26N 71°27W **175** D13
Maynard *Wash.,*
  U.S.A. 47°59N 122°55W **170** C4
Maynard Hills
  Australia 28°28S 119°49E **149** E2
Mayne → *Australia* 23°40S 141°55E **150** C3
Maynooth *Canada* 45°13N 77°56W **174** A7
Maynooth *Ireland* 53°23N 6°34W **64** C5
Mayo *Canada* 63°38N 135°57W **160** C6
Mayo *U.S.A.* 30°3N 83°10W **178** E6
Mayo □ *Ireland* 53°53N 9°3W **64** C2
Mayo → *Argentina* 45°45S 69°45W **192** C3
Mayo → *Peru* 6°58N 76°15W **188** B2
Mayo Daga *Nigeria* 6°59N 11°25E **139** D7
Mayo Faran *Nigeria* 8°57N 12°4E **139** D7
Mayon Volcano *Phil.* 13°15N 123°41E **119** B6
Mayor Buratovich
  Argentina 39°15S 62°37W **192** A4
Mayor I. *N.Z.* 37°16S 176°17E **154** D5
Mayorga *Spain* 42°10N 5°16W **88** C5
Mayotte ☑ *Ind. Oc.* 12°50S 45°10E **141** a
Mayqayyng *Kazakhstan* 51°27N 75°47E **109** B9
Maysän □ *Iraq* 31°55N 47°15E **128** D5
Mayskiy *Russia* 43°47N 44°2E **87** J7
Maysville *U.S.A.* 38°39N 83°46W **173** F12
Mayu *Indonesia* 1°30N 126°30E **119** D7
Mayuram = Mayiladuthurai
  India 11°3N 79°42E **127** J4
Mayville *N. Dak.,*
  U.S.A. 47°30N 97°20W **172** B5
Mayville *N.Y., U.S.A.* 42°15N 79°30W **174** D5
Mazabuka *Zambia* 15°52S 27°44E **143** F2
Mazagán = El Jadida
  Morocco 33°11N 8°17W **136** B2
Mazagão *Brazil* 0°7S 51°16W **189** D8
Mazamet *France* 43°30N 2°20E **72** E6
Mazán *Peru* 3°30S 73°0W **188** D4
Mãzandarãn □ *Iran* 36°30N 52°0E **129** B7
Mazapil *Mexico* 24°39N 101°34W **180** C4
Mazar *China* 36°32N 77°1E **109** E9
Mazar, O. → *Algeria* 31°50N 1°36E **136** B4
Mazär-e Sharïf *Afghan.* 36°41N 67°0E **109** F7
Mazara del Vallo *Italy* 37°39N 12°35E **94** E5
Mazarredo *Argentina* 47°10S 66°50W **192** C3
Mazarrón *Spain* 37°27N 1°19W **91** H3
Mazarrón, G. de *Spain* 37°27N 1°19W **91** H3
Mazaruni → *Guyana* 6°25N 58°35W **186** B7
Mazatán *Mexico* 29°0N 110°8W **180** B2
Mazatenango
  Guatemala 14°35N 91°30W **182** D1
Mazatlán *Mexico* 23°13N 106°25W **180** C3
Mažeikiai *Lithuania* 56°20N 22°20E **82** B9
Mãzhãn *Iran* 32°30N 59°0E **129** C8
Mazïdãgï *Turkey* 37°28N 40°29E **105** D9
Mazïnãn *Iran* 36°19N 56°56E **129** B8
Mazo Cruz *Peru* 16°45S 69°44W **188** D4
Mazoe *Mozam.* 16°42S 33°7E **143** F3
Mazoe → *Mozam.* 16°20S 33°30E **143** F3
Mazowe *Zimbabwe* 17°28S 30°58E **143** F3
Mazowieckie □ *Poland* 52°40N 21°0E **83** F8
Mazurski, Pojezierze
  Poland 53°50N 21°0E **82** E7
Mazyr *Belarus* 51°59N 29°15E **75** B15
Mba *Fiji* 17°33S 177°41E **154** a
Mbabane *Swaziland* 26°18S 31°6E **145** D5
Mbagne *Mauritania* 16°6N 14°47W **138** B2
M'bahiakro *Ivory C.* 7°33N 4°19W **138** D4
Mbaïki *C.A.R.* 3°53N 18°1E **140** D3
Mbala *Zambia* 8°46S 31°24E **143** D3
Mbalabala *Zimbabwe* 20°27S 29°3E **145** B4
Mbale *Uganda* 1°8N 34°12E **142** B3
Mbalmayo *Cameroon* 3°33N 11°33E **139** E7
Mbam → *Cameroon* 4°24N 11°17E **139** E7
Mbamba Bay *Tanzania* 11°13S 34°49E **143** E3
Mbandaka
  Dem. Rep. of the Congo 0°1N 18°18E **140** D3
Mbanga *Cameroon* 4°30N 9°33E **139** E6
Mbanza Congo *Angola* 6°18S 14°16E **142** D2
Mbanza Ngungu
  Dem. Rep. of the Congo 5°12S 14°53E **140** F2
Mbarangandu *Tanzania* 10°11S 36°48E **143** D4
Mbarara *Uganda* 0°35S 30°40E **142** C3
Mbatto *Ivory C.* 6°28N 4°22W **138** D4
Mbenge = Beqa *Fiji* 18°23S 178°8E **154** a
Mbenkuru → *Tanzania* 9°25S 39°50E **143** D4
Mberengwa *Zimbabwe* 20°29S 29°57E **143** G2
Mberengwa, Mt.
  Zimbabwe 20°37S 29°55E **143** G2
Mberubu *Nigeria* 6°10N 7°38E **139** D6
Mbesuma *Zambia* 10°0S 32°2E **143** D3
Mbeya *Tanzania* 8°54S 33°29E **143** D3
Mbeya □ *Tanzania* 8°15S 33°30E **143** D3
Mbhashe → *S. Africa* 32°15S 28°54E **145** D4
Mbinga *Tanzania* 10°50S 35°0E **143** E4
Mbini = Rio Muni □
  Eq. Guin. 1°30N 10°0E **140** D2
Mbizi *Zimbabwe* 21°23S 31°1E **143** G3

Mbombela *S. Africa* 25°29S 30°59E **145** C5
Mbomou = Bomu →
  C.A.R. 4°40N 22°30E **140** D4
M'bonge *Cameroon* 4°33N 9°5E **139** E6
Mboro *Senegal* 15°9N 16°54W **138** B1
Mbouda *Cameroon* 5°38N 10°15E **139** D7
M'boukou, L. de
  Cameroon 6°23N 12°50E **139** D7
Mboune *Senegal* 14°42N 13°34W **138** C2
Mbour *Senegal* 14°22N 16°54W **138** C1
Mbout *Mauritania* 16°1N 12°38W **138** B2
Mbuji-Mayi
  Dem. Rep. of the Congo 6°9S 23°40E **142** D1
Mbulu *Tanzania* 3°45S 35°30E **142** C4
Mburucuyá *Argentina* 28°1S 58°14W **190** B4
Mburucuyá △
  Argentina 28°1S 58°12W **190** B4
Mcherrah *Algeria* 27°0N 4°30W **136** C3
Mchinga *Tanzania* 9°44S 39°45E **143** D4
Mchinji *Malawi* 13°47S 32°58E **143** E3
Mdantsane *S. Africa* 32°56S 27°46E **145** D4
Mead, L. *U.S.A.* 36°0N 114°44W **171** J12
Meade *U.S.A.* 37°17N 100°20W **172** G3
Meade River = Atqasuk
  U.S.A. 70°28N 157°24W **166** A8
Meadow Lake *Canada* 54°10N 108°26W **163** C7
Meadow Lake ◯
  Canada 54°27N 109°0W **163** C7
Meadow Valley Wash →
  U.S.A. 36°40N 114°34W **171** J12
Meadville *U.S.A.* 41°39N 80°9W **174** E4
Meaford *Canada* 44°36N 80°35W **174** B4
Meakan Dake *Japan* 45°15N 144°0E **112** C11
Mealhada *Portugal* 40°22N 8°27W **88** E2
Mealy Mts. *Canada* 53°10N 58°0W **165** B8
Meander River *Canada* 59°2N 117°42W **162** B5
Meares, C. *U.S.A.* 45°37N 124°0W **168** D1
Mearim → *Brazil* 3°4S 44°35W **189** A2
Meath □ *Ireland* 53°40N 6°57W **64** C5
Meath Park *Canada* 53°27N 105°22W **163** C7
Meaulne *France* 46°36N 2°36E **71** F9
Meaux *France* 48°58N 2°50E **71** D9
Mebechi-Gawa →
  Japan 40°31N 141°31E **112** D10
Mebulu, Tanjung
  Indonesia 8°50S 115°5E **119** K18
Mecanhelas *Mozam.* 15°12S 35°54E **143** F4
Mecca = Makkah
  Si. Arabia 21°30N 39°54E **137** C4
Mecca *U.S.A.* 33°34N 116°5W **171** M10
Mechanicsburg *U.S.A.* 40°13N 77°1W **174** F8
Mechanicville *U.S.A.* 42°54N 73°41W **175** D11
Mechelen *Belgium* 51°2N 4°29E **69** C4
Mecheria *Algeria* 33°35N 0°18W **136** B3
Mechernich *Germany* 50°35N 6°39E **76** E2
Mechetinskaya *Russia* 46°45N 40°32E **87** G5
Mechra Bel Ksiri
  Morocco 34°34N 5°57W **136** B2
Mechra Benâbbou
  Morocco 32°39N 7°48W **136** B2
Mecidiye *Turkey* 40°38N 26°32E **97** F10
Mecitözü *Turkey* 40°32N 35°17E **104** B6
Mecklenburg *Germany* 53°33N 11°40E **74** B7
Mecklenburg-Vorpommern □
  Germany 53°45N 12°15E **76** B8
Mecklenburger Bucht
  Germany 54°20N 11°40E **76** A7
Meconta *Mozam.* 14°59S 39°50E **143** E4
Mecsek *Hungary* 46°10N 18°18E **80** D3
Mecubúri *Mozam.* 14°39S 38°54E **143** E4
Mecubúri → *Mozam.* 14°10S 40°32E **143** E5
Mecúfi *Mozam.* 13°20S 40°32E **143** E5
Méda *Portugal* 40°57N 7°18W **88** E3
Medak *India* 18°1N 78°15E **126** E4
Medan *Indonesia* 3°40N 98°38E **118** D1
Médanos *Argentina* 38°50S 62°42W **192** A4
Médanos de Coro △
  Venezuela 11°35N 69°44W **183** D6
Medanosa, Pta.
  Argentina 48°8S 66°0W **192** C3
Medart *U.S.A.* 30°5N 84°23W **178** E5
Medawachchiya
  Sri Lanka 8°30N 80°30E **127** K5
Medchal *India* 17°37N 78°29E **126** F4
Mede *Italy* 45°6N 8°44E **92** C5
Médéa *Algeria* 36°12N 2°50E **136** A5
Médéa □ *Algeria* 36°0N 2°50E **136** A5
Mededa *Bos.-H.* 43°44N 19°10E **80** G4
Medeiros Neto *Brazil* 17°20S 40°14W **189** D2
Medellín *Colombia* 6°15N 75°35W **186** B2
Medelpad *Sweden* 62°33N 16°30E **62** B10
Medemblik *Neths.* 52°46N 5°8E **69** B5
Médenine *Tunisia* 33°21N 10°30E **136** B6
Médenine □ *Tunisia* 32°0N 10°0E **136** B6
Mederdra *Mauritania* 17°0N 15°38W **138** B1
Medford *Mass., U.S.A.* 42°25N 71°7W **175** D13
Medford *Oreg., U.S.A.* 42°19N 122°52W **168** E2
Medford *Wis., U.S.A.* 45°9N 90°20W **172** C8
Medgidia *Romania* 44°15N 28°19E **81** F13
Media Agua *Argentina* 31°58S 68°25W **190** C3
Medianeira *Brazil* 25°17S 54°5W **191** B5
Mediaş *Romania* 46°9N 24°22E **81** D9
Medicina *Italy* 44°28N 11°38E **92** D8
Medicine Bow
  U.S.A. 41°54N 106°12W **168** F10
Medicine Bow Mts.
  U.S.A. 40°40N 106°0W **168** F10
Medicine Hat *Canada* 50°0N 110°45W **163** D6
Medicine Lake
  U.S.A. 48°30N 104°30W **168** B11
Medicine Lodge *U.S.A.* 37°17N 98°35W **172** G4
Medina = Al Madînah
  Si. Arabia 24°35N 39°52E **128** E3
Medina *Brazil* 16°15S 41°29W **189** D2
Medina *N. Dak., U.S.A.* 46°54N 99°18W **172** B4
Medina *N.Y., U.S.A.* 43°13N 78°23W **174** C6
Medina *Ohio, U.S.A.* 41°8N 81°52W **174** E3
Medina → *U.S.A.* 29°16N 98°29W **176** G5
Medina de Pomar *Spain* 42°56N 3°29W **88** C7
Medina de Ríoseco *Spain* 41°53N 5°3W **88** D5
Medina del Campo *Spain* 41°18N 4°55W **88** D6
Médina Gounas *Senegal* 13°8N 13°45W **138** C2
Medina L. *U.S.A.* 29°32N 98°56W **176** G5
Medina Sidonia *Spain* 36°28N 5°57W **89** J5
Medinaceli *Spain* 41°12N 2°30W **90** D2
Medinipur *India* 22°25N 87°21E **125** H12
Medio-Campidano □
  Italy 39°35N 8°30E **94** C1
Mediterranean Sea *Europe* 35°0N 15°0E **58** H7
Mednogorsk *Russia* 51°24N 57°37E **108** D5
Médoc *France* 45°10N 0°50W **72** C3

Medulin *Croatia* 44°49N 13°55E **93** D10
Medveda *Serbia* 42°50N 21°32E **96** D5
Medvedevo *Russia* 56°37N 47°47E **86** B8
Medveditsa → *Tver,*
  Russia 57°5N 37°30E **84** D9
Medveditsa → *Volgograd,*
  Russia 49°35N 42°41E **86** F6
Medvedok *Russia* 57°20N 50°1E **86** B10
Medvezhi, Ostrava
  Russia 71°0N 161°0E **107** B17
Medvezhyegorsk *Russia* 63°0N 34°25E **106** C4
Medway □ *U.K.* 51°25N 0°32E **67** F8
Medway → *U.K.* 51°27N 0°46E **67** F8
Medzev *Slovak Rep.* 48°43N 20°55E **79** C13
Medzilaborce
  Slovak Rep. 49°17N 21°52E **79** B14
Meda *China* 29°4N 77°42E **124** E7
Meekatharra *Australia* 26°32S 118°29E **149** E2
Meeker *U.S.A.* 40°2N 107°55W **168** F10
Meena *India* 29°1N 77°42E **124** E7
Meerhusen *Germany* 47°41N 9°16E **77** H5
Meerut *India* 29°1N 77°42E **124** E7
Meeteetse *U.S.A.* 44°9N 108°52W **168** D9
Mega *Ethiopia* 3°57N 38°19E **131** G2
Megalo Chorio *Greece* 36°27N 27°24E **99** E9
Megalopoli *Greece* 37°25N 22°7E **98** D4
Meganisi *Greece* 38°38N 20°46E **98** C2
Megara *Greece* 37°58N 23°22E **98** D5
Megasini *India* 21°38N 86°21E **125** J12
Megdova = Tavropos →
  Greece 39°10N 21°45E **98** B3
Megève *France* 45°51N 6°37E **73** C10
Meghalaya □ *India* 25°50N 91°0E **123** G17
Meghna → *Bangla.* 22°50N 90°50E **123** H17
Megion *Russia* 61°3N 76°6E **106** C8
Mégiscane, L. *Canada* 48°35N 75°55W **164** C4
Megisti *Greece* 36°8N 29°34E **99** E11
Megra *Russia* 60°11N 37°14E **84** B9
Mehadia *Romania* 44°56N 22°23E **80** F7
Mehaïguene, O. →
  Algeria 32°15N 2°59E **136** B4
Meharry, Mt.
  Australia 22°59S 118°35E **148** D2
Mehedeby *Sweden* 60°27N 17°25E **62** D11
Mehedinţi □ *Romania* 44°40N 22°45E **80** F7
Meheisa *Sudan* 19°38N 32°57E **137** D3
Mehekar *India* 20°9N 76°34E **126** D3
Mehlville *U.S.A.* 38°31N 90°19W **172** F8
Mehmetçik = Galateia
  Cyprus 35°25N 34°4E **101** D13
Mehndawal *India* 26°58N 83°5E **125** F10
Mehr Jãn *Iran* 33°50N 55°6E **129** C7
Mehrãbãd *Iran* 36°53N 47°55E **128** B5
Mehrãbãn *Iran* 38°4N 47°7E **105** C12
Mehrãn *Iran* 33°7N 46°10E **105** F12
Mehrãn → *Iran* 26°45N 55°26E **129** E7
Mehrgarh *Pakistan* 29°30N 67°30E **124** E2
Mehrïz *Iran* 31°35N 54°28E **129** D7
Mehun-sur-Yèvre *France* 47°10N 2°13E **71** E9
Mei Jiang → *China* 24°25N 116°35E **117** E11
Mei Xian *China* 34°18N 107°55E **116** C4
Meicheng *China* 29°29N 119°16E **117** C12
Meichengzhen *China* 28°9N 111°40E **117** C8
Meichuan *China* 30°8N 115°31E **117** B10
Meighen I. *Canada* 80°0N 99°30W **161** B12
Meiktila *Burma* 20°53N 95°54E **123** J19
Meili Xue Shan *China* 28°30N 98°39E **116** C2
Meimyo = Pyin-U-Lwin
  Burma 22°2N 96°28E **120** A1
Meinerzhagen *Germany* 51°6N 7°38E **76** D3
Meiningen *Germany* 50°34N 10°25E **76** E6
Meio → *Brazil* 13°36S 44°7W **189** C2
Meira, Serra de *Spain* 43°15N 7°15W **88** B3
Meiringen *Switz.* 46°43N 8°12E **77** J4
Meishan *China* 30°3N 103°23E **116** B4
Meissen *Germany* 51°9N 13°29E **76** D9
Meissner *Germany* 51°11N 9°50E **76** D5
Meissner-Kaufunger Wald ◯
  Germany 51°16N 9°45E **76** D5
Meitan *China* 27°45N 107°29E **116** D6
Meizhou *China* 24°16N 116°6E **117** E11
Meja *India* 25°9N 82°7E **125** G10
Mejillones *Chile* 23°10S 70°30W **190** A1
Mekele *Ethiopia* 13°33N 39°30E **131** G2
Mekerghene, Sebkra
  Algeria 26°21N 1°30E **136** C5
Mékhé *Senegal* 15°7N 16°38W **138** C1
Mekhtar *Pakistan* 30°30N 69°15E **122** D6
Meknès *Morocco* 33°57N 5°33W **136** B3
Meknès-Tafilalet □
  Morocco 33°30N 5°35W **136** B2
Meko *Nigeria* 7°27N 2°52E **139** D5
Mekongga *Indonesia* 3°39S 121°15E **119** E6
Mekrou → *Benin* 12°25N 2°50E **139** C5
Mekvari = Kür →
  Azerbaijan 39°29N 49°15E **105** C13
Mel *Italy* 46°4N 12°5E **93** B9
Melagiri Hills *India* 12°20N 77°30E **127** H3
Melah, Oued el →
  Algeria 32°20N 2°28E **136** B4
Melaka *Malaysia* 2°15N 102°15E **121** L4
Melaka □ *Malaysia* 2°15N 102°15E **121** L4
Melambes *Greece* 35°8N 24°40E **101** D6
Melanesia *Pac. Oc.* 4°0S 155°0E **156** H7
Melanesian Basin
  Pac. Oc. 0°5N 160°35E **156** G8
Melapalaiyam *India* 8°39N 77°44E **127** K3
Melaya *Indonesia* 8°17S 114°30E **119** J17
Melbourne *Australia* 37°48S 144°58E **153** D6
Melbourne *U.S.A.* 28°5N 80°37W **179** G6
Melchor Múzquiz
  Mexico 27°53N 101°31W **180** B4
Melchor Ocampo
  Mexico 24°51N 101°39W **180** C4

Melhus *Norway* 63°17N 10°18E **60** E14
Melide *Spain* 42°55N 8°1W **88** C2
Meligales *Greece* 37°15N 21°59E **98** D3
Melilla *N. Afr.* 35°21N 2°57W **134** A5
Melilli *Italy* 37°11N 15°7E **95** E8
Melipilla *Chile* 33°42S 71°15W **190** C1
Melissa *Canada* 45°24N 79°14W **174** A5
Melissa, Akra *Greece* 35°6N 24°33E **101** D6
Melissa Oros *Greece* 37°32N 26°4E **99** D8
Melita *Canada* 49°15N 101°0W **163** D8
Mélito di Porto Salvo
  Italy 37°55N 15°47E **95** E8
Melitopol *Ukraine* 46°50N 35°22E **85** J8
Melk *Austria* 48°13N 15°20E **78** C8
Mellan Fryken *Sweden* 59°45N 13°10E **62** E7
Mellansel *Sweden* 63°26N 18°19E **60** E18
Mellbystrand *Sweden* 56°30N 12°56E **63** H6
Melle *France* 46°14N 0°10W **72** B3
Melle *Germany* 52°12N 8°20E **76** C4
Mellègue, O. → *Tunisia* 36°36N 9°14E **136** A5
Mellerud *Sweden* 58°41N 12°28E **63** F6
Mellette *U.S.A.* 45°9N 98°30W **172** C4
Mellid = Melide *Spain* 42°55N 8°1W **88** C2
Mellieha *Malta* 35°57N 14°22E **101** D1
Mellizo Sur, Cerro
  Chile 48°33S 73°10W **192** C2
Mellrichstadt *Germany* 50°25N 10°17E **76** E6
Melnik *Bulgaria* 41°30N 23°25E **96** E7
Mělník *Czech Rep.* 50°22N 14°23E **78** A7
Melnytsya Podilska
  Ukraine 48°37N 26°10E **81** B11
Melo *Uruguay* 32°20S 54°10W **191** C5
Melolo *Indonesia* 9°53S 120°40E **119** F6
Melouprey *Cambodia* 13°48N 105°16E **120** F5
Melrhir, Chott *Algeria* 34°13N 6°30E **136** B5
Melrose *Australia* 32°42S 146°57E **153** B7
Melrose *U.K.* 55°36N 2°43W **65** F6
Melrose *Minn., U.S.A.* 45°40N 94°49W **172** C6
Melrose *N. Mex.,*
  U.S.A. 34°26N 103°38W **169** J12
Melstone *U.S.A.* 46°36N 107°52W **168** C10
Melsungen *Germany* 51°7N 9°32E **76** D5
Melton *Australia* 37°41S 144°35E **152** D6
Melton Mowbray *U.K.* 52°47N 0°54W **66** E7
Melun *France* 48°32N 2°39E **71** D9
Melung *Nepal* 27°31N 86°3E **125** F12
Melur *India* 10°2N 78°23E **127** J4
Melville *Canada* 50°55N 102°50W **163** C8
Melville, C. *Australia* 14°11S 144°30E **150** A3
Melville B. *Greenland* 75°30N 63°0W **167** B4
Melville I. *Australia* 11°30S 131°0E **148** B5
Melville I. *Canada* 75°30N 112°0W **161** B9
Melville Pen. *Canada* 68°0N 84°0W **161** D15
Melvin, Lough *Ireland* 54°26N 8°10W **64** B3
Mélykút *Hungary* 46°11N 19°25E **80** D4
Memaliaj *Albania* 40°25N 19°58E **96** J12
Memba *Mozam.* 14°11S 40°30E **143** E5
Memboro *Indonesia* 9°30S 119°30E **148** A2
Membrilla *Spain* 38°59N 3°21W **89** G7
Memel = Klaipėda
  Lithuania 55°43N 21°10E **82** C8
Memel *S. Africa* 27°38S 29°36E **145** C4
Memmingen *Germany* 47°58N 10°10E **77** H6
Mempawah *Indonesia* 0°30N 109°5E **118** D3
Memphis *Egypt* 29°50N 31°12E **137** D7
Memphis *Mich., U.S.A.* 42°54N 82°46W **174** D2
Memphis *Tenn., U.S.A.* 35°8N 90°2W **177** D9
Memphis *Tex., U.S.A.* 34°44N 100°33W **176** D4
Memphrémagog, L.
  N. Amer. 45°8N 72°17W **175** B12
Mena *Ukraine* 51°31N 32°13E **85** G7
Mena *U.S.A.* 34°35N 94°15W **176** D7
Menado = Manado
  Indonesia 1°29N 124°51E **119** D6
Menai Strait *U.K.* 53°11N 4°13W **66** D3
Ménaka *Mali* 15°59N 2°18E **139** B5
Menan = Chao Phraya →
  Thailand 13°40N 100°31E **120** F3
Menard *U.S.A.* 30°55N 99°47W **176** F5
Menard Fracture Zone
  Pac. Oc. 43°0S 97°0W **157** M18
Mendaña Fracture Zone
  Pac. Oc. 16°0S 91°0W **157** J18
Mendawai → *Indonesia* 3°30S 113°0E **118** E4
Mende *France* 44°31N 3°30E **72** D7
Mendeleyev Ridge
  Arctic 80°0N 178°0W **54** B17
Menden *Germany* 51°26N 7°47E **76** D3
Menderes *Turkey* 38°14N 27°8E **99** C9
Mendhar *India* 33°35N 74°10E **125** C6
Mendip Hills *U.K.* 51°17N 2°40W **67** F5
Mendocino *U.S.A.* 39°19N 123°48W **168** G2
Mendocino Fracture Zone
  Pac. Oc. 40°0N 142°0W **157** D12
Mendooran *Australia* 31°50S 149°6E **153** B8
Mendota *Calif., U.S.A.* 36°45N 120°23W **170** J6
Mendota *Ill., U.S.A.* 41°33N 89°7W **172** E8
Mendoyo *Indonesia* 8°23S 114°42E **119** J17
Mendoza *Argentina* 32°50S 68°52W **190** C3
Mendoza □ *Argentina* 33°0S 69°0W **190** C3
Mene Grande *Venezuela* 9°49N 70°56W **186** B4
Menemen *Turkey* 38°34N 27°3E **99** C9
Menen *Belgium* 50°47N 3°7E **69** D3
Menéndez, L. *Argentina* 42°40S 71°51W **192** B2
Menfi *Italy* 37°36N 12°58E **94** E5
Mengcheng *China* 33°12N 116°36E **116** H9
Mengdingjie *China* 23°31N 98°58E **116** F2
Mengeš *Slovenia* 46°10N 14°35E **93** D11
Menggala *Indonesia* 4°30S 105°15E **118** E3
Menghai *China* 21°54N 100°30E **116** F3
Mengibar *Spain* 37°58N 3°48W **89** H7
Mengjin *China* 22°21N 99°27E **116** F2
Mengshan *China* 24°14N 110°55E **117** E8
Mengyin *China* 35°40N 117°58E **116** G9
Mengzi *China* 23°20N 103°22E **116** F4
Menifee *U.S.A.* 33°41N 117°10W **171** M9
Menihek *Canada* 54°28N 56°36W **165** B6
Menihek L. *Canada* 54°0N 67°0W **165** B6
Menin = Menen *Belgium* 50°47N 3°7E **69** D3
Meninde *Australia* 32°20S 142°25E **153** B7
Meningie *Australia* 35°50S 139°18E **152** D3
Menjangan, Pulau
  Indonesia 8°7S 114°31E **119** J17
Menkrour *Algeria* 26°27N 8°9E **136** C6

Menlo Park *U.S.A.* 37°27N 122°12W **170** H4
Menngen ◯ *Australia* 15°21S 131°16E **148** C5
Menominee *U.S.A.* 45°6N 87°37W **172** C10
Menominee → *U.S.A.* 45°6N 87°35W **172** C10
Menomonie *U.S.A.* 44°53N 91°55W **172** C8
Menongue *Angola* 14°48S 17°52E **141** G3
Menorca *Spain* 40°0N 4°0E **100** B11
Menorca ✈ (MAH) *Spain* 39°50N 4°16E **100** F9
Mentakab *Malaysia* 3°29N 102°21E **121** L4
Mentawai, Kepulauan
  Indonesia 2°0S 99°0E **118** E1
Menton *France* 43°50N 7°29E **73** E11
Mentor *U.S.A.* 41°40N 81°21W **174** E3
Menzel-Bourguiba
  Tunisia 37°9N 9°49E **136** A5
Menzel-Chaker *Tunisia* 35°0N 10°26E **136** B6
Menzies *Australia* 29°40S 121°2E **149** E3
Meob B. *Namibia* 24°25S 14°34E **144** B1
Meoqui *Mexico* 28°17N 105°29W **180** B3
Mepaco *Mozam.* 15°57S 30°48E **143** F3
Meppel *Neths.* 52°42N 6°12E **69** B6
Meppen *Germany* 52°42N 7°17E **76** C3
Mequinenza *Spain* 41°22N 0°17E **90** D5
Mequinenza, Embalse de
  Spain 41°25N 0°15E **90** D5
Mer *France* 47°42N 1°30E **70** E8
Merak *Indonesia* 6°10N 106°26E **119** F12
Meramangye, L.
  Australia 28°25S 132°13E **149** E5
Meran = Merano *Italy* 46°40N 11°9E **93** B8
Merano *Italy* 46°40N 11°9E **93** B8
Merate *Italy* 45°42N 9°25E **92** C6
Merauke *Indonesia* 8°29S 140°24E **119** F10
Merca = Marka *Somalia* 1°48N 44°50E **131** G3
Mercantour △ *France* 44°16N 6°43E **73** D10
Mercato Saraceno *Italy* 43°57N 12°12E **93** E9
Merced *U.S.A.* 37°18N 120°29W **170** H6
Merced → *U.S.A.* 37°21N 120°59W **170** H6
Merced Pk. *U.S.A.* 37°36N 119°24W **170** H7
Mercedes *B. Aires,*
  Argentina 34°40S 59°30W **190** C4
Mercedes *Corrientes,*
  Argentina 29°10S 58°5W **190** B4
Mercedes *San Luis,*
  Argentina 33°40S 65°21W **190** C2
Mercedes *Uruguay* 33°12S 58°0W **190** C4
Merceditas *Chile* 28°20S 70°35W **190** B1
Mercer *N.Z.* 37°16S 175°5E **154** D4
Mercer *U.S.A.* 41°14N 80°15W **174** E4
Mercer Island *U.S.A.* 47°34N 122°13W **170** C4
Mercier *Bolivia* 10°42S 68°5W **188** C4
Mercury *U.S.A.* 36°40N 115°59W **171** J11
Mercury B. *N.Z.* 36°48S 175°45E **154** C4
Mercury Is. *N.Z.* 36°37S 175°52E **154** C4
Mercy, C. *Canada* 65°0N 63°30W **161** D17
Merdrignac *France* 48°11N 2°27W **70** D4
Mere *U.K.* 51°6N 2°16W **67** F5
Meredith, Akra *Greece* 38°16N 25°53E **99** D7
Meredith *Australia* 37°49S 144°5E **152** D6
Meredith, C. *Falk. Is.* 52°15S 60°40W **192** D4
Meredith, L. *U.S.A.* 35°43N 101°33W **176** D4
Merefa *Ukraine* 49°48N 36°3E **85** H9
Mereté, Espigão *Brazil* 12°30S 46°10W **189** C1
Merevári → *Venezuela* 5°15N 65°39W **186** B5
Merga = Nukheila
  Sudan 19°1N 26°21E **137** D2
Mergui *Burma* 12°26N 98°34E **120** F2
Mergui Arch. = Myeik Kyunzu
  Burma 11°30N 97°30E **121** G1
Méribel-les-Allues
  France 45°25N 6°34E **73** C10
Meriç *Turkey* 41°11N 26°25E **97** F10
Meriç → *Turkey* 40°52N 26°12E **97** F10
Mérida *Mexico* 20°58N 89°37W **181** C7
Mérida *Spain* 38°55N 6°25W **89** G4
Mérida *Venezuela* 8°24N 71°8W **186** B4
Mérida, Cord. de
  Venezuela 9°0N 71°0W **186** B4
Meriden *U.K.* 52°26N 1°38W **67** E6
Meriden *U.S.A.* 41°32N 72°48W **175** E12
Meridian *Calif., U.S.A.* 39°9N 121°55W **170** F5
Meridian *Ga., U.S.A.* 31°27N 81°23W **178** F8
Meridian *Idaho, U.S.A.* 43°37N 116°24W **168** E5
Meridian *Miss., U.S.A.* 32°22N 88°42W **177** E10
Mérignac *France* 44°50N 0°39W **72** D3
Merimbula *Australia* 36°53S 149°54E **153** D8
Merinda *Australia* 20°2S 148°11E **150** C4
Mering *Germany* 48°16N 10°59E **77** G6
Meringur *Australia* 34°20S 141°19E **152** C4
Merir *Palau* 4°10N 132°30E **156** D2
Merirumã *Brazil* 1°15N 54°50W **187** C8
Merkel *U.S.A.* 32°28N 100°1W **176** E4
Mermaid Reef *Australia* 17°6S 119°36E **148** C2
Meroe *Sudan* 16°56N 33°10E **137** D3
Merowe *Sudan* 18°29N 31°46E **137** D3
Merowe Dam *Sudan* 18°35N 31°56E **137** D3
Merredin *Australia* 31°28S 118°18E **149** F2
Merrick *U.K.* 55°8N 4°28W **65** F4
Merrickville *Canada* 44°55N 75°50W **174** B9
Merrill *Oreg., U.S.A.* 42°1N 121°36W **168** E3
Merrill *Wis., U.S.A.* 45°11N 89°41W **172** C8
Merriman *U.S.A.* 42°55N 101°42W **172** D3
Merritt *Canada* 50°10N 120°45W **162** C4
Merritt Island *U.S.A.* 28°21N 80°42W **179** G6
Merriwa *Australia* 32°6S 150°22E **153** B8
Merriwagga *Australia* 33°47S 145°43E **153** B7
Merry I. *Canada* 55°29N 77°31W **164** A4
Merryville *U.S.A.* 30°45N 93°33W **176** F8
Mersch *Lux.* 49°44N 6°7E **69** E6
Merseburg *Germany* 51°22N 11°59E **76** D7
Mersea I. *U.K.* 51°47N 0°58E **67** F8
Mersey → *U.K.* 53°25N 3°1W **66** D5
Merseyside □ *U.K.* 53°31N 3°2W **66** D5
Mersin *Turkey* 36°51N 34°36E **104** D6
Mersin □ *Turkey* 36°51N 34°36E **104** D6
Mersing *Malaysia* 2°25N 103°50E **121** L4
Merta *India* 26°39N 74°4E **124** F5
Merta Road *India* 26°43N 73°55E **124** F5
Merthyr Tydfil *U.K.* 51°45N 3°22W **67** F4
Merthyr Tydfil □ *U.K.* 51°46N 3°21W **67** F4
Mértola *Portugal* 37°40N 7°40W **89** H3
Merti *Kenya* 1°4N 38°40E **142** B4
Mértola *Portugal* 37°40N 7°40W **89** H3
Mertz Glacier
  Antarctica 67°30S 144°45E **55** C10
Merton □ *U.K.* 51°25N 0°12W **67** F7
Mertzon *U.S.A.* 31°16N 100°49W **176** F4
Méru *France* 49°13N 2°8E **71** C9

Meru *Kenya* 0°3N 37°40E 14
Meru *Tanzania* 3°15S 36°46E 14
Meru → *Kenya* 0°5N 38°10E 14
Meru Betiri △
  Indonesia 8°27S 113°51E 119
Merville *France* 50°38N 2°38E 6
Méry-sur-Seine *France* 48°31N 3°54E 71
Merzifon *Turkey* 40°53N 35°32E 104
Merzig *Germany* 49°26N 6°37E 6
Merzouga, Erg Tin
  Algeria 24°0N 11°4E 13
Mesa *U.S.A.* 33°25N 111°50W 169
Mesa Verde △ *U.S.A.* 37°11N 108°29W 169
Mesagne *Italy* 40°34N 17°48E 9
Mesanagros *Greece* 36°1N 27°49E 9
Mesaoria *Cyprus* 35°12N 33°14E 101
Mescit *Germany* 51°20N 41°11E 129
Mesgouez, L. *Canada* 51°20N 75°0W 16
Meshchovsk *Russia* 54°22N 35°17E 8
Meshchyora *Russia* 55°22N 40°12E 8
Meshchyorsky △ *Russia* 54°50N 41°0E 8
Meshed = Mashhad
  Iran 36°20N 59°35E 12
Meshgïn Shahr *Iran* 38°30N 47°45E 105
Meshoppen *U.S.A.* 41°36N 76°3W 175
Mesilinka → *Canada* 56°6N 124°30W 162
Meslay-du-Maine *France* 47°58N 0°33W 70
Mesocco *Switz.* 46°23N 9°12E 7
Mesolongi *Greece* 38°21N 21°28E 9
Mesongi *Greece* 39°29N 19°56E 9
Mesopotamia = Al Jazirah
  Iraq 33°30N 44°0E 108
Mesopotamia *U.S.A.* 41°27N 80°57W 17
Mesoraca *Italy* 39°5N 16°48E 9
Mésou Volimais = Volimes
  Greece 37°52N 20°39E 9
Mesquite *Nev., U.S.A.* 36°48N 114°4W 17
Mesquite *Tex., U.S.A.* 32°47N 96°36W 17
Messaad *Algeria* 34°8N 3°30E 13
Messac *France* 47°49N 1°50W 7
Messalo → *Mozam.* 12°25S 39°15E 14
Messaména *Cameroon* 3°48N 12°49E 13
Messara, Kolpos *Greece* 35°6N 24°47E 101
Messene *Greece* 37°4N 22°1E 9
Messier, Canal *Chile* 48°20S 74°33W 19
Messina = Musina
  S. Africa 22°20S 30°5E 14
Messina *Italy* 38°11N 15°34E 9
Messina, Str. di *Italy* 38°15N 15°35E 9
Messiniakos Kolpos
  Greece 36°45N 22°5E 9
Messkirch *Germany* 47°59N 9°7E 7
Messlingen *Sweden* 62°40N 12°50E 6
Mesta = Nestos →
  Europe 40°54N 24°49E 9
Mesta, Akra *Greece* 38°16N 25°53E 9
Mestanza *Spain* 38°35N 4°4W 8
Mestersvig *Greenland* 72°10N 23°40W 5
Mestre *Italy* 45°29N 12°15E 9
Mestre, Espigão *Brazil* 12°30S 46°10W 189
Mesudiye *Turkey* 40°48N 37°45E 104
Meta → *S. Amer.* 6°12N 67°28W 18
Meta Incognita Pen.
  Canada 62°45N 68°30W 16
Metabetchouan
  Canada 48°26N 71°52W 16
Metairie *U.S.A.* 29°59N 90°9W 17
Metaline Falls *U.S.A.* 48°52N 117°22W 16
Metán *Argentina* 25°30S 65°0W 19
Metangula *Mozam.* 12°40S 34°50E 14
Metauro → *Italy* 43°50N 13°8E 9
Metcalf *U.S.A.* 33°43N 83°59W 17
Metcalfe *Canada* 45°14N 75°28W 17
Metema *Ethiopia* 12°58N 36°12E 13
Metengobalame
  Mozam. 14°49S 34°30E 14
Meteora *Greece* 39°43N 21°31E 9
Methana *Greece* 37°35N 23°23E 9
Methoni *Greece* 36°49N 21°42E 9
Methven *N.Z.* 43°38S 171°40E 15
Metil *Mozam.* 16°24S 39°0E 14
Metkovets *Bulgaria* 43°37N 23°10E 9
Metković *Croatia* 43°6N 17°39E 9
Metlakatla *U.S.A.* 55°8N 131°35W 16
Metlaoui *Tunisia* 34°20N 8°24E 13
Metlika *Slovenia* 45°40N 15°20E 9
Metlili Chaamba *Algeria* 32°40N 3°30E 13
Metropolis *U.S.A.* 37°9N 88°44W 17
Metropolitana □ *Chile* 33°30S 70°50W 19
Metsovo *Greece* 39°48N 21°12E 9
Metter *U.S.A.* 32°24N 82°3W 17
Mettuppalayam *India* 11°18N 76°59E 1
Mettur *India* 11°48N 77°47E 1
Mettur *Ethiopia* 8°18N 35°35E 13
Metz *France* 49°8N 6°10E 7
Meulaboh *Indonesia* 4°11N 96°3E 11
Meung-sur-Loire *France* 47°50N 1°40E 7
Meureudu *Indonesia* 5°19N 96°10E 11
Meurthe → *France* 48°47N 6°9E 7
Meurthe-et-Moselle □
  France 48°52N 6°0E 7
Meuse □ *France* 49°8N 5°25E 7
Meuse → *Europe* 50°45N 5°41E 6
Meuselwitz *Germany* 51°3N 12°18E 7
Mexia *U.S.A.* 31°41N 96°29W 17
Mexiana, I. *Brazil* 0°0 49°30W 18
Mexicali *Mexico* 32°40N 115°30W 18
Mexican Plateau
  Mexico 25°0N 104°0W 18
Mexican Water
  U.S.A. 36°57N 109°32W 16
Mexico *Maine, U.S.A.* 44°34N 70°33W 17
Mexico *Mo., U.S.A.* 39°10N 91°53W 17
Mexico *N.Y., U.S.A.* 43°28N 76°14W 17
México □ *Mexico* 19°20N 99°30W 18
Mexico ■ *Cent. Amer.* 25°0N 105°0W 18
México, Ciudad de
  Mexico 19°24N 99°9W 18
Mexico, G. of *Cent. Amer.* 25°0N 90°0W 18
Mexico Beach *U.S.A.* 29°57N 85°25W 17
Meydan-e Naftün *Iran* 31°56N 49°18E 12
Meydani, Ra's-e *Iran* 25°24N 59°6E 12
Meyenburg *Germany* 53°19N 12°15E 7

vers Chuck U.S.A. 55°45N 132°15W 162 B2
mac France 45°32N 2°10E 72 C6
maneh Afghan. 35°53N 64°38E 108 E6
rueis France 44°12N 3°27E 72 D7
ssac France 45°31N 1°40E 72 C5
zieu France 45°46N 4°59E 73 C8
dra Bulgaria 43°12N 23°42E 96 C7
e France 43°27N 3°36E 72 E7
en Russia 65°50N 44°20E 106 C5
en → Russia 65°44N 44°22E 58 B14
enc, Mt. France 44°54N 4°11E 73 D8
eş, Munţii Romania 47°5N 23°5E 80 C8
ha → Russia 55°44N 31°33E 84 E6
hdurechensk
ussia 53°41N 88°3E 109 B11
hdurechenskiy
ussia 59°36N 65°56E 106 D7
idon-Canon France 49°5N 0°1W 70 C6
ières-en-Brenne
rance 46°49N 1°13E 72 B5
ilhac France 44°49N 4°21E 73 D8
in France 44°4N 0°16E 72 D4
öberény Hungary 46°49N 21°3E 80 D6
öfalva Hungary 46°55N 18°49E 80 D3
öhegyes Hungary 46°19N 20°49E 80 D5
ökövácsháza
ungary 46°25N 20°57E 80 D5
ökövesd Hungary 47°49N 20°35E 80 C5
os France 44°5N 1°10W 72 D2
ötúr Hungary 47°1N 20°41E 80 C5
quital Mexico 23°29N 104°23W 180 C4
zolombardo Italy 46°13N 11°5E 92 B8
lozi → S. Africa 28°25S 32°26E 145 C5
ta Tanzania 8°22S 32°50E 143 D4
in Russia 53°2N 32°50E 85 F7
amid Morocco 29°49N 5°43W 136 C2
aba Hills Zimbabwe 18°30S 30°30E 143 F3
ow India 22°33N 75°50E 124 H6
huatlán Mexico 16°20N 96°36W 181 D5
jadas Spain 39°9N 5°54W 89 F5
mi Fla., U.S.A. 25°46N 80°11W 179 K9
mi Okla., U.S.A. 36°53N 94°53W 176 C7
mi Tex., U.S.A. 35°42N 100°38W 176 D4
mi Beach U.S.A. 25°47N 80°7W 179 K9
mi Canal U.S.A. 25°45N 80°12W 179 K9
mi Gardens U.S.A. 25°56N 80°15W 179 C1
mi Int. ✈ (MIA)
S.A. 25°48N 80°17W 179 K9
mi Shores U.S.A. 25°51N 80°11W 179 K9
mi Springs U.S.A. 25°49N 80°17W 179 K9
n Xian China 33°10N 106°32E 116 A6
nchi China 34°48N 111°48E 114 G6
ndarreh Iran 35°37N 53°39E 129 C7
ndowāb Iran 37°0N 46°5E 105 D12
ndrivazo Madag. 19°31S 45°29E 141 H9
neh Iran 37°30N 47°40E 105 D12
nning China 28°32N 102°9E 116 C4
nwali Pakistan 32°38N 71°28E 124 C4
nyang China 31°22N 104°47E 116 B5
nzhu China 31°22N 104°7E 116 B5
o Ling China 26°5N 107°30E 116 D6
odao Qundao
ina 38°10N 120°45E 115 E11
oli Taiwan 24°37N 120°49E 117 E13
ss Russia 54°59N 60°6E 108 B6
steczko Krajeńskie
oland 53°7N 17°1E 83 E4
stko Poland 54°0N 16°58E 82 E3
a S. Africa 24°10S 30°48E 145 B5
anopy U.S.A. 29°30N 82°17W 179 F7
isasa Romania 46°7N 24°7E 81 D9
co U.S.A. 27°53N 80°30W 179 H9
cosukee U.S.A. 30°36N 84°3W 178 E5
cosukee, L. U.S.A. 30°33N 83°53W 178 E6
halovce Slovak Rep. 48°47N 21°58E 79 C14
higan ☐ U.S.A. 44°0N 85°0W 173 C11
higan, L. U.S.A. 44°0N 87°0W 172 D10
higan City U.S.A. 41°43N 86°54W 172 E10
hika Nigeria 10°36N 13°23E 139 C7
hipicoten I. Canada 47°40N 85°40W 164 C2
hoacán ☐ Mexico 19°10N 101°50W 180 D4
hurin Bulgaria 42°9N 27°51E 97 D11
hurinsk Russia 52°58N 40°27E 86 D5
oud St. Lucia 13°49N 60°54W 183 f
ronesia Pac. Oc. 11°0N 160°0E 156 G7
ronesia, Federated States of ■
ac. Oc. 9°0N 150°0E 156 G7
-Atlantic Ridge Atl. Oc. 0°0 20°0W 56 J10
-Indian Ocean Basin
nd. Oc. 10°0S 80°0E 146 F7
-Indian Ridge Ind. Oc. 30°0S 75°0E 146 H6
-Oceanic Ridge
nd. Oc. 42°0S 90°0E 156 M1
-Pacific Seamounts
ac. Oc. 18°0N 177°0W 156 F10
ai Indonesia 3°0N 107°47E 118 D3
ale Canada 49°25N 103°20W 163 D8
delburg Neths. 51°30N 3°36E 69 C3
delburg Eastern Cape,
Africa 31°30S 25°0E 144 D4
delburg Mpumalanga,
Africa 25°49S 29°28E 145 C4
delfart Denmark 55°30N 9°43E 63 J3
delpos S. Africa 31°55S 20°13E 144 D3
delwit S. Africa 24°51S 27°3E 144 B4
dle Alkali L. U.S.A. 41°27N 120°5W 168 F3
dle America Trench =
uatemala Trench
ac. Oc. 14°0N 95°0W 158 H10
dle Andaman I.
ndia 12°30N 92°50E 127 H11
dle Bass I. U.S.A. 41°41N 82°48W 174 E2
dle East Asia 35°0N 40°0E 102 E5
dle Fork Feather →
S.A. 38°33N 121°30W 170 F5
dle I. Australia 34°6S 123°11E 149 F3
dle Loup → U.S.A. 41°17N 98°24W 172 E4
ddleboro U.S.A. 41°54N 70°55W 175 E14
ddleburg Fla., U.S.A. 30°4N 81°52W 178 E8
ddleburg Pa., U.S.A. 40°47N 77°3W 174 F7
ddleburgh U.S.A. 42°36N 74°20W 175 D10
ddlebury U.S.A. 44°1N 73°10W 175 B11
ddlefield U.S.A. 41°27N 81°4W 174 E3
ddlemarch N.Z. 45°30S 170°9E 155 F5
ddlemount
ustralia 22°50S 148°40E 150 C4
ddleport N.Y.,
S.A. 43°13N 78°29W 174 C6
ddleport Ohio, U.S.A. 39°0N 82°3W 173 F12
ddlesboro U.S.A. 36°36N 83°43W 173 G12
ddlesbrough U.K. 54°35N 1°13W 66 C6
ddlesbrough ☐ U.K. 54°28N 1°13W 66 C6
Middlesex Belize 17°2N 88°31W 182 C2
Middlesex N.J., U.S.A. 40°36N 74°30W 175 F10
Middlesex N.Y., U.S.A. 42°42N 77°16W 174 D7
Middleton Australia 22°22S 141°32E 150 C3
Middleton Canada 44°57N 65°4W 165 D6
Middleton Cr. →
Australia 22°35S 141°51E 150 C3
Middleton I. U.S.A. 59°26N 146°20W 166 D10
Middletown U.K. 54°17N 6°51W 64 B5
Middletown Calif.,
U.S.A. 38°45N 122°37W 170 G4
Middletown Conn.,
U.S.A. 41°34N 72°39W 175 E12
Middletown N.Y.,
U.S.A. 41°27N 74°25W 175 E10
Middletown Ohio,
U.S.A. 39°31N 84°24W 173 F11
Middletown Pa., U.S.A. 40°12N 76°44W 175 F8
Midelt Morocco 32°46N 4°44W 136 B3
Midge Point Australia 20°39S 148°43E 150 b
Midhirst N.Z. 39°17S 174°18E 154 F3
Midhurst Canada 44°26N 79°43W 174 B5
Midhurst U.K. 50°59N 0°44W 67 G7
Midi, Canal du → France 43°45N 1°21E 72 E5
Midi d'Ossau, Pic du
France 42°50N 0°26W 72 F3
Midi-Pyrénées ☐ France 43°55N 1°45E 72 E5
Midland Australia 31°54S 116°1E 149 F2
Midland Canada 44°45N 79°50W 174 B5
Midland Calif.,
U.S.A. 33°52N 114°48W 171 M12
Midland Mich., U.S.A. 43°37N 84°14W 173 D11
Midland Pa., U.S.A. 40°39N 80°27W 174 F4
Midland Tex., U.S.A. 32°0N 102°3W 176 F3
Midlands ☐ Zimbabwe 19°40S 29°0E 143 F2
Midleton Ireland 51°55N 8°10W 64 E3
Midlothian ☐ U.K. 55°51N 3°5W 65 F5
Midnapore = Medinipur
India 22°25N 87°21E 125 H12
Midou → France 43°54N 0°30W 72 E3
Midouze → France 43°48N 0°51W 72 E3
Midtjylland ☐ Denmark 56°30N 9°0E 63 H2
Midu China 25°18N 100°30E 116 E3
Midville U.S.A. 32°49N 82°14W 178 C7
Midway Ala., U.S.A. 32°5N 85°31W 178 C4
Midway Fla., U.S.A. 30°30N 84°27W 178 E5
Midway Is. Pac. Oc. 28°13N 177°22W 167 K4
Midway Wells U.S.A. 32°41N 115°7W 171 N11
Midwest U.S.A. 42°0N 90°0W 167 G22
Midwest Wyo.,
U.S.A. 43°25N 106°16W 168 E10
Midwest City U.S.A. 35°27N 97°24W 176 D6
Midyat Turkey 37°25N 41°23E 105 D9
Midžor Bulgaria 43°24N 22°40E 96 C6
Mie ☐ Japan 34°30N 136°10E 113 G8
Miechów Poland 50°21N 20°5E 83 H7
Miedwie, Jezioro Poland 53°17N 14°54E 83 E1
Międzybórz Poland 51°25N 17°34E 83 G4
Międzychód Poland 52°35N 15°53E 83 F2
Międzylesie Poland 50°8N 16°40E 83 H3
Międzyrzec Podlaski
Poland 51°58N 22°45E 83 G9
Międzyrzecz Poland 52°26N 15°35E 83 F2
Międzyzdroje Poland 53°56N 14°26E 82 E1
Miejska Górka Poland 51°39N 16°58E 83 G3
Miélan France 43°27N 0°19E 72 E4
Mielec Poland 50°15N 21°25E 83 H8
Mienga Angola 17°12S 19°48E 144 A2
Miercurea-Ciuc
Romania 46°21N 25°48E 81 D10
Miercurea Sibiului
Romania 45°53N 23°48E 81 E8
Mieres Spain 43°18N 5°48W 88 B5
Mieroszów Poland 50°40N 16°11E 83 H3
Mieszkowice Poland 52°47N 14°30E 83 F1
Mifflintown U.S.A. 40°34N 77°24W 174 F7
Mifraz Hefa Israel 32°52N 35°0E 130 C4
Migang Shan China 35°32N 106°13E 114 G4
Migennes France 47°58N 3°31E 71 E10
Migliarino Italy 44°46N 11°56E 93 D8
Migliarino-San Rossore-
Massaciuccoli △ Italy 43°44N 10°20E 92 E7
Migori Kenya 1°4S 34°28E 142 C3
Miguasha △ Canada 48°5N 66°26W 165 C6
Miguel Alemán, Presa
Mexico 18°15N 96°32W 181 D5
Miguel Alves Brazil 4°11S 42°55W 189 A2
Miguel Calmon Brazil 11°26S 40°36W 189 C2
Miguel Hidalgo, Presa
Mexico 26°30N 108°34W 180 B3
Migueltura Spain 38°58N 3°53W 89 G7
Mihăileni Romania 47°58N 26°9E 81 C11
Mihăileşti Romania 44°20N 25°54E 81 F10
Mihailovca Moldova 46°33N 28°56E 81 D13
Mihalgazi Turkey 40°2N 30°34E 99 A12
Mihaliççık Turkey 39°53N 31°30E 104 C4
Mihara Japan 34°24N 133°5E 113 G6
Miheşu de Cîmpie
Romania 46°41N 24°9E 81 D9
Mijas Spain 36°36N 4°40W 89 J6
Mikese Tanzania 6°48S 37°55E 142 D4
Mikha-Tskhakaya = Senaki
Georgia 42°15N 42°1E 87 J6
Mikhailovka = Mykhaylivka
Ukraine 47°12N 35°15E 85 J8
Mikhaylov Russia 54°14N 39°0E 84 E10
Mikhaylovgrad = Montana
Bulgaria 43°27N 23°16E 96 C7
Mikhaylovka Russia 50°3N 43°5E 86 E6
Mikhaylovsk Russia 45°8N 42°0E 87 H5
Mikhnevo Russia 55°4N 37°59E 84 E9
Mikkeli Finland 61°43N 27°15E 84 B4
Mikkwa → Canada 58°25N 114°46W 162 B6
Mikolajki Poland 53°49N 21°37E 82 E8
Míkonos = Mykonos
Greece 37°30N 25°25E 99 D7
Mikri Prespa, L. Greece 40°47N 21°3E 96 F5
Mikro Derio Greece 41°19N 26°6E 97 E10
Mikstat Poland 51°32N 17°59E 83 G4
Mikulov Czech Rep. 48°48N 16°39E 79 C9
Mikumi Tanzania 7°26S 37°0E 142 D4
Mikumi △ Tanzania 7°35S 37°15E 142 D4
Mila Algeria 36°27N 6°16E 136 A5
Mila ☐ Algeria 36°25N 6°10E 136 A5
Milaca U.S.A. 45°45N 93°39W 172 C7
Milagro Ecuador 2°11S 79°36W 186 D3
Milan = Milano Italy 45°28N 9°10E 92 C6
Milan Mo., U.S.A. 40°12N 93°7W 172 E7
Milan Tenn., U.S.A. 35°55N 88°46W 177 D10
Milang Australia 35°24S 138°58E 152 C3
Milange Mozam. 16°3S 35°45E 143 F4
Milano Italy 45°28N 9°10E 92 C6
Milano Linate ✈ (LIN)
Italy 45°27N 9°16E 92 C6
Milâs Turkey 37°20N 27°50E 99 D9
Milatos Greece 35°18N 25°34E 101 D7
Milazzo Italy 38°13N 15°15E 95 D8
Milbank U.S.A. 45°13N 96°38W 172 C5
Milbanke Sd. Canada 52°19N 128°33W 162 C3
Milden Canada 51°29N 107°32W 163 C7
Mildenhall U.K. 52°21N 0°32E 67 E8
Mildmay Canada 44°3N 81°7W 174 B3
Mildura Australia 34°13S 142°9E 152 C5
Mile China 24°28N 103°20E 116 E4
Miles Australia 26°40S 150°9E 151 D5
Miles City U.S.A. 46°25N 105°51W 168 C11
Mileşti Moldova 47°13N 28°3E 81 C13
Milestone Canada 49°59N 104°31W 163 D8
Mileto Italy 38°36N 16°4E 95 D9
Miletto, Mte. Italy 41°27N 14°22E 95 A7
Miletus Turkey 37°30N 27°18E 99 D9
Milevsko Czech Rep. 49°27N 14°21E 78 B7
Milford Calif., U.S.A. 40°10N 120°22W 170 E6
Milford Conn., U.S.A. 41°14N 73°3W 175 E11
Milford Del., U.S.A. 38°55N 75°26W 173 F16
Milford Mass., U.S.A. 42°8N 71°31W 175 D13
Milford N.H., U.S.A. 42°50N 71°39W 175 D13
Milford N.Y., U.S.A. 42°35N 74°56W 175 D10
Milford Pa., U.S.A. 41°19N 74°48W 175 E10
Milford Utah, U.S.A. 38°24N 113°1W 168 G7
Milford Haven U.K. 51°42N 5°7W 67 F2
Milford Sd. N.Z. 44°41S 167°47E 155 E2
Milh, Bahr al = Razāzah,
Buhayrat ar Iraq 32°40N 43°35E 105 F10
Miliana Aïn Salah, Algeria 27°20N 2°32E 136 C4
Miliana Médéa, Algeria 36°20N 2°15E 136 A4
Milicz Poland 51°31N 17°19E 83 G4
Milies Greece 39°20N 23°9E 98 B5
Milikapiti Australia 11°26S 130°40E 148 B5
Miling Australia 30°30S 116°17E 149 F2
Militello in Val di Catánia
Italy 37°16N 14°48E 95 E7
Milk, Wadi el → Sudan 17°55N 30°20E 137 D3
Milk River Canada 49°10N 112°5W 162 D6
Mill → U.S.A. 42°57N 83°23W 174 D1
Mill I. Antarctica 66°0S 101°30E 55 C8
Mill I. Canada 63°58N 77°47W 161 E16
Mill Valley U.S.A. 37°54N 122°32W 170 H4
Millárs → Spain 39°55N 0°1W 90 F4
Millau France 44°8N 3°4E 72 D7
Millbridge Canada 44°41N 77°36W 174 B7
Millbrook Canada 44°10N 78°29W 174 B6
Millbrook Ala., U.S.A. 32°29N 86°22W 177 E11
Millbrook N.Y., U.S.A. 41°47N 73°42W 175 E11
Mille Lacs, L. des
Canada 48°45N 90°35W 164 C1
Mille Lacs L. U.S.A. 46°15N 93°39W 172 B7
Milledgeville U.S.A. 33°5N 83°14W 178 B6
Millen U.S.A. 32°48N 81°57W 178 C8
Millennium I. = Caroline I.
Kiribati 9°58S 150°13W 157 H12
Miller U.S.A. 44°31N 98°59W 172 C4
Miller Lake Canada 45°6N 81°26W 174 A3
Millerovo Russia 48°57N 40°28E 87 F5
Miller's Flat N.Z. 45°39S 169°23E 155 F4
Millersburg Ohio,
U.S.A. 40°33N 81°55W 174 F3
Millersburg Pa., U.S.A. 40°32N 76°58W 174 F8
Millerton N.Z. 41°39S 171°54E 155 B6
Millerton U.S.A. 41°57N 73°31W 175 E11
Millerton L. U.S.A. 37°1N 119°41W 170 J7
Millet St. Lucia 13°55N 60°59W 183 f
Millevaches, Plateau de
France 45°45N 2°0E 72 C6
Millheim U.S.A. 40°54N 77°29W 174 F7
Millicent Australia 37°34S 140°21E 152 D4
Milligan U.S.A. 30°45N 86°38W 179 E3
Millington U.S.A. 35°20N 89°53W 177 D10
Millinocket U.S.A. 45°39N 68°43W 173 C19
Millmerran Australia 27°53S 151°16E 151 D5
Millom U.K. 54°13N 3°16W 66 C4
Mills L. Canada 61°30N 118°20W 162 A5
Millsboro U.S.A. 40°0N 80°0W 174 G5
Millstream Chichester △
Australia 21°35S 117°6E 148 D2
Millstreet Ireland 52°4N 9°4W 64 D2
Millthorpe Australia 33°26S 149°12E 153 B8
Milltown Malbay Ireland 52°52N 9°24W 64 D2
Millville N.J., U.S.A. 39°24N 75°2W 173 F16
Millville Pa., U.S.A. 41°7N 76°32W 175 E8
Millwood L. U.S.A. 33°42N 93°58W 176 E8
Milna Croatia 43°20N 16°28E 93 E13
Milne → Australia 21°10S 137°33E 150 C2
Milne Land Greenland 70°40N 26°30W 57 C8
Milo U.S.A. 45°15N 68°59W 173 C19
Milo → Guinea 8°52N 9°0W 138 D3
Milon, Akra Greece 36°15N 28°11E 101 C10
Milos Greece 36°44N 24°25E 98 E6
Miłosław Poland 52°12N 17°32E 83 F4
Milot Albania 41°41N 19°43E 96 E3
Milparinka Australia 29°46S 141°57E 151 D3
Milpitas U.S.A. 37°26N 121°55W 170 H5
Miltenberg Germany 49°41N 9°16E 77 F5
Milton Australia 35°20S 150°27E 153 C9
Milton N.S., Canada 44°4N 64°45W 165 D7
Milton Ont., Canada 43°31N 79°53W 174 C5
Milton N.Z. 46°7S 169°59E 155 G4
Milton Calif., U.S.A. 38°3N 120°51W 170 G6
Milton Fla., U.S.A. 30°38N 87°3W 179 E2
Milton Pa., U.S.A. 41°1N 76°51W 174 F8
Milton Vt., U.S.A. 44°38N 73°7W 175 B11
Milton-Freewater
U.S.A. 45°56N 118°23W 168 D4
Milton Keynes U.K. 52°1N 0°44W 67 E7
Milton Keynes ☐ U.K. 52°1N 0°44W 67 E7
Miluo China 29°0N 112°59E 117 C9
Milverton Canada 43°34N 80°55W 174 C4
Milwaukee U.S.A. 43°2N 87°54W 172 D10
Milwaukee Deep
Atl. Oc. 19°50N 68°0W 183 C6
Milwaukie U.S.A. 45°26N 122°38W 170 E4
Mim Ghana 6°57N 2°33W 138 D4
Mimili Australia 27°0S 132°42E 149 E5
Mimizan France 44°12N 1°13W 72 D2
Mimoň Czech Rep. 50°38N 14°43E 78 A7
Mimoso Brazil 15°10S 48°5W 189 D1
Mims U.S.A. 28°40N 80°51W 179 G9
Min Jiang → Fujian,
China 26°0N 119°35E 117 E12
Min Jiang → Sichuan,
China 28°45N 104°40E 116 C5
Min Xian China 34°25N 104°5E 114 G3
Mīnā' al Aḥmadī Kuwait 29°5N 48°10E 129 D6
Mīnā' Jabal 'Alī U.A.E. 25°2N 55°8E 129 E7
Mina Pirquitas
Argentina 22°40S 66°30W 190 A2
Mīnā Su'ud Si. Arabia 28°45N 48°28E 129 D6
Minago → Canada 54°33N 98°59W 163 C9
Minaki Canada 49°59N 94°40W 163 D10
Minamata Japan 32°10N 130°30E 113 H5
Minami-Arapusa △
Japan 35°30N 138°9E 113 G9
Minami-Tori-Shima
Pac. Oc. 24°20N 153°58E 156 E7
Minamiaizu Japan 37°12N 139°46E 113 F9
Minamiawaji Japan 34°10N 134°42E 113 G7
Minamisōma Japan 37°38N 140°58E 112 F10
Minas Uruguay 34°20S 55°10W 191 C4
Minas, Sierra de las
Guatemala 15°9N 89°31W 182 C2
Minas Basin Canada 45°20N 64°12W 165 C7
Minas de Riotinto Spain 37°42N 6°35W 89 H4
Minas Gerais ☐ Brazil 18°50S 46°0W 189 D1
Minas Novas Brazil 17°15S 42°36W 189 D2
Minatitlán Mexico 17°59N 94°31W 181 D6
Minbu Burma 20°10N 94°52E 123 J19
Minchinabad Pakistan 30°10N 73°34E 124 D5
Mincio → Italy 45°4N 10°59E 92 C7
Minčol Slovak Rep. 49°15N 20°58E 79 B13
Mindanao Phil. 8°0N 125°0E 119 C7
Mindanao Sea = Bohol Sea
Phil. 9°0N 124°0E 119 C6
Mindanao Trench
Pac. Oc. 12°0N 126°6E 119 B7
Mindel → Germany 48°31N 10°23E 77 G6
Mindelheim Germany 48°2N 10°29E 77 G6
Mindelo C. Verde Is. 16°24N 25°0W 134 b
Minden Canada 44°55N 78°43W 174 B6
Minden Germany 52°17N 8°55E 76 C4
Minden La., U.S.A. 32°37N 93°17W 176 E8
Minden Nev., U.S.A. 38°57N 119°46W 170 G7
Mindibungu = Billiluna
Australia 19°37S 127°41E 148 C4
Mindiptana Indonesia 5°55S 140°22E 119 F10
Mindona L. Australia 33°6S 142°6E 152 B5
Mindoro Phil. 13°0N 121°0E 119 B6
Mindoro Str. Phil. 12°30N 120°30E 119 B6
Mine Japan 34°12N 131°7E 113 G5
Minehead U.K. 51°12N 3°29W 67 F4
Mineola N.Y., U.S.A. 40°44N 73°38W 175 F11
Mineola Tex., U.S.A. 32°40N 95°29W 176 E7
Mineral King U.S.A. 36°27N 118°36W 170 J8
Mineral Wells U.S.A. 32°48N 98°7W 176 E5
Mineralnyye Vody Russia 44°15N 43°8E 87 H6
Miners Bay Canada 44°49N 78°46W 174 B6
Minersville U.S.A. 40°41N 76°16W 175 F8
Minerva N.Y., U.S.A. 43°47N 73°59W 175 C11
Minerva Ohio, U.S.A. 40°44N 81°6W 174 F3
Minervino Murge Italy 41°5N 16°5E 95 A9
Minetto U.S.A. 43°24N 76°28W 175 C8
Minfeng China 37°4N 82°46E 109 E10
Ming-Kush Kyrgyzstan 41°40N 74°28E 109 D8
Mingäçevir Azerbaijan 40°45N 47°0E 87 K8
Mingäçevir Su Anbarı
Azerbaijan 40°57N 46°50E 87 K8
Mingan Canada 50°20N 64°0W 165 B7
Mingary Australia 32°8S 140°45E 152 B4
Mingechaur = Mingäçevir
Azerbaijan 40°45N 47°0E 87 K8
Mingechaurskoye Vdkhr. =
Mingäçevir Su Anbarı
Azerbaijan 40°57N 46°50E 87 K8
Mingela Australia 19°52S 146°38E 150 B4
Mingenew Australia 29°12S 115°21E 149 E2
Mingera Cr. →
Australia 20°38S 137°45E 150 C2
Minggang China 32°24N 114°3E 117 A10
Mingguang China 32°46N 117°59E 117 A11
Mingin Burma 22°50N 94°30E 123 H19
Mingir Moldova 46°40N 28°20E 81 D13
Minglanilla Spain 39°34N 1°38W 91 F3
Minglun China 25°10N 108°21E 116 E7
Mingo Junction U.S.A. 40°19N 80°37W 174 F4
Mingora Pakistan 34°48N 72°22E 125 B5
Mingorria Spain 40°45N 4°40W 88 E6
Mingshan China 30°6N 103°10E 116 B4
Mingteke Daban = Mintaka Pass
Pakistan 37°0N 74°58E 125 A6
Mingxi China 26°18N 117°12E 117 D11
Mingyuegue China 43°2N 128°50E 115 C15
Minhe China 36°9N 102°45E 110 D9
Minho = Miño → Spain 41°52N 8°40W 88 D2
Minhou China 26°0N 119°15E 117 E12
Miničevo Serbia 43°42N 22°18E 80 G7
Minicoy I. India 8°17N 73°2E 127 K1
Minidoka U.S.A. 42°45N 113°29W 168 E7
Minigwal, L. Australia 29°31S 123°14E 149 E3
Minilya → Australia 23°45S 114°0E 149 D1
Minilya Roadhouse
Australia 23°55S 114°0E 149 D1
Mininera Australia 37°37S 142°58E 152 D5
Minipi L. Canada 52°25N 60°45W 165 B7
Minjilang Australia 11°8S 132°33E 148 B5
Mink L. Canada 61°54N 117°40W 162 A5
Minlaton Australia 34°45S 137°35E 152 C2
Minna Nigeria 9°37N 6°30E 139 D6
Minneapolis Kans.,
U.S.A. 39°8N 97°42W 172 F5
Minneapolis Minn.,
U.S.A. 44°57N 93°16W 172 C7
Minneapolis-St. Paul Int. ✈ (MSP)
U.S.A. 44°53N 93°13W 172 C7
Minnedosa Canada 50°14N 99°50W 163 C9
Minnesota ☐ U.S.A. 46°0N 94°15W 172 B6
Minnesota → U.S.A. 44°54N 93°9W 172 C7
Minnewaukan U.S.A. 48°4N 99°15W 172 A4
Minnipa Australia 32°51S 135°9E 151 E2
Minnitaki L. Canada 49°57N 92°10W 164 C1
Miño = A Carreira Spain 43°21N 8°12W 88 B2
Mino Japan 35°32N 136°55E 113 G8
Miño → Spain 41°52N 8°40W 88 D2
Minoa Greece 35°6N 25°45E 99 F7
Minorca = Menorca
Spain 40°0N 4°0E 100 B11
Minore Australia 32°14S 148°27E 153 B8
Minot U.S.A. 48°14N 101°18W 172 A3
Minqin China 38°38N 103°20E 114 E2
Minqing China 26°15N 118°50E 117 D12
Minsen Germany 53°41N 7°58E 76 B3
Minsk Belarus 53°52N 27°30E 75 B14
Minsk ☐ Belarus 53°15N 27°30E 84 F4
Mińsk Mazowiecki
Poland 52°10N 21°33E 83 F8
Mintabie Australia 27°15S 133°7E 151 D1
Mintaka Pass Pakistan 37°0N 74°58E 125 A6
Minto Canada 46°5N 66°5W 165 C6
Minto, L. Canada 57°13N 75°0W 164 A5
Minton Canada 49°10N 104°35W 163 D8
Minturn U.S.A. 39°35N 106°26W 168 G10
Minturno Italy 41°15N 13°45E 94 A6
Minudasht Iran 37°17N 56°7E 129 B8
Minûf Egypt 30°26N 30°52E 137 E7
Minusinsk Russia 53°43N 91°20E 109 B12
Minutang India 28°15N 96°30E 123 E20
Minvoul Gabon 2°9N 12°8E 140 D2
Minya el Qamh Egypt 30°31N 31°21E 137 E7
Minya Konka = Gongga Shan
China 29°40N 101°55E 116 C3
Minyip Australia 36°29S 142°36E 152 D5
Minzhong China 22°37N 113°30E 111 a
Mionica Bos.-H. 44°51N 18°29E 80 F3
Mionica Serbia 44°14N 20°6E 96 B4
Mioveni Romania 44°56N 24°54E 81 F9
Miquan China 43°58N 87°42E 109 D11
Miquelon Canada 49°25N 76°27W 164 C4
Miquelon St-P. & M. 47°8N 56°22W 165 C8
Mir Belarus 53°27N 26°28E 75 B14
Mir Niger 14°5N 11°59E 139 C7
Mīr Kūh Iran 26°22N 58°55E 129 E8
Mīr Shahdād Iran 26°15N 58°29E 129 E8
Mira Italy 45°26N 12°8E 93 C9
Mira Portugal 40°26N 8°44W 88 E2
Mira → Portugal 37°43N 8°47W 89 H2
Mira por vos Cay
Bahamas 22°9N 74°30W 183 B5
Mirabella Eclano Italy 41°2N 14°59E 95 A7
Mirabello, Kolpos
Greece 35°10N 25°50E 101 D7
Miracema do Norte
Brazil 9°33S 48°24W 189 B1
Mirador Brazil 6°22S 44°22W 189 B2
Mirador-Río Azul △
Guatemala 17°45N 89°50W 182 C2
Miraj India 16°50N 74°45E 126 F2
Miram Shah Pakistan 33°0N 70°2E 124 C4
Miramar Argentina 38°15S 57°50W 190 D4
Miramar Mozam. 23°50S 35°35E 145 B6
Miramas France 43°33N 4°59E 73 E8
Mirambeau France 45°23N 0°35W 72 C3
Miramichi Canada 47°2N 65°28W 165 C6
Miramichi B. Canada 47°15N 65°0W 165 C7
Miramont-de-Guyenne
France 44°37N 0°21E 72 D4
Miranda Brazil 20°10S 56°15W 187 H7
Miranda → Brazil 19°25S 57°20W 186 G7
Miranda de Ebro Spain 42°41N 2°57W 90 C2
Miranda do Corvo
Portugal 40°6N 8°20W 88 E2
Miranda do Douro
Portugal 41°30N 6°16W 88 D4
Mirande France 43°31N 0°25E 72 E4
Mirandela Portugal 41°32N 7°10W 88 D3
Mirándola Italy 44°53N 11°4E 92 D8
Mirandópolis Brazil 21°9S 51°6W 191 A5
Mirango Malawi 13°32S 34°58E 143 E3
Mirani Australia 21°8S 148°53E 150 b
Mirano Italy 45°30N 12°7E 93 C9
Miras Albania 40°30N 20°56E 96 F4
Mirassol Brazil 20°46S 49°28W 191 A6
Mirbāṭ Oman 17°0N 54°45E 131 D5
Mirboo North
Australia 38°24S 146°10E 153 E7
Mirear Egypt 23°15N 35°41E 137 C4
Mirebeau France 46°49N 0°10E 70 F7
Mirebeau-sur-Bèze
France 47°25N 5°20E 71 E12
Mirecourt France 48°20N 6°10E 71 D13
Mires Greece 35°4N 24°56E 101 D6
Mirgorod = Myrhorod
Ukraine 49°58N 33°37E 85 H7
Miri Malaysia 4°23N 113°59E 118 D4
Mirialguda India 16°52N 79°35E 126 F4
Miriam Vale Australia 24°20S 151°33E 150 C5
Miribel France 45°50N 4°57E 71 G11
Mirigama Sri Lanka 7°15N 80°8E 127 L5
Mirim, L. S. Amer. 32°45S 52°50W 191 C5
Miriuwung Gajerrong ☼
Australia 15°0S 128°45E 148 C4
Mīrjāveh Iran 29°1N 61°30E 129 D9
Mirnyy Antarctica 66°50S 92°30E 55 C14
Mirnyy Russia 62°33N 113°53E 107 C12
Miroč Serbia 44°32N 22°16E 96 B6
Mirokhan Pakistan 27°46N 68°6E 124 F3
Mirond L. Canada 55°6N 102°47W 163 B8
Mirosławiec Poland 53°20N 16°5E 82 E3
Mirpur Pakistan 33°32N 73°56E 125 C5
Mirpur Batoro Pakistan 24°44N 68°16E 124 G3
Mirpur Bibiwari
Pakistan 28°33N 67°44E 124 E2
Mirpur Khas Pakistan 25°30N 69°0E 124 G3
Mirpur Sakro Pakistan 24°33N 67°41E 124 G2
Mirria Niger 13°43N 9°7E 139 C6
Mirrool Australia 34°19S 147°10E 153 C7
Mirs Bay = Tai Pang Wan
China 22°33N 114°24E 111 a
Mirsk Poland 50°58N 15°23E 83 H2
Mirtağ Turkey 38°23N 41°56E 128 B4
Mirtoo Sea Greece 37°0N 23°20E 98 D5
Miryang S. Korea 35°31N 128°44E 115 G15
Mirzaani Georgia 41°24N 46°5E 87 K8
Mirzapur India 25°10N 82°34E 125 G10
Mirzapur-cum-Vindhyachal =
Mirzapur India 25°10N 82°34E 125 G10
Misantla Mexico 19°56N 96°50W 181 D5
Misawa Japan 40°41N 141°24E 112 D10
Miscou I. Canada 47°57N 64°31W 165 C7
Misha India 7°59N 93°20E 127 L11
Mish'āb, Ra's al
Si. Arabia 28°15N 48°43E 129 D6
Mishagua → Peru 11°12S 72°58W 188 C3
Mishamo Tanzania 5°41S 30°41E 142 D3
Mishan China 45°37N 131°48E 112 B5
Mishawaka U.S.A. 41°40N 86°11W 172 E10
Mishbih, Gebel Egypt 22°38N 34°44E 137 C3
Mishima Japan 35°10N 138°52E 113 G9
Misión Mexico 32°6N 116°53W 171 N10
Misión Fagnano
Argentina 54°32S 67°17W 192 D3
Misiones ☐ Argentina 27°0S 55°0W 191 B5
Misiones ☐ Paraguay 27°0S 56°0W 190 B4
Miskah Si. Arabia 24°49N 42°56E 128 E4
Miskitos, Cayos Nic. 14°26N 82°50W 182 D3
Miskolc Hungary 48°7N 20°50E 80 B5
Misoke
Dem. Rep. of the Congo 0°42S 28°2E 142 C2
Misool Indonesia 1°52S 130°10E 119 E8
Mişr = Egypt ■ Africa 28°0N 31°0E 137 F7
Mişrātah Libya 32°24N 15°3E 135 B9
Missanabie Canada 48°20N 84°6W 164 C3
Missão Velha Brazil 7°15S 39°10W 189 B3
Missinaibi → Canada 50°43N 81°29W 164 B3
Missinaibi L. Canada 48°23N 83°40W 164 C3
Mission Canada 49°10N 122°15W 162 D4
Mission S. Dak.,
U.S.A. 43°18N 100°39W 172 D3
Mission Tex., U.S.A. 26°13N 98°20W 176 H5
Mission Beach Australia 17°53S 146°6E 150 B4
Mission Viejo U.S.A. 33°36N 117°40W 171 M9
Missirah Senegal 13°40N 16°30W 138 C1
Missisa L. Canada 52°20N 85°7W 164 B2
Missisicabi → Canada 51°14N 79°31W 164 B4
Mississagi → Canada 46°15N 83°9W 164 C3
Mississauga Canada 43°32N 79°35W 174 C5
Mississippi ☐ U.S.A. 33°0N 90°0W 177 E10
Mississippi → U.S.A. 29°9N 89°15W 177 G10
Mississippi L. Canada 45°5N 76°10W 175 A8
Mississippi River Delta
U.S.A. 29°10N 89°15W 177 G10
Mississippi Sd. U.S.A. 30°20N 89°0W 177 F10
Missoula U.S.A. 46°52N 114°1W 168 C6
Missour Morocco 33°3N 4°0W 136 B3
Missouri ☐ U.S.A. 38°25N 92°30W 172 F7
Missouri → U.S.A. 38°49N 90°7W 172 F8
Missouri City U.S.A. 29°37N 95°32W 176 G7
Missouri Valley U.S.A. 41°34N 95°53W 172 E6
Mist U.S.A. 45°59N 123°15W 170 E3
Mistassibi → Canada 48°53N 72°13W 165 B5
Mistassini Canada 48°53N 72°12W 165 C5
Mistassini → Canada 48°42N 72°20W 165 C5
Mistassini, L. Canada 51°0N 73°30W 164 B5
Mistastin L. Canada 55°57N 63°20W 165 A7
Mistelbach Austria 48°34N 16°34E 79 C9
Misterbianco Italy 37°31N 15°1E 95 E8
Misti, Volcán Peru 16°18S 71°24W 188 D3
Mistinibi, L. Canada 55°56N 64°17W 165 A7
Mistissini Canada 48°53N 72°12W 165 C5
Mistras = Mystras Greece 37°4N 22°22E 98 D4
Mistretta Italy 37°56N 14°22E 95 E7
Misty L. Canada 58°53N 101°40W 163 B8
Misurata = Mişrātah
Libya 32°24N 15°3E 135 B9
Mît Ghamr Egypt 30°42N 31°12E 137 E7
Mitande Mozam. 14°6S 35°58E 143 E4
Mitchell Australia 26°29S 147°58E 151 D4
Mitchell Canada 43°28N 81°12W 174 C3
Mitchell Ga., U.S.A. 33°13N 82°42W 178 B7
Mitchell Nebr., U.S.A. 41°57N 103°49W 172 E2
Mitchell Oreg., U.S.A. 44°34N 120°9W 168 D3
Mitchell S. Dak., U.S.A. 43°43N 98°2W 172 D4
Mitchell → Australia 15°12S 141°35E 150 B3
Mitchell, Mt. U.S.A. 35°46N 82°16W 177 D13
Mitchell-Alice Rivers △
Australia 15°28S 142°5E 150 B3
Mitchell Ra. Australia 12°49S 135°36E 150 A2
Mitchell River △
Australia 37°37S 147°22E 153 D7
Mitchelstown Ireland 52°15N 8°16W 64 D3
Mitha Tiwana Pakistan 32°13N 72°6E 124 C5
Mithi Pakistan 24°44N 69°48E 124 G3
Mithimna Greece 39°20N 26°12E 99 B8
Mithrao Pakistan 27°28N 69°40E 124 F3
Mitiamo Australia 36°12S 144°15E 152 D6
Mitilini Greece 39°6N 26°35E 99 B8
Mitilinii Greece 37°42N 26°56E 99 D8
Mitla Pass = Mamarr Mitlā
Egypt 30°2N 32°54E 130 E1
Mito Japan 36°20N 140°30E 113 F10
Mitre, Mt. N.Z. 40°50S 175°30E 154 G4
Mitrofanovka Russia 49°58N 39°42E 85 H10
Mitrovicë Kosovo 42°54N 20°52E 96 D4
Mitsamiouli Comoros Is. 11°20S 43°16E 141 a
Mitsiwa Eritrea 15°35N 39°25E 131 D2
Mitsukaidō Japan 36°1N 139°59E 113 F9
Mittagong Australia 34°28S 150°29E 153 C9
Mittelberg Austria 47°20N 10°10E 78 D3
Mittelfranken ☐
Germany 49°25N 10°40E 77 F6
Mittellandkanal →
Germany 52°20N 8°28E 76 C4
Mittenwalde Germany 52°15N 13°31E 76 C9
Mittersill Austria 47°16N 12°29E 78 D5
Mitterteich Germany 49°57N 12°14E 77 F8
Mittimatalik = Pond Inlet
Canada 72°40N 77°0W 161 C16
Mittweida Germany 50°59N 12°59E 76 E8
Mitú Colombia 1°15N 70°13W 186 C4
Mitumba Tanzania 7°8S 31°2E 142 D3
Mitumba, Mts.
Dem. Rep. of the Congo 7°0S 27°30E 142 D2
Mitwaba
Dem. Rep. of the Congo 8°2S 27°17E 143 D2
Mityana Uganda 0°23N 32°2E 142 B3
Mixteco → Mexico 18°11N 98°30W 181 D5
Miyagi ☐ Japan 38°15N 140°45E 112 E10
Miyāh, W. el → Egypt 25°0N 33°23E 137 C3
Miyāh, W. el → Syria 34°44N 39°57E 128 C3
Miyake-Jima Japan 34°5N 139°30E 113 G9
Miyako Japan 39°40N 141°59E 112 E10
Miyako-Jima Japan 24°45N 125°20E 113 M2
Miyako-Rettō Japan 24°24N 125°0E 113 M2
Miyakojima Japan 24°48N 125°17E 113 M2
Miyakonojō Japan 31°40N 131°5E 113 J5
Miyān Rahan Iran 34°34N 47°26E 105 E12
Miyani India 21°50N 69°26E 124 J3
Miyanoura-Dake
Japan 30°20N 130°31E 113 J5
Miyazaki Japan 31°56N 131°30E 113 J5
Miyazaki ☐ Japan 32°30N 131°30E 113 H5
Miyazu Japan 35°35N 135°10E 113 G7
Miyet, Bahr el = Dead Sea
Asia 31°30N 35°30E 130 D4
Miyi China 26°47N 102°9E 116 D4
Miyoshi Japan 34°48N 132°51E 113 G6
Miyun China 40°28N 116°50E 114 D9
Miyun Shuiku China 40°30N 117°0E 115 D9
Mizdah Libya 31°30N 13°0E 135 B8
Mizen Hd. Cork, Ireland 51°27N 9°50W 64 E2
Mizen Hd. Wicklow, Ireland 52°51N 6°4W 64 D5
Mizhhirya Ukraine 48°32N 23°30E 81 B8
Mizhi China 37°47N 110°12E 114 F6
Mizil Romania 44°59N 26°29E 81 F11
Mizoram ☐ India 23°30N 92°40E 123 H18
Mizpe Ramon Israel 30°34N 34°49E 130 E3
Mizuho Antarctica 70°30S 41°0E 55 D5
Mizusawa = Ōshū
Japan 39°8N 141°8E 112 E10
Mjällby Sweden 56°3N 14°40E 63 H8
Mjöbäck Sweden 57°28N 12°53E 63 G6
Mjölby Sweden 58°20N 15°10E 63 F9

Mjörn *Sweden* 57°55N 12°25E **63** G6
Mjøsa *Norway* 60°40N 11°0E **60** F14
Mkata *Tanzania* 5°45S 38°20E **142** D4
Mkhaya ⌓ *Swaziland* 26°34S 31°45E **145** C5
Mkhuze ⌓ *S. Africa* 29°27S 29°30E **145** C4
Mkoani *Tanzania* 5°22S 39°39E **142** D4
Mkokotoni *Tanzania* 5°55S 39°15E **142** D4
Mkomazi *Tanzania* 4°40S 38°7E **142** C4
Mkomazi → *S. Africa* 30°12S 30°50E **145** D5
Mkomazi ⌓ *Tanzania* 4°4S 30°2E **142** C3
Mkulwe *Tanzania* 8°37S 32°20E **143** D3
Mkumbi, Ras *Tanzania* 7°38S 39°55E **142** D4
Mkushi *Zambia* 14°25S 29°15E **143** E2
Mkushi River *Zambia* 13°32S 29°45E **143** E2
Mkuze *S. Africa* 27°10S 32°0E **145** C5
Mladá Boleslav
Czech Rep. 50°27N 14°53E **78** A7
Mladenovac *Serbia* 44°28N 20°44E **96** B4
Mlala Hills *Tanzania* 6°50S 31°40E **142** D3
Mlange = Mulanje, Mt.
Malawi 16°2S 35°33E **143** F4
Mlava → *Serbia* 44°45N 21°13E **96** B5
Mława *Poland* 53°9N 20°25E **83** E7
Mlawula ⌓ *Swaziland* 26°12S 32°2E **145** C5
Mliniště *Bos.-H.* 44°15N 16°50E **93** D13
Mljet *Croatia* 42°43N 17°30E **93** F14
Mljet △ *Croatia* 42°45N 17°25E **93** F14
Mljetski Kanal *Croatia* 42°48N 17°35E **93** F14
Młynary *Poland* 54°12N 19°46E **82** D6
Mmabatho *S. Africa* 25°49S 25°30E **144** C4
Mme *Cameroon* 6°18N 10°14E **139** D7
Mnichovo Hradiště
Czech Rep. 50°32N 14°59E **78** A7
Mo i Rana *Norway* 66°20N 14°7E **60** C16
Moa *Australia* 10°11S 142°16E **150** a
Moa *Cuba* 20°40N 74°56W **183** B4
Moa *Indonesia* 8°0S 128°0E **119** F7
Moa → *S. Leone* 6°59N 11°36W **138** D2
Moab *U.S.A.* 38°35N 109°33W **168** G9
Moaco → *Brazil* 7°41S 68°18W **188** B4
Moala *Fiji* 18°36S 179°53E **154** a
Moama *Australia* 36°7S 144°46E **151** F3
Moamba *Mozam.* 25°36S 32°15E **145** C5
Moapa *U.S.A.* 36°40N 114°37W **171** J12
Moate *Ireland* 53°24N 7°44W **64** C4
Moba
Dem. Rep. of the Congo 7°0S 29°48E **142** D2
Mobārakābād *Iran* 28°24N 53°20E **129** D7
Mobaye *C.A.R.* 4°25N 21°5E **140** D4
Moberly *U.S.A.* 39°25N 92°26W **172** F7
Moberly Lake *Canada* 55°50N 121°44W **162** B4
Mobile *U.S.A.* 30°41N 88°3W **177** F10
Mobile B. *U.S.A.* 30°30N 88°0W **177** F11
Mobridge *U.S.A.* 45°32N 100°26W **172** C3
Moc Chau *Vietnam* 20°50N 104°38E **120** B5
Moc Hoa *Vietnam* 10°46N 105°56E **121** G5
Mocabe Kasari
Dem. Rep. of the Congo 9°58S 26°12E **143** D2
Moçambique = Mozambique ■
Africa 19°0S 35°0E **143** F4
Moçambique *Mozam.* 15°3S 40°42E **143** F5
Mocanaqua *U.S.A.* 41°9N 76°8W **175** E8
Moce *Fiji* 18°40S 178°29W **154** a
Mocha, I. *Chile* 38°22S 73°56W **192** A2
Mochima △ *Venezuela* 10°30N 64°5W **183** D7
Mochos *Greece* 35°16N 25°27E **101** D7
Mochudi *Botswana* 24°27S 26°7E **144** B4
Mocimboa da Praia
Mozam. 11°25S 40°20E **143** E5
Mociu *Romania* 46°46N 24°3E **81** D9
Möckeln *Sweden* 56°40N 14°15E **63** H8
Mockfjärd *Sweden* 60°30N 14°57E **62** D8
Moclips *U.S.A.* 47°14N 124°13W **170** C2
Mocoa *Colombia* 1°7N 76°35W **186** C3
Mococa *Brazil* 21°28S 47°0W **191** A6
Mocorito *Mexico* 25°29N 107°55W **180** B3
Moctezuma *Mexico* 29°48N 109°42W **180** B3
Moctezuma → *Mexico* 21°59N 98°34W **181** C5
Mocuba *Mozam.* 16°54S 36°57E **143** F4
Modane *France* 45°12N 6°40E **73** C10
Modasa *India* 23°30N 73°21E **124** H5
Modder → *S. Africa* 29°2S 24°37E **144** C3
Modderrivier *S. Africa* 29°2S 24°38E **144** C3
Módena *Italy* 44°40N 10°55E **92** D7
Modena *U.S.A.* 37°48N 113°56W **169** H7
Modesto *U.S.A.* 37°39N 121°0W **170** H6
Módica *Italy* 36°52N 14°46E **95** F7
Modimolle *S. Africa* 24°42S 28°22E **145** B4
Modjadjiskloof *S. Africa* 23°42S 30°10E **145** B5
Mödling *Austria* 48°5N 16°17E **79** C9
Modoc *U.S.A.* 33°44N 82°13W **178** B7
Modra *Slovak Rep.* 48°19N 17°20E **79** C10
Modriča *Bos.-H.* 44°57N 18°17E **80** F3
Moe *Australia* 38°12S 146°19E **153** E7
Moebase *Mozam.* 17°3S 38°41E **143** F4
Moëlan-sur-Mer *France* 47°49N 3°38W **70** E3
Moengo *Suriname* 5°45N 54°20W **187** B8
Moenjodaro = Mohenjodaro
Pakistan 27°19N 68°7E **124** F3
Moerewa *N.Z.* 35°8S 174°1E **154** B3
Moers *Germany* 51°27N 6°36E **76** D2
Moffat *U.K.* 55°21N 3°27W **65** F5
Moga *India* 30°48N 75°8E **124** D6
Mogadishu = Muqdisho
Somalia 2°2N 45°25E **131** G4
Mogador = Essaouira
Morocco 31°32N 9°42W **136** B2
Mogadouro *Portugal* 41°22N 6°47W **88** D4
Mogalakwena →
S. Africa 22°38S 28°40E **145** B4
Mogami-Gawa →
Japan 38°45N 140°0E **112** E10
Mogán *Canary Is.* 27°53N 15°43W **100** G4
Mogaung *Burma* 25°20N 97°0E **123** G20
Mogente = Moixent
Spain 38°52N 0°45W **91** G4
Mogi-Mirim *Brazil* 22°29S 47°0W **187** H9
Mogielnica *Poland* 51°42N 20°41E **83** G7
Mogilev = Mahilyow
Belarus 53°55N 30°18E **75** B16
Mogilev-Podolskiy = Mohyliv-
Podilskyy *Ukraine* 48°26N 27°48E **81** B12
Mogilno *Poland* 52°39N 17°55E **83** F4
Mogincual *Mozam.* 15°35S 40°25E **143** F5
Mogliano Véneto *Italy* 45°33N 12°14E **93** C9
Mogocha *Russia* 53°40N 119°50E **107** D12
Mogoditshane
Botswana 24°37S 25°51E **144** B4
Mogok *Burma* 23°0N 96°40E **123** H20
Mogollon Rim *U.S.A.* 34°10N 110°50W **169** J8
Mógoro *Italy* 39°41N 8°47E **94** C1
Mograt *Sudan* 19°28N 33°16E **137** D3
Moguer *Spain* 37°15N 6°52W **89** H4
Mogumber *Australia* 31°2S 116°3E **149** F2
Mogwadi → *S. Africa* 23°4S 29°36E **145** B4
Mohács *Hungary* 45°58N 18°41E **80** E3
Mohaka → *N.Z.* 39°7S 177°12E **154** F6
Mohala *India* 20°35N 80°44E **126** D5
Mohales Hoek *Lesotho* 30°7S 27°26E **144** D4
Mohali = Ajitgarh
India 30°47N 76°41E **124** D7
Mohall *U.S.A.* 48°46N 101°31W **172** A3
Moḥammadābād *Iran* 37°52N 59°5E **129** B8
Mohammadia *Algeria* 35°33N 0°3E **136** A4
Mohammedia *Morocco* 33°44N 7°21W **136** B2
Mohana *India* 19°27N 84°16E **126** E7
Mohana → *India* 24°43N 85°0E **125** G11
Mohanlalganj *India* 26°41N 80°58E **125** F9
Mohave, L. *U.S.A.* 35°12N 114°34W **171** K12
Mohawk → *U.S.A.* 42°47N 73°41W **175** D11
Moheda *Sweden* 57°1N 14°35E **63** G8
Mohéli *Comoros Is.* 12°20S 43°40E **141** a
Mohenjodaro *Pakistan* 27°19N 68°7E **124** F3
Moher, Cliffs of *Ireland* 52°58N 9°27W **64** D2
Mohicanville Res.
U.S.A. 40°45N 82°9W **174** F2
Möhne → *Germany* 51°29N 7°57E **76** D3
Mohns Ridge *Arctic* 72°30N 5°0W **54** B7
Mohoro *Tanzania* 8°6S 39°8E **142** D4
Mohsenābād *Iran* 36°40N 59°35E **129** B8
Mohyliv-Podilskyy
Ukraine 48°26N 27°48E **81** B12
Moidart, L. *U.K.* 56°47N 5°52W **65** E3
Moinabad *India* 17°44N 77°16E **126** F3
Moinești *Romania* 46°28N 26°31E **81** D11
Moira → *Canada* 44°21N 77°24W **174** B7
Moirans *France* 45°20N 5°33E **73** C9
Moirans-en-Montagne
France 46°26N 5°43E **71** F12
Moisaküla *Estonia* 58°3N 25°12E **84** C3
Moisie *Canada* 50°12N 66°1W **165** B6
Moisie → *Canada* 50°14N 66°5W **165** B6
Moissac *France* 44°7N 1°5E **72** D5
Moita *Portugal* 38°38N 8°58W **89** G2
Moixent *Spain* 38°52N 0°45W **91** G4
Möja *Sweden* 59°26N 18°55E **62** E12
Mojácar *Spain* 37°6N 1°55W **91** H3
Mojados *Spain* 41°26N 4°40W **88** D6
Mojave *U.S.A.* 35°3N 118°10W **171** K8
Mojave ⌓ *U.S.A.* 35°7N 115°32W **171** K11
Mojave Desert *U.S.A.* 35°0N 116°30W **171** L10
Moji das Cruzes *Brazil* 23°31S 46°11W **191** A6
Moji-Guaçu → *Brazil* 20°53S 48°10W **191** A6
Mojiang *China* 23°37N 101°35E **116** F3
Mojkovac *Montenegro* 42°58N 19°35E **96** D3
Mojo *Bolivia* 21°48S 65°33W **190** A2
Mojokerto *Indonesia* 7°28S 112°26E **119** G15
Mokai *N.Z.* 38°32S 175°56E **154** E4
Mokala △ *S. Africa* 29°10S 24°10E **144** C3
Mokambo
Dem. Rep. of the Congo 12°25S 28°20E **143** E2
Mokameh *India* 25°24N 85°55E **125** G11
Mokau *N.Z.* 38°42S 174°39E **154** E3
Mokau → *N.Z.* 38°35S 174°35E **154** E3
Mokelumne →
U.S.A. 38°13N 121°28W **170** G5
Mokelumne Hill
U.S.A. 38°18N 120°43W **170** G6
Mokhotlong *Lesotho* 29°22S 29°2E **145** C4
Mokihinui → *N.Z.* 41°33S 171°58E **155** B6
Möklinta *Sweden* 60°4N 16°33E **62** D10
Moknine *Tunisia* 35°35N 10°58E **136** A6
Mokoan, L. *Australia* 36°27S 146°5E **153** D7
Mokokchung *India* 26°15N 94°30E **123** F19
Mokolo *Cameroon* 10°49N 13°54E **139** C7
Mokolo → *S. Africa* 23°14S 27°43E **145** B4
Mokopane *S. Africa* 24°10S 28°55E **145** B4
Mokpo *S. Korea* 34°50N 126°25E **115** G14
Mokra Gora *Europe* 42°50N 20°30E **96** D4
Mokronog *Slovenia* 45°57N 15°9E **93** C12
Moksha → *Russia* 54°45N 41°53E **86** C6
Mokshan *Russia* 53°25N 44°35E **86** D7
Mokwa *Nigeria* 9°19N 5°0E **139** D6
Mol *Belgium* 51°11N 5°5E **69** C5
Mola di Bari *Italy* 41°4N 17°5E **95** A10
Molai *Greece* 36°49N 22°56E **98** E4
Molakalmuru *India* 14°55N 76°50E **127** G3
Molaly *Kazakhstan* 45°27N 78°18E **109** C9
Molara *Italy* 40°52N 9°43E **94** B2
Molat *Croatia* 44°15N 14°50E **93** D11
Molchanovo *Russia* 57°40N 83°50E **106** D9
Mold *U.K.* 53°9N 3°8W **66** D4
Moldava nad Bodvou
Slovak Rep. 48°38N 21°0E **79** C14
Moldavia = Moldova ■
Europe 47°0N 28°0E **81** C13
Moldavia *Romania* 46°30N 27°0E **81** D12
Molde *Norway* 62°45N 7°9E **60** E12
Moldova ■ *Europe* 47°0N 28°0E **81** C13
Moldova Nouă *Romania* 44°45N 21°41E **80** F6
Moldoveanu, Vf.
Romania 45°36N 24°45E **81** E9
Moldovița *Romania* 47°41N 25°32E **81** C10
Mole → *U.K.* 51°24N 0°21W **67** F7
Mole △ *Ghana* 9°43N 1°44W **139** D4
Molepolole *Botswana* 24°28S 25°28E **144** B4
Molesworth *N.Z.* 42°5S 173°16E **155** C8
Molfetta *Italy* 41°12N 16°36E **95** A9
Molina de Aragón *Spain* 40°46N 1°52W **90** E3
Molina de Segura *Spain* 38°3N 1°12W **91** G3
Moline *U.S.A.* 41°30N 90°31W **172** E8
Molinella *Italy* 44°37N 11°40E **93** D8
Molino *U.S.A.* 30°43N 87°20W **179** E2
Molinos *Argentina* 25°28S 66°15W **190** B2
Moliro
Dem. Rep. of the Congo 8°12S 30°30E **142** D3
Moliterno *Italy* 40°14N 15°52E **95** B8
Molivos = Mithimna
Greece 39°20N 26°12E **99** B8
Molkom *Sweden* 59°37N 13°44E **62** E7
Mölle *Sweden* 56°17N 12°31E **63** H6
Molledo *Spain* 43°8N 4°6W **88** B6
Mollendo *Peru* 17°0S 72°0W **188** D3
Mollerin, L. *Australia* 30°30S 117°35E **149** F2
Mollerusa *Spain* 41°37N 0°54E **90** D5
Mollina *Spain* 37°8N 4°38W **89** H6
Mölln *Germany* 53°39N 10°32E **76** B6
Mölltorp *Sweden* 58°30N 14°26E **63** F8
Mölndal *Sweden* 57°40N 12°3E **63** G5
Mölnlycke *Sweden* 57°40N 12°8E **63** G6
Molo *Kenya* 0°15S 35°44E **142** C4
Molochansk *Ukraine* 47°15N 35°35E **85** J8
Molochnoye, Ozero
Ukraine 46°30N 35°20E **85** J8
Molodechno = Maladzyechna
Belarus 54°20N 26°50E **75** A14
Molodezhnaya
Antarctica 67°40S 45°51E **55** C9
Molodove *Ukraine* 46°13N 29°39E **81** D14
Moloka'i *U.S.A.* 21°8N 157°0W **167** L8
Molokai Fracture Zone
Pac. Oc. 28°0N 125°0W **157** E15
Molong *Australia* 33°5S 148°54E **153** B8
Molopo → *Africa* 28°30S 20°12E **144** C3
Molos *Greece* 38°47N 22°37E **98** C4
Molsheim *France* 48°33N 7°29E **71** D14
Molson L. *Canada* 54°22N 96°40W **163** C9
Molteno *S. Africa* 31°22S 26°22E **144** D4
Molu *Indonesia* 6°45S 131°40E **119** F8
Molucca Sea *Indonesia* 0°0 125°0E **119** E6
Moluccas = Maluku
Indonesia 1°0S 127°0E **119** E7
Moma
Dem. Rep. of the Congo 1°35S 23°52E **142** C1
Moma *Mozam.* 16°47S 39°4E **143** F4
Momba *Australia* 30°58S 143°30E **152** A5
Mombaça *Brazil* 5°43S 39°45W **189** B3
Mombasa *Kenya* 4°3S 39°40E **142** C4
Mombetsu *Japan* 44°21N 143°22E **112** B11
Mombuey *Spain* 42°3N 6°20W **88** C4
Momchilgrad *Bulgaria* 41°33N 25°23E **97** E9
Momi
Dem. Rep. of the Congo 1°42S 27°0E **142** C2
Mompós *Colombia* 9°14N 74°26W **186** B4
Møn *Denmark* 54°57N 12°20E **63** K6
Mon □ *Burma* 16°0N 97°30E **123** L20
Mona, Canal de la = Mona
Passage *W. Indies* 18°30N 67°45W **183** C6
Mona, Isla *Puerto Rico* 18°5N 67°54W **183** C6
Mona, Pta. *Costa Rica* 9°37N 82°36W **182** E3
Mona Passage
W. Indies 18°30N 67°45W **183** C6
Monaca *U.S.A.* 40°41N 80°17W **174** F4
Monaco ■ *Europe* 43°46N 7°23E **73** E11
Monadhliath Mts. *U.K.* 57°10N 4°4W **65** D4
Monadnock, Mt.
U.S.A. 42°52N 72°7W **175** D12
Monaghan *Ireland* 54°15N 6°57W **64** B5
Monaghan □ *Ireland* 54°11N 6°56W **64** B5
Monahans *U.S.A.* 31°36N 102°54W **176** F3
Monapo *Mozam.* 14°56S 40°19E **143** E5
Monar, L. *U.K.* 57°26N 5°8W **65** D3
Monaragala *Sri Lanka* 6°52N 81°22E **127** L5
Monarch Mt. *Canada* 51°55N 125°57W **162** C3
Monashee Mts. *Canada* 51°0N 118°43W **162** C5
Monasterevin *Ireland* 53°8N 7°4W **64** C4
Monastir = Bitola
Macedonia 41°1N 21°20E **96** E5
Monastir *Tunisia* 35°50N 10°49E **136** A6
Monastir □ *Tunisia* 35°37N 10°45E **136** A6
Monbetsu = Hidaka
Japan 42°30N 142°10E **112** C11
Moncalieri *Italy* 45°0N 7°41E **92** D4
Moncalvo *Italy* 45°3N 8°16E **92** C5
Monção *Portugal* 42°4N 8°27W **88** C2
Moncarapacho *Portugal* 37°5N 7°46W **89** H3
Moncayo, Sierra del
Spain 41°48N 1°50W **90** D3
Monchegorsk *Russia* 67°54N 32°58E **60** C25
Mönchengladbach
Germany 51°11N 6°27E **76** D2
Monchique *Portugal* 37°19N 8°38W **89** H2
Moncks Corner *U.S.A.* 33°12N 80°1W **178** B9
Monclova *Mexico* 26°54N 101°25W **180** B4
Moncontour *France* 48°22N 2°38W **70** D4
Moncton *Canada* 46°7N 64°51W **165** C7
Mondariz *Spain* 42°14N 8°27W **88** C2
Mondego → *Portugal* 40°9N 8°52W **88** E2
Mondego, C. *Portugal* 40°11N 8°54W **88** E2
Mondeodo *Indonesia* 3°34S 122°9E **119** E6
Mondeville *France* 49°10N 0°18W **70** C6
Mondlo *S. Africa* 27°59S 30°43E **145** C5
Mondolfo *Italy* 43°45N 13°6E **93** E10
Mondoñedo *Spain* 43°25N 7°23W **88** B3
Mondovì *Italy* 44°23N 7°49E **92** D4
Mondragon = Arrasate
Spain 43°4N 2°30W **90** B2
Mondragone *Italy* 41°7N 13°53E **94** A6
Mondrain I. *Australia* 34°9S 122°14E **149** F3
Moneague *Jamaica* 18°16N 77°7W **182** a
Monemvasia *Greece* 36°41N 23°3E **98** E5
Moneron, Ostrov
Russia 46°15N 141°16E **112** A10
Monessen *U.S.A.* 40°9N 79°54W **174** F5
Monesterio *Spain* 38°6N 6°15W **89** G4
Monestier-de-Clermont
France 44°55N 5°38E **73** D9
Monett *U.S.A.* 36°55N 93°55W **172** G7
Moneymore *U.K.* 54°41N 6°40W **64** B5
Monfalcone *Italy* 45°49N 13°32E **93** C10
Monflanquin *France* 44°32N 0°47E **72** D4
Monforte *Portugal* 39°6N 7°25W **89** F3
Monforte de Lemos *Spain* 42°31N 7°33W **88** C3
Monfragüe ⌓ *Spain* 39°48N 5°52W **88** F5
Mong Hpayak *Burma* 20°52N 99°55E **120** B2
Mong Hsat *Shan,*
Burma 21°54N 98°30E **116** G2
Mong Hsat *Shan,*
Burma 20°31N 99°15E **120** B2
Mong Kung *Burma* 21°35N 97°35E **123** J20
Mong Nai *Burma* 20°32N 97°46E **123** J20
Mong Ping *Burma* 21°22N 99°2E **116** G2
Mong Tai = Shan □
Burma 21°30N 98°30E **123** J21
Mong Ton *Burma* 20°17N 98°45E **123** J21
Mong Yai *Burma* 22°21N 98°3E **123** H21
Mong Yang *Burma* 21°50N 99°41E **120** B2
Mongalla *South Sudan* 5°8N 31°42E **135** G12
Mongers, L. *Australia* 29°25S 117°5E **149** E2
Monghyr = Munger
India 25°23N 86°30E **125** G12
Mongibello = Etna *Italy* 37°50N 14°55E **95** E7
Mongo *Chad* 12°14N 18°43E **135** F9
Mongo → *S. Leone* 9°35N 12°10W **138** D2
Mongolia ■ *Asia* 47°0N 103°0E **110** B9
Mongolia, Plateau of
Asia 45°0N 105°0E **102** D12
Mongonu *Nigeria* 12°40N 13°32E **139** C7
Mongu *Zambia* 15°16S 23°12E **141** H4
Môngua *Angola* 16°43S 15°20E **144** A2
Moniac *U.S.A.* 30°31N 82°14W **178** E7
Monifieth *U.K.* 56°30N 2°48W **65** E6
Monistrol-sur-Loire
France 45°17N 4°11E **73** C8
Monkey Bay *Malawi* 14°7S 35°1E **143** E4
Monkey Mia *Australia* 25°48S 113°43E **149** E1
Monkey River *Belize* 16°22N 88°29W **181** D7
Mońki *Poland* 53°23N 22°48E **82** E9
Monkland *Canada* 45°11N 74°52W **175** A10
Monkoto
Dem. Rep. of the Congo 1°38S 20°35E **140** E4
Monkton *Canada* 43°35N 81°5W **174** C3
Monmouth *U.K.* 51°48N 2°42W **67** F5
Monmouth *Ill., U.S.A.* 40°55N 90°39W **172** E8
Monmouth *Oreg.,*
U.S.A. 44°51N 123°14W **168** D2
Monmouthshire □ *U.K.* 51°48N 2°54W **67** F5
Mono → *Togo* 6°17N 1°51E **139** D5
Mono, Pta. *Nic.* 12°0N 83°30W **182** D3
Mono L. *U.S.A.* 38°1N 119°1W **170** H7
Monolith *U.S.A.* 35°7N 118°22W **171** K8
Monolithos *Greece* 36°7N 27°45E **101** C9
Monongahela *U.S.A.* 40°12N 79°56W **174** F5
Monópoli *Italy* 40°57N 17°18E **95** B10
Monor *Hungary* 47°21N 19°27E **80** C4
Monos I. *Trin. & Tob.* 10°42N 61°44W **187** K15
Monóvar *Spain* 38°28N 0°53W **91** G4
Monowai *N.Z.* 45°53S 167°31E **155** F2
Monowai, L. *N.Z.* 45°53S 167°25E **155** F2
Monreal del Campo
Spain 40°47N 1°20W **90** E3
Monreale *Italy* 38°5N 13°17E **94** D6
Monroe *Ga., U.S.A.* 33°47N 83°43W **178** B6
Monroe *La., U.S.A.* 32°30N 92°7W **176** E8
Monroe *Mich., U.S.A.* 41°55N 83°24W **173** E12
Monroe *N.C., U.S.A.* 34°59N 80°33W **177** D14
Monroe *N.Y., U.S.A.* 41°20N 74°11W **175** E10
Monroe *Utah, U.S.A.* 38°38N 112°7W **168** G7
Monroe *Wash., U.S.A.* 47°51N 121°58W **170** C5
Monroe *Wis., U.S.A.* 42°36N 89°38W **172** D9
Monroe, L. *U.S.A.* 28°50N 81°19W **179** G8
Monroe City *U.S.A.* 39°39N 91°44W **172** F8
Monroeton *U.S.A.* 41°43N 76°29W **175** E8
Monroeville *Ala.,*
U.S.A. 31°31N 87°20W **177** F11
Monroeville *Pa., U.S.A.* 40°26N 79°45W **174** F5
Monrovia *Liberia* 6°18N 10°47W **138** D2
Mons *Belgium* 50°27N 3°58E **69** D3
Møns Klint *Denmark* 54°57N 12°33E **63** K6
Monsaraz *Portugal* 38°28N 7°22W **89** G3
Monse *Indonesia* 4°7S 123°15E **119** E6
Monsefú *Peru* 6°52S 79°52W **188** B2
Monségur *France* 44°38N 0°4E **72** D4
Monsélice *Italy* 45°14N 11°45E **93** C8
Mönsterås *Sweden* 57°3N 16°26E **63** G10
Mont Cenis, Col du
France 45°15N 6°55E **73** C10
Mont-de-Marsan *France* 43°54N 0°31W **72** E3
Mont-Joli *Canada* 48°37N 68°10W **165** C6
Mont-Laurier *Canada* 46°35N 75°30W **164** C4
Mont-Louis *Canada* 49°15N 65°44W **165** C6
Mont Peko △ *Ivory C.* 9°5N 7°15W **138** D3
Mont-roig del Camp *Spain* 41°5N 0°58E **90** D5
Mont-St-Michel, Le
France 48°40N 1°30W **70** D5
Mont Sangbé △ *Ivory C.* 8°0N 7°10W **138** D3
Mont-Tremblant ⌓
Canada 46°30N 74°30W **164** C5
Montabaur *Germany* 50°25N 7°50E **76** E3
Montagnac *France* 43°29N 3°28E **72** E7
Montagnana *Italy* 45°14N 11°28E **93** C8
Montagne de Reims ⌓
France 49°8N 4°0E **71** C11
Montagnes □ *Ivory C.* 6°54N 7°50W **138** D3
Montagu *S. Africa* 33°45S 20°8E **144** D3
Montagu I. *Antarctica* 58°25S 26°20W **55** B1
Montague *Canada* 46°10N 62°39W **165** C7
Montague, I. *Mexico* 31°45N 114°48W **180** A2
Montague I. *Australia* 36°16S 150°13E **153** D9
Montague I. *U.S.A.* 60°0N 147°30W **166** D10
Montague Ra.
Australia 27°15S 119°30E **149** E2
Montague Sd.
Australia 14°28S 125°20E **148** B4
Montaigu *France* 46°59N 1°18W **70** F5
Montalbán *Spain* 40°50N 0°45W **90** E4
Montalbano Iónico *Italy* 40°17N 16°34E **95** B9
Montalbo *Spain* 39°53N 2°42W **90** F2
Montalcino *Italy* 43°3N 11°29E **93** E8
Montalegre *Portugal* 41°49N 7°47W **88** D3
Montalto *Italy* 38°10N 15°55E **95** D8
Montalto di Castro *Italy* 42°21N 11°37E **93** F8
Montalto Uffugo *Italy* 39°24N 16°9E **95** C9
Montalvo *U.S.A.* 34°15N 119°12W **171** L7
Montamarta *Spain* 41°39N 5°49W **88** D5
Montana *Bulgaria* 43°27N 23°16E **96** C7
Montaña *Peru* 6°0S 73°0W **188** B3
Montana □ *Bulgaria* 43°30N 23°10E **96** C7
Montana □ *U.S.A.* 47°0N 110°0W **168** C9
Montaña Clara, I.
Canary Is. 29°17N 13°33W **100** E6
Montañas de Malaga ⌓
Spain 36°48N 4°32W **89** J6
Montánchez *Spain* 39°15N 6°8W **89** F4
Montargil *Portugal* 39°5N 8°10W **89** F2
Montargis *France* 47°59N 2°43E **71** E9
Montauban *France* 44°2N 1°21E **72** D5
Montauk *U.S.A.* 41°3N 71°57W **175** E13
Montauk Pt. *U.S.A.* 41°4N 71°51W **175** E13
Montbard *France* 47°38N 4°20E **71** E11
Montbarrey *France* 47°1N 5°39E **71** E12
Montbéliard *France* 47°31N 6°48E **71** E13
Montblanc *Spain* 41°23N 1°4E **90** D6
Montbrison *France* 45°36N 4°3E **73** C8
Montcalm, Pic de *France* 42°40N 1°25E **72** F5
Montceau-les-Mines
France 46°40N 4°23E **71** F11
Montcenis *France* 46°47N 4°23E **73** B8
Montchanin *France* 46°45N 4°28E **73** B8
Montclair *U.S.A.* 40°49N 74°12W **175** F10
Montcornet *France* 49°40N 4°1E **71** C11
Montcuq *France* 44°21N 1°13E **72** D5
Montdidier *France* 49°38N 2°35E **71** C9
Monte Albán *Mexico* 17°2N 96°46W **181** D5
Monte Alegre *Brazil* 2°0S 54°0W **187** D8
Monte Alegre de Goiás
Brazil 13°14S 47°10W **189** C1
Monte Alegre do Piauí
Brazil 9°46S 45°18W **189** B1
Monte Azul *Brazil* 15°9S 42°53W **189** D2
Monte-Carlo *Monaco* 43°44N 7°25E **73** E11
Monte Carmelo *Brazil* 18°43S 47°29W **189** D1
Monte Caseros
Argentina 30°10S 57°50W **190** C4
Monte Comán
Argentina 34°40S 67°53W **190** C2
Monte Cristi *Dom. Rep.* 19°52N 71°39W **183** C5
Monte Cucco ⌓ *Italy* 43°22N 12°43E **93** E9
Monte Dinero
Argentina 52°18S 68°33W **192** D3
Monte León *Argentina* 50°15S 69°0W **192** D3
Monte Lindo →
Paraguay 23°56S 57°12W **190** A4
Monte Pascoal △
Brazil 16°51S 39°21W **189** D3
Monte Patria *Chile* 30°42S 70°58W **190** C1
Monte Quemado
Argentina 25°53S 62°41W **190** B3
Monte Redondo *Portugal* 39°53N 8°50W **88** F2
Monte Rio *U.S.A.* 38°28N 123°0W **170** G4
Monte San Giovanni Campano
Italy 41°38N 13°31E **94** A6
Monte San Savino *Italy* 43°20N 11°43E **93** E8
Monte Sant' Ángelo
Italy 41°42N 15°59E **93** G12
Monte Santu, C. di *Italy* 40°5N 9°44E **94** B2
Monte Subasio ⌓ *Italy* 43°5N 12°40E **93** E9
Monte Vista *U.S.A.* 37°35N 106°9W **169** H10
Monteagudo *Argentina* 27°14S 54°8W **191** B5
Montealegre del Castillo
Spain 38°48N 1°17W **91** G3
Montebello *Canada* 45°40N 74°55W **164** C5
Montebello Iónico *Italy* 37°59N 15°45E **95** E8
Montebello Is.
Australia 20°30S 115°45E **148** D2
Montebelluna *Italy* 45°47N 12°3E **93** C9
Montebourg *France* 49°30N 1°20W **70** C5
Montecarlo *Argentina* 26°34S 54°47W **191** B5
Montecastrilli *Italy* 42°39N 12°29E **93** F9
Montecatini Terme *Italy* 43°53N 10°46E **92** E7
Montecito *U.S.A.* 34°26N 119°40W **171** L7
Montecristo *Italy* 42°20N 10°19E **92** F7
Montefalco *Italy* 42°54N 12°39E **93** F9
Montefiascone *Italy* 42°32N 12°2E **93** F9
Montefrío *Spain* 37°20N 4°0W **89** H7
Montegiórgio *Italy* 43°6N 13°33E **93** E10
Montego Bay *Jamaica* 18°28N 77°55W **182** a
Montehermoso *Spain* 40°5N 6°21W **88** E4
Monteiro *Brazil* 7°48S 37°2W **189** B3
Montejícar *Spain* 37°33N 3°30W **89** H7
Montélimar *France* 44°33N 4°45E **73** D8
Montella *Italy* 40°51N 15°1E **95** B8
Montellano *Spain* 36°59N 5°29W **89** J5
Montello *U.S.A.* 43°48N 89°20W **172** D9
Montemayor, Meseta de
Argentina 44°20S 66°10W **192** B3
Montemor-o-Novo
Portugal 38°40N 8°12W **89** G2
Montemor-o-Velho
Portugal 40°11N 8°40W **88** E2
Montemorelos *Mexico* 25°12N 99°49W **181** B5
Montendre *France* 45°16N 0°26W **72** C3
Montenegro *Brazil* 29°39S 51°29W **191** B5
Montenegro ■ *Europe* 42°40N 19°20E **96** D3
Montenero di Bisáccia
Italy 41°57N 14°47E **93** G11
Montepuez *Mozam.* 13°8S 38°59E **143** E4
Montepuez → *Mozam.* 12°32S 40°27E **143** E5
Montepulciano *Italy* 43°5N 11°47E **93** E8
Montereale *Italy* 42°31N 13°15E **93** F10
Montereau-Faut-Yonne
France 48°22N 2°57E **71** D9
Monterey *U.S.A.* 36°37N 121°55W **170** J5
Monterey B. *U.S.A.* 36°45N 122°0W **170** J5
Montería *Colombia* 8°46N 75°53W **186** B3
Monteros *Argentina* 27°11S 65°30W **190** B2
Monterotondo *Italy* 42°3N 12°37E **93** F9
Monterrey *Mexico* 25°40N 100°19W **180** B4
Montes Altos *Brazil* 5°50S 47°4W **189** B1
Montes Azules ⌓
Mexico 16°21N 91°3W **181** D6
Montes Claros *Brazil* 16°30S 43°50W **189** D2
Montesano *U.S.A.* 46°59N 123°36W **170** D3
Montesano sulla Marcellana
Italy 40°16N 15°42E **95** B8
Montesárchio *Italy* 41°4N 14°38E **95** A7
Montescaglioso *Italy* 40°33N 16°40E **95** B9
Montesilvano *Italy* 42°29N 14°8E **93** F11
Montesinho ⌓ *Portugal* 41°54N 6°52W **88** D4
Montevarchi *Italy* 43°31N 11°34E **93** E8
Montevideo *Uruguay* 34°50S 56°11W **191** C4
Montevideo *U.S.A.* 44°57N 95°43W **172** C6
Montezuma *Ga., U.S.A.* 32°18N 84°2W **178** C5
Montezuma *Iowa,*
U.S.A. 41°35N 92°32W **172** E7
Montezuma Castle ⌓
U.S.A. 34°39N 111°45W **169** J8
Montfaucon *France* 47°6N 1°7W **70** E5
Montfaucon-d'Argonne
France 49°16N 5°8E **71** C12
Montfaucon-en-Velay
France 45°11N 4°20E **73** C8
Montfort-le-Gesnois
France 48°3N 0°25E **70** D7
Montfort-sur-Meu *France* 48°9N 1°58W **70** D5
Montgenèvre *France* 44°56N 6°43E **73** D10
Montgó ⌓ *Spain* 38°48N 0°7W **91** G5
Montgomery *U.K.* 52°34N 3°8W **67** E4
Montgomery *Ala.,*
U.S.A. 32°23N 86°19W **178** C3
Montgomery *Pa.,*
U.S.A. 41°10N 76°53W **174** E8
Montgomery *W. Va.,*
U.S.A. 38°11N 81°19W **173** F13
Montgomery City
U.S.A. 38°59N 91°30W **172** F8
Montguyon *France* 45°12N 0°12W **72** C3
Monthermé *France* 49°52N 4°42E **71** C11
Monthey *Switz.* 46°15N 6°56E **77** J2
Monthois *France* 49°19N 4°43E **71** C11
Monti *Italy* 40°49N 9°19E **94** B2
Monti Lucrétili ⌓ *Italy* 42°5N 12°50E **93** F9
Monti Picentini ⌓ *Italy* 40°45N 15°2E **95** B8
Monti Sibillini ⌓ *Italy* 42°55N 13°15E **93** F10
Monti Simbruini ⌓
Italy 41°55N 13°13E **93** G10
Monticelli d'Ongina *Italy* 45°5N 9°56E **92** C6
Monticello *Ark., U.S.A.* 33°38N 91°47W **176** E9
Monticello *Fla., U.S.A.* 30°33N 83°52W **178** E6
Monticello *Ga., U.S.A.* 33°18N 83°40W **178** B6
Monticello *Ind.,*
U.S.A. 40°45N 86°46W **172** E10
Monticello *Iowa,*
U.S.A. 42°15N 91°12W **172** D8
Monticello *Ky., U.S.A.* 36°50N 84°51W **173** G11
Monticello *Minn.,*
U.S.A. 45°18N 93°48W **172** C7
Monticello *Miss., U.S.A.* 31°33N 90°7W **177** F9
Monticello *N.Y.,*
U.S.A. 41°39N 74°42W **175** E10
Monticello *Utah,*
U.S.A. 37°52N 109°21W **16**
Montichiari *Italy* 45°25N 10°23E **9**
Montier-en-Der *France* 48°30N 4°45E **71**
Montignac *France* 45°4N 1°10E **7**
Montigny-les-Metz
France 49°7N 6°10E **71**
Montigny-sur-Aube
France 47°57N 4°45E **71**
Montijo *Portugal* 38°41N 8°54W **8**
Montijo *Spain* 38°52N 6°39W **8**
Montilla *Spain* 37°36N 4°40W **8**
Montivilliers *France* 49°33N 0°12E **7**
Montluçon *France* 46°22N 2°36E **7**
Montmagny *Canada* 46°58N 70°34W **16**
Montmarault *France* 46°19N 2°57E **7**
Montmartre *Canada* 50°14N 103°27W **16**
Montmédy *France* 49°30N 5°20E **71**
Montmélian *France* 45°30N 6°4E **73**
Montmirail *France* 48°51N 3°30E **71**
Montmoreau-St-Cybard
France 45°23N 0°8E **7**
Montmorillon *France* 46°26N 0°50E **7**
Montmort-Lucy *France* 48°55N 3°49E **71**
Monto *Australia* 24°52S 151°6E **15**
Montoire-sur-le-Loir
France 47°45N 0°52E **7**
Montongbuwoh
Indonesia 8°33S 116°4E **119**
Montório al Vomano
Italy 42°35N 13°38E **93**
Montoro *Spain* 38°1N 4°27W **8**
Montour Falls *U.S.A.* 42°21N 76°51W **17**
Montoursville *U.S.A.* 41°15N 76°55W **17**
Montpelier *Idaho,*
U.S.A. 42°19N 111°18W **16**
Montpelier *Vt., U.S.A.* 44°16N 72°35W **175**
Montpellier *France* 43°37N 3°52E **7**
Montpezat-de-Quercy
France 44°15N 1°30E **7**
Montpon-Ménestérol
France 45°0N 0°11E **7**
Montréal *Canada* 45°30N 73°33W **175**
Montréal *Aude, France* 43°13N 2°8E **7**
Montréal *Gers, France* 43°56N 0°11E **7**
Montreal → *Canada* 47°14N 84°39W **16**
Montréal L. *Canada* 54°20N 105°45W **16**
Montreal Lake *Canada* 54°3N 105°46W **16**
Montredon-Labessonnié
France 43°45N 2°18E **7**
Montrésor *France* 47°10N 1°10E **7**
Montret *France* 46°40N 5°7E **71**
Montreuil *Pas-de-Calais,*
France 50°27N 1°45E **7**
Montreuil *Seine-St-Denis,*
France 48°51N 2°27E **7**
Montreuil-Bellay *France* 47°8N 0°9W **7**
Montreux *Switz.* 46°26N 6°55E **7**
Montrevel-en-Bresse
France 46°21N 5°8E **71**
Montrichard *France* 47°20N 1°10E **7**
Montrose *U.K.* 56°44N 2°27W **6**
Montrose *Colo.,*
U.S.A. 38°29N 107°53W **168**
Montrose *Pa., U.S.A.* 41°50N 75°53W **17**
Monts, Pte. des *Canada* 49°20N 67°12W **16**
Montsalvy *France* 44°41N 2°30E **7**
Montsant, Serra de *Spain* 41°17N 1°0E **9**
Montsauche-les-Settons
France 47°13N 4°2E **71**
Montsec, Serra del *Spain* 42°5N 0°45E **9**
Montseny ⌓ *Spain* 41°43N 2°22W **9**
Montserrat *Spain* 41°36N 1°49E **9**
Montserrat ☑
W. Indies 16°40N 62°10W **18**
Montuenga *Spain* 41°3N 4°38W **8**
Montuiri *Spain* 39°34N 2°59E **10**
Monywa *Burma* 22°7N 95°11E **123**
Monza *Italy* 45°35N 9°16E **9**
Monza e Brianza □ *Italy* 45°30N 9°15E **9**
Monze *Zambia* 16°17S 27°29E **14**
Monze, C. *Pakistan* 24°47N 66°37E **12**
Monzón *Spain* 41°52N 0°10E **9**
Mooers *U.S.A.* 44°58N 73°35W **175**
Mooi → *S. Africa* 28°45S 30°34E **14**
Mooi River *S. Africa* 29°13S 29°50E **14**
Mookgopong *S. Africa* 24°31S 28°44E **14**
Moomba *Australia* 28°6S 140°12E **15**
Moonah → *Australia* 22°3S 138°33E **15**
Moonda, L. *Australia* 25°52S 140°25E **15**
Moonie *Australia* 27°46S 150°20E **15**
Moonie → *Australia* 29°19S 148°43E **15**
Moonta *Australia* 34°6S 137°32E **15**
Moora *Australia* 30°37S 115°58E **14**
Moorcroft *U.S.A.* 44°16N 104°57W **168**
Moore → *Australia* 31°22S 115°30E **14**
Moore, L. *Australia* 29°50S 117°35E **14**
Moore Falls *Canada* 44°48N 78°48W **17**
Moore Haven *U.S.A.* 26°50N 81°6W **17**
Moore Park *Australia* 24°43S 152°17E **15**
Moore Res. *U.S.A.* 44°20N 71°53W **175**
Moore River △
Australia 31°7S 115°39E **14**
Moorefield *U.S.A.* 39°4N 78°58W **173**
Moorfoot Hills *U.K.* 55°44N 3°8W **6**
Moorhead *U.S.A.* 46°53N 96°45W **17**
Moormerland *Germany* 53°20N 7°20E **7**
Moornanyah L.
Australia 33°15S 143°42E **15**
Mooroopna *Australia* 36°25S 145°22E **15**
Moorpark *U.S.A.* 34°17N 118°53W **17**
Moorreesburg *S. Africa* 33°6S 18°38E **14**
Moorrinya △ *Australia* 21°42S 144°58E **15**
Moosburg *Germany* 48°27N 11°56E **7**
Moose → *Canada* 51°20N 80°25W **16**
Moose → *U.S.A.* 43°38N 75°24W **17**
Moose Creek *Canada* 45°15N 74°58W **175**
Moose Factory *Canada* 51°16N 80°32W **16**
Moose Jaw *Canada* 50°24N 105°30W **16**
Moose Jaw → *Canada* 50°34N 105°18W **16**
Moose Lake *Canada* 53°46N 100°8W **16**
Moose Lake *U.S.A.* 46°27N 92°46W **17**
Moose Mountain ⌓
Canada 49°48N 102°25W **16**
Moosehead L. *U.S.A.* 45°38N 69°40W **173**
Mooselookmeguntic L.
U.S.A. 44°55N 70°49W **175**
Moosilauke, Mt.
U.S.A. 44°3N 71°40W **175**
Moosomin *Canada* 50°9N 101°40W **16**
Moosonee *Canada* 51°17N 80°39W **16**
Moosup *U.S.A.* 41°43N 71°53W **175**

ootwingee △
Australia 31°10S 142°30E **152** A5
opane _S. Africa_ 22°37S 29°52E **145** B4
opeia Velha _Mozam._ 17°30S 35°40E **143** F4
opipi _Botswana_ 21°6S 24°55E **144** B3
opoi _C.A.R._ 5°6N 26°54E **142** A2
opti _Mali_ 14°30N 4°0W **138** C4
opti □ _Mali_ 14°40N 4°0W **138** C4
oqor _Afghan._ 36°50N 67°42E **124** C2
oquegua _Peru_ 17°15S 70°46W **188** D3
oquegua □ _Peru_ 16°50S 70°55W **188** D3
or _Hungary_ 47°25N 18°12E **80** C3
ora _Cameroon_ 11°2N 14°7E **139** C7
ora _Portugal_ 38°55N 8°10W **89** G2
ora _Spain_ 39°41N 3°46W **89** F7
ora _Sweden_ 61°2N 14°38E **62** C8
ora _Minn., U.S.A._ 45°53N 93°18W **172** C7
ora _N. Mex., U.S.A._ 35°58N 105°20W **198** J11
ora de Rubielos _Spain_ 40°15N 0°45W **90** E4
ora d'Ebre _Spain_ 41°6N 0°38E **90** D5
ora la Nova _Spain_ 41°7N 0°39E **90** D5
oraća _Montenegro_ 42°20N 19°9E **96** C3
orada Nova _Brazil_ 5°7S 38°23W **189** B3
orada Nova de Minas
Brazil 18°37S 45°22W **189** D1
oradabad _India_ 28°50N 78°50E **125** E8
orafenobe _Madag._ 17°50S 44°53E **141** H8
orag _Poland_ 53°55N 19°56E **82** E6
oral de Calatrava
Spain 38°51N 3°33W **89** G7
oraleda, Canal _Chile_ 44°30S 73°30W **192** B2
oraleja _Spain_ 40°6N 6°43W **88** E4
oramanga _Madag._ 18°56S 48°12E **141** H9
oran _Kans., U.S.A._ 37°55N 95°10W **172** G6
oran _Wyo., U.S.A._ 43°50N 110°31W **168** E8
oranbah _Australia_ 22°1S 148°6E **150** C4
orang = Biratnagar
Nepal 26°27N 87°17E **125** F12
orano Cálabro _Italy_ 39°50N 16°8E **95** C9
orant Bay _Jamaica_ 17°53N 76°25W **182** a
orant Cays _Jamaica_ 17°22N 76°0W **182** C4
orant Pt. _Jamaica_ 17°55N 76°12W **182** a
orar _India_ 26°14N 78°14E **124** F8
orar, L. _U.K._ 56°57N 5°40W **65** E3
oratalla _Spain_ 38°14N 1°49W **91** G3
oratuwa _Sri Lanka_ 6°30N 79°58E **127** L4
orava = _Slovak Rep._ 48°10N 16°59E **79** C9
orava _U.S.A._ 42°43N 76°25W **175** D8
oravian Hts. = Českomoravská
Vrchovina _Czech Rep._ 49°30N 15°40E **78** B8
oravica → _Serbia_ 43°52N 20°8E **96** C4
oravița _Romania_ 45°17N 21°14E **80** E6
oravská Třebová
Czech Rep. 49°45N 16°40E **79** B9
oravské Budějovice
Czech Rep. 49°4N 15°49E **78** B8
oravskoslezský □
Czech Rep. 49°55N 17°58E **79** B10
orawa _Australia_ 29°13S 116°0E **149** E2
orawhanna _Guyana_ 8°30N 59°40W **186** B7
oray _U.S.A._ 57°31N 3°18W **65** D5
oray Firth _U.K._ 57°40N 3°52W **65** D5
orbach _Germany_ 49°48N 7°6E **77** F3
orbegno _Italy_ 46°8N 9°34E **92** B6
orbi _India_ 22°50N 70°42E **124** H4
orbihan □ _France_ 47°55N 2°50W **70** E4
orbihan □ _France_ 47°55N 2°50W **70** E4
orbylånga _Sweden_ 56°32N 16°22E **63** H10
orcenx _France_ 44°3N 0°55W **73** D3
orcone _Italy_ 41°20N 14°40E **95** A7
ordelles _France_ 48°4N 1°52W **70** D5
orden _Canada_ 49°15N 98°10W **163** D9
ordovian Republic =
Mordvinia □ _Russia_ 54°20N 44°30E **86** C7
ordovo _Russia_ 52°6N 40°50E **86** D5
ordvinia □ _Russia_ 54°20N 44°30E **86** C7
ordy _Poland_ 52°13N 22°31E **83** F9
oreau → _U.S.A._ 45°18N 100°43W **172** C3
oree _S. Africa_ 23°30S 29°55E **145** B4
orecambe _U.K._ 54°5N 2°52W **66** C5
orecambe B. _U.K._ 54°7N 3°0W **66** C5
oree _Australia_ 29°28S 149°54E **151** D4
orehead _Australia_ 38°11N 83°26W **173** F12
orehead City _U.S.A._ 34°43N 76°43W **177** D16
orel → _India_ 26°13N 76°36E **124** F7
oreland _U.S.A._ 33°17N 84°46W **178** D3
orelia _Mexico_ 19°42N 101°7W **180** D4
orella _Australia_ 23°0S 143°52E **150** C3
orella _Spain_ 40°35N 0°5W **90** E4
orelos _Mexico_ 26°42N 107°40W **180** B3
orelos □ _Mexico_ 18°45N 99°0W **181** D5
oremi △ _Botswana_ 19°18S 23°10E **144** A3
orena _India_ 26°30N 78°4E **124** F8
orena, Sierra _Spain_ 38°20N 4°0W **89** G7
orena _Romania_ 44°59N 25°36E **83** F10
oreno _Bolivia_ 11°9S 66°15W **188** C4
oreno Valley
_U.S.A._ 33°56N 117°14W **171** M10
oresby I. _Canada_ 52°30N 131°40W **162** C2
orestel _France_ 45°40N 5°28E **73** C9
oreton I. _Australia_ 27°10S 153°25E **151** D5
oreton Island △
Australia 27°2S 153°24E **151** D5
oreuil _France_ 49°46N 2°30E **71** C9
orez _France_ 46°31N 6°2E **71** F13
organ _Australia_ 34°2S 139°35E **152** C3
organ _Ga., U.S.A._ 31°32N 84°36W **178** D5
organ _Utah, U.S.A._ 41°2N 111°41W **168** F8
organ City _U.S.A._ 29°42N 91°12W **179** G9
organ Hill _U.S.A._ 37°8N 121°39W **170** H5
organfield _U.S.A._ 37°41N 87°55W **172** G10
organ's Port _U.S.A._ 35°45N 81°41W **177** D14
organton _U.S.A._ 39°38N 79°57W **173** F14
organzon _S. Africa_ 26°45S 29°36E **145** D4
orges _Switz._ 46°31N 6°29E **72** J2
orghak _Iran_ 29°7N 57°54E **129** D8
orgongagua _Sweden_ 48°55N 6°38E **71** D13
orhar → _India_ 25°29N 85°11E **125** G11
ori _China_ 43°49N 90°11E **109** D12
ori _India_ 42°6N 140°35E **112** C10
oriarty _U.S.A._ 34°55N 106°3W **169** J10
oribaya _Guinea_ 9°53N 9°52W **138** D3
orice L. _Canada_ 53°57N 127°40W **162** C3
oriki _Nigeria_ 12°52N 6°30E **139** C6
orioka _Japan_ 39°45N 141°8E **112** E10
oris _Russia_ 28°10N 108°32W **180** B3
orisset _Australia_ 33°6S 151°30E **153** B9
orlaàs _France_ 43°21N 0°18W **72** E3
orlaix _France_ 48°36N 3°52W **70** D3

Mörlunda _Sweden_ 57°19N 15°52E **63** G9
Mormanno _Italy_ 39°53N 15°59E **95** C8
Mormant _France_ 48°37N 2°52E **71** D9
Mormugao = Marmagao
India 15°25N 73°56E **127** G11
Mornington _Australia_ 38°15S 145°5E **153** E6
Mornington, I. _Chile_ 49°50S 75°30W **192** C1
Mornington I.
Australia 16°30S 139°30E **150** B2
Mornington Peninsula △
Australia 38°28S 144°53E **153** E6
Mornos → _Greece_ 38°25N 21°50E **98** C3
Moro _Pakistan_ 26°40N 68°0E **124** F2
Moro → _Pakistan_ 29°42N 67°22E **124** E2
Moro _G. U.S.A._ 36°20N 123°0E **119** C6
Morocco ■ _N. Afr._ 32°0N 5°50W **134** B4
Morococha _Peru_ 11°40S 76°5W **188** C2
Morogoro _Tanzania_ 6°50S 37°40E **142** D4
Morogoro □ _Tanzania_ 8°0S 37°0E **142** D4
Moroleón _Mexico_ 20°8N 101°12W **180** C4
Morombe _Madag._ 21°45S 43°22E **141** J8
Moron _Argentina_ 34°39S 58°37W **190** C4
Morón _Cuba_ 22°8N 78°39W **182** B4
Mörön _Mongolia_ 49°38N 100°9E **110** B9
Morón de Almazán
Spain 41°29N 2°27W **90** D2
Morón de la Frontera
Spain 37°6N 5°28W **89** H5
Morona → _Peru_ 4°40S 77°10W **186** D2
Morondava _Madag._ 20°17S 44°17E **141** J8
Morondo _Ivory C._ 8°57N 6°47W **138** D3
Morongo Valley
_U.S.A._ 34°3N 116°37W **171** L10
Moroni _Comoros Is._ 11°40S 43°16E **141** a
Moroni _U.S.A._ 39°32N 111°35W **168** G8
Moronou _Ivory C._ 6°16N 4°59W **138** D4
Morotai _Indonesia_ 2°10N 128°30E **119** D7
Moroto _Uganda_ 2°28N 34°42E **142** B3
Moroto, Mt. _Uganda_ 2°30N 34°43E **142** B3
Morozov _Bulgaria_ 42°30N 25°10E **97** D9
Morozovsk _Russia_ 48°25N 41°50E **87** F5
Morpeth _Canada_ 42°23N 81°50W **174** D3
Morpeth _U.K._ 55°10N 1°41W **66** B6
Morphou _Cyprus_ 35°12N 32°59E **101** D11
Morphou Bay _Cyprus_ 35°15N 32°50E **101** D11
Morrilton _U.S.A._ 35°9N 92°44W **176** D8
Morrinhos _Ceará, Brazil_ 3°14S 40°7W **189** A2
Morrinhos _Minas Gerais,
Brazil_ 17°45S 49°10W **187** G9
Morrinsville _N.Z._ 37°40S 175°32E **154** D4
Morris _Canada_ 49°25N 97°22W **163** D9
Morris _Ill., U.S.A._ 41°22N 88°26W **172** E9
Morris _Minn., U.S.A._ 45°35N 95°55W **172** C6
Morris _N.Y., U.S.A._ 42°33N 75°15W **175** D9
Morris _Pa., U.S.A._ 41°35N 77°17W **174** E7
Morris, Mt. _Australia_ 26°9S 131°4E **149** E5
Morris Jesup, Kap
Greenland 83°40N 34°0W **57** A7
Morrisburg _Canada_ 44°55N 75°7W **175** B9
Morristown _Ariz.,
U.S.A._ 33°51N 112°37W **169** K7
Morristown _N.J.,
U.S.A._ 40°48N 74°29W **175** F10
Morristown _N.Y.,
U.S.A._ 44°35N 75°39W **175** B9
Morristown _Tenn.,
U.S.A._ 36°13N 83°18W **177** C13
Morrisville _N.Y.,
U.S.A._ 42°53N 75°35W **175** D9
Morrisville _Pa., U.S.A._ 40°13N 74°47W **175** F10
Morrisville _Vt., U.S.A._ 44°34N 72°36W **175** B12
Morro, Pta. _Chile_ 27°6S 71°0W **190** B1
Morro Bay _U.S.A._ 35°22N 120°51W **170** K6
Morro Chico _Chile_ 52°2S 71°26W **192** D2
Morro del Jable
Canary Is. 28°3N 14°23W **100** F5
Morro do Chapéu _Brazil_ 11°33S 41°9W **189** C2
Morro Jable, Pta. de
Canary Is. 28°2N 14°20W **100** F5
Morrocoy ○ _Venezuela_ 10°48N 68°13W **183** D6
Morros _Brazil_ 2°52S 44°3W **189** A2
Morrosquillo, G. de
Colombia 9°35N 75°40W **182** C4
Mörrum _Sweden_ 56°12N 14°45E **63** H8
Morrumbene _Mozam._ 23°31S 35°16E **145** B6
Mörrumsån → _Sweden_ 56°10N 14°45E **63** H8
Mors _Denmark_ 56°50N 8°45E **63** H2
Morshansk _Russia_ 53°28N 41°50E **86** D5
Mörsil _Sweden_ 63°19N 13°40E **62** A7
Mortagne → _France_ 48°33N 6°27E **71** D13
Mortagne-au-Perche
France 48°31N 0°33E **70** D7
Mortagne-sur-Gironde
France 45°28N 0°47W **72** C3
Mortagne-sur-Sèvre
France 47°0N 0°59W **70** F5
Mortain _France_ 48°40N 0°57W **70** D6
Mortara _Italy_ 45°15N 8°44E **92** C5
Morteau _France_ 47°3N 6°35E **71** F13
Morteros _Argentina_ 30°50S 62°0W **190** C3
Mortlach _Canada_ 50°27N 106°4W **163** C7
Mortlake _Australia_ 38°5S 142°50E **152** E6
Morton _Tex., U.S.A._ 33°44N 102°46W **176** E3
Morton _Wash., U.S.A._ 46°34N 122°17W **170** D4
Morton △ _Australia_ 35°0S 150°12E **153** C9
Moruga _Trin. & Tob._ 10°4N 61°16W **187** K15
Morundah _Australia_ 34°57S 146°19E **153** E4
Moruya _Australia_ 35°58S 150°3E **153** C9
Morvan _France_ 47°5N 4°3E **71** E11
Morven _Australia_ 26°22S 147°5E **150** D4
Morven _N.Z._ 44°50S 171°6E **155** F4
Morven _U.S.A._ 34°50N 79°58W **177** D15
Morvern _U.K._ 56°38N 5°44W **65** E3
Morwell _Australia_ 38°10S 146°22E **153** E7
Morwell △ _Australia_ 38°14S 146°23E **153** E7
Moryń _Poland_ 52°51N 14°22E **83** F1
Morzine _France_ 46°11N 6°42E **71** F13
Mosakahiken = Moose Lake
Canada 53°46N 100°8W **163** C8
Mosalsk _Russia_ 54°30N 34°55E **84** E8
Mosbach _Germany_ 49°21N 9°9E **77** F5
Mošćenice _Croatia_ 45°17N 14°16E **93** C11
Mosciano Sant' Ángelo
Italy 42°42N 13°52E **93** F10
Moscos Is. _Burma_ 14°0N 97°30E **120** F1
Moscow = Moskva
Russia 55°45N 37°37E **84** E9
Moscow _Idaho, U.S.A._ 46°44N 117°0W **168** C5
Moscow _Pa., U.S.A._ 41°20N 75°31W **175** E9

Moscow Domodedovo Int. ✈
(DME) _Russia_ 55°24N 37°54E **84** E9
Mosel → _Europe_ 50°22N 7°36E **71** B14
Moselle = Mosel →
Europe 50°22N 7°36E **71** B14
Moselle □ _France_ 48°59N 6°33E **71** D13
Moses Lake _U.S.A._ 47°8N 119°17W **168** C4
Mosgiel _N.Z._ 45°53S 170°21E **155** F5
Moshaweng →
S. Africa 26°35S 22°50E **144** C3
Moshchnyy, Ostrov
Russia 60°1N 27°50E **84** B4
Moshi _Tanzania_ 3°22S 37°18E **142** C4
Moshi □ _Nigeria_ 9°18N 4°38E **139** D5
Moshupa _Botswana_ 24°46S 25°29E **144** B4
Mosi-oa-Tunya = Victoria Falls
Zimbabwe 17°58S 25°52E **143** F2
Mosina _Poland_ 52°15N 16°50E **83** F3
Mosjøen _Norway_ 65°51N 13°12E **60** D15
Moskenesøya _Norway_ 67°58N 13°0E **60** C15
Moskenstraumen
Norway 67°47N 12°45E **60** C15
Moskva _Russia_ 55°45N 37°37E **84** E9
Moskva □ _Russia_ 56°20N 37°20E **84** D9
Moskva → _Russia_ 55°5N 38°51E **84** E10
Moslavačka Gora
Croatia 45°40N 16°37E **93** C13
Mosomane _Botswana_ 24°2S 26°19E **144** B4
Mosonmagyaróvár
Hungary 47°52N 17°18E **80** C2
Mošorin _Serbia_ 45°19N 20°4E **80** E5
Mospyne _Ukraine_ 47°52N 38°0E **85** J9
Mosquera _Colombia_ 2°35N 78°24W **186** C2
Mosquero _U.S.A._ 35°47N 103°58W **169** J12
Mosqueruela _Spain_ 40°21N 0°27W **90** E4
Mosquitia _Honduras_ 15°20N 84°10W **182** C3
Mosquito Creek L.
_U.S.A._ 41°18N 80°46W **174** E4
Mosquito L. _Canada_ 62°35N 103°20W **163** A8
Mosquitos, G. de los
Panama 9°15N 81°10W **182** E3
Moss _Norway_ 59°27N 10°40E **61** G14
Moss Vale _Australia_ 34°32S 150°25E **153** C9
Mossaka _Congo_ 1°15S 16°45E **140** E3
Mossbank _Canada_ 49°56N 105°56W **163** D7
Mossburn _N.Z._ 45°41S 168°15E **155** F3
Mosselbaai _S. Africa_ 34°11S 22°8E **144** E3
Mossendjo _Congo_ 2°55S 12°42E **140** E2
Mossgiel _Australia_ 33°15S 144°5E **152** B6
Mossingen _Germany_ 48°24N 9°4E **77** G5
Mossman _Australia_ 16°21S 145°15E **150** B4
Mossoró _Brazil_ 5°10S 37°15W **189** B3
Mossuril _Mozam._ 14°58S 40°42E **143** E5
Mossy Head _U.S.A._ 30°45N 86°19W **179** E13
Mossy Point _Australia_ 35°50S 150°11E **153** C9
Most _Czech Rep._ 50°31N 13°38E **78** A6
Mosta _Malta_ 35°55N 14°26E **101** D1
Mostaganem _Algeria_ 35°54N 0°5E **136** A4
Mostaganem □ _Algeria_ 35°40N 0°15E **136** A4
Mostar _Bos.-H._ 43°22N 17°50E **80** G2
Mostardas _Brazil_ 31°2S 50°51W **191** C5
Mostiska = Mostyska
Ukraine 49°48N 23°4E **83** J10
Móstoles _Spain_ 40°19N 3°53W **88** B3
Mosty = Masty _Belarus_ 53°27N 24°38E **75** B13
Mostyska _Ukraine_ 49°48N 23°4E **83** J10
Mosul = Al Mawşil
Iraq 36°15N 43°5E **105** D10
Mota del Cuervo _Spain_ 39°30N 2°52W **91** F2
Mota del Marqués _Spain_ 41°38N 5°11W **88** D5
Motagua → _Guatemala_ 15°44N 88°14W **182** C2
Motala _Sweden_ 58°32N 15°1E **63** F9
Motaze _Mozam._ 24°48S 32°52E **145** B5
Moţca _Romania_ 47°15N 26°37E **81** C11
Moth _India_ 25°43N 78°57E **125** G8
Motherwell _U.K._ 55°47N 3°58W **65** F5
Motihari _India_ 26°30N 84°55E **125** F11
Motilla del Palancar
Spain 39°34N 1°55W **91** F3
Motiti I. _N.Z._ 37°38S 176°25E **154** D5
Motnik _Slovenia_ 46°14N 14°54E **93** B11
Motovun _Croatia_ 45°20N 13°50E **93** C10
Motozintla de Mendoza
Mexico 15°22N 92°14W **181** D6
Motril _Spain_ 36°31N 3°37W **89** J7
Motru _Romania_ 44°48N 22°59E **82** F7
Motru → _Romania_ 44°32N 23°31E **81** F8
Mott _U.S.A._ 46°23N 102°20W **172** B2
Mottama, G. of _Burma_ 16°5N 96°30E **123** L20
Móttola _Italy_ 40°38N 17°2E **95** B10
Motu _N.Z._ 37°52S 177°36E **154** D6
Motu → _N.Z._ 37°52S 177°36E **154** D6
Motueka _N.Z._ 41°7S 173°1E **155** B8
Motueka → _N.Z._ 41°5S 173°1E **155** B8
Motul _Mexico_ 21°6N 89°17W **181** C7
Mouchalagane →
Canada 50°56N 68°41W **165** B6
Mouding _China_ 25°20N 101°28E **116** E3
Moudjeria _Mauritania_ 17°50N 12°28W **138** B2
Moudon _Switz._ 46°40N 6°49E **72** J2
Moudros _Greece_ 39°50N 25°18E **99** B7
Mougins _France_ 43°36N 7°0E **73** E10
Mouhoun = Black Volta
→ _Africa_ 8°41N 1°33W **138** D4
Mouila _Gabon_ 1°50S 11°0E **140** E2
Moulamein _Australia_ 35°3S 144°1E **152** C6
Moule à Chique, C.
St. Lucia 13°43N 60°57W **183** f
Mouliana _Greece_ 35°10N 25°59E **101** D7
Moulins _France_ 46°35N 3°19E **71** F10
Moulmein = Mawlamyine
Burma 16°30N 97°40E **123** L20
Moulouya, O. →
Morocco 35°5N 2°25W **136** A3
Moultrie _U.S.A._ 31°11N 83°47W **178** E4
Moultrie, L. _U.S.A._ 33°20N 80°5W **178** D9
Mound City _Ill., U.S.A._ 40°7N 95°14W **172** F7
Mound City _S. Dak.,
U.S.A._ 45°44N 100°4W **172** C3
Moundou _Chad_ 8°10N 16°10E **135** G9
Moundsville _U.S.A._ 39°55N 80°44W **174** F4
Moung _Cambodia_ 12°46N 103°27E **120** F4
Mount Airy _U.S.A._ 36°31N 80°37W **177** C14
Mount Albert _Canada_ 44°8N 79°19W **174** B5
Mount Aspiring △
_N.Z._ 44°19S 168°47E **155** E3
Mount Barker _S. Austral.,
Australia_ 35°5S 138°52E **152** C3
Mount Barker _W. Austral.,
Australia_ 34°38S 117°40E **149** F2
Mount Barnett Roadhouse
Australia 16°39S 125°57E **148** C4

Mount Beauty
Australia 36°47S 147°10E **153** D7
Mount Brydges _Canada_ 42°54N 81°29W **174** D3
Mount Buffalo △
Australia 36°43S 146°46E **153** D7
Mount Burr _Australia_ 37°34S 140°26E **151** F3
Mount Carleton △
Canada 47°25N 66°55W **165** C6
Mount Carmel = Ha Karmel →
Israel 32°45N 35°5E **130** C4
Mount Carmel _Ill._
_U.S.A._ 38°25N 87°46W **172** F10
Mount Carmel _Pa._,
_U.S.A._ 40°47N 76°26W **175** F8
Mount Clemens _U.S.A._ 42°35N 82°53W **174** D1
Mount Cook _N.Z._ 43°44S 170°5E **155** D5
Mount Cook △ _N.Z._ 43°35S 170°15E **155** D5
Mount Coolon
Australia 21°25S 147°25E **150** C4
Mount Darwin
Zimbabwe 16°47S 31°38E **143** F3
Mount Desert I.
_U.S.A._ 44°21N 68°20W **173** C19
Mount Dora _U.S.A._ 28°48N 81°38W **179** G8
Mount Ebenezer
Australia 25°6S 132°34E **149** E5
Mount Eccles △
Australia 38°5S 141°54E **152** E4
Mount Edziza △
Canada 57°30N 130°45W **162** B2
Mount Elgon △ _E. Afr._ 1°4N 34°42E **142** B3
Mount Field △
Australia 42°39S 146°35E **151** G4
Mount Fletcher
S. Africa 30°40S 28°30E **145** D4
Mount Forest _Canada_ 43°59N 80°43W **174** C4
Mount Frankland △
Australia 31°47S 116°37E **149** F2
Mount Frederick ○
Australia 19°39S 129°18E **148** C4
Mount Gambier
Australia 37°50S 140°46E **152** D4
Mount Garnet _Australia_ 17°37S 145°6E **150** B4
Mount Holly _U.S.A._ 39°59N 74°47W **175** G10
Mount Holly Springs
_U.S.A._ 40°7N 77°12W **174** F7
Mount Hope _N.S.W._,
Australia 32°51S 145°51E **153** B6
Mount Hope _S. Austral._,
Australia 34°7S 135°23E **151** E2
Mount Isa _Australia_ 20°42S 139°26E **150** C2
Mount James ○
Australia 24°51S 116°54E **149** D2
Mount Jewett _U.S.A._ 41°44N 78°39W **174** E6
Mount Kaputar △
Australia 30°16S 150°10E **151** E5
Mount Kenya △ _Kenya_ 0°5S 37°21E **142** C4
Mount Kisco _U.S.A._ 41°12N 73°44W **175** E11
Mount Laguna
_U.S.A._ 32°52N 116°25W **171** N10
Mount Larcom
Australia 23°48S 150°59E **150** C5
Mount Lofty Ranges
Australia 34°35S 139°5E **152** C3
Mount Magnet
Australia 28°2S 117°47E **149** E2
Mount Manara
Australia 32°29S 143°58E **152** B5
Mount Maunganui
_N.Z._ 37°40S 176°14E **154** D5
Mount Molloy
Australia 16°42S 145°20E **150** B4
Mount Morgan
Australia 23°40S 150°25E **150** C5
Mount Morris _U.S.A._ 42°44N 77°52W **174** D7
Mount Pearl _Canada_ 47°31N 52°47W **165** C9
Mount Penn _U.S.A._ 40°20N 75°54W **175** F9
Mount Perry _Australia_ 25°13S 151°42E **151** D5
Mount Pleasant _Iowa,
U.S.A._ 40°58N 91°33W **172** E8
Mount Pleasant _Mich._,
_U.S.A._ 43°36N 84°46W **173** D11
Mount Pleasant _Pa._,
_U.S.A._ 40°9N 79°33W **174** F5
Mount Pleasant _S.C._,
_U.S.A._ 32°47N 79°52W **178** C10
Mount Pleasant _Tenn._,
_U.S.A._ 35°32N 87°12W **177** D11
Mount Pleasant _Tex._,
_U.S.A._ 33°9N 94°58W **176** E7
Mount Pleasant _Utah_,
_U.S.A._ 39°33N 111°27W **168** G8
Mount Pocono _U.S.A._ 41°7N 75°22W **175** E9
Mount Rainier △
_U.S.A._ 46°55N 121°50W **170** D5
Mount Remarkable △
Australia 32°47S 138°3E **152** B3
Mount Revelstoke △
Canada 51°5N 118°30W **162** C5
Mount Robson △
Canada 53°0N 119°0W **162** C5
Mount St. Helens ○
_U.S.A._ 46°14N 122°11W **170** D4
Mount Selinda
Zimbabwe 20°24S 32°43E **145** B5
Mount Shasta _U.S.A._ 41°19N 122°19W **168** F2
Mount Signal _U.S.A._ 32°39N 115°37W **171** N11
Mount Somers _N.Z._ 43°45S 171°27E **155** D6
Mount Sterling _Ill._,
_U.S.A._ 39°59N 90°45W **172** F8
Mount Sterling _Ky._,
_U.S.A._ 38°4N 83°56W **173** F12
Mount Surprise
Australia 18°10S 144°17E **150** B3
Mount Union _U.S.A._ 40°23N 77°53W **174** F7
Mount Upton _U.S.A._ 42°26N 75°23W **175** D9
Mount Vernon _Ga._,
_U.S.A._ 32°11N 82°36W **178** D4
Mount Vernon _Ill._,
_U.S.A._ 38°19N 88°55W **172** F9
Mount Vernon _Ind._,
_U.S.A._ 37°56N 87°54W **167** H22
Mount Vernon _N.Y._,
_U.S.A._ 40°54N 73°49W **175** F11
Mount Vernon _Ohio_,
_U.S.A._ 40°23N 82°29W **174** F2
Mount Vernon _Wash._,
_U.S.A._ 48°25N 122°20W **170** B4
Mount Victor
Australia 32°11S 139°44E **152** B3
Mount Wellington
_N.Z._ 36°55S 174°52E **154** C3

Mount William △
Australia 40°56S 148°14E **151** G4
Mounta, Akra _Greece_ 38°3N 20°47E **98** C2
Mountain Ash _U.K._ 51°40N 3°23W **67** F4
Mountain Center
_U.S.A._ 33°42N 116°44W **171** M10
Mountain City _Nev._,
_U.S.A._ 41°50N 115°58W **168** F6
Mountain City _Tenn._,
_U.S.A._ 36°29N 81°48W **177** C14
Mountain Dale
_U.S.A._ 41°41N 74°32W **175** E10
Mountain Grove _U.S.A._ 37°8N 92°16W **172** G7
Mountain Home _Ark._,
_U.S.A._ 36°20N 92°23W **176** C8
Mountain Home _Idaho,
U.S.A._ 43°8N 115°41W **168** E6
Mountain Iron _U.S.A._ 47°32N 92°37W **172** B7
Mountain Pass
_U.S.A._ 35°29N 115°35W **171** K11
Mountain View _Ark._,
_U.S.A._ 35°52N 92°7W **176** D8
Mountain View _Calif._,
_U.S.A._ 37°23N 122°5W **170** H4
Mountain Zebra △
S. Africa 32°14S 25°27E **144** D4
Mountainair _U.S.A._ 34°31N 106°15W **169** J10
Mountbellew _Ireland_ 53°28N 8°31W **64** C3
Mountlake Terrace
_U.S.A._ 47°47N 122°18W **170** C4
Mountmellick _Ireland_ 53°7N 7°20W **64** C4
Mountrath _Ireland_ 53°0N 7°28W **64** C4
Moura _Australia_ 24°35S 149°58E **150** C4
Moura _Brazil_ 1°32S 61°38W **186** D6
Moura _Portugal_ 38°7N 7°30W **89** G3
Mourão _Portugal_ 38°22N 7°22W **89** G3
Mourdi, Dépression du
Chad 18°10N 23°0E **135** E10
Mourdiah _Mali_ 14°35N 7°25W **138** C3
Mourenx _France_ 43°22N 0°38W **72** E3
Mouri _Ghana_ 5°6N 1°14W **139** D4
Mourilyan _Australia_ 17°35S 146°3E **150** B4
Mourmelon-le-Grand
France 49°8N 4°22E **71** C11
Mourne → _U.K._ 54°52N 7°26W **64** B4
Mourne Mts. _U.K._ 54°10N 6°0W **64** B5
Mournies _Greece_ 35°29N 24°1E **101** D6
Mouscron _Belgium_ 50°45N 3°12E **69** D3
Moussoro _Chad_ 13°41N 16°35E **135** F9
Mouthe _France_ 46°44N 6°12E **71** F13
Moutier _Switz._ 47°16N 7°21E **77** H3
Moûtiers _France_ 45°29N 6°32E **73** C10
Moutong _Indonesia_ 0°28N 121°13E **119** D6
Mouy _France_ 49°18N 2°20E **71** C9
Mouydir, Monts du
Algeria 25°30N 4°10E **134** D6
Mouzáki _Greece_ 39°25N 21°37E **98** B3
Mouzon _France_ 49°36N 5°3E **71** C12
Movas _Mexico_ 28°10N 109°25W **180** B3
Moville _Ireland_ 55°11N 7°3W **64** A4
Mowandjum _Australia_ 17°22S 123°38E **148** C3
Moxotó → _Brazil_ 9°19S 38°14W **189** B3
Moy → _Ireland_ 54°8N 9°8W **64** B2
Moya _Comoros Is._ 12°18S 44°18E **141** a
Moya _Ethiopia_ 3°34N 39°5E **142** B4
Moyale _Kenya_ 3°30N 39°4E **142** B4
Moyen Atlas _Morocco_ 33°0N 5°0W **136** B4
Moyo _Indonesia_ 8°10S 117°40E **118** F5
Moyobamba _Peru_ 6°0S 77°0W **188** B2
Moyowosi □ _Tanzania_ 3°50S 31°0E **142** C3
Moyynty → _Norway_ 68°32N 15°29E **60** B16
Moyu _China_ 37°15N 79°44E **109** D9
Moyyero → _Russia_ 68°44N 103°42E **107** C12
Moyynqum _Zhambyl,
Kazakhstan_ 44°17N 72°57E **109** D8
Moyynqum _Zhambyl,
Kazakhstan_ 44°12N 71°0E **109** D8
Moyynty _Kazakhstan_ 47°10N 73°18E **109** D8
Mozambique = Moçambique
Africa 15°3S 40°42E **143** F5
Mozambique ■ _Africa_ 19°0S 35°0E **143** F4
Mozambique Basin
Ind. Oc. 30°0S 40°0E **146** G2
Mozambique Chan.
Africa 17°30S 42°30E **145** A7
Mozdok _Russia_ 43°45N 44°48E **87** J7
Mozdūrān _Iran_ 36°9N 60°35E **129** B9
Mozhaysk _Russia_ 55°30N 36°2E **84** E9
Mozhga _Russia_ 56°26N 52°15E **86** B11
Mozhnābād _Iran_ 34°7N 60°6E **129** C9
Mozirje _Slovenia_ 46°22N 14°58E **93** B11
Mozyr = Mazyr _Belarus_ 51°59N 29°15E **75** B15
Mpanda _Tanzania_ 6°23S 31°1E **142** D3
Mpésoba _Mali_ 12°31N 5°39W **138** C3
Mphoeng _Zimbabwe_ 21°10S 27°51E **143** G2
Mpika _Zambia_ 11°51S 31°25E **143** E3
Mpulungu _Tanzania_ 8°51S 31°5E **143** D3
Mpumalanga _S. Africa_ 29°50S 30°33E **145** D5
Mpumalanga □ _S. Africa_ 26°0S 30°0E **145** D5
Mpwapwa _Tanzania_ 6°23S 36°30E **142** D4
Mqanduli _S. Africa_ 31°49S 28°45E **145** E4
Mqinvartsveri = Kazbek
Russia 42°42N 44°30E **87** J7
Mrągowo _Poland_ 53°52N 21°18E **82** E8
Mramor _Serbia_ 43°20N 21°45E **81** G8
Mrimina _Morocco_ 29°50N 7°9W **136** C3
Mrkonjić Grad _Bos.-H._ 44°26N 17°4E **80** F2
Mrkopalj _Croatia_ 45°21N 14°52E **93** C11
Mrocza _Poland_ 53°16N 17°35E **83** E4
Msaken _Tunisia_ 35°49N 10°33E **136** A6
Msambansovu _Zimbabwe_ 15°50S 30°3E **143** F3
M'sila _Algeria_ 35°46N 4°30E **136** A6
M'sila □ _Algeria_ 35°30N 4°50E **136** A6
Msoro → _Russia_ 58°25N 31°50E **84** C6
Mstislavl = Mstsislaw
Belarus 54°0N 31°50E **75** A16
Mstsislaw _Belarus_ 54°0N 31°50E **75** A16
Mszana Dolna _Poland_ 49°41N 20°5E **83** J7
Mszczonów _Poland_ 51°58N 20°33E **83** G7
Mtama _Tanzania_ 10°17S 39°21E **143** E4
Mtamvuna = Mthamvuna →
S. Africa 31°6S 30°12E **145** D5
Mthatha _S. Africa_ 31°36S 28°49E **145** D4
Mtilikwe → _Zimbabwe_ 21°9S 31°30E **143** G3
Mtirala △ _Georgia_ 41°50N 42°3E **87** K6
Mtito Andei _Kenya_ 2°41S 38°10E **142** C4
Mtsensk _Russia_ 53°17N 36°36E **84** F9
Mtskheta _Georgia_ 42°52N 44°45E **87** K7
Mtubatuba _S. Africa_ 28°30S 32°8E **145** D5

Mtwalume _S. Africa_ 30°30S 30°38E **145** D5
Mtwara _Tanzania_ 10°20S 39°9E **143** E4
Mtwara-Mikindani
Tanzania 10°20S 40°20E **143** E5
Mu Gia, Deo _Vietnam_ 17°40N 105°47E **120** D5
Mu Ko Chang △
Thailand 11°59N 102°22E **121** G4
Mu Ko Surin _Thailand_ 9°30N 97°55E **121** H1
Mu Us Shamo _China_ 39°0N 109°0E **114** E5
Muang Beng _Laos_ 20°23N 101°46E **116** G3
Muang Chiang Rai = Chiang Rai
Thailand 19°52N 99°50E **116** H2
Muang Et _Laos_ 20°49N 104°1E **120** B5
Muang Hiam _Laos_ 20°5N 103°22E **120** B4
Muang Hongsa _Laos_ 19°43N 101°20E **120** B3
Muang Houn _Laos_ 20°8N 101°23E **120** B3
Muang Kau _Laos_ 15°6N 105°47E **120** E5
Muang Khao _Laos_ 19°38N 101°32E **120** B3
Muang Khong _Laos_ 14°7N 105°51E **120** E5
Muang Khoua _Laos_ 21°5N 102°31E **116** G4
Muang Liap _Laos_ 18°29N 101°40E **120** C3
Muang Mai _Thailand_ 8°5N 98°21E **121** a
Muang May _Laos_ 14°49N 106°56E **120** E6
Muang Na Mo _Laos_ 21°3N 101°49E **116** G3
Muang Ngeun _Laos_ 20°36N 101°3E **116** G3
Muang Ngoi _Laos_ 20°43N 102°41E **116** G4
Muang Nong _Laos_ 16°22N 106°30E **120** D6
Muang Ou Neua _Laos_ 22°18N 101°48E **116** F3
Muang Ou Tay _Laos_ 22°7N 101°48E **116** F3
Muang Pak Beng _Laos_ 19°54N 101°8E **116** H3
Muang Phalane _Laos_ 16°39N 105°34E **120** D5
Muang Phiang _Laos_ 19°6N 101°32E **120** C3
Muang Phine _Laos_ 16°32N 106°2E **120** D6
Muang Phonhong
Laos 18°30N 102°25E **120** C4
Muang Saiapoun _Laos_ 18°24N 101°31E **120** C3
Muang Sing _Laos_ 21°11N 101°9E **116** G3
Muang Son _Laos_ 20°27N 103°19E **120** B4
Muang Soui _Laos_ 19°33N 102°52E **120** C4
Muang Va _Laos_ 21°53N 102°19E **116** F4
Muang Va _Laos_ 18°18N 101°20E **120** C3
Muang Xai _Laos_ 20°42N 101°59E **116** G3
Muang Xamteu _Laos_ 19°39N 104°27E **120** C5
Muar _Malaysia_ 2°3N 102°34E **121** L4
Muarabungo _Indonesia_ 1°28S 102°52E **118** E2
Muaraenim _Indonesia_ 3°40S 103°50E **118** E2
Muarajuloi _Indonesia_ 0°12S 114°3E **118** E4
Muarakaman _Indonesia_ 0°2S 116°45E **118** E5
Muaratebo _Indonesia_ 1°30S 102°26E **118** E2
Muaratembesi _Indonesia_ 1°42S 103°8E **118** E2
Muarateweh _Indonesia_ 0°58S 114°52E **118** E4
Mubarakpur _India_ 26°6N 83°18E **125** F10
Mubarraz = Al Mubarraz
Si. Arabia 25°30N 49°40E **129** E6
Mubende _Uganda_ 0°33N 31°22E **142** B3
Mubi _Nigeria_ 10°18N 13°16E **139** C8
Mucajaí → _Brazil_ 2°25S 60°52W **186** C6
Muchachos, Roque de los
Canary Is. 28°44N 17°52W **100** F2
Mücheln _Germany_ 51°17N 11°47E **76** D7
Muchinga □ _Zambia_ 12°0S 31°30E **143** E3
Muchinga Mts. _Zambia_ 11°30S 31°30E **143** E3
Muchkapskiy _Russia_ 51°52N 42°28E **86** E6
Muchuan _China_ 28°57N 103°55E **116** C5
Muck _U.K._ 56°50N 6°15W **65** E2
Muckadilla _Australia_ 26°35S 148°23E **151** D4
Muckalee Cr. → _U.S.A._ 31°38N 84°9W **178** D5
Muckaty ○ _Australia_ 18°37S 133°52E **150** B1
Muckle Flugga _U.K._ 60°51N 0°54W **65** A8
Mucktart _U.K._ 13°0S 41°23W **189** C2
Mucuci _Turkey_ 39°3N 34°22E **104** C6
Mucuri _Brazil_ 18°0S 39°36E **189** C3
Mucurici _Brazil_ 18°6S 40°31W **189** C3
Mucusso _Angola_ 18°1S 21°25E **144** A3
Muda _Canary Is._ 28°34N 13°57W **100** F6
Mudanjiang _China_ 44°38N 129°30E **115** B15
Mudanya _Turkey_ 40°25N 28°50E **97** F12
Muddebihal _India_ 16°20N 76°8E **127** L2
Muddus △ _Sweden_ 66°58N 20°15E **60** C19
Muddy Cr. → _U.S.A._ 38°24N 110°42W **168** G8
Mudgee _Australia_ 32°32S 149°31E **153** B8
Mudhol _Karnataka, India_ 16°21N 75°17E **127** L2
Mudhol _Telangana, India_ 18°58N 77°53E **127** K3
Mudigere _India_ 13°8N 75°38E **127** H2
Mudjatik → _Canada_ 56°1N 107°36W **163** B7
Mudon _Burma_ 16°15N 97°44E **123** L20
Mudurnu _Turkey_ 40°25N 31°12E **104** B5
Mudurnu → _Turkey_ 40°30N 31°12E **104** B5
Mudurnu _Turkey_ 14°55S 39°40E **143** E4
Mueda _Mozam._ 11°36S 39°28E **143** E4
Mueller Ranges
Australia 18°18S 126°46E **148** C4
Muende _Mozam._ 14°28S 33°0E **143** E3
Muerto, Mar _Mexico_ 16°10N 94°10W **181** D6
Mufu Shan _China_ 29°20N 114°30E **117** C10
Mufulira _Zambia_ 12°32S 28°15E **143** E2
Mufumbiro Range
Africa 1°25S 29°30E **142** C2
Mugardos _Spain_ 43°27N 8°15W **88** B2
Muge → _Portugal_ 39°8N 8°44W **89** F2
Múggia _Italy_ 45°36N 13°43E **93** C10
Mughal Sarai _India_ 25°18N 83°7E **125** G10
Mughalzhar Taūy
Kazakhstan 49°0N 58°40E **108** C5
Mughayrā' _Si. Arabia_ 29°17N 37°41E **128** D3
Mugi _Japan_ 33°40N 134°25E **113** H7
Mugia = Muxia _Spain_ 43°3N 9°10W **88** B1
Mugila, Mts.
Dem. Rep. of the Congo 7°0S 28°50E **142** D2
Muğla _Turkey_ 37°15N 28°22E **104** D3
Muğla □ _Turkey_ 37°15N 28°0E **99** D10
Müglizh _Bulgaria_ 42°37N 25°32E **97** D11
Mugodzhary = Mughalzhar Taūy
Kazakhstan 49°0N 58°40E **108** C5
Mugu _Nepal_ 29°45N 82°30E **125** E10
Mugu Karnali →
Nepal 29°38N 81°51E **125** E9
Muhala
Dem. Rep. of the Congo 5°40S 28°43E **142** D2
Muhammad, Râs _Egypt_ 27°44N 34°16E **128** E2
Muhammad Qol _Sudan_ 20°53N 37°9E **137** C4
Muhammadabad _India_ 26°4N 83°25E **125** F10
Muḩāyil _Si. Arabia_ 18°33N 42°3E **131** D3
Muhesi → _Tanzania_ 7°0S 35°20E **142** D4
Mühlacker _Germany_ 48°57N 8°51E **77** G4
Mühldorf _Germany_ 48°14N 12°32E **77** G8
Mühlhausen _Germany_ 51°12N 10°27E **76** D6
Mühlig Hofmann fjell
Antarctica 72°30S 5°0E **5** D3
Mühlviertel _Austria_ 48°30N 14°10E **78** C7
Muhos _Finland_ 64°47N 25°59E **60** D21
Muhu _Estonia_ 58°36N 23°11E **84** C2

Muhutwe Tanzania 1°35S 31°45E 142 C3
Mui Wo China 22°16N 114°0E 111 a
Muileann gCearr, An = Mullingar
  Ireland 53°31N 7°21W 64 C4
Muine Bheag = Bagenalstown
  Ireland 52°42N 6°58W 64 D5
Muineachán = Monaghan
  Ireland 54°15N 6°57W 64 B5
Muir, L. Australia 34°30S 116°40E 149 F2
Muir of Ord U.K. 57°32N 4°28W 65 D4
Mujeres, I. Mexico 21°13N 86°43W 182 B2
Muka, Tanjung
  Malaysia 5°28N 100°11E 121 c
Mukacheve Ukraine 48°27N 22°45E 80 B7
Mukachevo = Mukacheve
  Ukraine 48°27N 22°45E 80 B7
Mukah Malaysia 2°55N 112°5E 118 D4
Mukandwara India 24°49N 75°59E 124 G6
Mukawwa, Geziret
  Egypt 23°55N 35°53E 137 C4
Mukawwar Sudan 20°50N 37°17E 137 C4
Mukdahan Thailand 16°32N 104°43E 120 D5
Mukdahan □ Thailand 16°26N 104°40E 120 D5
Mukden = Shenyang
  China 41°48N 123°27E 115 D12
Mukerian India 31°57N 75°37E 124 D6
Mukhavyets → Belarus 52°5N 23°39E 83 F10
Mukher India 18°42N 77°22E 126 E3
Mukhtolovo Russia 55°29N 43°15E 86 C6
Mukinbudin Australia 30°55S 118°5E 149 F2
Mukishi
  Dem. Rep. of the Congo 8°30S 24°44E 143 D1
Muko Phetra △ Thailand 6°57N 99°33E 121 J2
Mukomuko Indonesia 2°30S 101°10E 118 E2
Mukomwenze
  Dem. Rep. of the Congo 6°49S 27°15E 142 D2
Mukono Uganda 0°21N 32°45E 142 B3
Muktinath Nepal 28°49N 83°53E 125 E10
Muktsar India 30°30N 74°30E 124 D6
Mukur = Moqor
  Afghan. 32°50N 67°42E 124 C2
Mukutuwa → Canada 53°10N 97°24W 163 C9
Mukwela Zambia 17°0S 26°40E 143 F2
Mul India 20°4N 79°40E 126 D4
Mula Spain 38°3N 1°33W 91 G3
Mula → India 18°34N 74°21E 126 E2
Mula → Pakistan 27°57N 67°36E 124 F2
Mulange
  Dem. Rep. of the Congo 3°40S 27°10E 142 D2
Mulanje, Mt. Malawi 16°2S 35°33E 143 F4
Mulbagal India 13°10N 78°24E 127 H4
Mulberry U.S.A. 27°54N 81°59W 179 H8
Mulchatna → U.S.A. 59°40N 157°7W 166 D8
Mulchén Chile 37°45S 72°20W 190 D1
Mulde → Germany 51°53N 12°15E 76 D8
Mule Creek Junction
  U.S.A. 43°23N 104°13W 168 E11
Muleba Tanzania 1°50S 31°37E 142 C3
Mulegé Mexico 26°53N 111°59W 180 B2
Muleshoe U.S.A. 34°13N 102°43W 176 D3
Mulgrave Canada 45°38N 61°31W 165 C7
Mulgrave I. = Badu
  Australia 10°7S 142°11E 150 a
Mulhacén Spain 37°4N 3°20W 89 H7
Mülheim Germany 51°25N 6°54E 76 D2
Mulhouse France 47°40N 7°20E 71 E14
Muli China 27°52N 101°8E 116 D3
Muling China 44°35N 130°10E 115 B16
Mulki India 13°6N 74°48E 127 H2
Mull U.K. 56°25N 5°56W 65 E3
Mull, Sound of U.K. 56°30N 5°50W 65 E3
Mullach Íde = Malahide
  Ireland 53°26N 6°9W 64 C5
Mullaittivu Sri Lanka 9°15N 80°49E 127 K5
Mullen U.S.A. 42°3N 101°1W 172 D3
Mullengudgery
  Australia 31°43S 147°23E 151 B4
Mullens U.S.A. 37°35N 81°23W 173 G13
Muller, Pegunungan
  Indonesia 0°30N 113°30E 118 D4
Mullet Pen. Ireland 54°13N 10°2W 64 B1
Mullewa Australia 28°29S 115°30E 149 E2
Möllheim Germany 47°47N 7°36E 77 H3
Mulligan → Australia 25°0S 139°0E 150 D2
Mullingar Ireland 53°31N 7°21W 64 C4
Mullins U.S.A. 34°12N 79°15W 177 D15
Mullsjö Sweden 57°56N 13°55E 63 G7
Mullumbimby
  Australia 28°30S 153°30E 151 D5
Mulobezi Zambia 16°45S 25°7E 143 F2
Mulonga Plain Zambia 16°20S 22°40E 141 H4
Mulroy B. Ireland 55°15N 7°46W 64 A4
Mulshi I. India 18°30N 73°48E 126 E1
Multai India 21°50N 78°21E 126 D4
Multan Pakistan 30°15N 71°36E 124 D4
Mulug India 18°11N 79°57E 126 E4
Mulumbe, Mts.
  Dem. Rep. of the Congo 8°40S 27°30E 143 D2
Mulungushi Dam
  Zambia 14°48S 28°48E 143 E2
Mululu L. Australia 33°15S 143°20E 152 B5
Mulvane U.S.A. 37°29N 97°15W 172 G5
Mulwad Sudan 18°45N 30°39E 137 D3
Mulwala Australia 35°59S 146°0E 153 C7
Mulwala, L. Australia 35°59S 146°1E 151 C4
Mumbai India 18°56N 72°50E 126 E1
Mumbwa Zambia 15°0S 27°0E 143 E2
Mumias Kenya 0°20N 34°29E 142 C4
Mummel Gulf △
  Australia 31°17S 151°51E 153 A9
Mumra Russia 45°45N 47°41E 87 H8
Mun → Thailand 15°19N 105°30E 120 E5
Muna Indonesia 5°0S 122°30E 119 F6
Munabao India 25°45N 70°17E 124 G4
Munamagi Estonia 57°43N 27°4E 84 D4
Munaung Burma 18°45N 93°40E 123 K18
Munaung I. = Cheduba I.
  Burma 18°45N 93°40E 123 K18
Muncan Indonesia 8°34S 115°11E 119 K18
Muncar Indonesia 8°26S 114°20E 119 J17
Münchberg Germany 50°11N 11°47E 77 E7
Müncheberg Germany 52°30N 14°9E 76 C10
Münchberg Germany 50°11N 11°47E 77 E7
München Franz Josef Strauss ✈
  (MUC) Germany 48°21N 11°47E 77 G7
Munchen-Gladbach = Mönchengladbach
  Germany 51°11N 6°27E 76 D2
Muncho Lake Canada 59°0N 125°50W 162 B3
Munch'ŏn N. Korea 39°14N 127°19E 115 E14
Muncie U.S.A. 40°12N 85°23W 173 E11

Muncoonie L. West
  Australia 25°12S 138°40E 150 D2
Mundabbera Australia 25°36S 151°18E 151 D5
Mundakayam India 9°30N 76°50E 127 K3
Mundal Sri Lanka 7°48N 79°48E 127 L4
Munday U.S.A. 33°27N 99°38W 176 E5
Mundemba Cameroon 4°57N 8°52E 139 E6
Münden Germany 51°25N 9°38E 76 D5
Münden □ Germany 51°28N 9°42E 76 D5
Mundiwindi Australia 23°47S 120°9E 148 D3
Mundo → Spain 38°30N 2°15W 91 G2
Mundo Novo Brazil 11°50S 40°29W 189 D22
Mundra India 22°54N 69°48E 124 H3
Mundrabilla Australia 31°52S 127°51E 149 F4
Munera Spain 39°2N 2°29W 91 F2
Muneru → India 16°45N 80°3E 126 F4
Mungallala Australia 26°28S 147°34E 151 D4
Mungallala Cr. →
  Australia 28°53S 147°5E 151 D4
Mungana Australia 17°8S 144°27E 150 B3
Mungaoli India 24°24N 78°7E 124 G8
Mungari Mozam. 17°12S 33°30E 143 F3
Mungbere
  Dem. Rep. of the Congo 2°36N 28°28E 142 B2
Mungeli India 22°4N 81°41E 125 H9
Munger India 25°23N 86°30E 125 G12
Mungerannie Australia 28°1S 138°39E 151 A2
Mungilli ○ Australia 25°14S 124°17E 149 E3
Mungkan Kandju △
  Australia 13°35S 142°52E 150 A3
Mungkarta ○ Australia 20°22S 134°2E 150 C1
Mungo, L. Australia 33°45S 143°0E 152 B5
Mungo △ Australia 33°44S 143°6E 152 B5
Munich = München
  Germany 48°8N 11°34E 77 G7
Munising U.S.A. 46°25N 86°40W 172 B10
Munka-Ljungby Sweden 56°16N 12°58E 63 H6
Munkebo Denmark 55°27N 10°34E 63 J4
Munkedal Sweden 58°28N 11°40E 63 F5
Munkfors Sweden 59°47N 13°30E 62 E7
Munku-Sardyk
  Russia 51°45N 100°20E 107 D11
Münnerstadt Germany 50°14N 10°12E 77 E6
Munnsville U.S.A. 42°58N 75°35W 175 D9
Muñoz Gamero, Pen.
  Chile 52°30S 73°5W 192 G2
Munroe L. Canada 59°13N 98°35W 163 B9
Munsan S. Korea 37°51N 126°48E 115 F14
Munster France 48°2N 7°8E 71 D14
Münster Niedersachsen,
  Germany 52°58N 10°5E 76 C6
Münster Nordrhein-Westfalen,
  Germany 51°58N 7°37E 76 D3
Munster □ Ireland 52°18N 8°44W 64 D3
Muntadgin Australia 31°45S 118°33E 149 F2
Muntele Mare, Vf.
  Romania 46°30N 23°12E 81 D8
Muntok Indonesia 2°5S 105°10E 118 E3
Munzur Dağları Turkey 39°30N 39°10E 105 C8
Muong Nhie Vietnam 22°12N 102°28E 116 F4
Muong Sen Vietnam 19°24N 104°8E 120 C5
Muong Xia Vietnam 20°19N 104°50E 120 B5
Muonio Finland 67°57N 23°40E 60 C20
Muonio älv = Muonionjoki →
  Finland 67°11N 23°34E 60 C20
Muonioälven = Muonionjoki →
  Finland 67°11N 23°34E 60 C20
Muonionjoki →
  Finland 67°11N 23°34E 60 C20
Mupa → Mozam. 18°58S 35°54E 143 F4
Muping China 37°22N 121°36E 115 F11
Muqdisho Somalia 2°2N 45°25E 131 G4
Mur → Austria 46°18N 16°52E 79 E9
Mûr-de-Bretagne France 48°12N 3°0W 70 D4
Muradiye Manisa, Turkey 38°39N 27°21E 99 C9
Muradiye Van, Turkey 39°0N 43°44E 105 C10
Murakami Japan 38°14N 139°29E 112 E9
Muralag = Prince of Wales I.
  Australia 10°40S 142°10E 150 A3
Murallón, Cerro Chile 49°48S 73°30W 192 C2
Muranda Rwanda 1°52S 29°20E 142 C2
Murang'a Kenya 0°45S 37°9E 142 C4
Murashi Russia 59°30N 49°0E 106 D5
Murat France 45°7N 2°53E 72 C6
Murat → Turkey 38°46N 40°0E 105 C9
Murat Dağı Turkey 38°55N 29°43E 99 C11
Murato France 42°35N 9°20E 73 F13
Murau Austria 47°6N 14°10E 78 D7
Murava Belarus 52°39N 24°15E 83 F11
Muravera Italy 39°25N 9°34E 94 C2
Murayama Japan 38°30N 140°25E 112 E10
Murça Portugal 41°24N 7°28W 88 D3
Murchison N.Z. 41°49S 172°21E 155 B7
Murchison → Australia 27°45S 114°0E 149 E1
Murchison, Mt. N.Z. 43°3S 171°2E 155 D6
Murchison, Mt.
  Antarctica 73°25S 166°20E 55 D11
Murchison Falls Uganda 2°15N 31°30E 142 B3
Murchison Falls △
  Uganda 2°17N 31°48E 142 B3
Murchison Mts. U.S.A. 45°13S 167°23E 155 F2
Murchison Ra.
  Australia 20°0S 134°10E 150 C1
Murchison Rapids
  Malawi 15°55S 34°35E 143 F3
Murchison Roadhouse
  Australia 27°39S 116°14E 149 E2
Murcia Spain 38°5N 1°10W 91 G3
Murcia □ Spain 37°50N 1°30W 91 H3
Murdo U.S.A. 43°53N 100°43W 172 D3
Murdoch Pt. Australia 14°37S 144°55E 150 A3
Mürefte Turkey 40°40N 27°4E 105 B10
Mureş □ Romania 46°45N 24°40E 81 D9
Mureş → Romania 46°15N 20°13E 80 D5
Mureşul = Mureş →
  Romania 46°15N 20°13E 80 D5
Muret France 43°30N 1°20E 72 E5
Murewa Zimbabwe 17°39S 31°47E 145 A5
Murfreesboro N.C.,
  U.S.A. 36°27N 77°6W 177 C16
Murfreesboro Tenn.,
  U.S.A. 35°51N 86°24W 177 D11
Murgap Tajikistan 38°10N 74°2E 109 E8
Murgap → Turkmenistan 38°18N 61°12E 129 B9
Murgenella Australia 11°34S 132°56E 148 B5
Murgeni Romania 46°12N 28°1E 81 D13
Murgha Kibzai
  Pakistan 30°44N 69°25E 124 D3

Murghob = Murgap
  Tajikistan 38°10N 74°2E 109 E8
Murgon Australia 26°15S 151°54E 151 D5
Muri India 23°22N 85°52E 125 H11
Muria Indonesia 6°36S 110°53E 119 G14
Muriaé Brazil 21°8S 42°23W 191 A7
Murias de Paredes Spain 42°52N 6°11W 88 C4
Murici Brazil 9°19S 35°56W 189 B3
Muriel Mine Zimbabwe 17°14S 30°40E 143 F3
Muriwai Beach N.Z. 36°50S 174°26E 154 C3
Murliganj India 25°54N 86°59E 125 G12
Murmansk Russia 68°57N 33°10E 60 B25
Murmashi Russia 68°47N 32°42E 60 B25
Muro France 42°34N 8°54E 73 F12
Muro Spain 39°44N 3°3E 90 B10
Muro, C. di France 41°44N 8°37E 73 G12
Muro de Alcoy Spain 38°46N 0°26W 91 G4
Murom Russia 55°35N 42°3E 86 C6
Muroran Japan 42°25N 141°0E 112 C10
Muros Spain 42°45N 9°5W 88 C1
Muros e Noya, Ría de →
  Spain 42°45N 9°0W 88 C1
Muroto Japan 33°18N 134°9E 113 H7
Muroto-Misaki Japan 33°15N 134°10E 113 H7
Murovani Kurylivtsi
  Ukraine 48°44N 27°31E 81 B12
Murowana Goślina
  Poland 52°35N 17°0E 83 F3
Murphy U.S.A. 43°13N 116°33W 168 E5
Murphys U.S.A. 38°8N 120°28W 170 G6
Murray Australia 9°56S 144°2E 150 a
Murray Ky., U.S.A. 36°37N 88°19W 172 G9
Murray Utah, U.S.A. 40°40N 111°53W 168 F8
Murray → Australia 35°20S 139°22E 152 C3
Murray, L. U.S.A. 34°3N 81°13W 178 A8
Murray Bridge
  Australia 35°6S 139°14E 152 C3
Murray Fracture Zone
  Pac. Oc. 35°0N 130°0W 157 D14
Murray Harbour
  Canada 46°0N 62°28W 165 C7
Murray River △
  Australia 34°23S 140°32E 151 E3
Murray-Sunset △
  Australia 34°45S 141°30E 152 C4
Murraysburg S. Africa 31°58S 23°47E 144 D3
Murree Pakistan 33°56N 73°28E 124 C5
Murrieta U.S.A. 33°33N 117°13W 171 M9
Murro di Porco, Capo
  Italy 37°0N 15°20E 95 F8
Murrumbateman
  Australia 34°58S 149°0E 153 C8
Murrumbidgee →
  Australia 34°43S 143°12E 152 C5
Murrumburrah
  Australia 34°32S 148°22E 153 C8
Murrurundi Australia 31°42S 150°51E 153 A9
Murshid Sudan 21°40N 31°10E 137 C3
Murshidabad India 24°11N 88°19E 125 G13
Murska Sobota
  Slovenia 46°39N 16°12E 93 B13
Murtazapur India 20°40N 77°25E 126 D3
Murtle L. Canada 52°8N 119°38W 162 C5
Murtoa Australia 36°35S 142°28E 152 D5
Murtosa Portugal 40°44N 8°40W 88 E2
Muru → Brazil 8°9S 70°45W 188 B3
Murud India 18°19N 72°58E 126 E1
Murunga Tanzania 4°12S 31°10E 142 C3
Murupara N.Z. 38°28S 176°42E 154 B5
Mururoa
  French Polynesia 21°52S 138°55W 157 K14
Murwara India 23°46N 80°28E 125 H9
Murwillumbah
  Australia 28°18S 153°27E 151 D5
Mürz → Austria 47°30N 15°25E 78 D8
Murzuq Libya 25°53N 13°57E 137 C8
Murzuq, Idehân Libya 24°50N 13°51E 135 D8
Mürzzuschlag Austria 47°36N 15°41E 78 D8
Mus India 7°59N 93°21E 123 K7
Muş Turkey 38°45N 41°30E 105 C9
Muş □ Turkey 38°45N 41°30E 105 C9
Mûsa, Gebel Egypt 28°33N 33°59E 128 D2
Musa Khel Pakistan 30°59N 69°52E 124 D3
Mûsa Qal'eh Afghan. 32°20N 64°50E 124 C4
Musafirkhana India 26°22N 81°48E 125 F9
Musala Bulgaria 42°13N 23°37E 96 D7
Musala Indonesia 1°41N 98°28E 118 D1
Musan N. Korea 42°12N 129°12E 115 C15
Musangu
  Dem. Rep. of the Congo 10°28S 23°55E 143 E1
Musasa Tanzania 3°25S 31°30E 142 C2
Muscat = Masqat
  Oman 23°37N 58°36E 131 C6
Muscatine U.S.A. 41°25N 91°3W 172 E8
Muscle Shoals U.S.A. 34°45N 87°40W 177 D11
Musengezi = Unsengedsi →
  Zimbabwe 15°43S 31°14E 143 F3
Musgrave Harbour
  Canada 49°27N 53°58W 165 C9
Musgrave Ranges
  Australia 26°0S 132°0E 149 E5
Mushie
  Dem. Rep. of the Congo 2°56S 16°55E 140 E3
Mushin Nigeria 6°31N 3°21E 139 D5
Musi → India 16°41N 79°40E 126 F4
Musi → Indonesia 2°20S 104°56E 118 E2
Musina S. Africa 22°20S 30°5E 145 B5
Musiri India 10°56N 78°27E 127 J4
Muskauer Park Europe 51°34N 14°43E 76 D10
Muskeg → Canada 60°20N 123°20W 162 A4
Muskegon U.S.A. 43°14N 86°16W 172 D9
Muskegon → U.S.A. 43°14N 86°21W 172 D9
Muskegon Heights
  U.S.A. 43°12N 86°16W 172 D9
Muskogee U.S.A. 35°45N 95°22W 176 D7
Muskoka, L. Canada 45°0N 79°25W 174 B5
Muskoka Falls Canada 44°59N 79°17W 174 B5
Muskwa → Canada 58°47N 122°48W 162 B4
Muslimiyah Syria 36°19N 37°12E 128 B3
Musmar Sudan 18°13N 35°40E 137 D4
Musofu Zambia 13°30S 29°0E 143 E2
Musoma Tanzania 1°30S 33°48E 142 C3
Musquaro, L. Canada 50°38N 61°5W 165 B7
Musquodoboit Harbour
  Canada 44°50N 63°9W 165 D7
Musselburgh U.K. 55°57N 3°2W 65 F5

Musselshell →
  U.S.A. 47°21N 107°57W 168 C10
Mussende Angola 10°32S 16°5E 140 G3
Mussidan France 45°2N 0°22E 72 C4
Mussomeli Italy 37°35N 13°45E 94 E6
Mussoorie India 30°27N 78°6E 124 D8
Mussuco Angola 17°2S 19°3E 144 A2
Mustafakemalpaşa
  Turkey 40°2N 28°24E 97 F12
Mustang Nepal 29°10N 83°55E 125 E10
Musters, L. Argentina 45°20S 69°25W 192 C3
Musudan N. Korea 40°50N 129°43E 115 D15
Muswellbrook
  Australia 32°16S 150°56E 153 B9
Muszyna Poland 49°22N 20°55E 83 J7
Müt Egypt 25°28N 28°58E 137 C5
Mut Turkey 36°40N 33°28E 104 D5
Mutanda Mozam. 21°0S 33°34E 145 B5
Mutanda Zambia 12°24S 26°13E 143 E2
Mutare Zimbabwe 18°58S 32°38E 143 F3
Mutawintji △
  Australia 31°10S 142°30E 151 E3
Mutha Kenya 1°48S 38°26E 142 C4
Muting Indonesia 7°23S 140°20E 119 F10
Mutirikwe Dam
  Zimbabwe 20°15S 31°0E 143 G3
Mutki = Mirtağ Turkey 38°23N 41°56E 128 B4
Mutoko Zimbabwe 17°24S 32°13E 145 A5
Mutomo Kenya 1°51S 38°12E 142 C4
Mutoray Russia 60°56N 101°0E 107 C11
Mutsamudu Comoros Is. 12°10S 44°25E 141 a
Mutshatsha
  Dem. Rep. of the Congo 10°35S 24°20E 143 E1
Mutsu Japan 41°5N 140°55E 112 D10
Mutsu-Wan Japan 41°5N 140°55E 112 D10
Muttaburra Australia 22°38S 144°29E 150 C3
Muttalip Turkey 39°50N 30°32E 99 B12
Mutton I. Ireland 52°49N 9°32W 64 D2
Muttukuru India 14°16N 80°6E 127 G5
Muttuáli Mozam. 14°55S 37°0E 143 E4
Mutum Biyu Nigeria 8°40N 10°50E 139 D7
Mutumba Burundi 3°25S 29°21E 142 C2
Mutur Sri Lanka 8°27N 81°16E 127 K5
Muweilih Egypt 30°42N 34°19E 130 E3
Muxía Spain 43°9N 9°10W 88 B1
Muy Muy Nic. 12°39N 85°36W 182 D2
Muyinga Burundi 3°14S 30°33E 142 C3
Mûynoq Uzbekistan 43°44N 59°10E 108 D5
Muyunkum, Peski = Moyynqum
  Kazakhstan 44°12N 71°0E 109 D8
Muz Tag China 36°25N 87°25E 109 E11
Muzaffarabad Pakistan 34°25N 73°30E 125 B5
Muzaffargarh Pakistan 30°5N 71°14E 124 D4
Muzaffarnagar India 29°26N 77°40E 124 E7
Muzaffarpur India 26°7N 85°23E 125 F11
Muzafirpur Pakistan 30°58N 69°9E 124 D3
Mużakowski, Park = Muskauer
  Park Europe 51°34N 14°43E 76 D10
Muzhi Russia 65°25N 64°40E 106 C7
Muzillac France 47°35N 2°30W 70 E4
Muztagh-Ata China 38°17N 75°7E 109 E9
Muzūra Egypt 30°26N 76°14E 124 D7
Mvuma Zimbabwe 19°16S 30°30E 143 F3
Mvurwi Zimbabwe 17°0S 30°57E 143 F3
Mwabvi △ Malawi 16°42S 35°0E 143 F3
Mwali = Mohéli
  Comoros Is. 12°20S 43°40E 141 a
Mwambo Tanzania 10°30S 40°22E 143 E5
Mwandi Zambia 17°30S 24°51E 143 F1
Mwanza
  Dem. Rep. of the Congo 7°55S 26°43E 142 D2
Mwanza Tanzania 2°30S 32°58E 142 C3
Mwanza Zambia 16°58S 24°28E 143 F1
Mwanza □ Tanzania 2°0S 33°0E 142 C3
Mwaya Tanzania 9°32S 33°55E 143 D3
Mweelrea Ireland 53°39N 9°49W 64 C2
Mweka
  Dem. Rep. of the Congo 4°50S 21°34E 140 E4
Mwene-Ditu
  Dem. Rep. of the Congo 6°35S 22°27E 140 F4
Mwenezi Zimbabwe 21°15S 30°48E 143 G3
Mwenezi → Mozam. 22°40S 31°50E 143 G3
Mwenga
  Dem. Rep. of the Congo 3°1S 28°28E 142 C2
Mweru, L. Zambia 9°0S 28°40E 143 D2
Mweru Wantipa △
  Zambia 8°39S 29°25E 143 D2
Mweza Range Zimbabwe 21°0S 30°0E 143 G3
Mwilambwe
  Dem. Rep. of the Congo 8°7S 25°5E 142 D2
Mwimbi Tanzania 8°38S 31°39E 143 D3
Mwingi Kenya 0°56S 38°4E 142 C4
Mwinilunga Zambia 11°43S 24°25E 143 E1
My Son Vietnam 15°48N 108°7E 120 E7
My Tho Vietnam 10°29N 106°23E 121 G6
Mya, O. → Algeria 30°46N 4°54E 136 B6
Myajlar India 26°15N 70°20E 124 F4
Myakka → U.S.A. 26°56N 82°11W 179 J7
Myall Lakes △
  Australia 32°25S 152°30E 153 B10
Myanaung Burma 18°18N 95°22E 123 K19
Myanmar = Burma ■
  Asia 21°0N 96°30E 123 J20
Myaungmya Burma 16°30N 94°40E 123 L19
Mycenae = Mykenes
  Greece 37°43N 22°46E 98 D4
Myedna Belarus 51°52N 23°42E 83 G10
Myeik = Mergui Burma 12°26N 98°34E 120 F2
Myeik Kyunzu Burma 11°30N 97°30E 121 G1
Myerstown U.S.A. 40°22N 76°19W 175 F8
Myingyan Burma 21°30N 95°20E 123 J19
Myitkyina Burma 25°24N 97°26E 123 G20
Myjava Slovak Rep. 48°41N 17°37E 79 G10
Mykines Greece 37°43N 22°46E 98 D4
Mykines Færoe Is. 62°7N 7°35W 60 E9
Mykolaiv Ukraine 46°58N 32°0E 85 J7
Mykolayiv □ Ukraine 47°35N 31°58E 85 J7
Mykolayiv Ukraine 47°30N 25°25E 99 D7
Mykonos Greece 37°30N 25°25E 99 D7
Mylius Erichsen Land
  Greenland 81°30N 27°0E 54 B6
Mymensingh Bangla. 24°45N 90°24E 123 G17
Mynydd Du U.K. 51°52N 3°50W 67 F4
Mýrdalsjökull Iceland 63°40N 19°6W 60 D4
Myrhorod Ukraine 49°58N 33°37E 85 H7
Myrina Greece 39°53N 25°4E 98 B7
Myrtle Beach U.S.A. 33°42N 78°53W 177 E15
Myrtle Creek U.S.A. 43°1N 123°17W 168 E2
Myrtle Grove U.S.A. 30°24N 87°19W 178 F9
Myrtle Point U.S.A. 43°4N 124°8W 168 E1
Myrtleford Australia 36°34S 146°44E 153 D7

Myrtoan Sea = Mirtoo Sea
  Greece 37°0N 23°20E 98 D5
Myrtou Cyprus 35°18N 33°4E 101 D12
Myrviken Sweden 62°58N 14°20E 62 B8
Mysia Turkey 39°50N 27°0E 97 G11
Myślenice Poland 49°51N 19°57E 83 J6
Myślibórz Poland 52°55N 14°50E 83 F1
Mysłowice Poland 50°15N 19°12E 83 H6
Mysore = Karnataka □
  India 13°15N 77°0E 127 H3
Mysore = Mysuru
  India 12°17N 76°41E 127 H3
Mystras Greece 37°4N 22°22E 98 D4
Mysuru India 12°17N 76°41E 127 H3
Myszków Poland 50°45N 19°22E 83 H6
Myszyniec Poland 53°23N 21°21E 82 E8
Mytilene = Mitilini
  Greece 39°6N 26°35E 99 B8
Mytishchi Russia 55°50N 37°50E 84 F9
Mývatn Iceland 65°36N 17°0W 60 D5
M'zab, Oued → Algeria 32°15N 5°0E 136 B5
M'Zab Valley = M'zab, Oued →
  Algeria 32°15N 5°0E 136 B5
Mže → Czech Rep. 49°46N 13°24E 78 B6
Mzimba Malawi 11°30S 33°55E 143 E3
Mzimkulu → S. Africa 30°44S 30°28E 145 E5
Mzimvubu → S. Africa 31°38S 29°33E 145 E4
Mzuzu Malawi 11°30S 33°55E 143 E3

N

Na Clocha Liatha = Greystones
  Ireland 53°9N 6°5W 64 C5
Na Haeo △ Thailand 17°31N 100°58E 120 D3
Na Hearadh = Harris
  U.K. 57°50N 6°55W 65 D2
Na Hearadh, Caolas = Harris, Sd.
  of U.K. 57°44N 7°6W 65 D1
Na Noi Thailand 18°19N 100°43E 120 C3
Na Phao Laos 17°35N 105°44E 120 D5
Na Sam Vietnam 22°3N 106°37E 116 F6
Na Sceirí = Skerries
  Ireland 53°35N 6°6W 64 C5
Na Thon Thailand 9°32N 99°56E 121 b
Naab → Germany 49°1N 12°2E 77 F8
Naama Algeria 33°16N 0°19E 136 B4
Naama □ Algeria 33°15N 0°45E 136 B4
Naantali Finland 60°29N 22°2E 64 B1
Naas Ireland 53°12N 6°40W 64 C5
Nababeep S. Africa 29°36S 17°46E 144 C2
Nabadwip = Navadwip
  India 23°34N 88°20E 125 H13
Nabawa Australia 28°30S 114°48E 149 E1
Nabberu, L. Australia 25°50S 120°30E 149 E3
Nabburg Germany 49°27N 12°11E 77 F8
Naberezhnyye Chelny
  Russia 55°42N 52°19E 86 C11
Nai Yong Thailand 8°14N 98°22E 121 a
Naicá Mexico 27°53N 105°31W 180 B3
Naicam Canada 52°30N 104°30W 163 C8
Naikoon □ Canada 53°55N 131°55W 162 C2
Naikul India 21°20N 84°58E 126 B7
Naila Germany 50°19N 11°42E 77 E7
Naimisharanya India 27°21N 80°30E 125 F9
Naimona'nyi Feng
  China 30°26N 81°18E 125 E9
Nain Canada 56°34N 61°40W 165 A7
Na'īn Iran 32°54N 53°0E 129 C7
Naini Tal India 29°30N 79°30E 125 E8
Nainpur India 22°30N 80°10E 125 H8
Naintré France 46°46N 0°29E 70 F7
Nainwa India 25°46N 75°51E 124 G6
Naipu Romania 44°12N 25°47E 81 E10
Nairai Fiji 17°49S 179°15E 155 a
Nairn U.K. 57°35N 3°53W 65 D5
Nairobi Kenya 1°17S 36°48E 142 C4
Nairobi □ Kenya 1°22S 36°50E 142 C4
Naissaar Estonia 59°34N 24°29E 84 A3
Naitaba Fiji 17°0S 179°16W 155 a
Naivasha Kenya 0°40S 36°30E 142 C4
Naivasha, L. Kenya 0°48S 36°30E 142 C4
Najac France 44°14N 1°58E 72 D5
Najaf = An Najaf Iraq 32°3N 44°15E 105 C4
Najafābād Iran 32°40N 51°15E 129 C6
Najd Si. Arabia 26°30N 42°0E 131 E5
Nájera Spain 42°26N 2°48W 89 C8
Najerilla → Spain 42°32N 2°48W 89 C8
Najibabad India 29°40N 78°20E 124 E8
Najin N. Korea 42°12N 130°15E 115 C16
Najmah Si. Arabia 26°42N 50°6E 129 E6
Najrān Si. Arabia 17°34N 44°18E 131 E5
Nakadōri-Shima Japan 32°57N 129°4E 113
Nakalagba
  Dem. Rep. of the Congo 2°50N 27°58E 142 B2
Nakambé = White Volta →
  Ghana 9°10N 1°15W 139 D4
Nakaminato Japan 36°21N 140°36E 113 F10
Nakamura = Shimanto
  Japan 32°59N 132°56E 113 H6
Nakano Japan 36°45N 138°22E 113 F9
Nakano-Shima Japan 29°51N 129°52E 113 K4
Nakashibetsu Japan 43°33N 144°59E 112 C12
Nakfa Eritrea 16°40N 38°32E 131 K1
Nakha Yai, Ko Thailand 8°3N 98°28E 121 a
Nakhichevan = Naxçıvan
  Azerbaijan 39°12N 45°15E 105 C11
Nakhichevan Rep. = Naxçıvan □
  Azerbaijan 39°25N 45°26E 105 C11
Nakhl Iran 29°55N 33°43E 130
Nakhl-e Taqī Iran 27°28N 52°36E 129
Nakhodka Russia 42°53N 132°54E 112
Nakhon Nayok
  Thailand 14°12N 101°13E 120 a
Nakhon Pathom
  Thailand 13°49N 100°3E 121 a
Nakhon Phanom
  Thailand 17°23N 104°43E 120 D5
Nakhon Ratchasima
  Thailand 14°59N 102°12E 120 D4
Nakhon Sawan
  Thailand 15°35N 100°10E 120 a
Nakhon Si Thammarat
  Thailand 8°29N 100°0E 121 b
Nakhon Thai Thailand 17°5N 100°44E 120
Nakhtarana India 23°20N 69°15E 124
Nakina Canada 50°10N 86°40W 164
Nakło nad Notecią Poland 53°9N 17°38E 83
Nako Burkina Faso 10°0N 3°0W 138
Nakodar India 31°8N 75°31E 124
Nakskov Denmark 54°50N 11°8E 63

Nagar Karnul India 16°29N 78°20E 127
Nagar Parkar Pakistan 24°28N 70°46E 124
Nagaram India 18°21N 80°26E 126
Nagarhole △ India 12°0N 76°14E 127
Nagari Hills India 13°3N 79°45E 127
Nagarjuna Sagar India 16°30N 79°13E 127
Nagasaki Japan 32°47N 129°50E 113
Nagasaki □ Japan 32°50N 129°40E 113
Nagato Japan 34°19N 131°5E 113
Nagaur India 27°15N 73°45E 124
Nagbhir India 20°34N 79°55E 126
Nagda India 23°27N 75°25E 124
Nagercoil India 8°12N 77°26E 127
Nagina India 29°30N 78°30E 124
Nagīneh Iran 34°20N 57°15E 128
Nagir Pakistan 36°12N 74°42E 125
Naglarby Sweden 60°25N 15°42E 62
Nagles Mts. Ireland 52°8N 8°30E 64
Nagod India 24°34N 80°36E 125
Nagold Germany 48°32N 8°43E 77
Nagold → Germany 48°52N 8°42E 77
Nagoorin Australia 24°17S 151°15E 150
Nagorno-Karabakh □
  Azerbaijan 39°55N 46°45E 105
Nagornyy Russia 55°58N 124°57E 107
Nagoya Japan 35°10N 136°50E 113
Nagoya ✈ (NGO)
  Japan 34°53N 136°45E 113
Nagpur India 21°8N 79°10E 126
Nagqu China 31°29N 92°3E 110
Nagua Dom. Rep. 19°23N 69°50W 183
Naguabo Puerto Rico 18°13N 65°44W 183
Nagurunguru ○
  Australia 16°45S 129°45E 148
Nagyatád Hungary 46°14N 17°22E 80
Nagyecsed Hungary 47°53N 22°24E 80
Nagykálló Hungary 47°53N 21°51E 80
Nagykanizsa Hungary 46°28N 17°0E 80
Nagykáta Hungary 47°25N 19°45E 80
Nagykőrös Hungary 47°5N 19°48E 80
Naha Japan 26°13N 127°42E 113
Nahan India 30°33N 77°18E 124
Nahanni → Canada 61°36N 125°41W 162
Nahanni Butte Canada 61°2N 123°31W 162
Nahargarh Mad. P.,
  India 24°10N 75°14E 124
Nahargarh Raj., India 24°55N 76°50E 124
Nahariyya Israel 33°1N 35°5E 130
Nahāvand Iran 34°10N 48°22E 128
Nahe → Germany 49°58N 7°54E 77
Nahīrne Ukraine 45°26N 28°27E 81
Nahiya, W. → Egypt 28°55N 31°0E 137
Nahuel Huapi, L.
  Argentina 41°0S 71°32W 192
Nahuel Huapi □
  Argentina 41°3S 71°59W 192
Nahuelbuta △ Chile 37°44S 72°57W 190
Nahunta U.S.A. 31°12N 81°59W 178
Nai Yong Thailand 8°14N 98°22E 121 a
Naicá Mexico 27°53N 105°31W 180
Naicam Canada 52°30N 104°30W 163
Naikoon △ Canada 53°55N 131°55W 162
Naikul India 21°20N 84°58E 126
Naila Germany 50°19N 11°42E 77
Naimisharanya India 27°21N 80°30E 125
Naimona'nyi Feng
  China 30°26N 81°18E 125
Nain Canada 56°34N 61°40W 165
Na'īn Iran 32°54N 53°0E 129
Naini Tal India 29°30N 79°30E 125
Nainpur India 22°30N 80°10E 125
Naintré France 46°46N 0°29E 70
Nainwa India 25°46N 75°51E 124
Naipu Romania 44°12N 25°47E 81
Nairai Fiji 17°49S 179°15E 155
Nairn U.K. 57°35N 3°53W 65
Nairobi Kenya 1°17S 36°48E 142
Nairobi □ Kenya 1°22S 36°50E 142
Naissaar Estonia 59°34N 24°29E 84
Naitaba Fiji 17°0S 179°16W 155
Naivasha Kenya 0°40S 36°30E 142
Naivasha, L. Kenya 0°48S 36°30E 142
Najac France 44°14N 1°58E 72
Najaf = An Najaf Iraq 32°3N 44°15E 105
Najafābād Iran 32°40N 51°15E 129
Najd Si. Arabia 26°30N 42°0E 131
Nájera Spain 42°26N 2°48W 89
Najerilla → Spain 42°32N 2°48W 89
Najibabad India 29°40N 78°20E 124
Najin N. Korea 42°12N 130°15E 115
Najmah Si. Arabia 26°42N 50°6E 129
Najrān Si. Arabia 17°34N 44°18E 131
Nakadōri-Shima Japan 32°57N 129°4E 113
Nakalagba
  Dem. Rep. of the Congo 2°50N 27°58E 142
Nakambé = White Volta →
  Ghana 9°10N 1°15W 139
Nakaminato Japan 36°21N 140°36E 113
Nakamura = Shimanto
  Japan 32°59N 132°56E 113
Nakano Japan 36°45N 138°22E 113
Nakano-Shima Japan 29°51N 129°52E 113
Nakashibetsu Japan 43°33N 144°59E 112
Nakfa Eritrea 16°40N 38°32E 131
Nakha Yai, Ko Thailand 8°3N 98°28E 121
Nakhichevan = Naxçıvan
  Azerbaijan 39°12N 45°15E 105
Nakhichevan Rep. = Naxçıvan □
  Azerbaijan 39°25N 45°26E 105
Nakhl Iran 29°55N 33°43E 130
Nakhl-e Taqī Iran 27°28N 52°36E 129
Nakhodka Russia 42°53N 132°54E 112
Nakhon Nayok
  Thailand 14°12N 101°13E 120
Nakhon Pathom
  Thailand 13°49N 100°3E 121
Nakhon Phanom
  Thailand 17°23N 104°43E 120
Nakhon Ratchasima
  Thailand 14°59N 102°12E 120
Nakhon Sawan
  Thailand 15°35N 100°10E 120
Nakhon Si Thammarat
  Thailand 8°29N 100°0E 121
Nakhon Thai Thailand 17°5N 100°44E 120
Nakhtarana India 23°20N 69°15E 124
Nakina Canada 50°10N 86°40W 164
Nakło nad Notecią Poland 53°9N 17°38E 83
Nako Burkina Faso 10°0N 3°0W 138
Nakodar India 31°8N 75°31E 124
Nakskov Denmark 54°50N 11°8E 63

ktong → S. Korea 35°7N 128°57E 115 G15
kuru Kenya 0°15S 36°4E 142 C4
kuru, L. Kenya 0°23S 36°5E 142 C4
kusp Canada 50°20N 117°45W 162 C5
l Pakistan 27°40N 66°12E 124 F2
l → Pakistan 25°20N 65°40E 124 E1
lázi India 24°3S 33°20E 145 B5
lchik Russia 43°30N 43°33E 87 J6
lerigu Ghana 10°35N 0°25W 139 C4
lgonda India 17°6N 79°15E 126 F4
lhati India 24°17N 87°52E 125 G12
liya India 23°16N 68°50E 124 H3
lumalai Hills India 15°30N 78°50E 127 J4
lhhan Turkey 40°11N 31°20E 104 B4
lón → Spain 43°32N 6°4W 88 B4
lubaale Dam Uganda 0°30N 33°5E 142 B3
lumasortoq Greenland 60°23N 44°28W 57 E6
m Can Vietnam 20°7S 106°40E 121 H5
m-ch'on N. Korea 38°15N 126°26E 115 E14
m Co China 30°30N 90°45E 110 E7
m Dinh Vietnam 20°25N 106°5E 116 G6
m Du, Quan Dao Vietnam 9°41N 104°21E 121 H5
m Hka → Burma 21°34N 95°41E 116 G2
m Loi → Burma 21°3N 98°27E 116 G3
m Nao △ Thailand 16°44N 101°32E 120 D3
m Ngum Res. Laos 18°35N 102°34E 120 C4
m Phan Vietnam 10°30N 106°0E 121 G6
m Phong Thailand 16°42N 102°52E 120 D3
m Theun Res. Laos 18°0N 104°48E 120 C4
m Tok Thailand 14°21N 99°4E 120 E2
m Un Res. Thailand 17°13N 103°44E 120 D4
macunde Angola 17°18S 15°50E 144 A2
macurra Mozam. 17°30S 36°50E 145 A6
madgi △ Australia 35°42S 149°0E 153 C8
mak, Daryācheh-ye Iran 34°30N 52°0E 129 C7
mak, Kavir-e Iran 34°30N 57°30E 129 C8
makkal India 11°13N 78°13E 127 J4
makzār, Daryācheh-ye Iran 34°0N 60°30E 129 C9
maland Namibia 20°5S 17°0E 144 B2
manga Kenya 2°33S 36°47E 142 C4
mangan Uzbekistan 41°0N 71°40E 109 D8
mangan □ Uzbekistan 41°0N 71°15E 109 D8
mapa Indonesia 13°43S 39°50E 143 E4
maqua △ S. Africa 30°37S 22°50E 144 D2
maqualand S. Africa 30°0S 17°25E 144 D2
masagali Uganda 1°2N 33°0E 142 B3
mber Indonesia 1°2S 134°49E 119 E8
mbour Australia 26°32S 152°58E 151 D5
mbouwalu = Nabouwalu Fiji 17°0S 178°45E 154 a
mbucca Heads Australia 30°37S 153°0E 153 A10
mbung △ Australia 30°30S 115°5E 149 F2
mcha Barwa China 29°40N 95°10E 110 F8
mche Bazar Nepal 27°51N 86°47E 125 F12
mchonjöm = Nam-ch'on N. Korea 38°15N 126°26E 115 E14
mecunda Mozam. 14°54S 37°37E 143 E4
menalala Fiji 17°8S 179°9E 154 a
meponda Mozam. 15°50S 39°50E 143 F4
mêst' nad Oslavou Czech Rep. 49°12N 16°10E 79 B9
mestovo Slovak Rep. 49°24N 19°25E 79 B12
metil Mozam. 16°24S 39°21E 143 F4
mew L. Canada 54°14N 101°50E 163 C8
mhkam Burma 23°50N 97°41E 116 E1
mialo Mozam. 14°55S 39°59E 143 E4
mib Desert Namibia 22°30S 15°0E 144 B2
mib-Naukluft △ Namibia 24°40S 15°16E 144 B2
mibe Angola 15°7S 12°11E 141 H2
mibe △ Angola 16°35S 12°30E 144 A1
mibia ■ Africa 22°0S 18°9E 144 B2
mibia Abyssal Plain Atl. Oc. 30°0S 5°30E 56 J12
mibwoestyn = Namib Desert Namibia 22°30S 15°0E 144 B2
mīn Iran 38°25N 48°30E 105 C13
minūs = Lubango Angola 14°55S 13°30E 141 G2
minūs = Lüderitz Angola 26°41S 15°8E 144 C2
mjeju S. Korea 33°14N 126°33E 115 H14
mlea Indonesia 3°18S 127°5E 119 E7
mous, O. en → Algeria 31°0N 0°15W 136 B3
mpa U.S.A. 43°34N 116°34W 168 E5
mpala Mali 15°20N 5°30W 138 B3
mp'o N. Korea 38°52N 125°10E 115 E13
mpula Mozam. 15°6S 39°15E 143 F4
mrole Indonesia 3°46S 126°46E 119 E7
mse Shankou China 30°0N 82°25E 125 D10
msen → Norway 64°28N 11°37E 60 D14
msos Norway 64°29N 11°30E 60 D14
mtok Chat Trakan △ Thailand 17°17N 100°40E 120 D3
mtok Huay Yang △ Thailand 11°35N 99°30E 121 G2
mtok Mae Surin △ Thailand 18°55N 98°2E 120 C2
mtok Ngao △ Thailand 9°58N 98°46E 121 H2
mtok Phlew △ Thailand 12°32N 102°13E 120 F4
mtok Yong △ Thailand 8°15N 98°45E 121 H2
mtsy Russia 62°43N 129°37E 107 C13
mtu Burma 25°10N 97°48E 116 E2
mtumbo Tanzania 10°30S 36°4E 143 E4
mu Australia 51°52S 178°57W 154 a
muka-i-Lau Fiji 18°53S 178°37W 154 a
mur Belgium 50°27N 4°52E 69 D4
mur □ Belgium 50°17N 5°0E 69 D4
muruputh Kenya 4°34N 35°57E 142 B4
mutoni Kenya 4°9S 39°15E 142 C4
mwala Zambia 15°44S 26°0E 143 F2
mwon S. Korea 42°57N 129°52E 115 C15
myang N. Korea 42°57N 129°52E 115 C15
mt, China Sea 10°45N 118°0E 118 B3
myłow Poland 51°16N 17°42E 83 G4
n □ Thailand 18°0N 98°59E 120 C2
n Ling China 25°0N 112°30E 117 F9
n Xian China 29°20N 112°22E 117 C9

Nana Romania 44°17N 26°34E 81 F11
Nana Kru Liberia 4°53N 8°45W 138 E3
Nanaimo Canada 49°10N 124°0W 162 D4
Nānākuli U.S.A. 21°24N 158°9W 167 L8
Nanam N. Korea 41°44N 129°40E 115 D15
Nan'an China 24°59N 118°21E 117 E12
Nanango Australia 26°40S 152°0E 151 D5
Nan'ao China 23°28N 117°5E 117 F11
Nanao Japan 37°0N 137°0E 113 F8
Nanbu China 31°18N 106°3E 116 B6
Nanchang China 28°42N 115°55E 117 C10
Nancheng China 27°33N 116°35E 117 D11
Nanching = Nanjing China 32°2N 118°47E 117 A12
Nanchong China 30°43N 106°2E 116 B6
Nanchuan China 29°9N 107°6E 116 C6
Nancowry India 7°59N 93°32E 127 L11
Nancy France 48°42N 6°12E 71 D13
Nanda Devi India 30°23N 79°59E 125 D8
Nanda Devi △ India 30°30N 79°50E 125 D8
Nanda Kot India 30°17N 80°5E 125 D9
Nandan = Minamiawaji Japan 34°10N 134°42E 113 G7
Nandan China 24°58N 107°29E 116 E6
Nanded India 19°10N 77°20E 126 E3
Nandewar Ra. Australia 30°15S 150°35E 151 E5
Nandgaon India 20°19N 74°39E 126 D2
Nandi = Nadi Fiji 17°42S 177°20E 154 a
Nandi Zimbabwe 20°58S 31°44E 143 G3
Nandi △ Kenya 0°10N 35°10E 142 B4
Nandigama India 16°47N 80°18E 126 F5
Nandigram India 22°1N 87°58E 125 H12
Nandikotkur India 15°52N 78°18E 127 G4
Nandura India 20°52N 76°25E 126 D3
Nandurbar India 21°20N 74°15E 126 D2
Nandyal India 15°30N 78°30E 127 G4
Nanfeng Guangdong, China 23°45N 111°47E 117 F8
Nanfeng Jiangxi, China 27°12N 116°28E 117 D11
Nang Rong Thailand 14°38N 102°48E 120 E4
Nanga-Eboko Cameroon 4°41N 12°22E 139 E7
Nanga Parbat Pakistan 35°10N 74°35E 125 B6
Nangade Mozam. 11°5S 39°36E 143 E4
Nangapinoh Indonesia 0°20S 111°44E 118 E4
Nangar △ Australia 33°23S 148°3E 153 B8
Nangarhār □ Afghan. 34°20N 70°0E 123 B5
Nangatayap Indonesia 1°32S 110°34E 118 E4
Nangbéto, L. de Togo 7°26N 1°25E 139 D5
Nangeya Mts. Uganda 3°30N 33°30E 142 B3
Nangis France 48°33N 3°1E 71 D10
Nangong China 37°23N 115°22E 114 F8
Nanguneri India 8°29N 77°40E 127 K3
Nanguwarry Australia 37°33S 140°48E 152 B4
Nanhua China 25°13N 101°21E 116 E3
Nanhuang China 36°58N 121°48E 115 F11
Nanhui China 30°53N 121°44E 117 B13
Nanisivik Canada 73°2N 84°33W 161 C15
Nanjangud India 12°6N 76°43E 127 H3
Nanji Shan China 27°27N 121°4E 117 D13
Nanjian China 25°2N 100°25E 116 E3
Nanjiang China 32°28N 106°51E 116 A6
Nanjing Fujian, China 24°25N 117°20E 117 E11
Nanjing Jiangsu, China 32°2N 118°47E 117 A12
Nanjirinji Tanzania 9°41S 39°5E 143 D4
Nankana Sahib Pakistan 31°27N 73°38E 124 D5
Nankang China 25°40N 114°45E 117 E10
Nanking = Nanjing China 32°2N 118°47E 117 A12
Nankoku Japan 33°39N 133°44E 113 H6
Nanlang China 22°30N 113°32E 111 a
Nanling China 30°55N 118°20E 117 B12
Nannial India 19°4N 79°38E 126 E4
Nannup Australia 33°59S 115°48E 149 F2
Nanortalik Greenland 60°10N 45°17W 57 E6
Nanpan Jiang → China 25°10N 106°5E 116 E6
Nanpara India 27°52N 81°33E 125 F9
Nanping Fujian, China 26°38N 118°10E 117 D12
Nanping Henan, China 29°55N 112°3E 117 C9
Nanri Dao China 25°15N 119°31E 117 E12
Nansei-Shotō = Ryūkyū-Rettō Japan 26°0N 126°0E 113 M3
Nansen Basin Arctic 84°0N 50°0E 54 A10
Nansen Land Greenland 83°0N 43°0W 57 A6
Nansen Sd. Canada 81°0N 91°0W 161 A13
Nansha China 22°45N 113°34E 111 a
Nansha Port China 22°40N 113°40E 111 a
Nanshan China 18°19N 109°10E 117 a
Nansha I. S. China Sea 10°45N 115°49E 118 B5
Nansio Tanzania 2°3S 33°4E 142 C3
Nant France 44°1N 3°18E 72 D7
Nantawarrinna ✪ Australia 30°49S 138°58E 151 B2
Nanterre France 48°53N 2°12E 71 D9
Nantes France 47°12N 1°33W 70 E5
Nantiat France 46°1N 1°11E 72 B5
Nanticoke U.S.A. 41°12N 76°0W 175 E8
Nanton Canada 50°21N 113°46W 162 C6
Nantong China 32°1N 120°52E 117 A13
Nantou China 22°32N 113°55E 111 a
Nant'ou Taiwan 23°55N 120°41E 117 F13
Nantua France 46°10N 5°35E 71 F12
Nantucket U.S.A. 41°17N 70°6W 173 E14
Nantucket I. U.S.A. 41°16N 70°5W 173 E14
Nantwich U.K. 53°4N 2°31W 66 D5
Nanty Glo U.S.A. 40°28N 78°50W 174 F6
Nanuque Brazil 17°50S 40°21W 189 D2
Nanusa, Kepulauan Indonesia 4°45N 127°1E 119 D7
Nanxi China 28°54N 104°59E 116 C5
Nanxiong China 25°6N 114°15E 117 E10
Nanyang China 33°11N 112°30E 114 H7
Nanyi Hu China 31°5N 119°0E 117 B12
Nanyuki Kenya 0°2N 37°4E 142 B4
Nanzhang China 31°45N 111°50E 116 B7
Nanzhao China 33°30N 112°20E 114 H7
Naococane, L. Canada 52°50N 70°45W 165 B5
Naoussa Cyclades, Greece 37°7N 25°14E 97 E6
Naoussa Imathia, Greece 40°42N 22°9E 96 C6
Naozhou Dao China 20°55N 110°20E 117 G8
Napa U.S.A. 38°18N 122°17W 170 G4

Napa → U.S.A. 38°10N 122°19W 170 G4
Napanee Canada 44°15N 77°0W 174 B8
Napanoch U.S.A. 41°44N 74°22W 175 E10
Nape Laos 18°18N 105°6E 120 C5
Nape Pass = Keo Neua, Deo Vietnam 18°23N 105°10E 120 C5
Napier N.Z. 39°30S 176°56E 154 F5
Napier Broome B. Australia 14°2S 126°37E 148 B4
Napier Pen. Australia 12°4S 135°43E 150 A2
Napierville Canada 45°11N 73°25W 175 A11
Naples = Nápoli Italy 40°50N 14°15E 95 B7
Naples U.S.A. 26°8N 81°48W 179 J8
Naples Park U.S.A. 26°16N 81°46W 179 J8
Napo China 23°22N 105°50E 116 F5
Napo → Peru 3°20S 72°40W 186 D4
Napoleon N. Dak., U.S.A. 46°30N 99°46W 172 B4
Napoleon Ohio, U.S.A. 41°23N 84°8W 173 E11
Nápoli Italy 40°50N 14°15E 95 B7
Nápoli, G. di Italy 40°40N 14°10E 95 B7
Nápoli Capodichino ✈ (NAP) Italy 40°53N 14°16E 95 B7
Napopo Dem. Rep. of the Congo 4°15N 28°0E 142 B2
Napperby Australia 33°9S 138°7E 152 B3
Naqadeh Iran 36°57N 45°23E 105 D11
Naqb, Ra's an Jordan 29°48N 35°44E 130 F4
Naqqāsh Iran 35°40N 49°6E 129 C6
Nār Sweden 57°15N 18°35E 63 G8
Nara Japan 34°40N 135°49E 113 G7
Nara Mali 15°10N 7°20W 138 B3
Nara → Japan 34°30N 136°0E 113 G8
Nara Canal Pakistan 24°30N 69°20E 124 G3
Nara Visa U.S.A. 35°37N 103°6W 169 J12
Naracoorte Australia 36°58S 140°45E 152 D4
Naradhan Australia 33°34S 146°17E 153 B7
Naraini India 25°11N 80°29E 125 G9
Naranjos Mexico 21°21N 97°41W 181 C5
Narasannapeta India 18°25N 84°3E 126 E7
Narasapur India 16°14N 81°40E 127 F5
Narasaraopet India 16°14N 80°4E 127 F5
Narathiwat Thailand 6°30N 101°48E 121 J3
Narayanapatnam India 18°53N 83°10E 126 E6
Narayangadh = Bharatpur Nepal 27°34N 84°10E 125 F11
Narayanganj Bangla. 23°40N 90°33E 123 H17
Narayanpet India 16°45N 77°30E 126 F3
Narberth U.K. 51°47N 4°44W 67 F3
Narbonne France 43°11N 3°0E 72 E7
Narcondam I. India 13°20N 94°16E 127 H12
Nardin Iran 37°3N 55°59E 129 B7
Nardò Italy 40°11N 18°2E 95 B11
Narembeen Australia 32°7S 118°24E 149 F2
Nares Abyssal Plain Atl. Oc. 22°0N 67°0W 56 D5
Nares Str. Arctic 80°0N 70°0W 57 B3
Naretha Australia 31°0S 124°45E 149 F3
Narew → Poland 52°26N 20°41E 83 F7
Nari → Pakistan 28°0N 67°40E 124 F2
Narin Afghan. 36°5N 69°0E 122 A6
Narita Japan 35°47N 140°19E 113 G10
Nariva Swamp Trin. & Tob. 10°26N 61°4W 187 K15
Närke Sweden 59°5N 15°0E 62 E8
Narmada → India 21°38N 72°36E 124 J5
Narmada Canal India 22°20N 73°45E 126 C1
Narman Turkey 40°26N 41°57E 105 B9
Narnaul India 28°5N 76°11E 124 E7
Narni Italy 42°30N 12°30E 93 F7
Naro Ghana 10°22N 2°27W 138 C4
Naro Fominsk Russia 55°23N 36°43E 84 E9
Narochanski △ Belarus 54°55N 26°50E 84 E4
Narodnaya Russia 65°5N 59°58E 58 B17
Narok Kenya 1°55S 35°52E 142 C4
Narok □ Kenya 1°15S 35°40E 142 C4
Narón Spain 43°32N 8°9W 88 B2
Narooma Australia 36°14S 150°4E 153 D9
Narowal Pakistan 32°6N 74°52E 124 C6
Narrabri Australia 30°19S 149°46E 151 E4
Narran → Australia 28°37S 148°12E 151 D4
Narrandera Australia 34°42S 146°31E 153 C7
Narrogin Australia 32°58S 117°14E 149 F2
Narromine Australia 32°12S 148°12E 153 B8
Narrow Hills △ Canada 54°0N 104°37W 163 C8
Narsampet India 17°57N 79°58E 126 F4
Narsaq Greenland 60°57N 46°4W 57 E6
Narsimhapur India 22°54N 79°14E 125 H8
Narsinghgarh India 23°45N 76°40E 124 H7
Narsinghpur India 20°28N 85°5E 126 C7
Narsipatnam India 17°40N 82°37E 126 F6
Nartes, L. e Albania 40°33N 19°25E 96 D1
Nartkala Russia 43°33N 43°51E 87 J6
Narutō = Sanmu Japan 35°36N 140°25E 113 G10
Narva Estonia 59°23N 28°12E 84 C5
Narva → Russia 59°27N 28°2E 84 C4
Narva Bay = Narva Laht Estonia 59°35N 27°35E 61 G22
Narva Laht Estonia 59°35N 27°35E 61 G22
Narvik Norway 68°28N 17°26E 60 B17
Narvskoye Vdkhr. Russia 59°18N 28°14E 84 C5
Narwana India 29°39N 76°6E 124 E7
Narwiński △ Poland 52°5N 22°53E 83 F9
Narwinbi ✪ Australia 16°7S 136°17E 150 B2
Naryan-Mar Russia 67°42N 53°12E 106 C6
Narym Russia 59°0N 81°30E 106 D9
Naryn Kyrgyzstan 41°26N 75°58E 109 D9
Naryn □ Kyrgyzstan 41°20N 76°0E 109 D9
Naryn → Uzbekistan 40°52N 71°36E 109 D8
Naryn Qum Kazakhstan 47°30N 49°0E 87 G9
Nás, An = Naas Ireland 53°12N 6°40W 64 C5
Nasa Norway 66°29N 15°23E 60 D16
Nasarawa Nigeria 8°32N 7°41E 139 D6
Nasarawa □ Nigeria 8°30N 8°20E 139 D6
Nasau U.S.A. 17°19S 179°27E 154 a
Năsăud Romania 47°19N 24°29E 81 E9
Nasca Peru 14°50S 74°57W 186 F4
Nasca Ridge Pac. Oc. 20°0S 80°0W 157 K19
Naseby N.Z. 45°1S 170°10E 155 F5
Naselle U.S.A. 46°22N 123°49W 170 D3
Naser, Buheirat en Egypt 23°0N 32°30E 137 C3
Nashik = Nasik India 19°58N 73°50E 126 E1
Nashua Mont., U.S.A. 48°8N 106°22W 171 B10
Nashua N.H., U.S.A. 42°45N 71°28W 175 D13
Nashville Ark., U.S.A. 33°57N 93°51W 176 E8
Nashville Ga., U.S.A. 31°12N 83°15W 178 D6
Nashville Tenn., U.S.A. 36°10N 86°47W 177 C11

Našice Croatia 45°32N 18°4E 80 E3
Nasielsk Poland 52°35N 20°50E 83 F7
Nasik India 19°58N 73°50E 126 E1
Nasirabad India 26°15N 74°45E 124 F6
Nasirabad Pakistan 28°23N 68°40E 124 F3
Nasiri = Ahvāz Iran 31°20N 48°40E 129 D6
Nasiriyah = An Nāşirīyah Iraq 31°0N 46°15E 128 D5
Naskaupi → Canada 53°47N 60°51W 165 B7
Naso Italy 38°7N 14°47E 95 D7
Naşrābād Iran 34°8N 51°26E 129 C6
Nasrian-e Pā'īn Iran 32°52N 46°52E 128 C5
Nass → Canada 55°0N 129°40W 162 C3
Nassau Bahamas 25°5N 77°20W 182 A4
Nassau U.S.A. 42°31N 73°37W 175 D11
Nassau, B. Chile 55°20S 68°0W 192 E3
Nasser, L. = Naser, Buheirat en Egypt 23°0N 32°30E 137 C3
Nassian Ivory C. 8°28N 3°28W 138 D4
Nässjö Sweden 57°39N 14°42E 63 G8
Nastapoka → Canada 56°55N 76°33W 164 A4
Nastapoka, Is. Canada 56°55N 76°50W 164 A4
Näsum Sweden 56°10N 14°29E 63 H7
Nasushiobara Japan 36°58N 140°3E 113 F10
Näsviken Sweden 61°46N 16°52E 62 C10
Nata Botswana 20°12S 26°12E 144 B4
Nata → Botswana 20°14S 26°10E 144 B4
Natal Brazil 5°47S 35°13W 189 B3
Natal Indonesia 0°35N 99°7E 118 D1
Natal Drakensberg = uKhahlamba Drakensberg △ S. Africa 29°27S 29°30E 145 C4
Natalinci Serbia 44°15N 20°49E 80 F5
Naţanz Iran 33°30N 51°55E 129 C6
Natashquan Canada 50°14N 61°46W 165 B7
Natashquan → Canada 50°7N 61°50W 165 B7
Natchez U.S.A. 31°34N 91°24W 176 F9
Natchitoches U.S.A. 31°46N 93°5W 176 F7
Natewa B. Fiji 16°35S 179°40E 154 a
Nathalia Australia 36°1S 145°13E 153 D6
Nathdwara India 24°55N 73°50E 124 G5
Nati, Pta. Spain 40°3N 3°50E 100 A11
Natimuk Australia 36°42S 142°0E 152 D5
Nation → Canada 55°30N 123°32W 162 B4
National City U.S.A. 32°40N 117°5W 171 N9
Natitingou Benin 10°20N 1°26E 139 C5
Natividad, I. Mexico 27°52N 115°11W 180 B1
Natkyizin Burma 14°57N 97°59E 120 E1
Natron, L. Tanzania 2°20S 36°0E 142 C4
Natrona Heights U.S.A. 40°37N 79°44W 174 F5
Natuna Besar, Kepulauan Indonesia 4°0N 108°15E 118 D3
Natuna Is. = Natuna Besar, Kepulauan Indonesia 4°0N 108°15E 118 D3
Natuna Selatan, Kepulauan Indonesia 2°45N 109°0E 118 D3
Natural Bridge U.S.A. 44°5N 75°30W 175 B9
Natural Bridges △ U.S.A. 37°36N 110°0W 169 H9
Naturaliste, C. Tas., Australia 40°50S 148°15E 151 G4
Naturaliste, C. W. Austral., Australia 33°32S 115°0E 149 F2
Naturaliste Plateau Ind. Oc. 34°0S 112°0E 156 L3
Nau Qala Afghan. 34°5N 68°5E 124 B3
Naucelle France 44°13N 2°20E 72 D6
Nauders Austria 46°54N 10°30E 78 E3
Nauen Germany 52°36N 12°52E 76 C8
Naugatuck U.S.A. 41°30N 73°3W 175 E11
Naujaat = Repulse Bay Canada 66°30N 86°30W 161 D14
Naujoji Akmenė Lithuania 56°19N 22°54E 82 B9
Naumburg Germany 51°9N 11°47E 76 D7
Nauru ■ Pac. Oc. 1°0S 166°0E 147 B9
Naushahra = Nowshera Pakistan 34°0N 72°0E 122 C4
Naushahro Pakistan 26°50N 68°7E 124 F3
Naushon I. U.S.A. 41°29N 70°45W 175 E14
Nausori Fiji 18°2S 178°32E 154 a
Nauta Peru 4°31S 73°35W 186 D4
Nautanwa India 27°20N 83°25E 125 F10
Naute □ Namibia 26°55S 17°57E 144 C2
Nautla Mexico 20°13N 96°47W 181 C5
Nava Mexico 28°25N 100°45W 180 B4
Nava Spain 43°21N 5°31W 88 B5
Nava del Rey Spain 41°22N 5°6W 88 D5
Navadwip India 23°34N 88°20E 125 H13
Navahermosa Spain 39°41N 4°28W 89 F6
Navahrudak Belarus 53°40N 25°50E 75 B13
Navajo Res. U.S.A. 36°48N 107°36W 169 H10
Navalcarnero Spain 40°17N 4°5W 88 E6
Navalgund India 15°34N 75°22E 127 G2
Navalmoral de la Mata Spain 39°52N 5°33W 88 F5
Navalvillar de Pela Spain 39°9N 5°24W 89 F5
Navan Ireland 53°39N 6°41W 64 C5
Navapolatsk Belarus 55°32N 28°37E 84 E5
Navarin, Mys Russia 62°15N 179°5E 107 C18
Navarino, I. Chile 55°0S 67°40W 192 E3
Navarra □ Spain 42°40N 1°40W 90 C3
Navarre Ohio, U.S.A. 40°43N 81°31W 174 F4
Navas de San Juan Spain 38°10N 3°19W 89 G7
Navasota U.S.A. 30°23N 96°5W 176 F6
Navassa I. W. Indies 18°30N 75°0W 183 C5
Nävekvarn Sweden 58°38N 16°49E 63 F10
Naver → U.K. 58°32N 4°14W 65 C4
Navi Mumbai India 19°2N 73°0E 126 E1
Navia Spain 43°35N 6°42W 88 B4
Navia → Spain 43°35N 6°42W 88 B4
Navia de Suarna = A Pobre Spain 42°58N 7°3W 88 B3
Navibandar India 21°26N 69°48E 124 J3
Navidad Chile 33°57S 71°50W 190 C1
Naviraí Brazil 23°8S 54°13W 190 A5
Naviti Fiji 17°7S 177°15E 154 a
Navlakhi India 22°58N 70°28E 124 H4
Navlya Russia 52°53N 34°30E 85 F8
Năvodari Romania 44°19N 28°36E 81 F8
Navoiy Uzbekistan 40°9N 65°22E 108 D7

Navojoa Mexico 27°6N 109°26W 180 B3
Navolato Mexico 24°47N 107°42W 180 C3
Navrongo Ghana 10°51N 1°3W 139 C4
Navsari India 20°57N 72°59E 126 D1
Nawa Kot Pakistan 28°21N 71°24E 124 E4
Nawab Khan Pakistan 30°17N 69°12E 124 D3
Nawabganj Ut. P., India 26°56N 81°14E 125 F9
Nawabganj Ut. P., India 28°32N 79°40E 125 E8
Nawabshah Pakistan 26°15N 68°25E 124 F3
Nawada India 24°50N 85°33E 125 G11
Nawakot Nepal 27°55N 85°10E 125 F11
Nawalgarh India 27°50N 75°15E 124 F6
Nawanshahr India 32°33N 74°48E 125 C6
Nawapara India 20°46N 82°33E 126 D6
Nawar, Dasht-i- Afghan. 33°52N 68°0E 124 C3
Nawāşīf, Ḥarrat Si. Arabia 21°20N 42°10E 128 C3
Nawi Sudan 18°32N 30°50E 137 D3
Naxçıvan Azerbaijan 39°12N 45°15E 105 C11
Naxçıvan □ Azerbaijan 39°25N 45°26E 105 C11
Naxos Greece 37°8N 25°25E 99 D7
Nay France 43°10N 0°18W 72 E3
Nāy Band Būshehr, Iran 27°20N 52°40E 129 E7
Nāy Band Khorāsān, Iran 32°20N 57°34E 129 C8
Nayagarh India 20°8N 85°5E 126 C7
Nayakhan Russia 61°56N 159°0E 107 C16
Nayarit □ Mexico 22°0N 105°0W 180 C4
Nayau Fiji 18°6S 178°10E 154 a
Nayé Senegal 14°28N 12°12W 138 C2
Nayong China 26°50N 105°20E 116 D5
Nayoro Japan 44°21N 142°28E 112 B11
Naypyidaw Burma 19°44N 96°12E 110 H8
Nayudupeta India 13°54N 79°54E 127 H4
Nayyāl, W. → Si. Arabia 28°35N 39°4E 128 D3
Nazar Kahrīzī Iran 37°20N 46°45E 105 D12
Nazaré Bahia, Brazil 13°2S 39°0W 189 D3
Nazaré Tocantins, Brazil 6°23S 47°40W 189 B1
Nazaré Portugal 39°36N 9°4W 89 F2
Nazareth = Nazerat Israel 32°42N 35°17E 130 C4
Nazareth U.S.A. 40°44N 75°19W 175 F9
Nazarovo Russia 57°0N 90°40E 107 D10
Nazas Mexico 25°14N 104°8W 180 B4
Nazas → Mexico 25°12N 104°12W 180 B4
Nazca = Nasca Peru 14°50S 74°57W 186 F4
Naze, The U.K. 51°53N 1°18E 67 F9
Nazerat Israel 32°42N 35°17E 130 C4
Nāzik Iran 39°1N 45°4E 105 C11
Nazilli Turkey 37°55N 28°15E 99 D10
Nazino = Red Volta → Africa 10°34N 0°30W 139 C4
Nazko Canada 53°1N 123°37W 162 C4
Nazko → Canada 53°7N 123°34W 162 C4
Nāzlū Iran 37°41N 45°0E 105 D11
Nazret Ethiopia 8°32N 39°22E 131 F2
Nchanga Zambia 12°30S 27°49E 143 E2
Ncheu Malawi 14°50S 34°47E 143 E3
Ndala Tanzania 4°45S 33°15E 142 C3
Ndalatando Angola 9°12S 14°48E 142 F2
Ndali Benin 9°50N 2°46E 139 D5
Ndareda Tanzania 4°12S 35°30E 142 C4
Ndélé C.A.R. 8°25N 20°36E 140 G4
Ndiael □ Senegal 16°15N 16°0W 138 B1
Ndikinimeki Cameroon 4°46N 10°50E 139 E7
N'Dioum Senegal 16°31N 14°39W 138 B2
Ndjamena Chad 12°10N 15°0E 141 F8
Ndola Zambia 13°0S 28°34E 143 E2
Ndomo → S. Africa 26°52S 32°15E 145 D5
Ndoto Mts. Kenya 2°0N 37°0E 142 B4
Nduguti Tanzania 4°18S 34°41E 142 C3
Nea Alikarnassos Greece 35°19N 25°11E 99 F7
Nea Anchialos Greece 39°16N 22°49E 98 B5
Nea Artaki Greece 38°31N 23°38E 98 C5
Nea Epidavros Greece 37°40N 23°7E 98 D5
Nea Ionia Greece 39°21N 22°56E 98 B5
Nea Kalikratia Greece 40°21N 23°3E 96 D7
Nea Makri Greece 38°5N 23°56E 98 C5
Nea Moudania Greece 40°15N 23°17E 96 D7
Nea Peramos Attiki, Greece 38°0N 23°24E 98 C5
Nea Peramos Kavala, Greece 40°50N 24°18E 97 B6
Nea Visa Greece 41°34N 26°33E 97 E10
Nea Zichni Greece 41°2N 23°49E 96 B6
Neagh, Lough U.K. 54°37N 6°25W 64 B5
Neah Bay U.S.A. 48°22N 124°37W 170 B2
Neale, L. Australia 24°15S 130°0E 148 D5
Neales → Australia 28°8S 136°47E 151 A2
Neamț □ Romania 47°0N 26°20E 81 C11
Neápoli Kozani, Greece 40°20N 21°24E 96 D5
Neápoli Kriti, Greece 35°15N 25°37E 99 F7
Neápoli Lakonia, Greece 36°27N 23°8E 98 E5
Near Is. U.S.A. 52°30N 174°0E 166 E2
Neath U.K. 51°39N 3°48W 67 F4
Neath Port Talbot □ U.K. 51°42N 3°45W 67 F4
Nebbi Uganda 2°28N 31°6E 142 B3
Nebbou Burkina Faso 11°9N 1°51W 139 C4
Nebine Cr. → Australia 29°27S 146°56E 151 D4
Nebitdag = Balkanabat Turkmenistan 39°30N 54°22E 108 F6
Nebka Algeria 27°28N 3°12W 136 C5
Nebo Australia 21°42S 148°20E 150 E4
Nebolchi Russia 59°8N 33°18E 84 C7
Nebraska □ U.S.A. 41°30N 99°30W 172 E5
Nebraska City U.S.A. 40°41N 95°52W 172 E6
Nébrodi, Monti Italy 37°54N 14°35E 95 E7
Necedah U.S.A. 44°2N 90°4W 172 C8
Nechako → Canada 53°30N 122°44W 162 C4
Neckar → Germany 49°27N 8°29E 77 F4
Neckartal-Odenwald △ Germany 49°30N 9°5E 77 F5
Necker I. U.S.A. 23°35N 164°42W 167 L7
Necochea Argentina 38°30S 58°50W 190 D5
Nectar Brook Australia 32°43S 137°57E 152 B2
Neda Spain 43°30N 8°9W 88 B2
Nedelino Bulgaria 41°26N 25°12E 97 B8
Nedelišće Croatia 46°23N 16°22E 93 B13
Nederland = Netherlands ■ Europe 52°0N 5°30E 69 B6
Nederland U.S.A. 29°58N 93°59W 176 G7
Nedroma Algeria 35°1N 1°45W 136 A5

Needles Canada 49°53N 118°7W 162 D5
Needles U.S.A. 34°51N 114°37W 171 L12
Needles, The U.K. 50°39N 1°35W 67 G6
Needles Pt. N.Z. 36°3S 175°25E 154 C4
Neembucú □ Paraguay 27°0S 58°0W 190 B4
Neemuch = Nimach India 24°30N 74°56E 124 G6
Neenah U.S.A. 44°11N 88°28W 172 C9
Neepawa Canada 50°15N 99°30W 163 C9
Neeses U.S.A. 33°33N 81°7W 178 D7
Nefta Tunisia 33°53N 7°50E 136 B7
Neftçala Azerbaijan 39°19N 49°12E 105 C13
Neftegorsk Krasnodar, Russia 44°25N 39°45E 87 H4
Neftegorsk Sakhalin, Russia 53°11N 142°58E 107 D15
Neftekumsk Russia 44°46N 44°50E 87 H7
Neftyugansk Russia 61°5N 72°42E 106 C8
Nefyn U.K. 52°56N 4°31W 66 E3
Négala Mali 12°52N 8°30W 138 C2
Negapatam = Nagapattinam India 10°46N 79°51E 127 J4
Negara Indonesia 8°22S 114°37E 119 J17
Negaunee U.S.A. 46°30N 87°36W 172 B10
Negele Ethiopia 5°20N 39°36E 131 F2
Negeri Sembilan □ Malaysia 2°45N 102°10E 121 L4
Negev Desert = Hanegev Israel 30°50N 35°0E 130 E4
Negoiul, Vf. Romania 45°38N 24°35E 81 F9
Negombo Sri Lanka 7°12N 79°50E 127 L4
Negotin Serbia 44°16N 22°37E 96 B6
Negotino Macedonia 41°29N 22°7E 96 E6
Negra, Peña Spain 42°11N 6°30W 88 C4
Negra, Pta. Mauritania 22°54N 16°18W 134 D2
Negra, Pta. Peru 6°6S 81°10W 188 B1
Negrais, C. = Maudin Sun Burma 16°0N 94°30E 123 M19
Negreşti Romania 46°50N 27°30E 81 D12
Negreşti-Oaş Romania 47°52N 23°26E 81 C8
Negril Jamaica 18°22N 78°20W 182 a
Négrine Algeria 34°30N 7°30E 136 B5
Negro → Argentina 41°2S 62°47W 192 B4
Negro → Brazil 3°0S 60°0W 186 D7
Negro → Uruguay 33°24S 58°22W 190 C4
Negro, C. = Tarf, Ras Morocco 35°40N 5°11W 136 A2
Negros Phil. 9°30N 122°40E 119 C6
Negru Vodă Romania 43°47N 28°21E 81 G13
Neguac Canada 47°15N 65°5W 165 C6
Nehalem → U.S.A. 45°40N 123°56W 170 E2
Nehāvand Iran 35°56N 49°31E 129 C6
Nehbandān Iran 31°35N 60°5E 129 D9
Nehe China 48°29N 124°50E 111 B13
Nehoiu Romania 45°24N 26°20E 81 E11
Nei Mongol Zizhiqu □ China 42°0N 112°0E 114 D7
Neiges, Piton des Réunion 21°5S 55°29E 141 c
Neijiang China 29°35N 104°55E 116 C5
Neilingding Dao China 22°25N 113°48E 111 a
Neill I. India 11°50N 93°3E 127 J11
Neillsville U.S.A. 44°34N 90°36W 172 C8
Neilton U.S.A. 47°25N 123°53W 170 C2
Neiqiu China 37°15N 114°30E 114 F8
Neiva Colombia 2°56N 75°18W 186 C3
Neixiang China 33°10N 111°52E 116 A7
Nejanilini L. Canada 59°33N 97°48W 163 B9
Nejd = Najd Si. Arabia 26°30N 42°0E 131 B3
Nekā Iran 36°39N 53°19E 129 B7
Nekemte Ethiopia 9°4N 36°30E 137 F3
Nékhel Egypt 29°55N 33°43E 130 F2
Neksø Denmark 55°4N 15°8E 63 J9
Nelamangala India 13°6N 77°22E 127 H3
Nelas Portugal 40°32N 7°52W 88 E3
Nelia Australia 20°39S 142°12E 150 D3
Nelidovo Russia 56°13N 32°49E 84 D7
Neligh U.S.A. 42°8N 98°2W 172 D5
Nelkan Russia 57°40N 136°4E 107 D14
Nellikuppam India 11°46N 79°43E 127 J4
Nellore India 14°27N 79°59E 127 G4
Nelson Canada 49°30N 117°20W 162 D5
Nelson N.Z. 41°18S 173°16E 155 D5
Nelson □ N.Z. 42°11S 172°15E 155 D5
Nelson → Canada 54°33N 98°2W 163 B9
Nelson, C. Australia 38°26S 141°32E 152 D4
Nelson, Estrecho Chile 51°30S 75°0W 192 D2
Nelson Bay Australia 32°43S 152°9E 153 B9
Nelson Forks Canada 59°30N 124°0W 162 B4
Nelson House Canada 55°47N 98°51W 163 B9
Nelson Lakes △ N.Z. 41°55S 172°44E 155 D5
Nelspoort S. Africa 32°7S 23°0E 144 D3
Nelspruit = Mbombela S. Africa 25°29S 30°59E 145 D5
Néma Mauritania 16°40N 7°15W 138 B3
Neman = Nemunas → Lithuania 55°25N 21°10E 82 C8
Neman Russia 55°2N 22°2E 82 C8
Nembe Nigeria 4°35N 6°24E 139 E6
Nembrala Indonesia 10°53S 122°50E 119 G6
Nemea Greece 37°49N 22°40E 98 D4
Nemeiben L. Canada 55°20N 105°20W 163 B7
Nemërçkë, Mal Albania 40°15N 20°15E 96 D2
Nemira, Vf. Romania 46°17N 26°19E 81 C11
Nemiscau Canada 51°18N 76°54W 164 B4
Nemiscau, L. Canada 51°25N 76°40W 164 B4
Nemours France 48°16N 2°40E 71 D9
Nemrut Dağı △ Turkey 38°39N 38°0E 105 B8
Nemšová Slovak Rep. 48°58N 18°7E 79 C11
Nemunas → Lithuania 55°25N 21°10E 82 C8
Nemuro Japan 43°20N 145°35E 112 C12
Nemuro-Kaikyō Japan 43°30N 145°30E 112 C12
Nemyriv Ukraine 50°7N 23°27E 83 H10
Nen Jiang → China 45°28N 124°30E 115 B13
Nenagh Ireland 52°52N 8°11W 64 D3
Nenana U.S.A. 64°34N 149°5W 166 C10
Nenasi Malaysia 3°9N 103°23E 121 L4
Nene → U.K. 52°49N 0°11E 67 E8
Nenita Greece 38°14N 26°9E 99 C9
Nenjiang China 49°10N 125°10E 111 B13
Neno Malawi 15°25N 34°40E 143 F3
Neo Chori Greece 38°35N 21°17E 98 C3
Neodesha U.S.A. 37°25N 95°41W 172 G6
Neon Petritsi Greece 41°16N 23°15E 96 C6
Neópolis Brazil 10°18S 36°35W 189 D3
Neora Valley △ India 27°0N 88°45E 125 F13
Neos Marmaras Greece 40°6N 23°47E 96 F7

Neosho U.S.A. 36°52N 94°22W 172 G6
Neosho → U.S.A. 36°48N 95°18W 176 C7
Nepal ■ Asia 28°0N 84°30E 125 F11
Nepalganj Nepal 28°5N 81°40E 125 E9
Nepalganj Road India 28°1N 81°41E 125 E9
Nepean B. Australia 35°42S 137°37E 152 C2
Nephi U.S.A. 39°43N 111°50W 168 G8
Nephin Ireland 54°1N 9°22W 64 B2
Nephin Beg Range Ireland 54°0N 9°40W 64 C2
Nepi Italy 42°14N 12°21E 93 F9
Nepomuk Czech Rep. 49°29N 13°35E 78 B6
Neptune U.S.A. 40°13N 74°2W 175 F10
Neptune Is. Australia 35°17S 136°10E 152 C2
Neqāb Iran 36°42N 57°25E 129 B8
Nera → Italy 42°26N 12°24E 93 F9
Nera → Romania 44°48N 21°25E 80 F6
Nérac France 44°8N 0°21E 72 D4
Nerang Australia 27°58S 153°20E 151 D5
Neratovice Czech Rep. 50°16N 14°31E 78 A7
Nerchinsk Russia 52°0N 116°39E 107 D12
Nereju Romania 45°43N 26°43E 81 E11
Nerekhta Russia 57°26N 40°38E 84 D11
Neresnytsya Ukraine 48°7N 23°46E 81 B8
Néret, L. Canada 54°45N 70°44W 165 B5
Neretvanski Kanal
Croatia 43°7N 17°10E 93 E14
Neringa Lithuania 55°20N 21°5E 82 C8
Neris → Lithuania 55°8N 24°16E 84 E3
Nerja Spain 36°43N 3°55W 89 J7
Nerl → Russia 56°11N 40°34E 84 D11
Nerpio Spain 38°11N 2°16W 91 G2
Nerva Spain 37°42N 6°30W 89 H4
Nervi Italy 44°23N 9°2E 92 D6
Neryungri Russia 57°38N 124°28E 107 D13
Nescopeck U.S.A. 41°3N 76°12W 175 E8
Nesebŭr Bulgaria 42°41N 27°46E 97 C11
Neskantaga Canada 52°14N 87°53W 164 B2
Neskaupstaður Iceland 65°9N 13°42W 60 D7
Ness, L. U.K. 57°15N 4°32W 65 D4
Ness City U.S.A. 38°27N 99°54W 172 F4
Nessebar = Nesebŭr
Bulgaria 42°41N 27°46E 97 D11
Nesterov = Zhovkva
Ukraine 50°4N 23°58E 75 C12
Nesterov Russia 54°38N 22°41E 82 D9
Nestorio Greece 40°24N 21°5E 96 F5
Nestos → Europe 40°54N 24°49E 97 F8
Nesvady Slovak Rep. 47°56N 18°7E 79 D11
Nesvizh = Nyasvizh
Belarus 53°14N 26°38E 75 B14
Netanya Israel 32°20N 34°51E 130 C3
Netarhat India 23°29N 84°16E 125 H11
Nete → Belgium 51°7N 4°14E 69 C4
Netherdale Australia 21°10S 148°33E 150 b
Netherlands ■ Europe 52°0N 5°30E 69 C5
Netherlands Antilles = ABC
Islands W. Indies 12°15N 69°0W 183 D6
Neto → Italy 39°12N 17°9E 95 C10
Netrang India 21°39N 73°21E 124 J5
Nettancourt France 48°51N 4°57E 71 D11
Nettilling L. Canada 66°30N 71°0W 161 D17
Nettuno Italy 41°27N 12°39E 94 A5
Netzahualcóyotl, Presa
Mexico 17°8N 93°35W 181 D6
Neu-Isenburg Germany 50°3N 8°42E 77 E4
Neu-Ulm Germany 48°22N 10°0E 77 G6
Neubrandenburg
Germany 53°33N 13°15E 76 B9
Neubukow Germany 54°2N 11°39E 76 A7
Neuburg Germany 48°44N 11°11E 77 G7
Neuchâtel Switz. 47°0N 6°55E 77 J2
Neuchâtel □ Switz. 47°0N 6°55E 77 J2
Neuchâtel, Lac de Switz. 46°53N 6°50E 77 J2
Neudau Austria 47°11N 16°6E 78 D9
Neuenhagen Germany 52°32N 13°38E 76 C9
Neuenhaus Germany 52°30N 6°58E 76 C2
Neuf-Brisach France 48°1N 7°30E 71 D14
Neufahrn Bayern,
Germany 48°41N 12°11E 77 G8
Neufahrn Bayern,
Germany 48°18N 11°40E 77 G7
Neufchâteau Belgium 49°50N 5°25E 69 E5
Neufchâteau France 48°21N 5°40E 71 D12
Neufchâtel-en-Bray
France 49°44N 1°26E 70 C8
Neufchâtel-sur-Aisne
France 49°26N 4°1E 71 C11
Neuhaus Germany 53°17N 10°56E 76 B6
Neuillé-Pont-Pierre
France 47°33N 0°33E 70 E7
Neuilly-St-Front France 49°10N 3°15E 71 C10
Neukalen Germany 53°49N 12°46E 76 B8
Neumarkt Germany 49°16N 11°27E 77 F7
Neumayer Antarctica 71°0S 68°30W 55 D17
Neumünster Germany 54°4N 9°58E 76 A5
Neung-sur-Beuvron
France 47°30N 1°50E 71 E8
Neunkirchen Austria 47°43N 16°4E 78 D9
Neunkirchen Germany 49°20N 7°9E 77 F3
Neuquén Argentina 38°55S 68°0W 192 A3
Neuquén □ Argentina 38°0S 69°50W 190 D2
Neuquén → Argentina 38°59S 68°0W 192 A3
Neuruppin Germany 52°55N 12°48E 76 C8
Neusäss Germany 48°24N 10°50E 77 G6
Neuse → U.S.A. 35°6N 76°29W 177 D16
Neusiedl Austria 47°57N 16°50E 78 D9
Neusiedler See Austria 47°50N 16°47E 78 D9
Neusiedler See-Seewinkel △
Austria 47°50N 16°45E 78 D9
Neuss Germany 51°11N 6°42E 76 D2
Neussargues-Moissac
France 45°9N 3°0E 72 C7
Neustadt Bayern,
Germany 49°34N 10°37E 77 F6
Neustadt Bayern, Germany 50°19N 11°7E 77 E7
Neustadt Brandenburg,
Germany 52°50N 12°27E 76 C8
Neustadt Hessen, Germany 50°51N 9°9E 76 E5
Neustadt Sachsen,
Germany 51°2N 14°12E 76 D10
Neustadt Schleswig-Holstein,
Germany 54°6N 10°49E 76 A6
Neustadt Thüringen,
Germany 50°45N 11°43E 76 E7
Neustadt am Rübenberge
Germany 52°30N 9°30E 76 C5
Neustadt an der Weinstrasse
Germany 49°21N 8°10E 77 F4

Neustrelitz Germany 53°21N 13°4E 76 B9
Neuvic France 45°23N 2°16E 72 C6
Neuville-sur-Saône
France 45°52N 4°51E 73 C8
Neuvy-le-Roi France 47°36N 0°36E 70 E7
Neuvy-St-Sépulchre
France 46°35N 1°48E 71 F8
Neuvy-sur-Barangeon
France 47°20N 2°15E 71 E9
Neuwerk Germany 53°55N 8°30E 76 B4
Neuwied Germany 50°26N 7°29E 76 E3
Neva → Russia 59°56N 30°20E 84 C6
Nevada Iowa, U.S.A. 42°1N 93°27W 172 D7
Nevada Mo., U.S.A. 37°51N 94°22W 172 G6
Nevada □ U.S.A. 39°0N 117°0W 168 G5
Nevada City U.S.A. 39°16N 121°1W 170 F6
Nevado, Cerro
Argentina 35°30S 68°32W 190 D2
Nevado de Colima = Volcán de
Colima △ Mexico 19°30N 103°40W 180 D4
Nevado de Tres Cruces △
Chile 27°13S 69°5W 190 B2
Nevasa India 19°34N 75°0E 124 E2
Nevel Russia 56°0N 29°55E 84 D5
Nevelsk Russia 46°40N 141°51E 107 E15
Nevers France 47°0N 3°9E 71 F10
Nevertire Australia 31°50S 147°44E 153 A7
Nevesinje Bos.-H. 43°14N 18°6E 96 C2
Neville Canada 49°58N 107°39W 163 D7
Nevinnomyssk Russia 44°40N 42°0E 87 H6
Nevis St. Kitts & Nevis 17°0N 62°30W 183 C7
Nevrokop = Gotse Delchev
Bulgaria 41°36N 23°46E 96 E7
Nevşehir Turkey 38°33N 34°40E 104 C6
Nevşehir □ Turkey 38°50N 34°40E 104 C6
Nevskoye Russia 54°32N 22°39E 82 D9
New → U.S.A. 38°10N 81°12W 173 F13
New Aiyansh Canada 55°12N 129°4W 162 B3
New Albany Ind.,
U.S.A. 38°18N 85°49W 173 F11
New Albany Miss.,
U.S.A. 34°29N 89°0W 177 D10
New Albany Pa.,
U.S.A. 41°36N 76°27W 175 E8
New Amsterdam
Guyana 6°15N 57°36W 186 B7
New Atlas = Akhali Atoni
Georgia 43°7N 40°50E 87 J5
New Baltimore U.S.A. 42°41N 82°44W 174 D2
New Bedford U.S.A. 41°38N 70°56W 175 E14
New Berlin N.Y.,
U.S.A. 42°37N 75°20W 175 D9
New Berlin Pa., U.S.A. 40°50N 76°57W 174 F8
New Bern U.S.A. 35°7N 77°3W 177 D16
New Bethlehem U.S.A. 41°0N 79°20W 174 F5
New Bight Bahamas 24°19N 75°24W 183 B4
New Bloomfield U.S.A. 40°25N 77°11W 174 F7
New Boston U.S.A. 33°28N 94°25W 176 E7
New Braunfels U.S.A. 29°42N 98°8W 176 G5
New Brighton N.Z. 43°29S 172°43E 155 D7
New Brighton U.S.A. 40°42N 80°19W 174 F4
New Britain Papua N. G. 5°50S 150°20E 147 B8
New Britain U.S.A. 41°40N 72°47W 175 E12
New Brockton U.S.A. 31°23N 85°56W 178 D4
New Brunswick
U.S.A. 40°30N 74°27W 175 F10
New Brunswick □
Canada 46°50N 66°30W 165 C6
New Bussa Nigeria 9°53N 4°31E 139 D5
New Caledonia ☑
Pac. Oc. 21°0S 165°0E 147 D9
New Caledonia Trough
Pac. Oc. 30°0S 165°0E 156 L8
New Castile = Castilla-La
Mancha □ Spain 39°30N 3°30W 89 F7
New Castle Ind.,
U.S.A. 39°55N 85°22W 173 F11
New Castle Pa., U.S.A. 41°0N 80°21W 174 F4
New Chitose ✈ (CTS)
Japan 42°46N 141°41E 112 C10
New City U.S.A. 41°9N 73°59W 175 E11
New Concord U.S.A. 39°59N 81°54W 174 G3
New Cumberland
U.S.A. 40°30N 80°36W 174 F4
New Cuyama U.S.A. 34°57N 119°38W 171 L7
New Delhi India 28°36N 77°11E 124 E7
New Denver Canada 50°0N 117°25W 162 D5
New Don Pedro Res.
U.S.A. 37°43N 120°24W 170 H6
New Ellenton U.S.A. 33°26N 81°41W 178 B8
New England N. Dak.,
U.S.A. 46°32N 102°52W 172 B2
New England △
Australia 30°25S 152°30E 153 A10
New England Ra.
Australia 30°20S 151°45E 151 C5
New England Seamounts
Atl. Oc. 38°0N 63°0W 154 C11
New Forest △ U.K. 50°53N 1°34W 67 G6
New Galloway U.K. 55°5N 4°9W 65 F4
New Glasgow Canada 45°35N 62°36W 165 C7
New Guinea Oceania 4°0S 136°0E 147 B6
New Hamburg Canada 43°23N 80°42W 174 C4
New Hampshire □
U.S.A. 44°0N 71°30W 175 C13
New Hampton U.S.A. 43°3N 92°19W 172 D7
New Hanover S. Africa 29°22S 30°31E 145 C5
New Hartford U.S.A. 43°4N 75°18W 175 C9
New Haven Conn.,
U.S.A. 41°18N 72°55W 175 E12
New Haven Mich.,
U.S.A. 42°44N 82°48W 174 D2
New Haven N.Y.,
U.S.A. 43°28N 76°18W 175 C8
New Hazelton Canada 55°20N 127°30W 162 B3
New Hebrides = Vanuatu ■
Pac. Oc. 15°0S 168°0E 147 C9
New Holland U.S.A. 40°6N 76°5W 175 F8
New Iberia U.S.A. 30°1N 91°49W 176 F9
New Ireland
Papua N. G. 3°20S 151°50E 147 B8
New Jersey □ U.S.A. 40°0N 74°30W 173 F16
New Kensington U.S.A. 40°34N 79°46W 174 F5
New Lexington U.S.A. 39°43N 82°13W 173 F12
New Liskeard Canada 47°31N 79°41W 164 C4
New London Conn.,
U.S.A. 41°22N 72°6W 175 E12
New London Ohio,
U.S.A. 41°5N 82°24W 174 E2

New London Wis.,
U.S.A. 44°23N 88°45W 172 C9
New Madrid U.S.A. 36°36N 89°32W 172 G9
New Martinsville
U.S.A. 39°39N 80°52W 173 F13
New Meadows U.S.A. 44°58N 116°18W 168 D5
New Melones L.
U.S.A. 37°57N 120°31W 170 H6
New Mexico □ U.S.A. 34°30N 106°0W 169 J11
New Milford Conn.,
U.S.A. 41°35N 73°25W 175 E11
New Milford Pa.,
U.S.A. 41°52N 75°44W 175 E9
New Mumbai = Navi Mumbai
India 19°5N 73°0E 124 E1
New Norcia Australia 30°57S 116°13E 149 F2
New Norfolk Australia 42°46S 147°2E 151 G4
New Orleans U.S.A. 29°57N 90°4W 177 G9
New Philadelphia
U.S.A. 40°30N 81°27W 174 F3
New Plymouth N.Z. 39°4S 174°5E 154 F3
New Plymouth
U.S.A. 43°58N 116°49W 168 E5
New Port Richey
U.S.A. 28°16N 82°43W 179 G7
New Providence
Bahamas 25°25N 77°35W 182 A4
New Quay U.K. 52°13N 4°21W 67 E3
New Radnor U.K. 52°15N 3°9W 67 E4
New Richmond
Canada 48°15N 65°45W 165 C6
New Richmond U.S.A. 45°7N 92°32W 172 C8
New River Gorge ☐
U.S.A. 37°53N 81°5W 173 G13
New Roads U.S.A. 30°42N 91°26W 176 F9
New Rochelle U.S.A. 40°55N 73°46W 175 F11
New Rockford U.S.A. 47°41N 99°8W 172 B4
New Romney U.K. 50°59N 0°57E 67 G8
New Ross Ireland 52°23N 6°57W 64 D5
New Salem U.S.A. 46°51N 101°25W 172 B3
New Scone = Scone U.K. 56°25N 3°24W 65 E5
New Siberian I. = Novaya Sibir,
Ostrov Russia 75°10N 150°0E 107 B16
New Siberian Is. = Novosibirskiye
Ostrova Russia 75°0N 142°0E 107 B15
New Smyrna Beach
U.S.A. 29°1N 80°56W 179 F9
New South Wales □
Australia 33°0S 146°0E 153 B7
New Tecumseth = Alliston
Canada 44°9N 79°52W 174 B5
New Town U.S.A. 47°59N 102°30W 172 B2
New Ulm U.S.A. 44°19N 94°28W 172 C6
New Waterford Canada 46°13N 60°4W 165 C7
New Westminster
Canada 49°13N 122°55W 170 A4
New York U.S.A. 40°43N 74°0W 175 F11
New York □ U.S.A. 43°0N 75°0W 175 D9
New York J.F. Kennedy Int. ✈
(JFK) U.S.A. 40°38N 73°47W 175 F11
New Zealand ■ Oceania 40°0S 176°0E 154 G5
Newaj → India 24°24N 76°49E 124 G7
Newala Tanzania 10°58S 39°18E 143 E4
Newark Del., U.S.A. 39°41N 75°46W 173 F16
Newark N.J., U.S.A. 40°44N 74°10W 175 F10
Newark N.Y., U.S.A. 43°3N 77°6W 174 C7
Newark Ohio, U.S.A. 40°3N 82°24W 174 F2
Newark Liberty Int. ✈ (EWR)
U.S.A. 40°42N 74°10W 175 F10
Newark-on-Trent U.K. 53°5N 0°48W 66 D7
Newark Valley U.S.A. 42°14N 76°11W 175 D8
Newberg U.S.A. 45°18N 122°58W 168 D2
Newberry Fla., U.S.A. 29°39N 82°37W 179 F7
Newberry Mich.,
U.S.A. 46°21N 85°30W 173 B11
Newberry S.C., U.S.A. 34°17N 81°37W 177 D14
Newberry Springs
U.S.A. 34°50N 116°41W 171 L10
Newboro L. Canada 44°38N 76°20W 175 B8
Newbridge Ireland 53°11N 6°48W 64 C5
Newburgh Canada 44°19N 76°52W 174 B7
Newburgh U.S.A. 41°30N 74°1W 175 E10
Newbury U.K. 51°24N 1°20W 67 F6
Newbury N.H., U.S.A. 43°19N 72°3W 175 B12
Newbury Vt., U.S.A. 44°5N 72°4W 175 B12
Newburyport U.S.A. 42°49N 70°53W 175 D14
Newcastle Australia 33°0S 151°46E 153 B9
Newcastle N.B., Canada 47°1N 65°38W 165 C6
Newcastle Ont., Canada 43°55N 78°35W 164 D4
Newcastle Ireland 52°27N 9°3W 64 D2
Newcastle S. Africa 27°45S 29°58E 145 C4
Newcastle U.K. 54°13N 5°54W 64 B6
Newcastle Calif., U.S.A. 38°53N 121°8W 170 G5
Newcastle Wyo., U.S.A. 43°50N 104°11W 168 E11
Newcastle Emlyn U.K. 52°2N 4°28W 67 E3
Newcastle Ra.
Australia 15°45S 130°15E 148 C5
Newcastle-under-Lyme
U.K. 53°1N 2°14W 66 D5
Newcastle-upon-Tyne
U.K. 54°58N 1°36W 66 C6
Newcastle Waters
Australia 17°30S 133°28E 150 B1
Newcomb U.S.A. 43°58N 74°10W 175 C10
Newcomerstown
U.S.A. 40°16N 81°36W 174 F3
Newdegate Australia 33°6S 119°0E 149 F2
Newell Australia 16°20S 145°16E 150 B4
Newell U.S.A. 44°43N 103°25W 172 C2
Newenham, C. U.S.A. 58°39N 162°11W 166 D7
Newfane U.S.A. 43°17N 78°43W 174 C6
Newfield U.S.A. 42°18N 76°33W 175 D8
Newfound L. U.S.A. 43°40N 71°47W 175 C13
Newfoundland Canada 41°18N 75°19W 175 E9
Newfoundland & Labrador □
Canada 52°0N 58°0W 165 B8
Newhaven U.K. 50°47N 0°3E 67 G8
Newington U.S.A. 32°35N 81°30W 178 C8
Newkirk U.S.A. 36°53N 97°3W 176 C6
Newlyn U.K. 50°6N 5°34W 67 G2
Newman Australia 23°18S 119°45E 148 D2
Newman U.S.A. 37°19N 121°1W 170 H5
Newmarket Canada 44°3N 79°48W 174 B5
Newmarket Ireland 52°13N 9°0W 64 D2
Newmarket U.K. 52°15N 0°25E 67 E8
Newmarket U.S.A. 43°5N 70°56W 175 C14
Newnan U.S.A. 33°23N 84°48W 178 B5
Newport Ireland 53°53N 9°33W 64 C2
Newport I. of W., U.K. 50°42N 1°17W 67 G6
Newport Newport, U.K. 51°35N 3°0W 67 F5

Newport Ark., U.S.A. 35°37N 91°16W 176 D9
Newport Fla., U.S.A. 30°11N 84°10W 178 E6
Newport Ky., U.S.A. 39°5N 84°29W 173 F11
Newport N.H., U.S.A. 43°22N 72°10W 175 C12
Newport N.Y., U.S.A. 43°11N 75°1W 175 C9
Newport Oreg., U.S.A. 44°39N 124°3W 168 D1
Newport Pa., U.S.A. 40°29N 77°8W 174 F7
Newport R.I., U.S.A. 41°29N 71°19W 175 E13
Newport Tenn., U.S.A. 35°58N 83°11W 177 D13
Newport Vt., U.S.A. 44°56N 72°13W 175 B12
Newport Wash., U.S.A. 48°11N 117°3W 168 B5
Newport □ U.K. 51°33N 3°1W 67 F4
Newport Beach
U.S.A. 33°37N 117°56W 171 M9
Newport News U.S.A. 36°58N 76°25W 173 G15
Newport Pagnell U.K. 52°5N 0°43W 67 E7
Newquay U.K. 50°25N 5°6W 67 G2
Newry U.K. 54°11N 6°21W 64 B5
Newry Islands △
Australia 20°51S 148°56E 150 b
Newton Ga., U.S.A. 31°19N 84°20W 178 D5
Newton Ill., U.S.A. 38°59N 88°10W 172 F9
Newton Iowa, U.S.A. 41°42N 93°3W 172 E7
Newton Kans., U.S.A. 38°3N 97°21W 172 F5
Newton Mass., U.S.A. 42°21N 71°12W 175 D13
Newton Miss., U.S.A. 32°19N 89°10W 177 E10
Newton N.C., U.S.A. 35°40N 81°13W 177 D14
Newton N.J., U.S.A. 41°3N 74°45W 175 E10
Newton Tex., U.S.A. 30°51N 93°46W 176 F8
Newton Abbot U.K. 50°32N 3°37W 67 G4
Newton Aycliffe U.K. 54°37N 1°34W 66 C6
Newton Falls N.Y.,
U.S.A. 44°12N 74°59W 175 B10
Newton Falls Ohio,
U.S.A. 41°11N 80°59W 174 E4
Newton Stewart U.K. 54°57N 4°30W 65 G4
Newtonmore U.K. 57°4N 4°8W 65 D4
Newtontoppen Svalbard 79°0N 17°30E 57 B12
Newtown U.K. 52°31N 3°19W 67 E4
Newtownabbey U.K. 54°40N 5°56W 64 B6
Newtownards U.K. 54°36N 5°42W 64 B6
Newtownbarry = Bunclody
Ireland 52°39N 6°40W 64 D5
Newtownstewart U.K. 54°43N 7°23W 64 B4
Newville U.S.A. 40°10N 77°24W 174 F7
Nexon France 45°41N 1°11E 72 C5
Neya Russia 58°21N 43°49E 86 A6
Neyrīz Iran 29°15N 54°19E 129 D7
Neyshābūr Iran 36°10N 58°50E 129 B8
Neyveli India 11°32N 79°29E 127 J4
Neyyattinkara India 8°26N 77°5E 127 K3
Nezhin = Nizhyn Ukraine 51°5N 31°55E 86 G6
Nezperce U.S.A. 46°14N 116°14W 168 C5
Nezvysko Ukraine 48°46N 25°15E 81 B10
Nga, Laem Thailand 7°55N 98°27E 121 a
Ngaanyatjarra ۞
Australia 22°40S 127°0E 148 D4
Ngabang Indonesia 0°23N 109°55E 118 D3
Ngabordamlu, Tanjung
Indonesia 6°56S 134°11E 119 F8
Ngala Nigeria 12°20N 14°11E 139 C7
Ngaliwurru Nungali ۞
Australia 15°42S 130°4E 148 C5
Ngalurrtju ۞ Australia 22°44S 132°5E 148 D5
Ngambé Centre,
Cameroon 5°48N 11°29E 139 D7
Ngambé Littoral,
Cameroon 4°21N 10°40E 139 E7
Ngami Depression
Botswana 20°30S 22°46E 144 B3
Ngamo Zimbabwe 19°3S 27°32E 143 F2
Ngamring China 29°14N 87°10E 110 F6
Nganglong Kangri China 33°0N 81°0E 125 C9
Ngao Thailand 18°46N 99°59E 120 C2
Ngaoundéré Cameroon 7°15N 13°35E 140 C2
Ngapara N.Z. 44°57S 170°46E 155 E5
Ngara Tanzania 2°29S 30°40E 142 C3
Ngaruawahia N.Z. 37°42S 175°11E 154 F4
Ngararoro → N.Z. 39°34S 176°56E 154 F5
Ngatapa N.Z. 38°32S 177°45E 154 F6
Ngauruhoe, Mt. N.Z. 39°13S 175°45E 154 F4
Ngawi Indonesia 7°24S 111°26E 119 G14
Ngcobo S. Africa 31°37S 28°0E 145 D4
Ngerulmut = Melekeok
Palau 7°27N 134°38E 156 G5
Nghia Lo Vietnam 21°33N 104°28E 116 G5
Ngoma Malawi 13°8S 33°45E 143 E3
Ngomahura Zimbabwe 20°26S 30°43E 143 G3
Ngomba Tanzania 8°20S 32°53E 143 D3
Ngomeni, Ras Kenya 2°59S 40°14E 142 C5
Ngong Kenya 1°22S 36°39E 142 C4
Ngongotaha N.Z. 38°5S 176°12E 154 F5
Ngoring Hu China 34°55N 97°5E 110 E8
Ngorkou Mali 15°40N 3°41W 138 B4
Ngorongoro Tanzania 3°11S 35°32E 142 C4
Ngorongoro △ Tanzania 2°40S 35°30E 142 C4
Ngozi Burundi 2°54S 29°50E 142 C2
Ngudu Tanzania 2°58S 33°25E 142 C3
Nguigmi Niger 14°20N 13°20E 139 C8
Nguila Cameroon 4°41N 11°43E 139 E7
Nguiu Australia 11°46S 130°38E 148 B5
Ngukurr Australia 14°44S 134°44E 150 A1
Ngum → Laos 18°31N 102°32E 120 C4
Ngundu Zimbabwe 18°11S 31°15E 143 G3
Ngunga Tanzania 3°37S 33°37E 142 C3
Nguru Nigeria 12°56N 10°29E 139 C7
Nguru Mts. Tanzania 6°0S 37°30E 142 D4
Ngusi Malawi 14°0S 34°50E 143 E3
Nguyen Binh Vietnam 22°39N 105°56E 116 F5
Ngwaketse → Botswana 25°0S 25°0E 144 C3
Nha Bang Vietnam 10°37N 105°0E 121 G5
Nha Trang Vietnam 12°16N 109°10E 121 F7
Nhacoongo Mozam. 24°18S 35°14E 145 C6
Nhamaabué Mozam. 17°25S 35°5E 143 F4
Nhamundá → Brazil 2°12S 56°41W 187 D7
Nhangulaze, L. Mozam. 24°0S 34°30E 145 C5
Nharnuwangu, Wajarri and
Ngarlawangga ۞
Australia 25°0S 118°0E 149 D2
Nhill Australia 36°18S 141°40E 152 C4
Nho Quan Vietnam 20°18N 105°45E 116 G5
Nhulunbuy Australia 12°10S 137°20E 150 A2
Nia-nia
Dem. Rep. of the Congo 1°30N 27°40E 142 B2
Niafounké Mali 16°0N 4°5W 138 B4
Niagara Falls Canada 43°7N 79°5W 174 C5
Niagara Falls U.S.A. 43°5N 79°4W 174 C6
Niagara-on-the-Lake
Canada 43°15N 79°4W 174 C5

Niah Malaysia 3°58N 113°46E 118 D4
Niamey Niger 13°27N 2°6E 139 C5
Niamtougou Togo 9°46N 1°6E 139 D5
Niandan-Koro Guinea 11°5N 9°15W 138 D3
Nianforando Guinea 9°37N 10°36W 138 D2
Niangara
Dem. Rep. of the Congo 3°42N 27°50E 142 B2
Niangoloko
Burkina Faso 10°15N 4°55W 138 C4
Niantic U.S.A. 41°20N 72°11W 175 E12
Nias Indonesia 1°0N 97°30E 118 D1
Niassa □ Mozam. 13°30S 36°0E 143 E4
Niassa, L. = Malawi, L.
Africa 12°30S 34°30E 143 E3
Niassa △ Mozam. 12°45S 36°57E 143 E4
Nibāk Si. Arabia 24°25N 50°50E 129 E7
Nibe Denmark 56°59N 9°38E 63 H3
Nicaragua ■
Cent. Amer. 11°40N 85°30W 182 D2
Nicaragua, L. de Nic. 12°0N 85°30W 182 D2
Nicastro Italy 38°59N 16°19E 95 D9
Nice France 43°42N 7°14E 73 E11
Nice-Côte-d'Azur ✈ (NCE)
France 43°41N 7°12E 73 E11
Niceville U.S.A. 30°31N 86°30W 179 E3
Nichicun, L. Canada 53°5N 71°0W 165 B5
Nichinan Japan 31°38N 131°23E 113 J5
Nicholás, Canal
Caribbean 23°30N 80°5W 182 B3
Nicholas Channel = Nicholás,
Canal Caribbean 23°30N 80°5W 182 B3
Nicholasville U.S.A. 37°53N 84°34W 173 G11
Nicholls U.S.A. 31°31N 82°38W 178 D7
Nichols U.S.A. 42°1N 76°22W 175 D8
Nicholson Australia 18°2S 128°54E 148 C4
Nicholson U.S.A. 41°37N 75°47W 175 E9
Nicholson L. Canada 62°40N 102°40W 163 A8
Nicholson Ra.
Australia 27°15S 116°45E 149 E2
Nicholville U.S.A. 44°41N 74°39W 175 B10
Nicobar Is. Ind. Oc. 8°0N 93°30E 127 L11
Nicola Canada 50°12N 120°40W 162 C4
Nicolls Town Bahamas 25°8N 78°0W 182 A4
Nicosia Cyprus 35°10N 33°25E 101 D12
Nicosia Italy 37°45N 14°24E 95 E7
Nicótera Italy 38°33N 15°56E 95 D8
Nicoya Costa Rica 10°9N 85°27W 182 D2
Nicoya, G. de Costa Rica 10°0N 85°0W 182 E3
Nicoya, Pen. de
Costa Rica 9°45N 85°40W 182 E2
Nida Lithuania 55°20N 21°4E 82 C8
Nidd → U.K. 53°59N 1°23W 66 D6
Nidda Germany 50°23N 9°1E 76 E5
Nidda → Germany 50°17N 8°48E 77 E4
Nidwalden □ Switz. 46°50N 8°25E 77 J4
Nidzica Poland 53°25N 20°28E 83 E7
Niebüll Germany 54°46N 8°48E 76 A4
Nied → Germany 49°23N 6°40E 71 C13
Niederbayern □
Germany 48°40N 12°50E 77 G8
Niederbronn-les-Bains
France 48°57N 7°39E 71 D14
Niedere Tauern Austria 47°20N 14°0E 78 D7
Niederlausitz Germany 51°42N 13°59E 76 D9
Niederösterreich □
Austria 48°25N 15°40E 78 C8
Niedersachsen □ Germany 52°50N 9°0E 76 C4
Niedersächsisches Wattenmeer △
Germany 53°45N 7°30E 76 B3
Niekerkshoop S. Africa 29°19S 22°51E 144 C3
Niellé Ivory C. 10°5N 5°38W 138 C3
Niemba
Dem. Rep. of the Congo 5°58S 28°24E 142 D2
Niemen = Nemunas →
Lithuania 55°25N 21°10E 82 C8
Niemodlin Poland 50°38N 17°38E 83 H4
Nienburg Germany 52°39N 9°13E 76 C5
Niepolomice Poland 50°3N 20°13E 83 J7
Niers → Germany 51°43N 5°57E 76 D1
Niesky Germany 51°17N 14°49E 76 D10
Nieszawa Poland 52°52N 18°50E 83 F5
Nieu Bethesda S. Africa 31°51S 24°34E 144 D3
Nieuw Amsterdam
Suriname 5°53S 55°5W 187 B7
Nieuw Nickerie Suriname 6°0N 56°59W 187 B7
Nieuwoudtville S. Africa 31°23S 19°7E 144 D2
Nieuwpoort Belgium 51°8N 2°45E 69 C2
Nieves, Pico de las
Canary Is. 27°57N 15°35W 100 G4
Nièvre □ France 47°10N 3°40E 71 E10
Niga Mali 13°38N 5°27E 138 C4
Niğde Turkey 37°58N 34°40E 104 D6
Niğde □ Turkey 38°0N 34°30E 104 D6
Nigel S. Africa 26°27S 28°25E 145 C4
Niger ■ W. Afr. 17°30N 10°0E 139 B7
Niger □ Nigeria 10°0N 5°30E 139 D6
Niger → W. Afr. 5°33N 6°33E 139 D6
Niger Delta Africa 4°50N 6°0E 139 E6
Nigeria ■ W. Afr. 8°30N 8°0E 139 D6
Nighasin India 28°14N 80°52E 125 E9
Nightcaps N.Z. 45°57S 168°2E 155 F3
Nihoa U.S.A. 23°6N 161°58W 166 L6
Nihon = Japan ■ Asia 36°0N 136°0E 113 G8
Nii-Jima Japan 34°20N 139°15E 113 G9
Niigata Japan 37°58N 139°0E 112 F9
Niigata □ Japan 37°15N 138°45E 112 F9
Niihama Japan 33°55N 133°16E 113 H6
Ni'ihau U.S.A. 21°54N 160°9W 166 L5
Niimi Japan 34°59N 133°28E 113 G6
Niitsu Japan 37°48N 139°7E 112 F9
Nijar Spain 36°53N 2°15W 91 J2
Nijil Jordan 30°32N 35°33E 130 E4
Nijkerk Neths. 52°13N 5°30E 69 C5
Nijmegen Neths. 51°50N 5°52E 69 D5
Nijverdal Neths. 52°22N 6°28E 69 B6
Nik Pey Iran 36°50N 48°10E 129 B6
Nikiniki Indonesia 9°49S 124°30E 119 G6
Nikiski U.S.A. 60°41N 151°18W 166 C9
Nikki Benin 9°58N 3°12E 139 D5
Nikkō Japan 36°45N 139°35E 113 F9
Nikkō △ Japan 36°56N 139°37E 113 F9

Nikolayev = Mykolayiv
Ukraine 46°58N 32°0E 85
Nikolayevsk Russia 50°0N 45°35E 86
Nikolayevsk-na-Amur
Russia 53°8N 140°44E 107
Nikolsk Russia 53°49N 46°4E 86
Nikolskoye Russia 55°12N 166°0E 107 D
Nikopol Bulgaria 43°43N 24°54E 97
Nikopol Ukraine 47°35N 34°25E 85
Nikopolis Greece 39°5N 20°43E 96
Niksar Turkey 40°31N 37°2E 104
Nīkshahr Iran 26°15N 60°10E 129
Nikšić Montenegro 42°50N 18°57E 96
Nīl, Nahr en → Africa 30°10N 31°6E 137
Nīl el Abyad → Sudan 15°38N 32°31E 135
Nīl el Azraq → Sudan 15°38N 32°31E 135
Nila Indonesia 6°44S 129°31E 119
Nilakkottai India 10°10N 77°52E 127
Niland U.S.A. 33°14N 115°31W 171
Nilanga India 18°6N 76°46E 126
Nile = Nīl, Nahr en →
Africa 30°10N 31°6E 137
Nile Delta Egypt 31°40N 31°0E 137
Niles Mich., U.S.A. 41°50N 86°15W 172
Niles Ohio, U.S.A. 41°11N 80°46W 174
Nileshwar India 12°15N 75°6E 127
Nilgiri Hills India 11°30N 76°30E 127
Nilo Peçanha Brazil 13°37S 39°6W 189
Nilüfer → Turkey 40°18N 28°27E 97
Nim Ka Thana India 27°44N 75°48E 124
Nimach India 24°30N 74°56E 124
Nimba, Mt. Africa 7°37N 8°25W 138
Nimbahera India 24°37N 74°45E 124
Nîmes France 43°50N 4°23E 73
Nimfaion, Ákra = Pines, Akra
Greece 40°5N 24°20E 97
Nimmitabel Australia 36°29S 149°15E 153
Nin Croatia 44°16N 15°12E 93
Nīnawā Iraq 36°25N 43°10E 105
Nīnawā □ Iraq 36°15N 43°0E 128
Nindigully Australia 28°21S 148°50E 151
Nine Degree Channel
India 9°0N 73°0E 127
Ninepin Group China 22°16N 114°21E 119
Ninety Mile Beach N.Z. 34°48S 173°0E 154
Ninety Mile Beach, The
Australia 38°15S 147°24E 153
Ninety Six U.S.A. 34°11N 82°1W 178
Nineveh = Nīnawā
Iraq 36°25N 43°10E 105
Ning Xian China 35°30N 107°58E 114
Ning'an China 44°22N 129°20E 115
Ningbo China 29°51N 121°28E 117
Ningcheng China 41°32N 119°53E 115
Ningde China 26°38N 119°23E 117
Ningdu China 26°38N 115°59E 117
Ningguo China 30°35N 119°0E 117
Ninghai China 29°15N 121°27E 117
Ninghua China 26°14N 116°45E 117
Ningi Nigeria 10°55N 9°30E 139
Ningjin China 37°35N 114°57E 114
Ningjing Shan China 31°0N 98°20E 116
Ningling China 34°25N 115°22E 114
Ningming China 22°8N 107°4E 116
Ningnan China 27°5N 102°36E 116
Ningpo = Ningbo
China 29°51N 121°28E 117
Ningqiang China 32°47N 106°15E 114
Ningshan China 33°21N 108°21E 116
Ningsia Hui A.R. = Ningxia Huizu
Zizhiqu □ China 38°0N 106°0E 114
Ningwu China 39°0N 112°18E 114
Ningxia Huizu Zizhiqu □
China 38°0N 106°0E 114
Ningxiang China 28°15N 112°30E 117
Ningyang China 35°47N 116°45E 114
Ningyuan China 25°37S 111°57E 117
Ninh Binh Vietnam 20°15N 105°55E 116
Ninh Giang Vietnam 20°44N 106°24E 120
Ninh Hoa Vietnam 12°30N 109°7E 120
Ninh Ma Vietnam 12°48N 109°21E 120
Nini-Suihen △ Ghana 5°20N 2°34W 138
Ninove Belgium 50°51N 4°2E 69
Nioaque Brazil 21°5S 55°50W 191
Niobrara U.S.A. 42°45N 98°2W 172
Niobrara → U.S.A. 42°46N 98°3W 172
Niokolo-Koba △ Senegal 13°3N 13°2W 138
Niono Mali 14°15N 6°0W 138
Nionsamoridougou
Guinea 8°45N 8°50W 138
Nioro du Rip Senegal 13°40N 15°50W 138
Nioro du Sahel Mali 15°15N 9°30W 138
Niort France 46°19N 0°29W 72
Nipani India 16°20N 74°25E 127
Nipawin Canada 53°20N 104°0W 163
Nipigon Canada 49°0N 88°17W 164
Nipigon, L. Canada 49°50N 88°30W 164
Nipishish L. Canada 54°12N 60°45W 165
Nipissing, L. Canada 46°20N 80°0W 164
Nipomo U.S.A. 35°3N 120°29W 171
Nippon = Japan ■ Asia 36°0N 136°0E 113
Nipton U.S.A. 35°28N 115°16W 171
Niquelândia Brazil 14°33S 48°23W 189
Nīr Iran 38°2N 47°59E 105
Nira → India 17°58N 75°8E 126
Nirasaki Japan 35°42N 138°27E 113
Nirmal India 19°3N 78°20E 126
Nirmali India 26°20N 86°35E 125
Niš Serbia 43°19N 21°58E 96
Nisa Portugal 39°30N 7°41W 89
Nisa Turkmenistan 37°59N 58°11E 129
Nişāb Si. Arabia 29°11N 44°43E 128
Nişāb Yemen 14°25N 46°29E 131
Nišava → Serbia 43°20N 21°46E 96
Niscemi Italy 37°9N 14°23E 95
Nishinomiya Japan 34°45N 135°20E 113
Nishino'omote Japan 30°43N 130°59E 113
Nishiwaki Japan 34°59N 134°58E 113
Niška Banja Serbia 43°18N 22°1E 96
Niskibi → Canada 56°29N 88°9W 164
Nisko Poland 50°35N 22°7E 83
Nisporeni Moldova 47°4N 28°10E 81
Nisqually → U.S.A. 47°7N 122°42W 170
Nissaki Greece 39°43N 19°52E 101
Nissan → Sweden 56°40N 12°51E 63
Nissiros Greece 36°35N 27°12E 97

sum Bredning
Denmark 56°40N 8°20E 63 H2
sum Fjord *Denmark* 56°20N 8°11E 63 H2
tru = Dnister ➤
Europe 46°18N 30°17E 75 E16
utlin ➤ *Canada* 60°14N 132°34W 162 A3
chequon *Canada* 53°10N 70°58W 165 B5
erói *Brazil* 22°53S 43°7W 191 A7
h ➤ *Canada* 43°12N 80°23W 174 C4
h ➤ *U.K.* 55°14N 3°33W 65 F5
miluk ➤ *Australia* 14°6S 132°15E 148 B5
ra *Slovak Rep.* 48°19N 18°4E 79 C11
ra ➤ *Slovak Rep.* 47°46N 18°10E 79 D11
riansky ➤
lovak Rep. 48°10N 18°30E 79 C11
enau *Germany* 49°12N 12°16E 77 F8
e ☒ *Pac. Oc.* 19°2S 169°54W 157 J11
lan Jiang ➤ *China* 27°30N 103°5E 116 D4
t *Indonesia* 0°55N 109°54E 118 D4
tou Shan *China* 29°5N 121°59E 117 C13
zhuang *China* 40°58N 122°28E 115 D12
a *Finland* 63°56N 24°57E 62 D10
ernais *France* 47°15N 3°30E 71 E10
erville *Canada* 49°36N 97°3W 163 D9
was *India* 23°3N 80°26E 125 H9
a *U.S.A.* 37°3N 93°18W 172 G7
on *U.S.A.* 29°16N 97°46W 176 G6
am Sagar *India* 18°10N 77°58E 126 E3
amabad *India* 18°45N 78°7E 126 E4
amghat *India* 28°20N 95°45E 123 E19
hne-Kolymsk
Russia 68°34N 160°55E 107 C17
hne-Svirskiy △
Russia 60°30N 32°55E 84 B7
hnegorskiy = Nyzhnohirskyy
Ukraine 45°27N 34°38E 85 K8
hnekamsk *Russia* 55°38N 51°49E 86 C10
hneudinsk *Russia* 54°54N 99°3E 107 D10
hnevartovsk *Russia* 56°56N 76°38E 106 C8
hniy Bestyakh
Russia 61°57N 129°54E 107 C13
hniy Chir *Russia* 48°22N 43°5E 87 F6
hniy Lomov *Russia* 53°34N 43°38E 86 D6
hniy Novgorod *Russia* 56°20N 44°0E 86 B7
hniy Novgorod □
Russia 56°30N 44°20E 86 B7
hniy Tagil *Russia* 57°55N 59°57E 106 D6
hyn *Ukraine* 51°5N 31°55E 85 G6
hna Mazowiecka
Poland 52°30N 21°0E 83 F8
ip *Turkey* 37°5N 37°50E 104 D7
ké Tatry *Slovak Rep.* 48°55N 19°30E 79 C12
ké Tatry △
lovak Rep. 48°55N 19°37E 79 C12
ký Jeseník
Czech Rep. 49°50N 17°30E 79 B10
wá *Oman* 22°56N 57°32E 131 C6
za Monferrato *Italy* 44°46N 8°21E 92 C5
kwa *Malawi* 11°1S 33°56E 143 E3
zidja = Grande Comore
Comoros Is. 11°35S 43°20E 141 a
goš *Montenegro* 42°53N 18°45E 96 C2
ru *Uganda* 0°27N 33°10E 142 B3
njo *Tanzania* 8°48S 38°54E 143 D4
mbe *Tanzania* 9°20S 34°50E 143 D3
mbe □ *Tanzania* 9°10S 34°50E 143 D3
mbe ➤ *Tanzania* 6°56S 35°6E 142 D4
arundabommen
Sweden 62°15N 17°25E 62 B11
ambe *Cameroon* 6°35N 10°40E 139 D7
ana *Zambia* 12°50S 28°8E 143 E2
andla *S. Africa* 28°37S 31°5E 145 D5
awkaw *Ghana* 6°36N 0°49W 139 D4
ayi *Zimbabwe* 19°41S 29°20E 143 F2
hotakota *Malawi* 12°55S 34°15E 143 E3
hotakota △ *Malawi* 12°50S 34°0E 143 E3
ondwe *Tanzania* 5°51S 30°51E 142 D3
ongsamba *Cameroon* 4°55N 9°55E 139 E6
oteng *Cameroon* 4°31N 12°2E 139 E7
urenkuru *Namibia* 17°42S 18°32E 144 A2
wanta *Ghana* 6°10N 2°10W 138 D4
ai ➤ *Burma* 25°30N 97°25E 116 F2
akhali *Bangla.* 22°48N 91°10E 123 H17
bel *Canada* 45°25N 80°6W 174 A4
beoka *Japan* 32°36N 131°41E 113 H5
blejas *Spain* 39°58N 3°26W 91 C7
blesville *U.S.A.* 40°3N 86°1W 172 E10
boribetsu *Japan* 42°24N 141°6E 112 C10
catee *U.S.A.* 27°10N 81°53W 179 H8
ccundara *Australia* 27°50S 142°36E 151 D3
ce ➤ *Italy* 46°9N 11°4E 92 B8
cera Inferiore *Italy* 40°44N 14°38E 95 B7
cera Umbra *Italy* 43°8N 12°50E 92 C5
ci *Italy* 40°48N 17°7E 95 B10
cona *U.S.A.* 33°47N 97°44W 176 E6
crich *Romania* 45°55N 24°26E 81 E13
da *Japan* 35°56N 139°52E 113 G9
gales *Mexico* 31°19N 110°56W 180 A2
gales *U.S.A.* 31°21N 110°56W 169 L8
garo *France* 43°45N 0°29W 72 E3
gat ➤ *Poland* 54°17N 19°17E 82 A6
gata *Japan* 34°38N 130°44E 113 H5
gent *France* 48°18N 0°20E 71 D12
gent *France* 48°11N 5°20E 71 D12
gent-sur-Seine
France 48°30N 3°30E 71 D10
gerup *Australia* 33°32S 116°5E 149 F2
ginsk *Russia* 64°30N 90°50E 107 C10
gliki *Russia* 51°50N 143°10E 107 D15
goa ➤ *Australia* 23°40S 147°55E 150 C4
goyá *Argentina* 32°24S 59°48W 190 C4
grád □ *Hungary* 48°0N 19°30E 80 A4
guera Pallaresa ➤
Spain 41°55N 0°55E 90 D5
guera Ribargorçana ➤
Spain 41°40N 0°43E 90 D5
har *India* 29°11N 74°49E 124 E6
thelden *Germany* 49°35N 7°7E 77 F3
hta *India* 24°55N 79°34E 125 H8
ia *India* 42°48N 8°53W 88 C2
ida *India* 28°36N 77°19E 124 E7
ire, Montagne *France* 43°28N 2°18E 72 E6
s, Mte. *France* 45°48N 3°46E 72 C7
irmoutier *France* 46°58N 2°10W 70 F4
irmoutier-en-l'Île
France 47°0N 2°14W 70 F4
jane *Botswana* 23°15S 20°14E 144 B3
ima-Zaki *Japan* 34°54N 139°53E 113 G9
h Kundi *Pakistan* 28°50N 62°45E 122 E3

Nok Ta Phao, Ko
Thailand 9°23N 99°40E 121 b
Nokaneng *Botswana* 19°40S 22°17E 144 A3
Nokia *Finland* 61°30N 23°30E 64 B2
Nokomis *Canada* 51°35N 105°0W 163 C8
Nokomis *U.S.A.* 27°7N 82°27W 179 H7
Nokomis L. *Canada* 57°0N 103°0W 163 B8
Nola *C.A.R.* 3°35N 16°4E 140 D3
Nola *Italy* 40°55N 14°33E 95 B7
Nolay *France* 46°58N 4°35E 71 F11
Noli, C. di *Italy* 44°12N 8°25E 92 D5
Nolinsk *Russia* 57°28N 49°57E 86 B9
Noma L. *Canada* 30°59N 85°37W 178 E4
Noma Omuramba ➤
Namibia 18°52S 20°53E 144 A3
Nombre de Dios *Panama* 9°34N 79°28W 182 E4
Nome *U.S.A.* 64°30N 165°25W 166 C6
Nomgon *Mongolia* 42°50N 105°8E 114 C3
Nomo-Zaki *Japan* 32°35N 129°44E 113 H4
Nonacho L. *Canada* 61°42N 109°40W 163 A7
Nonda *Australia* 20°40S 142°28E 150 C3
None *Italy* 44°56N 7°32E 92 D4
Nong Chang *Thailand* 15°23N 99°51E 120 E2
Nong Han Res.
Thailand 17°11N 104°9E 120 D5
Nong Het *Laos* 19°29N 103°59E 120 C4
Nong Khai *Thailand* 17°50N 102°46E 120 D4
Nong'an *China* 44°25N 125°5E 115 B13
Nongoma *S. Africa* 27°58S 31°35E 145 C5
Nongsa *Indonesia* 1°11N 104°8E 121 d
Nonoava *Mexico* 27°28N 106°44W 180 B3
Nonsan *S. Korea* 36°12N 127°5E 115 F14
Nonthaburi *Thailand* 13°50N 100°29E 120 D3
Nontron *France* 45°31N 0°40E 72 C4
Nonza *France* 42°47N 9°21E 73 F13
Noonamah *Australia* 12°40S 131°4E 148 B5
Noondie, L. *Australia* 28°30S 119°30E 149 E2
Noonkanbah ☼
Australia 18°30S 124°50E 148 C3
Noord Brabant □ *Neths.* 51°40N 5°0E 69 C5
Noord Holland □ *Neths.* 52°30N 4°45E 69 B4
Noordbeveland *Neths.* 51°35N 3°50E 69 C3
Noordoostpolder *Neths.* 52°45N 5°45E 69 B5
Noordwijk *Neths.* 52°14N 4°26E 69 B4
Nootka I. *Canada* 49°32N 126°42W 162 D3
Nopiming □ *Canada* 50°30N 95°37W 163 C9
Nora *Sweden* 59°32N 15°2E 62 E9
Noralee *Canada* 53°59N 126°26W 162 C3
Noranda = Rouyn-Noranda
Canada 48°20N 79°0W 164 C4
Norberg *Sweden* 60°4N 15°56E 62 D9
Nórcia *Italy* 42°48N 13°5E 93 F10
Norco *U.S.A.* 33°56N 117°33W 171 M9
Norcross *U.S.A.* 33°56N 84°13W 178 B5
Nord □ *Cameroon* 8°30N 14°0E 139 D7
Nord □ *France* 50°15N 3°30E 71 B10
Nord-Kivu □
Dem. Rep. of the Congo 1°0S 29°0E 142 C2
Nord-Ostsee-Kanal
Germany 54°12N 9°32E 76 A5
Nord-Ouest □ *Cameroon* 6°20N 10°30E 139 D7
Nord-Pas-de-Calais □
France 50°30N 2°50E 71 B9
Nordaustlandet *Svalbard* 79°14N 23°0E 54 B9
Nordborg *Denmark* 55°5N 9°50E 63 J3
Nordby *Denmark* 55°27N 8°24E 63 J2
Norddeich *Germany* 53°36N 7°9E 76 B3
Nordegg *Canada* 52°29N 116°5W 162 C5
Norden *Germany* 53°35N 7°12E 76 B3
Nordenham *Germany* 53°30N 8°30E 76 B4
Norderney *Germany* 53°42N 7°9E 76 B3
Norderstedt *Germany* 53°42N 10°1E 76 B6
Nordfjord *Norway* 61°55N 5°30E 60 F11
Nordfriesische Inseln
Germany 54°40N 8°20E 76 A4
Nordhausen *Germany* 51°30N 10°47E 76 D6
Nordhorn *Germany* 52°26N 7°4E 76 C3
Norðoyar *Færoe Is.* 62°17N 6°35W 60 E9
Nördinge-Nol *Sweden* 57°56N 12°5E 63 G6
Nordingrå *Sweden* 62°56N 18°17E 62 B12
Nordjylland □ *Denmark* 57°0N 9°30E 63 G3
Nordkapp *Norway* 71°10N 25°50E 60 A21
Nordkapp *Svalbard* 80°31N 20°0E 54 A9
Nordkinn *Norway* 71°8N 27°40E 60 A22
Nordkinnhalvøya
Norway 70°55N 27°40E 60 A22
Nördlicher Teutoburger
Wald-Wiehengebirge ◯
Germany 52°18N 8°10E 76 C4
Nördlingen *Germany* 48°48N 10°30E 77 G6
Nordstrundingen
Greenland 81°22N 11°40W 57 A9
Nordre Strømfjord
Greenland 67°10N 53°35W 57 D5
Nordrhein-Westfalen □
Germany 51°45N 7°30E 76 D3
Nordstrand *Germany* 54°30N 8°52E 76 A4
Nordvik *Russia* 74°2N 111°32E 107 B12
Nore ➤ *Ireland* 52°25N 6°58W 64 D4
Noreland *Canada* 44°43N 78°48W 174 B6
Norfolk = Simcoe
Canada 42°50N 80°23W 174 D4
Norfolk *N.Y., U.S.A.* 44°48N 74°59W 175 B10
Norfolk *Nebr., U.S.A.* 42°2N 97°25W 172 E5
Norfolk *Va., U.S.A.* 36°50N 76°17W 173 G15
Norfolk □ *U.K.* 52°39N 0°54E 67 E8
Norfolk Broads △ *U.K.* 52°45N 1°30E 67 E9
Norfolk I. *Pac. Oc.* 28°58S 168°3E 147 D9
Norfolk Ridge *Pac. Oc.* 30°0S 168°0E 156 L8
Norfork L. *U.S.A.* 36°15N 92°14W 176 C8
Norge = Norway ■
Europe 63°0N 11°0E 60 E14
Norilsk *Russia* 69°20N 88°6E 107 C9
Norma, Mt. *Australia* 20°55S 140°42E 150 C3
Normal *U.S.A.* 40°31N 88°59W 172 E9
Norman *U.S.A.* 35°13N 97°26W 176 D6
Norman ➤ *Australia* 19°18S 141°51E 150 B3
Norman Park *U.S.A.* 31°16N 83°41W 178 D6
Norman Wells
Canada 65°17N 126°51W 160 D6
Normanby *N.Z.* 39°32S 174°18E 154 F4
Normanby ➤
Australia 14°23S 144°10E 150 A3
Normandie-Maine ◯
France 48°30N 0°20W 70 D6
Normandin *Canada* 48°49N 72°31W 164 C5
Normanhurst, Mt.
Australia 25°4S 122°30E 149 E3
Normanton *Australia* 17°40S 141°10E 150 B3
Normanville *Australia* 35°27S 138°18E 152 C5

Normétal *Canada* 49°0N 79°22W 164 C4
Norquay *Canada* 51°53N 102°5W 163 C8
Norquinco *Argentina* 41°51S 70°55W 192 B2
Norra Kvill △ *Sweden* 57°46N 15°35E 63 G9
Norra Ulvön *Sweden* 63°3N 18°40E 62 A12
Norrahammar *Sweden* 57°43N 14°7E 63 G8
Norrbottens län □
Sweden 66°50N 20°0E 60 C19
Norrdellen *Sweden* 61°53N 16°43E 62 C10
Nørre Aaby *Denmark* 55°27N 9°52E 63 J3
Nørre Alslev *Denmark* 54°54N 11°52E 63 K5
Nørresundby *Denmark* 57°5N 9°52E 63 K5
Norrhult-Klavreström
Sweden 57°7N 15°10E 63 G9
Norris Point *Canada* 49°31N 57°53W 165 C8
Norristown, *Ga., U.S.A.* 32°30N 82°30W 178 C7
Norristown *Pa., U.S.A.* 40°7N 75°21W 175 F9
Norrköping *Sweden* 58°37N 16°11E 63 F10
Norrland *Sweden* 62°15N 15°45E 60 E16
Norrsundet *Sweden* 60°56N 17°8E 62 D11
Norrtälje *Sweden* 59°46N 18°42E 62 E12
Norseman *Australia* 32°8S 121°43E 149 F3
Norsewood *N.Z.* 40°3S 176°13E 154 G5
Norsk *Russia* 52°30N 130°5E 107 D14
Norte, Pta. *Argentina* 42°5S 63°46W 192 B4
Norte, Pta. del
Canary Is. 27°51N 17°57W 100 G3
Norte, Serra do *Brazil* 11°20S 59°0W 186 F7
North *U.S.A.* 33°37N 81°6W 178 B8
North, C. *Canada* 47°2N 60°20W 165 C7
North Adams *U.S.A.* 42°42N 73°7W 175 D11
North America 40°0N 100°0W 158 F10
North Andaman I.
India 13°15N 92°55E 127 H11
North Arm *Canada* 62°0N 114°30W 162 A5
North Augusta *U.S.A.* 33°30N 81°59W 178 B8
North Australian Basin
Ind. Oc. 14°30S 116°30E 146 F10
North Ayrshire □ *U.K.* 55°45N 4°44W 65 F4
North Bass I. *U.S.A.* 41°40N 82°56W 174 E2
North Battleford
Canada 52°50N 108°17W 163 C7
North Bay *Canada* 46°20N 79°30W 164 C4
North Belcher Is.
Canada 56°50N 79°50W 164 A4
North Bend *Oreg.,*
U.S.A. 43°24N 124°14W 168 E1
North Bend *Pa., U.S.A.* 41°20N 77°42W 174 E7
North Bend *Wash.,*
U.S.A. 47°30N 121°47W 170 C5
North Bennington
U.S.A. 42°56N 73°15W 175 D11
North Berwick *U.K.* 56°4N 2°42W 65 E6
North Berwick *U.S.A.* 43°18N 70°44W 175 C14
North Brother I. *India* 10°59N 92°40E 127 J11
North Bruce *Canada* 44°22N 81°26W 174 B3
North C. *Canada* 47°2N 60°20W 165 C7
North C. *N.Z.* 34°23S 173°4E 154 A2
North Canadian ➤
U.S.A. 35°22N 95°37W 176 D7
North Canton *U.S.A.* 40°53N 81°24W 174 F3
North Cape = Nordkapp
Norway 71°10N 25°50E 60 A21
North Caribou L.
Canada 52°50N 90°40W 164 B1
North Carolina □
U.S.A. 35°30N 80°0W 177 D15
North Cascades △
U.S.A. 48°45N 121°10W 168 B3
North Channel *Canada* 46°0N 83°0W 164 C3
North Channel *U.K.* 55°13N 5°52W 65 F3
North Charleston
U.S.A. 32°53N 79°58W 178 C10
North Chicago *U.S.A.* 42°19N 87°51W 172 D10
North Collins *U.S.A.* 42°35N 78°56W 174 D6
North Creek *U.S.A.* 43°42N 73°59W 175 C11
North Dakota □
U.S.A. 47°30N 100°15W 172 B3
North Downs *U.K.* 51°19N 0°21E 67 F8
North East *U.S.A.* 42°13N 79°50W 174 D5
North East □ *Botswana* 20°35S 27°30E 145 B4
North East Frontier Agency =
Arunachal Pradesh □
India 28°0N 95°0E 123 F19
North East Lincolnshire □
U.K. 53°34N 0°2W 66 D7
North Esk ➤ *U.K.* 56°46N 2°24W 65 E6
North European Plain
Europe 55°0N 25°0E 58 E10
North Foreland *U.K.* 51°22N 1°28E 67 F9
North Fork *U.S.A.* 37°14N 119°21W 170 H7
North Fork American ➤
U.S.A. 38°57N 120°59W 170 G5
North Fork Edisto ➤
U.S.A. 33°16N 80°54W 178 B9
North Fork Feather ➤
U.S.A. 38°33N 121°30W 170 F5
North Fork Grand ➤
U.S.A. 45°47N 102°16W 172 C2
North Fork Red ➤
U.S.A. 34°24N 99°14W 176 D5
North Fort Myers
U.S.A. 26°41N 81°53W 179 J8
North Frisian Is. = Nordfriesische
Inseln *Germany* 54°40N 8°20E 76 A4
North Gower *Canada* 45°8N 75°43W 175 B9
North Hd. *Australia* 30°14S 114°59E 149 F1
North Henik L. *Canada* 61°45N 97°40W 163 A9
North Highlands
U.S.A. 38°40N 121°23W 170 G5
North Horr *Kenya* 3°20N 37°8E 142 B4
North I. *India* 10°8N 72°20E 127 J1
North I. *Kenya* 4°5N 36°5E 142 B4
North I. *N.Z.* 38°0S 175°0E 154 E4
North I. *Seychelles* 4°25S 55°13E 141 b
North Kingsville
U.S.A. 41°54N 80°42W 174 E4
North Kitui △ *Kenya* 0°15S 38°29E 142 C4
North Knife ➤
Canada 58°53N 94°45W 163 B10
North Koel ➤ *India* 24°45N 83°50E 125 G10
North Korea ■ *Asia* 40°0N 127°0E 115 E14
North L. *Australia* 32°30S 143°45E 152 B5
North Lakhimpur *India* 27°14N 94°7E 123 F19
North Lanarkshire □
U.K. 55°52N 3°56W 65 F5
North Las Vegas
U.S.A. 36°11N 115°7W 171 J11
North Lincolnshire □
U.K. 53°36N 0°30W 66 D7
North Little Rock
U.S.A. 34°45N 92°16W 176 D8

North Loup ➤ *U.S.A.* 41°17N 98°24W 172 E4
North Luangwa △
Zambia 11°49S 32°9E 143 E3
North Magnetic Pole
Arctic 85°9N 149°0W 54 A1
North Mankato *U.S.A.* 44°10N 94°2W 172 D6
North Miami *U.S.A.* 25°53N 80°11W 179 K9
North Miami Beach
U.S.A. 25°55N 80°9W 179 K9
North Minch *U.K.* 58°5N 5°55W 65 C3
North Moose L. *Canada* 54°4N 100°12W 163 C8
North Myrtle Beach
U.S.A. 33°48N 78°42W 177 E15
North Nahanni ➤
Canada 62°15N 123°20W 162 A4
North Naples *U.S.A.* 26°12N 81°48W 179 J8
North New River Canal
U.S.A. 26°30N 80°30W 179 J9
North Ossetia-Alania □
Russia 43°30N 44°30E 87 J7
North Pagai, I. = Pagai Utara,
Pulau *Indonesia* 2°35S 100°0E 118 E2
North Palisade *U.S.A.* 37°6N 118°31W 170 H8
North Paravar *India* 10°13N 76°14E 127 J3
North Platte *U.S.A.* 41°8N 100°46W 172 E3
North Platte ➤ *U.S.A.* 41°7N 100°42W 172 E3
North Point *Canada* 27°4N 82°10W 179 H7
North Pole *Arctic* 90°0N 0°0 54 A
North Portal *Canada* 49°0N 102°33W 163 D8
North Powder *U.S.A.* 45°2N 117°55W 168 D5
North Pt. *Barbados* 13°20N 59°37W 183 g
North Pt. *Trin. & Tob.* 11°21N 60°31W 187 J16
North Pt. *U.S.A.* 45°2N 83°16W 174 A1
North Reef I. *India* 13°5N 92°43E 127 H11
North Rhine Westphalia =
Nordrhein-Westfalen □
Germany 51°45N 7°30E 76 D3
North River *Canada* 53°49N 57°6W 165 B8
North Rona *Atl. Oc.* 59°7N 5°49W 68 B4
North Ronaldsay *U.K.* 59°22N 2°26W 65 B6
North Saskatchewan ➤
Canada 53°15N 105°5W 163 C7
North Sea *Europe* 56°0N 4°0E 58 D6
North Seal ➤ *Canada* 58°50N 98°7W 163 B9
North Sentinel I. *India* 11°33N 92°15E 127 J11
North Shields
Australia 34°38S 135°52E 152 C1
North Shields *U.K.* 55°1N 1°26W 66 C6
North Slope *U.S.A.* 69°15N 152°0W 166 B9
North Somerset □ *U.K.* 51°24N 2°45W 67 F5
North Sydney *Canada* 46°12N 60°15W 165 C7
North Syracuse *U.S.A.* 43°8N 76°7W 175 C8
North Taranaki Bight
N.Z. 38°50S 174°15E 154 E3
North Thompson ➤
Canada 50°40N 120°20W 162 C4
North Tonawanda
U.S.A. 43°2N 78°53W 174 C6
North Troy *U.S.A.* 45°0N 72°24W 175 B12
North Twin I. *Canada* 53°20N 80°0W 164 B4
North Tyne ➤ *U.K.* 55°0N 2°8W 66 B5
North Uist *U.K.* 57°40N 7°15W 65 D1
North Vancouver
Canada 49°19N 123°4W 170 A3
North Vernon *U.S.A.* 39°0N 85°38W 173 F11
North Wabasca L.
Canada 56°0N 113°55W 162 B6
North Walsham *U.K.* 52°50N 1°22E 66 E9
North West = Severo-Zapadnyy □
Russia 65°0N 40°0E 106 C4
North West □ *Botswana* 19°20S 22°30E 144 A3
North-West □ *S. Africa* 27°0S 25°0E 145 D4
North West C. *Australia* 21°45S 114°9E 148 D1
North West Christmas I. Ridge
Pac. Oc. 6°30N 165°0W 157 F11
North West Frontier = Khyber
Pakhtunkhwa □
Pakistan 34°0N 72°0E 124 B5
North West Highlands
U.K. 57°33N 4°58W 65 D4
North West River
Canada 53°30N 60°10W 165 B7
North Western □
Zambia 13°30S 25°30E 143 E2
North Wildwood
U.S.A. 39°0N 74°48W 173 F16
North York Moors *U.K.* 54°23N 0°53W 66 C7
North York Moors △
U.K. 54°27N 0°51W 66 C7
North Yorkshire □
U.K. 54°15N 1°25W 66 C6
Northallerton *U.K.* 54°20N 1°26W 66 C6
Northam *Australia* 31°35S 116°42E 149 F2
Northam *S. Africa* 24°56S 27°18E 144 B4
Northampton
Australia 28°27S 114°33E 149 E1
Northampton *U.K.* 52°15N 0°53W 67 E7
Northampton *Mass.,*
U.S.A. 42°19N 72°38W 175 D12
Northampton *Pa.,*
U.S.A. 40°41N 75°30W 175 F9
Northamptonshire □
U.K. 52°16N 0°55W 67 E7
Northbridge *U.S.A.* 42°9N 71°39W 175 D13
Northbrook *Canada* 44°44N 77°9W 174 B7
Northcliffe *Australia* 34°39S 116°7E 149 F2
Northeast Pacific Basin
Pac. Oc. 32°0N 145°0W 157 D13
Northeast Providence Channel
W. Indies 26°0N 76°0W 182 A4
Northeim *Germany* 51°42N 10°0E 76 D6
Northern □ *Limpopo □*
S. Africa 24°5S 29°0E 145 B4
Northern □ *Malawi* 11°0S 34°0E 143 E3
Northern □ *S. Leone* 9°30N 11°50E 138 D2
Northern □ *Zambia* 10°30S 31°0E 143 E3
Northern Aral Sea
Kazakhstan 46°20N 60°30E 108 C6
Northern Areas = Gilgit-
Baltistan □ *Pakistan* 36°30N 73°0E 123 A5
Northern Cape □
S. Africa 30°0S 20°0E 144 C3
Northern Circars *India* 17°30N 82°30E 126 F6
Northern Dvina = Dvina,
Severnaya ➤ *Russia* 64°32N 40°30E 58 C14
Northern Indian L.
Canada 57°20N 97°20W 163 B9
Northern Ireland □ *U.K.* 54°45N 7°0W 64 B5
Northern Lau Group
Fiji 17°30S 178°59W 154 a
Northern Light L.
Canada 48°15N 90°39W 164 C1

Northern Marianas ☒
Pac. Oc. 17°0N 145°0E 156 F6
Northern Province □
S. Africa 24°0S 29°0E 145 B4
Northern Range
Trin. & Tob. 10°46N 61°15W 187 K15
Northern Sporades = Voreioi
Sporades *Greece* 39°15N 23°30E 98 B5
Northern Territory □
Australia 20°0S 133°0E 148 D5
Northfield *Minn., U.S.A.* 44°27N 93°9W 172 C7
Northfield *Vt., U.S.A.* 44°9N 72°40W 175 B12
Northgate *Canada* 49°0N 102°16W 163 D8
Northland □ *N.Z.* 35°30S 173°30E 154 B2
Northome *U.S.A.* 47°52N 94°17W 172 B6
Northport *Ala., U.S.A.* 33°14N 87°35W 177 E11
Northport *Wash.,*
U.S.A. 48°55N 117°48W 168 B5
Northumberland □ *U.K.* 55°12N 2°0W 66 B6
Northumberland, C.
Australia 38°5S 140°40E 152 E4
Northumberland Is.
Australia 21°30S 149°50E 150 C4
Northumberland Str.
Canada 46°20N 64°0W 165 C7
Northville *Canada* 43°10N 81°56W 174 C3
Northville *U.S.A.* 43°13N 74°11W 175 C10
Northwest Atlantic Mid-Ocean
Canyon *Atl. Oc.* 54°0N 48°0W 56 A7
Northwest Pacific Basin
Pac. Oc. 32°0N 165°0E 156 D8
Northwest Providence Channel
W. Indies 26°0N 78°0W 182 A4
Northwest Territories □
Canada 63°0N 118°0W 160 E8
Northwich *U.K.* 53°15N 2°31W 66 D5
Northwood *Iowa,*
U.S.A. 43°27N 93°13W 172 D7
Northwood *N. Dak.,*
U.S.A. 47°44N 97°34W 172 B5
Norton *U.S.A.* 39°50N 99°53W 172 F4
Norton *Zimbabwe* 17°52S 30°40E 143 F3
Norton Sd. *U.S.A.* 63°50N 164°0W 166 C7
Nortorf *Germany* 54°10N 9°50E 76 A5
Norwalk *Calif., U.S.A.* 33°54N 118°4W 171 M8
Norwalk *Conn., U.S.A.* 41°7N 73°22W 175 E11
Norwalk *Iowa, U.S.A.* 41°29N 93°41W 172 E7
Norwalk *Ohio, U.S.A.* 41°15N 82°37W 174 E2
Norway *Maine, U.S.A.* 44°13N 70°32W 173 C18
Norway *Mich., U.S.A.* 45°47N 87°55W 172 C10
Norway ■ *Europe* 63°0N 11°0E 60 E14
Norway House *Canada* 53°59N 97°50W 163 C9
Norwegian B. *Canada* 77°30N 90°0W 161 B14
Norwegian Basin *Atl. Oc.* 68°0N 2°0E 54 C8
Norwegian Sea *Atl. Oc.* 66°0N 1°0E 58 B6
Norwich *Canada* 42°59N 80°36W 174 D4
Norwich *U.K.* 52°38N 1°18E 67 E9
Norwich *Conn., U.S.A.* 41°31N 72°5W 175 E12
Norwich *N.Y., U.S.A.* 42°32N 75°32W 175 D9
Norwood *Canada* 44°23N 77°59W 174 B7
Norwood *U.S.A.* 44°45N 75°0W 175 B10
Nosappu-Misaki
Japan 45°26N 141°39E 112 C12
Noshiro *Japan* 40°12N 140°0E 112 D10
Nosivka *Ukraine* 50°50N 31°37E 85 G6
Nosovka = Nosivka
Ukraine 50°50N 31°37E 85 G6
Noṣratābād *Iran* 29°55N 60°0E 129 D8
Noss Hd. *U.K.* 58°28N 3°3W 65 C5
Nossa Senhora da Glória
Brazil 10°14S 37°25W 189 C3
Nossa Senhora das Dores
Brazil 10°29S 37°13W 189 C3
Nossa Senhora do Socorro
Brazil 10°52S 37°7W 189 C3
Nossebro *Sweden* 58°12N 12°43E 63 F6
Nossob ➤ *S. Africa* 26°55S 20°45E 144 D3
Nossombougou *Mali* 13°5N 7°55W 138 C3
Nosy Varika *Madag.* 20°35S 48°32E 141 J9
Noteć ➤ *Poland* 52°44N 15°26E 83 B8
Notikewin ➤ *Canada* 57°2N 117°38W 162 B5
Notio Aigaio □ *Greece* 36°52N 25°34E 99 F7
Notios Aiyaíon = Notio Aigaio □
Greece 36°52N 25°34E 99 F7
Notios Evvoikos Kolpos
Greece 38°20N 24°0E 98 C6
Noto *Italy* 36°53N 15°4E 95 F8
Noto, G. di *Italy* 36°50N 15°12E 95 F8
Noto, Val di *Italy* 37°14N 14°31E 95 F7
Noto-Hantō *Japan* 37°15N 136°40E 113 F8
Notodden *Norway* 59°35N 9°17E 61 G13
Notre Dame B. *Canada* 49°45N 55°30W 165 C8
Notre-Dame-de-Koartac =
Quaqtaq *Canada* 60°55N 69°40W 161 D13
Notre-Dame-des-Bois
Canada 45°24N 71°4W 175 A13
Notre-Dame-d'Ivugivic = Ivujivik
Canada 62°24N 77°55W 161 D12
Notre-Dame-du-Nord
Canada 47°36N 79°30W 164 C4
Notsé *Togo* 7°0N 1°17E 139 D5
Nottawasaga B. *Canada* 44°35N 80°15W 174 B4
Nottaway ➤ *Canada* 51°22N 78°55W 164 B4
Nottingham *U.K.* 52°58N 1°10W 66 E6
Nottingham, City of □
U.K. 52°58N 1°10W 66 E6
Nottinghamshire □ *U.K.* 53°10N 1°3W 66 D6
Nottoway ➤ *U.S.A.* 36°33N 76°55W 173 G15
Notwane ➤ *Botswana* 23°35S 26°58E 144 B4
Nouâdhibou *Mauritania* 20°54N 17°0W 138 D1
Nouâdhibou, Râs
Mauritania 20°50N 17°0W 134 D2
Nouakchott *Mauritania* 18°9N 15°58W 138 B1
Nouâmghâr
Mauritania 19°20N 16°20W 138 B1
Nouméa *N. Cal.* 22°17S 166°30E 147 D9
Nouna *Burkina Faso* 12°44N 3°54W 138 C4
Noupoort *S. Africa* 31°10S 24°57E 144 D3
Nouveau Comptoir = Wemindji
Canada 53°0N 78°49W 164 B4
Nouvelle Amsterdam, I.
Ind. Oc. 38°30S 77°30E 146 H10
Nouvelle-Calédonie = New
Caledonia ☒ *Pac. Oc.* 21°0S 165°0E 147 D9
Nouzonville *France* 49°48N 4°44E 71 C11
Nová Baňa *Slovak Rep.* 48°28N 18°39E 79 C11
Nová Bystřice *Czech Rep.* 49°2N 15°8E 78 B8

Nova Cruz *Brazil* 6°28S 35°25W 189 B3
Nova Era *Brazil* 19°45S 43°3W 189 D2
Nova Esperança *Brazil* 23°8S 52°24W 191 A5
Nova Friburgo *Brazil* 22°16S 42°30W 191 A7
Nova Gorica *Slovenia* 45°57N 13°39E 93 C10
Nova Gradiška *Croatia* 45°17N 17°28E 80 E2
Nova Iguaçu *Brazil* 22°45S 43°28W 191 A7
Nova Iorque *Brazil* 7°0S 44°5W 189 D2
Nova Kakhovka *Ukraine* 46°42N 33°27E 85 J7
Nova Lamego
Guinea-Biss. 12°19N 14°11W 138 C2
Nova Lusitânia *Mozam.* 19°50S 34°34E 143 F3
Nova Mambone *Mozam.* 21°0S 35°3E 145 B6
Nova Odesa *Ukraine* 47°19N 31°47E 85 J6
Nová Paka *Czech Rep.* 50°29N 15°30E 78 A8
Nova Pavova *Croatia* 44°56N 20°14E 80 F5
Nova Ponte *Brazil* 19°8S 47°41W 189 D1
Nova Russas *Brazil* 4°54S 40°58W 189 D3
Nova Scotia □ *Canada* 45°10N 63°0W 165 C7
Nova Siri *Italy* 40°10N 16°35E 95 B9
Nova Sofala *Mozam.* 20°7S 34°42E 145 B5
Nova Ushytsya *Ukraine* 48°50N 27°17E 81 B12
Nova Varoš *Serbia* 43°29N 19°48E 80 C3
Nova Venécia *Brazil* 18°45S 40°24W 189 D2
Nova Zagora *Bulgaria* 42°32N 26°1E 97 C10
Novaci *Macedonia* 41°5N 21°29E 96 E5
Novaci *Romania* 45°10N 23°42E 81 E12
Novafeltria *Italy* 43°53N 12°17E 93 E9
Novara *Italy* 45°28N 8°38E 92 C5
Novato *U.S.A.* 38°6N 122°35W 170 G4
Novaya Kakhovka = Nova
Kakhovka *Ukraine* 46°42N 33°27E 85 J7
Novaya Kazanka = Zhangqala
Kazakhstan 48°56N 49°36E 87 F9
Novaya Ladoga *Russia* 60°7N 32°16E 84 B7
Novaya Lyalya *Russia* 59°4N 60°45E 106 D7
Novaya Sibir, Ostrov
Russia 75°10N 150°0E 107 B16
Novaya Zemlya *Russia* 75°0N 56°0E 106 B6
Nové Město na Moravě
Czech Rep. 49°34N 16°5E 78 B9
Nové Město nad Metují
Czech Rep. 50°20N 16°10E 79 A9
Nové Město nad Váhom
Slovak Rep. 48°45N 17°50E 79 C10
Nové Zámky *Slovak Rep.* 48°2N 18°8E 79 C11
Novelda *Spain* 38°24N 0°45W 91 G4
Novellara *Italy* 44°51N 10°44E 92 D7
Noventa Vicentina *Italy* 45°18N 11°30E 92 C8
Novgorod = Velikiy Novgorod
Russia 58°30N 31°25E 84 C6
Novgorod □ *Russia* 58°50N 32°30E 84 C6
Novgorod-Severskiy = Novhorod-
Siverskyy *Ukraine* 52°2N 33°10E 85 G7
Novhorod-Siverskyy
Ukraine 52°2N 33°10E 85 G7
Novi Bečej *Serbia* 45°36N 20°10E 80 E5
Novi Grad *Bos.-H.* 45°2N 16°22E 93 C13
Novi Iskar *Bulgaria* 42°48N 23°21E 96 D7
Novi Kneževac *Serbia* 46°4N 20°8E 80 E5
Novi Ligure *Italy* 44°46N 8°47E 92 D5
Novi Pazar *Bulgaria* 43°25N 27°15E 97 C11
Novi Pazar *Serbia* 43°12N 20°28E 81 C4
Novi Sad *Serbia* 45°18N 19°52E 80 E4
Novi Slankamen *Serbia* 45°8N 20°15E 80 E5
Novi Travnik *Bos.-H.* 44°10N 17°40E 80 F2
Novi Vinodolski *Croatia* 45°10N 14°48E 93 C11
Novigrad *Zadar, Croatia* 44°11N 15°32E 93 D12
Novigrad *Istra, Croatia* 45°19N 13°33E 93 C10
Novigradsko More
Croatia 44°11N 15°32E 93 D12
Novo Acôrdo *Brazil* 10°10S 46°48W 189 C1
Novo Cruzeiro *Brazil* 17°25S 41°53W 189 D2
Novo Hamburgo *Brazil* 29°37S 51°7W 191 B5
Novo Ivânivka *Ukraine* 45°55N 29°5E 81 E14
Novo Mesto *Slovenia* 45°47N 15°12E 93 C12
Novo Miloševo *Serbia* 45°42N 20°18E 80 E5
Novoaleksandrovsk
Russia 45°29N 41°17E 87 H5
Novoaleksandrovskaya =
Novoaleksandrovsk
Russia 45°29N 41°17E 87 H5
Novoaltaysk *Russia* 53°30N 84°0E 109 B10
Novoanninskiy *Russia* 50°32N 42°39E 86 E6
Novoazovsk *Ukraine* 47°15N 38°4E 85 J10
Novocheboksarsk *Russia* 56°11N 47°27E 86 B8
Novocherkassk *Russia* 47°27N 40°15E 87 G5
Novodevichye *Russia* 53°37N 48°50E 86 D9
Novodvinsk *Russia* 64°25N 40°42E 106 C5
Novogrudok = Navahrudak
Belarus 53°40N 25°50E 75 D3
Novohrad-Volynskyy
Ukraine 50°34N 27°35E 75 C14
Novokachalinsk *Russia* 45°5N 132°0E 112 B5
Novokhopersk *Russia* 51°5N 41°39E 86 E6
Novokuybyshevsk
Russia 53°7N 49°58E 86 D9
Novolazarevskaya
Antarctica 71°0S 12°0E 55 D3
Novomoskovsk *Russia* 54°5N 38°15E 84 E6
Novomoskovsk *Ukraine* 48°33N 35°17E 85 H8
Novomyrhorod *Ukraine* 48°45N 31°33E 85 H6
Novopolotsk = Navapolatsk
Belarus 55°32N 28°37E 84 E5
Novorossiysk *Russia* 44°43N 37°46E 85 K9
Novorybnoye *Russia* 72°50N 105°50E 107 B11
Novorzhev *Russia* 57°3N 29°25E 84 D5
Novosej *Albania* 41°56N 20°35E 96 E4
Novoselytsya *Ukraine* 48°14N 26°15E 81 B13
Novoshakhtinsk *Russia* 47°46N 39°58E 85 J10
Novosibirsk *Russia* 55°0N 83°5E 109 B10
Novosibirskiye Ostrova
Russia 75°0N 142°0E 107 B15
Novosibirskoye Vdkhr.
Russia 54°35N 82°35E 109 B10
Novosil *Russia* 52°59N 37°2E 84 E6
Novosokolniki *Russia* 56°20N 30°2E 84 D6
Novotitarovskaya *Russia* 45°17N 39°2E 87 H4
Novotroitsk *Russia* 51°10N 58°15E 108 B5
Novotroitskoye = Tõle Bī
Kazakhstan 43°42N 73°46E 109 E8
Novoukrayinka *Ukraine* 48°25N 31°33E 85 H6
Novouljanovsk *Russia* 54°8N 48°17E 86 D9
Novouzensk *Russia* 50°32N 48°17E 86 E8
Novovolynsk *Ukraine* 50°45N 24°4E 81 A13
Novovoronezh *Russia* 51°19N 39°13E 85 G10
Novovyazniki *Russia* 56°6N 42°12E 86 B6
Novozybkov *Russia* 52°30N 32°0E 85 E6
Novska *Croatia* 45°19N 17°0E 93 C13
Nový Bor *Czech Rep.* 50°46N 14°35E 78 A7

Novy Bug = Novyy Buh
  Ukraine 47°34N 32°29E 85 J7
Nový Bydžov Czech Rep. 50°14N 15°29E 78 A8
Novy Dvor Belarus 52°50N 24°21E 83 F11
Novy Dwór Mazowiecki
  Poland 52°26N 20°44E 83 F7
Nový Jičín Czech Rep. 49°30N 18°2E 79 B11
Novyy Buh Ukraine 47°34N 32°29E 85 J7
Novyy Oskol Russia 50°44N 37°55E 85 G9
Novyy Port Russia 67°40N 72°30E 106 C8
Novyy Urengoy Russia 65°48N 76°52E 106 C8
Nowa Deba Poland 50°26N 21°41E 83 H8
Nowa Nowa Australia 37°44S 148°3E 153 D8
Nowa Ruda Poland 50°35N 16°30E 83 H3
Nowa Sarzyna Poland 50°21N 22°21E 83 H9
Nowa Sól Poland 51°48N 15°44E 83 G2
Nowata U.S.A. 36°42N 95°38W 176 C7
Nowbarān Iran 35°8N 49°42E 129 C6
Nowe Poland 53°41N 18°44E 82 E5
Nowe Miasteczko
  Poland 51°42N 15°42E 83 G2
Nowe Miasto Poland 51°38N 20°34E 83 G7
Nowe Miasto Lubawskie
  Poland 53°27N 19°33E 82 E6
Nowe Skalmierzyce
  Poland 51°43N 18°0E 83 G4
Nowe Warpno Poland 53°42N 14°18E 82 E1
Nowendoc Australia 31°32S 151°44E 153 A9
Nowendoc △ Australia 31°33S 151°45E 153 A9
Nowghāb Iran 33°53N 59°4E 129 C8
Nowgong = Nagaon
  India 26°20N 92°50E 123 F18
Nowgong India 25°4N 79°27E 125 G8
Nowogard Poland 53°41N 15°10E 82 E2
Nowogród Poland 53°14N 21°53E 83 E8
Nowogród Bobrzanski
  Poland 51°48N 15°15E 83 G2
Nowogrodziec Poland 51°12N 15°24E 83 G2
Nowra Australia 34°53S 150°35E 153 C9
Nowrangapur India 19°14N 82°33E 126 E6
Nowshera Pakistan 34°0N 72°0E 122 C8
Nowy Dwór Gdański
  Poland 54°13N 19°7E 82 D6
Nowy Sącz Poland 49°40N 20°41E 83 J7
Nowy Staw Poland 54°13N 19°2E 82 D6
Nowy Targ Poland 49°29N 20°2E 83 J7
Nowy Tomyśl Poland 52°19N 16°10E 83 F3
Nowy Wiśnicz Poland 49°55N 20°28E 83 J7
Noxen U.S.A. 41°25N 76°4W 175 E8
Noyabr'sk Russia 64°34N 76°21E 106 C8
Noyant France 47°30N 0°6E 70 E7
Noyers France 47°40N 4°0E 71 E10
Noyon France 49°34N 2°59E 71 C9
Noyon Mongolia 43°2N 102°4E 114 C2
Nozay France 47°34N 1°38W 70 E5
Nqutu S. Africa 28°13S 30°32E 145 C5
Nsa, O. en → Algeria 32°28N 5°24E 136 B5
Nsanje Malawi 16°55S 35°12E 143 F4
Nsawam Ghana 5°50N 0°24W 139 D4
Nseluka Zambia 9°58S 31°16E 143 D3
Nsomba Zambia 10°45S 29°51E 143 E2
Nsukka Nigeria 6°51N 7°29E 139 D6
Ntaria ○ Australia 24°0S 132°41E 148 D5
Ntui Cameroon 4°27N 11°38E 139 E7
Ntungamo Uganda 0°56S 30°17E 142 C3
Nu Jiang → China 29°58N 97°25E 116 E2
Nu Shan China 26°0N 99°20E 116 E2
Nuba Mts. = Nubah, Jibalan
  Sudan 12°0N 31°0E 135 F12
Nubah, Jibalan Sudan 12°0N 31°0E 135 F12
Nubia Africa 21°0N 32°0E 132 D7
Nubian Desert = Nûbiya, Es Sahrâ
  en Sudan 21°30N 33°30E 137 C3
Nûbiya, Es Sahrâ en
  Sudan 21°30N 33°30E 137 C3
Nubledo Spain 43°31N 5°52W 88 B5
Nuboai Indonesia 2°10S 136°30E 119 E9
Nubra → India 34°35N 77°35E 125 B7
Nucet Romania 46°28N 22°35E 80 D7
Nueces → U.S.A. 27°51N 97°30W 176 H6
Nueltin L. Canada 60°30N 99°30W 163 A9
Nuestra Señora del Rosario de
  Caá-Catí Argentina 27°45S 57°36W 190 B4
Nueva, I. Chile 55°13S 66°30W 192 E3
Nueva Carteya Spain 37°35N 4°28W 89 H6
Nueva Ciudad Guerrero
  Mexico 26°34N 99°12W 181 B5
Nueva Gerona Cuba 21°53N 82°49W 182 B3
Nueva Imperial Chile 38°45S 72°58W 192 A2
Nueva Palmira
  Uruguay 33°52S 58°20W 190 C4
Nueva Rosita Mexico 27°57N 101°13W 180 B4
Nueva San Salvador
  El Salv. 13°40N 89°18W 182 D2
Nuéve de Julio
  Argentina 35°30S 61°0W 190 D3
Nuevitas Cuba 21°30N 77°20W 182 B4
Nuevo, G. Argentina 43°0S 64°30W 192 B4
Nuevo Casas Grandes
  Mexico 30°25N 107°55W 180 A3
Nuevo Laredo Mexico 27°30N 99°31W 181 B5
Nuevo León □ Mexico 25°20N 100°0W 180 C5
Nuevo Mundo, Cerro
  Bolivia 21°55S 66°53W 188 E4
Nuevo Rocafuerte
  Ecuador 0°55S 75°27W 186 D3
Nugget Pt. N.Z. 46°27S 169°50E 155 G4
Nugrus, Gebel Egypt 24°47N 34°35E 137 C3
Nuhaka N.Z. 39°3S 177°45E 154 F6
Nuits-St-Georges France 47°10N 4°56E 71 E11
Nukey Bluff Australia 32°26S 135°29E 151 E2
Nukhayb Iraq 32°4N 42°3E 105 F10
Nukheila Sudan 19°1N 26°21E 137 D2
Nuku Hiva
  French Polynesia 8°54S 140°6W 157 H13
Nuku'alofa Tonga 21°10S 175°12W 147 D11
Nukus Uzbekistan 42°27N 59°41E 108 D5
Nulato U.S.A. 64°43N 158°6W 166 C8
Nules Spain 39°51N 0°9W 90 F4
Nullagine Australia 21°53S 120°7E 148 D3
Nullagine → Australia 21°20S 120°20E 148 D3
Nullarbor Australia 31°28S 130°55E 149 F5
Nullarbor △ Australia 32°39S 130°0E 149 F2
Nullarbor Plain
  Australia 31°10S 129°0E 149 F4
Numalla, L. Australia 35°28S 144°20E 151 D3
Numan Nigeria 9°29N 12°3E 139 D7
Numata Japan 36°45N 139°4E 113 F9
Numaykoos Lake ○
  Canada 57°50N 95°58W 163 B9
Numazu Japan 35°7N 138°51E 113 G9

Numbulwar Australia 14°15S 135°45E 150 A2
Numfoor Indonesia 1°0S 134°50E 119 E8
Numurkah Australia 36°5S 145°26E 153 D6
Nunakasaluk I. Canada 55°49N 60°20W 165 A7
Nunap Isua Greenland 59°48N 43°55W 57 F6
Nunatsiavut Canada 55°30N 62°0W 165 A7
Nunavik Canada 56°30N 71°0W 161 F17
Nunavik Greenland 71°50N 54°25W 57 C5
Nunavut □ Canada 66°0N 85°0W 161 D15
Nunda U.S.A. 42°35N 77°56W 174 D7
Nuneaton U.K. 52°32N 1°27W 67 E6
Nungarin Australia 31°12S 118°6E 149 F2
Nungo Mozam. 13°23S 37°43E 143 E4
Nungwe Tanzania 2°48S 32°2E 142 C3
Nunivak I. U.S.A. 60°10N 166°30W 166 C6
Nunkun India 33°57N 76°2E 125 C7
Núoro Italy 40°20N 9°20E 94 B2
Nuozhadu Dam China 22°39N 100°25E 119 F3
Nûr Iran 36°33N 52°1E 129 B7
Nura → Kazakhstan 50°30N 69°59E 109 B7
Nûrâbâd Hormozgân,
  Iran 27°47N 57°12E 129 E8
Nûrâbâd Lorestân, Iran 34°4N 47°58E 105 E12
Nure → Italy 45°3N 9°49E 92 C6
Nuremberg = Nürnberg
  Germany 49°27N 11°3E 77 F7
Nuri Mexico 28°5N 109°22W 180 B3
Nuri Sudan 18°29N 31°59E 137 D3
Nuriootpa Australia 34°27S 139°0E 152 C3
Nuristān □ Afghan. 35°20N 71°0E 109 E8
Nurlat Russia 54°29N 50°45E 86 C10
Nürnberg Germany 49°27N 11°3E 77 F7
Nurpur Pakistan 31°53N 71°54E 124 D4
Nurra, La Italy 40°45N 8°15E 94 B1
Nurran, L. = Terewah, L.
  Australia 29°52S 147°35E 151 D4
Nurrari Lakes Australia 29°1S 130°5E 149 E5
Nurri Italy 39°43N 9°14E 94 C2
Nürtingen Germany 48°37N 9°19E 77 G5
Nurzec → Poland 52°37N 22°25E 83 F9
Nus Italy 45°45N 7°28E 92 C4
Nusa Dua Indonesia 8°48S 115°14E 119 K18
Nusa Tenggara Barat □
  Indonesia 8°50S 117°30E 118 F5
Nusa Tenggara Timur □
  Indonesia 9°30S 122°0E 119 F6
Nusaybin Turkey 37°3N 41°10E 105 D9
Nuşeirat Gaza Strip 31°27N 34°24E 130 D3
Nushki Pakistan 29°35N 66°0E 124 E2
Nuuk Greenland 64°10N 51°35W 57 E5
Nuussuaq Greenland 74°8N 57°3W 57 C5
Nuwakot Nepal 28°10N 83°55E 125 E10
Nuwara Eliya Sri Lanka 6°58N 80°48E 127 L5
Nuwayb'ī, W. an →
  Si. Arabia 29°18N 34°57E 130 F3
Nuweiba' Egypt 28°59N 34°39E 128 D2
Nuwerus S. Africa 31°8S 18°24E 144 D2
Nuweveldberge
  S. Africa 32°10S 21°45E 144 D3
Nuyts, Pt. Australia 35°4S 116°38E 149 G2
Nuyts Arch. Australia 32°35S 133°20E 151 E1
Nxau Nxau Pan △ Botswana 25°50S 24°46E 144 A3
Nxaunxau Botswana 18°57S 21°4E 144 A3
Ny-Ålesund Svalbard 78°55N 11°56E 57 B12
Nyaake Liberia 4°52N 7°37W 138 E3
Nyabing Australia 33°33S 118°9E 149 F2
Nyack U.S.A. 41°5N 73°55W 175 E11
Nyagan Russia 62°30N 65°38E 106 C7
Nyah West Australia 35°16S 143°21E 152 C5
Nyahanga Tanzania 2°20S 33°37E 142 C3
Nyahua Tanzania 5°25S 33°23E 142 D3
Nyahururu Kenya 0°2N 36°27E 142 B4
Nyainqêntanglha Shan
  China 30°0N 90°0E 110 F7
Nyakanazi Tanzania 3°2S 31°10E 142 C3
Nyakrom Ghana 5°40N 0°50W 139 D4
Nyâlâ Sudan 12°2N 24°58E 135 F10
Nyalam China 28°32N 86°4E 125 E13
Nyamandhlovu
  Zimbabwe 19°55S 28°16E 143 F2
Nyambiti Tanzania 2°48S 33°27E 142 C3
Nyamira Kenya 0°36S 34°52E 142 B4
Nyamwaga Tanzania 1°27S 34°33E 142 C3
Nyandekwa Tanzania 3°57S 32°32E 142 C3
Nyandoma Russia 61°40N 40°12E 84 B11
Nyandrua △ Kenya 0°30S 36°35E 142 C4
Nyanga △ Kenya 0°30S 36°30E 142 C4
Nyanga Namibia 18°0S 20°40E 144 A3
Nyangana Namibia 18°0S 20°40E 144 A3
Nyanguge Tanzania 2°30S 33°12E 142 C3
Nyanji Zambia 14°25S 31°46E 143 E3
Nyankpala Ghana 9°21N 0°58W 139 D4
Nyanza Rwanda 2°20S 29°42E 142 C2
Nyanza-Lac Burundi 4°21S 29°36E 142 C2
Nyasa, L. = Malawi, L.
  Africa 12°30S 34°30E 143 E3
Nyasvizh Belarus 53°14N 26°38E 83 F4
Nyaungdon = Yandoon
  Burma 17°0N 95°40E 123 L19
Nyazura Zimbabwe 18°40S 32°16E 143 F3
Nyazwidzi → Zimbabwe 20°0S 31°17E 143 G3
Nyborg Denmark 55°18N 10°47E 63 A4
Nybro Sweden 56°44N 15°55E 63 H6
Nyda Russia 66°40N 72°58E 106 C8
Nyeboe Land Greenland 82°0N 57°0W 57 A5
Nyeri Kenya 0°23S 36°56E 142 C4
Nyhammar Sweden 60°17N 14°58E 62 D8
Nyika △ Malawi 10°30S 33°53E 143 E3
Nyimba Zambia 14°33S 30°50E 143 E3
Nyinahin Ghana 6°43N 2°3W 138 D4
Nyingchi China 29°32N 94°25E 110 F7
Nyíradony Hungary 47°41N 21°55E 80 C6
Nyíregyháza Hungary 47°58N 21°47E 80 C6
Nyiragongo
  Dem. Rep. of the Congo 1°30S 29°15E 142 C2
Nyírmártonfalva Hungary 47°49N 22°9E 80 C6
Nyíri Mt. Kenya 1°38N 36°50E 142 B4
Nykarleby = Uusikaarlepyy
  Finland 63°32N 22°31E 60 E20
Nykøbing Nordjylland,
  Denmark 56°48N 8°51E 63 H1
Nykøbing Sjælland,
  Denmark 54°56N 11°52E 63 K5
Nykøbing Sjælland,
  Denmark 55°55N 11°40E 63 J5
Nyköping Sweden 58°45N 17°1E 63 F11
Nykroppa Sweden 59°37N 14°18E 62 E8
Nykvarn Sweden 59°11N 17°25E 62 E11
Nylstroom = Modimolle
  S. Africa 24°42S 28°22E 145 B4
Nymagee Australia 32°7S 146°20E 153 B8

Nymboida → Australia 29°38S 152°29E 151 D5
Nymburk Czech Rep. 50°10N 15°1E 78 A8
Nynäshamn Sweden 58°54N 17°57E 63 F11
Nyngan Australia 31°30S 147°8E 153 A8
Nyoma Rap India 33°10N 78°40E 125 C8
Nyoman = Nemunas →
  Lithuania 55°25N 21°10E 82 C8
Nyon Switz. 46°23N 6°14E 77 J2
Nyong → Cameroon 3°17N 9°54E 139 E6
Nyons France 44°22N 5°10E 73 D9
Nyou Burkina Faso 12°42N 2°1W 139 C4
Nýrsko Czech Rep. 49°18N 13°9E 78 B6
Nysa Poland 50°30N 17°22E 83 H4
Nysa → Europe 52°4N 14°46E 76 C10
Nysa Kłodzka → Poland 50°49N 17°40E 83 H4
Nysäter Sweden 59°17N 12°47E 62 E6
Nyslott = Savonlinna
  Finland 61°52N 28°53E 84 B5
Nyssa U.S.A. 43°53N 117°0W 168 E5
Nystad = Uusikaupunki
  Finland 60°47N 21°25E 84 B1
Nysted Denmark 54°40N 11°44E 63 K5
Nyunzu
  Dem. Rep. of the Congo 5°57S 27°58E 142 D2
Nyurba Russia 63°17N 118°28E 107 C12
Nyzhankovychi Ukraine 49°40N 22°49E 83 J9
Nyzhnohirskyy Ukraine 45°27N 34°38E 85 K8
Nyzhny Vorota Ukraine 48°46N 23°6E 80 B8
Nzébéla Guinea 8°9N 9°7W 138 D3
Nzega Tanzania 4°10S 33°12E 142 C3
Nzérékoré Guinea 7°49N 8°48W 138 D3
Nzeto Angola 7°10S 12°52E 140 F2
Nzilo, Chutes de
  Dem. Rep. of the Congo 10°18S 25°27E 143 E2
N'zo → Ivory C. 6°15N 7°3W 138 D3
N'zo △ Ivory C. 6°15N 7°15W 138 D3
Nzubuka Tanzania 4°45S 32°50E 142 C3
Nzwani = Anjouan
  Comoros Is. 12°15S 44°20E 141 a

O

O Barco Spain 42°23N 6°58W 88 C4
O Carballiño Spain 42°26N 8°5W 88 C2
O Castro de Ferreira
  Spain 42°31N 7°37W 88 C3
O Convento Spain 42°28N 8°41W 88 C2
O Corgo Spain 42°56N 7°25W 88 C3
O Pedrouzo Spain 42°56N 8°20W 88 C2
O Pino = O Pedrouzo
  Spain 42°56N 8°20W 88 C2
O Porriño Spain 42°10N 8°37W 88 C2
O Real Spain 43°20N 8°19W 88 B2
O Seixo Spain 41°59N 8°46W 88 D2
Ô-Shima Hokkaidō,
  Japan 41°30N 139°22E 112 D9
Ô-Shima Shizuoka,
  Japan 34°44N 139°24E 113 G9
O.R. Tambo Int. ✈ (JNB)
  S. Africa 26°8S 28°15E 145 C4
Oa, Mull of U.K. 55°35N 6°20W 65 F2
Oacoma U.S.A. 43°48N 99°24W 172 D4
Oahe, L. U.S.A. 44°27N 100°24W 172 C3
Oahe Dam U.S.A. 44°27N 100°24W 172 C3
O'ahu U.S.A. 21°28N 157°58W 167 L8
Oak Hill Fla., U.S.A. 28°52N 80°51W 179 G9
Oak Hill W. Va., U.S.A. 37°59N 81°9W 173 G13
Oak Island U.S.A. 33°55N 78°10W 177 E15
Oak Park U.S.A. 32°52N 82°19W 178 D7
Oak Ridge U.S.A. 36°1N 84°16W 177 C12
Oak View U.S.A. 34°24N 119°18W 171 L7
Oakan-Dake Japan 43°27N 144°10E 112 C12
Oakbank Australia 34°4S 140°33E 152 B4
Oakdale Calif., U.S.A. 37°46N 120°51W 170 H6
Oakdale La., U.S.A. 30°49N 92°40W 176 F8
Oakes U.S.A. 46°8N 98°6W 172 B4
Oakesdale U.S.A. 47°8N 117°15W 168 C5
Oakey Australia 27°25S 151°43E 151 D5
Oakfield Calif., U.S.A. 31°47N 83°58W 178 D6
Oakfield N.Y., U.S.A. 43°4N 78°16W 174 C6
Oakham U.K. 52°40N 0°43W 67 E7
Oakhurst U.S.A. 37°19N 119°40W 170 H7
Oakland Calif., U.S.A. 37°48N 122°18W 170 H4
Oakland Oreg., U.S.A. 43°25N 123°18W 168 E2
Oakland Park U.S.A. 26°10N 80°7W 179 J9
Oaklands Australia 35°34S 146°10E 153 C7
Oakley Idaho, U.S.A. 42°15N 113°53W 168 E7
Oakley Kans., U.S.A. 39°8N 100°51W 172 F3
Oakover → Australia 21°0S 120°40E 148 D3
Oakridge U.S.A. 43°45N 122°28W 168 E2
Oaks, The Australia 34°3S 150°34E 153 C9
Oakville Canada 43°27N 79°41W 184 C5
Oakville U.S.A. 46°51N 123°14W 170 D3
Oamaru N.Z. 45°5S 170°59E 155 F5
Oancea Romania 45°21N 27°42E 81 E12
Oasis Calif., U.S.A. 37°29N 117°55W 170 H9
Oasis Calif., U.S.A. 33°28N 116°6W 171 M10
Oates Land Antarctica 69°0S 160°0E 55 C11
Oatman U.S.A. 35°1N 114°19W 171 K12
Oaxaca Mexico 17°3N 96°43W 181 D5
Oaxaca □ Mexico 17°0N 96°30W 181 D5
Ob → Russia 66°45N 69°30E 106 C7
Oba Canada 49°4N 84°7W 164 C3
Obala Cameroon 4°9N 11°32E 139 E7
Obama Japan 35°30N 135°45E 113 G7
Oban Nigeria 5°17N 8°33E 139 D6
Oban U.K. 56°25N 5°29W 65 E3
Obbia = Hobyo Somalia 5°25N 48°30E 131 F4
Oberá Argentina 27°21S 55°2W 191 B4
Oberammergau Germany 47°36N 11°4E 77 H7
Oberasbach Germany 49°25N 10°57E 77 F6
Oberbayern □ Germany 48°5N 11°50E 77 G7
Oberdrauburg Austria 46°44N 12°58E 76 E7
Obere Donau → Germany 48°5N 9°0E 77 G5
Oberer Bayerischer Wald △
  Germany 49°15N 12°40E 77 F8
Oberfranken □ Germany 50°10N 11°20E 77 E7
Oberhausen Germany 51°28N 6°51E 76 D2
Oberkirch Germany 48°31N 8°4E 77 G4
Oberlausitz Germany 51°16N 14°18E 76 D10
Oberlin Kans., U.S.A. 39°49N 100°32W 172 F3
Oberlin Ohio, U.S.A. 41°18N 82°13W 174 E2
Obernai France 48°28N 7°30E 71 D14
Oberndorf Germany 48°17N 8°34E 77 G4
Oberon Australia 33°45S 149°52E 153 B8
Oberösterreich □ Austria 48°10N 14°0E 78 C7
Oberpfalz □ Germany 49°20N 12°10E 77 F8
Oberpfälzer Wald
  Germany 49°30N 12°30E 77 F8

Oberpfälzer Wald △
  Germany 49°40N 12°20E 77 F8
Oberstdorf Germany 47°24N 10°15E 77 H6
Obertyn Ukraine 48°42N 25°10E 81 B10
Oberursel Germany 50°11N 8°35E 77 E4
Oberwart Austria 47°17N 16°12E 79 D9
Obi, Kepulauan
  Indonesia 1°23S 127°45E 119 E7
Obiaruku Nigeria 5°51N 6°9E 139 D6
Óbidos Brazil 1°50S 55°30W 187 D7
Óbidos Portugal 39°19N 9°10W 89 F1
Obihiro Japan 42°56N 143°12E 112 C11
Obilatu Indonesia 1°25S 127°20E 119 E7
Obilnoye Russia 47°32N 44°30E 87 G7
Obing Germany 48°0N 12°24E 77 G8
Objat France 45°16N 1°24E 72 C5
Obluchye Russia 49°1N 131°4E 107 E14
Obninsk Russia 55°8N 36°37E 84 E9
Obo C.A.R. 5°20N 26°32E 142 A2
Obodivka Ukraine 48°24N 29°15E 81 B14
Oborniki Poland 52°39N 16°50E 83 F3
Oborniki Śląskie Poland 51°17N 16°53E 83 G3
Oboyan Russia 51°15N 36°21E 85 G9
Obozerskaya = Obozerskiy
  Russia 63°34N 40°21E 106 C5
Obozerskiy Russia 63°34N 40°21E 106 C5
Obrenovac Serbia 44°40N 20°11E 96 B4
O'Brien U.S.A. 30°2N 82°57W 178 E7
Obrovac Croatia 44°11N 15°41E 93 D12
Obruk Turkey 38°7N 33°12E 104 C5
Obrzycko Poland 52°42N 16°32E 83 F3
Observatory Inlet
  Canada 55°10N 129°54W 162 B3
Obshchi Syrt Russia 52°0N 53°0E 58 E16
Obskaya Guba Russia 69°0N 73°0E 106 C8
Obuasi Ghana 6°17N 1°40W 139 D4
Obubra Nigeria 6°8N 8°20E 139 D6
Obudu Nigeria 6°38N 9°5E 139 D6
Obwalden □ Switz. 46°55N 8°15E 77 J4
Obzor Bulgaria 42°50N 27°52E 97 D11
Ocala U.S.A. 29°11N 82°8W 179 F7
Ocampo Chihuahua,
  Mexico 28°11N 108°23W 180 B3
Ocampo Tamaulipas,
  Mexico 22°50N 99°20W 181 C5
Ocaña Spain 39°55N 3°30W 88 F7
Occidental, Cordillera
  Colombia 5°0N 76°0W 186 C3
Occidental, Cordillera
  Peru 14°0S 74°0W 188 D3
Occidental, Grand Erg
  Algeria 30°20N 1°0E 136 B4
Ocean City Md., U.S.A. 38°20N 75°5W 173 F16
Ocean City N.J.,
  U.S.A. 39°17N 74°35W 173 F16
Ocean City Wash.,
  U.S.A. 47°4N 124°10W 170 C2
Ocean Falls Canada 52°18N 127°48W 162 C3
Ocean I. = Banaba
  Kiribati 0°45S 169°50E 156 H8
Ocean Park U.S.A. 46°30N 124°3W 170 D2
Oceano U.S.A. 35°6N 120°37W 171 K6
Oceanport U.S.A. 40°19N 74°3W 175 F10
Oceanside U.S.A. 33°12N 117°23W 171 M9
Ochagavía Spain 42°55N 1°5W 90 C3
Ochakiv Ukraine 46°37N 31°33E 85 J6
Ochamchire Georgia 42°46N 41°32E 87 J5
Ochil Hills U.K. 56°14N 3°40W 65 E5
Ochlocknee U.S.A. 30°58N 84°3W 178 E5
Ochlockonee →
  U.S.A. 29°59N 84°26W 178 F5
Ocho Rios Jamaica 18°24N 77°6W 182 a
Ochopee U.S.A. 25°54N 81°18W 179 K8
Ochsenfurt Germany 49°40N 10°4E 77 F6
Ochsenhausen Germany 48°4N 9°57E 77 G5
Ocilla U.S.A. 31°36N 83°15W 178 E6
Ockelbo Sweden 60°54N 16°45E 62 D10
Ocmulgee → U.S.A. 31°58N 82°33W 178 E6
Ocmulgee △ U.S.A. 32°38N 83°37W 178 D6
Ocna Mureş Romania 46°23N 23°55E 81 D8
Ocna Sibiului Romania 45°52N 24°2E 81 E9
Ocnele Mari Romania 45°8N 24°18E 81 E9
Ocniţa Moldova 48°25N 27°30E 81 B12
Ocoee U.S.A. 28°34N 81°32W 179 G8
Ocofia Peru 16°26S 73°8W 188 D3
Oconee → U.S.A. 31°58N 82°33W 178 E6
Oconee, L. U.S.A. 33°28N 83°15W 178 D6
Oconomowoc U.S.A. 43°7N 88°30W 172 D9
Oconto U.S.A. 44°53N 87°52W 172 C9
Oconto Falls U.S.A. 44°52N 88°9W 172 C9
Ocosingo Mexico 16°53N 92°6W 181 D6
Ocotal Nic. 13°41N 86°31W 182 D2
Ocotlán Jalisco,
  Mexico 20°21N 102°46W 180 C4
Ocotlán Oaxaca, Mexico 16°48N 96°40W 181 D5
Ocreza → Portugal 39°32N 7°50W 89 F3
Ócsa Hungary 47°17N 19°15E 80 C4
Oda Ghana 5°50N 0°51W 139 D4
Oda, J. Sudan 20°21N 36°39E 137 C4
Ōda Japan 35°11N 132°30E 113 G6
Ódáðahraun Iceland 65°5N 17°0W 60 D5
Ódaejin N. Korea 41°34N 129°40E 112 D4
Ódákra Sweden 56°7N 12°45E 63 H6
Odate Japan 40°16N 140°34E 112 D10
Odawara Japan 35°20N 139°6E 113 G9
Odda Norway 60°3N 6°35E 61 F12
Odder Denmark 55°58N 10°10E 63 J4
Odei → Canada 56°6N 96°54W 163 B9
Odemira Portugal 37°35N 8°40W 89 H2
Ödemiş Turkey 38°15N 28°0E 99 C9
Odendaalsrus S. Africa 27°48S 26°45E 145 D4
Odense Denmark 55°22N 10°23E 63 J4
Odensbacken Sweden 59°16N 15°39E 62 E9
Oder → Europe 53°33N 14°38E 76 B10
Oder-Havel Kanal
  Germany 52°52N 14°2E 76 C10
Oderzo Italy 45°47N 12°29E 93 C9
Odesa Ukraine 46°30N 30°45E 85 J6
Ödeshög Sweden 58°14N 14°38E 63 F9
Odessa = Odesa Ukraine 46°30N 30°45E 85 J6
Odessa Canada 44°17N 76°43W 175 B8
Odessa Tex., U.S.A. 31°52N 102°23W 176 F2
Odessa Wash., U.S.A. 47°20N 118°41W 168 C4
Odiakwe Botswana 20°12S 25°17E 144 B4
Odiel → Spain 37°10N 6°55W 89 H4
Odienné Ivory C. 9°30N 7°34W 138 D3
Odintsovo Russia 55°39N 37°16E 84 E9
Odisha □ India 20°0N 84°0E 126 D8

Odobești Romania 45°43N 27°4E 81 E12
Odolanów Poland 51°34N 17°40E 83 G4
O'Donnell U.S.A. 32°58N 101°50W 176 E4
O'Donnell Pt. Canada 45°5N 80°5W 174 A4
Odorheiu Secuiesc
  Romania 46°21N 25°21E 81 D10
Odra = Oder → Europe 53°33N 14°38E 76 B10
Odra → Spain 42°14N 4°17W 88 C6
Odum U.S.A. 31°40N 82°2W 178 D7
Odžaci Serbia 45°30N 19°17E 80 E4
Odžak Bos.-H. 45°3N 18°18E 80 E3
Odzi Zimbabwe 19°0S 32°20E 145 A5
Odzi → Zimbabwe 19°45S 32°23E 145 A5
Oecusse = Pante Macassar
  E. Timor 9°30S 123°58E 119 F6
Oeiras Brazil 7°0S 42°8W 189 D2
Oeiras Portugal 38°41N 9°18W 89 G1
Oelrichs U.S.A. 43°11N 103°14W 172 D2
Oelsnitz Germany 50°24N 12°11E 77 E8
Oelwein U.S.A. 42°41N 91°55W 172 D8
Oeno I. Pac. Oc. 24°0S 131°0W 157 K14
Oenpelli = Gunbalanya
  Australia 12°20S 133°4E 148 B5
Oetz Austria 47°13N 10°53E 78 D3
Of Turkey 40°59N 40°23E 105 B9
Ofanto → Italy 41°22N 16°13E 95 A9
Ofa Nigeria 8°13N 4°42E 139 D5
Offaly □ Ireland 53°15N 7°30W 64 C4
Offenbach Germany 50°6N 8°44E 77 E4
Offenburg Germany 48°28N 7°56E 77 G3
Officer Cr. → Australia 27°46S 132°30E 149 E5
Offida Italy 42°56N 13°41E 93 F10
Ofidousa Greece 36°33N 26°8E 99 E8
Ofotfjorden Norway 68°27N 17°0E 60 B17
Ōfunato Japan 39°4N 141°43E 112 E10
Oga Japan 39°55N 139°50E 112 E9
Oga-Hantō Japan 39°58N 139°47E 112 E9
Ōgaki Japan 35°21N 136°37E 113 G8
Ogallala U.S.A. 41°8N 101°43W 172 E3
Ogasawara Gunto
  Pac. Oc. 27°0N 142°0E 156 E6
Ogbomosho Nigeria 8°1N 4°11E 139 D5
Ogden U.S.A. 41°13N 111°58W 168 F8
Ogdensburg U.S.A. 44°42N 75°30W 175 B9
Ogea Driki Fiji 19°12S 178°27W 154 a
Ogea Levu Fiji 19°8S 178°24W 154 a
Ogilby U.S.A. 32°49N 114°50W 171 N12
Oglat Beraber Algeria 30°15N 3°34W 136 B3
Oglethorpe U.S.A. 32°18N 84°4W 178 D5
Ogliastra □ Italy 39°50N 9°35E 94 C2
Óglio → Italy 45°2N 10°39E 92 C7
Óglio Nord □ Italy 45°22N 9°54E 92 C6
Óglio Sud □ Italy 45°7N 10°24E 92 C7
Ogmore Australia 22°37S 149°35E 150 C4
Ognon → France 47°16N 5°28E 71 E12
Ogoja Nigeria 6°38N 8°39E 139 D6
Ogoki Canada 51°38N 85°58W 164 B2
Ogoki → Canada 51°38N 85°57W 164 B2
Ogoki L. Canada 50°50N 87°10W 164 B2
Ogoki Res. Canada 50°45N 88°15W 164 B2
Ogooué → Gabon 1°0S 9°0E 140 E1
Ogosta → Bulgaria 43°44N 23°55E 96 C7
Ogou → Togo 7°50N 1°19E 139 D5
Ogove = Ogooué → Gabon 1°0S 9°0E 140 E1
Ograzden Macedonia 41°30N 22°50E 96 E6
Ogre Latvia 56°49N 24°36E 84 D3
Ogulin Croatia 45°16N 15°16E 93 C12
Ogun □ Nigeria 7°0N 3°0E 139 D5
Ogurja Ada
  Turkmenistan 38°55N 53°2E 129 B7
Oguta Nigeria 5°44N 6°44E 139 D6
Óguzeli Turkey 36°57N 37°30E 104 D7
Ogwashi-Uku Nigeria 6°15N 6°30E 139 D6
Ogwe Nigeria 5°0N 7°14E 139 E6
Ohai N.Z. 45°55S 168°0E 155 F3
Ohakune N.Z. 39°24S 175°24E 154 F4
Ohanet Algeria 28°44N 8°46E 136 C6
Ohata Japan 41°24N 141°10E 112 D10
Ohau, L. N.Z. 44°15S 169°53E 155 E4
Ohaupo N.Z. 37°56S 175°20E 154 D4
Ohře → Czech Rep. 50°30N 14°10E 78 A7
Ohrid Macedonia 41°8N 20°52E 96 E4
Ohrid, L. Macedonia 41°8N 20°52E 96 E4
Ohridsko Jezero
  Macedonia 41°8N 20°52E 96 E4
Ohrigstad S. Africa 24°39S 30°36E 145 B5
Ohringen Germany 49°12N 9°31E 77 F5
Ohura N.Z. 38°51S 174°59E 154 E4
Oi Qu → China 28°37N 98°16E 116 C2
Oiapoque Brazil 3°50N 51°50W 187 C8
Oikou China 38°35N 117°42E 115 E9
Oil City U.S.A. 41°26N 79°42W 174 E5
Oil Springs Canada 42°47N 82°7W 174 D2
Oildale U.S.A. 35°25N 119°1W 171 K7
Oinousa = Inousses
  Greece 38°33N 26°14E 99 C8
Oise □ France 49°28N 2°30E 71 C9
Oise → France 49°0N 2°4E 71 C9
Oistins Barbados 13°4N 59°33W 183 g
Oistins B. Barbados 13°4N 59°33W 183 g
Ōita Japan 33°14N 131°36E 113 H5
Ōita □ Japan 33°15N 131°30E 113 H5
Oiticica Brazil 5°3S 41°5W 189 D3
Ojai U.S.A. 34°27N 119°15W 171 L7
Ojcowski □ Poland 50°15N 19°50E 83 H6
Ojhar India 20°6N 73°56E 126 D1
Ojinaga Mexico 29°34N 104°25W 180 B4
Ojiya Japan 37°18N 138°48E 113 F9
Ojo Caliente Mexico 22°34N 102°15W 180 C4
Ojo de Liebre, L.
  Mexico 27°50N 114°15W 180 B2
Ojos del Salado, Cerro
  Argentina 27°0S 68°40W 190 B3
Oka Nigeria 7°28N 5°48E 139 D5
Oka → Russia 56°20N 43°59E 86 B7
Oka Indonesia 8°6S 139°42E 119 F9
Okaba Indonesia 8°6S 139°42E 119 F9
Okahandja Namibia 22°0S 16°59E 144 B2
Okahukura N.Z. 38°48S 175°14E 154 E4
Okakarara Namibia 20°35S 17°27E 144 B2
Okanagan L. Canada 50°0N 119°30W 162 D5

Okanogan U.S.A. 48°22N 119°35W 166 B4
Okanogan → U.S.A. 48°6N 119°44W 166 B4
Okanogan Range
  N. Amer. 49°0N 119°55W 162 D5
Okány Hungary 46°52N 21°21E 80 D6
Okapi ○
  Dem. Rep. of the Congo 2°30N 27°20E 142 B2
Okaputa Namibia 20°5S 17°0E 144 B2
Okara Pakistan 30°50N 73°31E 124 D5
Okarito N.Z. 43°15S 170°9E 155 E3
Okarukambe = Steinhausen
  Namibia 21°49S 18°20E 144 B2
Okato N.Z. 39°12S 173°53E 154 E3
Okaukuejo Namibia 19°10S 16°0E 144 A1
Okavango = Cubango →
  Africa 18°50S 22°25E 144 A3
Okavango Delta
  Botswana 18°45S 22°45E 144 A3
Okavango Swamp = Okavango
  Delta Botswana 18°45S 22°45E 144 A3
Okaya Japan 36°5N 138°10E 113 F9
Okayama Japan 34°40N 133°54E 113 G6
Okayama □ Japan 35°0N 133°50E 113 G6
Okazaki Japan 34°57N 137°10E 113 G8
Oke-Iho Nigeria 8°1N 3°18E 139 D5
Okęcie, Warszawa ✈ (WAW)
  Poland 52°9N 20°59E 83 F7
Okeechobee U.S.A. 27°15N 80°50W 179 H9
Okeechobee, L. U.S.A. 27°0N 80°50W 179 H9
Okefenokee △ U.S.A. 30°45N 82°18W 178 E7
Okefenokee Swamp
  U.S.A. 30°40N 82°20W 178 E7
Okehampton U.K. 50°44N 4°0W 67 G4
Okene Nigeria 7°32N 6°11E 139 D6
Oker → Germany 52°32N 10°22E 76 C6
Okha India 22°27N 69°4E 124 H6
Okha Russia 53°40N 143°0E 107 D15
Okhotsk Russia 59°20N 143°10E 107 D15
Okhotsk, Sea of Asia 55°0N 145°0E 107 D15
Okhotskiy Perevoz
  Russia 61°52N 135°35E 107 C14
Okhtyrka Ukraine 50°25N 35°0E 85 G9
Oki-Shotō Japan 36°5N 133°15E 113 F6
Okiep S. Africa 29°39S 17°53E 144 D1
Okigwi Nigeria 5°52N 7°20E 139 D6
Okija Nigeria 5°54N 6°55E 139 D6
Okinawa Japan 26°19N 127°46E 113 L3
Okinawa □ Japan 26°40N 128°0E 113 L3
Okinawa-Guntō Japan 26°40N 128°0E 113 L3
Okinawa-Jima Japan 26°32N 128°0E 113 L4
Okino-erabu-Shima
  Japan 27°21N 128°33E 113 K4
Okitipupa Nigeria 6°31N 4°50E 139 D5
Oklahoma □ U.S.A. 35°20N 97°30W 176 D6
Oklahoma City U.S.A. 35°30N 97°30W 176 D6
Oklawaha → U.S.A. 29°28N 81°41W 179 F8
Okmulgee U.S.A. 35°37N 95°58W 176 C7
Oknitsa = Ocniţa
  Moldova 48°25N 27°30E 81 B12
Oko, W. → Sudan 21°15N 35°56E 137 C4
Okolo Uganda 2°37N 31°8E 142 B3
Okolona U.S.A. 34°0N 88°45W 177 D10
Okombahe Namibia 21°23S 15°22E 144 B1
Okonek Poland 53°32N 16°51E 82 E3
Okotoks Canada 50°43N 113°58W 162 D6
Okrika Nigeria 4°40N 7°10E 139 E6
Oktyabrsk = Qandyaghash
  Kazakhstan 49°28N 57°25E 108 C6
Oktyabrsk Russia 53°11N 48°40E 86 D9
Oktyabrskiy = Aktsyabrski
  Belarus 52°38N 28°53E 75 E5
Oktyabrskiy Bashkortostan,
  Russia 54°28N 53°28E 86 C5
Oktyabrskiy Kamchatka,
  Russia 52°39N 156°14E 107 D17
Oktyabrskiy Rostov,
  Russia 47°30N 40°4E 87 G5
Oktyabrskoy Revolyutsii, Ostrov
  Russia 79°30N 97°0E 107 B10
Oktyabrskoye = Zhovtneve
  Ukraine 46°54N 32°3E 85 J7
Okulovka Russia 58°25N 33°19E 84 C8
Okuru N.Z. 43°55S 168°55E 155 E3
Okushiri-Tō Japan 42°15N 139°30E 112 C9
Okuta Nigeria 9°14N 3°12E 139 D5
Okwa → Botswana 22°30S 23°0E 144 B3
Ola Russia 59°35N 151°17E 107 D16
Ola U.S.A. 35°2N 93°13W 176 D8
Ólafsfjörður Iceland 66°4N 18°39W 60 A4
Ólafsvík Iceland 64°53N 23°43W 60 D2
Olaine Latvia 56°47N 23°57E 84 D3
Olancha U.S.A. 36°17N 118°1W 171 J8
Olancha Pk. U.S.A. 36°16N 118°7W 171 J8
Olanchito Honduras 15°30N 86°30W 182 C2
Öland Sweden 56°45N 16°38E 63 H7
Ölands norra udde
  Sweden 57°22N 17°5E 63 G8
Ölands södra udde
  Sweden 56°12N 16°23E 63 H7
Olanta U.S.A. 33°56N 79°56W 178 D8
Olar U.S.A. 33°11N 81°11W 178 D7
Olargues France 43°34N 2°53E 72 E6
Olary Australia 32°18S 140°19E 152 B4
Olascoaga Argentina 35°15S 60°39W 190 D3
Olathe U.S.A. 38°53N 94°49W 172 F7
Olavarría Argentina 36°55S 60°20W 190 D3
Oława Poland 50°57N 17°20E 83 H4
Olbernhau Germany 50°40N 13°19E 76 E9
Ólbia Italy 40°55N 9°31E 94 B2
Ólbia, G. di Italy 40°55N 9°35E 94 B2
Olching Germany 48°12N 11°21E 77 G7
Olcott U.S.A. 43°20N 78°42W 174 C6
Old Bahama Chan. = Bahama,
  Canal Viejo de
  W. Indies 22°10N 77°30W 182 B4
Old Bar Australia 31°58S 152°35E 153 A9
Old Bridge U.S.A. 40°25N 74°22W 175 F10
Old Castile = Castilla y Leon □
  Spain 42°0N 5°0W 88 D6
Old Crow Canada 67°30N 139°55W 166 C4
Old Dale U.S.A. 34°8N 115°47W 171 L11
Old Forge N.Y., U.S.A. 43°43N 74°58W 175 C10
Old Forge Pa., U.S.A. 41°22N 75°45W 175 E9
Old Mapoon ○
  Australia 11°5S 142°22E 150 A3
Old Perlican Canada 48°5N 53°1W 165 C9
Old Shinyanga Tanzania 3°33S 33°27E 142 C3
Old Speck Mt. U.S.A. 44°34N 70°57W 175 B13
Old Town Fla., U.S.A. 29°36N 82°59W 178 F7

Town Maine,
  S.A. 44°56N 68°39W 173 C19
Washington U.S.A. 40°2N 81°27W 174 F3
Wives L. Canada 50°5N 106°0W 163 C17
bury U.K. 51°38N 2°33W 67 F5
astle Ireland 53°46N 7°10W 64 C4
ani Tanzania 3°22S 35°35E 142 C4
nburg Niedersachsen,
  rmany 53°9N 8°13E 76 B4
nburg Schleswig-Holstein,
  rmany 54°17N 10°52E 76 A6
nzaal Neths. 52°19N 6°53E 66 B6
am U.K. 53°33N 2°7W 66 D5
am → Canada 49°57N 111°42W 162 D6
neldrum U.K. 57°20N 2°19W 65 D6
mar U.S.A. 28°2N 82°39W 179 G7
vai Gorge Tanzania 2°57S 35°23E 142 C4
iyt Mongolia 44°40N 109°1E 114 B5
Romer Land
  reenland 74°10N 24°30W 57 C8
n U.S.A. 42°5N 78°26W 174 D6
y Sweden 60°8N 13°2E 62 D7
ko Poland 54°2N 22°31E 82 D9
gio Italy 45°36N 8°38E 92 C5
ros = O Real Spain 42°0N 7°40W 88 B3
ros Portugal 39°56N 7°56W 88 F3
ma → Russia 60°22N 120°42E 107 C13
minsk Russia 60°25N 120°30E 107 C13
ssandrivka Ukraine 48°55N 32°20E 85 H7
raine
  ssandriya Rivne,
  raine 48°42N 33°3E 85 H7
raine
  ssandriya Kirovohrad,
  raine 50°37N 26°19E 75 C14
sk U.S.A. 38°3N 122°47W 170 G4
aegorsk Russia 68°9N 33°18E 60 B25
ack Russia 68°28N 112°18E 107 C12
ck → Russia 73°0N 120°10E 107 B13
aino Russia 56°15N 33°30E 84 D7
on, Î. d' France 45°55N 1°15W 72 C2
k Ukraine 51°6N 24°11E 83 G11
nica Poland 51°13N 17°22E 83 G4
no Poland 50°51N 18°26E 83 H5
sk Ukraine 51°12N 27°39E 75 C14
ntshoek S. Africa 49°47N 77°15W 164 C14
a, The = Kata Tjuta
  ustralia 25°20S 130°50E 149 E5
y Mongolia 48°56N 89°57E 109 C11
d Denmark 55°49N 8°36E 63 J2
io Portugal 37°3N 7°48W 89 H3
tepa Italy 48°12N 29°30E 81 D14
io U.S.A. 42°29N 29°30E 81 D14
vatka Russia 54°30N 22°18E 82 D9
a Italy 40°16N 9°24E 94 B2
e Spain 41°1N 0°41W 90 D4
nts = Elefantes →
  rica 24°10S 32°40E 145 B5
nts → Namibia 25°30S 19°30E 144 B2
ntshoek S. Africa 27°57S 22°42E 144 C3
abos, Óros = Olymbos Oros
  reece 35°44N 27°11E 99 F9
abos Brazil 20°44S 48°54W 191 A6
apos-Beydaglari △
  rkey 36°36N 30°30E 99 E12
da Brazil 8°1S 34°51W 189 B4
e Spain 42°29N 1°40W 90 C3
a Argentina 32°0S 63°38W 190 C3
a Spain 38°58N 0°9W 91 G4
a de la Frontera
  ain 38°17N 6°54W 89 G4
ares, Cerro los
  rgentina 30°18S 69°55W 190 C2
ares de Júcar Spain 39°46N 2°20W 90 C2
e Branch U.S.A. 35°7N 89°49W 177 D10
ehurst U.S.A. 39°6N 121°34W 170 F5
eira Brazil 20°39S 44°50W 189 E2
e de Azeméis
  rtugal 40°49N 8°29W 88 E2
eira do Douro Portugal 41°5N 8°2W 88 D2
eira dos Brejinhos
  azil 12°19S 42°54W 189 D2
enza Spain 38°41N 7°9W 89 G3
er Canada 49°13N 119°37W 162 D5
er L. Canada 56°56N 103°22W 163 B8
et France 47°51N 1°55E 71 E8
ine Ra. N.Z. 44°15S 168°30E 155 E3
rva Russia 49°48N 44°32E 81 F7
asz Poland 50°18N 19°33E 83 H6
güe Chile 13°49S 70°29W 188 C3
ron, Gave d' France 43°33N 1°5W 72 E2
on-Ste-Marie France 43°11N 0°38W 72 E3
enga = Swains I.
  enga → Samoa 11°11S 171°4W 157 J11
s Spain 42°11N 2°30E 90 D7
vo Bos.-H. 44°8N 18°30E 80 F3
a → Russia 66°29N 159°29E 107 C16
erg Germany 51°21N 8°31E 76 D4
anka Ukraine 58°45N 14°48E 63 F8
anka Ukraine 48°16N 30°58E 85 H6
tyn Poland 53°48N 20°29E 82 E7
tynek Poland 53°48N 20°29E 82 E7
□ Romania 44°20N 24°30E 81 F9
a Russia 42°43N 24°51E 81 G9
niţa Romania 44°7N 26°42E 81 F11
n Switz. 47°21N 7°53E 77 H3
ja del Rio Spain 37°21N 7°28W 89 H3
Turkey 40°49N 42°8E 105 B10

Olustee U.S.A. 30°12N 82°26W 178 E7
Olvega Spain 41°47N 2°0W 90 D2
Olvera Spain 36°55N 5°18W 89 J5
Olymbos Cyprus 35°21N 33°45E 101 D12
Olymbos Oros Greece 40°6N 22°23E 96 F6
Olympia Greece 37°39N 21°39E 98 D3
Olympia U.S.A. 47°3N 122°53W 170 D4
Olympic △ U.S.A. 47°45N 123°43W 170 C3
Olympic Dam
  Australia 30°30S 136°55E 152 A2
Olympic Mts. U.S.A. 47°55N 123°45W 170 C3
Olympus Cyprus 34°56N 32°52E 101 E11
Olympus, Mt. = Olymbos Oros
  Greece 40°6N 22°23E 96 F6
Olympus, Mt. = Uludağ
  Turkey 40°4N 29°13E 97 F13
Olympus, Mt. U.S.A. 47°48N 123°43W 170 C3
Olyphant U.S.A. 41°27N 75°36W 175 E9
Olyutorskiy, Mys
  Russia 59°55N 170°27E 107 D18
Om → Russia 54°59N 73°22E 109 B8
Om Koi Thailand 17°48N 98°22E 120 D2
Ōma Japan 41°45N 141°5E 112 D10
Ōmachi Japan 36°30N 137°50E 113 F8
Omae-Zaki Japan 34°36N 138°14E 113 G9
Ōmagari = Daisen
  Japan 39°27N 140°29E 112 E10
Omagh U.K. 54°36N 7°19W 64 B4
Omagh □ U.K. 54°35N 7°15W 64 B4
Omaha U.S.A. 41°17N 95°58W 172 E6
Omaheke □ Namibia 21°30S 19°0E 144 B2
Omalos Greece 35°19N 23°55E 101 D5
Omalur India 11°44N 78°4E 127 J4
Oman ■ Asia 23°0N 58°0E 131 C6
Oman, G. of Asia 24°30N 58°30E 129 E8
Omapere N.Z. 35°37S 173°25E 154 B2
Omaruru Namibia 21°26S 16°0E 144 B2
Omaruru → Namibia 22°7S 14°15E 144 B1
Omate Peru 16°45S 71°0W 188 D3
Ombai, Selat Indonesia 8°30S 124°50E 119 F6
Ombeé Gabon 1°35S 9°15E 142 C1
Ombrone → Italy 42°42N 11°5E 92 F8
Omdurmân Sudan 15°40N 32°28E 135 E12
Omega Italy 31°21N 83°36W 178 D6
Omegna Italy 45°53N 8°24E 92 C5
Omemee Canada 44°18N 78°33W 174 B6
Omeo Australia 37°6S 147°36E 153 D7
Omeonga
  Dem. Rep. of the Congo 3°40S 24°22E 142 C1
Ometepe, I. de Nic. 11°32N 85°35W 182 D2
Ometepec Mexico 16°41N 98°25W 181 D5
Ominato Japan 41°17N 141°10E 112 D10
Omineca → Canada 56°3N 124°16W 162 B4
Omineca Mts. Canada 56°30N 125°30W 162 B3
Omiš Croatia 43°28N 16°40E 93 E13
Omišalj Croatia 45°13N 14°32E 93 C11
Omitara Namibia 22°16S 18°2E 144 B2
Ōmiya = Saitama
  Japan 35°54N 139°38E 113 G9
Omme Å → Denmark 55°56N 8°32E 63 J2
Ommen Neths. 52°31N 6°26E 66 B6
Ömnögovĭ □ Mongolia 43°15N 104°0E 114 C3
Omo → Ethiopia 6°25N 36°10E 131 F2
Omodeo, L. Italy 40°8N 8°56E 94 B1
Omodhos Cyprus 34°51N 32°48E 101 E11
Omoko Nigeria 5°19N 6°40E 139 D6
Omono-Gawa →
  Japan 39°46N 140°3E 112 E10
Ompha Canada 45°0N 76°50W 175 B8
Omsk Russia 55°0N 73°12E 109 B8
Omsukchan Russia 62°32N 155°48E 107 C16
Ōmu Japan 44°34N 142°58E 112 B11
Omul, Vf. Romania 45°27N 25°29E 81 E10
Omulew → Poland 53°5N 21°33E 83 E8
Ōmura Japan 32°56N 129°57E 113 H4
Omuramba Omatako →
  Namibia 17°45S 20°25E 144 A2
Omuramba Ovambo →
  Namibia 18°45S 16°59E 144 A2
Omurtag Bulgaria 43°8N 26°26E 97 C10
Omusati □ Namibia 18°30S 15°0E 144 A1
Ōmuta Japan 33°5N 130°26E 113 H5
Omuthiya Namibia 17°43S 16°13E 144 A2
Oña Spain 42°43N 3°25W 88 C7
Ona U.S.A. 27°29N 81°55W 179 H8
Onaga U.S.A. 39°29N 96°10W 172 F5
Onalaska U.S.A. 43°53N 91°14W 172 D8
Onancock U.S.A. 37°43N 75°45W 173 G16
Onangue, L. Gabon 0°57S 10°4E 140 E2
Onaping L. Canada 47°3N 81°30W 164 C3
Oñati Spain 43°3N 2°25W 90 B2
Onavas Mexico 28°31N 109°35W 180 B3
Onawa U.S.A. 42°2N 96°6W 172 D5
Oncócua Angola 16°30S 13°25E 144 A1
Onda Spain 39°55N 0°17W 90 F4
Ondangwa Namibia 17°57S 16°4E 144 A2
Ondarroa Spain 43°19N 2°25W 90 B2
Ondas → Brazil 12°8S 44°55W 189 C2
Ondaw → Slovak Rep. 48°27N 21°48E 79 C14
Ondjiva Angola 16°48S 15°50E 144 A2
Ondo Nigeria 7°4N 4°47E 139 D5
Ondo □ Nigeria 6°45N 5°0E 139 D6
Öndörhaan Mongolia 47°19N 110°39E 111 B11
Öndverðarnes Iceland 64°52N 24°0W 60 D2
One Arm Point
  Australia 16°26S 123°3E 148 C3
One Arm Point ◎
  Australia 16°31S 122°53E 148 C3
One Tree Australia 34°14S 144°13E 151 E3
Oneata Fiji 18°26S 178°25W 154 a
Oneco U.S.A. 27°25N 82°33W 179 H7
Onega Russia 64°0N 38°10E 106 C4
Onega → Russia 63°58N 38°2E 58 C13
Onega, L. = Onezhskoye Ozero
  Russia 61°44N 35°22E 84 B8
Onehunga N.Z. 36°55N 174°48E 154 B5
Oneida U.S.A. 43°6N 75°39W 175 C9
Oneida L. U.S.A. 43°12N 75°54W 175 D9
O'Neill U.S.A. 42°27N 98°39W 172 D4
Onekotan, Ostrov
  Russia 49°25N 154°45E 107 E16
Onema
  Dem. Rep. of the Congo 4°35S 24°30E 142 C1
Oneonta U.S.A. 42°27N 75°4W 175 D9
Onerahi N.Z. 35°45S 174°22E 154 a
Oneşti Romania 46°17N 26°47E 81 D11
Onezhskoye Ozero
  Russia 61°44N 35°22E 84 B8
Ongarue N.Z. 38°42S 175°19E 154 E4

Ongea Levu = Ogea Levu
  Fiji 19°8S 178°24W 154 a
Ongers → S. Africa 31°4S 23°13E 144 D3
Ongerup Australia 33°58S 118°28E 149 F2
Ongi N. Korea 45°27N 103°54E 114 B2
Ongjin N. Korea 37°56N 125°21E 115 F13
Ongkharak Thailand 14°8N 101°1E 120 E3
Ongniud Qi China 43°0N 118°38E 115 C10
Ongoka
  Dem. Rep. of the Congo 1°20S 26°0E 142 C2
Ongole India 15°33N 80°2E 127 G5
Ongon = Havirga
  Mongolia 45°41N 113°5E 114 B7
Ongtüstik Qazaqstan □
  Kazakhstan 43°0N 68°0E 109 D7
Ongwediva Namibia 17°47S 15°46E 144 A2
Oni Georgia 42°33N 43°26E 87 J6
Onida U.S.A. 44°42N 100°4W 172 C3
Onilahy → Madag. 23°34S 43°45E 145 C7
Onitsha Nigeria 6°6N 6°42E 139 D6
Onne Fiji 18°55S 178°29E 154 a
Onoda Japan 33°59N 131°11E 113 G5
Onoke, L. N.Z. 41°22S 175°8E 154 H4
Ons, I. de Spain 42°23N 8°55W 88 C2
Onsala Sweden 57°26N 12°0E 63 G6
Onslow Australia 21°40S 115°12E 148 D2
Onslow B. U.S.A. 34°20N 77°15W 177 D16
Ontake-San Japan 35°53N 137°29E 113 G8
Ontario Calif., U.S.A. 34°4N 117°39W 171 L9
Ontario Oreg., U.S.A. 44°2N 116°58W 168 D5
Ontario □ Canada 48°0N 83°0W 164 B2
Ontario, L. N. Amer. 43°20N 78°0W 174 C7
Ontinyent Spain 38°50N 0°35W 91 G4
Ontonagon U.S.A. 46°52N 89°19W 172 B9
Ontur Spain 38°38N 1°29W 91 G3
Onyx U.S.A. 35°41N 118°14W 179 K8
Oodaaq Greenland 83°40N 30°40W 57 A8
Oodnadatta Australia 27°33S 135°30E 151 D2
Ooldea Australia 30°27S 131°50E 149 F5
Oombulgurri
  Australia 15°15S 127°45E 148 C4
Oombulgurri ◎
  Australia 15°10S 127°50E 148 C4
Oorindi Australia 20°40S 141°1E 150 C3
Oost-Vlaanderen □
  Belgium 51°5N 3°50E 69 C3
Oostende Belgium 51°15N 2°54E 69 C2
Oosterhout Neths. 51°39N 4°47E 69 C4
Oosterschelde → Neths. 51°33N 4°0E 69 C4
Oosteschelde Neths. 53°0N 3°40E 69 C3
Oostvaardersplassen △
  Neths. 52°27N 5°22E 69 B5
Ootacamund = Udagamandalam
  India 11°30N 76°44E 127 J3
Ootha Australia 33°6S 147°29E 153 D7
Ootsa L. Canada 53°50N 126°2W 162 C3
Ooty = Udagamandalam
  India 11°30N 76°44E 127 J3
Op Luang △ Thailand 18°12N 98°32E 120 C2
Opaka Bulgaria 43°28N 26°10E 97 C10
Opala
  Dem. Rep. of the Congo 0°40S 24°20E 142 C1
Opâle, Côte d' France 50°30N 1°30E 70 B8
Opalenica Poland 52°18N 16°24E 83 B9
Opan Bulgaria 42°13N 25°41E 97 D9
Opanake Sri Lanka 6°35N 80°40E 127 L5
Opapa N.Z. 39°47S 176°42E 154 F5
Opasatika Canada 49°30N 82°50W 164 C3
Opasquia △ Canada 53°33N 93°5W 164 B1
Opatija Croatia 45°21N 14°17E 93 C11
Opatów Poland 50°50N 21°27E 83 H6
Opava Czech Rep. 49°57N 17°58E 79 B10
Opelika U.S.A. 32°39N 85°23W 178 C4
Opelousas U.S.A. 30°32N 92°5W 176 F8
Opémisca, L. Canada 49°56N 74°52W 164 C5
Opheim U.S.A. 48°51N 106°24W 168 B10
Ophthalmia Ra.
  Australia 23°15S 119°30E 148 D2
Opi Nigeria 6°36N 7°28E 139 D6
Opinaca → Canada 52°15N 78°2W 164 B4
Opinaca, Rés. Canada 52°39N 76°20W 164 B4
Opinnagau → Canada 54°12N 82°25W 164 B3
Opiscotéo, L. Canada 53°10N 68°10W 165 B6
Opobo Nigeria 4°35N 7°34E 139 E6
Opochka Russia 56°42N 28°45E 84 D5
Opoczno Poland 51°22N 20°18E 83 H7
Opole Poland 50°42N 17°58E 83 H4
Opole Lubelskie Poland 51°9N 21°58E 83 G8
Opolskie □ Poland 50°40N 17°58E 83 H5
Oponono L. Namibia 18°8S 15°45E 144 A2
Oporto = Porto Portugal 41°8N 8°40W 88 D2
Opotiki N.Z. 38°1S 177°19E 154 E6
Opp U.S.A. 31°17N 86°16W 178 D3
Oppdal Norway 62°35N 9°41E 60 E13
Óppido Mamertina Italy 38°16N 15°59E 95 D8
Opportunity U.S.A. 47°39N 117°15W 170 C5
Oprişor Romania 44°17N 23°5E 80 F8
Oprtalj Croatia 45°23N 13°50E 93 C10
Opua N.Z. 35°19S 174°9E 154 B5
Opunake N.Z. 39°26S 173°52E 154 F2
Opuwo Namibia 18°3S 13°45E 144 A1
Opuzen Croatia 43°1N 17°34E 93 E14
Or → Kazakhstan 51°11N 58°32E 108 D5
Or, Côte d' France 47°10N 4°50E 71 E11
Ora Cyprus 34°51N 33°12E 101 E12
Oracle U.S.A. 32°37N 110°46W 169 K8
Oradea Romania 47°2N 21°58E 80 C6
Öræfajökull Iceland 64°2N 16°39W 60 D5
Orahovac = Rahovec
  Kosovo 42°24N 20°40E 96 D4
Orahovica Croatia 45°35N 17°52E 80 E2
Oraison France 43°55N 5°55E 73 E9
Oral = Zhayyq →
  Kazakhstan 47°0N 51°48E 108 C4
Oral Kazakhstan 51°20N 51°20E 108 C4
Oran Algeria 35°45N 0°39W 136 A3
Oran □ Algeria 35°30N 0°35W 136 A3
Orange Australia 33°15S 149°7E 153 E8
Orange France 44°8N 4°47E 73 E8
Orange Calif., U.S.A. 33°47N 117°51W 171 M9
Orange Mass., U.S.A. 42°35N 72°19W 175 D13
Orange Tex., U.S.A. 30°6N 93°44W 176 F8
Orange → S. Africa 28°41S 16°28E 144 C2
Orange, C. Brazil 4°20N 51°30W 187 C8
Orange City U.S.A. 28°57N 81°18W 179 G8

Orange Cove U.S.A. 36°38N 119°19W 170 J7
Orange Free State = Free State □
  S. Africa 28°30S 27°0E 144 C4
Orange Grove U.S.A. 27°58N 97°56W 176 H6
Orange L. U.S.A. 29°25N 82°13W 179 F21
Orange Park U.S.A. 30°10N 81°42W 178 E8
Orange Walk Belize 18°6N 88°33W 181 D7
Orangeburg U.S.A. 33°30N 80°52W 178 B9
Orangeville Canada 43°55N 80°5W 174 C1
Orango Guinea-Biss. 11°5N 16°0W 138 C1
Orani Italy 40°15N 9°11E 94 B2
Oranienburg Germany 52°45N 13°14E 76 D9
Oranje = Orange →
  S. Africa 28°41S 16°28E 144 C2
Oranjemund Namibia 28°38S 16°29E 144 C2
Oranjerivier S. Africa 29°40S 24°12E 144 C3
Oranjestad Aruba 12°32N 70°2W 183 D5
Oras Phil. 12°9N 125°28E 117 E7
Orašje Bos.-H. 45°1N 18°42E 80 E3
Orăştie Romania 45°50N 23°10E 81 E8
Orava → Slovak Rep. 49°9N 19°8E 79 B12
Orava, Vodna nádrž
  Slovak Rep. 49°25N 19°35E 79 B12
Oraviţa Romania 45°2N 21°43E 80 E6
Orawia N.Z. 46°1S 167°50E 155 G2
Orb → France 43°15N 3°18E 72 E7
Orba → Italy 44°53N 8°37E 92 D5
Ørbæk Denmark 55°17N 10°39E 63 J4
Ørken Sweden 57°6N 15°1E 63 G9
Orkény Hungary 47°9N 19°26E 80 C4
Orbetello Italy 42°27N 11°13E 93 F8
Órbigo → Spain 42°5N 5°42W 88 C5
Orbisonia U.S.A. 40°15N 77°54W 174 F7
Orbost Australia 37°40S 148°29E 153 D8
Ørbyhus Sweden 60°15N 17°43E 62 D11
Orcadas Antarctica 60°44S 44°37W 55 C18
Orcas I. U.S.A. 48°42N 122°56W 170 B4
Orchard City U.S.A. 38°50N 107°58W 168 G10
Orchard Homes U.S.A. 46°55N 114°4W 168 C6
Orchid I. = Lan Yü
  Taiwan 22°4N 121°25E 117 F13
Orchies France 50°28N 3°14E 71 B10
Orchila, I. Venezuela 11°48N 66°10W 183 D6
Orchilla, Pta.
  Canary Is. 27°42N 18°10W 100 G1
Órcia → Italy 42°58N 11°21E 93 F8
Orco → Italy 45°10N 7°52E 92 C4
Orcopampa Peru 15°20S 72°23W 188 D3
Orcutt U.S.A. 34°52N 120°27W 171 L6
Ord → U.S.A. 36°30N 98°56W 172 E4
Ord → Australia 15°33S 128°15E 148 C4
Ord, Mt. Australia 17°20S 125°34E 148 C4
Ord Mts. U.S.A. 34°39N 116°45W 171 L10
Ordenes = Ordes Spain 43°5N 8°29W 88 B2
Orderville U.S.A. 37°17N 112°38W 169 H7
Ordes Spain 43°5N 8°29W 88 B2
Ordesa y Monte Perido △
  Spain 42°40N 0°10W 90 C4
Ording = Sankt Peter-Ording
  Germany 54°20N 8°36E 76 A4
Ordos = Mu Us Shamo
  China 39°0N 109°0E 114 E5
Ordos China 39°50N 110°0E 114 E6
Ordu Turkey 40°55N 37°53E 104 B7
Ordu □ Turkey 41°0N 37°50E 104 B7
Ordubad Azerbaijan 38°54N 46°1E 105 C12
Orduña Álava, Spain 42°58N 2°58W 90 C2
Orduña Granada, Spain 37°20N 3°30W 89 H7
Ordway U.S.A. 38°13N 103°46W 168 G12
Ordzhonikidze = Denisovka
  Kazakhstan 52°27N 61°39E 108 B6
Ordzhonikidze Ukraine 47°39N 34°3E 85 J8
Ore Dem. Rep. of the Congo 3°17N 29°30E 142 B2
Ore Mts. = Erzgebirge
  Germany 50°27N 12°55E 76 E8
Orebić Croatia 43°0N 17°11E 93 F14
Örebro Sweden 59°20N 15°18E 62 E9
Örebro □ Sweden 59°27N 15°0E 62 E8
Orecchiella △ Italy 44°16N 10°22E 92 D7
Oregon □ U.S.A. 44°0N 121°0W 168 E3
Oregon City U.S.A. 45°21N 122°36W 170 E4
Oregon Dunes △
  U.S.A. 43°40N 124°10W 168 E1
Öregrund Sweden 60°21N 18°30E 62 D12
Öregrundsgrepen
  Sweden 60°25N 18°15E 62 D12
Orekhov = Orikhiv
  Ukraine 47°30N 35°48E 85 J8
Orekhovo-Zuyevo
  Russia 55°50N 38°55E 84 E10
Orel Russia 52°57N 36°3E 85 F9
Orel □ Russia 52°30N 36°0E 84 E10
Orellana, Canal de Spain 39°2N 6°0W 89 F5
Orellana, Embalse de
  Spain 39°5N 5°10W 89 F5
Orellana la Vieja Spain 39°1N 5°32W 89 F5
Orem U.S.A. 40°19N 111°42W 168 F8
Ören Turkey 37°3N 27°57E 99 D9
Orenburg Russia 51°45N 55°6E 108 D6
Örencik Turkey 39°16N 29°33E 99 B11
Orense = Ourense Spain 42°19N 7°55W 88 C3
Orepuki N.Z. 46°19S 167°46E 155 G2
Orestes Pereyra
  Mexico 26°30N 105°39W 180 B3
Orestiada Greece 41°30N 26°33E 97 E10
Øresund Europe 55°45N 12°45E 63 J6
Oreti → N.Z. 46°28S 168°14E 155 G2
Orfanos Kolpos Greece 40°33N 24°0E 96 F7
Orford Ness U.K. 52°5N 1°35E 67 E9
Organ Pipe Cactus △
  U.S.A. 32°0N 112°52W 169 K7
Organos, Pta. de los
  Canary Is. 28°12N 17°17W 100 F2
Organyà Spain 42°13N 1°20E 90 C6
Orgaz Spain 39°39N 3°53W 89 F7
Orgeyev = Orhei
  Moldova 47°24N 28°50E 81 C13
Orgiva Spain 36°53N 3°24W 89 J7
Orhaneli → Turkey 39°54N 28°59E 99 B10
Orhangazi Turkey 40°29N 29°18E 99 F12
Orhangazi Turkey 40°30N 28°55E 99 F12
Orhaneli → Turkey 39°50N 28°35E 99 B10
Orhei Moldova 47°24N 28°50E 81 C13
Orhon Gol → Mongolia 50°21N 106°0E 110 A10
Óri Italy 40°30N 17°38E 95 B10
Oria Spain 37°30N 2°0W 89 H8
Oriental, Cordillera
  Colombia 6°0N 73°0W 186 B4

Oriental, Grand Erg
  Algeria 30°0N 6°30E 136 B5
Orientale □
  Dem. Rep. of the Congo 2°20N 26°0E 142 B2
Oriente Argentina 38°44S 60°37W 190 D3
Orihuela Spain 38°7N 0°55W 91 G4
Orihuela del Tremedal
  Spain 40°33N 1°39W 90 E3
Orikhiv Ukraine 47°30N 35°48E 85 J8
Orikum Albania 40°20N 19°26E 96 F3
Oril → Ukraine 48°40N 34°39E 85 H8
Orillia Canada 44°40N 79°24W 174 B5
Orinoco → Venezuela 9°15N 61°30W 186 B6
Orion Canada 49°27N 110°49W 163 D6
Orion U.S.A. 31°58N 86°0W 178 D4
Oriskany U.S.A. 43°10N 75°20W 175 C9
Orissa = Odisha □ India 20°0N 84°0E 126 E7
Orissaare Estonia 58°34N 23°5E 84 C2
Oristano Italy 39°54N 8°36E 94 C1
Oristano, G. di Italy 39°50N 8°29E 94 C1
Orizaba Mexico 18°51N 97°6W 181 D5
Orizaba, Pico de
  Mexico 18°58N 97°15W 181 D5
Orizare Bulgaria 42°44N 27°39E 97 D11
Orizona Brazil 17°3S 48°18W 189 D1
Orjen Bos.-H. 42°35N 18°34E 96 D2
Orjiva = Orgiva Spain 36°53N 3°24W 89 J7
Orkanger Norway 63°18N 9°51E 60 E13
Orkelljunga Sweden 56°17N 13°17E 63 H7
Orken Sweden 57°6N 15°1E 63 G9
Orkhon = Orhon Gol →
  Mongolia 50°21N 106°0E 110 A10
Orkla → Norway 63°18N 9°51E 60 E13
Orkney S. Africa 26°58S 26°40E 144 C4
Orkney □ U.K. 59°2N 3°13W 65 B5
Orkney Is. U.K. 59°0N 3°0W 65 B6
Orland U.S.A. 39°45N 122°12W 170 F4
Orlando U.S.A. 28°32N 81°22W 179 G8
Orlando, C. d' Italy 38°10N 14°43E 95 D7
Orlando Int. ✈ (MCO)
  U.S.A. 28°26N 81°19W 179 G8
Orléanais France 48°0N 2°0E 71 E9
Orléans France 47°54N 1°52E 71 E8
Orleans U.S.A. 44°49N 72°12W 175 B12
Orléans, Î. d' Canada 46°54N 70°58W 165 C5
Orlice → Czech Rep. 50°13N 15°50E 78 A8
Orlik Russia 52°30N 99°55E 110 D9
Orlivka Ukraine 45°19N 28°27E 81 E13
Orlov Slovak Rep. 49°17N 20°51E 79 B13
Orlov Gay Russia 50°56N 48°19E 86 E9
Orlová Czech Rep. 49°51N 18°26E 79 B11
Orlovat Serbia 45°14N 20°33E 80 E5
Orlovskoye Polesye △
  Russia 53°5N 35°45E 84 F7
Ormara Pakistan 25°16N 64°33E 122 G4
Ormea Italy 44°9N 7°54E 92 D4
Ormilia Greece 40°16N 23°39E 96 F7
Ormoc Phil. 11°0N 124°37E 119 B6
Ormond N.Z. 38°33S 177°56E 154 F6
Ormond Beach U.S.A. 29°17N 81°3W 179 F8
Ormond-by-the-Sea
  U.S.A. 29°21N 81°4W 179 F8
Ormondville N.Z. 40°5S 176°19E 154 G5
Ormož Slovenia 46°25N 16°10E 93 B13
Ormskirk U.K. 53°35N 2°54W 66 D5
Ormstown Canada 45°8N 74°0W 175 A11
Ornans France 47°7N 6°10E 71 E13
Orne □ France 48°40N 0°5W 70 D7
Orne → France 49°18N 0°15W 70 C6
Orneta Poland 54°8N 20°9E 82 D7
Ornö Sweden 59°4N 18°24E 62 E12
Örnsköldsvik Sweden 63°17N 18°40E 62 A12
Oro → Mexico 25°35N 105°2W 180 B3
Oro Grande U.S.A. 34°36N 117°20W 171 L9
Oro Valley U.S.A. 32°26N 110°58W 169 K8
Orobie, Alpi Italy 46°7N 10°0E 92 B6
Orobie Bergamasche △
  Italy 46°0N 9°45E 92 C6
Orobie Valtellinesi △ Italy 46°5N 9°45E 92 C6
Orocué Colombia 4°48N 71°20W 186 C4
Orodara Burkina Faso 11°0N 4°55W 138 C4
Orodo Nigeria 5°34N 7°4E 139 D6
Orofino U.S.A. 46°29N 116°15W 168 C5
Orohena, Mt. Tahiti 17°37S 149°28W 155 b
Orol Dengizi = Aral Sea
  Asia 45°0N 58°20E 108 C6
Oromocto Canada 45°54N 66°29W 165 C6
Oron Nigeria 4°48N 8°14E 139 E6
Orono Canada 43°59N 78°37W 174 C6
Orono U.S.A. 44°53N 68°40W 173 C19
Oronsay U.K. 56°1N 6°15W 65 C3
Oropesa Spain 39°57N 5°10W 88 F5
Oroquieta Phil. 8°32N 123°44E 119 C6
Orós Brazil 6°15S 38°55W 189 B3
Orosei Italy 40°23N 9°42E 94 B2
Orosei, G. di Italy 40°15N 9°44E 94 B2
Orosháza Hungary 46°32N 20°42E 80 D5
Oroszlány Hungary 47°29N 18°19E 80 C3
Orotukan Russia 62°16N 151°42E 107 C16
Oroville Calif., U.S.A. 39°31N 121°33W 170 F5
Oroville Wash., U.S.A. 48°56N 119°26W 168 B4
Oroville, L. U.S.A. 39°33N 121°29W 170 F5
Orr U.S.A. 48°3N 92°50W 172 B7
Orroroo Australia 32°43S 138°38E 152 B3
Orrville U.S.A. 40°50N 81°46W 174 F3
Orsa Sweden 61°7N 14°37E 62 C8
Orsara di Púglia Italy 41°17N 15°16E 95 A8
Orsasjön Sweden 61°7N 14°37E 62 C8
Orsha Belarus 54°30N 30°25E 84 D6
Orsjö Sweden 56°42N 15°43E 63 H8
Orsk Russia 51°12N 58°34E 108 D6
Orşova Romania 44°41N 22°25E 80 F8
Orta Turkey 40°38N 33°6E 104 B5
Orta, L. d' Italy 45°48N 8°21E 92 C5
Orta Nova Italy 41°19N 15°42E 95 A8
Ortaca Turkey 36°49N 28°32E 99 F10
Ortakent Turkey 37°5N 27°11E 99 D9
Ortaklar Turkey 37°53N 27°35E 99 D9
Ortaköy Çorum, Turkey 40°16N 35°15E 104 B6
Ortaköy Niğde, Turkey 38°44N 34°3E 104 B6
Orte Italy 42°28N 12°23E 93 F9
Ortegal, C. Spain 43°43N 7°52W 88 B3
Orthez France 43°29N 0°48W 72 E3
Ortigueira Spain 43°40N 7°50W 88 B3
Ortigueira, Ría de Spain 43°44N 7°45W 88 B3

Orting U.S.A. 47°6N 122°12W 170 C4
Ortisei Italy 46°34N 11°40E 93 B8
Ortles Italy 46°31N 10°33E 92 B7
Ortón → Bolivia 10°50S 67°0W 188 C4
Ortona Italy 42°21N 14°24E 93 F11
Ortonville U.S.A. 45°19N 96°27W 172 C5
Orūmīyeh Iran 37°40N 45°0E 105 D11
Orūmīyeh, Daryācheh-ye
  Iran 37°50N 45°30E 105 D11
Orune Italy 40°24N 9°22E 94 B2
Oruro Bolivia 18°0S 67°9W 188 D4
Orūzgān □ Afghan. 33°0N 66°0E 122 C5
Orvault France 47°17N 1°38W 70 E5
Orvieto Italy 42°43N 12°7E 93 F9
Orwell N.Y., U.S.A. 43°35N 75°50W 175 C9
Orwell Ohio, U.S.A. 41°32N 80°52W 174 E4
Orwell → U.K. 51°59N 1°18E 67 F9
Orwigsburg U.S.A. 40°38N 76°6W 175 F8
Oryakhovo Bulgaria 43°40N 23°57E 96 C7
Oryol = Orel Russia 52°57N 36°3E 85 F9
Orzinuovi Italy 45°24N 9°55E 92 C6
Orzyc → Poland 52°46N 21°14E 83 F8
Orzysz Poland 53°50N 21°58E 82 E8
Osa, Pen. de Costa Rica 8°0N 83°30W 182 E3
Osage U.S.A. 43°17N 92°49W 172 D7
Osage → U.S.A. 38°36N 91°57W 172 F8
Osage City U.S.A. 38°38N 95°50W 172 F6
Ōsaka Japan 34°42N 135°30E 113 G7
Osakarovka Kazakhstan 50°33N 72°34E 109 D8
Ōsaki Japan 38°34N 140°58E 112 E10
Osawatomie U.S.A. 38°31N 94°57W 172 F6
Osborn Plateau Ind. Oc. 14°45S 87°0E 146 F7
Osborne U.S.A. 39°26N 98°42W 172 F4
Osby Sweden 56°23N 13°59E 63 H7
Osceola Ark., U.S.A. 35°42N 89°58W 177 D10
Osceola Iowa, U.S.A. 41°2N 93°46W 172 E7
Oschatz Germany 51°17N 13°6E 76 D9
Oschersleben Germany 52°2N 11°14E 76 C7
Ōschiri Italy 40°43N 9°6E 94 B2
Oschri Italy 40°43N 9°6E 94 B2
Oscoda U.S.A. 44°26N 83°20W 174 B1
Ösel = Saaremaa
  Estonia 58°30N 22°30E 84 C2
Osery Russia 54°52N 38°28E 84 E10
Osgoode Canada 45°8N 75°36W 175 A9
Osh Kyrgyzstan 40°37N 72°49E 109 D8
Oshakati Namibia 17°45S 15°40E 144 A1
Oshana □ Namibia 17°50S 15°40E 144 A2
Oshawa Canada 43°50N 78°50W 174 C6
Oshigambo Namibia 17°45S 16°5E 144 A2
Oshika-Hantō Japan 38°20N 141°30E 112 E10
Oshikoto □ Namibia 18°30S 17°0E 144 A2
Oshivelo Namibia 18°37S 17°10E 144 A2
Oshkosh Nebr., U.S.A. 41°24N 102°21W 172 E2
Oshkosh Wis., U.S.A. 44°1N 88°33W 172 C9
Oshmyany = Ashmyany
  Belarus 54°26N 25°52E 75 A13
Oshnovīyeh Iran 37°2N 45°6E 105 D11
Oshogbo Nigeria 7°48N 4°37E 139 D5
Oshtorīnān Iran 34°1N 48°38E 105 C13
Ōshū Japan 39°8N 141°8E 112 E10
Oshwe
  Dem. Rep. of the Congo 3°25S 19°28E 140 E3
Osica de Sus Poland 51°55N 16°40E 83 G3
Osiecz Croatia 45°34N 18°41E 80 E3
Ōsijek Croatia 40°45N 8°40E 94 B1
Osilo Italy 43°28N 13°30E 93 G12
Osimo Italy 43°28N 13°30E 93 G12
Osintorf Belarus 54°40N 30°39E 84 E6
Osipovichi = Asipovichy
  Belarus 53°19N 28°33E 75 B15
Osiyan India 26°43N 72°55E 124 F5
Osizweni S. Africa 27°49S 30°7E 145 C5
Oskaloosa U.S.A. 41°18N 92°39W 172 E7
Oskarshamn Sweden 57°15N 16°27E 63 G10
Oskarström Sweden 56°48N 12°58E 63 H6
Öskemen Kazakhstan 50°0N 82°36E 109 C10
Oskol → Ukraine 49°6N 37°25E 85 H9
Oskū Iran 37°54N 46°9E 105 D12
Oslo Norway 59°54N 10°43E 61 G14
Oslofjorden Norway 59°20N 10°35E 61 G14
Osmanabad India 18°5N 76°10E 126 E3
Osmanck Turkey 40°58N 34°47E 104 B6
Osmaniye Turkey 37°5N 36°10E 104 D7
Osmannagar India 18°32N 79°0E 126 E4
Osmo Sweden 58°58N 17°55E 63 E11
Osnabrück Germany 52°17N 8°3E 76 C4
Ośno Lubuskie Poland 52°28N 14°51E 83 F1
Osoblaha Czech Rep. 50°17N 17°44E 79 A10
Osogbo = Oshogbo
  Nigeria 7°48N 4°37E 139 D5
Osogovska Planina
  Macedonia 42°10N 22°30E 96 D6
Osor Italy 44°42N 14°24E 93 D11
Ósorio Brazil 29°53S 50°17W 191 B5
Osorno Chile 40°25S 73°0W 192 E2
Osorno Spain 42°24N 4°22W 88 C6
Osorno, Vol. Chile 41°0S 72°30W 192 E2
Osoyoos Canada 49°0N 119°30W 162 D5
Osøyra Norway 60°9N 5°30E 60 F11
Ospika → Canada 56°20N 124°0W 162 B4
Osprey Reef Australia 13°52S 146°36E 150 A4
Oss Neths. 51°46N 5°32E 66 C5
Ossa → France 44°7N 0°17E 72 D4
Ossa → Nigeria 6°10N 5°20E 139 D6
Ossa, Mt. Australia 41°52S 146°3E 151 G4
Ossa, Oros Greece 39°47N 22°42E 96 E6
Ossa de Montiel Spain 38°58N 2°45W 91 G2
Ossabaw I. U.S.A. 31°50N 81°5W 178 D9
Ossabaw Sd. U.S.A. 31°50N 81°8W 178 D9
Osse → France 44°7N 0°17E 72 D4
Osse → Nigeria 6°10N 5°20E 139 D6
Ossi Italy 40°40N 8°35E 94 B1
Ossining U.S.A. 41°10N 73°55W 175 E11
Ossipee U.S.A. 43°41N 71°7W 175 C13
Ossokmanuan L.
  Canada 53°25N 65°0W 165 B7
Ossora Russia 59°20N 163°13E 107 D17
Ostashkov Russia 57°4N 33°2E 84 D7
Østavall Sweden 62°26N 15°29E 62 B9
Oste → Germany 53°30N 9°12E 76 B5
Ostend = Oostende
  Belgium 51°15N 2°54E 69 C2
Ostend N.Z. 36°48S 175°6E 154 C4
Oster Ukraine 50°57N 30°53E 75 C16

Österbotten = Pohjanmaa □
  Finland 62°58N 22°50E **60** E20
Osterburg Germany 52°47N 11°45E **76** C7
Osterburg U.S.A. 40°16N 78°31W **174** F6
Osterburken Germany 49°25N 9°26E **77** F5
Österbybruk Sweden 60°13N 17°55E **62** D11
Österbymo Sweden 57°49N 15°15E **63** G9
Österdalälven → Sweden 60°30N 15°7E **62** C7
Österdalen Norway 61°40N 10°50E **62** C4
Österfärnebo Sweden 60°19N 16°48E **62** D10
Österforse Sweden 63°9N 17°3E **62** A11
Östergötland □ Sweden 58°35N 15°45E **63** F9
Osterholz-Scharmbeck
  Germany 53°13N 8°47E **76** B4
Österild Denmark 57°2N 8°51E **63** G2
Östermyra = Seinäjoki
  Finland 62°40N 22°51E **60** E20
Osterode Germany 51°43N 10°15E **76** D6
Österreich = Austria ■
  Europe 47°0N 14°0E **78** E7
Östersund Sweden 63°10N 14°38E **62** A8
Östervåla Sweden 60°11N 17°11E **62** D11
Ostfriesische Inseln
  Germany 53°42N 7°0E **76** B3
Ostfriesland Germany 53°20N 7°30E **76** B3
Östhammar Sweden 60°16N 18°22E **62** D12
Östia, Lido di Italy 41°43N 12°17E **93** G9
Ostiglia Italy 45°4N 11°8E **93** C8
Östmark Sweden 60°17N 12°45E **62** C6
Östra Husby Sweden 58°35N 16°33E **63** F10
Ostrava Czech Rep. 49°51N 18°18E **79** B11
Ostróda Poland 53°42N 19°58E **82** E6
Ostrogozhsk Russia 50°55N 39°7E **85** G10
Ostroh Ukraine 50°20N 26°30E **75** C14
Ostrołęka Poland 53°4N 21°32E **83** E8
Ostrov Bulgaria 43°40N 24°9E **97** C8
Ostrov Czech Rep. 50°18N 12°57E **78** A5
Ostrov Romania 44°6N 27°24E **81** F12
Ostrov Russia 57°25N 28°20E **84** D5
Ostrów Lubelski Poland 51°29N 22°51E **83** G9
Ostrów Mazowiecka
  Poland 52°50N 21°51E **83** F8
Ostrów Wielkopolski
  Poland 51°36N 17°44E **83** G4
Ostrowiec-Świętokrzyski
  Poland 50°55N 21°22E **83** H8
Ostrožac Bos.-H. 43°43N 17°49E **80** G2
Ostrzeszów Poland 51°25N 17°52E **83** G4
Ostseebad Kühlungsborn
  Germany 54°8N 11°44E **76** A7
Osttirol □ Austria 46°50N 12°30E **78** E5
Ostuni Italy 40°44N 17°35E **95** B10
Osum → Albania 40°40N 20°10E **96** F4
Osŭm → Bulgaria 43°40N 24°50E **97** C8
Ōsumi-Kaikyō Japan 30°55N 131°0E **113** J5
Ōsumi-Shotō Japan 30°30N 130°0E **113** J5
Osun □ Nigeria 7°30N 4°30E **139** D5
Osuna Spain 37°14N 5°8W **89** H5
Oswegatchie →
  U.S.A. 44°42N 75°30W **175** B9
Oswego U.S.A. 43°27N 76°31W **175** C8
Oswego → U.S.A. 43°27N 76°30W **175** C8
Oswestry U.K. 52°52N 3°3W **66** E4
Oświęcim Poland 50°2N 19°11E **83** H6
Otaci Moldova 48°27N 27°47E **81** B12
Otago □ N.Z. 45°15S 170°0E **155** F5
Otago Harbour N.Z. 45°47S 170°42E **155** F5
Otago Pen. N.Z. 45°48S 170°39E **155** F5
Otaheite B.
  Trin. & Tob. 10°15N 61°30W **187** K15
Otahuhu N.Z. 36°56S 174°51E **154** C3
Ōtake Japan 34°12N 132°13E **113** G6
Otaki N.Z. 40°45S 175°10E **154** G4
Otane N.Z. 39°54S 176°39E **154** F5
Otaru Japan 43°10N 141°0E **112** C10
Otaru-Wan = Ishikari-Wan
  Japan 43°25N 141°1E **112** C10
Otautau N.Z. 46°9S 168°1E **155** G3
Otava → Czech Rep. 49°26N 14°12E **78** B7
Otavalo Ecuador 0°13N 78°20W **196** C3
Otavi Namibia 19°40S 17°24E **144** A2
Ōtawara Japan 36°50N 140°5E **113** F10
Otchinjau Angola 16°30S 13°56E **144** A1
Otego U.S.A. 42°23N 75°10W **175** D9
Otelec Romania 45°36N 20°50E **80** E5
Otelnuk, L. Canada 56°9N 68°12W **165** A6
Oțelu Roșu Romania 45°30N 22°22E **80** E7
Otero de Rey = Outeiro de Rei
  Spain 43°6N 7°36W **88** B3
Othello U.S.A. 46°50N 119°10W **168** C4
Othoni Greece 39°52N 19°22E **98** B1
Othris, Oros Greece 39°2N 22°37E **98** B4
Oti → Africa 7°48N 0°8E **139** D5
Oti □ Togo 8°40N 0°35E **139** C5
Otira N.Z. 42°49S 171°33E **155** C6
Otira Gorge N.Z. 42°53S 171°33E **155** C6
Otish, Mts. Canada 52°22N 70°30W **165** B5
Otishi △ Peru 11°40S 73°5W **188** C3
Otjinene Namibia 21°18S 18°44E **144** B2
Otjiwarongo Namibia 20°30S 16°33E **144** B2
Otjozondjupa □ Namibia 21°0S 17°0E **144** B2
Otmuchów Poland 50°28N 17°10E **83** H4
Otočac Croatia 44°53N 15°12E **93** D12
Otoineppu Japan 44°44N 142°16E **112** B11
Otok Croatia 45°42N 16°44E **93** E13
Otopeni, București × (OTP)
  Romania 44°30N 26°11E **81** F11
Otorohanga N.Z. 38°12S 175°14E **154** E4
Otoskwin → Canada 52°13N 88°6W **164** B2
Otra → Norway 58°9N 8°1E **61** G13
Otradniy Russia 53°22N 51°21E **86** D10
Otranto Italy 40°9N 18°28E **95** B11
Otranto, C. d' Italy 40°7N 18°30E **95** B11
Otranto, Str. of Italy 40°15N 18°40E **95** B11
Otrokovice Czech Rep. 49°12N 17°32E **79** B9
Otse S. Africa 25°2S 25°45E **144** C4
Otsego L. U.S.A. 44°25N 74°53W **175** D10
Ōtsu Japan 35°0N 135°50E **113** G7
Ōtsuki Japan 35°36N 138°57E **113** G9
Ottappalam India 10°46N 76°23E **127** J3
Ottawa = Outaouais →
  Canada 45°27N 74°8W **164** C7
Ottawa Canada 45°26N 75°42W **175** A9
Ottawa Ill., U.S.A. 41°21N 88°51W **172** E7
Ottawa Kans., U.S.A. 38°37N 95°16W **172** F6
Ottawa Is. Canada 59°35N 80°10W **161** F15
Ottélé Cameroon 3°38N 11°19E **139** E7
Ottensheim Austria 48°21N 14°12E **78** C7
Otter → U.K. 50°38N 3°17W **67** F5
Otter Cr. → U.S.A. 44°13N 73°17W **175** D11
Otter Creek U.S.A. 29°19N 82°46W **179** F7
Otter Lake Canada 45°17N 79°56W **174** A5

Otterbäcken Sweden 58°57N 14°3E **63** F8
Otterndorf Germany 53°48N 8°53E **76** B4
Otterup Denmark 55°30N 10°22E **63** J4
Otterville Canada 42°55N 80°36W **174** D4
Ottery St. Mary U.K. 50°44N 3°17W **67** G4
Otto Beit Bridge
  Zimbabwe 15°59S 28°56E **143** F2
Ottosdal S. Africa 26°46S 25°59E **144** C4
Ottumwa U.S.A. 41°1N 92°25W **172** E7
Otukpa Nigeria 7°9N 7°41E **139** D6
Oturkpo Nigeria 7°16N 8°8E **139** D6
Otway, B. Chile 53°30S 74°0W **192** D2
Otway, C. Australia 38°52S 143°30E **152** E5
Otway, Seno de Chile 53°0S 71°30W **192** D2
Otway □ Australia 38°47S 143°34E **152** E5
Otwock Poland 52°5N 21°20E **83** F8
Otyniya Ukraine 48°44N 24°51E **81** B9
Ötztal Ache →
  Austria 47°14N 10°50E **78** D3
Ötztaler Alpen Austria 46°56N 11°0E **78** E3
Ou → Laos 20°4N 102°13E **120** B4
Ou-Sammyaku Japan 39°20N 140°35E **112** E10
Ouachita → U.S.A. 31°38N 91°49W **176** F9
Ouachita, L. U.S.A. 34°34N 93°12W **176** D8
Ouachita Mts. U.S.A. 34°30N 94°30W **176** D7
Ouagadougou
  Burkina Faso 12°25N 1°30W **139** C4
Ouahigouya
  Burkina Faso 13°31N 2°25W **138** C4
Ouahran = Oran
  Algeria 35°45N 0°39W **136** A3
Oualâta Mauritania 17°20N 6°55W **138** B3
Ouallam Niger 14°23N 2°10E **139** C5
Ouallene Algeria 24°41N 1°11E **136** D4
Ouarâne Mauritania 21°0N 10°30W **134** D3
Ouargaye Burkina Faso 11°40N 0°5E **139** C5
Ouargla Algeria 31°59N 5°16E **136** B5
Ouargla □ Algeria 30°30N 6°10E **136** C5
Ouarkoye Burkina Faso 12°5N 3°40W **138** C4
Ouarkziz, Jebel Algeria 28°50N 8°0W **136** C2
Ouarra → C.A.R. 5°5N 24°26E **140** C4
Ouarzazate Morocco 30°55N 6°50W **136** B2
Ouassouas Mali 16°10N 1°23E **139** B5
Ouatagouna Mali 15°11N 0°43E **139** B5
Oubangi →
  Dem. Rep. of the Congo 0°30S 17°50E **140** E3
Oubarakai, O. → Algeria 27°20N 9°0E **136** C5
Ouche → France 47°6N 5°16E **71** E12
Ouddorp Neths. 51°50N 3°57E **69** C3
Oude Rijn → Neths. 52°12N 4°24E **69** B4
Oudeïka Mali 17°30N 1°40W **139** B4
Oudenaarde Belgium 50°50N 3°37E **69** D3
Oudon → France 47°41N 0°53W **70** E6
Oudtshoorn S. Africa 33°35S 22°14E **144** D3
Oued Zem Morocco 32°52N 6°34W **136** B2
Ouella Niger 14°48N 3°38E **139** C5
Ouellé Ivory C. 7°26N 4°1W **138** D4
Ouémé → Benin 6°30N 2°30E **139** D5
Ouenza Algeria 35°8N 8°8E **136** A5
Ouessa Burkina Faso 11°4N 2°47W **138** C4
Ouessant, Î. d' France 48°28N 5°6W **70** D1
Ouesso Congo 1°37N 16°5E **140** D3
Ouest, Pte. de l' Canada 49°52N 64°40W **165** C7
Ouezzane Morocco 34°51N 5°35W **136** B2
Ougarou Burkina Faso 12°10N 0°58E **139** C5
Oughter, L. Ireland 54°1N 7°28W **64** B4
Oughterard Ireland 53°26N 9°18W **64** C2
Ouidah Benin 6°25N 2°0E **139** D5
Ouidi Niger 14°10N 13°0E **139** C7
Ouistreham France 49°17N 0°18W **70** C6
Oujda Morocco 34°41N 1°55W **136** B3
Oujeft Mauritania 20°2N 13°0W **138** A2
Oulad-Teïma Morocco 30°24N 9°12W **136** B2
Oulainen Finland 64°17N 24°47E **60** D21
Oulanka △ Finland 66°26N 29°25E **60** C23
Ould Yenjé Mauritania 15°38N 12°16W **138** B2
Ouled Djellal Algeria 34°28N 5°2E **136** B5
Ouled Naïl, Mts. des
  Algeria 34°30N 3°30E **136** B4
Oullins France 45°43N 4°49E **73** C8
Oulmès Morocco 33°17N 6°0W **136** B2
Oulu Finland 65°1N 25°29E **60** D21
Oulujärvi Finland 64°25N 27°15E **60** D22
Oulujoki → Finland 65°1N 25°30E **60** D21
Oulx Italy 45°2N 6°50E **92** C4
Oum Chalouba Chad 15°48N 20°46E **135** E10
Oum-el-Bouaghi Algeria 35°55N 7°6E **136** A5
Oum-el-Bouaghi □
  Algeria 35°50N 7°5E **136** A5
Oum el Ksi Algeria 30°57S 152°12E **153** A10
Oum er-Rbia, O. →
  Morocco 33°19N 8°21W **136** B2
Oum Hadjer Chad 13°18N 19°41E **135** F9
Oumé Ivory C. 6°21N 5°27W **138** D3
Ounane, Dj. Algeria 25°4N 7°19E **136** C5
Ounasjoki → Finland 66°31N 25°40E **60** C21
Ounguati Namibia 22°0S 15°46E **144** B2
Ounianga Kébir Chad 19°4N 20°29E **135** E10
Our → Lux. 49°55N 6°5E **69** E6
Oura, Akra Greece 38°10N 26°2E **99** C8
Ouranoupoli Greece 40°20N 23°59E **96** F7
Ouarâne Niger 19°30N 7°10E **139** B6
Ouray U.S.A. 38°1N 107°40W **169** G10
Ourcq → France 49°1N 3°1E **71** C10
Ourém Portugal 39°40N 8°35W **88** F2
Ourense Spain 42°19N 7°55W **88** C3
Ourense □ Spain 42°15N 7°51W **88** C3
Ouricuri Brazil 7°53S 40°5W **189** D11
Ourinhos Brazil 23°0S 49°54W **191** A6
Ourique Portugal 37°38N 8°16W **89** H2
Ouro Fino Brazil 22°16S 46°25W **191** A6
Ouro-Ndia Mali 15°8N 4°35W **138** B4
Ouro Prêto Brazil 20°20S 43°30W **191** A7
Ouro Sogui Senegal 15°36N 13°19W **138** B2
Oursi Burkina Faso 14°41N 0°27W **139** B5
Ourthe → Belgium 50°29N 5°35E **69** D5
Ouse → E. Sussex, U.K. 50°47N 0°4E **67** G8
Ouse → N. Yorks., U.K. 53°44N 0°55W **66** D7
Oust France 42°52N 1°13E **72** F5
Oust → France 47°35N 2°6W **70** E4
Outamba-Kilimi △
  S. Leone 9°50N 12°40W **138** D2
Outaouais → Canada 45°27N 74°8W **164** C7
Outapi Namibia 17°30S 15°0E **144** A1
Outardes → Canada 49°24N 69°30W **165** C6
Outat Oulad el Haj
  Morocco 33°22N 3°42W **136** B3
Outeiro de Rei Spain 43°6N 7°36W **88** B3
Outer Hebrides U.K. 57°30N 7°15W **65** D1
Outes = A Serra de Outes
  Spain 42°52N 8°55W **88** C2

Outjo Namibia 20°5S 16°7E **144** B2
Outlook Canada 51°30N 107°0W **163** C7
Outokumpu Finland 62°43N 29°1E **60** E23
Outreau France 50°40N 1°36E **71** B8
Ouvèze → France 43°59N 4°51E **73** E8
Ouyen Australia 35°1S 142°22E **152** C5
Ouzouer-le-Marché
  France 47°54N 1°32E **71** E8
Ovada Italy 44°38N 8°38E **92** D5
Ovalau Fiji 17°40S 178°48E **154** a
Ovalle Chile 30°33S 71°18W **190** C1
Ovamboland Namibia 18°30S 16°0E **144** A2
Ovanåker Sweden 61°22N 15°53E **62** C9
Ovar Portugal 40°51N 8°40W **88** E2
Overath Germany 50°56N 7°17E **76** E3
Overflakkee Neths. 51°44N 4°10E **69** C4
Overijssel □ Neths. 52°25N 6°35E **69** B6
Overland Park U.S.A. 38°58N 94°40W **172** F6
Overlander Roadhouse
  Australia 26°19S 114°28E **149** E1
Overton U.S.A. 36°33N 114°27W **171** J12
Övertorneå Sweden 66°23N 23°38E **60** C20
Överum Sweden 58°0N 16°20E **63** F10
Ovid U.S.A. 42°41N 76°49W **175** D8
Ovidiopol Ukraine 46°15N 30°30E **85** J6
Ovidiu Romania 44°16N 28°34E **81** F13
Oviedo Spain 43°25N 5°50W **88** B5
Oviedo U.S.A. 28°40N 81°13W **179** G8
Oviksfjällen Sweden 63°0N 13°49E **62** A7
Ovišrags Latvia 57°33N 21°44E **82** A8
Ovoot Mongolia 45°21N 113°45E **114** B7
Övör Hangay □
  Mongolia 45°0N 102°30E **114** B2
Ovoro Nigeria 5°26N 7°16E **139** D6
Owaka N.Z. 46°27S 169°40E **155** G4
Owambo = Ovamboland
  Namibia 18°30S 16°0E **144** A2
Owasco L. U.S.A. 42°50N 76°31W **175** D8
Owase Japan 34°7N 136°12E **113** G8
Owatonna U.S.A. 44°5N 93°14W **172** C7
Owbeh Afghan. 34°28N 63°10E **128** B3
Owego U.S.A. 42°6N 76°16W **175** D8
Owen Australia 34°15S 138°32E **152** C3
Owen, Mt. N.Z. 41°35S 172°33E **155** B7
Owen Falls Dam = Nalubaale
  Dam Uganda 0°30N 33°5E **142** B3
Owen Sound Canada 44°35N 80°55W **174** B4
Owen Stanley Ra.
  Papua N. G. 8°30S 147°0E **147** B7
Oweniny → Ireland 54°8N 9°34W **64** B2
Owens → U.S.A. 36°32N 117°59W **170** J9
Owens L. U.S.A. 36°26N 117°57W **171** J9
Owensboro U.S.A. 37°46N 87°7W **172** G10
Owhango N.Z. 39°0S 175°23E **154** F5
Owl → Canada 57°51N 92°44W **163** B10
Owo Nigeria 7°10N 5°39E **139** D6
Owosso U.S.A. 43°0N 84°10W **173** D11
Owyhee U.S.A. 41°57N 116°6W **168** F5
Owyhee → U.S.A. 43°49N 117°2W **168** E5
Owyhee, L. U.S.A. 43°38N 117°14W **168** E5
Ox Mts. = Slieve Gamph
  Ireland 54°6N 9°0W **64** B3
Oxapampa Peru 10°33S 75°26W **188** C2
Öxarfjörður Iceland 66°15N 16°45W **60** C5
Oxbow Canada 49°14N 102°10W **163** D8
Oxelösund Sweden 58°43N 17°5E **63** F11
Oxford N.Z. 43°18S 172°11E **155** D7
Oxford U.K. 51°46N 1°15W **67** F6
Oxford Ala., U.S.A. 33°36N 85°51W **178** D4
Oxford Mass., U.S.A. 42°7N 71°52W **175** D13
Oxford Miss., U.S.A. 34°22N 89°31W **177** D10
Oxford N.C., U.S.A. 36°19N 78°35W **177** C15
Oxford N.Y., U.S.A. 42°27N 75°36W **175** D9
Oxford Ohio, U.S.A. 39°31N 84°45W **173** F11
Oxford L. Canada 54°51N 95°37W **163** C9
Oxfordshire □ U.K. 51°48N 1°16W **67** F6
Oxia Greece 38°18N 21°36E **98** C3
Oxie Sweden 55°33N 13°6E **63** J7
Oxilithos Greece 38°35N 24°7E **98** C6
Oxley Australia 34°11S 144°6E **152** C6
Oxley Wild Rivers △
  Australia 30°57S 152°12E **153** A10
Oxnard U.S.A. 34°12N 119°11W **171** L7
Oxsjövålen Sweden 62°34N 13°57E **62** B7
Oxus = Amudarya →
  Uzbekistan 43°58N 59°34E **108** D3
Oya Malaysia 2°55N 111°55E **118** D4
Oyama Japan 36°18N 139°48E **113** F9
Oyambre △ Spain 43°22N 4°21W **88** B6
Oyem Gabon 1°34N 11°31E **140** D2
Oyen Canada 51°22N 110°28W **163** C6
Oykel → U.K. 57°56N 4°26W **65** D4
Oymyakon Russia 63°25N 142°44E **107** C15
Oyo Nigeria 7°46N 3°56E **139** D5
Oyo Sudan 21°58N 36°10E **137** C4
Oyo □ Nigeria 8°15N 3°30E **139** D5
Oyón Peru 10°37S 76°47W **188** C2
Oyonnax France 46°16N 5°40E **71** F12
Ōyūbari Japan 43°1N 142°5E **112** C11
Oyyl → Kazakhstan 49°4N 54°0E **108** C4
Özalp Turkey 38°39N 43°59E **105** C10
Ozamiz Phil. 8°15N 123°50E **119** C6
Ozark Ala., U.S.A. 31°28N 85°39W **178** D4
Ozark Ark., U.S.A. 35°29N 93°50W **176** D8
Ozark Mo., U.S.A. 37°1N 93°12W **172** G7
Ozark Plateau U.S.A. 37°20N 91°40W **172** G8
Ozarks, L. of the U.S.A. 38°12N 92°38W **172** F7
Ozd Hungary 48°14N 20°15E **80** B5
Ozernovskiy Russia 51°30N 156°31E **107** D16
Ozernoye Russia 51°46N 51°12E **86** E10
Ozersk Russia 54°25N 22°0E **82** B8
Ozette, L. U.S.A. 48°6N 124°38W **170** B2
Ozieri Italy 40°35N 9°0E **94** B2
Ozinki Russia 51°12N 49°44E **86** E9
Ozona U.S.A. 30°43N 101°12W **176** G5
Ozorków Poland 51°57N 19°16E **83** G6
Ozren Bos.-H. 43°55N 18°29E **80** G3
Ozuluama Mexico 21°40N 97°50W **181** C5
Ozun Romania 45°47N 25°50E **81** E10
Ozurgeti Georgia 41°55N 42°0E **87** B5

P

Pa Burkina Faso 11°33N 3°19W **138** C4
Pa-an Burma 16°51N 97°40E **123** L20
Pa Mong Dam Thailand 18°0N 102°22E **120** D4
Pa Sak → Thailand 15°30N 101°0E **120** E3
Paamiut Greenland 62°0N 49°43W **57** E6
Paanayarvi △ Russia 66°16N 30°10E **60** C24
Paar → Germany 48°46N 11°36E **77** G7
Paarl S. Africa 33°45S 18°56E **144** D2
Pab Hills Pakistan 26°30N 66°45E **124** F2
Pabaidh = Pabbay U.K. 57°46N 7°14W **65** D1
Pabbay U.K. 57°46N 7°14W **65** D1
Pabianice Poland 51°40N 19°20E **83** G6
Pabna Bangla. 24°1N 89°18E **123** G16
Pabo Uganda 3°1N 32°10E **142** B3
Pacaipampa Peru 5°35S 79°39W **188** B2
Pacaja → Brazil 1°56S 50°50W **187** D8
Pacajus Brazil 4°0S 38°31W **189** A3
Pacaraima, Sa. S. Amer. 4°0N 62°30W **186** C6
Pacarán Peru 12°50S 76°3W **188** C2
Pacaraos Peru 11°12S 76°42W **188** C2
Pacasmayo Peru 7°20S 79°35W **188** B2
Pace U.S.A. 30°36N 87°10W **179** E12
Paceco Italy 37°59N 12°33E **94** E5
Pachacamac Peru 12°14S 77°53W **188** C2
Pachia Greece 36°17N 25°0E **99** E7
Pachino Italy 36°43N 15°5E **95** F8
Pachitea → Peru 8°46S 74°33W **188** B3
Pachiza Peru 7°16S 76°46W **188** B2
Pachmarhi India 22°28N 78°26E **125** H8
Pachnes Greece 35°16N 24°4E **101** D6
Pachora India 20°38N 75°29E **126** D2
Pachpadra India 25°58N 72°10E **124** G5
Pachuca Mexico 20°7N 98°44W **181** C5
Pacific Antarctic Ridge
  Pac. Oc. 43°0S 115°0W **55** B13
Pacific Grove U.S.A. 36°38N 121°56W **170** J5
Pacific Ocean 10°0N 140°0W **157** G14
Pacific Rim △ Canada 48°40N 124°45W **170** B2
Pacifica U.S.A. 37°37N 122°27W **170** H4
Pacitan Indonesia 8°12S 111°7E **119** H14
Packsaddle Australia 30°36S 141°58E **152** A4
Packwood U.S.A. 46°36N 121°40W **170** D5
Pacov Czech Rep. 49°27N 15°0E **78** B8
Pacuí → Brazil 16°46S 45°1W **189** D1
Pacy-sur-Eure France 49°1N 1°23E **70** C8
Padaido, Kepulauan
  Indonesia 1°5S 138°0E **119** E9
Padampur India 20°59N 83°4E **126** D6
Padang Riau, Indonesia 1°30N 102°30E **121** M4
Padang Sumatera Barat,
  Indonesia 1°0S 100°20E **118** E2
Padang Endau
  Malaysia 2°40N 103°38E **121** L4
Padangpanjang
  Indonesia 0°40S 100°20E **118** E2
Padangsidempuan
  Indonesia 1°30N 99°15E **118** D1
Padborg Denmark 54°49N 9°21E **63** K3
Paddle Prairie Canada 57°57N 117°29W **162** B5
Paderborn Germany 51°42N 8°45E **76** D4
Paderoo India 18°5N 82°40E **126** E6
Padeş, Vf. Romania 45°40N 22°22E **80** E7
Padina Romania 44°50N 27°8E **81** F12
Padjelanta △ Sweden 67°20N 16°35E **60** C17
Padma India 24°12N 85°22E **125** G11
Pádova Italy 45°25N 11°53E **93** C8
Padra India 22°15N 73°7E **124** H5
Padrauna India 26°54N 83°59E **125** F10
Padre I. U.S.A. 27°10N 97°25W **176** H6
Padre Island △ U.S.A. 27°0N 97°25W **176** H6
Padrón Spain 42°41N 8°39W **88** C2
Padstow U.K. 50°33N 4°58W **67** G3
Padthaway Australia 36°36S 140°31E **152** D4
Padua = Pádova Italy 45°25N 11°53E **93** C8
Paducah Ky., U.S.A. 37°5N 88°37W **172** G9
Paducah Tex., U.S.A. 34°1N 100°18W **176** D4
Padukka Sri Lanka 6°50N 80°5E **127** L5
Padul Spain 37°1N 3°38W **89** H7
Padwa India 18°27N 82°47E **126** D6
Paea Tahiti 17°41S 149°35W **155** b
Paekakariki N.Z. 40°59S 174°58E **154** E5
Paektu-san N. Korea 41°59N 128°4E **115** D15
Paengaroa N.Z. 37°49S 176°29E **154** G5
Paeroa N.Z. 37°23S 175°41E **154** D4
Paesana Italy 44°41N 7°16E **92** D4
Pafúri Mozam. 22°28S 31°17E **145** B5
Pag Croatia 44°25N 15°3E **93** D12
Paga Ghana 11°1N 1°8W **139** C4
Pagadian Phil. 7°55N 123°30E **119** C6
Pagai Selatan, Pulau
  Indonesia 3°0S 100°15E **118** E2
Pagai Utara, Pulau
  Indonesia 2°35S 100°0E **118** E2
Pagalu = Annobón
  Atl. Oc. 1°25S 5°36E **133** G4
Pagara India 24°22N 80°1E **125** G9
Pagastikos Kolpos Greece 39°15N 23°0E **98** B5
Pagatan Indonesia 3°33S 115°59E **118** E5
Page U.S.A. 36°57N 111°27W **169** H8
Pago Pago Amer. Samoa 14°16S 170°43W **154** b
Pagosa Springs
  U.S.A. 37°16N 107°1W **169** H10
Pagri China 27°45N 89°10E **123** F12
Pagwa River Canada 50°2N 85°14W **164** B2
Páhala U.S.A. 19°12N 155°29W **167** M8
Pahang □ Malaysia 3°30N 102°45E **121** L4
Pahang → Malaysia 3°30N 103°9E **121** L4
Pahia Pt. N.Z. 46°20S 167°42E **155** G2
Pahiatua N.Z. 40°27S 175°50E **154** G5
Pahokee U.S.A. 26°50N 80°40W **179** H8
Pahute Mesa U.S.A. 37°20N 116°45W **171** J11
Pai Thailand 19°19N 98°27E **120** C2
Paicines U.S.A. 36°44N 121°17W **170** J5
Paide Estonia 58°57N 25°31E **64** B4
Paignton U.K. 50°26N 3°35W **67** G4
Paihia N.Z. 35°17S 174°6E **154** B5
Paiho Taiwan 23°21N 120°25E **117** F13
Paiján Peru 7°42S 79°20W **188** B2
Päijänne Finland 61°30N 25°30E **63** E22
Pailani India 25°45N 80°26E **125** G9
Pailin Cambodia 12°46N 102°36E **120** F4
Paimpol France 48°48N 3°4W **70** C3
Painan Indonesia 1°21S 100°34E **118** E2

Paine Grande, Cerro
  Chile 50°59S 73°4W **192** D2
Painesville U.S.A. 41°43N 81°15W **174** E3
Paint Hills = Wemindji
  Canada 53°0N 78°49W **164** B4
Paint L. Canada 55°28N 97°57W **163** B9
Painted Desert U.S.A. 36°0N 111°0W **169** H8
Paintsville U.S.A. 37°49N 82°48W **173** G12
País Vasco □ Spain 42°50N 2°45W **90** C2
Paisley Canada 44°18N 81°16W **174** B3
Paisley U.K. 55°50N 4°25W **65** F4
Paisley U.S.A. 42°42N 120°32W **168** E3
Paita Peru 5°11S 81°9W **188** B1
Paithan India 19°29N 75°23E **126** E2
Paiva → Portugal 41°4N 8°16W **88** D2
Paizhou China 30°12N 113°55E **117** B9
Pajares Spain 43°1N 5°46W **88** B5
Pajares, Puerto de Spain 42°58N 5°46W **88** B5
Pajęczno Poland 51°10N 19°0E **83** G5
Pak Lay Laos 18°15N 101°27E **120** C3
Pak Ou Laos 20°3N 102°12E **120** B4
Pak Phanang Thailand 8°21N 100°12E **121** H3
Pak Sane Laos 18°22N 103°39E **120** C4
Pak Song Laos 15°11N 106°14E **120** E6
Pak Suang Laos 19°58N 102°15E **120** C4
Pak Tam Chung China 22°24N 114°19E **111** a
Pak Thong Chai
  Thailand 14°43N 102°1E **120** E4
Pakala India 13°29N 79°8E **127** H4
Pakaur India 24°38N 87°51E **125** G12
Pakenham Australia 38°6S 145°30E **153** F6
Pakenham Canada 45°18N 76°18W **175** A8
Pakhuis S. Africa 32°9S 19°5E **144** D2
Pakistan ■ Asia 30°0N 70°0E **124** E6
Pakkading Laos 18°19N 103°59E **120** C4
Paklenica △ Croatia 44°20N 15°39E **93** D12
Pakowki L. Canada 49°20N 111°0W **163** D6
Pakość Poland 52°48N 18°6E **83** F5
Pakpattan Pakistan 30°25N 73°27E **124** D5
Pakrac Croatia 45°27N 17°12E **80** E2
Pakruojis Lithuania 55°58N 23°52E **82** C10
Paks Hungary 46°38N 18°55E **80** D3
Paktīā □ Afghan. 33°0N 69°15E **122** C3
Paktīkā □ Afghan. 32°30N 69°0E **122** C3
Pakwach Uganda 2°28N 31°27E **142** B3
Pakxe Laos 15°5N 105°52E **120** E5
Pal Lahara India 21°27N 85°11E **125** J11
Pala Chad 9°25N 15°5E **135** G8
Pala
  Dem. Rep. of the Congo 6°45S 29°30E **142** D2
Pala U.S.A. 33°22N 117°5W **171** M9
Palabek Uganda 3°22N 32°33E **142** B3
Palacios U.S.A. 28°42N 96°13W **176** G6
Palafrugell Spain 41°55N 3°10E **90** D8
Palagiano Italy 40°35N 17°2E **95** B10
Palagonia Italy 37°19N 14°45E **95** E7
Palagruža Croatia 42°24N 16°15E **93** F13
Palaiseau France 48°42N 2°14E **71** D9
Palakkad India 10°46N 76°42E **127** J3
Palakol India 16°31N 81°46E **127** F5
Palalankwe India 10°52N 92°29E **127** J11
Palam India 19°0N 77°0E **126** E3
Palamás Greece 39°26N 22°4E **98** B4
Palamós Spain 41°50N 3°10E **90** D8
Palampur India 32°10N 76°30E **124** C7
Palamut Turkey 38°59N 27°41E **99** C9
Palana Australia 39°45S 147°55E **151** F4
Palana Russia 59°10N 159°59E **107** D16
Palanan Phil. 17°17N 122°30E **119** A6
Palanan Pt. Phil. 17°17N 122°30E **119** A6
Palandri Pakistan 33°42N 73°40E **125** B5
Palanga Lithuania 55°58N 21°3E **82** C8
Palangkaraya Indonesia 2°16S 113°56E **118** E4
Palani India 10°14N 77°33E **127** J3
Palani Hills India 10°14N 77°33E **127** J3
Palanpur India 24°10N 72°25E **124** G5
Palapye Botswana 22°30S 27°7E **144** B4
Palas Pakistan 35°4N 73°14E **125** B5
Palas de Rei Spain 42°52N 7°52W **88** C3
Palasponga India 21°47N 85°34E **125** J11
Palatka Russia 60°6N 150°54E **107** C16
Palatka U.S.A. 29°39N 81°38W **179** F8
Palau ■ Palau 7°30N 134°30E **156** G5
Palau Burma 13°10N 98°40E **120** F2
Palauk Burma 13°10N 98°40E **120** F2
Palaw Burma 12°58N 98°39E **120** F2
Palawan Phil. 9°30N 118°30E **118** C5
Palayankottai India 8°45N 77°45E **127** K3
Palazzo, Pte. France 42°28N 8°32E **73** F12
Palazzo San Gervásio
  Italy 40°56N 15°59E **95** B8
Palazzolo Acréide Italy 37°4N 14°54E **95** E7
Palca Chile 19°7S 69°9W **188** D3
Paldiski Estonia 59°23N 24°9E **64** B4
Palekastro Greece 35°12N 26°15E **101** D8
Palembang Indonesia 3°0S 104°50E **118** E2
Palena, L. Chile 43°55S 71°40W **192** B2
Palena → Chile 43°55S 71°40W **192** B2
Palencia Spain 42°1N 4°34W **88** C6
Palencia □ Spain 42°31N 4°33W **88** C6
Palenque Mexico 17°39N 91°58W **181** D6
Paleochóra Greece 35°16N 23°39E **101** D5
Paleokastritsa Greece 39°40N 19°41E **101** A3
Paleometokho Cyprus 35°7N 33°11E **101** D12
Paleopoli Greece 37°44N 24°50E **98** D6
Palermo Italy 38°7N 13°22E **94** D6
Palermo × (PMO) Italy 38°11N 13°5E **94** D6
Palermo U.S.A. 39°26N 121°33W **170** F5
Palestina Chile 23°50S 69°47W **190** A2
Palestine Asia 31°46N 35°2E **108** D11
Palestine U.S.A. 31°46N 95°38W **176** F7
Paletwa Burma 21°10N 92°50E **123** J18
Palghat = Palakkad
  India 10°46N 76°42E **127** J3

Palitana India 21°32N 71°49E **12**
Palizada Mexico 18°15N 92°5W **18**
Palk Bay Asia 9°30N 79°15E **12**
Palk Strait Asia 10°0N 79°45E **12**
Palkānah Iraq 35°49N 44°26E **12**
Palkonda India 18°36N 83°48E **12**
Palkonda Ra. India 13°50N 79°20E **12**
Palkot India 22°53N 84°39E **12**
Pallanza = Verbánia
  Italy 45°56N 8°33E **9**
Pallarenda Australia 19°12S 146°46E **15**
Pallas-Yllästunturi △
  Finland 68°8N 24°15E **60**
Pallasovka Russia 50°4N 47°0E **8**
Palleru → India 16°45N 80°2E **12**
Pallès, Bishti i Albania 41°24N 19°24E **9**
Pallinup → Australia 34°27S 118°50E **15**
Palliser, C. N.Z. 41°37S 175°14E **15**
Palliser B. N.Z. 41°26S 175°5E **15**
Pallu India 28°59N 74°14E **12**
Palm Bay U.S.A. 28°2N 80°35W **17**
Palm Beach U.S.A. 26°43N 80°2W **17**
Palm Coast U.S.A. 29°35N 81°12W **17**
Palm Desert U.S.A. 33°43N 116°22W **17**
Palm-Grove △
  Australia 24°5S 149°21E **15**
Palm Harbor U.S.A. 28°5N 82°46W **17**
Palm Is. Australia 18°40S 146°35E **15**
Palm Springs U.S.A. 33°50N 116°33W **17**
Palm Valley U.S.A. 30°11N 81°23W **17**
Palma Mozam. 10°46S 40°29E **14**
Palma → Brazil 12°33S 47°52W **18**
Palma, B. de Spain 39°30N 2°39E **9**
Palma de Mallorca
  Spain 39°35N 2°39E **9**
Palma de Mallorca × (PMI)
  Spain 39°33N 2°43E **9**
Palma del Río Spain 37°43N 5°17W **8**
Palma di Montechiaro
  Italy 37°11N 13°46E **9**
Palma Nova = Palmanova
  Spain 39°32N 2°34E **9**
Palma Soriano Cuba 20°15N 76°0W **18**
Palmaner India 13°12N 78°45E **12**
Palmanova Italy 39°32N 2°34E **9**
Palmares Brazil 8°41S 35°28W **18**
Palmarola Italy 40°56N 12°51E **9**
Palmas Paraná, Brazil 26°29S 52°0W **19**
Palmas Tocantins, Brazil 10°13S 48°16W **18**
Palmas, C. Liberia 4°27N 7°46W **13**
Palmas, G. di Italy 39°0N 8°30E **9**
Palmas de Monte Alto
  Brazil 14°16S 43°10W **18**
Palmdale Calif., U.S.A. 34°35N 118°7W **17**
Palmdale Fla., U.S.A. 26°57N 81°19W **17**
Palmeira das Missões
  Brazil 27°55S 53°17W **19**
Palmeira dos Índios
  Brazil 9°25S 36°37W **18**
Palmeirais Brazil 6°0S 43°0W **18**
Palmeiras → Brazil 12°31S 41°0W **18**
Palmeiras → Brazil 12°22S 47°8W **18**
Palmela Portugal 38°32N 8°57W **8**
Palmer Antarctica 64°35S 65°0W **5**
Palmer U.S.A. 61°36N 149°7W **16**
Palmer → Australia 16°0S 142°26E **15**
Palmer Arch. Antarctica 64°15S 65°0W **5**
Palmer Lake U.S.A. 39°7N 104°55W **16**
Palmer Land Antarctica 73°0S 63°0W **5**
Palmerston Australia 12°31S 130°59E **14**
Palmerston Canada 43°50N 80°51W **17**
Palmerston N.Z. 45°29S 170°43E **15**
Palmerston North
  N.Z. 40°21S 175°39E **15**
Palmerton U.S.A. 40°48N 75°37W **17**
Palmetto Fla., U.S.A. 27°31N 82°34W **17**
Palmetto Ga., U.S.A. 33°31N 84°40W **17**
Palmi Italy 38°21N 15°51E **9**
Palmira Argentina 32°59S 68°34W **19**
Palmira Colombia 3°32N 76°16W **18**
Palmyra = Tudmur
  Syria 34°36N 38°15E **10**
Palmyra Mo., U.S.A. 39°48N 91°32W **17**
Palmyra N.J., U.S.A. 40°0N 75°1W **17**
Palmyra N.Y., U.S.A. 43°5N 77°18W **17**
Palmyra Is. Pac. Oc. 5°52N 162°5W **15**
Palmyras Pt. India 20°46N 87°1E **12**
Palo Alto U.S.A. 37°27N 122°10W **17**
Palo Seco Trin. & Tob. 10°4N 61°36W **18**
Palo Verde U.S.A. 33°26N 114°44W **17**
Palo Verde △
  Costa Rica 10°21N 85°21W **18**
Palomar Mt. U.S.A. 33°22N 116°50W **17**
Palopo Indonesia 3°0S 120°16E **11**
Palos, C. de Spain 37°38N 0°40W **9**
Palos de la Frontera
  Spain 37°14N 6°53W **8**
Palos Verdes, Pt.
  U.S.A. 33°46N 118°25W **17**
Palos Verdes Estates
  U.S.A. 33°48N 118°23W **17**
Palpa Peru 14°30S 75°15W **18**
Pålsböda Sweden 59°3N 15°22E **6**
Palu Indonesia 1°0S 119°52E **11**
Palu Turkey 38°45N 40°0E **10**
Paluke Liberia 5°28N 9°3W **13**
Paluma Ra. Australia 19°9S 146°22E **15**
Paluzza Italy 46°32N 13°0E **9**
Palwal India 28°8N 77°19E **12**
Pama Burkina Faso 11°19N 0°44E **13**
Pama △ Burkina Faso 11°27N 0°40E **13**
Pamanukan Indonesia 6°16S 107°49E **11**
Pamban I. India 9°15N 79°20E **12**
Pamekasan Indonesia 7°10S 113°28E **11**
Pamenang Indonesia 8°24S 116°6E **11**
Pamiers France 43°7N 1°39E **7**
Pamir Tajikistan 37°40N 73°0E **10**
Pamlico → U.S.A. 35°20N 76°28W **17**
Pamlico Sd. U.S.A. 35°20N 76°0W **17**
Pampa U.S.A. 35°32N 100°58W **17**
Pampa de Agma
  Argentina 43°45S 69°40W **19**
Pampa Hermosa Peru 9°15S 74°50W **18**
Pampa de las Salinas
  Argentina 32°1S 66°58W **19**
Pampanua Indonesia 4°16S 120°8E **11**
Pampas Argentina 35°0S 63°0W **19**
Pampas Peru 12°20S 74°50W **18**
Pamphylia Turkey 37°0N 30°0E **10**

lona *Colombia* 7°23N 72°39W 186 B4
plona-Iruña *Spain* 42°48N 1°38W 90 C3
poenpoort *S. Africa* 31°3S 22°40E 144 D3
ukçu *Turkey* 39°3N 27°54E 99 B9
ukkale *Turkey* 37°55N 29°8E 99 D11
de Azúcar *Chile* 24°5S 68°10W 190 A2
de Azúcar *Chile*
Xian *China* 26°45N 104°38E 116 E5
a *U.S.A.* 37°47N 114°23W 169 H6
aca *U.S.A.* 30°2N 84°23N 178 F5
adura *Sri Lanka* 6°47N 79°53E 127 L4
agyurishte *Bulgaria* 42°30N 24°15E 97 D8
aitan *Indonesia* 6°36S 105°12E 119 G11
aji *India* 15°25N 73°50E 127 G1
ama *Panama* 9°0N 79°25N 182 E4
ama *Sri Lanka* 6°45N 81°48E 127 L5
amá ■ *Cent. Amer.* 8°48N 79°55W 182 E4
amá, G. de *Panama* 8°4N 79°20W 182 E4
ama, Isthmus of
nt. Amer. 9°0N 79°0W 182 E4
ama Basin *Pac. Oc.* 5°0N 83°30W 157 G19
ama Canal *Panama* 9°10N 79°37W 182 E4
ama City *U.S.A.* 30°10N 85°40W 178 E4
ama City Beach
S.A. 30°11N 85°48W 178 E4
mint Range
S.A. 36°20N 117°20W 171 J9
mint Springs
S.A. 36°20N 117°28W 171 J9
o *Peru* 9°55S 75°55W 188 B2
re *Thailand* 6°51N 101°30E 121 J3
rea *Italy* 38°38N 15°4E 95 D8
ro → *Italy* 44°55N 11°25E 93 D8
y *Phil.* 11°10N 122°30E 119 B6
y G. *Phil.* 11°0N 122°30E 119 B6
evo *Serbia* 44°25N 20°41E 80 F5
h'iao *Taiwan* 25°1N 121°27E 117 E13
u *Romania* 45°54N 27°8E 81 E12
orbo, Desfiladero
42°32N 3°5W 88 C7
ota *Romania* 46°20N 21°45E 80 D6
iu *Mozam.* 24°2S 34°45E 145 B5
lan *Malaysia* 1°32N 103°46E 121 d
lan *Phil.* 11°45N 122°10E 119 B6
lan, Selat *Singapore* 1°15N 103°44E 121 d
an Tampoi = Tampoi
laysia 1°30N 103°42E 121 d
egelang *Indonesia* 6°25S 106°5E 119 G12
hana *India* 21°42N 76°13E 124 J7
harkawada *India* 20°1N 78°32E 126 D4
harpur *India* 17°41N 75°20E 126 F2
hurna *India* 21°36N 78°35E 126 D4
o *Uruguay* 34°44S 56°10W 191 C4
o, L. = Hope, L.
o *Bolivia* 11°20S 67°40W 188 C4
okratoras
tralia 28°24S 139°18E 151 D2
okratoras *Greece* 39°45N 19°0E 101 A3
ora *Costa Rica* 9°43N 83°3W 182 E3
véggio-Pale di San
artino △ *Italy* 46°14N 11°46E 93 B8
vėžys *Lithuania* 55°42N 24°25E 84 E3
lovo *Russia* 50°25N 42°46E 86 E6
Sida △ *Thailand* 14°5N 102°17E 120 E4

Panna △ *India* 24°40N 80°0E 125 G8
Panna Hills *India* 24°40N 81°15E 125 G9
Pannawonica
Australia 21°39S 116°19E 148 D2
Pano Akil *Pakistan* 27°51N 69°7E 124 F3
Pano Lefkara *Cyprus* 34°53N 33°20E 101 E12
Pano Panayia *Cyprus* 34°55N 32°38E 101 E11
Panorama *Brazil* 21°21S 51°51W 191 A5
Panormos *Greece* 35°25N 24°41E 101 D6
Panruti *India* 11°46N 79°35E 127 J4
Pansemal *India* 21°39N 74°42E 124 J6
Panshan = Panjin
China 41°3N 122°2E 115 D12
Panshi *China* 42°58N 126°5E 115 C14
Pantanal *Brazil* 17°30S 57°40W 186 H7
Pantanos de Centla △
Mexico 18°25N 92°25W 181 D6
Pantar *Indonesia* 8°28S 124°10E 119 F6
Pante Macassar
E. Timor 9°30S 123°58E 119 F6
Pantelleria *Italy* 36°50N 11°57E 94 F4
Pánton = O Castro de Ferreira
Spain 42°31N 7°37W 88 C3
Pánuco *Mexico* 22°3N 98°10W 181 C5
Panvel *India* 18°59N 73°4E 126 E1
Panyam *Nigeria* 9°27N 9°8E 139 D6
Panyu *China* 23°1N 113°21E 117 F9
Panzhihua *China* 26°33N 101°44E 116 E1
Páola *Italy* 39°21N 16°2E 95 C9
Paola *Malta* 35°52N 14°30E 101 d
Paola *U.S.A.* 38°35N 94°53W 172 F6
Paonia *U.S.A.* 38°52N 107°36W 168 G10
Paoting = Baoding
China 38°50N 115°28E 114 E8
Paot'ou = Baotou
China 40°32N 110°2E 114 D6
Paoua *C.A.R.* 7°9N 16°20E 142 C4
Pápa *Hungary* 47°22N 17°30E 80 C2
Papa Stour *U.K.* 60°20N 1°42W 65 A7
Papa Westray *U.K.* 59°20N 2°55W 65 B6
Papagayo *Mexico* 16°46N 99°43W 181 D5
Papagayo, G. de
Costa Rica 10°30N 85°50W 182 D2
Papagni → *India* 15°35N 77°45E 126 E1
Papakura *N.Z.* 37°4S 174°59E 154 C5
Papantla *Mexico* 20°27N 97°19N 181 C5
Papar *Malaysia* 5°45N 116°0E 118 C5
Papara *Tahiti* 17°43S 149°31W 155 b
Paparoa *N.Z.* 36°6S 174°16E 154 C5
Paparoa Ra. *N.Z.* 42°7S 171°26E 155 C6
Papatoetoe *N.Z.* 36°59S 174°51E 154 C5
Papeete *Tahiti* 17°32S 149°34W 155 b
Papenburg *Germany* 53°5N 7°23E 76 B3
Papenoo *Tahiti* 17°30S 149°25W 155 b
Papenoo → *Tahiti* 17°30S 149°25W 155 b
Paphlagonia *Turkey* 41°30N 33°0E 104 B5
Paphos *Cyprus* 34°46N 32°25E 101 E11
Papikio Oros *Greece* 41°15N 25°13E 97 E9
Paposo *Chile* 25°0S 70°30W 190 B2
Papoutsa *Cyprus* 34°54N 33°4E 101 E12
Papua △ *Indonesia* 4°0S 137°0E 119 E9
Papua, G. of *Papua N. G.* 9°0S 144°50E 147 B7
Papua New Guinea ■
Oceania 8°0S 145°0E 147 B7
Papudo *Chile* 32°29S 71°27W 190 C1
Papuk *Croatia* 45°30N 17°30E 80 E2
Papun *Burma* 18°2N 97°30E 123 K20
Papunya *Australia* 23°15S 131°54E 148 D5
Pará = Belém *Brazil* 1°20S 48°30W 187 D9
Pará □ *Brazil* 3°20S 52°0W 187 D8
Paraburdoo *Australia* 23°14S 117°32E 148 D2
Paracas, Pen. de *Peru* 13°53S 76°20W 188 C2
Paracatu *Brazil* 17°10S 46°50W 189 D1
Paracatu → *Brazil* 16°30S 45°4W 189 D1
Paracel Is. *S. China Sea* 15°50N 112°0E 118 A4
Parachilna *Australia* 31°10S 138°21E 152 A3
Parachinar *Pakistan* 33°55N 70°5E 124 C4
Paraćin *Serbia* 43°54N 21°27E 96 C5
Paracuru *Brazil* 3°24S 39°4W 189 D3
Parada, Punta *Peru* 15°22S 75°11W 188 D2
Paradas *Spain* 37°18N 5°29W 89 H5
Paradela *Spain* 42°44N 7°37W 88 C3
Paradip *India* 20°15N 86°35E 126 E2
Paradise *Calif., U.S.A.* 39°46N 121°37W 170 F5
Paradise → *Canada* 53°27N 57°19W 165 B8
Paradise Hill *Canada* 53°32N 109°28W 163 C7
Paradise River *Canada* 53°27N 57°17W 165 B8
Paradise Valley
U.S.A. 41°30N 117°32W 168 F5
Paradisi *Greece* 36°18N 28°7E 101 C10
Paragould *U.S.A.* 36°3N 90°29W 177 C9
Paragua → *Venezuela* 6°55N 62°55W 186 B6
Paraguaçu → *Brazil* 12°45S 38°54W 189 C3
Paraguaçu Paulista
Brazil 22°22S 50°35W 191 A5
Paraguaná, Pen. de
Venezuela 12°0N 70°0W 186 A5
Paraguarí *Paraguay* 25°36S 57°0W 190 B4
Paraguarí □ *Paraguay* 26°0S 57°10W 190 B4
Paraguay ■ *S. Amer.* 23°0S 57°0W 190 A4
Paraguay → *Paraguay* 27°18S 58°38W 190 B4
Paraiba = João Pessoa
Brazil 7°10S 34°52W 189 B4
Paraíba □ *Brazil* 7°0S 36°0W 189 B3
Paraíba do Sul →
Brazil 21°37S 41°3W 191 A7
Paraíso *Mexico* 18°24N 93°14W 181 D6
Parak *Iran* 26°55N 53°25E 129 E7
Parakhino Paddubye
Russia 58°26N 33°10E 84 C7
Parakou *Benin* 9°25N 2°40E 139 D5
Parakylia *Australia* 30°24S 136°25E 152 A2
Paralimni *Cyprus* 35°2N 33°58E 101 D12
Paralio Astros *Greece* 37°25N 22°45E 98 D4
Páramo del Batallón y La
Negra △ *Venezuela* 8°2N 71°55W 183 D5
Paramushir, Ostrov
Russia 50°24N 156°0E 107 D16
Paran → *Israel* 30°20N 35°10E 130 E4
Paraná *Argentina* 31°45S 60°30W 190 C3
Paraná *Brazil* 12°30S 47°48W 187 F9
Paraná □ *Brazil* 24°30S 51°0W 191 A5
Paraná → *Argentina* 33°43S 59°15W 190 C4

Paraná → *Brazil* 12°30S 48°14W 189 C1
Paranaguá *Brazil* 25°30S 48°30W 191 B6
Paranaíba *Brazil* 19°40S 51°11W 187 G8
Paranaíba → *Brazil* 20°6S 51°4W 187 H8
Paranal, Cerro *Chile* 24°38S 70°24W 190 A1
Paranapanema →
Brazil 22°40S 53°9W 191 A5
Paranapiacaba, Serra do
Brazil 24°31S 48°35W 191 A6
Paranavaí *Brazil* 23°4S 52°56W 191 A5
Parang *Maguindanao,*
Phil. 7°23N 124°16E 119 C6
Parang *Sulu, Phil.* 5°55N 120°54E 119 C6
Parangippettai *India* 11°30N 79°38E 127 J4
Parângul Mare, Vf.
Romania 45°20N 23°37E 81 E8
Paranthan *Sri Lanka* 9°26N 80°24E 127 K5
Paraparaumu *N.Z.* 40°57S 175°3E 154 b
Paraspori, Akra *Greece* 35°55N 27°15E 99 F9
Paratinga *Brazil* 12°40S 43°10W 189 C2
Paratoo *Australia* 32°42S 139°20E 152 B2
Parauapebas *Brazil* 6°4S 49°54W 187 E9
Paray-le-Monial *France* 46°27N 4°7E 71 F11
Parbati →
India 25°50N 76°30E 124 G7
Parbati → *Raj., India* 26°54N 77°53E 124 F7
Parbhani *India* 19°8N 76°52E 126 E3
Parchim *Germany* 53°26N 11°52E 76 B7
Parczew *Poland* 51°40N 22°52E 83 G9
Pardes Hanna-Karkur
Israel 32°28N 34°57E 130 C3
Pardilla *Spain* 41°33N 3°43W 88 D7
Pardo → *Bahia, Brazil* 15°40S 39°0W 189 D3
Pardo → *Mato Grosso,*
Brazil 21°46S 52°9W 191 A5
Pardo → *Minas Gerais,*
Brazil 15°48S 44°48W 189 D2
Pardoo Roadhouse
Australia 20°6S 119°3E 148 D2
Pardubice *Czech Rep.* 50°3N 15°45E 78 A8
Pardubický □ *Czech Rep.* 50°0N 16°0E 78 B8
Pare *Indonesia* 7°43S 112°12E 119 G15
Pare Mts. *Tanzania* 4°0S 37°45E 142 C4
Parecis, Serra dos *Brazil* 13°0S 60°0W 186 F7
Paredes de Nava *Spain* 42°9N 4°42W 88 C6
Parelhas *Brazil* 6°41S 36°39W 189 B3
Paren *Russia* 62°30N 163°15E 107 C17
Parenda *India* 18°16N 75°28E 126 E2
Parengarenga Harbour
N.Z. 34°31S 173°0E 154 A2
Parent *Canada* 47°55N 74°35W 164 C5
Parent, L. *Canada* 48°31N 77°1W 164 C4
Parentis-en-Born *France* 44°21N 1°4W 72 D2
Parepare *Indonesia* 4°0S 119°40E 119 E5
Parfino *Russia* 57°59N 31°34E 84 D6
Parga *Greece* 39°15N 20°29E 98 B2
Pargas = Länsi-Turunmaa
Finland 60°18N 22°18E 84 B2
Pargi *India* 17°10N 77°53E 126 E3
Pargo, Pta. do *Madeira* 32°49N 17°17W 100 D2
Parham *Canada* 44°39N 76°43W 175 B8
Paria → *U.S.A.* 36°52N 111°36W 169 H8
Paria, G. de *Venezuela* 10°30N 61°40W 187 K14
Pariaguán *Venezuela* 8°51N 64°34W 186 B6
Paricutín, Cerro
Mexico 19°28N 102°15W 180 D4
Parigi *Indonesia* 0°50S 120°5E 119 E6
Parika *Guyana* 6°50N 58°20W 186 B7
Parikkala *Finland* 61°33N 29°31E 84 B5
Parima, Serra *Brazil* 2°30N 64°0W 186 C6
Parinari *Peru* 4°35S 74°25W 188 A3
Pariñas, Pta. *Peru* 4°30S 82°0W 188 A1
Parincea *Romania* 46°27N 27°9E 81 D12
Paringa *Australia* 34°10S 140°46E 152 B3
Parintins *Brazil* 2°40S 56°50W 187 D7
Pariparit Kyun *Burma* 14°52N 93°41E 127 G11
Paris *France* 48°53N 2°20E 71 D9
Paris *Idaho, U.S.A.* 42°14N 111°24W 168 E8
Paris *Ky., U.S.A.* 38°13N 84°15W 173 F11
Paris *Tenn., U.S.A.* 36°18N 88°19W 177 C10
Paris *Tex., U.S.A.* 33°40N 95°33W 176 E7
Paris, Ville de □ *France* 48°50N 2°20E 71 D9
Paris Charles de Gaulle ✈ (CDG)
France 49°0N 2°32E 71 D9
Paris Orly ✈ (ORY)
France 48°44N 2°23E 71 D9
Parish *U.S.A.* 43°25N 76°8W 175 C8
Parishville *U.S.A.* 44°38N 74°49W 175 B10
Pariti *Indonesia* 10°1S 123°45E 148 B3
Park → *U.S.A.* 48°45N 122°18W 170 B4
Park City *U.S.A.* 37°48N 97°20W 172 G5
Park Falls *U.S.A.* 45°56N 90°27W 172 C8
Park Head *Canada* 44°36N 81°9W 174 B3
Park Hills *U.S.A.* 37°51N 90°51W 172 G8
Park Range *U.S.A.* 40°14N 106°41W 168 F10
Park Rapids *U.S.A.* 46°55N 95°4W 172 B6
Park River *U.S.A.* 48°24N 97°45W 172 A5
Park Rynie *S. Africa* 30°25S 30°45E 145 E5
Parkā Bandar *Iran* 25°55N 59°35E 129 E8
Parkano *Finland* 62°1N 23°0E 84 A2
Parker *Ariz., U.S.A.* 34°9N 114°17W 171 L12
Parker *Pa., U.S.A.* 41°5N 79°41W 174 E5
Parker Dam *U.S.A.* 34°18N 114°8W 171 L12
Parkersburg *U.S.A.* 39°16N 81°34W 173 F13
Parkes *Australia* 33°9S 148°11E 153 B8
Parkfield *U.S.A.* 35°54N 120°26W 170 K6
Parkhill *Canada* 43°15N 81°38W 174 C3
Parkland *U.S.A.* 47°9N 122°26W 170 C4
Parkston *U.S.A.* 43°24N 97°59W 172 D5
Parksville *Canada* 49°20N 124°21W 162 D4
Parla *Spain* 40°14N 3°46W 88 E7
Parlakimidi *India* 18°45N 84°5E 126 E7
Parli *India* 18°50N 76°32E 126 E3
Pârlița *Moldova* 47°19N 27°52E 81 C12
Parma *Italy* 44°48N 10°20E 92 D7
Parma *Idaho, U.S.A.* 43°47N 116°57W 168 E5
Parma *Ohio, U.S.A.* 41°24N 81°43W 174 E3
Parma → *Italy* 44°56N 10°26E 92 D7
Parnaguá *Brazil* 10°10S 44°38W 189 C2
Parnaíba *Brazil* 2°54S 41°47W 189 A2
Parnaíba → *Brazil* 3°0S 41°50W 189 A2
Parnamirim *Pernambuco,*
Brazil 8°5S 39°34W 189 B3
Parnamirim *Rio Grande do N.,*
Brazil 5°55S 35°15W 189 B3
Parnarama *Brazil* 5°31S 43°6W 189 B2
Parnassós *Greece* 38°35N 22°30E 98 C4
Parnassus *N.Z.* 42°42S 173°23E 155 C8

Parndana *Australia* 35°48S 137°12E 152 C2
Parner *India* 19°0N 74°26E 126 E2
Parnitha *Greece* 38°14N 23°45E 98 C5
Parnitha △ *Greece* 38°12N 23°44E 98 C5
Parnonas Oros *Greece* 37°15N 22°45E 98 D4
Pärnu *Estonia* 58°28N 24°33E 84 C3
Pärnu → *Estonia* 58°28N 24°33E 84 C3
Paro Dzong *Bhutan* 27°32N 89°53E 125 F13
Parola *India* 20°47N 75°7E 126 D2
Paroo → *Australia* 31°28S 143°32E 152 A5
Paros *Greece* 37°5N 25°12E 99 D7
Parowan *U.S.A.* 37°51N 112°50W 169 H7
Parpaillon *France* 44°30N 6°40E 73 D10
Parral *Chile* 36°10S 71°52W 190 D1
Parramatta *Australia* 33°48S 151°1E 153 B9
Parras *Mexico* 25°25N 102°11W 180 B4
Parrett → *U.K.* 51°12N 3°1W 67 F4
Parris I. *U.S.A.* 32°20N 80°41W 178 C9
Parrsboro *Canada* 45°30N 64°25W 165 D7
Parry Channel *Canada* 74°15N 94°0W 161 C13
Parry I. *Canada* 45°18N 80°10W 174 A4
Parry Is. *Canada* 77°0N 110°0W 161 B10
Parry Sound *Canada* 45°20N 80°0W 174 A5
Parsābād *Iran* 39°39N 47°50E 105 C12
Parsberg *Germany* 49°10N 11°43E 77 D7
Parsęta → *Poland* 54°11N 15°34E 82 D2
Parsnip → *Canada* 55°10N 123°2W 162 B4
Parsons *U.S.A.* 37°20N 95°16W 172 G6
Parsons Ra. *Australia* 13°30S 135°15E 150 A2
Partabpur *India* 20°0N 80°42E 126 E5
Partanna *Italy* 37°43N 12°53E 94 E5
Partenio → *Italy* 40°56N 14°38E 95 B7
Parthenay *France* 46°38N 0°16W 70 F6
Partinico *Italy* 38°3N 13°7E 94 D6
Partizansk *Russia* 43°8N 133°9E 107 E14
Partizánske *Slovak Rep.* 48°38N 18°23E 79 C11
Partridge I. *Canada* 55°59N 87°37W 164 A2
Parry Mts. *Ireland* 53°40N 9°28W 64 C2
Partur *India* 19°40N 76°14E 126 E3
Paru → *Brazil* 1°33S 52°38W 187 D8
Paru = North Paravar
India 10°13N 76°14E 127 J3
Paruro *Peru* 13°45S 71°50W 188 C3
Parvān □ *Afghan.* 35°0N 69°0E 109 F7
Parvatipuram *India* 18°50N 83°25E 126 E6
Parvatsar *India* 26°52N 74°49E 124 F6
Påryd *Sweden* 56°34N 15°55E 63 H9
Parys *S. Africa* 26°52S 27°29E 144 C4
Pas, Pta. des *Spain* 38°46N 1°26E 100 C7
Pas, The *Canada* 53°45N 101°15W 163 C8
Pas-de-Calais □ *France* 50°30N 2°10E 71 B9
Pasada *Spain* 43°23N 5°40W 88 B5
Pasadena *Canada* 49°1N 57°36W 165 C8
Pasadena *Calif., U.S.A.* 34°9N 118°8W 171 L8
Pasadena *Tex., U.S.A.* 29°43N 95°13W 176 D7
Pasaje → *Argentina* 25°35S 63°56W 190 B3
Pasalimani *Turkey* 40°29N 27°36E 99 B10
Pasar *Indonesia* 8°27S 114°54E 119 J17
Pasargad *Iran* 30°11N 53°10E 129 D7
Pascagoula *U.S.A.* 30°21N 88°33W 177 F10
Pascagoula → *U.S.A.* 30°23N 88°37W 177 F10
Paşcani *Romania* 47°14N 26°45E 81 C11
Paschimbanga □ *India* 23°0N 88°0E 125 H13
Pasco □ *Peru* 10°40S 75°0W 188 C3
Pasco *U.S.A.* 46°14N 119°6W 168 C4
Pasco, I. *Chile* 27°7S 109°23W 157 K17
Pascoag *U.S.A.* 41°57N 71°42W 175 E13
Pascua, I. de *Chile* 27°7S 109°23W 157 K17
Pasewalk *Germany* 53°30N 13°58E 76 B9
Pasfield L. *Canada* 58°24N 105°20W 163 B7
Pasha → *Russia* 60°29N 32°55E 84 B7
Pashin *Turkey* 39°59N 41°41E 105 C9
Pasir Mas *Malaysia* 6°2N 102°8E 121 J4
Pasir Panjang *Singapore* 1°18N 103°46E 121 d
Pasir Putih *Malaysia* 5°50N 102°24E 121 J4
Pasirian *Indonesia* 8°13S 113°8E 119 H15
Paskallavik *Sweden* 57°10N 16°26E 63 G10
Paskūh *Iran* 27°34N 61°39E 129 E9
Pasłęk *Poland* 54°3N 19°41E 82 D6
Pasłęka → *Poland* 54°26N 19°46E 82 D6
Pasley, C. *Australia* 33°52S 123°35E 149 F3
Pašman *Croatia* 43°58N 15°20E 93 E12
Pasmore → *Australia* 31°5S 139°49E 152 A3
Pasni *Pakistan* 25°15N 63°27E 124 G3
Paso Bravo △ *Paraguay* 22°32S 57°5W 190 A4
Paso Cantinela
Mexico 32°33N 115°47W 171 N11
Paso de Indios *Argentina* 43°55S 69°0W 192 E3
Paso de los Indios
Argentina 38°32S 69°2W 192 A3
Paso de los Libres
Argentina 29°44S 57°10W 190 B4
Paso de los Toros
Uruguay 32°45S 56°30W 190 C4
Paso Flores *Argentina* 40°35S 70°38W 192 B2
Paso Robles *U.S.A.* 35°38N 120°41W 170 K6
Paspébiac *Canada* 48°3N 65°17W 165 C6
Pasrur *Pakistan* 32°16N 74°43E 126 C6
Passage East *Ireland* 52°14N 7°0W 64 D5
Passage West *Ireland* 51°52N 8°21W 64 E3
Passaic *U.S.A.* 40°51N 74°7W 175 F10
Passau *Germany* 48°34N 13°28E 77 G9
Passero, C. *Italy* 36°41N 15°10E 95 F8
Passo Fundo *Brazil* 28°10S 52°20W 191 B5
Passos *Brazil* 20°45S 46°37W 191 A6
Passow *Germany* 53°8N 14°6E 76 B9
Passy *France* 45°55N 6°41E 73 C10
Pastavy *Belarus* 55°4N 26°50E 84 E5
Pastaza → *Peru* 4°50S 76°52W 188 D3
Pasto *Colombia* 1°13N 77°17W 186 C3
Pastos Bons *Brazil* 6°36S 44°5W 189 B2
Pasuruan *Indonesia* 7°40S 112°44E 119 G15
Pasym *Poland* 53°48N 20°49E 82 E7
Pásztó *Hungary* 47°52N 19°43E 80 C4

Patagonia *U.S.A.* 31°33N 110°45W 171 L8
Patagonia *Argentina* 45°0S 69°0W 192 E3
Patambar *Iran* 29°45N 60°17E 129 D9
Patan = Lalitpur *Nepal* 27°40N 85°20E 125 F14
Patan = Somnath *India* 20°53N 70°22E 124 J4
Patan *Gujarat, India* 23°54N 72°14E 124 H5
Patan *Maharashtra,*
India 17°22N 73°57E 126 F1
Patani *Indonesia* 0°20N 128°50E 119 D7
Pătârlagele *Romania* 45°19N 26°21E 81 E11
Pataudi *India* 28°18N 76°48E 124 E7
Patchewollock
Australia 35°22S 142°12E 152 C5
Patchogue *U.S.A.* 40°46N 73°1W 175 F11
Pate *Kenya* 2°10S 41°0E 142 C5
Patea *N.Z.* 39°45S 174°30E 154 D5
Pategi *Nigeria* 8°50N 5°45E 139 D6
Patensie *S. Africa* 33°46S 24°49E 144 D3
Paterna *Spain* 39°30N 0°26W 91 F1
Paternion *Austria* 46°43N 13°38E 78 E6
Paternò *Italy* 37°34N 14°54E 95 E7
Pateros *U.S.A.* 48°3N 119°54W 168 B4
Paterson *U.S.A.* 40°54N 74°9W 175 F10
Paterson Inlet *N.Z.* 46°56S 168°5E 155 M1
Paterson Ra. *Australia* 21°45S 122°10E 148 D3
Pathankot *India* 32°18N 75°45E 124 C6
Pathardi *India* 19°10N 75°11E 126 E2
Pathein *Burma* 16°45N 94°30E 123 L19
Pathfinder Res.
U.S.A. 42°28N 106°51W 168 E10
Pathiu *Thailand* 10°42N 99°19E 121 H2
Pathri *India* 19°15N 76°27E 126 E3
Pathum Thani *Thailand* 14°1N 100°32E 120 E3
Pati *Indonesia* 6°45S 111°1E 119 G14
Patía → *Colombia* 2°13N 78°40W 186 C3
Patiala *Punjab, India* 30°23N 76°26E 124 D7
Patiala *Ut. P., India* 27°43N 79°1E 125 F8
Patine Kouka *Senegal* 12°45N 13°45W 138 C2
Patitiri *Greece* 39°8N 23°50E 98 B5
Patkai Bum *India* 27°0N 95°30E 123 F19
Patmos *Greece* 37°21N 26°36E 99 D8
Patna *India* 25°35N 85°12E 125 G11
Patnagarh *India* 20°43N 83°9E 126 D6
Patnos *Turkey* 39°13N 42°51E 105 C10
Pato Branco *Brazil* 26°13S 52°40W 191 B5
Patong, Ao *Thailand* 7°54N 98°17E 121 a
Patonga *Uganda* 2°45N 33°15E 142 B3
Patos *Albania* 40°42N 19°38E 96 F3
Patos *Brazil* 6°55S 37°16W 189 B3
Patos, L. dos *Brazil* 31°20S 51°0W 191 C5
Patos, Río de los →
Argentina 31°18S 69°25W 190 C2
Patos de Minas *Brazil* 18°35S 46°32W 189 D1
Patquía *Argentina* 30°2S 66°55W 190 C2
Patra *Greece* 38°14N 21°47E 98 C3
Patraikos Kolpos *Greece* 38°17N 21°30E 98 C3
Patras = Patra *Greece* 38°14N 21°47E 98 C3
Patricio Lynch, I. *Chile* 48°35S 75°30W 192 F1
Patriot Hills *Antarctica* 82°20S 81°25W 55 E16
Patrocínio *Brazil* 18°57S 47°0W 189 D1
Pattada *Italy* 40°35N 9°6E 94 B2
Pattadakal *India* 16°1N 75°42E 127 C7
Pattani *Thailand* 6°48N 101°15E 121 J3
Pattaya *Thailand* 12°52N 100°55E 120 E3
Patten *U.S.A.* 46°0N 68°38W 173 B19
Patterson *Calif., U.S.A.* 37°28N 121°8W 170 H5
Patterson *Ga., U.S.A.* 31°23N 82°8W 178 D7
Patterson *La., U.S.A.* 29°42N 91°18W 176 G9
Patterson, Mt. *U.S.A.* 38°29N 119°20W 170 G7
Patti *Punjab, India* 31°17N 74°54E 124 D6
Patti *Ut. P., India* 25°55N 82°12E 125 G10
Patti *Italy* 38°8N 14°58E 95 D7
Pattoki *Pakistan* 31°5N 73°52E 124 D5
Patton *U.S.A.* 40°38N 78°39W 174 F6
Pattukkattai *India* 10°25N 79°30E 127 J4
Patu *Brazil* 6°6S 37°38W 189 B3
Patuakhali *Bangla.* 22°20N 90°25E 125 H17
Patuanak *Canada* 55°55N 107°43W 163 B7
Patuca → *Honduras* 15°50N 84°18W 182 C3
Patuca, Punta
Honduras 15°49N 84°14W 182 C3
Patuca △ *Honduras* 14°30N 85°30W 182 D2
Pătulele *Romania* 44°21N 22°47E 80 F7
Patur *India* 20°27N 76°56E 126 D3
Patvinsuo △ *Finland* 63°7N 30°45E 60 E24
Pátzcuaro *Mexico* 19°31N 101°38W 180 D4
Pau *France* 43°19N 0°25W 72 E3
Pau, Gave de → *France* 43°33N 1°12W 72 E2
Pau dos Ferros *Brazil* 6°7S 38°10W 189 B3
Pauanui *N.Z.* 37°1S 175°52E 154 C4
Paucartambo *Peru* 13°19S 71°35W 188 C3
Paudash *Canada* 44°59N 77°58W 174 B7
Pauillac *France* 45°11N 0°46W 72 C3
Pauini *Brazil* 7°40S 66°58W 186 E5
Pauk *Burma* 21°27N 94°30E 123 J19
Paul I. *Canada* 56°30N 61°20W 165 A7
Paul Smiths *U.S.A.* 44°26N 74°15W 175 B10
Paulatuk *Canada* 69°25N 124°0W 160 D7
Paulding Bay *S. Ocean* 66°0S 118°0E 55 C8
Paulhan *France* 43°33N 3°28E 72 E7
Paulista *Brazil* 7°57S 34°53W 189 B4
Paulistana *Brazil* 8°9S 41°9W 189 B2
Paulín → *Sweden* 57°28N 15°31E 63 H9
Paulo Afonso *Brazil* 9°21S 38°15W 189 B3
Paulpietersburg
S. Africa 27°23S 30°50E 145 C5
Pauls Valley *U.S.A.* 34°44N 97°13W 176 D6
Pauma Valley
U.S.A. 33°16N 116°58W 171 M10
Pauni *India* 20°48N 79°40E 126 D4
Pauri *India* 30°9N 78°47E 125 D8
Pausa *Peru* 15°16S 73°22W 188 D3
Pavagada *India* 14°6N 77°16E 127 G3
Pāveh *Iran* 35°3N 46°22E 105 C12
Pavelets *Russia* 53°49N 39°14E 84 F10
Pavia *Italy* 45°7N 9°8E 92 C6
Pavilion *France* 43°19N 0°25W 72 E3
Pavilly *France* 49°34N 0°57E 70 C7
Pāvilosta *Latvia* 56°53N 21°14E 82 B8
Pavlikeni *Bulgaria* 43°14N 25°20E 97 C8
Pavlodar *Kazakhstan* 52°33N 77°0E 109 B9
Pavlograd = Pavlohrad
Ukraine 48°30N 35°52E 85 H8
Pavlohrad *Ukraine* 48°30N 35°52E 85 H8
Pavlovo *Russia* 55°58N 43°5E 86 C6
Pavlovsk *Russia* 50°26N 40°5E 85 G11
Pavlovskaya *Russia* 46°17N 39°47E 87 G4
Pavlovskiy-Posad
Russia 55°47N 38°42E 84 E10
Pavo *U.S.A.* 30°58N 83°45W 178 D7
Pavullo nel Frignano
Italy 44°20N 10°50E 92 D7
Pawai, Pulau *Singapore* 1°11N 103°44E 121 d
Pawayan *India* 28°4N 80°6E 125 E8
Pawhuska *U.S.A.* 36°40N 96°20W 176 C6
Pawling *U.S.A.* 41°34N 73°36W 175 E11
Pawnee *U.S.A.* 36°20N 96°48W 176 C6
Pawnee City *U.S.A.* 40°7N 96°9W 172 E5
Pawtucket *U.S.A.* 41°53N 71°23W 175 E13
Paxi *Greece* 39°14N 20°12E 98 B2
Paximadia *Greece* 35°0N 24°35E 101 E6
Paxton *U.S.A.* 40°27N 88°6W 172 E9
Payakumbuh *Indonesia* 0°20S 100°35E 118 E2
Payerne *Switz.* 46°49N 6°56E 77 J2

Payette *U.S.A.* 44°5N 116°56W 168 D5
Paymogo *Spain* 37°44N 7°21W 89 H3
Payne Bay = Kangirsuk
Canada 60°0N 70°0W 161 F18
Payne L. *Canada* 59°30N 74°30W 161 F17
Paynes Find *Australia* 29°15S 117°42E 149 E2
Paynesville *Liberia* 6°20N 10°45E 138 D2
Paynesville *U.S.A.* 45°23N 94°43W 172 C6
Pays de la Loire □ *France* 47°45N 0°25W 70 E6
Paysandú *Uruguay* 32°19S 58°8W 190 C4
Payson *Ariz., U.S.A.* 34°14N 111°20W 169 J8
Payson *Utah, U.S.A.* 40°3N 111°44W 168 F8
Paz → *Guatemala* 13°44N 90°10W 182 D1
Paz, B. de la *Mexico* 24°9N 110°25W 180 C2
Pazanān *Iran* 30°35N 49°59E 129 D6
Pazarcık *Turkey* 37°29N 37°17E 104 D7
Pazardzhik *Bulgaria* 42°12N 24°20E 97 D8
Pazardžik = Pazardzhik
Bulgaria 42°12N 24°20E 97 D8
Pazarköy *Turkey* 39°35N 27°24E 99 B9
Pazaryeri *Turkey* 40°0N 29°7E 99 C11
Pazaryolu *Turkey* 40°21N 40°47E 105 B9
Pazin *Croatia* 45°14N 13°56E 93 C10
Pazna *Bolivia* 18°36S 66°55W 188 D4
Pčinja → *Macedonia* 41°50N 21°45E 96 E5
Pe Ell *U.S.A.* 46°34N 123°18W 170 D3
Pea → *U.S.A.* 31°1N 85°51W 178 D4
Peabody *U.S.A.* 42°31N 70°56W 175 D14
Peace → *Canada* 59°0N 111°25W 162 B6
Peace Point *Canada* 59°7N 112°27W 162 B6
Peace River *Canada* 56°15N 117°18W 162 B5
Peach Springs *U.S.A.* 35°32N 113°25W 169 J7
Peachland *Canada* 49°47N 119°45W 162 D5
Peachtree City *U.S.A.* 33°25N 84°35W 178 D5
Peak, The = Kinder Scout
U.K. 53°24N 1°52W 66 D6
Peak Charles △
Australia 32°42S 121°10E 149 F3
Peak District △ *U.K.* 53°24N 1°46W 66 D6
Peak Hill *Australia* 32°47S 148°11E 153 B8
Peak Ra. *Australia* 22°50S 148°20E 150 C4
Peake *Australia* 35°25S 139°55E 152 C2
Peake Cr. → *Australia* 28°2S 136°7E 151 D2
Peal de Becerro *Spain* 37°55N 3°7W 89 H7
Peale, Mt. *U.S.A.* 38°26N 109°14W 168 G9
Pearblossom *U.S.A.* 34°30N 117°55W 171 L9
Pearl → *U.S.A.* 30°11N 89°32W 177 F10
Pearl and Hermes Reef
U.S.A. 27°55N 175°45W 167 K4
Pearl Banks *Sri Lanka* 8°45N 79°45E 127 K4
Pearl River = Zhu Jiang →
China 22°45N 113°37E 117 F9
Pearl River *China* 41°4N 74°2W 175 E10
Pearl River Bridge
China 22°15N 113°48E 111 a
Pearsall *U.S.A.* 28°54N 99°6W 176 G5
Pearson *U.S.A.* 31°18N 82°51W 178 D7
Pearson Int. Toronto ✈ (YYZ)
Canada 43°46N 79°35W 174 C5
Peary Chan. *Canada* 79°40N 101°30W 161 B11
Peary Land *Greenland* 82°40N 33°0W 57 A7
Pease → *U.S.A.* 34°12N 99°2W 176 E4
Peawanuck *Canada* 55°15N 85°12W 164 A2
Pebane *Mozam.* 17°10S 38°8E 143 F4
Pebas *Peru* 3°10S 71°46W 186 D4
Pebble, I. *Falk. Is.* 51°20S 59°40W 192 D5
Pebble Beach *U.S.A.* 36°34N 121°57W 170 J5
Peć = Pejë *Kosovo* 42°40N 20°17E 96 D4
Peçanha *Brazil* 18°35S 42°34W 189 D2
Péccioli *Italy* 43°33N 10°43E 92 E7
Pechea *Romania* 45°36N 27°49E 81 E12
Pechenga *Russia* 69°29N 31°4E 60 B24
Pechenizhyn *Ukraine* 48°30N 24°48E 81 B9
Pechiguera, Pta.
Canary Is. 28°51N 13°53W 100 F6
Pechnezhskoye Vdkhr.
Ukraine 50°5N 36°54E 85 G9
Pechora *Russia* 65°10N 57°11E 106 C6
Pechora → *Russia* 68°13N 54°15E 58 B16
Pechorskaya Guba
Russia 68°40N 54°0E 106 C6
Pechory *Russia* 57°48N 27°40E 84 D5
Pecica *Romania* 46°10N 21°3E 80 D6
Pecka *Serbia* 44°18N 19°33E 96 B3
Pécora, C. *Italy* 39°27N 8°23E 94 C1
Pecos *N. Mex., U.S.A.* 35°35N 105°41W 169 J11
Pecos *Tex., U.S.A.* 31°26N 103°30W 176 F3
Pecos → *U.S.A.* 29°42N 101°22W 176 G4
Pécs *Hungary* 46°5N 18°15E 80 D3
Pedasi *Panama* 7°32N 80°2W 182 E3
Pedda Bellala *India* 19°4N 78°49E 126 E4
Peddapalli *India* 18°40N 79°22E 126 E4
Peddapuram *India* 17°6N 82°8E 126 F6
Peddie *S. Africa* 33°14S 27°7E 145 D4
Pedernales *Dom. Rep.* 18°2N 71°44W 183 C5
Pedieos → *Cyprus* 35°10N 33°54E 101 D12
Pedirka Desert
Australia 26°47S 134°11E 151 D2
Pedra Azul *Brazil* 16°2S 41°17W 189 D2
Pedra Grande, Recifes de
Brazil 17°45S 38°58W 189 D3
Pedra Lume *C. Verde Is.* 16°40N 22°52W 134 b
Pedregal *Spain* 40°38N 0°3E 91 D2
Pedreiras *Brazil* 4°32S 44°40W 189 A2
Pedro Afonso *Brazil* 9°0S 48°10W 189 B1
Pedro Cays *Jamaica* 17°5N 77°48W 182 C4
Pedro de Valdivia *Chile* 22°55S 69°38W 190 A2
Pedro Juan Caballero
Paraguay 22°30S 55°40W 191 A4
Pedro Muñoz *Spain* 39°25N 2°56W 89 F7
Pee Dee = Great Pee Dee →
U.S.A. 33°21N 79°10W 177 E15
Peebinga *Australia* 34°52S 140°57E 152 C4
Peebles *U.K.* 55°40N 3°11W 65 F5
Peekskill *U.S.A.* 41°17N 73°55W 175 E11
Peel *I. of Man* 54°13N 4°40W 66 C3
Peel → *Australia* 31°22S 150°45E 153 B9
Peel → *Canada* 67°0N 135°0W 160 D6
Peel Sd. *Canada* 73°0N 96°0W 160 C10
Peene → *Germany* 54°9N 13°46E 76 A9
Peera Peera Poolanna L.
Australia 26°30S 138°0E 151 D2
Peerless Lake *Canada* 56°37N 114°40W 162 B6
Peery L. *Australia* 30°45S 143°35E 152 A4
Pegasus Bay *N.Z.* 43°20S 173°10E 155 D9
Peggau *Austria* 47°12N 15°21E 78 E8
Pegnitz *Germany* 49°44N 11°31E 77 F7

Pegnitz → Germany 49°30N 10°59E 77 F6
Pego Spain 38°51N 0°8W 91 G4
Pegu = Bago Burma 17°20N 96°29E 123 L20
Pegu Yoma Burma 19°0N 96°0E 123 K20
Pehčevo Macedonia 41°41N 22°55E 96 E5
Pehlivanköy Turkey 41°20N 26°55E 97 E10
Pehuajó Argentina 35°45S 62°0W 190 D3
Pei Xian China 34°44N 116°55E 114 G9
Peikang Taiwan 23°34N 120°18E 117 F13
Peine Chile 23°45S 68°8W 190 A2
Peine Germany 52°19N 10°14E 76 C6
Peip'ing = Beijing China 39°53N 116°21E 114 E9
Peipus, L. = Chudskoye, Ozero Russia 58°13N 27°30E 84 C4
Peissenberg Germany 47°48N 11°4E 77 H7
Peitz Germany 51°51N 14°24E 76 D10
Peixe Brazil 12°0S 48°40W 189 C1
Peixe → Brazil 21°31S 51°58W 187 H8
Pejë Kosovo 42°40N 20°17E 96 C4
Pek → Serbia 44°45N 21°29E 96 B5
Pekalongan Indonesia 6°53S 109°40E 118 F3
Pekan Malaysia 3°30N 103°25E 121 L4
Pekan Nenas Malaysia 1°31N 103°31E 121 d
Pekanbaru Indonesia 0°30N 101°15E 118 D2
Pekin U.S.A. 40°35N 89°40W 172 E9
Peking = Beijing China 39°53N 116°21E 114 E9
Pekutatan Indonesia 8°25S 114°49E 119 J17
Pela Guinea 40°46N 22°23E 96 F6
Pelabuhan Ratu, Teluk Indonesia 7°5S 106°30E 119 G12
Pélagos = Kira Panagia Greece 39°17N 24°4E 98 B6
Pelaihari Indonesia 3°55S 114°45E 118 E4
Pelat, Mt. France 44°16N 6°42E 73 D10
Pelczyce Poland 53°3N 15°16E 83 E2
Peleaga, Vf. Romania 45°22N 22°55E 80 E7
Pelechuco Bolivia 14°48S 69°4W 188 C4
Pelée, Mt. Martinique 14°48N 61°10W 182 c
Pelee, Pt. Canada 41°54N 82°31W 164 D3
Pelee I. Canada 41°47N 82°40W 174 C2
Pelejo Peru 6°10S 75°49W 188 B2
Pelekech Kenya 3°52N 35°8E 142 B4
Peleng Indonesia 1°20S 123°30E 119 E6
Pélézi Ivory C. 7°17N 6°54W 138 D3
Pelham U.S.A. 31°8N 84°9W 178 D5
Pelhřimov Czech Rep. 49°24N 15°12E 78 B8
Pelican U.S.A. 57°58N 136°14W 162 B1
Pelican L. Canada 52°28N 100°20W 163 C8
Pelican Narrows Canada 55°10N 102°56W 163 B8
Pelion U.S.A. 33°46N 81°15W 178 B8
Pelister △ Macedonia 41°0N 21°10E 96 F5
Peljesac Croatia 42°55N 17°25E 93 F14
Pelkosenniemi Finland 67°6N 27°28E 60 C22
Pell City U.S.A. 33°35N 86°17W 178 B3
Pella Greece 40°52N 22°0E 96 F6
Pella S. Africa 29°1S 19°6E 144 C2
Pella U.S.A. 41°25N 92°55E 172 E7
Pello Finland 66°47N 23°59E 60 C20
Pellworm Germany 54°31N 8°39E 76 A4
Pelly → Canada 62°47N 137°19W 162 A1
Pelly Bay Canada 68°38N 89°50W 161 D14
Peloponnesos □ Greece 37°10N 22°0E 98 D4
Peloritani, Monti Italy 38°3N 15°20E 95 D8
Pelorus → N.Z. 41°16S 173°45E 155 B8
Pelorus Sd. N.Z. 40°55S 173°59E 155 A8
Pelotas Brazil 31°42S 52°23W 191 C5
Pelotas → Brazil 27°28S 51°55W 191 B5
Pelovo Bulgaria 43°26N 24°17E 97 C8
Pelplin Poland 53°55N 18°42E 82 E5
Pelvoux, Massif du France 44°52N 6°20E 73 D10
Pemalang Indonesia 6°53S 109°23E 119 G13
Pemanggil, Pulau Malaysia 2°37N 104°21E 121 L5
Pematangsiantar Indonesia 2°57N 99°5E 118 D1
Pemba Mozam. 12°58S 40°30E 143 E5
Pemba Zambia 16°30S 27°28E 143 F2
Pemba Channel Tanzania 5°0S 39°37E 142 D4
Pemba I. Tanzania 5°0S 39°45E 142 D4
Pemberton Australia 34°30S 116°0E 149 F2
Pemberton Canada 50°25N 122°50W 162 C4
Pembina → Canada 54°45N 114°17W 162 C6
Pembroke Canada 45°50N 77°7W 164 C4
Pembroke U.K. 51°41N 4°55W 67 F3
Pembroke U.S.A. 32°8N 81°37W 178 C8
Pembroke Pines U.S.A. 26°0N 80°13W 179 H14
Pembrokeshire □ U.K. 51°52N 4°56W 67 F3
Pembrokeshire Coast △ U.K. 51°50N 5°2W 67 F2
Pen India 18°45N 73°5E 126 L1
Pen-y-bont ar Ogwr = Bridgend U.K. 51°30N 3°34W 67 F4
Pen-y-Ghent U.K. 54°10N 2°14W 66 C5
Peña, Sierra de la Spain 42°32N 0°45W 90 C4
Peña de Francia, Sierra de la Spain 40°32N 6°10W 88 E4
Peñafiel Portugal 41°12N 8°17W 88 D2
Peñafiel Spain 41°35N 4°7W 88 D6
Peñaflor Spain 37°43N 5°21W 89 H5
Penal Trin. & Tob. 10°9N 61°29W 187 K15
Peñalara Spain 40°51N 3°57W 88 E7
Penalva Brazil 3°18S 45°10W 189 A1
Penamacôr Portugal 40°10N 7°10W 88 E3
Penang = Pinang Malaysia 5°25N 100°15E 121 c
Penápolis Brazil 21°30S 50°0W 191 A6
Peñaranda de Bracamonte Spain 40°53N 5°13W 88 E5
Peñarroya Spain 40°5N 0°40W 90 E4
Peñarroya-Pueblonuevo Spain 38°19N 5°16W 89 G5
Penarth U.K. 51°26N 3°11W 67 F4
Peñas, C. de Spain 43°42N 5°52W 88 B5
Peñas, G. de Chile 47°0S 75°0W 192 C2
Peñas de San Pedro Spain 38°44N 2°0W 91 G3
Peñas del Chache Canary Is. 29°6N 13°33W 100 E6
Peñausende Spain 41°17N 5°52W 88 D5
Pench → India 21°17N 79°10E 126 J8
Pench △ India 21°50N 79°20E 125 J8
Pench'i = Benxi China 41°20N 123°48E 115 D12
Pend Oreille → U.S.A. 49°4N 117°37W 168 B5
Pend Oreille, L. U.S.A. 48°10N 116°21E 168 B5
Pendalofos Greece 40°14N 21°12E 96 F5

Pendembu Eastern, S. Leone 8°10N 10°42W 138 D2
Pendembu Northern, S. Leone 9°7N 11°14W 138 D2
Pendências Brazil 5°15S 36°43W 189 B3
Pender B. Australia 16°45S 122°42E 148 C3
Pendik Turkey 40°53N 29°13E 97 F13
Pendjari → Benin 10°55N 0°50E 139 C5
Pendjari △ Benin 11°15N 1°32E 139 C5
Pendleton U.S.A. 45°40N 118°47W 168 D4
Pendra India 22°46N 81°57E 125 H9
Pendzhikent = Panjakent Tajikistan 39°27N 67°37E 109 E7
Peneda-Gerês △ Portugal 41°57N 8°15W 88 D2
Penedo Brazil 10°15S 36°36W 189 C3
Penelokan Indonesia 8°17S 115°22E 119 J18
Penetanguishene Canada 44°50N 79°55W 174 B5
Penfield U.S.A. 41°13N 78°35W 174 E6
Penfro = Pembroke U.K. 51°41N 4°55W 67 F3
Peng Chau China 22°17N 114°2E 111 a
Peng'an China 31°2N 106°22E 116 B6
Penganga → India 19°53N 79°9E 126 E4
Penge Kasai-Or., Dem. Rep. of the Congo 5°30S 24°33E 142 D1
Penge Sud-Kivu, Dem. Rep. of the Congo 4°27S 28°25E 142 C2
P'enghu Ch'üntou Taiwan 23°34N 119°30E 117 F12
Penglai China 37°48N 120°42E 115 F11
Pengshan China 30°14N 103°58E 116 B4
Pengshui China 29°17N 108°12E 116 C7
Pengxi China 30°54N 105°45E 116 B5
Pengze China 29°52N 116°32E 117 C11
Pengzhou China 31°4N 103°32E 116 B4
Penhalonga Zimbabwe 18°52S 32°40E 143 F3
Peniche Portugal 39°19N 9°22W 89 F1
Penicuik U.K. 55°50N 3°13W 66 F5
Penida, Nusa Indonesia 8°45S 115°30E 118 F5
Peninnes, Alpes = Pennine, Alpi Alps 46°4N 7°30E 77 J3
Peninsular Malaysia □ Malaysia 4°0N 102°0E 121 L4
Peñiscola Spain 40°22N 0°24E 90 E5
Penitente, Serra do Brazil 8°45S 46°20W 189 B1
Pēnjwīn Iraq 35°37N 45°56E 105 E11
Penkridge U.K. 52°44N 2°6W 66 E5
Penmarch France 47°49N 4°21W 70 E2
Penmarch, Pte. de France 47°48N 4°22W 70 E2
Penn Hills U.S.A. 40°28N 79°52W 174 F5
Penn Yan U.S.A. 42°40N 77°3W 174 D7
Penna, Punta della Italy 42°10N 14°43E 93 F11
Pennant Canada 50°32N 108°14W 163 C7
Penne Italy 42°27N 13°55E 93 F10
Penner → India 14°35N 80°10E 127 G5
Penneshaw Australia 35°44S 137°56E 152 C2
Pennine, Alpi Alps 46°4N 7°30E 77 J3
Pennines U.K. 54°45N 2°27W 66 C5
Pennington U.S.A. 39°15N 121°47W 170 F5
Pennington → Nigeria 4°45N 5°35E 139 E6
Pennino, Mte. Italy 43°6N 12°53E 93 E9
Pennsburg U.S.A. 40°23N 75°29W 175 F9
Pennsylvania □ U.S.A. 40°45N 77°30W 173 E15
Penny Canada 53°51N 121°20W 162 C4
Peno Russia 57°2N 32°49E 84 D7
Penobscot → U.S.A. 44°30N 68°48W 173 C19
Penobscot B. U.S.A. 44°35N 68°50W 173 C19
Penola Australia 37°25S 140°48E 152 C4
Penong Australia 31°56S 133°1E 149 F5
Penonomé Panama 8°31N 80°21W 182 E3
Penrhyn Cook Is. 9°0S 158°0W 157 H12
Penrith Australia 33°43S 150°38E 153 B9
Penrith U.K. 54°40N 2°45W 66 C5
Penryn U.K. 50°9N 5°7W 67 G2
Pensacola U.S.A. 30°25N 87°13W 178 D3
Pensacola B. U.S.A. 30°25N 87°5W 179 E2
Pensacola Mts. Antarctica 84°0S 40°0W 55 E1
Pense Canada 50°25N 104°59W 163 C8
Penshurst Australia 37°49S 142°20E 152 D5
Pentadaktylos Cyprus 35°20N 33°20E 101 D12
Pentecoste Brazil 3°48S 39°17W 189 A3
Penticton Canada 49°30N 119°38W 162 D5
Pentland Australia 20°32S 145°25E 150 C4
Pentland Firth U.K. 58°43N 3°10W 65 C5
Pentland Hills U.K. 55°48N 3°25W 66 F5
Penukonda India 14°5N 77°38E 127 G3
Penza Russia 53°15N 45°5E 86 D7
Penza □ Russia 52°50N 44°50E 86 D7
Penzance U.K. 50°7N 5°33W 67 G2
Penzberg Germany 47°45N 11°22E 77 H7
Penzhino Russia 63°30N 167°55E 107 C17
Penzhinskaya Guba Russia 61°30N 163°0E 107 C17
Penzlin Germany 53°30N 13°5E 76 B9
Peoria Ariz., U.S.A. 33°43N 112°14W 169 K7
Peoria Ill., U.S.A. 40°42N 89°36W 172 E9
Pepacton Res. U.S.A. 42°5N 74°58W 175 D10
Pepani → S. Africa 25°49S 22°47E 144 C3
Pepel S. Leone 8°40N 13°5W 138 D2
Peqin Albania 41°3N 19°44E 96 E3
Pera Hd. Australia 12°55S 141°37E 150 A3
Perabumulih Indonesia 3°27S 104°15E 118 E2
Perachora Greece 38°2N 22°56E 98 C4
Perak □ Malaysia 5°0N 101°0E 121 K3
Perak → Malaysia 4°0N 100°50E 121 K3
Perales del Alfambra Spain 40°38N 1°0W 90 E4
Perales del Puerto Spain 40°10N 6°40W 88 E4
Peralta Spain 42°21N 1°49W 90 C3
Perama Epiros, Greece 39°42N 20°51E 98 B2
Perama Kerkyra, Greece 39°34N 19°56E 98 B1
Perama Kriti, Greece 35°20N 24°40E 101 D6
Perämeri △ Finland 65°35N 24°22E 60 D21
Perancak Indonesia 8°24S 114°37E 119 J17
Peräpohjola Finland 66°16N 26°10E 60 C22
Perast Montenegro 42°31N 18°42E 96 D2
Percé Canada 48°31N 64°13W 165 C7
Perche France 48°31N 1°1E 70 B8
Perche □ France 48°24N 0°46E 70 D7
Perchtoldsdorf Austria 48°7N 16°17E 79 C9
Percival Lakes Australia 21°25S 125°0E 148 D4
Percy France 48°55N 1°11W 70 B4
Percy Is. Australia 21°39S 150°16E 150 C5
Perdido, Mte. Spain 42°40N 0°5E 90 C6
Perdu, Mt. = Perdido, Mte. Spain 42°40N 0°5E 90 C6

Perechyn Ukraine 48°44N 22°28E 80 B7
Perehinske Ukraine 48°49N 24°11E 81 B9
Pereira Colombia 4°49N 75°43W 186 C3
Perejil Spain 35°55N 5°25W 89 K5
Perelazovskiy Russia 49°8N 42°35E 87 F6
Peremul Par India 11°10N 72°4E 127 J1
Perené → Peru 11°9S 74°14W 188 C3
Perenjori Australia 29°26S 116°16E 149 E2
Peresecina Moldova 47°16N 28°46E 81 C13
Pereslavl-Zalesskiy Russia 56°45N 38°50E 84 D10
Pereyra Romania 44°3N 25°5E 81 F10
Pereyma Ukraine 48°4N 29°30E 81 B14
Pereyaslav-Khmelnytskyy Ukraine 50°3N 31°28E 85 G6
Perg Austria 48°15N 14°38E 78 C7
Pergamino Argentina 33°52S 60°30W 190 C3
Pergamon Turkey 39°8N 27°11E 99 B9
Pergau → Malaysia 5°23N 102°2E 121 K3
Pérgine Valsugana Italy 46°4N 11°14E 93 B8
Pérgola Italy 43°34N 12°50E 93 E9
Perham U.S.A. 46°36N 95°34W 172 B6
Perhentian, Kepulauan Malaysia 5°54N 102°42E 121 K4
Peri → Turkey 38°53N 39°52E 105 C8
Periam Romania 46°2N 20°52E 80 D5
Péribonka → Canada 48°45N 72°5W 165 C5
Péribonka, L. Canada 50°1N 71°10W 165 B5
Péribonka, La Centrale de Canada 50°0N 71°10W 165 C5
Perico Argentina 24°20S 65°5W 190 A2
Pericos Mexico 25°3N 107°42W 180 B3
Périers France 49°11N 1°25W 70 C5
Périgord France 45°0N 0°40E 72 D4
Périgord-Limousin △ France 45°40N 0°50E 72 C4
Périgueux France 45°10N 0°42E 72 C4
Perijá, Sierra de Colombia 9°30N 73°3W 186 B4
Perijá △ Venezuela 9°30N 72°55W 183 E5
Peringat Malaysia 6°2N 102°17E 121 J4
Perisher Valley Australia 36°27S 148°25E 153 D8
Peristera Greece 39°15N 23°58E 98 B5
Peristerona → Cyprus 35°8N 33°5E 101 D12
Perito Moreno Argentina 46°36S 70°56W 192 C2
Perito Moreno △ Argentina 47°49S 72°17W 192 C2
Peritoró Brazil 4°20S 44°18W 189 A2
Perivol = Dragovishtitsa Bulgaria 42°22N 22°39E 96 D6
Periyakulam India 10°5N 77°30E 127 J3
Periyar → India 10°15N 76°10E 127 J3
Periyar □ India 9°25N 77°10E 127 K3
Periyar △ India 9°25N 77°10E 127 K3
Perkasie U.S.A. 40°22N 75°18W 175 F9
Perković Croatia 43°41N 16°10E 93 E13
Perlas, Arch. de las Panama 8°41N 79°7W 182 E4
Perlas, Punta de Nic. 12°30N 83°30W 182 D3
Perleberg Germany 53°5N 11°52E 76 B7
Perlez Serbia 45°11N 20°22E 96 B4
Perlis □ Malaysia 6°30N 100°15E 121 J2
Perm Russia 58°0N 56°10E 106 D6
Përmet Albania 40°15N 20°21E 96 F4
Pernambuco = Recife Brazil 8°0S 35°0W 189 B4
Pernambuco □ Brazil 8°0S 37°0W 189 B3
Pernambuco Abyssal Plain Atl. Oc. 5°0S 24°0W 56 G9
Pernatty Lagoon Australia 31°30S 137°12E 152 A2
Pernik Bulgaria 42°35N 23°2E 96 D7
Pernik □ Bulgaria 42°35N 23°2E 96 D7
Peron Is. Australia 13°9S 130°4E 148 B5
Péronne France 49°55N 2°57E 71 C9
Perosa Argentina Italy 44°58N 7°10E 92 D4
Perow Canada 54°35S 126°10W 162 C3
Perpignan France 42°42N 2°53E 72 F6
Perrine U.S.A. 25°36N 80°21W 179 H9
Perris U.S.A. 33°47N 117°14W 171 M9
Perros-Guirec France 48°49N 3°28W 70 D3
Perry Fla., U.S.A. 30°7N 83°35W 178 C6
Perry Ga., U.S.A. 32°28N 83°44W 178 C6
Perry Iowa, U.S.A. 41°51N 94°6W 172 E6
Perry N.Y., U.S.A. 42°42N 78°0W 174 D7
Perry Okla., U.S.A. 36°17N 97°14W 176 C6
Perryton U.S.A. 36°24N 100°48W 176 C4
Perryville U.S.A. 37°43N 89°52W 172 G9
Persan France 49°9N 2°16E 71 C9
Persberg Sweden 59°47N 14°15E 62 E8
Persepolis Iran 29°55N 52°50E 129 D7
Pershore U.K. 52°11N 2°2W 66 E5
Pershotravensk Ukraine 50°13N 27°40E 75 C14
Persia = Iran ■ Asia 33°0N 53°0E 129 C7
Persian Gulf Asia 27°0N 50°0E 129 E6
Perstorp Sweden 56°10N 13°25E 63 H7
Pertek Turkey 38°51N 39°19E 105 C7
Perth Australia 31°57S 115°52E 149 F2
Perth Canada 44°55N 76°15W 175 B8
Perth U.K. 56°24N 3°26W 66 E5
Perth & Kinross □ U.K. 56°45N 3°55W 66 E5
Perth Amboy U.S.A. 40°30N 74°15W 175 F10
Perth-Andover Canada 46°44N 67°42W 165 C6
Perth Basin Ind. Oc. 30°0S 108°0E 156 L2
Pertuis France 43°42N 5°30E 73 E9
Pertusato, C. France 41°21N 9°11E 73 G13
Peru Ind., U.S.A. 40°45N 86°4W 172 E10
Peru N.Y., U.S.A. 44°35N 73°32W 175 B11
Peru ■ S. Amer. 4°0S 75°0W 186 D4
Peru Basin Pac. Oc. 20°0S 95°0W 157 J18
Peru-Chile Trench Pac. Oc. 20°0S 72°0W 186 G3
Perúgia Italy 43°7N 12°23E 93 E9
Perušić Croatia 44°40N 15°22E 93 D12
Pervomaysk Russia 54°56N 43°58E 86 D7
Pervomaysk Ukraine 48°10N 30°46E 85 H6
Pervomayskiy Kazakhstan 50°16N 82°0E 109 B10
Pervouralsk Russia 56°59N 59°59E 106 D6
Pésaro Italy 43°54N 12°55E 93 E9
Pésaro e Urbino □ Italy 43°45N 12°40E 93 E9
Pescadores = P'enghu Ch'üntou Taiwan 23°34N 119°30E 117 F12
Pescara Italy 42°28N 14°13E 93 F11
Pescara → Italy 42°28N 14°13E 93 F11
Peschanokopskoye Russia 46°14N 41°4E 87 G5
Péscia Italy 43°54N 10°41E 92 E7

Pescina Italy 42°2N 13°39E 93 F10
Peshawar Pakistan 34°2N 71°37E 124 B4
Peshkopi Albania 41°41N 20°25E 96 E4
Peshtera Bulgaria 42°2N 24°18E 97 D8
Peshtigo U.S.A. 45°3N 87°45W 172 C10
Peski Russia 51°14N 42°29E 86 E6
Peski Turkmenistan 38°11N 62°59E 108 E6
Pêso da Régua Portugal 41°10N 7°47W 88 D3
Pesqueira Brazil 8°20S 36°42W 189 B3
Pessac France 44°48N 0°37W 72 D3
Pest □ Hungary 47°29N 19°5E 80 C4
Pestovo Russia 58°33N 35°42E 84 C8
Pestravka Russia 52°28N 49°57E 86 D9
Petah Tiqwa Israel 32°6N 34°53E 130 C3
Petal U.S.A. 31°21N 89°18W 179 E10
Petalidi Greece 36°57N 21°55E 98 E3
Petaling Jaya Malaysia 3°4N 101°42E 121 L3
Petalioi Greece 36°18N 25°52E 101 C10
Petaluma U.S.A. 38°14N 122°39W 170 G4
Pétange Lux. 49°33N 5°55E 69 E5
Petatlán Mexico 17°31N 101°16W 180 D4
Petatlán → Mexico 24°58S 130°0E 149 E4
Petawawa Canada 45°54N 77°17W 164 C4
Petén Itzá, L. Guatemala 16°58N 89°50W 182 C2
Peter I. Br. Virgin Is. 18°22N 64°35W 183 e
Peter I. Øy Antarctica 69°0S 91°0W 55 C16
Peter Pond L. Canada 55°55N 108°44W 163 B7
Peterbell Canada 48°36N 83°21W 164 C3
Peterborough Australia 32°58S 138°51E 152 B3
Peterborough Canada 44°20N 78°20W 174 B6
Peterborough U.K. 52°35N 0°15W 67 E7
Peterborough U.S.A. 42°53N 71°57W 175 D13
Peterborough □ U.K. 52°35N 0°15W 67 E7
Peterculter U.K. 57°6N 2°16W 65 D6
Peterhead U.K. 57°31N 1°48W 65 D7
Peterlee U.K. 54°47N 1°20W 66 C6
Petermann ◎ Australia 24°58S 130°0E 149 E4
Petermann Bjerg Greenland 73°7N 28°25W 57 C8
Petermann Gletscher Greenland 80°30N 60°0W 57 A4
Petermann Ranges Australia 26°0S 130°30E 149 E5
Petersburg Alaska, U.S.A. 56°46N 132°58W 160 F5
Petersburg Ind., U.S.A. 38°30N 87°17W 172 F9
Petersburg Va., U.S.A. 37°14N 77°24W 173 G15
Petersburg W. Va., U.S.A. 39°1N 79°5W 173 F14
Petersfield U.K. 51°1N 0°56W 67 F7
Petershagen Germany 52°23N 8°58E 76 C4
Petilia Policastro Italy 39°7N 16°48E 95 C9
Petit-Canal Guadeloupe 16°25N 61°31W 182 b
Petit-Goâve Haiti 18°27N 72°51W 183 C5
Petit Lac Manicouagan Canada 51°25N 67°40W 165 B6
Petit-Mécatina → Canada 50°40N 59°30W 165 B8
Petit-Mécatina, Î. du Canada 50°30N 59°25W 165 B8
Petit Piton St. Lucia 13°51N 61°5W 183 f
Petit-Saguenay Canada 48°15N 70°4W 165 C5
Petit Saint Bernard, Col du Italy 45°40N 6°52E 73 C10
Petitcodiac Canada 45°57N 65°11W 165 C6
Petite Terre, Îles de la Guadeloupe 16°13N 61°9W 182 b
Petitot → Canada 60°14N 123°29W 162 A4
Petitsikapau L. Canada 54°37N 66°25W 165 B6
Petlad India 22°30N 72°45E 124 H5
Peto Mexico 20°8N 88°55W 181 C7
Petone N.Z. 41°13S 174°53E 154 H3
Petorca Chile 32°15S 70°56W 190 C1
Petoskey U.S.A. 45°22N 84°57W 173 C11
Petra Jordan 30°20N 35°22E 130 E4
Petra, Ostrov Russia 76°15N 118°30E 107 B12
Petra Velikogo, Zaliv Russia 42°40N 132°0E 112 C6
Petre, Pt. Canada 43°50N 77°9W 174 C7
Petrel = Petrer Spain 38°30N 0°46W 91 G4
Petrella, Monte Italy 41°18N 13°40E 94 A6
Petrer Spain 38°30N 0°46W 91 G4
Petreto-Bicchisano France 41°47N 8°58E 73 G12
Petrich Bulgaria 41°24N 23°13E 96 E7
Petrified Forest △ U.S.A. 35°0N 109°30W 169 J9
Petrikov = Pyetrikaw Belarus 52°11N 28°29E 75 B15
Petrila Romania 45°29N 23°29E 81 E8
Petrinja Croatia 45°28N 16°18E 93 C13
Petrolândia Brazil 9°5S 38°20W 189 B3
Petrolia Canada 42°54N 82°9W 174 D2
Petrolina Brazil 9°24S 40°30W 189 B2
Petropavl Kazakhstan 54°53N 69°13E 108 D7
Petropavlovsk = Petropavl Kazakhstan 54°53N 69°13E 108 D7
Petropavlovsk-Kamchatskiy Russia 53°3N 158°43E 107 D16
Petropavlovskiy = Akhtubinsk Russia 48°13N 46°7E 87 E8
Petrópolis Brazil 22°33S 43°9W 191 A7
Petroşani Romania 45°28N 23°20E 81 E8
Petrova Gora Croatia 45°15N 15°45E 93 C12
Petrovac Montenegro 42°13N 18°57E 96 D2
Petrovaradin Serbia 45°16N 19°55E 96 B3
Petrovsk Russia 52°22N 45°19E 86 D7
Petrovsk-Zabaykalskiy Russia 51°20N 108°55E 107 D11
Petrovskaya Russia 45°31N 37°58E 85 K9
Petrozavodsk Russia 61°41N 34°20E 84 B8
Petrus Steyn S. Africa 27°38S 28°8E 145 C4
Petrusburg S. Africa 29°4S 25°6E 144 C4
Petukhovo Russia 55°6N 67°55E 108 D7
Petzeck Austria 46°57N 12°48E 78 B5
Peumo Chile 34°21N 71°12W 190 C1
Peureulak Indonesia 4°48N 97°45E 118 D1
Pevek Russia 69°41N 171°19E 107 C18
Peyrehorade France 43°34N 1°7W 72 E2
Peyruis France 44°1N 5°56E 73 D9
Pézenas France 43°28N 3°24E 72 E7
Pezinok Slovak Rep. 48°17N 17°17E 79 C10

Pfaffenhofen Germany 48°31N 11°31E 77 G7
Pfälzerwald △ Germany 49°18N 9°55E 77 F5
Pfarrkirchen Germany 48°25N 12°56E 77 G8
Pfeffenhausen Germany 48°39N 11°58E 77 G7
Pforzheim Germany 48°52N 8°41E 77 G4
Pfullendorf Germany 47°55N 9°15E 77 H5
Pfungstadt Germany 49°48N 8°35E 77 F4
Pha Taem △ Thailand 15°32N 105°30E 120 E5
Phagwara India 31°10N 75°40E 124 D6
Phala Botswana 23°45S 26°50E 144 C4
Phalaborwa S. Africa 23°57S 31°7E 145 B5
Phalera = Phulera India 26°52N 75°16E 124 F6
Phalodi India 27°12N 72°24E 124 F5
Phalsbourg France 48°46N 7°15E 71 D14
Phaltan India 17°59N 74°26E 126 F2
Phalui, Ko Thailand 9°9N 99°51E 121 b
Phan Thailand 19°28N 99°43E 120 C2
Phan Rang-Thap Cham Vietnam 11°34N 109°0E 120 G7
Phan Ri Cua Vietnam 11°16N 108°40E 120 G7
Phan Si Pan Vietnam 22°18N 103°46E 120 A4
Phan Thiet Vietnam 11°1N 108°9E 120 G7
Phan Thiet, Vinh Vietnam 10°53N 108°5E 120 G7
Phanae Greece 38°8N 25°52E 99 C11
Phanat Nikhom Thailand 13°27N 101°11E 120 F3
Phangan, Ko Thailand 9°45N 100°0E 121 H3
Phangnga Thailand 8°28N 98°30E 121 H2
Phangnga, Ao Thailand 8°16N 98°33E 121 a
Phanom Sarakham Thailand 13°45N 101°21E 120 F3
Phaphund India 26°36N 79°28E 125 F8
Pharenda India 27°5N 83°17E 125 F10
Pharr U.S.A. 26°12N 98°11W 176 H5
Phatthalung Thailand 7°39N 100°6E 121 J3
Phayam, Ko Thailand 9°44N 98°25E 121 H2
Phayao Thailand 19°11N 99°55E 120 C2
Phelps U.S.A. 42°58N 77°3W 174 D7
Phelps L. U.S.A. 59°15N 103°15W 163 B8
Phenix City U.S.A. 32°28N 85°1W 178 C4
Phet Buri = Phetchaburi Thailand 13°1N 99°55E 120 F2
Phetchabun Thailand 16°25N 101°8E 120 D3
Phetchabun, Thiu Khao Thailand 16°0N 101°20E 120 E3
Phetchaburi Thailand 13°1N 99°55E 120 F2
Phi Phi, Ko Thailand 7°45N 98°46E 121 J2
Phiafay Laos 14°48N 106°0E 120 E6
Phibun Mangsahan Thailand 15°14N 105°14E 120 E5
Phichai Thailand 17°22N 100°10E 120 D3
Phichit Thailand 16°26N 100°22E 120 D3
Philadelphia Miss., U.S.A. 32°46N 89°7W 177 E10
Philadelphia N.Y., U.S.A. 44°9N 75°43W 175 B9
Philadelphia Pa., U.S.A. 39°57N 75°9W 175 G9
Philadelphia Int. ✈ (PHL) U.S.A. 39°51N 75°18W 175 G9
Philip U.S.A. 44°2N 101°40W 172 D3
Philip Smith Mts. U.S.A. 68°0N 148°0W 166 B10
Philippeville Belgium 50°12N 4°33E 69 D4
Philippi U.S.A. 39°9N 80°3W 173 F13
Philippi L. Australia 24°20S 138°55E 150 C2
Philippine Basin Pac. Oc. 17°0N 130°0E 72 F4
Philippine Sea Pac. Oc. 18°0N 125°0E 156 F4
Philippine Trench = Mindanao Trench Pac. Oc. 12°0N 126°6E 119 B7
Philippines ■ Asia 12°0N 123°0E 119 E6
Philippolis S. Africa 30°15S 25°16E 144 C4
Philippopolis = Plovdiv Bulgaria 42°8N 24°44E 97 D8
Philipsburg Canada 45°2N 73°5W 175 A11
Philipsburg Mont., U.S.A. 46°20N 113°18W 168 C7
Philipstown = Daingean Ireland 53°18N 7°17W 64 C4
Philipstown S. Africa 30°28S 24°30E 144 C3
Phillip I. Australia 38°30S 145°12E 153 E6
Phillips U.S.A. 45°42N 90°24W 172 C8
Phillipsburg Ga., U.S.A. 31°35N 83°30W 178 D5
Phillipsburg Kans., U.S.A. 39°45N 99°19W 176 A5
Phillipsburg N.J., U.S.A. 40°42N 75°12W 175 F9
Philmont U.S.A. 42°15N 73°39W 175 D11
Philomath U.S.A. 44°32N 123°22W 168 D2
Philomath Ga., U.S.A. 33°44N 82°59W 178 B7
Philomath Oreg., U.S.A. 44°32N 123°22W 168 D2
Phimai Thailand 15°13N 102°30E 120 E4
Phitsanulok Thailand 16°50N 100°12E 120 D3
Phnom Kulen △ Cambodia 13°38N 104°15E 120 F5
Phnom Penh Cambodia 11°33N 104°55E 120 G5
Phnum Penh = Phnom Penh Cambodia 11°33N 104°55E 120 G5
Pho, Laem Thailand 6°55N 101°19E 121 J3
Phocaea = Fokida Greece 38°30N 22°15E 98 C4
Phoenicia U.S.A. 42°5N 74°14W 175 D10
Phoenix Mauritius 20°17S 57°30E 145 d
Phoenix Ariz., U.S.A. 33°26N 112°4W 169 K7
Phoenix N.Y., U.S.A. 43°14N 76°18W 175 C9
Phoenix Is. Kiribati 3°30S 172°0W 156 H10
Phoenix Sky Harbour Int. ✈ (PHX) U.S.A. 33°26N 112°1W 169 K7
Phoenixville U.S.A. 40°8N 75°31W 175 F9
Phon Thailand 15°49N 102°30E 120 E4
Phong → Thailand 16°23N 102°56E 120 D4
Phong Nha -Ke Bang △ Vietnam 17°30N 106°10E 120 D6
Phong Saly Laos 21°42N 102°9E 116 G4
Phong Tho Vietnam 22°32N 103°21E 120 A4
Phonsavan Vietnam 19°27N 103°4E 120 C4
Phonum Thailand 8°49N 98°48E 121 H2
Phosphate Hill Australia 21°53S 139°58E 150 C2
Phra Nakhon Si Ayutthaya Thailand 14°25N 100°30E 120 E3
Phra Pradaeng Thailand 13°40N 100°30E 120 F3
Phra Thong, Ko Thailand 9°5N 98°17E 121 H2
Phrae Thailand 18°7N 100°9E 120 C3

Phrom Phiram Thailand 17°2N 100°12E 1
Phrom Thep, Laem Thailand 7°45N 98°19E 1
Phrygia Turkey 38°40N 30°0E 1
Phthiotis = Fthiotida Greece 38°50N 22°25E 1
Phu Bia Laos 19°10N 103°0E 1
Phu Chong -Na Yoi △ Thailand 14°25N 105°30E 1
Phu Hin Rong Kla △ Thailand 17°0N 100°59E 1
Phu Kao -Phu Phan Kham △ Thailand 16°53N 102°13E 1
Phu Kradung △ Thailand 17°2N 101°44E 1
Phu Loi Laos 20°14N 103°14E 1
Phu Luang △ Thailand 17°15N 101°29E 1
Phu Ly Vietnam 20°35N 105°50E 1
Phu My Vietnam 14°15N 109°5E 1
Phu Pha Man △ Thailand 16°44N 101°50E 1
Phu Phan △ Thailand 17°0N 103°56E 1
Phu Quoc, Dao Vietnam 10°20N 104°0E 1
Phu Sa Dok Bua △ Thailand 16°11N 104°45E 1
Phu Sang △ Thailand 19°35N 100°19E 1
Phu Tho Vietnam 21°24N 105°13E 1
Phu Wiang △ Thailand 16°39N 102°20E 1
Phuc Yen Vietnam 21°16N 105°45E 1
Phuket Thailand 7°53N 98°24E 1
Phuket, Ko Thailand 8°0N 98°22E 1
Phul India 30°19N 75°14E 1
Phulad India 25°38N 73°49E 1
Phulbani India 20°28N 84°14E 1
Phulchari Bangla. 25°11N 89°37E 1
Phulera India 26°52N 75°16E 1
Phulpur India 25°31N 82°49E 1
Phunphin Thailand 9°7N 99°12E 1
Phuntsholing Bhutan 26°51N 89°23E 1
Phuphrabat Thailand 17°40N 102°45E 1
Phuthaditjhaba S. Africa 28°29S 28°48E 1
Phyu = Pyu Burma 18°30N 96°28E 1
Pia ◎ Australia 27°7S 116°23E 1
Piaçabuçu Brazil 10°24S 36°25W 1
Piacenza Italy 45°1N 9°40E 1
Piai, Tanjung Malaysia 1°17N 103°30E 1
Piako → N.Z. 37°12S 175°30E 1
Pian-Upe ◎ Uganda 1°44N 34°20E 1
Piana France 42°15N 8°34E 1
Pianella Italy 42°24N 14°2E 1
Piangil Australia 35°5S 143°20E 1
Pianosa Toscana, Italy 42°35N 10°5E 1
Piao'ertun China 41°50N 123°47E 1
Piapot Canada 49°59N 109°8W 1
Pias Portugal 38°1N 7°29W 1
Piaseczno Poland 52°5N 21°2E 1
Piaski Poland 51°8N 22°52E 1
Piastów Poland 52°12N 20°48E 1
Piatã Brazil 13°9S 41°48W 1
Piatra Romania 43°51N 25°9E 1
Piatra Craiului △ Romania 45°30N 25°12E 1
Piatra Neamț Romania 46°56N 26°21E 1
Piatra Olt Romania 44°22N 24°16E 1
Piauí □ Brazil 7°0S 43°0W 1
Piauí → Brazil 6°38S 42°42W 1
Piave → Italy 45°32N 12°44E 1
Piazza Ármerina Italy 37°23N 14°22E 1
Pibor Post South Sudan 6°47N 33°3E 1
Pic St-Loup France 43°47N 3°48E 1
Pica Chile 20°35S 69°25W 1
Picardie, Plaine de France 50°0N 2°0E 1
Picardy = Picardie □ France 49°50N 3°0E 1
Picayune U.S.A. 30°32N 89°41W 1
Picerno Italy 40°38N 15°38E 1
Pichhor India 25°58N 78°20E 1
Pichilemu Chile 34°22S 72°0W 1
Pichor India 25°11N 78°11E 1
Pickerel L. Canada 48°40N 91°25W 1
Pickering U.K. 54°15N 0°46W 1
Pickering, Vale of U.K. 54°14N 0°45W 1
Pickle Lake Canada 51°30N 90°12W 1
Pickwick L. U.S.A. 35°4N 88°15W 1
Pico Azores 38°28N 28°20W 1
Pico Bonito △ Honduras 15°34N 86°48W 1
Pico Truncado Argentina 46°40S 68°0W 1
Picos Brazil 7°5S 41°28W 1
Picos, Pta. dos Spain 41°52N 8°53W 1
Picos de Europa △ Spain 43°14N 4°59W 1
Picota Peru 6°54S 76°24W 1
Picton Australia 34°12S 150°34E 1
Picton Canada 44°1N 77°9W 1
Picton N.Z. 41°18S 174°3E 1
Picton, I. Chile 55°2S 66°57W 1
Pictou Canada 45°41N 62°42W 1
Picture Butte Canada 49°55N 112°45W 1
Pictured Rocks △ U.S.A. 46°30N 86°30W 1
Picuí Brazil 6°31S 36°21W 1
Picún Leufú Argentina 39°30S 69°5W 1
Pidbuzh Ukraine 49°19N 23°14E 1
Pidurutalagala Sri Lanka 7°10N 80°50E 1
Piechowice Poland 50°51N 15°36E 1
Piedimonte Matese Italy 41°22N 14°22E 1
Piedmont = Piemonte □ Italy
Piedmont Ala., U.S.A. 33°55N 85°37W 1
Piedmont S.C., U.S.A. 34°42N 82°28W 1
Piedra → Spain 41°18N 1°47W 1
Piedra del Águila Argentina 40°2S 70°4W 1
Piedra del Águila, Embalse Argentina
Piedrabuena Spain 39°0N 4°10W 1
Piedrahita Spain 40°28N 5°23W 1
Piedralaves Spain 40°19N 4°42W 1
Piedras, R. de las → Peru 12°30S 69°15W 1
Piedras Blancas Spain 43°33N 5°59W 1
Piedras Negras Mexico 28°42N 100°31W 1
Piekary Śląskie Poland 50°24N 18°57E 1

...käsmäki *Finland* 62°18N 27°10E **84** A4
...linen *Finland* 63°15N 29°40E **60** E23
...jekaise △ *Sweden* 66°20N 16°45E **60** C17
...monte □ *Italy* 45°0N 8°0E **92** D5
...naarsrivier *S. Africa* 25°15S 28°18E **145** C4
...niezno *Poland* 54°14N 20°8E **82** D7
...ainský △ *Europe* 49°25N 20°28E **79** B13
...fisk *Poland* 51°16N 15°2E **83** G2
...rcefield *U.S.A.* 44°13N 74°35W **175** B10
...rceland *Canada* 54°20N 109°46W **163** C7
...ria *Greece* 40°33N 22°25E **96** F6
...rpont *U.S.A.* 41°45N 80°34W **174** E4
...re *U.S.A.* 44°22N 100°21W **172** C3
...re-Bufflière *France* 45°41N 1°22E **72** C5
...re-de-Bresse *France* 46°54N 5°13E **71** F12
...refonds *Canada* 45°29N 73°51W **175** A11
...rance 47°14N 6°32E **71** E13
...refort *France* 44°55N 2°50E **72** D6
...rrelatte *France* 44°23N 4°43E **73** D8
...rson *U.S.A.* 29°14N 81°28W **179** F8
...st'any *Slovak Rep.* 48°38N 17°55E **79** C10
...sting → *Austria* 48°6N 16°40E **79** C9
...szyce *Poland* 50°43N 16°33E **83** H3
...Retief *S. Africa* 27°1S 30°50E **145** C5
...arsainá *Finland* 63°40N 22°43E **60** E20
...ermaritzburg
...Africa 29°35S 30°25E **145** C5
...ersburg = Polokwane
...Africa 23°54S 29°25E **145** B4
...ragalla *Italy* 40°45N 15°53E **95** B8
...rasanta *Italy* 43°57N 10°14E **92** E7
...roșița *Romania* 45°11N 25°26E **81** E10
...rosul, Vf. *Maramureș,*
...omania 47°35N 24°43E **81** C9
...rosul, Vf. *Suceava,*
...omania 47°12N 25°18E **81** C10
...re di Cadore *Italy* 46°26N 12°22E **93** B9
...re di Teco *Italy* 44°3N 7°56E **92** D4
...repélago *Italy* 44°12N 10°37E **92** D7
...aditsa *Greece* 39°59N 21°03E **96** G5
...eon I. *India* 14°2N 74°20E **127** G2
...eon L. *Canada* 44°27N 78°30W **174** B6
...es *Greece* 39°17N 21°25E **98** H3
...gott *U.S.A.* 36°23N 90°11W **177** C9
...na *Italy* 43°56N 7°40E **92** E4
...ie *Argentina* 37°36S 62°25W **190** D3
...a *N.Z.* 36°57S 174°28E **154** C3
...ni *India* 27°36N 80°15E **125** F9
...ajavesi *Finland* 61°45N 28°45E **84** B5
...iapan *Mexico* 15°42N 93°14W **181** D6
...alevo *Russia* 59°37N 34°9E **84** C8
...angikum *Canada* 51°49N 94°0W **163** C10
...s Peak *U.S.A.* 38°50N 105°3W **168** G11
...etberg *S. Africa* 32°55S 18°40E **144** D2
...eville *U.S.A.* 37°29N 82°31W **173** G12
...ou *China* 39°18N 122°22E **115** E12
...switonei *Canada* 55°35N 97°9W **163** B9
...Poland 53°10N 16°48E **83** E3
...Spain 38°16N 1°11W **91** G3
...nesberg △ *S. Africa* 25°15S 27°4E **144** C4
...ni *India* 28°22N 75°33E **124** E6
...raj *Paraguay* 9°36S 35°56W **189** B6
...r *Paraguay* 26°50S 58°20W **190** B4
...r de la Horadada
...pain 37°52N 0°47W **91** H4
...t, Dune du *France* 44°35N 1°13W **72** D2
...r *France* 45°20N 4°30E **73** C8
...wa *Poland* 51°57N 21°32E **83** G8
...ya → *Bolivia* 20°55S 64°4W **186** H6
...ara *Australia* 21°15S 118°16E **148** D2
...omaya →
...araguay 25°21S 57°42W **190** B4
...s Sweden 62°57N 15°2E **62** B9
...rim's Rest *S. Africa* 24°55S 30°44E **145** B5
...rimstad *Sweden* 62°57N 15°2E **62** B9
...Greece 39°19N 22°59E **98** B4
...phit *India* 28°40N 79°50E **125** E8
..., Oros *Greece* 39°27N 23°3E **98** B5
...dinas = Philippines ■
...sia 12°0N 123°0E **119** B6
...s Hungary 47°1N 19°35E **80** C4
...svörösvár *Hungary* 47°38N 18°56E **80** C3
...hawa *India* 28°43N 77°42E **124** E7
...ga *Australia* 30°21S 148°54E **151** E4
...es *Greece* 36°55N 21°42E **98** E3
...t Mound *U.S.A.* 49°15N 98°54W **163** D9
...t Point *U.S.A.* 33°24N 96°58W **176** E6
...t Rock *U.S.A.* 45°29N 118°50W **168** D4
...stanj *Slovenia* 46°8N 15°39E **93** B12
...ene *Latvia* 57°13N 21°40E **82** A8
...no *Australia* 28°43N 21°16E **83** J8
...a *U.S.A.* 32°54N 109°50W **169** K9
...abala *U.S.A.* 38°15N 136°46E **152** A2
...enta Bueno *Brazil* 11°35S 61°10W **186** F6
...entel *Peru* 6°45S 79°55W **188** B2
...pri Chinchwad
...ndia 18°37N 73°47E **126** E1
...Valley → *India* 31°50N 77°0E **124** D7
...a de Ebro *Spain* 41°29N 0°33W **90** D4
...ang *Malaysia* 5°25N 100°15E **121** K3
...ang □ *Malaysia* 5°20N 100°12E **121** K3
...no Cuba 39°53N 3°12E **180** D3
...ar del Rio *Cuba* 22°26N 83°40W **182** B3
...arbaşı *Çanakkale,*
...urkey 39°23N 26°15E **99** B8
...arbaşı *Kayseri,*
...urkey 38°43N 36°23E **104** C7
...arhisar *Turkey* 41°37N 27°30E **97** E11
...atubo, Mt. *Phil.* 15°8N 120°21E **119** A6
...awa *Canada* 50°9N 95°50W **163** D9
...awa *India* 26°41N 18°27E **80** D3
...ehely *Hungary* 46°14N 18°58E **80** E3
...chang *China* 31°36N 107°38E **116** B6
...her Creek *Canada* 49°30N 113°57W **162** D6
...s L. *Canada* 54°38N 124°30W **162** C4
...ckard *U.S.A.* 31°19N 85°33W **178** D4
...ckneyville *U.S.A.* 38°5N 89°23W **172** F9
... czów *Poland* 50°32N 20°32E **83** H7
...l Dadan Khan
...akistan 32°36N 73°7E **109** F8
...dar *Australia* 34°15S 145°47E **149** F7
...daré → *Brazil* 3°17S 45°21W **189** A2
...daré-Mirim *Brazil* 3°37S 45°21W **189** A1
...ustralia 29°24S 142°37E **151** A3
...di Gheb *Pakistan* 33°14N 72°21E **124** C5
...diga *Nigeria* 9°58N 10°53E **139** D7
...dos △ *Greece* 39°52N 21°11E **98** B3
...dos Oros *Greece* 40°0N 21°0E **98** B3

Pindus Mts. = Pindos Oros
Greece 40°0N 21°0E **98** B3
Pine → *B.C., Canada* 56°8N 120°43W **162** B4
Pine → *Sask., Canada* 58°50N 105°38W **163** B7
Pine Bluff *U.S.A.* 34°13N 92°1W **176** D8
Pine Bluffs *U.S.A.* 41°11N 104°4W **168** F11
Pine City *U.S.A.* 45°50N 92°59W **172** C7
Pine Cr. → *U.S.A.* 41°10N 77°16W **174** E7
Pine Creek *Australia* 13°50S 131°50E **148** B5
Pine Falls *Canada* 50°34N 96°11W **163** C9
Pine Flat L. *U.S.A.* 36°50N 119°20W **170** J7
Pine Grove *U.S.A.* 40°33N 76°23W **175** F8
Pine Hill *Australia* 23°38S 146°57E **150** C4
Pine Hills *U.S.A.* 28°33N 81°27W **179** G8
Pine I. *U.S.A.* 26°36N 82°7W **179** J7
Pine Island Glacier
Antarctica 76°0S 100°0W **55** D15
Pine Level *U.S.A.* 35°30N 78°14W **177** H7
Pine Mountain *U.S.A.* 32°49N 84°51W **178** C5
Pine Pass *Canada* 55°25N 122°42W **162** B4
Pine Ridge *Australia* 31°30S 150°28E **153** A9
Pine Ridge *U.S.A.* 43°2N 102°33W **172** D2
Pine River *Canada* 51°45N 100°30W **163** C8
Pine River *U.S.A.* 46°43N 94°24W **172** B6
Pine Valley *U.S.A.* 32°50N 116°32W **171** N10
Pinecrest *U.S.A.* 38°12N 120°1W **170** G6
Pineda de Mar *Spain* 41°37N 2°42E **90** D7
Pinedale *Calif., U.S.A.* 36°50N 119°48W **170** J7
Pinedale *Wyo., U.S.A.* 42°52N 109°52W **168** E9
Pinega → *Russia* 64°30N 44°19E **106** C5
Pinehouse L. *Canada* 55°32N 106°35W **163** B7
Pineimuta → *Canada* 52°8N 88°33W **164** B1
Pinellas Park *U.S.A.* 27°50N 82°41W **179** H7
Pinerolo *Italy* 44°53N 7°21E **92** D4
Pines, Akra *Greece* 40°5N 24°20E **98** F8
Pineto *Italy* 42°36N 14°4E **93** F11
Pinetop-Lakeside
U.S.A. 34°9N 109°58W **169** A9
Pinetown *S. Africa* 29°48S 30°54E **145** C5
Pinetta *U.S.A.* 30°36N 83°21W **178** E6
Pineview *U.S.A.* 32°7N 83°30W **178** C6
Pineville *La., U.S.A.* 31°19N 92°26W **176** F8
Pineville *S.C., U.S.A.* 33°26N 80°1W **178** B9
Pinewood *U.S.A.* 33°44N 80°27W **178** B9
Piney *France* 48°22N 4°21E **71** D11
Ping → *Thailand* 15°42N 100°9E **120** E3
Pingaring *Australia* 32°40S 118°32E **149** F2
Pingba *China* 26°23N 106°12E **116** D6
Pingbian *China* 23°0N 103°45E **116** F4
Pingchuan *China* 27°35N 101°55E **116** D3
Pingding *China* 37°47N 113°38E **114** F7
Pingdingshan *China* 33°43N 113°27E **114** H7
Pingdu *China* 36°42N 119°59E **115** F10
Pingelly *Australia* 32°35S 117°5E **149** F2
Pingguo *China* 23°19N 107°36E **116** F6
Pinghe *China* 24°17N 117°21E **117** E11
Pinghu *China* 30°40N 121°2E **117** B13
Pingjiang *China* 28°45N 113°36E **117** C9
Pingle *China* 24°40N 110°40E **117** E8
Pingli *China* 32°27N 109°22E **116** A7
Pingliang *China* 35°35N 106°31E **114** G4
Pinglu *China* 39°31N 112°30E **114** E7
Pingluo *China* 38°52N 106°30E **114** E4
Pingnan *Fujian, China* 26°55N 119°0E **117** D12
Pingnan *Guangxi Zhuangzu,*
China 23°33N 110°22E **117** F8
Pingquan *China* 41°1N 118°37E **115** D10
Pingrup *Australia* 33°32S 118°29E **149** F2
Pingshan *China* 28°39N 104°3E **116** C5
Pingtan *China* 25°31N 119°47E **117** E12
Pingtang *China* 25°49N 107°17E **116** E6
P'ingtung *Taiwan* 22°38N 120°30E **117** F13
Pingwu *China* 32°25N 104°30E **114** H3
Pingxiang *Guangxi Zhuangzu,*
China 22°6N 106°46E **116** F6
Pingxiang *Jiangxi,*
China 27°43N 113°48E **117** D9
Pingyao *China* 37°12N 112°10E **114** F7
Pingyi *China* 35°30N 117°35E **115** G9
Pingyin *China* 36°30N 116°25E **114** F9
Pingyuan *Guangdong,*
China 24°37N 115°57E **117** E10
Pingyuan *Shandong,*
China 37°10N 116°22E **114** F9
Pingyuanjie *China* 23°45N 103°48E **116** F4
Pinhal Novo *Portugal* 38°38N 8°55W **89** G2
Pinheiro *Brazil* 2°31S 45°5W **189** A1
Pinheiro Machado
Brazil 31°34S 53°23W **191** C5
Pinhel *Portugal* 40°50N 7°1W **88** E3
Pini *Indonesia* 0°10N 98°40E **118** D1
Pinios → *Ilia, Greece* 37°48N 21°20E **98** D3
Pinios → *Trikala, Greece* 39°55N 22°41E **98** B4
Pinjarra *Australia* 32°37S 115°52E **149** F2
Pink → *Canada* 57°3N 122°52W **162** B4
Pinkafeld *Austria* 47°22N 16°9E **79** D9
Pinnacle Is. = Senkaku-Shotō
E. China Sea 25°45N 123°30E **113** M1
Pinnacles *U.S.A.* 36°25N 121°12W **170** J5
Pinnaroo *Australia* 35°17S 140°53E **152** C4
Pinneberg *Germany* 53°40N 9°48E **76** B5
Pino Hachado, Paso
S. Amer. 38°39S 70°54W **192** A2
Pinon Hills *U.S.A.* 34°26N 117°39W **171** L9
Pinos *Mexico* 22°18N 101°34W **180** C4
Pinos, Mt. *U.S.A.* 34°49N 119°8W **171** L7
Pinos Pt. *U.S.A.* 36°38N 121°57W **169** H3
Pinos Puente *Spain* 37°15N 3°45W **89** H7
Pinrang *Indonesia* 3°46S 119°41E **119** E5
Pins, Pte. aux *Canada* 42°15N 81°51W **174** D3
Pinsk *Belarus* 52°10N 26°1E **75** B14
Pintados *Chile* 20°35S 69°40W **188** H4
Pinturas → *Argentina* 36°15S 66°0W **192** C2
Pinyang *China* 27°42N 120°31E **117** D13
Pinyug *Russia* 60°5N 48°0E **106** D6
Pio XII *Brazil* 3°53S 45°17W **189** A1
Pioche *U.S.A.* 37°56N 114°27W **169** H6
Piombino *Italy* 42°55N 10°32E **92** F7
Piombino, Canale di
Italy 42°53N 10°30E **92** F7
Pioner, Ostrov *Russia* 79°50N 92°0E **107** B10
Pionerskiy *Russia* 54°56N 20°14E **82** D7
Pionki *Poland* 51°29N 21°28E **83** G8
Piopiotaki = Milford Sd.
N.Z. 44°41S 167°47E **155** E2
Piorini, L. *Brazil* 3°15S 62°35W **186** D6
Piotrków Trybunalski
Poland 51°23N 19°43E **83** G6
Piove di Sacco *Italy* 45°18N 12°2E **93** C9
Pīp *Iran* 26°45N 60°10E **129** E9
Pipar *India* 26°25N 73°31E **124** F5
Pipar Road *India* 26°27N 73°27E **124** F5

Piparia *Mad. P., India* 22°45N 78°23E **124** H8
Piparia *Mad. P., India* 21°49N 77°37E **124** J7
Piperi *Greece* 39°20N 24°19E **98** B8
Pipestone *U.S.A.* 44°0N 96°19W **172** D6
Pipestone → *Canada* 52°53N 89°23W **164** B2
Pipestone Cr. →
Canada 49°38N 100°15W **163** D8
Pipiriki *N.Z.* 39°28S 175°5E **154** F4
Piplan *Pakistan* 32°17N 71°21E **124** C4
Piploda *India* 23°37N 74°56E **124** H6
Pipmuacan, Rés.
Canada 49°45N 70°30W **165** C5
Pippingarra *Australia* 20°27S 118°42E **148** D2
Pipriac *France* 47°59N 1°58W **70** E5
Piqua *U.S.A.* 40°9N 84°15W **173** E11
Piquet Carneiro *Brazil* 5°48S 39°25W **189** B3
Piquiri → *Brazil* 24°3S 54°14W **191** A5
Piracanjuba *Brazil* 17°20S 49°2W **191** A6
Piracicaba *Brazil* 22°45S 47°40W **191** A6
Piracuruca *Brazil* 3°50S 41°50W **189** A2
Pirae *Tahiti* 17°33S 149°32W **155** b
Pirajuí *Brazil* 21°59S 49°29W **191** A6
Piram I. *India* 21°36N 72°21E **124** J8
Piran *Slovenia* 45°31N 13°33E **93** C10
Pirané *Argentina* 25°42S 59°6W **190** B4
Piranhas *Brazil* 9°27S 37°46W **189** B3
Pirano = Piran *Slovenia* 45°31N 13°33E **93** C10
Pirānshahr *Iran* 36°41N 45°8E **105** D11
Pirapemas *Brazil* 3°43S 44°14W **189** A2
Pirapora *Brazil* 17°20S 44°56W **189** D2
Pirawa *India* 24°10N 76°2E **124** G7
Pirdop *Bulgaria* 42°40N 24°10E **97** D8
Pireas *Greece* 37°57N 23°42E **98** D5
Pires do Rio *Brazil* 17°18S 48°17W **189** D1
Pirgi *Greece* 38°13N 25°59E **99** C7
Pirgos *Ilia, Greece* 37°40N 21°27E **98** D3
Pirgos *Kriti, Greece* 35°0N 25°9W **99** F7
Pirgovo *Bulgaria* 43°44N 25°43E **97** C9
Piribebuy *Paraguay* 25°26S 57°2W **190** B4
Pirimapun *Indonesia* 6°20S 138°24E **119** F9
Pirin *Bulgaria* 41°48N 23°22E **96** E7
Pirin Planina *Bulgaria* 41°40N 23°30E **96** E7
Pirineos = Pyrénées
Europe 42°45N 0°18E **72** F4
Piripiri *Brazil* 4°15S 41°46W **189** A2
Pirlangimpi *Australia* 11°24S 130°26E **148** B5
Pirmasens *Germany* 49°12N 7°36E **77** F3
Pirna *Germany* 50°57N 13°57E **76** E9
Pirot *Serbia* 43°9N 22°33E **96** C6
Piru *Indonesia* 3°4S 128°12E **119** E7
Piru *U.S.A.* 34°25N 118°48W **171** L8
Piryatin = Pyryatyn
Ukraine 50°15N 32°25E **85** G7
Pisa *Italy* 43°43N 10°23E **92** E7
Pisa → *Poland* 53°14N 21°52E **83** E8
Pisa, Firenze ✈ (PSA)
Italy 43°40N 10°22E **92** E7
Pisa Ra. *N.Z.* 44°52S 169°12E **155** E4
Pisac *Peru* 13°25S 71°50W **188** D4
Pisagua *Chile* 19°40S 70°15W **188** G4
Pisarovina *Croatia* 45°35N 15°50E **93** C12
Pisco *Peru* 13°50S 76°12W **188** D2
Piscu *Romania* 45°30N 27°43E **81** E12
Písek *Czech Rep.* 49°19N 14°10E **78** B7
Pishan *China* 37°30N 78°33E **109** E9
Pishchanka *Ukraine* 51°35N 23°50E **83** G10
Pishchanka *Ukraine* 48°12N 28°54E **81** B13
Pishin *Iran* 26°6N 61°47E **129** E9
Pishin *Pakistan* 30°35N 67°0E **124** D2
Pishin Lora → *Pakistan* 29°9N 64°5E **124** E1
Pisidia *Turkey* 37°30N 31°40E **104** D4
Pising *Indonesia* 5°8S 121°53E **119** F6
Pismo Beach *U.S.A.* 35°9N 120°38W **171** K6
Piso, L. *Liberia* 6°50N 11°15W **138** D2
Pisogne *Italy* 45°49N 10°10E **92** C7
Pissila *Burkina Faso* 13°7N 0°50W **138** C4
Pissis, Cerro *Argentina* 27°45S 68°48W **190** B3
Pissos *France* 44°19N 0°49W **72** D3
Pissouri *Cyprus* 34°40N 32°42E **101** E11
Pisticci *Italy* 40°23N 16°33E **95** B9
Pistóia *Italy* 43°55N 10°54E **92** E7
Pisuerga → *Spain* 41°33N 4°52W **88** D6
Pisz *Poland* 53°38N 21°49E **83** E8
Pit → *U.S.A.* 40°47N 122°6W **168** F2
Pita *Guinea* 11°5N 12°15W **138** C2
Pitangui *Brazil* 19°40S 44°54W **189** D2
Pitarpunga L.
Australia 34°24S 143°30E **152** C5
Pitcairn I. *Pac. Oc.* 25°5S 130°5W **157** K14
Pitch L. *Trin. & Tob.* 10°14N 61°39W **187** K15
Piteå *Sweden* 65°20N 21°25E **60** D19
Piteälven → *Sweden* 65°20N 21°25E **60** D19
Piterka *Russia* 50°41N 47°29E **86** G8
Pitești *Romania* 44°52N 24°54E **81** F9
Pithapuram *India* 17°10N 82°15E **126** F6
Pithara *Australia* 30°20S 116°35E **149** F2
Pithio *Greece* 41°24N 26°40E **97** E10
Pithiviers *France* 48°10N 2°13E **71** D9
Pithora *India* 21°6N 82°31E **126** D6
Pithoragarh *India* 29°35N 80°13E **125** E9
Pithoro *Pakistan* 25°31N 69°23E **124** G3
Pitigliano *Italy* 42°38N 11°40E **93** F8
Pitkyaranta *Russia* 61°34N 31°37E **84** B6
Pitlochry *U.K.* 56°42N 3°44W **65** E5
Pitrufquén *Chile* 38°59S 72°39W **192** A2
Pitsilia *Cyprus* 34°55N 33°0E **101** E12
Pitsunda = Bichvinta
Georgia 43°9N 40°21E **87** J5
Pitt I. *Canada* 53°30N 129°50W **162** C3
Pitti I. *India* 10°49N 72°39E **127** G2
Pittsburg *Calif., U.S.A.* 38°2N 121°53W **170** G5
Pittsburg *Kans., U.S.A.* 37°25N 94°42W **172** G6
Pittsburg *Tex., U.S.A.* 33°0N 94°59W **176** E6
Pittsburgh *U.S.A.* 40°26N 79°58W **174** F5
Pittsfield *Ill., U.S.A.* 39°36N 90°49W **172** F8
U.S.A. 44°47N 69°23W **173** C19
Pittsfield *Mass., U.S.A.* 42°27N 73°15W **175** D11
Pittsfield *N.H.,*
U.S.A. 43°18N 71°20W **175** C13
Pittston *U.S.A.* 41°19N 75°47W **175** E9
Pittsworth *Australia* 27°41S 151°37E **151** D5
Pituri → *Australia* 22°35S 138°30E **150** C2
Piumhi *Brazil* 20°28S 45°58W **189** D2
Piura *Peru* 5°15S 80°38W **188** B1
Piura □ *Peru* 5°15S 80°0W **188** B2
Piuthan *Nepal* 28°7N 82°56E **125** E10

Piva → *Montenegro* 43°20N 18°50E **96** C2
Piwniczna *Poland* 49°28N 20°42E **83** J7
Pixian *China* 30°48N 103°52E **116** B4
Pixley *U.S.A.* 35°58N 119°18W **170** K7
Pizhou = Pei Xian
China 34°44N 116°55E **114** G9
Pizhou *China* 34°18N 117°57E **115** G9
Pizzo *Italy* 38°44N 16°10E **95** D9
Placentia *Canada* 47°20N 54°0W **165** C9
Placentia B. *Canada* 47°0N 54°40W **165** C9
Placerville *U.S.A.* 38°44N 120°48W **170** G6
Placetas *Cuba* 22°15N 79°44W **182** B4
Plácido de Castro
Brazil 10°20S 67°11W **188** C4
Plačkovica *Macedonia* 41°45N 22°30E **96** E6
Plaine des Jarres *Laos* 19°27N 103°10E **120** C4
Plainfield *N.J., U.S.A.* 40°37N 74°25W **175** F10
Plainfield *Ohio, U.S.A.* 40°13N 81°43W **174** F3
Plainfield *Vt., U.S.A.* 44°17N 72°26W **175** B12
Plains *Ga., U.S.A.* 32°2N 84°24W **178** C5
Plains *Mont., U.S.A.* 47°28N 114°53W **168** C6
Plains *Tex., U.S.A.* 33°11N 102°50W **176** E3
Plainview *Nebr., U.S.A.* 42°21N 97°47W **172** D5
Plainview *Tex., U.S.A.* 34°11N 101°43W **176** D4
Plainwell *U.S.A.* 42°27N 85°38W **173** D11
Plaisance *France* 43°36N 0°3E **72** E4
Plaistow *U.S.A.* 42°50N 71°6W **175** D13
Plaka *Greece* 40°0N 25°24E **99** B7
Plaka, Akra *Greece* 35°11N 26°19E **101** D8
Plakenska Planina
Macedonia 41°14N 21°2E **96** E5
Planá *Czech Rep.* 49°50N 12°44E **78** B5
Plana Cays *Bahamas* 22°38N 73°30W **183** B5
Planada *U.S.A.* 37°16N 120°19W **170** H6
Planchón *Peru* 12°14S 69°11W **188** C4
Plancoët *France* 48°32N 2°13W **70** D4
Plandište *Serbia* 45°16N 21°10E **96** B6
Plano *U.S.A.* 33°1N 96°42W **176** E6
Plant City *U.S.A.* 28°1N 82°7W **179** G7
Plantation *U.S.A.* 26°7N 80°14W **179** J8
Plaquemine *U.S.A.* 30°17N 91°14W **176** F9
Plasencia *Spain* 40°3N 6°8W **88** E4
Plaški *Croatia* 45°4N 15°22E **93** C12
Plast *Russia* 54°22N 60°28E **106** D11
Plaster City *U.S.A.* 32°47N 115°51W **171** N11
Plaster Rock *Canada* 46°53N 67°22W **165** C6
Plastun *Russia* 44°45N 136°19E **112** B8
Plasy *Czech Rep.* 49°56N 13°24E **78** B6
Plata, Río de la →
S. Amer. 34°45S 57°30W **190** C4
Plátani → *Italy* 37°23N 13°16E **94** F6
Platanos *Greece* 35°28N 23°33E **101** D5
Plateau □ *Nigeria* 8°30N 9°0E **139** D6
Platja d'Aro *Spain* 41°49N 3°4E **90** D8
Plato *Colombia* 9°47N 74°47W **186** B3
Platte → *Mo., U.S.A.* 39°16N 94°50W **172** F6
Platte → *Nebr., U.S.A.* 41°4N 95°53W **172** E6
Platteville *U.S.A.* 42°44N 90°29W **172** D8
Plattling *Germany* 48°46N 12°53E **77** G8
Plattsburgh *U.S.A.* 44°42N 73°28W **175** B11
Plattsmouth *U.S.A.* 41°1N 95°53W **172** E6
Plauen *Germany* 50°30N 12°8E **76** E8
Plauer See *Germany* 53°28N 12°17E **76** B8
Plavinas *Latvia* 56°35N 25°46E **84** D3
Plavnica *Montenegro* 42°20N 19°13E **96** D3
Plavno *Croatia* 44°9N 16°10E **93** D13
Play Cu *Vietnam* 13°57N 108°0E **120** F7
Playa Blanca *Canary Is.* 28°51N 13°50W **100** F6
Playa de las Americas
Canary Is. 28°5N 16°43W **100** F3
Playa de Mogán
Canary Is. 27°48N 15°47W **100** G4
Playa del Carmen
Mexico 20°37N 87°4W **181** C7
Playa del Inglés
Canary Is. 27°45N 15°33W **100** G4
Playgreen L. *Canada* 54°0N 98°15W **163** C9
Pleasant Bay *Canada* 46°51N 60°48W **165** C7
Pleasant Hill *U.S.A.* 37°57N 122°4W **170** H4
Pleasant Mount *U.S.A.* 41°44N 75°26W **175** E9
Pleasanton *Calif.,*
U.S.A. 37°39N 121°52W **170** H5
Pleasanton *Tex., U.S.A.* 28°58N 98°29W **176** G5
Pleasantville *N.J.,*
U.S.A. 39°24N 74°32W **173** F11
Pleasantville *Pa.,*
U.S.A. 41°35N 79°34W **174** E5
Pléaux *France* 45°8N 2°13E **72** C6
Plei Ku *Vietnam* 13°57N 108°0E **120** F7
Plélan-le-Grand *France* 48°0N 2°7W **70** D4
Plenița *Romania* 44°14N 23°10E **81** F8
Plenty → *Australia* 23°25S 136°31E **150** C2
Plenty, B. of *N.Z.* 37°45S 177°0E **154** D6
Plentywood *U.S.A.* 48°47N 104°34W **168** B11
Plérin *France* 48°32N 2°46W **70** D4
Pleshcheyevo Ozero △
Russia 56°45N 38°50E **84** D10
Plessisville *Canada* 46°14N 71°47W **165** C5
Plestin-les-Grèves *France* 48°40N 3°39W **70** D3
Pleszew *Poland* 51°53N 17°47E **83** G4
Pleternica *Croatia* 45°17N 17°48E **80** E2
Plétipi, L. *Canada* 51°44N 70°6W **165** B5
Pleven *Bulgaria* 43°26N 24°37E **97** C8
Plevna *Canada* 44°58N 76°59W **174** B8
Plevna = Pleven *Bulgaria* 43°26N 24°37E **97** C8
Plitvice Lakes = Plitvička Jezera △
Croatia 44°54N 15°36E **93** D12
Plitvička Jezera △
Croatia 44°54N 15°36E **93** D12
Pljevlja *Montenegro* 43°21N 19°21E **96** C3
Ploaghe *Italy* 40°40N 8°45E **94** B1
Ploče *Croatia* 43°4N 17°26E **93** E14
Płock *Poland* 52°32N 19°40E **83** F6
Plöckenpass *Italy* 46°37N 12°57E **76** E7
Plöckenstein *Germany* 48°46N 13°51E **77** G9
Ploemeur *France* 47°55N 3°26W **70** E3
Ploërmel *France* 47°55N 2°26W **70** E4
Ploiești *Romania* 44°57N 26°5E **81** F10
Plomári *Greece* 38°58N 26°24E **99** C9
Plomb du Cantal *France* 45°2N 2°48E **72** C6
Plombières-les-Bains
France 47°58N 6°27E **71** E13
Plomin *Croatia* 45°8N 14°10E **93** C11
Plonge, Lac la *Canada* 55°8N 107°20W **163** B7
Płońsk *Poland* 52°37N 20°21E **83** F7
Płopeni *Romania* 45°4N 25°59E **81** E10
Plopșoru *Romania* 44°54N 23°18E **81** F8
Plopșului, Munții
Romania 47°5N 22°30E **80** C7

Ploty *Poland* 53°48N 15°18E **82** E2
Plouaret *France* 48°37N 3°28W **70** D3
Plouay *France* 47°55N 3°21W **70** E3
Ploučnice → *Czech Rep.* 50°46N 14°13E **78** A7
Ploudalmézeau *France* 48°34N 4°41W **70** D2
Plouescat *France* 48°39N 4°10W **70** D2
Plougasnou *France* 48°42N 3°49W **70** D3
Plougastel-Daoulas
France 48°22N 4°17W **70** D2
Plouguerneau *France* 48°36N 4°30W **70** D2
Plouha *France* 48°41N 2°57W **70** D4
Plouhinec *France* 48°0N 4°29W **70** E2
Plovdiv *Bulgaria* 42°8N 24°44E **97** D8
Plovdiv □ *Bulgaria* 42°15N 24°30E **97** D8
Plover Cove Res. *China* 22°28N 114°15E **111** a
Plum *U.S.A.* 40°29N 79°47W **174** F5
Plum I. *U.S.A.* 41°11N 72°12W **175** E12
Plumas *U.S.A.* 39°45N 120°4W **170** F6
Plummer *U.S.A.* 47°20N 116°53W **168** C5
Plumridge Lakes
Australia 29°26S 125°16E **149** E4
Plumtree *Zimbabwe* 20°27S 27°55E **143** G2
Plungė *Lithuania* 55°53N 21°59E **82** C8
Plužine *Montenegro* 43°8N 18°51E **96** C2
Plymouth *Trin. & Tob.* 11°14N 60°48W **187** J16
Plymouth *U.K.* 50°22N 4°10W **67** G3
Plymouth *Calif.,*
U.S.A. 38°29N 120°51W **170** G6
Plymouth *Ind., U.S.A.* 41°21N 86°19W **172** E10
Plymouth *Mass.,*
U.S.A. 41°57N 70°40W **175** E14
Plymouth *N.C.,*
U.S.A. 35°52N 76°43W **177** D16
Plymouth *N.H.,*
U.S.A. 43°46N 71°41W **175** C13
Plymouth *Pa., U.S.A.* 41°14N 75°57W **175** E9
Plymouth *Wis.,*
U.S.A. 43°45N 87°59W **172** D10
Plympton-Wyoming = Wyoming
Canada 42°57N 82°7W **174** D2
Plynlimon = Pumlumon Fawr
U.K. 52°28N 3°46W **67** E4
Plyusa *Russia* 58°28N 29°27E **84** C5
Plyusa → *Russia* 58°40N 29°20E **84** C5
Plzeň *Czech Rep.* 49°45N 13°22E **78** B6
Plzeňský □ *Czech Rep.* 49°35N 13°0E **78** B6
Pmere Nyente ☉
Australia 24°15S 136°10E **150** C2
Pniewy *Poland* 52°31N 16°16E **83** F3
Pô *Burkina Faso* 11°14N 1°5W **139** C4
Po → *Italy* 44°57N 12°4E **93** C9
Po, Delta del *Italy* 44°55N 12°30E **93** C9
Pô △ *Burkina Faso* 11°25N 1°5W **139** C4
Po Hai = Bo Hai *China* 39°0N 119°0E **115** E10
Po Toi *China* 22°10N 114°16E **111** a
Pobé *Benin* 7°0N 2°56E **139** D5
Pobé *Burkina Faso* 13°53N 1°42W **139** C4
Pobeda *Russia* 65°12N 146°12E **107** C15
Pobedy, Pik *Asia* 42°0N 79°58E **109** C9
Pobiedziska *Poland* 52°29N 17°11E **83** F4
Pobladura del Valle *Spain* 42°6N 5°44W **88** C5
Poblet, Monasterio de
Spain 41°22N 1°4E **90** D6
Pobra de Trives *Spain* 42°20N 7°10W **88** C3
Pocahontas *Ark.,*
U.S.A. 36°16N 90°58W **177** C9
Pocahontas *Iowa,*
U.S.A. 42°44N 94°40W **172** D6
Pocatello *U.S.A.* 42°52N 112°27W **168** E7
Počátky *Czech Rep.* 49°15N 15°14E **78** B8
Pochep *Russia* 52°58N 33°29E **84** E7
Pochinki *Russia* 54°41N 44°59E **86** C7
Pochinok *Russia* 54°28N 32°29E **84** E7
Pöchlarn *Austria* 48°12N 15°12E **78** C8
Pocinhos *Brazil* 7°4S 36°3W **189** B3
Pocking *Germany* 48°24N 13°19E **77** G8
Poções *Brazil* 14°31S 40°21W **189** D2
Pocomoke City *U.S.A.* 38°5N 75°34W **173** F16
Poços de Caldas *Brazil* 21°50S 46°33W **191** A6
Poddębice *Poland* 51°54N 18°58E **83** G5
Podbořany *Czech Rep.* 50°9N 13°18E **78** A6
Poddębice *Poland* 51°54N 18°58E **83** G5
Poddorie *Russia* 57°30N 31°8E **84** D6
Podensac *France* 44°40N 0°22W **72** D3
Podenzano *Italy* 44°57N 9°41E **92** D6
Podgorač *Croatia* 45°27N 18°24E **80** E3
Podgorica *Montenegro* 42°30N 19°19E **96** D3
Podgorie *Albania* 40°36N 20°49E **96** F4
Podile *India* 15°37N 79°37E **127** G4
Podlaskie □ *Poland* 53°0N 23°0E **83** E10
Podilska Vysočina
Ukraine 49°0N 28°0E **81** B13
Podkarpackie □ *Poland* 50°0N 22°0E **83** H9
Podkova *Bulgaria* 41°24N 25°24E **97** E9
Podlapača *Croatia* 44°37N 15°47E **93** D12
Podlaskie □ *Poland* 53°30N 23°0E **83** E10
Podoleni *Romania* 46°46N 26°39E **81** C11
Podolínec *Romania* 49°16N 20°31E **83** J7
Podolsk *Russia* 55°25N 37°30E **84** D9
Podor *Senegal* 16°40N 15°2W **138** B1
Podporozhye *Russia* 60°55N 34°2E **84** B8
Podravska Slatina *Croatia* 45°42N 17°45E **80** E2
Podu Iloaiei *Romania* 47°13N 27°16E **81** C12
Podu Turcului *Romania* 46°11N 27°25E **81** C12
Podujevo = Besianë
Kosovo 42°54N 21°10E **96** D6
Podyjí △ *Czech Rep.* 48°51N 15°57E **78** D5
Poel *Germany* 54°0N 11°25E **76** A7
Pofadder *S. Africa* 29°10S 19°22E **144** C2
Poggiardo *Italy* 40°3N 18°21E **95** B11
Poggibonsi *Italy* 43°28N 11°9E **92** E8
Pöggio Mirteto *Italy* 42°16N 12°41E **93** F9
Pogoanele *Romania* 44°55N 27°0E **81** F11
Pogorzela *Poland* 51°50N 17°12E **83** G4
Pogradec *Albania* 40°57N 20°37E **96** F4
Pogranichnyy *Russia* 44°25N 131°24E **112** B5
Poh *Indonesia* 0°46S 122°51E **119** E6
Pohang *S. Korea* 36°1N 129°23E **115** F15
Pohjanmaa □ *Finland* 62°58N 22°50E **60** E20
Pohnpei *Micronesia* 6°55N 158°10E **156** G7
Pohorelá *Slovak Rep.* 48°50N 20°2E **83** J6
Pohořelice *Czech Rep.* 48°59N 16°31E **79** C9
Pohorje *Slovenia* 46°30N 15°0E **78** E8
Poiana Mare *Romania* 43°57N 23°5E **81** G8
Poiana Ruscăi, Munții
Romania 45°45N 22°25E **80** E7
Poiana Stampei *Romania* 47°19N 25°8E **81** C10
Poinsett, C. *Antarctica* 65°42N 113°18W **55** C8
Point Arena *U.S.A.* 38°55N 123°41W **170** G3
Point Baker *U.S.A.* 56°21N 133°37W **162** B2
Point Calimere *India* 10°11N 79°49E **127** G4
Point Fortin
Trin. & Tob. 10°10N 61°42W **187** K15

Point Hope *U.S.A.* 68°21N 166°47W **166** B6
Point L. *Canada* 65°15N 113°4W **160** D9
Point Lisas
Trin. & Tob. 10°24N 61°29W **187** K15
Point Pedro *Sri Lanka* 9°50N 80°15E **127** K5
Point Pelee △ *Canada* 41°57N 82°31W **174** E2
Point Pleasant *N.J.,*
U.S.A. 40°5N 74°4W **175** F10
Point Pleasant *W. Va.,*
U.S.A. 38°51N 82°8W **173** F12
Point Reyes *U.S.A.* 38°10N 122°55W **170** G2
Pointe-à-Pitre
Guadeloupe 16°15N 61°32W **182** b
Pointe-Claire *Canada* 45°26N 73°50W **175** A11
Pointe-Gatineau
Canada 45°27N 75°41W **175** A9
Pointe-Noire *Congo* 4°48S 11°53E **140** E2
Pointe-Noire *Guadeloupe* 16°14N 61°47W **182** b
Poio = O Convento *Spain* 38°41W **88** C2
Poipet *Cambodia* 13°39N 102°33E **120** F4
Poirino *Italy* 44°56N 7°48E **92** D4
Poisonbush Ra.
Australia 22°30S 121°30E **148** D3
Poissonnier Pt.
Australia 19°57S 119°10E **148** C2
Poitiers *France* 46°35N 0°20E **70** F7
Poitou *France* 46°40N 0°10W **72** B3
Poitou-Charentes □
France 46°10N 0°15E **72** B4
Poix-de-Picardie *France* 49°47N 1°58E **71** C8
Poix-Terron *France* 49°38N 4°38E **71** C11
Pojoaque *U.S.A.* 35°54N 106°1W **169** J10
Pokaran *India* 27°0N 71°50E **124** F4
Pokataroo *Australia* 29°30S 148°36E **151** D4
Pokhara *Nepal* 28°14N 83°58E **125** E10
Pokhvistnevo *Russia* 53°36N 52°0E **86** D9
Poko
Dem. Rep. of the Congo 3°7N 26°52E **142** B2
Pokrov *Russia* 55°55N 39°7E **84** E10
Pokrovka = Kyzyl-Suu
Kyrgyzstan 42°20N 78°0E **109** C9
Pokrovsk *Russia* 61°29N 129°0E **107** C13
Pokrovskoye *Russia* 47°25N 38°54E **85** J10
Pol-e Dokhtar *Iran* 33°9N 47°42E **105** C12
Pol-e Zahāb *Iran* 34°27N 45°51E **105** C11
Pola = Pula *Croatia* 44°54N 13°57E **93** D10
Pola *Russia* 57°55N 32°0E **84** D7
Pol'ana *Slovak Rep.* 48°38N 19°29E **79** C12
Poland *Europe* 52°0N 20°0E **83** G8
Pola de Allande *Spain* 43°16N 6°37W **88** B4
Pola de Lena *Spain* 43°10N 5°49W **88** B5
Pola de Siero *Spain* 43°24N 5°39W **88** B5
Pola de Somiedo *Spain* 43°5N 6°15W **88** B4
Polacca *U.S.A.* 35°50N 110°23W **169** J8
Polan *Iran* 25°30N 61°10E **129** E9
Pol'ana *Slovak Rep.* 48°38N 19°29E **79** C12
Poland ■ *Europe* 52°0N 20°0E **83** G8
Polanica-Zdrój *Poland* 50°26N 16°37W **83** H3
Polaniec *Poland* 50°26N 21°17E **83** H8
Polar Bear △ *Canada* 55°0N 83°45W **164** A2
Polatlı *Turkey* 39°36N 32°9E **104** C5
Polatsk *Belarus* 55°30N 28°50E **84** E5
Polavaram *India* 17°15N 81°38E **126** F5
Polcura *Chile* 37°17S 71°43W **190** D2
Połczyn-Zdrój *Poland* 53°47N 16°5E **82** E2
Poldasht *Iran* 39°20N 45°4E **105** C11
Poleski △ *Poland* 51°29N 23°5E **83** G10
Polessk *Russia* 54°50N 21°8E **82** D8
Polesye = Pripet Marshes
Europe 52°10N 27°10E **75** B15
Polgár *Hungary* 47°54N 21°6E **80** D6
Poli *Cameroon* 8°34N 13°15E **139** D7
Policastro, G. di *Italy* 40°0N 15°35E **95** C8
Police *Poland* 53°33N 14°33E **82** E1
Police, Pte. *Seychelles* 4°51S 55°32E **141** b
Polichnitos *Greece* 39°6N 26°10E **99** B9
Polička *Czech Rep.* 49°43N 16°15E **79** B9
Policoro *Italy* 40°13N 16°41E **95** B9
Poliegos *Greece* 36°45N 24°38E **99** E6
Poligiros *Greece* 40°23N 23°25E **96** D6
Polignano a Mare *Italy* 41°0N 17°13E **95** A10
Poligny *France* 46°50N 5°42E **71** F12
Polillo Is. *Phil.* 14°56N 122°0E **119** B6
Polis *Cyprus* 35°2N 32°26E **101** D11
Polistena *Italy* 38°24N 16°4E **95** D9
Polk *U.S.A.* 41°22N 79°56W **174** E5
Polkowice *Poland* 51°29N 16°3E **83** G3
Polla *Italy* 40°31N 15°28E **95** B8
Pollachi *India* 10°35N 77°0E **127** J3
Pollença *Spain* 39°54N 3°1E **90** B10
Pollensa, B. de *Spain* 39°53N 3°8E **90** B10
Póllica *Italy* 40°13N 15°0E **95** B8
Pollino, Mte. *Italy* 40°0N 16°12E **95** C9
Pollino △ *Italy* 40°0N 16°13E **95** C9
Polna *Russia* 58°31N 28°5E **84** C5
Polnovat *Russia* 63°50N 65°54E **106** C7
Pology □ *Ukraine* 47°29N 36°15E **85** J8
Polokwane *S. Africa* 23°54S 29°25E **145** B4
Polokwane → *S. Africa* 22°25S 30°5E **145** B5
Polonne *Ukraine* 50°6N 27°30E **75** C14
Polonnaruwa *Sri Lanka* 7°56N 81°0E **127** L5
Polonnoye = Polonne
Ukraine 50°6N 27°30E **75** C14
Polski Trümbesh
Bulgaria 43°20N 25°38E **97** C9
Polsko Kosovo *Bulgaria* 43°23N 25°38E **97** C9
Polson *U.S.A.* 47°41N 114°9W **168** C6
Poltár *Slovak Rep.* 48°26N 19°48E **79** C12
Poltava □ *Ukraine* 49°35N 34°35E **85** H8
Poltava □ *Ukraine* 50°15N 33°31E **85** H8
Põltsamaa *Estonia* 58°39N 25°58E **84** C3
Põltsamaa → *Estonia* 58°41N 26°58E **84** C4
Polunochnoye *Russia* 60°52N 60°25E **106** C7
Põlva *Estonia* 58°3N 27°3E **84** C4
Polyana *Ukraine* 48°41N 22°58E **80** B7
Polyarny Zori *Russia* 67°22N 32°30E **60** C25
Polyarnyye Zori *Russia* 67°22N 32°30E **60** C25
Polynésie française = French
Polynesia ☐ *Pac. Oc.* 20°0S 145°0W **157** J13
Pomabamba *Peru* 8°50S 77°28W **188** B2
Pomarance *Italy* 43°18N 10°52E **92** E7
Pomarico *Italy* 40°31N 16°33E **95** B9
Pombal *Brazil* 6°45S 37°50W **189** B3
Pombal *Portugal* 39°55N 8°40W **88** F2
Pomene *Mozam.* 22°53S 35°33E **145** B6
Pomeroy *Ohio, U.S.A.* 39°2N 82°2W **173** F12
Pomeroy *Wash.,*
U.S.A. 46°28N 117°36W **168** C5

Pomézia *Italy* 41°40N 12°30E **94** A5
Pomichna *Ukraine* 48°13N 31°36E **85** H6
Pomona *Australia* 26°22S 152°52E **151** D5
Pomona *U.S.A.* 34°4N 117°45W **171** L9
Pomona Park *U.S.A.* 29°30N 81°36W **179** F8
Pomorie *Bulgaria* 42°32N 27°41E **97** D11
Pomorskie □ *Poland* 53°40N 18°0E **82** D5
Pomorskie, Pojezierze *Poland* 53°40N 16°37E **82** E3
Pomos *Cyprus* 35°9N 32°33E **101** D11
Pomos, C. *Cyprus* 35°10N 32°33E **101** D11
Pompano Beach *U.S.A.* 26°14N 80°7W **179** J9
Pompei *Italy* 40°45N 14°30E **95** B7
Pompey *France* 48°46N 6°6E **71** D13
Pompeys Pillar *U.S.A.* 45°59N 107°57W **168** D10
Pompeys Pillar △ *U.S.A.* 46°0N 108°0W **168** D10
Pompton Lakes *U.S.A.* 41°0N 74°17W **175** F10
Ponape = Pohnpei *Micronesia* 6°55N 158°10E **156** G7
Ponask L. *Canada* 54°0N 92°41W **164** B1
Ponca *U.S.A.* 42°34N 96°43W **172** D5
Ponca City *U.S.A.* 36°42N 97°5W **176** C6
Ponce *Puerto Rico* 18°1N 66°37W **183** d
Ponce de Leon *U.S.A.* 30°44N 85°56W **178** E4
Ponce de Leon B. *U.S.A.* 25°15N 81°10W **179** K8
Ponchatoula *U.S.A.* 30°26N 90°26W **177** F9
Poncheville, L. *Canada* 50°10N 76°55W **164** B4
Pond *U.S.A.* 35°43N 119°20W **171** K7
Pond Inlet *Canada* 72°40N 77°0W **161** C16
Pondicherry = Puducherry *India* 11°59N 79°50E **127** J4
Ponds, I. of *Canada* 53°27N 55°52W **165** B8
Ponferrada *Spain* 42°32N 6°35W **88** C4
Poniatowa *Poland* 51°11N 22°3E **83** G9
Poniec *Poland* 51°48N 16°50E **83** G3
Ponikva *Slovenia* 46°16N 15°26E **93** B12
Ponnaiyar → *India* 11°50N 79°45E **127** J4
Ponnani *India* 10°45N 75°59E **127** J2
Ponneri *India* 13°20N 80°15E **127** H5
Ponnuru *India* 16°5N 80°34E **127** M3
Ponoka *Canada* 52°42N 113°40W **162** C6
Ponorogo *Indonesia* 7°52S 111°27E **119** G14
Pons = Ponts *Spain* 41°55N 1°12E **90** D6
Pons *France* 45°35N 0°34W **72** C3
Ponsul → *Portugal* 39°40N 7°31W **88** F3
Pont-à-Mousson *France* 48°54N 6°1E **71** D13
Pont-Audemer *France* 49°21N 0°30E **70** C7
Pont-Aven *France* 47°51N 3°47W **70** E3
Pont Canavese *Italy* 45°25N 7°36E **92** C4
Pont-d'Ain *France* 46°3N 5°21E **71** F12
Pont-de-Roide *France* 47°23N 6°45E **71** E13
Pont-de-Salars *France* 44°18N 2°44E **72** D6
Pont-de-Vaux *France* 46°26N 4°56E **71** F11
Pont-de-Veyle *France* 46°17N 4°53E **71** F11
Pont-du-Château *France* 45°47N 3°15E **71** G10
Pont du Gard *France* 43°57N 4°32E **73** E8
Pont-l'Abbé *France* 47°52N 4°15W **70** E2
Pont-l'Évêque *France* 49°18N 0°11E **70** C7
Pont-St-Esprit *France* 44°16N 4°40E **73** D8
Pont-St-Martin *Italy* 45°36N 7°48E **92** C4
Pont-Ste-Maxence *France* 49°18N 2°36E **71** C9
Pont-sur-Yonne *France* 48°18N 3°10E **71** D10
Ponta Delgada *Azores* 37°44N 25°40W **134** a
Ponta do Sol *Madeira* 32°42N 17°7W **100** D2
Ponta Grossa *Brazil* 25°7S 50°10W **191** B5
Ponta Porã *Brazil* 22°20S 55°35W **191** A4
Pontacq *France* 43°11N 0°8W **72** E3
Pontailler-sur-Saône *France* 47°13N 5°25E **71** E12
Pontal → *Brazil* 9°8S 40°12W **189** B2
Pontardawe *U.K.* 51°43N 3°51W **67** F3
Pontarlier *France* 46°54N 6°20E **71** F13
Pontassieve *Italy* 43°46N 11°26E **93** E8
Pontaumur *France* 45°52N 2°40E **72** C6
Pontcharra *France* 45°26N 6°1E **73** C10
Pontchartrain, L. *U.S.A.* 30°5N 90°5W **177** F9
Pontchâteau *France* 47°25N 2°5W **70** E4
Ponte Alta, Serra do *Brazil* 19°42S 47°40W **189** D1
Ponte Alta do Norte *Brazil* 10°45S 47°34W **189** C1
Ponte da Barca *Portugal* 41°48N 8°25W **88** D2
Ponte de Lima *Portugal* 41°46N 8°35W **88** D2
Ponte de Sor *Portugal* 39°17N 8°1W **89** F2
Ponte dell'Ólio *Italy* 44°52N 9°39E **92** D6
Ponte di Legno *Italy* 46°16N 10°31E **92** B7
Ponte do Pungué *Mozam.* 19°30S 34°33E **143** F3
Ponte-Leccia *France* 42°28N 9°13E **73** F13
Ponte nelle Alpi *Italy* 46°11N 12°16E **93** B9
Ponte Nova *Brazil* 20°25S 42°54W **189** E2
Ponte Vedra Beach *U.S.A.* 30°15N 81°23W **178** E8
Ponteareas *Spain* 42°11N 8°28W **88** C2
Pontebba *Italy* 46°30N 13°18E **93** B10
Ponteceso *Spain* 43°15N 8°54W **88** B2
Pontecorvo *Italy* 41°27N 13°40E **94** A6
Pontedeume *Spain* 43°24N 8°10W **88** B2
Ponteix *Canada* 49°46N 107°29W **163** D7
Pontevedra *Spain* 42°26N 8°40W **88** C2
Pontevedra □ *Spain* 42°25N 8°39W **88** C2
Pontevedra, R. de → *Spain* 42°22N 8°45W **88** C2
Pontevico *Italy* 45°16N 10°5E **92** C7
Pontiac *Ill., U.S.A.* 40°53N 88°38W **172** E9
Pontiac *Mich., U.S.A.* 42°38N 83°18W **173** D12
Pontian Kechil *Malaysia* 1°29N 103°23E **121** d
Pontianak *Indonesia* 0°3S 109°15E **118** E3
Pontine Is. = Ponziane, Ísole *Italy* 40°55N 12°57E **94** B5
Pontine Mts. = Kuzey Anadolu Dağları *Turkey* 41°0N 36°45E **104** B7
Pontínia *Italy* 41°25N 13°2E **94** A6
Pontoise *France* 48°5N 2°58W **70** D4
Ponton → *Canada* 58°27N 116°11W **162** B5
Pontorson *France* 48°34N 1°30W **70** D5
Pontrémoli *Italy* 44°22N 9°52E **92** D6
Pontrieux *France* 48°42N 3°10W **70** D3
Ponts *Spain* 41°55N 1°12E **90** D6
Pontypool *Canada* 44°6N 78°38W **174** B6
Pontypool *U.K.* 51°42N 3°2W **67** F4
Pontypridd *U.K.* 51°36N 3°20W **67** F4
Ponza *Italy* 40°54N 12°57E **94** B5
Ponziane, Ísole *Italy* 40°55N 12°57E **94** B5
Poochera *Australia* 32°43S 134°51E **151** E1
Poole *U.K.* 50°43N 1°59W **67** G6
Poole □ *U.K.* 50°43N 1°59W **67** G6
Pooler *U.S.A.* 32°7N 81°15W **178** C8

Poona = Pune *India* 18°29N 73°57E **126** E1
Poonamallee *India* 13°3N 80°10E **127** H5
Pooncarie *Australia* 33°22S 142°31E **152** B5
Poopelloe L. *Australia* 31°40S 144°0E **152** A6
Poopó *Bolivia* 18°23S 66°59W **188** D4
Poopó, L. de *Bolivia* 18°30S 67°35W **188** D4
Poor Knights Is. *N.Z.* 35°29S 174°43E **154** B3
Popayán *Colombia* 2°27N 76°36W **186** C3
Poperinge *Belgium* 50°51N 2°42E **69** D2
Popiltah L. *Australia* 33°10S 141°42E **152** B4
Popina *Bulgaria* 44°7N 26°57E **97** B10
Popio L. *Australia* 33°10S 141°52E **152** B4
Poplar *U.S.A.* 48°7N 105°12W **168** B11
Poplar → *Canada* 53°0N 97°19W **163** C9
Poplar Bluff *U.S.A.* 36°46N 90°24W **172** G8
Poplarville *U.S.A.* 30°51N 89°32W **177** F10
Popocatépetl, Volcán *Mexico* 19°2N 98°38W **181** D5
Popokabaka *Dem. Rep. of the Congo* 5°41S 16°40E **140** F3
Pópoli *Italy* 42°10N 13°50E **93** F10
Popovača *Croatia* 45°30N 16°41E **93** C13
Popovo *Bulgaria* 43°21N 26°18E **97** C10
Poppberg *Germany* 49°26N 11°37E **77** F7
Poppi *Italy* 43°43N 11°46E **93** E8
Poprad *Slovak Rep.* 49°3N 20°18E **79** B13
Poprad → *Slovak Rep.* 49°38N 20°42E **79** B13
Porali → *Pakistan* 25°58N 66°26E **124** G2
Porangahau *N.Z.* 40°17S 176°37E **154** G5
Porangatu *Brazil* 8°48S 70°36W **188** B3
Porbandar *India* 21°44N 69°43E **124** J3
Porcher I. *Canada* 53°50N 130°30W **162** C2
Porcos → *Brazil* 12°42S 45°7W **189** C1
Porcuna *Spain* 37°52N 4°11W **89** H6
Porcupine → *Canada* 59°11N 104°46W **163** B8
Porcupine → *U.S.A.* 66°34N 145°19W **160** D2
Porcupine Abyssal Plain *Atl. Oc.* 48°0N 8°0W **56** B10
Porcupine Gorge △ *Australia* 20°22S 144°26E **150** C3
Pordenone *Italy* 45°57N 12°39E **93** C9
Pordim *Bulgaria* 43°23N 24°51E **97** C8
Poreč *Croatia* 45°14N 13°36E **93** C10
Poretskoye *Russia* 55°9N 46°21E **86** C8
Pori *Finland* 61°29N 21°48E **84** B1
Pori *Greece* 35°58N 23°13E **98** F5
Porkhov *Russia* 57°45N 29°38E **84** D5
Porlamar *Venezuela* 10°57N 63°51W **186** A6
Porlezza *Italy* 46°2N 9°7E **92** B6
Porma → *Spain* 42°49N 5°28W **88** C5
Pornic *France* 47°7N 2°5W **70** E4
Poronaysk *Russia* 49°13N 143°0E **111** B17
Poroszló *Hungary* 47°39N 20°40E **80** C5
Poroto Mts. *Tanzania* 9°0S 33°30E **143** D3
Porpoise B. *Antarctica* 66°0S 127°0E **5** C9
Porquerolles, Î. de *France* 43°0N 6°13E **73** F10
Porrentruy *Switz.* 47°25N 7°6E **71** H3
Porreres *Spain* 39°31N 3°2E **100** B10
Porsangerfjorden *Norway* 70°40N 25°40E **60** A21
Porsgrunn *Norway* 59°10N 9°40E **61** G13
Port Adelaide *Australia* 34°50S 138°30E **152** C3
Port Alberni *Canada* 49°14N 124°50W **162** D4
Port Albert *Australia* 38°42S 146°42E **153** E7
Port Alfred *S. Africa* 33°36S 26°55E **144** D4
Port Alice *Canada* 50°20N 127°25W **162** C3
Port Allegany *U.S.A.* 41°48N 78°17W **174** E6
Port Allen *U.S.A.* 30°27N 91°12W **176** F9
Port Alma *Australia* 23°38S 150°53E **150** C5
Port Alma *Canada* 42°10N 82°14W **174** D2
Port Angeles *U.S.A.* 48°7N 123°27W **170** B3
Port Antonio *Jamaica* 18°10N 76°26W **182** a
Port Aransas *U.S.A.* 27°50N 97°4W **176** M6
Port Arthur *Australia* 43°7S 147°50E **151** G4
Port Arthur *U.S.A.* 29°54N 93°56W **176** G8
Port au Choix *Canada* 50°43N 57°22W **165** B8
Port au Port B. *Canada* 48°40N 58°50W **165** C8
Port-au-Prince *Haiti* 18°40N 72°20W **183** C5
Port Augusta *Australia* 32°30S 137°50E **152** B2
Port Austin *U.S.A.* 44°3N 83°1W **174** B2
Port-aux-Français *Kerguelen* 49°21S 70°13E **146** J6
Port Blair *India* 11°40N 92°12E **127** J11
Port Blandford *Canada* 48°20N 54°10W **165** C9
Port-Bouët *Ivory C.* 5°16N 3°57W **138** D4
Port Bradshaw *Australia* 12°30S 137°20E **150** A2
Port Broughton *Australia* 33°37S 137°56E **152** B2
Port Bruce *Canada* 42°39N 81°0W **174** D4
Port Burwell *Canada* 42°40N 80°48W **174** D4
Port Campbell *Australia* 38°37S 143°1E **152** E5
Port Campbell *India* 11°56N 92°37E **127** J11
Port Campbell △ *Australia* 38°8S 143°6E **152** E5
Port Canning *India* 22°23N 88°40E **125** H13
Port Carling *Canada* 45°7N 79°35W **174** A5
Port-Cartier *Canada* 50°2N 66°50W **165** B6
Port Chalmers *N.Z.* 45°49S 170°30E **155** F5
Port Charles *N.Z.* 36°33S 175°30E **154** C4
Port Charlotte *U.S.A.* 26°59N 82°6W **179** J7
Port Chester *U.S.A.* 41°0N 73°40W **175** F11
Port Clements *Canada* 53°40N 132°10W **162** C2
Port Clinton *U.S.A.* 41°31N 82°56W **173** E12
Port Colborne *Canada* 42°50N 79°10W **174** D5
Port Coquitlam *Canada* 49°15N 122°45W **170** A4
Port Cornwallis *India* 13°17N 93°5E **127** H11
Port Credit *Canada* 43°33N 79°35W **174** C5
Port Curtis △ *France* 43°0N 6°24E **73** F10
Port d'Alcúdia *Spain* 39°50N 3°7E **100** B10
Port Dalhousie *Canada* 43°13N 79°16W **174** C5
Port d'Andratx *Spain* 39°32N 2°23E **100** B9
Port Darwin *Australia* 12°24S 130°45E **148** B5
Port Darwin *Falk. Is.* 51°50S 59°0W **192** D5
Port Davey *Australia* 43°16S 145°55E **151** G4
Port-de-Bouc *France* 43°24N 4°59E **73** E8
Port-de-Paix *Haiti* 19°50N 72°50W **183** C5
Port Dickson *Malaysia* 2°30N 101°49E **121** L3
Port Douglas *Canada* 42°41N 80°12W **174** D4
Port Dover *Canada* 42°47N 80°12W **174** D4
Port Edward *Canada* 54°12N 130°10W **162** C2
Port Elgin *Canada* 44°25N 81°25W **174** B3

Port Elizabeth *S. Africa* 33°58S 25°40E **144** E4
Port Ellen *U.K.* 55°38N 6°11W **65** F2
Port Elliot *Australia* 35°32S 138°41E **152** C3
Port-en-Bessin-Huppain *France* 49°21N 0°45W **70** C6
Port Erin *I. of Man* 54°5N 4°45W **66** C3
Port Essington *Australia* 11°15S 132°10E **148** B5
Port Ewen *U.S.A.* 41°54N 73°59W **175** E11
Port Fairy *Australia* 38°22S 142°12E **152** E5
Port Fitzroy *N.Z.* 36°8S 175°20E **154** C4
Port Fouâd = Bûr Fuad *Egypt* 31°15N 32°20E **137** E8
Port Gamble *U.S.A.* 47°51N 122°34W **170** C4
Port-Gentil *Gabon* 0°40S 8°50E **140** E1
Port Ghalib *Egypt* 25°20N 34°58E **128** C2
Port Gibson *U.S.A.* 31°58N 90°59W **176** F9
Port Glasgow *U.K.* 55°56N 4°41W **65** F4
Port Harcourt *Nigeria* 4°40N 7°10E **139** E6
Port Hardy *Canada* 50°41N 127°30W **162** C3
Port Harrison = Inukjuak *Canada* 58°25N 78°15W **161** F16
Port Hawkesbury *Canada* 45°36N 61°22W **165** C7
Port Hedland *Australia* 20°25S 118°35E **148** D2
Port Henry *U.S.A.* 44°3N 73°28W **175** B11
Port Hood *Canada* 46°0N 61°32W **165** C7
Port Hope *Canada* 43°56N 78°20W **174** C6
Port Hope *U.S.A.* 43°57N 82°43W **174** C2
Port Hope Simpson *Canada* 52°33N 56°18W **165** B8
Port Hueneme *U.S.A.* 34°7N 119°12W **171** L7
Port Huron *U.S.A.* 42°58N 82°26W **174** D2
Port Iliç = Liman *Azerbaijan* 38°53N 48°47E **105** C13
Port Jefferson *U.S.A.* 40°57N 73°3W **175** F11
Port Jervis *U.S.A.* 41°22N 74°41W **175** E10
Port Kembla *Australia* 34°52S 150°49E **153** C9
Port Kenny *Australia* 33°10S 134°41E **151** E1
Port Klang *Malaysia* 3°0N 101°23E **121** L3
Port-la-Nouvelle *France* 43°1N 3°3E **72** E7
Port Láirge = Waterford *Ireland* 52°15N 7°8W **64** D4
Port Lavaca *U.S.A.* 28°37N 96°38W **176** G6
Port Leyden *U.S.A.* 43°35N 75°21W **175** C9
Port Lincoln *Australia* 34°42S 135°52E **152** C1
Port Loko *S. Leone* 8°48N 12°46W **138** D2
Port Louis *France* 47°42N 3°22W **70** E3
Port-Louis *Guadeloupe* 16°28N 61°32W **182** b
Port Louis *Mauritius* 20°10S 57°30E **141** d
Port MacDonnell *Australia* 38°5S 140°48E **152** C4
Port McNeill *Canada* 50°35N 127°6W **162** C3
Port Macquarie *Australia* 31°25S 152°25E **153** A10
Port Maria *Jamaica* 18°22N 76°54W **182** a
Port Mathurin *Rodrigues* 19°41S 63°22E **146** F5
Port Matilda *U.S.A.* 40°48N 78°3W **174** F6
Port Mayaca *U.S.A.* 26°59N 80°36W **179** J9
Port McNicoll *Canada* 44°44N 79°48W **174** B5
Port Mellon *Canada* 49°32N 123°31W **162** D4
Port-Menier *Canada* 49°51N 64°15W **165** C7
Port Moody *Canada* 49°17N 122°51W **170** A4
Port Morant *Jamaica* 17°54N 76°19W **182** a
Port Moresby *Papua N. G.* 9°24S 147°8E **147** B7
Port Muhammed Bin Qasim = Port Qasim *Pakistan* 24°46N 67°20E **124** G2
Port Musgrave *Australia* 11°55S 141°50E **150** A3
Port-Navalo *France* 47°34N 2°54W **70** E4
Port Neches *U.S.A.* 30°0N 93°59W **176** G8
Port Nicholson *N.Z.* 41°20S 174°52E **154** H3
Port Nolloth *S. Africa* 29°17S 16°52E **144** C2
Port Nouveau-Québec = Kangiqsualujjuaq *Canada* 58°30N 65°59W **161** F18
Port of Climax *Canada* 49°10N 108°20W **163** D7
Port of Coronach *Canada* 49°7N 105°31W **163** D7
Port of Spain *Trin. & Tob.* 10°40N 61°31W **183** D7
Port Orange *U.S.A.* 29°9N 80°59W **179** F9
Port Orchard *U.S.A.* 47°32N 122°38W **170** C4
Port Orford *U.S.A.* 42°45N 124°30W **168** E1
Port Pegasus *N.Z.* 47°12S 167°41E **155** H2
Port Perry *Canada* 44°6N 78°56W **174** B6
Port Phillip B. *Australia* 38°10S 144°50E **153** E6
Port Pirie *Australia* 33°10S 138°1E **152** B3
Port Qasim *Pakistan* 24°46N 67°20E **124** G2
Port Renfrew *Canada* 48°30N 124°20W **170** B2
Port Roper *Australia* 14°45S 135°25E **150** A2
Port Rowan *Canada* 42°40N 80°30W **174** D4
Port Royal Sd. *U.S.A.* 32°15N 80°40W **178** C9
Port Safaga = Bûr Safâga *Egypt* 26°43N 33°57E **128** C2
Port Said = Bûr Sa'îd *Egypt* 31°16N 32°18E **137** E8
Port St. Joe *U.S.A.* 29°49N 85°18W **178** G4
Port St. John *U.S.A.* 28°29N 80°47W **179** G9
Port St. Johns = Umzimvubu *S. Africa* 31°38S 29°33E **145** D4
Port-St-Louis-du-Rhône *France* 43°23N 4°49E **73** E8
Port St. Lucie *U.S.A.* 27°18N 80°21W **179** H9
Port-Ste-Marie *France* 44°15N 0°25E **72** D4
Port Salerno *U.S.A.* 27°9N 80°12W **179** H9
Port Sanilac *U.S.A.* 43°26N 82°33W **174** C2
Port Severn *Canada* 44°48N 79°43W **174** B5
Port Shepstone *S. Africa* 30°44S 30°28E **145** D5
Port Simpson *Canada* 54°30N 130°20W **162** C2
Port Stanley = Stanley *Falk. Is.* 51°40S 59°51W **192** D5
Port Stanley *Canada* 42°40N 81°10W **174** D3
Port Sudan = Bûr Sûdân *Sudan* 19°32N 37°9E **137** D4
Port Sulphur *U.S.A.* 29°29N 89°42W **177** G10
Port-sur-Saône *France* 47°42N 6°2E **71** E13
Port Talbot *U.K.* 51°35N 3°47W **67** F4
Port Taufiq = Bûr Taufiq *Egypt* 29°54N 32°32E **137** E8
Port Townsend *U.S.A.* 48°7N 122°45W **170** B4
Port-Vendres *France* 42°32N 3°8E **72** F7
Port Victoria *Australia* 34°30S 137°29E **152** C2
Port Vila *Vanuatu* 17°45S 168°18E **147** D9
Port Vladimir *Russia* 69°25N 33°6E **60** B25

Port Wakefield *Australia* 34°12S 138°10E **152** C3
Port Washington *U.S.A.* 43°23N 87°53W **172** D10
Port Wentworth *U.S.A.* 32°9N 81°10W **178** C8
Porta Orientalis *Romania* 45°6N 22°18E **75** F12
Portacloy *Ireland* 54°20N 9°46W **64** B2
Portadown *U.K.* 54°25N 6°27W **64** B5
Portaferry *U.K.* 54°23N 5°33W **64** B6
Portage *Pa., U.S.A.* 40°23N 78°41W **174** F6
Portage *Wis., U.S.A.* 43°33N 89°28W **172** D9
Portage la Prairie *Canada* 49°58N 98°18W **163** D9
Portageville *U.S.A.* 36°26N 89°42W **172** G9
Portal *U.S.A.* 32°33N 81°56W **178** C8
Portalegre *Portugal* 39°19N 7°25W **89** F3
Portalegre □ *Portugal* 39°20N 7°40W **89** F3
Portales *U.S.A.* 34°11N 103°20W **169** J12
Portarlington *Ireland* 53°9N 7°14W **64** C4
Portbou *Spain* 42°25N 3°9E **90** C8
Porteirinha *Brazil* 15°44S 43°2W **189** D2
Portel *Portugal* 38°19N 7°41W **89** G3
Portela, Lisboa ✈ (LIS) *Portugal* 38°46N 9°8W **89** G1
Porter L. *N.W.T., Canada* 61°41N 108°5W **163** A7
Porter L. *Sask., Canada* 56°20N 107°20W **163** B7
Porterville *S. Africa* 33°0S 19°0E **144** D2
Porterville *U.S.A.* 36°4N 119°1W **170** J8
Portes-lès-Valence *France* 44°52N 4°54E **73** D8
Porth Tywyn = Burry Port *U.K.* 51°41N 4°15W **67** F3
Porthcawl *U.K.* 51°29N 3°42W **67** F4
Porthill *U.S.A.* 48°59N 116°30W **168** B5
Porthmadog *U.K.* 52°55N 4°8W **66** E3
Portile de Fier *Europe* 44°44N 22°30E **80** F7
Portimão *Portugal* 37°8N 8°32W **89** H2
Portishead *U.K.* 51°29N 2°46W **67** F5
Portiței, Gura *Romania* 44°41N 29°0E **81** F14
Portknockie *U.K.* 57°42N 2°51W **65** D6
Portland *N.S.W., Australia* 33°20S 150°0E **153** B9
Portland *Vic., Australia* 38°20S 141°35E **152** E4
Portland *Canada* 44°42N 76°12W **175** B8
Portland *Conn., U.S.A.* 41°34N 72°38W **175** E12
Portland *Fla., U.S.A.* 30°31N 86°12W **178** E3
Portland *Maine, U.S.A.* 43°39N 70°16W **173** D18
Portland *Mich., U.S.A.* 42°52N 84°54W **173** D11
Portland *Oreg., U.S.A.* 45°32N 122°37W **170** E4
Portland *Pa., U.S.A.* 40°55N 75°6W **175** F9
Portland *Tex., U.S.A.* 27°53N 97°20W **176** M6
Portland, I. of *U.K.* 50°33N 2°26W **67** G5
Portland B. *Australia* 38°15S 141°45E **152** E4
Portland Bight *Jamaica* 17°52N 77°5W **182** a
Portland Bill *U.K.* 50°31N 2°28W **67** G5
Portland Canal *U.S.A.* 55°56N 130°0W **162** B2
Portland I. *N.Z.* 39°20S 177°51E **154** F6
Portland Int. ✈ (PDX) *U.S.A.* 45°35N 122°36W **170** E4
Portland Pt. *Jamaica* 17°42N 77°11W **182** a
Portlaoise *Ireland* 53°2N 7°18W **64** C4
Portmadoc = Porthmadog *U.K.* 52°55N 4°8W **66** E3
Portmore *Jamaica* 17°53N 76°53W **182** a
Porto *Brazil* 3°54S 42°42W **189** A2
Porto *France* 42°16N 8°42E **73** F12
Porto □ *Portugal* 41°8N 8°40W **88** D2
Porto, G. de *France* 42°17N 8°34E **73** F12
Porto Acre *Brazil* 9°34S 67°31W **188** B4
Pôrto Alegre *Brazil* 30°5S 51°10W **191** C5
Porto Azzurro *Italy* 42°46N 10°24E **92** F7
Porto Cervo *Italy* 41°8N 9°33E **94** A2
Porto Colom *Spain* 39°26N 3°15E **100** B10
Porto Cristo *Spain* 39°33N 3°20E **100** B10
Pôrto da Fôlha *Brazil* 9°55S 37°17W **189** B3
Porto de Moz *Brazil* 1°41S 52°13W **187** D8
Porto de Pedras *Brazil* 9°10S 35°17W **189** B3
Porto Empédocle *Italy* 37°17N 13°32E **94** E6
Pôrto Esperança *Brazil* 19°37S 57°29W **188** D6
Porto Franco *Brazil* 6°20S 47°24W **189** B1
Pôrto Inglês = Vila do Maio *C. Verde Is.* 15°21N 23°10W **134** b
Porto Mendes *Brazil* 24°30S 54°15W **191** A5
Porto Moniz *Madeira* 32°52N 17°11W **100** D2
Pôrto Murtinho *Brazil* 21°45S 57°55W **188** E6
Porto Nacional *Brazil* 10°40S 48°30W **189** C1
Porto-Novo *Benin* 6°23N 2°42E **139** D5
Porto Primavera, Represa *Brazil* 22°50S 52°45W **191** A5
Porto San Giórgio *Italy* 43°11N 13°48E **93** E10
Porto Santo, I. de *Madeira* 33°45N 16°25W **134** D2
Porto Sant' Elpídio *Italy* 43°15N 13°43E **93** E10
Pôrto São José *Brazil* 22°43S 53°10W **191** A5
Porto Seguro *Brazil* 16°26S 39°5W **189** D3
Porto Tolle *Italy* 44°56N 12°22E **93** D9
Porto Tórres *Italy* 40°50N 8°24E **94** A1
Pôrto União *Brazil* 26°10S 51°10W **191** B5
Porto-Vecchio *France* 41°35N 9°16E **73** G13
Porto Velho *Brazil* 8°46S 63°54W **186** E6
Porto Viro *Italy* 45°1N 12°13E **93** D9
Portobelo *Panama* 9°35N 79°42W **182** E4
Portoferráio *Italy* 42°48N 10°20E **92** F7
Portofino *Italy* 44°18N 9°12E **92** D6
Portogruaro *Italy* 45°47N 12°50E **93** C9
Portola *U.S.A.* 39°49N 120°28W **170** F6
Portomaggiore *Italy* 44°42N 11°48E **93** D8
Portopetro *Spain* 39°22N 3°13E **100** B10
Portoscuso *Italy* 39°12N 8°24E **94** C1
Portree *U.K.* 57°25N 6°12W **65** D2
Portreath *U.K.* 50°13N 5°18W **67** G2
Portroe *Ireland* 52°53N 8°20W **64** D3
Portrush *U.K.* 55°12N 6°40W **64** A5
Portsmouth *Dominica* 15°34N 61°27W **183** C7
Portsmouth *U.K.* 50°48N 1°6W **67** G6
Portsmouth *N.H., U.S.A.* 43°5N 70°45W **175** C14
Portsmouth *Ohio, U.S.A.* 38°44N 82°57W **173** F12
Portsmouth *R.I., U.S.A.* 41°36N 71°15W **175** E13
Portsmouth *Va., U.S.A.* 36°50N 76°18W **174** G7
Portsmouth □ *U.K.* 50°48N 1°6W **67** G6
Portsoy *U.K.* 57°41N 2°41W **65** D6
Portstewart *U.K.* 55°11N 6°43W **64** A5

Porttipahdan tekojärvi *Finland* 68°5N 26°40E **60** B22
Portugal ■ *Europe* 40°0N 8°0W **88** F3
Portugalete *Spain* 43°19N 3°4W **90** B1
Portumna *Ireland* 53°6N 8°14W **64** C3
Portville *U.S.A.* 42°3N 78°20W **174** D6
Porvenir *Bolivia* 11°10S 68°50W **188** C4
Porvenir *Chile* 53°10S 70°16W **192** D2
Porvoo *Finland* 60°24N 25°40E **84** B3
Porzuna *Spain* 39°9N 4°9W **89** F6
Posada *Italy* 40°38N 9°43E **94** B2
Posada → *Italy* 40°39N 9°45E **94** B2
Posadas *Argentina* 27°30S 55°50W **191** B4
Posadas *Spain* 37°47N 5°11W **89** H5
Poschiavo *Switz.* 46°19N 10°4E **77** J6
Posets *Spain* 42°39N 0°25E **90** C5
Posht-e Badam *Iran* 33°2N 55°23E **129** C7
Posidium *Greece* 35°30N 27°10E **99** F9
Poso *Indonesia* 1°20S 120°55E **119** E6
Poso, Danau *Indonesia* 1°52S 120°35E **119** E6
Posof *Turkey* 41°30N 42°43E **104** B9
Pospelikha *Russia* 51°57N 81°46E **109** B10
Posse *Brazil* 14°4S 46°18W **189** C1
Possession I. *Antarctica* 72°4S 172°0E **5** D11
Pössneck *Germany* 50°42N 11°35E **76** E7
Possum Kingdom L. *U.S.A.* 32°52N 98°26W **176** E5
Post *U.S.A.* 33°12N 101°23W **176** E4
Post Falls *U.S.A.* 47°43N 116°57W **168** C5
Postavy = Pastavy *Belarus* 55°4N 26°50E **84** E4
Poste-de-la-Baleine = Kuujjuarapik *Canada* 55°20N 77°35W **164** A4
Postmasburg *S. Africa* 28°18S 23°5E **144** C3
Postojna *Slovenia* 45°46N 14°12E **93** C11
Postville *U.S.A.* 54°54N 59°47W **165** B8
Posyet *Russia* 42°39N 130°48E **112** C5
Potamós *Antikythira, Greece* 35°52N 23°15E **98** F5
Potamós *Kythira, Greece* 36°15N 22°58E **98** E5
Potchefstroom *S. Africa* 26°41S 27°7E **144** C4
Potcoava *Romania* 44°30N 24°39E **81** F9
Poté *Brazil* 17°49S 41°49W **189** D2
Poteau *U.S.A.* 35°3N 94°37W **176** D7
Poteet *U.S.A.* 29°2N 98°35W **176** G5
Potenza *Italy* 40°38N 15°48E **95** B8
Potenza → *Italy* 43°26N 13°40E **93** E10
Potenza Picena *Italy* 43°22N 13°37E **93** E10
Poteriteri, L. *N.Z.* 46°5S 167°10E **155** G2
Potgietersrus = Mokopane *S. Africa* 24°10S 28°55E **145** B4
Poti *Georgia* 42°10N 41°38E **87** J5
Potiraguá *Brazil* 15°36S 39°53W **189** D3
Potiskum *Nigeria* 11°39N 11°2E **139** C7
Potlogi *Romania* 44°34N 25°34E **81** F10
Potomac → *U.S.A.* 38°0N 76°23W **173** F14
Potosí *Bolivia* 19°38S 65°50W **186** G5
Potosi Mt. *U.S.A.* 35°57N 115°29W **171** K11
Pototan *Phil.* 10°54N 122°38E **119** B6
Potrerillos *Chile* 26°30S 69°30W **190** B2
Potsdam *Germany* 52°23N 13°3E **76** C9
Potsdam *U.S.A.* 44°40N 74°59W **175** B10
Pottangi *India* 18°34N 82°58E **126** B6
Pottenstein *Germany* 49°46N 11°24E **77** F7
Pottersville *U.S.A.* 43°43N 73°50W **175** C11
Pottstown *U.S.A.* 40°15N 75°39W **175** F9
Pottsville *U.S.A.* 40°41N 76°12W **175** F8
Pottuvil *Sri Lanka* 6°55N 81°50E **127** L5
Pouancé *France* 47°44N 1°10W **70** E5
Pouce Coupé *Canada* 55°40N 120°10W **162** B4
Poughkeepsie *U.S.A.* 41°42N 73°56W **175** E11
Pouilly-sur-Loire *France* 47°18N 2°57E **71** E9
Poulaphouca Res. *Ireland* 53°8N 6°30W **64** C5
Poulsbo *U.S.A.* 47°44N 122°38W **170** C4
Poultney *U.S.A.* 43°31N 73°14W **175** C11
Poulton-le-Fylde *U.K.* 53°51N 2°58W **66** D5
Pouso Alegre *Brazil* 22°14S 45°57W **191** A6
Pout *Senegal* 14°45N 17°0W **138** C1
Pouthisat *Cambodia* 12°34N 103°50E **120** F4
Pouytenga *Burkina Faso* 12°15N 0°25W **138** C4
Pouzauges *France* 46°47N 0°50W **72** B3
Považská Bystrica *Slovak Rep.* 49°8N 18°27E **79** B11
Poverty B. *N.Z.* 38°43S 178°2E **154** E7
Poverty Point Nat. Monument △ *U.S.A.* 32°38N 91°25W **176** E9
Povlen *Serbia* 44°9N 19°44E **96** B3
Póvoa de Lanhosa *Portugal* 41°33N 8°15W **88** D2
Póvoa de Santa Iria *Portugal* 38°51N 9°4W **89** G1
Póvoa de Varzim *Portugal* 41°25N 8°46W **88** D2
Povorino *Russia* 51°12N 42°5E **86** E6
Povorotnyy, Mys *Russia* 42°40N 133°2E **112** C6
Povungnituk = Puvirnituq *Canada* 60°2N 77°10W **161** E16
Powassan *Canada* 46°5N 79°25W **164** B4
Powder → *U.S.A.* 46°45N 105°26W **168** C11
Powder River *U.S.A.* 43°2N 106°59W **168** E10
Powell *U.S.A.* 44°45N 108°46W **168** D9
Powell, L. *U.S.A.* 36°57N 111°29W **169** H8
Powell River *Canada* 49°50N 124°35W **162** D4
Powers *U.S.A.* 45°40N 124°4W **168** E1
Powers Lake *U.S.A.* 48°34N 102°39W **168** B2
Pownal *U.S.A.* 42°45N 73°14W **175** D11
Powys □ *U.K.* 52°20N 3°20W **67** E4
Poyang Hu *China* 29°5N 116°20E **117** C11
Poyarkovo *Russia* 49°36N 128°41E **107** E13
Poygan, L. *U.S.A.* 44°9N 88°49W **172** C9
Poza de la Sal *Spain* 42°35N 3°30W **89** A7
Poza Rica *Mexico* 20°33N 97°27E **181** C5
Pozantı *Turkey* 37°25N 34°50E **104** D6
Pozazal, Puerto *Spain* 42°56N 4°10W **88** C6
Požega *Croatia* 45°20N 17°15E **93** C14
Požega *Serbia* 43°53N 20°2E **96** C4
Poznań *Poland* 52°25N 16°55E **83** F3
Poznań ✈ (POZ) *Poland* 52°25N 16°50W **83** F3
Pozo *U.S.A.* 35°20N 120°24W **171** K6
Pozo Almonte *Chile* 20°10S 69°50W **188** G4
Pozo Colorado *Paraguay* 23°30S 58°45W **190** A4

Pozo Negro *Canary Is.* 28°19N 13°55W **100**
Pozoblanco *Spain* 38°23N 4°51W **89**
Pozuzo *Peru* 10°5S 75°35W **186**
Pozzallo *Italy* 36°43N 14°51E **94**
Pozzomaggiore *Italy* 40°24N 8°39E **94**
Pozzuoli *Italy* 40°49N 14°7E **95**
Pra → *Ghana* 5°1N 1°37W **139**
Prabuty *Poland* 53°47N 19°15E **83**
Prača *Bos.-H.* 43°47N 18°43E **96**
Prachatice *Czech Rep.* 49°1N 14°0E **76**
Prachin Buri *Thailand* 14°0N 101°25E **120**
Prachuap Khirikhan *Thailand* 11°49N 99°48E **121**
Pradelles *France* 44°46N 3°52E **72**
Prades *France* 42°38N 2°23E **72**
Prado *Brazil* 17°20S 39°13W **189**
Prado del Rey *Spain* 36°48N 5°33W **89**
Præstø *Denmark* 55°8N 12°2E **63**
Pragersko *Slovenia* 46°27N 15°42E **93**
Prague = Praha *Czech Rep.* 50°4N 14°25E **76**
Praha *Czech Rep.* 50°4N 14°25E **76**
Praha ✈ (PRG) *Czech Rep.* 50°6N 14°16E **76**
Prahecq *France* 46°19N 0°26W **72**
Prahita → *India* 19°0N 79°55E **127**
Prahova □ *Romania* 45°10N 26°0E **81**
Prahova → *Romania* 44°50N 25°50E **81**
Prahovo *Serbia* 44°18N 22°39E **96**
Praia *C. Verde Is.* 15°2N 23°34W **134**
Praia a Mare *Italy* 39°50N 15°45E **95**
Praid *Romania* 46°32N 25°10E **81**
Prainha *Brazil* 1°45S 53°30W **187**
Prainha Nova *Brazil* 7°10S 60°30W **187**
Prairie *Australia* 20°50S 144°35E **150**
Prairie City *U.S.A.* 44°28N 118°43W **168**
Prairie Dog Town Fork Red → *U.S.A.* 34°30N 99°58W **176**
Prairie du Chien *U.S.A.* 43°3N 91°9W **172**
Prairies, L. of the *Canada* 51°16N 101°32W **163**
Pramanda *Greece* 39°32N 21°8E **98**
Prambanan △ *Indonesia* 7°45S 110°28E **119**
Prampram *Ghana* 5°43N 0°8E **139**
Pran Buri *Thailand* 12°23N 99°55E **121**
Prang *Ghana* 8°1N 0°56E **139**
Prapat *Indonesia* 2°41N 98°58E **118**
Praslin *Seychelles* 4°18S 55°45E **145**
Prasonísi, Ákra *Greece* 35°42N 27°46E **101**
Praszka *Poland* 51°5N 18°31E **83**
Prata *Brazil* 19°25S 48°54W **189**
Pratabpur *India* 23°28N 83°15E **125**
Pratapgarh *Raj., India* 24°2N 74°40E **124**
Pratapgarh *Ut. P., India* 25°56N 81°59E **125**
Pratas I. = Dongsha Dao *S. China Sea* 20°35N 116°43E **111**
Prato *Italy* 43°53N 11°6E **93**
Prátola Peligna *Italy* 42°6N 13°52E **93**
Prats-de-Mollo-la-Preste *France* 42°25N 2°27E **72**
Pratt *U.S.A.* 37°39N 98°44W **172**
Prattville *U.S.A.* 32°28N 86°29W **177**
Pravara → *India* 19°35N 74°45E **126**
Pravdinsk *Kaliningrad, Russia* 54°27N 21°1E **82**
Pravdinsk *Nizhniy Novgorod, Russia* 56°29N 43°28E **86**
Pravets *Bulgaria* 42°53N 23°55E **96**
Pravia *Spain* 43°30N 6°12W **88**
Praya *Indonesia* 8°39S 116°17E **118**
Prayag = Allahabad *India* 25°25N 81°58E **125**
Pre-delta △ *Argentina* 32°10S 60°40W **190**
Pré-en-Pail *France* 48°28N 0°12W **70**
Preah Seihanu = Kampong Saom *Cambodia* 10°38N 103°30E **121**
Preah Vihear *Cambodia* 14°23N 104°41E **120**
Preble *U.S.A.* 42°44N 76°8W **175**
Precipice △ *Australia* 25°18S 150°5E **151**
Precordillera *Argentina* 30°0S 69°1W **190**
Predáppio *Italy* 44°6N 11°59E **93**
Predazzo *Italy* 46°19N 11°36E **93**
Predeal *Romania* 45°30N 25°34E **81**
Predejane *Serbia* 42°51N 22°9E **96**
Preeceville *Canada* 51°57N 102°40W **163**
Preetz *Germany* 54°14N 10°16E **76**
Pregolya → *Russia* 54°41N 20°22E **82**
Pregrada *Croatia* 46°11N 15°45E **93**
Preiļi *Latvia* 56°18N 26°43E **84**
Preko *Croatia* 44°7N 15°10E **93**
Prelog *Croatia* 46°18N 16°32E **93**
Premer *Australia* 31°29S 149°56E **153**
Prémery *France* 47°10N 3°18E **71**
Premià de Mar *Spain* 41°29N 2°22E **90**
Premont *U.S.A.* 27°22N 98°7W **176**
Premuda *Croatia* 44°20N 14°36E **93**
Prentice *U.S.A.* 45°33N 90°17W **172**
Prenzlau *Germany* 53°19N 13°51E **76**
Preobrazheniye *Russia* 42°54N 133°54E **112**
Preparis I. = Paripariti Kyun *Burma* 14°52N 93°41E **127**
Preparis North Channel *Ind. Oc.* 15°27N 94°5E **127**
Preparis South Channel *Ind. Oc.* 14°33N 93°30E **127**
Přerov *Czech Rep.* 49°28N 17°27E **79**
Prescott *Canada* 44°45N 75°30W **175**
Prescott *Ariz., U.S.A.* 34°33N 112°28W **169**
Prescott *Ark., U.S.A.* 33°48N 93°23W **176**
Prescott Valley *U.S.A.* 34°40N 112°18W **169**
Preservation Inlet *N.Z.* 46°8S 166°35E **155**
Preševo *Serbia* 42°19N 21°39E **96**
Presho *U.S.A.* 43°54N 100°3W **172**
Presicce *Italy* 39°54N 18°16E **95**
Presidencia de la Plaza *Argentina* 27°0S 59°50W **190**
Presidencia Roque Saenz Peña *Argentina* 26°45S 60°30W **190**
Presidente Dutra *Brazil* 5°15S 44°30W **189**
Presidente Epitácio *Brazil* 21°56S 52°6W **191**
Presidente Hayes □ *Paraguay* 24°0S 59°0W **190**
Presidente Prudente *Brazil* 22°5S 51°25W **191**
Presidente Ríos, L. *Chile* 46°28S 74°25W **192**
Presidio *U.S.A.* 29°34N 104°22W **176**
Preslav *Bulgaria* 43°10N 26°52E **97**

slavska Planina
Bulgaria 43°10N 26°45E **97** C10
sov *Slovak Rep.* 49°0N 21°15E **79** B14
sovský □ *Slovak Rep.* 49°10N 21°0E **79** B13
spa *Bulgaria* 41°44N 24°55E **97** E8
spa, L. = Prespansko Jezero
Macedonia 40°55N 21°0E **96** F5
stea *Ghana* 5°22N 2°7W **138** D4
steigne *U.K.* 52°17N 3°0W **67** E5
stice *Czech Rep.* 49°34N 13°20E **78** B6
ston *Canada* 43°23N 80°21W **174** C4
ston *U.K.* 53°46N 2°42W **66** D5
ston *Ga., U.S.A.* 32°4N 84°32W **178** C5
ston *Idaho, U.S.A.* 42°6N 111°53W **168** E8
ston *Minn., U.S.A.* 43°40N 92°5W **172** D7
ston, C. *Australia* 20°51S 116°12E **148** D2
stonsburg *U.S.A.* 37°40N 82°47W **176** G4
stranda *Norway* 59°6N 9°4E **62** E3
stwick *U.K.* 55°29N 4°37W **66** F4
sto → *Brazil* 11°21S 43°52W **189** C22
stória *S. Africa* 25°44S 28°12E **145** D4
suilly-sur-Claise *France* 46°51N 0°56E **70** F7
sweza *Greece* 38°57N 20°45E **98** C2
Veng *Cambodia* 13°35N 105°29E **121** G5
stavozskoye *Ukraine* 46°44N 35°40E **85** J8

russia 52°30N 106°0E **107** D11
ilof I. *U.S.A.* 57°0N 170°0W **166** D6
oj *Serbia* 43°35N 19°32E **96** C3
ram *Czech Rep.* 49°41N 14°2E **78** B7
e *U.S.A.* 39°36N 110°49W **168** G8
he, C. *India* 13°34N 93°3E **127** H11
e I. *Canada* 52°23N 128°41W **162** C3
shard *U.S.A.* 30°44N 88°5W **177** F10
go *Spain* 40°26N 2°21W **90** E2
go de Córdoba *Spain* 37°27N 4°12W **89** H6
ikule *Latvia* 56°26N 21°35E **82** B8
ikule *Lithuania* 55°33N 21°17E **82** B8
ibrusye △ *Russia* 43°20N 42°37E **87** J6
n *Germany* 47°51N 12°20E **78** C7
mai *Lithuania* 54°38N 23°57E **82** D10
ska *S. Africa* 29°40S 22°4E **144** C3
st L. *U.S.A.* 48°35N 116°52W **168** B5
st River *U.S.A.* 48°11N 116°55W **168** B5
st Valley *U.S.A.* 36°10N 120°39W **170** J6
vidza *Slovak Rep.* 48°46N 18°36E **79** C11
gnitz *Germany* 53°6N 11°45E **78** B7
edor *Bos.-H.* 44°58N 16°41E **93** D13
epolje *Serbia* 43°27N 19°40E **96** C3
ussia* 52°30N 106°0E **107** D11
aspiyskaya Nizmennost =
aspian Depression
Eurasia 47°0N 48°0E **87** G9
cro *Ivory C.* 7°40N 3°59W **138** D4
ubanskaya Nizmennost =
ubanskaya Depression
Russia 45°39N 38°33E **87** H4
ep *Macedonia* 41°21N 21°32E **96** E5
aki = Pryluky
Ukraine 50°30N 32°24E **85** G7
ne Hd. *Antarctica* 63°12S 48°57W **55** C18
ne Seal I. *Australia* 40°3S 147°43E **150** A4
neira Cruz *Brazil* 2°30S 43°26W **189** A22
no Tapia *Mexico* 32°16N 116°54W **171** N10
norsk *Kaliningrad,*
Russia 54°44N 20°0E **82** D6
norsk *St. Petersburg,*
Russia 60°22N 28°37E **84** B5
norskiy Kray □
Russia 45°0N 135°0E **112** B7
norsko *Russia* 42°15N 27°44E **97** D11
norsko-Akhtarsk
Russia 46°2N 38°10E **85** J10
ace L. *Canada* 54°55N 109°45W **163** C7
ace Albert *Canada* 53°15N 105°50W **163** C7
ace Albert *S. Africa* 33°12S 22°2E **144** D3
ace Albert △
Canada 54°0N 106°25W **163** C7
ace Albert Mts.
Antarctica 76°0S 161°30E **55** D11
ace Albert Pen.
Canada 72°30N 116°0W **160** C8
ace Albert Sd.
Canada 70°25N 115°0W **160** C9
ace Alfred, C.
Canada 74°20N 124°40W **54** B1
ace Charles I.
Antarctica 67°47N 76°12W **161** D16
ace Charles Mts.
Antarctica 72°0S 67°0E **55** D6
ace Edward Fracture Zone
Ind. Oc. 46°0S 35°0E **55** A4
ace Edward I. □
ace Edward Is.
Ind. Oc. 46°35S 38°0E **146** J2
ace George *Canada* 53°55N 122°50W **162** C4
ace of Wales, C.
U.S.A. 65°36N 168°5W **166** B6
ace of Wales I.
Australia 10°40S 142°10E **150** A3
ace of Wales I.
Canada 73°0N 99°0W **160** C12
ace of Wales I.
U.S.A. 55°47N 132°50W **160** F5
ace of Wales Icefield
Canada 78°15N 79°0W **161** B16
ace of Wales Str.
Canada 73°0N 117°0W **160** C8
ace Patrick I. *Canada* 77°0N 120°0W **161** B8
ace Regent Inlet
Canada 73°0N 90°0W **161** C14
ace Rupert *Canada* 54°20N 130°20W **162** C2
ace William Sd.
U.S.A. 60°40N 147°0W **160** E2
ces Town
Br. Virgin Is. 18°16N 64°37W **187** K15
ncesa Isabel *Brazil* 7°44S 38°0W **189** B33
ncess Charlotte B.
Australia 14°25S 144°0E **150** A3
ncess Elizabeth Trough
Ind. Oc. 64°10S 83°0E **55** C7
ncess May Ranges
Australia 15°30S 125°30E **148** C4
ncess Royal I.
Canada 52°30N 128°40W **162** C3
nceton *Canada* 49°27N 120°30W **162** D4
nceton *Calif., U.S.A.* 39°24N 122°1W **170** F4

Princeton *Ill., U.S.A.* 41°23N 89°28W **172** E9
Princeton *Ind., U.S.A.* 38°21N 87°34W **172** F10
Princeton *Ky., U.S.A.* 37°7N 87°53W **172** G10
Princeton *Mo., U.S.A.* 40°24N 93°35W **172** E7
Princeton *N.J., U.S.A.* 40°21N 74°39W **175** F10
Princeton *W. Va.,*
U.S.A. 37°22N 81°6W **173** G13
Principe
São Tomé & Príncipe 1°37N 7°25E **132** F4
Principe da Beira
Brazil 12°20S 64°30W **186** F6
Prineville *U.S.A.* 44°18N 120°51W **168** D3
Prins Christian Sund
Greenland 60°4N 43°10W **57** E6
Prins Harald Kyst
Antarctica 70°0S 35°1E **55** D4
Prins Karls Forland
Svalbard 78°30N 11°0E **57** B12
Prinsesse Astrid Kyst
Antarctica 70°45S 12°30E **55** D3
Prinsesse Ragnhild Kyst
Antarctica 70°15S 27°30E **55** D4
Prinzapolca *Nic.* 13°20N 83°35W **182** D3
Prior, C. *Spain* 43°34N 8°17W **88** B2
Priozersk *Russia* 61°2N 30°7E **84** B6
Pripet = Prypyat →
Europe 51°20N 30°15E **75** C16
Pripet Marshes *Europe* 52°10N 27°10E **75** B15
Pripyat = Prypyat →
Europe 51°20N 30°15E **75** C16
Pripyat Marshes = Pripet Marshes
Europe 52°10N 27°10E **75** B15
Pripyats = Prypyat →
Europe 51°20N 30°15E **75** C16
Prishtinë *Kosovo* 42°40N 21°13E **96** D5
Prislop, Pasul *Romania* 47°37N 24°48E **81** C9
Pristen *Russia* 51°15N 36°44E **85** G9
Priština = Prishtinë
Kosovo 42°40N 21°13E **96** D5
Pritzwalk *Germany* 53°9N 12°10E **76** B8
Privas *France* 44°45N 4°37E **73** D8
Priverno *Italy* 41°28N 13°11E **94** A6
Privolzhsk *Russia* 57°23N 41°16E **86** B5
Privolzhskaya Vozvyshennost
Russia 51°0N 46°0E **86** E7
Privolzhskiy *Russia* 51°25N 46°3E **86** E8
Privolzhskiy □ *Russia* 56°0N 50°0E **106** D6
Priyutnoye *Russia* 46°12N 43°40E **87** G6
Prizren *Kosovo* 42°13N 20°45E **96** D4
Prizzi *Italy* 37°43N 13°26E **94** E6
Prnjavor *Bos.-H.* 44°52N 17°43E **82** D7
Probolinggo *Indonesia* 7°46S 113°13E **119** G15
Prochowice *Poland* 51°17N 16°20E **83** G3
Proctor *U.S.A.* 43°40N 73°2W **175** C11
Proddatur *India* 14°45N 78°30E **127** G4
Prodhromos *Cyprus* 34°57N 32°50E **101** E11
Proença-a-Nova *Portugal* 39°45N 7°54W **88** F3
Profília *Greece* 36°5N 27°51E **101** C9
Profondeville *Belgium* 50°23N 4°52E **69** D4
Progreso *Coahuila,*
Mexico 27°28N 100°59W **180** B4
Progreso *Yucatán,*
Mexico 21°20N 89°40W **181** C7
Progress *Antarctica* 66°22S 76°22E **55** C12
Progress *Russia* 49°45N 129°37E **107** E13
Prokhladnyy *Russia* 43°50N 44°2E **87** J7
Prokhorovka *Russia* 51°2N 36°44E **86** E3
Prokletije *Albania* 42°30N 19°45E **96** D3
Prokopyevsk *Russia* 54°0N 86°45E **109** B11
Prokuplje *Serbia* 43°16N 21°36E **96** C5
Proletarsk *Russia* 46°42N 41°50E **87** G5
Prome = Pye *Burma* 18°49N 95°13E **123** K19
Prophet → *Canada* 58°48N 122°40W **162** B4
Prophet River *Canada* 58°6N 122°43W **162** B4
Proprié *Brazil* 10°13S 36°51W **189** C23
Propriano *France* 41°41N 8°52E **73** G12
Proserpine *Australia* 20°21S 148°36E **150** b
Prosna → *Poland* 52°6N 17°44E **83** F4
Prospect *U.S.A.* 43°18N 75°9W **175** C9
Prosperity *U.S.A.* 30°15N 85°56W **178** D5
Prosser *U.S.A.* 46°12N 119°46W **168** C4
Prostějov *Czech Rep.* 49°30N 17°9E **79** B10
Prostki *Poland* 53°42N 22°25E **82** E9
Proston *Australia* 26°8S 151°32E **151** D5
Proszowice *Poland* 50°13N 20°16E **83** H7
Proti *Greece* 37°5N 21°32E **98** D3
Provadiya *Bulgaria* 43°12N 27°30E **97** C11
Provadiya →
Bulgaria 43°12N 27°42E **97** C11
Provence *France* 43°40N 5°46E **73** E9
Provence-Alpes-Côte d'Azur □
France 44°0N 6°15E **73** E10
Providence *Ky.,*
U.S.A. 37°24N 87°46W **172** G10
Providence *R.I.,*
U.S.A. 41°49N 71°24W **175** E13
Providence, C. *N.Z.* 45°59S 166°29E **155** F1
Providence Bay
Canada 45°41N 82°15W **164** C3
Providence Mts.
U.S.A. 35°10N 115°15W **171** K11
Providencia, I. de
Caribbean 13°25N 81°26W **182** D3
Provideniya *Russia* 64°23N 173°18W **107** C19
Provincetown *U.S.A.* 42°3N 70°11W **173** D18
Provins *France* 48°33N 3°15E **71** D10
Provo *U.S.A.* 40°14N 111°39W **168** F8
Provost *Canada* 52°25N 110°20W **163** C6
Prozor *Bos.-H.* 43°50N 17°34E **80** G2
Prrenjas *Albania* 41°4N 20°32E **96** E4
Prudhoe Bay *U.S.A.* 70°18N 148°22W **166** A10
Prudhoe I. *Australia* 21°19S 149°41E **150** C4
Prud'homme *Canada* 52°20N 105°54W **163** C7
Prudnik *Poland* 50°20N 17°38E **83** H4
Prüm *Germany* 50°12N 6°25E **69** E6
Prundu *Romania* 44°6N 26°14E **81** F11
Prundu Bârgăului
Romania 47°13N 24°46E **81** C9
Pruszcz Gdański *Poland* 54°17N 18°40E **82** D5
Pruszków *Poland* 52°9N 20°49E **83** F7
Prut → *Romania* 45°28N 28°10E **81** E13
Pruzhany *Belarus* 52°33N 24°28E **82** F11
Prvić *Croatia* 44°55N 14°47E **93** D11
Prydz B. *Antarctica* 69°0S 74°0E **55** C6
Pryluky *Ukraine* 50°30N 32°24E **85** G7
Prymorske *Ukraine* 46°58N 36°20E **85** J9
Pryor *U.S.A.* 36°19N 95°19W **176** C7
Prypyat → *Europe* 51°20N 30°15E **75** C16
Prypyatsky △ *Belarus* 52°0N 28°0E **75** C14
Przasnysz *Poland* 53°2N 20°54E **83** E7
Przedbórz *Poland* 51°6N 19°53E **83** G6
Przedecz *Poland* 52°20N 18°53E **83** F5
Przemków *Poland* 51°31N 15°48E **83** G2

Przemyśl *Poland* 49°50N 22°45E **83** J9
Przeworsk *Poland* 50°6N 22°32E **83** H9
Przewóz *Poland* 51°28N 14°57E **83** G1
Przhevalsk = Karakol
Kyrgyzstan 42°30N 78°20E **109** D9
Przysucha *Poland* 51°22N 20°38E **83** G7
Psachna *Greece* 38°34N 23°35E **98** C5
Psara *Greece* 38°37N 25°38E **99** C7
Psathoura *Greece* 39°30N 24°12E **98** B6
Pserimos *Greece* 36°56N 27°8E **99** E9
Psíloritis, Oros *Greece* 35°15N 24°45E **101** D6
Psíra *Greece* 35°12N 25°52E **101** D7
Pskem → *Uzbekistan* 41°38N 70°1E **109** D7
Pskov *Russia* 57°50N 28°25E **84** D5
Pskov □ *Russia* 57°20N 29°0E **84** D5
Pskovskoye, Ozero
Russia 58°0N 27°58E **84** D5
Psol → *Ukraine* 49°10N 33°37E **85** H7
Psunj *Croatia* 45°25N 17°19E **80** E2
Pteleos *Greece* 39°3N 22°57E **98** B4
Ptich = Ptsich →
Belarus 52°9N 28°52E **75** B15
Ptichia = Vídos *Greece* 39°38N 19°55E **101** A3
Ptolemaída *Greece* 40°30N 21°43E **96** F5
Ptsich → *Belarus* 52°9N 28°52E **75** B15
Ptuj *Slovenia* 46°28N 15°50E **93** B12
Ptujska Gora *Slovenia* 46°23N 15°47E **93** B12
Pu Xian *China* 36°24N 111°6E **114** F6
Pua *Thailand* 19°11N 100°55E **120** C3
Puán *Argentina* 37°30S 62°45W **190** D3
Pu'an *China* 25°46N 104°57E **116** E5
Pubei *China* 22°16N 109°31E **116** F7
Pucallpa *Peru* 8°25S 74°30W **188** B3
Pucará *Cajamarca, Peru* 6°0S 79°7W **188** B2
Pucará *Puno, Peru* 15°5S 70°24W **188** C3
Pucarani *Bolivia* 16°23S 68°30W **188** D4
Pucheng *China* 27°59N 118°31E **117** D12
Pucheni *Romania* 45°12N 25°17E **81** E10
Puchheim *Germany* 48°9N 11°21E **77** G7
Puch'on = Bucheon
S. Korea 37°28N 126°45E **115** F14
Púchov *Slovak Rep.* 49°8N 18°20E **79** B11
Pucioasa *Romania* 45°5N 25°25E **81** E10
Pučišća *Croatia* 43°22N 16°43E **93** E13
Puck *Poland* 54°45N 18°23E **82** D5
Pucka, Zatoka *Poland* 54°30N 18°40E **82** D5
Puçol *Spain* 39°37N 0°18W **91** F4
Pudasjärvi *Finland* 65°23N 26°53E **60** D22
Puding *China* 26°18N 105°44E **116** D5
Pudozh *Russia* 61°48N 36°32E **84** B9
Pudu = Suizhou *China* 31°42N 113°24E **117** B9
Pudukkottai *India* 10°28N 78°47E **127** J4
Puebla *Mexico* 19°3N 98°12W **181** D5
Puebla □ *Mexico* 18°50N 98°0W **181** D5
Puebla de Alcocer *Spain* 38°59N 5°14W **89** G5
Puebla de Don Fadrique
Spain 37°58N 2°25W **91** H2
Puebla de Don Rodrigo
Spain 39°5N 4°37W **89** F6
Puebla de Guzmán *Spain* 37°37N 7°15W **89** H3
Puebla de la Calzada
Spain 38°54N 6°37W **89** G4
Puebla de Sanabria *Spain* 42°4N 6°38W **88** C4
Puebla de Trives = Pobra de
Trives *Spain* 42°20N 7°10W **88** C3
Pueblo *U.S.A.* 38°16N 104°37W **168** G12
Puelches *Argentina* 38°5S 65°51W **190** D3
Puelén *Argentina* 37°32S 67°38W **190** D3
Puente Alto *Chile* 33°32S 70°35W **190** C1
Puente-Genil *Spain* 37°22N 4°47W **89** H6
Puente la Reina *Spain* 42°40N 1°49W **90** C3
Puente San Miguel *Spain* 43°21N 4°5W **88** B6
Puenteareas = Ponteareas
Spain 42°10N 8°28W **88** C2
Puentedeume = Pontedeume
Spain 43°24N 8°10W **88** B2
Puentes de García Rodríguez = As
Pontes de García Rodríguez
Spain 43°27N 7°51W **88** B3
Puerca, Pta. *Puerto Rico* 18°13N 65°36W **183** d
Puerco → *U.S.A.* 34°22N 107°50W **169** J10
Puerto Acosta *Bolivia* 15°32S 69°15W **188** D4
Puerto Aisén *Chile* 45°27S 73°0W **192** C2
Puerto Arista *Mexico* 15°56N 93°48W **181** D6
Puerto Armuelles
Panama 8°20N 82°51W **182** E3
Puerto Ayacucho
Venezuela 5°40N 67°35W **186** B5
Puerto Barrios
Guatemala 15°40N 88°32W **182** C2
Puerto Bermejo
Argentina 26°55S 58°34W **190** B4
Puerto Bermúdez *Peru* 10°20S 74°58W **188** B3
Puerto Bolívar *Ecuador* 3°19S 79°55W **186** D3
Puerto Cabello
Venezuela 10°28N 68°1W **186** A5
Puerto Cabezas *Nic.* 14°0N 83°30W **182** D3
Puerto Cabo Gracias á Dios
Nic. 15°0N 83°10W **182** D3
Puerto Carreño
Colombia 6°12N 67°22W **186** B5
Puerto Castilla *Honduras* 16°0N 86°0W **182** C2
Puerto Chicama *Peru* 7°45S 79°20W **188** B2
Puerto Cisnes *Chile* 44°45S 72°42W **192** C2
Puerto Coig *Argentina* 50°54S 69°15W **192** D3
Puerto Cortés *Honduras* 15°51N 88°0W **182** C2
Puerto Cumarebo
Venezuela 11°29N 69°30W **186** A5
Puerto de Alcudia = Port
d'Alcúdia *Spain* 39°50N 3°7E **100** B10
Puerto de Cabrera *Spain* 39°8N 2°56E **100** B9
Puerto de la Cruz
Canary Is. 28°24N 16°32W **100** F3
Puerto de los Angeles △
Mexico 23°39N 105°45W **180** C3
Puerto de Mazarrón
Spain 37°34N 1°15W **91** H3
Puerto de Sóller = Port de Sóller
Spain 39°48N 2°42E **100** B9
Puerto de Somosierra
Spain 41°9N 3°35W **88** D7
Puerto del Carmen
Canary Is. 28°55N 13°38W **100** F6
Puerto del Rosario
Canary Is. 28°30N 13°52W **100** F6
Puerto Deseado
Argentina 47°55S 66°0W **192** C3
Puerto Escondido
Mexico 15°50N 97°3W **181** D5

Puerto Heath *Bolivia* 12°34S 68°39W **188** C4
Puerto Inca *Peru* 9°22S 74°54W **188** B3
Puerto Inírida *Colombia* 3°53N 67°52W **186** C5
Puerto Juárez *Mexico* 21°11N 86°49W **181** C7
Puerto La Cruz
Venezuela 10°13N 64°38W **186** A6
Puerto Leguizamo
Colombia 0°12S 74°46W **186** D4
Puerto Lempira
Honduras 15°16N 83°46W **182** C3
Puerto Libertad
Mexico 29°55N 112°43W **180** B2
Puerto Limón *Colombia* 3°23N 73°30W **186** C4
Puerto Lobos *Argentina* 42°0S 65°3W **192** B3
Puerto Lumbreras *Spain* 37°34N 1°48W **91** H3
Puerto Madryn
Argentina 42°48S 65°4W **192** B3
Puerto Maldonado
Peru 12°30S 69°10W **188** C4
Puerto Manatí *Cuba* 21°22N 76°50W **182** B4
Puerto Montt *Chile* 41°28S 73°0W **192** B2
Puerto Morazán *Nic.* 12°51N 87°11W **182** D2
Puerto Morelos *Mexico* 20°50N 86°52W **181** C7
Puerto Natales *Chile* 51°45S 72°15W **192** D2
Puerto Oscuro *Chile* 31°24S 71°35W **190** C1
Puerto Padre *Cuba* 21°13N 76°35W **182** B4
Puerto Páez *Venezuela* 6°13N 67°28W **186** B5
Puerto Peñasco
Mexico 31°20N 113°33W **180** A2
Puerto Pinasco
Paraguay 22°36S 57°50W **190** A4
Puerto Pirámides
Argentina 42°35S 64°20W **192** B4
Puerto Plata *Dom. Rep.* 19°48N 70°45W **183** C5
Puerto Pollensa = Port de
Pollença *Spain* 39°54N 3°4E **100** B10
Puerto Portillo *Peru* 9°55S 72°42W **188** B3
Puerto Princesa *Phil.* 9°46N 118°45E **119** C5
Puerto Quepos *Costa Rica* 9°29N 84°6W **182** E3
Puerto Real *Spain* 36°33N 6°12W **89** J4
Puerto Rico *Bolivia* 11°55S 67°38W **188** C4
Puerto Rico ■ *W. Indies* 18°15N 66°45W **183** d
Puerto Rico ☑ *W. Indies* 18°15N 66°45W **183** d
Puerto Rico Trench
Atl. Oc. 19°50N 66°0W **183** C6
Puerto Saavedra *Chile* 38°47S 73°24W **192** A2
Puerto San Julián
Argentina 49°15S 67°45W **192** C3
Puerto Santa Cruz
Argentina 50°0S 68°32W **192** D3
Puerto Sastre *Paraguay* 22°2S 57°55W **190** A4
Puerto Serrano *Spain* 36°56N 5°33W **89** J5
Puerto Suárez *Bolivia* 18°58S 57°52W **188** G7
Puerto Supe *Peru* 11°0S 77°30W **188** C2
Puerto Vallarta
Mexico 20°37N 105°15W **180** C3
Puerto Varas *Chile* 41°19S 72°59W **192** B2
Puerto Wilches
Colombia 7°21N 73°54W **186** B4
Puerto Williams *Chile* 54°56S 67°37W **192** D3
Puertollano *Spain* 38°43N 4°7W **89** G6
Pueu *Tahiti* 17°44S 149°13W **155** b
Pueyrredón, L.
Argentina 47°20S 72°0W **192** C2
Púez Odle △ *Italy* 46°37N 11°48E **93** B8
Puffin I. *Ireland* 51°50N 10°24W **64** E1
Pugachev *Russia* 52°0N 48°49E **86** D9
Pugal *India* 28°30N 72°48E **124** E5
Puge *China* 27°20N 102°31E **116** D4
Puge *Tanzania* 4°45S 33°11E **142** C3
Puget Sound *U.S.A.* 47°50N 122°30W **170** C4
Puget-Théniers *France* 43°58N 6°53E **73** E10
Púglia □ *Italy* 41°15N 16°15E **95** A9
Pugödong *N. Korea* 42°5N 130°0E **115** C16
Pugu *Tanzania* 6°55S 39°4E **142** D4
Pūgünzī *Iran* 25°49N 59°10E **129** E8
Puha *N.Z.* 38°30S 177°50E **154** E6
Pui *Romania* 45°30N 23°4E **80** E8
Puica *Peru* 15°0S 72°33W **188** D3
Puiești *Romania* 46°25N 27°33E **81** D12
Puig Major *Spain* 39°48N 2°47E **100** B9
Puigcerdà *Spain* 42°24N 1°50E **90** C6
Puigmal *Spain* 42°23N 2°7E **90** C7
Puijpunyent *Spain* 39°38N 2°32E **100** B9
Puisaye, Collines de la
France 47°37N 3°2E **71** E10
Puiseaux *France* 48°11N 2°30E **71** D9
Pujehun *S. Leone* 7°23N 11°45W **138** D2
Pujiang *China* 29°29N 119°54E **117** C12
Pujols *France* 44°48N 0°22W **72** D3
Pujon-ho *N. Korea* 40°35N 127°35E **115** D14
Pukaki, L. *N.Z.* 44°4S 170°1E **155** F3
Pukapuka *Cook Is.* 10°53S 165°49W **157** J11
Pukaskwa △ *Canada* 48°20N 86°0W **164** C2
Pukatawagan *Canada* 55°45N 101°20W **163** B8
Pukchin *N. Korea* 40°12N 125°45E **115** D13
Pukch'ŏng *N. Korea* 40°14N 128°19E **115** D15
Pukë *Albania* 42°2N 19°53E **96** D3
Pukearuhe *N.Z.* 38°55S 174°31E **154** E3
Pukekohe *N.Z.* 37°12S 174°55E **154** D4
Puketeraki Ra. *N.Z.* 42°58S 172°13E **155** C7
Puketoi Ra. *N.Z.* 40°30S 176°5E **154** G6
Puketui *N.Z.* 45°4S 171°2E **155** F6
Pukhrayan *India* 26°14N 79°51E **125** F8
Puksubaek-san
N. Korea 40°42N 127°45E **115** D14
Pula *Croatia* 44°54N 13°57E **93** D10
Pula *Italy* 39°1N 9°0E **94** D2
Pulacayo *Bolivia* 20°55S 66°41W **188** E4
Pulandian *China* 39°25N 121°58E **115** E11
Pulaski *N.Y., U.S.A.* 43°34N 76°8W **175** C8
Pulaski *Tenn., U.S.A.* 35°12N 87°2W **177** D11
Pulaski *Va., U.S.A.* 37°3N 80°47W **173** G13
Pulau → *Indonesia* 5°50S 138°15E **119** F9
Pulau Gili *Indonesia* 8°21S 116°1E **119** J19
Puławy *Poland* 51°23N 21°59E **83** G8
Pulga *U.S.A.* 39°48N 121°29W **170** F5
Pulgaon *India* 20°44N 78°21E **126** D4
Pulicat L. *India* 13°25N 80°19E **127** H5
Pulicat L. *India* 13°40N 80°15E **127** H5
Pulivendla *India* 14°25N 78°15E **127** G4
Puliyangudi *India* 9°11N 77°24E **127** K3
Pullman *U.S.A.* 46°44N 117°10W **168** C5
Pulog, Mt. *Phil.* 16°40N 120°50E **119** A6
Pulpí *Spain* 37°24N 1°44W **91** H3
Pultusk *Poland* 52°43N 21°6E **83** F8
Pülümür *Turkey* 39°30N 39°51E **105** C8
Pumlumon Fawr *U.K.* 52°28N 3°46W **67** E4
Puná, I. *Ecuador* 2°55S 80°5W **186** D2
Punaauia *Tahiti* 17°37S 149°34W **155** b

Punakha Dzong
Bhutan 27°42N 89°52E **123** F16
Punalur *India* 9°0N 76°56E **127** K3
Punasar *India* 27°6N 73°6E **124** F5
Punata *Bolivia* 17°32S 65°50W **188** G5
Punch *India* 33°48N 74°4E **125** C6
Punch → *Pakistan* 33°12N 73°40E **124** C5
Punda Maria *S. Africa* 22°40S 31°5E **145** B5
Pune *India* 18°29N 73°57E **126** E1
P'ungsan *N. Korea* 40°50N 128°9E **115** D15
Pungue, Ponte de *Mozam.* 19°0S 34°0E **143** F3
Puning *China* 23°20N 116°12E **117** F11
Punjab □ *India* 31°0N 76°0E **124** D7
Punjab □ *Pakistan* 32°0N 72°30E **124** E6
Puno *Peru* 15°55S 70°3W **188** D3
Puno □ *Peru* 15°0S 70°0W **188** D3
Punpun → *India* 25°31N 85°18E **125** G11
Punta, Cerro de
Puerto Rico 18°10N 66°37W **183** d
Punta Alta *Argentina* 38°53S 62°4W **192** A4
Punta Arenas *Chile* 53°10S 71°0W **192** D2
Punta Coles *Peru* 17°43S 71°23W **188** D3
Punta de Bombón
Peru 17°10S 71°48W **188** D3
Punta del Díaz *Chile* 28°0S 70°45W **190** B1
Punta del Hidalgo
Canary Is. 28°33N 16°19W **100** F3
Punta Delgada
Argentina 42°43S 63°38W **192** B4
Punta Gorda *Belize* 16°10N 88°45W **182** D2
Punta Gorda *U.S.A.* 26°56N 82°3W **179** J7
Punta Prieta *Mexico* 28°58N 114°17W **180** B2
Punta Prima *Spain* 39°48N 4°16E **100** B11
Punta Umbría *Spain* 37°10N 6°56W **89** H4
Puntarenas *Costa Rica* 10°0N 84°50W **182** E3
Puntland *Somalia* 9°0N 50°0E **131** F4
Punto Fijo *Venezuela* 11°50N 70°13W **186** A4
Punxsutawney *U.S.A.* 40°57N 78°59W **174** F6
Pupuan *Indonesia* 8°19S 115°0E **119** J18
Puqi *China* 29°40N 113°50E **117** C9
Puquio *Peru* 14°45S 74°10W **188** C3
Pur → *Russia* 67°31N 77°55E **106** C8
Puracé, Vol. *Colombia* 2°21N 76°23W **186** C3
Puračić *Bos.-H.* 44°33N 18°28E **80** F3
Puralia = Puruliya
India 23°17N 86°24E **125** H12
Puranpur *India* 28°31N 80°9E **125** E9
Purbalingga *Indonesia* 7°23S 109°21E **119** G13
Purbeck, Isle of *U.K.* 50°39N 1°59W **67** G5
Purcell *U.S.A.* 35°1N 97°22W **176** D6
Purcell Mts. *Canada* 49°55N 116°15W **162** D5
Purdy *Canada* 45°19N 77°44W **174** A7
Puri *India* 19°50N 85°58E **126** E7
Purmerend *Neths.* 52°32N 4°58E **69** B4
Purna → *India* 19°6N 77°2E **126** E3
Purnia *India* 25°45N 87°31E **125** G12
Purnululu △ *Australia* 17°20S 128°20E **148** C4
Pursat = Pouthisat
Cambodia 12°34N 103°50E **120** F4
Purukcahu *Indonesia* 0°35S 114°35E **118** E4
Puruliya *India* 23°17N 86°24E **125** H12
Purus → *Brazil* 3°42S 61°28W **186** D6
Puruvesi *Finland* 61°50N 29°30E **84** B5
Pūrvomay *Bulgaria* 42°8N 25°17E **97** D9
Purwa *India* 26°28N 80°47E **125** F9
Purwakarta *Indonesia* 6°35S 107°29E **119** G12
Purwo, Tanjung
Indonesia 8°44S 114°21E **119** K18
Purwodadi *Indonesia* 7°7S 110°55E **119** G14
Purwokerto *Indonesia* 7°25S 109°14E **119** G13
Puryŏng *N. Korea* 42°5N 129°43E **115** C15
Pus → *India* 19°55N 77°55E **126** E3
Pusa *India* 25°59N 85°41E **125** G11
Pusad *India* 19°56N 77°36E **126** E3
Pusan = Busan
S. Korea 35°5N 129°0E **115** G15
Pushkin *Russia* 59°45N 30°25E **84** C6
Pushkino *Moskva, Russia* 56°2N 37°49E **84** D9
Pushkino *Saratov, Russia* 51°16N 47°0E **86** E8
Püspökladány *Hungary* 47°19N 21°6E **80** D6
Pustoshka *Russia* 56°20N 29°30E **84** D5
Puszczykowo *Poland* 52°18N 16°49E **83** F3
Put-in-Bay *U.S.A.* 41°39N 82°49W **174** E2
Putahow L. *Canada* 59°54N 100°40W **163** B8
Putao *Burma* 27°28N 97°30E **123** F20
Putaruru *N.Z.* 38°2S 175°50E **154** E4
Putbus *Germany* 54°22N 13°28E **76** A9
Puteran *Indonesia* 7°5S 114°0E **119** G16
Putian *China* 25°23N 119°0E **117** D12
Putignano *Italy* 40°51N 17°7E **95** B10
Putina *Peru* 14°55S 69°55W **188** C4
Puting, Tanjung
Indonesia 3°31S 111°46E **118** E4
Putlitz *Germany* 53°15N 12°3E **76** B8
Putna *Romania* 47°50N 25°33E **81** C10
Putna → *Romania* 45°45N 27°24E **81** E11
Putnam *U.S.A.* 41°55N 71°55W **175** E13
Putney *U.S.A.* 42°59N 84°8W **178** D5
Putnok *Hungary* 48°18N 20°26E **80** D5
Putorana, Gory *Russia* 69°0N 95°0E **107** C10
Putorino *N.Z.* 39°3S 176°58E **154** F5
Putrajaya *Malaysia* 2°55N 101°40E **121** L3
Putre *Chile* 18°12S 69°35W **188** G5
Puttalam *Sri Lanka* 8°1N 79°55E **127** K5
Puttalam Lagoon
Sri Lanka 8°15N 79°45E **127** K4
Puttgarden *Germany* 54°30N 11°10E **76** A7
Püttlingen *Germany* 49°17N 6°53E **77** F2
Puttur *Karnataka, India* 12°46N 75°12E **127** H2
Putty *Australia* 32°57S 150°52E **151** E5
Putumayo → *S. Amer.* 3°7S 67°58W **186** D5
Putusibau *Indonesia* 0°50N 112°56E **118** D4
Pututahi *N.Z.* 38°39S 177°53E **154** F6
Putyla *Ukraine* 48°0N 25°5E **81** B9
Puvirnituq *Canada* 60°2N 77°10W **161** E16
Puy-de-Dôme □ *France* 45°40N 3°0E **72** C6
Puy-de-Dôme *France* 45°46N 2°57E **72** C6
Puy-l'Évêque *France* 44°31N 1°9E **72** D5
Puyallup *U.S.A.* 47°12N 122°18W **170** C4
Puyang *China* 35°40N 115°1E **114** G8
Puyehue *Chile* 40°40S 72°37W **192** B2
Puyehue △ *Chile* 40°27S 72°7W **192** B2
Puylaurens *France* 43°35N 2°0E **72** E5
Puysegur Pt. *N.Z.* 46°9S 166°37E **155** G1
Püzeh Rīg *Iran* 27°20N 58°40E **129** E8
Puzhayka *Ukraine* 48°7N 29°50E **81** A13
Pwani □ *Tanzania* 7°0S 39°0E **142** D4

Pweto
Dem. Rep. of the Congo 8°25S 28°51E **143** D2
Pwllheli *U.K.* 52°53N 4°25W **66** E3
Pyana → *Russia* 55°43N 46°1E **86** C8
Pyaozero, Ozero *Russia* 66°5N 30°58E **60** C24
Pyapon *Burma* 16°20N 95°40E **123** L19
Pyasina → *Russia* 73°30N 87°0E **107** B9
Pyatigorsk *Russia* 44°2N 43°6E **87** H6
Pyatykhatky *Ukraine* 48°28N 33°38E **85** H7
Pyay = Pye *Burma* 18°49N 95°13E **123** K19
Pydna *Greece* 40°20N 22°34E **96** F6
Pye *Burma* 18°49N 95°13E **123** K19
Pyeongchang
S. Korea 37°22N 128°23E **115** F15
Pyeongtaek *S. Korea* 37°1N 127°4E **115** F14
Pyetrikaw *Belarus* 52°11N 28°29E **75** B15
Pyhäjoki *Finland* 64°28N 24°14E **60** D21
Pyhätunturi △ *Finland* 66°58N 27°55E **60** C22
Pyin-U-Lwin *Burma* 22°2N 96°28E **123** H20
Pyinmana *Burma* 19°45N 96°12E **123** K20
Pyla, C. *Cyprus* 34°56N 33°51E **101** E12
Pymatuning Res.
U.S.A. 41°30N 80°28W **174** E4
P'yŏktong *N. Korea* 40°50N 125°50E **115** D13
P'yŏnggang *N. Korea* 38°24N 127°17E **115** E14
P'yŏngsong *N. Korea* 39°14N 125°52E **115** E13
P'yŏngyang *N. Korea* 39°0N 125°30E **115** E13
Pyote *U.S.A.* 31°32N 103°8W **176** F3
Pyramid L. *U.S.A.* 40°1N 119°35W **168** F4
Pyramid Pk. *U.S.A.* 36°25N 116°37W **171** J10
Pyramids *Egypt* 29°58N 31°9E **137** C7
Pyrénées *Europe* 42°45N 0°18E **72** F4
Pyrénées □ *France* 42°52N 0°10W **72** F3
Pyrénées-Atlantiques □
France 43°10N 0°50W **72** E3
Pyrénées-Orientales □
France 42°35N 2°26E **72** F6
Pyrzyatyn *Ukraine* 50°15N 32°25E **85** G7
Pyrzyce *Poland* 53°10N 14°55E **83** E1
Pyskowice *Poland* 50°23N 18°38E **83** H5
Pytalovo *Russia* 57°5N 27°55E **84** D4
Pyu *Burma* 18°30N 96°28E **123** K20
Pyzdry *Poland* 52°11N 17°42E **83** F4

Q

Qaanaaq *Greenland* 77°30N 69°10W **57** B4
Qaasuitsup □ *Greenland* 74°0N 52°0W **57** C5
Qābālā *Azerbaijan* 40°58N 47°47E **87** K8
Qabanbay *Kazakhstan* 45°50N 80°37E **109** C10
Qabirri → *Azerbaijan* 41°3N 46°17E **87** K8
Qachasnek *S. Africa* 30°6S 28°42E **145** D4
Qādisiyah, Buhayrat al
Iraq 34°20N 42°12E **105** C10
Qa'el Jafr *Jordan* 30°20N 36°25E **130** E5
Qa'emābād *Iran* 31°44N 60°2E **129** D9
Qā'emshahr *Iran* 36°30N 52°53E **129** B7
Qagan Nur *Jilin,*
China 45°15N 124°18E **115** B13
Qagan Nur *Nei Monggol Zizhiqu,*
China 43°30N 114°55E **114** C8
Qahar Youyi Zhongqi
China 41°12N 112°40E **114** C7
Qahremānshahr = Kermānshāh
Iran 34°23N 47°0E **105** C12
Qaidam Pendi *China* 37°0N 95°0E **110** D8
Qa'jarīyeh *Iran* 31°1N 48°22E **129** D6
Qala, Ras il *Malta* 36°2N 14°20E **101** C1
Qala-i-Jadid = Spīn Būldak
Afghan. 31°1N 66°25E **124** D2
Qala Point = Qala, Ras il
Malta 36°2N 14°20E **101** C1
Qala Viala *Pakistan* 30°49N 67°17E **124** D2
Qala Yangi *Afghan.* 34°20N 66°30E **124** B2
Qalaikhum = Kalaikhum
Tajikistan 38°28N 70°46E **109** F8
Qal'at al Akhḍar
Si. Arabia 28°4N 37°9E **128** E3
Qal'at Bīshah *Si. Arabia* 20°0N 42°36E **137** D5
Qal'at Dizah *Iraq* 36°11N 45°7E **105** D11
Qal'at Ṣāliḥ *Iraq* 31°31N 47°16E **128** D5
Qal'at Sukkar *Iraq* 31°51N 46°5E **105** D12
Qal'eh-ye Now *Afghan.* 35°0N 63°5E **108** F6
Qalyûb *Egypt* 30°12N 31°11E **137** E7
Qamani'tuaq = Baker Lake
Canada 64°20N 96°3W **160** E12
Qamdo *China* 31°15N 97°6E **116** B1
Qamea *Fiji* 16°45S 179°45W **154** a
Qamruddin Karez
Pakistan 31°45N 68°20E **124** D3
Qandahār = Kandahār
Afghan. 31°32N 65°43E **124** D2
Qandahār = Kandahār □
Afghan. 31°0N 65°0E **124** D2
Qandyagbash
Kazakhstan 49°28N 57°25E **108** C5
Qapān *Iran* 37°40N 55°47E **128** B7
Qapqal *China* 43°48N 81°5E **109** D10
Qapshagbay
Kazakhstan 43°51N 77°14E **109** D8
Qapshagbay Bögeni
Kazakhstan 43°45N 77°0E **109** D8
Qaqortoq *Greenland* 60°43N 46°0W **57** E6
Qâra *Egypt* 29°38N 26°30E **137** C11
Qara Dāgh *Iraq* 35°18N 45°18E **105** C11
Qara Qash → *India* 35°0N 78°30E **125** B8
Qarabalyq *Kazakhstan* 53°50N 62°0E **108** D7
Qarabutaq *Kazakhstan* 50°0N 60°14E **108** C6
Qaraçala *Azerbaijan* 39°45N 48°53E **87** L9
Qaraçuxur *Azerbaijan* 40°25N 50°1E **87** K10
Qaraghandy
Kazakhstan 49°50N 73°10E **109** C8
Qārah *Si. Arabia* 29°55N 40°3E **128** D4
Qaraoba *Kazakhstan* 47°6N 54°15E **108** C5
Qaraqiya Oyysy
Kazakhstan 43°27N 51°45E **108** E3
Qaraqosh *Iraq* 36°16N 43°22E **105** B10
Qaratoū Ongtüstik Qazaqstan,
Kazakhstan 43°30N 69°30E **108** F7
Qarataū *Zhambyl,*
Kazakhstan 43°10N 70°28E **109** D8
Qarazhal *Kazakhstan* 48°2N 70°49E **108** D8
Qarchak *Iran* 35°25N 51°34E **129** C6
Qardho *Somalia* 9°30N 49°6E **131** F4
Qareh → *Iran* 39°25N 47°22E **128** B5
Qareh Tekān *Iran* 36°38N 49°29E **128** B6
Qarnein *U.A.E.* 24°56N 52°52E **129** E7

Qarokŭl = Karakul, Ozero
  Tajikistan 39°5N 73°25E **109** E8
Qarqan He → China 39°30N 88°30E **109** E11
Qarqaraly Kazakhstan 49°26N 75°30E **109** C9
Qarshi Uzbekistan 38°53N 65°48E **109** E7
Qartabā Lebanon 34°4N 35°50E **130** A4
Qārūh Kuwait 28°49N 48°46E **129** D6
Qaryat al Gharab Iraq 31°27N 44°48E **128** D5
Qaryat al 'Ulyā
  Si. Arabia 27°33N 47°42E **128** E5
Qarynzharyq Oyysy
  Kazakhstan 42°55N 54°25E **108** D4
Qashqadaryo □
  Uzbekistan 38°35N 66°0E **109** E7
Qasigiannguit
  Greenland 68°50N 51°18W **57** D5
Qasr 'Amra Jordan 31°48N 36°35E **128** D3
Qasr-e Qand Iran 26°15N 60°45E **129** E9
Qasr-e Shīrīn Iran 34°31N 45°35E **105** E11
Qasr Farâfra Egypt 27°0N 28°1E **137** B2
Qasuittuq = Resolute
  Canada 74°42N 94°54W **161** C13
Qatanā Syria 33°26N 36°4E **130** B5
Qatar ■ Asia 25°30N 51°15E **129** E6
Qatlīsh Iran 37°50N 57°19E **129** B8
Qattâra Egypt 30°12N 27°3E **137** A2
Qattâra, Munkhafed el
  Egypt 29°30N 27°30E **137** B2
Qattâra Depression = Qattâra,
  Munkhafed el Egypt 29°30N 27°30E **137** B2
Qawâm al Ḥamzah = Al Ḥamzah
  Iraq 31°43N 44°58E **128** D5
Qāyen Iran 33°40N 59°10E **129** C8
Qaynar Kazakhstan 49°12N 77°22E **109** C9
Qazaly Kazakhstan 45°45N 62°6E **108** C6
Qazaqstan = Kazakhstan ■
  Asia 50°0N 70°0E **109** C8
Qazaqtyng Usaqshogylyghy
  Kazakhstan 50°0N 72°0E **109** C8
Qazax Azerbaijan 41°5N 45°21E **87** K7
Qazimämmäd Azerbaijan 40°3N 49°0E **87** K9
Qazvīn Iran 36°15N 50°0E **129** B6
Qazvīn □ Iran 36°20N 50°0E **129** B6
Qazyghurt Kazakhstan 41°45N 69°23E **109** D7
Qena Egypt 26°10N 32°43E **137** B3
Qena, W. → Egypt 26°12N 32°44E **137** B3
Qeqertarsuaq Qaasuitsup,
  Greenland 69°45N 53°30W **57** D5
Qeqertarsuaq Qaasuitsup,
  Greenland 69°15N 53°38W **57** D5
Qeqertarsuatsiaat
  Greenland 63°5N 50°45W **57** E5
Qeqqata □ Greenland 66°30N 48°0W **57** D6
Qeshlāq Iran 34°55N 46°28E **105** E12
Qeshm Iran 26°55N 56°10E **129** E8
Qeydār Iran 36°6N 48°35E **105** D13
Qeys Iran 26°32N 53°58E **129** E7
Qezel Owzen → Iran 36°45N 49°22E **129** B6
Qez'ot Israel 30°52N 34°26E **130** E3
Qi Xian China 34°40N 114°48E **114** G8
Qian Gorlos China 45°5N 124°42E **115** B13
Qian Hai China 22°32N 113°54E **111** a
Qian Xian China 34°31N 108°15E **114** G5
Qian'an China 40°0N 118°41E **115** E10
Qiancheng China 27°12N 109°50E **116** D7
Qianjiang Guangxi Zhuangzu,
  China 23°38N 108°58E **116** F7
Qianjiang Hubei, China 30°24N 112°55E **117** B9
Qianjiang Sichuan,
  China 29°33N 108°47E **116** C7
Qianjin China 47°34N 133°4E **111** B15
Qianshan Anhui,
  China 30°37N 116°35E **117** B11
Qianshan Guangdong,
  China 22°15N 113°31E **111** a
Qianwei China 29°1N 103°39E **116** C4
Qianxi China 27°3N 106°3E **116** D6
Qianyang Hunan,
  China 27°18N 110°10E **117** D8
Qianyang Shaanxi,
  China 34°40N 107°8E **114** G4
Qianyang Zhejiang,
  China 30°11N 119°25E **117** B12
Qi'ao China 22°25N 113°39E **111** a
Qi'ao Dao China 22°25N 113°39E **111** a
Qiaocun China 39°56N 112°55E **114** E7
Qiaojia China 26°56N 102°58E **116** D4
Qichun China 30°18N 115°25E **117** B10
Qidong Hunan, China 26°49N 112°7E **117** D9
Qidong Jiangsu, China 31°48N 121°40E **117** B13
Qiemo China 38°8N 85°32E **109** L11
Qijiang China 29°1N 106°35E **116** C6
Qijiaojing China 43°28N 91°36E **109** C12
Qikiqtaaluk = Baffin I.
  Canada 68°0N 75°0W **161** C17
Qikiqtarjuaq Canada 67°33N 63°0W **161** D19
Qila Saifullāh Pakistan 30°45N 68°17E **124** D3
Qilian Shan China 38°30N 96°0E **114** D1
Qimen China 30°50N 117°42E **117** C11
Qin He → China 35°1N 113°22E **114** G7
Qin Jiang → Guangxi Zhuangzu,
  China 21°53N 108°35E **116** F7
Qin Jiang → Jiangxi,
  China 26°15N 115°55E **117** D10
Qin Ling = Qinling Shandi
  China 33°50N 108°10E **114** H5
Qin'an China 34°48N 105°40E **114** G3
Qing Xian China 38°35N 116°45E **114** E9
Qingcheng China 37°15N 117°40E **115** F9
Qingcheng Shan
  China 30°58N 103°31E **116** B4
Qingchuan China 32°36N 105°9E **114** H3
Qingfeng China 35°52N 115°8E **114** G8
Qinghai □ China 36°0N 98°0E **110** D8
Qinghai Hu China 36°40N 100°10E **114** D1
Qinghe China 46°37N 90°25E **109** C12
Qinghecheng China 41°28N 124°15E **115** D13
Qinghemen China 41°48N 121°25E **115** D11
Qingjian China 37°8N 110°8E **114** F6
Qingjiang = Huaiyin
  China 33°30N 119°2E **115** H10
Qingliu China 26°11N 116°48E **117** D11
Qinglong China 25°49N 105°12E **116** E5
Qingping China 28°49N 104°47E **116** D6
Qingshui China 34°48N 106°8E **114** G4
Qingshuihe China 39°55N 111°35E **114** E6
Qingtian China 28°12N 120°15E **117** C13
Qingtongxia China 38°2N 106°3E **114** E4
Qingtongxia Shuiku
  China 37°50N 105°58E **114** F3
Qingxi China 27°8N 108°43E **116** D7

Qingxu China 37°34N 112°22E **114** F7
Qingyang Anhui,
  China 30°38N 117°50E **117** B11
Qingyang Gansu, China 36°2N 107°55E **114** F4
Qingyi Jiang → China 29°32N 103°44E **116** C4
Qingyuan Guangdong,
  China 23°40N 112°59E **117** F9
Qingyuan Liaoning,
  China 42°10N 124°55E **115** C13
Qingyuan Zhejiang,
  China 27°36N 119°3E **117** D12
Qingyun China 37°45N 117°20E **115** F9
Qingzhen China 26°31N 106°25E **116** D6
Qinhuangdao China 39°56N 119°30E **115** E10
Qinling Shandi China 33°50N 108°10E **114** H5
Qinshui China 35°40N 112°8E **114** G7
Qinyang = Jiyuan
  China 35°7N 112°57E **114** G7
Qinyang China 35°5N 112°56E **114** G7
Qinyuan China 36°29N 112°20E **114** F7
Qinzhou China 21°58N 108°38E **116** G7
Qionghai China 19°15N 110°26E **117** a
Qionglai China 30°25N 103°31E **116** B4
Qionglai Shan China 31°0N 102°30E **116** B4
Qiongshan China 19°51N 110°26E **117** a
Qiongzhou Haixia
  China 20°10N 110°15E **117** a
Qiqihar China 47°26N 124°0E **111** B13
Qira China 37°0N 80°48E **109** E10
Qiraîya, W. → Egypt 30°27N 34°0E **130** E3
Qiryat Ata Israel 32°47N 35°6E **130** C4
Qiryat Gat Israel 31°32N 34°46E **130** D3
Qiryat Mal'akhi Israel 31°44N 34°44E **130** D3
Qiryat Shemona Israel 33°13N 35°35E **130** B4
Qiryat Yam Israel 32°51N 35°4E **130** C4
Qishan China 34°25N 107°38E **114** G4
Qitai China 44°2N 89°35E **109** C11
Qitaihe China 45°48N 130°51E **112** B5
Qiubei China 24°2N 104°12E **116** E5
Qixia China 37°17N 120°52E **115** F11
Qiyang China 26°35N 111°50E **117** D8
Qızılağac Körfäzi
  Azerbaijan 39°9N 49°0E **105** C13
Qobda Kazakhstan 50°55N 54°31E **108** B4
Qods Iran 35°45N 51°15E **129** C6
Qojūr Iran 36°12N 47°55E **128** B5
Qom Iran 34°40N 51°0E **129** C6
Qom □ Iran 34°40N 51°0E **129** C6
Qomolangma Feng = Everest, Mt.
  Nepal 28°5N 86°58E **125** E12
Qomsheh Iran 32°0N 51°55E **129** D6
Qong Muztag China 35°42N 82°22E **109** E10
Qoqek = Tacheng
  China 46°40N 82°58E **109** C10
Qo'qon Uzbekistan 40°31N 70°56E **109** D8
Qorako'l Uzbekistan 39°32N 63°50E **108** E6
Qoraqalpog'iston □
  Uzbekistan 43°0N 58°0E **108** D5
Qorghalzhyn
  Kazakhstan 50°25N 69°11E **109** B7
Qorveh Iran 35°10N 47°48E **105** E12
Qosshaghyl Kazakhstan 46°40N 54°0E **108** C4
Qostanay Kazakhstan 53°10N 63°35E **108** B6
Qotanqaraghay
  Kazakhstan 49°10N 85°36E **109** C11
Qoţūr Iran 38°28N 44°25E **105** C11
Qu Jiang → China 30°1N 106°24E **116** B6
Qu Xian China 30°48N 106°58E **116** B6
Quabbin Res. U.S.A. 42°20N 72°20W **175** D12
Quairading Australia 32°0S 117°21E **149** F2
Quakenbrück Germany 52°41N 7°57E **76** B3
Quakertown U.S.A. 40°26N 75°21W **175** F9
Qualicum Beach
  Canada 49°22N 124°26W **162** D4
Quambatook Australia 35°49S 143°34E **152** C5
Quambone Australia 30°57S 147°53E **153** A7
Quamby Australia 20°22S 140°17E **150** C3
Quan Long = Ca Mau
  Vietnam 9°7N 105°8E **121** H5
Quanah U.S.A. 34°18N 99°44W **176** D5
Quandialla Australia 34°1S 147°47E **153** C7
Quang Ngai Vietnam 15°13N 108°58E **120** E7
Quang Tri Vietnam 16°45N 107°13E **120** D6
Quang Yen Vietnam 20°56N 106°52E **116** G6
Quannan China 24°45N 114°33E **117** E10
Quanyang China 42°21N 127°32E **115** C14
Quanzhou Fujian,
  China 24°55N 118°34E **117** E12
Quanzhou Guangxi Zhuangzu,
  China 25°57N 111°5E **117** E8
Qu'Appelle →
  Canada 50°33N 103°53W **163** C8
Quaqtaq Canada 60°55N 69°40W **161** E18
Quaraí Brazil 30°15N 56°20W **190** C4
Quarré-les-Tombes
  France 47°21N 4°0E **71** E11
Quarteira Portugal 37°4N 8°6W **89** H2
Quartu Sant'Élena Italy 39°15N 9°10E **94** C2
Quartzsite U.S.A. 33°40N 114°13W **171** M12
Quatre Bornes Mauritius 20°15S 57°28E **141** d
Quatsino Sd. Canada 50°25N 127°58W **162** C3
Quba Azerbaijan 41°21N 48°32E **87** K9
Qūchān Iran 37°10N 58°27E **129** B8
Queanbeyan Australia 35°17S 149°14E **153** C8
Québec Canada 46°52N 71°13W **165** C5
Québec □ Canada 48°0N 74°0W **164** B6
Quebo Guinea-Biss. 11°20N 14°56W **138** C2
Quebrada del Condorito △
  Argentina 31°49S 64°40W **190** C4
Quedlinburg Germany 51°47N 11°8E **76** D7
Queen Alexandra Ra.
  Antarctica 85°0S 170°0E **55** E11
Queen Charlotte B.
  Falk. Is. 51°50S 60°40W **192** G4
Queen Charlotte City
  Canada 53°15N 132°2W **162** C2
Queen Charlotte Is. = Haida Gwaii
  Canada 53°20N 132°10W **162** C2
Queen Charlotte Sd.
  Canada 51°0N 128°0W **162** C3
Queen Charlotte Sd.
  N.Z. 41°10S 174°15E **155** B9
Queen Charlotte Strait
  Canada 50°45N 127°10W **162** C3
Queen Elizabeth △ Uganda 0°0 30°0E **142** C3
Queen Elizabeth Is.
  Canada 76°0N 95°0W **161** B13
Queen Elizabeth Land
  Antarctica 85°0S 60°0W **55** E17
Queen Mary Land
  Antarctica 70°0S 95°0E **55** D7

Queen Maud G.
  Canada 68°15N 102°30W **160** D11
Queen Maud Land = Dronning
  Maud Land Antarctica 72°30S 12°0E **55** D3
Queen Maud Mts.
  Antarctica 86°0S 160°0W **55** E12
Queens Channel
  Australia 15°0S 129°30E **148** C4
Queenscliff Australia 38°16S 144°39E **152** E6
Queensland □ Australia 22°0S 142°0E **150** C3
Queenstown Australia 42°4S 145°35E **151** G4
Queenstown N.Z. 45°1S 168°40E **155** F3
Queenstown Singapore 1°18N 103°48E **121** d
Queenstown S. Africa 31°52S 26°52E **144** D4
Queets U.S.A. 47°32N 124°19W **170** C2
Queguay Grande →
  Uruguay 32°9S 58°9W **190** C4
Queimadas Brazil 11°0S 39°38W **189** D3
Quelimane Mozam. 17°53S 36°58E **143** F4
Quellón Chile 43°7S 73°37W **192** B2
Quelpart = Jeju-do
  S. Korea 33°29N 126°34E **115** H14
Queluz Portugal 38°45N 9°14W **89** G1
Quemado N. Mex.,
  U.S.A. 34°20N 108°30W **169** J9
Quemado Tex., U.S.A. 28°56N 100°37W **176** G4
Quemoy = Chinmen
  Taiwan 24°26N 118°19E **117** E12
Quemú-Quemú
  Argentina 36°3S 63°36W **190** D3
Quepem India 15°13N 74°3E **127** G2
Quequén Argentina 38°30S 58°30W **190** D4
Querco Peru 13°50S 74°52W **188** C3
Querétaro Mexico 20°36N 100°23W **180** C4
Querétaro □ Mexico 21°0N 99°55W **180** C5
Querfurt Germany 51°23N 11°35E **76** D7
Quérigut France 42°42N 2°6E **72** F6
Querqueville France 49°40N 1°42W **70** C5
Quesada Spain 37°51N 3°4W **89** H7
Queshan China 32°55N 114°2E **117** A10
Quesnel Canada 53°0N 122°30W **162** C4
Quesnel → Canada 52°58N 122°29W **162** C4
Quesnel L. Canada 52°30N 121°20W **162** C4
Questa U.S.A. 36°42N 105°36W **169** H11
Questembert France 47°40N 2°28W **70** E4
Quetico △ Canada 48°30N 91°45W **164** C1
Quetrequile Argentina 41°33S 69°22W **192** B3
Quetta Pakistan 30°15N 66°55E **124** D2
Quetzaltenango
  Guatemala 14°50N 91°30W **182** D1
Queuls Indonesia 7°8S 114°13E **119** G16
Quealat △ Chile 44°29S 72°24W **192** B2
Queyras → France 44°45N 6°50E **73** D10
Quezon City Phil. 14°37N 121°2E **119** B6
Qufār Si. Arabia 27°26N 41°37E **128** E4
Qufu China 35°36N 116°58E **114** G9
Qui Nhon Vietnam 13°40N 109°13E **120** F7
Quibala Angola 10°46S 14°59E **140** G2
Quibaxe Angola 8°24S 14°27E **140** F2
Quibdó Colombia 5°42N 76°40W **186** B3
Quiberon France 47°29N 3°9W **70** E3
Quiberon, Presqu'île de
  France 47°30N 3°8W **70** E3
Quickborn Germany 53°42N 9°52E **76** B5
Quiet L. Canada 61°5N 133°5W **162** A2
Quiindy Paraguay 25°58S 57°14W **190** B4
Quilá Mexico 24°23N 107°13W **180** C3
Quilán, C. Chile 43°15S 74°30W **192** B2
Quilcene U.S.A. 47°49N 122°53W **170** C4
Quilimarí Chile 32°5S 71°30W **190** C1
Quilino Argentina 30°14S 64°29W **190** C3
Quillabamba Peru 12°50S 72°50W **188** C3
Quillagua Chile 21°40S 69°40W **190** A2
Quillan France 42°53N 2°10E **72** F6
Quillota Chile 32°54S 71°16W **190** C1
Quilmes Argentina 34°43S 58°15W **190** C4
Quilon = Kollam India 8°50N 76°38E **127** K3
Quilpie Australia 26°35S 144°11E **151** D3
Quilpué Chile 33°5S 71°33W **190** C1
Quilua Mozam. 16°17S 39°54E **143** F4
Quime Bolivia 17°2S 67°15W **188** D4
Quimili Argentina 27°40S 62°30W **190** B3
Quimper France 48°0N 4°9W **70** D2
Quimperlé France 47°53N 3°33W **70** E3
Quinault → U.S.A. 47°21N 124°18W **170** C2
Quince Mil Peru 13°15S 70°40W **188** C3
Quincy Calif., U.S.A. 39°56N 120°57W **170** F6
Quincy Fla., U.S.A. 30°35N 84°34W **178** E5
Quincy Ill., U.S.A. 39°56N 91°23W **174** F8
Quincy Mass., U.S.A. 42°14N 71°0W **175** D14
Quincy Wash., U.S.A. 47°14N 119°51W **168** C4
Quines Argentina 32°13S 65°48W **190** C2
Quinga Mozam. 15°49S 40°15E **143** F5
Quingey France 47°7N 5°52E **71** E12
Quinhámel
  Guinea-Biss. 11°53N 15°51W **138** C1
Quintana de la Serena
  Spain 38°45N 5°40W **89** G5
Quintana Roo □
  Mexico 19°40N 88°30W **181** D7
Quintana Roo △ Quintana Roo,
  Mexico 18°35N 87°45W **181** C7
Quintanar de la Orden
  Spain 39°36N 3°5W **89** F7
Quintanar de la Sierra
  Spain 41°57N 2°55W **90** D2
Quintanar del Rey Spain 39°21N 1°56W **91** F3
Quintero Chile 32°45S 71°30W **190** C1
Quintin France 48°26N 2°56W **70** D4
Quinto Spain 41°25N 0°32W **90** D4
Quipar → Spain 38°15N 1°40W **91** G3
Quirihue Chile 36°15S 72°35W **190** D1
Quirimbas △ Mozam. 12°30S 40°15E **143** E5
Quirindi Australia 31°28S 150°40E **153** B9
Quirinópolis Brazil 18°32S 50°30W **187** B3
Quiroga Spain 42°28N 7°18W **89** B3
Quiruvilca Peru 8°1S 78°19W **186** C2
Quissanga Mozam. 12°24S 40°28E **143** E5
Quissico Mozam. 24°42S 34°44E **145** C5
Quitilipi Argentina 26°50S 60°13W **190** B3
Quitman U.S.A. 30°47N 83°34W **178** E6
Quito Ecuador 0°15S 78°35W **186** D2
Quixadá Brazil 4°55S 39°0W **189** D3
Quixaxe Mozam. 15°17S 40°4E **143** F5
Quixeramobim Brazil 5°12S 39°17W **189** D3
Qujing China 25°32N 103°41E **116** E4
Qulan Kazakhstan 42°55N 72°43E **108** E8
Qul'ān, Jazā'ir Egypt 24°22N 35°31E **128** C2
Qulsary Kazakhstan 46°59N 54°1E **108** C3
Qumbu S. Africa 31°10S 28°48E **145** D4

Quneitra = Al Qunayţirah
  Syria 33°5N 35°45E **130** B4
Qŭnghirot Uzbekistan 43°2N 58°50E **108** D5
Qu'nyido China 31°15N 98°6E **116** B2
Quoin I. Australia 14°54S 129°32E **148** B4
Quoin Pt. S. Africa 34°46S 19°37E **144** D2
Quorn Australia 32°25S 138°5E **152** B3
Qŭrghonteppa
  Tajikistan 37°50N 68°47E **109** E7
Qurnat as Sawdā'
  Lebanon 34°18N 36°6E **130** A5
Qŭryq Kazakhstan 43°12N 51°39E **108** D4
Qūs Egypt 25°55N 32°50E **137** B3
Qusar Azerbaijan 41°25N 48°26E **87** K9
Quşaybā' Si. Arabia 26°53N 43°35E **128** E4
Qusaybah Iraq 34°24N 40°59E **105** E9
Quseir Egypt 26°7N 34°16E **128** C2
Quseir Amra = Qasr 'Amra
  Jordan 31°48N 36°35E **128** D3
Qüshchī Iran 37°59N 45°3E **105** D11
Qusmuryn Kazakhstan 52°27N 64°36E **108** B6
Qusmuryn Köli
  Kazakhstan 52°41N 64°48E **108** B6
Qutang Gorge = Qutang Xia
  China 31°0N 109°40E **116** B7
Qutang Xia China 31°0N 109°40E **116** B7
Quthing Lesotho 30°25S 27°36E **145** E4
Qūţīābād Iran 35°47N 48°30E **105** E13
Quttinirpaaq = Ellesmere I.
  Canada 79°30N 80°0W **161** B16
Quttinirpaaq △
  Canada 82°13N 72°13W **161** A17
Quwo China 35°38N 111°25E **114** G6
Quyang China 38°35N 114°40E **114** E8
Quynh Nhai Vietnam 21°49N 103°33E **120** B4
Quyon Canada 45°31N 76°14W **175** A8
Quzhou China 28°57N 118°54E **117** C12
Quzi China 36°20N 107°20E **114** F4
Qvareli Georgia 41°57N 45°47E **87** K7
Qyzylorda Kazakhstan 44°48N 65°28E **108** D6
Qyzylorda □ Kazakhstan 45°0N 65°0E **108** D6
Qyzylzhar Kazakhstan 48°17N 69°38E **109** C7

R

Ra, Ko Thailand 9°13N 98°16E **121** H2
Raab Austria 48°21N 13°39E **78** C6
Raahe Finland 64°40N 24°28E **60** D21
Raalte Neths. 52°23N 6°16E **69** B6
Raas Indonesia 7°8S 114°33E **119** G16
Raasay U.K. 57°25N 6°4W **65** D2
Raasay, Sd. of U.K. 57°30N 6°8W **65** D2
Rab Croatia 44°45N 14°45E **93** D11
Rába → Hungary 47°38N 17°38E **80** C2
Raba → Poland 50°8N 20°30E **83** H7
Rabaçal → Portugal 41°30N 7°12W **88** D3
Rabah Nigeria 13°5N 5°30E **139** C6
Rabai Kenya 3°50S 39°31E **142** C4
Rabastens France 43°50N 1°43E **72** E5
Rabastens-de-Bigorre
  France 43°23N 0°9E **72** E4
Rabat = Victoria Malta 36°3N 14°14E **101** C1
Rabat Malta 35°53N 14°24E **101** D1
Rabat Morocco 34°2N 6°48W **136** B2
Rabat □ Morocco 34°2N 6°48W **136** B2
Rabaul Papua N. G. 4°24S 152°18E **147** M8
Rabbah Nigeria 13°5N 5°30E **139** C6
Rabi Fiji 16°30S 179°59W **154** a
Rābigh Si. Arabia 22°50N 39°5E **131** C2
Rabka Poland 49°37N 19°59E **83** J6
Rābniţa = Rîbniţa
  Moldova 47°45N 29°0E **81** C14
Rābor Iran 29°17N 56°55E **129** D8
Rabwah = Chenab Nagar
  Pakistan 31°45N 72°55E **124** D5
Rača Serbia 44°14N 21°0E **96** B4
Răcăciuni Romania 46°20N 26°59E **81** D11
Răcăşdia Romania 44°59N 21°36E **80** F6
Racconigi Italy 44°46N 7°46E **92** D4
Race, C. Canada 46°40N 53°5W **165** C9
Race Pond U.S.A. 30°55N 82°0W **178** F6
Rach Gia Vietnam 10°5N 105°5E **121** G5
Rach Soi Vietnam 9°57N 105°7E **121** H5
Racha Noi, Ko Thailand 7°30N 98°19E **121** J2
Racha Yai, Ko Thailand 7°36N 98°21E **121** J2
Rachid Mauritania 18°45N 11°35W **138** B2
Raciąż Poland 52°46N 20°10E **83** F7
Racibórz Poland 50°7N 18°18E **83** H5
Racichy Belarus 53°44N 23°42E **82** E10
Racine U.S.A. 42°44N 87°47W **172** D10
Rackerby U.S.A. 39°26N 121°22W **170** F5
Råda Sweden 60°0N 13°36E **62** E7
Radan Serbia 42°59N 21°29E **96** C5
Rădăuţi Romania 47°50N 25°59E **81** C10
Rădăuţi-Prut Romania 48°14N 26°48E **81** B11
Radbuza → Czech Rep. 49°45N 13°22E **78** B6
Radcliff U.S.A. 37°51N 85°57W **173** G11
Radeberg Germany 51°7N 13°55E **76** D9
Radebeul Germany 51°6N 13°39E **76** D9
Radeče Slovenia 46°5N 15°14E **93** B12
Radekhiv Ukraine 50°25N 24°32E **75** C13
Radekhov = Radekhiv
  Ukraine 50°25N 24°32E **75** C13
Radenthein Austria 46°48N 13°43E **78** E6
Radew → Poland 54°2N 15°52E **82** D2
Radford U.S.A. 37°8N 80°34W **173** G8
Radhanpur India 23°50N 71°38E **124** H4
Radhwa, Jabal
  Si. Arabia 24°34N 38°18E **128** E3
Radika → Macedonia 41°38N 20°37E **96** A4
Radisson Qué., Canada 53°47N 77°37W **164** B4
Radisson Sask.,
  Canada 52°30N 107°20W **163** C7
Radium Hot Springs
  Canada 50°35N 116°2W **162** C5
Radje ob Dravi
  Slovenia 46°38N 15°13E **93** B12
Radnevo Bulgaria 42°17N 25°58E **99** G11
Radnice Czech Rep. 49°51N 13°35E **78** B6
Radnor Forest U.K. 52°17N 3°10W **67** E4
Radolfzell Germany 47°44N 8°58E **79** E4
Radom Poland 51°23N 21°12E **83** G8
Radom □ Poland 51°30N 21°0E **83** G8
Radomka → Poland 51°32N 21°28E **83** G8
Radomsko Poland 51°5N 19°28E **83** G6
Radomyshl Ukraine 50°30N 29°12E **75** C5
Radomyśl Wielki Poland 50°14N 21°15E **83** H8

Radoszyce Poland 51°4N 20°15E **83** G7
Radoviš Macedonia 41°38N 22°28E **96** E6
Radovljica Slovenia 46°22N 14°12E **93** B11
Radstadt Austria 47°24N 13°28E **78** D6
Radstock, C. Australia 33°12S 134°20E **151** E1
Raduša Macedonia 42°7N 21°15E **96** D5
Raduzhnyy Russia 62°5N 77°28E **106** C8
Radvanichy Belarus 52°1N 24°0E **83** F11
Radviliškis Lithuania 55°49N 23°33E **82** C10
Radville Canada 49°30N 104°15W **163** D8
Radwą, J. Si. Arabia 24°34N 38°18E **137** C4
Radymno Poland 49°59N 22°52E **83** J9
Radzanów Poland 52°56N 20°8E **83** F7
Radziejów Poland 52°40N 18°30E **83** F5
Radzyń Chelmiński
  Poland 53°23N 18°55E **82** E5
Radzyń Podlaski Poland 51°47N 22°37E **83** G9
Rae = Behchoko
  Canada 62°50N 116°3W **162** A5
Rae Bareli India 26°18N 81°20E **125** F8
Rae Isthmus Canada 66°40N 87°30W **161** D14
Raeren Belgium 50°41N 6°7E **69** D6
Raeside, L. Australia 29°20S 122°0E **149** E3
Raetihi N.Z. 39°25S 175°17E **154** F4
Rafaela Argentina 31°10S 61°30W **190** C3
Rafah Gaza Strip 31°18N 34°14E **130** D3
Rafaï C.A.R. 4°59N 23°58E **142** B1
Raffadali Italy 37°24N 13°32E **94** E6
Rafḥā Si. Arabia 29°35N 43°35E **128** D4
Rafina Greece 38°2N 24°0E **98** C6
Rafsanjän Iran 30°30N 56°5E **129** D8
Raft Pt. Australia 16°4S 124°26E **148** C3
Raga South Sudan 8°28N 25°41E **135** G11
Ragachow Belarus 53°8N 30°5E **75** B16
Ragama Sri Lanka 7°0N 79°50E **122** R11
Ragged, Mt. Australia 33°27S 123°25E **149** F3
Ragged Pt. Barbados 13°10N 59°26W **183** g
Raghunathpalli India 22°14N 84°48E **125** H11
Raghunathpur India 23°33N 86°40E **125** H12
Raglan N.Z. 37°55S 174°55E **154** D3
Raglan Harbour N.Z. 37°47S 174°50E **154** D3
Ragland U.S.A. 33°45N 86°9W **178** B3
Ragusa Italy 36°55N 14°44E **95** F7
Raha Indonesia 4°55S 123°0E **119** E6
Rahaeng = Tak Thailand 16°52N 99°8E **120** D2
Rahat, Ḥarrat Si. Arabia 23°0N 40°5E **137** C5
Rahatgarh India 23°47N 78°22E **125** H8
Rahden Germany 52°26N 8°36E **76** C4
Rahimyar Khan
  Pakistan 28°30N 70°25E **124** E4
Rähjerd Iran 34°22N 50°22E **129** C6
Rahole △ Kenya 0°5N 38°57E **142** B4
Rahon India 31°3N 76°7E **124** D7
Rahotu N.Z. 39°20S 173°49E **154** F2
Rahovec Kosovo 42°24N 20°40E **96** D4
Rahuri India 19°23N 74°39E **126** E2
Rai, Hon Vietnam 9°48N 104°38E **121** H5
Raiatéa, Î.
  French Polynesia 16°50S 151°25W **157** J12
Raichur India 16°10N 77°20E **127** E3
Raïgarh India 21°56N 83°25E **125** D9
Raighar India 19°51N 82°6E **126** E6
Raijua Indonesia 10°37S 121°36E **119** F6
Raikot India 30°41N 75°42E **124** D6
Railton Australia 41°25S 146°28E **151** G4
Rainbow Bridge △
  U.S.A. 37°5N 110°58W **169** H8
Rainbow City U.S.A. 33°57N 86°5W **178** B3
Rainbow Lake Canada 58°30N 119°23W **162** B5
Rainier U.S.A. 46°53N 122°41W **170** D4
Rainier, Mt. U.S.A. 46°52N 121°46W **170** D4
Rainy L. Canada 48°42N 93°10W **163** D10
Rainy River Canada 48°43N 94°29W **163** D10
Raippaluoto Finland 63°13N 21°14E **62** E19
Raipur India 21°17N 81°45E **125** D8
Raïrakhol India 21°4N 84°21E **125** D7
Ra'is Si. Arabia 23°33N 38°43E **137** C4
Raisen India 23°20N 77°48E **124** H7
Raisio Finland 60°28N 22°11E **63** E12
Raj Nandgaon India 21°5N 81°5E **125** D8
Raj Nilgiri India 21°28N 86°46E **125** D12
Raja, Ujung Indonesia 3°40N 96°25E **120** D1
Raja Ampat, Kepulauan
  Indonesia 0°30S 130°0E **119** E8
Rajahmundry India 17°1N 81°48E **127** C5
Rajaji △ India 30°10N 78°20E **124** D8
Rajajinagar India 30°10N 78°20E **124** D8
Rajampet India 14°11N 79°5E **127** F4
Rajang → Malaysia 2°30N 112°0E **118** D4
Rajapalaiyam India 9°25N 77°35E **127** K3
Rajasthan □ India 26°45N 73°30E **124** F5
Rajasthan Canal = Indira Gandhi
  Canal India 28°0N 72°0E **124** F5
Rajauri India 33°25N 74°21E **124** C5
Rajendranagar India 17°18N 78°22E **124** F6
Rajgangpur India 22°18N 84°33E **125** H11
Rajgarh Mad. P., India 24°2N 76°45E **124** G7
Rajgarh Raj., India 28°40N 75°25E **124** E6
Rajgarh Raj., India 27°14N 76°38E **124** F6
Rajgir India 25°2N 85°11E **125** G11
Rajkot India 22°15N 70°56E **124** H4
Rajmahal Hills India 24°30N 87°30E **125** G12
Rajpipla India 21°50N 73°30E **124** J5
Rajpur India 22°18N 74°21E **124** H6
Rajpura India 30°25N 76°32E **124** D7
Rajsamand = Kankroli
  India 25°4N 73°53E **124** G5
Rajshahi Bangla. 24°22N 88°39E **125** G16
Rajshahi □ Bangla. 25°0N 89°0E **125** G16
Rajula India 21°3N 71°26E **124** J4
Rajura India 19°47N 79°22E **126** E4
Rakai Uganda 0°45S 31°30E **142** C3
Rakaia N.Z. 43°45S 172°1E **155** E4
Rakaposhi Pakistan 36°10N 74°25E **125** A6
Rakata, Pulau
  Indonesia 6°10S 105°20E **118** G3
Rakitnoye Russia 45°36N 134°17E **112** —
Rakh Pakistan 41°40N 111°11W **108** —
Rakhiv Ukraine 48°3N 24°12E **75** C13
Rakhni Pakistan 30°4N 69°56E **124** D3
Rakhny-Lisovi Ukraine 48°47N 28°19E **81** B13
Rakiraki Fiji 17°22S 178°11E **154** a

Rakitnoye Russia 45°36N 134°17E **112** —
Rakitnoye Russia 50°57N 35°56E **97** —
Rakitovo Bulgaria 41°59N 24°5E **97** —
Rakiura = Stewart I.
  N.Z. 46°58S 167°54E **155** —
Rakoniewice Poland 52°10N 16°16E **83** —
Rakops Botswana 21°1S 24°28E **144** —
Rakovica Croatia 44°59N 15°38E **93** —
Rakovník Czech Rep. 50°6N 13°42E **78** —
Rakovski Bulgaria 42°21N 24°57E **97** —
Rakvere Estonia 59°20N 26°25E **64** —
Raleigh Fla., U.S.A. 29°25N 82°32W **179** —
Raleigh N.C., U.S.A. 35°47N 78°39W **177** —
Ralik Chain Pac. Oc. 8°0N 160°0E **146** —
Ralja Serbia 44°33N 20°34E **96** —
Rälla Sweden 56°40N 16°30E **63** —
Ralls U.S.A. 33°41N 101°24W **176** —
Ralston U.S.A. 41°30N 76°57W **174** —
Ram → Canada 62°1N 123°41W **162** —
Rām Allāh West Bank 31°55N 35°10E **130** —
Rama Nic. 12°9N 84°15W **182** —
Ramacca Italy 37°23N 14°42E **95** —
Ramachandrapuram
  India 16°50N 82°4E **126** —
Ramagiri Udayagiri
  India 19°5N 84°18E **126** —
Ramagundam India 18°55N 79°15E **126** —
Ramakona India 21°43N 78°50E **125** —
Ramalho, Serra do
  Brazil 13°45S 44°0W **189** —
Rāmallāh = Rām Allāh
  West Bank 31°55N 35°10E **130** —
Raman Thailand 6°29N 101°18E **121** —
Ramanathapuram India 9°25N 78°55E **127** —
Ramanujganj India 23°48N 83°42E **125** —
Ramas C. India 15°5N 73°55E **127** —
Ramat Gan Israel 32°4N 34°48E **130** —
Ramatlhabama
  S. Africa 25°37S 25°33E **144** —
Ramban India 33°14N 75°12E **125** —
Rambervillers France 48°20N 6°38E **71** —
Rambi = Rabi Fiji 16°30S 179°59W **154** —
Rambipuji Indonesia 8°12S 113°37E **119** —
Rambouillet France 48°39N 1°50E **70** —
Ramdurg India 15°58N 75°22E **127** —
Rame Hd. Australia 37°47S 149°30E **153** —
Ramechhap Nepal 27°25N 86°10E **125** —
Ramenskoye Russia 55°32N 38°15E **84** —
Ramer U.S.A. 9°17N 79°18E **127** —
Rameswaram India 9°17N 79°18E **127** —
Ramganga → India 27°5N 79°58E **125** —
Ramgarh Jharkhand,
  India 23°40N 85°35E **125** —
Ramgarh Raj., India 27°16N 75°14E **124** —
Ramgarh Raj., India 27°30N 70°36E **124** —
Rāmhormoz Iran 31°15N 49°35E **129** —
Ramīān Iran 37°3N 55°16E **129** —
Ramingining Australia 12°19S 135°3E **150** —
Ramla Israel 31°55N 34°52E **130** —
Ramm = Rum Jordan 29°35N 35°24E **130** —
Ramm, Jabal Jordan 29°35N 35°24E **130** —
Râmna → Romania 45°26N 27°3E **81** —
Ramnad = Ramanathapuram
  India 9°25N 78°55E **127** —
Ramnagar Jammu & Kashmir,
  India 32°47N 75°18E **125** —
Ramnagar Uttarakhand,
  India 29°24N 79°7E **125** —
Ramnäs Sweden 59°46N 16°12E **62** —
Râmnicu Sărat Romania 45°26N 27°3E **81** —
Râmnicu Vâlcea Romania 45°9N 24°21E **81** —
Ramon Russia 51°55N 39°21E **85** —
Ramona U.S.A. 33°2N 116°52W **171** —
Ramonville-St-Agne
  France 43°33N 1°28E **72** —
Ramore Canada 48°30N 80°25W **164** —
Ramos → Mexico 5°8N 52°23E **180** —
Ramotswa Botswana 24°50S 25°52E **144** —
Rampur H.P., India 31°26N 77°43E **124** —
Rampur Mad. P., India 23°25N 73°53E **124** —
Rampur Odisha, India 28°50N 79°5E **125** —
Rampur Ut. P., India 28°50N 79°5E **125** —
Rampur Hat India 24°10N 87°50E **125** —
Rampura India 24°30N 75°27E **124** —
Ramrama Tola India 21°52N 79°55E **125** —
Ramree I. Burma 19°0N 93°40E **123** —
Rāmsar Iran 36°53N 50°41E **129** —
Ramsey I. of Man 54°20N 4°22W **66** —
Ramsey U.S.A. 41°4N 74°9W **175** —
Ramsey L. Canada 47°13N 82°15W **164** —
Ramsgate U.K. 51°20N 1°25E **67** —
Ramsjö Sweden 62°11N 15°37E **62** —
Ramstein Germany 49°27N 7°36E **64** —
Ramtek India 21°20N 79°15E **125** —
Ramu Kenya 3°55N 41°10E **142** —
Ramvik Sweden 62°49N 17°51E **62** —
Rana Pratap Sagar Dam
  India 24°58N 75°38E **124** —
Ranaghat India 23°15N 88°35E **125** —
Ranahu Pakistan 25°55N 69°45E **124** —
Ranau Malaysia 6°2N 116°40E **118** —
Rancagua Chile 34°10S 70°50W **190** —
Rance → France 48°34N 1°59W **70** —
Rancheria → Canada 60°13N 129°7W **162** —
Ranchester U.S.A. 44°54N 107°10W **168** —
Ranchi India 23°19N 85°27E **125** —
Rancho Cordova
  U.S.A. 38°36N 121°18W **172** —
Rancho Cucamonga
  U.S.A. 34°10N 117°30W **171** —
Ranco, L. Chile 40°15S 72°25W **192** —
Rand Australia 35°33S 146°32E **153** —
Randalstown U.K. 54°45N 6°19W **64** —
Randan France 46°2N 3°21E **72** —
Randazzo Italy 37°53N 14°56E **95** —
Randers Denmark 56°29N 10°1E **63** —
Randers Fjord Denmark 56°37N 10°20E **63** —
Randfontein S. Africa 26°8S 27°45E **145** —
Randle U.S.A. 46°32N 121°57W **170** —
Randolph Mass.,
  U.S.A. 42°10N 71°2W **175** —
Randolph N.Y., U.S.A. 42°10N 78°59W **174** —
Randolph Utah,
  U.S.A. 41°40N 111°11W **168** —
Randsburg U.S.A. 35°22N 117°39W **171** —
Râneälven → Sweden 65°50N 22°20E **62** —
Ranfurly N.Z. 45°7S 170°6E **155** —
Rangae Thailand 6°19N 101°44E **121** —
Rangataua N.Z. 39°26S 175°28E **154** —

hgaunu B. N.Z. 34°51S 173°15E 154 A2
geley, The Zimbabwe 19°2S 31°2E 143 F3
geley L. U.S.A. 44°58N 70°39W 175 B14
geley L. U.S.A. 44°55N 70°43W 175 B14
gely U.S.A. 40°5N 108°48W 168 F9
ager U.S.A. 32°28N 98°41W 176 E5
gia India 26°28N 91°38E 123 F17
giora N.Z. 43°19S 172°36E 155 D7
gitaiki N.Z. 38°52S 176°4E 154 C5
gitaiki → N.Z. 37°54S 176°49E 154 C5
gitikei → N.Z. 40°17S 175°15E 154 G4
gitoto ke te tonga = D'Urville
  N.Z. 40°50S 173°55E 155 A8
gitoto Ra. N.Z. 38°25S 175°35E 154 E4
gkasbitung
  ndonesia 6°21S 106°15E 119 G12
gaon = Yangôn
  urma 16°45N 96°20E 123 L20
gsang Indonesia 1°20N 103°5E 121 M4
ai-ki-Vav India 23°51N 72°6E 124 H4
ibennur India 14°35N 75°30E 127 G2
ganj Paschimbanga,
  adia 23°40N 87°5E 123 H15
igani Ut. P., India 27°3N 82°13E 125 F9
gitata → N.Z. 29°39N 79°25E 125 E8
ikhet India 29°39N 79°25E 125 E8
gippettai India 12°56N 79°23E 127 H4
giwara India 24°50N 72°10E 124 G8
giyah Iraq 36°15N 44°53E 105 C11
aka India 23°59N 83°47E 125 H13
ken → Australia 20°31S 137°36E 150 C2
akin U.S.A. 31°13N 101°56W 176 F4
akin Inlet Canada 62°30N 93°0W 160 E13
akins Springs
  ustralia 33°49S 146°14E 153 B7
akweil Austria 47°17N 9°39E 78 D2
anoch, L. U.K. 56°38N 4°20W 65 E4
anoch Moor U.K. 56°38N 4°48W 65 E4
aohira Madag. 22°29S 45°24E 141 J9
aong Thailand 9°56N 98°40E 121 H2
apur India 20°5N 85°20E 126 D7
asa Iran 33°39N 48°18E 129 C6
asiki Indonesia 1°30S 134°10E 119 E8
atau Abang
  Malaysia 4°52N 103°24E 121 K4
ataupraprat Indonesia 2°15N 99°50E 118 D1
atemario Indonesia 3°15S 119°57E 119 E5
athambore △ India 26°10N 76°30E 124 F7
atoul U.K. 40°19N 88°9W 172 E10
aum Denmark 56°54N 9°14E 63 H3
ayah, W. →
  Arabia 21°18N 43°20E 137 C5
he China 46°47N 134°0E 112 A7
n l'Étape France 48°24N 6°50E 71 D13
ping China 23°42N 117°1E 117 F11
i, Er Algeria 29°0N 2°0W 136 C3
yang China 38°15N 115°45E 114 E8
, Ko Thailand 9°19N 99°58E 121 b
a French Polynesia 27°35S 144°20W 157 K13
Nui = Pascua, I. de
  hile 27°7S 109°23W 157 K17
allo Italy 44°21N 9°14E 92 D6
ar India 23°34N 70°38E 124 H4
ch Iran 25°40N 59°15E 129 E8
er, Lago Chile 34°20S 71°14W 190 C1
er, C. Canada 69°44N 67°6W 161 D18
id City U.S.A. 44°5N 103°14W 172 C2
id River U.S.A. 45°55N 86°59W 172 C10
a Estonia 59°1N 24°52E 84 C3
ti → India 26°18N 83°41E 125 F10
quette → U.S.A. 45°0N 74°42W 175 B10
a → Nepal 29°30N 82°0E 125 E10
a Cook Is. 21°30S 160°0W 157 K12
otonga Cook Is. 21°30S 160°0W 157 K12
s al 'Ayn Syria 36°45N 40°12E 105 D9
s Al Khair Si. Arabia 27°27N 49°18E 129 E6
s al Khaymah
  U.A.E. 25°50N 55°59E 129 E7
s at Tib Tunisia 37°1N 11°2E 136 A6
el Ma Algeria 36°22N 0°50W 136 B3
el Mâ Mali 16°35N 4°20W 138 B4
el Oued Algeria 35°57N 5°2E 136 A5
Ghârib Egypt 28°6N 33°18E 137 F8
Muhammad △
  gypt 27°45N 34°16E 137 B3
Sudr Egypt 29°40N 32°42E 137 F8
Argentina 36°20S 56°41W 190 D4
a, Pta. Río Negro,
  rgentina 40°50S 62°15W 192 B4

Rathdrum Ireland 52°56N 6°14W 64 D5
Rathenow Germany 52°37N 12°19E 76 C8
Rathkeale Ireland 52°32N 8°56W 64 D3
Rathlin I. U.K. 55°18N 6°14W 64 A5
Rathmelton Ireland 55°2N 7°39W 64 A4
Ratibor = Racibórz
  Poland 50°7N 18°18E 83 H5
Rätikon Austria 47°0N 9°55E 78 D2
Ratingen Germany 51°18N 6°52E 76 D2
Ratlam India 23°20N 75°0E 124 H6
Ratmanova, Ostrov
  Russia 65°46N 169°6W 166 B6
Ratnagiri India 16°57N 73°18E 126 F1
Ratnapura Sri Lanka 6°40N 80°20E 127 L5
Ratodero Pakistan 27°48N 68°18E 124 F3
Raton U.S.A. 36°54N 104°24W 169 H11
Rattaphum Thailand 7°8N 100°16E 121 J3
Ratten Austria 47°28N 15°44E 78 D8
Rattray Hd. U.K. 57°38N 1°50W 65 D7
Rättvik Sweden 60°52N 15°7E 62 D9
Ratz, Mt. Canada 57°23N 132°12W 162 B2
Ratzeburg Germany 53°40N 10°46E 76 B6
Raub Malaysia 3°47N 101°52E 121 L3
Rauch Argentina 36°45S 59°5W 190 D4
Raudales Mexico 17°27N 93°39W 181 D6
Raufarhöfn Iceland 66°27N 15°57W 60 C6
Raufoss Norway 60°44N 10°37E 60 F14
Raukumara Ra. N.Z. 38°5S 177°55E 154 E6
Raul Soares Brazil 20°5S 42°22W 189 E2
Rauma Finland 61°10N 21°30E 84 B1
Raumo = Rauma
  Finland 61°10N 21°30E 84 B1
Raung, Gunung
  Indonesia 8°8S 114°3E 119 J17
Raurkela India 22°14N 84°50E 125 H11
Rausu-Dake Japan 44°4N 145°7E 112 B12
Räut → Moldova 47°15N 29°9E 81 C14
Rava-Ruska Ukraine 50°15N 23°42E 83 H10
Rava Russkaya = Rava-Ruska
  Ukraine 50°15N 23°42E 83 H10
Ravalli U.S.A. 47°17N 114°11W 168 C6
Ravānsar Iran 34°43N 46°40E 105 E12
Ravanusa Italy 37°16N 13°58E 94 E6
Rāvar Iran 31°20N 56°51E 129 D8
Ravena U.S.A. 42°28N 73°49W 175 D11
Ravenel U.S.A. 32°46N 80°15W 178 C9
Ravenna Italy 44°25N 12°12E 93 D9
Ravenna Nebr., U.S.A. 41°1N 98°55W 172 E4
Ravenna Ohio, U.S.A. 41°9N 81°15W 174 E3
Ravensburg Germany 47°46N 9°36E 77 H5
Ravenshoe Australia 17°37S 145°29E 150 D4
Ravensthorpe Australia 33°35S 120°2E 149 F3
Ravenswood Australia 20°6S 146°54E 150 D4
Ravenswood U.S.A. 38°57N 81°46W 173 F13
Ravensworth Australia 32°26S 151°4E 153 B9
Raver India 21°15N 76°2E 126 D3
Ravi → Pakistan 30°35N 71°49E 124 D4
Ravna Gora Croatia 45°24N 14°50E 93 C11
Ravna Reka Serbia 44°1N 21°33E 96 B5
Ravne na Koroškem
  Slovenia 46°36N 14°59E 93 B11
Rawa Mazowiecka
  Poland 51°46N 20°12E 83 G7
Rawalpindi Pakistan 33°38N 73°8E 124 C5
Rawang Malaysia 3°20N 101°35E 121 L3
Rawene N.Z. 35°25S 173°32E 154 B2
Rawi, Ko Thailand 6°33N 99°14E 121 J2
Rawicz Poland 51°36N 16°52E 83 G3
Rawka → Poland 52°9N 20°8E 83 F7
Rawlinna Australia 30°58S 125°28E 149 F4
Rawlins U.S.A. 41°47N 107°14W 168 F10
Rawlinson Ra.
  Australia 24°40S 128°30E 149 D4
Rawson Argentina 43°15S 65°5W 192 B3
Raxaul India 26°59N 84°51E 125 F11
Raxaul U.S.A. 48°21N 103°0W 172 A2
Ray, C. Canada 47°33N 59°15W 165 C8
Ray City U.S.A. 31°5N 83°11W 178 D6
Ray Mts. U.S.A. 66°0N 152°0W 166 B9
Rayachoti India 14°4N 78°50E 127 G4
Rayadurg India 14°40N 76°50E 127 G3
Rayagada India 19°15N 83°20E 126 E6
Raychikhinsk Russia 49°46N 129°25E 107 E13
Rāyen Iran 29°34N 57°26E 129 D8
Rayle U.S.A. 33°48N 82°54W 178 B7
Rayleigh U.K. 51°36N 0°37E 67 F8
Raymond Calif.,
  U.S.A. 37°13N 119°54W 170 H7
Raymond N.H., U.S.A. 43°2N 71°11W 175 C13
Raymond Wash.,
  U.S.A. 46°41N 123°44W 170 D3
Raymond Terrace
  Australia 32°45S 151°44E 153 B9
Raymondville U.S.A. 26°29N 97°47W 176 H6
Raymore Canada 51°25N 104°31W 163 C8
Rayón Mexico 29°43N 110°35W 180 B2
Rayong Thailand 12°40N 101°20E 120 F3
Rayville U.S.A. 32°29N 91°46W 176 E9
Raz, Pte. du France 48°2N 4°47W 70 D2
Razan Iran 35°23N 49°2E 105 E13
Ražana Serbia 44°6N 19°55E 96 B3
Ražanj Serbia 43°40N 21°31E 96 C5
Razāzah, Buḩayrat ar
  Iraq 32°40N 43°35E 105 F10
Razdelna Bulgaria 43°13N 27°41E 97 C11
Razdel'naya = Rozdilna
  Ukraine 46°50N 30°2E 81 D15
Razdolnoye Russia 43°30N 131°52E 112 C5
Razdolnoye Ukraine 45°46N 33°28E 85 K7
Razeh Iran 31°20N 49°59E 129 D6
Razgort Russia 62°4N 52°46E 86 B9
Razgrad Bulgaria 43°33N 26°34E 97 C10
Razim, Lacul Romania 44°50N 29°0E 81 F16
Razlog Bulgaria 41°53N 23°28E 96 E7
Razmak Pakistan 32°45N 69°50E 124 C3
Razzaza, L. = Razāzah, Buḩayrat
  ar Iraq 32°40N 43°35E 105 F10
Re, Cu Lao Vietnam 15°22N 109°8E 120 E7
Ré, Î. de France 46°12N 1°30W 70 F5
Reading U.K. 51°27N 0°58W 67 F7
Reading U.S.A. 40°20N 75°56W 175 F9
Reading □ U.K. 51°27N 0°58W 67 F7
Real, Cordillera Bolivia 17°0S 67°10W 188 G5
Realicó Argentina 35°0S 64°15W 190 D3
Réalmont France 43°48N 2°10E 72 E6
Ream Cambodia 10°34N 103°39E 121 G4
Ream △ Cambodia 10°30N 103°45E 121 G4
Reay Forest U.K. 58°22N 4°55W 65 C4

Rebais France 48°50N 3°10E 71 D10
Rebecca, L. Australia 30°0S 122°15E 149 F3
Rebi Indonesia 6°23S 134°7E 119 F8
Rebiana, Sahrâ' Libya 24°30N 21°0E 135 D10
Rebun-Tō Japan 45°23N 141°2E 112 B10
Recanati Italy 43°24N 13°32E 93 C10
Recaş Romania 45°46N 21°30E 80 E6
Recco Italy 44°22N 9°9E 92 D6
Recherche, Arch. of the
  Australia 34°15S 122°50E 149 F3
Rechna Doab Pakistan 31°35N 73°30E 124 D5
Rechytsa Belarus 52°21N 30°24E 75 E6
Recife Brazil 8°0S 35°0W 189 B4
Recife Seychelles 4°36S 55°42E 141 b
Recklinghausen Germany 51°37N 7°12E 76 D3
Reckong Peo India 31°32N 78°16E 124 D8
Reconquista Argentina 29°10S 59°45W 190 B4
Recreo Argentina 29°25S 65°10W 190 B3
Recuay Peru 9°43S 77°28W 188 B2
Recz Poland 53°16N 15°31E 83 E2
Red → Hong → Asia 20°16N 106°34E 120 B5
Red →, U.S.A. 31°1N 91°45W 176 F9
Red Bank U.S.A. 40°21N 74°5W 175 F10
Red Bay Canada 51°44N 56°25W 165 B8
Red Bluff U.S.A. 40°11N 122°15W 168 F2
Red Bluff Res. U.S.A. 31°54N 103°55W 169 L12
Red Cliffs Australia 34°19S 142°11E 152 C5
Red Cloud U.S.A. 40°5N 98°32W 172 E4
Red Creek U.S.A. 43°14N 76°45W 175 C8
Red Deer Canada 52°20N 113°50W 162 C6
Red Deer → Alta.,
  Canada 50°58N 110°0W 163 C7
Red Deer → Man.,
  Canada 52°53N 101°1W 163 C8
Red Deer L. Canada 52°55N 101°20W 163 C8
Red Hook U.S.A. 41°55N 73°53W 175 E11
Red Indian L. Canada 48°35N 57°0W 165 C8
Red L. Canada 51°3N 93°49W 163 C10
Red Lake Canada 51°3N 93°49W 163 C10
Red Lake Falls U.S.A. 47°53N 96°16W 172 B5
Red Lake Road
  Canada 49°59N 93°25W 163 D10
Red Lodge U.S.A. 45°11N 109°15W 168 D9
Red Mountain U.S.A. 35°37N 117°38W 171 K9
Red Oak U.S.A. 41°1N 95°14W 172 E6
Red River of the North →
  N. Amer. 49°0N 97°15W 172 A5
Red Rock Canada 48°55N 88°15W 164 C2
Red Rock, L. U.S.A. 41°22N 92°59W 172 E7
Red Rocks Pt.
  Australia 32°13S 127°32E 149 F4
Red Sea Asia 25°0N 36°0E 131 C2
Red Slate Mt. U.S.A. 37°31N 118°52W 170 H8
Red Sucker L. Canada 54°9N 93°40W 164 B1
Red Tower Pass = Turnu Roşu, P.
  Romania 45°33N 24°17E 81 E9
Red Volta → Africa 10°34N 0°30W 139 C4
Red Wing U.S.A. 44°34N 92°31W 172 C7
Reda Poland 54°40N 18°19E 82 D5
Redang, Pulau Malaysia 5°49N 103°2E 121 K4
Redange Lux. 49°46N 5°52E 69 E5
Redcar U.K. 54°37N 1°4W 66 C6
Redcar & Cleveland □
  U.K. 54°29N 1°0W 66 C7
Redcliff Canada 50°10N 110°50W 168 A8
Redcliffe Australia 27°12S 153°6E 151 D5
Redcliffe, Mt. Australia 28°30S 121°30E 149 E3
Reddersburg S. Africa 29°41S 26°10E 144 C4
Reddick U.S.A. 29°22N 82°12W 178 F7
Redding U.S.A. 40°35N 122°24W 168 F2
Redditch U.K. 52°18N 1°55W 67 E6
Redenção Brazil 4°13S 38°43W 189 A3
Redfield U.S.A. 44°53N 98°31W 172 C4
Redford U.S.A. 44°38N 73°48W 175 B11
Redhead Trin. & Tob. 10°44N 60°58W 187 K16
Redkino Russia 56°39N 36°16E 84 D9
Redlands U.S.A. 34°4N 117°11W 171 M9
Redmond Oreg.,
  U.S.A. 44°17N 121°11W 168 D3
Redmond Wash.,
  U.S.A. 47°40N 122°7W 170 C4
Redon France 47°40N 2°6W 70 E4
Redonda Antigua & B. 16°58N 62°19W 183 C7
Redondela Spain 42°15N 8°38W 88 C2
Redondo Portugal 38°39N 7°37W 89 C3
Redondo Beach
  U.S.A. 33°50N 118°23W 171 M8
Redoubt Volcano
  U.S.A. 60°29N 152°45W 166 C9
Redruth U.K. 50°14N 5°14W 67 G2
Redvers Canada 49°35N 101°40W 163 D8
Redwater Canada 53°55N 113°6W 162 C6
Redwood U.S.A. 44°18N 75°48W 175 B9
Redwood □ U.S.A. 41°40N 124°5W 168 F1
Redwood City U.S.A. 37°30N 122°15W 170 H4
Redwood Falls U.S.A. 44°32N 95°7W 172 C6
Ree, L. Ireland 53°35N 8°0W 64 C3
Reed City U.S.A. 43°53N 85°31W 173 D11
Reed L. Canada 54°38N 100°30W 163 B8
Reedley U.S.A. 36°36N 119°27W 170 J7
Reedsburg U.S.A. 43°32N 90°0W 172 D8
Reedsport U.S.A. 43°42N 124°6W 168 E1
Reedsville U.S.A. 44°9N 87°57W 172 C10
Reedy Creek Australia 36°58S 140°2E 152 D4
Reefton N.Z. 42°6S 171°51E 155 C6
Rees Germany 51°46N 6°24E 76 D2
Reese → U.S.A. 40°48N 117°4W 168 F5
Refahiye Turkey 39°54N 38°47E 105 C8
Reftele Sweden 57°11N 13°35E 63 G7
Refugio U.S.A. 28°18N 97°17W 176 G6
Rega → Poland 54°10N 15°18E 82 D2
Regalbuto Italy 37°39N 14°38E 95 E7
Regana, C. de Spain 39°25N 2°43E 100 B9
Regen Germany 48°58N 13°8E 77 G9
Regen → Germany 49°1N 12°6E 77 F8
Regensburg Germany 49°1N 12°6E 77 F8
Regenstauf Germany 49°7N 12°6E 77 F8
Reggâne = Zaouiet Reggâne
  Algeria 26°32N 0°3E 136 C4
Reggello Italy 43°41N 11°32E 93 C8
Réggio di Cálabria Italy 38°6N 15°39E 95 D8
Réggio nell'Emília Italy 44°43N 10°36E 92 D7
Reghin Romania 46°46N 24°42E 80 D9
Regina Canada 50°27N 104°35W 163 C8
Regina Beach Canada 50°47N 105°0W 163 C8
Register U.S.A. 32°13N 81°53W 178 C8
Registro Brazil 24°29S 47°49W 191 A6
Reguengos de Monsaraz
  Portugal 38°25N 7°32W 89 C3

Rehli India 23°38N 79°5E 125 H8
Rehoboth Namibia 23°15S 17°4E 144 B2
Rehovot Israel 31°54N 34°48E 130 D3
Rei, Costa Italy 39°15N 9°40E 94 C2
Reichenbach Germany 50°37N 12°17E 76 E8
Reid Australia 30°49S 128°26E 149 F4
Reidsville Ga., U.S.A. 32°6N 82°7W 178 C7
Reidsville N.C., U.S.A. 36°21N 79°40W 177 C15
Reigate U.K. 51°14N 0°12W 67 F7
Reillo Spain 39°54N 1°53W 90 F3
Reims France 49°15N 4°1E 71 C11
Reina Adelaida, Arch.
  Chile 52°20S 74°0W 192 D2
Reina Sofía, Tenerife ✈ (TFS)
  Canary Is. 28°3N 16°33W 100 F3
Reindeer → Canada 55°36N 103°11W 163 B8
Reindeer I. Canada 52°30N 98°0W 163 C9
Reindeer L. Canada 57°15N 102°15W 163 B8
Reinga, C. N.Z. 34°25S 172°43E 154 A1
Reinheimen △ Norway 62°10N 7°45E 60 E12
Reinosa Spain 43°2N 4°15W 88 B6
Reitz S. Africa 27°48S 28°29E 145 C4
Reivilo S. Africa 27°36S 24°8E 144 C3
Rejmyre Sweden 58°50N 15°55E 63 F9
Reka → Slovenia 45°40N 14°0E 93 C11
Rekovac Serbia 43°51N 21°3E 96 C5
Reliance Canada 63°0N 109°20W 163 A7
Relizane Algeria 35°44N 0°31E 136 A4
Remad, Oued →
  Algeria 33°28N 1°20W 136 B3
Rémalard France 48°26N 0°47E 70 D7
Remanso Brazil 9°41S 42°4W 189 B2
Remarkable, Mt.
  Australia 32°48S 138°10E 152 B3
Remarkables, The
  N.Z. 45°10S 168°50E 155 F3
Rembang Indonesia 6°42S 111°21E 119 G14
Rembert U.S.A. 34°6N 80°32W 178 A9
Remchi Algeria 35°2N 1°26W 136 A3
Remedios Panama 8°15N 81°50W 182 E3
Remeshk Iran 26°55N 58°50E 129 E8
Remetea Romania 46°45N 25°29E 81 D10
Remich Lux. 49°32N 6°22E 69 E6
Remiremont France 48°2N 6°36E 71 D13
Remontnoye Russia 46°34N 43°37E 87 G6
Remoulins France 43°55N 4°35E 73 E8
Remscheid Germany 51°11N 7°12E 76 D3
Ren Xian China 37°8N 114°40E 114 F8
Rendang Indonesia 8°26S 115°25E 119 J18
Rende Italy 39°20N 16°11E 95 C9
Rendina Greece 39°4N 21°58E 98 B3
Rendsburg Germany 54°17N 9°39E 76 A5
René-Levasseur, Î.
  Canada 51°20N 68°40W 165 B6
Renfrew Canada 45°30N 76°40W 175 B8
Renfrewshire □ U.K. 55°49N 4°38W 65 F4
Renfroe U.S.A. 32°14N 84°43W 178 C5
Rengat Indonesia 0°30S 102°45E 118 E2
Rengo Chile 34°24S 70°50W 190 C1
Renhua China 25°5N 113°40E 117 E9
Renhuai China 27°48N 106°24E 116 D6
Reni → Taranagar India 28°43N 74°50E 124 E6
Reni Ukraine 45°28N 28°15E 81 E13
Renigunta India 13°38N 79°30E 127 H4
Renland Greenland 71°10N 26°30W 57 C8
Renmark Australia 34°11S 140°43E 152 C4
Rennell Sd. Canada 53°23N 132°35W 162 C2
Renner Springs
  Australia 18°20S 133°47E 150 B1
Rennes France 48°7N 1°41W 70 D5
Rennick Glacier
  Antarctica 70°30S 161°45E 55 D11
Rennie L. Canada 45°30N 105°39W 163 A7
Reno U.S.A. 39°31N 119°48W 170 F7
Reno → Italy 44°38N 12°16E 93 D9
Renovo U.S.A. 41°20N 77°45W 174 E7
Renqiu China 38°43N 116°5E 114 E9
Rens China 25°59N 104°9E 116 E5
Renshou China 29°59N 104°19E 116 C5
Rensselaer Ind., U.S.A. 40°57N 87°9W 172 E9
Rensselaer N.Y.,
  U.S.A. 42°38N 73°45W 175 D11
Renton U.S.A. 47°28N 122°12W 170 C4
Renukoot India 24°13N 83°2E 125 G10
Renwick N.Z. 41°30S 173°51E 155 B8
Réo Burkina Faso 12°28N 2°35W 138 C4
Reocín = Puente San Miguel
  Spain 43°21N 4°5W 88 B6
Reotipur India 25°33N 83°45E 125 G10
Repalle India 16°2N 80°45E 127 F5
Répcelak Hungary 47°24N 17°1E 80 C2
Republic Mo., U.S.A. 37°7N 93°29W 172 G7
Republic Wash.,
  U.S.A. 48°39N 118°44W 168 B4
Republican → U.S.A. 39°4N 96°48W 172 F5
Republika Srpska □
  Bos.-H. 44°56N 17°11E 93 D14
Repulse B. Australia 20°35S 148°46E 150 b
Repulse Bay Canada 66°30N 86°30W 161 C14
Requena Peru 5°5S 73°52W 188 B3
Requena Spain 39°30N 1°4W 91 F3
Réquista France 44°1N 2°32E 72 D6
Reşadiye Muğla, Turkey 36°45N 27°39E 104 D7
Reşadiye Tokat, Turkey 40°23N 37°20E 104 B7
Reşadiye Yarımadası
  Turkey 36°40N 27°45E 99 E9
Resavica Serbia 44°4N 21°31E 96 B5
Reserve U.S.A. 33°43N 108°45W 169 K9
Resht = Rasht Iran 37°20N 49°40E 105 D13
Resistencia Argentina 27°30S 59°0W 190 B4
Reşiţa Romania 45°18N 21°53E 80 E6
Resko Poland 53°47N 15°25E 82 E2
Reso = Raisio Finland 60°28N 22°11E 84 B2
Resolute Canada 74°42N 94°54W 161 C12
Resolution I. Canada 61°30N 65°0W 161 D19
Resolution I. N.Z. 45°40S 166°40E 155 F1
Resplandes Brazil 6°17S 45°13W 189 B3
Resplendor Brazil 19°20S 41°15W 189 D2
Ressano Garcia Mozam. 25°25S 32°0E 145 C5
Reston Canada 49°33N 101°6W 163 D8
Reszel Poland 54°4N 21°10E 82 D8
Retalhuleu Guatemala 14°33N 91°46W 182 C1
Retenue, L. de
  Dem. Rep. of the Congo 11°0S 27°0E 143 E2
Retezat, Munţii Romania 45°25N 23°0E 80 E7
Retezat △ Romania 45°23N 22°56E 80 E7

Rethel France 49°30N 4°20E 71 C11
Rethem Germany 52°47N 9°25E 76 C5
Rethimno Greece 35°18N 24°30E 101 D6
Reti Pakistan 28°5N 69°48E 124 E3
Retiche, Alpi Switz. 46°30N 10°0E 77 J6
Retiers France 47°55N 1°23W 70 E5
Retortillo Spain 40°48N 6°21W 88 E4
Retournac France 45°12N 4°2E 73 D8
Rétság Hungary 47°58N 19°10E 80 C4
Réunion ☑ Ind. Oc. 21°0S 56°0E 141 c
Reus Spain 41°10N 1°5E 90 D6
Reuterstadt Stavenhagen
  Germany 53°42N 12°54E 76 B8
Reutlingen Germany 48°29N 9°12E 77 G5
Reutte Austria 47°29N 10°42E 78 D3
Reval = Tallinn Estonia 59°22N 24°48E 84 C3
Revel France 43°28N 2°1E 72 E6
Revelganj India 25°50N 84°40E 125 G11
Revelstoke Canada 51°0N 118°10W 162 C5
Reventazón Peru 6°10S 80°58W 188 B1
Revigny-sur-Ornain
  France 48°49N 4°59E 71 D11
Revilla Gigedo, Is. de
  Pac. Oc. 18°40N 112°0W 180 D2
Revin France 49°56N 4°39E 71 C11
Revúca Slovak Rep. 48°41N 20°7E 78 C13
Revuè → Mozam. 19°50S 34°0E 143 F3
Rewa India 24°33N 81°25E 125 G9
Rewari India 28°15N 76°40E 124 E7
Rexburg U.S.A. 43°49N 111°47W 168 E8
Rey Iran 35°35N 51°25E 108 E4
Rey, I. del Panama 8°20N 78°30W 182 E4
Rey, L. del Mexico 27°1N 103°26W 180 B4
Rey Malabo Eq. Guin. 3°45N 8°50E 139 E6
Reyðarfjörður Iceland 65°2N 14°13W 60 D6
Reyes Bolivia 14°19S 67°23W 188 C4
Reyes, Pt. U.S.A. 38°0N 123°0W 170 H3
Reyhanlı Turkey 36°16N 36°35E 104 D7
Reykjahlíð Iceland 65°40N 16°55W 60 D5
Reykjanes Iceland 63°48N 22°40W 60 E2
Reykjanes Ridge Atl. Oc. 59°0N 31°0W 56 A8
Reykjavík Iceland 64°10N 21°57W 60 D3
Reynolds U.S.A. 32°33N 84°6W 178 C5
Reynolds Ra. Australia 22°30S 133°0E 148 D5
Reynoldsville Ga.,
  U.S.A. 30°51N 84°47W 178 E5
Reynoldsville Pa.,
  U.S.A. 41°6N 78°53W 174 E6
Reynosa Mexico 26°7N 98°18W 181 B5
Rēzekne Latvia 56°30N 27°17E 84 D4
Rezina Moldova 47°50N 28°50E 81 C13
Rezovo Bulgaria 42°0N 28°0E 97 D12
Rezvān Iran 27°34N 56°6E 129 E8
Rezvānshahr Iran 37°30N 49°7E 105 D13
Rgotina Serbia 44°1N 22°18E 96 B6
Rharbi, Zahrez Algeria 34°50N 2°55E 136 B4
Rharis, O. → Algeria 26°0N 5°4E 136 C5
Rhayader U.K. 52°18N 3°29W 67 E4
Rheda-Wiedenbrück
  Germany 51°50N 8°20E 76 D4
Rhede Germany 51°50N 6°42E 76 D2
Rhein → Europe 51°52N 6°2E 76 D2
Rhein-Main-Donau-Kanal
  Germany 49°1N 11°27E 77 F7
Rhein-Ruhr, Düsseldorf ✈ (DUS)
  Germany 51°17N 6°46E 76 D2
Rhein-Taunus △
  Germany 50°10N 8°10E 77 E4
Rhein-Westerwald △
  Germany 50°32N 7°20E 76 E3
Rheinbach Germany 50°38N 6°57E 76 E2
Rheine Germany 52°17N 7°26E 76 C3
Rheinfelden Germany 47°33N 7°47E 77 H3
Rheinland-Pfalz □ Germany 50°0N 7°0E 77 E2
Rheinsberg Germany 53°6N 12°54E 76 B8
Rheris, Oued →
  Morocco 30°50N 4°34W 136 B3
Rhin = Rhein → Europe 51°52N 6°2E 76 D2
Rhine = Rhein → Europe 51°52N 6°2E 76 D2
Rhinebeck U.S.A. 41°56N 73°55W 175 E11
Rhineland-Palatinate =
  Rheinland-Pfalz □
  Germany 50°0N 7°0E 77 E2
Rhinelander U.S.A. 45°38N 89°25W 172 C9
Rhinns Pt. U.K. 55°40N 6°29W 65 F2
Rhino Camp Uganda 3°0N 31°22E 142 B3
Rhir, Cap Morocco 30°38N 9°54W 136 B2
Rho Italy 45°31N 9°2E 92 C6
Rhode Island □
  U.S.A. 41°40N 71°30W 175 E13
Rhodes Greece 36°15N 28°10E 101 D6
Rhodes ✈ (RHO) Greece 36°23N 28°12E 99 E10
Rhodope Mts. = Rodopi Planina
  Bulgaria 41°40N 24°20E 97 E8
Rhön Germany 50°24N 9°58E 76 E5
Rhondda U.K. 51°39N 3°31W 67 F4
Rhondda Cynon Taff □
  U.K. 51°42N 3°27W 67 F4
Rhône □ France 45°54N 4°35E 73 C8
Rhône → France 43°28N 4°42E 73 E8
Rhône-Alpes □ France 45°40N 6°0E 73 D9
Rhum = Rùm U.K. 57°0N 6°20W 65 E2
Rhydaman = Ammanford
  U.K. 51°48N 3°59W 67 F4
Rhyl U.K. 53°20N 3°29W 66 D4
Ri-Aba Eq. Guin. 3°28N 8°40E 139 E6
Ria Formosa △ Portugal 37°0N 7°49W 89 D2
Riachão Brazil 7°20S 46°37W 189 B1
Riacho de Santana
  Brazil 13°37S 42°57W 189 C2
Riang, Laem Thailand 8°7N 98°27E 121 a
Riaño Spain 42°59N 4°59W 88 B6
Rians France 43°37N 5°44E 73 E9
Riansáres → Spain 39°32N 3°18W 89 C7
Riasi India 33°10N 74°50E 125 C5
Riau, Kepulauan □
  Indonesia 0°0 102°45E 118 D2
Riau Arch. = Riau, Kepulauan □
  Indonesia 0°30N 104°20E 118 D2
Riaza Spain 41°18N 3°30W 88 D7
Riaza → Spain 41°42N 3°55W 88 D7
Riba de Saelices Spain 40°55N 2°17W 90 E2
Riba-roja de Túria Spain 39°33N 0°34W 91 F4
Ribadavia Spain 42°17N 8°8W 88 C2
Ribadeo Spain 43°35N 7°5W 88 A3
Ribadesella Spain 43°30N 5°7W 88 A5
Ribado Nigeria 9°16N 12°47E 139 D7

Ribas = Ribes de Freser
  Spain 42°19N 2°15E 90 C7
Ribas do Rio Pardo
  Brazil 20°27S 53°46W 187 H8
Ribauê Mozam. 14°57S 38°17E 143 E4
Ribble → U.K. 53°52N 2°25W 66 D5
Ribe Denmark 55°19N 8°44E 63 J2
Ribeauvillé France 48°10N 7°20E 71 D14
Ribécourt-Dreslincourt
  France 49°30N 2°55E 71 C9
Ribeira Brava Madeira 32°41N 17°4W 100 D2
Ribeira do Pombal
  Brazil 10°50S 38°32W 189 C3
Ribeira Grande C. Verde Is. 17°0N 25°4W 134 b
Ribeirão Prêto Brazil 21°10S 47°50W 191 A6
Ribeiro Gonçalves
  Brazil 7°32S 45°14W 189 B1
Ribemont France 49°47N 3°27E 71 C10
Ribera Italy 37°30N 13°16E 94 E6
Ribérac France 45°15N 0°20E 72 C4
Riberalta Bolivia 11°0S 66°0W 188 C4
Ribes de Freser Spain 42°19N 2°15E 90 C7
Ribnica Slovenia 45°45N 14°45E 93 C11
Ribniţa Moldova 47°45N 29°0E 81 C14
Ribnitz-Damgarten
  Germany 54°15N 12°27E 76 A8
Ričany Czech Rep. 50°0N 14°40E 78 B7
Riccarton N.Z. 43°32S 172°37E 155 D7
Riccia Italy 41°30N 14°50E 95 A7
Riccione Italy 43°59N 12°39E 93 E9
Rice L. Canada 34°5N 114°51W 171 L12
Rice L. Canada 44°12N 78°10W 174 B6
Rice Lake U.S.A. 45°30N 91°44W 172 C8
Riceboro U.S.A. 31°44N 81°26W 178 D8
Rich, C. Canada 44°43N 80°38W 174 B4
Richards Bay S. Africa 28°48S 32°6E 145 C5
Richardson →
  Canada 58°25N 111°14W 163 B6
Richardson Lakes
  U.S.A. 44°46N 70°58W 173 C18
Richardson Mts. N.Z. 44°49S 168°34E 155 E3
Richardson Springs
  U.S.A. 39°51N 121°46W 170 F5
Riche, C. Australia 34°36S 118°47E 149 F2
Richelieu France 47°1N 0°20E 70 E7
Richey U.S.A. 47°39N 105°4W 168 C11
Richfield U.S.A. 38°46N 112°5W 168 G7
Richfield Springs
  U.S.A. 42°51N 74°59W 175 D10
Richford U.S.A. 45°0N 72°40W 175 B12
Richibucto Canada 46°42N 64°54W 165 C7
Richland Ga., U.S.A. 32°5N 84°40W 178 C5
Richland Wash.,
  U.S.A. 46°17N 119°18W 168 C4
Richland Center
  U.S.A. 43°21N 90°23W 172 D8
Richlands U.S.A. 37°6N 81°48W 173 G13
Richmond N.S.W.,
  Australia 33°35S 150°42E 153 B9
Richmond Queens.,
  Australia 20°43S 143°8E 150 D3
Richmond N.Z. 41°20S 173°12E 155 B8
Richmond U.K. 54°25N 1°43W 66 C6
Richmond Calif.,
  U.S.A. 37°56N 122°21W 170 H4
Richmond Ind., U.S.A. 39°50N 84°53W 173 F11
Richmond Ky., U.S.A. 37°45N 84°18W 173 G11
Richmond Mich.,
  U.S.A. 42°49N 82°45W 174 D2
Richmond Mo., U.S.A. 39°17N 93°58W 172 F7
Richmond Tex., U.S.A. 29°35N 95°46W 176 G7
Richmond Utah,
  U.S.A. 41°56N 111°48W 168 F8
Richmond Va., U.S.A. 37°33N 77°27W 173 G15
Richmond Vt., U.S.A. 44°24N 72°59W 175 B12
Richmond, Mt. N.Z. 41°32S 173°22E 155 B8
Richmond Hill Canada 43°52N 79°27W 174 C5
Richmond Hill U.S.A. 31°56N 81°18W 178 D8
Richmond Ra. Australia 29°0S 152°45E 151 D5
Richmondville U.S.A. 42°38N 74°33W 175 D10
Richtersveld △ S. Africa 28°15S 17°10E 144 C2
Richville U.S.A. 44°25N 75°23W 175 B9
Richwood U.S.A. 38°14N 80°32W 173 F13
Ricla Spain 41°31N 1°24W 90 D3
Ridder Kazakhstan 50°20N 83°30E 109 B10
Riddlesburg U.S.A. 40°9N 78°15W 174 F6
Rideau → Canada 45°27N 75°42W 175 A9
Ridge Spring U.S.A. 33°51N 81°40W 178 B8
Ridgecrest U.S.A. 35°38N 117°40W 171 K9
Ridgefield Conn.,
  U.S.A. 41°17N 73°30W 175 E11
Ridgefield Wash.,
  U.S.A. 45°49N 122°45W 170 D4
Ridgeland Miss., U.S.A. 32°26N 90°8W 177 E9
Ridgeland S.C., U.S.A. 32°29N 80°59W 178 D8
Ridgetown Canada 42°26N 81°52W 174 D3
Ridgeville U.S.A. 33°6N 80°19W 178 D8
Ridgewood U.S.A. 40°59N 74°7W 175 F10
Ridgway U.S.A. 41°25N 78°44W 174 E6
Riding Mountain △
  Canada 50°50N 100°0W 163 C9
Ridley, Mt. Australia 33°12S 122°7E 149 F3
Riebeek-Oos S. Africa 33°10S 26°10E 144 D4
Ried Austria 48°14N 13°30E 78 D6
Riedlingen Germany 48°9N 9°28E 77 G5
Riesa Germany 51°17N 13°17E 76 D9
Rienza → Italy 46°49N 11°47E 93 B8
Riesco, I. Chile 52°55S 72°40W 192 D2
Riesi Italy 37°17N 14°5E 95 E7
Riet → S. Africa 29°0S 23°54E 144 C3
Rietavas Lithuania 55°44N 21°56E 82 D8
Rietbron S. Africa 32°54S 23°10E 144 D3
Rietfontein Namibia 21°58S 20°58E 144 B3
Rieti Italy 42°24N 12°51E 93 C9
Rieupeyroux France 44°19N 2°12E 72 D6
Rieux France 43°15N 1°12E 72 E5
Rif = Er Rif Morocco 35°1N 4°1W 136 A3
Rifle U.S.A. 39°32N 107°47W 168 G10
Rift Valley Africa 7°0N 30°0E 142 C3
Riga Latvia 56°53N 24°8E 82 B10
Riga, G. of Latvia 57°40N 23°45E 82 A10
Riga ✈ (RIX) Latvia 56°54N 23°59E 82 B10
Rīgas Jūras Līcis = Riga, G. of
  Latvia 57°40N 23°45E 82 A10
Rigachikun Nigeria 10°40N 7°50E 139 D6
Rīgān Iran 28°37N 58°58E 129 D8
Rigaud Canada 45°29N 74°18W 175 A10

Rigby *U.S.A.* 43°40N 111°55W **168 E8**
Rīgestān *Afghan.* 30°15N 65°0E **122 D4**
Riggins *U.S.A.* 45°25N 116°19W **168 D5**
Rignac *France* 44°25N 2°16E **72 D6**
Rigolet *Canada* 54°10N 58°23W **165 B8**
Rigu *Ghana* 9°59N 0°48W **139 D4**
Rihand Dam *India* 24°9N 83°2E **125 G10**
Riihimäki *Finland* 60°45N 24°48E **84 B3**
Riiser-Larsen-halvøya
Antarctica 68°0S 35°0E **55 C4**
Riiser-Larsen Ice Shelf
S. Ocean 74°0S 19°0W **55 D2**
Riiser-Larsen Sea *S. Ocean* 67°30S 22°0E **55 C4**
Riisitunturi △ *Finland* 66°27N 28°27E **60 C23**
Rijau *Nigeria* 11°8N 5°17E **139 C6**
Rijeka *Croatia* 45°20N 14°21E **93 C11**
Rijeka Crnojevića
Montenegro 42°24N 19°1E **96 D3**
Rijssen *Neths.* 52°19N 6°31E **69 B6**
Rika → *Ukraine* 48°11N 23°16E **81 B8**
Rikuchū-Kaigan △
Japan 39°20N 142°0E **112 E11**
Rikuzentakata *Japan* 39°0N 141°40E **112 E10**
Rila *Bulgaria* 42°7N 23°7E **96 D7**
Rila Planina *Bulgaria* 42°10N 23°20E **96 D7**
Riley *U.S.A.* 43°32N 119°28W **168 E4**
Rima → *Nigeria* 13°4N 5°10E **139 C6**
Rimah, Wadi ar →
Si. Arabia 26°5N 41°30E **128 E4**
Rimau, Pulau *Malaysia* 5°15N 100°16E **121 c**
Rimavská Sobota
Slovak Rep. 48°22N 20°2E **79 C13**
Rimbey *Canada* 52°35N 114°15W **162 C6**
Rimbo *Sweden* 59°44N 18°21E **62 E12**
Rimersburg *U.S.A.* 41°3N 79°30W **174 E5**
Rimforsa *Sweden* 58°6N 15°43E **63 F9**
Rimini *Italy* 44°3N 12°33E **93 D9**
Rimouski *Canada* 48°27N 68°30W **165 C6**
Rimrock *U.S.A.* 46°40N 121°7W **170 D5**
Rinca *Indonesia* 8°45S 119°35E **119 F5**
Rincon *U.S.A.* 32°18N 81°14W **178 C8**
Rincón de Anchuras = Anchuras
Spain 39°29N 4°50W **89 F6**
Rincón de la Victoria
Spain 36°43N 4°18W **89 J6**
Rincón de Romos
Mexico 22°14N 102°18W **180 C4**
Rinconada *Argentina* 22°26S 66°10W **190 A2**
Rind → *India* 25°53N 80°33E **125 G9**
Ringarum *Sweden* 58°21N 16°26E **63 F10**
Ringas *India* 27°21N 75°34E **124 F6**
Ringe *Denmark* 55°13N 10°28E **63 J4**
Ringgold Is. *Fiji* 16°15S 179°25W **154 a**
Ringim *Nigeria* 12°13N 9°10E **139 C6**
Ringkøbing *Denmark* 56°5N 8°15E **63 H7**
Ringkøbing Fjord *Denmark* 56°0N 8°15E **63 H7**
Ringsjön *Sweden* 55°55N 13°30E **63 J7**
Ringsted *Denmark* 55°25N 11°46E **63 J5**
Ringvassøya *Norway* 69°56N 19°15E **60 B18**
Ringwood *U.S.A.* 41°7N 74°15W **175 E10**
Rinia *Greece* 37°23N 25°13E **99 D7**
Rinjani, Gunung
Indonesia 8°24S 116°28E **118 F5**
Rinteln *Germany* 52°10N 9°8E **76 C5**
Rinyirru △ *Australia* 15°24S 144°26E **150 B3**
Rio, *real del Spain* 36°49N 2°24W **91 J2**
Rio Branco *Brazil* 9°58S 67°49W **188 B4**
Rio Branco *Uruguay* 32°40S 53°40W **191 C5**
Río Bravo *Mexico* 25°59N 98°6W **181 B5**
Río Bravo → *N. Amer.* 29°2N 102°45W **180 B4**
Río Bravo del Norte →
Mexico 25°57N 97°9W **181 B5**
Rio Brilhante *Brazil* 21°48S 54°33W **191 A5**
Rio Bueno *Chile* 40°19S 72°58W **192 D2**
Rio Claro *Brazil* 22°19S 47°35W **191 A6**
Rio Claro *Trin. & Tob.* 10°20N 61°10W **183 D7**
Rio Colorado *Argentina* 39°0S 64°0W **192 A4**
Rio Cuarto *Argentina* 33°10S 64°25W **190 C3**
Rio das Pedras *Mozam.* 23°8S 35°28E **145 B6**
Rio de Contas *Brazil* 13°36S 41°48W **189 C2**
Rio de Janeiro *Brazil* 22°54S 43°12W **191 A7**
Rio de Janeiro □ *Brazil* 22°50S 43°0W **191 A7**
Rio do Prado *Brazil* 16°35S 40°34W **189 D2**
Rio do Sul *Brazil* 27°13S 49°37W **191 B6**
Río Dulce △ *Guatemala* 15°43N 88°50W **182 C2**
Río Gallegos *Argentina* 51°35S 69°15W **192 D3**
Rio Grande *Argentina* 53°50S 67°45W **192 D3**
Rio Grande *Bolivia* 20°51S 67°17W **188 E4**
Rio Grande *Brazil* 32°0S 52°20W **191 C5**
Río Grande *Mexico* 23°50N 103°2W **180 C4**
Río Grande *Puerto Rico* 18°23N 65°50W **183 d**
Rio Grande → *N. Amer.* 25°58N 97°9W **176 H5**
Rio Grande City *U.S.A.* 26°23N 98°49W **176 H5**
Rio Grande de Santiago →
Mexico 21°36N 105°26W **180 C3**
Rio Grande do Norte □
Brazil 5°40S 36°0W **189 B3**
Rio Grande do Sul □
Brazil 30°0S 53°0W **191 C5**
Rio Grande Rise *Atl. Oc.* 31°0S 35°0W **56 K8**
Río Hato *Panama* 8°22N 80°10W **182 E3**
Río Lagartos *Mexico* 21°36N 88°10W **181 C7**
Rio Largo *Brazil* 9°28S 35°50W **189 B3**
Río Maior *Portugal* 39°19N 8°57W **89 F2**
Rio Marina *Italy* 42°49N 10°25E **92 F7**
Rio Mayo *Argentina* 45°40S 70°15W **192 C2**
Rio Mulatos *Bolivia* 19°40S 66°50W **188 D4**
Río Muni □ *Eq. Guin.* 1°30N 10°0E **140 D2**
Rio Negro *Brazil* 26°0S 49°55W **191 B6**
Río Negro *Chile* 40°47S 73°14W **192 D2**
Rio Pardo *Brazil* 30°0S 52°30W **191 C5**
Río Pico *Argentina* 44°0S 70°22W **192 B2**
Rio Pilcomayo △
Argentina 25°5S 58°5W **190 B4**
Río Plátano △ *Honduras* 15°45N 85°0W **182 C3**
Rio Rancho *U.S.A.* 35°14N 106°41W **169 J10**
Rio Real *Brazil* 11°28S 37°56W **189 C3**
Rio Segundo *Argentina* 31°40S 63°59W **190 C3**
Rio Simpson △ *Chile* 45°27S 73°30W **192 C2**
Rio Tercero *Argentina* 32°15S 64°8W **190 C3**
Rio Tinto *Brazil* 6°48S 35°5W **189 B3**
Rio Tinto *Portugal* 41°11N 8°34W **88 D2**
Rio Turbio *Argentina* 51°35S 72°15W **192 D2**
Rio Verde *Brazil* 17°50S 51°0W **187 D8**
Río Verde *Mexico* 21°56N 99°59W **181 C5**
Rio Vista *U.S.A.* 38°10N 121°42W **170 G5**
Ríobamba *Ecuador* 1°50S 78°45W **186 D3**
Ríohacha *Colombia* 11°33N 72°55W **186 A4**
Rioja *Peru* 6°11S 77°5W **188 B2**
Riom *France* 45°54N 3°7E **72 C7**
Riom-ès-Montagnes
France 45°17N 2°39E **72 C6**

Rion-des-Landes *France* 43°55N 0°56W **72 E3**
Rionero in Vúlture *Italy* 40°55N 15°40E **95 B8**
Rioni → *Georgia* 42°14N 41°44E **87 A5**
Ríos *Spain* 41°58N 7°16E **88 D3**
Riosucio *Colombia* 7°27N 77°7W **186 B3**
Riou L. *Canada* 59°7N 106°25W **163 B7**
Rioz *France* 47°26N 6°5E **71 E13**
Ripatransone *Italy* 42°59N 13°46E **93 F10**
Ripley *Canada* 44°4N 81°35W **174 B3**
Ripley *Calif., U.S.A.* 33°32N 114°39W **171 M12**
Ripley *N.Y., U.S.A.* 42°16N 79°43W **174 D5**
Ripley *Tenn., U.S.A.* 35°45N 89°32W **177 D10**
Ripley *W. Va., U.S.A.* 38°49N 81°43W **173 F13**
Ripoll *Spain* 42°15N 2°13E **90 C7**
Ripon *U.K.* 54°9N 1°31W **66 C6**
Ripon *Calif., U.S.A.* 37°44N 121°7W **170 H5**
Ripon *Wis., U.S.A.* 43°51N 88°50W **172 D9**
Riposto *Italy* 37°44N 15°12E **95 E8**
Risan *Montenegro* 42°32N 18°42E **96 D2**
Rishā', W. ar →
Si. Arabia 25°33N 44°5E **128 E5**
Rishikesh *India* 30°7N 78°19E **124 D8**
Rishiri-Rebun-Sarobetsu △
Japan 45°26N 141°30E **112 B10**
Rishiri-Tō *Japan* 45°11N 141°15E **112 B10**
Rishon le Ziyyon *Israel* 31°58N 34°48E **130 D3**
Risle → *France* 49°26N 0°23E **70 C7**
Risnjak △ *Croatia* 45°25N 14°36E **93 C11**
Rison *U.S.A.* 33°58N 92°11W **176 E8**
Risør *Norway* 58°43N 9°13E **61 G13**
Rissani *Morocco* 31°18N 4°12W **136 B3**
Rita Blanca Cr. →
U.S.A. 35°40N 102°29W **176 D3**
Ritchie's Arch. *India* 12°14N 93°10E **127 H11**
Riti *Nigeria* 7°57N 9°41E **139 D6**
Ritter, Mt. *U.S.A.* 37°41N 119°12W **170 H7**
Ritzville *U.S.A.* 47°8N 118°23W **168 C4**
Riva del Garda *Italy* 45°53N 10°50E **92 C7**
Riva Lígure *Italy* 43°50N 7°50E **92 E4**
Rivadavia *B. Aires,
Argentina* 35°29S 62°59W **190 D3**
Rivadavia *Mendoza,
Argentina* 33°13S 68°30W **190 C2**
Rivadavia *Salta,
Argentina* 24°5S 62°54W **190 A3**
Rivadavia *Chile* 29°57S 70°35W **190 B1**
Rivarolo Canavese *Italy* 45°19N 7°43E **92 C4**
Rivas *Nic.* 11°30N 85°50W **182 D2**
Rive-de-Gier *France* 45°32N 4°37E **73 C8**
River Cess *Liberia* 5°30N 9°32W **138 D3**
River Jordan *Canada* 48°26N 124°3W **170 B2**
Rivera *Argentina* 37°12S 63°14W **190 D3**
Rivera *Uruguay* 31°0S 55°50W **191 C4**
Riverbank *U.S.A.* 37°44N 120°56W **170 H6**
Riverdale *Calif., U.S.A.* 36°26N 119°52W **170 J7**
Riverdale *Ga., U.S.A.* 33°34N 84°25W **178 B5**
Riverhead *U.S.A.* 40°55N 72°40W **175 F12**
Riverhurst *Canada* 50°55N 106°50W **163 C7**
Rivers *Canada* 50°2N 100°14W **163 C8**
Rivers □ *Nigeria* 4°30N 7°10E **139 E6**
Rivers Inlet *Canada* 51°42N 127°15W **162 C3**
Riverside *Canada* 44°5N 81°20W **174 B3**
Riverside *N.Z.* 45°54S 168°44E **155 F3**
Riverside *S. Africa* 27°1S 21°15E **144 D3**
Riverside *U.S.A.* 33°59N 117°22W **171 M9**
Riversleigh *Australia* 19°5S 138°40E **150 B2**
Riverton *Australia* 34°10S 138°46E **152 C3**
Riverton *Canada* 51°1N 97°0W **163 C9**
Riverton *N.Z.* 46°21S 168°0E **155 G3**
Riverton *U.S.A.* 43°2N 108°23W **168 E9**
Riverview *Fla., U.S.A.* 27°52N 82°20W **179 H7**
Riverview *Fla., U.S.A.* 30°32N 87°12W **179 E2**
Rives *France* 45°21S 5°31E **73 C9**
Rivesaltes *France* 42°47N 2°50E **72 F6**
Riviera = Azur, Côte d'
France 43°25N 7°10E **73 E11**
Riviera *U.S.A.* 35°4N 114°35W **171 K12**
Riviera Beach *U.S.A.* 26°47N 80°3W **179 J9**
Riviera di Levante *Italy* 44°15N 9°30E **92 D5**
Riviera di Ponente *Italy* 44°10N 8°20E **92 D5**
Rivière-au-Renard
Canada 48°59N 64°23W **165 C7**
Rivière-du-Loup
Canada 47°50N 69°30W **165 C6**
Rivière-Pentecôte
Canada 49°57N 67°1W **165 C6**
Rivière-Pilote
Martinique 14°26N 60°53W **182 c**
Rivière St-Paul *Canada* 51°28N 57°45W **165 B8**
Rivière-Salée *Martinique* 14°31N 61°0W **182 c**
Rivne *Odesa, Ukraine* 46°1N 29°10E **81 C14**
Rivne *Rivne, Ukraine* 50°40N 26°10E **75 C14**
Rivne □ *Ukraine* 51°15N 26°30E **75 C14**
Rívoli *Italy* 45°3N 7°31E **92 C4**
Rívoli B. *Australia* 37°32S 140°3E **152 D4**
Riwaka *N.Z.* 41°5S 172°59E **155 B7**
Rixheim *France* 47°40N 7°24E **71 E14**
Riyadh = Ar Riyāḍ
Si. Arabia 24°41N 46°42E **128 E5**
Riza *Greece* 40°31N 23°15E **96 F7**
Rize *Turkey* 41°0N 40°30E **105 B9**
Rize □ *Turkey* 41°0N 40°30E **105 B9**
Rizhao *China* 35°25N 119°30E **115 G10**
Rizokarpaso *Cyprus* 35°36N 34°23E **101 D13**
Rizzuto, C. *Italy* 38°53N 17°5E **95 D10**
Rjukan *Norway* 59°54N 8°33E **61 G13**
Rkîz, L. *Mauritania* 16°50N 15°23W **138 B1**
Ro *Greece* 36°9N 29°33E **99 E11**
Roa *Spain* 41°42N 3°55W **88 D7**
Road Town *Br. Virgin Is.* 18°27N 64°37W **183 e**
Roan Plateau *U.S.A.* 39°20N 109°20W **168 G9**
Roanne *France* 46°3N 4°4E **71 F11**
Roanoke *Ala., U.S.A.* 33°9N 85°22W **178 B4**
Roanoke *Va., U.S.A.* 37°16N 79°56W **173 G7**
Roanoke → *U.S.A.* 35°57N 76°42W **177 D16**
Roanoke I. *U.S.A.* 35°53N 75°39W **177 D17**
Roanoke Rapids
U.S.A. 36°28N 77°40W **177 C16**
Roatán *Honduras* 16°18N 86°35W **182 C2**
Robāt *Iran* 34°16N 46°47E **105 E12**
Robāt Sang *Iran* 35°35N 59°10E **129 C8**
Robāṭkarīm *Iran* 35°25N 50°59E **129 C6**
Robben I. *S. Africa* 33°46S 18°22E **144 D2**
Robbins I. *Australia* 40°42S 145°0E **151 G4**
Róbbio *Italy* 45°17N 8°35E **92 C5**
Robe *Australia* 37°11S 139°45E **152 D3**
Robe → *Australia* 21°42S 116°15E **148 D2**
Röbel *Germany* 53°22N 12°35E **76 B8**

Robert Bourassa, Rés.
Canada 53°40N 76°55W **164 B4**
Robert Lee *U.S.A.* 31°54N 100°29W **176 F4**
Roberta *U.S.A.* 32°43N 84°1W **178 D3**
Robertsdale *U.S.A.* 40°11N 78°6W **174 F6**
Robertsganj *India* 24°44N 83°4E **125 G10**
Robertson *S. Africa* 33°46S 19°50E **144 D2**
Robertson I. *Antarctica* 65°15S 59°30W **55 C18**
Robertson Ra. *Australia* 23°15S 121°0E **148 D3**
Robertsport *Liberia* 6°45N 11°26W **138 D2**
Robertstown *Australia* 33°58S 139°5E **152 B3**
Roberval *Canada* 48°32N 72°15W **165 C5**
Robeson Chan. *N. Amer.* 82°0N 61°30W **57 A4**
Robesonia *U.S.A.* 40°21N 76°8W **175 F8**
Robinson *Australia* 16°3S 137°16E **150 B2**
Robinson *U.S.A.* 39°0N 87°44W **172 F10**
Robinson → *Australia* 16°3S 137°16E **150 B2**
Robinson Crusoe I.
Pac. Oc. 33°38S 78°52W **184 F2**
Robinson Ra. *Australia* 25°40S 119°0E **149 E2**
Robinvale *Australia* 34°40S 142°45E **152 C5**
Robledo *Spain* 38°46N 2°26W **91 G2**
Roboré *Bolivia* 18°10S 59°45W **186 G7**
Robson, Mt. *Canada* 53°10N 119°10W **162 C5**
Robstown *U.S.A.* 27°47N 97°40W **176 H6**
Roca, C. da *Portugal* 38°40N 9°31W **89 G1**
Roca Partida, I. *Mexico* 19°1N 112°2W **180 D2**
Rocamadour *France* 44°48N 1°37E **72 D5**
Rocas, Atol das *Brazil* 4°0S 34°1W **187 D12**
Rocca San Casciano *Italy* 44°3N 11°50E **93 D8**
Roccadáspide *Italy* 40°27N 15°10E **95 B8**
Roccastrada *Italy* 43°0N 11°10E **93 F8**
Roccella Iónica *Italy* 38°19N 16°24E **95 D9**
Rocciamelone, Mte. *Italy* 45°12N 7°5E **73 C11**
Rocha *Uruguay* 34°30S 54°25W **191 C5**
Rochdale *U.K.* 53°38N 2°9W **66 D5**
Roche Melon = Rocciamelone,
Mte. *Italy* 45°12N 7°5E **73 C11**
Rochechouart *France* 45°50N 0°49E **72 C4**
Rochefort *Belgium* 50°9N 5°12E **69 D5**
Rochefort *France* 45°56N 0°57W **72 C3**
Rochefort-en-Terre
France 47°42N 2°22W **70 E4**
Rochelle *Ga., U.S.A.* 31°57N 83°27W **178 D6**
Rochelle *Ill., U.S.A.* 41°56N 89°4W **172 E9**
Rocher River *Canada* 61°23N 112°44W **162 A6**
Rocheservière *France* 46°57N 1°30W **70 F5**
Rochester *Australia* 36°22S 144°41E **152 D6**
Rochester *U.K.* 51°23N 0°31E **67 F8**
Rochester *Ind., U.S.A.* 41°4N 86°13W **172 E10**
Rochester *Minn., U.S.A.* 44°1N 92°28W **172 C7**
Rochester *N.H.,
U.S.A.* 43°18N 70°59W **175 C14**
Rochester *N.Y., U.S.A.* 43°10N 77°37W **174 C7**
Rociu *Romania* 44°43N 25°2E **81 F10**
Rock → *Canada* 60°7N 127°7W **162 A3**
Rock, The *Australia* 35°15S 147°2E **153 C7**
Rock Creek *U.S.A.* 41°40N 80°52W **174 E4**
Rock Falls *U.S.A.* 41°47N 89°41W **172 E9**
Rock Flat *Australia* 36°21S 149°13E **153 D8**
Rock Hill *U.S.A.* 34°56N 81°1W **177 D14**
Rock Island *U.S.A.* 41°30N 90°34W **172 E8**
Rock Port *U.S.A.* 40°25N 95°31W **172 E6**
Rock Rapids *U.S.A.* 43°26N 96°10W **172 D5**
Rock Sound *Bahamas* 24°54N 76°12W **182 B4**
Rock Springs *Mont.,
U.S.A.* 46°49N 106°15W **168 C10**
Rock Springs *Wyo.,
U.S.A.* 41°35N 109°14W **168 F9**
Rock Valley *U.S.A.* 43°12N 96°18W **172 D5**
Rockall *Atl. Oc.* 57°37N 13°42W **58 D3**
Rockall Trough *Atl. Oc.* 57°0N 12°0W **56 A10**
Rockdale *Wash.,
U.S.A.* 47°22N 121°28W **170 C5**
Rockeby = Mungkan Kandju △
Australia 13°35S 142°52E **150 A3**
Rockefeller Plateau
Antarctica 76°0S 130°0W **55 E14**
Rockford *Ala., U.S.A.* 32°53N 86°13W **178 C3**
Rockford *Ill., U.S.A.* 42°16N 89°6W **172 D9**
Rockglen *Canada* 49°11N 105°57W **163 D7**
Rockhampton
Australia 23°22S 150°32E **150 C5**
Rockingham *Australia* 32°15S 115°38E **149 F2**
Rockingham *N.C.,
U.S.A.* 34°57N 79°46W **177 D15**
Rockingham *Vt.,
U.S.A.* 43°11N 72°29W **175 C12**
Rockingham B.
Australia 18°5S 146°10E **150 B4**
Rocklake *U.S.A.* 48°47N 99°15W **172 A4**
Rockland *Canada* 45°33N 75°17W **175 A9**
Rockland *Idaho,
U.S.A.* 42°34N 112°53W **168 E7**
Rockland *Maine, U.S.A.* 44°6N 69°7W **173 C19**
Rockland *Mich., U.S.A.* 46°44N 89°11W **172 B9**
Rocklands Reservoir
Australia 37°15S 142°5E **152 D5**
Rockledge *U.S.A.* 28°20N 80°43W **179 G9**
Rocklin *U.S.A.* 38°48N 121°14W **170 G5**
Rockly B. *Trin. & Tob.* 11°9N 60°46W **187 J16**
Rockmart *U.S.A.* 34°1N 85°3W **178 B3**
Rockport *Mass.,
U.S.A.* 42°39N 70°37W **175 D14**
Rockport *Tex., U.S.A.* 28°2N 97°3W **176 G6**
Rocksprings *U.S.A.* 30°1N 100°13W **176 F4**
Rockville *Conn.,
U.S.A.* 41°52N 72°28W **175 E12**
Rockville *Md., U.S.A.* 39°5N 77°9W **173 F15**
Rockwall *U.S.A.* 32°56N 96°28W **176 E6**
Rockwell City *U.S.A.* 42°24N 94°38W **172 D6**
Rockwood *Canada* 43°37N 80°8W **174 C4**
Rockwood *Maine,
U.S.A.* 45°41N 69°45W **173 C19**
Rockwood *Tenn.,
U.S.A.* 35°52N 84°41W **177 D12**
Rocky Ford *U.S.A.* 38°3N 103°43W **168 G12**
Rocky Gully *Australia* 34°30S 116°57E **149 F2**
Rocky Harbour
Canada 49°36N 57°55W **165 C8**
Rocky Island L. *Canada* 46°55N 83°0W **164 C3**
Rocky Lane *Canada* 58°31N 116°22W **162 B5**
Rocky Mountain △
U.S.A. 40°25N 105°45W **168 F11**
Rocky Mountain House
Canada 52°22N 114°55W **162 C6**
Rocky Mts. *N. Amer.* 49°0N 115°0W **168 B6**
Rocky Point *Namibia* 19°3S 12°30E **144 A1**
Rocroi *France* 49°55N 4°30E **71 C11**
Rod *Pakistan* 28°10N 63°5E **122 E3**

Roda *Greece* 39°48N 19°46E **101 A3**
Rødby *Denmark* 54°41N 11°23E **63 K5**
Rødbyhavn *Denmark* 54°39N 11°22E **63 K5**
Roddickton *Canada* 50°51N 56°8W **165 B8**
Rødding *Denmark* 55°23N 9°3E **63 J3**
Rödeby *Sweden* 56°15N 15°37E **63 H9**
Rodekro *Denmark* 55°4N 9°20E **63 J3**
Rodenkirchen *Germany* 53°23N 8°26E **76 B4**
Rodez *France* 44°21N 2°33E **72 D6**
Rodholivos *Greece* 40°55N 24°0E **96 F7**
Ródhos = Rhodes
Greece 36°15N 28°10E **101 C10**
Rodi Gargánico *Italy* 41°55N 15°53E **93 G12**
Rodia *Greece* 35°22N 25°1E **101 D7**
Rodina *Kazakhstan* 50°16N 66°53E **109 B7**
Rodna *Romania* 47°25N 24°50E **81 C9**
Rodna ○ *Australia* 23°45S 132°4E **148 D5**
Rodnei, Munţii *Romania* 47°35N 24°35E **81 C9**
Rodney *Canada* 42°34N 81°41W **174 D3**
Rodney, C. *N.Z.* 36°17S 174°50E **154 C3**
Rodniki *Russia* 57°7N 41°47E **86 B5**
Rodotopa *Greece* 40°55N 24°0E **96 F7**
Rodopi □ *Greece* 41°5N 25°30E **97 E9**
Rodopi Planina *Bulgaria* 41°40N 24°20E **97 E8**
Rodopos *Greece* 35°34N 23°45E **101 D5**
Rodrigues *Ind. Oc.* 19°45S 63°20E **146 F5**
Roe → *U.K.* 55°6N 6°59W **64 A5**
Roebling *U.S.A.* 40°7N 74°47W **175 F10**
Roebourne *Australia* 20°44S 117°9E **148 D2**
Roebuck *S. Africa* 18°5S 122°20E **148 C3**
Roebuck Roadhouse
Australia 17°59S 122°36E **148 C3**
Roermond *Neths.* 51°12N 6°0E **69 C6**
Roes Welcome Sd.
Canada 65°0N 87°0W **161 E14**
Roeselare *Belgium* 50°57N 3°7E **69 D3**
Rogachev = Ragachow
Belarus 53°8N 30°5E **75 B16**
Rogačica *Serbia* 45°50N 0°49E **72 C4**
Rogagua, L. *Bolivia* 13°43S 66°50W **188 C4**
Rogaška Slatina
Slovenia 46°15N 15°42E **93 B12**
Rogatec *Slovenia* 46°15N 15°46E **93 B12**
Rogatica *Bos.-H.* 43°47N 19°0E **80 G4**
Rogatyn *Ukraine* 49°24N 24°36E **75 D13**
Rogen *Sweden* 62°20N 12°20E **62 B6**
Rogers *U.S.A.* 36°20N 94°7W **176 C7**
Rogers City *U.S.A.* 45°25N 83°49W **173 C12**
Rogersville *Canada* 46°44N 65°26W **165 C6**
Roggan → *Canada* 54°24N 79°25W **164 B4**
Roggan L. *Canada* 54°8N 77°50W **164 B4**
Roggeveen Basin
Pac. Oc. 31°30S 95°30W **157 L18**
Roggeveldberge
S. Africa 32°10S 20°10E **144 D3**
Roggiano Gravina *Italy* 39°37N 16°9E **95 C9**
Rogliano *France* 42°57N 9°30E **73 E13**
Rogliano *Italy* 39°10N 16°19E **95 C9**
Rogoaguado, L. *Bolivia* 13°0S 65°30W **188 F5**
Rogojampi *Indonesia* 8°19S 114°17E **119 J17**
Rogozno *Poland* 52°45N 16°59E **83 F3**
Rogue → *U.S.A.* 42°26N 124°26W **168 E1**
Roha *India* 18°26N 73°7E **126 E1**
Rohan *France* 48°4N 2°45W **70 D4**
Rohnert Park *U.S.A.* 38°16N 122°40W **170 G4**
Rohri *Pakistan* 27°45N 68°51E **124 F3**
Rohri Canal *Pakistan* 26°15N 68°27E **124 F3**
Rohtak *India* 28°55N 76°43E **124 E7**
Roi Et *Thailand* 16°4N 103°40E **120 D4**
Roja *Latvia* 57°29N 22°43E **82 A9**
Rojas *Argentina* 34°10S 60°45W **190 C3**
Rojo, C. *Mexico* 21°33N 97°20W **181 C5**
Rokan → *Indonesia* 2°0N 100°50E **118 D2**
Rokel → *S. Leone* 8°30N 12°48W **138 D2**
Rokiškis *Lithuania* 55°55N 25°35E **84 E3**
Rokua △ *Finland* 64°36N 26°50E **60 D22**
Rokycany *Czech Rep.* 49°43N 13°35E **78 B6**
Rolândia *Brazil* 23°18S 51°23W **191 A5**
Rolla *N. Dak., U.S.A.* 48°52N 99°37W **172 A4**
Rolla *U.S.A.* 37°57N 91°46W **172 G8**
Rolleston *Australia* 24°28S 148°35E **150 C4**
Rolleston *N.Z.* 43°35S 172°24E **155 D7**
Rollingstone *Australia* 19°2S 146°24E **150 B4**
Roma *Australia* 26°32S 148°49E **150 C4**
Roma *Italy* 41°54N 12°28E **93 G9**
Roma *Sweden* 57°32N 18°26E **63 G13**
Roma = Rome *Italy* 41°54N 12°28E **93 G9**
Roma Fiumicino ✈ (FCO)
Italy 41°48N 12°15E **93 G9**
Roma-Los Saenz *U.S.A.* 26°24N 99°1W **176 H5**
Romain, C. *U.S.A.* 33°0N 79°22W **177 E15**
Romaine → *Canada* 50°18N 63°47W **165 B7**
Roman *Romania* 43°8N 23°54W **96 C7**
Roman *Romania* 46°57N 26°55E **81 D11**
Roman-Kosh, Gora
Ukraine 44°37N 34°15E **85 K8**
Romanche → *France* 45°5N 5°43E **73 C9**
Romang *Indonesia* 7°30S 127°20E **119 F7**
Români *Egypt* 30°59N 32°38E **130 E1**
Romania ■ *Europe* 46°0N 25°0E **81 D10**
Romanija *Bos.-H.* 43°50N 18°45E **80 G3**
Romano, C. *U.S.A.* 25°51N 81°41W **179 H8**
Romano, Cayo *Cuba* 22°0N 77°30W **182 B4**
Romans-sur-Isère *France* 45°3N 5°3E **73 C9**
Romanshorn *Switz.* 47°33N 9°22E **75 H9**
Romanzof C. *U.S.A.* 61°49N 166°6W **166 C6**
Romblon *Phil.* 12°33N 122°17E **119 B6**
Rome = Roma *Italy* 41°54N 12°28E **93 G9**
Rome *Ga., U.S.A.* 34°15N 85°10W **178 B3**
Rome *N.Y., U.S.A.* 43°13N 75°27W **175 C9**
Rome *Pa., U.S.A.* 41°51N 76°21W **175 E8**
Rometta *Italy* 38°10N 15°25E **95 D8**
Romilly-sur-Seine
France 48°31N 3°44E **71 D10**
Romiton *Uzbekistan* 39°56N 64°23E **108 E6**
Rommani *Morocco* 33°31N 6°40W **136 B4**
Romney *U.S.A.* 39°21N 78°45W **173 F14**
Romney Marsh *U.K.* 51°2N 0°54E **67 F8**
Rømø *Denmark* 55°10N 8°30E **63 J2**
Romodan *Ukraine* 50°6N 33°15E **85 G7**
Romodanovo *Russia* 54°26N 45°23E **86 C8**
Romont *Switz.* 46°42N 6°54E **75 J3**
Romorantin-Lanthenay
France 47°21N 1°45E **71 E8**
Rompin → *Malaysia* 2°49N 103°29E **121 L4**
Romsdalen *Norway* 62°25N 7°52E **62 E5**
Romsey *U.K.* 51°0N 1°29W **67 G6**
Ron *India* 15°40N 75°44E **127 G2**
Ron *Vietnam* 17°53N 106°27E **120 D6**
Rona *U.K.* 57°34N 5°59W **65 D3**
Ronan *U.S.A.* 47°32N 114°6W **168 C6**

Roncador, Cayos
Caribbean 13°32N 80°4W **182 D3**
Roncador, Serra do
Brazil 12°30S 52°30W **187 F8**
Ronciglione *Italy* 42°17N 12°13E **93 F9**
Ronco → *Italy* 44°24N 12°12E **93 D9**
Ronda *Spain* 36°46N 5°12W **89 J5**
Ronda, Serranía de *Spain* 36°44N 5°3W **89 J5**
Rondane *Norway* 61°57N 9°50E **60 F13**
Rondônia □ *Brazil* 11°0S 63°0W **186 F6**
Rondonópolis *Brazil* 16°28S 54°38W **187 G8**
Rondu *Pakistan* 35°32N 75°10E **125 B6**
Rong, Koh *Cambodia* 10°45N 103°15E **121 G4**
Rong Jiang → *China* 24°35N 109°20E **116 E7**
Rong Xian *China* 22°50N 110°31E **117 F8**
Rong'an *China* 25°14N 109°22E **116 E7**
Rongchang *China* 29°20N 105°32E **116 C5**
Rongcheng *China* 37°9N 122°23E **115 F12**
Ronge, L. la *Canada* 55°6N 105°17W **163 B7**
Rongjiang *China* 25°59N 108°18E **116 E6**
Rongotea *N.Z.* 40°19S 175°25E **154 D4**
Rongshui *China* 25°5N 109°12E **116 E7**
Rongxian *China* 29°23N 104°22E **116 C5**
Rønne *Denmark* 55°6N 14°43E **63 J8**
Ronne Ice Shelf
Antarctica 77°30S 60°0W **55 D18**
Ronneby *Sweden* 56°12N 15°17E **63 H9**
Ronnebyån → *Sweden* 56°16N 15°18E **63 H9**
Rönneshytta *Sweden* 58°56N 15°2E **63 F9**
Ronsard, C. *Australia* 24°46S 113°10E **149 D1**
Ronse *Belgium* 50°45N 3°35E **69 D3**
Roodepoort *S. Africa* 26°11S 27°54E **145 C4**
Roof Butte *U.S.A.* 36°28N 109°5W **169 H9**
Rooiboklaagte →
Namibia 20°50S 21°0E **144 B3**
Rooniu, Mt. *Tahiti* 17°49S 149°12W **155 b**
Roopville *U.S.A.* 33°27N 85°8W **178 B4**
Roorkee *India* 29°52N 77°59E **124 E7**
Roosendaal *Neths.* 51°32N 4°29E **69 C4**
Roosevelt *U.S.A.* 40°18N 109°59W **168 F9**
Roosevelt → *Brazil* 7°35S 60°20W **186 E6**
Roosevelt, Mt. *Canada* 58°26N 125°20W **162 B3**
Roosevelt I. *Antarctica* 79°30S 162°0W **55 D12**
Ropczyce *Poland* 50°4N 21°38E **83 H8**
Roper → *Australia* 14°43S 135°27E **150 B2**
Roper Bar *Australia* 14°44S 134°44E **150 B1**
Roper River = St. Vidgeon's ○
Australia 14°43S 134°53E **150 A1**
Roque Pérez *Argentina* 35°25S 59°24W **190 D4**
Roquefort *France* 44°2N 0°20W **72 D3**
Roquemaure *France* 44°3N 4°48E **73 D8**
Roquetas de Mar *Spain* 36°46N 2°36W **91 J2**
Roquetes *Spain* 40°50N 0°30E **90 E5**
Roraima □ *Brazil* 2°0N 61°30W **186 C6**
Roraima, Mt. *Venezuela* 5°10N 60°40W **186 B6**
Rorketon *Canada* 51°24N 99°35W **163 C8**
Røros *Norway* 62°35N 11°23E **60 E14**
Rorschach *Switz.* 47°28N 9°28E **77 H5**
Ros Comáin = Roscommon
Ireland 53°38N 8°11W **64 C3**
Ros Mhic Thriúin = New Ross
Ireland 52°23N 6°57W **64 D5**
Rosa *Zambia* 9°33S 31°15E **143 D3**
Rosa, C. *Algeria* 37°0N 8°16E **136 A5**
Rosa, Monte *Europe* 45°57N 7°53E **92 C4**
Rosal de la Frontera
Spain 37°59N 7°13W **89 H3**
Rosalia *U.S.A.* 47°14N 117°22W **168 C5**
Rosamond *U.S.A.* 34°52N 118°10W **171 L8**
Rosans *France* 44°24N 5°29E **73 D9**
Rosario *Argentina* 33°0S 60°40W **190 C3**
Rosário *Brazil* 3°0S 44°15W **189 A2**
Rosario *Mexico* 22°58N 105°53W **180 C3**
Rosario *Paraguay* 24°30S 57°35W **190 A4**
Rosario de la Frontera
Argentina 25°50S 65°0W **190 B3**
Rosario de Lerma
Argentina 24°59S 65°35W **190 A3**
Rosario del Tala
Argentina 32°20S 59°10W **190 C4**
Rosário do Sul *Brazil* 30°15S 54°55W **191 C5**
Rosarito *Baja Calif.,
Mexico* 32°20N 117°2W **171 N9**
Rosarito *Baja Calif.,
Mexico* 28°38N 114°1W **180 B2**
Rosarno *Italy* 38°29N 15°58E **95 D8**
Rosas = Roses *Spain* 42°19N 3°10E **90 C8**
Roscoe *U.S.A.* 41°56N 74°55W **175 D10**
Roscoff *France* 48°44N 3°59W **70 C3**
Roscommon *Ireland* 53°38N 8°11W **64 C3**
Roscommon □ *Ireland* 53°49N 8°23W **64 C3**
Roscrea *Ireland* 52°57N 7°49W **64 D4**
Rose → *Australia* 14°16S 135°45E **150 B2**
Rose, L. *Bahamas* 21°0N 73°30W **183 B5**
Rose Belle *Mauritius* 20°24S 57°36E **147 d**
Rose Blanche *Canada* 47°38N 58°45W **165 C8**
Rose Hill *Mauritius* 20°14S 57°27E **147 d**
Rose Valley *Canada* 52°19N 103°49W **163 C8**
Roseau *Dominica* 15°17N 61°24W **183 D7**
Roseau *U.S.A.* 48°51N 95°46W **172 A6**
Rosebery *Australia* 41°46S 145°33E **151 G4**
Rosebud *Australia* 38°21S 144°54E **152 E6**
Rosebud *S. Dak.,
U.S.A.* 43°14N 100°51W **172 D3**
Rosebud *Tex., U.S.A.* 31°4N 96°59W **176 F6**
Roseburg *U.S.A.* 43°13N 123°20W **168 E2**
Rosedale *U.S.A.* 33°51N 91°2W **176 E8**
Rosehearty *U.K.* 57°42N 2°7W **65 D6**
Roseires Res. *Sudan* 11°51N 34°23E **135 F12**
Roses *Spain* 42°19N 3°10E **90 C8**
Roses, G. de *Spain* 42°10N 3°15E **90 C8**
Rosetown *Canada* 51°35N 107°59W **163 C7**
Rosetta = Rashîd *Egypt* 31°21N 30°22E **137 F12**
Roseville *Calif., U.S.A.* 38°45N 121°17W **170 G5**
Roseville *Mich., U.S.A.* 42°30N 82°56W **174 D1**
Rosewood *Australia* 27°38S 152°36E **153 A5**
Roshkhvār *Iran* 34°58N 59°37E **129 C8**
Rosignano Maríttimo
Italy 43°24N 10°28E **92 E7**
Rosignol *Guyana* 6°15N 57°30W **186 B7**
Roşiori de Vede *Romania* 44°9N 25°0E **81 F10**

Rositsa *Bulgaria* 43°57N 27°57E **97**
Rositsa → *Bulgaria* 43°10N 25°30E **97**
Roskilde *Denmark* 55°38N 12°3E **63**
Roskovec *Albania* 40°44N 19°43E **96**
Roslavl *Russia* 53°57N 32°55E **86**
Rosmaninhal *Portugal* 39°44N 7°5W **89**
Rosmead *S. Africa* 31°29S 25°8E **144**
Røsnæs *Denmark* 55°44N 10°55E **63**
Rosolini *Italy* 36°49N 14°57E **95**
Rosporden *France* 47°57N 3°50W **70**
Ross *N.Z.* 42°53S 170°49E **155**
Ross Béthio *Mauritania* 16°15N 16°8W **138**
Ross Dependency
Antarctica 76°0S 170°0W **55**
Ross I. *Antarctica* 77°30S 168°0E **55**
Ross Ice Shelf *Antarctica* 80°0S 180°0E **55**
Ross L. *U.S.A.* 48°44N 121°4W **168**
Ross-on-Wye *U.K.* 51°54N 2°34W **67**
Ross River *Australia* 19°15S 146°49E **150**
Ross River *Canada* 62°30N 131°30W **166**
Ross Sea *Antarctica* 74°0S 178°0E **55**
Rossan Pt. *Ireland* 54°42N 8°47W **64**
Rossano *Italy* 39°36N 16°39E **95**
Rossburn *Canada* 50°40N 100°49W **163**
Rosseau *Canada* 45°16N 79°39W **174**
Rosseau, L. *Canada* 45°10N 79°35W **174**
Rosses, The *Ireland* 55°2N 8°20W **64**
Rossignol, L. *Canada* 52°43N 73°40W **164**
Rossignol L. *Canada* 44°12N 65°10W **165**
Rossiya = Russia ■
Eurasia 62°0N 105°0E **107**
Rossland *Canada* 49°6N 117°50W **162**
Rosslare *Ireland* 52°17N 6°24W **64**
Rosslare Europort = Rosslare
Harbour *Ireland* 52°15N 6°20W **64**
Rosslare Harbour *Ireland* 52°15N 6°20W **64**
Rosslau *Germany* 51°52N 12°15E **76**
Rossmore *Canada* 44°8N 77°23W **174**
Rossosh *Russia* 16°40N 15°45W **138**
Rosso *Mauritania* 16°40N 15°45W **138**
Rosso, C. *France* 42°13N 8°32E **73**
Rossosh *Russia* 50°15N 39°28E **85**
Rossvatnet *Norway* 65°45N 14°5E **60**
Røst *Norway* 67°32N 12°0E **60**
Rosthern *Canada* 52°40N 106°20W **163**
Rostock *Germany* 54°5N 12°8E **76**
Rostov *Don, Russia* 47°15N 39°45E **85**
Rostov *Yaroslavl, Russia* 57°14N 39°25E **84**
Rostov □ *Russia* 48°50N 41°10E **85**
Rostrenen *France* 48°14N 3°21W **70**
Roswell *Ga., U.S.A.* 34°2N 84°22W **178**
Roswell *N. Mex.,
U.S.A.* 33°24N 104°32W **169**
Rota *Spain* 36°37N 6°20W **89**
Rotan *U.S.A.* 32°51N 100°28W **176**
Rote *Indonesia* 10°50S 123°0E **118**
Rotenburg *Hessen,
Germany* 50°59N 9°44E **76**
Rotenburg *Niedersachsen,
Germany* 53°6N 9°24E **76**
Roth *Germany* 49°15N 11°5E **77**
Rothaargebirge *Germany* 51°2N 8°13E **76**
Rothaargebirge △
Germany 51°0N 8°15E **76**
Rothenburg ob der Tauber
Germany 49°23N 10°11E **77**
Rother → *U.K.* 50°59N 0°45E **67**
Rotherham *U.K.* 53°26N 1°20W **66**
Rothes *U.K.* 57°32N 3°13W **65**
Rothesay *Canada* 45°23N 66°0W **165**
Rothesay *U.K.* 55°50N 5°3W **65**
Roti = Rote *Indonesia* 10°50S 123°0E **118**
Rotja, Pta. *Spain* 38°38N 1°35E **91**
Roto *Australia* 33°0S 145°30E **153**
Rotoaira, L. *N.Z.* 39°3S 175°45E **154**
Rotoehu, L. *N.Z.* 38°1S 176°32E **154**
Rotoiti, L. *Bay of Plenty,
N.Z.* 38°2S 176°26E **154**
Rotoiti, L. *W. Coast,
N.Z.* 41°51S 172°49E **155**
Rotoma, L. *N.Z.* 38°5S 176°35E **154**
Rotondo, Mte. *France* 42°14N 9°8E **73**
Rotorua *N.Z.* 38°9S 176°16E **154**
Rotorua, L. *N.Z.* 38°5S 176°18E **154**
Rott → *Germany* 48°26N 13°26E **77**
Rottenburg *Germany* 48°28N 8°55E **77**
Rottenmann *Austria* 47°31N 14°22E **77**
Rotterdam *Neths.* 51°55N 4°30E **69**
Rotterdam *U.S.A.* 42°48N 74°1W **175**
Rottne *Sweden* 57°1N 14°54E **63**
Rottnest I. *Australia* 32°0S 115°27E **149**
Rottumeroog *Neths.* 53°33N 6°34E **69**
Rottweil *Germany* 48°9N 8°37E **77**
Rotuma *Fiji* 12°25S 177°5E **147**
Roubaix *France* 50°40N 3°10E **71**
Roudnice nad Labem
Czech Rep. 50°25N 14°15E **78**
Rouen *France* 49°27N 1°4E **70**
Rouergue *France* 44°15N 2°0E **72**
Rough Ridge *N.Z.* 45°10S 169°55E **155**
Rouillac *France* 45°47N 0°4W **72**
Rouïssat *Algeria* 31°55N 5°20E **136**
Rouleau *Canada* 50°10N 104°56W **163**
Roulpmaulpma ○
Australia 23°25S 133°0E **148**
Round I. *Mauritius* 19°51S 57°45E **147**
Round Mountain
U.S.A. 38°43N 117°4W **168**
Round Mt. *Australia* 30°26S 152°16E **153**
Round Rock *U.S.A.* 30°31N 97°41W **176**
Roundup *U.S.A.* 46°27N 108°33W **168**
Rousay *U.K.* 59°10N 3°2W **65**
Rouses Point *U.S.A.* 44°59N 73°22W **175**
Rouseville *U.S.A.* 41°28N 79°42W **174**
Rousse = Ruse *Bulgaria* 43°48N 25°59E **97**
Roussenski Lom →
Bulgaria 43°40N 26°10E **97**
Roussillon *Isère, France* 45°24N 4°49E **73**
Roussillon *Pyrénées-Or.,
France* 42°30N 2°35E **72**
Rouxville *S. Africa* 30°25S 26°50E **144**
Rouyn-Noranda *Canada* 48°20N 79°0W **164**
Rovaniemi *Finland* 66°29N 25°41E **60**
Rovato *Italy* 45°34N 10°0E **92**
Rovenki *Ukraine* 48°5N 39°21E **85**
Rovereto *Italy* 45°53N 11°3E **92**
Rovigo *Italy* 45°4N 11°47E **92**
Rovinj *Croatia* 45°5N 13°40E **93**
Rovno = Rivne *Ukraine* 50°40N 26°10E **75**

noye Russia 50°52N 46°3E **86** E8
vuma = Ruvuma →
Tanzania 10°29S 40°28E **143** E5
w'ān Iran 35°8N 48°51E **128** C4
wena Australia 29°48S 148°55E **151** D4
wley I. Canada 69°6N 77°52W **161** D16
wkas Phil. 11°36N 122°49E **119** B6
kboro U.S.A. 36°24N 78°59W **177** C15
rin. & Tob. 11°15N 60°35W **187** D7
borough
Australia 30°43S 136°46E **151** E2
cen Sweden 58°30N 15°40E **63** F9
w' Mont., U.S.A. 47°20N 108°58W **168** C9
N. Mex., U.S.A. 35°57N 104°12W **169** J11
Utah, U.S.A. 41°10N 112°2W **168** F7
Hill Australia 22°41S 119°57E **148** D3
val △ Australia 34°5S 151°5E **153** C9
val Bardia △ Nepal 28°20N 81°20E **125** E9
val Canal Ireland 53°30N 7°13W **64** C4
val Chitawan △
Nepal 26°30N 84°30E **125** F11
val Geographical Society Is.
Canada 68°50N 100°15W **160** D11
val Leamington Spa
U.K. 52°18N 1°31W **67** E6
val Natal △ S. Africa 28°43S 28°51E **145** C4
val Palm Beach
U.S.A. 26°42N 80°14W **179** J9
val Tunbridge Wells
U.K. 51°7N 0°16E **67** F8
vale, Isle U.K. 48°0N 88°54W **172** B9
valla Australia 35°3S 149°9E **153** C8
van France 45°37N 1°2W **72** C2
ye France 49°42N 2°48E **71** C9
yston U.K. 52°3N 0°0 **67** E7
kan Montenegro 42°50N 20°11E **96** D4
tan Poland 52°52N 21°25E **83** F8
zay-en-Brie France 48°41N 2°58E **71** D9
adilna Ukraine 46°50N 30°2E **81** D15
thnyativ Ukraine 48°56N 24°9E **81** B9
thyshche Ukraine 50°54N 25°15E **75** C13
mitál pod Třemšínem
Czech Rep. 49°36N 13°53E **78** B6
thava Slovak Rep. 48°37N 20°35E **79** C13
zogi Poland 53°28N 21°19E **82** E8
tov-sur-Serre France 49°40N 4°8E **71** C11
rtoczański △ Poland 50°37N 23°0E **83** H10
zzano Italy 45°22N 9°10E **92** C6
shen Albania 41°47N 19°49E **96** E3
gozhine Albania 41°4N 19°50E **96** E3
arij Serbia 43°45N 21°0E **96** C5
m, O. er →' Algeria 33°29N 5°38E **136** B5
shchevo Russia 52°18N 43°46E **86** D6
a = Ruka Spain 17°27S 14°21E **144** A1
acaná Namibia
aha △ Tanzania 7°41S 34°30E **142** D3
ahine Ra. N.Z. 39°55S 176°2E **154** F5
amahanga →' N.Z. 41°24S 175°8E **154** H4
apehu N.Z. 39°17S 175°35E **154** F5
apuke I. N.Z. 46°46S 168°31E **155** G3
āq, W. →' Egypt 30°0N 33°49E **130** F2
atoria N.Z. 37°55S 178°20E **154** G7
awai N.Z. 36°8S 173°59E **154** D4
b' al Khāli Si. Arabia 19°0N 48°0E **131** D4
beho Mts. Tanzania 6°50S 36°25E **142** D4
bezhnoye = Rubizhne
Ukraine 49°6N 38°25E **85** H10
bh a' Mhail U.K. 55°56N 6°8W **65** F2
bha Hunish U.K. 57°42N 6°20W **65** D2
bha Robhanais = Lewis, Butt of
U.K. 58°31N 6°16W **65** C2
bi Spain 41°29N 2°0E **90** D7
bicon →' Italy 38°53N 121°4W **170** G5
bicone → Italy 44°8N 12°28E **93** D9
bik Albania 41°46N 19°4E **96** E3
bino Ivory C. 6°4N 4°18W **138** D4
bizhne Venezuela 7°43N 72°22W **186** B4
bizhne Ukraine 49°6N 38°25E **85** H10
bondo a Tanzania 2°18S 31°58E **142** C3
btsovsk Russia 51°30N 81°10E **109** B10
by L. U.S.A. 40°10N 115°28W **168** F6
by Mts. U.S.A. 40°30N 115°20W **168** F6
byvale Australia 33°25S 147°42E **150** C4
bcheng China 33°25S 113°38E **117** E9
ciane-Nida Poland 53°40N 21°32E **82** E8
d Sar Iran 37°8N 50°18E **128** B6
da Sweden 57°6N 16°7E **63** G10
da Śląska Poland 50°16N 18°50E **83** H5
dall U.K. 52°27N 13°47E **152** B2
dall →' Australia 22°34S 122°13E **148** D3
d River △
Australia 22°38S 122°30E **148** A3
dbar Iran 36°48N 49°23E **128** B6
dersdorf Germany 52°27N 13°47E **76** C9
dewa Tanzania 10°7S 34°40E **143** E3
dkobing Denmark 54°56N 10°41E **63** K4
dky Ukraine 49°38N 23°29E **83** J10
dna Poland 51°30N 16°17E **83** G3
dnik Bulgaria 42°36N 27°30E **97** D11
dnik Poland 50°26N 22°15E **83** H9
dnik Serbia 44°7N 20°35E **96** B4
dnytsa Ukraine 54°55N 31°7E **84** B6
dnyy Uzbekistan 48°16N 28°54E **81** B13
do Bos.-H. 43°41N 19°23E **96** C3
dolfa, Ostrov Russia 81°45N 58°30E **106** A6
dolstadt Germany 50°44N 11°19E **76** E7
dong China 32°20N 121°12E **117** A13
dozm Bulgaria 28°59N 79°24E **125** E8
dyard U.S.A. 46°14N 84°36W **173** B11
ne France 50°15N 1°40E **71** B8
kenya →' Africa 16°24S 33°48E **143** H5
ffling Pt. Br. Virgin Is. 18°44N 64°27W **183** e
fiji →' Fiji 17°20S 177°5E **155** a
fino Argentina 34°20S 62°50W **190** C3
fufunsa Zambia 15°4S 29°34E **143** F2
gao China 32°20N 120°31E **117** A13
gby U.K. 52°23N 1°16W **67** E6
geley U.S.A. 48°22N 100°0W **172** A4
rgen →' Germany 54°22N 13°25E **76** A9
igen Germany 54°25N 13°25E **76** A9
gles France 48°50N 0°40E **70** D7

Ruhengeri Rwanda 1°30S 29°36E **142** C2
Ruhla Germany 50°54N 10°23E **76** E6
Ruhland Germany 51°27N 13°51E **76** D9
Ruhnu Estonia 57°48N 23°15E **82** A10
Ruhr →' Germany 51°27N 6°43E **76** D2
Ruhuhu →' Tanzania 10°31S 34°34E **143** E3
Rui Barbosa Brazil 12°18S 40°27W **189** D2
Rui'an China 27°47N 120°40E **117** D13
Ruichang China 29°40N 115°39E **117** C10
Ruidoso U.S.A. 33°20N 105°41W **169** K11
Ruijin China 25°48N 116°0E **117** D10
Ruili China 24°6N 97°46E **116** E1
Ruiru Kenya 1°9S 36°58E **142** C4
Ruivo, Pico Madeira 32°45N 16°56W **100** D3
Rujen Macedonia 42°9N 22°34E **96** D6
Rujm Tal'at al Jamā'ah
Jordan 30°24N 35°30E **130** E4
Ruk Pakistan 27°50N 68°42E **124** F3
Rukhla Pakistan 32°27N 71°57E **124** C4
Ruki →'
Dem. Rep. of the Congo 0°5N 18°17E **140** E3
Rukumkot Nepal 28°37N 82°37E **125** E10
Rukwa □ Tanzania 7°0S 31°30E **142** D3
Rukwa, L. Tanzania 8°0S 32°20E **142** D3
Rulenge Burundi 2°43S 30°37E **142** C3
Rulhieres, C. Australia 13°56S 127°22E **148** B4
Rum Jordan 29°39N 35°26E **130** F4
Rum U.K. 57°0N 6°20W **65** E2
Rum Cay Bahamas 23°40N 74°58W **183** B5
Rum Jungle Australia 13°0S 130°59E **148** B5
Ruma Serbia 45°0N 19°50E **80** E4
Ruma a Kenya 0°39S 34°18E **142** C3
Rumāḥ Si. Arabia 25°29N 47°10E **128** E5
Rumania = Romania ■
Europe 46°0N 25°0E **81** D10
Rumaylah Iraq 30°47N 47°37E **128** D5
Rumaylah, 'Urūq ar
Si. Arabia 22°0N 48°30E **131** C4
Rumbek South Sudan 6°54N 29°37E **135** G11
Rumburk Czech Rep. 50°57N 14°32E **78** A7
Rumford U.S.A. 44°33N 70°33W **175** B14
Rumia Poland 54°37N 18°25E **82** D5
Rumilly France 45°53N 5°56E **73** C9
Rumoi Japan 43°56N 141°39E **112** C10
Rumonge Burundi 3°59S 29°26E **142** C2
Rumpi N.Z. 42°25S 171°15E **155** C6
Rumson U.S.A. 40°22N 74°0W **175** F11
Runan China 33°0N 114°30E **117** A10
Runanga N.Z. 42°25S 171°15E **155** C6
Runaway, C. N.Z. 37°32S 177°59E **154** D6
Runaway Bay Jamaica 18°27N 77°20W **182** a
Runcorn U.K. 53°21N 2°44W **66** D5
Rundu Namibia 17°52S 19°43E **144** A2
Rungwa Tanzania 6°55S 33°32E **142** D3
Rungwa →' Tanzania 7°36S 31°50E **142** D3
Rungwa △ Tanzania 6°53S 34°2E **142** D3
Rungwe Tanzania 9°11S 33°32E **143** D3
Rungwe, Mt. Tanzania 9°8S 33°40E **140** F6
Runka Nigeria 12°28N 7°20E **139** C6
Runn Sweden 60°30N 15°40E **62** D9
Runton Ra. Australia 23°31S 123°6E **148** D3
Ruo Shui →' China 41°0N 100°16E **110** C9
Ruokolahti Finland 61°17N 28°50E **84** B5
Ruoqiang China 38°55N 88°10E **109** E11
Rupa India 27°15N 92°21E **123** F18
Rupar India 31°2N 76°38E **124** D7
Rupat Indonesia 1°45N 101°40E **118** D2
Rupea Romania 46°2N 25°13E **81** D10
Rupen →' India 23°28N 71°31E **124** H4
Rupert U.S.A. 42°37N 113°41W **168** E7
Rupert →' Canada 51°29N 78°45W **164** B4
Rupert B. Canada 51°35N 79°0W **164** B4
Rupert House = Waskaganish
Canada 51°30N 78°40W **164** B4
Rupnagar = Rupar
India 31°2N 76°38E **124** D7
Rupsa India 21°37N 87°1E **125** J12
Rur →' Germany 51°11N 5°59E **76** D1
Rurrenabaque Bolivia 14°30S 67°32W **188** C4
Rus →' Spain 39°30N 2°30W **91** F2
Rusambo Zimbabwe 16°30S 32°4E **143** F3
Rusape Zimbabwe 18°35S 32°8E **143** F3
Ruschuk = Ruse
Bulgaria 43°48N 25°59E **97** C9
Ruse Bulgaria 43°48N 25°59E **97** C9
Ruse □ Bulgaria 43°35N 25°40E **97** C9
Ruşeţu Romania 44°57N 27°14E **81** F12
Rush Ireland 53°31N 6°6W **64** C5
Rushan China 36°56N 121°30E **115** F11
Rushikulya →' India 19°23N 85°5E **126** E7
Rushmore, Mt.
U.S.A. 43°53N 103°28W **172** D2
Rushville Ill., U.S.A. 40°7N 90°34W **172** E8
Rushville Ind., U.S.A. 39°37N 85°27W **173** F11
Rushville Nebr.,
U.S.A. 42°43N 102°28W **172** D2
Rushworth Australia 36°32S 145°1E **153** D6
Ruskin U.S.A. 27°43N 82°26W **179** H7
Russas Brazil 4°55S 37°50W **189** A3
Russell Canada 50°50N 101°20W **163** C8
Russell N.Z. 35°16S 174°10E **154** B3
Russell Fla., U.S.A. 38°31N 81°45W **178** F8
Russell Kans., U.S.A. 38°54N 98°52W **172** F4
Russell N.Y., U.S.A. 44°27N 75°9W **175** B9
Russell Pa., U.S.A. 41°56N 79°8W **174** E5
Russell Cave △
U.S.A. 34°59N 85°49W **177** D12
Russell I. Man.,
Canada 56°15N 101°30W **163** B8
Russell I. N.W.T.,
Canada 63°5N 115°44W **162** A5
Russellkonda India 19°57N 84°42E **126** E7
Russellville
U.S.A. 34°30N 87°44W **177** D11
Russellville Ark., U.S.A. 35°17N 93°8W **176** D8
Russellville Ky.,
U.S.A. 36°51N 86°53W **172** G10
Rüsselsheim Germany 49°59N 8°25E **77** F4
Russi Italy 44°22N 12°2E **93** D9
Russian ■ Eurasia 62°0N 105°0E **107** C11
Russian →' U.S.A. 38°27N 123°8W **170** G3
Russian Arktika △
Russia 73°40N 55°55E **106** B6
Russkiy, Ostrov Russia 43°0N 131°50E **117** D15
Russkiy Sever △ Russia 59°57N 38°34E **84** B10
Rust Austria 47°48N 16°42E **79** D9
Rustam Shahr Pakistan 26°58N 66°6E **124** F2
Rustenburg S. Africa 25°41S 27°14E **144** C4

Ruston U.S.A. 32°32N 92°38W **176** E8
Rutana Burundi 3°55S 30°0E **142** C3
Rute Spain 37°19N 4°23W **89** H6
Ruteng Indonesia 8°35S 120°30E **119** F6
Rutenga Zimbabwe 21°15S 30°44E **143** G3
Ruth U.S.A. 43°42N 82°45W **174** C2
Rutherford U.S.A. 38°26N 122°24W **170** G4
Rutherglen Australia 36°5S 146°29E **153** D7
Rutland □ U.K. 52°38N 0°40W **67** E7
Rutland I. U.K. 11°25N 92°10E **127** J11
Rutland Water U.K. 52°39N 0°38W **67** E7
Rutledge →' Canada 61°4N 112°0W **163** A6
Rutledge L. Canada 61°33N 110°47W **163** A6
Rutog China 33°27N 79°42E **109** F9
Rutqa, W. →' Syria 34°30N 41°3E **105** C9
Rutshuru
Dem. Rep. of the Congo 1°13S 29°25E **142** C2
Ruvo di Púglia Italy 41°7N 16°29E **95** A9
Ruvu Tanzania 6°23S 38°52E **142** D4
Ruvu →' Tanzania 6°23S 38°52E **142** D4
Ruvuba □ Burundi 3°10S 30°0E **142** C2
Ruvuma □ Tanzania 10°20S 36°0E **143** E4
Ruvuma →' Tanzania 10°29S 40°28E **143** E5
Ruwais U.A.E. 24°5N 52°50E **129** E7
Ruwenzori Africa 0°30N 29°55E **142** B2
Ruwenzori △ Uganda 0°20N 30°0E **142** B2
Ruya →' Zimbabwe 16°27S 32°5E **145** A5
Ruyang China 34°9N 112°27E **116** A7
Ruyigi Burundi 3°29S 30°15E **142** C3
Ruyuan China 24°46N 113°16E **117** E9
Růzaevka Kazakhstan 52°49N 66°56E **109** B7
Ruzhevo Konare
Bulgaria 42°23N 24°46E **97** D8
Ruzhou China 34°11N 112°52E **114** C7
Ružomberok Slovak Rep. 49°3N 19°17E **79** B12
Ruzyně, Praha ✈ (PRG)
Czech Rep. 50°6N 14°16E **78** A7
Rwanda ■ Africa 2°0S 30°0E **142** C3
Ryakhovo Bulgaria 43°58N 26°18E **97** C10
Ryan, L. U.K. 55°0N 5°2W **65** G5
Ryazan Russia 54°40N 39°40E **84** D10
Ryazan □ Russia 54°50N 39°30E **86** C4
Ryazhsk Russia 53°45N 40°3E **84** F11
Rybachiy Russia 55°10N 20°50E **82** C7
Rybachiy Poluostrov
Russia 69°43N 32°0E **60** B25
Rybachye = Balykchy
Kyrgyzstan 42°26N 76°12E **109** D9
Rybinsk Russia 58°5N 38°50E **84** C10
Rybinskoye Vdkhr.
Russia 58°30N 38°25E **84** C10
Rybnik Poland 50°6N 18°32E **83** H5
Rybnitsa = Rîbniţa
Moldova 47°45N 29°0E **81** E15
Rybnoye Russia 54°45N 39°30E **84** E10
Rychnov nad Kněžnou
Czech Rep. 50°10N 16°17E **79** A9
Rychwał Poland 52°4N 18°10E **83** F5
Rycroft Canada 55°45N 118°40W **162** B5
Ryd Sweden 56°27N 14°42E **63** H8
Rydaholm Sweden 56°59N 14°18E **63** H8
Ryde U.K. 50°43N 1°9W **67** G6
Ryderwood U.S.A. 46°23N 123°3W **170** D3
Rydzyna Poland 51°47N 16°39E **83** G3
Rye U.K. 50°57N 0°45E **67** G8
Rye →' U.K. 54°11N 0°44W **66** C7
Rye Bay U.K. 50°52N 0°49E **67** G8
Rye Patch Res. U.S.A. 40°28N 118°19W **168** F4
Ryegate U.S.A. 46°18N 109°15W **168** C9
Ryki Poland 51°38N 21°56E **83** G8
Ryley Canada 53°17N 112°26W **162** C6
Rylsk Russia 51°36N 34°43E **85** E8
Rylstone Australia 32°46S 149°58E **153** B8
Rymanów Poland 49°35N 21°51E **83** J8
Ryn Poland 53°57N 21°34E **82** E8
Ryn Peski = Naryn Qum
Kazakhstan 47°30N 49°0E **87** E9
Ryōtsu Japan 38°5N 138°26E **112** E9
Rypin Poland 53°3N 19°25E **83** E6
Ryssby Sweden 56°52N 14°10E **63** H8
Rysy Europe 49°10N 20°4E **79** B13
Ryūgasaki Japan 35°54N 140°11E **113** G10
Ryukyu Is. = Ryūkyū-Rettō
Japan 26°0N 126°0E **113** M3
Ryūkyū-Rettō Japan 26°0N 126°0E **113** M3
Rzepin Poland 52°20N 14°49E **83** F1
Rzeszów Poland 50°5N 21°58E **83** H8
Rzhev Russia 56°20N 34°20E **84** D8

S

Sa Cabaneta Spain 39°37N 2°45E **100** B9
Sa Canal Spain 38°51N 1°23E **100** C7
Sa Conillera Spain 38°59N 1°13E **100** C7
Sa Dec Vietnam 10°20N 105°46E **121** G5
Sa Dragonera Spain 39°35N 2°19E **100** B9
Sa Kaeo Thailand 13°49N 102°4E **120** F4
Sa Mesquida Spain 39°55N 4°16E **100** B11
Sa Pa Vietnam 22°20N 103°47E **120** A4
Sa Pobla Spain 39°46N 3°1E **90** F8
Sa Savina Spain 38°44N 1°25E **100** C7
Sa'ādat Shahr Iran 30°10N 53°5E **129** D7
Sa'ādatābād Hormozgān,
Iran 28°3N 55°53E **129** D7
Sa'ādatābād Kermān,
Iran 29°40N 55°51E **129** D7
Saale →' Germany 51°56N 11°54E **76** D7
Saaler Bodden Germany 54°20N 12°27E **76** A8
Saalfeld Germany 50°38N 11°21E **76** E7
Saalfelden Austria 47°25N 12°51E **78** D5
Saane →' Switz. 47°8N 7°10E **77** H3
Saanich Canada 48°29N 123°26W **170** B3
Saar →' Europe 49°41N 6°32E **69** E6
Saar-Hunsrück △
Germany 49°30N 6°50E **77** F2
Saarbrücken Germany 49°14N 6°59E **77** F2
Saarburg Germany 49°36N 6°32E **77** F2
Saaremaa Estonia 58°30N 22°30E **84** C2
Saarijärvi Finland 62°43N 25°16E **60** E21
Saarland □ Germany 49°20N 6°45E **77** F2
Saarlouis Germany 49°19N 6°45E **77** F2
Saath Azerbaijan 39°55N 48°22E **105** C13
Sab 'Ābar Syria 33°46N 37°41E **104** F4
Saba W. Indies 17°38N 63°14W **183** C7
Šabac Serbia 44°48N 19°42E **96** B3
Sabadell Spain 41°28N 2°7E **90** D7
Sabah □ Malaysia 6°0N 117°0E **118** C5

Sabak Bernam
Malaysia 3°46N 100°58E **121** L3
Sabalān, Kūhhā-ye
Iran 38°15N 47°45E **105** C12
Sabalana, Kepulauan
Indonesia 6°45S 118°50E **119** F5
Sabanalarga Colombia 10°38N 74°55W **186** A4
Sabang Indonesia 5°50N 95°15E **118** C1
Sābāoani Romania 47°1N 26°51E **81** C11
Sabará Brazil 19°55S 43°46W **189** E2
Sabarania Indonesia 2°5S 138°18E **119** E9
Sabarmati →' India 22°18N 72°22E **124** H5
Sabattis U.S.A. 44°6N 74°40W **175** B10
Sábáudia Italy 41°18N 13°1E **94** A6
Sabaya Bolivia 19°1S 68°23W **188** D4
Saberania Indonesia 2°5S 138°18E **119** E9
Sabhā Libya 27°9N 14°29E **135** C8
Sabhah Si. Arabia 28°29N 76°44E **124** E7
Sabie →' S. Africa 25°10S 30°48E **145** C5
Sabie S. Africa 25°10S 30°48E **145** C5
Sabinal U.S.A. 29°19N 99°28W **176** G5
Sabinánigo Spain 42°31N 0°22W **90** C4
Sabinas Mexico 27°51N 101°7W **180** B4
Sabinas →' Mexico 27°37N 100°42W **180** B4
Sabinas Hidalgo
Mexico 26°30N 100°10W **180** B4
Sabine →' U.S.A. 29°59N 93°47W **176** G8
Sabine L. U.S.A. 29°53N 93°51W **176** G8
Sabine Pass U.S.A. 29°44N 93°54W **176** G8
Sabinópolis Brazil 18°40S 43°6W **189** D2
Sabinov Slovak Rep. 49°6N 21°5E **79** B14
Sable Canada 55°30N 68°21W **165** A6
Sable, C. Canada 43°29N 65°38W **165** D6
Sable, C. U.S.A. 25°9N 81°8W **179** K8
Sable I. Canada 44°0N 60°0W **165** D8
Sablé-sur-Sarthe France 47°50N 0°20W **70** E6
Saboeiro Brazil 6°32S 39°54W **189** B3
Sabonkafi Niger 14°40N 8°45E **139** C6
Sabor →' Portugal 41°10N 7°7W **88** D3
Sabou Burkina Faso 12°1N 2°15W **138** C4
Sabrés France 44°9N 0°43W **72** D3
Sabrina Coast Antarctica 68°0S 120°0E **5** C9
Sabugal Portugal 40°20N 7°5W **88** E3
Sabulubek Indonesia 1°36S 98°40E **118** E1
Sabuncu Turkey 39°33N 30°12E **99** B12
Sabzevār Iran 36°15N 57°40E **129** B8
Sabzvārān = Jiroft Iran 28°45N 57°50E **129** D8
Sac City U.S.A. 42°25N 95°0W **172** D6
Sacedón Spain 40°29N 2°41W **90** E2
Săcele Romania 45°37N 25°41E **81** E10
Sacheon S. Korea 35°0N 128°6E **115** G15
Sachigo →' Canada 55°6N 88°58W **164** A2
Sachigo, L. Canada 53°50N 92°12W **164** B1
Sachimbo Angola 9°14S 20°16E **140** F4
Sachin India 21°5N 72°53E **126** D7
Sachkhere Georgia 42°25N 43°28E **87** J6
Sachsen □ Germany 50°55N 13°10E **76** E9
Sachsen-Anhalt □
Germany 52°0N 12°0E **76** D7
Sächsische Schweiz △
Germany 50°55N 14°10E **76** E10
Sacile Italy 45°57N 12°30E **93** C9
Sackets Harbor U.S.A. 43°57N 76°7W **175** C8
Sackville Canada 45°54N 64°22W **165** C7
Saco Maine, U.S.A. 43°30N 70°27W **175** C14
Saco Mont., U.S.A. 48°28N 107°21W **168** B10
Sacramento Brazil 19°53S 47°27W **189** D1
Sacramento U.S.A. 38°35N 121°29W **170** G5
Sacramento →' U.S.A. 38°3N 121°56W **170** G5
Sacramento Mts.
U.S.A. 32°30N 105°30W **169** K11
Sacramento Valley
U.S.A. 39°30N 122°0W **170** G5
Săcueni Romania 47°20N 22°5E **80** C7
Sada, C. Spain 36°42N 3°28W **89** J7
Sada-Misaki Japan 33°20N 132°5E **113** H6
Sádaba Spain 42°19N 1°12W **90** C3
Sadani □ Tanzania 6°3S 38°47E **142** D4
Sadao Thailand 6°38N 100°26E **121** J3
Sadaseopet India 17°38N 77°59E **126** F3
Sadd el Aali Egypt 23°54N 32°54E **137** D3
Saddle Mt. U.S.A. 45°58N 123°41W **170** E3
Saddle Pk. India 13°9N 93°1E **127** H11
Sade Nigeria 11°22N 10°45E **139** C7
Sadimi
Dem. Rep. of the Congo 9°25S 23°32E **143** D1
Sadiola Mali 13°50N 11°40W **138** C2
Sa'dīyah, Hawr as
Iraq 32°15N 46°30E **105** F12
Sado Japan 38°0N 138°25E **112** F9
Sado →' Portugal 38°29N 8°55W **89** G2
Sadon Russia 42°52N 43°58E **87** J6
Sadovoye Russia 47°47N 44°31E **87** G7
Sadra India 23°21N 72°43E **124** H5
Sadrazamköy = Livera
Cyprus 35°23N 32°57E **101** D11
Sadri India 25°11N 73°26E **124** G5
Sæby Denmark 57°21N 10°30E **63** G4
Saegertown U.S.A. 41°43N 80°9W **174** E4
Saelices Spain 39°55N 2°49W **90** F2
Safaalan Turkey 41°26N 28°6E **97** E12
Safājah Si. Arabia 26°25N 39°0E **128** E3
Šafárikovo = Tornaľa
Slovak Rep. 48°25N 20°20E **79** C13
Safed Dasht Iran 33°27N 48°11E **129** C6
Safed Kūh Afghan. 34°15N 64°0E **128** C6
Safed Rūd →' Iran 37°23N 50°11E **129** B6
Safipur India 26°44N 80°21E **125** F9
Ṣāfītā Syria 34°48N 36°7E **104** E4
Safonovo Russia 55°4N 33°16E **84** D7
Safranbolu Turkey 41°20N 32°39E **104** A2
Saft Morocco 32°18N 9°20W **136** B4
Safwān Iraq 30°7N 47°43E **128** D5
Sag Harbor U.S.A. 41°0N 72°18W **175** E12
Saga Indonesia 2°40S 132°55E **119** E8
Saga □ Japan 33°15N 130°16E **113** H5
Saga Japan 33°15N 130°20E **113** H5
Saga Burma 21°52N 95°59E **123** J19

Sagala Mali 14°9N 6°38W **138** C3
Sagamore U.S.A. 40°46N 79°14W **174** F5
Saganaga L. Canada 48°14N 90°52W **172** A8
Saganthit Kyun Burma 11°56N 98°29E **121** G2
Sagar Karnataka, India 16°38N 76°48E **126** F3
Sagar Karnataka, India 14°14N 75°6E **127** G2
Sagar Mad. P., India 23°50N 78°44E **125** H8
Sagara, L. Tanzania 5°20S 31°0E **142** D3
Sagarejo Georgia 41°44N 45°19E **87** K7
Sagarmatha = Everest, Mt.
Nepal 28°5N 86°58E **125** E12
Sagarmatha △ Nepal 27°55N 86°45E **125** E12
Saginaw U.S.A. 43°26N 83°56W **173** D12
Saginaw B. U.S.A. 43°50N 83°40W **173** D12
Saglouc = Salluit
Canada 62°14N 75°38W **161** E16
Sagone France 42°7N 8°42E **73** F12
Sagone, G. de France 42°4N 8°40E **73** F12
Sagres Portugal 37°0N 8°58W **89** J2
Sagua la Grande Cuba 22°50N 80°10W **182** B3
Saguache U.S.A. 38°5N 106°8W **168** G10
Saguaro △ U.S.A. 32°12N 110°38W **169** K8
Saguenay →' Canada 48°22N 71°0W **165** C5
Sagunt = Sagunto Spain 39°42N 0°18W **90** F4
Sagunto = Sagunt Spain 39°42N 0°18W **90** F4
Sagwara India 23°41N 74°1E **124** H6
Sahaba Sudan 18°57N 30°25E **137** D3
Sahagún Spain 42°18N 5°2W **88** C5
Saham al Jawlān Syria 32°45N 35°55E **130** C4
Sahand, Kūh-e Iran 37°44N 46°27E **105** C12
Sahara Africa 23°0N 5°0E **134** D6
Saharan Atlas = Saharien, Atlas
Algeria 33°30N 1°0E **136** B6
Saharanpur India 29°58N 77°33E **124** E7
Saharien, Atlas Algeria 33°30N 1°0E **136** B6
Saharsa India 25°53N 86°36E **125** G12
Sahaswan India 28°5N 78°45E **125** E8
Saheira, W. el →' Egypt 30°5N 33°25E **130** E2
Sahel Africa 16°0N 5°0E **134** E5
Sahel, Canal du Mali 14°20N 6°0W **138** C3
Sahibganj India 25°12N 87°40E **125** G12
Sāhilīyah Iraq 33°43N 42°42E **105** F10
Sahiwal Pakistan 30°45N 73°8E **124** D5
Ṣahneh Iran 34°29N 47°41E **105** E12
Sahrawi = Western Sahara ■
Africa 25°0N 13°0W **134** D3
Sahuaripa Mexico 29°0N 109°13W **180** B3
Sahuarita U.S.A. 31°57N 110°58W **169** L8
Sahuayo de Díaz
Mexico 20°4N 102°43W **180** C4
Sai →' India 25°39N 82°47E **125** G10
Sai Buri Thailand 6°43N 101°45E **121** J3
Sai Kung China 22°23N 114°16E **111** a
Sai Thong △ Thailand 15°56N 101°10E **120** E3
Sai Yok △ Thailand 14°25N 98°40E **120** E1
Saibai I. Australia 9°25S 142°40E **150** a
Sa'id Bundas
South Sudan 8°24N 24°48E **135** G10
Saïda Algeria 34°50N 0°11E **136** B4
Saïda □ Algeria 34°40N 0°20E **136** B4
Sa'īdābād = Sirjān Iran 29°30N 55°45E **129** D7
Sa'īdābād Iran 36°8N 54°11E **129** B7
Saïdia Morocco 35°5N 2°14W **136** A3
Saidpur Bangla. 25°48N 89°0E **123** G16
Saidpur India 25°33N 83°11E **125** G10
Saidu Sharif Pakistan 34°43N 72°24E **125** B5
Saignes France 45°20N 2°31E **72** C6
Saigō Japan 36°12N 133°20E **113** F6
Saigon = Thanh Pho Ho Chi Minh
Vietnam 10°58N 106°40E **121** G6
Saijō Japan 33°55N 133°11E **113** H6
Saikai △ Japan 33°12N 129°36E **113** H4
Saikhoa Ghat India 27°50N 95°40E **123** F19
Saiki Japan 32°58N 131°51E **113** H5
Sailana India 23°28N 74°55E **124** H6
Saillans France 44°42N 5°12E **73** D9
Sailolof Indonesia 1°15S 130°46E **119** E8
Sailu India 19°28N 76°28E **126** E3
Saimaa Finland 61°15N 28°15E **84** B5
Saimbeyli Turkey 37°59N 36°6E **104** D7
Saimen = Saimaa
Finland 61°15N 28°15E **84** B5
Şa'in Dezh Iran 36°40N 46°25E **105** C12
St. Abb's Head U.K. 55°55N 2°9W **65** F6
St-Affrique France 43°57N 2°53E **72** E6
St-Agrève France 45°0N 4°23E **73** C8
St-Aignan France 47°16N 1°22E **70** E8
St. Alban's Canada 47°51N 55°50W **165** C8
St. Albans U.K. 51°45N 0°19W **67** F7
St. Albans Vt., U.S.A. 44°49N 73°5W **175** B11
St. Albans W. Va.,
U.S.A. 38°23N 81°50W **173** F13
St. Alban's Head U.K. 50°34N 2°4W **67** G5
St. Albert Canada 53°37N 113°32W **162** C6
St-Amand-en-Puisaye
France 47°32N 3°5E **71** E10
St-Amand-les-Eaux
France 50°27N 3°25E **71** B10
St-Amand-Montrond
France 46°43N 2°30E **71** F9
St-Amarin France 47°54N 7°2E **71** E14
St-Amour France 46°26N 5°21E **71** F12
St-André Réunion 20°57S 55°39E **141** c
St. André-de-Cubzac
France 44°59N 0°26W **72** D3
St-André-les-Alpes
France 43°58N 6°30E **73** E10
St. Andrew Sd. U.S.A. 30°58N 81°25W **178** F8
St. Andrew's Canada 47°45N 59°15W **165** C8
St. Andrews N.Z. 44°33N 171°10E **155** D5
St. Andrews U.K. 56°20N 2°47W **65** E6
St. Andrews N.B. 45°8N 67°3W **165** C6
St. Andrews U.S.A. 32°47N 80°0W **178** C9
St-Anicet Canada 45°8N 74°22W **175** A10
St. Annes Canada 49°40N 96°39W **163** D9
St. Ann's Canada 43°14N 79°37W **174** D5
St. Ann's Bay Jamaica 18°26N 77°12W **182** a
St-Anthème France 45°31N 3°55E **72** C7
St. Anthony Canada 51°22N 55°35W **165** B8
St. Anthony U.S.A. 43°58N 111°41W **168** E8
St-Antoine Canada 46°22N 64°45W **165** C7
St-Antonin-Noble-Val
France 44°10N 1°45E **72** D5
St-Astier France 45°8N 0°31E **72** C4
St-Aubin-du-Cormier
France 48°15N 1°26W **70** D5
St-Augustin Canada 51°13N 58°38W **165** B8

St-Augustin →'
Canada 51°16N 58°40W **165** B8
St. Augustine U.S.A. 29°54N 81°19W **178** F8
St. Augustine Beach
U.S.A. 29°51N 81°16W **178** F8
St-Aulaye France 45°12N 0°9E **72** C4
St. Austell U.K. 50°20N 4°47W **67** G3
St-Avold France 49°6N 6°43E **71** C13
St-Barthélemy ☑
W. Indies 17°50N 62°50W **183** C7
St. Barts = St-Barthélemy ☑
W. Indies 17°50N 62°50W **183** C7
St. Bathans N.Z. 44°53S 169°50E **155** E4
St. Bathan's, Mt. N.Z. 44°45S 169°15E **155** E4
St-Béat France 42°55N 0°41E **72** F4
St. Bees Hd. U.K. 54°31N 3°38W **66** C4
St. Bees I. Australia 20°56S 149°28E **150** b
St-Benoît Réunion 21°2S 55°43E **141** c
St-Benoît-du-Sault
France 46°26N 1°24E **72** B4
St-Bonnet-en-Champsaur
France 44°40N 6°5E **73** D10
St-Brevin-les-Pins France 47°14N 2°10W **70** E4
St-Brice-en-Coglès
France 48°25N 1°22W **70** D5
St. Bride's U.K. 46°56N 54°10W **165** C9
St. Brides B. U.K. 51°49N 5°9W **67** F2
St-Brieuc France 48°30N 2°46W **70** D4
St-Calais France 47°55N 0°45E **70** E7
St-Cast-le-Guildo France 48°37N 2°18W **70** D4
St. Catharines Canada 43°10N 79°15W **174** C5
St. Catherines I. U.S.A. 31°40N 81°10W **178** D8
St. Catherine's Pt. U.K. 50°34N 1°18W **67** G6
St-Céré France 44°51N 1°54E **72** D5
St-Cergue Switz. 46°27N 6°10E **77** J2
St-Cernin France 45°5N 2°25E **72** C6
St-Chamond France 45°28N 4°31E **73** C8
St. Charles Ill., U.S.A. 41°54N 88°19W **172** E9
St. Charles Md.,
U.S.A. 38°36N 76°56W **173** F15
St. Charles Mo., U.S.A. 38°47N 90°29W **172** F8
St. Charles C. Africa 34°14S 24°49E **144** D3
St-Chély-d'Apcher France 44°48N 3°17E **72** D7
St-Chinian France 43°25N 2°56E **72** E6
St. Christopher-Nevis = St. Kitts &
Nevis ■ W. Indies 17°20N 62°40W **183** C7
St-Ciers-sur-Gironde
France 45°17N 0°37W **72** C3
St. Clair, Ga., U.S.A. 33°9N 82°13W **178** B7
St. Clair Mich., U.S.A. 42°50N 82°30W **174** D2
St. Clair Pa., U.S.A. 40°43N 76°12W **175** F8
St. Clair →' U.S.A. 42°38N 82°31W **174** D2
St. Clair, L. Australia 37°20S 139°55E **152** B3
St. Clair, L. N. Amer. 42°30N 82°45W **174** D2
St. Clairsville U.S.A. 40°5N 80°54W **174** F4
St-Claud France 45°54N 0°28E **72** C4
St-Claude Canada 49°40N 98°20W **163** D9
St-Claude France 46°22N 5°52E **71** F12
St. Clears U.K. 51°49N 4°31W **67** F3
St-Clet Canada 45°21N 74°13W **175** A10
St. Cloud Fla., U.S.A. 28°15N 81°17W **179** G8
St. Cloud Minn., U.S.A. 45°34N 94°10W **172** C7
St-Cricq, C. Australia 25°17S 113°6E **149** E1
St. Croix U.S. Virgin Is. 17°45N 64°45W **183** C7
St. Croix →' U.S.A. 44°45N 92°48W **172** C7
St. Croix Falls U.S.A. 45°24N 92°38W **172** C7
St-Cyprien France 42°37N 3°2E **72** F7
St-Cyr-sur-Mer France 43°11N 5°43E **73** E9
St. David's Canada 48°12N 58°52W **165** C8
St. David's U.K. 51°53N 5°16W **67** F2
St. David's Head U.K. 51°54N 5°19W **67** F2
St-Denis Canada 48°56N 2°20E **71** D9
St-Denis Réunion 20°52S 55°27E **141** c
St-Denis ✈ (RUN)
Réunion 20°53S 55°32E **141** c
St-Dié-en-Vosges France 48°17N 6°56E **71** D13
St-Dizier France 48°38N 4°56E **71** D11
St-Égrève France 45°14N 5°41E **73** C9
St. Elias, Mt. U.S.A. 60°18N 140°56W **160** B11
St. Elias Mts. N. Amer. 60°33N 139°28W **162** A1
St-Éloy-les-Mines France 46°10N 2°51E **71** F9
St-Émilion France 44°53N 0°9W **72** D3
St-Étienne France 45°27N 4°22E **73** C8
St-Étienne-de-Tinée
France 44°16N 6°56E **73** D10
St-Étienne-du-Rouvray
France 49°23N 1°6E **70** C8
St. Eugène Canada 45°30N 74°28W **175** A10
St. Eustatius ✈ Indies 17°20N 63°0W **183** C7
St-Exupéry, Lyon ✈ (LYS)
France
St-Fargeau France 47°39N 3°4E **71** E10
St-Félicien Canada 48°40N 72°25E **165** C5
St-Florent France 42°41N 9°18E **73** F13
St-Florent, G. de France 42°47N 9°12E **73** F13
St-Florent-sur-Cher
France 46°59N 2°15E **71** F9
St-Florentin France 48°0N 3°45E **71** D10
St-Flour France 45°2N 3°5E **72** C7
St. Francis U.S.A. 39°47N 101°48W **172** F3
St. Francis →' U.S.A. 34°38N 90°36W **177** D9
St. Francis, C. S. Africa 34°14S 24°49E **144** D3
St-François, L. Canada 45°10N 74°22W **175** A10
St-Fulgent France 46°50N 1°10W **70** F5
St-Gabriel Canada 46°17N 73°24W **164** C5
St. Gallen = Sankt Gallen
Switz. 47°26N 9°22E **77** H5
St-Galmier France 45°35N 4°19E **71** C8
St-Gaudens France 43°6N 0°44E **72** E4
St-Gaultier France 46°39N 1°26E **70** F8
St-Gengoux-le-National
France 46°37N 4°40E **71** F11
St-Geniez-d'Olt France 44°27N 2°58E **72** D6
St. George Australia 28°1S 148°30E **153** A8
St. George N.B. 45°11N 66°50W **165** C6
St. George S.C., U.S.A. 33°11N 80°35W **178** C8
St. George Utah, U.S.A. 37°6N 113°35W **169** H7
St. George, C. Canada 48°30N 59°16W **165** C8
St. George, C. U.S.A. 29°40N 85°5W **178** G5
St. George I. Alaska,
U.S.A. 56°35N 169°35W **166** D6
St. George I. Fla.,
U.S.A. 29°36N 84°55W **178** F5
St. George Ra. Australia 18°40S 125°0E **148** C4
St-Georges Canada 46°8N 70°40W **165** C5
St. George's Grenada 12°5N 61°43W **183** D7
St. George's B. Canada 48°24N 58°53W **165** C8

St. Georges Basin N.S.W.,
Australia 35°7S 150°36E **153** C9
St. Georges Basin W. Austral.,
Australia 15°23S 125°2E **148** C4
St. George's Channel
Europe 52°0N 6°0W **64** E6
St. George's Channel
India 7°15N 93°43E **127** L11
St. Georges Hd.
Australia 35°12S 150°42E **153** C9
St-Georges-lès-Baillargeaux
France 46°41N 0°22E **72** B4
St-Germain-de-Calberte
France 44°13N 3°48E **72** D7
St-Germain-en-Laye
France 48°53N 2°4E **71** D9
St-Germain-Lembron
France 45°27N 3°14E **72** C7
St-Gervais-d'Auvergne
France 46°4N 2°50E **71** F9
St-Gervais-les-Bains
France 45°53N 6°42E **73** C10
St-Gildas, Pte. de France 47°8N 2°14W **70** E4
St-Gilles France 43°40N 4°26E **73** E8
St-Girons France 42°59N 1°8E **72** F5
St. Gotthard P. = San Gottardo, P.
del Switz. 46°33N 8°33E **77** J4
St. Helena Atl. Oc. 15°58S 5°42W **132** H3
St. Helena U.S.A. 38°30N 122°28W **170** G4
St. Helena U.S.A. 38°40N 122°36W **170** G4
St. Helena B. S. Africa 32°40S 18°10E **144** D2
St. Helena Sd. U.S.A. 32°15N 80°25W **178** C19
St. Helens Australia 41°20S 148°15E **151** G4
St. Helens U.K. 53°27N 2°44W **66** D5
St. Helens, U.S.A. 45°52N 122°48W **170** E4
St. Helens, Mt. U.S.A. 46°12N 122°12W **170** D4
St. Helier U.K. 49°10N 2°7W **67** H5
St-Herblain France 47°13N 1°40W **70** E5
St-Hilaire-du-Harcouët
France 48°35N 1°5W **70** D5
St-Hilaire-de-Riez
France 46°43N 1°57W **72** B2
St-Hippolyte France 47°19N 6°50E **71** E13
St-Hippolyte-du-Fort
France 43°58N 3°52E **72** E7
St-Honoré-les-Bains
France 46°54N 3°50E **71** F10
St-Hubert Canada 45°29N 73°25W **175** A11
St-Hyacinthe Canada 45°40N 72°58W **164** C5
St. Ignace U.S.A. 45°52N 84°44W **173** C11
St. Ignace I. U.S.A. 48°45N 88°0W **164** C2
St. Ignatius U.S.A. 47°19N 114°6W **168** C6
St-Imier Switz. 47°9N 6°58E **77** H2
St. Ives Cambs., U.K. 52°20N 0°4W **67** E7
St. Ives Corn., U.K. 50°12N 5°30W **67** G2
St-James France 48°31N 1°20W **70** D5
St. James U.S.A. 43°59N 94°38W **172** D6
St-Jean → Canada 50°17N 64°20W **165** B7
St-Jean, L. Canada 48°40N 72°0W **165** C5
St-Jean-d'Angély France 45°57N 0°31W **72** C3
St-Jean-de-Braye France 47°53N 1°58E **71** E8
St-Jean-de-Luz France 43°23N 1°39W **72** E2
St-Jean-de-Maurienne
France 45°16N 6°21E **73** C10
St-Jean-de-Monts France 46°47N 2°4W **70** F4
St-Jean-du-Gard France 44°7N 3°52E **72** D7
St-Jean-en-Royans France 45°1N 5°18E **73** C9
St-Jean-Pied-de-Port
France 43°10N 1°14W **72** E2
St-Jean-Port-Joli
Canada 47°15N 70°13W **165** C5
St-Jean-sur-Richelieu
Canada 45°20N 73°20W **175** A11
St-Jérôme Canada 45°47N 74°0W **164** C5
St. John Canada 45°20N 66°8W **165** C6
St. John U.S.A. 38°0N 98°46W **172** F4
St. John → Liberia 6°40N 9°10W **138** D2
St. John → N. Amer. 45°12N 66°5W **173** C20
St. John, C. Canada 50°0N 55°32W **165** C8
St. John I. U.S. Virgin Is. 18°20N 64°42W **183** e
St. John's Antigua & B. 17°6N 61°51W **183** C7
St. John's Canada 47°35N 52°40W **165** C6
St. Johns Ariz., U.S.A. 34°30N 109°22W **169** J9
St. Johns Mich., U.S.A. 43°0N 84°33W **173** D11
St. Johns → U.S.A. 30°24N 81°24W **178** E8
St. John's Pt. Ireland 54°34N 8°27W **64** B3
St. Johnsbury U.S.A. 44°25N 72°1W **175** B12
St. Johnsville U.S.A. 43°0N 74°43W **175** C10
St. Joseph Canada 43°24N 81°42W **172** D3
St. Joseph Martinique 14°39N 61°4W **182** c
St-Joseph Réunion 21°22S 55°37E **141** c
St. Joseph La., U.S.A. 31°55N 91°14W **176** F9
St. Joseph Mo., U.S.A. 39°46N 94°50W **172** F6
St. Joseph → U.S.A. 42°7N 86°29W **172** D10
St. Joseph, I. Canada 46°12N 83°58W **164** C3
St. Joseph, L. Canada 51°10N 90°35W **164** B1
St. Joseph Pt. U.S.A. 29°52N 85°24W **178** F4
St-Juéry France 43°57N 2°12E **72** E6
St-Julien-Chapteuil France 45°2N 4°4E **73** C8
St-Julien-de-Vouvantes
France 47°38N 1°13W **70** E5
St-Julien-en-Genevois
France 46°9N 6°5E **71** F13
St-Junien France 45°53N 0°55E **72** C4
St-Just-en-Chaussée
France 49°30N 2°25E **71** C9
St-Just-en-Chevalet
France 45°55N 3°50E **72** C7
St. Kilda N.Z. 45°53S 170°31E **155** F5
St. Kilda U.K. 57°49N 8°34W **68** C2
St. Kitts & Nevis ■
W. Indies 17°20N 62°40W **183** C7
St. Laurent Canada 50°25N 97°58W **163** C9
St-Laurent-de-la-Salanque
France 42°46N 2°59E **72** F6
St-Laurent-du-Pont
France 45°23N 5°45E **73** C9
St-Laurent-en-Grandvaux
France 46°35N 5°58E **71** F12
St-Laurent-Médoc France 45°8N 0°49W **72** C3
St. Lawrence Australia 22°16S 149°31E **150** C4
St. Lawrence Canada 46°54N 55°23W **165** C8
St. Lawrence → Canada 49°30N 66°0W **165** C6
St. Lawrence, Gulf of
Canada 48°25N 62°0W **165** C7
St. Lawrence I. U.S.A. 63°30N 170°30W **166** C5
St. Lawrence Islands △
Canada 44°27N 75°52W **175** B9
St. Léonard Canada 47°12N 67°58W **165** C6
St-Léonard-de-Noblat
France 45°49N 1°29E **72** C5
St-Leu Réunion 21°9S 55°18E **141** c

St. Lewis → Canada 52°26N 56°11W **165** B8
St-Lô France 49°7N 1°5W **70** C5
St-Louis France 47°30N 7°34E **71** E14
St-Louis Guadeloupe 15°56N 61°19W **182** b
St-Louis Réunion 21°16S 55°25E **141** c
St. Louis Senegal 16°8N 16°27W **138** B1
St. Louis U.S.A. 38°37N 90°11W **172** F8
St. Louis → U.S.A. 46°44N 92°9W **172** B7
St-Louis □ Senegal 16°20N 15°0W **138** B2
St-Loup-sur-Semouse
France 47°53N 6°16E **71** E14
St-Luc Canada 45°22N 73°18W **175** A11
St. Lucia ■ W. Indies 14°0N 60°57W **183** f
St. Lucia, L. S. Africa 28°5S 32°30E **145** C5
St. Lucia △ S. Africa 28°6S 32°27E **145** C5
St. Lucia Channel
W. Indies 14°15N 61°0W **183** D7
St. Lucie U.S.A. 27°29N 80°20W **179** H9
St. Lucie Canal U.S.A. 27°10N 80°18W **179** H9
St. Maarten ☑ W. Indies 18°5N 63°5W **183** C7
St. Magnus B. U.K. 60°25N 1°35W **65** A7
St-Maixent-l'École
France 46°24N 0°12W **72** B3
St-Malo France 48°39N 2°1W **70** D4
St-Malo, G. de France 48°50N 2°10W **70** D4
St-Mandrier-sur-Mer
France 43°4N 5°57E **73** E9
St-Marc Haiti 19°10N 72°41W **183** C5
St-Marcellin France 45°9N 5°20E **73** C9
St-Marcouf, Îs. France 49°30N 1°10W **70** C5
St. Maries U.S.A. 47°19N 116°35W **168** C5
St. Marks U.S.A. 30°9N 84°12W **178** E5
St-Martin, Martinique 14°41N 61°14W **182** c
St-Martin, L. Canada 51°40N 98°30W **163** C9
St-Martin-de-Crau France 43°38N 4°48E **73** E8
St-Martin-de-Ré France 46°12N 1°21W **72** B2
St-Martin-d'Hères France 45°9N 5°45E **73** C9
St-Martin-Vésubie France 44°4N 7°15E **73** D11
St. Martins Barbados 13°5N 59°28W **183** g
St-Martory France 43°9N 0°56E **72** E4
St. Mary Is. India 13°20N 74°35E **127** H2
St. Mary Pk. Australia 31°32S 138°34E **152** A4
St. Marys Australia 41°35S 148°11E **151** G4
St. Marys Canada 43°20N 81°10W **174** C3
St. Mary's Corn., U.K. 49°55N 6°18W **67** H1
St. Mary's Orkney, U.K. 58°54N 2°54W **65** C6
St. Marys Ga., U.S.A. 30°44N 81°33W **178** E8
St. Marys Pa., U.S.A. 41°26N 78°34W **174** E6
St. Mary's, C. Canada 46°50N 54°12W **165** C9
St. Mary's B. Canada 46°50N 53°50W **165** C9
St. Mary's Bay Canada 44°25N 66°10W **165** D6
St-Mathieu, Pte. France 48°20N 4°45W **70** D2
St. Matthew I. U.S.A. 60°24N 172°42W **166** C5
St. Matthews U.S.A. 33°40N 80°46W **178** D5
St-Maurice → Canada 46°21N 72°31W **164** C5
St. Mawes U.K. 50°10N 5°2W **67** G2
St-Maximin-la-Ste-Baume
France 43°27N 5°52E **73** E9
St-Médard-en-Jalles
France 44°53N 0°43W **72** D3
St-Méen-le-Grand
France 48°11N 2°12W **70** D4
St-Mihiel France 48°54N 5°32E **71** D12
St-Nazaire France 47°17N 2°12W **70** E4
St. Neots U.K. 52°14N 0°15W **67** E7
St-Nicolas-de-Port
France 48°38N 6°18E **71** D13
St-Omer France 50°45N 2°15E **71** B9
St-Palais-sur-Mer France 45°38N 1°5W **72** C2
St-Pamphile Canada 46°58N 69°48W **165** C6
St-Pardoux-la-Rivière
France 45°29N 0°45E **72** C4
St-Pascal Canada 47°32N 69°48W **165** C6
St. Paul Canada 54°0N 111°17W **162** C6
St-Paul Réunion 20°59S 55°17E **141** c
St. Paul Minn., U.S.A. 44°56N 93°5W **172** C8
St. Paul Nebr., U.S.A. 41°13N 98°27W **172** E4
St-Paul → Canada 51°27N 57°42W **165** B8
St. Paul → Liberia 6°25N 10°48W **138** D2
St. Paul, Î. Ind. Oc. 38°55N 77°34E **146** H6
St-Paul-de-Fenouillet
France 42°48N 2°30E **72** F6
St. Paul I. Canada 47°12N 60°9W **165** C7
St. Paul I. U.S.A. 57°10N 170°15W **166** D5
St-Paul-lès-Dax France 43°44N 1°3W **72** E2
St-Paul-sur-Ubaye
France 44°31N 6°45E **73** D10
St-Péray France 44°57N 4°50E **73** D8
St. Pete Beach U.S.A. 27°43N 82°44W **179** H7
St. Peter U.S.A. 44°20N 93°57W **172** C7
St. Peter Port U.K. 49°26N 2°33W **67** H5
St. Peters N.S., Canada 45°40N 60°53W **165** C7
St. Peters P.E.I., Canada 46°25N 62°35W **165** C7
St. Petersburg = Sankt-Peterburg
Russia 59°55N 30°20E **84** C6
St. Petersburg U.S.A. 27°46N 82°40W **179** H7
St-Philbert-de-Grand-Lieu
France 47°2N 1°39W **70** E5
St-Phillippe Réunion 21°21S 55°44E **141** c
St-Pie Canada 45°30N 72°54W **175** A12
St-Pierre Martinique 14°45N 61°10W **182** c
St-Pierre Réunion 21°19S 55°28E **141** c
St-Pierre St-P. & M. 46°46N 56°12W **165** C8
St-Pierre, L. Canada 46°12N 72°52W **164** C5
St-Pierre-d'Oléron
France 45°57N 1°19W **72** C2
St-Pierre-en-Port France 49°48N 0°30E **70** C7
St-Pierre-et-Miquelon ☑
N. Amer. 46°55N 56°10W **165** C8
St-Pierre-le-Moûtier
France 46°47N 3°7E **71** F10
St-Pol-de-Léon France 48°41N 4°0W **70** D3
St-Pol-sur-Mer France 51°1N 2°20E **71** A9
St-Pol-sur-Ternoise
France 50°23N 2°20E **71** B9
St-Pons France 43°30N 2°45E **72** E6
St-Pourçain-sur-Sioule
France 46°18N 3°18E **71** F10
St-Priest France 45°42N 4°57E **73** C8
St-Quay-Portrieux
France 48°39N 2°51W **70** D4
St-Quentin France 49°50N 3°16E **71** C10
St-Quentin Canada 47°30N 67°23W **165** C6
St-Rambert-d'Albon
France 45°17N 4°49E **73** C8
St-Raphaël France 43°25N 6°46E **73** E10
St. Regis U.S.A. 47°18N 115°6W **168** C6
St. Regis Falls U.S.A. 44°40N 74°32W **175** B10
St-Renan France 48°26N 4°37W **70** D2

St-Saëns France 49°41N 1°16E **70** C8
St-Savin France 46°34N 0°53E **72** B4
St-Savinien France 45°53N 0°42W **72** C3
St-Seine-l'Abbaye
France 47°26N 4°47E **71** E11
St-Sernin-sur-Rance
France 43°54N 2°35E **72** E6
St-Sever France 43°45N 0°35W **72** E3
St-Siméon Canada 47°51N 69°54W **165** C6
St. Simons I. U.S.A. 31°12N 81°15W **178** D8
St. Simons Island
U.S.A. 31°9N 81°22W **178** D8
St. Stephen Canada 45°16N 67°17W **165** C6
St. Stephen U.S.A. 33°24N 79°55W **178** B10
St-Sulpice France 43°46N 1°41E **72** E5
St-Sulpice-Laurière France 46°3N 1°29E **72** B5
St-Sulpice-les-Feuilles
France 46°19N 1°21E **72** B5
St-Syprien = St-Cyprien
France 42°37N 3°2E **72** F7
Ste. Teresa U.S.A. 29°55N 84°27W **178** F5
St-Thégonnec France 48°31N 3°57W **70** D3
St. Thomas Canada 42°45N 81°10W **172** D3
St. Thomas I.
U.S. Virgin Is. 18°20N 64°55W **183** e
St-Tite Canada 46°45N 72°34W **164** C5
St-Trond = Sint-Truiden
Belgium 50°48N 5°10E **69** D5
St-Tropez France 43°17N 6°38E **73** E10
St-Vaast-la-Hougue
France 49°35N 1°17W **70** C5
St-Valery-en-Caux
France 49°52N 0°43E **70** C7
St-Valéry-sur-Somme
France 50°11N 1°38E **71** B8
St-Vallier France 46°38N 4°22E **71** F11
St-Vallier-de-Thiey
France 43°42N 6°51E **73** E10
St-Varent France 46°53N 0°13W **70** F6
St-Vaury France 46°12N 1°46E **72** B5
St. Vidgeon's ○
Australia 14°47S 134°53E **150** A1
St. Vincent = São Vicente
C. Verde Is. 17°0N 25°0W **134** b
St. Vincent Italy 45°45N 7°39E **92** C4
St. Vincent, G. Australia 35°0S 138°0E **152** C3
St. Vincent & the Grenadines ■
W. Indies 13°0N 61°10W **183** D7
St-Vincent-de-Tyrosse
France 43°39N 1°19W **72** E2
St. Vincent I. U.S.A. 29°42N 85°3W **179** F4
St. Vincent Passage
W. Indies 13°30N 61°0W **183** D7
St-Vith Belgium 50°17N 6°9E **69** D6
St-Vivien-de-Médoc
France 45°25N 1°2W **72** C2
St. Walburg Canada 53°39N 109°12W **163** C7
St-Yrieix-la-Perche
France 45°31N 1°12E **72** C5
Saintala India 20°26N 83°20E **126** D6
Ste-Adresse France 49°31N 0°5E **70** C7
Ste-Agathe-des-Monts
Canada 46°3N 74°17W **164** C5
Ste-Anne Guadeloupe 16°13N 61°24W **182** b
Ste-Anne Seychelles 4°36S 55°31E **141** b
Ste-Anne, L. Canada 50°0N 67°42W **165** B6
Ste-Anne-des-Monts
Canada 49°8N 66°30W **165** C6
Ste-Croix Switz. 46°49N 6°34E **77** J2
Ste-Énimie France 44°22N 3°26E **72** D7
Ste-Foy-la-Grande France 44°50N 0°13E **72** D4
Ste. Genevieve U.S.A. 37°59N 90°2W **172** G8
Ste-Hermine France 46°32N 1°4W **72** B2
Ste-Livrade-sur-Lot
France 44°24N 0°36E **72** D4
Ste-Marguerite →
Canada 50°9N 66°36W **165** B6
Ste-Marie Canada 46°26N 71°0W **165** C5
Ste-Marie Martinique 14°48N 61°1W **182** c
Ste-Marie Réunion 20°53S 55°33E **141** c
Ste-Marie, Île = Boraha, Nosy
Madag. 16°50S 49°55E **141** H9
Ste-Marie-aux-Mines
France 48°15N 7°12E **71** D14
Ste-Maure-de-Touraine
France 47°7N 0°37E **70** E7
Ste-Maxime France 43°19N 6°39E **73** E10
Ste-Menehould France 49°5N 4°54E **71** C11
Ste-Mère-Église France 49°24N 1°19W **70** C5
Ste-Rose Guadeloupe 16°20N 61°45W **182** b
Ste-Rose Réunion 21°8S 55°44E **141** c
Ste. Rose du Lac Canada 51°4N 99°30W **163** C9
Ste-Savine France 48°18N 4°3E **71** D11
Ste-Sigolène France 45°15N 4°14E **73** C8
Saintes France 45°45N 0°37W **72** C3
Saintes, Îs. des
Guadeloupe 15°50N 61°35W **182** b
Stes-Maries-de-la-Mer
France 43°26N 4°26E **73** E8
Saintfield U.K. 54°28N 5°49W **64** B6
Saintonge France 45°40N 0°50W **72** C3
Saipal Nepal 29°50N 81°40E **125** E9
Saipan N. Marianas 15°12N 145°45E **156** F6
Sairang India 23°50N 92°45E **123** H18
Sairecábur, Cerro
Bolivia 22°43S 67°54W **190** A2
Sāitah Si. Arabia 16°36N 42°56E **131** D3
Saitama Japan 35°54N 139°38E **113** G9
Saitama □ Japan 36°25N 139°30E **113** F9
Saiteli = Kadınhanı
Turkey 38°14N 32°13E **104** C5
Saïti Moldova 46°30N 29°24E **81** D14
Saiyid Pakistan 33°7N 73°2E **124** C5
Saja-Besaya △ Spain 43°10N 4°0W **88** B6
Sajama Bolivia 18°7S 69°0W **188** D4
Sajama, Nevado Bolivia 18°6S 68°54W **188** D4
Sajan Serbia 45°50N 20°20E **88** B5
Sajó → Hungary 47°56N 21°7E **80** C6
Sajószentpéter Hungary 48°12N 20°44E **80** B5
Sajum India 33°20N 79°0E **125** C8
Sak → S. Africa 30°52S 20°25E **144** D3
Saka Kenya 0°11S 39°3E **142** C5
Sakaba Nigeria 11°4N 5°57E **139** C6
Sakai Japan 34°30N 135°30E **113** G7
Sakaide Japan 34°19N 133°50E **113** G6
Sakaiminato Japan 35°38N 133°11E **113** G6
Sakakah Si. Arabia 30°0N 40°8E **128** D4
Sakakawea, L. U.S.A. 47°30N 101°25W **172** B3
Sakami → Canada 53°40N 76°40W **164** B4
Sakami, L. Canada 53°15N 77°0W **164** B4
Sâkâne, 'Erg i-n Mali 20°30N 1°30W **139** A4

Sakania
Dem. Rep. of the Congo 12°43S 28°30E **143** E2
Sakartvelo = Georgia ■
Asia 42°0N 43°0E **87** J6
Sakarya Turkey 40°48N 30°25E **104** B4
Sakarya □ Turkey 40°45N 30°25E **104** B4
Sakarya → Turkey 41°7N 30°39E **104** B4
Sakashima-Guntō
Japan 24°46N 124°0E **113** M2
Sakata Japan 38°55N 139°50E **112** E9
Sakchu N. Korea 40°23N 125°2E **115** D13
Sakété Benin 6°40N 2°45E **139** D5
Sakha □ Russia 66°0N 130°0E **107** C14
Sakhalin Russia 51°0N 143°0E **107** D15
Sakhalinskiy Zaliv
Russia 54°0N 141°0E **107** D15
Sakhi Gopal India 19°58N 85°50E **126** E7
Šaki Azerbaijan 41°10N 47°5E **87** K8
Šakiai Lithuania 54°59N 23°2E **82** D10
Sakmara → Russia 51°46N 55°1E **108** B5
Sakon Nakhon
Thailand 17°10N 104°9E **120** D5
Sakrand Pakistan 26°10N 68°15E **124** F3
Sakri Maharashtra, India 26°13N 86°5E **125** F12
Sakri Maharashtra, India 21°2N 74°20E **124** D2
Sakrivier S. Africa 30°54S 20°28E **144** E3
Saksköbing Denmark 54°49N 11°39E **63** K5
Sakti India 22°2N 82°58E **125** H10
Sakuma Japan 35°3N 137°49E **113** G8
Sakurai Japan 34°30N 135°51E **113** G7
Saky Ukraine 45°9N 33°34E **85** K7
Sal C. Verde Is. 16°45N 22°55W **134** b
Sal → Russia 47°31N 40°45E **87** G5
Sal Rei C. Verde Is. 16°11N 22°53W **134** b
Sala Slovak Rep. 48°10N 17°50E **79** C10
Sala Sweden 59°58N 16°35E **63** E10
Sala Consilina Italy 40°23N 15°36E **95** B8
Sala-y-Gómez
Pac. Oc. 26°28S 105°28W **157** K17
Sala-y-Gómez Ridge
Pac. Oc. 25°0S 98°0W **157** K18
Salaberry-de-Valleyfield
Canada 45°15N 74°8W **175** A10
Salacgrīva Latvia 57°45N 24°21E **82** A11
Salada, L. Mexico 32°20N 115°40W **169** K6
Saladas Argentina 28°15S 58°40W **190** B4
Saladillo Argentina 35°40S 59°55W **190** D4
Salado → B. Aires,
Argentina 35°44S 57°22W **190** D4
Salado → La Pampa,
Argentina 37°30S 67°0W **192** A3
Salado → Río Negro,
Argentina 41°34S 65°3W **192** B3
Salado → Santa Fe,
Argentina 31°40S 60°41W **190** C3
Salado → Mexico 26°52N 99°19W **176** H5
Salaga Ghana 8°31N 0°31W **138** D4
Sālah Syria 32°40N 36°45E **130** C5
Salāh ad Dīn □ Iraq 34°35N 43°35E **128** C4
Sălaj □ Romania 47°15N 23°0E **80** B8
Salakos Greece 36°17N 27°57E **101** C9
Salala Liberia 6°42N 10°7W **138** D2
Salala Sudan 21°17N 36°16E **137** C4
Salālah Oman 16°56N 53°59E **135** D5
Salamajärvi △ Finland 63°12N 24°50E **60** E21
Salamanca Chile 31°46S 70°59W **190** C1
Salamanca Spain 40°58N 5°39W **88** E5
Salamanca U.S.A. 42°10N 78°43W **174** D6
Salamanca □ Spain 40°57N 5°40W **88** E5
Salāmatābād Iran 35°39N 47°50E **128** C5
Salamina Greece 37°56N 23°30E **98** D5
Salamis Cyprus 35°11N 33°54E **101** D12
Salar de Atacama
Chile 23°30S 68°25W **190** A2
Salar de Uyuni Bolivia 20°30S 67°45W **188** E4
Sālard Romania 47°12N 22°3E **80** C7
Salas Spain 43°25N 6°15W **88** B4
Salas de los Infantes Spain 42°2N 3°17W **88** C7
Salatiga Indonesia 7°19S 110°30E **119** G14
Salavat Russia 53°21N 55°55E **108** B5
Salaverry Peru 8°15S 79°0W **188** B2
Salawati Indonesia 1°7S 130°52E **119** E8
Salawin △ Thailand 18°18N 97°40E **120** C1
Salaya India 22°19N 69°35E **124** H3
Salazar → Spain 42°40N 1°20W **88** C2
Salbris France 47°25N 2°3E **71** E9
Salcacate Argentina 31°20S 65°5W **190** C2
Salcantay, Nevado
Peru 13°19S 72°33W **188** C3
Salcia Romania 43°56N 24°55E **83** G13
Salcíua Romania 46°24N 23°26E **81** D8
Salcombe U.K. 50°14N 3°47W **67** G4
Saldaña Spain 42°32N 4°48W **88** C6
Saldanha S. Africa 33°0S 17°58E **144** D2
Saldanha B. S. Africa 33°6S 18°0E **144** D2
Saldus Latvia 56°38N 22°30E **82** B9
Sale Australia 38°6S 147°6E **153** F4
Sale Italy 44°59N 8°48E **92** D5
Salé Morocco 34°3N 6°48W **136** B4
Sale U.K. 53°26N 2°19W **66** D5
Salekhard Russia 66°30N 66°35E **106** C7
Salem India 11°40N 78°11E **127** J4
Salem Ill., U.S.A. 38°38N 88°57W **172** F9
Salem Ind., U.S.A. 38°36N 86°6W **172** F10
Salem Mass., U.S.A. 42°31N 70°53W **175** D14
Salem Mo., U.S.A. 37°39N 91°32W **172** G8
Salem N.H., U.S.A. 42°45N 71°12W **175** D13
Salem N.J., U.S.A. 39°34N 75°28W **173** F16
Salem N.Y., U.S.A. 43°10N 73°20W **175** C11
Salem Ohio, U.S.A. 40°54N 80°52W **174** E4
Salem Oreg., U.S.A. 44°56N 123°2W **168** D2
Salem S. Dak., U.S.A. 43°44N 97°23W **172** D5
Salem Va., U.S.A. 37°18N 80°3W **173** G13
Salemi Italy 37°49N 12°48E **94** E5
Sälen Sweden 61°20N 13°10E **62** C7
Salernes France 43°34N 6°15E **73** E10
Salerno Italy 40°41N 14°47E **95** B7
Salerno, G. di Italy 40°35N 14°45E **95** B7
Salford U.K. 53°30N 2°18W **66** D5
Salgótarján Hungary 48°5N 19°47E **80** B4
Salgueiro Brazil 8°4S 39°6W **189** B3
Salher India 20°40N 73°55E **126** D5
Salhyr → Ukraine 45°30N 34°30E **85** K8
Salibabu Indonesia 3°51N 126°40E **119** D7
Salibea = Salybia
Trin. & Tob. 10°43N 61°2W **187** K15
Salida U.S.A. 38°32N 106°0W **168** G11

Salies-de-Béarn France 43°28N 0°56W **72** E3
Salihli Turkey 38°28N 28°8E **104** C3
Salihorsk Belarus 52°51N 27°27E **75** B14
Salima Malawi 13°47S 34°28E **141** G6
Salina Italy 38°34N 14°50E **95** D7
Salina Kans., U.S.A. 38°50N 97°37W **172** F5
Salina Utah, U.S.A. 38°58N 111°51W **168** G8
Salina Cruz Mexico 16°10N 95°12W **181** D5
Salina di Margherita di Savóia △
Italy 41°23N 16°4E **95** A9
Salinas Brazil 16°10S 42°10W **189** D2
Salinas Ecuador 2°10S 80°58W **186** D2
Salinas U.S.A. 36°40N 121°39W **170** J5
Salinas → Guatemala 16°28N 90°31W **181** D6
Salinas → U.S.A. 36°45N 121°48W **170** J5
Salinas, B. de Nic. 11°4N 85°45W **182** D2
Salinas, Pampa de las
Argentina 31°58S 66°42W **190** C2
Salinas Ambargasta
Argentina 29°0S 65°0W **190** B3
Salinas de Hidalgo
Mexico 22°38N 101°43W **180** C4
Salinas Grandes
Argentina 30°0S 65°0W **190** C3
Salinas Pueblo Missions △
U.S.A. 34°6N 106°4W **169** J10
Salinas Valley U.S.A. 36°15N 121°15W **170** J5
Salines, C. de ses Spain 39°16N 3°4E **100** B10
Salinópolis Brazil 0°40S 47°20W **187** D9
Salins-les-Bains France 46°58N 5°52E **71** F12
Salir Portugal 37°14N 8°2W **89** H2
Salisbury Australia 34°46S 138°38E **152** C3
Salisbury U.K. 51°4N 1°47W **67** F6
Salisbury Md., U.S.A. 38°22N 75°36W **173** F16
Salisbury N.C., U.S.A. 35°40N 80°29W **177** D5
Salisbury I. Canada 63°30N 77°0W **161** E16
Salisbury Plain U.K. 51°14N 1°55W **67** F6
Săliste Romania 45°45N 23°56E **81** E8
Salitre → Brazil 9°29S 40°39W **189** B2
Salkehatchie →
U.S.A. 32°37N 80°53W **178** E7
Salkhad Syria 32°29N 36°43E **130** C5
Salkove Ukraine 48°15N 29°59E **81** D14
Salla Finland 66°50N 28°49E **60** C23
Sallanches France 45°55N 6°38E **73** C10
Sallent Spain 41°49N 1°54E **90** D6
Salles France 44°33N 0°52W **72** D3
Salles-Curan France 44°11N 2°48E **72** D6
Salliq = Coral Harbour
Canada 64°8N 83°10W **161** E15
Sallisaw U.S.A. 35°28N 94°47W **176** D7
Sallom Sudan 19°17N 37°6E **137** D4
Salluit Canada 62°14N 75°38W **161** E16
Sallyana Nepal 28°22N 82°10E **125** E10
Salmān Pak Iraq 33°6N 44°57E **105** C11
Salmās Iran 38°11N 44°47E **128** C11
Salmo Canada 49°10N 117°20W **162** D5
Salmon U.S.A. 45°11N 113°54W **168** C7
Salmon → Canada 54°3N 122°40W **162** C4
Salmon → U.S.A. 45°51N 116°47W **168** D5
Salmon Arm Canada 50°40N 119°15W **162** C5
Salmon Gums
Australia 32°59S 121°38E **149** F3
Salmon Pt. Canada 43°52N 77°15W **174** C7
Salmon River Mts.
U.S.A. 44°50N 115°30W **168** D6
Salmon River Res.
U.S.A. 43°32N 75°55W **175** C9
Salo Finland 60°22N 23°10E **64** B2
Salò Italy 45°36N 10°31E **92** C7
Salobreña Spain 36°44N 3°35W **89** J7
Salon India 26°2N 81°27E **125** F9
Salon-de-Provence France 43°39N 5°6E **73** E9
Salonica = Thessaloniki
Greece 40°38N 22°58E **98** D4
Salonta Romania 46°49N 21°42E **80** C8
Saloum → Senegal 13°50N 16°45W **138** C1
Salou Spain 41°4N 1°8E **90** D6
Salou, C. de Spain 41°3N 1°10E **90** D6
Salpausselkä Finland 61°3N 26°15E **64** B4
Salsacate Argentina 31°20S 65°5W **190** C2
Salsette I. India 19°12N 72°58E **124** K8
Salsk Russia 46°28N 41°30E **87** G5
Salso → Italy 37°6N 13°57E **94** E6
Salsomaggiore Terme
Italy 44°49N 9°59E **92** D6
Salt → Canada 60°0N 112°25W **162** B6
Salt → U.S.A. 33°23N 112°19W **169** K7
Salt Fork Red →
U.S.A. 34°27N 99°21W **176** D5
Salt L. Australia 30°6S 142°8E **153** E3
Salt Lake City U.S.A. 40°45N 111°53W **168** F8
Salt Lake City Int. ✈ (SLC)
U.S.A. 40°47N 111°58W **168** F7
Salt Range Pakistan 32°30N 72°25E **124** C5
Salt Springs U.S.A. 29°21N 81°44W **179** F8
Salta Argentina 24°57S 65°25W **190** A2
Salta □ Argentina 24°48S 65°30W **190** A2
Saltara Italy 43°45N 12°50E **93** E9
Saltash U.K. 50°24N 4°14W **67** G3
Saltburn-by-the-Sea
U.K. 54°35N 0°58W **66** C7
Saltcoats U.K. 55°38N 4°47W **65** F4
Saltee Is. Ireland 52°7N 6°37W **64** D5
Salters → U.S.A. 33°36N 79°51W **178** B10
Saltfjellet-Svartisen △
Norway 66°45N 15°10E **60** C16
Saltfjorden Norway 67°15N 14°10E **60** C16
Saltholm Denmark 55°38N 12°43E **63** J6
Saltillo Mexico 25°24N 101°0W **180** B4
Salto Argentina 34°20S 60°15W **190** C3
Salto Uruguay 31°27S 57°50W **190** C4
Salto da Divisa Brazil 16°0S 39°57W **189** D3
Salto del Guairá
Paraguay 24°3S 54°17W **191** A5
Salton City U.S.A. 33°18N 115°57W **171** M11
Salton Sea U.S.A. 33°15N 115°45W **171** M11
Saltpond Ghana 5°15N 1°3W **139** D4
Saltsjöbaden Sweden 59°15N 18°20E **62** E18
Saluda → U.S.A. 34°1N 81°4W **177** D5

Saluda → U.S.A. 34°1N 81°4W **177** D5
Salue Timpaus, Selat
Indonesia 1°50S 123°50E **119** E6
Salûm Egypt 31°31N 25°7E **137** B13
Salûm, Khâlig el Egypt 31°35N 25°24E **137** B13
Salur India 18°27N 83°18E **126** E5
Saluzzo Italy 44°39N 7°29E **92** D4
Salvación, B. Chile 50°50S 75°10W **192** D1
Salvador Brazil 13°0S 38°30W **189** D3
Salvador Canada 52°10N 109°32W **163** C7
Salvador, El ■
Cent. Amer. 13°50N 89°0W **182** D2
Salvador, L. U.S.A. 29°43N 90°15W **176** G9
Salvaterra de Magos
Portugal 39°1N 8°47W **89** F2
Sálvora, I. de Spain 42°30N 8°58W **88** C2
Salween → Burma 16°31N 97°37E **122** D2
Salyan Azerbaijan 39°33N 48°59E **87** K9
Salybia Trin. & Tob. 10°43N 61°2W **187** K15
Salza → Austria 47°40N 14°43E **81** E4
Salzach → Austria 48°12N 12°56E **81** D3
Salzburg Austria 47°48N 13°2E **81** D3
Salzburg □ Austria 47°15N 13°0E **81** D3
Salzgitter Germany 52°9N 10°19E **74** C6
Salzwedel Germany 52°52N 11°10E **74** C7
Sam India 26°50N 70°31E **124** F4
Sam Neua Laos 20°29N 104°5E **120** B5
Sam Ngao Thailand 17°18N 99°0E **120** D2
Sam Rayburn Res.
U.S.A. 31°4N 94°5W **176** F7
Sam Rong, Laem Thailand 9°35N 100°4E **121** b
Sam Son Vietnam 19°44N 105°54E **122** C5
Sama de Langreo = Langreo
Spain 43°18N 5°40W **88** B5
Šamac Bos.-H. 45°3N 18°29E **81** E8
Samagaltay Russia 50°36N 95°3E **109** D10
Samales Group Phil. 6°0N 122°0E **119** C6
Samalga Pass U.S.A. 52°50N 169°0W **166** E6
Samalkot India 17°3N 82°13E **126** F5
Samālūt Egypt 28°20N 30°42E **137** C12
Samana India 30°10N 76°13E **124** D7
Samana Cays Bahamas 23°3N 73°45W **183** B5
Samandağ Turkey 36°5N 35°59E **104** D6
Samandira Turkey 40°59N 29°13E **97** F13
Samanga Tanzania 8°20S 39°13E **142** D7
Samangān □ Afghan. 36°15N 68°3E **104** B9
Samani Japan 42°7N 142°56E **112** C11
Samanli Dağları Turkey 40°32N 29°10E **97** F13
Samar Phil. 12°0N 125°0E **115** G7
Samara Russia 53°8N 50°6E **86** D9
Samara → Russia 53°10N 50°4E **86** D9
Samaria = Shomron
West Bank 32°15N 35°13E **130** C4
Samaria △ Greece 35°17N 23°58E **101** E6
Samarinda Indonesia 0°30S 117°9E **119** E5
Samarkand = Samarqand
Uzbekistan 39°40N 66°55E **106** F7
Samarqand Uzbekistan 39°40N 66°55E **106** F7
Samarqand □
Uzbekistan 39°35N 66°35E **106** F7
Sāmarrā' Iraq 34°12N 43°52E **105** C10
Samarskaya Luka △
Russia 53°30N 49°30E **86** D9
Samastipur India 25°50N 85°50E **125** G11
Samaxı Azerbaijan 40°38N 48°37E **87** K9
Samba
Dem. Rep. of the Congo 4°38S 26°22E **142** D2
Samba India 32°32N 75°10E **124** C9
Sambaíba Brazil 7°8S 45°21W **189** B1
Sambalpur India 21°28N 84°4E **125** J11
Sambar, Tanjung
Indonesia 2°59S 110°19E **119** E4
Sambas Indonesia 1°20N 109°20E **119** D3
Sambawizi Zimbabwe 18°24S 26°13E **143** C3
Sambhajinagar = Aurangabad
India 19°50N 75°23E **124** K9
Sambhal India 28°35N 78°37E **125** E8
Sambhar India 26°52N 75°6E **124** F6
Sambhar L. India 26°55N 75°12E **124** F6
Sambir Ukraine 49°30N 23°10E **85** G2
Sambor Cambodia 12°46N 106°0E **120** F6
Sambor Prei Kuk
Cambodia 12°46N 105°58E **120** F6
Samborombón, B.
Argentina 36°5S 57°20W **190** D4
Sambuca di Sicília Italy 37°39N 13°7E **94** E6
Samburu □ Kenya 1°10N 36°40E **142** B4
Samburu □ Kenya 0°37N 37°31E **142** B4
Samchok S. Korea 37°26N 129°10E **115** F15
Same Tanzania 4°2S 37°38E **142** E7
Samer France 50°38N 1°44E **71** B8
Samet, Ko Thailand 12°34N 101°27E **120** F3
Samfya Zambia 11°22S 29°31E **142** E5
Šamkir Azerbaijan 40°50N 46°0E **87** K8
Samland = Zemlandskiy
Poluostrov Russia 54°50N 20°20E **82** D8
Şamlı Turkey 39°48N 27°51E **99** E9
Sammanturai Sri Lanka 7°36N 81°39E **127** F4
Samnah Si. Arabia 25°10N 37°15E **128** E3
Samo Alto Chile 30°22S 71°0W **190** C1
Samoa ■ Pac. Oc. 14°0S 172°0W **147** J8
Samobor Croatia 45°47N 15°44E **93** C12
Samoëns France 46°5N 6°45E **71** F13
Samokov Bulgaria 42°18N 23°35E **98** B5
Šamorín Slovak Rep. 48°2N 17°19E **79** E4
Samorogouan
Burkina Faso 11°21N 4°57W **138** C4
Samos Greece 37°45N 26°50E **99** F8
Samoš Serbia 45°13N 20°48E **81** E10
Samoset U.S.A. 27°20N 82°26W **179** H7
Samothráki = Mathraki
Greece 39°48N 19°31E **101** A3
Samothraki Greece 40°28N 25°28E **99** D8
Samoylovka Russia 51°12N 43°43E **86** E6
Sampa Ghana 8°0N 2°36W **138** D4
Sampacho Argentina 33°20S 64°50W **190** C3
Sampalan Indonesia 8°35S 115°34E **119** b
Sampang Indonesia 7°11S 113°13E **119** G15
Samper de Calanda
Spain 41°11N 0°28W **90** D4
Sampéyre Italy 44°34N 7°11E **92** D4
Sampit Indonesia 2°34S 113°0E **119** E4
Sampit, Teluk Indonesia 3°5S 113°3E **119** E4
Samrong Cambodia 14°15N 103°30E **120** E4
Samsø Denmark 55°50N 10°35E **63** J4
Samsø Bælt Denmark 55°45N 10°45E **63** J4
Samson U.S.A. 31°7N 86°3W **178** F3
Samsun Turkey 41°15N 36°22E **104** B6

insun □ *Turkey* 41°10N 36°10E **104** B7
ntredia *Georgia* 42°7N 42°24E **87** J6
nui, Ko *Thailand* 9°30N 100°0E **121** b
nur → *Russia* 41°53N 48°32E **87** K9
nurskiy Khrebet
 ussia 41°55N 47°11E **87** K8
nusole
 em. Rep. of the Congo 10°2S 24°0E **143** E1
nut Prakan
 hailand 13°40N 100°36E **120** F3
nut Sakhon
 hailand 13°32N 100°17E **120** F3
nut Songkhram
 hailand 13°24N 100°1E **120** F3
nwari *Pakistan* 28°30N 66°46E **124** E2
 Mali 13°15N 4°57W **138** C4
 → *Cambodia* 13°32N 105°57E **120** F5
 → *Poland* 50°45N 21°51E **83** H8
Adrián *Spain* 42°20N 1°56W **90** C3
Adrián, C. de *Spain* 43°21N 8°50W **88** B2
Agustín
 rgentina 30°35S 67°30W **190** C2
Agustín de Valle Fértil
 rgentina 30°35S 67°30W **190** C2
Ambrosio *Pac. Oc.* 26°28S 79°53W **184** F3
Andreas *U.S.A.* 38°12N 120°41W **170** G6
Andrés, I. de
 aribbean 12°42N 81°46W **182** D3
Andrés del Rabanedo
 pain 42°37N 5°36W **88** C5
Andres Mts.
 .S.A. 33°0N 106°30W **169** K10
Andrés Tuxtla
 Mexico 18°27N 95°13W **181** D5
Angelo *U.S.A.* 31°28N 100°26W **176** F4
Anselmo *U.S.A.* 37°59N 122°34W **170** H4
Antonio *Belize* 16°15N 89°2W **181** D7
Antonio *Chile* 33°40S 71°40W **190** C1
Antonio *N. Mex.,*
 .S.A. 33°55N 106°52W **169** K10
Antonio *Tex.,*
 .S.A. 29°25N 98°29W **176** G5
Antonio →
 .S.A. 28°30N 96°54W **176** G6
Antonio, C.
 rgentina 36°15S 56°40W **190** D4
Antonio, C. de
 uba 21°50N 84°57W **182** B3
Antonio, C. de *Spain* 38°48N 0°12E **91** G5
Antonio, Mt.
 .S.A. 34°17N 117°38W **171** L9
Antonio de los Baños
 uba 22°54N 82°31W **182** B3
Antonio de los Cobres
 rgentina 24°10S 66°17W **190** A2
Antonio Oeste
 rgentina 40°40S 65°0W **192** B4
Arcángelo *Italy* 40°14N 16°14E **95** B9
Ardo *U.S.A.* 36°1N 120°54W **170** J6
Augustín
 anary Is. 27°47N 15°32W **90** G4
Augustine *U.S.A.* 31°32N 94°7W **176** F7
Bartolomé
 anary Is. 28°59N 13°37W **100** F6
Bartolomé de Tirajana
 anary Is. 27°54N 15°34W **100** G4
Bartolomeo in Galdo
 aly 41°24N 15°1E **95** A8
Benedetto del Tronto
 aly 42°57N 13°53E **93** F10
Benedetto Po *Italy* 45°2N 10°55E **92** C7
Benedicto, I.
 Mexico 19°18N 110°49W **180** D2
Benito *U.S.A.* 26°8N 97°38W **176** H6
Benito → *U.S.A.* 36°53N 121°34W **170** J5
Benito Mt. *U.S.A.* 36°22N 120°37W **170** J6
Bernardino *U.S.A.* 34°7N 117°19W **171** L9
Bernardino Mts.
 .S.A. 34°10N 116°45W **171** L10
Bernardino Str.
 hil. 12°30N 124°10E **119** B7
Bernardo *Chile* 33°40S 70°50W **190** C1
Bernardo, I. de
 olombia 9°45N 75°50W **186** B3
Blas *Mexico* 26°5N 108°46W **180** B3
Blas, Arch. de
 anama 9°50N 78°31W **182** E4
Blas, C. *U.S.A.* 29°40N 85°21W **178** F3
Bonifacio *Italy* 45°24N 11°16E **93** C8
Borja *Bolivia* 14°50S 66°52W **188** C4
Buenaventura = Ventura
 .S.A. 34°17N 119°18W **171** L7
Buenaventura
 olivia 14°28S 67°35W **188** C4
Buenaventura
 Mexico 27°5N 101°32W **180** B4
Carlos = San Carles
 pain 39°3N 1°34E **100** B8
Carlos *Argentina* 33°50S 69°0W **190** C2
Carlos *Chile* 36°10S 72°0W **190** D1
Carlos *Baja Calif. S.,*
 Mexico 24°47N 112°7W **180** C2
Carlos *Coahuila,*
 Mexico 29°1N 100°51W **180** B4
Carlos *Nic.* 11°12N 84°50W **182** D3
Carlos *Phil.* 10°29N 123°25E **119** B6
Carlos *Uruguay* 34°46S 54°58W **191** C5
Carlos *U.S.A.* 33°21N 110°27W **171** K8
Carlos *Venezuela* 9°40S 68°36W **186** B5
Carlos de Bariloche
 rgentina 41°10S 71°25W **192** B2
Carlos de Bolívar
 rgentina 36°15S 61°6W **190** D3
Carlos de la Rápita = Sant
 arles de la Rápita
 . 40°37N 0°35E **90** E5
Carlos del Zulia
 enezuela 9°1N 71°55W **186** B4
Carlos L. *U.S.A.* 33°11N 110°32W **169** K8
Carlos Park *U.S.A.* 26°28N 81°49W **179** J8
Cataldo *Italy* 37°29N 13°59E **94** E6
Celoni = Sant Celoni
 pain 41°42N 2°30E **90** D7
Clemente *Chile* 35°30S 71°29W **190** D1
Clemente *Spain* 39°24N 2°25W **91** F2
Clemente *U.S.A.* 33°26N 117°37W **171** M9
Clemente I.
 .S.A. 32°53N 118°29W **171** N8
Cristóbal = Es Migjorn Gran
 . 39°57N 4°3E **100** B11
Cristóbal *Argentina* 30°20S 61°10W **190** C3
Cristóbal *Dom. Rep.* 18°25N 70°6W **183** C5

San Cristóbal
 Solomon Is. 10°30S 161°0E **147** C9
San Cristóbal *Venezuela* 7°46N 72°14W **186** B4
San Cristóbal de La Laguna
 Canary Is. 28°28N 16°18W **100** F3
San Cristóbal de las Casas
 Mexico 16°45N 92°38W **181** D6
San Damiano d'Asti *Italy* 44°50N 8°4E **92** D5
San Daniele del Friuli
 Italy 46°9N 13°1E **93** B10
San Diego *Calif., U.S.A.* 32°42N 117°9W **171** N9
San Diego *Tex., U.S.A.* 27°46N 98°14W **176** H5
San Diego, C. *Argentina* 54°40S 65°10W **192** D3
San Diego de la Unión
 Mexico 21°28N 100°52W **180** C4
San Diego Int. ✈ (SAN)
 . 32°44N 117°11W **171** N9
San Dimitri, Ras *Malta* 36°4N 14°11E **101** C1
San Dimitri Point = San Dimitri,
 Ras *Malta* 36°4N 14°11E **101** C1
San Donà di Piave *Italy* 45°38N 12°34E **93** C9
San Estanislao
 Paraguay 24°39S 56°26W **190** A4
San Esteban de Gormaz
 Spain 41°34N 3°13W **90** D1
San Felice Circeo *Italy* 41°14N 13°5E **94** A6
San Felice sul Panaro
 Italy 44°50N 11°8E **92** C8
San Felipe *Chile* 32°43S 70°42W **190** C1
San Felipe *Mexico* 31°1N 114°52W **180** A2
San Felipe *Venezuela* 10°20N 68°44W **186** A5
San Felipe → *U.S.A.* 33°10N 115°49W **171** M11
San Félix *Chile* 28°56S 70°28W **190** B1
San Félix *Pac. Oc.* 26°23S 80°0W **184** F2
San Fernando = Sant Ferran
 Spain 38°42N 1°28E **100** C7
San Fernando *Chile* 34°30S 71°0W **190** C1
San Fernando *Mexico* 24°51N 98°10W **181** C5
San Fernando *La Union,*
 Phil. 16°40N 120°23E **119** A6
San Fernando *Pampanga,*
 Phil. 15°5N 120°37E **119** A6
San Fernando *Spain* 36°28N 6°17W **89** J4
San Fernando
 Trin. & Tob. 10°16N 61°28W **183** D7
San Fernando *U.S.A.* 34°17N 118°26W **171** L8
San Fernando de Apure
 Venezuela 7°54N 67°15W **186** B5
San Fernando de Atabapo
 Venezuela 4°3N 67°42W **186** C5
San Fernando di Púglia
 Italy 41°18N 16°5E **95** A9
San Francisco *Argentina* 31°30S 62°5W **190** C3
San Francisco *Peru* 12°36S 73°49W **188** C3
San Francisco *U.S.A.* 37°46N 122°23W **170** H4
San Francisco →
 U.S.A. 32°59N 109°22W **169** K9
San Francisco, C. de
 Colombia 6°18N 77°29W **184** C3
San Francisco, Paso de
 S. Amer. 27°0S 68°0W **190** B2
San Francisco de Macorís
 Dom. Rep. 19°19N 70°15W **183** C5
San Francisco del Monte de Oro
 Argentina 32°36S 66°8W **190** C2
San Francisco del Oro
 Mexico 26°52N 105°51W **180** B3
San Francisco Int. ✈ (SFO)
 U.S.A. 37°37N 122°22W **170** H4
San Francisco Javier = Sant
 Francesc de Formentera
 Spain 38°42N 1°26E **100** C7
San Fratello *Italy* 38°1N 14°36E **95** D7
San Gabriel *Chile* 33°47S 70°15W **190** C1
San Gabriel Chilac
 Mexico 18°19N 97°21W **181** D5
San Gabriel Mts.
 U.S.A. 34°17N 117°38W **171** L9
San Gavino Monreale
 Italy 39°33N 8°47E **94** C1
San German *Puerto Rico* 18°4N 67°4W **183** d
San Gimignano *Italy* 43°28N 11°2E **92** E8
San Giórgio di Nogaro
 Italy 45°50N 13°13E **93** C10
San Giórgio Iónico
 Italy 40°27N 17°23E **95** B10
San Giovanni Bianco
 Italy 45°52N 9°39E **92** C6
San Giovanni in Fiore
 Italy 39°15N 16°42E **95** C9
San Giovanni in Persiceto
 Italy 44°38N 11°11E **93** D8
San Giovanni Rotondo
 Italy 41°42N 15°44E **93** G12
San Giovanni Valdarno
 Italy 43°34N 11°32E **93** E8
San Giuliano Terme
 Italy 43°46N 10°26E **92** E7
San Gorgonio Mt.
 U.S.A. 34°6N 116°50W **171** L10
San Gottardo, P. del
 Switz. 46°33N 8°33E **77** J4
San Gregorio *Uruguay* 32°37S 55°40W **191** C4
San Gregorio *U.S.A.* 37°20N 122°23W **170** H4
San Guillermo →
 Argentina 27°50S 69°45W **190** B2
San Giuseppe Jato *Italy* 37°57N 13°11E **94** E6
San Ignacio *Belize* 17°10N 89°5W **181** D7
San Ignacio *Bolivia* 16°20S 60°55W **186** G6
San Ignacio *Mexico* 27°27N 112°51W **180** B2
San Ignacio *Paraguay* 26°52S 57°3W **190** B4
San Ignacio *Peru* 5°8S 78°59W **188** B2
San Ignacio, L.
 Mexico 26°54N 113°13W **180** B2
San Ildefonso, C. *Phil.* 16°0N 122°1E **119** A6
San Isidro *Argentina* 34°29S 58°31W **190** C4
San Jacinto *U.S.A.* 33°47N 116°57W **171** M10
San Jaime = Sant Jaume
 Spain 39°54N 4°4E **100** B11
San Javier *Misiones,*
 Argentina 27°55S 55°5W **191** B4
San Javier *Santa Fe,*
 Argentina 30°40S 59°55W **190** C4
San Javier *Bolivia* 16°18S 62°30W **186** G6
San Javier *Chile* 35°40S 71°45W **190** D1
San Javier *Spain* 37°49N 0°50W **91** H4
San Jerónimo Taviche
 Mexico 16°44N 96°35W **181** D5
San Joaquín *Bolivia* 13°4S 64°49W **186** F5
San Joaquín *U.S.A.* 36°36N 120°11W **170** J6
San Joaquín → *U.S.A.* 38°4N 121°51W **170** G5
San Joaquin Valley
 U.S.A. 37°20N 121°0W **170** J6

San Jon *U.S.A.* 35°6N 103°20W **169** J12
San Jordi = Sant Jordi
 Spain 39°33N 2°46E **100** B9
San Jorge *Argentina* 31°54S 61°50W **190** C3
San Jorge, B. *Mexico* 31°20N 113°20W **180** A2
San Jorge, G. *Argentina* 46°0S 66°0W **192** C3
San José = San Josep
 Spain 38°55N 1°18E **100** C7
San José *Argentina* 32°12S 58°15W **190** C4
San José *Costa Rica* 9°55N 84°2W **182** E3
San José *Guatemala* 14°0N 90°50W **182** D1
San José *Mind. Occ.,*
 Phil. 12°27N 121°4E **119** B6
San Jose *Nueva Ecija,*
 Phil. 15°45N 120°55E **119** A6
San Jose *U.S.A.* 37°20N 121°53W **170** H5
San Jose → *U.S.A.* 34°25N 106°45W **169** J10
San José, G. *Argentina* 42°20S 64°18W **192** B4
San José, I. *Mexico* 25°0N 110°38W **180** C2
San Jose de Buenavista
 Phil. 10°45N 121°56E **119** B6
San José de Chiquitos
 Bolivia 17°53S 60°50W **186** G6
San José de Feliciano
 Argentina 30°26S 58°46W **190** C4
San José de Jáchal
 Argentina 30°15S 68°46W **190** C3
San José de Mayo
 Uruguay 34°27S 56°40W **190** C4
San José de Uchapiamonas
 Bolivia 14°13S 68°5W **188** C4
San José del Cabo
 Mexico 23°3N 109°41W **180** C3
San José del Guaviare
 Colombia 2°35N 72°38W **186** C4
San Josep *Spain* 38°55N 1°18E **100** C7
San Juan *Argentina* 31°30S 68°30W **190** C2
San Juan *Peru* 15°22S 75°7W **188** D2
San Juan *Puerto Rico* 18°28N 66°7W **183** d
San Juan *Trin. & Tob.* 10°39N 61°29W **187** K15
San Juan □ *Argentina* 31°9S 69°0W **190** C2
San Juan → *Argentina* 32°20S 67°25W **190** C2
San Juan → *Nic.* 10°56N 83°42W **182** D3
San Juan → *U.S.A.* 37°16N 110°26W **169** H8
San Juan, C. *Argentina* 54°44S 63°44W **192** D4
San Juan Bautista = Sant Joan de
 Labritja *Spain* 39°5N 1°31E **100** B8
San Juan Bautista
 Paraguay 26°37S 57°6W **190** B4
San Juan Bautista
 U.S.A. 36°51N 121°32W **170** J5
San Juan Capistrano
 U.S.A. 33°30N 117°40W **171** M9
San Juan Cr. →
 U.S.A. 35°40N 120°22W **170** J5
San Juan de Guadelupe
 Mexico 24°38N 102°44W **180** C4
San Juan de la Costa
 Mexico 24°20N 110°41W **180** C2
San Juan de los Lagos
 Mexico 21°15N 102°18W **180** C4
San Juan de los Morros
 Venezuela 9°55N 67°21W **186** B5
San Juan del Norte
 Nic. 10°58N 83°40W **182** D3
San Juan del Norte, B. de
 Nic. 11°0N 83°40W **182** D3
San Juan del Río
 Mexico 20°23N 100°0W **181** C5
San Juan del Sur *Nic.* 11°20N 85°51W **182** D2
San Juan I. *U.S.A.* 48°32N 123°5W **170** B3
San Juan Island △
 U.S.A. 48°35N 123°8W **170** B4
San Juan Mts. *U.S.A.* 37°30N 107°0W **169** H10
San Just, Sierra de *Spain* 40°45N 0°49W **90** E4
San Justo *Argentina* 30°47S 60°30W **190** C3
San Kamphaeng
 Thailand 18°45N 99°8E **120** C2
San Lázaro, C. *Mexico* 24°50N 112°18W **180** C2
San Leandro *U.S.A.* 37°42N 122°9W **170** H4
San Leonardo de Yagüe
 Spain 41°51N 3°5W **90** D1
San Lorenzo = Sant Llorenç des
 Cardassar *Spain* 39°37N 3°17E **100** B10
San Lorenzo *Argentina* 32°45S 60°45W **190** C3
San Lorenzo *Ecuador* 1°15N 78°50W **186** C3
San Lorenzo *Paraguay* 25°20S 57°32W **190** B4
San Lorenzo →
 Mexico 24°15N 107°24W **180** C3
San Lorenzo, I.
 Mexico 28°38N 112°51W **180** B2
San Lorenzo, I. *Peru* 12°7S 77°15W **188** D2
San Lorenzo, Mte.
 Argentina 47°40S 72°20W **192** C2
San Lorenzo de la Parrilla
 Spain 39°51N 2°22W **90** F2
San Lorenzo de Morunys = Sant
 Llorenç de Morunys
 Spain 42°8N 1°35E **90** C6
San Lucas = Cabo San Lucas
 Mexico 22°53N 109°54W **180** C3
San Lucas *Bolivia* 20°5S 65°7W **186** H5
San Lucas *Mexico* 27°10N 112°14W **180** B2
San Lucas *U.S.A.* 36°8N 121°1W **170** J5
San Lucas, C. *Mexico* 22°52N 109°53W **180** C3
San Lúcido *Italy* 39°18N 16°3E **95** C9
San Luis *Argentina* 33°20S 66°20W **190** C2
San Luis *Cuba* 22°17N 83°46W **182** B3
San Luis *Guatemala* 16°14N 89°27W **182** C2
San Luis *Ariz., U.S.A.* 32°29N 114°47W **169** K6
San Luis *Colo., U.S.A.* 37°12N 105°25W **169** H11
San Luis □ *Argentina* 34°0S 66°0W **190** C2
San Luis, I. *Mexico* 29°58N 114°26W **180** B2
San Luis, Sierra de
 Argentina 32°30S 66°10W **190** C2
San Luis de la Paz
 Mexico 21°18N 100°31W **180** C4
San Luis Obispo
 U.S.A. 35°17N 120°40W **171** K6
San Luis Potosí *Mexico* 22°9N 100°59W **180** C4
San Luis Potosí □
 Mexico 23°0N 101°0W **180** C4
San Luis Res. *U.S.A.* 37°4N 121°5W **170** H5
San Luis Río Colorado
 Mexico 32°29N 114°58W **180** A2
San Manuel *U.S.A.* 32°36N 110°38W **169** K8
San Marco, C. *Italy* 39°51N 8°26E **94** C1
San Marco Argentano
 Italy 39°33N 16°7E **95** C9
San Marco in Lámis
 Italy 41°43N 15°38E **93** G12

San Marcos *Calif.,*
 U.S.A. 33°9N 117°10W **171** M9
San Marcos *Tex.,*
 U.S.A. 29°53N 97°56W **176** G6
San Marcos, I. *Mexico* 27°13N 112°6W **180** B2
San Marino *San Marino* 43°55N 12°30E **93** E9
San Marino ■ *Europe* 43°56N 12°25E **93** E9
San Martín *Antarctica* 68°11S 67°0W **55** C17
San Martín *Argentina* 33°5S 68°28W **190** C2
San Martín □ *Peru* 7°0S 76°50W **188** E3
San Martín → *Bolivia* 13°8S 63°43W **186** F6
San Martín, L.
 Argentina 48°50S 72°50W **192** C2
San Martín de la Vega
 Spain 40°13N 3°34W **88** E7
San Martín de los Andes
 Argentina 40°10S 71°20W **192** B2
San Martín de Valdeiglesias
 Spain 40°21N 4°24W **88** E6
San Mateo = Sant Mateu *Baleares,*
 Spain 39°3N 1°23E **100** B7
San Mateo = Sant Mateu *Valencia,*
 Spain 40°28N 0°10E **90** E5
San Mateo *U.S.A.* 37°34N 122°19W **170** H4
San Matías *Bolivia* 16°25S 58°20W **186** G7
San Matías, G.
 Argentina 41°30S 64°0W **192** B4
San Miguel = Sant Miquel
 Spain 39°3N 1°26E **100** B7
San Miguel *Brazil* 28°35S 54°33W **190** B5
San Miguel *El Salv.* 13°30N 88°12W **182** D2
San Miguel *Panama* 8°27N 78°55W **182** E4
San Miguel *U.S.A.* 35°45N 120°42W **170** K6
San Miguel → *Bolivia* 13°52S 63°56W **186** F6
San Miguel de Huachi
 Bolivia 15°40S 67°15W **188** D4
San Miguel de Tucumán
 Argentina 26°50S 65°20W **190** B2
San Miguel del Monte
 Argentina 35°23S 58°50W **190** D4
San Miguel I. *U.S.A.* 34°2N 120°23W **171** L6
San Millán de la Cogolla
 Spain 42°19N 2°51W **90** C2
San Miniato *Italy* 43°41N 10°51E **92** E7
San Nicandro Gargánico
 Italy 41°50N 15°34E **93** G12
San Nicolás *Canary Is.* 27°58N 15°47W **100** G4
San Nicolás de los Arroyos
 Argentina 33°25S 60°10W **190** C3
San Nicolas I. *U.S.A.* 33°15N 119°30W **171** M7
San Onofre *U.S.A.* 33°22N 117°34W **171** M9
San Pablo *Bolivia* 21°43S 66°38W **190** A2
San Pablo *U.S.A.* 37°58N 122°21W **170** H4
San Páolo di Civitate
 Italy 41°44N 15°15E **93** G12
San Pedro *B. Aires,*
 Argentina 33°40S 59°40W **190** C4
San Pedro *Misiones,*
 Argentina 26°30S 54°10W **191** B5
San Pedro *Chile* 33°54S 71°28W **190** C1
San Pedro *Ivory C.* 4°50N 6°33W **138** E3
San Pedro *Mexico* 23°55N 110°17W **180** C2
San Pedro *Peru* 14°49S 74°5W **188** D3
San Pedro □ *Paraguay* 24°0S 57°0W **190** A4
San Pedro → *Chihuahua,*
 Mexico 28°21N 105°25W **180** B3
San Pedro → *Nayarit,*
 Mexico 21°45N 105°30W **180** C3
San Pedro de Atacama
 Chile 22°55S 68°15W **190** A2
San Pedro de Jujuy
 Argentina 24°12S 64°55W **190** A3
San Pedro de las Colonias
 Mexico 25°45N 102°59W **180** B4
San Pedro de Lloc *Peru* 7°15S 79°28W **188** E2
San Pedro de Macorís
 Dom. Rep. 18°30N 69°18W **183** C6
San Pedro del Norte
 Nic. 13°4N 84°33W **182** D3
San Pedro del Paraná
 Paraguay 26°43S 56°13W **190** B4
San Pedro del Pinatar
 Spain 37°50N 0°50W **91** H4
San Pedro Mártir, Sa. de
 Mexico 30°45N 115°13W **180** A1
San Pedro Ocampo = Melchor
 Ocampo *Mexico* 24°51N 101°39W **180** C4
San Pedro Pochutla
 Mexico 15°44N 96°28W **181** D5
San Pedro Sula
 Honduras 15°30N 88°0W **182** C2
San Pedro Tututepec
 Mexico 16°9N 97°38W **181** D5
San Pietro *Italy* 39°8N 8°17E **94** C1
San Pietro Vernótico
 Italy 40°29N 18°0E **95** B11
San Rafael *Argentina* 34°40S 68°21W **190** C2
San Rafael *Calif.,*
 U.S.A. 37°58N 122°32W **170** H4
San Rafael *N. Mex.,*
 U.S.A. 35°7N 107°53W **169** J10
San Rafael Mt. *U.S.A.* 34°41N 119°52W **171** L7
San Rafael Mts.
 U.S.A. 34°40N 119°50W **171** L7
San Ramón de la Nueva Orán
 Argentina 23°10S 64°20W **190** A3
San Remo *Italy* 43°49N 7°46E **92** E4
San Roque *Argentina* 28°25S 58°45W **190** B4
San Roque *Spain* 36°17N 5°21W **89** J5
San Rosendo *Chile* 37°16S 72°43W **190** D1
San Saba *U.S.A.* 31°12N 98°43W **176** F5
San Salvador *El Salv.* 13°40N 89°10W **182** D2
San Salvador de Jujuy
 Argentina 24°10S 64°48W **190** A3
San Salvador I.
 Bahamas 24°0N 74°30W **183** B5
San Salvo *Italy* 42°3N 14°44E **93** F11
San Sebastián = Donostia-San
 Sebastián *Spain* 43°17N 1°58W **90** B3
San Sebastián
 Argentina 53°10S 68°30W **192** D3
San Sebastián
 Puerto Rico 18°20N 66°59W **183** d
San Sebastián de la Gomera
 Canary Is. 28°5N 17°7W **100** F2

San Serra = Son Serra
 Spain 39°43N 3°13E **100** B10
San Severino Marche
 Italy 43°13N 13°10E **93** E10
San Severo *Italy* 41°41N 15°23E **93** G12
San Simeon *U.S.A.* 35°39N 121°11W **170** K5
San Simon *U.S.A.* 32°16N 109°14W **169** K9
San Stéfano di Cadore
 Italy 46°34N 12°33E **93** B9
San Telmo = Sant Elm
 Spain 45°44N 12°41E **93** C9
San Telmo *Mexico* 30°58N 116°6W **180** A1
San Teodoro *Italy* 40°46N 9°40E **94** B2
San Tiburcio *Mexico* 24°8N 101°32W **180** C4
San Valentin, Mte.
 Chile 46°30S 73°30W **192** C2
San Vicente de Alcántara
 Spain 39°22N 7°8W **89** F3
San Vicente de Cañete
 Peru 13°8S 76°30W **188** C2
San Vicente de la Barquera
 Spain 43°23N 4°29W **88** B6
San Vicenzo *Spain* 42°58N 8°46W **88** C2
San Vincenzo *Italy* 43°6N 10°32E **92** E7
San Vito *Costa Rica* 8°50N 82°58W **182** E3
San Vito *Italy* 39°26N 9°32E **94** C2
San Vito, C. *Italy* 38°11N 12°41E **94** D5
San Vito al Tagliamento
 Italy 45°54N 12°52E **93** C9
San Vito Chietino *Italy* 42°18N 14°27E **93** F11
San Vito dei Normanni
 Italy 40°39N 17°42E **95** B10
Sana' = Şan'ā' *Yemen* 15°27N 44°12E **131** D3
Saña *Peru* 6°54S 79°36W **188** B2
Şan'ā' *Yemen* 15°27N 44°12E **131** D3
Sanaa = Şan'ā' *Yemen* 15°27N 44°12E **131** D3
Sanaba *Burkina Faso* 12°25N 3°47W **138** C4
Sanae IV *Antarctica* 70°20S 9°0W **5** D2
Sanaga → *Cameroon* 3°35N 9°38E **139** E6
Sanak I. *U.S.A.* 54°25N 162°40W **166** E7
Sanalona, Presa
 Mexico 24°49N 107°7W **180** C3
Sanana *Indonesia* 2°4S 125°58E **119** E7
Sanand *India* 22°59N 72°25E **124** H8
Sanandaj *Iran* 35°18N 47°1E **105** E12
Sanandita *Bolivia* 21°40S 63°45W **190** A3
Sanary-sur-Mer *France* 43°7N 5°49E **73** E9
Sanawad *India* 22°11N 76°5E **124** H7
Sancellas = Sencelles
 Spain 39°39N 2°54E **100** B9
Sancergues *France* 47°10N 2°54E **71** E9
Sancerre *France* 47°20N 2°50E **71** E9
Sancerrois, Collines du
 France 47°20N 2°40E **71** E9
Sancha He → *China* 26°48N 106°7E **116** D7
Sanchahe *China* 44°50N 126°2E **115** B14
Sánchez *Dom. Rep.* 19°15N 69°36W **183** C6
Sanchi *India* 23°28N 77°44E **124** H7
Sanchor *India* 24°45N 71°55E **124** G4
Sancoins *France* 46°47N 2°55E **71** F9
Sancti Spíritus *Cuba* 21°52N 79°33W **182** B4
Sancy, Puy de *France* 45°32N 2°50E **72** C6
Sand = Polokwane →
 S. Africa 22°25S 30°5E **145** B5
Sand Hills *U.S.A.* 42°10N 101°30W **172** D3
Sand Lakes △ *Canada* 57°51N 98°32W **163** B9
Sand Springs *U.S.A.* 36°9N 96°7W **176** C6
Sanda *Japan* 34°53N 135°14E **113** G7
Sandakan *Malaysia* 5°53N 118°4E **121** C5
Sandalwood *Australia* 34°55S 140°9E **152** C4
Sandan = Sambor
 Cambodia 12°46N 106°0E **120** F6
Sandanski *Bulgaria* 41°35N 23°16E **96** E7
Sandaré *Mali* 14°40N 10°15W **138** C2
Sandared *Sweden* 57°43N 12°47E **63** G6
Sandarne *Sweden* 61°16N 17°9E **62** C11
Sanday *U.K.* 59°16N 2°31W **65** B6
Sande *Norway* 59°36N 10°12E **64** E4
Sandefjord *Norway* 59°10N 10°15E **61** G14
Sanders *U.S.A.* 35°13N 109°20W **169** J9
Sanderson *Fla., U.S.A.* 30°15N 82°16W **178** F7
Sanderson *Tex., U.S.A.* 30°9N 102°24W **176** F3
Sandersville *U.S.A.* 32°59N 82°48W **179** J6
Sandfire Roadhouse
 Australia 19°45S 121°15E **148** C3
Sandfly L. *Canada* 55°43N 106°6W **163** B7
Sandfontein *Namibia* 23°48S 19°1E **142** B2
Sandhammaren *Sweden* 55°23N 14°14E **63** J8
Sandheads, The *India* 21°10N 88°20E **125** J13
Sandia *Peru* 14°10S 69°30W **188** C4
Sandıklı *Turkey* 38°28N 30°17E **99** C12
Sandila *India* 27°5N 80°31E **125** F9
Sandnes *Norway* 58°50N 5°45E **61** G11
Sandnessjøen *Norway* 66°2N 12°38E **60** C15
Sandoa
 Dem. Rep. of the Congo 9°41S 23°0E **140** F4
Sandomierz *Poland* 50°40N 21°43E **83** H8
Sândominic *Romania* 46°35N 25°47E **81** D10
Sandover → *Australia* 21°43S 136°32E **150** C2
Sandoway = Thandwe
 Burma 18°20N 94°30E **123** K19
Sandoy *Færoe Is.* 61°52N 6°46W **60** F9
Sandpoint *U.S.A.* 48°17N 116°33W **168** B5
Sandray *U.K.* 56°53N 7°31W **65** E1
Sandringham *U.K.* 52°51N 0°31E **66** E8
Sandstone *Australia* 27°59S 119°16E **149** E2
Sandu *China* 26°0N 107°52E **116** E6
Sandur *India* 15°6N 76°33E **127** G3
Sandusky *Mich.,*
 U.S.A. 43°25N 82°50W **174** C2
Sandusky *Ohio, U.S.A.* 41°27N 82°42W **174** E2
Sandveld *Namibia* 21°25S 20°0E **142** A3
Sandvig *Denmark* 55°18N 14°47E **63** J8
Sandviken *Sweden* 60°38N 16°46E **62** A10
Sandwich, C. *Australia* 18°14S 146°18E **150** B4
Sandwich B. *Canada* 53°40N 57°15W **165** B8
Sandwich B. *Namibia* 23°25S 14°20E **144** B1
Sandy *Oreg., U.S.A.* 45°24N 122°16W **170** E4
Sandy *Pa., U.S.A.* 41°6N 78°46W **174** E6
Sandy *Utah, U.S.A.* 40°32N 111°50W **168** F8
Sandy Bay *Canada* 55°31N 102°19W **163** B8
Sandy Bight *Australia* 33°50S 123°20E **149** F3
Sandy C. *Queens.,*
 Australia 24°42S 153°15E **150** C5
Sandy C. *Tas., Australia* 41°25S 144°45E **150** G3
Sandy Cay *Bahamas* 23°13N 75°18W **183** B4
Sandy Cr. → *Australia* 31°54S 145°19E **151** B4
Sandy Cr. → *U.S.A.* 41°51N 109°47W **168** F9

Sandy Creek *U.S.A.* 43°38N 76°5W **175** C8
Sandy L. *Canada* 53°2N 93°0W **164** B1
Sandy Lake *Canada* 53°0N 93°15W **164** B1
Sandy Point *India* 10°32N 92°22E **127** J11
Sandy Valley *U.S.A.* 35°49N 115°38W **171** K11
Sånfjället △ *Sweden* 62°17N 13°35E **188** B5
Sanford *Fla., U.S.A.* 28°48N 81°16W **179** G8
Sanford *Maine, U.S.A.* 43°27N 70°47W **175** C14
Sanford *N.C., U.S.A.* 35°29N 79°10W **178** D5
Sanford *Australia* 27°22S 115°53E **149** E2
Sanford, Mt. *U.S.A.* 62°13N 144°8W **166** C5
Sang-i-Masha *Afghan.* 33°8N 67°27E **124** C2
Sanga *Mozam.* 12°22S 35°21E **143** A4
Sanga → *Congo* 1°5S 17°0E **140** E3
Sangamner *India* 19°37N 74°15E **126** E2
Sangān *Iran* 34°23N 60°15E **129** C9
Sanganeb Atoll △
 Sudan 19°33N 37°11E **137** D13
Sangar *Afghan.* 32°56N 65°30E **124** C1
Sangar *Russia* 64°2N 127°31E **107** C13
Sangar Sarai *Afghan.* 34°27N 70°35E **124** B4
Sangaredi *Guinea* 11°7N 13°53E **138** C2
Sangarh → *Pakistan* 30°43N 70°44E **124** D4
Sangasso *Mali* 12°5N 5°35W **138** C3
Sangatte *France* 50°56N 1°44E **71** B8
Sangay *Ecuador* 2°0S 78°20W **186** D3
Sangbé *Cameroon* 6°3N 12°28E **139** D7
Sange
 Dem. Rep. of the Congo 6°58S 28°21E **142** D2
Sangeang *Indonesia* 8°12S 119°6E **119** F5
Sângeorz-Băi *Romania* 47°22N 24°41E **81** C9
Sanger *U.S.A.* 36°42N 119°33W **170** J7
Sangerhausen *Germany* 51°28N 11°18E **76** D7
Sanggan He → *China* 38°12N 117°15E **114** E9
Sanggau *Indonesia* 0°5N 110°30E **118** D4
Sanghar *Pakistan* 26°2N 68°57E **124** F3
Sangihe, Kepulauan
 Indonesia 3°0N 125°30E **119** D7
Sangihe, Pulau
 Indonesia 3°35N 125°30E **119** D7
Sangiran △ *Indonesia* 7°27S 110°50E **119** G14
Sangju *S. Korea* 36°25N 128°10E **115** F15
Sangkapura *Indonesia* 5°52S 112°40E **118** F4
Sangkha *Thailand* 14°37N 103°52E **120** E4
Sangkhla Buri *Thailand* 14°57N 98°28E **120** E2
Sangkulirang *Indonesia* 0°59N 117°58E **118** D5
Sangla *Pakistan* 31°43N 73°23E **124** D5
Sangli *India* 16°55N 74°33E **126** F2
Sangmélima *Cameroon* 2°57N 12°1E **139** E7
Sangod *India* 24°55N 76°17E **124** G7
Sangole *India* 17°26N 75°12E **126** F2
Sangre de Cristo Mts.
 U.S.A. 37°30N 105°20W **169** H11
Sangre Grande
 Trin. & Tob. 10°35N 61°8W **187** K15
Sangro → *Italy* 42°14N 14°32E **93** F11
Sangrur *India* 30°14N 75°50E **124** D6
Sangudo *Canada* 53°50N 114°54W **162** C6
Sangue → *Brazil* 11°1S 58°39W **186** F7
Sanguinaires, Îs. *France* 41°51N 8°36E **73** G12
Sanghi *China* 29°25N 110°12E **117** C8
Sanhala *Ivory C.* 10°3N 6°51W **138** C3
Sanibel *U.S.A.* 26°27N 82°1W **179** J7
Sanibel I. *U.S.A.* 26°26N 82°6W **179** J7
Sanikluaq *Canada* 56°32N 79°14W **164** A4
Sanin-Kaigan △ *Japan* 35°39N 134°37E **113** G7
Sanirajak = Hall Beach
 Canada 68°46N 81°12W **161** D15
Sanjawi *Pakistan* 30°17N 68°21E **124** D3
Sanje *Uganda* 0°49S 31°30E **142** C3
Sanjiang *China* 25°48N 109°37E **116** E7
Sanjo *Japan* 37°37N 138°57E **112** F9
Sankarankovil *India* 9°10N 77°35E **127** K3
Sankeshwar *India* 16°23N 74°32E **127** F2
Sankh → *India* 22°15N 84°48E **125** H11
Sankt Andrä *Austria* 46°46N 14°50E **78** E7
Sankt Anton *Austria* 47°8N 10°16E **77** H6
Sankt Augustin *Germany* 50°45N 7°10E **76** E3
Sankt Blasien *Germany* 47°47N 8°7E **77** H4
Sankt Gallen *Switz.* 47°26N 9°22E **77** H5
Sankt Gallen □ *Switz.* 47°25N 9°22E **77** H5
Sankt Goar *Germany* 50°12N 7°43E **77** E3
Sankt Ingbert *Germany* 49°16N 7°6E **77** F3
Sankt Johann im Pongau
 Austria 47°22N 13°12E **78** D6
Sankt Johann in Tirol
 Austria 47°30N 12°25E **78** D5
Sankt Michel = Mikkeli
 Finland 61°43N 27°15E **84** A4
Sankt Moritz *Switz.* 46°30N 9°51E **77** J5
Sankt Peter-Ording
 Germany 54°20N 8°36E **76** A4
Sankt-Peterburg *Russia* 59°55N 30°20E **84** C6
Sankt Pölten *Austria* 48°12N 15°38E **78** C8
Sankt Ulrich = Ortisei
 Italy 46°34N 11°40E **93** B8
Sankt Valentin *Austria* 48°1N 14°33E **78** C7
Sankt Veit an der Glan
 Austria 46°47N 14°22E **78** E7
Sankt Wendel *Germany* 49°27N 7°9E **77** F3
Sankt Wolfgang *Austria* 47°43N 13°27E **78** D6
Sankuru →
 Dem. Rep. of the Congo 4°17S 20°25E **140** E4
Sanliurfa *Turkey* 37°12N 38°50E **105** D8
Şanlıurfa □ *Turkey* 37°0N 39°0E **105** D8
Sanlúcar de Barrameda
 Spain 36°46N 6°21W **89** J4
Sanlúcar la Mayor
 Spain 37°26N 6°18W **89** H4
Sanluri *Italy* 39°34N 8°54E **94** C1
Sânmartin *Romania* 46°19N 25°58E **81** D10
Sanmen *China* 29°5N 121°35E **117** C13
Sanmenxia *China* 34°47N 111°12E **114** G6
Sanmu *Japan* 34°11N 134°37E **113** G7
Sanndraigh = Sandray
 U.K. 56°53N 7°31W **65** E1
Sânnicolau Mare
 Romania 46°5N 20°39E **80** D5
Sannieshof *S. Africa* 26°30S 25°47E **142** D4
Sannin, J. *Lebanon* 33°57N 35°52E **130** B4
Sannūr, W. → *Egypt* 28°59N 31°3E **137** F7
Sano *Japan* 36°19N 139°35E **113** F9
Sanok *Poland* 49°35N 22°10E **83** J9
Sanquhar *U.K.* 55°22N 3°54W **65** F5

Sanremo = San Remo
Italy 43°49N 7°46E **92** E4
Sans Souci Trin. & Tob. 10°50N 61°0W **187** K16
Sansanding Mali 13°48N 6°0W **138** C3
Sansané Niger 13°50N 1°36E **139** C5
Sansepolcro Italy 43°34N 12°8E **93** E9
Sansha China 26°58N 120°12E **117** D13
Sanshui China 23°10N 112°56E **117** F9
Sanski Most Bos.-H. 44°46N 16°40E **93** D13
Sansui China 26°58N 108°39E **116** D7
Sant Antoni de Portmany
Spain 38°59N 1°19E **100** C7
Sant Boi de Llobregat
Spain 41°20N 2°2E **90** D7
Sant Carles Spain 39°3N 1°34E **100** B8
Sant Carles de la Ràpita
Spain 40°37N 0°35E **90** E5
Sant Celoni Spain 41°42N 2°30E **90** D7
Sant Elm Spain 39°35N 2°21E **100** B9
Sant Feliu de Guíxols
Spain 41°45N 3°1E **90** D8
Sant Feliu de Llobregat
Spain 41°22N 2°2E **90** D7
Sant Ferran Spain 38°42N 1°28E **100** C7
Sant Francesc de Formentera
Spain 38°42N 1°26E **100** C7
Sant Jaume Spain 39°54N 4°4E **100** B11
Sant Joan Spain 39°36N 3°4E **100** B10
Sant Joan d'Alacant
Spain 38°24N 0°26W **91** G4
Sant Joan de Labritja
Spain 39°5N 1°31E **100** B8
Sant Jordi Ibiza, Spain 38°53N 1°24E **100** C7
Sant Jordi Mallorca, Spain 39°33N 2°46E **100** B9
Sant Jordi, G. de Spain 40°53N 1°2E **90** E6
Sant Llorenç de Morunys
Spain 42°8N 1°35E **90** C6
Sant Llorenç del Munt y l'Obac ○
Spain 41°39N 1°55W **90** D3
Sant Llorenç des Cardassar
Spain 39°37N 3°17E **100** B10
Sant Mateu Baleares,
Spain 39°3N 1°23E **100** B7
Sant Mateu Valencia,
Spain 40°28N 0°10E **90** E5
Sant Miquel Spain 39°3N 1°26E **100** B7
Sant Pere de Ribes Spain 41°16N 1°46E **90** D6
Sant Salvador Spain 39°27N 3°11E **100** B10
Sant Vicent del Raspeig
Spain 38°24N 0°31W **91** G4
Santa Peru 8°59S 78°40W **188** E2
Sant' Ágata Militello Italy 38°2N 14°8E **95** D7
Santa Agnès Spain 39°3N 1°21E **100** B7
Santa Ana Beni, Bolivia 13°50S 65°40W **186** F5
Santa Ana La Paz,
Bolivia 15°31S 67°30W **188** D4
Santa Ana El Salv. 14°0N 89°31W **182** D2
Santa Ana Mexico 30°33N 111°7W **180** A2
Santa Ana U.S.A. 33°46N 117°52W **171** M9
Santa Ana de los Rios de Cuenca
= Cuenca Ecuador 2°50S 79°9W **186** D3
Santa Bárbara Chile 37°40S 72°1W **190** D1
Santa Bárbara
Honduras 14°53N 88°14W **182** D2
Santa Bárbara Mexico 26°48N 105°49W **180** B3
Santa Bárbara Spain 40°42N 0°29E **90** E5
Santa Bárbara U.S.A. 34°25N 119°42W **171** L7
Santa Bárbara, Mt.
Spain 37°23N 2°50W **91** H2
Santa Barbara Channel
U.S.A. 34°15N 120°0W **171** L7
Santa Barbara I.
U.S.A. 33°29N 119°2W **171** M7
Santa Catalina, Gulf of
U.S.A. 33°10N 117°50W **171** N9
Santa Catalina, I.
Mexico 25°40N 110°47W **180** B2
Santa Cataliña de Armada
Spain 43°2N 8°49W **88** B2
Santa Catalina I.
U.S.A. 33°23N 118°25W **171** M8
Santa Catarina □
Brazil 27°25S 48°30W **191** B6
Santa Catarina, I. de
Brazil 27°30S 48°40W **191** B6
Santa Caterina di Pittinuri
Italy 40°6N 8°27E **94** B1
Santa Caterina Villarmosa
Italy 37°35N 14°2E **95** E7
Santa Cecília Brazil 26°56S 50°18W **191** B5
Santa Clara Cuba 22°20N 80°0W **182** B4
Santa Clara Calif.,
U.S.A. 37°21N 121°57W **170** H5
Santa Clara N.Y.,
U.S.A. 44°38N 74°27W **175** B10
Santa Clara Utah,
U.S.A. 37°8N 113°39W **169** H7
Santa Clara → Mexico 29°51N 107°6W **180** A3
Santa Clara de Olimar
Uruguay 32°50S 54°54W **191** C5
Santa Clara Valley
U.S.A. 36°50N 121°30W **170** J5
Santa Clarita U.S.A. 34°24N 118°33W **171** L8
Santa Clotilde Peru 2°33S 73°45W **186** D4
Santa Coloma de Farners
Spain 41°50N 2°39E **90** D7
Santa Coloma de Gramenet
Spain 41°27N 2°13E **90** D7
Santa Comba = Santa Cataliña de
Armada Spain 43°2N 8°49W **88** B2
Santa Croce Camerina
Italy 36°50N 14°31E **95** F7
Santa Croce di Magliano
Italy 41°42N 14°59E **93** G11
Santa Cruz Bolivia 17°43S 63°10W **186** G6
Santa Cruz Brazil 6°13S 36°1W **189** D11
Santa Cruz Chile 34°38S 71°27W **190** C1
Santa Cruz Costa Rica 10°15N 85°35W **182** D2
Santa Cruz Madeira 32°42N 16°46E **100** D3
Santa Cruz Peru 5°40S 75°56W **188** D2
Santa Cruz Phil. 14°20N 121°24E **119** B6
Santa Cruz U.S.A. 36°58N 122°1W **170** J4
Santa Cruz □ Argentina 49°0S 70°0W **192** D3
Santa Cruz →
Argentina 50°10S 68°20W **192** D3
Santa Cruz Cabrália
Brazil 16°17S 39°2W **189** D3
Santa Cruz de la Palma
Canary Is. 28°41N 17°46W **100** F2
Santa Cruz de la Palma ✈ (SPC)
Canary Is. 28°40N 17°45W **100** F2

Santa Cruz de Mompox =
Mompós Colombia 9°14N 74°26W **186** B4
Santa Cruz de Mudela
Spain 38°39N 3°28W **89** G7
Santa Cruz de Tenerife
Canary Is. 28°28N 16°15W **100** F3
Santa Cruz del Norte
Cuba 23°9N 81°55W **182** B3
Santa Cruz del Retamar
Spain 40°8N 4°14W **88** E6
Santa Cruz del Sur Cuba 20°44N 78°0W **182** B4
Santa Cruz do Rio Pardo
Brazil 22°54S 49°37W **191** A6
Santa Cruz do Sul
Brazil 29°42S 52°25W **191** B5
Santa Cruz I. U.S.A. 34°1N 119°43W **171** M7
Santa Cruz Is.
Solomon Is. 10°30S 166°0E **147** C9
Santa Cruz Mts. Jamaica 17°58N 77°43W **182** a
Santa Elena Argentina 30°58S 59°47W **190** C4
Santa Elena, C.
Costa Rica 10°54N 85°56W **182** D2
Sant' Eufémia, G. di Italy 38°51N 16°4E **95** D9
Santa Eulària des Riu
Spain 38°59N 1°32E **100** C8
Santa Fé Argentina 31°35S 60°41W **190** C3
Santa Fé Spain 37°11N 3°43W **89** H7
Santa Fe U.S.A. 35°41N 105°57W **169** J11
Santa Fé □ Argentina 31°50S 60°55W **190** C3
Santa Fé do Sul Brazil 20°13S 50°56W **189** H8
Santa Filomena Brazil 9°6S 45°50W **189** B1
Santa Fiora Italy 42°50N 11°35E **93** E8
Santa Gertrudis Spain 39°0N 1°26E **100** C7
Santa Giulia France 41°32N 9°17E **73** G13
Santa Giustina Italy 46°10N 12°5E **93** B9
Santa Helena Brazil 2°14S 45°18W **189** A1
Santa Inês Bahia, Brazil 13°17S 39°48W **189** C3
Santa Inés Maranhão,
Brazil 3°39S 45°20W **189** A1
Santa Inés Spain 38°32N 5°37W **89** G5
Santa Inés, I. Chile 54°0S 73°0W **192** D2
Santa Isabel Argentina 36°10S 66°54W **190** D2
Santa Isabel do Morro
Brazil 11°34S 50°40W **187** F8
Santa Lucía Corrientes,
Argentina 28°58S 59°5W **190** B4
Santa Lucía San Juan,
Argentina 31°30S 68°30W **190** C2
Santa Lucia Spain 37°35N 0°58W **91** H4
Santa Lucia Uruguay 34°27S 56°24W **190** C4
Santa Lucia Range
U.S.A. 36°0N 121°20W **170** K5
Santa Luzia Brazil 19°47S 43°57W **189** E2
Santa Luzia C. Verde Is. 16°50N 24°35W **134** b
Santa Margalida Spain 39°42N 3°6E **100** B10
Santa Margarita
Argentina 38°28S 61°35W **190** D3
Santa Margarita
U.S.A. 35°23N 120°37W **170** K6
Santa Margarita →
U.S.A. 33°13N 117°23W **171** M9
Santa Margarita, I.
Mexico 24°27N 111°50W **180** C2
Santa Margherita Italy 38°58N 8°58E **94** D1
Santa Margherita Ligure
Italy 44°20N 9°11E **92** D6
Santa María Argentina 26°40S 66°0W **190** B2
Santa Maria Azores 36°58N 25°6W **134** a
Santa Maria Brazil 29°40S 53°48W **191** B5
Santa Maria C. Verde Is. 16°31N 22°53W **134** b
Santa Maria U.S.A. 34°57N 120°26W **171** L6
Santa María →
Mexico 31°0N 107°14W **180** A3
Santa María, B. de
Mexico 25°4N 108°6W **180** B3
Santa Maria, C. de
Portugal 36°58N 7°53W **89** J3
Santa María, Vol.
Guatemala 14°45N 91°33W **182** D1
Santa Maria Cápua Vétere
Italy 41°5N 14°15E **95** A7
Santa Maria da Feira
Portugal 40°55N 8°35W **88** E2
Santa Maria da Vitória
Brazil 13°24S 44°12W **189** C2
Santa María de Guadalupe =
Guadalupe Spain 39°27N 5°17W **89** F5
Santa María del Camí
Spain 39°38N 2°47E **100** B9
Santa Maria di Léuca, C.
Italy 39°47N 18°22E **95** C11
Santa María do Suaçuí
Brazil 18°12S 42°25W **189** D2
Santa María la Real de Nieva
Spain 41°4N 4°24W **88** D6
Santa Marinella Italy 42°2N 11°52E **93** F8
Santa Marta Colombia 11°15N 74°13W **186** A4
Santa Marta, Sierra Nevada de
Colombia 10°55N 73°50W **186** A4
Santa Marta de Tormes
Spain 40°57N 5°38W **88** E5
Santa Marta Grande, C.
Brazil 28°43S 48°50W **191** B6
Santa Maura = Lefkada
Greece 38°40N 20°43E **98** C2
Santa Monica U.S.A. 34°1N 118°29W **171** M8
Santa Monica Mts. ○
U.S.A. 34°4N 118°44W **171** L8
Santa Olalla Spain 40°2N 4°25W **88** E6
Santa Olalla del Cala
Spain 37°54N 6°14W **89** H4
Santa Paula U.S.A. 34°21N 119°4W **171** L7
Santa Pola Spain 38°13N 0°35W **91** G4
Santa Ponça Spain 39°30N 2°28E **100** B9
Santa Quitéria Brazil 4°20S 40°10W **189** D10
Santa Rita de Cássia
Brazil 11°0S 44°32W **189** C2
Santa Rosa La Pampa,
Argentina 36°40S 64°17W **190** D3
Santa Rosa San Luis,
Argentina 32°21S 65°10W **190** C2
Santa Rosa Beni,
Bolivia 14°10S 66°53W **188** F5
Santa Rosa Pando,
Bolivia 10°36S 67°20W **188** F5
Santa Rosa Brazil 27°52S 54°29W **191** B5
Santa Rosa Puno, Peru 14°30S 70°50W **188** G4
Santa Rosa San Martin,
Peru 6°41S 76°37W **188** B2
Santa Rosa Calif.,
U.S.A. 38°26N 122°43W **170** G4

Santa Rosa N. Mex.,
U.S.A. 34°57N 104°41W **169** J11
Santa Rosa and San Jacinto
Mts. ○ U.S.A. 33°28N 116°20W **171** M10
Santa Rosa Beach
U.S.A. 30°22N 86°14W **178** E3
Santa Rosa de Copán
Honduras 14°47N 88°46W **182** D2
Santa Rosa de Río Primero
Argentina 31°8S 63°20W **190** C3
Santa Rosa del Sara
Bolivia 17°7S 63°35W **186** G6
Santa Rosa I. Calif.,
U.S.A. 33°58N 120°6W **171** M6
Santa Rosa I. Fla.,
U.S.A. 30°20N 86°50W **179** E3
Santa Rosa Range
U.S.A. 41°45N 117°40W **168** F5
Santa Rosalía Mexico 27°19N 112°17W **180** B2
Santa Sylvina
Argentina 27°50S 61°10W **190** B3
Santa Tecla = Nueva San
Salvador El Salv. 13°40N 89°18W **182** D2
Santa Teresa Argentina 33°25S 60°47W **190** C3
Santa Teresa Australia 24°8S 134°22E **150** C1
Santa Teresa Brazil 19°55S 40°36W **189** D2
Santa Teresa Mexico 25°17N 97°51W **181** B5
Santa Teresa △
Uruguay 33°57S 53°31W **191** C5
Santa Teresa di Riva
Italy 37°57N 15°22E **95** E8
Santa Teresa Gallura
Italy 41°14N 9°11E **94** A2
Santa Teresita
Argentina 36°32S 56°41W **190** D4
Santa Uxía de Ribeira = Ribeira
Spain 42°36N 8°58W **88** C2
Santa Vitória do Palmar
Brazil 33°32S 53°25W **191** C5
Santa Ynez → U.S.A. 34°41N 120°36W **171** L6
Santa Ynez Mts.
U.S.A. 34°30N 120°0W **171** L6
Santa Ysabel U.S.A. 33°7N 116°40W **171** M10
Santadi Italy 39°5N 8°43E **94** C1
Santaella Spain 37°34N 4°51W **89** H6
Santai China 31°5N 104°58E **116** B5
Santaluz Brazil 11°15S 39°22W **189** C3
Santana Brazil 12°2S 44°5W **189** C2
Santana Madeira 32°48N 16°52W **100** D3
Sântana Romania 46°20N 21°30E **80** D6
Santana, Coxilha de
Brazil 30°50S 55°35W **191** C4
Santana da Ipanema
Brazil 9°22S 37°14W **189** B3
Santana do Livramento
Brazil 30°55S 55°30W **191** C4
Santander Spain 43°27N 3°51W **88** B7
Santander Jiménez
Mexico 24°13N 98°28W **181** C5
Santanilla, Is.
Honduras 17°22N 83°57W **182** C3
Santanyí Spain 39°20N 3°5E **100** B10
Santaquin U.S.A. 39°59N 111°47W **168** G8
Santarcángelo di Romagna
Italy 44°4N 12°26E **93** D9
Santarém Brazil 2°25S 54°42W **187** D8
Santarém Portugal 39°12N 8°42W **89** F2
Santarém □ Portugal 39°10N 8°40W **89** F2
Santaren Channel
W. Indies 24°0N 79°30W **182** B4
Santee U.S.A. 32°50N 116°58W **171** N10
Santee → U.S.A. 33°7N 79°17W **177** E15
Santéramo in Colle Italy 40°49N 16°45E **95** B9
Santerno → Italy 44°34N 11°58E **93** D8
Santhià Italy 45°22N 8°10E **92** C5
Santi-Quaranta = Sarandë
Albania 39°52N 19°55E **96** G3
Santiago = Río Grande de
Santiago →
Mexico 21°36N 105°26W **180** C3
Santiago = São Tiago
C. Verde Is. 15°0N 23°40W **134** b
Santiago Brazil 29°11S 54°52W **191** B5
Santiago Canary Is. 28°2N 17°12W **100** F2
Santiago Chile 33°26S 70°40W **190** C1
Santiago Panama 8°0N 81°0W **182** E3
Santiago Peru 4°27S 77°38W **186** D3
Santiago Phil. 16°41N 121°33E **119** A6
Santiago → Peru 4°27S 77°38W **186** D3
Santiago, C. Chile 50°46S 75°7W **192** D1
Santiago, Punta de
Eq. Guin. 3°12N 8°40E **139** E6
Santiago de Chuco Peru 8°9S 78°11W **188** E2
Santiago de Compostela
Spain 42°52N 8°37W **88** C2
Santiago de Cuba Cuba 20°0N 75°49W **182** C4
Santiago de los Caballeros
Dom. Rep. 19°30N 70°40W **183** C5
Santiago del Estero
Argentina 27°50S 64°15W **190** B3
Santiago del Estero □
Argentina 27°40S 63°15W **190** B3
Santiago del Teide
Canary Is. 28°17N 16°48W **100** F3
Santiago do Cacém
Portugal 38°1N 8°42W **89** G2
Santiago Ixcuintla
Mexico 21°49N 105°13W **180** C3
Santiago Jamiltepec
Mexico 16°17N 97°49W **181** D5
Santiago Papasquiaro
Mexico 25°3N 105°25W **180** C3
Santiago Pinotepa Nacional
Mexico 16°19N 98°1W **181** D5
Santiaguillo, L. de
Mexico 24°48N 104°48W **180** C4
Santiguila Mali 11°0S 44°32W **138** C3
Santillana del Mar Spain 43°24N 4°6W **88** B6
Santisteban del Puerto
Spain 38°17N 3°15W **89** G7
Santo → Peru 8°56S 78°37W **188** E2
Santo Amaro Brazil 12°30S 38°43W **189** C3
Santo Anastácio Brazil 21°58S 51°39W **191** A5
Santo André Brazil 23°39S 46°29W **191** A6
Santo Ângelo Brazil 28°15S 54°15W **191** B5
Sant' Ángelo Lodigiano
Italy 45°14N 9°25E **92** C6
Santo Antão C. Verde Is. 16°52N 25°10W **134** b
Sant' Antíoco Italy 39°4N 8°27E **94** C1
Santo Antônio de Jesus
Brazil 12°58S 39°16W **189** C3

Santo Antônio do Içá
Brazil 3°5S 67°57W **186** D5
Santo Antônio do Leverger
Brazil 15°52S 56°5W **187** G7
Santo Domingo
Dom. Rep. 18°30N 69°59W **183** C6
Santo Domingo
Mexico 25°29N 111°55W **180** B2
Santo Domingo Nic. 12°14N 84°59W **182** D3
Santo Domingo, Cay
Bahamas 21°25N 75°45W **182** B4
Santo Domingo de la Calzada
Spain 42°26N 2°57W **90** C2
Santo Domingo de los Colorados
Ecuador 0°15S 79°9W **186** D3
Santo Domingo Pueblo
U.S.A. 35°31N 106°22W **169** J10
Santo Domingo Tehuantepec =
Tehuantepec
Mexico 16°21N 95°13W **181** D5
Sant' Egídio alla Vibrata
Italy 42°49N 13°42E **93** F10
Santo Stéfano di Camastro
Italy 38°1N 14°22E **95** D7
Santo Tirso Portugal 41°21N 8°28W **88** D2
Santo Tomás Mexico 31°33N 116°24W **180** A1
Santo Tomás Peru 14°26S 72°8W **188** C3
Santo Tomé Argentina 28°16S 56°5W **191** B4
Santo Tomé de Guayana = Ciudad
Guayana Venezuela 8°0N 62°30W **186** B6
Santomera Spain 38°4N 1°3W **91** G3
Santoña Spain 43°29N 3°27W **88** B7
Santorini Greece 36°23N 25°27E **99** E7
Santos Brazil 24°0S 46°20W **191** A6
Santos, Sierra de los Spain 38°7N 5°12W **89** G5
Santos Dumont Brazil 22°55S 43°10W **191** A7
Santuario de Aves Laguna
Colorada △ Bolivia 22°10S 67°45W **190** A2
Sanuki Japan 34°19N 134°10E **113** G7
Sanur Indonesia 8°41S 115°15E **119** K18
Sanwer India 22°59N 75°50E **124** H6
Sanxenxo Spain 42°24N 8°49W **88** C2
Sanxia Shuiku China 30°3N 107°58E **116** B6
Sanxiang China 22°21N 113°25E **111** a
Sanya China 18°14N 109°29E **117** a
Sanyuan China 34°35N 108°58E **114** G5
São Bartolomeu de Messines
Portugal 37°15N 8°17W **89** H2
São Benedito Brazil 4°3S 40°53W **189** D10
São Bento Brazil 2°42S 44°50W **189** A2
São Bento do Norte Brazil 5°4S 36°2W **189** B3
São Bernardo do Campo
Brazil 23°45S 46°34W **191** A6
São Borja Brazil 28°39S 56°0W **191** B4
São Brás de Alportel
Portugal 37°8N 7°37W **89** H3
São Caitano Brazil 8°21S 36°6W **189** B3
São Carlos Brazil 22°0S 47°50W **191** A6
São Cristóvão Brazil 11°1S 37°15W **189** C3
São Domingos Brazil 13°25S 46°19W **189** C1
São Domingos
Guinea-Biss. 12°19N 16°13W **138** C1
São Domingos do Maranhão
Brazil 5°42S 44°22W **189** B2
São Filipe C. Verde Is. 15°2N 24°30W **134** b
São Francisco Brazil 16°0S 44°50W **189** C2
São Francisco →
Brazil 10°30S 36°24W **189** C3
São Francisco do Maranhão
Brazil 6°15S 42°52W **189** B2
São Francisco do Sul
Brazil 26°15S 48°36W **191** B6
São Gabriel Brazil 30°20S 54°20W **191** B5
São Gabriel da Palha
Brazil 18°47S 40°39W **189** D2
São Gonçalo Brazil 22°48S 43°5W **191** A7
São Gotardo Brazil 19°19S 46°3W **189** D1
São Hill Tanzania 8°20S 35°12E **143** D4
São João da Boa Vista
Brazil 22°0S 46°52W **191** A6
São João da Madeira
Portugal 40°54N 8°30W **88** E2
São João da Pesqueira
Portugal 41°8N 7°24W **88** D3
São João da Ponte
Brazil 15°56S 44°1W **189** D2
São João del Rei Brazil 21°8S 44°15W **191** A7
São João do Araguaia
Brazil 5°23S 48°46W **187** E9
São João do Paraíso
Brazil 15°19S 42°1W **189** D2
São João do Piauí Brazil 8°21S 42°15W **189** B2
São João dos Patos
Brazil 6°30S 43°42W **189** B2
São Joaquim Brazil 28°18S 49°56W **191** B6
São Joaquim □ Brazil 28°12S 49°37W **191** B6
São Joaquim da Barra
Brazil 20°35S 47°53W **189** E1
São Jorge Azores 38°38N 28°3W **134** a
São Jorge, Pta. de
Madeira 32°50N 16°53W **100** D3
São José Brazil 27°38S 48°39W **191** B6
São José da Laje Brazil 9°1S 36°3W **189** B3
São José de Mipibu Brazil 6°5S 35°15W **189** B3
São José do Norte Brazil 32°1S 52°3W **191** C5
São José do Peixe Brazil 7°24S 42°34W **189** B2
São José do Rio Preto
Brazil 20°50S 49°20W **191** A6
São José dos Campos
Brazil 23°7S 45°52W **191** A6
São Leopoldo Brazil 29°50S 51°10W **191** B5
São Lourenço Brazil 22°7S 45°3W **191** A6
São Lourenço →
Brazil 17°53S 57°27W **187** G7
São Lourenço, Pta. de
Madeira 32°44N 16°24W **100** D3
São Lourenço do Sul
Brazil 31°22S 51°58W **191** C5
São Luís Brazil 2°39S 44°15W **189** A2
São Luís do Curu Brazil 3°40S 39°14W **189** A3
São Luís Gonzaga Brazil 28°25S 55°0W **191** B5
São Marcos → Brazil 18°15S 47°37W **189** D1
São Marcos, B. de Brazil 2°0S 44°0W **189** A2
São Martinho da Cortiça
Portugal 40°18N 8°9W **88** E2
São Mateus Brazil 18°44S 39°50W **189** D3
São Mateus → Brazil 18°35S 39°44W **189** D3
São Mateus do Sul
Brazil 25°52S 50°23W **191** B5
São Miguel Azores 37°47N 25°30W **134** a

São Miguel do Oeste
Brazil 26°45S 53°34W **191** B5
São Miguel dos Campos
Brazil 9°47S 36°5W **189** B3
São Nicolau C. Verde Is. 16°20N 24°20W **134** b
São Nicolau → Brazil 5°45S 42°2W **189** B2
São Paulo Atl. Oc. 0°56N 29°22W **56** F9
São Paulo Brazil 23°32S 46°38W **191** A6
São Paulo □ Brazil 22°0S 49°0W **191** A6
São Paulo de Olivença
Brazil 3°27S 68°48W **186** D5
São Pedro Atl. Oc. 0°56N 29°22W **56** F9
São Pedro do Sul Portugal 40°46N 8°4W **88** E2
São Rafael Brazil 5°47S 36°55W **189** B3
São Raimundo das Mangabeiras
Brazil 7°1S 45°29W **189** B1
São Raimundo Nonato
Brazil 9°1S 42°42W **189** B2
São Romão Brazil 16°22S 45°4W **189** D1
São Roque Madeira 32°46N 16°48W **100** D3
São Roque, C. de Brazil 5°30S 35°16W **189** B3
São Sebastião, I. de
Brazil 23°50S 45°18W **191** A6
São Sebastião do Paraíso
Brazil 20°54S 46°59W **191** A6
São Teotónio Portugal 37°30N 8°42W **89** H2
São Tiago C. Verde Is. 15°0N 23°40W **134** b
São Tomé C. Verde Is. 5°58S 36°4W **189** B3
São Tomé
São Tomé & Príncipe 0°10N 6°39E **132** F4
São Tomé, C. de Brazil 22°0S 40°59W **189** E2
São Tomé & Príncipe ■
Africa 0°12N 6°39E **133** F4
São Vicente Brazil 23°57S 46°23W **191** A6
São Vicente C. Verde Is. 17°0N 25°0W **134** b
São Vicente Madeira 32°48N 17°3W **100** D2
São Vicente, C. de Portugal 37°0N 9°0W **89** H1
Saona, I. Dom. Rep. 18°10N 68°40W **183** C6
Saône → France 45°44N 4°50E **71** C6
Saône-et-Loire □ France 46°30N 4°50E **71** F11
Saonek Indonesia 0°22S 130°55E **119** E8
Saoura, O. → Algeria 29°0N 0°55W **136** C3
Sapam, Ao Thailand 8°0N 98°26E **121** a
Sápanca Turkey 40°41N 30°16E **104** B4
Sápão → Brazil 11°1S 45°32W **189** C1
Saparua Indonesia 3°33S 128°40E **119** E7
Sapé Brazil 7°6S 35°13W **189** B3
Sape Indonesia 8°34S 118°59E **119** F5
Sapele Nigeria 5°50N 5°40E **139** D6
Sapelo I. U.S.A. 31°25N 81°12W **178** D8
Sapelo Sound U.S.A. 31°30N 81°10W **178** D8
Sapes Greece 41°2N 25°43E **97** E9
Saphane Turkey 39°1N 29°13E **99** B11
Sapi △ Zimbabwe 15°48S 29°42E **143** F2
Sapienza Greece 36°45N 21°43E **98** E3
Sapo △ Liberia 5°15N 8°30W **138** D3
Sapo, Serra do Burkina Faso 12°3N 1°35W **139** C4
Saposoa Peru 6°55S 76°45W **188** E2
Sapotskina Belarus 53°49N 23°40E **82** E10
Sapouy Burkina Faso 11°34N 1°44W **139** C4
Sapozhok Russia 53°59N 40°41E **86** D5
Sapphire Australia 23°28S 147°43E **154** C4
Sappho U.S.A. 48°4N 124°16W **170** B2
Sapporo Japan 43°0N 141°21E **112** C10
Sapporo New Chitose ✈ (CTS)
Japan 42°46N 141°41E **112** C10
Sapri Italy 40°4N 15°38E **95** B8
Sapt Kosi → Nepal 26°32N 86°56E **125** F12
Sapudi Indonesia 7°6S 114°20E **119** G16
Sapulpa U.S.A. 35°59N 96°5W **176** D6
Saqqez Iran 36°15N 46°20E **105** D12
Sar Dasht Āzarbāyjān-e Gharbī,
Iran 36°9N 45°28E **105** D11
Sar Dasht Khuzestān,
Iran 32°32N 48°52E **129** C6
Sar-e Pol Afghan. 36°10N 66°0E **109** E7
Sar-e Pol □ Afghan. 36°20N 65°50E **109** E7
Sar Gachineh = Yāsūj
Iran 30°31N 51°31E **129** D6
Sar Planina Macedonia 42°0N 21°0E **96** G4
Sara Burkina Faso 11°40N 3°53W **138** C4
Šara → Serbia 42°12N 21°0E **96** D5
Sara Buri = Saraburi
Thailand 14°30N 100°55E **120** E3
Sarāb Iran 37°55N 47°40E **105** D12
Sarābādī Iraq 33°1N 44°48E **128** C5
Saraburi Thailand 14°30N 100°55E **120** E3
Saradiya India 21°34N 70°2E **124** J4
Saraféré Mali 15°50N 3°40W **138** B4
Saragossa = Zaragoza
Spain 41°39N 0°53W **90** D4
Saraguro Ecuador 3°35S 79°16W **186** D3
Sarahs Turkmenistan 36°32N 61°13E **129** B9
Sarai Naurang Pakistan 32°50N 70°47E **124** C4
Saraikela India 22°42N 85°56E **125** H11
Saraipali India 21°20N 82°59E **125** D7
Saraiu Romania 44°43N 28°10E **81** B8
Sarajevo Bos.-H. 43°52N 18°26E **80** G3
Sarakhs = Sarahs
Turkmenistan 36°32N 61°13E **129** B9
Sarakhs Iran 36°32N 61°9E **108** B8
Saran, Gunung
Indonesia 0°30S 111°25E **118** E4
Saranac Lake U.S.A. 44°20N 74°10W **175** B10
Saranac Lakes U.S.A. 44°20N 74°28W **175** B10
Saranda Tanzania 5°45S 34°59E **142** D3
Sarandë Albania 39°52N 19°55E **96** G3
Sarandi del Yi Uruguay 33°18S 55°38W **191** C4
Sarandí Grande
Uruguay 33°44S 56°20W **190** C4
Sarangani B. Phil. 6°0N 125°13E **119** C7
Sarangani Is. Phil. 5°25N 125°25E **119** C7
Sarangarh India 21°30N 83°5E **125** D7
Saransk Russia 54°10N 45°10E **86** D8
Sarapul Russia 56°28N 53°48E **86** C9
Sarasota U.S.A. 27°20N 82°32W **179** H7
Sarata Ukraine 46°1N 29°40E **81** E14
Saratoga Calif.,
U.S.A. 37°16N 122°2W **170** H4
Saratoga Wyo.,
U.S.A. 41°27N 106°49W **168** F10
Saratoga L. U.S.A. 43°5N 73°47W **175** C11
Saratoga Springs
U.S.A. 43°5N 73°47W **175** C11
Saratov Russia 51°30N 46°2E **86** E8
Saravan Laos 15°43N 106°25E **12**
Sarawak □ Malaysia 2°0N 113°0E **12**
Saray Tekirdağ, Turkey 41°26N 27°55E **97**
Saray Van, Turkey 38°38N 44°9E **105**
Saraya Senegal 12°50N 11°45W **13**
Saraycık Turkey 39°1N 29°49E **99**
Sarayköy Turkey 37°55N 28°54E **99**
Saraylar Turkey 40°30N 27°40E **97**
Sarayönü Turkey 38°16N 32°24E **10**
Sarbāz Iran 26°38N 61°19E **12**
Sarbīsheh Iran 32°30N 59°40E **12**
Sárbogárd Hungary 46°50N 18°40E **8**
Sarca → Italy 45°52N 10°52E **9**
Sarcelles France 49°1N 2°23E **7**
Sarda → India 27°21N 81°23E **12**
Sardar Sarovar Dam
India 21°50N 73°50E **12**
Sardarshahr India 28°30N 74°29E **12**
Sardegna □ Italy 40°0N 9°0E **9**
Sardhana India 29°9N 77°39E **12**
Sardina, Pta. Canary Is. 28°9N 15°44W **10**
Sardinia = Sardegna □
Italy 40°0N 9°0E **9**
Sardis Turkey 38°28N 27°58E **99**
Sardīs Turkey 38°28N 27°58E **17**
Sārdūīyeh = Dar Mazār
Iran 29°14N 57°20E **12**
Sarek △ Sweden 67°22N 17°55E **6**
Saren Indonesia 8°26S 115°34E **119**
S'Arenal Spain 39°30N 2°45E **10**
Sarentino Italy 46°38N 11°21E **9**
Sarera, G. of Indonesia 2°0S 135°0E **14**
Saréyamou Mali 16°7N 3°10W **13**
Sargasso Sea Atl. Oc. 27°0N 72°0W **158**
Sargent U.S.A. 33°26N 84°52W **17**
Sargodha Pakistan 32°10N 72°40E **12**
Sarh Chad 9°5N 18°23E **13**
Sarhala Ivory C. 8°22N 6°8W **13**
Sarhro, Jebel Morocco 31°6N 5°0W **13**
Sārī Iran 36°30N 53°4E **12**
Sari d'Orcino France 42°3N 8°49E **7**
Saria India 21°38N 83°22E **125**
Sariab Pakistan 30°6N 66°59E **12**
Saribeyler Turkey 39°24N 27°35E **9**
Sarıcakaya Turkey 39°59N 30°22E **10**
Sarıgöl Turkey 38°14N 28°41E **10**
Sarıkamış Turkey 40°22N 42°35E **10**
Sarikaya Turkey 39°29N 35°22E **10**
Sarikei Malaysia 2°8N 111°30E **11**
Sarıköy Turkey 40°12N 27°37E **9**
Sarila India 25°46N 79°41E **12**
Sarina Australia 21°22S 149°13E **15**
Sariñena Spain 41°47N 0°10W **9**
Sarıoğlan Turkey 39°5N 35°59E **10**
Sarita U.S.A. 27°13N 97°47W **18**
Sariwŏn N. Korea 38°31N 125°46E **115**
Sariyar Barajı Turkey 40°2N 31°33E **10**
Sarıyer Turkey 41°10N 29°3E **9**
Sarız Turkey 38°28N 36°30E **10**
Sarju → India 27°21N 81°23E **12**
Sark U.K. 49°25N 2°22E **7**
Sarkad Hungary 46°47N 21°23E **8**
Sarkari Tala India 27°39N 70°52E **12**
Şarkışla Turkey 39°21N 36°25E **10**
Sarlat-la-Canéda France 44°54N 1°13E **7**
Sărmăşag Romania 47°21N 22°50E **8**
Sărmaşu Romania 46°45N 24°13E **8**
Sarmi Indonesia 1°49S 138°44E **14**
Sarmiento Argentina 45°35S 69°5W **19**
Sarmiento, Mt. Chile 54°27S 70°50W **19**
Sarmizegetusa Romania 45°31N 22°47E **8**
Särna Sweden 61°41N 13°8E **6**
Sarnen Switz. 46°53N 8°13E **7**
Sarnia Canada 42°58N 82°23W **17**
Sarno Italy 40°49N 14°37E **9**
Sarnthein = Sarentino
Italy 46°38N 11°21E **9**
Särö Sweden 57°31N 11°57E **6**
Sarolangun Indonesia 2°19S 102°42E **11**
Saronikos Kolpos Greece 37°45N 23°45E **9**
Saronno Italy 45°38N 9°2E **9**
Saros Körfezi Turkey 40°30N 26°15E **97**
Sárospatak Hungary 48°18N 21°33E **8**
Sarov Russia 54°56N 43°19E **8**
Sarpsborg Norway 59°16N 11°7E **6**
Sarqan Kazakhstan 45°24N 79°55E **10**
Sarracín Spain 42°15N 3°45W **8**
Sarralbe France 49°0N 7°1E **7**
Sarre = Saar → Europe 49°41N 6°32E **6**
Sarre Italy 45°40N 7°15E **9**
Sarre-Union France 48°57N 7°4E **7**
Sarrebourg France 48°43N 7°3E **7**
Sarreguemines France 49°5N 7°4E **7**
Sarria Spain 42°49N 7°29W **8**
Sarrión Spain 40°9N 0°49W **9**
Sarro Mali 13°40N 5°15W **13**
Sarroch Italy 39°4N 9°8E **9**
Sarsing Iraq 37°2N 43°20E **10**
Sarstedt Germany 52°14N 9°52E **6**
Sartell U.S.A. 45°37N 94°12W **17**
Sartène France 41°38N 8°58E **7**
Sarthe □ France 48°0N 0°10E **7**
Sarthe → France 47°33N 0°31W **7**
Sartilly France 48°45N 1°13E **7**
Saruhanlı Turkey 38°44N 27°34E **9**
Sărulești Romania 44°25N 26°39E **8**
Saruna → Pakistan 26°31N 67°7E **12**
Sārūr Azerbaijan 39°32N 45°5E **105**
Sárvár Hungary 47°15N 16°56E **8**
Sarvar India 26°4N 75°0E **12**
Sarvestān Iran 29°20N 53°10E **12**
Särvfjället Sweden 62°42N 13°30E **6**
Sárviz → Hungary 46°24N 18°41E **8**
Sary-Tash Kyrgyzstan 39°44N 73°15E **10**
Sarych, Mys Ukraine 44°25N 33°45E **8**
Saryesik-Atyraū Qumy
Kazakhstan 45°30N 76°0E **10**
Sarykamyshskoye, Ozero □
Turkmenistan 41°56N 57°15E **8**
Sarykemer Kazakhstan 42°55N 71°15E **10**
Sarykenggir →
Kazakhstan 48°22N 67°59E **10**
Saryköl Kazakhstan 53°4N 64°18E **10**
Sarykolskiy Khrebet
Tajikistan 38°30N 74°40E **10**
Saryözek Kazakhstan 44°22N 77°59E **10**
Saryqamysh Köli
Turkmenistan 41°56N 57°15E **8**

...yshaghan
...azakhstan 46°12N 73°38E **109** C8
...ysū ➤ Kazakhstan 45°12N 66°36E **109** C10
...eau France 44°7N 9°58E **92** D6
...ana Italy 47°31N 2°48W **70** E4
...an Gir India 21°10N 70°36E **124** J4
...aram India 24°57N 84°5E **125** G11
...ebo Japan 33°10N 129°43E **113** H4
...er Kangri India 34°50N 77°50E **125** B7
...katchewan □
...anada 54°40N 106°0W **163** C7
...katchewan ➤
...anada 53°37N 100°40W **163** C8
...katoon Canada 52°10N 106°38W **163** C6
...kylakh Russia 71°55N 114°1E **107** B12
...aya △ Nic. 13°45N 85°4W **182** D2
...lburg S. Africa 26°46S 27°49E **145** C4
...on Turkey 38°19N 41°24E **105** C9
...avo Russia 54°25N 41°55E **86** C5
...sandra △ Ivory C. 4°55N 6°58E **138** E3
...sandra ➤ Ivory C. 4°58N 6°5W **138** E3
...sandra-Marahoué □
...ory C. 6°58N 6°26W **138** D3
...sari Italy 40°43N 8°34E **94** B1
...sia Australia 10°2S 142°51E **150** a
...snitz Germany 54°29N 13°39E **76** A9
...so Marconi Italy 44°24N 11°15E **93** D8
...socorvaro Italy 43°47N 12°3E **93** E9
...soferrato Italy 43°26N 12°51E **93** E9
...suolo Italy 44°33N 10°47E **92** D7
...ago Spain 41°19N 0°21W **90** D4
...amala Finland 61°20N 22°54E **63** E12
...own Liberia 4°45N 8°27W **138** E3
...vad India 18°20N 74°2E **126** E2
...vk, Ozero Ukraine 45°45N 29°40E **81** E14
...vkol Kazakhstan 46°35N 81°0E **109** C10
...-Misaki Japan 31°0N 130°40E **113** J5
...dougou Mali 12°25N 11°25W **138** C2
...kunta □ Finland 61°45N 23°0E **60** F20
...ama-Soukoura
...ory C. 7°55N 4°27W **138** D4
...ara India 17°44N 73°58E **126** F1
...ara S. Africa 24°29S 31°47E **145** B5
...arwa India 23°55N 84°16E **125** H11
...ellite Beach U.S.A. 28°10N 80°36W **179** G6
...r Sweden 60°21N 15°45E **62** D9
...vó Mexico 27°57N 106°7W **180** B3
...lla ➤ U.S.A. 30°59N 81°29W **178** E8
...po Peru 11°15S 74°25W **188** C3
...ca Russia 55°3N 59°1E **108** A5
...aj = Sutlej ➤
...akistan 29°23N 71°3E **124** E4
...nala Hills Maharashtra,
...dia 20°15N 74°40E **126** D2
...nala Hills Telangana,
...dia 19°45N 78°45E **126** E4
...a India 24°35N 80°50E **125** G9
...r Bos.-H. 44°11N 16°37E **93** D13
...raljaújhely Hungary 48°25N 21°41E **80** B6
...ura India 22°40N 78°15E **124** H8
...ura Ra. India 21°25N 76°10E **126** D3
...up Germany 54°41N 9°36E **76** A5
...una-Sendai Japan 31°50N 130°20E **113** J5
...unan-Shotō Japan 30°0N 130°0E **113** K5
...ahip Thailand 12°41N 100°54E **120** F3
...enapalle India 16°25N 80°6E **127** F5
...n Mare Romania 47°46N 22°55E **80** C7
...n Mare □ Romania 47°45N 23°0E **80** D8
...ai Indonesia 3°50S 115°27E **125** F5
...n Thailand 6°43N 100°2E **121** J3
...rnina ➤ Brazil 12°15S 58°10W **186** F7
...ce Argentina 30°5S 58°46W **190** C4
...ceda Mexico 25°46N 101°19W **180** B4
...cillo Mexico 28°1N 105°17W **180** B3
...da Norway 59°40N 6°20E **61** G12
...e Brazil 10°30S 40°24W **189** C12
...ðarkrókur Iceland 65°45N 19°40W **60** D4
...r Arabia ⊡ Asia 26°0N 44°0E **128** C4
...erland Germany 51°12N 7°59E **74** C3
...geen ➤ Canada 44°30N 81°22W **174** B3
...gues U.S.A. 42°5N 73°57W **175** D11
...gues France 44°58N 3°32E **72** D7
...gus U.S.A. 34°25N 118°32W **171** L8
...ion France 45°41N 0°55W **72** C3
...k Centre U.S.A. 45°44N 94°57W **172** C6
...k Rapids U.S.A. 45°35N 94°10W **172** C6
...da Germany 51°1N 9°29E **74** C5
...ieu France 47°17N 4°14E **71** E11
...lt France 44°6N 5°24E **73** D9
...anada 46°30N 84°20W **164** C3
...lt Ste. Marie
...anada 46°30N 84°20W **164** C3
...lt Ste. Marie
...S.A. 46°30N 84°21W **173** B11
...malkol Kazakhstan 53°17N 68°6E **109** B7
...mlaki Indonesia 7°55S 131°0E **119** F8
...mur France 47°15N 0°5W **70** E6
...ndatti India 15°45N 75°7E **127** G2
...nders, C. N.Z. 45°53S 170°45E **155** F5
...nders I. Antarctica 57°48S 26°28W **55** B1
...nders Pt. Australia 27°52S 125°38E **149** E4
...ni Nigeria 11°42N 6°44E **138** C3
...rimo Angola 9°40S 20°12E **140** F4
...salito U.S.A. 37°51N 122°29W **170** H4
...vage, Côte France 45°50N 1°30W **72** C2
...veterre-de-Béarn
...France 43°24N 0°57W **72** E3
...é-Vaussais France 46°8N 0°8E **72** B4
...a Honduras 15°32N 86°15W **182** D2
...a Italy 40°24N 17°35E **95** B10
...a Serbia 44°10N 20°50E **85** C9
...age U.S.A. 47°27N 104°21W **168** C11
...age I. = Niue ⊡
...ic. Oc. 19°2S 169°54W **157** J11
...age River Australia 41°31S 145°14E **151** G4
...ai'i Samoa 13°28S 172°24W **157** C13
...alou Benin 7°57N 1°58E **139** D5
...anes □ Ivory C. 9°30N 6°0W **138** D3
...anna-la-Mar
...maica 18°10N 78°10W **182** a
...annah U.S.A. 32°5N 81°6W **178** C8
...annah Ga., U.S.A. 32°5N 81°6W **178** C8
...annah Mo., U.S.A. 39°56N 94°50W **172** F6
...annah Tenn.,
...S.A. 35°14N 88°15W **177** D10
...annah ➤ U.S.A. 32°2N 80°53W **178** C9
...annah Beach = Tybee Island
...S.A. 32°1N 80°51W **178** C9
...annakhet Laos 16°30N 104°49E **120** D5
...ant L. Canada 50°16N 90°44W **164** B1
...ant Lake U.S.A. 50°14N 90°40W **164** B1

Savantvadi India 15°55N 73°54E **127** G1
Savanur India 14°59N 75°21E **127** G2
Savarkundla = Kundla
India 21°21N 71°25E **124** J4
Savaştepe Turkey 39°22N 27°42E **99** B9
Savda India 21°9N 75°56E **126** D2
Savé Benin 8°2N 2°29E **139** D5
Save ➤ France 43°47N 1°17E **72** E5
Save ➤ Mozam. 21°16S 34°0E **145** B5
Sāveh Iran 35°2N 50°20E **129** C6
Savelugu Ghana 9°38N 0°54W **139** D4
Savenay France 47°20N 1°55W **70** E5
Săveni Romania 47°57N 26°52E **81** C11
Saverdun France 43°14N 1°34E **72** E5
Saverne France 48°43N 7°20E **71** D14
Savigliano Italy 44°38N 7°40E **92** D4
Savigny-sur-Braye
France 47°53N 0°49E **70** E7
Sávio ➤ Italy 44°19N 12°20E **93** D9
Šavnik Montenegro 42°59N 19°10E **96** D3
Savo Finland 62°45N 27°30E **60** E22
Savoie □ France 45°26N 6°25E **73** C10
Savona Italy 44°17N 8°30E **92** D5
Savona U.S.A. 42°17N 77°13W **174** D7
Savonlinna Finland 61°52N 28°53E **84** B5
Savoy = Savoie □ France 62°45N 27°30E **60** E22
Savsat Turkey 41°15N 42°20E **105** B10
Sävsjö Sweden 57°20N 14°40E **63** G8
Savur Turkey 37°34N 40°53E **105** C9
Savusavu Fiji 16°34S 179°15E **154** a
Savusavu B. Fiji 16°45S 179°15E **154** a
Savuti Botswana 18°37S 24°5E **144** A3
Sawahlunto Indonesia 0°40S 100°52E **118** E2
Sawai Indonesia 3°0S 129°5E **119** E7
Sawai Madhopur India 26°0N 76°25E **124** F7
Sawahklok Thailand 17°19N 99°50E **120** D2
Sawang Daen Din
Thailand 17°28N 103°28E **120** D4
Sawankhalok Thailand 17°19N 99°50E **120** D2
Sawara Japan 35°55N 140°30E **113** G10
Sawatch Range
U.S.A. 39°0N 106°30W **168** G10
Sawel Mt. U.K. 54°50N 7°2W **64** B4
Sawi Thailand 10°14N 99°5E **121** G2
Sawla Ghana 9°17N 2°25W **138** D4
Sawmills Zimbabwe 19°30S 28°2E **143** F2
Sawtell Australia 30°19S 153°6E **153** A10
Sawtooth △ U.S.A. 44°0N 114°50W **168** D6
Sawtooth Range
U.S.A. 44°3N 114°58W **168** D6
Sawu Indonesia 10°35S 121°50E **119** F6
Sawu Sea Indonesia 9°30S 121°50E **119** F6
Saxby ➤ Australia 18°25S 140°53E **150** B3
Saxmundham U.K. 52°13N 1°30E **67** E9
Saxon Switzerland = Sächsische
Schweiz △ Germany 50°55N 14°10E **76** E10
Saxony = Sachsen □
Germany 50°55N 13°10E **76** E9
Saxony, Lower =
Niedersachsen □
Germany 52°50N 9°0E **76** C4
Saxton U.S.A. 40°13N 78°15W **174** F6
Say Mali 13°50N 4°57W **138** C4
Say Niger 13°8N 2°22E **139** C5
Saya Nigeria 9°30N 3°18E **139** D5
Sayabec Canada 48°35N 67°41W **165** C6
Sayaboury Laos 19°15N 101°45E **120** C3
Sayán Peru 11°8S 77°12W **188** C2
Sayan, Vostochnyy
Russia 54°0N 96°0E **107** D10
Sayan, Zapadnyy
Russia 52°30N 94°0E **107** D10
Sayano-Shushenskoye Vdkhr.
Russia 52°50N 91°22E **107** D10
Sayanogorsk Russia 53°5N 91°23E **107** D10
Saydā Lebanon 33°35N 35°25E **130** B4
Sayhandulaan = Öldziyt
Mongolia 44°40N 109°1E **114** B5
Sayhūt Yemen 15°12N 51°10E **131** D5
Saykhin Kazakhstan 48°50N 46°47E **87** F8
Saylac Somalia 11°21N 43°30E **131** E3
Saynshand = Buyant-Uhaa
Mongolia 44°55N 110°11E **114** B6
Sayre Okla., U.S.A. 35°18N 99°38W **176** D5
Sayre Pa., U.S.A. 41°59N 76°32W **175** E8
Sayreville U.S.A. 40°28N 74°22W **175** F10
Sayula Mexico 19°52N 103°36W **180** D4
Say'ün Yemen 15°56N 48°47E **131** D4
Sayward Canada 50°21N 125°55W **162** C3
Sazanit Albania 40°30N 19°20E **96** F3
Sázava ➤ Czech Rep. 49°53N 14°24E **76** B7
Sazin Pakistan 35°35N 73°30E **125** B5
Sazlika ➤ Bulgaria 41°59N 25°50E **97** E9
Sbeïtla Tunisia 35°12N 9°7E **136** A5
Scaër France 48°2N 3°42W **70** D3
Scalea Italy 39°49N 15°47E **95** C8
Scalloway U.K. 60°9N 1°17W **65** A7
Scalpay U.K. 57°18N 6°0W **65** D3
Scandia Canada 50°20N 112°2W **162** C6
Scandiano Italy 44°36N 10°43E **92** D7
Scandicci Italy 43°45N 11°11E **93** E8
Scandinavia Europe 64°0N 12°0E **60** E15
Scansano Italy 42°41N 11°20E **93** F8
Scapa Flow U.K. 58°53N 3°3W **65** C5
Scappoose U.S.A. 45°45N 122°53W **170** E4
Scarámia, Capo Italy 36°47N 14°29E **95** F7
Scarborough
Trin. & Tob. 11°11N 60°42W **183** D7
Scarborough U.K. 54°17N 0°24W **66** C7
Scargill N.Z. 42°56S 172°58E **155** D4
Scarisoara △ Romania 46°34N 24°33E **81** F9
Scartaglin Ireland 51°44N 10°15W **64** E1
Scarp U.K. 58°1N 7°8W **65** C1
Scarpe-Escaut ⊂ France 50°23N 3°2E **71** B10
Scarsdale Australia 37°41S 143°39E **152** D5
Scebeli = Shabeelle ➤
Somalia 2°0N 44°0E **131** G3
Scedro Croatia 43°6N 16°43E **93** E13
Schaal See Germany 53°40N 10°57E **76** B6
Schaalsee ⊂ Germany 53°40N 10°57E **76** B6
Schaffhausen Switz. 47°42N 8°39E **74** E4
Schagen Neths. 52°49N 4°48E **69** B4
Schaghticoke U.S.A. 42°54N 73°35W **175** D11
Schärding Austria 48°27N 13°27E **78** D6
Scharhörn Germany 53°58N 8°24E **76** B4
Scheessel Germany 53°10N 9°29E **76** B5
Schefferville Canada 54°48N 66°50W **165** B6
Scheibbs Austria 48°1N 15°9E **78** C8

Schelde ➤ Belgium 51°15N 4°16E **69** C4
Schell Creek Ra.
U.S.A. 39°25N 114°40W **168** G6
Schellsburg U.S.A. 40°3N 78°39W **174** F6
Schenectady U.S.A. 42°49N 73°57W **175** D11
Schenevus U.S.A. 42°33N 74°50W **175** D10
Scherfede Germany 51°32N 9°2E **76** D5
Schesslitz Germany 49°58N 11°1E **77** F7
Schiedam Neths. 51°55N 4°25E **69** C4
Schiermonnikoog Neths. 53°30N 6°15E **69** A6
Schiermonnikoog △
Neths. 53°30N 6°15E **69** A6
Schiltigheim France 48°35N 7°45E **71** D14
Schinousa Greece 36°53N 25°31E **99** F7
Schio Italy 45°43N 11°21E **93** C8
Schiphol, Amsterdam ✈ (AMS)
Neths. 52°18N 4°45E **69** B4
Schiza Greece 36°41N 21°40E **98** E3
Schladming Austria 47°23N 13°41E **78** D6
Schlanders = Silandro
Italy 46°38N 10°46E **92** B7
Schlei ➤ Germany 54°40N 10°0E **76** A5
Schleiden Germany 50°31N 6°29E **76** E2
Schleiz Germany 50°35N 11°49E **76** E7
Schleswig Germany 54°31N 9°34E **76** A5
Schleswig-Holstein □
Germany 54°30N 9°30E **76** A5
Schlüchtern Germany 50°20N 9°32E **77** E5
Schmalkalden Germany 50°44N 10°26E **76** E6
Schmölln Germany 50°54N 12°19E **76** E8
Schneeberg Austria 47°47N 15°48E **78** D8
Schneeberg Germany 50°35N 12°38E **76** E8
Schneverdingen Germany 53°7N 9°48E **76** B5
Schoelcher Martinique 14°36N 61°7W **182** c
Schoharie U.S.A. 42°40N 74°19W **175** D10
Schoharie Cr. ➤
U.S.A. 42°57N 74°18W **175** D10
Schokland Neths. 52°38N 5°46E **69** B5
Scholls U.S.A. 45°24N 122°56W **170** E4
Schönberg
Mecklenburg-Vorpommern,
Germany 53°52N 10°56E **76** B6
Schönberg Schleswig-Holstein,
Germany 54°23N 10°21E **76** A6
Schönbuch ⊂ Germany 48°35N 9°2E **77** G5
Schönebeck Germany 52°2N 11°44E **76** C7
Schongau Germany 47°47N 10°53E **77** H6
Schöningen Germany 52°8N 10°56E **76** C6
Schopfheim Germany 47°38N 7°50E **77** H3
Schorndorf Germany 48°47N 9°32E **77** G5
Schortens Germany 53°31N 7°56E **76** B3
Schouten I. Australia 42°20S 148°20E **151** G4
Schouten Is. = Supiori
Indonesia 1°0S 136°0E **119** E9
Schouwen Neths. 51°43N 3°45E **69** C3
Schramberg Germany 48°13N 8°22E **77** G4
Schrankogel Austria 47°3N 11°7E **78** D4
Schreiber Canada 48°45N 87°20W **164** C2
Schrems Austria 48°47N 15°4E **78** C8
Schrobenhausen
Germany 48°34N 11°16E **77** G7
Schroffenstein Namibia 27°11S 18°42E **144** C2
Schroon Lake U.S.A. 43°50N 73°46W **175** C11
Schruns Austria 47°5N 9°56E **78** D2
Schuler Canada 50°20N 110°6W **163** C6
Schumacher Canada 48°30N 81°16W **164** C3
Schurz U.S.A. 38°57N 118°49W **168** G4
Schuyler U.S.A. 41°27N 97°4W **172** E5
Schuylerville U.S.A. 43°6N 73°35W **175** C11
Schuylkill ➤ U.S.A. 39°53N 75°12W **175** G9
Schuylkill Haven
U.S.A. 40°37N 76°11W **175** F8
Schwabach Germany 49°19N 11°2E **77** F7
Schwaben □ Germany 48°20N 10°30E **77** G6
Schwäbisch-Fränkischer Wald ⊂
Germany 49°0N 9°30E **77** G5
Schwäbisch Gmünd
Germany 48°48N 9°47E **77** G5
Schwäbisch Hall Germany 49°6N 9°44E **77** F5
Schwäbische Alb
Germany 48°20N 9°30E **77** G5
Schwabmünchen
Germany 48°11N 10°46E **77** G6
Schwandorf Germany 49°20N 12°7E **77** F8
Schwaner, Pegunungan
Indonesia 1°0S 112°30E **118** E4
Schwanewede Germany 53°14N 8°35E **76** B4
Schwarmstedt Germany 52°39N 9°38E **76** C5
Schwarze Elster ➤
Germany 51°48N 12°50E **76** D8
Schwarzenberg Germany 50°32N 12°47E **76** E8
Schwarzrand Namibia 25°37S 16°50E **144** C2
Schwarzwald ⊂ Germany 48°30N 8°20E **77** G4
Schwatka Mts.
U.S.A. 67°20N 156°30W **166** B8
Schwaz Austria 47°20N 11°44E **78** D4
Schwechat Austria 48°9N 16°28E **79** C9
Schwechat, Wien ✈ (VIE)
Austria 48°7N 16°35E **79** C9
Schwedt Germany 53°3N 14°16E **76** B10
Schweinfurt Germany 50°3N 10°14E **77** E6
Schweiz = Switzerland ■
Europe 46°30N 8°0E **77** J4
Schweizer-Reneke
S. Africa 27°11S 25°18E **144** C3
Schwenningen = Villingen-
Schwenningen Germany 48°3N 8°26E **77** G4
Schwerin Germany 53°36N 11°22E **76** B7
Schweriner See Germany 53°45N 11°26E **76** B7
Schwetzingen Germany 49°22N 8°35E **77** F4
Schwyz Switz. 47°2N 8°39E **77** H4
Schwyz □ Switz. 47°2N 8°39E **77** H4
Sciacca Italy 37°31N 13°3E **94** E6
Scicli Italy 36°47N 14°42E **95** F7
Sciliar-Catinaccio △
Italy 46°28N 11°35E **93** B8
Scilla Italy 38°15N 15°43E **95** D8
Scilly, Isles of U.K. 49°56N 6°22W **67** H1
Ścinawa Poland 51°25N 16°26E **83** D9
Scione Greece 39°57N 23°36E **96** G7
Scioto ➤ U.S.A. 38°44N 83°1W **173** F12
Scituate U.S.A. 42°12N 70°44W **175** D13
Scobey U.S.A. 48°47N 105°25W **168** B11
Scone Australia 32°5S 150°52E **153** B9
Scone U.K. 56°25N 3°24W **65** E5
Scordia Italy 37°18N 14°51E **95** E7
Scoresby Sund
Greenland 70°20N 23°0W **57** C6
Scoresbysund = Ittoqqortoormiit
Greenland 70°20N 23°0W **57** C6
Scornicești Romania 44°34N 24°33E **81** F9

Sedziszów Małopolski
Poland 50°5N 21°45E **83** H8
Seebad Ahlbeck
Germany 53°56N 14°10E **76** B10
Seefeld in Tirol Austria 47°19N 11°13E **78** D4
Seehausen Germany 52°54N 11°45E **76** C7
Seeheim Namibia 26°50S 17°45E **144** D2
Seeheim-Jugenheim
Germany 49°49N 8°40E **77** F4
Seekoei ➤ S. Africa 30°18S 25°1E **144** E4
Seeley's Bay Canada 44°29N 76°14W **175** B8
Seelow Germany 52°32N 14°23E **76** C10
Seemandra = Andhra Pradesh □
India 18°0N 79°0E **126** F4
Sées France 48°38N 0°10E **70** D7
Seesen Germany 51°54N 10°10E **76** D6
Seevetal Germany 51°25N 10°11E **76** B6
Seewinkel = Neusiedler See-
Seewinkel △ Austria 47°50N 16°45E **79** D9
Sefadu Turkey 38°10N 26°50E **99** C8
Seferihisar Turkey 38°10N 26°50E **99** C8
Séféto Mali 14°8N 9°49W **138** C3
Sefophe Botswana 22°11S 27°58E **145** B4
Sefrou Morocco 33°52N 4°52W **136** B3
Sefton N.Z. 43°15S 172°41E **155** D4
Sefwi Bekwai Ghana 6°10N 2°25W **138** D4
Segamat Malaysia 2°30N 102°50E **121** L4
Segarcea Romania 44°6N 23°43E **81** F8
Ségbana Benin 10°55N 3°42E **139** C5
Segbwema S. Leone 8°0N 11°0W **138** D2
Segebarg Germany 53°7N 9°48E **76** B5
Segersta Sweden 61°16N 16°39E **62** C10
Segesta Italy 37°56N 12°50E **94** E5
Seget Indonesia 1°24S 130°58E **119** E8
Seggueur, O. ➤ Algeria 32°14N 1°48E **136** B4
Segmon Sweden 59°17N 13°3E **62** E7
Segonzac France 45°36N 0°14W **72** C3
Segorbe Spain 39°50N 0°30W **90** F4
Ségou Mali 13°30N 6°16W **138** C3
Ségou □ Mali 14°0N 6°0W **138** C3
Segovia = Coco ➤
Cent. Amer. 15°0N 83°8W **182** D3
Segovia Spain 40°57N 4°10W **88** E6
Segovia □ Spain 40°55N 4°10W **88** E6
Segré France 47°40N 0°52W **70** E6
Segre ➤ Spain 41°40N 0°43E **90** D5
Séguéla Ivory C. 7°55N 6°40W **138** D3
Séguélon Ivory C. 9°13N 7°7W **138** D3
Séguénéga Burkina Faso 13°25N 1°58W **138** C4
Seguin U.S.A. 29°34N 97°58W **176** G6
Segundo ➤ Argentina 30°53S 62°44W **190** C3
Segura ➤ Spain 38°3N 0°44W **91** G4
Segura, Sierra de Spain 38°5N 2°45W **91** G2
Seh Konj, Kūh-e Iran 30°6N 57°30E **129** D8
Seh Qal'eh Iran 33°40N 58°24E **129** C8
Sehitwa Botswana 20°30S 22°30E **144** B3
Sehlabathebe △ Lesotho 29°53S 29°7E **145** C4
Sehore India 23°10N 77°5E **124** H7
Sehwan Pakistan 26°28N 67°53E **124** F2
Seia Portugal 40°25N 7°43W **88** E3
Seica Mare Romania 46°1N 24°7E **81** D9
Seikan Tunnel Japan 41°28N 140°10E **112** D10
Seil U.K. 56°18N 5°38W **65** E3
Seiland Norway 70°25N 23°15E **60** A20
Seilhac France 45°22N 1°43E **72** C5
Seiling U.S.A. 36°9N 98°56W **176** C5
Seille ➤ Moselle, France 49°7N 6°11E **71** C13
Seille ➤ Saône-et-Loire,
France 46°31N 4°57E **71** F11
Sein, Î. de France 48°2N 4°52W **70** D2
Seinäjoki Finland 62°40N 22°51E **60** E20
Seine ➤ France 49°26N 0°26E **70** C7
Seine, B. de la France 49°40N 0°40W **70** C6
Seine-et-Marne □ France 48°35N 3°0E **70** D10
Seine-Maritime □ France 49°40N 1°0E **70** C7
Seine-St-Denis □ France 48°58N 2°24E **70** D9
Seini Romania 47°44N 23°21E **81** C8
Seirijai Lithuania 54°14N 23°49E **82** D10
Seistan = Sīstān Asia 30°50N 61°0E **129** D9
Seistan, Daryācheh-ye = Sīstān,
Daryācheh-ye Iran 31°0N 61°0E **129** D9
Seitseminen △ Finland 61°52N 23°25E **60** E20
Sejerø Denmark 55°54N 11°9E **63** J5
Sejerø Bugt Denmark 55°53N 11°15E **63** J5
Sejny Poland 54°6N 23°21E **82** D10
Sejong S. Korea 36°35N 127°15E **115** F14
Sekayu Indonesia 2°51S 103°51E **118** E2
Seke Tanzania 3°20S 33°31E **142** C3
Sekenke Tanzania 4°18S 34°11E **142** C3
Sekhira Tunisia 34°20N 10°5E **136** B6
Seki Turkey 36°40N 29°30E **99** E11
Sekondi-Takoradi Ghana 4°58N 1°45W **138** E4
Sekseüil Kazakhstan 47°58N 61°10E **108** C6
Seksna Russia 59°13N 38°30E **84** C6
Sekudai Malaysia 1°33N 103°39E **121** d
Sekuma Botswana 24°36S 23°50E **144** B3
Selah U.S.A. 46°39N 120°32W **168** C3
Selama Malaysia 5°12N 100°42E **121** K3
Selangor □ Malaysia 3°10N 101°30E **121** L3
Selárgius Italy 39°16N 9°10E **94** C2
Selaru Indonesia 8°9S 131°0E **119** F8
Selatan, Selat Malaysia 5°15N 100°20E **121** c
Selawik L. U.S.A. 66°30N 160°45W **166** B7
Selb Germany 50°10N 12°7E **76** E8
Selby U.K. 53°47N 1°5W **66** E6
Selca Croatia 43°20N 16°50E **93** E13
Selçuk Turkey 37°56N 27°22E **99** D9
Selden U.S.A. 39°33N 100°34W **172** F3
Sele ➤ Italy 40°29N 14°56E **95** B7
Selebi-Phikwe
Botswana 21°58S 27°48E **145** B4
Selemdzha ➤ Russia 51°42N 128°53E **107** D13
Selendi Manisa, Turkey 38°43N 28°50E **99** C11
Selendi Manisa, Turkey 38°46N 27°53E **99** C10
Selenga = Selenge Mörön ➤
Asia 52°16N 106°16E **110** A10
Selenge Mörön ➤
Asia 52°16N 106°16E **110** A10
Selenicë Albania 40°33N 19°39E **96** F3
Selenter See Germany 54°18N 10°26E **76** A6
Sélestat France 48°16N 7°26E **71** D14
Seletan, Tanjung
Indonesia 4°10S 114°40E **118** E4
Sélibabi Mauritania 15°10N 12°15E **138** B2
Seliger, Ozero Russia 57°15N 33°0E **84** D5
Seligman U.S.A. 35°20N 112°53W **174** J7
Selima, Pik Russia 73°29N 54°0E **106** B6
Selim Turkey 40°30N 42°46E **105** B10
Šelima Sudan 21°22N 29°19E **137** C12
Senj Croatia 45°0N 14°58E **93** D11

Selinda Spillway ➤
Botswana 18°35S 23°10E **144** A3
Sélingué, L. de Mali 11°37N 8°14W **138** C3
Selinsgrove U.S.A. 40°48N 76°52W **174** F8
Selizharovo Russia 56°51N 33°27E **84** D7
Selkirk Man., Canada 50°10N 96°55W **163** C9
Selkirk Ont., Canada 42°49N 79°56W **174** D5
Selkirk U.K. 55°33N 2°50W **65** F6
Selkirk I. = Horse I.
Canada 53°20N 99°6W **163** C9
Selkirk Mts. Canada 51°15N 117°40W **160** D8
Sellafield U.K. 54°25N 3°29W **66** C4
Sellia Greece 35°12N 24°23E **101** D6
Sellières France 46°50N 5°32E **71** F12
Sells U.S.A. 31°55N 111°53W **169** L8
Sellye Hungary 45°52N 17°51E **80** E2
Selma Ala., U.S.A. 32°25N 87°1W **177** E11
Selma Calif., U.S.A. 36°34N 119°37W **168** H4
Selma N.C., U.S.A. 35°32N 78°17W **177** D15
Selmer U.S.A. 35°10N 88°36W **177** D10
Selongey France 47°36N 5°11E **71** E12
Selouane Morocco 35°7N 2°57W **136** A3
Selous □ Tanzania 8°37S 37°42E **143** D4
Selowandoma Falls
Zimbabwe 21°15S 31°50E **143** G3
Selpele Indonesia 0°1S 130°5E **119** E8
Selsey Bill U.K. 50°43N 0°47W **67** G7
Selsø Russia 53°22N 34°4E **84** F8
Seltz France 48°54N 8°4E **71** D15
Sélune ➤ France 48°38N 1°22W **70** D5
Selva = La Selva del Camp
Spain 41°13N 1°8E **90** D6
Selva Argentina 29°50S 62°0W **190** B3
Selva Spain 39°46N 2°54E **100** B9
Selva Lancandona = Montes
Azules △ Mexico 16°21N 91°3W **181** D6
Selvagens, Ilhas
Madeira 30°5N 15°55W **134** B2
Selvas Brazil 6°30S 67°0W **188** B4
Selwyn L. Canada 60°0N 104°30W **163** B8
Selwyn Mts. Canada 63°0N 130°0W **160** C5
Selyatyn Ukraine 47°50N 25°12E **81** C10
Seman ➤ Albania 40°47N 19°30E **96** F3
Semarang Indonesia 7°0S 110°26E **118** F4
Semarapura = Klungkung
Indonesia 8°32S 115°24E **119** K18
Sembabule Uganda 0°4S 31°25E **142** C3
Sembawang Singapore 1°27N 103°50E **121** d
Sembiang Indonesia 8°28S 115°11E **119** J18
Şemdinli Turkey 37°18N 44°35E **105** D11
Sémé Senegal 15°4N 13°41W **138** C2
Semenic-Cheile Caraşului △
Romania 45°8N 22°5E **80** E7
Semenivka Chernihiv,
Ukraine 52°8N 32°36E **85** F7
Semenivka Kremenchuk,
Ukraine 49°37N 33°10E **85** H7
Semenov Russia 56°43N 44°30E **86** B7
Semeru Indonesia 8°4S 112°55E **119** H15
Semey Kazakhstan 50°30N 80°10E **109** D10
Semiluki Russia 51°41N 39°2E **85** G10
Seminoe Res. U.S.A. 42°9N 106°55W **168** E10
Seminole Fla., U.S.A. 27°50N 82°47W **179** F7
Seminole Okla., U.S.A. 35°14N 96°41W **176** D6
Seminole Tex., U.S.A. 32°43N 102°39W **176** E3
Seminole, L. U.S.A. 30°43N 84°52W **178** F3
Seminole Draw ➤
U.S.A. 32°27N 102°20W **176** E3
Semipalatinsk = Semey
Kazakhstan 50°30N 80°10E **109** D10
Semirara Is. Phil. 12°0N 121°20E **119** E6
Semisopochnoi I.
U.S.A. 51°55N 179°36E **166** E3
Semitau Indonesia 0°29N 111°57E **118** D4
Semiyarka Kazakhstan 50°55N 78°23E **109** D10
Semmering P. Austria 47°41N 15°45E **78** D8
Semnān Iran 35°40N 53°23E **129** C7
Semnān □ Iran 36°0N 54°0E **129** C7
Sempoorna Malaysia 4°30N 118°33E **119** D5
Semuda Indonesia 2°51S 112°58E **118** E4
Semur-en-Auxois France 47°30N 4°20E **71** E11
Sena Bolivia 11°32S 67°11W **188** C4
Sena Iran 28°27N 51°36E **129** D6
Sena Mozam. 17°30N 35°0E **143** F4
Sena ➤ Bolivia 11°31S 67°11W **188** C4
Sena Madureira Brazil 9°5S 68°45W **188** B4
Senador Pompeu Brazil 5°40S 39°20W **189** B3
Senaki Georgia 42°15N 42°1E **87** B7
Senang, Pulau Singapore 1°11N 103°52E **121** d
Senanga Zambia 16°7S 23°16E **141** H4
Senatobia U.S.A. 34°37N 89°58W **177** D10
Sencelles Spain 39°39N 2°54E **100** B9
Sendai = Satsuma-Sendai
Japan 31°50N 130°20E **113** J5
Sendai Japan 38°15N 140°53E **112** E10
Sendai-Wan Japan 38°15N 141°0E **112** E10
Sendenhorst Germany 51°50N 7°47E **76** D3
Senden Nordrhein-Westfalen,
Germany 51°52N 7°22E **76** D3
Sendhwa India 21°41N 75°6E **124** J6
Sendurjana India 21°32N 78°17E **126** D4
Sene ➤ Ghana 8°2N 1°13W **138** D4
Senec Slovak Rep. 48°12N 17°23E **77** G10
Seneca U.S.A. 34°41N 82°57W **177** D13
Seneca Falls U.S.A. 42°55N 76°48W **175** D8
Seneca L. U.S.A. 42°40N 76°54W **175** D8
Senecaville L. U.S.A. 39°55N 81°25W **174** G3
Senegal ■ W. Afr. 14°30N 14°30W **138** C2
Senegal ➤ W. Afr. 15°48N 16°32W **138** B1
Senegambia Africa 12°45N 12°0W **130** E2
Senekal S. Africa 28°20S 27°36E **145** C4
Senftenberg Germany 51°30N 14°1E **76** D9
Senga Hill Zambia 9°19S 31°11E **143** D3
Senge Khambab = Indus ➤
Pakistan 24°20N 67°47E **124** G2
Sengerema Tanzania 2°43S 32°30E **142** C3
Senggigi Indonesia 8°29S 116°2E **119** J19
Sengiley Russia 53°58N 48°46E **86** D8
Senguerr ➤ Argentina 45°35S 68°55W **192** C3
Senhor-do-Bonfim
Brazil 10°30S 40°10W **189** D3
Senica Slovak Rep. 48°41N 17°25E **77** G10
Sengília Italy 43°43N 13°13E **93** E9
Senio ➤ Italy 44°35N 12°15E **93** D9
Senirkent Turkey 38°6N 30°34E **99** C12
Senise Italy 40°9N 16°17E **95** B9

Senja Norway 69°25N 17°30E 60 B17
Senkaku-Shotō
  E. China Sea 25°45N 123°30E 113 M1
Senlis France 49°13N 2°35E 71 C9
Senmonorom
  Cambodia 12°27N 107°12E 120 F6
Senneterre Canada 48°25N 77°15W 164 C4
Senno Belarus 54°45N 29°43E 84 E5
Sénnori Italy 40°47N 8°35E 94 B1
Seno Laos 16°35N 104°50E 120 D5
Senoia U.S.A. 33°18N 84°33W 178 B5
Senonches France 48°34N 1°2E 70 D8
Senorbì Italy 39°32N 9°8E 94 C2
Senožeče Slovenia 45°43N 14°3E 93 C11
Senqu = Orange →
  S. Africa 28°41S 16°28E 144 C2
Sens France 48°11N 3°15E 71 D10
Senta Serbia 45°55N 20°3E 80 E5
Sentery = Lubao
  Dem. Rep. of the Congo 5°17S 25°42E 142 D2
Sentinel U.S.A. 32°52N 113°13W 169 K7
Šentjur Slovenia 46°14N 15°24E 93 B12
Sentosa Singapore 1°16N 103°50E 121 d
Senwabarana S. Africa 23°17S 29°7E 145 B4
Senya Beraku Ghana 5°28N 0°31W 139 D4
Seo de Urgel = La Seu d'Urgell
  Spain 42°22N 1°23E 90 C6
Seogwipo S. Korea 33°13N 126°34E 115 H14
Seohara India 29°15N 78°33E 125 E8
Seonath → India 21°44N 82°28E 125 J10
Seondha India 26°9N 78°48E 125 F8
Seongnam S. Korea 37°26N 127°8E 115 F14
Seoni India 22°5N 79°30E 125 H8
Seoni Malwa India 22°27N 77°28E 124 H8
Seonsan S. Korea 36°14N 128°17E 115 F15
Seoriuarayan India 21°45N 82°34E 126 D6
Seosan S. Korea 36°47N 126°27E 115 F14
Seoul S. Korea 37°31N 126°58E 115 F14
Sepang Malaysia 2°49N 101°44E 121 L3
Separation Pt. N.Z. 40°47S 172°59E 155 A7
Sepīdān Iran 30°20N 52°5E 129 D7
Sepo-ri N. Korea 38°57N 127°25E 115 E14
Sępólno Krajeńskie
  Poland 53°26N 17°30E 82 E4
Sepone Laos 16°45N 106°13E 120 D6
Sępopol Poland 54°16N 21°2E 82 D8
Sept-Îles Canada 50°13N 66°22W 165 B6
Septemvri Bulgaria 42°13N 24°6E 97 D8
Sepúlveda Spain 41°18N 3°45W 88 D7
Sequeros Spain 40°31N 6°2W 88 E4
Sequim U.S.A. 48°5N 123°6W 170 B3
Sequoia △ U.S.A. 36°30N 118°30W 170 J8
Serafimovich Russia 49°36N 42°43E 86 F6
Seraing Belgium 50°35N 5°32E 69 D5
Serakhis → Cyprus 35°13N 32°55E 101 D11
Seram Indonesia 3°10S 129°0E 119 E7
Seram Sea Indonesia 2°30S 128°30E 119 E7
Serampore = Shrirampur
  India 22°44N 88°21E 125 H13
Serang Indonesia 6°8S 106°10E 119 G12
Serangoon Singapore 1°23N 103°54E 121 d
Serasan Indonesia 2°29N 109°4E 118 D3
Seravezza Italy 43°59N 10°13E 92 E7
Şerbettar Turkey 41°27N 26°46E 97 E10
Serbia ■ Europe 43°20N 20°0E 96 C4
Şercaia Romania 45°49N 25°9E 81 E10
Serdar Turkmenistan 39°4N 56°23E 129 B8
Serdobsk Russia 52°28N 44°10E 86 D7
Serebryansk
  Kazakhstan 49°41N 83°17E 109 C10
Sered' Slovak Rep. 48°17N 17°44E 79 C10
Seredka Russia 58°12N 28°10E 84 C5
Serednye Ukraine 48°32N 22°30E 80 B7
Şereflikoçhisar Turkey 38°56N 33°32E 104 C5
Seregno Italy 45°39N 9°12E 92 C6
Seremban Malaysia 2°43N 101°53E 121 L3
Serengeti △ Tanzania 2°11S 35°0E 142 C3
Serengeti Plain Tanzania 2°40S 35°0E 142 C4
Serenje Zambia 13°14S 30°15E 143 E3
Seret → Ukraine 48°37N 25°52E 81 B10
Sereth = Siret →
  Romania 45°24N 28°1E 81 E12
Sergach Russia 55°30N 45°30E 86 C7
Sergeevka Kazakhstan 53°52N 67°24E 109 B7
Sergen Turkey 41°41N 27°42E 97 E11
Sergeya Kirova, Ostrova
  Russia 77°30N 89°0E 107 B10
Sergino Russia 62°25N 65°12E 106 C7
Sergipe □ Brazil 10°30S 37°30W 189 C3
Sergiyev Posad Russia 56°20N 38°10E 84 D10
Serhetabat
  Turkmenistan 35°20N 62°18E 129 C9
Seria Brunei 4°37N 114°23E 118 D4
Serian Malaysia 1°10N 110°31E 118 D4
Seriate Italy 45°41N 9°43E 92 C6
Sericho Kenya 1°5N 39°5E 142 B4
Sérifontaine France 49°20N 1°45E 71 C8
Sérifos Greece 37°9N 24°30E 98 D6
Sérignan France 43°17N 3°17E 72 E7
Sérigny → Canada 56°47N 66°0W 165 A6
Serik Turkey 36°55N 31°7E 104 D4
Seringapatam Reef
  Australia 13°38S 122°5E 148 B3
Serinhisar Turkey 37°36N 29°18E 99 D11
Seririt Indonesia 8°12S 114°56E 119 J17
Serishâbâd Iran 35°14N 47°36E 105 C12
Serkout Algeria 23°56N 6°47E 136 D5
Sermaize-les-Bains
  France 48°47N 4°54E 71 D11
Sermata Indonesia 8°15S 128°50E 119 F7
Sermersooq □ Greenland 68°0N 40°0W 57 D7
Sermersuaq Greenland 50°0N 111°18E 93 D8
Sérmide Italy 45°0N 11°18E 92 C8
Sernovodsk Russia 53°58N 51°16E 86 D10
Sernur Russia 56°52N 49°2E 86 C8
Sernur Russia 56°52N 49°2E 86 C8
Serock Poland 52°31N 21°4E 83 F8
Serón Spain 37°20N 2°29W 91 H2
Seròs Spain 41°27N 0°24E 90 D5
Serouenout Algeria 24°18N 7°25E 136 D5
Serov Russia 59°29N 60°35E 106 D7
Serowe Botswana 22°25S 26°43E 144 B4
Serpa Portugal 37°57N 7°38W 89 H3
Serpeddi, Pta. Italy 39°22N 9°18E 94 C2
Serpentara Italy 39°8N 9°36E 94 C2
Serpentine Lakes
  Australia 28°30S 129°10E 149 E4
Serpent's Mouth = Sierpe, Bocas
  de la Venezuela 10°0N 61°30W 187 L15
Serpis → Spain 38°59N 0°9W 91 G4
Serpneve Ukraine 46°18N 29°1E 81 D14
Serpukhov Russia 54°55N 37°28E 84 E9
Serra Brazil 20°7S 40°18W 189 E2

Serra da Canastra △
  Brazil 20°3S 46°50W 189 E1
Serra da Capivara △
  Brazil 8°42S 42°15W 189 B2
Serra da Estrela ○
  Portugal 40°27N 7°33W 88 E3
Serra das Confusões □
  Brazil 8°50S 43°50W 189 B2
Serra de Mesa, Barragem de
  Brazil 14°30S 48°30W 189 C1
Serra do Cipó △ Brazil 19°14S 43°23W 189 D2
Serra do Divisor △ Brazil 8°3S 73°29W 188 B3
Serra do Navio Brazil 0°59N 52°3W 187 C8
Serra do Salitre Brazil 19°6S 46°41W 189 D1
Serra San Bruno Italy 38°35N 16°20E 95 D9
Serra Talhada Brazil 7°59S 38°18W 189 B3
Serradilla Spain 39°50N 6°9W 88 F4
Serramanna Italy 39°25N 8°55E 94 C1
Serrania San Luís △
  Paraguay 22°35S 57°22W 190 A4
Serrania San Rafael △
  Paraguay 25°30S 56°0W 191 B4
Serras d'Aire e Candeeiros ○
  Portugal 39°31N 8°48W 89 F2
Serrat, C. Tunisia 37°14N 9°10E 136 A5
Serravalle Scrivia Italy 44°43N 8°51E 92 D5
Serre-Ponçon, L. de
  France 44°22N 6°20E 73 D10
Serrejón Spain 39°49N 5°48W 88 F5
Serres France 44°26N 5°43E 73 D9
Serres Greece 41°5N 23°31E 96 E7
Serrezuela Argentina 30°40S 65°20W 190 C2
Serrinha Brazil 11°39S 39°0W 189 C3
Serrita Brazil 7°56S 39°19W 189 B3
Sersale Italy 39°1N 16°43E 95 C9
Sertã Portugal 39°48N 8°6W 88 F2
Sertânia Brazil 8°5S 37°20W 189 B3
Sertanópolis Brazil 23°4S 51°2W 191 A5
Sêrtar China 32°20N 100°41E 116 A3
Serua Indonesia 6°18S 130°1E 119 F8
Serui Indonesia 1°53S 136°10E 119 E9
Serule Botswana 21°57S 27°20E 144 B4
Servia Greece 40°11N 22°0E 96 F6
Serzedelo Portugal 41°24N 8°14W 88 D2
Ses Salines Spain 39°21N 3°3E 100 B10
Sese Is. Uganda 0°20S 32°20E 142 C3
Sesepe Indonesia 1°30S 127°59E 119 E7
Sesfontein Namibia 19°7S 13°39E 144 A1
Sesheke Zambia 17°29S 24°13E 144 A3
Sésia → Italy 45°5N 8°37E 92 C5
Sesimbra Portugal 38°28N 9°6W 89 G1
S'Espalmador Spain 38°47N 1°26E 100 C7
S'Espardell Spain 38°48N 1°29E 100 C7
Sessa Aurunca Italy 41°14N 13°56E 94 A6
S'Estanyol Spain 39°22N 2°54E 100 B9
Sestao Spain 43°18N 3°0W 90 B2
Sesto San Giovanni Italy 45°31N 9°13E 92 C6
Sestri Levante Italy 44°16N 9°24E 92 D6
Sestriere Italy 44°57N 6°53E 92 D3
Sestroretsk Russia 60°5N 29°58E 84 B6
Sestrunj Croatia 44°10N 15°0E 93 D11
Sestu Italy 39°18N 9°5E 94 C2
Setana Japan 42°26N 139°51E 112 C9
Sète France 43°25N 3°42E 72 E7
Sete Cidades △ Brazil 4°0S 41°37W 189 A2
Sete Lagoas Brazil 19°27S 44°16W 189 D2
Seti → Nepal 28°59N 81°8E 125 E9
Sétif Algeria 36°9N 5°26E 136 A5
Sétif □ Algeria 36°10N 5°30E 136 A5
Seto Japan 35°14N 137°6E 113 G8
Setonaikai Japan 34°20N 133°30E 113 G6
Setonaikai △ Japan 34°15N 133°15E 113 G6
Settat Morocco 33°0N 7°40W 136 B2
Séttimo Torinese Italy 45°9N 7°46E 92 C4
Setting L. Canada 55°0N 98°38W 163 C9
Settle U.K. 54°5N 2°16W 66 C5
Settlement, The
  Br. Virgin Is. 18°43N 64°22W 183 e
Settlers S. Africa 25°2S 28°30E 145 C4
Setúbal Portugal 38°30N 8°58W 89 G2
Setúbal □ Portugal 38°25N 8°35W 89 G2
Setúbal, B. de Portugal 38°40N 8°56W 89 G2
Seugne → France 45°42N 0°32W 72 C3
Seul, Lac Canada 50°20N 92°30W 164 B1
Seurre France 47°0N 5°8E 71 F12
Sevan Armenia 40°33N 44°56E 87 K7
Sevan, Ozero = Sevana Lich
  Armenia 40°30N 45°20E 87 K7
Sevana Lich Armenia 40°30N 45°20E 87 K7
Sevastopol Ukraine 44°35N 33°30E 85 K7
Seven Sisters Canada 54°56N 128°10W 162 C3
Sever → Spain 39°40N 7°32W 89 F3
Sévérac-le-Château France 44°20N 3°5E 72 D7
Severn → Canada 56°2N 87°36W 164 B2
Severn → U.K. 51°35N 2°40W 67 F5
Severnaya Zemlya
  Russia 79°0N 100°0E 107 B11
Severo Kosovo Kosovo 43°29N 21°27E 96 C4
Severo-Kurilsk Russia 50°40N 156°8E 107 D16
Severo-Yeniseyskiy
  Russia 60°22N 93°1E 107 C10
Severo-Zapadnyy □
  Russia 65°0N 40°0E 106 C4
Severobaykalsk
  Russia 55°39N 109°19E 107 D11
Severočeský □ Czech Rep. 50°30N 14°0E 78 A7
Severodonetsk = Syeverodonetsk
  Ukraine 48°58N 38°35E 85 H10
Severodvinsk Russia 64°27N 39°58E 106 C4
Severomoravský □
  Czech Rep. 49°38N 17°40E 79 B10
Severomorsk Russia 69°5N 33°27E 60 B25
Seversk Russia 56°36N 84°49E 106 D9
Sevier → U.S.A. 39°4N 113°6W 168 G7
Sevier Desert U.S.A. 39°40N 112°45W 168 G7
Sevier L. U.S.A. 38°54N 113°9W 168 G7
Sevilla Spain 37°23N 5°58W 89 H5
Sevilla □ Spain 37°25N 5°30W 89 H5
Seville = Sevilla Spain 37°23N 5°58W 89 H5
Seville Fla., U.S.A. 29°19N 81°30W 179 F14
Seville Ga., U.S.A. 31°58N 83°36W 178 D6
Sevlievo Bulgaria 43°2N 25°6E 97 C9
Sevnica Slovenia 46°2N 15°19E 93 B12
Sèvre-Nantaise →
  France 47°12N 1°33W 70 E5
Sèvre-Niortaise →
  France 46°28N 0°50W 72 B3
Sevsk Russia 52°10N 34°30E 85 F8
Sewa → S. Leone 7°20N 12°10W 138 D2
Sewani India 28°58N 75°39E 124 E6
Seward Alaska, U.S.A. 60°7N 149°27W 160 D2

Seward Nebr., U.S.A. 40°55N 97°6W 172 E5
Seward Pa., U.S.A. 40°25N 79°1W 174 F5
Seward Peninsula
  U.S.A. 65°30N 166°0W 166 B6
Sewell Chile 34°10S 70°23W 190 C1
Sewer Indonesia 5°53S 134°40E 119 F8
Sewickley U.S.A. 40°32N 80°12W 174 F4
Sexsmith Canada 55°21N 118°47W 162 B5
Seychelles ■ Ind. Oc. 5°0S 56°0E 141 b
Seyðisfjörður Iceland 65°16N 13°57W 60 D7
Seydişehir Turkey 37°25N 31°51E 104 D4
Seydvān Iran 38°34N 45°2E 105 C11
Seyhan → Turkey 36°43N 34°53E 104 D6
Seyhan Barajı Turkey 37°2N 35°18E 104 D6
Seyitgazi Turkey 39°27N 30°43E 99 B12
Seyitömer Turkey 39°34N 29°52E 99 B11
Seym → Ukraine 51°27N 32°34E 85 G7
Seymen Turkey 41°6N 27°57E 97 E11
Seymour Australia 37°2S 145°10E 153 D6
Seymour S. Africa 32°33S 26°46E 145 D4
Seymour Conn., U.S.A. 41°24N 73°4W 175 E11
Seymour Ind., U.S.A. 38°58N 85°53W 173 F11
Seymour Tex., U.S.A. 33°35N 99°16W 176 E5
Seyne France 44°21N 6°22E 73 D10
Seyssel France 45°57N 5°50E 73 C9
Sežana Slovenia 45°43N 13°41E 93 C10
Sézanne France 48°40N 3°40E 71 D10
Sezze Italy 41°30N 13°3E 94 A6
Sfântu Gheorghe Covasna,
  Romania 45°52N 25°48E 81 E10
Sfântu Gheorghe Tulcea,
  Romania 44°53N 29°36E 81 F14
Sfântu Gheorghe, Brațul →
  Romania 45°1N 29°36E 81 F14
Sfax Tunisia 34°49N 10°48E 136 B6
Sfax □ Tunisia 34°40N 10°20E 136 B6
Sha Tau Kok China 22°33N 114°13E 111 a
Sha Tin China 22°23N 114°12E 111 a
Sha Xi → China 26°35N 118°0E 117 D12
Sha Xian China 26°23N 117°45E 117 D11
Shaanxi □ China 35°0N 109°0E 114 G5
Shaba = Katanga □
  Dem. Rep. of the Congo 8°0S 25°0E 142 D2
Shaba □ Kenya 0°38N 37°48E 142 B4
Shabeelle → Somalia 2°0N 44°0E 131 G3
Shabestar Iran 38°11N 45°41E 105 C11
Shabla Bulgaria 43°31N 28°32E 97 C12
Shabogamo L. Canada 53°15N 66°30W 165 B6
Shabunda
  Dem. Rep. of the Congo 2°40S 27°16E 142 C2
Shache China 38°20N 77°10E 109 E9
Shackleton Fracture Zone
  S. Ocean 60°0S 60°0W 55 B18
Shackleton Ice Shelf
  Antarctica 66°0S 100°0E 55 C8
Shackleton Inlet
  Antarctica 83°0S 160°0E 55 E11
Shādegān Iran 30°40N 48°38E 129 D6
Shadi China 26°7N 114°47E 117 D10
Shadi India 33°24N 77°14E 125 C7
Shadrinsk Russia 56°5N 63°32E 106 D7
Shady Dale U.S.A. 33°24N 83°36W 178 B6
Shady Grove U.S.A. 30°17N 83°38W 178 E6
Shadyside U.S.A. 39°58N 80°45W 174 G4
Shaffa Nigeria 10°30N 12°6E 139 C7
Shafter U.S.A. 35°30N 119°16W 171 K7
Shaftesbury U.K. 51°0N 2°11W 67 F5
Shaftsbury U.S.A. 43°0N 73°11W 175 D11
Shag Pt. N.Z. 45°29S 170°52E 155 F5
Shag Rocks Atl. Oc. 53°0S 41°0W 56 M7
Shagamu Nigeria 6°51N 3°39E 139 D5
Shagram Pakistan 36°24N 72°20E 125 A5
Shah Alam Malaysia 3°5N 101°32E 121 L3
Shah Alizai Pakistan 29°25N 66°33E 124 E2
Shah Bunder Pakistan 24°13N 67°56E 124 G2
Shahabad Karnataka,
  India 17°10N 76°54E 126 F3
Shahabad Punjab, India 30°10N 76°55E 124 D7
Shahabad Raj., India 25°15N 77°11E 124 G7
Shahabad Ut. P., India 27°36N 79°56E 125 F8
Shahada India 21°33N 74°30E 126 D2
Shahadpur Pakistan 25°55N 68°35E 124 G3
Shahapur India 15°50N 74°43E 127 G2
Shahbā' Syria 32°52N 36°38E 130 C5
Shahdād Iran 30°30N 57°40E 129 D8
Shahdād, Namakzār-e
  Iran 30°20N 58°20E 129 D8
Shahdadkot Pakistan 27°50N 67°55E 124 F2
Shahdol India 23°19N 81°26E 125 H9
Shahe China 37°0N 114°32E 114 F8
Shahganj India 26°3N 82°44E 125 F10
Shahgarh India 27°15N 69°50E 124 F3
Shahid Rajaee Port = Bandar
  Shahid Rajaee Iran 27°7N 56°4E 129 E8
Shāhīn Shahr Iran 32°49N 51°32E 129 C6
Shahjahanpur India 27°54N 79°57E 125 F8
Shahpur = Salmās
  Iran 38°11N 44°47E 105 C11
Shahpur Karnataka,
  India 16°40N 76°48E 126 F3
Shahpur Mad. P., India 22°12N 77°58E 124 H7
Shahpur Baluchistan,
  Pakistan 28°46N 68°27E 124 E3
Shahpur Punjab,
  Pakistan 32°17N 72°26E 124 C5
Shahpur Chakar
  Pakistan 26°9N 68°39E 124 F3
Shahpura Mad. P., India 23°10N 80°45E 125 H9
Shahpura Raj., India 25°38N 74°56E 124 G6
Shahr-e Bābak Iran 30°7N 55°9E 129 D7
Shahr-e Kord Iran 32°15N 50°55E 129 C6
Shahr-i Sokhta Iran 30°34N 61°21E 129 D9
Shāhrakht Iran 33°38N 60°16E 129 C9
Shāhrezā = Qomsheh
  Iran 32°0N 51°55E 129 D6
Shahrig Pakistan 30°15N 67°40E 124 D2
Shahrisabz Uzbekistan 39°3N 66°50E 109 E7
Shahrud = Emāmrūd
  Iran 36°30N 55°0E 129 B7
Shahukou China 40°20N 112°18E 114 D7
Shaikhabad Afghan. 34°2N 68°45E 124 B3
Shajapur India 23°27N 76°21E 124 H6
Shajing China 22°44N 113°48E 111 a
Shakargarh Pakistan 32°17N 75°10E 124 C6
Shakawe Botswana 18°28S 21°49E 144 A3
Shaker Heights U.S.A. 41°28N 81°32W 174 E3
Shakhrisyabz = Shahrisabz
  Uzbekistan 39°3N 66°50E 109 E7
Shakhtersk Russia 49°10N 142°8E 107 E15
Shakhtinsk Kazakhstan 49°42N 72°35E 109 C8
Shakhty Russia 47°40N 40°16E 87 G5
Shakhunya Russia 57°40N 46°46E 86 B8

Shaki Nigeria 8°41N 3°21E 139 D5
Shākir Egypt 27°30N 33°59E 137 B3
Shakotan-Hantō
  Japan 43°10N 140°30E 112 C10
Shaksam Valley Asia 36°0N 76°20E 125 A7
Shali Russia 43°9N 45°55E 87 J7
Shalkar Köli
  Kazakhstan 50°35N 51°47E 86 E10
Shallow Lake Canada 44°36N 81°5W 174 B3
Shalqar Kazakhstan 47°48N 59°39E 108 C5
Shalqar Köli Kazakhstan 50°33N 51°40E 108 B4
Shalskiy Russia 61°48N 35°58E 84 B8
Shaluli Shan China 30°40N 99°55E 116 B2
Shām Iran 26°39N 57°21E 129 E8
Shām, Bādiyat ash Asia 32°0N 40°0E 128 C3
Shamāl Sīnī □ Egypt 30°0N 33°30E 130 E2
Shamattawa Canada 55°51N 92°5W 164 A1
Shamattawa → Canada 55°1N 85°23W 164 A2
Shamīl Iran 27°30N 56°55E 129 E8
Shamkhor = Şämkir
  Azerbaijan 40°50N 46°0E 87 K8
Shāmkūh Iran 35°47N 57°50E 129 C8
Shamli India 29°32N 77°18E 124 E7
Shammar, Jabal
  Si. Arabia 27°40N 41°0E 128 E4
Shamo = Gobi Asia 44°0N 110°0E 114 C6
Shamo, L. Ethiopia 5°45N 37°30E 131 F2
Shamokin U.S.A. 40°47N 76°34W 175 F8
Shamrock Canada 45°23N 76°59W 175 A8
Shamrock U.S.A. 35°13N 100°15W 176 D4
Shamva Zimbabwe 17°20S 31°32E 143 F3
Shan □ Burma 21°30N 98°30E 123 J21
Shan Xian China 34°50N 116°5E 114 G9
Shanchengzhen
  China 42°20N 125°20E 115 C13
Shāndak Iran 28°28N 60°27E 129 D9
Shandan China 38°45N 101°15E 110 D9
Shandong □ China 36°0N 118°0E 115 G10
Shandong Bandao
  China 37°0N 121°0E 115 F11
Shandur Pass Pakistan 36°4N 72°31E 125 A5
Shang Xian = Shangzhou
  China 33°50N 109°58E 114 H5
Shangalowe
  Dem. Rep. of the Congo 10°50S 26°30E 143 E2
Shangani Zimbabwe 19°41S 29°20E 145 A4
Shangani → Zimbabwe 18°41S 27°10E 143 F2
Shangbancheng
  China 40°50N 118°1E 115 D10
Shangcheng China 31°47N 115°26E 117 B10
Shangchuan Dao
  China 21°40N 112°50E 117 G9
Shangdu China 41°30N 113°30E 114 D7
Shanggao China 28°17N 114°55E 117 C10
Shanghai China 31°15N 121°26E 117 B13
Shanghai Shi □ China 31°0N 121°30E 117 B13
Shanghang China 25°2N 116°23E 117 E11
Shanghe China 37°20N 117°10E 115 F9
Shanglin China 23°27N 108°33E 116 F7
Shangnan China 33°32N 110°50E 114 H6
Shangqiu China 34°26N 115°36E 114 G8
Shangrao China 28°25N 117°59E 117 C11
Shangri-La = Zhongdian
  China 27°48N 99°42E 116 D2
Shangshui China 33°32N 114°35E 114 H8
Shangsi China 22°8N 107°58E 116 F6
Shangyi China 41°4N 113°57E 114 D7
Shangyou China 25°48N 114°32E 117 E10
Shangzhi China 45°22N 127°56E 115 B14
Shangzhou China 33°50N 109°58E 114 H5
Shanhetun China 44°33N 127°15E 115 B14
Shani Nigeria 10°14N 12°2E 139 C7
Shāniān Iraq 36°48N 44°14E 105 D11
Shanklin U.K. 50°38N 1°11W 67 G6
Shannon N.Z. 40°33S 175°25E 154 G4
Shannon → Ireland 52°35N 9°30W 64 D2
Shannon ✕ (SNN)
  Ireland 52°42N 8°57W 64 D3
Shannon, Mouth of the
  Ireland 52°30N 9°55E 64 D2
Shannon △ Australia 34°35S 116°25E 149 F2
Shannon Ø Greenland 75°10N 18°30W 57 B9
Shannonbridge Ireland 53°17N 8°3W 64 C3
Shannontown U.S.A. 33°53N 80°21W 178 B9
Shanshan China 42°20N 90°10E 109 D12
Shansi = Shanxi □
  China 37°0N 112°0E 114 F7
Shantar, Ostrov Bolshoy
  Russia 55°9N 137°40E 107 D14
Shantipur India 23°17N 88°25E 125 H13
Shantou China 23°18N 116°40E 117 F11
Shantung = Shandong □
  China 36°0N 118°0E 115 G10
Shanwei China 22°48N 115°20E 117 F10
Shanxi □ China 37°0N 112°0E 114 F7
Shanyang China 33°31N 109°55E 114 H5
Shanyin China 39°25N 112°56E 114 E7
Shaodong China 27°15N 111°43E 117 D8
Shaoguan China 24°48N 113°35E 117 E9
Shaoshan China 27°55N 112°33E 117 D9
Shaowu China 27°22N 117°28E 117 D11
Shaoxing China 30°0N 120°35E 117 C13
Shaoyang China 27°14N 111°25E 117 D8
Shap U.K. 54°32N 2°40W 66 C5
Shapinsay U.K. 59°3N 2°51W 65 B6
Shaqlāwah Iraq 36°23N 44°20E 105 C11
Shaqra' Si. Arabia 25°15N 45°16E 128 E5
Shar Kazakhstan 49°35N 81°0E 109 C10
Sharafkhāneh Iran 38°11N 45°29E 105 C11
Sharashova Belarus 52°34N 24°12E 83 F11
Sharavati → India 14°20N 74°25E 127 G2
Sharbaqty Kazakhstan 52°48N 78°17E 109 C9
Sharbot Lake Canada 44°46N 76°41W 175 B8
Shardara, Step
  Kazakhstan 42°20N 68°0E 109 D7
Sharhorod Ukraine 48°45N 28°5E 81 B13
Shari Japan 43°55N 144°40E 112 C12
Sharjah = Ash Shāriqah
  U.A.E. 25°23N 55°26E 129 E7
Shark B. Australia 25°30S 113°32E 149 E1
Shark Bay △ Australia 25°30S 113°0E 149 E1
Sharm el Sheikh Egypt 27°53N 34°18E 137 B3
Sharon Canada 44°6N 79°26W 174 B5
Sharon Mass., U.S.A. 42°7N 71°11W 175 D13
Sharon Pa., U.S.A. 41°14N 80°31W 174 E4
Sharon Springs Kans.,
  U.S.A. 38°54N 101°45W 172 F3
Sharon Springs N.Y.,
  U.S.A. 42°48N 74°37W 175 D10
Sharp Pt. Australia 10°58S 142°43E 150 A3

Sharpe L. Canada 54°24N 93°40W 164 B1
Sharpes U.S.A. 28°26N 80°46W 179 G9
Sharpsville U.S.A. 41°15N 80°29W 174 E4
Sharqi, Al Jabal ash
  Lebanon 33°40N 36°10E 130 B5
Sharqīya, Es Sahrâ esh
  Egypt 27°30N 32°30E 137 B3
Sharr Kosovo 42°5N 20°41E 96 D4
Sharya Russia 58°22N 45°20E 86 C7
Shashemene Ethiopia 7°13N 38°33E 131 F2
Shashi Botswana 21°15S 27°27E 145 B4
Shashi → Africa 21°14S 29°20E 143 G2
Shasta, Mt. U.S.A. 41°25N 122°12W 168 F2
Shasta L. U.S.A. 40°43N 122°25W 168 F2
Shatsk Russia 54°5N 41°45E 86 C5
Shatsk Ukraine 51°29N 23°55E 83 G10
Shatsky Rise Pac. Oc. 34°0N 157°0E 156 D7
Shatskyy △ Ukraine 51°30N 23°52E 83 G10
Shatt al Arab Asia 29°57N 48°34E 129 D6
Shatura Russia 55°33N 39°21E 84 E10
Shaumyani = Shulaveri
  Georgia 41°22N 44°45E 87 K7
Shaunavon Canada 49°35N 108°25W 163 D7
Shaver L. U.S.A. 37°9N 119°18W 170 H7
Shaw → Australia 20°21S 119°17E 148 D2
Shaw I. Australia 20°30S 149°2E 150 b
Shawanaga Canada 45°31N 80°17W 174 A4
Shawangunk Mts.
  U.S.A. 41°35N 74°30W 175 E10
Shawano U.S.A. 44°47N 88°36W 172 C9
Shawinigan Canada 46°35N 72°50W 164 C5
Shawmari, J. ash
  Jordan 30°35N 36°35E 130 E5
Shawnee Okla., U.S.A. 35°20N 96°55W 176 D6
Shawnee Wyo., U.S.A. 42°45N 105°1W 168 E11
Shay Gap Australia 20°30S 120°10E 148 D3
Shayang China 30°42N 112°29E 117 B9
Shaybārā Si. Arabia 25°26N 36°47E 128 E3
Shayib el Banat, Gebel
  Egypt 26°59N 33°29E 137 B3
Shaykh, J. ash Lebanon 33°25N 35°50E 130 B4
Shaykh Miskīn Syria 32°49N 36°9E 130 C5
Shaykh Sa'd Iraq 32°34N 46°17E 105 F12
Shaykh 'Uthmān Yemen 12°52N 44°59E 131 E3
Shāzand Iran 33°56N 49°24E 129 C6
Shazud Tajikistan 37°45N 72°25E 109 F8
Shchekino Russia 54°1N 37°34E 84 E9
Shchigry Russia 51°55N 36°58E 85 G9
Shchors Ukraine 51°48N 31°56E 85 G6
Shchuchinsk
  Kazakhstan 52°56N 70°12E 109 B8
She Xian Anhui,
  China 29°50N 118°25E 117 C12
She Xian Hebei, China 36°30N 113°40E 114 F7
Shebekino Russia 50°28N 36°54E 85 G9
Shebele = Shabeelle →
  Somalia 2°0N 44°0E 131 G3
Sheberghān Afghan. 36°40N 65°48E 127 A11
Sheboygan U.S.A. 43°46N 87°45W 172 D9
Shebshi Mts. Nigeria 8°30N 11°0E 139 D7
Shediac Canada 46°14N 64°32W 165 C7
Sheelin, L. Ireland 53°48N 7°20W 64 C4
Sheenjek → U.S.A. 66°45N 144°33W 161 B11
Sheep Haven Ireland 55°11N 7°52W 64 A4
Sheep Range U.S.A. 36°35N 115°15W 171 J11
Sheerness U.K. 51°26N 0°47E 67 F8
Sheet Harbour Canada 44°56N 62°31W 165 D7
Sheffield U.K. 53°23N 1°28W 66 D6
Sheffield Ala., U.S.A. 34°46N 87°41W 177 D11
Sheffield Mass., U.S.A. 42°5N 73°21W 175 D11
Sheffield Pa., U.S.A. 41°42N 79°3W 174 E5
Sheffield Tex., U.S.A. 30°41N 101°49W 176 F4
Shegaon India 20°48N 76°47E 126 D3
Shehong China 30°55N 105°18E 116 B5
Shehuen → Argentina 49°35S 69°34W 192 C3
Sheikh Zayed Canal
  Egypt 23°30N 30°17E 137 C3
Sheikhpura India 25°9N 85°53E 125 G11
Shekhupura Pakistan 31°42N 73°58E 124 D5
Sheki = Şaki Azerbaijan 41°10N 47°5E 87 K8
Shekou China 22°29N 113°55E 111 a
Shelburne N.S., Canada 43°47N 65°20W 165 D6
Shelburne Ont., Canada 44°4N 80°15W 174 B4
Shelburne B. Australia 11°50S 142°50E 150 A3
Shelburne Falls
  U.S.A. 42°36N 72°45W 175 D12
Shelby Mich., U.S.A. 43°37N 86°22W 172 D8
Shelby Miss., U.S.A. 33°57N 90°46W 177 E8
Shelby Mont., U.S.A. 48°30N 111°51W 168 B8
Shelby N.C., U.S.A. 35°17N 81°32W 178 C8
Shelby Ohio, U.S.A. 40°53N 82°40W 174 F3
Shelbyville Ill., U.S.A. 39°24N 88°48W 172 F9
Shelbyville Ind.,
  U.S.A. 39°31N 85°47W 173 F11
Shelbyville Ky., U.S.A. 38°13N 85°14W 173 F11
Shelbyville Tenn.,
  U.S.A. 35°29N 86°28W 177 D11
Sheldon Iowa, U.S.A. 43°11N 95°51W 172 D6
Sheldon S.C., U.S.A. 32°36N 80°48W 178 C9
Sheldrake Canada 50°20N 64°51W 165 B7
Shelek Kazakhstan 43°33N 78°17E 109 D9
Shelikhova, Zaliv
  Russia 59°30N 157°0E 107 D16
Shelikof Strait U.S.A. 57°30N 155°0W 166 D9
Shell Lakes Australia 29°20S 127°30E 149 E4
Shellbrook Canada 53°13N 106°24W 163 C7
Shellharbour Australia 34°31S 150°51E 153 E5
Shelter B. Australia 31°46N 84°37W 178 D6
Shelter I. U.S.A. 41°4N 72°20W 175 E12
Shelton Conn., U.S.A. 41°19N 73°5W 175 E11
Shelton Wash., U.S.A. 47°13N 123°6W 170 C3
Shemakha = Şamaxı
  Azerbaijan 40°38N 48°37E 87 K9
Shemonaïkha
  Kazakhstan 50°37N 81°54E 109 B10
Shëmri Albania 42°7N 20°13E 96 D4
Shemsi Sudan 19°26N 29°57E 137 D2
Shen Xian China 36°15N 115°40E 114 F8
Shenandoah Iowa,
  U.S.A. 40°46N 95°22W 172 E6
Shenandoah Pa.,
  U.S.A. 40°49N 76°12W 175 F8
Shenandoah Va.,
  U.S.A. 38°29N 78°37W 174 F6
Shenandoah → U.S.A. 39°19N 77°44W 175 F15
Shenandoah △
  U.S.A. 38°35N 78°22W 174 F6
Shenchi China 39°8N 112°10E 114 E7

Shencottah India 8°59N 77°18E 127
Shendam Nigeria 8°49N 9°30E 139
Shendi Sudan 16°46N 33°22E 135
Shendurni India 20°39N 75°36E 126
Shenge S. Leone 7°54N 12°55W 138
Shengfang China 39°3N 116°42E 114
Shēngjergj Albania 41°17N 20°10E 96
Shëngjin Albania 41°50N 19°35E 96
Shengzhou China 29°35N 120°50E 117
Shenjingzi China 44°40N 124°30E 115
Shenmu China 38°50N 110°29E 114
Shennongjia China 31°43N 110°44E 117
Shenqiu China 33°25N 115°5E 114
Shensi = Shaanxi □
  China 35°0N 109°0E 114
Shenyang China 41°48N 123°27E 115
Shenzhen China 22°32N 114°5E 114
Shenzhen Bao'an Int. ✕ (SZX)
  China 22°41N 113°49E 111
Shenzhen Wan China 22°27N 113°55E 111
Shenzhou China 38°9N 115°2E 114
Sheopur Kalan India 25°40N 76°40E 124
Shepetivka Ukraine 50°10N 27°10E 75
Shepparton Australia 36°23S 145°26E 155
Sheppey, I. of U.K. 51°25N 0°48E 67
Shepton Mallet U.K. 51°11N 2°33W 67
Sheqi China 33°12N 112°57E 117
Sher Qila Pakistan 36°7N 74°2E 125
Sherborne U.K. 50°57N 2°31W 67
Sherbro → S. Leone 7°45N 12°55W 138
Sherbro I. S. Leone 7°30N 12°40W 138
Sherbrooke N.S., Canada 45°8N 61°59W 165
Sherbrooke Qué.,
  Canada 45°28N 71°57W 175
Sherburne U.S.A. 42°41N 75°30W 175
Shereik Sudan 18°44N 33°47E 135
Shergarh India 26°20N 72°18E 124
Sherghati India 24°34N 84°47E 125
Sheridan Ark., U.S.A. 34°19N 92°24W 177
Sheridan Wyo.,
  U.S.A. 44°48N 106°58W 168
Sheringham U.K. 52°56N 1°13E 66
Sherkin I. Ireland 51°28N 9°26W 64
Sherkot India 29°22N 78°35E 125
Sherlovaya Gora
  Russia 50°34N 116°15E 107
Sherman N.Y., U.S.A. 42°9N 79°35W 174
Sherman Tex., U.S.A. 33°38N 96°36W 176
Sherobod Uzbekistan 37°40N 67°1E 109
Sherpur India 25°34N 83°47E 125
Sherridon Canada 55°8N 101°5W 163
Shertallai = Cherthala
  India 9°42N 76°20E 127
Sherwood Forest U.K. 53°6N 1°7W 66
Sherwood Park
  Canada 53°31N 113°19W 162
Sheslay → Canada 58°48N 132°5W 162
Shethanei L. Canada 58°48N 97°50W 163
Shetland □ U.K. 60°30N 1°30W 65
Shetland Is. U.K. 60°30N 1°30W 65
Shetpe Kazakhstan 44°10N 52°7E 108
Shetrunji → India 21°19N 72°7E 124
Sheung Shui China 22°31N 114°7E 111
Shevaroy Hills India 11°58N 78°12E 127
Shevchenkovo Ukraine 45°33N 29°20E 81
Shevgaon India 19°21N 75°14E 124
Shevisheh Iran 35°21N 46°40E 105
Shey-Phoksundo △
  Nepal 29°30N 82°45E 125
Sheyang China 33°48N 120°29E 115
Sheyenne → U.S.A. 47°2N 96°50W 172
Shiashkotan, Ostrov
  Russia 48°49N 154°6E 107
Shibām Yemen 15°59N 48°36E 131
Shibata Japan 37°57N 139°20E 112
Shibecha Japan 43°17N 144°36E 112
Shibetsu Hokkaidō,
  Japan 43°30N 145°10E 112
Shibetsu Hokkaidō,
  Japan 44°10N 142°23E 112
Shibīn el Kôm Egypt 30°31N 30°55E 137
Shibīn el Qanātir Egypt 30°19N 31°19E 137
Shibing China 27°2N 108°5E 116
Shibogama L. Canada 53°35N 88°15W 164
Shibushi Japan 31°25N 131°8E 113
Shicheng China 26°22N 116°20E 117
Shickshinny U.S.A. 41°9N 76°9W 175
Shickshock Mts. = Chic-Chocs,
  Mts. Canada 48°55N 66°0W 165
Shidao China 36°50N 122°25E 115
Shiderty → Kazakhstan 52°32N 74°50E 109
Shidian China 24°40N 99°5E 116
Shido = Sanuki Japan 34°19N 134°10E 113
Shiel, L. U.K. 56°48N 5°34W 65
Shield, C. Australia 13°20S 136°20E 150
Shīeli Kazakhstan 44°20N 66°15E 108
Shifang China 31°18N 104°10E 116
Shiga □ Japan 35°20N 136°0E 113
Shigu China 26°51N 99°56E 116
Shiguaigou China 40°52N 110°15E 114
Shihchiachuang = Shijiazhuang
  China 38°2N 114°28E 114
Shihezi China 44°15N 86°2E 109
Shijak Albania 41°21N 19°33E 96
Shijiazhuang China 38°2N 114°28E 114
Shijiu Hu China 31°25N 118°50E 117
Shikarpur India 28°17N 78°7E 124
Shikarpur Pakistan 27°57N 68°39E 124
Shikohabad India 27°6N 78°36E 125
Shikokuchō Japan 34°1N 133°34E 113
Shikoku □ Japan 33°30N 133°30E 113
Shikoku-Sanchi Japan 33°30N 133°30E 113
Shikotan, Ostrov
  Asia 43°47N 146°44E 112
Shikotsu-Ko Japan 42°45N 141°25E 112
Shikotsu-Tōya △ Japan 44°4N 145°8E 112
Shiliguri India 26°45N 88°25E 125
Shiliu = Changjiang
  China 19°20N 108°55E 116
Shilka Russia 52°0N 115°55E 107
Shilka → Russia 53°20N 121°26E 107
Shillelagh Ireland 52°45N 6°32W 64
Shillington U.S.A. 40°18N 75°58W 175
Shillong India 25°35N 91°53E 125
Shilo West Bank 32°3N 35°18E 130
Shilong China 23°5N 113°52E 111
Shilou China 37°0N 110°48E 114
Shilovo Russia 54°25N 40°57E 86
Shimabara Japan 32°48N 130°20E 113
Shimada Japan 34°49N 138°10E 113
Shimane □ Japan 35°0N 132°30E 113

manovsk Russia 52°15N 127°30E 107 D13
manto Kōchi, Japan 33°12N 133°8E 113 H6
manto Kōchi, Japan 32°59N 132°56E 113 H6
mba Hills ⌂ Kenya 4°14S 39°25E 142 C4
mbiris Somalia 10°44N 47°14E 131 E4
men China 29°35N 111°20E 117 C8
menjie China 29°29N 116°48E 117 C11
mian China 29°17N 102°23E 116 C4
mizu Japan 35°0N 138°30E 113 G9
nla India 31°2N 77°9E 124 D7
nodate Japan 36°20N 139°55E 113 F9
noga = Shivamogga
ndia 13°57N 75°32E 127 H2
nokita-Hantō
apan 41°20N 141°0E 112 D10
noni Kenya 4°38S 39°20E 142 C4
nonoseki Japan 33°58N 130°55E 113 H5
npuru Rapids
amibia 17°45S 19°55E 144 A2
nsha → India 13°15N 77°10E 127 H3
nsk Russia 58°15N 30°50E 84 C6
ı, L. U.K. 58°5N 4°30W 65 C4
nan China 22°44N 109°53E 116 F7
nano-Gawa →
apan 36°50N 138°30E 113 F9
nâş Oman 24°46N 56°28E 129 E8
ndand Afghan. 33°12N 62°8E 122 C3
nglehouse U.S.A. 41°58N 78°12W 174 E6
ngū Japan 33°40N 135°55E 113 H7
ngwidzi S. Africa 23°5S 31°25E 145 B5
njō Japan 38°46N 140°18E 112 E10
nkafe Nigeria 13°8N 6°29E 139 C6
nkolobwe
em. Rep. of the Congo 11°10S 26°40E 140 G5
nshâr Syria 34°36N 36°43E 130 A5
ntuya Peru 12°41S 71°15W 188 C3
nyanga Tanzania 3°45S 33°27E 142 C3
nyanga □ Tanzania 3°50S 33°30E 142 C3
o-no-Misaki Japan 33°25N 135°45E 113 H7
ogama Japan 38°19N 141°1E 112 E10
ojiri Japan 36°6N 137°58E 113 F8
ochenski Prokhod
ulgaria 42°45N 25°15E 97 D9
ohoirt, L. = Seaforth, L.
.K. 57°52N 6°36W 65 D2
oing China 23°45N 102°23E 116 F4
opagan Canada 47°45N 64°45W 165 C7
opensburg U.S.A. 40°3N 77°31W 174 F7
openville U.S.A. 41°15N 79°28W 174 E5
orock U.S.A. 36°47N 108°41W 169 H9
qian China 27°32N 108°13E 116 D7
qma, N. → Israel 31°37N 34°30E 130 D3
quan China 33°5N 108°15E 116 A7
quan He = Indus →
akistan 24°20N 67°47E 124 G2
Kūh Iran 31°39N 54°3E 129 D7
a'awh Qatar 25°2N 52°14E 129 E7
abad = Sherobod
zbekistan 37°40N 67°1E 109 E7
agami-Misaki
apan 41°24N 140°12E 112 D10
akawa Fukushima,
apan 37°7N 140°13E 113 F10
akawa Gifu, Japan 36°17N 136°56E 113 F8
ane-San Gumma,
apan 36°48N 139°22E 113 F9
ane-San Yamanashi,
apan 35°42N 138°9E 113 G9
aoi Japan 42°33N 141°21E 112 C10
āz Iran 29°42N 52°30E 129 D7
bīn Egypt 31°11N 31°32E 137 E7
e → Africa 17°42S 35°19E 143 F4
en China 41°57N 126°34E 115 D14
etoko □ Japan 44°15N 145°15E 112 B12
etoko-Misaki
apan 44°21N 145°20E 112 B12
inab → Pakistan 30°15N 66°28E 124 D2
iya-Zaki Japan 41°25N 141°30E 112 D10
oishi Japan 38°0N 140°37E 112 F10
ol India 16°47N 74°41E 126 F2
oro Res. Nigeria 9°56N 6°54E 139 D6
pur India 21°21N 74°57E 126 D2
shov Ridge Pac. Oc. 58°0N 170°0E 156 B8
vān Iran 37°30N 57°50E 129 B8
wa, L. = Chilwa, L.
Ialawi 15°15S 35°40E 143 F4
shaldin Volcano
.S.A. 54°45N 163°58W 166 E7
shi China 24°44N 118°37E 117 E12
shou China 29°38N 112°22E 117 C9
ai China 30°12N 117°25E 117 B11
hāthah Iraq 32°34N 43°28E 105 G10
vamogga India 13°57N 75°32E 127 H2
vpuri India 25°26N 77°42E 124 G7
kian China 43°5N 129°50E 115 C15
king China 24°46N 114°5E 117 E10
yan Guangdong,
hina 22°42N 113°56E 111 a
yan Hubei, China 32°35N 110°45E 117 A8
yan Shuiku China 22°42N 113°54E 111 a
vata Egypt 29°25N 25°7E 137 B2
hu China 29°58N 108°7E 116 C7
ong China 24°50N 104°0E 116 E5
uishan China 39°15N 106°50E 114 E4
uoka Japan 34°57N 138°24E 113 G9
uoka □ Japan 35°15N 138°40E 113 G9
ha Georgia 43°0N 43°8E 105 A10
lov = Shklow
elarus 54°16N 30°15E 75 A16
low Belarus 54°16N 30°15E 75 A16
odër Albania 42°4N 19°32E 96 D3
umbini → Albania 41°2N 19°31E 96 E3
nidta, Ostrov Russia 81°0N 91°0E 107 A10
-Gawa → Japan 36°47N 137°4E 113 F8
al L. Canada 49°33N 95°1W 163 D9
al Lake Canada 50°30N 100°35W 163 C8
alhaven →
ustralia 34°54S 150°42E 153 C9
do-Shima Japan 34°30N 134°15E 113 G7
lapur = Solapur
ndia 17°43N 75°56E 126 F2
nrōn West Bank 32°15N 35°13E 130 C4
nzhy Kazakhstan 43°32N 79°28E 109 D9
ranur India 10°46N 76°19E 127 J3
rapur India 16°31N 76°48E 127 F3
reham U.S.A. 43°53N 73°18W 175 C11
reham-by-Sea U.K. 50°50N 0°16W 67 G7
ri → Pakistan 28°29N 69°44E 124 E3
rkot Pakistan 30°50N 72°0E 124 D4
rkot Road Pakistan 30°47N 72°15E 124 D5
rsky ⌂ Russia 52°40N 88°0E 109 B11
rter U.S.A. 32°24N 85°57W 178 C4
Shorterville U.S.A. 31°34N 85°6W 178 D4
Shortt's I. India 20°47N 87°4E 126 D8
Shoshone Calif., U.S.A. 35°58N 116°16W 171 K10
Shoshone Idaho, U.S.A. 42°56N 114°25W 168 E6
Shoshone L. U.S.A. 44°22N 110°43W 168 D8
Shoshone Mts. U.S.A. 39°20N 117°25W 168 G5
Shoshong Botswana 22°56S 26°31E 144 B4
Shoshoni U.S.A. 43°14N 108°7W 168 E9
Shostka Ukraine 51°57N 33°32E 85 G7
Shotover → N.Z. 44°59S 168°41E 155 E3
Shou Xian China 32°37N 116°42E 117 A11
Shouchang China 29°18N 119°12E 117 C12
Shouguang China 37°52N 118°45E 115 F10
Shouning China 27°27N 119°31E 117 D12
Shouyang China 37°54N 113°8E 114 F7
Show Low U.S.A. 34°15N 110°2W 169 J8
Showt Iran 39°12N 44°49E 105 C11
Shpola Ukraine 49°1N 31°30E 85 H6
Shpykiv Ukraine 48°47N 28°34E 81 B13
Shqipëria = Albania ■ Europe 41°0N 20°0E 96 E4
Shreveport U.S.A. 32°31N 93°45W 176 E8
Shrewsbury U.K. 52°43N 2°45W 67 E5
Shri Mohangarh India 27°17N 71°18E 124 F4
Shrigonda India 18°37N 74°41E 126 E2
Shrirampur India 22°44N 88°21E 125 H13
Shropshire □ U.K. 52°36N 2°45W 67 E5
Shtërpcë Kosovo 42°14N 21°1E 96 D5
Shū Kazakhstan 43°36N 73°42E 109 D8
Shū → Kazakhstan 45°0N 67°44E 109 D7
Shuangbai China 24°42N 101°38E 116 E3
Shuangcheng China 45°20N 126°15E 115 B14
Shuangfeng China 27°29N 112°11E 117 D9
Shuanggou China 34°2N 117°30E 115 G9
Shuangjiang China 23°26N 99°58E 116 F2
Shuangliao China 43°29N 123°30E 115 C12
Shuangshanzi China 40°20N 119°8E 115 D10
Shuangyang China 43°28N 125°40E 115 C13
Shuangyashan China 46°28N 131°5E 111 B15
Shubarqudyq Kazakhstan 49°13N 56°34E 108 C5
Shubarshī Kazakhstan 48°39N 57°11E 108 C5
Shubrâ el Kheima Egypt 30°4N 31°14E 137 E7
Shubrâ Khit Egypt 31°2N 30°42E 137 E7
Shucheng China 31°28N 116°57E 117 B11
Shugozero Russia 59°54N 34°10E 84 C8
Shuguri Falls Tanzania 8°33S 37°22E 143 D4
Shuiding = Huocheng China 44°0N 80°48E 109 D10
Shuiji China 27°13N 118°20E 117 D12
Shujalpur India 23°18N 76°46E 124 H7
Shukpa Kunzang India 34°22N 78°22E 125 B8
Shulan China 44°28N 127°0E 115 B14
Shulaveri Georgia 41°22N 44°45E 87 K7
Shule China 39°25N 76°3E 109 E9
Shule He → China 40°20N 92°50E 110 C7
Shumagin Is. U.S.A. 55°7N 160°30W 166 D7
Shumanay Uzbekistan 42°38N 58°55E 108 D5
Shumen Bulgaria 43°18N 26°55E 97 C10
Shumerlya Russia 55°30N 46°25E 86 C8
Shumikha Russia 55°10N 63°15E 106 D7
Shunān Japan 34°3N 131°50E 113 G5
Shunchang China 26°54N 117°48E 117 D11
Shunde China 22°42N 113°14E 117 F9
Shungay Kazakhstan 48°30N 46°45E 87 F8
Shungnak U.S.A. 66°52N 157°9W 166 B8
Shuo Xian = Shuozhou China 39°20N 112°33E 114 E7
Shuozhou China 39°20N 112°33E 114 E7
Shuqrā' Yemen 13°22N 45°44E 131 E4
Shūr → Fārs, Iran 28°30N 55°0E 129 D7
Shūr → Kermān, Iran 30°52N 57°37E 129 D8
Shūr → Yazd, Iran 31°45N 55°15E 129 D7
Shūr Āb Iran 34°23N 51°11E 129 C6
Shūr Gaz Iran 29°10N 59°20E 129 D8
Shūrāb Iran 33°43N 56°29E 129 C8
Shūrjestān Iran 31°24N 52°25E 129 D7
Shurugwi Zimbabwe 19°40S 30°0E 143 F3
Shūsf Iran 31°50N 60°5E 129 D9
Shūsh Iran 32°11N 48°15E 105 F13
Shushenskoye Russia 53°19N 91°56E 109 B12
Shushensky Bor ⌂ Russia 52°40N 91°15E 109 B12
Shūshtar Iran 32°0N 48°50E 129 D6
Shuswap L. Canada 50°55N 119°3W 162 C5
Shute Harbour △ Australia 20°17S 148°47E 150 b
Shuya Russia 56°50N 41°28E 86 B5
Shuyang China 34°10N 118°42E 115 G10
Shūzū Iran 29°52N 54°30E 129 D7
Shwebo Burma 22°30N 95°45E 123 H19
Shwegu Burma 24°15N 96°26E 123 G20
Shweli → Burma 23°45N 96°45E 123 H20
Shyamnagar India 13°21N 92°57E 127 H11
Shyghanaq Kazakhstan 45°6N 73°59E 109 C8
Shyghys Qazaqstan □ Kazakhstan 48°30N 82°0E 109 D10
Shymkent Kazakhstan 42°18N 69°36E 109 D7
Shyok India 34°13N 78°12E 125 B8
Shyok → Pakistan 35°13N 75°53E 125 B6
Shyroke Odesa, Ukraine 45°59N 30°5E 81 E15
Shyroke Ternopil, Ukraine 48°13N 23°6E 80 B8
Si Kiang = Xi Jiang → China 22°5N 113°20E 117 F9
Si Lanna △ Thailand 19°17N 99°12E 120 C2
Si Nakarin Res. Thailand 14°35N 99°0E 120 E2
Si-ngan = Xi'an China 34°15N 109°0E 114 G5
Si Phangnga Thailand 9°8N 98°29E 121 H2
Si Prachan Thailand 14°37N 100°9E 120 E3
Si Racha Thailand 13°10N 100°48E 120 F3
Si Sa Ket Thailand 15°8N 104°23E 120 E5
Siachen Glacier Asia 35°20N 77°30E 125 B7
Sīah Cheshmeh Iran 39°3N 44°25E 105 C11
Siahaf → Pakistan 29°3N 68°57E 124 E3
Siahan Range Pakistan 27°30N 64°40E 122 F4
Siak Sri Indrapura Indonesia 0°51N 102°0E 118 D2
Sialkot Pakistan 32°32N 74°30E 124 C6
Siam = Thailand ■ Asia 16°0N 102°0E 120 E4
Sian = Xi'an China 34°15N 109°0E 114 G5
Sian Ka'an ⌂ Mexico 19°35N 87°40W 181 D7
Sianów Poland 54°13N 16°18E 82 D3
Siantan Indonesia 3°10N 106°15E 118 D3
Sīāreh Iran 28°5N 60°14E 129 D9
Siargao I. Phil. 9°52N 126°3E 119 C7
Siasi Phil. 5°34N 120°50E 119 C6
Siatista Greece 40°15N 21°33E 96 F5
Siau Indonesia 2°50N 125°25E 119 D7
Šiauliai Lithuania 55°56N 23°15E 82 C10
Šiauliai □ Lithuania 55°56N 23°19E 82 C10
Siavonga Zambia 16°33S 28°42E 145 A4
Siaya Kenya 0°4N 34°17E 142 B3
Siazan = Siyäzän Azerbaijan 41°3N 49°10E 87 K9
Sibâi, Gebel el Egypt 25°45N 34°10E 128 E2
Sibang Indonesia 8°34S 115°13E 119 K18
Sibay Russia 52°42N 58°39E 108 B5
Sibayi, L. S. Africa 27°20S 32°45E 145 C5
Šibenik Croatia 43°48N 15°54E 93 E12
Siberia = Sibirskiy □ Russia 58°0N 90°0E 107 D10
Siberia Russia 60°0N 100°0E 102 B12
Siberut Indonesia 1°30S 99°0E 118 E1
Sibi Pakistan 29°30N 67°54E 124 E2
Sibiloi △ Kenya 4°0N 36°20E 142 B4
Sibirskiy □ Russia 58°0N 90°0E 107 D10
Sibirtsevo Russia 44°12N 132°26E 112 B5
Sibiti Congo 3°38S 13°19E 140 E2
Sibiu Romania 45°45N 24°9E 81 E9
Sibiu □ Romania 45°50N 24°15E 81 E9
Sibley U.S.A. 43°24N 95°45W 172 D6
Sibo Sweden 61°13N 16°37E 62 C10
Sibolga Indonesia 1°42N 98°45E 118 D1
Siborongborong Indonesia 2°13N 98°58E 121 L2
Sibsagar = Sivasagar India 27°0N 94°36E 123 F19
Sibu Malaysia 2°18N 111°49E 118 D4
Sibuco Phil. 7°20N 122°10E 119 C6
Sibuguey B. Phil. 7°50N 122°45E 119 C6
Sibut C.A.R. 5°46N 19°10E 140 C3
Sibutu Phil. 4°45N 119°30E 119 D5
Sibutu Passage E. Indies 4°50N 120°0E 119 D6
Sibuyan I. Phil. 12°25N 122°40E 119 B6
Sibuyan Sea Phil. 12°30N 122°20E 119 B6
Sic Romania 46°56N 23°53E 81 D8
Sicamous Canada 50°49N 119°0W 162 C5
Sicasica Bolivia 17°22S 67°45W 188 D4
Siccus → Australia 31°55S 139°17E 152 A3
Sichon Thailand 9°0N 99°54E 121 H2
Sichuan □ China 30°30N 103°0E 116 B5
Sichuan Pendi China 31°0N 105°0E 116 B5
Sicilia Italy 37°30N 14°30E 95 E7
Sicily = Sicilia Italy 37°30N 14°30E 95 E7
Sicily, Str. of Medit. S. 37°35N 11°56E 94 E4
Sico → Honduras 15°58N 84°58W 182 C3
Sicuani Peru 14°21S 71°10W 188 C3
Šid Serbia 45°8N 19°14E 80 E4
Sidaouet Niger 18°34N 8°3E 139 B6
Sidari Greece 39°47N 19°41E 101 A3
Siddapur India 14°20N 74°53E 127 G2
Siddhapur India 23°56N 72°25E 124 H5
Siddipet India 18°5N 78°51E 126 E4
Sidensjö Sweden 63°18N 18°17E 62 A12
Sidéradougou Burkina Faso 10°42N 4°12W 138 C4
Siderno Italy 38°16N 16°18E 95 D9
Sideros, Akra Greece 35°19N 26°19E 101 D8
Sidhauli India 27°17N 80°50E 125 F9
Sidhi India 24°25N 81°53E 125 G9
Sîdi Abd el Rahmân Egypt 30°55N 29°44E 137 E6
Sîdi Barrâni Egypt 31°38N 25°58E 137 A2
Sidi-bel-Abbès Algeria 35°13N 0°39W 136 A3
Sidi-bel-Abbès □ Algeria 34°50N 0°30W 136 B3
Sidi Bennour Morocco 32°40N 8°25W 136 B2
Sidi Boubekeur Algeria 35°1N 0°4E 136 A4
Sidi Bouzid Tunisia 35°1N 9°16E 136 B5
Sidi Bouzid □ Tunisia 35°0N 9°30E 136 B5
Sîdi Haneish Egypt 31°10N 27°35E 137 A2
Sidi Ifni Morocco 29°29N 10°12W 134 C3
Sidi Kacem Morocco 34°12N 5°42W 136 B2
Sîdi Omar Egypt 31°24N 24°57E 137 A1
Sidi Slimane Morocco 34°16N 5°56W 136 B2
Sidi Smaïl Morocco 32°50N 8°31W 136 B2
Sidikalang Indonesia 2°45N 98°19E 121 L2
Sidirokastro Greece 41°13N 23°24E 96 E7
Sidlaw Hills U.K. 56°32N 3°2W 65 E5
Sidley, Mt. Antarctica 77°2S 126°2W 55 D14
Sidmouth U.K. 50°40N 3°15W 67 G4
Sidmouth, C. Australia 13°25S 143°36E 150 A3
Sidney Canada 48°39N 123°24W 170 B3
Sidney Mont., U.S.A. 47°43N 104°9W 168 C11
Sidney N.Y., U.S.A. 42°19N 75°24W 175 D9
Sidney Nebr., U.S.A. 41°8N 102°59W 172 E2
Sidney Ohio, U.S.A. 40°17N 84°9W 173 E11
Sidney Lanier, L. U.S.A. 34°10N 84°4W 178 A5
Sido Mali 11°37N 7°29W 138 C3
Sidoarjo Indonesia 7°27S 112°43E 119 G15
Sidon = Saydā Lebanon 33°35N 35°25E 130 B4
Sidra = Surt Libya 31°11N 16°39E 135 B9
Sidra, G. of = Surt, Khalīj Libya 31°40N 18°30E 135 B9
Siedlce Poland 52°10N 22°20E 83 F9
Sieg → Germany 50°46N 7°6E 76 E3
Siegburg Germany 50°47N 7°12E 76 E3
Siegen Germany 50°51N 8°0E 76 E4
Siem Pang Cambodia 14°7N 106°23E 120 E6
Siem Reap = Siemreab Cambodia 13°20N 103°52E 120 F4
Siemiatycze Poland 52°27N 22°53E 83 F9
Siemreab Cambodia 13°20N 103°52E 120 F4
Siena Italy 43°19N 11°21E 93 E8
Sieniawa Poland 50°11N 22°38E 83 H9
Sieradz Poland 51°37N 18°41E 83 G5
Sieraków Poland 52°39N 16°2E 83 F3
Sierck-les-Bains France 49°26N 6°20E 71 C13
Sierning Austria 48°2N 14°18E 78 C7
Sierpc Poland 52°55N 19°43E 83 F6
Sierpe, Bocas de la Venezuela 10°0N 61°30W 187 L15
Sierra Blanca U.S.A. 31°11N 105°22W 176 F2
Sierra Blanca Peak U.S.A. 33°23N 105°49W 169 K11
Sierra City U.S.A. 39°34N 120°38W 170 F6
Sierra Colorada Argentina 40°35S 67°50W 192 B3
Sierra de Agalta △ Honduras 15°1N 85°48W 182 C2
Sierra de Andújar ⌂ Spain 38°20N 3°50W 89 G7
Sierra de Aracena y Picos de Aroche ⌂ Spain 37°53N 6°41W 89 H4
Sierra de Bahoruco △ Dom. Rep. 18°10N 71°25W 183 C5
Sierra de Baza ⌂ Spain 37°20N 2°48W 91 H2
Sierra de Castril ⌂ Spain 37°54N 2°50W 91 H2
Sierra de Espuña ⌂ Spain 37°50N 1°31W 91 H3
Sierra de Grazalema ⌂ Spain 36°31N 5°28W 89 J5
Sierra de Gredos ⌂ Spain 40°17N 5°17W 88 E5
Sierra de Guadarrama △ Spain 40°50N 4°0W 88 E6
Sierra de Hornachuelos ⌂ Spain 37°56N 5°14W 89 H5
Sierra de Huétor ⌂ Spain 37°14N 3°30W 89 H7
Sierra de La Culata △ Venezuela 8°45N 71°10W 183 E5
Sierra de Lancandón △ Guatemala 16°59N 90°23W 182 C1
Sierra de las Nieves ⌂ Spain 36°42N 5°0W 89 J6
Sierra de las Quijadas △ Argentina 32°29S 67°5W 190 C2
Sierra de María-Los Vélez ⌂ Spain 37°41N 2°10W 91 H2
Sierra de San Luis △ Venezuela 11°20N 69°43W 183 D6
Sierra de San Pedro Mártir △ Mexico 31°10N 115°30W 180 A1
Sierra de Yeguas Spain 37°7N 4°52W 89 H6
Sierra del São Mamede ⌂ Portugal 39°17N 7°18W 89 F3
Sierra Gorda Chile 22°50S 69°15W 190 A2
Sierra Grande Argentina 41°36S 65°22W 192 B3
Sierra Leone ■ W. Afr. 9°0N 12°0W 138 D2
Sierra Leone Basin Atl. Oc. 5°0N 17°0W 56 F10
Sierra Leone Rise Atl. Oc. 7°0N 22°0W 56 F9
Sierra Madre Mexico 16°0N 93°0W 181 D6
Sierra Madre Occidental Mexico 27°0N 107°0W 180 B3
Sierra Madre Oriental Mexico 25°0N 100°0W 180 C5
Sierra Mágina ⌂ Spain 37°44N 3°28W 89 H7
Sierra Mojada Mexico 27°18N 103°41W 180 B4
Sierra Nevada Spain 37°3N 3°15W 89 H7
Sierra Nevada U.S.A. 39°0N 120°30W 170 H8
Sierra Nevada ⌂ Spain 37°4N 3°7W 89 H7
Sierra Nevada △ Venezuela 8°35N 70°45W 183 E5
Sierra Nevada de Santa Marta △ Colombia 10°56N 73°36W 183 D5
Sierra Norte de Sevilla ⌂ Spain 37°55N 5°46W 89 H5
Sierra Subbéticas ⌂ Spain 37°26N 4°18W 89 H6
Sierra Vista U.S.A. 31°33N 110°18W 169 L8
Sierras de Cardeña y Montoro ⌂ Spain 38°13N 4°15W 89 G6
Sierras de Cazorla, Segura y las Villas ⌂ Spain 37°0N 2°45W 91 J2
Sierraville U.S.A. 39°36N 120°22W 170 F6
Sierre Switz. 46°17N 7°31E 77 J3
Sifié Ivory C. 8°0N 7°5W 138 D3
Sifnos Greece 37°0N 24°45E 98 E6
Sifton Canada 51°21N 100°8W 163 C8
Sifton Pass Canada 57°52N 126°15W 162 B3
Sig Algeria 35°32N 0°12W 136 A3
Sigatoka Fiji 18°8S 177°32E 154 a
Sigean France 43°2N 2°58E 72 E6
Sighetu-Marmaţiei Romania 47°57N 23°52E 81 C8
Sighişoara Romania 46°12N 24°50E 81 D9
Sigiriya Sri Lanka 7°57N 80°45E 127 L5
Sigli Indonesia 5°25N 96°0E 118 C1
Siglufjörður Iceland 66°12N 18°55W 60 C4
Sigmaringen Germany 48°5N 9°12E 77 G5
Signa Italy 43°45N 11°10E 92 E8
Signakhi = Tsnori Georgia 41°40N 45°57E 87 K7
Signal de Botrang Belgium 50°29N 6°4E 69 D6
Signal Pk. U.S.A. 33°20N 114°2W 171 M12
Signy I. Antarctica 60°43S 45°36W 55 C18
Signy-l'Abbaye France 49°40N 4°25E 71 C11
Sigsbee U.S.A. 31°16N 83°52W 178 D6
Sigsbee Deep Gulf of Mexico 25°0N 92°0W 56 D1
Sigsig Ecuador 3°0S 78°50W 186 D3
Sigtuna Sweden 59°36N 17°44E 62 E11
Sigüenza Spain 41°3N 2°40W 90 D2
Siguiri Guinea 11°31N 9°10W 138 C3
Sigulda Latvia 57°10N 24°55E 84 D3
Siguniangshan China 31°15N 103°10E 116 B4
Sihawa India 20°19N 81°55E 126 D5
Sihong China 33°27N 118°16E 115 H10
Sihora India 23°29N 80°6E 125 H9
Sihuas Peru 8°40S 77°40W 188 B2
Sihui China 23°20N 112°40E 117 F9
Siikajoki → Finland 64°50N 24°43E 60 D21
Siilinjärvi Finland 63°4N 27°39E 60 E22
Siirt Turkey 37°57N 41°55E 105 D9
Siirt □ Turkey 37°55N 41°55E 105 D9
Sijarira Ra. = Chizarira Ra. Zimbabwe 17°36S 27°45E 143 F2
Sika India 22°26N 69°47E 124 H3
Sikanni Chief → Canada 57°47N 122°15W 162 B4
Sikao Thailand 7°34N 99°21E 121 J2
Sikar India 27°33N 75°10E 124 F6
Sikasso Mali 11°18N 5°35W 138 C3
Sikasso □ Mali 10°55N 7°0W 138 C3
Sikeston U.S.A. 36°53N 89°35W 172 G9
Sikhote Alin, Khrebet Russia 45°0N 136°0E 112 B8
Sikhote Alin Ra. = Sikhote Alin, Khrebet Russia 45°0N 136°0E 112 B8
Sikia Greece 40°2N 23°56E 96 F7
Sikinos Greece 36°40N 25°8E 99 E7
Sikkim □ India 27°50N 88°30E 123 F16
Siklós Hungary 45°50N 18°19E 80 E3
Sil → Spain 42°27N 7°43W 88 C3
Silacayoapan Mexico 17°30N 98°9W 181 D5
Šilalė Lithuania 55°28N 22°12E 82 C9
Silandro Italy 46°38N 10°46E 92 B7
Silawad India 21°54N 74°54E 124 J6
Silba Croatia 44°24N 14°41E 93 D11
Silchar India 24°49N 92°48E 123 G18
Şile Turkey 41°10N 29°37E 97 E13
Silent Valley △ India 11°10N 76°20E 127 J3
Siler City U.S.A. 35°44N 79°28W 177 D15
Silera → India 17°49N 81°24E 126 F5
Silesia = Śląsk Poland 51°0N 16°30E 74 C9
Siletitengiz Köli Kazakhstan 53°20N 73°10E 109 B8
Silgarhi Doti Nepal 29°15N 81°0E 125 E9
Silghat India 26°35N 93°0E 123 F18
Silhouette Seychelles 4°29S 55°12E 141 b
Sili Burkina Faso 11°37N 2°30W 138 C4
Siliana Tunisia 36°5N 9°22E 136 A5
Siliana □ Tunisia 36°0N 9°20E 136 A5
Silicon Valley = Santa Clara Valley U.S.A. 36°50N 121°30W 170 J5
Silifke Turkey 36°22N 33°58E 104 D5
Siliguri = Shiliguri India 26°45N 88°25E 123 F16
Siling Co China 31°50N 89°20E 110 E6
Silistea Nouă Romania 44°23N 25°1E 81 F10
Silistra Bulgaria 44°6N 27°19E 97 B11
Silistra □ Bulgaria 44°6N 27°19E 97 B11
Silivri Turkey 41°4N 28°14E 97 E12
Siljan Sweden 60°55N 14°45E 62 D8
Siljansnäs Sweden 60°47N 14°52E 62 D8
Silkeborg Denmark 56°10N 9°32E 63 H3
Silkwood Australia 17°45S 146°2E 150 B4
Silla Spain 39°22N 0°25W 91 F4
Sillajhuay, Cordillera Chile 19°46S 68°40W 188 D4
Sillamäe Estonia 59°24N 27°45E 84 C4
Sillé-le-Guillaume France 48°10N 0°8W 70 D6
Silleda Spain 42°42N 8°14W 88 C2
Sillod India 20°18N 75°39E 126 D2
Silloth U.K. 54°52N 3°23W 66 C4
Sillustani Peru 15°50S 70°7W 188 D3
Silo Greece 41°10N 25°53E 97 E9
Siloam Springs U.S.A. 36°11N 94°32W 176 C7
Silopi Turkey 37°15N 42°27E 105 D10
Siluko Nigeria 6°35N 5°10E 139 D6
Šilutė Lithuania 55°21N 21°33E 82 C8
Silvan Turkey 38°7N 41°2E 105 C9
Silvani India 23°18N 78°25E 125 H8
Silvassa India 20°16N 73°1E 126 D1
Silver City U.S.A. 32°46N 108°17W 169 K9
Silver Cr. → U.S.A. 43°16N 119°13W 168 E4
Silver Creek U.S.A. 42°33N 79°10W 174 D5
Silver L. U.S.A. 38°39N 120°6W 170 G6
Silver Lake Calif., U.S.A. 35°21N 116°7W 171 K10
Silver Lake Oreg., U.S.A. 43°8N 121°3W 168 E3
Silver Springs U.S.A. 29°13N 82°3W 179 F7
Silverdalen Sweden 57°32N 15°45E 63 G9
Silvermine Mts. Ireland 52°47N 8°15W 64 D3
Silverton Australia 31°52S 141°10E 152 A4
Silverton Colo., U.S.A. 37°49N 107°40W 169 H10
Silverton Tex., U.S.A. 34°28N 101°19W 176 D4
Silves Portugal 37°11N 8°26W 89 H2
Silvi Marina Italy 42°34N 14°5E 93 F11
Silvies → U.S.A. 43°34N 119°2W 168 E4
Silvrettahorn Switz. 46°50N 10°6E 92 B7
Silwa Bahari Egypt 24°45N 32°55E 137 C3
Silz Austria 47°16N 10°56E 78 D3
Sim, C. Morocco 31°26N 9°51W 136 B2
Simaltala India 24°43N 86°33E 125 G12
Simanggang = Bandar Sri Aman Malaysia 1°15N 111°32E 118 D4
Simao China 22°47N 101°5E 116 F3
Simão Dias Brazil 10°44S 37°49W 189 C3
Simard, L. Canada 47°40N 78°40W 164 C4
Şimareh → Iran 33°9N 47°41E 105 F12
Simav Turkey 39°4N 28°58E 99 B10
Simav → Turkey 40°23N 28°31E 97 F12
Simav Dağları Turkey 39°10N 28°30E 99 B10
Simba Tanzania 2°10S 37°36E 142 C4
Simbach Germany 48°16N 13°2E 77 G9
Simbirsk = Ulyanovsk Russia 54°20N 48°25E 86 C9
Simbo Tanzania 4°51S 29°41E 142 C2
Simcoe Canada 42°50N 80°23W 174 D4
Simcoe, L. Canada 44°25N 79°20W 174 B5
Simdega India 22°37N 84°31E 125 H11
Simeonovgrad Bulgaria 42°1N 25°50E 97 D9
Simeria Romania 45°51N 23°1E 80 E8
Simeto → Italy 37°24N 15°6E 95 E8
Simeulue Indonesia 2°45N 95°45E 118 D1
Simferopol Ukraine 44°55N 34°3E 85 K8
Simi Greece 36°35N 27°50E 99 E9
Simi Valley U.S.A. 34°16N 118°47W 171 L8
Simikot Nepal 30°0N 81°50E 125 E9
Simineh → Iran 36°59N 45°54E 105 D11
Simitli Bulgaria 41°52N 23°7E 96 E7
Simiyu □ Tanzania 2°55S 34°20E 142 C3
Simla = Shimla India 31°2N 77°9E 124 D7
Simlångsdalen Sweden 56°43N 13°6E 63 H7
Şimleu-Silvaniei Romania 47°17N 22°50E 80 C7
Simlipal △ India 21°45N 86°30E 125 J12
Simmern Germany 49°58N 7°30E 77 F3
Simmie Canada 49°56N 108°6W 163 D7
Simmler U.S.A. 35°21N 119°59W 171 K7
Simnas Lithuania 54°24N 23°39E 82 D10
Simo älv = Simojoki → Finland 65°35N 25°1E 60 D21
Simões Brazil 7°36S 40°49W 189 B2
Simojoki → Finland 65°35N 25°1E 60 D21
Simojovel Mexico 17°12N 92°38W 181 D6
Simonette → Canada 55°9N 118°15W 162 B5
Simonstown S. Africa 34°14S 18°26E 144 D2
Simontornya Hungary 46°45N 18°33E 80 D3
Simpang Empat Malaysia 5°27N 100°29E 121 c
Simplício Mendes Brazil 7°51S 41°54W 189 B2
Simplonpass Switz. 46°15N 8°3E 77 J4
Simplontunnel Switz. 46°15N 8°7E 77 J4
Simpson Desert Australia 25°0S 137°0E 150 D2
Simpson Desert △ Australia 24°59S 138°21E 150 C2
Simpson Pen. Canada 68°34N 88°45W 161 D14
Simrishamn Sweden 55°33N 14°22E 63 J8
Simsbury U.S.A. 41°53N 72°48W 175 E12
Simushir, Ostrov Russia 46°50N 152°30E 107 E16
Sin Cowe I. S. China Sea 9°53N 114°19E 118 C4
Sina → India 17°30N 75°55E 126 F2
Sina Dhago Somalia 5°50N 47°0E 131 F4
Sinabang Indonesia 2°30N 96°24E 118 D1
Sinai = Es Sînâ' Egypt 29°0N 34°0E 130 F2
Sinai, Mt. = Mûsa, Gebel Egypt 28°33N 33°59E 128 D2
Sinaia Romania 45°21N 25°38E 81 E10
Sinaloa □ Mexico 25°0N 107°30W 180 C3
Sinaloa de Leyva Mexico 25°50N 108°14W 180 B3
Sinalunga Italy 43°12N 11°44E 93 E8
Sinan China 27°56N 108°13E 116 D7
Sînandrei Romania 45°52N 21°13E 80 E6
Sinarades Greece 39°34N 19°51E 101 A3
Sincan Turkey 40°0N 32°36E 104 B5
Sincanlı Turkey 38°45N 30°15E 99 C12
Sincelejo Colombia 9°18N 75°24W 186 B3
Sinch'ang N. Korea 40°7N 128°28E 115 D15
Sinch'ŏn N. Korea 38°17N 125°21E 115 E13
Sinclair U.S.A. 41°47N 107°7W 168 F10
Sinclair, L. U.S.A. 33°8N 83°12W 178 B6
Sinclair Mills Canada 54°5N 121°40W 162 C4
Sinclair's B. U.K. 58°31N 3°5W 65 C5
Sinclairville U.S.A. 42°16N 79°16W 174 D5
Sincorá, Serra do Brazil 13°10S 41°20W 189 C2
Sind = Sindh □ Pakistan 26°0N 69°0E 124 G3
Sind → Jammu & Kashmir, India 34°18N 74°45E 125 B6
Sind → Mad. P., India 26°26N 79°13E 125 F8
Sind Sagar Doab Pakistan 32°0N 71°30E 124 D4
Sindal Denmark 57°28N 10°10E 63 G4
Sindangan Phil. 8°10N 123°5E 119 C6
Sindangbarang Indonesia 7°27S 107°1E 119 G12
Sinde Zambia 17°28S 25°51E 143 F2
Sindelfingen Germany 48°42N 9°0E 77 G4
Sindewahi India 20°17N 79°39E 126 D4
Sindgi India 16°55N 76°14E 126 F3
Sindh = Indus → Pakistan 24°20N 67°47E 124 G2
Sindh □ Pakistan 26°0N 69°0E 124 G3
Sindhnur India 15°47N 76°46E 127 G3
Sindhuli Garhi Nepal 27°16N 85°58E 125 F11
Sindi India 20°48N 78°52E 126 D4
Sındırgı Turkey 39°13N 28°10E 99 B10
Sindou Burkina Faso 10°35N 5°4W 138 C3
Sindri India 23°45N 86°42E 125 H12
Sine → Senegal 14°10N 16°28W 138 C1
Sinegorskiy Russia 47°55N 40°52E 87 G5
Sinekli Turkey 41°14N 28°12E 97 E12
Sinelnikovo = Synelnykove Ukraine 48°25N 35°30E 85 H8
Sinendé Benin 10°20N 2°22E 139 C5
Sines Portugal 37°56N 8°51W 89 H2
Sines, C. de Portugal 37°58N 8°53W 89 H2
Sineu Spain 39°38N 3°1E 100 B10
Sinfra Ivory C. 6°35N 5°56W 138 D3
Sing Buri Thailand 14°53N 100°25E 120 E3
Singa Sudan 13°10N 33°57E 135 F12
Singalila △ India 27°10N 88°5E 125 F13
Singanallur India 11°2N 77°1E 127 J3
Singapore ■ Asia 1°17N 103°51E 121 d
Singapore, Straits of Asia 1°15N 104°0E 121 d
Singapore Changi ✕ (SIN) Singapore 1°23N 103°59E 121 M4
Singaraja Indonesia 8°7S 115°6E 118 F5
Singatoka = Sigatoka Fiji 18°8S 177°32E 154 a
Singen Germany 47°45N 8°50E 77 H4
Singida Tanzania 4°49S 34°48E 142 C3
Singida □ Tanzania 6°0S 34°30E 142 D3
Singkang Indonesia 4°8S 120°1E 119 E6
Singkawang Indonesia 1°0N 108°57E 118 D3
Singkep Indonesia 0°30S 104°25E 118 E2
Singkil Indonesia 2°17N 97°49E 121 L1
Singkuang Indonesia 1°3N 98°55E 121 L1
Singleton Australia 32°33S 151°10E 153 B9
Singleton, Mt. N. Terr., Australia 22°0S 130°46E 148 D5
Singleton, Mt. W. Austral., Australia 29°27S 117°15E 149 E2
Singö Sweden 60°12N 18°45E 62 D12
Singoli India 25°0N 75°22E 124 G6
Singora = Songkhla Thailand 7°13N 100°37E 121 J3
Singrauli India 24°7N 82°23E 125 G10
Sinh Ton, Dao = Sin Cowe I. S. China Sea 9°53N 114°19E 118 C4
Sinharaja Sri Lanka 6°25N 80°30E 127 L5
Sinhgarh India 18°22N 73°45E 126 E1
Sinhŭng N. Korea 40°11N 127°34E 115 D14
Sinis Italy 38°55N 8°25E 94 C1
Siniscóla Italy 40°34N 9°41E 94 B2
Sinj Croatia 43°42N 16°39E 93 E13
Sinjai Indonesia 5°7S 120°20E 119 F6
Sinjajevina Montenegro 42°57N 19°22E 96 D3
Sinjār Iraq 36°19N 41°52E 105 D9
Sinjār, Jabal Iraq 36°23N 41°47E 105 D9
Sinkat Sudan 18°55N 36°49E 137 D4
Sinkiang = Xinjiang Uygur Zizhiqu □ China 42°0N 86°0E 109 D11
Sinko Guinea 8°53N 8°16W 138 D3
Sinmak N. Korea 38°25N 126°14E 115 E14
Sinmi-do N. Korea 39°33N 124°53E 115 E13
Sinnai Italy 39°18N 9°13E 94 C2
Sinnamary Fr. Guiana 5°25N 53°0W 187 B8
Sinnar India 19°48N 74°0E 126 E2
Sinni → Italy 40°8N 16°41E 95 B9
Sinnuris Egypt 29°26N 30°31E 137 F7
Sinoie, Lacul Romania 44°35N 28°50E 81 F13
Sinop Turkey 42°1N 35°11E 104 A6
Sinop □ Turkey 42°0N 35°0E 104 B6
Sinor India 21°55N 73°20E 124 J5
Sinp'o N. Korea 40°0N 128°13E 115 E15
Sinsheim Germany 49°15N 8°52E 77 F4
Sinsk Russia 61°8N 126°48E 107 C13
Sint-Hubert Belgium 50°2N 5°23E 69 D5
Sint-Niklaas Belgium 51°10N 4°8E 69 C4
Sint-Truiden Belgium 50°48N 5°10E 69 D5
Sintang Indonesia 0°5N 111°35E 118 D4
Sinton U.S.A. 28°2N 97°31W 176 G6
Sintra Portugal 38°47N 9°25W 89 G1
Sintra-Cascais ⌂ Portugal 38°50N 9°25W 89 G1
Sinŭiju N. Korea 40°5N 124°24E 115 D13
Sinyukha → Ukraine 48°3N 30°51E 85 H6
Sinzig Germany 50°32N 7°14E 76 E3
Sio → Hungary 46°20N 18°53E 80 D3
Siocon Phil. 7°40N 122°10E 119 C6
Siófok Hungary 46°54N 18°3E 80 D3
Sion Switz. 46°14N 7°20E 77 J3
Sion Mills U.K. 54°48N 7°29W 64 B4
tSionainn, An = Shannon → Ireland 52°35N 9°30W 64 D2
Sioux Center U.S.A. 43°5N 96°11W 172 D5
Sioux City U.S.A. 42°30N 96°24W 172 D5
Sioux Falls U.S.A. 43°33N 96°44W 172 D5
Sioux Lookout Canada 50°10N 91°50W 164 B1
Sioux Narrows Canada 49°25N 94°10W 163 D10
Sipadan Malaysia 4°6N 118°38E 119 D5
Šipan Croatia 42°45N 17°52E 96 D1
Siparia Trin. & Tob. 10°8N 61°31W 187 K15
Sipil Dağı △ Turkey 38°35N 27°30E 99 C9
Siping China 43°8N 124°21E 115 C13
Sipiwesk L. Canada 55°5N 97°35W 163 B9
Siple I. Antarctica 73°40S 125°10W 55 D14
Šipovo Bos.-H. 44°16N 17°6E 80 F2
Sipra → India 23°55N 75°28E 124 H6

Sipsongpanna = Xishuangbanna
China 22°5N 101°1E 116 F3
Sipur India 21°11N 85°9E 126 D7
Sipura Indonesia 2°18S 99°40E 118 E1
Siquia → Nic. 12°10N 84°20W 182 D3
Siquijor Phil. 9°12N 123°35E 119 C6
Siquirres Costa Rica 10°6N 83°30W 182 D3
Šīr Abū Nu'ayr U.A.E. 25°20N 54°20E 129 E7
Šīr Banī Yās U.A.E. 24°19N 52°37E 129 E7
Sir Edward Pellew Group
Australia 15°40S 137°10E 150 B2
Sir Graham Moore Is.
Australia 13°53S 126°34E 148 B4
Sir James MacBrien, Mt.
Canada 62°7N 127°41W 160 E6
Sira India 13°41N 76°49E 127 H3
Sira → Norway 58°23N 6°34E 61 G12
Siracusa Italy 37°4N 15°17E 95 E8
Sirajganj Bangla. 24°25N 89°47E 125 G13
Sirakoro Mali 12°41N 9°14W 138 C3
Şiran Turkey 40°11N 39°7E 105 B8
Sirasso Ivory C. 9°16N 6°6W 138 D3
Sirathu India 25°39N 81°19E 125 G9
Sīrdān Iran 36°39N 49°12E 105 D13
Sirdaryo □ Uzbekistan 40°30N 68°45E 109 D7
Siren U.S.A. 45°47N 92°24W 172 C7
Sirente-Velino △ Italy 42°10N 13°32E 93 F10
Sirer Spain 38°56N 1°22E 100 C7
Siret Romania 47°55N 26°5E 81 C11
Siret → Romania 45°24N 28°1E 81 E12
Sirghāyā Syria 33°51N 36°8E 130 B5
Şiria Romania 46°16N 21°38E 80 D6
Sirikit Res. Thailand 17°45N 100°34E 120 C3
Sirinat △ Thailand 8°6N 98°17E 121 a
Sirino, Mte. Italy 40°7N 15°50E 95 B8
Sīrjān Iran 29°30N 55°45E 129 D7
Sirkali = Sirkazhi India 11°15N 79°41E 127 J4
Sirkazhi India 11°15N 79°41E 127 J4
Sırmans U.S.A. 30°21N 83°39W 178 E6
Sirmaur India 24°51N 81°23E 125 G9
Sirmilik △ Canada 72°50N 80°35W 161 C15
Sirmione Italy 45°30N 10°36E 92 C7
Sirna Greece 36°22N 26°42E 99 E8
Şırnak Turkey 37°32N 42°28E 105 D10
Sirohi India 24°52N 72°53E 124 G5
Sironj India 24°5N 77°39E 124 G7
Siros = Ermoupoli
Greece 37°28N 24°57E 98 D6
Sirpur India 19°29N 79°36E 126 E4
Sirr, Nafud as Si. Arabia 25°33N 44°35E 128 E5
Sirretta Pk. U.S.A. 35°56N 118°19W 171 K8
Sīrrī Iran 25°55N 54°32E 129 E7
Sirsa India 29°33N 75°4E 124 E6
Sirsa → India 26°51N 79°4E 125 F8
Sirsi India 14°40N 74°49E 127 G2
Sirsilla India 18°23N 78°50E 126 E4
Sirte = Surt Libya 31°11N 16°39E 135 B9
Siruela Spain 38°58N 5°3W 89 G5
Siruguppa India 15°38N 76°54E 127 F3
Sirur India 18°50N 74°23E 126 E2
Şirvan Azerbaijan 39°59N 48°52E 87 L9
Sirvān → India 35°4N 46°50E 105 C12
Sisak Croatia 45°30N 16°21E 93 C13
Sisante Spain 39°25N 2°12W 91 F2
Sisargas, Is. Spain 43°21N 8°50W 88 B2
Sishen S. Africa 27°47S 22°59E 144 C3
Sishui China 35°42N 117°18E 115 G9
Sisian Armenia 39°31N 46°1E 105 C12
Sisimiut Greenland 66°40N 53°30W 57 D5
Sisipuk L. Canada 55°45N 101°50W 163 B8
Sisophon Cambodia 13°38N 102°59E 120 F4
Sisseton U.S.A. 45°40N 97°3W 172 C5
Sissonne France 49°34N 3°51E 71 C10
Sīstān Asia 30°50N 61°0E 129 D9
Sīstān, Daryācheh-ye
Iran 31°0N 61°0E 129 D9
Sīstān va Balūchestān □
Iran 27°0N 62°0E 129 E9
Sisteron France 44°12N 5°57E 73 D9
Sisters U.S.A. 44°18N 121°33W 168 D3
Sisters, The Seychelles 4°16S 55°52E 141 b
Siswa Bazar India 27°9N 83°46E 125 F10
Sitakili Mali 13°7N 11°14W 138 C2
Sitamarhi India 26°37N 85°30E 125 F11
Sitapur India 27°38N 80°45E 125 F9
Siteki Swaziland 26°32S 31°58E 145 C5
Sitges Spain 41°17N 1°47E 90 D6
Sithonia Greece 40°0N 23°45E 96 F7
Sitia Greece 35°13N 26°6E 101 D8
Sitio da Abadia Brazil 14°48S 46°16W 189 C1
Sitito-Ozima Ridge
Pac. Oc. 23°0N 143°0E 156 E6
Sitka U.S.A. 57°3N 135°20W 162 B1
Sitkaing = Sagaing
Burma 21°52N 95°59E 123 J19
Sitoti Botswana 23°15S 23°40E 144 B3
Sitra Egypt 28°40N 26°53E 137 B2
Sittang Myit →
Burma 17°20N 96°45E 123 L20
Sittard Neths. 51°0N 5°52E 69 C5
Sittensen Germany 53°17N 9°32E 76 B5
Sittingbourne U.K. 51°21N 0°45E 67 F8
Sittoung = Sittang Myit →
Burma 17°20N 96°45E 123 L20
Sittwe Burma 20°18N 92°45E 123 J18
Situbondo Indonesia 7°42S 113°56E 119 G16
Siuna Nic. 13°37N 84°45W 182 D3
Siuri India 23°50N 87°34E 125 H12
Siutghiol, Lacul
Romania 44°15N 28°35E 81 F13
Sivaganga India 9°50N 78°28E 127 K4
Sivagiri India 9°16N 77°26E 127 K3
Sivakasi India 9°24N 77°47E 127 K3
Sivand Iran 30°5N 52°55E 129 D7
Sivas Turkey 38°31N 36°58E 104 C7
Sivas □ Turkey 39°45N 37°0E 104 C7
Sivasagar India 27°0N 94°36E 123 F19
Sivasamudram India 12°16N 77°10E 127 H3
Sivasli Turkey 38°31N 29°42E 99 C11
Siverek Turkey 37°50N 39°19E 105 D8
Sivrihisar Turkey 39°30N 31°35E 104 C4
Siwa Egypt 29°11N 25°31E 137 B2
Siwa, El Wâhât es
Egypt 29°10N 25°30E 137 B2
Siwa Oasis = Siwa, El Wâhât es
Egypt 29°10N 25°30E 137 B2
Siwalik Range Nepal 28°0N 83°0E 125 F10
Siwan India 26°13N 84°21E 125 F11
Siwana India 25°38N 72°25E 124 G5
Six Cross Roads Barbados 13°7N 59°28W 183 g
Six-Fours-les-Plages
France 43°6N 5°49E 73 E9

Sixian China 33°30N 117°50E 115 H9
Sixmilebridge Ireland 52°44N 8°46W 64 D3
Sixth Cataract Sudan 16°20N 32°42E 135 E12
Siyabuswa S. Africa 25°7S 29°3E 145 C4
Siyah Kuh, Kavīr-e
Iran 32°55N 53°55E 129 C7
Siyâl, Jazâ'ir Egypt 22°49N 36°12E 137 C4
Siyang China 33°42N 118°40E 115 H10
Siyäzän Azerbaijan 41°3N 49°10E 87 K9
Siziwang Qi China 41°25N 111°40E 114 D6
Sjælland Denmark 55°30N 11°30E 63 J5
Sjælland □ Denmark 55°30N 11°30E 63 J5
Sjællands Odde Denmark 55°58N 11°24E 63 J5
Sjenica Serbia 43°16N 20°0E 96 C3
Sjeverni Velebit △
Croatia 44°30N 15°15E 93 D12
Sjöbo Sweden 55°37N 13°45E 63 J7
Sjötofta Sweden 57°22N 13°17E 63 H7
Sjötorp Sweden 58°50N 14°0E 63 F8
Sjumen = Shumen
Bulgaria 43°18N 26°55E 97 C10
Sjuntorp Sweden 58°12N 12°13E 63 F6
Skadarsko Jezero Europe 42°10N 19°20E 96 D3
Skadarsko Jezero △
Montenegro 42°10N 19°20E 96 D3
Skadovsk Ukraine 46°17N 32°52E 85 J7
Skælskør Denmark 55°15N 11°18E 63 J5
Skærbæk Denmark 55°9N 8°45E 63 J2
Skagafjörður Iceland 65°54N 19°35W 60 D4
Skagastølstindane
Norway 61°28N 7°52E 60 F12
Skagaströnd Iceland 65°50N 20°19W 60 D3
Skagen Denmark 57°43N 10°35E 63 G4
Skagern Sweden 59°0N 14°20E 62 E8
Skagerrak Denmark 57°30N 9°0E 63 G3
Skagit → U.S.A. 48°23N 122°22W 170 B4
Skagway U.S.A. 59°28N 135°19W 160 F4
Skala-Podilska Ukraine 48°50N 26°15E 81 B11
Skalat Ukraine 49°23N 25°55E 75 D13
Skalbmierz Poland 50°20N 20°25E 83 H7
Skälderviken Sweden 56°22N 12°30E 63 H6
Skalica Slovak Rep. 48°50N 17°15E 79 C10
Skallingen Denmark 55°32N 8°13E 63 J2
Skalni Dol = Kamenyak
Bulgaria 43°24N 26°57E 97 C10
Skanderborg Denmark 56°2N 9°55E 63 H3
Skåne Sweden 55°59N 13°30E 63 J7
Skåne □ Sweden 56°15N 14°0E 63 J7
Skaneateles U.S.A. 42°57N 76°26W 175 D8
Skaneateles L. U.S.A. 42°51N 76°22W 175 D8
Skänninge Sweden 58°24N 15°5E 63 F9
Skanör med Falsterbo
Sweden 55°24N 12°50E 63 J6
Skantzoura Greece 39°5N 24°6E 98 B6
Skara Sweden 58°25N 13°30E 63 F7
Skärblacka Sweden 58°35N 15°54E 63 F9
Skardu Pakistan 35°20N 75°44E 125 B6
Skåre Sweden 59°26N 13°26E 62 E7
Skärhamn Sweden 57°59N 11°34E 63 G5
Skarszewy Poland 54°4N 18°25E 82 D5
Skarvan og Roltdalen △
Norway 63°16N 11°31E 60 E14
Skaryszew Poland 51°19N 21°15E 83 G8
Skarżysko-Kamienna
Poland 51°7N 20°52E 83 G7
Skattkärr Sweden 59°25N 13°40E 62 E7
Skattungbyn Sweden 61°10N 14°56E 62 C8
Skawina Poland 49°59N 19°50E 83 J6
Skebobruk Sweden 59°58N 18°36E 62 E12
Skee Sweden 58°56N 11°19E 63 F5
Skeena → Canada 54°9N 130°5W 162 C2
Skeena Mts. Canada 56°40N 128°30W 162 B3
Skegness U.K. 53°9N 0°20E 66 D8
Skeleton Coast Namibia 20°0S 13°0E 141 J2
Skeleton Coast △
Namibia 20°0S 13°20E 144 B1
Skellefteå Sweden 64°45N 20°50E 60 D19
Skellefteälven →
Sweden 64°45N 21°10E 60 D19
Skelleftehamn Sweden 64°40N 21°9E 60 D19
Skellig Michael = Great Skellig
Ireland 51°47N 10°33W 64 E1
Skender Vakuf Bos.-H. 44°29N 17°22E 80 F2
Skerries Ireland 53°35N 6°8W 64 C5
Skerries, The U.K. 53°25N 4°36W 66 D3
Skhidnytsya Ukraine 49°25N 23°21E 81 B10
Ski Norway 59°43N 10°52E 63 G14
Skiathos Greece 39°12N 23°30E 98 B5
Skibbereen Ireland 51°33N 9°16W 64 E2
Skiddaw U.K. 54°39N 3°9W 66 C4
Skidegate Canada 53°15N 132°1W 162 C2
Skidra Greece 40°46N 22°10E 96 F6
Skien Norway 59°12N 9°35E 61 G13
Skierniewice Poland 51°58N 20°10E 83 G7
Skihist, Mt. Canada 50°12N 121°54W 162 C4
Skikda Algeria 36°50N 6°58E 136 A5
Skikda □ Algeria 36°38N 6°40E 136 A5
Skillingaryd Sweden 57°27N 14°5E 63 G8
Skillinge Sweden 55°30N 14°16E 63 J8
Skilloura Cyprus 35°14N 33°10E 101 D12
Skinari, Akra Greece 37°56N 20°42E 98 D2
Skinnskatteberg Sweden 59°50N 15°42E 62 E9
Skipton Australia 37°39S 143°40E 152 D5
Skipton U.K. 53°58N 2°3W 66 D5
Skiring, C. Senegal 12°26N 16°46W 138 C1
Skirmish Pt. Australia 11°59S 134°17E 150 A1
Skíros = Skyros Greece 38°55N 24°34E 98 B6
Skivarp Sweden 55°26N 13°34E 63 J7
Skive Denmark 56°33N 9°2E 63 H3
Skjálfandafljót →
Iceland 65°59N 17°25W 60 D5
Skjálfandi Iceland 66°5N 17°30W 60 C5
Skjern Denmark 55°57N 8°30E 63 J2
Skjern Å → Denmark 55°59N 8°30E 63 H2
Škocjanske Jame
Slovenia 45°40N 14°0E 93 C10
Skoczów Poland 49°49N 18°45E 83 J5
Škofja Loka Slovenia 46°9N 14°19E 93 B11
Skoghall Sweden 59°20N 13°30E 62 E7
Skogstorp Sweden 59°19N 16°29E 62 E10
Skoki Poland 52°40N 17°11E 83 F4
Skole Ukraine 49°3N 23°30E 75 D12
Skopelos Greece 39°9N 23°47E 98 B5
Skopi Greece 35°11N 26°1E 101 D8
Skopin Russia 53°55N 39°32E 84 F10
Skopje Macedonia 42°1N 21°26E 96 D5
Skopje ✈ (SKP)
Macedonia 41°59N 21°29E 96 E5
Skórcz Poland 53°47N 18°30E 82 E5

Skørping Denmark 56°50N 9°53E 63 H3
Skövde Sweden 58°24N 13°50E 63 F7
Skovorodino Russia 54°0N 124°0E 107 D13
Skowhegan U.S.A. 44°46N 69°43W 173 C19
Skradin Croatia 43°52N 15°53E 93 E12
Skrea Sweden 56°53N 12°34E 63 H6
Skrunda Latvia 56°41N 22°1E 62 B9
Skull Ireland 51°32N 9°34W 64 E2
Skultorp Sweden 58°24N 13°51E 63 F7
Skultuna Sweden 59°43N 16°25E 62 E10
Skunk → U.S.A. 40°42N 91°7W 172 E8
Skuodas Lithuania 56°16N 21°33E 62 B8
Skurup Sweden 55°28N 13°30E 63 J7
Skutskär Sweden 60°37N 17°25E 62 D11
Skvyra Ukraine 49°44N 29°40E 75 D15
Skwierzyna Poland 52°33N 15°30E 83 F2
Sky Harbour Int., Phoenix ✈
(PHX) U.S.A. 33°26N 112°5W 169 K7
Skye U.K. 57°15N 6°10W 65 D2
Skykomish U.S.A. 47°42N 121°22W 168 C3
Skyring, Seno Chile 52°35S 72°0W 192 D3
Skyropoula Greece 38°50N 24°21E 98 C6
Skyros Greece 38°55N 24°34E 98 B6
Skyttorp Sweden 60°5N 17°44E 62 D11
Slade Point Australia 21°4S 149°13E 150 b
Slade Pt. Australia 21°5S 149°13E 150 b
Slættaratindur Føroe Is. 62°18N 7°1W 60 E9
Slagelse Denmark 55°23N 11°19E 63 J5
Slamet Indonesia 7°16S 109°8E 119 G13
Slaney → Ireland 52°26N 6°33W 64 D5
Slangberge S. Africa 31°32S 20°48E 144 D3
Slânic Romania 45°14N 25°58E 81 E10
Slano Croatia 42°48N 17°53E 96 D1
Slantsy Russia 59°7N 28°5E 64 A5
Slaný Czech Rep. 50°13N 14°6E 78 A7
Ślask Poland 51°0N 16°30E 74 C9
Śląskie □ Poland 50°30N 19°0E 83 H6
Slätbaken Sweden 58°25N 16°45E 63 F10
Slate Is. Canada 48°40N 87°0W 164 C2
Slatina Croatia 45°42N 17°45E 80 E2
Slatina Romania 44°28N 24°22E 81 F9
Slatina Timiş Romania 45°15N 22°17E 80 E7
Slatington U.S.A. 40°45N 75°37W 175 F9
Slaton U.S.A. 33°26N 101°39W 176 E4
Slave → Canada 61°18N 113°39W 162 A6
Slave Coast W. Afr. 6°0N 2°30E 139 D5
Slave Lake Canada 55°17N 114°43W 162 B6
Slave Pt. Canada 61°11N 115°56W 162 A5
Slavgorod Russia 53°1N 78°37E 108 D8
Slavinja Serbia 43°9N 22°50E 96 C6
Slavkov u Brna
Czech Rep. 49°10N 16°52E 79 B9
Slavkovský Les △
Czech Rep. 50°5N 12°44E 78 A5
Slavonia Europe 45°0N 17°40E 80 E2
Slavonski Brod Croatia 45°11N 18°1E 80 E3
Slavsk Russia 55°3N 21°41E 82 C8
Slavske Ukraine 48°51N 23°27E 81 B8
Slavskoye Russia 54°30N 20°27E 82 D7
Slavuta Ukraine 50°15N 27°2E 75 C14
Slavyanka Russia 42°53N 131°21E 112 C5
Slavyanovo Bulgaria 43°28N 24°52E 97 C8
Slavyansk = Slovyansk
Ukraine 48°55N 37°36E 85 H9
Slavyansk-na-Kubani
Russia 45°15N 38°11E 85 K10
Sława Poland 51°52N 16°2E 83 G3
Sławharad Belarus 53°27N 31°0E 75 B16
Sławno Poland 54°20N 16°41E 82 D3
Sławoborze Poland 53°55N 15°42E 82 E2
Slea Hd. Ireland 52°6N 10°27W 64 D1
Sleaford U.K. 53°0N 0°24W 66 D7
Sleaford B. Australia 34°55S 135°45E 151 E2
Sleat, Sd. of U.K. 57°5N 5°47W 65 D3
Sleeper Is. Canada 58°30N 81°0W 161 F15
Sleeping Bear Dunes △
U.S.A. 44°50N 86°5W 172 C10
Sleepy Eye U.S.A. 44°18N 94°43W 172 C6
Slemon L. Canada 63°13N 116°4W 162 A5
Ślesin Poland 52°22N 18°14E 83 F5
Slide Mt. U.S.A. 42°0N 74°25W 175 E10
Slidell U.S.A. 30°17N 89°47W 177 F10
Sliema Malta 35°55N 14°30E 101 D2
Slieve Aughty Ireland 53°4N 8°30W 64 C3
Slieve Bloom Ireland 53°4N 7°40W 64 C4
Slieve Donard U.K. 54°11N 5°55W 64 B6
Slieve Gamph Ireland 54°6N 9°0W 64 B3
Slieve Gullion U.K. 54°7N 6°26W 64 B5
Slieve Mish Ireland 52°12N 9°50W 64 D2
Slieve League Ireland 54°40N 8°42W 64 B3
Slievenamon Ireland 52°25N 7°34W 64 D4
Sligeach = Sligo Ireland 54°16N 8°28W 64 B3
Sligo Ireland 54°16N 8°28W 64 B3
Sligo □ Ireland 54°8N 8°42W 64 B3
Sligo B. Ireland 54°18N 8°40W 64 B3
Slippery Rock U.S.A. 41°4N 80°3W 174 E4
Slite Sweden 57°42N 18°48E 63 G12
Sliven Bulgaria 42°42N 26°19E 97 D10
Sliven □ Bulgaria 42°42N 26°19E 97 D10
Slivnitsa Bulgaria 42°50N 23°2E 96 D7
Sljeme Croatia 45°57N 15°58E 93 C12
Sloan U.S.A. 35°57N 115°13W 171 K11
Sloansville U.S.A. 42°45N 74°22W 175 D10
Slobidka Ukraine 47°54N 29°12E 81 B14
Slobozia Moldova 46°45N 29°42E 81 D14
Slobozia Argeş, Romania 44°30N 25°14E 81 F10
Slobozia Ialomiţa,
Romania 44°34N 27°23E 81 F11
Slocan Canada 49°48N 117°28W 162 D5
Slocomb U.S.A. 31°7N 85°36W 178 D4
Slomniki Poland 50°16N 20°4E 83 H7
Słonim Belarus 53°4N 25°19E 75 B13
Slough U.K. 51°30N 0°36W 67 F7
Slough □ U.K. 51°30N 0°36W 67 F7
Sloughhouse U.S.A. 38°26N 121°12W 170 G5
Slovak Rep. ■ Europe 48°30N 20°0E 79 C12
Slovakia = Slovak Rep. ■
Europe 48°30N 20°0E 79 C12
Slovakian Ore Mts. = Slovenské
Rudohorie Slovak Rep. 48°45N 20°0E 79 C12
Slovenia ■ Europe 45°58N 14°30E 93 C11
Slovenija = Slovenia ■
Europe 45°58N 14°30E 93 C11
Slovenj Gradec Slovenia 46°31N 15°5E 93 B12
Slovenska = Slovak Rep. ■
Europe 48°30N 20°0E 79 C12

Slovenska Bistrica
Slovenia 46°24N 15°35E 93 B12
Slovenské Konjice
Slovenia 46°20N 15°28E 93 B12
Slovenské Rudohorie
Slovak Rep. 48°45N 20°0E 79 C12
Slovenský Raj △
Slovak Rep. 48°53N 20°25E 79 C13
Slovyansk Ukraine 48°55N 37°36E 85 H9
Słowiński △ Poland 54°43N 17°26E 82 D4
Słubice Poland 52°22N 14°35E 83 F1
Sluch → Ukraine 51°37N 26°38E 75 C14
Sluis Neths. 51°18N 3°23E 69 C3
Slunj Croatia 45°6N 15°33E 93 C12
Słupca Poland 52°15N 17°52E 83 F4
Słupia → Poland 54°35N 16°51E 82 D3
Słupsk Poland 54°30N 17°3E 82 D4
Slurry S. Africa 25°49S 25°42E 144 C4
Slutsk Belarus 53°2N 27°31E 75 B14
Slyne Hd. Ireland 53°25N 10°10W 64 C1
Slyudyanka Russia 51°40N 103°40E 107 D11
Småland Sweden 57°15N 15°25E 63 G9
Smålandsfarvandet
Denmark 55°10N 11°20E 63 J5
Smålandsstenar Sweden 57°10N 13°25E 63 G7
Smalltree L. Canada 61°0N 105°0W 163 A8
Smallwood Res. Canada 54°5N 64°30W 165 B7
Smarhon Belarus 54°20N 26°24E 75 A14
Smarje Slovenia 46°15N 15°34E 93 B12
Smartt Syndicate Dam
S. Africa 30°45S 23°10E 144 D3
Smartville U.S.A. 39°13N 121°18W 170 F5
Smeaton Canada 53°30N 104°49W 163 C8
Smedby Sweden 56°41N 16°13E 63 H10
Smederevo Serbia 44°40N 20°57E 96 B4
Smederevska Palanka
Serbia 44°22N 20°58E 96 B4
Smedjebacken Sweden 60°8N 15°25E 62 D9
Smela = Smila Ukraine 49°15N 31°58E 85 H6
Smeralda, Costa Italy 41°5N 9°35E 94 A2
Smerwick Harbour
Ireland 52°12N 10°23W 64 D1
Smethport U.S.A. 41°49N 78°27W 174 E6
Smidovich Russia 48°36N 133°49E 107 E14
Śmigiel Poland 52°1N 16°32E 83 F3
Smila Ukraine 49°15N 31°58E 85 H6
Smilyan Bulgaria 41°29N 24°46E 97 E8
Smith Canada 55°10N 114°0W 162 B6
Smith Center U.S.A. 39°47N 98°47W 172 F4
Smith I. Canada 60°45N 78°25W 161 E16
Smith I. India 13°20N 93°4E 127 H11
Smith Islands △
Australia 20°40S 149°9E 150 b
Smith River △ U.S.A. 41°55N 124°0W 168 F2
Smith Sd. N. Amer. 78°25N 74°0W 57 B3
Smithburne →
Australia 17°3S 140°57E 150 B3
Smithers Canada 54°45N 127°10W 162 C3
Smithfield S. Africa 30°9S 26°30E 145 D4
Smithfield N.C.,
U.S.A. 35°31N 78°21W 177 D15
Smithfield Utah,
U.S.A. 41°50N 111°50W 168 F8
Smiths Canada 32°32N 85°6W 178 C4
Smiths Falls Canada 44°55N 76°0W 175 B9
Smithton Australia 40°53S 145°6E 151 G4
Smithville Canada 43°6N 79°33W 177 C5
Smithville Ga., U.S.A. 31°54N 84°15W 178 D5
Smithville Tex., U.S.A. 30°1N 97°10W 176 F6
Smoke Creek Desert
U.S.A. 40°30N 119°40W 168 F4
Smoky → Canada 56°10N 117°21W 162 B5
Smoky Bay Australia 32°22S 134°13E 151 E1
Smoky Hill → U.S.A. 39°4N 96°48W 172 F5
Smoky Hills U.S.A. 39°15N 99°30W 172 F4
Smoky Lake Canada 54°10N 112°30W 162 C6
Smøla Norway 63°23N 8°3E 60 E13
Smolensk Russia 54°45N 32°5E 84 E7
Smolensk □ Russia 55°20N 33°0E 84 E7
Smolenskoye Poozerye △
Russia 55°35N 31°50E 84 E7
Smolikas, Oros Greece 40°9N 20°58E 96 F4
Smolník Slovak Rep. 48°43N 20°44E 79 C13
Smolny △ Russia 54°50N 47°10E 86 C9
Smolyan Bulgaria 41°36N 24°38E 97 E8
Smolyan □ Bulgaria 41°36N 24°38E 97 E8
Smooth Rock Falls
Canada 49°17N 81°37W 164 C3
Smoothstone L.
Canada 54°40N 106°50W 163 C7
Smorgon = Smarhon
Belarus 54°20N 26°24E 75 A14
Smotrych Ukraine 48°37N 26°33E 81 B11
Smotrych → Ukraine 48°34N 26°39E 81 B11
Smulţi Romania 45°57N 27°44E 81 E11
Smyadovo Bulgaria 43°2N 27°1E 97 C11
Smygehamn Sweden 55°21N 13°22E 63 J7
Smygehuk Sweden 55°20N 13°23E 63 J7
Smyley I. Antarctica 72°55S 78°0W 55 D17
Smyrna = İzmir Turkey 38°25N 27°8E 99 C9
Smyrna Del., U.S.A. 39°18N 75°36W 173 F16
Smyrna Ga., U.S.A. 33°53N 84°31W 178 B5
Snæfell Iceland 64°48N 15°34W 60 D6
Snaefell I. of Man 54°16N 4°27W 66 C3
Snæfellsjökull Iceland 64°49N 23°46W 60 D2
Snake I. = Zmiinyi, Ostriv
Black Sea 45°15N 30°12E 85 K6
Snake I. Australia 38°47S 146°33E 153 E7
Snake Range U.S.A. 39°0N 114°20W 168 G6
Snake River Plain
U.S.A. 42°50N 114°0W 168 E7
Snasahögarna Sweden 63°13N 12°21E 62 A6
Snåsavatnet Norway 64°12N 12°0E 60 D15
Snedsted Denmark 56°55N 8°32E 63 H2
Sneek Neths. 53°2N 5°40E 69 A5
Sneem Ireland 51°50N 9°54W 64 E2
Sneeuberge S. Africa 31°46S 24°20E 144 D3
Snejbjerg Denmark 56°8N 8°54E 63 H2
Snelling Calif., U.S.A. 37°31N 120°26W 170 H6
Snelling S.C., U.S.A. 33°15N 81°27W 178 C8
Snells Beach N.Z. 36°25S 174°44E 154 C3
Snežnik Slovenia 45°36N 14°35E 93 C11
Śniardwy, Jezioro Poland 53°48N 21°50E 82 E8
Śnieżka Europe 50°41N 15°50E 83 H3
Śnieżnik Poland 50°12N 16°44E 83 H3
Snigirevka = Snihurivka
Ukraine 47°2N 32°49E 85 J7

Snihurivka Ukraine 47°2N 32°49E 85 J7
Snina Slovak Rep. 48°58N 22°9E 79 C15
Snizort, L. U.K. 57°33N 6°28W 65 D2
Snøhetta Norway 62°19N 9°16E 60 E13
Snohomish U.S.A. 47°55N 122°6W 170 C4
Snoqualmie U.S.A. 47°31N 121°49W 170 C5
Snoqualmie Pass
U.S.A. 47°25N 121°25W 170 C5
Snoul Cambodia 12°4N 106°26E 121 F6
Snover U.S.A. 43°27N 82°58W 174 C2
Snow Hill U.S.A. 38°11N 75°24W 173 F16
Snow Lake Canada 54°52N 100°3W 163 C8
Snow Mt. Calif.,
U.S.A. 39°23N 122°45W 170 F4
Snow Mt. Maine,
U.S.A. 45°18N 70°48W 175 A14
Snow Shoe U.S.A. 41°2N 77°57W 174 E7
Snowbird L. Canada 60°45N 103°0W 163 A8
Snowdon △ U.K. 53°4N 4°5W 66 D3
Snowdonia △ U.K. 53°7N 3°59W 66 D4
Snowdoun U.S.A. 32°15N 86°18W 178 C3
Snowdrift = Lutsel K'e
Canada 62°24N 110°44W 163 A6
Snowdrift → Canada 62°24N 110°44W 163 A6
Snowflake U.S.A. 34°30N 110°5W 169 J8
Snowtown Australia 33°46S 138°14E 152 B3
Snowville U.S.A. 41°58N 112°43W 168 F7
Snowy → Australia 37°46S 148°30E 153 D8
Snowy Mt. U.S.A. 43°42N 74°23W 175 C10
Snowy Mts. Australia 36°30S 148°20E 153 D8
Snowy River △
Australia 37°15S 147°29E 153 D7
Snug Corner Bahamas 22°33N 73°52W 183 B5
Snug Harbour Canada 45°22N 80°17W 174 B7
Snyatyn Ukraine 48°27N 25°38E 81 B10
Snyder Okla., U.S.A. 34°40N 98°57W 176 D5
Snyder Tex., U.S.A. 32°44N 100°55W 176 E4
Soahanina Madag. 16°6S 45°20E 141 H9
Soalala Madag. 16°6S 45°20E 141 H9
Soan → Pakistan 33°1N 71°44E 124 C4
Soanierana-Ivongo
Madag. 16°55S 49°35E 141 H9
Soap Lake U.S.A. 47°23N 119°29W 168 C4
Soasiu Indonesia 0°48N 127°34E 119 D7
Soata Colombia 6°20N 72°35W 184 B3
Soavinandriana
Madag. 19°9S 46°45E 141 H9
Sobat, Nahr → Sudan 8°32N 32°40E 135 G12
Sobhapur India 22°47N 78°17E 124 H8
Sobinka Russia 56°0N 40°0E 84 E11
Sobótka Poland 50°54N 16°44E 83 H3
Sobradinho, Represa de
Brazil 9°30S 42°0W 189 B2
Sobral Brazil 3°50S 40°20W 189 A2
Sobrance Slovak Rep. 48°45N 22°11E 79 C15
Sobreira Formosa
Portugal 39°46N 7°51W 88 F3
Soc Giang Vietnam 22°54N 106°1E 116 F6
Soc Trang Vietnam 9°37N 105°50E 121 H5
Soča → Europe 46°20N 13°40E 78 E6
Socastee U.S.A. 33°41N 78°59W 177 E15
Sochaczew Poland 52°15N 20°13E 83 F7
Soch'e = Shache China 38°20N 77°10E 109 E9
Sochi Russia 43°35N 39°40E 87 J4
Sochi ✈ (AER) Russia 43°27N 39°57E 87 J4
Sochos Greece 40°48N 23°22E 96 F7
Social Circle U.S.A. 33°39N 83°43W 178 B6
Société, Îs. de la
French Polynesia 17°0S 151°0W 157 J12
Society Hill U.S.A. 32°26N 85°27W 178 C4
Society Is. = Société, Îs. de la
French Polynesia 17°0S 151°0W 157 J12
Socompa, Portezuelo de
Chile 24°27S 68°18W 190 A2
Socorro N. Mex.,
U.S.A. 34°4N 106°54W 169 J10
Socorro Tex., U.S.A. 31°39N 106°18W 176 F2
Socorro, I. Mexico 18°30N 111°0W 180 D2
Socotra Yemen 12°30N 54°0E 131 E5
Socovos Spain 38°20N 1°56W 91 G3
Socuéllamos Spain 39°16N 2°47W 91 F2
Soda L. U.S.A. 35°10N 116°4W 171 K10
Soda Plains India 35°30N 79°0E 125 B8
Soda Springs U.S.A. 42°39N 111°36W 168 E8
Sodankylä Finland 67°29N 26°40E 60 C22
Soddy-Daisy U.S.A. 35°17N 85°10W 178 B3
Söderala Sweden 61°18N 17°10E 62 C11
Söderbärke Sweden 60°5N 15°35E 62 D9
Söderfors Sweden 60°23N 17°25E 62 D11
Söderhamn Sweden 61°18N 17°10E 62 C11
Söderköping Sweden 58°31N 16°35E 63 F10
Södermanland □
Sweden 59°10N 16°30E 62 E10
Södertälje Sweden 59°12N 17°39E 62 E11
Södra Finnskoga Sweden 60°42N 12°42E 62 D6
Södra Sandby Sweden 55°43N 13°21E 63 J7
Södra Ulvön Sweden 63°0N 18°38E 62 B12
Södra Vi Sweden 57°45N 15°45E 63 G9
Sodražica Slovenia 45°45N 14°39E 93 C11
Sodus U.S.A. 43°14N 77°4W 174 C7
Sodwana Bay △
S. Africa 27°35S 32°43E 145 C6
Soe Indonesia 9°52S 124°17E 148 A3
Soekmekaar = Morebeng
S. Africa 23°30S 29°55E 145 A4
Soest Neths. 52°9N 5°19E 69 B5
Soest Germany 51°34N 8°7E 76 D4
Sofades Greece 39°18N 22°4E 98 B4
Sofala □ Mozam. 19°30S 34°30E 143 H6
Sofara Mali 13°59N 4°9W 138 C4
Sofia = Sofiya Bulgaria 42°45N 23°20E 96 D7
Sofia → Madag. 15°27S 47°23E 141 H9
Sofievka Ukraine 37°47N 37°32E 85 J8
Sofiko Greece 37°46N 23°3E 98 D5
Sofiya Bulgaria 42°45N 23°20E 96 D7
Sofiya ✈ (SOF) Bulgaria 42°42N 23°18E 96 D7
Sofu-Gan Japan 29°49N 140°21E 113 K10
Sogaer Germany 52°59N 8°26E 76 B4
Sogakofe Ghana 6°2N 0°39E 139 D5
Sogamoso Colombia 5°43N 72°56W 184 B3
Sogār Iran 25°53N 58°6E 129 E8
Sogdalsfjora Norway 61°14N 7°5E 60 F12
Sognefjorden Norway 61°10N 5°50E 61 F11
Sogn og Fjordane □
Norway 61°40N 6°0E 61 F11
Sögütlü Turkey 40°46N 30°25E 104 B4
Soh Iran 33°26N 51°27E 129 C6

Sohâg Egypt 26°33N 31°43E 1
Sohagpur India 22°42N 78°12E 1
Sohar = Şuḩār Oman 24°20N 56°40E 1
Sohela India 21°18N 83°24E 1
Soheuksando S. Korea 34°4N 125°7E 11
Sohm Abyssal Plain
Atl. Oc. 36°0N 55°0W
Soignies Belgium 50°35N 4°5E
Soin Burkina Faso 12°47N 3°50W 1
Soissons France 49°25N 3°19E 7
Söja Japan 34°40N 133°45E 1
Sojat India 25°55N 73°45E 1
Sok → Russia 53°24N 50°8E 8
Sokal Ukraine 50°31N 24°15E 7
Sokcho S. Korea 38°12N 128°36E 11
Söke Turkey 37°48N 27°28E
Sokelo
Dem. Rep. of the Congo 9°55S 24°36E 1
Sokhumi Georgia 43°0N 41°0E
Sokki, Oued In →
Algeria 29°30N 3°...E 1
Soko Banja Serbia 43°40N 21°51E 1
Soko Is. China 22°10N 113°54E
Sokodé Togo 9°0N 1°11E 1
Sokol Russia 59°30N 40°5E 8
Sokolac Bos.-H. 43°56N 18°48E
Sokółka Poland 53°25N 23°30E 8
Sokolo Ségou, Mali 14°53N 6°8W 1
Sokolo Sikasso, Mali 10°52N 6°59W 1
Sokołów Malpolski
Poland 50°12N 22°7E 8
Sokołów Podlaski
Poland 52°25N 22°15E 8
Sokoły Poland 52°59N 22°42E 8
Sokoto Nigeria 13°2N 5°16E 1
Sokoto □ Nigeria 12°30N 6°0E 1
Sokoto → Nigeria 11°20N 4°10E 1
Sokyrnytsya Ukraine 48°7N 23°23E
Sokyryany Ukraine 48°27N 27°25E 8
Sol, Costa del Spain 36°30N 4°30W
Sol Iletsk Russia 51°10N 55°0E 1
Sola → Poland 50°4N 19°15E
Solai Kenya 0°2N 36°12E 1
Solan India 30°55N 77°7E 1
Solana Beach U.S.A. 32°58N 117°16W 1
Solander I. N.Z. 46°34S 166°54E 1
Solapur India 17°43N 75°56E 1
Solca Romania 47°40N 25°50E 8
Solda Gölü Turkey 37°33N 29°42E 9
Soldăneşti Moldova 47°49N 28°48E 8
Soldeu Andorra 42°35N 1°40E
Soldotna U.S.A. 60°29N 151°3W 1
Soléa Cyprus 35°5N 33°4E 10
Solec Kujawski Poland 53°5N 18°14E
Soledad Colombia 10°55N 74°46W 1
Soledad Venezuela 8°10N 63°34W 1
Solent, The U.K. 50°45N 1°25W
Solenzara France 41°53N 9°23E 7
Solesmes France 50°10N 3°30E
Solferino Italy 45°22N 10°34E
Solfonntaggen Norway 60°2N 6°57E 6
Solhan Turkey 38°57N 41°3E 1
Soligorsk = Salihorsk
Belarus 52°51N 27°27E 7
Solihull U.K. 52°26N 1°47W
Solikamsk Russia 59°38N 56°50E 1
Solimões = Amazonas →
S. Amer. 0°5S 50°0W 1
Solin Croatia 43°33N 16°30E 9
Solingen Germany 51°10N 7°5E 7
Söll Austria 47°30N 12°11E 7
Sollebrunn Sweden 58°8N 12°32E
Solleftea Sweden 63°12N 17°20E 6
Sollentuna Sweden 59°26N 17°56E
Sóller Spain 39°46N 2°43E 1
Solling Germany 51°45N 9°38E
Solling-Vogler △
Germany 51°45N 9°32E
Solnechnogorsk Russia 56°10N 36°57E 8
Solo → Indonesia 6°47S 112°22E 1
Solofra Italy 40°50N 14°51E
Sologne France 47°40N 1°45E
Solok Indonesia 0°45S 100°40E 1
Solola Guatemala 14°49N 91°10W 1
Sololo Kenya 3°33N 38°39E 1
Solomon, N. Fork →
U.S.A. 39°29N 98°26W 1
Solomon, S. Fork →
U.S.A. 39°25N 99°12W 1
Solomon Is. ■ Pac. Oc. 6°0S 155°0E 1
Solomon Rise Pac. Oc.
Solon China 46°32N 121°10E 11
Solon Springs U.S.A. 46°22N 91°49W 1
Solonópole Brazil 5°44S 39°1W 1
Solor Indonesia 8°27S 123°0E 1
Solotcha Russia 54°48N 39°53E 8
Solothurn Switz. 47°13N 7°32E
Solothurn □ Switz. 47°18N 7°40E
Solotvyn Ukraine 48°42N 24°25E 8
Solsona Spain 42°0N 1°31E
Solt Hungary 46°45N 19°1E
Šolta Croatia 43°24N 16°15E 9
Solţānābād Khorāsān,
Iran 34°13N 59°58E 1
Solţānābād Khorāsān,
Iran 36°29N 58°5E 1
Soltāniyeh Iran 36°20N 48°47E 10
Soltau Germany 52°59N 9°51E
Soltsy Russia 58°10N 30°13E 8
Soltüstik Qazaqstan □
Kazakhstan 53°0N 70°0E 1
Solund Norway 61°5N 4°50E
Solunska Glava
Macedonia 41°44N 21°31E 9
Solvay U.S.A. 43°3N 76°13W 1
Sölvesborg Sweden 56°5N 14°35E
Solway Firth U.K. 54°49N 3°35W
Solwezi Zambia 12°11S 26°21E 1
Sōma Japan 37°40N 140°50E 11
Soma Turkey 39°10N 27°35E
Somabhula Zimbabwe 19°42S 29°40E 1
Somali Pen. Africa 7°0N 46°0E 1
Somali Rep. ■ Africa 7°0N 47°0E 1
Somalia ■ Africa 7°0N 47°0E 1
Somaliland □ Somalia 9°0N 46°0E 1
Sombernon France 47°20N 4°40E
Sombo Angola 7°22S 21°15E 1
Sombor Serbia 45°46N 19°9E
Sombra Canada 42°43N 82°29W 1
Sombrerete Mexico 23°38N 103°39W 1
Sombrero Anguilla 18°37N 63°30W 1

NDEX TO WORLD MAPS
Stanley Mission 273

brero Channel
dia 7°41N 93°35E 127 L11
cuta Mare Romania 47°31N 23°28E 81 C8
dari India 25°47N 72°38E 124 G5
eido ⌂ Spain 43°5N 6°11W 88 B4
ers U.S.A. 48°5N 114°13W 168 B6
erset Ky., U.S.A. 37°5N 84°36W 173 G11
erset Mass., U.S.A. 41°47N 71°8W 175 E13
erset Pa., U.S.A. 40°1N 79°5W 174 F5
erset □ U.K. 51°9N 3°0W 67 F5
erset East S. Africa 32°42S 25°35E 144 D4
erset I. Canada 73°30N 93°0W 160 C13
erset West S. Africa 34°8S 18°50E 144 D2
ersworth U.S.A. 43°16N 70°52W 175 C14
erton U.S.A. 32°36N 114°43W 169 K6
erville U.S.A. 40°35N 74°38W 175 F10
eş → Romania 47°49N 22°43E 80 C7
eşul Mare →
mania 47°9N 23°55E 81 C8
me □ France 49°57N 2°20E 71 C9
me → France 50°11N 1°38E 71 B8
me, B. de la France 50°14N 1°33E 70 B8
men Jönköping,
eden 58°12N 14°58E 63 F8
men Östergötland,
eden 58°0N 15°15E 63 F9
mepy-Tahure
ance 49°15N 4°31E 71 C11
merda Germany 51°9N 11°7E 76 D7
mesous France 48°44N 4°12E 71 D11
mières France 43°47N 4°6E 73 E8
nath India 20°53N 70°22E 124 J4
ogy □ Hungary 46°19N 17°30E 80 D2
ogyszob Hungary 46°18N 17°20E 80 D2
osomo Fiji 16°47S 179°58W 154 a
osomo Str. Fiji 16°0S 180°0E 154 a
oto Nic. 13°28N 86°37W 182 D2
polno Poland 52°26N 18°30E 83 F5
port, Túnel de Spain 42°48N 0°31W 90 C4
uncurá, Meseta de
gentina 41°30S 67°0W 192 B3
warpet India 12°36N 75°52E 127 H2
→ India 25°42N 84°52E 125 G11
Laem Thailand 7°59N 98°16E 121 a
Ha Vietnam 15°3N 108°34E 120 E7
La Vietnam 21°20N 103°50E 116 G4
Morrell Spain 39°44N 3°20E 100 B10
Rapinya Spain 39°35N 2°37E 100 B9
Sardina Spain 39°37N 2°40E 100 B9
Serra Spain 39°43N 3°13E 100 B10
Servera Spain 39°37N 3°21E 90 F8
Tay Vietnam 21°8N 105°30E 116 G5
Tinh Vietnam 15°10N 108°40E 120 E7
Panama 8°0N 81°20W 182 E3
marg India 34°18N 75°21E 125 B6
mukhi India 23°18N 87°27E 125 H12
r → India 24°24N 79°56E 125 G8
h'ŏn N. Korea 39°48N 124°55E 115 E13
ags → S. Africa 33°44S 25°51E 144 D4
alo Italy 46°20N 10°19E 92 B7
er Felding Denmark 55°57N 8°47E 63 J2
er Omme Denmark 55°50N 8°54E 63 J2
erborg Denmark 54°55N 9°49E 63 K3
ershausen Germany 51°22N 10°51E 76 D6
er Strømfjord =
angerlussuaq
eenland 66°59N 50°40W 57 D5
rio Italy 46°10N 9°52E 92 B6
ur → India 20°40N 82°1E 126 D6
Mozam. 17°23S 34°55E 143 F3
pur India 20°55N 83°50E 126 D6
m Brazil 6°0S 67°52W 188 B4
Nigeria 9°49N 12°39E 139 D7
Thailand 18°28N 100°11E 120 C3
Cau Vietnam 13°27N 109°18E 120 F7
-Köl Kyrgyzstan 41°50N 75°12E 109 D9
Ma Vietnam 20°56N 103°53E 116 G4
Xian China 34°12N 112°8E 114 G7
adh India 21°9N 73°33E 126 D1
an Indonesia 8°13S 115°24E 119 J18
ea Tanzania 10°40S 35°40E 143 E4
ens France 49°32N 1°50E 71 C8
gang China 22°46N 113°50E 111 a
Hu China 43°35N 126°50E 115 C14
hua Jiang →
ina 47°45N 132°30E 111 B15
jimvelo ⌂ S. Africa 25°50S 31°2E 145 C5
jiang China 31°1N 121°12E 117 B13
jianghe China 42°10N 127°29E 115 C14
jin = Kimch'aek
Korea 40°40N 129°10E 115 D15
kan China 28°35N 106°52E 116 C6
khla Thailand 7°13N 100°37E 121 J3
ming China 25°12N 103°2E 116 E4
nim N. Korea 38°45N 125°39E 115 E13
o Mozam. 15°34S 32°38E 145 A5
pan China 32°40N 103°30E 116 A4
tao China 28°11N 109°10E 116 C7
we
m. Rep. of the Congo 3°20S 26°16E 142 C2
we → Africa 9°44S 33°58E 143 D3
xi China 27°31N 118°44E 117 D12
zi China 30°12N 111°45E 117 B8
at India 23°29N 82°31E 125 H10
d Youqi China 42°45N 112°48E 114 C7
d Zuoqi China 43°50N 113°42E 114 C7
at India 29°0N 77°5E 124 E7
ach India 22°59N 76°21E 124 H7
covo Russia 57°50N 37°5E 84 D9
niani Pakistan 25°25N 66°40E 124 G2
niani B. Pakistan 25°15N 66°30E 124 G2
aeberg Germany 50°21N 11°10E 77 F7
nino Italy 41°25N 13°14E 94 A6
→ Minas Gerais,
azil 17°2S 45°32W 189 D1
→ Tocantins, Brazil 9°58S 48°11W 189 B1
oma U.S.A. 38°18N 122°28W 170 G4
ra Calif., U.S.A. 37°59N 120°23W 170 H6
ra Tex., U.S.A. 30°34N 100°39W 176 F4
ra □ Mexico 29°20N 110°40W 180 B2
ra → Mexico 29°5N 110°55W 180 B2
ran Desert
.S.A. 33°40N 113°30W 171 L12
yta Mexico 31°51N 112°50W 180 A2
or Iran 34°47N 47°36E 105 E12
eca Spain 39°42N 3°57W 89 F7
onate El Salv. 13°43N 89°44W 182 D2
torp Sweden 58°44N 15°38E 63 F9
hofen Germany 47°30N 10°16E 77 H6
how = Suzhou
ina 31°19N 120°38E 117 B13
e Canada 48°13N 123°43W 170 B3
Soomaa △ Estonia 58°30N 28°5E 84 C3
Soomaaliya = Somalia ■
Africa 7°0N 47°0E 131 F4
Sop Hao Laos 20°33N 104°27E 116 G5
Sop Prap Thailand 17°53N 99°20E 120 D2
Sopchoppy U.S.A. 30°4N 84°29W 178 E5
Sopelana Spain 43°23N 2°58W 90 B2
Soperton U.S.A. 32°23N 82°35W 178 C7
Sopi Indonesia 2°34N 128°28E 119 D7
Sopot Bulgaria 42°39N 24°45E 97 D8
Sopot Poland 54°27N 18°31E 82 D5
Sopot Serbia 44°29N 20°36E 96 B4
Sopotnica Macedonia 41°18N 21°13E 96 E5
Sopron Hungary 47°45N 16°32E 80 C1
Sopur India 34°18N 74°27E 125 B6
Sør-Rondane Antarctica 72°0S 25°0E 55 D4
Sora Italy 41°43N 13°37E 93 G10
Sorab India 14°23N 75°6E 127 G2
Sorada India 19°45N 84°26E 126 E7
Sorah Pakistan 27°13N 68°56E 124 F3
Söråker Sweden 62°30N 17°32E 62 B11
Sorang Kazakhstan 49°46N 72°51E 109 C8
Sorano Italy 42°41N 11°43E 93 F8
Soraon India 25°37N 81°51E 125 G9
Sorata Bolivia 15°50S 68°40W 188 D4
Sorbas Spain 37°6N 2°7W 91 H2
Sörbygden Sweden 62°48N 16°12E 62 B10
Sord = Swords Ireland 53°28N 6°13W 64 C5
Sordellen Sweden 61°48N 16°43E 62 C10
Sore France 44°18N 0°35W 72 D3
Sorel-Tracy Canada 46°0N 73°10W 164 C5
Soresina Italy 45°17N 9°51E 92 C6
Sörforsa Sweden 61°43N 16°58E 62 C10
Sórgono Italy 40°1N 9°6E 94 B2
Sorgues France 44°1N 4°53E 73 D8
Sorgun Turkey 39°46N 35°11E 104 C6
Soria Spain 41°43N 2°32W 90 D2
Soria □ Spain 41°46N 2°28W 90 D2
Soriano Uruguay 33°24S 58°19W 190 C4
Soriano nel Cimino Italy 42°25N 12°14E 93 F9
Sorkh, Kuh-e Iran 35°40N 58°30E 129 C8
Sorø Denmark 55°26N 11°32E 63 J5
Soro Guinea 10°9N 9°48W 138 C3
Soroca Moldova 48°8N 28°12E 81 B13
Sorocaba Brazil 23°31S 47°27W 191 A6
Sorochinsk Russia 52°26N 53°10E 108 B4
Soroki = Soroca
Moldova 48°8N 28°12E 81 B13
Sorong Indonesia 0°55S 131°15E 119 E8
Soroni Greece 36°21N 28°1E 101 C10
Soroti Uganda 1°43N 33°35E 142 B3
Sørøya Norway 70°40N 22°30E 60 A20
Sørøysundet Norway 70°25N 23°0E 60 A20
Sorraia → Portugal 38°55N 8°53W 89 G2
Sorrell Australia 42°47S 147°34E 151 G4
Sorrento Italy 40°37N 14°22E 95 B7
Sorsele Sweden 65°31N 17°30E 60 D17
Sörsjön Sweden 61°24N 13°5E 62 C7
Sorso Italy 40°48N 8°34E 94 B1
Sorsogon Phil. 13°0N 124°0E 119 B6
Sortavala Russia 61°42N 30°41E 84 B6
Sortino Italy 37°9N 15°2E 95 E8
Sortland Norway 68°42N 15°25E 60 B16
Sortot Sudan 19°30N 30°28E 137 D3
Sørvågen Norway 67°53N 13°1E 60 C15
Sorvizhi Russia 57°52N 48°32E 86 B9
Sos del Rey Católico
Spain 42°30N 1°13W 90 C3
Soscumica, L. Canada 50°15N 77°27W 164 B4
Sösdala Sweden 56°2N 13°41E 63 H7
Sosna → Russia 52°42N 38°55E 85 F10
Sosnovka Kirov, Russia 56°17N 51°17E 86 B10
Sosnovka Tambov, Russia 53°13N 41°24E 86 D5
Sosnovyy Bor Russia 59°55N 29°6E 84 C5
Sosnowiec Poland 50°20N 19°10E 83 H6
Sospel France 43°52N 7°27E 73 E11
Sossus Vlei Namibia 24°40S 15°23E 144 B2
Šoštanj Slovenia 46°23N 15°4E 93 B12
Sŏsura N. Korea 42°16N 130°36E 115 C16
Sot → India 27°27N 79°37E 125 F8
Sotavento C. Verde Is. 15°0N 24°0W 134 b
Sotik Kenya 0°41S 35°7E 142 C4
Sotkamo Finland 64°8N 28°23E 60 D23
Soto Spain 43°32N 6°4W 88 B4
Soto la Marina Mexico 23°46N 98°13W 181 C5
Soto la Marina →
Mexico 23°45N 97°45W 181 C5
Soto y Amío Spain 42°46N 5°53W 88 C5
Sotouboua Togo 8°34N 0°59E 139 D5
Sotrondio Spain 43°17N 5°36W 88 B5
Sotuta Mexico 20°36N 89°1W 181 C7
Souanké Congo 2°10N 14°3E 140 D2
Soubré Ivory C. 5°50N 6°35W 138 D3
Souda Greece 35°29N 24°4E 101 D6
Soudas, Ormos Greece 35°25N 24°10E 101 D6
Souderton U.S.A. 40°19N 75°19W 175 F9
Soufli Greece 41°12N 26°18E 97 E10
Soufrière Guadeloupe 16°5N 61°40W 182 b
Soufrière St. Lucia 13°51N 61°3W 183 f
Soufrière Bay Dominica 15°13N 61°22W 183 f
Souillac France 44°53N 1°29E 72 D5
Souilly France 49°3N 5°17E 71 C12
Souk-Ahras Algeria 36°23N 7°57E 136 A5
Souk-Ahras □ Algeria 36°10N 7°55E 136 A5
Souk el Arba du Rharb
Morocco 34°43N 5°59W 136 B2
Soukhouma Laos 14°38N 105°48E 120 E5
Sŏul = Seoul S. Korea 37°31N 126°58E 115 F14
Soulac-sur-Mer France 45°30N 1°7W 72 C2
Soulougou Burkina Faso 13°1N 0°25E 139 C5
Soultz-sous-Forêts
France 48°57N 7°52E 71 D14
Sound, The = Øresund
Europe 55°45N 12°40E 63 J6
Sound, The U.K. 50°20N 4°10W 67 G3
Sound I. India 12°58N 92°59E 127 H11
Sounio, Akra Greece 37°37N 24°1E 98 D6
Sour el Ghozlane Algeria 36°10N 3°45E 136 A4
Sources, Mt. aux
Lesotho 28°45S 28°50E 145 C4
Soure Brazil 0°35S 48°30W 187 D9
Soure Portugal 40°4N 8°38W 88 E2
Souris Man., Canada 49°40N 100°20W 163 D8
Souris P.E.I., Canada 46°21N 62°15W 165 C7
Souris → N. Amer. 49°40N 99°34W 172 A4
Sourou → Africa 12°45N 3°25W 138 C4
Sourpi Greece 39°6N 22°54E 98 B4
Sous, O. → Morocco 30°27N 9°31W 136 B2
Sous-Massa △ Morocco 30°26N 9°35W 136 B2
Sous-Massa-Drâa □
Morocco 30°45N 6°30W 136 B2
Sousa Brazil 6°45S 38°10W 189 B3
Sousel Portugal 38°57N 7°40W 89 G3
Sousse Tunisia 35°50N 10°38E 136 A6
Sousse □ Tunisia 35°40N 10°30E 136 A6
Soustons France 43°45N 1°19W 72 E2
Sout → S. Africa 31°35S 18°24E 144 D2
South Africa ■ Africa 32°0S 23°0E 144 D3
South America 10°0S 60°0W 184 E5
South Andaman India 11°45N 92°10E 127 J11
South Aulatsivik I.
Canada 56°45N 61°30W 165 A7
South Australia □
Australia 32°0S 139°0E 152 B3
South Australian Basin
Ind. Oc. 38°0S 126°0E 156 L4
South Ayrshire □ U.K. 55°18N 4°41W 65 F4
South Baldy Pk.
U.S.A. 34°6N 107°11W 169 J10
South Bass I. U.S.A. 41°39N 82°49W 174 E2
South Bay U.S.A. 26°40N 80°43W 179 J9
South Bend Ind.,
U.S.A. 41°41N 86°15W 172 E10
South Bend Wash.,
U.S.A. 46°40N 123°48W 170 D3
South Boston U.S.A. 36°42N 78°54W 173 G14
South Branch Canada 47°55N 59°2W 165 C8
South Brook Canada 49°26N 56°5W 165 C8
South Brother I. India 10°56N 92°37E 127 J11
South Bruny I.
Australia 43°20S 147°15E 151 G4
South Carolina □
U.S.A. 34°0N 81°0W 177 E14
South Charleston
U.S.A. 38°22N 81°44W 173 F13
South China Sea Asia 10°0N 113°0E 118 C4
South Congaree U.S.A. 33°53N 81°9W 178 B8
South Cumberland Is. △
Australia 20°42S 149°11E 150 b
South Dakota □
U.S.A. 44°15N 100°0W 172 C4
South Dayton U.S.A. 42°21N 79°3W 174 D5
South Daytona U.S.A. 29°10N 81°0W 179 F8
South Deerfield
U.S.A. 42°29N 72°37W 175 D12
South Downs U.K. 50°52N 0°25W 67 G7
South Downs △ U.K. 50°50N 0°50W 67 G7
South Dublin □ Ireland 53°16N 6°24W 64 C5
South East □ Botswana 25°0S 25°40E 144 C4
South East C. Australia 43°40S 146°50E 151 G4
South East Forest △
Australia 37°0S 149°30E 153 D8
South East Is. Australia 34°17S 123°30E 149 F3
South Esk → U.K. 56°43N 2°31W 65 E6
South Fiji Basin Pac. Oc. 26°0S 175°0E 156 K9
South Foreland U.K. 51°8N 1°24E 67 F9
South Fork American →
U.S.A. 38°57N 120°59W 170 G5
South Fork Edisto →
U.S.A. 33°16N 80°54W 178 B9
South Fork Feather →
U.S.A. 39°17N 121°36W 170 F5
South Fork Grand →
U.S.A. 45°43N 102°17W 172 C2
South Fork Milk →
U.S.A. 48°4N 106°19W 168 B10
South Fork Republican →
U.S.A. 40°3N 101°31W 172 E3
South Georgia Antarctica 54°30S 37°0W 55 B1
South Gloucestershire □
U.K. 51°32N 2°28W 67 F5
South Hadley U.S.A. 42°16N 72°35W 175 D12
South Haven U.S.A. 42°24N 86°16W 172 D10
South Henik L. Canada 61°30N 97°20W 163 A9
South Horr Kenya 2°12N 36°56E 142 B4
South I. India 10°3N 72°17E 127 J1
South I. Kenya 2°35N 36°35E 142 B4
South I. N.Z. 44°0S 170°0E 155 E5
South Indian Lake
Canada 56°47N 98°56W 163 B9
South Invercargill
N.Z. 46°26S 168°23E 155 G3
South Island △ Kenya 2°39N 36°35E 142 B4
South Kitui ⌂ Kenya 1°48S 38°46E 142 C4
South Knife →
Canada 58°55N 94°37W 163 B10
South Koel → India 22°32N 85°14E 125 H11
South Korea ■ Asia 36°0N 128°0E 115 G15
South Lake Tahoe
U.S.A. 38°57N 119°59W 170 G6
South Lanarkshire □
U.K. 55°37N 3°53W 65 F5
South Loup → U.S.A. 41°4N 98°39W 172 E4
South Luangwa △
Zambia 13°0S 31°20E 143 E3
South Magnetic Pole
Antarctica 64°8S 138°8E 55 C9
South Miami U.S.A. 25°42N 80°17W 179 K9
South Milwaukee
U.S.A. 42°55N 87°52W 172 D10
South Molton U.K. 51°1N 3°51W 67 F4
South Moose L. Canada 53°49N 100°1W 163 C8
South Nahanni →
Canada 61°3N 123°21W 162 A4
South Nation →
Canada 45°34N 75°6W 175 A9
South Natuna Is. = Natuna
Selatan, Kepulauan
Indonesia 2°45N 109°0E 118 D3
South Negril Pt. Jamaica 18°16N 78°22W 182 a
South Newport U.S.A. 31°38N 81°24W 178 D8
South Orkney Is.
Antarctica 63°0S 45°0W 55 C18
South Ossetia □ Georgia 42°21N 44°2E 87 J7
South Otselic U.S.A. 42°38N 75°46W 175 D9
South Pagai, I. = Pagai Selatan,
Pulau Indonesia 3°0S 100°15E 118 E2
South Paris U.S.A. 44°14N 70°31W 175 B14
South Pittsburg U.S.A. 35°1N 85°42W 177 D12
South Platte → U.S.A. 41°7N 100°42W 172 E3
South Pole Antarctica 90°0S 0°0 55 E
South Ponte Vedra Beach
U.S.A. 30°3N 81°20W 178 E8
South Porcupine
Canada 48°30N 81°12W 164 C3
South Portland
U.S.A. 43°38N 70°15W 173 D18
South Pt. Barbados 13°2N 59°32W 183 g
South Pt. U.S.A. 44°52N 83°19W 174 B1
South River Canada 45°52N 79°23W 164 C4
South River U.S.A. 40°27N 74°23W 175 F10
South Ronaldsay U.K. 58°48N 2°58W 65 C6
South Rukuru →
Malawi 10°44S 34°14E 143 E3
South Sandwich Is.
Antarctica 57°0S 27°0W 55 B1
South Sandwich Trench
Atl. Oc. 56°0S 24°0W 55 B1
South Saskatchewan →
Canada 53°15N 105°5W 163 C7
South Seal → Canada 58°48N 98°8W 163 B9
South Sentinel I. India 10°59N 92°14E 127 J11
South Shetland Is.
Antarctica 62°0S 59°0W 55 C18
South Shields U.K. 55°0N 1°25W 66 C6
South Sioux City
U.S.A. 42°28N 96°24W 172 D5
South Sister U.S.A. 44°4N 121°51W 168 D3
South Sudan ■ Africa 8°0N 30°0E 135 G11
South Taranaki Bight
N.Z. 39°40S 174°5E 154 F3
South Tasman Rise
S. Ocean 48°0S 146°0E 55 A10
South Thompson →
Canada 50°40N 120°20W 162 C4
South Twin I. Canada 53°7N 79°52W 164 B4
South Tyne → U.K. 54°59N 2°8W 66 C5
South Uist U.K. 57°20N 7°15W 65 D1
South Valley U.S.A. 35°1N 106°41W 169 J10
South Venice U.S.A. 27°3N 82°25W 179 H7
South Wellesley Is.
Australia 16°58S 139°17E 150 B2
South West C. Australia 43°34S 146°3E 151 G4
South West C. N.Z. 47°17S 167°28E 155 H2
South West Rocks
Australia 30°52S 153°3E 153 A10
South Williamsport
U.S.A. 41°13N 77°0W 174 E8
South Yorkshire □ U.K. 53°27N 1°36W 66 D6
Southampton Canada 44°30N 81°25W 174 B3
Southampton U.K. 50°54N 1°23W 67 G6
Southampton U.S.A. 40°53N 72°23W 175 F12
Southampton □ U.K. 50°54N 1°23W 67 G6
Southampton I.
Canada 64°30N 84°0W 161 E15
Southaven U.S.A. 34°59N 90°0W 177 D9
Southbank Canada 54°2N 125°46W 162 C3
Southbridge N.Z. 43°48S 172°16E 155 D7
Southbridge U.S.A. 42°5N 72°2W 175 D12
Southeast Indian Ridge
Ind. Oc. 43°0S 80°0E 146 J10
Southend Canada 56°19N 103°22W 163 B8
Southend-on-Sea U.K. 51°32N 0°44E 67 F8
Southend-on-Sea □ U.K. 51°32N 0°44E 67 F8
Southern = Yuzhnyy □
Russia 44°0N 40°0E 106 E5
Southern □ Malawi 15°0S 35°0E 143 F4
Southern □ S. Leone 8°0N 12°30W 138 D2
Southern □ Zambia 16°20S 26°20E 143 F2
Southern Alps N.Z. 43°41S 170°11E 155 D5
Southern Aral Sea Asia 45°0N 58°0E 108 D5
Southern Cross
Australia 31°12S 119°15E 149 F2
Southern Indian L.
Canada 57°10N 98°30W 163 B9
Southern Lau Group
Fiji 18°40S 178°40W 154 a
Southern Ocean 62°0S 60°0E 55 C6
Southern Pines
U.S.A. 35°11N 79°24W 177 D15
Southern Uplands U.K. 55°28N 3°52W 65 F5
Southington U.S.A. 41°36N 72°53W 175 E12
Southland □ N.Z. 45°30S 168°0E 155 F3
Southold U.S.A. 41°4N 72°26W 175 E12
Southport Australia 27°58S 153°25E 151 D5
Southport U.K. 53°39N 3°0W 66 D4
Southport Fla., U.S.A. 30°17N 85°38W 178 E4
Southport N.Y., U.S.A. 42°3N 76°49W 174 D8
Southwest △ Australia 43°8S 146°5E 151 G4
Southwest Pacific Basin
Pac. Oc. 40°0S 140°0W 55 A12
Southwold U.K. 52°20N 1°41E 67 E9
Southwood △ Australia 27°48S 150°8E 151 D5
Soutpansberg S. Africa 23°0S 29°30E 145 B4
Souvigny France 46°33N 3°10E 71 F10
Sovata Romania 46°35N 25°3E 81 D10
Soverato Italy 38°41N 16°33E 95 D9
Sovetsk Kaliningrad,
Russia 55°6N 21°50E 82 C8
Sovetsk Kirov, Russia 57°38N 48°53E 86 B9
Sovetskaya Gavan
Russia 48°58N 140°18E 107 E15
Sovicille Italy 43°17N 11°13E 93 E8
Soweto S. Africa 26°14S 27°52E 145 C4
Sowma'eh Sarā Iran 37°17N 49°18E 105 D13
Sōya-Kaikyō = La Perouse Str.
Asia 45°40N 142°0E 112 B11
Sōya-Misaki Japan 45°30N 141°55E 112 B10
Soyaux France 45°39N 0°12E 72 C4
Soyo Angola 6°13S 12°20E 140 F2
Sozaq Kazakhstan 44°8N 68°28E 109 D7
Sozh → Belarus 51°57N 30°48E 75 B16
Sozopol Bulgaria 42°23N 27°42E 97 D11
Spa Belgium 50°29N 5°53E 69 D5
Spaatz I. Antarctica 73°10S 75°0W 55 D17
Spain ■ Europe 39°0N 4°0W 59 H5
Spalding Australia 33°30S 138°37E 152 B3
Spalding U.K. 52°48N 0°9W 66 E7
Spanaway U.S.A. 47°6N 122°26W 170 C4
Spangler U.S.A. 40°39N 78°48W 174 F6
Spanish Canada 46°12N 82°20W 164 C3
Spanish Fork U.S.A. 40°7N 111°39W 168 F8
Spanish Town
Br. Virgin Is. 18°26N 64°26W 183 e
Spanish Town Jamaica 18°0N 76°57W 182 a
Sparks Ga., U.S.A. 31°11N 83°26W 178 D6
Sparks Nev., U.S.A. 39°32N 119°45W 170 F7
Sparreholm Sweden 59°4N 16°49E 62 E10
Sparta = Sparti Greece 37°5N 22°25E 98 D4
Sparta Ga., U.S.A. 33°17N 82°58W 178 B7
Sparta Mich., U.S.A. 43°10N 85°42W 173 D11
Sparta N.J., U.S.A. 41°2N 74°38W 175 E10
Sparta Wis., U.S.A. 43°56N 90°49W 172 D8
Spartanburg U.S.A. 34°56N 81°57W 177 D14
Spartel, C. Morocco 35°47N 5°56W 136 A2
Sparti Greece 37°5N 22°25E 98 D4
Spartivento, C. Calabria,
Italy 37°55N 16°4E 95 E9
Spartivento, C. Sard.,
Italy 38°53N 8°50E 94 D1
Sparwood Canada 49°44N 114°53W 162 D6
Spas-Demensk Russia 54°20N 34°0E 84 E7
Spas-Klepiki Russia 55°10N 40°10E 84 E11
Spassk-Dalniy Russia 44°40N 132°48E 112 B6
Spassk-Ryazanskiy
Russia 54°24N 40°25E 84 E11
Spatha, Akra Greece 35°42N 23°43E 101 D5
Spatsizi → Canada 57°42N 128°7W 162 B3
Spatsizi Plateau Wilderness ⌂
Canada 57°40N 128°0W 162 B3
Spean → U.K. 56°55N 4°59W 65 E4
Spearfish U.S.A. 44°30N 103°52W 172 C2
Spearman U.S.A. 36°12N 101°12W 176 C4
Speculator U.S.A. 43°30N 74°22W 175 C10
Speed Australia 35°21S 142°27E 152 C5
Speia Moldova 46°59N 29°19E 81 D14
Speightstown Barbados 13°15N 59°39W 183 g
Speke Gulf Tanzania 2°20S 32°50E 142 C3
Spello Italy 42°59N 12°40E 93 F9
Spence Bay = Taloyoak
Canada 69°32N 93°32W 160 D13
Spencer Idaho, U.S.A. 44°22N 112°11W 168 D7
Spencer Iowa, U.S.A. 43°9N 95°9W 172 D6
Spencer N.Y., U.S.A. 42°13N 76°30W 175 D8
Spencer Nebr., U.S.A. 42°53N 98°42W 172 D4
Spencer, C. Australia 35°20S 136°53E 152 C2
Spencer B. Namibia 25°30S 14°47E 144 C1
Spencer G. Australia 34°0S 137°20E 152 C2
Spencerville Canada 44°51N 75°33W 175 B9
Spences Bridge
Canada 50°25N 121°20W 162 C4
Spennymoor U.K. 54°42N 1°36W 66 C6
Spenser Mts. N.Z. 42°15S 172°45E 155 C7
Spentrup Denmark 56°33N 10°2E 63 H4
Sperchios → Greece 38°57N 22°3E 98 C4
Sperrgebiet △ Namibia 27°38S 15°56E 144 C2
Sperrin Mts. U.K. 54°50N 7°0W 64 B5
Spessart Germany 49°56N 9°18E 77 F5
Spetses Greece 37°15N 23°10E 98 D5
Spey → U.K. 57°40N 3°6W 65 D5
Speyer Germany 49°29N 8°25E 77 F4
Spezand Pakistan 29°59N 67°0E 124 E2
Spezzano Albanese Italy 39°40N 16°19E 95 C9
Spiddle Ireland 53°15N 9°18W 64 C2
Spiekeroog Germany 53°46N 7°42E 76 B3
Spiez Switz. 46°40N 7°40E 77 J3
Spili Greece 35°13N 24°31E 101 D6
Spilimbergo Italy 46°7N 12°54E 93 B9
Spīn Būldak Afghan. 31°1N 66°25E 124 D2
Spinalonga Greece 35°18N 25°44E 101 D7
Spinazzola Italy 40°58N 16°5E 95 B9
Spineni Romania 44°43N 24°37E 81 F9
Spinifex ✪ Australia 28°30S 128°30E 149 E4
Spirit Lake U.S.A. 46°15N 122°9W 170 D4
Spirit River Canada 55°45N 118°50W 162 B5
Spiritwood Canada 53°24N 107°33W 163 C7
Spišská Nová Ves
Slovak Rep. 48°58N 20°34E 79 C13
Spišské Podhradie
Slovak Rep. 49°0N 20°48E 79 B13
Spital Austria 47°42N 14°18E 78 D7
Spithead U.K. 50°45N 1°10W 67 G6
Spitsbergen = Svalbard
Arctic 78°0N 17°0E 57 B12
Spittal an der Drau
Austria 46°48N 13°31E 78 E6
Spjelkavik Norway 62°28N 6°22E 60 E12
Split Croatia 43°31N 16°26E 93 E13
Split ✈ (SPU) Croatia 43°33N 16°15E 93 E13
Split L. Canada 56°8N 96°15W 163 B9
Split Lake Canada 56°8N 96°15W 163 B9
Splitski Kanal Croatia 43°31N 16°20E 93 E13
Splügenpass Switz. 46°30N 9°20E 77 J5
Spofford U.S.A. 29°10N 100°25W 176 G4
Spokane U.S.A. 47°40N 117°24W 168 C5
Spoleto Italy 42°44N 12°44E 93 F9
Spooner U.S.A. 45°50N 91°53W 172 C8
Sporyy Navolok, Mys
Russia 75°50N 68°40E 106 B7
Sprague U.S.A. 47°18N 117°59W 168 C5
Spratly I. S. China Sea 8°38N 111°55E 118 C4
Spratly Is. S. China Sea 8°20N 112°0E 118 C4
Spray U.S.A. 44°50N 119°48W 168 D4
Spreča → Bos.-H. 44°44N 18°6E 80 F3
Spree → Germany 52°32N 13°12E 76 C9
Spreewald Germany 51°58N 13°51E 76 D9
Spremberg Germany 51°34N 14°22E 76 D10
Sprengisandur Iceland 64°52N 18°7W 60 D4
Spring City U.S.A. 40°11N 75°33W 175 F9
Spring Cr. → U.S.A. 30°54N 84°45W 178 E5
Spring Creek U.S.A. 40°44N 115°35W 168 F6
Spring Garden U.S.A. 39°52N 120°47W 170 F6
Spring Hall Barbados 13°18N 59°36W 183 g
Spring Hill Ala., U.S.A. 31°42N 85°58W 178 D4
Spring Hill Fla., U.S.A. 28°27N 82°41W 179 G7
Spring Mts. U.S.A. 36°0N 115°45W 171 J11
Spring Temple Buddha
China 33°46N 112°27E 114 H7
Spring Valley Calif.,
U.S.A. 32°44N 116°59W 171 N10
Spring Valley Nev.,
U.S.A. 36°6N 115°14W 171 J11
Springbok S. Africa 29°42S 17°54E 144 C2
Springboro U.S.A. 41°48N 80°22W 174 E4
Springdale Canada 49°30N 56°6W 165 C8
Springdale U.S.A. 36°11N 94°8W 176 C7
Springe Germany 52°13N 9°33E 76 C5
Springer U.S.A. 36°22N 104°36W 169 H11
Springerville U.S.A. 34°8N 109°17W 169 J9
Springfield Canada 42°50N 80°56W 174 D4
Springfield N.Z. 43°19S 171°56E 155 D6
Springfield Colo.,
U.S.A. 37°24N 102°37W 169 H12
Springfield Fla., U.S.A. 30°10N 85°37W 178 E4
Springfield Ga., U.S.A. 32°22N 81°18W 178 C8
Springfield Ill., U.S.A. 39°48N 89°39W 172 F9
Springfield Mass.,
U.S.A. 42°6N 72°35W 175 D12
Springfield Mo., U.S.A. 37°13N 93°17W 172 G7
Springfield Ohio,
U.S.A. 39°55N 83°49W 173 F12
Springfield Oreg., U.S.A. 44°3N 123°1W 168 D2
Springfield S.C., U.S.A. 33°30N 81°17W 178 B8
Springfield Tenn.,
U.S.A. 36°31N 86°53W 177 C11
Springfield Vt., U.S.A. 43°18N 72°29W 175 C12
Springfontein S. Africa 30°15S 25°40E 144 D4
Springhill Canada 45°40N 64°4W 165 C7
Springhill U.S.A. 33°0N 93°28W 176 E8
Springhouse Canada 51°56N 122°7W 162 C4
Springlands = Corriverton
Guyana 5°55N 57°20W 186 B7
Springs S. Africa 26°13S 28°25E 145 C4
Springsure Australia 24°8S 148°6E 150 C4
Springvale Ga., U.S.A. 31°50N 84°53W 178 D5
Springvale Maine,
U.S.A. 43°28N 70°48W 175 C14
Springville Calif.,
U.S.A. 36°8N 118°49W 170 J8
Springville N.Y., U.S.A. 42°31N 78°40W 174 D6
Springville Utah,
U.S.A. 40°10N 111°37W 168 F8
Springwater U.S.A. 42°38N 77°35W 174 D7
Spruce-Creek U.S.A. 40°36N 78°9W 174 F6
Spruce Knob-Seneca Rocks ⌂
U.S.A. 38°50N 79°30W 173 F14
Spruce Mt. U.S.A. 44°12N 72°19W 175 B12
Sprucedale Canada 45°29N 79°28W 174 A5
Spur U.S.A. 33°28N 100°52W 176 E4
Spurn Hd. U.K. 53°35N 0°8E 66 D8
Spuž Montenegro 42°32N 19°10E 96 D3
Spuzzum Canada 49°37N 121°23W 162 D4
Squam L. U.S.A. 43°45N 71°32W 175 C13
Squamish Canada 49°45N 123°10W 162 D4
Square Islands Canada 52°47N 55°47W 165 B8
Squillace, G. di Italy 38°45N 16°50E 95 D9
Squinzano Italy 40°26N 18°2E 95 B11
Squires, Mt. Australia 26°14S 127°28E 149 E4
Srbac Bos.-H. 45°7N 17°30E 80 E2
Srbica = Skënderaj
Kosovo 42°45N 20°47E 96 D4
Srbija = Serbia ■ Europe 43°20N 20°0E 96 C4
Srbobran Serbia 45°32N 19°48E 80 E4
Sre Ambel Cambodia 11°8N 103°46E 121 G4
Sre Khtum Cambodia 12°10N 106°52E 121 F6
Sre Umbell = Sre Ambel
Cambodia 11°8N 103°46E 121 G4
Srebarna Bulgaria 44°6N 27°4E 97 B11
Srebrenica Bos.-H. 44°6N 19°18E 80 F4
Sredinnyy Khrebet
Russia 57°0N 160°0E 107 D17
Sredinnyy Ra. = Sredinnyy
Khrebet Russia 57°0N 160°0E 107 D17
Središče Slovenia 46°24N 16°17E 93 B13
Sredna Gora Bulgaria 42°40N 24°20E 97 D8
Srednekolymsk
Russia 67°27N 153°40E 107 C16
Sredni Rodopi Bulgaria 41°40N 24°45E 97 E8
Srednogorie Bulgaria 42°43N 24°10E 97 D8
Śrem Poland 52°6N 17°2E 83 F4
Sremska Mitrovica
Serbia 44°59N 19°38E 80 F4
Sremski Karlovci Serbia 45°12N 19°56E 80 E4
Srepok → Cambodia 13°33N 106°16E 120 F6
Sretensk Russia 52°10N 117°40E 107 D12
Sri Aman = Bandar Sri Aman
Malaysia 1°15N 111°32E 118 D4
Sri Kalahasti India 13°45N 79°44E 127 H4
Sri Lanka ■ Asia 7°30N 80°50E 127 L5
Sri Pada = Adam's Peak
Sri Lanka 6°48N 80°30E 127 L5
Sriharikota I. India 13°40N 80°20E 127 H5
Srikakulam India 18°14N 83°58E 126 E6
Srinagar India 34°5N 74°50E 125 B6
Srivardhan India 18°4N 73°3E 126 E1
Srivilliputtur India 9°31N 77°40E 127 K3
Środa Śląska Poland 51°10N 16°36E 83 G3
Środa Wielkopolski
Poland 52°15N 17°19E 83 F4
Srono Indonesia 8°24S 114°16E 119 J17
Srpska Crnja Serbia 45°38N 20°44E 80 E5
Srpski Itebej Serbia 45°35N 20°44E 80 E5
Srungavarapukota India 18°7N 83°10E 126 E6
Ssese Is. = Sese Is.
Uganda 0°20S 32°20E 142 C3
Staaten → Australia 16°24S 141°17E 150 B3
Staaten River △
Australia 16°15S 142°40E 150 B3
Stabbursdalen △
Norway 70°5N 24°15E 60 A21
Staberhuk Germany 54°23N 11°18E 76 A7
Stade Germany 53°35N 9°29E 76 B5
Stadskanaal Neths. 53°4N 6°55E 69 A6
Stadtallendorf Germany 50°48N 9°1E 76 E5
Stadthagen Germany 52°19N 9°13E 76 C5
Stadtlohn Germany 51°59N 6°55E 76 D2
Stadtroda Germany 50°52N 11°44E 76 E7
Staffa U.K. 56°27N 6°21W 65 E2
Staffanstorp Sweden 55°39N 13°13E 63 J7
Stafford U.K. 52°49N 2°7W 66 E5
Stafford U.S.A. 37°58N 98°36W 172 G4
Stafford, L. U.S.A. 29°20N 82°29W 179 F7
Stafford Springs
U.S.A. 41°57N 72°18W 175 E12
Staffordshire □ U.K. 52°53N 2°10W 66 E5
Stagnone Italy 37°53N 12°26E 94 E5
Stagnone di Marsala ⌂
Italy 37°52N 12°26E 94 E5
Staines-upon-Thames
U.K. 51°26N 0°29W 67 F7
Stainz Austria 46°53N 15°17E 78 E8
Stakhanov Ukraine 48°35N 38°40E 85 H10
Stalać Serbia 43°43N 21°28E 96 C5
Stalida Greece 35°17N 25°25E 101 D7
Stallarholmen Sweden 59°22N 17°12E 62 E11
Ställdalen Sweden 59°56N 14°56E 62 E8
Stalowa Wola Poland 50°34N 22°3E 83 H9
Stalybridge U.K. 53°28N 2°3W 66 D5
Stamford Australia 21°15S 143°46E 150 C3
Stamford U.K. 52°39N 0°29W 67 E7
Stamford Conn., U.S.A. 41°3N 73°32W 175 E11
Stamford N.Y., U.S.A. 42°25N 74°38W 175 D10
Stamford Tex., U.S.A. 32°57N 99°48W 176 E5
Stampriet Namibia 24°20S 18°28E 144 B2
Stamps U.S.A. 33°22N 93°30W 176 E8
Stančevo = Kalipetrovo
Bulgaria 44°5N 27°14E 97 B11
Standerton S. Africa 26°55S 29°7E 145 C4
Standish U.S.A. 43°59N 83°57W 173 D12
Stanford S. Africa 34°26S 19°29E 144 D2
Stanford U.S.A. 47°9N 110°13W 168 C8
Stånga Sweden 57°17N 18°29E 63 G12
Stanger S. Africa 29°27S 31°14E 145 C5
Stängselåsen = Salpausselkä
Finland 61°3N 26°15E 84 B4
Stanhope Australia 36°27S 144°59E 153 D6
Stanišić Serbia 45°56N 19°10E 80 E4
Stanislaus → U.S.A. 37°40N 121°14W 170 H5
Stanisławów Poland 52°18N 21°33E 83 F8
Stanley Australia 40°46S 145°19E 151 G4
Stanley China 22°13N 114°12E 111 a
Stanley Falk. Is. 51°40S 59°51W 192 D5
Stanley U.K. 54°53N 1°41W 66 C6
Stanley Idaho, U.S.A. 44°13N 114°56W 168 D6
Stanley N. Dak.,
U.S.A. 48°19N 102°23W 172 A2
Stanley N.Y., U.S.A. 42°48N 77°6W 174 D7
Stanley Mission
Canada 55°25N 104°33W 163 B8

Stanley Res. India 11°50N 77°40E 127 J3
Stannards U.S.A. 42°5N 77°55W 174 D7
Stanovoy Khrebet Russia 55°0N 130°0E 107 D14
Stanovoy Ra. = Stanovoy Khrebet Russia 55°0N 130°0E 107 D14
Stansmore Ra. Australia 21°23S 128°33E 148 D4
Stansted, London ✈ (STN) U.K. 51°54N 0°14E 67 F8
Stanthorpe Australia 28°36S 151°59E 151 D5
Stanton U.S.A. 32°8N 101°48W 176 E4
Stanwood U.S.A. 48°15N 122°23W 170 B4
Staples Canada 42°10N 82°35W 174 D2
Staples U.S.A. 46°21N 94°48W 172 B6
Stapleton U.S.A. 41°29N 100°31W 172 E3
Stapodia Greece 37°24N 25°34E 99 D7
Staporków Poland 51°9N 20°31E 83 G7
Star City Canada 52°50N 104°20W 163 C8
Star Lake U.S.A. 44°10N 75°2W 175 B9
Stará L'ubovňa Slovak Rep. 49°18N 20°42E 79 B13
Stara Moravica Serbia 45°50N 19°30E 80 E4
Stara Pazova Serbia 44°58N 20°10E 80 F5
Stara Planina Bulgaria 43°15N 23°0E 96 C7
Stara Sil Ukraine 49°29N 22°58E 83 J9
Stará Turá Slovak Rep. 48°47N 17°42E 79 C10
Stara Ushytsya Ukraine 48°35N 27°8E 81 B12
Stara Zagora Bulgaria 42°26N 25°39E 97 D9
Stara Zagora □ Bulgaria 42°26N 25°39E 97 D9
Starachowice Poland 51°3N 21°2E 83 G8
Staraya Russa Russia 57°58N 31°23E 84 D6
Starbuck I. Kiribati 5°37S 155°55W 157 H12
Starchiojd Romania 45°19N 26°11E 81 E11
Starcke △ Australia 14°56S 145°2E 150 A4
Stargard Szczeciński Poland 53°20N 15°0E 82 E2
Stari Bar Montenegro 42°7N 19°10E 96 D3
Stari Grad Croatia 43°10N 16°38E 93 E13
Stari Trg Slovenia 45°29N 15°7E 93 C12
Staritsa Russia 56°33N 34°55E 84 D8
Starke U.S.A. 29°57N 82°7W 178 F7
Starkville U.S.A. 33°28N 88°49W 177 E10
Starnberg Germany 48°0N 11°21E 77 H7
Starnberger See Germany 47°54N 11°19E 77 H7
Staro Oryakhovo Bulgaria 42°59N 27°47E 97 D11
Starobilsk Ukraine 49°16N 39°0E 85 H10
Starodub Russia 52°30N 32°50E 85 F7
Starogard Gdański Poland 53°59N 18°30E 82 E5
Starokonstantinov = Starokonstyantyniv Ukraine 49°48N 27°10E 75 D14
Starokonstyantyniv Ukraine 49°48N 27°10E 75 D14
Starokozache Ukraine 46°20N 29°59E 81 D14
Starominskaya Russia 46°33N 39°0E 87 G4
Staroshcherbinovskaya Russia 46°40N 38°53E 87 G4
Starrs Mill U.S.A. 33°19N 84°31W 178 B5
Start Pt. U.K. 50°13N 3°39W 67 G4
Stary Sącz Poland 49°33N 20°35E 83 J7
Staryy Biryuzyak Russia 44°46N 46°50E 87 H18
Staryy Chartoriysk Ukraine 51°15N 25°54E 75 C13
Staryy Krym Ukraine 45°3N 35°8E 85 K8
Staryy Oskol Russia 51°19N 37°55E 85 G9
Staryy Sambir Ukraine 49°27N 22°59E 83 J9
Stassfurt Germany 51°51N 11°35E 76 D7
Staszów Poland 50°33N 21°10E 83 H8
State College U.S.A. 40°48N 77°52W 174 F7
Stateline U.S.A. 38°57N 119°56W 170 G7
Staten, I. = Estados, I. de Los Argentina 54°40S 64°30W 192 D4
Staten I. U.S.A. 40°35N 74°9W 175 F10
Statenville U.S.A. 30°42N 83°2W 178 E6
Statesboro U.S.A. 32°27N 81°47W 178 C8
Statesville U.S.A. 35°47N 80°53W 177 D14
Statham U.S.A. 33°58N 83°35W 178 B6
Statia = St. Eustatius W. Indies 17°20N 63°0W 183 C7
Stauffer U.S.A. 34°45N 119°3W 171 L7
Staunton Ill., U.S.A. 39°1N 89°47W 173 F14
Staunton Va., U.S.A. 38°9N 79°4W 174 F6
Stavanger Norway 58°57N 5°40E 61 G11
Stavelot Belgium 50°23N 5°55E 69 D5
Stavern Norway 59°0N 10°1E 61 G14
Stavoren Neths. 52°53N 5°22E 69 B5
Stavropol Russia 45°5N 42°0E 87 H6
Stavropol □ Russia 47°20N 42°50E 87 G6
Stavros Cyprus 35°1N 32°38E 101 D11
Stavros Kriti, Greece 35°12N 24°45E 101 D6
Stavros Thessaloniki, Greece 40°39N 23°43E 96 F7
Stavros, Akra Greece 35°26N 24°58E 101 D6
Stavroupoli Greece 41°12N 24°45E 97 E8
Stawell Australia 37°5S 142°47E 152 D5
Stawell → Australia 20°20S 142°55E 150 C3
Stawiski Poland 53°22N 22°9E 82 E9
Stawiszyn Poland 51°56N 18°4E 83 G5
Stayner Canada 44°25N 80°5W 174 B4
Stayton U.S.A. 44°48N 122°48W 168 D2
Steamboat Springs U.S.A. 40°29N 106°50W 168 F10
Steblevë Albania 41°23N 20°33E 96 E4
Steele Ala., U.S.A. 33°56N 86°12W 178 B3
Steele N. Dak., U.S.A. 46°51N 99°55W 172 B4
Steelton U.S.A. 40°14N 76°50W 174 F8
Steen River Canada 59°40N 117°12W 162 B5
Steens Mt. U.S.A. 42°35N 118°40W 168 E4
Steenstrup Gletscher Greenland 75°15N 57°0W 57 B5
Steenwijk Neths. 52°47N 6°7E 69 B6
Steep Pt. Australia 26°8S 113°8E 149 E1
Steep Rock Canada 51°30N 98°48W 163 C9
Ştefan Vodă Moldova 46°27N 29°42E 81 D14
Ştefăneşti Romania 47°44N 27°15E 81 C12
Stefanie L. = Chew Bahir Ethiopia 4°40N 36°50E 131 G2
Stefansson Bay Antarctica 67°20S 59°8E 55 C5
Stefansson I. Canada 73°20N 105°45W 161 C10
Stege Denmark 54°59N 12°18E 63 K6
Ştei Romania 46°32N 22°27E 80 D7
Steiermark □ Austria 47°26N 15°0E 78 D8
Steigerwald Germany 49°44N 10°26E 77 F6
Steigerwald △ Germany 49°45N 10°30E 77 F6
Steilacoom U.S.A. 47°12N 122°36W 170 C4
Steilrandberge Namibia 17°45S 13°20E 144 A1
Steinbach Canada 49°32N 96°40W 163 D9
Steinfort Germany 52°9N 7°26E 76 C3

Steinhatchee U.S.A. 29°40N 83°23W 178 F6
Steinhausen Namibia 21°49S 18°20E 144 B2
Steinheim Germany 51°51N 9°5E 76 D5
Steinhuder Meer Germany 52°29N 9°21E 76 C5
Steinhuder Meer ○ Germany 52°30N 9°16E 76 C5
Steinkjer Norway 64°1N 11°31E 60 D14
Steinkopf S. Africa 29°18S 17°43E 144 C2
Steinwald △ Germany 49°55N 12°8E 77 F8
Stellarton Canada 45°32N 62°30W 165 C7
Stellenbosch S. Africa 33°58S 18°50E 144 D2
Stélvio, Paso dello Italy 46°32N 10°27E 92 B7
Stenay France 49°29N 5°12E 71 C12
Stendal Germany 52°36N 11°53E 76 C7
Stende Latvia 57°11N 22°33E 62 A9
Stenhamra Sweden 59°20N 17°41E 62 E11
Stenshuvud △ Sweden 55°39N 14°15E 63 J8
Stenstorp Sweden 58°17N 13°45E 63 F7
Stenungsund Sweden 58°6N 11°50E 63 F5
Steornabhaigh = Stornoway U.K. 58°13N 6°23W 65 C2
Stepanakert = Xankändi Azerbaijan 39°52N 46°49E 105 C12
Stepanavan Armenia 41°1N 44°23E 87 K7
Stephens, C. N.Z. 40°42S 173°58E 155 A8
Stephens Creek Australia 31°50S 141°30E 152 A4
Stephens I. Canada 54°10N 130°45W 162 C2
Stephens I. N.Z. 40°40S 174°1E 155 A8
Stephens L. Canada 56°32N 95°0W 163 B9
Stephenville Canada 48°31N 58°35W 165 C8
Stephenville U.S.A. 32°13N 98°12W 176 E5
Stepnica Poland 53°38N 14°36E 82 E1
Stepnogorsk Kazakhstan 52°21N 71°53E 109 B8
Steppe Asia 50°0N 50°0E 102 C7
Sterea Ellas □ Greece 38°50N 23°0E 98 C4
Sterkstroom S. Africa 31°32S 26°32E 144 D4
Sterling Colo., U.S.A. 40°37N 103°13W 168 F12
Sterling Ga., U.S.A. 31°16N 81°34W 178 D8
Sterling Ill., U.S.A. 41°48N 89°42W 172 E9
Sterling Kans., U.S.A. 38°13N 98°12W 172 F4
Sterling City U.S.A. 31°51N 101°0W 176 F4
Sterling Heights U.S.A. 42°35N 83°2W 173 D12
Sterling Run U.S.A. 41°25N 78°12W 174 E6
Sterlitamak Russia 53°40N 56°0E 108 B5
Sternberg Germany 53°42N 11°50E 76 B7
Šternberk Czech Rep. 49°45N 17°15E 79 B10
Sternes Greece 35°30N 24°9E 101 D6
Sterzing = Vipiteno Italy 46°54N 11°26E 92 B8
Stettin = Szczecin Poland 53°27N 14°27E 82 E1
Stettiner Haff Germany 53°47N 14°15E 76 B10
Stettler Canada 52°19N 112°40W 162 C6
Steubenville U.S.A. 40°22N 80°37W 174 F4
Stevenage U.K. 51°55N 0°13W 67 F7
Stevens Point U.S.A. 44°31N 89°34W 172 C9
Stevens Pottery U.S.A. 32°57N 83°17W 178 C6
Stevenson U.S.A. 45°42N 121°53W 170 E5
Stevenson → Australia 27°6S 135°33E 151 D2
Stevenson L. Canada 53°55N 96°0W 163 C9
Stevensville U.S.A. 46°30N 114°5W 168 C6
Stevns Klint Denmark 55°17N 12°28E 63 J6
Stewart Canada 55°56N 129°57W 162 B3
Stewart Ga., U.S.A. 32°35N 83°57W 178 B6
Stewart Nev., U.S.A. 39°5N 119°46W 170 F7
Stewart → Canada 63°19N 139°26W 160 E4
Stewart, C. Australia 11°57S 134°56E 150 A1
Stewart, I. Chile 54°50S 71°15W 192 D2
Stewart I. N.Z. 46°58S 167°54E 155 F1
Stewarts Point U.S.A. 38°39N 123°24W 170 G3
Stewartville U.S.A. 43°51N 92°29W 172 D7
Stewiacke Canada 45°9N 63°22W 165 C7
Steynsburg S. Africa 31°15S 25°49E 144 D4
Steyr Austria 48°3N 14°25E 78 C7
Steyr → Austria 48°3N 14°25E 78 C7
Steytlerville S. Africa 33°17S 24°19E 144 D3
Stia Italy 43°48N 11°42E 93 E8
Stigler U.S.A. 35°15N 95°8W 176 D7
Stigliano Italy 40°24N 16°14E 95 B9
Stigtomta Sweden 58°47N 16°48E 63 F10
Stikine → Canada 56°40N 132°30W 162 B2
Stilfontein S. Africa 26°51S 26°50E 144 C4
Stilida Greece 38°55N 22°47E 98 C4
Stillmore U.S.A. 32°27N 82°13W 178 C7
Stillwater N.Y., U.S.A. 42°55N 73°41W 175 D11
Stillwater Okla., U.S.A. 36°7N 97°4W 176 D6
Stillwater Range U.S.A. 39°50N 118°5W 168 G4
Stillwater Res. U.S.A. 43°54N 75°3W 175 C9
Stilo, Pta. Italy 38°27N 16°35E 95 D9
Stilwell U.S.A. 35°49N 94°38W 176 D7
Stînga Nistrului = Transnistria □ Moldova 47°20N 29°15E 81 C14
Štip Macedonia 41°42N 22°10E 96 E6
Stira Greece 38°9N 24°14E 98 C6
Stirling Canada 44°18N 77°33W 174 B7
Stirling N.Z. 46°14S 169°49E 155 G4
Stirling U.K. 56°8N 3°57W 65 E5
Stirling □ U.K. 56°12N 4°18W 65 E4
Stirling Ra. Australia 34°23S 118°0E 149 F2
Stirling Range △ Australia 34°26S 118°20E 149 F2
Stittsville Canada 45°15N 75°55W 175 A9
Stjernøya Norway 70°20N 22°40E 60 A20
Stjørdalshalsen Norway 63°29N 10°51E 60 E14
Stock Island U.S.A. 24°32N 81°43W 179 L8
Stocka Sweden 61°53N 17°20E 62 C11
Stockach Germany 47°50N 9°1E 77 H5
Stockbridge Sweden 57°19N 14°36E 63 H8
Stockbridge U.S.A. 33°33N 84°14W 178 B5
Stockerau Austria 48°24N 16°12E 79 C9
Stockholm Sweden 59°19N 18°4E 62 E12
Stockholm Arlanda ✈ (ARN) Sweden 59°41N 17°56E 62 E11
Stockport U.K. 53°25N 2°9W 66 D5
Stocksbridge U.K. 53°29N 1°35W 66 D6
Stockton Calif., U.S.A. 37°58N 121°17W 170 H5
Stockton Kans., U.S.A. 39°26N 99°16W 172 F4
Stockton-on-Tees □ U.K. 54°35N 1°19W 66 C6
Stockton Plateau U.S.A. 30°30N 102°30W 176 F3
Stockton-on-Tees □ U.K.
Stoczek Łukowski Poland 51°58N 21°58E 83 G8
Stöde Sweden 62°28N 16°35E 62 B10
Stoeng Treng Cambodia 13°31N 105°58E 120 F5

Stoer, Pt. of U.K. 58°16N 5°23W 65 C3
Stogovo Macedonia 41°31N 20°38E 96 E4
Stoholm Denmark 56°30N 9°8E 63 H3
Stoke N.Z. 41°19S 173°14E 155 B8
Stoke-on-Trent U.K. 53°1N 2°11W 66 D5
Stoke-on-Trent □ U.K. 53°1N 2°11W 66 D5
Stokes △ Australia 33°45S 121°11E 149 F3
Stokes Bay Canada 45°0N 81°28W 174 B3
Stokes Pt. Australia 40°10S 143°56E 151 G3
Stokes Ra. Australia 15°50S 130°50E 148 C5
Stokksnes Iceland 64°14N 14°58W 60 D6
Stokmarknes Norway 68°34N 14°54E 60 B16
Stolac Bos.-H. 43°5N 17°59E 96 C1
Stolberg Germany 50°47N 6°13E 76 E2
Stolbovoy, Ostrov Russia 74°44N 135°14E 107 B14
Stolbtsy = Stowbtsy Belarus 53°30N 26°43E 75 B14
Stolin Belarus 51°53N 26°50E 75 C14
Stöllet Sweden 60°26N 13°15E 62 D7
Stolnici Romania 44°31N 24°48E 81 F9
Stomio Greece 35°21N 23°32E 101 D5
Ston Croatia 42°51N 17°43E 93 F14
Stone U.K. 52°55N 2°9W 66 E5
Stone Mountain U.S.A. 33°49N 84°10W 178 B5
Stoneboro U.S.A. 41°20N 80°7W 174 E4
Stonehaven U.K. 56°59N 2°12W 65 E6
Stonehenge Australia 24°22S 143°17E 150 C3
Stonehenge U.K. 51°9N 1°45W 67 F6
Stonewall Canada 50°10N 97°19W 163 C9
Stony L. Canada 43°53N 76°19W 175 C8
Stony L. Man., Canada 58°51N 98°40W 163 B9
Stony L. Ont., Canada 44°30N 78°5W 174 B6
Stony Point U.S.A. 41°14N 73°59W 175 E11
Stony Pt. U.S.A. 43°50N 76°18W 175 C8
Stony Rapids Canada 59°16N 105°50W 163 B7
Stony Tunguska = Tunguska, Podkamennaya → Russia 61°50N 90°13E 107 C10
Stonyford U.S.A. 39°23N 122°33W 170 F4
Stopnica Poland 50°27N 20°57E 83 H7
Storå Sweden 59°42N 15°6E 62 E9
Storå → Denmark 56°20N 8°19E 63 H2
Stora Gla Sweden 59°30N 12°30E 62 E6
Stora Le Sweden 59°5N 11°55E 62 E5
Stora Lulevatten Sweden 67°10N 19°30E 60 C18
Stora Sjöfallet △ Sweden 67°36N 17°45E 60 C17
Storavan Sweden 65°45N 18°10E 60 D18
Stord Norway 59°52N 5°23E 61 G11
Store Bælt Denmark 55°20N 11°0E 63 J4
Store Heddinge Denmark 55°18N 12°23E 63 J6
Store Koldewey Greenland 76°30N 19°0W 57 B9
Store Mosse △ Sweden 57°18N 13°55E 63 G7
Storebro Sweden 57°35N 15°52E 63 G9
Storfors Sweden 59°32N 14°17E 62 E8
Storkerson Pen. Canada 72°30N 106°30W 160 C10
Storlien Sweden 63°19N 12°6E 62 A6
Stormberg S. Africa 31°16S 26°17E 144 D4
Stormsrivier S. Africa 33°59S 23°52E 144 E3
Stornoway U.K. 58°13N 6°23W 65 C2
Storo Italy 45°51N 10°35E 92 C7
Storozhinets = Storozhynets Ukraine 48°14N 25°45E 81 B10
Storozhynets Ukraine 48°14N 25°45E 81 B10
Storrs U.S.A. 41°49N 72°15W 175 E12
Storsjön Gävleborg, Sweden 60°35N 16°45E 62 D10
Storsjön Jämtland, Sweden 62°48N 13°7E 62 B7
Storsjön Jämtland, Sweden 63°12N 14°18E 62 A8
Storstrømmen Greenland 76°17N 22°25W 57 B8
Storuman Sweden 65°5N 17°10E 60 D17
Storuman, L. Sweden 65°13N 16°50E 60 D17
Storvik Sweden 60°35N 16°33E 62 D10
Storvreta Sweden 59°58N 17°44E 62 E11
Stouffville Canada 43°58N 79°15W 174 C5
Stoughton Canada 49°40N 103°0W 163 D8
Stour → Dorset, U.K. 50°43N 1°47W 67 G6
Stour → Kent, U.K. 51°18N 1°22E 67 F9
Stour → Suffolk, U.K. 51°57N 1°4E 67 F9
Stourbridge U.K. 52°28N 2°8W 67 E5
Stout L. Canada 52°0N 94°40W 163 C10
Stove Pipe Wells Village U.S.A. 36°35N 117°11W 171 J9
Støvring Denmark 56°54N 9°50E 63 H3
Stow U.S.A. 41°10N 81°27W 174 E4
Stowbtsy Belarus 53°30N 26°43E 75 B14
Stowmarket U.K. 52°12N 1°0E 67 E9
Strabane U.K. 54°50N 7°27W 64 B4
Stracin Macedonia 42°13N 22°2E 96 D6
Stradella Italy 45°5N 9°18E 92 C6
Strahan Australia 42°9S 145°20E 151 G4
Strahitsa Bulgaria 43°14N 25°58E 97 C9
Strakonice Czech Rep. 49°15N 13°53E 78 B6
Straldzha Bulgaria 42°35N 26°40E 97 D10
Stralsund Germany 54°18N 13°4E 76 A9
Strand S. Africa 34°9S 18°48E 144 D2
Stranda Møre og Romsdal, Norway 62°19N 6°58E 60 E12
Stranda Nord-Trøndelag, Norway 63°33N 10°14E 60 E14
Strandby Denmark 57°30N 10°29E 63 H4
Strangford L. U.K. 54°30N 5°37W 64 B6
Strängnäs Sweden 59°23N 17°2E 62 E11
Stranorlar Ireland 54°48N 7°46W 64 B4
Stranraer U.K. 54°54N 5°1W 66 G3
Strasbourg Canada 51°4N 104°55W 163 C8
Strasbourg France 48°35N 7°42E 71 D14
Strasburg U.S.A. 38°59N 78°22W 174 F6
Strășeni Moldova 47°8N 28°35E 81 C14
Stråssa Sweden 59°44N 15°12E 62 E9
Stratford N.S.W., Australia 32°7S 151°55E 153 B6
Stratford Vic., Australia 37°59S 147°7E 153 D7
Stratford Canada 43°23N 81°0W 174 C3
Stratford N.Z. 39°20S 174°19E 154 F3
Stratford Calif., U.S.A. 36°11N 119°49W 170 J7
Stratford Conn., U.S.A. 41°12N 73°8W 175 E11
Stratford Tex., U.S.A. 36°20N 102°4W 176 C3
Stratford-upon-Avon U.K. 52°12N 1°42W 67 E6
Strath Spey U.K. 57°9N 3°49W 65 D5
Strathalbyn Australia 35°13S 138°53E 152 C3
Strathaven U.K. 55°40N 4°5W 65 F4

Strathcona △ Canada 49°38N 125°40W 162 D3
Strathmore Canada 51°5N 113°18W 162 C6
Strathmore U.K. 56°37N 3°7W 65 E5
Strathmore U.S.A. 36°9N 119°4W 170 J7
Strathnaver Canada 53°20N 122°33W 162 C4
Strathpeffer U.K. 57°35N 4°32W 65 D4
Strathroy Canada 42°58N 81°38W 174 D3
Strathy Pt. U.K. 58°36N 4°1W 65 C4
Stratoni Greece 40°31N 23°49E 96 F7
Strattanville U.S.A. 41°12N 79°19W 174 E5
Stratton U.S.A. 45°8N 70°26W 175 A14
Stratton Mt. U.S.A. 43°4N 72°55W 175 C12
Straubing Germany 48°52N 12°34E 77 G8
Straumnes Iceland 66°26N 23°8W 60 C2
Strausberg Germany 52°35N 13°54E 76 C9
Strawberry → U.S.A. 40°10N 110°24W 168 F8
Stráznice Czech Rep. 48°54N 17°19E 79 C10
Streaky B. Australia 32°48S 134°13E 151 E1
Streaky Bay Australia 32°51S 134°18E 151 E1
Streator U.S.A. 41°8N 88°50W 172 E9
Středočeský □ Czech Rep. 49°55N 14°30E 78 B7
Streetsboro U.S.A. 41°14N 81°21W 174 E3
Streetsville Canada 43°35N 79°42W 174 C5
Strehaia Romania 44°37N 23°10E 81 F8
Strelcha Bulgaria 42°25N 24°19E 97 D8
Strésa Italy 45°52N 8°28E 92 C5
Streymoy Færoe Is. 62°8N 7°5W 60 E9
Strezhevoy Russia 60°42N 77°34E 106 C8
Stříbro Czech Rep. 49°44N 13°0E 78 A6
Strilky Ukraine 49°20N 22°59E 83 J9
Strimonas → Greece 40°46N 23°51E 96 F7
Strœder Argentina 40°12S 62°37W 192 B4
Strofades Greece 37°15N 21°0E 98 D3
Strokestown Ireland 53°47N 8°5W 64 C3
Stroma U.K. 58°41N 3°7W 65 C5
Stromberg-Heuchelberg △ Germany 49°2N 8°50E 77 F4
Strómboli Italy 38°47N 15°13E 95 D8
Stromeferry U.K. 57°21N 5°33W 65 D3
Stromness U.K. 58°58N 3°17W 65 C5
Strömsbruk Sweden 61°52N 17°18E 62 C11
Stromsburg U.S.A. 41°7N 97°36W 172 E5
Strömsnäsbruk Sweden 56°35N 13°45E 63 H7
Strömstad Sweden 58°56N 11°10E 62 E4
Strömsund Sweden 63°51N 15°33E 60 E16
Strongili Greece 36°6N 29°42E 99 E11
Stróngoli Italy 39°16N 17°3E 95 C10
Strongsville U.S.A. 41°19N 81°50W 174 E3
Stronie Śląskie Poland 50°18N 16°53E 83 H3
Stronsay U.K. 59°7N 2°35W 65 B6
Stropkov Slovak Rep. 49°13N 21°39E 79 B14
Stroud U.K. 51°45N 2°13W 67 F5
Stroud Road Australia 32°18S 151°57E 153 B6
Stroudsburg U.S.A. 40°59N 75°12W 175 F9
Stroumbi Cyprus 34°53N 32°29E 101 E11
Strpce = Shtërpcë Kosovo 42°14N 21°1E 96 D5
Struer Denmark 56°30N 8°35E 63 H2
Struga Macedonia 41°11N 20°44E 96 E4
Strugi Krasnyye Russia 58°21N 29°1E 84 C5
Strumica Macedonia 41°28N 22°41E 96 E6
Strumica → Europe 41°20N 23°22E 96 E7
Strumok Ukraine 45°43N 29°27E 81 E14
Struthers U.S.A. 41°4N 80°39W 174 E4
Stryama Bulgaria 42°16N 24°54E 97 D8
Stryi Ukraine 49°16N 23°48E 75 D12
Stryków Poland 51°55N 19°33E 83 G6
Stryy Ukraine 49°16N 23°48E 75 D12
Strzegom Poland 50°58N 16°20E 83 H3
Strzelce Krajeńskie Poland 52°52N 15°33E 83 F2
Strzelce Opolskie Poland 50°31N 18°18E 83 H5
Strzelecki Cr. → Australia 29°37S 139°59E 151 D2
Strzelecki Desert Australia 29°30S 140°0E 151 D3
Strzelin Poland 50°46N 17°2E 83 H4
Strzelno Poland 52°35N 18°9E 83 F5
Strzybnica Poland 50°28N 18°48E 83 H5
Strzyżów Poland 49°52N 21°47E 83 J8
Stuart Fla., U.S.A. 27°12N 80°15W 179 M9
Stuart Nebr., U.S.A. 42°36N 99°8W 172 D4
Stuart → Canada 54°0N 123°35W 162 C4
Stuart Bluff Ra. Australia 22°50S 131°52E 148 D5
Stuart I. U.S.A. 63°35N 162°30W 160 D3
Stuart L. Canada 54°30N 124°30W 162 C4
Stuart Mts. N.Z. 45°2S 167°39E 155 F2
Stuart Ra. Australia 29°10S 134°56E 151 D1
Stuben Austria 47°10N 10°8E 78 D3
Stubbeköbing Denmark 54°53N 12°9E 63 K6
Studen Kladenets, Yazovir Bulgaria 41°37N 25°30E 97 E9
Studenica Serbia 43°29N 20°32E 96 C4
Studénka Czech Rep. 49°44N 18°5E 79 B11
Studholme N.Z. 44°42S 171°9E 155 E6
Stugun Sweden 63°10N 15°40E 62 A9
Stuhr Germany 53°5N 8°44E 76 B4
Stull L. Canada 54°24N 92°34W 163 B10
Stung Treng = Stoeng Treng Cambodia 13°31N 105°58E 120 F5
Stupart → Canada 56°0N 93°25W 163 B10
Stupava Slovak Rep. 48°17N 17°2E 79 C10
Stupino Russia 54°57N 38°2E 84 E10
Sturge I. Antarctica 67°26S 164°47E 55 C11
Sturgeon B. Canada 52°0N 97°50W 163 C9
Sturgeon Bay U.S.A. 44°50N 87°23W 172 C10
Sturgeon Falls Canada 46°25N 79°57W 164 B6
Sturgeon L. Alta., Canada 55°6N 117°32W 162 B5
Sturgeon L. Ont., Canada 50°0N 90°45W 164 C1
Sturgeon L. Ont., Canada 44°28N 78°43W 174 B6
Sturgis Mich., U.S.A. 41°48N 85°25W 173 E11
Sturgis S. Dak., U.S.A. 44°25N 103°31W 172 C2
Sturkö Sweden 56°5N 15°42E 63 H9
Štúrovo Slovak Rep. 47°48N 18°41E 79 D11
Sturt → Australia 28°30S 141°31E 150 C2
Sturt Cr. → Australia 19°8S 127°50E 148 C4
Sturt Stony Desert Australia 28°30S 141°0E 151 D2
Sturts Meadows Australia 31°18S 141°42E 152 A4
Stutterheim S. Africa 32°33S 27°28E 144 D4
Stuttgart Germany 48°48N 9°11E 77 G5
Stuttgart U.S.A. 34°30N 91°33W 176 D8
Stuttgart Echterdingen ✈ (STR) Germany 48°42N 9°11E 77 G5
Stuyvesant U.S.A. 42°23N 73°45W 175 D11
Stykkishólmur Iceland 65°2N 22°40W 60 D2

Styria = Steiermark □ Austria 47°26N 15°0E 78 D8
Styrsö Sweden 57°37N 11°46E 63 G5
Su Xian = Suzhou China 33°41N 116°59E 114 H9
Suakin Sudan 19°8N 37°20E 137 D4
Suakin Archipelago Sudan 18°42N 38°30E 137 D4
Suamico U.S.A. 44°38N 88°2W 172 C9
Suan N. Korea 38°42N 126°22E 115 E14
Suana Indonesia 8°44S 115°36E 119 K18
Suar India 29°2N 79°3E 125 E8
Subā Si. Arabia 27°10N 35°40E 128 E3
Subang Indonesia 6°34S 107°45E 119 G12
Subansiri → India 26°48N 93°50E 125 F18
Subarnagiri India 19°50N 83°51E 126 E6
Subarnarekha → India 22°34N 87°24E 125 H12
Subay', Urūq Si. Arabia 22°15N 43°5E 137 C3
Subayhah Si. Arabia 30°2N 38°50E 128 D3
Subcetate Romania 45°36N 23°0E 80 E8
Subi Indonesia 2°58N 108°50E 118 D3
Subiaco Italy 41°56N 13°5E 93 G10
Subotica Serbia 46°6N 19°39E 80 D4
Suceava Romania 47°38N 26°16E 81 C11
Suceava □ Romania 47°37N 25°40E 81 C11
Suceava → Romania 47°39N 26°32E 81 C11
Sucha-Beskidzka Poland 49°44N 19°35E 83 J6
Suchan = Partizansk Russia 43°8N 133°9E 107 E14
Suchań Poland 53°18N 15°18E 83 E2
Suchedniów Poland 51°3N 20°49E 83 G7
Suchil Mexico 23°39N 103°54W 180 C4
Suchou = Suzhou China 31°19N 120°38E 117 B13
Süchow = Xuzhou China 34°18N 117°10E 115 G9
Suchowola Poland 53°33N 23°3E 82 E10
Suck → Ireland 53°17N 8°3W 64 C3
Sucre Bolivia 19°0S 65°15W 187 G5
Sucuraj Croatia 43°10N 17°8E 93 E14
Sucuriú → Brazil 20°47S 51°38W 187 H8
Sud, Pte. du Canada 49°3N 62°14W 165 C7
Sud-Kivu □ Dem. Rep. of the Congo 3°0S 28°30E 142 C2
Sud-Ouest □ Cameroon 5°25N 9°20E 146 D6
Sud-Ouest, Pte. Canada 49°23N 63°36W 165 C7
Sud-Ouest, Pte.
Suda → Russia 59°0N 37°40E 84 C9
Sudak Ukraine 44°51N 34°57E 85 K8
Sudan U.S.A. 34°4N 102°31W 176 E3
Sudan ■ Africa 15°0N 30°0E 135 E11
Sudbury Canada 46°30N 81°0W 164 C3
Sudbury U.K. 52°2N 0°45E 67 E8
Sudd South Sudan 8°20N 30°0E 135 G12
Sudeten = Sudety Europe 50°20N 16°45E 79 A9
Sudeten Mts. = Sudety Europe 50°20N 16°45E 79 A9
Sudety Europe 50°20N 16°45E 79 A9
Südheide ○ Germany 52°46N 10°10E 76 C6
Suðuroy Færoe Is. 61°32N 6°50W 60 F9
Sudi Tanzania 10°11S 39°57E 143 E4
Sudirman, Pegunungan Indonesia 4°30S 137°0E 119 E9
Sudiți Romania 44°35N 27°38E 81 F12
Sudogda Russia 55°55N 40°50E 84 D6
Sudong, Pulau Singapore 1°13N 103°44E 121 d
Sudova Vyshnya Ukraine 49°46N 23°22E 83 J10
Sudzha Russia 51°14N 35°17E 85 G8
Sueca Spain 39°12N 0°21W 91 F4
Suedinenie Bulgaria 42°16N 24°33E 97 D8
Suemez I. U.S.A. 55°15N 133°20W 162 B2
Suez = El Suweis Egypt 29°58N 32°31E 137 F8
Suez, G. of = Suweis, Khalig el Egypt 28°40N 33°0E 137 F8
Suez Canal = Suweis, Qanâ es Egypt 31°0N 32°20E 137 H8
Suffield Canada 50°12N 111°10W 162 C6
Suffolk U.S.A. 36°44N 76°35W 173 G15
Suffolk □ U.K. 52°16N 1°0E 67 E9
Sufián Iran 38°16N 45°58E 105 C11
Şugag Romania 45°47N 23°37E 81 E8
Sugar Grove U.S.A. 41°59N 79°20W 174 E5
Sugar Hill U.S.A. 34°6N 84°2W 178 A5
Sugarcreek U.S.A. 41°25N 79°52W 174 E5
Sugargrove → India 26°16N 86°24E 125 F12
Sughd □ Tajikistan 40°0N 69°0E 109 E7
Suğla Gölü Turkey 37°20N 32°0E 104 D4
Sugluk = Salluit Canada 62°14N 75°38W 161 E16
Sugun China 39°28N 76°47E 116 C2
Suhaia, Lacul Romania 43°45N 25°15E 81 G10
Suhār Oman 24°20N 56°40E 129 E8
Sühbaatar Mongolia 50°17N 106°10E 110 A10
Sühbaatar □ Mongolia 45°30N 114°0E 114 B8
Suheli Par India 10°5N 72°17E 127 J1
Suhl Germany 50°36N 10°42E 76 E6
Suhut Turkey 38°31N 30°32E 104 C4
Sui Pakistan 28°37N 69°19E 126 E3
Sui Xian China 34°25N 115°2E 114 G8
Suibin China 47°15N 131°50E 115 B16
Suichang China 28°29N 119°15E 117 D12
Suichuan China 26°20N 114°32E 117 D10
Suide China 37°30N 110°12E 114 F6
Suifenhe China 44°25N 131°10E 115 B16
Suihua China 46°32N 126°55E 111 B14
Suijiang China 28°41N 104°2E 116 D5
Suining Hunan, China 26°35N 110°10E 117 C8
Suining Jiangsu, China 33°56N 117°58E 115 H9
Suining Sichuan, China 30°26N 105°35E 116 C5
Suiping China 33°10N 113°59E 114 H7
Suippes France 49°8N 4°30E 71 C11
Suir → Ireland 52°16N 7°9W 64 D4
Suixi China 21°19N 110°10E 117 G8
Suiyang Guizhou, China 27°58N 107°11E 116 D6

Suiyang Heilongjiang, China 44°30N 130°56E 115 B16
Suizhong China 40°21N 120°20E 115 D11
Sujangarh India 27°42N 74°31E 126 F6
Sujiatun China 41°39N 123°20E 115 D12
Sukabumi Indonesia 6°56S 106°50E 119 G12
Sukadana Indonesia 1°10S 110°0E 119 E4
Sukagawa Japan 37°17N 140°23E 119 E7
Sukamade Indonesia 8°30S 113°52E 119 H15
Sukaraja Indonesia 2°28S 110°25E 119 E4
Sukarno-Hatta Int., Jakarta ✈ (CGK) Indonesia 6°7S 106°40E 119 G12
Sukawati Indonesia 8°35S 115°17E 119 K18
Sukch'ŏn N. Korea 39°22N 125°35E 115 E13
Sukhindol Bulgaria 43°11N 25°10E 97 C9
Sukhinichi Russia 54°8N 35°10E 84 E9
Sukhothai Thailand 17°1N 99°49E 120 D2
Sukhumi = Sokhumi Georgia 43°0N 41°0E 85 J5
Sukkertoppen = Maniitsoq Greenland 65°26N 52°55W 57 C5
Sukkur Pakistan 27°42N 68°54E 126 F3
Sukkur Barrage Pakistan 27°40N 68°50E 126 F3
Sukma India 18°24N 81°45E 127 K5
Sukovo Serbia 43°4N 22°37E 96 C7
Sukri → India 25°4N 71°43E 126 G4
Sukumo Japan 32°56N 132°44E 118 H6
Sukunka → Canada 55°45N 121°15W 162 B4
Sula → Ukraine 49°40N 32°41E 85 H7
Sula, Kepulauan Indonesia 1°45S 125°0E 119 E7
Sulaco → Honduras 15°2N 87°44W 182 C2
Sulaiman Range Pakistan 30°30N 69°50E 126 D3
Sulaiman-Too Kyrgyzstan 40°31N 72°46E 108 C6
Sulak → Russia 43°20N 47°34E 87 J8
Sulakyurt Turkey 40°10N 33°43E 104 B5
Sülär Iran 31°53N 51°54E 129 D6
Sulawesi □ Indonesia 2°0S 120°0E 119 E6
Sulawesi Barat □ Indonesia 2°30S 119°0E 119 E5
Sulawesi Sea = Celebes Sea Indonesia 3°0N 123°0E 119 D6
Sulawesi Selatan □ Indonesia 2°30S 120°0E 119 E6
Sulawesi Tengah □ Indonesia 1°30S 121°0E 119 E6
Sulawesi Tenggara □ Indonesia 3°50S 122°0E 119 E6
Sulawesi Utara □ Indonesia 1°0N 124°0E 119 D6
Sulechów Poland 52°5N 15°40E 82 F2
Sulęcin Poland 52°26N 15°10E 82 F2
Sulejów Poland 51°26N 19°53E 83 G6
Sulejówek Poland 52°13N 21°17E 83 F8
Süleymanlı Turkey 38°58N 27°47E 104 C2
Sulima S. Leone 6°58N 11°32W 150 ...
Sulina Romania 45°10N 29°40E 81 E14
Sulina, Brațul → Romania 45°10N 29°40E 81 E14
Sulingen Germany 52°41N 8°48E 76 C4
Sulița Romania 47°39N 26°59E 81 C11
Sulitjelma Norway 67°9N 16°3E 60 C17
Sulkowice Poland 49°50N 19°49E 83 J6
Sullana Peru 4°52S 80°39W 186 D1
Säller Turkey 38°9N 29°29E 104 C3
Sullivan Ill., U.S.A. 39°36N 88°37W 172 F9
Sullivan Ind., U.S.A. 39°6N 87°24W 172 F9
Sullivan Mo., U.S.A. 38°13N 91°10W 172 F8
Sullivan Bay Canada 50°55N 126°50W 162 C3
Sullivan I. = Lanbi Kyun Burma 10°50N 98°20E 121 ...
Sullom Voe U.K. 60°27N 1°20W 65 A7
Sullorsuaq Greenland 70°56N 53°0W 57 ...
Sully-sur-Loire France 47°45N 2°20E 70 E5
Sulmierzyce Poland 51°37N 17°32E 83 G4
Sulmona Italy 42°3N 13°55E 93 G10
Süloğlu Turkey 41°44N 26°53E 97 F10
Sulphur La., U.S.A. 30°14N 93°23W 176 F7
Sulphur Okla., U.S.A. 34°31N 96°58W 176 D6
Sulphur Pt. Canada 60°56N 114°48W 162 A5
Sulphur Springs U.S.A. 33°8N 95°36W 176 E7
Sultan Canada 47°36N 82°47W 164 C3
Sultan U.S.A. 47°52N 121°49W 170 C5
Sultan Dağları Turkey 38°20N 31°20E 104 C4
Sultan Hamud Kenya 2°1S 37°20E 142 C4
Sultanabad = Arāk Iran 34°0N 49°40E 128 C6
Sultanhanı Turkey 37°53N 33°36E 104 C5
Sultaniça Turkey 40°37N 26°8E 97 F10
Sultanpur Mad. P., India 23°9N 77°56E 126 H7
Sultanpur Punjab, India 31°13N 75°11E 126 D6
Sultanpur Ut. P., India 26°18N 82°4E 125 F10
Sulu Arch. Phil. 6°0N 121°0E 113 C6
Sulu Sea E. Indies 8°0N 120°0E 113 C6
Sülüklü Turkey 38°53N 32°20E 104 C5
Suluova Turkey 40°50N 35°32E 104 B6
Sulūq Libya 31°44N 20°14E 135 B10
Suluru India 13°42N 80°1E 127 H5
Sulzbach Germany 49°18N 7°3E 77 F3
Sulzbach-Rosenberg Germany 49°30N 11°44E 77 F7
Sulzberger Ice Shelf Antarctica 78°0S 150°0W 55 E13
Sumalata Indonesia 1°0N 122°31E 119 D6
Sumampa Argentina 29°25S 63°29W 190 B3
Sumava Czech Rep. 49°0N 13°20E 78 B6
Sumba Indonesia 9°45S 119°35E 119 F5
Sumba, Selat Indonesia 9°0S 118°40E 119 F5
Sumbawa Indonesia 8°26S 117°30E 119 F5
Sumbawa Besar Indonesia 8°30S 117°26E 119 F5
Sumbawanga □ Tanzania 8°0S 31°30E 142 D3
Sumbe Angola 11°10S 13°48E 144 A1
Sumbu △ Zambia 8°43S 30°22E 142 D3
Sumburgh Hd. U.K. 59°52N 1°17W 65 B7
Sumdeo India 31°26N 78°44E 126 D8

o China 35°6N 78°41E 125 B8
Brazil 7°39S 36°55W 189 B3
dang Indonesia 6°52S 107°55E 119 G12
g Hungary 46°59N 17°20E 80 D2
n = Shumen
garia 43°18N 26°55E 97 C10
nep Indonesia 7°1S 113°52E 119 G15
ait = Sumqayıt
rbaijan 40°34N 49°38E 87 K9
ner L. U.S.A. 42°50N 120°45W 168 E3
nerland Canada 49°32N 119°41W 162 D5
nerland Key
.A. 24°40N 81°27W 179 L8
nerside Canada 46°24N 63°47W 165 C7
nersville U.S.A. 38°17N 80°51W 173 F13
nerton U.S.A. 33°36N 80°20W 178 B9
nertown U.S.A. 32°45N 82°16W 178 C7
nerville Ga.,
.A. 34°29N 85°21W 177 D12
nerville S.C.,
.A. 33°1N 80°11W 178 B9
nit Lake Canada 54°20N 122°40W 162 C4
nit Peak U.S.A. 37°21N 106°42W 169 H10
ner N.Z. 43°35S 172°48E 155 D7
ner Iowa, U.S.A. 42°51N 92°6W 172 D7
ner Wash., U.S.A. 47°12N 122°14W 170 C4
ner, L. N.Z. 42°42S 172°15E 155 C7
oto Japan 34°21N 134°54E 113 G7
perk Czech Rep. 49°59N 16°59E 79 B9
qayıt Azerbaijan 40°34N 49°38E 87 K9
er U.S.A. 33°55N 80°21W 178 B9
i China 34°35N 80°22E 109 F10
Ukraine 50°57N 34°50E 85 G8
☐ Ukraine 50°50N 33°50E 85 G7
ity S. Africa 25°17S 27°3E 144 C4
ity Center U.S.A. 27°43N 82°21W 179 H7
Kosi ➔ Nepal 26°59N 87°8E 125 F12
akes U.S.A. 33°10N 111°52W 169 K8
Valley U.S.A. 43°42N 114°21W 168 E6
gawa Japan 43°29N 141°55E 112 C10
n N. Korea 39°15N 125°40E 115 E13
t, L. U.K. 56°42N 5°43W 65 E3
rt, L. U.K. 51°15N 0°31W 67 F7
urst U.S.A. 48°53N 111°55W 168 B8
ury Australia 37°35S 144°44E 153 D6
ury U.S.A. 40°52N 76°48W 175 F8
nales Argentina 30°58S 61°35W 190 C3
heon S. Korea 34°52N 127°31E 115 G14
ho Corral
entina 27°55S 63°27W 190 B3
h'on N. Korea 39°25N 125°56E 115 E13
ook U.S.A. 43°8N 71°27W 175 C13
a, Selat Indonesia 6°20S 105°30E 118 F3
a Is. Indonesia 5°0S 105°0E 156 H2
a Str. = Sunda, Selat
onesia 6°20S 105°30E 118 F3
a Trench = Java Trench
Oc. 9°0S 105°0E 118 F3
ance Canada 56°32N 94°4W 163 B10
ance U.S.A. 44°24N 104°23W 168 D11
ar Nagar India 31°32N 76°53E 124 D7
arbans Asia 22°0N 89°0E 123 J16
arbans △ India 22°0N 88°45E 125 J13
argarh India 22°4N 84°5E 126 C7
ays = Sondags ➔
frica 33°44S 25°51E 144 D4
erland Canada 44°16N 79°4W 174 B5
erland U.K. 54°55N 1°23W 66 C6
own △ Australia 28°49S 151°38E 151 D5
re Canada 51°49N 114°38W 162 C6
s Denmark 56°13N 9°1E 63 H3
svall Sweden 62°23N 17°17E 62 B11
svallsbukten
eden 62°21N 17°25E 62 B11
ai Acheh Malaysia 5°8N 100°30E 121 c
ai Kolok Thailand 6°2N 101°58E 121 J3
ai Lembing
laysia 3°55N 103°3E 121 L4
ai Petani Malaysia 5°37N 100°30E 121 K3
aigerong Indonesia 2°59S 104°52E 118 E2
ailiat Indonesia 1°51S 106°8E 118 E3
aipenuh Indonesia 2°1S 101°20E 118 E2
ari = Songhua Jiang ➔
na 47°45N 132°30E 111 B15
hua Chiang = Songhua
ng ➔ China 47°45N 132°30E 111 B15
urlu Turkey 40°12N 34°21E 104 B6
ja Croatia 45°21N 16°35E 93 C13
and Park U.S.A. 31°50N 106°40W 169 L10
ansjö Sweden 60°13N 14°58E 62 D8
dalsøra Norway 62°40N 8°33E 60 E13
e Sweden 59°52N 13°5E 62 E7
e Sweden 59°53N 13°44E 62 E7
yside U.S.A. 46°20N 120°0W 168 C4
yvale U.S.A. 37°23N 122°2W 170 H4
se U.S.A. 26°8N 80°14W 179 J9
se Manor U.S.A. 36°12N 115°4W 171 J11
ar Russia 62°15N 117°30E 107 C12
ani Ghana 7°21N 2°22W 138 D4
enselkä Finland 62°52N 24°0E 60 E21
= Finland ■
rope 63°0N 27°0E 60 E22
ussalmi Finland 64°54N 29°10E 60 D23
arvi Russia 62°3N 32°20E 84 A7
i U.S.A. 36°15N 112°41W 169 H7
ul India 26°10N 86°40E 125 F12
rior Ariz., U.S.A. 33°18N 111°6W 169 K8
rior Mont., U.S.A. 47°12N 114°53W 168 C6
rior Nebr., U.S.A. 40°1N 98°4W 172 E4
rior Wis., U.S.A. 46°44N 92°6W 172 B7
rior, L. N. Amer. 47°0N 87°0W 164 C2
tar Croatia 43°25N 16°32E 93 E13
an Buri Thailand 14°14N 100°10E 120 E3
an Dağı Turkey 38°54N 42°48E 105 C10
ori Indonesia 1°0S 136°0E 119 E9
asl Poland 53°13N 23°19E 83 E10
asl ➔ Poland 53°11N 22°57E 83 E9
a Georgia 42°2N 41°49E 87 J5
ng Shuiku
ina 40°35N 124°50E 115 D13
sh Shuyūkh Iraq 30°53N 46°28E 128 D5
uwayq Si. Arabia 24°23N 38°27E 128 E3
an China 33°54N 118°8E 115 H10
ıtra = Socotra
nen 12°30N 54°0E 131 E5
Lebanon 33°19N 35°16E 130 B4
Oman 22°34N 59°32E 131 C6
Pt. U.S.A. 36°18N 121°54W 170 J5
➔ Russia 56°6N 46°0E 86 C8
b Pakistan 28°25N 66°15E 124 E2
baja = Surabaya
donesia 7°17S 112°45E 118 F4
baya Indonesia 7°17S 112°45E 118 F4
Surahammar Sweden 59°43N 16°13E 62 E10
Suraia Romania 45°40N 27°25E 81 E12
Surakarta Indonesia 7°35S 110°48E 118 F4
Šurany Slovak Rep. 48°6N 18°10E 79 C11
Surat Australia 27°10S 149°6E 151 D4
Surat India 21°12N 72°55E 126 D1
Surat Thani Thailand 9°6N 99°20E 121 H2
Suratgarh India 29°18N 73°55E 124 E5
Surathkal India 12°58N 74°46E 127 H2
Suraxanı = Qaraçuxar
Azerbaijan 40°25N 50°1E 87 K10
Şuraymilā Si. Arabia 25°7N 46°7E 128 E5
Suraż Poland 52°57N 22°57E 83 F9
Surazh Belarus 55°25N 30°44E 84 E6
Surazh Russia 53°5N 32°27E 85 F7
Surduc Romania 47°15N 23°25E 81 C8
Surduc Pasul Romania 45°21N 23°23E 81 E8
Surdulica Serbia 42°41N 22°11E 96 D6
Surendranagar India 22°45N 71°40E 124 H4
Surf U.S.A. 34°41N 120°36W 171 L6
Surfers Paradise
Australia 28°0S 153°25E 151 D5
Surfside U.S.A. 25°52N 80°7W 179 K9
Surgana India 20°34N 73°37E 126 D1
Surgères France 46°7N 0°47W 72 B3
Surgut Russia 61°14N 73°20E 106 C8
Sùria Spain 41°50N 1°45E 90 D6
Suriapet India 17°10N 79°40E 126 F4
Surigao Phil. 9°47N 125°29E 119 C7
Surin Thailand 14°50N 103°34E 120 E4
Surinam = Suriname ■
S. Amer. 4°0N 56°0W 187 C7
Suriname ■ S. Amer. 4°0N 56°0W 187 C7
Suriname ➔ Suriname 5°50N 55°15W 187 B7
Surjagarh India 19°36N 80°25E 126 E5
Sūrmaq Iran 31°3N 52°48E 129 D7
Sürmene Turkey 41°0N 40°1E 105 B9
Surovikino Russia 48°32N 42°55E 87 F6
Surprise U.S.A. 33°38N 112°19W 169 K7
Surrency U.S.A. 31°44N 82°12W 178 D7
Surrey Canada 49°7N 122°45W 170 A4
Surrey ☐ U.K. 51°15N 0°31W 67 F7
Sursand India 26°39N 85°43E 125 F11
Sursar ➔ India 26°14N 87°3E 125 F12
Sursee Switz. 47°11N 8°6E 77 H4
Sursk Russia 53°3N 45°40E 86 D7
Surskoye Russia 54°30N 46°44E 86 C8
Surt Libya 31°11N 16°39E 135 B9
Surt, Khalīj Libya 31°40N 18°30E 135 B9
Surtanahu Pakistan 26°22N 70°0E 124 F4
Surte Sweden 57°50N 12°1E 63 G6
Surtsey Iceland 63°20N 20°30W 60 E3
Surubim Brazil 7°50S 35°45W 189 B3
Sürüç Turkey 36°58N 38°25E 105 D8
Suruga-Wan Japan 34°45N 138°30E 113 G9
Surxondaryo ☐
Uzbekistan 38°0N 67°30E 109 E7
Şuşa Azerbaijan 39°46N 46°45E 105 C12
Susa Italy 45°8N 7°3E 92 C4
Suså ➔ Denmark 55°12N 11°42E 63 J5
Sušac Croatia 42°46N 16°30E 93 F13
Sūsah Libya 32°52N 21°59E 135 B10
Susak Croatia 44°30N 14°18E 93 D11
Susaki Japan 33°22N 133°17E 113 H6
Sūsangerd Iran 31°35N 48°6E 105 G13
Susanville U.S.A. 40°25N 120°39W 168 F3
Susch Switz. 46°46N 10°5E 77 J6
Suşehri Turkey 40°10N 38°6E 105 B8
Sušice Czech Rep. 49°17N 13°30E 78 B6
Susleni Moldova 47°25N 28°59E 81 C13
Susner India 23°57N 76°5E 124 H7
Susong China 30°10N 116°5E 117 B11
Susquehanna U.S.A. 41°57N 75°36W 175 E9
Susquehanna ➔
U.S.A. 39°33N 76°5W 175 G8
Susques Argentina 23°35S 66°25W 190 A2
Sussex Canada 45°45N 65°37W 165 C6
Sussex U.S.A. 41°13N 74°37W 175 E10
Sussex, East ☐ U.K. 51°0N 0°20E 67 G8
Sussex, West ☐ U.K. 51°0N 0°30W 67 G7
Sussex Inlet Australia 35°10S 150°36E 153 C9
Sustut ➔ Canada 56°20N 127°30W 162 B3
Susuman Russia 62°47N 148°10E 107 C15
Susunu Indonesia 3°7S 133°39E 119 E8
Susurluk Turkey 39°54N 28°8E 99 B10
Susuz Turkey 40°46N 43°8E 105 B10
Susz Poland 53°44N 19°20E 82 E6
Sutay Uul Asia 46°35N 93°38E 110 B7
Sütçüler Turkey 37°29N 30°57E 104 D4
Şuţeşti Romania 45°13N 27°27E 81 E12
Sutherland Australia 34°2S 151°4E 153 C9
Sutherland S. Africa 32°24S 20°40E 144 D3
Sutherland U.K. 58°12N 4°50W 65 C4
Sutherland U.S.A. 41°10N 101°8W 172 E3
Sutherland Falls N.Z. 44°48S 167°46E 155 E2
Sutherlin U.S.A. 43°23N 123°19W 168 E2
Suthri India 23°3N 68°55E 124 H3
Sutjeska △ Bos.-H. 43°50N 18°32E 80 G3
Sutlej ➔ Pakistan 29°23N 71°3E 124 E4
Sutter U.S.A. 39°10N 121°45W 170 F5
Sutter Buttes U.S.A. 39°12N 121°49W 170 F5
Sutter Creek U.S.A. 38°24N 120°48W 170 G6
Sutton Canada 45°6N 72°37W 175 A12
Sutton N.Z. 45°34S 170°8E 155 F5
Sutton Nebr., U.S.A. 40°36N 97°52W 172 E5
Sutton W. Va., U.S.A. 38°40N 80°43W 173 F13
Sutton ➔ Canada 55°15N 83°45W 164 A3
Sutton Coldfield U.K. 52°35N 1°49W 67 E6
Sutton in Ashfield U.K. 53°8N 1°16W 66 D6
Sutton L. Canada 54°15N 84°42W 164 B3
Suttor ➔ Australia 21°36S 147°2E 150 C4
Suttsu Japan 42°48N 140°14E 112 C10
Sutwik I. U.S.A. 56°34N 157°12W 166 D8
Suva Fiji 18°6S 178°30E 154 a
Suva Gora Macedonia 41°45N 21°3E 96 E5
Suva Planina Serbia 43°10N 22°5E 96 C6
Suva Reka = Therandë
Kosovo 42°21N 20°50E 96 D4
Suvorov Russia 54°7N 36°30E 84 E9
Suvorov Is. = Suwarrow Is.
Cook Is. 13°15S 163°5W 157 J11
Suvorove Ukraine 45°35N 28°59E 81 E13
Suvorovo Bulgaria 43°20N 27°35E 97 C11
Suwałki Poland 54°8N 22°59E 82 D9
Suwannaphum
Thailand 15°33N 103°47E 120 E4
Suwannee U.S.A. 29°20N 83°9W 179 F6
Suwannee ➔ U.S.A. 29°17N 83°10W 179 F6
Suwannee Sd. U.S.A. 29°20N 83°15W 179 F6
Suwanose-Jima Japan 29°38N 129°43E 113 K4
Suwarrow Is. Cook Is. 13°15S 163°5W 157 J11
Suwayqīyah, Hawr as
Iraq 32°40N 46°3E 105 G12
Suweis, Khalîg el Egypt 28°40N 33°0E 137 F8
Suweis, Qanâ es Egypt 31°0N 32°20E 137 E8
Suwon S. Korea 37°17N 127°1E 115 F14
Suzdal Russia 56°29N 40°26E 84 D11
Suzhou Anhui, China 33°41N 116°59E 114 H9
Suzhou Jiangsu, China 31°19N 120°38E 117 B13
Suzu Japan 37°25N 137°17E 113 F8
Suzu-Misaki Japan 37°31N 137°21E 113 F8
Suzuka Japan 34°55N 136°36E 113 G8
Suzun Russia 53°47N 82°18E 109 B10
Suzzara Italy 44°59N 10°45E 92 D7
Svalbard Arctic 78°0N 17°0E 57 B12
Svalbard Radio = Longyearbyen
Svalbard 78°13N 15°40E 54 B8
Svalöv Sweden 55°57N 13°8E 63 J7
Svalyava Ukraine 48°33N 22°59E 80 B7
Svaneke Denmark 55°8N 15°8E 63 J9
Svaneti Georgia 42°50N 42°45E 105 A10
Svängsta Sweden 56°16N 14°47E 63 H8
Svanskog Sweden 59°11N 12°33E 62 E6
Svappavaara Sweden 67°40N 21°3E 60 C19
Svärdsjö Sweden 60°45N 15°54E 62 D9
Svartå Sweden 59°8N 14°32E 62 E8
Svartisen Norway 66°40N 13°59E 60 C15
Svartvik Sweden 62°19N 17°24E 62 B11
Svatove Ukraine 49°22N 38°15E 85 H10
Svatovo = Svatove
Ukraine 49°22N 38°15E 85 H10
Svay Chek Cambodia 13°48N 102°58E 120 F4
Svay Rieng Cambodia 11°9N 105°45E 121 G5
Svealand Sweden 60°20N 15°0E 62 D9
Svedala Sweden 55°30N 13°15E 63 J7
Sveg Sweden 62°2N 14°21E 62 B8
Svendborg Denmark 55°4N 10°35E 63 J4
Svenljunga Sweden 57°29N 13°5E 63 G7
Svenstavik Sweden 62°45N 14°26E 62 B8
Svenstrup Denmark 56°58N 9°50E 63 H3
Svenyhorodka Ukraine 49°4N 30°56E 85 H6
Sverdlovsk Ukraine 48°5N 39°47E 85 H10
Sverdrup Chan.
Canada 79°56N 96°25W 161 B12
Sverdrup Is. Canada 79°0N 97°0W 158 B10
Sverige = Sweden ■
Europe 57°0N 15°0E 61 H16
Sveshtari Bulgaria 43°40N 26°40E 97 C10
Svetac Croatia 43°3N 15°43E 93 E12
Sveti Nikola, Prokhad
Europe 43°27N 22°6E 96 C6
Sveti Nikole Macedonia 41°51N 21°56E 96 E5
Sveti Rok Croatia 44°22N 15°39E 93 D12
Svetlaya Russia 46°33N 138°18E 112 A9
Svetlogorsk = Svyetlahorsk
Belarus 52°38N 29°46E 75 B15
Svetlogorsk Russia 54°56N 20°10E 82 D7
Svetlograd Russia 45°25N 42°58E 87 H6
Svetlovodsk = Svitlovodsk
Ukraine 49°2N 33°13E 85 H7
Svetlyy Kaliningrad, Russia 54°41N 20°8E 82 D7
Svetlyy Orenburg, Russia 50°48N 60°51E 108 B6
Svidník Slovak Rep. 49°20N 21°37E 79 B14
Svilaja Planina Croatia 43°49N 16°31E 93 E13
Svilajnac Serbia 44°15N 21°11E 96 B5
Svilengrad Bulgaria 41°49N 26°12E 97 E10
Svir ➔ Russia 60°30N 32°48E 84 B7
Sviritsa Russia 60°29N 32°51E 84 B7
Svishtov Bulgaria 43°36N 25°23E 97 C9
Svislach Belarus 53°3N 24°2E 83 E11
Svitava ➔ Czech Rep. 49°11N 16°37E 79 B9
Svitavy Czech Rep. 49°47N 16°28E 79 B9
Svitlovodsk Ukraine 49°2N 33°13E 85 H7
Svityaz, Ozero Ukraine 51°30N 23°50E 83 G10
Svizzera = Switzerland ■
Europe 46°30N 8°0E 77 J4
Svobodnyy Russia 51°20N 128°0E 107 D13
Svoge Bulgaria 42°59N 23°23E 96 D7
Svolvær Norway 68°15N 14°34E 60 B16
Svratka ➔ Czech Rep. 49°11N 16°38E 79 B9
Svrljig Serbia 43°25N 22°6E 96 C6
Svyetlahorsk Belarus 52°38N 29°46E 75 B15
Swabian Alps = Schwäbische Alb
Germany 48°20N 9°30E 77 G5
Swaffham U.K. 52°39N 0°42E 67 E8
Swains I. Amer. Samoa 11°11S 171°4W 157 J11
Swainsboro U.S.A. 32°36N 82°20W 178 C7
Swakop ➔ Namibia 22°38S 14°36E 144 B1
Swakopmund Namibia 22°37S 14°30E 144 B1
Swale ➔ U.K. 54°5N 1°20W 66 C6
Swamihalli India 14°52N 76°38E 127 G3
Swan ➔ Australia 32°3S 115°45E 149 F2
Swan ➔ Canada 52°30N 100°45W 163 C8
Swan Hill Australia 35°20S 143°33E 152 C5
Swan Hills Canada 54°43N 115°24W 162 C5
Swan Is. = Santanilla, Is.
Honduras 17°22N 83°57W 182 C3
Swan L. =
Kalajun-Ku'erdening ⌂
China 43°10N 81°50E 109 D10
Swan L. Man., Canada 52°30N 100°40W 163 C8
Swan L. Ont., Canada 54°16N 91°11W 164 B1
Swan Ra. U.S.A. 48°0N 113°45W 168 C7
Swan Reach Australia 34°35S 139°37E 152 C3
Swan River Canada 52°10N 101°16W 163 C8
Swanage U.K. 50°36N 1°58W 67 G6
Swansea N.S.W.,
Australia 33°3S 151°35E 153 B9
Swansea Tas., Australia 42°8S 148°4E 151 G4
Swansea Canada 43°38N 79°28W 174 C5
Swansea U.K. 51°37N 3°57W 67 F4
Swansea U.S.A. 33°44N 81°6W 178 B8
Swansea ☐ U.K. 51°38N 4°3W 67 F3
Swartberge S. Africa 33°20S 22°0E 144 D3
Swartmodder S. Africa 28°1S 20°32E 144 C3
Swartnossob ➔ Namibia 23°8S 18°42E 144 B2
Swartruggens S. Africa 25°39S 26°42E 144 C4
Swarzędz Poland 52°25N 17°4E 83 F4
Swastika Canada 48°7N 80°6W 164 C3
Swat ➔ Pakistan 34°40N 72°5E 125 B5
Swatow = Shantou
China 23°18N 116°40E 117 F11
Swaziland ■ Africa 26°30S 31°30E 145 C5
Sweden ■ Europe 57°0N 15°0E 61 H16
Swedru Ghana 5°32N 0°41W 139 D4
Sweet Grass U.S.A. 48°59N 111°58W 168 B8
Sweet Home U.S.A. 44°24N 122°44W 168 D2
Sweetwater Nev.,
U.S.A. 38°27N 119°9W 170 G7
Sweetwater Tenn.,
U.S.A. 35°36N 84°28W 177 D12
Sweetwater Tex.,
U.S.A. 32°28N 100°25W 176 E4
Sweetwater ➔
U.S.A. 42°31N 107°2W 168 E10
Swellendam S. Africa 34°1S 20°26E 144 D3
Swider ➔ Poland 52°6N 21°14E 83 F8
Świdnica Poland 50°50N 16°30E 83 H3
Świdnik Poland 51°13N 22°39E 83 G9
Świdwin Poland 53°47N 15°49E 82 E2
Świebodzice Poland 50°51N 16°20E 83 H3
Świebodzin Poland 52°15N 15°31E 83 F2
Świecie Poland 53°25N 18°30E 82 E5
Świerzawa Poland 51°1N 15°54E 83 G2
Świętokrzyski △ Poland 50°53N 20°59E 83 H7
Świętokrzyskie ☐
Poland 50°45N 20°45E 83 H7
Świętokrzyskie, Góry
Poland 51°0N 20°30E 83 H7
Swift Current Canada 50°20N 107°45W 163 C7
Swift Current ➔
Canada 50°38N 107°44W 163 C7
Swifts Creek Australia 37°17S 147°44E 153 D7
Swilly, L. Ireland 55°12N 7°33W 64 A4
Swindon U.K. 51°34N 1°46W 67 F6
Swindon ☐ U.K. 51°34N 1°46W 67 F6
Swinemünde = Świnoujście
Poland 53°54N 14°16E 82 E1
Swinford Ireland 53°57N 8°58W 64 C3
Świnoujście Poland 53°54N 14°16E 82 E1
Switzerland ■ Europe 46°30N 8°0E 77 J4
Swords Ireland 53°28N 6°13W 64 C5
Swoyerville U.S.A. 41°18N 75°53W 175 E9
Syasstroy Russia 60°9N 32°33E 84 B7
Sychevka Russia 55°59N 34°16E 84 E8
Syców Poland 51°19N 17°40E 83 G4
Syddanmark ☐ Denmark 55°30N 9°0E 63 J2
Sydenham ➔ Canada 42°33N 82°25W 174 D2
Sydney Australia 33°52S 151°12E 153 B9
Sydney Canada 46°7N 60°7W 165 C7
Sydney L. Canada 50°41N 94°25W 163 C10
Sydney Mines Canada 46°18N 60°15W 165 C7
Sydprøven = Alluitsup Paa
Greenland 60°30N 45°35W 57 E6
Sydra, G. of = Surt, Khalīj
Libya 31°40N 18°30E 135 B9
Syeverodonetsk
Ukraine 48°58N 38°35E 85 H10
Syke Germany 52°55N 8°50E 76 C4
Sykesville U.S.A. 41°3N 78°50W 174 E6
Syktyvkar Russia 61°45N 50°40E 106 C6
Sylacauga U.S.A. 33°10N 86°15W 178 B3
Sylarna Sweden 63°2N 12°13E 60 E15
Sylhet Bangla. 24°54N 91°52E 123 G17
Sylhet ☐ Bangla. 24°50N 91°50E 123 G17
Sylt Germany 54°54N 8°22E 76 A4
Sylvan Beach U.S.A. 43°12N 75°44W 175 C9
Sylvan Lake Canada 52°20N 114°3W 162 C6
Sylvania Ga., U.S.A. 32°45N 81°38W 178 C8
Sylvania Ohio, U.S.A. 41°43N 83°42W 173 E12
Sylvester U.S.A. 31°32N 83°50W 178 D6
Sym Russia 60°20N 88°18E 106 C9
Synelnykove Ukraine 48°25N 35°30E 85 H8
Synevyr △ Ukraine 48°30N 23°40E 81 B8
Synevyrska Polyana
Ukraine 48°35N 23°41E 81 B8
Synnot Ra. Australia 16°30S 125°20E 148 C4
Synyak Ukraine 48°35N 22°51E 80 B7
Syöte △ Finland 65°44N 27°58E 60 D22
Syowa Antarctica 68°50S 12°0E 55 C5
Syracuse Kans.,
U.S.A. 37°59N 101°45W 172 G3
Syracuse N.Y., U.S.A. 43°3N 76°9W 175 C8
Syracuse Nebr., U.S.A. 40°39N 96°11W 172 E5
Syrdarya ➔ Kazakhstan 46°3N 61°0E 108 C6
Syria ■ Asia 35°0N 38°0E 105 E8
Syrian Desert = Shām, Bādiyat
ash Asia 32°0N 40°0E 128 C3
Syros = Ermoupoli
Greece 37°28N 24°57E 98 D6
Sysslebäck Sweden 60°44N 12°52E 62 D6
Syzran Russia 53°12N 48°30E 86 D9
Szabolcs-Szatmár-Bereg ☐
Hungary 48°2N 21°45E 80 B6
Szadek Poland 51°41N 18°59E 83 G5
Szamocin Poland 53°2N 17°7E 83 E4
Szamos ➔ Hungary 48°7N 22°20E 80 B7
Szamotuły Poland 52°37N 16°33E 83 F3
Száraz ➔ Hungary 46°10N 21°15E 80 D6
Szarvas Hungary 46°50N 20°38E 80 D5
Százhalombatta
Hungary 47°20N 18°58E 80 C3
Szczawnica Poland 49°26N 20°30E 83 J7
Szczebrzeszyn Poland 50°42N 22°59E 83 H9
Szczecin Poland 53°27N 14°27E 82 E1
Szczecinek Poland 53°43N 16°41E 82 E3
Szczeciński, Zalew = Stettiner Haff
Germany 53°47N 14°15E 76 B10
Szczekociny Poland 50°38N 19°48E 83 H6
Szczucin Poland 50°18N 21°4E 83 H8
Szczuczyn Poland 53°36N 22°19E 82 E9
Szczyrk Poland 49°43N 19°2E 83 J6
Szczytna Poland 50°25N 16°28E 83 H3
Szczytno Poland 53°33N 21°0E 82 E7
Szechuan = Sichuan ☐
China 30°30N 103°0E 116 B5
Szechuan Basin = Sichuan Pendi
China 31°0N 105°0E 116 B5
Szécsény Hungary 48°7N 19°30E 80 B4
Szeged Hungary 46°16N 20°10E 80 D5
Szeghalom Hungary 47°1N 21°10E 80 C6
Székesfehérvár Hungary 47°15N 18°25E 80 C3
Szekszárd Hungary 46°22N 18°42E 80 D3
Szendrő Hungary 48°24N 20°41E 80 B5
Szentendre Hungary 47°39N 19°4E 80 C4
Szentes Hungary 46°39N 20°21E 80 D5
Szentgotthárd Hungary 46°58N 16°19E 80 D1
Szentlőrinc Hungary 46°3N 18°1E 80 D3
Szerencs Hungary 48°10N 21°12E 80 B6
Szigetszentmiklós
Hungary 47°21N 19°3E 80 C4
Szigetvár Hungary 46°3N 17°46E 80 D2
Szikszó Hungary 48°12N 20°56E 80 B5
Szklarska Poręba Poland 50°50N 15°33E 83 H2
Szkwa ➔ Poland 53°11N 21°43E 83 E8
Szlichtyngowa Poland 51°42N 16°15E 83 G3
Szob Hungary 47°48N 18°53E 80 C3
Szolnok Hungary 47°10N 20°15E 80 C5
Szombathely Hungary 47°14N 16°38E 80 C1
Szprotawa Poland 51°33N 15°35E 83 G2
Sztum Poland 53°55N 19°1E 82 E6
Sztutowo Poland 54°20N 19°15E 82 D6
Szubin Poland 53°1N 17°45E 83 E4
Szydłowiec Poland 51°15N 20°51E 83 G7
Szypliszki Poland 54°17N 23°2E 82 D10

T

Ta Khli Thailand 15°15N 100°21E 120 E3
Ta Lai Vietnam 11°24N 107°23E 121 G6
Ta Phraya △ Thailand 14°11N 102°49E 120 E4
Taal Volcano Phil. 14°2N 120°59E 119 B6
Taamisaari = Raasepori
Finland 60°0N 23°26E 84 B2
Tab Hungary 46°44N 18°2E 80 D3
Tabacal Argentina 23°15S 64°15W 190 A3
Tabaco Phil. 13°22N 123°44E 119 B6
Tabagné Ivory C. 7°59N 3°4W 138 D4
Ţābah Si. Arabia 26°55N 42°38E 128 E4
Tabalos Peru 6°26S 76°37W 188 B2
Tabanan Indonesia 8°32S 115°8E 119 K18
Tabankort Niger 17°44N 0°20E 139 B5
Tabarka Tunisia 36°56N 8°46E 136 A5
Ţabas Khorāsān, Iran 32°48N 60°12E 129 C9
Ţabas Yazd, Iran 33°35N 56°55E 129 C8
Tabasará, Serranía de
Panama 8°35N 81°40W 182 E3
Tabasco ☐ Mexico 18°0N 92°40W 181 D6
Tabāsīn Iran 31°12N 57°54E 129 D8
Tabatinga Brazil 4°16S 69°56W 188 A4
Tabatinga, Serra da
Brazil 10°30S 44°0W 189 C2
Tabelbala Algeria 29°24N 3°15W 136 C3
Tabelbala, Kahal de
Algeria 28°47N 2°0W 136 C3
Tabelembila Algeria 24°43N 4°16E 136 D4
Taber Canada 49°47N 112°8W 162 D6
Taberg Sweden 57°40N 14°6E 63 G8
Tabira Brazil 7°35S 37°33W 189 B3
Tabla Niger 13°46N 3°1E 139 C5
Tablas de Daimiel △ Spain 39°9N 3°40W 89 F7
Tablas I. Phil. 12°25N 122°2E 119 B6
Table, Pte. de la Réunion 21°14S 55°48E 141 c
Table B. Canada 53°40N 56°25W 165 B8
Table B. S. Africa 33°35S 18°25E 144 D2
Table C. N.Z. 39°6S 178°0E 154 F7
Table I. Burma 14°12N 93°22E 127 G11
Table Mountain △
S. Africa 33°58S 18°28E 144 D2
Table Mt. S. Africa 33°58S 18°26E 144 D2
Table Rock L. U.S.A. 36°36N 93°19W 172 G7
Tabletop, Mt. Australia 23°24S 147°11E 150 C4
Tábor Czech Rep. 49°25N 14°39E 78 B7
Tabora Tanzania 5°2S 32°50E 142 D3
Tabora ☐ Tanzania 5°0S 33°0E 142 D3
Tabou Ivory C. 4°30N 7°20W 138 E3
Tabrīz Iran 38°7N 46°20E 105 C12
Tabuaeran Kiribati 3°51N 159°22W 157 G12
Tabuenca Spain 41°42N 1°33W 90 D3
Tabūk Si. Arabia 28°23N 36°36E 128 D3
Tabūk ☐ Si. Arabia 27°40N 36°50E 128 E3
Taburno-Camposauro ⌂
Italy 41°8N 14°37E 95 A7
Täby Sweden 59°26N 18°2E 62 E12
Tacámbaro de Codallos
Mexico 19°14N 101°28W 180 D4
Tacheng China 46°40N 82°58E 109 C10
Tach'i Taiwan 24°53N 121°17E 117 E13
Tachia Taiwan 24°25N 120°28E 117 E13
Tachilek Burma 20°26N 99°52E 120 B2
Tach'ing Shan = Daqing Shan
China 40°40N 111°0E 114 D6
Tachov Czech Rep. 49°47N 12°39E 78 B5
Tácina ➔ Italy 38°57N 16°55E 95 D9
Tacloban Phil. 11°15N 124°58E 119 B6
Tacna Peru 18°0S 70°20W 188 D3
Tacna ☐ Peru 17°40S 70°20W 188 D3
Tacoma U.S.A. 47°14N 122°26W 170 C4
Tacuarembó Uruguay 31°45S 56°0W 191 C4
Tademaït, Plateau du
Algeria 28°30N 2°30E 136 C4
Tādepallegudem India 16°50N 81°30E 126 F5
Tadio, L. Ivory C. 5°10N 5°15W 138 D3
Tadjerdjeri, O. ➔ Algeria 26°0N 8°0E 136 C5
Tadjerouna Algeria 33°31N 2°3E 136 B4
Tadjmout Laghouat,
Algeria 33°52N 2°30E 136 B4
Tadjmout Saoura, Algeria 25°37N 3°48E 136 C4
Tadjourah Djibouti 11°50N 42°55E 131 E3
Tadla-Azilal ☐ Morocco 32°0N 6°30W 136 B2
Tadmor N.Z. 41°27S 172°45E 155 B7
Tadoba △ India 20°30N 78°20E 126 D4
Tadoule L. Canada 58°36N 98°20W 163 B9
Tadoussac Canada 48°11N 69°42W 165 C6
Tadpatri India 14°55N 78°1E 127 G4
Tadrés ⌂ Niger 16°0N 7°10E 139 B6
Tadzhikistan = Tajikistan ■
Asia 38°30N 70°0E 109 E8
Taegu = Daegu
S. Korea 35°50N 128°37E 115 G15
Taegwan N. Korea 40°13N 125°12E 115 D13
Taejŏn = Daejeon
S. Korea 36°20N 127°28E 115 F14
Taen, Ko Thailand 9°22N 99°57E 121 b
Tafalla Spain 42°30N 1°41W 90 C3
Tafelbaai = Table B.
S. Africa 33°35S 18°25E 144 D2
Tafelney, C. Morocco 31°3N 9°51W 136 B2
Tafermaar Indonesia 6°47S 134°10E 119 F8
Taffermit Morocco 29°37N 9°15W 136 C2
Tafí Viejo Argentina 26°43S 65°17W 190 B2
Tafīhān Iran 29°25N 52°39E 129 D7
Tafilalet Morocco 31°20N 4°45W 136 B3
Tafiré Ivory C. 9°4N 5°4W 138 D3
Tafo Ghana 6°15N 0°20W 139 D4
Tafraoute Morocco 29°50N 8°58W 136 C2
Tafresh Iran 34°45N 49°57E 129 C6
Taft Iran 31°45N 54°14E 129 D7
Taft Phil. 11°57N 125°30E 119 B7
Taft U.S.A. 35°8N 119°28W 171 K7
Taftan Pakistan 29°0N 61°30E 122 E2
Taftān, Kūh-e Iran 28°40N 61°0E 129 D9
Tafwap India 7°23N 93°43E 127 L11
Taga Dzong Bhutan 27°5N 89°55E 123 F16
Taganay △ Russia 55°15N 59°48E 108 B5
Taganrog Russia 47°12N 38°50E 85 J10
Taganrogskiy Zaliv
Russia 47°0N 38°30E 85 J10
Tagânt ☐ Mauritania 19°0N 10°0W 138 B3
Tagbilaran Phil. 9°39N 123°51E 119 C6
Tàggia Italy 43°52N 7°51E 92 E4
Taghit Algeria 30°58N 2°0W 136 B3
Tagish Canada 60°19N 134°16W 162 A2
Tagish L. Canada 60°10N 134°20W 162 A2
Tagliacozzo Italy 42°4N 13°14E 93 F10
Tagliamento ➔ Italy 45°38N 13°6E 93 C10
Táglio di Po Italy 45°0N 12°12E 93 D9
Tagomago Spain 39°2N 1°39E 100 B8
Tagourāret Mauritania 17°45N 7°45W 138 B3
Taguatinga Distrito Federal,
Brazil 15°51S 48°4W 189 D1
Taguatinga Tocantins,
Brazil 12°27S 46°22W 189 C1
Tagum Phil. 7°33N 125°53E 119 C7
Tagus = Tejo ➔ Europe 38°40N 9°24W 89 F2
Tahakopa N.Z. 46°30S 169°23E 155 G4
Tahala Morocco 34°0N 4°28W 136 B3
Tahan, Gunung
Malaysia 4°34N 102°17E 121 K4
Tahat Algeria 23°18N 5°33E 136 D5
Tāherī Iran 27°43N 52°20E 129 E7
Tahifet Algeria 22°58N 6°0E 136 D5
Tahiti French Polynesia 17°37S 149°27W 155 b
Tahiti, I. Tahiti 17°37S 149°27W 155 b
Tahlequah U.S.A. 35°55N 94°58W 176 D7
Tahoe, L. U.S.A. 39°6N 120°2W 170 G6
Tahoe City U.S.A. 39°10N 120°9W 170 F6
Tahoka U.S.A. 33°10N 101°48W 176 E4
Taholah U.S.A. 47°21N 124°17W 170 C2
Tahora N.Z. 39°2S 174°49E 154 F3
Tahoua Niger 14°57N 5°16E 139 C6
Tahrūd Iran 29°26N 57°49E 129 D8
Tahsis Canada 49°55N 126°40W 162 D3
Tahta Egypt 26°44N 31°32E 137 B3
Tahtaköprü Turkey 39°57N 29°39E 97 G13
Tahtalı Dağları Turkey 38°20N 36°0E 104 C7
Tahuamanú ➔ Bolivia 11°6S 67°36W 188 C4
Tahulandang Indonesia 2°27N 125°23E 119 D7
Tahuna Indonesia 3°38N 125°30E 119 D7
Taï Ivory C. 5°55N 7°30W 138 D3
Taï △ Ivory C. 5°25N 7°5W 138 D3
Tai Hu China 31°5N 120°10E 117 B13
Tai Mo Shan China 22°25N 114°7E 111 a
Tai O China 22°15N 113°52E 111 a
Tai Pang Wan China 22°33N 114°24E 111 a
Tai Po China 22°27N 114°10E 111 a
Tai Rom Yen △ Thailand 8°45N 99°30E 121 H2
Tai Shan China 36°25N 117°20E 115 F9
Tai Yue Shan = Lantau I.
China 22°15N 113°56E 111 a
Tai'an China 36°12N 117°8E 115 F9
Taiarapu, Presqu'île de
Tahiti 17°47S 149°14W 155 b
Taibai Shan China 33°57N 107°45E 114 H4
Taibique Canary Is. 27°42N 17°58W 100 G2
Taibus Qi China 41°54N 115°22E 114 D8
Taicang China 31°30N 121°5E 117 B13
T'aichung Taiwan 24°9N 120°37E 117 E13
Taieri ➔ N.Z. 46°3S 170°12E 155 G5
Taigu China 37°28N 112°30E 114 F7
Taihang Shan China 36°0N 113°30E 114 G7
Taihape N.Z. 39°41S 175°48E 154 F4
Taihe Anhui, China 33°20N 115°42E 114 H8
Taihe Jiangxi, China 26°47N 114°52E 117 D10
Taihu China 30°22N 116°20E 117 B11
Taijiang China 26°39N 108°21E 116 D7
Taikang China 34°5N 114°50E 114 G8
Tailem Bend Australia 35°12S 139°29E 152 C3
Tailfingen Germany 48°15N 9°1E 77 G5
T'ailuko Taiwan 24°9N 121°37E 117 E13
Taimyr Peninsula = Taymyr,
Poluostrov Russia 75°0N 100°0E 107 B11
Tain U.K. 57°49N 4°4W 65 D4
T'ainan Taiwan 23°0N 120°10E 117 F13
Taining China 26°54N 117°9E 117 D11
Taiobeiras Brazil 15°49S 42°14W 189 D2
Taipa China 22°10N 113°35E 111 a
T'aipei Taiwan 25°4N 121°29E 117 E13
Taiping China 30°15N 118°6E 117 B12
Taiping Malaysia 4°51N 100°44E 121 K3
Taiping Dao = Itu Aba I.
S. China Sea 10°23N 114°21E 118 B4
Taipingchuan China 44°23N 123°11E 115 B12
Taipingzhen China 33°35N 111°42E 114 H6
Taipu Brazil 5°37S 35°36W 189 B3
Tairua N.Z. 37°0S 175°51E 154 D4
Taishan China 22°14N 112°41E 117 F9
Taishun China 27°30N 119°42E 117 D12
Taita Hills Kenya 3°25S 38°15E 142 C4
Taita-Taveta ☐ Kenya 3°20S 38°15E 142 C4
Taitao, C. Chile 45°53S 75°5W 192 C1
Taitao, Pen. de Chile 46°30S 75°0W 192 C2
T'aitung Taiwan 22°43N 121°4E 117 F13
Taivalkoski Finland 65°33N 28°12E 60 D23
Taiwan ■ Asia 23°30N 121°0E 117 F13
Taiwan Strait Asia 24°40N 120°0E 117 E12
Taixing China 32°11N 120°0E 117 A13
Taiyiba Israel 32°36N 35°27E 130 C4
Taiyuan China 37°52N 112°33E 114 F7
Taizhou Jiangsu,
China 32°28N 119°55E 117 A12
Taizhou Zhejiang,
China 28°40N 121°24E 117 C13
Taizhou Liedao China 28°30N 121°55E 117 C13
Ta'izz Yemen 13°35N 44°2E 131 E3
Taj Mahal India 27°10N 78°2E 124 F8
Tājābād Iran 30°2N 54°24E 129 D7
Tajikistan ■ Asia 38°30N 70°0E 109 E8
Tajima = Minamiaizu
Japan 37°12N 139°46E 113 F9
Tajo = Tejo ➔ Europe 38°40N 9°24W 89 F2
Tajrīsh Iran 35°48N 51°25E 129 C6
Tak Thailand 16°52N 99°8E 120 D2
Takāb Iran 36°24N 47°7E 105 D12
Takachiho Japan 32°42N 131°18E 113 H5
Takachu Botswana 22°37S 21°58E 144 B3
Takada Japan 37°7N 138°15E 113 F9
Takahagi Japan 36°43N 140°45E 113 F10
Takaka N.Z. 40°51S 172°50E 155 A7
Takamaka Seychelles 4°50S 55°30E 141 b
Takamatsu Japan 34°20N 134°5E 113 G7
Takaoka Japan 36°47N 137°0E 113 F8
Takapau N.Z. 40°2S 176°21E 154 G5
Takapuna N.Z. 36°47S 174°47E 154 C3
Takasaki Japan 36°20N 139°0E 113 F9
Takatsuki Japan 34°51N 135°37E 113 G7
Takaungu Kenya 3°38S 39°52E 142 C4
Takayama Japan 36°18N 137°11E 113 F8
Take-Shima Japan 30°49N 130°26E 113 J5
Takefu = Echizen
Japan 35°50N 136°10E 113 G8
Takengon Indonesia 4°45N 96°50E 118 D1
Takeo Cambodia 10°59N 104°47E 121 G5
Takeo Japan 33°12N 130°1E 113 H5
Tåkern Sweden 58°22N 14°45E 63 F8
Takeshima = Liancourt Rocks
Asia 37°15N 131°52E 113 F5
Tākestān Iran 36°0N 49°40E 129 C6

Taketa *Japan* 32°58N 131°24E **113** H5
Takh *India* 33°6N 77°32E **125** C7
Takhär □ *Afghan.* 36°40N 70°0E **109** E7
Takhiyatas *Uzbekistan* 42°20N 59°33E **108** D5
Takhmau *Cambodia* 11°29N 104°57E **121** G5
Takht-e Soleyman
  Iran 36°36N 47°14E **105** D12
Takht-Sulaiman
  Pakistan 31°40N 69°58E **124** D3
Takiéta *Niger* 13°41N 8°32E **139** C6
Takikawa *Japan* 43°33N 141°54E **112** C10
Takla L. *Canada* 55°15N 125°45W **162** B3
Takla Landing
  Canada 55°30N 125°50W **162** B3
Taklamakan *China* 38°0N 83°0E **109** E10
Taklamakan Shamo =
  Taklamakan *China* 38°0N 83°0E **109** E10
Taksimo *Russia* 56°20N 114°52E **107** D12
Taku → *Canada* 58°30N 133°50W **162** B2
Takua Thung *Thailand* 8°24N 98°27E **121** a
Takum *Nigeria* 7°18N 9°36E **139** D6
Tal Halâl *Iran* 28°54N 55°1E **129** D7
Tala *Uruguay* 34°21S 55°46W **191** C4
Talachyn *Belarus* 54°25N 29°42E **84** E5
Talagang *Pakistan* 33°5N 72°25E **124** C5
Talagante *Chile* 33°40S 70°50W **190** C1
Talahouhait *Algeria* 24°52N 1°5E **136** D4
Talaimannar *Sri Lanka* 9°6N 79°43E **127** K4
Talaïnt *Morocco* 29°41N 9°40W **136** C2
Talak *Niger* 18°0N 5°0E **139** B6
Talamanca, Cordillera de
  Cent. Amer. 9°20N 83°20W **182** E3
Talampaya △
  Argentina 29°43S 67°42W **190** B2
Talant *France* 47°19N 4°58E **71** E11
Talara *Peru* 4°38S 81°18W **188** A1
Talas *Kyrgyzstan* 42°30N 72°13E **109** D8
Talas *Turkey* 38°41N 35°33E **104** C6
Talas □ *Kyrgyzstan* 42°20N 72°0E **109** D8
Talas → *Kazakhstan* 44°0N 70°20E **109** D8
Talas Ala Too
  Kyrgyzstan 42°15N 72°0E **109** D8
Talasskiy Alatau = Talas Ala Too
  Kyrgyzstan 42°15N 72°0E **109** D8
Talâta *Egypt* 30°36N 32°20E **130** E1
Talata Mafara *Nigeria* 12°38N 6°4E **139** C6
Talaud, Kepulauan
  Indonesia 4°30N 126°50E **119** D7
Talaud Is. = Talaud, Kepulauan
  Indonesia 4°30N 126°50E **119** D7
Talavera de la Reina
  Spain 39°55N 4°46W **88** F6
Talavera la Real *Spain* 38°53N 6°46W **89** G4
Talayan *Phil.* 6°52N 124°24E **119** C6
Talayuela *Spain* 39°59N 5°36W **88** F5
Talbandh *India* 22°3N 86°20E **125** H12
Talbert, Sillon de *France* 48°53N 3°5W **70** D3
Talbot *Australia* 37°10S 143°44E **152** D5
Talbotton *U.S.A.* 32°41N 84°32W **178** C5
Talbragar → *Australia* 32°12S 148°37E **153** B8
Talca *Chile* 35°28S 71°40W **190** D1
Talcahuano *Chile* 36°40S 73°10W **190** D1
Talcher *India* 21°0N 85°18E **126** D7
Talcho *Niger* 14°44N 3°28E **139** C5
Taldy Kurgan = Taldyqorghan
  Kazakhstan 45°10N 78°45E **109** C9
Taldyqorghan
  Kazakhstan 45°10N 78°45E **109** C9
Tälesh *Iran* 37°58N 48°58E **105** D13
Tälesh, Kühhä-ye
  Iran 37°42N 48°55E **105** D13
Talgar *= Talghar
  Kazakhstan 43°19N 77°15E **109** D9
Talghar *Kazakhstan* 43°19N 77°15E **109** D9
Talguharai *Sudan* 18°19N 35°56E **137** D4
Talguppa *India* 14°13N 74°56E **127** G2
Tali Post *South Sudan* 5°55N 30°44E **135** G12
Taliabu *Indonesia* 1°50S 125°0E **119** E6
Talibon *Phil.* 10°9N 124°20E **119** B6
Talihina *U.S.A.* 34°45N 95°3W **176** D7
Talikota *India* 16°29N 76°17E **127** F3
Talipparamba *India* 12°3N 75°21E **127** H2
Taliwang *Indonesia* 8°50S 116°55E **118** F5
Talkha *Egypt* 31°3N 31°22E **137** E7
Talkot *Nepal* 29°37N 81°19E **125** E9
Tall 'Afar *Iraq* 36°22N 42°27E **105** D10
Tall Kalakh *Syria* 34°41N 36°15E **130** A5
Tall Kayf *Iraq* 36°29N 43°7E **105** D10
Talla *Egypt* 28°5N 30°43E **137** F7
Talladega *U.S.A.* 33°26N 86°6W **178** B3
Tallaganda △
  Australia 35°29S 149°37E **153** C8
Tallahassee *U.S.A.* 30°27N 84°17W **178** E5
Tallangatta *Australia* 36°15S 147°19E **153** D7
Tallapoosa *U.S.A.* 33°45N 85°17W **178** B4
Tallapoosa → *U.S.A.* 32°30N 86°16W **178** C3
Tallard *France* 44°28N 6°3E **73** D10
Tallarook *Australia* 37°5S 145°6E **153** D6
Tallassee *U.S.A.* 32°32N 85°54W **178** C4
Tällberg *Sweden* 60°51N 15°2E **62** D9
Tallering Pk. *Australia* 28°6S 115°37E **149** E2
Talli *Pakistan* 29°32N 68°8E **124** E3
Tallinn *Estonia* 59°22N 24°48E **64** C3
Tallmadge *U.S.A.* 41°6N 81°27W **174** E3
Tallulah *U.S.A.* 32°25N 91°11W **176** E9
Tălmaciu *Romania* 45°38N 24°19E **81** E8
Talmest *Morocco* 31°48N 9°21W **136** B2
Talmont-St-Hilaire
  France 46°27N 1°37W **72** B2
Talnakh *Russia* 69°29N 88°22E **107** C9
Talne *Ukraine* 48°50N 30°44E **85** H6
Talnoye = Talne *Ukraine* 48°50N 30°44E **85** H6
Taloda *India* 21°34N 74°11E **126** D2
Täloqän *Afghan.* 36°44N 69°37E **108** E6
Talovaya *Russia* 51°6N 40°45E **86** E5
Taloyoak *Canada* 69°32N 93°32W **160** D13
Talpa de Allende
  Mexico 20°23N 104°51W **180** C4
Talparo *Trin. & Tob.* 10°30N 61°17W **187** K15
Talquin, L. *U.S.A.* 30°23N 84°39W **178** E5
Talsi *Latvia* 57°10N 22°30E **64** B3
Talsint *Morocco* 32°33N 3°27W **136** B3
Taltal *Chile* 25°23S 70°33W **190** B1
Taltson → *Canada* 61°24N 112°46W **162** A6
Talwood *Australia* 28°29S 149°29E **151** D4
Talyawalka Cr. →
  Australia 32°28S 142°22E **152** B5
Tam Dao △ *Vietnam* 21°45N 105°40E **120** B5
Tam Ky *Vietnam* 15°34N 108°12E **120** E7
Tam Quan *Vietnam* 14°34N 109°3E **120** E7

Tama *U.S.A.* 41°58N 92°35W **172** E7
Tama Abu, Banjaran
  Malaysia 3°50N 115°5E **118** D5
Tamale *Ghana* 9°22N 0°50W **139** D4
Taman *Russia* 45°14N 36°41E **85** K9
Taman Negara △
  Malaysia 4°38N 102°26E **121** K4
Tamanar *Morocco* 31°1N 9°46W **136** B2
Tamani *Mali* 13°20N 6°50W **138** C3
Tamano *Japan* 34°29N 133°59E **113** G6
Tamanrasset *Algeria* 22°50N 5°30E **136** D5
Tamanrasset □ *Algeria* 22°45N 4°40E **136** D4
Tamaqua *U.S.A.* 40°48N 75°58W **175** F9
Tamar → *U.K.* 50°27N 4°15W **67** G3
Tamarac *U.S.A.* 26°12N 80°15W **179** J9
Tamarin *Mauritius* 20°19S 57°20E **141** d
Tamarinda *Spain* 39°55N 3°49E **100** B10
Tamarite de Litera *Spain* 41°52N 0°25E **90** D5
Tamashima *Japan* 34°32N 133°40E **113** G6
Tamási *Hungary* 46°40N 18°18E **80** D3
Tamaské *Niger* 14°49N 5°43E **139** C6
Tamatave = Toamasina
  Madag. 18°10S 49°25E **141** H9
Tamaulipas □ *Mexico* 24°0N 98°45W **181** C5
Tamaulipas, Sierra de
  Mexico 23°30N 98°20W **181** C5
Tamazula *Mexico* 24°57N 106°57W **180** C3
Tamazunchale *Mexico* 21°16N 98°47W **181** C5
Tamba-Dabatou
  Guinea 11°50N 10°40W **138** C2
Tambach *Kenya* 0°36N 35°31E **142** B4
Tambacounda *Senegal* 13°45N 13°40W **138** C2
Tambacounda □ *Senegal* 14°0N 13°0W **138** C2
Tambaram *India* 12°55N 80°7E **127** H5
Tambelan, Kepulauan
  Indonesia 1°0N 107°30E **118** D3
Tambellup *Australia* 34°4S 117°37E **149** F2
Tambo *Australia* 24°54S 146°14E **150** C4
Tambo *Peru* 12°57S 74°1W **188** D3
Tambo → *Peru* 10°42S 73°47W **188** C3
Tambo de Mora *Peru* 13°30S 76°8W **188** C2
Tambobamba *Peru* 13°54S 72°9W **188** C3
Tambopata → *Peru* 13°21S 69°36W **188** C4
Tambora *Indonesia* 8°12S 118°5E **118** F5
Tamboritha, Mt.
  Australia 37°31S 146°40E **153** D7
Tamboura *C.A.R.* 5°10N 25°12E **142** A2
Tambov *Russia* 52°45N 41°28E **86** D5
Tambov □ *Russia* 52°50N 41°20E **86** D5
Tambre → *Spain* 42°49N 8°53W **88** C2
Tambuku *Indonesia* 7°8S 113°40E **119** G15
Tâmchekket
  Mauritania 17°25N 10°40W **138** B2
Tâmega → *Portugal* 41°5N 8°21W **88** D2
Tamegroute *Morocco* 30°15N 5°39W **136** B2
Tamelelt *Morocco* 31°50N 7°32W **136** B2
Tamenglong *India* 25°0N 93°35E **123** G18
Tamerza *Tunisia* 34°23N 7°58E **136** B5
Tamgué, Massif du
  Guinea 12°0N 12°18W **138** C2
Tamiahua, L. de
  Mexico 21°35N 97°35W **181** C5
Tamiami Canal *U.S.A.* 25°50N 81°0W **179** K8
Tamil Nadu □ *India* 11°0N 77°0E **127** J3
Tamis → *Serbia* 44°51N 20°39E **80** F5
Tamiya *Egypt* 29°29N 30°58E **137** F7
Tamlett, Plaine de
  Morocco 32°30N 2°20W **136** B3
Tamluk *India* 22°18N 87°58E **125** H12
Tammerfors = Tampere
  Finland 61°30N 23°50E **84** B2
Tämnaren *Sweden* 60°10N 17°25E **62** D11
Tampa *U.S.A.* 27°56N 82°27W **179** H7
Tampa, Tanjung
  Indonesia 8°55S 116°12E **119** K19
Tampa B. *U.S.A.* 27°50N 82°30W **179** H7
Tampa Int. ✈ (TPA)
  U.S.A. 27°59N 82°32W **179** H7
Tampere *Finland* 61°30N 23°50E **84** B2
Tampico *Mexico* 22°13N 97°51W **181** C5
Tampin *Malaysia* 2°28N 102°13E **121** L4
Tampoi *Malaysia* 1°30N 103°39E **121** d
Tamri *Morocco* 30°49N 9°50W **136** B2
Tamsagbulag
  Mongolia 47°14N 117°21E **111** B12
Tamsweg *Austria* 47°7N 13°49E **78** D6
Tamu *Burma* 24°13N 94°12E **123** G19
Tamuja → *Spain* 39°38N 6°29W **89** F4
Tamworth *Australia* 31°7S 150°58E **153** B9
Tamworth *Canada* 44°29N 77°0W **174** B8
Tamworth *U.K.* 52°39N 1°41W **67** E6
Tan An *Vietnam* 10°32N 106°25E **121** G6
Tan Chau *Vietnam* 10°48N 105°12E **121** G5
Tan Hiep *Vietnam* 10°27N 106°21E **121** G6
Tan Iddah *Algeria* 26°33N 9°49E **136** C7
Tan-Tan *Morocco* 28°29N 11°1W **134** C3
Tan Yen *Vietnam* 22°4N 105°3E **120** A5
Tana → *Kenya* 2°32S 40°31E **142** C5
Tana → *Norway* 70°30N 28°14E **60** A23
Tana, L. *Ethiopia* 13°5N 37°30E **131** E2
Tana River *Kenya* 2°0S 40°0E **142** C5
Tana River Primate △
  Kenya 1°55S 40°7E **142** C5
Tanabe *Japan* 33°44N 135°22E **113** H7
Tanafjorden *Norway* 70°45N 28°25E **60** A23
Tanaga I. *U.S.A.* 51°48N 177°53W **166** E4
Tanah Merah *Malaysia* 5°48N 102°9E **121** K4
Tanahbala *Indonesia* 0°30S 98°30E **118** E1
Tanahgrogot *Indonesia* 1°55S 116°15E **118** E5
Tanahjampea *Indonesia* 7°10S 120°35E **119** F6
Tanahmasa *Indonesia* 0°12S 98°39E **118** E1
Tanahmerah *Indonesia* 6°5S 140°16E **119** F10
Tanakpur *India* 29°5N 80°7E **125** E9
Tanamalwila *Sri Lanka* 6°26N 81°8E **127** L5
Tanami Desert
  Australia 18°50S 132°0E **148** C5
Tanana *U.S.A.* 65°10N 152°4W **166** B9
Tanana → *U.S.A.* 65°10N 151°58W **160** D1
Tananarive = Antananarivo
  Madag. 18°55S 47°31E **141** H9
Tanannt *Morocco* 31°54N 6°56W **136** B2
Táncaro → *Italy* 40°25N 18°4E **77** B10
Tancheng *China* 34°25N 118°20E **115** G10
Tanch'ŏn N. Korea 40°27N 128°54E **115** D15
Tanda Ut. P., *India* 26°33N 82°35E **125** F10
Tanda Ut. P., *India* 28°57N 78°56E **125** E8
Tanda *Ivory C.* 7°48N 3°10W **138** D4
Tandag *Phil.* 9°4N 126°9E **119** C7
Tandaia *Tanzania* 9°25S 34°15E **143** D3

Tăndărei *Romania* 44°39N 27°40E **81** F12
Tandaué *Angola* 16°58S 18°5E **144** A2
Tandil *Argentina* 37°15S 59°6W **190** D4
Tandil, Sa. del *Argentina* 37°30S 59°0W **190** D4
Tandlianwala *Pakistan* 31°3N 73°9E **124** D5
Tando Adam *Pakistan* 25°45N 68°40E **124** G3
Tando Allahyar
  Pakistan 25°28N 68°43E **124** G3
Tando Bago *Pakistan* 24°47N 68°58E **124** G3
Tando Mohommed Khan
  Pakistan 25°8N 68°32E **124** G3
Tandou L. *Australia* 32°40S 142°5E **152** B5
Tandoureh △ *Iran* 37°50N 59°0E **129** B8
Tandragee *U.K.* 54°21N 6°24W **64** B5
Tandsjöborg *Sweden* 61°42N 14°43E **62** C8
Tandula → *India* 21°6N 81°14E **126** D5
Tandula Tank *India* 20°40N 81°12E **126** D5
Tandur Telangana, *India* 19°11N 79°30E **126** E4
Tandur Telangana, *India* 17°14N 77°35E **126** F3
Tane-ga-Shima *Japan* 30°30N 131°0E **113** J5
Tandragee *U.K.* 54°21N 6°24W **64** B5
Tanen Tong Dan = Dawna Ra.
  Burma 16°30N 98°30E **120** D2
Tanew → *Poland* 50°29N 22°16E **83** H9
Tanezrouft *Algeria* 23°9N 0°11E **134** D6
Tang, Koh *Cambodia* 10°16N 103°7E **121** G4
Tang, Ra's-e *Iran* 25°21N 59°52E **129** E8
Tang Krasang
  Cambodia 12°34N 105°3E **120** F5
Tanga *Tanzania* 5°5S 39°2E **142** D4
Tanga □ *Tanzania* 5°20S 38°0E **142** D4
Tangalla *Sri Lanka* 6°1N 80°48E **127** L5
Tanganyika, L. *Africa* 6°40S 30°0E **142** D3
Tangasseri *India* 8°53N 76°35E **127** K3
Tangaza *Nigeria* 13°19N 4°55E **139** C5
Tanger *Morocco* 35°50N 5°49W **136** A2
Tanger-Med *Morocco* 35°53N 5°30W **89** K5
Tanger-Tétouan □
  Morocco 35°50N 5°50W **136** A2
Tangerang *Indonesia* 6°11S 106°37E **119** G12
Tangerhütte *Germany* 52°26N 11°48E **76** C7
Tangermünde *Germany* 52°33N 11°58E **76** C7
Tanggu *China* 39°2N 117°40E **115** E9
Tanggula Shan *China* 32°40N 92°10E **110** E7
Tanggula Shankou
  China 32°42N 92°27E **110** E7
Tanghe *China* 32°47N 112°50E **117** A9
Tangi *India* 19°56N 85°24E **126** E7
Tangier = Tanger
  Morocco 35°50N 5°49W **136** A2
Tangjia *China* 22°22N 113°35E **111** a
Tangjia Wan *China* 22°21N 113°33E **111** a
Tangorin *Australia* 21°47S 144°12E **150** C3
Tangra Yumco *China* 31°0N 86°38E **110** E6
Tangshan *China* 39°38N 118°10E **115** E10
Tangtou *China* 35°50N 118°30E **115** G10
Tanguen-Dassour
  Burkina Faso 12°16N 1°42W **139** C4
Tanguiéta *Benin* 10°35N 1°21E **139** C5
Tangxi *China* 29°3N 119°25E **118** C5
Tangyan He → *China* 28°54N 108°19E **116** C7
Tangyin *China* 35°54N 114°21E **116** G8
Taniantaweng Shan
  China 31°20N 98°0E **116** B2
Tanimbar, Kepulauan
  Indonesia 7°30S 131°30E **119** F8
Tanimbar Is. = Tanimbar,
  Kepulauan *Indonesia* 7°30S 131°30E **119** F8
Tanintharyi = Taninthayi
  Burma 12°6N 99°3E **121** F2
Taninthayi *Burma* 12°6N 99°3E **121** F2
Tanjay *Phil.* 9°30N 123°5E **119** C6
Tanjore = Thanjavur
  India 10°48N 79°12E **127** J4
Tanjung *Kalimantan Selatan,*
  Indonesia 2°10S 115°25E **118** E5
Tanjung *Nusa Tenggara Barat,*
  Indonesia 8°21S 116°9E **119** J19
Tanjung Malim
  Malaysia 3°42N 101°31E **121** L3
Tanjung Pelepas
  Malaysia 1°21N 103°33E **121** d
Tanjung Tokong
  Malaysia 5°28N 100°18E **121** c
Tanjungbalai *Indonesia* 2°55N 99°44E **118** D1
Tanjungbatu *Indonesia* 2°23N 118°3E **118** D5
Tanjungkarang Telukbetung =
  Bandar Lampung
  Indonesia 5°20S 105°10E **118** F3
Tanjungpinang
  Indonesia 1°5N 104°30E **118** D2
Tanjungredeb *Indonesia* 2°9N 117°29E **118** D5
Tanjungselor *Indonesia* 2°55N 117°25E **118** D5
Tank *Pakistan* 32°14N 70°25E **124** C4
Tankhala *India* 21°58N 73°47E **124** J5
Tankwa-Karoo △
  S. Africa 32°14S 19°50E **148** E2
Tännäs *Sweden* 62°26N 12°42E **62** B6
Tannersville *U.S.A.* 41°3N 75°18W **175** E9
Tannis Bugt *Denmark* 57°40N 10°15E **63** G4
Tannu Ola *Asia* 51°0N 94°0E **109** B12
Tannum Sands
  Australia 23°57S 151°22E **150** C5
Tano → *Ghana* 5°7N 2°56W **138** D4
Tanombella *Algeria* 25°30N 5°49E **136** D5
Tanout *Niger* 14°50N 8°55E **139** C6
Tanquinho *Brazil* 11°58S 39°6W **189** C3
Tanshui *Taiwan* 25°10N 121°28E **117** E13
Tansilla *Burkina Faso* 12°25N 4°23W **138** C4
Tansing *Nepal* 52°9N 83°33E **125** F10
Tantoyuca *Mexico* 21°21N 98°14W **181** C5
Tantung = Dandong
  China 40°10N 124°20E **115** D13
Tanumshede *Sweden* 58°42N 11°20E **63** F5
Tanunda *Australia* 34°30S 139°0E **152** B2
Tanur *India* 11°1N 75°52E **127** J2
Tanus *France* 44°8N 2°19E **72** D6
Tanzania ■ *Africa* 6°0S 34°0E **142** D3
Tanzhou *China* 22°16N 113°28E **111** a
Tanzilla → *Canada* 58°8N 130°43W **162** B2
Tao, Ko *Thailand* 10°5N 99°52E **121** G2
Tao'an = Taonan
  China 45°22N 122°40E **115** B12
Tao'er He → *China* 45°45N 124°5E **115** B13
Taohua Dao *China* 29°50N 122°20E **117** C14

Taolanaro *Madag.* 25°2S 47°0E **141** K9
Taole *China* 38°48N 106°40E **114** E4
Taonan *China* 45°22N 122°40E **115** B12
Taormina *Italy* 37°51N 15°17E **95** E8
Taos *U.S.A.* 36°24N 105°35W **169** H11
Taoudenni *Mali* 22°40N 3°55W **134** D5
Taoudrart, Adrar
  Algeria 24°25N 2°24E **136** D4
Taounate *Morocco* 34°25N 4°41W **136** B3
Taourirt *Algeria* 26°37N 0°20E **136** C4
Taourirt *Morocco* 34°25N 2°53W **136** B3
Taouz *Morocco* 30°53N 4°0W **136** B3
Taoyuan *China* 28°55N 111°16E **117** C8
T'aoyüan *Taiwan* 25°0N 121°4E **117** E13
Tapa *Estonia* 59°15N 25°50E **61** G21
Tapa Shan = Daba Shan
  China 32°0N 109°0E **116** B7
Tapachula *Mexico* 14°54N 92°17W **181** E6
Tapah *Malaysia* 4°12N 101°15E **121** K3
Tapajós → *Brazil* 2°24S 54°41W **187** D8
Tapaktuan *Indonesia* 3°15N 97°10E **118** D1
Tapanahoni →
  Suriname 4°20N 54°25W **187** C8
Tapanui *N.Z.* 45°56S 169°18E **155** F4
Tapauá *Brazil* 5°40S 64°21W **186** E6
Tapes *Brazil* 30°40S 51°23W **191** C5
Tapeta *Liberia* 6°29N 8°52W **138** D3
Taphan Hin *Thailand* 16°13N 100°26E **120** D3
Tapia de Casariego *Spain* 43°34N 6°56W **88** B4
Tapirai *Brazil* 19°52S 46°1W **189** D1
Tapirapecó, Serra
  Venezuela 1°10N 65°0W **186** C6
Taplan *Australia* 34°33S 140°52E **152** C4
Taplejung *Nepal* 27°1N 88°16E **125** F12
Tapo-Capara △
  Venezuela 7°55N 71°15W **183** E5
Tapolca *Hungary* 46°53N 17°29E **80** D2
Tapti → *India* 21°8N 72°41E **126** D1
Tapuae-o-Uenuku N.Z. 42°0S 173°39E **155** C8
Tapul Group *Phil.* 5°35N 120°50E **119** C6
Tapurucuará *Brazil* 0°24S 65°2W **186** D5
Taqtaq *Iraq* 35°53N 44°35E **105** E11
Taquara *Brazil* 29°36S 50°46W **191** B5
Taquari → *Brazil* 19°15S 57°17W **187** G7
Tara *Australia* 27°17S 150°31E **151** D5
Tara *Canada* 44°28N 81°9W **174** B3
Tara *Russia* 56°55N 74°24E **106** D8
Tara *Zambia* 16°58S 26°45E **143** F2
Tara → *Montenegro* 43°21N 18°51E **96** C2
Tara △ *Serbia* 43°55N 19°30E **96** C3
Taraba □ *Nigeria* 8°0N 10°30E **139** D7
Taraba → *Nigeria* 8°30N 10°15E **139** D7
Tarābulus *Lebanon* 34°31N 35°50E **130** A4
Tarābulus *Libya* 32°49N 13°7E **135** B8
Tarābulus *Libya* 31°0N 13°0E **135** B8
Taraclia, Taraclia,
  Moldova 45°54N 28°40E **81** E13
Taraclia Tighina, Moldova 46°34N 29°7E **81** D14
Taradale *N.Z.* 39°33S 176°53E **154** F5
Taradehi *India* 23°18N 79°21E **125** H8
Tarajalejo *Canary Is.* 28°12N 14°7W **100** F5
Tarakit, Mt. *Kenya* 2°2N 35°10E **142** B4
Taralga *Australia* 34°26S 149°52E **153** C8
Tarama-Jima *Japan* 24°42N 124°42E **113** M2
Taramakau → *N.Z.* 42°34S 171°8E **155** C6
Taran, Mys *Russia* 54°56N 19°59E **82** D6
Taranagar *India* 28°43N 74°50E **124** E6
Taranaki □ *N.Z.* 39°25N 174°30E **154** F3
Taranaki, Mt. *N.Z.* 39°17S 174°5E **154** F3
Tarancón *Spain* 40°1N 3°1W **90** E1
Tarangire △ *Tanzania* 4°21S 36°7E **142** C4
Taransay *U.K.* 57°54N 7°0W **65** D1
Táranto *Italy* 40°28N 17°14E **95** B10
Táranto, G. di *Italy* 40°8N 17°20E **95** B10
Tarapacá *Colombia* 2°56S 69°46W **186** D5
Tarapacá □ *Chile* 20°45S 69°30W **190** A2
Tarapoto *Peru* 6°30S 76°20W **188** B2
Tarare *France* 45°54N 4°26E **73** C8
Tararua Ra. *N.Z.* 40°45S 175°25E **154** G4
Tarasaigh = Taransay
  U.K. 57°54N 7°0W **65** D1
Tarascon *France* 43°48N 4°39E **73** E8
Tarascon-sur-Ariège
  France 42°50N 1°36E **72** F5
Tarashcha *Ukraine* 49°30N 30°31E **75** D16
Tarata *Peru* 17°27S 70°2W **188** D3
Tarauacá *Brazil* 8°6S 70°48W **188** B3
Tarauacá → *Brazil* 6°42S 69°48W **188** B4
Taravao *Tahiti* 17°43S 149°18W **155** b
Taravao, Isthme de
  Tahiti 17°43S 149°19W **155** b
Taravo → *France* 41°42N 8°49E **73** G12
Tarawa *Kiribati* 1°30N 173°0E **156** G9
Tarawera *N.Z.* 39°2S 176°36E **154** F5
Tarawera, L. *N.Z.* 38°13S 176°27E **154** F5
Tarawera, Mt. *N.Z.* 38°14S 176°32E **154** F5
Taraz *Kazakhstan* 42°54N 71°22E **109** D8
Tarazona *Spain* 41°55N 1°43W **90** D3
Tarazona de la Mancha
  Spain 39°16N 1°55W **91** F3
Tarbagatay, Khrebet
  Kazakhstan 48°0N 83°0E **109** C10
Tarbat Ness *U.K.* 57°52N 3°47W **65** D5
Tarbela Dam *Pakistan* 34°8N 72°52E **124** B5
Tarbert *Argyll & Bute,*
  U.K. 55°52N 5°25W **64** B3
Tarbert *W. Isles, U.K.* 57°54N 6°49W **65** D2
Tarbes *France* 43°15N 0°3E **72** E4
Tarboro *U.S.A.* 35°54N 77°32W **177** D16
Tarbu *Libya* 26°0N 15°5E **137** C3
Tarcento *Italy* 46°13N 13°13E **85** K5
Tarcoola *Australia* 30°44S 134°36E **151** E1
Tarcutta *Australia* 35°16S 147°44E **153** C7
Tardets-Sorholus *France* 43°8N 0°52W **72** E3
Tardoire → *France* 45°52N 0°14E **72** C4
Taree *Australia* 31°50S 152°30E **153** A10
Tarella *Australia* 31°2S 143°26E **152** A5
Tarf, W. el → *Egypt* 30°4S 51°10W **136** A2
Tarfa, W. el → *Egypt* 28°36N 30°50E **137** C7
Tarfaya *Morocco* 27°55N 12°55W **134** C3
Târgovişte *Romania* 44°55N 25°27E **81** F10
Târgu Bujor *Romania* 45°52N 27°54E **81** E12
Târgu Cărbuneşti
  Romania 44°57N 23°31E **81** F8
Târgu Frumos *Romania* 47°12N 27°2E **81** C12
Târgu Jiu *Romania* 45°5N 23°19E **81** E8
Târgu Lăpuş *Romania* 47°27N 23°52E **81** C8

Târgu Mureş *Romania* 46°31N 24°38E **81** D9
Târgu Neamţ *Romania* 47°12N 26°25E **81** C11
Târgu Ocna *Romania* 46°16N 26°39E **81** D11
Târgu Secuiesc *Romania* 46°0N 26°10E **81** D11
Targuist *Morocco* 34°59N 4°14W **136** B3
Tärhäus, Vf. *Romania* 46°40N 26°8E **81** D11
Tarhbalt *Morocco* 30°39N 5°20W **136** B2
Tarhûna *Libya* 32°33N 13°42E **135** B8
Tarfa *Spain* 36°1N 5°36W **89** K5
Tarija *Bolivia* 21°30S 64°40W **190** A3
Tarija □ *Bolivia* 21°30S 63°30W **190** A3
Tariku → *Indonesia* 2°55S 138°26E **119** E9
Tarim Basin = Tarim Pendi
  China 40°0N 84°0E **109** E11
Tarim He → *China* 39°30N 88°30E **109** E11
Tarim Pendi *China* 40°0N 84°0E **109** E11
Taritatu → *Indonesia* 2°54S 138°27E **119** E9
Tarka → *S. Africa* 32°10S 26°0E **144** D4
Tarka La *Bhutan* 27°12N 89°45E **125** F16
Tarkastad *S. Africa* 32°0S 26°16E **144** D4
Tarkhankut, Mys
  Ukraine 45°25N 32°30E **85** K7
Tarko Sale *Russia* 64°55N 77°50E **106** C8
Tarkwa *Ghana* 5°20N 2°0W **138** D4
Tarlac *Phil.* 15°29N 120°35E **119** B4
Tarm *Denmark* 55°56N 8°31E **63** J2
Tarma *Peru* 11°25S 75°45W **188** C2
Tarn □ *France* 43°49N 2°8E **72** E6
Tarn → *France* 44°5N 1°6E **72** D5
Tarn-et-Garonne □
  France 44°8N 1°20E **72** D5
Tarna → *Hungary* 47°31N 19°59E **80** C4
Târnava Mare →
  Romania 46°10N 23°43E **81** D8
Târnava Mică →
  Romania 46°9N 23°55E **81** D8
Târnăveni *Romania* 46°19N 24°13E **81** D9
Tarnica *Poland* 49°4N 22°44E **83** J9
Tarnobrzeg *Poland* 50°35N 21°41E **83** H8
Tarnogród *Poland* 50°22N 22°45E **83** H9
Tarnos *France* 43°32N 1°28E **72** E2
Târnova *Moldova* 48°10N 27°40E **81** B12
Târnova *Romania* 46°23N 21°59E **80** E6
Tarnów *Poland* 50°3N 21°0E **83** H8
Tarnowskie Góry *Poland* 50°27N 18°54E **83** H5
Tärnsjö *Sweden* 60°9N 16°56E **62** D10
Táro → *Italy* 45°2N 10°15E **92** C7
Ţärom *Iran* 28°11N 55°46E **129** D7
Taroom *Australia* 25°36S 149°48E **151** D4
Taroudannt *Morocco* 30°30N 8°52W **136** B2
Tarp *Germany* 54°39N 9°24E **76** A5
Tarpeena *Australia* 37°35S 140°47E **152** D4
Tarpon Springs *U.S.A.* 28°9N 82°45W **179** G7
Tarqüinia *Italy* 42°15N 11°45E **93** F8
Tarra Bulga △
  Australia 38°27S 146°31E **153** E7
Tarrafal *C. Verde Is.* 15°18N 23°39W **134** b
Tarragona *Spain* 41°5N 1°17E **90** D6
Tarragona □ *Spain* 41°5N 1°0E **90** D6
Tarraleah *Australia* 42°17S 146°26E **151** G4
Tarrasa = Terrassa *Spain* 41°34N 2°1E **90** D7
Tàrrega *Spain* 41°39N 1°9E **90** D6
Tarrytown Ga., *U.S.A.* 32°19N 82°34W **178** C7
Tarrytown N.Y., *U.S.A.* 41°4N 73°52W **175** E11
Tårs *Denmark* 57°23N 10°7E **63** G4
Tarsus *Turkey* 36°58N 34°55E **106** G6
Tartagal *Argentina* 22°30S 63°50W **190** A3
Tärtär *Azerbaijan* 40°26N 46°58E **87** K8
Tärtär → *Azerbaijan* 40°26N 47°2E **87** K8
Tartas *France* 43°50N 0°49W **72** E3
Tartu *Estonia* 58°20N 26°44E **84** C4
Tarţüs *Syria* 34°55N 35°55E **104** E6
Tarţüs □ *Syria* 35°0N 36°0E **104** E6
Tarumirim *Brazil* 19°16S 41°59W **189** D2
Tarumizu *Japan* 31°29N 130°42E **113** K5
Tarussa *Russia* 54°44N 37°10E **84** E9
Tarutao = Ko Tarutao △
  Thailand 6°31N 99°26E **121** J2
Tarutao, Ko *Thailand* 6°33N 99°40E **121** J2
Tarutung *Indonesia* 2°0N 98°54E **118** D1
Tarutyne *Ukraine* 46°12N 29°9E **81** D14
Tarvísio *Italy* 46°30N 13°35E **93** B10
Tarzaret, O. → *Algeria* 26°25N 1°59E **136** D4
Tasböget *Kazakhstan* 44°46N 65°33E **108** D7
Taseko → *Canada* 52°6N 123°45W **162** C4
Tash-Kömür
  Kyrgyzstan 41°40N 72°10E **109** D8
Tashauz = Daşoguz
  Turkmenistan 41°49N 59°58E **108** E6
Tashi Chho Dzong = Thimphu
  Bhutan 27°31N 89°45E **125** F16
Ţashk, Daryächeh-ye
  Iran 29°45N 53°35E **129** D7
Tashkent = Toshkent
  Uzbekistan 41°20N 69°10E **108** E7
Tashtagol *Russia* 52°47N 87°53E **109** B11
Tasiilaq *Greenland* 65°40N 37°20W **101** C6
Tasikmalaya *Indonesia* 7°18S 108°12E **119** G13
Tasjön *Sweden* 64°15N 16°0E **60** D16
Task *Niger* 14°56N 10°46E **139** C7
Tasman □ *N.Z.* 41°3N 172°25E **155** D4
Tasman B. *N.Z.* 40°59S 173°25E **155** D4
Tasman Basin *Pac. Oc.* 46°0S 158°0E **156** M4
Tasman Glacier *N.Z.* 43°37S 170°12E **155** F3
Tasman Mts. = Toros Dağları
  Turkey 37°0N 32°30E **106** G5
Tasman Pen. *Australia* 43°10S 148°0E **151** G4
Tasman Sea *Pac. Oc.* 36°0S 160°0E **158** M8
Tasmania □ *Australia* 42°0S 146°30E **151** G4
Tasmanian Wilderness World
  Heritage Area △
  Australia 43°0S 146°0E **151** G4
Taşova *Turkey* 40°45N 36°19W **106** F6
Tasra → *Canada* 70°58N 115°46W **162** A8

Tasüj *Iran* 38°18N 45°23E **10**
Tat Ton △ *Thailand* 15°57N 102°2E **1**
Tata *Hungary* 47°37N 18°19E **8**
Tata *Morocco* 29°46N 7°56W **1**
Tatabánya *Hungary* 47°32N 18°25E **8**
Tataouine *Tunisia* 32°57N 10°29E **1**
Tatar Republic = Tatarstan □
  Russia 55°30N 51°30E **8**
Tatarbunary *Ukraine* 45°50N 29°39E **8**
Tatarsk *Russia* 55°14N 76°0E **1**
Tatarskiy Proliv *Russia* 50°0N 141°0E **1**
Tatarstan □ *Russia* 55°30N 51°30E **8**
Tatatua, Pte. *Tahiti* 17°44S 149°8W **1**
Tateyama *Japan* 34°58N 139°50E **1**
Tathlina L. *Canada* 60°33N 117°39W **1**
Tathra *Australia* 36°44S 149°59E **1**
Tatinnai L. *Canada* 60°55N 97°40W **1**
Tatla Lake *Canada* 52°0N 124°20W **1**
Tatlïsu = Akanthou
  Cyprus 35°22N 33°45E **10**
Tatlïsu *Turkey* 40°24N 27°55E **9**
Tatnam, C. *Canada* 57°16N 91°0W **16**
Tatra = Tatry
  Slovak Rep. 49°20N 20°0E **7**
Tatranský △ *Slovak Rep.* 49°10N 20°0E **7**
Tatry *Slovak Rep.* 49°20N 20°0E **7**
Tatshenshini →
  Canada 59°28N 137°45W **16**
Tatshenshini-Alsek △
  Canada 59°55N 137°45W **16**
Tatsuno *Japan* 34°52N 134°33E **11**
Tatta = Thatta *Pakistan* 24°42N 67°55E **12**
Tatuí *Brazil* 23°25S 47°53W **19**
Tatum *U.S.A.* 33°16N 103°19W **16**
Tat'ung = Datong
  China 40°6N 113°18E **11**
Tatura *Australia* 36°29S 145°16E **15**
Tatvan *Turkey* 38°31N 42°15E **10**
Tauá *Brazil* 6°1S 40°26W **18**
Taubaté *Brazil* 23°0S 45°36W **19**
Tauberbischofsheim
  Germany 49°37N 9°39E **7**
Taucha *Germany* 51°23N 12°29E **7**
Tauern *Austria* 47°15N 12°40E **7**
Tauern-tunnel *Austria* 47°0N 13°12E **7**
Taulé *France* 48°37N 3°55W **7**
Taumarunui *N.Z.* 38°53S 175°15E **15**
Taumaturgo *Brazil* 8°54S 72°51W **18**
Taung *S. Africa* 27°33S 24°47E **14**
Taungdwingyi *Burma* 20°1N 95°40E **12**
Taunggyi *Burma* 20°50N 97°0E **12**
Taungoo = Toungoo
  Burma 19°0N 96°30E **12**
Taungup *Burma* 18°51N 94°14E **12**
Taunsa *Pakistan* 30°42N 70°39E **12**
Taunsa Barrage
  Pakistan 30°42N 70°50E **12**
Taunton *U.K.* 51°1N 3°5W **6**
Taunton *U.S.A.* 41°54N 71°6W **17**
Taunus *Germany* 50°13N 8°34E **7**
Taupo *N.Z.* 38°41S 176°7E **15**
Taupo, L. *N.Z.* 38°46S 175°55E **15**
Taurage *Lithuania* 55°14N 22°16E **6**
Tauramena *Colombia* 5°1N 72°45W **18**
Tauranga *N.Z.* 37°42S 176°11E **15**
Tauranga Harb. *N.Z.* 37°30S 176°5E **15**
Taureau, Rés. *Canada* 46°46N 73°50W **17**
Taurianova *Italy* 38°21N 16°1E **9**
Tauroa Pt. *N.Z.* 35°10S 173°4E **15**
Taurus Mts. = Toros Dağları
  Turkey 37°0N 32°30E **10**
Tauste *Spain* 41°58N 1°18W **9**
Tautira *Tahiti* 17°44S 149°9W **1**
Tauyskaya Guba
  Russia 59°20N 150°20E **10**
Tauz = Tovuz *Azerbaijan* 41°0N 45°40E **8**
Tavan Bogd Uul
  Mongolia 49°10N 87°49E **10**
Tavares *U.S.A.* 28°48N 81°44W **17**
Tavas *Turkey* 37°35N 29°8E **10**
Tavastehus = Hämeenlinna
  Finland 61°0N 24°28E **6**
Tavda *Russia* 58°7N 65°8E **10**
Tavda → *Russia* 57°47N 67°18E **10**
Tavernes de la Valldigna
  Spain 39°5N 0°13W **9**
Tavernier *U.S.A.* 25°1N 80°31W **17**
Taveta *Kenya* 3°23S 37°37E **14**
Taveuni *Fiji* 16°51S 179°58W **1**
Taviano *Italy* 39°59N 18°5E **9**
Tavignano → *France* 42°7N 9°33E **7**
Tavira *Portugal* 37°8N 7°40W **8**
Tavistock *Canada* 43°19N 80°50W **17**
Tavistock *U.K.* 50°33N 4°9W **6**
Tavolara *Italy* 40°54N 9°42E **9**
Távora → *Portugal* 41°8N 7°35W **8**
Tavoy = Dawei *Burma* 13°2N 98°12E **12**
Tavoy Pt. *Burma* 13°32N 98°10E **12**
Tavricbanka *Russia* 43°18N 131°59E **11**
Tavropós → *Greece* 39°10N 21°45E **9**
Tavşanlı *Turkey* 39°32N 29°45E **10**
Tavua *Fiji* 17°37S 177°5E **1**
Tavuki *Fiji* 19°7S 178°8E **1**
Taw → *U.K.* 51°4N 4°4W **6**
Tawa → *India* 22°48N 77°48E **12**
Tawa Res. *India* 22°35N 78°5E **12**
Tawas City *U.S.A.* 44°16N 83°31W **17**
Tawau *Malaysia* 4°20N 117°55E **11**
Tawi-tawi I. *Phil.* 5°10N 120°0E **11**
Tāwūq *Iraq* 35°18N 44°30E **10**
Tawūq *Iraq* 22°58N 120°54E **11**
Taxco *Mexico* 18°33N 99°36W **18**
Taxila *Pakistan* 33°42N 72°52E **12**
Taxkorgan Tajik Zizhixian
  China 37°49N 75°14E **10**
Tay → *U.K.* 56°37N 3°38W **6**
Tay, Firth of *U.K.* 56°25N 3°8W **6**
Tay, L. *Australia* 33°15S 120°48E **14**
Tay, L. *U.K.* 56°32N 4°8W **6**
Tay Ninh *Vietnam* 11°20N 106°5E **12**
Tayabamba *Peru* 8°15S 77°16W **18**
Taygetos Oros *Greece* 37°0N 22°23E **9**
Taylakova *Russia* 59°13N 74°0E **10**
Taylakovo = Taylakova
  Russia 59°13N 74°0E **10**
Taylor *Canada* 56°13N 120°40W **16**
Taylor Fla., *U.S.A.* 30°2N 82°18W **17**
Taylor Nebr., *U.S.A.* 41°46N 99°23W **17**
Taylor Pa., *U.S.A.* 41°23N 75°43W **17**
Taylor Tex., *U.S.A.* 30°34N 97°25W **17**

lor, Mt. N.Z. 43°30S 171°20E 155 D6
lor, Mt. U.S.A. 35°14N 107°37W 169 J10
lorville U.S.A. 39°33N 89°18W 172 F9
mā Si. Arabia 27°35N 38°45E 128 E3
myr, Oz. Russia 74°20N 102°0E 107 B11
myr, Poluostrov
  Russia 75°0N 100°0E 107 B11
port U.K. 56°27N 2°52W 65 E6
rona ▪ Colombia 11°20N 74°2W 183 D5
shet Russia 55°58N 98°1E 107 D10
tay Phil. 10°45N 119°33E 119 B5
yebād Iran 34°45N 60°45E 129 C9
yebād ← Iran 34°44N 60°44E 129 C9
ynsha Kazakhstan 53°50N 69°45E 108 B7
  ← Russia 67°32N 78°40E 106 C8
a Morocco 34°6N 4°6W 136 B3
-Al Hoceïma-Taounate □
  Morocco 34°15N 3°20W 136 B3
-Khurmātū Iraq 35°18N 44°20E 105 E11
-Taou □ Morocco 34°15N 4°10W 136 B3
awa-Ko Japan 39°43N 140°40E 112 E10
erbo Libya 25°45N 21°0E 135 C10
n ← Canada 59°48N 109°55W 163 B7
ona L. Canada 59°44N 108°42W 136 A5
ult Algeria 35°29N 6°11E 136 A5
ovskiy Russia 67°30N 78°44E 106 C8
rouk Algeria 23°24N 6°15E 136 D6
asi Georgia 41°43N 44°50E 87 K7
ed = Chad ■ Africa 15°0N 17°15E 135 F8
ad, L. Chad 13°30N 14°30E 135 F8
aourou Benin 8°58N 2°40E 139 D5
ngtou = Chengdu
  China 30°38N 104°2E 116 B5
ento L. Canada 55°15N 125°0W 162 B4
tti Benin 7°50N 1°40E 139 D5
banga Gabon 2°45S 11°0E 140 E2
en Liberia 5°59N 8°15W 138 D3
n Tabaraden Niger 15°58N 5°56E 139 B6
ogha Zanbil = Choghā Zanbīl
  Iran 32°1N 48°32E 129 C6
ong-k'ing = Chongqing
  China 29°35N 106°25E 116 C6
w Poland 54°8N 18°50E 82 D5
anau N.Z. 45°25S 167°43E 155 F2
arau N.Z. 45°15S 167°45E 155 F2
rraroa N.Z. 37°39S 178°25E 154 D7
aroha N.Z. 37°32S 175°44E 154 D4
ka a Maui = North I.
  N.Z. 38°0S 175°0E 154 E4
aha N.Z. 37°44S 177°53E 154 D6
araka N.Z. 38°26S 177°53E 154 E6
auwhata N.Z. 37°25S 175°9E 154 D4
opuru N.Z. 36°2S 173°54E 154 C4
wamutu N.Z. 38°1S 175°19E 154 E4
Waewae B. N.Z. 46°13S 167°33E 155 G2
ai Pounamu = South I.
  Canada 44°0S 170°0E 155 E5
ca Romania 46°55N 24°30E 81 D9
gue U.S.A. 31°38N 96°17W 176 F6
hupoo Tahiti 17°50S 149°16W 155 b
o Italy 41°15N 14°4E 95 A7
pa Mexico 17°33N 92°57W 181 D6
a Spain 36°59N 4°55W 89 C6
akang Malaysia 1°6N 110°30E 118 D4
arat Niger 14°49N 4°27E 139 C5
x ← Malaysia 1°30N 103°42E 121 d
erda Russia 43°30N 41°46E 87 J5
essa □ Algeria 35°22N 8°8E 136 A5
essa Algeria 35°0N 7°50E 136 B5
essa □ Algeria 35°0N 7°50E 136 B5
cuary ← Paraguay 26°36S 58°16W 190 B4
donesia 1°0N 102°45E 118 E2
donesia 3°20N 99°9E 118 D1
urba Tunisia 36°49N 9°51E 136 A5
oursouk Tunisia 36°29N 9°10E 136 A5
los Georgia 42°36N 45°17E 87 J7
ate Mexico 32°34N 116°38W 171 N10
er Dağları Turkey 39°27N 37°27E 104 C7
← France 47°36N 3°3E 72 F7
himan Ghana 7°35N 1°58W 138 D4
iroani Romania 44°4N 28°32E 81 F13
ka Argentina 43°29S 70°48W 192 B2
uba U.S.A. 18°55N 103°53W 180 D4
pa U.S.A. 35°51N 116°13W 171 K10
uala Mexico 28°37N 109°57W 180 B3
uci Canada 45°51N 27°27E 81 E12
imseh Canada 42°19N 82°54W 174 D2
imseh Mich.,
  U.S.A.
imseh Okla., U.S.A. 35°15N 96°56W 176 D5
= Tejen
urkmenistan 37°23N 60°31E 108 E6
s ← U.K. 54°37N 1°10W 66 C6
B. U.K. 54°40N 1°9W 66 C6
swater Canada 43°59N 81°17W 174 C3
Brazil 3°25S 64°50W 186 D6
ni Turkey 37°18N 29°45E 99 D11
allalang Indonesia 6°52S 109°8E 118 F3
el, Berlin ✈ (TXL)
ernsee Germany 47°43N 11°46E 77 H7
giano Italy 40°23N 15°32E 95 B8
Nigeria 6°53N 3°37W 66 E4
idal, L. = Bala, L. U.K. 52°53N 3°37W 66 E4
ucigalpa Honduras 14°5N 87°14W 182 D2
uidda i-n-Tessoum 14°50N 6°37E 139 B6
achapi U.S.A. 35°8N 118°27W 171 K8
achapi Mts. U.S.A. 35°0N 118°30W 171 L8
amiyam Sudan 18°20N 36°34E 137 D4
eran = Tehrān Iran 35°41N 51°25E 129 C6
oru Indonesia 3°23S 129°30E 119 E7
rān Iran 35°30N 51°30E 129 C6
uacán Mexico 18°27N 97°23W 181 D5
uantepec Mexico 16°21N 95°13W 181 D5
uantepec, G. de 15°50N 95°12W 181 D5
uantepec, Istmo de

Mexico 17°15N 94°30W 181 D6
Teide, Pico del
  Canary Is. 28°15N 16°38W 100 F3
Teifi ← U.K. 52°5N 4°41W 67 E3
Teigebyen Norway 60°12N 11°0E 62 D5
Teign ← U.K. 50°32N 3°32W 67 G4
Teignmouth U.K. 50°33N 3°31W 67 G4
Teinainano = Tarawa
  Kiribati 1°30N 173°0E 156 G9
Teius Romania 46°12N 23°40E 81 D8
Teixeira Brazil 7°13S 37°15W 189 B3
Teixeira Pinto
  Guinea-Biss. 12°3N 16°0W 138 C1
Tejakula Indonesia 8°8S 115°20E 119 J18
Tejen Turkmenistan 37°23N 60°31E 108 E6
Tejen ← Turkmenistan 37°24N 60°38E 129 B9
Tejo ← Europe 38°40N 9°24W 89 C2
Tejon Pass U.S.A. 34°49N 118°53W 171 L8
Tekamah U.S.A. 41°47N 96°13W 172 E5
Tekapo, L. N.Z. 43°53S 170°33E 155 F5
Tekax Mexico 20°12N 89°17W 181 C7
Teke Turkey 41°4N 29°39E 97 F13
Tekeli Kazakhstan 44°50N 79°0E 109 D9
Tekeze Dam Ethiopia 13°10N 38°45E 131 E2
Tekija Serbia 44°42N 22°26E 96 B6
Tekirdağ Turkey 40°58N 27°30E 97 F11
Tekirdağ □ Turkey 41°0N 27°0E 97 F11
Tekirova Turkey 36°30N 30°32E 99 E12
Tekkali India 18°37N 84°15E 126 E7
Tekke Turkey 40°42N 36°12E 104 B7
Tekman Turkey 39°38N 41°29E 105 C10
Tekoa U.S.A. 47°14N 117°4W 168 C5
Tekong Besar, Pulau
  Singapore 1°25N 104°3E 121 d
Tel ← India 20°50N 83°54E 126 D6
Tel Aviv ✈ (TLV) Israel 32°5N 34°49E 130 C3
Tel Aviv-Yafo Israel 32°4N 34°48E 130 C3
Tel Lakhish Israel 31°34N 34°51E 130 D3
Tel Megiddo Israel 32°35N 35°11E 130 C4
Tela Honduras 15°40N 87°28W 182 C2
Télagh Algeria 34°51N 0°32W 136 B3
Telanaipura = Jambi
  Indonesia 1°38S 103°30E 118 E2
Telangana □ India 17°30N 78°30E 126 F4
Telašćica ← Croatia 43°55N 15°10E 93 G12
Telavi Georgia 42°0N 45°30E 87 J7
Telč Czech Rep. 49°11N 15°28E 78 B8
Telciu Romania 47°25N 24°24E 81 C9
Telde Canary Is. 27°59N 15°25W 100 G4
Telegraph Creek
  Canada 58°0N 131°10W 162 B2
Telekhany = Tsyelyakhany
  Belarus 52°30N 25°46E 75 B13
Telemark Norway 59°15N 7°40E 61 G12
Télemsès Niger 15°37N 4°44E 139 B5
Telén Argentina 36°15S 65°31W 190 D2
Teleneşti Moldova 47°30N 28°22E 81 C13
Teleng Iran 25°47N 61°3E 129 E9
Teleño Spain 42°23N 6°22W 88 C4
Teleorman □ Romania 44°0N 25°0E 81 G10
Teleorman ← Romania 43°52N 25°26E 81 G10
Telerhteba, Djebel
  Algeria 24°10N 6°51E 136 D5
Teles Pires ← Brazil 7°21S 58°3W 186 E7
Telescope Pk. U.S.A. 36°10N 117°5W 171 J9
Teletaye Mali 16°31N 1°30E 139 B5
Teletskoye, Oz. Russia 51°40N 87°30E 109 B11
Telford and Wrekin □
  U.K. 52°45N 2°27W 66 E5
Telfs Austria 47°19N 11°4E 78 D4
Télimélé Guinea 10°54N 13°2W 138 C2
Telkwa Canada 54°41N 127°5W 162 C3
Tell City U.S.A. 37°57N 86°46W 172 G10
Teller U.S.A. 65°16N 166°22W 166 B6
Tellicherry = Thalassery
  India 11°45N 75°30E 127 J2
Telluride U.S.A. 37°56N 107°49W 169 H10
Teloloapán Mexico 18°21N 99°51W 181 D5
Telpos Iz Russia 63°16N 59°13E 58 C17
Telsen Argentina 42°30S 66°50W 192 D3
Telšiai Lithuania 55°59N 22°14E 82 C9
Telšiai □ Lithuania 55°59N 22°25E 82 C9
Teltow Germany 52°23N 13°17E 76 C9
Teluk Anson = Teluk Intan
  Malaysia 4°3N 101°0E 121 K3
Teluk Bahang Malaysia 5°28N 100°13E 121 c
Teluk Betung = Bandar Lampung
  Indonesia 5°20S 105°10E 118 F3
Teluk Intan Malaysia 4°3N 101°0E 121 K3
Teluk Kumbar Malaysia 5°18N 100°12E 121 c
Telukbutun Indonesia 4°13N 108°12E 118 D3
Telukdalam Indonesia 0°33N 97°50E 118 D1
Tema Ghana 5°41N 0°0 139 D5
Temagami, L. Canada 47°0N 80°10W 164 C7
Temax Mexico 21°9N 88°56W 181 C7
Temba S. Africa 25°20S 28°17E 145 D4
Tembagapura Indonesia 4°20S 137°0E 119 E9
Tembe
  Dem. Rep. of the Congo 0°16S 28°14E 142 C2
Tembe ← S. Africa 26°51S 32°24E 145 D5
Tembleque Spain 39°41N 3°30W 88 F7
Temblor Range
  U.S.A. 35°20N 119°50W 171 K7
Teme ← U.K. 52°11N 2°13W 67 E5
Temecula U.S.A. 33°30N 117°9W 171 N9
Temengor, Tasik
  Malaysia 5°24N 101°18E 121 K3
Temerloh Malaysia 3°27N 102°25E 121 L4
Teminabuan Indonesia 1°26S 132°1E 119 E8
Temir Kazakhstan 49°1N 57°14E 108 D5
Temirtau Kazakhstan 50°5N 72°56E 108 D8
Témiscamie ← Canada 50°59N 73°5W 165 B5
Témiscamingue, L.
  Canada 47°10N 79°25W 164 C4
Temnikov Russia 54°40N 43°11E 86 D6
Temo ← Italy 40°17N 8°28E 94 B1
Temora Australia 34°30S 147°30E 153 C7
Temosachic Mexico 28°57N 107°51W 180 B3
Tempe U.S.A. 33°24N 111°54W 169 E8
Témpio Pausánia Italy 40°54N 9°6E 94 B2
Tempiute U.S.A. 37°38N 115°38W 170 H11
Temple U.S.A. 31°6N 97°21W 176 F6
Temple B. Australia 12°15S 143°3E 150 A3
Temple Terrace U.S.A. 28°2N 82°23W 179 G7
Templemore Ireland 52°47N 7°51W 64 D4
Templeton U.S.A. 35°33N 120°42W 170 K6
Templeton ← Australia 21°0S 138°40E 150 C2
Templin Germany 53°7N 13°28E 76 B9

Tempoal de Sánchez
  Mexico 21°31N 98°23W 181 C5
Temryuk Russia 45°15N 37°24E 85 K9
Temska ← Serbia 43°17N 22°33E 96 C6
Temuco Chile 38°45S 72°40W 192 A2
Temuka N.Z. 44°14S 171°17E 155 E6
Ten Degree Channel
  India 10°0N 92°30E 127 K11
Ten Thousand Is.
  U.S.A. 25°55N 81°45W 179 K8
Tenabo Mexico 20°3N 90°14W 181 C6
Tenaha U.S.A. 31°57N 94°15W 176 F7
Tenakee Springs
  U.S.A. 57°47N 135°13W 162 B1
Tenali India 16°15N 80°35E 127 F5
Tenancingo Mexico 18°58N 99°38W 181 D5
Tenango del Valle
  Mexico 19°7N 99°33W 181 D5
Tenaro, Akra Greece 36°22N 22°27E 98 E4
Tenasserim = Taninthayi
  Burma 12°6N 99°3E 121 F2
Tenasserim □ Burma 14°0N 98°30E 120 F2
Tenasserim ← Burma 12°24N 98°37E 120 F2
Tenby U.K. 51°40N 4°42W 67 F3
Tenda, Colle di France 44°7N 7°36E 73 D11
Tendaho Ethiopia 11°48N 40°54E 131 E3
Tende France 44°5N 7°35E 73 D11
Tendjedi, Adrar Algeria 23°41N 7°32E 136 D5
Tendō Japan 38°20N 140°30E 112 E10
Tendrara Morocco 33°3N 1°58W 136 B3
Tendrovskaya Kosa
  Ukraine 46°16N 31°35E 85 J6
Tendukhera India 23°24N 79°33E 125 H8
Teneguía, Volcán
  Canary Is. 28°28N 17°51W 100 F2
Teneida Egypt 25°30N 29°19E 137 B2
Tenenkou Mali 14°28N 4°55W 138 C4
Ténéré Niger 19°0N 10°30E 139 B7
Ténéré, Erg du Niger 17°35N 10°55E 135 E8
Tenerife Canary Is. 28°15N 16°35W 100 F3
Tenerife, Pico Canary Is. 27°43N 18°1W 100 G1
Tenerife Norte ✈ (TFN)
  Canary Is. 28°28N 16°17W 100 F3
Tenerife Sur ✈ (TFS)
  Canary Is. 28°3N 16°33W 100 F3
Ténès Algeria 36°31N 1°14E 136 A4
Teng Xian Guangxi Zhuangzu,
  China 23°21N 110°56E 117 F8
Teng Xian Shandong,
  China 35°5N 117°10E 115 G9
Tengah, Kepulauan
  Indonesia 7°5S 118°15E 118 F5
Tengchong China 25°0N 98°28E 116 E2
Tengchowfu = Penglai
  China 37°48N 120°42E 115 F11
Tenggarong Indonesia 0°24S 116°58E 118 E5
Tengger Feng China 43°12N 86°48E 109 D11
Tengger Shamo China 38°0N 104°10E 114 F3
Tenggol, Pulau
  Malaysia 4°48N 103°41E 121 K4
Tengiz Köli Kazakhstan 50°30N 69°0E 108 D7
Tengzhou China 35°12N 117°10E 115 G9
Tenhult Sweden 57°41N 14°20E 63 G8
Teniente Enciso △
  Paraguay 21°5S 61°8W 190 A3
Tenille U.S.A. 29°46N 83°19W 178 F6
Tenino U.S.A. 46°51N 122°51W 170 D4
Tenkasi India 8°55N 77°20E 127 K3
Tenke Katanga,
  Dem. Rep. of the Congo 11°22S 26°40E 143 E2
Tenke Katanga,
  Dem. Rep. of the Congo 10°32S 26°7E 143 E2
Tenkodogo Burkina Faso 11°54N 0°19W 139 C4
Tenna ← Italy 43°14N 13°47E 93 E10
Tennant Creek
  Australia 19°30S 134°15E 150 B1
Tennessee □ U.S.A. 36°0N 86°30W 177 D11
Tennessee ← U.S.A. 37°4N 88°34W 177 C10
Tennille U.S.A. 32°56N 82°48W 178 C7
Teno, Pta. de Canary Is. 28°21N 16°55W 100 F3
Tenojoki ← Tana ←
  Norway 70°30N 28°14E 60 A23
Tenom Malaysia 5°4N 115°57E 118 C5
Tenosique Mexico 17°29N 91°26W 181 D6
Tenryū-Gawa ←
  Japan 35°39N 137°48E 113 G8
Tensift, Oued ← Morocco 32°3N 9°28W 136 B2
Tenterden U.K. 51°4N 0°42E 67 F8
Tenterfield Australia 29°0S 152°0E 151 D5
Teo = A Ramallosa Spain 42°45N 8°30W 88 C2
Teófilo Otoni Brazil 17°50S 41°30W 189 D2
Tepa Indonesia 7°52S 129°31E 119 F7
Tepalcatepec ←
  Mexico 18°35N 101°59W 180 D4
Tepecik Bursa, Turkey 40°7N 28°57E 97 F13
Tepecik Kütahya, Turkey 39°32N 29°28E 99 E13
Tepehuanes Mexico 25°21N 105°44W 180 B3
Tepelenë Albania 40°17N 20°2E 96 F4
Tepetongo Mexico 22°28N 103°9W 180 C4
Tepic Mexico 21°30N 104°54W 180 C4
Teplá Czech Rep. 49°59N 12°52E 78 B5
Teplice Czech Rep. 50°40N 13°48E 76 C8
Teplyk Ukraine 48°40N 29°44E 81 B14
Tequila Mexico 20°54N 103°47W 180 C4
Ter ← Spain 42°2N 3°12E 90 C8
Ter Apel Neths. 52°53N 7°5E 69 B7
Téra Niger 14°0N 0°45E 139 C5
Tera ← Spain 41°54N 5°44W 88 D5
Teraina Kiribati 4°43N 160°25W 157 G12
Téramo Italy 42°39N 13°42E 93 F10
Terang Australia 38°15S 142°55E 152 E5
Terawhiti, C. N.Z. 41°16S 174°38E 154 H3
Terazit, Massif de Niger 20°2N 8°30E 139 A6
Tercan Turkey 39°47N 40°23E 105 C9
Terceira Azores 38°43N 27°13W 134 a
Tercero ← Argentina 32°58S 61°47W 190 C3
Terdal India 16°33N 75°3E 127 F2
Terebovlya Ukraine 49°18N 25°44E 75 D13
Teregova Romania 45°10N 22°16E 80 E7
Terek ← Russia 44°0N 47°30E 87 J8
Terengganu □ Malaysia 4°55N 103°0E 121 K4
Terepaima △ Venezuela 9°58N 69°17W 183 E6
Tereshka ← Russia 51°48N 46°26E 86 E8
Teresina Brazil 5°9S 42°45W 189 B2
Terespol Poland 52°5N 23°37E 83 F10
Teressa Island India 8°15N 93°10E 127 G11
Teresva ← Ukraine 48°0N 23°42E 81 B8
Terewah, L. Australia 29°52S 147°35E 151 D4
Terges ← Portugal 37°49N 7°41W 89 H3

Tergnier France 49°40N 3°17E 71 C10
Teridgerie Cr. ←
  Australia 30°25S 148°50E 153 A8
Terlizzi Italy 41°8N 16°32E 95 A9
Termas de Río Hondo
  Argentina 27°29S 64°52W 190 B3
Terme Turkey 41°11N 37°0E 104 B7
Términi Imerese Italy 37°59N 13°42E 94 E6
Términos, L. de Mexico 18°37N 91°33W 181 D6
Termiz Uzbekistan 37°15N 67°15E 109 E7
Térmoli Italy 42°0N 15°0E 93 F12
Ternate Indonesia 0°45N 127°25E 119 D7
Terneuzen Neths. 51°20N 3°50E 69 C3
Terney Russia 45°3N 136°37E 116 C1
Terni Italy 42°34N 12°37E 93 F9
Ternitz Austria 47°43N 16°2E 78 D9
Ternopil Ukraine 49°30N 25°40E 75 D13
Ternopil □ Ukraine 49°30N 25°40E 75 D13
Ternopol = Ternopil
  Ukraine 49°30N 25°40E 75 D13
Terowie Australia 33°8S 138°55E 152 B3
Terpni Greece 40°55N 23°26E 96 F7
Terra Bella U.S.A. 35°58N 119°3W 171 K7
Terra Nova △ Canada 48°33N 53°55W 165 C9
Terrace Canada 54°30N 128°35W 162 C3
Terrace Bay Canada 48°47N 87°5W 164 C2
Terracina Italy 41°17N 13°15E 94 A6
Terralba Italy 39°43N 8°39E 94 C1
Terrasini Italy 38°10N 13°4E 94 D6
Terrassa Spain 41°34N 2°1E 90 D7
Terrasson-la-Villedieu
  France 45°8N 1°18E 72 C5
Terre Haute U.S.A. 39°28N 87°25W 172 F10
Terrebonne B. U.S.A. 29°5N 90°35W 177 E9
Terrell U.S.A. 32°44N 96°17W 176 E6
Terrenceville Canada 47°40N 54°44W 165 C9
Terrick Terrick △
  Australia 36°8S 144°13E 152 D6
Terry U.S.A. 46°47N 105°19W 168 C11
Terryville U.S.A. 41°41N 73°3W 175 E11
Terschelling Neths. 53°25N 5°20E 69 A5
Tersko-Kumskiy Kanal
  Russia 44°32N 44°38E 87 H7
Tertenia Italy 39°42N 9°34E 94 C2
Terter = Tärtär ←
  Azerbaijan 40°26N 47°20E 87 K8
Teruel Spain 40°22N 1°8W 90 E3
Teruel □ Spain 40°48N 1°0W 90 E4
Tervel Bulgaria 43°45N 27°28E 97 C11
Tervola Finland 66°6N 24°49E 60 C21
Teryaweynya L.
  Australia 32°18S 143°22E 152 B5
Tešanj Bos.-H. 44°38N 18°1E 80 F3
Tesha ← Russia 55°38N 42°9E 86 C6
Teshio Japan 44°53N 141°44E 112 B10
Teshio-Gawa ←
  Japan 44°53N 141°45E 112 B10
Tešica Serbia 43°27N 21°45E 96 C5
Tesiyn Gol ← Mongolia 50°40N 93°20E 110 A7
Teslić Bos.-H. 44°37N 17°54E 80 F7
Teslin Canada 60°10N 132°43W 162 A2
Teslin ← Canada 61°34N 134°35W 162 A2
Teslin L. Canada 60°15N 132°57W 162 A2
Tessalit Mali 20°12N 1°0E 139 A5
Tessaoua Niger 13°47N 7°56E 139 C6
Tessin Germany 54°2N 12°28E 76 B8
Tessit Mali 15°13N 0°18E 139 B5
Test ← U.K. 50°56N 1°29W 67 G6
Testa del Gargano Italy 41°50N 16°10E 93 G13
Testigos, Is. Los
  Venezuela 11°23N 63°7W 183 D7
Tét Hungary 47°30N 17°33E 80 C2
Tét ← France 42°44N 3°2E 72 F7
Tetachuck L. Canada 53°18N 125°55W 162 C3
Tetas, Pta. Chile 23°31S 70°38W 190 A1
Tete Mozam. 16°13S 33°33E 143 F3
Tete □ Mozam. 15°15S 32°40E 143 F3
Teteven Bulgaria 42°58N 24°17E 97 D8
Teterev ← Ukraine 51°1N 30°5E 75 C16
Teterow Germany 53°46N 12°34E 76 B8
Tetiyev Ukraine 49°22N 29°38E 75 D15
Tetlin Junction ←
  Canada 67°30N 134°55W 160 D5
Teton ← U.S.A. 47°56N 110°31W 168 C8
Tétouan Morocco 35°35N 5°21W 136 A2
Tetovo Macedonia 42°1N 20°59E 96 D4
Tetufera, Mt. Tahiti 17°40S 149°26W 155 b
Tetyushi Russia 54°55N 48°49E 86 C9
Teuco ← Argentina 25°35S 60°11W 190 B3
Teulada Italy 38°58N 8°46E 94 D1
Teulon Canada 50°23N 97°16W 163 C9
Teun Indonesia 6°59S 129°8E 119 F7
Teuri-Tō Japan 44°26N 141°19E 112 B10
Teutoburger Wald
  Germany 52°5N 8°22E 76 C4
Tevere ← Italy 41°44N 12°14E 93 G9
Teverya Israel 32°47N 35°32E 130 C4
Teviot ← U.K. 55°29N 2°38W 65 F6
Tewantin Australia 26°27S 153°3E 151 D5
Tewkesbury U.K. 51°59N 2°9W 67 F5
Texada I. Canada 49°40N 124°25W 162 D4
Texarkana Ark., U.S.A. 33°26N 94°2W 176 E7
Texarkana Tex., U.S.A. 33°26N 94°3W 176 E7
Texas Australia 28°49S 151°9E 151 D5
Texas □ U.S.A. 31°40N 98°30W 176 F5
Texas City U.S.A. 29°24N 94°54W 176 G7
Texel Neths. 53°5N 4°50E 69 A4
Texhoma U.S.A. 36°30N 101°47W 176 C4
Texline U.S.A. 36°23N 103°2W 176 C3
Texoma, L. U.S.A. 33°50N 96°34W 176 E6
Teyateyaneng Lesotho 29°7S 27°34E 145 D4
Teykovo Russia 56°50N 40°30E 84 D11
Tezin Afghan. 34°24N 69°30E 124 B3
Teziutlán Mexico 19°50N 97°21W 181 D5
Tezpur India 26°40N 92°45E 123 F18
Tezzeron L. Canada 54°43N 124°30W 162 C4
Tha-anne ← Canada 60°31N 94°37W 163 A10
Tha Deua Laos 17°57N 102°53E 120 D4
Tha Deua Laos 19°26N 101°50E 120 C3
Tha Li Thailand 17°37N 101°25E 120 D3
Tha Pla Thailand 17°48N 100°32E 120 D3
Tha Rua Thailand 14°34N 100°44E 120 E3
Tha Sala Thailand 8°40N 99°56E 121 H2
Tha Song Yang
  Thailand 17°34N 97°55E 120 D1
Thaba Putsoa Lesotho 29°45S 28°0E 145 D4
Thaba-Tseka Lesotho 29°32S 28°56E 145 D4

Lesotho 29°30S 29°16E 145 C4
Thabazimbi S. Africa 24°40S 27°21E 145 B4
Thādiq Si. Arabia 25°18N 45°52E 128 E5
Thai Binh Vietnam 20°35N 106°1E 116 D6
Thai Muang Thailand 8°24N 98°16E 121 H2
Thai Nguyen Vietnam 21°35N 105°55E 116 D5
Thailand ■ Asia 16°0N 102°0E 120 D4
Thailand, G. of Asia 11°30N 101°0E 121 G3
Thakhek Laos 17°25N 104°45E 120 D5
Thal Pakistan 33°28N 70°33E 124 C4
Thal Desert Pakistan 31°10N 71°30E 124 D4
Thala Tunisia 35°35N 8°40E 136 A5
Thala La = Hkakabo Razi
  Burma 28°25N 97°23E 116 C1
Thalabarivat Cambodia 13°33N 105°57E 120 F5
Thalang = Amphoe Thalang
  Thailand 8°1N 98°20E 121 a
Thalara Nepal 29°28N 80°59E 125 E9
Thalassery India 11°45N 75°30E 127 J2
Thale Sap Songkhla
  Thailand 7°12N 100°28E 121 J3
Thallon Australia 28°39S 148°49E 151 D4
Thalu, Ko Thailand 9°26N 99°54E 121 b
Thalwil Switz. 47°17N 8°35E 77 H4
Tham Lot Thailand 19°34N 98°16E 120 C2
Thamarīt Oman 17°39N 54°2E 133 D5
Thames N.Z. 37°7S 175°34E 154 D4
Thames ← Canada 42°20N 82°25W 174 D2
Thames ← U.K. 51°29N 0°34E 67 F8
Thames, Firth of N.Z. 37°0S 175°25E 154 D4
Thames Estuary U.K. 51°29N 0°52E 67 F8
Thamesford Canada 43°4N 81°0W 174 C3
Thamesville Canada 42°33N 81°59W 174 D3
Than India 22°34N 71°11E 124 H6
Than Kyun Burma 9°49N 98°4E 121 H1
Than Uyen Vietnam 22°0N 103°54E 120 B4
Thana Gazi India 27°25N 76°19E 124 F7
Thandla India 23°0N 74°34E 124 H6
Thandwe Burma 18°20N 94°30E 123 K19
Thane India 19°12N 72°59E 126 E1
Thanesar India 30°1N 76°52E 124 D7
Thanet, I. of U.K. 51°21N 1°20E 67 F9
Thangool Australia 24°38S 150°42E 150 C5
Thanh Hoa Vietnam 19°48N 105°46E 116 D5
Thanh Thuy Vietnam 22°55N 104°51E 120 A5
Thanh Pho Ho Chi Minh
  Vietnam 10°58N 106°40E 121 G6
Thanjavur India 10°48N 79°12E 127 J4
Thanlwin = Salween ←
  Burma 16°31N 97°37E 123 L20
Thann France 47°48N 7°5E 71 E14
Thano Bula Khan
  Pakistan 25°22N 67°50E 124 G2
Thanya Buri Thailand 14°1N 100°33E 120 E3
Thaoge ← Botswana 20°27S 22°36E 144 B3
Thaolintoa L. Canada 61°30N 96°25W 163 A9
Thaon-les-Vosges
  France 48°15N 6°24E 71 D13
Thap Lan △ Thailand 14°15N 102°10E 120 E4
Thap Sakae Thailand 11°30N 99°37E 121 G2
Thap Than Thailand 15°27N 99°54E 120 E2
Thar Desert India 28°0N 72°0E 124 F5
Tharad India 24°30N 71°44E 124 G4
Tharaka-Nithi □ Kenya 0°20S 38°0E 142 C4
Thargomindah
  Australia 27°58S 143°46E 151 D3
Tharp Fracture Zone
  S. Ocean 54°0S 135°0W 55 B14
Tharrawaddy Burma 17°38N 95°48E 123 L19
Tharthār, Buḩayrat ath
  Iraq 34°0N 43°15E 105 E10
Tharthār, L. = Tharthār,
  Buḩayrat ath Iraq 34°0N 43°15E 105 E10
Tharthār, W. ath ←
  Iraq 34°32N 43°4E 105 E10
Thasopoula Greece 40°49N 24°45E 97 F8
Thasos Greece 40°40N 24°40E 97 F8
That Khe Vietnam 22°16N 106°28E 116 F6
Thatcher Ariz., U.S.A. 32°51N 109°46W 169 E9
Thatcher Colo., U.S.A. 37°33N 104°7W 169 H11
Thaton Burma 16°55N 97°22E 123 L20
Thatta Pakistan 24°42N 67°55E 124 G2
Thau, Bassin de France 43°23N 3°36E 72 E7
Thaungdut Burma 24°30N 94°40E 123 G19
Thayawthadangy Kyun
  Burma 12°19N 98°0E 120 F1
Thayer U.S.A. 36°31N 91°33W 172 G8
Thayetmyo Burma 19°20N 95°18E 123 K19
Thazi Burma 20°49N 96°55E 123 J20
Thbeng Meanchey
  Cambodia 13°49N 104°58E 120 F5
The Bahamas ■
  N. Amer. 24°0N 75°0W 183 B5
The Broads U.K. 52°45N 1°30E 66 E9
The Everglades U.S.A. 25°50N 81°0W 179 K9
The Gambia ■ W. Afr. 13°25N 16°0W 138 C1
The Gulf = Persian Gulf
  Asia 27°0N 50°0E 129 E6
The Hague = 's-Gravenhage
  Neths. 52°7N 4°17E 69 B4
The Pas Canada 53°45N 101°15W 163 C8
The Wash U.K. 52°58N 0°20E 66 E8
The Weald U.K. 51°4N 0°20E 67 F8
Thebes = Thiva Greece 38°19N 23°19E 98 C5
Thebes Egypt 25°40N 32°35E 137 C4
Thedford Canada 43°9N 81°51W 174 C3
Theebine Australia 25°57S 152°34E 151 D5
Thekulthili L. Canada 61°3N 110°0W 163 A7
Thelon ← Canada 62°35N 104°3W 163 A8
Thénezay France 46°44N 0°2W 72 B3
Thénon France 45°9N 1°4E 72 C5
Theodore Australia 24°55S 150°3E 150 C5
Theodore Canada 51°26N 102°55W 163 C8
Theodore U.S.A. 30°33N 88°10W 177 F10
Theodore Roosevelt △
  U.S.A. 47°0N 103°25W 168 C12
Theodore Roosevelt L.
  U.S.A. 33°40N 111°10W 169 K8
Thepha Thailand 6°52N 100°58E 121 J3
Thérain ← France 49°15N 2°27E 71 C9
Therandê Kosovo 42°21N 20°50E 96 D4
Theresa U.S.A. 44°13N 75°48W 175 C9
Theressa U.S.A. 29°50N 82°4W 178 F7
Thermaïkos Kolpos
  Greece 40°15N 22°45E 96 F6
Thermopolis U.S.A. 43°39N 108°13W 168 E9
Thermopylæ Greece 38°48N 22°35E 98 C4
Thesprotia □ Greece 39°27N 20°22E 98 B2
Thessalon Canada 46°20N 83°30W 164 C3

Thessalonica, Gulf of =
  Thermaïkos Kolpos
  Greece 40°15N 22°45E 96 F6
Thessaloniki Greece 40°38N 22°58E 96 F6
Thessaloniki ✈ (SKG)
  Greece 40°30N 23°0E 96 F7
Thessaly □ Greece 39°25N 22°0E 98 B4
Thetford U.K. 52°25N 0°45E 67 E8
Thetford Mines Canada 46°8N 71°18W 165 C5
Theun ← Laos 18°19N 104°0E 120 C5
Theunissen S. Africa 28°26S 26°43E 144 C4
Thevenard Australia 32°9S 133°38E 151 E1
Thiamis ← Greece 39°15N 20°6E 98 B2
Thiberville France 49°8N 0°27E 70 C7
Thibodaux U.S.A. 29°48N 90°49W 177 G9
Thicket Portage
  Canada 55°19N 97°42W 163 B9
Thief River Falls U.S.A. 48°7N 96°10W 172 A5
Thiel Mts. Antarctica 85°15S 91°0W 55 E16
Thiene Italy 45°42N 11°29E 93 C8
Thiérache France 49°51N 3°45E 71 C11
Thiers France 45°52N 3°33E 72 C7
Thiès □ Senegal 14°50N 16°51W 138 C1
Thiès ▪ Senegal 14°45N 16°50W 138 C1
Thiesi Italy 40°31N 8°43E 94 B1
Thika Kenya 1°1S 37°5E 142 C4
Thille-Boubacar Senegal 16°31N 15°5W 138 B1
Thimphu Bhutan 27°31N 89°45E 123 F16
Thina ← S. Africa 31°18S 29°13E 145 D4
Þingvallavatn Iceland 64°11N 21°9W 60 D3
Thionville France 49°20N 6°10E 71 C13
Thira = Santorini Greece 36°23N 25°27E 99 E7
Thirasia Greece 36°26N 25°21E 99 E7
Third Cataract Sudan 19°42N 30°20E 137 D3
Thiruvananthapuram
  India 8°41N 77°0E 127 K3
Thiruvarur India 10°46N 79°38E 127 J4
Thisted Denmark 56°58N 8°40E 63 H2
Thistle I. Australia 35°0S 136°8E 152 C2
Thithia = Cicia Fiji 17°45S 179°18W 154 a
Thitu I. S. China Sea 11°3N 114°17E 118 B4
Thiva Greece 38°19N 23°19E 98 C5
Thivai = Thiva Greece 38°19N 23°19E 98 C5
Thiviers France 45°25N 0°54E 72 C4
Thizy France 46°2N 4°18E 71 F11
Þjórsá ← Iceland 63°47N 20°48W 60 E3
Thlewiaza ← Canada 60°29N 94°40W 163 A10
Thmar Puok Cambodia 13°57N 103°4E 120 F4
Tho Chu, Dao Vietnam 9°20N 103°28E 121 H4
Tho Vinh Vietnam 19°16N 105°42E 120 C5
Thoa ← Canada 60°31N 109°47W 163 A8
Thoen Thailand 17°43N 99°12E 120 D2
Thoeng Thailand 19°41N 100°12E 120 C3
Thohoyandou S. Africa 22°58S 30°29E 141 A8
Thomas U.S.A. 35°45N 98°45W 176 D5
Thomas, L. Australia 26°4S 137°58E 151 D2
Thomas Hubbard, C.
  Canada 82°0N 94°25W 161 A13
Thomaston U.S.A. 32°53N 84°20W 178 C5
Thomasville Ala.,
  U.S.A. 31°55N 87°44W 177 F11
Thomasville Ga.,
  U.S.A. 30°50N 83°59W 178 F6
Thomasville N.C.,
  U.S.A. 35°53N 80°5W 177 D14
Thompson Canada 55°45N 97°52W 163 B9
Thompson U.S.A. 41°52N 75°31W 175 E9
Thompson ← Canada 50°15N 121°24W 162 C4
Thompson ← U.S.A. 39°46N 93°37W 172 F7
Thompson Falls
  U.S.A. 47°36N 115°21W 168 C6
Thompson Pk. U.S.A. 41°0N 123°2W 168 F2
Thompson Sd. N.Z. 45°9S 166°46E 155 F1
Thompson Springs
  U.S.A. 38°58N 109°43W 168 G9
Thompsontown U.S.A. 40°33N 77°14W 174 F7
Thomson U.S.A. 33°28N 82°30W 178 C6
Thomson ← Australia 25°11S 142°53E 150 C3
Thôn Buri Thailand 13°43N 100°29E 120 F3
Thônes France 45°54N 6°18E 73 C10
Thong Yang Thailand 9°30N 99°56E 121 b
Thonon-les-Bains
  France 46°22N 6°29E 71 F13
Thoothukudi = Tuticorin
  India 8°50N 78°12E 127 K4
Thorez Ukraine 48°4N 38°34E 85 H10
Þórisvatn Iceland 64°20N 18°55W 60 D4
Thornaby on Tees U.K. 54°33N 1°18W 66 C6
Thornbury Canada 44°34N 80°26W 174 B4
Thornbury N.Z. 46°17S 168°9E 155 G2
Thorne U.K. 53°37N 0°57W 66 D7
Thornton Canada 44°16N 79°43W 174 B5
Thornton U.S.A. 39°52N 104°58W 168 G11
Thorold Canada 43°7N 79°12W 174 C5
Þórshöfn Iceland 66°12N 15°20W 60 D6
Thouarcé France 47°17N 0°30W 70 E6
Thouars France 47°0N 0°13W 70 F6
Thouet ← France 47°17N 0°6W 70 E6
Thouin, C. Australia 20°20S 118°10E 148 D2
Thousand Islands
  U.S.A. 44°20N 76°0W 175 B9
Thousand Oaks
  U.S.A. 34°10N 118°50W 171 L8
Thrace Europe 41°0N 27°0E 97 F10
Thrace, Sea of Greece 40°30N 25°0E 98 B7
Thredbo Australia 36°31S 148°22E 153 D8
Three Forks U.S.A. 45°54N 111°33W 168 D8
Three Gorges Dam
  China 30°45N 111°15E 117 B8
Three Gorges Res. = Sanxia
  Shuiku China 30°40N 109°58E 116 B8
Three Hills Canada 51°43N 113°15W 162 C6
Three Hummock I.
  Australia 40°25S 144°55E 151 G3
Three Pagodas Pass
  Asia 15°20N 98°30E 120 E2
Three Points, C. Ghana 4°42N 2°6W 138 E4
Three Rivers Calif.,
  U.S.A. 36°26N 118°54W 170 J8
Three Rivers Tex.,
  U.S.A. 28°28N 98°11W 176 G5
Three Springs
  Australia 29°32S 115°45E 149 E2
Thrissur India 10°30N 76°18E 127 J3
Throssell, L. Australia 27°33S 124°14E 149 E3
Throssell Ra. Australia 17°24S 126°4E 148 D4
Thrushton △ Australia 27°47S 147°147E 151 D4
Thu Dau Mot Vietnam 10°58N 106°40E 121 G6
Thua ← Kenya 1°5S 40°30E 142 C5
Thuamal Rampur India 19°23N 82°6E 126 E6
Thuan Hoa Vietnam 8°58N 105°30E 121 H5

Thubun Lakes *Canada* 61°30N 112°0W **163** A6
Thueyts *France* 44°41N 4°9E **73** D8
Thugga = Dougga
  Tunisia 36°25N 9°13E **136** A5
Thuin *Belgium* 50°20N 4°17E **69** D4
Thuir *France* 42°38N 2°45E **72** F6
Thule = Qaanaaq
  Greenland 77°30N 69°10W **57** B4
Thule Air Base = Uummannaq
  Greenland 77°33N 68°52W **57** B4
Thun *Switz.* 46°45N 7°38E **77** J3
Thunder B. *U.S.A.* 45°0N 83°20W **174** B1
Thunder Bay *Canada* 48°20N 89°15W **164** C2
Thunderbolt *U.S.A.* 32°3N 81°4W **178** C8
Thunersee *Switz.* 46°43N 7°39E **77** J3
Thung Salaeng Luang △
  Thailand 16°43N 100°50E **120** D3
Thung Song *Thailand* 8°10N 99°40E **121** H2
Thungyai △ *Thailand* 15°20N 98°55E **120** E2
Thunkar *Bhutan* 27°55N 91°0E **123** F17
Thuong Tra *Vietnam* 16°2N 107°42E **120** D6
Thur → *Switz.* 47°32N 9°10E **77** H5
Thurgau □ *Switz.* 47°34N 9°10E **77** H5
Thüringen □ *Germany* 51°0N 11°0E **76** D6
Thüringer Wald *Germany* 50°35N 11°0E **76** E6
Thuringowa △
  Australia 19°18S 146°43E **150** B4
Thurles *Ireland* 52°41N 7°49W **64** D4
Thurn P. *Austria* 47°20N 12°25E **78** D5
Thurrock □ *U.K.* 51°31N 0°23E **67** F8
Thursday I. *Australia* 10°30S 142°3E **150** A3
Thurso *Canada* 45°36N 75°15W **144** C4
Thurso *U.K.* 58°36N 3°32W **65** C5
Thurso → *U.K.* 58°36N 3°32W **65** C5
Thurston I. *Antarctica* 72°0S 100°0W **55** D16
Thury-Harcourt *France* 48°59N 0°30W **70** D6
Thutade L. *Canada* 57°0N 126°55W **162** B3
Thy *Denmark* 56°52N 8°25E **63** H2
Thy △ *Denmark* 56°55N 8°25E **63** H2
Thyborøn *Denmark* 56°42N 8°12E **63** H2
Thyolo *Malawi* 16°7S 35°5E **143** F4
Ti-n-Amzi → *Niger* 18°20N 4°32E **139** B5
Ti-n-Barraouene, O. →
  Africa 18°40N 4°5E **139** B5
Ti-n-Tanezrouft *Algeria* 24°49N 3°48E **136** D4
Ti-n-Zaouatene *Algeria* 19°55N 2°55E **139** B5
Ti-Tree *Australia* 22°5S 133°22E **150** C1
Tiadiaye *Senegal* 14°25N 16°40W **138** C1
Tiahuanaco *Bolivia* 16°33S 68°42W **188** D5
Tian Shan *Asia* 40°30N 76°0E **109** D9
Tianchang *China* 32°40N 119°0E **117** A12
Tiandeng *China* 23°6N 107°7E **116** F6
Tiandong *China* 23°36N 107°8E **116** F6
Tian'e *China* 25°1N 107°9E **116** F6
Tianguá *Brazil* 3°44S 40°59W **189** A2
Tianhe *China* 24°48N 108°40E **116** E7
Tianjin *China* 39°7N 117°12E **115** E9
Tianjin Shi □ *China* 39°8N 117°12E **115** E9
Tianjun *China* 38°0N 98°30E **110** D8
Tiankoura *Burkina Faso* 10°47N 3°17W **138** C4
Tianlin *China* 24°21N 106°12E **116** E6
Tianmen *China* 30°39N 113°9E **117** B9
Tianquan *China* 30°7N 102°43E **116** B4
Tianshifu *China* 41°17N 124°22E **115** D13
Tianshui *China* 34°32N 105°40E **114** D3
Tiantai *China* 29°10N 121°2E **117** C13
Tianyang *China* 23°42N 106°53E **116** F6
Tianzhen *China* 40°24N 114°5E **114** D8
Tianzhu *China* 26°54N 109°11E **116** D7
Tianzhuangtai *China* 40°43N 122°5E **115** D12
Tiarei *Tahiti* 17°32S 149°20W **155** b
Tiaret *Algeria* 35°20N 1°21E **136** A4
Tiaret □ *Algeria* 34°30N 1°30E **136** B4
Tiassalé *Ivory C.* 5°58N 4°57W **138** D4
Tibagi *Brazil* 24°30S 50°24W **191** A5
Tibagi → *Brazil* 22°47S 51°1W **191** A5
Tibastī, Sarīr *Libya* 22°50N 18°30E **135** D9
Tibati *Cameroon* 6°22N 12°30E **139** D7
Tiber = Tevere → *Italy* 41°44N 12°14E **93** G9
Tiber Res. *U.S.A.* 48°19N 111°6W **168** B8
Tiberias = Teverya
  Israel 32°47N 35°32E **130** C4
Tiberias, L. = Yam Kinneret
  Israel 32°45N 35°35E **130** C4
Tibesti *Chad* 21°0N 17°30E **135** D9
Tibet = Xizang Zizhiqu □
  China 32°0N 88°0E **110** E6
Tibet, Plateau of *Asia* 32°0N 86°0E **102** E10
Tibiri *Niger* 13°34N 7°4E **139** C6
Ţibleş, Vf. *Romania* 47°32N 24°15E **81** C9
Ţibleşului, Munţii
  Romania 47°38N 24°5E **81** C9
Tibnī *Syria* 35°36N 39°50E **108** C3
Tibooburra *Australia* 29°26S 142°1E **151** D3
Tibrikot *Nepal* 29°3N 82°48E **125** E10
Tibro *Sweden* 58°28N 14°10E **63** F8
Tiburón, I. *Mexico* 29°0N 112°25W **180** B2
Tice *U.S.A.* 26°40N 81°49W **179** J8
Tichît *Mauritania* 18°21N 9°29W **138** B3
Ticino □ *Switz.* 46°20N 8°45E **77** J4
Ticino → *Italy* 45°9N 9°14E **92** C6
Ticleni *Romania* 44°53N 23°24E **81** F8
Ticonderoga *U.S.A.* 43°51N 73°26W **175** C11
Ticul *Mexico* 20°24N 89°32W **181** C7
Tidaholm *Sweden* 58°12N 13°58E **63** F7
Tidan *Sweden* 58°34N 14°1E **63** F8
Tiddim *Burma* 23°28N 93°45E **123** H18
Tiden *India* 7°15N 93°33E **127** L11
Tidikelt *Algeria* 26°58N 1°30E **136** C6
Tidioute *U.S.A.* 41°41N 79°24W **174** E5
Tidjikja *Mauritania* 18°29N 11°35W **138** B2
Tidore *Indonesia* 0°40N 127°25E **119** D7
Tiébissou *Ivory C.* 7°9N 5°10W **138** D4
Tiefa *China* 42°28N 123°26E **115** C12
Tiegang Shuiku *China* 22°37N 113°53E **111** a
Tiel *Neths.* 51°53N 5°26E **69** C5
Tiel *Senegal* 14°55N 15°5W **138** C1
Tieli *China* 46°57N 128°3E **111** B14
Tieling *China* 42°20N 123°55E **115** C12
Tielt *Belgium* 51°0N 3°20E **69** C3
Tiemenguan *China* 41°49N 85°39E **109** D11

Tiénigbé *Ivory C.* 8°11N 5°43W **138** D3
Tientsin = Tianjin
  China 39°7N 117°12E **115** E9
Tieri *Australia* 23°2S 148°21E **150** C4
Tierp *Sweden* 60°20N 17°30E **62** D11
Tierra Amarilla *Chile* 27°28S 70°18W **190** B1
Tierra Amarilla
  U.S.A. 36°42N 106°33W **169** H10
Tierra Colorada
  Mexico 17°11N 99°32W **181** D5
Tierra de Barros *Spain* 38°40N 6°30W **89** G4
Tierra de Campos *Spain* 42°10N 4°50W **88** C6
Tierra del Fuego □
  Argentina 54°0S 67°45W **192** D3
Tierra del Fuego, I. Grande de
  Argentina 54°0S 69°0W **192** D3
Tierra del Fuego △
  Argentina 54°50S 68°23W **192** D3
Tiétar → *Spain* 39°50N 6°1W **88** F4
Tieté → *Brazil* 20°40S 51°35W **191** A5
Tiffin *U.S.A.* 41°7N 83°11W **173** E12
Tiflèt *Morocco* 33°54N 6°20W **136** B4
Tifton *U.S.A.* 31°27N 83°31W **178** D6
Tifu *Indonesia* 3°39S 126°24E **119** E7
Tiga Res. *Nigeria* 11°35N 8°30E **139** C6
Tiger Leaping Gorge = Hutiao Xia
  China 27°13N 100°9E **116** D3
Tigharghar, Adrar *Mali* 19°30N 1°13E **139** B5
Tigil *Russia* 57°49N 158°40E **107** D16
Tigiria *India* 20°29N 85°31E **126** D7
Tignall *U.S.A.* 33°52N 82°44W **178** B7
Tignish *Canada* 46°58N 64°2W **165** C7
Tigre → *Peru* 4°30S 74°10W **188** D3
Tigre → *Venezuela* 9°20N 62°30W **186** B6
Tigris = Dijlah, Nahr →
  Asia 31°0N 47°25E **128** D5
Tiguentourine *Algeria* 27°52N 9°8E **136** C5
Tigveni *Romania* 45°10N 24°31E **81** E9
Tigyaing *Burma* 23°45N 96°10E **123** H20
Tīh, Gebel el *Egypt* 29°32N 33°26E **137** F8
Tihāmah *Asia* 15°3N 41°55E **131** D3
Tihodaine, Erg de
  Algeria 25°15N 7°15E **136** C5
Tiilikka △ *Finland* 63°40N 28°15E **62** D23
Tijara *India* 27°56N 76°31E **124** F7
Tijuana *Mexico* 32°32N 117°1W **171** N9
Tikal *Guatemala* 17°13N 89°24W **182** C2
Tikal △ *Guatemala* 17°23N 89°34W **182** C2
Tikamgarh *India* 24°44N 78°50E **125** G8
Tikaré *Burkina Faso* 13°15N 1°43W **139** C4
Tikchik Lakes *U.S.A.* 60°0N 159°0W **166** D8
Tikhoretsk *Russia* 45°56N 40°5E **87** H5
Tikhvin *Russia* 59°35N 33°30E **84** C7
Tikirarjuaq = Whale Cove
  Canada 62°10N 92°34W **163** A10
Tikkadouine, Adrar
  Algeria 24°28N 1°30E **136** D4
Tikmehdāsh *Iran* 37°16N 46°54E **105** D12
Tiko *Cameroon* 4°4N 9°20E **139** E6
Tikrīt *Iraq* 34°35N 43°37E **105** E10
Tiksi *Russia* 71°40N 128°45E **107** B13
Tilā' al 'Alī *Jordan* 32°0N 35°52E **130** D4
Tilamuta *Indonesia* 0°32N 122°23E **119** D6
Tilburg *Neths.* 51°31N 5°6E **69** C5
Tilbury *Canada* 42°17N 82°23W **174** D2
Tilbury *U.K.* 51°27N 0°22E **67** F8
Tilcara *Argentina* 23°36S 65°23W **190** A2
Tilden *U.S.A.* 42°33N 97°50W **172** D5
Tilemsi, Vallée du *Mali* 17°42N 0°15E **139** B5
Tilhar *India* 28°0N 79°45E **125** F8
Tilia, O. → *Algeria* 27°32N 0°55E **136** C4
Tilichiki *Russia* 60°27N 166°5E **107** C17
Tililane *Algeria* 27°49N 0°6W **136** C3
Tilissos *Greece* 35°20N 25°1E **101** D7
Tillamook *U.S.A.* 45°27N 123°51W **168** D2
Tillanchong I. *India* 8°30N 93°37E **127** K11
Tillberga *Sweden* 59°48N 16°39E **62** E10
Tillia *Niger* 16°8N 4°47E **139** B5
Tillsonburg *Canada* 42°53N 80°44W **174** D4
Tillyeria *Cyprus* 35°6N 32°40E **101** D11
Tilogne *Senegal* 16°0N 13°40W **138** B2
Tilos *Greece* 36°27N 27°27E **99** E9
Tilpa *Australia* 30°57S 144°24E **152** A6
Tilrhemt *Algeria* 33°9N 3°22E **136** B6
Tilt → *U.K.* 56°46N 3°51W **65** E5
Tilton *U.S.A.* 43°27N 71°36W **175** C13
Tiltonsville *U.S.A.* 40°10N 80°41W **174** F4
Tim *Denmark* 56°12N 8°19E **63** H2
Tima *Egypt* 26°54N 31°25E **137** C12
Timanfaya △ *Canary Is.* 29°0N 13°46W **100** F6
Timaru *N.Z.* 44°23S 171°14E **155** F4
Timashevo *Russia* 53°22N 51°9E **86** D10
Timashevsk *Russia* 45°35N 39°0E **87** H4
Timau *Kenya* 0°4N 37°15E **142** B4
Timbaki *Greece* 35°4N 24°45E **101** D6
Timbaúba *Brazil* 7°31S 35°19W **189** B3
Timbedgha *Mauritania* 16°17N 8°16W **138** B3
Timber Creek
  Australia 15°40S 130°29E **148** C5
Timber Lake *U.S.A.* 45°26N 101°5W **172** C3
Timber Mt. *U.S.A.* 37°6N 116°28W **170** H10
Timbo *Guinea* 10°30N 11°50W **138** C2
Timbo *Liberia* 5°35N 9°45W **138** D3
Timboon *Australia* 38°30S 142°58E **152** E5
Timbué, Ponta *Mozam.* 18°47S 36°22E **143** F4
Timbuktu = Tombouctou
  Mali 16°50N 3°0W **138** B4
Timeïaouine *Algeria* 20°56N 1°0E **139** A5
Timellouline *Algeria* 29°22N 8°55E **136** C5
Timétrine, Mts. *Mali* 19°25N 1°10W **138** B4
Timfi Oros *Greece* 39°59N 20°45E **98** B2
Timgad *Algeria* 35°29N 6°28E **136** A6
Timhadit *Morocco* 33°15N 5°4W **136** B2
Timi *Cyprus* 34°44N 32°31E **101** E11
Tīmia *Niger* 18°4N 8°40E **139** B6
Timika *Indonesia* 4°47S 136°32E **119** E9
Timimoun *Algeria* 29°14N 0°16E **136** C4
Timimoun, Sebkha de
  Algeria 28°0N 0°46E **136** C4
Timiris, Râs *Mauritania* 19°21N 16°30W **138** B1
Timiş = Tamiş → *Serbia* 44°51N 20°39E **80** E5
Timiş □ *Romania* 45°30N 21°30E **80** E6
Timiskaming, L. =
  Témiscamingue, L.

  Canada 47°10N 79°25W **164** C4
Timişoara *Romania* 45°43N 21°15E **80** E6
Timmersdala *Sweden* 58°32N 13°46E **63** F7
Timmins *Canada* 48°28N 81°25W **164** C3
Timmonsville *U.S.A.* 34°8N 79°57W **178** A10
Timok → *Serbia* 44°10N 22°40E **96** B6
Timoleague *Ireland* 51°39N 8°46W **64** E3
Timon *Brazil* 5°8S 42°52W **189** B2
Timor *Asia* 9°0S 125°0E **119** F7
Timor Leste = East Timor ■
  Asia 8°50S 126°0E **119** F7
Timor Sea *Ind. Oc.* 12°0S 127°0E **148** B4
Timrå *Sweden* 62°29N 17°18E **62** B11
Timucuan △ *U.S.A.* 30°28N 81°27W **178** E8
Tin Alkoum *Algeria* 24°42N 10°17E **136** D6
Tin Atanai *Algeria* 25°52N 1°37E **136** C4
Tin Can Bay *Australia* 25°56S 153°0E **151** D5
Tin Ethisane *Mali* 19°3N 0°52W **139** B4
Tin Gornai *Mali* 20°31N 0°57W **139** B4
Tin Mt. *U.S.A.* 36°50N 117°10W **170** J9
Tin Shui Wai *China* 22°28N 114°0E **111** a
Tina = Thina →
  S. Africa 31°18S 29°13E **145** D4
Tina, Khalig el *Egypt* 31°10N 32°40E **130** D1
Tinaca Pt. *Phil.* 5°30N 125°25E **119** C7
Tinajo *Canary Is.* 29°4N 13°42W **100** E6
Tinca *Romania* 46°46N 21°58E **80** D6
Tindal *Australia* 14°31S 132°22E **148** B5
Tindivanam *India* 12°15N 79°41E **127** H4
Tindouf *Algeria* 27°42N 8°10W **136** C2
Tindouf □ *Algeria* 27°25N 5°50W **136** C2
Tinée → *France* 43°55N 7°11E **73** E11
Tineo *Spain* 43°21N 6°27W **88** B4
Tinerhir *Morocco* 31°29N 5°31W **136** B2
Tinfouchy *Algeria* 28°52N 5°49W **136** C2
Tinfunque △ *Paraguay* 23°55S 60°17W **190** A3
Ting Jiang → *China* 24°45N 116°35E **117** E11
Tingi, Pulau *Malaysia* 2°18N 104°7E **121** L5
Tingi Mts. *S. Leone* 8°55N 10°47W **138** D2
Tinglev *Denmark* 54°57N 9°13E **63** K3
Tingo María *Peru* 9°10S 75°54W **188** E3
Tingrela *Ivory C.* 10°27N 6°25W **138** C3
Tingri *China* 28°34N 86°38E **110** F6
Tingsryd *Sweden* 56°31N 15°0E **63** H9
Tingstäde *Sweden* 57°44N 18°37E **63** G12
Tinh Bien *Vietnam* 10°36N 104°57E **121** G5
Tinharé, I. de *Brazil* 13°30S 38°58W **189** C3
Tinian *N. Marianas* 15°0N 145°38E **156** F6
Tinkisso → *Guinea* 11°21N 9°10W **138** C3
Tinnevelly = Tirunelveli
  India 8°45N 77°45E **127** K3
Tinogasta *Argentina* 28°5S 67°32W **190** B2
Tinos *Greece* 37°33N 25°8E **99** D7
Tiñoso, C. *Spain* 37°32N 1°6W **91** H3
Tinpahar *India* 24°59N 87°44E **125** G12
Tinrhert, Plateau du
  Algeria 29°30N 9°0E **136** C6
Tinta *Peru* 14°3S 71°20W **188** C3
Tîntâne *Mauritania* 16°18N 10°10W **138** B2
Tintinara *Australia* 27°2S 62°45W **190** B3
Tintinara *Australia* 35°48S 140°2E **152** C4
Tintioulé *Guinea* 10°13N 9°12W **138** C3
Tinto → *Spain* 37°12N 6°55W **89** H4
Tinui *N.Z.* 40°52S 176°5E **154** G5
Tinwald *N.Z.* 43°55S 171°43E **155** D6
Tiobraid Árann = Tipperary
  Ireland 52°28N 8°10W **64** D3
Tioga *N. Dak., U.S.A.* 48°24N 102°56W **172** A2
Tioga *Pa., U.S.A.* 41°55N 77°8W **174** E7
Tioman, Pulau
  Malaysia 2°50N 104°10E **121** L5
Tione di Trento *Italy* 46°2N 10°43E **92** B7
Tionesta *U.S.A.* 41°30N 79°28W **174** E5
Tiou *Burkina Faso* 13°38N 2°28W **138** C4
Tioulilin *Algeria* 27°1N 0°2W **136** C3
Tipaza *Algeria* 36°35N 2°26E **136** A4
Tipaza □ *Algeria* 36°35N 2°25E **136** A4
Tipperary *Ireland* 52°28N 8°10W **64** D3
Tipperary □ *Ireland* 52°37N 7°55W **64** D4
Tipton *Calif., U.S.A.* 36°4N 119°19W **170** J7
Tipton *Iowa, U.S.A.* 41°46N 91°8W **172** E8
Tipton *Mt., U.S.A.* 35°32N 114°12W **171** K12
Tiptonville *U.S.A.* 36°23N 89°29W **177** C10
Tiptur *India* 13°15N 76°26E **127** H3
Tiquina *Bolivia* 16°13S 68°50W **188** D4
Tiracambu, Serra do
  Brazil 3°15S 46°30W **189** A1
Tirahart, O. → *Algeria* 23°45N 3°10E **136** D4
Tīrān *Iran* 32°45N 51°8E **129** C6
Tīrān *Si. Arabia* 27°57N 34°32E **137** B3
Tirane ✠ (TIA) *Albania* 41°57N 19°49E **96** E3
Tirano *Italy* 46°13N 10°10E **92** B7
Tirari Desert *Australia* 28°22S 138°7E **151** D2
Tiraspol *Moldova* 46°55N 29°35E **81** D14
Tiratimine *Algeria* 25°56N 3°37E **136** D4
Tirdout *Mali* 16°7N 1°5W **139** B4
Tire *Turkey* 38°5N 27°45E **99** D9
Tirebolu *Turkey* 38°58N 38°45E **105** B8
Tiree *U.K.* 56°31N 6°55W **65** E2
Tiree, Passage of *U.K.* 56°30N 6°30W **65** E2
Tîrgovişte = Târgovişte
  Romania 44°55N 25°27E **81** F10
Tirgu Jiu = Târgu Jiu
  Romania 45°5N 23°19E **81** E8
Tirgu Mureş = Târgu Mureş
  Romania 46°31N 24°38E **81** D9
Tirich Mir *Pakistan* 36°15N 71°55E **123** A4
Tiriolo *Italy* 38°57N 16°30E **95** D9
Tiririca, Serra da *Brazil* 17°6S 47°6W **189** D1
Tiriro *Guinea* 10°27N 9°40W **138** C3
Tiritiri o te Moana = Southern
  Alps *N.Z.* 43°41S 170°11E **155** E3
Tirna → *India* 18°4N 76°57E **126** E3
Tirnavos *Greece* 39°45N 22°18E **98** B4
Tirodi *India* 21°40N 79°44E **126** D4
Tirol □ *Austria* 47°3N 10°43E **78** D4
Tiros *Brazil* 19°0S 45°58W **189** D1
Tirrukkovil *Sri Lanka* 7°7N 81°51E **127** L5
Tirschenreuth *Germany* 49°53N 12°19E **77** F8
Tirso → *Italy* 39°53N 8°32E **94** C1
Tirstrup *Denmark* 56°18N 10°42E **63** H4
Tirtagangga *Indonesia* 8°24S 115°35E **119** J18
Tirthahalli *India* 13°45N 75°14E **127** H2
Tirua Pt. *N.Z.* 38°25S 174°40E **154** E3
Tiruchchendur *India* 8°30N 78°11E **127** K4
Tiruchchirappalli *India* 10°45N 78°45E **127** J4
Tiruchirappalli *India* 10°45N 78°45E **127** J4
Tirukkoyilur *India* 11°57N 79°22E **127** J4
Tirumangalam *India* 9°49N 77°58E **127** K3
Tirumayam *India* 10°14N 78°45E **127** J4
Tirunelveli *India* 8°45N 77°45E **127** K3

Tirupati *India* 13°39N 79°25E **127** H4
Tiruppattur *Tamil Nadu,*
  India 10°8N 78°37E **127** J4
Tiruppattur *Tamil Nadu,*
  India 12°30N 78°30E **127** H4
Tiruppur *India* 11°5N 77°22E **127** J3
Tirur *India* 10°54N 75°55E **127** J2
Tiruttani *India* 13°11N 79°58E **127** H4
Tirutturaippundi *India* 10°32N 79°41E **127** J4
Tiruvadaimarudur *India* 11°3N 79°27E **127** J4
Tiruvalla *India* 9°23N 76°34E **127** K3
Tiruvallar *India* 13°9N 79°57E **127** H4
Tiruvannamalai *India* 12°15N 79°5E **127** H4
Tiruvettipuram *India* 12°39N 79°33E **127** H4
Tiruvottiyur *India* 13°10N 80°22E **127** H5
Tisa *India* 32°50N 76°9E **124** C7
Tisa → *Serbia* 45°15N 20°17E **80** E5
Tisdale *Canada* 52°50N 104°0W **163** C8
Tishomingo *U.S.A.* 34°14N 96°41W **176** D6
Tisjön *Sweden* 60°56N 13°0E **62** D7
Tisnaren *Sweden* 58°58N 15°56E **63** F9
Tišnov *Czech Rep.* 49°21N 16°25E **79** B9
Tisovec *Slovak Rep.* 48°41N 19°56E **79** C12
Tissamaharama
  Sri Lanka 6°17N 81°17E **127** L5
Tissemsilt *Algeria* 35°35N 1°50E **136** A4
Tissemsilt □ *Algeria* 35°45N 1°45E **136** A4
Tissint *Morocco* 29°57N 7°16W **136** C3
Tisza = Tisa → *Serbia* 45°15N 20°17E **80** E5
Tiszaföldvár *Hungary* 46°58N 20°14E **80** D5
Tiszafüred *Hungary* 47°38N 20°50E **80** C5
Tiszalök *Hungary* 48°1N 21°20E **80** B6
Tiszavasvári *Hungary* 47°58N 21°18E **80** C6
Tit *Ahaggar, Algeria* 23°0N 5°10E **136** D5
Tit *Tademait, Algeria* 27°0N 1°29E **136** C4
Tit-Ary *Russia* 71°55N 127°2E **107** B13
Titaguas *Spain* 39°53N 1°6W **90** F3
Titao *Burkina Faso* 13°45N 2°5W **139** C4
Titel *Serbia* 45°10N 20°18E **80** E5
Tithwal *Pakistan* 34°21N 73°50E **125** B5
Titicaca, L. *S. Amer.* 15°30S 69°30W **188** D4
Titisee *Germany* 47°54N 8°10E **77** H4
Titititra Hd. *N.Z.* 34°35S 169°25E **155** D4
Titiwa *Nigeria* 12°14N 12°53E **139** C7
Titlagarh *India* 20°15N 83°11E **126** D6
Tito *Italy* 40°35N 15°40E **95** B8
Titova Korenica
  Croatia 44°45N 15°41E **93** D12
Titu *Romania* 44°39N 25°32E **81** F10
Titule
  Dem. Rep. of the Congo 3°15N 25°31E **142** B2
Titusville *Fla., U.S.A.* 28°37N 80°49W **179** G9
Titusville *Pa., U.S.A.* 41°38N 79°41W **174** E5
Tivaouane *Senegal* 14°56N 16°45W **138** C1
Tivat *Montenegro* 42°43N 18°43E **96** D2
Tiverton *Canada* 44°16N 81°32W **174** B3
Tiverton *U.K.* 50°54N 3°29W **67** G4
Tívoli *Italy* 41°58N 12°45E **93** G9
Tiwanaku = Tiahuanaco
  Bolivia 16°33S 68°42W **188** D4
Tiwi ◊ *Australia* 11°33S 130°42E **148** B5
Tizga *Morocco* 32°1N 5°9W **136** B2
Ti'zi N'Isli *Morocco* 32°28N 5°47W **136** B2
Tizi-Ouzou *Algeria* 36°42N 4°3E **136** A4
Tizi-Ouzou □ *Algeria* 36°35N 4°5E **136** A4
Tizimín *Mexico* 21°9N 88°9W **181** C7
Tiznap He → *China* 38°21N 77°26E **109** E9
Tiznit *Morocco* 29°48N 9°45W **136** C2
Tjæreborg *Denmark* 55°28N 8°36E **63** J2
Tjällmo *Sweden* 58°43N 15°21E **63** F9
Tjeggelvas *Sweden* 66°37N 17°45E **60** C17
Tjeggelvas = Tjeggelvas
  Sweden 66°37N 17°45E **60** C17
Tjirebon = Cirebon
  Indonesia 6°45S 108°32E **118** F3
Tjirkarli ◊ *Australia* 26°0S 125°28E **149** E4
Tjluring *Indonesia* 8°25S 114°13E **119** J17
Tjörn *Sweden* 58°0N 11°35E **63** F5
Tjukayirla Roadhouse
  Australia 27°9S 124°34E **149** E3
Tjurabalan ◊ *Australia* 19°50S 128°0E **148** C4
Tkibuli = Tqibuli *Georgia* 42°26N 43°0E **87** J6
Tkvarcheli = Tqvarcheli
  Georgia 42°47N 41°42E **87** J5
Tlacotalpan *Mexico* 18°37N 95°40W **181** D5
Tlahualilo de Zaragoza
  Mexico 26°7N 103°27W **180** B4
Tlaquepaque *Mexico* 20°39N 103°19W **180** C4
Tlaxcala *Mexico* 19°19N 98°14W **181** D5
Tlaxcala □ *Mexico* 19°25N 98°10W **181** D5
Tlaxiaco *Mexico* 17°25N 97°35W **181** D5
Tlemcen *Algeria* 34°52N 1°21W **136** B3
Tlemcen □ *Algeria* 34°38N 1°30W **136** B3
Tleta Sidi Bouguedra
  Morocco 32°16N 9°59W **136** B2
Tlokweng *Botswana* 24°40S 25°58E **144** B4
Tlumach *Ukraine* 48°51N 25°0E **81** B10
Tłuszcz *Poland* 52°25N 21°25E **81** B9
Tlyarata *Russia* 42°9N 46°26E **87** J8
To Bong *Vietnam* 12°45N 109°16E **120** F7
Toa Payoh *Singapore* 1°20N 103°51E **121** d
Toad → *Canada* 59°25N 124°57W **162** B4
Toad River *Canada* 58°51N 125°14W **162** B3
Toamasina *Madag.* 18°10S 49°25E **141** H9
Toay *Argentina* 36°43S 64°38W **190** D3
Toba *China* 31°19N 97°42E **116** B1
Toba *Japan* 34°30N 136°51E **113** G8
Toba, Danau *Indonesia* 2°30N 98°30E **118** D1
Toba Kakar *Pakistan* 31°30N 69°0E **124** D3
Toba Tek Singh
  Pakistan 30°55N 72°25E **124** D5
Tobago *Trin. & Tob.* 11°10N 60°30W **183** D7
Tobarra *Spain* 38°37N 1°44W **91** G3
Tobelo *Indonesia* 1°45N 127°56E **119** D7
Tobercurry *Ireland* 54°3N 8°44W **64** B3
Tobermory *Canada* 45°12N 81°40W **174** A3
Tobermory *U.K.* 56°38N 6°5W **65** E2
Tobi *Palau* 3°1N 131°10E **119** D8
Tobi-Shima *Japan* 41°12N 139°34E **112** D9
Tobin, L. *Australia* 21°45S 125°49E **148** D4
Tobin L. *Canada* 53°35N 103°30W **163** C8
Toblach = Dobbiaco
  Italy 46°44N 12°14E **93** B9
Toboali *Indonesia* 3°0S 106°25E **118** E3
Tobol → *Russia* 58°10N 68°12E **106** D7
Tobol *Kazakhstan* 52°40N 62°39E **106** D7
Toboli *Indonesia* 0°38S 120°5E **119** E6
Tobolsk *Russia* 58°15N 68°10E **106** D7
Tobor *Senegal* 12°40N 16°15W **138** C1
Tobruk = Tubruq
  Libya 32°7N 23°55E **135** B10
Tobyhanna *U.S.A.* 41°11N 75°25W **175** E9

Tobyl = Tobol →
  Russia 58°10N 68°12E **106** D7
Tobyl *Kazakhstan* 52°41N 62°34E **108** B6
Tocache Nuevo *Peru* 8°9S 76°26W **188** B2
Tocantínia *Brazil* 9°33S 48°22W **189** B1
Tocantinópolis *Brazil* 6°20S 47°25W **189** B1
Tocantins □ *Brazil* 10°0S 48°0W **187** F9
Tocantins → *Brazil* 1°45S 49°10W **187** D9
Toccoa *U.S.A.* 34°35N 83°19W **177** D13
Toce → *Italy* 45°56N 8°29E **92** C5
Tochi → *Pakistan* 32°49N 70°41E **124** C4
Tochigi *Japan* 36°25N 139°45E **113** F9
Tochigi □ *Japan* 36°45N 139°45E **113** F9
Tocina *Spain* 37°37N 5°44W **89** H5
Töcksfors *Sweden* 59°31N 11°52E **62** E5
Toco *Chile* 22°5S 69°35W **190** A2
Toco *Trin. & Tob.* 10°49N 60°57W **187** K16
Toconao *Chile* 23°11S 68°1W **190** A2
Tocopilla *Chile* 22°5S 70°10W **190** A1
Tocumwal *Australia* 35°51S 145°31E **153** E4
Tocuyo → *Venezuela* 11°3N 68°23W **186** A5
Todd → *Australia* 24°52S 135°48E **150** C2
Todeli *Indonesia* 1°40S 124°29E **119** E6
Todenyang *Kenya* 4°35N 35°56E **142** B4
Todgarh *India* 25°42N 73°58E **124** G5
Todi *Italy* 42°47N 12°24E **93** F9
Todos os Santos, B. de
  Brazil 12°48S 38°38W **189** C3
Todos Santos *Mexico* 23°26N 110°13W **180** C2
Todtnau *Germany* 47°49N 7°56E **77** H3
Toe Hd. *U.K.* 57°50N 7°8W **65** D1
Toecé *Burkina Faso* 11°50N 1°16W **139** C4
Toetoes B. *N.Z.* 46°42S 168°41E **155** G3
Tofield *Canada* 53°25N 112°40W **162** C6
Tofino *Canada* 49°11N 125°55W **162** D3
Tōsingdalen △ *Sweden* 62°10N 12°28E **62** B6
Tōgane *Japan* 35°33N 140°22E **113** G10
Togba *Mauritania* 17°26N 10°12W **138** B2
Togian, Kepulauan
  Indonesia 0°20S 121°50E **119** E6
Togliatti *Russia* 53°32N 49°24E **86** D9
Togo ■ *W. Afr.* 8°30N 1°35E **139** D5
Tögrög *Mongolia* 47°25N 92°13E **109** C12
Togtoh *China* 40°15N 111°10E **114** D6
Tohma → *Turkey* 38°29N 38°23E **104** C8
Tōhoku □ *Japan* 39°50N 141°45E **112** D10
Tōhōm *Mongolia* 44°27N 108°2E **114** B5
Tohopekaliga, East L.
  U.S.A. 28°18N 81°15W **179** G8
Tohopekaliga, L.
  U.S.A. 28°12N 81°24W **179** E8
Toibalewe *India* 10°32N 92°30E **127** J11
Toinya *South Sudan* 6°17N 29°46E **135** G11
Toiyabe Range *U.S.A.* 39°30N 117°0W **168** G5
Tojikiston = Tajikistan ■
  Asia 38°30N 70°0E **109** E8
Tōjō *Japan* 34°53N 133°16E **113** G6
Tok *U.S.A.* 63°20N 142°59W **166** D3
Tokachi → *Japan* 42°44N 143°42E **112** C11
Tokaj *Hungary* 48°8N 21°27E **80** B6
Tokala *Indonesia* 1°30S 121°40E **119** E6
Tōkamachi *Japan* 37°8N 138°43E **113** F9
Tokanui *N.Z.* 46°34S 168°56E **155** G3
Tokara-Rettō *Japan* 29°37N 129°43E **113** K4
Tokarahi *N.Z.* 44°56S 170°39E **155** E3
Tokashiki-Shima
  Japan 26°11N 127°21E **113** L3
Tokat *Turkey* 40°22N 36°35E **104** B7
Tokat □ *Turkey* 40°15N 36°30E **104** B7
Tŏkch'ŏn *N. Korea* 39°45N 126°18E **115** E14
Tokdo = Liancourt Rocks
  Asia 37°15N 131°52E **113** F5
Tokelau *Is.* ◊ *Pac. Oc.* 9°0S 171°45W **156** H10
Tokmak *Kyrgyzstan* 42°49N 75°15E **109** D9
Tokmak *Ukraine* 47°16N 35°42E **85** J8
Toko Ra. *Australia* 23°5S 138°20E **150** C2
Tokomaru Bay *N.Z.* 38°8S 178°22E **154** E7
Tokoro-Gawa → *Japan* 44°7N 144°5E **112** B12
Tokoroa *N.Z.* 38°13S 175°56E **154** E4
Tokorozawa *Japan* 35°47N 139°28E **113** G9
Toktogul *Kyrgyzstan* 41°50N 72°50E **109** D8
Tokuno-Shima *Japan* 27°56N 128°55E **113** L4
Tokushima *Japan* 34°4N 134°34E **113** G7
Tokushima □ *Japan* 33°55N 134°0E **113** H7
Tokuyama = Shūnan
  Japan 34°3N 131°50E **113** G5
Tōkyō *Japan* 35°43N 139°45E **113** G9
Tolaga Bay *N.Z.* 38°21S 178°20E **154** E7
Tolbo *Mongolia* 48°25N 90°10E **109** C12
Tolbukhin = Dobrich
  Bulgaria 43°37N 27°49E **97** C11
Toledo *Brazil* 24°44S 53°45W **191** A5
Toledo *Spain* 39°50N 4°2W **88** F6
Toledo *Ohio, U.S.A.* 41°39N 83°33W **173** E12
Toledo *Oreg., U.S.A.* 44°37N 123°56W **168** D2
Toledo *Wash., U.S.A.* 46°26N 122°51W **170** D4
Toledo, Montes de *Spain* 39°33N 4°20W **89** F6
Toledo Bend Res.
  U.S.A. 31°11N 93°34W **176** F8
Tolentino *Italy* 43°12N 13°17E **93** E10
Tolfa *Italy* 42°9N 11°56E **93** F8
Tolga *Algeria* 34°40N 5°22E **136** B6
Tolga *Australia* 17°15S 145°29E **150** B4
Tolhuaca △ *Chile* 38°15S 71°50W **190** D2
Toli *China* 45°57N 83°37E **109** C10
Toliara *Madag.* 23°21S 43°40E **141** J8
Tolima *Colombia* 4°40N 75°19W **186** C3
Tolitoli *Indonesia* 1°5N 120°50E **119** D6
Tollarp *Sweden* 55°55N 13°58E **63** J7
Tollensesee *Germany* 53°30N 13°15E **76** B9
Tollhouse *U.S.A.* 37°1N 119°24W **170** H7
Tolmachevo *Russia* 58°56N 29°51E **84** C5
Tolmezzo *Italy* 46°24N 13°1E **93** B10
Tolmin *Slovenia* 46°11N 13°45E **93** B10
Tolna *Hungary* 46°25N 18°48E **80** E3
Tolna □ *Hungary* 46°30N 18°30E **80** E3
Tolo *Dem. Rep. of the Congo* 2°55S 18°34E **140** E3
Tolo, Teluk *Indonesia* 2°20S 122°10E **119** E6
Toló *China* 33°55N 103°30W **163** C8
Tolochin = Talachyn
  Belarus 54°25N 29°42E **84** C5
Tolosa *Spain* 43°8N 2°5W **89** A7
Tolox *Spain* 36°41N 4°54W **89** J6
Toltén *Chile* 39°13S 73°44W **190** D2
Toluca *Mexico* 19°17N 99°40W **181** D5

Tolyatti = Togliatti
  Russia 53°32N 49°24E **86**
Tom Burke *S. Africa* 23°5S 28°0E **14**
Tom Price *Australia* 22°40S 117°48E **14**
Toma *Burkina Faso* 12°45N 2°53W **13**
Tomah *U.S.A.* 43°59N 90°30W **17**
Tomahawk *U.S.A.* 45°28N 89°44W **17**
Tomai *Moldova* 46°34N 28°19E **8**
Tomakomai *Japan* 42°38N 141°36E **112**
Tomales *U.S.A.* 38°15N 122°53W **17**
Tomales B. *U.S.A.* 38°15N 123°58W **17**
Tomanivi *Fiji* 17°37S 178°1E *
Tomar *Portugal* 39°36N 8°25W **8**
Tómaros, Oros *Greece* 39°29N 20°48E **9**
Tomarza *Turkey* 38°27N 35°48E **10**
Tomás Barrón *Bolivia* 17°35S 67°31W **18**
Tomashevka *Belarus* 51°33N 23°36E **83**
Tomashpil *Ukraine* 48°32N 28°31E **81**
Tomaszów Lubelski
  Poland 50°27N 23°25E **8**
Tomaszów Mazowiecki
  Poland 51°30N 20°2E **8**
Tomatlán *Mexico* 19°56N 105°15W **18**
Tombadónkéa *Guinea* 10°30N 13°30W **13**
Tombador, Serra do
  Brazil 12°0S 58°0W **18**
Tombigbee → *U.S.A.* 31°8N 87°57W **17**
Tombouctou *Mali* 16°50N 3°0W **13**
Tombouctou □ *Mali* 20°0N 3°0W **13**
Tombstone *U.S.A.* 31°43N 110°4W **16**
Tombua *Angola* 15°55S 11°55E **14**
Tomé *Chile* 36°36S 72°57W **19**
Tome *Japan* 38°40N 141°20E **11**
Tomelilla *Sweden* 55°33N 13°58E **6**
Tomelloso *Spain* 39°10N 3°2W **8**
Tomingley *Australia* 32°26S 148°16E **15**
Tomini *Indonesia* 0°30N 120°30E **11**
Tomini, Teluk *Indonesia* 0°10S 121°0E **11**
Tominian *Mali* 13°17N 4°35W **13**
Tomiño = O Seixo *Spain* 41°59N 8°46W **8**
Tomintoul *U.K.* 57°15N 3°23W **6**
Tomislavgrad *Bos.-H.* 43°42N 17°13E **8**
Tomkinson Ranges
  Australia 26°11S 129°5E **14**
Tommot *Russia* 59°4N 126°20E **107**
Tomnop Ta Suos
  Cambodia 11°20N 104°15E **12**
Tomo → *Colombia* 5°20N 67°48W **18**
Toms Place *U.S.A.* 37°34N 118°41W **17**
Toms River *U.S.A.* 39°58N 74°12W **175**
Tomsk *Russia* 56°30N 85°5E **10**
Tomtabacken *Sweden* 57°30N 14°30E **6**
Tomür Feng = Pobedy, Pik
  Asia 42°0N 79°58E **10**
Tona *Spain* 41°51N 2°14E **9**
Tonalá *Chiapas, Mexico* 16°4N 93°45W **18**
Tonalá *Jalisco, Mexico* 20°37N 103°14W **18**
Tonale, Passo del *Italy* 46°16N 10°35E **9**
Tonantins *Brazil* 2°45S 67°45W **18**
Tonasket *U.S.A.* 48°42N 119°26W **16**
Tonawanda *U.S.A.* 43°1N 78°53W **17**
Tonb *U.A.E.* 26°15N 55°15E **1**
Tonbridge *U.K.* 51°11N 0°17E **6**
Tondano *Indonesia* 1°35N 124°54E **11**
Tondela *Portugal* 40°31N 8°5W **8**
Tønder *Denmark* 54°58N 8°50E **6**
Tondi *India* 9°45N 79°4E **12**
Tondi Kiwindi *Niger* 14°28N 2°2E **13**
Tondibi *Mali* 16°39N 0°14W **13**
Tondoro *Namibia* 17°45S 18°50E **14**
Tone → *Australia* 34°25S 116°25E **14**
Tone-Gawa → *Japan* 35°44N 140°51E **11**
Tonekābon *Iran* 36°45N 51°12E **12**
Tong Xian *China* 39°55N 116°35E **11**
Tong-yeong *S. Korea* 34°50N 128°20E **11**
Tonga *Cameroon* 4°58N 10°42E **13**
Tonga ■ *Pac. Oc.* 19°50S 174°30W **14**
Tonga Trench *Pac. Oc.* 18°0S 173°0W **15**
Tongaat *S. Africa* 29°33S 31°9E **14**
Tongala *Australia* 36°14S 144°56E **15**
Tong'an *China* 24°37N 118°8E **11**
Tongareva = Penrhyn
  Cook Is. 9°0S 158°0W **15**
Tongariro, Mt. *N.Z.* 39°8S 175°38E **15**
Tongariro △ *N.Z.* 39°5S 175°50E **15**
Tongatapu Group
  Tonga 21°0S 175°0W **14**
Tongbai *China* 32°20N 113°23E **11**
Tongcheng *Anhui,*
  China 31°4N 116°56E **11**
Tongcheng *Hubei,*
  China 29°15N 113°50E **11**
Tongchuan *China* 35°6N 109°3E **11**
Tongdao *China* 26°10N 109°42E **11**
Tongeren *Belgium* 50°47N 5°28E **6**
Tonggu *China* 28°31N 114°20E **11**
Tonggu Jiao *China* 22°20N 113°37E **11**
Tongguan *China* 34°40N 110°25E **11**
Tonghai *China* 24°6N 102°48E **11**
Tonghua *China* 41°42N 125°58E **115**
Tongjiang *Heilongjiang,*
  China 47°40N 132°27E **11**
Tongjiang *Sichuan,*
  China 31°58N 107°11E **11**
Tongioson-man
  N. Korea 39°30N 128°0E **11**
Tongking, G. of = Tonkin, G. of
  Asia 20°0N 108°0E **12**
Tongliang *China* 29°50N 106°20E **11**
Tongliao *China* 43°38N 122°18E **11**
Tongling *China* 30°55N 117°48E **11**
Tonglu *China* 29°45N 119°37E **11**
Tongnan = Anyue
  China 30°9N 105°0E **11**
Tongoy *Chile* 30°16S 71°31W **19**
Tongren *Guizhou,*
  China 27°43N 109°11E **11**
Tongren *Qinghai, China* 35°25N 102°5E **11**
Tongres = Tongeren
  Belgium 50°47N 5°28E **6**
Tongsa Dzong *Bhutan* 27°31N 90°31E **12**
Tongshi *China* 18°50N 109°20E **12**
Tongue *U.K.* 58°29N 4°25W **6**
Tongue → *U.S.A.* 46°25N 105°52W **16**
Tongwei *China* 35°0N 105°5E **11**
Tongxiang *China* 30°38N 120°23E **11**
Tongxin *China* 36°59N 105°58E **11**
Tongyang *N. Korea* 39°9N 126°53E **11**
Tongyu *China* 44°45N 123°4E **11**

igzhou China 32°12N 121°2E 117 A13
gzi China 28°9N 106°49E 116 C6
j South Sudan 7°20N 28°44E 135 U11
k India 26°6N 75°54E 124 F6
akawa U.S.A. 36°41N 97°18W 176 C6
akin = Bac Phan
ietnam 22°0N 105°0E 116 G5
lé Sap Cambodia 13°0N 104°0E 120 C7
nay-Charente France 45°56N 0°55W 72 C3
neins France 44°23N 0°19E 72 C4
nerre France 47°51N 3°59E 71 E10
ning Germany 54°19N 8°56E 76 A4
o Japan 39°19N 141°32E 112 E10
opah U.S.A. 38°4N 117°14W 169 G5
o Panama 7°20N 80°20W 182 E3
s → Haryana, India 30°30N 77°39E 124 D7
sosi Panama
s → Ut. P., India 26°1N 83°33E 125 F10
sberg Norway 59°19N 10°25E 61 G14
ya Turkey 40°53N 39°16E 105 B8
banna Australia 18°42S 146°9E 150 B4
dyay Australia 31°34S 116°0E 149 F2
ele U.S.A. 40°32N 112°18W 168 F7
mpine Australia 27°15S 144°19E 151 D3
ra Australia 38°39S 146°23E 153 E7
ra-Khem Russia 52°28N 96°17E 109 B13
woomba Australia 27°32S 151°56E 151 D5
Springs Australia 16°37S 131°51E 148 C5
alu Romania 44°31N 28°3E 81 F13
az U.S.A. 38°41N 119°30W 172 F6
eka U.S.A. 39°3N 95°40W 172 F6
d'a → Slovak Rep. 48°45N 21°45E 79 C14
ley Canada 54°54N 126°18W 162 C3
lica → Serbia 43°15N 21°49E 96 C5
liţa Romania 46°55N 25°20E 81 D10
ocalma, Pta. Chile 34°10S 72°2W 190 C1
ock U.S.A. 34°46N 114°29W 171 L12
ola Serbia 44°17N 20°41E 96 B4
olčani Macedonia 41°14N 21°25E 96 E5
ol'čany Slovak Rep. 48°35N 18°12E 79 C11
olnitsa → Bulgaria 42°11N 24°18E 97 D8
olobampo Mexico 25°36N 109°3W 180 B3
oloveni Romania 44°49N 25°5E 81 F10
olovgrad Bulgaria 42°5N 26°20E 97 D10
olvăţu Mare
omania 45°46N 21°41E 80 E6
ozero, Ozero Russia 65°35N 32°0E 60 D25
penish U.S.A. 46°23N 120°19W 168 C3
raisar Romania 44°1N 28°27E 81 F13
usko Croatia 45°18N 15°59E 93 C12
uepala Peru 17°24S 70°1W 188 D3
yraûyn →
azakhstan 46°48N 75°24E 109 C9
à Spain 41°49N 1°25E 90 B6
ata Peru 17°23S 70°1W 188 D3
bah Turkey 38°10N 27°21E 99 C9
bat-e Heydāriyeh
Iran 35°15N 59°12E 129 C8
bat-e Jām Iran 35°16N 60°35E 129 C9
bay Canada 47°40N 52°42W 165 C9
bay U.K. 50°26N 3°31W 67 G4
björntorp Sweden 58°12N 13°36E 63 F7
desillas Spain 41°30N 5°0W 88 D6
eboda Sweden 58°41N 14°7E 63 F8
ekov Sweden 56°26N 12°37E 63 H6
ello Spain 42°3N 2°16E 90 C7
eno Spain 42°42N 6°30W 88 C4
faen U.K. 51°43N 3°3W 67 F4
gau Germany 51°34N 13°0E 76 D8
gelow Germany 53°37N 14°1E 76 B10
ghay → Kazakhstan 48°1N 62°45E 108 C6
ghay Ustirti Asia 51°0N 63°0E 108 C6
ghay Zhylghasy
azakhstan 52°0N 64°30E 108 B6
hamn Sweden 56°6N 15°50E 63 H9
hout Belgium 51°5N 3°7E 69 C3
hovytsya Ukraine 50°25N 26°2E 81 B10
-Shima Japan 30°29N 140°19E 113 J10
nghay-Sur-Vire France 49°5N 0°58W 70 C6
ja Spain 40°44N 3°2W 90 E1
ino Italy 45°3N 7°40E 92 C4
ß South Sudan 4°27N 32°13E 135 H12
kamān Iran 37°35N 47°23E 105 D12
kovichi Russia 58°51N 30°21E 84 C6
mac Romania 45°30N 21°30E 80 E6
mes → Spain 41°18N 6°29W 88 D4
oada Mt. Canada 49°55N 114°40W 162 D6
nal'a Slovak Rep. 48°25N 20°0E 79 C13
→ Tornio
inland 65°50N 24°12E 60 D21
neälven → Europe 65°50N 24°12E 50 D21
neträsk Sweden 68°24N 19°15E 60 B18
ngat Mountains Nat. Park △
anada 53°0N 63°40W 161 F19
ngat Mts. Canada 53°0N 63°40W 161 F19
io Finland 65°50N 25°0E 60 D21
nionjoki = Torneälven →
urope 65°50N 24°12E 60 D21
nquist Argentina 38°8S 62°15W 190 D3
o Baleares, Spain 39°59N 4°8E 100 B11
oro Spain 41°35N 5°24W 88 D5
ö Sweden 58°48N 17°50E 63 F11
o, Cerro del Chile 30°50N 69°50W 190 B2
o → Uganda 1°5N 30°22E 142 C3
ío Pk. U.S.A. 33°34N 116°24W 171 M10
odi Niger 17°1N 7°47E 139 C5
ökszentmiklós
ungary 47°11N 20°27E 80 C5
onto Australia 30°3S 151°30E 153 B9
onto Canada 43°39N 79°20W 174 C5
onto Canada 40°28N 80°36W 174 D5
onto Lester B. Pearson Int. ✈
YYZ] Canada 43°37N 79°37W 174 C5
opets Russia 56°30N 31°40E 84 D6
oro Uganda 0°45N 34°12E 142 B3
os Dağları Turkey 37°0N 32°30E 104 D5
pa India 22°57N 85°6E 125 H11
quay Australia 38°20S 144°19E 152 E6
quay U.K. 50°27N 3°32W 67 G4
quemada Spain 42°2N 4°19W 88 D6
rão Portugal 38°10N 8°11W 89 G2
re Annunziata Italy 40°45N 14°27E 95 B7
re di Moncorvo
ortugal 41°12N 7°8W 88 D3
re del Campo Spain 37°46N 3°53W 89 H7
re del Greco Italy 40°47N 14°22E 95 B7
re del Mar Spain 36°44N 4°6W 89 J6

Torre-Pacheco Spain 37°44N 0°57W 91 H4
Torre Péllice Italy 44°49N 7°13E 92 D4
Torreblanca Spain 40°14N 0°12E 90 E5
Torrecampo Spain 38°29N 4°41W 89 G6
Torrecilla en Cameros
Spain 42°15N 2°38W 90 C2
Torredembarra Spain 41°9N 1°24E 90 D6
Torredonjimeno Spain 37°46N 3°57W 89 H7
Torrejón de Ardoz Spain 40°27N 3°29W 88 B7
Torrejoncillo Spain 39°54N 6°28W 88 F4
Torrelaguna Spain 40°50N 3°38W 88 E7
Torrelavega Spain 43°20N 4°5W 88 B6
Torremaggiore Italy 41°41N 15°17E 93 G12
Torremolinos Spain 36°38N 4°30W 89 J6
Torrens, L. Australia 31°0S 137°50E 152 A2
Torrens Cr. →
Australia 22°23S 145°9E 150 C4
Torrens Creek Australia 20°48S 145°3E 150 C4
Torrent Spain 39°27N 0°28W 91 F4
Torrenueva Spain 38°38N 3°22W 89 G7
Torreón Mexico 25°33N 103°26W 180 B4
Torreperogil Spain 38°2N 3°17W 89 G7
Torres Brazil 29°21S 49°44W 191 B5
Torres Mexico 28°46N 110°47W 180 B2
Torres del Paine △
Chile 51°3S 72°58W 192 D2
Torres Novas Portugal 39°27N 8°33W 89 F2
Torres Strait Australia 9°50S 142°20E 150 a
Torres Vedras Portugal 39°5N 9°15W 89 F1
Torrevieja Spain 37°59N 0°42W 91 H4
Torrey U.S.A. 38°18N 111°25W 168 G8
Torridge → U.K. 51°0N 4°13W 67 G3
Torridon, L. U.K. 57°35N 5°50W 66 D3
Torrijos Spain 39°59N 4°18W 88 F6
Torring Denmark 55°52N 9°29E 63 J3
Torrington Conn.,
U.S.A. 41°48N 73°7W 175 E11
Torrington Wyo.,
U.S.A. 42°4N 104°11W 168 E11
Torroella de Montgrí Spain 42°2N 3°8E 90 C8
Torrox Spain 36°46N 3°57W 89 J7
Torsås Sweden 56°24N 16°0E 63 H9
Torsby Sweden 60°7N 13°0E 62 D6
Torshälla Sweden 59°25N 16°28E 62 A10
Tórshavn Faroe Is. 62°5N 6°56W 60 E9
Torslanda Sweden 57°44N 11°45E 63 G5
Torsö Sweden 58°48N 13°45E 63 F7
Tortola Br. Virgin Is. 18°19N 64°45W 183 e
Tórtoles de Esgueva Spain 41°49N 4°2W 88 D6
Tortolì Italy 39°55N 9°39E 94 C2
Tortona Italy 44°54N 8°52E 92 D5
Tortorici Italy 38°2N 14°49E 95 D7
Tortosa Spain 40°49N 0°31E 90 E5
Tortosa, C. Spain 40°41N 0°52E 90 E5
Tortosendo Portugal 40°15N 7°31W 88 E3
Tortue, Î. de la Haiti 20°5N 72°57W 183 B5
Tortuguero △
Costa Rica 10°31N 83°29W 182 D3
Tortum Turkey 40°19N 41°35E 105 B9
Torūd Iran 35°25N 55°5E 129 C7
Torul Turkey 40°34N 39°18E 105 B8
Toruń Poland 53°2N 18°39E 85 E6
Torun Ukraine 48°40N 23°34E 81 B8
Tory Hill Canada 44°58N 78°16W 174 B6
Tory I. Ireland 55°16N 8°14W 64 A3
Torysa → Slovak Rep. 48°39N 21°21E 79 C14
Torzhok Russia 57°5N 34°55E 84 B8
Torzym Poland 52°19N 15°5E 83 F2
Tosa Japan 33°24N 133°23E 113 H6
Tosa-Shimizu Japan 32°52N 132°58E 113 H6
Tosa-Wan Japan 33°15N 133°30E 113 H6
Toscana □ Italy 43°25N 11°0E 92 E8
Toscano, Arcipelago
Italy 42°30N 10°30E 92 F7
Toshka Egypt 22°50N 31°0E 137 C3
Toshka, Buheirat en
Egypt 22°50N 31°0E 137 C3
Toshkent Uzbekistan 41°20N 69°10E 109 D7
Toshkent □ Uzbekistan 41°0N 69°40E 109 D7
Tosno Russia 59°38N 30°46E 84 C6
Tossa de Mar Spain 41°43N 2°56E 90 D7
Tösse Sweden 58°55N 12°26E 63 F6
Tostado Argentina 29°15S 61°50W 190 B3
Tostón, Pta. de
Canary Is. 28°42N 14°2W 100 F5
Tosu Japan 33°22N 130°31E 113 H5
Tosya Turkey 41°1N 34°2E 104 B6
Toszek Poland 50°27N 18°32E 83 H5
Totana Spain 37°45N 1°30W 91 H3
Totebo Sweden 57°38N 16°12E 63 G10
Toteng Botswana 20°22S 22°58E 144 B3
Totma Russia 60°0N 42°40E 106 D5
Totnes U.K. 50°26N 3°42W 67 G4
Totness Suriname 5°53N 56°19W 187 B7
Toto Nigeria 8°26N 7°25E 139 D6
Totonicapán
Guatemala 14°58N 91°12W 182 D1
Totoya, I. Fiji 18°57S 179°50W 154 a
Totten Glacier
Antarctica 66°45S 116°10E 55 C8
Tottenham Australia 32°14S 147°21E 153 B7
Tottenham Canada 44°1N 79°49W 174 B5
Tottori Japan 35°30N 134°15E 113 G7
Tottori □ Japan 35°30N 134°12E 113 G7
Touáret Algeria 20°17N 7°8E 139 A6
Touat Algeria 27°27N 0°30E 138 C4
Touba Ivory C. 8°22N 7°40W 138 D3
Touba Senegal 14°50N 15°55W 138 C1
Toubkal, Djebel Morocco 31°0N 8°0W 136 B2
Toubkal △ Morocco 31°0N 8°0W 136 B2
Toucy France 47°44N 3°15E 71 E10
Tougan Burkina Faso 13°11N 2°58E 138 C4
Touggourt Algeria 33°6N 6°4E 138 B6
Tougué Guinea 11°25N 11°50W 138 C2
Toukoto Mali 13°27N 9°52W 138 C3
Toul France 48°40N 5°53E 71 D12
Toulepleu Ivory C. 6°32N 8°24W 138 D3
Touliu Taiwan 23°42N 120°31E 117 F13
Toulon France 43°10N 5°55E 73 E9
Toulon U.S.A. 41°6N 89°52W 172 E9
Toulouse France 43°37N 1°27E 72 E5
Toulouse Blagnac ✈ (TLS)
France 43°38N 1°21E 72 E5
Toummo Niger 22°45N 14°8E 135 D8
Toumodi Ivory C. 6°32N 5°4W 138 D3
Tounan Taiwan 23°41N 120°28E 117 F13

Tounassine, Hamada
Algeria 28°48N 5°0W 136 C3
Tounggoo Burma 19°0N 96°30E 123 K20
Toungo Nigeria 8°20N 12°3E 139 D7
Touques → France 49°22N 0°8E 70 C7
Touraine France 47°20N 0°30E 70 E7
Touran = Tūrān △
Iran 35°45N 56°30E 129 C8
Tourcoing France 50°42N 3°10E 71 B10
Touriñán, C. Spain 43°3N 9°18W 88 B1
Tournai Belgium 50°35N 3°25E 69 D3
Tournan-en-Brie France 48°44N 2°46E 71 D9
Tournon-St-Martin
France 46°45N 0°58E 70 F7
Tournon-sur-Rhône
France 45°4N 4°50E 73 C8
Tournus France 46°35N 4°54E 71 F11
Touros Brazil 5°12S 35°28W 189 B3
Tours France 47°22N 0°40E 70 E7
Toussoro, Mt. C.A.R. 9°7N 23°14E 140 C4
Touws → S. Africa 33°45S 21°11E 144 D3
Touwsrivier S. Africa 33°20S 20°2E 144 D3
Tovarkovskiy Russia 53°40N 38°14E 84 F10
Tovste Ukraine 48°50N 25°44E 81 B9
Tovuz Azerbaijan 41°0N 45°40E 87 K7
Towada Japan 40°37N 141°13E 112 D10
Towada-Hachimantai △
Japan 40°20N 140°55E 112 D10
Towada-Ko Japan 40°28N 140°55E 112 D10
Towanda U.S.A. 41°46N 76°27W 175 E8
Towarri △ Australia 31°50S 150°37E 153 B9
Tower U.S.A. 47°48N 92°17W 172 B7
Towerhill Cr. →
Australia 22°28S 144°35E 150 C3
Towner U.S.A. 48°21N 100°25W 172 A3
Townsend U.S.A. 46°19N 111°31W 168 C8
Townsend Ga., U.S.A. 31°33N 81°31W 178 D8
Townsend Mont.,
U.S.A. 46°19N 111°31W 168 C8
Townshend I.
Australia 22°10S 150°31E 150 C5
Townsville Australia 19°15S 146°45E 150 B4
Towot South Sudan 6°12N 34°25E 142 A4
Towraghondī Afghan. 35°13N 62°16E 108 B3
Towson U.S.A. 39°24N 76°36W 173 F15
Towuti, Danau
Indonesia 2°45S 121°32E 119 E6
Toxkan He → China 40°8N 80°11E 109 D10
Tōya-Ko Japan 42°35N 140°51E 112 C10
Toyama Japan 36°40N 137°15E 113 F8
Toyama □ Japan 36°45N 137°30E 113 F8
Toyama-Wan Japan 37°0N 137°30E 113 F8
Toyapakeh Indonesia 8°41S 115°29E 119 K18
Toyohashi Japan 34°45N 137°25E 113 G8
Toyokawa Japan 34°48N 137°27E 113 G8
Toyonaka Japan 34°46N 135°28E 113 G7
Toyooka Japan 35°35N 134°48E 113 G7
Toyota Japan 35°3N 137°7E 113 G8
Tozeur Tunisia 33°56N 8°0E 138 B6
Tozeur □ Tunisia 34°0N 8°5E 136 B5
Tqibuli Georgia 42°26N 43°0E 87 J6
Tqvarcheli Georgia 42°47N 41°42E 87 J5
Trá Lí = Tralee Ireland 52°16N 9°42W 64 D2
Trá Mhór = Tramore
Ireland 52°10N 7°10W 64 D4
Tra On Vietnam 9°58N 105°55E 121 H5
Tra Vinh Vietnam 9°50N 106°15E 121 H6
Trabancos → Spain 41°36N 5°15W 88 D5
Traben-Trarbach Germany 49°57N 7°7E 77 F3
Trabzon Turkey 41°0N 39°45E 105 B8
Trabzon □ Turkey 41°0N 39°45E 105 B8
Tracadie Canada 47°30N 64°55W 165 C7
Tracy Calif., U.S.A. 37°44N 121°26W 170 H5
Tracy Minn., U.S.A. 44°14N 95°37W 172 C6
Tradate Italy 45°43N 8°54E 92 C5
Trade Town Liberia 5°50N 9°58W 138 D3
Trafalgar Australia 38°14S 146°12E 153 E7
Trafalgar, C. Spain 36°10N 6°2W 89 J4
Tragonisi Greece 37°27N 25°29E 99 D7
Traian Brăila, Romania 45°11N 27°44E 81 E12
Traian Tulcea, Romania 45°2N 28°15E 81 E13
Traiguén Chile 38°15S 72°41W 192 A2
Trail Canada 49°5N 117°40W 162 D5
Traill Ø Greenland 72°30N 23°0W 57 C8
Trainor L. Canada 60°24N 120°17W 162 A4
Trakai Lithuania 54°30N 25°10E 61 J21
Trákhonas Cyprus 35°12N 33°21E 101 D12
Tralee Ireland 52°16N 9°42W 64 D2
Tralee B. Ireland 52°17N 9°55W 64 D2
Tram Chim △ Vietnam 10°43N 105°31E 121 G5
Tramore Ireland 52°10N 7°10W 64 D4
Tramore B. Ireland 52°9N 7°10W 64 D4
Tramuntana, Serra de
Spain 39°48N 2°54E 100 B9
Tranås Sweden 58°3N 14°59E 63 F8
Tranbjerg Denmark 56°6N 10°9E 63 H4
Trancas Argentina 26°11S 65°20W 190 B2
Trancoso Portugal 40°49N 7°21W 88 E3
Tranebjerg Denmark 55°51N 10°36E 63 J4
Tranemo Sweden 57°30N 13°20E 63 H7
Trang Thailand 7°33N 99°38E 121 J2
Trangan Indonesia 6°40S 134°20E 119 F8
Trangie Australia 32°4S 148°0E 153 B8
Trångsviken Sweden 63°19N 13°59E 62 A7
Trani Italy 41°17N 16°25E 95 A9
Tranoroa Madag. 24°42S 45°4E 141 J9
Tranqueras Uruguay 31°13S 55°45W 191 C4
Trans-Nzoia □ Kenya 1°10S 35°0E 142 B3
Transantarctic Mts.
Antarctica 85°0S 170°0W 55 E12
Transcarpathia = Zakarpattya □
Ukraine 48°30N 23°0E 81 D8
Transilvania Romania 46°30N 24°0E 81 D9
Transilvanian Alps = Carpaţii
Meridionali Romania 45°30N 25°0E 81 E9
Transnistria □ Moldova 47°20N 29°15E 81 C14
Transtrand Sweden 61°6N 13°20E 62 C6
Transtrandsfjällen Sweden 61°8N 13°0E 62 C6
Transylvania = Transilvania
Romania 46°30N 24°0E 81 D9
Trápani Italy 38°1N 12°29E 94 D5
Trapper Pk. U.S.A. 45°54N 114°18W 168 D6
Traralgon Australia 38°12S 146°34E 153 E7
Traryd Sweden 56°35N 13°45E 63 H7
Trarza □ Mauritania 18°0N 15°0W 138 B2
Trasacco Italy 41°57N 13°32E 93 G10
Trăscău, Munţii
Romania 46°14N 23°14E 81 D8

Trasimeno, L. Italy 43°8N 12°6E 93 E9
Träslövsläge Sweden 57°4N 12°16E 63 G6
Trasvase Tajo-Segura, Canal de
Spain 40°15N 2°55W 90 E2
Trat Thailand 12°14N 102°33E 121 F4
Tratani → Pakistan 29°19N 68°20E 124 E3
Traun Austria 48°14N 14°15E 78 C7
Traunreut Germany 47°57N 12°36E 77 H8
Traunsee Austria 47°55N 13°50E 78 D6
Traunstein Germany 47°52N 12°37E 77 H8
Travellers L. Australia 33°20S 142°0E 152 B5
Travemünde Germany 53°57N 10°52E 76 B6
Travers, Mt. N.Z. 42°1S 172°45E 155 C7
Traverse City U.S.A. 44°46N 85°38W 173 C11
Travis, L. U.S.A. 30°24N 97°55W 176 F6
Travnik Bos.-H. 44°17N 17°39E 80 F7
Trawbreaga B. Ireland 55°20N 7°25W 64 A4
Trbovlje Slovenia 46°12N 15°5E 93 B12
Treasure Island U.S.A. 27°46N 82°46W 179 H7
Trébbia → Italy 45°4N 9°41E 92 C6
Trebbin Germany 52°13N 13°13E 76 B9
Trébeurden France 48°46N 3°35W 70 D3
Trebević △ Bos.-H. 43°20N 18°45E 80 G3
Trebíč Czech Rep. 49°14N 15°55E 78 B8
Trebinje Bos.-H. 42°44N 18°22E 96 D2
Trebišacce Italy 39°52N 16°32E 95 C9
Trebišnjica → Bos.-H. 42°47N 18°8E 96 C3
Trebišov Slovak Rep. 48°38N 21°41E 79 C14
Trebižat → Bos.-H. 43°15N 17°30E 93 E14
Trebnje Slovenia 45°54N 15°1E 93 C12
Trebonne Australia 18°37S 146°5E 150 B4
Třebon Czech Rep. 49°1N 14°48E 78 B7
Trebujena Spain 36°52N 6°11W 89 J4
Trecate Italy 45°26N 8°44E 92 C5
Trefaldwyn = Montgomery
U.K. 52°34N 3°8W 67 E4
Trefynwy = Monmouth
U.K. 51°48N 2°42W 67 F5
Tregaron U.K. 52°14N 3°56W 67 E4
Tregnago Italy 45°31N 11°10E 93 C8
Tregrosse Is. Australia 17°41S 150°43E 150 B5
Tréguier France 48°47N 3°16W 70 D3
Trégunc France 47°51N 3°51W 70 E3
Treherne Canada 49°38N 98°42W 163 D9
Tréia Italy 43°19N 13°19E 93 E10
Treignac France 45°32N 1°48E 72 C5
Treinta y Tres Uruguay 33°16S 54°17W 191 C5
Treis-karden Germany 50°10N 7°18E 77 E3
Treklyano Bulgaria 42°33N 22°36E 96 D6
Trelawney Zimbabwe 17°30S 30°30E 145 A5
Trelawny France 47°26N 0°30W 70 E6
Trelew Argentina 43°10S 65°20W 192 B3
Trélissac France 45°11N 0°47E 72 C4
Trelleborg Sweden 55°20N 13°10E 63 J7
Tremadog Bay U.K. 52°51N 4°18W 66 E3
Trémiti Italy 42°8N 15°30E 93 F12
Tremonton U.S.A. 41°43N 112°10W 168 F7
Tremp Spain 42°10N 0°52E 90 C6
Trenche → Canada 47°46N 72°53W 164 C5
Trenčiansky □
Slovak Rep. 48°45N 18°20E 79 C11
Trenčín Slovak Rep. 48°52N 18°4E 79 C11
Trenggalek Indonesia 8°3S 111°43E 119 H14
Trento Italy 46°30N 11°20E 93 B8
Trenton Canada 44°10N 77°34W 174 B7
Trenton Fla., U.S.A. 29°37N 82°49W 179 F7
Trenton Mo., U.S.A. 40°5N 93°37W 172 E7
Trenton N.J., U.S.A. 40°14N 74°46W 175 D10
Trenton Nebr., U.S.A. 40°11N 101°1W 172 E3
Trenton S.C., U.S.A. 33°45N 81°51W 178 D8
Trepassey Canada 46°43N 53°25W 165 C9
Trepuzzi Italy 40°24N 18°4E 95 B11
Tres Arroyos Argentina 38°26S 60°20W 190 D3
Três Corações Brazil 21°44S 45°15W 191 A6
Três Lagoas Brazil 20°50S 51°43W 187 H8
Três Lagos Argentina 49°35S 71°29W 192 D2
Tres Lomas Argentina 36°27S 62°51W 190 D3
Três Marias, Represa
Brazil 18°12S 45°15W 189 D1
Tres Montes, C. Chile 46°50S 75°30W 192 C1
Três Pinos U.S.A. 36°48N 121°19W 170 J5
Três Pontas Brazil 21°23S 45°29W 191 A6
Tres Puentes Chile 27°50S 70°15W 190 B1
Tres Puntas, C. Argentina 47°0S 66°0W 192 C3
Três Rios Brazil 22°6S 43°15W 191 A7
Tres Valles Mexico 18°15N 96°8W 181 D5
Tresco U.K. 49°57N 6°20W 67 H1
Treska → Macedonia 42°0N 21°20E 96 E5
Treskavica Bos.-H. 43°40N 18°20E 80 G3
Trespaderne Spain 42°47N 3°24W 88 C7
Tresticklan △ Sweden 59°0N 11°42E 63 F5
Trets France 43°27N 5°41E 73 E9
Treuchtlingen Germany 48°58N 10°54E 77 G6
Treuenbrietzen Germany 52°5N 12°52E 76 B8
Trevi Italy 42°53N 12°45E 93 F9
Treviglio Italy 45°31N 9°35E 92 C6
Treviño, Peña Spain 42°15N 6°46W 88 C4
Treviño Spain 42°44N 2°45W 88 C2
Treviso Italy 45°40N 12°15E 93 C9
Trévoux France 45°57N 4°47E 73 C8
Treysa Serbia 42°20N 22°10E 96 D6
Triabunna Australia 42°30S 147°55E 151 G4
Triangle Zimbabwe 21°2S 31°28E 145 B5
Triaucourt-en-Argonne
France 48°59N 5°2E 71 D12
Tribal Areas □ Pakistan 33°0N 70°0E 124 C4
Tribsees Germany 54°5N 12°44E 76 A8
Tribulation, C. Australia 16°5S 145°29E 150 B4
Tribune U.S.A. 38°28N 101°45W 172 F3
Tricárico Italy 40°37N 16°9E 95 B9
Tricase Italy 39°56N 18°22E 95 C11
Trichinopoly = Tiruchchirappalli
India 10°45N 78°45E 127 J4
Trichonida, L. Greece 38°34N 21°30E 98 C3
Trichur = Thrissur
India 10°30N 76°18E 127 J3
Trichy = Tiruchchirappalli
India 10°45N 78°45E 127 J4
Trida Australia 33°1S 145°1E 153 B7
Trier Germany 49°45N 6°38E 77 F2
Trieste Italy 45°40N 13°46E 93 C10
Trieste, G. di Italy 45°40N 13°35E 93 C10
Trieux → France 48°50N 3°3W 70 D3
Triggiano Italy 41°4N 16°55E 95 A9

Triglav Slovenia 46°21N 13°50E 93 B10
Triglavski △ Slovenia 46°20N 13°50E 93 B10
Trigno → Italy 42°4N 14°48E 93 F11
Trigueros Spain 37°24N 6°50W 89 H4
Trikala Greece 39°34N 21°47E 98 B3
Trikeri Greece 39°6N 23°5E 98 B5
Trikomo Cyprus 35°17N 33°52E 101 D12
Trikora, Puncak
Indonesia 4°15S 138°45E 119 E9
Trilby U.S.A. 28°28N 82°12W 179 G7
Trilj Croatia 43°38N 16°42E 93 E13
Trillo Spain 40°42N 2°35W 90 E2
Trim Ireland 53°33N 6°48W 64 C5
Trimbak India 19°56N 73°33E 126 D8
Trimmu Dam Pakistan 31°10N 72°8E 124 D5
Trincomalee Sri Lanka 8°38N 81°15E 127 K5
Trindade Brazil 16°40S 49°30W 187 G9
Trindade Bolivia 14°46S 64°50W 188 C5
Trindade Paraguay 27°7S 55°47W 191 B4
Trindade Cuba 21°48N 80°0W 182 B4
Trinidad Uruguay 33°30S 56°50W 190 C4
Trinidad U.S.A. 37°10N 104°31W 169 H11
Trinidad Tri.-T. 10°30S 64°55W 188 C5
Trinidad, G. Chile 49°55S 75°25W 192 C1
Trinidad, I. Argentina 39°10S 62°0W 192 A4
Trinidad & Tobago ■
W. Indies 10°30N 61°20W 186 A6
Trinitápoli Italy 41°21N 16°5E 95 A9
Trinity Canada 48°59N 53°55W 165 C9
Trinity U.S.A. 30°57N 95°22W 176 F7
Trinity → Calif.,
U.S.A. 41°11N 123°42W 168 F2
Trinity → Tex., U.S.A. 29°45N 94°43W 176 G7
Trinity B. Canada 48°20N 53°10W 165 C9
Trinity Hills Trin. & Tob. 10°7N 61°7W 187 K15
Trinity Is. U.S.A. 56°33N 154°25W 166 D9
Trinity Range U.S.A. 40°10N 118°40W 168 F4
Trinkat India 8°5N 93°30E 127 K11
Trinkitat Sudan 18°45N 37°51E 137 D4
Trino Italy 45°12N 8°18E 92 C5
Trinway U.S.A. 40°9N 82°1W 174 F2
Triolet Mauritius 20°4S 57°32E 141 d
Trionto, C. Italy 39°37N 16°43E 95 C9
Triora Italy 44°1N 7°46E 92 D4
Tripoli = Tarābulus
Lebanon 34°31N 35°50E 130 A4
Tripoli = Tarābulus
Libya 32°49N 13°7E 135 B8
Tripoli Greece 37°31N 22°25E 98 D4
Tripolis = Tarābulus
Libya 32°49N 13°7E 135 B8
Tripolitania = Tarābulus
Libya 31°0N 13°0E 135 B8
Tripura □ India 24°0N 92°0E 123 H18
Tripylos Cyprus 34°59N 32°41E 101 E11
Trischen Germany 54°4N 8°40E 76 A4
Tristan da Cunha
Atl. Oc. 37°6S 12°20W 133 K2
Trisul India 30°19N 79°47E 125 D8
Triton I. S. China Sea 15°47N 111°12E 118 A4
Trivandrum =
Thiruvananthapuram
India 8°41N 77°0E 127 K3
Trivento Italy 41°47N 14°33E 93 G11
Trizina Greece 37°25N 23°15E 98 D5
Trnava Slovak Rep. 48°23N 17°35E 79 C10
Trnavský □ Slovak Rep. 48°30N 17°45E 79 C10
Troarn France 49°11N 0°11W 70 C6
Trochu Canada 51°50N 113°13W 162 C6
Trodely I. Canada 52°15N 79°26W 164 B4
Troebratskīy Kazakhstan 54°25N 66°4E 109 B7
Trogir Croatia 43°32N 16°15E 93 E13
Troglav Croatia 43°56N 16°36E 80 G7
Tróia Italy 41°22N 15°18E 95 A8
Troilus, L. Canada 50°50N 74°35W 164 B5
Troina Italy 37°47N 14°36E 95 E7
Trois Fourches, Cap des
Morocco 35°26N 2°58W 136 A3
Trois-Pistoles Canada 48°5N 69°10W 165 C6
Trois-Rivières Canada 46°25N 72°34W 164 C5
Trois-Rivières
Guadeloupe 15°57N 61°40W 182 b
Troisdorf Germany 50°48N 7°11E 76 E3
Troitsk Russia 54°10N 61°35E 108 D7
Troitsko Pechorsk
Russia 62°40N 56°10E 106 C6
Troitskoye Russia 46°26N 44°15E 87 G7
Troll Antarctica 72°0S 2°30E 55 D3
Tröllaskagi Iceland 64°54N 17°16W 60 D5
Trollhättan Sweden 58°17N 12°20E 63 F6
Trollheimen Norway 62°46N 9°1E 62 B3
Trombetas → Brazil 1°55S 55°35W 187 D7
Tromelin I. Ind. Oc. 15°52S 54°25E 146 F4
Troms Norway 69°57N 19°0E 60 B17
Tromsø Norway 69°40N 18°56E 60 B18
Tron Thailand 17°28N 100°7E 120 D3
Trona U.S.A. 35°46N 117°23W 171 K9
Tronador, Mte.
Argentina 41°10S 71°50W 192 B2
Trondheim Norway 63°36N 10°25E 60 E14
Trondheimsfjorden
Norway 63°35N 10°30E 60 E14
Trönninge Sweden 56°37N 12°51E 63 H6
Tronto → Italy 42°54N 13°55E 93 F10
Troodos Cyprus 34°55N 32°52E 101 E11
Troon U.K. 55°33N 4°39W 66 F4
Tropea Italy 38°41N 15°54E 95 D8
Tropic U.S.A. 37°37N 112°5W 168 H7
Tropojë Albania 42°23N 20°10E 96 d4
Trosa Sweden 58°54N 17°33E 63 F11
Trostan U.K. 55°3N 6°10W 64 A5
Trostberg Germany 48°1N 12°33E 77 G8
Trostyanets Sumy,
Ukraine 50°50N 34°59E 85 G10
Trostyanets Vinnyts'ka,
Ukraine 48°31N 29°11E 81 B14
Trou Gras Pt. St. Lucia 13°51N 60°53W 183 f
Trout → Canada 61°19N 119°51W 162 A5
Trout L. N.W.T.,
Canada 60°40N 121°14W 162 A4
Trout L. Ont., Canada 51°20N 93°15W 163 C10
Trout Lake Canada 56°30N 114°32W 162 B6
Trout Lake U.S.A. 46°0N 121°32W 170 E5
Trout River Canada 49°29N 58°8W 165 C8
Trout Run U.S.A. 41°23N 77°3W 174 E7

Troy Mont., U.S.A. 48°28N 115°53W 168 B6
Troy N.Y., U.S.A. 42°44N 73°41W 175 D11
Troy Ohio, U.S.A. 40°2N 84°12W 173 E11
Troy Pa., U.S.A. 41°47N 76°47W 175 E8
Troyan Bulgaria 42°57N 24°43E 97 D8
Troyes France 48°19N 4°3E 71 D11
Trpanj Croatia 43°1N 17°15E 93 E14
Trstenik Serbia 43°36N 21°0E 96 C5
Trubchevsk Russia 52°33N 33°47E 85 F7
Truchas Pk. U.S.A. 35°58N 105°39W 169 J11
Trucial States = United Arab
Emirates ■ Asia 23°50N 54°0E 129 F7
Truckee U.S.A. 39°20N 120°11W 170 F6
Trudfront Russia 45°56N 47°40E 87 G8
Trudovoye Russia 43°17N 132°5E 112 C6
Trujillo Honduras 16°0N 86°0W 182 C2
Trujillo Peru 8°6S 79°0W 188 B2
Trujillo Spain 39°28N 5°55W 89 F5
Trujillo U.S.A. 35°32N 104°42W 169 J11
Trujillo Venezuela 9°22N 70°38W 186 B4
Truk Micronesia 7°25S 151°46E 156 G7
Trumann U.S.A. 35°41N 90°31W 177 D9
Trumansburg U.S.A. 42°33N 76°40W 175 D8
Trumbull, Mt. U.S.A. 36°25N 113°19W 169 H7
Trŭn Bulgaria 42°51N 22°38E 96 C6
Trun France 48°50N 0°2E 70 D7
Trundle Australia 32°53S 147°35E 153 B8
Trung Lon, Hon Vietnam 8°36N 106°8E 121 H6
Trung Phan Vietnam 17°0N 109°0E 120 D6
Truong Sa, Dao = Spratly I.
S. China Sea 8°38N 111°55E 118 C4
Truro Canada 45°21N 63°14W 165 C7
Truro U.K. 50°16N 5°4W 67 G2
Truskavets Ukraine 49°17N 23°30E 75 D12
Trŭstenik Bulgaria 43°31N 24°28E 97 C8
Trustrup Denmark 56°20N 10°46E 63 H4
Trutch Canada 57°44N 122°57W 162 B4
Truth or Consequences
U.S.A. 33°8N 107°15W 169 K10
Trutnov Czech Rep. 50°37N 15°54E 78 A8
Truyère → France 44°38N 2°34E 72 D6
Tryavna Bulgaria 42°54N 25°25E 97 D10
Tryonville U.S.A. 41°42N 79°48W 174 E5
Tryphena N.Z. 36°18S 175°28E 154 C4
Trzcianka Poland 53°3N 16°25E 83 E3
Trzciel Poland 52°23N 15°50E 83 F2
Trzcińsko Zdrój Poland 52°58N 14°35E 83 F1
Trzebiatów Poland 54°3N 15°18E 82 D2
Trzebiez Poland 53°38N 14°31E 82 E1
Trzebnica Poland 51°20N 17°1E 83 G4
Trzemeszno Poland 52°33N 17°48E 83 F4
Tržič Slovenia 46°22N 14°18E 93 B11
Tsagaannur Mongolia 49°32N 89°42E 109 C13
Tsagan Aman Russia 47°34N 46°43E 87 G8
Tsala Apopka L.
U.S.A. 28°53N 82°19W 179 G7
Tsamandas Greece 39°46N 20°21E 98 B2
Tsandi Namibia 17°42S 14°50E 144 A1
Tsaratanana Madag. 16°47S 47°39E 141 G9
Tsarevo Bulgaria 42°28N 27°51E 97 D12
Tsaritsani Greece 39°53N 22°14E 98 B4
Tsau Botswana 20°8S 22°22E 144 B3
Tsavo Kenya 2°59S 38°28E 142 C4
Tsavo East △ Kenya 2°44S 38°47E 142 C4
Tsavo West △ Kenya 3°19S 37°57E 142 C4
Tsentralen Balkan △
Bulgaria 42°40N 24°45E 97 D8
Tsentralnyy □ Russia 52°0N 40°0E 106 D4
Tses Namibia 25°58S 18°8E 144 C2
Tsetserleg Mongolia 47°36N 101°32E 110 B9
Tseung Kwan China 22°19N 114°15E 111 a
Tsévié Togo 6°25N 1°20E 139 D5
Tshabong Botswana 26°2S 22°29E 144 C3
Tshane Botswana 24°5S 21°54E 144 B3
Tshela
Dem. Rep. of the Congo 4°57S 13°4E 140 F2
Tshesebe Botswana 21°51S 27°32E 145 B4
Tshibeke
Dem. Rep. of the Congo 2°40S 28°35E 142 C2
Tshibinda
Dem. Rep. of the Congo 2°23S 28°43E 142 C2
Tshikapa
Dem. Rep. of the Congo 6°28S 20°48E 140 F4
Tshilenge
Dem. Rep. of the Congo 6°17S 23°48E 142 D1
Tshinsenda
Dem. Rep. of the Congo 12°20S 28°0E 143 G2
Tshofa
Dem. Rep. of the Congo 5°13S 25°16E 142 D2
Tshwane = Pretoria
S. Africa 25°44S 28°12E 145 D4
Tshwane Botswana 22°24S 22°1E 144 B3
Tsigara Botswana 20°22S 25°54E 144 B4
Tsihombe Madag. 25°10S 45°41E 141 K9
Tsiigehtchic Canada 67°15N 134°0W 160 D5
Ts'il-os △ Canada 51°9N 123°59W 162 C4
Tsimlyansk Russia 47°40N 42°6E 87 G6
Tsimlyansk Res. = Tsimlyanskoye
Vdkhr. Russia 48°0N 43°0E 87 G7
Tsimlyanskoye Vdkhr.
Russia 48°0N 43°0E 87 G7
Tsinan = Jinan China 36°38N 117°1E 114 F9
Tsineng S. Africa 27°5S 23°5E 144 C3
Tsing Yi China 22°21N 114°6E 111 a
Tsingtao = Qingdao
China 36°5N 120°20E 115 F11
Tsiteli-Tsqaro = Dedoplis Tsqaro
Georgia 41°33N 46°0E 87 K8
Tsitsikamma △ S. Africa 34°0S 24°40E 144 E3
Tsivilsk Russia 55°50N 47°25E 86 C9
Tskhinvali Georgia 42°14N 44°1E 87 J7
Tsna → Russia 54°55N 41°58E 86 C6
Tso Moriri, L. India 32°50N 78°20E 125 C8
Tsobis Namibia 19°27S 17°30E 144 A2
Tsodilo Hills Botswana 18°49S 21°43E 144 A3
Tsogttsetsiy = Baruunsuu
Mongolia 43°43N 105°35E 114 C3
Tsolo S. Africa 31°18S 28°37E 145 E4
Tsomo S. Africa 32°0S 27°42E 145 E4
Tsu Japan 34°45N 136°25E 113 G8
Tsu L. Canada 60°40N 111°52W 162 A6
Tsuchiura Japan 36°5N 140°15E 113 F10
Tsuen Wan China 22°22N 114°6E 111 a
Tsugaru-Hantō Japan 41°0N 140°30E 112 D10
Tsugaru-Kaikyō
Japan 41°35N 141°0E 112 D10

Tsumeb *Namibia* 19°9S 17°44E **144** A2
Tsumis *Namibia* 23°39S 17°29E **144** B2
Tsuruga *Japan* 35°45N 136°2E **113** G8
Tsurugi-San *Japan* 33°51N 134°6E **113** H7
Tsuruoka *Japan* 38°44N 139°50E **112** E9
Tsushima *Gifu, Japan* 35°10N 136°43E **113** G8
Tsushima *Nagasaki, Japan* 34°20N 129°20E **113** G4
Tsuyama *Japan* 35°3N 134°0E **113** G7
Tsvetkovo *Ukraine* 49°8N 31°33E **85** H6
Tsyelyakhany *Belarus* 52°30N 25°46E **75** B13
Tua → *Portugal* 41°13N 7°26W **88** D3
Tuaheni Pt. *N.Z.* 38°43S 178°4E **154** E7
Tuai *N.Z.* 38°47S 177°10E **154** E6
Tuaim = Tuam *Ireland* 53°31N 8°51W **64** C3
Tuakau *N.Z.* 37°16S 174°59E **154** D3
Tual *Indonesia* 5°38S 132°44E **119** F8
Tualatin *U.S.A.* 45°23N 122°45W **170** E4
Tuam *Ireland* 53°31N 8°51W **64** C3
Tuamarina *N.Z.* 41°25S 173°59E **155** B8
Tuamotu, Ís. *French Polynesia* 17°0S 144°0W **157** J13
Tuamotu Arch. = Tuamotu, Ís. *French Polynesia* 17°0S 144°0W **157** J13
Tuamotu Ridge *Pac. Oc.* 20°0S 138°0W **157** K14
Tuan Giao *Vietnam* 21°35N 103°25E **120** B4
Tuanfeng *China* 30°38N 114°52E **117** B10
Tuanxi *China* 27°28N 107°8E **116** D6
Tuao *Phil.* 17°45N 121°22E **119** A6
Tuapse *Russia* 44°5N 39°10E **87** H4
Tuas *Singapore* 1°19N 103°39E **121** d
Tuatapere *N.Z.* 46°8S 167°41E **155** G2
Tuba City *U.S.A.* 36°8N 111°14W **169** H8
Tuban *Indonesia* 6°54S 112°3E **119** G15
Tubani *Botswana* 24°46S 24°18E **144** B3
Tubarão *Brazil* 28°30S 49°0W **191** B6
Tûbâs *West Bank* 32°20N 35°22E **130** C4
Tubas → *Namibia* 22°54S 14°35E **144** B2
Tübingen *Germany* 48°31N 9°4E **77** G5
Tubmanburg = Bomi *Liberia* 7°1N 10°38W **138** D2
Tubou *Fiji* 18°13S 178°48W **154** a
Tubruq *Libya* 32°7N 23°55E **135** B10
Tubuaï, Ís. *French Polynesia* 25°0S 150°0W **157** K13
Tuc Trung *Vietnam* 11°1N 107°12E **121** G6
Tucacas *Venezuela* 10°48N 68°19W **186** A5
Tucano *Brazil* 10°58S 38°48W **189** C3
T'uch'ang *Taiwan* 24°35N 121°29E **117** E13
Tuchitua *Canada* 60°55N 129°13W **162** A3
Tuchodi → *Canada* 58°17N 123°42W **162** B4
Tuchola *Poland* 53°33N 17°52E **82** E4
Tuchów *Poland* 49°54N 21°1E **83** J8
Tuckanarra *Australia* 27°7S 118°5E **149** E2
Tucker *U.S.A.* 33°51N 84°13W **178** B5
Tucson *U.S.A.* 32°13N 110°58W **169** K8
Tucumán □ *Argentina* 26°48S 66°2W **190** B2
Tucumcari *U.S.A.* 35°10N 103°44W **169** J12
Tucupita *Venezuela* 9°2N 62°3W **186** B6
Tucuruí *Brazil* 3°42S 49°44W **187** D9
Tucuruí, Represa de *Brazil* 4°0S 49°30W **187** D9
Tuczno *Poland* 53°13N 16°10E **83** E3
Tudela *Spain* 42°4N 1°39W **90** C3
Tudmur *Syria* 34°36N 38°15E **105** E8
Tudor, L. *Canada* 55°50N 65°25W **165** A6
Tudora *Romania* 47°31N 26°45E **81** C11
Tuella → *Portugal* 41°30N 7°12W **88** D3
Tuen Mun *China* 22°23N 113°57E **111** a
Tufanbeyli *Turkey* 38°15N 36°13E **104** C7
Tug Hill Plateau *U.S.A.* 43°45N 75°50W **175** C9
Tugela → *S. Africa* 29°14S 31°30E **145** C5
Tugela Falls *S. Africa* 28°42S 29°51E **145** C4
Tuguegarao *Phil.* 17°35N 121°42E **119** A6
Tugur *Russia* 53°44N 136°45E **107** D14
Tui *Spain* 42°3N 8°39W **88** C2
Tuineje *Canary Is.* 28°19N 14°3W **100** F5
Tukangbesi, Kepulauan *Indonesia* 6°0S 124°0E **119** F6
Tukarak I. *Canada* 56°15N 78°45W **164** A4
Tukayyid *Iraq* 29°47N 45°36E **128** D5
Tûkh *Egypt* 30°21N 31°12E **137** E7
Tukhlya *Ukraine* 48°55N 23°28E **81** B8
Tukituki → *N.Z.* 39°36S 176°56E **154** F5
Tukobo *Ghana* 5°1N 2°47W **138** D4
Tuktoyaktuk *Canada* 69°27N 133°2W **160** D5
Tuktut Nogait △ *Canada* 69°15N 122°0W **160** D7
Tukums *Latvia* 56°58N 23°10E **82** B10
Tukuyu *Tanzania* 9°17S 33°35E **143** D3
Tula *Hidalgo, Mexico* 20°3N 99°21W **181** C5
Tula *Tamaulipas, Mexico* 23°0N 99°43W **181** C5
Tula *Nigeria* 9°51N 11°27E **139** D7
Tula *Russia* 54°13N 37°38E **84** E9
Tula △ *Russia* 53°45N 37°30E **84** E9
Tulach Mhór = Tullamore *Ireland* 53°16N 7°31W **64** C4
Tulancingo *Mexico* 20°5N 98°22W **181** C5
Tulare *Serbia* 42°48N 21°28E **96** D5
Tulare *U.S.A.* 36°13N 119°21W **170** J7
Tulare Lake Bed *U.S.A.* 36°0N 119°48W **170** K7
Tularosa *U.S.A.* 33°5N 106°1W **169** K10
Tulbagh *S. Africa* 33°16S 19°6E **144** D2
Tulcán *Ecuador* 0°48N 77°43W **186** C3
Tulcea *Romania* 45°13N 28°46E **81** E13
Tulcea □ *Romania* 45°0N 29°0E **81** E13
Tulchyn *Ukraine* 48°41N 28°49E **81** B13

Tulsa *U.S.A.* 36°10N 95°55W **176** C7
Tulsequah *Canada* 58°39N 133°35W **162** B2
Tuluá *Colombia* 4°6N 76°11W **186** C3
Tulucești *Romania* 45°34N 28°2E **81** E13
Tulum *Mexico* 20°13N 87°28W **181** C7
Tulun *Russia* 54°32N 100°35E **107** D11
Tulungagung *Indonesia* 8°5S 111°54E **119** H14
Tuma → *Russia* 55°10N 40°30E **84** E11
Tuma → *Nic.* 13°6N 84°35W **182** D3
Tumacacori △ *U.S.A.* 31°35N 111°6W **169** L8
Tumaco *Colombia* 1°50N 78°45W **186** C3
Tumakuru *India* 13°18N 77°6E **127** H3
Tumatumari *Guyana* 5°20N 58°55W **186** B7
Tumba *Sweden* 59°12N 17°48E **62** E11
Tumba, L. *Dem. Rep. of the Congo* 0°50S 18°0E **140** E3
Tumbarumba *Australia* 35°44S 148°0E **153** C8
Tumbaya *Argentina* 23°50S 65°26W **190** A2
Tumbes *Peru* 3°37S 80°27W **188** A1
Tumbes □ *Peru* 3°50S 80°30W **188** A1
Tumbler Ridge *Canada* 55°8N 121°0W **162** B4
Tumbwe *Dem. Rep. of the Congo* 11°25S 27°15E **143** E2
Tumby Bay *Australia* 34°21S 136°8E **152** C2
Tumd Youqi *China* 40°30N 110°30E **114** D6
Tumen *China* 43°0N 129°50E **112** C4
Tumen Jiang → *China* 42°20N 130°35E **115** C16
Tumeremo *Venezuela* 7°18N 61°30W **186** B6
Tumiritinga *Brazil* 18°58S 41°38W **189** D2
Tumkur = Tumakuru *India* 13°18N 77°6E **127** H3
Tump *Pakistan* 26°7N 62°16E **122** F3
Tumpat *Malaysia* 6°11N 102°10E **121** J4
Tumsar *India* 21°26N 79°45E **126** D4
Tumu *Ghana* 10°56N 1°56W **138** C4
Tumucumaque, Serra *Brazil* 2°0N 55°0W **187** C8
Tumupasa *Bolivia* 14°9S 67°55W **188** C4
Tumut *Australia* 35°16S 148°13E **153** C8
Tumwater *U.S.A.* 47°1N 122°54W **170** C4
Tumxuk *China* 41°22N 79°58E **109** D9
Tun *Sweden* 58°26N 12°43E **63** F6
Tuna *India* 22°59N 70°5E **124** H4
Tunapuna *Trin. & Tob.* 10°38N 61°24W **187** K15
Tunas de Zaza *Cuba* 21°39N 79°34W **182** B4
Tunbridge Wells = Royal Tunbridge Wells *U.K.* 51°7N 0°16E **67** F8
Tunçbilek *Turkey* 39°37N 29°29E **99** B11
Tunceli *Turkey* 39°6N 39°31E **105** C8
Tunceli □ *Turkey* 39°5N 39°35E **105** C8
Tunchang *China* 19°21N 110°5E **117** a
Tuncurry *Australia* 32°17S 152°29E **153** B10
Tundla *India* 27°28N 78°17E **124** F8
Tundubai *Sudan* 18°36N 28°35E **137** D2
Tunduru *Tanzania* 11°8S 37°25E **143** E4
Tundzha → *Bulgaria* 41°40N 26°35E **97** C10
Tung Chung *China* 22°17N 113°57E **111** a
Tung Lung Chau *China* 22°15N 114°17E **111** a
Tunga → *India* 15°0N 75°50E **127** G2
Tungabhadra → *India* 15°57N 78°15E **127** G4
Tungabhadra Dam *India* 15°0N 75°50E **127** G2
Tungla *Nic.* 13°24N 84°21W **182** D3
Tungsha Tao = Dongsha Dao *S. China Sea* 20°45N 116°43E **111** G12
Tungshih *Taiwan* 24°12N 120°43E **117** E13
Tungsten *Canada* 61°57N 128°16W **162** A3
Tunguska, Nizhnyaya → *Russia* 65°48N 88°4E **107** C9
Tunguska, Podkamennaya → *Russia* 61°50N 90°13E **107** C10
Tuni *India* 17°22N 82°36E **126** F6
Tunica *U.S.A.* 34°41N 90°23W **177** D9
Tunis *Tunisia* 36°50N 10°11E **136** A6
Tunis × (TUN) *Tunisia* 36°52N 10°14E **94** F3
Tunis, Golfe de *Tunisia* 37°0N 10°30E **136** A6
Tunisia ■ *Africa* 33°30N 9°10E **136** B5
Tunja *Colombia* 5°33N 73°25W **186** B4
Tunkhannock *U.S.A.* 41°32N 75°57W **175** E9
Tunkinsky △ *Russia* 51°30N 102°0E **107** D11
Tunliu *China* 36°13N 112°52E **114** F7
Tunnel Creek △ *Australia* 17°41S 125°18E **148** C4
Tunnsjøen *Norway* 64°45N 13°25E **60** D15
Tunø *Denmark* 55°57N 10°27E **63** J4
Tunungayualok I. *Canada* 56°0N 61°0W **165** A7
Tunuyán *Argentina* 33°35S 69°0W **190** C2
Tunuyán → *Argentina* 33°33S 67°30W **190** C2
Tunxi = Huangshan *China* 29°42N 118°25E **117** C12
Tuo Jiang → *China* 28°50N 105°35E **116** C5
Tuolumne *U.S.A.* 37°58N 120°15W **170** H6
Tuolumne → *U.S.A.* 37°36N 121°13W **170** H5
Tüp *Kyrgyzstan* 42°45N 78°20E **109** D9
Tüp Âghâj *Iran* 36°3N 47°50E **105** C12
Tupã *Brazil* 21°57S 50°28W **191** A5
Tupaciguara *Brazil* 18°35S 48°43W **191** D1
Tupelo *U.S.A.* 34°16N 88°43W **177** D10
Tupik *Russia* 55°42N 33°22E **84** E7
Tupinambarana, I. *Brazil* 3°0S 58°0W **186** D7
Tupirama *Brazil* 8°3S 48°0W **187** D9
Tupiratins *Brazil* 8°23S 48°8W **189** B1
Tupiza *Bolivia* 21°30S 65°40W **190** A2
Tupižnica *Serbia* 43°43N 22°10E **96** C6
Tupman *U.S.A.* 35°18N 119°21W **171** K7
Tupper *Canada* 55°32N 120°1W **162** B4
Tupper L. *U.S.A.* 44°10N 74°32W **175** B10
Tupper Lake *U.S.A.* 44°14N 74°28W **175** B10
Tüpqarghan Muyis *Kazakhstan* 44°40N 50°19E **87** H10
Tupungato, Cerro *S. Amer.* 33°15S 69°50W **190** C2
Túquerres *Colombia* 1°5N 77°37W **186** C3
Tura *Russia* 64°20N 100°17E **107** C11
Turabah *Ḥāʾil, Si. Arabia* 28°20N 43°15E **128** D4
Turabah *Makkah, Si. Arabia* 21°15N 41°34E **137** C5
Turakina *N.Z.* 40°3S 175°16E **154** G4
Turakina → *N.Z.* 40°5S 175°8E **154** G4
Turakirae Hd. *N.Z.* 41°26S 174°56E **154** H3
Tûrân *Iran* 35°39N 56°42E **128** B8
Turan *Russia* 51°55N 95°0E **109** A10
Tūrān △ *Iran* 35°45N 56°30E **129** C8
Turan Lowland *Asia* 43°0N 62°0E **108** D6
Turangi *N.Z.* 38°59S 175°48E **154** E4

Ṭurayf *Si. Arabia* 31°41N 38°39E **128** D3
Turbacz *Poland* 49°30N 20°8E **83** J7
Turbe *Bos.-H.* 44°15N 17°35E **80** F7
Turbeville *U.S.A.* 33°54N 80°1W **178** B9
Turčianske Teplice *Slovak Rep.* 48°52N 18°52E **79** C11
Turco *Bolivia* 18°10S 68°11W **188** D4
Turcoaia *Romania* 45°7N 28°11E **81** E13
Turda *Romania* 46°34N 23°47E **81** D8
Turek *Poland* 52°3N 18°30E **83** F5
Turén *Venezuela* 9°17N 69°6W **186** B5
Turfan = Turpan *China* 43°58N 89°10E **109** D11
Turfan Basin = Turpan Pendi *China* 42°40N 89°25E **109** D11
Turfan Depression = Turpan Pendi *China* 42°40N 89°25E **109** D11
Turgashkaya Stolovaya Strana = Torghay Ustirti *Asia* 51°0N 63°0E **108** B6
Turgeon → *Canada* 50°0N 78°56W **164** C4
Türgovishte *Bulgaria* 43°17N 26°38E **97** C10
Türgovishte □ *Bulgaria* 43°17N 26°38E **97** C10
Turgut *Turkey* 37°22N 28°4E **99** D10
Turgutlu *Turkey* 38°30N 27°43E **99** C9
Turgutreis *Turkey* 37°2N 27°15E **99** D9
Turgwe → *Zimbabwe* 21°31S 32°15E **145** B5
Turhal *Turkey* 40°24N 36°5E **104** B7
Turia → *Spain* 39°27N 0°19W **91** F4
Turiaçu *Brazil* 1°40S 45°19W **187** D9
Turiaçu → *Brazil* 1°36S 45°19W **187** D9
Turiec → *Slovak Rep.* 49°7N 18°55E **79** B11
Turin = Torino *Italy* 45°3N 7°40E **92** C4
Turka *Ukraine* 49°10N 23°2E **83** J10
Turkana □ *Kenya* 3°0N 35°20E **142** B4
Turkana, L. *Africa* 3°30N 36°5E **142** B4
Türkeli *Turkey* 40°30N 27°30E **97** F11
Turkestan = Türkistan *Kazakhstan* 43°17N 68°16E **109** D7
Turkestan Range = Türkiston Range *Asia* 39°35N 69°0E **109** D7
Türkeve *Hungary* 47°6N 20°44E **80** C5
Turkey ■ *Eurasia* 39°0N 36°0E **104** C7
Turkey Creek = Warmun *Australia* 17°2S 128°12E **148** C4
Türki *Russia* 52°0N 43°15E **86** D6
Türkistan *Kazakhstan* 43°17N 68°16E **109** D7
Turkmenabat *Turkmenistan* 39°6N 63°34E **129** B9
Türkmenbashi *Turkmenistan* 40°5N 53°5E **129** A7
Türkmenli *Turkey* 39°45N 26°30E **99** B8
Türkoğlu *Turkey* 37°23N 36°50E **104** D7
Turks & Caicos Is. ☑ *W. Indies* 21°20N 71°20W **183** B5
Turks Island Passage *Turks & Caicos* 21°25N 71°19W **183** B5
Turku *Finland* 60°30N 22°19E **84** B2
Turkwel → *Kenya* 3°6N 36°6E **142** B4
Turlock *U.S.A.* 37°30N 120°51W **170** H6
Turnagain *Australia* 9°34S 142°17E **150** a
Turnagain → *Canada* 59°12N 127°35W **162** B3
Turnagain, C. *N.Z.* 40°28S 176°38E **154** G5
Turneffe Is. *Belize* 17°20N 87°50W **181** D7
Turner *U.S.A.* 48°51N 108°24W **166** B9
Turner Pt. *Australia* 11°47S 133°32E **150** A1
Turner Valley *Canada* 50°40N 114°17W **162** C6
Turners Falls *U.S.A.* 42°36N 72°33W **175** D12
Turner's Pen. *S. Leone* 7°22N 12°24W **138** D2
Turnhout *Belgium* 51°19N 4°57E **69** C4
Túrnor L. *Canada* 56°35N 108°35W **163** B7
Turnov *Czech Rep.* 50°34N 15°10E **78** A8
Turnovo = Veliko Tŭrnovo *Bulgaria* 43°5N 25°41E **97** C9
Turnu Măgurele *Romania* 43°46N 24°56E **81** G9
Turnu Roşu, P. *Romania* 45°33N 24°17E **81** E9
Turobin *Poland* 50°50N 22°44E **83** H9
Tuross Head *Australia* 36°3S 150°8E **153** D9
Turpan *China* 43°58N 89°10E **109** D11
Turpan Pendi *China* 42°40N 89°25E **109** D11
Turrawan *Australia* 30°28S 149°53E **153** A8
Turrës, Kala e *Albania* 41°10N 19°28E **96** E3
Turriff *U.K.* 57°32N 2°27W **65** D6
Tursāq *Iraq* 33°27N 45°47E **105** F11
Tursi *Italy* 40°15N 16°28E **95** B9
Tursunzoda *Tajikistan* 38°30N 68°14E **109** F7
Turtle Head I. *Australia* 10°56S 142°37E **150** A3
Turtle Is. *S. Leone* 7°40N 13°0W **138** D2
Turtle L. *Canada* 53°36N 108°38W **163** C7
Turtle Lake *U.S.A.* 47°31N 100°53W **172** B3
Turtleford *Canada* 53°23N 108°57W **162** C7
Turua *N.Z.* 37°14S 175°35E **154** D4
Turuépano △ *Venezuela* 10°34N 62°43W **183** D7
Turukhansk *Russia* 65°21N 88°5E **107** C9
Turzovka *Slovak Rep.* 49°25N 18°35E **79** B11
Tuscaloosa *U.S.A.* 33°12N 87°34W **177** E11
Tuscania *Italy* 42°25N 11°55E **92** A4
Tuscany = Toscana □ *Italy* 43°25N 11°0E **92** C4
Tuscarawas → *U.S.A.* 40°24N 81°25W **174** F3
Tuscarora Mt. *U.S.A.* 40°55N 77°55W **174** F7
Tuscola *Ill., U.S.A.* 39°48N 88°17W **172** F10
Tuscola *Tex., U.S.A.* 32°12N 99°48W **176** E5
Tuscumbia *U.S.A.* 34°44N 87°42W **177** D11
Tuskegee *U.S.A.* 32°25N 85°42W **178** C4
Tuszyn *Poland* 51°36N 19°33E **83** G6
Tutak *Turkey* 39°31N 42°46E **105** C10
Tutayev *Russia* 57°53N 39°32E **84** D10
Tuticorin *India* 8°50N 78°12E **127** K4
Tutin *Serbia* 43°0N 20°20E **96** C4
Tutóia *Brazil* 2°45S 42°20W **189** A2
Tutong *Brunei* 4°47N 114°40E **118** D4
Tutova → *Romania* 46°7N 27°30E **81** D12
Tutrakan *Bulgaria* 44°2N 26°40E **97** B10
Tuttle Creek L. *U.S.A.* 39°15N 96°36E **172** F5
Tuttlingen *Germany* 47°58N 8°48E **77** H4
Tutuala *E. Timor* 8°25S 127°15E **119** F7
Tutuko, Mt. *N.Z.* 44°35S 168°1E **155** D2
Tutume *Botswana* 20°30S 27°5E **141** J5
Tutun *Egypt* 29°9N 30°46E **137** F7
Tuul Gol → *Mongolia* 48°30N 104°25E **110** B9
Tuva □ *Russia* 51°30N 95°0E **109** A10
Tuvalu ■ *Pac. Oc.* 8°0S 178°0E **147** B10
Tuvuca *Fiji* 17°40S 178°48W **154** a
Tuxer Alpen *Austria* 47°10N 11°45E **78** D4
Tuxpan *Mexico* 20°57N 97°24W **181** C5

Tuxtla Gutiérrez *Mexico* 16°45N 93°7W **181** D6
Tuy = Tui *Spain* 42°3N 8°39W **88** C2
Tuy Duc *Vietnam* 12°15N 107°27E **121** F6
Tuy Hoa *Vietnam* 11°14N 108°43E **121** F7
Tuy Phong *Vietnam* 11°14N 108°43E **121** G7
Tuya L. *Canada* 59°7N 130°35W **162** B2
Tuyen Hoa *Vietnam* 17°50N 106°10E **120** D6
Tuyen Quang *Vietnam* 21°50N 105°10E **116** G5
Tüysarkān *Iran* 34°33N 48°27E **105** C13
Tūz Khurmātū *Iraq* 34°56N 44°38E **105** C11
Tuzi *Montenegro* 42°22N 19°20E **96** C3
Tuzigoot △ *U.S.A.* 34°46N 112°2W **169** J7
Tuzla *Bos.-H.* 44°34N 18°41E **80** F3
Tuzla *Turkey* 47°1N 39°57E **85** J10
Tuzluca *Turkey* 40°3N 43°39E **105** C10
Tuzly *Ukraine* 45°54N 30°6E **81** E15
Tvååker *Sweden* 57°4N 12°25E **63** G6
Tvardița *Moldova* 46°9N 28°58E **81** E13
Tver *Russia* 56°55N 35°55E **84** D9
Tver □ *Russia* 56°50N 35°0E **84** D8
Tvrdošín *Slovak Rep.* 49°21N 19°35E **79** B12
Tvrdošovce *Slovak Rep.* 48°6N 18°4E **79** C11
Tvŭrditsa *Bulgaria* 42°42N 25°53E **97** D9
Twain *U.S.A.* 40°1N 121°3W **170** E5
Twain Harte *U.S.A.* 38°2N 120°14W **170** G6
Twardogóra *Poland* 51°23N 17°28E **83** G4
Twee River *Namibia* 25°27S 19°27E **144** C2
Tweed *Canada* 44°29N 77°19W **174** B7
Tweed → *U.K.* 55°45N 2°0W **66** F6
Tweed Heads *Australia* 28°10S 153°31E **155** D5
Tweedsmuir △ *Canada* 53°0N 126°20W **162** C3
Twentynine Palms *U.S.A.* 34°8N 116°3W **171** L10
Twillingate *Canada* 49°42N 54°45W **165** C9
Twin Bridges *U.S.A.* 45°33N 112°20W **168** D7
Twin City *U.S.A.* 32°35N 82°10W **178** C7
Twin Falls *Canada* 53°30N 64°32W **165** B7
Twin Falls *U.S.A.* 42°34N 114°28W **168** E6
Twin Lakes *U.S.A.* 30°43N 83°13W **178** G6
Twin Valley *U.S.A.* 47°16N 96°16W **172** B5
Twinsburg *U.S.A.* 41°19N 81°26W **174** E3
Twistringen *Germany* 52°48N 8°37E **76** C4
Twitchell Res. *U.S.A.* 34°59N 120°19W **171** L6
Two Harbors *U.S.A.* 47°2N 91°40W **172** B8
Two Hills *Canada* 53°43N 111°52W **162** C6
Two Rivers *U.S.A.* 44°9N 87°34W **172** C10
Two Rocks *Australia* 31°30S 115°35E **149** F2
Two Thumb Ra. *N.Z.* 43°45S 170°44E **155** D5
Twofold B. *Australia* 37°8S 149°59E **153** D8
Twyfelfontein *Namibia* 20°34S 14°22E **144** B1
Ty Ty *U.S.A.* 31°28N 83°39W **178** D6
Tyachiv *Ukraine* 48°1N 23°35E **75** D12
Tybee Island *U.S.A.* 32°1N 80°51W **178** C9
Tychy *Poland* 50°9N 18°59E **83** H5
Tyczyn *Poland* 49°58N 22°2E **83** J9
Tykocin *Poland* 53°13N 22°46E **83** E9
Tyler *Minn., U.S.A.* 44°17N 96°8W **172** C5
Tyler *Tex., U.S.A.* 32°21N 95°18W **176** E7
Tyligul → *Ukraine* 47°4N 30°57E **85** J6
Tymanivka *Ukraine* 48°34N 28°52E **81** B13
Týn nad Vltavou *Czech Rep.* 49°13N 14°26E **78** B7
Tynda *Russia* 55°10N 124°43E **107** D13
Tyndall *U.S.A.* 42°59N 97°50W **172** D5
Tyne → *U.K.* 54°59N 1°32W **66** C6
Tyne & Wear □ *U.K.* 55°6N 1°17W **66** B6
Týnec nad Sázavou *Czech Rep.* 49°13N 14°26E **78** B7
Tynemouth *U.K.* 55°1N 1°26W **66** B6
Tyre = Sūr *Lebanon* 33°19N 35°16E **130** B4
Tyresta △ *Sweden* 59°12N 18°14E **62** E12
Tyrifjorden *Norway* 60°2N 10°8E **61** F14
Tyringe *Sweden* 56°9N 13°35E **63** H7
Tyrnyauz *Russia* 43°21N 42°45E **87** J6
Tyrol = Tirol □ *Austria* 47°3N 10°43E **78** D3
Tyrone *U.S.A.* 40°40N 78°14W **174** F6
Tyrone □ *U.K.* 54°38N 7°11W **64** B4
Tyrrell → *Australia* 35°26S 142°51E **152** C5
Tyrrell, L. *Australia* 35°20S 142°50E **152** C5
Tyrrell L. *Canada* 63°7N 105°27W **163** A7
Tyrrhenian Sea *Medit.* 40°0N 12°30E **58** G8
Tysfjorden *Norway* 68°7N 16°25E **60** B17
Tysmenytsya *Ukraine* 48°54N 24°51E **81** B9
Tystberga *Sweden* 58°51N 17°15E **63** F11
Tytuvėnai *Lithuania* 55°36N 23°12E **82** C10
Tyub Karagan, Mys = Tüpqarghan Muyis *Kazakhstan* 44°40N 50°19E **87** H10
Tyuleni, Ostrova = Tüledi Araldary *Kazakhstan* 45°2N 50°16E **87** H10
Tyuleniy *Russia* 44°28N 47°30E **87** H8
Tyuleniy, Mys *Azerbaijan* 40°12N 50°22E **87** K10
Tyumen *Russia* 57°11N 65°29E **108** D7
Tyup = Tüp *Kyrgyzstan* 42°45N 78°20E **109** D9
Tywi → *U.K.* 51°48N 4°21W **67** F3
Tywyn *U.K.* 52°35N 4°5W **67** E3
Tzaneen *S. Africa* 23°47S 30°9E **145** B5
Tzermiado *Greece* 35°12N 25°29E **101** D7
Tzoumérka, Óros = Athamanon Óros *Greece* 39°30N 21°26E **98** B3
Tzukong = Zigong *China* 29°15N 104°48E **116** C5

U

U.S.A. = United States of America ■ *N. Amer.* 37°0N 96°0W **167** H20
U.S. Virgin Is. ☑ *W. Indies* 18°20N 65°0W **183** e
Uaimh, An = Navan *Ireland* 53°39N 6°41W **64** C5
Uanle Uen = Wanleweyne *Somalia* 2°37N 44°54E **131** G3
Uasin Gishu □ *Kenya* 0°30N 35°15E **142** B4
Uatumã → *Brazil* 2°26S 57°37W **186** D7
Uauá *Brazil* 9°50S 39°28W **189** D3
Uaupés *Brazil* 0°8S 67°5W **186** D5
Uaupés → *Brazil* 0°2N 67°16W **186** C5
Uaxactún *Guatemala* 17°25N 89°29W **182** C2
Ubá *Brazil* 21°8S 43°0W **191** A7
Ubá *Nigeria* 10°29N 13°13E **139** C8
Ubaitaba *Brazil* 14°18S 39°20W **189** D3
Ubajara *Brazil* 3°55S 40°50W **189** A2
Ubangi = Oubangi → *Dem. Rep. of the Congo* 0°30S 17°50E **140** E3
Ubauro *Pakistan* 28°15N 69°45E **124** E3
Ubaye → *France* 44°28N 6°18E **73** D7
Ubayyid, W. al → *Iraq* 32°34N 43°48E **105** F10

Ube *Japan* 33°56N 131°15E **113** H5
Úbeda *Spain* 38°3N 3°23W **89** G7
Uberaba *Brazil* 19°50S 47°55W **189** D1
Uberlândia *Brazil* 19°0S 48°20W **189** D1
Überlingen *Germany* 47°46N 9°10E **77** H5
Ubiaja *Nigeria* 6°41N 6°22E **139** D6
Ubin, Pulau *Singapore* 1°24N 103°57E **121** d
Ubly *U.S.A.* 43°42N 82°55W **174** C2
Ubolratna Res. *Thailand* 16°45N 102°30E **120** D4
Ubombo *S. Africa* 27°31S 32°4E **145** C5
Ubon Ratchathani *Thailand* 15°15N 104°50E **120** E5
Ubondo *Dem. Rep. of the Congo* 0°55S 25°42E **142** C2
Ubort → *Belarus* 52°6N 28°30E **75** B15
Ubrique *Spain* 36°41N 5°27W **89** J5
Ubud *Indonesia* 8°30S 115°16E **119** J18
Ubundu *Dem. Rep. of the Congo* 0°22S 25°30E **142** C2
Ucar *Azerbaijan* 40°31N 47°39E **87** K8
Ucayali → *Peru* 4°30S 73°30W **188** A3
Uchab *Namibia* 19°47S 17°42E **144** A2
Uchiura-Wan *Japan* 42°25N 140°40E **112** C10
Uchiza *Peru* 8°25S 76°20W **188** B2
Uchquduq *Uzbekistan* 41°50N 62°50E **108** D6
Uchte *Germany* 52°30N 8°54E **76** C4
Uchur → *Russia* 58°48N 130°35E **107** D14
Uckermark *Germany* 53°5N 13°30E **76** B9
Ucluelet *Canada* 48°57N 125°32W **162** D3
Uda → *Russia* 54°42N 135°14E **107** D14
Uda Walawe △ *Sri Lanka* 6°20N 81°0E **127** L5
Udachnyy *Russia* 66°25N 112°24E **107** C12
Udagamandalam *India* 11°30N 76°44E **127** J3
Udainagar *India* 22°33N 76°13E **124** H7
Udaipur *India* 24°36N 73°44E **124** G5
Udaipur Garhi *Nepal* 27°0N 86°35E **125** F12
Udala *India* 21°35N 86°34E **125** J12
Udayagiri *Andhra Pradesh, India* 14°52N 79°19E **127** G4
Udayagiri *Odisha, India* 20°8N 84°23E **126** D7
Udbina *Croatia* 44°31N 15°47E **80** F4
Uddeholm *Sweden* 60°1N 13°38E **62** D7
Uddevalla *Sweden* 58°21N 11°55E **63** F5
Uddheden *Sweden* 59°57N 12°54E **62** E6
Uddjaure *Sweden* 65°56N 17°49E **60** D17
Udgir *India* 18°25N 77°5E **126** E3
Udhampur *India* 33°0N 75°5E **126** C6
Udi *Nigeria* 6°17N 7°21E **139** D6
Údine *Italy* 46°3N 13°14E **93** B10
Udintsev Fracture Zone *S. Ocean* 57°0S 145°0W **55** B13
Udmurtia □ *Russia* 57°30N 52°30E **86** C9
Udon Thani *Thailand* 17°29N 102°46E **120** D4
Udong *Cambodia* 11°48N 104°45E **121** G5
Udskaya Guba *Russia* 54°50N 135°45E **107** D14
Udu Pt. *Fiji* 16°9S 179°57W **154** a
Udumalaippettai *India* 10°35N 77°15E **127** J3
Udupi *India* 13°25N 74°42E **127** H2
Udvoy Balkan *Bulgaria* 42°50N 26°50E **97** D10
Udzungwa Range *Tanzania* 9°30S 35°10E **143** D4
Udzungwa △ *Tanzania* 7°52S 36°35E **142** D4
Ueckermünde *Germany* 53°44N 14°1E **76** B10
Ueda *Japan* 36°24N 138°16E **113** F9
Uedineniya, Os. *Russia* 78°0N 85°0E **54** B12
Uele → *Dem. Rep. of the Congo* 3°45N 24°45E **140** D4
Uelen *Russia* 66°10N 170°0W **107** C19
Uelzen *Germany* 52°57N 10°32E **76** C6
Uetersen *Germany* 53°40N 9°40E **76** B5
Uetze *Germany* 52°28N 10°11E **76** C6
Ufa *Russia* 54°45N 55°55E **86** D10
Ufa → *Russia* 54°40N 56°0E **86** D10
Uffenheim *Germany* 49°33N 10°14E **77** F6
Ugab → *Namibia* 20°55S 13°30E **144** B1
Ugalla → *Tanzania* 5°8S 30°42E **142** D3
Ugalla River △ *Tanzania* 5°50S 31°54E **142** D3
Uganda ■ *Africa* 2°0N 32°0E **142** B3
Ugchin *Russia* 59°33N 38°18E **84** C10
Ugep *Nigeria* 5°53N 8°2E **139** D6
Ughelli *Nigeria* 5°30N 6°0E **139** D6
Ugie *S. Africa* 31°10S 28°13E **145** D4
Ugijar *Spain* 36°58N 3°7W **89** J7
Ugine *France* 45°45N 6°25E **73** C10
Uglegorsk *Russia* 49°5N 142°2E **107** E15
Uglich *Russia* 57°33N 38°20E **84** D10
Ugljan *Croatia* 44°12N 15°10E **80** G4
Ugljane *Croatia* 43°35N 16°46E **93** E13
Ugolnye Kopi *Russia* 64°44N 177°42E **107** C18
Ugra → *Russia* 54°30N 36°7E **84** E9
Ugürchin *Bulgaria* 43°6N 24°26E **97** C8
Uh → *Slovak Rep.* 48°7N 22°0E **79** C15
Uherské Hradiště *Czech Rep.* 49°4N 17°30E **79** B9
Uherský Brod *Czech Rep.* 49°1N 17°40E **79** B9
Uhlava → *Czech Rep.* 49°45N 13°24E **78** B6
Uhlenhorst *Namibia* 23°45S 17°55E **144** B2
Uhrichsville *U.S.A.* 40°24N 81°21W **174** F3

Uka *Russia* 57°50N 162°0E **107** D17
Ukai Sagar *India* 21°20N 73°43E **126** D1
Ukara I. *Tanzania* 1°50S 33°0E **142** C3
Uke-Shima *Japan* 28°2N 129°14E **113** a
Ukerewe I. *Tanzania* 2°0S 33°0E **142** C3
uKhahlamba Drakensberg □ *S. Africa* 29°27S 29°30E **145** D4
Ukholovo *Russia* 53°47N 40°30E **86** D7
Ukhrul *India* 25°10N 94°25E **123** G7
Ukhta *Russia* 63°34N 53°41E **106** C9
Ukiah *U.S.A.* 39°9N 123°13W **170** F3
Ukkusiksalik △ *Canada* 65°20N 89°30W **160** D7
Ukmergė *Lithuania* 55°15N 24°45E **84** D4
Ukraine ■ *Europe* 49°0N 32°0E **85** H6
Ukwi *Botswana* 23°29S 20°30E **144** C3
Ula *Turkey* 37°6N 28°25E **99** D10
Ulaan Nuur *Mongolia* 44°30N 103°40E **114** C2
Ulaan-Uul *Mongolia* 46°40N 92°10E **110** B7
Ulaanbaatar *Mongolia* 47°55N 106°53E **110** B9
Ulaangom *Mongolia* 50°5N 92°10E **110** A7
Ulaanjirem *Mongolia* 45°5N 105°30E **114** B3
Ulak I. *U.S.A.* 51°22N 178°57W **166** d
Ulamambri *Australia* 31°19S 149°23E **153** B8
Ulamba *Dem. Rep. of the Congo* 9°3S 23°38E **143** D1
Ulan Bator = Ulaanbaatar *Mongolia* 47°55N 106°53E **110** B9
Ulan Erge *Russia* 46°19N 44°53E **87** H7
Ulan Khol *Russia* 45°18N 47°4E **87** J8
Ulan Ude *Russia* 51°45N 107°40E **111** A9
Ulanhad = Chifeng *China* 42°18N 118°58E **115** C6
Ulanów *Poland* 50°30N 22°16E **83** H9
Ulansuhai Nur *China* 40°53N 108°51E **114** D5
Ulaş *Sivas, Turkey* 39°26N 37°2E **104** C7
Ulaş *Tekirdağ, Turkey* 41°14N 27°42E **97** E11
Ulaya *Morogoro, Tanzania* 7°3S 36°55E **142** D4
Ulaya *Tabora, Tanzania* 4°25S 33°30E **142** C3
Ulcinj *Montenegro* 41°58N 19°10E **96** D3
Ulco *S. Africa* 28°21S 24°15E **144** D3
Ule älv = Oulujoki → *Finland* 65°1N 25°30E **60** D21
Ule träsk = Oulujärvi *Finland* 64°25N 27°15E **60** D22
Uleåborg = Oulu *Finland* 65°1N 25°29E **60** D21
Ulefoss *Norway* 59°17N 9°16E **61** G6
Uleşa *Albania* 41°46N 19°54E **96** E4
Ulfborg *Denmark* 56°16N 8°20E **63** H2
Ulhasnagar *India* 19°15N 73°10E **126** F1
Uliastay *Mongolia* 47°56N 97°28E **110** B8
Uljin *S. Korea* 36°59N 129°24E **115** F15
Uljma *Serbia* 45°2N 21°10E **80** D5
Ülken Kazakhstan *Kazakhstan* 46°51N 73°58E **109** D8
Ülken Borsyq Qumy *Kazakhstan* 47°50N 59°11E **108**
Ulla → *Spain* 42°39N 8°44W **88** C2
Ulladulla *Australia* 35°21S 150°29E **153** C9
Ullal *India* 12°48N 74°51E **127**
Ullapool *U.K.* 57°54N 5°9W **65** D3
Ullared *Sweden* 57°8N 12°42E **63**
Ulldecona *Spain* 40°36N 0°20E **90**
Ulleungdo *S. Korea* 37°30N 130°30E **113**
Ullswater *Canada* 45°12N 79°29W **174**
Ullswater *U.K.* 54°34N 2°52W **66**
Ulm *Germany* 48°23N 9°58E **77**
Ulmarra *Australia* 29°37S 153°4E **155**
Ulmeni *Buzău, Romania* 45°4N 26°42E **81**
Ulmeni *Maramureș, Romania* 47°28N 23°18E **81**
Ulonguè *Mozam.* 14°37S 34°19E **143**
Ulricehamn *Sweden* 57°46N 13°26E **63**
Ulrika *Sweden* 58°5N 15°23E **63**
Ulsan *S. Korea* 35°20N 129°15E **115**
Ulsta *U.K.* 60°30N 1°9W **65**
Ulster □ *U.K.* 54°35N 6°30W **64**
Ulstrem *Bulgaria* 42°1N 26°27E **97**
Ultima *Australia* 35°30S 143°18E **152**
Ulubat Gölü *Turkey* 40°9N 28°35E **97**
Ulubey *Turkey* 38°25N 29°29E **99**
Uluborlu *Turkey* 38°5N 30°27E **99**
Uluçinar *Turkey* 36°24N 35°53E **104**
Uludağ *Turkey* 40°4N 29°13E **97**
Uludağ △ *Turkey* 40°8N 29°10E **99**
Ulugqat *China* 39°48N 74°15E **109**
Uluguru Mts. *Tanzania* 7°15S 37°40E **142**
Ulukhaktok *Canada* 70°44N 117°44W **160**
Ulukışla = Marathóvounos *Cyprus* 35°13N 33°37E **101**
Ulukışla *Turkey* 37°34N 34°28E **104**
Ulundi *S. Africa* 28°21S 31°23E **145**
Ulungur He → *China* 47°1N 87°24E **110**
Ulungur Hu *China* 47°20N 87°10E **110**
Uluru *Australia* 25°23S 131°5E **149**
Uluru-Kata Tjuta △ *Australia* 25°19S 131°1E **149**
Uluwatu *Indonesia* 8°50S 115°5E **119**
Ulva *U.K.* 56°29N 6°13W **66**
Ulverston *U.K.* 54°13N 3°5W **66**
Ulverstone *Australia* 41°11S 146°11E **151**
Ulya → *Russia* 59°11N 142°0E **107**
Ulyanovo *Russia* 54°9N 20°40E **82**
Ulyanovsk *Russia* 54°20N 48°25E **86**
Ulyanovsk □ *Russia* 54°5N 48°5E **86**
Ulyasutay = Uliastay *Mongolia* 47°56N 97°28E **110**
Ulysses *Kans., U.S.A.* 37°35N 101°22W **172**
Ulysses *Pa., U.S.A.* 41°54N 77°46W **174**
Ulysses, Mt. *Canada* 57°20N 124°5W **162**
Uŋia Mts. *Russia* 64°10N 62°0E **108**
Uŋia *Namibia* 21°8S 14°49E **144**
Uŋzhylanshyq → *Kazakhstan* 48°51N 63°46E **108**
Umag *Croatia* 45°26N 13°31E **93**
Umala *Bolivia* 17°25S 68°5W **188**
'Umān = Oman ■ *Asia* 23°0N 58°0E **132**
Umán *Mexico* 20°53N 89°44W **181**
Umaria *India* 23°35N 80°50E **125**
Umarkhed *India* 19°37N 77°46E **126**
Umarkot *Pakistan* 25°15N 69°40E **124**
Umarpada *India* 21°27N 73°30E **126**
Umatilla *U.S.A.* 28°56N 81°40W **178**
Umba *Russia* 66°50N 34°20E **58**
Umbagog L. *U.S.A.* 44°46N 71°4W **175**
Umbakumba *Australia* 13°47S 136°50E **150**
Umbértide *Italy* 43°18N 12°20E **92**
Umbrella Mts. *N.Z.* 45°35S 169°5E **155**
Umbria □ *Italy* 42°43N 12°30E **92**
Umeå *Sweden* 63°45N 20°20E **60**

ëlven → Sweden 63°45N 20°20E 60 E19
era Indonesia 0°12S 129°37E 119 E7
uli → Zimbabwe 17°30S 29°23E 143 F2
urudzi → Zimbabwe 17°6S 31°40E 143 F3
gusa Zimbabwe 19°29S 27°52E 143 F2
gwenya → Mozam. 25°14S 32°18E 145 C5
ujaq Canada 56°33N 76°33W 164 A4
cka Serbia 44°40N 20°19E 96 B4
azi S. Africa 30°13S 30°48E 145 D5
azi S. Africa 29°59S 30°54E 141 L6
n ad Daraj, J. Libya 32°18N 35°48E 130 C4
n al Khashab Jordan 17°23N 42°32E 137 D5
n al Qaywayn U.A.E. 25°30N 55°35E 129 E7
n al Qittayn Jordan 32°18N 36°40E 130 C5
n al Rasas Jordan 31°30N 35°55E 130 D4
n Bāb Qatar 25°12N 50°48E 129 E6
n Birkah Si. Arabia 27°44N 36°31E 137 B4
n Durman = Omdurmân Sudan 15°40N 32°28E 135 E12
n el Fahm Israel 32°31N 35°9E 130 C4
n el Ketef, Khalig Egypt 23°40N 35°35E 128 F2
n Keddada Sudan 13°33N 26°35E 135 F11
n Lajj Si. Arabia 25°0N 37°23E 128 D3
n Qasr Iraq 30°1N 47°58E 128 D5
n Ruwaba Sudan 12°50N 31°20E 135 F12
n Sa'id Qatar 25°0N 51°33E 129 E6
n Tais □ Qatar 26°7N 51°15E 129 E6
n Urūmah . Arabia 25°43N 36°35E 137 B4
n Zehetir Egypt 28°48N 32°31E 137 B8
miati → Zimbabwe 16°49S 28°45E 143 F2
qua → U.S.A. 43°40N 124°12W 168 E1
red India 20°51N 79°18E 126 D4
reth India 22°41N 73°4E 124 H5
ri India 19°2N 77°39E 126 E4
tata = Mthatha Africa 31°36S 28°49E 145 D4
uahia Nigeria 5°31N 7°26E 139 D6
uarama Brazil 23°45S 53°0W 191 A4
urbey Turkey 40°13N 26°36E 97 F10
yukwe Ra. Africa 16°45S 30°45E 143 F3
zimvubu S. Africa 31°38S 29°33E 145 D4
zingwane → mbabwe 22°12S 29°56E 143 G2
zinto = eMuziwezinto Africa 30°15S 30°45E 145 D5
India 20°46N 71°8E 124 J4
→ Bos.-H. 45°0N 16°20E 93 D13
Bos.-H. 44°30N 16°9E 93 D13
dilla Ga., U.S.A. 32°16N 83°44W 178 D6
dilla N.Y., U.S.A. 42°20N 75°19W 175 D9
haí Brazil 16°23S 46°53W 189 D7
lakleet U.S.A. 63°52N 160°47W 166 C7
laska U.S.A. 53°53N 166°32W 166 E6
laska I. U.S.A. 53°35N 166°50W 166 E6
layhah, J. Asia 26°6N 43°58E 128 E4
layzah, J. Asia 32°12N 39°18E 105 F8
castillo Spain 42°21N 1°8W 90 C3
a Bolivia 18°25S 66°40W 186 G5
ompahgre Peak .S.A. 38°4N 107°28W 168 G10
ompahgre Plateau .S.A. 38°20N 108°15W 168 G9
lara Volcanic △ stralia 18°14S 144°41E 150 B3
len Sweden 58°45N 14°25E 63 F8
lerbool Australia 35°10S 141°51E 152 C4
lersaker Sweden 63°19N 13°21E 62 A7
lerwood Canada 44°18N 81°29W 174 B3
echa Russia 52°50N 32°37E 85 F7
garie Australia 33°38S 146°56E 153 B7
cha Australia 34°12S 136°2E 152 C2
gava, Pén. d' Canada 60°0N 74°0W 161 F17
gava B. Canada 59°30N 67°30W 161 F18
= Ungheni Moldova 47°11N 27°51E 81 C12
gi N. Korea 42°16N 130°28E 115 C16
gheni Moldova 47°11N 27°51E 81 C12
guja = Zanzibar anzania 6°12S 39°12E 142 D4
gwana B. Kenya 2°45S 40°20E 142 C5
Russia 57°46N 51°13E 86 B10
ão Brazil 4°35S 42°52W 189 A2
ão dos Palmares Brazil 9°10S 36°2W 189 B3
čov Czech Rep. 49°46N 17°58E 79 B10
ejów Poland 51°59N 18°46E 83 G5
je Croatia 44°40N 14°15E 93 D11
mak I. U.S.A. 54°45N 164°0W 166 E7
imak Pass. U.S.A. 54°15N 164°30W 166 E7
on Miss., U.S.A. 32°34N 89°7W 177 E11
on Mo., U.S.A. 38°27N 91°0W 172 F8
on S.C., U.S.A. 34°43N 81°37W 177 D14
on City Calif., .S.A. 37°36N 122°1W 170 H4
on City Ga., U.S.A. 33°35N 84°33W 178 B5
on City N.J., U.S.A. 40°45N 74°2W 175 F10
on City Pa., .S.A. 41°54N 79°51W 174 E5
ion City Tenn., .S.A. 36°26N 89°3W 177 C10
ion Gap U.S.A. 46°33N 120°28W 168 C3
ion Park U.S.A. 28°34N 81°17W 178 G5
ion Point U.S.A. 38°37N 83°44W 178 B6
ion Springs Ala., .S.A. 32°9N 85°43W 178 C4
ion Springs N.Y., .S.A. 32°50N 85°43W 178 C4
iondale S. Africa 33°39S 23°7E 144 D3
iontown U.S.A. 34°5N 79°44W 173 F14
ionville Ga., U.S.A. 31°26N 83°30W 178 D6
ionville Mo., U.S.A. 40°29N 93°1W 172 E7
irea Indonesia 8°4S 139°9E 81 F12
ited Arab Emirates ■ Asia 23°50N 54°0E 129 F7
ited Kingdom ■ Europe 53°0N 2°0W 68 E6
ited States of America ■ N. Amer. 37°0N 96°0W 167 H20
iv Canada 52°30N 109°5W 163 C7
iversales, Mtes. Spain 40°18N 1°33W 90 E3
iversity Park .S.A. 32°17N 106°45W 169 K10
iversity Place .S.A. 47°14N 122°33W 170 C4

Unjha India 23°46N 72°24E 124 H5
Unna Germany 51°32N 7°42E 76 D3
Unnao India 26°35N 80°30E 125 F9
Uno, Ilha Guinea-Biss. 11°15N 16°13W 138 C1
Unsengedsi → Zimbabwe 15°43S 31°14E 143 F3
Unst U.K. 60°44N 0°53W 65 A8
Unstrut → Germany 51°10N 11°48E 76 D7
Unterfranken □ Germany 50°0N 10°0E 77 F5
Unterschleissheim Germany 48°17N 11°34E 77 G7
Unuk → Canada 56°5N 131°3W 162 B2
Ünye Turkey 41°5N 37°15E 104 B7
Unzen-Amakusa △ Japan 32°15N 130°10E 113 H5
Unzha Russia 58°0N 44°0E 86 A7
Unzha → Russia 57°49N 43°47E 86 B6
Uong Bi Vietnam 21°2N 106°47E 120 B6
Uotsuri-Shima E. China Sea 25°45N 123°29E 113 M1
Uozu Japan 36°48N 137°24E 113 F8
Upata Venezuela 8°1N 62°24W 186 B6
Upatoi Cr. → U.S.A. 32°22N 84°58W 178 C5
Upemba, L. Dem. Rep. of the Congo 8°30S 26°20E 143 D2
Upemba △ Dem. Rep. of the Congo 9°0S 26°35E 143 D2
Upernavik Greenland 72°49N 56°20W 57 C5
Upington S. Africa 28°25S 21°15E 144 C3
Upleta India 21°46N 70°16E 124 J4
'Upolu Samoa 13°58S 172°0W 147 C11
Upper Alkali L. U.S.A. 41°47N 120°8W 168 F3
Upper Arrow L. Canada 50°30N 117°50W 162 C5
Upper Daly ☉ Australia 14°26S 131°3E 148 B5
Upper Darby U.S.A. 39°55N 75°16W 173 F16
Upper East □ Ghana 10°30N 1°0W 139 C4
Upper Foster L. Canada 56°47N 105°20W 163 B7
Upper Hutt N.Z. 41°8S 175°5E 154 H4
Upper Klamath L. U.S.A. 42°25N 121°55W 168 E3
Upper Lake U.S.A. 39°10N 122°54W 170 F4
Upper Liard Canada 60°3N 128°54W 162 A3
Upper Manilla Australia 30°38S 150°40E 153 A9
Upper Manzanilla Trin. & Tob. 10°31N 61°4W 187 K15
Upper Missouri Breaks △ U.S.A. 47°50N 109°55W 168 C9
Upper Musquodoboit Canada 45°10N 62°58W 165 C7
Upper Red L. U.S.A. 48°8N 94°45W 172 A6
Upper Sandusky U.S.A. 40°50N 83°17W 173 E12
Upper Volta = Burkina Faso ■ Africa 12°0N 1°0W 138 C4
Upper West □ Ghana 10°30N 2°0W 138 C4
Upphärad Sweden 58°9N 12°19E 63 F6
Uppland Sweden 59°59N 17°48E 62 D12
Upplands-Väsby Sweden 59°31N 17°54E 62 E11
Uppsala Sweden 59°53N 17°38E 62 D11
Uppsala □ Sweden 60°0N 17°30E 62 D11
Upshi India 33°48N 77°52E 125 C7
Upton U.S.A. 44°6N 104°38W 168 D11

Urkiola △ Spain 43°6N 1°2W 90 B3
Urla Turkey 38°20N 26°47E 99 C8
Urlaţi Romania 44°59N 26°15E 81 F11
Urmia = Orūmīyeh Iran 37°40N 45°0E 105 D11
Uromi Nigeria 6°42N 6°20E 139 D6
Uroševac = Ferizaj Kosovo 42°23N 21°10E 96 C5
Ürotteppa = Istaravshan Tajikistan 39°55N 69°1E 109 E7
Uroyan, Montanas de Puerto Rico 18°12N 66°50W 183 d
Urrampinyi Iltjiltarri ☉ Australia 24°20S 132°10E 148 D5
Urshult Sweden 56°31N 14°50E 63 H8
Uru Uru, L. Bolivia 18°6S 67°8W 186 H4
Uruaçu Brazil 14°30S 49°10W 187 F9
Uruapan Mexico 19°24N 102°3W 180 D4
Urubamba Peru 13°20S 72°10W 188 C3
Urubamba → Peru 10°43S 73°48W 188 B3
Urucará Brazil 2°32S 57°45W 186 D7
Uruçuí Brazil 7°20S 44°28W 189 B2
Uruçuí, Serra do Brazil 9°0S 44°45W 189 B2
Uruçuí Prêto → Brazil 7°20S 44°38W 189 B2
Urucuia → Brazil 16°8S 45°5W 191 B5
Uruguai → Brazil 26°0S 53°30W 191 B5
Uruguaiana Brazil 29°50S 57°0W 190 B4
Uruguay ■ S. Amer. 32°30S 56°30W 190 C4
Uruguay → S. Amer. 34°12S 58°18W 190 C4
Urumchi = Ürümqi China 43°45N 87°45E 109 D11
Ürümqi China 43°45N 87°45E 109 D11
Uruna ☉ Australia 24°3S 133°1E 148 D5
Urup → Russia 46°0N 41°10E 87 H5
Urup, Ostrov Russia 46°0N 151°0E 107 E16
Urus-Martan Russia 43°8N 45°33E 87 J7
Urutai Brazil 17°28S 48°12W 189 D1
Uryupinsk Russia 50°45N 41°58E 86 E5
Ürzhar Kazakhstan 47°5N 81°38E 109 C10
Urzhum Russia 57°10N 49°56E 86 B9
Urziceni Romania 44°40N 26°42E 81 F11
Usa → Russia 66°16N 59°49E 106 C6
Uşak Turkey 38°43N 29°28E 99 C11
Uşak □ Turkey 38°30N 29°0E 99 C11
Usakos Namibia 21°54S 15°31E 144 B2
Usborne, Mt. Falk. Is. 51°35S 59°5W 192 D5
Ušče Serbia 43°30N 20°39E 96 C4
Usedom Germany 53°55N 14°2E 76 B10
Usedom △ Germany 53°55N 14°0E 76 B10
Useless Loop Australia 26°8S 113°23E 149 E1
'Usfān Si. Arabia 21°58N 39°27E 137 C4
Ushakova, Ostrov Russia 82°0N 80°0E 107 A8
Ushakovo Russia 54°37N 20°16E 82 D7
Ushant = Ouessant, Î. d' France 48°28N 5°6W 70 D1
Ushʿal Kazakhstan 46°10N 80°56E 109 C10
Ushashi Tanzania 1°59S 33°57E 142 C3
'Ushayrah Ar Riyāḍ, Si. Arabia 25°35N 45°47E 128 E5
'Ushayrah Makkah, Si. Arabia 21°46N 40°42E 128 E3
Ushibuka Japan 32°11N 130°1E 113 H5
Üshtöbe Kazakhstan 45°16N 78°0E 109 C9
Ushuaia Argentina 54°50S 68°23W 192 D3
Ushumun Russia 52°47N 126°32E 107 D13
Ushytsya → Ukraine 48°35N 27°8E 81 B12
Usinsk Russia 65°57N 57°27E 106 C6
Usk Canada 54°38N 128°26W 162 C3
Usk → U.K. 51°33N 2°58W 67 F5
Uska India 27°12N 83°7E 125 F10
Üsküdar Turkey 41°1N 29°0E 97 F13
Uslar Germany 51°39N 9°38E 76 D5
Usman Russia 52°5N 39°48E 85 F10
Usoke Tanzania 5°8S 32°24E 142 D3
Usolye-Sibirskoye Russia 52°48N 103°40E 107 D11
Usoro Nigeria 5°33N 6°11E 139 D6
Uspallata, P. de Argentina 32°37S 69°22W 190 C2
Ussel France 45°32N 2°18E 72 D6
Usson-du-Poitou France 46°16N 0°31E 72 B4
Ussuriysk Russia 43°48N 131°59E 112 C5
Ussurka Russia 45°12N 133°31E 112 B6
Ust-Buzulukskaya Russia 50°8N 42°11E 86 E6
Ust-Chaun Russia 68°47N 170°30E 107 C18
Ust-Chorna Ukraine 48°19N 23°56E 81 B8
Ust-Donetskiy Russia 47°35N 40°55E 87 G5
Ust-Dzheguta Russia 44°5N 41°58E 87 H5
Ust-Ilimsk Russia 58°3N 102°39E 107 D11
Ust-Ishim Russia 57°45N 71°10E 106 D8
Ust-Kamchatsk Russia 56°10N 162°28E 107 D17
Ust-Kamenogorsk = Öskemen Kazakhstan 50°0N 82°36E 109 C10
Ust-Khayryuzovo Russia 57°15N 156°45E 107 D16
Ust-Kut Russia 56°50N 105°42E 107 D11
Ust-Kuyga Russia 70°1N 135°43E 107 B14
Ust-Labinsk Russia 45°15N 39°41E 87 H4
Ust-Luga Russia 59°35N 28°20E 84 C5
Ust-Maya Russia 60°30N 134°28E 107 C14
Ust-Mil Russia 59°40N 133°11E 107 D14
Ust-Nera Russia 64°35N 143°0E 107 C15
Ust-Nyukzha Russia 56°34N 121°37E 107 D13
Ust-Olenek Russia 73°0N 120°5E 107 B12
Ust-Omchug Russia 61°9N 149°38E 107 C15
Ust-Port Russia 69°40N 84°26E 106 C9
Ust-Tsilma Russia 65°28N 52°11E 106 C6
Ust-Urt = Ustyurt Plateau Asia 44°0N 55°0E 108 D6
Ustaritz France 43°24N 1°27W 72 E2
Ustecký □ Czech Rep. 50°30N 14°0E 78 A7
Uster Switz. 47°22N 8°43E 77 H4
Ústí nad Labem Czech Rep. 50°41N 14°3E 78 A7
Ústí nad Orlicí Czech Rep. 49°58N 16°24E 78 B9
Ústica Italy 38°42N 13°11E 94 D6
Ustinov = Izhevsk Russia 56°51N 53°14E 106 D6
Ustka Poland 54°35N 16°55E 82 D3
Ustroń Poland 49°43N 18°48E 83 D5
Ustrzyki Dolne Poland 49°27N 22°40E 83 J9
Ustyluh Ukraine 50°51N 24°10E 83 H11
Ustyurt Plateau Asia 44°0N 55°0E 108 D6
Ustyuzhna Russia 58°50N 36°32E 84 B10
Usu China 44°27N 84°40E 109 D10
Usuki Japan 33°8N 131°49E 113 H5
Usulután El Salv. 13°25N 88°28W 182 D2
Usumacinta → Mexico 18°24N 92°38W 181 D6
Usumbura = Bujumbura Burundi 3°16S 29°18E 142 C2

Usure Tanzania 4°40S 34°22E 142 D3
Usutuo → Mozam. 26°48S 32°7E 145 D5
Uta Indonesia 4°33S 136°0E 119 E9
Utah □ U.S.A. 39°20N 111°30W 168 G8
Utah L. U.S.A. 40°12N 111°48W 168 F8
Utarakhand □ India 30°0N 79°6E 125 D8
Utara, Selat Malaysia 5°28N 100°20E 121 c
Utarni India 26°5N 71°58E 124 F4
Utatlan Guatemala 15°2N 91°11W 182 C1
Ute Creek → U.S.A. 35°21N 103°50W 169 J12
Utebo Spain 41°43N 1°0W 90 D3
Utena Lithuania 55°27N 25°40E 84 E3
Utete Tanzania 8°0S 38°45E 142 D4
Uthai Thani Thailand 15°22N 100°3E 120 E3
Uthal Pakistan 25°44N 66°40E 124 G2
Utiariti Brazil 13°0S 58°10W 186 F7
Utica N.Y., U.S.A. 43°6N 75°14W 175 C9
Utica Ohio, U.S.A. 40°14N 82°27W 174 F2
Utiel Spain 39°37N 1°11W 91 F3
Utikuma L. Canada 55°50N 115°30W 162 B5
Utila Honduras 16°6N 86°56W 182 C2
Utinga Brazil 12°6S 41°5W 189 d
Utkela India 20°6N 83°10E 126 D6
Utlängen Sweden 56°2N 15°48E 63 H9
Utnur India 19°22N 78°46E 126 E4
Utō Sweden 58°56N 18°16E 62 F12
Utopia Australia 22°14S 134°33E 150 C1
Utraula India 27°19N 82°25E 125 F10
Utrecht Neths. 52°5N 5°8E 69 B5
Utrecht S. Africa 27°38S 30°20E 145 C5
Utrecht □ Neths. 52°6N 5°7E 69 B5
Utrera Spain 37°12N 5°48W 89 H5
Utsjoki → Finland 69°51N 26°59E 60 B22
Utsunomiya Japan 36°30N 139°50E 113 F9
Uttar Pradesh □ India 27°0N 80°0E 125 F9
Uttaradit Thailand 17°36N 100°5E 120 D3
Uttarakhand □ India 30°0N 79°30E 125 D8
Utterson Canada 45°12N 79°19W 174 A5
Uttoxeter U.K. 52°54N 1°52W 66 E6
Utuado Puerto Rico 18°16N 66°42W 183 d
Uummannaq Qaasuitsup, Greenland 70°58N 52°17W 54 B5
Uummannaq Qaasuitsup, Greenland 77°33N 68°52W 57 B4
Uummannarsuaq = Nunap Isua Greenland 59°48N 43°55W 57 F6
Uunartoq Qeqertaq Greenland 71°33N 21°47W 57 C8
Uusikaarlepyy Finland 63°32N 22°31E 60 E20
Uusikaupunki Finland 60°47N 21°25E 84 B1
Uva Russia 56°59N 52°13E 86 B11
Uvac → Serbia 43°35N 19°30E 96 C3
Uvalda U.S.A. 32°2N 82°31W 178 C7
Uvalde U.S.A. 29°13N 99°47W 176 G5
Uvarovo Russia 51°59N 42°14E 86 E6
Uvat Russia 59°5N 68°50E 106 D7
Uvinza Tanzania 5°5S 30°24E 142 D3
Uvira Dem. Rep. of the Congo 3°22S 29°3E 142 C2
Uvs □ Mongolia 49°38N 93°0E 109 C12
Uvs Nuur Mongolia 50°20N 92°30E 109 B12
'Uwairidh, Ḥarrat al Si. Arabia 26°50N 38°0E 128 E3
Uwajima Japan 33°10N 132°35E 113 H6
Uwanda ○ Tanzania 7°46S 32°0E 142 D3
Uweinat, Jebel Sudan 21°54N 24°58E 137 C1
Uxbridge Canada 44°6N 79°7W 174 B5
Uxin Qi China 38°50N 109°5E 114 E5
Uxmal Mexico 20°22N 89°46W 181 C7
Üydzin Mongolia 44°9N 107°0E 114 B4
Uyo Nigeria 5°1N 7°53E 139 D6
Üyüklü Tepe Turkey 37°5N 27°21E 99 D9
Uyūn Mūsa Egypt 29°53N 32°40E 130 F1
Uyuni Bolivia 20°28S 66°47W 188 E4
Uzbekistan ■ Asia 41°30N 65°0E 109 D7
Uzboy → Turkmenistan 39°30N 55°0E 129 B7
Uzen, Mal → Kazakhstan 49°4N 49°44E 87 F9
Uzerche France 45°25N 1°34E 72 C5
Uzès France 44°1N 4°26E 73 D8
Uzh → Ukraine 51°15N 30°12E 75 C16
Uzhgorod = Uzhhorod Ukraine 48°36N 22°18E 80 B7
Uzhhorod Ukraine 48°36N 22°18E 80 B7
Uzhok Ukraine 48°59N 22°52E 80 B7
Užice Serbia 43°55N 19°50E 96 C3
Üzümlü Turkey 36°44N 29°14E 99 E11
Uzunköprü Turkey 41°16N 26°43E 97 F10
Uzunkuyu Turkey 38°17N 26°33E 99 C8

V

Vaal → S. Africa 29°4S 23°38E 144 C3
Vaal Dam S. Africa 27°0S 28°14E 145 C4
Vaalwater S. Africa 24°15S 28°8E 145 B4
Vaasa Finland 63°6N 21°38E 60 E19
Vabre France 43°42N 2°24E 72 E6
Vác Hungary 47°49N 19°10E 80 C4
Vacaria Brazil 28°31S 50°52W 191 B5
Vacaville U.S.A. 38°21N 121°59W 170 G5
Vaccarès, Étang de France 43°32N 4°34E 73 E8
Vach = Vakh → Russia 60°45N 76°45E 106 C8
Vache, Î. à Haiti 18°2N 73°35W 183 C5
Väckelsång Sweden 56°37N 14°58E 63 H8
Vacoas Mauritius 20°18S 57°29E 144 d
Vada India 19°39N 73°8E 126 E1
Vadakara India 11°35N 75°40E 127 J2
Väddö Sweden 60°0N 18°50E 62 D12
Vadheim Norway 61°12N 5°49E 63 D2
Vadnagar India 23°47N 72°40E 124 H5
Vado Lígure Italy 44°16N 8°26E 92 D5
Vadodara India 22°20N 73°10E 124 H5
Vadsø Norway 70°3N 29°50E 60 A23
Vadstena Sweden 58°28N 14°54E 63 F8
Vaduj India 17°36N 74°27E 126 F2
Vaduz Liech. 47°8N 9°31E 77 H4
Vadvetjåkka △ Sweden 68°30N 18°28E 60 B18
Vágar Færoe Is. 62°5N 7°15W 60 E9
Vaggeryd Sweden 57°30N 14°10E 63 H8
Vaghia Greece 38°19N 23°11E 98 C5
Vagia, Ákra Greece 36°15N 28°11E 99 E10
Vagney France 48°1N 6°43E 71 D13
Vagnhärad Sweden 58°57N 17°33E 62 F11
Vágsfjorden Norway 68°50N 16°50E 60 B17
Váh → Slovak Rep. 47°43N 18°7E 79 D11

Vahsel B. Antarctica 75°0S 35°0W 55 D1
Váhtjer = Gällivare Sweden 67°9N 20°40E 60 C19
Vaï Greece 35°15N 26°18E 101 D8
Vaiaku = Fongafale Tuvalu 8°31S 179°13E 147 B10
Vaigai → India 9°15N 79°10E 127 K4
Vaihingen Germany 48°54N 8°57E 77 G4
Vaihiria, L. Tahiti 17°40S 149°25W 155 b
Vaijapur India 19°58N 74°45E 126 E2
Vaikam India 9°45N 76°25E 127 K3
Vail U.S.A. 39°40N 106°20W 168 G10
Vailly-sur-Aisne France 49°24N 3°31E 71 C10
Vaippar → India 9°0N 78°25E 127 K4
Vairao Tahiti 17°47S 149°17W 155 b
Vaisali → India 26°28N 78°53E 125 F8
Vaison-la-Romaine France 44°14N 5°4E 73 D9
Vajpur India 21°24N 73°17E 126 D1
Vakarai Sri Lanka 8°8N 81°26E 127 K5
Vakarel Bulgaria 42°35N 23°40E 96 D7
Vakfikebir Turkey 41°2N 39°17E 105 B8
Vakh → Russia 60°45N 76°45E 106 C8
Vakhsh → Tajikistan 37°6N 68°18E 109 E7
Vakhtan Russia 57°3N 46°47E 86 B8
Vál Hungary 47°22N 18°40E 80 C3
Val Camónica Italy 45°57N 10°17E 92 C7
Val-de-Marne □ France 48°45N 2°28E 71 D9
Val-d'Isère France 45°27N 6°59E 73 C10
Val-d'Oise □ France 49°5N 2°0E 71 C9
Val-d'Or Canada 48°7N 77°47W 164 C4
Val Grande ○ Italy 46°4N 8°30E 92 B5
Val Marie Canada 49°15N 107°45W 163 D7
Val Thorens France 45°20N 6°33E 73 C10
Valaam Russia 61°22N 30°57E 84 B6
Valadares Portugal 41°5N 8°38W 88 D2
Valahia Romania 44°35N 25°0E 83 F9
Valaichenai Sri Lanka 7°54N 81°32E 127 L5
Valais □ Switz. 46°12N 7°45E 77 J3
Valais, Alpes du Switz. 46°5N 7°35E 77 J3
Valandovo Macedonia 41°19N 22°34E 96 E6
Valašské Meziříčí Czech Rep. 49°29N 17°59E 79 B10
Valatie U.S.A. 42°25N 73°40W 175 D11
Valaxa Greece 38°50N 24°29E 98 C6
Vålberg Sweden 59°23N 13°11E 62 E7
Valbo Sweden 60°40N 17°2E 62 D11
Valbondione Italy 46°0N 10°1E 92 B7
Valcani Romania 46°0N 20°26E 80 D5
Vâlcea □ Romania 45°0N 24°10E 81 F9
Valcheta Argentina 40°40S 66°8W 192 B3
Valdagno Italy 45°39N 11°18E 93 C8
Valdahon France 47°9N 6°21E 71 E13
Valdai Hills = Valdayskaya Vozvyshennost Russia 57°0N 33°30E 84 D7
Valday Russia 57°58N 33°9E 84 D7
Valdayskaya Vozvyshennost Russia 57°0N 33°30E 84 D7
Valdecañas, Embalse de Spain 39°45N 5°0W 89 F5
Valdemarsvik Sweden 58°14N 16°40E 63 F10
Valdemoro Spain 40°12N 3°40W 88 E7
Valdepeñas Spain 38°43N 3°25W 89 G7
Valderaduey → Spain 41°31N 5°42W 88 D5
Valderrobres Spain 40°53N 0°9E 90 E5
Valdés, Pen. Argentina 42°30S 63°45W 192 B4
Valdez U.S.A. 61°7N 146°16W 160 E2
Valdivia Chile 39°50S 73°14W 192 A2
Valdivia Abyssal Plain S. Ocean 62°30S 70°0E 55 C6
Valdobbiádene Italy 45°54N 12°0E 93 C8
Valdosta U.S.A. 30°50N 83°17W 178 E6
Valdoviño = Aviño Spain 43°36N 8°9W 88 B2
Valdres Norway 61°5N 9°5E 60 F13
Vale Georgia 41°30N 42°58E 87 K6
Vale U.S.A. 43°59N 117°15W 168 E5
Vale of Glamorgan □ U.K. 51°28N 3°25W 67 F4
Valea lui Mihai Romania 47°32N 22°11E 80 C7
Valea Mărului Romania 45°49N 27°42E 81 E12
Valemount Canada 52°50N 119°18W 162 C5
Valença Brazil 13°20S 39°5W 189 C3
Valença Portugal 42°1N 8°34W 88 C2
Valença do Piauí Brazil 6°20S 41°45W 189 B2
Valençay France 47°9N 1°34E 71 E8
Valence France 44°57N 4°54E 73 D8
Valence d'Agen France 44°6N 0°53E 72 D4
Valencia Spain 39°27N 0°23W 91 F4
Valencia Trin. & Tob. 10°39N 61°11W 187 K15
Valencia Venezuela 10°11N 68°0W 186 A5
Valencia U.S.A. 34°48N 106°43W 169 J10
Valencia □ Spain 39°20N 0°40W 91 F4
Valencia, G. de Spain 39°30N 0°20E 91 F5
Valencia de Alcántara Spain 39°25N 7°14W 89 F3
Valencia de Don Juan Spain 42°17N 5°31W 88 C5
Valencia I. Ireland 51°54N 10°22W 64 E1
Valenciennes France 50°20N 3°34E 71 B10
Vălenii de Munte Romania 45°11N 26°3E 81 E11
Valensole France 43°50N 5°59E 73 E9
Valentigney France 47°28N 6°50E 71 E13
Valentin Russia 43°8N 134°17E 112 C7
Valentine Nebr., U.S.A. 42°52N 100°33W 172 D3
Valentine Tex., U.S.A. 30°35N 104°30W 176 F2
Valenza Italy 45°1N 8°38E 92 C5
Valera Venezuela 9°19N 70°37W 186 B4
Valga Estonia 57°47N 26°2E 84 D4
Valguarnera Caropepe Italy 37°30N 14°23E 95 E7
Valier U.S.A. 48°18N 112°16W 168 B7
Valinco, G. de France 41°40N 8°52E 73 G12
Valjevo Serbia 44°18N 19°53E 96 B4
Valka Latvia 57°42N 25°57E 84 D4
Valkeakoski Finland 61°16N 24°2E 84 B2
Vall de Uxó = La Vall d'Uixó Spain 39°49N 0°15W 91 F4
Valla Sweden 60°42N 16°48E 62 C10
Valladolid Mexico 20°41N 88°12W 181 C7
Valladolid Spain 41°38N 4°43W 88 D6

Valladolid □ Spain 41°38N 4°43W 88 D6
Vallata Italy 41°2N 15°15E 95 A8
Valldemossa Spain 39°43N 2°37E 100 B9
Valle d'Aosta □ Italy 45°45N 7°15E 92 C4
Valle de la Pascua Venezuela 9°13N 66°0W 186 B5
Valle de las Palmas Mexico 32°20N 116°43W 171 N10
Valle de Santiago Mexico 20°23N 101°12W 180 C4
Valle de Villaverde Spain 43°15N 3°15W 88 B7
Valle de Zaragoza Mexico 27°25N 105°50W 180 B3
Valle del Ticino ○ Italy 45°22N 9°0E 92 C6
Valle Fértil, Sierra del Argentina 30°20S 68°0W 190 C2
Valle Gran Rey Canary Is. 28°5N 17°20W 100 F2
Valle Hermoso Mexico 25°35N 97°40W 181 B5
Valle Nacional Mexico 17°47N 96°18W 181 D5
Valledupar Colombia 10°29N 73°15W 186 A4
Vallée du Bandama □ Ivory C. 8°0N 5°0W 138 D3
Vallehermoso Canary Is. 28°10N 17°15W 100 F2
Vallejo U.S.A. 38°7N 122°14W 170 G4
Vallenar Chile 28°30S 70°50W 190 B1
Vallentuna Sweden 59°32N 18°5E 62 E12
Valleraugue France 44°6N 3°39E 72 D7
Vallet France 47°10N 1°15W 70 E5
Valletta Malta 35°54N 14°31E 101 D2
Valley Center U.S.A. 33°13N 117°2W 171 M9
Valley City U.S.A. 46°55N 98°0W 172 B5
Valley Falls Oreg., U.S.A. 42°29N 120°17W 168 E3
Valley Falls R.I., U.S.A. 41°54N 71°24W 175 E13
Valley of Flowers △ India 30°50N 79°40E 125 D8
Valley of the Kings Egypt 25°41N 32°34E 137 B3
Valley Springs U.S.A. 38°12N 120°50W 170 G6
Valley View U.S.A. 39°36N 76°33W 173 F8
Valley Wells U.S.A. 35°27N 115°46W 171 K11
Valleyview Canada 55°5N 117°17W 162 B5
Valli di Comácchio Italy 44°40N 12°15E 93 D9
Vallimanca, Arroyo Argentina 35°40S 59°10W 190 D4
Vallo della Lucánia Italy 40°14N 15°16E 95 B8
Vallon-Pont-d'Arc France 44°24N 4°24E 73 D8
Vallorbe Switz. 46°42N 6°20E 77 J2
Valls Spain 41°18N 1°15E 90 D6
Vallvik Sweden 61°11N 17°10E 62 C11
Valmaseda = Balmaseda Spain 43°11N 3°12W 90 B1
Valmiera Latvia 57°37N 25°29E 84 D3
Valnera Spain 43°9N 3°40W 88 B7
Valognes France 49°30N 1°28W 70 C5
Valona = Vlorë Albania 40°32N 19°28E 96 F1
Valozhyn Belarus 54°3N 26°30E 75 A14
Valparai India 10°22N 76°58E 127 J3
Valparaíso Chile 33°2S 71°40W 190 C1
Valparaíso Mexico 22°46N 103°34W 180 C4
Valparaiso Fla., U.S.A. 30°29N 86°30W 179 F3
Valparaiso Ind., U.S.A. 41°28N 87°4W 172 E10
Valparaíso □ Chile 33°2S 71°40W 190 C1
Valpovo Croatia 45°39N 18°25E 84 E3
Valpoy India 15°32N 74°8E 127 G2
Valréas France 44°24N 5°0E 73 D9
Vals Switz. 46°39N 9°11E 77 J5
Vals → S. Africa 27°23S 26°30E 144 C4
Vals, Tanjung Indonesia 8°26S 137°25E 119 F9
Vals-les-Bains France 44°42N 4°24E 73 D8
Valsad India 20°40N 72°58E 124 J5
Valtellina Italy 46°11N 9°55E 92 B6
Valujki Russia 50°10N 38°55E 85 G10
Valverde Canary Is. 27°48N 17°55W 100 G2
Valverde del Camino Spain 37°35N 6°47W 89 H4
Valverde del Fresno Spain 40°15N 6°51W 88 E4
Vama Romania 47°34N 25°42E 81 C10
Vamberi India 19°17N 74°44E 126 E2
Vamdrup Denmark 55°25N 9°17E 63 J3
Vámhus Sweden 61°7N 14°29E 62 C8
Vamizi, I. Mozam. 11°2S 40°40E 143 E5
Vammala = Sastamala Finland 61°20N 22°54E 84 B2
Vamos Greece 35°24N 24°13E 101 D6
Vamsadhara → India 18°21N 84°8E 126 E8
Van Turkey 38°30N 43°20E 105 C10
Van, L. = Van Gölü Turkey 38°30N 43°0E 105 C10
Van Alstyne U.S.A. 33°25N 96°35W 176 E6
Van Blommestein Meer Surinam 4°45N 55°5W 187 C7
Van Buren Canada 47°10N 67°55W 165 C6
Van Buren Ark., U.S.A. 35°26N 94°21W 176 D7
Van Buren Maine, U.S.A. 47°10N 67°58W 173 B20
Van Buren Mo., U.S.A. 37°0N 91°1W 172 G8
Van Canh Vietnam 13°37N 109°0E 120 F7
Van Diemen, C. N. Terr., Australia 11°9S 130°24E 148 B5
Van Diemen, C. Queens., Australia 16°30S 139°46E 150 B2
Van Diemen G. Australia 11°45S 132°0E 148 B5
Van Gölü Turkey 38°30N 43°0E 105 C10
Van Horn U.S.A. 31°3N 104°50W 176 F2
Van Ninh Vietnam 12°42N 109°14E 120 F7
Van Rees, Pegunungan Indonesia 2°35S 138°15E 119 E9
Van Tivu India 8°51N 78°15E 127 K4
Van Wert U.S.A. 40°52N 84°35W 173 E11
Van Yen Vietnam 21°4N 104°42E 116 B8
Van Zylsrus S. Africa 26°52S 22°4E 144 C3
Vanadzor Armenia 40°48N 44°30E 87 K7
Vanavara Russia 60°22N 102°16E 107 C11
Vancouver Canada 49°15N 123°7W 170 A3
Vancouver U.S.A. 45°38N 122°40W 170 E4
Vancouver, C. Australia 35°2S 118°11E 149 G2
Vancouver I. Canada 49°50N 126°0W 162 D3
Vancouver Int. ✈ (YVR) Canada 49°10N 123°10W 170 A3
Vanda = Vantaa Finland 60°18N 24°56E 84 B3
Vandalia Ill., U.S.A. 38°58N 89°6W 172 F9
Vandalia Mo., U.S.A. 39°19N 91°29W 172 F8

282 Vandavasi
INDEX TO WORLD MAPS

Vandavasi India 12°30N 79°30E 127 H4
Vandellòs Spain 41°1N 0°55E 90 E5
Vandeloos B. Sri Lanka 8°0N 81°45E 127 L5
Vandenberg Village U.S.A. 34°43N 120°28W 171 L6
Vanderbijlpark S. Africa 26°42S 27°54E 145 C4
Vandergrift U.S.A. 40°36N 79°34W 174 F5
Vanderhoof Canada 54°0N 124°0W 162 C4
Vanderkloof Dam S. Africa 30°4S 24°40E 144 D3
Vanderlin I. Australia 15°44S 137°2E 150 B2
Vänern Sweden 58°47N 13°30E 63 F6
Vänersborg Sweden 58°26N 12°19E 63 F6
Vang Vieng Laos 18°58N 102°32E 120 C4
Vanga Kenya 4°35S 39°12E 142 C4
Vangaindrano Madag. 23°21S 47°36E 141 J9
Vänge Sweden 59°50N 17°20E 62 E11
Vanguard Canada 49°55N 107°20W 163 D7
Vanino Russia 48°50N 140°5E 107 E15
Vanivilasa Sagara India 13°45N 76°30E 127 H3
Vaniyambadi India 12°46N 78°44E 127 H4
Vânju Mare Romania 44°25N 22°52E 80 F7
Vankleek Hill Canada 45°32N 74°40W 175 A10
Vännäs Sweden 63°58N 19°48E 60 E18
Vannes France 47°40N 2°47W 70 E4
Vannøya Norway 70°6N 19°50E 60 A18
Vanoise, Massif de la France 45°25N 6°40E 73 C10
Vanrhynsdorp S. Africa 31°36S 18°44E 144 D2
Vansada India 20°47N 73°25E 126 D1
Vansbro Sweden 60°32N 14°15E 62 D8
Vansittart B. Australia 14°3S 126°17E 148 B4
Vansittart I. Canada 65°50N 84°0W 161 D15
Vantaa Finland 60°18N 24°56E 84 B3
Vanua Balavu Fiji 17°12S 178°55W 154 a
Vanua Levu Fiji 16°33S 179°15E 154 a
Vanua Vatu Fiji 18°22S 179°15W 154 a
Vanuatu ■ Pac. Oc. 15°0S 168°0E 147 C9
Vanwyksvlei S. Africa 30°18S 21°49E 144 D3
Vapi India 20°22N 72°54E 126 D1
Vapnyarka Ukraine 48°32N 28°45E 81 B13
Var □ France 43°27N 6°18E 73 E10
Var ➝ France 43°39N 7°12E 73 E11
Vara Sweden 58°16N 12°55E 63 F6
Varada ➝ India 15°0N 75°40E 127 G2
Varades France 47°25N 1°1W 70 E5
Varáita ➝ Italy 44°9N 7°53E 92 D4
Varalé Ivory C. 9°40N 3°17W 138 D4
Varallo Italy 45°49N 8°15E 92 C5
Varāmīn Iran 35°20N 51°39E 129 C6
Varāmīn □ Iran 35°18N 51°35E 129 B6
Varanasi India 25°22N 83°0E 125 G10
Varangerfjorden Norway 70°3N 29°25E 60 A23
Varangerhalvøya Norway 70°25N 29°30E 60 A23
Varano, Lago di Italy 41°53N 15°45E 93 G12
Varaždin Croatia 46°20N 16°20E 93 B13
Varazze Italy 44°22N 8°34E 92 D5
Varberg Sweden 57°6N 12°20E 63 G6
Vardak □ Afghan. 34°0N 68°0E 122 B6
Vardar = Axios ➝ Greece 40°57N 22°35E 96 F6
Varde Denmark 55°38N 8°29E 63 J2
Varde Å ➝ Denmark 55°35N 8°19E 63 J2
Vardenis Armenia 40°10N 45°43E 87 K7
Vardø Norway 70°23N 31°5E 60 A24
Varel Germany 53°23N 8°8E 76 B4
Varella, Mui = Nay, Mui Vietnam 12°54N 109°26E 120 F7
Varėna Lithuania 54°12N 24°30E 84 E3
Varennes-sur-Allier France 46°19N 3°24E 71 F10
Varennes-Vauzelles France 47°3N 3°9E 71 E10
Vareš Bos.-H. 44°12N 18°23E 80 F3
Varese Italy 45°48N 8°50E 92 C5
Vârfurile Romania 46°19N 22°31E 80 D7
Vårgårda Sweden 58°2N 12°49E 63 F6
Vargem Bonita Brazil 20°20S 46°22W 189 E1
Vargem Grande Brazil 3°33S 43°56W 189 A2
Varginha Brazil 21°33S 45°25W 191 A6
Vargön Sweden 58°22N 12°20E 63 F6
Varillas Chile 24°0S 70°10W 190 A1
Varkaus Finland 62°19N 27°50E 84 A4
Värmdölandet Sweden 59°20N 18°33E 62 E12
Värmeln Sweden 59°35N 12°54E 62 E6
Värmland □ Sweden 60°0N 13°20E 62 E6
Värmlandsbro Sweden 59°11N 13°0E 62 E7
Varna Bulgaria 43°13N 27°56E 97 C11
Varna □ Bulgaria 43°20N 27°30E 97 C11
Varna ➝ India 16°48N 74°32E 126 F2
Värnamo Sweden 57°10N 14°3E 63 G8
Várnjárga = Varangerhalvøya Norway 70°25N 29°30E 60 A23
Varnsdorf Czech Rep. 50°55N 14°35E 78 A7
Várpalota Hungary 47°12N 18°8E 80 C3
Vars Canada 45°21N 75°21W 175 A9
Vars France 44°37N 6°42E 73 D10
Varto Turkey 39°10N 41°27E 105 C9
Varvarin Serbia 43°43N 21°20E 96 C5
Varysburg U.S.A. 42°46N 78°19W 174 D6
Varzaneh Iran 32°25N 52°40E 129 C7
Varzaqān Iran 38°29N 46°40E 105 C12
Várzea Alegre Brazil 6°47S 39°17W 189 B3
Várzea da Palma Brazil 17°36S 44°44W 189 D2
Varzi Italy 44°49N 9°12E 92 D6
Varzo Italy 46°12N 8°15E 92 B5
Varzy France 47°22N 3°20E 71 E10
Vas □ Hungary 47°10N 16°55E 80 C1
Vasa = Vaasa Finland 63°6N 21°38E 60 E19
Vasa Barris ➝ Brazil 11°10S 37°10W 189 C3
Vasai-Virar India 19°28N 72°48E 126 E1
Vásárosnamény Hungary 48°9N 22°19E 80 B7
Vascão ➝ Portugal 37°31N 7°31W 89 H3
Vaşcău Romania 46°28N 22°30E 80 D7
Vascongadas = País Vasco □ Spain 42°50N 2°45W 90 C2
Vashkivtsi Ukraine 48°23N 25°31E 81 B10
Vasht = Khāsh Iran 28°15N 61°15E 129 D9
Vasilevichi Belarus 52°15N 29°50E 75 B16
Vasilika Greece 40°29N 23°8E 96 F7
Vasiliki Greece 38°37N 20°36E 98 C2
Vasiliko Greece 38°25N 23°40E 98 C5
Vasilkov = Vasylkiv Ukraine 50°7N 30°15E 75 C16
Väskinde Sweden 57°40N 18°20E 63 G10
Vaslui Romania 46°38N 27°42E 81 D12
Vaslui □ Romania 46°30N 27°45E 81 D12
Väsman Sweden 60°9N 15°5E 62 D9
Vassar Canada 49°10N 95°55W 163 D9
Vassar U.S.A. 43°22N 83°35W 173 D12
Västerås Sweden 59°37N 16°38E 62 E10
Västerbotten Sweden 64°36N 20°4E 60 D19
Västerdalälven ➝ Sweden 60°30N 15°7E 62 D8
Västergötland Sweden 58°0N 13°10E 63 F7
Västerhaninge Sweden 59°7N 18°6E 62 E12
Västervik Sweden 57°43N 16°33E 63 G10
Västmanland Sweden 59°45N 16°20E 61 G17
Västmanland □ Sweden 59°45N 16°20E 62 E10
Vasto Italy 42°8N 14°40E 93 F11
Västra Götaland □ Sweden 58°0N 13°0E 63 F6
Vasvár Hungary 47°3N 16°47E 80 C1
Vasylivka Ukraine 45°38N 28°50E 81 E13
Vasylkiv Ukraine 50°7N 30°15E 75 C16
Vat Phou Laos 14°51N 105°49E 120 E5
Vatan France 47°4N 1°50E 71 E8
Vatersay U.K. 56°55N 7°32W 65 E1
Vathia Greece 36°29N 22°29E 98 E4
Vati Greece 36°3N 27°53E 101 C9
Vatican City ■ Europe 41°54N 12°27E 93 G9
Vaticano, C. Italy 38°37N 15°50E 95 D8
Vatili Cyprus 35°6N 33°40E 101 D12
Vatin Serbia 45°12N 21°20E 80 E6
Vatiu = Atiu Cook Is. 20°0S 158°10W 157 J12
Vatnajökull Iceland 64°30N 16°48W 60 D5
Vatnajökull △ Iceland 64°24N 16°48W 60 D5
Vätö Sweden 59°50N 19°0E 62 E12
Vatolakkos Greece 35°27N 23°53E 101 D5
Vatra-Dornei Romania 47°22N 25°22E 81 C10
Vatrak ➝ India 23°9N 73°2E 124 H5
Vättern Sweden 58°25N 14°30E 63 F8
Vatu Vara Fiji 17°26S 179°31W 154 a
Vatulele Fiji 18°33S 177°37E 154 a
Vaucluse □ France 43°50N 5°20E 73 E9
Vaucouleurs France 48°37N 5°40E 71 D12
Vaud □ Switz. 46°35N 6°30E 77 J2
Vaudreuil-Dorion Canada 45°23N 74°3W 175 A10
Vaughn Mont., U.S.A. 47°33N 111°33W 168 C8
Vaughn N. Mex., U.S.A. 34°36N 105°13W 169 J11
Vaujours L. Canada 55°27N 74°15W 164 A5
Vaupés = Uaupés ➝ Brazil 0°2N 67°16W 186 C5
Vaupés □ Colombia 1°0N 71°0W 186 C4
Vauvert France 43°42N 4°17E 73 E8
Vauxhall Canada 50°5N 112°9W 162 C6
Vav India 24°22N 71°31E 124 G4
Vavoua Ivory C. 7°23N 6°29W 138 D3
Vavuniya Sri Lanka 8°45N 80°30E 127 K5
Vawkavysk Belarus 53°9N 24°30E 75 B13
Vaxholm Sweden 59°25N 18°20E 62 E12
Växjö Sweden 56°52N 14°50E 63 H8
Våxtorp Sweden 56°25N 13°8E 63 H7
Vayalpad India 13°39N 78°38E 127 H4
Vaygach, Ostrov Russia 70°0N 60°0E 106 C7
Veadeiros Brazil 14°7S 47°31W 189 C1
Veaikevárri = Svappavaara Sweden 67°40N 21°3E 60 C19
Vechelde Germany 52°16N 10°22E 76 C6
Vechta Germany 52°44N 8°17E 76 C4
Vechte ➝ Neths. 52°34N 6°6E 69 B6
Vecsés Hungary 47°26N 19°19E 80 C4
Vedaranniyam India 10°25N 79°50E 127 J4
Veddige Sweden 57°17N 12°20E 63 G6
Vedea ➝ Romania 43°42N 25°41E 81 G10
Vedi Armenia 39°54N 44°43E 105 C11
Vedia Argentina 34°30S 61°31W 190 C3
Vedrette di Ries-Aurina △ Italy 46°54N 12°5E 93 B9
Vedum Sweden 58°11N 13°0E 63 F7
Veendam Neths. 53°5N 6°52E 69 A6
Veenendaal Neths. 52°2N 5°34E 69 B5
Vefsna ➝ Norway 65°48N 13°10E 60 D15
Vega Norway 65°40N 11°55E 60 D14
Vega U.S.A. 35°15N 102°26W 176 D3
Vega Baja Puerto Rico 18°27N 66°23W 183 d
Vegadeo Spain 43°27N 7°4W 88 B3
Vegoritida, L. Greece 40°45N 21°45E 96 F5
Vegreville Canada 53°30N 112°5W 162 C6
Veinge Sweden 56°33N 13°4E 63 H7
Veisiejai Lithuania 54°6N 23°42E 82 D10
Vejbystrand Sweden 56°19N 12°45E 63 H6
Vejen Denmark 55°30N 9°9E 63 J3
Vejer de la Frontera Spain 36°15N 5°59W 89 J5
Vejle Denmark 55°43N 9°30E 63 J3
Vejle Fjord Denmark 55°40N 9°50E 63 J3
Vela Luka Croatia 42°59N 16°44E 93 F13
Velachha India 21°26N 73°1E 126 D1
Velanai I. Sri Lanka 9°45N 79°45E 127 K4
Velas, C. Costa Rica 10°21N 85°52W 182 D2
Velasco, Sierra de Argentina 29°20S 67°10W 190 B2
Velay, Mts. du France 45°0N 3°40E 72 D7
Velbert Germany 51°20N 7°3E 76 D3
Velddrif S. Africa 32°42S 18°11E 144 D2
Velebit Planina Croatia 44°50N 15°20E 93 D12
Velebitski Kanal Croatia 44°45N 14°55E 93 D11
Veleka ➝ Bulgaria 42°4N 27°58E 97 D11
Velencei-tó Hungary 47°13N 18°36E 80 C3
Velenje Slovenia 46°23N 15°8E 93 B12
Veles Macedonia 41°46N 21°47E 96 E5
Velestino Greece 39°23N 22°43E 98 B4
Vélez-Málaga Spain 36°48N 4°5W 89 J6
Vélez Rubio Spain 37°41N 2°5W 91 H2
Velhas ➝ Brazil 17°13S 44°49W 189 D2
Velika Croatia 45°27N 17°40E 80 E2
Velika Gorica Croatia 45°44N 16°5E 93 C13
Velika Kapela Croatia 45°10N 15°5E 93 C12
Velika Kladuša Bos.-H. 45°11N 15°48E 93 C12
Velika Kruša = Krushë e Madhe Kosovo 42°19N 20°39E 96 D4
Velika Morava ➝ Serbia 44°43N 21°3E 96 B5
Velika Plana Serbia 44°20N 21°4E 96 B5
Velikaya ➝ Russia 57°48N 28°10E 84 D5
Velikaya Kema Russia 45°30N 137°12E 112 B8
Velikaya Lepetikha Ukraine 47°2N 33°58E 85 J7
Velike Lašče Slovenia 45°49N 14°45E 93 C11
Veliki Jastrebac Serbia 43°25N 21°30E 96 C5
Veliki Kanal Serbia 45°45N 19°15E 80 E4
Veliki Popović Serbia 44°8N 21°18E 96 B5
Velikiy Novgorod Russia 58°30N 31°25E 84 C6
Velikiye Luki Russia 56°25N 30°32E 84 D6
Veliko Gradište Serbia 44°46N 21°29E 96 B5
Veliko Tŭrnovo Bulgaria 43°5N 25°41E 97 C9
Veliko Tŭrnovo □ Bulgaria 43°5N 25°41E 97 C9
Velikonda Range India 14°45N 79°10E 127 G4
Vélingara Kolda, Senegal 13°12N 14°5W 138 C2
Vélingara Louga, Senegal 15°0N 14°40W 138 B2
Velingrad Bulgaria 42°4N 23°58E 96 D7
Velino, Mte. Italy 42°9N 13°23E 93 F10
Velizh Russia 55°36N 31°11E 84 E6
Vel'ké Kapušany Slovak Rep. 48°34N 22°5E 79 C15
Velké Karlovice Czech Rep. 49°20N 18°17E 79 B11
Velké Meziříčí Czech Rep. 49°21N 16°1E 78 B9
Vel'ký Javorník Slovak Rep. 49°19N 18°22E 79 B11
Vel'ký Krtíš Slovak Rep. 48°12N 19°21E 79 C12
Vel'ký Meder Slovak Rep. 47°52N 17°46E 79 D10
Vel'ký Tribeč Slovak Rep. 48°28N 18°15E 79 C11
Vellar ➝ India 11°30N 79°36E 127 J4
Velletri Italy 41°41N 12°47E 94 A5
Vellinge Sweden 55°29N 13°2E 63 J6
Vellmar Germany 51°22N 9°28E 76 D5
Vellore India 12°57N 79°10E 127 H4
Velopoula Greece 36°55N 23°27E 98 E5
Velsk Russia 61°10N 42°0E 84 B11
Velten Germany 52°42N 13°10E 76 C9
Veluwezoom △ Neths. 52°5N 6°0E 69 B6
Velva U.S.A. 48°4N 100°56W 172 A3
Velvendos Greece 40°15N 22°6E 96 F6
Velyka Mykhaylivka Ukraine 47°4N 29°52E 81 C14
Velyki Luchky Ukraine 48°25N 22°34E 80 B7
Velykyy Bereznyy Ukraine 48°54N 22°28E 80 B7
Velykyy Bychkiv Ukraine 47°58N 24°1E 81 C9
Vemb Denmark 56°21N 8°21E 63 H2
Vembanad L. India 9°36N 76°15E 127 K3
Vemdalen Sweden 62°27N 13°51E 62 B7
Ven Sweden 55°55N 12°45E 63 J6
Venaco France 42°14N 9°11E 73 F13
Venado Mexico 22°56N 101°6W 180 C4
Venado Tuerto Argentina 33°50S 62°0W 190 C3
Venafro Italy 41°29N 14°2E 95 A7
Venarey-les-Laumes France 47°32N 4°26E 71 E11
Venaria Italy 45°8N 7°38E 92 C4
Venčane Serbia 44°24N 20°28E 96 B4
Vence France 43°43N 7°6E 73 E11
Vendas Novas Portugal 38°39N 8°27W 89 G2
Vendée □ France 46°50N 1°35W 70 F5
Vendée ➝ France 46°20N 1°10W 70 F5
Vendéen, Bocage France 46°40N 1°20W 72 B2
Vendeuvre-sur-Barse France 48°14N 4°28E 71 D11
Vendicari △ Italy 36°49N 15°6E 95 F8
Vendôme France 47°47N 1°3E 70 E8
Vendrell = El Vendrell Spain 41°10N 1°30E 90 D6
Vendsyssel Denmark 57°22N 10°0E 63 G4
Vendychany Ukraine 48°38N 27°48E 81 B12
Venelles France 43°35N 5°28E 73 E9
Véneta, L. Italy 45°23N 12°25E 93 C9
Véneto □ Italy 45°30N 12°0E 93 C9
Venev Russia 54°22N 38°17E 84 E10
Venézia Italy 45°27N 12°21E 93 C9
Venézia, G. di Italy 45°15N 13°0E 93 C10
Venézia Lido Italy 45°25N 12°22E 93 C9
Venezuela ■ S. Amer. 8°0N 66°0W 186 B5
Venezuela, G. de Venezuela 11°30N 71°0W 186 A4
Vengurla India 15°53N 73°45E 127 G1
Vengurla Rocks India 15°55N 73°22E 127 G1
Venice = Venézia Italy 45°27N 12°21E 93 C9
Venice U.S.A. 27°6N 82°27W 179 H7
Vénissieux France 45°42N 4°53E 73 C8
Venjan Sweden 60°57N 13°55E 62 D7
Venjansjön Sweden 60°54N 14°0E 62 D8
Venkatagiri India 14°0N 79°35E 127 H4
Venkatapuram India 18°20N 80°30E 126 E5
Venlo Neths. 51°22N 6°11E 69 C6
Vennachar Junction Canada 45°5N 77°14W 174 A7
Vennesla Norway 58°15N 7°59E 61 G12
Venosa Italy 40°58N 15°49E 95 B8
Venray Neths. 51°31N 6°0E 69 C6
Venta Lithuania 56°12N 22°42E 82 B9
Venta ➝ Latvia 57°24N 21°33E 82 A8
Venta de Baños Spain 41°55N 4°30W 88 D6
Venta de Cardeña = Cardeña Spain 38°16N 4°20W 89 G6
Ventana, Sa. de la Argentina 38°0S 62°30W 190 D3
Ventersburg S. Africa 28°7S 27°9E 144 C4
Venterstad S. Africa 30°47S 25°48E 144 D4
Ventimíglia Italy 43°47N 7°36E 92 E4
Ventnor U.K. 50°36N 1°12W 67 G6
Ventotène Italy 40°47N 13°25E 94 B6
Ventoux, Mt. France 44°10N 5°17E 73 D9
Ventspils Latvia 57°25N 21°32E 82 A8
Ventuari ➝ Venezuela 3°58N 67°2W 186 C5
Ventucopa U.S.A. 34°50N 119°29W 171 L7
Ventura U.S.A. 34°17N 119°18W 171 L7
Venus U.S.A. 27°4N 81°22W 179 H8
Vénus, Pte. Tahiti 17°29S 149°29W 155 b
Venus B. Australia 38°40S 145°42E 153 E6
Venustiano Carranza Mexico 30°25N 115°53W 180 A1
Venustiano Carranza, Presa Mexico 27°30N 100°37W 180 B4
Vera Argentina 29°30S 60°20W 190 B3
Vera Spain 37°15N 1°51W 91 H3
Veracruz Mexico 19°11N 96°8W 181 D5
Veracruz □ Mexico 19°0N 96°15W 181 D5
Veraval India 20°53N 70°27E 124 J4
Verbánia Italy 45°56N 8°33E 92 C5
Verbano, L. di = Maggiore, L. Italy 45°57N 8°39E 92 B5
Verbano Cusio Ossola □ Italy 46°15N 8°20E 92 B5
Verbicaro Italy 39°45N 15°55E 95 C8
Verbier Switz. 46°6N 7°13E 77 J3
Vercelli Italy 45°19N 8°25E 92 C5
Verchovchevo Ukraine 48°32N 34°10E 85 H8
Vercors △ France 45°5N 5°25E 73 D9
Verdalsøra Norway 63°48N 11°30E 60 E14
Verde ➝ Argentina 41°56S 65°5W 192 B3
Verde ➝ Goiás, Brazil 18°1S 50°14W 187 G8
Verde ➝ Mato Grosso do Sul, Brazil 21°25S 52°20W 187 H8
Verde ➝ Chihuahua, Mexico 26°39N 107°11W 180 B3
Verde ➝ Jalisco, Mexico 20°42N 103°14W 180 C4
Verde ➝ Oaxaca, Mexico 15°59N 97°50W 181 D5
Verde ➝ Paraguay 23°9S 57°37W 190 A4
Verde ➝ U.S.A. 33°33N 111°40W 169 K8
Verde, Cay Bahamas 23°0N 75°5W 182 B4
Verde Grande ➝ Brazil 16°13S 43°49W 189 D2
Verde Pequeno ➝ Brazil 14°48S 43°31W 189 C2
Verden Germany 52°55N 9°14E 76 C5
Verdi U.S.A. 39°31N 119°59W 170 F7
Verdikoussa Greece 39°47N 21°59E 98 B3
Verdon ➝ France 43°43N 5°46E 73 E9
Verdon △ France 43°50N 6°5E 73 E10
Verdun France 49°9N 5°24E 71 C12
Verdun-sur-le-Doubs France 46°54N 5°2E 71 F12
Vereeniging S. Africa 26°38S 27°57E 145 C4
Verga, C. Guinea 10°30N 14°10W 138 C2
Vergara = Bergara Spain 43°9N 2°28W 90 B2
Vergara Uruguay 32°56S 53°57W 191 C5
Vergato Italy 44°17N 11°7E 92 D8
Vergemont Cr. ➝ Australia 24°16S 143°16E 150 C3
Vergennes U.S.A. 44°10N 73°15W 175 B11
Vergina = Aigai Greece 40°28N 22°19E 96 F6
Vergt France 45°2N 0°43E 72 C4
Veria Greece 40°34N 22°12E 96 F6
Verín Spain 41°57N 7°27W 88 D3
Verkhnedvinsk = Vyerkhnyadzvinsk Belarus 55°45N 27°58E 84 E4
Verkhnetulomskoye Vdkhr. Russia 68°36N 31°12E 60 B24
Verkhnevilyuysk Russia 63°27N 120°18E 107 C13
Verkhniy Baskunchak Russia 48°14N 46°44E 87 F8
Verkhovye Russia 52°55N 37°15E 85 F9
Verkhovyna Ukraine 48°9N 24°47E 81 B9
Verkhoyansk Russia 67°35N 133°25E 107 C14
Verkhoyansk Ra. = Verkhoyanskiy Khrebet Russia 66°0N 129°0E 107 C13
Verkhoyanskiy Khrebet Russia 66°0N 129°0E 107 C13
Vermeille, Côte France 42°50N 3°20E 72 F7
Vermenton France 47°40N 3°42E 71 E10
Vermilion Canada 53°20N 110°50W 163 C6
Vermilion U.S.A. 41°25N 82°22W 174 E2
Vermilion ➝ Canada 53°22N 110°51W 163 C6
Vermilion B. U.S.A. 29°42N 92°0W 176 G9
Vermilion Bay Canada 49°51N 93°34W 163 D10
Vermilion Cliffs Nat. Monument △ U.S.A. 36°54N 112°5W 169 H8
Vermilion L. U.S.A. 47°53N 92°26W 172 B7
Vermillion U.S.A. 42°47N 96°56W 172 D5
Vermillion ➝ Canada 47°38N 72°56W 164 C5
Vermont □ U.S.A. 44°0N 73°0W 175 C12
Vermosh Albania 42°35N 19°42E 96 D3
Verna U.S.A. 27°23N 82°16W 179 H7
Vernadsky Antarctica 65°0S 64°0W 55 C17
Vernal U.S.A. 40°27N 109°32W 168 F9
Vernalis U.S.A. 37°36N 121°17W 170 H5
Vernazza Italy 44°10N 9°45E 92 D6
Verner Canada 46°25N 80°8W 164 C3
Verneuil-sur-Avre France 48°45N 0°55E 70 D7
Verneukpan S. Africa 30°0S 21°0E 144 D3
Vernier Switz. 46°11N 6°12E 77 J2
Vérnio Italy 44°3N 11°9E 92 D8
Vernon Canada 50°20N 119°15W 162 C5
Vernon France 49°5N 1°30E 70 C8
Vernon U.S.A. 34°9N 99°17W 176 D5
Vernonia U.S.A. 45°52N 123°11W 170 E3
Vero Beach U.S.A. 27°38N 80°24W 179 H9
Véroia = Veria Greece 40°34N 22°12E 96 F6
Véroli Italy 41°41N 13°25E 93 G10
Verona Canada 44°29N 76°42W 175 B8
Verona Italy 45°27N 10°59E 92 C7
Verrès Italy 45°40N 7°42E 92 C4
Versailles France 48°48N 2°7E 71 D9
Versmold Germany 52°2N 8°9E 76 C4
Vert, C. Senegal 14°45N 17°30W 138 C1
Vertou France 47°10N 1°28W 70 E5
Vertus France 48°54N 4°2E 71 D11
Verulam S. Africa 29°38S 31°2E 145 C5
Verviers Belgium 50°37N 5°52E 69 D5
Vervins France 49°50N 3°53E 71 C10
Veržej Slovenia 46°34N 16°13E 93 B13
Verzy France 49°9N 4°10E 71 C11
Vescovato France 42°30N 9°27E 73 F13
Veseli nad Lužnicí Czech Rep. 49°12N 14°43E 78 B7
Veselie Bulgaria 42°18N 27°38E 97 D11
Veselovskoye Vdkhr. Russia 46°58N 41°25E 87 G5
Veshenskaya Russia 49°35N 41°44E 86 F5
Vesle ➝ France 49°23N 3°28E 71 C10
Vesoul France 47°40N 6°11E 71 E13
Vessigebro Sweden 56°58N 12°40E 63 H6
Vesterålen Norway 68°45N 15°0E 60 B16
Vestfjorden Norway 67°55N 14°0E 60 C16
Vestmannaeyjar Iceland 63°27N 20°15W 60 E3
Vestvågøya Norway 68°18N 13°50E 60 B15
Vesuvio Italy 40°49N 14°26E 95 B7
Vesuvius, Mt. = Vesuvio Italy 40°49N 14°26E 95 B7
Vesyegonsk Russia 58°40N 37°16E 84 C9
Veszprém Hungary 47°8N 17°57E 80 C2
Veszprém □ Hungary 47°5N 17°55E 80 C2
Vésztő Hungary 46°55N 21°16E 80 D6
Vetapalem India 15°47N 80°18E 127 G5
Vetlanda Sweden 57°24N 15°3E 63 G9
Vetluga Russia 57°53N 45°45E 86 B8
Vetlugu ➝ Russia 56°36N 46°4E 86 B8
Vetluzhskiy Kostroma, Russia 58°23N 45°26E 86 A7
Vetluzhskiy Nizhniy Novgorod, Russia 57°17N 45°12E 86 B7
Vetovo Bulgaria 43°42N 26°16E 97 C10
Vetralla Italy 42°20N 12°2E 93 F9
Vetren Bulgaria 42°15N 24°3E 97 D8
Vettore, Mte. Italy 42°49N 13°16E 93 F10
Veurne Belgium 51°5N 2°40E 69 C2
Vevey Switz. 46°28N 6°51E 77 J2
Vevi Greece 40°47N 21°38E 96 F5
Veynes France 44°32N 5°49E 73 D9
Veys Iran 31°30N 49°0E 129 D6
Vézelay France 47°27N 3°45E 71 E10
Vézelise France 48°30N 6°5E 71 D13
Vézère ➝ France 44°53N 0°53E 72 D4
Vezhen Bulgaria 42°50N 24°20E 97 D8
Vezirköprü Turkey 41°8N 35°27E 104 B6
Vezzani France 42°10N 9°15E 73 F13
Vi Thanh Vietnam 9°42N 105°26E 121 H5
Viacha Bolivia 16°39S 68°18W 188 D4
Viadana Italy 44°56N 10°31E 92 D7
Viamão Brazil 30°5S 51°0W 191 C5
Viana Brazil 3°13S 44°55W 189 A2
Viana Spain 42°31N 2°22W 90 C2
Viana do Alentejo Portugal 38°17N 7°59W 89 G3
Viana do Bolo Spain 42°11N 7°6W 88 C3
Viana do Castelo Portugal 41°42N 8°50W 88 D2
Viana do Castelo □ Portugal 41°50N 8°30W 88 D2
Vianden Lux. 49°56N 6°12E 69 E6
Viangchan = Vientiane Laos 17°58N 102°36E 120 D4
Vianópolis Brazil 16°40S 48°35W 189 D1
Vianos Greece 35°2N 25°21E 101 D7
Viar ➝ Spain 37°36N 5°50W 89 H5
Viaréggio Italy 43°52N 10°14E 92 E7
Viaur ➝ France 44°8N 1°58E 72 D5
Vibble Sweden 57°37N 18°16E 63 G12
Vibo Valéntia Italy 38°40N 16°6E 95 D9
Viborg Denmark 56°27N 9°23E 63 H3
Vibraye France 48°3N 0°44E 70 D7
Vic Spain 41°58N 2°19E 90 D7
Vic, Étang de France 43°29N 3°50E 72 E7
Vic-en-Bigorre France 43°24N 0°3E 72 E4
Vic-Fezensac France 43°47N 0°19E 72 E4
Vic-le-Comte France 45°39N 3°14E 71 G10
Vic-sur-Cère France 44°59N 2°38E 72 D6
Vicar Spain 36°50N 2°38W 91 J2
Vicente Pérez Rosales △ Chile 41°11S 72°12W 192 B2
Vicenza Italy 45°33N 11°33E 93 C8
Vich = Vic Spain 41°58N 2°19E 90 D7
Vichada ➝ Colombia 4°55N 67°50W 186 C5
Vichuga Russia 57°12N 41°55E 86 B5
Vichy France 46°9N 3°26E 71 F10
Vicksburg Ariz., U.S.A. 33°45N 113°45W 171 M13
Vicksburg Miss., U.S.A. 32°21N 90°53W 177 E9
Vico France 42°10N 8°49E 73 F12
Vico, L. di Italy 42°19N 12°10E 93 F9
Vico del Gargano Italy 41°54N 15°57E 93 G12
Viçosa Brazil 9°28S 36°14W 189 B3
Viçosa do Ceará Brazil 3°34S 41°5W 189 A2
Vicovu de Sus Romania 47°56N 25°41E 81 C10
Victor India 21°0N 71°30E 124 J4
Victor Harbor Australia 35°30S 138°37E 152 C3
Victoria Argentina 32°40S 60°10W 190 C3
Victoria Canada 48°30N 123°25W 170 B3
Victoria Chile 38°13S 72°20W 192 A2
Victoria China 22°17N 114°11E 111 a
Victoria Guinea 10°50N 14°32W 138 C2
Victoria Malta 36°3N 14°14E 101 C1
Victoria Romania 45°44N 24°41E 81 E9
Victoria Seychelles 4°38S 55°28E 141 b
Victoria Kans., U.S.A. 38°52N 99°9W 172 F4
Victoria Tex., U.S.A. 28°48N 97°0W 176 G6
Victoria □ Australia 37°0S 144°0E 152 D6
Victoria ➝ Australia 15°10S 129°40E 148 C4
Victoria, Grand L. Canada 47°31N 77°30W 164 C4
Victoria, L. Africa 1°0S 33°0E 142 C3
Victoria, L. Australia 33°57S 141°15E 152 B4
Victoria, Mt. Burma 21°14N 93°55E 123 J18
Victoria Beach Canada 50°40N 96°35W 163 C9
Victoria de Durango = Durango Mexico 24°3N 104°39W 180 C4
Victoria de las Tunas = Las Tunas Cuba 20°58N 76°59W 182 B4
Victoria Falls Zimbabwe 17°58S 25°52E 143 F2
Victoria Fjord Greenland 82°10N 46°0W 57 A6
Victoria Harbour Canada 44°45N 79°45W 174 B5
Victoria I. Canada 71°0N 111°0W 160 C9
Victoria L. Canada 48°20N 57°27W 165 C8
Victoria Ld. Antarctica 75°0S 160°0E 55 D11
Victoria Nile ➝ Uganda 2°14N 31°26E 142 B3
Victoria Pk. Belize 16°48N 88°37W 181 D7
Victoria Ra. N.Z. 42°12S 172°7E 155 C7
Victoria River Australia 16°25S 131°0E 148 C5
Victoria Str. Canada 69°31N 100°30W 160 D11
Victoria West S. Africa 31°25S 23°4E 144 D3
Victoriaville Canada 46°4N 71°56W 165 C5
Victorica Argentina 36°20S 65°30W 190 D2
Victorville U.S.A. 34°32N 117°18W 171 L9
Vicuña Chile 30°0S 70°50W 190 C1
Vicuña Mackenna Argentina 33°53S 64°25W 190 C3
Vidal U.S.A. 34°7N 114°31W 171 L12
Vidalia U.S.A. 32°13N 82°25W 178 C7
Vidamlya Belarus 52°19N 23°47E 83 F10
Vidauban France 43°25N 6°27E 73 E10
Viddolatno = Vindelälven ➝ Sweden 63°55N 19°50E 60 E18
Videbæk Denmark 56°6N 8°38E 63 H2
Videle Romania 44°17N 25°31E 81 F10
Vidette U.S.A. 33°2N 82°15W 178 B7
Vidigueira Portugal 38°12N 7°48W 89 G3
Vidin Bulgaria 43°59N 22°50E 96 C6
Vidin □ Bulgaria 43°59N 22°50E 96 C6
Vidio, C. Spain 43°35N 6°14W 88 B4
Vidisha India 23°28N 77°53E 124 H7
Vidos Greece 39°38N 19°55E 101 A3
Vidra Romania 45°56N 26°55E 81 E11
Viduša Bos.-H. 42°55N 18°21E 96 D2
Vidzy Belarus 55°23N 26°37E 84 E4
Viechtach Germany 49°4N 12°53E 77 F8
Viedma Argentina 40°50S 63°0W 192 B4
Viedma, L. Argentina 49°30S 72°30W 192 C2
Vieira do Minho Portugal 41°38N 8°8W 88 D2
Vielha Spain 42°43N 0°44E 90 C5
Viella = Vielha Spain 42°43N 0°44E 90 C5
Vielle St-Girons France 43°56N 1°18W 72 E2
Vielsalm Belgium 50°17N 5°54E 69 D5
Vienenburg Germany 51°57N 10°34E 76 D6
Vieng Pou Kha Laos 20°41N 101°4E 116 G3
Vienna = Wien Austria 48°12N 16°22E 79 C9
Vienna Canada 42°41N 80°48W 174
Vienna Ga., U.S.A. 32°6N 83°47W 178
Vienna Ill., U.S.A. 37°25N 88°54W 172
Vienna Mo., U.S.A. 38°11N 91°57W 172
Vienne France 45°31N 4°53E 73
Vienne □ France 46°30N 0°42E 72
Vienne ➝ France 47°13N 0°5E 70
Vientiane Laos 17°58N 102°36E 120
Vientos, Paso de los Caribbean 20°0N 74°0W 183
Vieques Puerto Rico 18°8N 65°25W 18
Vierge Pt. St. Lucia 13°49N 60°53W 1
Viernheim Germany 49°31N 8°35E 7
Viersen Germany 51°15N 6°23E 76
Vierwaldstättersee Switz. 47°0N 8°30E 7
Vierzon France 47°13N 2°5E 71
Vieste Italy 41°53N 16°10E 93
Viet Quang Vietnam 22°30N 104°48E 116
Viet Tri Vietnam 21°18N 105°25E 12
Vietnam ■ Asia 19°0N 106°0E 120
Vieux-Boucau-les-Bains France 43°48N 1°23W 72
Vieux Fort St. Lucia 13°46N 60°58W 1
Vif France 45°5N 5°41E 73
Vigan Phil. 17°35N 120°28E 119
Vigévano Italy 45°19N 8°51E 92
Vigia Brazil 0°50S 48°5W 187
Viglas, Akra Greece 35°54N 27°51E 101
Vignemale France 42°47N 0°10W 72
Vigneulles-lès-Hattonchâtel France 48°59N 5°43E 71
Vignola Italy 44°29N 11°1E 92
Vigo Spain 42°12N 8°41W 88
Vigo, Ría de Spain 42°15N 8°45W 88
Vigsø Bugt Denmark 57°8N 8°47E 63
Vihiers France 47°10N 0°30W 70
Vihiga Kenya 0°3N 34°44E 142
Vihowa Pakistan 31°8N 70°30E 124
Vihowa ➝ Pakistan 31°8N 70°41E 124
Vijayadurg India 16°30N 73°25E 126
Vijayapura India 16°50N 75°55E 126
Vijayawada India 16°31N 80°39E 126
Vijosë ➝ Albania 40°37N 19°24E 96
Vík Iceland 63°25N 19°1W 60
Vika Sweden 60°57N 14°28E 62
Vikarabad India 17°20N 77°54E 126
Vikarbyn Sweden 60°55N 15°1E 62
Vikeke = Viqueque E. Timor 8°52S 126°23E 119
Viken Skåne, Sweden 56°9N 12°34E 63
Viken Västra Götaland, Sweden 58°39N 14°20E 63
Viking Canada 53°7N 111°50W 162
Vikmanshyttan Sweden 60°18N 15°50E 62
Vikna Norway 64°55N 10°58E 60
Vikos-Aoos △ Greece 40°0N 20°45E 98
Vila Bela da Santissima Trindade Brazil 15°0S 59°57W 186
Vila da Maganja Mozam. 17°18S 37°30E 143
Vila da Ribeira Brava C. Verde Is. 16°32N 24°25W 13
Vila de Rei Portugal 39°41N 8°9W 88
Vila do Bispo Portugal 37°5N 8°53W 89
Vila do Conde Portugal 41°21N 8°45W 88
Vila do Maio C. Verde Is. 15°21N 23°10W 13
Vila Franca de Xira Portugal 38°57N 8°59W 89
Vila Gamito Mozam. 14°12S 33°0E 143
Vila Gomes da Costa Mozam. 24°20S 33°37E 145
Vila Machado Mozam. 19°15S 34°14E 143
Vila Mouzinho Mozam. 14°48S 34°25E 143
Vila Nova de Famalicão Portugal 41°25N 8°32W 88
Vila Nova de Foz Côa Portugal 41°5N 7°9W 88
Vila Nova de Gaia Portugal 41°8N 8°37W 88
Vila Pouca de Aguiar Portugal 41°30N 7°38W 88
Vila Real Portugal 41°17N 7°48W 88
Vila-Real Spain 39°55N 0°3W 90
Vila Real □ Portugal 41°36N 7°35W 88
Vila Real de Santo António Portugal 37°10N 7°28W 89
Vila-seca Spain 41°7N 1°9E 90
Vila Vasco da Gama Mozam. 14°54S 32°14E 143
Vila Velha Espírito Santo, Brazil 20°20S 40°17W 189
Vila Velha Sergipe, Brazil 11°20S 38°9W 189
Vila Viçosa Portugal 38°45N 7°27W 89
Vilafranca del Maestrat = Villafranca del Cid Spain 40°26N 0°16W 90
Vilafranca del Penedès Spain 41°21N 1°40E 90
Vilagarcía de Arousa Spain 42°34N 8°46W 88
Vilaine ➝ France 47°30N 2°27W 70
Vilanandro, Tanjona Madag. 16°11S 44°27E 141
Vilanculos Mozam. 22°1S 35°17E 145
Vilanova i la Geltrú Spain 41°13N 1°40E 90
Vilar Formoso Portugal 40°38N 6°45W 88
Vilaseca-Salou = Vila-seca Spain 41°7N 1°9E 90
Vilbjerg Denmark 56°12N 8°46E 63
Vilcabamba, Cordillera Peru 13°0S 73°0W 188
Vilcanchos Peru 13°40S 74°25W 188
Vilcheka, Ostrov Russia 80°0N 58°31E 106
Vilcheka, Zemlya Russia 80°30N 60°30E 54
Vilches Spain 38°12N 3°30W 89
Vileyka Belarus 54°30N 26°53E 75
Vilhelmina Sweden 64°35N 16°39E 60
Vilhena Brazil 12°40S 60°5W 186
Viliya = Neris ➝ Lithuania 55°8N 24°16E 84
Viljandi Estonia 58°28N 25°30E 84
Vilkaviškis Lithuania 54°39N 23°2E 82
Vilkija Lithuania 55°3N 23°35E 82
Vilkitskogo, Proliv Russia 78°0N 103°0E 107
Vilkovo = Vylkove Ukraine 45°28N 29°32E 81
Villa Abecia Bolivia 21°0S 68°18W 190
Villa Ana Argentina 28°28S 59°40W 190
Villa Angela Argentina 27°34S 60°45W 190

a Bella *Bolivia* 10°25S 65°22W **186 F5**
a Cañas *Argentina* 34°0S 61°35W **190 C3**
la Constitución *Argentina* 33°15S 60°20W **190 C3**
a de Arriaga *Mexico* 21°56N 101°20W **180 C4**
a de María *Argentina* 29°55S 63°43W **190 B3**
a de Méndez *Mexico* 25°7N 98°34W **181 B5**
a del Rio *Spain* 37°59N 4°17W **89 H6**
a Dolores *Argentina* 31°58S 65°15W **190 C2**
a Gesell *Argentina* 37°15S 56°55W **190 D4**
a Guillermina *Argentina* 28°15S 59°29W **190 B4**
a Hayes *Paraguay* 25°5S 57°20W **190 B4**
a Hidalgo *Mexico* 24°15N 99°26W **181 C5**
a Iris *Argentina* 38°12S 63°12W **190 D3**
a Las Estrellas = Frei *Antarctica* 62°30S 58°0W **55 C18**
a María *Argentina* 32°20S 63°10W **190 C3**
a Mazán *Argentina* 28°40S 66°30W **190 B2**
a Minozzo *Italy* 44°22N 10°28E **92 D7**
a Montes *Bolivia* 21°10S 63°30W **190 A3**
a Ocampo *Argentina* 28°30S 59°20W **190 B4**
a Ocampo *Mexico* 26°27N 105°31W **180 B3**
a Ojo de Agua *Argentina* 29°30S 63°44W **190 B3**
a Regina *Argentina* 39°6S 67°4W **192 A3**
a Rica *Italy* 33°44N 84°55W **178 B5**
a San Giovanni 38°13N 15°38E **95 D8**
a San Martín *Argentina* 28°15S 64°9W **190 B3**
a Santina *Italy* 46°24N 12°55E **93 B9**
a Unión *Argentina* 23°12N 106°14W **180 C4**
ablino *Spain* 42°57N 6°19W **88 C4**
acarlos *Spain* 39°53N 4°17E **100 B11**
acarriedo *Spain* 43°14N 3°48W **88 B7**
acarrillo *Spain* 38°7N 3°3W **89 G7**
acastín *Spain* 40°46N 4°25W **88 E6**
ach *Austria* 46°37N 13°51E **78 E6**
acido *Italy* 39°27N 8°44E **94 C1**
ada *Spain* 42°15N 4°59W **88 C6**
adiego *Spain* 42°31N 4°1W **88 C6**
adóssola *Italy* 46°4N 8°16E **92 B5**
afeliche *Spain* 41°10N 1°30W **90 D3**
afranca *Spain* 42°17N 1°46W **90 C3**
afranca de Bonany *Spain* 39°34N 3°5E **100 B11**
afranca de los Barros *Spain* 38°35N 6°18W **89 G4**
afranca de los Caballeros *Spain* 39°26N 3°21W **89 F7**
afranca del Cid *Spain* 40°26N 0°16W **90 E4**
afranca del Panadés = Vilafranca del Penedès *Spain* 41°21N 1°40E **90 D6**
afranca di Verona *Italy* 45°21N 10°50E **92 C7**
afranca Tirrena *Italy* 45°21N 10°50E **92 C7**
agrán *Mexico* 24°29N 99°29W **181 C5**
aguay *Argentina* 32°0S 59°0W **190 C4**
aharta *Spain* 38°9N 4°54W **89 G6**
ahermosa *Mexico* 17°59N 92°55W **180 D6**
aines-la-Juhel *France* 48°21N 0°20W **70 D6**
ajoyosa *Spain* 38°30N 0°12W **91 G4**
alba *Spain* 42°32N 7°40W **88 B3**
alba de Guardo *Spain* 42°42N 4°49W **88 C6**
alón de Campos *Spain* 42°5N 5°4W **88 C5**
alpando *Spain* 41°51N 5°25W **88 D5**
aluenga de la Sagra *Spain* 40°2N 3°54W **88 E7**
amanán *Spain* 42°19N 5°35W **88 D5**
amartín *Spain* 36°52N 5°38W **89 J5**
amayor de Santiago *Spain* 39°50N 2°59W **90 F2**
amblard *France* 45°2N 0°32E **72 C4**
anova Monteleone *Italy* 40°30N 8°28E **94 B1**
anueva *U.S.A.* 35°16N 105°22W **169 J11**
anueva de Castellón *Spain* 39°5N 0°31W **91 F4**
anueva de Córdoba *Spain* 38°20N 4°38W **89 G6**
anueva de la Fuente *Spain* 38°42N 2°42W **91 G2**
anueva de la Serena *Spain* 38°59N 5°50W **89 G5**
anueva de la Sierra *Spain* 40°12N 6°24W **88 E4**
anueva de los Castillejos *Spain* 37°30N 7°15W **89 H3**
anueva de los Infantes *Spain* 38°43N 3°1W **89 G7**
anueva del Arzobispo *Spain* 38°10N 3°0W **91 G2**
anueva del Fresno *Spain* 38°23N 7°10W **89 G3**
anueva y Geltrú = Vilanova i la Geltrú *Spain* 41°13N 1°40E **90 D6**
aputzu *Italy* 39°26N 9°34E **94 C2**
aquilambre *Spain* 42°39N 5°33W **88 C5**
lar del Arzobispo *Spain* 39°44N 0°50W **90 F4**
lar del Rey *Spain* 39°7N 6°50W **89 F4**
lard-de-Lans *France* 45°3N 5°33E **73 C9**
larreal = Vila-Real *Spain* 39°55N 0°3W **90 F4**
larrica *Chile* 39°15S 72°15W **192 A2**
larrica *France* 24°45S 67°46W **192 A2**
larrobledo *Spain* 39°18N 2°36W **91 F2**
arroya de la Sierra *Spain* 41°27N 1°46W **90 D3**
larrubia de los Ojos *Spain* 39°14N 3°36W **89 F7**
lars-les-Dombes *France* 46°3N 5°3E **71 F12**
lasayas *Spain* 41°24N 2°39W **90 D2**
laseco de los Gamitos *Spain* 41°2N 6°7W **88 D4**
lasimius *Italy* 39°8N 9°31E **94 C2**
lastar *Spain* 40°17N 1°9W **90 E3**
latobas *Spain* 39°54N 3°20W **88 F7**
lavicencio *Argentina* 32°28S 69°0W **190 C2**
lavicencio *Colombia* 3°9N 73°37W **186 C4**
laviciosa *Spain* 43°32S 65°35W **190 A2**
lazón *Bolivia* 22°0S 65°35W **190 A2**
le-Marie *Canada* 47°20N 79°30W **164 C4**
le Platte *U.S.A.* 30°41N 92°17W **176 F8**

Villedieu-les-Poêles *France* 48°50N 1°13W **70 D5**
Villefort *France* 44°28N 3°56E **72 D7**
Villefranche-de-Lauragais *France* 43°25N 1°44E **72 E5**
Villefranche-de-Rouergue *France* 44°21N 2°2E **72 D6**
Villefranche-du-Périgord *France* 44°38N 1°5E **72 D5**
Villefranche-sur-Saône *France* 45°59N 4°43E **73 C8**
Villel *Spain* 40°14N 1°12W **90 E3**
Villena *Spain* 38°39N 0°52W **91 G4**
Villenauxe-la-Grande *France* 48°35N 3°33E **71 D10**
Villenave-d'Ornon *France* 44°46N 0°33W **72 D3**
Villeneuve-d'Ascq *France* 50°38N 3°9E **71 B10**
Villeneuve-l'Archevêque *France* 48°14N 3°32E **71 D10**
Villeneuve-lès-Avignon *France* 43°58N 4°49E **73 E8**
Villeneuve-sur-Allier *France* 46°40N 3°13E **71 F10**
Villeneuve-sur-Lot *France* 44°24N 0°42E **72 D4**
Villeneuve-sur-Yonne *France* 48°5N 3°18E **71 D10**
Villeréal *France* 44°38N 0°45E **72 D4**
Villers-Bocage *France* 49°3N 0°40W **70 C6**
Villers-Cotterêts *France* 49°15N 3°4E **71 C10**
Villers-sur-Mer *France* 49°21N 0°2W **70 C6**
Villersexel *France* 47°33N 6°26E **71 E13**
Villerupt *France* 49°28N 5°55E **71 C12**
Villeurbanne *France* 45°46N 4°55E **73 C8**
Villiers *S. Africa* 27°2S 28°36E **145 C4**
Villingen-Schwenningen *Germany* 48°3N 8°26E **77 G4**
Villmanstrand = Lappeenranta *Finland* 61°3N 28°12E **84 B5**
Villupuram *India* 11°59N 79°31E **127 J4**
Vilna *Canada* 54°7N 111°55W **162 C6**
Vilnius *Lithuania* 54°38N 25°19E **84 E3**
Vils *Austria* 47°33N 10°38E **78 D3**
Vils → *Bayern, Germany* 48°37N 13°11E **77 G9**
Vils → *Bayern, Germany* 49°11N 11°57E **77 F7**
Vilsandi *Estonia* 58°23N 21°52E **84 C1**
Vilsbiburg *Germany* 48°26N 12°22E **77 G8**
Vilshofen *Germany* 48°37N 13°11E **77 G9**
Vilusi *Montenegro* 42°44N 18°34E **96 D2**
Vilvoorde *Belgium* 50°56N 4°26E **69 D4**
Vilyuchinsk *Russia* 52°55N 158°24E **107 D16**
Vilyuy → *Russia* 64°24N 126°26E **107 C13**
Vilyuysk *Russia* 63°40N 121°35E **107 C13**
Vilyuyskoye Vdkhr. *Russia* 63°0N 112°0E **107 C12**
Vimianzo *Spain* 43°7N 9°2W **88 B1**
Vimioso *Portugal* 41°35N 6°31W **88 D4**
Vimmerby *Sweden* 57°40N 15°55E **63 G9**
Vimoutiers *France* 48°57N 0°10E **70 D7**
Vimperk *Czech Rep.* 49°3N 13°46E **78 B6**
Viña del Mar *Chile* 33°0S 71°30W **190 C1**
Vinarós *Spain* 40°30N 0°27E **90 E5**
Vincennes *U.S.A.* 38°41N 87°32W **172 F10**
Vincennes Bay *S. Ocean* 66°0S 109°0E **55 C8**
Vinchina *Argentina* 28°45S 68°15W **190 B2**
Vindelälven → *Sweden* 63°55N 19°50E **60 E18**
Vindeln *Sweden* 64°12N 19°43E **60 D18**
Vinderup *Denmark* 56°29N 8°45E **63 H2**
Vindhya Ra. *India* 22°50N 77°0E **124 H7**
Vineland *U.S.A.* 39°29N 75°2W **173 F16**
Vineuil *France* 47°35N 1°22E **70 E8**
Vinga *Romania* 46°1N 21°14E **80 D6**
Vingåker *Sweden* 59°2N 15°52E **62 E9**
Vinh *Vietnam* 18°45N 105°38E **120 C5**
Vinh Long *Vietnam* 10°16N 105°57E **121 G5**
Vinh Moc *Vietnam* 21°18N 105°1E **120 B5**
Vinh Yen *Vietnam* 21°21N 105°35E **116 G5**
Vinhais *Portugal* 41°50N 7°5W **88 D3**
Vinica *Croatia* 46°20N 16°9E **93 B13**
Vinica *Macedonia* 41°53N 22°30E **96 E6**
Vinica *Slovenia* 45°28N 15°16E **93 C12**
Vinita *U.S.A.* 36°39N 95°9W **176 C7**
Vinkovci *Croatia* 45°19N 18°48E **80 E3**
Vinnitsa = Vinnytsya *Ukraine* 49°15N 28°30E **75 D15**
Vinnytsya *Ukraine* 49°15N 28°30E **75 D15**
Vinnytsya □ *Ukraine* 49°20N 28°15E **75 D15**
Vinslöv *Sweden* 56°7N 13°55E **63 H6**
Vinson Massif *Antarctica* 78°35S 85°25W **55 D18**
Vintjärn *Sweden* 60°50N 16°4E **62 D10**
Vinton *Calif., U.S.A.* 39°48N 120°10W **170 F6**
Vinton *Iowa, U.S.A.* 42°10N 92°1W **172 D7**
Vinton *La., U.S.A.* 30°11N 93°35W **176 F8**
Vinţu de Jos *Romania* 46°0N 23°30E **81 D8**
Vinukonda *India* 16°4N 79°45E **127 F4**
Viöl *Germany* 54°34N 9°11E **76 A5**
Violet Town *Australia* 36°38S 145°42E **153 D6**
Violet Valley ○ *Australia* 17°10S 127°55E **148 C4**
Viooolsdrif *S. Africa* 28°46S 17°39E **144 C2**
Viotia □ *Greece* 38°20N 23°0E **98 C5**
Vipava *Slovenia* 45°51N 13°58E **93 C10**
Vipiteno *Italy* 46°54N 11°26E **93 B8**
Viqueque *E. Timor* 8°52S 126°23E **119 F7**
Vir *Croatia* 13°30N 124°20E **119 B6**
Virac *Phil.* 13°30N 124°20E **119 B6**
Virachey *Cambodia* 13°59N 106°49E **120 F6**
Virachey △ *Cambodia* 14°14N 106°55E **120 E6**
Virago Sd. *Canada* 54°0N 132°30W **162 C2**
Virajpet = Virarajendrapet *India* 12°10N 75°50E **127 J2**
Viramgam *India* 23°5N 72°0E **124 H7**
Virananşehir *Turkey* 37°13N 39°45E **105 D8**
Virarajendrapet *India* 12°10N 75°50E **127 J2**
Virawah *Pakistan* 24°31N 70°46E **124 G4**
Virbalis *Lithuania* 54°39N 22°50E **84 D4**
Virden *Canada* 49°50N 100°56W **163 D8**
Vire *France* 48°50N 0°53W **70 D6**
Vire → *France* 49°20N 1°7W **70 C5**
Virgem da Lapa *Brazil* 16°49S 42°27W **189 H9**
Virgenes, C. *Argentina* 52°19S 68°21W **192 D3**
Virgin → *U.S.A.* 36°28N 114°21W **169 H6**
Virgin Gorda *Br. Virgin Is.* 18°30N 64°26W **183 a**
Virgin Is. (British) ○ *W. Indies* 18°30N 64°30W **183 a**
Virgin Is. (U.S.) ○ *W. Indies* 18°20N 65°0W **183 a**

Virgin Islands △ *U.S. Virgin Is.* 18°21N 64°43W **183 C7**
Virginia *S. Africa* 28°8S 26°55E **144 C4**
Virginia *U.S.A.* 47°31N 92°32W **172 B7**
Virginia □ *U.S.A.* 37°30N 78°45W **173 G14**
Virginia Beach *U.S.A.* 36°49N 76°9W **173 F16**
Virginia City *Mont., U.S.A.* 45°18N 111°56W **168 D8**
Virginia City *Nev., U.S.A.* 39°19N 119°39W **170 F7**
Virginia Falls *Canada* 61°38N 125°42W **162 A3**
Virginiatown *Canada* 48°9N 79°36W **164 C4**
Virje *Croatia* 46°4N 16°59E **93 B13**
Viroqua *U.S.A.* 43°34N 90°53W **172 D8**
Virovitica *Croatia* 45°51N 17°21E **80 E2**
Virpazar *Montenegro* 42°14N 19°6E **96 D3**
Virpur *India* 21°51N 70°42E **124 J4**
Virsbo *Sweden* 59°52N 16°12E **62 E10**
Virserum *Sweden* 57°20N 15°35E **63 G9**
Virton *Belgium* 49°35N 5°32E **69 E5**
Virú *Peru* 8°25S 78°45W **188 E2**
Virudhunagar *India* 9°30N 77°58E **127 K3**
Virunga △ *Dem. Rep. of the Congo* 0°5N 29°38E **142 B2**
Vis *Croatia* 43°4N 16°10E **93 E13**
Visalia *U.S.A.* 36°20N 119°18W **170 J7**
Visayan Sea *Phil.* 11°30N 123°30E **119 B6**
Visby *Sweden* 57°37N 18°18E **63 G12**
Viscount Melville Sd. *Canada* 74°10N 108°0W **161 C10**
Visé *Belgium* 50°44N 5°41E **69 D5**
Vise, Ostrov *Russia* 79°33N 76°50E **106 B8**
Višegrad *Bos.-H.* 43°47N 19°17E **80 G4**
Viseu *Brazil* 1°10S 46°5W **187 D9**
Viseu *Portugal* 40°40N 7°55W **88 E3**
Viseu □ *Portugal* 40°40N 7°55W **88 E3**
Vişeu de Sus *Romania* 47°45N 24°25E **81 C8**
Vishakhapatnam *India* 17°45N 83°20E **126 F6**
Vişina *Romania* 43°52N 24°27E **81 D9**
Vişineşti *Moldova* 46°20N 28°27E **81 D13**
Visingsö *Sweden* 58°2N 14°20E **63 F8**
Viskafors *Sweden* 57°37N 12°50E **63 G6**
Viskan → *Sweden* 57°14N 12°12E **63 G6**
Viški Kanal *Croatia* 43°4N 16°5E **93 E13**
Vislanda *Sweden* 56°46N 14°30E **63 H8**
Visnagar *India* 23°45N 72°32E **124 H5**
Višnja Gora *Slovenia* 45°58N 14°45E **93 C11**
Viso, Mte. *Italy* 44°38N 7°5E **92 D4**
Viso del Marqués *Spain* 38°32N 3°34W **89 G7**
Visoko *Bos.-H.* 43°58N 18°10E **80 G3**
Visokoi I. *Antarctica* 56°43S 27°15W **55 B1**
Visp *Switz.* 46°17N 7°52E **77 J3**
Vissefjärda *Sweden* 56°32N 15°35E **63 H9**
Visselhövede *Germany* 52°59N 9°34E **76 C5**
Vissenbjerg *Denmark* 55°23N 10°8E **63 C4**
Vista *U.S.A.* 33°12N 117°14W **171 M9**
Vistonida, L. *Greece* 41°0N 25°7E **97 E9**
Vistonikos, Ormos = Vistonida. L. *Greece* 41°0N 25°7E **97 E9**
Vistula = Wisła → *Poland* 54°22N 18°55E **82 D5**
Vistula Spit *Europe* 54°25N 19°32E **82 D5**
Vit → *Bulgaria* 43°30N 24°30E **97 C8**
Vita *India* 17°17N 74°33E **126 F2**
Vitanje *Slovenia* 46°25N 15°18E **93 B12**
Vitebsk = Vitsyebsk *Belarus* 55°10N 30°15E **84 E6**
Viterbo *Italy* 42°25N 12°6E **93 F9**
Vitez *Bos.-H.* 44°10N 17°48E **80 F2**
Viti Levu *Fiji* 17°30S 177°30E **154 a**
Vitigudino *Spain* 41°1N 6°26W **88 D4**
Vitim *Russia* 59°28N 112°35E **107 D12**
Vitim → *Russia* 59°26N 112°34E **107 D12**
Vitina *Greece* 37°40N 22°10E **98 D4**
Vitkov *Czech Rep.* 49°46N 17°45E **79 B10**
Vitória *Brazil* 20°20S 40°22W **189 E2**
Vitória da Conquista *Brazil* 14°51S 40°51W **189 C2**
Vitória de Santo Antão *Brazil* 8°10S 35°20W **189 B3**
Vitoria-Gasteiz *Spain* 42°50N 2°41W **90 C2**
Vitória Seamount *Atl. Oc.* 20°0S 40°0W **56 G8**
Vitorino Freire *Brazil* 4°45S 45°10W **189 A1**
Vitosha △ *Bulgaria* 42°36N 23°18E **96 G7**
Vitré *France* 48°8N 1°12W **70 D5**
Vitry-le-François *France* 48°43N 4°33E **71 D11**
Vitry-sur-Seine *France* 48°47N 2°23E **71 D9**
Vitsand *Sweden* 60°20N 13°0E **62 D7**
Vitsi, Oros *Greece* 40°40N 21°25E **98 F5**
Vitsyebsk *Belarus* 55°10N 30°15E **84 E6**
Vitsyebsk □ *Belarus* 55°10N 29°30E **84 E5**
Vittaryd *Sweden* 57°24N 14°30E **63 H7**
Vitteaux *France* 47°24N 4°30E **71 E11**
Vittel *France* 48°12N 5°57E **71 D12**
Vittória *Italy* 36°57N 14°32E **95 F7**
Vittório Véneto *Italy* 45°59N 12°18E **93 C9**
Vittsjö *Sweden* 56°20N 13°40E **63 H6**
Viveiro *Spain* 43°39N 7°38W **88 B3**
Vivian *U.S.A.* 32°53N 93°59W **176 E8**
Viviers *France* 44°30N 4°43E **73 D8**
Vivonne *Australia* 35°59S 137°9E **152 C2**
Vivonne *France* 46°25N 0°15E **72 B4**
Vivonne B. *Australia* 35°59S 137°9E **152 C2**
Viwa *Fiji* 17°10S 177°58E **154 a**
Vizcaíno, Desierto de *Mexico* 27°30N 113°45W **180 B2**
Vizcaíno, Sierra *Mexico* 27°30N 114°0W **180 B2**
Vize *Turkey* 41°34N 27°45E **97 E11**
Vizianagaram *India* 18°6N 83°30E **126 E6**
Vizille *France* 45°5N 5°46E **73 C9**
Viziñada *Croatia* 45°20N 13°46E **93 C10**
Viziru *Romania* 45°0N 27°43E **81 D11**
Vizzini *Italy* 37°10N 14°45E **95 F7**
Vlaardingen *Neths.* 51°55N 4°21E **69 C4**
Vlachiotis *Greece* 36°52N 22°42E **98 D4**
Vlădeasa, Vf. *Romania* 46°47N 22°50E **80 D7**
Vladičin Han *Serbia* 42°42N 22°1E **96 D6**
Vladikavkaz *Russia* 43°0N 44°35E **87 J7**
Vladimir *Russia* 56°15N 40°30E **86 B5**
Vladimir □ *Russia* 56°5N 40°10E **86 B5**
Vladimir Volynskiy = Volodymyr-Volynskyy *Ukraine* 50°50N 24°18E **75 C13**
Vladimirci *Serbia* 44°36N 19°50E **96 B3**
Vladimirovac *Serbia* 45°1N 20°53E **80 E5**
Vladimirovo *Bulgaria* 43°32N 23°22E **96 C7**
Vladislavovka *Ukraine* 45°12N 35°29E **85 K8**
Vladivostok *Russia* 43°10N 131°53E **112 C5**
Vlăhiţa *Romania* 46°25N 25°31E **81 D10**

Vlasenica *Bos.-H.* 44°11N 18°59E **80 F3**
Vlašić *Bos.-H.* 44°19N 17°37E **80 F2**
Vlašim *Czech Rep.* 49°40N 14°53E **78 B7**
Vlasinsko Jezero *Serbia* 42°44N 22°22E **96 D6**
Vlasotince *Serbia* 42°59N 22°7E **96 D6**
Vlieland *Neths.* 53°16N 4°55E **69 A4**
Vlissingen *Neths.* 51°26N 3°34E **69 C3**
Vlkolínec *Slovak Rep.* 49°1N 19°16E **79 B12**
Vlorë *Albania* 40°32N 19°28E **96 F3**
Vlorës, Gjiri i *Albania* 40°29N 19°27E **96 F3**
Vltava → *Czech Rep.* 50°21N 14°30E **78 A7**
Vo Dat *Vietnam* 11°9N 107°31E **121 G6**
Voćin *Croatia* 45°37N 17°33E **80 E2**
Vöcklabruck *Austria* 48°1N 13°39E **78 D6**
Vodice *Croatia* 43°47N 15°47E **93 E12**
Vodlozersky △ *Russia* 62°35N 37°5E **106 C1**
Vodňany *Czech Rep.* 49°9N 14°11E **78 B7**
Vodnjan *Croatia* 44°59N 13°52E **93 D10**
Voe *U.K.* 60°21N 1°16W **65 A7**
Vogan *Togo* 6°23N 1°30E **139 D5**
Vogel Pk. *Nigeria* 7°24N 11°47E **139 D7**
Vogelkop = Doberai, Jazirah *Indonesia* 1°25S 133°0E **119 E8**
Vogelsberg *Germany* 50°31N 9°12E **76 E5**
Voghera *Italy* 44°59N 9°1E **92 D6**
Vohibinany *Madag.* 18°49S 49°4E **141 H9**
Vohimarina = Iharana *Madag.* 13°25S 50°0E **141 G10**
Vohimena, Tanjon' i *Madag.* 25°36S 45°8E **141 K9**
Vohipeno *Madag.* 22°22S 47°51E **141 J9**
Voi *Kenya* 3°25S 38°32E **142 C4**
Void-Vacon *France* 48°40N 5°36E **71 D12**
Voinești *Iași, Romania* 47°5N 27°27E **81 C12**
Voinești *Prahova, Romania* 45°5N 25°14E **81 D10**
Voinjama *Liberia* 8°25N 9°44W **138 D3**
Voiron *France* 45°22N 5°35E **73 C9**
Voisey B. *Canada* 56°15N 61°50W **165 A7**
Voitsberg *Austria* 47°3N 15°9E **78 D8**
Vojens *Denmark* 55°16N 9°18E **63 J3**
Vojmsjön *Sweden* 65°0N 16°24E **60 D17**
Vojnić *Croatia* 45°19N 15°43E **93 C12**
Vojnik *Slovenia* 46°18N 15°19E **93 B12**
Vojvodina □ *Serbia* 45°20N 20°0E **80 E5**
Vokhtoga *Russia* 58°46N 41°8E **84 C11**
Volary *Czech Rep.* 48°54N 13°52E **78 C6**
Volborg *U.S.A.* 45°51N 105°41W **168 D11**
Volcán de Colima △ *Mexico* 19°30N 103°40W **180 D4**
Volcano Is. = Kazan-Rettō *Pac. Oc.* 25°0N 141°0E **156 E6**
Volcans d'Auvergne △ *France* 45°20N 2°40E **72 C6**
Volchansk = Vovchansk *Ukraine* 50°17N 36°58E **85 G9**
Volchikha *Russia* 52°20N 80°23E **109 B10**
Volchya → *Ukraine* 48°32N 36°0E **85 H8**
Volda *Norway* 62°9N 6°5E **60 E12**
Volga = Privolzhskiy □ *Russia* 56°0N 50°0E **106 D6**
Volga → *Russia* 55°58N 38°16E **84 C10**
Volga → *Russia* 46°0N 48°30E **87 G9**
Volga Hts. = Privolzhskaya Vozvyshennost *Russia* 51°0N 46°0E **86 E7**
Volgo-Baltiyskiy Kanal *Russia* 60°0N 38°0E **84 B9**
Volgo-Donskoy Kanal *Russia* 48°40N 43°37E **87 F7**
Volgodonsk *Russia* 47°33N 42°5E **87 G6**
Volgograd *Russia* 48°40N 44°25E **87 F7**
Volgograd □ *Russia* 49°30N 44°30E **86 F7**
Volgogradskoye Vdkhr. *Russia* 50°0N 45°20E **86 E8**
Volgorechensk *Russia* 57°28N 41°14E **86 B5**
Volimes *Greece* 37°52N 20°38E **98 D2**
Volintiri *Moldova* 46°26N 29°37E **81 D14**
Volissos *Greece* 38°29N 25°54E **99 C7**
Volkach *Germany* 49°52N 10°14E **77 F6**
Völkermarkt *Austria* 46°39N 14°39E **78 E7**
Volkhov *Russia* 59°55N 32°15E **84 C7**
Volkhov → *Russia* 60°8N 32°20E **84 B7**
Völklingen *Germany* 49°15N 6°50E **77 F2**
Volkovysk = Vawkavysk *Belarus* 53°9N 24°30E **75 B13**
Volksrust *S. Africa* 27°24S 29°53E **145 C4**
Volnovakha *Ukraine* 47°35N 37°30E **85 J9**
Volochanka *Russia* 71°0N 94°28E **107 B10**
Volodarsk *Russia* 56°12N 43°15E **86 B6**
Volodymyr-Volynskyy *Ukraine* 50°50N 24°18E **75 C13**
Vologda *Russia* 59°10N 39°45E **84 C10**
Vologda □ *Russia* 60°15N 39°0E **84 C10**
Volokolamsk *Russia* 56°5N 35°57E **84 D8**
Volokonovka *Russia* 50°33N 37°52E **85 G9**
Volos *Greece* 39°24N 22°59E **98 E5**
Volosovo *Russia* 59°27N 29°32E **84 C5**
Volovets *Ukraine* 48°43N 23°11E **81 B8**
Volovo *Russia* 53°35N 38°1E **84 F10**
Volozhin = Valozhyn *Belarus* 54°3N 26°30E **75 A14**
Volsk *Russia* 52°5N 47°22E **86 D8**
Volta □ *Ghana* 7°0N 0°30E **139 D5**
Volta → *Ghana* 5°46N 0°41E **139 D5**
Volta, L. *Ghana* 7°30N 0°0 **139 D5**
Volta Blanche = White Volta → *Ghana* 9°10N 1°15W **139 D4**
Volta Redonda *Brazil* 22°31S 44°5W **191 A7**
Voltaire, C. *Australia* 14°16S 125°35E **148 B4**
Volterra *Italy* 43°24N 10°51E **92 E7**
Voltri *Italy* 44°26N 8°45E **92 D5**
Volturno → *Italy* 41°1N 13°55E **94 A6**
Volubilis *Morocco* 34°2N 5°33W **136 B4**
Voluntari *Romania* 44°30N 26°11E **81 F11**
Volvi, L. *Greece* 40°40N 23°34E **96 F7**
Volyně *Czech Rep.* 49°10N 13°53E **78 B6**
Volzhsk *Russia* 55°57N 48°23E **86 A6**
Volzhskiy *Russia* 48°56N 44°46E **87 F7**
Vomo *Fiji* 17°30S 177°15E **154 a**
Vonitsa *Greece* 38°55N 20°58E **98 E3**
Vopnafjörður *Iceland* 65°45N 14°50W **60 D6**
Vorarlberg □ *Austria* 47°20N 10°0E **78 D2**
Voras Oros *Greece* 40°57N 21°45E **96 F5**
Vorbasse *Denmark* 55°39N 9°6E **63 J3**
Vorchdorf *Austria* 48°0N 13°55E **78 D6**
Vordingborg *Denmark* 55°0N 11°54E **63 J5**
Vorë *Albania* 41°23N 19°40E **96 G3**
Voreio Aigaio □ *Greece* 38°50N 25°30E **99 C7**

Voreios Sporades *Greece* 39°15N 23°30E **98 B5**
Voreppe *France* 45°18N 5°39E **73 C9**
Vori *Greece* 35°4N 24°49E **98 F6**
Vorios Evoikos Kolpos *Greece* 38°45N 23°15E **98 C5**
Vorkuta *Russia* 67°48N 64°20E **106 C7**
Vormsi *Estonia* 59°1N 23°13E **84 C2**
Vorona → *Russia* 51°22N 42°3E **86 E6**
Voronezh *Russia* 51°40N 39°10E **85 G10**
Voronezh *Ukraine* 51°47N 33°28E **85 G7**
Voronezh □ *Russia* 51°30N 39°30E **86 E4**
Vorontsovo-Aleksandrovskoye = Zelenokumsk *Russia* 44°24N 44°0E **87 H6**
Vorpommersche Boddenlandschaft △ *Germany* 54°25N 12°32E **76 A8**
Vorskla → *Ukraine* 48°50N 34°10E **85 H8**
Võrts järv *Estonia* 58°16N 26°3E **84 C4**
Võru *Estonia* 57°48N 26°54E **84 D4**
Vosges □ *France* 48°20N 7°10E **71 D14**
Vosges □ *France* 48°12N 6°20E **71 D13**
Vosges du Nord △ *France* 49°0N 7°30E **71 D14**
Voskopojë *Albania* 40°35N 20°33E **96 F4**
Voskresensk *Russia* 55°19N 38°43E **84 E10**
Voskresenskoye *Russia* 56°51N 45°30E **86 B7**
Voss *Norway* 60°38N 6°26E **60 F12**
Vostochnyy Port *Russia* 42°44N 133°4E **112 C6**
Vostok *Antarctica* 78°30S 106°50E **55 D8**
Vostok I. *Kiribati* 10°5S 152°23W **157 J12**
Votice *Czech Rep.* 49°38N 14°39E **78 B7**
Vouga → *Portugal* 40°41N 8°40W **88 E2**
Vouillé *France* 46°38N 0°10E **72 B4**
Vouxa, Akra *Greece* 35°37N 23°32E **101 D5**
Vouzela *Portugal* 40°43N 8°7W **88 E2**
Vouziers *France* 49°22N 4°40E **71 C11**
Vovchansk *Ukraine* 50°17N 36°58E **85 G9**
Vowchyn *Belarus* 52°18N 23°18E **75 B12**
Voyageurs △ *U.S.A.* 48°32N 93°0W **172 A7**
Voynitsa *Russia* 65°10N 30°20E **60 D24**
Voyvozh *Russia* 62°56N 54°56E **106 C6**
Vozhe, Ozero *Russia* 60°45N 39°0E **84 B10**
Vozhega *Russia* 60°29N 40°12E **84 B11**
Voznesensk *Ukraine* 47°35N 31°21E **85 J6**
Voznesenye *Russia* 61°0N 35°28E **84 B8**
Vozrozhdeniya I. *Asia* 45°10N 59°20E **108 C5**
Vrå *Denmark* 57°21N 9°56E **63 G3**
Vráble *Slovak Rep.* 48°15N 18°16E **79 C11**
Vraćevsnica *Serbia* 44°2N 20°34E **96 B4**
Vrachneika *Greece* 38°10N 21°40E **98 C3**
Vrancea □ *Romania* 45°50N 26°45E **81 E11**
Vrancei, Munţii *Romania* 46°0N 26°30E **81 E11**
Vrangel *Russia* 42°43N 133°5E **112 C6**
Vrangelya, Ostrov *Russia* 71°0N 180°0E **107 B18**
Vranica *Bos.-H.* 43°55N 17°50E **80 G2**
Vranje *Serbia* 42°34N 21°54E **96 D6**
Vranjska Banja *Serbia* 42°34N 22°1E **96 D6**
Vranov nad Topľou *Slovak Rep.* 48°53N 21°40E **79 C14**
Vransko *Slovenia* 46°17N 14°58E **93 B11**
Vransko Jezero *Croatia* 43°53N 15°34E **93 E12**
Vrapčište *Macedonia* 41°50N 20°53E **96 E4**
Vratsa *Bulgaria* 43°15N 23°30E **96 C7**
Vratsa □ *Bulgaria* 43°15N 23°30E **96 C7**
Vrbas *Serbia* 45°40N 19°40E **80 E4**
Vrbas → *Bos.-H.* 45°8N 17°29E **80 E2**
Vrbnik *Croatia* 45°4N 14°40E **93 C11**
Vrbovec *Croatia* 45°53N 16°28E **93 C13**
Vrbovsko *Croatia* 45°24N 15°5E **93 C12**
Vrchlabí *Czech Rep.* 50°38N 15°37E **78 A8**
Vrede *S. Africa* 27°24S 29°6E **145 C4**
Vredefort *S. Africa* 27°0S 27°22E **144 C4**
Vreden *Germany* 52°2N 6°50E **76 C2**
Vredenburg *S. Africa* 32°56S 18°0E **144 E2**
Vredendal *S. Africa* 31°41S 18°35E **144 D2**
Vretstorp *Sweden* 59°1N 14°53E **62 E8**
Vrgorac *Croatia* 43°12N 17°20E **93 E14**
Vrhnika *Slovenia* 45°58N 14°15E **93 C11**
Vriddhachalam *India* 11°30N 79°20E **127 J4**
Vrīdi *Ivory C.* 5°15N 4°3W **138 D4**
Vrigstad *Sweden* 57°21N 14°28E **63 H8**
Vrindavan *India* 27°37N 77°40E **124 F7**
Vrisses *Greece* 35°23N 24°13E **101 D6**
Vrnograč *Bos.-H.* 45°10N 15°57E **93 C12**
Vrondados *Greece* 38°25N 26°7E **99 C8**
Vrpolje *Croatia* 45°13N 18°24E **80 E3**
Vršac *Serbia* 45°8N 21°20E **80 E6**
Vrsacki Kanal *Serbia* 45°15N 21°0E **80 E5**
Vrútky *Slovak Rep.* 49°7N 18°55E **79 B11**
Vryburg *S. Africa* 26°55S 24°45E **144 C3**
Vryheid *S. Africa* 27°45S 30°47E **145 C5**
Vsetín *Czech Rep.* 49°20N 18°0E **79 B10**
Vu Liet *Vietnam* 18°43N 105°23E **120 C5**
Vúcha → *Bulgaria* 42°10N 24°26E **97 D8**
Vučitrn = Vushtrri *Kosovo* 42°49N 20°59E **96 D4**
Vukovar *Croatia* 45°21N 18°59E **80 E4**
Vuktyl *Russia* 63°52N 57°20E **106 C6**
Vulcan *Canada* 50°25N 113°15W **162 D6**
Vulcan *Romania* 45°23N 23°17E **81 E8**
Vulcăneşti *Moldova* 45°41N 28°18E **81 E13**
Vulcano *Italy* 38°24N 14°58E **95 D7**
Vulkaneshty = Vulcăneşti *Moldova* 45°41N 28°18E **81 E13**
Vunduzi → *Mozam.* 18°56S 34°1E **143 B3**
Vung Tau *Vietnam* 10°21N 107°4E **121 G6**
Vunidawa *Fiji* 17°50S 178°21E **154 a**
Vunisea *Fiji* 19°3S 178°10E **154 a**
Vuntut △ *Canada* 68°25N 139°46W **166 C4**
Vürbitsa *Bulgaria* 42°59N 26°40E **97 D10**
Vushtrri *Kosovo* 42°49N 20°59E **96 D4**
Vutcani *Romania* 46°26N 27°59E **81 D12**
Vvedenskoye *Russia* 55°43N 64°8E **108 D7**
Vwaza △ *Malawi* 10°58S 33°25E **143 E3**
Vyara *India* 21°8N 73°28E **124 J5**
Vyartsilya *Russia* 62°8N 30°45E **84 A5**
Vyatka = Kirov *Russia* 58°35N 49°40E **86 B8**
Vyatka → *Russia* 55°37N 51°28E **86 C10**
Vyatskiye Polyany *Russia* 56°14N 51°5E **86 B10**
Vyazemskiy *Russia* 47°32N 134°45E **107 E14**
Vyazma *Russia* 55°10N 34°15E **84 E8**
Vyazniki *Russia* 56°10N 42°10E **86 B6**
Vyborg *Russia* 60°43N 28°47E **84 B5**
Vychegda → *Russia* 61°18N 46°36E **106 C5**
Vychodné Beskydy *Europe* 49°20N 22°0E **79 B15**

Vyerkhnyadzvinsk *Belarus* 55°45N 27°58E **84 E4**
Vyhoda *Ukraine* 48°56N 23°55E **81 B8**
Vyksa *Russia* 55°19N 42°11E **86 C6**
Vylkove *Ukraine* 45°28N 29°32E **81 E14**
Vylok *Ukraine* 48°8N 22°50E **80 B7**
Vynohradiv *Ukraine* 48°9N 23°2E **80 B7**
Vypin *India* 10°10N 76°15E **127 J3**
Vyrnwy, L. *U.K.* 52°48N 3°31W **66 E4**
Vyshkiv *Ukraine* 48°44N 23°39E **81 B8**
Vyshkove *Ukraine* 48°3N 23°25E **81 B8**
Vyshniy Volochek *Russia* 57°30N 34°30E **84 D8**
Vyshzha = imeni 26 Bakinskikh Komissarov *Turkmenistan* 39°22N 54°10E **129 B7**
Vyškov *Czech Rep.* 49°17N 17°0E **79 B9**
Vysočina □ *Czech Rep.* 49°30N 15°30E **78 B8**
Vysoké Mýto *Czech Rep.* 49°58N 16°10E **79 B9**
Vysokaye *Belarus* 52°23N 23°27E **83 F10**
Vyšší Brod *Czech Rep.* 48°37N 14°19E **78 C7**
Vytegra *Russia* 61°0N 36°27E **84 B9**
Vyzhnytsya *Ukraine* 48°15N 25°11E **81 B10**
Vyzhnytsya △ *Ukraine* 48°7N 25°15E **81 B10**

W

W du Benin △ *Benin* 11°57N 2°43E **139 C5**
W du Burkina Faso △ *Burkina Faso* 11°52N 2°50E **139 C5**
W du Niger △ *Niger* 13°31N 2°28E **139 C5**
W.A.C. Bennett Dam *Canada* 56°2N 122°6W **162 B4**
Wa *Ghana* 10°7N 2°25W **138 C4**
Waal → *Neths.* 51°37N 5°0E **69 C5**
Waalwijk *Neths.* 51°42N 5°4E **69 C5**
Waanyi-Garawa ○ *Australia* 18°2S 137°33E **150 B2**
Wabakimi △ *Canada* 50°38N 89°45W **164 B2**
Wabana *Canada* 47°40N 53°0W **165 C9**
Wabasca → *Canada* 58°22N 115°20W **162 B5**
Wabasca-Desmarais *Canada* 55°57N 113°56W **162 B6**
Wabash *U.S.A.* 40°48N 85°49W **173 E11**
Wabash → *U.S.A.* 37°48N 88°2W **172 G9**
Wabasso *U.S.A.* 27°45N 80°26W **179 H9**
Wabigoon L. *Canada* 49°44N 92°44W **163 D10**
Wabowden *Canada* 54°55N 98°38W **163 C9**
Wąbrzeźno *Poland* 53°16N 18°57E **83 E5**
Wabu Hu *China* 32°20N 116°45E **117 A11**
Wabuk Pt. *Canada* 55°20N 85°5W **164 A2**
Wabush *Canada* 52°55N 66°52W **165 B6**
Waccasassa B. *U.S.A.* 29°10N 82°50W **179 G7**
Wachau *Austria* 48°21N 15°26E **78 C8**
Wąchock *Poland* 51°4N 21°1E **83 G8**
Wächtersbach *Germany* 50°14N 9°17E **77 E5**
Wacissa *U.S.A.* 30°22N 83°59W **178 E6**
Waco *U.S.A.* 31°33N 97°9W **176 F6**
Waconichi, L. *Canada* 50°8N 74°0W **164 B5**
Wad Hamid *Sudan* 16°30N 32°45E **135 E12**
Wad Medani *Sudan* 14°28N 33°30E **135 F12**
Wad Thana *Pakistan* 27°22N 66°23E **124 F5**
Wadayama *Japan* 35°19N 134°52E **113 G7**
Wadbilliga △ *Australia* 36°25S 149°35E **153 D8**
Waddeneilanden *Neths.* 53°25N 5°10E **69 A5**
Waddenzee *Neths.* 53°6N 5°10E **69 A5**
Waddi, Chappal *Nigeria* 7°11N 11°43E **139 D7**
Waddington *U.S.A.* 44°52N 75°12W **173 C9**
Waddington, Mt. *Canada* 51°23N 125°15W **162 C3**
Waddy Pt. *Australia* 24°58S 153°21E **151 C5**
Wadebridge *U.K.* 50°31N 4°51W **67 G3**
Wadena *Canada* 51°57N 103°47W **163 C8**
Wadena *U.S.A.* 46°26N 95°8W **172 B6**
Wädenswil *Switz.* 47°14N 8°40E **77 H4**
Wadern *Germany* 49°32N 6°53E **77 F2**
Wadeye *Australia* 14°28S 129°52E **148 B4**
Wadgaon *India* 18°44N 73°39E **126 E1**
Wadhams *Canada* 51°30N 127°30W **162 C3**
Wadhwan *India* 22°42N 71°41E **124 H4**
Wadi *India* 17°4N 76°59E **126 F3**
Wādī as Sīr *Jordan* 31°56N 35°49E **130 D4**
Wādī Gemāl, J. *Egypt* 24°35N 35°10E **130 C4**
Wadi Halfa *Sudan* 21°53N 31°19E **137 D12**
Wādī Rum △ *Jordan* 29°30N 35°20E **130 F4**
Wadian *China* 32°42N 112°29E **117 A9**
Wadlew *Poland* 51°31N 19°23E **83 G6**
Wadley *Ala., U.S.A.* 33°7N 85°34W **178 B4**
Wadley *Ga., U.S.A.* 32°52N 82°24W **178 D7**
Wadowice *Poland* 49°52N 19°30E **83 J6**
Wadsworth *Nev., U.S.A.* 39°38N 119°17W **168 G4**
Wadsworth *Ohio, U.S.A.* 41°2N 81°44W **174 E7**
Waegwan *S. Korea* 35°59N 128°23E **115 G15**
Wafangdian *China* 39°38N 121°58E **115 C11**
Wafrah *Kuwait* 28°33N 47°56E **128 D5**
Wagait ○ *Australia* 13°1S 130°5E **148 B5**
Wagener *U.S.A.* 33°39N 81°22W **178 D8**
Wageningen *Neths.* 51°58N 5°40E **69 C5**
Wager B. *Canada* 65°26N 88°40W **161 D14**
Wagga Wagga *Australia* 35°7S 147°24E **153 C7**
Waghai *India* 20°46N 73°28E **124 H4**
Waghete *Indonesia* 4°10S 135°50E **119 E9**
Wagin *Australia* 33°17S 117°25E **149 F2**
Wagner *U.S.A.* 43°5N 98°18W **172 D4**
Wagon Mound *U.S.A.* 36°1N 104°42W **169 H11**
Wagoner *U.S.A.* 35°58N 95°22W **176 D7**
Wagrowiec *Poland* 52°48N 17°11E **83 F4**
Wah *Pakistan* 33°45N 72°40E **124 C5**
Wahai *Indonesia* 2°48S 129°35E **119 E7**
Wāhāt al Kharga, El = El Kharga *Egypt* 25°25N 30°33E **135 C12**
Waharoa *N.Z.* 37°46S 175°45E **154 D4**
Wāhāt Wafra *Egypt* 30°19N 67°52E ...
Wahai *U.S.A.* 32°40N 65°50E **124 C1**
Wahnai *Afghan.* 32°40N 65°50E **124 C1**
Wahoo *U.S.A.* 41°13N 96°37W **172 E5**
Wahpeton *U.S.A.* 46°16N 96°36W **172 B5**
Wai *India* 17°56N 73°57E **126 F1**
Waialua *U.S.A.* 21°34N 158°8W **167 L8**
Waiapu → *N.Z.* 37°47S 178°29E **154 C8**
Waiau → *N.Z.* 42°39S 173°5E **155 C8**
Waiau → *Canterbury, N.Z.* 42°47S 173°22E **155 C8**
Waiau → *Southland, N.Z.* 46°12S 167°38E **155 G2**
Waiawe Ganga → *Sri Lanka* 6°15N 81°0E **127 L5**
Waibeem *Indonesia* 0°30S 132°59E **119 E8**
Waiblingen *Germany* 48°49N 9°18E **77 G5**

284 Waidhofen an der Thaya INDEX TO WORLD MAPS

Waidhofen an der Thaya Austria 48°49N 15°17E 78 C8
Waidhofen an der Ybbs Austria 47°57N 14°46E 78 D7
Waigeo Indonesia 0°20S 130°40E 119 E8
Waihao → N.Z. 44°47S 171°10E 155 E6
Waihao Downs N.Z. 44°48S 170°55E 155 E5
Waiheke I. N.Z. 36°48S 175°6E 154 C4
Waihi N.Z. 37°23S 175°52E 154 D4
Waihi Beach N.Z. 37°25S 175°57E 154 D4
Waihola N.Z. 46°1S 170°8E 155 G5
Waihola L. N.Z. 45°59S 170°8E 155 F5
Waihou → N.Z. 37°15S 175°40E 154 D4
Waika Dem. Rep. of the Congo 2°22S 25°42E 142 C2
Waikabubak Indonesia 9°45S 119°25E 119 F5
Waikaia N.Z. 45°44S 168°51E 155 F3
Waikaka N.Z. 45°55S 169°1E 155 F4
Waikare, L. N.Z. 37°26S 175°13E 154 D4
Waikareiti, L. N.Z. 38°43S 177°10E 154 E6
Waikaremoana N.Z. 38°42S 177°12E 154 E6
Waikaremoana, L. N.Z. 38°49S 177°9E 154 E6
Waikari N.Z. 42°58S 172°41E 155 C7
Waikato → N.Z. 37°23S 174°43E 154 D3
Waikelo Indonesia 9°24S 119°19E 148 A2
Waikerie Australia 34°9S 140°0E 152 C4
Waikiekie N.Z. 35°57S 174°16E 154 B3
Waikokopu N.Z. 39°3S 177°52E 154 F6
Waikouaiti N.Z. 45°36S 170°41E 155 F5
Waikouaiti Downs N.Z. 45°30S 170°30E 155 F5
Waimakariri → N.Z. 43°24S 172°42E 155 D7
Waimangaroa N.Z. 41°43S 171°46E 155 B6
Waimarie N.Z. 41°35S 171°58E 155 B6
Waimate N.Z. 44°45S 171°3E 155 E6
Waimea Plain N.Z. 45°55S 168°35E 155 F3
Wainganga → India 18°50N 79°55E 126 E4
Waingapu Indonesia 9°35S 120°11E 119 F6
Waini → Guyana 8°20N 59°50W 186 B7
Wainuiomata N.Z. 41°17S 174°56E 154 H3
Wainwright Canada 52°50N 110°50W 163 C6
Wainwright U.S.A. 70°38N 160°2W 166 A7
Waiotapu N.Z. 38°21S 176°25E 154 E5
Waiouru N.Z. 39°28S 175°41E 154 F4
Waipa → N.Z. 38°16S 175°21E 154 E4
Waipahi N.Z. 46°6S 169°15E 155 G4
Waipapa Pt. N.Z. 46°40S 168°51E 155 G3
Waipara N.Z. 43°3S 172°46E 155 D7
Waipawa N.Z. 39°56S 176°38E 154 F5
Waipiro N.Z. 38°2S 178°22E 154 E7
Waipiro Bay N.Z. 38°1S 178°21E 154 E7
Waipoua Forest N.Z. 35°39S 173°33E 154 B2
Waipu N.Z. 35°59S 174°29E 154 B3
Waipukurau N.Z. 40°1S 176°33E 154 G5
Wairakei N.Z. 38°37S 176°6E 154 E5
Wairarapa, L. N.Z. 41°14S 175°15E 154 H4
Wairau → N.Z. 41°32S 174°7E 155 B9
Wairio N.Z. 45°59S 168°3E 155 F3
Wairoa N.Z. 39°3S 177°25E 154 F6
Wairoa → Hawke's Bay, N.Z. 39°4S 177°25E 154 F6
Wairoa → Northland, N.Z. 36°5S 173°59E 154 C2
Waitaki → N.Z. 44°56S 171°7E 155 E6
Waitaki Plains N.Z. 44°22S 170°0E 155 E5
Waitangi N.Z. 35°16S 174°5E 154 B3
Waitara N.Z. 38°59S 174°15E 154 E3
Waitara → N.Z. 38°59S 174°14E 154 E3
Waitiki Landing N.Z. 34°31S 172°50E 154 A1
Waitoa N.Z. 37°37S 175°35E 154 D4
Waitomo Caves N.Z. 38°16S 175°7E 154 E4
Waitotara N.Z. 39°49S 174°44E 154 F3
Waitotara → N.Z. 39°51S 174°41E 154 F3
Waitsburg U.S.A. 46°16N 118°9W 168 C4
Waiuku N.Z. 37°15S 174°45E 154 D3
Wajima Japan 37°30N 137°0E 113 F8
Wajir Kenya 1°42N 40°5E 142 B5
Wajir □ Kenya 1°45N 40°5E 142 B5
Wakasa Japan 35°20N 134°24E 113 G7
Wakasa-Wan Japan 35°40N 135°30E 113 G7
Wakatipu, L. N.Z. 45°5S 168°33E 155 F3
Wakaw Canada 52°39N 105°44W 163 C7
Wakaya Fiji 17°37S 179°0E 154 a
Wakayama Japan 34°15N 135°15E 113 G7
Wakayama □ Japan 33°50N 135°30E 113 H7
Wake Forest U.S.A. 35°59N 78°30W 177 D15
Wake I. Pac. Oc. 19°18N 166°36E 156 F8
WaKeeney U.S.A. 39°1N 99°53W 172 F4
Wakefield Jamaica 18°26N 77°42W 182 a
Wakefield N.Z. 41°24S 173°5E 155 B8
Wakefield U.K. 53°41N 1°29W 66 D6
Wakefield Mass., U.S.A. 42°30N 71°5W 175 D13
Wakefield Mich., U.S.A. 46°29N 89°56W 172 B9
Wakkanai Japan 45°28N 141°35E 112 B10
Wakkerstroom S. Africa 27°24S 30°10E 145 C5
Wakool Australia 35°28S 144°23E 152 C6
Wakool → Australia 35°5S 143°33E 152 C5
Wakre Indonesia 0°19S 131°5E 119 E8
Wakuach, L. Canada 55°34N 67°32W 165 A6
Wakulla U.S.A. 30°14N 84°14W 178 E5
Walagunya ✪ Australia 23°10S 120°50E 148 D3
Walamba Zambia 13°30S 28°42E 143 E2
Wałbrzych Poland 50°45N 16°18E 83 H3
Walbury Hill U.K. 51°21N 1°28W 67 F6
Walcha Australia 30°55S 151°31E 153 A9
Walcheren Neths. 51°30N 3°35E 69 C3
Walcott U.S.A. 41°46N 106°51W 168 F10
Wałcz Poland 53°17N 16°27E 83 E3
Waldbröl Germany 50°52N 7°37E 76 E3
Waldburg Ra. Australia 24°40S 117°35E 149 D2
Waldeck Germany 51°12N 9°4E 76 D5
Walden Colo., U.S.A. 40°44N 106°17W 168 F10
Walden N.Y., U.S.A. 41°34N 74°11W 175 E10
Waldkirch Germany 48°5N 7°58E 77 G3
Waldkirchen Germany 48°43N 13°36E 77 G9
Waldkraiburg Germany 48°11N 12°24E 77 G8
Waldo U.S.A. 29°48N 82°10W 178 F7
Waldport U.S.A. 44°26N 124°4W 168 D1
Waldron U.S.A. 34°54N 94°5W 176 D7
Waldviertel Austria 48°30N 15°30E 78 C8
Walebing Australia 30°41S 116°13E 149 F2
Walembele Ghana 10°30N 1°58W 138 C4
Walensee Switz. 47°7N 9°13E 77 H5
Wales □ U.K. 52°19N 4°43W 67 E3
Wales I. Canada 68°1N 86°40W 161 D14
Walewale Ghana 10°21N 0°50W 139 C4
Walgett Australia 30°0S 148°5E 151 E4
Walgreen Coast Antarctica 75°15S 105°0W 55 D15
Walhalla Australia 37°56S 146°29E 153 D7
Walhalla U.S.A. 34°46N 83°4W 177 D13
Walker U.S.A. 47°6N 94°35W 172 B6
Walker, L. Canada 50°20N 67°11W 165 B6
Walker L. Canada 54°42N 95°57W 163 C9
Walker L. U.S.A. 38°42N 118°43W 168 G4
Walkerston Australia 21°11S 149°8E 150 b
Walkerton Canada 44°10N 81°10W 174 B3
Wall U.S.A. 44°0N 102°8W 172 C2
Walla Walla Australia 35°45S 146°54E 153 C7
Walla Walla U.S.A. 46°4N 118°20W 168 C4
Wallace Idaho, U.S.A. 47°28N 115°56W 168 C6
Wallace N.C., U.S.A. 34°44N 77°59W 177 D16
Wallaceburg Canada 42°34N 82°23W 174 D2
Wallacetown N.Z. 46°21S 168°19E 155 G3
Wallachia = Valahia Romania 44°35N 25°0E 81 F9
Wallal Australia 26°32S 146°7E 151 D4
Wallam Cr. → Australia 28°40S 147°20E 151 D4
Wallambin, L. Australia 30°57S 117°35E 149 F2
Wallan Australia 37°26S 144°59E 153 D6
Wallangarra Australia 28°56S 151°58E 151 D5
Wallaroo Australia 33°56S 137°39E 152 B2
Wallasey U.K. 53°25N 3°2W 66 D4
Walldürn Germany 49°34N 9°22E 77 F5
Wallenhorst Germany 52°21N 8°1E 76 C4
Wallenpaupack, L. U.S.A. 41°25N 75°15W 175 E9
Wallerawang Australia 33°25S 150°4E 153 B9
Wallingat △ Australia 32°14S 152°25E 153 B10
Wallingford Conn., U.S.A. 41°27N 72°50W 175 E12
Wallingford Vt., U.S.A. 43°28N 72°58W 175 C12
Wallis & Futuna, Îs. ☑ Pac. Oc. 13°18S 176°10W 147 C11
Wallowa U.S.A. 45°34N 117°32W 168 D5
Wallowa Mts. U.S.A. 45°20N 117°30W 168 D5
Walls U.K. 60°14N 1°33W 65 A7
Walls of Jerusalem △ Australia 41°56S 146°15E 151 G4
Wallsend Australia 32°55S 151°40E 153 B9
Wallula U.S.A. 46°5N 118°54W 168 C4
Wallumbilla Australia 26°33S 149°9E 151 D4
Walmsley L. Canada 63°25N 108°36W 163 A7
Walney, I. of U.K. 54°6N 3°15W 66 C4
Walnut Canyon ⌂ U.S.A. 35°15N 111°20W 169 J8
Walnut Creek U.S.A. 37°54N 122°4W 170 H4
Walnut Grove U.S.A. 34°4N 86°18W 178 A3
Walnut Hill U.S.A. 30°53N 87°30W 179 E2
Walnut Ridge U.S.A. 36°4N 90°57W 177 C9
Walpeup Australia 35°7S 142°2E 152 C5
Walpole Australia 34°58S 116°44E 149 F2
Walpole U.S.A. 42°9N 71°15W 175 D13
Walpole-Nornalup △ Australia 35°0S 116°45E 149 G2
Wals Austria 47°47N 12°58E 78 D5
Walsall U.K. 52°35N 1°58W 67 E6
Walsenburg U.S.A. 37°38N 104°47W 169 H11
Walsh U.S.A. 37°23N 102°17W 169 H12
Walsh → Australia 16°31S 143°42E 150 B3
Walsingham Canada 42°40N 80°31W 174 D4
Walsrode Germany 52°51N 9°35E 76 C5
Walt Disney World Resort U.S.A. 28°22N 81°33W 179 G8
Waltair India 17°44N 83°23E 126 F6
Walter F. George Res. U.S.A. 31°38N 85°4W 178 D4
Walterboro U.S.A. 32°55N 80°40W 178 C9
Walters U.S.A. 34°22N 98°19W 176 D5
Waltershausen Germany 50°54N 10°33E 76 E6
Waltershausen Gletscher Greenland 73°54N 24°25W 57 C8
Waltham U.S.A. 42°23N 71°14W 175 D13
Waltman U.S.A. 43°4N 107°12W 168 E10
Walton U.S.A. 42°10N 75°8W 175 D9
Walton-on-the-Naze U.K. 51°51N 1°17E 67 F9
Walvis Bay Namibia 23°0S 14°28E 144 B1
Walvis Ridge Atl. Oc. 26°0S 5°0E 56 J12
Walvisbaai = Walvis Bay Namibia 23°0S 14°28E 144 B1
Walwa Australia 35°59S 147°44E 153 C7
Wamba Dem. Rep. of the Congo 2°10N 27°57E 142 B2
Wamba Kenya 0°58N 37°19E 142 B4
Wamba Nigeria 8°57N 8°42E 139 D6
Wambardi ✪ Australia 16°2S 130°55E 148 C5
Wamego U.S.A. 39°12N 96°18W 172 F5
Wamena Indonesia 4°4S 138°57E 119 E9
Wampana Karlantijpa ✪ Australia 17°45S 132°10E 148 C5
Wampaya ✪ Australia 17°20S 135°0E 150 B2
Wampsville U.S.A. 43°4N 75°42W 175 C9
Wamsutter U.S.A. 41°40N 107°58W 168 F10
Wamulan Indonesia 3°27S 126°7E 119 E7
Wan Tup Burma 21°13N 98°42E 116 G2
Wan Xian China 38°47N 115°7E 114 E8
Wana Pakistan 32°20N 69°32E 124 C3
Wanaaring Australia 29°38S 144°9E 151 D3
Wanaka N.Z. 44°42S 169°9E 155 E4
Wanaka, L. N.Z. 44°33S 169°7E 155 E4
Wan'an China 26°26N 114°49E 117 D10
Wanapitei L. Canada 46°45N 80°40W 164 C3
Wanbi Australia 34°46S 140°17E 152 C4
Wandel Sea = McKinley Sea Arctic 82°0N 0°0 57 A11
Wandérama Ivory C. 8°37N 4°25W 138 D4
Wandhari Pakistan 27°42N 66°48E 124 F2
Wanding China 24°5N 98°4E 116 E2
Wandoan Australia 26°5S 149°55E 151 D4
Wandur Marine △ India 11°30N 92°30E 127 J11
Wanfu China 40°8N 122°38E 115 D12
Wang → Thailand 17°8N 99°2E 120 D2
Wang Noi Thailand 14°13N 100°44E 120 E3
Wang Saphung Thailand 17°18N 101°46E 120 D3
Wang Thong Thailand 16°50N 100°26E 120 D3
Wanga Dem. Rep. of the Congo 2°58N 29°12E 142 B2
Wanganella Australia 35°6S 144°49E 153 C6
Wanganui N.Z. 39°56S 175°3E 154 F4
Wanganui → W. Coast, N.Z. 43°3S 170°26E 155 D5
Wanganui → Wanganui-Manawatu, N.Z. 39°55S 175°4E 154 F4
Wangaratta Australia 36°21S 146°19E 153 D7
Wangary Australia 34°35S 135°29E 151 E2
Wangcang China 32°18N 106°20E 116 A6
Wangcheng China 28°22N 112°49E 117 C9
Wangcun China 36°41N 117°41E 115 F9
Wangdu China 38°40N 115°7E 114 E8
Wangen Germany 47°41N 9°50E 77 H5
Wangerooge Germany 53°47N 7°54E 76 B3
Wangiwangi Indonesia 5°22S 123°37E 119 F6
Wangjiang China 30°10N 116°42E 117 B11
Wangmo China 25°11N 106°5E 116 E6
Wangolodougou Ivory C. 9°55N 5°10W 138 D3
Wangqing China 43°12N 129°42E 115 C15
Wani India 20°5N 78°55E 126 D4
Wanimiyn ✪ Australia 15°55S 130°49E 148 C5
Wanjina Wunggurr Wilinggin ✪ Australia 16°0S 127°0E 148 C4
Wankaner India 22°35N 71°0E 124 H4
Wanless Canada 54°11N 101°21W 163 C8
Wanleweyne Somalia 2°37N 44°54E 131 G3
Wanneroo Australia 31°42S 115°46E 149 F2
Wannian China 28°42N 117°4E 117 C11
Wanning China 18°48N 110°22E 117 a
Wannoo Billabong Roadhouse Australia 27°25S 115°49E 149 E2
Wanon Niwat Thailand 17°38N 103°46E 120 D4
Wanqinsha China 22°43N 113°33E 111 a
Wanquan China 40°50N 114°40E 114 D8
Wanrong China 35°25N 110°50E 114 G6
Wanshan China 27°30N 109°12E 116 D7
Wanshan Qundao China 21°57N 113°45E 111 a
Wansheng China 28°57N 106°53E 116 C6
Wanstead N.Z. 40°8S 176°30E 154 G5
Wantage U.K. 51°35N 1°25W 67 F6
Wanxian China 30°42N 108°20E 116 B7
Wanyuan China 32°4N 108°3E 116 A7
Wanzai Guangdong, China 22°12N 113°31E 111 a
Wanzai Jiangxi, China 28°7N 114°30E 117 C10
Wapakoneta U.S.A. 40°34N 84°12W 173 E11
Wapato U.S.A. 46°27N 120°25W 168 C3
Wapawekka L. Canada 54°55N 104°40W 163 C8
Wapikopa L. Canada 52°56N 87°53W 164 B2
Wapiti → Canada 55°5N 118°18W 162 B5
Wappingers Falls U.S.A. 41°36N 73°55W 175 E11
Wapsipinicon → U.S.A. 41°44N 90°19W 172 E8
Wapusk △ Canada 57°46N 93°22W 163 B10
Warakurna Australia 24°59S 128°17E 149 D4
Warangal India 17°58N 79°35E 126 F4
Waraseoni India 21°45N 80°2E 125 J9
Waratah Australia 41°30S 145°30E 151 G4
Waratah B. Australia 38°54S 146°5E 153 E7
Warburg Germany 51°28N 9°11E 76 D5
Warburton Vic., Australia 37°47S 145°42E 153 D6
Warburton W. Austral., Australia 26°8S 126°35E 149 E4
Warburton ✪ Australia 26°7S 126°34E 149 E4
Warburton → Australia 28°4S 137°28E 151 D2
Warburton Groove Australia 28°18S 137°8E 151 A2
Warburton Ra. Australia 25°55S 126°28E 149 E4
Ward N.Z. 41°49S 174°11E 155 B9
Ward → Australia 26°28S 146°6E 151 D4
Ward Mt. U.S.A. 37°12N 118°54W 170 H8
Wardang I. Australia 34°30S 137°20E 152 C2
Warden S. Africa 27°50S 29°0E 145 C4
Wardha India 20°45N 78°39E 126 D4
Wardha → India 19°57N 79°11E 126 E4
Wardsville Canada 42°39N 81°45W 174 D3
Ware U.K. 51°49N 0°0 67 F8
Ware U.S.A. 42°16N 72°14W 175 D12
Waregem Belgium 50°53N 3°27E 69 D3
Wareham U.S.A. 41°46N 70°43W 175 E14
Waremme Belgium 50°43N 5°15E 69 D5
Waren Germany 53°31N 12°40E 76 B8
Warendorf Germany 51°57N 8°1E 76 D4
Waresboro U.S.A. 31°15N 82°29W 178 D7
Warialda Australia 29°29S 150°33E 151 D5
Warin Chamrap Thailand 15°12N 104°53E 120 E5
Warka Poland 51°47N 21°12E 83 G8
Warkopi Indonesia 1°12S 134°9E 119 E8
Warkworth N.Z. 36°24S 174°41E 154 C3
Warm Springs Ga., U.S.A. 32°53N 84°41W 178 C5
Warm Springs Nev., U.S.A. 38°10N 116°20W 169 G5
Warman Canada 52°19N 106°30W 163 C7
Warmbad = Bela Bela S. Africa 24°51S 28°19E 145 B4
Warmbad Namibia 28°25S 18°42E 144 C2
Warming I. = Uunartoq Qeqertoq Greenland 71°33N 21°47W 57 C8
Warmińsko-Mazurskie □ Poland 54°0N 21°0E 82 D8
Warminster U.K. 51°12N 2°10W 67 F5
Warminster U.S.A. 40°12N 75°6W 175 F9
Warmun Australia 17°2S 128°12E 148 C4
Warnemünde Germany 54°10N 12°4E 76 A8
Warner Mts. U.S.A. 41°40N 120°15W 168 F3
Warner Robins U.S.A. 32°37N 83°36W 178 C6
Warnow → Germany 54°6N 12°9E 76 A8
Waroona Australia 32°50S 115°58E 149 F2
Warora India 20°14N 79°1E 126 D4
Warrabah △ Australia 30°31S 150°56E 153 A10
Warrabri ✪ Australia 21°1S 134°19E 150 C1
Warracknabeal Australia 36°9S 142°26E 152 D5
Warragul Australia 38°10S 145°58E 153 E6
Warrego → Australia 30°24S 145°21E 151 E4
Warrego Ra. Australia 24°58S 146°0E 150 C4
Warren Australia 31°42S 147°51E 153 A7
Warren Ark., U.S.A. 33°37N 92°4W 176 E8
Warren Mich., U.S.A. 42°28N 83°1W 173 D12
Warren Minn., U.S.A. 48°12N 96°46W 172 A5
Warren Ohio, U.S.A. 41°14N 80°49W 174 E4
Warren Pa., U.S.A. 41°51N 79°9W 174 E5
Warrenpoint U.K. 54°6N 6°15W 64 B5
Warrensburg Mo., U.S.A. 38°46N 93°44W 172 F7
Warrensburg N.Y., U.S.A. 43°29N 73°46W 175 C11
Warrenton S. Africa 28°9S 24°47E 144 C3
Warrenton Ga., U.S.A. 33°24N 82°40W 178 B7
Warrenton Oreg., U.S.A. 46°10N 123°56W 170 D3
Warrenville U.S.A. 33°33N 81°48W 178 B8
Warri Nigeria 5°30N 5°41E 139 D6
Warrington N.Z. 45°43S 170°35E 155 F5
Warrington U.K. 53°24N 2°35W 66 D5
Warrington U.S.A. 30°23N 87°17W 179 E2
Warrington □ U.K. 53°24N 2°35W 66 D5
Warrnambool Australia 38°25S 142°30E 152 E5
Warroad U.S.A. 48°54N 95°19W 172 A6
Warrumbungle △ Australia 31°18S 149°1E 153 A8
Warruwi Australia 11°36S 133°20E 150 A1
Warsak Dam Pakistan 34°11N 71°19E 124 B4
Warsaw = Warszawa Poland 52°14N 21°0E 83 F8
Warsaw Ind., U.S.A. 41°14N 85°51W 173 E11
Warsaw N.Y., U.S.A. 42°45N 78°8W 174 D6
Warsaw Ohio, U.S.A. 40°20N 82°0W 174 F3
Warsaw Chopin ✕ (WAW) Poland 52°9N 20°59E 83 F7
Warstein Germany 51°26N 8°22E 76 D4
Warszawa Poland 52°14N 21°0E 83 F8
Warta Poland 51°43N 18°38E 83 G5
Warta → Poland 52°35N 14°39E 83 F1
Warthe = Warta → Poland 52°35N 14°39E 83 F1
Warthen U.S.A. 33°6N 82°48W 178 B7
Waru Indonesia 3°30S 130°36E 119 E8
Warud India 21°30N 78°16E 126 D4
Warumungu ✪ Australia 19°15S 134°44E 150 B1
Warwick Australia 28°10S 152°1E 151 D5
Warwick U.K. 52°18N 1°35W 67 E6
Warwick Ga., U.S.A. 31°50N 83°57W 178 D6
Warwick N.Y., U.S.A. 41°16N 74°22W 175 E10
Warwick R.I., U.S.A. 41°42N 71°28W 175 E13
Warwickshire □ U.K. 52°14N 1°38W 67 E6
Wasaga Beach Canada 44°31N 80°1W 174 B4
Wasagaming Canada 50°39N 99°58W 163 C9
Wasatch Ra. U.S.A. 40°0N 111°30W 168 F8
Wasbank S. Africa 28°15S 30°9E 145 C5
Wasco Calif., U.S.A. 35°36N 119°20W 171 K7
Wasco Oreg., U.S.A. 45°36N 120°42W 168 D3
Wase Nigeria 9°4N 9°54E 139 D6
Waseca U.S.A. 44°5N 93°30W 172 C7
Wasekamio L. Canada 56°45N 108°45W 163 B7
Wasgomuwa △ Sri Lanka 7°45N 81°0E 127 L5
Wash, The U.K. 52°58N 0°20E 66 E8
Washago Canada 44°45N 79°20W 174 B5
Washburn N. Dak., U.S.A. 47°17N 101°2W 172 B3
Washburn Wis., U.S.A. 46°40N 90°54W 172 B8
Washim India 20°3N 77°0E 126 D3
Washington U.K. 54°55N 1°30W 66 C6
Washington D.C., U.S.A. 38°53N 77°2W 173 F15
Washington Ga., U.S.A. 33°44N 82°44W 178 B7
Washington Ind., U.S.A. 38°40N 87°10W 172 F10
Washington Iowa, U.S.A. 41°18N 91°42W 172 E8
Washington Mo., U.S.A. 38°33N 91°1W 172 F8
Washington N.C., U.S.A. 35°33N 77°3W 177 D16
Washington N.J., U.S.A. 40°46N 74°59W 175 F10
Washington Pa., U.S.A. 40°10N 80°15W 174 F4
Washington Utah, U.S.A. 37°8N 113°31W 169 H7
Washington □ U.S.A. 47°30N 120°30W 168 C3
Washington, Mt. U.S.A. 44°16N 71°18W 175 B13
Washington Court House U.S.A. 39°32N 83°26W 173 F12
Washington Dulles Int. ✕ (IAD) U.S.A. 38°57N 77°27W 173 F15
Washington I. U.S.A. 45°23N 86°54W 172 C10
Washington Land Greenland 80°30N 66°0W 57 A4
Washougal U.S.A. 45°35N 122°21W 170 E4
Washpool △ Australia 29°22S 152°20E 151 D5
Wasian Indonesia 1°47S 133°19E 119 E8
Wasilków Poland 53°12N 23°13E 83 E10
Wasilla U.S.A. 61°35N 149°26W 160 E2
Wasini Marine ⌂ Kenya 4°33S 39°14E 142 C4
Wasior Indonesia 2°43S 134°30E 119 E8
Wasiri Indonesia 7°30S 126°30E 119 F7
Wāsiţ □ Iraq 32°50N 45°50E 105 F11
Waskaganish Canada 51°30N 78°40W 164 B4
Waskaiowaka L. Canada 56°33N 96°23W 163 B9
Waskesiu Lake Canada 53°55N 106°5W 163 C7
Wassaw I. U.S.A. 31°53N 80°58W 178 D9
Wassaw Sd. U.S.A. 31°55N 80°55W 178 D9
Wasserburg Germany 48°3N 12°14E 77 G8
Wasserkuppe Germany 50°29N 9°55E 76 E5
Wassy France 48°30N 4°58E 71 D11
Wasur △ Indonesia 8°41S 140°44E 119 F10
Waswanipi Canada 49°40N 76°29W 164 C4
Waswanipi, L. Canada 49°35N 76°40W 164 C4
Watagans △ Australia 33°0S 151°28E 153 B9
Watampone Indonesia 4°29S 120°25E 119 E6
Watamu Kenya 3°23S 40°0E 142 C5
Watarrka △ Australia 24°20S 131°30E 148 D5
Water Park Pt. Australia 22°56S 150°47E 150 C5
Water Valley U.S.A. 34°10N 89°38W 177 D10
Waterberg Plateau ⌂ Namibia 20°25S 17°18E 144 B2
Waterberge S. Africa 24°10S 28°0E 145 B4
Waterbury Conn., U.S.A. 41°33N 73°3W 175 E11
Waterbury Vt., U.S.A. 44°20N 72°46W 175 B12
Waterbury L. Canada 58°10N 104°22W 163 B8
Waterdown Canada 43°20N 79°53W 174 C5
Wateree → U.S.A. 33°45N 80°37W 178 B9
Waterford Canada 42°56N 80°17W 174 D4
Waterford Ireland 52°15N 7°8W 64 D4
Waterford Calif., U.S.A. 37°38N 120°46W 170 H6
Waterford Pa., U.S.A. 41°57N 79°59W 174 E5
Waterford □ Ireland 52°10N 7°40W 64 D4
Waterford Harbour Ireland 52°8N 6°58W 64 D5
Waterhen L. Canada 52°10N 99°40W 163 C9
Waterloo Belgium 50°43N 4°25E 69 D4
Waterloo Ont., Canada 43°30N 80°32W 174 C4
Waterloo Qué., Canada 45°22N 72°32W 175 A12
Waterloo S. Leone 8°26N 13°8W 138 D2
Waterloo Ill., U.S.A. 38°20N 90°9W 172 F8
Waterloo Iowa, U.S.A. 42°30N 92°21W 172 D7
Waterloo N.Y., U.S.A. 42°54N 76°52W 174 D8
Watersmeet U.S.A. 46°16N 89°11W 172 B9
Waterton Lakes △ Canada 48°45N 115°0W 162 D6
Watertown Conn., U.S.A. 41°36N 73°7W 175 E11
Watertown Fla., U.S.A. 30°11N 82°36W 178 E7
Watertown N.Y., U.S.A. 43°59N 75°55W 175 C9
Watertown S. Dak., U.S.A. 44°54N 97°7W 172 C5
Watertown Wis., U.S.A. 43°12N 88°43W 172 D9
Waterval-Boven = Emgwenya S. Africa 25°40S 30°18E 145 C5
Waterville Canada 45°16N 71°54W 175 A13
Waterville Maine, U.S.A. 44°33N 69°38W 173 C19
Waterville N.Y., U.S.A. 42°56N 75°23W 175 D9
Waterville Pa., U.S.A. 41°19N 77°21W 174 E7
Waterville Wash., U.S.A. 47°39N 120°4W 168 C3
Watervliet U.S.A. 42°44N 73°42W 175 D11
Wates Indonesia 7°51S 110°10E 119 G14
Watford Canada 42°57N 81°53W 174 D3
Watford U.K. 51°40N 0°24W 67 F7
Watford City U.S.A. 47°48N 103°17W 172 B2
Wathaman → Canada 57°16N 102°59W 163 B8
Wathaman L. Canada 56°58N 103°44W 163 B8
Watheroo Australia 30°15S 116°5E 149 F2
Watheroo △ Australia 30°19S 115°48E 149 F2
Wating China 35°40N 106°38E 114 G4
Watkins Glen U.S.A. 42°23N 76°52W 174 D8
Watkinsville U.S.A. 33°52N 83°25W 178 B6
Watling I. = San Salvador I. Bahamas 24°0N 74°30W 183 B5
Watonga U.S.A. 35°51N 98°25W 176 D5
Watrous Canada 51°40N 105°25W 163 C7
Watrous U.S.A. 35°48N 104°59W 169 J11
Watsa Dem. Rep. of the Congo 3°4N 29°30E 142 B2
Watseka U.S.A. 40°47N 87°44W 172 E10
Watson Canada 52°10N 104°30W 163 C8
Watson Lake Canada 60°6N 128°49W 162 A3
Watsontown U.S.A. 41°5N 76°52W 174 E8
Watsonville U.S.A. 36°55N 121°45W 170 J5
Wattiwarriganna Cr. → Australia 28°57S 136°10E 151 D2
Wattwil Switz. 47°18N 9°6E 77 H5
Watuata = Batuata Indonesia 6°12S 122°42E 119 F6
Watubela, Kepulauan Indonesia 4°28S 131°35E 119 E8
Watubela Is. = Watubela, Kepulauan Indonesia 4°28S 131°35E 119 E8
Wau South Sudan 7°45N 28°1E 135 G11
Waubamik Canada 45°27N 80°1W 174 A4
Waubay U.S.A. 45°20N 97°18W 172 C5
Waubra Australia 37°21S 143°39E 152 D5
Wauchope N.S.W., Australia 31°28S 152°45E 153 A10
Wauchope N. Terr., Australia 20°36S 134°15E 150 C1
Wauchula U.S.A. 27°33N 81°49W 179 H8
Waukarlycarly, L. Australia 21°18S 121°56E 148 D3
Waukeenah U.S.A. 30°25N 83°57W 178 E6
Waukegan U.S.A. 42°22N 87°50W 172 D10
Waukesha U.S.A. 43°1N 88°14W 172 D9
Waukon U.S.A. 43°16N 91°29W 172 D8
Waupaca U.S.A. 44°21N 89°5W 172 C9
Waupun U.S.A. 43°38N 88°44W 172 D9
Waurika U.S.A. 34°10N 98°0W 176 D6
Wausau Fla., U.S.A. 30°38N 85°35W 178 E4
Wausau Wis., U.S.A. 44°58N 89°38W 172 C9
Wautoma U.S.A. 44°4N 89°18W 172 C9
Wauwatosa U.S.A. 43°2N 88°0W 172 D9
Wave Hill = Kalkarindji Australia 17°30S 130°47E 148 C5
Wave Rock ⌂ Australia 32°26S 118°53E 149 F2
Waveney → U.K. 52°35N 1°39E 67 E9
Waverley N.Z. 39°46S 174°37E 154 F3
Waverly Ala., U.S.A. 32°44N 85°35W 178 C4
Waverly Fla., U.S.A. 27°59N 81°37W 179 H8
Waverly Ga., U.S.A. 31°6N 81°43W 178 D8
Waverly Iowa, U.S.A. 42°44N 92°29W 172 D7
Waverly N.Y., U.S.A. 42°1N 76°32W 175 E8
Waverly Hall U.S.A. 32°41N 84°44W 178 C5
Wavre Belgium 50°43N 4°38E 69 D4
Wâw = Wau South Sudan 7°45N 28°1E 135 G11
Wāw al Kabīr Libya 25°20N 16°43E 135 C9
Wawa Canada 47°59N 84°47W 164 C3
Wawa Nigeria 9°54N 4°27E 139 D5
Wawa Sudan 20°30N 30°22E 137 C3
Wawanesa Canada 49°36N 99°40W 163 D9
Wawona U.S.A. 37°32N 119°39W 170 H7
Waxahachie U.S.A. 32°24N 96°51W 176 E6
Waxxari China 38°42N 87°19E 109 E11
Way, L. Australia 26°45S 120°16E 149 E3
Waya Fiji 17°19S 177°10E 154 a
Waycross U.S.A. 31°13N 82°21W 178 D7
Wayland U.S.A. 42°34N 77°35W 174 D7
Wayne Nebr., U.S.A. 42°14N 97°1W 172 D5
Wayne W. Va., U.S.A. 38°13N 82°27W 173 F12
Waynesboro Ga., U.S.A. 33°6N 82°1W 178 B7
Waynesboro Miss., U.S.A. 31°40N 88°39W 177 F10
Waynesboro Pa., U.S.A. 39°45N 77°35W 173 F15
Waynesboro Va., U.S.A. 38°4N 78°53W 173 F14
Waynesburg U.S.A. 39°54N 80°11W 173 F13
Waynesville U.S.A. 35°28N 82°58W 177 D13
Waynoka U.S.A. 36°35N 98°53W 176 C5
Wayside U.S.A. 33°4N 83°37W 178 B6
Wazirabad Pakistan 32°30N 74°8E 124 C6
Waziristan Pakistan 33°0N 70°0E 124 C4
Wda → Poland 53°25N 18°29E 82 E5
We Indonesia 5°51N 95°18E 118 C1
Weald, The U.K. 51°4N 0°20E 67 F8
Wear → U.K. 54°55N 1°23W 66 C6
Weatherford Okla., U.S.A. 35°32N 98°43W 176
Weatherford Tex., U.S.A. 32°46N 97°48W 176
Weaverville U.S.A. 40°44N 122°56W 168
Webb City U.S.A. 37°9N 94°28W 172
Webequie Canada 52°59N 87°21W 164
Weber N.Z. 40°24S 176°20E 154
Webo = Nyaake Liberia 4°52N 7°37W 138
Webster Mass., U.S.A. 42°3N 71°53W 175 D
Webster N.Y., U.S.A. 43°13N 77°26W 174
Webster S. Dak., U.S.A. 45°20N 97°31W 172
Webster City U.S.A. 42°28N 93°49W 172
Webster Springs U.S.A. 38°29N 80°25W 173 F
Webuye Kenya 0°37N 34°46E 142
Weda Indonesia 0°21N 127°50E 119
Weda, Teluk Indonesia 0°20N 128°0E 119
Weddell Abyssal Plain S. Ocean 65°0S 20°0W 55
Weddell I. Falk. Is. 51°50S 61°0W 192
Weddell Sea Antarctica 72°30S 40°0W 55
Wedderburn Australia 36°26S 143°33E 152
Weddin Mts. △ Australia 33°59S 148°0E 153
Wedel Germany 53°34N 9°42E 76
Wedemark Germany 52°32N 9°43E 76
Wedgeport Canada 43°44N 65°59W 165
Wedowee U.S.A. 33°19N 85°29W 178
Wedza Zimbabwe 18°40S 31°33E 143
Wee Waa Australia 30°11S 149°26E 151
Weed U.S.A. 41°25N 122°23W 168
Weed Heights U.S.A. 38°59N 119°13W 170
Weedsport U.S.A. 43°2N 76°33W 175
Weedville U.S.A. 41°17N 78°30W 174
Weeki Wachee U.S.A. 28°32N 82°35W 179
Weenen S. Africa 28°48S 30°7E 145
Weener Germany 53°9N 7°20E 76
Weerribben △ Neths. 52°47N 5°58E 69
Weert Neths. 51°15N 5°43E 69
Węgierska-Górka Poland 49°36N 19°7E 83
Węgliniec Poland 51°18N 15°10E 83
Węgorzewo Poland 54°13N 21°43E 82
Węgorzyno Poland 53°32N 15°33E 82
Węgrów Poland 52°24N 22°0E 83
Wei He → Hebei, China 36°10N 115°45E 114
Wei He → Shaanxi, China 34°38N 110°15E 114
Weichang China 41°58N 117°49E 115
Weichuan China 34°20N 113°59E 114
Weida Germany 50°46N 12°2E 76
Weiden Germany 49°41N 12°10E 77
Weifang China 36°44N 119°7E 115 F
Weihai China 37°30N 122°6E 115 F
Weihui China 35°25N 114°3E 114
Weil Germany 47°35N 7°37E 77
Weilburg Germany 50°28N 8°17E 76
Weilheim Germany 47°50N 11°9E 77
Weimar Germany 50°58N 11°19E 76
Weinan China 34°31N 109°29E 114
Weingarten Germany 49°3N 8°31E 77
Weinheim Germany 49°32N 8°39E 77
Weining China 26°50N 104°17E 116
Weipa Australia 12°40S 141°50E 150
Weir → Australia 28°20S 149°50E 151
Weir → Canada 56°54N 93°21W 163 B
Weir, L. U.S.A. 29°0N 81°57W 179
Weir River Canada 56°49N 94°6W 163 B
Weirsdale U.S.A. 28°59N 81°55W 179
Weirton U.S.A. 40°24N 80°35W 174
Weiser U.S.A. 44°15N 116°58W 168
Weishan Shandong, China 34°47N 117°5E 115
Weishan Yunnan, China 25°12N 100°20E 116
Weishan Hu China 34°35N 117°14E 115
Weissenburg Germany 49°2N 10°58E 77
Weissenfels Germany 51°11N 12°0E 76
Weisswasser Germany 51°30N 14°36E 76 D
Weitra Austria 48°41N 14°54E 78
Weixi China 27°10N 99°10E 116
Weixin China 27°48N 105°3E 116
Weiyuan Gansu, China 35°7N 104°10E 114
Weiyuan Sichuan, China 29°35N 104°36E 116
Weiz Austria 47°13N 15°39E 78
Weizhou Dao China 21°0N 109°5E 116
Wejherowo Poland 54°35N 18°12E 82
Wekusko L. Canada 54°40N 99°50W 163
Welch U.S.A. 37°26N 81°35W 173 G
Welford △ Australia 25°5S 143°16E 150
Weligama Sri Lanka 5°58N 80°25E 127
Welkom S. Africa 28°0S 26°46E 144
Welland Canada 43°0N 79°15W 174
Welland → U.K. 52°51N 0°5W 67
Wellawaya Sri Lanka 6°44N 81°6E 127
Wellesley Is. Australia 16°42S 139°30E 150
Wellesley Islands ✪ Australia 16°32S 139°23E 150
Wellingborough U.K. 52°19N 0°41W 67
Wellington Australia 32°35S 148°59E 153
Wellington Canada 43°57N 77°20W 174
Wellington N.Z. 41°19S 174°46E 154
Wellington S. Africa 33°38S 19°1E 144
Wellington Somst., U.K. 50°58N 3°13W 67
Wellington Telford & Wrekin, U.K. 52°42N 2°30W 67
Wellington Colo., U.S.A. 40°42N 105°0W 168 F
Wellington Fla., U.S.A. 26°39N 80°15W 179
Wellington Kans., U.S.A. 37°16N 97°24W 172
Wellington Nev., U.S.A. 38°45N 119°23W 170
Wellington Ohio, U.S.A. 41°10N 82°13W 174
Wellington Tex., U.S.A. 34°51N 100°13W 176
Wellington □ N.Z. 41°0S 175°30E 154
Wellington, I. Chile 49°30S 75°0W 192
Wellington, L. Australia 38°6S 147°20E 153
Wellington Chan. Canada 75°0N 93°0W 161 C
Wells U.K. 51°13N 2°39W 67
Wells Maine, U.S.A. 43°20N 70°35W 175 C
Wells N.Y., U.S.A. 43°24N 74°17W 175 C
Wells Nev., U.S.A. 41°7N 114°58W 168
Wells, L. Australia 26°44S 123°15E 149
Wells, Mt. Australia 17°25S 127°8E 148
Wells Gray ⌂ Canada 52°30N 120°15W 162

ls-next-the-Sea U.K. 52°57N 0°51E 66 E8
ls River U.K. 44°9N 72°4W 175 B12
lsboro U.S.A. 41°45N 77°18W 174 E7
lsford N.Z. 36°16S 174°42E 154 C3
lsville N.Y., U.S.A. 42°7N 77°57W 174 D7
lsville Ohio, U.S.A. 40°16N 80°39W 174 F4
lsville Utah, U.S.A. 41°38N 111°56W 168 F8
lton U.S.A. 32°40N 114°8W 169 K6
n Austria 48°9N 14°1E 78 C7
shpool England 38°42S 146°26E 153 F4
shpool U.K. 52°39N 3°8W 67 E4
wyn Garden City
U.K. 51°48N 0°12W 67 F7
n U.K. 52°52N 2°44W 66 E5
nbere → Tanzania 4°10S 34°15E 142 C3
mindji Canada 53°0N 78°49W 164 B4
nyss Canada 44°52N 76°23W 175 B8
n Xian Gansu,
China 28°0N 120°38E 117 D13
n Xian Henan, China 34°55N 113°5E 114 C7
natchee U.S.A. 47°25N 120°19W 168 C3
nchang China 19°38N 110°42E 117 a
ncheng China 27°46N 120°4E 117 D13
nchow = Wenzhou
China 28°0N 120°38E 117 D13
nchuan China 31°22N 103°35E 116 B4
nden U.S.A. 33°49N 113°33W 171 M13
ndeng China 37°15N 122°5E 115 F12
ndover U.S.A. 40°44N 114°2W 168 F6
ng'an China 27°5N 107°25E 116 D6
ngcheng China 24°22N 113°50E 117 F9
ngen Switz. 46°37N 7°55E 71 F14
ngyuan China 24°20N 114°9E 117 E10
nling China 28°21N 121°20E 117 C13
nlock → Australia 12°2S 141°55E 150 A3
nshan China 23°20N 104°18E 116 F5
nshang China 35°45N 116°30E 114 G9
nshui China 37°26N 112°1E 114 F7
nsleydale U.K. 54°17N 2°0W 66 C6
nsu U.K. 41°15N 80°10E 109 D10
nsum → U.K. 52°40N 1°15E 66 E8
ntworth Australia 34°2S 141°54E 152 C4
ntzel L. Canada 59°2N 114°28W 162 B6
nut Indonesia 3°11S 133°19E 119 E8
nzhou China 35°20N 111°10E 114 G6
xxi China 28°0N 120°38E 117 D13
ott U.S.A. 40°20N 123°55W 168 F2
ener S. Africa 29°42S 27°3E 144 C4
rda Botswana 25°24S 23°15E 144 C3
rdau Germany 50°44N 12°22E 76 E8
rder Germany 52°23N 12°55E 76 C8
i Indonesia 3°10S 132°38E 119 E8
rneck Germany 49°58N 10°5E 77 F6
rnigerode Germany 51°50N 10°47E 76 D6
rra → Germany 51°24N 9°39E 76 D5
rikimbe △
Australia 31°11S 152°15E 153 A10
rimull Australia 34°25S 141°38E 152 C4
rris Creek Australia 31°18S 150°38E 153 A9
rtach → Germany 48°24N 10°54E 77 G6
rtheim Germany 49°45N 9°32E 77 F5
rttingen Germany 48°33N 10°41E 77 G6
ssel Germany 51°39N 6°37E 76 D2
sser → Germany 53°36N 8°28E 76 B4
serbergland Germany 52°12N 9°7E 76 C5
serbergland Schaumburg
ameln □ Germany 52°8N 9°20E 76 C5
slaco U.S.A. 26°10N 97°58W 176 H6
slemkoon L. Canada 45°7N 77°25W 174 A7
sleyville Canada 49°9N 53°33W 165 C9
sleyville U.S.A. 42°9N 80°1W 174 D4
ssel Is. Australia 11°10S 136°45E 150 A2
sselburen Germany 54°13N 8°54E 76 A4
ssex U.K. 51°0N 2°0W 67 F5
ssington Springs
U.S.A. 44°5N 98°34W 172 C4
st U.S.A. 31°48N 97°6W 176 F6
st → U.S.A. 42°52N 72°33W 175 D12
st Allis U.S.A. 43°1N 88°0W 172 D9
st Antarctica
Antarctica 80°0S 90°0W 55 D15
st Baines →
Australia 15°38S 129°59E 148 C4
st Bank ■ Asia 32°6N 35°13E 130 C4
st Bend U.S.A. 43°25N 88°11W 172 D9
st Bengal □ India 23°0N 88°0E 125 H13
st Berkshire □ U.K. 51°25N 1°17W 67 F6
st Branch U.S.A. 44°17N 84°14W 173 C11
st Branch Susquehanna
U.S.A. 40°53N 76°48W 175 F8
st Bromwich U.K. 52°32N 1°59W 67 E6
st Burra U.K. 60°5N 1°21W 65 A7
st Canada Cr. →
U.S.A. 43°1N 74°58W 175 C10
st Caroline Basin
Pac. Oc. 4°0N 138°0E 156 G5
st Chazy U.S.A. 44°49N 73°28W 175 B11
st Chester U.S.A. 39°58N 75°36W 175 G9
st Coast □ N.Z. 43°15S 170°30E 155 D5
st Coast △ Namibia 21°53S 14°14E 144 B1
st Coast △ S. Africa 33°13S 18°0E 144 D2
st Columbia S.C.,
U.S.A. 33°59N 81°4W 178 B8
st Columbia Tex.,
U.S.A. 29°9N 95°39W 176 G7
st Covina U.S.A. 34°4N 117°54W 171 L9
st Des Moines
U.S.A. 41°35N 93°43W 172 E7
st Dunbartonshire □
U.K. 55°59N 4°30W 65 F4
st End Bahamas 26°41N 78°58W 182 A4
st Falkland Falk. Is. 51°40S 60°0W 192 G5
st Fargo U.S.A. 46°52N 96°54W 172 B5
st Fiji Basin Pac. Oc. 15°0S 173°0E 156 J9
st Fjord = Vestfjorden
Norway 67°55N 14°0E 60 C16
st Fork Trinity →
U.S.A. 32°48N 96°54W 176 E6
st Frankfort U.S.A. 37°54N 88°55W 172 G9
st Grand L. U.S.A. 45°14N 67°51W 173 C20
st Green U.S.A. 31°37N 82°44W 178 D7
st Hartford U.S.A. 41°45N 72°44W 175 E12

West Haven U.S.A. 41°17N 72°57W 175 E12
West Hazleton U.S.A. 40°58N 76°0W 175 F9
West Hurley U.S.A. 41°59N 74°7W 175 E10
West I. India 13°35N 92°54E 127 H11
West Ice Shelf Antarctica 67°0S 85°0E 55 C7
West Indies Cent. Amer. 15°0N 65°0W 183 D7
West Jordan U.S.A. 40°36N 111°56W 168 F8
West Kavango □
Namibia 18°0S 18°30E 144 A2
West Lamma Channel
China 22°14N 114°4E 111 a
West Linn U.S.A. 45°21N 122°36W 170 E4
West Lorne Canada 42°36N 81°36W 174 D3
West Lothian □ U.K. 55°54N 3°36W 65 F5
West Lunga → Zambia 13°6S 24°39E 143 E1
West MacDonnell △
Australia 23°38S 132°59E 148 D5
West Mariana Basin
Pac. Oc. 15°0N 137°0E 156 F5
West Memphis U.S.A. 35°8N 90°10W 177 D9
West Midlands □ U.K. 52°26N 2°0W 67 E6
West Mifflin U.S.A. 40°21N 79°52W 174 F5
West Milford U.S.A. 41°8N 74°22W 175 E10
West Milton U.S.A. 41°1N 76°50W 174 E8
West Monroe U.S.A. 32°31N 92°9W 176 F8
West Newton U.S.A. 40°14N 79°46W 174 F5
West Nicholson
Zimbabwe 21°2S 29°20E 143 G2
West Odessa U.S.A. 31°50N 102°30W 176 F3
West Palm Beach
U.S.A. 26°43N 80°3W 179 J9
West Palm Beach Canal
U.S.A. 26°40N 80°15W 179 J9
West Pensacola U.S.A. 30°25N 87°16W 179 E2
West Plains U.S.A. 36°44N 91°51W 172 G8
West Point Ga., U.S.A. 32°53N 85°11W 178 C4
West Point Miss.,
U.S.A. 33°36N 88°39W 177 E10
West Point N.Y.,
U.S.A. 41°24N 73°58W 175 E11
West Point Nebr.,
U.S.A. 41°51N 96°43W 172 E5
West Point Va.,
U.S.A. 37°32N 76°48W 173 G15
West Pokot □ Kenya 1°15N 35°10E 142 B4
West Pt. = Ouest, Pte. de l'
Canada 49°52N 64°40W 165 C7
West Pt. Australia 35°1S 135°56E 152 C1
West Road → Canada 53°18N 122°53W 162 C4
West Rutland U.S.A. 43°36N 73°3W 175 C11
West Schelde = Westerschelde →
Neths. 51°25N 3°25E 69 C3
West Seneca U.S.A. 42°51N 78°48W 174 D6
West Siberian Plain
Russia 62°0N 75°0E 102 B9
West Sussex □ U.K. 50°55N 0°30W 67 G7
West-Terschelling Neths. 53°22N 5°13E 69 A5
West Valley City
U.S.A. 40°42N 111°58W 168 F8
West Virginia □
U.S.A. 38°45N 80°30W 173 F13
West-Vlaanderen □
Belgium 51°0N 3°0E 69 D2
West Walker →
U.S.A. 38°54N 119°9W 170 G7
West Wyalong
Australia 33°56S 147°10E 153 B7
West Yellowstone
U.S.A. 44°40N 111°6W 168 D8
West Yorkshire □ U.K. 53°45N 1°40W 66 D6
Westall, Pt. Australia 32°55S 134°4E 151 E1
Westbay U.S.A. 30°18N 85°52W 178 E4
Westbrook U.S.A. 43°41N 70°22W 173 D18
Westbury Australia 41°30S 146°51E 151 G4
Westby U.S.A. 48°52N 104°3W 168 B11
Westend U.S.A. 35°42N 117°24W 171 K9
Westerland Germany 54°54N 8°17E 76 A4
Westerly U.S.A. 41°22N 71°50W 175 E13
Western □ Ghana 5°30N 2°30W 138 D4
Western □ S. Leone 8°30N 13°20W 138 D2
Western □ Zambia 15°0S 24°4E 143 F1
Western Australia □
Australia 25°0S 118°0E 149 E2
Western Cape □ S. Africa 34°0S 20°0E 144 E3
Western Dvina = Daugava →
Latvia 57°4N 24°3E 84 D3
Western Ghats India 14°0N 75°0E 127 H2
Western Isles = Eilean Siar □
U.K. 57°30N 7°10W 65 D1
Western Sahara ■
Africa 25°0N 13°0W 134 D3
Western Samoa = Samoa ■
Pac. Oc. 14°0S 172°0W 147 C11
Western Sierra Madre = Madre
Occidental, Sierra
Mexico 27°0N 107°0W 180 B3
Westernport U.S.A. 39°29N 79°3W 173 F14
Westerschelde → Neths. 51°25N 3°25E 69 C3
Westerstede Germany 53°15N 7°55E 76 B3
Westerwald Germany 50°38N 7°56E 76 E3
Westfield Mass., U.S.A. 42°7N 72°45W 175 D12
Westfield N.Y., U.S.A. 42°20N 79°35W 174 D5
Westfield Pa., U.S.A. 41°55N 77°32W 174 E7
Westhill U.K. 57°9N 2°19W 65 D6
Westhope U.S.A. 48°55N 101°1W 172 A3
Westland □ N.Z. 43°16S 170°16E 155 D5
Westland Bight N.Z. 42°55S 170°5E 155 D5
Westlock Canada 54°9N 113°55W 162 C6
Westmar Australia 27°55S 149°44E 151 D4
Westmeath □ Ireland 53°33N 7°34W 64 C4
Westminster Calif.,
U.S.A. 33°45N 118°0W 171 M8
Westminster Colo.,
U.S.A. 39°50N 105°2W 168 G11
Westminster Md.,
U.S.A. 39°34N 76°59W 173 F15
Westmont U.S.A. 40°19N 78°58W 174 F6
Westmoreland Barbados 13°13N 59°37W 183 d
Westmorland U.S.A. 33°2N 115°37W 171 M11
Weston Oreg., U.S.A. 45°49N 118°26W 168 D4
Weston W. Va., U.S.A. 39°2N 80°28W 173 F13
Weston I. Canada 52°33N 79°36W 164 B4
Weston-super-Mare
U.K. 51°21N 2°58W 67 F5
Westover U.S.A. 40°45N 78°40W 174 F6
Westport Canada 44°40N 76°25W 175 B8
Westport Ireland 53°48N 9°31W 64 C2
Westport N.Z. 41°46S 171°37E 155 D4
Westport N.Y., U.S.A. 44°11N 73°26W 175 B11
Westport Oreg., U.S.A. 46°8N 123°23W 170 D3

Westport Wash., U.S.A. 46°53N 124°6W 170 D2
Westray Canada 53°36N 101°24W 163 C8
Westray U.K. 59°18N 3°0W 65 B5
Westree Canada 47°26N 81°34W 164 C3
Westville Calif., U.S.A. 39°8N 120°42W 170 F6
Westville Fla., U.S.A. 30°46N 85°51W 178 E4
Westwood U.S.A. 40°18N 121°0W 170 F5
Westwood Lake U.S.A. 25°44N 80°23W 179 K9
Wetar Indonesia 7°48S 126°30E 119 F7
Wetaskiwin Canada 52°55N 113°24W 162 C6
Wete Tanzania 5°4S 39°43E 140 F7
Wetherby U.K. 53°56N 1°23W 66 D6
Wethersfield U.S.A. 41°42N 72°40W 175 E12
Wetteren Belgium 51°0N 3°53E 69 D3
Wetumpka U.S.A. 32°32N 86°13W 178 C3
Wetzlar Germany 50°32N 8°31E 76 E4
Wewahitchka U.S.A. 30°7N 85°12W 178 E4
Wewoka U.S.A. 35°9N 96°30W 176 D6
Wexford Ireland 52°20N 6°28W 64 D5
Wexford □ Ireland 52°20N 6°25W 64 D5
Wexford Harbour Ireland 52°20N 6°25W 64 D5
Weyburn Canada 49°40N 103°50W 163 D8
Weyer Markt Austria 47°51N 14°40E 78 D7
Weyhe Germany 52°58N 8°49E 76 C4
Weymouth Canada 44°30N 66°1W 165 D6
Weymouth U.K. 50°37N 2°28W 67 G5
Weymouth U.S.A. 42°13N 70°58W 175 D14
Weymouth, C.
Australia 12°37S 143°27E 150 A3
Wha Ti Canada 63°8N 117°16W 160 E8
Whakaari N.Z. 37°30S 177°13E 154 D6
Whakamaru N.Z. 38°23S 175°50E 154 E4
Whakatane N.Z. 37°57S 177°1E 154 D6
Whakatane → N.Z. 37°57S 177°1E 154 D6
Whale = Baleine →
Canada 58°15N 67°40W 165 A6
Whale B. Burma 11°37N 98°38E 121 G2
Whale Cove Canada 62°10N 92°34W 163 A10
Whale Valley = Hitan, W. el
Egypt 29°1N 30°10E 137 F7
Whales, B. of Antarctica 78°0S 160°0W 55 D12
Whalsay U.K. 60°22N 0°59W 65 A8
Whangaehu → N.Z. 40°3S 175°5E 154 C4
Whangamata N.Z. 37°12S 175°53E 154 D4
Whangamomona N.Z. 39°8S 174°44E 154 F3
Whanganui → N.Z. 39°1'S 174°53E 154 F3
Whangaparaoa Pen.
N.Z. 36°35S 174°45E 154 C3
Whangarei N.Z. 35°43S 174°21E 154 B3
Whangarei Harb. N.Z. 35°45S 174°28E 154 B3
Whangaroa Harb. N.Z. 35°4S 173°46E 154 B2
Whangaruru Harb.
N.Z. 35°24S 174°23E 154 B3
Wharanui N.Z. 41°55S 174°6E 155 B9
Wharekauri = Chatham Is.
Pac. Oc. 44°0S 176°40W 155 c
Wharfe → U.K. 53°51N 1°9W 66 D6
Wharfedale U.K. 54°6N 2°1W 66 C5
Wharton N.J., U.S.A. 40°54N 74°35W 175 F10
Wharton Pa., U.S.A. 41°31N 78°1W 174 E6
Wharton Tex., U.S.A. 29°19N 96°6W 176 G6
Wharton Basin Ind. Oc. 20°0S 99°0E 146 G9
Whataroa N.Z. 43°18S 170°22E 155 D5
Whataroa → N.Z. 43°7S 170°16E 155 D5
Wheatland Calif.,
U.S.A. 39°1N 121°25W 170 F5
Wheatland Wyo.,
U.S.A. 42°3N 104°58W 168 E11
Wheatley Canada 42°6N 82°27W 174 D2
Wheaton Md., U.S.A. 39°3N 77°3W 173 F15
Wheaton Minn., U.S.A. 45°48N 96°30W 172 C5
Wheelbarrow Pk.
U.S.A. 37°26N 116°5W 170 H10
Wheeler Oreg., U.S.A. 45°41N 123°53W 168 D2
Wheeler Tex., U.S.A. 35°27N 100°16W 176 D4
Wheeler → Canada 57°2N 67°13W 165 A6
Wheeler L. U.S.A. 34°48N 87°23W 177 D11
Wheeler Pk. N. Mex.,
U.S.A. 36°34N 105°25W 169 H11
Wheeler Pk. Nev.,
U.S.A. 38°57N 114°15W 168 G6
Wheeler Ridge U.S.A. 35°0N 118°57W 171 L8
Wheelersburg U.S.A. 38°44N 82°51W 173 F12
Wheeling U.S.A. 40°4N 80°43W 174 F4
Whernside U.K. 54°14N 2°24W 66 C5
Whiddy I. Ireland 51°41N 9°31W 64 E2
Whim Creek Australia 20°50S 117°49E 148 D2
Whiskey Jack L.
Canada 58°23N 101°55W 163 B8
Whiskeytown-Shasta-Trinity △
U.S.A. 40°45N 122°15W 168 F2
Whistleduck Cr. →
Australia 20°15S 135°18E 150 C2
Whistler Canada 50°7N 122°58W 162 C4
Whitby Canada 43°52N 78°56W 174 C6
Whitby U.K. 54°29N 0°37W 66 C7
Whitcombe Pass N.Z. 43°13S 170°55E 155 D5
White → Ark., U.S.A. 33°57N 91°5W 176 E9
White → Ind., U.S.A. 38°25N 87°45W 172 F10
White → S. Dak.,
U.S.A. 43°42N 99°27W 172 D4
White → Tex., U.S.A. 33°14N 100°56W 176 E4
White → Utah, U.S.A. 40°4N 109°41W 168 F9
White → Vt., U.S.A. 43°37N 72°20W 175 C12
White → Wash.,
U.S.A. 47°12N 122°15W 170 C4
White B. Canada 50°0N 56°35W 165 C8
White Bird U.S.A. 45°46N 116°18W 168 D5
White Butte U.S.A. 46°23N 103°18W 172 B2
White City Fla., U.S.A. 29°53N 85°13W 178 F4
White City Oreg.,
U.S.A. 42°26N 122°51W 168 E2
White Cliffs Australia 30°50S 143°10E 152 A5
White Desert = Beida, Es Sahrâ al
Egypt 27°28N 28°45E 137 B2
White Hall U.S.A. 39°26N 90°24W 172 F8
White Haven U.S.A. 41°4N 75°47W 175 E9
White Horse, Vale of
U.K. 51°37N 1°30W 67 F6
White I. = Whakaari
N.Z. 37°30S 177°13E 154 D6
White L. Canada 45°18N 76°31W 175 A8
White L. U.S.A. 29°44N 92°30W 176 G8
White Lake Canada 45°21N 76°29W 175 A8
White Mountain Peak
U.S.A. 37°38N 118°15W 170 H8
White Mts. Calif.,
U.S.A. 37°30N 118°15W 170 H8
White Mts. N.H.,
U.S.A. 44°15N 71°15W 175 B13

White Mts. △
Australia 20°43S 145°12E 150 C4
White Nile = Nil el Abyad →
Sudan 15°38N 32°31E 135 E12
White Oak U.S.A. 31°2N 81°43W 178 D8
White Otter L. Canada 49°5N 91°55W 164 C1
White Pass U.S.A. 46°38N 121°24W 170 D5
White Plains Ga., U.S.A. 33°28N 83°1W 178 B6
White Plains N.Y.,
U.S.A. 41°2N 73°46W 175 E11
White River Canada 48°35N 85°20W 164 C2
White River U.S.A. 43°34N 100°45W 172 D3
White Rock Canada 49°2N 122°48W 170 A4
White Rock U.S.A. 35°50N 106°12W 169 J10
White Rocks Nat. Recr. Area △
U.S.A. 43°22N 72°55W 175 C12
White Russia = Belarus ■
Europe 53°30N 27°0E 75 B14
White Sands △
U.S.A. 32°46N 106°20W 169 K10
White Sea = Beloye More
Russia 66°30N 38°0E 58 B13
White Springs U.S.A. 30°20N 82°45W 178 E7
White Sulphur Springs Mont.,
U.S.A. 46°33N 110°54W 168 C8
White Sulphur Springs W. Va.,
U.S.A. 37°48N 80°18W 173 G13
White Swan U.S.A. 46°23N 120°44W 170 D5
White Volta → Ghana 9°10N 1°15W 139 D4
Whitecliffs N.Z. 43°26S 171°55E 155 D5
Whitecourt Canada 54°10N 115°45W 162 C5
Whiteface Mt. U.S.A. 44°22N 73°54W 175 B11
Whitefield U.S.A. 44°23N 71°37W 175 B13
Whitefish U.S.A. 48°25N 114°20W 168 B6
Whitefish B. U.S.A. 46°40N 84°55W 164 C3
Whitefish L. Canada 62°41N 106°48W 163 A7
Whitefish Pt. U.S.A. 46°45N 84°59W 173 B11
Whitegull, L. = Goélands, L. aux
Canada 55°27N 64°17W 165 A7
Whitehall Mich.,
U.S.A. 43°24N 86°21W 172 D10
Whitehall Mont.,
U.S.A. 45°52N 112°6W 168 D7
Whitehall N.Y.,
U.S.A. 43°33N 73°24W 175 C11
Whitehall Wis., U.S.A. 44°22N 91°19W 172 C8
Whitehaven U.K. 54°33N 3°35W 66 C4
Whitehorse Canada 60°43N 135°3W 162 A1
Whitemark Australia 40°7S 148°3E 151 G4
Whiteplains Liberia 6°28N 10°40W 138 D2
Whiteriver U.S.A. 33°50N 109°58W 169 K9
Whitesand → Canada 60°9N 115°45W 162 A5
Whitesands S. Africa 34°23S 20°50E 144 E3
Whitesboro N.Y., U.S.A. 43°7N 75°18W 175 C9
Whitesboro Tex.,
U.S.A. 33°39N 96°54W 176 E6
Whiteshell △ Canada 49°50S 95°40W 163 D9
Whiteside, Canal Chile 53°55S 70°15W 192 D2
Whiteville U.S.A. 34°20N 78°42W 177 D15
Whitewater U.S.A. 42°50N 88°44W 172 D9
Whitewater B. U.S.A. 25°15N 81°0W 179 K9
Whitewater Baldy
U.S.A. 33°20N 108°39W 169 K9
Whitewood Australia 21°28S 143°30E 150 C3
Whitewood Canada 50°20N 102°20W 163 C8
Whitfield Australia 36°42S 146°24E 153 D7
Whithorn U.K. 54°44N 4°26W 65 G4
Whitianga N.Z. 36°47S 175°41E 154 C4
Whitman U.S.A. 42°5N 70°56W 175 D14
Whitmore Mts.
Antarctica 82°35S 104°30W 55 E15
Whitney, Mt. U.S.A. 36°35N 118°18W 170 J8
Whitney Point U.S.A. 42°20N 75°58W 175 D9
Whitstable U.K. 51°21N 1°3E 67 F9
Whitsunday I. Australia 20°15S 149°4E 150 b
Whitsunday Islands △
Australia 20°15S 149°0E 150 b
Whittier Alaska,
U.S.A. 60°47N 148°41W 166 C10
Whittier Calif., U.S.A. 33°58N 118°2W 171 M8
Whittlesea Australia 37°27S 145°9E 153 D6
Wholdaia L. Canada 60°43N 104°20W 163 A8
Whyalla Australia 33°2S 137°30E 152 B2
Wiang Kosai △
Thailand 17°54N 99°29E 120 D2
Wiang Sa Thailand 18°34N 100°45E 120 C3
Wiarton Canada 44°40N 81°10W 174 B3
Wiawso Ghana 6°10N 2°25W 138 D4
Wiay U.K. 57°24N 7°13W 65 D1
Wiązów Poland 50°50N 17°10E 83 H4
Wibaux U.S.A. 46°59N 104°11W 168 C11
Wichian Buri Thailand 15°39N 101°7E 120 E3
Wichita U.S.A. 37°42N 97°20W 172 G5
Wichita Falls U.S.A. 33°54N 98°30W 176 E5
Wick U.K. 58°26N 3°5W 65 C5
Wickenburg U.S.A. 33°58N 112°44W 169 K7
Wickepin Australia 32°50S 117°30E 149 F2
Wickham Australia 20°42S 117°11E 148 D2
Wickham, C. Australia 39°35S 143°57E 151 F3
Wickliffe U.S.A. 41°36N 81°28W 174 E3
Wicklow Ireland 52°59N 6°3W 64 D5
Wicklow □ Ireland 52°57N 6°25W 64 D5
Wicklow Hd. Ireland 52°58N 6°0W 64 D6
Wicklow Mts. Ireland 52°58N 6°26W 64 C5
Wicklow Mts. △ Ireland 53°6N 6°21W 64 C5
Widawa Poland 51°27N 18°51E 83 G5
Widawka → Poland 51°27N 18°52E 83 G5
Widgeegoara Cr. →
Australia 28°51S 146°34E 151 D4
Widgiemooltha
Australia 31°30S 121°34E 149 F3
Widnes U.K. 53°23N 2°45W 66 D5
Widrefk Poland 51°30N 17°30E 83 G4
Wiehengebirge = Nördlicher
Teutoburger
Wald-Wiehengebirge △
Germany 52°18N 8°10E 76 C4
Wiehl Germany 50°56N 7°34E 76 E3
Wiek Germany 54°37N 13°17E 76 A9
Wielbark Poland 53°24N 20°55E 82 E7
Wielcń Poland 52°53N 16°9E 83 F3
Wielichowo Poland 52°5N 16°31E 83 F3
Wieliczka Poland 50°0N 20°5E 83 J7
Wielkopolski △ Poland 52°18N 16°45E 83 F3
Wielkopolskie □ Poland 52°10N 17°30E 83 F4
Wieluń Poland 51°15N 18°34E 83 G5
Wien Austria 48°12N 16°22E 79 C9
Wien-Schwechat ✈ (VIE)
Austria 48°7N 16°35E 79 C9

Wiener Neustadt
Austria 47°49N 16°16E 79 D9
Wieprz → Poland 51°34N 21°49E 83 G8
Wieprza → Poland 54°26N 16°25E 82 D3
Wieruszów Poland 51°19N 18°9E 83 G5
Wiesbaden Germany 50°4N 8°14E 77 E4
Wiesental Germany 49°13N 8°31E 77 F4
Wiesloch Germany 49°18N 8°41E 77 F4
Wiesmoor Germany 53°24N 7°47E 76 B3
Więżyca Poland 54°14N 18°8E 82 D5
Wigan U.K. 53°33N 2°38W 66 D5
Wiggins Colo., U.S.A. 40°14N 104°4W 168 E11
Wiggins Miss., U.S.A. 30°51N 89°8W 177 F10
Wight, I. of U.K. 50°41N 1°17W 67 G6
Wigierski △ Poland 54°2N 23°8E 82 D10
Wigry, Jezioro Poland 54°2N 23°8E 82 D10
Wigston U.K. 52°35N 1°6W 67 E6
Wigton U.K. 54°50N 3°10W 66 C4
Wigtown U.K. 54°53N 4°27W 65 G4
Wigtown B. U.K. 54°46N 4°15W 65 G4
Wik and Wikway People ☉
Australia 13°55S 142°28E 150 A3
Wil Switz. 47°28N 9°3E 71 H5
Wilamowice Poland 49°55N 19°9E 83 J6
Wilber U.S.A. 40°29N 96°58W 172 E5
Wilberforce Canada 45°2N 78°13W 174 A6
Wilberforce, C.
Australia 11°54S 136°35E 150 A2
Wilburton U.S.A. 34°55N 95°19W 176 D7
Wilcannia Australia 31°30S 143°26E 152 B5
Wilcox U.S.A. 41°35N 78°41W 174 E6
Wildbad Germany 48°44N 8°33E 77 G4
Wildeshausen Germany 52°54N 8°27E 76 C4
Wildhauser Geest ☉
Germany 52°54N 8°30E 76 C4
Wildomar U.S.A. 33°36N 117°16W 171 M9
Wildon Austria 46°52N 15°31E 78 E8
Wildrose U.S.A. 36°14N 117°11W 171 J9
Wildspitze Austria 46°53N 10°53E 78 E5
Wildwood U.S.A. 28°52N 82°2W 179 G7
Wilga → Poland 51°52N 21°18E 83 G8
Wilge → S. Africa 27°3S 28°20E 145 C4
Wilhelm II Coast
Antarctica 68°0S 90°0E 55 C7
Wilhelmsburg Austria 48°6N 15°36E 78 C8
Wilhelmshaven Germany 53°31N 8°7E 76 B4
Wilhelmstal Namibia 21°58S 16°21E 144 B2
Wilis Indonesia 7°51S 111°48E 119 G15
Wilkes-Barre U.S.A. 41°15N 75°53W 175 E9
Wilkes Land Antarctica 69°0S 120°0E 55 D9
Wilkie Canada 52°27N 108°42W 163 C7
Wilkins Ice Shelf
Antarctica 70°30S 72°0W 55 C17
Wilkinsburg U.S.A. 40°26N 79°52W 174 F5
Wilkinson Lakes
Australia 29°40S 132°39E 149 E5
Willacoochee U.S.A. 31°20N 83°3W 178 D6
Willandra △ Australia 33°12S 145°0E 153 B6
Willandra Creek →
Australia 33°22S 145°52E 153 B6
Willapa B. U.S.A. 46°40N 124°0W 170 D3
Willapa Hills U.S.A. 46°35N 123°25W 170 D3
Willard U.S.A. 41°3N 82°44W 174 E2
Willare Bridge Roadhouse
Australia 17°43S 123°38E 148 C3
Willbriggie Australia 34°28S 146°2E 153 C7
Willcox U.S.A. 32°15N 109°50W 169 K9
Willemstad Curaçao 12°5N 68°55W 183 D6
Willi Willi △
Australia 30°57S 152°27E 153 A10
William → Canada 59°8N 109°19W 163 B7
William, Mt. Australia 37°17S 142°35E 152 D5
William 'Bill' Dannelly Res.
U.S.A. 32°8N 87°24W 177 E11
William Creek
Australia 28°58S 136°22E 151 D2
Williams Australia 33°2S 116°52E 149 F2
Williams Ariz., U.S.A. 35°15N 112°11W 169 J7
Williams Calif., U.S.A. 39°9N 122°9W 170 F4
Williams Harbour
Canada 52°33N 55°47W 165 B8
Williams Lake Canada 52°10N 122°10W 162 C4
Williamsburg Ky.,
U.S.A. 36°44N 84°10W 173 G11
Williamsburg Pa.,
U.S.A. 40°28N 78°12W 174 F6
Williamsburg Va.,
U.S.A. 37°16N 76°43W 173 G15
Williamson N.Y., U.S.A. 43°14N 77°11W 174 C7
Williamson W. Va.,
U.S.A. 37°41N 82°17W 173 G12
Williamsport U.S.A. 41°15N 77°1W 174 E7
Williamston U.S.A. 35°51N 77°4W 177 D16
Williamstown
Australia 37°51S 144°52E 151 F3
Williamstown Mass.,
U.S.A. 42°43N 73°12W 175 D11
Williamstown N.Y.,
U.S.A. 43°26N 75°53W 175 C9
Willimantic U.S.A. 41°43N 72°13W 175 E12
Willingboro U.S.A. 40°3N 74°54W 173 E16
Williston S. Africa 31°20S 20°53E 144 D3
Williston Fla., U.S.A. 29°23N 82°27W 179 F7
Williston N. Dak.,
U.S.A. 48°9N 103°37W 172 A2
Williston S.C., U.S.A. 33°24N 81°25W 178 B8
Williston L. Canada 56°0N 124°0W 162 B4
Willits U.S.A. 39°25N 123°21W 168 G2
Willmar U.S.A. 45°7N 95°3W 172 C6
Willmore Wilderness △
Canada 53°45N 119°30W 162 C5
Willoughby U.S.A. 41°39N 81°24W 174 E3
Willow Bunch
Canada 49°20N 105°35W 163 D7
Willow L. Canada 62°10N 119°8W 162 A5
Willow Tree Australia 31°40S 150°45E 153 A9
Willow Wall, The
China 42°10N 122°0E 115 C12
Willowick U.S.A. 41°38N 81°28W 174 E3
Willowlake → Canada 62°42N 123°8W 162 A4
Willowmore S. Africa 33°15S 23°30E 144 E3
Willows U.S.A. 39°31N 122°12W 170 F4
Willowvale = Gatyana
S. Africa 32°16S 28°31E 145 E4
Wills, L. Australia 21°25S 128°51E 148 D4
Wills Cr. → Australia 22°43S 140°2E 150 C3
Willsboro U.S.A. 44°21N 73°24W 175 B11
Willunga Australia 35°15S 138°30E 152 C2

Wilma U.S.A. 30°9N 84°58W 178 E5
Wilmette U.S.A. 42°4N 87°42W 172 D10
Wilmington Australia 32°39S 138°7E 152 B3
Wilmington Del.,
U.S.A. 39°45N 75°33W 173 F16
Wilmington N.C.,
U.S.A. 34°14N 77°55W 177 D16
Wilmington Ohio,
U.S.A. 39°27N 83°50W 173 F12
Wilmington Vt.,
U.S.A. 42°52N 72°52W 175 D12
Wilmslow U.K. 53°19N 2°13W 66 D5
Wilpattu △ Sri Lanka 8°20N 79°50E 127 K4
Wilpena Australia 31°33S 138°37E 152 A3
Wilpena Cr. →
Australia 31°25S 139°29E 152 A3
Wilsall U.S.A. 45°59N 110°38W 168 D8
Wilson N.C., U.S.A. 35°44N 77°55W 177 D16
Wilson N.Y., U.S.A. 43°19N 78°50W 174 C6
Wilson Pa., U.S.A. 40°41N 75°15W 175 F9
Wilson → Australia 16°48S 128°16E 148 C4
Wilson Bluff Australia 31°41S 129°0E 149 F4
Wilson Inlet Australia 35°0S 117°22E 149 G2
Wilsons Promontory
Australia 38°59S 146°23E 153 E7
Wilsons Promontory △
Australia 38°59S 146°23E 153 E7
Wilster Germany 53°55N 9°23E 76 B5
Wilton U.S.A. 47°10N 100°47W 172 B3
Wilton → Australia 14°45S 134°33E 150 A1
Wiltshire □ U.K. 51°18N 1°53W 67 F6
Wiltz Lux. 49°57N 5°55E 69 E5
Wiluna Australia 26°36S 120°14E 149 E3
Wimborne Minster U.K. 50°48N 1°59W 67 G6
Wimereux France 50°45N 1°37E 71 B8
Wimmera → Australia 36°8S 141°56E 152 D4
Winam G. Kenya 0°20S 34°15E 142 C7
Winburg S. Africa 28°30S 27°2E 144 D4
Winchelsea Australia 38°10S 144°1E 153 E6
Winchendon U.S.A. 42°41N 72°3W 175 D12
Winchester N.Z. 44°11S 171°17E 155 D6
Winchester U.K. 51°4N 1°18W 67 F6
Winchester Conn.,
U.S.A. 41°53N 73°9W 175 E11
Winchester Idaho,
U.S.A. 46°14N 116°38W 168 C5
Winchester Ind.,
U.S.A. 40°10N 84°59W 173 E11
Winchester Ky.,
U.S.A. 37°59N 84°11W 173 G11
Winchester N.H.,
U.S.A. 42°46N 72°23W 175 D12
Winchester Nev.,
U.S.A. 36°7N 115°7W 171 J11
Winchester Tenn.,
U.S.A. 35°11N 86°7W 177 D11
Winchester Va.,
U.S.A. 39°11N 78°10W 173 F14
Wind → U.S.A. 43°12N 108°12W 168 E9
Wind Cave △ U.S.A. 43°32N 103°17W 172 D2
Wind River Range
U.S.A. 43°0N 109°30W 168 E9
Windamere, L.
Australia 32°48S 149°51E 153 B8
Windau = Ventspils
Latvia 57°25N 21°32E 82 A10
Windber U.S.A. 40°14N 78°50W 174 F6
Winder U.S.A. 34°0N 83°45W 178 B6
Windermere U.K. 54°23N 2°55W 66 C5
Windermere U.S.A. 28°29N 81°32W 179 G8
Windhoek Namibia 22°35S 17°4E 144 B2
Windidda ☉ Australia 26°23S 122°12E 149 E3
Windischgarsten
Austria 47°42N 14°21E 78 D7
Windjana Gorge △
Australia 17°51S 125°0E 148 C3
Windom U.S.A. 43°52N 95°7W 172 D6
Windorah Australia 25°24S 142°36E 150 D3
Window Rock U.S.A. 35°41N 109°3W 169 J9
Windrush → U.K. 51°43N 1°24W 67 F6
Windsor Australia 33°37S 150°50E 153 B9
Windsor N.S., Canada 44°59N 64°5W 165 D7
Windsor Ont., Canada 42°18N 83°0W 174 D2
Windsor N.Z. 44°59S 170°49E 155 E6
Windsor U.K. 51°29N 0°36W 67 F7
Windsor Colo., U.S.A. 40°29N 104°54W 168 E11
Windsor Conn., U.S.A. 41°50N 72°39W 175 E12
Windsor Mo., U.S.A. 38°32N 93°31W 172 F7
Windsor N.Y., U.S.A. 42°5N 75°37W 175 D9
Windsor Vt., U.S.A. 43°29N 72°24W 175 C12
Windsor & Maidenhead □
U.K. 51°29N 0°40W 67 F7
Windsorton S. Africa 28°16S 24°44E 144 D3
Windward Is. W. Indies 13°0N 61°0W 183 D7
Windward Passage = Vientos,
Paso de los Caribbean 20°0N 74°0W 183 C5
Winefred L. Canada 55°30N 110°30W 163 B6
Winfield U.S.A. 37°15N 96°59W 172 G5
Wingate Mts.
Australia 14°25S 130°40E 148 B5
Wingellina = Irrunytju
Australia 26°3S 128°56E 149 E4
Wingham Australia 31°48S 152°22E 153 A10
Wingham Canada 43°55N 81°20W 174 C3
Winisk → Canada 55°17N 85°5W 164 A2
Winisk L. Canada 52°55N 87°22W 164 B2
Wink U.S.A. 31°45N 103°9W 176 F3
Winkler Canada 49°10N 97°56W 163 D9
Winklern Austria 46°52N 12°52E 78 E5
Winlock U.S.A. 46°30N 122°56W 170 D4
Winneba Ghana 5°25N 0°36W 139 D4
Winnebago, L. U.S.A. 44°0N 88°26W 172 D9
Winnecke Cr. →
Australia 18°35S 131°34E 148 C5
Winnemucca U.S.A. 40°58N 117°44W 168 F5
Winnemucca L. U.S.A. 40°7N 119°21W 168 F4
Winner U.S.A. 43°22N 99°52W 172 D4
Winnett U.S.A. 47°0N 108°21W 168 C9
Winnfield U.S.A. 31°56N 92°38W 176 F8
Winnibigoshish, L.
U.S.A. 47°27N 94°13W 172 B7
Winnipeg Canada 49°54N 97°9W 163 D9
Winnipeg → Canada 50°38N 96°19W 163 C9
Winnipeg, L. Canada 52°0N 97°0W 163 C9
Winnipeg Beach
Canada 50°30N 96°58W 163 C9
Winnipegosis Canada 51°39N 99°55W 163 C8
Winnipegosis L.
Canada 52°30N 100°0W 163 C8
Winnipesaukee, L.
U.S.A. 43°38N 71°21W 175 C13

Winnisquam L.
U.S.A. 43°33N 71°31W **175** C13
Winnsboro La., U.S.A. 32°10N 91°43W **176** E9
Winnsboro S.C., U.S.A. 34°23N 81°5W **177** D14
Winnsboro Tex., U.S.A. 32°58N 95°17W **176** E7
Winokapau, L. Canada 53°15N 62°50W **165** B7
Winona Minn., U.S.A. 44°3N 91°39W **172** C8
Winona Miss., U.S.A. 33°29N 89°44W **177** E10
Winooski U.S.A. 44°29N 73°11W **175** B11
Winooski → U.S.A. 44°32N 73°17W **175** B11
Winschoten Neths. 53°9N 7°3E **69** A7
Winsen Germany 52°32N 10°13E **76** B6
Winsford U.K. 53°12N 2°31W **66** D5
Winslow = Bainbridge Island
U.S.A. 47°38N 122°32W **170** C4
Winslow U.S.A. 35°2N 110°42W **199** E8
Winsted U.S.A. 41°55N 73°4W **175** E11
Winston-Salem U.S.A. 36°6N 80°15W **177** C14
Winter Garden U.S.A. 28°34N 81°35W **179** G8
Winter Haven U.S.A. 28°1N 81°44W **179** G8
Winter Park U.S.A. 28°36N 81°20W **179** G8
Winterberg Germany 51°11N 8°33E **76** D4
Winterhaven U.S.A. 32°44N 114°38W **171** N12
Winters U.S.A. 38°32N 121°58W **170** G5
Winterset U.S.A. 41°20N 94°1W **172** E6
Wintersville U.S.A. 40°23N 80°42W **174** F4
Winterswijk Neths. 51°58N 6°43E **69** C6
Winterthur Switz. 47°30N 8°44E **77** H4
Winthrop U.S.A. 48°28N 120°10W **168** B3
Winton Australia 22°24S 143°3E **150** C3
Winton N.Z. 46°8S 168°20E **155** G3
Wipper → Germany 51°16N 11°12E **76** D7
Wirlyajarrayi ○
Australia 21°45S 132°35E **148** D5
Wirraminna Australia 31°12S 136°13E **152** A2
Wirrulla Australia 32°24S 134°31E **151** E1
Wisbech U.K. 52°41N 0°9E **67** E8
Wisconsin □ U.S.A. 44°45N 89°30W **172** C9
Wisconsin → U.S.A. 43°0N 91°15W **172** D8
Wisconsin Rapids
U.S.A. 44°23N 89°49W **172** C9
Wisdom U.S.A. 45°37N 113°27W **168** D7
Wiseman U.S.A. 67°25N 150°6W **166** B9
Wishaw U.K. 55°46N 3°54W **65** F5
Wishek U.S.A. 46°16N 99°33W **172** B4
Wisła Poland 49°38N 18°53E **83** J5
Wisła → Poland 54°22N 18°55E **82** D5
Wiślany, Zalew Poland 54°20N 19°50E **82** D6
Wisłok → Poland 50°13N 22°32E **83** H9
Wisłoka → Poland 50°27N 21°23E **83** H8
Wismar Germany 53°54N 11°29E **76** B7
Wisner U.S.A. 41°59N 96°55W **172** E5
Wissant France 50°52N 1°40E **71** B8
Wissembourg France 49°2N 7°57E **71** C14
Wisznice Poland 51°48N 23°13E **83** G10
Witbank = eMalahleni
S. Africa 25°51S 29°14E **145** C4
Witches Gorge = Wu Xia
China 31°2N 110°10E **117** B8
Witdraai S. Africa 26°58S 20°48E **144** C3
Witham U.K. 51°48N 0°40E **67** F8
Witham → U.K. 52°59N 0°2W **66** E7
Withernsea U.K. 53°44N 0°1E **66** D8
Withlacoochee → Fla.,
U.S.A. 30°24N 83°10W **178** E6
Withlacoochee → Fla.,
U.S.A. 29°0N 82°45W **179** G7
Witjira △ Australia 26°22S 135°37E **151** D2
Witkowo Poland 52°26N 17°45E **83** F4
Witless Bay Canada 47°17N 52°50W **165** C9
Witney U.K. 51°48N 1°28W **67** F6
Witnica Poland 52°40N 14°54E **83** F1
Witnossob → Namibia 23°55S 18°45E **144** C3
Witriver S. Africa 25°20S 31°0E **145** C5
Wittdün Germany 54°38N 8°23E **76** A4
Wittelsheim France 47°48N 7°14E **71** E14
Witten Germany 51°26N 7°20E **76** D3
Wittenberge Germany 53°0N 11°45E **76** B7
Wittenburg Germany 53°31N 11°4E **76** B7
Wittenoom Australia 22°15S 118°20E **148** D2
Wittingen Germany 52°44N 10°44E **76** C6
Wittlich Germany 49°59N 6°53E **77** F2
Wittmund Germany 53°34N 7°46E **76** B3
Wittow Germany 54°38N 13°20E **76** A9
Wittstock Germany 53°10N 12°28E **76** B8
Witu Kenya 2°23S 40°26E **142** C5
Witvlei Namibia 22°23S 18°32E **144** B2
Witzenhausen Germany 51°20N 9°51E **76** D5
Wiwon N. Korea 40°54N 126°3E **115** D14
Wkra → Poland 52°27N 20°44E **83** F7
Władysławowo Poland 54°48N 18°25E **82** D5
Wleń Poland 51°2N 15°39E **83** G2
Wlingi Indonesia 8°5S 112°25E **119** H15
Włocławek Poland 52°40N 19°3E **83** F6
Włodawa Poland 51°33N 23°31E **83** G10
Włoszczowa Poland 50°50N 19°55E **83** H6
Woburn U.S.A. 42°29N 71°9W **175** D13
Wodian China 32°50N 112°35E **114** H7
Wodonga Australia 36°5S 146°50E **153** D7
Wodzisław Śląski Poland 50°1N 18°26E **83** H5
Woerth France 48°57N 7°45E **71** D14
Woinbogoin China 32°31N 98°39E **116** A2
Woippy France 49°10N 6°8E **71** C13
Wojcieszow Poland 50°58N 15°55E **83** H2
Wokam Indonesia 5°45S 134°28E **119** F8
Woking U.K. 51°19N 0°34W **67** F7
Wokingham U.K. 51°24N 0°49W **67** F7
Wokingham □ U.K. 51°25N 0°51W **67** F7
Woko △ Australia 31°46S 151°49E **153** A9
Wolbrom Poland 50°24N 19°45E **83** H6
Wolczyn Poland 51°1N 18°3E **83** G5
Woldegk Germany 53°27N 13°34E **76** B9
Wolf → Canada 60°17N 132°33W **162** A2
Wolf Creek U.S.A. 47°0N 112°4W **168** C7
Wolf L. Canada 60°24N 131°40W **162** A2
Wolf Point U.S.A. 48°5N 105°39W **168** B11
Wolfe Creek Crater △
Australia 19°10S 127°47E **148** C4
Wolfe I. Canada 44°7N 76°20W **175** B8
Wolfeboro U.S.A. 43°35N 71°13W **175** C13
Wolfenbüttel Germany 52°10N 10°33E **76** C6
Wolfratshausen
Germany 47°54N 11°24E **77** H7
Wolfsberg Austria 46°50N 14°52E **78** E7
Wolfsburg Germany 52°25N 10°48E **76** C6
Wolgast Germany 54°3N 13°44E **76** A9
Wolhusen Switz. 47°4N 8°4E **77** H4
Wolin Poland 53°50N 14°37E **82** B1
Woliński △ Poland 53°57N 14°28E **82** B1
Wollaston, Is. Chile 55°40S 67°30W **192** E3
Wollaston Forland
Greenland 74°25N 19°40W **57** C9

Wollaston L. Canada 58°7N 103°10W **163** B8
Wollaston Lake
Canada 58°3N 103°33W **163** B8
Wollaston Pen. Canada 69°30N 115°0W **160** D9
Wollemi △ Australia 33°0S 150°30E **153** B9
Wollongong Australia 34°25S 150°54E **153** C9
Wolmaransstad
S. Africa 27°12S 25°59E **144** C4
Wolmirstedt Germany 52°14N 11°37E **76** C7
Wołomin Poland 52°19N 21°15E **83** F8
Wołów Poland 51°20N 16°38E **83** G3
Wolseley Australia 36°23S 140°54E **152** D4
Wolseley S. Africa 33°26S 19°7E **144** D2
Wolsey U.S.A. 44°25N 98°28W **172** C4
Wolstenholme, C.
Canada 62°35N 77°30W **158** C12
Wolsztyn Poland 52°8N 16°5E **83** F3
Wolvega Neths. 52°52N 6°0E **69** B6
Wolverhampton U.K. 52°35N 2°7W **67** E5
Wondai Australia 26°20S 151°49E **151** D5
Wongalarroo L.
Australia 31°32S 144°0E **152** A6
Wongan Hills
Australia 30°51S 116°37E **149** F2
Wonju S. Korea 37°22N 127°58E **115** F14
Wonosari Indonesia 7°58S 110°36E **119** G14
Wonosobo Indonesia 7°22S 109°54E **119** G13
Wonowon Canada 56°44N 121°48W **162** B4
Wŏnsan N. Korea 39°11N 127°27E **115** E14
Wonthaggi Australia 38°37S 145°37E **153** E6
Wood Buffalo △
Canada 59°0N 113°41W **162** B6
Wood Is. Australia 16°24S 123°19E **148** C3
Wood L. Canada 55°17N 103°17W **163** B8
Woodah, I. Australia 13°27S 136°10E **150** A2
Woodbine U.S.A. 30°58N 81°44W **178** E8
Woodbourne U.S.A. 41°46N 74°36W **175** E10
Woodbridge Canada 43°47N 79°36W **174** C5
Woodbridge U.K. 52°6N 1°20E **67** E9
Woodburn Australia 29°6S 153°23E **151** A5
Woodburn U.S.A. 45°9N 122°51W **168** D2
Woodbury U.S.A. 32°59N 84°4W **178** D5
Woodenbong
Australia 28°24S 152°39E **151** D5
Woodend Australia 37°20S 144°33E **152** D6
Woodford Australia 26°58S 152°47E **151** D5
Woodfords U.S.A. 38°47N 119°50W **170** G7
Woodlake U.S.A. 36°25N 119°6W **170** J7
Woodland Calif.,
U.S.A. 38°41N 121°46W **170** G5
Woodland Maine,
U.S.A. 45°9N 67°25W **173** C20
Woodland Pa., U.S.A. 41°0N 78°21W **174** F6
Woodland Wash.,
U.S.A. 45°54N 122°45W **170** E4
Woodland Caribou △
Canada 51°0N 94°45W **163** C10
Woodlands Singapore 1°26N 103°46E **121** d
Woodlands, The U.S.A. 30°9N 95°29W **176** F7
Woodonga Australia 36°10S 146°50E **151** F4
Woodroffe, Mt.
Australia 26°20S 131°45E **149** E5
Woods, L. Australia 17°50S 133°30E **150** B1
Woods, L. of the
N. Amer. 49°15N 94°45W **163** D10
Woods Bay Canada 45°8N 79°59W **174** A5
Woodside S. Austral.,
Australia 34°58S 138°52E **152** C3
Woodside Vic.,
Australia 38°31S 146°52E **153** E7
Woodstock N.S.W.,
Australia 33°45S 148°53E **153** B8
Woodstock Queens.,
Australia 19°35S 146°50E **150** B4
Woodstock N.B.,
Canada 46°11N 67°37W **165** C6
Woodstock Ont.,
Canada 43°10N 80°45W **174** C4
Woodstock U.K. 51°51N 1°20W **67** F6
Woodstock Ill., U.S.A. 42°19N 88°27W **172** D9
Woodstock N.Y., U.S.A. 42°2N 74°7W **175** D10
Woodstock Vt.,
U.S.A. 43°37N 72°31W **175** C12
Woodsville U.S.A. 44°9N 72°2W **175** B13
Woodview Canada 44°35N 78°8W **174** B6
Woodville N.Z. 40°20S 175°53E **154** G4
Woodville Fla., U.S.A. 30°19N 84°15W **178** E5
Woodville Ga., U.S.A. 33°40N 83°7W **178** B6
Woodville Miss., U.S.A. 31°6N 91°18W **176** F9
Woodville Tex., U.S.A. 30°47N 94°25W **176** F7
Woodward U.S.A. 36°26N 99°24W **176** C5
Woody U.S.A. 35°42N 118°50W **171** K8
Woody → Canada 52°31N 100°51W **163** C8
Woody I. S. China Sea 16°50N 112°20E **118** A4
Woolacombe U.K. 51°10N 4°13W **67** F3
Woolamai, C. Australia 38°30S 145°23E **153** E6
Woolbrook Australia 30°56S 151°25E **153** A9
Wooler U.K. 55°33N 2°1W **66** B5
Woolgoolga Australia 30°6S 153°11E **151** E5
Woomargama △
Australia 35°50S 147°15E **153** C7
Woomera Australia 31°5S 136°50E **152** A2
Woonsocket R.I.,
U.S.A. 42°0N 71°31W **175** E13
Woonsocket S. Dak.,
U.S.A. 44°3N 98°17W **172** C4
Wooramel →
Australia 25°47S 114°10E **149** E1
Wooramel Roadhouse
Australia 25°45S 114°17E **149** E1
Wooroonooran △
Australia 16°25S 146°1E **150** B4
Wooster U.S.A. 40°48N 81°56W **174** F3
Worcester S. Africa 33°39S 19°27E **144** D2
Worcester U.K. 52°11N 2°12W **67** E5
Worcester Mass.,
U.S.A. 42°16N 71°48W **175** D13
Worcester N.Y.,
U.S.A. 42°36N 74°45W **175** D10
Worcestershire □ U.K. 52°13N 2°10W **67** E5
Wörgl Austria 47°29N 12°3E **78** D5
Workington U.K. 54°39N 3°33W **66** C4
Worksop U.K. 53°18N 1°7W **66** D6
Workum Neths. 52°59N 5°26E **69** B5
Worland U.S.A. 44°1N 107°57W **168** D10
Wormhout France 50°52N 2°28E **71** B9
Worms Germany 49°37N 8°21E **77** F4
Woroba △ Ivory C. 8°9N 7°54W **138** D3
Worsley Canada 56°31N 119°8W **162** B5
Wörth Germany 49°1N 12°24E **77** F8

Wortham U.S.A. 31°47N 96°28W **176** F6
Wörther See Austria 46°37N 14°10E **78** E7
Worthing Barbados 13°5N 59°35W **183** g
Worthing U.K. 50°49N 0°21W **67** G7
Worthington Minn.,
U.S.A. 43°37N 95°36W **172** D6
Worthington Pa.,
U.S.A. 40°50N 79°38W **174** F5
Wosi Indonesia 0°15S 128°0W **119** E7
Wote Kenya 1°47S 37°38E **142** C4
Wotjalum ○ Australia 16°30S 123°45E **148** C3
Wotjobaluk ○ Australia 37°0S 142°0E **151** C3
Wou-han = Wuhan
China 30°31N 114°18E **117** B10
Wousi = Wuxi China 31°33N 120°18E **117** B13
Wowoni Indonesia 4°5S 123°5E **119** E6
Woy Woy Australia 33°30S 151°19E **153** B9
Wrangel I. = Vrangelya, Ostrov
Russia 71°0N 180°0E **107** B18
Wrangell U.S.A. 56°28N 132°23W **162** B2
Wrangell Mts. U.S.A. 61°30N 142°0W **160** D5
Wrath, C. U.K. 58°38N 5°1W **65** C3
Wray U.S.A. 40°5N 102°13W **168** F12
Wrekin, The U.K. 52°41N 2°32W **67** E5
Wrens U.S.A. 33°12N 82°23W **178** B7
Wrexham U.K. 53°3N 3°0W **66** D4
Wrexham □ U.K. 53°1N 2°58W **66** D5
Wriezen Germany 52°42N 14°7E **76** C10
Wright Fla., U.S.A. 30°27N 86°38W **179** E3
Wright Wyo., U.S.A. 43°45N 105°28W **168** D11
Wright Pt. Canada 43°48N 81°44W **174** C3
Wrightmyo India 11°47N 92°43E **127** J11
Wrightson, Mt.
U.S.A. 31°42N 110°51W **169** L8
Wrightsville U.S.A. 32°44N 82°43W **178** C7
Wrightwood U.S.A. 34°22N 117°38W **171** L9
Wrigley Canada 63°16N 123°37W **160** D7
Wrocław Poland 51°5N 17°5E **83** G4
Wronki Poland 52°41N 16°21E **83** F3
Września Poland 52°21N 17°36E **83** F4
Wschowa Poland 51°48N 16°20E **83** G3
Wu Jiang → China 29°40N 107°20E **116** C6
Wu Kau Tang China 22°30N 114°14E **111** a
Wu Xia China 31°2N 110°10E **117** B8
Wu'an China 36°40N 114°15E **114** F8
Wubalawun ○
Australia 15°28S 133°1E **148** C5
Wubin Australia 30°6S 116°37E **149** F2
Wubu China 37°28N 110°42E **114** F6
Wuchang China 44°55N 127°5E **115** B14
Wucheng China 37°12N 116°20E **114** F8
Wuchuan Guangdong,
China 21°33N 110°43E **117** G8
Wuchuan Guizhou,
China 28°25N 108°3E **116** C7
Wuchuan Nei Monggol Zizhiqu,
China 41°5N 111°28E **114** D6
Wuda China 39°29N 106°42E **114** E4
Wudang Shan China 32°23N 111°2E **117** A8
Wudi China 37°40N 117°35E **115** F9
Wuding China 25°24N 102°21E **116** E4
Wuding He → China 37°2N 110°23E **114** F6
Wudinna Australia 33°0S 135°22E **152** B2
Wudongde Dam
China 26°20N 102°15E **116** D4
Wudu China 33°22N 104°54E **114** H3
Wufeng China 30°12N 110°42E **117** B8
Wugang China 26°44N 110°35E **117** C8
Wugong Shan China 27°30N 114°0E **117** D9
Wuguishan China 22°25N 113°25E **111** a
Wugullar = Beswick
Australia 14°34S 132°53E **148** B5
Wuhai China 39°39N 106°48E **114** E4
Wuhan China 30°31N 114°18E **117** B10
Wuhe China 33°10N 117°50E **115** H9
Wuhsi = Wuxi China 31°33N 120°18E **117** B13
Wuhu China 31°22N 118°21E **117** B12
Wujiang China 31°10N 120°38E **117** B13
Wujiaqu China 44°12N 87°33E **109** D11
Wukari Nigeria 7°51N 9°42E **139** D6
Wulanbulang China 41°5N 110°55E **114** D6
Wular L. India 34°20N 74°30E **126** B6
Wulehe Ghana 8°39N 0°0 **139** D5
Wulff Land Greenland 82°0N 49°0W **57** A6
Wulian China 35°40N 119°12E **115** G10
Wulian Feng China 24°0N 103°0E **116** D4
Wuliang Shan China 24°30N 100°40E **116** E3
Wuliaru Indonesia 7°27S 131°0E **119** F8
Wuling Shan China 29°30N 110°0E **116** C7
Wulingyuan □ China 29°20N 110°30E **117** C8
Wulong China 29°21N 107°43E **116** C6
Wulsin → Greenland 71°8N 103°5E **116** B4
Wulumuchi = Ürümqi
China 43°45N 87°45E **109** D11
Wum Cameroon 6°24N 10°2E **139** D7
Wumeng Shan China 26°48N 104°0E **116** D5
Wuming China 23°12N 108°18E **116** F7
Wundanyi Kenya 3°24S 38°22E **142** C4
Wuning China 29°17N 115°5E **117** C10
Wunna → India 20°18N 78°48E **126** D4
Wunnummin L.
Canada 52°55N 89°10W **164** B2
Wunsiedel Germany 50°2N 12°0E **77** E8
Wunstorf Germany 52°25N 9°26E **76** C5
Wuntho Burma 23°55N 95°45E **123** H19
Wupatki □ U.S.A. 35°35N 111°20W **169** H8
Wuping China 25°5N 116°5E **117** E11
Wuppertal Germany 51°16N 7°12E **76** D3
Wuppertal S. Africa 32°13S 19°12E **144** D2
Wuqia China 39°40N 75°7E **109** E9
Wuqing China 39°23N 117°1E **115** E9
Wurralibi ○ Australia 15°43S 137°1E **150** B2
Würzburg Germany 49°46N 9°55E **77** F5
Wurzen Germany 51°23N 12°44E **76** D8
Wushan China 31°24N 109°33E **116** B7
Wushi China 41°9N 79°13E **109** D9
Wushishi Nigeria 9°46N 6°7E **139** D6
Wutach → Germany 47°37N 8°15E **77** H4
Wutai China 38°40N 113°12E **114** E7
Wutai Shan China 39°3N 113°23E **114** E7
Wuting = Huimin
China 37°27N 117°28E **115** F9
Wutong China 25°20N 110°4E **117** E8
Wutonghaolai China 42°50N 120°5E **115** C11
Wutongqiao China 29°22N 103°50E **116** C4
Wuwei Anhui, China 31°18N 117°54E **117** B11
Wuwei Gansu, China 37°57N 102°34E **114** F9
Wuxi Jiangsu, China 31°33N 120°18E **117** B13
Wuxi Sichuan, China 31°23N 109°35E **116** B7

Wuxiang China 36°49N 112°50E **114** F7
Wuxuan China 23°34N 109°38E **116** F7
Wuxue China 29°52N 115°30E **117** C10
Wuyang China 33°25N 113°35E **114** H7
Wuyi Hebei, China 37°46N 115°56E **114** F8
Wuyi Zhejiang, China 28°52N 119°50E **117** C12
Wuyi Shan China 27°0N 117°0E **117** D11
Wuyishan China 27°45N 118°0E **117** D12
Wuyishan △ China 27°55N 117°54E **117** D11
Wuyo Nigeria 10°23N 11°50E **139** C7
Wuyuan Jiangxi,
China 29°15N 117°50E **117** C11
Wuyuan Nei Monggol Zizhiqu,
China 41°2N 108°20E **114** D5
Wuzhai China 38°54N 111°48E **114** E6
Wuzhi Shan China 18°45N 109°45E **117** a
Wuzhishan = Tongshi
China 18°50N 109°20E **117** a
Wuzhong China 38°2N 106°12E **114** E4
Wuzhou China 23°30N 111°18E **117** F8
Wyaaba Cr. →
Australia 16°27S 141°35E **150** B3
Wyalkatchem Australia 31°8N 117°22E **149** F2
Wyalusing U.S.A. 41°40N 76°16W **175** E8
Wyandotte U.S.A. 42°12N 83°9W **173** D12
Wyandra Australia 27°12S 145°56E **151** D4
Wyangala, L. Australia 33°54S 149°0E **153** B8
Wyara, L. Australia 28°42S 144°14E **151** D3
Wycheproof Australia 36°5S 143°17E **152** D5
Wycliffe Well Australia 20°48S 134°14E **150** C1
Wye → U.K. 51°38N 2°40W **67** F5
Wyemandoo Australia 28°28S 118°29E **149** E2
Wyk Germany 54°41N 8°33E **76** A4
Wymondham U.K. 52°39N 1°7E **67** E9
Wymore U.S.A. 40°7N 96°40W **172** E5
Wyndham Australia 15°33S 128°3E **148** C4
Wyndham N.Z. 46°20S 168°51E **155** G2
Wynne U.S.A. 35°14N 90°47W **177** D9
Wynyard Australia 41°5S 145°44E **151** G4
Wynyard Canada 51°45N 104°10W **163** C8
Wyola L. Australia 29°8S 130°17E **149** E5
Wyoming Canada 42°57N 82°7W **174** D2
Wyoming □ U.S.A. 43°0N 107°30W **168** E10
Wyomissing U.S.A. 40°20N 75°59W **175** F9
Wyong Australia 33°14S 151°24E **153** B9
Wyperfeld △ Australia 35°30S 141°42E **152** C4
Wyrzysk Poland 53°10N 17°17E **83** E4
Wyśmierzyce Poland 51°37N 20°50E **83** G7
Wysoka Poland 53°13N 17°2E **83** E4
Wysokie Mazowieckie
Poland 52°55N 22°40E **83** F9
Wyszków Poland 52°36N 21°25E **83** F8
Wyszogród Poland 52°23N 20°9E **83** F7
Wytheville U.S.A. 36°57N 81°5W **173** G13
Wyżyna Małopolska
Poland 50°45N 20°0E **83** H7

X

Xaafuun Somalia 10°25N 51°16E **131** E5
Xaafuun, Ras Somalia 10°27N 51°24E **131** E5
Xàbia = Jávea Spain 38°48N 0°10E **91** G5
Xaçmaz Azerbaijan 41°31N 48°42E **87** K9
Xai-Xai Mozam. 25°6S 33°31E **145** D5
Xaidulla China 36°28N 77°59E **109** E8
Xaignabouri = Sayaboury
Laos 19°15N 101°45E **120** C3
Xainza China 30°58N 88°35E **110** E6
Xalapa Mexico 19°32N 96°55W **181** D5
Xallas → Spain 42°54N 9°8W **88** C1
Xangongo Angola 16°45S 15°5E **144** B2
Xankändi Azerbaijan 39°52N 46°49E **105** C12
Xanlar = Goygöl
Azerbaijan 40°37N 46°12E **87** K8
Xanten Germany 51°39N 6°26E **76** D2
Xanthi Greece 41°10N 24°58E **97** E8
Xanthos Turkey 36°19N 29°18E **99** E11
Xanxerê Brazil 26°53S 52°23W **191** B5
Xapuri Brazil 10°35S 68°35W **189** F5
Xar Moron He →
China 43°25N 120°35E **115** C11
Xarrë Albania 39°44N 20°3E **96** G4
Xàtiva Spain 38°59N 0°32W **91** G4
Xau, L. Botswana 21°15S 24°44E **144** B3
Xavantina Brazil 21°15S 52°48W **191** A5
Xayar China 41°31N 82°48E **109** D10
Xebert China 44°2N 122°0E **115** B12
Xenia U.S.A. 39°41N 83°56W **173** F12
Xeraco Spain 39°2N 0°13W **91** F4
Xeropotamos →
Cyprus 34°42N 32°33E **101** E11
Xertigny France 48°3N 6°24E **71** D13
Xhora S. Africa 31°55S 28°38E **145** D4
Xhumo Botswana 21°7S 24°35E **144** B3
Xi Jiang → China 22°5N 113°20E **117** F9
Xi Ujimqin Qi China 44°32N 117°40E **115** B9
Xi Xian Henan, China 32°20N 114°43E **117** A10
Xi Xian Shanxi, China 36°41N 110°58E **114** F6
Xia Xian China 35°8N 111°12E **114** G6
Xiachengzi China 44°40N 130°18E **115** B16
Xiachuan Dao China 21°40N 112°40E **117** G9
Xiaguan China 25°32N 100°16E **110** F9
Xiajiang China 27°30N 115°10E **117** D10
Xiajin China 36°56N 116°0E **114** F9
Xiamen China 24°25N 118°4E **117** E12
Xiamen Gaoqi Int. ✈ (XMN)
China 24°33N 118°8E **117** E12
Xi'an China 34°15N 109°0E **114** G5
Xian Xian China 38°12N 116°6E **114** E9
Xian Xianyang Int. ✈ (XIY)
China 34°20N 108°45E **114** G5
Xianfeng China 29°40N 109°8E **116** C7
Xiang Jiang → China 28°55N 112°50E **117** C9
Xiang Khouang Laos 19°17N 103°25E **120** C4
Xiangcheng Henan,
China 33°50N 113°27E **114** H7
Xiangcheng Sichuan,
China 28°53N 99°47E **116** C2
Xiangdu China 23°13N 106°58E **116** F6
Xiangfan China 32°2N 112°8E **117** A9
Xianggang = Hong Kong □
China 22°11N 114°14E **111** a
Xianghuang Qi China 42°2N 113°50E **114** C7
Xiangjiaba Dam China 28°37N 104°17E **116** C5
Xiangning China 35°58N 110°50E **114** G6
Xiangquan China 36°30N 113°1E **114** F7
Xiangquan He → = Sutlej →
Pakistan 29°23N 71°3E **124** E4
Xiangshan China 29°29N 121°51E **117** C13

Xiangshui China 34°12N 119°33E **115** G10
Xiangtan China 27°51N 112°54E **117** D9
Xiangxiang China 27°43N 112°28E **117** D9
Xiangyin China 28°38N 112°54E **117** C9
Xiangyun China 25°34N 100°35E **116** E3
Xiangzhou China 23°58N 109°40E **116** F7
Xianju China 28°51N 120°44E **117** C13
Xianning China 29°51N 114°16E **117** C10
Xianshui He → China 30°10N 100°59E **116** B3
Xiantao China 30°25N 113°25E **117** B9
Xianyang China 34°20N 108°40E **114** G5
Xianyou China 25°22N 118°33E **117** E12
Xiao Hinggan Ling
China 49°0N 127°0E **115** B14
Xiaofeng China 30°35N 119°37E **117** B12
Xiaogan China 30°55N 113°50E **117** B9
Xiaojin China 30°59N 102°21E **116** B4
Xiaolan China 22°38N 113°13E **117** F9
Xiaoshan China 30°12N 120°18E **117** B13
Xiaowan Dam China 24°42N 100°5E **116** E3
Xiaowutai Shan China 39°51N 114°59E **114** E8
Xiaoxian China 34°15N 116°10E **114** G9
Xiaoyi China 37°8N 111°48E **114** F6
Xiapu China 26°54N 119°59E **117** D12
Xiashan = Zhanjiang
China 21°15N 110°20E **117** G8
Xiawa China 42°35N 120°38E **115** C11
Xiayi China 34°15N 116°10E **114** G9
Xichang China 27°51N 102°19E **116** D4
Xichou China 30°57N 105°54E **116** B5
Xichuan China 33°0N 111°30E **117** A8
Xide China 28°8N 102°19E **116** C4
Xiemahe China 31°38N 111°12E **117** B8
Xifei He → China 32°45N 116°40E **117** A11
Xifeng Gansu, China 35°40N 107°40E **114** G4
Xifeng Guizhou, China 27°7N 106°42E **116** D6
Xifeng Liaoning, China 42°42N 124°45E **115** C13
Xifengzhen = Xifeng
China 35°40N 107°40E **114** G4
Xigazê China 29°5N 88°45E **110** F6
Xihe China 34°2N 105°20E **114** G3
Xihua China 33°45N 114°30E **114** H8
Xilaganı Greece 40°58N 25°28E **97** F9
Xiliao He → China 43°32N 123°35E **115** C12
Xilin China 24°30N 105°6E **116** E5
Xiling Gorge = Xiling Xia
China 30°50N 110°48E **117** B8
Xilinhot China 43°52N 116°2E **114** C9
Xilokastro Greece 38°5N 22°38E **98** C4
Xima Mozam. 19°24S 33°58E **143** F3
Ximeng China 22°50N 99°27E **116** F2
Xin Jiang → China 40°59N 100°12E **114** C9
Xin Xian = Xinzhou
China 38°22N 112°46E **114** E7
Xin'anjiang Shuiku
China 29°33N 118°56E **117** C12
Xinavane Mozam. 25°2S 32°47E **145** C5
Xinbin China 41°40N 125°2E **115** D13
Xincai China 32°43N 114°58E **117** A10
Xincheng Guangxi Zhuangzu,
China 24°5N 108°39E **116** E7
Xincheng Jiangxi,
China 26°48N 114°6E **117** D10
Xinfeng Guangdong, China 24°5N 114°16E **117** E10
Xinfeng Jiangxi, China 27°7N 116°11E **117** D11
Xinfeng Jiangxi, China 25°27N 114°58E **117** D10
Xinfengjiang Shuiku
China 23°52N 114°30E **117** F10
Xing Xian China 38°27N 111°7E **114** E6
Xing'an Guangxi Zhuangzu,
China 25°38N 110°40E **117** E8
Xingan Jiangxi, China 27°46N 115°20E **117** D10
Xingcheng China 40°40N 120°45E **115** D11
Xingguo China 26°21N 115°21E **117** D10
Xinghe China 40°55N 113°55E **114** D7
Xinghua China 32°58N 119°48E **117** A12
Xinghua Wan China 25°15N 119°20E **117** D12
Xinglong China 40°25N 117°30E **115** D9
Xingping China 34°25N 108°28E **114** G5
Xingren China 25°24N 105°11E **116** E5
Xingshan China 31°15N 110°45E **117** B8
Xingtai China 37°3N 114°32E **114** F8
Xingu → Brazil 1°30S 51°53W **187** D8
Xingwen China 28°22N 104°50E **116** C5
Xingxingxia China 41°47N 95°0E **110** C7
Xingyang China 34°45N 112°52E **114** G7
Xinhe Hebei, China 37°30N 115°15E **114** F8
Xinhe Xinjiang Uygur,
China 41°33N 82°37E **109** D10
Xinhua China 27°42N 111°13E **117** D8
Xinhuang China 27°21N 109°12E **116** D7
Xinhui China 22°25N 113°0E **117** F9
Xining China 36°34N 101°40E **110** D9
Xinji China 37°54N 115°22E **114** F8
Xinjiang China 35°34N 111°11E **114** G6
Xinjiang Uygur Zizhiqu □
China 42°0N 86°0E **109** D11
Xinjin = Pulandian
China 39°25N 121°58E **115** E11
Xinjin China 34°15N 109°0E **116** B4
Xinkai He → China 43°32N 123°35E **115** C12
Xinken China 22°39N 113°36E **111** a
Xinle China 38°25N 114°40E **114** E8
Xinlitun China 42°0N 122°8E **115** C12
Xinlong China 30°57N 100°12E **116** B3
Xinmin China 41°59N 122°50E **115** D12
Xinning China 26°28N 110°50E **117** D8
Xinping China 24°5N 101°59E **116** E3
Xinshao China 27°20N 111°26E **117** D8
Xintai China 35°55N 117°45E **115** G9
Xintian China 25°55N 112°15E **117** D9
Xinwan China 22°47N 113°40E **111** a
Xinxiang China 35°18N 113°50E **114** G7
Xinxing China 22°47N 112°13E **117** F9
Xinyang China 32°6N 114°3E **117** A10
Xinye China 32°30N 112°20E **114** H7
Xinyi Guangdong, China 22°25N 110°58E **117** F8
Xinyi Nei Monggol Zizhiqu,
China 34°23N 118°21E **115** G10

Xinyu China 27°49N 114°58E **117**
Xinzhan China 43°50N 127°18E **115**
Xinzheng China 34°20N 113°45E **114**
Xinzhou Hainan, China 19°43N 109°17E **117**
Xinzhou Hubei, China 30°50N 114°48E **117**
Xinzhou Shanxi, China 38°22N 112°46E **114**
Xinzo de Limia Spain 42°3N 7°47W **88**
Xiongyuecheng China 40°12N 122°5E **115**
Xiping Henan, China 33°22N 114°5E **114**
Xiping Henan, China 33°25N 111°8E **114**
Xiping China 28°16N 119°29E **117**
Xianyou China 25°22N 118°33E **117** E12
Xique-Xique Brazil 10°50S 42°40W **189**
Xırdalan Azerbaijan 40°27N 49°45E **105**
Xiruá → Brazil 6°3S 67°50W **188**
Xisha Qundao = Paracel Is.
S. China Sea 15°50N 112°0E **118**
Xishuangbanna China 22°5N 101°1E **116**
Xishui Guizhou, China 28°19N 106°9E **116**
Xishui Hubei, China 30°30N 115°15E **117**
Xitole Guinea-Biss. 11°43N 14°50W **138**
Xiu Shui → China 29°45N 116°10E **117**
Xiuning China 29°45N 118°0E **117**
Xiuren China 24°27N 110°12E **117**
Xiushan China 28°25N 108°57E **116**
Xiushui China 29°2N 114°33E **117**
Xiuwen China 26°49N 106°32E **116**
Xiuyan China 40°18N 123°11E **115**
Xiva Uzbekistan 41°30N 60°18E **108**
Xixabangma Feng
China 28°20N 85°40E **125**
Xixia China 33°25N 111°29E **114**
Xixiang Guangdong,
China 22°34N 113°52E **111**
Xixiang Shaanxi, China 33°0N 107°44E **114**
Xixón = Gijón Spain 43°32N 5°42W **88**
Xiyang China 37°38N 113°38E **114**
Xizang Zizhiqu □ China 32°0N 88°0E **110**
Xlendi Malta 36°1N 14°12E **101**
Xochob Mexico 19°21N 89°48W **181**
Xo'jayli Uzbekistan 42°29N 59°33E **108**
Xorazm □ Uzbekistan 43°0N 60°0E **108**
Xu Jiang → China 28°0N 116°25E **117**
Xuan Loc Vietnam 10°56N 107°14E **121**
Xuan'en China 30°0N 109°30E **116**
Xuanhan China 31°18N 107°38E **116**
Xuanhua China 40°40N 115°2E **114**
Xuanwei China 26°15N 103°59E **116**
Xuanzhou China 30°56N 118°43E **117**
Xuchang China 34°2N 113°48E **114**
Xudat Azerbaijan 41°38N 48°41E **87**
Xuefeng Shan China 27°30N 110°40E **117**
Xuejiaping China 31°39N 110°6E **117**
Xun Jiang → China 23°35N 111°30E **117**
Xun Xian China 35°42N 114°33E **114**
Xundian China 25°36N 103°15E **116**
Xunwu China 24°54N 115°37E **117**
Xunyang China 32°48N 109°22E **114**
Xunyi China 35°8N 108°20E **114**
Xupu China 27°53N 110°32E **117**
Xúquer → Spain 39°5N 0°10W **91**
Xushui China 39°2N 115°40E **114**
Xuwen China 20°20N 110°10E **117**
Xuyi China 32°55N 118°32E **117**
Xuyong China 28°10N 105°22E **116**
Xuzhou China 34°18N 117°10E **115**
Xylophagou Cyprus 34°54N 33°51E **101**

Y

Y Drenewydd = Newtown
U.K. 52°31N 3°19W **67**
Y Fenni = Abergavenny
U.K. 51°49N 3°1W **67**
Y Gelli Gandryll = Hay-on-Wye
U.K. 52°5N 3°8W **67**
Y Trallwng = Welshpool
U.K. 52°39N 3°8W **67**
Ya Xian = Sanya China 18°14N 109°29E **118**
Yaamba Australia 23°8S 150°22E **150**
Ya'an China 29°58N 103°5E **116**
Yaapeet Australia 35°45S 142°3E **152**
Yabassi Cameroon 4°30N 9°57E **139**
Yabayo Ivory C. 5°56N 6°36W **138**
Yablanitsa Bulgaria 43°2N 24°5E **97**
Yablonovskiy Russia 44°59N 38°57E **87**
Yablonovyy Khrebet
Russia 53°0N 114°0E **107**
Yablonovyy Ra. = Yablonovyy
Khrebet Russia 53°0N 114°0E **107**
Yabrūd Syria 33°58N 36°39E **94**
Yabucoa Puerto Rico 18°3N 65°53W **183**
Yacambú △ Venezuela 9°42N 69°27W **183**
Yacata Fiji 17°15S 179°31W **155**
Yacheng China 18°22N 109°6E **118**
Yackandandah
Australia 36°18S 146°52E **153**
Yacuiba Bolivia 22°0S 63°43W **190**
Yacuma → Bolivia 13°38S 65°23W **190**
Yacurí □ Ecuador 4°42S 79°20W **188**
Yadgir India 16°45N 77°5E **126**
Yadkin → U.S.A. 35°23N 80°4W **177**
Yadrin Russia 55°57N 46°12E **86**
Yadua Fiji 16°49S 178°18E **155**
Yaeyama-Rettō Japan 24°30N 123°40E **113**
Yagaba Ghana 10°14N 1°20W **139**
Yagasa Cluster Fiji 18°57S 178°28W **155**
Yağcılar Turkey 39°25N 28°23E **99**
Yagodnoye Russia 62°33N 149°40E **107**
Yahila
Dem. Rep. of the Congo 0°13N 24°28E **142**
Yahk Canada 49°6N 116°10W **162**
Yahotyn Ukraine 50°17N 31°46E **86**
Yahuma
Dem. Rep. of the Congo 1°0N 23°10E **142**
Yahyalı Turkey 38°5N 35°18E **104**
Yaita Japan 36°48N 139°56E **113**
Yaiza Canary Is. 28°57N 13°46W **100**
Yajiang China 30°2N 100°58E **116**
Yajua Nigeria 11°27N 12°49E **139**
Yakeshi China 49°17N 120°44E **115**
Yakima U.S.A. 46°36N 120°31W **168**
Yakima → U.S.A. 47°0N 120°30W **168**
Yakishiri-Jima Japan 44°26N 141°25E **112**
Yako Burkina Faso 12°59N 2°15W **138**
Yakobi I. U.S.A. 58°0N 136°30W **162**
Yakoruda Bulgaria 42°1N 23°39E **97**
Yakovlevka Russia 44°26N 133°28E **112**

-Shima *Japan* 30°20N 130°30E **113** J5
..mo *Japan* 42°15N 140°16E **112** C10
..tat *U.S.A.* 59°33N 139°44W **160** F4
..tat B. *U.S.A.* 59°45N 140°45W **166** D11
..ssia 66°0N 130°0E **107** C14
..tsk *Russia* 62°5N 129°50E **107** C13
..rmivka *Ukraine* 46°44N 35°0E **85** J8
.. *Thailand* 6°33N 101°18E **121** J3
.. *Sri Lanka* 6°20N 81°30E **127** L5
..ta *Australia* 31°59S 132°26E **149** F5
..aga ○ *Australia* 31°35S 132°7E **149** F5
..oroo *Australia* 20°50S 148°40E **150** b
..ta *Australia* 43°8N 82°48W **174** C2
..orup △ *Australia* 32°39S 115°38E **149** F2
..aga *C.A.R.* 6°33N 23°10E **140** C4
..roi *Australia* 24°3S 145°42E **150** C4
..busha ← *U.S.A.* 33°33N 90°10W **177** E9
..ng *China* 18°12N 109°42E **117** a
..ng Jiang ←
..ina 26°40N 101°55E **116** D3
..wa *Turkey* 40°41N 29°15E **97** F13
..irakinu ◎
..stralia 22°24S 132°15E **148** D5
..uh, Ozero *Ukraine* 45°30N 28°41E **81** E13
..t Ukraine 44°30N 34°10E **85** K8
.. Jiang ← *China* 39°55N 124°19E **115** E13
..ac *Turkey* 38°17N 31°10E **104** C4
.. *Australia* 9°54S 142°46E **150** a
..Ha Melaḥ = Dead Sea
..la 31°30N 35°30E **130** D4
.. Kinneret *Israel* 32°45N 35°35E **130** C4
..ada = Kama
..agata *Japan* 33°33N 130°49E **113** H5
..agata *Japan* 38°15N 140°15E **112** E10
..agata *Japan* 38°30N 140°0E **112** E10
..aguchi *Japan* 34°10N 131°32E **113** G5
..aguchi ○ *Japan* 34°20N 131°40E **113** G5
..al, Poluostrov *Russia* 71°0N 70°0E **106** B8
..al Pen. = Yamal, Poluostrov
..ssia 71°0N 70°0E **106** B8
..anashi ○ *Japan* 35°40N 138°40E **113** G9
..antau, Gora *Russia* 54°15N 58°6E **108** B5
..ato Ridge
..r of Japan 39°20N 135°0E **112** F7
..ba *Australia* 29°26S 153°23E **151** D5
..stralia 15°10S 130°25E **148** C5
..béring *Guinea* 11°50N 12°18W **138** C2
..bio *South Sudan* 4°35N 28°16E **135** H11
..bol *Bulgaria* 42°30N 26°30E **97** D10
..bol ○ *Bulgaria* 42°30N 26°30E **97** D10
..burg *Russia* 68°21N 77°8E **106** C8
..dena *Indonesia* 7°45S 131°20E **119** F8
..ie *Japan* 33°13N 130°35E **113** H5
..ethin *Burma* 20°29N 96°18E **123** J20
..ma Yamma, L.
..stralia 26°16S 141°20E **151** D3
..oussoukro *Ivory C.* 6°49N 5°17W **138** D3
..oussoukro □
..ry C. 6°47N 5°14W **138** D3
..pa ← *U.S.A.* 40°32N 108°59W **168** F9
..pi Sd. *Australia* 16°8S 123°38E **148** C3
..pol *Moldova* 48°15N 28°15E **75** D15
..pol = Yampil
..ldova 48°15N 28°15E **75** D15
..rat *Nigeria* 10°11N 9°55E **139** C6
..rukchal = Botev
..lgaria 42°44N 24°52E **97** D8
..u, Laem *Thailand* 7°59N 98°26E **121** a
..→ *India* 30°7N 77°17E **124** D7
..zho Yumco *China* 28°48N 90°35E **110** F7
..Nigeria 10°5N 8°2E **139** C7
..Oya ← *Sri Lanka* 9°0N 81°10E **127** K5
.. ← *Russia* 71°30N 136°0E **107** B14
..agawa *Japan* 33°10N 130°24E **113** H5
..agawa *Japan* 33°58N 132°7E **113** H6
..an *China* 36°35N 109°26E **114** F5
..bian *China* 26°47N 101°31E **116** D3
..bu 'al Baḥr *Si. Arabia* 36°43N 110°1E **128** E3
..cheng *Henan, China* 34°30N 114°0E **114** H8
..cheng *Jiangsu,*
..ina 33°23N 120°8E **115** H11
..chep *Australia* 31°33S 115°37E **149** F2
..chuan *China* 37°48N 107°20E **114** F4
..chuan *China* 36°51N 110°10E **114** F5
..co *Australia* 34°38S 146°27E **153** C7
..co Cr. ← *Australia* 35°14S 145°35E **153** C6
..dang Shan *China* 28°0N 120°25E **117** D13
..deyarra ◎
..stralia 21°17S 118°24E **148** D2
..dicoogina
..stralia 22°49S 119°12E **148** D2
..doon *Burma* 17°0N 95°40E **123** L19
..feng *China* 25°52N 101°8E **116** E3
..folila *Mali* 11°11N 8°9W **138** C3
..g *China* 33°15N 107°30E **116** A6
..gambi
..em. Rep. of the Congo 0°47N 24°24E **142** B1
..gbi *China* 37°58N 113°31E **114** F7
..gcheng *China* 35°28N 112°22E **114** G7
..ch'ü = Taiyuan
..ina 37°52N 112°33E **114** F7
..gchun *China* 22°11N 111°48E **117** F8
..ggao *China* 36°58N 114°0E **114** F7
..gshan *Shanghai,*
..ina 30°37N 122°4E **117** B14
..gshuo *China* 24°48N 110°29E **117** E8
..gtse = Chang Jiang ←
..ina 31°48N 121°10E **117** B13
..gtze Kiang = Chang Jiang ←
..ina 31°48N 121°10E **117** B13
..gxin *China* 29°50N 115°12E **117** C10
..gyuan *China* 40°1N 114°10E **114** D8
..gzhou *China* 32°21N 119°22E **117** A12
..gzhou *China* 32°21N 119°22E **117** A12

Yanhe *China* 28°31N 108°32E **116** C7
Yanji *China* 42°59N 129°30E **115** C15
Yanjing *China* 29°5N 104°18E **116** C5
Yanjing *China* 29°7N 98°33E **116** C2
Yankari △ *Nigeria* 9°50N 10°28E **139** D7
Yankton *U.S.A.* 42°53N 97°23W **172** D5
Yankunytjatjara-Antakirinja ◎
Australia 27°20S 134°30E **151** A1
Yanonge
Dem. Rep. of the Congo 0°35N 24°38E **142** B1
Yanqi *China* 42°5N 86°35E **109** D11
Yanqing *China* 40°30N 115°58E **114** D8
Yanshan *Hebei, China* 38°4N 117°22E **115** E9
Yanshan *Jiangxi,*
China 28°15N 117°41E **117** C11
Yanshan *Yunnan,*
China 23°35N 104°20E **116** F5
Yanshou *China* 45°28N 128°22E **115** B15
Yantabulla *Australia* 29°21S 145°0E **151** D4
Yantai *China* 37°34N 121°22E **115** F11
Yantarnyy *Russia* 54°52N 19°57E **82** D6
Yantian *China* 22°35N 114°16E **111** a
Yanting *China* 31°11N 105°24E **116** B5
Yantongshan *China* 43°17N 126°0E **115** C14
Yantra ← *Bulgaria* 43°40N 25°37E **97** C9
Yanuca *Fiji* 18°24S 178°0E **154** a
Yanununbeyan △
Australia 35°29S 149°24E **153** C8
Yanwa *China* 27°35N 98°55E **116** D2
Yanyuan *China* 27°25N 101°30E **116** D3
Yanzhou *China* 35°35N 116°49E **114** G9
Yao Xian *China* 34°55N 108°59E **114** G5
Yao Yai, Ko *Thailand* 8°7N 98°37E **121** a
Yao'an *China* 25°31N 101°18E **116** E3
Yaoundé *Cameroon* 3°50N 11°35E **139** D7
Yaowan *China* 34°15N 118°3E **115** G10
Yap *Pac. Oc.* 9°30N 138°10E **156** G5
Yapei *Ghana* 9°10N 1°10W **139** D4
Yapen *Indonesia* 1°50S 136°0E **119** E9
Yapen, Selat *Indonesia* 1°20S 136°10E **119** E9
Yapero *Indonesia* 4°59S 137°11E **119** F9
Yappar ← *Australia* 18°22S 141°16E **150** B3
Yapuparra ◎ *Australia* 27°25S 126°0E **149** E4
Yaqaga *Fiji* 16°35S 178°36E **154** a
Yaqui ← *Mexico* 27°37N 110°39W **180** B2
Yar Çalli = Naberezhnyye Chelny
Russia 55°42N 52°19E **86** C11
Yar-Sale *Russia* 66°50N 70°50E **106** C8
Yaraka *Australia* 24°53S 144°3E **150** C3
Yaransk *Russia* 57°22N 47°49E **86** B8
Yarbasan *Turkey* 38°35N 28°10E **99** E11
Yardımcı Burnu *Turkey* 36°13N 30°25E **99** E12
Yare ← *U.K.* 52°35N 1°38E **67** E9
Yaremcha *Ukraine* 48°27N 24°33E **81** B9
Yarensk *Russia* 62°11N 49°15E **106** C5
Yarfa *Si. Arabia* 24°37N 38°35E **137** C4
Yarí ← *Colombia* 0°20S 72°20W **186** D4
Yarkand = Shache
China 38°20N 77°10E **109** E9
Yarkant He ← *China* 38°40N 76°46W **175** B8
Yarker *Canada* 44°23N 76°46W **175** B8
Yarkhun ← *Pakistan* 36°17N 72°30E **125** A5
Yarlung Ziangbo Jiang =
Brahmaputra ←
Asia 23°40N 90°35E **125** H13
Yarmouth *Canada* 43°50N 66°7W **165** D6
Yarmūk ← *Syria* 32°42N 35°40E **130** C4
Yaroslavl *Russia* 57°35N 39°55E **84** C10
Yaroslavl □ *Russia* 59°20N 38°50E **84** C10
Yarqa, W. ← *Egypt* 30°0N 33°49E **130** F2
Yarra Ranges △
Australia 37°40S 146°3E **153** D7
Yarra Yarra Lakes
Australia 29°40S 115°45E **149** E2
Yarram *Australia* 38°29S 146°39E **153** E7
Yarraman *Australia* 26°50S 152°0E **151** D5
Yarras *Australia* 31°25S 152°20E **153** A10
Yarrawonga *Australia* 36°0S 146°0E **153** C7
Yarrie *Australia* 20°40S 120°12E **148** D3
Yartsevo *Sib., Russia* 60°20N 90°0E **107** C10
Yartsevo *Smolensk, Russia* 55°6N 32°43E **84** D7
Yarumal *Colombia* 6°58N 75°24W **186** B3
Yasawa *Fiji* 16°47S 177°31E **154** a
Yasawa Group *Fiji* 17°0S 177°23E **154** a
Yaselda *Belarus* 52°7N 26°28E **75** B14
Yashi *Nigeria* 12°23N 7°54E **139** C6
Yashikera *Nigeria* 9°44N 3°29E **139** D5
Yashkul *Russia* 46°11N 45°21E **87** G7
Yasinovataya *Ukraine* 48°7N 37°57E **85** H9
Yasinski, L. *Canada* 53°16N 77°35W **164** B4
Yasinya *Ukraine* 48°24N 24°21E **81** B9
Yasnyy *Russia* 51°1N 59°58E **108** B5
Yasothon *Thailand* 15°50N 104°10E **120** E5
Yass *Australia* 34°49S 148°54E **153** C8
Yāsūj *Iran* 30°31N 51°31E **129** D6
Yatağan *Turkey* 37°20N 28°10E **99** D10
Yatakala *Niger* 14°50N 0°22E **139** C5
Yates Center *U.S.A.* 37°53N 95°44W **172** G6
Yates Pt. *N.Z.* 44°29S 167°49E **155** E2
Yathkyed L. *Canada* 62°40N 98°0W **163** A9
Yathong *Australia* 32°37S 145°33E **153** B6
Yatsushiro *Japan* 32°30N 130°40E **113** H5
Yatta Plateau *Kenya* 2°0S 38°0E **142** C4
Yauca *Peru* 15°39S 74°35W **188** C2
Yauco *Puerto Rico* 18°2N 66°51W **183** d
Yauri *Peru* 14°47S 71°25W **188** C3
Yauya *Peru* 8°59S 77°17W **188** B2
Yauyos *Peru* 12°19S 75°50W **188** C2
Yaval *India* 21°10N 75°42E **126** D2
Yavari ← *Peru* 4°21S 70°2W **188** A3
Yávaros *Mexico* 26°42N 109°31W **180** B3
Yavatmal *India* 20°20N 78°15E **126** D4
Yavero ← *Peru* 12°6S 72°57W **188** C3
Yavne *Israel* 31°52N 34°45E **130** D3
Yavoriv *Ukraine* 49°55N 23°20E **75** D12
Yavorov = Yavoriv
Ukraine 49°55N 23°20E **75** D12
Yavuzeli *Turkey* 37°18N 37°24E **104** D7
Yawatahama *Japan* 33°27N 132°24E **113** H6
Yawri B. *S. Leone* 8°22N 13°0W **138** D2
Yaxi *China* 27°33N 106°10E **116** D6
Yaxian = Sanya *China* 18°14N 109°29E **117** a
Yayladağı *Turkey* 35°54N 36°3E **104** C7
Yazd *Iran* 31°55N 54°27E **129** D7
Yazd □ *Iran* 32°0N 55°0E **129** D7
Yazd-e Khvāst *Iran* 31°31N 52°7E **129** D7
Yazköy *Turkey* 36°40N 27°20E **99** E9
Yazman *Pakistan* 29°8N 71°45E **124** E4
Yazoo ← *U.S.A.* 32°22N 90°54W **177** E9

Yazoo City *U.S.A.* 32°51N 90°25W **177** E9
Ybbs *Austria* 48°12N 15°4E **78** C8
Ybycuí △ *Paraguay* 26°5S 56°46W **190** B4
Ybytyruzú △ *Paraguay* 25°51S 56°11W **191** B4
Ye *Burma* 15°15N 97°15E **120** E1
Ye Xian *China* 33°35N 113°25E **114** H7
Yea *Australia* 37°14S 145°26E **153** D6
Yebyu *Burma* 14°15N 98°13E **120** E2
Yecheng *China* 37°54N 77°26E **109** E9
Yecheon *S. Korea* 36°39N 128°27E **115** F15
Yecla *Spain* 38°35N 1°5W **91** G3
Yécora *Mexico* 28°20N 108°58W **180** B3
Yedigöllar △ *Turkey* 40°55N 31°55E **104** B4
Yedintsy = Edineţ
Moldova 48°9N 27°18E **81** B12
Yedseram ← *Nigeria* 12°30N 14°5E **139** C7
Yefremov *Russia* 53°8N 38°3E **84** F10
Yeghegnadzor
Armenia 39°44N 45°19E **105** C11
Yegorlyk ← *Russia* 46°35N 41°57E **87** G5
Yegorlykskaya *Russia* 46°35N 40°35E **87** G5
Yegoryevsk *Russia* 55°27N 38°55E **84** C10
Yehbuah *Indonesia* 8°23S 114°45E **119** J17
Yehuda, Midbar *Israel* 31°35N 35°15E **130** D4
Yei *South Sudan* 4°9N 30°40E **135** H12
Yeji *Ghana* 8°13N 0°39W **139** D4
Yejmiadzin = Ejmiatsin
Armenia 40°12N 44°19E **87** K7
Yekaterinburg *Russia* 56°50N 60°30E **106** D7
Yekateriny, Proliv
Russia 44°30N 146°30E **107** E15
Yelabuga *Russia* 55°46N 52°2E **86** C11
Yelan *Russia* 50°55N 43°43E **86** E6
Yelandur *India* 12°6N 77°0E **127** H3
Yelarbon *Australia* 28°33S 150°38E **151** D5
Yelatma *Russia* 55°0N 41°45E **84** C11
Yelcho, L. *Chile* 43°18S 72°18W **192** B2
Yelets *Russia* 52°40N 38°30E **84** F10
Yélimané *Mali* 15°9N 10°34W **138** B2
Yelin = Lingshui *China* 18°27N 110°0E **117** a
Yelizavetgrad = Kirovohrad
Ukraine 48°35N 32°20E **85** H7
Yelizovo *Russia* 53°11N 158°23E **107** D16
Yell *U.K.* 60°35N 1°5W **65** A7
Yell Sd. *U.K.* 60°33N 1°15W **65** A7
Yellamanchilli = Elamanchili
India 17°33N 82°50E **126** F6
Yellandu *India* 17°39N 80°23E **126** F5
Yellapur *India* 14°58N 74°43E **127** G2
Yellareddi *India* 18°12N 78°2E **126** E4
Yellow = Huang He ←
China 37°55N 118°50E **115** F10
Yellow ← *U.S.A.* 30°30N 87°0W **179** E3
Yellow Sea *China* 35°0N 123°0E **115** G12
Yellowhead Pass
Canada 52°53N 118°25W **162** C5
Yellowknife *Canada* 62°27N 114°29W **162** A6
Yellowknife ←
Canada 62°31N 114°19W **162** A6
Yellowstone ←
U.S.A. 47°59N 103°59W **168** C12
Yellowstone △ *U.S.A.* 44°40N 110°30W **168** D8
Yellowstone L. *U.S.A.* 44°27N 110°22W **168** D8
Yelnya *Russia* 54°35N 33°15E **84** E7
Yelsk *Belarus* 51°50N 29°10E **75** C15
Yelwa *Nigeria* 10°49N 4°41E **139** C5
Yemanzhelinsk *Russia* 54°58N 61°18E **108** B6
Yemassee *U.S.A.* 32°41N 80°51W **178** D9
Yemen ■ *Asia* 15°0N 44°0E **131** E3
Yemmiganur *India* 15°44N 77°29E **127** G3
Yen Bai *Vietnam* 21°42N 104°52E **116** G5
Yenagoa *Nigeria* 4°58N 6°16E **139** E6
Yenakiyeve *Ukraine* 48°15N 38°15E **85** H10
Yenakiyevo = Yenakiyeve
Ukraine 48°15N 38°15E **85** H10
Yenangyaung *Burma* 20°30N 95°0E **123** J19
Yenbo = Yanbu 'al Baḥr
Si. Arabia 24°5N 38°5E **128** E3
Yenda *Australia* 34°13S 146°14E **153** C7
Yende Millimou *Guinea* 8°55N 10°10W **138** D2
Yendéré *Burkina Faso* 10°12N 4°59W **138** C4
Yendi *Ghana* 9°29N 0°1W **139** D4
Yengisar *China* 37°36N 76°9E **109** E9
Yengo □ *Australia* 33°0S 150°55E **153** B9
Yéni *Niger* 13°30N 3°1E **139** C5
Yeni Erenköy = Yialousa
Cyprus 35°32N 34°10E **101** D13
Yenibaşak *China* 30°41N 115°32E **117** B10
Yenibogaziçi = Áyios Seryios
Cyprus 35°12N 33°53E **101** D12
Yenice *Ankara, Turkey* 39°14N 32°42E **104** C5
Yenice *Aydın, Turkey* 37°49N 28°35E **99** D10
Yenice *Çanakkale, Turkey* 39°55N 27°17E **99** B9
Yenice *Edirne, Turkey* 40°42N 26°9E **97** B10
Yenice ← *Turkey* 37°37N 35°33E **104** D6
Yenifoça *Turkey* 38°44N 26°51E **99** C8
Yenihisar = Didim
Turkey 37°22N 27°16E **99** D9
Yeniköy *Bursa, Turkey* 40°31N 29°22E **97** F13
Yeniköy *Çanakkale,*
Turkey 39°55N 26°10E **99** B8
Yeniköy *Kütahya,*
Turkey 38°55N 29°17E **99** C11
Yenişehir *Turkey* 40°16N 29°38E **97** F13
Yenisey ← *Russia* 71°50N 82°40E **106** B9
Yeniseysk *Russia* 58°27N 92°13E **107** D10
Yeniseyskiy Zaliv *Russia* 72°20N 81°0E **106** B9
Yenne *France* 45°43N 5°44E **73** C9
Yenotayevka *Russia* 47°15N 47°0E **87** G8
Yenyuka *Russia* 57°57N 121°15E **107** D13
Yeo ← *U.K.* 51°2N 2°49W **67** G5
Yeo, L. *Australia* 28°0S 124°30E **149** E3
Yeo I. *Canada* 45°24N 81°48W **174** A3
Yeola *India* 20°2N 74°30E **126** D2
Yeon-do = Sejong
S. Korea 36°35N 127°15E **115** F14
Yeong-wol *S. Korea* 37°11N 128°28E **115** F15
Yeongcheon *S. Korea* 35°58N 128°56E **115** G15
Yeongdeok *S. Korea* 36°24N 129°22E **115** F15
Yeongdong *S. Korea* 36°10N 127°46E **115** F14
Yeongju *S. Korea* 36°50N 128°40E **115** F15
Yeosu *S. Korea* 34°47N 127°45E **115** G14
Yeotmal = Yavatmal
India 20°20N 78°15E **126** D4
Yeovil *U.K.* 50°57N 2°38W **67** G5
Yepes *Spain* 39°55N 3°39W **88** F7
Yeppoon *Australia* 23°5S 150°47E **150** C5
Yerbent *Turkmenistan* 39°19N 58°36E **129** B8
Yerbogachen *Russia* 61°16N 108°0E **107** C11
Yerevan *Armenia* 40°10N 44°31E **87** K7

Yerington *U.S.A.* 38°59N 119°10W **168** G4
Yerkesik *Turkey* 37°7N 28°19E **99** D10
Yerköy *Turkey* 39°38N 34°28E **104** C6
Yerla ← *India* 16°50N 74°30E **126** F2
Yermo *U.S.A.* 34°54N 116°50W **175** L10
Yerolakkos *Cyprus* 35°11N 33°15E **101** D12
Yeropol *Russia* 65°15N 168°40E **107** C17
Yeroskipos *Cyprus* 34°46N 32°28E **101** E11
Yershov *Russia* 51°23N 48°27E **86** E9
Yerushalayim = Jerusalem
Israel/West Bank 31°47N 35°10E **130** D4
Yes Tor *U.K.* 50°41N 4°0W **67** G4
Yesan *S. Korea* 36°41N 126°51E **115** F14
Yesilhisar *Turkey* 38°20N 35°5E **104** C6
Yeşilırmak ← *Turkey* 41°22N 36°37E **104** B7
Yeşilkent *Turkey* 36°57N 36°12E **104** D7
Yeşilova *Azerbaijan* 37°31N 29°46E **99** D11
Yeşilyurt *Manisa,*
Turkey 38°22N 28°40E **99** C10
Yeşilyurt *Muğla, Turkey* 37°10N 28°20E **99** D10
Yesnogorsk *Russia* 54°32N 37°38E **84** D9
Yeso *U.S.A.* 34°26N 104°37W **169** J11
Yessentuki *Russia* 44°5N 42°53E **87** H6
Yessey *Russia* 68°29N 102°10E **107** C11
Yeste *Spain* 38°22N 2°19W **91** G2
Yetman *Australia* 28°56S 150°48E **151** D5
Yeu, Î. d' *France* 46°42N 2°20W **70** F4
Yevlax *Azerbaijan* 40°39N 47°7E **87** K8
Yevpatoriya *Ukraine* 45°15N 33°20E **85** K7
Yeya ← *Russia* 46°40N 38°40E **87** G4
Yeysk *Russia* 46°40N 38°12E **85** H10
Yezd = Yazd *Iran* 31°55N 54°27E **129** D7
Yezerishche *Belarus* 55°50N 30°0E **84** E5
Ygatimi *Paraguay* 24°5S 55°40W **191** A4
Yhati *Paraguay* 25°45S 56°35W **190** B4
Yhú *Paraguay* 25°0S 56°0W **191** A4
Yi ← *Uruguay* 33°7S 57°8W **190** C4
Yi 'Allaq, G. *Egypt* 30°22N 33°31E **130** E2
Yi He ← *China* 34°10N 118°8E **115** G10
Yi Xian *Anhui, China* 29°55N 117°57E **117** C11
Yi Xian *Hebei, China* 39°20N 115°30E **114** E8
Yi Xian *Liaoning,*
China 41°30N 121°22E **115** D11
Yialiás ← *Cyprus* 35°9N 33°44E **101** D12
Yialousa *Cyprus* 35°32N 34°10E **101** D13
Yibin *China* 28°45N 104°32E **116** C5
Yichang *China* 30°40N 111°20E **117** B8
Yicheng *Henan, China* 31°41N 112°12E **117** B9
Yicheng *Shanxi, China* 35°42N 111°40E **114** G6
Yichuan *China* 36°2N 110°10E **114** F6
Yichun *Heilongjiang,*
China 47°44N 128°52E **111** B14
Yichun *Jiangxi, China* 27°48N 114°22E **117** D10
Yidu *China* 36°43N 118°28E **115** F10
Yidun *China* 30°22N 99°21E **116** B2
Yifeng *China* 28°24N 114°45E **117** C10
Yihuang *China* 27°30N 116°12E **117** D11
Yijun *China* 35°28N 109°8E **114** G5
Yıldız Dağları *Turkey* 41°48N 27°36E **97** E11
Yıldızeli *Turkey* 39°51N 36°36E **104** C7
Yilehuli Shan *China* 51°20N 124°20E **111** A13
Yiliang *Yunnan, China* 27°38N 104°2E **116** D5
Yiliang *Yunnan, China* 24°56N 103°11E **116** E4
Yilong *China* 31°34N 106°23E **116** B6
Yima *China* 34°44N 111°53E **114** G6
Yimen *China* 24°40N 102°10E **116** E4
Yimianpo *China* 45°7N 128°2E **115** B15
Yin Xu *China* 36°7N 114°18E **114** F8
Yi'nan *China* 35°31N 118°24E **115** G10
Yinchuan *China* 38°30N 106°15E **114** E4
Yindarlgooda, L.
Australia 30°40S 121°52E **149** F3
Ying He ← *China* 32°30N 116°30E **117** A11
Ying Xian *China* 39°32N 113°10E **114** E7
Yingcheng *China* 30°56N 113°35E **117** B9
Yingde *China* 24°10N 113°25E **117** E9
Yingjiang *China* 24°41N 97°55E **116** E1
Yingkou *China* 40°37N 122°18E **115** D12
Yingpanshui *China* 37°26N 104°18E **114** F3
Yingshan *Hubei,*
China 30°41N 115°32E **117** B10
Yingshan *Sichuan,*
China 31°4N 106°35E **116** B6
Yingshang *China* 32°38N 116°12E **117** A11
Yingtan *China* 28°12N 117°0E **117** C11
Yingualyalya ◎
Australia 18°49S 129°12E **148** C4
Yining *China* 43°58N 81°10E **109** D10
Yinjiang *China* 28°1N 108°21E **116** C7
Yinmabin *Burma* 22°10N 94°55E **123** H19
Yioúra = Giaros *Greece* 37°32N 24°40E **98** D6
Yipinglang *China* 25°10N 101°52E **116** E3
Yirga Alem *Ethiopia* 6°48N 38°22E **131** F2
Yirrkala *Australia* 12°14S 136°56E **150** A2
Yishan *China* 24°28N 108°38E **116** E7
Yishui *China* 35°47N 118°30E **115** G10
Yishun *Singapore* 1°26N 103°51E **121** d
Yitong *China* 43°13N 125°20E **115** C13
Yiwu *China* 29°20N 120°3E **117** C13
Yixing *China* 31°21N 119°48E **117** B12
Yiyang *Henan, China* 34°27N 112°10E **114** G7
Yiyang *Hunan, China* 28°35N 112°18E **117** C9
Yiyang *Jiangxi, China* 28°21N 117°20E **117** C11
Yizhang *China* 25°27N 112°57E **117** E9
Yizheng *China* 32°18N 119°10E **117** A12
Yli-Kitka *Finland* 66°8N 28°30E **60** C23
Yli-Li *Finland* 65°24N 25°28E **60** D21
Ylitornio *Finland* 66°19N 23°39E **60** C20
Ylivieska *Finland* 64°4N 24°28E **60** D21
Ymer Ø *Greenland* 73°9N 24°20W **57** C8
Ynarmen *Sweden* 58°50N 16°35E **63** F10
Yoakum *U.S.A.* 29°17N 97°9W **176** G6
Yobe □ *Nigeria* 12°0N 11°30E **139** C7
Yogpi Pt. *Phil.* 14°6N 124°12E **119** B5
Yoğuntaş *Turkey* 41°50N 27°41E **97** E11
Yogyakarta *Indonesia* 7°49S 110°22E **118** F4
Yogyakarta □
Indonesia 7°49S 110°20E **118** F4
Yoho △ *Canada* 51°25N 116°30W **162** C5
Yojoa, L. de *Honduras* 14°53N 88°0W **182** D2
Yok Don △ *Vietnam* 12°50N 107°40E **120** F6
Yokadouma *Cameroon* 3°26N 14°55E **140** D2

Yokkaichi *Japan* 34°55N 136°38E **113** G8
Yoko *Cameroon* 5°32N 12°20E **139** D7
Yokohama *Japan* 35°27N 139°28E **113** G9
Yokosuka *Japan* 35°20N 139°40E **113** G9
Yokote *Japan* 39°20N 140°30E **112** E10
Yola *Nigeria* 9°10N 12°29E **139** D7
Yolaina, Cordillera de
Nic. 11°30N 84°0W **182** D3
Yom ← *Thailand* 15°35N 100°1E **120** E3
Yonago *Japan* 35°25N 133°19E **113** G6
Yonaguni-Jima *Japan* 24°27N 123°0E **117** F12
Yōnan *N. Korea* 37°55N 126°11E **115** F14
Yonezawa *Japan* 37°57N 140°4E **112** F10
Yong Peng *Malaysia* 2°0N 103°3E **121** M4
Yong Sata *Thailand* 7°8N 99°41E **121** J2
Yong'an *China* 25°59N 117°25E **117** E11
Yongchang *China* 38°17N 102°7E **110** D9
Yongcheng *China* 33°55N 116°20E **114** H9
Yongchuan *China* 29°17N 105°55E **116** C5
Yongchun *China* 25°16N 118°20E **117** E12
Yongde *China* 24°5N 99°25E **116** E2
Yongdeng *China* 36°38N 103°25E **114** F2
Yongding *China* 24°43N 116°45E **117** E11
Yongfeng *China* 27°20N 115°22E **117** D10
Yongfu *China* 24°59N 109°59E **116** E7
Yonghe *China* 36°46N 110°38E **114** F6
Yongjeong *N. Korea* 39°31N 127°18E **115** E14
Yongji *Jilin, China* 43°33N 126°13E **115** C14
Yongji *Shanxi, China* 34°52N 110°28E **114** G6
Yongjia *China* 28°5N 120°52E **117** C13
Yongkang *Yunnan, China* 24°9N 99°20E **116** E2
Yongkang *Zhejiang,*
China 28°55N 120°2E **117** C13
Yongnian *China* 36°47N 114°29E **114** F8
Yongning *Guangxi Zhuangzu,*
China 22°44N 108°28E **116** F7
Yongning *Ningxia Huizu,*
China 38°15N 106°14E **114** E4
Yongqing *China* 39°25N 116°28E **114** E9
Yongren *China* 26°4N 101°40E **116** D3
Yongshan *China* 28°11N 103°15E **116** C4
Yongsheng *China* 26°38N 100°46E **116** D3
Yongshun *China* 29°2N 109°51E **116** C7
Yongtai *China* 25°49N 118°58E **117** E12
Yongxin = Jinggangshan
S. China Sea 16°50N 112°20E **118** A4
Yongxiu *China* 29°2N 115°42E **117** C10
Yongzhou *China* 26°17N 111°37E **117** D8
Yonibana *S. Leone* 8°30N 12°19W **138** D2
Yonkers *U.S.A.* 40°56N 73°52W **175** F11
Yonne □ *France* 47°50N 3°40E **71** E10
Yonne ← *France* 48°23N 2°58E **71** D9
York *Australia* 31°52S 116°47E **149** F2
York *U.K.* 53°58N 1°6W **66** D6
York, Kap *Greenland* 75°55N 66°25W **57** B4
York, Vale of *U.K.* 54°15N 1°25W **66** D6
York, City of □ *U.K.* 53°58N 1°6W **66** D6
York Sd. *Australia* 15°0S 125°5E **148** C4
Yorke Pen. *Australia* 34°50S 137°40E **152** C2
Yorketown *Australia* 35°0S 137°33E **152** C2
Yorkshire Dales △ *U.K.* 54°12N 2°10W **66** C5
Yorkshire Wolds *U.K.* 54°8N 0°31W **66** C7
Yorkton *Canada* 51°11N 102°28W **163** C8
Yorkville *Calif., U.S.A.* 38°52N 123°13W **170** G3
Yorkville *Ill., U.S.A.* 41°38N 88°27W **172** E9
Yoro *Honduras* 15°9N 87°7W **182** C2
Yoron-Jima *Japan* 27°2N 128°26E **113** L4
Yorosso *Mali* 12°17N 4°55W **138** C4
Yos Sudarso, Pulau = Dolak,
Pulau Indonesia 8°0S 138°30E **119** F9
Yosemite △ *U.S.A.* 37°45N 119°40W **170** H7
Yosemite Village
U.S.A. 37°45N 119°35W **170** H7
Yoshino-Kumano △
Japan 34°12N 135°55E **113** H8
Yoshkar Ola *Russia* 56°38N 47°55E **86** B8
Yotvata *Israel* 29°55N 35°2E **130** F4
You Jiang ← *China* 22°50N 108°6E **116** F7
You Xian *China* 27°1N 113°17E **117** D9
Youbou *Canada* 48°53N 124°13W **170** B2
Youghal *Ireland* 51°56N 7°52W **64** E4
Youghal B. *Ireland* 51°55N 7°49W **64** E4
Youkounkoun *Guinea* 12°35N 13°11W **138** C2
Young *Australia* 34°19S 148°18E **153** C8
Young *Canada* 51°47N 105°45W **163** C7
Young *Uruguay* 32°44N 57°36W **190** C4
Young I. *Antarctica* 66°24S 162°24E **55** C11
Young Ra. *N.Z.* 44°10S 169°30E **155** E4
Younghusband, L.
Australia 30°50S 136°5E **152** A2
Younghusband Pen.
Australia 36°0S 139°25E **152** C3
Youngstown *Canada* 51°35N 111°10W **163** C6
Youngstown *Fla.,*
U.S.A. 30°22N 85°26W **178** E4
Youngstown *N.Y.,*
U.S.A. 43°15N 79°3W **174** C5
Youngstown *Ohio,*
U.S.A. 41°6N 80°39W **174** E4
Youngsville *U.S.A.* 41°51N 79°19W **174** E4
Youngwood *U.S.A.* 40°14N 79°34W **174** F5
Youssoufia *Morocco* 32°16N 8°31W **136** B4
Youxi *China* 26°10N 118°13E **117** D12
Youyang *China* 28°47N 108°42E **117** C7
Youyu *China* 40°10N 112°20E **114** D7
Yozgat *Turkey* 39°51N 34°47E **104** C6
Yozgat □ *Turkey* 39°30N 35°0E **104** C6
Ypacaraí △ *Paraguay* 25°20S 57°19W **190** B4
Ypané ← *Paraguay* 23°29S 57°19W **190** A4
Yport *France* 49°44N 0°15E **70** B7
Ypres = Ieper *Belgium* 50°51N 2°53E **69** D2
Yr Wyddgrug = Mold *U.K.* 53°9N 3°8W **66** D4
Yreka *U.S.A.* 41°44N 122°38W **168** F2
Yrghyz *Kazakhstan* 48°37N 61°16E **108** D10
Yrghyz ← *Kazakhstan* 48°6N 62°2E **108** D10
Yssingeaux *France* 45°9N 4°8E **73** C6
Ystad *Sweden* 55°26N 13°50E **63** D6
Ystradgynlais *U.K.* 51°47N 3°46W **67** F4
Ysyk-Köl = Balykchy
Kyrgyzstan 42°26N 76°12E **108** D9
Ysyk-Köl *Kyrgyzstan* 42°25N 77°15E **108** D9

Ysyk-Köl □ *Kyrgyzstan* 42°0N 78°0E **108** D9
Ythan ← *U.K.* 57°19N 1°59W **65** D7
Ytteran *Sweden* 63°16N 14°7E **62** A8
Ytterhogdal *Sweden* 62°12N 14°56E **62** B8
Yttermalung *Sweden* 60°35N 13°47E **62** D7
Ytyk-Kyuyel *Russia* 62°30N 133°45E **107** C14
Yu Jiang ← *China* 23°22N 110°3E **116** F7
Yu Shan *Taiwan* 23°25N 120°52E **117** F13
Yu Xian = Yuzhou
China 34°10N 113°28E **114** G7
Yu Xian *Hebei, China* 39°50N 114°35E **114** E8
Yu Xian *Shanxi, China* 38°5N 113°20E **114** E7
Yuan Jiang = Hong ←
Asia 20°16N 106°34E **120** B5
Yuan Jiang ← *Hunan,*
China 28°55N 111°50E **117** C8
Yuan Jiang ← *Yunnan,*
China 22°20N 103°59E **116** F4
Yuan'an *China* 31°3N 111°34E **117** B8
Yuanjiang *Hunan,*
China 28°47N 112°21E **117** C9
Yuanjiang *Yunnan,*
China 23°36N 102°0E **116** E4
Yuanli *Taiwan* 24°27N 120°39E **117** E13
Yuanlin *Taiwan* 23°58N 120°30E **117** F13
Yuanling *China* 28°29N 110°22E **117** C8
Yuanmou *China* 25°42N 101°53E **116** E3
Yuanping *China* 38°42N 112°46E **114** E7
Yuanqu *China* 35°18N 111°42E **114** G6
Yuanyang *Henan, China* 35°3N 113°58E **114** G7
Yuanyang *Yunnan,*
China 23°10N 102°43E **116** F4
Yuba ← *U.S.A.* 39°8N 121°36W **170** F5
Yuba City *U.S.A.* 39°8N 121°37W **170** F5
Yūbari *Japan* 43°4N 141°59E **112** C10
Yūbetsu *Japan* 44°13N 143°50E **112** B11
Yucatán □ *Mexico* 20°50N 89°0W **181** C7
Yucatán, Canal de
Caribbean 22°0N 86°30W **182** B2
Yucatán, Peninsula de
Mexico 19°30N 89°0W **158** H11
Yucatan Basin
Cent. Amer. 19°0N 86°0W **181** D7
Yucatan Channel = Yucatán,
Canal de Caribbean 22°0N 86°30W **182** B2
Yucca *U.S.A.* 34°52N 114°9W **171** L12
Yucca Valley *U.S.A.* 34°8N 116°27W **171** L10
Yucheng *China* 36°55N 116°32E **114** F9
Yuci = Jinzhong *China* 37°42N 112°46E **114** F7
Yudu *China* 25°59N 115°30E **117** E10
Yuechi *China* 30°34N 106°25E **116** B6
Yuen Long *China* 22°26N 114°2E **111** a
Yuendumu *Australia* 22°16S 131°49E **148** D5
Yuendumu ◎
Australia 22°21S 131°40E **148** D5
Yueqing *China* 28°9N 120°59E **117** C13
Yueqing Wan *China* 28°5N 121°20E **117** C13
Yuexi *Anhui, China* 30°50N 116°20E **117** B11
Yuexi *Sichuan, China* 28°37N 102°26E **116** C4
Yueyang *China* 29°21N 113°5E **117** C9
Yugan *China* 28°43N 116°37E **117** C11
Yugorenok *Russia* 59°47N 137°40E **107** D14
Yugyd Va △ *Russia* 62°25N 58°45E **106** C6
Yuhuan *China* 28°9N 121°12E **117** C13
Yuhuan Dao *China* 28°5N 121°15E **117** C13
Yujiang *China* 28°10N 116°43E **117** C11
Yukhary Askipara
Azerbaijan 41°4N 45°1E **105** B11
Yukhnov *Russia* 54°44N 35°15E **84** E8
Yukon *U.S.A.* 35°31N 97°45W **176** D6
Yukon ← *U.S.A.* 62°32N 163°54W **166** E5
Yukon Flats *U.S.A.* 66°40N 145°45W **166** B10
Yukon Territory □
Canada 63°0N 135°0W **160** E5
Yüksekova *Turkey* 37°34N 44°16E **105** D11
Yukta *Russia* 63°26N 105°42E **107** C11
Yukuhashi *Japan* 33°44N 130°59E **113** H5
Yulara *Australia* 25°10S 130°55E **149** E5
Yule ← *Australia* 20°41S 118°17E **148** D2
Yuleba *Australia* 26°37S 149°24E **151** D4
Yulee *U.S.A.* 30°38N 81°36W **178** E8
Yuli *China* 41°19N 86°15E **109** E7
Yüli *Taiwan* 23°20N 121°18E **117** F13
Yulin *Guangxi Zhuangzu,*
China 22°40N 110°8E **117** F8
Yulin *Hainan, China* 18°10N 109°31E **117** a
Yulin *Shaanxi, China* 38°20N 109°30E **114** E5
Yulong Xueshan *China* 27°14N 100°12E **116** D3
Yuma *Ariz., U.S.A.* 32°43N 114°37W **171** N12
Yuma *Colo., U.S.A.* 40°8N 102°43W **168** F12
Yuma, B. de *Dom. Rep.* 18°20N 68°35W **183** C6
Yumali *Australia* 35°32S 139°45E **152** C2
Yumbe
Dem. Rep. of the Congo 1°12S 26°15E **142** C2
Yumen *China* 39°50N 97°30E **110** D8
Yumurtalık *Turkey* 36°45N 35°48E **104** D6
Yun Gui Gaoyuan *China* 27°0N 107°0E **116** D6
Yun Ling Shan *China* 27°0N 99°20E **116** D2
Yun Xian *Hubei, China* 32°50N 110°46E **114** H6
Yun Xian *Yunnan,*
China 24°54N 100°1E **116** E3
Yuna *Australia* 28°20S 114°0E **149** E2
Yunak *Turkey* 38°49N 31°43E **104** C4
Yunan *China* 23°13N 111°32E **117** F8
Yuncheng *Henan,*
China 35°36N 115°57E **114** G8
Yuncheng *Shanxi, China* 35°3N 111°0E **114** G6
Yunfu *China* 22°50N 112°0E **117** F9
Yungang Shiku *China* 40°6N 113°7E **114** D7
Yungas *Bolivia* 17°0S 66°0W **188** G5
Yungay *China* 37°10S 72°5W **190** D1
Yunhe *China* 28°8N 119°33E **117** C12
Yunkai Dashan *China* 22°30N 111°0E **117** F8
Yunlin □ *Taiwan* 23°44S 120°30E **117** F13
Yunling Shan *China* 28°0N 98°50E **116** C2
Yunmeng *China* 31°2N 113°43E **117** B9
Yunnan □ *China* 25°0N 102°0E **116** E4
Yunquera de Henares
Spain 40°47N 3°11W **90** E1
Yunt Dağı *Turkey* 38°47N 27°13E **99** C9
Yunta *Australia* 32°34S 139°36E **152** B2
Yunxi *China* 33°0N 110°22E **114** H6
Yunxiao *China* 23°59N 117°18E **117** F11
Yunyang *Chongqing,*
China 31°2N 108°52E **117** B7
Yunyang *Henan, China* 33°26N 112°42E **114** H7
Yupanqui Basin
Pac. Oc. 19°0S 101°0W **157** J17

Yuping China 27°13N 108°56E 116 D7
Yuqing China 27°13N 107°53E 116 D6
Yuraygir △ Australia 29°45S 153°15E 151 D5
Yurga Russia 55°42N 84°51E 106 D9
Yurihonjō Japan 39°23N 140°3E 112 E10
Yurimaguas Peru 5°55S 76°7W 188 B2
Yurkiyka Ukraine 48°42N 28°35E 81 B13
Yurubí △ Venezuela 10°26N 68°42W 183 D6
Yurungkax He →
  China 38°5N 80°34E 109 E10
Yuryev-Polskiy Russia 56°30N 39°40E 84 D10
Yuryevets Russia 57°25N 43°2E 86 B6
Yuscarán Honduras 13°58N 86°45W 182 D2
Yûsef, Bahr → Egypt 28°25N 30°35E 137 F7
Yushan China 28°42N 118°10E 117 C12
Yushanzhen China 29°28N 108°22E 116 C7
Yushe China 37°4N 112°58E 114 F7
Yushu Jilin, China 44°43N 126°38E 115 B14
Yushu Qinghai, China 33°5N 96°55E 110 E8
Yusufeli Turkey 40°50N 41°33E 105 B9
Yutai China 35°0N 116°45E 114 G9
Yutian Hebei, China 39°53N 117°45E 115 E9
Yutian Sinkiang-Uigur,
  China 36°52N 81°42E 109 E10
Yuxarı Qarabağ =
  Nagorno-Karabakh □
  Azerbaijan 39°55N 46°45E 105 C12
Yuxi China 24°30N 102°35E 116 E4
Yuyao China 30°3N 121°10E 117 B13
Yuzawa Japan 39°10N 140°30E 112 E10
Yuzha Russia 56°34N 42°1E 86 B6
Yuzhno-Kurilsk
  Russia 44°1N 145°51E 107 E15
Yuzhno-Sakhalinsk
  Russia 46°58N 142°45E 111 B17
Yuzhno-Sukhokumsk
  Russia 44°40N 45°35E 87 H7
Yuzhnoukrainsk
  Ukraine 47°49N 31°11E 85 J6
Yuzhnouralsk Russia 54°26N 61°15E 108 B6
Yuzhnyy □ Russia 44°0N 40°0E 106 E5
Yuzhou China 34°10N 113°28E 114 G7
Yvelines □ France 48°40N 1°45E 71 D8
Yverdon-les-Bains Switz. 46°47N 6°39E 77 J2
Yvetot France 49°37N 0°44E 70 C7
Yzeure France 46°33N 3°22E 71 F10

Z

Zaanstad Neths. 52°27N 4°50E 69 B4
Zab, Monts du Algeria 34°55N 5°0E 136 B5
Zāb al Kabīr → Iraq 36°1N 43°24E 105 D10
Zāb aş Şaghīr → Iraq 35°17N 43°29E 105 E10
Žabalj Serbia 45°21N 20°5E 80 E5
Žabari Serbia 44°22N 21°15E 96 B5
Zabarjad Egypt 23°40N 36°12E 137 C4
Zabaykalsk Russia 49°40N 117°25E 107 E12
Zabaykalsky △ Russia 53°40N 109°0E 107 D11
Ząbki Poland 52°17N 21°6E 83 F8
Ząbkowice Śląskie
  Poland 50°35N 16°50E 83 H3
Žabljak Montenegro 43°18N 19°5E 96 C3
Zabludów Poland 53°0N 23°19E 83 F9
Żabno Poland 50°9N 20°53E 83 H7
Zabol Iran 31°0N 61°32E 129 D9
Zābol □ Afghan. 32°0N 67°0E 122 D5
Zābolī Iran 27°10N 61°35E 129 E9
Zabolotiv Ukraine 48°28N 25°18E 81 B10
Zabolottya Ukraine 51°38N 24°16E 83 G11
Zabré Burkina Faso 11°12N 0°36W 139 C4
Zábřeh Czech Rep. 49°53N 16°52E 79 B9
Zabrze Poland 50°18N 18°50E 83 H5
Zabuzhzhya Ukraine 51°21N 23°42E 83 G10
Zabzuga Ghana 9°20N 0°30E 139 D5
Zacapa Guatemala 14°59N 89°31W 182 D2
Zacapu Mexico 19°50N 101°43W 180 D4
Zacatecas Mexico 22°47N 102°35W 180 C4
Zacatecas □ Mexico 23°0N 103°0W 180 C4
Zacatecoluca El Salv. 13°29N 88°51W 182 D2
Zacharo Greece 37°30N 21°39E 98 D3
Zachary U.S.A. 30°39N 91°9W 176 F9
Zachodnio-Pomorskie □
  Poland 53°40N 15°50E 82 E2
Zacoalco de Torres
  Mexico 20°14N 103°35W 180 C4
Zacualtipán Mexico 20°39N 98°36W 181 C5
Zadawa Nigeria 11°33N 10°19E 139 C7
Zadetkyi Kyun Burma 10°0N 98°25E 121 G2
Zadonsk Russia 52°25N 38°56E 85 F10
Zafarqand Iran 33°11N 52°29E 129 C7
Zafra Spain 38°26N 6°30W 89 G4
Żagań Poland 51°39N 15°22E 83 G2
Zagaoua Chad 15°30N 22°24E 135 E10
Žagarė Lithuania 56°21N 23°15E 88 B10
Zagazig Egypt 30°40N 31°30E 137 E7
Zāghén Iran 33°30N 48°42E 129 C6
Zaghouan Tunisia 36°23N 10°10E 136 A6
Zaghouan □ Tunisia 36°20N 10°0E 136 A6
Zaglou Algeria 27°17N 0°3W 136 C3
Zagnanado Benin 7°18N 2°28E 139 D5
Zagora Greece 39°27N 23°6E 98 B5
Zagora Morocco 30°22N 5°51W 136 B2
Zagorje ob Savi Slovenia 46°8N 15°0E 93 B11
Zagórów Poland 52°10N 17°54E 83 F4
Zagórz Poland 49°30N 22°14E 83 J9
Zagreb Croatia 45°50N 15°58E 93 C12
Zagreb ✈ (ZAG) Croatia 45°45N 16°4E 93 C13
Zagros, Kūhhā-ye Iran 33°45N 48°5E 129 C6
Zagros Mts. = Zagros, Kūhhā-ye
  Iran 33°45N 47°0E 129 C6
Žagubica Serbia 44°15N 21°47E 96 B5
Zaguinaso Ivory C. 9°14N 6°14W 138 C3
Zagyva → Hungary 47°5N 20°4E 80 C5
Zāhedān Fārs, Iran 28°46N 53°52E 129 D7
Zāhedān Sīstān va Balūchestān,
  Iran 29°30N 60°50E 129 D9
Zahirabad India 17°43N 77°37E 126 F3
Zahlah Lebanon 33°52N 35°50E 130 B4
Zahna Germany 51°54N 12°47E 76 C8
Zāhran al Janub
  Si. Arabia 17°40N 43°30E 131 D3
Zainsk Russia 55°18N 52°4E 86 C11
Zaïre = Congo → Africa 6°4S 12°24E 140 F2
Zaječar Serbia 43°53N 22°18E 96 C6
Zaka Zimbabwe 20°20S 31°29E 145 B5
Zakamensk Russia 50°23N 103°17E 107 D11
Zakarpattya □ Ukraine 48°20N 23°20E 81 B8
Zakataly = Zaqatala
  Azerbaijan 41°38N 46°35E 87 K8

Zakhodnaya Dzvina =
  Daugava → Latvia 57°4N 24°3E 84 D3
Zākhū Iraq 37°10N 42°50E 105 D10
Zakinthos = Zakynthos
  Greece 37°47N 20°54E 98 D2
Zakopane Poland 49°18N 19°57E 83 J6
Zakroczym Poland 52°26N 20°38E 83 F7
Zakros Greece 35°6N 26°10E 101 D8
Zakynthos Greece 37°47N 20°54E 98 D2
Zala □ Hungary 46°42N 16°50E 80 D1
Zala → Hungary 46°43N 17°16E 80 D2
Zalaegerszeg Hungary 46°53N 16°47E 80 D1
Zalakomár Hungary 46°33N 17°10E 80 D2
Zalalövő Hungary 46°51N 16°35E 80 D1
Zalamea de la Serena
  Spain 38°40N 5°38W 89 G5
Zalamea la Real Spain 37°41N 6°38W 89 H4
Zalantun China 48°0N 122°43E 111 B13
Zalari Russia 53°33N 102°30E 107 D11
Zalău Romania 47°12N 23°3E 80 C8
Žalec Slovenia 46°16N 15°10E 93 B12
Zaleshchiki = Zalishchyky
  Ukraine 48°45N 25°45E 81 B10
Zalesye Russia 54°50N 21°31E 82 D8
Zalewo Poland 53°50N 19°41E 82 E6
Zalingei Sudan 12°51N 23°29E 135 F10
Zalishchyky Ukraine 48°45N 25°45E 81 B10
Zama L. Canada 58°45N 119°5W 162 B5
Zambeke
  Dem. Rep. of the Congo 2°8N 25°17E 142 B2
Zambeze → Africa 18°35S 36°20E 143 F4
Zambezi = Zambeze →
  Africa 18°35S 36°20E 143 F4
Zambezi Zambia 13°30S 23°15E 141 G4
Zambezi □ Namibia 18°0S 23°30E 144 A3
Zambezi △ Zimbabwe 17°54S 25°41E 143 F2
Zambezia □ Mozam. 16°15S 37°30E 143 F4
Zambia ■ Africa 15°0S 28°0E 143 F2
Zamboanga Phil. 6°59N 122°3E 119 C6
Zambrów Poland 52°59N 22°14E 83 F9
Zamfara □ Nigeria 12°10N 6°0E 139 C6
Zamfara → Nigeria 12°5N 4°2E 139 C5
Zamora Mexico 19°59N 102°16W 180 D4
Zamora Spain 41°30N 5°45W 88 D5
Zamora □ Spain 41°30N 5°46W 88 D5
Zamość Poland 50°43N 23°15E 83 H10
Zamtang China 32°26N 101°6E 116 A3
Zan Ghana 9°26N 0°17W 139 D4
Záncara → Spain 39°18N 3°18W 91 F1
Zanda China 31°32N 79°50E 110 E4
Zandvoort Neths. 52°22N 4°32E 69 B4
Zanesville U.S.A. 39°56N 82°1W 174 F4
Zangābād Iran 38°26N 46°44E 128 B5
Zangliveri Greece 40°36N 23°15E 96 F7
Zangoza = Sangüesa
  Spain 42°37N 1°17W 90 D3
Zangue → Mozam. 17°50S 35°21E 143 F4
Zanjān Iran 36°40N 48°35E 105 D13
Zanjān □ Iran 37°20N 49°30E 129 B6
Zanjān → Iran 37°8N 47°47E 129 B6
Zannone Italy 40°58N 13°3E 94 B6
Zante = Zakynthos
  Greece 37°47N 20°54E 98 D2
Zanthus Australia 31°2S 123°34E 149 F3
Zanzan □ Ivory C. 8°30N 3°30W 138 C3
Zanzibar Tanzania 6°12S 39°12E 142 D4
Zaouatallaz Algeria 24°52N 8°26E 136 D7
Zaouiet El-Kala = Bordj Omar
  Driss Algeria 28°10N 6°40E 136 C5
Zaouiet Reggâne Algeria 26°32N 0°3E 136 C4
Zaoyang China 32°10N 112°45E 117 A9
Zaozernyy Kazakhstan 52°6N 71°9E 109 B8
Zaozhuang China 34°50N 117°35E 115 G9
Zap Suyu = Zāb al Kabīr →
  Iraq 36°1N 43°24E 105 D10
Zapadna Morava →
  Serbia 43°38N 21°30E 96 C5
Zapadnaya Dvina = Daugava →
  Latvia 57°4N 24°3E 84 D3
Zapadnaya Dvina Russia 56°15N 32°3E 84 D7
Západné Beskydy
  Europe 49°30N 19°0E 79 B12
Zapadni Rodopi Bulgaria 41°50N 24°0E 96 E7
Západočeský □
  Czech Rep. 49°35N 13°0E 78 B6
Zapala Argentina 39°0S 70°5W 192 A2
Zapaleri, Cerro Bolivia 22°49S 67°11W 190 A2
Zapata U.S.A. 26°55N 99°16W 176 H5
Zapatón → Spain 39°0N 6°49W 89 F4
Zapiga Chile 19°40S 69°55W 188 D4
Zapolyarnyy Russia 69°26N 30°51E 60 B24
Zapopán Mexico 20°43N 103°24W 180 C4
Zaporizhzhya Ukraine 47°50N 35°10E 85 J8
Zaporizhzhya □ Ukraine 46°55N 35°50E 85 J8
Zaporozhye = Zaporizhzhya
  Ukraine 47°50N 35°10E 85 J8
Zaqatala Azerbaijan 41°38N 46°35E 87 K8
Zara Turkey 39°58N 37°43E 104 C7
Zarafshon Uzbekistan 41°34N 64°12E 108 D6
Zaragoza Coahuila,
  Mexico 28°29N 100°55W 180 B4
Zaragoza Nuevo León,
  Mexico 23°58N 99°46W 181 C5
Zaragoza Spain 41°39N 0°53W 90 D4
Zaragoza □ Spain 41°35N 1°0W 90 D4
Zarand Kermān, Iran 30°46N 56°34E 129 D8
Zarand Markazī, Iran 35°18N 50°25E 129 C6
Zărandului, Munții
  Romania 46°14N 22°7E 80 D7
Zaranj Afghan. 30°55N 61°55E 122 D2
Zarasai Lithuania 55°40N 26°20E 84 E4
Zárate Argentina 34°7S 59°0W 190 C4
Zarautz Spain 43°17N 2°10W 90 B2
Zaraysk Russia 54°48N 38°53E 84 E10
Zard, Kūh-e Iran 32°22N 50°4E 129 C6
Zarechniy Russia 53°49N 61°2E 108 B4
Zāreh Iran 35°7N 49°9E 129 C6
Zari Nigeria 12°43N 7°40E 139 C6
Zaria Nigeria 11°0N 7°40E 139 C6
Zarineh → Iran 37°17N 46°26E 105 D12
Zarinsk Russia 53°34N 84°55E 109 B10
Zarki Poland 50°38N 19°23E 83 H6
Zarko Greece 39°38N 22°6E 98 B4
Zarneh Iran 33°55N 46°10E 128 C5
Žarnești Romania 45°33N 25°18E 81 D10
Zaros Greece 35°8N 24°54E 101 D6
Żarów Poland 50°56N 16°29E 83 H3
Zarqā' → Jordan 32°10N 35°37E 130 C4
Zarqā', Nahr az →
  Jordan 32°10N 35°37E 130 C4
Zarrīnābād Iran 36°25N 48°17E 129 C6
Zarrīneh → Iran 37°17N 47°22E 129 B6
Zaruma Ecuador 3°40S 79°38W 186 D3

Žary Poland 51°37N 15°10E 83 G2
Zarza de Granadilla Spain 40°14N 6°3W 88 E4
Zarzaitine Algeria 28°15N 9°34E 136 C5
Zarzis Tunisia 33°31N 11°2E 136 B6
Zas Spain 43°4N 8°53W 88 B2
Zashaghan Kazakhstan 51°11N 51°20E 108 B4
Zaskar → India 34°13N 77°20E 125 B7
Zaskar Mts. India 33°15N 77°30E 125 C7
Zastavna Ukraine 48°31N 25°51E 81 B10
Zastron S. Africa 30°18S 27°7E 144 D4
Žatec Czech Rep. 50°20N 13°32E 78 A6
Zaterechnyy Russia 44°48N 45°11E 87 H7
Zator Poland 49°59N 19°28E 83 J6
Zatyshshya Ukraine 47°20N 29°51E 81 C14
Zavala Bos.-H. 42°50N 17°59E 96 D1
Zavāreh Iran 33°29N 52°28E 129 C7
Zave Zimbabwe 17°6S 30°1E 145 A5
Zavetnoye Russia 47°13N 43°50E 87 H7
Zavidovići Bos.-H. 44°27N 18°10E 80 F3
Zavitinsk Russia 50°10N 129°20E 107 D13
Zavodovski I. Antarctica 56°0S 27°45W 55 B1
Zavolzhsk Russia 57°30N 42°3E 86 B6
Zavolzhye Russia 56°37N 43°28E 86 B6
Zawadzkie Poland 50°37N 18°28E 83 H5
Zawichost Poland 50°48N 21°51E 83 H8
Zawidów Poland 51°1N 15°1E 83 G2
Zawiercie Poland 50°30N 19°24E 83 H6
Zāwiyat al Bayḍā = Al Bayḍā
  Libya 32°50N 21°44E 135 B10
Zāwyet Shammas
  Egypt 31°30N 26°37E 137 A2
Zāwyet Um el Rakham
  Egypt 31°18N 27°1E 137 A2
Zāwyet Ungeîla Egypt 31°23N 26°42E 137 A2
Zāyā Iraq 33°33N 44°13E 128 C5
Zāyandeh → Iran 32°35N 52°0E 129 C7
Zaysan Kazakhstan 47°28N 84°52E 109 C10
Zaysan Köli Kazakhstan 48°0N 83°0E 109 C10
Zayü China 28°48N 97°27E 123 E20
Zázrivá Slovak Rep. 49°16N 19°7E 79 B12
Zbarazh Ukraine 49°43N 25°44E 75 D13
Zbąszyń Poland 52°14N 15°56E 83 F2
Zbąszynek Poland 52°16N 15°51E 83 F2
Zblewo Poland 53°56N 18°19E 82 E5
Zbruch → Ukraine 48°32N 26°27E 81 B11
Ždár nad Sázavou
  Czech Rep. 49°34N 15°57E 78 B8
Zdolbuniv Ukraine 50°30N 26°15E 75 D14
Ždrelo Serbia 44°16N 21°28E 96 B5
Zduńska Wola Poland 51°37N 18°59E 83 G5
Zduny Poland 51°39N 17°21E 83 G4
Zeballos Canada 49°59N 126°50W 162 D3
Zebediela S. Africa 24°20S 29°17E 145 B4
Zebila Ghana 10°55N 0°30W 139 C4
Zebulon U.S.A. 33°6N 84°21W 178 B5
Zeebrugge Belgium 51°19N 3°12E 69 B3
Zeehan Australia 41°52S 145°25E 151 G4
Zeeland □ Neths. 51°30N 3°50E 69 C3
Zeerust S. Africa 25°31S 26°4E 144 C4
Zefat Israel 32°58N 35°29E 130 C4
Zegdou Algeria 29°51N 4°45W 136 C3
Zeggerene, Iracher Mali 16°49N 2°16E 139 B5
Zégoua Mali 10°32N 5°35W 138 C3
Zehak Iran 30°53N 61°42E 129 D9
Zehdenick Germany 52°58N 13°20E 76 C9
Zeil, Mt. Australia 23°30S 132°23E 148 D5
Zeila = Saylac Somalia 11°21N 43°30E 131 E3
Zeist Neths. 52°5N 5°15E 69 B5
Zeitz Germany 51°2N 12°7E 76 C8
Żelechów Poland 51°49N 21°54E 83 G8
Żelena Ukraine 48°3N 24°45E 81 B9
Zelená Hora Czech Rep. 49°34N 15°56E 78 B8
Zelengora Bos.-H. 43°22N 18°30E 96 C2
Zelenodolsk Russia 55°55N 48°30E 86 C9
Zelenogorsk Russia 60°12N 29°43E 84 B5
Zelenograd Russia 56°1N 37°12E 84 D9
Zelenogradsk Russia 54°53N 20°29E 82 D7
Zelenokumsk Russia 44°24N 44°0E 87 H6
Železná Ruda Czech Rep. 49°8N 13°15E 78 B6
Železnik Serbia 44°43N 20°23E 96 B4
Zelfana Algeria 32°27N 4°15E 136 B4
Zelienople U.S.A. 40°48N 80°8W 174 F4
Želiezovce Slovak Rep. 48°3N 18°40E 79 C11
Zelina Croatia 45°57N 16°16E 93 C13
Zell Baden-W., Germany 47°42N 7°52E 77 H3
Zell Rhld-Pfz., Germany 50°1N 7°10E 77 E3
Zell am See Austria 47°19N 12°47E 78 D5
Zella-Mehlis Germany 50°39N 10°40E 76 E6
Želów Poland 51°28N 19°14E 83 G6
Zeltweg Austria 47°11N 14°45E 78 D7
Žemaitijos □ Lithuania 55°55N 22°0E 84 D3
Zemetchino Russia 53°30N 42°30E 86 D6
Zémio C.A.R. 5°2N 25°5E 142 A2
Zemlandskiy Poluostrov
  Russia 54°50N 20°20E 82 D7
Zemmora Algeria 35°44N 0°51E 136 A4
Zemoul, O. → Algeria 29°15N 7°0W 136 C2
Zemplení-hegység
  Hungary 48°25N 21°25E 80 B6
Zemplínska širava
  Slovak Rep. 48°48N 22°0E 79 C15
Zempoala Mexico 19°27N 96°23W 181 D5
Zemun Serbia 44°51N 20°25E 96 B4
Zengbé Cameroon 5°46N 13°4E 139 D7
Zengcheng China 23°13N 113°52E 117 F9
Zenica Bos.-H. 44°10N 17°57E 80 F2
Žepče Bos.-H. 44°28N 18°10E 80 F3
Zepu China 38°11N 77°16E 109 E9
Zerbst Germany 51°58N 12°5E 76 C8
Zerhamra Algeria 29°58N 2°30W 136 C3
Żerków Poland 52°4N 17°32E 83 F4
Zermatt Switz. 46°2N 7°46E 77 J3
Zernez Switz. 46°42N 10°1E 73 C10
Zernograd Russia 46°52N 40°19E 87 G5
Zêrqan → Iran 36°29N 48°42E 129 C6
Zestaponi Georgia 42°6N 43°0E 87 J6
Zetel Germany 53°25N 7°58E 76 B3
Zeulenroda-Triebes
  Germany 50°39N 11°59E 76 E7
Zevenaar Neths. 51°56N 6°5E 69 C6
Zevenbergen Neths. 51°37N 4°38E 69 C4
Zévio Italy 45°23N 11°10E 92 C8
Zeya Russia 53°48N 127°14E 107 D13
Zeya → Russia 51°42N 128°53E 107 D13
Zeyskoye Vdkhr.
  Russia 54°30N 127°30E 107 D13
Zeytinbaği Turkey 40°24N 28°47E 97 F12
Zeytindağ Turkey 38°58N 27°4E 99 E9
Zgharta Lebanon 34°21N 35°53E 130 A4
Zgierz Poland 51°50N 19°27E 83 G6
Zgorzelec Poland 51°10N 15°0E 83 G2

Zguriţa Moldova 48°8N 28°1E 81 B13
Zhabinka Belarus 52°13N 24°2E 83 F11
Zhabokrych Ukraine 48°32N 28°59E 81 B13
Zhalaghash Kazakhstan 45°5N 64°40E 108 C6
Zhalpaqtal Kazakhstan 49°42N 49°25E 86 E9
Zhaltyr Kazakhstan 51°37N 69°44E 109 B7
Zhambyl = Taraz
  Kazakhstan 42°54N 71°22E 109 D8
Zhambyl □ Kazakhstan 44°0N 72°0E 109 D8
Zhanatas Kazakhstan 43°36N 69°35E 109 D7
Zhangaly Kazakhstan 47°1N 50°37E 87 G10
Zhangaqala Kazakhstan 48°56N 49°36E 87 F9
Zhangatas = Zhanatas
  Kazakhstan 43°36N 69°35E 109 D7
Zhangbei China 41°10N 114°45E 114 D8
Zhangguangcai Ling
  China 45°0N 129°0E 115 B15
Zhangjiabian China 22°33N 113°28E 111 a
Zhangjiagang China 31°55N 120°30E 117 B13
Zhangjiajie China 29°11N 110°30E 117 C8
Zhangjiakou China 40°48N 114°55E 114 D8
Zhangping China 25°17N 117°23E 117 E11
Zhangpu China 24°8N 117°35E 117 E11
Zhangshu China 28°4N 115°29E 117 C10
Zhangye China 38°50N 100°23E 110 D9
Zhangzhou China 24°30N 117°35E 117 E11
Zhanhua China 37°40N 118°8E 115 F10
Zhänibek Kazakhstan 49°25N 46°50E 86 F8
Zhanjiang China 21°15N 110°20E 117 G8
Zhannetty, Ostrov
  Russia 76°43N 158°0E 107 B16
Zhanyi China 25°38N 103°48E 116 E4
Zhanyu China 44°30N 122°30E 115 B12
Zhao Xian China 37°43N 114°45E 114 F8
Zhao'an China 23°41N 117°10E 117 F11
Zhaocheng China 36°22N 111°38E 114 F6
Zhaodong China 46°4N 125°59E 111 B13
Zhaojue China 28°1N 102°49E 116 C4
Zhaoping China 24°11N 110°48E 117 E8
Zhaoqing China 23°0N 112°20E 117 F9
Zhaotong China 27°20N 103°44E 116 D4
Zhaoyang Hu China 35°4N 116°47E 114 G9
Zhaoyuan Heilongjiang,
  China 45°27N 125°0E 115 B13
Zhaoyuan Shandong,
  China 37°20N 120°23E 115 F11
Zhar, Mali Kosovo 42°20N 21°0E 96 D5
Zhari Namco China 31°6N 85°36E 110 E6
Zharkent Kazakhstan 44°10N 80°0E 109 D10
Zharkovskiy Russia 55°56N 32°19E 84 E7
Zhashkiv Ukraine 49°15N 30°5E 75 D16
Zhashui China 33°40N 109°8E 114 H5
Zhaslyk = Jasliq
  Uzbekistan 43°58N 57°10E 108 D5
Zhayrang Kazakhstan 48°20N 70°10E 109 D8
Zhayylma Kazakhstan 51°37N 61°33E 108 B4
Zhayyq → Kazakhstan 47°0N 51°48E 108 C4
Zhdanov = Mariupol
  Ukraine 47°5N 37°31E 85 J9
Zhecheng China 34°7N 115°20E 114 G8
Zhegao China 31°46N 117°45E 117 B11
Zhejiang □ China 29°0N 120°0E 117 C13
Zheleznodorozhnyy
  Russia 54°22N 21°19E 82 D8
Zheleznogorsk Russia 52°22N 35°23E 85 F8
Zheleznogorsk-Ilimskiy
  Russia 56°34N 104°8E 107 D11
Zheltye Vody = Zhovti Vody
  Ukraine 48°21N 33°31E 85 H7
Zhen'an China 33°27N 109°9E 116 A7
Zhenba China 32°34N 107°58E 116 A6
Zhenfeng China 25°22N 105°40E 116 E5
Zheng'an China 28°32N 107°27E 116 C6
Zhengding China 38°8N 114°32E 114 E8
Zhenghe China 27°20N 118°50E 117 D12
Zhengyang China 32°37N 114°22E 117 A10
Zhengzhou China 34°45N 113°34E 114 G7
Zhenhai China 29°59N 121°42E 117 C13
Zhenjiang China 32°11N 119°26E 117 A12
Zhenkang China 23°58N 99°0E 116 E2
Zhenlai China 45°50N 123°5E 115 B12
Zhenning China 26°4N 105°45E 116 D5
Zhenping Henan, China 33°10N 112°16E 114 H7
Zhenping Shaanxi,
  China 31°59N 109°31E 116 B7
Zhenxiong China 27°27N 104°50E 116 D5
Zhenyuan Gansu,
  China 35°35N 107°30E 114 G4
Zhenyuan Guizhou,
  China 27°4N 108°21E 116 D7
Zhenyuan Yunnan,
  China 23°51N 100°59E 116 F3
Zherdevka Russia 51°56N 41°29E 86 E5
Zherebkove Ukraine 47°30N 29°52E 81 C14
Zherong China 27°15N 119°52E 117 D12
Zhetiqara Kazakhstan 52°11N 61°12E 108 B6
Zhezdi Kazakhstan 48°8N 67°53E 109 D7
Zhezqazghan
  Kazakhstan 47°44N 67°40E 109 D7
Zhicheng China 30°25N 111°27E 116 B8
Zhidan China 36°48N 108°48E 114 F5
Zhigansk Russia 66°48N 123°27E 107 C13
Zhigulevsk Russia 53°28N 49°30E 86 D9
Zhijiang Hubei, China 30°28N 111°45E 116 B8
Zhijiang Hunan, China 27°7N 109°42E 116 D7
Zhijin China 26°38N 105°45E 116 D5
Zhilinda Russia 70°0N 114°20E 107 C12
Zhilino Russia 54°54N 21°54E 82 D8
Zhirnovsk Russia 50°57N 44°49E 86 E7
Zhitomir = Zhytomyr
  Ukraine 50°20N 28°40E 81 A13
Zhizdra Russia 53°45N 34°40E 84 F8
Zhlobin Belarus 52°55N 30°0E 81 B16
Zhmerynka Ukraine 49°2N 28°2E 75 D15
Zhob Pakistan 31°20N 69°31E 128 D6
Zhob → Pakistan 32°4N 69°50E 128 D6
Zhodino = Zhodzina
  Belarus 54°5N 28°17E 75 A15
Zhokhova, Ostrov
  Russia 76°4N 152°40E 107 B16
Zhongba China 29°40N 84°10E 110 F6
Zhongdian China 27°48N 99°42E 116 D2
Zhongdong China 24°40N 109°40E 116 E7
Zhongjian Dao = Triton I.
  S. China Sea 15°47N 111°12E 118 A4
Zhongning China 37°18N 105°40E 114 F3
Zhongsha Qundao = Macclesfield
  Bank S. China Sea 16°0N 114°30E 118 A4

Zlatni Pyasŭtsi Bulgaria 43°17N 28°3E 97
Zlatograd Bulgaria 41°22N 25°7E
Zlatoust Russia 55°10N 59°40E 108
Zletovo Macedonia 41°59N 22°17E
Zlín Czech Rep. 49°14N 17°40E 79
Zlínský □ Czech Rep. 49°20N 17°40E 79
Złocieniec Poland 53°30N 16°1E
Złoczew Poland 51°24N 18°35E 8
Złot Serbia 44°1N 21°58E 9
Złotoryja Poland 51°8N 15°55E 8
Złotów Poland 53°22N 17°2E 8
Zmeinogorsk
  Kazakhstan 51°10N 82°13E 109
Żmigród Poland 51°28N 16°53E 8
Zmiinyi, Ostriv Black Sea 45°15N 30°12E
Znamenka = Znamyanka
  Ukraine 48°45N 32°30E 8
Znamensk Russia 54°37N 21°10E 8
Znamensk = Kapustin Yar
  Russia 48°37N 45°40E
Znamyanka Ukraine 48°45N 32°30E 8
Znin Poland 52°51N 17°44E
Znojmo Czech Rep. 48°50N 16°2E 7
Zobeyrī Iran 34°10N 46°40E 1
Zobia
  Dem. Rep. of the Congo 3°0N 25°59E 1
Zoetermeer Neths. 52°3N 4°30E
Zogang China 29°55N 97°42E 1
Zogno Italy 45°48N 9°40E
Zohreh → Iran 30°16N 51°15E 1
Zolfo Springs U.S.A. 27°30N 81°48W 1
Zolochiv Ukraine 49°39N 24°51E 7
Zolotonosha Ukraine 49°39N 32°5E 8
Zolotyy Potik Ukraine 48°54N 25°20E 8
Zomba Malawi 15°22S 35°19E 1
Zomba
  Dem. Rep. of the Congo 3°20N 18°35E 1
Zongo
  Dem. Rep. of the Congo 4°20N 18°35E 1
Zonguldak Turkey 41°28N 31°50E 1
Zonguldak □ Turkey 41°30N 31°45E 1
Zongor Pt. Malta 35°52N 14°34E 1
Zonza France 41°45N 9°11E 7
Zorgo Burkina Faso 12°15N 0°35W 1
Zorita Spain 39°17N 5°39W
Zorleni Romania 46°14N 27°44E 8
Zornitsa Bulgaria 42°23N 26°58E 9
Zorritos Peru 3°43S 80°40W 1
Żory Poland 50°3N 18°44E 8
Zo, Oued → Morocco 31°40N 4°15W 136
Zossen Germany 52°13N 13°27E
Zou Xiang China 35°30N 116°58E 1
Zouan-Hounien Ivory C. 6°55N 8°15W 1
Zouar Chad 20°30N 16°32E 1
Zouérate = Zouîrât
  Mauritania 22°44N 12°21W 1
Zouîrât Mauritania 22°44N 12°21W 1
Zourika Niger 19°16N 7°52E 1
Zourma Burkina Faso 11°20N 0°50W 1
Zousfana, O. → Algeria 31°28N 2°17W 1
Zoutkamp Neths. 53°20N 6°18E
Zov Tigra △ Russia 43°25N 134°10E 1
Zrenjanin Serbia 45°22N 20°23E
Zuba Nigeria 9°11N 7°12E 1
Zubin Potok Kosovo 42°54N 20°41E 9
Zubtsov Russia 56°10N 34°34E 8
Zuénoula Ivory C. 7°34N 6°3W 1
Zuera Spain 41°51N 0°49W
Zufâr Oman 17°40N 54°0E 1
Zug Switz. 47°10N 8°31E 7
Zugdidi Georgia 42°30N 41°55E 8
Zugersee Switz. 47°7N 8°35E 7
Zuid-Holland □ Neths. 52°0N 4°35E
Zuidbeveland Neths. 51°30N 3°50E
Zuidhorn Neths. 53°15N 6°23E
Zújar Spain 37°34N 2°50W
Zújar → Spain 39°1N 5°47W
Żukowo Poland 54°21N 18°22E
Zula Eritrea 15°17N 39°40E 1
Zülpich Germany 50°41N 6°39E
Zumaia Spain 43°19N 2°15W
Zumárraga Spain 43°8N 2°15W
Zumbo Mozam. 15°35S 30°26E 1
Zummo Nigeria 9°51N 12°59E 1
Zumpango Mexico 19°48N 99°6W 1
Zungeru Nigeria 9°48N 6°8E 1
Zunhua China 40°18N 117°58E 1
Zuni Pueblo U.S.A. 35°4N 108°51W 1
Zunyi China 27°42N 106°53E 1
Zuo Jiang → China 22°50N 108°6E 1
Zuoquan China 37°5N 113°22E 1
Zuozhou China 22°36N 107°18E 1
Županja Croatia 45°4N 18°43E
Zurbātīyah Iraq 33°9N 46°3E 1
Zürich Switz. 47°22N 8°32E 7
Zürich □ Switz. 47°26N 8°40E 7
Zürich ✈ (ZRH) Switz. 47°27N 8°33E 7
Zürichsee Switz. 47°18N 8°43E 7
Zuromin Poland 53°4N 19°51E
Zut Croatia 43°52N 15°17E 9
Zutphen Neths. 52°9N 6°12E
Zuurberg △ S. Africa 33°12S 25°32E 1
Zuwārah Libya 32°58N 12°1E 1
Zūzan Iran 34°22N 59°53E 1
Žužemberk Slovenia 45°52N 14°56E 9
Zvečan Kosovo 42°54N 20°49E 9
Zvenigorodka = Svenyhorodka
  Ukraine 49°4N 30°56E 8
Zvezdets Bulgaria 42°6N 27°26E 9
Zvishavane Zimbabwe 20°17S 30°2E 1
Zvolen Slovak Rep. 48°33N 19°10E 7
Zvonce Serbia 42°57N 22°34E 9
Zvornik Bos.-H. 44°26N 19°7E 9
Zwedru = Tchien Liberia 5°59N 8°15W 1
Zweibrücken Germany 49°15N 7°20E 7
Zwettl Austria 48°35N 15°9E 7
Zwickau Germany 50°44N 12°30E 7
Zwierzyniec Poland 50°36N 22°58E 8
Zwiesel Germany 49°1N 13°14E 7
Zwoleń Poland 51°21N 21°28E 8
Zwolle Neths. 52°31N 6°6E
Zwolle U.S.A. 31°38N 93°39W 1
Żychlin Poland 52°15N 19°37E 8
Zyrardów Poland 52°3N 20°28E 8
Zyryanka Russia 65°45N 150°51E 1
Zyryanovsk = Zyryan
  Kazakhstan 49°43N 84°20E 109
Žywiec Poland 49°42N 19°10E 8